# THE
# ALL ENGLAND
# LAW REPORTS

# 1989

## Volume 2

*Editor*
PETER HUTCHESSON LL M
Barrister, New Zealand

*Assistant Editor*
BROOK WATSON
of Lincoln's Inn, Barrister
and of the New South Wales Bar

*Consulting Editor*
WENDY SHOCKETT
of Gray's Inn, Barrister

London
BUTTERWORTHS

| | |
|---|---|
| UNITED KINGDOM | Butterworth & Co (Publishers) Ltd, 88 Kingsway, **London** WC2B 6AB and 4 Hill Street, **Edinburgh** EH2 3JZ |
| AUSTRALIA | Butterworths Pty Ltd, **Sydney, Melbourne, Brisbane, Adelaide, Perth, Canberra** and **Hobart** |
| CANADA | Butterworths Canada Ltd, **Toronto** and **Vancouver** |
| IRELAND | Butterworth (Ireland) Ltd, **Dublin** |
| MALAYSIA | Malayan Law Journal Pte Ltd, **Kuala Lumpur** |
| NEW ZEALAND | Butterworths of New Zealand Ltd, **Wellington** and **Auckland** |
| PUERTO RICO | Equity de Puerto Rico Inc, **Hato Rey** |
| SINGAPORE | Malayan Law Journal Pte Ltd, **Singapore** |
| USA | Butterworth Legal Publishers, **Austin**, Texas, **Boston**, Massachusetts, **Clearwater**, Florida (D & S Publishers), **Orford**, New Hampshire (Equity Publishing), **St Paul**, Minnesota, **Seattle**, Washington |

ISBN 0 406 85168 9

**Butterworths**

PART OF REED INTERNATIONAL P.L.C.

# House of Lords

The Lord High Chancellor: Lord Mackay of Clashfern

## Lords of Appeal in Ordinary

Lord Keith of Kinkel
Lord Bridge of Harwich
Lord Brandon of Oakbrook
Lord Templeman
Lord Griffiths

Lord Ackner
Lord Oliver of Aylmerton
Lord Goff of Chieveley
Lord Jauncey of Tullichettle
Lord Lowry

# Court of Appeal

The Lord High Chancellor

The Lord Chief Justice of England: Lord Lane
(President of the Criminal Division)

The Master of the Rolls: Lord Donaldson of Lymington
(President of the Civil Division)

The President of the Family Division: Sir Stephen Brown

The Vice-Chancellor: Sir Nicolas Christopher Henry Browne-Wilkinson

## Lords Justices of Appeal

Sir Tasker Watkins VC
(Deputy Chief Justice)
Sir Patrick McCarthy O'Connor
Sir Michael John Fox
Sir Michael Robert Emanuel Kerr
(retired 9 June 1989)
Sir John Douglas May
(retired 9 June 1989)
Sir Christopher John Slade
Sir Francis Brooks Purchas
Sir George Brian Hugh Dillon
Sir Roger Jocelyn Parker
Sir David Powell Croom-Johnson
Sir Anthony John Leslie Lloyd
Sir Brian Thomas Neill
Sir Michael John Mustill
Sir Martin Charles Nourse

Sir Iain Derek Laing Glidewell
Sir Alfred John Balcombe
Sir Ralph Brian Gibson
Sir John Dexter Stocker
Sir Harry Kenneth Woolf
Sir Donald James Nicholls
Sir Thomas Henry Bingham
Sir Thomas Patrick Russell
Dame Ann Elizabeth Oldfield Butler-Sloss
Sir Peter Murray Taylor
Sir Murray Stuart-Smith
Sir Christopher Stephen Thomas Jonathan
Thayer Staughton
Sir Michael Mann
Sir Donald Henry Farquharson
(appointed 12 June 1989)

## Chancery Division

The Lord High Chancellor

The Vice-Chancellor

Sir John Evelyn Vinelott
Sir Douglas William Falconer
Sir Jean-Pierre Frank Eugene Warner
Sir Peter Leslie Gibson
Sir David Herbert Mervyn Davies
Sir Jeremiah LeRoy Harman
Sir Richard Rashleigh Folliott Scott
  (Vice-Chancellor of the County Palatine
  of Lancaster)

Sir Leonard Hubert Hoffmann
Sir John Leonard Knox
Sir Peter Julian Millett
Sir Robert Andrew Morritt
Sir William Aldous

## Queen's Bench Division

The Lord Chief Justice of England

Sir William Lloyd Mars-Jones
Sir Leslie Kenneth Edward Boreham
Sir Alfred William Michael Davies
Sir Haydn Tudor Evans
Sir Kenneth Graham Jupp
Sir Walter Derek Thornley Hodgson
Sir Ronald Gough Waterhouse
Sir Frederick Maurice Drake
Sir Barry Cross Sheen
Sir David Bruce McNeill
Sir Christopher James Saunders French
Sir Peter Edlin Webster
Sir Donald Henry Farquharson
  (appointed Lord Justice of Appeal 12
  June 1989)
Sir Anthony James Denys McCowan
Sir Iain Charles Robert McCullough
Sir Hamilton John Leonard
Sir Alexander Roy Asplan Beldam
Sir David Cozens-Hardy Hirst
Sir John Stewart Hobhouse
Sir Andrew Peter Leggatt
Sir Michael Patrick Nolan
Sir Oliver Bury Popplewell
Sir William Alan Macpherson
Sir Philip Howard Otton
Sir Paul Joseph Morrow Kennedy
Sir Michael Hutchison
Sir Simon Denis Brown
Sir Anthony Howell Meurig Evans

Sir Mark Oliver Saville
Sir Johan Steyn
Sir Christopher Dudley Roger Rose
Sir Richard Howard Tucker
Sir Robert Alexander Gatehouse
Sir Patrick Neville Garland
Sir John Ormond Roch
Sir Michael John Turner
Sir Harry Henry Ognall
Sir John Downes Alliott
Sir Konrad Hermann Theodor Schiemann
Sir John Arthur Dalziel Owen
Sir Denis Robert Maurice Henry
Sir Francis Humphrey Potts
Sir Richard George Rougier
Sir Ian Alexander Kennedy
Sir Nicholas Addison Phillips
Sir Robin Ernest Auld
Sir Malcolm Thomas Pill
Sir Stuart Neill McKinnon
Sir Mark Howard Potter
Sir Henry Brooke
Sir Igor Judge
Sir Edwin Frank Jowitt
Sir Michael Morland
  (appointed 18 May 1989)
Sir Mark Waller
  (appointed 26 May 1989)
Sir Roger John Buckley
  (appointed 20 July 1989)

## Family Division

The President of the Family Division

Sir Alfred Kenneth Hollings
Sir John Kember Wood
Sir Thomas Michael Eastham
Dame Margaret Myfanwy Wood Booth
Sir Anthony Leslie Julian Lincoln
Sir Anthony Bruce Ewbank
Sir John Douglas Waite
Sir Anthony Barnard Hollis

Sir Swinton Barclay Thomas
Sir Mathew Alexander Thorpe
Sir Edward Stephen Cazalet
Sir Alan Hylton Ward
Sir Thomas Scott Gillespie Baker
Sir Robert Lionel Johnson
Sir Douglas Dunlop Brown
Sir Donald Keith Rattee
  (appointed 23 May 1989)

# CITATION

## These reports are cited thus:

## [1989] 2 All ER

## REFERENCES

These reports contain references to the following major works of legal reference described in the manner indicated below.

## Halsbury's Laws of England

The reference 26 Halsbury's Laws (4th edn) para 577 refers to paragraph 577 on page 296 of volume 26 of the fourth edition of Halsbury's Laws of England.

The reference 7(1) Halsbury's Laws (4th edn reissue) para 267 refers to paragraph 267 on page 177 of reissue volume 7(1) of the fourth edition of Halsbury's Laws of England.

## Halsbury's Statutes of England and Wales

The reference 27 Halsbury's Statutes (4th edn) 208 refers to page 208 of volume 27 of the fourth edition of Halsbury's Statutes of England and Wales.

The reference 4 Halsbury's Statutes (4th edn) (1987 reissue) 953 refers to page 953 of the 1987 reissue of volume 4 of the fourth edition of Halsbury's Statutes of England and Wales.

The reference 45 Halsbury's Statutes (3rd edn) 1196 refers to page 1196 of volume 45 of the third edition of Halsbury's Statutes of England.

## The Digest

References are to the green band reissue volumes of The Digest (formerly the English and Empire Digest).

The reference 36(2) Digest (Reissue) 764, 1398 refers to case number 1398 on page 764 of Digest Green Band Reissue Volume 36(2).

The reference 27(1) Digest (2nd reissue) 330, 2849 refers to case number 2849 on page 330 of Digest Green Band Second Reissue Volume 27(1).

## Halsbury's Statutory Instruments

The reference 1 Halsbury's Statutory Instruments (Grey Volume) 278 refers to page 278 of Grey Volume 1 of Halsbury's Statutory Instruments.

The reference 17 Halsbury's Statutory Instruments (4th reissue) 256 refers to page 256 of the fourth reissue of volume 17 of Halsbury's Statutory Instruments.

# Cases reported in volume 2

# Digest of cases reported in volume 2

xv

xvi

# House of Lords petitions

This list, which covers the period 22 April 1989 to 11 August 1989, sets out all cases which have formed the subject of a report in the All England Law Reports in which an Appeal Committee of the House of Lords has, subsequent to the publication of that report, dismissed a petition or refused leave to appeal on a perusal of the papers or after an oral hearing. Where the result of a petition for leave to appeal was known prior to the publication of the relevant report a note of that result appears at the end of the report.

**Kleinwort Benson Ltd v Malaysia Mining Corp Bhd** [1989] 1 All ER 785, CA. Leave to appeal refused 10 May 1989 (Lord Keith, Lord Griffiths and Lord Goff) (oral hearing)

**R v Secretary of State for Foreign and Commonwealth Affairs, ex p Everett** [1989] 1 All ER 655, CA. Leave to appeal refused 6 June 1989 (Lord Keith, Lord Brandon and Lord Lowry) (oral hearing)

## CORRIGENDUM

[1989] 2 All ER

p 444. **Janred Properties Ltd v Ente Nazionale Italiano per il Turismo.** Line *c* 2 should read '... Repudiation by *purchaser* ...'.

# Attorney General's Reference (No 1 of 1988)

HOUSE OF LORDS

LORD KEITH OF KINKEL, LORD TEMPLEMAN, LORD ACKNER, LORD OLIVER OF AYLMERTON AND LORD LOWRY

1 MARCH, 13 APRIL 1989

*Company – Insider dealing – Prohibition on stock exchange deals by insiders etc – Person who obtains insider information – Obtain – Whether 'obtains' restricted to acquiring by purpose and effort – Whether person who receives unsolicited inside information prohibited from dealing in company's securities – Company Securities (Insider Dealing) Act 1985, s 1(3)(4)(a).*

The appellant contemplated making a take-over offer for a publicly-quoted company and had discussions with the company's merchant bankers. Shortly afterwards, the company's chairman agreed to the company being taken over by another company. The merchant bankers informed the appellant of the proposed take-over and told him that a public announcement would be made shortly but that until then the information was sensitive and highly confidential. The appellant promptly purchased 6,000 shares in the company and, following the announcement of the take-over, made a substantial profit. He was charged with two offences of dealing in the securities of a company as a prohibited person, contrary to s 1(3) and (4)(a)[a] of the Company Securities (Insider Dealing) Act 1985. The trial judge directed the jury to acquit the appellant on the ground that there was no evidence that he had 'obtained' the information, for the purposes of s 1(3), since it had been given to him unsolicited. The Attorney General then referred to the Court of Appeal for its opinion the question of the meaning of 'obtained' in s 1(3) of the 1985 Act. The Court of Appeal held that a person obtained information for the purposes of s 1(3) and (4)(a) of the 1985 Act even if he came by it without any positive action on his part. On the appellant's application the Court of Appeal referred the point to the House of Lords.

**Held** – For the purposes of the offence of insider dealing contrary to s 1(3) and (4)(a) of the 1985 Act a person 'obtained' confidential information about a company if he acquired or got it without any effort on his part. Accordingly, the recipient of confidential information about a company who used it to deal in the company's shares committed an offence under s 1(3) and (4) of the 1985 Act even if the information was volunteered to him (see p 2 *g*, p3 *a b d* to *f*, p 4 *g*, p 5 *d* and p 8 *f*, post).

Per Lord Keith, Lord Ackner, Lord Oliver and Lord Lowry. For a person to be guilty of 'knowingly' obtaining confidential information about a company for the purposes of ss 1(3)(a) and 2(1)(a) of the 1985 Act he has to know from whom he obtained it (see p 2 *g*, p 3 *e f* and p 7 *a*, post).

Decision of the Court of Appeal [1989] 1 All ER 321 affirmed.

**Notes**

For insider dealing, see 7(1) Halsbury's Laws (4th edn reissue) paras 1060–1068.

---

*a* Section 1, so far as material, is set out at p 3 *g* to *j*, post

For the Company Securities (Insider Dealing) Act 1985, ss 1, 2, see 8 Halsbury's Statutes (4th edn) 829, 831.                                                                                          *a*

**Cases referred to in opinions**
*Black-Clawson International Ltd v Papierwerke Waldhof-Aschaffenburg AG* [1975] 1 All ER 810, [1975] AC 591, [1975] 2 WLR 513, HL.
*Customs and Excise Comrs v Top Ten Promotions Ltd* [1969] 3 All ER 39, [1969] 1 WLR 1163, HL.                                                                                                        *b*
*DPP v Ottewell* [1968] 3 All ER 153, [1970] AC 642, [1968] 3 WLR 621, HL.
*Fisher v Raven* [1963] 2 All ER 389, [1964] AC 210, [1963] 2 WLR 1137, HL.
*R v Hayat* (1976) 63 Cr App R 181, CA.
*Spillers Ltd v Cardiff (Borough) Assessment Committee* [1931] 2 KB 21, [1931] All ER Rep 524, DC.
*Tuck & Sons v Priester* (1887) 19 QBD 629, CA.                                                      *c*

**Reference**
On 14 April 1988 the appellant was acquitted at the Crown Court at Southwark before his Honour Judge Butler QC and a jury on two counts of an indictment which charged him with dealing in the securities of a company as a prohibited person, contrary to ss 1(3) and (4)(a) and 8(1) of the Company Securities (Insider Dealing) Act 1985. The Attorney   *d* General referred to the Court of Appeal, Criminal Division, pursuant to s 36(1) of the Criminal Justice Act 1972, two points of law (set out at p 4 d e, post) for its consideration. On 18 October 1988 that court (Lord Lane CJ, Hutchison and Tucker JJ) ([1989] 1 All ER 321, [1989] 2 WLR 195), having given its opinion on the points of law referred to, on the application of the appellant under s 36(3) of the 1972 Act, referred the points to the House of Lords for its consideration. The facts are set out in the opinion of Lord   *e* Templeman.

*Roger Buckley QC* and *Antony White* for the appellant.
*Nicholas Purnell QC* and *Timothy Nash* for the Attorney General.

Their Lordships took time for consideration.                                                       *f*

13 April. The following opinions were delivered.

**LORD KEITH OF KINKEL.** My Lords, I have had the opportunity of considering in draft the speech to be delivered by my noble and learned friend Lord Lowry. I agree   *g* with it, and for the reasons he gives would affirm the decision of the Court of Appeal.

**LORD TEMPLEMAN.** My Lords, by ss 1(3) and (4) and 8 of the Company Securities (Insider Dealing) Act 1985 a criminal offence is committed, subject to exceptions and conditions not here material, where 'an individual has information which he knowingly obtained (directly or indirectly) from' a person connected with a company and then deals   *h* on the Stock Exchange with shares in that company knowing that the information is confidential unpublished price sensitive information in relation to those shares.
    The appellant was informed by a merchant bank connected with a company that a take-over bid had been agreed and that this information was confidential. The appellant promptly purchased 6,000 shares in the company on the Stock Exchange and, following the announcement of the take-over, made a profit of £3,000. If a member of the police   *j* force, after studying the 1985 Act, had asked the appellant whether he had obtained information and, if so, from whom, a truthful appellant would have answered that he had obtained information from the merchant bank. Yet, when the appellant was tried for an offence under the Act, the trial judge held that the appellant had not obtained any information.

The argument is that, according to the dictionary, information is not 'obtained' if the
a information is volunteered. The object of the 1985 Act was to prevent insider dealing.
The appellant became an insider when he learnt of the take-over agreement and he
became an insider dealer when he bought 6,000 shares. Parliament cannot have intended
that a man who asks for information which he then misuses should be convicted of an
offence while a man who, without asking, learns the same information which he also
misuses should be acquitted.

b    In *Customs and Excise Comrs v Top Ten Promotions Ltd* [1969] 3 All ER 39, [1969] 1 WLR
1163 this House construed a taxing statute and reached a conclusion adverse to the
taxpayer. Lord Upjohn said ([1969] 3 All ER 39 at 90, [1969] 1 WLR 1163 at 1171):

> 'It is highly dangerous, if not impossible, to attempt to place an accurate definition
> on a word in common use; you can look up examples of its many uses if you want
c > to in the *Oxford Dictionary* but that does not help on definition; in fact it probably
> only shows that the word normally defies definition. The task of the court in
> construing statutory language such as that which is before your Lordships is to look
> at the mischief at which the Act is directed and then, in that light, to consider
> whether as a matter of common sense and everyday usage the known, proved or
> admitted or properly inferred facts of the particular case bring the case within the
d > ordinary meaning of the words used by Parliament.'

My Lords, without troubling any dictionary, I am satisfied that the appellant obtained
information which he made no effort to obtain and that his subsequent misuse of that
information was in breach of the 1985 Act.

**LORD ACKNER.** My Lords, I have had the advantage of reading in draft the speech
e prepared by my noble and learned friend Lord Lowry. For the reasons which he has
given, I, too, would answer the questions posed by the reference in the same way as the
Court of Appeal.

**LORD OLIVER OF AYLMERTON.** My Lords, I have had the advantage of reading
f in draft the speech prepared by my noble and learned friend Lord Lowry. For the reasons
which he has given, I, too, would answer the questions posed by the reference in the
same way as the Court of Appeal.

**LORD LOWRY.** My Lords, this appeal is concerned with the meaning of the word
'obtained' in s 1(3) of the Company Securities (Insider Dealing) Act 1985, which, with
g sub-s (4)(a), provides:

> '(3) The next subsection applies where—(a) an individual has information which
> he knowingly obtained (directly or indirectly) from another individual who—(i) is
> connected with a particular company, or was at any time in the 6 months preceding
> the obtaining of the information so connected, and (ii) the former individual knows
> or has reasonable cause to believe held the information by virtue of being so
h > connected, and (b) the former individual knows or has reasonable cause to believe
> that, because of the latter's connection and position, it would be reasonable to expect
> him not to disclose the information except for proper performance of the functions
> attaching to that position.
> (4) Subject to section 3, the former individual in that case—(a) shall not himself
> deal on a recognised stock exchange in securities of that company if he knows that
j > the information is unpublished price sensitive information in relation to those
> securities...'

On 11 April 1988 at the Crown Court at Southwark an accused person, whom for the
purpose of these proceedings I shall call 'the appellant', pleaded not guilty to two charges
laid against him as a prohibited person dealing in the securities of a company contrary to

the above provisions and to s 8(1) of the 1985 Act, which alleged that on or about
5 December 1985, (1) having information which he knowingly obtained from an    *a*
employee of the company's merchant bankers who was connected with the company
and whom he knew or had reasonable cause to believe held that information by virtue of
being so connected, (2) knowing or having reasonable cause to believe that because of the
said employee's connection and position it would be reasonable to expect her not to
disclose that information except for the proper performance of the functions attaching
to that position and (3) knowing that that information was unpublished price sensitive    *b*
information in relation to the securities of the comany, he purchased in one instance
5,000 and, in another, 1,000 ordinary shares in the company on a recognised stock
exchange, namely the Stock Exchange.

The prosecution conceded that the appellant had taken no step directly or indirectly to
secure, procure or acquire the information (which had been given to him quite properly)
and at the conclusion of the prosecution case his counsel submitted, inter alia, that there    *c*
was no evidence that the appellant *obtained* information, that he merely *received* it and
that the prohibition in s 1(4) did not operate against him, since the proper construction
of the word 'obtained' in s 1(3) connoted active conduct. The trial judge upheld this
submission and directed the jury to acquit the appellant on both counts in the indictment.

The Attorney General then referred the following points of law to the Court of Appeal
under s 36(1) of the Criminal Justice Act 1972:    *d*

> '(a) Whether or not the word "obtained" in section 1(3) of the Company Securities
> (Insider Dealing) Act 1985 has the restricted meaning of "acquired by purpose and
> effort" or whether it has a wider meaning.
> (b) Whether or not any individual who has, from another, information within
> the scope of the Act and is otherwise within the scope of the prohibitions contained    *e*
> in sections 1(4), 1(6) and 2 of the Act, may be an individual who has "obtained"
> within the terms of sections 1(3), 1(6) and 2 of that Act.'

The Court of Appeal (Lord Lane CJ, Hutchison and Tucker JJ) ([1989] 1 All ER 321,
[1989] 2 WLR 195) gave its opinion on the points of law referred to it by saying that (a)
the word 'obtained' in s 1(3) has a wider meaning than 'acquired by purpose and effort'    *f*
and (b) an individual who has, from another, information within the scope of the Act
may be an individual who has 'obtained' within the meaning of ss 1(4), (6) and 2. Then,
in pursuance of an application by the appellant under s 36(3) of the 1972 Act, it referred
the points to your Lordships' House. (A full statement of the facts and also the Attorney
General's reference may be found at [1989] 2 WLR 196–200).

It would, I believe, suffice to say that I agree with the reasoning and conclusions
contained in the judgment of the court delivered by Lord Lane CJ, which I would be    *g*
more than content to adopt as my own. But I feel that the persuasive and helpful
arguments of counsel for the appellant before your Lordships deserve and require a
positive response. Accordingly, I venture to express my own view of the matter.

The immediately relevant provisions set out above apply to what is conveniently
termed a secondary insider (because his information is derived from another individual).    *h*
They are logically preceded by s 1(1) and (2), which apply to a primary insider, being 'an
individual who is, or at any time in the preceding 6 months has been, knowingly
connected with a company'. Section 1(5) inhibits dealing by an individual who is
contemplating or has contemplated making a take-over offer for a company and s 1(6)
applies to an individual who has *knowingly obtained* information from an individual to
whom sub-s (5) applies. Section 2 deals with abuse of information held by or *knowingly*    *j*
*obtained* from a Crown servant (now a 'public servant': see the Financial Services Act 1986,
s 173). The prohibitions in ss 1 and 2 are expressly subject to s 3 of the 1985 Act:

> '(1) Sections 1 and 2 do not prohibit an individual by reason of his having any
> information from—(a) doing any particular thing otherwise than with a view to the
> making of a profit or the avoidance of a loss (whether for himself or another person)

a  by the use of that information; (b) entering into a transaction in the course of the exercise in good faith of his functions as liquidator, receiver or trustee in bankruptcy; or (c) doing any particular thing if the information—(i) was obtained by him in the course of a business of a jobber in which he was engaged or employed, and (ii) was of a description which it would be reasonable to expect him to obtain in the ordinary course of that business, and he does that thing in good faith in the course of that business. "Jobber" means an individual, partnership or company dealing in securities

b  on a recognised stock exchange and recognised by the Council of The Stock Exchange as carrying on the business of a jobber.

(2) An individual is not, by reason only of his having information relating to any particular transaction, prohibited—(a) by section 1(2), (4)(b), (5) or (6) from dealing on a recognised stock change in any securities, or (b) by section 1(7) or (8) from doing any other thing in relation to securities which he is prohibited from dealing in by

c  any of the provisions mentioned in paragraph (a), or (c) by section 2 from doing anything, if he does that thing in order to facilitate the completion or carrying out of the transaction.'

The answer depends on the meaning in context of the word 'obtained'. The first meaning in the Oxford English Dictionary is:

d  'To come into the possession or enjoyment of (something) by one's own effort, or by request; to procure or gain, as the result of purpose and effort: hence, generally, to acquire, get.'

The primary meaning of 'obtain', which stems from the Latin, is consistent, and consistent only, with the appellant's case; but the words following the colon and

e  commencing 'hence, generally' clearly denote a general meaning derived from the primary meaning: the words 'acquire' and 'get', unaccompanied by any adverb or adverbial phrase, are wide enough to cover both the primary meaning and the secondary meaning of coming into possession of a thing without effort on one's own part. Linguistic research need go no further to establish this fact; there is no point in considering the four other meanings in the Oxford English Dictionary, which are mainly obsolete, or in shopping

f  around among a variety of dictionaries and phrasebooks.

The appellant relies on the principle that any ambiguity in a penal statute should be resolved in favour of the defence (see Tuck & Sons v Priester (1887) 19 QBD 629 at 638 per Lord Esher MR) and says that the statute is, at best from the Crown's point of view, ambiguous. This submission must be qualified by Lord Reid's observation, on which the Court of Appeal relied ([1989] 1 All ER 321 at 326–327, [1989] 2 WLR 195 at 206), in

g  DPP v Ottewell [1968] 3 All ER 153 at 157, [1970] AC 642 at 649:

'I would never seek to diminish in any way the importance of that principle within its proper sphere; but it only applies where after full enquiry and consideration one is left in real doubt. It is not enough that the provision is ambiguous in the sense that it is capable of having two meanings. The impression

h  of the English language (and, so far as I am aware, of any other language) is such that it is extremely difficult to draft any provision which is not ambiguous in that sense. This section is clearly ambiguous in that sense: the Court of Appeal (Criminal Division) attach one meaning to it, and your lordships are attaching a different meaning to it. But if, after full consideration, your lordships are satisfied, as I am, that the latter is the meaning which Parliament must have intended the words to

j  convey, then this principle does not prevent us from giving effect to our conclusions.'

The next step, therefore, is to decide whether Parliament must have intended the word 'obtained' to convey and include its secondary or general meaning. If so, the offence is made out; if, however, one cannot be satisfied of that, then the ambiguity remains and the Tuck & Sons v Priester principle compels your Lordships to adopt the primary or narrow meaning.

The following points assist the Crown.

(1) The offence is dealing on a stock exchange in securities of a company in defined *a* circumstances. It can be committed by a primary insider or by a secondary insider who has knowingly obtained information (directly or indirectly) from a primary insider. Whether the secondary insider solicited the information or merely received it does not increase or diminish the undesirability of his making use of it or the ultimate effect on the other party to his dealing.

(2) It is permissible to look at circumstances preceding the legislation in order to see *b* what was considered to be the mischief in need of a remedy: see *Black-Clawson International Ltd v Papierwerke Waldhof-Aschaffenburg AG* [1975] 1 All ER 810 at 814, 842–845, [1975] AC 591 at 614, 645–658 per Lord Reid and Lord Simon. I draw attention to para 22 of the White Paper entitled *The Conduct of Company Directors* (Cmnd 7037 (1977)):

> 'Insider dealing is understood broadly to cover situations where a person buys or *c* sells securities when he, but not the other party to the transaction, is in possession of confidential information which affects the value to be placed on those securities. Furthermore the confidential information in question will generally be in his possession because of some connection which he has with the company whose securities are to be dealt in (e g he may be a director, employee or professional adviser of that company) or because someone in such a position has provided him, directly *d* or indirectly, with the information. Public confidence in directors and others closely associated with companies requires that such people should not use insider information to further their own interests. Furthermore, if they were to do so, they would frequently be in breach of their obligations to the companies, and could be held to be taking an unfair advantage of the people with whom they were dealing.'

This tends to show that the mischief consists of dealing in securities while in possession *e* of the confidential information. The words above, 'because someone . . . has provided him, directly or indirectly, with the information', cannot of course be used as a guide to the meaning of the word 'obtained' in the legislation which followed, but they look to the possession of the crucial information and not to the method of its acquisition. The same White Paper, having dealt with the position of primary insiders, goes on to say in *f* para 28:

> 'However, in addition to the specific list of persons who are to be treated as insiders, the Government proposes that anyone who receives information which he knows to be price sensitive and not generally available and which he realises has come directly or indirectly from an insider should also refrain from dealing.'

The majority view and, as I accept, the preferable view in the *Black-Clawson* case (the *g* effect of which is analysed in *Cross on Statutory Interpretation* (2nd edn, 1987) pp 158–161) was that an observation like this cannot be used as a guide to the meaning of the word 'obtained' in the subsequent legislation, but para 28 still confirms that the use of sensitive information by a secondary insider was regarded as one of the evils to be dealt with. (A further White Paper, *Changes in Company Law* (Cmnd 7291 (1978)), incorporated *h* a draft Bill. This was the basis for sections of the Companies Act 1980 which were consolidated in the 1985 Act.)

(3) A primary insider is forbidden to use any information of the specified description. One may properly ask why a secondary insider should be prohibited *only* from using part of the information which may come to his hands, namely that which he has procured by his own efforts: the procurement is not the guilty act. In this connection, ss 1(8), 2(1)(*a*) *j* and 5(1) are worthly of consideration.

(4) The object of the legislation must be partially defeated if the narrow meaning of 'obtained' is adopted.

(5) That meaning would create a need to make fine distinctions, which will not arise if the wider meaning prevails (see [1989] 1 All ER 321 at 327, [1989] 2 WLR 195 at 206 per Lord Lane CJ).

At first I thought that the word 'knowingly' might further support the Crown's
*a* interpretation, but I accept as correct the explanation of counsel for the appellant that its
use in ss 1(3)(*a*) and 2(1)(*a*) denotes that, to be guilty, the user of the confidential
information has to know from whom he has obtained it.

Against these points the appellant advanced arguments which it is necessary to take
account of before reaching a conclusion. They were as follows.

(1) 'Obtain' is used in its primary sense in the statutory provisions which were
*b* considered in cases like *Fisher v Raven* [1963] 2 All ER 389, [1964] AC 210 and *R v Hayat*
(1976) 63 Cr App R 181 and also in s 15 of the Theft Act 1968. It is easy to see why this
is so, because the examples given can only arise from situations in which the active
procurement of a thing constitutes the guilty act. More potent, though less specific, is
counsel's observation that, whenever a criminal statute uses the word 'obtain', it uses that
word in the primary sense. The reason for this, however, is not hard to understand.

*c* (2) Relying on what he called a family relationship between the 1985 Act and the
Insolvency Act 1986, counsel pointed to the word 'obtains' used in its primary meaning
in s 360 of the 1986 Act which, as s 155 of the Bankruptcy Act 1914, was considered in
*Fisher v Raven* [1963] 2 All ER 389, [1964] AC 210. But the words 'obtains' and 'obtained'
are used in different contexts with a difference, I would suggest, in meaning which the
'relationship' is powerless to annul.

*d* (3) By reference to Lord Diplock's test in *Black-Clawson's* case [1975] 1 All ER 810 at
836, [1975] AC 591 at 638 of 'what the words of the statute would be reasonably
understood to mean by those whose conduct it regulates', it was suggested that someone
in the position of a secondary insider would (particularly if he consulted a dictionary) feel
safe in using confidential information which he had acquired unsolicited from the
forbidden source. With respect, I feel that it could as easily be asserted that someone in
*e* that position would feel far from safe, particularly if his dictionary contained the words
'hence, generally, to acquire, get'.

(4) It was further submitted that words ought to be given their natural and ordinary
meaning, and *Spillers Ltd v Cardiff (Borough) Assessment Committee* [1931] 2 KB 21, [1931]
All ER Rep 524 was strongly relied on for the proposition that words must be construed
in their ordinary and proper sense and not in their loose sense. But the word to be
*f* construed in that case was 'contiguous' and the court held that it ought to be construed
in its ordinary and proper sense as meaning 'touching' and not in its loose sense as
meaning 'neighbouring'. I shall quote two short extracts from the judgment of Lord
Hewart CJ ([1931] 2 KB 21 at 42–43, [1931] All ER Rep 524 at 528–529):

*g* 'Does it mean, as the Recorder of Plymouth held, "touching or in contact with,"
or does it mean, as the other Courts have held, "neighbouring or in proximity to'?
As to the proper meaning of the word "contiguous" there can, we think, be no
doubt. Dr. Johnson, of whom it may probably be said that he employed the English
language with a more anxious precision than any other man that ever lived, defines
"contiguous" in his dictionary thus: "Meeting so as to touch; bordering upon each
*h* other; not separate," and he gives no other definition. The Oxford English Dictionary
gives five definitions. The first and principal one is: "Touching, in actual contact,
next in space; meeting at a common boundary, bordering, adjoining." The second
and third deal only with variants of that meaning, in the application of the word,
not to space, but to time and thought. The fourth refers to a use now and long
obsolete. The fifth is this: "*loosely.* Neighbouring, situated in close proximity
*j* (though not in contact)" . . . It ought to be the rule, and we are glad to think that it
is the rule, that words are used in an Act of Parliament correctly and exactly, and
not loosely and inexactly. Upon those who assert that that rule has been broken the
burden of establishing their proposition lies heavily. And they can discharge it only
by pointing to something in the context which goes to show that the loose and
inexact meaning must be preferred. This, indeed, must be not merely the legal, but
also the literary canon of interpretation. No person of education or intelligence

would understand, or suspect, that a writer or speaker was using the word "contiguous" in its loose sense of "neighbouring," unless there was something in the context that compelled that conclusion. If a man spoke or wrote of "contiguous islands" he must necessarily mean "neighbouring," because one island must be separated by water from another. But if he spoke of "contiguous houses" it would be difficult to suppose that he meant anything but houses touching each other.'

Thus in the *Spillers Ltd* case the choice was between the proper and ordinary meaning of a word and its loose and inaccurate meaning; whereas in this case the choice is between the primary meaning and the secondary but correct and acceptable meaning.

(5) The appellants' next argument was based on para 14 of his printed case:

'Even if the Attorney General is right to suggest that the word "obtained" is capable of meaning no more than "has", the rules of construction still require the word to be given its natural and ordinary meaning where it appears in Section 1 of the Act.'

This point relies on the words used in the reference 'who has, from another, information'. But the question of law for your Lordships would still have been the same if the reference had said 'who has received from another information'. It is the Act, and not the reference, which has to be construed.

(6) Finally, by reference to the change of wording from 'information which . . . he holds' in s 1(1) and (2) to 'information which he knowingly obtained' in s 1(3), it has been submitted that, unless the word 'obtained' connotes effort on the part of the individual concerned, it adds nothing to the requirement of having or holding information which applies in the case of the earlier subsections. I cannot accept this reasoning; the addition of the relative clause ('which he knowingly obtained' etc) in s 1(3) is due to the need to describe the forbidden *source* from which a secondary insider must have obtained the information. The *grammatical* construction of s 1(3)(*a*) is equally consistent with both meanings of the word 'obtained'. Therefore this argument does not help the appellant.

Having carefully weighed the points on either side, and not forgetting that we are dealing with a penal statute, I am, in the words of Lord Reid in *DPP v Ottewell* [1968] 3 All ER 153 at 157, [1970] AC 642 at 649, satisfied that the wider meaning is the meaning which Parliament must have intended the word 'obtained' to have in this Act and that, accordingly, there is no room for the kind of ambiguity on which the appellant has attempted to rely.

Therefore I would answer the questions posed by the reference in the same way as the Court of Appeal.

*Reference answered accordingly.*

Solicitors: *Offenbach & Co* (for the appellant); *Solicitor to the Department of Trade and Industry.*

Mary Rose Plummer     Barrister.

*a*

# R v Hennessy

COURT OF APPEAL, CRIMINAL DIVISION
LORD LANE CJ, ROSE AND PILL JJ
27 JANUARY 1989

*b*   *Criminal law – Automatism – Insanity distinguished – Diabetic hyperglycaemia – Diabetic failing to take proper dose of insulin and suffering from hyperglycaemia – Appellant taking car and driving while disqualified – Appellant claiming to be suffering from hyperglycaemia and in a state of automatism – Whether appellant entitled to rely on defence of automatism.*

The appellant, a diabetic, was charged with taking a car and driving while disqualified.
*c* At his trial he pleaded not guilty, his defence being that at the relevant time he had failed to take his proper dose of insulin because of stress, anxiety and depression, and was suffering from hyperglycaemia and in a state of automatism when the offences occurred. The trial judge rejected the defence of automatism on the ground that if it existed the appellant's mental condition was caused by disease, namely diabetes, and therefore fell within the legal definition of 'insanity' under the M'Naghten rules. Following the judge's
*d* ruling the appellant changed his plea to guilty and was convicted. He appealed on the grounds that the judge's ruling was wrong, contending that the stress, anxiety and depression which had caused or contributed to his state of mind were external factors and were not caused by a disease of the mind.

**Held** – Stress, anxiety and depression were not in themselves, either separately or
*e* together, external factors of the kind capable in law of causing or contributing to a state of automatism since they were neither unique nor accidental factors but constituted a state of mind which was prone to recur. Accordingly, since hyperglycaemia caused by an inherent defect and not corrected by insulin was a disease and since the functioning of the appellant's mind was disturbed by disease and not by some external factor the judge's ruling had been correct. The appeal would therefore be dismissed (see p 13 *c* and p 14 *h*
*f* to p 15 *a*, post).
    *M'Naghten's Case* [1843–60] All ER Rep 229, dicta of Devlin J in *Hill v Baxter* [1958] 1 All ER 193 at 197, of Lawton LJ in *R v Quick* [1973] 3 All ER 347 at 356 and of Lord Diplock in *R v Sullivan* [1983] 2 All ER 673 at 677 applied.

**Notes**
*g* For automatism as a defence to a criminal charge, see 11 Halsbury's Laws (4th edn) paras 6–7, and for cases on the subject, see 14(1) Digest (Reissue) 14–16, 31–34.

**Cases referred to in judgment**
*Hill v Baxter* [1958] 1 All ER 193, [1958] 1 QB 277, [1958] 2 WLR 76, DC.
*M'Naghten's Case* (1843) 10 Cl & Fin 200, [1843–60] All ER Rep 229, 8 ER 718, HL.
*h* *R v Bailey* [1983] 2 All ER 503, [1983] 1 WLR 760, CA.
*R v Kemp* [1956] 3 All ER 249, [1957] 1 QB 399, [1956] 3 WLR 724, Assizes.
*R v Quick, R v Paddison* [1973] 3 All ER 347, [1973] QB 910, [1973] 3 WLR 26, CA.
*R v Sullivan* [1983] 2 All ER 673, [1984] AC 156, [1983] 3 WLR 123, HL.

*j* **Appeal against conviction**
On 15 January 1988 in the Crown Court at Lewes before His Honour Judge Birks, the appellant, Andrew Michael Hennessy, pleaded guilty to taking a conveyance (count 1) and to driving while disqualified (count 2) following a ruling by the trial judge that the defence of non-insane automatism was not open to him. He was sentenced to nine months' imprisonment suspended for two years on count 1 and to six months' imprisonment concurrent, also suspended for two years, on count 2. He was also

disqualified from holding or obtaining a driving licence for two years and his driving
licence was endorsed. A community service order imposed on 25 March 1988 was      *a*
ordered to continue. He appealed against his conviction by way of a certificate granted
by the trial judge pursuant to s 1(2) of the Criminal Appeal Act 1968, on the grounds (1)
that the judge erred in holding that he was not entitled to have his defence of non-insane
automatism left to the jury because any impairment of his consciousness was the result
of a disease of the mind and thus amounted to a defence of insanity, and (2) that the
judge erred in holding that the stress and anxiety from which the appellant claimed to     *b*
be suffering was not an external factor and in holding that the sole cause of the appellant's
temporary impairment of consciousness was a 'disease of the mind'. The appellant also
sought leave to call further medical evidence on the issue of diabetes and hyperglycaemia.
The facts are set out in the judgment of the court.

*Timothy Owen* (assigned by the Registrar of Criminal Appeals) for the appellant.           *c*
*Bernard Phelvin* for the Crown.

**LORD LANE CJ** delivered the following judgment of the court. On 15 January 1988,
on the second day of a trial in the Crown Court at Lewes before his Honour Judge Birks
and a jury, following a ruling on the defence of non-insane automatism, this appellant,
Andrew Michael Hennessy, now 27 years of age, pleaded guilty and was sentenced as     *d*
follows: first of all on count 1, for taking a conveyance without authority, nine months'
imprisonment suspended for two years; count 2, driving while disqualified, six months'
imprisonment to run concurrently, also suspended for two years. He was disqualified
from holding or obtaining a driving licence for two years and his driving licence was
endorsed. Also a community service order made in March 1988 was ordered to continue.

He now appeals against conviction by a certificate of the trial judge. The judge's     *e*
certificate, to read it somewhat out of chronological order, was as follows:

'The defendant, who is diabetic, claimed that he did not know what he was doing
when the offence was committed because he was suffering from hyperglycaemia,
having failed to take insulin for some days. He sought to raise the defence of
automatism. I rejected this on the ground that his alleged mental condition, if it     *f*
existed, was caused by disease, namely diabetes.'

The facts which gave rise to the charges, in so far as material, were these. On Thursday,
28 May 1987, two police constables, Barnes and Grace, were on duty in St Leonards-on-
Sea on the Sussex coast, among other things looking for a Ford Granada car which had
been stolen. They found the car. It was unattended. They kept it under watch. As they
watched they saw the appellant get into the car, switch on the headlights and ignition,     *g*
start the car and drive off. The appellant at the wheel of the car correctly stopped the car
at a set of traffic lights which were showing red against him. Pc Grace then went over to
the car as it was stationary, removed the ignition keys from the ignition lock, but not
before the appellant had tried to drive the motor car away and escape from the attention
of the policeman. The appellant was put in the police car. On the way to the police     *h*
station an informal conversation about motor vehicles took place between the appellant
and the police officers, in particular about the respective merits of the new Rover motor
car and the Ford Sierra. Indeed, the appellant appeared to Pc Barnes not only to be fully
in possession of his faculties but to be quite cheerful and intelligent. Indeed he went so
far as to say to the police officer that if he had only got the car, which he was in the
process of removing, onto the open road, he would have given the policemen a real run     *j*
for their money.

However after having been at the police station for a time, the appellant was at a later
stage escorted by Pc Barnes to hospital. He seemed to be normal when he left the cell
block at the police station, but when he arrived at the hospital he appeared to be dazed
and confused. He complained to the sister in the casualty ward that he had failed to take

a his insulin and indeed had had no insulin since the previous Monday when he should have had regular self-injected doses. He was given insulin, with which he injected himself, and the hospital discharged him and he was taken back to the police station.

The appellant gave evidence to the effect that he had been a diabetic for about ten years. He needed, in order to stabilise his metabolism, two insulin injections on a daily basis, morning and afternoon. The amount required would depend on factors such as stress and eating habits. He was on a strict carbohydrate diet. At the time of the offence
b he said he had been having marital and employment problems. His wife had submitted a divorce petition some time shortly before, and he was very upset. He had not been eating and he had not been taking his insulin. He remembered very few details of the day. He could recall being handcuffed and taken to the chargeroom at the police station. He remembered being given insulin at the hospital and injecting himself and he remembers feeling better when he got back to the police station afterwards. He said he
c did not recall taking the car.

When cross-examined he agreed that he had understood proceedings at the police station and what had gone on there. Indeed he had given the name and address of his solicitor. That was a considerable time before he had had his insulin at the hospital.

His general practitioner, Dr Higginson, was called to give evidence. He spoke as to the appellant's medical condition. He described in broad outlines the effect of diabetes: it is a
d deficiency in the system of the production of hormones which should balance the sugar metabolism. The lacking hormone is of course insulin. In the absence of the hormone the blood sugar rises and that results in hyperglycaemia. If the patient does not take his insulin and does not stick to the proper diet, then hyperglycaemia will supervene. If unchecked, the liver will become affected and the increasingly high level of sugar makes the patient drowsy and he will ultimately go into a coma.
e If on the other hand the balance tips the other way, if too much insulin is taken, then the blood sugar will fall and hypoglycaemia, that is to say too little sugar in the blood, will supervene.

According to the hospital notes, on the evening in question the appellant's blood sugar had been high at 22 plus millimolecules per litre, the normal being 8 or 9. According to Dr Higginson one would expect to see some physical manifestation of hyperglycaemia at
f that level. So the doctor was saying in short that eventually hyperglycaemia can result in drowsiness, loss of consciousness and coma, greater or less unresponsiveness to stimuli according to the degree of hyperglycaemia present. He added, I will read a passage from his evidence in a moment, that anxiety or depression can increase the blood sugar level, a person's ability and awareness of what is going on could be impaired if there were 'associated symptoms and he had other conditions and worries at the same time . . .'
g If one reads a passage from Dr Higginson's evidence, it says:

'Q. What if a person was in a state of anxiety or depression at the same time as having high blood sugar? A. The blood sugar tends to be increased in the ordinary diabetic by any trauma or psychological stress, so the answer to your question is yes, it would go up.
h Q. What about the person's ability and awareness of what was going on, would that be impaired or could it be impaired? A. I think if there was associated symptoms and he had other conditions and worries at the same time, yes it could be impaired.'

Then in answer to a question by the trial judge the doctor said:

j 'There is a great individual variability in this situation, and it is difficult to be dogmatic, but I think that would be a reasonable explanation of someone who is under a lot of stress and had a very high level of blood sugar . . . He might not be clear about what he was doing; he might be a bit befuddled. It is well known that the reverse condition, hypoglycaemia produces these symptoms very markedly. From time to time people are arrested for being drunk.'

The defence to these charges accordingly was that the appellant had failed to take his proper twice a day dose of insulin for two or three days and at the time the events in question took place he was in a state of automatism and did not know what he was doing. Therefore it is submitted that the guilty mind, which is necessary to be proved by the prosecution, was not proved, and accordingly that he was entitled to be acquitted.

The judge took the view, rightly in our view, that the appellant, having put his state of mind in issue, the preliminary question which he had to decide was whether this was truly a case of automatism or whether it was a case of legal 'insanity' within the M'Naghten rules (see M'Naghten's Case (1843) 10 Cl & Fin 200, [1843–60] All ER Rep 229). He concluded that it was the latter, and he so ruled, whereupon the appellant changed his plea to guilty and was sentenced to the terms of imprisonment suspended which we have already mentioned. The judge then certified the case fit for appeal in the terms which I have already described.

The M'Naghten rules in the earlier part of the last century have in many ways lost their importance; they certainly have lost the importance they once had, but they are still relevant in so far as they may affect the defence of automatism. Although the rules deal with what they describe as insanity, it is insanity in the legal sense and not in the medical or psychological sense. The rules were, as is well known, embodied in replies given by the judges of the day to certain abstract questions which were placed before them. The historical reasons for the questions being posed it is not necessary for us to describe, interesting though they are.

The answers to the questions were: first of all that—

> 'every man is to be presumed to be sane, and to possess a sufficient degree of reason to be responsible for his crimes, until the contrary be proved to [the] satisfaction of [the jury] . . .'

The second rule is that—

> 'to establish a defence on the ground of insanity, it must be clearly proved that, at the time of the committing of the act, the party accused was labouring under such a defect of reason, from disease of the mind, as not to know the nature and quality of the act he was doing; or, if he did know it, that he did not know he was doing what was wrong.'

(See 10 Cl & Fin 200 at 210, [1843–60] All ER Rep 229 at 233.)

The importance of the rules in the present context, namely the context of automatism, is this. If the defendant did not know the nature and quality of his act because of something which *did not* amount to defect of reason from disease of the mind then he will probably be entitled to be acquitted on the basis that the necessary criminal intent which the prosecution has to prove is not proved. But, if, on the other hand, his failure to realise the nature and quality of his act was due to a defect of reason from disease of the mind, then in the eyes of the law he is suffering from insanity, albeit M'Naghten insanity.

It should perhaps be added, in order to complete the picture, though it is not relevant to the present situation, that where a defendant's failure to appreciate what he was doing was wrong (that is the second part of the second of the M'Naghten rules) where that failure is due to some reason other than a defect of reason from disease of the mind he will generally have no valid defence at all.

If one wants any confirmation, it is to be found, if we may respectfully say so, in Smith and Hogan Criminal Law (6th edn, 1988) p 186, where these matters are very helpfully and clearly set out. If we may just cite the passage from that page, it runs as follows:

> 'When a defendant puts his state of mind in issue, the question whether he has raised the defence of insanity is one of law for the judge. Whether D, or indeed his medical witnesses, would call the condition on which he relies "insanity", is

immaterial. The expert witnesses may testify as to the factual nature of the condition but it is for the judge to say whether that is evidence of "a defect of reason, from disease of the mind", because, as will appear, these are legal, not medical, concepts.'

Then by s 2 of the Trial of Lunatics Act 1883, as amended, it is provided as follows:

'(1) Where in any indictment or information any act or omission is charged against any person as an offence, and it is given in evidence on the trial of such person for that offence that he was insane, so as not to be responsible according to law, for his actions at the time when the act was done or omission made, then, if it appears to the jury before whom such person is tried that he did the act or made the omission charged, but was insane as aforesaid at the time when he did or made the same, the jury shall return a *special verdict that the accused is not guilty by reason of insanity*.'

In the present case, therefore, what had to be decided was whether the defendant's condition was properly described as a disease of the mind. That does not mean any disease of the brain. It means a disease which affects the proper functioning of the mind. There have been a series of authorities on that particular subject. One such instance is *R v Kemp* [1956] 3 All ER 249, [1957] 1 QB 399 and the judgment of Devlin J therein.

The question in many cases, and this is one such case, is whether the function of the mind was disturbed on the one hand by disease or on the other hand by some external factor. The matter was discussed, as counsel for the appellant has helpfully pointed out to us, by the House of Lords in *R v Sullivan* [1983] 2 All ER 673 at 677–678, [1984] AC 156 at 172 in the speech of Lord Diplock, which reads as follows:

'I agree with what was said by Devlin J in *R v Kemp* [1956] 3 All ER 249 at 253, [1957] 1 QB 399 at 407 that "mind" in the M'Naghten Rules is used in the ordinary sense of the mental faculties of reason, memory and understanding. If the effect of a disease is to impair these faculties so severely as to have either of the consequences referred to in the latter part of the rules, it matters not whether the aetiology of the impairment is organic, as in epilepsy, or functional, or whether the impairment itself is permanent or is transient and intermittent, provided that it subsisted at the time of commission of the act. The purpose of the legislation relating to the defence of insanity, ever since its origin in 1880, has been to protect society against recurrence of the dangerous conduct. The duration of a temporary suspension of the mental faculties of reason, memory and understanding, particularly if, as in the appellant's case, it is recurrent, cannot on any rational ground be relevant to the application by the courts of the M'Naghten Rules, though it may be relevant to the course adopted by the Secretary of State, to whom the responsibility for how the defendant is to be dealt with passes after the return of the special verdict of not guilty by reason of insanity.'

The point was neatly raised in *R v Quick, R v Paddison* [1973] 3 All ER 347, [1973] QB 910, also referred to us by counsel for the appellant, in which Lawton LJ reviewed the authorities. It might perhaps help if I read a short passage from the headnote ([1973] QB 910):

'The defendants, Q and P, nurses at a mental hospital, were jointly and severally charged with assaulting a patient occasioning actual bodily harm. Both pleaded not guilty. Q, a diabetic, relied on the defence of automatism. He gave evidence that he had taken insulin as prescribed on the morning of the assault, had drunk a quantity of spirits and eaten little food thereafter and had no recollection of the assault. He called medical evidence to the effect that his condition at the material time was consistent with that of hypoglycaemia. The judge ruled that that evidence could only support a defence of insanity, not automatism. Q then pleaded guilty and P was convicted of aiding and abetting Q by encouragement. The defendants appealed against conviction.'  *a*

I turn to the passage in the judgment where Lawton LJ said ([1973] 3 All ER 347 at 356, [1973] QB 910 at 922–923):

'A malfunctioning of the mind of transitory effect caused by the application to the body of some external factor such as violence, drugs, including anaesthetics, alcohol and hypnotic influences cannot fairly be said to be due to disease. Such  *b*
malfunctioning, unlike that caused by a defect of reason from disease of the mind, will not always relieve an accused from criminal responsibility ... In this case Quick's alleged mental condition, if it ever existed, was not caused by his diabetes but by his use of the insulin prescribed by his doctor. Such malfunctioning of his mind as there was, was caused by an external factor and not by a bodily disorder in the nature of a disease which disturbed the working of his mind. It follows in our  *c*
judgment that Quick was entitled to have his defence of automatism left to the jury and that Bridge J's ruling as to the effect of the medical evidence called by him was wrong.'

Thus in *R v Quick* the fact that his condition was, or may have been, due to the injections of insulin meant that the malfunction was due to an external factor and not to  *d*
the disease. The drug it was that caused the hypoglycaemia, the low blood sugar. As suggested in another passage of the judgment of Lawton LJ, hyperglycaemia, high blood sugar, caused by an inherent defect and not corrected by insulin is a disease, and if, as the defendant was asserting here, it does cause a malfunction of the mind, then the case may fall within the M'Naghten rules.

The burden of the argument of counsel for the appellant to us is this. It is that the  *e*
appellant's depression and marital troubles were a sufficiently potent external factor in his condition to override, so to speak, the effect of the diabetic shortage of insulin on him. He refers us not only to the passage which I have already cited in *R v Quick*, but also to a further passage in *Hill v Baxter* [1958] 1 All ER 193 at 197, [1958] 1 QB 277 at 285 which is part of the judgment of Devlin J, sitting with Lord Goddard CJ and Pearson J, in the Divisional Court of Queen's Bench Division. It reads as follows:  *f*

'I have drawn attention to the fact that the accused did not set up a defence of insanity. For the purposes of the criminal law there are two categories of mental irresponsibility, one where the disorder is due to disease and the other where it is not. The distinction is not an arbitrary one. If disease is not the cause, if there is some temporary loss of consciousness arising accidentally, it is reasonable to hope  *g*
that it will not be repeated and that it is safe to let an acquitted man go entirely free. If, however, disease is present, the same thing may happen again and therefore since 1800 the law has provided that persons acquitted on this ground should be subject to restraint.'

That is the submission made by counsel as a basis for saying the judge's decision was  *h*
wrong and that this was a matter which should have been decided by the jury.

In our judgment, stress, anxiety and depression can no doubt be the result of the operation of external factors, but they are not, it seems to us, in themselves separately or together external factors of the kind capable in law of causing or contributing to a state of automatism. They constitute a state of mind which is prone to recur. They lack the feature of novelty or accident, which is the basis of the distinction drawn by Lord Diplock  *j*
in *R v Sullivan*. It is contrary to the observations of Devlin J, to which we have just referred in *Hill v Baxter*. It does not, in our judgment, come within the scope of the exception 'some external physical factor such as a blow on the head ... or the administration of an anaesthetic ...' (see *R v Sullivan* [1983] 2 All ER 673 at 678, [1984] AC 156 at 172).

For those reasons we reject the arguments, able though they were, of counsel for the
*a* appellant. It is not in those circumstances necessary for us to consider the further
arguments which he addressed to us based on the decision in *R v Bailey* [1983] 2 All ER
503, [1983] 1 WLR 760. In our judgment the reasoning and judgment of the circuit
judge were correct.

Accordingly this appeal must be dismissed.

*b  Appeal dismissed.*

Solicitors: *Crown Prosecution Service*, Lewes.

N P Metcalfe Esq    Barrister.

*c*   # R v Chief Constable of the Avon and Somerset Constabulary, ex parte Robinson

QUEEN'S BENCH DIVISION

WATKINS, MANN LJJ AND AULD J

*d* 1 DECEMBER 1988, 12 JANUARY, 2 FEBRUARY 1989

*Solicitor – Access to – Right of person in custody – Access by solicitor's clerk – Solicitor employing
unqualified clerks to visit clients held in police custody – Chief constable issuing instructions that
presence of such clerks at police interviews with suspects undesirable – Instructions leaving decision
on access by clerks in particular cases to individual custody officers – Whether chief constable's
e instructions contrary to code of practice for detention of suspects – Code of Practice for the
Detention, Treatment and Questioning of Persons by Police Officers, para 6.9.*

The applicant solicitor, whose firm specialised in legal aid defences in criminal cases
concerning the black community, employed several clerks, who were not legally
qualified, to visit on his behalf clients held in police custody. The chief constable for the
*f* police area in which the applicant practised issued instructions to his police force to the
effect that the character and antecedents of various unqualified clerks employed by the
applicant was such as to make their presence at police interviews with suspects
undesirable. In a general instruction issued in 1988 the chief constable stated that the
presumption of integrity applicable to solicitors did not apply to clerks and that he
intended to circulate to custody officers details of clerks thought to be undesirable to
*g* enable them to decide whether those clerks should be allowed access to persons in
custody, and in four particular instructions issued shortly thereafter relating to clerks
employed by the applicant he stated that although he could not impose on custody
officers a decision restricting access by the applicant's clerks it was his opinion that there
would be very few occasions on which it would be appropriate to allow those clerks access
to persons in custody. The applicant applied for judicial review of the chief constable's
*h* instructions, contending that they were in breach of para 6.9[a] of the Code of Practice for
the Detention, Treatment and Questioning of Persons by Police Officers issued by the
Secretary of State under s 66 of the Police and Criminal Evidence Act 1984. Paragraph
6.9 provided that a solicitor's clerk was to be admitted to a police station for the purpose
of seeing a person held in custody unless a police officer of the rank of inspector or above
considered 'that such a visit will hinder the investigation of crime'.

*j*

**Held** – Although a genuine solicitor's clerk who was competent to give advice on behalf
of the solicitor could not be refused access to a person in custody on the ground that his
advice was likely to be bad, the police were entitled to refuse access to persons in custody

_____

*a*  Paragraph 6.9 is set out at p 17 *e*, post

by a clerk who was not a genuine clerk or whose visit the police knew or believed, from
his criminal record or associations, would hinder the investigation of crime or who the     *a*
police knew or believed was not capable of providing advice on behalf of the solicitor.
Whether such a visit might hinder the investigation of a crime was a matter for the
subjective judgment of an officer of the rank of inspector or above based on any
knowledge he might have of the clerk in question. Since the chief constable had left the
actual decision whether to deny the applicant's clerks access to persons in custody to
individual custody officers or their inspectors and had not imposed a blanket ban on the     *b*
applicant's clerks the chief constable's instructions were not contrary to para 6.9 of the
code of practice. The application would therefore be dismissed (see p 17 *f* to p 18 *b* and
p 21 *b* to *d*, post).

**Notes**
For the right of a detained person to access to legal advice, see Supplement to 11     *c*
Halsbury's Laws (4th edn) para 120B.5.
    For the Police and Criminal Evidence Act 1984, s 66, see 12 Halsbury's Statutes (4th
edn) 1019.

**Case referred to in judgment**
*R v Samuel* [1988] 2 All ER 135, [1988] QB 615, [1988] 2 WLR 920, CA.     *d*

**Cases also cited**
*B (solicitor's clerk), Re* (1988) Times, 19 April, DC.
*R v Pollumn* (1 November 1983, unreported), SC Taxing Office.
*R v Sherratt* (19 June 1986, unreported), Crown Ct at Stafford.

**Application for judicial review**     *e*
Timothy Morgan Robinson, a solicitor practising as Robinsons in Bristol, applied with
the leave of Roch J given on 7 June 1988 for judicial review by way of, inter alia, (i) an
order of mandamus quashing a directive issued by or on behalf of the respondent, the
Chief Constable of the Avon and Somerset Constabulary, relating to access by clerks
employed by the applicant to persons held in police custody, (ii) a declaration that issuing     *f*
such directives was unlawful and (iii) an injunction restraining the issuing of such
directives. The facts are set out in the judgment of the court.

*David Elfer QC* and *Bernard Buckley* for the applicant.
*R N Titheridge QC* and *Malcolm Cotterill* for the respondent.
*Andrew Nicol* for the Law Society.     *g*

                                                            *Cur adv vult*

2 February. The following judgment of the court was delivered.

**MANN LJ.** The judgment which I am about to give was prepared by me and has been     *h*
agreed by Watkins LJ and Auld J, neither of whom, for differing reasons, is able to be
present today. There is before the court an application for judicial review. Leave to move
was granted by Roch J after an oral hearing on 7 June 1988.
    The applicant is a solicitor whose firm specialises in legal aid defences in criminal cases
concerning the black community in Bristol. This is not a remunerative field of activity.
Many solicitors will not contemplate it and we were told by counsel who helpfully     *j*
appeared for the Law Society that there is an economic necessity to employ persons who
have no professional qualifications to attend at the interview of suspects. The applicant
employs such persons. Among the persons he has used are Junior Benjamin, Anthony
Campbell, Paul Whitcliffe, Rodney Wilson and Damian Whitlow. Junior Benjamin is no
longer relevant to these proceedings because the applicant has accepted that Benjamin is

an unsuitable person to attend any interview. The five whom we have named are not
*a* employed by the applicant but they are employed by either Southmead Law Services Ltd
or Bristol Law Services Ltd. Those are two companies controlled by the applicant and
which have no purpose other than that of providing staff and services to the applicant's
firm. The reason for the formation of these service companies is a fiscal one. No objection
is taken by the Revenue and the Law Society approves of service companies providing a
firm with services and staff. In those circumstances we do not comment on the
*b* arrangement which has been made and are prepared for present purposes to assume
without deciding that the persons in question are 'in effect' employed by the applicant.

The respondent to this application does not require any description.

The application arises in the context of Code C, which is the *Code of Practice for the
Detention, Treatment and Questioning of Persons by Police Officers* which has been issued by
the Secretary of State for the Home Department in pursuance of his duty under s 66 of
*c* the Police and Criminal Evidence Act 1984. Section 58 of that Act provides:

'(1) A person arrested and held in custody in a police station or other premises
shall be entitled, if he so requests, to consult a solicitor privately at any time . . .'

There are elaborate provisions governing the circumstances in which delay in
complying with a request is justified. Paragraphs 6.1 to 6.8 of Code C further fill out the
*d* position in regard to solicitors. We need not recite those provisions. The critical provision
for our purposes is para 6.9:

'In this code "solicitor" means a solicitor qualified to practise in accordance with
the Solicitors Act 1974. If a solicitor wishes to send a clerk or legal executive to
provide advice on his behalf, then the clerk or legal executive shall be admitted to
*e* the police station for this purpose unless an officer of the rank of inspector or above
considers that such a visit will hinder the investigation of crime and directs
otherwise. Once admitted to the police station, the provisions of paragraphs 6.3 to
6.7 apply.'

It is apparent that there is only one ground on which the clerk or legal executive can
*f* be excluded from the police station and that is that his visit would hinder the investigation
of crime. That, of course, is a matter for the subjective judgment of the officer being an
officer of the rank of inspector or above. However, although there is but one express
reason justifying exclusion there is a prefatory question which must be asked, that is to
say is the person who seeks admission 'a clerk or legal executive'? There should be no
difficulty in identifying a legal executive, but who is a 'clerk'? The expression 'clerk to a
*g* solicitor' occurs in the Solicitors Act 1974 (see for example s 43) but nowhere in either
statute or case law is the expression 'clerk' defined. Leaving aside for the moment the
question whether the inspector may not be entitled to exclude an obviously incompetent
person on the basis that he is likely to 'hinder', it seems to us that there are certain matters
which are necessarily implicit in the words of para 6.9.

The first of those implicit matters is that the clerk must be sent by the solicitor to
*h* provide 'advice on his behalf', and if the police know or believe that the person is not
capable of providing advice on behalf of the solicitor, whether because of his appearance,
his age, his mental capacity or because of the police knowledge of him, they are entitled
to refuse to allow him to enter the police station.

The second implicit matter, which is perhaps the same point differently expressed, is
that the person must be a 'clerk' genuinely so-called and not someone recruited, so to
*j* speak, off the streets masquerading as a clerk. In this case also, if the police know or
believe that the person is merely a colourable pretence of a clerk, they are entitled to
exclude him from the station.

We return to the hindering point. There may be circumstances where the police know
that the person has a record of convictions, they may know that he is criminally
orientated if unsullied by detection. In those circumstances, likewise, they will be entitled

to conclude that to admit such a person to the station to tender advice would hinder the investigation of crime.                                                                          *a*

If a person is ostensibly capable of giving advice then we do not think that the police could refuse admission on the basis that the quality of the advice would be poor. We see no objection to the police forming a view on capacity but we think it would be unfortunate if the police were also to form a view on quality. That being said, we are anxious about quality. Under the Law Society's Legal Aid (Duty Solicitor) Scheme 1985, as amended, there are in para 47 detailed provisions about duty solicitors' representatives. *b* For example, if the representative is a solicitor's clerk he must have had at least three years' experience of criminal defence work. No such provisions apply where a solicitor is privately chosen. We think it is of importance that a person sent by a solicitor should be competent. We think the Law Society should consider urgently whether or not the situation envisaged by para 6.9 of Code C does not deserve some provision similar to that in the duty solicitor scheme. In each case competence should be required.                    *c*

We turn now to the instant case. The decision impugned is 'directive issued by or on behalf of the Chief Constable of the Avon and Somerset Constabulary relating to access by Defendants to their Solicitors and other Legal Representatives'. We do not consider there was any directive but there were a number of instructions issued by the deputy chief constable. There was a general instruction, dated 31 March 1988, in the following terms:                                                                               *d*

> 'This instruction replaces paragraphs 3 to 5 of my instruction dated 31st January 1986, and the whole of my later instructions dated May 1986 and 18th December 1987.
>
> *General Princicples*
> 2. A person in custody has the legal right to consult a solicitor privately at any *e* time. However, it should be noted that: (a) The right is that of the prisoner, and not of the solicitor. (b) If the nominated solicitor chooses to employ a clerk different considerations apply (see later).
> 3. Access to a solicitor cannot be denied, but may be delayed in accordance with section 58 of the Police and Criminal Evidence Act and section 6 of Code C.
> 4. Delay can only be authorised: (i) By an officer of Superintendent rank. (ii) *f* Where the person is detained for a "Serious Arrestable Offence".
>
> *Denial of Access to a Solicitor's Clerk*
> 5. Section 58 confers the right to consult a solicitor. In the first instance there is no *right* to consult a solicitor's clerk but if the solicitor, once contacted, decides to send a clerk, access will be permitted in accordance with Code C paragraph 6.9.     *g*
> 6. It follows that access to a clerk may not be "delayed" under section 58 but could, instead, be *denied* under paragraphs 6.9 and 6.10 of Code C.
> 7. A decision to deny access to a clerk must be taken by an officer of Inspector rank or above and there is no obligation to give reasons. As a matter of policy reasons will not be given.                                                                        *h*
>
> *Further Considerations regarding Solicitors*
> 8. Case law has established that police officers must assume that solicitors will act with professional integrity. The most recent case is that of SAMUEL [see [1988] 2 All ER 135, [1988] QB 615] and a copy of the case report is attached at "A".
> 9. A decision to delay access can only be justified where a Superintendent has reasonable grounds for believing that access *will* lead to one of the consequences *j* listed in section 58(8). It is not sufficient to believe that such consequences may arise.
> 10. Where one solicitor represents more than one suspect in a particular case it cannot be *assumed* that there will be any transference of information between those suspects. If access is to be delayed in such circumstances it must be because of facts specific to that case, or to that individual solicitor.

11. In practice access will rarely be delayed merely because one solicitor acts for more than one suspect. Case law has determined that the officers involved should merely remind the solicitor to be careful. If access is delayed on these grounds, it is open to the suspect to nominate an alternative solicitor.

*Further Consideration Regarding Clerks*

12. The same presumption of "integrity" does not apply to Clerks. Where two or more suspects are in custody, and it is feared that information may pass between them, a Clerk will not normally be permitted access to any prisoner in the first instance. Access will be denied and the solicitor concerned informed in accordance with paragraph 6.10 of Code C.

13. In the general case the grounds on which access may be denied are much broader than those in section 58. An officer of Inspector rank must "consider that such a visit will hinder the investigation of crime."

14. Officers who do not know whether or not a particular individual is a solicitor, or merely a clerk, are quite entitled to ask such a person for that information. They may also, if necessary, ask for proof of identification.

*Special Procedure Regarding Clerks*

15. I am very concerned about the increasing use of unqualified Clerks whose character and antecedents is such as to make their presence at interviews undesirable. There have, in particular, been examples of Clerks with previous criminal convictions.

16. I have considered the possibility of issuing a "blanket ban" on Clerks whom I consider to be undesirable. I believe, however, that such a ban would be inappropriate because: (a) The Code of Practice places the decision with individual Inspectors to make, on the merits of the particular case. (Code C 6.9). (b) However undesirable a Clerk may be there might be occasion when access to a prisoner would be of no conceivable harm—for example where the prisoner has already been charged and no further enquiries are in being.

17. I intend, in future, to circulate details of such Clerks who come to my attention. Those details will include character, antecedents and behaviour in earlier cases. In so doing I would hope that Custody Officers, and their Inspectors will be better equipped to decide whether or not a Clerk should be admitted.

18. Where officers have reason to believe that a Clerk should be identified in this way, they should report the details to me through their Divisional Commanders.

19. There have been several occasions when police officers have been confronted with quite disgraceful behaviour by Solicitors' Clerks, and I am determined that such instances will not be tolerated. Individual Inspectors who decide to exercise their authority under paragraph 6.9 of Code C, may be assured of my full support.

20. It must be emphasised that when a Clerk is excluded, the solicitor concerned will be informed immediately in accordance with paragraph 6.10 of Code C, and given the opportunity to make alternative arrangements.'

This general instruction was followed by a number of particular instructions dated 29 April 1988. In regard to Rodney Wilson the instruction was in these terms:

'1. I refer to my instruction of 31st March, 1988 which deals with access by persons in custody to legal advice.

2. Mr. Wilson appears to be a Clerk employed by Messrs. Robinsons, Solicitors and I attach a report from Police Constable 639 Dalley which describes his conduct on 17th March, 1988.

3. Whilst I cannot, for the reasons given in my instruction impose decisions of this kind upon individual officers, it is my opinion that there will be very few occasions on which it would be appropriate to allow this man access to persons in custody.

4. Divisional Commanders must ensure that this information is circulated to

officers of their Divisions, and that copies are retained *inconspicuously* in custody offices.

     5. Details of each occasion when Wilson is denied entry will be reported to Chief Superintendent "K" Division who will collate that information, and deal with any correspondence received from the solicitors concerned.'

In regard to Anthony Campbell the instruction was in these terms:

     '1. I refer to my instruction of 31st March, 1988 which deals with access by persons in custody to legal advice.

     2. Mr. Campbell, whose full name has not yet been ascertained, will be well known to officers of the Bristol Division. He is employed as a Clerk by Robinsons, Solicitors and I have received a number of reports concerning his conduct which are attached.

     3. Whilst I cannot, for the reasons given in my instructions impose decisions of this kind upon individual officers, it is my opinion that there will be very few occasions on which it would be appropriate to allow this man access to persons in custody.

     4. Divisional Commanders must ensure that this information is circulated to officers of their Divisions, and that copies are retained *inconspicuously* in custody offices.

     5. Details of each occasion when Campbell is denied entry will be reported to Chief Superintendent "K" Division who will collate that information, and deal with any correspondence received from the solicitors concerned.'

In regard to Paul Whitcliffe the instruction was in these terms:

     '1. I refer to my instruction of 31st March, 1988 which deals with access by persons in custody to legal advice.

     2. Paul Anthony Whitcliffe appears to be a Clerk employed by Messrs. Robinsons, Solicitors and it will be seen from the attached report of Detective Constable Audus that he has one previous conviction for conspiracy to defraud.

     3. Whilst I cannot, for the reasons given in my instruction impose decisions of this kind upon individual officers, it is my opinion that there will be very few occasions on which it would be appropriate to allow this man access to persons in custody.

     4. Divisional Commanders must ensure that this information is circulated to officers of their Divisions, and that copies are retained *inconspicuously* in custody offices.

     5. Details of each occasion when Whitcliffe is denied entry will be reported to Chief Superintendent "K" Division who will collate that information, and deal with any correspondence received from the solicitors concerned.'

Somewhat later on 6 June 1988 the deputy chief constable circulated to the divisional commanders the following memorandum in regard to Damian Whitlow:

     '1. I refer to my instruction of 31st March, 1988 which deals with access by persons in custody to legal advice.

     2. Damian Whitlow will be well known to officers of the Bristol Division. He is employed as a clerk by Robinsons, Solicitors.

     3. I have received a report from W.P.C. Holt of "C" Division which is attached. I also attach comments made by the Force Solicitor in relation to that matter.

     4. I have also now received a report from Constable 3249 Spokes of "A" Division which is attached and contains further evidence of Mr. Whitlow's conduct.

     5. Whilst I cannot, for the reasons given in my instruction impose decisions of this kind upon individual officers, it is my opinion that there will be very few occasions on which it would be appropriate to allow this man access to persons in custody.

a
    6. Divisional Commanders must ensure that this information is circulated to officers of their Divisions, and that copies are retained *inconspicuously* in custody offices.

    7. Details of each occasion when Whitlow is denied entry will be reported to Chief Superintendent "K" Division who will collate that information, and deal with any correspondence received from the solicitors concerned.'

b
    We regard the general and particular instructions as paying scrupulous regard to the 1984 Act and to Code C. As is recognised in the instructions it is a matter for the individual police officer to decide in regard to admission but we see no reason why senior officers should not advise their subordinates of the activities or proclivities of clerks. That advice must not and cannot derogate from the individual responsibilities of the officer concerned with the investigation. He must make his own decision within the area with

c which he is empowered to do so and which we have endeavoured to describe earlier in this judgment.

    There was in this case no complaint by any suspect. There was in this case no direction how a discretion in regard to presence at interview should be exercised. It is quite plain on the evidence that police officers concerned with interview have been exercising an individual discretion in each case which comes before them because there has been no

d blanket ban on the clerks in question. The same or different officers have made the same or different decisions on different occasions, having regard, no doubt, to the information about the clerk in question to hand and the nature and circumstances of the investigation. We would accordingly and do dismiss this application.

    We would, however, add this. Pargraph 6.10 of Code C provides as follows:

e
    'If the inspector refuses access to a clerk or legal executive or a decision is taken that such a person should not be permitted to remain at an interview, he must forthwith notify a solicitor on whose behalf the clerk or legal executive was to have acted or was acting, and give him an opportunity of making alternative arrangements.'

    There has been no suggestion that this sub-paragraph has not been complied with in

f relation to the applicant's clerks. However, inspectors do not inform the solicitor why his clerk was refused an attendance. This seems to us to be a wise practice because of the risks of an action for defamation. A result of the present proceedings has been that the chief constable has undertaken to inform a solicitor why a particular clerk has been refused presence at an interview. We think it appropriate that such information should be given at chief officer level, or failing that by his deputy. How the information is given

g must be a matter for the chief constable to decide.

*Application dismissed.*

Solicitors: *Robinsons*, Bristol (for the applicant); *Susan A Dauncey*, Bristol (for the respondent); *Eric Hiley* (for the Law Society).

                                                               Sophie Craven   Barrister.

# Customs and Excise Commissioners v Air Canada

QUEEN'S BENCH DIVISION

TUCKER J

26 OCTOBER, 7 NOVEMBER 1988

*Customs and excise – Forfeiture – Aircraft used for carriage of thing liable to forfeiture – Used for carriage – Prohibited drugs discovered in container carried by aircraft on commercial scheduled flight – Proceedings by commissioners to forfeit aircraft – Whether carriage of prohibited goods per se rendering aircraft liable to forfeiture – Whether aircraft liable to forfeiture only if airline knew or ought to have known that prohibited goods were on board – Customs and Excise Management Act 1979, s 141(1)(a).*

An aircraft owned and operated by a commercial airline made a regular scheduled flight from Singapore to Toronto via Bombay and London. Cargo unloaded at London from the aircraft was found to include a container holding 331 kg of cannabis resin with an estimated street value of £800,000. After the aircraft's departure from Heathrow it made several international flights, including flights to the United Kingdom, before it was seized by the Customs and Excise, who claimed it was liable to forfeiture under s 141(1)(a)ᵃ of the Customs and Excise Management Act 1979 because carriage of the container constituted 'use of the aircraft for the carriage of a thing liable for forfeiture'. On the same day the aircraft was delivered up to the airline on payment of £50,000, pursuant to s 139(5) of the 1979 Act. The Commissioners of Customs and Excise subsequently commenced proceedings for an order for condemnation of the aircraft under para 6 of Sch 3 to the 1979 Act or, alternatively, an order under s 144 that there were reasonable grounds for its seizure. The master ordered trial of certain preliminary issues, including (i) whether the fact that cannabis resin was found in a container which had been carried by an aircraft on a scheduled flight constituted 'use of the aircraft for the carriage of a thing liable for forfeiture' within s 141(1)(a) of the 1979 Act such as to justify its subsequent seizure and (ii) whether there could be a defence on the part of the airline to the action brought by the commissioners.

**Held** – The offence in s 141(1)(a) of the 1979 Act of using an aircraft 'for the carriage of a thing liable to forfeiture', thereby making the aircraft itself liable to forfeiture, was not an absolute offence and the mere fact that prohibited drugs were found in a container which had been carried by a commercial aircraft on a scheduled flight did not per se constitute an offence under s 141(1)(a) since it was a defence to a claim by the commissioners to seize the aircraft for the airline to establish that it did not know and was not reckless in failing to discover that the container contained prohibited drugs or that it could not with reasonable diligence have discovered the drugs or prevented them from being secreted in the container. The preliminary issues would therefore be determined in favour of the airline (see p 33 *b* to *h*, post).

Dicta of Lord Reid in *Warner v Metropolitan Police Comr* [1968] 2 All ER 356 at 366–367 and of Lord Reid in *Sweet v Parsley* [1969] 1 All ER 347 at 349 applied.

*De Keyser v British Railway Traffic and Electric Co Ltd* [1936] 1 KB 224 and *Customs and Excise Comrs v Jack Bradley (Accrington) Ltd* [1958] 3 All ER 487 distinguished.

**Notes**

For the power of the Commissioners of Customs and Excise to seize aircraft etc, see 12 Halsbury's Laws (4th edn) para 626.

---

ᵃ    Section 141(1), so far as material, is set out at p 25 *b c*, post

a   For the Customs and Excise Management Act 1979, s 141, see 13 Halsbury's Statutes
(4th edn) 410.

### Cases referred to in judgment
A-G v Lockwood (1842) 9 M & W 378, 152 ER 160.
Associated Provincial Picture Houses Ltd v Wednesbury Corp [1947] 2 All ER 680, [1948] 1
KB 223, CA.
b   Customs and Excise Comrs v Jack Bradley (Accrington) Ltd [1958] 3 All ER 487, [1959] 1 QB
219, [1958] 3 WLR 639.
De Keyser v British Railway Traffic and Electric Co Ltd [1936] 1 KB 224, DC.
Denton v John Lister Ltd [1971] 3 All ER 669, [1971] 1 WLR 1426, DC.
Gammon (Hong Kong) Ltd v A-G of Hong Kong [1984] 2 All ER 503, [1985] AC 1, [1984] 3
WLR 437, PC.
c   Lim Chin Aik v R [1963] 1 All ER 223, [1963] AC 160, [1963] 2 WLR 42, PC.
Sweet v Parsley [1969] 1 All ER 347, [1970] AC 132, [1969] 2 WLR 470, HL.
Warner v Metropolitan Police Comr [1968] 2 All ER 356, [1969] 2 AC 256, [1968] 2 WLR
1303, HL.
Yeandel v Fisher [1965] 3 All ER 158, [1966] 1 QB 440, [1965] 3 WLR 1002, DC.

d   ### Case also cited
Allgemeine Gold- und Silberscheideanstalt AG v UK (1986) 9 EHRR 1, E Ct HR.

### Preliminary issues
The Commissioners of Customs and Excise issued a writ on 27 August 1987 against the
defendants, Air Canada, claiming an order for condemnation of an aircraft which was
e   found to have carried in its cargo a container with 331 kg of cannabis resin with an
estimated street value of £800,000, pursuant to para 6 of Sch 3 to the Customs and Excise
Management Act 1979, or, alternatively, an order under s 144 of that Act that there were
reasonable grounds for the seizure of the aircraft. On 8 June 1988 Master Hodgson made
a consent order that there should be a determination of four preliminary issues:
f   (1) whether the facts (a) that cannabis resin was found in the container and (b) that that
container had been carried by the aircraft alone constituted 'use of the aircraft for the
carriage of a thing liable to forfeiture' within s 141(1)(a) of the 1979 Act such as to justify
its subsequent seizure; (2) whether it was a defence to the commissioners' claim if the
defendants established that they did not know that the container contained cannabis
resin and were not reckless in failing so to discover; (3) whether it was a defence if the
g   defendants established that they could not with reasonable diligence have discovered that
cannabis had been secreted and hidden or was being carried in the container nor by
reasonable diligence could they have prevented its being secreted; and (4) whether it was
necessary for the commissioners to prove (i) that the defendants knew or ought to have
known that cannabis resin was on board and/or (ii) that the aircraft was on other than a
regular scheduled flight. The facts are set out in the judgment.
h
Roger Ter Haar for the Crown.
Robert Webb QC and David Fisher for the defendants.

Cur adv vult

j   7 November. The following judgment was delivered.

**TUCKER J.** On 26 April 1987 a Tristar aeroplane owned and operated by the
defendants, Air Canada, landed at Heathrow Airport. The aircraft had made a regular
scheduled timetabled flight from Singapore via Bombay to Heathrow and was bound
from there to Toronto. It carried fare-paying members of the public as passengers and

also some cargo. The passengers were disembarked and the cargo was unloaded on arrival
at Heathrow. At about 9.20 am on the same day the aircraft continued its scheduled   a
flight to Toronto.

The unloading of the cargo took place under the supervision of HM Customs and
Excise. A number of containers were identified and were taken to the cargo area of the
airport. One of these containers was opened and it was found to contain a total of 331 kg
of cannabis resin, with an estimated street value of £800,000.

The importation of cannabis resin is prohibited under s 3(1) of the Misuse of Drugs   b
Act 1971. The cannabis resin was liable to forfeiture by virtue of s 49(1)(b) of the Customs
and Excise Management Act 1979.

After its departure from Heathrow on 26 April 1987 the aircraft made several
international flights, including flights to the United Kingdom.

On 1 May 1987 the aircraft was seized by representatives of the Customs and Excise as
liable to forfeiture under s 141(1) of the 1979 Act. On the same date, under the powers   c
contained in s 139(5) of and para 16 of Sch 3 to the 1979 Act, the aircraft was delivered
up on payment by the defendants of £50,000.

On 20 May 1987 solicitors acting on behalf of the defendants gave notice of claim
under para 3 of Sch 3, on the grounds that the aircraft was not liable to forfeiture.

The plaintiffs, the Commissioners of Customs and Excise, have now commenced
proceedings, claiming an order for condemnation of the aircraft, pursuant to para 6 of   d
Sch 3 or, in the alternative, an order pursuant to s 144 of the 1979 Act that there were
reasonable grounds for seizure of the aircraft. By their defence, the defendants contend
that the aircraft was not liable to forfeiture pursuant to s 141(1) of the Act or at all, by
reason of the following facts.

(a) It was not used for the carriage of cannabis resin. The defendants admit that a
substance alleged to be cannabis resin was found in the container referred to, and that the   e
container had been on the flight from Bombay to Heathrow, but they deny that those
facts alone constitute use of the aircraft, whether by the defendants or at all, for the
carriage of cannabis resin.

(b) The defendants did not know that the container contained cannabis resin nor were
they reckless in failing so to discover.

(c) Further or alternatively, the defendants could not with reasonable diligence have   f
discovered that cannabis had been secreted and hidden, or was being carried on the
container, if such was the case, nor could they by the exercise of reasonable diligence
have prevented it being secreted and hidden there.

The defendants accordingly deny that the aircraft was liable to forfeiture or that there
were any reasonable grounds for its seizure. The cannabis was found on 26 April 1987.
The aircraft was seized on 1 May 1987. They contend that at no time was it alleged that   g
the defendants knew or ought to have known that cannabis had been on board on 26
April 1987, nor was it alleged that the aircraft was on other than a regular scheduled and
legitimate flight.

On 8 June 1988 Master Hodgson made an order in the following agreed terms:
1. There should be a determination of the following as preliminary issues, on the   h
assumption that the facts and matters set out in paras 1 to 5, 7 and 8 of the statement of
claim and paras 1 and 2 of the defence are correct. (1) Whether the facts (a) that cannabis
resin was found in the container and (b) that that container had been carried by the
aircraft on the relevant flight on 26 April 1987 alone constitute 'use of the aircraft for the
carriage of a thing liable for forfeiture' within the meaning of s 141(1)(a) of the Customs
and Excise Management Act 1979 such as to justify its subsequent seizure on 1 May   j
1987. (2) Whether it is a defence to the commissioners' claim in this action if the
defendants establish that they did not know that the aforesaid container contained
cannabis resin and were not reckless in failing so to discover. (3) Whether it is a defence
to the commissioners' claim in this action if the defendants establish that they could not
with reasonable diligence have discovered that cannabis had been secreted and hidden or
was being carried in the container nor could they by the exercise of reasonable diligence

have prevented its being secreted in the container. (4) Whether it is necessary for the
commissioners to prove in this action (i) that the defendants knew or ought to have
known that cannabis resin was on board the aircraft on 26 April 1987 and/or (ii) that the
aircraft was on other than a regular scheduled and legitimate flight.

I am now asked to decide these preliminary issues and have heard submissions based
on the agreed facts which I have already recited in this judgment.

Section 141 of the 1979 Act provides as follows, so far as is material:

'(1) ... where any thing has become liable to forfeiture under the customs and
excise Acts—(a) any ship, aircraft, vehicle, animal, container (including any article
of passengers' baggage) or other thing whatsoever which has been used for the
carriage, handling, deposit or concealment of the thing so liable to forfeiture, either
at a time when it was so liable or for the purposes of the commission of the offence
for which it later became so liable ... shall also be liable to forfeiture ...

(3) Where any of the following, that is to say—(a) any ship not exceeding
100 tons register; (b) any aircraft; or (c) any hovercraft, becomes liable to forfeiture
under this section by reason of having been used in the importation, exportation or
carriage of goods contrary to or for the purpose of contravening any prohibition or
restriction for the time being in force with respect to those goods ... the owner and
the master or commander shall each be liable on summary conviction to a penalty
equal to the value of the ship, aircraft or hovercraft or level 5 on the standard scale,
whichever is the less.'

The level referred to is now £2,000.

Under s 139 of the 1979 Act it is provided:

'(1) Any thing liable to forfeiture under the customs and excise Acts may be
seized or detained by any officer or constable or any member of Her Majesty's armed
forces or coastguard ...

(5) Subject to subsections (3) and (4) above and to Schedule 3 to this Act, any thing
seized or detained under the customs and excise Acts shall, pending the determination
as to its forfeiture or disposal, be dealt with, and, if condemned or deemed to have
been condemned or forfeited, shall be disposed of in such manner as the
Commissioners may direct.

(6) Schedule 3 to this Act shall have effect for the purpose of forfeitures, and of
proceedings for the condemnation of any thing as being forfeited, under the customs
and excise Acts ...'

Schedule 3 contains the provisions relating to forfeiture. Paragraph 1 deals with notice
of seizure, and by sub-para (1) it is provided:

'The Commissioners shall, except as provided in sub-paragraph (2) below, give
notice of the seizure of any thing as liable to forfeiture and of the grounds therefor
to any person who to their knowledge was at the time of the seizure the owner or
one of the owners thereof.'

Paragraph 3 deals with notice of claim, and provides:

'Any person claiming that any thing seized as liable to forfeiture is not so liable
shall, within one month of the date of the notice of seizure or, where no such notice
has been served on him, within one month of the date of seizure, give notice of his
claim in writing to the Commissioners at any office of customs and excise.'

Paragraphs 5 and 6 deal with condemnation, and provide:

'5. If on the expiration of the relevant period under paragraph 3 above for the
giving of notice of claim in respect of any thing no such notice has been given to
the Commissioners, or if, in the case of any such notice given, any requirement of
paragraph (4) is not complied with, the thing in question shall be deemed to have
been duly condemned as forfeited.

6. Where notice of claim in respect of any thing is duly given in accordance with [the preceding paragraphs] the Commissioners shall take proceedings for the condemnation of that thing by the court, and if the court finds that the thing was at the time of seizure liable to forfeiture the court shall condemn it as forfeited.'

By para 8 it is provided:

'Proceedings for condemnation shall be civil proceedings . . .'

Paragraph 16 empowers the Commissioners to deal with seizures before condemnation, and gives them a discretion in the following terms:

'Where any thing has been seized as liable to forfeiture the Commissioners may at any time if they see fit and notwithstanding that the thing has not yet been condemned, or is not yet deemed to have been condemned, as forfeited—(a) deliver it up to any claimant upon his paying to the Commissioners such sum as they think proper, being a sum not exceeding that which in their opinion represents the value of the thing, including any duty or tax chargeable thereon which has not been paid . . .'

As I have already indicated, the commissioners exercised their discretion under the provisions of this paragraph and delivered the aircraft to the defendants on payment of the sum of £50,000.

Counsel for the Crown submits that s 141(1) is absolute in its terms, and provides a remedy in rem. In his submission the sole test is: was the aircraft used for the carriage of the drug? He submits that s 141(3) provides for a similar liability for the commander of the aircraft. There is no doubt that sub-s (3) at least is a penal provision. It creates a summary offence with a monetary penalty.

In support of his contention, counsel for the Crown submits, first, that there is nothing in the section to suggest that there is any requirement of knowledge, actual or presumed, that there is no provision that the owner of the aircraft should act with due care or that if he proves he acted with due care he has a defence and, second, that sub-s (1) of the section is concerned with the aircraft, irrespective of who the owner might be.

Counsel contrasts the provisions of s 141 with the special provisions of s 142, relating to the forfeiture of larger ships. In this latter section there is express reference to the object of the voyage: it might under that section be material to ascertain whether or not it was scheduled. But there is no such reference in s 141, and counsel submits that there is no requiremen; that the plaintiffs should establish that the aircraft was on anything other than a regular flight.

Counsel draws attention to ss 88, 89 and 90 of the 1979 Act. These sections provide for the forfeiture of a ship, aircraft or other vehicle if they are constructed or adapted for the purpose of concealing goods, for the forfeiture of a ship from which cargo is jettisoned to avoid seizure and for the forfeiture of a ship or aircraft whose master or commander fails to account for missing cargo. Counsel submits that in those cases too the remedy is against the ship or aircraft regardless of whether or not its owner has any knowledge of the acts giving rise to the power of forfeiture.

Counsel also draws attention to the provisions of s 170 of the 1979 Act. This section creates an offence punishable on summary conviction with a fine or imprisonment for a term not exceeding six months or both, and on conviction on indictment to a fine of any amount or to imprisonment for a term not exceeding two years or to both. But in order to establish an offence under this section it has to be shown that the person charged (a) knowingly acquires possession of the goods or (b) is in any way knowingly concerned in carrying, removing, depositing, harbouring, keeping or concealing or in any manner dealing with the goods and that he does so with intent to defraud Her Majesty or to evade any such prohibition or restriction with respect to the goods. Counsel contrasts the provisions of this section with those of s 141(3), where any requirement of knowledge on the part of the owner, master or commander is (he submits) irrelevant.

Counsel urges me to look at the overall purpose of the 1979 Act, which is to prevent
a smuggling and to impose severe penalties in order to deter any person from attempting
to commit such an offence. He submits that, if a defence can be made out, the Act points
out what it can be, as for example under s 90, where it is open to the master of the ship
or commander of the aircraft to account for the missing cargo to the satisfaction of the
commissioners, or under s 142, where it is a defence to show that the carriage of the
offending goods was not substantially the object of the voyage during which the offence
b was committed.

The 1979 Act is the latest in a series of Acts regulating the importation of goods into
the United Kingdom and intended to prevent smuggling. The preamble to the 1979 Act
states that it is:

c
'An Act to consolidate the enactments relating to the collection and management
of the revenues of customs and exercise and in some cases to other matters in relation
to which the Commissioners of Customs and Excise for the time being perform
functions, with amendments to give effect to recommendations of the Law
Commission and the Scottish Law Commission.'

The earliest Act to which counsel for the plaintiffs drew attention was the Customs
d Consolidation Act 1876. Section 202 of that Act provided, so far as is material, as follows:

'All ships, boats, carriages or other conveyances made use of in the importation,
landing, removal, or conveyance of any uncustomed, prohibited, restricted, or other
goods liable to forfeiture under the Customs Acts shall be forfeited . . .'

e This section was considered in *De Keyser v British Railway Traffic and Electric Co Ltd*
[1936] 1 KB 224. The facts of the case, taken from the headnote, were these:

'A motor tank wagon was seized by officers of Customs and Excise on the ground
that it was being used in the conveyance of goods liable to forfeiture under the
Customs Acts. The owners claimed the vehicle under s. 207 of the Customs
Consolidation Act, 1876, and an information was exhibited before justices on behalf
f of the Commissioners of Customs and Excise for the forfeiture and condemnation
of the vehicle . . . *Held*, that, it having been admitted that the vehicle had been used
in the conveyance of goods liable to forfeiture (in which case s. 202 of the Act
provides that the vehicle itself shall be forfeited), the justices were bound to
condemn the vehicle, s . 226 giving them no discretion to refuse to do so on the
g ground, for example, of hardship on an innocent owner.'

In the course of his judgment Lord Hewart CJ said (at 229–231):

'It seems to me that in the present case the power of the justices is coupled with a
duty and that, when once the necessary facts have been established, and an
application has been made for the condemnation of the property in question, the
h justices have no choice but to condemn . . . It seems to me that on a true construction
of this statute, where certain events have happened—and in the present case there is
no dispute that those events have happened—the property in question is labelled
"forfeited" under s. 202. There may be, where the owner of the property or other
person authorized by him gives notice of a claim, an inchoate forfeiture which is to
be completed by the combined forfeiture and condemnation contemplated by
j s. 226. What is it that is open to the claimant on such proceedings? In my opinion,
nothing more is open to him than to contend, and, if need be, to offer evidence to
prove, that, on a true view of the facts, the conveyance in question does not come
within the class of things which, by s. 202, are forfeited. He may contend with
success, for instance, that through error or otherwise a conveyance not liable to be
forfeited has been seized. He may say in whatever form is suitable to the relevant

facts that the conveyance does not come within the class of things forfeited. But once it is established that the conveyance does come within that class, this *a* undoubtedly rigorous statute gives the claimant no opportunity of asking the Court to take into consideration mitigating circumstances with the effect of removing the conveyance from that class. There is no opportunity for mercy with regard to a conveyance which has been forfeited, although there may be grounds for contending that the conveyance does not come within the class of forfeited property. In the present case no such contention was advanced. All that was argued on behalf of the *b* [owners] was that they did not know of the wrongful use for which the lorry was being employed. That circumstance was wholly irrelevant to the proceedings before the justices. It did not affect the purpose for which the lorry had been used. If that sort of argument were to be open to the owner of a conveyance in such a case as the present, the result might be, in the case of two partners, where one was aware of the wrongful use to which the vehicle was being put and the other was not, that the *c* vehicle might be excused from condemnation because of the innocent mind of one of the partners, that result enuring for the benefit of the guilty partner. In the present case the argument adduced before the justices, which was really an argument in mercy, that the owner of the vehicle was not aware of the illegal use to which it was being put, was wholly irrelevant to the only question which the justices had to consider.'          *d*

In the course of his judgment, Humphreys J said (at 232):

'Sect. 202 is free from ambiguity. It is perfectly clear and direct in its terms. It provides that (inter alia) all conveyances used in various illegal ways, including the conveyance of goods liable to forfeiture, shall be forfeited. On the plain terms of that section, as soon as it is ascertained that a conveyance has been used in the *e* conveyance of goods liable to forfeiture, ipso facto that conveyance is forfeited. It would be remarkable if one found in subsequent sections something which cut down that plain statement of the result of certain facts, and I do not find anything of the sort.'

It will be noticed that the words used in the 1876 Act were 'made use of'.          *f*

The next statute was the Customs and Excise Act 1952, and the relevant section was s 277, which provided as follows:

'(1) Without prejudice to any other provision of this Act, where any thing has become liable to forfeiture under the customs or excise Acts—(a) any ship, aircraft, vehicle, animal, container (including any article of passengers' baggage) or other thing whatsoever which has been used for the carriage, handling, deposit or *g* concealment of the thing so liable to forfeiture, either at a time when it was so liable or for the purposes of the commission of the offence for which it later became so liable . . . shall also be liable to forfeiture . . .'

The words used in this section were 'has been used', which are the same as those in s 141(1) of the 1979 Act.          *h*

Section 277 of the 1952 Act was considered in *Customs and Excise Comrs v Jack Bradley (Accrington) Ltd* [1958] 3 All ER 487, [1959] 1 QB 219. The facts taken from the headnote (see [1959] 1 QB 219 at 219–220) are that kerosine which had been delivered to the defendants for home use and on which a rebate of duty had been allowed under the 1952 Act was found in the fuel tanks of a number of the defendants' motor vehicles. No amount equal to the rebate on the oil had been paid by the defendants to the *j* commissioners and accordingly the oil used in the tanks was liable to forfeiture under s 200(2) of the Act. On the question whether the vehicles themselves became liable to forfeiture under s 277(1), it was held that the vehicles had been used for the carriage of the oil within s 277(1)(a) for the purposes of the commission of the offence, namely

consumption of the oil in the vehicles, for which the oil later became liable to forfeiture.
a  Accordingly, the vehicles were also liable to forfeiture. In the course of his judgment in
that case Lord Parker CJ said ([1958] 3 All ER 487 at 489–490, [1959] 1 QB 219 at 223–
224):

'The question then becomes whether, under s. 277, the vehicles had been used for
the carriage of that oil, either at a time when it was liable to forfeiture, or for the
b  purposes of the commission of the offence for which it later became liable to
forfeiture. It is not an easy point and one must bear in mind that powers such as
these, if they are to be taken and exercised by the commissioners, must be in clear
language ... I think that the crux of this case is the construction of the words
"which has been used for" that carriage. If that meant that a vehicle must be one
which has been used with the object of carrying something from "A" to "B"—if the
c  question is "What was the object of the journey, was it to carry goods from 'A' to
'B'?" or "What was the intention, was the intention to carry them from 'A' to 'B'?"—
then clearly, approached in that way, it was only incidentally that the vehicles were
carrying at the time oil. The purposes for which these vehicles were being used
were purposes in connexion with the docks. They were carrying oil for consumption
and not for the purpose of taking the oil from one place to another. I do not think,
d  however, that the words used are used in that sense. It seems to me that they are
used, as one would expect them to be used in a statute of this sort, to mean "where
use has been made of the vehicle to carry", or "where a vehicle has been made use of
in the carriage of". Some support for that view is to be obtained from considering
the very next section, s. 278, which is dealing with forfeiture of large vessels, and
there forfeiture cannot take place unless the offence in connexion with which the
e  forfeiture is claimed was substantially the object of the voyage during which the
offence was committed. Looked at in that way it seems to me that, as a matter of
English, what happened here comes directly within the words in s. 277, because it
can be said that use was made of these vehicles for carrying the oil for the purposes
of the commission of the offence for which the oil later became liable to forfeiture.
The offence is the use of oil. I am not deciding whether it may not be right to say
f  that use is made of oil when it is appropriated to a particular purpose, the
unauthorised purpose. One thing, at least, is clear, viz., that oil is used when it is
consumed; and, that being so, I cannot see why, as an ordinary matter of language,
use was not being made of the vehicles to carry oil for the purposes of that oil being
consumed ...'

g  Counsel for the Crown also relies on *Denton v John Lister Ltd* [1971] 3 All ER 669, [1971]
1 WLR 1426. That case concerned postage stamps which had been imported from
Southern Rhodesia at a time when such imports were prohibited. It was a case where the
Rhodesian Post Office had sent the respondent companies unsolicited samples of their
new issue postage stamps. These were seized by an officer of the Customs and Excise.
h  The Divisional Court was concerned with proceedings brought for their forfeiture and
condemnation, pursuant to s 275 of and Sch 7 to the 1952 Act.
The judgment of the court was delivered by Lord Widgery CJ, who said ([1971] 3 All
ER 669 at 673, [1971] 1 WLR 1426 at 1431):

'It seems to me quite clear that the forfeiture proceedings in Sch 7 are ...
j  proceedings in rem and not in personam, that is to say the issue which is to be dealt
with in forfeiture proceedings is whether the goods in question are liable to be
forfeited. If they are liable to be forfeited then those proceedings are not interested
in the identity of the person who imported them. Forfeiture or no depends on
whether the goods were imported contrary to a prohibition. The identity of the
importer is not a relevant factor as I see it.'

Counsel for the Crown concedes that the provisions of the 1979 Act are draconian. But he submits that they can be mitigated by the discretion given to the commissioners *a* under para 16 of Sch 3. He submits that there is available to any aggrieved person the remedy of judicial review, so that if the commissioners should refuse to listen to reasonable submissions or, in other words, should fail to act with 'Wednesbury reasonableness', then there is a remedy in the courts (see *Associated Provincial Picture Houses Ltd v Wednesbury Corp* [1947] 2 All ER 680, [1948] 1 KB 223). He submits that the decisions which he has cited show that the courts have upheld what was the clear *b* intention of Parliament in each of those Acts. He concedes that in the present case there is nothing to indicate that the defendants knew of the existence of the offending container or its contents, or that they were reckless about it. But he submits that the issues raised in paras 2 and 3 of the master's order are attempts to write into the 1979 Act defences which are not there.

Counsel for the defendants on the other hand submits that the function of the court *c* in construing s 141 of the 1979 Act is to give effect to the will of Parliament, and that it is unlikely as a matter of common sense that Parliament intended the section to have the width contended for by the Crown. He argues that the scheduled journeys made by the defendants' aircraft are to be made whether the aircraft is full or empty, in fair weather or foul. If someone hides cannabis in a sealed container which is then put on the aircraft unknown to the carrier, its servants or agents, who then make the scheduled journey, *d* that cannot make the aircraft 'used for the carriage' so as to render it liable to forfeiture. Counsel makes a number of analogies, e g the passenger who takes two litre bottles of duty-free liquor instead of the permitted one on board Concorde, or the Post Office van which carries dutiable goods in a packet.

Counsel submits that the aircraft is not 'used for the carriage' in a situation where the journey is going to be made anyway, unless those who have its management know of or *e* are reckless as to its use. Counsel relies on passages in the dissenting speech of Lord Reid in *Warner v Metropolitan Police Comr* [1968] 2 All ER 356 at 366–367, [1969] 2 AC 256 at 279 where, dealing with regulations made under the Dangerous Drugs Act 1965, he said:

'These regulations purport to make any ordinary member of the public guilty of a very serious offence if a drug within the meaning of the Act is "in his actual *f* custody". Any person may, and most people do, from time to time take into their custody an apparently innocent package without ascertaining what it contains, without having the slightest reason to suspect that it may contain anything out of the ordinary, and indeed without having any right to open the package and see what is in it. If every person who takes such a package into his custody must do so at his peril, then this goes immensely farther than any enactment imposing absolute *g* liability has yet been held to go, and I refuse to believe that Parliament can ever have intended such an oppressive result. Normally the plain ordinary grammatical meaning of the words of an enactment affords the best guide. But in cases of this kind the question is not what the words mean but whether there are sufficient grounds for inferring that Parliament intended to exclude the general rule that mens rea is an essential element in every offence; and the authorities show that it is *h* generally necessary to go behind the words of the enactment and take other factors into consideration.'

Counsel also relied on passages in the speech of Lord Morris where he said ([1968] 2 All ER 356 at 372, [1969] 2 AC 256 at 286):

'A useful start in considering an Act of Parliament is to take the plain literal and *j* grammatical meaning of the words used. In *A.-G. v. Lockwood* ((1842) 9 M & W 378 at 398, 152 ER 160 at 168) ALDERSON, B., said: "The rule of law, I take it, upon the construction of all statutes . . . is, whether they be penal or remedial, to construe them according to the plain, literal and grammatical meaning of the words in which they are expressed, unless that construction leads to a plain and clear contradiction of the apparent purpose of the Act, or to some palpable and evident absurdity." On this basis I think that the notion of having something in one's possession involves a mental element. It involves in the first place that one knows that one has something in one's possession. It does not, however, involve that one knows precisely what it is that one has got.'

Counsel also relied on the decision of the House of Lords in *Sweet v Parsley* [1969] 1 All ER 347 at 349, [1970] AC 132 at 148, where Lord Reid said:

'But this was held to be an absolute offence following the earlier decision in *Yeandel v. Fisher* ([1965] 3 All ER 158, [1966] 1 QB 440). How has it come about that the Divisional Court has felt bound to reach such an obviously unjust result? It has, in effect, held that it was carrying out the will of Parliament because Parliament has chosen to make this an absolute offence. And, of course, if Parliament has so chosen, the courts must carry out its will, and they cannot be blamed for any unjust consequences. But has Parliament so chosen? I dealt with this matter at some length in *Warner v. Metropolitan Police Comr.* ([1968] 2 All ER 356 at 366–367, [1969] 2 AC 256 at 279–280). On reconsideration I see no reason to alter anything which I there said. But I think that some amplification is necessary. Our first duty is to consider the words of the Act; if they show a clear intention to create an absolute offence, that is an end of the matter. But such cases are very rare. Sometimes the words of the section which creates a particular offence make it clear that mens rea is required in one form or another. Such cases are quite frequent. But in a very large number of cases there is no clear indication either way. In such cases there has for centuries been a presumption that Parliament did not intend to make criminals of persons who were in no way blameworthy in what they did. That means that, whenever a section is silent as to mens rea, there is a presumption that, in order to give effect to the will of Parliament, we must read in words appropriate to require mens rea.'

Having referred to the decision of Alderson B in *A-G v Lockwood* (1842) 9 M & W 378 at 398, 152 ER 160 at 168, Lord Reid continued ([1969] 1 All ER 347 at 350, [1970] AC 132 at 149):

'That is perfectly right as a general rule and where there is no legal presumption. But what about the multitude of criminal enactments where the words of the Act simply make it an offence to do certain things but where everyone agrees that there cannot be a conviction without proof of mens rea in some form? This passage, if applied to the present problem, would mean that there is no need to prove mens rea unless it would be "a plain and clear contradiction of the apparent purpose of the Act" to convict without proof of mens rea. But that would be putting the presumption the wrong way round; for it is firmly established by a host of authorities that mens rea is an essential ingredient of every offence unless some reason can be found for holding that that is not necessary. It is also firmly established that the fact that other sections of the Act expressly require mens rea, for example because they contain the word "knowingly", is not in itself sufficient to justify a decision that a section which is silent as to mens rea creates an absolute offence. In the absence of a clear indication in the Act that an offence is intended to be an absolute offence, it is necessary to go outside the Act and examine all relevant circumstances in order to establish that this must have been the intention of Parliament. I say "must have been", because it is a universal principle that if a penal provision is reasonably capable of two interpretations, that interpretation which is most favourable to the accused must be adopted.'

In the speech of Lord Diplock this passage occurs ([1969] 1 All ER 347 at 362, [1970] AC 132 at 163):

'Where penal provisions are of general application to the conduct of ordinary
citizens in the course of their everyday life, the presumption is that the standard of  *a*
care required of them in informing themselves of facts which would make their
conduct unlawful, is that of the familiar common law duty of care. But where the
subject-matter of a statute is the regulation of a particular activity involving potential
danger to public health, safety or morals, in which citizens have a choice whether
they participate or not, the court may feel driven to infer an intention of Parliament
to impose, by penal sanctions, a higher duty of care on those who choose to  *b*
participate and to place on them an obligation to take whatever measures may be
necessary to prevent the prohibited act, without regard to those considerations of
cost or business practicability which play a part in the determination of what would
be required of them in order to fulfil the ordinary common law duty of care. But
such an inference is not lightly to be drawn, nor is there any room for it unless there
is something that the person on whom the obligation is imposed can do directly or  *c*
indirectly, by supervision or inspection, by improvement of his business methods
or by exhorting those whom he may be expected to influence or control, which will
promote the observance of the obligation (see *Lim Chin Aik* v. *Reginam* ([1963] 1 All
ER 223 at 228, [1963] AC 160 at 174)).'

Basing himself on these passages, counsel for the defendants submits that the word  *d*
'used' in s 141(1) must infer knowledge, either because this is a criminal provision or
because an absurd result would otherwise follow. Counsel further submits that to give
s 141(1) the interpretation sought by the Crown would mean that the section was in
conflict with art 6 of the European Convention on Human Rights (Convention for the
Protection of Human Rights and Fundamental Freedoms (Rome, 4 November 1950;
TS 71 (1953); Cmd 8969)), the material part of which is as follows:  *e*

'(1) In the determination of his civil rights and obligations or of any criminal
charge against him, everyone is entitled to a fair and public hearing within a
reasonable time by an independent and impartial tribunal established by law . . .'

I agree with counsel for the defendants that there is something wrong about a provision
which entitles the commissioners to a right of forfeiture in rem without recourse to the  *f*
courts. Even though they have a discretion under para 16 of Sch 3 they are not bound to
exercise it, and it is only if they fail to do so in a reasonable manner that the owner or
operator of the forfeited vehicle has any right to seek judicial review. It seems to me to
be unlikely that Parliament intended that such power should be given to the Crown
without proper supervision by the courts in situations such as the present.

Counsel for the defendants also relies on the judgment of the Privy Council in *Gammon*  *g*
*(Hong Kong) Ltd* v *A-G of Hong Kong* [1984] 2 All ER 503 at 508, [1985] AC 1 at 14, which
is in these terms.

'. . . (1) there is a presumption of law that mens rea is required before a person
can be held guilty of a criminal offence; (2) the presumption is particularly strong
where the offence is "truly criminal" in character; (3) the presumption applies to  *h*
statutory offences, and can be displaced only if this is clearly or by necessary
implication the effect of the statute; (4) the only situation in which the presumption
can be displaced is where the statute is concerned with an issue of social concern;
public safety is such an issue; (5) even where a statute is concerned with such an
issue, the presumption of mens rea stands unless it can also be shown that the
creation of strict liability will be effective to promote the objects of the statute by  *j*
encouraging greater vigilance to prevent the commission of the prohibited act.'

Counsel for the Crown submits in reply that the whole purpose of the 1979 Act and of
the statutes which preceded it is to prevent smuggling and to deter those who are minded
to engage in it. These are of course highly commendable and important objectives, but I

*a* cannot see how the forfeiture of an aircraft belonging to an operator who has no knowledge of, and can have no knowledge of, the contents of a container being carried in its cargo hold can possibly deter the operators of aircraft or any potential smuggler from an illegal act or that the operators can be required to take any stricter methods of control than those which they already exercise. Operators cannot be expected to open every container that is sought to be placed aboard their aircraft and to search it for contraband goods in fear that if they do not do so and contraband goods are found therein *b* their aircraft may be forfeited.

I have set out the submissions of counsel at some length in order to show that I have them well in mind, and that I have had all relevant authorities brought to my attention.

I cannot think that the draftsman of the 1979 Act had the present situation in mind. I cannot believe that it was the intention of Parliament that the innocent and bona fide operator of an extremely valuable aircraft on an international scheduled flight should be *c* at risk of having the aircraft forfeited if, unknown to him and without any recklessness on his part, some evil-minded person smuggles contraband or prohibited goods aboard the aircraft. It cannot sensibly be said that in such circumstances the aircraft 'has been used for the carriage'. What has been used is no more than the opportunity afforded by the availability of cargo space on an already scheduled flight which was going to be made in any event.

*d* In my judgment, s 141(1) of the 1979 Act is *not* one of the very rare cases referred to by Lord Reid in *Sweet v Parsley* [1969] 1 All ER 347 at 349, [1970] AC 132 at 148. I do not interpret it as being absolute in its terms. I agree with counsel for the defendants that the word 'used' in s 141(1) of the 1979 Act must infer knowledge. I do not feel myself bound by the decisions in *De Keyser v British Railway Traffic and Electric Co Ltd* [1936] 1 KB 224 or *Customs and Excise Comrs v Jack Bradley (Accrington) Ltd* [1958] 3 All ER 487, *e* [1959] 1 QB 219, and counsel for the Crown does not suggest that I am, however persuasive those decisions may be. They were decisions under different statutes. In *De Kayser's* case it seems to have been conceded that the wagon was made use of, and no argument was heard on this point. The facts of that case, and of the *Bradley* case, were very different from the facts of the case before me. Counsel for the defendants reserves *f* the right to argue, if need be, that both cases were wrongly decided, and observes that they were decided before *Warner v Metropolitan Police Comr* [1968] 2 All ER 356, [1969] 2 AC 256 and *Sweet v Parsley* [1969] 1 All ER 347, [1970] AC 132.

The draconian effect of the 1979 Act has already been referred to. If counsel for the Crown is right, the effect of forfeiture on the owners and operators is obvious. It can also have a serious effect on innocent passengers and consignors of legitimate cargo. I *g* respectfully adopt the words of Lord Reid in *Warner v Metropolitan Police Comr* [1968] 2 All ER 356 at 366, [1969] 2 AC 256 at 279: 'I refuse to believe that Parliament can ever have intended such an oppressive result.' It would in my view be disproportionate.

Accordingly, I determine the preliminary issues as follows. (1) No; those facts alone do not constitute 'use of the aircraft for the carriage of a thing liable to forfeiture' within the meaning of s 141(1)(*a*).' (2) Yes; it is a defence. (3) Yes; it is a defence. (4) It is *h* necessary for the commissioners to prove in this action: (i) that the defendants knew or ought to have known that cannabis resin was on board the aircraft on 26 April 1987; or (but *not* 'and') (ii) that the aircraft was on other than a regular scheduled and legitimate flight.

*Order accordingly.*

Solicitors: *Solicitor for the Customs and Excise ; Beaumont & Son* (for the defendants).

K Mydeen Esq   Barrister.

# Belcourt v Belcourt

*a*

CHANCERY DIVISION
MORRITT J
24, 25 OCTOBER 1988

*b*

*Land registration – Caution against dealings – Notice of appeal – Appeal from 'decision or order
... of the Court' – Entry of notice of appeal from decision or order of court in register – Whether
only notice of appeal from decision of court on appeal from registrar need be entered in register –
Whether any notice of appeal affecting property required to be registered – Land Registration
Rules 1925, r 301.*

*c*

The plaintiff, claiming to be entitled to a beneficial interest in the proceeds of sale of a
property which was registered in the name of the defendant and which the defendant
wished to sell, registered a caution against the property. At the hearing of the plaintiff's
originating summons the judge dismissed her claim and ordered that the caution be
vacated and also refused a stay pending an appeal. The plaintiff lodged an appeal and
served notice of the appeal on the land registrar, who entered a caution against the
property under r 301[a] of the Land Registration Rules 1925, which provided that notice
of appeal 'from a decision or order . . . of the Court . . . shall be entered in the register'.
The defendant applied for the caution to be vacated.

*d*

**Held** – Rule 301 of the 1925 rules was of general application and was not restricted to
appeals from the decision of the court on appeals from the registrar. Accordingly, the
plaintiff, who was entitled to appeal from the order of the county court judge, was
entitled to serve notice of the appeal on the registrar who was obliged to enter a caution
against the property under r 301. The defendant's application would therefore be
dismissed (see p 38 *c* to *e*, post).

*e*

**Notes**
For entering notice of an appeal from a court order, see 26 Halsbury's Laws (4th edn)
para 1469.
    For the Land Registration Rules 1925, r 301, see 18 Halsbury's Statutory Instruments
(4th reissue) 290.

*f*

**Case referred to in judgment**
*Elias v Mitchell* [1972] 2 All ER 153, [1972] Ch 652, [1972] 2 WLR 740.

*g*

**Case also cited**
*Heywood v BDC Properties Ltd (No 2)* [1964] 2 All ER 702, [1964] 1 WLR 971, CA.

**Appeal**
On 21 June 1988 his Honour Judge Paul Baker QC sitting as a judge of the High Court
ordered on the hearing of an originating summons filed by the plaintiff, Vivienne Rachel
Augusta Belcourt, that the plaintiff's claim for a beneficial interest in the property at 15
Westbury Lodge Close, Pinner, which was registered in the sole name of the defendant,
Sandra Vivienne Belcourt, be dismissed, and the caution registered by the plaintiff against
the property on 7 May 1987 be vacated. On 19 July 1988 the plaintiff issued a notice of
appeal from the order of 21 June 1988 seeking an order declaring that she held the
property on trust for herself and the defendant as beneficial tenants-in-common or
alternatively that the defendant held the property on trust to permit the plaintiff to reside

*h*

*j*

---

*a*   Rule 301 is set out at p 37 *f*, post

there for her life and that the proceeds of sale were likewise so held, and that the plaintiff
a  was entitled to protect her interest by registering a caution. On 17 October 1988 the
defendant by motion sought an order that unless and until a stay of the order of 21 June
1988 be ordered the plaintiff be restrained from lodging a further caution or other
restriction and that the entry in the register of 22 June 1988 recording the notice of
appeal be vacated and no further entry be made without leave of the court. The facts are
set out in the judgment.
b

*Charles Purle* for the plaintiff.
*Irvine MacCabe* for the defendant.

**MORRITT J.** By this motion the defendant seeks orders in the following terms:

c          '1. Until or unless a stay of the Order made by His Honour Paul Baker sitting as
a Judge of the High Court on 21st June 1988 be ordered by this Court or the Court
of Appeal or a single judge thereof, the Plaintiff whether by herself, her servants or
agents, be restrained from lodging any further caution, Notice of Appeal or other
Notice, restriction or inhibition whatsoever upon Her Majesty's Land Registry in
respect of title number NGL 336055 without leave of this Court or the Court of
d          Appeal or a single Judge thereof.
2. That the entry in the Charges Register of title number NGL 336055 made on
the 22nd June 1988 recording that a Notice of Appeal has been lodged against the
Order of the 21st June 1988 made in the High Court of Justice be vacated forthwith
and that no further entry relating to the Notice of Appeal be entered upon Her
Majesty's Land Registry without leave of this Court or the Court of Appeal or a
e          single Judge thereof.'

The background is as follows. In 1987 the plaintiff (who is the defendant's mother)
registered a caution under s 54 of the Land Registration Act 1925 against the title to 15
Westbury Lodge Close, Pinner, a property which was then registered in the name of the
defendant alone. The plaintiff instituted proceedings against the defendant, claiming to
have a beneficial interest in the proceeds of sale of the property which, as shown by *Elias
f  v Mitchell* [1972] 2 All ER 153, [1972] Ch 652, is a minor interest properly protected by a
caution. That action came before his Honour Judge Paul Baker QC, who, after a five-day
hearing, dismissed the plaintiff's claim. By his order it was provided, inter alia:

'2 that the caution in favour of the Plaintiff registered on the 7th May 1987 in
the register of Title Number NGL 336055 at Her Majesty's Land Registry (being the
g          Title relating to the freehold property known as and situate at 15 Westbury Lodge
Close Pinner Middlesex) be vacated . . .
5 that leave to the Plaintiff for a stay of paragraph 2 of this Order pending any
appeal therefrom to the Court of Appeal be refused.'

In the transcript of his judgment the judge observed:

h          'And in due course a caution was registered against dealings on 7 May, which
frustrated the sale. It seems, I am bound to say, a most unfortunate move this, to
frustrate the sale in the circumstances I have recounted, but that is what happened.
It would have been far better to have sought to attach, pending the resolution of any
legal claim, the proceeds of sale or part of them by some sort of Mareva or other
injunction. As it was, the proceedings were not started until getting on for a year
j          later. It may be that legal aid had something to do with that, but it was not until the
following February that the originating summons was issued. In the meantime the
position has stagnated.'

After certain submissions made to the judge after his judgment, counsel for the plaintiff
is recorded as stating:

'My Lord, I obviously cannot resist the application to vacate the caution. Obviously
I am going to consider whether or not to appeal the matter and I would ask that the *a*
caution not be vacated pending appeal, bearing in mind that we have a right to
register (a) [and then the transcript records a question mark] and obviously we
would be prepared to vacate it if appeal was not considered to be advisable or if there
was an undertaking given in relation to the proceeds of sale. Obviously we would
be prepared to give an undertaking that, subject to obtaining legal aid for appeal,
we would proceed with all due diligence and there will not be any delay on the *b*
plaintiff's part.'

To which the judge observed: 'I am afraid I must refuse that. I think that throughout
the caution was ill-judged.'

The plaintiff served notice of appeal and I understand that there is also pending before
the Court of Appeal an application for leave to adduce fresh evidence on the hearing of
the appeal. It may be, but I cannot say, that the fresh evidence if admitted would *c*
undermine the judge's observations which I have quoted based on the evidence which
was before him.

A copy of the notice of appeal was served on the registrar of Her Majesty's Land
Registry and he took the view that, pursuant to the Land Registration Rules 1925, SR &
O 1925/1093, r 301, the notice should be entered in the register. Accordingly, there is *d*
now entered in the Land Registry against the title to the property a note in the following
terms:

'22 July 1988—Notice of Appeal against the Order dated 21 June 1988 made in
the High Court of Justice, Chancery Division (Action Ch 8 1988 B 1046) directing
that the caution in favour of Vivienne Rachel Belcourt be vacated.'
*e*
The consequence is that a further attempt by the defendant to sell the property has
been frustrated because the prospective purchaser declined to proceed when apprised of
the entry.

The defendant contends that r 301 does not apply in respect of appeals from the High
Court acting under its general original jurisdiction. The defendant contends that it is
absurd if the mere service of a notice of appeal on the registrar should provide a de facto *f*
stay on the order appealed from, particularly when a stay was sought and refused.

Notice of this application was served on the registrar. He indicated that his position
was made plain in the correspondence and that he had no wish to appear at the hearing.
His position as so revealed is that:

'I have considered in the light of your arguments whether the notice of the *g*
intention to appeal has been correctly entered. The Registry's view is that Rule 301
is not confined to appeals from an order of the registrar. The rule itself refers to an
appeal from a decision or order of the court. Although the rule falls within the
section headed "Hearing before the Registrar", this heading is for guidance only and
does not affect the interpretation of the rules. This must clearly be so if you look at
the following Rule 302. A notice of intention to appeal has been delivered to the *h*
Registry and the rule is framed in mandatory terms regarding the entry thereof on
the register.'

Then later in a letter dated 12 August 1988 the Chief Land Registrar wrote:

'In addition to proceedings in which the Courts are asked to decide matters under
the Land Registration Acts and Rules, there are those relating to registered land *j*
which are brought under some other provision and in which the fact of registration
is purely incidental. Such proceedings may, however, result in an alteration of the
register and the Registry's view is that Rule 301 covers these proceedings. There is
certainly nothing in the Rule which limits its operation to proceedings brought
under Land Registration Acts and Rules. The Rule does not stipulate the manner in

which the appeal is to be conducted. It is by way of an ancillary provision governing
the effect of appeal on dealings with registered land.'

These and other arguments have been espoused by the plaintiff.

The question, therefore, is the proper construction of r 301. The rule comes within a
section headed 'Hearings before the Registrar'. This is not strictly a marginal note, which,
by r 1(6), is not to affect the construction of the 1925 rules. But, even if it is a correct
description of the contents of r 298, it would be a misdescription of rr 299 and 302.
Accordingly, I do not find it of any assistance on the construction of r 302. Rule 298
provides:

'(1) If any question, doubt, dispute, difficulty or complaint arises before the
Registrar upon any application or during any investigation of title [and then there
are set out five topics] (whether such questions relate to the construction, validity,
or effect of any instrument, or the persons interested, or the nature or extent of their
respective interests or powers, or as to order of priority, or the mode in which any
entry should be made or dealt with in the register or otherwise), the Registrar shall
hear and determine the matter and, subject to appeal to the Court, make such order
in the matter as he shall think just.

(2) But the Registrar may, if he thinks fit, instead of deciding the question
himself, refer the matter at any stage, or any question thereon, for the decision of
the Court.'

Rule 299 provides: 'Any person aggrieved by an order or decision of the Registrar may
appeal to the Court.' Such an appeal would be governed by RSC Ord 93, r 10(3), which
provides, in relation to such an appeal:

'No appeal shall lie from the decision of the Court on an appeal under any of the
enactments mentioned in [and then material exceptions are set out] except with the
leave of the Court or of the Court of Appeal.'

I need not refer to r 300 of the 1925 rules. Rule 301 provides as follows:

'No appeal from a decision or order of the Registrar, or (unless otherwise ordered)
of the Court, shall affect any dealing for valuable consideration which has been duly
registered before a notice in writing of the intention to appeal has been delivered at
the registry on the part of the appellant. Such notice shall be entered in the register.'

And r 302 provides:

'(1) Service on the Registrar of any order or office copy of any order of any Court
shall be made by delivering the same at the Registry.

(2) When the order directs rectification of the register to be made, or any other
act to be done, an application therefor shall be delivered at the same time and the
matter shall be proceeded with as the registrar shall direct: Provided that no such
rectification, or act, shall be completed until the expiration of four clear days from
the day on which the order is made.'

It will be noticed that r 302 is entirely general, referring as it does to 'any order of any
Court' and it was presumably pursuant to that provision that the original caution was
vacated subject to Judge Baker's order.

The question is, therefore, should the reference in r 302 to an 'appeal from ... a
decision of the Court' be restricted by reference to rr 298 and 299 to appeals from the
decision of the court on appeal from the registrar or on a reference from him? Or, should
the apparently unrestricted words be left with an unrestricted meaning, confirmed by
the general provisions of r 302?

The defendant claims that unless the former construction is preferred the rule will
permit abuse of the court's procedure, as he claims has happened in this case, and set up
a conflict with Ord 59, r 13(1), which provides:

'Except so far as the court below or the Court of Appeal or a single judge may direct—(a) an appeal shall not operate as a stay of execution of proceedings under the decision of the court below; (b) no intermediate act or proceedings shall be invalidated by an appeal.'

As to the first point, I do not think that there has been an abuse of the court's procedure, unless I construe the rule as the defendant claims I should. So this point does not advance the argument on the question of construction.

As to the second point, there is no actual conflict because the appeal did not strictly operate as a stay on Judge Baker's judgment and order and the original caution has been vacated, though no doubt in practice the entry purportedly made pursuant to r 301 has the same effect as the original caution.

In my judgment, r 301 is of general application. It is concerned with the position of third parties and the effect on dealings for valuable consideration which are duly registered in the event of an appeal, by inference, subsequently succeeding. The dividing line which was adopted was delivery to the registrar of notice in writing of the intention to appeal and placing the registrar under an obligation to enter such notice on the register. Dealings already registered before the entry of such a notice would be unaffected by the subsequent fate of the appeal. Dealings not registered could be affected.

If this is, as I think, the purpose of the rule, then there is no need to confine its operation to some only of the appeals which might affect intermediate registered dealings for value by third parties.

Accordingly, in my judgment both the wording and the apparent purpose of r 301 show that it is unlimited in its application. It follows from this that the plaintiff, who was entitled to appeal from the order of Judge Baker, was also entitled to give notice thereof to the registrar. The registrar was then obliged to make the appropriate entry in the register.

Accordingly, in view of my decision on the question of construction, I see no ground for making an order as sought under para 2 of the notice of motion and no need to make an order as sought under para 1 of the notice of motion.

It was also submitted by the plaintiff that as the order of Judge Baker was a final order and that the relief now sought was sought in the same action and was not for the purpose of working out Judge Baker's order, I had no jurisdiction to entertain the application. In the light of my decision on the question of construction, I need not and do not express any view on this submission.

*Motion dismissed.*

Solicitors: *Camerons*, Harrow (for the plaintiff); *Woolf Seddon Roscoe Phillips* (for the defendant).

Hazel Hartman    Barrister.

a   # Re a debtor (No 10 of 1988, Aylesbury), ex parte Lovell Construction (Southern) Ltd v The debtor

CHANCERY DIVISION
b   HOFFMANN J
2 DECEMBER 1988

*Insolvency – Statutory demand – Setting aside statutory demand – Grounds on which statutory demand may be set aside – Debt disputed on substantial grounds – Whether court having power to set aside demand if part of debt demanded is disputed – Insolvency Rules 1986, r 6.5(4)(b).*

c
The court's power under r 6.5(4)(b)ᵃ of the Insolvency Rules 1986 to set aside a statutory demand if 'the debt is disputed on grounds that appear to the court to be substantial' includes the power to set aside a statutory demand if part of the debt demanded is disputed on substantial grounds (see p 41 *a b f*, post).

d   **Notes**
For setting aside a statutory demand, see 3(2) Halsbury's Laws (4th edn reissue) paras 148–149.
    For the Insolvency Rules 1986, r 6.5, see 3 Halsbury's Statutory Instruments (Grey Volume) 364.

e   **Cases referred to in judgment**
*Cardiff Preserved Coal and Coke Co v Norton* (1867) LR 2 Ch App 405.
*Company, Re a* [1984] 3 All ER 78, [1984] 1 WLR 1090.

**Cases also cited**
*Foulds (R A) Ltd, Re* (1986) 2 BCC 99269.
f   *Practice Direction (Bankruptcy 1/87)* [1987] 1 All ER 607, [1987] 1 WLR 119.
*Tweed's Garages Ltd, Re* [1962] 1 All ER 121, [1962] Ch 406.

**Appeal**
By notice of appeal dated 29 September 1988 the appellants, Lovell Construction (Southern) Ltd, appealed against an order made by Mr Registrar Smee in the Aylesbury
g   County Court on 8 September 1988 setting aside a statutory demand served on the respondent debtor by the appellants.

*D R J Alexander* for the appellants.
The respondent appeared in person.

h   **HOFFMANN J.** This is an appeal from an order of the registrar in the Aylesbury County Court setting aside a statutory demand under the Insolvency Act 1986. The demand was made by the appellants, a firm of builders, against the respondent for whom they had performed building work on her house. The demand was in the sum of £15,727·17. The application to set aside the demand was made under the Insolvency
j   Rules 1986, SI 1986/1925, r 6.5(4)(b) on the grounds that the debt was disputed. The respondent swore an affidavit in which she said that the builders had done a very bad

---

a   Rule 6.5(4), so far as material, provides: 'The court may grant the application [to set aside a statutory demand] if . . . (b) the debt is disputed on grounds which appear to the court to be substantial . . .'

job, that they had overcharged her in relation to their estimate and that she proposed to make a counterclaim against them.

*a*

Counsel for the appellants concedes that there is a triable issue as to a substantial part of the amount included in the demand; but, he says, the respondent in her own affidavit says that on 12 April 1988 she attended a meeting with the appellants at which the accounts were gone through that showed the outstanding work which she had not paid for to be £2,426·26, and that, accordingly, at least that sum, together with value added tax, is owing. It is true that the respondent alleges that she has a counterclaim, but the

*b*

grounds on which her counterclaim is stated in her affidavit are somewhat lacking in particularity, and counsel for the appellants said that I should not treat it as raising a seriously triable issue.

The position therefore is that part of the sum demanded is admitted to be disputed on substantial grounds within the meaning of r 6.5(4)(b), and the question is whether on that ground alone the respondent is entitled to have the demand set aside.

*c*

The procedure of statutory demand introduced by the 1986 Act is modelled on that which previously existed in relation to companies. By s 123(1)(a) of the 1986 Act, which reproduces earlier provisions going back a very long way, a company is deemed to be unable to pay its debts if a creditor to whom the company is indebted has served on the company a written demand requiring it to pay the sum so due and the company has for three weeks thereafter neglected to pay the sum.

*d*

In *Cardiff Preserved Coal and Coke Co v Norton* (1867) LR 2 Ch App 405 the question arose of whether the equivalent presumption in the Joint Stock Companies Act 1856 would apply in a case where the demand was for a sum in excess of the sum due. There the demand had been for £628 but the actual debt was only £411. Lord Chelmsford LC said in that case that there was a debt due to the petitioner (at 410):

*e*

'He made, it is true, a demand upon the company for payment of more than was due, but of course the amount due was known to the company, and was included in the demand, and the company neglected to pay "such sum", which means not the sum demanded, but the sum due, which they might have paid, and so have prevented the order being made.'

On that basis it has since been held that where it is clear that a definite sum is owing,

*f*

although less than the amount stated in the statutory demand, the statutory presumption of insolvency will nonetheless apply if the company was in a position to know exactly what it ought to pay: see *Re a company* [1984] 3 All ER 78 at 82, [1984] 1 WLR 1090 at 1095.

Under s 267(2)(c) of the 1986 Act a creditor's petition in bankruptcy may be presented in respect of a debt if, at the time the petition is presented, the debt is a debt which the debtor appears either to be unable to pay or to have no reasonable prospect of being able to pay. By s 268 it is provided:

*g*

'(1) For the purposes of section 267(2)(c), the debtor appears to be unable to pay a debt if, but only if, the debt is payable immediately and [I read one of the two alternative conditions]—(a) the petitioning creditor to whom the debt is owed has served on the debtor a demand (known as "the statutory demand") in the prescribed form requiring him to pay the debt or to secure or compound for it to the satisfaction of the creditor, at least 3 weeks have elapsed since the demand was served and the demand has been neither complied with nor set aside in accordance with the rules...'

*h*

It appears therefore that, unlike the position in the case of companies to which Lord Chelmsford LC referred in *Cardiff Preserved Coal and Coke Co v Norton*, the ground on which the bankruptcy petition may be presented is not that the debtor has failed to pay the sum actually due to the creditor, but that he has failed to comply with the terms of the bankruptcy notice. Thus in the case of a bankruptcy notice which was for a greater

*j*

a    amount than that actually owed, the creditor could not avert a petition merely by paying
    the amount actually owing. He would have to either pay the whole sum demanded or
    have the statutory demand set aside. That being the case it seems to me that the debtor
    must, under r 6.5(4)(b), be entitled to have the demand set aside unless the whole of the
    debt demanded in the statutory demand is in fact undisputed.

    Counsel for the appellants said that if that were the case, creditors who were not
    confident of being able to establish beyond doubt the full amount which they were
b    claiming would have to take care to formulate a bankruptcy notice in a sum which was
    within the limit which they felt sure that they could substantiate; if they demanded
    more than that sum and the debtor was able to show that there was a bona fide dispute as
    to any additional amount, then the notice would be liable to be set aside. That does
    indeed appear to be the consequence of the construction which I have given to the rule,
    but I do not necessarily regard this as being contrary to the policy of the statute. The
c    service of the statutory demand is a serious matter and it seems to me right that creditors
    should confine it to the amounts as to which there can be no substantial dispute.

    Counsel for the appellants drew attention to r 6.5(4)(a) of the 1986 rules, under which
    the court may set aside the statutory demand if the debtor appears to have a counterclaim,
    set-off or cross-demand which equals or exceeds the amount of the debt. He submitted
    that it was anomalous that a debtor could have the statutory demand set aside by showing
d    a dispute as to only part of it but that he could not have it set aside on the grounds of a
    counterclaim unless that counterclaim were in excess of the whole amount of the debt
    due. Similarly he referred me to r 6.5(5), which deals with the case in which the creditor
    has, in formulating the demand, undervalued any security which he holds. In that case
    the result is not to have the statutory notice set aside but to give the debtor the right to
    require him to amend it so as to reduce the amount to the level which is truly unsecured.
e    I accept that the first provision means that to avoid a petition the debtor may have to
    pay the whole sum demanded even though he had a cross-claim for part. But cross-claims
    have always been treated somewhat differently from disputes over the debt itself. The
    second provision presents no similar difficulty.

    Accordingly, it seems to me that on the true construction of the rule the debt in respect
f    of which the demand was made in this case was disputed on grounds which appear to be
    substantial and the debtor was entitled to have the demand set aside.

    The appeal must therefore be dismissed.

*Order accordingly.*

Solicitors: *Cripps & Shone*, High Wycombe (for the appellants).

                                                    Evelyn M C Budd    Barrister.

# Re a debtor (No 310 of 1988), ex parte the debtor v Arab Bank Ltd

CHANCERY DIVISION
KNOX J
9 DECEMBER 1988

*Insolvency – Statutory demand – Setting aside statutory demand – Debt disputed on substantial grounds – Security in respect of debt – Debtor's claim against third party assigned to creditor – Whether security in respect of debt restricted to debts secured over debtor's property – Whether security in respect of debt including claim against third party assigned to creditor – Insolvency Act 1986, s 383(2) – Insolvency Rules 1986, rr 6.1(5), 6.5(4)(c).*

The debtor guaranteed a debt amounting to $ US227,580 plus interest owed to the creditor bank by a company of which he was a director and shareholder. The debtor admitted liability under the terms of the guarantee for the debt. However, a claim which the company had against a third party had been assigned to the bank and when the bank issued a statutory demand against the debtor for the full amount of the debt the debtor applied under r 6.5(4)(c)[a] of the Insolvency Rules 1986 to have the demand set aside on the ground that the assigned claim against the third party constituted 'security in respect of the debt' and therefore the demand did not comply with r 6.1(5)[b] because the amount claimed in the demand should have been the amount of the debt less the security, ie the value of the assigned claim. The registrar dismissed the application and the debtor appealed.

**Held** – The term 'security' in the 1986 rules was to be construed in accordance with the definition of that term contained in s 383(2)[c] of the Insolvency Act 1986, which provided that a debt was secured to the extent that security was held over any property of the debtor whether by way of mortgage, charge, lien or other security, and since the claim against the third party assigned to the bank was not secured over the debtor's property there had been no failure to comply with r 6.1(5) of the 1986 rules and the statutory demand could not be set aside under r 6.5(4)(c). The appeal would therefore be dismissed (see p 44 c j to p 45 b d, post).

**Notes**
For setting aside a statutory demand, see 3(2) Halsbury's Laws (4th edn reissue) paras 148–149.

For the Insolvency Act 1986, s 383, see 4 Halsbury's Statutes (4th edn) (1987 reissue) 1010.

For the Insolvency Rules 1986, rr 6.1, 6.5, see 3 Halsbury's Statutory Instruments (Grey Volume) 362, 364.

**Appeal**
The debtor appealed against the decision of Mr Registrar Dewhurst on 11 October 1988 refusing to set aside a statutory demand served on the debtor by the respondent, Arab Bank Ltd, on the ground that the statutory demand did not comply with r 6.1(5) of the Insolvency Rules 1986, SI 1986/1925, because the amount claimed should have been the

---

a  Rule 6.5(4), so far as material, is set out at p 44 *d e*, post
b  Rule 6.1(5) is set out at p 43 *j*, post
c  Section 383(2) is set out at p 44 *b*, post

amount of the debt less security, ie the value of a claim against a third party which the
*a*  debtor had assigned to the bank. The facts are set out in the judgment.

*Andrew Munday* for the debtor.
*Hugh Tomlinson* for the creditor bank.

**KNOX J.** This is an appeal from a decision of Mr Registrar Dewhurst whereby on 11
*b*  October 1988 he dismissed an application to set aside a statutory demand.

The statutory demand was made by the respondent bank on the debtor, and it claimed
the sum of £107,994·16. The way the matter was set out in the statutory demand was
that it was described as a debt arising out of the agreement evidenced by a letter of 18
December 1987. That is a reference (it is not in dispute) to a letter by which a previous
application to set aside a statutory demand by the same creditor against the same debtor
*c*  was compromised. The letter is in fact in evidence. It is dated 18 December and it records
the compromise. In para 1 there was confirmation that the debtor admitted that he was
liable to the bank under the terms of a guarantee dated 26 September 1980 in the sum of
$ US227,580·28 plus some interest. Paragraph 2 records an agreement between the
parties' solicitors that that sum, together with interest, should be paid in certain
*d*  instalments, the first one of $ US50,000 which was in fact paid, and the balance of
$ US177,000 to be paid on 18 June and 18 December of this year, of which the first was
not paid; the second, of course, has not become due yet.

Then the letter provides that if any of the instalments are not paid the remaining
balance becomes due and payable. Paragraph 4 disposes of the then existing statutory
demand. Then para 5 says:

*e*       'Subject to [the debtor] complying with his aforesaid obligations to make payment
      to our client, our client shall forebear from pursuing any legal remedies against [the
      debtor in his capacity as guarantor] or against [the company guaranteed] in relation
      to the above indebtedness. In the event [that ] there is any default of any of the
      above obligations our client reserves the right to pursue any proceedings against
*f*     [the debtor], or against [the company] which we may deem appropriate without
      giving notice to [the debtor] or [the company].'

In relation to that, it is said that the effect of this compromise was not to release all pre-
existing claims, but rather to put a temporary stop on the rights that the creditor had
under the status quo ante before the compromise was reached; and it seems to me that
there is considerable force in that submission, because para 5 does contemplate the
*g*  survival of the original cause of action. Otherwise it is difficult to see what rights to
pursue proceedings there were that were being reserved as against the debtor.

In relation to those antecedent rights it is claimed, and not as I understand it disputed,
that the original liability of the debtor was under a guarantee of certain obligations of a
company in which he evidently was interested as a director and shareholder; and in
respect of those, there are claims outstanding against the Export Credit Guarantee
*h*  Department which have been assigned to the respondent bank, the creditor in this case.
That raises the issue which it seems to me does arise for decision, namely, whether the
assigned rights against the Export Credit Guarantee Department constitute security for
the purposes of r 6.1(5) of the Insolvency Rules 1986, SI 1986/1925. The rule reads:

*j*      'If the creditor holds any security in respect of the debt, the full amount of the
      debt shall be specified, but—(a) there shall in the demand be specified the nature of
      the security, and the value which the creditor puts upon it as at the date of the
      demand, and (b) the amount of which payment is claimed by the demand shall be
      the full amount of the debt, less the amount specified as the value of the security.'

That is what is to go into the statutory demand, r 6 being headed, 'Form and content of

statutory demand', a heading which is amply justified by the subsequent provisions of
the rule which I need not read, except for r 6.1(5).                                    *a*
    The Insolvency Act 1986 itself has definitions. Section 385(1) contains, inter alia, the
following, '"secured" and related expressions are to be construed in accordance with
section 383.' That throws one back to that section which contains in sub-s (2) the
following:

> 'Subject to the next two subsections and any provision of the rules requiring a    *b*
> creditor to give up his security for the purposes of proving a debt, a debt is secured
> for the purposes of this Group of Parts to the extent that the person to whom the
> debt is owed holds any security for the debt (whether a mortgage, charge, lien or
> other security) over any property of the person by whom the debt is owed.'

    It is not disputed by counsel for the debtor in his very clear submissions but that that
definition, if it is applicable, does not extend to the export credit guarantee rights which  *c*
were assigned to the creditor in this case, because it is self-evident that that was not over
any property of the person by whom the debt was owed. The question is whether that
definition is one which forms a guide to the interpretation that one should put on
r 6.1(5), because if it is not, and if a wider construction can be put on the provisions of
r 6.1(5), wide enough to let in the Export Credit Guarantee Department security, to use
a prejudicial expression, then it would be a ground for setting aside the statutory demand,  *d*
because, under r 6.5(4)(c) of the 1986 rules it is specifically provided that the court may
grant an application to set a statutory demand aside if it appears that inter alia, 'the
creditor holds some security in respect of the debt claimed by the demand, and . . .
Rule 6.1(5) is not complied with in respect of it . . .' So that a default in complying with
r 6.1(5) is, possibly subject to the discretion of the court, a ground for setting aside the
statutory demand.                                                                        *e*
    It is to be noted that the definition in s 383(2) is subject to any provision of the 1986
rules requiring a creditor to give up his security for the purposes of proving a debt. That
seems to me to reflect forward to the provisions of the rules in Pt 6, and in particular the
one that I have already read, and r 6.5.
    The other provision in the 1986 Act as opposed to the rules to which it seems to me    *f*
that it would be right to have regard in this context is s 267(2), which, near the outset of
Pt IX of the Act, dealing with bankruptcy petitions states what the grounds of a creditor's
petition must be. In particular, one of the qualifications that a creditor's petition has to
satisfy is this:

> 'Subject to the next three sections, a creditor's petition may be presented to the
> court in respect of a debt or debts only if at the time the petition is presented—[then  *g*
> I can pass over para (a), which requires the bankruptcy level to be reached] (b) the
> debt, or each of the debts, is for a liquidated sum payable to the petitioning creditor,
> or one or more of the petitioning creditors, either immediately or at some certain,
> future time, and is unsecured . . .'

    I do not think counsel for the debtor contended significantly to the contrary that      *h*
'unsecured' in that particular context was something which was governed by the
definition section in s 383, more especially with the assistance of s 385(1), which makes
it clear I think beyond any sort of argument that 'secured' is to be construed in much the
same way as 'unsecured', and vice versa. So that so far as the petition is concerned, and
this was accepted, it is clear that 'security' and 'secured' have the narrow sense which one
derives from the definitions in ss 383(2) and 385(1). But what is urged on me is that it is  *j*
not exactly the same turn of phrase that is used in the 1986 rules, and that in r 6.1(5) the
phrase is a wider one, 'If the creditor holds any security in respect of the debt . . .' then
certain consequences follow. The submission is made that because a different and wider
turn of expression is used, one should look for a different and wider meaning. That
seems to me the point at which I part company with the argument. It seems to me that

one has to read the rules in the context of the requirements of the 1986 Act, and it does
*a* seem to me to follow that the word 'security' and the conception of an unsecured debt all
hold together, and that the requirement that value should be placed on a security, and
that the amount to be claimed shall be the amount less the amount specified as the value
of the security, is closely tied to the way in which the grounds for a creditor's petition are
set out in s 267(2).

It seems to me, therefore, that although the turn of phrase is not exactly the same, and
*b* although the definition is in the 1986 Act and not in the 1986 rules, the two ought to be
read so that they mesh together and operate hand in hand. It was submitted to me that it
might be a matter for the exercise of the court's discretion under the fourth of the
grounds that are specified in r 6.5(4) as the bases on which a statutory demand may be set
aside, that there was security in the wider sense of the word that is to say, a security from
a third person and not on the debtor's property, and that to enable that to be taken into
*c* consideration it was desirable that there should be an obligation on the creditor when
serving the statutory demand to put, in the phrase that was used, all the cards on the
table, including any third party rights with which the creditor was armed.

I do not reach that conclusion on the terms of r 6.5(4)(*d*). Indeed, it looks to me, from
that particular paragraph, that it is r 6.5(4)(*c*) that one needs to look at to see whether or
not the creditor has done what he ought to have done under r 6.1(5), and I do not see any
*d* space for implying a wider obligation than there otherwise would be in respect of para
(*d*) than is expressly stated in para (*c*).

For those reasons, I have reached the conclusion that 'security' in r 6.1(5) is governed
by the definition in the 1986 Act, and on that basis counsel for the debtor accepts that
this appeal must fail.

*e*  *Appeal dismissed.*

Solicitors: *Brooke Blain Russell* (for the debtor); *Denton Hall Burgin & Warrens* (for the
bank).

Evelyn M C Budd   Barrister.

# Re a debtor (No 1 of 1987, Lancaster), ex parte the debtor v Royal Bank of Scotland plc

COURT OF APPEAL, CIVIL DIVISION

SIR STEPHEN BROWN P, GLIDEWELL AND NICHOLLS LJJ

16 JANUARY 1989

*Insolvency – Statutory demand – Setting aside statutory demand – Grounds on which statutory demand may be set aside – Other grounds – Statutory demand deficient – Whether debtor prejudiced by deficiencies – Whether statutory demand containing deficiencies should be set aside – Insolvency Rules 1986, r 6.5(4)(d).*

The creditor bank issued a bankruptcy notice against the debtor in respect of his failure to clear a judgment debt which was outstanding. The bank subsequently served a statutory demand on the debtor under s 268ᵃ of the Insolvency Act 1986 and r 6.1ᵇ of the Insolvency Rules 1986 requiring immediate payment of the outstanding debt. Under r 6.5(4)ᶜ the court could set aside a statutory demand on the grounds specified in r 6.5(4)(a) to (c) or 'on other grounds' under r 6.5(4)(d) if it was 'satisfied . . . that the demand ought to be set aside'. The debtor sought to have the statutory demand set aside under r 6.5(4)(d) on the ground that it was defective because it was not in the form prescribed for a judgment debt, it overstated the amount of the debt and the particulars of the calculation of the amount claimed set out in the affidavit in support were perplexing and inconsistent with the supporting exhibits. The registrar refused the application and his decision was upheld by the judge, who ruled that for a statutory demand to be set aside on 'other grounds' within r 6.5(4)(d) those grounds had to be of the same degree of substance as the grounds specified in r 6.5(4)(a), (b) and (c), and that it was not sufficient for the debtor merely to show that the statutory demand served on him was perplexing or contained technical deficiencies, but instead he had to explain the true position between him and the creditor or justify his inability to give such explanation. The debtor appealed.

**Held** – The court would only exercise its discretionary power under r 6.5(4)(d) of the 1986 rules to set aside a statutory demand 'on other grounds' if the circumstances were such that it would be unjust for the creditor to present a bankruptcy petition founded on the debtor's non-compliance with the demand. Although the deficiencies in the demand made it technically defective, there was no evidence of prejudice to the debtor, who had been given all the information which would have been supplied to him had the correct form been completed, and no evidence to suggest that he would have taken steps to satisfy a non-defective demand, and in those circumstances justice did not require that the demand should be set aside. Accordingly, in the absence of injustice to the debtor, the demand would be allowed to stand and his appeal would be dismissed (see p 50 c to e, p 51 h j and p 52 g j to p 53 b e h, post).

*Per curiam.* While the new insolvency code contained in the 1986 Act affords the court a degree of flexibility when confronted with an application to set aside a defective statutory demand, that is not to be taken by creditors as a charter for the slipshod preparation of statutory demands. The making of a bankruptcy order remains a serious step in relation to the debtor and the prescribed preliminaries are intended to afford protection to him (see p 53 f, post).

Decision of Warner J [1988] 1 All ER 959 affirmed.

---

a    Section 268, so far as material, is set out at p 47 h, post

b    Rule 6.1, so far as material, is set out at p 48 a to c, post

c    Rule 6.5(4) is set out at p 50 a b, post

**Notes**

For setting aside a statutory demand, see 3(2) Halsbury's Laws (4th edn reissue) paras 148–149.

For the Insolvency Act 1986, s 268, see 4 Halsbury's Statutes (4th edn) (1987 reissue) 911.

For the Insolvency Rules 1986, rr 6.1, 6.5, see 3 Halsbury's Statutory Instruments (Grey Volume) 362, 364.

**Cases referred to in judgments**

Debtor (No 21 of 1950), Re a, ex p the debtor v Bowmaker Ltd [1950] 2 All ER 1129, [1951] Ch 313, DC.

Debtor (No 190 of 1987), Re a (1988) Times, 21 May.

Pillai v Comptroller of Income Tax [1970] AC 1124, [1970] 2 WLR 1053, PC.

**Appeal**

The debtor appealed with leave against the decision of Warner J ([1988] 1 All ER 959, [1988] 1 WLR 419) on 12 October 1987 dismissing his appeal against the refusal of the registrar in the Lancaster County Court to set aside a statutory demand dated 14 April 1987 served on him by the plaintiff creditor, Royal Bank of Scotland plc, under s 268(1)(a) of the Insolvency Act 1986 and r 6.1 of the Insolvency Rules 1986, SI 1986/1925. The facts are set out in the judgment of Nicholls LJ.

Nigel Joseph Ley for the debtor.
Peter Griffiths for the bank.

**NICHOLLS LJ** (delivering the first judgment at the invitation of Sir Stephen Brown P). The Insolvency Act 1986 contains the new insolvency code. Section 264 provides that one of the classes of persons who may present a petition for a bankruptcy order to be made against an individual comprises his creditors.

Section 267(2) sets out four conditions which must be satisfied in the case of a creditors' petition presented in respect of a debt. One of these conditions, contained in para (c), is that the debt is one which the debtor appears either to be unable to pay or to have no reasonable prospect of being able to pay.

The tests to be applied in determining whether, for this purpose, a debtor appears to be unable to pay a debt which is immediately payable are stated in s 268(1). Two tests are prescribed, fulfilment of either of which is sufficient for a creditor's purpose. The first, stated in para (a), is:

> 'the petitioning creditor to whom the debt is owed has served on the debtor a demand (known as "the statutory demand") in the prescribed form requiring him to pay the debt or to secure or compound for it to the satisfaction of the creditor, at least 3 weeks have elapsed since the demand was served and the demand has been neither complied with nor set aside in accordance with the rules.'

The second test, stated in para (b), is of an unsatisfied return to 'execution or other process issued in respect of the debt on a judgment or order of any court . . .'

The prescribed form for a statutory demand is set out, so far as applicable in the present case, in the Insolvency Rules 1986, SI 1986/1925. We were told that certain amendments have been made in respect of the prescribed forms under amending regulations, namely the Insolvency (Amendment) Rules 1987, SI 1987/1919, but they are not applicable in this case having regard to the relevant dates. Rule 6.1(1) of the 1986 rules provides that the demand must be dated and appropriately signed. Under para (2):

'The statutory demand must specify whether it is made under section 268(1) (debt payable immediately) or section 268(2) (debt not so payable).'

The material part of r 6.1(3) reads as follows:

'The demand must state the amount of the debt, and the consideration for it (or, if there is no consideration, the way in which its arises) and—(a) if made under section 268(1) and founded on a judgment or order of a court, it must give details of the judgment or order . . .'

Rule 6.1(4) provides:

'If the amount claimed in the demand includes—(a) any charge by way of interest not previously notified to the debtor as a liability of his . . . the amount or rate of the charge must be separately identified, and the grounds on which payment of it is claimed must be stated.'

Rule 6.2(1) provides that the statutory demand must include an explanation to the debtor of, amongst other matters:

'(a) the purpose of the demand, and the fact that, if the debtor does not comply with the demand, bankruptcy proceedings may be commenced against him; (b) the time within which the demand must be complied with, if that consequence is to be avoided . . .'

Rule 12.7 provides that the forms contained in Sch 4 to the rules shall be used in, and in connection with, insolvency proceedings, and that the forms shall be used with such variations, if any, as the circumstances may require. The two forms material for the purposes of this appeal are Forms 6.1 and 6.2 (not to be confused with rr 6.1 and 6.2). Both forms are headed 'Statutory Demand under section 268(1)(a) of the Insolvency Act 1986'. In the case of Form 6.1 the heading continues: 'Debt for Liquidated Sum Payable Immediately.' In the case of Form 6.2 the equivalent part of the heading reads: 'Debt for Liquidated Sum Payable Immediately Following a Judgment or Order of the Court.'

The body of the two forms is substantially identical save that Form 6.2 contains spaces which, when completed appropriately, will identify the judgment or order of the court and the amount ordered to be paid thereby to the creditor. There are notes on the forms telling the debtor that, if he wishes to avoid a bankruptcy petition being presented against him, he must pay the debt demanded within 21 days and that if he disputes the demand, in whole or in part, he should contact the creditor or his representative whose name, address and telephone number are stated on the form.

One difference between the two forms is that the notes to Form 6.2 provide that, in the case of a judgment or order of a county court, payment must be made to that court. That is not a difference material in the present case.

Inevitably, of course, mistakes will be made from time to time by creditors, or their advisers, in selecting the correct form to be used, or in completing the Form. That is what happened in the present case. On 1 May 1987 the debtor was served with a statutory demand dated 14 April 1987. The form used was the printed form 6.1. In the body of the form, in the space intended to be completed with details of when the debt was incurred, the description of the debt and the amount due, were typed these words: '6/1/1982 judgment debt plus interest at the statutory rate less monies paid by [the debtor] and interest accrued thereon. See copy affidavit annexed hereto.' The amount of the debt was specified as the sum of £7,286·04.

The copy affidavit annexed to the demand was not a happily drawn document. It harked back to the old bankruptcy procedures. The affidavit purported to be made in support of an application to the Lancaster County Court to issue a bankruptcy notice against the debtor. Paragraph (2) of the affidavit stated that on 7 January 1982 the bank obtained judgment in the Manchester District Registry of the Queen's Bench Division of a the High Court against the debtor and his wife in the sum of £7,857, £155 interest and £110 costs. (In stating those sums, I have ignored pence, and for convenience I shall continue to do so throughout this judgment.)

The affidavit continued by stating that a bankruptcy notice had subsequently been issued by the Blackpool County Court against the debtor. At that time the debtor was living in the Fylde. The bankruptcy notice was issued on 26 October 1982 and was served a few days later. The debtor made proposals for payment by instalments, and he then b made regular and satisfactory payments to the bank until 17 January 1985. Thereafter nothing further was paid. Paragraph 5 exhibited a bundle of bank statements which purported to show that the amount outstanding under the judgment, including interest at the statutory rate up to 3 March 1987, was £15,184. Paragraph 6 exhibited a further bundle of bank statements showing the amounts paid by the debtor since the judgment. With interest credited thereon at the statutory rate, the amount to be credited to 3 March c 1987 totalled £7,898. Hence, arithmetically, the balance due, according to the affidavit, was £7,286.

On 12 May 1987 the debtor applied for an order setting aside the statutory demand. The ground specified in the supporting affidavit made by him was that in four respects the demand did not comply with the provisions of the 1986 rules. The four respects were these: (1) the notice was defective in that it was not in the form prescribed for a judgment d debt; (2) that neither the demand nor the accompanying affidavit identified the judgment relied on; (3) that the Royal Bank of Scotland plc had never obtained a judgment against the debtor in the sum claimed in the demand; and (4) that the form did not give, in Pt C, details of any assignment of the debt of the Royal Bank of Scotland even though on the face of the form the creditor serving the demand was described as 'the Royal Bank of Scotland plc (formerly Williams and Glyn's Bank Limited)'.

e The deputy registrar declined to set aside the demand. In particular, he took the view that, although strictly Form 6.2 was the appropriate form, the form used (Form 6.1) as completed gave the debtor the further information which Form 6.2 envisages will be supplied in the case of a judgment debt. The necessary information concerning the judgment debt was set out in the copy affidavit annexed to the demand.

The debtor appealed, and his appeal was dismissed by Warner J on 12 October 1987 f (see [1988] 1 All ER 959, [1988] 1 WLR 419). The judge found the demand to be perplexing. He said ([1988] 1 All ER 959, [1988] 1 WLR 419 at 420):

> 'There is no doubt in my mind that, if this statutory demand had been a bankruptcy notice under the old legislation, I would have had to set it aside because it is perplexing, so perplexing indeed that counsel who appeared for the creditor g had to ask for an adjournment before he could understand it himself, or rather understand what lay behind it. There are any number of defects in this demand, the gravest of which is that it refers to an affidavit which was served with it as particularising the way in which the amount claimed was ascertained; but there is inconsistency between that affidavit and the exhibits to it as to how that amount was reached.'

h

The judge went on to say that under the new legislation it is not enough for a debtor merely to show that a statutory demand served on him is perplexing, he must go further and show what he says is the true position as between himself and the creditor, or explain why he cannot say what it is (see [1988] 1 All ER 959 at 960, [1988] 1 WLR 419 at 421). The judge noted that there had been no attempt by the debtor to do that. On the j contrary, in his affidavit in support of the application, he had taken only technical points. The debtor has now appealed against Warner J's decision.

Rule 6.5(4) sets out the circumstances in which the court, in the exercise of its discretion, may make an order setting aside a statutory demand. The rule provides as follows:

'The court may grant the application if—(a) the debtor appears to have a counterclaim, set-off or cross demand which equals or exceeds the amount of the *a* debt or debts specified in the statutory demand; or (b) the debt is disputed on grounds which appear to the court to be substantial; or (c) it appears that the creditor holds some security in respect of the debt claimed by the demand, and either Rule 6.1(5) is not complied with in respect of it, or the court is satisfied that the value of the security equals or exceeds the full amount of the debt; or (d) the court is satisfied, on other grounds, that the demand ought to be set aside.'          *b*

The question arising on this appeal concerns the exercise by the court of its power to set aside a statutory demand 'on other grounds' within sub-para (d). In my view, the right approach to para (4) of r 6.5 is this. Under the 1986 Act, a statutory demand which is not complied with founds the consequence that the debtor is regarded as being unable to pay the debt in question or, if the debt is not immediately payable, as having no reasonable prospect of being able to pay the debt when it becomes due. That consequence, in turn, *c* founds the ability of the creditor to present a bankruptcy petition because, under s 268(1), in the absence of an unsatisfied return to execution or other process a debtor's inability to pay the debt in question is established if, but only if, the appropriate statutory demand has been served and not complied with.

When therefore the rules provide, as does r 6.5(4)(d), for the court to have a residual *d* discretion to set aside a statutory demand, the circumstances which normally will be required before a court can be satisfied that the demand 'ought' to be set aside, are circumstances which would make it unjust for the statutory demand to give rise to those consequences in the particular case. The court's intervention is called for to prevent that injustice.

This approach to sub-para (d) is in line with the particular grounds specified in sub- *e* paras (a) to (c) of r 6.5(4). Normally it would be unjust that an individual should be regarded as unable to pay a debt if the debt is disputed on substantial grounds (sub-para (b)); likewise if the debtor has a counterclaim, set-off or cross-demand which equals or exceeds the amount of the debt (sub-para (a)); again, if the creditor is fully secured (sub-para (c)).

Counsel for the debtor submitted that the test to be applied by the court in determining *f* whether a statutory demand ought to be set aside is the objective one of whether the demand is calculated to perplex, formerly applied on applications to set aside bankruptcy notices.

I am unable to accept this. I do not think that on this the new bankruptcy code simply incorporates and adopts the same approach as the old code. The new code has made many changes in the law of bankruptcy, and the court's task, with regard to the new code, must *g* be to construe the new statutory provisions in accordance with the ordinary canons of construction, unfettered by previous authorities. Those authorities on the setting aside of bankruptcy notices were concerned with a different scheme, in that the operation of a bankruptcy notice was not, in all respects, the same as the effect of the new statutory demand. For example, unlike bankruptcy notices, the statutory demand can be relied on only by the creditor serving it.          *h*

I am fortified in this approach to the new bankruptcy code by certain observations made by Vinelott J, who has a particularly intimate acquaintance with the new bankruptcy scheme. In *Re a debtor (No 190 of 1987)* (1988) Times, 21 May Vinelott J was concerned with an application to set aside a statutory demand in which the date of a guarantee had been misstated. In upholding the registrar's refusal to set aside the statutory demand, the judge made observations to the effect that one of the purposes of *j* the new legislation was to avoid the technicalities which grew up around the bankruptcy law when framed as penal proceedings, and that it would be unfortunate if the new provisions were to become enmeshed in the technical objections which disfigures the old law.

In my view, applying the ordinary principles of construction to the new statutory
*a* provisions, the court's task under r 6.5(4) is as I have sought to state.

Before proceeding further, I should note a submission made on behalf of the debtor
that, in the light of the totality of the errors in this statutory demand, the document
served was not in law a statutory demand at all. Counsel referred us to *Pillai v Comptroller
of Income Tax* [1970] AC 1124. In that case the advice of the Board was given by Lord
Diplock. The question in that case concerned a bankruptcy notice which was, as required,
*b* signed by the registrar, sealed with the seal of the court and expressed to be issued by the
court (there, the High Court in Malaya) but which, as also required, did not mention the
Chief Justice of that court, or the Yang di-Pertuan Agong.

Lord Diplock said (at 1135):

'But there is relevant authority upon the construction of the identical words in
*c* section 147(1) of the English Bankruptcy Act, 1914. It is implicit in the section that
proceedings in bankruptcy may be so defective as to render them a nullity
notwithstanding that no substantial and irremedial injustice has in fact been caused
by the defect. The section draws a distinction between such a defect and a "formal
defect or irregularity". It is only the latter which are validated by the section,
provided that no substantial and irremedial injustice has been caused. What, then,
*d* is a "formal defect or irregularity" within the meaning of the section? This was
discussed in relation to a bankruptcy notice in *In re A Debtor (No. 21 of 1950), Ex
parte the Debtor v. Bowmaker Ltd.* ([1950] 2 All ER 1129, [1951] Ch 313), in which
the earlier authorities were considered. The test there laid down was whether the
defect in the notice was of such a kind as could reasonably mislead a debtor upon
whom it was served. If it was, the notice was not validated by the section
*e* notwithstanding that the particular debtor upon whom it was served was not in fact
misled. If, on the other hand, it could not reasonably mislead the debtor it was a
formal defect and validated by the section. Their Lordships are here only concerned
with the application of the section to a bankruptcy notice. They are not concerned
with whether the same test is appropriate to determine the validity of subsequent
steps in bankruptcy proceedings. In their view any failure to comply with the
*f* statutory provisions as to the form of a bankruptcy notice of a kind which could not
reasonably mislead a debtor upon whom it is served is a "formal defect" and
validated by the section.'

Like the judge I am not persuaded by this argument even though s 147(1) of the
Bankruptcy Act 1914 is reproduced in substantially identical terms in r 7.55 of the 1986
*g* rules. No doubt there may still be cases where the document served as a statutory demand
is so defective that it cannot sensibly be regarded as a statutory demand at all. That is not
this case. The essentials required of a statutory demand were present in this case. The
deficiencies in the demand make this indeed a defective demand, but I do not think that
they are sufficient to deprive the document altogether of its character of a statutory
demand.

*h* I turn therefore to consider whether the deficiencies make this a case in which it would
be unjust for the demand to be allowed to stand. As to that I say at once that, in
agreement with the deputy registrar and with the judge, I see nothing in any of the four
points set out in the affidavit sworn in support of the application. In particular, the copy
affidavit annexed to the statutory demand and to which the statutory demand referred
sufficiently identified the 1982 judgment and gave the debtor the information which
*j* would have been supplied to him had Form 6.2 been used and appropriately completed.

In this court, however, the debtor made an application for leave to adduce further
evidence, to the effect that he does not know the amount, if any, still owed by him to the
bank, and he explains with reference to the documents why this is so. His explanation
for not having made an affidavit to this effect previously is that he was advised by his

solicitor that, in accordance with the old law relating to bankruptcy notices, his own state of mind, having received a statutory demand, was irrelevant. This latter explanation, it *a* seems to me, is all very well as far as it goes, but it cannot conceal that the debtor is seeking in substance to take on appeal a new point regarding the statutory demand. Neither before the judge, nor before the deputy registrar, was the point taken that the amount specified by the bank in its statutory demand as the sum currently due must be materially wrong and that the debtor did not know the true amount, if any, of the debt.

In the exercise of our discretion we admitted the further evidence and permitted the *b* new point to be taken. Over the period of three years from January 1982 to January 1985 the debtor paid to the bank sums of varying amounts and at irregular intervals. So the calculation of the balance due to the bank, under the judgment debt with interest, is not altogether straightforward. Indeed, the bank itself got the calculation wrong. It would not be at all surprising, therefore, that the debtor should be ignorant of the precise amount still due from him to the bank, and it would not be right for this appeal, *c* concerned as it is with bankruptcy proceedings, to proceed on what in the circumstances would be likely to be a false factual footing.

In the event the debtor, as I have already said, was served, along with the statutory demand, with a calculation which was confusing. It was confusing in particular in that the opening entry was not the amount of the judgment debt, but a much smaller sum, to which was added a substantial sum of interest expressed to be payable for a short *d* period prior to the date of the judgment. The interest calculation for that period, as set out, was manifestly wrong. Further, the calculation of subsequent interest did not follow the pattern of the sums paid in being credited to the account, with interest at the appropriate rate being calculated on the reducing balance. Instead, the sums paid in were totted up in a separate account, with interest thereon. That of course achieved the same arithmetical result but, given the other elements of confusion, this was not a helpful *e* method of presentation of the account to the debtor.

Not only was the calculation sent with the statutory demand confusing; the amount specified was wrong. The interest calculations were made on the basis of compound interest being payable at varying rates, whereas only simple interest was payable on the judgment debt, and that at the rate of 15% per annum applicable when the judgment debt arose. The correct amount, put forward by the bank in affidavit evidence sworn on *f* 9 December 1988, is £6,746.

Nevertheless, applying the approach which I have indicated above as the correct approach to these statutory provisions, in my view it by no means follows from the existence of those defects that this statutory demand ought to be set aside. The court will exercise its discretion on whether or not to set aside a statutory demand having regard to all the circumstances. That must require the court to have regard to all the circumstances *g* as they are at the time of the hearing before the court. There may be cases where the terms of the statutory demand are so confusing or misleading that, having regard to all the circumstances, justice requires that the demand should not be allowed to stand. There will be other cases where, despite such defects in the contents of the statutory demand, those defects have not prejudiced and will not prejudice the debtor in any way, *h* and to set aside the demand in such a case would serve no useful purpose. For example, a debtor may be wholly unable to pay a debt which is immediately payable, either out of his own resources or with financial assistance from others. In such a case the only practical consequence of setting aside a statutory demand would be that the creditor would promptly serve a revised statutory demand, which also and inevitably would not be complied with. In such a case the need for a further statutory demand would serve only *j* to increase costs. Such a course would not be in the interests of anyone.

In the present case the amount stated was wrong, but in my view the mere overstatement of the amount of the debt in a statutory demand is not, by itself and without more, a ground for setting aside a statutory demand. This is implicit, first, in the provisions in r 6.5(4)(a) to (c), which envisage that the counterclaim, set-off, cross-

claim, dispute or security, will extend to the full amount of the debt, and, second, in the terms of r 6.25(3). In the present case there is no evidence that the error as to the amount due or the misleading features of the calculation have resulted or will result in the debtor being prejudiced in any way. There is, for example, no evidence that had the correct amount been stated in the statutory demand, the debtor would have taken steps to satisfy the demand, or that he has been deprived of this or any other opportunity by his perplexity, either as to the precise amount of the debt due or as to anything else contained
b in the demand. Indeed, the debtor's affidavit admitted on this appeal, and setting out his perplexity, is in some respects a disingenuous document. Thus in para 5 he makes submissions as to why he found the bank's statement of account perplexing. He makes a calculation which is based on the judgment debt being in the sum of £3,379, and concludes that on that footing, and having regard to the payments he has made, the bank would be indebted to him. But it is clear that the order of the court dated 7 January
c 1982, ordering payment of the sum of £8,012, inclusive of interest plus costs, was served on the debtor, albeit a long time ago. This sum of £8,012 is the sum which appears near the top of the bank's statement, below the first of the erroneous calculations.

Moreover, had the debtor genuinely been perplexed on some point which actually affected what he did after he was served with the statutory demand, he, or the solicitor who on his behalf made the application to set aside the statutory demand, would surely
d have approached the bank for clarification. Instead, this point, of the debtor genuinely being misled and perplexed, was not even taken before the deputy registrar or the judge.

In these circumstances I am in no doubt that, despite the mistakes in this statutory demand and the use strictly of the incorrect form, and despite the debtor not being aware of the precise amount of the debt when the demand was served on him, justice does not require that this statutory demand should be set aside. I can see no injustice in the
e consequences which flow from non-compliance with a statutory demand being permitted to flow in this case, despite the existence of those features.

I add a footnote. The new statutory code affords the court a desirable degree of flexibility when confronted with an application to set aside a statutory demand containing one or more defects. But this is not to be taken by banks or others as a charter for the slipshod preparation of statutory demands. The making of a bankruptcy order remains a
f serious step so far as a debtor is concerned, and the prescribed preliminaries are intended to afford protection to him. If a statutory demand is served in an excessive amount or is otherwise defective, the court will be alert to see whether those mistakes have caused or will cause any prejudice to the debtor. In the present case no prejudice has resulted, or will result, and hence it is right that the statutory demand should be allowed to stand. But if there had been prejudice, the bank would only have had itself to blame if the court
g had set aside the statutory demand.

I would dismiss this appeal.

**GLIDEWELL LJ.** I agree.

h **SIR STEPHEN BROWN P.** I also agree that the appeal should be dismissed for the reasons given by Nicholls LJ.

*Appeal dismissed. Leave to appeal to the House of Lords refused.*

Solicitors: *J S Siergant & Co*, Chorley (for the debtor); *Cobbett Leak Almond*, Manchester (for the bank).

Bebe Chua    Barrister.

# Cia Portorafti Commerciale SA v Ultramar Panama Inc and others

# The Captain Gregos

QUEEN'S BENCH DIVISION (COMMERCIAL COURT)
HIRST J
14, 21 DECEMBER 1988

*Shipping – Carriage by sea – Damages for breach of contract – Time limit for bringing action – Misdelivery of cargo – Cargo interests bringing action against carrier claiming damages for misdelivery of part of cargo – Cargo interests alleging theft by carrier – Action brought outside one-year limitation period prescribed by Hague Visby Rules for claims in respect of carriage of goods – Whether claim for misdelivery subject to one-year limitation period – Carriage of Goods by Sea Act 1971, Sch, art II, art III, para 6.*

The owners of a cargo of crude oil which was to be shipped from Egypt to Rotterdam sold it to P, which then resold the cargo under a processing deal to B. The cargo was subsequently loaded at an Egyptian port onto a vessel chartered from the carrier. The contract of carriage contained in the two bills of lading incorporated the Hague Visby Rules, as set out in the schedule to the Carriage of Goods by Sea Act 1971. More than one year after the cargo had been discharged in Rotterdam, the cargo interests, P and B, brought an action for damages against the carrier, claiming that the carrier had stolen a quantity of the oil by diverting it into a gathering space on board the vessel and not delivering it to B, the party entitled to it. The carrier issued an originating summons against the cargo interests, seeking the determination of the court on the question whether the one-year limitation period prescribed by art III, para 6[a] of the Hague Visby Rules discharged the carrier from all liability in respect of the misdelivery of the cargo arising out of the alleged theft because the action was brought more than one year after the cargo should have been delivered and was therefore extinguished.

**Held** – Since delivery and the concepts of possessory or proprietary rights associated with it were outside the scope of art II[b] of the Hague Visby Rules, which provided that the carrier was subject to the responsibilities and liabilities set out in art III of those rules 'in relation to the loading, handling, stowage, carriage, custody, care and discharge' stages in the transportation of a cargo, it followed that misdelivery of any kind, whether made honestly, dishonestly or arising out of an alleged theft by the carrier, was outside the scope of art III, para 6, and accordingly a carrier could not rely on that paragraph to defeat a claim by cargo interests for misdelivery of the cargo. The claim for misdelivery was therefore not subject to the one-year limitation period, and the carrier's summons would accordingly be dismissed (see p 62 b to d g j to p 63 a, post).

Dictum of Kerr LJ in *D/S A/S Idaho v Peninsular and Oriental Steam Navigation Co, The Strathnewton* [1983] 1 Lloyd's Rep 219 at 223 applied.

### Notes

For time limits for bringing actions for loss or damage under the Hague Visby Rules, see 43 Halsbury's Laws (4th edn) para 773, and for cases on the subject, see 43 Digest (Reissue) 597, 11084–11086.

For the Carriage of Goods by Sea Act 1971, Sch, arts II, III, see 39 Halsbury's Statutes (4th edn) 836.

---

a Article III, para 6, so far as material, is set out at p 57 a b, post
b Article II is set out at p 56 j, post

**Cases referred to in judgment**

a  *Brown & Co Ltd v Harrison, Hourani v Harrison* (1927) 96 LJKB 1025, [1927] All ER Rep 195, CA.

*D/S A/S Idaho v Peninsular and Oriental Steam Navigation Co, The Strathnewton* [1983] 1 Lloyd's Rep 219, CA.

*Fothergill v Monarch Airlines Ltd* [1980] 2 All ER 696, [1981] AC 251, [1980] 3 WLR 209, HL.

b  *Gatoil International Inc v Arkwright-Boston Manufacturers Mutual Insurance Co* [1985] 1 All ER 129, [1985] AC 255, [1985] 2 WLR 74, HL.

*Hollandia, The* [1982] 3 All ER 1141, [1983] 1 AC 565, [1982] 3 WLR 1111, HL.

*Jade, The, The Eschersheim* [1976] 1 All ER 920, [1976] 1 WLR 430, HL.

**Originating summons**

c  By a summons dated 28 January 1987, as amended on 27 November 1987, the plaintiff, Cia Portorafti Commerciale SA of Panama, sought as against the defendants, Ultramar Panama Inc of Panama, Phibro Energy AG of Switzerland and BP Oil International Ltd, the determination of the court of the question whether a claim in tort by the defendants, who were the owners of a cargo of crude oil carried by the plaintiff on board the vessel Captain Gregos pursuant to a contract of carriage contained in or evidenced by two bills d  of lading (ref no LN-A-84-42) dated 31 May and 1 June 1984 which incorporated the Hague Visby Rules for damages arising out of an alleged theft of part of the cargo had been extinguished by art III, para 6 of the Hague Visby Rules on the ground that suit was not brought within one year of the date when the cargo should have been delivered. The first defendant took no part in the summons since it had sold its interest in the cargo of oil to the second defendant on 25 May 1984, several days prior to the date of the contract e  of carriage. The facts are set out in the judgment.

Nigel Teare for the plaintiff.
Iain Milligan for the defendants.

f
*Cur adv vult*

21 December. The following judgment was delivered.

**HIRST J.**
g  *Introduction*
    The central issue in the present case is whether the one-year time bar in favour of the carrier laid down by art III, para 6 of the Hague Visby Rules applies to a claim by the cargo owners in conversion based on the alleged theft of the cargo by the carrier himself.
    If this point is resolved against the carrier, it is common ground in the present case h  that the defendant cargo owners are entitled to succeed. If the point is resolved in favour of the plaintiff carrier, other issues arise which I shall refer to very briefly at the end of this judgment.

*Factual background*
    By a voyage charterparty dated 24 May 1984 a company called Scandports Shipping j  Ltd chartered a vessel called the Captain Gregos from the plaintiff carrier, Cia Portorafti Commerciale SA of Panama, to carry a cargo of crude oil from an Egyptian Red Sea port to Rotterdam.
    On 25 May 1984 the cargo was sold by the first defendant, Ultramar Panama Inc (which has not been served and which has played no part in the case), to the second defendant, Phibro Energy AG.

On the same day Phibro resold the cargo under a processing deal to the third defendant, BP Oil International Ltd. On 31 May and 1 June 1984 the cargo was loaded at an *a* Egyptian port and was discharged to BP in Rotterdam on 16 and 17 June 1984.

On 17 June 1985, as is common ground, the time period (if it applies) for commencing suit under art III, para 6 expired. On 5 December 1985 solicitors on behalf of the defendant cargo interests, now effectively identified as Phibro and BP, claimed that the plaintiff carrier had stolen a quantity of oil valued at $US261,000 by diverting that amount of the cargo into a gathering space on board and not delivering it to the party *b* entitled to it. This was alleged to be part of a course of conduct also involving other voyages by the same vessel which are not in issue in the present case. On 27 June 1986 security was given for the claim to avoid arrest of the vessel.

On 28 January 1987 the plaintiff carrier issued the present originating summons claiming the following relief, it not being disputed that the bills of lading signed by the vessel's master on 31 May and 1 June respectively under the reference number cited in *c* the originating summons incorporated the Hague Visby Rules:

> 'whether a claim in tort by the owners of a cargo of crude oil carried on board the vessel CAPTAIN GREGOS pursuant to the contract of carriage contained in or evidenced by 2 bills of lading ref. no. LN-A-84-42 dated 31 May 1984 and 1 June 1984 which incorporate the Hague-Visby rules for damages arising out of an alleged theft of part *d* of the said cargo has been extinguished by Article III rule 6 of the said Rules on the grounds that suit was not brought within one year of the date when the cargo should have been delivered.'

*The relevant Hague Visby Rules*

These rules were, of course, enacted into English law by the Carriage of Goods by Sea *e* Act 1971, repealing its 1924 counterpart which enshrined the original Hague Rules. The amendments came about as a result of a conference which was held in Stockholm in 1963, the proceedings of which it will be necessary to refer to later in this judgment.

These rules are to be applied as if they were part of 'directly enacted statute law' (see *The Hollandia* [1982] 3 All ER 1141 at 1145, [1983] 1 AC 565 at 572 per Lord Diplock in a speech with which all the others members of the Appellate Committee agreed). *f*

The relevant rules for present purposes are the following:

> 'ARTICLE I
> In these Rules the following words are employed, with the meanings set out below—(*a*) "Carrier" includes the owner or the charterer who enters into a contract of carriage with a shipper. (*b*) "Contract of carriage" applies only to contracts of *g* carriage covered by a bill of lading or any similar document of title, in so far as such document relates to the carriage of goods by sea, including any bill of lading or any similar document as aforesaid issued under or pursuant to a charter party from the moment at which such bill of lading or similar document of title regulates the relations between a carrier and a holder of the same. (*c*) "Goods" includes goods, wares, merchandise, and articles of every kind whatsoever except live animals and *h* cargo which by the contract of carriage is stated as being carried on deck and is so carried. (*d*) "Ship" means any vessel used for the carriage of goods by sea. (*e*) "Carriage of goods" covers the period from the time when the goods are loaded on to the time they are discharged from the ship.
>
> ARTICLE II
> [Risks] *j*
> Subject to the provisions of Article VI, under every contract of carriage of goods by sea the carrier, in relation to the loading, handling, stowage, carriage, custody, care and discharge of such goods, shall be subject to the responsibilities and liabilities, and entitled to the rights and immunities hereinafter set forth.

ARTICLE III

a

[Responsibilities and liabilities]

... 2. Subject to the provisions of Article IV, the carrier shall properly and carefully load, handle, stow, carry, keep, care for, and discharge the goods carried ...

6 ... the carrier and the ship shall in any event be discharged from all liability whatsoever in respect of the goods, unless suit is brought within one year of their

b

delivery or of the date when they should have been delivered. This period may, however, be extended if the parties so agree after the cause of action has arisen ...

ARTICLE IV

... 5. [Laying down a limitation per unit or package] ... (e) Neither the carrier nor the ship shall be entitled to the benefit of the limitation of liability provided for in this paragraph if it is proved that the damage resulted from an act or omission of

c

the carrier done with intent to cause damage, or recklessly and with knowledge that damage would probably result ...

ARTICLE IV BIS

1. The defences and limits of liability provided for in these Rules shall apply in any action against the carrier in respect of loss or damage to goods covered by a

d

contract of carriage whether the action be founded in contract or in tort ...'

*The plaintiff's submissions*

On behalf of the plaintiff carrier, counsel submitted that the allegation as to the theft of the goods plainly concerned the carrier's custody, care and discharge of the cargo under art II, and that the theft of the goods during discharge was a breach of the obligation

e

under art III, para 2 properly to discharge. The wording of art III, para 6 on its proper construction, particularly having regard to the wide language of the words 'all liability whatsoever in respect of the goods', was apt to include all claims of any kind against the carrier, including claims for wrongful delivery or non-delivery, whether or not these involved allegations of deliberate theft by the carrier himself. In support of this argument counsel submitted (as was common ground) that he was entitled to invite consideration

f

of the proceedings of the Stockholm Conference as an aid to interpretation and construction under the authority of the decision of the House of Lords in *Gatoil International Inc v Arkwright-Boston Manufacturers Mutual Insurance Co* [1985] 1 All ER 129, [1985] AC 255. In the leading judgment (with which Lord Fraser, Lord Scarman and Lord Roskill agreed) Lord Wilberforce stated the principle as follows in relation to a comparable convention ([1985] 1 All ER 129 at 132, [1985] AC 255 at 263):

g

'My Lords, there is here, no doubt, no more than a degree of doubt as to the meaning of statutory words not significantly greater than often arises, particularly in such cases as reach this House. They can be, and are, solved by a judicial process of interpretation. My noble and learned friend Lord Keith has followed this path, and if there were no other material to help us, I would be content to follow him.

h

However, I believe that contentment can be converted to conviction by legitimate reinforcement ab extra, namely by resort to the travaux préparatoires of the International Convention Relating to the Arrest of Sea-going Ships (Brussels, 10 May 1952; TS 47 (1960); Cmnd 1128). The case for a cautious use of travaux préparatoires in aid of the interpretation of conventions or treaties of private law received some acceptance in this House in *Fothergill v Monarch Airlines Ltd* [1980] 2 All ER 696,

j

[1981] AC 251. I there suggested that two conditions must be fulfilled before they can be used: first, that the material is public and accessible; second, that it clearly and indisputably points to a definite legislative intention. The case for resort to them here is, in my opinion, a strong one. The Administration of Justice Act 1956, Pt V (which included s 47) was enacted to give effect to the obligations of the United

Kingdom consequent on its accession to the 1952 convention (see *The Jade, The Eschersheim* [1976] 1 All ER 920 at 923, [1976] 1 WLR 430 at 434 per Lord Diplock), and in particular to displace, in Scotland, the wide common law powers of arrestment in favour of statutory provisions which were narrower and precisely defined. The situation is slightly more complex in that the list of maritime claims set out in art 1 of the 1952 convention was, in fact, based on the list of such claims then applicable in *England* under s 22 of the Supreme Court of Judicature (Consolidation) Act 1925 (see particularly sub-s (1)(*a*)(xii)). This list was adopted, as part of a compromise, in the 1952 convention, and was then made applicable (with minor variations) to England and to Scotland by ss 1 and 47 of the 1956 Act respectively. This derivation provides a clear justification for attributing to the provisions in the Scottish portion of the 1956 Act the meaning which they ought to receive under the convention, if that can be ascertained.' (Lord Wilberforce's emphasis.)

Lord Wilberforce then proceeded to recite the course of the relevant proceedings of the conference which led to that convention, and concluded as follows ([1985] 1 All ER 129 at 133, [1985] AC 255 at 265):

'The conclusion from the above is clear. The conference decided not to include premiums on policies of insurance among the maritime claims justifying arrest. It did so, moreover, not because it thought that these premiums were already covered (so that explicit reference was unnecessary) but because it considered it unnecessary as a mater of policy to provide for their protection by means of arrestment. The legislative intention is manifest: not by any provision in art 1 to provide for the inclusion of premiums among arrestable maritime claims. In the face of this legislative intention the adoption of the provisions of art 1 of the convention in the 1956 Act must be treated as carrying the same meaning as that evidently placed on them in the convention and as not extending to premiums on insurance policies. My Lords, I respectfully think that the interpretation of the 1956 Act is legitimately aided by consideration of this extrinsic material, and that we should not deny ourselves this reinforcement to our conclusions. With that reinforcement I am of opinion that this appeal must be allowed and the arrestment recalled.'

Lord Scarman stated that the court should not deny itself the 'reinforcement' which the travaux préparatoires provide to 'the interpretation which . . . we hold to be correct' (see [1985] 1 All ER 129 at 131, [1985] AC 255 at 262).

The relevant portion of the proceedings of the Stockholm Conference, which have been published by the International Maritime Committee, consists first of a report of a sub-committee, which was in the following terms (pp 77–78):

'3. *Time limit in respect of claims for wrong delivery (Art. III(6) third para).* Article III(6) third paragraph of the 1924 Convention provides that "in any event the carrier and the ship shall be discharged from all liability in respect of loss or damage unless suit is brought within one year after delivery of the goods or the date when the goods should have been delivered". The Sub-Committee discussed at some length whether and to what extent the expression "the liability in respect of loss or damage" also covers the carrier's liability for wrong delivery. Whereas it was felt that in some countries wrong delivery caused by mere negligence on the part of the carrier's servant falls within the terms of the Convention it was generally agreed that intentional delivery of the goods to a person who is not a bearer of the B/L is not covered by the Convention. Therefore, it is held in most countries that neither the limitation amount nor the time limit for action provided for in the Convention applies when the carrier has delivered the goods to a person not entitled to them. Were the Convention to contain a rule laying down that a time limit should operate also in respect of claims based upon wrong delivery of the goods such a rule would solve a recurrent practical problem: How long should a person who has received the a    goods without producing the B/L and who therefore has had to put a bank guarantee be obliged to keep the guarantee running? If a time limit for the claim is definitely fixed this would also determine the necessary duration of the bank guarantee. The Sub-Committee felt that it would be useful and practical to have a rule on this particular point. One great advantage would undoubtedly be that a bank guarantee given against claims for wrong delivery would be reduced to more reasonable periods and would thus actually operate to the benefit of consignees as well as

b    carriers. The Sub-Committee considered whether the 1 year time limit should be made to apply also in cases of wrong delivery. However the Sub-Committee believed that the carrier should not have the benefit of such a short prescription period in that case and that a 2 years limit would be fair to both the carrier and the consignee who has put up a bank guarantee. A period of 2 years would also appear fair in respect of a person who might actually hold the B/L but fails to produce it. In order

c    to fix the date when the two years should start running the Sub-Committee recommends that the date of the Bill of Lading be taken as the point of departure for the 2 years period. The attention of the Sub-Committee was also drawn to the distinction between goods being lost or damaged, on the one hand, and goods not being delivered—though neither lost nor damaged—on the other. The Sub-Committee accepted that a technical distinction could be drawn but the majority

d    were of the opinion that this was not really a major practical issue and that, indeed, to introduce this distinction into the Convention would necessitate amendments of many provisions in it.

     DECISION:
     The majority of the Sub-Committee makes the following recommendation to the

e    I.M.C. in respect of Article III(6) third paragraph (new text in italics): "In any event the carrier and the ship shall be discharged from all liability in respect of loss or damage unless suit is brought within one year after delivery of the goods or the date when the goods should have been delivered; *provided that in the event of delivery of the goods to a person not entitled to them the above period of one year shall be extended to two years from the date of the Bill of Lading.*" When coming forward with this

f    recommandation [sic] the Sub-Committee wishes to state that in formulating this amendment it is not intended to give the impression that the Sub-Committee has expressed an opinion upon whether and to what extent wrong delivery may be covered by the Convention. In fact the Sub-Committee has passed a formal resolution to that effect reading thus: "This amendment does not imply that the Sub-Committee expresses its view on the question whether delivery to a person not

g    entitled to the goods is covered by the expression 'loss or damage' in the Convention."'

     This was then discussed by the various delegations, and at the plenary session of the conference the present rule was adopted, i e in line with the recommendation of the sub-committee, other than the proviso for an extended period of limitation.
     The relevant wording in the original Hague Rules was: 'shall be discharged from all

h    liability in respect of loss or damage unless suit is brought . . .' Thus the effective change was the introduction of the word 'whatsoever' and the replacement of the words 'in respect of loss or damage' by the words 'in respect of the goods'.
     Counsel submitted that the above-quoted proceedings demonstrated a very clear legislative intention to include within the time bar claims in respect of intentional wrong delivery, and he submitted that this was to be interpreted broadly so as to include all

j    types of delivery, including theft by the carrier himself; there was no reason, he submitted, to differentiate between different types of conversion.
     Counsel sought to reinforce his submissions by drawing a contrast with art VI, para 5(e), and suggested that if it had been intended to except theft from the scope of art III, para 6, a similar saving provision should have been included there.
     Finally, counsel relied on the decision of the Court of Appeal in *Brown & Co Ltd v*

*Harrison, Hourani v Harrison* (1927) 96 LJKB 1025, [1927] All ER Rep 195, where the
court appeared to have assumed that a theft which occurred during discharge was a    *a*
breach of the duties laid down under art III, para 2 of the original Hague Rules, though
he recognised that the point was not specifically argued.

### The defendants' submissions

Counsel on behalf of the defendant cargo interests submitted that the essential starting
point was the wording of art II. This, he submitted, did not apply to possessory or    *b*
proprietory rights at all, but essentially to the standards of care of the carrier qua carrier
from the inception of loading through the various intermediate stages up to discharge.
None of the language of art II, he submitted, was in any way appropriate to embrace
obligations as to delivery of the goods.

In support of this argument counsel relied on the description of the nature of the rules
given by Kerr LJ in *D/S A/S Idaho v Peninsular and Oriental Steam Navigation Co, The*    *c*
*Strathnewton* [1983] 1 Lloyd's Rep 219 at 223, with which Sir John Donaldson MR and
Sir Sebag Shaw agreed, as follows:

'As is of course well known, the rules emerged in an international convention
which embodied a compromise between the desire of carriers by sea for maximum
freedom to contract out of responsibility for cargo and the desire of cargo-owners to    *d*
subject the carriers to maximum responsibility for cargo: see, e.g., Carver [*Carriage
by Sea* (13th edn, 1982)] pars. 441 to 450, and Scrutton [*Charterparties* (18th edn,
1974)] at p. 405. The rules are accordingly something in the nature of a "package"—
the phrase which [counsel for the charterers] appropriately used in his argument—
a balance of "Responsibilities and Liabilities of carrier and ship", which is the
heading of art. III, and of "Rights and Immunities of carrier and ship", the heading    *e*
of art. IV. The general nature and effect of this "package" is clearly stated in art. II.
Thus, the carrier's duty to exercise due diligence to make the ship seaworthy, etc.
under art. III(1), and his duties in relation to the cargo under art. III(2), are balanced
or mitigated, in particular, by the provisions of art. IV. As regards claims against the
carrier, his liability is also balanced or mitigated by art. III(6) headed "Notice of loss
or damage; limitation of actions". This includes the time bar which I have already    *f*
quoted, and the time bar forms part of the "package".'

Counsel submitted that this 'package', terminating with discharge, had no bearing on
delivery. It followed that delivery was also outside the scope of art III, para 6, since 'all
liability whatsoever' under the rules could not extend beyond or outside the art II
package. There was thus no need for a counterpart to art IV, para 5(*e*) since misdelivery,    *g*
whether intentional or otherwise, was entirely outside the scope of the rules. In view of
this very clear wording, counsel contended, there was no warrant for recourse to the
proceedings of the Stockholm Conference for the purpose of interpreting art III, para 6;
in the light of Lord Wilberforce's speech in the *Gatoil* case [1981] 1 All ER 129 at 132–
133, [1985] AC 255 at 263–265, he submitted, such recourse should only be undertaken
cautiously, and for no greater purpose than to reinforce a prima facie conclusion. Here,    *h*
on the clear construction of the language itself, there was no such prima facie conclusion.

Counsel sought to strengthen his construction of the extent of the 'package' by
reference to the definition of 'carriage of goods' in art I, para (*e*), and he submitted that
support was to be found for his contention that delivery is outside the scope of the
'package' in the commentary on para (*e*) in *Scrutton on Charterparties* (19th edn, 1984)
p 431 as follows:    *j*

'The function of this sub-rule is to assist in the definition of the contract of carriage
by identifying the first and last operations of those which together constitute the
carriage of goods by sea. The words "*loaded on*" do not mean that the rights and
liabilities referred to in Article II apply only to that part of the operation of loading

a that takes place after the goods cross the ship's rail. Similarly goods are not
"*discharged*" before they have been put into a lighter alongside. It is clear from
Article III, Rules 1 and 3, that the carrier may have obligations before the operation
of loading begins.'

He further relied on a footnote in *Scrutton* to the commentary on art III, para 6 which
is in the following terms (p 441, footnote 32):

b 'One purpose of the amendment was to apply the time limit to cases of delivery
without production of bills of lading, and hence to enable banks and other parties
issuing letters of indemnity to regard themselves as discharged after the expiry of
one year. We submit that it is at least doubtful whether the Rules apply at all to
cases of this nature, or whether if they do, the words of the new Rule are strong
enough to cover such a claim. But there are understandably arguments in favour of
c the opposite view: see Diamond ['The Hague-Visby Rules' [1978] Lloyd's MCLQ
225 at 256].'

He also cited an article by Mr Michael Mustill QC entitled 'Carriage of Goods by Sea
Act 1971' (1972) 11 Arkiv Sjorett 684 at 706 as follows:

d '"*All liability whatsoever*" It cannot be an accident that the word "whatsoever" has
been added to Article III Rule 6, although no such addition has been made to the
limitation provisions of Article IV Rule 5, or to the other places in the Hague Rules
where the expression "loss or damage" appears—e.g. Article III Rules 5 and 8, and
Article IV Rules 1 and 2. Presumably the reason is that the parties to the Convention
intended the limit to apply even in case of deviations. If this is correct, the monetary
e limit will be opened by "wilful misconduct" and possibly also by deviation as well,
whereas the time limit will not. It is possible that the word "whatsoever" was also
intended to cover liabilities arising from the delivery of goods without production
of bills of lading, the intention being that the ship-owner or counter-signing banker
would not have to keep open indefinitely the letter of indemnity customarily
obtained on such occasions. If this was indeed the intention, it must be doubted
f whether the desired result has been achieved. It is very questionable whether a
deliberate mis-delivery after the completion of the transit is subject to the Hague
Rules at all: see Article II. And even if it were, the English Court treats delivery
without production of bills as a serious tort and breach of contract, and it is unlikely
that any limitation of the cargo-owner's rights of action for such an act would be
effective, unless very clear words are used. I suggest that "whatsoever" is not
g sufficiently clear for this purpose.'

Counsel for the plaintiff countered by relying on an article by Mr Anthony Diamond
QC entitled 'The Hague-Visby Rules' [1978] Lloyd's MCLQ 225 at 256 as follows:

'*IV The Time-Bar*. The only important question arising on the Visby amendments
h relating to the time-bar is whether the substitution of the words "discharged from
all liability whatsoever in respect of the goods" for the former expression "discharged
from all liability in respect of loss or damage" has the effect of making the one-year
time-bar applicable where the carrier has misdelivered the goods. There is the
clearest possible evidence that the sole or main purpose of this amendment was to
make the time limit apply where the goods had been delivered without production
j of bills of lading and so to make it unnecessary to require an indemnity given by
the receiver to be kept open indefinitely. Although the editors of Scrutton
[Charterparties (18th edn, 1974)] knew that this was one of the intentions, they
considered that the amendment did not have the desired effect. I submit, albeit
with considerable doubt, that as the first paragraph of art. III, r. 6 is dealing with the
effect of delivery of the goods, so also the time-bar should be construed as applying

to events taking place after discharge. If so, I submit, again with doubt, that the limit should apply.'

Finally (and this was not contested by counsel for the plaintiff) counsel pointed out that the use of the word 'delivery' in art III, para 6 itself has no bearing on the question, since it is there used simply and solely for the purpose of fixing the inception of the one-year limitation period.

*Conclusions*
The first question which I have to decide is whether delivery is in any way within the scope of the art II 'package'. Article II describes the various stages at which the carrier bears responsibilities and liabilities, and is entitled to rights and immunities; this begins with loading and ends with discharge of goods, with the intermediate stages of handling, stowage, carriage, custody and care in between. All these are functions of transportation, beginning at the moment when the goods start to be put on board and ending with the moment when they are finally unloaded. The 'package' so described thus seem to me inherently inapt to embrace delivery, which imports concepts of possessory or proprietory rights, alien in my judgment to these carefully listed transportational stages. This view seems to me to be reinforced by the definition of "Carriage of goods' in art I, para (*e*). Once the conclusion is reached that delivery is outside the scope of art II, which is of course the key article, it must inexorably follow that misdelivery of whatever kind is outside the scope of art III, para 6, since the carrier is under no 'liability' in that respect. There is, moreover, in consequence no need for any saving clause comparable to art IV, para 5(*e*).

In reaching this conclusion as to the correct construction of the relevant articles I have fully borne in mind the need to adopt a broad and purposive approach in construing a convention of this kind.

This view is in my judgment strongly supported by Mustill 'Carriage of Goods by Sea Act 1971' (1972) 11 Arkiv Sjorett 684 at 706, with which I respectfully agree, and by the footnote in *Scrutton*. Mr Diamond's very hesitant and tentative comments to the contrary in 'The Hague-Visby Rules' [1978] Lloyd's MCLQ 225 at 256 do not in my judgment carry similar weight. Nor do I think that *Brown & Co Ltd v Harrison, Hourani v Harrison* (1927) 96 LJKB 1025, [1927] All ER Rep 195 gives the plaintiff any assistance, since the point in issue was never argued.

Once this conclusion is reached it seems to me that the discussions at the Stockholm Conference cannot possibly be invoked to support a contrary view, having regard to the cautions criteria laid down by Lord Wilberforce and agreed to by Lord Scarman in *Gatoil International Inc v Arkwright-Boston Manufacturers Mutual Insurance Co* [1985] 1 All ER 129 at 132–133, 131, [1985] AC 255 at 263–265, 262.

Thus I hold as a matter of construction that misdelivery, whether dishonest, honestly intentional or merely mistaken, is entirely outside the scope of the rule.

If, however, I am wrong in this main conclusion, and, either because the rules are ambiguous or for any other reason, it is appropriate to have recourse to the discussions of the Stockholm Conference, then I recognise that they tend to demonstrate a legislative intention to apply the time limit to cases of wrong delivery. There is, however, no mention throughout the whole of the discussions of cases of theft by the carrier, and therefore nothing in those discussions which tends in the slightest degree to support a view that there was a legislative intention that the time limit should apply in such cases, of which the present case is alleged to be an instance.

Consequently, even if, contrary to my main conclusion, wrong delivery was within the scope of the rules, I should have still declined to hold that theft by the carrier himself was within their scope. As Mr Mustill stated in his article, very clear words would be required to cover even 'deliberate misdelivery by the carrier'; a fortiori very clear words would be necessary to cover theft by the carrier. No such clear words are to be found in

the rules, nor is any support to be found in the Stockholm discussions that such was the
*a* legislative intent.

For the above reasons the plaintiff fails on the crucial point.

*Remaining issues*

If the plaintiff had succeeded the following further issues would have arisen.

(a) Is the plaintiff right in its contention that under the Hague Visby Rules a carrier
*b* can rely on the art III, para 6 exception against a claimant who is not a party to a contract
with the carriers to which those rules apply? This turns on the resolution of the rival
constructions put forward by the parties of art IV bis, and in particular whether this
article gives the claimant an unrestricted right to sue in tort as well as in contract. This is
a pure question of construction of the rules, and since it is unnecessary for the purposes
of my present decision I do not propose to embark on it.

*c* (b) If a contractual nexus is required, is the plaintiff carrier able to establish it on the
basis either (i) that there was an implied contract between the defendants Phibro and BP
respectively and the plaintiff or (ii) that the plaintiff is entitled to invoke the so-called
'wide construction' of the Bills of Lading Act 1855, so that the defendants became parties
to a contract of carriage contained in or evidenced by the bills of lading or (iii) that, even
if there was no strictly contractual nexus, the defendants are still bound by the bills of
*d* lading by reason of their being a bailment to the plaintiff on the terms of the bills of
lading.

All these points turn partly on questions of pure law and partly on the construction of
the relevant documents (which is also an issue of law) and there are no issues of disputed
fact to be resolved; indeed, there was no oral evidence at the trial. It therefore seems to
me to be equally inappropriate to attempt to resolve these issues, which are also
*e* unnecessary for the purpose of my decision.

It goes without saying that, should my decision on the main question be wrong, all
these points are open for consideration at any later stage in the case, including of course
all the arguments addressed to me.

There will therefore be judgment for the defendants.

*f* *Judgment for the defendants.*

Solicitors: *Lewis Moore* (for the plaintiff); *Clyde & Co* (for the defendants).

K Mydeen Esq    Barrister.

# Practice Direction

COURT OF PROTECTION

*Power of attorney – Enduring power of attorney – Form – Explanatory information and marginal notes – Necessity for inclusion – Enduring Powers of Attorney Act 1985, s 2(6) – Enduring Powers of Attorney (Prescribed Form) Regulations 1987, reg 2(1)(2).*

The Enduring Powers of Attorney (Prescribed Form) Regulations 1987, SI 1987/1612, came into force on 1 November 1987 and any enduring power of attorney executed on or after 1 July 1988 has to be in the form prescribed by those regulations in order to be a valid enduring power of attorney.

Regulation 2(1) of the regulations provides that a valid form must include the requisite explanatory information and all the relevant marginal notes. Regulation 2(2) refers to omissions or deletions of one of the various pairs of alternatives given in the form and allows omission or deletion of the corresponding marginal note.

Section 2(6) of the Enduring Powers of Attorney Act 1985 provides that an instrument differing in an immaterial respect in form or mode of expression from the prescribed form shall be treated as sufficient in point of form and expression.

Consequently, marginal notes may only be omitted if they are irrelevant (reg 2(1)), correspond to the omitted or deleted one of a pair of alternatives (reg 2(2)) or constitute an immaterial difference from the prescribed form (s 2(6)).

On several occasions recently, solicitors have submitted for registration enduring powers of attorney bearing no marginal notes at all, on the basis that the instrument had in each case been drawn up by the solicitors after the various choices had been explained to the donor and he had selected the options he wished to include and had decided the precise terms of the power.

There is no provision in the regulations for differences in form where donors prepare the form themselves and where solicitors prepare the form. Solicitors should therefore include in the forms to be completed by their client all marginal notes unless they come within one of the exceptions already mentioned.

A B MACFARLANE
28 February 1989                                    Master of the Court of Protection.

# Lonrho plc v Fayed and others

COURT OF APPEAL, CIVIL DIVISION
DILLON, RALPH GIBSON AND WOOLF LJJ
28 FEBRUARY, 1, 2 MARCH 1989

*Tort – Interference with trade or business – Take-over bid – False statements made to third party to prevent rival's take-over bid succeeding – No predominant purpose to injure rival – No complete tort vis-à-vis third party – Whether false statements giving rise to cause of action.*

The plaintiffs and the defendants were competing bidders to take over a public company. By 1979 the plaintiffs had acquired 29·9% of the share capital of the company and their bid was referred to the Monopolies and Mergers Commission by the Secretary of State. In 1981, at his request, the plaintiffs gave an undertaking to the Secretary of State not to purchase any more shares in the company. In 1985 the defendants made a bid for the company while the plaintiffs were still subject to their undertaking. The defendants' bid was not referred by the Secretary of State to the commission. The plaintiffs alleged that the Secretary of State had been influenced in his decision not to refer the defendants' bid by fraudulent misrepresentations made to him by the defendants about their own commercial standing and worth. The plaintiffs brought an action against the defendants claiming, inter alia, that the defendants had thereby committed the tort of wrongful interference with the plaintiffs' trade or business. The judge, on the defendants' application, struck out the claim as disclosing no reasonable cause of action. The plaintiffs appealed. The defendants contended that the essential elements of the tort included a predominant purpose on the part of the tortfeasor to injure the victim and the existence of a complete tort between the tortfeasor and the third party against whom the wrong was committed, neither of which had been pleaded by the plaintiffs. The defendants further contended that there had been no causation since what had deprived the plaintiffs of the opportunity to bid in 1985 was not anything done by the defendants, but the undertaking given by the plaintiffs to the Secretary of State in 1981, and that the plaintiffs had not shown that they had suffered sufficient damage to a business interest to support a cause of action.

**Held** – In order to establish the tort of wrongful interference with trade or business it was not necessary to prove either a predominant purpose to injure the plaintiff or the existence of a complete tort between the tortfeasor and the third party against whom the wrong was committed. On the other hand, it was necessary to prove that the unlawful act was directed against the plaintiff or was intended to harm the plaintiff. However, it was only in plain and obvious cases that recourse should be had to the striking out procedure and on the facts the case was not suitable for disposal by the summary process of striking out since although wrongful interference with trade or business was a recognised tort its ambit was uncertain, and the application of the tort and the issues of fraud, causation and damage to a business interest which had been raised could only be determined on the actual facts as they emerged at the trial. Accordingly, the appeal would be allowed and the plaintiffs' claim reinstated (see p 69 d to j, p 70 c to e, p 71 c to f j to p 72 c g j to p 73 b f to h, post).

*Lonrho Ltd v Shell Petroleum Co Ltd* [1981] 2 All ER 456 applied.
Decision of Pill J [1988] 3 All ER 464 reversed.

**Notes**
For damage arising out of trade rivalry and damage to and interference with business by unlawful means, see 45 Halsbury's Laws (4th edn) paras 1206, 1525, and for a case on the subject, see 46 Digest (Reissue) 589, 6396.

**Cases referred to in judgments**

*Allen v Flood* [1898] AC 1, [1895–9] All ER Rep 52, HL.
*Cutler v Wandsworth Stadium Ltd* [1949] 1 All ER 544, [1949] AC 398, HL.
*Dyson v A-G* [1911] 1 KB 410, CA.
*Hadmor Productions Ltd v Hamilton* [1982] 1 All ER 1042, [1983] 1 AC 191, [1982] 2 WLR 322, HL; *rvsg* [1981] 2 All ER 724, [1983] 1 AC 191, [1981] 3 WLR 139, CA.
*Lonrho Ltd v Shell Petroleum Co Ltd* [1981] 2 All ER 456, [1982] AC 173, [1981] 3 WLR 33, HL.
*Merkur Island Shipping Corp v Laughton* [1983] 2 All ER 189, [1983] 2 AC 570, [1983] 2 WLR 778, HL.
*Metall und Rohstoff AG v Donaldson Lufkin & Jenrette Inc* (1989) Times, 2 February, CA; *rvsg in part* [1988] 3 All ER 116, [1988] 3 WLR 548.
*National Phonograph Co Ltd v Edison-Bell Consolidated Phonograph Co Ltd* [1908] 1 Ch 335, [1904–7] All ER Rep 116, CA.
*RCA Corp v Pollard* [1982] 3 All ER 771, [1983] Ch 135, [1982] 3 WLR 1007, CA.
*Stratford (J T) & Son Ltd v Lindley* [1964] 3 All ER 102, [1965] AC 269, [1964] 3 WLR 541, HL.
*Union Carbide Corp v Naturin Ltd* [1987] FSR 538, CA.

**Appeal**

The plaintiffs, Lonrho plc (Lonrho), appealed against the decision of Pill J ([1988] 3 All ER 464, [1989] 2 WLR 356) on 22 June 1988 allowing an appeal by the defendants, Mohamed Fayed, Salah Fayed, Ali Fayed, House of Fraser Holdings plc (Holdings), John MacArthur and Kleinwort Benson Ltd (Kleinworts), against the decision of Master Topley on 30 July 1987 and striking out Lonrho's statement of claim in which they alleged that they had suffered loss and damage by reason of false statements made by the defendants or a conspiracy between the defendants or the negligence of the sixth defendants which had deprived the plaintiffs of the opportunity to acquire House of Fraser plc, on the ground that it disclosed no reasonable cause of action. The facts are set out in the judgment of Dillon LJ.

*John Beveridge QC* and *Edward Bannister* for Lonrho.
*David Oliver QC* and *Alastair Walton* for the Fayeds and Holdings.
*Anthony Grabiner QC* and *Nicolas Bratza QC* for Mr MacArthur and Kleinworts.

**DILLON LJ.** This is an appeal by the plaintiffs in the action, Lonrho plc, against an order of Pill J made on 22 June 1988 ([1988] 3 All ER 464, [1989] 2 WLR 356) whereby he struck out the statement of claim as disclosing no cause of action, and he dismissed the action with costs as against all six defendants. Any striking out case is dealt with on the footing that the allegations of fact in the statement of claim are true, but the general background in the present case is not in dispute.

Lonrho by 1979 had acquired some 29·9% of the share capital of House of Fraser plc, a company which owned various department stores including Harrods. Lonrho desired to acquire control of the whole share capital of House of Fraser, but there were various successive references to the Monopolies and Mergers Commission (the MMC) as to the merger situation which would be involved if Lonrho did acquire the share capital of House of Fraser, and, at the request of the Secretary of State for Trade and Industry, Lonrho gave an undertaking not to acquire shares in House of Fraser which would take its holding up to 30% or more. That was given on 15 December 1981. A third and so far final reference to the MMC in relation to Lonrho and House of Fraser was made on 31 May 1984. On 30 October 1984 the Secretary of State extended the time for the MMC to report to 28 February 1985. No further extension was possible beyond that, and it was accordingly obvious that, if the report was favourable to Lonrho's acquisition of control of House of Fraser, the undertaking would be likely to be released, but equally obvious

that the undertaking would not be likely to be released until the MMC's report had been
a received.

The first three defendants in this action, the Fayeds, are brothers said to hail from
Egypt. The fourth defendant, House of Fraser Holdings plc (Holdings), is a company
acquired ad hoc by the Fayeds to acquire for them the share capital of House of Fraser. It
is alleged in the statement of claim that from at latest November 1984 the Fayeds
intended and planned to acquire through the medium of Holdings all the issued share
b capital of House of Fraser.

On 2 November 1984 Lonrho sold to Holdings all but 1,200 shares of its 29·9%
holding in House of Fraser, but shortly afterwards Lonrho acquired shares bringing its
holding up to 6%.

On 3 March 1985 Holdings, on behalf of the Fayeds, made a cash offer for the issued
share capital of House of Fraser. The sixth defendants Kleinwort Benson Ltd (Kleinworts),
c a well-known merchant banker in the City of London, acted as merchant bank and
adviser of the Fayeds and Holdings in relation to that offer. The fifth defendant, Mr John
MacArthur, was a director of Kleinworts who acted in the matter.

On 4 March 1985 the offer by Holdings was announced publicly after the directors of
House of Fraser had agreed to recommend it. On 7 March 1985 the report of the MMC
in relation to the Lonrho reference was published. It gave clearance for Lonrho's
d acquisition of the share capital of House of Fraser, but for the moment the undertaking
to the Secretary of State against acquiring further shares was not released. By 11 March
1985 Holdings had acquired more than 50% of the issued share capital of House of Fraser.
This was achieved by purchase from Lonrho, the 29% purchased on 2 November 1984
and by purchases in the market which were not conditional, including purchases of
Lonrho's 6%.

e        On 14 March 1985 the Secretary of State released Lonrho from the 1981 undertaking.
On the same day the Secretary of State announced that the bid by Holdings for the share
capital of House of Fraser would not be referred to the MMC. The bid therefore went
ahead, and Holdings acquired 100% of the share capital of House of Fraser.

I pass now to matters of fact alleged in the statement of claim which are strongly
disputed. It is fair to all the defendants to emphasise that they are very strongly disputed.
f It is said by Lonrho in the statement of claim that the Secretary of State's decision not to
refer the bid by Holdings to the MMC was procured by fraud on the part of the Fayeds
and Holdings and on the part of Kleinworts and Mr MacArthur on their behalf.

The nature of the fraud by the Fayeds and Holdings is said to have been a complete
misrepresentation of the commercial standing and worth of the Fayeds, including
representations contrary to the fact that the Fayeds had money from their own resources
g to pay for the share capital of the House of Fraser. It is not said that the nature of the
representations was to run down Lonrho, but to puff up the position of the Fayeds so that
there would be no reference to the MMC of the bid by Holdings or, indeed, of any bid
by Holdings and the Fayeds. It is said that, if the truth had been disclosed, there would
probably have been a reference to the MMC and the outcome would probably have been
h that the Fayeds would have been barred from acquiring control of the House of Fraser
and would have been required to divest themselves of the 50% plus interest which they
had acquired.

If Lonrho is right on the facts pleaded, it is obvious that there was deliberate fraud on
the Secretary of State at least on the part of the Fayeds. In justice to Kleinworts and Mr
MacArthur it is not said that they knew that the facts told them by their clients, which
j they relayed to the Secretary of State, to the directors of the House of Fraser, and by press
announcements to the general public, were false. It is said that they had a duty to satisfy
themselves as to the truth of what their clients told them, that they failed to do so, and
that it is to be inferred accordingly that they acted recklessly, careless whether what they
said was true or false, and therefore that they acted in that sense fraudulently.
Accordingly, at a trial of the action the position of Kleinworts and Mr MacArthur in

relation to the allegations of fraud may be very different from the position of the Fayeds and Holdings. But that is not a difference which is relevant on the present application. No distinction has been taken on the hearing of this appeal in relation to the alleged cause of action with which we are concerned between the position of Kleinworts and Mr MacArthur and the position of the Fayeds and Holdings.

Lonrho issued a writ claiming damages. The statement of claim is lengthy and contains detailed allegations of alleged fact in over 50 paragraphs. All the defendants applied to strike out the statement of claim in toto. Pill J had to deal with three alleged causes of action in the statement of claim. In this court we have only had to deal with one.

So far as the other two are concerned, the position is as follows. First, there was an allegation against Kleinworts alone of the tort of negligence. It was said that they acted negligently in breach of a duty of care which they were said to have owed to Lonrho. That was struck out by the judge with the rest of the statement of claim, but his decision on that cause of action is not challenged and the notice of appeal did not seek to restore that alleged cause of action. Second, there was an allegation in the statement of claim against all the defendants of the tort of conspiracy. That also was struck out by the judge, and counsel for Lonrho accepts that the judge's decision on that cannot be challenged in this court in the light of the decision of the House of Lords in *Lonrho Ltd v Shell Petroleum Co Ltd* [1981] 2 All ER 456, [1982] AC 173, as interpreted by this court in *Metall und Rohstoff AG v Donaldson Lufkin & Jenrette Inc* (1989) Times, 2 February; *rvsg in part* [1988] 3 All ER 116, [1988] 3 WLR 548. The point here is that for the tort of conspiracy to lie, the predominant purpose of the conspirators must have been to injure the plaintiff rather than to further their own commercial interests. Here, the predominant purpose was to further the Fayeds' own commercial interests by acquiring the share capital of House of Fraser. However, counsel for Lonrho seeks to keep open the possible resuscitation of the allegation of conspiracy should this application reach the House of Lords and the decision of this court in *Metall und Rohstoff*, which binds us, become susceptible of review.

Because those two causes of action are not pursued in this court, we approach this appeal on the basis that paras 42 to 47, 55 and 56 of the statement of claim and the words 'and/or conspiracy and/or breach of duty' in para 57 stay struck out.

The third cause of action alleged in the statement of claim is the common law tort of wrongful interference with trade or business. The existence of such a tort is conceded by the defendants. Reference can be made to the speech of Lord Diplock in *Merkur Island Shipping Corp v Laughton* [1983] 2 All ER 189 at 196–197, [1983] 2 AC 570 at 609–610, where he said:

> 'In anticipation of an argument that was addressed to your Lordships on the stage 3 point, I should mention that the evidence also establishes a prima facie case of the common law tort, referred to in s 13(2) and (3) of the [Trade Union and Labour Relations Act 1974], of interfering with the trade or business of another person by doing unlawful acts. To fall within this genus of torts the unlawful act need not involve procuring another person to break a subsisting contract or to interfere with the performance of a subsisting contract. The immunity granted by s 13(2) and (3) I will call the "genus immunity". Where, however, the procuring of another person to break a subsisting contract *is* the unlawful act involved, as it is in s 13(1), this is but one species of the wider genus of tort. This I will call the "species immunity".' (Lord Diplock's emphasis.)

There are also references to this tort in *J T Stratford & Son Ltd v Lindley* [1964] 3 All ER 102, [1965] AC 269. Lord Reid said ([1964] 3 All ER 102 at 106, [1965] AC 269 at 324):

> 'In addition to interfering with existing contracts the respondents' action made it practically impossible for the appellants to do any new business with the barge-hirers. It was not disputed that such interference with business is tortious, if any unlawful means are employed.'

Viscount Radcliffe said ([1964] 3 All ER 102 at 109, [1965] AC 269 at 328):

'The case comes before us as one in which the respondents have inflicted injury
a     on the appellants in the conduct of their business and have resorted to unlawful
means to bring this about.'

But, although those statements indicate that the tort is a recognised tort, they cannot be
taken as comprehensive definitions of what constitutes that tort.

There are several what may be called established exceptions to the generality of those
b   definitions. In particular, although it is not relevant on the facts of the present case, the
speech of Lord Diplock in Lonrho Ltd v Shell Petroleum Co Ltd [1981] 2 All ER 456 at 463,
[1982] AC 173 at 187 establishes that the mere fact that a person has suffered injury in
his business by an act of the defendant which is illegal in the sense of being in breach of
a statutory prohibition does not automatically entitle the injured person to bring an
action within this tort to recover damages for the injury. The complainant still has to
c   show that on its true construction the statute which imposed the prohibition gave rise to
a civil remedy. That has to be considered in the light of the principles examined in Cutler
v Wandsworth Stadium Ltd [1949] 1 All ER 544, [1949] AC 398. Furthermore, in RCA
Corp v Pollard [1982] 3 All ER 771 at 781, [1983] Ch 135 at 153 Oliver LJ sets out
cogently that the action does not lie where the damage complained of is merely economic
damage as an incidental result of the breach of a prohibition in a statute not designed to
d   protect the interests of a class to which the plaintiff belongs.

It is submitted to us that, even with this tort, it must, as with the tort of conspiracy,
have been the predominant purpose of the tortfeasor to injure the victim rather than to
further the tortfeasor's own financial ends. I do not accept that. It would be inconsistent
with the way Lord Diplock treated this tort and the tort of conspiracy differently in his
speech in Lonrho Ltd v Shell Petroleum Co Ltd and in Hadmor Productions Ltd v Hamilton
e   [1982] 1 All ER 1042 at 1052–1053, [1983] 1 AC 191 at 228- 229. No predominant
purpose to injure is required where the tortious act relied on is injury by wrongful
interference with a third party's contract with the victim or by intimidation of a third
party to the detriment of the victim, nor should it in my view be required where the
wrongful interference has been by the practice of fraud on a third party, aimed specifically
at the plaintiff, as it was put by Oliver LJ in RCA Corp v Pollard [1982] 3 All ER 771 at
f   780, [1983] Ch 135 at 151.

It is also submitted for the defendants that for this tort of wrongful interference with
business to apply there must have been a complete tort as between the alleged wrongdoer
and the third party against whom the wrong was practised to the detriment of the
plaintiff in the action. It is said that that is not the case here, because though fraud was
practised, if the allegations of Lonrho are correct, on the Secretary of State to achieve the
g   end that the Secretary of State did not refer Holdings' bid to the MMC, the tort of deceit
requires that the plaintiff should have suffered damage, and the Secretary of State
suffered, it is said, no actionable damage. I, for my part, can see no valid reason why the
tort should need, as against the third party, to have been complete to the extent that the
third party had himself suffered damage. The distinction drawn by Lord Diplock
h   elsewhere between primary and secondary obligations may be relevant. Apart from that,
the need to show that the injured third party had suffered damage, as opposed to the
plaintiff having suffered damage, was not a factor in the decision of the majority of this
court in National Phonograph Co Ltd v Edison-Bell Consolidated Phonograph Co Ltd [1908] 1
Ch 335, [1904–7] All ER Rep 116. Causation has of course to be proved, but that is a
different matter.

j     It also has to be proved by a plaintiff who seeks to rely on this tort, as counsel conceded
for Lonrho, that the unlawful act was in some sense directed against the plaintiff or
intended to harm the plaintiff. The origin of those phrases is the oft-quoted passage in
the speech of Lord Watson in Allen v Flood [1898] AC 1 at 96, [1895–9] All ER Rep 52 at
69, which was applied by the majority of this court (Buckley and Kennedy LJJ) in National
Phonograph Co Ltd v Edison-Bell Consolidated Phonograph Co Ltd. In that case the fraud was
clearly directed against the plaintiff.

I have to bear in mind, however, as I have endeavoured to bear in mind throughout the hearing of this appeal, that this court has before it not the trial of the action or an  *a* appeal from a decision of the judge at the trial of the action, but an appeal on a striking out application. The rule is well known and clearly stated in *The Supreme Court Practice* 1988, vol 1, para 18/19/3 that it is only in plain and obvious cases that recourse should be had to the summary process of striking out, and a little later:

> 'The summary remedy under this rule is only to be implied in plain and obvious  *b* cases when the action is one which cannot succeed or is in some way an abuse of the process or the case unarguable . . .'

Furthermore, as Cozens-Hardy MR pointed out in *Dyson v A-G* [1911] 1 KB 410 at 414, in a passage cited by Slade LJ in his judgment in *RCA Corp v Pollard* [1982] 3 All ER 771 at 783, [1983] Ch 135 at 155, the striking out procedure 'ought not to be applied to an action involving serious investigation of ancient law and questions of general  *c* importance . . .'

Here the existence of this tort is recognised, but the detailed limits of it have to be refined. I regard it as right and, indeed, essential that this should be done on the actual facts as they emerge at the trial rather than on a set of hypotheses, more or less wide, in very comprehensive pleadings. This is very far from being a case in which there is no conflict as to the facts, and the matters in conflict involve questions of intention, purpose,  *d* motive or probability. We have the general framework of the law which falls to be applied to this case laid down, and to a considerable extent refined as a result of this application. But the actual application of that law to the facts of the case should, in my judgment, be a matter for the trial of the action.

However, there is one further point which I ought to mention before concluding this judgment. It is submitted for the defendants, and particularly by counsel for the Fayeds  *e* and Holdings, that what deprived Lonrho of the opportunity to bid in March 1985 was not anything done by or on behalf of the Fayeds, but the undertaking given by Lonrho to the Secretary of State in 1981. There were in truth two things which realistically, by their combined effect, prevented Lonrho from bidding for the share capital of House of Fraser in March 1985. One was that the 1981 undertaking was not released by the Secretary of State until 14 March. The other was that before that date Holdings had, by  *f* purchases in the market in addition to its purchase from Lonrho, achieved an unconditional majority holding of over 50% of the share capital in House of Fraser. There is no suggestion at all that the Fayeds achieved by fraud that the release by the Secretary of State of the undertaking was deferred until later than would otherwise have been the case or too late for the release to do Lonrho any good. Equally, there is no suggestion in the statement of claim, so far as I have seen, that the acquisition of over  *g* 50% in total by purchases in the market was procured by the pleaded fraud on the part of the Fayeds and the other defendants. Prima facie, therefore, the pleaded fraud was not causative of the deferment of the release of the undertaking or of the acquisition by Holdings of over the 50% level of the share capital of House of Fraser. Counsel for the Fayeds and Holdings submits, therefore, that there is no case on causation for the  *h* defendants to meet.

But the matter does not end at 11 March, when Holdings acquired more than 50% of House of Fraser, or on 14 March, when the Secretary of State released Lonrho from the undertaking. The powers of the Secretary of State under the Fair Trading Act 1973 can still be exercised even if a bidder has acquired control of a company before there has been any reference to the MMC. Within the statutory time limit, even after 50% control has  *j* been achieved, the merger situation may be referred to the MMC, and if the MMC report that the merger situation or its consequences may be expected to operate against the public interest, there are powers for the Secretary of State to order the successful bidder to divest himself of all shares in the target company concerned.

It is pleaded in the present case that the fraudulent misrepresentations relied on, and in particular those made in March 1985 to influence the Secretary of State, were intended

to have continuing effect. The continuing situation is dealt with in paras 48 and 49 of
*a* the statement of claim. Those paragraphs may not perhaps be worded as clearly as they
might be, but the situation, as I understand it, that they are seeking to deal with is that
by the fraud alleged in the statement of claim, if it was directed against Lonrho in the
sense of that requirement which will have to be explored at the trial, Lonrho has been
deprived of the opportunity of bidding, not merely at or before 14 March 1985, but at
any time when there would have been a divestment order as a probable consequence of a
*b* reference to the MMC, which would probably have been made if the truth had been
disclosed to the Secretary of State at the outset before 14 March 1985, or, if the truth had
become known to the Secretary of State, at a stage when to direct a reference was still
within his powers under the 1973 Act. In other words, what is alleged is a continued
deprivation, not merely of a right to bid at the outset, but of a right to bid if there were
to be directions to Holdings and the Fayeds to divest themselves of what they had
*c* acquired.
   Whether or not that can be made out is a matter for investigation, in my judgment, at
the trial of the action. It is not right to endeavour to try complicated issues of causation
on a striking out application on what might or might not appear to be on paper, on the
balance of probabilities, the foreseeable outcome of a trial.
   There are many other issues which fall to be investigated, which are also, in my
*d* judgment, matters for investigation at the trial, such as whether the business interest
which Lonrho claims to have had and which it claims has been injured by the allegedly
tortious acts is a sufficient business interest to support the tort which is alleged, and
whether the nature of the damage which Lonrho claims to have suffered is damage
properly recoverable for that tort in the particular circumstances of this case. I have no
doubt at all that these are all matters which must be investigated at the trial of the action.
*e* I underline that this tort is still in the process of judicial definition. This is not, therefore,
so far as this cause of action is concerned, a proper case for striking out.
   I would, accordingly, allow this appeal, and set aside the order of the judge save in so
far as the judge's order struck out paras 42 to 47, 55 and 56 of the statement of claim and
the words which I have mentioned in para 57.

*f* **RALPH GIBSON LJ.** I agree that the appeal should be allowed to the extent indicated
by Dillon LJ and for the reasons which he has given. I have very little to add.
   The tort of unlawful interference in business may still be described in our law as new.
Lord Denning MR in *Hadmor Productions Ltd v Hamilton* [1981] 2 All ER 724, [1983] 1
AC 191 so referred to it. It is, of course, more familiar to us when the unlawful means
used is intimidation or procuring the breach of or interference with a contract. It is not,
*g* I think, disputed by the defendants that if the unlawful means alleged in this case had
been fraudulent misstatements made to the Secretary of State for Trade and Industry and
denigrating the plaintiffs, Lonrho plc, the action might arguably fall within the definition
of the tort, but it was contended that the use of fraudulent misstatements to the Secretary
of State, which served only to improve the reputation and standing and the supposed
*h* assets of the Fayed brothers could not, as a matter of law, be held to have been directed
against Lonrho.
   It is submitted for the defendants that there was no sufficient pleading of sufficient
intention in the defendants to ground any tort, even the tort of unlawful interference
with business, and that an essential element of that specific tort must be that of
predominant intention to injure the plaintiffs. There is no allegation of such predominant
*j* intention. It is a question of law whether proof of such an element is required. That
point is plainly for decision on an application to strike out, because, if it was right, it
would bring the action to an end. But for my part, and in agreement with Dillon LJ, I do
not accept it. It is not a requirement, as I understand the cases, of the tort when the
unlawful means employed is intimidation or procuring a breach of contract. I see no
reason to introduce such a requirement where the unlawful means employed is
fraudulent misrepresentation, and such a requirement does not appear to be necessary

from the decision or reasoning in *Lonrho Ltd v Shell Petroleum Co Ltd* [1981] 2 All ER 456, [1982] AC 173.

It was also contended that the unlawful means used to the Secretary of State must be itself demonstrably actionable as a complete cause; and that in this case that is not pleaded as an alleged fact, because it is not said that there was any financial loss suffered by the Secretary of State. For my part I do not accept that fraudulent misrepresentations used to a public official in the circumstances alleged in this case cease to be unlawful means for the purposes of the tort of unlawful interference with business because there is no identifiable financial loss caused in addition to the fact that a public official has been caused to do by the fraud what otherwise he would not have done, or not to do what otherwise he would have done.

There were other points urged on the court for the defendants, which have been described by Dillon LJ, but I would hold that they are not such as to justify striking out this action. This is a comparatively new tort of which the precise boundaries must be established from case to case. Those points include, first, the nature of the intention which is required to satisfy the requirement that the conduct be 'directed against' the plaintiffs, in particular where the fraudulent misstatement is made by A to B about A himself in order to cause B to act in such a way that A obtains or retains a commercial advantage over C or deprives C of a commercial advantage; second, the nature of the business interest by reference to which the plaintiff must prove that he has been damaged; third, whether there is sufficient nexus or directness of impact and consequence between the unlawful means employed and the alleged loss causing effect on the plaintiffs; and, fourth, whether the damage alleged is sufficient to support the existence of a cause of action.

I would apply to these matters the long-established principle, to which Dillon LJ has referred and which was well expressed in *Union Carbide Corp v Naturin Ltd* [1987] FSR 538 at 544, where Slade LJ said:

'A long line of authority, of which examples are to be found in the notes at 18/19/ 3 in The Supreme Court Practice 1985, shows that the jurisdiction to strike out will be exercised only in plain and obvious cases. There is at least one good reason why in particular, in my judgment, the court hearing a striking out application should be slow to commit itself to stating principles of law which are not clearly covered by previous authority. *Ex hypothesi* it has to deal with the application on assumed facts. General statements of legal principle made on assumed facts are, in my experience, a perilous exercise, since they may well require addition or qualification when applied to the facts as actually found on the evidence in a particular case.'

I am not concerned to say that the points raised are particularly obscure, but they may be difficult of application in this case. In my view, it is better to deal with the remaining points on facts determined on evidence rather than on the statements in the statement of claim which are of some width and generality.

There were, as Dillon LJ has pointed out, powerful submissions both by counsel for the Fayeds and House of Fraser Holdings plc and by counsel for Mr MacArthur and Kleinwort Benson Ltd to the effect that the facts alleged in the statement of claim on proper analysis do not enable this court to hold that there is any arguable case that the loss of opportunity or damage alleged by Lonrho were in fact caused by any unlawful means employed by the defendants, or by the alleged response of the Secretary of State or anyone else thereto. I mean no disrespect to the submissions made when I say that I am not going to express any detailed view on the points raised for the reason that this case, in my view, must proceed to trial. I say only that I was not persuaded that the facts alleged could not support a conclusion that Lonrho were injured by the alleged wrongdoing.

For the reasons that I have given, and those given by Dillon LJ, I would allow this appeal.

**WOOLF LJ.** I agree with both judgments and the order proposed. The tort relied on by
a  Lonrho plc of unlawful interference is still, in my view, of uncertain ambit, albeit that
its existence is now beyond doubt and certain of its features are clearly defined. This
coupled with the fact that in this case fraud is pleaded and relied on by Lonrho are
matters which have influenced me into coming to my conclusion that I agree that this
appeal should be allowed for the reasons given.

That said, I should make it clear that I have two reservations. My first reservation is
b  whether the fraudulent misrepresentations relied on by Lonrho are sufficiently direct to
be capable of amounting to the interference with the plaintiffs' business which is needed
for the purposes of the tort. I say this for two reasons: (1) the fraud relied on consisted of
alleged misrepresentations as to the qualities of the Fayed brothers and not as to the
shortcomings of Lonrho; (2) it is not suggested that the misrepresentations caused the
Secretary of State for Trade and Industry to take any action or to desist from any action as
c  against Lonrho. Instead it is alleged that the Secretary of State was influenced not to take
action against the Fayeds.

My second reservation is whether the business asset which Lonrho alleges has been
damaged is in fact capable of being a business interest for the purpose of a tort of unlawful
interference. The business asset identified in para 16(1) of the statement of claim is
Lonrho's desire to exploit an opportunity to acquire House of Fraser plc by bidding for
d  shares in the company without 'competition' from the Fayeds. Whether or not particular
conduct is capable of amounting to interference and what is or is not capable of being a
business asset which is protected by the tort is very much a question of fact and degree
subject to parameters which are in the process of being settled by the courts as a matter
of law.

Having considered what is pleaded in the statement of claim in very broad terms, I do
e  not feel it would be right to hold that it is clear that the plaintiffs could not succeed in
bringing within those parameters the two matters about which I have indicated I have
reservations. Particularly in cases involving allegations of fraud, it appears to me
preferable for a decision to be reached after all the evidence has been heard and Lonrho
have had an opportunity of arguing that on that evidence they should succeed in their
claim.
f       As to the question of predominant intent, I agree with both judgments. So far as
conspiracy is concerned, there is good reason for requiring that predominant intent
should be an ingredient of the tort. Great difficulty would, in my view, arise if a
requirement of predominant intent to injure were to be introduced into the tort with
which we are concerned here. This tort is not based on any agreement, but interference,
and frequently it will be fully appreciated by a defendant that a course of conduct that he
g  is embarking on will have a particular consequence to a plaintiff, and the defendant will
have decided to pursue that course of conduct knowing what the consequence will be.
Albeit that he may have no desire to bring about that consequence in order to achieve
what he regards as his ultimate ends, from the point of view of the plaintiff, whatever
the motive of the defendant, the damage which he suffers will be the same. If a defendant
h  has deliberately embarked on a course of conduct, the probable consequence of which on
the plaintiff he appreciated, I do not see why the plaintiff should not be compensated.

For those reasons, in addition to those given by Dillon and Ralph Gibson LJJ, I agree
that this appeal should be allowed.

*Appeal allowed. Leave to appeal to the House of Lords refused.*
j
Solicitors: *Stephenson Harwood* (for Lonrho); *Herbert Smith* (for the Fayeds and Holdings);
*Slaughter & May* (for Mr MacArthur and Kleinworts).

L I Zysman Esq   Barrister.

# R v Westminster City Council, ex parte Monahan and another

QUEEN'S BENCH DIVISION
WEBSTER J
3, 4, 5, 8 FEBRUARY 1988

COURT OF APPEAL, CIVIL DIVISION
KERR, NICHOLLS AND STAUGHTON LJJ
19, 20, 21 SEPTEMBER, 19 OCTOBER 1988

*Town and country planning – Permission for development – Material consideration – Financial considerations – Planning proposal combining improvements to opera house and substantial office accommodation – Commercial development undesirable but necessary to finance improvements to opera house – Whether financial considerations of planning proposal a material consideration – Whether planning authority entitled to take into account that undesirable development would benefit desirable development – Whether planning authority entitled to take into account that commercial development would fund improvements to opera house – Town and Country Planning Act 1971, s 29(1).*

The charitable company responsible for operating and administering an opera house applied to the respondent council, as the local planning authority, for permission to redevelop its existing site. The proposals for which permission was sought included plans to modernise and improve the opera house, which was accepted by the council as being a desirable and necessary development if the opera house was to maintain its international standing, and also included substantial office accommodation, which the opera house company maintained was necessary to fund the improvements to the opera house. The council accepted that argument and granted permission even though the commercial development involved a departure from the development plan for the area and would otherwise have been considered undesirable in the area. The applicant community association, which objected to the proposed office development, sought judicial review of the council's decision on the ground, inter alia, that the opera house company's financial reasons for seeking to carry out commercial development which would otherwise have been impermissible were not a 'material consideration' which the council was entitled to take into account under s 29(1)[a] of the Town and Country Planning Act 1971. The judge dismissed the application. The community association appealed.

**Held** – Financial considerations which fairly and reasonably related to a permitted development were a 'material consideration' which a planning authority was entitled to take into account under s 29(1) of the 1971 Act when considering an application for development and therefore when considering an application for development which was contrary to planning policy it was permissible for the planning authority to have regard to the fact that the financial gains from that development would enable a related and desirable development to proceed. It followed that the council had been entitled to take into account when considering the opera house company's proposals the fact that the commercial development would fund the improvements to the opera house and to grant permission for the proposed office accommodation even though by itself it would have been considered undesirable development. The council's decision was accordingly not invalid and the appeal would be dismissed (see p 96 a to d, p 98 g to j, p 99 j, p 100 f to h, p 101 h j, p 102 b j and p 103 b c h to p 104 a f to h, post).

**Notes**

For material considerations to which a local planning authority must have regard in

---

a   Section 29, so far as material, is set out at p 88 b c, post

dealing with applications for the grant of planning permission for development, see 46
a Halsbury's Laws (4th edn) para 139, and for cases on the subject, see 47(1) Digest (Reissue)
100–108, 377–409.

For the Town and Country Planning Act 1971, s 29, see 46 Halsbury's Statutes (4th
edn) 273.

**Cases referred to in judgments**

b *Bradford City Metropolitan Council v Secretary of State for the Environment* [1986] 1 EGLR
199, CA.
*Brighton BC v Secretary of State for the Environment* (1978) 39 P & CR 46.
*East Barnet UDC v British Transport Commission* [1961] 3 All ER 878, [1962] 2 QB 484,
[1962] 2 WLR 134, DC.
*Great Portland Estates plc v Westminster City Council* [1984] 3 All ER 744, [1985] AC 661,
c [1984] 3 WLR 1035, HL.
*Hall & Co Ltd v Shoreham-by-Sea UDC* [1964] 1 All ER 1, [1964] 1 WLR 240, CA.
*Newbury DC v Secretary of State for the Environment* [1980] 1 All ER 731, [1981] AC 578,
[1980] 2 WLR 379, HL.
*Niarchos (London) Ltd v Secretary of State for the Environment* (1977) 35 P & CR 259.
*Prest v Secretary of State for Wales* (1982) 81 LGR 193, CA.
d *Pyx Granite Co Ltd v Ministry of Housing and Local Government* [1958] 1 All ER 625, [1958]
1 QB 554, [1958] 2 WLR 371, CA; *rvsd* [1959] 3 All ER 1, [1960] AC 260, [1959] 3
WLR 346, HL.
*Sosmo Trust Ltd v Secretary of State for the Environment* [1983] JPL 806.
*Sovmots Investments Ltd v Secretary of State for the Environment* [1976] 1 All ER 178, [1977]
QB 411, [1976] 2 WLR 73; *rvsd* [1976] 3 All ER 720, [1977] QB 411, [1976] 3 WLR
e 597, CA; *rvsd* [1977] 2 All ER 385, [1979] AC 144, [1977] 2 WLR 951, HL.
*Stringer v Minister of Housing and Local Government* [1971] 1 All ER 65, [1970] 1 WLR
1281.
*Westminster City Council v British Waterways Board* [1984] 3 All ER 737, [1985] AC 676,
[1984] 3 WLR 1047, HL.

f **Cases also cited**
*Bushell v Secretary of State for the Environment* [1980] 2 All ER 608, [1981] AC 75, HL.
*Hanks v Minister of Housing and Local Government* [1963] 1 All ER 47, [1963] 1 QB 999.
*New Forest DC v Secretary of State for the Environment* [1984] JPL 178.
*Puhlhofer v Hillingdon London BC* [1986] 1 All ER 467, [1986] AC 484, HL.
g *R v Bowman* [1898] 1 QB 663, DC.
*R v Hillingdon London Borough, ex p Royco Homes Ltd* [1974] 2 All ER 643, [1974] QB 720,
DC.
*R v Sheffield Justices, ex p T Rawson & Co Ltd* (1927) 44 TLR 43, [1927] All ER Rep 477,
DC.
*Tameside Metropolitan BC v Secretary of State for the Environment* [1984] JPL 180.
h *Westminster Renslade Ltd v Secretary of State for the Environment* (1983) 48 P & CR 255.

**Application for judicial review**
James Monahan and Ginny Scott, on behalf of themselves and all other members of the
Covent Garden Community Association, applied, with the leave of Roch J given on
13 October 1987, for judicial review by way of an order of certiorari to quash a resolution
j of the planning and development committee of the Westminster City Council made on
30 June 1987 granting planning permission and listed building consents to the Royal
Opera House Covent Garden Ltd (the ROH) for redevelopment of the Royal Opera
House, the Floral Hall, 2 Bow Street, 17–21 Russell Street, 2–6 Mart Street, 45–51 Floral
Street, 51–54 Long Acre and land fronting James Street, Covent Garden, London WC2.
The facts are set out in the judgment.

*Robert Carnwath QC* and *Alice Robinson* for the association.
*Jeremy M Sullivan QC* and *David Mole* for the council.                          *a*
*Peter Boydell QC* and *Charles George* for the ROH.

*Cur adv vult*

8 February. The following judgment was delivered.                               *b*

**WEBSTER J.** This is an application by James Monahan and Ginny Scott on behalf of
the Covent Garden Community Association (the association), of which they are members,
to quash a resolution of the planning and development committee of the Westminster
City Council made on 30 June 1987, and adopted by the council on 29 July 1987, that
planning permission and listed building consents be granted for the redevelopment of  *c*
the Royal Opera House, the Floral Hall, 2 Bow Street, 17–21 Russell Street, 2–6 Mart
Street, 45–51 Floral Street, 51–54 Long Acre and land fronting James Street, Covent
Garden, London WC2 subject to the fulfilment of three conditions referred to in the
resolution.

The principal ground on which the application is based is that, as the proposal involved
substantial office development and the demolition of listed buildings, it constituted a  *d*
major departure from the development plan, which it is alleged the council had been
persuaded to permit, in principle, because it believed that it was the only way for the
Royal Opera House Covent Garden Ltd (the ROH) to finance improvements that would
maintain its international standing, and that the council had no power to grant permission
for that reason. The second main ground is that if, contrary to the applicants' submission,
the council were entitled to have regard to the need to finance improvements for the  *e*
Opera House they failed to consider, or to take reasonable steps to inform themselves of,
other methods of financing those improvements without major departures from the
plan.

The association is an unincorporated association which was formed in 1971 to safeguard
and protect the interests of residents and businesses in the Covent Garden area. Among  *f*
the purposes for which the association was established are the promotion of high
standards of planning and architecture in the area and to secure the preservation,
protection, development and improvement of buildings or features of historic or public
interest. The area plan, to which I refer below, acknowledges at para A4.34 the 'substantial
and constructive contribution to the public debate on the Plan' made by the association.

The first of the two grounds on which the association relies is a very short point of law,  *g*
but the second could in principle involve quite a close consideration of the circumstances
leading up to the resolution in question. Moreover, the subject matter of that resolution
is of general interest to many people. For these reasons it is necessary for me to relate the
history of, and background to, the matter in some detail.

The ROH is a company limited by guarantee and a registered charity. It is responsible
for the day-to-day administration and operation of the Royal Opera House situated in  *h*
Covent Garden. The Royal Opera House was designed by E M Barrie and opened in
1858. The stage and its equipment were modernised in 1902 and new dressing rooms
were added in an annexe in 1932. Since 1946 the theatre has housed two internationally
renowned companies, the Royal Opera and the Royal Ballet; and Sadlers Wells Royal
Ballet has been administered from the Royal Opera House since 1957. As with many
similar European theatres, the stage arrangements were never designed to accommodate  *j*
present day performance and rehearsal requirements. The Royal Opera House has
therefore felt it essential to undertake a programme of modernisation and reconstruction
to ensure its future as a major international house. The association acknowledges that it
is widely accepted that further improvements are necessary if the Royal Opera House is
to maintain and improve its standing as one of the leading opera houses in the world.

In order to meet the most pressing needs of the Royal Opera House for additional and
*a* improved facilities a first phase of expansion was completed in 1982 when the Royal
Opera House was extended westward along its axis, enabling rehearsal studios, chorus
and dressing rooms and other offices to be added. The cost of that phase was £10m,
mainly financed by money raised by public appeal. But the carrying out of the first phase
of development did not alleviate all the problems. Accordingly, in October 1986 the
ROH applied for outline planning permission to redevelop the Royal Opera House, and
*b* surrounding land and buildings. Applications for listed building consents were also
made. I will consider the details of those applications later in this judgment.

But in the mean time I must go back a few years and explain the town and country
planning background against which those applications were made. Section 29(1) of the
Town and Country Planning Act 1971 requires a planning authority dealing with an
application for planning permission to have regard 'to the provisions of the development
*c* plan, so far as material to the application, and to any other material considerations . . .'
The development plan for the area is the Covent Garden action area plan (the area plan),
which was adopted by the Greater London Council (the GLC) on 20 January 1978. Prior
to its demise the GLC was the local planning authority, although the majority of the
planning applications in the Covent Garden area were dealt with by the council under a
designated authority from the GLC; since the GLC's demise, the council has been the
*d* sole planning authority for that part of the area which falls within its boundaries.

A number of paragraphs of the area plan should be quoted. As to land use, the policy
is to promote mixed use. Paragraph B1.2 reads:

*e* 'The [GLC] is keen to retain and promote the mixed use character of the whole of
Covent Garden, even within buildings and in those areas where short term action is
planned. It considers that a mixed-use approach to development control will provide
the best possible way of achieving the Plan's total aims . . .'

The policy for offices is expressed at the end of section B6 in these terms:

*f* 'It will be the normal policy to control any increase in office floor-space in
accordance with office policy contained in GLDP [the Greater London development
plan] as supplemented from time to time. No special case is seen for Covent Garden
as a whole to be treated differently from the rest of the Central Area and each
proposal should be treated on its merits.'

Earlier in this section it had been noted that 'the overall [office] policy will be one of
restraint consistent with the Council's strategic aims for the Central Area' (para B6.21);
*g* and para B6.23 should be quoted in full. It reads:

'Each case will therefore be assessed on its merits with continuous monitoring of
overall decisions with reference to the basic planning aims of the area. The following
factors will be taken into account when considering planning applications for office
development: 1 The type of office activity and its linkage with Covent Garden and
the Central Area. 2 The degree of benefit to the community office development
*h* would produce by way of: (a) provision of residential accommodation in conjunction
with the development; (b) provision of specific benefits in the form of buildings,
land or other facilities for use of the public; (c) conservation of buildings or places of
architectural or historic interest; (d) provision of small office suites; (e) provision of
land or buildings for other employment generating uses, for instance, small
industrial units.'

*j*
Counsel for the council has submitted, as it seems to me with some force, that this
paragraph contemplates that an office development might produce a benefit to the
community by, in a sense, subsidising benefits or amenities not necessarily directly
related to the office development itself. But I do not purport to decide whether or not
that submission is correct, and I do not rely on it in reaching my decision. If the

submission is substantially correct it seems to me probable that the benefits contemplated must all be matters regarded as beneficial in planning terms.

Policy with regard to theatres is expressed at para B7.16 in these terms:

'The theatre plays a very major economic role in the area and the Council consider that its continued existence and expansion should be encouraged to enhance the economic vitality of Covent Garden, to increase employment opportunities and to retain and increase the viability of other activities such as theatre support industries, pubs, restaurants and clubs. The economic spin-off effect would have more than local significance in view of the importance of theatres as a tourist attraction and as a means of earning foreign exchange.'

Finally, the area plan refers expressly to the extension of the Royal Opera House. Part of para C1.22 reads:

'The proposal [to extend the Royal Opera House], probably the most significant single project in the area is for extensions to the west and south of the existing building. On the move of the market the opportunity arose to safeguard the site required for this extension and in early 1975 the Government purchased the adjoining land westwards as far as Russell Street, the Piazza and Bow Street. It is the intention that the development be undertaken in phases. The extension of the backstage facilities to James Street will be the first part of the project to be undertaken and it is anticipated that this could be completed by 1981. The Opera House's overall scheme includes in addition to a major extension to the stage area, accommodation for the Royal Ballet School, the London Opera Centre and administrative offices and for a new raised flytower facilitating productions and giving better sight lines from the amphitheatre.'

As I have already said, the first phase has already been completed, in 1982 not in 1981; this application relates to the 'overall scheme', although the details of that scheme are not now precisely the same as they were at the date of the area plan.

The centre of Covent Garden is a conservation area designated as one of outstanding 'status' and the Royal Opera House's development proposals fall entirely within the area. Moreover, the Royal Opera House itself (Grade I), the Floral Hall, 46–47 Floral Street and 51–52 Long Acre (Grade II) are all listed buildings. In addition, consideration has been given by the Historical Buildings and Monuments Commission to listing 18 and 19 Russell Street. Long Acre, Floral Street and Russell Street have attractive frontages of eighteenth and nineteenth century buildings of architectural merit.

The latest government policy on listed buildings is contained in Department of the Environment circular 1987/8. Paragraph 91 reads:

'Generally it should be remembered that the number of buildings of special architectural and historic interest is limited. Accordingly the Secretary of State is of the view that the presumption should be in favour of preservation except where a strong case can be made out for granting consent after application of the criteria mentioned.'

In 1984 the ROH instructed architects to prepare proposals for a comprehensive redevelopment of the Royal Opera House and the surrounding area which would meet the needs not met by the first phase of development. Those proposals included a large element of commercial office development intended to finance the improvements as a whole; and they included a proposal to demolish the Floral Hall. On 26 April 1985 the GLC's planning committee met and considered a report of the director of architecture and controller of transportation and development. The report included the following paragraph:

'... on its merits the scheme will ensure the completion of an undoubted a prestigious project. As such it will also comply with criteria (b) of para B.6.23 [that is to say of the area plan, the paragraph which I have already quoted in full] in that it will result in the "provision of special benefits in the form of buildings, land or other facilities for use of the public".'

The report concluded:

b 'Whilst it may be considered desirable to encourage a mixed use scheme on the site, for example, shopping fronting the [piazza], the principle of office development funding the project must be considered undesirable. Leaving aside matters of policy and precedent, the site is obviously sensitive in townscape terms, and it will be difficult enough to incorporate the required uses in a satisfactory civic design solution, without the added impact of a significant level of office space . . . In terms of listed buildings there is no doubt that no case has been made for the demolition

c of the Floral Hall . . .'

Having received that report the planning committee of the GLC resolved:

'That the Project Director of the Royal Opera House be informed: (i) Whilst the Council would be prepared to accept at this initial stage the principle of Opera House uses and other uses on the site, it would not accept the principle that sufficient

d commercial development should be included within the development to fund works to the Opera House. Besides being contrary to statutory and current Council policies such a development concept would put at risk the potential to secure a scheme that would be sympathetic to the well-established character of Covent Garden; (ii) That the Project Director be further informed that the Council is not satisfied that a case has been made for the demolition of the Floral Hall and therefore

e it would not at this stage authorise the grant of listed building consent for such demolition.'

Two points should be noted about that resolution of the planning committee of the GLC. First, it was not put before the planning committee of the council which later made the decisions now under review, although counsel on behalf of the association does

f not rely on that omission as a ground to support these applications but merely as part of the background. Second, the commercial development forming part of the proposals now under consideration are not sufficient to fund all the work that is proposed, as will be seen in a moment.

The applications made on 3 October 1986, which were later amended in June 1987, provide, after those amendments, for the demolition in whole or in part of the Floral

g Hall (although the Floral Hall is to be rebuilt) and of 51–52 Long Acre, for approximately 16,000 sq m of office floor space and for a 300-space underground car park entered from Bow Street. The proposals will also involve the demolition of other listed and unlisted buildings. The proposal for the underground car park was not initiated by the ROH but by the council itself; and the council will own and operate that car park if it is built. But it must be noted that the proposal was a long way from being a proposal simply for the

h development of offices and car park. To make good this point, it is necessary to recite the details of the proposal contained in the application, which are as follows:

'Comprehensive development comprising alteration of, extensions to and partial demolition of the Royal Opera House, demolition of listed buildings at the Floral Hall, 46–47 Floral Street and 51–52 Long Acre and new development, to provide:

j improved Opera, Ballet and ancillary facilities; office; shops; restaurants; car parking; pedestrian and vehicular ways'

The proposals relate to a number of sites, which include the whole of the area bounded by Floral Street, Bow Street, Russell Street and James Street, an area on the corner of Hanover Street and Floral Street, and about half of the area bounded by Long Acre,

Hanover Place, Floral Street and James Street. The buildings which it is proposed to demolish so as to provide the main commercial development are 17–21 Russell Street and 2 Bow Street, on the corner of those two streets.

In a letter dated 30 September 1986 accompanying the application the ROH stated:

'The financing of the scheme will not be easily achieved. No grant aid from Government sources has been offered. This means that the cultural benefits from the Royal Opera House improvements will not be completed within an acceptable timescale unless they can, to a substantial degree, be financed from the overall project.'

The ROH has estimated that the improvements would cost £56m, that £33m of this amount would be met by profits from the commercial element of the proposed development and that the balance of £23m would be privately raised. Those were the figures which related to the application as it was originally made. As will be seen, they have been slightly amended in view of the subsequent variation.

An architects' report, which was made available to each individual member of the committee both for the February and the June meetings, was included with the application. Some passages of this report must be quoted. First (p 2, second and third paragraphs):

'As with many such European theatres, the stage arrangements were never designed to accommodate present day performance and rehearsal requirements, and the stage machinery itself is now at the end of its useful life. The Royal Opera House is therefore compelled to undertake a programme of modernisation and reconstruction to ensure its future as a major international house.

It has been made clear that any such project would not be able to rely on public money and that part of the site available would have to generate income towards the cost of the theatre's requirements. The project, therefore, consists of improvements to the theatre and a series of buildings on adjacent sites, notably those bounding the Covent Garden Market Square, that generate the greater part of the income to pay for the theatre works.'

Also on the same page Sir John Tooley, the General Director of the Royal Opera House, who has sworn an affidavit in this application, is quoted as having said:

'It is our belief that the Royal Opera House should be an integral part of Covent Garden, and an essential aspect of the proposals is the re-establishment of the missing frontages to the Market Square with generous shopping arcades which lead to a new second entrance to the theatre. This entrance, the arcades, and an open loggia at roof level will give the Royal Opera House a positive presence in the Square. The proposed scheme thus offers an opportunity to combine the interests of the theatre with those of the area at large, ensuring the future of the Royal Opera House and the completion of an important piece of London's Townscape.'

Later on the same page, the introduction reads:

'The scheme is a mixture of new buildings for the Opera House, refurbishment of existing Opera House premises, and new offices, shops and public parking. This report deals in functional terms with each of these categories. However, when considering the appearance of the buildings and their relationship to the surrounding area, the whole project is brought together so that it can be seen as a coherent part of the city.'

Under the heading 'The Site: Proposed' the report reads (p 10):

'The project has to find a balance between commercial and arts uses. The disposition of the site in relation to the present theatre happens to allow the project

a

to maximise the benefit to the Royal Opera House without necessarily undermining commercial potential.'

Later on the same page reference is made to the complete rebuilding of the fly tower. The report deals with the new arcade, saying (p 30):

b

'The arcade building unifies the theatre and commercial parts of the scheme. It marks the second entrance to the Opera House, provides an opportunity for a continuous elegant shopping frontage at ground level and offers at roof level the loggia, a promenade which connects directly to the new amphitheatre foyer . . .'

In a letter dated 30 September 1986 accompanying the application the ROH stated:

c

'The financing of the scheme will not be easily achieved. No grant aid from Government sources has been offered. This means that the cultural benefits from the Royal Opera House improvements will not be completed within an acceptable timescale unless they can, to a substantial degree, be financed from the overall project.'

I have already read out that passage of the letter and the estimated costs.

d

The association accepts that the proposals include elements of architectural merit and some mixed uses; but they point out that the principal land use applied for outside the Royal Opera House itself is for commercial offices, mostly in one large block designed to be let in large units, that the proposals involve the demolition of large numbers of buildings in the area both listed and unlisted and that only the Royal Opera House itself would remain externally in its present form. They point out that the proposed development before the amendments were made in June 1987 included no residential

e

accommodation, although 3,660 sq ft of residential accommodation exist in the area at present; and in their view many architectural features would be totally out of keeping with other buildings in the conservation area and the size of the office units would be out of keeping with units existing at present. Whether there is force in that criticism is not for me to say. Unless it comes to the exercise of my discretion I am not concerned with the merits of the application, and even if it does come to that I shall certainly not

f

take into account aesthetic considerations of that kind. On 3 February 1987 the planning and development committee of the council (the committee) considered the proposed development and a report of the council's director of planning and transportation. I must quote a number of passages from this long and detailed report. It was stated that the key objectives of the project are (para 4.3):

g

'—to modernise the stage —to provide a permanent home for the Royal Ballet —to provide greater public accessibility to the theatre.'

Under the heading 'The Opera House Improvements' the report continues:

h

'. . . Externally, the most obvious manifestations of these works will be the new fly tower and paint frame studio. Internally, the [new] alterations provide for greatly improved and enlarged stage areas, new ballet studios, orchestra facilities and support facilities.

4.4 Greater public accessibility is achieved by providing a new entrance to be located in the Market Square. This and the retained Bow Street entrance are linked to a new foyer system and to an open air loggia at roof level overlooking the Square. The foyer system incorporates two new performance spaces capable of accommodat-

j

ing audiences of 300 & 250 people.

4.5 Additional support facilities are provided north of Floral Street. The larger site bounded by Floral Street, Hanover Place and Long Acre, which is to be completely redeveloped, will on its Floral Street frontage provide a new rehearsal studio ballet dressing rooms and administrative offices. These facilities will be linked directly to the Royal Opera House by 2 high level bridges. The buildings at

48–51 Floral Street will be refurbished to provide workshops for the Royal Opera House wardrobe production centre.'

Under the heading 'Shops and Offices' the report states that the project incorporates a substantial commercial element to generate a part of the income to pay for the theatre works and a table of the various existing and proposed uses in the area demonstrates that the originally proposed office development of approximately 16,000 sq m would involve an addition of about 14,500 sq m to the existing area of office use (para 4.6). The report summarises the responses received by many interested parties and under the heading 'Office and Residential Policy', it having been noted that the application site is subject to the policies contained in the area plan and that the office policy of that plan is one of restraint which emphasises the importance of providing small office units, reads (paras 6.4–6.6):

'6.4 . . . The Director of Property Services considers that the commercial content of the proposed development maximises the financial return that can be achieved from this element of the development within the townscape constraints, even though the commercial content will not fully subsidise the cost of the improvements to the Opera House.

6.5 The compelling functional needs for the modernisation of the Opera House cannot be disputed. It is clear that the stage arrangements and rehearsal facilities are wholly unsatisfactory and that the stage machinery is at the end of its useful life. It also has to be accepted that in the current climate the project will not be able to rely on public funds.

6.6 It is considered that in principle the proposed office content could be justified on the basis of the special needs of the Royal Opera House and the uniqueness of the application . . .'

Under the heading 'Character and Function' the report reads:

'6.7 The proposals will introduce a major office use into an area where none exists to any significant degree. Many of the responses received from the public and amenity groups consider that this would have a serious detrimental effect on the special character and function of this part of Covent Garden.

6.8 The architects anticipating this criticism state in their report that the offices "take an appropriately restrained position in the street scene" and suggest that the main office building fronting the Square should be used for individual rooms rather than general office space. They also state that the building will be suitable for occupancy by either single or multiple tenants providing office suites ranging from 350 m² upwards.

6.9 Notwithstanding the attempts made by the architects to lessen the impact it is inevitable that a major effect on the character and function of the area will result. On balance however it is not considered that the effect would be so detrimental as to outweigh the benefits of the overall scheme.'

Under the heading 'Implementation and Financial Considerations' the report reads:

'6.12 The very significant office content proposed could only be considered acceptable in policy terms if the Council were convinced that the development would be completed in its entirety within a reasonable period of time, and that all of the improvements and community benefits associated with the scheme could be provided.

6.13 The applicants have indicated their willingness to enter into legal agreements to safeguard the full implementation of the scheme. The [ROH] are offering assurances that all monies raised from the development would be committed to arts improvements and that the development would be undertaken in one continuous phased building programme . . .'

Under the heading 'Demolition of the Floral Hall' the report reads (para 6.18):

a

'The proposed near total demolition of E M Barrie's Floral Hall ... is clearly contentious in principle. However given, once again, the special need to provide first rate stage, back stage and other ancillary facilities commensurate with an opera house of international standing, the loss of the greater part of the building might be reasonably regarded as sustainable ... In addition, the taking down of the iron and glass frontage to the north-east corner of the Piazza and the adjacent part of the Hall, enables the original Inigo Jones architectural concept of the Piazza to be substantially reinstated by the restoration of one continuous, colonnaded building around the North and Eastern sides of the square ...'

Under the heading 'The loss of other buildings' the report reads (para 6.20):

c

'Except for the group of buildings in Floral Street to the west of Hanover Place (ie. nos. 45, 46 and 47 Floral Street), which are proposed for demolition and redevelopment for further ancillary accommodation for the Opera House, the proposed demolition and redevelopment of other listed buildings and unlisted buildings of townscape value in Long Acre, Hanover Place, and Russell Street is related to the "commercial" part of the scheme, as distinct from that part which provides functional accommodation for the Opera House. The case for demolition and redevelopment for commercial uses would not normally be acceptable but in the unique context of the Opera House is on balance considered acceptable.'

The amendments to the proposal made in June 1987, which I have already mentioned, took out from the application the proposal to demolish 46–47 Floral Street.

Under the heading 'The New Buildings' the report reads (para 6.23):

'There is little doubt that the design of the new buildings in the proposed development is of considerable architectural quality and urban design interest. Indeed that part of the proposed development fronting the Piazza provides a most welcome restatement of the original Inigo Jones concept and a singularly positive contribution to and enhancement of the character and appearance of this part of Covent Garden Conservation Area.'

Under the heading 'Conclusions' appear the following paragraphs:

'9.1 The details of this scheme are very complex. However, the planning issue can be simply stated. That is, do the special circumstances of the Royal Opera House justify the provision of a major commercial development in this part of Covent Garden? ...

9.4 The final decision must be balanced against the wider considerations, in particular the impact of the development on the special character and function of Covent Garden, the creation of a major speculative office development in the context of a restrictive office policy and the loss of buildings of special architectural and historic importance in the absence of good evidence to support their demolition as opposed to retention and adoption. These factors are compounded by the uncertainties which exist with regard to the Royal Opera House securing the substantial amount of additional funding required over and above the income generated by the scheme, and the difficulty of securing concrete assurances which could form the basis of an acceptable legal agreement to ensure the implementation of the scheme in its entirety.

9.5 The proposals have to be seen against the need to enhance the functioning of the Royal Opera House and to improve and update its facilities to a standard commensurate with its place as a premier European Opera House. It is in this context that the Committee is, despite some of the less welcome aspects of the package, on balance recommended to approve the proposals in principle and to

authorise the Director to seek a resolution of a number of design issues raised and to
secure amendments safeguarding the amenities of adjoining residential occupiers   *a*
...'

The committee, having received that report, by no means slavishly followed its
recommendations. On 3 February 1987 it took its own line and it resolved:

'That the decision be referred to the June meeting of the Planning and
Development Committee for the following reasons:—1. The Committee is willing   *b*
to contemplate in principle a major departure from the Covent Garden Action Area
Plan, but wishes to be absolutely convinced that the commercial development of
the site is the only way of achieving the Royal Opera House improvements.
Accordingly, while welcoming the application in principle, the Committee would
wish there to be an opportunity for future discussion on this crucial aspect. 2. That
in the meantime discussions be held with [the ROH] regarding the principle of the   *c*
demolition of listed buildings and buildings in a conservation area, the design of the
frontages to Russell and Bow Streets and the reinstatement or possible gain of
residential accommodation.'

In response to that decision and resolution the ROH prepared certain amendments to
the proposed development. Apart from a number of design amendments to the exterior   *d*
of the proposed new buildings, they abandoned the proposal to demolish 46–47 Floral
Street, one of the listed buildings, and they proposed an amendment to the reconstruction
of the Floral Hall which would include reinstatement of a section of the glazed barrel
vault roof which had been lost in a fire 30 years ago. They also considered five alternative
options, each involving less office space; and shortly before the next meeting of the
committee, held on 30 June, they proposed a sixth alternative the effect of which would   *e*
be to provide between 20 and 25 flats on the upper floors of the building as proposed for
the Long Acre frontage, instead of the previously proposed offices, an amendment which
would reduce the office floor space content by just over 2,000 sq m, reducing the overall
total to about 14,000 sq m, and which would increase the estimated deficit of £23m by
between £2m and £2·5m to about £25m. The proposal approved on 30 June included
this option.   *f*

Before the next meeting of the committee, on 30 June, a further report by the acting
director of planning and transportation was circulated. Since at its previous meeting the
committee had accepted the proposal in principle subject to its being convinced that the
commercial development was the only way of achieving the improvements to the Royal
Opera House, this report was not unnaturally concentrated primarily on that aspect of
the matter. The committee were reminded that they had indicated their willingness to   *g*
accept in principle a major departure from the action area plan (para 1.2). The next few
paragraphs of the report, so far as material, read as follows:

'1.3 In response to the Committee request the Royal Opera House have carried
out studies which show that other alternative land uses would produce considerably
lower development receipts. They therefore adhere to the view that the proposals as   *h*
submitted represent the only means of financing the essential improvements to the
Royal Opera House.'

Paragraph 1.4 refers to the retention of 46–47 Floral Street and the reinstatement of the
barrel vault roof of the Floral Hall, para 1.5 refers to the public response and para 1.6, so
far as material, reads:   *j*

'On balance, and having regard to the uniqueness of the project, it is considered
that the proposals can be recommended in principle ...'

Paragraph 5 consisted of an examination of the first five of the six options to which I
have referred. It was stated (para 5.1):

a   '. . . The detailed financial information has been submitted on a confidential basis
to the Assistant Director (Valuation), Property Services Department, who has
undertaken a financial assessment in respect of the Russell Street block as being
indicative of the various changes in the overall scheme.'

Those five options included an increase in the retail accommodation, an increase in the
retail and leisure facilities, an increase in the retail and residential accommodation, an
b   increase in the retail accommodation together with a hotel and an increase in the retail
and residential accommodation on a larger scale than the earlier option. Not surprisingly,
in view of the fact that each of the options involved less office accommodation, the
assistant director (valuation) considered that each of those alternatives would provide a
lower financial contribution towards the cost of the Royal Opera House improvement,
adding to the estimated deficit of £23m varying amounts ranging from £7·5m to £21m
c   the additional deficit which would result if all office development were to be deleted
from the proposals.

Dealing with 'The Demolition of Buildings', the first two paragraphs under that
heading read as follows:

'5.8 The revised proposals at present involve the same degree of demolition as
the scheme previously considered by the Committee. The applicants contend that
d   the demolition of the listed buildings is justified by the benefits provided by the
improvements to the Opera House, the Floral Hall reconstruction involving the
reinstatement of a small section of the barrel vault and the completion of the Covent
Garden Piazza with architecture of a high quality.

5.9 With respect to the listed building at 51–52 Long Acre and the unlisted
properties in Russell Street the applicant's case is that the replacement buildings arc
e   of equal or greater architectural or townscape merit than those currently existing.'

Further on under the same heading the report reads:

'5.10 . . . The retention of 46/47 Floral Street would obviously be warmly
welcomed and would go a considerable way towards overcoming the concern
expressed both by the City Council and others regarding the extent of demolition
f   involved in the proposals.'

The conclusions contain the following paragraphs:

'5.14 In summary, the Royal Opera House have demonstrated to the satisfaction
of the Assistant Director (Valuation) that no other combination of land uses could
g   provide as high a financial contribution to the Opera House improvement as could
an office based commercial scheme.

5.17 It is considered that the architects, working within the brief presented by
the Royal Opera House, have produced an imaginative and sensitive example of
urban renewal in the important context of Covent Garden. It is on this basis that
the proposals are recommended for approval subject to the subsequent agreement
h   of detailed planning conditions . . .'

In a supplementary report added to that report shortly before the meeting the acting
director of planning and transportation referred to the sixth option, the effect of which I
have already described.

The minutes of the meeting of the committee held on 30 June 1987, having
j   summarised those passages of the officers' report to which I have already referred,
including in para 5.2 a reference back to their conclusion on 3 February 1987 that the
proposal represented a major departure from the area plan and that commercial
development of the site was the only way of achieving the Royal Opera House
improvements and having noted also in para 5.4 that—

'Other possible alternative ways of financing the improvements and extensions to the Opera House put forward by third parties had not come to fruition'

records resolutions of the committee in the following terms:

'Resolved—1. That, subject to a) any direction by the Historic Buildings and Monuments Commission and Department of the Environment, and b) satisfactory legal agreements to include the completion of the development in its entirety, the provision and mode of operation of the car park, the pedestrian walkways, the relocation of the Piazza frontage of the Floral Hall and the type and management policy of the retail provision, conditional permission and listed building consent be granted.
2. That the conditions to be attached to the permission and listed building consent be determined by the Town Planning (Applications) Sub-Committee by way of the Chairman's recommendations procedure.'

That decision was referred to the meeting of the council on 27 July 1987, when it was adopted. It is those two decisions, that of the committee and that of the council, which are the subject matter of this application. It should be noted that no planning permission has yet been granted. Unless this application succeeds, it will be granted when the two conditions referred to in the resolution have been fulfilled, and when it is granted it will be subject to such conditions as may be determined by the town planning (applications) sub-committee.

I have set out the background to this application in much greater detail than is strictly necessary for the purpose of considering the points of law which arise. But I have been encouraged to take this course not only because the matter is one of considerable public interest but also because all three parties, by their counsel, have directed me to, and asked me to take into account, the details of the history which I have just described. It has been necessary in any event to examine fairly closely the written material which was before the committee, specifically the architects' report and the council officers' reports, because there can be no doubt but that that written material was available and before the committee when it made its decisions. In making those decisions it is common ground that it had to consider the applications 'on their merits', that is to say taking into account all aspects of the applications known to it which were material. Of course the association is entitled for the purposes of this application to concentrate only on one or two of those aspects. But the committee, if its decisions are to be fairly judged, is entitled to ask the court to take into account many more than just those one or two aspects. Even though it may be the case that a decision can be invalidated if only one consideration taken into account was not material, none the less in deciding whether or not in such circumstances to quash the decision the court might well need to take into account all the considerations which the committee had in mind and took into account when making its decisions.

I described in general terms, at the beginning of this judgment, the two grounds on which the association relies in seeking to quash the committee's decisions and that of the council. The first ground, as formally expressed in the amended notice of motion, is:

'The provision of finance to maintain the international status of the Opera House was not a material planning consideration which could lawfully justify development regarded by the Committee as involving a major departure from the development plan.'

This is a reference to what has been described in this judgment as the area plan.

To assess the validity of that ground it is necessary to examine it carefully in order to see whether it accurately expresses a consideration which the committee did in fact take into account. The consideration which it is contended the committee took into account can be seen to fall into two parts: (i) that the committee regarded the proposals as constituting a major departure from planning control and (ii) that such departure was

justified by the fact that it would provide finance to maintain the international status of
a the Royal Opera House.

It is quite clear that the committee did regard the proposals as constituting a major
departure from planning control: see para 1 of its resolution of 3 February 1987 and para
5.2 of the minutes of its meeting of 30 June 1987; and it is equally clear that the features
which constituted the major departure were primarily the commercial development,
that is to say the area of office accommodation which was originally to have been about
b 16,000 sq m, reduced before the June meeting to about 14,000 sq m, and to a lesser
extent the demolition of listed and unlisted buildings in a conservation area. But it is
much less clear that, as the minutes express its decisions, the committee considered that
such departure was justified by the fact that it would provide finance to maintain the
international status of the Royal Opera House. Nor is it by any means clear that the
committee considered that the departure was justified by the fact that the profits from
c the commercial development would 'finance opera', or a 'socially desirable objective'. I
refer to two of the expressions used by counsel on behalf of the association in his
submissions in seeking to challenge the legality of the decision.

If one examines the precise terms of the decision of 3 February 1987 (repeated in the
same terms in para 5.2 of the minutes of the meeting of 30 June 1987) they are that the
committee wished to be convinced that the commercial development was the only way
d of achieving the Royal Opera House *improvements*. It decided, therefore, that the major
departure from the area plan was justified not by the fact that it would provide finance
to maintain the international status of the Royal Opera House, still less that profits from
it would finance opera, or a socially desirable objective, but that it would finance the
Royal Opera House *improvements*, that is to say the improvement of the Royal Opera
House which could not otherwise be achieved.

e The last stage therefore in this analysis of the committee's decision is to identify those
improvements. They were clearly identified in paras 4.3 to 4.5 of the report of the
officers to the meeting of 3 February 1987, which I have quoted in full; they include the
modernisation of the stage, a new fly tower, additional studios and rehearsal rooms, a
new entrance to the opera house to give improved access, a new foyer system, new
f dressing rooms, workshops, offices and other support facilities.

The question of law which I have to consider therefore is whether the committee was
entitled to take into account, in deciding whether or not to give planning permission,
the fact that the finance made available from a commercial development which formed
part of the proposals would enable other improvements, also forming part of the
proposals, to be carried out, or, put more narrowly, the fact that unless the commercial
development were to be approved those other improvements could not be achieved.

g Before considering that central question of law, namely whether or not that fact,
whichever way it is expressed, was material and therefore a legal consideration, it is
important to note the limits of that question and the limits of this court's powers in
relation to it.

The limits of the question are that it is confined to the legality of the committee's
h decisions. It does not extend to the reasonableness or rationality of those decisions, an
issue which is raised by the association under the second main ground of challenge. But
if, as a matter of law, a particular consideration is material, this court is not concerned,
when considering the legality of the decision, with the weight which ought to be given
to the consideration. On the other hand, in considering the rationality as distinct from
the legality of the decision, which I will have to do when considering the second ground,
j the court must expressly or by implication consider and give effect to the relative weight
of different material considerations.

I should add for completeness that, although the court when ruling on the legality of
a decision never has to decide what weight ought to have been given to any particular
consideration, it may, at least on one view of the law, have to decide what weight was
given to particular considerations by the decision-making body if one consideration
which it took into account was material and therefore legal but another was not.

Finally, before returning to the immediate question before me, I should clarify precisely my function, which is to decide not whether the consideration taken into *a* account by the committee is in fact material, but whether as a matter of law it is capable of being material.

I have already cited a few words from s 29 of the Town and Country Planning Act 1971. I must now cite it more fully, omitting immaterial words. It reads:

'(1) . . . where an application is made to a local planning authority for planning *b* permission, that authority, in dealing with the application, shall have regard to the . . . development plan, so far as material to the application, and to any other material considerations, and—(a) . . . may grant planning permission, either unconditionally or subject to such conditions as they think fit; or (b) may refuse planning permission . . .'

There is no appeal, under the legislation, against a grant of planning permission, but *c* there is one against a refusal of planning permission or against a condition of its grant.

The leading authority on the expression 'material considerations' in s 29 is *Stringer v Minister of Housing and Local Government* [1971] 1 All ER 65 at 77, [1970] 1 WLR 1281 at 1294–1295, where Cooke J decided that the expression 'material considerations' was not limited to amenity, but that 'material considerations' must be considerations of a planning nature, and that 'all considerations relating to the use and development of land *d* are considerations which may, in a proper case, be regarded as planning considerations . . .' In *Great Portland Estates plc v Westminster City Council* [1984] 3 All ER 744 at 750, [1985] AC 661 at 670 Lord Scarman, having cited a dictum of Viscount Dilhorne in *Newbury DC v Secretary of State for the Environment* [1980] 1 All ER 731 at 738, [1981] AC 578 at 599 that the test for whether a consideration was a material consideration was whether it served a planning purpose, said that a planning purpose was one which related to the *e* character of the use of the land.

It seems to me to be quite beyond doubt but that the fact that the finances made available from the commercial development would enable the improvements to be carried out was capable of being a material consideration, that is to say that it was a consideration which related to the use or development of the land, that it related to a planning purpose and to the character of the use of the land, namely the improvements *f* to the Royal Opera House which I have already described, particularly as the proposed commercial development was on the same site as the Royal Opera House and as the commercial development and the proposed improvements to the Royal Opera House all formed part of one proposal.

Counsel for the association has submitted that the width of Cooke J's definition of material consideration has been judicially cut down in two ways. First he submits that *g* the decision of the House of Lords in the *Newbury DC* case is authority for the proposition that a material consideration must satisfy two tests: first that it must serve a planning purpose and second that it must fairly and reasonably relate to the permitted development. The proposition expressed in that way is an elision of the dicta of Viscount Dilhorne, of Lord Fraser and of Lord Scarman (see [1980] 1 All ER 731 at 739, 745, 754, [1981] AC *h* 578 at 599, 607, 618). That case was concerned with the question whether a condition subject to which planning permission had been granted was legal, not whether an unconditional permission was legal, which is the question of principle raised in this case. I do not propose to decide whether the same test applies for both purposes. It may be that the test of a material consideration in the context of a condition imposed has been more tightly drawn, perhaps because of the penal consequences of a breach of a condition and *j* perhaps because of the statutory right of appeal against the imposition of a condition. But whether or not that is so it seems to be equally beyond doubt but that the consideration taken into account by this committee, as I have analysed it to be, is capable of having satisfied each of those two tests.

Second, counsel for the association submitted that, by giving effect to this consideration, the committee was giving effect to purely financial considerations or to considerations purely personal to the Royal Opera House. For the reasons which I have already expressed,

in analysing the committee's reasons, I cannot accept that that is an accurate description
*a* of its decisions. But even if it can be properly said that it was taking into account the
personal or financial circumstances of the Royal Opera House it does not follow that the
decision was illegal because those considerations were not capable of being material. Lord
Scarman in the *Westminster City Council* case [1984] 3 All ER 744 at 750, [1985] AC 661
at 670 said:

*b*       'Personal circumstances . . . personal hardship . . . are not to be ignored . . . The
          human factor . . . can . . . and sometimes should, be given direct effect as an
          exceptional or special circumstance.'

Counsel for the council and for the ROH ask, rhetorically, what could be a more special
or exceptional case than this? In my judgment the respondents could properly have
relied on that dictum of Lord Scarman even if there was not such a close relationship
*c* between the proposed commercial development and the improvements to the Royal
Opera House. Sir Douglas Frank QC applied the same sort of principle in *Brighton BC v
Secretary of State for the Environment* (1978) 39 P & CR 46, where he refused to quash a
decision to allow a proposal by a school to develop playing fields adjacent to the school,
which had been made because the profit from the development would enable the school
building to be kept up, even though there was no immediate proposal relating to those
*d* school buildings.
          Counsel for the council also submitted that the effect of Department of the
Environment circular 1980/22 is to widen the scope of material considerations so as to
have the effect of including in that category, if they were not already included, financial
and economic considerations. Although that circular may well have the effect of
encouraging local planning authorities to treat, as a question of fact, as material
*e* considerations considerations which they might otherwise have ignored, or to give to
such considerations more weight, I do not think that the circular can have the effect of
enlarging the scope of or category of considerations which, as a matter of law, are capable
of being material.
          Although therefore I do not accept that final submission of counsel for the council, in
*f* my judgment the committee did not take into account a consideration which was not
capable of being material, so that the association's first ground of challenge fails.
          The second ground is that the committee, it is contended, failed to consider or to take
reasonable steps to inform itself of other methods of financing the opera house
improvements without major departures from the plan, or to balance the different
financial contributions produced by different combinations of uses against the respective
*g* degree of impact of each such combination of uses on the planning of the area. Counsel
for the association did not pursue in his submissions the contention that the committee
did not balance the different financial considerations produced by different combinations
of uses. The history which I have cited, particularly the officers' report which was before
the committee on 30 June 1987, demonstrates that it did so. His submission in argument
was that the committee did not make sufficient inquiries to enable it to be satisfied that
*h* the whole of the cost of the proposal could not be funded otherwise than by means of the
commercial development.
          In support of that submission he sought to rely on the decision of the Court of Appeal
in *Prest v Secretary of State for Wales* (1982) 81 LGR 193, where the court held that it was
the duty of the Secretary of State before making a compulsory purchase order to take
reasonable steps to acquaint himself with all the relevant information to enable him to
*j* reach his decision. But in my view a decision to grant planning permission is not to be
equated with a decision to make a compulsory purchase order, for the purposes of this
point. I doubt whether a planning committee has a duty to make inquiries at all, even
though if it makes or has made no inquiries its decision may in certain circumstances be
illegal on the ground of irrationality if it was made in the absence of information without
which no reasonable planning authority would have granted permission. So counsel for
the association's submission becomes, as is reflected in his skeleton argument, a
submission that goes to that issue. I quote from his skeleton argument:

'. . . the information put before the Committee . . . was not such as to enable it
rationally to conclude that the proposal was the only way of achieving the Opera    *a*
House improvements.'

In my judgment this second ground is not made out. The committee had been told
that the project would not be able to rely on public funds (see para 6.5 of the officers'
report of 3 February 1987). Mr Sporle, the council's acting director of planning and
transportation, took the members of the committee through the officers' reports and told    *b*
them that the commercial element was necessary so as to generate income to enable the
improvements to be carried out. And the committee was aware that even with that
income a deficit of about £25m would remain. The ROH raised the better part of £10m
to finance the first phase of the improvement, a demonstration, if demonstration was
necessary, that it is capable of raising money. But the money it raised then was a small
fraction of the amount needed to fund these proposals. And I am satisfied that there was    *c*
sufficient material information and general knowledge in the possession of the committee
to enable it rationally to conclude, as it implicitly did, that about £25m was the
maximum that the ROH could raise to fund the proposed improvements. For that
reason, in my judgment, the second of the association's grounds is not established.

But even if that last conclusion of mine were to be wrong I would not, in the exercise
of my discretion, quash the decision on that ground alone, partly because of the obvious    *d*
merits of the decision in the light of the history I have described (when I say that I am
not talking about aesthetic merits), partly because of the material before the committee,
which included the ROH's willingness to enter into a legal agreement which is a
condition of approval to safeguard the full implementation of the scheme, partly because
it is apparent that the committee applied itself, as indeed did its officers, conscientiously
to the issues and that the committee did not just slavishly adopt its officers'    *e*
recommendation, but primarily because the association has not made any specific
suggestion of any sort as to how the ROH could raise the whole cost of the development
in excess of £50m, that is to say about twice the amount which apparently it believes
that it can raise through the commercial development in any other way.

For all these reasons I dismiss this application.

*f*

*Application dismissed.*

K Mydeen Esq    Barrister.

**Appeal**
The association appealed.    *g*

*Robert Carnwath QC* and *Alice Robinson* for the association.
*Jeremy M Sullivan QC* and *David Mole* for the council.
*Peter Boydell QC* and *Charles George* for the ROH.

Cur adv vult    *h*

19 October. The following judgments were delivered.

**KERR LJ.**
*Introduction*
    This is an appeal on behalf of the Covent Garden Community Association (the    *j*
association) against a judgment of Webster J given on 8 February 1988 whereby he
refused to quash a planning decision of the Westminster City Council made in June/July
1987. Its effect was to grant permission to the Royal Opera House Covent Garden Ltd
(the ROH) to carry out a far-reaching redevelopment of Covent Garden. The central
objective of the application was to extend and improve the Opera House by reconstruction

and modernisation to bring it up to a standard consistent with its national and
*a* international reputation and to develop the surrounding area consistently with this
project. The decision to permit the development of the site in the manner proposed in
the application, after some modifications of the original scheme, involved a departure
from the relevant development plan by permitting the use of parts of the site for the
erection of office accommodation. The council was reluctant to permit this, but
ultimately accepted the need for it on the ground that the balance of the funds necessary
*b* to carry out the desired improvements to the Opera House was unobtainable by any
other means.

That decision was challenged by an application for judicial review on behalf of the
association instituted by two of its members. There are two grounds of challenge. First
and mainly it is said that the inclusion of office accommodation for financial reasons is
impermissible, even though the ROH is ready to enter into a binding agreement to use
*c* the proceeds from the commercial development for the benefit of the opera. It is said
that to permit the commercial development of part of the site for purely financial reasons,
whatever their nature or purpose, is not a 'material consideration' which the council was
entitled to take into account under s 29(1) of the Town and Country Planning Act 1971
in granting planning permission for the development as a whole. That raises an issue of
law of general importance on which there has been considerable discussion. Alternatively,
*d* if the challenge on that ground fails, then it is said that the council was bound to
investigate the financial aspects sufficiently to entitle it rationally to conclude that the
provision of office accommodation, by way of departure from the development plan,
was in fact necessary to achieve the objectives relating to the Opera House, that it failed
to do so and that its conclusion was accordingly irrational.

Webster J rejected both of these contentions and the association now appeals. The only
*e* issue before him and us is whether the planning permission for the proposed development
was invalid in law on either or both of these grounds. The courts are not concerned, in
the sense of having no right to concern themselves, with the planning merits or demerits
of the development in any respect. It is important to emphasise this, because many
controversial views are held about the scheme, and a number of press comments have
*f* referred to these proceedings in ways which might well give the false impression that
the courts are somehow involved in taking sides in the discussions.


*The legislation*

It is only necessary to refer to a few of the provisions of the 1971 Act. The project
formed part of an 'action area' local plan prepared pursuant to s 11 which falls within the
*g* definition of 'development plan' in s 20. This was the Covent Garden action area plan
adopted by the Greater London Council (the GLC) in 1978. When the GLC disappeared
the planning authority became the Westminster City Council, whose planning and
development committee passed the relevant resolution which the council subsequently
adopted. It is necessary to quote the material part of s 29(1):

*h*        '... where an application is made to a local planning authority for planning
permission, that authority, in dealing with the application, shall have regard to the
provisions of the development plan, so far as material to the application, and to any
other material considerations ...'

The effect of the words 'shall have regard to' is that the contents of the development plan
are deemed to be material considerations, but not that they *must* necessarily be followed.
*j* Moreover, under s 31(1)(b) the Secretary of State is empowered to authorise planning
authorities 'to grant planning permission for development which does not accord with
the provisions of the development plan', and this was done in the present case by art 14
of the Town and Country Planning General Development Order 1977, SI 1977/289.

The other provision which is of some relevance is s 52, dealing with agreements
regulating development or use of land, since the conclusion of such an agreement formed

an integral part of the planning permission granted in this case. Subsection (1) is in the
following terms:                                                                                 *a*

'A local planning authority may enter into an agreement with any person
interested in land in their area for the purpose of restricting or regulating the
development or use of the land, either permanently or during such period as may
be prescribed by the agreement; and any such agreement may contain such
incidental and consequential provisions (including provisions of a financial character)  *b*
as appear to the local planning authority to be necessary or expedient for the
purposes of the agreement.'

It should also be noted that the scheme involved the demolition and reconstruction of a
substantial number of listed buildings in relation to which special planning controls are
imposed by ss 55 to 58A; but it is unnecessary to quote from these provisions. Finally,
counsel who appeared on behalf of the association drew attention to s 145 of the Local  *c*
Government Act 1972, which empowers a local authority to contribute financially to the
promotion of entertainment.

*The facts*
The Covent Garden Community Association is an unincorporated association which
was formed in 1971 to safeguard and protect the interests of residents and businesses in  *d*
the Covent Garden area. Its purposes include the promotion of high standards of planning
and architecture and to secure the preservation, protection, development and
improvement of buildings or features of historical public interest in the area. The action
area plan acknowledges in para A4.34 the 'substantial and constructive contribution to
the public debate on the Plan' made by the association.

The application for judicial review seeks to quash a resolution of the planning and  *e*
development committee of the Westminster City Council passed on 30 June 1987 and
adopted by the council on 29 July 1987 that planning permission and listed building
consents be granted for the redevelopment of the Royal Opera House, the Floral Hall, 2
Bow Street, 17–21 Russell Street, 2–6 Mart Street, 45–51 Floral Street, 51–54 Long Acre
and land fronting James Street, Covent Garden, London WC2 subject to the fulfilment  *f*
of three conditions referred to in the resolution. The permitted development included a
substantial block of office accommodation along Russell Street and part of Bow Street
and two smaller blocks along parts of James Street and Long Acre. These were decisions
taken in principle only; the relevant permissions and consents are still in draft. But rather
than wait for the formalities to be completed it was thought convenient to challenge the
decisions at this stage, and no objection has been taken to this course. On the other hand,  *g*
counsel for the council and for the ROH do not accept a submission on behalf of the
association that the court can therefore have regard to changes in circumstances which
have taken place since July 1987 when the decisions were taken in principle.

The ROH is a company limited by guarantee and a registered charity. It is responsible
for the day-to-day administration and operation of the Royal Opera House. This was
designed by E M Barrie and opened in 1858. Its stage and equipment were modernised  *h*
in 1902 and new dressing rooms were added in an annexe in 1932. Since 1946 the theatre
has housed two internationally renowned companies, the Royal Opera and the Royal
Ballet, and the Sadlers Wells Royal Ballet has also been administered from there since
1957. In the same way as many similar European theatres, the stage and other
arrangements were never designed to accommodate present day performance and
rehearsal requirements. The ROH therefore felt it essential to undertake a programme  *j*
of modernisation and reconstruction to ensure the opera's future national and international
reputation. The association does not dispute that further improvements are necessary if
the Royal Opera is to maintain and improve its standing as one of the leading opera
houses in the world.

The Covent Garden action area plan issued in 1978, to which I must refer in some
detail hereafter, accepted the need to improve the Opera House and regarded the proposal

to extend it as 'probably the most significant single project in the area'. It envisaged that
a  this development would be carried out in phases. In order to meet the most pressing
needs for additional and improved facilities a first phase of expansion was completed in
1982 when the Opera House was extended westward along its axis, enabling rehearsal
studios, chorus and dressing rooms and other offices to be added. The cost of that phase
was £10m, mainly financed by money raised by public appeal. But this was considered
to be far from sufficient, and in the result the ROH applied in October 1986 for outline
b  planning permission and listed building consents to carry out a far-reaching
redevelopment of the Opera House and parts of the surrounding land and buildings.

Before coming to the subsequent history I must refer to a number of provisions of the
action area plan. In para B1.2 it was made clear that the policy was to continue to promote
the mixed use of land within the area. For present purposes we are concerned with
theatres, including of course the Opera House itself, on the one hand, and office
c  accommodation on the other. I will therefore deal with these aspects in that order.

The plan contains numerous passages acknowledging the importance of theatres, both
from the point of view of the public interest in entertainment and also for economic
reasons. Thus, para B7.16 stated:

'The theatre plays a very major economic role in the area and the Council consider
d      that its continued existence and expansion should be encouraged to enhance the
economic vitality of Covent Garden, to increase employment opportunities and to
retain and increase the viability of other activities such as theatre support industries,
pubs, restaurants and clubs. The economic spin-off effect would have more than
local significance in view of the importance of theatres as a tourist attraction and as
a means of earning foreign exchange.'

e  The proposed extension of the Royal Opera House was dealt with in para C1.22:

'The proposal, probably the most significant single project in the area is for
extensions to the west and south of the existing building. On the move of the
market the opportunity arose to safeguard the site required for this extension and
in early 1975 the Government purchased the adjoining land westwards as far as
f      Russell Street, the Piazza and Bow Street.

It is the intention that the development be undertaken in phases. The extension
of the backstage facilities to James Street will be the first part of the project to be
undertaken and it is anticipated that this could be completed by 1981.   ·

The Opera House's overall scheme includes in addition to a major extension to
the stage area, accommodation for the Royal Ballet School, the London Opera Centre
g      and administrative offices and for a new raised flytower facilitating productions and
giving better sight lines from the amphitheatre.

As only part of the proposed extension will be undertaken during the Plan period,
it is important that each phase is acceptable as an entity and that the remainder of
the site be given sympathetic treatment and used appropriately on an interim basis.
As a matter of urgency proposals for using part of the site as open space in the short
h      term should be brought forward.'

The land referred to in the first paragraph was subsequently transferred by the
government to the ROH in order to enable it to carry out the development. The first
phase referred to in the second paragraph comprised the extensions and alterations
completed in 1982 which I have already mentioned. In connection with the second far
j  more important phase, which is now under consideration, it must be borne in mind that
the centre of Covent Garden is a conservation area designated as one of outstanding
'status' and that the proposals concerning this phase fall entirely within that area.

As regards the policies concerning office accommodation, counsel on behalf of the
council placed some reliance on para B6.23, both below and again before us. But in order
to deal with this submission it is necessary to quote this together with the two preceding
paragraphs:

'B6.21 The amount of existing and proposed office floorspace should be sufficient to contain the estimated future demand for office accommodation in the area. There *a* is therefore no reason to relax the Council's office policy for the Central Area. Thus the overall policy will be one of restraint consistent with the Council's strategic aims for the Central Area.

B6.22 It is essential, however, to ensure that new office developments, replacement offices and the modernisation of existing buildings contain a preponderance of small office units to provide a supply of units which meet the demand and to prevent the *b* creation of large unlettable units which could remain vacant for long periods.

B6.23 Each case will therefore be assessed on its merits with continuous monitoring of overall decisions with reference to the basic planning aims of the area. The following factors will be taken into account when considering planning applications for office development: 1 The type of office activity and its linkage with Covent Garden and the Central Area. 2 The degree of benefit to the community *c* office development would produce by way of: (a) provision of residential accommodation in conjunction with the development; (b) provision of specific benefits in the form of buildings, land or other facilities for use of the public; (c) conservation of buildings or places of architectural or historic interest; (d) provision of small office suites; (e) provision of land or buildings for other employment generating uses, for instance, small industrial units.' *d*

Counsel's submission, though only subsidiary to his main arguments, was that these references in the plan could be placed in the balance in support of the validity of the resolutions. Although they contain no direct reference to the financial benefits for other parts of the development which might be derived from the provision of some office accommodation, he said that the second part of para B6.23 clearly implied that this had *e* been in the mind of the GLC committee. So he submitted, in effect, that the proposal which was ultimately accepted went no further than to differ in degree from what had been contemplated throughout. Webster J saw some force in this argument but declined to base any reliance on it in reaching his decision. I would adopt the same approach. As counsel for the association pointed out, it is perfectly clear that the planning and development committee regarded the ultimate acceptance of the proposals for office *f* accommodation as involving a radical departure from the action plan. It did not base itself on para B6.23 in any way, and I am also doubtful whether any particular consideration was given to para B6.22. I therefore disregard these references to office accommodation in the plan.

It is then necessary to review the subsequent lengthy history. The judgment does so in considerable detail, and I have already gratefully drawn on parts of it. Webster J said that *g* he had taken this course 'not only because the matter is one of considerable public interest but also because all three parties, by their counsel, have directed me to, and asked me to take into account, the details of the history . . .' (see p 86 *e*, ante).

There has been no criticism of anything in this lengthy review, for which the court and the parties are greatly indebted. If the judgment of Webster J had been reported I would have incorporated these passages by reference. But they should not be lost, and *h* since I cannot improve on them I set them out verbatim. [His Lordship then set out the passage at p 78 *h* to p 86 *d*, ante, of the judgment of Webster J and continued:]

*The issues*
I have already mentioned these briefly at the beginning of this judgment. The first *j* raises the question whether financial considerations can properly be regarded as material in granting permission for a development which would otherwise have been rejected on planning policy grounds or would only have been allowed to be carried out in some different way. For the purposes of that submission there is no challenge to the committee's conclusion, which it clearly accepted on the facts, that the proposed extension and

improvements to the Opera House could only be carried out if the funds generated by
a  the proposed office accommodation will be available to make up the anticipated deficit.
The second issue is put in the alternative. It challenges the rationality of this assumption
on the facts, but accepts for that purpose that the decision would have been legally valid
if the assumption had been rationally justifiable. On that issue it will be necessary to
supplement the judge's review of the history to some extent in the light of counsel for
the association's passing references to subsequent events.

b    For the sake of completeness I should briefly mention three other matters to which
reference was made in the judgment, but they have not played any part on this appeal.
First, in answer to an argument raised below the judgment points out that the funds
generated by the office accommodation were to be used for physical purposes, viz the
extension of and improvements to the Opera House and not, as had been suggested on
behalf of the applicants, as a '[provision of] finance to maintain the international status
c  of the Royal Opera House' (see p 87 c, ante). This attempted distinction was rightly not
pursued before us. Second, the judgment points out that the ultimate decision of the
committee was clearly based on a balance of many factors, and it therefore poses the
question whether it is really fair to judge its validity solely by reference to the inclusion
of the office accommodation in question. That aspect has also played no part in the
d  argument before us. Third, the judge cites a passage from the speech of Lord Scarman in
Great Portland Estates plc v Westminster City Council [1984] 3 All ER 744 at 750, [1985] AC
661 at 670, which I will also cite later on, to suggest that the decision of the committee
may in any event be justified on the ground that the needs of the Royal Opera House
constitute 'an exceptional or special circumstance'. That aspect was not abandoned on
behalf of the respondents, but it was not felt necessary to develop it and I therefore
express no opinion about it.
e    Finally, it was faintly submitted on behalf of the respondents, in particular by counsel
for the ROH, that the conclusion of a 's 52 agreement' between the ROH and the council,
as a condition designed to ensure that all aspects of the permitted development, including
the office accommodation, were in fact carried out, could have an effect on the validity
of the committee's decision. I will briefly refer to this aspect later on.

f
*The first issue: can 'any other material considerations' in s 29(1) properly include
financial considerations?*
This issue can of course be phrased in many differently contentious ways. If one seeks
a negative answer one might pose the question whether it can possibly be permissible to
authorise a development which, in planning terms, is undesirable or even indefensible
in order to provide funds for some other desirable development. On the other hand, a
g  more moderate way of putting the issue would be to ask whether, as a matter of common
sense, there could be any reason why the financial viability of a desirable development,
and the means of achieving it, must necessarily be immaterial considerations in
determining applications for planning permission. Similarly, one can argue by giving
illustrations at different points of the spectrum. For instance it was said on behalf of the
h  association that it would be inconceivable that if the ROH happened to own a site near
Victoria it would be allowed to use it for the erection of an undesirable office block on
the basis that the profits would be used to extend and improve the Royal Opera House.
The respondents did not accept that this was self-evident if no other means were available
and countered with more realistic illustrations to demonstrate the fallacy of the
proposition that purely financial considerations can never be material. For instance, if it
j  is uneconomic to restore a derelict listed building for its original residential or other use,
then it would be perfectly proper and an everyday situation for a planning authority to
allow it to be used wholly or partly for commercial purposes, if its restoration cannot in
practice be achieved in any other way. Or, to take an example given by counsel for the
ROH, in the case of a landmark or tourist attraction such as a derelict old windmill, a
planning authority might well decide to permit the owner to put up an otherwise

undesirable kiosk to sell postcards and souvenirs if this is the only viable way of obtaining
a desirable restoration.                                                                    *a*
   This was the nature of the opposing contentions. In my view, for the reasons which
follow, I have no doubt that the respondents' approach is correct in principle, and I would
summarise it in the following way. Financial constraints on the economic viability of a
desirable planning development are unavoidable facts of life in an imperfect world. It
would be unreal and contrary to common sense to insist that they must be excluded
from the range of considerations which may properly be regarded as material in  *b*
determining planning applications. Where they are shown to exist they may call for
compromises or even sacrifices in what would otherwise be regarded as the optimum
from the point of view of the public interest. Virtually all planning decisions involve
some kind of balancing exercise. A commonplace illustration is the problem of having
to decide whether or not to accept compromises or sacrifices in granting permission for
developments which could, or would in practice, otherwise not be carried out for  *c*
financial reasons. Another, no doubt rarer, illustration would be a similar balancing
exercise concerning composite or related developments, ie related in the sense that they
can and should properly be considered in combination, where the realisation of the main
objective may depend on the financial implications or consequences of others. However,
provided that the ultimate determination is based on planning grounds and not on some
ulterior motive, and that it is not irrational, there would be no basis for holding it to be  *d*
invalid in law solely on the ground that it has taken account of, and adjusted itself to, the
financial realities of the overall situation.
   This approach is consistent with the authorities and with good sense. There is no
legislative definition of 'other material considerations' in s 29(1). In passages from two
decisions of the House of Lords the scope of these words has merely been circumscribed
in wide terms, but these would not exclude financial considerations from being treated  *e*
as material in appropriate cases. In *Newbury DC v Secretary of State for the Environment*
[1980] 1 All ER 731 at 739, [1981] AC 578 at 599 Viscount Dilhorne dealt with this
aspect. He referred to s 29(1) and then quoted the following well-known passage from
the judgment of Lord Denning in *Pyx Granite Co Ltd v Ministry of Housing and Local
Government* [1958] 1 All ER 625 at 633, [1958] 1 QB 554 at 572:                             *f*

   'Although the planning authorities are given very wide powers to impose "such
   conditions as they think fit", nevertheless the law says that those conditions, to be
   valid, must fairly and reasonably relate to the permitted development. The planning
   authority are not at liberty to use their powers for an ulterior object, however
   desirable that object may seem to them to be in the public interest.'

Having pointed out that this statement had already been approved by the House of Lords  *g*
he went on:

   'It follows that the conditions imposed must be for a planning purpose and not
   for any ulterior one, and that they must fairly and reasonably relate to the
   development permitted. Also they must not be so unreasonable that no reasonable
   planning authority could have imposed them . . .'                                        *h*

This passage was taken a little further in the speech of Lord Scarman in *Great Portland
Estates plc v Westminster City Council* [1984] 3 All ER 744 at 750, [1985] AC 661 at 670,
with which the other members of the House of Lords expressed agreement. The appeal
had been concerned with a development plan whose validity was challenged on the
ground that it contained proposals for the protection of specific industrial activities; it  *j*
was said that these were concerned with the interests of particular users of land rather
than the development and use of land in itself. In that context Lord Scarman cited a
sentence from an earlier judgment of Lord Parker CJ in which he had said that 'what one
is really considering is the character of the use of the land, not the particular purpose of a
particular occupier' (see *East Barnet UDC v British Transport Commission* [1961] 3 All ER

878 at 884, [1962] 2 QB 484 at 491). Then Lord Scarman went on ([1984] 3 All ER 744
a   at 750, [1985] AC 661 at 670):

> 'It is a logical process to extend the ambit of Lord Parker CJ's statement so that it
> applies not only to the grant or refusal of planning permission and to the imposition
> of conditions but also to the formulation of planning policies and proposals. The
> test, therefore, of what is a material "consideration" in the preparation of plans or in
> the control of development (see s 29(1) of the 1971 Act in respect of planning
b   permission and s 11(9) and Sch 4, para 11(4) in respect of local plans) is whether it
> serves a planning purpose: see *Newbury DC v Secretary of State for the Environment*
> [1980] 1 All ER 731 at 739, [1981] AC 578 at 599 per Viscount Dilhorne. And a
> planning purpose is one which relates to the character of the use of land. Finally,
> this principle has now the authority of the House. It has been considered and, as I
c   understand the position, accepted by your Lordships not only in this appeal but also
> in *Westminster City Council v British Waterways Board* [1984] 3 All ER 737, [1985] AC
> 676, a case in which argument was heard by your Lordships immediately following
> argument in this appeal. However, like all generalisations Lord Parker CJ's statement
> has its own limitations. Personal circumstances of an occupier, personal hardship,
> the difficulties of businesses which are of value to the character of a community are
d   not to be ignored in the administration of planning control. It would be inhuman
> pedantry to exclude from the control of our development the human factor. The
> human factor is always present, of course, indirectly as the background to the
> consideration of the character of land use. It can, however, and sometimes should,
> be given direct effect as an exceptional or special circumstance. But such
> circumstances, when they arise, fall to be considered not as a general rule but as
e   exceptions to a general rule to be met in special cases. If a planning authority is to
> give effect to them, a specific case has to be made and the planning authority must
> give reasons for accepting it. It follows that, though the existence of such cases may
> be mentioned in a plan, this will only be necessary where it is prudent to emphasise
> that, notwithstanding the general policy, exceptions cannot be wholly excluded
> from consideration in the administration of planning control.'

f       Admittedly, neither of these cases was concerned directly with financial considerations
similar to the present case. And it is no doubt true that planning authorities must be
particularly careful not to give way too readily to assertions of financial constraints as a
ground for relaxing policies which have been formulated in the public interest. Thus,
take another illustration given by counsel for the ROH. Suppose that an urban authority
g   had a policy of requiring the use of green tiles, which are substantially more expensive
than others, in areas of residential developments bordering on the countryside. If a
developer who wished to erect an otherwise highly desirable housing estate claimed that
this would be uneconomic if green tiles had to be used, then the authority would clearly
not be bound to reject his application out of hand. It would be bound to consider it on
its merits, although it might well be highly sceptical about the assertion that the
h   economic viability of the project would founder if green tiles had to be used. But if, after
proper consideration, this were indeed the conclusion reached on a basis which would
not admit of a charge of irrationality, then there could be no question about the validity
of a decision which permitted the use of red or black tiles in the circumstances.
    This takes one to the authorities in which financial considerations have played a direct
part. In *Bradford City Metropolitan Council v Secretary of State for the Environment* [1986] 1
j   EGLR 199 at 202 Lloyd LJ said that it has usually been regarded as axiomatic that
planning consent cannot be bought or sold and that this must be true as a general
proposition. However, the reported cases which can properly be described as falling
within this class were concerned with situations in which planning and other consents
had been granted for ulterior, and therefore impermissible, motives. *Hall & Co Ltd v
Shoreham-by-Sea UDC* [1964] 1 All ER 1, [1964] 1 WLR 240 is a well-known example, to

which Lloyd LJ referred at length in the *Bradford* case. In granting permission for a
housing development the authority had imposed a condition that an adjoining highway,  *a*
which was already overloaded and due to be widened by the authority, was to be widened
at the expense of the applicant and by the use of a strip of his land, which would
otherwise have had to have been acquired for the purpose. As Willmer LJ said in holding
with the other members of the court that the condition was invalid ([1964] 1 All ER 1 at
9, [1964] 1 WLR 240 at 250–251):

> 'The defendants would thus obtain the benefit of having the road constructed for  *b*
> them at the plaintiffs' expense, on the plaintiffs' land, and without the necessity of
> paying any compensation in respect thereof.'

That was a clear instance of a grant of planning permission coupled with a condition
based on an ulterior motive. And in most such instances, though not necessarily, the
motive will no doubt be financial or have some financial implications. The facts in the  *c*
*Bradford* case were similar, although less extreme, and were judged to fall on the same
side of the line. In both cases a condition with financial implications had been imposed
with the ulterior motive of furthering the purposes of the local authority. In the result
both decisions were held to be 'manifestly unreasonable', to use the words of Lloyd LJ,
which he understandably preferred to 'irrational'.

Situations such as those in the present case and in the earlier illustrations to which I  *d*
have referred are obviously quite different from cases like *Hall & Co Ltd v Shoreham-by-Sea
UDC* and *Bradford City Metropolitan Council v Secretary of State for the Environment*. They
do not involve the imposition of a condition to serve the purposes of the local authority.
They involve the acceptance, faute de mieux, of a relatively undesirable feature of a
development as a compromise or sacrifice in order to ensure the viability of the main
project which is judged to be sufficiently desirable to warrant a partial relaxation of  *e*
policy. But counsel for the association challenged this analysis. While agreeing that no
ulterior motive was involved in the present case, he did not accept what he called the 'but
for' argument, that but for the permission for the undesired office accommodation the
desired development of the Opera House could or would not take place. He pointed out
that under the Local Government Act 1972 the council had the necessary power to make  *f*
up any financial deficiency and claimed that the situation was therefore no different from
the *Hall & Co Ltd* and *Bradford* cases in principle.

I cannot agree with this analysis. There are few, if any, situations in which the 'but for'
argument could not be countered by pointing to alternatives, but alternatives of a nature
which the relevant authority may reasonably consider to be uneconomic and therefore
impracticable. Such situations do not invalidate the 'but for' argument. If sufficient  *g*
money is made available almost anything can be done. But this approach provides no
test for the balancing exercise involved in the realistic determination of most planning
applications. In the present case, subject to the association's second submission, to which
I come shortly, the council was entitled to proceed on the basis that, but for the
permission to the ROH to include the office accommodation in the proposed development,
this would not proceed at all. The association's first submission, with which I am dealing  *h*
now, assumes this as a fact while challenging the decision in law. On that basis the
situation is wholly different from cases such as the *Hall & Co Ltd* and *Bradford* cases where
the economic viability of the proposed developments was not dependent on the financial
conditions imposed by the authorities.

To the extent that situations similar to the present case have been considered by the
courts, the trend of authority has been in line with the foregoing approach and with the  *j*
respondents' submissions. In *Niarchos (London) Ltd v Secretary of State for the Environment*
(1977) 35 P & CR 259 Sir Douglas Frank QC held that it was impossible to decide whether
premises could reasonably be adapted for residential occupation unless the cost of the
adaptation was taken into account. He quashed a rejection of a planning application for
office use of the premises, which would have been contrary to the local development

plan, on the ground that no account had been taken of the financial considerations. He
a followed that decision in *Brighton BC v Secretary of State for the Environment* (1978) 39
P & CR 46 on facts which lie closer to the present case. An inspector had allowed an
appeal against a refusal by a local authority of planning permission to a school, situated
in a conservation area, to put up houses in a part of its playing fields which lay outside
this area. The basis of the application had been that the proceeds from selling the houses
were to be used for the improvement of the school buildings for which no funds would
b otherwise have been available. It is true that the first ground of the inspector's decision
was that there were no amenity objections to the development. But the materiality of
the financial considerations figured large in the ratio of the judgment. For the reasons
already discussed I do not accept the submission of counsel for the association that on this
aspect the decision was wrong in principle.

The third in this line of cases is the important decision of Woolf J in *Sosmo Trust Ltd v*
c *Secretary of State for the Environment* [1983] JPL 806. The appellants put forward three
schemes for the development of a site which would otherwise have remained derelict.
Two were shown to produce an uneconomic return; the third was for a six-storey office
development which would produce a profit. The planning authority opposed the third
scheme on the ground that it was contrary to its planning policy for the area and refused
permission. An appeal to an inspector on behalf of the Secretary of State was dismissed.
d He had accepted that the site would remain derelict if the rejection of the third alternative
was upheld, but he dismissed the appeal, saying:

> 'However as a generality, the financial aspects of a development are not a relevant
> planning consideration. A planning permission runs with the land and in my
> opinion it would not be appropriate for the grant of permission to be dependent on
e the resources or intentions of a particular developer to carry out a development . . .
> I am of the opinion that there are no compelling reasons in favour of allowing the
> appeal proposal contrary to the office policy of the district plan.'

The developers successfully applied to the High Court to quash the inspector's decision.
Woolf J pointed out (at 807) that—

f > 'what could be significant was not the financial or lack of financial viability of a
> particular project but the consequences of that financial viability or lack of financial
> viability.'

He went on to follow a passage from the judgment of Forbes J in *Sovmots Investments Ltd
v Secretary of State for the Environment* [1976] 1 All ER 178 at 186, [1977] QB 411 at 425
g in which references to the minister equally apply to planning authorities:

> '. . . all that the court can do is to say that cost can be a relevant consideration and
> leave it to the Minister to decide whether in any circumstances it is or is not. Of
> course it follows that the weight to be given to cost, if it is a relevant factor, is also a
> matter for the Minister and not one in respect of which any court is entitled to
> substitute its opinion . . . I would conclude that it is impossible to say that cost can
h never be a relevant consideration either in a planning matter or in a compulsory
> purchase matter. It can be in both or either and it will depend in every case on the
> circumstances of the case. It is then a matter for the Minister to decide whether or
> not in any particular instance cost is in fact a relevant consideration.'

Adopting that passage and quashing the inspector's decision Woolf J held (at 808) that—

j > 'no Secretary of State could reasonably come to the conclusion that the economic
> factor was not relevant. He could, however, subject to that, have decided what
> weight was to be attached to it.'

For the reasons already stated I am in full agreement with that approach, and in my
view it determines the first issue of this appeal. Counsel for the ROH raised an additional

point in submitting that the present case was in any event distinguishable from *Hall &* *a*
*Co Ltd v Shoreham-by-Sea UDC* [1964] 1 All ER 1, [1964] 1 WLR 240 and *Bradford City*
*Metropolitan Council v Secretary of State for the Environment* [1986] 1 EGLR 199, because
there was no question of the imposition of any condition by the planning authority, but
a situation in which the developer, the ROH, was only too willing to erect the office
accommodation in order to provide the necessary balance of finance required for the
development of the Opera House, and willing to conclude a s 52 agreement to that effect,
as the council required. He submitted that the powers of a planning authority under *b*
such an agreement were wider than under s 29(1) and that the contrary view indicated
by Lloyd LJ in an obiter passage in the *Bradford* case [1986] 1 EGLR 199 at 202 was
incorrect and should not be followed. While it is equally unnecessary to express any
concluded view on this question in the present case, I would certainly not accept that
submission as a general proposition. Section 52 agreements undoubtedly facilitate the
formulation of qualified planning permissions in comparison with the imposition of *c*
express conditions, and no doubt they also simplify the procedural aspects of the planning
process in many ways. They have the advantages of the flexibility of a negotiable
agreement in contrast to a process of unilateral imposition; and they are therefore no
doubt far less vulnerable to the risk of successful appeals or applications for judicial
review, which is to be welcomed. But if a particular condition would be illegal, on the
ground of manifest unreasonableness or otherwise, if it were imposed on an applicant for *d*
planning permission then it cannot acquire validity if it is embodied in a s 52 agreement,
whether at the instance of the applicant himself or not. That, in effect, was equally the
conclusion of Lloyd LJ in the *Bradford* case.

That leaves counsel for the association's extreme hypothetical illustration of the
undesirable office block in Victoria which is claimed to be necessary to generate the
finance for a desirable development in Covent Garden. A combination of this nature *e*
would be unlikely to be properly entertained as a single planning application or as an
application for one composite development, as in the present case. I therefore say no
more about it save that all such cases would in my view involve considerations of fact
and degree rather than of principle.

Having already referred to so much from the judgment of Webster J, it is only right *f*
to quote the passage in which he expressed his conclusion on this issue (see p 88 *e* to *g*,
ante), with which I entirely agree:

'It seems to me to be quite beyond doubt but that the fact that the finances made
available from the commercial development would enable the improvements to be
carried out was capable of being a material consideration, that is to say that it was a
consideration which related to the use or development of the land, that it related to *g*
a planning purpose and to the character of the use of the land, namely the
improvements to the Royal Opera House which I have already described, particularly
as the proposed commercial development was on the same site as the Royal Opera
House and as the commercial development and the proposed improvements to the
Royal Opera House all formed part of one proposal.'

*h*

*The second issue: was the council entitled to conclude that but for the office accommodation*
*the development of the Opera House would not proceed?*

In the same way as the judge, I can deal with this issue more shortly. On the basis of
the decision of this court in *Prest v Secretary of State for Wales* (1982) 81 LGR 193 counsel
for the association submitted that the planning and development committee had been
under a positive duty to investigate all aspects relevant to its determination before *j*
reaching a conclusion. That was a case concerning the confirmation of a compulsory
purchase order, not an application for planning permission, in which the relevant
financial aspect, the relative land cost of alternative sites, had not been considered at all.
Watkins LJ said that the Secretary of State had not even given it 'a passing thought' (at

211). That is miles away from the present case. As will be remembered, before its final
*a* resolution on 30 June 1987, the planning and development committee had resolved on
3 February that it—

'wishes to be absolutely convinced that the commercial development of the site is
the only way of achieving the Royal Opera House improvements. Accordingly,
while welcoming the application in principle, the Committee would wish there to
*b* be an opportunity for future discussion on this crucial aspect.'

The judge rightly said (p 89 *j*, ante) that if a planning committee—

'makes or has made no inquiries its decision may in certain circumstances be
illegal on the ground of irrationality if it was made in the absence of information
without which no reasonable planning authority would have granted permission.'

*c* The association's contention on this issue had therefore been correctly formulated in
their skeleton argument that—

'. . . the information put before the Committee . . . was not such as to enable it
rationally to conclude that the proposal was the only way of achieving the Opera
House improvements.'
*d*
That submission turns on the facts. The history has been set out in the lengthy extract
from the judgment below, and I have already quoted the committee's resolution on 3
February 1987 that it wished to be 'absolutely convinced' about the need to include the
office accommodation which it described as the 'crucial aspect'. Further investigations
and discussions then followed until the meeting on 30 June 1987, when the committee
*e* resolved to accept the proposal subject to the conditions already mentioned. Counsel for
the association criticised that decision on three grounds. First, he submitted that the
committee could not have been satisfied that further funds could not have been raised in
other ways, for instance by lotteries which might soon be legalised by legislation, as in
other countries. Second, he said that no account appears to have been taken of a forecast
in a report prepared for the association that the level of commercial rents was likely to
*f* rise so as to reduce the financial deficit from about £22m to about £10m. As a separate
point counsel also relied on the fact that by April 1988, some nine months after the
committee's decision, this forecast was proved to have been correct. Finally, he submitted
that the information before the committee had been insufficient to entitle it rationally
to reach the conclusion embodied in the resolution which has already been set out. In
support of this submission he relied on the contents of the further and supplementary
*g* reports by the acting director of planning and transportation which had been placed
before the committee for the purposes of the meeting on 30 June and on the minutes of
that meeting.
In my view there is no substance in these contentions. On 16 February 1987 the
Minister for the Arts had again made it clear in the House of Commons that no further
financial assistance would be available from government sources, and there was ample
*h* material before the committee, both before and after its preliminary decision in February
1987, that there was every probability of a deficit which could not be bridged by any
appeal or other foreseeable means. As regards the size of the deficit, the material placed
before the committee showed that careful consideration had been given to six options of
mixed uses, but that even the most favourable of these still left a substantial unbridgeable
deficit. On this material it is clearly impossible to describe the committee's acceptance of
*j* a solution involving the most favourable of these options as manifestly unreasonable.
As regards the third point of counsel for the association, this is not borne out by the
evidence. As one knows, the bare written record of the minutes of a meeting and of the
papers placed before it often fail to provide a fair impression of the matters which
informed the minds of the participants before they reached their decision. In the present

case the reality was described in affidavits sworn by two officers of the council and by a
chartered surveyor which show the degree of discussion, questioning and consideration    *a*
which took place before the outcome of the meeting on 30 June. To suggest that the
conclusion which was then reached was irrational or manifestly unreasonable, or based
on information which was, or should reasonably have been regarded as, inadequate, is in
my view untenable.

*Conclusion*                                                                            *b*
    It follows that I agree with the conclusions of Webster J and that I have no doubt that
this appeal must be dismissed. It remains to mention, for the sake of completeness, that
in referring to events which have occurred since 30 June 1987 counsel for the association
stressed, as already briefly mentioned, that by April 1988 commercial rents had in fact
risen to a level which confirmed the earlier forecast, that on this basis the unbridged
deficit would be reduced to £10m and that this was now admitted on behalf of the    *c*
council. Pointing out that the formal planning permissions and listing consents were
still in draft, he said that an opportunity, and perhaps a duty, to reconsider remained.
But this is not an aspect which we can consider on this appeal. As has been said, keeping
track of changing circumstances in planning situations is like trying to hit a moving
target in the dark. Many variables must inevitably enter into any assessment, and the
rises in interest and mortgage rates during the summer of 1988 may well have falsified    *d*
estimates made as recently as last April. Moreover, the desirability of finality is no doubt
also an important factor. We cannot enter into considerations of this nature. We can only
say that, if it is considered by the council that the circumstances warrant some
modification of the development as presently resolved, then there is clearly no legal
impediment in the way.

                                                                                        *e*


**NICHOLLS LJ.** On 30 June 1987 the planning and development committee of the
Westminster City Council decided in principle to grant planning permission for a scheme
of development proposed by the Royal Opera House Covent Garden Ltd (the ROH). The
scheme involved improvements and alterations to the Opera House itself and also a
substantial element of office development on adjacent land. The decision of the    *f*
committee was adopted by the council on 29 July 1987. The Covent Garden Community
Association is seeking to impeach that decision. It objects to the office element. It says
that the decision was invalid in law.
    The primary line of attack of the association is that when deciding to approve the
office element in the overall scheme the committee took into account a matter it ought
not to have taken into account. It exercised a statutory power for a purpose for which it    *g*
was not intended. The office element was approved by the committee as a source of
finance for the other works. Permitting the financially profitable office development
would make it possible for the ROH to proceed with much-needed alterations and
improvements to the Opera House. Otherwise the ROH could not afford to go ahead.
The association's case is that that was not a proper reason for granting permission for a    *h*
commercial development which would otherwise have been refused. Counsel crystallised
the association's submission thus: if permission for development A would be refused on
its individual planning merits, the fact that the profits of that development are to be used
to finance development B is not a sufficient reason for granting permission for
development A. The financial purpose is extraneous to a proper consideration of the
planning merits of development A.                                                        *j*
    That a planning authority may properly take into account as a material consideration
within s 29 of the Town and Country Planning Act 1971 the practical consequences
likely to follow if permission for a particular development is refused seems to me to be
self-evident. For example, take a run-down site, littered with derelict buildings. The soil
is contaminated from previous industrial use. Preparation of the site for development

a will be expensive. The planning authority is anxious that such an eyesore shall be removed, and housing is the preferred use. An application is submitted for development with high-density housing. In my view it is clear that in considering this application the planning authority is entitled to take into account, first, that a lower density of housing will not be commercially viable, having regard to the heavy cost of site clearance, so that, second, the probable consequence of refusing to permit the development sought will be the absence of any development for the foreseeable future, in which event the eyesore

b will remain.

   Likewise if what is sought is a mixed development, mostly of houses but including some offices. The planning authority prefers no offices on the particular site. But I can see no reason, in logic or in policy, why the planning authority should not be able to opt for what it considers, in planning terms, to be the best development obtainable in practice: some offices, thus making a development of the rest of the site for housing

c purposes commercially possible. The authority can prefer this to no development at all. I cannot accept that granting permission for offices in such a case would be an exercise of the statutory power for a purpose for which it cannot have been intended. Of course, it is for the planning authority to determine how much importance, or weight, to attach to the various factors such as the likelihood of there being no development if the application is refused, the likely consequences in the neighbourhood if there is no

d development and the likely consequences if a mixed development is permitted.

   The strongest point of counsel for the association was that if what I have said above is correct one is on a slippery slope on which there is no stopping short of a conclusion which would embrace and accept as valid other cases from which one instinctively recoils. If the purpose of granting permission for development A is to finance development B, that purpose can equally exist and be fulfilled if the two developments

e have no physical contiguity at all. They can be miles apart. A hypothetical example mentioned in argument was of the ROH owning land elsewhere in London, in Victoria for instance. Could permission for a commercial development of land in Victoria have been properly granted solely to finance alterations to the Opera House situated in Covent Garden? Counsel for the council, for his part, frankly accepted that he could discern no

f legal principle which distinguished between (a) what happens within one building, (b) what happens on two adjoining sites and (c) what happens on two sites which are miles away from each other.

   Other examples spring to mind. Could permission for an otherwise unacceptable development in Victoria, or elsewhere in London, or yet further afield, properly be granted because the site owner is prepared to give a substantial sum towards the cost of the Opera House works? If it could, could the local planning authority impose a condition

g to that effect when granting permission?

   I am not persuaded by this reductio ad absurdum argument. Circumstances vary so widely that it may be unsatisfactory and unwise to attempt to state a formula which is intended to provide a definitive answer in all types of case. All that need be said to decide this appeal is that the sites of the commercial development approved in principle are

h sufficiently close to the Opera House for it to have been proper for the local planning authority to treat the proposed development of the office sites, in Russell Street and elsewhere, and the proposed improvements to the Opera House as forming part of one composite development project. As such it was open to the planning authority to balance the pros and cons of the various features of the scheme. It was open to the authority to treat the consequence, for the Opera House works, of granting or withholding permission

j for offices as a material consideration in considering the part of the application which related to offices.

   For this reason I too would reject the association's primary ground of appeal. As to its second ground of appeal I have nothing to add to the reasons, with which I agree, given by Kerr LJ.

   I also would dismiss this appeal.

**STAUGHTON LJ.** I agree that this appeal must be dismissed. On the first issue, the major difficulty seems to me to lie in drawing a line between obvious extremes. It may *a* be sufficient for the decision in this case to say on which side of the line it lies. But in my view the court ought, if it can, to give some indication where the line should be drawn. In *Erewhon* Samuel Butler wrote:

'Extremes are alone logical, but they are always absurd; the mean is illogical, but an illogical mean is better than the sheer absurdity of an extreme.'
*b*

Those propositions were attributed to the School of Unreasoning. But they appear to me to demonstrate both the difficulty and also the necessity of drawing a line.

The question here is whether a planning authority can permit undesirable development A as a means of securing desirable development B. It is the same question, whether it comes in the shape of a 'material consideration' within s 29(1) of the Town and Country Planning Act 1971 or of conditions which a planning authority may lawfully impose on *c* the grant of planning permission. One extreme is the example given by Kerr LJ of a derelict listed building which the planning authority wishes to see restored. In principle it would be wholly proper to consider partial office development A, if that were the only means by which restoration and partial residential occupation B could be made financially viable.

The other extreme arises from the axiom of Lloyd LJ that planning permission cannot *d* be bought and sold. Suppose that a developer wished to erect an office building at one end of the town, A, and offered to build a swimming-pool at the other end, B. It would in my view be wrong for the planning authority to regard the swimming-pool as a material consideration, or to impose a condition that it should be built. That case seems to me little different from the developer who offers the planning authority a cheque so that it can build the swimming-pool for itself, provided he has permission for his office *e* development. *Brighton BC v Secretary of State for the Environment* (1978) 39 P & CR 46 may have come close to infringing that principle. But I do not say that, on its own facts, it was wrongly decided.

Where then is the line to be drawn between those extremes? In my judgment the answer lies in the speech of Viscount Dilhorne in *Newbury DC v Secretary of State for the Environment* [1980] 1 All ER 731 at 739, [1981] AC 578 at 599, which Kerr LJ has quoted. *f* Conditions imposed must 'fairly and reasonably relate to the development permitted', if they are to be valid. So must considerations, if they are to be material.

In the present case, the improvement of the Royal Opera House, B, is a development which the Westminster City Council considers to be desirable, for valid planning reasons. The building of office premises in close proximity, A, is necessary if development B is to occur. It can fairly and reasonably be said to relate to the proposed development which *g* ought to be permitted. The whole is, to quote the words of Kerr LJ, a composite or related development. The offices are not ulterior or extraneous: they are part of the whole.

On the second issue, there is nothing which I would add to the judgment of Kerr LJ.

*h*
*Appeal dismissed. Leave to appeal to House of Lords refused.*

19 December. The Appeal Committee of the House of Lords (Lord Keith of Kinkel, Lord Griffiths and Lord Oliver of Aylmerton) refused a petition for leave to appeal.

Solicitors: *Gouldens* (for the association); *G Matthew Ives* (for the council); *Linklaters &* *j* *Paines* (for the ROH).

Kate O'Hanlon   Barrister.

# *a* Minories Finance Ltd v Arthur Young (a firm) (Bank of England, third party)
# Johnson Matthey plc v Arthur Young (a firm) (Bank of England, third party)

*b* QUEEN'S BENCH DIVISION

SAVILLE J

11, 12, 13, 18 JULY 1988

*Negligence – Duty to take care – Existence of duty – Bank of England – Bank's supervisory role*
*c* *over commercial banks in United Kingdom – Commercial bank incurring substantial losses on loan*
*portfolio – Bank of England joined as third party by auditors in actions brought against them by*
*bank and its parent company for damages in negligence – Whether Bank of England under legal*
*obligation to individual bank to exercise reasonable care and skill in carrying out supervisory*
*functions – Whether Bank of England owing duty of care to bank to protect it from financial losses*
*resulting from imprudent dealings.*

*d*
*Bank – Deposit-taking business – Control by Bank of England – Bank's supervisory role over*
*commercial banks in United Kingdom – Parent company lodging funds with bank operated by*
*subsidiary – Bank incurring substantial losses on loan portfolio – Whether funds lodged with bank*
*a 'deposit' – Whether Bank of England owing duty of care to parent company as depositor –*
*Banking Act 1979, s 1(5)(d).*

*e*
Following the insolvency of JMB's commercial banking business and its financial rescue
by the Bank of England, MF Ltd, the successor to JMB, claimed damages in negligence
against JMB's auditors, alleging that the auditors should have discovered and reported on
the state of JMB's loan portfolio and that had they done so much of the loss sustained by
the insolvency of JMB's bank would have been avoided. JMB's parent company, which
*f* had lodged funds with JMB's bank, also claimed damages against the auditors for, inter
alia, breach of their duty as auditors to the parent group of companies. The auditors
denied any breach of duty on their part and asserted in third party proceedings that, if
they were under any liability, they were entitled to an indemnity or contribution from
the Bank of England in respect of that liability on the basis that the Bank of England, as
the body responsible for the supervision of banks in the United Kingdom, owed a duty
*g* of care to JMB and its parent company to carry out its investigations and checks of JMB
with reasonable care and skill and had failed to do so. The auditors further claimed that,
given the clear history of reliance by JMB on advice given by the Bank of England, the
close relationship between the two banks, together with the foreseeability of loss and
damage to JMB resulting from the Bank of England's failure to exercise its supervisory
functions with due care and skill, satisfied the requirement of proximity necessary to
*h* establish the existence of a duty of care. The Bank of England sought to strike out the
third party notices, contending that they owed no duty to JMB and therefore the notices
disclosed no reasonable cause of action.

**Held** – The Bank of England was not under a legal obligation to an individual
commercial bank to exercise reasonable care and skill in carrying out its function of
*j* supervising the operations of commercial banks, since it would be contrary to common
sense and reason to suggest that an individual bank, as a commercial profit-making
enterprise, could look to the Bank of England to make good losses arising from its own
imprudent conduct on the ground that the Bank of England should have discovered and
dealt with those shortcomings. Furthermore, the Bank of England did not owe a duty of

care to JMB's parent company as a depositor, since sums of money paid by a parent to a subsidiary company or vice versa were excluded by s 1(5)(d)ᵃ of the Banking Act 1979 *a* from the definition of 'deposit' and therefore were outside the scope of the Bank of England's statutory powers and responsibilities in respect of deposit-taking businesses. Accordingly, since the third party notices disclosed no reasonable cause of action, the applications to strike out would be granted (see p 110 *f* to *h* and p 111 *h* to p 112 *d g*, post).

Dictum of Lord Morris in *Home Office v Dorset Yacht Co Ltd* [1970] 2 All ER 294 at 307– *b* 308, *Governors of the Peabody Donation Fund v Sir Lindsay Parkinson & Co Ltd* [1984] 3 All ER 529 and *Investors in Industry Commercial Properties Ltd v South Bedfordshire DC (Ellison & Partners (a firm) third parties)* [1986] 1 All ER 787 applied.

**Notes**
For the duty to take care, see 34 Halsbury's Laws (4th edn) paras 5–6, and for cases on the *c* subject, see 36(1) Digest (Reissue) 17–32, 34–103.

For the functions and duties of the Bank of England, see 3(1) Halsbury's Laws (4th edn reissue) para 17, and for protected deposits, see ibid para 116.

For the Banking Act 1979, s 1, see 4 Halsbury's Statutes (4th edn) (1987 reissue) 459.

As from 1 October 1987 s 1(5) of the 1979 Act was replaced by s 5(3) of the Banking Act 1987.          *d*

**Cases referred to in judgment**
*Baird v R* (1983) 148 DLR (3d) 1, Can Fed CA.
*Donoghue (or M'Alister) v Stevenson* [1932] AC 562, [1932] All ER Rep 1, HL.
*Home Office v Dorset Yacht Co Ltd* [1970] 2 All ER 294, [1970] AC 1004, [1970] 2 WLR 1140, HL.
*Investors in Industry Commercial Properties Ltd v South Bedfordshire DC (Ellison & Partners (a* *e* *firm), third parties)* [1986] 1 All ER 787, [1986] QB 1034, [1986] 2 WLR 937, CA.
*Peabody Donation Fund (Governors) v Sir Lindsay Parkinson & Co Ltd* [1984] 3 All ER 529, [1985] AC 210, [1984] 3 WLR 953, HL.
*Rowling v Takaro Properties Ltd* [1988] 1 All ER 163, [1988] AC 473, [1988] 2 WLR 418, PC.
*Williams & Humbert v W & H Trade Marks (Jersey) Ltd* [1986] 1 All ER 129, [1986] AC *f* 368, [1986] 2 WLR 24, HL.
*Yuen Kun-yeu v A-G of Hong Kong* [1987] 2 All ER 705, [1988] AC 175, [1987] 3 WLR 776, PC.

**Applications to strike out**
          *Minories Finance Ltd v Arthur Young (a firm) (Bank of England, third party)*          *g*
Minories Finance Ltd, formerly Johnson Matthey Bankers Ltd (JMB), brought an action against Arthur Young, a firm of chartered accountants, claiming damages of over £100m in negligence for breach of duty on the ground that Arthur Young in the course of their audits between 1981 and 1985 should have discovered and reported on the state of JMB's loan portfolio and that had they done so much of the loss sustained by JMB on that portfolio would have been avoided. Arthur Young denied any breach of duty and served *h* a third party notice dated 14 July 1986 on the Bank of England, claiming that the Bank of England owed a duty to JMB to exercise reasonable care and skill in carrying out its supervisory functions which it had failed to do, and that if Arthur Young were under any liability, they were entitled to an indemnity or contribution from the Bank of England pursuant to s 1 of the Civil Liability (Contributions) Act 1978. On 29 February 1988 the Bank of England applied to strike out the third party notice, contending that *j* the alleged duty did not exist as a matter of English law and that therefore the notice disclosed no reasonable cause of action. The application was heard in chambers and judgment was delivered in open court. The facts are set out in the judgment.

--------

*a*  Section 1(5), so far as material, is set out at p 111 *h*, post

*Johnson Matthey plc v Arthur Young (a firm) (Bank of England, third party)*

a   Johnson Matthey plc (PLC), the parent company of Johnson Matthey Bankers Ltd (JMB) at the time of the latter's insolvency, brought an action against Arthur Young, a firm of chartered accountants, claiming damages of over £100m in negligence for (i) breach of duty as auditors to the Johnson Matthey group of companies on the ground that Arthur Young in the course of their audits between 1981 and 1985 should have discovered and reported on the state of JMB's loan portfolio and that had they done so much of the loss

b   sustained by JMB on that portfolio would have been avoided, and (ii) breach of duty of care owed to PLC as a shareholder in JMB. Arthur Young denied any breach of duty and served a third party notice dated 17 November 1986 on the Bank of England, claiming that the Bank of England owed a duty to PLC, as the parent company of the Johnson Matthey group of companies and a depositor in JMB, to exercise reasonable care and skill in carrying out its supervisory functions which it had failed to do, and that if Arthur

c   Young were under any liability, they were entitled to an indemnity or contribution from the Bank of England pursuant to s 1 of the Civil Liability (Contributions) Act 1978. On 29 February 1988 the Bank of England applied to strike out the third party notice, contending that the alleged duty did not exist as a matter of law and that therefore the notice disclosed no reasonable cause of action. The application was heard in chambers but judgment was given by Saville J in open court. The facts are set out in the judgment.

d
*Gordon Langley QC* and *Richard Siberry* for the Bank of England.
*Timothy Walker QC* and *Andrew Smith* for Arthur Young.

*Cur adv vult*

e   18 July. The following judgment was delivered.

**SAVILLE J.** In these proceedings the Bank of England seeks to strike out third party notices served on it by Arthur Young, a firm of chartered accountants, on the grounds that the notices disclose no reasonable cause of action. There are two actions which have been ordered to be heard together. In the first action Minories Finance Ltd (formerly

f   Johnson Matthey Bankers Ltd) claims damages against Arthur Young for alleged breach of duty as its auditors. In the second action Johnson Matthey plc (which at the material time was the parent company of Johnson Matthey Bankers Ltd) claims damages against Arthur Young for alleged breach of duty as auditors to the Johnson Matthey group of companies and also on the grounds that Arthur Young were in breach of a duty of care owed to it as the shareholders of Johnson Matthey Bankers Ltd. For ease of reference I

g   shall refer to the parent company as PLC and to the subsidiary as JMB.

The case arises out of the conduct of JMB's commercial loan banking business between 1980 and 1984. In essence it is claimed that over that period this business was conducted in such an imprudent and careless way that JMB became insolvent and had to be rescued by the Bank of England which, in October 1984, acquired the share capital of JMB from

h   PLC for £1 on terms that the latter lent £50m to JMB and waived repayment of this sum. JMB and PLC claim, in effect, that in the course of their audits between 1981 and 1985 Arthur Young should have discovered and reported what was going on, and that had they done so much of the loss sustained by JMB and PLC would have been avoided. The damages claimed by JMB and PLC exceed in each case £100m.

Arthur Young deny any breach of duty on their part; and further join issue on many

j   other aspects of the claims made against them. In the third party proceedings with which I am concerned they assert that if they are under any liability in the actions then they are entitled to an indemnity or contribution from the Bank of England under the Civil Liability (Contribution) Act 1978, s 1 of which provides that any person liable in respect of any damage suffered by another person may recover contribution from any other person liable in respect of the same damage.

The basis of Arthur Young's claim in the third party proceedings is that the Bank of
England as the body responsible for the supervision of banks in the United Kingdom   *a*
owed a duty of care both to JMB and to PLC to carry out its supervisory functions with
reasonable skill and care; that it failed so to do, and that if JMB and PLC are right in
asserting that losses could have been avoided had Arthur Young discovered and reported
what was going on, then by the same token such losses would also have been avoided or
at least reduced had the Bank of England fulfilled this duty. The Bank of England
submits that the duty alleged does not exist as a matter of English law and that   *b*
accordingly the third party notices (which have been ordered to stand as the statements
of claim in the third party proceedings and amended with my leave) disclose no
reasonable cause of action.

By way of preliminary objection to the applications, counsel for Arthur Young
submitted that they had been made too late in the history of the proceedings; the Bank
of England had been joined in 1986, on the summons for directions the solicitors for the   *c*
Bank of England had in effect abandoned a suggestion that the existence of the alleged
duties should be tried in advance as preliminary issues, discovery has not taken place, and
in April 1987 the date for trial was fixed for January 1989 with the agreement of all
parties that the Bank of England should take part. The applications to strike out were not
issued until February 1988.

I am not persuaded that the applications have come too late. It is clear that the case   *d*
made by Arthur Young could not be fully pleaded by them until after discovery; when
this had occurred and the pleadings put in their final (or at least present) form the Bank
of England issued the summonses. In applications of this kind made under RSC Ord 18,
r 19, the allegations in the pleading under attack are all important, since they are to be
treated as true and since no evidence or other factual material is admissible. It is thus in
the nature of things likely to be difficult properly to mount (or indeed to counter) an   *e*
attack on the pleadings at a stage when further material averments are likely to be
forthcoming after discovery. It is true that as a general proposition applications under
Ord 18, r 19 should be made promptly but this can only mean as soon as reasonably
possible, for the rule itself empowers the court to strike out or amend pleadings at 'any
stage of the proceedings' (see *The Supreme Court Practice 1988* vol 1, para 18/19/2). In my   *f*
mind there are two main reasons why such applications should generally be made as
soon in the litigation as reasonably possible. Firstly, the object of the rule is to enable the
court to put an end to hopeless or objectionable litigation and obviously the earlier that
happens the better; while, secondly, if the matter is left until later than it should be, then
time and money are likely to be unnecessarily wasted, or other avoidable prejudice likely
to occur.

In my judgment, these applications were made as soon as reasonably possible after the   *g*
pleading under attack had been completed by the supply of particulars etc, which had
awaited discovery. It is further suggested that the effect of hearing the applications now
may jeopardise the trial date, but in my view this is most unlikely; it seems to me that
any appeals from my judgment can be heard and determined early enough to enable the
parties, whatever the ultimate result, to prepare for the trial in January 1989.

The second preliminary objection raised to the applications is that Ord 18, r 19 should   *h*
only be invoked in plain and obvious cases, i e where the claim is obviously unsustainable;
and that in any event the present cases do not fall within that category. In *Williams &
Humbert Ltd v W & H Trade Marks (Jersey) Ltd* [1986] 1 All ER 129 at 139, [1986] AC 368
at 435 Lord Templeman said:

*j*

  'My Lords, if an application to strike out involves a prolonged and serious
  argument the judge should, as a general rule, decline to proceed with the argument
  unless he not only harbours doubts about the soundness of the pleading but, in
  addition, is satisfied that striking out will obviate the necessity for a trial or will

substantially reduce the burden of preparing for trial or the burden of the trial
*a* itself.'

Lord Mackay made very similar observations (see [1986] 1 All ER 129 at 143, [1986] AC
368 at 441).

Applying this approach, I can say that at the outset I did entertain doubts about the
validity of the assertion that the Bank of England owed a duty of care to JMB and PLC
respectively, and I was also satisfied that were I to conclude after argument that those
*b* doubts were well founded, to the extent that I was persuaded that the claims were simply
unsustainable on any view, then to strike out the third party proceedings would be likely
substantially to reduce the burden of the trial. Accordingly, I took the view that I should
hear the substantive argument on the applications, which in the event took some two
and a half days.

*c* Finally, by way of preliminary submissions counsel for Arthur Young took the point
that since in order to determine whether or not a duty of care existed it was necessary to
look at all the circumstances of the case (for which proposition reliance was placed on the
speech of Lord Keith in *Rowling v Takaro Properties Ltd* [1988] 1 All ER 163 at 172, [1988]
AC 473 at 501) it would be inappropriate for the matters to be dealt with on the pleadings
under Ord 18, r 19. I am not persuaded by this submission. Given that the court must
*d* proceed not only on the assumption that all the facts and matters alleged in the pleading
are true, but also on the basis that the case should be allowed to proceed unless the court
is satisfied that the claim is unsustainable even on that assumption, I see no difficulty or
injustice in dealing with the matter under Ord 18, r 19. It is for the party concerned to
assert in his pleading all the facts and matters on which he proposes to rely at the trial, ie
all the factual circumstances which he deems material to his case. At the trial he would
*e* not, without leave, be permitted to enlarge his case. Often on applications of the present
kind the party concerned is not struck out but is given leave to amend his pleadings so as
to seek to remedy any defects or omissions that have become apparent. That is not this
case. At no stage has it been suggested that there are or might be other facts and matters
which could have been pleaded and which might have made a difference. Whether or
not the suggested duties of care exist is a matter which to my mind can properly be
*f* considered on the basis of what is alleged in the third party notices and the particulars
given of them. I turn therefore to consider the substantive issues between the parties.

Arthur Young allege in their third party notice that the Bank of England as the central
bank of the United Kingdom has for a very long time indeed asserted power and
authority over the United Kingdom banking system, in particular by assuming
responsibility for the supervision of banks carrying on business in this country. It is
*g* alleged that the Bank of England exercises supervisory functions both in the interests of
depositors and in order to safeguard the stability of individual banks; and that the Bank
of England was well aware that the individual banks looked to it to carry out such
supervisory functions. It is also alleged that so far as JMB itself is concerned there is a
clear history of reliance by JMB on advice given to it by the Bank of England and of
compliance with that advice, of a close relationship between the two banks, with
*h* representatives of the Bank of England visiting JMB and discussing its banking business,
and of the Bank of England seeking and obtaining information from JMB concerning its
banking operations. It is alleged that such a close relationship, together with foreseeability
of loss and damage to JMB resulting from a failure by the Bank of England to exercise its
functions of supervision with reasonable care and skill, fully satisfies the 'proximity' or
'neighbour' requirements for the existence of a duty of care. It is further alleged that the
*j* failure of the Bank of England to act with reasonable care and skill lay not so much in
areas in which it might be said to have customary or statutory discretionary powers, but
in simply carelessly carrying out or failing to carry out the very investigations and checks
which it had itself already decided were appropriate things to be done in the course of
exercising its supervisory functions. Arthur Young allege that the specific shortcomings

in the conduct of JMB's banking business asserted against them were the very matters with which the Bank of England was particularly concerned and which were *a* comprehended within the supervisory functions which the Bank of England assumed and exercised. Thus, it is alleged, had the Bank of England exercised reasonable care and skill the losses claimed against Arthur Young would not have occurred or would have been substantially reduced.

It is clear from recent authorities such as *Governors of the Peabody Donation Fund v Sir Lindsay Parkinson & Co Ltd* [1984] 3 All ER 529, [1985] AC 210, and *Investors in Industry* *b* *Commercial Properties Ltd v South Bedfordshire DC (Ellison & Partners (a firm), third parties)* [1986] 1 All ER 787, [1986] QB 1034 that it is not enough merely to establish that as between the alleged wrongdoer and the person who has suffered damage there is a sufficient relationship of proximity or neighbourhood such that, in the reasonable contemplation of the former, carelessness on his part may be likely to cause damage to the latter. Quite apart from possible considerations of public policy, the court must be *c* satisfied that in the circumstances it is fair and reasonable for a duty of care to be owed to the person concerned. As is clear from Lord Atkin's speech in *Donoghue v Stevenson* [1932] AC 562 at 599, [1932] All ER Rep 1 at 20 and Lord Morris's speech in *Home Office v Dorset Yacht Co Ltd* [1970] 2 All ER 294 at 307–308, [1970] AC 1004 at 1039, this requirement is really one of ordinary reason and common sense.

In the present case it is important to bear in mind that the negligence alleged against *d* the Bank of England is not that wrong or misleading advice or instructions were given in the course of supervision. What is alleged is that the Bank of England negligently failed to discover or comment on or take any appropriate action in relation to the imprudent and careless manner in which JMB was conducting its commercial loan portfolio.

In relation to JMB therefore, the proposition is that the Bank of England was under a *e* legal obligation to JMB to exercise reasonable care and skill in its supervision of this bank, so as to avoid financial loss accruing to JMB from its own imprudent or careless conduct.

In my judgment principles of common sense and reason do not indicate that such an obligation should exist. On the contrary, it seems to offend these principles to suggest that a commercial concern such as JMB can look to the Bank of England to make good its *f* losses arising from its own imprudence or carelessness, on the basis that the Bank of England should have discovered and dealt with those shortcomings. It was suggested in argument on behalf of JMB that a true analogy with the relationship between the Bank of England and JMB was one of nurse and mental patient. That cannot be right. Private banks in this country are commercial enterprises whose raison d'être is to make profits through providing financial services. They may act prudently or imprudently, carefully *g* or carelessly, and depending on how good or bad they are as bankers they will make profits or losses. Unlike the mental patient, whose responsibility for himself is diminished to such an extent that others must assume that responsibility, there is nothing in the alleged relationship between the Bank of England and private banks (or even JMB in particular) to suggest that the latter should be protected from themselves by the former. I take the view that there is nothing just or fair or reasonable in making the Bank of *h* England assume or share any part of the commercial responsibilities which it can be said private banks owe to themselves to conduct their commercial dealings prudently and carefully so as to make profits and avoid losses. It follows that, in my judgment, the third party notice alleging a duty owed to JMB truly discloses no reasonable cause of action.

So far as PLC is concerned, the claim is based on the proposition that PLC was a depositor in JMB and that the Bank of England owed a duty to depositors to exercise *j* reasonable care and skill in its supervision of banks such as JMB.

On behalf of the Bank of England counsel argued that since the losses claimed by PLC against Arthur Young were not in respect of deposits made with JMB, on no view could it be said that the Bank of England was liable to PLC in respect of the same damage as that claimed from Arthur Young, so that the matter fell outside the 1978 Act. In my

view, however, this argument is far from conclusive. Given the existence of a duty of
a care owed by the Bank of England to depositors and a breach of that duty, the question is
whether the loss claimed is a reasonably foreseeable consequence of the breach and is
otherwise not too remote. I can see no reason, other things being equal, why damages for
breach of duty owed to a depositor should be limited to the deposits in question, or
should somehow exclude other reasonably foreseeable losses flowing from the breach.

Counsel's principle submission was that the Bank of England owed no duty of care to
b depositors and he placed great reliance on the decision of the Privy Council in *Yuen Kun-
yeu v A-G of Hong Kong* [1987] 2 All ER 705, [1988] AC 175. In that case the Privy Council
held that the Hong Kong Commissioner of Deposit-taking Companies owed no duty of
care to persons who might make deposits in companies subject to the licensing and
registration provisions of the Deposit-taking Companies Ordinance. There it was alleged
that the commissioner had been negligent in registering the company concerned or in
c failing to revoke that registration in circumstances where it was alleged the commissioner
should have appreciated that the company was not fit to carry on a deposit-taking
business.

Counsel submitted that this case was conclusive authority against the proposition that
the Bank of England owed a duty of care to depositors in this country. Although this
submission is formidable, I am not persuaded that it is so strong that the contrary
d argument can simply be dismissed as unsustainable. The Privy Council were concerned
with a Hong Kong ordinance; the present case concerns a different supervisory banking
authority in a different country exercising, according to the third party notices, powers
and functions over and above those to be found in the Banking Act 1979, the then
equivalent in this country of the Deposit-taking Companies Ordinance. It is noteworthy
that the Privy Council itself distinguished the Canadian case of *Baird v R* (1983) 148 DLR
e (3d) 1, where the Federal Court of Appeal concluded that a similar claim should not be
struck out as disclosing no reasonable cause of action, on the ground that the legislation
and circumstances under consideration in Canada were different from those in the Hong
Kong case.

Having said this, however, it seems to me that there is an insuperable barrier against
f arguing for a duty of care owed by the Bank of England to PLC as a depositor. The
Banking Act 1979 (now replaced by the Banking Act 1987) for the first time established
a formal scheme for the recognition and licensing by the Bank of England of banks and
other institutions carrying on deposit-taking business. It is clear that one of the principle
purposes of this Act was to provide protection for depositors. Under this Act the Bank of
England is given statutory powers and responsibilities, and the Act sets out the criteria
g which the Bank of England must employ in considering whether or not to recognise or
licence an institution or whether to revoke recognition or a licence previously granted.
Included in the matters to which the Bank of England is to have regard is whether the
institution concerned is or will be carrying on its deposit-taking business 'with integrity
and prudence and with those professional skills which are consistent with the range and
scale of the institution's activities': see Pt I of Sch 2 to and ss 3 and 6 of the 1979 Act.
h However, s 1(5)(d) of the Act excludes from the definition of 'deposit' a 'sum which is
paid by one company to another at a time when one is a subsidiary of the other or both
are subsidiaries of another company'. The statutory prohibition on accepting deposits in
the course of a deposit-taking business without a licence or recognition does not therefore
apply to any money deposited by PLC with JMB. It is noteworthy that previous (and
different) statutory protection for depositors to be found in the now repealed Protection
j of Depositors Act 1963 does not include this limitation. It seems clear to me that
Parliament did not regard parent companies making deposits with their subsidiaries (or
vice versa) as requiring the protection of the licensing and recognition system set up by
the 1979 Act. In those circumstances, whatever the position with regard to those making
deposits which do fall within this statutory definition, I take the view that in the light of
the Act it cannot seriously be argued that the Bank of England owes a common law duty

of care to persons making deposits not falling within its statutory remit. Counsel for
Arthur Young submitted that his client's claim was not based (or solely based) on the    *a*
powers and duties given to and imposed on the Bank of England under the 1979 Act,
but on the customary powers which the Bank of England has asserted and exercised both
before and after the passage of the Act. However, even on this assumption, the submission
seems to me to be beside the point. As counsel was himself correctly at pains to point
out, in considering whether a duty of care exists in a body such as the Bank of England
the court should look at all the circumstances. One of those circumstances is the fact that    *b*
there was in force at the material time the Banking Act 1979. One of the features of that
Act is that in effect the protection afforded by it to depositors does not, by express
provision, extend to deposits made by parent companies with subsidiaries. In that
circumstance, a suggestion that nevertheless the Bank of England owes a duty of care at
common law to such depositors once again seems to me to be unsustainable. One of the
reasons for the exclusion (at least so far as subsidiaries accepting deposits is concerned) is    *c*
doubtless because, unlike ordinary depositors, a parent company, (or another subsidiary
through the common parent) has ample means itself to investigate, monitor and control
the activities of the subsidiary concerned, which is itself a reason for resisting the
suggestion that it is just or fair or reasonable that the Bank of England should nevertheless
owe common law duties of care to such depositors. For these reasons I conclude that the
assertion that the Bank of England owed a duty of care to PLC in respect of its supervision    *d*
of JMB cannot be sustained. It follows that, in my judgment, the third party notice
alleging such a duty also discloses no reasonable cause of action.

In these circumstances it is not necessary for me to deal with other arguments advanced
by counsel on behalf of the Bank of England, chief among which was the submission
that the alleged common law duties were inconsistent with the provisions of the 1979
Act, which in his submission gave the Bank of England policing powers and sanctions    *e*
which simply could not work alongside the suggested duty of care. In an application of
this kind, having reached the conclusions stated, I do not regard it as appropriate to
consider those submissions in this judgment.

It remains to say that although in both the third party notices Arthur Young alleged
that the Bank of England owed statutory as well as common law duties to, respectively,
JMB and PLC, no attempt was made before me to assert that those allegations provided    *f*
Arthur Young with a reasonable cause of action; counsel acknowledged (in my view
rightly) that if he could not sustain the alleged common law duties, he could not defend
the pleadings on the basis of the alleged statutory duties.

For the reasons given in this judgment I order that the third party notices in both the
JMB and the PLC cases be struck out.
                                                                                          *g*

*Order accordingly.*

Solicitors: *Freshfields* (for the Bank of England); *McKenna & Co* (for Arthur Young).

                                                            K Mydeen Esq    Barrister.

# *a* R v Licensing Authority, ex parte Smith Kline & French Laboratories Ltd (Generics (UK) Ltd and another intervening) (No 2)

COURT OF APPEAL, CIVIL DIVISION

*b* DILLON, WOOLF AND TAYLOR LJJ

28, 29 JULY 1988

*Crown – Relief against the Crown – Interlocutory relief – Jurisdiction – Injunction against officer of the Crown – Interim injunction – Judicial review proceedings – Application for interim injunction against statutory body pending determination of petition for leave to appeal – Whether*
*c* *court having jurisdiction to grant interim injunction against statutory body – Supreme Court Act 1981, s 31 – RSC Ord 53, r 3(10)(b).*

The applicant pharmaceutical company applied in 1972 for a product licence in respect of a drug developed by it for controlling the secretion of gastric acid and treating peptic ulcers. The applicant supplied the licensing authority (which was in effect the Minister
*d* of Health) with details of its research and testing in the development of the drug and was duly granted a licence. Under Council Directive (EEC) 87/21 other pharmaceutical companies were entitled to apply to the licensing authority for a product licence for a similar generic product after the lapse of ten years from the grant of a licence to the applicant. In 1987 two firms (the generic companies) applied for product licences to market generic forms of the applicant's drug. Under art 4(8)(*a*)(ii) of Council Directive
*e* (EEC) 65/65 (as replaced by Directive 87/21) an applicant for a product licence in a member state was not required to supply results of tests on his drugs if he could 'demonstrate' that his product was essentially similar to a product which had been authorised within the Community for ten years and was marketed in that member state. The generic companies claimed that the essential similarity could be demonstrated by reference to the research and testing details supplied by the applicant in support of its
*f* application for a product licence. The applicant opposed the use by the licensing authority of the information supplied by it to determine the essential similarity of the generic companies' drugs, on the grounds that the applicant's information was confidential, and it was granted an injunction restraining the authority from so using the information. On appeal to the Court of Appeal, the licensing authority's appeal was granted, and the applicant was refused leave to appeal to the House of Lords. Pending the applicant's
*g* petition for leave to appeal to the House of Lords, the applicant sought an interim injunction restraining the licensing authority from using the applicant's confidential information. The licensing authority contended that there was no jurisdiction to grant such relief against it.

**Held** (Dillon LJ dissenting) – On its true construction s 31[a] of the Supreme Court Act
*h* 1981 extended the jurisdiction of the court, thereby enabling it in its discretion to grant injunctive relief against the Crown on an application for judicial review. Furthermore, there was under RSC Ord 53, r 3(10)(*b*)[b] power to grant interim relief against officers of the Crown by way of injunction. However, in exercising its discretion in the instant case the court would have regard to the facts that the Court of Appeal had unanimously allowed the appeal of the licensing authority, that the licensing authority was performing
*j* a statutory duty which it was required to perform and that the court should be hesitant in granting relief which interfered, even on an interim basis, with the performance by the statutory authority of that role. Accordingly, (Dillon LJ concurring), in the exercise

---

*a* Section 31, so far as material, is set out at p 119 *a* to *c*, post
*b* Rule 3, so far as material, is set out at p 119 *d*, post

of its discretion the court would refuse the relief sought (see p 121 *e*, p 123 *b g h*, p 124 *e f*, p 125 *c d*, p 126 *c* to *h* and p 127 *c* to *f*, post).

*R v Secretary of State for the Home Dept, ex p Herbage* [1986] 3 All ER 209 applied.
*IRC v Rossminster Ltd* [1980] 1 All ER 80 distinguished.

**Notes**
For restriction on granting injunctions against an officer of the Crown, see 11 Halsbury's Laws (4th edn) para 1435.
For the Supreme Court Act 1981, s 31, see 11 Halsbury's Statutes (4th edn) 782.

**Cases referred to in judgments**
*Anisminic Ltd v Foreign Compensation Commission* [1967] 3 All ER 986, [1968] 2 QB 862, [1976] 3 WLR 382, CA; *rsvd* [1969] 1 All ER 208, [1969] 2 AC 147, [1969] 2 WLR 162, HL.
*Gouriet v Union of Post Office Workers* [1977] 3 All ER 70, [1978] AC 435, [1977] 3 WLR 300, HL.
*International General Electric Co of New York Ltd v Customs and Excise Comrs* [1962] 2 All ER 398, [1962] Ch 784, [1962] 3 WLR 20, CA.
*IRC v Rossminster Ltd* [1980] 1 All ER 80, [1980] AC 952, [1980] 2 WLR 1, HL.
*Law v National Greyhound Racing Club Ltd* [1983] 3 All ER 300, [1983] 1 WLR 1302, CA.
*O'Reilly v Mackman* [1982] 3 All ER 1124, [1983] 2 AC 237, [1982] 3 WLR 1096, HL.
*R v Licensing Authority, ex p Smith Kline & French Laboratories Ltd (Generics (UK) Ltd intervening)* [1989] 1 All ER 175, [1988] 3 WLR 896, CA.
*R v Powell* (1841) 1 QB 352, 113 ER 1166.
*R v Secretary of State for the Home Dept, ex p Ganeshanathan* [1988] CA Transcript 680.
*R v Secretary of State for the Home Dept, ex p Herbage* [1986] 3 All ER 209, [1987] QB 872, [1986] 3 WLR 504.
*Ridge v Baldwin* [1963] 2 All ER 66, [1964] AC 40, [1963] 3 WLR 935, HL.
*Underhill v Ministry of Food* [1950] 1 All ER 591.

**Interlocutory application**
The licensing authority under the Medicines Act 1968 appealed against the decision of Henry J on 21 December 1987 whereby on an application by Smith Kline & French Laboratories Ltd (SKF) for judicial review he declared that the licensing authority, when considering an application under the abridged procedure set out in item 8(*a*)(ii) of the second paragraph of art 4 of Council Directive (EEC) 65/65, as replaced by Council Directive (EEC) 87/21, for product licences by third parties in respect of generic versions of the pharmaceutical product cimetidine originated by SKF, was not permitted to use, refer to or have recourse to any confidential information supplied by SKF except with their express consent. At the hearing of the appeal leave was given to Generics (UK) Ltd and Harris Pharmaceuticals Ltd to intervene. On 29 June 1988 the Court of Appeal (Dillon, Balcombe and Staughton LJJ) ([1989] 1 All ER 175, [1988] 3 WLR 896) allowed the appeal and refused SKF leave to appeal to the House of Lords. SKF sought an injunction restraining the licensing authority, whether by itself, its officers, employees, agents or otherwise howsoever, when determining applications made by persons other than SKF for product licences in respect of medicinal products containing cimetidine from making use of or having regard to, otherwise than with the consent of SKF, any confidential information supplied to the licensing authority by them in connection with applications by SKF for product licences in respect of such products, pending the determination of SKF's petition for leave to appeal to the House of Lords against the decision of the Court of Appeal dated 29 June 1988. The facts are set out in the judgment of Dillon LJ.

*Sydney Kentridge QC* and *Derrick Turriff* for SKF.
*Andrew Collins QC* and *Helen Rogers* for the licensing authority.

*Jonathan Sumption QC* for the first intervener.
a *Henry Carr* for the second intervener.

**DILLON LJ.** The background to the applications with which we have been concerned yesterday and today is that Smith Kline & French Laboratories Ltd (SKF) are a pharmaceutical company which manufacture various drugs, and one of their products is an extremely successful drug called cimetidine, which they have marketed under the
b brand name Tagamet. They hold a patent in respect of cimetidine and they also hold necessary product licences under the Medicines Act 1968, without which it is not permissible to market a drug or pharmaceutical product in this country.

To obtain those product licences SKF have to supply a lot of information about the drug to the licensing authority under the 1968 Act who is the Minister of Health. It is not in doubt that the information so supplied goes far beyond anything disclosed in the
c patent specification and is confidential information which SKF would not gladly see disclosed to any trade rivals.

As a result of the provisions of the Patents Act 1977 the cimetidine patents are now marked 'licences of right' and the two interveners in these proceedings, Generics (UK) Ltd and Harris Pharmaceuticals Ltd, have obtained licences of right under the patent. However, they also need product licences in respect of their generic cimetidine or any
d formulations of it under the 1968 Act and for these they have applied. Apparently there are some eight other companies which have also applied for product licences and there may in the future be others. The licences of right only apply during the final four years of the 20-year life of the patent under the 1977 Act. The product licences under the 1968 Act will continue to be required even after the patent has finally expired.

In these circumstances SKF applied for leave to move for judicial review and in their
e notice of application, Form 86A, they set out as the judgment, order, decision or other proceeding in respect of which relief was sought:

'The performance by the licensing authority, as defined in section 6 of the Medicines Act 1968, of its functions under that Act in relation to the grant of product licences for pharmaceutical products: in particular, the policy and/or
f practice of the licensing authority ... with regard to the use by the licensing authority, in the assessment of applications by third parties for product licences in respect of generic versions of a pharmaceutical product, of confidential information supplied to it by the originator of the product in support of the originator's own application for a product licence in respect of that product.'

g The relief sought was a declaration that the licensing authority might not lawfully grant product licences to a third party in respect of a cimetidine product where the third party's application, if read without recourse to one or more of the applicant's product licence applications, (i) is deficient with regard to the results of physico-chemical, biological or microbiological tests, and/or (ii) in so far as the third party relies on evidence relating to pharmacological and/or toxicological tests and/or clinical trials carried out
h with one of the applicant's products, fails to establish the essential similarity of its product to the applicant's said product, unless the applicant expressly consents to the authority having recourse to its application or applications to make good such deficiency and/or to establish such essential similarity.

The declaration was formulated alternatively and in support of it an order of prohibition restraining the licensing authority from granting product licences in the
j circumstances mentioned, or an injunction to restrain the licensing authority from having recourse without the express consent of the applicant to any of its product licence applications, was sought.

Leave to apply for judicial review was granted and the initial position was covered, under an order of Schiemann J of 30 October 1987, by certain assurances given by the licensing authority and a certain undertaking given by SKF. The assurances were that the licensing authority, in effect, would not grant any licence without giving seven days notice in writing to SKF and the applicant for the licence and would make no use of any data submitted to it by SKF in connection with SKF's application for any grant of cimetidine product licences without giving 14 days' notice in writing to SKF and the relevant applicant for a licence.

The application for judicial review came for hearing before Henry J and by an order of 23 February 1988 he acceded to that application and made an order declaring that in considering an application for a product licence in respect of a medicinal product containing cimetidine made pursuant to the abridged procedure provided for by art 4(8)(a)(iii) of Council Directive (EEC) 65/65 as amended the licensing authority may not for the purpose of such application use refer to or have recourse to any confidential information supplied to it by SKF in connection with any application by SKF for a product licence in respect of such a product except with the express consent of SKF.

The licensing authority appealed against that order and on 29 June 1988 a division of this court consisting of Staughton, Balcombe LJJ and myself allowed that appeal and discharged the order of Henry J. On that occasion the two generic companies whom I have mentioned, Generics (UK) Ltd and Harris Pharmaceuticals Ltd, were given leave to appear and be heard in support of the licensing authority as they had been allowed to be heard before Henry J.

On 29 June 1988 leave to SKF to appeal to the House of Lords was refused. The court took the view that it was appropriate that their Lordships should decide if they wanted to entertain an appeal in this case. A petition for leave to appeal to the House of Lords has now been lodged by SKF. The possible timetables, as I see them, raise three main alternatives. The first and shortest timetable is if leave to appeal is refused by their Lordships. The second alternative is that leave is granted and the appeal is either allowed or dismissed by their Lordships without reference to the Court of Justice of the European Communities at Luxembourg. The third alternative, which would lead to the longest time-lag in the disposal of the proceedings, is that leave to appeal is granted and their Lordships' House then directs a reference to Luxembourg before deciding to allow or dismiss the appeal. This would be likely to take a very considerable time[1].

When the judgments of the Court of Appeal were handed down on 29 June, leading counsel for SKF asked for interim protection against the use by the licensing authority of SKF's confidential information pending disposal of the application for leave to appeal or possibly pending final disposal of the appeal if leave was granted.

It was intimated to the court that questions of principle and jurisdiction would be raised, but the division of the court which had decided the appeal was committed in other matters and had no time to proceed to hear the application for interim relief that day. Consequently interim assurances were given by the licensing authority until the end of July, that is the present month, while the parties sought to see if there was any solution acceptable to them all.

The application was then renewed yesterday and today, coming before this division of the court, it being still impossible for reasons of listing to reassemble the court as originally constituted for the hearing of the appeal.

What is now sought, as set out in the skeleton argument of leading counsel for SKF, is as follows: (1) an injunction restraining the licensing authority whether by itself, its officers, employees, agents or otherwise howsoever, when determining applications, made by persons other than SKF, for product licences in respect of medicinal products containing cimetidine from making use of or having regard to, otherwise than with the consent of SKF, any confidential information supplied to the licensing authority by SKF in connection with applications by SKF for product licences in respect of such products,

---

1  Editor's note: On 10 October 1988 the Appeal Committee of the House of Lords gave SKF leave to appeal against the Court of Appeal's decision, but on 9 February 1989 the appeal was dismissed: see [1989] 1 All ER 578, [1989] 2 WLR 397.

pending the determination of SKF's petition for leave to appeal to the House of Lords
*a* from the decision of the Court of Appeal given on 29 June 1988 or further order; (2) a
stay of proceedings in relation to the determination by the licensing authority of such
applications for product licences made by persons other than SKF to the same effect as (1)
above and for the same period.

Although relief is only sought pending the determination of SKF's petition for leave
to appeal to the House of Lords, it is necessary, I think, to bear in mind that any interim
*b* protection granted over that period may well, if leave to appeal is granted and if there is
a reference to the European Court in Luxembourg, have to last very much longer.

The objection is taken by the licensing authority, supported by the two interveners,
that there is no jurisdiction to grant any such relief against the licensing authority, it
begin a representative of the Crown. Alternatively it is said that in the circumstances and
in the light of certain proposals put forward by the licensing authority, with the
*c* agreement of the interveners, as a matter of discretion it would not be right to grant any
interim relief as sought.

Any consideration of a question of jurisdiction in relation to relief against the Crown
will necessarily start with reference to the Crown Proceedings Act 1947. Section 1 of that
Act provided that where a person had a claim against the Crown, and, if the 1947 Act
had not been passed, the claim might have been enforced, subject to the grant of His
*d* Majesty's fiat, by petition of right, or a proceeding provided by any statutory provision
repealed by the 1947 Act, then, the claim might, subject to the proceedings of the 1947
Act, be enforced as of right, and without the fiat by proceedings taken against the Crown.

Section 2 provided that the Crown should be subject to liabilities in tort. Section 13
provided that subject to the provisions of the 1947 Act, all such civil proceedings by or
against the Crown as were mentioned in Sch 1 to the 1947 Act were abolished, and all
*e* civil proceedings by or against the Crown in the High Court should be instituted and
proceeded with in accordance with rules of court and not otherwise. The civil proceedings
mentioned in Sch 1 were various proceedings by what are now, at any rate, regarded as
very archaic procedures.

Section 21 of the 1947 Act is concerned with the nature of relief. It provides by sub-s
*f* (1):

> 'In any civil proceedings by or against the Crown the court shall, subject to the
> provisions of this Act, have power to make all such orders as it has power to make
> in proceedings between subjects, and otherwise to give such appropriate relief as the
> case may require; Provided that:—(*a*) where in any proceedings against the Crown
> any such relief is sought as might in proceedings between subjects be granted by
*g* > way of injunction or specific performance, the court shall not grant an injunction
> or make an order for specific performance, but may in lieu thereof make an order
> declaratory of the rights of the parties . . .'

Paragraph (*b*) contains provisions as to orders against the Crown for the recovery of land
or other property. Subsection (2) provides:
*h*

> 'The court shall not in any civil proceedings grant any injunction or make any
> order against an officer of the Crown if the effect of granting the injunction or
> making the order would be to give any relief against the Crown which could not
> have been obtained in proceedings against the Crown.'

*j* In relation to the proviso (*a*) to s 21(1) it was held that an interim injunction could not
be granted against the Crown and an interim declaration could not be made against the
Crown because an interim declaration is an animal that the courts do not recognise. This
was held by Romer J in *Underhill v Ministry of Food* [1950] 1 All ER 591. His view was
approved by this court in *International General Electric Co of New York Ltd v Customs and
Excise Comrs* [1962] 2 All ER 398, [1962] Ch 784, and the same view was strongly

indorsed by the majority of the House of Lords at any rate, that is to say Lord Wilberforce, Lord Diplock and Lord Scarman, in *IRC v Rossminster Ltd* [1980] 1 All ER 80, [1980] AC  **a** 952.

The 1947 Act proceeds in s 22 to deal with stays of execution and provides that, subject to the provisions of the Act, all enactments, rules of court and county court rules relating to appeals and stay of execution shall, with any necessary modifications, apply to civil proceedings by or against the Crown as they apply to proceedings between subjects. It is, however, common ground in the present case that the ordinary stay of execution under  **b** RSC Ord 59, r 13, which is the stay of execution with which s 22 is concerned, is not appropriate.

It has been pointed out in the argument on the present application that under s 32(2) of the 1947 Act the term 'civil proceedings against the Crown' is limited to certain particular types of proceeding under the former archaic procedure and to such other proceedings as any person is entitled to bring against the Crown by virtue of the 1947  **c** Act. The definition section, that is s 38(2) in the 1947 Act, expressly provides that 'Civil proceedings' does not include 'proceedings on the Crown side of the King's Bench Division'.

In 1947, when the Act was passed, the procedure by what is now called judicial review was, under the Administration of Justice (Miscellaneous Provisions) Act 1938, a procedure by way of application for an order of mandamus, prohibition or certiorari. No relief by  **d** way of injunction in any relevant sense or declaration was possible in such proceedings; a fortiori, there was no question of an interlocutory injunction or declaration being granted.

Rules made to give effect to the provisions of the 1938 Act shortly after that Act was enacted include provisions corresponding to the present Ord 53, r 3(10)(a) which provides:  **e**

'Where leave to apply for judicial review is granted, then—(a) if the relief sought is an order of prohibition or certiorari and the Court so directs, the grant shall operate as a stay of the proceedings to which the application relates until the determination of the application or until the Court otherwise orders . . .'

However, a parallel procedure developed of seeking to challenge administrative  **f** decisions by an action for a declaration and/or injunction brought very often in the Chancery Division. Instances are afforded by *Anisminic Ltd v Foreign Compensation Commission* [1967] 3 All ER 986, [1968] 2 QB 862 and *IRC v Rossminster Ltd*, which I have already mentioned. Obviously in such an action no injunction could be obtained against the Crown: see *Rossminster* and the other cases which I have mentioned.

Apart from that procedural development, the scope of the remedy available by way of  **g** the prerogative orders was extended. The history is recorded in the speech of Lord Diplock in *O'Reilly v Mackman* [1982] 3 All ER 1124, [1983] 2 AC 237; the decision of the House of Lords in *Ridge v Baldwin* [1963] 2 All ER 66, [1964] AC 40 established that judicial review was not confined to decisions or actions of bodies performing judicial or quasi-judicial functions.  **h**

In 1977 the Rules of the Supreme Court were amended to introduce the present Ord 53. The objectives as I see them were, firstly, to streamline the procedure, that is make various other forms of interim relief available and to provide for discovery and the hearing of evidence, but also to bring the claims for declarations and injunctions within the scope of the procedure under the order and within the range of relief obtainable on judicial review. It was obviously undesirable that the fairly summary procedure by way  **j** of judicial review should have still running in parallel with it the slower procedure by writ for a declaration.

The statutory authority for judicial review is now s 31 of the Supreme Court Act 1981, which provides, so far as material:

'(1) An application to the High Court for one or more of the following forms of relief, namely—(a) an order of mandamus, prohibition or certiorari; (b) a declaration or injunction under subsection (2); or (c) an injunction under section 30 restraining a person not entitled to do so from acting in an office to which that section applies, shall be made in accordance with rules of court by a procedure to be known as an application for judicial review.

(2) A declaration may be made or an injunction granted under this subsection in any case where an application for judicial review, seeking that relief, has been made and the High Court considers that, having regard to [certain matters, including all the circumstances of the case] it would be just and convenient for the declaration to be made or the injunction to be granted, as the case may be.

(3) No application for judicial review shall be made unless the leave of the High Court has been obtained in accordance with rules of court . . .'

Order 53 and its rules previously made now have effect by virtue of s 17(2)(b) of the Interpretation Act 1978 as if made under the rule-making power in the 1981 Act. Order 53, r 3, besides the provision that I have just read from para (10)(a) of r 3, provides by para (10)(b):

'Where leave to apply for judicial review is granted, then . . . (b) if any other relief is sought, the Court may at any time grant in the proceedings such interim relief as could be granted in an action begun by writ.'

That seems to me to underline that what was being done was to blend together in the one procedure the old procedure for a prerogative order and the newly developing procedure of the action by writ for a declaration or injunction.

Against that background, Hodgson J had to decide *R v Secretary of State for the Home Dept, ex p Herbage* [1986] 3 All ER 209, [1987] QB 872. In that case he considered the jurisdiction of the court, though in the event he held that the relief sought should not be granted for reasons that are not material to the present case. However, he held (see [1987] QB 872):

'(1)  that, although s 21(2) of the Crown Proceedings Act 1947 had been construed as prohibiting the grant of an injunction against an officer of the Crown in civil proceedings, the subsection was not applicable to proceedings on the Crown side of the Queen's Bench Division and did not affect the jurisdiction of the court to grant prerogative orders against officers of the Crown; that the provisions of section 31 of the Supreme Court Act 1981 and R.S.C., Ord. 53, r. 3(10) gave the court power to grant injunctive and interim relief in proceedings for judicial review and, therefore, the court now had jurisdiction to grant an interim injunction against an officer of the Crown on an application for judicial review . . .'

The judge had *IRC v Rossminster Ltd* referred to him in argument, though I have not noticed any citation of it in his judgment. He said ([1986] 3 All ER 209 at 212, [1987] QB 872 at 881): 'The immunity of the Crown and its officers from injunctive relief is to be found in s 21 of the Crown Proceedings Act 1947.'

It has to be borne in mind that the 1947 Act was an enabling Act enabling certain proceedings to be brought against the Crown in the ordinary way under the Rules of the Supreme Court, and s 21, prohibiting the grant of an injunction against the Crown, was an exemption from that enabling provision. It is not the case that there was any prior right to injunctive relief against the Crown which was only cut down in a limited field by the 1947 Act.

As to r 3(10)(b) of Ord 53, Hodgson J's view was that that provision was a mere enabling power allowing the court to grant to an applicant for judicial review all the interlocutory remedies available in an action begun by writ (see [1986] 3 All ER 209 at 215, [1987] QB

872 at 885–886). He rejected the argument to the contrary presented on behalf of the Crown that the injunction would not lie against a servant of the Crown in proceedings brought by writ and that, accordingly, it could not, on the wording of Ord 53, r 3(10)(*b*), be granted against the Crown in proceedings for judicial review.

I have to say that my personal opinion on that question is with all respect to Hodgson J to the contrary. It seems to me, and again I state my personal view, that the direct effect of para (10)(*b*) of r 3 is to make the position in respect of interlocutory relief such as it would have been if an action had been brought against the Crown; if such an action had been brought, then the action would plainly be within the 1947 Act and on the basis of *IRC v Rossminster Ltd* no interim injunction could have been obtained.

I should add in respect of *IRC v Rossminster Ltd* that it appears that although there had been an action brought in the Chancery Division for a declaration, that had been transferred to the Queen's Bench Division and had not proceeded further. What the House of Lords were actually considering was an application for judicial review or at least the appeal by the Crown against the order of the Court of Appeal granting a final declaration on an interlocutory application for relief in respect of judicial review proceedings. It was, I would have thought, necessary for their Lordships to explain why the procedure adopted in the Court of Appeal was not a permissible procedure on a judicial review application.

There is, therefore, in my judgment no doubt that interim injunctions cannot be granted against the Crown even in proceedings for judicial review. I turn, therefore, to consider the application for a stay of proceedings as put in the second part of SKF's application, that is to say a stay of the proceedings to which the application for judicial review under Ord 53, r 3(10)(*a*) relates.

I do not doubt that s 31 of the 1981 Act and Ord 53 bind the Crown in the sense that judicial review can be obtained against the Crown and a final declaration can be made against the Crown. Indeed, no procedural objection was raised to the declaration which Henry J made on the view of the law which he took. I see no need to consider the granting of a final injunction against the Crown rather than a declaration because I cannot see that that is ever likely in practice to be granted.

I do not for my part see why para (10)(*a*) of Ord 53, r 3 should not bind the Crown in an appropriate case. It goes back historically to the rules made after the enactment of the 1938 Act which was concerned only with the prerogative orders. I would myself construe the words 'the proceedings' in para (10)(*a*) widely as having effect in the light of the modern scope of judicial review. The paragraph has effect under the 1981 Act, as I have endeavoured to explain. I see no basis for construing it narrowly as suggested by counsel for the licensing authority by reference to the antithesis in the phrase 'proceedings or matters' in s 7(2) of the 1938 Act. The 1938 Act has been repealed by the 1981 Act.

However, in my judgment, what SKF are seeking in the second limb of their application is essentially an injunction which cannot be granted and not a mere stay within para (10)(*a*) of r 3. SKF do not seek to stop the licensing authority from proceeding with the examination of applications for product licences in respect of cimetidine, but they seek to stop the licensing authority from doing certain things which, in the view of this court in the judgments handed down at the end of June, the licensing authority are entitled to do in the proper exercise of their statutory functions. It seems to me that that is really a matter of injunction rather than stay of proceedings.

Apart from that, a stay of the applications by the licensing authority, however curtailed in its wording, is, in my judgment, far too drastic relief. What this application is about is, of course, competition in the market. SKF are seeking, so far as they lawfully can, to keep generic companies out of the market in cimetidine, even though the monopoly protection accorded by their patent is now by the 1977 Act, which itself was enacted as a result of the Convention on the Grant of European Patents (Munich, 5 October 1973; TS 20 (1978); Cmnd 7090), subject to licences of right, and even if the patent finally expires.

Against that background certain proposals were put forward by the Treasury Solicitor

on behalf of the licensing authority in correspondence. What was suggested was that
a licences issued by the licensing authority should contain the following conditions to
cover the situation which would arise should any appeal by SKF be successful. The
conditions are:

'(a) A reference has been made by the licensing authority to data supplied in
support of applications for licences for Cimetidine products by Smith Kline and
French Laboratories Ltd for the purpose of ascertaining whether the applicant had
b demonstrated that [this medicinal product] is essentially similar to a product
authorised and marketed within the European Community for not less than ten
years. (b) It is subject to the condition that if on the determination of any appeal by
Smith Kline & French Laboratories Ltd against the decision of the Court of Appeal
dated 29th June 1988 in the case of *The Queen v The Licensing Authority established*
*under the Medicines Act 1968, Ex parte Smith Kline & French Laboratories Ltd*, it shall be
c held that reference to the data of Smith Kline & French Laboratories Ltd for such
purpose was unlawful this licence shall forthwith determine and cease to have
effect.'

It is impossible to provide a completely satisfactory interim solution to the rival
demands of SKF and the generic companies pending the ultimate decision of the House
d of Lords at whichever stage that may be reached. Also, there is the difficulty that there
are the other companies which I have mentioned which have applied for product licences
from the licensing authority but which are not parties to these proceedings and would
not have the protection of the cross-undertaking in damages which SKF has offered both
to the licensing authority and to the two interveners in these proceedings.

Bearing all these factors in mind, I take the view that even if para (2) of the relief
e sought by the licensing authority could be said to be within para (10)(a) of Ord 53, r 3, or
otherwise relief which the court had power to grant, it would not be appropriate as a
matter of discretion to grant it.

Accordingly, I would for my part reject this application by SKF for interim relief.

f **WOOLF LJ.** Although this is only an application pending an appeal or possible appeal
to the House of Lords, it raises a point of considerable importance as to the powers and
the jurisdiction of the court to grant an interim injunction or stay against the Crown.

It may well be that in practice the issue, although important, will not prove to be one
which frequently troubles the court. However, having regard to the decision of Hodgson
J in *R v Secretary of State for the Home Dept, ex p Herbage* [1986] 3 All ER 209, [1987] QB
g 872, although I have come to the same conclusion as Dillon LJ as to the outcome of this
application, it is desirable that I should also deal with the question of jurisdiction as I
differ from Dillon LJ on the extent of the court's jurisdiction in one important respect.

It has always generally been understood that the court's powers to make peremptory
orders in the form of injunctions or the equivalent against the Crown are restricted.
Earliest authorities on this subject indicate the problem. As an example I refer to *R v*
h *Powell* (1841) 1 QB 352 at 361, 113 ER 1166 at 1170, where Lord Denman CJ said:

'That there can be no mandamus to the Sovereign there can be no doubt, both
because there would be an incongruity in the Queen commanding herself to do an
act, and also because the disobedience to a writ of mandamus is to be enforced by
attachment.'

j However, the precise ambit of the principle to which Lord Denman CJ referred has
never been clearly defined. In *de Smith's Judicial Review of Administrative Action* (4th edn,
1980) p 445, in dealing with injunctions and the Crown, it is stated:

'Before the Crown Proceedings Act 1947 an injunction would lie against an officer
of the Crown if he committed a civil wrong in his personal capacity; it would never

lie against the Crown; but whether it would lie against a government department, or against an officer of the Crown for a wrongful act done in his official capacity, *a* was uncertain.'

The learned editors then go on to consider the position in greater detail, and in the notes draw attention to the fact that conflicting views are taken by distinguished academic writers as to the extent of the principle.

The situation on applications for judicial review has been altered by the passing of the *b* Supreme Court Act 1981. It is to be noted that while that Act was a consolidating Act, it was also an amending Act.

In so far as judicial review is concerned, to an extent, the Act codified the provisions which had existed and had been in force (although subsequently amended) since 1977, which are contained in RSC Ord 53. Order 53 had transformed the position with regard to the obtaining of public law remedies.

The extent to which Ord 53 altered the jurisdiction of the courts was in doubt until *c* the 1981 Act was enacted. Indeed, it may be fortunate that prior to that Act coming into force the vires of certain of its provisions was never fully considered by the courts. That question now becomes academic in consequence of the 1981 Act. Pursuant to s 17(2)(*b*) of the Interpretation Act 1978, Ord 53 in its present form has to be treated as though it had been brought into existence under the 1981 Act. *d*

Turning to consider the provisions of the 1981 Act, it is important to note that there is a distinction between the way that the Act deals with the power of the courts to grant relief by way of injunction or by way of declaration from that which exists in relation to damages. Here s 31(2) and (4) is important. Section 31(2) provides:

'A declaration may be made or an injunction granted under this subsection in any *e* case where an application for judicial review, seeking that relief, has been made and the High Court consider that, having regard to—(*a*) the nature of the matters in respect of which relief may be granted by orders of mandamus, prohibition or certiorari; (*b*) the nature of the persons and bodies against whom relief may be granted by such orders; and (*c*) all the circumstances of the case, it would be just and convenient for the declaration to be made or the injunction to be granted, as the *f* case may be.'

The effect of s 31(2), read literally, is that the court has a discretion to grant a declaration or grant an injunction at least in that class of cases where it was the practice previously to grant an order of mandamus, prohibition or certiorari, subject to the qualification that the application is against the type of body or persons in relation to whom those orders *g* normally would be available. This is a different basis of jurisdiction from that which previously existed. Turning to sub-s (4), that provides:

'On an application for judicial review the High Court may award damages to the applicant if—(*a*) he has joined with his application a claim for damages arising from any matter to which the application relates; and (*b*) the court is satisfied that, if the *h* claim had been made in an action begun by the applicant at the time of making his application, he would have been awarded damages.'

The position with regard to a claim for damages, therefore, is quite distinct from that in relation to a claim for a declaration or injunction because in respect of a claim for damages it has to be a situation where if the claim had been included in an action *j* damages would be awarded. The key to the distinction between sub-s (2) and sub-s (4) is that sub-s (2) has the innovative effect of making a declaration or injunction for the first time a public law remedy in addition to being a private law remedy which could be used to obtain relief on the same basis against private bodies and public bodies, which was the position prior to the coming into force of the new procedure of judicial review.

However, in the case of damages the situation is otherwise. Damages could previously
*a* only be obtained in private law proceedings against a public body if private law, common
law or statutory rights were breached and now the same restrictions apply in judicial
review, that is public law proceedings, where damages are claimed.

In my view, looking at the language of s 31 alone, it is quite clear that the court's
jurisdiction was being extended in relation to declarations and injunctions, but that its
jurisdiction was not being extended in relation to damages, and in relation to damages
*b* all that has happened is that there is a procedural change, whereas in relation to
declarations and injunctions not only has there been a procedural change there has also
been a jurisdictional change.

That that is the position with regard to a declaration or injunction is in my view made
abundantly clear when one considers the entitlement to a declaration rather than an
injunction that existed prior to the changes to which I have referred. In order to obtain a
*c* declaration in private law proceedings, it was and still is necessary to establish that you
have some private interest which was threatened with infringement or had clearly been
infringed. You either had to show that you had a private right or that you had some
other interest which had resulted in or could result in your suffering damage.

I do not propose to lengthen this judgment, especially bearing in mind the stage of the
term at which it is given, by exploring this subject, apart from drawing attention to the
*d* speeches in the House of Lords in *Gouriet v Union of Post Office Workers* [1977] 3 All ER 70
esp at 85–86, 99, [1978] AC 435 esp at 484, 500 per Lord Wilberforce and Lord Diplock.

Nowadays on an application for judicial review declarations are regularly being granted
in circumstances where a declaration could not prior to the change in the law be obtained.
There is no need for an applicant to concern himself with the question whether he could
bring himself within the private law limits to which I have been referring. One of the
*e* most beneficial effects of the changes which have occurred as a result of the new remedy
of judicial review is the growth in the circumstances where it is not only possible for the
courts to intervene but appropriate for the courts to intervene in consequence of its
power to grant declaratory relief.

The test that exists in seeing whether or not an application is appropriate to be before
the court is one which is decided by looking, first of all, at the nature of the body who is
*f* the subject matter of the application, secondly, the nature of the function that body
performs, and, thirdly, the interest of the applicant. With regard to the last matter a
generous view is now appropriately being taken by the courts having regard to the
safeguards which exist in relation to an application for judicial review which do not exist
in the case of private law proceedings.

Against that background to the statutory provisions I ask myself whether or not there
*g* is a power to grant an injunction against the Crown, and subject to what I have to say
hereafter I conclude that there clearly is such a power under the new procedure. It is not
challenged that there is the power to grant a declaration against the Crown. The same
statutory provisions which create the power to grant a declaration apply equally to an
injunction, and I cannot see how, on the language of the Act, it is possible to draw any
*h* distinction between a declaration or an injunction.

This is not, in my view, an astonishing result because an order of mandamus was
always available, although it was used with great circumspection against public bodies,
including officers or ministers of the Crown, subject to the qualification that they must
not be acting as the alter ego of the sovereign or indeed be said to be acting in such
circumstances where to grant relief would offend the statement which I cited earlier by
*j* Lord Denman CJ so that the courts would be giving relief against the sovereign: see *R v
Powell* (1841) 1 QB 352 at 361, 113 ER 1166 at 1170.

When one comes to look at the matter on authority, the only authority which is
directly applicable to this issue which is in any way inconsistent with the approach that I
have taken, apart from the speeches in *IRC v Rossminster Ltd* [1980] 1 All ER 80, [1980]
AC 952, is the case to which counsel referred us, i e *Law v National Greyhound Racing Club*

*Ltd* [1983] 3 All ER 300 at 304, [1983] 1 WLR 1302 at 1308, where Lawton LJ said: 'The purpose of s 31 is to regulate procedure in relation to judicial reviews, not to extend the *a* jurisdiction of the court.'

However, that statement of Lawton LJ has to be read in the context of that case. What the court was there considering was whether or not judicial review was the appropriate procedure in relation to domestic tribunals and, of course, with regard to that situation it can be fairly said, as Lawton LJ did, that there had been a change of procedure but not a change of jurisdiction. If one looks at the other judgments in that case, they do not repeat *b* the same approach indicated by Lawton LJ and I do not regard that case as being any authority inconsistent with the approach that I have indicated.

So far as any other statutory provision which impinges on this approach is concerned, one immediately, of course, considers the Crown Proceedings Act 1947, the terms of which have been referred to by Dillon LJ. So far as s 21 of that Act is concerned, which was relied on by counsel for the licensing authority with his characteristic force and *c* clarity, I have no difficulty in coming to the conclusion that that Act cannot alter the view that I have formed as to the application of s 31 of the 1981 Act.

The 1947 Act was not dealing with injunctions on applications for judicial review because, of course, you could not get injunctions on the Crown side in 1947. It was as a result of the change in procedure that they became available for the first time on the Crown side, and in my view it is quite clear that although the proviso to s 21(1) refers to *d* 'any proceedings against the Crown', that proviso has to be read subject to the opening words of s 21(1), and I am wholly in agreement with Dillon LJ in rejecting the argument of counsel for the licensing authority in this regard. In so far as it had been necessary, I would have referred to ss 23, 38(2) and 40(5) in support of that conclusion.

It seems, therefore, clear to me that injunctive relief is available against the Crown on an application for judicial review. The next question, therefore, which is important to be *e* answered here is whether interim relief is available against the Crown in the form of an injunction. It is here that I have the misfortune to differ from the view expressed by Dillon LJ.

I start off by saying that if you are entitled to have a final injunction against the Crown in proceedings for judicial review, it is difficult to see what good reason there should be *f* for not having interim relief in the form of an injunction against the Crown. I then remind myself that in what is sometimes called 'statutory certiorari' (and here I refer to the many different Acts which provide for statutory appeals to the High Court against orders by ministers) there is a power to grant interim relief, at least in the form of a stay.

Taking one example, in s 245(4) of the Town and Country Planning Act 1971 it is provided that the court may by interim order suspend the operation of the order of the *g* minister which is subject to challenge. If this formula has been statutorily recognised time after time going back for many years, long before the change in judicial review, one asks oneself: if the minister can be subject to an order in that situation, why should he not, in appropriate circumstances on an application for judicial review, be subject to the same type of order? Of course, one would always bear in mind that it is a power which the court would not exercise other than when it was warranted by the *h* circumstances.

However, it is difficult to envisage that you can have an interim declaration, although it is right to point out that in other jurisdictions, and I have particularly in mind the jurisdiction in Israel which is based on our own system, I understand they now do grant interim declarations, but certainly the problems with regard to interim declarations do not apply to interim injunctions. *j*

Furthermore, subject to the arguments advanced by counsel for the licensing authority, if the court has power to grant a stay on an application for judicial review that is, in effect, identical to an injunction, one asks oneself: if it was intended that there should be, as against the Crown, a power to grant a stay by way of interim relief why should it not also be available in relation to injunctions?

The difficulty arises, however, because of the wording of Ord 53, r 3(10)(b). So far as
a Ord 53, r 3(10)(a) is concerned Dillon LJ has indicated why he rejects the arguments of
counsel for the licensing authority that there should be no power to grant a stay against
the Crown, and I respectfully adopt that reasoning. In so far as para (b) is concerned, the
wording is capable of more than one interpretation.

The differing interpretations were canvassed before Hodgson J in R v Secretary of State
for the Home Dept, ex p Herbage [1986] 3 All ER 209, [1987] QB 872 and I can only say that
b because I can see no purpose in restrictively interpreting para (10)(b) and no basis for
depriving the court of a jurisdiction, however sparingly it may be exercised, to grant
interim relief by way of injunction, I would adopt the reasoning of Hodgson J which
appears in his judgment (see [1986] 3 All ER 209 at 215–216, [1987] QB 872 at 886).

It, therefore, seems to me that this is a case where there is jurisdiction to grant both a
stay and interim relief in the form of an injunction. I would emphasise here that Mr
c Collins submitted that there was no jurisdiction even to grant a stay and so far as that is
concerned it has been the practice, so far as my knowledge goes, for stays to be regularly
granted by High Court judges and by the Court of Appeal against the Crown, and
although there may never have been an opportunity for the Crown to properly contest
the matter before now it seems to me that this is a most important and appropriate
jurisdiction.
d Indeed, two members of this court two days ago granted a stay pending the
consideration of an application for leave to apply for judicial review in R v Secretary of
State for the Home Dept, ex p Ganeshanathan [1988] CA Transcript 680, and the facts of this
case are worth recording in the course of considering this matter very briefly because
they reflect the importance of the jurisdiction. In that case there was a Tamil about to be
removed from this country at one o'clock on the day the matter came before the court.
e It came before the court at half past twelve. We were told that the Home Office had been
asked to hold their hand pending an application for judicial review. Bearing in mind the
circumstances, not unnaturally, the Home Office were not prepared to hold their hand.
When the matter came before the court, we were not able to deal with it within the time
available before one o'clock, so we granted a short stay to enable us to deal with it. Of
course, there is a long tradition, which I hope will be maintained, of the Crown respecting
f the courts and avoiding the necessity for stays being granted by indicating that without
any order of the court they will await the outcome.

However, there are situations where it is important for the Crown to know what the
attitude is of the court, otherwise it is left in a situation where it holds its hand quite
needlessly. It is the experience of those who are engaged in the immigration field that
would-be immigrants into this country were languishing in custodial establishments
g merely because they were making applications for judicial review which were doomed
to failure and once the Crown was told that an application was intended to be made the
Crown felt it had to hold its hand.

If, on the other hand, the matter can be brought to the court and the court can in the
appropriate cases grant stays, that would avoid that sort of problem. Of course, where
h there is good reason for the Crown not holding its hand and where the Crown is not
content to leave it to the applicant to pursue any remedies, then the court has to consider
any arguments advanced by the Crown for saying that interim relief should not be
granted.

In my view, the court should always bear in mind the language of Lord Scarman on
this subject expressed in IRC v Rossminster Ltd [1980] 1 All ER 80 at 105–106, [1980] AC
j 952 at 1027. I am afraid that I am at fault in not referring earlier to the speeches of the
House of Lords in the Rossminster case. Those speeches have been referred to by Dillon
LJ. Those speeches did cause me considerable concern. I accept that in relation to interim
relief they indicated that there was no jurisdiction to grant injunctive relief on an interim
application.

However, I draw comfort from the fact that the case was being considered prior to the

passing of the 1981 Act. At that stage, of course, the argument that there was a new
power to grant interim relief by way of injunction in public law proceedings against the    *a*
Crown depended on a new rule of the Supreme Court alone. In my view their Lordships
would not have made the same comments now having regard to the passing of the 1981
Act. In particular Lord Scarman who dealt with the issue most fully would not, for
reasons I have indicated, have said Ord 53, r 2 has not altered the substantive law if that
rule had already been given the statutory backing of the 1981 Act.

When the report of the arguments are looked at in *IRC v Rossminster Ltd*, it is clear that    *b*
the matter was not fully canvassed before their Lordships' House. It was being considered
by them obiter, and therefore as I have formed such a clear view as to the effect of s 31 of
the 1981 Act and Ord 53 I am not deterred from expressing the views which I have by
the contents of those speeches.

I, therefore, turn to the question of discretion in this case on the basis that it would be
appropriate to grant injunctive relief and also that it would be appropriate to grant a stay    *c*
if in the court's discretion it was thought right to do so. However here Lord Scarman's
comments in the *Rossminster* case [1980] 1 All ER 80 at 105–106, [1980] AC 952 at 1027
are highly pertinent. Dealing with the question of discretion, I start off with the fact that
a decision of this court has unanimously allowed the appeal of the licensing authority. I
also bear in mind that the licensing authority is performing a statutory duty. It is a duty
which it is required to perform and the court, in my view, should be hesitant in granting    *d*
relief which interferes, even on an interim basis, with the performance by the statutory
authority of this role.

When one contemplates the problems involved in granting the sort of interim relief
which the applicants seek, I have come to the conclusion that as a matter of discretion
this court should refuse that relief. Dillon LJ has drawn attention to the fact that a stay
would not be an appropriate machinery for bringing about that which the applicants    *e*
seek because they do not wish to stop the licensing authority considering an application,
but only the manner in which the application is considered.

It is also to be noted that although two interveners are before the court, there are
apparently eight other applications pending. There are problems so far as they are
concerned of achieving a satisfactory result by consent and speaking for myself, having    *f*
paid attention to the offers which have been made on behalf of the licensing authority to
the applicants in the correspondence to which Dillon LJ has referred, the conclusion
which I have come to as a matter of discretion is that this is not a case where interim
relief should be granted.

**TAYLOR LJ.** I concur in the outcome proposed by Dillon LJ and Woolf LJ, but since    *g*
they are not in agreement as to the jurisdiction of the court to grant an interim injunction
against the licensing authority, I should very briefly express my reasons for agreeing, as I
do, with the judgment and reasoning of Woolf LJ, and the decision of Hodgson J in *R v
Secretary of State for the Home Dept, ex p Herbage* [1986] 3 All ER 209, [1987] QB 872.

In my view, RSC Ord 53, r 3(10)(a) would apply since there was here an application
for prohibition to permit the court to grant a stay. Counsel for the licensing authority    *h*
opposed that conclusion on two grounds. First he says that 'proceedings' in the paragraph
referred only to judicial or quasi-judicial proceedings. I do not consider that can be so in
view of the way in which judicial review has developed following *Ridge v Baldwin* [1963]
2 All ER 66, [1964] AC 40. 'Proceedings', in my view, include any procedure by which a
decision challengeable on judicial review is reached and implemented. Second, he
submits, that the paragraph does not bind the Crown. However, it is clear that the    *j*
prerogative orders are available against officers and ministers of the Crown. Here the
licensing authority is, in effect, the Minister of Health. Section 31 of the Supreme Court
Act 1981, which currently gives the Rules of the Supreme Court statutory force, is in the
very widest terms, and sub-s (2) of that section extended the scope of judicial review to

include the grant of declaratory and injunctive relief. That statute came into force after
*a*  *IRC v Rossminster Ltd* [1980] 1 All ER 80, [1980] AC 952.

However, counsel for the licensing authority relies on the Crown Proceedings Act
1947, s 21(1)(*a*) of which, he says, excludes the grant of injunctions against officers of the
Crown. He argues that a stay, particularly in the circumstances of this case, is tantamount
to an injunction and the court has no power to grant it. This is a startling proposition for
reasons which Woolf LJ has already developed. The court has, in fact, granted stays in
*b*  many judicial review cases where justice seemed to require it, especially, as in the
example given by Woolf LJ, in immigration cases.

Counsel for the licensing authority grasps that nettle and says that such stays have been
ultra vires. The fallacy in his argument, in my view, is that s 21 is concerned with civil
proceedings which by the definition contained in s 38(2) of the 1947 Act excludes
proceedings on the Crown's side of the Queen's Bench Division. Accordingly, the 1947
*c*  Act does not apply to judicial review.

As to Ord 53, r 3(10)(*b*), I agree with Woolf LJ that there is power to grant an interim
injunction against officers of the Crown. The contrary argument is that the final words
of the paragraph should be construed as requiring the court to ask whether, against the
particular respondent, an interim injunction could be granted in an action commenced
by writ. Since such a remedy could not be granted in such an action against officers of
*d*  the Crown by reason of s 21 of the 1947 Act, it cannot be granted under the paragraph in
judicial review proceedings.

I prefer the construction which appealed to Hodgson J and to Woolf LJ, that those final
words of the paragraph are merely descriptive of the types of relief which have now been
made available to the court on judicial review. That construction is fortified by
contrasting the wording of the paragraph with the wording of s 31(4)(*b*) of the 1981 Act
*e*  to which Woolf LJ has referred.

Accordingly, I consider that this court has power to grant either a stay under para
(10)(*a*) or an interim injunction under para (10)(*b*). However, for the reasons given by
Dillon and Woolf LJJ I do not think it appropriate here, as a matter of discretion, to grant
either.

*f*
*Application dismissed. Leave to appeal to the House of Lords refused.*

Solicitors: *Simmons & Simmons* (for SKF); *Treasury Solicitor*; *S J Berwin & Co* (for the first
intervener); *Roiter Zucker* (for the second intervener).

                                                         Radhika Edwards   Barrister.

# Practice Note          *a*

QUEEN'S BENCH DIVISION
MICHAEL DAVIES J
17 APRIL 1989

*County court – Transfer of action – Transfer from High Court – Transfer from Queen's Bench* *b*
*Division – Cases suitable for transfer – Jury cases – Actions for malicious prosecution, false*
*imprisonment and assault – Cases in which modest damages likely to be awarded – Cases not*
*involving difficult questions of law or fact – Opportunity to be heard on question of transfer –*
*Scale of costs – RSC Ord 107, r 2(1).*

**MICHAEL DAVIES J** gave the following direction at the sitting of the court. As a *c*
result of the heavy and increasing demands on High Court judges trying civil actions in
the Royal Courts of Justice, procedures for the remission to the county court of the less
serious cases in the non-jury list have been successfully operated for some time.

Experience has demonstrated that in most (not of course all) actions for malicious
prosecution, false imprisonment and assault in the jury list the plaintiff if successful is
awarded by the jury damages less than by current practices would in a non-jury case *d*
justify trial in the High Court; in a substantial number of these cases the damages have
been such that the action ought to have been started in the county court. Such cases do
not often involve difficult questions of law or fact.

In these circumstances, the judge in charge of the jury list will in future review all
cases of this nature as and when they are set down. Suitable cases will be transferred to
the county court. *e*

Two points must be emphasised. Transfer to the county court will not affect the mode
of trial, which will be by judge and jury as it would have been in the High Court.
Secondly, as provided for by RSC Ord 107, r 2(1), the parties will have the opportunity
of being heard on the question of transfer.

In any case remaining in the High Court in which in the result only modest damages
are awarded, the plaintiff may find that costs on the appropriate county court scale and *f*
not on the High Court scale will be ordered.

Remitted cases will generally go to the Croydon Combined County and Crown Court,
where jurors are always readily available.

The above procedure is introduced with the approval of the Lord Chief Justice and the
presiding judges of the South Eastern Circuit. Any necessary modifications will be
introduced in the light of experience. The judge in charge of the jury list will be glad at *g*
any time to receive comments from interested parties.

K Mydeen Esq    Barrister.

*a*    # Re Hetherington (deceased)
       # Gibbs v McDonnell and another

CHANCERY DIVISION

SIR NICOLAS BROWNE-WILKINSON V-C

*b*    18, 19, 20, 23 JANUARY 1989

*Charity – Religion – Charitable or religious purposes – Gift for saying of Masses – Whether gift for religious purposes – Whether gift establishing valid charitable trust.*

*Precedent – Ratio decidendi – Binding effect of decision – Legal principles which are binding.*

*c*
By a holograph will dated 17 November 1980 the testatrix, who was a Roman Catholic, left £2,000 to the Roman Catholic Bishop of Westminster for 'masses for the repose of the souls of my husband and my parents and my sisters and also myself when I die'. The will further provided that the residue was to be given to a named church for 'masses for my soul'. By an originating summons the administrator of the will of the deceased
*d*  sought, inter alia, the determination of the court on the question whether those gifts established valid charitable trusts.

**Held** – A gift for the saying of Masses was prima facie charitable because it was for a religious purpose and contained the necessary element of public benefit, since in practice the Masses would be celebrated in public and the provision of stipends for priests saying
*e*  the Masses relieved the Roman Catholic Church of the liability to provide such stipends to that extent (see p 134 *f* to *h* and p 135 *e f*, post).

*Re Caus, Lindeboom v Camille* [1933] All ER Rep 818 followed.

*Bourne v Keane* [1918–19] All ER Rep 167 and *Gilmour v Coats* [1949] 1 All ER 848 considered.

*f*      Per curiam. Where a decision on a point of law in a particular sense was essential to an earlier decision of a superior court, but that court had merely assumed the correctness of the law on a particular issue, a judge in a later case is not bound to hold that the law is as decided in that sense by the superior court (see p 133 *g*, post); dictum of May LJ in *Ashville Investments Ltd v Elmer Contractors Ltd* [1988] 2 All ER 577 at 582 applied.

*g*  **Notes**

For gifts for religious purposes, see 5 Halsbury's Laws (4th edn) paras 529, 555, and for cases on the subject, see 8(1) Digest (Reissue) 403–419, *2643–2818*.

**Cases referred to in judgment**

*Ashville Investments Ltd v Elmer Contractors Ltd* [1988] 2 All ER 577, [1988] 3 WLR 867,
*h*    CA.

*Baker v R* [1975] 3 All ER 55, [1975] AC 774, [1975] 3 WLR 113, PC.

*Banfield (decd), Re, Lloyds Bank Ltd v Smith* [1968] 2 All ER 276, [1968] 1 WLR 846.

*Barrs v Bethell* [1982] 1 All ER 106, [1982] Ch 294, [1981] 3 WLR 874.

*Bourne v Keane* [1919] AC 815, [1918–19] All ER Rep 167, HL; *rvsg sub nom Re Egan,*
       *Keane v Hoare* [1918] 2 Ch 350, CA.

*j*  *Caus, Re, Lindeboom v Camille* [1934] Ch 162, [1933] All ER Rep 818.

*Gilmour v Coats* [1949] 1 All ER 848, [1949] AC 426, HL; *affg* [1948] 1 All ER 521, [1948]
       Ch 340, CA; *affg* [1947] 2 All ER 422, [1948] Ch 1.

*Heath v Chapman* (1854) 2 Drew 417, 61 ER 781.

*Hoare v Hoare* (1886) 56 LT 147, [1886–90] All ER Rep 553.

*National Anti-Vivisection Society v IRC* [1947] 2 All ER 217, [1948] AC 31, HL.
*West v Shuttleworth* (1835) 2 My & K 684, 39 ER 1106.
*White, Re, White v White* [1893] 2 Ch 41, [1891–4] All ER Rep 242, CA.
*Yeap Cheah Neo v Ong Cheng Neo* (1875) LR 6 PC 381.

**Cases also cited**
*Barclay, Re, Gardner v Barclay, Steuart v Barclay* [1929] 2 Ch 173, [1929] All ER Rep 272, Ch D and CA.
*Close v Steel Co of Wales Ltd* [1961] 2 All ER 953, [1962] AC 367, HL.
*Cocks v Manners* (1871) LR 12 Eq 574.
*Delany, Re, Conoley v Quick* [1902] 2 Ch 642.
*Dingle v Turner* [1972] 1 All ER 878, [1972] AC 601, HL.
*FA & AB Ltd v Lupton (Inspector of Taxes)* [1971] 3 All ER 948, [1972] AC 634, HL.
*Guaranty Trust Co of New York v Hannay & Co* [1918] 2 KB 623, [1918–19] All ER Rep 151, CA.
*Hallisy, Re* [1932] 4 DLR 516, Ont CA.
*King, Re, Kerr v Bradley* [1923] 1 Ch 243, [1923] All ER Rep 688.
*Monk, Re, Giffen v Wedd* [1927] 2 Ch 197, [1927] All ER Rep 157, CA.
*Straus v Goldsmid* (1837) 8 Sim 614, 59 ER 243.
*Watson (decd), Re, Hobbs v Smith* [1973] 3 All ER 678, [1973] 1 WLR 1472.

**Originating summons**
By an originating summons dated 12 November 1987 the plaintiff, John William Barratt Gibbs, the administrator of the will of Margaret Josephine Hetherington deceased, sought, inter alia, the determination of the court on the question whether on the true construction of the will the gifts of £2,000 to 'the Roman Catholic Church Bishop of Westminster for the repose of the souls of my husband and my parents and my sisters and also myself when I die' and 'Whatever is left over of my estate is to be given to the Roman Catholic Church St Edwards Golders Green for masses for my soul' constituted an absolute immediate gift, a gift subject to a valid condition, a gift imposing a valid charitable trust or a gift void as contrary to public policy. The respondents were Deirdre McDonnell, who was one of the next-of-kin of the deceased, and the Attorney General. The facts are set out in the judgment.

*J H G Sunnucks* for the plaintiff.
*J G Ross Martyn* for the first defendant.
*Peter Crampin* for the Attorney General.

**SIR NICOLAS BROWNE-WILKINSON V-C.** This case raises a question on the will of Mrs Hetherington dated 17 November 1980 which she made in her own hand. The testatrix was a devout Roman Catholic. At the date of her will she worshipped regularly at a church, St Edward's, Golders Green. The two gifts in the will which are relevant are as follows:

'I wish to leave two thousand pounds to the Roman Catholic Church Bishop of Westminster for masses for the repose of the souls of my husband and my parents and my sisters and also myself when I die.'

The other gift is:

'Whatever is left over of my estate is to be given to the Roman Catholic Church St. Edwards, Golders Green for masses for my soul.'

The question which arises is whether or not those gifts being gifts for the saying of Masses establish valid charitable trusts.

The first defendant is one of the next of kin of the testatrix. Her own personal wish is
*a* that the gifts contained in those trusts should take effect. However, she has been joined
as a representative defendant and represented by counsel who has put forward all the
arguments in favour of the trusts failing.

The nature of the Mass in the doctrine of the Roman Catholic Church was summarised
by Luxmoore J in *Re Caus, Lindeboom v Camille* [1934] Ch 162 at 167–168, [1933] All ER
Rep 818 at 820 in these terms:

*b*
'According to the doctrines of the Roman Catholic Church the Mass is a true and
real sacrifice offered to God by the priest, not in his own person only, but in the
name of the church whose minister he is. Every Mass, on whatever occasion used, is
offered to God in the name of the church, to propitiate His anger, to return thanks
for His benefits, and to bring down His blessings upon the whole world. Some
portions of the Mass are invariable and some are variable. Amongst those invariable
*c*
"are an offering of the Host by the priest for his own sins and for all present, and also
for all faithful Christians both living and dead, and the sacrifice is offered for the
church, and the granting to it of peace, and its preservation and union. It includes
commemoration of the living and of the dead; and he states that it is impossible,
according to the doctrine of the church, that a Mass can be offered for the benefit of
*d*
one or more individuals living or dead to the exclusion of the general objects
included by the church. When an honorarium is given, for the purpose of saying a
Mass for a departed soul, the priest is bound to say it with that intention, but that
obligation may be discharged by a mental act of the priest, but it cannot be
discharged by the ordinary parochial Mass which he says on Sundays and holy days.
Such honoraria for Masses form a portion of the ordinary income and means of
*e*
livelihood of priests, and are generally in Ireland distributed by those to whom the
distribution is entrusted among priests whose circumstances are such that they stand
in need of the assistance offered."'

That that summary is applicable to the Roman Catholic Church in this country is
broadly confirmed by the evidence before me from Mgr Brown. In addition, he adds
certain other matters. First, Mgr Brown states that the Mass for departed souls is
*f* invariably celebrated in public in the sense that the public are free to attend. There is no
obligation to celebrate the Mass in public as a matter of canon law. Second, Mgr Brown
states that a stipend is payable to the priest for each Mass said with the intention of
benefiting the soul of a departed individual. Such payments received by the celebrant
relieve the funds of the diocese pro tanto from the cost of providing for the maintenance
of that priest.

*g*
Mgr Brown's evidence further raised some question whether the regulations applicable
within the Archdiocese of Westminster operated so as to prevent the application of the
substantial funds contained in this residuary gift wholly in the payment of stipends for
the saying of Masses for the departed. However, in the course of the evidence it became
plain that in a case where a separate trust such as the residuary gift in this case is
*h* established, there is no reason either in the practice of the Church or in canon law to
prevent the whole of the residue being used for the stated purposes. Counsel for the first
defendant accepted in the light of Mgr Brown's extended evidence that there was here no
question of impracticability in carrying out the trust.

The first point that was argued was that there was here no trust for the saying of Masses
but either an outright gift or a gift conditional on the saying of Masses. I have no doubt
*j* that those submissions are wrong. It is true that in certain cases where precatory words
are used it is a question whether or not the intention of the testator was to impose a
mandatory trust. That kind of question arises where there is a gift to an individual and
then a super-added requirement prefaced by such words as 'in the confidence that' he
will do certain things. In neither of the gifts here in question are there any precatory
words. It is simply a gift for Masses. In my judgment those words are mandatory and

impose a trust. Quite apart from that, in the case of the residuary gift, there is no legatee
to whom it can be said that there was an absolute gift or a conditional gift. The gift is to   *a*
a church, not an individual.

The question therefore is whether a trust for Masses is or is not charitable. In *Re Caus*
Luxmoore J decided that trusts for Masses for the repose of souls were charitable, and he
held that notwithstanding the fact that in *Re Caus* there was no specific requirement that
such Masses should be celebrated in public. In *Gilmour v Coats* [1949] 1 All ER 848,
[1949] AC 426 comments were made on *Re Caus*, some of them adverse. It is therefore   *b*
said that the decision in *Gilmour v Coats* has cast doubt on the validity of the decision in
*Re Caus*. In order to understand the position it is necessary to say something of the
historical development of the law on this subject.

In the nineteenth century it was established by authority at Appeal Court level that a
gift for Masses was void as being for a superstitious use rendered illegal under the
Dissolution of Colleges Act 1547: see *West v Shuttleworth* (1835) 2 My & K 684, 39 ER   *c*
1106 and *Heath v Chapman* (1854) 2 Drew 417, 61 ER 781. The further question arose in
those earlier cases whether, even assuming that the gift was void as being for a
superstitious use, the gift being for a charitable purpose was applicable cy-près for other
charitable purposes. It was therefore necessary for the decision in both these cases to
decide whether or not the trusts were charitable. In both cases the trusts were held to be
not only void for illegality but also not charitable.   *d*

The matter came before the House of Lords in *Bourne v Keane* [1919] AC 815, [1918–
19] All ER Rep 167. The simple question was whether a gift or trust for Masses for the
repose of souls was valid. In that case there were a number of pecuniary legacies to
Roman Catholic communities for Masses and the residue was given to the Jesuit Fathers
at Farm Street for Masses. In the Court of Appeal, sub nom *Re Egan, Keane v Hoare* [1918]
2 Ch 350, the legatees argued not only that the gifts were not illegal under the 1547 Act   *e*
but also that they were valid charitable trusts. In the Court of Appeal the next of kin also
argued the charity point, contending that the trusts were not charitable. The Court of
Appeal in very short judgments held the trusts void.

When the case went to the House of Lords the legatees in argument submitted that
not only were the gifts for Masses lawful but also that they were good charitable gifts (see
[1919] AC 815 at 817, 825). The argument of the next of kin as reported was confined   *f*
simply to the point of illegality, no reference being made to any submissions on the
question whether the gifts were charitable. The House of Lords held that the gift was
not void as being for a superstitious use rendered illegal by the 1547 Act. However, with
the possible exception of Lord Buckmaster (see [1919] AC 815 at 875, [1918–19] All ER
Rep 167 at 193), the speeches made no clear reference to the charity point. The House of
Lords declared that all the gifts in that case were valid gifts (see [1919] AC 815 at 926).   *g*

There was considerable argument before me whether the decision in *Bourne v Keane*
binds me to hold that a trust for Masses is a valid trust. That conclusion might have been
reached either on the basis that a trust for Masses is a valid charitable trust or on the basis
that a trust for Masses is one of that anomalous class of case where a trust for a non-
charitable purpose is valid (see the discussion in Morris and Leach *The Rule against*   *h*
*Perpetuities* (2nd edn, 1962) p 307–321).

In *Bourne v Keane* on the facts there was no question of perpetuity: the gifts were
outright gifts. The rule of law that non-perpetuitous gifts for non-charitable purposes are
void has developed since the House of Lords decided *Bourne v Keane* in 1919. This
probably accounts for the submission made by counsel for the legatees which implied
that, since the gifts were not perpetuitous, it was irrelevant whether or not the trusts   *j*
were charitable (see [1919] AC 815 at 825). It probably also accounts for the fact that the
speeches in the House of Lords did not deal with the charity question.

However, the fact remains that the House of Lords did decide that a trust for Masses
was a valid trust and that under the law as we know it now to be such trusts cannot be
valid unless (a) they were not illegal under the 1547 Act and (b) they were either

charitable trusts or trusts of the anomalous class. The question therefore is whether I am
*a* bound by the decision made by the House of Lords to hold that in the present case the
claim of the next of kin must fail.

In my judgment, I am not so bound. In *Baker v R* [1975] 3 All ER 55 at 64, [1975] AC
774 at 788 Lord Diplock, after mentioning that the Judicial Committee of the Privy
Council does not normally allow parties to raise for the first time on appeal a point of law
not argued in the court below, said:

*b*
'A consequence of this practice is that in its opinions delivered on an appeal the
Board may have assumed, without itself deciding, that a proposition of law which
was not disputed by the parties in the court from which the appeal is brought is
correct. The proposition of law so assumed to be correct may be incorporated,
whether expressly or by implication, in the ratio decidendi of the particular appeal;
but because it does not bear the authority of an opinion reached by the Board itself
*c* it does not create a precedent for use in the decision of other cases.'

That decision was applied in *Barrs v Bethell* [1982] 1 All ER 106 at 116, [1982] Ch 294
at 308, where after quoting the passage I have read from Lord Diplock, Warner J
continued:

*d*
'In my judgment, the principle that, where a court assumes a proposition of law
to be correct without addressing its mind to it, the decision of that court is not
binding authority for that proposition applies generally. It is not confined to
decisions of the Judicial Committee of the Privy Council . . .'

That approach coincides with some words of May LJ in the recent Court of Appeal case
of *Ashville Investments Ltd v Elmer Contractors Ltd* [1988] 2 All ER 577 at 582, [1988] 3
*e* WLR 867 at 873 where he said:

'In my opinion the doctrine of precedent only involves this: that when a case has
been decided in a court it is only the legal principle or principles on which that
court has so decided that bind courts of concurrent or lower jurisdictions and require
them to follow and adopt them when they are relevant to the decision in later cases
*f* before those courts. The ratio decidendi of a prior case, the reason why it was
decided as it was, is in my view only to be understood in this somewhat limited
sense.'

In my judgment the authorities therefore clearly establish that even where a decision
of a point of law in a particular sense was essential to an earlier decision of a superior
*g* court, but that superior court merely assumed the correctness of the law on a particular
issue, a judge in a later case is not bound to hold that the law is decided in that sense. So
therefore, in my judgment, *Bourne v Keane* is not decisive of the case before me.

I turn then to *Re Caus* [1934] Ch 162, [1933] All ER Rep 818. In that case there were
two gifts for foundation Masses for the repose of souls. Foundation Masses are perpetual
income trusts. It was argued that the trusts for Masses for the repose of souls were not
*h* charitable and that accordingly the gifts were void for perpetuity. Luxmoore J held that
the trusts were charitable. He noted that the earlier decisions in *West v Shuttleworth* (1835)
2 My & K 684, 39 ER 1106 and *Heath v Chapman* (1854) 2 Drew 417, 61 ER 781 that such
trusts were illegal, had been overruled by *Bourne v Keane*. However, he treated those two
earlier decisions as still subsisting authority on the question whether trusts for Masses
were or were not charitable.

*j* He distinguished the earlier cases on the basis that the evidence before him (which is
the evidence I have already read) showed that the earlier decisions proceeded on an
erroneous assumption of fact. He decided that the gifts were charitable on the following
grounds ([1934] Ch 162 at 170, [1933] All ER Rep 818 at 821):

'. . . first, that it enables a ritual act to be performed which is recognised by a large

proportion of Christian people to be the central act of their religion, and, secondly,
because it assists in the endowment of priests whose duty it is to perform that ritual   *a*
act.'

Earlier in his judgment, however, after quoting the evidence which I have read, he
said ([1934] Ch 162 at 168, [1933] All ER Rep 818 at 820):

> 'On that evidence, apart from the decisions in *West* v. *Shuttleworth* and *Heath* v.
> *Chapman*, could there be any real doubt but that a gift for Masses was charitable in   *b*
> the sense which is derived [from the Charitable Uses Act 1601], because the object
> must necessarily be one which is not only for the public benefit, but for the
> advancement of religion.'

It is that statement that it must necessarily be for the public benefit that gave rise to
difficulty in the later House of Lords decision of *Gilmour v Coats* [1949] 1 All ER 848,   *c*
[1949] AC 426. *Re Caus* has stood now for over 50 years and I would certainly follow it
unless it has been undermined by the decision of the House of Lords in *Gilmour v Coats*.

In the latter case there was gift on trust to apply income for the purposes of a Roman
Catholic community of cloistered nuns who devoted their lives to prayer, contemplation,
penance and self-sanctification within their convent, from which the public was wholly
excluded. The nuns did not engage in any work outside their convent. The House of   *d*
Lords held that the trusts were not valid charitable trusts since they lacked any element
of public benefit. The only benefits alleged to accrue to the public at large were said to
accrue through the effects of intercessory prayer, which the House of Lords said were
incapable of proof, or by edification by example which the House of Lords held to be too
intangible.

In argument before the House of Lords *Re Caus* was relied on. Lord Simonds pointed   *e*
out that the actual grounds for decision in *Re Caus* did not rely on the public benefiting
by means of intercessory prayer and example (see [1949] 1 All ER 848 at 855, [1949] AC
426 at 447–448). He reserved the question whether the decision in *Re Caus* was itself
right on other grounds. Lord du Parcq also reserved the same question. Lord Reid
pointed out that there were grounds, other than the alleged public benefit by means of
prayer, on which it could be argued that *Re Caus* was rightly decided, but he too expressed   *f*
no opinion on the point (see [1949] 1 All ER 848 at 863, [1949] AC 426 at 460).

In my judgment *Gilmour v Coats* does not impair the validity of the decision in *Re Caus*.
Certainly the passage from the judgment of Luxmoore J which I have quoted which
suggests that public benefit can be shown from the mere celebration of a religious rite is
no longer good law. The same in my judgment is true of Luxmoore J's first ground of
decision, if it suggests that the performance *in private* of a religious ritual act is charitable   *g*
as being for the public benefit. But in my judgment there is nothing in the House of
Lords decision which impugns Luxmoore J's second ground of decision, namely that the
public benefit was to be found in the endowment of the priesthood. Therefore the
decision in *Re Caus* is still good law and I must follow it.

I do so without reluctance because it accords with my own views on the matter,
though the reasoning by which I reach that conclusion is rather different.   *h*

The grounds on which the trust in the present case can be attacked are that there is no
*express* requirement that the Masses for souls which are to be celebrated are to be
celebrated in public. The evidence shows that celebration in public is the invariable
practice but there is no requirement of canon law to that effect. Therefore it is said the
money could be applied to saying Masses in private which would not be charitable since
there would be no sufficient element of public benefit.   *j*

In my judgment the cases establish the following propositions. (1) A trust for the
advancement of education, the relief of poverty or the advancement of religion is prima
facie charitable and assumed to be for the public benefit: see *National Anti-Vivisection
Society v IRC* [1947] 2 All ER 217 at 220, 233, [1948] AC 31 at 42, 65. This assumption of

public benefit can be rebutted by showing that in fact the particular trust in question
*a* cannot operate so as to confer a legally recognised benefit on the public, as in *Gilmour v Coats*. (2) The celebration of a religious rite in public does confer a sufficient public benefit because of the edifying and improving effect of such celebration on the members of the public who attend. As Lord Reid said in *Gilmour v Coats* [1949] 1 All ER 848 at 862, [1949] AC 426 at 459:

*b*      'A religion can be regarded as beneficial without it being necessary to assume that all its beliefs are true, and a religious service can be regarded as beneficial to all those who attend it without it being necessary to determine the spiritual efficacy of that service or to accept any particular belief about it.'

(3) The celebration of a religious rite in private does not contain the necessary element of public benefit since any benefit by prayer or example is incapable of proof in the legal *c* sense, and any element of edification is limited to a private, not public, class of those present at the celebration: see *Gilmour v Coats* itself; *Yeap Cheah Neo v Ong Cheng Neo* (1875) LR 6 PC 381 and *Hoare v Hoare* (1886) 56 LT 147, [1886–90] All ER Rep 553. (4) Where there is a gift for a religious purpose which could be carried out in a way which is beneficial to the public (ie by public Masses) but could also be carried out in a way which would not have sufficient element of public benefit (ie by private Masses) the *d* gift is to be construed as a gift to be carried out only by the methods that are charitable, all non-charitable methods being excluded: see *Re White, White v White* [1893] 2 Ch 41 at 52–53, [1891–4] All ER Rep 242 at 244–245 and *Re Banfield (decd), Lloyds Bank Ltd v Smith* [1968] 2 All ER 276, [1968] 1 WLR 846.

Applying those principles to the present case, a gift for the saying of Masses is prima facie charitable, being for a religious purpose. In practice, those Masses will be celebrated *e* in public, which provides a sufficient element of public benefit. The provision of stipends for priests saying the Masses, by relieving the Roman Catholic Church pro tanto of the liability to provide such stipends, is a further benefit. The gift is to be construed as a gift for public Masses only on the principle of *Re White*, private Masses not being permissible since it would not be a charitable application of the fund for a religious purpose.

I will therefore declare that both gifts are valid charitable trusts for the saying of Masses *f* in public. The pecuniary legacy should be paid to the Archbishop of Westminster, who is plainly the person referred to as the Bishop of Westminster, to be held by him on those trusts. Since the will appoints no trustee of the residuary gift, the residuary gift will be dealt with by the Crown under a scheme made under the sign manual.

*g* *Order accordingly.*

Solicitor: *Witham Weld* (for the plaintiff and the first defendant): *Treasury Solicitor.*

Celia Fox   Barrister.

# Rome and another v Punjab National Bank

*a*

QUEEN'S BENCH DIVISION (COMMERCIAL COURT)
HIRST J
27, 28 JUNE, 6 JULY 1988

*Discovery – Production of documents – Jurisdiction – Jurisdiction of court in action disputed –* *b*
*Plaintiffs serving writ on bank – Bank disputing jurisdiction of court and applying to set aside*
*service of writ because of irregularity in service – Plaintiffs applying for discovery of documents*
*held by bank – Whether court having power to order discovery when jurisdiction in issue –*
*Whether discovery necessary for fair disposal of bank's application – RSC Ord 12, r 8(5),*
*Ord 24, r 8.*

*c*
The plaintiffs, acting on behalf of themselves and a number of other Lloyd's syndicates,
brought an action against an Indian bank, PNB, seeking (i) a declaration that two
insurance policies under which PNB was the assured party had been validly avoided and
(ii) repayment of over $US28m paid out under those policies. The writ was served at the
address of the London offices of SBI, another Indian bank. PNB disputed the jurisdiction
of the court in the proceedings and sought an order under RSC Ord 12, r 8ᵃ setting aside  *d*
the writ for irregularity of service, alleging that by the time the plaintiffs had commenced·
their action it had already closed down its United Kingdom banking business, and that
the address at which the writ had been served was not its business address but simply the
offices from which it had co-ordinated the winding down operation. The plaintiffs came
into possession of three letters, the first of which concerned the winding up of PNB's
pension scheme 'consequent upon closure of [PNB's] UK operations' and was written on  *e*
SBI notepaper to a former employee and signed by S as 'Manager—PNB Cell'. The second
was the employee's response and the third was addressed to the employee's financial
adviser and was also written on SBI notepaper and signed by S under the same description.
On the basis of those letters the plaintiffs claimed that PNB continued to perform business
functions within the United Kingdom and to maintain a business address at the London
offices of SBI. The plaintiffs sought discovery of all documents authorising S to act as  *f*
'Manager—PNB Cell' and defining the capacity of that position and all documents signed
by S in that capacity. The issue arose whether the court could order discovery if the
defendant disputed the jurisdiction of the court under Ord 12, r 8.


**Held** – The court had the power to order discovery of documents on a defendant's  *g*
application to set aside a writ for irregularity of service since such an order was an
appropriate direction for disposal of the application under Ord 12, r 8(5), but the court
would exercise that power only very rarely and in exercising its discretion would,
pursuant to RSC Ord 24, r 8ᵇ, require a clear demonstration that discovery was 'necessary'
for the fair disposal' of the application. On the facts, the plaintiffs had failed to show that
discovery was necessary for the fair disposal of PNB's application since nothing in the  *h*
three letters raised any suspicion that the information supplied by PNB was other than
full and frank. Accordingly, the application would be dismissed (see p 141 *d e h j* and
p 142 *b f g j*, post).

**Notes**
For the discretion of the court in granting discovery, see 13 Halsbury's Laws (4th edn)  *j*
para 5, and for cases on the subject, see 18 Digest (Reissue) 44–45, 302–312.

---

*a*   Rule 8, so far as material, is set out at p 139 *h j*, post
*b*   Rule 8, so far as material, is set out at p 140 *e*, post

**Case referred to in judgment**

a *Bekhor (A J) & Co Ltd v Bilton* [1981] 2 All ER 565, [1981] QB 923, [1981] 2 WLR 601, CA.

**Application**

The plaintiffs, Christopher William Rome and Andrew Bathurst, acting on their own behalf and on behalf of a number of other Lloyd's syndicates, by a writ issued on 24 February 1988 sought as against the defendant, Punjab National Bank, (i) a declaration
b that two insurance policies under which the defendant was the assured party had been validly avoided and (ii) repayment of over $US28m paid to the defendant pursuant to those policies. The writ was served at 1 Milk Street, London EC2, being the London offices of the State Bank of India. By a summons dated 7 April 1988 the defendant sought an order under RSC Ord 12, r 8 that service be set aside, and/or a declaration that the writ had not been duly served on the ground that it had no place of business in the United
c Kingdom. By a summons dated 17 June 1988 the plaintiffs sought discovery of certain classes of documents held by the defendant, claiming that the defendant had an established place of business at 1 Milk Street when the writ was served. The plaintiffs' application was heard in chambers but judgment was given by Hirst J in open court. The facts are set out in the judgment.

d *Stephen Ruttle* for the plaintiffs.
*Michael Brindle* for the defendant.

*Cur adv vult*

6 July. The following judgment was delivered.

e
**HIRST J.**

*Introduction*

This case raises the question as to the powers of the court to order discovery of documents in a case where the defendant disputes the jurisdiction of the court under RSC Ord 12, r 8 by reason of an alleged irregularity in the service of the writ on him.
f     Counsel agree that the point is not covered by authority, and for that reason have jointly requested me to give this judgment in open court.

Counsel for the defendant invited me to avoid identification of the parties, but, in view of the special factual features of the case on which my decision will eventually turn, this is not really practicable, as I think counsel himself in the end recognised.

g *Factual background*

The plaintiffs, Mr Christopher William Rome and Mr Adrew Bathurst, sue on their own behalf and on behalf of a number of other Lloyd's syndicates claiming a declaration that two policies of insurance under which the defendant, Punjab National Bank, was the assured have been validly avoided, and also claiming repayment of a sum in excess of $US28m which was paid pursuant to a claim under these policies. The detailed basis of
h the plaintiffs' claim and the issues which arise are immaterial for present purposes.

The writ was issued in the Commercial Court on 24 February 1988 and was served or purportedly served at Fourth Floor, State Bank House, 1 Milk Street, London EC2P 2JP.

By summons dated 7 April 1988 the defendant seeks an order pursuant to Ord 12, r 8 that the service of the writ on the defendant be set aside and/or it be declared that the writ had not been duly served on the defendant.
j     In essence, the grounds of this application are that at the date of the commencement of the action the defendant, which is of course a foreign corporation whose head office is in New Delhi, India, had no place of business in Great Britain, and that the address at which the writ was served was not the defendant's address but that of the State Bank of India.

The evidence in support of this application is contained in an affidavit of Mr Nicholas Jeremy Archer, an assistant solicitor in Messrs Slaughter & May, who have been instructed by the defendant in connection with its application. Much of his evidence is not in dispute and may be summarised as follows. (a) Until 1986 the defendant carried on banking business at Moor House, London Wall, and at other branches elsewhere in the United Kingdom. (b) By late 1986 the defendant resolved that no further business should be done in Great Britain, and that consequently all its offices in this country should be closed. (c) Pursuant to various agreements, the bulk of its assets were transferred to the State Bank of India during 1987. (d) However, during that year the defendant retained some business presence in Great Britain, although it carried out no new business. (e) In December 1987 those of its assets which had not been transferred to the State Bank of India were transferred back to the defendant's own head office in India. (f )By the end of 1987 the transitional period was over and the defendant surrendered its authorisation under the Banking Act 1987 to the Bank of England with effect from 31 December 1987. (g)The winding down operation during 1987 was carried out by two employees of the defendant, one of whom was a Mr Golani, from the offices of the State Bank of India at the address at 1 Milk Street.

I now come to the more controversial part of Mr Archer's evidence, which I wish to quote verbatim:

'Since early 1988 the Defendant has had no employees working for it in Great Britain and has not rented any accommodation of any kind here. It owns no office accommodation; it owned the house which used to be occupied by Mr Golani before he left. This was sold on 4 March, 1988. The Defendant conducts no form of public relations and there is no gathering or disseminating of any financial information in Great Britain at all. No new banking business has been done since the end of 1986, and all accounts then open have either been transferred to the State Bank of India or have been transferred back to the Defendant's head office in India. No formal representation is made, by name-plate or otherwise, at the offices of State Bank of India. Nothing remains. State Bank of India is effecting the detailed working out of the machinery of completion of the transfer of the 1987 assets. This is, however, a mere matter of machinery, in order to give effect to the discontinuance by the Defendant of all business activity in Great Britain as from, at the latest, the end of 1987. As regards State Bank of India, it merely provides a point of contact in London for the Defendant's solicitors in order to enable instructions easily to be obtained from the Defendant's head office in India. So far as the Defendant is concerned it does not consider that it now carries on any business in Great Britain.'

In support of the validity of the service, the plaintiffs have two strings to their bow. First, they rely on formal documents which were undoubtedly filed by the defendant in the Companies Registry on 13 August 1987 giving the address in Milk·Street and, inter alios, Mr Golani's name as a person resident in Great Britain authorised to accept service on behalf of the company pursuant to s 692(1)(c) of the Companies Act 1985. The defendant disputes the plaintiffs' claim under this heading, and the point will in due course have to be resolved at the hearing of the summons, but for present purposes it can be disregarded since it does not give rise to any claim for discovery. The second string to the plaintiffs' bow is a submission that, contrary to the evidence of Mr Archer, the defendant indeed had at the time when the writ was served an established place of business at 1 Milk Street.

The present basis of this part of their case, and also of the application for discovery, is three documents which have recently come into the plaintiffs' hands. These are crucial to the issue I have to decide, and it is necessary to quote at least one of them, namely a letter dated 19 May 1988 written on the notepaper of the State Bank of India at the Milk Street address and signed, 'Harwant Singh Manager—PNB Cell' to a Mr Peter Scrivens under the heading, 'Our reference PNB/Pension'. The text of the letter is as follows:

'*Re: Punjab National Bank Superplan 157291 Pension Scheme*

a    You are already aware that consequent upon closure of Punjab National Bank's UK operations on 31st December 1986, the above Pension Scheme is in the process of being wound up. As per the Pension Scheme rule, you now have the following two options: 1. Obtain Crown Financial Management's Certificate of Entitlement to Benefits; or 2. Get transfer into another Company's Pension Scheme/Contract with another Insurer (Section 32). The required documentation for the above

b    mentioned two options is ready with us. We request you to elect from one of these options immediately and confirm the same either in writing or on the telephone, but in no case later than 20 days from the date of this letter, to enable us to send you the required documents for further action.'

The second letter is Mr Scrivens's reply dated 26 May electing to opt for the second of

c    the two options suggested, and giving the name and address of his financial adviser.

The third letter, also on State Bank of India notepaper and signed under the same description by Mr Harwant Singh, is dated 8 June and is addressed to Mr Scrivens's financial advisers giving them the requisite details.

The essence of the plaintiffs' case, based on these letters, is that the fact that Mr Harwant Singh signed himself as 'Manager—PNB Cell' is a clear indication that the

d    defendant continues to perform business functions within the United Kingdom, and maintain an established business at the Milk Street address. As a result, by the present summons for discovery, the plaintiffs seek discovery of the following classes of documents:

'All documents defining the capacity and/or authorising Mr Harwant Singh and/or any other individual to act as Manager of the Punjab National Bank Cell, London.

e    All documents or correspondence signed by Mr Harwant Singh and/or any other individual, in the capacity of Manager of the Punjab National Bank Cell, London. All documents brought into being as a result of an act or acts performed by Mr Harwant Singh or any other individual in the capacity of Manager of the Punjab National Bank Cell, London.'

f    *The relevant rules of procedure*

Order 12, rr 7 and 8, which are the basis of the present application, provide as follows, so far as relevant, particular attention being directed to para (5) of Ord 12, r 8:

'*Acknowledgment not to constitute waiver*

7. The acknowledgment by a defendant of service of a writ shall not be treated as a waiver by him of any irregularity in the writ or service thereof or in any order

g    giving leave to serve the writ out of the jurisdiction or extending the validity of the writ for the purpose of service.

*Dispute as to jurisdiction*

8.—1(1) A defendant who wishes to dispute the jurisdiction of the court in the proceedings by reason of any such irregularity as is mentioned in rule 7 or on any

h    other ground shall give notice of intention to defend the proceedings and shall, within the time limited for service of a defence, apply to the Court for—(a) an order setting aside the writ or service of the writ on him, or (b) an order declaring that the writ has not been duly served on him, or (c) the discharge of any order giving leave to serve the writ on him out of the jurisdiction, or (d) the discharge of any order extending the validity of the writ for the purpose of service, or (e) the protection or

j    release of any property of the defendant seized or threatened with seizure in the proceedings, or (f) the discharge of any order made to prevent any dealing with any property of the defendant, or (g) a declaration that in the circumstances of the case the court has no jurisdiction over the defendant in respect of the subject matter of the claim or the relief or remedy sought in the action, or (h)such other relief as may be appropriate . . .

(5) Upon hearing an application under paragraph (1), the Court, if it does not dispose of the matter in dispute, may give such directions for its disposal as may be *a* appropriate, including directions for the trial thereof as a preliminary issue . . .'.

The general rules covering applications for discovery for specific documents are contained in Ord 24, rr 7 and 8, which so far as relevant provide as follows:

'*Order for discovery of particular documents*
7.—(1) Subject to rule 8, the Court may at any time, on the application of any *b* party to a cause or matter, make an order requiring any other party to make an affidavit stating whether any document specified or described in the application or any class of document so specified or described is, or has at any time been, in his possession, custody or power, and if not then in his possession, custody or power when he parted with it and what has become of it.
(2) An order may be made against a party under this rule notwithstanding that *c* he may already have made or been required to make a list of documents or affidavits under rule 2 or rule 3.
(3) An application for an order under this rule must be supported by an affidavit stating the belief of the dependent that the party from whom discovery is sought under this rule has, or at some time had, in his possession, custody or power the document, or class of document, specified or described in the application and that it *d* relates to one or more of the matters in question in the cause or matter.

*Discovery to be ordered only if necessary*
8. On the hearing of an application for an order under rule 3, 7 or 7A the Court, if satisfied that discovery is not necessary, or not necessary at that stage of the cause or matter, may dismiss or, as the case may be, adjourn the application and shall in *e* any case refuse to make such an order if and so far as it is of opinion that discovery is not necessary either for disposing fairly of the cause or matter or for saving costs.'

*Jurisdiction*
Counsel for the plaintiffs submits that the court has jurisdiction to make the order *f* sought under both these rules on the footing that an order for discovery is, in a proper case, an appropriate direction for disposal of the application under Ord 12, r 8(5), and that this present application is within Ord 24, r 7 since the affidavit of Mr John Simon Todd, as assistant solicitor employed by Messrs Ince & Co, the plaintiffs' solicitors, in support of the application demonstrates by reference to the three above-mentioned letters that the discovery sought relates to one or more of the matters in question in the present *g* cause or matter, namely the question whether the court has jurisdiction.
Counsel for the defendant accepts that the wording of Ord 12, r 8(5) is capable of bearing the construction put forward by the plaintiffs, but submits that the preferable interpretation is a much narrower meaning, namely that it is limited to directions of an administrative character, eg as to the date, place and mode of resolution of the issues at stake. He points out that nothing is said about discovery and he submits, as a matter of *h* basic principle, that, on an application where the very existence of the court's jurisdiction is put in issue, it is inappropriate for the court to impose its own special procedures for discovery which are not universally reflected in other jurisdictions elsewhere in the world.
On Ord 24, r 7 he submits that the present application does not relate to 'one or more of the matters in question in the cause or matter', relying for this proposition on the *j* decision of the Court of Appeal in *A J Bekhor & Co Ltd v Bilton* [1981] 2 All ER 565, [1981] QB 923.
In that case the question arose as to the jurisdiction of the court to grant orders for discovery in aid of a Mareva injunction. The court held that such jurisdiction was properly based on the predecessor of the present s 37(3) of the Supreme Court Act 1981,

but not under Ord 24, r 7. The basis of this decision was that on their proper construction
*a* 'matters in question in the cause or matter' meant matters in issue in the action itself,
and that the matters in question in the Mareva injunction were not in issue in the action,
for the following reasons epitomised in the judgment of Stephenson LJ, which are
reflected in similar passages in the judgments of Ackner and Griffiths LJJ ([1981] 2 All
ER 565 at 585, [1981] QB 923 at 952):

*b*      'The matters in question in the Mareva injunction are not in issue in the action.
The plaintiffs do not have to prove the existence of assets of the defendant within
the jurisdiction and the risk of their being removed out of the jurisdiction in order
to prove their case or obtain judgment; the plaintiffs want the injunction and
discovery in aid of it in order to preserve something out of which any judgment
they may obtain on proving their case can be executed and satisfied. That is the
*c*      matter in question to which this discovery relates.'

While counsel accepts that the present case is not on all fours with a Mareva injunction,
he argues that, on the proper interpretation of the rule in the light of the *Bekhor* case,
discovery is limited to matters which need to be proved in a properly constituted action,
thus excluding issues as to jurisdiction.

*d*      In my judgment, jurisdiction exists under both headings. So far as Ord 12, r 8 is
concerned, it seems to me that on their natural construction the words 'such directions'
are apt to include orders for discovery. Such an order, coupled with one for inspection of
disclosed documents, is an everyday occurrence within the ambit of a summons for
directions in almost every action in every division of the court; indeed, by Ord 25,
r 8(1)(a), an order for discovery of documents is the first item in the list of 'the following
directions' which take effect automatically in personal injury actions.

*e*      This also seems to me to be inherent in the express power contained in Ord 12, r 8(5),
albeit very rarely exercised, to direct a trial of an application under the rule as a
preliminary issue, since it seems inconceivable that the rule-makers can have envisaged a
trial of a preliminary issue bereft of discovery. On the other hand, nothing in the
wording supports counsel's submission that directions should be narrowly interpreted as
*f*  comprising nothing more than administrative orders.

So far as Ord 24, r 7 is concerned, a question as to the jursidiction of the court, such as
is raised in any application under Ord 12, r 8, seems to me without doubt to raise an issue
in the action, and thus fall within the criteria laid down in the *Bekhor* case. This is fully
in accordance with the closing words of Ord 12, r 8(5), to which I have just referred,
which speak of the trial of 'a preliminary *issue*'. Once the question is raised by the
*g*  defendant as it has been here, it is incumbent on the plaintiff to establish as an essential
first step in his action that service has been properly effected, so as to give the court the
necessary jurisdiction. This is in complete contrast to the situation in a Mareva
application, where, as is shown by the above quotation from Stephenson LJ, the issues
which arise have no bearing at all on success or failure in the action itself, but only come
into play when a successful plaintiff seeks to enforce his judgment. I should add for
*h*  completeness that it is common ground between counsel that at the present juncture
both the plaintiffs and the defendant are 'parties to the action' within the meaning of
Ord 24, r 7(1).

It follows that I hold as a matter of principle that the court has jursidiction to make the
order sought here. That being said, however, I wish to stress that, as counsel for the
plaintiffs himself accepts, the court will only exercise its powers under this heading very
*j*  rarely, and will require the clearest possible demonstration from the party seeking
discovery that it is necessary for the fair disposal of the application. I say this for two
reasons. In the first place, the court is naturally reluctant to place such a burden on a
defendant who disputes the basic jurisdiction of the court, for the reasons put forward by
counsel for the defendant. Secondly, applications under Ord 12, r 8 are a fairly common
feature of court business, most particularly in the Commercial Court when dealing with

applications to set aside leave granted ex parte under Ord 11 for service out of the
jurisdiction, and they are normally dealt with by a hearing on affidavit evidence (see *The*
*Supreme Court Practice 1988* vol 1, para 12/7–8/5). It would be most undesirable, and
productive of extra delay and unnecessary expense, if applications for discovery were to
become a common feature in such cases.

*Exercise of my discretion*
Here the cardinal consideration is that prescribed by Ord 24, r 8, namely whether the
court is of the opinion that the discovery sought is necessary for the fair disposal of this
application.

Counsel for the plaintiffs submits that the three letters raise a reasonable suspicion that
the defendant has been less than full and frank in the information it has given to Mr
Archer, and that the discovery sought is consequently necessary for the fair disposal of
the Ord 12, r 8 application in order to enable the plaintiffs to pursue a case that Mr
Harwant Singh is continuing to conduct business on behalf of the defendant at 1 Milk
Street, under authority conferred on him by the defendant.

In considering this submission, the three documents themselves deserve close scrutiny.
It is manifest that they relate to the pension arrangements of a past employee of the
defendants. Obviously, even after the complete closure of a business, there will remain a
number of loose ends which have to be tied up, and pension arrangements such as these
are an obvious instance in this category; another might be an Inland Revenue or Customs
and Excise query concerning past PAYE or VAT payments, or any outstanding steps
required for the transfer of the United Kingdom assets of the business which has ceased
to be conducted here. This last aspect is expressly referred to by Mr Archer in his affidavit
in the above quotation when he says:

'State Bank of India is effecting the detailed working out of the machinery of
completion of the transfer of the 1987 assets; this is, however, a mere matter of
machinery in order to give effect to the discontinuance by the defendants of all
business activity in Great Britain as from, at the latest, the end of 1987.'

In my judgment these pension arrangements are no more than another aspect of the
machinery in order to give effect to the discontinuance by the defendant of its United
Kingdom business, so that nothing in these three letters is in any way inconsistent with
the evidence presented by Mr Archer on behalf of the defendant bank. They thus raise
in my mind no vestige of a suspicion that the information that the defendant has supplied
to Mr Archer is other than full and frank.

This is underlined by the fact that the letter is written on State Bank of India notepaper,
thus suggesting that they and not the defendant are the effective authors, and the
description 'Manager—PNB Cell' seems to me perfectly apt to connote the office entity
within the State Bank of India which is, as Mr Archer testifies, handling the loose ends of
the defendant's now defunct United Kingdom business.

Finally, and this is by no means the least telling point, the opening sentence of the first
of the three letters, which I have quoted in full, states in terms that the pension scheme
is in the process of being wound up 'consequent upon closure of Punjab National Bank's
UK operations on 31st December 1986'.

If (which there is not) there had been any evidence produced by the plaintiffs of a
continuance in some shape or form of the defendant's banking business in 1988, I should
have been not unsympathetic to the application for discovery, even bearing in mind the
need to grant such orders only very sparingly.

But as it is, for the reasons given above, the plaintiffs have completely failed to satisfy
me that this discovery is necessary for the fair disposal of this application, and for that
reason, in the exercise of my discretion, and as expressly enjoined by Ord 24, r 8, I shall
dismiss this application. Counsel for the defendant raised a number of other matters
connected with the question of discretion, but in view of the clear conclusion which I

a have reached as expressed above there is no need for me to consider these additional points.

*Application dismissed.*

Solicitors: *Ince & Co* (for the plaintiffs); *Slaughter & May* (for the defendant).

b
K Mydeen Esq   Barrister.


# Behbehani and others v Salem and others

c COURT OF APPEAL, CIVIL DIVISION
NOURSE AND WOOLF LJJ
9, 10, 11 SEPTEMBER 1987

*Practice – Pre-trial or post-judgment relief – Mareva injunction – Ex parte application – Duty of applicant to disclose material facts – Non-disclosure of material facts – Consequences of non-*
d *disclosure – Grant of fresh injunction – Plaintiff failing to disclose existence of proceedings in another jurisdiction when applying for injunction – Judge discharging injunction and immediately regranting fresh injunction in substantially same terms – Test to be applied in discharging and regranting Mareva injunctions – Whether injunction should have been regranted.*

The first plaintiff, a wealthy Kuwaiti national, owned two companies, the second and
e third plaintiffs, which were used by him in his property transactions. In 1976 he met the first defendant, a real estate agent, and began making substantial property investments in England, France, Spain and Canada through the first defendant as his agent. The plaintiffs alleged that the first defendant had acted fraudulently in those transactions and made substantial secret profits, and that the conduct of the other five defendants, who were involved in the transactions or were associated with the first defendant, was also
f fraudulent. Early in 1987 cross-claims were brought in Spain by the first defendant against the first plaintiff and by the first plaintiff against the first and sixth defendants. Each side was granted an embargo preventivo (the Spanish equivalent of a Mareva injunction) by the court. On 31 March notice of the first plaintiff's proceedings, including a notice of the embargo preventivo, were served at the first defendant's Spanish offices. On 8 April notice of the defendants' proceedings were formally served at the plaintiffs'
g Spanish office together with the embargo preventivo which the defendants had obtained. On 9 April 1987 the plaintiffs brought an action in England against the defendants claiming sums in excess of £17m and on the same day they were granted ex parte a Mareva injunction restraining the defendants from dealing with or disposing of their assets within the jurisdiction. The defendants applied for the discharge of the injunction
h on the ground that when applying for the injunction there had been material non-disclosure by the plaintiffs, namely failure to disclose the existence of the Spanish proceedings and other material matters, including the fact that a settlement of part of the action had been reached between the various parties and that the defendants had a counterclaim exceeding £3.2m. The judge discharged the injunction but, on a renewed application made by the plaintiffs, immediately regranted substantially the same
j injunction against each of the defendants. The defendants appealed against the regranting of the injunction.

**Held** – In deciding whether to discharge an existing injunction and grant a fresh injunction where there had been non-disclosure of material matters the court had to consider each case on its own merits, taking into account the considerable public interest

in ensuring that full disclosure was made on ex parte applications for Mareva injunction
and Anton Piller orders. The court had to assess for itself the degree and extent of the *a*
culpability of the non-disclosure and the importance and significance of the matters
which were not disclosed in the light of that public interest, rather than either merely
determining whether the original judge who granted the ex parte injunction would have
been likely to arrive at a different decision if the material matters had been placed before
him or merely balancing the harm that could be caused to the plaintiff if a fresh
injunction was not granted against the matters that were not disclosed. The fact that *b*
proceedings were taking place or were contemplated in another jurisdiction was a highly
material matter to be put before the judge when applying for a Mareva injunction since
the court had to be satisfied that it would not be oppressive for the defendant to be
subject to Mareva-type relief in more than one jurisdiction. The plaintiffs' failure to
disclose the existence of the Spanish proceedings and the settlement was sufficiently
serious for a fresh injunction not to be granted against the defendants especially since the *c*
defendants were prepared to give an undertaking not to dispose of property assets within
the jurisdiction without 28 days' notice to the plaintiffs. The appeal would accordingly
be allowed (see p 149 *e h j*, p 150 *j* to p 151 *a*, p 154 *f* to *h*, p 155 *e g j*, p 156 *a*, p 157 *d* and
p 158 *c* to *g*, post).

> *Brink's-MAT Ltd v Elcombe* [1988] 3 All ER 188 applied.
> *Eastglen International Corp v Monpare SA* (1986) 137 NLJ 56 considered. *d*
> Per Woolf LJ. Quaere whether it is appropriate to regard a disclosure as being deliberate
> when the facts not disclosed were not known to be material at the time albeit that they
> ought to have been known to be material (see p 148 *j* to p 149 *a*, post).

### Notes

For Mareva injunctions, see 37 Halsbury's Laws (4th edn) para 362, and for cases on the *e*
subject, see 37(2) Digest (Reissue) 474–476, 2947–2962.

### Cases referred to in judgments

*Bank Mellat v Nikpour* [1985] FSR 87, CA.
*Brink's-MAT Ltd v Elcombe* [1988] 3 All ER 188, [1988] 1 WLR 1350, CA.
*Columbia Picture Industries Inc v Robinson* [1986] 3 All ER 338, [1987] Ch 38, [1986] 3 *f*
    WLR 542.
*Dalglish v Jarvie* (1850) 2 Mac & G 231, 42 ER 89.
*Eastglen International Corp v Monpare SA* (1986) 137 NLJ 56, CA.
*Lloyds Bowmaker Ltd v Britannia Arrow Holdings plc (Lavens, third party)* [1988] 3 All ER
    178, [1988] 1 WLR 1337, CA.
*R v Kensington Income Tax Comrs, ex p Princess Edmond de Polignac* [1917] 1 KB 486, CA. *g*
*Siporex Trade SA v Comdel Commodities Ltd* [1986] 2 Lloyd's Rep 428.
*Thermax Ltd v Schott Industrial Glass Ltd* [1981] FSR 289.

### Interlocutory appeal

By a writ issued on 9 April 1987 the plaintiffs, (1) Hussain Sayed Hashim Behbehani,
(2) Behbehani Buildings Ltd and (3) Behbehani France SA, a body corporate, brought an *h*
action against the defendants, (1) Maurice Salem, (2) Maurice Salem Investments Ltd,
(3) Camille Salem, (4) Philip Harold Frederick, (5) Philip Frederick (Investments) Ltd and
(6) Bassam Edward Kirreh, for moneys had and received by the defendants and each of
them to the plaintiffs' use, damages for conspiracy to cheat and defraud the plaintiffs and
each of them, damages for deceit, declarations that certain assets were held by the first
defendant and the sixth defendant in trust for the first plaintiff absolutely, a declaration *j*
that the defendants and each of them held on trust for the plaintiffs absolutely all moneys
and assets being the proceeds of moneys had and received by the defendants to the
plaintiffs' use, all necessary accounts and inquiries, and orders for payment of the sums
due. On the same day Roch J, on an ex parte application made by the plaintiffs, granted
a Mareva injunction against the defendants restraining each of them until two weeks

a  after trial or further order from dealing with or otherwise disposing of any of their assets situate within the jurisdiction. The defendants applied for the discharge of the injunction. On 7 May 1987, by order dated 15 May 1987, Rougier J in chambers granted their application but, on the cross-application of the plaintiffs, he granted a fresh Mareva injunction on substantially the same terms against each of the defendants. The defendants appealed. The facts are set out in the judgment of Woolf LJ.

b  *Michael Burton QC, Richard Slowe* and *Stuart Isaacs* for the first, second, fourth, fifth and sixth defendants.
*Murray Rosen* for the third defendant.
*Stanley Brodie QC, Roydon Thomas QC* and *Jeremy Nicholson* for the plaintiffs.

c  **WOOLF LJ** (delivering the first judgment at the invitation of Nourse LJ). This appeal raises the question as to the circumstances in which it is appropriate, having discharged a Mareva and Anton Piller injunction because of the failure of the applicant for that injunction to make proper disclosure to the court, for the court to then immediately regrant substantially the same injunction.

In this case the original injunctions were granted by Roch J on 9 April 1987 in the usual way on an ex parte application. Those injunctions were discharged and regranted d  by Rougier J on 7 May, the order being drawn up on 15 May. The material before this court indicates that the first plaintiff is a Kuwaiti national who is extremely affluent; the second plaintiff is a company (the shares of which are owned by the first plaintiff) and which was used by the first plaintiff in connection with his property transactions (principally or in respect of property situated in England); and the third plaintiff is a French company also owned by the first plaintiff which was used by him in connection e  with his French property transactions.

The first defendant is not without means. He apparently has not always been as wealthy as he is now. The first plaintiff says of him in para 3 of this first affidavit:

'I met the First Defendant for the first time in about 1976 in London. The First Defendant was introduced to me as a real estate agent. He said he specialised in f  acquiring substantial residential properties and land for residential purposes on behalf of his clients. He told me that he had a number of respectable and very wealthy clients from the Middle East for whom he had made substantial profits. I arranged for the First Defendant to purchase some small residential properties in England on my behalf and from 1978 onwards I began making more substantial investments through the First Defendant as my agent. Investments were made in g  England, France, Spain and Canada.'

The second defendant is a company controlled by the first defendant. The third defendant is a son of the first defendant and a director of the second defendant. He assisted in the management of at least two properties acquired on behalf of the plaintiffs in England. The fourth defendant is the chairman and managing director of the fifth defendant, and the fourth and fifth defendants were involved in certain of the plaintiff's h  property transactions. The sixth defendant is closely associated with the first defendant in Spain and held powers of attorney to act on behalf of the plaintiff in Spain. It is alleged that he received money on behalf of the first plaintiff in Spain and in England.

The third defendant was separately represented and separate arguments were to be advanced on his behalf before this court. Before the judge he was not separately j  represented. So far as the remaining defendants are concerned, it was suggested by counsel on their behalf that in addition to the general argument he presented there were arguments that he could advance in respect of individual defendants which would make it possible to distinguish their cases. However, as the argument proceeded, it was possible to dispose of this appeal without dealing with the possible differences in the positions of the defendants, and the separate arguments can be gone into hereafter if and in so far as

it is necessary to do so. We have also not heard the separate arguments which counsel
wished to advance in relation to the third defendant.                                        a
    Counsel for the defendants other than the third defendant also wanted to rely on fresh
evidence that was not before the judge and, although we did not finally rule on the
application to adduce that evidence, having regard to the lack of welcome this court was
displaying towards the idea of fresh evidence being introduced on this appeal, counsel
has deferred reliance on that fresh evidence for consideration, if need be, on a fresh
application for discharge of the injunction granted by the judge.                            b
    The case for the plaintiffs in summary is that after the first plaintiff met the first
defendant he was induced, primarily by the first defendant, to make substantial property
investments in England, France, Spain and Canada, and with regard to those investments
substantial secret profits were made by the first defendant. The first plaintiff alleges that
he used to be told the purchase price of a property, which was substantially in excess of
the actual purchase price, that he paid the inflated price, but the properties were acquired  c
at a lower price, and that the first defendant obtained substantial benefits in consequence.
The first defendant was then acting as his agent, and he was making the secret profits
fraudulently.
    Other misconduct is also alleged against the first defendant and the other defendants.
It is alleged that the first defendant sold properties in which he was interested to the
plaintiffs without disclosing that fact, and indeed suggesting that they were owned by      d
others. Certain of the properties, it is alleged, were not, as they should have been, placed
in the plaintiffs' name, and after the properties had been acquired it is alleged they were
managed in such a way that the plaintiffs were deprived of the income which they should
have received. No proper accounts were provided to the plaintiffs, and it is alleged that
the defendants abused the trust which was placed on them. It is contended that this        e
conduct of the defendants was fraudulent.
    The total amount claimed to have been fraudulently obtained as a result of this conduct
is in excess of £17m.
    Before Rougier J the ground which was primarily advanced for discharging the
injunctions was non-disclosure. In the first defendant's first affidavit he makes it clear
that he did, however, also argue that the injunctions should be discharged because there    f
was no evidence of risk of removal or dissipation of assets, and other defendants rely on a
similar ground.
    It was accepted before the judge that the plaintiffs had made out a sufficient prima
facie case. On my reading of the evidence, I should make it clear that I am satisfied that
there is a strong prima facie case of fraud as against the first defendant and the fourth
defendant involving large sums of money, although they are not necessarily as large as     g
those alleged in the statement of claim.
    The law with regard to the non-disclosure of material matters on an application for an
ex parte injunction has now been clearly stated in a series of cases. In the course of helpful
arguments by counsel for both the defendants and the plaintiffs, we were referred to the
most helpful authorities. However, for the purposes of this appeal, I need do no more
than refer to the decision of this court in *Brink's-MAT Ltd v Elcombe* [1988] 3 All ER 188,   h
[1988] 1 WLR 1350, when on 12 June 1987 this court allowed an appeal from Alliott J.
It is not necessary to go into the facts of the *Brink's-MAT* case. It suffices if I refer to the
following passages in the judgments of the court, starting with the judgment of Ralph
Gibson LJ where he said ([1988] 3 All ER 188 at 192–193, [1988] 1 WLR 1350 at 1356–
1357):                                                                                        j

    'In considering whether there has been relevant non-disclosure and what
    consequence the court should attach to any failure to comply with the duty to make
    full and frank disclosure, the principles relevant to the issues in these appeals appear
    to me to include the following. (i) The duty of the applicant is to make "a full and
    fair disclosure of all the material facts": see *R v Kensington Income Tax Comrs, ex p*

*Princess Edmond de Polignac* [1917] 1 KB 486 at 514 per Scrutton LJ. (ii) The material
facts are those which it is material for the judge to know in dealing with the
application as made; materiality is to be decided by the court and not by the
assessment of the applicant or his legal advisers: see the *Kensington Income Tax Comrs*
case [1917] 1 KB 486 at 504 per Lord Cozens-Hardy MR, citing *Dalglish v Jarvie*
(1850) 2 Mac & G 231 at 238, 42 ER 89 at 92, and *Thermax Ltd v Schott Industrial
Glass Ltd* [1981] FSR 289 per Browne-Wilkinson J. (iii) The applicant must make
proper inquiries before making the application: see *Bank Mellat v Nikpour* [1985]
FSR 87. The duty of disclosure therefore applies not only to material facts known to
the applicant but also to any additional facts which he would have known if he had
made such inquiries. (iv) The extent of the inquiries which will be held to be proper,
and therefore necessary, must depend on all the circumstances of the case including
(a) the nature of the case which the applicant is making when he makes the
application, (b) the order for which application is made and the probable effect of
the order on the defendant: see, for example, the examination by Scott J of the
possible effect of an Anton Piller order in *Columbia Picture Industries Inc v Robinson*
[1986] 3 All ER 338, [1987] Ch 38, and (c) the degree of legitimate urgency and the
time available for the making of inquiries: see *Bank Mellat v Nikpour* [1985] FSR 87
at 92–93 per Slade LJ. (v) If material non-disclosure is established the court will be
"astute to ensure that a plaintiff who obtains . . . an ex parte injunction without full
disclosure is deprived of any advantage he may have derived by that breach of
duty . . .": see *Bank Mellat v Nikpour* (at 91) per Donaldson LJ, citing Warrington LJ
in the *Kensington Income Tax Comrs* case. (vi) Whether the fact not disclosed is of
sufficient materiality to justify or require immediate discharge of the order without
examination of the merits depends on the importance of the fact to the issues which
were to be decided by the judge on the application. The answer to the question
whether the non-disclosure was innocent, in the sense that the fact was not known
to the applicant or that its relevance was not perceived, is an important consideration
but not decisive by reason of the duty on the applicant to make all proper inquiries
and to give careful consideration to the case being presented. (vii) Finally "it is not
for every omission that the injunction will be automatically discharged. A locus
poenitentiae may sometimes be afforded": see *Bank Mellat v Nikpour* [1985] FSR 87
at 90 per Lord Denning MR. The court has a discretion, notwithstanding proof of
material non-disclosure which justifies or requires the immediate discharge of the
ex parte order, nevertheless to continue the order, or to make a new order on terms:
". . . when the whole of the facts, including that of the original non-disclosure, are
before it, [the court] may well grant such a second injunction if the original non-
disclosure was innocent and if an injunction could properly be granted even had the
facts been disclosed." (See *Lloyds Bowmaker Ltd v Britannia Arrow Holdings plc (Lavens,
third party)* [1988] 3 All ER 178 at 183, [1988] 1 WLR 1337 at 1343–1344 per
Glidewell LJ.)'

Balcombe LJ said ([1988] 3 All ER 188 at 193–194, [1988] 1 WLR 1350 at 1358):

'The courts today are frequently asked to grant ex parte injunctions, either because
the matter is too urgent to await a hearing on notice or because the very fact of
giving notice may precipitate the action which the application is designed to
prevent. On any ex parte application, the fact that the court is asked to grant relief
without the person against whom the relief is sought having the opportunity to be
heard makes it imperative that the applicant should make full and frank disclosure
of all facts known to him or which should have been known to him had he made all
such inquiries as were reasonable and proper in the circumstances. The rule that an
ex parte injunction will be discharged if it was obtained without full disclosure has
a twofold purpose. It will deprive the wrongdoer of an advantage improperly
obtained: see *R v Kensington Income Tax Comrs, ex p Princess Edmond de Polignac*

[1917] 1 KB 486 at 509. But it also serves as a deterrent to ensure that persons who make ex parte applications realise that they have this duty of disclosure and of the *a* consequence (which may include a liability in costs) if they fail in that duty. Nevertheless, this judge-made rule cannot be allowed itself to become an instrument of injustice. It is for this reason that there must be a discretion in the court to continue the injunction, or to grant a fresh injunction in its place, notwithstanding that there may have been non-disclosure when the original ex parte injunction was obtained: see in general *Bank Mellat v Nikpour* [1985] FSR 87 at 90 and *Lloyds* *b* *Bowmaker Ltd v Britannia Arrow Holdings plc (Lavens, third party)* [1988] 3 All ER 178, [1988] 1 WLR 1337, a recent decision of this court in which the authorities are fully reviewed. I make two comments on the exercise of this discretion. (i) Whilst, having regard to the purpose of the rule, the discretion is one to be exercised sparingly, I would not wish to define or limit the circumstances in which it may be exercised. (ii) I agree with the views of Dillon LJ in the *Lloyds Bowmaker* case [1988] 3 All ER *c* 178 at 187, [1988] 1 WLR 1337 at 1349 that, if there is jurisdiction to grant a fresh injunction, then there must also be a discretion to refuse, in an appropriate case, to discharge the original injunction.'

Slade LJ said ([1988] 3 All ER 188 at 194–195, [1988] 1 WLR 1350 at 1359):

'The principle is, I think, a thoroughly healthy one. It serves the important *d* purposes of encouraging persons who are making ex parte applications to the court diligently to observe their duty to make full disclosure of all material facts and to deter them from any failure to observe this duty, whether through deliberate lack of candour or innocent lack of due care. Nevertheless, the nature of the principle, as I see it, is essentially penal and in its application the practical realities of any case before the court cannot be overlooked. By their very nature, ex parte applications *e* usually necessitate the giving and taking of instructions and the preparation of the requisite drafts in some haste. Particularly in heavy commercial cases, the borderline between material facts and non-material facts may be a somewhat uncertain one. While in no way discounting the heavy duty of candour and care which falls on persons making ex parte applications, I do not think the application of the principle *f* should be carried to extreme lengths. In one or two other recent cases coming before this court, I have suspected signs of a growing tendency on the part of some litigants against whom ex parte injunctions have been granted, or of their legal advisers, to rush to the *R v Kensington Income Tax Comrs* principle as a tabula in naufragio, alleging material non-disclosure on sometimes rather slender grounds, as represent- ing substantially the only hope of obtaining the discharge of injunctions in cases *g* where there is little hope of doing so on the substantial merits of the case or on the balance of convenience.'

The only other passage in those judgments to which I need refer is to a short statement in Ralph Gibson LJ's judgment (which is not included in either report), where he makes it clear what he, at any rate, means with regard to 'a failure to disclose which is innocent'. There he says: *h*

'. . . the failure to disclose these matters was, in my judgment, innocent in the sense that the plaintiffs did not intentionally omit information which they thought to be material.'

I refer to that last passage from the judgment of Ralph Gibson LJ because counsel for the *j* defendants submitted that a failure to disclose is not innocent, but deliberate, if the situation is one where material which ought to have been disclosed is not disclosed deliberately, and it is not disclosed in circumstances where it was known to be material or it *ought* to have been known that it was material. I am not happy about the suggestion that it is appropriate to regard a disclosure as not innocent when the facts not disclosed

were not known at the time to be material, albeit that it ought to have been known they
*a* were material. In practice in most cases it will be extremely difficult for a defendant who
is applying to discharge injunctions which have been granted ex parte to show that the
matters which were not disclosed, but which should have been disclosed, were the subject
of any decision not to disclose which was made in circumstances where it was appreciated
that there should have been disclosure. In the majority of cases the matter has to be
approached on the basis of considering the quality of the material which was not disclosed
*b* without making any final decision whether or not there has in fact been bad faith. If, of
course, it can be established that there has been bad faith, either on behalf of the parties
or their legal advisers, that will be a most material matter in considering whether
injunctions which have been granted should be discharged, and, if they are discharged,
whether it is appropriate in the circumstances to regrant injunctions either in the same
terms or in similar terms.

*c*    Counsel for the plaintiffs, in the course of his submissions, attached great importance
to the earlier decision of this court in *Eastglen International Corp v Monpare SA* 137 NLJ
56 of 17 September 1986, of which we were provided with a Lexis transcript. In that
case this court, presided over by Sir John Donaldson MR, came to the conclusion that, as
the fault was that of the solicitor alone, it was possible and appropriate in the
circumstances which there existed to regrant an injunction, although certainly so far as
*d* the solicitor was concerned it cannot be said that he was innocent in the way that term
was used in the *Brink's-MAT* case. However, I regard the *Eastglen International* case as
being very much an exceptional case, and one which should not be regarded as having
application in respect of the different facts and in the different circumstances which exist
here. Indeed, I regard it as undesirable to apply hard and fast rules. It is preferable, in my
view, for each case to be considered on its own merits, taking into account the public
*e* interest which exists in protecting the administration of justice from the harm that will
be caused if applicants for the draconian relief of Mareva and Anton Piller orders do not,
on an ex parte application, make disclosure of all the material facts, whether or not the
non-disclosure is innocent. I recognise the strain placed on legal advisers and the pressure
under which they have to work, especially in large commercial actions, where prompt
steps sometimes have to be taken in order to protect their clients' interests. However, if
*f* the court does not approach the question of the non-disclosure of material matters in the
way that has been indicated in earlier decisions, there will be little hope of solicitors who
are subjected to such pressures appreciating the importance of making full disclosure
and, more important, bringing home to the clients the serious consequences of non-
disclosure.

*g*    In deciding in a case where there has undoubtedly been non-disclosure whether or not
there should be a discharge of an existing injunction and a regrant of fresh injunctions,
it is most important that the court assesses the degree and extent of the culpability with
regard to the non-disclosure, and the importance and significance to the outcome of the
application for an injunction of the matters which were not disclosed to the court.

    In this connection counsel for the plaintiff at one stage of his argument submitted that
*h* the acid test was whether or not the original judge who granted the injunction ex parte
would have been likely to have arrived at a different decision if the material matters had
been before him. I do not regard that as being the acid test. Indeed, although I regard it
as a relevant matter when considering the question of discharge and regrant of
injunctions, I do not regard it as a matter of great significance unless the facts which were
not disclosed would have resulted in the refusal of an injunction.

*j*    Turning to the facts of the present appeal, it is important to note that, although at one
time there were very close business relations between the plaintiffs and the defendants,
since December 1984 those relations have deteriorated and the plaintiffs have at least had
some knowledge of some default on the part of the defendants, if their contentions are
correct.

    According to the first plaintiff, in his first affidavit, in December 1984 the first defendant did make an admission of overcharging in respect of one matter. However, the history of the present proceedings starts at either the end of 1986 or the beginning of *a* 1987. In September 1986 a letter was sent by the first defendant's Spanish lawyer, making reference to the possibility of proceedings in Spain. On 14 November a letter with regard to conciliation proceedings was sent by the Marbella court in Spain to the first plaintiff. On 15 January 1987 there was a conciliation hearing by the Marbella court in relation to proposed Spanish proceedings by the first defendant. The plaintiffs did not attend, but they did subseqsuently receive notice of the existence of those proceedings. On 12 *b* February the first plaintiff filed proceedings against the first and sixth defendants in the Marbella court. On 16 February the first defendant's proceedings against the first plaintiff were filed in the same court. On 23 February the first plaintiff was granted an embargo preventivo by the Marbella court, which is the equivalent of a Mareva injunction granted in this jurisdiction. On 11 March the first and sixth defendants became aware of the first plaintiff's proceedings against them. On 31 March those proceedings were served at the *c* first defendant's office in Marbella. The first plaintiff's Spanish lawyer, at any rate, must have been aware of the service of those proceedings, which included a notice of the embargo preventivo, since, although service is by a court officer in Spain, in fact the Spanish lawyer of the plaintiff or his representative was in attendance. On 8 April, the day before the ex parte order was granted by Roch J, the defendants' proceedings were formally served at the Marbella office of the plaintiff, together with the embargo *d* preventivo which the defendants had obtained.

When the ex parte application came before Roch J it is not in dispute that material matters which should have been disclosed to him were not disclosed to him. The order which Roch J made was extensive in its terms.

On 7 May, as I have already said, the application came before Rougier J for the discharge of those injunctions. The matters which were relied on by the defendants as *e* amounting to non-disclosure were, first of all, the plaintiffs' proceedings in Spain, including the grant of the embargo preventivo. Second, it was contended that it should have been disclosed to Roch J, and it was not, that the Spanish proceedings, as I will call them, by the plaintiffs duplicated to some extent at any rate the proceedings in this country. Third, there was a failure to disclose the Spanish proceedings brought by the *f* first defendant (and again there is no dispute that they were not drawn to the judge's attention). Fourth, it is contended that it should have been disclosed to the judge that in respect of one of the property transactions on which the first plaintiff was relying, namely that involving Scala House, the defendants had written letters to the first plaintiff and his solicitors intimating a claim for just over £500,000 in consequence of the sale of that property. Finally, it was contended that there should have been disclosure that a *g* settlement was reached between various parties, including certain of the parties who are the subject matter of the English proceedings, relating to the management of the properties which the plaintiffs owned in Warwick Square. Not only is it accepted that the matters to which I have made reference should have been disclosed, but it is accepted that when looked at collectively, at any rate, their materiality was such that the decision which Rougier J came to, to discharge the injunction which was granted by Roch J, was *h* one which was correct and which cannot be challenged before this court. I am not surprised that that should be the position which is now adopted by the plaintiffs.

So far as the Spanish proceedings brought by the plaintiffs are concerned, I accept the submission of counsel for the plaintiffs that it can be quite proper to bring proceedings in more than one jurisdiction, although those proceedings overlap. Furthermore, I accept that it is quite in order to seek in more than one jurisdiction orders equivalent to our *j* Mareva and Anton Piller orders. However, as counsel for the plaintiffs concedes, although it is proper to bring proceedings in more than one jurisdiction, it is a highly material matter to be considered by a judge when granting relief in this jurisdiction on an ex parte application that there are proceedings either actually taking place or contemplated within another jurisdiction. It is, in my view, of great importance that that should be the

position, because clearly, in exercising his discretion whether or not to grant the
a  draconian remedies which such injunctions amount to, the judge should be satisfied that
the case warrants the granting of such relief, and in particular that it is not oppressive for
the defendants to be subject to orders of the court in more than one jurisdiction.

So far as the issue of the Spanish proceedings by the defendants is concerned, it is in
my view equally important that the court should be aware of this, because the fact that
there are proceedings being brought or about to be brought by a defendant is a matter
b  which the court would want to investigate since the defendants' proceedings could be
the trigger for proceedings which are being brought for some improper purpose by a
plaintiff within this jurisdiction. The defendants' proceedings may also throw light on
the true nature of the relations between the parties. If the court is only told about part of
the dispute between the parties this could give a wholly misleading picture.

So far as the Scala property transaction is concerned, and the counterclaim with regard
c  to that transaction, counsel for the plaintiffs submits that before the judge this was
regarded (and rightly so regarded) as a matter of limited significance. The position is that
the proposed counterclaim in connection with this was first raised in a letter to the
plaintiff dated 1 April 1987, but there is no evidence that the first plaintiff actually
received that letter. Communications were also sent to the plaintiffs' solicitors and were
undoubtedly received. However, they were not addressed to the solicitor who was
d  handling the plaintiffs' litigation at that time and, although I consider it would have been
preferable for the solicitor who was handling the plaintiffs' litigation to have filed an
affidavit deposing to the fact that he had no knowledge of the notice that had been given
of the proposed counterclaim, I would regard it as right not to infer such knowledge. In
addition, I accept that the judge was perfectly correct as counsel for the plaintiffs submits
to regard the Scala property matter as being one which really was not of any signficiance.
e  So far as the settlement is concerned in connection with the Warwick Square
transaction I will draw attention as to how Rougier J dealt with this when considering
whether to discharge and regrant the injunction. However, I should make it clear that
although the settlement covers only a very small part of the plaintiffs' proceedings as a
whole, I do regard it as a material matter which should have been brought to the attention
f  of Roch J and which should have been appreciated to be material. The fact of the matter
is that, if the plaintiff was carrying on, as he apparently was, investigations into large-
scale frauds which he thought had been carried out by the defendants, a judge, on an
application for an ex parte injunction, could regard it as strange and require an
explanation as to why a settlement of the sort contained in the agreement was being
entered into in December 1986.

g  In considering the materiality of that matter, I do not accept the contention of counsel
for the plaintiffs that you can look merely at the terms of the agreement in relation to
the size of the plaintiffs' claim as a whole.

So far as there has been non-disclosure it is, of course, for the plaintiffs to explain that
non-disclosure. For the explanation as to the principal non-disclosure which has occurred
in this case, one is confined to the evidence which is provided by Mr Hughes, who was
h  the solicitor acting on behalf of the plaintiffs at the material times. Mr Hughes has
deposed to a series of affidvits, but the most important is his second affidavit where he
frankly explains his approach to the non-disclosure of the Spanish proceedings brought
by the plaintiffs. He deals with this matter in para 6(ii) of that affidavit, where he says:

'It is misleading to say that the Spanish proceedings were started on 16th February
j  1987. Mr. Soler and Mr. Queral, the Plaintiffs' lawyers in Spain having conduct of
the action there, inform me that the papers were lodged with the Court on 12th
February 1987. It took about two weeks before the papers were issued by the Court
and the application for a freezing order considered. Once the freezing order was
made the Plaintiffs had to provide a bank guarantee as security which took about
one week. Unlike this country, service of civil proceedings in Spain are effected by

the Courts and it took several weeks thereafter for the Courts to serve the Defendants
and, more importantly, the banks. In the event the Defendants were not served  *a*
until 31st March 1987 and the banks were not notified of the freezing order until
1st April 1987. This was not communicated to [the first plaintiff,] [who at about
this time was in Paris and thereafter in London] or to me until after the Order in
England had been obtained on 9th April. I was, of course, aware that proceedings
were being taken in Spain and the intention was to have contemporaneous service
of the two freezing orders; because of the uncertainties of the date of service  *b*
inherent under the Spanish procedure this was impractical. It would of course have
been folly for me to have disclosed the fact that proceedings were being taken in
Spain since if I had disclosed this before the Spanish procedings were served it would
have been a short step from that to surmise that a freezing order was being sought
there. The First and Sixth Defendants would then have had every opportunity to
remove their assets from Spain before the freezing order could bite. For the same  *c*
reason the Spanish lawyers agreed not to disclose the existence of the English
proceedings. There is of course nothing unusual in bringing two sets of proceedings
in different jurisdictions where Defendants maintain their assets and there is nothing
adversely material in omitting to mention this.'

The most charitable view which can be taken of the explanation which Mr Hughes  *d*
gives for not disclosing the Spanish proceedings by the plaintiffs is that it portrays a
fundamental misunderstanding of his duty with regard to the court. It is right that I
should make it clear that in the course of argument some doubt arose as to the extent to
which Mr Hughes in fact was not relying on his own judgment but relying on the advice
of counsel who was then appearing for the plaintiffs, but who is not now representing
them. We have no evidence as to this, but not having investigated this possibility I do  *e*
not propose to make any personal criticism of Mr Hughes as to what happened, other
than making it clear, as I have already, that the affidavit to which I have made reference
discloses a fundamental misunderstanding of the position. In my view, not only should
Mr Hughes have taken steps to ensure that the nature of the Spanish proceedings was
brought to the attention of the court, but he was under an obligation to ascertain exactly
what the position was in relation to those proceedings before the application was made  *f*
in this country. In particular, he should have found out, as he obviously could easily have
found out, that the proceedings had already been served in Spain prior to the date of the
application, and that the protective relief which was granted by the Spanish court had
been extended to the plaintiffs.

In the subsequent paragraphs of his affidavit Mr Hughes deals with the other
explanations which are advanced for not disclosing matters which I regard as material.  *g*
Again suffice it to say that I see no satisfactory explanation in that affidavit which justifies
the existence of the Spanish proceedings which were brought by the defendants also not
being disclosed to the court, and I take the same view with regard to the settlement
agreement.

However, in his argument before this court, counsel for the plaintiffs submits that,
notwithstanding that there has been serious non-disclosure, the judge in his approach to  *h*
the matter has dealt with the appropriate steps which should be taken in an exemplary
manner, and it is not possible for this court to criticise or indeed interfere with the way
he decided that the matter should be dealt with.

I turn therefore to consider the approach of Rougier J, bearing in mind as this is a
matter of discretion the limited powers which this court has to interfere with the proper
exercise of a discretion by a judge. It is right that I should begin by making it clear that  *j*
it is apparent from the judgment of Rougier J that he gave very careful consideration to
the issues which were before him. He set out clearly the background to the applications
of the defendants and summarised shortly, but accurately, the matters relied on by the
defendants in support of the application and the arguments which were made on both

sides. He also referred in the course of his judgment to a number of authorities, and in
a particularly referred to a passage of a judgment of Bingham J in *Siporex Trade SA v Comdel
Commodities Ltd* [1986] 2 Lloyd's Rep 428 at 437, which correctly sets out the approach
which the court should adopt to the question of non-disclosure. Basing himself on the
principles of Bingham J, which he cited, he said:

'. . . in my opinion this order was obtained partly as a result of deliberate non-
disclosure of facts which were material and I have very little hesitation in saying
b that up to that moment it should be discharged, not varied but discharged, and,
moreover, discharged against all the defendants.'

He then goes on to indicate that he does not regard that as being the end of the matter,
and he refers to two authorities, and in particular a passage from the judgment of
Glidewell LJ in *Lloyds Bowmaker Ltd v Britannia Arrow Holdings plc (Lavens, third party)*
c [1988] 3 All ER 178 at 183, [1988] 1 WLR 1337 at 1343–1344 which indicates that in
appropriate circumstances, although a judge has come to a decision that an injunction
should be discharged for non-disclosure, it is proper for an injunction to be regranted.
Although his reasoning so far is accepted on both sides, it is important that I should just
refer to one of the matters that he dealt with in coming to the first part of his decision.
Having set out the various arguments relied on by the defendants and having referred in
d particular to the Spanish procedings, he then proceeded to set out, among other matters,
the Scala House and the settlement matters. With regard to those matters he said:

'As I indicated to [counsel for the defendants] towards the end of the hearing, I do
not, myself, consider that the fact that the defendant has an embargo preventivo
against the first plaintiff in relation to his claim is of particular relevance here, nor
e the counterclaim for £½m, in the English action. The settlement agreement, when
it is looked at, does not seem to me to have any bearing on the present dispute
between the parties and I do not think on the evidence I have seen and read that the
plaintiffs can be blamed for not anticipating that the first defendant would start
raising the point that he was not properly served within the jurisdiction in view of
the presence he keeps here.'

f In relation to that passage, as will be apparent from what I have already said about the
settlement, I do disagree with his treatment of the settlement. However, it is the passage
in his judgment where he deals with the question of the regrant of the injunction which
is most important.
Having set out the submissions on behalf of the defendants, he went on to say:

g 'What features ought I to consider? I agree with [counsel for the defendants] that
the first thing one has to do is to consider the nature of the non-disclosure. Was it
what has been called an "innocent non-disclosure" or not? Now, as to that I do not
think that the word "innocent" or its antithesis "guilty" are particularly apt to
describe the reasons which led the plaintiffs, through their solicitor, not to make
this disclosure. That it was deliberate and conscious is apparent, but it was made for
h reasons which one can understand on the material which was available to Mr
Hughes although his fault really lay in a failure to see that the difficulties could be
circumvented while still obeying the duty of the utmost frankness. Secondly, and I
think this is allied to the first, one needs to consider the reasons for the non-
disclosure and I have already dealt with those. I should perhaps add, under number
one, the nature of the non-disclosure. I find it was, in case there should be any doubt
j about this, deliberate. I find it was mistaken, but I do not find that it was
contumacious in the sense that there was a knowledge and a certainty amongst those
who chose to conceal the fact that this would necessarily have an effect on the judge's
mind. That is the third question which [counsel for the defendants] suggested,
rightly in my view, that I should consider: what would have been the effect on the

judge had the Spanish action been disclosed to him? In my estimation, faced with
the very strong evidence which the plaintiffs had been able to adduce, it seems to   a
me that the judge might well have taken the view that because of the extreme
danger of dissipation of assets he should grant the Mareva as a temporary measure
at least leaving open and pending the determination of the question of which was
the convenient forum and the discovery of the true nature and extent of the claims
being made under the Spanish action. Where I cannot agree with [counsel for the
defendants] is that the conduct of the defendant is not a relevant consideration for   b
me attempting to decide whether or not I should renew the Mareva. It seems to me
that if it is relevant in determining whether the original grant of the injunction
should be made it must be relevant in determining what one might call a regrant.
It is noticeable that there has not really been, on the part of the defendants, any
convincing attempt in their affidavits, nor in some rather emotional pleadings I
have read in the Spanish action, to refute by facts and documents the details of the   c
plaintiffs' case. All that has been done is a mere blanket denial and in those
circumstances it seems to me that the prima facie evidence adduced on behalf of the
plaintiffs is of such a strength and discloses such a type of conduct that there must
be an enormous risk from the very nature of the facts giving rise to the plaintiffs'
claim that if the court relaxes its grip for one instant any assets which the defendants
may have in this country will melt like snow on the desert's dusty face. This, in my   d
judgment, is a most relevant consideration and although, as I have said, I think that
the decision not to disclose was in fact wholly misguided and mistaken I think it is
outweighed as a balancing factor by those matters which originally persuaded Roch
J to grant the injunction and I propose to regrant it in precisely the same terms.'

With regard to that passage of the judge's judgment, I would draw attention to the   e
fact that the judge adopts a more charitable view with regard to the failure to disclose the
Spanish proceedings of the plaintiffs than I would consider to be appropriate. With the
greatest respect to Mr Hughes, and taking into account the fact that he may have been
advised, the fact of the matter is that I do not regard it as understandable that the view
should have been taken that those proceedings should not have been disclosed. In that   f
passage to which I have made reference the judge does not refer to the obligation to make
inquiries so as to ascertain the material facts or to the Spanish proceedings brought by
the defendant. He concludes by approaching the matter as being one of balance, and he
puts in the scales on one side the strength of the plaintiffs' claim and on the other side he
puts the matters which were not disclosed. It is in the performance of that balancing
exercise where the judge has gone wrong to a critical extent, and come to a conclusion
which I can only regard as being wholly wrong.   g

I sought to indicate earlier that in my view there is a considerable public interest in
the court ensuring that full disclosure is made on ex parte applications of this sort. If it is
to be sufficient to outweigh that public interest to point to the harm that could befall
plaintiffs if an injunction is not regranted, then the whole policy which has been adopted
by the court in this field in my view would be undermined. Injunctions in the nature of   h
Marevas and Anton Piller orders should not be granted unless the plaintiff can show a
substantial case for saying that unless they are granted they will be under serious risk of
assets which might otherwise be available to meet the judgment being dissipated or
evidence which might otherwise be available disappearing. In my view it cannot be
sufficient to carry out a balancing exercise in the way it was carried out by the judge. It
would seem to me that, if that approach were adopted, a judge would inevitable come to   j
the conclusion that the injunction must be regranted.

I am very conscious of the passages which I have cited, particularly from the judgments
of Balcombe and Slade LJJ which refer to the danger of applications to discharge
injunctions which have been granted resulting in injustice if the court refuses all relief
to a plaintiff. It is true here, as I have sought to indicate, that, if the plaintiffs are right,

there has been large-scale fraud. It is, however, at this stage only a prima facie case.

*a* Counsel for the plaintiffs substantially criticised the defendants for the fact that in their affidavit evidence they have not dealt satisfactorily with the allegations of fraud which are made against them. In regard to that criticism (and I am not here referring to the defence, to which different considerations might apply, but I draw attention to the fact that the defence was not before the judge), I can well understand that in a case of this sort, where the plaintiff has undoubtedly a strong prima facie case, the defendants should

*b* take the view that they are not going to deal with the merits of the plaintiff's claim on interlocutory matter of this sort. If they deal with the merits of the plaintiff's claim it may well not assist the court, because there would still be the position that there is a strong prima facie case. Quite clearly, as the proceedings are before us, the situation is one where the action is being contested. There are with regard to certain of the transactions undoubtedly matters which will require considerable investigation. The

*c* judge referred to the fact that the claim may be inflated. There is the position that in relation to the Spanish proceedings there is a remarkable contrast between those proceedings and the English proceedings as they are framed at present. There may be an innocent explanation for that, there may not be. But that is a matter which, like many other matters, is to be investigated before the court at the trial.

When one looks at this case, with regard to the Spanish proceedings there was a

*d* remarkable failure to make disclosure to this court in respect of the plaintiffs' proceedings. In my view there was also a serious failure both in regard to the defendants' proceedings and in relation to the settlement. If the right approach is one which requires the court to measure the materiality of the non-disclosure looked at cumulatively, then it cannot be right just to sweep that aside on the basis of the strength of the plaintiffs' case against the defendants. In my view it is important that this court should uphold the policy which I

*e* detect indicated by the cases to which I have made reference, and the cases in particular which were cited by this court in *Brink's-MAT Ltd v Elcombe* [1988] 3 All ER 188, [1988] 1 WLR 1350 and not approach the matter in the way which was indicated by the judge. It is for that reason that I would allow this appeal.

However, bearing in mind the importance of not allowing the non-disclosure of the

*f* material matters to which I have made reference to result in injustice, I thought it right to inquire of the defendants whether or not they were prepared to give an undertaking in a form that I sought, that being an undertaking not to dispose of an asset which consists of a freehold or leasehold interest in property within this jurisdiction without giving reasonable notice, which I would regard as being 28 days' notice, of the intention of making such disposal. I was informed by counsel that they are prepared to give such an undertaking subject to the position of the third defendant, where the undertaking is

*g* limited to what I would call 'his new property', which can be identified hereafter. In case there is any requirement hereafter to make reference to the undertaking, I should make it clear why, speaking for myself, I regard the giving of that undertaking as being of some materiality to the outcome of this appeal.

The object of requiring the undertaking which I had in mind was that the plaintiffs

*h* should at least have this limited protection, that they should have notice before the defendants dispose of their principal assets within the jurisdiction, so that if they choose to do so, on receiving notice of a proposed disposal, they can make an application to the court for protection with regard to the proceeds of such disposal, if it takes place, or indeed to restrain that disposal. On such an application, of course, the court would have to look at the whole history. However, I make it clear that I would not, in relation to an

*j* application with regard to reasonable protection for the plaintiffs, regard it as right to hold against them as debarring them from protection the fact that at the outset of these proceedings the non-disclosure which was the subject matter of this appeal occurred. That would by then probably be a background matter of little importance. Accordingly, subject to the undertakings to which I have made reference being made, I would allow this appeal and discharge the orders made by Rougier J.

**NOURSE LJ.** I agree that for the reasons given by Woolf LJ this appeal must be allowed. At the risk of some repetition, I add some views of my own.

    I agree that in order to get at the principles of discretion on which the court acts in a case of this kind we need not now look further than the decision of this court in *Brink's-MAT Ltd v Elcombe* [1988] 3 All ER 188 at 193, [1988] 1 WLR 1350 at 1357, where they are summarised in the passage in the judgment of Ralph Gibson LJ which Woolf LJ has read. In para (vii) of that summary we find that:

    'The court has a discretion, notwithstanding proof of material non-disclosure which justifies or requires the immediate discharge of the ex parte order, nevertheless to continue the order, or to make a new order on terms: ". . . when the whole of the facts, including that of the original non-disclosure are before it, [the court] may well grant such a second injunction if the original non-disclosure was innocent and if an injunction could properly be granted even had the facts been disclosed." (See *Lloyds Bowmaker Ltd v Britannia Arrow Holdings plc (Lavens, third party)* [1988] 3 All ER 178 at 183, [1988] 1 WLR 1337 at 1343–1344 per Glidewell LJ.)'

    Although it would not be correct to treat Glidewell LJ's statement of the circumstances in which the court may exercise its discretion as being exhaustive, it is, I think, likely to have relevance in many of these cases, and it is certainly a useful starting point in this. I should add that in the *Brink's-MAT* case all three members of this court defined an innocent non-disclosure as one where there was no intention to omit or withhold information which was thought to be material.

    Since it is accepted both that the non-disclosure justified or required the immediate discharge of the ex parte order and that the whole of the facts are now before the court, the questions to which we should start by addressing ourselves are, first, whether it was innocent and, second, whether an injunction could properly have been granted if full disclosure had been made to Roch J.

    In deciding whether there was an intention to omit or withhold information which was thought to be material, it is first necessary to establish what the plaintiffs and their advisers knew on 9 April 1987, the date of the application before Roch J. I would concentrate on (1) the existence of the plaintiffs' Spanish proceedings, (2) the grant of an embargo preventivo in those proceedings and (3) the existence or imminence of the first defendant's Spanish proceedings. The existence of the plaintiffs' Spanish proceedings and the grant of the embargo preventivo therein were known or must be taken to have been known both to the plaintiffs themselves and to their English solicitor, Mr Hughes. We have also been told informally that counsel then acting for the plaintiffs on the application before Roch J was informed of the existence of the plaintiffs' Spanish proceedings, but that is a matter which has not been investigated and must therefore be disregarded. Mr Hughes did not know of the existence or imminence of the first defendant's Spanish proceedings.

    It has been accepted throughout that information on all these material matters was omitted or withheld from Roch J. The question then is whether they were thought to be material. Here it is necessary to deal with the plaintiffs separately from Mr Hughes. No explanatory affidavit has been sworn by the first plaintiff or indeed by his Spanish lawyer on his behalf. We cannot know whether they thought that the information in their possession was material in the English proceedings or not. As I see it, the onus being on the plaintiffs, that means that we cannot assume that they thought that it was immaterial. No doubt because they were relying on their English advisers to conduct the application before Roch J the plaintiffs' cannot seriously be criticised for omitting or withholding information which was already in the possession of those advisers. But there still remains the important matter of the existence of the first defendant's Spanish proceedings. It must be material for the court to have before it information of that kind because it goes directly to the question whether the defendants have a defence to the English proceedings.

    Turning to Mr Hughes, I repeat that he knew both of the existence of the plaintiffs'

Spanish proceedings and of the grant of the embargo preventivo therein, although he did
*a* not know either of the service of the embargo preventivo on 31 March or of the existence
or imminence of the first defendant's Spanish proceedings. He has frankly accepted
throughout that he made a deliberate decision not to disclose what he did know, because
if that information had been contained in his affidavit and had come to the notice of the
defendants before the embargo preventivo had been served, it would have been a short
step for them to surmise what was intended in Spain, and they would then have had an
*b* opportunity to remove their Spanish assets from that jurisdiction. That decision was
therefore made in what he thought were the best interests of his clients, and I will
certainly accept for present purposes that he thought that the information was not
material and that his non-disclosure was therefore innocent.

However, that cannot in my judgment conclude the question. I wish to adopt
everything which Woolf LJ has said in general about Mr Hughes's failure to disclose the
*c* existence of the plaintiffs' Spanish proceedings. I would myself go somewhat further. It
is well established by the authorities that all proper inquiries must be made before the ex
parte application is launched, their extent depending on all the circumstances, including
the nature of the case which the applicant is making when he makes his application. This
requirement is stated in paras (iii) and (iv) of Ralph Gibson LJ's summary in the *Brink's-
MAT* case [1988] 3 All ER 188 at 192, [1988] 1 WLR 1350 at 1356–1357.
*d* Although Mr Hughes knew of the existence of the plaintiff's Spanish proceedings, he
did not know how the claim was put. In my view he ought to have inquired about that.
Without that knowledge his decision whether or not it was material to disclose the
existence of those proceedings could not be soundly based. Furthermore, if he had made
the inquiry, he would necessarily have seen the Spanish pleading dated 12 February
1987, from which he would have seen that there were some material discrepancies in the
*e* plaintiffs' case as it was then put, in particular the failure to give the defendants' credit
for the investment of moneys in the properties outside Spain and the inflation in value
of one or more of the Spanish properties over those which were being put forward in
England. If he had known that, I do not think that he could or would have decided that
the information was not material, because the most important duty of an ex parte
applicant is to disclose to the court anything which may be material to the defendant's
*f* defence. It must be the duty of the applicant's advisers to tell the court of material which
suggests that the case which he is putting forward in the foreign jurisdiction differs in
not insignificant respects from that which he is putting forward in England.

In the *Brink's-MAT* case [1988] 3 All ER 188 at 194, [1988] 1 WLR 1350 at 1359 Slade
LJ said this of the rule or principle of policy which the court applies in cases of this kind:

*g*       'The principle is, I think, a thoroughly healthy one. It serves the important
purposes of encouraging persons who are making ex parte applications to the court
diligently to observe their duty to make full disclosure of all material facts and to
deter them from any failure to observe this duty, whether through deliberate lack
of candour or innocent lack of due care.'

*h* I have to say that I think that Mr Hughes was guilty of an innocent lack of due care in
a material and important respect is not making the inquiries which he could have made.
Furthermore, the failure of the first plaintiff or his Spanish lawyers to disclose the
existence of the first defendant's Spanish proceedings constituted another failure to
observe the duty of disclosure in a material and important respect. It may be that that
duty did not necessarily extend to putting the information on affidavit for the benefit of
*j* the English court. However that may be, I think that it did extend to informing the
plaintiffs' English advisers of that important matter and, furthermore, that, in the absence
of evidence put in either by the first plaintiff or by his Spanish lawyer, this court cannot
make any assumption in favour of the plaintiffs.

Counsel for the plaintiffs has strongly urged on us that Rougier J took all these matters
into account, together with the other matters to which Woolf LJ has referred, in

particular the settlement agreement. Certain it is that he took account both of Mr Hughes's failure to make inquiries and of the failure of the first plaintiff and his Spanish *a* lawyer to disclose the existence of the defendant's Spanish proceedings, as well as the general failure to refer to the existence of the plaintiff's Spanish proceedings. What I respectfully think that he did not take into account were the important consequences which would necessarily have flowed from making the necessary inquiries as to the plaintiff's Spanish proceedings. Nor do I think that Rougier J attached anywhere near the correct importance to telling the court of the existence of the defendant's Spanish *b* proceedings, which by itself could only suggest that there might be a defence to the plaintiffs' claims. Certain it is that, although he took them into account to some extent, the judge did not give the defendant's Spanish proceedings any consideration separate from the plaintiffs' Spanish proceedings.

The fact that at the end of the day Roch J might nevertheless have made the orders sought, which I am perfectly prepared to assume that he would, is, as Woolf LJ has said, *c* entirely beside the point. That is not a consideration which can relieve an ex parte applicant of the duty of disclosure.

While I take full account of all the points which counsel for the plaintiffs has made to us, including his submissions on the depth and scale of the defendants' iniquity, as it was seen by the judge, particularly perhaps in Canada and France, and also the requirement that the rule of policy should not become an instrument of injustice, I am in the end *d* satisfied that Rougier J's decision cannot be sustained. I certainly do not say that a judge's view of the general merits of the plaintiff's case is a consideration which cannot be weighed in the balance, although my clear impression of the cases is that it has never played the same part on an application for discharge as it does on the initial ex parte application. Indeed, I do not see how it could play such a part if the rule of policy is to be maintained, as it is essential that it should be. Be that as it may, I am entirely satisfied *e* that, on the facts of this case and on the material before him, the judge was in error in allowing that consideration to outweight the rule of policy. Whether it is more correct to say that he erred in applying established principles of discretion on which the court acts or that he failed to take into account important matters which he ought to have taken into account or that his decision was plainly wrong may not matter very much. *f*

If I had been left entirely to myself, I think it likely that I would have allowed this appeal without requiring the undertakings which counsel for the defendants has now offered. However, since they have been offered and since it is a matter to which Woolf LJ attaches importance, I certainly do not wish to differ on that point. In the circumstances and subject to those undertakings, the form of which can now be discussed further, I too agree that this appeal must be allowed. *g*

*Appeal allowed. Leave to appeal to House of Lords refused.*

Solicitors: *Theodore Goddard* (for the first, second, fourth, fifth and sixth defendants); *Harris Rosenblatt & Kramer* (for the third defendant); *Oppenheimers* (for the plaintiffs).

Mary Rose Plummer   Barrister.

# Pacific Associates Inc and another v Baxter and others

COURT OF APPEAL, CIVIL DIVISION

PURCHAS, RALPH GIBSON AND RUSSELL LJJ

24, 26, 27, 28, 31 OCTOBER, 2 NOVEMBER, 15 DECEMBER 1988

*Negligence – Duty to take care – Consultant engineer – Consultant engineer retained by employer to supervise contract works – Contractor making claims for additional payments – Engineer rejecting claims – Contractor claiming engineer negligent in rejecting claims – Whether engineer owing duty of care to contractor.*

The plaintiff contractor was the successful tenderer for dredging and reclamation work in Dubai for the employer, the ruler of Dubai. The contractor tendered in the knowledge that the work would be supervised by a consultant engineer retained by the employer, and the contract between the employer and the contractor provided that the contractor would only be paid sums on account of the contract price when they were certified by the engineer. The contractor claimed that inaccurate information provided by the engineer at the tender stage had resulted in the work being more difficult than expected and that in consequence its tender price had been too low. The contract provided that the contractor was entitled to additional payment if it encountered hard material in the course of dredging which could not have been reasonably foreseen by an experienced contractor, and in the course of the work the contractor made repeated claims for additional payments for hard materials. Those claims were consistently rejected by the engineer on the ground that the hard materials should have been foreseen by the contractor from the data supplied to it. The contractor brought an action against the engineer claiming £45m, alleging that the engineer had acted negligently or was in breach of its duty to act fairly and impartially in administering the contract by its continual failure to certify the contractor's claims for additional payments for hard materials and its final rejection of those claims. On the trial of a preliminary issue the judge held that the contractor could not recover damages from the engineer. The contractor appealed to the Court of Appeal.

**Held** – Where an engineer was employed or retained by a person, such as a building owner, to oversee the work of a contractor in circumstances where the engineer was under a duty to the employer to exercise care and skill in overseeing the contractor's work and was liable to the employer if the employer was sued by the contractor for economic loss which the contractor had suffered as the result of the engineer's negligence and where there was no direct contractual relationship between the contractor and the engineer or any assumption by the engineer of direct responsibility to the contractor for economic loss caused to the latter, the engineer owed no duty of care directly to the contractor coterminous with the contractor's rights against the employer. Accordingly, since there was no direct contractual relationship between the contractor and the engineer and since the contractor was entitled under its contract with the employer to claim the additional payments for hard materials from the employer, the engineer owed no duty of care to the contractor. The appeal would therefore be dismissed (see p 170 *f g*, p 171 *b c*, p 179 *b* to *d j* to p 180 *g j*, p 182 *d*, p 183 *e f*, p 184 *d f*, p 185 *b c f* to *h*, p 187 *b c* and p 191 *d* to *g*, post).

*Hedley Byrne & Co Ltd v Heller & Partners Ltd* [1963] 2 All ER 575 and *Sutcliffe v Thackrah* [1974] 1 All ER 859 considered.

**Notes**

For when a duty of care arises, see 35 Halsbury's Laws (4th edn) para 5, and for cases on the subject, see 36(1) Digest (Reissue) 17–19, 34–123.

**Cases referred to in judgments**

*Anns v Merton London Borough* [1977] 2 All ER 492, [1978] AC 728, [1977] 2 WLR 1024, *a*
HL.

*Arenson v Casson Beckman Rutley & Co* [1975] 3 All ER 901, [1977] AC 405, [1975] 3 WLR
815, HL; *rvsg* sub nom *Arenson v Arenson* [1973] 2 All ER 235, [1973] Ch 346, [1973]
2 WLR 553, CA.

*Banque Financière de la Cité SA v Westgate Insurance Co Ltd* (1988) Financial Times, 12
August, [1988] CA Transcript 658; *rvsg* sub nom *Banque Keyser Ullmann SA v Skandia* *b*
*(UK) Insurance Co Ltd* [1987] 1 Lloyd's Rep 69.

*Caparo Industries plc v Dickman* [1989] 1 All ER 798, [1989] 2 WLR 316, CA.

*Chambers v Goldthorpe* [1901] 1 KB 624, [1900–3] All ER Rep 969, CA.

*D & F Estates Ltd v Church Comrs for England* [1988] 2 All ER 992, [1988] 3 WLR 368,
HL.

*Davis Contractors Ltd v Fareham UDC* [1956] 2 All ER 145, [1956] AC 696, [1956] 3 WLR *c*
37, HL.

*Donoghue (or M'Alister) v Stevenson* [1932] AC 562, [1932] All ER Rep 1, HL.

*Ernst & Whinney v Willard Engineering (Dagenham) Ltd* (1987) 3 Const LJ 292.

*Esso Petroleum Co Ltd v Mardon* [1976] 2 All ER 5, [1976] QB 801, [1976] 2 WLR 583, CA.

*Glanzer v Shepard* (1922) 233 NY 236, NY Ct of Apps.

*Gleeson v J Wippell & Co Ltd* [1977] 3 All ER 54, [1977] 1 WLR 510.                    *d*

*Goldberg v Housing Authority of Newark* (1962) 38 NJ 578, NJ SC.

*Greater Nottingham Co-op Society Ltd v Cementation Piling and Foundations Ltd* [1988] 2 All
ER 971, [1989] QB 71, [1988] 3 WLR 396, CA.

*Hedley Byrne & Co Ltd v Heller & Partners Ltd* [1963] 2 All ER 575, [1964] AC 465, [1963]
3 WLR 101, HL.

*Hirachand Punamchand v Temple* [1911] 2 KB 330, CA.                                   *e*

*Home Office v Dorset Yacht Co Ltd* [1970] 2 All ER 294, [1970] AC 1004, [1970] 2 WLR
1140, HL.

*Junior Books Ltd v Veitchi Co Ltd* [1982] 3 All ER 201, [1983] 1 AC 520, [1982] 3 WLR 477,
HL.

*Leigh & Sillavan Ltd v Aliakmon Shipping Co Ltd, The Aliakmon* [1986] 2 All ER 145, [1986] *f*
AC 785, [1986] 2 WLR 902, HL.

*Lubenham Fidelities and Investment Co Ltd v South Pembrokeshire DC* (1986) 33 Build LR 39,
CA; *affg* [1985] CILL 214.

*Minister of Pensions v Chennell* [1946] 2 All ER 719, [1947] KB 250.

*Ministry of Housing and Local Government v Sharp* [1970] 1 All ER 1009, [1970] 2 QB 223,
[1970] 2 WLR 802, CA.
*g*
*Muirhead v Industrial Tank Specialities Ltd* [1985] 3 All ER 705, [1986] QB 507, [1985] 3
WLR 993, CA.

*Nocton v Lord Ashburton* [1914] AC 932, [1914–15] All ER Rep 45, HL.

*Peabody Donation Fund (Governors) v Sir Lindsay Parkinson & Co Ltd* [1984] 3 All ER 529,
[1985] AC 210, [1984] 3 WLR 953, HL.

*Ranger v Great Western Rly Co* (1854) 5 HL Cas 72, [1843–60] All ER Rep 321, 10 ER 824. *h*

*Ross v Caunters (a firm)* [1979] 3 All ER 580, [1980] Ch 297, [1979] 3 WLR 605.

*Rutter v Palmer* [1922] 2 KB 87, [1922] All ER Rep 367, CA.

*Salliss (Michael) & Co Ltd v Calil* (3 July 1987, unreported), QBD.

*Shui On Construction Co Ltd v Shui Kay Co Ltd* (1985) 1 Const LJ 305, Hong Kong SC.

*Simaan General Contracting Co v Pilkington Glass Ltd (No 2)* [1988] 1 All ER 791, [1988] QB
758, [1988] 2 WLR 761, CA.                                                            *j*

*Smith v Cox* [1940] 3 All ER 546, [1940] 2 KB 558.

*Stevenson v Watson* (1879) 4 CPD 148.

*Sutcliffe v Thackrah* [1974] 1 All ER 859, [1974] AC 727, [1974] 2 WLR 295, HL.

*Tai Hing Cotton Mill Ltd v Liu Chong Hing Bank Ltd* [1985] 2 All ER 947, [1986] AC 80,
[1985] 3 WLR 317, PC.

*Townsend v Stone Toms & Partners* (1984) 27 Build LR 26, CA.
a   *Welby v Drake* (1825) 1 C & P 557, 171 ER 1315, NP.
*Woods v Martins Bank Ltd* [1958] 3 All ER 166, [1959] 1 QB 55, [1958] 1 WLR 1018,
   Assizes.
*Yuen Kun-yeu v A-G of Hong Kong* [1987] 2 All ER 705, [1988] AC 175, [1987] 3 WLR 776,
   PC.

b **Appeal**
The plaintiffs, Pacific Associates Inc and RB Construction Ltd (together referred to as 'the
contractor'), appealed against the decision of his Honour Judge John Davies QC hearing
official referees' business on 1 December 1987 whereby he ordered on the trial of a
preliminary issue that the contractor's claim for damages against the defendants, Ronald
Stafford Baxter and 12 other named partners comprising the Halcrow International
c  Partnership (collectively referred to as 'the engineer'), be struck out on the ground that it
disclosed no reasonable cause of action. The facts are set out in the judgment of
Purchas LJ.

*Anthony Scrivener QC, Andrew Burr* and *N Mark Hill* for the contractor.
*Simon Tuckey QC* and *Elizabeth Davies* for the engineer.
d

                                                                    *Cur adv vult*

15 December. The following judgments were delivered.

**PURCHAS LJ.** These appeals raise important issues relating to the duty owed, if any,
e  by an engineer appointed to supervise construction works. Pacific Associates Inc (the
contractor) and RB Construction Ltd (the sub-contractor) claimed against Halcrow
International Partnership and 13 individual partners (hereinafter collectively referred to
as 'the engineer') by writ and statement of claim damages alleged to have been caused by
breach of duty by the engineer. For the purposes of the appeals the position of the
f  contractor and the sub-contractor are equivalent. I propose to use the word 'contractor'
to include 'sub-contractor' where appropriate after the date of the sub-contract, 13 April
1977.
    The appeals relate both to a determination of a preliminary issue and to an order to
strike out the amended statement of claim by his Honour Judge John Davies QC hearing
official referees' business on 1 December 1987. The works out of which the claim arose
g  were dredging and reclamation work in Dubai Creek Lagoon in the Persian Gulf (the
works) to be carried out by the contractor pursuant to a contract dated 25 February 1975
(the contract) between the contractor and His Highness the Ruler of Dubai (the employer).
The matter first came before the judge on an application by the engineer under RSC
Ord 18, r 19 to strike out the contractor's claims on the grounds that they did not disclose
a reasonable cause of action and were an abuse of the process of the court. By consent, it
h  was ordered that at the same time the judge should consider as a preliminary issue the
following question:

    'Assuming, without deciding, the facts pleaded in the amended statement of
    claim whether in law the [contractor] can recover damages from the [engineer] and
    if so what damages?'

j      The background can be shortly stated. Invitations to tender for the works were issued
at some date prior to February 1975 by predecessors of the engineer, Halcrow (Middle
East) Ltd, consultant engineers. Nothing turns on the change of formal identity which
took place in July 1978. We have been told that there were some 20 tenderers of which
the contractor was the successful one. The tender was made after examining, inter alia,
the 'drawings, conditions of contract, specification and bill of quantities', and in the light

of borehole reports and other geological information. The contractor tendered in the
knowledge that the work would be supervised by the engineer in accordance with the    a
conditions of contract.

It is not necessary to consider the details of the work involved, save to say that they
were extensive. A central matter for consideration was the nature of the bed of the creek,
the dredging of which was the subject matter of the contract. The borehole reports
which had been provided by the engineer disclosed that of the materials to be found on
the floor of the lagoon a certain percentage would consist, or was expected to consist, of    b
'hard materials'. Again, it is only necessary to know that the presence of these materials
rendered the dredging more difficult and expensive. In particular, it required more
powerful dredging equipment. The contractor's case was that the information imparted
at the tender stage was inaccurate and, as a result, the tender price on which the contract
sum was based was too low. The following provisions of the contract are relevant:

c

'PART I—GENERAL CONDITIONS

... 11. The Tender shall be deemed to have been based on such data regarding
hydrological climatic and physical conditions as shall have been supplied by the
Employer in the documents furnished to the Contractor by the Employer for the
purpose of tendering. The Contractor shall nevertheless inspect and examine the
Site and its surroundings and shall satisfy himself ...    d

12. The Contractor shall be deemed to have satisfied himself before tendering as
to the correctness and sufficiency of his Tender for the Works ... cover all his
obligations under the Contract and all matters and things necessary for the proper
completion and maintenance of the Works. If however during the execution of the
Works the Contractor shall encounter physical conditions or artificial obstructions
which conditions or obstructions could not have been reasonably foreseen by an    e
experienced contractor the Contractor shall forthwith give written notice thereof to
the Engineer's Representative and if in the opinion of the Engineer such conditions
or artificial obstructions could not have been reasonably foreseen by an experienced
contractor then the Engineer shall certify and the Employer shall pay the additional
expense to which the Contractor shall have been put by reason of such conditions    f
including the proper and reasonable expense ...

46. The whole of the materials plant and labour to be provided by the Contractor
under Clause 5 hereof and the mode manner and speed of execution and
maintenance of the Works are to be of a kind and conducted in a manner to the
satisfaction of the Engineer. Should the rate of progress of the Works or any part
thereof be at any time in the opinion of the Engineer too slow to ensure the
completion of the Works by the prescribed time or extended time for completion    g
the Engineer shall so notify the Contractor in writing and the Contractor shall
thereupon take such steps as the Contractor may think necessary and the Engineer
may approve to expedite progress so as to complete the Works by the prescribed
time or extended time for completion ...

56. The engineer shall except as otherwise stated ascertain and determine by    h
admeasurement the value in accordance with the Contract of work done in
accordance with the Contract ... If after examination of such records and drawings
the Contractor does not agree the same or does not sign the same as agreed they shall
nevertheless be taken to be correct unless the Contractor shall within 14 days of such
examination lodge with the Engineer's Representative for decision by the Engineer
notice in writing of the respects in which such records and drawings are claimed by    j
him to be incorrect ...

60. (1) Unless otherwise provided payments shall be made at monthly intervals
in accordance with the conditions set out in Part II in the Clause numbered 60 ...

67. If any dispute or difference of any kind whatsoever shall arise between the
Employer or the Engineer and the Contractor in connection with or arising out of
the Contract or the carrying out of the Works (whether during the progress of the

a     Works or after their completion and whether before or after the termination abandonment or breach of the Contract) it shall in the first place be referred to and settled by the Engineer who within a period of 90 days after being requested by either party to do so shall give written notice of his decision to the Employer and the Contractor. Save as hereinafter provided such decision in respect of every matter so referred shall be final and binding upon the Employer and the Contractor until the completion of the work and shall forthwith be given effect to by the Contractor

b     who shall proceed with the Works with all due diligence whether he or the Employer requires arbitration as hereinafter provided or not. If the Engineer has given written notice of his decision to the Employer and the Contractor and no claim to arbitration has been communicated to him by either the Employer or the Contractor within a period of 90 days from receipt of such notice the said decision shall remain final and binding upon the Employer and the Contractor. If the

c     Engineer shall fail to give notice of his decision as aforesaid within a period of 90 days after being requested as aforesaid or if either the Employer or the Contractor be dissatisfied with any such decision then and in any such case either the Employer or the Contractor may within 90 days after receiving notice of such decision or within 90 days after the expiration of the first named period of 90 days (as the case may be) require that the matter or matters in dispute be referred to arbitration as

d     hereinafter provided. All disputes or differences in respect of which the decision (if any) of the Engineer has not become final and binding as aforesaid shall be finally settled under the Rules of Conciliation and Arbitration of the International Chamber of Commerce by one or more arbitrators appointed in accordance with the said Rules. The said arbitrator/s shall have full power to open up review and revise any decision opinion direction certificate or valuation of the Engineer and neither party

e     shall be limited in the proceedings before such arbitrator/s to the evidence or arguments put before the Engineer for the purpose of obtaining his said decision. No decision given by the Engineer in accordance with the foregoing provisions shall disqualify him from being called as a witness and giving evidence before the arbitrator/s on any matter whatsoever relevant to the dispute or difference referred to the arbitrator/s as aforesaid. The arbitrator/s shall not enter on the reference until

f     after the completion or alleged completion of the Works unless with the written consent of the Employer and the Contractor provided always (i) that such reference may be opened before such completion or alleged completion in respect of the withholding by the Engineer of any certificate or the withholding of any portion of the retention money to which the Contractor claims in accordance with the conditions set out in Part II in the Clause numbered 60 to be entitled or in respect

g     of the exercise of the Engineer's power to give a certificate under Clause 63(1) hereof or in respect of a dispute arising under Clause 71 hereof (ii) that the giving of a Certificate of Completion under Clause 48 hereof shall not be a condition precedent to the opening of any such reference . . .

h     PART II—CONDITIONS OF PARTICULAR APPLICATION
      . . . 60. (4) The Contractor shall submit to the Engineer after the end of each month a statement showing the estimated contract value of the permanent work executed up to the end of the month . . . and the Contractor will be paid monthly on the certificate of the Engineer the amount due to him on account of the estimated contract value of the permanent work executed up to the end of the previous month

j     subject to a retention . . .
      (6) Payment upon each of the Engineer's Certificates shall be made by the Employer within 30 days after such certificate has been delivered to the Employer and in the event of failure by The Employer to comply with the provisions of this sub-clause he shall pay to the Contractor interest at the rate of 9% per annum . . .
      (7) The Engineer may by any certificate make any correction or modification in any previous certificate which shall have been issued by him and shall have power

to withhold any certificate if the Works or any part thereof are not being carried out
to his satisfaction . . .

    84. The Engineer in giving his decision with respect to a claim or in respect of
any matter mentioned in the last preceding clause or in respect of all other matters
in which his decision is made final by the terms of the Contract or any of them will
act independently of and entirely unfettered by the Employer.

    85. In measuring, valuing, deciding or certifying the Engineer is not intended to
act as arbitrator but as an Engineer acts by his skill and from his knowledge of any
fact and incidents connected with the Works and in so far as any facts are not within
his own knowledge, he shall be at liberty to inform his mind by enquiring of the
Engineer's Representative assistant engineers, inspectors and others. The Engineer
shall at all times be considered seized of all the facts necessary for him to form his
opinion, make his measurements or valuation, give his decision or order, make his
requisition or give or refuse his certificate and he shall be at liberty to certify at such
time and in such manner as in his discretion he shall think proper and he shall not
be bound to give any reason for or any particulars of his certificate or any reason for
his not certifying.

    86. Neither any member of the Employer's staff nor the Engineer nor any of his
staff, nor the Engineer's Representative shall be in any way personally liable for the
acts or obligations under the Contract, or answerable for any default or omission on
the part of the Employer in the observance or performance of any of the acts,
matters or things which are herein contained . . .'

Work started in the summer of 1975. By letter of 10 November the engineer gave
notice under cl 46 of the general conditions (to which I shall refer as 'GC 46') that they
were not satisfied with the progress of the dredging. In a reply two weeks later the
contractor referred to damage to the dredgers caused by hard rock which had been
encountered. Meetings and correspondence concerned with the progress of the dredging
continued into 1976 between the contractor and the engineer. By an agreement made as
of 2 October 1976 and signed on 13 April 1977 the contractor sub-contracted part of the
work to RB Construction Ltd.

By letter dated 9 July 1977 the contractor first intimated a claim under GC52(5) for
additional expenses in accordance with GC12. This was rejected by letter dated 10 August
1977 from the engineer which stated that if the contractor wished to pursue the claim it
would be necessary to establish an agreed set of observation data'. At a meeting on 14
December 1977 the contractor's representative indicated that the work could only be
completed by a much larger dredging plant than originally envisaged; that the contractor
was incurring considerable losses and that it was going to seek an increase in the rates for
the contract. The engineer's representative pointed out that as a matter of grace the
employer had already agreed to one year's extension of time; that nothing had been
shown that had not been indicated by the borehole reports at tender stage and repeated
that a claim would have to be supported by full details which could be the basis for
recommendations to the employer.

Under cover of a letter dated 7 June 1980 the contractor sent to the engineer three
volumes comprising a 'Summary Presentation of Claim', which included the formal
claim under GC12 for additional expenses. This claim was rejected by the engineer in a
letter dated 25 June 1980:

    'So far as your claims relate to an assertion that the materials to be dredged were
different to those which might reasonably have been assumed at the date of tender
in terms of dredgeability and cost of removal, transportation and effect on
overdredging they are rejected.'

The contractor made formal submissions in accordance with GC67 of a number of
claims including, inter alia, the hard material claim to which on 13 December 1980 the
engineer made a formal rejection in accordance with the terms of the clause. On 12

a March 1981 the matter was referred to the International Chamber of Commerce in the form of an arbitration between the contractor and the employer. The engineer was not, of course, formally a party to this arbitration although its representatives would clearly play a part as witnesses. The points of claim were delivered with the request for arbitration. The defence in those proceedings was dated 29 October 1981. The next relevant event was on 2 July 1985 when by a formal agreement between the contractor and the employer the arbitration was settled in consideration for the payment by the

b employer to the contractor of the equivalent of £10m in consideration for the agreement by the contractor that—

'such payment and agreement by the Defendant [the employer] constitutes full and final settlement of all its and their claims against the Defendant and bears its and their own costs in connection therewith.'

c There was a reciprocal agreement by the employer acknowledging that the settlement was in full and final settlement of all claims by the employer against the contractor and those claiming under him.

On 24 March 1986 the contractor issued a writ naming the 14 defendants but this was not served until 5 March in the following year when it was served together with a statement of claim on the first 13 defendants. This prompted the application to strike

d out the claim to which I have already referred and which was heard on 9, 20, 21 and 22 October 1987. The hard materials claim was for £31m plus interest. The facts in the statement of claim which in the terms of the consent order for the trial of the preliminary issue are assumed to be correct were set out in the judgment in the following terms:

'*Statement of claim*  I can summarise the essential basis of the plaintiff's claims as follows without distinguishing between them since the parties have agreed that I

e should treat the sub-contractor's claim on a par with that of the contractor. It was entitled under cll 11 and 12 of the contract to additional payment for hard materials. It was the duty of the engineer in administering the contract and in particular in issuing interim certificates and in deciding claims under cl 67 of the contract to act with the care and skill, fairness and impartiality to be expected of engineers of their high standing and repute; the [contractor], to the engineer's knowledge, relied on it

f to do so. As part of its duties the engineer was obliged to consider the [contractor's] hard material claims and, if it considered them valid to certify them for interim payment when they were originally submitted or if not, then by the adjustment of later certificates, or ultimately by decision under cl 67. Throughout the duration of the works the [contractor] made repeated claims for additional payment for hard materials, but notwithstanding the validity of its claims the engineer invariably

g maintained that "the hard materials should have been foreseen by the [contractor]" from the data supplied to it and consistently rejected its claims right up to and including the time when it finally rejected them under cl 67 in December 1980. By its continual failure to certify and by its final rejection of the [contractor's] claims the engineer acted negligently and alternatively was in breach of its duty to act fairly

h and impartially in administering the contract. As a result the [contractor] suffered the following loss and damage:

| | |
|---|---|
| Entitlement (that is to say its entitlement to be paid extra for hard materials under the terms of the contract) | £31m |
| Interest | £22m |
| Arbitration costs (due to the fact that "the rejection of Pacific's claim forced it to commence arbitration proceedings as required by cl 67") | £2m |
| *Less* credit (for the amount recovered in the arbitration proceedings) | £10m |
| Net total | £45m' |

By the contract between the employer and the contractor the latter can only recover sums of money on account of the contract price when these are certified by the engineer. In the end, subject to retention money, the ultimate sum earned by the contractor is the initial contract price as varied under the terms of the contract. The terms of GC12 clearly provided that the additional sum to be paid by the employer shall represent the additional expense to which the contractor had been put by reason of the unexpected circumstances together with the proper and reasonable expense of complying with instructions which the engineer might issue and of any proper, reasonable measures approved by the engineer which the contractor might take in the absence of specified instructions. The contractor, therefore, was to be protected against being out of pocket, but was not entitled to any profit on the additional work involved.

Describing the position of the engineer the judge said:

'He was the agent of the employer for those purposes [ie the administration of the contract]; he was contractually bound to his principal, the employer, and the terms and scope of his agency would be those to be inferred from what he was employed to do under the terms of the contract. It also follows that, short of any fraud or dishonesty on his part, which would be manifestly outside the scope of his agency, his principal would be liable for the acts of his agent, subject to any right of recourse he might have against his agent for indemnity.'

The amended statement of claim asserted in para 7 that—

'the Engineer held itself out, and was expected to, and the Plaintiffs relied on (the engineer) so to perform the Engineer's obligations with the skill, etc . . .'

Although these facts are to be assumed for the purpose of the trial of the preliminary issue, they are not determinative of the existence of 'proximity' for the purpose of liability in tort for the damage claimed.

On the question of liability the judge took as his starting point the quotation from the speech of Lord Keith in *Governors of the Peabody Donation Fund v Sir Lindsay Parkinson & Co Ltd* [1984] 3 All ER 529 at 534, [1985] AC 210 at 241:

'So in determining whether or not a duty of care of particular scope was incumbent on a defendant it is material to take into consideration whether it is just and reasonable that it should be so.'

The judge continued:

'This, in my view, is especially so where the duties on which a plaintiff relies to found a case in tort arise out of a contract, and there would seem to be no reason why the defendant should not have been made a party to the contract if that was the intention of the parties and he had been prepared to assume a liability similar to that now sought to be attached to him in tort.'

He then referred to *Tai Hing Cotton Mill Ltd v Liu Chong Hing Bank Ltd* [1985] 2 All ER 947 at 957, [1986] AC 80 at 107 per Lord Scarman:

'Their Lordships do not believe that there is anything to the advantage of the law's development in searching for a liability in tort where the parties are in a contractual relationship. This is particularly so in a commercial relationship. Though it is possible as a matter of legal semantics to conduct an analysis of the rights and duties inherent in some contractual relationships including that of banker and customer either as a matter of contract law when the question will be what, if any, terms are to be implied or as a matter of tort law when the task will be to identify a duty arising from the proximity and character of the relationship between the parties, their Lordships believe it to be correct in principle and necessary for the avoidance of confusion in the law to adhere to the contractual analysis: on principle

because it is a relationship in which the parties have, subject to a few exceptions, the
a    right to determine their obligations to each other ...'

The judge continued:

'He [Lord Scarman] was there dealing with the liability in negligence of a banker
to his customer. However, his words are in my view equally pertinent to the
situation one has here, where the duties alleged arise out of the participation of the
b    engineer in a contract, although he was not a party to it, but the person who seeks
to make him liable in tort for his acts under the contract was a party to it. More
than that, the damage which the [contractor alleges is wholly comprehended within
the ambit of the contract, and the action in tort is based on the [contractor's]
entitlement to what [it claims was [its] due from the employer under that
contract ... Just as the implications of the agency relationship between the engineer
c    and the employer depend on the terms of the contract between the employer and
the contractor (see Lord Morris in *Sutcliffe v Thackrah* [1974] 1 All ER 859 at 872,
876, [1974] AC 727 at 747, 752), so also, in my view, must those of the relationship
between the contractor and the engineer. More than that, the [contractor's] whole
case is based on the contract and on the alleged breach of a duty of care by the
engineer in performing [its] functions under it. The damage relied on is, and can
d    only be the infringement by the engineer of a right which the contractor had against
the employer under the contract. The paradox at the root of this claim seems to me
to be that it postulates the continuing validity of the contractor's claim against the
employer while seeking to impose a commensurate liability on the latter's agent on
the ground that in the course of [its] administration of the contract [it] negligently
failed to give proper or timeous effect to its terms. [After reviewing the relevant
e    terms of the contract, the judge commented] I cannot with respect see how the
question of the existence, nature and scope of such a duty or of its breach can be
divorced from the question of the nature of the function which the engineer was
employed to perform with the knowledge and agreement of the contractor: the
provisions of conditions 67, 85 and 86 are integral parts of the nature of [its]
function.'
f
Asking himself the question—

'whether it accords with good sense for the law to intervene in a commercial
relationship like this to impose on the agent of one party to the contract a duty of
care towards the other party to that contract in respect of administrative acts for the
consequences of which his principal would in any case be liable under the contract'
g
the judge came to the firm conclusion that the answer was No. On this basis, he answered
the question posed in the preliminary issue in the negative.

The judge then turned to the question of the 'balance of the application to strike out
the writ and the statement of claim' on the ground that they were an abuse of the process
of the court. The settlement of the arbitration on 2 July 1985 was the basis of his
h    approach to this problem in the light of two authorities: *Welby v Drake* (1825) 1 C & P
557, 171 ER 1315 and *Hirachand Punamchand v Temple* [1911] 2 KB 330. These cases
concerned actions in debt. The judge said:

'In my view, however, the principle which they express is equally applicable to
the circumstances of this case, which is concerned with principal and agent, where
j    the contract between the principal and the third party expressly excludes the
personal liability of the agent, and the settlement made by the principal was on the
terms which I have already mentioned. I would, therefore, strike out the claim in
this case, both on the ground that it discloses no reasonable cause of action, that it is
unconscionable and an abuse of the process of the court.'

In support of his appeal counsel for the contractor submitted that on the assumptions made for the purposes of the trial of the preliminary issue the three criteria necessary to *a* establish liability which appear from the authorities and which were marshalled in the judgment of Bingham LJ in *Caparo Industries plc v Dickman* [1989] 1 All ER 798, [1989] 2 WLR 316 were established. These were (1) foreseeability of harm, (2) proximity, (3) that as a matter of policy it is just and reasonable to impose a duty of care on the engineer in favour of the contractor. He submitted that a failure on the part of the engineer properly to discharge its duty under the contract must be taken to cause *b* foreseeable harm to the contractor which was, under the terms of its contract with the employer dependent on the proper discharge by the engineer of his duties, inter alia, to certify the moneys due to the contractor under the contract. In addition counsel for the contractor emphasised that the employer had a right of action outside the contract and the arbitration provision in GC67 against the engineer in negligence or breach of duty (see *Sutcliffe v Thackrah* [1974] 1 All ER 859, [1974] AC 727) and that, therefore, it would *c* not be just and reasonable if a similar right against the engineer was not enjoyed by the other party to the contract, namely the contractor. The contractor's claim, counsel submitted, was covered entirely by the principles in *Hedley Byrne & Co Ltd v Heller & Partners Ltd* [1963] 2 All ER 575, [1964] AC 465 and was not affected by any of the subsequent authorities in which this case was considered.

Further, counsel distinguished *Welby v Drake* and the *Hirachand Punamchand* case *d* which he said were both accord and satisfaction cases. The settlement which was achieved with the employer, including the mutual releases of all outstanding claims etc, he submitted, did not involve the engineer at all and the latter was not entitled to rely on any accord and satisfaction which formed the basis of the settlement of the arbitration with the employer. He referred to *Smith v Cox* [1940] 3 All ER 546, [1940] 2 KB 558. In further submissions counsel relied on *Townsend v Stone Toms & Partners* (1984) 27 Build *e* LR 26.

Counsel for the engineer in support of the judgment relied on the well-established proposition that there was no general liability in tort for foreseeable economic loss dissociated from physical damage. He relied on the proposition that the terms of the contract sufficiently defined the rights and liabilities arising between the engineer and the two parties to the contract; and that there was no justification for any extension of *f* this position by superimposing a duty in tort. Furthermore, counsel relied on the disclaimer contained in cl 86 of the conditions of particular application (to which I shall refer as 'PC86') as a disclaimer on which the engineer could rely to disprove that element of acceptance of a duty of care necessary to establish liability under the principle in *Hedley Byrne*. In this case, it was submitted, the contractor's rights of protection in relation to any loss which might ensue from a failure on the part of the engineer either properly to *g* certify or to accept a claim under GC67 were catered for under the arbitration provisions and a right of recovery against the employer under that clause. Counsel submitted that the remote possibility of an employer becoming bankrupt or unable to meet the liability for any damages flowing from the conduct of his agent, the engineer, was too remote a consideration to affect a general principle of whether or not liability in tort should be *h* superimposed on the contractual position. If there was any appreciable danger of the employer failing to meet his obligations under the contract it would be open to the contractor to stipulate for a separate contractual right of action against the engineer.

On the question of reasonableness, counsel for the engineer submitted that the mere fact that the engineer accepted appointment by the employer to act under the contract was not sufficient to impose a duty in tort in favour of the contractor who had its own *j* remedies under the contract. Furthermore, in the face of the commercial relationship and the detailed provisions of the contract, it was not just and reasonable but rather undesirable to import into a carefully structured contractual arrangement added obligations in tort. This was particularly the case where those provisions expressly

provided an exclusion from liability protecting the engineer or any of its staff from
*a* liability for their acts or obligations under the contract. In support of his respondent's
notice counsel submitted that in any event the engineer was entitled to immunity from
suit in respect of the decision under GC67 because any miscertification at an earlier stage
could then have been corrected at the GC67 stage and that in acting in pursuance of its
duties under GC67 the engineer was acting in a quasi-arbitral role.

The sheet-anchor for the consideration of the main issue raised in this appeal is still
*b* *Hedley Byrne & Co Ltd v Heller & Partners Ltd* [1963] 2 All ER 575, [1964] AC 465. The
central issue in that case was, of course, whether a duty of care could arise in relation to
spoken or written words. At the risk of making a dangerous generalisation, the effect of
the authority for the present purposes can be culled from the following short extracts
from the speech of Lord Devlin ([1963] 2 All ER 575 at 610–611, [1964] AC 465 at 528–
530):
*c*
> 'I think, therefore, that there is ample authority to justify your lordships in saying
> now that the categories of special relationships, which may give rise to a duty to take
> care in word as well as in deed, are not limited to contractual relationships or to
> relationships of fiduciary duty, but include also relationships which in the words of
> LORD SHAW in *Nocton* v. *Lord Ashburton* ([1914] AC 932 at 972, [1914–15] All ER
*d* Rep 45 at 62) are "equivalent to contract" that is, where there is an assumption of
> responsibility in circumstances in which, but for the absence of consideration, there
> would be a contract . . . I shall therefore content myself with the proposition that
> wherever there is a relationship equivalent to contract there is a duty of care. Such a
> relationship may be either general or particular. Examples of a general relationship
> are those of solicitor and client and of banker and customer. For the former *Nocton*
*e* v. *Lord Ashburton* has long stood as the authority and for the latter there is the
> decision of SALMON, J., in *Woods* v. *Martins Bank, Ltd.* ([1958] 3 All ER 166, [1959] 1
> QB 55) which I respectfully approve. There may well be others yet to be established.
> Where there is a general relationship of this sort it is unnecessary to do more than
> prove its existence and the duty follows. Where, as in the present case, what is relied
> on is a particular relationship created ad hoc, it will be necessary to examine the
*f* particular facts to see whether there is an express or implied undertaking of
> responsibility.'

Of course, there has not only to be an acceptance of responsibility to take care on the part
of the potential tortfeasor but also a reliance on that duty by the alleged victim. If it were
otherwise the damage would not have flowed from the breach if established. The
engineer is a professional body and in the context of the contract assumes a responsibility
*g* towards the employer to execute its duties in a professional manner. It remains, however,
to consider whether beyond this the engineer accepted a direct duty towards the
contractor and whether on its part the contractor relied on the due performance of its
duties under the contract by the engineer beyond giving rights to it to proceed against
the employer under the contract. This question lies at the heart of this appeal and
*h* depends on whether an appropriate degree of proximity between the engineer and the
contractor beyond the terms of contract is established. As I have already commented the
assumption of the truth of the facts pleaded in the amended statement of claim does not
determine this issue.

During the course of argument the court has been referred to a large number of
authorities many of which have considered a duty in tort based on the *Hedley Byrne* duty
*j* or extensions thereto. It is clear from these authorities that there is no one touchstone
with which to determine the existence or otherwise of a duty of care in any particular
circumstances. Various criteria emerge which are capable of adaptation to the particular
circumstances of the case under review. As a generalisation before a duty can be found to
exist the circumstances in which the parties find themselves must establish a proximity

of some kind that would demonstrate that the lack of care of the one will foreseeably
cause pecuniary loss to the other in the context where the first has accepted responsibility  *a*
for such loss, if occasioned by his negligence, and the second has in the same context
relied on the exercise of due care and skill by the first so as to give rise to a direct duty to
be responsible for that loss. The matter does not end there, however, because
superimposed on the foregoing criteria is what has been called a policy aspect, namely
that before a duty of care will be held to exist the court should find it just and reasonable
to impose such a duty (see per Lord Keith in *Governors of the Peabody Donation Fund v Sir*  *b*
*Lindsay Parkinson & Co Ltd* [1984] 3 All ER 529 at 534, [1985] AC 210 at 241). This aspect
was also discussed in the judgments in *Greater Nottingham Co-op Society Ltd v Cementation
Piling and Foundations Ltd* [1988] 2 All ER 971, [1989] QB 71. In this case there was a sub-
contract between the parties in which certain liabilities in contract were accepted, namely
to exercise skill and care in the design of the concrete piling but nothing mentioned in
the contract of executing the work with care and skill. In those circumstances it was held  *c*
that no duty of care would be superimposed on the existing contractual relationship
([1988] 2 All ER 971 at 984–985, [1989] QB 71 at 100 per Purchas LJ):

> 'In order to establish what might be called the *Hedley Byrne* type of liability, it
> must be possible to cull from the close relationship of the parties the assumption by
> the tortfeasor of a duty not to cause pecuniary loss to the victim. In the *Hedley Byrne*  *d*
> case the relationship was not affected by a direct contractual relationship and this
> was also the position in [*Junior Books Ltd v Veitchi Co Ltd* [1982] 3 All ER 201, [1983]
> 1 AC 520], and there was, therefore, no contractual influence on the relationship. In
> the present case the tortfeasor had contracted to be liable for failure to use reasonable
> skill and care in the design of the pile driving operation and in the selection of
> materials and goods (cl A(1)(a) and (b)) but, the contract was significantly silent as to  *e*
> liability for the manner in which the work was executed. Once it is established that
> there is no general liability in tort for pecuniary loss dissociated from physical
> damage (see per Robert Goff and Bingham LJJ in [*Muirhead v Industrial Tank
> Specialities Ltd* [1985] 3 All ER 705, [1986] QB 507 and *Simaan General Contracting Co
> v Pilkington Glass Ltd (No 2)* [1988] 1 All ER 791, [1988] QB 758]) it would be difficult
> to construct a special obligation of this nature in tort to which liabilities created by  *f*
> a collateral contract did not extend.'

The facts of the present case are, of course, clearly distinguishable from those in the
*Greater Nottingham Co-op* case but from the policy point of view there may be a useful
analogy, namely that, where the parties have come together against a contractual
structure which provides for compensation in the event of a failure of one of the parties
involved, the court will be slow to superimpose an added duty of care beyond that which  *g*
was in the contemplation of the parties at the time that they came together. I acknowledge
at once the distinction, namely where obligations are founded in contract they depend
on the agreement made and the objective intention demonstrated by that agreement
whereas the existence of a duty in tort may not have such a definitive datum point.
However, I believe that in order to determine whether a duty arises in tort it is necessary  *h*
to consider the circumstances in which the parties came together in the initial stages at
which time it should be considered what obligations, if any, were assumed by the one in
favour of the other and what reliance was placed by the other on the first. The obligations
do not, however, remain fixed subject only to specific variations as in the case of contract.
I would not exclude a change in the relationship affecting the existence or nature of a
duty of care in tort. This situation, however, does not arise in the present case.  *j*
The contractual structure against which the engineer and the contractor came into
contact was substantially provided by the terms of the contract which, of course, were
part of the background against which the tender was made. The contract in its general
conditions contained a large number of provisions by reason of which the contractor was

in a direct relationship with the engineer; examples are to be found in GC46 and GC56
*a* and numerous other certifying conditions such as GC52, GC60 and PC60 etc. In other
aspects the engineer worked solely as the agent for the employer. Instances of this were,
of course, the preparation of the invitations to tender and the contract document, bills of
quantities etc which accompanied it. We were told that there was no record available of
any specific contract between the employer and the engineer in relation to the contract.
The best information was that the engineer had for a considerable time prior to 1974
*b* acted in relation to other contracts for the employer and that the position between them
was most probably one similar to a general retainer. For the purposes of this appeal I do
not think that the precise contractual arrangement between the employer and the
engineer is relevant. It is sufficient to notice that there must have been some contract,
expressed or implied, between the two a term of which must have been that the engineer
would carry out its function with due skill and care.
*c*     It is now necessary to turn to consider some of the authorities relating to the specific
position as between the contractor and the engineer. It is immediately apparent that
there is no simple unqualified answer to the question 'Does the engineer owe a duty to
the contractor in tort to exercise reasonable skill and care?' but that this question can only
be answered in the context of the factual matrix including especially the contractual
structure against which such duty is said to arise.
*d*     The central question which arises here is: against the contractual structure of the
contract into which the contractor was prepared to enter with the employer, can it be
said that it looked to the engineer by way of reliance for the proper execution of the
latter's duties under the contract in extension of the rights which would accrue to it
under the contract against the employer? In other words, although the parties were
brought into close proximity in relation to the contract, was it envisaged that a failure to
*e* carry out its duties under the contract by the engineer would foreseeably cause any loss
to the contractor which was not properly recoverable by it under its rights against the
employer under the contract? Although this is distinguishable from the position in the
*Greater Nottingham Co-op* case it may be argued that it would not be just and reasonable to
impose on the engineer by way of liability in tort rights in favour of the contractor in
*f* excess of those rights which the contractor was content to acquire against the employer
under the contract.
    A start can be made with *Ranger v Great Western Rly Co* (1854) 5 HL Cas 72, [1843–60]
All ER Rep 321, which was cited in *Sutcliffe v Thackrah* [1974] 1 All ER 859, [1974] AC
727. This case has the distinction of antiquity but the facts involved bear an uncanny
resemblance to those in the present case. Ranger was the contractor engaged on the
*g* construction of works including, inter alia, the Avon bridge. The engineer was Brunel.
Ranger's bills asserted fraud on the part of the company through their engineer in two
relevant respects. The first was that inspection pits misled the contractor into
underestimating the hardness of the rock to be excavated in the cutting and tunnel and
he was thereby induced to tender an uneconomically low price. The second point of
greater subtlety was that unbeknown to the contractor Brunel was a shareholder in the
*h* company. It is on the second point that Lord Cranworth LC said (5 HL Cas 72 at 88–89,
[1843–60] All ER Rep 321 at 326):

> 'It is not necessary to state the duties of the engineer in detail: he was, in truth,
> made the absolute judge, during the progress of the works, of the mode in which
> the Appellant was discharging his duties; he was to decide how much of the contract
> price of £63,028 from time to time had become payable; and how much was due
*j*    > for extra works; and from his decision, so far, there was no appeal. After all the
> works should have been completed, the Appellant might call in a referee of his own
> as to any question as to the amount (if any) then due beyond what had been certified.

The contention now made by the Appellant is, that the duties thus confided to the principal engineer were of a judicial nature; that Mr. Brunel was the principal engineer by whom those duties were to be performed, and that he was himself a *a* shareholder in the Company; that he was thus made a judge, or arbitrator, in what was, in effect, his own cause. That until the month of July 1838 the Appellant was unaware of the fact of Mr. Brunel having any interest in the Company, except as the engineer, and so ought not to be bound by any of his decisions. [Lord Cranworth LC then considered an authority to the effect that the decision of a judge made in a cause in which he has an interest is voidable and continued:] I think the principle *b* has no application here; a judge ought to be, and is supposed to be, indifferent between the parties. He has, or is supposed to have, no bias inducing him to lean to the one side rather than to the other. In ordinary cases it is a just ground of exception to a judge that he is not indifferent, and the fact that he is himself a party, or interested as a party, affords the strongest proof that he cannot be indifferent. But here the whole tenor of the contract shows it was never intended that the engineer *c* should be indifferent between the parties. When it is stipulated that certain questions shall be decided by the engineer appointed by the Company, this is, in fact, a stipulation that they shall be decided by the Company. It is obvious that there never was any intention of leaving to third persons the decision of questions arising during the progress of the works. The Company reserved the decision to itself, acting however, as from the nature of things it must act, by an agent, and that agent *d* was, for this purpose, the engineer. His decisions were, in fact, those of the Company. The contract did not hold out, or pretend to hold out, to the Appellant, that he was to look to the engineer in any other character than as the impersonation of the Company: in fact, the contract treats his acts and the acts of the Company, for many purposes, as equivalent, or rather identical. I am therefore of opinion that the principle on which the doctrine as to a judge rests, wholly fails in its application to *e* this case.'

Of course, the contract in the present case specifically included provisions whereby the engineer's decisions could be challenged (GC67) and which placed a duty on the engineer while acting as agent of the employer to be fair as between the employer and the contractor (PC84) and to that extent that it should be objective in the discharge of its *f* duties.

In *Sutcliffe v Thackrah* [1974] 1 All ER 859, [1974] AC 727 their Lordships were concerned with a claim by an employer against the architect whom he had employed to design a house. There was a contract between the building owner and the architect which acknowledged that, inter alia, the latter would be concerned with a RIBA form of contract. Subsequently the employer entered into a contract with a firm of builders *g* which was in a standard RIBA form. The architects were appointed architects and quantity surveyors and during the course of the works issued interim certificates to the builders. The builders failed and were removed from site and another firm completed the work at higher cost. The original builders went into liquidation and the employer brought an action against the architects in negligence and breach of duty. The RIBA *h* form contained a condition 35(x) providing for arbitration. In his speech Lord Reid drew the distinction between the function of an arbitrator to form a judgment having heard the evidence and contentions of each party in dispute from the role of an architect ([1974] 1 All ER 859 at 862–863, [1974] AC 727 at 735–737):

'In other forms of professional activity the professional man is generally left to *j* make his own investigation. In the end he must make a decision but it is a different kind of decision. He is not determining a dispute: he is deciding what to do in all the circumstances . . . Now I can come to the position of an architect. He is employed by the building owner but has no contract with the contractor. *We do not in this case have occasion to consider whether nevertheless he may have some duty to the contractor: I do*

*not think that a consideration of that matter would help in the present case.* The RIBA form
a      of contract sets out the architect's functions in great detail. It has often been said, I
think rightly, that the architect has two different types of function to perform. In
many matters he is bound to act on his client's instructions, whether he agrees with
them or not; but in many other matters requiring professional skill he must form
and act on his own opinion. Many matters may arise in the course of the execution
of a building contract where a decision has to be made which will affect the amount
b      of money which the contractor gets. Under the RIBA contract many such decisions
have to be made by the architect and the parties agree to accept his decisions. For
example, he decides whether the contractor should be reimbursed for loss under
cl 11 (variation), cl 24 (disturbance) or cl 34 (antiquities); whether he should be
allowed extra time (cl 23); or where work ought reasonably to have been completed
(cl 22). And, perhaps most important, he has to decide whether work is defective.
c      These decisions will be reflected in the amounts contained in certificates issued by
the architect. The building owner and the contractor make their contract on the
understanding that in all such matters the architect will act in a fair and unbiased
manner and it must therefore be implicit in the owner's contract with the architect
that he shall not only exercise due care and skill but also reach such decisions fairly
holding the balance between his client and the contractor.' (My emphasis.)
d
Lord Reid then continued firmly to dismiss the suggestion that architects acting in
accordance with an RIBA form of contract could enjoy immunity as 'quasi-arbitrators'
and said ([1974] 1 All ER 859 at 864, [1974] AC 727 at 737–738):

'One might almost suppose that to be based on the completely illogical
argument—all persons carrying out judicial functions must act fairly, therefore all
e      persons who must act fairly are carrying out judicial functions. There is nothing
judicial about an architect's function in determining whether certain work is
defective. There is no dispute. He is not jointly engaged by the parties. They do not
submit evidence as contentious to him. He makes his own investigations and comes
to a decision. It would be taking a very low view to suppose that without being put
in a special position his employer would wish him to act unfairly or that a
f      professional man would be willing to depart from the ordinary honourable standard
of professional conduct.'

Lord Morris approached the position in similar terms with a difference in contrasting
the rights accruing to the employer with those accruing to the contractor. I would not,
however, with respect over-emphasise this distinction, which I do not think was
g      necessarily to the mind of Lord Morris ([1974] 1 All ER 859 at 869–870, [1974] AC 727
at 744–745):

'If there is no arbitration to which the provisions of the Arbitration Act 1950
apply but if two or more people informally agree to refer a disputed matter to the
decision of some person of their own selection they may place him in the position
h      of quasi-arbitrator and the common understanding of them all may be that the
chosen person in accepting the charge does not expressly or implicitly undertake to
do more than to give his honest opinion. Were the respondents in the present case
in that position? They were employed and paid by the appellant. The duties
involved that the architect would act fairly: he was to act fairly in ensuring that the
provisions of the building contract were faithfully carried out. He was to exercise
j      his care and skill in so ensuring. But his function differed from that of one who had
to decide disputes between a building owner and a contractor. When interim
certificates were issued it was necessary to have regard to the contract terms and to
exercise care and skill in certifying the value of work done. *If the contractor thought
that the sum certified was too little the contractor could call for arbitration. If the employer
paid the amount certified and later found that there was over-certification as a result of the*

*architect's negligence I can see no reason why, if loss resulted to him, he should not sue his architect.* As parties to a building contract or to a contract of sale are in general free  **a**
to introduce whatever terms they wish into their contract it follows that it is quite possible for them to arrange that someone who at one stage is the agent of one party may at another stage become an arbitrator as between the parties. But this must be a definite arrangement. *The mere fact that an architect must act fairly as between a building owner and a contractor does not of itself involve that the architect is discharging arbitral functions.'* (My emphasis.)          **b**

Lord Morris continued ([1974] 1 All ER 859 at 876–877, [1974] AC 727 at 752–753):

'In summarising my conclusions I must preface them by the observation that each case will depend on its own facts and circumstances and on the particular provisions of the relevant contract. But in general any architect or surveyor or valuer will be liable to the person who employs him if he causes loss by reason of his  **c**
negligence. There will be an exception to this and judicial immunity will be accorded if the architect or surveyor or valuer has by agreement been appointed to act as an arbitrator. There may be circumstances in which what is in effect an arbitration is not one that is within the provisions of the Arbitration Act. The expression quasi-arbitrator should only be used in that connection. A person will only be an arbitrator or quasi-arbitrator if there is a submission to him either of a  **d**
specific dispute or of present points of difference or of defined differences that may in future arise and if there is agreement that his decision will be binding. The circumstance that an architect in valuing work must act fairly and impartially does not constitute him either an arbitrator or a quasi-arbitrator. The circumstance that a building owner and contractor agree between themselves that a certificate of an architect showing a balance due is to be conclusive evidence of the works having  **e**
been duly completed and that the contractor is entitled to receive payment does not of itself involve that the architect is an arbitrator or quasi-arbitrator in giving his certificate.'

Viscount Dilhorne adopted the same approach and made no specific reference to the existence or otherwise of any duty owed by the architect to the contractor. He referred  **f**
to the effect of the arbitration clause, however, in the following terms ([1974] 1 All ER 859 at 880, [1974] AC 727 at 757):

'It began with the words "Provided always that in case any dispute or difference shall arise between the employer or the Architect on his behalf and the contractor". That, to my mind, shows that the parties to the contract recognised that the architect in performing his duties under the contract would be acting on behalf of the  **g**
employer. The inclusion of this arbitration clause of itself makes it highly improbable that the parties to the contract agreed that the architect should act as an arbitrator between them for then there might be an arbitration on an arbitration.'

Lord Salmon, in his speech in *Arenson v Casson Beckman Rutley & Co* [1975] 3 All ER 901 at 924, [1977] AC 405 at 438 in dismissing a submission made that there should not  **h**
be a duty owed by the architect to the contractor since it would put the former in the risk of being 'shot at from both sides', said:

'In spite of the remarkable skill with which this argument was developed, I cannot accept it. Were it sound, it would be just as relevant in *Sutcliffe v Thackrah* as in the present case. The architect owed a duty to his client, the building owner, arising out  **j**
of the contract between them to use reasonable care in issuing his certificates. He also, however, owed a similar duty of care to the contractor arising out of their proximity: see the *Hedley Byrne* case. In *Sutcliffe v Thackrah* the architect negligently certified that more money was due than was in fact due; and he was successfully sued for the damage which this had caused his client. He might, however, have

a    negligently certified less money was payable than was in fact due and thereby starved the contractor of money. In a trade in which cash flow is especially important, this might have caused the contractor serious damage for which the architect could have been successfully sued. He was thus exposed to the dual risk of being sued in negligence but this House unanimously held that he enjoyed no immunity from suit.'

b    However, in *Sutcliffe v Thackrah* [1974] 1 All ER 859 at 882, [1974] AC 727 at 759 Lord Salmon concentrated on the position of the architect quâ the employer:

    'No one denies that the architect owes a duty to his client to use proper care and skill in supervising the work and in protecting his client's interests. That, indeed, is what he is paid to do. Nevertheless, it is suggested that because, in issuing the certificates, he must act fairly and impartially as between his client and the
c    contractor, he is immune from being sued by his client if, owing to his negligent supervision (or as in the present case) other negligent conduct, he issues a certificate for far more than the proper amount, and thereby causes his client a serious loss.'

    During the remainder of his speech Lord Salmon dealt in considerable detail with the position of valuers and others in the context of arbitral immunity. He referred to the
d    'trilogy of cases' by which the majority of the Court of Appeal in *Chambers v Goldthorpe* [1901] 1 KB 624, [1900–3] All ER Rep 969 were so influenced but did not return specifically to consider the question of a duty arising between the architect and the contractor in circumstances akin to those prevailing in *Sutcliffe v Thackrah*. In referring to *Stevenson v Watson* (1879) 4 CPD 148, the third case of the trilogy, however, Lord Salmon said ([1974] 1 All ER 859 at 886, [1974] AC 727 at 763–764):

e
    'Under the very special terms of the contract in *Stevenson v Watson* "all questions or matters in dispute which [might] arise during the progress of the works or in settlement of the account" had to be left to the architect "whose decisions [were to be] final and binding upon all parties". It seems to me that this architect may well have been put in the position of an arbitrator under the exceptional terms of the
f    contract. Moreover, since there was no contractual relationship between the architect and the builder, it is difficult to see how any action based on a duty of care could be got up on its feet against him; in those days, the law of negligence was in a very early stage of its development.'

    With great deference to Lord Salmon the reference to his view of the position which
g    would have arisen in *Sutcliffe v Thackrah*, had there been undercertification rather than overcertification, may not be of such compelling authority as if it had been a central matter for consideration when delivering his speech in the earlier case.
    This analysis of *Sutcliffe v Thackrah* would, in my judgment, dispose of two submissions that were made during the course of argument, namely the submission by counsel for the engineer that when refusing to review the contractor's application under GC 67 the
h    engineer was acting in an arbitral role. I am quite unable to accept the proposition that the role played by the engineer under GC67 was anything other than a review of an earlier executive decision made in the course of its function as supervising engineer and subject to arbitration under the latter provisions of GC67. To adopt the words of Viscount Dilhorne in a similar position in *Sutcliffe v Thackrah*, to view the function of the engineer under GC67 as an arbitral function would be to construct an arbitration on an arbitration.
j    The second submission which I think is at least damaged by the attitude taken by their Lordships in *Sutcliffe v Thackrah* was that made by counsel for the contractor in pursuit of the 'just and reasonable approach' that if there was a duty in tort owed by the engineer to the employer so there ought also to be a similar duty owed by the engineer to the contractor. Counsel relied on the dismissal by Lord Salmon in *Arenson v Casson Beckman Rutley & Co* of the 'shot at from both sides' argument In my judgment, however, this

submission is flawed because it ignores the contractual basis of the relationship between
the employer and the engineer as opposed to the relationship which can only be    a
constructed in tort arising out of the contractual structure accepted by the contractor to
determine the duty, if any, owed by the engineer to the contractor. Although not central
to the considerations with which Lord Morris was concerned in his speech the extract
already cited in this judgment in which Lord Morris refers to a right to sue the architect
enjoyed by the employer arising out of his duties to the employer and the right of the
contractor to go to arbitration if he disputed any certification or action which affected    b
him in a financial way points the distinction between the remedies available to each.

Counsel in support of his submission that a duty of care was owed by the engineer to
the contractor referred to a number of decisions at first instance. These emanate from
judges of great experience and merit consideration. They are conveniently assembled in
the judgment of his Honour Judge Fox-Andrews QC, hearing official referees' business,
in *Michael Salliss & Co Ltd v Calil* (3 July 1987, unreported), of which we have been given    c
a transcript. The first of the other two cases was *Lubenham Fidelities and Investment Co Ltd
v South Pembrokeshire DC* (1986) 33 Build LR 39, on appeal from his Honour Judge John
Newey QC (see [1985] CILL 214). The third case was *Shui On Construction Co Ltd v Shui
Kay Co Ltd* (1985) 1 Const LJ 305, a judgment of Hunter J in the Supreme Court of Hong
Kong. Judge John Newey came to the conclusion that the architects, the Wigley Fox
Partnership, as they were the architects appointed under the contract, owed a duty of    d
care to Lubenham (the contractors) as well as to the council. There was an alternative
claim in tort based on an assertion that by issuing certain certificates the architects were
liable to the contractors for procuring a breach of contract by the council. It was this
latter issue, apart from the construction of the contract itself, which attracted the
attention of the Court of Appeal and to a large extent the attention of the official referee.
The question of a duty of care in tort received only passing reference in the judgment of    e
May LJ (see 33 Build LR 39 at 61). This issue does not appear to have been argued in any
detail in the Court of Appeal.

The judgment of Hunter J in *Shui On Construction Co Ltd v Shui Kay Co Ltd* (1985) 1
Const LJ 305 is a skilfully structured and careful judgment. After rehearsing the two
questions posed by Lord Wilberforce in *Anns v Merton London Borough* [1977] 2 All ER    f
492 at 498, [1978] AC 728 at 751, and considering other cases 'in the wake of', the *Hedley
Byrne* case', the judge took comfort from the decision of the Court of Appeal in *Esso
Petroleum Co Ltd v Mardon* [1976] 2 All ER 5, [1976] QB 801 on the question of legal
proximity (1 Const LJ 305 at 307). Turning to the second question, the judge considered
*Sutcliffe v Thackrah* with particular attention to the reference to that case made by Lord
Salmon in *Arenson v Casson Beckman Rutley & Co* and described Lord Salmon's remark as    g
'admittedly an obiter but in my judgment a plainly considered view of a very
distinguished judge in this field' (at 308). Hunter J also relied on the views of Lord
Denning MR in the Court of Appeal in the *Arenson* case [1973] 2 All ER 235 at 243–244,
[1973] Ch 346 at 365. However, Lord Denning MR at the passage to which reference is
made was dealing with the position of a professional man carrying out a valuation or a
weighing operation (see *Glanzer v Shepard* (1922) 233 NY 236 per Cardozo J). With    h
respect to Hunter J this latter reference is of little assistance to the application of the
second question in *Anns* as it is now applied in the circumstances of the present case.
Summarising the position in what may well be a sage comment, Hunter J said (1 Const
LJ 305 at 309):

'One is minded to suspect that architects will prove to be unable to resist the tide    
which in the last twenty or thirty years has successively submerged accountants,    j
solicitors, barristers, surveyors and valuers in the sense that they have all been held
to owe duties of care to persons other than their own clients. When one adds that
support to the statute [sic] of Lord Salmon and Lord Denning, it does seem to me
impossible for me to conclude that the case advanced on the pleading is unarguable.'

Hunter J was dealing with an application to strike out the claim. In fairness to Hunter J
a  since he delivered his judgment in 1985 there has been an extensive and dramatic
reconsideration of the whole area of tortious liability for pecuniary loss arising from
negligent misstatements and the like (see the judgment of Bingham LJ in *Caparo
Industries plc v Dickman* [1989] 1 All ER 798, [1989] 2 WLR 316). With respect to
Hunter J, in my view his judgment was not supported by the judgment of Lord Denning
MR or the speech of Lord Salmon to which he referred.

b          I come now to the third of the judgments at first instance, *Michael Salliss & Co Ltd v
Calil*. Here again in a careful judgment, Judge Fox-Andrews considered the well-trodden
path of authority leading up to *Junior Books Ltd v Veitchi & Co Ltd* [1982] 3 All ER 201,
[1983] 1 AC 520 and the judgment of Hunter J to which I have just referred, together
with the judgment of Robert Goff LJ in *Muirhead v Industrial Tank Specialities Ltd* [1985]
3 All ER 705 esp at 715, [1986] QB 507 esp at 527–528. Judge Fox-Andrews considered
c  the passage in the latter judgment and came to the following conclusion:

> 'But it is self-evident that a contractor who is a party to a JCT contract looks to the
> architect/supervising officer to act fairly as between him and the building employer
> in matters such as certificates and extensions of time. Without a confident belief
> that that reliance will be justified, in an industry where cash flow is so important to
> d  the contractor, contracting could be a hazardous operation. If the architect unfairly,
> promotes the building employers' interest by low certification or merely fails
> properly to exercise reasonable care and skill in his certification it is reasonable that
> the contractor should not only have the right as against the owner to have the
> certificate reviewed in arbitration, but also should have the right to recover damages
> against the unfair architect. I find that to the extent that the plaintiffs are able to
> e  establish damage resulting from the architects' unfairness in respect of matters in
> which under the contract the architects were required to act impartially damages
> are recoverable and are not too remote.'

If I may say so, I find Judge Fox-Andrews's comment of not a little force and in my
judgment it isolates an aspect of this case over which I have had a good deal of doubt.
f  However, the judge formed his conclusion against an understanding that one of three
critical factors mentioned by Robert Goff LJ in *Muirhead v Industrial Tank Specialities Ltd*
[1985] 3 All ER 705 at 715, [1986] QB 507 at 527–528 was absent in the *Salliss* case:

> '. . . that the defendant may be able to rely on contractual terms with a third party
> in order to defeat the plaintiff's claim against him, is that, on the facts in *Junior Books*,
> it was considered by a majority of the House of Lords that the nominated sub-
> g  contractor had assumed a direct responsibility to the building owner.'

Robert Goff LJ continued:

> 'Voluntary assumption of responsibility, in circumstances akin to contract, was
> the basis of liability in the *Hedley Byrne* case, which Lord Roskill regarded as relevant
> in *Junior Books* both to the invocation by the defendant of contractual terms with a
> h  third party and to reliance.'

With respect to the judge in ignoring the third criterion I am forced to the conclusion
that a question mark must reside over his conclusion in the *Salliss* case. It apparently
overlooks the contractual structure against which any reliance placed by the victim on
the assumption of liability demonstrated by the proposed tortfeasor depends.
j          Bearing these authorities in mind it is now necessary to consider the position of the
contractor against the circumstances prevailing at the time when its relationship with
the engineer was established, namely at tender stage, and to pose the question: did the
contractor rely on any assumption of liability in tort appearing to be accepted on the part
of the engineer which would afford to it remedies beyond those which it acquired under

the terms of the contract in respect of which it was to tender? One must start with the
proposition that if it had required an indemnity or extra-contractual protection in respect   a
of defaults by the engineer or insolvency on the part of the employer then it was open to
the contractor to have stipulated for such protection. On the contrary, by accepting the
invitation to tender on the terms disclosed in the document 'Instructions to Tenderers'
and the contractual documents submitted therewith it must be taken to accept the role
to be played by the engineer as defined in the contract.

The terms of the contract provided a three-stage process under which the contractor   b
obtained payment for its work, the third stage of which (GC67) included a reference to
one or more independent arbitrators who are given the power 'to open up review and
revise any decision opinion direction certificate or valuation of the Engineer'. In the case
of withholding by the engineer of any certificate, the resort to arbitration is not postponed
until after completion of the works. However in this case, as a matter of history, the
claim under GC67 was not made until after the second certificate of completion. The   c
opening words of GC67 are extremely wide: 'If any dispute or difference of any kind
whatsoever shall arise between the Employer or Engineer and the Contractor . . .' No
function of the engineer under or in connection with the contract was mentioned in the
court during the course of argument which would escape this clause. PC84 refers to
PC83 (deduction of sums certified due from the contractor to the employer) and other
matters in which the engineer's decision is made final by the contract but the purpose of   d
the clause is to ensure that the engineer 'will act independently of and entirely unfettered
by the Employer'. It was not argued that this clause affected in any way the operation of
the arbitration provisions in GC67.

PC85 gives very wide discretionary powers to the engineer in the discharge of its
function under the contract which are quite incompatible with the role of an arbitrator.
Wide as they may be, however, they are subject to the provisions of GC67, and it is under   e
this clause that arbitration is introduced. In my judgment, as I have already indicated,
there is no question of arbitral immunity being enjoyed under the terms of this contract
by the engineer.

It remains only to consider shortly the significance of PC86. This is admittedly an
important part of the contractual structure against which the contractor accepted the   f
engineer in its role under the contract. The clause provides specifically that 'neither . . .
the Engineer nor any of his staff . . . shall be in any way personally liable for the acts or
obligations under the Contract . . .' This can only refer to their own acts in performing
the obligations imposed on the engineer under the contract. The question is whether the
protection of this clause extends to the negligent performance of those functions. In this
context it is not necessary to establish that the negligence on the part of the person   g
relying on the exclusion clause is the only negligence to which reference can be made as
is the case with such a clause in ordinary contracts. The presence of the reservation is
given its normal role to play in the overall consideration of what responsibility was
accepted by the proposed tortfeasor. This is dealt with in the speech of Lord Reid in
*Hedley Byrne & Co Ltd v Heller & Partners Ltd* [1963] 2 All ER 575 at 586–587, [1964] AC
465 at 492 –493:   h

'It appears to me that the only possible distinction in the present case is that here
there was no adequate disclaimer of responsibility. Here, however, the appellants'
bank, who were their agents in making the enquiry, began by saying that "they
wanted to know in confidence and without responsibility on our part ", i.e. on the
part of the respondents. So I cannot see how the appellants can now be entitled to
disregard that and maintain that the respondents did incur a responsibility to them.   j
The appellants founded on a number of cases in contract where very clear words
were required to exclude the duty of care which would otherwise have flowed from
the contract. To that argument there are, I think, two answers. In the case of a
contract it is necessary to exclude liability for negligence, but in this case the

a question is whether an undertaking to assume a duty to take care can be inferred; and that is a very different matter. Secondly, even in cases of contract general words may be sufficient if there was no other kind of liability to be excluded except liability for negligence: the general rule is that a party is not exempted from liability for negligence "unless adequate words are used"—per SCRUTTON, L.J., in *Rutter* v. *Palmer* ([1922] 2 KB 87 at 92). It being admitted that there was here a duty to give an honest reply, I do not see what further liability there could be to exclude except

b liability for negligence: there being no contract there was no question of warranty.'

In accepting the invitation to tender with the complete contractual framework including the disclaimer in PC86, it would, in my judgment, be impossible to support the contention that either the engineer was holding itself out to accept a duty of care with the consequential liability for pecuniary loss outside the provisions afforded to the

c contractor under the contract, or to support the contention that the contractor relied in any way on such an assumption of responsibility on the part of the engineer in any way to bolster or extend its rights. I think that I should say that even if PC86 were not included in the contract in this case, the provisions of GC67 would, in my view, be effective to exclude the creation of any direct duty on the engineer towards the contractor.

Before leaving the question of disclaimer I should refer to the speech of Lord Brandon

d in *Leigh & Sillavan Ltd v Aliakmon Shipping Co Ltd, The Aliakmon* [1986] 2 All ER 145 at 155, [1986] AC 785 at 817. Lord Brandon was commenting on the speech of Lord Roskill in *Junior Books Ltd v Veitchi Co Ltd* [1982] 3 All ER 201 at 214, [1983] 1 AC 520 at 546 in which he was considering whether an exclusion clause in the main contract might affect the position as between one party to that contract and a third party:

e 'My Lords, that question does not arise for decision in the instant appeal, but in principle I would venture the view that such a clause according to the manner in which it was worded might in some circumstances limit the duty of care just as in the *Hedley Byrne* case the plaintiffs were ultimately defeated by the defendants' disclaimer of responsibility.'

f With reference to this passage Lord Brandon said:

'As is apparent this observation was no more than an obiter dictum. Moreover, with great respect to Lord Roskill there is no analogy between the disclaimer in *Hedley Byrne & Co Ltd v Heller & Partners Ltd* [1963] 2 All ER 575, [1964] AC 465, which operated directly between the plaintiffs and the defendants, and an exclusion of liability clause in a contract to which the plaintiff is a party but the defendant is

g not. I do not therefore find in the observation of Lord Roskill relied on any convincing legal basis for qualifying a duty of care owed by A to B by reference to a contract to which A is, but B is not, a party.'

There can be no doubt of the force of Lord Brandon's comment as it stands. However, with great respect to the learned and noble Lord the absence of a direct contractual nexus between A and B does not necessarily exclude the recognition of a clause limiting liability

h to be imposed on A in a contract between B and C, when the existence of that contract is the basis of the creation of a duty of care asserted to be owed by A to B. The presence of such an exclusion clause while not being directly binding between the parties, cannot be excluded from a general consideration of the contractual structure against which the contractor demonstrates reliance on, and the engineer accepts responsibility for, a duty in tort, if any, arising out of the proximity established between them by the existence of

j that very contract.

I have come to the conclusion, for the reasons already stated, that no liability can be established in tort under which the engineer owed a direct duty to the contractor in the circumstances disclosed in this case. I emphasise, however, that in coming to this conclusion it does depend on the particular circumstances of the case not the least of

which were the contractual provisions in the contract which afforded an avenue enabling
the contractor to recover from the employer. I see no justification for superimposing on    *a*
this contractual structure an additional liability in tort as between the engineer and the
contractor. In coming to this conclusion I have taken into account (1) that although there
was a degree of proximity established in the obvious sense that the contractor under the
terms of the contract relied on the engineer performing its duties in supervising the
execution of the works, this is not the same quality of proximity required to establish a
duty of care in the Hedley Byrne sense, (2) that the duty on the engineer to perform in    *b*
accordance with the contract arose out of some contractual relationship, unspecified,
existing between the employer and the engineer, which gave rise to that duty, (3) that
there was no direct contractual relationship between the engineer and the contractor, (4)
that under the contract, the contractor could challenge in the fullest sense the performance
of its duties by the engineer by claiming against the employer for sums due to it
including extra expenses and interest on outstanding sums due; (5) that the contractor,    *c*
when tendering for the contract, was content to offer for the works on the terms set out
in the invitation to tender which incorporated the full terms of the proposed contract.

In these circumstances the following propositions appear to me to be established. (1)
The engineer remains under contractual obligations to the employer, which give rise to
a duty to exercise skill and care and in appropriate circumstances to act fairly between
the employer and the contractor. If the engineer is in breach of this duty it is liable to the   *d*
employer for economic loss directly flowing from the breach. Whether this action lies in
contract or tort or both will only be a relevant question in very exceptional circumstances.
Their Lordships did not specifically consider this question in Sutcliffe v Thackrah. (2)
There is no reason to infer that the contractor was relying on any right to recover damages
in the form of economic loss arising from any breach of duty in (1) above, other than by
pursuing its remedies against the employer under the contract. (3) There is no reason to   *e*
infer that the engineer ever assumed or appeared to assume a direct responsibility to the
contractor for any economic loss that might be occasioned to the contractor as a result of
any breach of his duty as in (1) above. (4) There is, therefore, no basis on which a duty of
care to prevent economic loss can be imposed on the engineer in favour of the contractor
which would be for all practical purposes coterminous with the rights to be enjoyed by   *f*
the contractor under the contract.

Whether it is said that in the above circumstances there was not proximity between
the parties and, therefore, no duty of care, or whether it is said that no economic loss in
the sense of loss not recoverable under GC67 is foreseeable; or whether it is said that to
allow the existence of such a duty would not be just and reasonable may not in the
present case matter very much. The result will be the same. The position might well   *g*
have been otherwise if GC67 or some other provision for arbitration had not been
included in the contract. The position of the engineer, if the contract so provided, might
well be arbitral or quasi-arbitral: see per Lord Morris in Sutcliffe v Thackrah [1974] 1 All
ER 859 at 875, [1974] AC 727 at 751. On the other hand, he might well owe a duty to
exercise skill and care to a contractor who relies on his valuations and certificates just as
the person operating the weighbridge was found to be liable in Glanzer v Shepard (1922)   *h*
233 NY 236 or even to be shot at from both sides as envisaged by Lord Salmon in Arenson
v Casson Beckman Rutley & Co [1975] 3 All ER 901 at 924, [1977] AC 405 at 438. These
are all exceptional cases. It will be rare in these days for a contract for engineering works
of any substance in which a consulting engineer is appointed not to have an arbitration
clause.

In my judgment, therefore, Judge John Davies was correct in ruling that the statement   *j*
of claim disclosed no cause of action. It remains, however, to consider the other aspects
of the case on which counsel for the engineer relied in support of his submission that in
any event the claim was an abuse of the process of the court which should be struck out
on those grounds. I have already touched on the submission that the function of the
engineer was a quasi-arbitral function and have expressed the view that the duty to

a reconsider the matter under GC67 was not such a function. There is no reason to suggest that both contesting parties submitted evidence in support of their respective cases in a dispute or difference submitted for arbitration or quasi arbitration by the engineer at this stage. All the contemporary documents and the conduct by the contractor and the reaction by the engineer show that the latter was, while acting inpartially under GC67, acting in pursuance of its contract with the employer. I do not think it is necessary to deal further with this aspect of the case. As I have already said, no question of arbitral
b immunity can arise in this case.

Counsel for the engineer referred to Spencer Bower and Turner *Res judicata* (2nd edn, 1969) App A, paras 503–505. The burden of these paragraphs is to the effect that the court, in the exercise of its inherent jurisdiciton to prevent vexatious or oppressive litigation, in earlier times exercised this jurisdiction very sparingly; but that in modern practice the jurisdiction has been resorted to with increasing frequency. The modern
c exercise of this jurisdiction is no longer restricted to cases where estoppel per rem judicatam is established but in appropriate circumstances will be used where they are such as to render any reagitation of the questions formerly adjudicated on being a scandal or abuse. Counsel's submission was that although the determination by settlement of the arbitration proceedings under GC67 could not raise a formal estoppel, nevertheless, under this extension the court should exercise its inherent jurisdiction. Counsel
d submitted that three conditions must be satisfied in order to establish a true issue estoppel, namely: (a) final judgment in earlier proceedings, (b) where the subject matter was identical and (c) there was an identity of parties. In the present case the settlement of the arbitration satisfied the first condition. Certainly it could be said that the subject matter was the same in the sense that all the issues which would have been relevant had the arbitration run its full course would be those which would be litigated in the action.
e Although the litigating parties were not the same there was a degree of privity of interest between the employer, who was respondent to the arbitration, and the engineer, his agent, who was the defendant in the High Court action, and the contractors in both proceedings. The question of privity, which is the central one in issue, is clearly a very difficult area of the law. It was the subject of a critical and detailed analysis by Megarry
f V-C in *Gleeson v J Wippell & Co Ltd* [1977] 3 All ER 54 at 59–60, [1977] 1 WLR 510 at 515–516. The privity between the engineer, the contractor and the employer arising out of the contractual structure against which they came together over the works involved is clearly one of some relevance. The issues will be very similar if not the same as those raised in the arbitration. The question is: should the contractor be prevented from proceeding on similar grounds against the engineer in these circumstances? In one sense
g it is a bare reagitation of the same issues on the part of the contractor. The difficulty is, the proposition mentioned by Megarry V-C in considering what he described as his third point, that if there is to be privity it cannot depend on the success of the earlier proceedings out of which the estoppel arises and the concept that a defendant is entitled to rely on his own defence rather than be prejudiced by someone else's defence. Thus, had the arbitration been successful in favour of the contractor, would the fact that the
h employer's defence failed prevent the engineer from constructing its own defence? It would appear to be unjust that this should be the case. I have made it clear that to my mind this is a very difficult aspect of this case. Had I been obliged in order to determine this appeal to reach a firm conclusion in the circumstances I would have been minded to sustain what would be a small extension of the principle already established; but fortunately it is not necessary for me to arrive at a firm conclusion on this subject.
j Finally, counsel for the engineer submitted that any damages which might have been suffered by the contractor in this case did not flow from the breach of the duty, if such existed, owed by the engineer to the contractor. His submission was that the event of the arbitration and its settlement constituted a novus actus interveniens. The engineer's breach, if any, must have arisen out of a failure to perform the duty imposed on it by GC67. Any pre-existing breach in failing to grant interim certificates was capable of

remedy under the review provided by the clause. Any damage suffered by the contractor
resulting from such a breach was recoverable in the arbitration proceedings provided for   a
by the clause. These proceedings were instituted by the contractor and were the subject
matter of a settlement. The reasons behind, or the cause for, that settlement cannot be
related back to any breach on the part of the engineer either in failing to certify under
GC12, GC52 or GC67, but must arise out of the circumstances in which the settlement
was achieved. The circumstances in which the settlement was achieved were not fully
deployed either before the official referee or before this court. It is worthy of note in this   b
respect that in the amended statement of claim the costs of the arbitration are claimed
but the fact of the compromise is pleaded as narrative but not as being caused by the
breach of duty of the defendants. It was indicated, however, that there were fears about
the health and continued existence of the employer; and this may well be so, but there
was also clearly a serious dispute as to any right of certification under GC12 which was
fully deployed in the correspondence which took place between the contractor and the   c
engineer almost from the beginning of the work up to the time when the formal GC67
application was made. In my judgment there is considerable force in counsel's submissions
that the settlement occurring in the context of the arbitration constituted a novus actus
interveniens and would prevent the recovery of any loss occurring to the contractor as a
result of the settlement in that arbitration. For these reasons I would dismiss both appeals.
                                                                                         d

**RALPH GIBSON LJ.** I agree that these appeals should be dismissed. Purchas LJ has
stated the terms of the contract between the contractor and the employer as a result of
which the relationship between the contractor and the engineer came into existence.

As I understood the submissions of counsel for the contractor he placed primary
reliance on the application to the facts of this case of the principles established by *Hedley*   e
*Byrne & Co Ltd v Heller & Partners Ltd* [1963] 2 All ER 575, [1964] AC 465. In short, he
said that this is a case of the engineer, as a professional man, acting with knowledge that
his skill and judgment were being relied on so that he is to be treated as having
voluntarily assumed responsibility to the contractor for exercising that skill and judgment
with due care. Counsel pointed to and relied on the passages in the speeches of their
Lordships (see [1963] 2 All ER 575 at 583, 589–590, 594, 598, 601, 602–603, 608, 610–   f
611, 616, [1964] AC 465 at 486, 495, 497, 502, 509, 514, 517, 525–526, 528–530, 538
per Lord Reid, Lord Morris, Lord Hodson, Lord Devlin and Lord Pearce). He contended
that the comments, in the cases following the decision in *Junior Books Ltd v Veitchi Co Ltd*
[1982] 3 All ER 201, [1983] 1 AC 520, have not been directed to and have had no effect
on the position and responsibility of the professional man as explained in the *Hedley*
*Byrne* case. Counsel was referring in this context to such cases as *D & F Estates Ltd v*   g
*Church Comrs for England* [1988] 2 All ER 992, [1988] 3 WLR 368, *Greater Nottingham Co-*
*op Society Ltd v Cementation Piling and Foundations Ltd* [1988] 2 All ER 971, [1989] QB 71,
*Ernst & Whinney v Willard Engineering (Dagenham) Ltd* (1987) 3 Const LJ 292, *Simaan*
*General Contracting Co v Pilkington Glass Ltd (No 2)* [1988] 1 All ER 791, [1988] QB 758,
*Muirhead v Industrial Tank Specialities Ltd* [1985] 3 All ER 705, [1986] QB 507 and
*Governors of the Peabody Donation Fund v Sir Lindsay Parkinson & Co Ltd* [1984] 3 All ER   h
529, [1985] AC 210.

Counsel for the contractor also contended that this was a case in which, even if the
engineer could not be treated as having voluntarily assumed a responsibility to the
contractor to use proper care, and therefore could not be treated as having known that
the contractor was relying on that assumption of responsibility, nevertheless the
relationship between the contractor and engineer was so close and so direct that a duty to   j
take care, owed by the engineer to the contractor, must be imposed by the law.

There are, in my judgment, two main questions to be answered in this case. The first
is whether the relationship between the contractor and the engineer, as alleged in the
statement of claim, was such that the engineer became under a duty to the contractor to
act with due care to avoid economic loss to the contractor under the contract with the

employer, assuming for that purpose, in the first instance, that there was no such
*a* exemption clause or statement as is contained in cl 86 of the conditions of particular
application (PC86). The text of it has been set out by Purchas LJ. The second main
question is whether any such duty of care is to be imposed having regard to the presence
of that exemption clause even if the answer to the first question is that, in the absence of
such a clause, the engineer would have become under such a duty. Since the exemption
clause is present in the contract, and since, for reasons which I shall give, it would be
*b* decisive against the imposition of any such duty of care, in my judgment, even if, in its
absence, the law would impose such a duty of care on the engineer, there is no necessity
for this court to reach a final conclusion on the first question.

  This court should, however, I think, express its view as to what the answer to that first
question should be. The professional firms engaged in construction work as architects or
engineers or surveyors, and the companies which carry out such work, are concerned to
*c* know whether in the relationships between contractor, employer and engineer under a
contractual relationship like that set out in this contract, but ignoring the disclaimer
clause, the law imposes a duty of care on the engineer to the contractor not to cause
economic loss to the contractor in the process of certifying and of accepting or rejecting
claims under the contract. Of course, each case will depend on its own facts and
circumstances and on the particular provisions of the relevant contract (see *Sutcliffe v*
*d* *Thackrah* [1974] 1 All ER 859 at 876, [1974] AC 727 at 752 per Lord Morris) but it is
likely that a large number of contracts are placed for construction or engineering works
in which the contractual relationship of contractor and employer and the contractual
duties of the engineer are substantially similar to those present in this case; and it should
be possible to determine whether in general a duty of care does or does not arise in such
a case. Further, in considering the effect which may properly be given to the exemption
*e* clause it is relevant to know whether there would be a duty of care but for the presence
of that clause.

  For my part, I would answer the first question by saying that, on the facts as they are
in this case assumed to be, there was no 'express or implied undertaking of responsibility'
on which the alleged liability of the engineer could be founded, according to the primary
submission by counsel for the contractor based on the *Hedley Byrne* [1963] 2 All ER 575
*f* at 611, [1965] AC 465 at 530 per Lord Devlin. It seems to me that the facts in *Hedley*
*Bryne* were markedly different and that the principle there applied is not capable of direct
application in this case. A feature of *Hedley Byrne*, in my judgment, is that there was an
approach, made to the defendant bank by or on behalf of the plaintiffs, inviting the bank
to provide a service of advice and information directly to them. Hence it was, to deal
with some of the passages relied on by counsel, that Lord Reid said ([1963] 2 All ER 575
*g* at 583, [1964] AC 465 at 486):

  'A reasonable man, knowing that he was being trusted or that his skill and
  judgment were being relied on, would, I think, have three courses open to him. He
  could keep silent or decline to give the information or advice sought: or he could
  give an answer with a clear qualification that he accepted no responsibility for it or
*h*  that it was given without that reflection or inquiry which a careful answer would
  require: or he could simply answer without any such qualification. If he chooses to
  adopt the last course he must, I think, be held to have accepted some responsibility
  for his answer being given carefully, or to have accepted a relationship with the
  inquirer which requires him to exercise such care as the circumstances require.'

*j*  Hence it was, also, that Lord Morris said ([1963] 2 All ER 575 at 589, [1964] AC 465 at
495):

  'If someone who was not a customer of a bank made a formal approach to the
  bank with a definite request that the bank would give him deliberate advice as to
  certain financial matters of a nature with which the bank ordinarily dealt the bank
  would be under no obligation to accede to the request: if however they undertook,

though gratuitously, to give deliberate advice (I exclude what I might call casual and perfunctory conversations) they would be under a duty to exercise reasonable care *a* in giving it. They would be liable if they were negligent although, there being no consideration, no enforceable contractual relationship was created.'

Further, Lord Devlin said ([1963] 2 All ER 575 at 608, [1964] AC 465 at 525–526):

'It would be surprising if the sort of problem that is created by the facts of this case had never until recently arisen in English law. As a problem it is a by-product *b* of the doctrine of consideration. If the [bank] had made a nominal charge for the reference, the problem would not exist. If it were possible in English law to construct a contract without consideration, the problem would move at once out of the first and general phase into the particular; and the question would be, not whether on the facts of the case there was a special relationship, but whether on the facts of the case there was a contract. The [bank] in this case cannot deny that they *c* were performing a service. Their sheet anchor is that they were performing it gratuitously and therefore no liability for its performance can arise. My lords, in my opinion this is not the law.'

In this case there was no request to the engineer by or on behalf of the contractor for the engineer to render any service of any kind to the contractor. The contractor came *d* into that relationship with the engineer, as Purchas LJ has demonstrated, which was the result of the contractor entering into the contract with the employer and of the engineer having been engaged by agreement with the employer to perform the functions of the engineer under the contract. The engineer assumed the obligation under its agreement with the employer to act fairly and impartially in performing its functions. It was under a contractual duty to the employer to act with proper care and skill. Such risk as the *e* engineer could reasonably foresee of the contractor suffering loss as a result of any want of care on the part of the engineer is, in my judgment, remote: the contract provided for the correction by the process of arbitration of any error on the part of the engineer and it has not been suggested that there is any real scope for an error on the part of the engineer which would not be at once detected by the contractor. The court should, I think, at least in the absence of any factual basis for the engineer to have foreseen any other outcome, *f* proceed on the basis that the contractor would recover by arbitration the sums which it ought to recover under the contract. It is, I acknowledge, foreseeable that a contractor under such an arrangement may suffer loss by being deprived of prompt payment as a result of negligent undercertification or negligent failure to certify by the engineer but arbitration should secure interest on the unpaid sums.

The contractual duty of the engineer, owed to the employer, to act fairly and *g* impartially is a duty in the performance of which the employer has a real interest. If the engineer should act unfairly to the detriment of the contractor claims will be made by the contractor to get the wrong decisions put right. If arbitration proceedings are necessary the employer will be exposed to the risk of costs in addition to being ordered to pay the sums which the engineer should have allowed. If the decisions and advice of *h* the engineer, which caused the arbitration proceedings to be taken, were shown by the employer to have been made and given by the engineer in breach of the engineer's contractual duty to the employer, the employer would recover its losses from the engineer. There is, therefore, not only an interest on the part of the employer in the due performance by the engineer of the duty to act fairly and impartially but also a sanction which would operate, in addition to the engineer's sense of professional obligation, to *j* deter the engineer from the careless making of unfair or unsustainable decisions adverse to the contractor.

I have had in mind the submission of counsel for the contractor based on the opinions of Lord Salmon and Lord Fraser in *Arenson v Casson Beckman Rutley & Co* [1975] 3 All ER 901 at 924, 927, [1977] AC 405 at 438, 442 and on the decisions of the judges at first

instance which have been reviewed by Purchas LJ. It is, nevertheless, in my judgment,
*a* plain that, assuming the truth of the allegations set out in the statement of claim, there
is no material on which it could properly be said that the engineer voluntarily assumed
any responsibility to the contractor to take care in the discharge of the duties of the
engineer under the contract.

There was, as I have said, nothing in the nature of the engineer being asked to render
any service to the contractor, or of undertaking to do so. As must have been obvious, in
*b* my judgment, to the contractor, the position was that the engineer had agreed with the
employer to perform the functions of engineer under the contract and the proper
performance of those functions required that the engineer act fairly and impartially. I
find it impossible to hold that the engineer in fact assumed any relevant responsibility to
the contractor or that it said or did anything which objectively considered could properly
be regarded as an express or implied assumption of such responsibility. The law may
*c* impose a duty in the absence of any actual assumption of responsibility by a defendant
in a case of economic loss but, if it is to do so, it should in my judgment be on the basis
of an imposed duty and not by the assertion of an implied assumption when there was in
fact none.

I have, in reaching that conclusion, also had in mind the decision of this court in
*Caparo Industries plc v Dickman* [1989] 1 All ER 798, [1989] 2 WLR 316, which was a case
*d* concerned with the relationship of a statutory auditor of a company to a shareholder and
to an investor in the company. Bingham LJ said ([1989] 1 All ER 798 at 806, [1989] 2
WLR 316 at 326):

'*Hedley Byrne & Co Ltd v Heller & Partners Ltd* [1963] 2 All ER 575, [1964] AC 465
shows that the relationship of A and B may be sufficiently proximate if,
*e* independently of contract, A assumes the responsibility of giving B deliberate
advice; if A engages B contractually to give advice to C, the relationship of B and C
is no less proximate, however that expression is interpreted.'

The statutory auditors had been retained by contract by the company to give an
independent report to shareholders about the financial state of the company. Bingham
*f* LJ concluded that it was inescapable that the auditor had voluntarily assumed direct
responsibility to individual shareholders (see [1989] 1 All ER 798 at 807, [1989] 2 WLR
316 at 327). I cannot regard the engineer as being in a similar position to that of the
statutory auditors. In agreement with Purchas LJ, I would hold that the engineer was not
employed by the employer to exercise due care in the interest of the contractor, so that
the engineer could be regarded as assuming responsibility to the contractor so to act. The
*g* engineer was employed by the employer to act for the employer as engineer under the
contract and the duty thereby assumed by the engineer to act fairly and impartially was
a responsibility assumed only to the employer.

As to the second basis of the argument of counsel for the contractor, I would again, for
the following reasons, answer the first question by saying that, if the disclaimer clause
were not present, the law should not, on the facts set out in the statement of claim,
*h* impose a duty of care on the engineer owed to the contractor in respect of the matters set
out in the statement of claim. It has been accepted that in a case of pure economic loss
there may be imposed by the law a duty to take care although there has been no
'voluntary assumption of responsibility': see per Bingham LJ in *Caparo Industries plc v
Dickman* [1989] 1 All ER 798 at 807, [1989] 2 WLR 316 at 326–327, citing *Ministry of
Housing and Local Government v Sharp* [1970] 1 All ER 1009 at 1018–1019, 1027–1028,
*j* 1038, [1970] 2 QB 223 at 268–269, 279, 291 per Lord Denning MR, Salmon and Cross
LJJ. Further, in *Ross v Caunters (a firm)* [1979] 3 All ER 580, [1980] Ch 297 the defendant's
solicitors had undertaken to their client, the testator, to act with care with reference to
the effective making of the testator's will, including the conferring of a benefit on a
named beneficiary. That beneficiary was held entitled to recover against the solicitors in
respect of the benefit lost through the solicitors' negligence although there had been no

direct assumption of responsibility by the solicitors to the beneficiary or reliance by the beneficiary. It was common ground on the argument of this appeal that, for imposition *a* of such a duty of care, the three requirements must be satisfied, namely of foreseeability, of proximity, and that it is just and reasonable to impose the duty. In considering whether it is just and reasonable to impose the duty it is necessary, of course, to take into account the nature, extent and likelihood of any harm foreseeably resulting from any want of care.

As to foresight of harm, I have stated above that such risk as the engineer could *b* reasonably foresee of the contractor suffering loss, as a result of any want of care on the part of the engineer such as is alleged in the statement of claim, is, in my judgment, remote, because the contract provided for the correction of any such mistake by the process of arbitration; and any risk of loss through an event such as the insolvency of the employer, causing the contractor not to recover some payment which he would have recovered if such payment had been earlier certified by the engineer, was at least equally *c* remote. No allegation is made that such insolvency or other event should have been in contemplation by any party.

Next, as to proximity, namely 'such close and direct relations that the act complained of directly affects a person whom the person alleged to be bound to take care would know would be directly affected by his careless Act' (per Lord Atkin in *Donoghue v Stevenson* [1932] AC 562 at 580, [1932] All ER Rep 1 at 11–12, cited by Lord Keith in *Yuen Kun-yeu* *d* *v A-G of Hong Kong* [1987] 2 All ER 705 at 711, [1988] AC 175 at 192), it is clear that the contractor in entering into the contract placed reliance on the engineer performing properly its obligations under the contract and the engineer knew that the contractor would be initially affected by the way in which the engineer performed those obligations; but, for the reasons already stated, the engineer would not expect the contractor to be in the end directly affected by the careless act of the engineer in performing those obligations *e* because of the way in which the contract provisions would be expected to operate. The engineer is not giving an opinion, or advising, on matters on which it has information, or access to documents, not available to the contractor as in the case of the bankers in *Hedley Byrne* and of the certifying accountants in such cases as *Caparo Industries plc v Dickman* [1989] 1 All ER 798, [1989] 2 WLR 316. In such a case as this, the contractor *f* will know at once whether he agrees with the action of the engineer and the contractor has the information on which to judge whether it can or sensibly should dispute the engineer's decision. That fact, not unlike the expected intermediate examination before use of a defective chattel which may be sufficient to negative any duty of care in a producer of the chattel to the injured user (see the cases cited in *Charlesworth and Percy on Negligence* (7th edn, 1983) para 8–33), seems to me to be of importance. The producer, *g* when that principle is applied, is not under a duty of care to the ultimate user because he is entitled to suppose that the defective state of the chattel, resulting from any want of care on his part, would be detected and any risk of injury thereby prevented. Similarly, the engineer in this case should be entitled to suppose that the contractor will detect any error on the part of the engineer, caused by want of care, and take appropriate action. Further, the engineer has an opportunity to correct any error which it has made and *h* which is pointed out to it by the contractor. If the engineer persists in its error the process of arbitration should correct it and provide to the contractor the reward which should have been allowed by the engineer together with appropriate interest.

As to the third requirement, namely that it should be just and reasonable in all the circumstances to impose liability, I have no doubt that, assuming the disclaimer clause to be absent, it would not be just and reasonable. Counsel for the contractor drew attention *j* to the fact that in certain textbooks the existence of a duty of care on the part of an engineer or architect to the contractor, in the circumstances of contractual structures similar to that in this case, has been considered or assumed. The presence of the disclaimer in PC86 in this case indicates that attention has been given to the possibility. I will assume that the engineer could, and perhaps did, obtain such insurance cover as was

thought to be necessary. Counsel also asserted that, if a duty of care should be imposed
a in such a case as this, it is unlikely that attempts will be made with any frequency to
pursue similar claims hereafter because of the great difficulty of proving that a decision
made by a professional man is capable of being characterised as negligent, in the sense of
being outside the range of opinion open to a competent member of the relevant
profession. I see force in these submissions. The fact that most contractors are in ordinary
circumstances sufficiently protected by recourse to the contractual obligations of the
b employer does not wholly preclude the risk, in a small number of cases, of a contractor
suffering severe loss as a result of the sort of conduct of which the engineer is here alleged
to have been guilty. Nevertheless, in agreement with Purchas LJ, it seems to me to be
neither just nor reasonable in the circumstances of the contractual terms existing between
the contractor and the employer (absent the disclaimer clause) to impose a duty of care
on the engineer to the contractor in respect of the matters alleged in the statement of
c claim, namely the alleged failure to certify and final rejection of the plaintiff contractor's
claims. So to do would be to impose, in my judgment, a duty which would cut across
and be inconsistent with the structure of relationships created by the contracts, into
which the parties had entered, including in particular the machinery for settling disputes.
    It may be that, if the court upheld the submission that such a duty of care should be
imposed on the architect or engineer in a case where the contractual structure is generally
d as it is in this case, but without any disclaimer clause, the professions and those in the
construction industries would devise effective contractual structures to contain or deal
with the potential existence of such a duty. Suitable exclusion clauses would be employed
or omitted as thought to be appropriate. Provision could be made as to when claims
against the engineer or architect may proceed. A separate arbitration clause could be
included or provision made for joint arbitration when necessary. Nevertheless, in my
e judgment, assuming the absence of the disclaimer clause, in the light of the other
contractual provisions, it would be unreasonable and unjust to impose the duty of care.
If the contractor accepted the terms set out in the tender document, without the presence
of the disclaimer clause, the contractor should, with reference to certification and
admission or rejection of claims, be limited to such relief as it can obtain through
f operation of the terms of the contract and the court should not impose a duty of care on
the engineer which would be additional to the relationship between the parties set out in
the contract, and which is unnecessary for the fair working of that relationship as, in my
judgment, the parties expected and intended it to work.
    As to the second question, if, contrary to my view, the correct answer to the first
question were that, without the disclaimer, the engineer would be under a duty to the
contractor to take care, I would hold that the presence of the disclaimer clause should
g prevent the imposition on the engineer of any duty to take care in the circumstances set
out in the statement of claim. Firstly, as to the plaintiff contractor's reliance on the *Hedley
Byrne* case, it seems to me to be impossible to argue that the engineer can be treated as
having assumed responsibility to the contractor. In the *Hedley Byrne* case [1963] 2 All ER
575 at 613, [1964] AC 465 at 533 Lord Devlin said:

h      'A man cannot be said voluntarily to be undertaking a responsibility if at the very
      moment when he is said to be accepting it he declares that in fact he is not. The
      problem of reconciling words of exemption with the existence of a duty arises only
      when a party is claiming exemption from a responsibility which he has already
      undertaken or which he is contracting to undertake.'

j The words of PC86 contain a provision in the contract documents prepared on behalf of
the employer and given to the contractor for the preparation of his tender. The contractor
knew at the time who the engineer would be. In the context, those words, in my
judgment, are to be treated as put forward by the employer, but with the knowledge and
approval of the engineer, for the purpose and with the effect of showing that, in
performing its functions under the contract contemplated by the contract documents,

the engineer was not accepting or assuming any responsibility directly to the contractor.

Next, as to proof of a relationship so close and direct that a duty to take care should be *a* imposed despite the absence of any voluntary assumption of responsibility on the part of the engineer, the presence of the disclaimer clause would be equally effective, in my judgment, even if, without it, a duty of care would be imposed by law on the engineer in the circumstances and with reference to the matters set out in the statement of claim. The effect of the clause would still be sufficient to prevent the alleged duty of care from arising, because there is no factor present of such force as could render it just and *b* equitable to impose that duty of care on the engineer whose freedom from liability 'for the acts or obligations under the Contract' is declared by PC86. All the matters alleged against the engineer are, as it seems to me, acts of the engineer under the contract between the employer and the contractor and are acts, namely certification and acceptance or rejection of claims, falling within the intended scope of that clause. The fact that the clause is contained in a contract to which the engineer is not a party should not, in my *c* judgment, prevent the words having the effect which all the parties to this arrangement, namely the contractor, employer and engineer, plainly expected and intended them to have.

As to the alternative ground advanced by counsel for the engineer, namely that the engineer could not be liable because it was acting as an arbitrator or quasi arbitrator, I agree that the point fails for the reasons given by Purchas LJ.        *d*

I would not uphold the additional ground on which the judge relied and which was based on the principles expressed in *Welby v Drake* (1825) 1 C & P 557, 171 ER 1315 and *Hirachand Punamchand v Temple* [1911] 2 KB 330. In the latter case the plaintiffs were treated as having accepted money from the father of the defendant on the terms proposed, namely that it be accepted in satisfaction of all sums due from the defendant. By so accepting the father's payment, the son's debt became extinct or the situation was *e* created in which it would be an abuse of the process of the court for the plaintiff to pursue the claim further against the son: see per Fletcher Moulton and Farwell LJJ ([1911] 2 KB 330 at 339, 340). In that case the payment was offered and retained on terms that the son was to have the benefit of the payment and to procure his release. There is nothing to show that the settlement between the contractor and the employer in this *f* case, and the payment by the employer to the contractor under that settlement, were to be in any way for the benefit of the engineer or that they were to procure any protection or release for the engineer from any liability under which it might be.

As to the contention that the court should not permit the reopening and reagitation of the claim of the contractor, on the ground that what it seeks to raise against the engineer is the same claim as that advanced against the employer in the arbitration and finally settled in those proceedings, I would prefer to express no concluded view. On the *g* assumption that the contractor had in law a valid basis of claim against the engineer, I would have difficulty in accepting that the settlement of its claim against the employer could provide the basis for holding that the contractor should be prevented from pursuing that claim against the engineer.

Lastly, as to the contention that the loss alleged in the statement of claim could not, on *h* the facts pleaded, be held to have been caused by any negligence alleged against the engineer, I agree with Purchas LJ that there is much force in the submissions made by counsel for the engineer. The statement of claim sets out the alleged acts of negligence in failing to allow the plaintiff contractor appropriate additional compensation, extensions of time and the other relief claimed by it under the contract. It is then alleged that, by reason of matters set out in the statement of claim, the contractor has suffered loss and *j* damage. Under the particulars, it is alleged that the rejection of the contractor's claim forced it to commence arbitration proceedings against the employer. There is then the bare statement that those proceedings were settled on the terms described by Purchas LJ. Nothing suggests that the alleged negligence of the engineer was a cause of the contractor choosing to settle its claim as it did. If the engineer was not to blame for the circumstances

which caused the contractor to choose to settle the claim for a fraction of what was
*a* properly due to the contractor, and if such an outcome was not a foreseeable consequence
of any negligence on the part of the engineer in dealing with the contractor's claims, and
it is not alleged that it was, the negligence of the engineer in rejecting the contractor's
claims could be regarded as relegated to no more than part of the history and
circumstances in which the contractor's decision was made to settle those arbitration
proceedings: see *Minister of Pensions v Chennell* [1946] 2 All ER 719, [1947] KB 250, cited
*b* in *Banque Financière de la Cité SA v Westgate Insurance Co Ltd* [1988] CA Transcript 658.
Since, for the reasons given, the contractor has failed to demonstrate any arguable cause
of action against the engineers it is not necessary to decide whether this point of lack of
proof of causation could be held by itself to justify striking out the contractor's claim.

**RUSSELL LJ.** This case is concerned with (a) the existence and (b) the extent of any
*c* tortious duty owed, where purely economic loss has resulted from negligent conduct on
the part of an expert professional. In this field *Hedley Byrne & Co Ltd v Heller & Partners
Ltd* [1963] 2 All ER 575, [1964] AC 465 was a watershed and since that case the problem
has crystallised in a number of authorities in the Court of Appeal and the House of Lords.
The instant appeal is yet another illustration of the problem.
     As my starting point I take what is to be gleaned from the *Hedley Byrne* case. The
*d* headnote reads ([1964] AC 465 at 466):

> '. . . a negligent, though honest, misrepresentation, spoken or written, may give
> rise to an action for damages for financial loss caused thereby, apart from any
> contract or fiduciary relationship, since the law will imply a duty of care when a
> party seeking information from a party possessed of a special skill trusts him to
*e* > exercise due care, and that party knew or ought to have known that reliance was
> being placed on his skill and judgment . . .'

Lord Morris said ([1963] 2 All ER 575 at 594, [1964] AC 465 at 502–503):

> 'My lords, I consider that it follows and that it should now be regarded as settled
> that if someone possessed of a special skill undertakes, quite irrespective of contract,
*f* > to apply that skill for the assistance of another person who relies on such skill, a duty
> of care will arise. The fact that the service is to be given by means of or by the
> instrumentality of, words can make no difference. Furthermore if, in a sphere in
> which a person is so placed that others could reasonably rely on his judgment or his
> skill or on his ability to make careful inquiry, a person takes it on himself to give
> information or advice to, or allows his information or advice to be passed on to,
*g* > another person who, as he knows or should know, will place reliance on it, then a
> duty of care will arise.'

     A succession of cases in the years since the *Hedley Byrne* case have recognised the
necessity to put a brake on these developments relating to the existence of a duty of care,
*h* so that in addition to what was subsequently to be described as the tests of proximity and
foreseeability, there has to be grafted on a third test which must be satisfied before a duty
of care can arise. That third test is whether, in the circumstances of the individual case, it
is just and reasonable that the duty should be imposed. In agreement with Bingham LJ
in *Caparo Industries plc v Dickman* [1989] 1 All ER 798, [1989] 2 WLR 316, I think this
third test was admirably put by Weintraub CJ in *Goldberg v Housing Authority of Newark*
*j* (1962) 38 NJ 578 at 583 when he said:

> 'Whether a *duty* exists is ultimately a question of fairness. The inquiry involves a
> weighing of the relationship of the parties, the nature of the risk, and the public
> interest in the proposed solution.' (Weintraub CJ's emphasis.)

In my judgment it is this third test which is at the heart of this appeal.

I entertain no doubt but that the engineer, when it prepared tenders and contract documents, held itself out as an expert on whom the contractor was entitled to rely in the administration of the contract. Throughout its operation it was plainly contemplated that the engineer would supervise the activities of the contractor and would bring to bear its expertise, as well as fairness, in determining the extent of the work to be certified. Its position, which has been fully described in the judgment of Purchas LJ was, vis-à-vis the contractor, a very close one, albeit falling short of any direct contractual relationship. In my judgment the proximity test was satisfied.

I am less certain that the engineer, when it assumed its position under the contract between the employer and the contractor, reasonably contemplated that in the event of its negligence in the way of undercertification, or indeed of undercertification without negligence, economic damage would, or at least could, ensue. Counsel for the engineer submitted that because the contractor had a remedy for non-certification or undercertification against the employer, no damage was to be foreseen by the engineer. On this aspect of the case I entertain some reservation. The non-certification or undercertification by an engineer might lead, in an individual case, to such financial embarrassment for the contractor that withdrawal from the contract might become necessary. In such a situation the fact that subsequently the contractor would be able to recoup its loss via arbitration (weeks, months or years ahead) would be cold comfort to it. The loss in the meantime would have been real. In a less extreme case the contractors would simply be kept out of working capital which, but for it being withheld, would be available to it. But, having recognised these possibilities, the circumstances in the instant case were such that the possibility of damage being suffered by this contractor beyond what could be recouped in arbitration has to be regarded as remote, and I believe that this remoteness is a factor to be taken into account when one comes to consider the third test.

That third test was considered by Lord Keith in *Governors of the Peabody Donation Fund v Sir Lindsay Parkinson & Co Ltd* [1984] 3 All ER 529 at 534, [1985] AC 210 at 240–241 when he said:

'The true question in each case is whether the particular defendant owed to the particular plaintiff a duty of care having the scope which is contended for, and whether he was in breach of that duty with consequent loss to the plaintiff. A relationship of proximity in Lord Atkin's sense must exist before any duty of care can arise, but the scope of the duty must depend on all the circumstances of the case. In *Home Office v Dorset Yacht Co Ltd* [1970] 2 All ER 294 at 307–308, [1970] AC 1004 at 1038–1039 Lord Morris, after observing that at the conclusion of his speech in *Donoghue v Stevenson* [1932] AC 562 at 599, [1932] All ER Rep 1 at 20 Lord Atkin said that it was advantageous if the law "is in accordance with sound common sense" and expressing the view that a special relation existed between the prison officers and the yacht company which gave rise to a duty on the former to control their charges so as to prevent them doing damage, continued: "Apart from this I would conclude that in the situation stipulated in the present case it would not only be fair and reasonable that a duty of care should exist but that it would be contrary to the fitness of things were it not so. I doubt whether it is necessary to say, in cases where the court is asked whether in a particular situation a duty existed, that the court is called on to make a decision as to policy. Policy need not be invoked where reasons and good sense will at once point the way. If the test whether in some particular situation a duty of care arises may in some cases have to be whether it is fair and reasonable that it should so arise the court must not shrink from being the arbiter. As Lord Radcliffe said in his speech in *Davis Contractors Ltd v Fareham Urban District Council* [1956] 2 All ER 145 at 160, [1956] AC 696 at 728, the court is 'the spokesman of the fair and reasonable man'." So in determining whether or not a duty of care of a    particular scope was incumbent on a defendant it is material to take into consideration whether it is just and reasonable that it should be so.'

With those words in mind I examine some of the facts in the instant case. The engineeer presented the contractor with the contract documents, and the contractor freely chose to enter into the contract with the employer. The contractor was aware that the engineer was not a party to the contract and that, accordingly, any complaint that
b    might arise against the engineer at the suit of the contractor would be an extra-contractual one which would have to be resolved by a process other than a claim for breach of contract.

In the event of non-certification or undercertification the contractor was entitled to arbitrate along the well-defined processes to be found in cl 67 of the general conditions (GC67). Although for the reasons given by Purchas LJ in his judgment the engineer is
c    not able to claim immunity from suit as a result of any arbitral or quasi-arbitral role under the terms of the contract, in my judgment the presence of GC67, freely accepted by the contractor and agreed to by it without stipulation that the engineer should be a party to the contract or to any arbitration pursuant to the clause, does not merely define the ambit of the duty owed; it goes to its very existence.

In my opinion the following question is worthy of being posed. Given the contractual
d    structure between the contractor and the employer, can it be fairly said that it was ever within the contemplation of the contractor that, outside the contract, it could pursue a remedy against the engineer? I do not believe that any representative of the contractor would have thought so for one moment, nor do I believe that from an entirely objective point of view the answer could be anything other than in the negative. The contractor in reality had its rights adequately protected by the terms of its bilateral contract with the
e    employer. If it had thought not, then it was at liberty to insist on a tripartite contract before embarking on the work.

The very existence of GC67 in the form in which it is drafted is, in my judgment, sufficient to dispose of this appeal in favour of the engineer. I would hold that, the parties having sought to regulate their relationships the one with the other by a contractual process, the law should be very cautious indeed before grafting on to the contractual
f    relationships what might be termed a parasitic duty, unnecessary for the protection of the interests of the parties and, as will appear when reference is made to cl 86 of the conditions of particular application (PC86), contrary to the express declarations of the engineer.

PC86 is worth setting out in full. It provides:

g    'Neither any member of the Employer's staff nor the Engineer nor any of his staff, nor the Engineer's Representative shall be in any way personally liable for the acts or obligations under the Contract, or answerable for any default or omission on the part of the Employer in the observance or performance of any of the acts, matters or things which are herein contained.'

h    Of course, the engineer cannot rely on the clause as a binding contractual term between itself and the contractor for there was no contract between them. But, in my view, there must be a presumption against the clause being present for no purpose. In my opinion the purpose of the clause was, inter alia, to eliminate the possibility of the contractor pursuing a remedy of whatever kind, save fraud, against the engineers.

Counsel for the contractor argued that the clause had nothing other than administrative
j    significance. I do not agree. True it is that the clause did not specifically refer to negligence, and that in contractual cases such a requirement has been shown to be essential. But this, vis-à-vis the engineer and the contractor, is not a contractual case. The clause, in my opinion, destroys the duty of the engineer, if duty there ever was.

As to the wording of the clause, reference can usefully be made to Lord Reid's

observations in *Hedley Byrne & Co Ltd v Heller & Partners Ltd* [1963] 2 All ER 575 at 586–
587, [1964] AC 465 at 492–493:

> 'The appellants founded on a number of cases in contract where very clear words
> were required to exclude the duty of care which would otherwise have flowed from
> the contract. To that argument there are, I think, two answers. In the case of a
> contract it is necessary to exclude liability for negligence, but in this case the
> question is whether an undertaking to assume a duty to take care can be inferred;
> and that is a very different matter. Secondly, even in cases of contract general words
> may be sufficient if there was no other kind of liability to be excluded except
> liability for negligence: the general rule is that a party is not exempted from liability
> for negligence "unless adequate words are used"—per Scrutton, L.J., in *Rutter* v.
> *Palmer* ([1922] 2 KB 87 at 92, cf [1922] All ER Rep 367 at 370). It being admitted
> that there was here a duty to give an honest reply, I do not see what further liability
> there could be to exclude except liability for negligence: there being no contract
> there was no question of warranty.'

In my judgment the words of PC86 effectively exclude, and were intended to exclude,
the liability of the engineer for its negligence. The word 'liable' to be found in the clause
can relate only to negligence. The absence of the word 'negligence' does not destroy, in
the circumstances of this case, the efficacy of the clause. It is effective against the
contractor in so far as they were on notice as to the terms of the clause, appearing as it did
in a contract to which it, the contractor, was a party. The clause being present in a
contract freely entered into by the contractor, I do not think that it is just and reasonable
that the contractor should be permitted to go behind it and, despite its existence, take
proceedings against the engineer on the very basis which the clause seeks to exclude.

I summarise my conclusions on the existence or otherwise of a duty owed by the
engineer to the contractor as follows. The parties so chose to structure their relationships
that there was no contract between the engineer and the contractor, although there were
contracts between the employer and the contractor and the employer and the engineer.
The absence of any contract between the engineer and the contractor is not without
significance. The tests of proximity and foreseeability may be satisfied, but it is not just
and reasonable that there should be imposed on the engineer a duty which the contractor
chose not to make a contractual one because (a) PC86 is part of the relationship between
the parties and (b) GC67 provides for the contractor an adequate remedy in the event of
non-certification or undercertification. The existence of these clauses in my judgment
eliminates any duty of care on the part of the engineer.

Purchas and Ralph Gibson LJJ have both referred to the submissions made by counsel
for the engineer that the loss alleged in the statement of claim could not be held to have
been caused by any negligence alleged against the engineer. I think there is much to be
said for this submission based on novus actus interveniens but, because I am firmly of
the opinion that the contractor has failed to establish an arguable cause of action against
the engineer, I find it unnecessary to express any definitive view. For the reasons that I
have indicated and those expressed by his Honour Judge John Davies QC, to whose
judgment I would wish to pay tribute, I would dismiss these appeals.

*Appeal dismissed. Leave to appeal to the House of Lords refused.*

Solicitors: *Lovell White Durrant* (for the contractor); *Davies Arnold & Cooper* (for the
engineer).

June Meader   Barrister.

# Jeyaretnam v Law Society of Singapore

PRIVY COUNCIL
LORD BRIDGE OF HARWICH, LORD TEMPLEMAN, LORD ACKNER, LORD OLIVER OF AYLMERTON AND
LORD JAUNCEY OF TULLICHETTLE
24, 25 OCTOBER, 21 NOVEMBER 1988

*Singapore – Appeal – High Court – Appeal from district court – Function of appellate judge – Appellate judge deciding that evidence accepted by district court judge untrue – Appellate judge refusing to reserve questions of law to Court of Appeal – Whether appellate judge exceeding proper function – Supreme Court of Judicature Act (Singapore), s 60.*

*Singapore – Criminal law – False statutory declaration – Declaration as evidence of fact – Accused signing statement which omitted words of solemn declaration – Statement exhibited to affidavit by official – Affidavit filed with court – Whether statement admissible as evidence of facts stated – Whether statement a declaration which court bound to receive as evidence of any fact – Penal Code (Singapore), s 199.*

*Singapore – Criminal law – Fraudulent disposal of property to prevent distribution to creditor – Cheque – Donation by way of cheque to political party – Receiver of party's assets appointed – Party officials diverting donation cheques with donors' approval before cheques paid into party's bank account – Whether officials guilty of fraudulent disposal of property to prevent distribution to party's creditor – Penal Code (Singapore), s 421.*

*Singapore – Advocate and solicitor – Disciplinary proceedings – Conviction of criminal offence implying defect of character making person unfit for profession – Solicitor convicted of criminal offences – Solicitor struck off – Convictions vitiated by errors of law – Whether striking off should be revoked – Legal Profession Act (Singapore), ss 80, 95(6).*

The appellant was a solicitor, a member of the Singapore Law Society, the only opposition member of Parliament in Singapore and the secretary general of his political party. The party owed a judgment debt to a government member of Parliament arising out of an unsuccessful slander action and one of its supporters owed a debt arising out of an unsuccessful election petition brought on behalf of the party. As a result a receiver of the party's assets was appointed on the application of the government member, and the supporter was threatened with bankruptcy proceedings. In order to assist the supporter in discharging her liability the appellant and the chairman of the party, with the knowledge of the donor, signed over to her solicitors a cheque for a donation made out to the party. Two other donors were invited to change cheques for donations made out to the party to cash and did so. The proceeds of one of those cheques was given to the supporter's solicitors. Those actions frustrated the attempts of the receiver to get in assets to satisfy the judgment debt and he requested the treasurer of the party to supply him with the party's accounts, which showed no record of the three cheques. The receiver then required the appellant and the chairman to sign a statutory declaration that the accounts were true and in an affidavit filed with the court in the receivership proceedings the receiver exhibited that document in support of his statement of information and belief that the accounts were true. Although purporting to be a statutory declaration the document omitted any words of solemn declaration. The appellant and the chairman were jointly charged with fraudulently disposing of the three cheques with the intention of defeating payment to the party's creditors, contrary to s 421[a] of the Penal Code (the cheque charges) and were each charged with making a false statutory declaration

---

a   Section 421 is set out at p 197 j, post

veryifying the accounts which the official receiver was authorised to receive as 'evidence
of any fact', contrary to s 199[b] of the Penal Code (the accounts charges). At their trial the  a
district court judge held that there was no case to answer on the accounts charge because
the document signed by the appellant and the chairman was not a statutory declaration
and he acquitted both accused on two of the cheque charges because he found that the
relevant cheques were not the property of the party and the actions of the appellant and
the chairman were not done with the fraudulent intention of preventing the distribution
of the proceeds to the creditors of the party. He convicted the accused on the third  b
cheque charge and fined them $S1,000 each. The appellant and the chairman appealed
against their conviction on the one cheque charge, while the public prosecutor appealed
against their acquittal on the other cheque charges and the accounts charge and against
the sentence imposed on the cheque charge on which they were found guilty. The
appeals were heard by the Chief Justice, who (i) allowed the public prosecutor's appeal
against the acquittals of the accused on the accounts charges and ordered a retrial, on the  c
ground that the document signed by the appellant and the chairman was, for the
purposes of s 199 of the Penal Code, a declaration which the receiver and the court were
authorised to receive as evidence in the receivership proceedings, (ii) allowed the public
prosecutor's appeal against the acquittal of the accused on the two cheque charges and
fined them $S1,000 each, on the ground that evidence accepted by the district court
judge was untrue and the actions of the appellant and the chairman were done with the  d
fraudulent intention of preventing the distribution of assets to the party's creditors, (iii)
dismissed the public prosecutor's and the accused's appeals on the third cheque charge
and (iv) dismissed applications by the accused under s 60(1)[c]of the Supreme Court of
Judicature Act to reserve to the Court of Criminal Appeal questions raised by the accused,
on the ground that they were not 'questions of law' and were not 'of public interest'. The
appellant and the chairman applied to have the retrial of the accounts charges transferred  e
from the district court to the High Court so that if necessary they could appeal to the
Court of Criminal Appeal and the Privy Council on the question whether the document
signed by them was a declaration for the purposes of s 199 of the Penal Code but that
application was refused by a High Court judge, on the ground that any attempt to reopen that issue or to go behind the Chief Justice's ruling would be an abuse of process.
On the retrial the district court judge followed the Chief Justice's ruling, convicted the  f
accused and sentenced them to three month's imprisonment. On appeal the convictions
were upheld but sentences of one month's imprisonment and a fine of $5,000 were
substituted. However, a fine of that amount meant that the appellant was automatically
disqualified from being a member of Parliament for five years. A further application by
the accused that the judge reserve to the Court of Criminal Appeal questions raised by
the accused was refused, again on the ground that they were not 'questions of law' and  g
were not 'of public interest'. Following the conviction of the appellant the Attorney
General reported him to the Law Society submitting that the appellant should be struck
off the roll under s 80[d] of the Legal Profession Act because he had been 'convicted of a
criminal offence implying a defect of character which [made] him unfit for his profession'.
The appellant was summoned to show cause why he should not be struck off. Section  h
95(6)[e] of the Legal Profession Act stated that the summons 'shall be heard by a court of
three judges of whom the Chief Justice shall be one'. The summons against the appellant
was heard by a court consisting of the Chief Justice and two High Court judges. At the
outset the appellant objected to the Chief Justice sitting since his defence was based on
persuading the court that the convictions were wrong but the court refused the
application on the ground that s 95(6) was mandatory and therefore the Chief Justice  j
could not disqualify himself from sitting. The court found the charges preferred by the

b   Section 199 is set out at p 198 c, post
c   Section 60(1) is set out at p 200 g h, post
d   Section 80, so far as material, is set out at p 202 e, post
e   Section 95(6), so far as material, is set out at p 202 h, post

a Attorney General against the appellant proved and ordered him to be struck off the roll. The appellant appealed to the Privy Council against that decision.

**Held** – (1) The High Court judge hearing the application for the transfer of the retrial from the district court to the High Court had been wrong to hold that any attempt to reopen the issue of whether the document signed by the accused was a declaration for the purposes of s 199 of the Penal Code or to go behind the Chief Justice's ruling on that issue would be an abuse of process (see p 201 *f* to *h*, post).

b (2) On its true construction s 95(6) of the Legal Profession Act, stating that the Chief Justice was to be a member of any court hearing a summons to show cause why a solicitor should not be struck off, was clearly directory rather than mandatory, since it would be absurd if the Chief Justice could not disqualify himself from sitting when there was good reason for him to disqualify himself. Furthermore, the Chief Justice ought to have

c disqualified himself since it was the impeachment of his own previous ruling that formed the foundation of the appellant's defence and in those circumstances it was unacceptable that the Chief Justice should preside as justice could not be seen to be done (see p 202 *h j* and p 203 *a b*, post).

(3) The convictions of the appellant and the chairman were flawed and vitiated by errors of law since (a) a statement which was not a statutory declaration but which was

d exhibited to an affidavit, although receivable in evidence, was not admissible as evidence of the facts stated and therefore the accounts charges under s 199 of the Penal Code were misconceived in law, (b) the Chief Justice had exceeded the proper function of an appellate court and had ignored the advantage which the district court judge had had of seeing and hearing the witnesses when he held that the evidence accepted by the district court judge was untrue, (c) the cheques on which the cheque charges were based were

e revocable mandates to the drawer's banks and therefore, each drawer could at any time before the cheque was presented for payment give authority to the person holding the cheque to dispose of it as the drawer wished, and on the evidence accepted by the district court judge the cheques had been lawfully disposed of in accordance with the drawer's instructions before the party obtained title. In those circumstances the appellant and the chairman were innocent of the cheque charges under s 421 of the Penal Code and also

f had a good defence on the merits to the accounts charges (see p 204 *e* to p 205 *a g h*, p 206 *h j* and p 207 *b* to *e*, post).

(4) Although a court hearing a summons to strike a solicitor off the roll for disciplinary reasons could only go behind the convictions which were the basis of the disciplinary charge if there were exceptional circumstances, the fact that the convictions of the appellant were vitiated by errors of law and the judges' refusal to reserve questions of law

g to the Court of Criminal Appeal thereby depriving the appellant of the right of appeal were such circumstances and accordingly the appeal would be allowed and the appellant's name ordered to be restored to the roll (see p 203 *h* to p 204 *d*, *post*); *Ratnam v Law Society of Singapore* [1976] 1 MLJ 195 applied.

**Notes**

h For removal from the roll of solicitors on conviction of a criminal offence, see 44 Halsbury's Laws (4th edn) para 298, and for cases on the subject, see 44 Digest (Reissue) 491–493, 5335–5367.

For false statutory declarations, see 11 Halsbury's Laws (4th edn) para 944.

For the nature of cheques, see 3(1) Halsbury's Laws (4th edn reissue) para 210, and for cases on the subject, see 6 Digest (Reissue) 9–10, 5–22.

j **Case referred to in judgment**

*Ratnam v Law Society of Singapore* [1976] 1 MLJ 195, PC.

**Cases also cited**

*Baban Singh v Jagdish Singh* AIR 1967 SC 68.

*Mahbub Shah v Emperor* AIR 1945 PC 118.

*Teh Kim Chooi v R* (1955) 21 MLJ 37.
*Velumailum v Public Prosecutor* (1947) 13 MLJ 152.                                    *a*

**Appeal**
Joshua Benjamin Jeyaretnam appealed with leave granted by the High Court of Singapore
against the decision of the High Court (Wee Chong Jin CJ, Chua J and Chan Sek Keong
JC) on 19 October 1987 ordering that the appellant's name be struck off the roll of
advocates and solicitors of the Supreme Court of Singapore. The applicant in the striking *b*
off application and the respondent to the appeal was the Law Society of Singapore. The
facts are set out in the judgment of the Board.

Martin Thomas QC and Robert Britton for the appellant.
Robert Reid QC and Goh Joon Seng (of the Singapore Bar) for the Law Society.
                                                                                        *c*

At the conclusion of the argument the Board announced that the appeal should be
allowed for reasons to be given later.

21 November. The following judgment of the Board was delivered.

**LORD BRIDGE OF HARWICH.** On 19 October 1987 the High Court of Singapore *d*
ordered that the appellant be struck off the roll of advocates and solicitors of the Supreme
Court of Singapore. On 25 October 1988 their Lordships allowed the appellant's appeal
from that order indicating that they would give the reasons for their decision later. This
they now do.

*The background*                                                                       *e*
  The Workers' Party of Singapore is a political party in the ordinary sense, but is also,
unlike English political parties, a body having legal personality under Singapore law.
The appellant is the secretary general of the Workers' Party. In 1972 the Workers' Party
sued Tay Boon Too (Tay), a member of Parliament, for slander in respect of words spoken
in the 1972 general election campaign. The action failed and the Workers' Party were *f*
ordered to pay Tay's costs. A liability under this order for a sum exceeding $S17,000
remained unsatisfied.
  In the 1980 general election the appellant himself stood unsuccessfully as a Workers'
Party candidate for Parliament. Madam Chiew Kim Kiat (Madam Chiew), the mother of
the appellant's election agent, brought an election petition against the appellant's
successful opponent alleging electoral irregularities. The petition was dismissed with *g*
costs.
  In 1981 the appellant was elected to Parliament in a by-election and became the sole
member in opposition to the ruling People's Action Party. At the general election in
1984 he was re-elected.

*The crucial events of 1982*                                                           *h*
  By the beginning of 1982 the judgment debt for the balance of Tay's costs, after the
lapse of more than six years, had become unenforceable by execution without the leave
of the court. Early in 1982 bankruptcy proceedings were instituted against Madam
Chiew in respect of the unpaid balance of her liability for costs incurred in the
unsuccessful election petition proceedings. The salient events in 1982 are best recounted
in chronological order.                                                                *j*
  On 19 January the appellant received by post a cheque drawn by Dr Ivy Chew Wan
Heong (Dr Chew) for $2,000 made payable to the Workers' Party (the $2,000 cheque).
This was then indorsed by the appellant and Wong Hong Toy (Wong), the chairman of
the Workers' Party, in favour of Madam Chiew's solicitors as a contribution to help meet
her liability for costs in respect of the election petition proceedings. On 23 January Tay's

solicitor wrote to the appellant's firm, as solicitors for the Workers Party, demanding
a  payment of the costs due to Tay. On 3 February Tay applied to the court for leave to
execute for the unpaid costs. On 17 February the $2,000 cheque was handed to Madam
Chiew's solicitors. On 22 February Tay was granted leave to execute and the court made
a garnishee order in his favour on the Workers' Party's bank account. On 8 March the
garnishee order was made absolute and the bank paid over the balance of $18·47 standing
to the credit of the Workers' Party's account. On 10 March the appellant and Wong
b  received a cheque for $200 (the $200 cheque) drawn by Ping Koon Yam (Ping) in favour
of the Workers' Party with the word 'bearer' crossed out. Ping then altered the cheque to
a bearer cheque by overriding the cancellation of the word 'bearer'. The cheque was paid
into Wong's personal account. Wong drew $200 in cash from the account and handed it
to Madam Chiew's solicitors as a contribution towards her liability for costs. On 12
March, the date fixed for the hearing of the bankruptcy petition against Madam Chiew,
c  her solicitors were able to discharge her outstanding liability for costs by handing over to
the petitioner's solicitors $2,655, including the proceeds of the $2,000 and $200 cheques
and other money collected for her by the Workers' Party.

On 22 May Tay applied to the court for the appointment of a receiver by way of
equitable execution. On the same day Willie Lim Tian Sze (Willie Lim) made a donation
to the Workers' Party in the form of a crossed cheque for $400 (the $400 cheque) payable
d  to the Workers' Party. On 1 June the Official Receiver was appointed by the court as
receiver of the Workers' Party's assets. Some days later Willie Lim was invited by Wong
in the presence of the appellant to alter the $400 cheque and agreed to do so. He
uncrossed the cheque and made it payable not to the Workers' Party but to cash.

On 21 July the Official Receiver wrote to A Balakrishnan, the treasurer of the Workers'
Party, asking for the accounts of the Workers' Party for 1980, 1981 and up to 3 June
e  1982, and for all the relevant account books, vouchers and other accounting documents
for this period. Balakrishnan complied with this request and, in response to a further
request, filed an affidavit verifying the accounts for the period 1 January to 16 June 1982.
The accounts contained no entries referring to the transactions represented by the
cheques previously referred to.

The Official Receiver then requested the appellant and Wong, as secretary general and
f  chairman of the Workers' Party, to make a statutory declaration to confirm the accounts.
A document purporting to be a joint statutory declaration verifying the accounts was
submitted to the appellant and Wong in a form drafted by the Official Receiver and they
duly went through the formalities of making the declaration. It is common ground,
however, that the document was not a statutory declaration at all, since it did not contain
the vital words 'and I make this solemn declaration conscientiously believing the same to
g  be true, and by virtue of the Statutory Declarations Act 1835'. On 6 August the Official
Receiver swore his own affidavit, which was duly lodged in the court, verifying his own
account of the receivership and exhibiting, inter alia, the declaration by the appellant
and Wong in support of his own statement of information and belief that the exhibited
accounts of the Workers' Party were true.

h

*The criminal proceedings*

Arising out of these events the appellant and Wong were jointly charged with three
offences and each was separately charged with a fourth offence. The three joint charges
were laid under s 421 of the Singapore Penal Code, which provides:

j  'Whoever dishonestly or fraudulently removes, conceals, or delivers to any peson,
or transfers or causes to be transferred to any person without adequate consideration,
any property, intending thereby to prevent, or knowing it to be likely that he will
thereby prevent, the distribution of that property according to law among his
creditors or the creditors of any other person, shall be punished with imprisonment
for a term which may extend to two years, or with fine, or with both.'

These charges (the cheque charges) related to the disposal of the $2,000, $200 and $400 cheques respectively. The ingredients of each of these offences which the prosecution needed to prove were: (1) that the cheque was the property of the Workers' Party; (2) that the accused jointly transferred it without adequate consideration; (3) that they did so intending or knowing that it would be likely to prevent the distribution of the property according to law amongst the creditors of the Workers' Party, meaning thereby the payment of the proceeds of the cheque to the creditor Tay; (4) that in so doing they acted fraudulently.

The fourth separate charge against each accused was laid under s 199 of the Penal Code, which provides:

'Whoever, in any declaration made or subscribed by him, which declaration any court of justice, or any public servant or other person, is bound or authorized by law to receive as evidence of any fact, makes any statement which is false, and which he either knows or believes to be false or does not believe to be true, touching any point material to the object for which the declaration is made or used, shall be punished in the same manner as if he gave false evidence.'

These charges (the accounts charges) related to the purported statutory declaration. The falsity alleged was the omission in the accounts which the declaration verified of any entry relating to the cheques which were the subject of the cheque charges. In this sense the accounts charges were parasitic on the cheque charges. It was alleged that the accused had, so to speak, compounded their fraudulent dealings with the cheques by failing to own up to them when they were required to verify the accounts. But an offence under s 199 is much graver than an offence under s 421. It is treated as equivalent to an offence of perjury under s 193 and is punishable by up to seven years' imprisonment.

*The first trial*

These charges came for trial before Senior District Judge Michael Khoo. He gave written reasons for his decision on 30 March 1984.

Judge Khoo ruled at the close of the prosecution case that there was no case to answer on the accounts charges on the ground that the purported statutory declaration, lacking the essential words of affirmation, was not within s 199. He rejected a submission that it was a document which 'any court of justice' was 'bound or authorized ... to receive as evidence of any fact' because it could be, as it was, exhibited to the affidavit of the Official Receiver in the receivership proceedings in support of his own accounts. Judge Khoo refused various applications by the prosecution to substitute amended charges for the accounts charges under s 199.

Judge Khoo acquitted both accused of the charges in respect of the $2,000 and $200 cheques. He held that in each case the prosecution had failed to prove that the cheque was, at the material time, the property of the Workers' Party. In the case of the $2,000 cheque he accepted the evidence of the appellant that he had received a note from Dr Chew with the cheque authorising him to use it a he thought fit, and that after deciding to use the money to help Madam Chiew meet her liability for costs he had confirmed with Dr Chew that he could use the money as he wished. The receipt and disposal of the $2,000 cheque were reported to a meeting of the executive council of the Workers' Party on 16 February 1982 and recorded in the minutes. In the case of the $200 cheque Judge Khoo accepted the evidence of both accused that Ping, the donor, had agreed that the proceeds of the cheque should be used to help Madam Chiew and, instead of making out a further cheque payable to Madam Chiew, had altered the cheque to make it payable to bearer.

Judge Khoo found confirmation of these findings in two statutory declarations by Dr Chew which had been tendered in evidence (presumably without objection) and in a contemporary record kept by Wong of money collected for Madam Chiew, which included a reference to Ping's $200 and which the judge accepted as genuine.

a The explanations given by the defence in relation to the $2,000 and $200 cheques accorded with what they had told the police when first questioned. Judge Khoo noted that the prosecution had taken statements from Dr Chew and Ping and subpoenaed them but had elected not to call them to testify.

Independently of his findings that these two cheques were not the property of the Workers' Party, Judge Khoo carefully analysed the evidence bearing on the chronology of the steps taken to enforce Tay's judgment for the balance of the costs of the 1972

b action in relation to the actions of the accused in their dealings with the two cheques. He expressed his conclusion thus:

'Having regard therefore to all the circumstances surrounding the receipt of the cheques, the time of their receipt and their eventual disbursement to the solicitors of Madam Chiew and the reasons therefore, I was not satisfied that the acts of the
c       accused in the delivery of the cheques were done with a fraudulent intention to prevent their distribution according to law, amongst the creditors of the Party.'

Judge Khoo convicted both accused of the $400 cheque charge. He accepted the evidence of Willie Lim, disputed by the defence, that it was on a date after the appointment of the receiver that he agreed, at the invitation of Wong and in the presence of the appellant, to alter his cheque to make it payable to cash and that this was done
d expressly to prevent the proceeds reaching the receiver on behalf of Tay. The judge drew the inference from this evidence and the subsequent encashment of the cheque that Wong and the appellant had acted jointly in transferring the property of the Workers' Party in the $400 cheque without adequate consideration and with the fraudulent intention of preventing the property being distributed according to law amongst the party's creditors, sc by payment to the receiver for the creditor Tay. Each accused was
e sentenced to pay a fine of $1,000.

*The first appeal*

Under the Singapore Criminal Procedure Code appeal lies from the district court to the High Court against conviction or sentence by the accused and against acquittal or
f sentence by the public prosecutor: ss 245 and 247. The appeal is ordinarily to be heard by a single judge: s 252(3). The grounds on which the High Court is to act are indicated, somewhat obliquely, by s 261, which povides:

'No judgment, sentence or order of a District Council . . . shall be reversed or set aside unless it is shown to the satisfaction of the High Court that the judgment, acquittal, sentence or order was either wrong in law or against the weight of the
g       evidence, or, in the case of a sentence, manifestly excessive or inadequate in the circumstances of the case.'

In this case the public prosecutor appealed against the acquittals on the accounts charges and the first two cheque charges and also against sentence on the $400 cheque charge. The appellant and Wong appealed against conviction on the $400 cheque charge. These
h appeals were heard by Wee Chong Jin CJ in May 1984. He gave judgment in writing on 18 April 1985.

Dealing with the accounts charges, Wee Chong Jin CJ reasoned as follows. Under RSC Ord 30 the receiver appointed by the court was required to submit accounts to the court and to verify them by affidavit. Under Ord 41, r 5(2) an affidavit sworn for the purpose of being used in interlocutory proceedings may contain statements of information or
j belief with the sources and grounds thereof. Wee Chong Jin CJ concluded:

'In my judgment, the declaration, being a document which was permitted by Ord 41, r 5(2) to form part of the affidavit accompanying the receiver's own account presented to the High Court for passing and certification, was a declaration which the court was authorised by the Rules of the Supreme Court to receive as evidence in the receivership proceedings.'

He therefore set aside the acquittal and ordered a retrial of both accused on the accounts charges.

The judgment of the Chief Justice dealing with the charges relating to the $2,000 and $200 cheques is extremely long and their Lordships find some of the reasoning difficult to follow. Since it will be necessary later in this judgment to return to examine this part of the judgment of the Chief Justice to see whether it can be supported, their Lordships will not at this point attempt to do more than summarise its salient features. The Chief Justice began with an unexceptionable statement of the principles governing his appellate jurisdiction under the Criminal Procedure Code as follows:

'It is settled law that this court in the exercise of its statutory appellate criminal jurisdiction has full power to review at large the evidence on which an order of conviction or acquittal was founded and to reach the conclusion that on that evidence the order should be reversed. In reviewing the evidence and before reaching its conclusions on fact this court should always give proper weight and consideration to such matters as (1) the views of the trial judge as to the credibility of witnesses, (2) the presumption of innocence in favour of the accused, (3) the right of the accused to the benefit of the doubt and (4) the slowness of an appellate court in disturbing a finding of fact arrived at by a judge who had the advantage of seeing the witnesses.'

He went on, however, to reject as untrue the evidence which the trial judge had accepted as true given by the appellant and Wong in the two vital areas, namely with respect to their communications with Dr Chew and Ping, the donors of the two cheques, regarding the donor's intentions with respect to the disposal of the proceeds of the cheques. He held, in effect, that the cheques themselves were so made out as to found an inference that they were the property of the Workers' Party and that this could only be rebutted by the defence calling Dr Chew and Ping to give evidence. He further declared himself satisfied, contrary to the view of the trial judge, that the transfers had been fraudulently intended to prevent the distribution of the property according to law amongst the creditors of the Workers' Party. He therefore allowed the public prosecutor's appeal against acquittal on both these charges and sentenced each of the accused to pay a fine of $1,000 on each charge.

On the $400 charge Wee Cheong Jin CJ dismissed both the appeals of the accused against conviction and that of the public prosecutor against sentence.

On 21 June 1985 the appellant and Wong applied to the Chief Justice pursuant to s 60(1) of the Supreme Court of Judicature Act that he should reserve certain questions of law arising from his decision on the appeals from Judge Khoo for the decision of the Court of Criminal Appeal. Section 60(1) provides:

'When an appeal from a decision of a subordinate court in a criminal matter has been determined by the High Court the Judge may on the application of any party and shall on the application of the Public Prosecutor reserve for the decision of the Court of Criminal Appeal any question of law of public interest which has arisen in the course of the appeal and the determination of which by the Judge has affected the event of the appeal.'

The questions of law which the Chief Justice was asked to reserve include the following.
(1) On the accounts charges:

'Whether the declaration by the respondents was a declaration within the scope and and meaning of section 199 of the Penal Code.'

(2) On the $2,000 and $200 cheque charges:

'(a) whether the property in the cheques for $2,000 and $200 was in the Workers' Party before the cheques were negotiated; (b) on whom was the onus to prove the

a    property of the cheques in the Workers' Party and whether such onus was discharged
     by the party on whom it lay on the whole of the evidence adduced before the court;
     (c) whether the said onus shifted at any time from one party to the other, alternatively
     whether there was any onus on the respondents at any stage of the trial to prove that
     the property in the said cheques was not in the Workers' Party; (d) whether on the
     whole of the evidence adduced before the court the prosecution had discharged the
     onus on it to satisfy the court that the respondents fraudulently transferred the
b    property in the said cheques assuming the property in the said cheques was in the
     Workers' Party; (e) whether the High Court was right and justified on well
     established principles of law in disturbing the very careful findings of fact made by
     the trial judge before acquitting the respondents on the charges.'

     (3)  On the $400 cheque charge:

c         'Whether the property in the cheque for $400 remained with the Workers' Party
     after the end of May 1982 and in particular was it so on the 2nd of July 1982 when
     the proceedings of the cheque were realised.'

     The Chief Justice refused this application on the ground that none of these questions
     were questions of law and that, even if they were, they were not of public interest.
d    The appellant and Wong nevertheless sought to appeal to the Court of Criminal Appeal
     but failed, as they were bound to, because s 44(1) only gives jurisdiction to the Court of
     Criminal Appeal to hear an appeal 'against any decision by the High Court in the exercise
     of its original criminal jurisdiction . . .' There is thus no avenue of appeal from the
     decision of a High Court judge exercising appellate jurisdiction from the district court
     under s 247 of the Criminal Procedure Code unless that judge has reserved a question of
e    law for decision by the Court of Criminal Appeal pursuant to s 60(1) of the Supreme
     Court of Judicature Act. It was so held by the Court of Criminal Appeal (Lai Kew Chai,
     Thean and Chua JJ) dismissing the appeals of the appellant and Wong on 9 October 1985.
     This decision was, in effect, affirmed when special leave to appeal to the Judicial
     Committee of the Privy Council was refused on 6 March 1986.

f    *The retrial on the accounts charges*
     Having failed to persuade the Chief Justice to reserve the question of law arising on
     the contruction of s 199 of the Penal Code, it is not surprising that the appellant and
     Wong then applied to have the retrial transferred from the district court to the High
     Court pursuant to s 184 of the Criminal Procedure Code. If this application had
     succeeded, it would have opened up an avenue of appeal on the issue whether the joint
g    declaration was a document which a 'court of justice . . . is bound or authorized by law
     to receive as evidence of any fact' to the Court of Criminal Appeal in the first instance
     and, if necessary, to the Judicial Committee of the Privy Council. This was the manifest
     purpose of the application. Their Lordships must confess their astonishment that Thean
     J, in refusing this application, held that any attempt to reopen this issue and or go behind
     the Chief Justice's ruling would be an abuse of the process of the court. It was further
h    urged that, as secretary general and chairman of a political party in opposition to the
     party in power facing a charge with such serious implications, the appellant and Wong
     should, in any event, be tried by the High Court, not the district court. Thean J dismissed
     this consideration as irrelevant.
     Retrial accordingly took place before Judge Foenander, who had now replaced Judge
     Khoo as senior district judge. He gave judgment convicting both accused on 8 April
j    1986 and sentenced both to three months' imprisonment. Both appealed to the High
     Court against conviction and sentence. The appeal was heard by Lai Kew Chai J. On 10
     November 1986 he dismissed the appeals against conviction, but allowed the appeals
     against sentence to the extent of substituting for the sentence of three months'
     imprisonment in each case a sentence of one month's imprisonment plus a fine of $5,000.

For the appellant this was indeed a Pyrrhic victory, since a person sentenced to pay a fine of $5,000 or more on any single criminal charge is automatically disqualified for five *a* years from membership of Parliament. The appellant thus lost his seat as the single opposition member and was unable to stand at the next general election in 1988.

The proceedings on the retrial and appeal followed a predictable course. Both Judge Foenander at first instance and Lai Kew Chai J on appeal applied the reasoning of Wee Chong Jin CJ in holding that the declaration verifying the accounts fell within s 199 of the Penal Code and found that the accounts were false in omitting reference to the *b* cheques which had been the subject of the cheque charges. On the retrial neither the appellant nor Wong gave evidence.

An application to Lai Kew Chai J under s 60(1) of the Supreme Court of Judicature Act to reserve, inter alia, a question of law whether, on its true construction, s 199 of the Penal Code applied to the joint declaration verifying the accounts was refused on 11 November 1986. The question, although more elaborately formulated, was essentially *c* the same as the question which the Chief Justice had refused to reserve in June 1985. Again predictably, Lai Kew Chai J echoed, albeit at greater length, the view of the Chief Justice that the question was not one of law or, if it was, was not of public interest. No question having been reserved, further attempts by Wong and the appellant to challenge their convictions on the accounts charges before the Court of Criminal Appeal and by way of application for special leave to appeal to the Judicial Committee of the Privy *d* Council failed, as they were bound to, for want of jurisdiction.

*The disciplinary proceedings*

Under s 80 of the Legal Profession Act an advocate and solicitor is liable to be struck off the roll, suspended or censured on the ground, inter alia, that he 'has been convicted of a criminal offence, implying a defect of character which makes him unfit for his *e* profession'. On 14 November 1986 the Attorney General reported to the Law Society of Singapore that the appellant had been convicted of three offences under s 421 and one offence under s 199 of the Penal Code, asserted that the offences implied a defect of character which made him unfit for his profession and requested that the matter be referred to a disciplinary committee. Thereafter the disciplinary proceedings followed a *f* course which, save in one respect, was inevitable. The disciplinary committee reported that the appellant had been convicted of criminal offences implying a defect of character which made him unfit for his profession and that cause of sufficient gravity existed for disciplinary action to be taken. The appellant was thereupon summoned to show cause why he should not be struck off, suspended or censured. Realistically the only chance that the appellant had of avoiding being struck off was if the court could be persuaded to go behind the convictions. The matter came before Wee Chong Jin CJ, Chua J and Chan *g* Sek Keong JC. At the outset objection was taken to the Chief Justice sitting on the ground that it would be inappropriate in the light of the history, although no bias or prejudice was alleged against him. The court rejected the objection. Section 95(6) of the Legal Profession Act provides that the proceedings on the summons to show cause 'shall be heard by a court of three judges of whom the Chief Justice shall be one'. The court held *h* this provision to be mandatory. The court went on to hold that there were no exceptional circumstances to justify going behind the convictions and that, in any event, the convictions were unimpeachable. Given offences of such gravity, an order that the appellant be struck off the roll of advocates and solicitors inexorably followed.

Their Lordships must record their opinion that the refusal of the appellant's objection to the Chief Justice sitting was both erroneous and unfortunate. It was erroneous because, *j* in their Lordships' judgment, the relevant provision of s 95(6) is clearly not mandatory but directory only. Section 95(8) in terms provides:

> 'The Chief Justice or any other judge of the Supreme Court shall not be a member of the court of three judges when the application under sub-section (6) is in respect of a complaint made or information referred to the Society by him.'

It would be absurd that the Chief Justice should not be able to disqualify himself from
a  sitting if the advocate and solicitor facing disciplinary charges was either a close relative
or a sworn enemy or for any other good reason. The refusal of the objection was
unfortunate because the court was to be invited to go behind and condemn the Chief
Justice's own decision on the appeals from Judge Khoo and his later refusal to reserve
questions of law for the Court of Criminal Appeal. It was quite unacceptable that he
should preside. Justice might be done, but certainly could not be seen to be done.
b       The order that the appellant be struck off was made on 19 October 1987. The court
refused a stay of execution. Leave to appeal to the Judicial Committee of the Privy
Council was granted pursuant to s 3(1)(a) of the Judicial Committee Act on 4 November
1987. An application to the Board for a stay of execution was refused on 21 December
1987. The judgment giving the court's reasons for the decision that the appellant should
be struck off was delivered on 12 January 1988.
c

*The issues in the appeal*
A number of grounds were advanced in the appellant's written case. Their Lordships
only found it necessary to examine two questions. First, were there exceptional
circumstances which justified the court in the disciplinary proceedings, and the Board on
d  appeal, in going behind the convictions? Second, if so, were the convictions flawed?
Inevitably the two questions overlap since any conclusion as to the propriety of going
behind the convictions depends to an extent on the nature of the attack on the convictions.
The question whether it is possible in disciplinary proceedings under the Singapore
Legal Profession Act to go behind convictions relied on as the basis of a disciplinary
charge was considered in *Ratnam v Law Society of Singapore* [1976] 1 MLJ 195. Delivering
e  the judgment of the Board, Lord Simon said (at 200–201):

> 'There is a preliminary point which arises—namely, whether in disciplinary
> proceedings under the Legal Profession Act it is open, for the purposes of section
> 84(2)(a) (conviction implying a defect of character), to go behind the conviction and
> enquire whether it was correctly made. The Disciplinary Committee held that it
> f       was not open to them to go behind the conviction. The High Court assumed that it
> was open to them to go behind the conviction. Though, having done so, they held
> that the appellant was rightly convicted. It is, strictly, unnecessary for their Lordships
> to express an opinion on this point . . . But, since the matter was fully argued before
> their Lordships, they think it proper to state that they agree with the view of the
> High Court. They would, however, add this rider. Although it is open to go behind
> the conviction, this would only be justified in exceptional circumstances. Their
> g       Lordships will not attempt to lay down what circumstances should be considered so
> exceptional as to permit the question whether the accused had been rightly convicted
> to be raised, beyond saying that an important consideration would be whether an
> appeal against the conviction had been available. For example if a plea of guilty had
> been made under a misunderstanding, and there was no opportunity of rectifying
> h       it on appeal, justice would demand that the conviction should not be conclusive
> against the accused in the course of disciplinary proceedings, the object of which
> themselves is, after all, to promote justice.'

In the instant case their Lordships consider the following circumstances sufficiently
exceptional at least to warrant examination of the grounds on which the convictions are
attacked as bad in law. The conviction of the appellant on the accounts charge depends
j  on a construction of s 199 of the Penal Code first propounded by the Chief Justice sitting
as a single judge and later adopted by Judge Foenander and Lai Kew Chai J which is
attacked as bad in law. The convictions on the $2,000 and $200 cheque charges depend
on findings of fact by the Chief Justice reversing the primary findings of the trial Judge
on grounds which are attacked as bad in law. The affirmation by the Chief Justice of the
conviction by Judge Khoo of the $400 cheque charge is attacked as bad in law. The

appellant has had no opportunity to test any of the questions of law which he claims are involved by appeal to the Court of Criminal Appeal of Singapore or, if necessary, by *a* further appeal to the Board, because the Chief Justice and Lai Kew Chai J refused to reserve any questions of law pursuant to s 60 of the Supreme Court of Judicature Act and, in the absence of such reservation, neither the Court of Criminal Appeal nor the Board had any jurisdiction to entertain any appeal. If it can be shown that there were questions of law of public interest which should have been reserved for decision by the Court of Criminal Appeal and that this would have led to the quashing of the convictions *b* either by the Court of Criminal Appeal or on appeal by the Board, it must surely be appropriate, to quote Lord Simon's words, 'that the [convictions] should not be conclusive against the accused in the course of disciplinary proceedings, the object of which themselves is, after all, to promote justice'.

Their Lordships have from the outset entertained no doubt that these convictions do indeed raise serious questions of law and they find it difficult to understand how any *c* serious question of law arising in a criminal case on which a person's conviction of a grave offence may depend can be said not to be 'of public interest' within the meaning of s 60(1) of the Supreme Court of Judicature Act. In the end, therefore, the determination of the appeal turns on the question whether the convictions are vitiated by errors of law.

*The accounts charge*                                               *d*

Section 199 of the Penal Code, as already pointed out, creates an offence of the same gravity as perjury under s 193. The language, if in any way ambiguous, should be construed narrowly to restrict the ambit of the criminal net which the section casts. But, in their Lordships' judgment, there is really no ambiguity. What is required is a declaration which is per se admissible 'as evidence of any fact'. A statement which is not a statutory declaration but which is relied on by the deponent to an affidavit containing *e* a statement of information and belief and is exhibited to the affidavit to show the source of the deponent's information and belief is not admissible *as* evidence of the facts stated, although it may be received *in* evidence. The evidence admissible to prove the facts stated is the deponent's affidavit of his information and belief, not the statement relied on as the source of it. Any other construction of s 199 would create a potential offence of *f* perjury by the maker of a casual statement to a third party who later relied on it in an affidavit of information and belief or, to take another example canvassed in argument, by a witness who gave a proof of evidence to a solicitor which was later put in evidence by agreement of the parties. It can make no difference whether or not the maker of the statement or the witness who signed the statement or the witness who signed his proof knew that the statement or proof was likely to be put in evidence.

It follows, in their Lordships' judgment, that the charges against the appellant and *g* Wong under s 199 were misconceived in law, as Judge Khoo held, quite apart from any question on the merits whether the accounts verified by the declaration ought to have included reference to the transactions which were the subject of the cheque charges. The appellant's conviction on this charge was fatally flawed.

*The cheque charges*                                               *h*

It is fundamental to a proper understanding of the transactions which gave rise to the cheque charges to appreciate the legal implications of the fact that the three cheques were given by way of voluntary donation. Each cheque made payable to the Workers' Party was a revocable mandate to the drawer's bank to pay the amount shown and a revocable promise to the Workers' Party that the amount would be paid. At any time before the *j* cheque was presented for payment or negotiated by the Workers' Party the drawer could revoke the mandate and the promise by stopping payment of the cheque. The Workers' Party could not sue on the cheque because it was given for no consideration. It follows that the drawer, as donor, could at any time before the cheque was presented for payment or negotiated by the Workers' Party give authority to any person holding the cheque to

dispose of it as the donor wished. It is fair to all concerned to point out that these
*a* important considerations do not appear to have been fully appreciated at any stage in the
criminal proceedings or to have been adequately formulated in argument until the
matter reached the Board.


*The $2,000 and $200 cheque charges*
*b*   As related earlier in this judgment, the evidence of the appellant was to the effect that
the $2,000 cheque had been indorsed over to Madam Chiew's solicitors with the full
authority of the drawer, Dr Chew. Judge Khoo pointed out that this was the only
evidence of Dr Chew's intention, that it was substantially confirmed by Dr Chew's
statutory declarations and that the prosecution had had every opportunity to call Dr
Chew but had not done so. As their Lordships read Judge Khoo's judgment, he accepted
*c* the appellant's evidence on this issue without reserve or qualification.
   On appeal the Chief Justice quoted two short passages from the judgment of Judge
Khoo which read as follows:

   'At the conclusion of the trial, the only evidence I had concerning the intentions
   of both Dr Chew and Ping when donating their respective cheques were the
   testimonies of both accused, although in the course of the prosecution's case the
*d*   defence had tendered two statutory declarations sworn to by Dr. Chew, albeit in
   another (the receivership) proceeding (exhibits D4 and D5) which substantially
   confirmed what the second accused had said regarding her donation . . . In respect
   of these two charges, the prosecution had to my mind failed to prove an essential
   ingredient of the offence, namely that the $2,000 and $200 cheques were the
   property of the Workers' Party.'
*e*
The Chief Justice went on:

   'It seems to me implicit in these two passages that the trial judge's finding that
   the prosecution had failed to prove that the $2,000 cheque was the property of the
   Workers' Party was because he construed the contents of Dr Chew's two statutory
   declarations as "substantially confirming" [the appellant's] evidence and *not because*
*f*   *he found [the appellant] to be a credible witness whose evidence he accepted.*' (Our
   emphasis.)

   Their Lordships can find no warrant whatever for the view that Judge Khoo did *not*
find the appellant to be a credible witness whose evidence on this issue he accepted. But
this was the cornerstone of the Chief Justice's judgment on this charge. As an appellate
*g* judge who had not seen or heard the witnesses, it was only if he could validly reject the
trial judge's finding of primary fact based on acceptance of witnesses whose evidence he
had seen and heard that he, the appellate judge, could substitute his own findings of fact.
This the Chief Justice then proceeded to do. He ignored the fact that the prosecution had
taken a statement from Dr Chew and subpoenaed her as a witness, but elected not to call
her. He repeatedly referred to the failure of the defence to call Dr Chew. Two key
*h* passages in his judgment read as follows. The first is:

   'I am unable to accept [the appellant's] evidence that there was a note to him from
   Dr Chew and consequently I do not accept his evidence of their subsequent
   telephone conversation for the following reasons. It was highly unlikely that Dr
   Chew would write the words "Workers' Party" on the face of the cheque and send it
*j*   to [the appellant] with a note, the contents of which were as related to [the appellant],
   if she did not intend to donate the sum specified on its face to the Workers' Party. If
   her intention was different from that as expressed on the face of the cheque, *her*
   evidence was *necessary* to explain why she wrote the words "Workers' Party" on the
   face of the cheque when she intended someone else to be the donee of her $2,000
   gift and, if her intention was to donate the $2,000 to [the appellant] to be used by

him for any purposes he thought fit, it was *essential* for *her* to give an explanation
why she named the Workers' Party and not [the appellant] as the payee on the face    a
of the cheque . . .' (Our emphasis.)

The second is:

'. . . In my judgment, it was sufficient for the prosecution to rely on the cheque
itself as proof that the cheque was the property of the Workers' Party but, having
regard to the nature and content of the defence on the issue of Dr Chew's intention,    b
the defence should have called her as a witness who could give evidence in support
of [the appellant's] evidence.'

This judgment starts from a false premise with respect to the trial judge's assessment
of the evidence he had heard and proceeds on a clear misdirection with respect to the
onus of proof. It cannot be supported.

On the $200 cheque charge the trial judge again clearly accepted the evidence of Wong    c
as to the circumstances in which the donor, Ping, had altered his cheque to make it
payable to bearer. The Chief Justice, after citing a lengthy passage from the judgment of
Judge Khoo, said:

'If the correct inference from that passage was that the trial judge accepted Wong's
account of what Ping said, it is clear that he did not base it on his acceptance of    d
Wong as a reliable and credible witness and that he failed to observe, analyse or
consider the undisputed facts and material probabilities.'

Beyond this their Lordships need only quote two other critical passages from the Chief
Justice's judgment as follows. The first is:

'It seems to me to be plain that, by naming the Workers' Party as the payee in his    e
cheque, Ping's intention must be taken to have been that the property in the cheque
should pass to the Workers' Party as a donation from him . . .'

The second is:

'In my judgment, on a full consideration of the material evidence and the    f
circumstances and bearing in mind that an appellate court should be slow in
disturbing a finding of fact arrived at by a judge who had the advantage of seeing
the witnesses but is none the less duty bound to review at large the evidence on
which that finding was reached, I am satisfied that the trial judge was wrong in
accepting Wong's account and in finding that Ping had no intention of transferring
the property in his cheque to the Workers' Party. I am also satisfied that Wong's    g
account of what Ping said when he handed his cheque to Wong was untrue. It
follows, in my opinion inescapably, that [the appellant's] recollections, as given in
evidence by him, that Wong told him Ping wanted to give something for Madam
Chiew's costs must also be untrue as was his recollection that he indorsed it so that
they could get the money for Madam Chiew. Accordingly, I find that at all material
times Ping's cheque was the property of the Workers' Party.'    h

There is much besides by way of a purported analysis of the evidence by which the
Chief Justice seeks to justify his direct rejection of the evidence which the trial judge had
plainly accepted. But their Lordships find the reasoning wholly unconvincing. On this
issue the trial judge *did* accept Wong as a reliable and credible witness and found his
evidence to be corroborated by a genuine contemporary document which the prosecution
had vainly sought to challenge and which the Chief Justice ignored. In setting out to    j
controvert the trial judge's primary findings of fact on this central issue, the Chief Justice
patently exceeded the proper function of an appellate court and wholly ignored the
advantage enjoyed by the trial judge who had seen and heard the witnesses. This
amounted to a serious error of law which vitiated the Chief Justice's decision.

Having reached these conclusions, it is unnecessary for their Lordships to examine the
a further question whether it was open to the Chief Justice to reverse the finding of the
trial judge on the issue of the fraudulent intent of the accused.

*The $400 cheque charge*
This was perhaps the simplest case of all and here it was the trial judge who fell into
error, probably because the right point was never clearly taken. On the prosecution's
b own evidence, the case against the accused was bound to fail. Willie Lim's cheque made
payable to the Workers' Party had never been negotiated or presented for payment. It
remained, therefore, an imperfect gift which Willie Lim was fully entitled to withdraw.
That is just what he did. On his own evidence, led for the prosecution, precisely in order
to prevent the proceeds of the cheque going to the receiver for Tay, to whom he obviously
did not want to make a voluntary gift, he altered the cheque to make it payable to cash.
c It was just as if he had stopped payment of the cheque or torn it up and made a gift of
cash to Wong. In the circumstances no offence by Wong or the appellant was committed.

*Conclusion*
The Workers' Party never had more than a defeasible title to the proceeds of the
  cheques. Before the title was perfected the cheque was in each case lawfully disposed of
d in accordance with the donor's instructions. The appellant and Wong were innocent of
any offence under s 421 and, even if the declaration verifying the accounts had been one
to which s 199 applied, they had a good defence on the merits to the accounts charges.
It was for these reasons that their Lordships allowed the appeal. The Law Society must
pay the appellant's costs of and occasioned by the disciplinary proceedings and of the
  appeal to the Board.
e
Their Lordships have to record their deep disquiet that by a series of misjudgments
the appellant and his co-accused Wong have suffered a grievous injustice. They have been
fined, imprisoned and publicly disgraced for offences of which they were not guilty. The
appellant, in addition, has been deprived of his seat in Parliament and disqualified for a
year from practising his profession. Their Lordships' order restores him to the roll of
f advocates and solicitors of the Supreme Court of Singapore, but, because of the course
taken by the criminal proceedings, their Lordships have no power to right the other
wrongs which the appellant and Wong have suffered. Their only prospect of redress,
their Lordships understand, will be by way of petition for pardon to the President of the
Republic of Singapore.

g *Appeal allowed.*

Solicitors: *Penningtons* (for the appellant); *Linklaters & Paines* (for the Law Society).

Mary Rose Plummer   Barrister.

# R v Minors
# R v Harper

COURT OF APPEAL, CRIMINAL DIVISION
WATKINS LJ, BUSH AND STEYN JJ
7, 8 NOVEMBER, 14 DECEMBER 1988

*Criminal evidence – Document – Computer print-out – Admissibility – Evidence of accuracy and functioning of computer – Admissibility of documentary records where person who supplied information unable to give oral evidence – Whether prosecution required to produce evidence of accuracy and functioning of computer to establish admissibility of documentary record – Police and Criminal Evidence Act 1984, ss 68, 69, Sch 3, Pt II.*

At separate trials of the two defendants, M and H, the Crown sought to rely on the evidence of a computer print-out. In the first case, M was charged with attempting to obtain money from a building society by deception and using a passbook in which the last four entries purporting to show deposits totalling £510 were false. The Crown sought to rely on the evidence of a computer print-out of the account which showed the earlier transactions recorded in the passbook but not the last four entries. The Crown also relied on the evidence of an auditor employed by the building society who stated that, having worked regularly with the particular computer, he had no reason to believe that the computer was not operating properly and that, although there were occasional mistakes, it was improbable that there would be four mistakes in a row on the same account. In the second case, H was charged with handling stolen goods by travelling on a bus with a stolen season-ticket. The Crown sought to rely on the evidence of a computer print-out made by the bus company listing the number of the season-ticket in question, and on the evidence of an employee who stated that she regularly used print-outs from the same computer in the course of tracing and recovering stolen season-tickets and that she had no reason to doubt the reliability of that computer. In both cases the trial judge determined that the requirements of s 69[a] of the Police and Criminal Evidence Act 1984 regarding the accuracy and functioning of the computer which produced the print-out had been satisfied since the employee who gave the evidence on the reliability of the computer was properly qualified to do so, and he accordingly ruled that the computer evidence was admissible. M and H were both convicted. They appealed on the ground that the computer print-outs had been wrongly admitted in evidence.

**Held** – A computer record was only admissible in evidence in criminal proceedings if it satisfied the requirements of both s 68[b] of the 1984 Act, which was wide enough to encompass a computer print-out and provided for the admissibility of documentary records only where the person who supplied the information was unable to give oral evidence, and s 69 of that Act, which laid down further requirements for the admissibility of computer records relating to the accuracy and functioning of the computer. Furthermore, although the requirements of s 69 could be proved by a certificate under Pt II[c] of Sch 3 to the 1984 Act the requirements of s 68 had to be proved by oral evidence unless admissions were made by the defence or the defence allowed a statement to be read. In deciding whether to admit a disputed computer record the appropriate course for the trial judge to adopt was to hold a trial within a trial to determine whether the prosecution had established that the requirements of ss 68 and 69 were satisfied according to the ordinary standard of criminal proof. Accordingly, since both trial judges had failed to consider whether the oral evidence satisfied the requirements of s 68 and, in particular,

---

a Section 68 is set out at p 210 *j* to p 211 *b*, *post*
b Section 69 is set out at p 210 *e* to *h*, *post*
c Part II, so far as material, is set out at p 211 *e* to *g*, *post*

a whether the employees giving the oral evidence had direct or indirect 'personal knowledge' of the operation of the computers which produced the print-outs, the computer print-outs relied on in each case had been wrongly admitted in evidence. The appeal would be allowed in the second case, but dismissed in the first case since, even without the computer evidence, any jury would have concluded that the Crown's case had been proved (see p 213 *b c e*, p 214 *c d*, p 215 *c* to *h* and p 216 *c* to *e*, post).

b **Notes**
For the admissibility of statements produced by computers, see 17 Halsbury's Laws (4th edn) para 59.

For the Police and Criminal Evidence Act 1984, ss 68, 69, Sch 3, Pt II, see 17 Halsbury's Statutes (4th edn) 208, 209, 222.

c As from 3 April 1989 Pt II (ss 23–28) of and Sch 2 to the Criminal Justice Act 1988 made fresh provision in relation to documentary evidence in criminal proceedings in place of s 68 of the 1984 Act.

**Cases referred to in judgment**
*R v Bray* (1988) 153 JP 11, CA.
*R v Ewing* [1983] 2 All ER 645, [1983] QB 1039, [1983] 3 WLR 1, CA.
d *R v Gorman* [1987] 2 All ER 435, [1987] 1 WLR 545, CA.
*R v Wood* (1983) 76 Cr App R 23, CA.
*Sophocleous v Ringer* [1988] RTR 52, DC.

**Cases also cited**
*R v Gainsborough Justices, ex p Green* (1984) 78 Cr App R 9, DC.
*R v McKenna* (1956) 40 Cr App R 65, CA.
e *R v Day* (1940) 27 Cr App R 168, CA.

**Appeals against conviction**

*R v Minors*

Craig Minors appealed with leave of a single judge against his conviction on 7 October
f 1987 at the Crown Court at Acton before his Honour Judge Clarke and a jury of two charges of attempted deception and using a false instrument, on the ground, inter alia, that a computer print-out had been wrongly admitted in evidence because it did not comply with s 69 of the Police and Criminal Evidence Act 1984 since it was not given by a person occupying a responsible position in relation to the operation of the computer and was therefore hearsay. The facts are set out in the judgment of the court.

g
*R v Harper*

Giselle Gaile Harper appealed with leave of a single judge against her conviction on 4 August 1987 at the Crown Court at Wood Green before Mr Recorder Goldstein and a jury of handling stolen goods, on the ground that a computer print-out had been wrongly admitted in evidence because it did not comply with s 69 of the Police and Criminal
h Evidence Act 1984 since it was not given by a person occupying a responsible position in relation to the operation of the computer and was therefore hearsay. The facts are set out in the judgment of the court.

The appeals were specially listed together for hearing.

j *Robert Temblett* (assigned by the Registrar of Criminal Appeals) for the appellant Minors.
*Walter Bealby* for the Crown in *R v Minors*.
*Robert Meikle* (assigned by the Registrar of Criminal Appeals) for the appellant Harper.
*Warwick McKinnon* for the Crown *R v Harper*.

*Cur adv vult*

14 December. The following judgment of the court was delivered.

**STEYN J.** The law of evidence must be adapted to the realities of contemporary business practice. Mainframe computers, minicomputers and microcomputers play a pervasive *a* role in our society. Often the only record of a transaction, which nobody can be expected to remember, will be in the memory of a computer. The versatility, power and frequency of use of computers will increase. If computer output cannot relatively readily be used as evidence in criminal cases, much crime (and notably offences involving dishonesty) will in practice be immune from prosecution. On the other hand, computers are not infallible. They do occasionally malfunction. Software systems often have 'bugs'. *b* Unauthorised alteration of information stored on a computer is possible. The phenomenon of a 'virus' attacking computer systems is also well established. Realistically, therefore, computers must be regarded as imperfect devices. The legislature no doubt had in mind such countervailing considerations when it enacted ss 68 and 69 of the Police and Criminal Evidence Act 1984. At first glance these two sections of the Act do not appear to be of undue complexity. But in two criminal appeals which we recently heard, it *c* became obvious that in each case prosecuting counsel, defence counsel and the judge fundamentally misunderstood the meaning of these statutory provisions in their application to the admissibility of computer print-outs. It is our impression that this misunderstanding may not be restricted to those who were involved in the two appeals before us. There is also very little authority on the interpretation of ss 68 and 69. It may therefore be helpful if we set out our understanding of the meaning of these sections, *d* and the procedure to be adopted in applying them, not exhaustively but in broad outline, before we turn to the particular facts of the two appeals.

*The relevant statutory provisions*

Section 68 of the 1984 Act provides for the admissibility of documentary records in criminal proceedings. It reads as follows: *e*

'(1) Subject to section 69 below, a statement in a document shall be admissible in any proceedings as evidence of any fact stated therein of which direct oral evidence would be admissible if—(*a*) the document is or forms part of a record compiled by a person acting under a duty from information supplied by a person (whether acting under a duty or not) who had, or may reasonably be supposed to have had, personal *f* knowledge of the matters dealt with in that information; and (*b*) any condition relating to the person who supplied the information which is specified in subsection (2) below is satisfied.

(2) The conditions mentioned in subsection (1)(*b*) above are—(*a*) that the person who supplied the information—(i) is dead or by reason of his bodily or mental condition unfit to attend as a witness; (ii) is outside the United Kingdom and it is *g* not reasonably practicable to secure his attendance; or (iii) cannot reasonably be expected (having regard to the time which has elapsed since he supplied or acquired the information and to all the circumstances) to have any recollection of the matters dealt with in that information; (*b*) that all reasonable steps have been taken to identify the person who supplied the information but that he cannot be identified; and (*c*) that, the identity of the person who supplied the information being known, *h* all reasonable steps have been taken to find him, but that he cannot be found.

(3) Nothing in this section shall prejudice the admissibility of any evidence that would be admissible apart from this section.'

Section 69 of the 1984 Act deals specifically with evidence from computer records in criminal proceedings. It reads as follows: *j*

'(1) In any proceedings, a statement in a document produced by a computer shall not be admissible as evidence of any fact stated therein unless it is shown—(*a*) that there are no reasonable grounds for believing that the statement is inaccurate because of improper use of the computer; (*b*) that at all material times the computer a  was operating properly, or if not, that any respect in which it was not operating properly or was out of operation was not such as to affect the production of the document or the accuracy of its contents; and (c) that any relevant conditions specified in rules of court under subsection (2) below are satisfied.

(2) Provision may be made by rules of court requiring that in any proceedings where it is desired to give a statement in evidence by virtue of this section such information concerning the statement as may be required by the rules shall be
b  provided in such form and at such time as may be so required.'

No rules of court have been made under sub-s (2) of s 69. By virtue of s 70 of the Act, ss 68 and 69 must be read with Sch 3, the provisions of which have the same force in effect as ss 68 and 69. Part I of Sch 3 supplements s 68. Notwithstanding the importance of Pt I, we propose to refer to only two provisions of it, namely:

c  '1. Section 68(1) above applies whether the information contained in the document was supplied directly or indirectly but, if it was supplied indirectly, only if each person through whom it was supplied was acting under a duty; and applies also where the person compiling the record is himself the person by whom the information is supplied . . .

d  6. Any reference in section 68 above or this Part of this Schedule to a person acting under a duty includes a reference to a person acting in the course of any trade, business, profession or other occupation in which he is engaged or employed or for the purposes of any paid or unpaid office held by him . . .'

Part II supplements s 69 in important respects. We propose to refer to only two provisions of it, namely:

e  '8. In any proceedings where it is desired to give a statement in evidence in accordance with section 69 above, a certificate—(a) identifying the document containing the statement and describing the manner in which it was produced; (b) giving such particulars of any device involved in the production of that document as may be appropriate for the purpose of showing that the document was produced
f  by a computer; (c) dealing with any of the matters mentioned in subsection (1) of section 69 above; and (d) purporting to be signed by a person occupying a responsible position in relation to the operation of the computer, shall be evidence of anything stated in it; and for the purposes of this paragraph it shall be sufficient for a matter to be stated to the best of the knowledge and belief of the person stating it.

9. Notwithstanding paragraph 8 above, a court may require oral evidence to be
g  given of anything of which evidence could be given by a certificate under that paragraph.'

The making of a false statement is a criminal offence: see Sch 3, Pt II, para 10. Part III supplements both ss 68 and 69. Paragraph 14 in Pt III reads as follows:

h  'For the purpose of deciding whether or not a statement is so admissible the court may draw any reasonable inference—(a) from the circumstances in which the statement was made or otherwise came into being; or (b) from any other circumstances, including the form and contents of the document in which the statement is contained.'

j  Paragraph 15 provides that rules of court may supplement ss 68 and 69 and Sch 3. No such rules have been made.

Turning back to the main body of the relevant part of the 1984 Act we draw attention to the fact that s 71 authorises the use in criminal proceedings of copies of documents, subject to the court's approval. Finally, s 72(2) preserves the court's power, in relation to documents within the scope of ss 68 and 69, to exclude evidence at its discretion.

In 1986 the Fraud Trials Committee Report made a number of recommendations for
the relaxation of the stringent requirements of s 68 of the 1984 Act in relation to fraud  *a*
trials. The observations of the Roskill Committee (as it is commonly known in deference
to the fact that Lord Roskill was its chairman) were, however, of wider import, and led
to the repeal of s 68 and to the substitution of a less stringent provision by the Criminal
Justice Act 1988. The new provision is contained in s 24 of the 1988 Act. Notably, there
is absent from the new provision a requirement that the document should have been
compiled by a person 'acting under a duty'. The repeal of s 68 of the 1984 Act will be  *b*
effected by s 170(2) of and Sch 6 to the 1988 Act. The provisions of s 24 of the 1988 Act
have not yet been brought into operation. While some of the observations in this
judgment will be equally applicable to s 24 of the 1988 Act, we will make only minimal
reference, and in obvious respects, to a statute which is not directly relevant to the appeals
before us. Turning now to the requirements of ss 68 and 69 of the 1984 Act, we will
state our general observations in a series of numbered paragraphs.  *c*

*The requirements of ss 68 and 69 of the 1984 Act*
  1. At the outset it must be remembered that documentary records of transactions or
events are a species of hearsay, which are not admissible unless they come within the
scope of a common law or statutory exception to the hearsay rule. For example, at
common law certain public documents were admissible and proved themselves. An  *d*
instance of a statutory exception is provided by the Banking Act 1979, Sch 6. We do not
propose to list other exceptions. But s 68 of the 1984 Act was designed to create a further
exception to the hearsay rule and does not render inadmissible computer evidence which
is otherwise admissible (see s 68(3)).
  Two comments are pertinent. First, to the extent to which a computer is merely used
to perform functions of calculation, no question of hearsay is involved and the  *e*
requirements of ss 68 and 69 do not apply: see *R v Wood* (1983) 76 Cr App R 23,
*Sophocleous v Ringer* [1988] RTR 52. It is probably right to say that such calculations do
not constitute evidence in any strict sense of the word. In a jury trial this exception, if it
be a true exception, is subject to the judge's overriding discretion to exclude material
which in his judgment ought not to be placed before the jury. Second, the question arises  *f*
whether computer print-outs may sometimes be admissible as real or original evidence.
With characteristic incisiveness Professor J C Smith has argued that where a computer
operator, by hitting the appropriate keys, *credits an account*, the print-out provides the
thing done because it was the thing done or, at least, a copy of the thing done: see his
note on *R v Ewing* [1983] Crim LR 472, and the same author's earlier article 'The
Admissibility of Statements by a Computer' [1981] Crim LR 387. In such a case, it was  *g*
argued, no hearsay is involved. We respectfully agree. But, although ss 68 and 69 are
inapplicable, it will still be necessary in such a case, in the absence of agreement on the
point, to prove the provenance of the computer print-out. Moreover, it seems to us in
practice that there will be much scope for serious argument whether a particular print-
out does amount to real evidence and the usefulness of this exception is therefore limited.
In any event, neither of these two exceptions are relevant to the two appeals before us.  *h*
  2. In the courts below it was assumed by all concerned that s 69 constitutes a self-
contained code governing the admissibility of computer records in criminal proceedings.
Undoubtedly, that is a legislative technique which Parliament could have adopted. The
question is whether Parliament *did* adopt it. There is some tenuous textual support for
the view taken in the lower courts. Section 69(2) which created the power to make the
relevant rules, refers to cases 'where it is desired to give a statement in evidence *by virtue*  *j*
*of this section*'. Arguably, this language suggests that a computer record may be admissible
solely by reason of the provisions of s 69. We are satisfied, however, that such an
argument must fail. The wording of s 68 is wide enough to cover a computer print-out
of, for example, a building society account. Indeed in *R v Ewing* [1983] 2 All ER 645,
[1983] QB 1039 it was held that a computer print-out of the appellant's bank account was

admissible in evidence under s 1 of the Criminal Evidence Act 1965. The latter provision

*a* is in material respects in substantially the same terms as s 68, the main difference being that the 1965 reform applied to records compiled by persons in the course of a private business, whereas s 68 of the 1984 Act extended this exception to the hearsay rule to records kept by anyone acting under a duty, whether in the private or public sector. Section 68 is therefore not only *apt* to apply to computer records, but it was enacted against the background of a decision of the Court of Appeal, on materially similar

*b* wording, holding that it is wide enough to cover computer records. The question is, therefore, simply whether against this background s 69 is to be regarded as a separate code exclusively governing computer records. Section 69 is, however, entirely negative in form. It lays down additional requirements for the admissibility of a computer record which has already passed the hurdle of s 68. In other words, such a document will only be admissible if it satisfies the foundation requirements of both ss 68 and 69. And in

*c* passing we note that when s 24 of the 1988 Act comes into operation there will be two hurdles to clear in relation to computer records, viz the new s 24 and s 69.

3. The method of proving the foundation requirements of ss 68 and 69 requires some comment. The additional requirements of s 69 can be proved by an appropriate certificate, complying with the provisions of Pt II of Sch 3, subject to the judge's power to require oral evidence to be given. There is no such general provision in relation to

*d* s 68. There is only a restricted right to prove medical unfitness to testify by a certificate: see Sch 3, Pt I, para 5. A computer print-out does not prove itself. It follows therefore that the foundation requirements of s 68 cannot (except in the case of medical unfitness to testify) be proved by a certificate. The requirements of s 68 must therefore be proved by oral evidence unless admissions are made by the defence or the defence allows a statement to be read. This result severely reduces, in relation to computers, the utility of

*e* the provisions allowing the requirements of s 69 to be proved by a certificate. It is, however, the inevitable result of the way in which the relevant statutory provisions have been drafted. And in passing we note that the foundation requirements of s 24 of the 1988 Act will also not be susceptible of proof by certificate.

4. Turning now to the requirements of s 68(1), it seems to us that the requirement

*f* which may sometimes prove troublesome in practice is the need to prove 'personal knowledge' of the person who supplied the information. In relation to records produced by computer technology, both in the public and private sectors, the 'information' will often have passed through the hands of a chain of employees. But it is important to bear in mind that para 1 of Pt I of Sch 3 extends the application of s 68 to the *indirect* supply of knowledge. Moreover, in a great many cases the necessary evidence could be supplied

*g* by circumstantial evidence of the usual habit or routine regarding the use of the computer. Sometimes this is referred to as the presumption of regularity. We prefer to describe it as a commonsense inference, which may be drawn where appropriate. That leaves for consideration the requirements of s 68(2). In relation to computer records, it seems likely that the condition of admissibility which will most frequently be involved is that—

*h*
'the person who supplied the information . . . (iii) cannot reasonably be expected (having regard to the time which has elapsed since he supplied or acquired the information and to all the circumstances) to have any recollection of the matters dealt with in that information . . .'

*j* While we do not propose to examine this particular requirement in detail, we draw attention to the fact that it has been held by the Court of Appeal that the criterion of reasonableness is not merely to be examined at the moment the trial opens but against the whole background of the case: see *R v Bray* (1988) 153 JP 11. And this provision is mirrored by a provision in s 24(4) of the 1988 Act to which the same comment will apply.

5. The requirements of s 69 speak for themselves. The only comment we would make is that the failure of a computer, or a software programme, may occasionally result in a *a* total failure to supply the required information, or in the supply of unintelligible or obviously wrong information. It will be a comparatively rare case where the computer supplies wrong and intelligible information, which pertinently answers the questions posed. Nevertheless, such cases could occur. In the light of these considerations trial judges who are called on to decide whether the foundation requirements of s 69 have been fulfilled, ought perhaps to examine critically a suggestion that any prior malfunction *b* of the computer, or software, has any relevance to the reliability of the *particular* computer record tendered in evidence.

6. The course adopted by the judge in one of the two appeals before us prompts us to refer to the procedure which ought to be adopted in a case where there is a disputed issue as to the admissibility of a computer print-out. It is clear that in such a case a judge ought to adopt the procedure of embarking on a trial within a trial. It is the judge's function to *c* decide whether the prosecution has established the foundation requirements of ss 68 and 69. In coming to that conclusion he ought to apply the ordinary criminal standard of proof: see *R v Ewing* [1983] 2 All ER 645, [1983] QB 1039. He ought to bear in mind his power to exclude in his discretion prejudicial evidence which ought not to be admitted. And, in relation to computer records which are admitted in evidence, he will no doubt often find it necessary to give a specific direction to the jury that the weight to be attached *d* to such documentary evidence is entirely a matter for them to assess.

We now turn to the facts of the two appeals before us.

*R v Minors*

On 6 May 1986 a man with a passbook of the Alliance Building Society presented it at *e* the counter of the newly merged Alliance and Leicester Building Society at Kilburn. The passbook purported to show a credit balance of £510. He wanted to withdraw £250. He was asked for means of identification but he had none. When he left the counter the cashier operated the security camera. The same man returned with means of identification and renewed his request. The cashier thought that the last four entries in the passbook were suspect because in each case the logo stamp was drawn by hand and was one which *f* was no longer used by the building society. A check on the computer revealed that there was only about £1 in the account. The camera was operated again. The passbook was retained. But the man disappeared.

In due course the appellant, the owner of the passbook, was arrested and charged. After a trial lasting five days he was convicted by majority of 10:1 of offences of attempted deception and using a false instrument. He was sentenced to concurrent terms *g* of 12 months' imprisonment suspended for two years. He now appeals with the leave of the single judge.

A bewildering number of points of criticism were advanced in the grounds of appeal. Counsel had the good sense to abandon some of the grounds of appeal. But a number of hopeless grounds were still advanced. We will deal with them quite shortly. First, attention was drawn to the fact that when the judge quite properly discharged a juror he *h* said: 'I am sorry that you will not be in at the kill, so to speak.' From the context in which that was said no juror could possibly have inferred a bias against the appellant. In any event, the judge subsequently apologised, and corrected what was alleged to be a wrong impression which he had created. The point is without merit. Second, it was said that the judge failed to warn a witness not to speak to other witnesses and in consequence she did speak to other witnesses. Counsel did not intervene to remind the judge of the usual *j* practice. The fact is, however, that counsel fully exploited this factor in cross-examination. It is a hopeless ground of appeal. Third, complaint was made of the fact that, when a note was sent by the jury to the judge, the judge failed to read it to the jury. We are satisfied, however, that counsel for the prosecution and the defence, expressly or by conduct,

indicated to the judge that the note should not be read to the jury. In any event, the note
a revealed the processes of reasoning of some of the jurors and on the authority of *R v
Gorman* [1987] 2 All ER 435, [1987] 1 WLR 545 ought not to have been revealed to
counsel. This point is also without merit.

Among all the bad points there was, however, a matter of substance. It related to a
computer print-out which on its face showed that the last four entries in the passbook
were false. The judge had to rule on the admissibility of this document but he failed to
b conduct a trial within a trial on the issue. Mr Abbot, an auditor in the audit investigation
department of the building society, produced the computer record of the complete
history of the appellant's account. The last four entries in the passbook were not recorded
in the computer. Counsel for the appellant argued that Mr Abbot was not qualified to
give evidence about the reliability of the computer. He had 14 years' relevant experience,
and regularly worked with this particular computer. In our judgment he was properly
c qualified to testify as to the reliability of the computer. His evidence was, however, solely
directed to the requirements of s 69. No attempt was made to satisfy the requirements
of s 68. Everybody assumed that s 68 was irrelevant. Accordingly, the judge never
considered whether the foundation requirements of s 68 were fulfilled. It follows that
the evidence of the computer print-out was wrongly admitted. It is therefore unnecessary
to consider a further argument that the judge erred in ruling that such evidence could
d be led after the close of the prosecution case.

The question is whether the conviction is nevertheless safe and satisfactory. We have
come to the firm conclusion that this is a classic case for the application of the proviso.
The real issue was one of identity. The appellant faced a strong circumstantial case. In
the act of attempted deception his passbook was used. That passbook had been in his
possession a few days before the offence. He did not testify. There was therefore no
e evidence that the passbook had been stolen, and no such report had been made. Moreover,
the man who perpetrated the act of attempted deception returned to the cashier on the
second occasion with satisfactory means of identification bearing the name and address
of the appellant. Finally, the photographs, although not conclusive by themselves,
identified a man of the appearance of the appellant. On the issue of identity there was
f therefore an overwhelming prosecution case and the computer print-out was irrelevant
to that issue. It could only be relevant to the subsidiary questions whether there was in
fact only a balance of about £1 in the account and whether the appellant knew it. It is
important to bear in mind that the appellant did not testify and that his case was
conducted on the basis that he did not make the four disputed entries. On his case they
were false entries. On that basis there were plainly insufficient funds in the account to
g accommodate the request for a withdrawal of funds. The prosecution called Mr Abbot
from the audit investigation department and Mr Stevenson, the branch manager, and
they testified that the last four entries were false not because of the handwriting but
because each had next to it a hand drawn logo instead of an official stamp. That is obvious
on an inspection of the passbook. Once the last four entries are found to be forgeries, and
that is an inevitable finding of fact, it follows that there was only £1 in the account and
h the appellant (who tendered the passbook to the cashier) must have known that those
entries were false. In our judgment, even without the computer evidence, any jury
would without doubt have concluded that the unanswered prosecution case had been
clearly proved. This appeal is dismissed.

*R v Harper*

j     On 20 February 1987 the appellant, who was travelling on a London Regional
Transport bus, presented a Capitalcard and photocard for inspection. The revenue
protection official identified the number as one of a list of stolen cards. According to this
official the appellant said that she got the card from Edgware Road Station and 'that her
work got it for her'. That was the shape of the prosecution case which after a short trial

resulted in the appellant's conviction by an 11:1 majority of handling stolen goods. The appellant was conditionally discharged. She now appeals with the leave of the single a judge.

The real problem at the trial was to prove that the card had been stolen. The relevant sequence of events was as follows. (a) In February 1985 a batch of cards were stolen at Alexandra Palace railway station. (b) Appropriate entries were made in the lost book at Alexandra Palace railway station. At the time of the trial that book was missing. (c) The relevant entries were transferred to a British Rail computer at the British Rail station at b King's Cross. (d) From the latter computer the entries were transferred to a London Regional Transport computer at Waterloo.

The prosecution relied on a computer print-out from the latter computer. The computer print-out was produced by Mrs Alcock, a revenue protection official, who worked in offices in Baker Street. She was not a computer technologist. She said that she had no reason to doubt the reliability of the London Regional Transport computer and c she said that she regularly relied on print-outs from it. The judge ruled that her evidence satisfied the requirements of s 69 of the 1984 Act. In our judgment he erred: Mrs Alcock could not from her own knowledge testify as to the reliability of the computer. In any event, no attempt had been made to satisfy the requirements of s 68. The computer print-out was therefore inadmissible.

Counsel for the prosecution has asked us to apply the proviso. He emphasises that the d appellant testified in her defence and that the jury must have disbelieved her. But in this case the inadmissible computer print-out was a major plank in the prosecution case. It served to prove that the card was stolen, and to controvert the defence suggestion that the appellant might innocently have acquired a forged card. Without the computer evidence the judge may have stopped the case at the end of the prosecution case, or, in any event, the appellant may not have testified. The prosecution case, without the e computer evidence, was by no means overwhelming. It is impossible to say that the jury would inevitably have convicted if the computer print-out had been ruled inadmissible.

This appeal is allowed and the conviction is quashed.

*Appeal in R v Minors dismissed. Appeal in R v Harper allowed.*        f

Solicitors: *Crown Prosecution Service*, North London.

Kate O'Hanlon   Barrister.

a # Customs and Excise Commissioners v Bell Concord Educational Trust Ltd

COURT OF APPEAL, CIVIL DIVISION
SIR NICOLAS BROWNE-WILKINSON V-C, WOOLF AND STAUGHTON LJJ
23, 24 NOVEMBER 1988, 3 FEBRUARY 1989

b
*Value added tax – Exemptions – Education – Provision of education otherwise than for profit – Charitable company providing educational courses – Company charging such fees as would achieve surplus income in order to maintain and improve facilities offered – Company required to apply income and property solely to its objects and prohibited from paying profits to its members – Whether company providing education 'otherwise than for profit' – Value Added Tax Act* c *1983, Sch 6, Group 6, item 2(a) – Council Directive (EEC) 77/388, art 13(A)(1)(i)(2)(a).*

The appellant company was a company limited by guarantee and was a registered charity. Its objects were to promote the advancement of education and to carry on, acquire and develop schools. Its memorandum of association expressly provided that its income and d property were to be applied solely towards the promotion of its objects and that no portion thereof was to be paid or transferred by way of dividend, bonus or otherwise by way of profit to its members. The company acquired and carried on as its only activity an educational establishment, and in fixing the fees payable for courses there it budgeted for, and achieved, a substantial surplus of income over expenditure, with the intention of using the excess to maintain and improve the quality of facilities offered to students. e The question arose whether the company was registerable for value added tax or whether it was exempt because it provided the courses 'otherwise than for profit' within the Value Added Tax Act 1983, Sch 6, Group 6, item 2(a)[a]. A value added tax tribunal held that the company was not so registrable but that decision was reversed by the judge, who held that the exemption in item 2(a), which was intended to give effect to the exemption provided for by art 13(A)(1)(i)[b] of Council Directive (EEC) 77/388, did not apply where f for the time being the organisation in question was aiming to make a surplus or profit on current account. The company appealed, contending that, since the surplus could never redound to the profit of any individual but had to be applied for the educational charitable purposes of the company, the services were being provided otherwise than for profit. The Crown contended that, so long as the company was pursuing a policy of making a surplus on the provison of educational services, those services were being g provided for profit.

**Held** – The phrase 'otherwise than for profit' in item 2(a) of Group 6 of Sch 6 to the 1983 Act, construed in the light of art 13(A)(2)(a) of Council Directive (EEC) 77/388, referred to the objects for which an organisation was established and not to the budgeting policy being pursued for the time being by the organisation in question. If the constitution of h the organisation was looked at to discover the purposes for which it was established, that provided a clear and unambiguous test whether the supplies made by it were for profit. Since the company's charitable educational objects prevented the distribution of its profits to private individuals and since the making of a surplus was incidental to and not an object of the company, it followed that the company provided educational services 'otherwise than for profit' and was therefore not registrable for value added tax. The j appeal would accordingly be allowed (see p 219 h j, p 220 a to d g h, p 221 d, p 223 c to e and p 224 d e g h, post).

---

a   Item 2, so far as material, is set out at p 219 a, post
b   Article 13(A), so far as material, is set out at p 221 h j and p 222 a b, post

**Notes**

For the exemption of education from liability for value added tax, see 12 Halsbury's Laws *a* (4th edn) para 901 and 52 ibid para 20–27, and for cases on the subject, see 49 Digest (Reissue) 20, 59–60.

For the Value Added Tax Act 1983, Sch 6, Group 6, see 48 Halsbury's Statutes (4th edn) 688.

**Cases referred to in judgments** *b*

*Buchanan (James) & Co Ltd v Babco Forwarding and Shipping (UK) Ltd* [1977] 3 All ER 1048, [1978] AC 141, [1977] 3 WLR 907, HL.

*Garland v British Rail Engineering Ltd* [1982] 2 All ER 402, [1983] 2 AC 751, [1982] 2 WLR 918, HL.

*National Deposit Friendly Society (Trustees) v Skegness UDC* [1958] 2 All ER 601, [1959] AC 293, [1958] 3 WLR 172, HL. *c*

**Cases also cited**

*Becker v Finanzamt Münster-Innenstadt* Case 8/81 [1982] ECR 53.

*Beswick v Beswick* [1967] 2 All ER 1197, [1968] AC 58, HL.

*Customs and Excise Comrs v Apple and Pear Development Council* [1984] STC 296; *affd* [1985] STC 383, CA; *on appeal* [1986] STC 192, HL; *on reference* Case 102/86 [1988] 2 All ER *d* 922, CJEC.

*Gilbert v Gilbert and Boucher* [1928] P 1, CA.

*IRC v Hinchy* [1960] 1 All ER 505, [1960] AC 748, HL.

*International Bible Students Association v Customs and Excise Comrs* [1988] STC 412.

*Kirkness (Inspector of Taxes) v John Hudson & Co Ltd* [1955] 2 All ER 345, [1955] AC 696, HL. *e*

*Yoga for Health Foundation v Customs and Excise Comrs* [1984] STC 630.

**Appeal**

Bell Concord Educational Trust Ltd (the company) appealed with leave of the judge against the decision of Taylor J ([1988] STC 143) on 17 December 1987 reversing the decision of the Manchester Value Added Tax Tribunal (chairman Mr A W Simpson) *f* ([1986] VATTR 165) dated 28 August 1986 that the company had not made taxable supplies of education and therefore was not required to be registered for value added tax. The facts are set out in the judgment of Sir Nicolas Browne-Wilkinson V-C.

*Frederic Reynold QC* and *Roderick Cordara* for the company.
*Guy Sankey* for the Crown. *g*

*Cur adv vult*

3 February. The following judgments were delivered.

*h*

**SIR NICOLAS BROWNE-WILKINSON V-C.** This is an appeal by Bell Concord Educational Trust Ltd (the company) from a decision of Taylor J ([1988] STC 143), who held that the company was registerable for value added tax with effect from 1 September 1983. The judge allowed an appeal by the Crown from a decision of the Manchester Value Added Tax Tribunal ([1986] VATTR 165) that the company was not so registerable.

The company is a company limited by guarantee and is a registered charity. Its objects *j* are to promote the advancement of education and to carry on, acquire and develop boarding or day schools. The company's memorandum and articles expressly provide that its income and property are to be applied solely towards the promotion of its objects and that no portion thereof shall be paid or transferred directly or indirectly by way of dividend, bonus or otherwise by way of profit to its members. The company acquired and carries on as its only activity an educational establishment known as Concord College.

The question whether or not the company is registerable for value added tax depends
*a* on whether the services it supplies are exempted under s 17(1) of the Value Added Tax
Act 1983. Under that section a supply of services is exempt if it is of a description for the
time being specified in Sch 6 to the 1983 Act. Item 2(a) of Group 6 of Sch 6 is as follows:

'The provision, otherwise than for profit, of—(a) education or research of a kind
provided by a school or university . . .'

*b* The sole question in this case is whether the provision of education by the company is or
was 'otherwise than for profit' within the meaning of Group 6 of Sch 6.

The value added tax tribunal made the following findings of fact. In fixing the fees
payable for its courses the company budgets for, and achieves, a substantial surplus of
income over expenditure. Its purpose is to maintain and improve the quality of the
facilities offered to students by increasing the number of teachers and by improving and
*c* adding to the buildings. It intends, when such purposes have been achieved, to reduce its
fees in real terms and, if possible, to establish scholarships for gifted children in need.
Like many other well-managed charities which run a continuing operation, the company
must plan and budget for the future. From the start it has budgeted for and achieved a
substantial surplus of income over expenditure. In the year ending on 31 August 1984
the surplus was nearly £216,000 and in the following year it was over £232,000,
*d* representing in each case a little over a fifth of the company's total turnover. The
company intended, for the next two years at least, to continue to budget for surpluses of
that order. The company's purpose in building up a cash reserve in that manner was to
maintain and improve the quality of the facilities which the company offers to its
students, by increasing the number of teachers (and thus reducing the size of classes) and,
more importantly, by improving and adding to the buildings.
*e* The question, therefore, is whether the fact that the company was budgeting to make
a surplus each year with a view to applying such accumulated surpluses in the future for
its charitable purposes means that at the relevant time it was not providing its educational
services 'otherwise than for profit' within the meaning of Sch 6.

The judge construed the 1983 Act in the light of an EEC Directive, Council Directive
*f* (EEC) 77/388 (the Sixth Directive), and on that basis found that the exemption did not
apply where, for the time being, an organisation was aiming to make a surplus or profit
on current account. I will have to consider the directive hereafter, but I will first seek to
find the proper construction of the 1983 Act apart from any guidance to be gathered
from the directive.

Under the 1983 Act value added tax is chargeable on the supply of goods and services:
*g* s 17 exempts supplies of a description specified in Sch 6. Applying the conventional
approach, therefore, one would have to look at each provision of services by the company
and ask of it: was such supply otherwise than for profit? That would plainly be
impracticable and the Crown does not contend for that view. It is common ground
between the parties that one has to look at the organisation providing the services to
discover whether such services were provided otherwise than for profit. It is also common
*h* ground that the answer to that question lies in the purpose, intention or motive of the
company. There are two possible views: (a) that, notwithstanding that the surplus will
never be applied otherwise than for the educational charitable purposes of the company,
so long as the company is pursuing a policy of making a surplus on the provision of
educational services, those services are being provided for profit. This is the Crown's
contention and focuses on the policy for the time being pursued by the organisation,
*j* irrespective of the objects for which it is established; (b) that, since the surplus can never
redound to the profit of any individual but must be applied for the educational charitable
purposes of the company, the services are being provided otherwise than for profit. This
is the company's contention, which focuses on the objects for which the organisation is
established, irrespective of its budgeting policy from time to time.

In my judgment, the phrase 'otherwise than for profit' is ambiguous and is capable of
bearing either of the meanings contended for. I will first consider how I would construe

the paragraph apart from any guidance to be gained from the Sixth Directive, and then consider what light, if any, that directive casts on the matter.

Apart from the Sixth Directive, I would construe the phrase in the sense contended for by the company. There is nothing in the context which throws any light on the meaning of the words and my reasons for favouring the company's contention are primarily practical. If the phrase 'otherwise than for profit' requires one to look at the constitution of the organisation to discover the purposes for which it is established, there is a clear and unambiguous test whether the supply is made for profit. If the Crown's test is correct the consequential difficulties are formidable.

If the phrase 'otherwise than for profit' implies that a charitable organisation can carry on a business for 'profit', the question at once arises: what is meant by 'profit'? In relation to what period does one assess the profit? How often does one have to ask the question: is the organisation providing its services otherwise than for profit? Counsel for the Crown suggested that the matter could be considered quarterly, that is to say on each occasion when the organisation is liable to make a value added tax return. I find it inconceivable that Parliament could have intended the question of exemption to depend on ascertaining the subjective state of mind of an educational body at such short intervals. Common sense suggests the exemption should depend on some long-lasting and objective yardstick rather than on this frequent review of the state of mind of those running the organisation.

If the profit is not to be taken on a quarterly basis, what other period is to be taken? Although the 1983 Act does not say so, let us assume (as did the judge) that the question whether or not the organisation is conducted for profit has to be answered by reference to the excess in any year of receipts over expenses. This would require every educational charity, in order to be exempt from value added tax, to budget precisely in order to cover expenditure of one year out of the income of the same year. Quite apart from being a hopeless task, this would cut across the well-known policy of many educational charities. Is it really the intention that an organisation which aims to make a surplus in year 1 in order to provide the funds necessary to meet a known liability falling payable in year 2 is not to be a body supplying services 'otherwise than for profit'? If exemption is not lost by budgeting to cover known liabilities arising in the following year, at what stage does such surplus become a profit? If the organisation seeks to pitch its fees at a level sufficient to cover known expenditure in year 3 or year 6 or year 10, is that sufficient?

If, on the other hand, one has to look to see if the intention was to make a surplus in any one year, if the organisation seeks to make a surplus in year 1 in order to cover a liability in year 2, then the organisation will be registerable in year 1 but cease to be registerable in year 2. Again, I find it difficult to believe that Parliament intended this exemption to be such a transitory matter.

In my judgment, Parliament is far more likely to have considered that the phrase 'otherwise than for profit' meant bodies which were non-profit-making bodies in the ordinary sense of the word rather than bodies which, from time to time, aimed to make a surplus on revenue account. The administration of the tax for educational charities would become so complex on any other view that, apart from any guidance from the Sixth Directive, I would reject the Crown's construction.

My view receives some support from the speech of Lord Denning in *Trustees of the National Deposit Friendly Society v Skegness UDC* [1958] 2 All ER 601, [1959] AC 293. That case concerned entitlement to rating relief for hereditaments 'occupied for the purposes of an organisation . . . which is not established or conducted for profit'. The society was the occupier of a convalescent home but also made a substantial surplus on income it received from its investments after paying the interests on monies deposited by its members. The House of Lords held that, despite such surplus, the society was not established or conducted for profit. Lord Denning said ([1958] 2 All ER 601 at 612, [1959] AC 293 at 319–320):

'Looking at the way in which the society has conducted its affairs, I am of opinion that it has made profits. It has not distributed those profits like a commercial

a    company. Nor has it returned them to members. It has used them to build up large
and accumulating reserve funds. But the fact that the society has made profits does
not mean that it is "conducted for profit", which I take to mean "conducted for the
purpose of making profit". Many charitable bodies, such as colleges and religious
foundations, have large funds which they invest at interest in stocks and shares, or
purchase land which they let at a profit. Yet they are not established or conducted

b    for profit. The reason is because their objects are to advance education or religion, as
the case may be. The investing of funds is not one of their objects properly so called,
but only a means of achieving those objects. So here, it seems to me, that, if the
making of profit is not one of the main objects of an organisation, but is only a
subsidiary object—that is to say, if it is only a means whereby its main objects can
be furthered or achieved—then it is not established or conducted for profit . . .

c    Applied to this case, I think that the building up of a reserve fund—despite its size—
is not one of the main objects of this society. It is only incidental—a consequence of
the wise investment policy it has pursued. The main object of the society is to
provide security for people of small means against the risks which life holds for
them—and not to make a profit therefrom. It is, therefore, not conducted for profit.'

d    So in this case, the question is whether the supply is 'for profit'. The answer, in my
judgment, is No, the making of a surplus is incidental to, and not an object of, the
company and it is therefore not supplying its educational services for profit.

Is the position altered by the Sixth Directive? That directive came into force on
1 January 1978. Under art 189 of the EEC Treaty the directive is binding on this country
as to the result to be achieved. Pursuant to that treaty obligation, the Value Added Tax

e    (Education) Order 1977, SI 1977/1787 (which came into operation on 1 January 1978),
was made, substituting a new Group 6 of Sch 5 to the Finance Act 1972, which was the
Act then regulating value added tax. Group 6 as enacted by the 1977 order is in the same
terms as Group 6 of Sch 6 to the 1983 Act, which is a consolidating Act.

If there is an ambiguity in the domestic United Kingdom legislation on value added
tax, it is permissible and necessary to seek to construe Group 6 of Sch 6 to the 1983 Act

f    so as to produce compliance by the United Kingdom with its treaty obligations by
making the United Kingdom provisions accord, so far as possible, with the provisions of
the Sixth Directive: see Garland v British Rail Engineering Ltd [1982] 2 All ER 402 at 415,
[1983] 2 AC 751 at 771. Counsel for the company submitted that such aid to construction
was not permissible in the present case since the exemption for educational services
provided otherwise than for profit was first introduced by the Finance Act 1972, ie at a

g    time before the Sixth Directive was in force. I do not accept this submission. The 1977
order and the 1983 Act were both approved by Parliament in their present form after the
Sixth Directive was made and in force; the presumption that Parliament intends to
comply with United Kingdom's treaty obligations is equally applicable in such a case.

What light then is cast by the Sixth Directive on the problem? The English text of
art 13(A)(1) of the directive imposes a mandatory duty on member states to exempt from

h    value added tax—

'(i) children's or young people's education, school or university education,
vocational training or retraining, including the supply of services and of goods
closely related thereto, provided by bodies governed by public law having such as
their aim or by other organizations defined by the Member State concerned as

j    having similar objects.'

Such mandatory exemptions are to be given by the member states 'under conditions
which they shall lay down for the purpose of ensuring the correct and straightforward
application of such exemptions'. Article 13(A)(2), however, gives member states a limited
right to impose conditions on such exemptions. So far as relevant art 13(A)(2) provides
as follows:

'(a) Member States may make the granting to bodies other than those governed by public law of each exemption provided for in 1 ... (i) ... of this Article subject    *a*
in each individual case to one or more of the following conditions: —they shall not systematically aim to make a profit, but any profits nevertheless arising shall not be distributed, but shall be assigned to the continuance or improvement of the services supplied, —they shall be managed and administered on an essentially voluntary basis by persons who have no direct or indirect interest, either themselves or through intermediaries, in the results of the activities concerned ...'     *b*

I would note in passing that art 13(A)(1) stresses that the conditions which are to be laid down under that paragraph are for the purpose of ensuring the 'straightforward application' of such exemptions. The complexities which would arise if the Crown's contention is correct are hard to reconcile with this provision.

Under the Sixth Directive the company (having been treated as having educational    *c*
purposes) is entitled to mandatory exemption under art 13(A)(1)(i) but the United Kingdom legislature was entitled to refuse such relief unless the company is an organisation which does not 'systematically aim to make a profit, but any profits nevertheless arising [are] not [to] be distributed etc'. It is the Crown's contention that those words in art 13(A)(2) are the basis on which Group 6 of Sch 6 is founded. Those words are themselves very obscure. As to the second requirement (namely the ban on    *d*
the distribution of profits), it is clear from the memorandum and articles of the company that that requirement is in any event satisfied. But what is meant by the words 'systematically aim to make a profit'?

Counsel for the Crown submits that the words 'systematically aim' require one to look at the budgeting policy from time to time being adopted. He prays in aid the second clause of art 13(A)(2), which refers to profits 'nevertheless arising'. He says that the words    *e*
of the article are looking to the aim for the time being and the incidental production of profit from time to time. He further submits that, in order to qualify for exemption under art 13(A)(1), the organisations have to have educational objects. Article 13(A)(2) therefore presupposes that there can be an organisation having educational objects which can nevertheless systematically aim to make, and in fact makes, a profit. Therefore, says counsel for the Crown, art 13(A)(2) cannot be referring to the objects for which the    *f*
organisation is established but must be looking at the way in which it carries on its business and in particular its budgetary policy.

Although there is much force in this submission, I do not regard the matter as being clear on the English text. It is perfectly possible to have an organisation which has been established with dual objects, one of providing education and the other of making a private profit, ie the privately owned school. Therefore there is nothing impossible in    *g*
the concept of a body having both educational and profit-making objects. Moreover, the system referred to in the words 'systematically aimed' is perfectly capable of referring to the system established by the regulating documents themselves, eg the memorandum and articles of the company. Therefore, in my judgment, the English text of the Sixth Directive (read in isolation) is itself ambiguous and throws no clear light on the true construction of Group 6 of Sch 6 to the 1983 Act.     *h*

In such circumstances, it is legitimate to look at the French text of the Sixth Directive to see if it clarifies the position: see *James Buchanan & Co Ltd v Babco Forwarding and Shipping (UK) Ltd* [1977] 3 All ER 1048 at 1052, 1060, 1065, [1978] AC 141 at 152, 161, 167. In the French text, art 13(A)(2), so far as relevant, reads as follows:

'... les organismes en question ne doivent pas avoir pour but la recherche    *j*
systématique du profit, les bénéfices éventuels ne devant jamais être distribués mais devant être affectés au maintien ou à l'amélioration des prestations fournies ...'

This is, in my judgment, illuminating in a number of different respects. First, unlike the English text, the word 'systématique' does not limit the word 'but'. It is clear that the aim or object ('but') referred to is the aim of the organisation itself, ie the object for

which it is constituted. Nothing corresponding to the English words 'but' and
*a* 'nevertheless' appear in the French text at all. As a result, in the French text there are not
two conditions but simply one description of the organisation: an organisation not
established with a view to systematic profit, any profit arising being applicable to the
furtherance of its objects. Moreover, the use of the words 'ne doivent pas' and 'ne devant
jamais' and 'devant', involving as they do the concept of an outside legal requirement to
do or not to do something, are to be contrasted with the corresponding words in the
*b* English text, 'shall not', which do not necessarily look to there being any legal
requirement as to the application of moneys but may be looking to what in fact is done
with such moneys. Although my knowledge of French is far from commanding, the
French text appears to be providing clearly as follows: the organisations shall not have as
their object the systematic pursuit of profit, any beneficial out-turn being required not
to be distributed but required to be applied to the maintenance or improvement of the
*c* services provided. If, as I believe, that is a correct translation, in the French text 'the
systematic pursuit of profit' is explained by the latter words of the clause as meaning an
organisation which cannot apply any profits arising otherwise than for its purposes. It
follows that on this basis the United Kingdom government could only withhold the
exemption from organisations which have the power to distribute profits for private
gain. In my judgment, it is legitimate to construe the English text, which is capable of
*d* bearing this meaning, in that sense also.

Accordingly, I reach the view that, to the extent that the Sixth Directive assists in the
construction of the 1983 Act, it points in favour of the view that I would in any event
prefer, namely that the words 'otherwise than for profit' refer to the objects for which an
organisation is established and not to the budgeting policy being pursued for the time
being by the organisation in question. I would therefore allow the appeal and restore the
*e* decision of the value added tax tribunal.


**WOOLF LJ.** I agree that this appeal should be allowed. I also agree with the reasoning
of Sir Nicolas Browne-Wilkinson V-C set out in his judgment, subject to two points to
which I will now refer, which I do not consider it is necessary to decide for the purposes
*f* of this appeal and on which I would prefer to express no concluded view, although I
regard it as important to draw attention to them since otherwise our decision could be
considered to have wider application than I would wish.

The first point is whether item 2 of Group 6 of Sch 6 to the Value Added Tax Act 1983
can only apply to a supply by a charity or other body whose constitution prevents it from
being conducted with a view to profit. In this case the appellant company is a charity and
*g* its articles and memorandum of association make it clear that supplies which it makes
will inevitably be 'otherwise than for profit'. However, I would regard it as open to
argument whether the terms of item 2 of Group 6 are confined to bodies whose powers
are limited so as to prevent their activities resulting in personal profit. I draw attention
to the fact that, for example, you have in Group 10 express reference to supplies by 'a
non-profit-making body' and in Sch 5, Group 16, you have references specifically to
*h* supplies by 'charities'; while item 2 only appears to place a restriction on the purpose for
which the supplies are made and does not place limitations on the nature of the body
which has to make the supplies before the supplies will be exempt as is the case with
items 1 and 3 of Group 6. Against this I do appreciate the desirability of avoiding the
undesirable consequences, to which Sir Nicolas Browne-Wilkinson V-C refers, which
would arise in administering the tax if it is necessary to consider the motives with which
*j* supplies are made in order to decide whether or not they are exempt.

Therefore in particular I would wish to leave open for decision when it arises whether
an individual or individuals could take advantage of Group 6, item 2. Clearly, it would
be more difficult for an unincorporated body to establish that it was carrying on the
activities in question 'otherwise than for profit' if 'profits' were made which were not
required to be ploughed back by the constitution which controls the body. However, I

would regard it as arguable that an individual can be treated as making supplies otherwise than for profit if, but only if, he can establish that any difference between the price charged and the gross cost of a supply or supplies was intended to be used broadly for the purposes identified in item 2. In this case this was clearly the policy of the company in relation to the supplies which it made.

The second point on which I would prefer not to express any conclusion is as to the position of a charity which carries on educational activities which are within item 2 and other non-educational charitable activities. Would supplies still fall within item 2 if 'profits' which result from making educational supplies are intended to be used to subsidise the other non-educational activities of the charity? Here again I would regard it as being at least arguable that if the proceeds of the provision of supplies which otherwise fall within item 2 are to be used for non-educational purposes the provision would not be otherwise than for profit and not therefore within item 2.

Finally, I should indicate that I am far from satisfied that any issue as to the interpretation of item 2 which I have identified could result in a conflict between item 2 and the requirements of the French or English version of Council Directive (EEC) 77/388 (the Sixth Directive).

**STAUGHTON LJ.** Save in one minor respect, I wholly agree with the judgment delivered by Sir Nicolas Browne-Wilkinson V-C. Looking first at the Value Added Tax Act 1983 on its own, I consider that the words 'otherwise than for profit' in Sch 6, Group 6, item 2, refer to the motive of the supplier. If he effects the supply with the motive of making a profit, the supply is not exempt; if his motive is the advancement of education but a surplus of income over expenditure nevertheless results, it is exempt.

Even if that is not the only possible construction, it is in my judgment plainly one that the statute is capable of bearing. Can reference then be made to Council Directive (EEC) 77/388 (the Sixth Directive) to resolve the ambiguity?

It was conceded that a taxpayer can rely directly on a Council directive, whether or not the commissioners could do so.

If reference is made only to the English text of the Sixth Directive, I would be inclined to agree with Taylor J that a company which deliberately planned to make a large surplus, whether or not for the benefit of its members, would be infringing a condition that it should not 'systematically aim to make a profit'. In those circumstances, the directive would be of no assistance to the company in this case: either the United Kingdom has enacted one of the conditions which it may lawfully impose under the directive, viz that the supplier shall not systematically aim to make a profit, or, if it has not but has enacted some different condition in the 1983 Act by the words 'otherwise than for profit', one is no nearer ascertaining what that condition means.

But when one turns to the French text it is to my mind plain, for the reasons given by Sir Nicolas Browne-Wilkinson V-C, that the words 'otherwise than for profit' in the 1983 Act are a condition authorised by the Sixth Directive, because they refer to the activities of an organisation with an objective other than profit, which retains any profits incidentally made within its business. The company can accordingly rely on the Sixth Directive as resolving the ambiguity in the 1983 Act (if there were one, which in my opinion there is not) in their favour. We have not looked beyond the French text, at that in the other languages of the European Community. For my part, I would not be competent to do so without expert assistance.

I too would allow this appeal.

*Appeal allowed. Leave to appeal to the House of Lords refused.*

Solicitors: *H H Mainprice* (for the company); *Solicitor for the Customs and Excise.*

Heather Whicher   Barrister.

# Buckinghamshire County Council v Moran

COURT OF APPEAL, CIVIL DIVISION
SLADE, NOURSE AND BUTLER-SLOSS LJJ
12, 13 JANUARY, 13 FEBRUARY 1989

*Limitation of action – Land – Adverse possession – Dispossession of true owner – Acts amounting to possession – Land held by owner for purpose of future road development – Owner having no immediate use for land – Occupier of neighbouring house maintaining land as part of his garden – Land not fenced off from garden – Whether occupier's acts amounting to dispossession of owner – Whether occupier having adverse possession for requisite period – Whether occupier prevented from claiming adverse possession by owner's plans for its future use – Limitation Act 1980, s 15(1).*

In 1955 the plaintiff council acquired a plot of land adjacent to some houses with a view to carrying out a road diversion at some time in the future. It was envisaged that the proposed diversion would not take place for many years and in the mean time the council, which had no use for the land, left it vacant. The plot adjoined the garden of a house owned by the defendant's predecessors in title and, although the council fenced the roadside boundary of the plot, no fence was put up between the plot and the garden of the house. The defendant's predecessors in title maintained the plot and treated it as part of their garden. The only access to the plot was through the garden. In 1971 the defendant purchased the house and continued to maintain the plot as if it was part of his garden. The defendant was aware that the plot belonged to the council. On 18 December 1975 the council wrote to the defendant asking him to supply details of the basis on which he was exercising rights over the plot. On 20 January 1976 the defendant replied in a letter stated to be 'Without prejudice' that he understood that he was entitled to use the land until the proposed road diversion was built. The council replied by refuting the defendant's right to use the land but made no attempt to assert physical ownership of the plot until 28 October 1985, when it issued a writ claiming possession of the plot. The defendant by his defence claimed that since he and his predecessors in title had been in adverse possession of the plot for more than 12 years the council's claim was barred by s 15(1)[a] of the Limitation Act 1980. The judge held that the defendant's letter of 20 January 1976 was inadmissible in evidence because the fact that it had been written 'Without prejudice' showed that it was intended by the defendant to be part of negotiations with the council and was therefore privileged. On the substantive issue the judge upheld the defendant's claim of adverse possession and dismissed the council's claim. The council appealed, contending that the letter was admissible in evidence and that where land was acquired or retained by the true owner for a specific future purpose he could not be dispossessed by acts of trespass which were not inconsistent with that purpose.

**Held** – (1) The defendant's letter of 20 January 1976 was not an offer to negotiate but an assertion of the defendant's right and therefore it could not fairly and properly be read as the opening of negotiations. Accordingly, it was not privileged despite the fact that it had been written 'Without prejudice' and was therefore admissible in evidence (see p 231 *f* to *j*, p 238 *f* and p 240 *b*, post); *South Shropshire DC v Amos* [1987] 1 All ER 340 distinguished.

(2) There was no special rule of law that an owner of land who intended to use it for a particular purpose at some future date could not lose title to it by adverse possession to a squatter whose acts did not substantially interfere with the owner's plans for future use of the land but who was nevertheless able to show the requisite factual possession and

---

*a   Section 15(1) is set out at p 231 j to p 232 a, post*

intention to establish adverse possession. Instead, if in such a case the squatter was aware that the true owner, although having no present use for the land, had plans for its future use the court would require very clear evidence that the squatter had not only established factual possession of the land but also the requisite intention to exclude the world at large, including the true owner, before deciding that the owner's claim to the land was barred. Since the defendant had acquired complete and exclusive physical control of the plot by 28 October 1973, ie 12 years before the council issued its writ, and intended for the time being to possess the land to the exclusion of all other persons including the true owner he had established the necessary adverse possession to defeat the council's claim. The appeal would therefore be dismissed (see p 234 g j to p 235 g j to p 236 a c to e, p 238 b c e f, p 239 a to e and p 240 h to p 241 a, post); *Powell v McFarlane* (1977) 38 P & CR 452 applied; *Leigh v Jack* (1879) 5 Ex D 264 not followed.

**Notes**
For the meaning and effect of adverse possession, see 28 Halsbury's Laws (4th edn) paras 768–769, and for cases on the subject, see 32 Digest (Reissue) 612, 4542–4543.

For the Limitation Act 1980, s 15, see 24 Halsbury's Statutes (4th edn) 642.

**Cases referred to in judgments**
*Daintrey, Re, ex p Holt* [1893] 2 QB 116, [1891–4] All ER Rep 209, DC.
*Gray v Wykeham-Martin* [1977] CA Transcript 10A.
*Leigh v Jack* (1879) 5 Ex D 264, CA.
*Littledale v Liverpool College* [1900] 1 Ch 19, CA.
*Marshall v Taylor* [1895] 1 Ch 641, CA.
*Powell v McFarlane* (1977) 38 P & CR 452.
*Rains v Buxton* (1880) 14 Ch D 537.
*Rush & Tompkins Ltd v Greater London Council* [1988] 3 All ER 737, [1988] 3 WLR 939, HL.
*Seddon v Smith* (1877) 36 LT 168, CA.
*South Shropshire DC v Amos* [1987] 1 All ER 340, [1986] 1 WLR 1271, CA.
*Tecbild Ltd v Chamberlain* (1969) 20 P & CR 633, CA.
*Treloar v Nute* [1977] 1 All ER 230, [1976] 1 WLR 1295, CA.
*Wallis's Cayton Bay Holiday Camp Ltd v Shell-Mex and BP Ltd* [1974] 3 All ER 575, [1975] QB 94, [1974] 3 WLR 387, CA.
*Williams Bros Direct Supply Stores Ltd v Raftery* [1957] 3 All ER 593, [1958] 1 QB 159, [1957] 3 WLR 931, CA.
*Wimpey (George) & Co Ltd v Sohn* [1966] 1 All ER 232, [1967] Ch 487, [1966] 2 WLR 414, CA.

**Case also cited**
*Bligh v Martin* [1968] 1 All ER 1157, [1968] 1 WLR 804.

**Appeal**
Buckinghamshire County Council appealed with the leave of the judge against the decision of Hoffmann J on 19 February 1988 dismissing the council's claim against the defendant, Christopher John Moran, for possession of land situated at Chenies Avenue, Amersham, Buckinghamshire. The facts are set out in the judgment of Slade LJ.

*Michael Douglas* for the council.
*Peter R Griffiths* for the defendant.

*Cur adv vult*

13 February. The following judgments were delivered.

**SLADE LJ.** This is an appeal by the Buckinghamshire County Council from a judgment
a of Hoffmann J given on 19 February 1988, whereby he dismissed the claim by the
council to recover possession of a plot of land situated at Chenies Avenue, Amersham,
Buckinghamshire (the plot). By a conveyance of 12 October 1955 the plot was conveyed
to the council, which indisputably still has the paper title to it. However, the judge held
that Mr Christopher Moran, the defendant to the action and respondent to this appeal,
had been in adverse possession of it for more than 12 years before the proceedings were
b commenced on 28 October 1985, and that the council's title to it had therefore been
extinguished under ss 15 and 17 of the Limitation Act 1980.

I can take the primary facts of the case largely from the judge's judgment, where they
are stated very clearly. The plot fronts onto Chenies Avenue, which runs from north to
south. It is one of a number of plots of roughly equal size on the west side of the road.
By 1955 houses had been built on the plots immediately to the north and south of the
c plot, but the plot itself remained vacant. The house immediately to the north was called
Westwood Way; the house immediately to the south was called Croft Edge. The council
acquired the plot for a proposed diversion of the A404 road around Amersham, but it
was contemplated that the construction of that road would not take place for many years.
Meantime, the council had no use for the land.

In 1955 there was a laurel hedge separating the plot from the garden of Croft Edge, a
d chain link fence and a privet hedge along the western boundary and a fence in poor
condition with an old iron gate along the road frontage. There was no fence between the
plot and Westwood Way.

In 1962 the council acquired Croft Edge also for the purposes of the proposed new
road. It let the house to a tenant. At about the same time, Mr Builth, the then owner of
Westwood Way, complained about the state of the fence on the road frontage to the plot.
e He said that children were using the plot as a playground and as a means of access to
some recreation grounds beyond the western boundary and that they were causing him
annoyance. In response to his complaint the council put up a chestnut paling fence along
the whole length of the road frontage and re-erected the gate at the road, which had
fallen down. Mr Wherry, the district surveyor at the time, said in evidence that, when
f making inspections during the 1960s, he used occasionally to climb over the gate or
fence; he thought that the gate was wired up, but not locked.

On 15 June 1965 Mr Builth wrote another letter of complaint to the council and
suggested that the only solution was for the council to fence off the plot completely from
his garden. The council, however, declined to do so. At about the same time, Mr Builth
built another house on the western side of his plot, which was Dolphin Place.

g Early in 1966 Mr Builth sold off Dolphin Place, together with most of the garden, to a
Mr and Mrs Swaby. The southern boundary of their garden abutted the north boundary
of the plot along the whole of its length. Mr and Mrs Swaby, in turn, conveyed Dolphin
Place to a Mr and Mrs Wall. They took over the maintenance of the plot, mowing the
grass, trimming the hedges and treating it as part of their garden. In August 1970 the
divisional road surveyor noted in a memorandum to the county surveyor that the plot
h was being cut and maintained in a tidy condition by Mr Wall. Thereafter, the road
surveyor's department, being spared the need to maintain the plot itself, did no more
than inspect it regularly by looking over the fence from the road, usually from a car
window. Mr Wherry, who was responsible for these inspections in the 1960s and early
1970s, said that so far as he knew no one from the council had gone on the land since the
late 1960s.

j In 1971 Mr and Mrs Wall sold Dolphin Place to the defendant, Mr Moran. The judge
found that there had not been any substantial change in appearance of the house and
garden since the time when Mr Moran bought it. On inspection, he said, the plot would
appear to be part of the garden enclosed on all sides except the north, where there is
nothing to indicate any boundary between it and the garden contained within the paper
title of Dolphin Place. He also found, however, that Mr Moran was aware that the paper

title to the plot was vested in the council, and that the council had acquired the land in order to construct a road at some time in the future.      *a*

It seems fairly clear that, at the time of his purchase of Dolphin Place, Mr Moran and his legal advisers were well aware of the possibility that Mr and Mrs Wall had acquired, or were in the course of acquiring, a possessory title to the plot. They procured the making of a statutory declaration by Mr and Mrs Wall dated 15 July 1971, in which they said that since 1967 they had occupied the plot and cultivated it to the extent of tending and cutting the grass and trimming hedges and had from time to time parked a horse   *b* box on the plot. They said that no person had challenged their right to occupy it, and their permission had been requested for the laying of an electricity supply across it, by parties owning or occupying the tennis courts at the rear. The conveyance of Dolphin Place to the defendant dated 28 July 1971 was expressed to include not only the land comprised in the vendor's paper title, but also 'all such estate right title and interest that the Vendors may have in or over the remaining part of the plot formerly numbered 206   *c* as aforesaid [ie the plot]'.

Following the conveyance to him of Dolphin Place, the defendant took possession of that property and for the next 18 months or so lived there with his mother, Mrs Moran. After that time he moved out, but his mother has remained there ever since and he returns occasionally for weekends and other visits. In argument on this appeal no reliance has been placed on the fact that since about 1973 the defendant has not been personally   *d* residing at Dolphin Place.

The defendant said in evidence that he thought that the gate which the council had re-erected in the early 1960s might have had a lock which had been placed on it by Mr Wall. Subject to this, the judge found that the state of the fences when the defendant bought the property was as has been described earlier in this judgment. Whether or not there was already a lock on the gate when the defendant bought the property, the judge   *e* accepted the defendant's evidence that when he moved in he bought a new lock and chain and fastened the gate; he also found that he kept the key. The judge also found that since then there has been no access to the plot other than by climbing over the fence or through the hedges, except via the driveway of Chenies Avenue and through the garden of Dolphin Place.

In 1975 the local tennis club, whose courts lay over the boundary to the west of the   *f* plot, had a scheme for laying a drain which would be connected with the drainage arrangements of Dolphin Place. They applied to the council for permission. As a result, the council got in touch with the defendant. A telephone conversation took place between the defendant and Mr Harris of the county valuer's department on 10 November 1975. Mr Harris made an attendance note of that conversation which, so far as material,   *g* reads as follows:

'[The defendant] . . . discussed with [Mr Harris] the use of the land immediately to the north of the property known as "Croft Edge". [The defendant] indicated that he had been the owner of Dolphin Place for five years and that the land in question . . . was incorporated within the garden of his property. He indicated that he had purchased the property from a Mr. Wall of Westwood Way in whose garden   *h* Dolphin Place was built. He stated that the previous owner had obtained a right to use the County Council land when Dolphin Place was built and that this right had been passed on to himself. He believed that the right to use this land had been arranged as part of the granting of planning permission for the erection of Dolphin Place. He also stated that he was of the opinion that he had first option to purchase the land if the road was not constructed. He believes that the County Council had   *j* asked the previous owners for permission to lay an electricity cable across the land. This was actually carried out by the Tennis Club. [The defendant] requested details of the works proposed by the Tennis Club.'

The defendant said in evidence that, while he did not remember this conversation, he

had no reason to believe that it had not taken place. He did not accept some of the things
*a* which Mr Harris recorded him as having said. The judge, however, thought it right to
treat the attendance note as representing a substantially accurate account of the
conversation and it has not been suggested that he was wrong to do so.

Correspondence between the defendant and the council followed that telephone
conversation. On 18 December 1975 the county secretary and solicitor wrote to the
defendant a letter saying:
*b*
'I understand from the County Valuer and Land Agent that you have been
exercising certain rights over the Council's land shown coloured pink on the attached
plan [the plot], and that you have laid this land to grass and planted trees thereon.
Would you please let me know how long you have been exercising this right, and
also let me have a copy of the document granting you permission to use the same.
*c* The County Valuer and Land Agent informs me that you were going to send him a
copy of the document granting you permission to use the land, but to date he has
not heard from you. I await hearing from you as soon as possible.'

Following a reminder the defendant, on 20 January 1976, wrote to the county secretary
and solicitor a letter acknowledging the letter of 18 December 1975 and saying:

*d* 'I enclose herewith a copy of the sale agreement between myself and Mr. G. Wall
dated 28th July 1971, upon which I have marked the relevant part which I believe
relates to the piece of land in question. I also enclose herewith, a copy of a signed
statement regarding the piece of land, which I obtained from the Vendor at the
time of the sale. You will notice from the Documents, that the previous owner laid
the land to grass in April 1967 and ever since then either the previous owner or
*e* myself have occupied the land and it has therefore, been kept as part of the garden
for the last eleven years. It was my understanding with Mr. Wall, that he had the
right to this ground and that he only lost this right, if and when the Little Chalfont
By-pass was built, so much so that as you can see I went to the trouble to get an extra
declaration document from him. I notice your enclosed plan is to do with an
Underground Cable and I believe that Mr. Wall was asked for and had given
*f* permission for this to be put under the land concerned. I do not know whether you
know the property itself, but the piece of land concerned forms an integral part of
the garden and the whole situation of the house itself, in fact, without it, the house
I think, would be unbearable to live in. I would reiterate, that it has always been my
firm understanding that the land should be kept by the owner of Dolphin Place, if
and until the proposed Little Chalfont By-pass was built. Since the owner of Dolphin
*g* Place has been the occupier of the land for the last eleven years, I have never had any
doubt as to the situation indeed many local functions, mainly Conservative Party
ones, which local Councillors have attended, have been held there. I have not
discussed this matter with my Solicitor as yet and I await your reply before doing
so.'

*h* After the defendant's signature, this letter appended the words 'Without prejudice'.

On 3 February 1976 the county secretary and solicitor wrote to the defendant
acknowledging his letter of 20 January, and continued as follows:

'The Council purchased [the plot] in 1955, for an estate in fee simple. At no time
since that date has the Council given any permission for the land to be used for any
*j* purposes whatsoever, except for the laying of an electricity cable by the Little
Chalfont Sports Club. The Council totally disclaims your purported right to use the
land, and admits that at no time have you been entitled to the use and occupation of
the land. I note you claim that the land has been kept as part of the garden of
Dolphin Place for the last eleven years, but the statutory declaration made by Mr.
and Mrs. Wall states that the land has only [been] used since 4th April, 1967. This

is, therefore, a period of nine years at the present time. No doubt you will be consulting your Solicitor in this matter, and I await hearing from you further as soon as possible.'

The defendant then consulted solicitors, who on 22 March wrote a letter to the council making a claim that he had acquired title to the plot by adverse possession, a claim which was debated in further correspondence during 1976.

However, the council allowed a further nine years or so to elapse before it took any steps with a view to excluding the defendant from the plot. At last, on 28 October 1985, it issued proceedings seeking an order for possession and ancillary injunctions.

During the course of the trial a question arose as to the admissibility in evidence of the letter of 20 January 1976. The judge held that it was inadmissible in evidence on the basis that it was written 'Without prejudice'. He gave his reasons in a short judgment on this point delivered in the course of the trial in which he said:

'In the recent case of *South Shropshire DC v Amos* [1987] 1 All ER 340, [1986] 1 WLR 1271 Parker LJ, giving the judgment of the Court of Appeal, said that the use of the words "without prejudice" prima facie meant that the letter was intended to be a part of negotiation. It would not, of course, be conclusive because it might be plain from the contents of the letter that it was not so intended and, in addition, the rule that "without prejudice" documents are inadmissible is qualified by, for example, the ruling in *Re Daintrey, ex p Holt* [1893] 2 QB 116, [1891–4] All ER Rep 209, that a document which might prejudicially affect the recipient cannot be excluded from evidence. The letter in question does not specifically propose any terms of settlement to the council but it is clear that [the defendant] recognised that the council might be making claims adverse to those which he was putting forward and therefore that there was a possibility of dispute. That is, of course, confirmed by his statement that he might have to go to his solicitor. The *South Shropshire* case also decided that a letter which purported to initiate some sort of negotiation ("an opening shot") is not necessarily excluded from the privilege. Negotiations have to begin somewhere. The question really is whether this letter contemplated any kind of negotiation at all. It did not, as I have said, put forward any offers or make any proposals of compromise. It merely stated what [the defendant], without yet having obtained legal advice, thought that his rights might be. I do not think that a letter of that kind can be characterised as incapable of being a negotiating document. Looking at the public policy expressed in the privilege, it would seem to me advantageous that parties should, under cover of the privilege, be able to offer to discuss the case, not necessarily putting forward any immediate compromise terms for settlement but with a view to seeing whether either side can persuade the other that he is right. I think that that was what [the defendant] was trying to do and I think it is clear from the last line of his letter that he was telling the council that, if as a result of this correspondence neither side could persuade the other, he would have to seek legal advice. In my view, the prima facie inference that the document was intended to be a negotiating document which is derived from the "without prejudice" label has not been displaced in this case and the document is therefore not admissible.'

In his judgment on the substantive issue the judge held in effect that the defendant had for more than 12 years before the institution of proceedings had sufficient physical control of the plot and sufficient animus possidendi to constitute possession in law and that such possession had been adverse within the meaning of the Limitation Act 1980. He accordingly held that the defence based on ss 15 and 17 of the 1980 Act succeeded.

With the leave of the judge, the council now appeals from his order made during the course of the trial whereby he held that the letter of 20 January 1976 written by the

defendant to the council was inadmissible in evidence. The council further appeals from
*a* his judgment on the substantive issue relating to the 1980 Act.

*The letter of 20 January 1976*
In *Re Daintrey, ex p Holt* [1893] 2 QB 116 at 119–120, [1891–4] All ER Rep 209 at 211
Vaughan Williams J, delivering the judgment of the court, stated the conditions for the
application of the 'without prejudice' rule as follows:

*b*
'In our opinion the rule which excludes documents marked "without prejudice"
has no application unless some person is in dispute or negotiation with another, and
terms are offered for the settlement of the dispute or negotiation, and it seems to us
that the judge must necessarily be entitled to look at the document in order to
determine whether the conditions, under which alone the rule applies, exist. The
rule is a rule adopted to enable disputants without prejudice to engage in discussion
*c* for the purpose of arriving at terms of peace, and unless there is a dispute or
negotiations and an offer the rule has no application.'

If this statement represented the outer limits of the 'without prejudice' rule, there
could be no question of its availing the defendant, since by his letter of 20 January 1976,
he was not offering terms for the settlement of any dispute or negotiation subsisting
*d* between him and the council. Later authorities, however, have expressed the principle
in rather wider terms. This court in *South Shropshire DC v Amos* [1987] 1 All ER 340,
[1986] 1 WLR 1271 held that privilege can attach to a document headed 'without
prejudice' even if it is merely an 'opening shot' in negotiations. As Parker LJ said ([1987]
1 All ER 340 at 344, [1986] 1 WLR 1271 at 1277–1278):

*e*
'It attaches to all documents which are marked "without prejudice" and form part
of negotiations, whether or not they are themselves offers, unless the privilege is
defeated on some other ground as was the case in *Re Daintrey, ex p Holt.*'

More recently, the House of Lords in *Rush & Tompkins Ltd v Greater London Council*
[1988] 3 All ER 737 at 740, [1988] 3 WLR 939 at 942 per Lord Griffiths has stated the
general principle that the rule applies 'to exclude all negotiations genuinely aimed at
*f* settlement whether oral or in writing from being given in evidence'.
I think the judge was right to regard the relevant question as being whether or not the
letter of 20 January 1976 could properly be regarded as a negotiating document. But I
respectfully disagree with his conclusion that it could. As the judge himself said, and as
the letter itself indicated, the defendant was writing the letter in an attempt to persuade
the council that his case was well founded. As I read the letter, it amounted not to an
*g* offer to negotiate, but to an assertion of the defendant's rights, coupled with an intimation
that he contemplated taking his solicitor's advice unless the council replied in terms
recognising his asserted rights. I cannot derive from the letter any indication, or at least
any clear indication, of any willingness whatever to negotiate.
If, as is my view, the letter of 20 January 1976 cannot fairly and properly be read as an
*h* 'opening shot' in negotiations, the attribution of the protection of 'without prejudice'
privilege to it would in my opinion go beyond the bounds of that privilege established
by existing authority and would not in my opinion be justifiable. The public policy on
which the privilege rests does not in my judgment justify giving protection to a letter
which does not unequivocally indicate the writer's willingness to negotiate. Though I
think this will make no difference to the result on the substantive issue, this head of
*j* appeal is in my judgment, accordingly, well founded.

*The substantive issue*
Section 15(1) of the 1980 Act provides:

'No action shall be brought by any person to recover any land after the expiration of twelve years from the date on which the right of action accrued to him or, if it first accrued to some person through whom he claims, to that person.'

Subject to certain irrelevant exceptions, s 17 of the 1980 Act provides for the extinction of a person's title to land after the expiration of the relevant time limit.

As is stated in s 15(6), Pt I of Sch 1 to the 1980 Act contains provisions for determining the date of accrual of rights of action to recover land in the cases there mentioned. Paragraph 1 of Sch 1 provides:

'Where the person bringing an action to recover land, or some person through whom he claims, has been in possession of the land, and has while entitled to the land been dispossessed or discontinued his possession, the right of action shall be treated as having accrued on the date of the dispossession or discontinuance.'

It is clear that, under the 1980 Act as under the previous law, the person claiming a possessory title must show either (1) discontinuance by the paper owner followed by possession or (2) dispossession (or, as it sometimes called, ouster) of the paper owner: cf *Treloar v Nute* [1977] 1 All ER 230 at 234, [1976] 1 WLR 1295 at 1300. As Fry J said in *Rains v Buxton* (1880) 14 Ch D 537 at 539–540:

'... the difference between dispossession and the discontinuance of possession might be expressed in this way—the one is where a person comes in and drives out the others from possession, the other case is where the person in possession goes out and is followed into possession by other persons.'

In the present case the judge found that the council had never discontinued its possession of the plot, and this finding is not challenged on this appeal. The defendant's claim is that the council had been dispossessed of the plot by him more than 12 years before it instituted its proceedings.

If the law is to attribute possession of land to a person who can establish no paper title to possession, he must be shown to have both factual possession and the requisite intention to possess (animus possidendi). A person claiming to have dispossessed another must similarly fulfil both these requirements. However, a further requirement which the alleged dispossessor claiming the benefit of the 1980 Act must satisfy is to show that his possession has been adverse within the meaning of the Act. Paragraph 8(1) of Sch 1 defines 'adverse possession' as follows:

'No right of action to recover land shall be treated as accruing unless the land is in the possession of some person in whose favour the period of limitation can run (referred to below in this paragraph as "adverse possession"); and where under the preceding provisions of this Schedule any such right of action is treated as accruing on a certain date and no person is in adverse possession on that date, the right of action shall not be treated as accruing unless and until adverse possession is taken of the land.'

Paragraph 8(2) of Sch 1 provides:

'Where a right of action to recover land has accrued and after its accrual, before the right is barred, the land ceases to be in adverse possession, the right of action shall no longer be treated as having accrued and no fresh right of action shall be treated as accruing unless and until the land is again taken into adverse possession.'

On this appeal counsel for the council has accepted that if the plot was in adverse possession of the defendant more than 12 years before action was brought (ie on 28 October 1973) it has not ceased to be in adverse possession since that time. Ultimately, therefore, the crucial question will be: was the defendant in adverse possession of the plot on 28 October 1973?

Possession is never 'adverse' within the meaning of the 1980 Act if it is enjoyed under

a lawful title. If, therefore, a person occupies or uses land by licence of the owner with
*a* the paper title and his licence has not been duly determined, he cannot be treated as
having been in 'adverse possession' as against the owner with the paper title.

Before the passing of the 1980 Act certain decisions of this court, in particular *Wallis's
Cayton Bay Holiday Camp Ltd v Shell-Mex and BP Ltd* [1974] 3 All ER 575, [1975] QB 94
and *Gray v Wykeham-Martin* [1977] CA Transcript 10A, were thought to have established
a general doctrine that in one special type of case there would be implied in favour of the
*b* would-be adverse possessor, *without any specific factual basis for such implication*, a licence
permitting him to commit the acts of possession on which he sought to rely; the effect
of implying such a licence would, of course, be to prevent the squatter's possession from
being 'adverse'. That special type of case was broadly one where the acts of an intruder,
however continuous and far-reaching, did not substantially interfere with any plans
which the owners might have for the future use of undeveloped land.
*c*      The doctrine of implied licence, in my view, raised substantial conceptual difficulties
as a matter of law for reasons which I stated in *Powell v McFarlane* (1977) 38 P & CR 452
at 484:

> 'I do not find it easy to see how the words "possession" or "dispossess" can properly
> be given anything but their ordinary meaning in the context of the [Limitation Act
*d*   > 1939] and I doubt whether this has been done in any decisions before the *Wallis*
> case. I am not sure how one can justify the imputation of an implied or hypothetical
> licence for the purpose of applying or defeating the provisions of that Act in
> circumstances where the facts would not admit the imputation of a licence for any
> other purposes.'

The doctrine has now been abrogated by para 8(4) of Sch 1 to the 1980 Act, which
*e* provides:

> 'For the purpose of determining whether a person occupying any land is in
> adverse possession of the land it shall not be assumed by implication of law that his
> occupation is by permission of the person entitled to the land merely by virtue of
> the fact that his occupation is not inconsistent with the latter's present or future
*f*   > enjoyment of the land. This provision shall not be taken as prejudicing a finding to
> the effect that a person's occupation of any land is by implied permission of the
> person entitled to the land in any case where such a finding is justified on the actual
> facts of the case.'

In the light of this provision, it would at first sight appear that there is now no reason
*g* why the words 'possess' and 'dispossess' or similar expressions should not be given their
ordinary legal meaning in the context of the 1980 Act. However, counsel for the council,
while accepting that the implied licence doctrine is now abrogated, nevertheless submits
that para 8(4) (I quote from his skeleton argument)—

> 'leaves intact the special rule formulated by Bramwell LJ in *Leigh v Jack* ((1879) 5
> Ex D 264) and Sir John Pennycuick in *Treloar v Nute* ([1977] 1 All ER 230, [1976]
*h*   > 1 WLR 1295) that where land is acquired or retained by the owner for a specific
> future purpose then acts of trespass which are not inconsistent with such purpose
> do not amount to dispossession.'

The origin of the suggested 'special rule' is said to be the often-cited statement of
Bramwell LJ in *Leigh v Jack* 5 Ex D 264 at 273:

*j*   > '... in order to defeat a title by dispossessing the former owner, acts must be done
> which are inconsistent with his enjoyment of the soil for the purposes for which he
> intended to use it: that is not the case here, where the intention of the plaintiff and
> her predecessors in title was not either to build upon or to cultivate the land, but to
> devote it at some future time to public purposes.'

Superficial support for the existence of the 'special rule' is to be found in a passage in the judgment of this court delivered by Sir John Pennycuick in *Treloar v Nute* [1977] 1    a All ER 230 at 235, [1976] 1 WLR 1295 at 1300–1301, where he said:

'The literal application of the statutory provisions has been adapted by this court to meet one special type of case. It sometimes happens that the owner of a piece of land retains it with a view to its utilisation for some specific purpose in the future and that meanwhile some other person has physical possession of it. When that state    b of affairs exists, the owner is not treated as dispossessed. See *Leigh v Jack* where factory materials were placed on a strip of land intended by the owner to be dedicated as a road . . .'

Sir John Pennycuick went on to refer to the judgment of Cockburn CJ in *Leigh v Jack* 5 Ex D 264 at 271 and cited the passage from Bramwell LJ's judgment cited above. He also referred very briefly to the decision of this court in *Williams Bros Direct Supply Stores Ltd*    c *v Raftery* [1957] 3 All ER 593, [1958] 1 QB 159.

All the observations of Sir John Pennycuick to which I have referred were obiter because they were made in the absence of any evidence of 'special purpose' on the part of the plaintiff (see [1977] 1 All ER 230 at 236, [1976] 1 WLR 1295 at 1302). The court below had found that the defendant's father took possession of the disputed land outside the limitation period, but that this possession was not adverse by reason that it caused no    d inconvenience to the plaintiff. The actual decision of this court was that, in the absence of any evidence of special purpose, the absence of inconvenience to the plaintiff was an irrelevant consideration, and that time began from the taking of possession by the father, whether or not the plaintiff suffered inconvenience from such possession.

The other members of this court in *Treloar v Nute* were Ormrod LJ, who had been one of the majority in the *Wallis* case [1974] 3 All ER 575, [1975] QB 94, in which Lord    e Denning MR had introduced the doctrine of implied licence, and Stamp LJ, who had dissented in that case. In giving judgment, the court referred to the considerable disadvantage which it had suffered from the absence of any legal argument on behalf of the defendant (see [1977] 1 All ER 230 at 236, [1977] 1 WLR 1295 at 1302). It was faced with a further difficulty that the ratio of the majority decision in *Wallis's* case, so far as    f that ratio extended, was binding on it, since the 1980 Act had not been passed. I respectfully agree with the actual decision in *Treloar v Nute*, but respectfully disagree with the obiter dicta to which I have referred.

On any footing, it must, in my judgment, be too broad a proposition to suggest that an owner who retains a piece of land with a view to its utilisation for a specific purpose in the future can never be treated as dispossessed, however firm and obvious the intention    g to dispossess, and however drastic the acts of dispossession of the person seeking to dispossess him may be. Furthermore, while it may well be correct to say that the implied licence doctrine (so long as it survived) itself involved the 'adaptation' of the literal application of the statutory provisions 'to meet one special type of case', I do not think it correct to suggest that the decisions in *Leigh v Jack* or *Williams Bros Direct Supply Stores Ltd v Raftery* (or indeed any other decisions prior to *Wallis's* case) authorise or justify an    h application of the statutory provisions otherwise than in accordance with their ordinary and natural meaning.

In the course of my judgment in *Powell v McFarlane* (1977) 38 P & CR 452 at 472–474 I considered in some detail the decisions in *Leigh v Jack* and the *Williams* case and *Tecbild Ltd v Chamberlain* (1969) 20 P & CR 633. I do not propose to embark on a similar analysis in this judgment, but would venture to repeat certain conclusions about these cases    j which I expressed (at 484–485):

'I incline to the view that the *ratio decidendi* of all the various judgments in cases such as *Leigh v. Jack*, the *Williams* case and *Tecbild Ltd. v. Chamberlain* was either (a) that the necessary *animus possidendi* had not been shown or (b) that the acts relied on

had been too trivial to amount to the taking of actual possession; some members of
*a* each court seem to have relied on the first ground and others on the second. I
venture to think that all these three decisions are readily explicable, not so much on
the basis of any imputed licence, but merely on the grounds that in circumstances
where an owner has no present use for his land but has future plans for its use (for
example by development or by dedication to the public as a highway), then the
court will, on the facts, readily treat a trespasser, whose acts have not been
*b* inconsistent with such future plans, as having not manifested the requisite *animus
possidendi* or alternatively, as not having acquired a sufficient degree of exclusive
occupation to constitute possession.'

On rereading the relevant authorities, the view to which I then inclined has become a
firm one. The statement of Bramwell LJ in *Leigh v Jack* (1879) 5 Ex D 264 at 273 on
*c* which so much reliance has been placed on this appeal was made in the context of a case
in which, it would appear, the defendant would have had knowledge of the intention of
the owner to dedicate it to the public as a highway. (It was marked as a street on a plan of
his estate, which he hung up in his estate office and this fact was presumably common
knowledge among those interested in the property.) If in any given case the land in
dispute is unbuilt land and the squatter is aware that the owner, while having no present
*d* use for it, has a purpose in mind for its use in the future, the court is likely to require
very clear evidence before it can be satisfied that the squatter who claims a possessory
title has not only established factual possession of the land, but also the requisite intention
to exclude the world at large, including the owner with the paper title, so far as is
reasonably practicable and so far as the processes of the law will allow. In the absence of
clear evidence of this nature, the court is likely to infer that the squatter neither had had
*e* nor had claimed any intention of asserting a right to the possession of the land.

I agree entirely with the following passage from the dissenting judgment of Stamp LJ
in *Wallis's Cayton Bay Holiday Camp Ltd v Shell-Mex and BP Ltd* [1974] 3 All ER 575 at 585,
[1975] QB 94 at 109–110:

'Reading the judgments in *Leigh v Jack* and *Williams Brothers Direct Supply Store
*f*    Ltd v Raftery*, I conclude that they establish that in order to determine whether the
acts of user do or do not amount to dispossession of the owner, the character of the
land, the nature of the acts done on it and the intention of the squatter fall to be
considered. Where the land is waste land and the true owner cannot and does not
for the time being use it for the purpose for which he acquired it, one may more
readily conclude that the acts done on the waste land do not amount to dispossession
*g*    of the owner. But I find it impossible to regard those cases as establishing that so
long as the true owner cannot use his land for the purpose for which he acquired it
the acts done by the squatter do not amount to possession of the land. One must
look at the facts and circumstances and determine whether what has been done in
relation to the land constitutes possesion.'

In the present case, the defendant was well aware that the council had acquired the
*h* plot in order to construct a road on it at some time in the future and meantime had no
present use for the land. This factor, which counsel for the council naturally stressed in
the course of his argument, should make the court the more cautious before holding that
the defendant had had both a factual possession and animus possidendi sufficient to
confer on him a possessory title. Nevertheless, every *Leigh v Jack* type of case such as this
*j* must involve questions of fact and degree. I would, for my part, reject the submission
that since the 1980 Act there remains any 'special rule' which requires the words
'possessed' and 'dispossessed' or similar words to be given anything other than their
natural and ordinary meaning in the *Leigh v Jack* type of case.

Thus far, therefore, I conclude that (1) if by 28 October 1973 the defendant had taken
possession of the plot, his possession must have been adverse to the council, and (2) the

question whether or not the defendant had taken possession of the plot by 28 October
1973 falls to be decided by reference to conventional concepts of possession and     *a*
dispossession and not by departing from the ordinary and natural meaning of the relevant
statutory provisions merely because this is a *Leigh v Jack* type of case.

I turn then to consider the first of the two requisite elements of possession. First, as at
28 October 1973 did the defendant have factual possession of the plot? I venture to repeat
what I said in *Powell v McFarlane* (1977) 38 P & CR 452 at 470–471:

> 'Factual possession signifies an appropriate degree of physical control. It must be     *b*
> a single and [exclusive] possession . . . Thus an owner of land and a person intruding
> on that land without his consent cannot both be in possession of the land at the same
> time. The question what acts constitute a sufficient degree of exclusive physical
> control must depend on the circumstances, in particular the nature of the land and
> the manner in which land of that nature is commonly used or enjoyed.'     *c*

On evidence it would appear clear that by 28 October 1973 the defendant had acquired
complete and exclusive physical control of the plot. He had secured a complete enclosure
of the plot and its annexation to Dolphin Place. Any intruder could have gained access to
the plot only by way of Dolphin Place, unless he was prepared to climb the locked gate
fronting the highway or to scramble through one or other of the hedges bordering the
plot. The defendant had put a new lock and chain on the gate and had fastened it. He     *d*
and his mother had been dealing with the plot as any occupying owners might have been
expected to deal with it. They had incorporated it into the garden of Dolphin Place. They
had planted bulbs and daffodils in the grass. They had maintained it as part of that garden
and had trimmed the hedges. I cannot accept counsel's submission for the council that
the defendant's acts of possession were trivial. It is hard to see what more he could have
done to acquire complete physical control of the plot by October 1973. In my judgment,     *e*
he had plainly acquired factual possession of the plot by that time.

However, as the judge said, the more difficult question is whether the defendant had
the necessary animus possidendi. As to this, counsel for the council accepted the
correctness of the following statement (so far as it went) which I made in *Powell v
McFarlane* (at 471–472):     *f*

> '. . . the *animus possidendi* involves the intention, in one's own name and on one's
> own behalf, to exclude the world at large, including the owner with the paper title
> if he be not himself the possessor, so far as is reasonably practicable and so far as the
> processes of the law will allow.'

At least at first sight the following observations of Lord Halsbury in *Marshall v Taylor*
[1895] 1 Ch 641 at 645 (which were referred to by Hoffmann J in his judgment) are very     *g*
pertinent to the present case:

> 'The true nature of this particular strip of land is that it is inclosed. It cannot be
> denied that the person who now says he owns it could not get to it in any ordinary
> way. I do not deny that he could have crept through the hedge, or, if it had been a
> brick wall, that he could have climbed over the wall; but that was not the ordinary     *h*
> and usual mode of access. That is the exclusion—the dispossession—which seems to
> me to be so important in this case.'

As a number of authorities indicate, inclosure by itself prima facie indicates the
requisite animus possidendi. As Cockburn CJ said in *Seddon v Smith* (1877) 36 LT 168 at
169: 'Enclosure is the strongest possible evidence of adverse possession . . .' Russell LJ in     *j*
*George Wimpey & Co Ltd v Sohn* [1966] 1 All ER 232 at 240, [1967] Ch 487 at 511 similarly
observed: 'Ordinarily, of course, enclosure is the most cogent evidence of adverse
possession and of dispossession of the true owner.' While counsel for the council pointed
out that the plot was always accessible from the north where no boundary demarcation

existed, it was only accessible from the defendant's own property, Dolphin Place. In my
*a* judgment, therefore, he must be treated as having inclosed it.

Counsel for the council, however, submitted that, even if inclosure had occurred, the
defendant's intention must be assessed in the light of the particular circumstances of this
case. The defendant knew that the council had acquired and retained the plot with the
specific intention of building a road across it at some future time. The council had no use
for the land in the interim. It was for all practical purposes waste land. None of the
*b* defendant's acts, he submitted, were inconsistent with the council's known future
intentions. He invoked, inter alia, the words of Cockburn CJ in *Leigh v Jack* (1879) 5 Ex D
264 at 271, which, he submitted, applied in the present case:

> 'I do not think that any of the defendant's acts were done with the view of
> defeating the purpose of the parties to the conveyances; his acts were those of a man
> who did not intend to be a trespasser, or to infringe upon another's right. The
*c* > defendant simply used the land until the time should come for carrying out the
> object originally contemplated.'

If the defendant had stopped short of placing a new lock and chain on the gate, I might
perhaps have felt able to accept these submissions. Counsel for the council submitted
that this act did not unequivocally show an intention to exclude the council as well as
*d* other people. It is well established that it is no use for an alleged adverse possessor to rely
on acts which are merely equivocal as regards the intention to exclude the true owner:
see for example *Tecbild Ltd v Chamberlain* (1969) 20 P & CR 633 at 642 per Sachs LJ. In
my judgment, however, the placing of the new lock and chain and gate did amount to a
final unequivocal demonstration of the defendant's intention to possess the land. I agree
with the judge in his saying:
*e*
> '. . . I do not think that if the council, on making an inspection, had found the
> gate newly padlocked, they could have come to any conclusion other than that [the
> defendant] was intending to exclude everyone, including themselves, from the
> land.'

*f* The other main point which counsel for the council has argued in support of this
appeal has caused me slightly more difficulty. In his submission there can be no sufficient
animus possidendi to constitute adverse possession for the purpose of the 1980 Act unless
there exists the intention to exclude the owner with the paper title in *all* future
circumstances. The defendant's oral statements to Mr Harris in the conversation of
10 November 1975, as recorded in the attendance note, do appear to have constituted an
implicit acknowledgment by the defendant that he would be obliged to leave the plot if
*g* in the future the council required it for the purpose of constructing the proposed new
road. The letter of 18 December 1975, which I have concluded should be admitted in
evidence, contains an express acknowledgment of this nature. If the intention to exclude
the owner with the paper title in *all* future circumstances is a necessary constituent of the
animus possidendi, the attendance notice and the letter of 18 December 1975 show that
*h* this constituent was absent in the present case.

There are some dicta in the authorities which might be read as suggesting that an
intention to *own* the land is required. Lindley MR, for example, in *Littledale v Liverpool
College* [1900] 1 Ch 19 at 23, referred to the 'acts of ownership' relied on by the plaintiffs.
Russell LJ in *George Wimpey & Co Ltd v Sohn* [1966] 1 All ER 232 at 240, [1967] Ch 487 at
510 said:

*j*
> '. . . I am not satisfied that the actions of the *predecessors* in bricking up the
> doorway and maintaining a lock on the gate to the roadway were necessarily
> referable to an intention to occupy the [land] as their own absolute property.'
> (Russell LJ's emphasis.)

At one point in my judgment in *Powell v McFarlane* (1977) 38 P & CR 452 at 478 I
suggested that:                                                                                    *a*

'... any objective informed observer might probably have inferred that the
plaintiff was using the land simply for the benefit of his family's cow or cows,
during such periods as the absent owner took no steps to stop him, without any
intention to appropriate the land as his own.'

Nevertheless, I agree with the judge that 'What is required for this purpose is not an  *b*
intention to own or even an intention to acquire ownership but an intention to possess',
that is to say an intention *for the time being* to possess the land to the exclusion of all other
persons, including the owner with the paper title. No authorities cited to us establish the
contrary proposition. The conversation with Mr Harris, as recorded in the attendance
note and the letter of 18 December 1975, to my mind demonstrate the intention of the
defendant for the time being to continue in possession of the plot to the exclusion of the  *c*
council unless and until the proposed bypass is built. The form of the conveyance to the
defendant and of the contemporaneous statutory declaration which he obtained from Mr
and Mrs Wall are, of course, entirely consistent with the existence of an intention on his
part to take and keep adverse possession of the plot, at least unless and until that event
occurred.

In the light of the line of authorities to which we have been referred, beginning with  *d*
*Leigh v Jack*, I have already accepted that the court should be slow to make a finding of
adverse possession in a case such as the present. However, as the judge pointed out, in
none of those earlier cases, where the owner with the paper title successfully defended
his title, was there present the significant feature of complete inclosure of the land in
question by the trespasser. On the evidence in the present case he was, in my judgment,
right in concluding that the defendant had acquired adverse possession of the plot by  *e*
28 October 1973 and had remained in adverse possession of it ever since. There is no
evidence that any representative of the council has even set foot on the plot since that
date.

This appeal, which has been well argued on both sides, should in my judgment be
dismissed.                                                                                         *f*

**NOURSE LJ.** I agree. I add some views of my own on the substantive issue.

Under most systems of law a squatter who has been in long possession of land can
acquire title to it in the place of the true owner. The Scots and continental systems, more
faithful to the Roman law, have opted for prescription, a doctrine founded on the fiction
that the land has been granted to the squatter. In England, prescription, although a shoot
well favoured by the common law, was stunted in its lateral growth by the statutes of  *g*
limitation, being confined in its maturity to the acquisition of easements and profits à
prendre over another's land. Limitation, so far from being founded on some fictional
grant, extinguishes the right of the true owner to recover the land, so that the squatter's
possession becomes impregnable, giving him a title superior to all others.

The essential difference between prescription and limitation is that in the former case  *h*
title can be acquired only by possession as of right. That is the antithesis of what is
required for limitation, which perhaps can be described as possession as of wrong. It can
readily be understood that with prescription the intention of the true owner may be of
decisive importance, it being impossible to presume a grant by someone whose intention
is shown to have been against it. But with limitation it is the intention of the squatter
which is decisive. He must intend to possess the land to the exclusion of all the world,  *j*
including the true owner, while the intention of the latter is, with one exception, entirely
beside the point.

In order that title to land may be acquired by limitation, (1) the true owner must
either (a) have been dispossessed or (b) have discontinued his possession, of the land and
(2) the squatter must have been in adverse possession of it for the statutory period before

action brought. Adopting the distinction between dispossession and discontinuance
*a* which was suggested by Fry J in *Rains v Buxton* (1880) 14 Ch D 537 at 539, I take the first
case to be one where the squatter comes in and drives out the true owner from possession
and the second to be one where the true owner goes out of possession and is followed in
by the squatter. In the light of that distinction, a very fine one, it is sometimes said that
the intention of the true owner may be material in this way. If he intends to use the land
for a particular purpose at some future date, a discontinuance of possession can be
*b* prevented by the slightest acts of ownership on his part, even by none at all. That no
doubt is perfectly correct, but nothing follows from it except that the case becomes one
where the true owner must be dispossessed before his title can be lost. He can only be
dispossessed if the squatter performs sufficient acts and has a sufficient intention to
constitute adverse possession. Those acts and that intention are no different from those
which are required in a case of discontinuance, there being no practical distinction
*c* between what is necessary to exclude all the world in a case where the true owner has
retained possession and in one where he has discontinued it.

By this route I have come to a belief that the intention of the true owner, although it
may have some influence in theory, is irrelevant in practice. To that I would make one
exception. If an intention on the part of the true owner to use the land for a particular
purpose at some future date is known to the squatter, then his knowledge may affect the
*d* quality of his own intention, reducing it below that which is required to constitute
adverse possession. To say that is only to emphasise that it is adverse possession on which
everything depends. I think it very doubtful whether the distinction between
dispossession and a discontinuance of possession can ever have decisive consequences, a
consideration which is perhaps confirmed by the confusion between them which is
found in some of the decided cases.
*e* For over a hundred years the leading case on adverse possession in English law has
been the decision of this court in *Leigh v Jack* (1879) 5 Ex D 264 at 273, where Bramwell
LJ said:

> 'I do not think that there was any dispossession of the plaintiff by the acts of the
> defendant: acts of user are not enough to take the soil out of the plaintiff and her
*f* > predecessors in title and to vest it in the defendant; in order to defeat a title by
> dispossessing the former owner, acts must be done which are inconsistent with his
> enjoyment of the soil for the purposes for which he intended to use it: that is not
> the case here, where the intention of the plaintiff and her predecessors in title was
> not either to build upon or to cultivate the land, but to devote it at some future time
> to public purposes.'

*g* These observations suppose that the intention of the true owner may, in the circumstances
stated, defeat what would, without the intention, constitute adverse possession. They
would, for example, allow a true owner to recover land, even against a squatter who had
inclosed it for a garden with the intention of excluding all the world, by claiming that
that use was not inconsistent with the future residential development which he had
*h* always intended.

For the reasons already expressed, I cannot accept Bramwell LJ's observations to have
been a correct statement of the law. Moreover, the decision in *Leigh v Jack* can be
satisfactorily explained on the grounds that there was no inclosure of the land by the
defendant, that his acts of possession were trivial and, more significantly, that his
knowledge of the plaintiff's intention prevented him from having a sufficient intention
*j* himself. Thus Cockburn CJ said (at 271):

> 'I do not think that any of the defendant's acts were done with the view of
> defeating the purpose of the parties to the conveyances; his acts were those of a man
> who did not intend to be a trespasser, nor to infringe upon another's right. The
> defendant simply used the land until the time should come for carrying out the

object originally contemplated. If a man does not use his land, either by himself or by some person claiming through him, he does not necessarily discontinue *a* possession of it.'

Cotton LJ was of the opinion that there had been no dispossession of the plaintiff or her predecessors by the acts of the defendant (at 274). He went on to hold that there had also been no discontinuance of possession. Although in that he based himself in part on the fact that the land was not capable of use for the purpose intended by the plaintiff, I *b* do not read his judgment, any more than that of Cockburn CJ, as subscribing to the view of Bramwell LJ that the intention of the true owner can withstand what would otherwise be sufficient acts of possession and a sufficient intention on the part of the squatter. To that extent, and while the judgments are not at all clear, I think that the views of Bramwell LJ were obiter.

In *Williams Bros Direct Supply Stores Ltd v Raftery* [1957] 3 All ER 593 at 597, [1958] 1 *c* QB 159 at 169 Hodson LJ rejected a submission by counsel that in *Leigh v Jack*—

'BRAMWELL, L.J., was striking out on his own unsupported by the other members of the court, when he spoke of acts having to be done inconsistent with the enjoyment of the soil for the purposes for which the plaintiff intended to use it.'

*d*

For myself, I respectfully think that the submission was correct. However, it is not clear how far Hodson LJ or the other members of the court (Morris and Sellers LJJ) relied on Bramwell LJ's dictum for the purpose of making a decision in that case. Again, it can be satisfactorily explained on the grounds that there was no inclosure of the land, that the defendant's acts of possession were trivial and that he did not have a sufficient animus possidendi. *e*

The decision in *Williams Bros Direct Supply Stores Ltd v Raftery* was given at a time when many plots of waste land had been brought under the spade in digging for victory during the second world war and afterwards. The problem was a very familiar one and this court's indorsement of Bramwell LJ's dictum gave county court judges all round the country a simple and straightforward basis for rejecting unmeritorious claims to *f* squatters' titles, even, we may be sure, where the land had been inclosed. By 1976 the dictum had assumed the dignity of a special rule, although it was recognised by this court that it carried with it an adaptation of the literal application of the statutory provisions in order to meet a special type of case: see *Treloar v Nute* [1977] 1 All ER 230 at 235, [1976] 1 WLR 1295 at 1300. Before that, it had been effectively rejected in the dissenting judgment of Stamp LJ in *Wallis's Cayton Bay Holiday Camp Ltd v Shell-Mex and* *g* *BP Ltd* [1974] 3 All ER 575 at 585, [1975] QB 94 at 109–110, a case in which Lord Denning MR propounded an original heresy of his own, the implied licence theory. That has now been put to rest by para 8(4) of Sch 1 to the Limitation Act 1980, a provision which did not have any wider effect. The argument of counsel for the council has shown us that the dictum of Bramwell LJ rides on.

The whole of this troubled subject was carefully considered by Slade J in *Powell v* *h* *MacFarlane* (1977) 38 P & CR 452. In my opinion that judgment accurately stated the law in all material respects and I speak from my own experience in saying that it has consistently been treated as having done so. There can be no doubt that the view of the difficult cases from *Leigh v Jack* onwards to which the judge inclined is correct (at 484–485). Those authorities can be satisfactorily explained on conventional grounds without reliance on the dictum of Bramwell LJ. We should now say that it must no longer be *j* followed, so that the decision of these cases can be returned to the paths of orthodoxy, without, I am confident, any increase in the success rate amongst unmeritorious claims.

For these reasons I am of the opinion that Hoffmann J was right to approach this case, albeit that it is in the classical *Leigh v Jack* mould, by looking no further than the principles stated in *Powell v McFarlane*. He correctly applied those principles to the facts which he

found. I would affirm his decision accordingly. On this part of the case I do not wish to
add anything to the judgment of Slade LJ, with which I am in complete agreement.
I too would dismiss this appeal.

**BUTLER-SLOSS LJ.** I agree with both judgments.

*Appeal dismissed. Leave to appeal to the House of Lords refused.*

Solicitors: *Sharpe Pritchard*, agents for *C R Hetherington*, Aylesbury (for the council);
*Memery Crystal* (for the defendant).

Celia Fox    Barrister.

# Rubin v Director of Public Prosecutions

QUEEN'S BENCH DIVISION
WATKINS LJ AND POTTER J
10 OCTOBER, 13 DECEMBER 1988

*Magistrates – Jurisdiction – Trial of information – Validity of information – Laying of information
– Identity of informant – Information stated to have been preferred by named police force –
Identity of informant not stated in information – Whether information invalid.*

The appellant was charged with exceeding the speed limit on a motorway. The
information preferred against him was stated to have been preferred by a named police
force. At the hearing of the charge the appellant contended that the information was bad
because the identity of the informant was not stated in the information. The magistrates
convicted the appellant. He appealed by way of case stated.

**Held** – Although when the police brought a prosecution it had to be commenced by an
information laid by a member of the relevant police force, ie the officer reporting the
offence and the person accused of committing it or the chief constable or some other
member of the force authorised by him to lay an information, the failure to name the
police officer laying the information did not invalidate it. Since it was clear that a police
officer had laid the information against the appellant and since that officer's identity was
easily ascertainable the appellant had not been misled and could not challenge the officer's
authority to prosecute. The appeal would therefore be dismissed (see p 247 *b d e g* to *j* and
p 248 *a b*, post).

**Notes**
For who may lay an information, see 29 Halsbury's Laws (4th edn) para 317, and for cases
on the subject, see 33 Digest (Reissue) 122, 810–812.

**Cases referred to in judgments**
*Garfield v Maddocks* [1973] 2 All ER 303, [1974] QB 7, [1973] 2 WLR 888, DC.
*Hawkins v Bepey* [1980] 1 All ER 797, [1980] 1 WLR 419, DC.
*Hill v Anderton* [1982] 2 All ER 963, [1983] 1 AC 328, [1982] 3 WLR 331, HL.
*R v Gateshead Justices, ex p Tesco Stores Ltd, R v Birmingham Justices, ex p D W Parkin
Construction Ltd* [1981] 1 All ER 1027, [1981] QB 470, [1981] 2 WLR 419, DC.

**Case also cited**
*R v Brentford Justices, ex p Catlin* [1975] 2 All ER 201, [1975] QB 455, DC.

**Case stated**

Howard Jeffrey Rubin appealed by way of a case stated by the justices for the county of a
Berkshire acting in and for the petty sessional division of Maidenhead in respect of their
adjudication as a magistrates' court sitting at Maidenhead on 15 September 1987 whereby
they convicted the appellant on an information preferred by the Thames Valley Police of
contravening reg 3 of the Motorways Traffic (Speed Limit) Regulations 1974, SI 1974/
502, by driving a motor vehicle at a speed exceeding 70 mph on a motorway, contrary to
s 17(4) of the Road Traffic Regulation Act 1984. The respondent to the appeal was the b
Director of Public Prosecutions. The facts are set out in the judgment of Watkins LJ.

*R Alun Jones* for the appellant.
*Rhodri Price Lewis* for the respondent.

*Cur adv vult* c

13 December. The following judgments were delivered.

**WATKINS LJ.** This is an appeal by case stated from a decision of the justices for the
county of Berkshire acting in and for the petty sessional division of Maidenhead when
sitting as a magistrates' court at Maidenhead on 15 September 1987.                    d
    They had before them an information stated to be preferred by the 'Thames Valley
Police' against the appellant which alleged that on 7 November 1986 at Bray and
Burnham he contravened reg 3 of the Motorways Traffic (Speed Limit) Regulations 1974,
SI 1974/502, by driving a motor vehicle at a speed exceeding 70 mph on the M4
motorway contrary to s 17(4) of the Road Traffic Regulations Act 1984.
    At the hearing the appellant, who is a solicitor, argued a preliminary point. The e
decision of the justices as to that went against him. Thereupon he pleaded guilty and was
fined £90, his licence was endorsed and he was disqualified from holding or obtaining a
licence for 30 days.
    The preliminary point taken concerned the identity of the informant as named in the
information.
    As to that point the justices say they found that the police force for the Thames Valley f
area is a statutory body created under the provisions of s 21(2) of the Police Act 1964 and
the Thames Valley Police (Amalgamation) Order 1968, SI 1968/496. That order created
three bodies, namely the Thames Valley Police Authority, the Thames Valley Police
Fund and the Thames Valley Constabulary, of which the Thames Valley Constabulary is
the only body relevant to the proceedings. A constabulary is an organised body of
constables or police.                                                                 g
    The appellant, who was not represented, submitted that (1) there was no such body as
the Thames Valley Police and that therefore the information had not been validly laid,
(2) if he was wrong about that then the informant was not sufficiently identified because
he should be a named person so that he could be easily identified by the accused, (3) as
the informant was not sufficiently identified he, the appellant, suffered a substantial h
injustice because he did not know which of the three bodies created under the order was
laying the information and it was therefore impossible for him to ascertain whether or
not that particular body had the necessary authority to lay an information, (4) the duties
of a constable are individual to the constable and cannot be exercised by the constabulary
at large, (5) the Thames Valley Constabulary therefore did not have authority to lay an
information which could and should be exercised by an individual constable.           j
    For the respondent it was contended that (1) the police force for the Thames Valley
area had long been known as the Thames Valley Police, which title was referred to in the
order, but if the official title should be the Thames Valley Constabulary, the words
'police' and 'constabulary' are interchangeable, (2) it was unnecessary for the informant
to be a named individual person and if the appellant required the name of the actual

a informant, that was easily obtainable and in any case, if the informant was named, it would be the chief inspector of the relevant prosecutions department and not the officer involved in the case, (3) it could not be said that the appellant had suffered any injustice by the so-called failure to have the actual informant identified on the information because an inquiry of the Thames Valley Police would have revealed it, (4) the information could properly have been laid in the name of the chief constable and, if it had been, that would not have assisted the appellant without inquiry to know the name of the officer who had

b reported him for speeding.

The justices were referred to a number of cases, including *R v Gateshead Justices, ex p Tesco Stores Ltd, R v Birmingham Justices, ex p D W Parkin Construction Ltd* [1981] 1 All ER 1027, [1981] QB 470.

They were of the opinion that (1) an information may validly be laid in the name of the Thames Valley Constabulary, which is the title given to the police force in the order,

c (2) the words 'police' and 'constabulary' have the same meaning and are interchangeable, and thus an information laid in the name of the Thames Valley Police is valid, (3) while the person who had actually laid the information was not named, he could have been identified from the information given, (4) the appellant had not suffered a substantial injustice.

d They ask us the following questions:

'(1) Whether in the laying of an information before the Magistrate the informant must either (a) be an individual using his true name; or (b) if a statutory or other corporate body use the name by which it was enacted or incorporated? (2) Can an information be laid by a group of police officers under the name "Constabulary" or must an information, if being laid by a police officer, be laid by the individual police

e officer?'

It needs to be said at the outset, I think, that this is an appeal without any merit whatsoever. The contention that the appellant suffered any kind of injustice by the information being laid in the name of the Thames Valley Police is in my view unmeritorious and unworthy of serious consideration. I agree with the justices that,

f while the actual police officer who caught the appellant speeding was not named in the information, a simple inquiry would have led to his identification.

I also agree with them that the words 'police' and 'constabulary' have for present purposes the same meaning and are interchangeable. Thus the use of the word 'police' instead of 'constabulary' as appears in the information as a description of the police force created by the order could not possibly be said to have been misleading or in any way have served for that reason to affect the validity of the information.

g The single issue in this appeal to which we have to address ourselves in my view is whether an information has inevitably to be laid by a named person such as, in the case of a police prosecution, the chief constable himself or any other authorised member of his force, including, of course, the officer who reports the alleged commission of an offence. Counsel for the appellant agrees that the information would have been correctly

h laid if the informant had been named as the chief constable or a named inspector, for example, authorised for such a purpose.

There is no statutory definition of an information, the laying of which is the beginning of the prosecution process, as was clearly stated in *Hill v Anderton* [1982] 2 All ER 963 at 973–974, [1983] 1 AC 328 at 345–346 by Lord Roskill, with whom all other of their Lordships agreed. He said:

j

'My Lords, if your Lordships agree with me that an information is laid when it is received at the office of the magistrates' court and is the first step to be taken towards the initiation of a prosecution irrespective of whether it is after receipt the basis of an application for a summons, it follows that in the case of the present appeals each of the informations in question was timeously laid ... In the result I would dismiss all these appeals. I would answer the certified question by saying that "an information is laid for the purpose of s 127 of the Magistrates' Courts Act 1980 when it is received at the office of the clerk to the justices for the relevant area". I would add that it is not necessary for the information to be personally received by a justice of the peace or by the clerk to the justices. It is enough that it is received by any member of the staff of the clerk to the justices, expressly or impliedly authorised to receive it, for onward transmission to a justice of the peace or to the clerk to the justices. The same applies to the making of a complaint.'

Counsel for the appellant began his submissions by contending that in this case the information is bad and the summons issued thereupon void in consequence. The use of the words 'Thames Valley Police' in the information and summons leaves it unclear, he said, whether the informant or prosecutor purports to be (a) the body of constables known as the Thames Valley Constabulary, (b) the Thames Valley Police Authority, (c) the Thames Valley Police Fund, (d) an unknown constable who is a member of the Thames Valley Constabulary or (e) a civilian clerk or computer operator employed by one of the bodies mentioned.

The justices, he asserted, found that the informant was the Thames Valley Constabulary, which he maintained is no more than a collection of individuals and does not have legal capacity to lay an information. On the other hand, the prosecution had contended, he said, that the informant was (d) but, he submitted, it is contrary to authority and convention that a prosecution can be started anonymously. A suspect is entitled to know who his accuser is either by name or by description, for he may wish to address an immediate inquiry to him.

In my view, to suggest that anyone might think from reading the information that the informant was any one of (b), (c) or (e) is fanciful. It cannot be denied, of course, that a suspect is entitled to know who his accuser is. However, there could have been no room for doubt in anyone's mind in this case that the actual informant was a police officer and a member of the Thames Valley Police, from which force his identity could easily be ascertained.

It is, I believe, well established that an information may be oral or in writing (when a warrant to arrest is required, it should be in writing and on oath). There are no prescribed forms for an information, which should, as I have already indicated, identify the informant and also the defendant and give particulars of the offence and any relevant statute or regulation. The laying of an information is an administrative act by whoever prosecutes but the issue of a summons, which is the immediately following process, is a judicial act which can only be performed by a justice or a clerk to the justices.

Counsel for the appellant contends that as well as a defendant so does a justice or a clerk to justices require to know the identity of an informant and that neither should be expected to make inquiries as to the identity of the actual informant. This should be obvious on the face of the information.

It is, I also believe, equally well established that, generally speaking, any member of the public may lay an information. There are statutory exceptions to that right and in some instances consent to prosecute has to be obtained from a specified authority. But in the vast majority of cases it is a member of the public who informs and with rare exceptions that member of the public is a constable.

Obviously a constable is no ordinary member of the public. A member of a police force, though he be of the rank of sergeant or above, including chief constable, is nevertheless a constable: see 36 Halsbury's Laws (4th edn) para 201, where it is stated:

'The common law constable. The history of the police is the history of the office of constable and, notwithstanding that present day police forces are the creation of statute and that the police have numerous statutory powers and duties, in essence a police force is neither more nor less than a number of individual constables, whose status derives from the common law, organised together in the interests of efficiency . . .'

The jurisdiction and function of a constable is just as clearly stated (para 319):

a    'Jurisdiction. The jurisdiction of a member of a police force is not limited to his
     police area; he has all the powers and privileges of a constable throughout England
     and Wales . . .'

It is also stated (para 320):

b    'General functions of constables. The primary function of the constable remains, as
     in the seventeenth century, the preservation of the Queen's peace. From this general
     function stems a number of particular duties additional to those conferred by statute
     and including those mentioned hereafter. The first duty of a constable is always to
     prevent the commission of a crime. If a constable reasonably apprehends that the
     action of any person may result in a breach of the peace it is his duty to prevent that
c    action. It is his general duty to protect life and property. The general function of
     controlling traffic on the roads is derived from this duty . . .'

Furthermore, it cannot I think be doubted that it is the duty of every chief officer of
police (the chief constable) to enforce the law of the land. It is for him to decide, subject
to certain exceptions, whether or not there should be a criminal prosecution following
apprehension of a suspected offender in the circumstances of any particular case or in
d accordance with a policy adopted or devised or formulated by him.
   So the constable's duty is to strive to keep the peace, to enforce the law and to prosecute
suspected offenders. It needs hardly to be said that the chief constable delegates much of
his power to decide whether there shall be a prosecution to other constables in his force
of lower rank. But the power so delegated remains his power. Hence, there can be no
denying his right to lay an information no matter who is the actual informant from
e within his force, likewise the right of any of his officers to perform that act who have the
requisite delegated power from him. Such a person may be of any rank from constable
upwards.
   Since the introduction of the Crown Prosecution Service, by s 3 of the Prosecution of
Offences Act 1985 the duty of a chief constable to continue or not a prosecution begun
f by information has passed to the Director of Public Prosecutions, but otherwise his duty
to prosecute is unaffected and the power to decide whether to lay an information is not
affected at all by the 1985 Act.
   Rule 4(1) of the Magistrates Courts' Rules 1981, SI 1981/552, provides:

     'An information may be laid or complaint made by the prosecutor or complainant
     in person or by his counsel or solicitor or other person authorised in that behalf.'

g    A like provision is to be found as long ago as 1848 in s 1 of the Summary Jurisdiction
Act 1848. This provision, it is submitted, makes it crystal clear that an information can
only be laid by a person, whether on his own behalf or on behalf of another person.
Wherever one looks, it is said, in the Magistrates' Courts Act 1980 at any relevant matter,
the appropriate reference is to a person and nowhere is there to be found in the Act an
h indication that a body, an unincorporated one especially, such as the Thames Valley
Police, may begin the prosecution process by laying an information. While it has to be
acknowledged that an information if written need not take any prescribed form, the
essential contents of it must be apparent with clarity, it is contended, on the face of it, the
name of the informant especially, for, in addition to other reasons, a justice or the clerk
to the justices required to issue a summons needs to know whether the informant has
j the authority to prosecute: see R v Gateshead Justices, ex p Tesco Stores Ltd [1981] 1 All ER
1027 at 1030, [1981] QB 470 at 474.
   It does not assist the respondent, it is argued, to endeavour to rely as he does on s 5 of
and Sch 1 to the Interpretation Act 1978. Section 5 provides:

     'In any Act, unless the contrary intention appears, words and expressions listed in
     Schedule 1 to this Act are to be construed according to that Schedule.'

Schedule 1 provides:

> '. . . "Person" includes a body of persons corporate or unincorporate . . .'          *a*

It cannot, counsel for the appellant submits, have been the intention of the Magistrates' Courts Act 1980 that any person referred to in r 4(1) of the rules made under that Act can be taken to refer, inter alia, to an unincorporated body.

Moreover, he says the respondent is not assisted by the terms of s 123 of the 1980 Act, which provides:          *b*

> '*Defect in process.*—(1) No objection shall be allowed to any information or complaint, or to any summons or warrant to procure the presence of the defendant, for any defect in it in substance or in form, or for any variance between it and the evidence adduced on behalf of the prosecutor or complainant at the hearing of the information or complaint.
>
> (2) If it appears to a magistrates' court that any variance between a summons or          *c* warrant and the evidence adduced on behalf of the prosecutor or complainant is such that the defendant has been misled by the variance, the court shall, on the application of the defendant, adjourn the hearing.'

The name of the informant, he argues, affects neither the form nor the substance of an information. None of the cases decided under this section suggests anything to the          *d* contrary.

He places reliance also on the appearance of the words 'any other person' in s 3(2)(*a*) of the Prosecution of Offences Act 1985 as follows:

> 'It shall be the duty of the Director—(*a*) to take over the conduct of all criminal proceedings, other than specified proceedings, instituted on behalf of a police force          *e* (whether by a member of that force or by any other person) . . .'

This is another plain indication, it is maintained, especially as those words are allied to 'a member of that force', that the layer of an information, unless a statute otherwise provides, must be a person and in no circumstances a body, corporate or unincorporate.

A like indication, it is urged, appears in s 145 of the Customs and Excise Management          *f* Act 1979, which provides:

> '*Institution of proceedings.*—(1) Subject to the following provisions of this section, no proceedings for an offence under the customs and excise Acts or for condemnation under Schedule 3 to this Act shall be instituted exempt by order of the Commissioners.
>
> (2) Subject to the following provisions of this section, any proceedings under the          *g* customs and excise Acts instituted in a magistrates' court, and any such proceedings instituted in a court of summary jurisdiction in Northern Ireland, shall be commenced in the name of an officer . . .
>
> (4) In the case of the death, removal, discharge or absence of the officer in whose name any proceedings were commenced under subsection (2) above, those          *h* proceedings may be continued by any officer authorised in that behalf by the Commissioners.
>
> (5) Nothing in the foregoing provisions of this section shall prevent the institution of proceedings for an offence under the customs and excise Acts by order and in the name of a law officer of the Crown in any case in which he thinks it proper that proceedings should be so instituted.          *j*
>
> (6) Notwithstanding anything in the foregoing provisions of this section, where any person has been detained for any offence for which he is liable to be detained under the customs and excise Acts, any court before which he is brought may proceed to deal with the case although the proceedings have not been instituted by order of the Commissioners or have not been commenced in the name of an officer.'

a   I should interpolate here that I have already adverted to the absence of a prescribed
form for an information, but I should in this context refer to Form 1 in Sch 2 to the
Magistrates' Courts (Forms) Rules 1981, SI 1981/553, which is stated in r 2 to be a form
or something to the like effect which an information may take. However, the form in
Sch 2 does nothing to assist on the issue here.

The view I formed about the main issue is that the arguments of counsel for the
appellant persuade me that when the police bring a prosecution it has to be commenced
b   by an information which has been laid by a member of the force, that is to say by that
member who reported the offence and the person accused of committing it or by the
chief constable himself or some other member of the force authorised by him to lay an
information.

I cannot accept that Parliament intended the definition of 'person' in Sch 1 to the 1978
Act to apply to the laying of informations. The terms of r 4(1) militate strongly against
c   any other view in my opinion. In any event, I do not see from where a chief constable
could derive the power to, so to speak, delegate his authority to commence a prosecution
by laying an information to an inanimate body, corporate or unincorporate.

I take the additional view that the terms of s 123 of the 1980 Act did not prevent the
appellant from objecting to the information. The wrong description of the person
entitled to prosecute was not, I think, a defect either in form or in substance. For the
d   kind of matter which is involved in that, see the judgment of Lord Widgery CJ in *Garfield
v Maddocks* [1973] 2 All ER 303 at 306, [1974] QB 7 at 12.

But, having said that, what I cannot accept is that the failure of the chief constable or
one of his officers to ensure that a person laid the information in his own name (whether
on behalf of another officer or not is immaterial) and which allowed the prosecutor to be
called the Thames Valley Police necessarily created an invalid information, i e one that
e   could not lawfully be proceeded on.

Although it was not cited to us, we have borne in mind *Hawkins v Bepey* [1980] 1 All
ER 797, [1980] 1 WLR 419, where the prosecutor was held either to have been the chief
constable or the Kent police force but assumed to be the former. However, the case is of
little direct assistance because the reference to the Kent police force was made without
f   the benefit of the argument we have heard in the present case and was, in any event,
unnecessary for the purposes of the decision in that case, which was not concerned with
the precise question of who has the authority to lay an information. I, in fact, gave a
judgment in that case.

Unquestionably, an accused is entitled to know the identity of who it is who accuses
him of an offence and that person must have authority to lay an information. Within the
Thames Valley Constabulary, two persons at least had that authority: the chief constable
g   and the person who caught the appellant speeding. Unfortunately because of some
maladministration, due possibly to the use of computers for laying informations, the
essential requirement surely well known to the chief constable that the information
should reveal the identity of the informant was not conformed to on the material
occasion. The identity of the actual informant was masked by the title used for him,
h   namely the Thames Valley Police.

But no one could have been in doubt that it was a police officer who had in fact laid
the information. This is not a case in which any challenge could have been mounted to
his authority to prosecute; no such thing is suggested. The actual identity of that person
could, if needs be, easily have been revealed.

Where, in my judgment, the erroneous title is given in an information, as here, to a
j   person who has a right to prosecute and no one is misled as to the status of that person,
such an error does not have the effect of rendering an information invalid. The
paramount considerations are the authority to prosecute and the right to know the
prosecutor. As to the former, there can in the present case be no doubt. As to the latter,
it was clear that a police officer was prosecuting. All that was lacking was his easily
ascertainable name.

I would dismiss this appeal but in so doing advise that, no matter what sophisticated aids are used for laying informations, care should be taken to ensure that modern *a* technology be not allowed to cause departure from what should be, and I feel sure is, customary police practice, which is to lay informations by a named person.

**POTTER J.** I agree.

*Appeal dismissed.*        *b*

Solicitors: *Sheridans* (for the appellant); *Crown Prosecution Service,* Reading.

Raina Levy    Barrister.

*c*

# Re a company's application

CHANCERY DIVISION
SCOTT J
7 FEBRUARY 1989        *d*

*Employment – Duty of employee – Confidential information – Confidential information acquired by employee in course of employment – Disclosure to regulatory authorities and Inland Revenue – Disclosure alleged to be motivated by malice on part of employee – Whether abuse of confidential information – Whether employer entitled to injunction restraining employee from disclosing confidential information to regulatory authorities and Inland Revenue.*        *e*

The defendant was employed as its compliance officer by the plaintiff, a financial services company which was subject to regulation by the Financial Intermediaries, Managers and Brokers Regulatory Association (FIMBRA). In October 1988 the defendant was dismissed with one month's notice. His compensation for unfair dismissal and the amount were a *f* matter of dispute between the defendant and the plaintiff, and in the course of a telephone conversation between the defendant and the plaintiff's chief executive the defendant said that he thought that £10,000 was the right amount and also referred to various breaches of the FIMBRA regulations and tax irregularities which had in his view been committed by the plaintiff. The plaintiff's chief executive took the view that the defendant's statements amounted to blackmail and that any disclosure to FIMBRA or the Inland Revenue would be based on confidential documents belonging to the plaintiff and *g* held by the defendant. The plaintiff accordingly obtained an Anton Piller order to retrieve its documents from the defendant and an ex parte injunction restraining the defendant from disclosing any confidential documents belonging to the plaintiff. On the inter partes hearing of the plaintiff's application for a continuation of the injunction,

*h*

**Held** – The court would not grant an injunction preventing an employee of a financial services company from disclosing confidential information about the company to a regulatory authority such as FIMBRA or to the Inland Revenue, notwithstanding that the disclosure might be motivated by malice on the part of the employee, because the employee's undoubted duty of confidence did not prevent him disclosing to regulatory authority or the Inland Revenue matters which it was the province of those authorities *j* to investigate, and because it would be contrary to the public interest if employees of such companies were inhibited in reporting possible breaches of the regulatory system or fiscal irregularities. The plaintiff's application for an injunction would therefore be granted subject to the qualification that it would not apply to communications to FIMBRA or the Inland Revenue (see p 251 *h j* and p 252 *a b j* to p 253 *c*, post).

Dictum of Lord Keith in *A-G v Guardian Newspapers Ltd (No 2)* [1988] 3 All ER 545 at
*a* 644 distinguished.

**Notes**
For an employee's duty not to disclose confidential information after the termination of
his employment, see 16 Halsbury's Laws (4th edn) para 549 and for cases on the subject,
see 20 Digest (Reissue) 284–288, *2618–2633.*
*b*

**Case referred to in judgment**
*A-G v Guardian Newspapers Ltd (No 2)* [1988] 3 All ER 545, [1988] 3 WLR 776, Ch D, CA
and HL.

**Motion**
*c* The plaintiff, a financial services company the identity of which the judge ordered should
not be revealed, applied by motion seeking, inter alia, an injunction restraining the
defendant, a former employee, from making use of any confidential information or
confidential documents in his possession which were the property of the plaintiff. The
facts are set out in the judgment.

*d* *Graham Shipley* for the plaintiff.
*Mark Warby* for the defendant.

**SCOTT J.** I make an order under s 4 of the Contempt of Court Act 1981 so that the
identity of the plaintiff company and of the defendant should not be revealed.
      The plaintiff is a company that carries on business in the supply of financial advice and
*e* financial management of clients' investment portfolios. As it carries on business of that
character, it is subject to the regulatory scheme imposed by the Financial Intermediaries,
Managers and Brokers Regulatory Association (FIMBRA), pursuant to the provisions of
the Financial Services Act 1986.
      The defendant was, until fairly recently, an employee of the plaintiff in a fairly senior
*f* position. He was, among other things, the compliance officer within the plaintiff whose
duty it was to supervise the procedures and practices of the plaintiff so as to secure
compliance with the regulatory requirements imposed from time to time by FIMBRA.
      I have been told, and it seems sensible, that FIMBRA is entitled at its discretion from
time to time to make spot checks on companies subject to its regulatory umbrella for the
purpose of ensuring compliance with its regulations. It follows therefore that the details
of the businesses carried on by these companies may at any time become known to
*g* FIMBRA and those acting on behalf of FIMBRA. Of course it would be expected, and it
may for all I know be expressly so provided, that any details which come to the attention
of FIMBRA in the discharge of its regulatory role would be kept confidential by FIMBRA.
      In October 1988 the plaintiff gave the defendant a month's notice, effective from
1 November 1988. However, it was agreed, in circumstances which are not entirely
*h* without dispute, that the defendant would not sever entirely his connection with the
plaintiff but would act as a self-employed consultant in connection with the business of
the plaintiff. He would, I suppose it was envisaged, continue to introduce clients to the
plaintiff and would receive some form of remuneration for his services.
      For a time, following the cesser of his employment with the plaintiff, the defendant
acted in that self-employed capacity. In the course of so acting, it was natural that he
*j* would have in his possession documents containing confidential information about the
plaintiff, its clients and its business and which were the property of the plaintiff.
      On Monday, 12 December 1988 a telephone conversation took place between the
defendant and a gentleman who is either the chief executive or one of the chief executives
of the plaintiff. The content of that telephone conversation and the detail of what passed
between the two men is in dispute. It is alleged on behalf of the plaintiff that the

defendant sought to extract from the plaintiff the sum of £10,000 under threat that if he
were not paid that sum he would report the plaintiff to FIMBRA for breaches of the  *a*
FIMBRA regulations and to the Inland Revenue for misfeasances on the part of some of
the directors of the plaintiff and some of its clients in respect of their obligations under
the Taxes Acts. In short, blackmail is alleged.

The defendant denies that there was any blackmailing attempt at all. He contends that
he indicated his intention to seek compensation for unfair dismissal, and indicated that
he thought £10,000 was the right amount for him to receive.                    *b*

He then, he says, went on to raise with the gentleman with whom he was speaking,
the senior executive of the plaintiff, various misfeasances in connection with the plaintiff's
carrying on of business which represented, in his view, breaches of the FIMBRA
regulations and improprieties in regard to tax.

So while there is some agreement as to the matters referred to in the course of this
telephone conversation, the parties are miles apart as to the tenor and the implications of  *c*
what was said.

The plaintiff concluded that in order to make the disclosures to FIMBRA and to the
tax authorities that had been threatened, the defendant would be making use of
confidential information and confidential documents. An ex parte application was
therefore made for injunctions to restrain any disclosure based on confidential
information or confidential documents and for an Anton Piller order entitling the  *d*
plaintiff by its solicitors and representatives to attend the defendant's home and remove
all the plaintiff's documents there found as well as documents which those searching
might reasonably believe to be the plaintiff's documents.

An order to that effect was made by Knox J on 14 December 1988. The hearing before
me is the inter partes hearing of the plaintiff's application for a continuance of the ex
parte interlocutory relief granted by Knox J. There is also before me an application by  *e*
the defendant to have the ex parte order set aside on the ground that it was obtained by
inadequate disclosure and misrepresentation, and for an inquiry as to the damage caused
to the defendant by that order. It is agreed that the defendant's application shall stand
over until trial. It is not possible, it is realistically accepted by counsel for the defendant,
for the defendant to establish at this interlocutory stage that the order made by Knox J  *f*
was improperly obtained.

I omitted to say, but it is perhaps implicit in what I have said, that the Anton Piller
order was executed shortly after it was granted. A volume of documents was removed
from the defendant's house by those executing the search. They included some
documents which it is now accepted were not the plaintiff's documents but were the
defendant's documents. Those have been returned. A number of the documents removed  *g*
from the defendant's premises are documents as to which there is no question but that
they are the plaintiff's documents. Any question as to the impropriety of the defendant
having them in his possession must await trial, and one of the matters before me today is
an application by the plaintiff under RSC Ord 14 for final judgment in respect of those
documents. As I understand it, agreement has been reached between counsel for the
plaintiff and counsel for the defendant as to what order I should make on that application.  *h*

The final matter outstanding before me with which I must deal in this judgment
concerns the questions as to what if any negative injunction should, pending trial or
further order, be made against the defendant for the purpose of restraining him from
making any use of confidential documents or of confidential information. The motion is
argued before me at a stage when, commendably, a statement of claim and a defence
thereto have already been served. The defendant has therefore specified in his defence  *j*
what use he proposes to make of such confidential information or copies of confidential
documents as he may have in his possession.

He denies, of course, that he made any attempt at blackmail in the course of the
telephone conversation to which I have referred, but he accepts that he did indicate on

that occasion his intention to communicate information to FIMBRA and to the Inland
*a* Revenue, and in his defence he repeats and to some extent amplifies that intention.

I am therefore, on this interlocutory application, faced with the need to consider the
extent to which it would be right to grant an interlocutory application to restrain the
defendant from making communications to FIMBRA, the regulatory authority, of
alleged breaches by the plaintiff of FIMBRA regulations, or communications to the
Inland Revenue of alleged improprieties in respect of tax concerning some of the
*b* plaintiff's directors and clients.

Counsel for the plaintiff has suggested that I ought to grant a full injunction against
the defendant restraining any use of confidential documents or confidential information
pending trial, subject only to an undertaking by the plaintiff itself to place before
FIMBRA and the Inland Revenue respectively such documents as it may have relating to
the specific matters identified by the defendant in his affidavits or defence as being, in
*c* his view, matters which merit investigation.

I do not think, however, that that is the right approach. I must ask myself what cause
of action the plaintiff is pursuing in seeking this interlocutory relief. The case has been
based by counsel for the plaintiff on the duty of confidentiality that undoubtedly was
owed by the defendant to the plaintiff in the course of and arising out of his employment.
It is easy to agree that details about the plaintiff's clients' personal affairs should be
*d* regarded as confidential information and should be so treated by all the plaintiff's
employees.

If this were a case in which there were any question or threat of general disclosure by
the defendant of confidential information concerning the way in which the plaintiff
carries on its business or concerning any details of the affairs of any of its clients, there
could be no answer to the claim for an injunction; but it is not general disclosure that the
*e* defendant has in mind. He has in mind only disclosure to FIMBRA, the regulatory
authority, and, in relation to a particular case that he has identified in his affidavit, the
Inland Revenue. I ask myself whether an employee of a company carrying on the
business of giving financial advice and of financial management to members of the
public under the regulatory umbrella provided by FIMBRA owes a duty of confidentiality
*f* that extends to barring disclosure of information to FIMBRA.

It is part of the plaintiff's case, although not essential to its confidential information
cause of action, that the defendant in communicating with FIMBRA will be motivated
by malice. The defendant's professed intention is, in the plaintiff's view, associated with
the blackmail attempt made by the defendant. At the present stage, and until cross-
examination, I must accept that that may be true. It is not necessarily true. The
*g* defendant's explanation may be a genuine one. But the plaintiff's case may be true. It
may be the case that the information proposed to be given, the allegations proposed to be
made by the defendant to FIMBRA, and for that matter by the defendant to the Inland
Revenue, are allegations made out of malice and based on fiction or invention.

But, if that is so, then I ask myself what harm will be done. FIMBRA may decide that
the allegations are not worth investigating. In that case, no harm will have been done.
*h* Or FIMBRA may decide that an investigation is necessary. In that case, if the allegations
turn out to be baseless, nothing will follow the investigation. And, if harm is caused by
the investigation itself, it is harm which is implicit in the regulatory role of FIMBRA. It
may be that what is put before FIMBRA includes some confidential information. But
that information would, as it seems to me, be information which FIMBRA could at any
time obtain by the spot checks that it is entitled to carry out. I doubt whether an
*j* employee of a financial services company such as the plaintiff owes a duty of confidence
which extends to an obligation not to disclose information to the regulatory authority
FIMBRA.

So far as the Inland Revenue is concerned, the point is a narrower one. The Inland
Revenue is not concerned in any general way with the business of a financial services

company. It is concerned with tax. It is concerned with assets, with capital and income.
If confidential details which did not relate to fiscal matters were disclosed to the Inland   *a*
Revenue, that would, in my opinion, be as much a breach of the duty of confidentiality
as the disclosure of that information to any other third party. But, if what is disclosed to
the Inland Revenue relates to fiscal matters that are the concern of the Inland Revenue, I
find it difficult to accept that the disclosure would be in breach of a duty of confidentiality.

Counsel for the plaintiff submitted that it was for me now, on this interlocutory
application, to conduct some sort of preliminary investigation into the substance of the   *b*
allegations proposed to be made by the defendants to FIMBRA and to the Inland Revenue
respectively, for the purpose of deciding whether there was any case warranting
investigation either by FIMBRA or by the Inland Revenue. I am unable to accept that
that is a proper function for me to discharge.

Counsel for the plaintiff supported his submission by referring me to a part of the
speech made by Lord Keith in the *Spycatcher* case, *A-G v Guardian Newspapers Ltd (No 2)*   *c*
[1988] 3 All ER 545 at 644, [1988] 3 WLR 776 at 787:

> 'As to just cause or excuse, it is not sufficient to set up the defence merely to show
> that allegations of wrongdoing have been made. There must be at least a prima facie
> case that the allegations have substance.'

But that remark was in the context of a disclosure threatened to be made to the world   *d*
at large, a disclosure which would have taken place in the national press. Where the
disclosure which is threatened is no more than disclosure to a recipient which has a duty
to investigate matters within its remit, it is not, in my view, for the court to investigate
the substance of the proposed disclosure unless there is ground for supposing that the
disclosure goes outside the remit of the intended recipient of the information.

In the present case, in my opinion, it is for FIMBRA, on receiving whatever information   *e*
the defendant puts before it, to decide whether there is a matter for investigation. If
there is not, then I cannot see that any harm has been done to the plaintiff. If there is,
then it is right for FIMBRA rather than the court to investigate. Similarly, it is not for
the court but for the Inland Revenue, if information is placed before them by the
defendant, to decide whether there is material that warrants investigation or explanation.   *f*

Counsel for the plaintiff suggested that if the allegations were insubstantial and based
on moonshine harm would flow in that management of the plaintiff would have to
spend time in dealing with the investigations. That, of course, presupposes that at least
the allegations would have sufficient substance to prompt some investigation. He
suggested also, and this I thought had more substance, that public knowledge that
investigations were being conducted by FIMBRA or the Inland Revenue would damage   *g*
its credibility and injure it in its business prospects.

It was not suggested that public knowledge of an investigation would come about
through any lack of discretion on the part of FIMBRA or the Inland Revenue. It is,
however, feared that the defendant (be it remembered that the plaintiff regards him as
maliciously motivated) might spread around the story of the investigations that he had
prompted. I thought, when this point was raised by counsel for the plaintiff, that it   *h*
might well be right to impose an injunction on the defendant restraining him, in the
event that he does provide information to FIMBRA or to the Inland Revenue, from
communicating to anyone other than to his legal advisers the fact that he has done so. I
was anticipated, however, by counsel for the defendant, who offered an undertaking on
the part of the defendant that he would not disclose publicly the fact that he had placed
information before FIMBRA or the Inland Revenue or that in consequence thereof any   *j*
investigation was continuing.

I think it would be contrary to the public interest for employees of financial services
companies who thought that they ought to place before FIMBRA information of possible
breaches of the regulatory system, or information about possible fiscal irregularities
before the Inland Revenue, to be inhibited from so doing by the consequence that they

might become involved in legal proceedings in which the court would conduct an
*a* investigation with them as defendants into the substance of the information they were
minded to communicate.

If it turns out that the defendant's allegations are groundless and that he is motivated
by malice then, as it seems to me, he will be at serious risk of being found liable in
damages for defamation or malicious falsehood. But that is for the future. The plaintiff's
application before me for an injunction is based on the proposition that the disclosure by
*b* the defendant of the information will be in breach of his duty of confidence. In my
judgment, however, the defendant's undoubted duty of confidence does not extend so as
to bar the disclosures to FIMBRA and the Inland Revenue of matters that it is the province
of those authorities to investigate.

Accordingly, I propose to grant an injunction in the form sought in para 1 of the
plaintiff's notice of motion but to qualify the injunction so as not to apply to
*c* communications made by the defendant either to FIMBRA or to the Inland Revenue in
respect of the matters identified in his defence. I propose also to accept the undertaking
offered by the defendant not to reveal to anyone other than to his legal advisers the fact
that he has made these communications to FIMBRA or to the Inland Revenue. These
orders will be until trial or further order in the mean time. I would expect that it would
be possible for counsel to draw up a suitable injunction to give effect to what I have
*d* decided.

*Order accordingly.*

Solicitors: *Booth & Co*, Leeds (for the plaintiff); *Hammond Suddards*, Leeds (for the
defendant).

Jacqueline Metcalfe     Barrister.

# R v Inner London North District Coroner, ex parte Linnane

QUEEN'S BENCH DIVISION
TAYLOR LJ AND HENRY J
19, 20 JANUARY 1989

*Coroner – Inquest – Jury – Circumstances in which coroner should sit with jury – Death occurring while deceased in police custody – Police custody – Deceased serving sentence of imprisonment at police station – Deceased suffering inflammation of heart and admitted to hospital – Deceased dying in hospital – Whether deceased dying in police custody – Coroners Act 1988, s 8(3)(b).*

*Coroner – Inquest – Jury – Circumstances in which coroner should sit with jury – Circumstances the continuance or possible recurrence of which would be prejudicial to the health or safety of the public – Deceased serving sentence of imprisonment at police station – Deceased suffering inflammation of heart and admitted to hospital – Deceased dying in hospital – Whether deceased dying in circumstances which would be prejudicial to health or safety of public if they continued or recurred – Coroners Act 1988, s 8(3)(d).*

The deceased was an epileptic and alcoholic who was convicted of theft and sentenced to a term of imprisonment. Because of overcrowding in the prisons he was taken to a police station to serve his sentence. Two days after being sentenced he was visited by the applicant, his son, who suggested to the police that his father was ill and ought to be taken to hospital. Four hours later he was found to be unconscious and was taken to hospital, where he died the next day. Pathologists' reports indicated that he had died of inflammation of the heart caused by a virus, possibly aggravated by alcohol withdrawal symptoms. The coroner opened an inquest but decided not to empanel a jury. The applicant sought judicial review of his decision not to empanel a jury. Under s 8(3)(b) and (d)ᵃ of the Coroners Act 1988 the coroner was required to summon a jury if there was reason to suspect that the death 'occurred while the deceased was in police custody' or 'occurred in circumstances the continuance or possible recurrence of which is prejudicial to the health or safety of the public'. In reaching his decision the coroner formed the view that since the deceased had died in hospital without being under the physical control of the police he had not died in police custody for the purposes of s 8(3)(b) and since his death had not been caused by circumstances prejudicial to public health or safety his death had not occurred in circumstances prejudicial to public health or safety for the purposes of s 8(3)(d).

**Held** – The application would be granted and mandamus issued directing the coroner to summon a jury, for the following reasons—
(1) For the purposes of s 8(3)(b) of the 1988 Act the deceased had died in the legal custody of the police even though he was not at the time being held by a specific officer, and the coroner if he had properly directed himself ought to have had reason to suspect that the deceased was in police custody (see p 258 g to j and p 261 b, post).
(2) For the purposes of s 8(3)(d) of the 1988 Act it was not necessary for there to be a causative link between the death of the deceased and the circumstances in which his death occurred. Instead, a coroner was required to summon a jury if the deceased had died when there were circumstances present the continuance or possible recurrence of which were prejudicial to public health or safety even though they may not have caused his death (see p 260 h j and p 261 a b, post).

---

a   Section 8(3), so far as material, is set out at p 256 f to h, post

**Notes**

a For the circumstances in which a coroner must summon a jury when holding an inquest, see 9 Halsbury's Laws (4th edn) 1082.

As from 10 July 1988 s 8 of the Coroners Act 1988 replaced s 3A(1) to (7) of the Coroners Act 1887 (as inserted by the Coroners' Juries Act 1983, s 1). For s 3A of the 1887 Act, see 11 Halsbury's Statutes (4th edn) 356.

b **Case referred to in judgments**

R v Hammersmith Coroner, ex p Peach [1980] 2 All ER 7, [1980] QB 211, [1980] 2 WLR 496, CA.

**Cases also cited**

Nicoll v Catron (1985) 81 Cr App R 339, DC.
c R v Moss (1986) 82 Cr App R 116, CA.
R v Walthamstow Coroner, ex p Rubenstein [1982] Crim LR 509, DC.
R v West Yorkshire Coroner, ex p National Union of Mineworkers (Yorkshire Area) (1985) Times, 22 October, DC.

**Application for judicial review**

d Gregory John Linnane, the son of Anthony Linnane deceased, applied with the leave of Henry J given on 8 December 1988 for judicial review of the decision of Douglas Robert Chambers, the coroner for the district of Inner London North, to hold an inquest without a jury into the death of the deceased at St Pancras Coroner's Court on 12 December 1988. The relief sought was (i) an order of prohibition to prohibit the coroner from holding the inquest without a jury, (ii) a stay of the inquest pending the determination of the
e application for judicial review and (iii) an order of mandamus requiring the coroner to summon a jury for the inquest. The facts are set out in the judgment of Taylor LJ.

R Alun Jones for the applicant.
Charles Flint for the coroner.

f **TAYLOR LJ.** This is an application for judicial review of a decision of the coroner for Inner London North, sitting at St Pancras, to hold an inquest without a jury. The application is made by Mr Gregory Linnane, the son of the deceased, Anthony Linnane.

The deceased was only 41 years of age at the time of his death, which was on 19 October 1988. He was an epileptic and an alcoholic. Unfortunately his alcoholism led him into crime. On 7 October 1988 he was sentenced at Camberwell Green Magistrates' Court to
g ten weeks' imprisonment for theft. According to an affidavit from the solicitor who represented him at that hearing he looked unwell at that time. Due to overcrowding in the prisons, the deceased was taken to Albany Street police station and began to serve his sentence there. He arrived at about 6.30 pm.

At 8.15 pm the deceased was seen by a Dr O'Halloran at the police station. The doctor
h examined him and his report queries whether the deceased may have had an epileptic fit. On the next day, 8 October, the deceased was seen by a Dr Barnett, who visited him at the police station. Dr Barnett reported that the deceased was behaving very strangely. There was a question on the pro forma the doctor had to fill in which gave the opportunity for him to say whether the deceased was fit to be detained or not. That part of the form was not answered.

j At some time on 8 October the deceased soiled his clothes with both urine and faeces and those clothes were removed. One of the police officers, whose statement was before the coroner, expressed the view that he attributed that behaviour to the deceased's unstable intelligence.

At 6.30 pm on 8 October the deceased was visited by the applicant, aged 18. The applicant found his father to be in a poor state. He had a paper towel wrapped around his waist. It was saturated, presumably with urine. He had no other covering on him at all. He was shaking and his lips were blue. The applicant suggested to the police that he *a* ought to be removed to hospital.

At 9.10 pm the divisional police surgeon was recalled to see the deceased, but it does not appear from the papers before us that he arrived. A note was made that, having regard to the deceased's condition, he ought to be visited regularly. At 10.40 pm when he was visited in his cell he was found to be unconscious, face down on the stone floor, not breathing and cyanosed. An ambulance was called. It did not arrive. Eventually, *b* some 25 minutes later at 11.05 pm a police van was brought, the deceased was carried, wrapped in a blanket, to the van and was transported to University College Hospital, where he arrived at 11.10 pm. He was put into intensive care although the indications were that, if he had recovered, he would have been severely brain damaged. He died at 8.20 pm on 9 October. Therefore, he was sentenced by the court on 7 October and was dead by the evening of 9 October.     *c*

There were two pathologist's reports which agree as to the principal cause of death. One pathologist simply said that it was due to acute myocarditis. That is an inflammation of the heart muscles which was probably due, in the pathologist's opinion, to a viral infection. The other pathologist agreed with that, but added that in his view, the condition was aggravated by withdrawal symptoms in an alcoholic. Neither doctor expressly made any reference to, or still less criticism of, the way in which the deceased *d* had been cared for and handled.

It is necessary next to look at the statutory provisions relating to the holding of an inquest. They are to be found in s 8 of the Coroners Act 1988, which, so far as material, provides:

'(1) Where a coroner is informed that the body of a person ("the deceased") is *e* lying within his district and there is reasonable cause to suspect that the deceased— (a) has died a violent or an unnatural death; (b) has died a sudden death of which the cause is unknown; or (c) has died in prison or in such a place or in such circumstances as to require an inquest under any other Act, then, whether the cause of death arose within his district or not, the coroner shall as soon as practicable hold an inquest into the death of the deceased either with or, subject to subsection (3) below, without *f* a jury . . .

(3) If it appears to a coroner, either before he proceeds to hold an inquest or in the course of an inquest begun without a jury, that there is reason to suspect—(a) that the death occurred in prison or in such a place or in such circumstances as to require an inquest under any other Act; (b) that the death occurred while the deceased was in police custody, or resulted from an injury caused by a police officer *g* in the purported execution of his duty; (c) that the death was caused by an accident, poisoning or disease notice of which is required to be given . . . or (d) that the death occurred in circumstances the continuance or possible recurrence of which is prejudicial to the health or safety of the public or any section of the public, he shall proceed to summon a jury in the manner required by subsection (2) above . . .'

In this case the coroner opened an inquest on the deceased under the provisions of *h* s 8(1)(b), that is to say because there was reasonable cause to suspect that he had died a sudden death of which the cause was unknown. The coroner came to the view that he was not bound by any of the matters set out in s 8(3) to empanel a jury and, although sub-s (4) gives him discretion to summon a jury, he decided not to do so.

Before proceeding to the submissions which have been made by counsel for the *j* applicant as to two grounds under s 8(3) on which he submits that the coroner was bound to call a jury, there are two preliminary matters which are common ground and which can be mentioned straight away. The first is this. The phrase 'If it appears to the coroner', which governs the whole of s 8(3), leaves the decision of whether to summon a jury

under that subsection solely to the coroner. His decision can only be overturned if he has
*a* misdirected himself in some material respect.

Second, the phrase which is the preamble to the specific provisions of sub-s (3), 'there
is reason to suspect', does not require positive proof or even formulated evidence. The
question is usually to be decided at a preliminary stage, although, as indicated in the
subsection, it may arise for decision during the inquest. Therefore, any information
giving 'reason to suspect' will suffice.

*b*    I turn now to the two arguments which have been addressed by counsel for the
applicant. He submits that the coroner is bound to call a jury in this case under sub-s
(3)(*b*) and (*d*). Paragraph (*b*) relates to a death occurring while the deceased was in police
custody. Counsel for the applicant submits that this deceased was in police custody at the
time of his death. He was a prisoner who had been sentenced to a term of imprisonment.
He had begun to serve it. Due to the unusual circumstances in the prisons he was serving
*c* it in a police cell. He was therefore in police custody. He clearly remained, and there is
no dispute about this, in police custody until he arrived at the hospital. Counsel for the
applicant submits that he remained in police custody until his death. He says that, merely
because the deceased was taken to hospital by the police owing to his condition, the police
did not, by leaving him there, abandon their legal custody of him. He submits by way of
analogy that s 13 of the Prison Act 1952 is relevant. Section 13 provides:
*d*
'(1) Every prisoner shall be deemed to be in the legal custody of the governor of
the prison.
(2) A prisoner shall be deemed to be in legal custody while he is confined in, or is
being taken to or from, any prison and while he is working, or is for any other
reason, outside the prison in the custody or under the control of an officer of the
*e* prison and while he is being taken to any place to which he is required or authorised
by or under this Act or the Criminal Justice Act 1982 to be taken, or is kept in
custody in pursuance of any such requirement or authorisation.'

Under s 13, which relates to prison and not to police custody, a prisoner who is taken
to a funeral, for example, from the prison is deemed to be in the legal custody of the
governor of the prison. By analogy, so would a prisoner taken to hospital, submits
*f* counsel for the applicant, and by a further analogy so would this deceased remain in
custody when taken by the police from their physical custody to the hospital for
treatment.

Counsel for the applicant also referred to the Imprisonment (Temporary Provisions)
Act 1980, which is the statute enacted to deal with the sort of situation which existed in
this case, namely where a prisoner could not be accommodated in a prison and had to be
*g* accommodated elsewhere. Section 6 of that statute, under the heading 'Detention in the
custody of a constable', provides as follows:

'(1) This section applies to any person in the custody of a constable whose duty it
is to take him to a prison . . . and shall be deemed always to have applied to persons
in the custody of a constable in those circumstances.
*h*        (2) It is hereby declared that where it is for any reason not practicable to secure
the admission of a person to whom this section applies to the prison . . . in which
his detention is so authorised, he may lawfully be detained in the custody of a
constable until such time as he can be admitted there or is required to appear before
a court.'

*j* Section 6 would seem, where someone cannot be admitted to prison, to put him into the
custody of a constable until such time as he can be admitted to prison or is required to
attend before the court.

Although it has no statutory force, counsel for the applicant referred the court to a
Home Office circular 109/1982, dated 20 December 1982, which deals with the practical

considerations. Guidance is given therein to those dealing with prisoners in custody. The
relevant passage reads as follows:

    *a*

> 'Guidance was given in Home Office circulars 35/1969 and 23/1981 as to the
> Secretary of State's view that it was desirable for an inquest to be held, with a jury,
> in all cases of deaths occurring in any form of legal custody, even though the death
> may have occurred in hospital or elsewhere and even though it may have been due
> to natural causes.'

    *b*

The submission on behalf of the coroner is that the question of whether someone is in
police custody or not is a question of fact and that such custody must amount to physical
control. There is no room for what counsel referred to as 'notional custody'. Accordingly,
in this case, since there was no information to suggest that the police had remained at the
hospital in close proximity to the deceased, there was not physical police custody.

The coroner approached the matter in this way, as appears from his affidavit. In para 6   *c*
he said:

> 'It did not appear to me that there was reason to suspect that the death occurred
> while the deceased was in police custody. The death indisputably occurred in
> University College Hospital. I could see no evidence to suggest that the deceased,
> whilst in hospital, was in the custody of the police. There was no evidence that the
> police were present at the hospital at any time after Mr Linnane was admitted, nor   *d*
> was there any evidence that the hospital was in any way holding Mr Linnane in
> custody on behalf of the police.'

Accordingly, it would seem that the coroner's approach was one based on a narrow
view of physical custody. In effect, putting it in homely terms, he was saying that there
was no police officer holding his arm or within a sufficiently short distance to lay an arm   *e*
on him should it become necessary to do so. That is a somewhat narrow concept of
custody.

In this case, one has to ask the question: what was the deceased's status at the time that
he was in hospital? He was a sentenced prisoner serving his sentence. The argument on
behalf of the coroner really amounts to this. From the moment he got into the hospital,
the deceased was no longer a prisoner in the sense of being in the custody of the police   *f*
serving his sentence, but was simply a patient at the hospital. Had he made a miraculous
recovery, there would have been nothing in those circumstances, as counsel for the
coroner conceded, to prevent him walking out. He would not have been escaping from
custody in doing that although the police could no doubt come and rearrest him. The
question also arises whether, if he was to be detained for any period in the hospital,
having got there whilst serving a sentence, the period he was there was to be subtracted   *g*
from his sentence.

Looking at this matter, I hope, with common sense, I take the view that he was in
police custody. He was not in the physical custody in the sense of being physically held
by, or arranged to be physically held by, any specific officer, but he was in the legal
custody of the police or at any rate (and this is sufficient) there must have been, to anyone
properly directing themselves on the circumstances then existing, reason to suspect that   *h*
he was in police custody.

That in itself would be sufficient to dispose of this application, for, once it is decided
that the coroner did not direct himself correctly on the question of whether there was
reason to suspect that the deceased was in police custody, then his decision is flawed. As I
have indicated, there was clearly, in my view, had the coroner properly directed himself,
reason to suspect that the deceased was in police custody at the relevant time.   *j*

I turn to the other argument raised by counsel for the applicant, which is based on
s 8(3)(*d*). That provides that there must be a jury empanelled when it appears to the
coroner that there is reason to suspect—

a
'that the death occurred in circumstances the continuance or possible recurrence of which is prejudicial to the health or safety of the public or any section of the public.'

The argument presented on this paragraph has turned on whether there has to be causation as between the circumstances mentioned in the paragraph and the death, for that paragraph to apply. Counsel for the applicant says quite simply that one looks at the wording of the paragraph and sees the words used are not 'caused by', but 'occurred in'.

b It is not said that the death has to be 'caused by circumstances the continuance or possible recurrence of which is prejudicial . . .' The phrase used is that the death 'occurred in circumstances the continuance or possible recurrence of which is prejudicial . . .'

Counsel for the applicant relies on R v Hammersmith Coroner, ex p Peach [1980] 2 All ER 7, [1980] QB 211. That was a case in which the Divisional Court refused an application for judicial review where a coroner had declined to have a jury, but the Court of Appeal

c reversed that decision. It was a case in which the argument was conducted on a hypothesis, which was common ground, that there was evidence that Mr Peach was struck by a policeman with something more harmful that a police truncheon. The 'circumstances' in that case were those in which the officer gained possession of that weapon. It is therefore a case in which the question of causation was not specifically in issue. However, there are observations of Lord Denning MR, Bridge LJ and Sir David

d Cairns in the Court of Appeal which are helpful in considering what is the purpose of this paragraph in s 8(3).

Lord Denning MR said ([1980] 2 All ER 7 at 10, [1980] QB 211 at 226):

e
'Having regard to these illustrations, it seems to me that the suggestions made by Bridge LJ in the course of the argument gives a good indication of the "circumstances" in which a jury must be summoned. It is when the circumstances are such that similar fatalities may possibly recur in the future, and it is reasonable to expect that some action should be taken to prevent their recurrence.'

Bridge LJ said ([1980] 2 All ER 7 at 10, [1980] QB 211 at 226):

f
'The key to the nature of that limitation is to be found, I think, in the paragraph's concern with the continuance or possible recurrence of the circumstances in question. This indicates to my mind that the paragraph applies to circumstances of such a kind that their continuance or recurrence may reasonably and ought properly to be avoided by the taking of appropriate steps which it is in the power of some responsible body to take.'

g Sir David Cairns said ([1980] 2 All ER 7 at 11, [1980] QB 211 at 228):

'The reference to "continuance or possible recurrence" indicates to my mind that the provision was intended to apply only to circumstances the continuance or recurrence of which was preventable or to some extent controllable. Moreover, since it is prejudice to the health or safety of the public or a section of the public that is referred to, what is envisaged must, I think, be something which might be

h
prevented or safeguarded by a public authority or some other person or body whose activities can be said to affect a substantial section of the public.'

The argument which has been addressed on behalf of the coroner is that there must be some causative link between the circumstances in question and the death. The argument proceeds that, in the present case, the coroner, on reviewing the evidence before him,

j whatever view he may have taken about the circumstances at the police station and the timing of the deceased's removal to hospital, was faced with the medical opinions that the death was due to a viral infection, namely myocarditis. The coroner said:

'There was no evidence contained in the report of either pathologist to the effect

that any treatment or lack of treatment whilst in police custody had affected the
infective process which caused the death . . . In any event I considered that the *a*
circumstances of the case were quite exceptional, given the rarity of the disease . . .
It did not appear to me that there was any significant possibility of such unusual
circumstances recurring, so as to require an examination of the system under which
Mr Linnane was held in police custody.'

The riposte of the applicant to that is that it may be that acute myocarditis is very rare, *b*
it may be quite exceptional and it may be that it is unlikely to recur in prison, but the
circumstances of somebody falling obviously ill in prison could recur. The way in which
the system operates where a sentenced prisoner is being held in a police station as opposed
to a prison is something which could be prejudicial to the health or safety of that section
of the public which is formed by the prison population. Accordingly, the paragraph is
brought into play.
                                                                                              *c*
Counsel for the coroner referred the court to certain provisions which he submits
show that causation is required. He referred to s 11(5) of the Coroners Act 1988, which
deals with the procedures at an inquest and in particular with the inquisition. Section
11(5) provides as follows:

'An inquisition—(a) shall be in writing under the hand of the coroner and, in the
case of an inquest held with a jury, under the hands of the jurors who concur in the *d*
verdict; (b) shall set out, so far as such particulars have been proved—(i) who the
deceased was; and (ii) how, when and where the deceased came by his death . . .'

Counsel for the coroner also referred to the Coroners Rules 1985, SI 1984/552, and
particularly r 36, which provides, under the heading 'Matters to be ascertained at inquest':

'(1) The proceedings and evidence at an inquest shall be directed solely to *e*
ascertaining the following matters, namely—(a) who the deceased was; (b) how,
when and where the deceased came by his death; (c) the particulars for the time
being required by the Registration Acts to be registered concerning the death.
(2) Neither the coroner nor the jury shall express any opinion on any other
matters.'                                                                                     *f*

There is a provision under r 43, headed 'Prevention of similar fatalities', which states:

'A coroner who believes that action should be taken to prevent the recurrence of
fatalities similar to that in respect of which the inquest is being held may announce
at the inquest that he is reporting the matter in writing to the person or authority
who may have power to take such action and he may report the matter accordingly.' *g*

Those provisions relied on by counsel for the coroner are concerned with the verdict
and they are not, in my judgment, directly germane to the question whether or not to
call a jury in the first place and in particular under s 8(3)(d).

I am persuaded by the argument of counsel for the applicant that one ought to look
simply at the words of that paragraph. They are striking in that the phrase used is
'occurred in' and not 'caused by'. I therefore come to the conclusion that if before the *h*
coroner there are circumstances the continuance or possible recurrence of which is
prejudicial to the health or safety of any section of the public, and those are circumstances
in which the death occurred in the sense of being circumstances present where there has
been a death, then causation is not essential. In those circumstances, in the public interest,
the paragraph requires that a jury should be called.

One does not know from the medical evidence here, which has not been subjected to *j*
any forensic testing, whether the views that the pathologist expressed about the
aggravation due to withdrawal symptoms may involve criticism of the treatment of this
deceased at the police station or whether it may have accelerated death. There was
nothing that specifically dealt with that matter in the material before the coroner. It

might be that there was some causative connection, but even without that, for the reasons
*a* that I have endeavoured to express, I take the view that para (*d*) is in point here and that
the test which the coroner applied of looking simply at the cause of death was too narrow
a test to apply.

I conclude that under both paras (*b*) and (*d*) the coroner asked himself the wrong
questions and that the right conclusion would be that there ought to be a jury summoned
in this case. Accordingly, I would order that mandamus should go to achieve that result.
*b*

**HENRY J.** I agree.

*Application granted. No order as to costs.*

*Solicitors: J B Wheatley & Co (for the applicant); Beachcroft Stanleys (for the coroner).*
*c*

Dilys Tausz    Barrister.


# Pidduck v Eastern Scottish Omnibuses Ltd
*d*
QUEEN'S BENCH DIVISION
SHEEN J
14, 17, 27 OCTOBER 1988

*Fatal accident – Damages – Benefits excluded in assessing damages – Pension – Widow's*
*e* *allowance – Payments made to widow from husband's pension fund consequent on husband's death*
*– Whether payments to widow 'benefits' accruing to her as result of husband's death – Whether*
*payments to widow to be disregarded in assessing damages for husband's death – Fatal Accidents*
*Act 1976, s 4.*

The plaintiff was the widow of the deceased, who was a retired bank employee who
*f* received a monthly pension from his former employer's pension fund. Under the rules
of the fund the plaintiff was entitled to a lump sum and payment of certain allowances
linked to the deceased's pension if the deceased died within five years of retiring. The
deceased was killed within two years of retiring when a bus owned and operated by the
defendants in which he was travelling was involved in a collision. In an action for
damages brought by the plaintiff in respect of the deceased's death, the defendants
admitted liability and judgment was entered for the plaintiff for damages to be assessed.
*g* On the issue of damages the plaintiff claimed, inter alia, £17,057, being the loss of
dependency received up to the date of trial. The defendants contended that that claim
was subject to the deduction of the amount which the plaintiff had received from the
deceased's pension fund. Under s 4[a] of the Fatal Accidents Act 1976 'benefits' which
accrued to a person as the result of a deceased person's death were to be disregarded in
*h* assessing damages for that person's death. The question arose whether the amounts
received by the plaintiff from the pension fund were 'benefits' for the purposes of s 4.

**Held** – For the purposes of s 4 of the 1976 Act a pension and a widow's allowance
received from an employer's pension fund were 'benefits' and were therefore to be
disregarded in assessing damages for the deceased's death. Accordingly no deduction
*j* would be made from the claim for loss of dependency up to the date of trial (see p 264 *g*
*h* and p 265 *e*, post).

Dictum of Oliver LJ in *Auty v National Coal Board* [1985] 1 All ER 930 at 944
considered.

---

*a*  Section 4 is set out at p 264 *c*, post

**Notes**

For deduction from damages under the Fatal Accidents Act 1976, see 34 Halsbury's Laws  *a*
(4th edn) para 97, and for cases on the subject, see 36(1) Digest (Reissue) 360–362, 1456–
1469.

For the Fatal Accidents Act 1976, s 4, see 31 Halsbury's Statutes (4th edn) 210.

**Cases referred to in judgment**

*Auty v National Coal Board* [1985] 1 All ER 930, [1985] 1 WLR 784, CA.　　　　　　　　　　*b*
*Cookson v Knowles* [1978] 2 All ER 604, [1979] AC 556, [1978] 2 WLR 978, HL.
*Davies v Whiteways Cyder Co Ltd* [1974] 3 All ER 168, [1975] QB 262, [1974] 3 WLR 597.

**Assessment of damages**

The plaintiff, Elizabeth Muriel Pidduck, suing on her own behalf and on behalf of the
estate of her husband, John Walter Furnivall Pidduck deceased, brought an action against  *c*
the defendants, Eastern Scottish Omnibuses Ltd, alleging negligence on the part of an
employee of the defendants and claiming damages under the Fatal Accidents Act 1976
and the Law Reform (Miscellaneous Provisions) Act 1934 arising out of the death of the
plaintiff's husband while travelling in a bus owned and operated by the defendants. The
defendants admitted liability and judgment was entered for the plaintiff for damages to
be assessed. The facts are set out in the judgment.　　　　　　　　　　　　　　　　　　　*d*

*Oliver Ticciati* for the plaintiff.
*Anthony Temple QC* and *D M Harris* for the defendants.

　　　　　　　　　　　　　　　　　　　　　　　　　　　　　　　　　　　　*Cur adv vult*
　　　　　　　　　　　　　　　　　　　　　　　　　　　　　　　　　　　　　　　　　*e*

27 October. The following judgment was delivered.

**SHEEN J.** The plaintiff is the widow and executrix of the will of John Walter Furnivall
Pidduck who was killed on 21 October 1985 as a result of a collision on the M6 motorway
when he was a passenger in a coach owned and operated by the defendants and driven by  *f*
one of their servants. On 7 October 1987 judgment was entered for the plaintiff against
the defendants with damages to be assessed. The court must now assess the damages.

John Pidduck was 61½ years of age when he died. The defendants and the plaintiff
agree that at the time of his death the deceased was in a state of health reasonably
described as average for his age and condition in life, and that his expectation of life was
the expectation of life of a man in such a state of health. The person for whose benefit  *g*
this action is brought as a dependant is the plaintiff, who is now aged 64 years.

On behalf of the plaintiff a schedule of damages was produced. The parties are in
agreement that the plaintiff is entitled to recover the following sums: (a) bereavement
£3,500; (b) funeral expenses £896; (c) loss and damage to personal effects £550; and
(d) loss of deceased's services (based on a multiplicand of £500 and a multiplier of 7)
£3,500.　　　　　　　　　　　　　　　　　　　　　　　　　　　　　　　　　　　*h*

The next two items in the schedule are in dispute. The plaintiff claims the sum of
£17,057 for loss of dependency for the three years which have elapsed between the date
on which her husband died and the date of the trial, and the further sum of £46,287 for
future loss of dependency. These claims give rise to two disputes, the first of which is
whether, in assessing the damages for dependency, account should be taken of the
'widow's allowance' or 'pension' which the plaintiff is receiving, and the second is the  *j*
question: what is the appropriate multiplier in this case?

*The relevant facts*

The deceased had been in the employment of the Bank of England. In 1984 the
deceased voluntarily took early retirement. At the time of his death his sole source of
income was a pension of £820·42 gross per month, which represented a net monthly
income of £646·32 or £7,759 per annum. If the deceased had lived until the date of the

trial, his net income would have increased to £9,257 per annum. The parties have agreed
*a* that if the deceased had lived until the date of the trial (1) he would have been paid by
way of pension in the intervening three years the sum of £25,585 and (2) that during
that period his wife, the plaintiff, would have had the benefit of two-thirds of his income,
namely £17,057.

Counsel for the plaintiff contends that Mrs Pidduck is entitled to recover £17,057 in
respect of her loss of dependency up to the date of the trial. The defendants contend that
*b* under this part of the claim Mrs Pidduck is only entitled to £7,015, because she must
give credit for the sum of £10,042 which she received from the Bank of England during
this period.

*The pension fund*
The Bank of England maintains for the benefit of its employees a pension fund, which
*c* is non-contributory. Any member of the fund could expect on retirement to receive a
pension, with the option of taking part of the pension as a tax-free lump sum, and
pension increases based on the rate of inflation. On the death of the member of the fund
there would be paid a lump sum if he died in service or during the first five years on
pension and, in addition, allowances for his widow and children and perhaps other
dependants. There would also be annual increases in these allowances based on the rate
*d* of inflation. The widow's allowance is based on the employee's pension entitlement,
which depends on the length of the employee's service with the bank. Rule E of the
pension fund's rules is entitled 'Widows and Dependants Allowances'. Rule E2 deals with
allowances payable on the death of pensioner. Rule E2(a)(i) provides:

'On the death of a male Pensioner whose widow was married to him at the date
*e*     on which he ceased Employment his widow shall be paid an annual widow's
allowance which shall be made up of the following parts (to the extent that they are
applicable):—(1) One half of that element of the Base Pension attributable to the
period of the Pensioner's employment from 1st March 1974 ... To this must be
added various other items including an allowance for contributions made towards
the Widow's Annuity Fund.'
*f*
By rule E3 an allowance payable to a widow under rule E2(a) shall be paid to the
widow until her death.

The deceased had elected to make additional contributions to the widow's annuity
fund. When the widow's allowance was calculated in October 1985 in the sum of
£5,568·05 there was attributable to Mr Pidduck's contributions to the widow's annuity
*g* fund the sum of £1,444·44, which is 26% of the allowance granted. The defendants
concede that in assessing damages in this case they are not entitled to claim any
diminution in the damages by reason of this part of the widow's allowance received by
the plaintiff. On the basis of the rules of the Bank of England pension fund, it seems to
me that the pension of an employee and the allowance which will be made to his widow
after his death are all part of the reward for his services to the bank. Before his retirement
*h* the deceased was an employee, whose services were rewarded by (a) the immediate
payment of a salary, together with (b) the prospect of the payment of a pension for life
after retirement and (c) an allowance to his widow if he predeceased her, thereby reducing
the need for him to make provision for her to that extent. As I have already pointed out,
he had the option, which he exercised, of making voluntary payments in order to make
further provision for his widow.
*j*
*The statutory provisions*
The Administration of Justice Act 1982 substituted five new sections for ss 1 to 4 of
the Fatal Accidents Act 1976. The new s 3(1) provides:

'In the action such damages, other than damages for bereavement, may be
awarded as are proportioned to the injury resulting from the death to the dependants
respectively.'

The wording of that subsection may appear somewhat archaic in its use of the word 'injury', particularly because s 1(6) provides that any reference in the Act to injury  *a* includes disease and any impairment of a person's physical or mental condition. But in s 3 of the 1976 Act Parliament has reverted to the wording of s 2 of the Fatal Accidents Act 1846 (Lord Campbell's Act).

When Lord Campbell's Act came into force the injury referred to in s 2 was assessed on a balance of loss and gain. If one had then asked the question, 'Was there a reasonable probability of pecuniary advantage to the plaintiff from the continuance of the life of the  *b* deceased?' that question would have been answered by taking account of the financial gains accruing to the plaintiff as a result of the death of the deceased and setting them off against the losses occasioned by his death.

The same process would be applied in assessing damages under s 3(1) of the 1976 Act, if it were not for the provisions of s 4 of the Act, which now provides;

*c*

> 'In assessing damages in respect of a person's death in an action under this Act, benefits which have accrued or will or may accrue to any person from his estate or otherwise as a result of his death shall be disregarded.'

It is the plaintiff's case that the widow's allowance paid by the Bank of England and received by her must be disregarded by reason of s 4. On behalf of the plaintiff it is said that the widow's allowance is a benefit which has accrued to her 'as a result of the death'  *d* of her husband. The defendants contend that the plaintiff must give credit for the sums which she has received and will continue to receive from the bank by way of widow's allowance.

By the Fatal Accidents Act 1959, s 2 Parliament enacted that in assessing damages in respect of a person's death there shall not be taken into account any pension which will be paid as a result of the death. That was repeated in s 4 of the 1976 Act, which was a  *e* consolidating statute.

In *Cookson v Knowles* [1968] 2 All ER 604 at 608, [1979] AC 556 at 568 Lord Diplock said:

> 'Today the assessment of damages in fatal accident cases has become an artificial and conjectural exercise. Its purpose is no longer to put dependants, particularly  *f* widows, into the same economic position as they would have been in had their late husband lived. Section 4 of the Fatal Accidents Act 1976 requires the court in assessing damages to leave out of account any insurance money or benefit under national insurance or social security legislation or other pension or gratuity which becomes payable to the widow on her husband's death . . .'

*g*

The wording of s 4 of the 1976 Act was changed by the Administration of Justice Act 1982, and is now as set out above. Benefits which have accrued to a person as a result of the death are to be disregarded. There is no definition of 'benefits'. It seems to me that the word 'benefits' is apt to include a pension. If Parliament had intended to make such a fundamental change in the law relating to the assessment of damages in fatal accident cases as would be involved if the word 'benefits' in s 4 does not include a pension, I would  *h* have expected that change in the law to be made clear beyond doubt.

Counsel for the defendants drew my attention to *Auty v National Coal Board* [1985] 1 All ER 930 at 944, [1985] 1 WLR 784 at 806. Counsel sought to rely on two passages in the judgment of Oliver LJ where he said:

> 'There are thus two stages in the inquiry. Firstly there must be ascertained what  *j* "injury . . . to the dependants" has resulted from the death. Secondly, there must be assessed the damages which are to be awarded for that injury. No doubt in ascertaining the extent of the injury suffered (for instance, the loss of dependency or of the estate duty advantage with which *Davies v Whiteways Cyder Co Ltd* [1974] 3 All ER 168, [1975] QB 262 was concerned) you do not take into account any

a    countervailing advantage which may have resulted to the dependant from the death
in the form of pension or insurance benefit. In other words, it is no doubt right to
observe the provisions of s 4(1) at both stages of the inquiry.'

And he later said:

'But it is still necessary to establish that the dependant has in fact suffered an
injury (ie lost something) as a result of the death. Here what is claimed as the injury
b    is the loss of the very thing (ie a widow's pension) that the widow in fact has gained
as a result of the fulfilment of the conditions of the scheme earlier rather than later,
and whilst s 4 precludes setting the benefit of the pension against damage suffered
under some other head, there is nothing in that section which requires one to
assume, in ascertaining whether there has been any injury at all, that that which has
happened in fact has not happened.'

c
The defendants contend that before the death of the deceased the plaintiff was
dependent on the pension paid to her husband. After his death she received support
from precisely the same source in the form of an allowance to her. It was argued that this
change does not alter the underlying reality that the only injury which she has suffered
is the difference between the monetary advantage to her of her husband's pension and
d    the allowance which she received from the bank after his death. Counsel for the
defendants submitted that it is still permissible to compare like with like, and that in this
case the type of loss under consideration is a loss of pension benefits against which should
be set the receipt of pension benefits.

This is an attractive argument. Indeed if it is not acceptable to the court the result may
well be regarded as an anomaly. The result would be that the plaintiff is financially better
e    off as a result of the death of her husband to the extent of the widow's allowance. But it
seems to me that that is the effect of the provisions of the Fatal Accidents Act 1976, as
amended in 1982, and this court must give effect to it.

*Future loss of dependency*
For the reasons given above the appropriate multiplicand is £6,171·60, which is two-
f    thirds of the pension which would have been received by the deceased at the date of trial.
There is an issue as to what is an appropriate multiplier. At the date of his death the
deceased was 61½ years of age. As he had already retired, it was submitted by the plaintiff
that the court should ignore many of the vicissitudes of life such as the possibility of
redundancy, ill health and injury. The only relevant contingencies are the death of the
deceased and the death of the plaintiff. I have already referred to the agreement between
g    the parties as to the state of health of the deceased. It seems to me that if I were
considering his life alone the appropriate multiplier would have been ten at the date of
his death. But some allowance has to be made for the contingency of the death of the
plaintiff, because two lives were at risk. In the circumstances, the appropriate multiplier
seems to me to be nine. Three years have elapsed since the death of the deceased, so that
the figure appropriate for future loss of dependency must be reached by multiplying the
h    multiplicand by six. That produces the sum of £37,030. All the other figures have been
agreed. Accordingly, there will be judgment for the plaintiff for the sum of £67,481.

*Judgment for the plaintiff accordingly.*

Solicitors: *Hughes Hooker & Co* (for the plaintiff); *Davis Campbell*, Liverpool (for the
defendants).

K Mydeen Esq    Barrister.

# Director General of Fair Trading v Tobyward Ltd and another

CHANCERY DIVISION

HOFFMANN J

16, 17 NOVEMBER 1988

*Advertising – Control – Misleading advertisements – Advertisement in similar terms – Injunction – Terms of injunction – Respondents publishing misleading advertisements to sell slimming aid – Whether court having jurisdiction to grant interlocutory injunction restraining respondents from publishing misleading advertisements – Whether injunction restraining respondents from publishing advertisements in similar terms or likely to convey a similar impression too vague – Control of Misleading Advertisements Regulations 1988, reg 6(2).*

*Injunction – Interlocutory – Undertaking as to damages – Undertaking by Director General of Fair Trading – Injunction sought in attempt to enforce law – Control of misleading advertisements – Director General seeking interlocutory injunction to restrain publication of misleading advertisements – Whether Director General should be required to give cross-undertaking in damages.*

The respondents advertised and marketed a product which was claimed to be a slimming aid. In their advertisements the respondents claimed, inter alia, (1) that use of their product could result in permanent weight loss, (2) that success was guaranteed, (3) that the product contained an ingredient which represented a medical or scientific breakthrough, (4) that the product prevented fats entering the bloodstream, (5) that the product enabled the user to lose a specific amount of weight in a specified time and (6) that the product was 100% safe in all cases. The Advertising Standards Authority received complaints about the respondents' advertisements and found the advertisements to be contrary to the British Code of Advertising Practice in that the six claims were misleading. The authority gave the respondents advice on how to comply with the code but the respondents continued to publish advertisements which the authority considered to be misleading. The authority referred the breaches of the code to the Director General of Fair Trading, who applied under reg 6 of the Control of Misleading Advertisements Regulations 1988 for an interlocutory injunction to restrain the respondents from publishing misleading advertisements in relation to their product. Under reg 6(2)[a] an injunction could be issued to restrain not only a particular advertisement but also 'any advertisement in similar terms or likely to convey a similar impression' and the Director General sought an injunction in those terms. The respondents contended that an injunction in those terms would be too vague. The respondents also contended that if an injunction were to be granted the Director General should be required to give a cross-undertaking in damages.

**Held** – The court had jurisdiction under reg 6 of the 1988 regulations to grant the interlocutory injunction sought because there was a strong prima facie case that the respondents' advertisements were likely to deceive the persons to whom they were addressed by making false claims for the respondents' product and were likely to induce those persons to buy the product. In granting an injunction the court had to avoid the extremes of granting an injunction which was so specific that the advertiser could escape its effect and still publish a misleading advertisement merely by making a small alteration in the terms of the advertisement or of granting an injunction which was so general that the advertiser had no clear idea of what he was not allowed to do. Since the respondents' advertisements contained a large amount of material it would place the respondents in difficulty if, without more, an injunction were to be granted simply restraining the

---

a   Regulation 6(2), so far as material, is set out at p 271 *f*, post

particular advertisements about which complaint had been made and advertisements in
*a* similar terms or likely to convey a similar impression. Accordingly, an injunction would
be granted restraining the particular advertisements about which complaint had been
made and advertisements which were in similar terms or likely to convey a similar
impression in respect of the six specific misleading claims. The injunction would not be
subject to a condition that the Director General give the usual cross-undertaking in
damages because in seeking the injunction the Director General was attempting to
*b* enforce the law on behalf of the Crown and given the Director General's strong prima
facie case there was no reason to require him to give such a cross-undertaking (see p 270
*e f*, p 271 *d e g h*, p 272 *b e f h* to p 273 *a*, post).
    *F Hoffmann-La Roche & Co AG v Secretary of State for Trade and Industry* [1974] 2 All ER
1128 applied.

*c* **Notes**
For the European policy on the control of misleading advertising, see 51 Halsbury's Laws
(4th edn) para 8.92.
    For an undertaking in damages as a condition of being granted an interlocutory
injunction, see 24 ibid paras 1072–1076, and for cases on the subject, see 28(2) Digest
*d* (Reissue) 1133–1136, *1332–1377*.

**Cases referred to in judgment**
*Hoffmann-La Roche (F) & Co AG v Secretary of State for Trade and Industry* [1974] 2 All ER
    1128, [1975] AC 295, [1974] 3 WLR 104, HL.
*National Daily and Sunday Newspapers Proprietors' Agreement, Re* [1986] ICR 44, RPC.

*e* **Cases also cited**
*Rochdale BC v Anders* [1988] 3 All ER 490.
*Staver Co Inc v Digitext Display Ltd* [1984] FSR 512.

**Appeal**
*f* By motion dated 27 October 1988 the Director General of Fair Trading sought an
interlocutory injunction to restrain the respondents, Tobyward Ltd and Robert Johnson,
a director of the company, from publishing or disseminating or permitting or being
concerned with publishing or disseminating (i) three advertisements published on 24
July 1988, 31 July 1988 and 22 August 1988 in the Sunday Sport newspaper and '9 to 5'
magazine and (ii) any advertisement in similar terms or likely to convey a similar
*g* impression in respect of the product 'SpeedSlim' which was the subject of the three
advertisements. The facts are set out in the judgment.

*S P Richards* for the Director General.
*T M B Higginson* for the first respondent.
*N M Peters* for the second respondent.

*h*
**HOFFMANN J.** There is before the court a motion by the Director General of Fair
Trading for an interlocutory injunction to restrain the publication of misleading
advertisements. The first respondent is a company which markets and has extensively
advertised a product called 'SpeedSlim'. The product is sold in the form of tablets and is
claimed to cause loss of weight. The second respondent is the sole director of the first
*j* respondent.
    The Director General applies under reg 5 of the Control of Misleading Advertisements
Regulations 1988, SI 1988/915, which came into force on 20 June 1988. These regulations
were made to implement Council Directive (EEC) 84/450. For the purposes of reg 2(2)
of the 1988 regulations, an advertisement is misleading if—

    'in any way, including its presentation, it deceives or is likely to deceive the
    persons to whom it is addressed or whom it reaches and if, by reason of its deceptive
    nature, it is likely to affect their economic behaviour or, for those reasons, injures or

is likely to injure a competitor of the persons whose interests the advertisement
seeks to promote.'

The director has a duty under reg 4(1) to consider any complaints that advertisements are
misleading. A duty expressed in such broad terms might impose on the director's office
an unacceptable volume of work but it is qualified in two respects. First, he need not
consider complaints which appear to be frivolous or vexatious; second, and much more
important, he need not consider any complaint until the complainant has invoked what
the regulations describe as 'such established means of dealing with such complaints as
the Director may consider appropriate'.

The British advertising industry has a system of self-regulation which has been
established under the auspices of its voluntary regulatory body, the Advertising Standards
Authority (the ASA). There is a British Code of Advertising Practice which is administered
by the code of advertising practice committee, and the committee and the ASA deal with
complaints of breaches of the code. They are also willing to give guidance to advertisers
on whether a proposed advertisement would be regarded as acceptable. So the proper
working of the self-regulatory system is essential to the overall scheme of control, which
contemplates that the director will deal only with exceptional cases in which for one
reason or another self-regulation has proved inadequate.

If a complaint is referred to the director and he considers the advertisement to be
misleading, he may apply to the court for an injunction. The regulations provide no
other legal remedy. They do not make the publication of misleading advertisements
unlawful. The only sanction is that, once an injunction has been made, the publication
of an advertisement in breach of its terms will be a contempt of court and punishable as
such. Under reg 6(1) the court may grant a final injunction only if it is satisfied that the
advertisement in question is misleading, but this degree of persuasion is not required at
the present interlocutory stage. In exercising this jurisdiction, the court must have
'regard to all the interests involved and in particular the public interest'.

In January 1988 the ASA received a number of complaints about the first respondent's
advertising. The code has a specific section dealing with the advertisement of slimming
products, which recognises that this is a particularly sensitive area of advertising. As
Professor Bender, a distinguished nutritionist who has sworn an affidavit in these
proceedings, deposes:

'... people who are overweight are often anxious about their condition, and ...
their anxiety makes them ready, even against their better judgement, to believe
extravagant claims about slimming products.'

The code therefore goes into considerable detail about the kind of claims which an
advertisement can properly make. For example, it says in para 5.4 2 of the section in
question, which is section C.IV of the code:

'Care should be taken not to suggest that particular methods *cannot fail, must work.*
Because of the enormous variations between individuals in terms of weight, build
and physical condition as well as in psychological preparedness, the most that can be
claimed for any method is a high probability of success.'

And in para 5.2:

'Claims in the form (*you can*) *lose* (*up to*) *X pounds* (*or Y inches*), *look X pounds lighter,*
(*you can*) *start to slim in X days, how to slim in less than X weeks, lose X inches immediately*
*etc,* should not be made, since the measurements and weights of individuals and
their degrees of application vary too widely for such unqualified promises to be
capable of fulfilment.'

There was correspondence between the ASA and the first respondent's advertising
agents after the complaints were made in January and going on, including meetings
between them, until August 1988. The council of the ASA upheld the complaints against
the advertisements, and the secretariat gave the advertising agents detailed advice on

what was necessary to comply with the code. The first respondent nevertheless continued
*a* to publish advertisements in terms which the ASA considered to be misleading. In
August 1988 (the regulations having, as I have said, come into force in June) the ASA
referred the matter to the director. The director invited the respondents to comment and
there followed some discussions, during which the respondents through their solicitors
offered the director undertakings. He considered the terms of these undertakings to be
inadequate. The proceedings were commenced by originating motion on 27 October
*b* 1988 and the motion for an interlocutory injunction was issued on the same day.

The main ingredient in SpeedSlim is guar gum, which is obtained by hot water
extraction from the Indian cluster bean. Its principal chemical material is galactomannan,
a substance which slows down the emptying of the bowels and may therefore make one
feel less hungry. In consequence one may eat less and so lose weight. In the end, however,
the only way in which a healthy person can lose weight is by eating less calories than his
*c* body consumes. Galactomannan may make it easier to follow such a diet. On the other
hand, there is also some evidence to suggest that in tablet form it can occasionally swell
up while still in the throat and cause unpleasant obstructions.

The director complains of three specific advertisements for SpeedSlim, of which copies
marked A, B and C are annexed to the originating motion. Advertisement A was
published in the 'Sunday Sport' on 24 July 1988, B in the same newspaper on 31 July and
*d* C in a publication called '9 to 5' on 22 August. These advertisements are said to be
misleading in respect of six claims which are contained in them and I will deal briefly
with each of these claims.

(1) The use of the product can result in permanent weight loss. Thus A says, 'the ALL
NATURAL proven weight-loss powers of SpeedSlim have made it possible for almost anyone
to lose weight quickly and permanently—yet safely . . .' and 'SpeedSlim is an awesome
*e* discovery that will enable you to lose weight easily and, most importantly—permanently'.
Advertisement B says, 'LOSE YOUR FAT—NOW AND FOREVER'. Professor Bender, whose
expert evidence is at present uncontradicted, says that one cannot say that weight will be
lost permanently by using the product. Any weight lost by any dietary regime can be,
and usually is, restored when food intake again exceeds expenditure.

(2) The product carries a guarantee of success. Thus advertisement A says 'It is virtually
*f* impossible not to lose weight when you take the SpeedSlim Course', and 'You cannot
fail'. Advertisement B says, 'GRAPEFRUIT SPEEDSLIM—[a grapefruit flavoured variety] A
100% GUARANTEE OF SUCCESS'. Professor Bender says that trials with guar gum as reported
in the literature have shown that, while some patients did indeed lose weight, others did
not and some even gained weight. The claim is also patently in breach of the terms of
para 5.4 2 of section C.IV of the code to which I have already referred.
*g*
(3) The product, or some ingredient of it, represents a medical or scientific
breakthrough save where the claims can be substantiated. I have read one example of
such a claim in advertisement A already. It and advertisement B have a box headed in
large type 'A NEW MEDICAL BREAKTHROUGH!' Professor Bender says that the effects of
galactomannan have become known gradually over a number of years and similar
*h* products have been on sale for some time.

(4) The product places a lining on the stomach or other part of the alimentary canal so
that fats that cause the gaining of weight cannot enter the bloodstream. This claim is
made in advertisements A and B. Professor Bender says that it is simply untrue and the
respondents have not produced evidence to substantiate it.

(5) The product will enable users to lose specific amounts of weight in specified
*j* periods of time. Advertisements A and B say, 'HOW MUCH WEIGHT DO YOU WANT TO LOSE?'
and offer alternatives from 10 lb in 10 days to 50 lb in 60 days. Advertisement C says
that SpeedSlim 'lets you set your weight loss with complete confidence', although it does
suggest that losing weight at too great a rate can be corrected by ceasing to take the tablets
for a few days. Professor Bender says that the suggestion that rapid weight loss can be
sustained over lengthy periods by any person is wrong and misleading, and the suggestion
that one could lose at the rate of 1 lb a day over a period exceeding one or two weeks is in

his opinion simply impossible. Claims of this kind are also contrary to the provisions of
para 5.2 of section C.IV of the code which I have quoted.

(6) The product is 100% safe in all cases. Advertisement C says that 'SpeedSlim is the
*reliable and safe* way to help you lose those *hunger cravings . . .*' and advertisements A and
B say that it places a 'totally natural and 100% safe lining in your stomach'. I have already
referred to the evidence that SpeedSlim or products of that kind may cause swelling and
blocking of the oesophagus. Counsel for the respondents say that these claims really
meant no more than that the product was safe in its effects on the stomach and that they
were not inconsistent with the possibility of choking when ingested in tablet form.
SpeedSlim is sold in tablet form and I do not think the ordinary reader of the
advertisement would think that a reference to it being safe was as limited as counsel
suggests.

Those are the six respects in which it is alleged that the advertisement is misleading.

'Misleading', as I have said, is defined in the regulations as involving two elements:
first, that the advertisement deceives or is likely to deceive the persons to whom it is
addressed and, second, that it is likely to affect their economic behaviour. In my judgment
in this context there is little difficulty about applying the concept of deception. An
advertisement must be likely to deceive the persons to whom it is addressed if it makes
false claims on behalf of the product. It is true that many people read advertisements
with a certain degree of scepticism. For the purposes of applying the regulations,
however, it must be assumed that there may be people who will believe what the
advertisers tell them, and in those circumstances the making of a false claim is likely to
deceive. Having regard to the evidence of Professor Bender, which at present is the only
scientific evidence before the court, there is in my judgment a strong prima facie case
that these advertisements were likely to deceive in each of the six respects of which
complaint is made. The other element, namely that the advertisement is likely to affect
the economic behaviour of the persons to whom it is addressed, means in this context no
more than that it must make it likely that they will buy the product. As that was no
doubt the intention of the advertisement, it is reasonable to draw the inference that it
would have such a result. I am therefore satisfied that the court has jurisdiction under
reg 6 to make an injunction in this case.

The making of the injunction is, however, a matter of discretion, and I must consider
whether in this case it would be appropriate to do so. There are two reasons why I think
I should. First, the regulations contemplate that there will only be intervention by the
director when the voluntary system has failed. It is in my judgment desirable and in
accordance with the public interest to which I must have regard that the courts should
support the principle of self-regulation. I think that advertisers would be more inclined
to accept the rulings of their self-regulatory bodies if it were generally known that in
cases in which their procedures had been exhausted and the advertiser was still publishing
an advertisement which appeared to the court to be prima facie misleading an injunction
would ordinarily be granted. The respondents did offer undertakings to the director
which could not have been enforced by any legal process other than the making of an
application such as this for an injunction. But they were in terms which the director
thought to be inadequate. For example, the respondents were unwilling to give
undertakings in respect of advertisements which the director thought to be misleading
but which had already been booked into the magazines or newspapers, notwithstanding
that it was known for some time that the director considered them to be objectionable.
Then the respondents required qualifications to the wording of certain of the
undertakings. For example, the undertaking not to claim that the use of the product can
result in permanent weight loss was to be qualified by adding the words 'after cessation
of the use of the product'. In my view the director was reasonable in objecting to that
qualification, since the objectionable feature of the claim is the use of the word permanent
in any circumstances. There are other qualifications with which it is not necessary for
me to deal in detail, but I do not think that the terms of the undertakings which were
offered were such as to make it inappropriate for the director to apply for an injunction
today.

Second, in my view the interests of consumers require the protection of an injunction
*a*  pending trial of the action. It does not seem to me that the respondents could complain
of any legitimate interference with their business if they were restrained from making
claims of the kind to which the director is here taking objection.

I turn therefore to the terms of the injunction. Counsel for the respondents said that
on the footing that, contrary to their primary submissions, an injunction was granted
they would have no objection to its formulation in terms of the restraint on them of
*b*  publishing advertisements which made claims of the six kinds to which I have referred.
The director also asks for a restraint on publication of the three specific advertisements to
which I have referred. Again the respondents make no objection to that part of the order.
But the director then asks that the respondents be restrained from publishing any
advertisement 'in similar terms or likely to convey a similar impression' to any of the
said advertisements in respect of 'any of the following claims in relation to any slimming
*c*  product', and then listing the six claims.

The respondents say that an injunction expressed in those terms is far too vague and
would not satisfy the essential requirement in formulating any injunction, namely that
it should make clear to the respondents what they can lawfully do and what they must
refrain from doing. 'In similar terms or likely to convey a similar impression' is said to
be so uncertain a matter that it should not form part of the terms of the injunction.

*d*  In a case like this the formulation of the injunction must avoid extremes on either
side. On the one hand it must not be so specific that by a small variation in the terms of
the advertisement the advertiser can escape its effect and publish an advertisement which
is nevertheless misleading in the same kind of way. On the other hand, it must not be in
terms so general that the advertiser does not have a clear idea of what he is not allowed to
do.

*e*  In the regulations themselves it is provided in reg 6(1) that the court may grant an
injunction if it is satisfied that the advertisement to which the application relates is
misleading. The primary ground for the application must therefore be a specific
advertisement. But by reg 6(2) it is provided that the—

*f*  'injunction may relate not only to a particular advertisement but to any
advertisement in similar terms or likely to convey a similar impression'.

It is that language which the director has adopted in his formulation of the proposed
injunction.

The advertisements in this case contain a good deal of material, and simply to prohibit
advertisements in similar terms or likely to convey a similar impression without more
would in my judgment place the respondents in a very considerable difficulty. In that
*g*  respect the case would be similar to *Re National Daily and Sunday Newspapers Proprietors'
Agreement* [1986] ICR 44, in which the Restrictive Trade Practices Court had accepted an
undertaking that the defendants in that case would not enter into a particular kind of
agreement or 'agreements or arrangements to the like effect'. The agreement in question
was a fairly complex one and it was therefore not easy to tell what would be an agreement
which was, for relevant purposes, 'to the like effect'. In order to remove that uncertainty,
*h*  what the director proposes is that the statutory language 'in similar terms or likely to
convey a similar impression' should be made more specific by spelling out the six
headings under which an advertisement should not be in similar terms or convey a
similar impression. The effect of such an injunction is, in my judgment, precisely the
same as an injunction which merely prohibits any advertisement making the six claims
to which I have referred, but has these further advantages. First, it follows the statutory
*j*  scheme in reg 6(1) and (2). Second, it makes it clear that the court regards the three
specified advertisements as containing examples of claims which fall within the six
categories. It does not, in my view, create any difficulties for the respondents which
would not exist in an injunction framed in the terms which they say they would prefer.
Counsel objected in particular to the words 'or likely to convey a similar impression',
which he said were inappropriate to a case in which what was objected to was the
language used in the advertisement. That, he said, was simply a matter of the *terms* of

the advertisement and not the *impression* which it conveys. It seems to me, however, that that point is fallacious. The purpose of reg 6(2) is to prohibit advertisements which are *a* not precisely the same as those which have been brought before the court, and it should not matter whether the alternative advertisement presents itself in the form of texts or pictures or in any other way, provided that in the impression it conveys it makes a claim of a nature which has been held to be prohibited.

For those reasons I would propose to make an injunction in the revised terms which were put before me by counsel for the director.          *b*

That leaves one final question, namely whether the director ought to be required as a condition of obtaining an interlocutory injunction to give the usual cross-undertaking in damages.

The position at this interlocutory stage is that, although I have found that the director has a strong prima facie case that the advertisements in question were misleading, that point will not be finally determined until the trial, and it may be that the judge at the *c* trial will hold that my prima facie view was wrong. In those circumstances the respondents will turn out to have been restrained from publishing advertisements which they ought to have been allowed to publish. As Lord Diplock said in F *Hoffmann-La Roche & Co AG v Secretary of State for Trade and Industry* [1974] 2 All ER 1128 at 1150, [1975] AC 295 at 361:
*d*
'... at the time of the application it is not possible for the court to be absolutely certain that the plaintiff will succeed at the trial in establishing his legal right to restrain the defendant from what he is threatening to do. If he should fail to do so the defendant may have suffered loss as a result of having been prevented from doing it while the interim injunction was in force ... So unless some other means is provided in this event for compensating the defendant for his loss there is a risk that *e* injustice may be done.'

That is the basis of a normal cross-undertaking in damages. There is, however, an established exception to which effect was given in the *Hoffmann-La Roche* case, namely that when the Crown is seeking an interlocutory injunction in an action in which it is attempting to enforce the law the usual practice is that no cross-undertaking is required. The way Lord Cross justified the practice of *Hoffmann-La Roche* was ([1974] 2 All ER 1128 *f* at 1158, [1975] AC 295 at 371):

'To make the granting of an interim injunction conditional on the giving of an undertaking in damages may deter the Crown from asking for one. The Attorney-General may say to himself: "I think we are right – but one never knows; and if we get an interim injunction and it turns out that we are wrong we may be held liable *g* to pay very heavy damages ..."'

Whatever one may say about the policy in question it is, in my judgment, well established. I must therefore ask myself two questions. First, is this a law enforcement action? There is no right for anybody else to take proceedings to enforce the regulations, and the director has no remedy except the injunction which is sought here. It seems to *h* me therefore that this is plainly a law enforcement claim.

The second question is whether there is any reason in this case why the Crown should, contrary to the normal practice, be required to give a cross-undertaking in damages. Counsel for the respondents said that this case was different from the *Hoffmann-La Roche* case because the House of Lords in that case plainly considered that the Crown had a very strong case indeed, whereas in this case he submits that the matter is still one to be tried. *j* Lord Diplock, however, said that to displace the Crown's right to an injunction without a cross-undertaking it was for the respondents to show a strong prima facie case that their proposed conduct was lawful (see [1974] 2 All ER 1128 at 1155, [1975] AC 295 at 367). As in this case it appears to me that it is the director who has a strong prima facie case, I think that the normal practice should apply and the director should be entitled to his

injunction without a cross-undertaking. I will therefore grant the injunction in those
a terms.

*Order accordingly.*

Solicitors: *Treasury Solicitor; Kaye Tesler & Co* (for the first and second respondents).

b
Evelyn M C Budd   Barrister.


# Harris v Newcastle Health Authority

c
COURT OF APPEAL, CIVIL DIVISION
KERR, MANN LJJ AND SIR JOHN MEGAW
2 NOVEMBER 1988

*Discovery – Production of documents – Production before commencement of proceedings – Claim*
d *in respect of personal injuries – Production where claim likely to be made in subsequent proceedings
– Likely to be made – Limitation defence – Relevance of proposed limitation defence to application
for pre-trial discovery – Plaintiff applying 22 years after operation for pre-trial disclosure of
medical records – Whether limitation defence should be taken into account in determining whether
plaintiff likely to become party to proceedings – Supreme Court Act 1981, s 33(2).*

e The plaintiff was born in 1959 suffering from a squint in her eye. In 1961 and 1965 she
had operations at hospitals administered by the defendant health authority but they were
not successful and she continued to suffer from pain and a partly closed eye. The plaintiff
was advised in 1987 that she might have a claim against the health authority for personal
injuries and for the purpose of bringing such proceedings she applied pursuant to s 33(2)[a]
of the Supreme Court Act 1981 for pre-trial disclosure of the medical records relating to
f her treatment at the authority's hospitals on the basis that she was a person who appeared
'to be likely to be a party to . . . proceedings' in respect of a claim for personal injuries.
The health authority intended to plead that the claim was time-barred and contended
that because of the probability of that defence succeeding at the trial the court ought to
exercise its discretion under s 33(2) by refusing the application. The district registrar and
on appeal the judge held that, although they had jurisdiction under s 33(2) to order the
g pre-trial disclosure requested, the strength of the limitation defence was such that the
action was doomed to failure and the application should be refused. The plaintiff
appealed, contending that on an application for pre-trial disclosure the court should have
no regard to the prospects of a proposed limitation defence.

**Held** – (1) The court had jurisdiction under s 33(2) of the 1981 Act to order the pre-trial
h disclosure on the basis that the plaintiff was a person who appeared 'to be likely to be a
party to . . . proceedings' in respect of a claim for personal injuries if there was a reasonable
prospect that the plaintiff would become a party. Where it was plain beyond doubt that
a proposed limitation defence would succeed the court was entitled to take that defence
into account when considering an application for pre-trial disclosure both when
determining whether there was jurisdiction under s 33(2) to make an order and also
j when deciding as matter of discretion whether an order should be made. Normally,
however, the court ought not to consider the merits of a proposed limitation defence on
the hearing of an application for pre-trial disclosure since at that stage the court would

---

*a  Section 33(2), so far as material, is set out at p 274 j to p 275 a, post*

usually not have sufficient material before it to come to a proper decision on the defence
(see p 277 *e* to p 278 *a f g* and p 279 *b c*, post).          *a*

(2) Although the health authority's limitation defence had very strong prospects of
succeeding, nevertheless,since it was likely that proceedings would be instituted by the
plaintiff regardless of the outcome of the application for pre-trial disclosure and since it
could not be said that such proceedings would be doomed to failure because pre-trial
disclosure of the hospital records might reveal facts relevant to the prospects of the
limitation defence not succeeding, it followed that the court ought to exercise its          *b*
discretion by making an order for the pre-trial disclosure of the hospital records. The
appeal would therefore be allowed (see p 278 *b* to *d f h j* and p 279 *e f h*, post).

**Notes**

For discovery in personal injury claims before proceedings are begun, see 13 Halsbury's
Laws (4th edn) para 14, and for cases on the subject, see 18 Digest (Reissue) 33, *218–219*.          *c*

For the Supreme Court Act 1981, s 33, see 11 Halsbury's Statutes (4th edn) 786.

**Cases referred to in judgment**

*Dunning v Board of Governors of United Liverpool Hospitals* [1973] 2 All ER 454, [1973] 1
WLR 586, CA.

*Kennett v Brown* [1988] 2 All ER 600, [1988] 1 WLR 582, CA.          *d*

*Shaw v Vauxhall Motors Ltd* [1974] 2 All ER 1186, CA.

*Victoria Laundry Ltd v Newman Industries Ltd* [1949] 1 All ER 997, [1949] 2 KB 528, CA.

**Cases also cited**

*Davies v Ministry of Defence* [1985] CA Transcript 413.

*Hall v Wadsworth Health Authority* (1985) Times, 16 February.          *e*

*Organsanya v Lambeth Area Health Authority* (3 July 1985, unreported), QBD.

*Riches v DPP* [1974] 2 All ER 935, [1973] 1 WLR 1019, CA.

**Interlocutory appeal**

The plaintiff, Veronica Kim Harris, appealed against the decision of Staughton J sitting          *f*
in the Queen's Bench Division at Newcastle upon Tyne on 25 November 1987 dismissing
her appeal from the order of Mr District Registrar Ward made on 30 June 1987 dismissing
her application by summons dated 28 May 1987 for pre-trial disclosure by the defendants,
the Newcastle Health Authority, of the plaintiff's medical records, pursuant to s 33(2) of
the Supreme Court Act 1981. The facts are set out in the judgment of Kerr LJ.

          *g*

*Michael Powers* for the plaintiff.

*Richard Dening* for the defendants.

**KERR LJ.** This is an appeal from a judgment given at Newcastle by Staughton J on 25
November 1987. It raises a point of importance for potential proceedings for personal          *h*
injury in which a defence of limitation is likely to be raised. The appeal has come into
our list unexpectedly, and since this constitution will not be sitting together after today
we propose to give judgment now because it would be difficult to leave it until another
date.

The matter concerned an application for pre-trial discovery under s 33(2) of the
Supreme Court Act 1981. That provides:          *j*

'On the application, in accordance with rules of court, of a person who appears to
the High Court to be likely to be a party to subsequent proceedings in that court in
which a claim in respect of personal injuries to a person . . . is likely to be made, the
High Court shall, in such circumstances as may be specified in the rules, have power
to order a person who appears to the court to be likely to be a party to the proceedings

a and to be likely to have or to have had in his possession, custody or power any documents which are relevant to an issue arising or likely to arise out of that claim (a) to disclose whether those documents are in his possession, custody or power; and (b) to produce such of those documents . . .'

I need not read the remainder of that provision.

b The rules of court do not take its application much further. RSC Ord 24, r 7A merely prescribes the procedural steps which have to be taken to make the application. Order 24, r 8, headed 'Discovery to be ordered only if necessary', is of some limited assistance. It provides:

c 'On the hearing of an application for an order under rule . . . 7A the Court, if satisfied that discovery is not necessary, or not necessary at that stage of the cause or matter, may dismiss or, as the case may be, adjourn the application and shall in any case refuse to make such an order if and so far as it is of opinion that discovery is not necessary either for disposing fairly of the cause or matter or for saving costs.'

d The issue in the present case turns on the relevance, and, if relevant, on the weight that is to be given to it at the stage of an application under this provision, of a defence of limitation which will clearly be raised. That does not appear to be an issue which has arisen in any previously reported case. Indeed, counsel for the plaintiff has told us that in his considerable experience he has not previously encountered a refusal of an application under s 33(2) of the 1981 Act. As I understood him, he has also not previously encountered any argument about limitation being raised at this stage.

What happened was this. The district registrar said: 'I consider that the plaintiff has no prospect of overcoming the limitation point, and s 33 of the Supreme Court Act 1981 e gives me a discretion.' At the end of the day that was the conclusion which Staughton J equally reached on appeal. He refused the application on the facts of the case in the light of what he considered to be the prospects on the limitation issue. The plaintiff now appeals against that refusal.

Before referring to the facts I should briefly mention such authorities as we have had drawn to our attention, in which the practice under this provision has arisen for f consideration. The leading case is *Dunning v Board of Governors of the United Liverpool Hospitals* [1973] 2 All ER 454, [1973] 1 WLR 586. That decided by a majority of Lord Denning MR and James LJ, with Stamp LJ dissenting, that an application for pre-trial discovery was not to be denied solely on the ground that it was quite uncertain, before the result of the application was known, before one would know what documents were available and what they contained, whether or not there might be a cause of action. That g was held not to be a ground for refusing the application. The court took the view that, although the effect of the requested documents on the prospects of the action was quite uncertain, nevertheless the word 'likely' in s 31 of the Administration of Justice Act 1970 was satisfied if the position was that the action might, or might well, proceed in the unknown circumstances of what discovery might reveal.

The only indication which one gets from that case about the circumstances in which h an application for pre-trial discovery should be refused is a short passage in the judgment of James LJ in which he said ([1973] 2 All ER 454 at 460, [1973] 1 WLR 586 at 593):

'In order to take advantage of the section [ie s 31 of the Administration of Justice Act 1970, the wording of which is no different from that of s 33(2) of the 1981 Act] the applicant for relief must disclose the nature of the claim he intends to make and j show not only the intention of making it but also that there is a reasonable basis for making it. Ill-founded, irresponsible and speculative allegations or allegations based merely on hope, would not provide a reasonable basis for an intended claim in subsequent proceedings.'

In another case in the following year, *Shaw v Vauxhall Motors Ltd* [1974] 2 All ER 1185, the appropriate procedure to be operated by would-be plaintiffs seeking discovery before

action was considered, and in effect laid down. It resulted in what has since become
known as a 'Shaw letter' asking for the discovery. And, since the normal practice is that  *a*
the applicant will be obliged to pay the costs of compliance with the request, we are told
that there have been very few cases, and none reported, which have come before the
courts since then. The fact that the costs of and occasioned by the application will
normally fall on the applicant is referred to in *The Supreme Court Practice 1988* vol 1, para
24/7A/8.

The only other matters with regard to the general practice which I think I ought to  *b*
mention are the advantages of granting applications of this kind, relying, as one must,
on the responsibility of counsel not to advise actions to proceed when they have no
reasonable prospect of success, and of course equally where there is legal aid. These
aspects were stressed in the judgments of Buckley and Ormrod LJJ in *Shaw's* case [1974]
2 All ER 1185 at 1188–1189. The effect of these passages is that applications under this
provision, if properly used, are obviously useful and particularly desirable in legal aid  *c*
cases. Since these applications can only be made in personal injury cases, many of which
are of course legally aided, as in this case, that is an important matter to bear in mind
with regard to the desirability of granting such orders.

In the present case, however, the proposed defendants, the Newcastle Health Authority,
declined to comply with the request made in a Shaw letter sent on behalf of the proposed
plaintiff. They did so, in my view quite understandably, because of the very ancient  *d*
history of this matter, or rather the antiquity of the alleged cause of action if there be
one.

The facts briefly are as follows. The plaintiff is now just 29 having been born on 30
October 1959. She suffered from a squint, or cast, in her left eye when she was a baby. In
about April 1961 (though the date is uncertain) her parents evidently consulted a Mr
Lake about this. He conducted an operation either at the Fleming Memorial Hospital or  *e*
at the Royal Victoria Infirmary. The result was that her eyelid became nearly closed. Her
parents were reassured (I am taking the recital of events from the judgment), but some
three or four years later she was again taken to see Mr Lake and her parents were told
that nothing could be done.

Mr Lake then died, in 1964 or 1965. Then in about 1965, when the plaintiff was about
six, a Mr Howard was consulted on her behalf and she had a further operation. This  *f*
resulted in some improvement cosmetically, the eyelid was opening more, but since then
she has suffered pain, which has become progressively worse.

There was then total silence in the history until February 1987. In the course of a
medical examination for a job, it was then suggested to her by a nurse that the problem
was not of natural origin. That is how the judge saw the position at the time. But we
now know that in fact she has always known that her condition was connected (to put it  *g*
neutrally) with the operation which she had as a small child. The judge did not know
that, because he had no evidence relevant to the issue of limitation, and the question of
knowledge under the Limitation Act 1980 was not before him. But before us there has
been an application to admit evidence on that aspect. The ground was that it had not
been expected by those advising the plaintiff that issues of limitation would be gone into  *h*
on an application for pre-action discovery because they considered that these were not
relevant at that stage. Having looked at the evidence by consent we now know that the
plaintiff has always known that there was some connection between the condition of her
eye and one or other, or both, of these operations. But it was only in February 1987 that
it was suggested to her that she might have a claim for compensation. I put these matters
deliberately somewhat vaguely because in my view it is not appropriate to consider them  *j*
in any detail at this stage.

The position so far as limitation is concerned is that the plaintiff has attained her
majority and has been under no disability for many years. It may well be that she would
have great difficulty in overcoming the obstacle of knowledge within ss 11 and 14 of the
Limitation Act 1980, but of course there remains the question of the court's discretion
under s 33 of that Act to disapply the provisions of s 11.

Having regard to the antiquity of the history of this matter, the defendants have made
a it very clear that they intend to rely on limitation. They have also taken the view, again
understandably, that to search for documents and seek to ascertain what documents may
have been in their possession or power in the early 1960s is a very heavy burden, even on
the basis that the costs are going to be borne by the plaintiff, or in practice by the legal
aid fund in this case. Accordingly, they have taken the view that the facts of this case are
so strong in the context of limitation that they should contest this application under
b s 33(2) of the Supreme Court Act 1981.

The judge considered that, if the question of likelihood of ensuing proceedings was to
be considered apart from any question of limitation, then it was likely that proceedings
would ensue, in which case it is of course perfectly clear that Mrs Harris would be the
plaintiff and the Newcastle Health Authority would be the defendants. Accordingly, so
far as jurisdiction was concerned, he took the view that the provisions of s 33(2) of the
c 1981 Act were satisfied.

But on the question of discretion he thought on the material before him, in the same
way as the district registrar, that the plaintiff had virtually no prospect of succeeding
under ss 11 and 14 of the Limitation Act 1980 or of having the effect of these provisions
disapplied under s 33 of that Act. He concluded his judgment by saying:

d      'Accordingly, I conclude that this action is doomed to failure if the defendants
take the limitation point; and they have indicated, more or less in plain terms, that
they will. In those circumstances, I think that the district registrar was right, in the
exercise of his discretion, not to grant pre-trial discovery. There was no point in
doing so.'

The main point argued by counsel for the plaintiff was that it is always wrong for the
e court to pay any regard to the prospects of a limitation defence succeeding, and therefore
to the prospects of an action being doomed to failure, on an application of this nature. I
would not accept an extreme submission on those lines. If it is plain beyond doubt that a
defence of limitation will be raised and will succeed, then it seems to me that the court
must be entitled to take that matter into account. It would then say that no responsible
counsel would advise the institution of proceedings and that there would accordingly be
f no likelihood of proceedings taking place. That would oust the jurisdiction under s 33(2)
of the 1981 Act. Or it would say in such a case that, even if an action were to be instituted
in the face of the limitation defence, it would be a waste of time and costs to order
discovery because the action would be ill-founded, irresponsible, speculative or otherwise
within the spirit of the passage from the judgment of James LJ in *Dunning v Board of
Governors of United Liverpool Hospitals* [1973] 2 All ER 454 at 460, [1973] 1 WLR 586 at
g 593 which I have read. That would involve the rejection of the application on the ground
of discretion, and the result would be the same. However, since s 33 of the Limitation
Act 1980 applies to all personal injury actions and is therefore always a long-stop to a plea
of limitation in such actions, and since applications for pre-trial discovery can also only
be made in claims for personal injury (apart from death), one must obviously take
h account of s 33 of the 1980 Act before one can conclude that an action is so clearly bound
to be defeated by a plea of limitation as to be within the kind of situation which James LJ
envisaged in that passage.

Counsel for the plaintiff submitted that there can be no such situation because there is
always a residual discretion under s 33 of the Limitation Act 1980. He therefore says that
one can never say with certainty in a personal injury case that a defence of limitation
j must succeed. I think that goes too far. But I would accept that in the normal run of
cases, even where a defence of limitation has a strong prospect of success, like here, it is
very difficult for a court, on limited material, before pleadings and discovery, to conclude
at that stage that the situation is such that the proposed action is bound to fail and
therefore frivolous, vexatious or otherwise ill-founded. So in general I would accept the
submission of counsel that issues relevant to limitation should not enter into consideration
on applications for pre-trial discovery.

There are at least two good policy reasons for adopting that general approach. First, the court will not usually have the full material at that stage which may be relevant to *a* the matters raised by s 33 of the Limitation Act 1980. Second, the contrary approach would involve the need, at any rate to some extent, to examine issues as to limitation which will arise again at a later stage.

In the light of these comments I turn to this appeal on its facts as presently known. Certainly they are exceptionally strong from the point of view of antiquity, without prejudice to whatever may emerge on the issues relevant to limitation. However, this is *b* a case in which it is likely, having regard to what we have been told by counsel for the plaintiff, that proceedings will in fact be instituted irrespective of the outcome of this. application. I accept, coming from him, that this is a decision taken with full responsibility towards his client and the legal aid fund. On that basis the jurisdictional requirements of s 33(2) of the Supreme Court Act 1981 are satisfied and it is undesirable to say more than is necessary about the prospects of the limitation defence on the question of discretion. *c* All that I would say is that, although this is a very strong case, it is not clearly doomed to failure. The claim is not frivolous etc, within the passage in the judgment of James LJ in *Dunning's* case which I have read so as to require the refusal of this application.

On that basis the advantages of this pre-trial application are obvious, as illustrated by the two cases to which I have referred. I think that it should be granted on the basis that the most careful consideration will be given to the question whether it is proper to *d* institute proceedings thereafter.

For the sake of completeness I should add that we were also referred to the decision of this court in *Kennett v Brown* [1988] 2 All ER 600. That involved the question in a different context, whether or not the merits of a defence of limitation should be considered at an early stage. I derived some assistance by way of analogy from the remarks of Lord Donaldson MR in favour of the view that limitation should be *e* considered at its appropriate stage (see [1988] 2 All ER 600 at 602–603, [1988] 1 WLR 582 at 585). Furthermore, I was much impressed throughout by the consideration, which was substantially undisputed, that it would be unusual in practice for issues under ss 11, 14 and 33 of the Limitation Act 1980 to be heard and decided prior to discovery.

Accordingly, while I have full sympathy for the view expressed by the judge, I would allow this appeal. *f*

**MANN LJ.** I agree; I also would allow this appeal. As it seems to me, a court confronted with an application under s 33(2) of the Supreme Court Act 1981 has to ask itself two questions. The first is jurisdictional; the second is as to discretion.

The jurisdictional question is resolved by determining the likelihood of participation in proceedings and, as James LJ said in *Dunning v Board of Governors of the United Liverpool* *g* *Hospitals* [1973] 2 All ER 454 at 460, [1973] 1 WLR 586 at 594, likelihood of participation means a reasonable prospect of participation in the proceedings.

It may well be that questions of limitation could bear on reasonable prospect. However, if satisfied that there is reasonable prospect, the court then must decide how, as a matter of discretion, to exercise it. I would not wish to lay down any general rule as to the *h* exercise of discretion; to do so would be plainly undesirable. But on the facts of this particular case I am of the diffident view that it was wrong for the judge to say that the action was doomed to failure. With respect, I think he was wrong in the sense that he was pre-supposing a decision under s 33 of the Limitation Act 1980.

On that very narrow ground I would allow the appeal.

*j*

**SIR JOHN MEGAW.** I agree with the order proposed by Kerr LJ.

I have felt very considerable difficulty in two aspects in particular of this appeal. The first is as to the approach to the interpretation of the words in s 33(2) of the Supreme Court Act 1981, which refer to the application being made by a 'person who appears to the High Court to be likely to be a party to subsequent proceedings' in the court in which

a claim for personal injuries is likely to be made. The word 'likely' to my mind, in its
*a* ordinary and sensible meaning, involves something which is not unlikely, which is more
probable than not.

If that were the position, then I think it would be difficult, on the material in this case,
to say that it is likely that there would be subsequent proceedings if the position were
that those proceedings were certain, or almost certain, to be defeated by a defence under
the Limitation Act 1980.

*b* However, on the authority of this court in *Dunning v Board of Governors of the United
Liverpool Hospitals* [1973] 2 All ER 454 esp at 460, [1973] 1 WLR 586 esp at 594 per James
LJ, I have come to the conclusion that we are bound by that authority to construe the
word 'likely', in the context of the section to which I have referred, as having the meaning
which James LJ gives to it when he says: 'I would construe "likely" . . . as meaning a
"reasonable prospect".' You can have a reasonable prospect even though you may fall
*c* considerably short of a 50% chance. Another phrase which might be used to describe the
same effect is one which was used long ago by Asquith LJ 'on the cards': see *Victoria
Laundry Ltd v Newman Industries Ltd* [1949] 1 All ER 997 at 1003, [1949] 2 KB 528 at 540.

Staughton J in his judgment in this case accepted that the requirement of s 33(2) of the
1981 Act, which may be a jurisdictional requirement, of its being 'likely' had been
fulfilled.

*d* The other difficulty which I have felt is as to the discretion exercised by Staughton J. I
have not found it easy to come to a conclusion whether it is proper to say in this case that
Staughton J erred in principle in the exercise of his discretion, which he undoubtedly
had in this case. However, I am satisfied in the end by the submissions of counsel for the
plaintiff that it cannot be said with any certainty that on discovery facts would not
emerge which would be relevant to the issue of limitation. That is with reference in
*e* particular to s 11 of the Limitation Act 1980 and with reference to the criteria set out in
ss 33(1)(a), (b) and (3)(a) to (f) of the 1980 Act, which are relevant to the discretionary
exclusion of the time limit for actions in respect of personal injury or death.

In those circumstances I do not think that it can be said in this case that the criterion
laid down by James LJ in his judgment in *Dunning v Board of Governors of United Liverpool
Hospitals* [1973] 2 All ER 454 at 460, [1973] 1 WLR 586 at 594 has been fulfilled, that is
*f* the criterion for refusing an application of this sort. Kerr LJ has already read that, but I
will repeat it:

> 'In order to take advantage of the section the applicant for relief must disclose the
> nature of the claim he intends to make and show not only the intention of making
> it but also that there is reasonable basis for making it. Ill-founded, irresponsible and
*g* > speculative allegations or allegations based merely on hope would not provide a
> reasonable basis for an intended claim in subsequent proceedings.'

I am satisfied that in the end this case cannot be said to fall within the condemnation
of that sentence and accordingly I agree that the appeal should be allowed.

*h* *Appeal allowed. No order as to costs.*

Solicitors: *Peter Maughan & Co*, Gateshead (for the plaintiff); *Wilkinson Maughan*,
Newcastle upon Tyne (for the defendant).

Wendy Shockett    Barrister.

# Dimino v Dimino

a

COURT OF APPEAL, CIVIL DIVISION
PURCHAS LJ AND SIR DENYS BUCKLEY
7 OCTOBER 1988

*Divorce – Custody – Custody proceedings – Procedure – Proposed order – Judge receiving court* b
*welfare officer's report and indorsing proposed order on it – Parties notified of proposed order –*
*Whether judge prejudging issues before hearing evidence – Whether judge's order invalid.*

Following the divorce of the parties the father applied for custody of the four children of
the marriage who were still minors. The court welfare officer prepared a report which
was referred to the judge who had granted the decree nisi. The judge indorsed the report  c
with his proposed order, which was that custody of the children be given to the mother
and that no order be made as to access. The court office, in accordance with its usual
practice, then sent a pro forma form to both parties which stated that the judge had read
the court welfare officer's report and set out the judge's proposed order. The form
requested the parties to notify the court whether they agreed with the proposal or
whether a hearing would be required. The father requested a hearing, at which the judge  d
heard evidence from the parties and the welfare officer and saw three of the children in
his room. The judge then made an order in the same terms as his proposed order. The
father appealed to the Court of Appeal, contending that the judge's order should be set
aside and a new trial ordered because he had prejudged the issue when he read the court
welfare officer's report and indorsed his proposed order on it.

e

**Held** – Although the practice of the judge indorsing his proposed order on the court
welfare officer's report before the hearing of the application for custody was a serious
irregularity, it had not caused a substantial wrong or miscarriage since there had been a
full and detailed investigation of the matter at the hearing and on the facts before him
the judge had reached the right decision. The appeal would therefore be dismissed (see
p 284 c, p 286 b j to p 287 c f h j, post).    f
*Fowler v Fowler and Sines* [1963] 1 All ER 119 distinguished.
Per curiam. The practice of notifying the parties of the form of order which the judge,
having seen the court welfare officer's report, is minded to make is highly irregular since
it can give the impression that the judge has predetermined the issues before hearing the
evidence (see p 282 d e and p 287 c to e j, post).

g

**Notes**
For the procedure on the hearing of an application for custody of children of the
marriage, see 13 Halsbury's Laws (4th edn) para 942.

**Cases referred to in judgments**
*Banbury v Bank of Montreal* [1918] AC 626, [1918–19] All ER Rep 1, HL.    h
*Fowler v Fowler and Sines* [1963] 1 All ER 119, [1963] P 311, [1963] 2 WLR 155, CA.
*H v H (irregularity: effect on order)* (1983) 4 FLR 119.
*K (infants), Re* [1962] 3 All ER 1000, [1963] Ch 381, [1962] 3 WLR 1517, CA; *rvsg* [1962]
     3 All ER 178, [1963] Ch 381, [1962] 3 WLR 752.
*Smith v Charles Baker & Sons* [1891] AC 325, [1891–4] All ER Rep 69, HL.

j

**Interlocutory appeal**
Lucio Dimino (the father) appealed from the order made by his Honour Judge Hutton
in the Gloucester County Court on 4 February 1988 granting custody of the minor

children of the marriage to Anne Jacqueline Dimino (the mother) and refusing the
a  father's application for access. The facts are set out in the judgment of Purchas LJ.

*Charles Geekie* for the father.
*Alicia Collinson* for the mother.

**PURCHAS LJ.** This is an appeal by Lucio Dimino (to whom I shall refer as 'the father')
b  against an order made by his Honour Judge Hutton in the Gloucester County Court on 4
February 1988. In that order the judge refused an application made by the father for
access to four of the five children of the family resulting from his marriage to the
respondent, Anne Jacqueline Dimino (to whom I shall refer as 'the mother').
   The appeal has raised unusual and important points with which this court has been
asked to deal.
c     The history, so far as it is relevant to the appeal and the issues raised, can be shortly
stated. The parties were married on 12 November 1969. There were five children: A,
who was born on 13 February 1970, and so is 18 years of age and with whom the court is
not concerned; M, born on 20 June 1972; L, born on 30 November 1974; V, born on
14 August 1979; and L, born on 24 September 1985. The marriage came into difficulties
in the mid-1970s.
d     Affidavit evidence in the file, with which we have not been concerned in detail,
disclosed allegations, denials and counter-allegations. There was a petition in October
1975 which was dismissed in February of the following year, followed by another
petition (the effective petition in this matter) filed by the father and dated 18 September
1985. Decree nisi was pronounced by Judge Hutton on 4 February 1988.
   The father applied for custody of the children in February 1986. A report by the court
e  welfare officer was ordered in March 1986, but the report was not presented until August
1987 because for some reason, undisclosed, the documents required by Mr Swan, the
court welfare officer, did not reach him until June 1987. I mention this to indicate that
nothing can be said against Mr Swan for any delay which occurred.
   The parties separated in May 1985 when the mother left the matrimonial home in
f  Aylesbury taking the children with her. After a short stay in a refuge she established a
home for herself and the children in Elkstone, Gloucestershire. She did not tell the father
where she had gone. It is not necessary to consider the reasons for that, but it was some
time before the father discovered their whereabouts.
   There was access between the father and the children which took place in Aylesbury,
but the evidence is that it was not satisfactory from the point of view of the children.
g  Again, that is a matter of background.
   Having received the documents, which included an affidavit from the mother in June
1987, Mr Swan prepared his report of August 1987. From a document which is in the
court file it is clear that the report, when received, was referred to the judge by a clerk in
the Gloucester County Court office with the request: 'Your Honour, do you make a
proposed order?' and the judge indorsed that report with the following: 'C of M, L, V
h  and L to P. No order A. No order for access.' That indorsement was dated 2 September
1987. On a pro forma document headed with the names of the parties and date-stamped
16 December 1987 there is the following:

   'TAKE NOTICE THAT pursuant to an Order, a Court Welfare Officer's Report has
   been filed a copy of which is enclosed herewith. The Judge has read the Report and
   proposes that an Order be made in the following terms: 1. Custody of [M, L, V and
j     L] be granted to [the mother]. 2. There be no order regarding the child [A]. 3. There
   be no order for access. Please notify the Court by the 30th Day of September 1987
   whether: (A) The parties agree to this proposal, or (B) A hearing will be required. *In
   the event of (B) you should* (1) Supply an agreed time estimate, and (2) Comply with

paragraphs 3 and 4 of Practice Direction dated 16th July 1981 [[1981] 2 All ER 1056, [1981] 1 WLR 1162, the details of which are not germane to this appeal].'     *a*

This pro forma form contains the names of the parties together with the details of the proposed order completed in manuscript. Counsel has informed the court that this is a routine procedure followed in the Gloucestershire County Court, the idea behind the form being an invitation to the parties to agree and thereby save the time and costs of litigation.

The sending of the order in this case is relied on as being the corner-stone of the appeal.     *b* Counsel for the father, who has argued this appeal with skill and attraction, says that this is an irregularity of such dimension that it is incurable. He says that 'The Judge' is not identified. In practice, from what I have said earlier in this judgment, it is clear 'The Judge' refers to Judge Hutton who tried the matter.

Secondly, counsel submits that on its face this document discloses that the judge has prejudged the issues which are due to be litigated before him. Therefore this is a travesty     *c* of justice.

Thirdly, it imposes an intolerable burden on the party against whom the effect of the order will run, and that he can never be satisfied that justice has been done.

For my part I see there is great force in those submissions, had the matter ended there. In any event in this case (and in almost all but the most exceptional circumstances) an     *d* indication of a prejudging of issues of this kind would be an irregularity of great significance, and is a procedure (if it be one regularly adopted in this county court) which ought not to be followed.

We have been informed by counsel for the mother that in her experience this is the only county court where this procedure is adopted. I think I have said sufficient to make it clear that my view is that it is highly undesirable that this procedure should be     *e* continued.

It is now necessary to consider what happened thereafter. There was a hearing before the judge. The parties neither knew nor inquired whether the hearing was to be before the same judge. Counsel for the father has informed the court that this procedure has caused a great deal of anxiety to litigants, including his client in this case, but a considered view was taken (rightly or wrongly) that it would be disadvantageous to his client, the     *f* father, to take a point at the beginning of the trial that the irregularity which had occurred was such that it would not be possible for the issues to be tried with justice. That was a tactical decision made in the context of uncertainty as to the way in which the judge might have decided the issue. The judge therefore continued to hear the application without submissions being made by the complaining party. Indeed, at the end of the hearing, when it was clear that the judge had not departed in any way from the order     *g* proposed in the pro forma form of 16 September, no objection was taken, and no application was made for a new trial or that the order should be set aside.

The rules applicable in the county court have not been argued before this court, but in my view such an application would have been open to the parties at that stage.

Concerning the welfare report, that came down firmly against custody being granted to the father. Indeed, at the outset of the hearing before the judge it was made clear that     *h* the father was in fact only seeking access. However, as to that, the report was by no means unequivocal. Referring to the children with whom we are concerned it indicates that V would see her father if he visits, but the impression was that such a visit would have to fit in with her village activities. So far as L is concerned, the report says: 'She is ready to see her father here but indicates no interest in staying access.' Then, so far as M is concerned: 'He is also prepared to see his father but he has a job at a nearby farm which     *j* seems to take precedence in his thinking. I rather suspect it is more important to him than school.'

In an interview with Mr Swan, the court welfare officer, the father gave him this impression:

*a*
'He is of the opinion that he and his co-habitee could look after and raise the children responsibly. He is certainly not interested in visiting access and if he were not to be granted custody, I am quite sure that staying access (with the children making the journey to Aylesbury) would be the minimum requirement.'

As part of his conclusion Mr Swan said:

*b*
'I have attempted to outline the conflicting attitudes of the parties towards [M, L, V and L] but do not doubt that the custody of these happy children should be granted to the petitioner mother. Access is another matter. The apparent lack of interest by the children in visiting their father is matched by his resistance to visiting Elkstone to see them. The court will have to decide what is to happen, bearing in mind the respondent's feelings with regard to the restraints of the law. Supervision is not recommended.'

*c*
It is necessary to mention one further matter, and that is that, so far as visiting access in Gloucestershire is concerned, the mother's attitude was that such visiting access in her home was not practicable because of the difficulties she alleges that the father makes on such visits; but her view was that, if he wished to come to Gloucestershire and take the children out, she would not object to that, or to any other visiting access with which the *d* children would co-operate.

Another matter to mention concerning the history of this case is the decision by Mr Swan to write a letter to the three middle children, M, L and V. That letter is dated 25 August 1987, addressed to the three children, and it reads as follows:

*e*
'When I called to see you on 16th June none of you seemed to be very interested in seeing your father and when he called at Elkstone on 23rd July he did not get to see you except through the window. I have asked your mother to try to get you to write a letter to your father or at least telephone him. If you do not want to see your father it will be best if you tell him. At the moment your father thinks your mother is stopping you from seeing him and that is not very fair to your mother. Finally, if you do write to your father, keep a copy of the letters for your mother's solicitor.'

*f*
That letter has been strongly criticised by counsel for the father on the ground that the welfare officer was in fact descending into the dispute between the parties and thereby disentitling himself from taking an objective position on the issue of access. I find it impossible to follow counsel in that submission because in my view this was a very genuine letter, written with every intention of helping to restore some contact between the father and the children. The final paragraph of the letter, which has attracted *g* criticism, in my judgment has no sinister connotation attaching to it. It was important that both parties should be aware of what was happening and that the mother should know if the children wrote to their father as a result of Mr Swan's intervention.

Counsel also complains that the writing of this letter by Mr Swan was not disclosed to the father. It may have been better if Mr Swan had informed the father, but I see no prejudice to the father resulting from such an omission.

*h*
The children wrote letters which are before the court, which I found to be charming letters. I do not propose to read them, considering the age of the writers. It is quite clear they were not dictated by anyone. They are genuine letters, and they show a degree of sympathy with their father. The letter sent by the welfare officer has not generated any antipathy in these children because they explain why they are not anxious to go to see their father in Aylesbury and they have made comments as to other matters which they *j* found embarrassing or distressing. They are frank, friendly letters. Inasmuch as any criticism has been made of Mr Swan, I find such criticism unjustified. In my opinion Mr Swan acted perfectly properly in these circumstances. Moreover, so far as this court is concerned, it is significant evidence of the genuine attitude of these children in relation to the question of access to their father.

In fairness to Mr Swan, I should also refer to the fact that he was challenged in cross-examination concerning this letter and he dealt fully and frankly with that challenge. *a*
He said:

'I agree it is unusual to address children in this way in a letter, but the wife has not been able to persuade them to write. I wanted to encourage them at least to write. It seemed likely that the letters would confirm their previous views. Frankly, I did not think they would actually write. I do not think my position was *b* compromised.'

If the judge formed the view (as I believe he did) that those answers given by Mr Swan were genuine and impressive, he was fully entitled to take that view. For my own part, had I been in his position, I would have taken the same view.

It is therefore necessary to consider the hearing itself in the context of what I find was a serious irregularity, to see whether or not a retrial should be ordered. The appropriate *c* order in this matter is RSC Ord 59, r 11(2), which reads:

'The Court of Appeal shall not be bound to order a new trial on the ground of misdirection, or of the improper admission or rejection of evidence, or because the verdict of the jury was not taken upon a question which the judge at the trial was not asked to leave to them, unless in the opinion of the Court of Appeal some *d* substantial wrong or miscarriage has been thereby occasioned.'

The question in the particular context of this case is: has that irregularity caused a substantial wrong or miscarriage?

Counsel for the father has referred the court to two authorities in particular in support of his submission that, whatever happened at the trial, such was the gravity of this irregularity that it was incurable. He relied on *Fowler v Fowler and Sines* [1963] 1 All ER *e* 119, [1963] P 311. That was a case in which, after the conclusion of argument, the judge requested the parties and their legal representatives to leave the court, but invited the welfare officer to remain and interviewed her for some minutes privately. Without disclosing to the parties, or giving them an opportunity to make submissions on the matter, the judge decided the summons. This court held that that was such an irregularity *f* that a retrial should be ordered. Willmer LJ said ([1963] 1 All ER 119 at 123, [1963] P 311 at 319):

'For those reasons, as well as for the reason that, in my judgment this case is really covered by the ratio of the decision in *Re K. (infants)* ([1962] 3 All ER 1000, [1963] Ch 381), I am satisfied that the learned judge here took an irregular and objectionable course when he interviewed the welfare officer privately and in the absence of the *g* parties. The effect of that was, in my view, to vitiate the decision at which he arrived.'

Counsel for the father also referred the court to *H v H (irregularity: effect on order)* (1983) 4 FLR 119. In that case, before the hearing between the parties, the judge had a private conversation with the welfare officer in which the case was discussed. The judge *h* stated that nothing which was said had influenced his decision, although it was alleged that the discussion had prompted the welfare officer to make a comment to one of the parties as to a possible favourable outcome. The party not granted care and control appealed on the merits of the case and also on the basis that misleading information had been given by the welfare officer which had led to insufficient evidence being given.

On the general principle rather than on the details, counsel particularly relied on the *j* short judgment delivered by Eveleigh LJ, which agreed with the leading judgment of Arnold P. Eveleigh LJ said (at 121):

'I agree. The unsatisfactory nature of the situation is reinforced when one sees the ground of appeal which was originally pleaded, namely that, as a result of a *a* communication from the officer concerned, one of the parties refrained from adducing evidence which might otherwise have been adduced. One has to consider these irregularities in relation to the facts of the case, but it would take very strong considerations to the contrary to cause me to refrain from saying that this irregularity is fatal and that the matter should be tried again.'

Earlier, in the leading judgment, Arnold P said (at 120):

*b*        'Any private conversation between the judge and a person concerned with the case, such as, for example, a reporting officer, which is not disclosed to the parties, or of which the parties would not otherwise know in detail, must involve an infraction of that principle, whether it takes place before or after the witnesses have been heard and whether it is possible, however improbable, that the judge might have been influenced in his decision by what had passed, or whether that matter *c*        could be safely ignored as a possibility in spite of the irregularity.'

Counsel submitted that the burden of those two authorities was such that, having prejudged this matter and apparently considering only the court welfare officer's report, which as I have said was equivocal on the question of access, Judge Hutton had disqualified himself from thereafter doing justice between the parties. Counsel for the *d* mother distinguished the present case on the basis that, after the irregularity had occurred, there was a full hearing of this matter in which the judge heard evidence from the parties, from the welfare officer, at length, and saw the three middle children, M, L and V. She submitted that, had there been any prejudging of the issues involved, this was wholly displaced by the very careful investigation of the facts and issues given in evidence before the judge.

*e* Counsel for the mother also referred the court to the note to RSC Ord 59, r 11 in *The Supreme Court Practice 1988* vol 1, para 59/11/10, which reads as follows:

        'It is not now ever a complete answer to an application for a new trial that the point of law relied on was not raised in the Court below, it is a matter for the discretion of the Court to allow it to be raised [and then *Banbury v Bank of Montreal* [1918] AC 626, [1918–19] All ER Rep 1 is referred to]. If the complaint is of a defect *f*        in the proceedings, which could have been remedied if attention had been drawn to it below, the Court of Appeal will commonly not give effect to the application . . . and a party may preclude himself, as a matter of justice by his course of conduct of the action, from complaining of the decision—for example [and then an example is given].'

*g* In support of that, counsel referred the court to *Smith v Charles Baker & Sons* [1891] AC 325, [1891–4] All ER Rep 69 and to the speech of Lord Halsbury LC, dealing with the question of the failure to take a point of law below. Lord Halsbury LC said ([1891] AC 325 at 333, [1891–4] All ER Rep 69 at 73):

        'My Lords, I think there are good reasons for the enactment which has so limited *h*        an appeal, and in truth even where written pleadings render such precautions as the statute has enforced in the county court less necessary, the same precaution has been constantly enforced where applications for a new trial have been made in the Superior Courts. It is obvious that it would be unjust to one of the parties if the other could lie by and afterwards, having failed on the contention that he in fact set up, be permitted to rely on some other point not suggested at the trial, but which if *j*        had been suggested might have been answered by evidence . . .'

In this case, as counsel for the father has very frankly informed the court, there was a deliberate decision not to apply to the judge on the basis that he should disqualify himself from doing justice at the trial because of his prejudging of the issues after receiving only the welfare officer's report. The decision was a tactical one. It was thought that such an application, if refused, would antagonise the judge.

In those circumstances I would be of the opinion it would be wrong to permit this point to be taken on this appeal in the absence of an application to the judge for an adjournment for a trial before a different judge. But I do not have to rely on that decision because, had such an application been made and refused by the judge, in my view the position would have remained the same on an appeal against his refusal on the basis that here his refusal, if it were wrong, would not have caused a miscarriage of justice in the light of the detailed investigation and the evidence led before him. In my judgment his conclusion was inevitable in all the circumstances of the case.

It is clear from the evidence adduced before the judge that at least two of these children are capable of expressing views of their own, and that they in fact did so. The youngest of them, however, expressed no view at all, but the judge, on all the evidence before him (including the views of the children expressed in their letters), came to the conclusion it would not be right to make an order for access and that to make an order which forced access would be detrimental to the welfare of the children themselves.

Reverting to the evidence given by the welfare officer, Mr Swan was examined and cross-examined at some length on this aspect. His evidence was important. The fact that he gave such evidence disperses any criticism that could be levied against him concerning the delay which occurred between the ordering of the report and its preparation.

The reason for such delay has not been identified. When questioned by counsel for the father, Mr Swan said:

'I have formed the impression of children settled in an idyllic situation. They have shut out their previous life to some extent. I do not get the impression that the wife is opposed to access if the children desire it. She adopts a neutral stance. I do not think she has either encouraged or discouraged. All the children are well able to express themselves, even the 8-year-old.'

He then deals with the question of access at Aylesbury, for which the father was pressing: 'Aylesbury involves bus journeys and they lack the interest in seeing him.' Then he deals with the letters, to which I have already referred. Counsel for the mother then asked him:

'Q. What are your views on the husband seeing [L]? A. I would have strong opposition. I do wonder what benefit it would be to her. It is the three central children that are vitally important to this question.'

Then counsel invited the judge to see the three middle children, M, L and V, in his room. Counsel for the father then submitted that it was not appropriate to see the children, given the suspicion about why they think what they do. I take it that is a reference to the letter written by Mr Swan, but it may not be. Counsel said: 'There is a severe danger that the views do not come from the hearts of the children.'

Deciding on those submissions, the judge said: 'It will be a disappointment for the children not to have their say. It will not harm them. It might be helpful. I will see the three [M, L and V].' Having seen them the judge then said: 'I have briefly seen them. [M and L] say they do not want to see their father. [V] says nothing. I can see no advantage in these children seeing their father.' He was then addressed by both counsel and gave his judgment.

Counsel for the father, very properly if I may say so, in his skeleton argument does not attack the exercise of the discretion of the judge in the context of the evidence which was before him. His attack centres on the assertion that the judge had disqualified himself by previously prejudging the matter, and that therefore there should be a retrial before another judge.

I hope I have already made clear in this judgment the reasons why I consider this submission must fail. In my judgment there is no evidence of any kind to indicate that a the careful investigation carried out by the judge, taking into account all the evidence, including his seeing the children, and bearing in mind no application was made that he should not try the case, led to a miscarriage of justice.

Having said this, I sympathise with the father, who feels that at one stage there was a prejudging of the issue without his having a chance to put his case to the judge. However, Judge Hutton is an experienced and skilful judge, and, although the father may genuinely hold a suspicion that the judge did not fairly try these issues, I have no doubt in my mind b that the judge applied a perfectly judicial approach to this matter and, moreover, reached the only conclusion to which he could properly come, on the body of evidence placed before him. In those circumstances, this case is distinguishable from *Fowler v Fowler and Sines* [1963] 1 All ER 119, [1963] P 311 and *H v H* (1983) 4 FLR 119.

Exercising the discretion which is open to this court granted by RSC Ord 59, r 11, I would dismiss this appeal, and would not order a retrial.

c

**SIR DENYS BUCKLEY.** I agree, and I do not wish to add anything to what Purchas LJ has said on the general issues arising in this matter between the parties and affecting the children who are concerned. But I would wish to say something about the criticism that has been made of the procedure adopted in this particular county court by which d parties in proceedings of this kind are notified of the form of order which a judge who has seen a welfare officer's report, but who has not yet had an opportunity of considering any of the evidence in the case, is minded to make in the light of that report.

It is, I think, of the highest importance that a judge before whom issues are to come for determination should avoid any suggestion, before he has had an opportunity of hearing or reading the evidence involved, that he has reached a view as to the relief which he is likely to give in determining the matter. Not only is it desirable that the e court should avoid any such suggestion, but it is desirable that there should be no grounds for any of the parties concerned to think that the judge may have arrived at even a preliminary view as to the order which he will ultimately make.

That the practice adopted in the present case is likely to offend against that consideration is I think quite clear. Purchas LJ has read the communication dated 16 September 1987 f which was involved in this case, but I would read it again, so far as is appropriate:

'TAKE NOTICE THAT pursuant to an Order, a Court Welfare Officer's Report has been filed a copy of which is enclosed herewith. The Judge has read the Report and proposes that an Order may be made in the following terms . . .'

Then is set out the order which in the particular case the judge has it in mind to make.

g It is possible and perhaps probable that a lawyer would appreciate that that is no more than an indication of the kind of relief that the judge thinks may turn out, on consideration of the facts, to be the kind of order which he will make. But I think that is not the impression which would be given to a litigant who is not an experienced litigant or lawyer.

If the judge says that he proposes to make a particular order, unless the parties require h a hearing, it must necessarily suggest to a party in the proceedings that he has arrived at a conclusion as to the type of order he is disposed or likely to make. It is true that the document in question uses the expression 'may be made', but in my view it is clearly a document which is likely to convey to the mind of the recipient that the judge has taken a preliminary view. In my view that must necessarily give rise to the difficulty that the recipient of the document will think that the judge has predetermined the case, and that, j as I say, is something which it is of the highest importance should be avoided.

Consequently, I entirely concur in what Purchas LJ has said with regard to this practice. One can see that, from a practical administrative point of view, the use of a document in this form may have been intended merely to save time and expense and, in those ways, to benefit litigants, but it is a practice which has inherent defects of such a nature that it is a thoroughly unsatisfactory practice to adopt.

I do not wish to add anything to what Purchas LJ has said concerning other matters which have arisen for consideration in this case. I am in entire agreement with what he *a* has said.

*Appeal dismissed. No order as to costs.*

Solicitors: *Parrott & Coales*, Aylesbury (for the father); *Linda Stapleton & Co*, Gloucester (for the mother). *b*

Bebe Chua  Barrister.

# Practice Note *c*

COURT OF APPEAL, CIVIL DIVISION
LORD DONALDSON OF LYMINGTON MR, WOOLF LJ AND SIR DENYS BUCKLEY
9 MAY 1989

*Counsel – Fees – Note of judgment – Brief fee including remuneration for taking note of judgment,* *d*
*having it transcribed, submitting it to judge for approval and revising it if required, and providing*
*copies to Court of Appeal, solicitors and client.*

**LORD DONALDSON OF LYMINGTON MR** made the following statement at the sitting of the court. For the avoidance of doubt I wish, in agreement with the General Council of the Bar, to make it clear that counsel's brief fee includes his remuneration for *e* taking a note of the judgment of the court, having the note transcribed accurately, submitting the note to the judge for approval where appropriate, revising it if so required by the judge, and providing any copies required to the Court of Appeal, his instructing solicitors and his lay client. Accordingly, save in exceptional circumstances, there can be no justification for charging any additional fee for such work.

*f*

Mary Rose Plummer  Barrister.

a   **Dawson v Inland Revenue Commissioners**

HOUSE OF LORDS
LORD KEITH OF KINKEL, LORD TEMPLEMAN, LORD ACKNER, LORD OLIVER OF AYLMERTON AND
LORD LOWRY
4 APRIL, 4 MAY 1989

b
*Income tax – Foreign possessions – Income arising from possessions out of United Kingdom –
Trustee – Liability – Discretionary settlement – Principal beneficiaries not resident in United
Kingdom – No beneficiary entitled to income as it accrued – Trust assets and income administered
outside United Kingdom – No income remitted to United Kingdom – Three trustees of whom only
one resident in United Kingdom – Whether United Kingdom resident trustee liable for assessment
c  to income tax on income derived from trust assets – Income and Corporation Taxes Act 1970,
s 108, Sch D, para 1(a), s 114(1).*

Three trusts were made, on dates between 1946 and 1965, by settlors who were domiciled
and resident in the United Kingdom, the principal beneficiaries under each being
members of the family of C, who in 1969 emigrated to Switzerland and became
d  permanently resident there with his family. Between 12 February 1974 and 14 March
1977 the taxpayer was the only trustee of the trusts who was resident in the United
Kingdom, the other trustees being a Swiss bank and a Liechtenstein company. During
that period most of the trust assets were invested in securities of non-United Kingdom
companies, the income therefrom being paid into accounts of the trustees maintained in
the Swiss bank. Distributions of income were decided at meetings of the trustees held in
e  Switzerland, no beneficiary having any absolute vested interest in any of the trust income,
and none of that income was remitted to the United Kingdom. The taxpayer was assessed
for the year 1975–76 to income tax in respect of the trust income under Sch D, Case V
on income arising from possessions out of the United Kingdom. The taxpayer appealed,
contending that, even if it were accepted that the trust income arose or accrued to him,
no assessment could be made on him because he was not a person 'receiving or entitled
f  to' that income within s 114(1)[a] of the Income and Corporation Taxes Act 1970 and that
income did not arise or accrue to him within s 108, Sch D, para 1(a)[b] of that Act and was
not within the charge to tax under that schedule. A Special Commissioner upheld the
assessments but, on appeal, the judge reversed his determination. The Crown appealed
to the Court of Appeal, which dismissed its appeal. The Crown appealed to the House of
Lords.
g
**Held** – Where trustees of a settlement were jointly entitled to income of the settlement
which arose from assets situated outside the United Kingdom, and only one of them was
resident within the United Kingdom, that trustee was not a person to whom annual
profits or gains arose or accrued within para 1(a) of Sch D in s 108 of the 1970 Act, nor
was he a person 'receiving or entitled to' the income within s 114 of that Act. He was
h  therefore not a person liable for income tax on such income. Accordingly, the taxpayer
was not liable to tax on the income of the three settlements and the Crown's appeal
would therefore be dismissed (see p 291 h j and p 292 a e to h, post).
   Decision of the Court of Appeal [1988] 3 All ER 753 affirmed.

j   **Notes**
For tax in respect of income arising from possessions out of the United Kingdom, see 23
Halsbury's Laws (4th edn) paras 611–618, and for cases on the subject, see 28(1) Digest
(2nd reissue) 436–449, 2103–2156.

---

a   Section 114(1), so far as material, is set out at p 291 e, post
b   Section 108, so far as material, is set out at p 291 c d, post

For the liability to tax of non-resident trustees, see 23 Halsbury's Laws (4th edn) para
850.

In relation to tax for the year 1988–89 and subsequent years of assessment and for
companies' accounting periods ending after 5 April 1988 ss 108 and 114 of the Income
and Corporation Taxes Act 1970 were replaced by ss 18 and 59 of the Income and
Corporation Taxes Act 1988. For ss 18 and 59 of the 1988 Act, see 44 Halsbury's Statutes
(4th edn) 47, 96.

## Appeal

The Commissioners of Inland Revenue appealed, with leave of the Appeal Committee of
the House of Lords given on 26 October 1988 on terms as to costs, against the decision of
the Court of Appeal (Kerr, Dillon and Nicholls LJJ) ([1988] 3 All ER 753, [1988] 1 WLR
930) on 25 May 1988 dismissing an appeal by the commissioners against an order of
Vinelott J ([1987] STC 371, [1987] 1 WLR 716) dated 10 March 1987 allowing an appeal
by Oliver Nainby Dawson (the taxpayer) by way of case stated (set out at [1987] STC 372–
378) by a Commissioner for the Special Purposes of the Income Tax Acts upholding
assessments to income tax made on the taxpayer for the year 1975–76 on income of a
trust fund, arising to him and two non-resident trustees of a settlement comprising
foreign investments, to which he and they were jointly entitled. The facts are set out in
the opinion of Lord Keith.

*John Mummery* for the Crown.
*Stephen Oliver QC* and *James Kessler* for the taxpayer.

Their Lordships took time for consideration.

4 May. The following opinions were delivered.

**LORD KEITH OF KINKEL.** My Lords, the respondent in this appeal (the taxpayer)
was, until he resigned in 1977, a trustee under each of three discretionary settlements
governed by English law made at various dates between 1946 and 1965 by members of a
family called Cotton, who were on these dates domiciled and resident in England. The
principal beneficiaries under each trust were the issue of a Mr Gordon Cotton, one of the
settlors. In 1969 Mr Gordon Cotton emigrated to Switzerland with his immediate family
and became permanently resident there. Up until 12 February 1974 each trust had three
trustees all resident in the United Kingdom, including the taxpayer. On that date the
two other trustees resigned and there were assumed in their place an individual residing
in Switzerland and a Liechtenstein company.

During the fiscal year 1975–76 the trust assets consisted principally in holdings of
securities of non-United Kingdom companies, though there were also some small
holdings in United Kingdom companies and some land in England. The certificates for
the foreign company securities were in the name of a Swiss bank or other foreign
nominees, and the income from these securities was paid into accounts in the name of
the trustees at the same Swiss bank. In the year in question certain small sums were paid
by the trustees out of income to Mr Gordon Cotton for the benefit of his infant children,
and all the rest of the income was accumulated. The distributions were decided on at a
meeting of the trustees held in Switzerland.

Further details about the three settlements are to be found in the judgment of Vinelott
J in the Chancery Division (see [1987] STC 371, [1987] 1 WLR 716), and it is unnecessary
for present purposes to recapitulate them.

In respect of that fiscal year 1975–76 the appellants, the Commissioners of Inland
Revenue, assessed the taxpayer to basic rate tax and additional rate tax on the whole
income of the three settlements, including that arising from the foreign assets comprised
therein.

The taxpayer accepted liability for tax on the income from United Kingdom assets,
a but disputed liability for tax on income from the foreign assets. He appealed to a single
Special Commissioner, who decided against him. That decision was reversed by Vinelott
J on 10 March 1987, and the reversal was affirmed by the Court of Appeal (Kerr, Dillon
and Nicholls LJJ) on 25 May 1988 (see [1988] 3 All ER 753, [1988] 1 WLR 930). The
Crown now appeals, with leave given here, to your Lordships' House.

The issue in the appeal, which has not been considered in any previous reported case,
b is whether, where one of a number of trustees of a settlement resides in the United
Kingdom but the other or others reside abroad, the one who resides in the United
Kingdom is liable for income tax on income of the settlement which arises from assets
situated outside the United Kingdom. Resolution of that issue turns on the proper
construction of part of the Sch D provisions contained in s 108 of the Income and
Corporation Taxes Act 1970. Paragraph 1(a) of those provisions enacts:
c
'Tax under this Schedule shall be charged in respect of—(a) the annual profits or
gains arising or accruing—(i) to any person residing in the United Kingdom from
any kind of property whatever, whether situated in the United Kingdom or
elsewhere, and (ii) to any person residing in the United Kingdom from any trade,
profession or vocation, whether carried on in the United Kingdom or elsewhere,
d            and (iii) to any person, whether a British subject or not, although not resident in the
United Kingdom, from any property whatever in the United Kingdom, or from
any trade, profession or vocation exercised within the United Kingdom . . .'

The persons chargeable to tax under Sch D are identified by s 114, of which only sub-s
(1) is relevant for present purposes. So far as material, it provides:

e            '. . . income tax under Schedule D shall be charged on and paid by the persons
receiving or entitled to the income in respect of which the tax is directed by the
Income Tax Acts to be charged.'

The argument for the Crown accepts that the income of the settlements arose or
accrued to the three trustees jointly, and not jointly and severally, so that none of them
f was entitled in law separately to any particular share or fraction of the income. It is
contended, however, that the whole income from the foreign investments did, on a
proper construction of para 1(a)(i) of s 108, arise or accrue to the taxpayer as a person
residing in the United Kingdom, and that the circumstance that it did so to him jointly
with two co-trustees resident abroad is irrelevant. However, the word 'person' in para (i)
must include the plural 'persons' by virtue of s 6(c) of the Interpretation Act 1978. If all
three trustees had been resident in the United Kingdom application of the enactment
g would have been such that the income would have been treated as arising or accruing to
all three, and all three would have been jointly assessable to tax. In the situation which
prevails here, namely that one of the trustees is resident in the United Kingdom but the
other two are resident abroad, the income likewise arises or accrues to all three, but all
three cannot be jointly assessed to tax. There can be no justification for assessing to tax
h the taxpayer alone, on the ground that he is resident in the United Kingdom, because the
income does not arise or accrue to him personally. He has no right of control over the
income. His only interest in it is a right and duty to secure, in conjunction with his co-
trustees, that it is applied in accordance with the directions of the trust deeds. Similarly,
when one turns to s 114(1) of the 1970 Act it is found that the persons receiving or
entitled to the income are the three trustees jointly. Should the plural 'persons' be turned
j into the singular 'person' it is found that the taxpayer as an individual cannot properly be
described as the person receiving or entitled to the income. Reference was made to certain
other provisions of the 1970 Act, in particular s 153, which relates to partnerships
controlled abroad. I have not, however, been able to gather any assistance from elsewhere
in the Act towards the true construction of the enactments under immediate consideration.

I have reached the conclusion, as did the Court of Appeal, that these enactments do not have the effect of imposing on the taxpayer, in the circumstances of the case, liability to *a* tax on the foreign income of the three settlements.

Much was made, on either side of the bar, of the anomalies which would arise if the competing argument was successful. For the taxpayer it was urged that if the Crown's argument was correct the income arising from foreign sources to the trustees of a settlement made by a settlor domiciled abroad and administered abroad would, if no beneficiary had a vested right to the income and if one of several co-trustees happened to *b* be resident in the United Kingdom, properly be liable to be assessed to United Kingdom taxation on that one trustee. That trustee would be unable to obtain any indemnity out of the trust funds. It was stated that in practice the Revenue did not seek to raise any assessments to tax in such situations. The anomalous legal position must, however, prevail whatever the Revenue practice might be. Counsel for the Crown, for his part, observed that if the taxpayer's argument were correct the foreign income of an *c* accumulation trust administered in England and governed by English law could be made to avoid taxation by the simple expedient of appointing one co-trustee resident abroad. He further maintained that the anti-avoidance provisions of s 478 of the 1970 Act and s 45 of the Finance Act 1981, relating to the transfer of assets abroad, could in the case of trusts be sidestepped by a similar expedient.

The issue cannot be resolved by a balancing of the anomalies which would arise on *d* either view. It is sufficient to say that the enactments directly in point do not, on a sound analysis, support the construction contended for by the Crown. It can be perceived that there would be much to be said for making the liability to tax depend on the centre of administration of the trust and the place of residence of the majority of the trustees, as is the position with capital gains tax: see s 52 of the Capital Gains Tax Act 1979. But Parliament has not so far chosen to do that. *e*

My Lords, for these reasons, which are in substance the same as those favoured by the Court of Appeal, with whose judgments I entirely agree, I would dismiss the appeal.

**LORD TEMPLEMAN.** My Lords, for the reasons given by my noble and learned friend Lord Keith, I would dismiss this appeal. *f*

**LORD ACKNER.** My Lords, I have had the advantage of reading the judgment prepared by my noble and learned friend Lord Keith. I agree with it and would dismiss the appeal for the reasons which he has given.

**LORD OLIVER OF AYLMERTON.** My Lords, I have had the advantage of reading in draft the speech delivered by my noble and learned friend Lord Keith. I agree with it *g* and would dismiss the appeal for the reasons which he has given.

**LORD LOWRY.** My Lords, I have had the advantage of reading in draft the speech of my noble and learned friend Lord Keith. I agree with it and, for the reasons which he gives, I, too, would dismiss this appeal. *h*

*Appeal dismissed.*

Solicitors: *Solicitor of Inland Revenue; Simmons & Simmons* (for the taxpayer).

Rengan Krishnan Esq   Barrister. *j*

# Hayes v Bowman

COURT OF APPEAL, CIVIL DIVISION,
SLADE, CROOM-JOHNSON AND LLOYD LJJ
30 JUNE, 1, 27 JULY 1988

*Practice – Dismissal of action for want of prosecution – Inordinate delay without excuse – Prejudice to defendant – Admission of liability – Size of claim increased by delay – Whether financial prejudice due to delay sufficient to justify striking out.*

In August 1981 the plaintiff, who had been unemployed for a year but who was about to commence work as a self-employed carpenter, suffered serious injuries, including the permanent loss of the use of his right arm, as a result of a motor accident when his motorcycle collided with the defendant's car. On 5 April 1984 the plaintiff issued a writ against the defendant and on 16 July served a statement of claim. The defendant admitted liability on 24 July. On 13 August the plaintiff's solicitor sent to the defendant's solicitor all the medical reports in his possession. On 10 September the defendant's solicitor wrote asking for the plaintiff's previous working history. That was eventually sent on 9 May 1985 and on 24 May the defendant's solicitor requested a schedule of the special damage relating to loss of earnings. That was never sent. On 23 July the defendant requested further and better particulars of the statement of claim so that the plaintiff's prospects could be evaluated and his loss of profit assessed. The plaintiff's solicitor replied by letter on 13 December stating that counsel had advised that there should be a further medical report. There was no further communication from the plaintiff's solicitor and in March 1987 the defendant applied for the action to be struck out for want of prosecution. The registrar struck out the plaintiff's claim but on appeal the judge reversed his decision, on the ground that although the plaintiff and his advisers had been guilty of inordinate and inexcusable delay the defendant had not established a sufficient degree of prejudice to justify striking out the action. The defendant appealed, contending that he had been prejudiced because the size of the claim had been increased by the delay.

**Held** – Although the fact that a defendant had suffered financial prejudice as a result of the plaintiff's inordinate and inexcusable delay in prosecuting an action might justify striking out the action for want of prosecution on the grounds of serious prejudice, it would not be regarded as a sufficient ground of prejudice in every case. On the facts, the judge had been entitled to hold that the defendant had failed to establish a sufficient degree of prejudice to justify striking out and the court would not interfere with the exercise of his discretion. The appeal would therefore be dismissed (see p 299 *a*, p 300 *h j*, p 301 *a b*, p 303 *h* and p 304 *a f g*, post).

Dicta of Lord Diplock in *Birkett v James* [1977] 2 All ER 801 at 805, 809 and *Pritchard v J H Cobden Ltd* [1987] 1 All ER 300 considered.

Per curiam. The defendant may in a future case where there has been inordinate and inexcusable delay in prosecuting a claim for personal injuries by a living plaintiff be in a position on the particular facts to produce compelling evidence of substantial financial prejudice due to the delay sufficient to justify the dismissal of the proceedings for want of prosecution (see p 298 *g h*, p 301 *a*, p 302 *d* and p 304 *g*, post).

## Notes

For dismissal of actions for want of prosecution, see 37 Halsbury's Laws (4th edn) paras 447–450, and for cases on the subject, see 37(3) Digest (Reissue) 67–78, 3293–3341.

## Cases referred to in judgments

*Allen v Sir Alfred McAlpine & Sons Ltd* [1968] 1 All ER 543, [1968] 2 QB 229, [1968] 2 WLR 366, CA.

*Birkett v Hayes* [1982] 2 All ER 710, [1982] 1 WLR 816, CA.

*Birkett v James* [1977] 2 All ER 801, [1978] AC 297, [1977] 3 WLR 38, HL.

*Biss v Lambeth Southwark and Lewisham Health Authority* [1978] 2 All ER 125, [1978] 1 WLR 382, CA.

*Cookson v Knowles* [1978] 2 All ER 604, [1979] AC 556, [1978] 2 WLR 978, HL; *affg* [1977] 2 All ER 820, [1977] QB 913, [1977] 3 WLR 279, CA.

*Gloria v Sokoloff* [1969] 1 All ER 204, CA.

*Graham v Dodds* [1983] 2 All ER 953, [1983] 1 WLR 808, HL.

*Martin v Turner* [1970] 1 All ER 256, [1970] 1 WLR 82, CA.

*National Insurance and Guarantee Corp Ltd v Robert Bradford & Co Ltd* (1970) 114 SJ 436, CA.

*Pritchard v J H Cobden Ltd* [1987] 1 All ER 300, [1988] Fam 22, [1987] 2 WLR 627, CA.

**Appeal**

The defendant, Richard Edward Bowman, appealed with the leave of Parker LJ against the judgment of Otton J given in chambers on 28 July 1987 whereby he allowed an appeal by the plaintiff, Brian Hayes, from the order of Mr Registrar Horsey dated 28 April 1987 dismissing the plaintiff's claim for want of prosecution. The facts are set out in the judgment of Croom-Johnson LJ.

*Piers Ashworth QC* and *Simon King* for the defendant.
*I A B McLaren* for the plaintiff.

*Cur adv vult*

27 July. The following judgments were delivered.

**CROOM-JOHNSON LJ** (giving the first judgment at the invitation of Slade LJ). This is an appeal by the defendant from the refusal by Otton J to dismiss the action for want of prosecution. In so doing the judge reversed the decision of the registrar.

On 2 August 1981 the plaintiff, then aged 39, was riding a motor cycle when he was in collision with the defendant's motor car. He suffered bad injuries, involving the right arm and hand, both feet, the neck, the pelvis and the brachial plexus. The permanent and serious result has been the loss of the use of his right arm, coupled with some neck pain.

He issued a writ on 5 April 1984, two and a half after the accident, and a statement of claim was served on 16 July 1984. A defence was immediately put in, and liability was admitted by letter on 24 July 1984. The statement of claim, after setting out the plaintiff's injuries, alleges that by reason of his injuries the plaintiff is unable to pursue his occupation as a carpenter.

There is then a section headed 'Particulars of Special Damage'. It reads:

'At the time of the accident the Plaintiff was about to commence work as a self-employed carpenter. He was unable to do so and lost the profits which he would have made in that business. The Plaintiff is still unable to pursue that occupation and the loss is continuing. Further particulars hereof will be provided upon discovery.'

There follow particulars of out-of-pocket losses from damage to clothing and the motor cycle, and continuing travelling expenses, totalling £570.

On 13 August 1984 the plaintiff's solicitor sent to the defendant's solicitor all the medical reports then in his possession. The latest was dated 24 July 1984 and was from Mr Whatmore, a consultant neurosurgeon, who had been seeing whether the neck pain could be relieved. It ended:

a 'I think the prognosis for this gentleman is very poor. I cannot see him returning to any form of occupation which involves either dextrous or heavy use of his right upper limb, or any occupation which imposes any undue stress or strain on his cervical spine.'

Discussions between the parties were clearly contemplated, and on 10 September 1984 the defendant's solicitor wrote asking for the plaintiff's previous working history.
b Nothing happened, and the request was repeated on 16 April 1985. The history was sent on 9 May 1985. It showed that the plaintiff had been unemployed for a year before the accident. The defendant was also told that there was available for inspection a folder of documents relating to carpentry jobs which the plaintiff had undertaken during that year, in anticipation of setting up his own business, and a short but inconclusive letter from the Institute of Carpenters about rates of pay for carpenters. In addition, there was
c sent a letter written by Mr Whatmore the previous September painting a very gloomy picture of the plaintiff's employability and in effect relegating him to what used to be known as the 'odd-lot' category.

On 24 May 1985 the defendant's solicitor asked for a schedule of the special damage relating to loss of earnings, together with vouchers in support. On 5 June the plaintiff's solicitor replied:

d 'Special damage is somewhat complicated in this case and our papers at the moment are with Counsel to advise particularly on this aspect. As soon as we hear from him we will endeavour to let you have the schedule you refer to.'

The schedule was not sent, and never has been.

On 23 July 1985 a formal request for further and better particulars of the statement of
e claim was made. What it was concerned with was the allegation that the plaintiff had been about to begin work as a self-employed carpenter. The defendant specially wanted to know what it was alleged the plaintiff's prospects had been, so that his pleaded loss of profit could be assessed and a value placed on the claim. The defendant wanted to know how the plaintiff was putting his case in view of the vague way in which the claim had been pleaded. He also wanted to know what was alleged to be his post-accident earning
f capacity.

The only reply to that request was a letter dated 13 December 1985 stating that counsel had advised there should be a further medical report as—

'the question of continuing loss is a most material point of the case and if that is to be affected you will clearly wish to know. We will be in touch with you as quickly as possible therefore.'
g
That was the last communication from the plaintiff's solicitors until the defendant took out a summons in March 1987 to dismiss for want of prosecution. During the hearing of these proceedings it has emerged that in the mean time the plaintiff had had some medical examinations, including a short but fruitless admission to hospital in January 1987 for rehabilitation. The medical position has therefore not altered since Mr
h Whatmore's report in 1984. None of this had been communicated to the defence, although under RSC Ord 25, r 8 automatic directions should have come into existence in August 1984. No time summons was ever issued. No consent for the delay was sought.

Whatever the plaintiff's advisers were doing, there was no further prosecution of the action because the defendant's advisers were being left out in the cold, and this was so in spite of the fact that on 1 August 1984 and 16 April 1985 the defendant's solicitors had
j expressly written to say that they wanted to ensure that 'the matter kept moving'.

An instance of the plaintiff's dilatoriness is that, although the last advice from leading counsel was received by his solicitors on 15 October 1986, it was not until 27 March 1987, four days before the summons to dismiss was served, that accountants were first instructed on his behalf. In a last minute attempt to show activity, on 24 April 1987, at

the hearing before the registrar, there was served a reply to the defendant's request for
further and better particulars dated 23 July 1985. It was a worthless and possibly window-   *a*
dressing document and it may be disregarded.

On 28 April 1987 the registrar dismissed the action for want of prosecution. He held
that there had been inordinate and inexcusable delay, and that the defendant had been
prejudiced by his inability to evaluate the claim and protect himself by settling or
making a payment into court. The court is loth to dismiss where there has been an
admission of liability, but such inability may cause prejudice: see *Gloria v Sokoloff* [1969]   *b*
1 All ER 204 and *Martin v Turner* [1970] 1 All ER 256, [1970] 1 WLR 82.

The plaintiff appealed to Otton J. On 8 June 1987 he adjourned the hearing on the
terms that the plaintiff served a schedule of damages within 14 days, which has still not
been done. The judge also ordered that a list of supporting documents should be served
within the same time, and gave further directions.

The accountants concluded that no claim for loss of earning could be based on anything   *c*
which the plaintiff had earned since he left Jaguar Cars Ltd a year before the accident.
Accordingly, on 16 June 1987 they submitted a long report, in which they set out their
view that as a self-employed joiner the plaintiff had at the time of the accident a net
earning capacity of £3,846 pa. They used national average figures for the construction
industry which showed year by year a gross increase of between £500 and £600 and
calculated on that basis that up to the time of a trial in August 1987 the plaintiff would   *d*
have lost net earnings as special damage totalling £33,610.

Taking the last annual net figure of £6,946 as a multiplicand and giving 12 years'
purchase they calculated future loss of earnings at £83,362. This meant a total loss of
earnings of £116,972. It was wholly unrealistic to assume a trial in August 1987. A trial
by August 1988 was a possibility and this has meant amending the above figures, which
produces a figure of £41,212 in place of the figure of £33,610 and a figure of £124,574   *e*
for aggregate loss of earnings. It also produces a multiplicand of £7,602. The accountant's
report has been described as the schedule ordered by the judge, although it is evidence
and not pleading, and is inconsistent with the original statement of claim.

On 28 July 1987 Otton J resumed the hearing of the summons. He held that the
plaintiff and his advisers had been guilty of inordinate and inexcusable delay, a finding   *f*
with which I agree. There has been no cross-notice of appeal against that. The judge then
considered the question of prejudice to the defendant. He found it a difficult matter, and
finely balanced. He took into account the considerably changed nature of the basis of the
claim and that the defendant had been deprived of the right to make a payment into
court. So far as loss of future earnings was concerned, the judge was aware that the effect
of special damage accumulating over seven years, followed by a multiplier of 12 years for
future loss, meant that the loss 'will be spread over 19 years'. There then followed a   *g*
consideration of the medical reports, expressed as follows:

> 'There have been and are still difficulties on the medical side and that situation
> has always existed throughout the period of delay. That is not sufficient to amount
> to substantial prejudice. The claim for loss of earnings hinges on the assessment of
> the medical issue.'   *h*

With respect to the judge, that was not an accurate account of the full medical reports,
all of which were before him. The medical position has not changed since 1984. The
judge then went on to hold that 'taking the matter overall the defendant has not
established a sufficient degree of prejudice' and he allowed the plaintiff's appeal.

The judge was entitled to disregard (as he did) the 19 years. That had recently been   *j*
decided in *Pritchard v J H Cobden Ltd* [1987] 1 All ER 300, [1988] Fam 22. That was an
action for personal injuries in which there had been great delay. The trial came on nine
years after the accident, and an attempt was made by the defendant to have the claim for
loss of earnings dealt with in the same way as loss of dependency is dealt with in cases
under the Fatal Accidents Act 1976, where the date of the death is the starting point for

calculating the future loss. Thus an attempt was made to start the clock ticking at the
a   accident, so that a long period of accumulating special damage should not increase the
amount awarded. This court held that damages for loss of earnings of a living plaintiff
should continue to be assessed as special damages for the earnings lost between the
accident and the date of the trial and a calculation of the future loss of earnings from the
date of the trial by selecting an adequate multiplier for the multiplicand to compensate
the plaintiff for the likely loss of earnings for the remainder of his working life.
b       In the joint judgment of O'Connor LJ and myself is a passage which I will quote
([1987] 1 All ER 300 at 307, [1988] Fam 22 at 36):

'The defendants have advanced their argument in another way. It is based on the
delay which has occurred in the present case in bringing it to trial, and the argument
is that where there is such a long period policy requires that there should be a
reduction in the multiplier. Otherwise, delay means larger damages, and injustice
c       to the defendant. But the whole of the time occupied before trial is not "delay". In
every contested action there is an interval of time between the arising of the cause
of action and trial. That interval may in some cases be lengthened by unnecessary
delay, which should be prevented wherever possible. Sometimes a longer interval
works in favour of justice, as where what was only a risk of epilepsy becomes a fact
d       of epilepsy. But the plaintiff is not to be deprived of his proper sum of compensation
because his case takes a long time, even an unnecessarily long time, to come to trial.
The weapons to be used against too long an interval of time are striking out for want
of prosecution, or in some cases depriving the plaintiff of part of the interest on his
special damage, or in bringing on the hearing in good time.'

It has long been said that delay in bringing a case on for trial favours the plaintiff and
e   leads to larger awards of damages. This may happen for two reasons. One is that the
simple passage of time causes the damages to pile up, as in *Pritchard's* case. The other is
that by the time of trial the multiplicand has become larger because of increases in wage
rates due to negotiated increases or the decline in the value of money. In *Pritchard's* case
the multiplicand was an agreed figure, so that problem did not arise. But it is said in the
present case there was an annual increase alleged in the wage rates reaching from £3,846
f   in 1982 to £7,602 in 1988, and had the case come on for trial or been settled in, say,
1985, instead of probably three years later, the award for loss of future earnings would
have been much less and the capital sum likely then to be awarded would have been
available for investment by the plaintiff in the ordinary way. Otton J did not consider
that point.

Counsel for the plaintiff has conceded that delay which increases the size of the claim
g   is prejudicial to the defendant, but that the increase must not be one which is attributable
to inflation. Accordingly, we have been supplied with two sets of calculations showing
the effect of delay on the ultimate award if the case came on for hearing seven years after
the accident. The defendant's calculations make use of the actual figures set out in the
report of the plaintiff's accountants, showing a loss of earnings increasing each year and
h   the special damage mounting over seven years. The plaintiff's calculations assume a
notional net earning of £5,999 pa with no increases at all. Both sets of calculations make
allowance for the fact that in the meantime the defendant's insurers will have had the
use of the money eventually awarded, and accordingly reduce the total sum to be found
by the insurers.

The plaintiff's calculation proceeds on the assumption that any annual increase in
j   earnings is wholly due to inflation. The purpose of the assumption is to show that if
inflationary increases are taken out of the special damage then the insurers do not end up
out of pocket at all, and consequently there is no prejudice to them. That is an assumption
which cannot be made. For some years wages have been increasing at a faster rate than
the rate of inflation, reflecting the bargaining power of the workforce. Among the
documents annexed to the accountants' report was a table of increases in the retail price

index. It shows that the increase in suggested earnings from £3,846 in 1982 to £6,946
in 1987 was by no means entirely due to inflation.                                    *a*

Moreover, the answer to this proposition is that the plaintiff's claim for loss of wages
as special damage is for money of which he has been deprived and which, but for the
accident, he would have received year by year in the money of the day to spend on his
needs. There is some element of inflation in the special damage, but it is not all of it. In
that way the multiplicand is arrived at, to the benefit of a plaintiff.

Not only is there an unavoidable element of inflation in the money receivable by the  *b*
plaintiff, but it is also in the money payable by the defendant, also in the money of the
day. I have no hesitation in accepting the calculations put forward by the defendant.
They make use of the actual figures set out in the accountants' report and which, it seems,
now form the basis of the plaintiff's claim. They add in the interest payable on the special
damage year by year, and also make the assumption, against the defence, that the trial
judge would exercise his discretion to deprive the plaintiff of two years' interest in  *c*
accordance with the guidelines set out in *Birkett v Hayes* [1982] 2 All ER 710, [1982] 1
WLR 816 and applied in *Pritchard*'s case.

The original calculation used a 12-year multiplier for future loss, because that was the
figure used in the accountants' report, but the defendant has reduced it to 11 because the
accountants had assumed a trial in 1987 and not 1988. Allowance has also been made, as
it must be made, for the fact that until trial the defendant's insurers have the use of the  *d*
money, and so will have the benefit of what it earns.

There has been some argument about the rate of interest which the insurers would
earn on the money, but I am satisfied that the rate of 7·5% net put forward is a fair one.
The result of these calculations is that the net value of the claim (as it is now put) is
£16,637 more in 1988 than it was in 1985. In 1987 it was £7,727 more than in 1985.

The question to be answered in this appeal is therefore this: does delay which increases  *e*
the size of the claim amount to prejudice entitling the defendant to have the action
struck out if it drags on?

There have been numbers of cases where the facts have been held to involve prejudice.
They have not all been cases where the defendant has been prejudiced in his ability to
fight the case, such as by the disappearance of evidence, or his being unable to test that of  *f*
the plaintiff. We have been told that there has been no case where the present point has
arisen.

The court is not construing a statute. It is using its discretion in the exercise of its
inherent jurisdiction. The statement by Lord Diplock in *Birkett v James* [1977] 2 All ER
801 at 805, [1978] AC 297 at 318 is that the action will be struck out if the delay gives
rise to a substantial risk that it is not possible to have a fair trial of the issues in the action
or is such as is likely to cause or to have caused serious prejudice to the defendant. It gives  *g*
no hint as to what is meant by 'prejudice'.

For my part, if 'prejudice' is given its ordinary meaning of 'detriment', I do not see
why delay which has caused the claim to grow in the course of three years by £16,637
has not caused prejudice to the defendant, and serious prejudice at that. The question is
whether the court should exercise its discretion to strike out. RSC Ord 25, r 1(4) expressly  *h*
gives power to strike out if the timetables laid down in the rules are not obeyed and in
the present case they seem to have been ignored.

This power of striking out is discretionary and, as Lord Diplock said in *Birkett v James*,
the prejudice which has been caused must be 'serious'. One must also bear in mind that
in this case liability has been admitted. We have been urged not to interfere with the
judge's discretion.                                                                   *j*

It is at this point that I have reservations. Otton J did not consider the point about the
multiplicand. All that was argued before him was the point about the 'spread of earnings
over 19 years'. Counsel for the defendant has told us that the calculations which have
been supplied to this court to show the possible increase in the damages because of the
increase in the multiplicand were not before the judge.

I do not regard the misunderstanding of the medical evidence as justifying us in
*a* interfering with the judge's discretion on a point which was not argued before him. If it
had been I would have been minded to allow this appeal, but in the result, in spite of the
force of counsel's submissions for the defendant, I have reluctantly concluded that it
should be dismissed.

**LLOYD LJ.** When the layman criticises the law's delays, it is usually the deserving
*b* plaintiff whom he has in mind. But a glance at some recent law reports would prove him
wrong, at any rate in personal injuries litigation. It is the defendant insurer who now
complains loudest. The advent of the interim payment under RSC Ord 29, r 9 has solved
the plaintiff's short term need for cash. It follows that he no longer has anything much
to gain from an early trial. The defendant, on the other hand, stands to lose with every
year that passes. The reasons for this phenomenon have been explored in great detail on
*c* this appeal.

In *Cookson v Knowles* [1978] 2 All ER 604, [1979] AC 556, a Fatal Accidents Act case, it
was held that the appropriate multiplier should be taken as at the death of the deceased,
not as at the date of trial, on the assumption that the deceased had survived. I need not
go over the reasons. They are very clearly set out in the speech of Lord Fraser (see [1978]
2 All ER 604 at 613, [1979] AC 556 at 574). Lord Fraser acknowledged that the practice
*d* in personal injuries actions was different. There the appropriate multiplier is taken at the
date of trial. But Lord Fraser held that the different approach was justified by the differing
nature of the actions.

On the facts of *Cookson v Knowles*, the trial judge had taken a multiplier of 11 at the
date of death. The case took $2\frac{1}{2}$ years to come on. So the Court of Appeal deducted $2\frac{1}{2}$
from 11 and thereby arrived at $8\frac{1}{2}$ as the appropriate multiplier for future loss. The
*e* House of Lords approved this course. Had it been a personal injuries action the multiplier
for future loss would have been greater.

In *Graham v Dodds* [1983] 2 All ER 953, [1983] 1 WLR 808 the House of Lords
expressly approved Lord Fraser's speech in *Cookson v Knowles*. Lord Bridge observed that
any other solution—

*f*          'would lead to the highly undesirable anomaly that in fatal accident cases the
          longer the trial of the dependants' claims could be delayed the more they would
          eventually recover.'

(See [1983] 2 All ER 953 at 958, [1983] 1 WLR 808 at 815.)

In *Pritchard v J H Cobden Ltd* [1987] 1 All ER 300, [1988] Fam 22, a personal injuries
*g* case, the defendants argued, reasonably enough, that, if it would be a 'highly undesirable
anomaly' in fatal accident cases that delay in bringing the case to trial should increase the
amount eventually recovered, so also must it be a highly undesirable anomaly in personal
injury cases. But the Court of Appeal rejected the defendant's argument. On the facts in
*Pritchard*'s case the trial judge had taken a multiplier of 14 as at the date of trial. The
Court of Appeal regarded 14 as high, but declined to interfere. The case had taken nine
*h* years to come to trial. In the event, therefore, the plaintiff recovered 23 times his annual
loss of earnings. The defendants argued that this was obviously too high for a man of 39
at the date of trial. But, as O'Connor and Croom-Johnson LJJ observed, five years'
purchase for loss of future earnings (14 years less 9 years) would have been obviously too
low (see [1987] 1 All ER 300 at 307, [1988] Fam 22 at 35). As for the argument that the
multiplier should be reduced, as in Fatal Accident Act cases, in order to encourage speedy
*j* trials, the court held that the best remedy lay in an application to strike out. They said
([1987] 1 All ER 300 at 307, [1988] Fam 22 at 36):

          '. . . the plaintiff is not to be deprived of his proper sum of compensation because
          his case takes a long time, even an unnecessarily long time, to come to trial. The
          weapons to be used against too long an interval of time are striking out for want of

prosecution, or in some cases depriving the plaintiff of part of the interest on his special damage, or in bringing on the hearing in good time.'

In the present case the defendant has accepted the invitation proffered in *Pritchard's* case. He applied to strike out. Mr Registrar Horsey granted the application. But his decision was reversed by Otton J. Otton J's reasons are important. He held that there had been inordinate and inexcusable delay on the part of the plaintiff. As for prejudice, he referred to the two arguments advanced on the part of the defendant, first, that he had been deprived of the opportunity to make a payment into court and, second, that the sum for which he would now be liable had been increased by reason of delay. Otton J continued:

'It seems to me that taking the matter overall the defendant has not established a sufficient degree of prejudice to justify exercising my discretion to dismiss the case for want of prosecution. In my judgment the action should be allowed to proceed and the appeal will be allowed.'

Thus the judge accepted that there had been some prejudice to the defendant, but insufficient to justify the drastic course of striking out.

Before us, counsel for the defendant did not press the first of the two arguments advanced before the judge. He conceded that it would be difficult for us to interfere with the judge's discretion in that regard. But he developed the second argument in much greater depth. He said that if the trial had taken place in 1985 the net loss to date of trial would have been £18,546. If the trial had taken place two years later, in 1987, the net loss to date of trial would have been £38,800. As for future loss, he took a multiplier of 12 in each case. But the multiplicand had increased between 1985 and 1987 from £5,960 to £6,946, in line with the increase in average wages in the construction industry. Thus, if the trial had taken place in 1985, future loss would have amounted to £71,520, giving a total of £90,066. For a trial taking place in 1987 future loss would have been £83,352, giving a total of £122,152. Counsel accepted that, in order to make a fair comparison, the defendant's insurers should give credit for their use of the money between 1985 and 1987. Taking 8% compound interest, £90,066 would have become just over £105,000 by 1987. So the comparison is between £105,000 and £122,152, a difference of £17,000. Counsel submitted that, on any view, that is substantial prejudice to the defendant, and justifies an order to strike out.

Counsel for the plaintiff criticises the defendant's figures. He demonstrated that, if you take a multiplier of 11 for a trial in 1987, instead of 12, and if you deprive the plaintiff of two years' interest to account for the delay, as envisaged in *Pritchard's* case, you get a total award of £111,807, instead of £122,152. Although there is still a margin of about £7,000 in favour of the plaintiff, it is by no means so great.

But counsel's main argument for the plaintiff was that it is impossible to make a precise comparison between a trial in 1985 and a trial in 1987, first, because the 8% compound interest assumed in the calculation is an arbitrary figure; the defendant's insurers might earn more, or they might earn less. Second, the comparison ignores the fall in the value of money between 1985 and 1987. Although the insurers would be paying out a larger sum in 1987, they would be paying out in depreciated currency.

In my judgment, counsel's argument for the plaintiff is well founded. I would accept that, so long as the present practice in awarding damages in personal injuries actions remains as it is, delay will favour the plaintiff, at least in nominal terms. The reason is that multiplicands are likely to increase each year, so long as average earnings increase; and multipliers, based on 4½% rate of interest, do not decrease pari passu. But the fact that defendant suffers financial prejudice from delay does not mean that in every case of inordinate delay there is 'serious prejudice' so as to justify striking out. (I leave on one side the ordinary factors which arise where liability is in issue, such as the death or disappearance of witnesses. In the present case liability is admitted and we are concerned with financial prejudice only.)

It seems to me that the degree of financial prejudice will vary from case to case. It will
a usually be difficult to prove, since it involves so many uncertainties. I would not myself
rule out the possibility of showing serious financial prejudice so as to justify striking out
in some future case. But here the judge held that the defendant had failed to establish 'a
sufficient degree of prejudice' to justify striking out. I can see no ground on which we
could, or should, disagree with that view. I would therefore dismiss the appeal.

b **SLADE LJ.** I gratefully adopt Croom-Johnson LJ's statement of the facts of this case.
The two principles governing the dismissal of actions for want of prosecution are set out
in the often-cited passage from Lord Diplock's speech in *Birkett v James* [1977] 2 All ER
801 at 805, [1978] AC 297 at 318. In the present case, since contumelious default is not
relied on, we are concerned with principle (2), namely:

c      '(a) that there has been inordinate and inexcusable delay on the part of the
       plaintiff or his lawyers, and (b) that such delay will give rise to a substantial risk that
       it is not possible to have a fair trial of the issues in the action or is such as is likely to
       cause or to have caused serious prejudice to the defendants either as between
       themselves and the plaintiff or between each other or between them and a third
       party.'
d
The finding of Otton J that there has been inordinate and inexcusable delay on the
part of the plaintiff or his lawyers has not been challenged on this appeal. The timetable
set out by Croom-Johnson LJ speaks for itself.
The defendant does not argue that it is now impossible to have a fair trial of the issues
in the action. His point, as presented by counsel, is that the delay is likely to have caused
e him prejudice. There was some brief debate before us as to the degree of prejudice which
is required before an action can properly be struck out. In *Birkett v James* [1977] 2 All ER
801 at 809, [1978] AC 297 at 323 Lord Diplock said:

       'To justify dismissal of an action for want of prosecution some prejudice to the
       defendant additional to that inevitably flowing from the plaintiff's tardiness in
f      issuing his writ must be shown to have resulted from his subsequent delay (beyond
       the period allowed by rules of court) in proceeding promptly with the successive
       steps in the action. The additional prejudice need not be great compared with that
       which may have been already caused by the time elapsed before the writ was issued;
       but it must be more than minimal; and the delay in taking a step in the action if it
       is to qualify as inordinate as well as prejudicial must exceed the period allowed by
g      rules of court for taking that step.'

Counsel for the defendant relied on this passage in support of a submission that all he
had to show was 'more than minimal' additional prejudice to the defendant resulting
from the post-writ delay, beyond that already caused by the delay of two and a half years
in issuing the writ. We must not read Lord Diplock's speech as if it were a statute.
h Nevertheless, I have little doubt that counsel was right in submitting on behalf of the
plaintiff that the sense of Lord Diplock's statement of the relevant principles is that a
defendant seeking the dismissal of an action for want of prosecution on grounds of delay
must show overall serious prejudice *plus* more than minimal additional prejudice
resulting from the post-writ delay. This is the basis on which I proceed in this judgment.
       *The Supreme Court Practice 1988* vol 1, para 25/1/6 deals with the question of prejudice
j as follows:

       'This is a matter of fact and degree and has been discussed in *Allen* v. *McAlpine*
       ([1968] 1 All ER 543, [1968] 2 QB 229), and in a large number of reported cases.
       The effect of the lapse of time on the memory of witnesses or [because] of their
       death or disappearance are the most usual factors. Their importance depends upon

the circumstances, the issues and the other evidence that can be given. Thus the
lapse of time may be very prejudicial if the circumstances of an accident or oral *a*
contracts or representations are in issue, but is of much less importance in a heavy,
well-documented commercial action (*National Insurance Guarantee Corporation Ltd.*
v. *Robert Bradford & Co. Ltd.* ((1970) 114 SJ 436)). But prejudice is not limited to
matters affecting proof; a defendant, particularly a professional man, may be made
prejudiced by having an action hanging over his head indefinitely (*Biss* v. *Lambeth,
Southwark and Lewisham Health Authority (Teaching)* ([1978] 2 All ER 125, [1978] 1 *b*
WLR 382)).'

In the present case the prejudice alleged by the defendant is of a nature which, so far
as I know, has never been relied on in any previous reported case dealing with an
application to dismiss for want of prosecution. It is submitted that, because of the
plaintiff's (now accepted) inordinate and inexcusable delay in prosecuting the proceedings, *c*
the defendant, who admitted liability as long ago as 1984, will find himself with a
substantially larger bill to pay by way of damages if the action is now allowed to proceed
to trial than he would have had to pay if the trial had taken place a few years earlier.
Provided that it is shown that the defendant will have a substantially larger bill to pay in
terms of the spending power of his money, which I will call 'real money', I can see no
reason why this should not constitute serious prejudice to the defendant within the *d*
principles enunciated by Lord Diplock, even though the prejudice relied on in earlier
cases may not have been of this nature.

It is common ground that, if this case proceeds to trial, the judge will have to assess the
loss of earnings caused to the plaintiff by his injury *as at the date of the trial*. The calculation
for the years preceding the trial could be made on a fairly realistic basis in the light of
what has actually happened since the accident. The calculation for the post-trial years *e*
would fall to be made on the conventional basis well summarised in *McGregor on Damages*
(15th edn, 1988) para 1453 as follows:

'This amount is calculated by taking the figure of the plaintiff's present annual
earnings less the amount, if any, which he can now earn annually, and multiplying
this by a figure which, while based upon the number of years during which the loss *f*
of earning power will last, is discounted so as to allow for the fact that a lump sum
is being given now instead of periodical payments over the years. This latter figure
has long been called the multiplier; the former figure has come to be referred to as
the multiplicand. Further adjustments, however, may have to be made to
multiplicand or multiplier on account of a variety of factors, *viz.* the probability of
future increase or decrease in the annual earnings, the so-called contingencies of life, *g*
and the incidence of inflation and taxation.'

In *Pritchard v J H Cobden Ltd* [1987] 1 All ER 300, [1988] Fam 22 this court held in
effect that in the case of a living plaintiff the appropriate multiplier had to be ascertained
as at the date of trial, having regard to the factors affecting the future as at that date and *h*
that it does not fall to be reduced merely on account of the delay, whether avoidable or
unavoidable, in bringing the case on for trial. Particularly in the light of this decision,
counsel for the defendant made the broad submission that in any personal injury case
where a living plaintiff is claiming compensation for loss of wages and liability is
admitted, delay in bringing the case on for trial is bound to prejudice the defendant, by
subjecting him to a higher award than he would have had to pay if the trial had happened *j*
at the proper time. While the multiplicand will increase over the years along with rises
in wage levels, the court will not be in a position to reduce the multiplier by a similar
proportion. When the sum of multiplier and multiplicand is added to the compensation
attributable to the years preceding the trial, the defendant, it is said, will inevitably find
himself with a larger bill to pay. True it is that, where there has been delay, the defendant

will have had the use of the money ultimately payable by way of damages during the
*a* period of the delay. Furthermore, as counsel for the defendant accepted, the trial judge
might, if he thought fit, properly penalise the dilatory plaintiff by depriving him of part
of the interest on his damages (though never, it was submitted, for a period exceeding
the period of unjustifiable delay). Nevertheless, so the broad argument runs, largely
because of the limits on the ability of the court to adjust the multiplier, delay will
inevitably leave the defendant out of pocket.

*b*      In response to counsel's broad submission for the defendant, counsel for the plaintiff
made an equally broad submission to the opposite effect. He suggested that the only
financial prejudice to a defendant which may be caused by a delayed trial in a personal
injuries case flows from a full award of interest. He sought to demonstrate this by a
schedule of statistics. In his submission, the remedy available for a defendant when
needed is simply to invite the court to exercise its discretion to reduce the interest
*c* element of the award: see *Birkett v Hayes* [1982] 2 All ER 710 at 717, [1982] 1 WLR 816
at 825 and *Pritchard v J H Cobden Ltd* [1987] 1 All ER 300 at 307, [1988] Fam 22 at 36. He
rightly stressed that any hypothetical figures must take into account the fact that, because
of inflation, an award of damages which a defendant has to meet in year B will be worth
in terms of real money less than the same sum paid in an earlier year A. In his submission,
all the delay does is to enable the court to award a plaintiff a figure more nearly
*d* approximating to the amount of his true loss.

       I do not accept counsel's broad submission for the plaintiff, if only for this reason. In
some, perhaps many, cases, during the period of relevant delay rates of wage settlements
will have substantially outstripped the rate of inflation so that the multiplicand will be
proportionately higher than any increase simply aligned to inflation. At least if this is so,
I see a strong possibility that delay will subject the defendant to a greater liability in
*e* terms of real money. Merely because the plaintiff will at the trial receive a sum
representing what the court considers is then fairly and properly due to him in respect of
loss of earnings, it does not follow that the defendant will not in terms of real money
have a larger bill to pay than would have been the case if the trial had happened earlier.

       Counsel for the defendant has convinced me that at least in the great majority of cases
*f* delay of the trial from year A to a later year B will result in the defendant having to pay
an award of £x + y rather than £x, for the reasons which he gives. Nevertheless, I am
not satisfied that this will necessarily leave the defendant out of pocket in terms of real
money. Whether or not it does so, it seems to me, will depend largely on two factors,
namely: (a) whether £x + y exceeds £x by an amount exceeding the rate of inflation
operating during the period from year A to year B, and (b) the amount of interest which
*g* the defendant has been able to earn on the £x retained by him during that period.

       In the present case, I understand, the submission made to the judge in this context
more or less followed the lines of the broad submission of counsel for the defendant
which I have summarised above. We were told that no argument was submitted to him
based on the available figures relating to this plaintiff. The argument was based on the
broad submission that, because the defendant, by slippage of time, was now faced with
*h* special damages over a period of seven years and a claim that there should be a 12-year
multiplier, this inevitably indicated prejudice to the defendant. For the reasons already
appearing, I would not accept this argument and think the judge was right to hold that
by itself it did not establish (in his words) 'sufficient degree of prejudice to justify
exercising [his] discretion to dismiss the case for want of prosecution.'

       On this appeal, however, counsel for the defendant, though making the broad
*j* submission already mentioned, primarily based his case on a number of calculations
seeking to demonstrate the probable effect on the quantum of *this* defendant's liability of
the lapse of time between the accident of this plaintiff and the trial. The calculations
were helpful and illuminating because they were, so far as possible, based on the figures
appearing in the report of the accountants very belatedly obtained and dated 16 June
1987 setting out the basis of the plaintiff's claim for loss of earnings.

Even if I had myself been convinced that those calculations demonstrated a sufficient degree of prejudice in this particular instance to justify dismissing the case for want of *a* prosecution, I would not for my part have thought it right to interfere with the exercise of the judge's discretion on this account, when the case had been presented to him on the different basis of the broader proposition which I have summarised and rejected.

However, out of deference to counsel's powerful argument for the defendant, I will make the following brief comments on his calculations, the correctness of which I am for present purposes prepared to assume. I think they show the following. (1) Assuming *b* the adoption of a 12-year multiplier (which I think is a fair assumption) the plaintiff would have been likely to obtain an award of £90,066 in respect of lost earnings on a trial in August 1985. (2) Assuming the adoption of an 11-year multiplier and the reduction of the interest element by two years (which I think are fair assumptions) the plaintiff would have been likely to obtain an award of £111,807 on a trial in August 1987. (3) Assuming the adoption of an 11-year multiplier and a similar reduction of the *c* interest element (which I think are fair assumptions) the plaintiff would have been likely to obtain an award of £128,526 on a trial in August 1988.

Now, on the face of it, £111,807 is a substantially higher figure than £90,066 and £128,526 is an even more substantially higher figure. But, if the true prejudice to the defendant or his insurers is to be ascertained, there have to be set against the higher figures of £111,807 and £128,526 (a) the fall in the spending power of money between *d* 1985 and 1987 or 1988, as the case may be, (b) the interest and/or capital appreciation which the defendant or his insurers would have been able to earn in respect of the £90,066 if they had retained it in their hands over the period between 1985 and 1987 or 1988 as the case might be.

Our attention has been drawn to no figures in respect of (a). As to (b), counsel for the defendant has invited us to assume that interest would have been earned at a maximum *e* rate of 7·5% net compound, producing an interest figure of £14,016 for 1987 and £21,823 for 1988. This may be a reasonable assumption, but the figures can be no more than speculative. In any event, they would absorb a large part of the difference between £90,066 and £111,807 or £128,526 as the case might be.

In all the circumstances, I conclude that, even if the judge had had all counsel's calculations before him, but had then expressed the view that he was not satisfied that *f* sufficient degree of prejudice had been established to justify the dismissal of the case for want of prosecution, we could not properly have interfered with the exercise of his discretion.

For these reasons, I would dismiss this appeal. I would, however, add this warning. On the particular facts of other future cases, where there has been inordinate and inexcusable delay in prosecuting a claim for personal injuries by a living plaintiff, defendants may be *g* in a position to produce compelling evidence of substantial financial prejudice due to the delay (more compelling than that available in the present case) sufficient to justify the dismissal of the proceedings for want of prosecution. This could provide a salutary precedent for the reasons counsel for the defendant has eloquently urged on us.

*h*

*Appeal dismissed. Leave to appeal to the House of Lords refused.*

Solicitors: *Browne Jacobson,* Nottingham (for the defendant); *Headleys,* Hinckley (for the plaintiff).

Celia Fox    Barrister.

# Scott and another v R
# Barnes and others v R

PRIVY COUNCIL

LORD BRIDGE OF HARWICH, LORD GRIFFITHS, LORD ACKNER, LORD GOFF OF CHIEVELEY AND LORD
LOWRY

30 JANUARY, 13 MARCH 1989

*Criminal law – Trial – Depositions as evidence – Exclusion of deposition – Deposition of deceased witness – Deposition containing uncorroborated identification evidence – Whether trial judge having discretion to exclude admission of deposition in evidence.*

In two separate appeals from Jamaica the questions arose whether a trial judge in a criminal case had a discretion to refuse to admit the sworn deposition of a witness who had died before trial and, if so, in what circumstances that discretion should be exercised and what direction the judge should give on the issue of identification.

In the first case the two appellants were charged with murdering a special constable in a bar. The only evidence of identification was that contained in the deposition of a witness who deposed that he had seen the appellants' faces as they ran from the bar and had subsequently pointed out the appellants to the police when they were at a bingo game before they were arrested. The witness died before the trial. The appellants both gave evidence at their trial that they had been elsewhere on the day of the shooting and that at the time of their arrest they had not been singled out by the witness. In the second case the three appellants were charged with shooting dead the driver of a van and stealing a factory payroll which he was carrying. A witness gave evidence at the preliminary inquiry but was murdered before the trial. In his deposition he had stated that he saw the shooting and that it had been done by the three appellants, all of whom he knew. The only other eye witness was unable to recognise anyone. All three appellants raised an alibi defence. In each case, without the evidence in the deposition, there would have been insufficient evidence to put any of the appellants on trial. In each case the trial judge admitted the depositions in evidence. In the first case the judge in his summing up implied to the jury that the fact that the witness had picked out the appellants to the police when they were amongst others at a bingo game authenticated the identification itself. In the second case the judge gave no direction on the issue of identification and did not warn the jury of the danger of a mistaken identification or draw their attention to the circumstances in which the identification was made or to the fact that it differed from the evidence of the other eye witness. In each case the appellants were convicted. The Court of Appeal of Jamaica refused the appellants leave to appeal against their convictions and they appealed to the Privy Council.

**Held** – (1) A judge in a criminal trial had a discretion to exclude the admission of a sworn deposition of a deceased witness so as to ensure a fair trial, notwithstanding that the deposition was relevant and admissible evidence, but that discretion should be exercised with great restraint. Provided that (a) the jury were warned that they had not had the benefit of hearing the deponent's evidence tested in cross-examination, (b) particular features of the evidence in the deposition which conflicted with other evidence and which could have been explored in cross-examination were pointed out where appropriate, (c) the appropriate warning of the danger of identification evidence was given in an identification case and (d) inadmissible matters such as hearsay or matters which were prejudicial rather than probative were excluded from the deposition before it was read to the jury, the deposition should be admitted in evidence. Neither the inability to cross-examine nor the fact that the deposition contained the only evidence against the accused nor the fact that it was identification evidence was of itself sufficient to justify the exclusion of a deposition. The crucial factor was the quality of the evidence in the deposition and if the deposition contained evidence of reasonable quality, even if *a* it was the only evidence against the accused, the deposition should be admitted and the interests of the accused protected in the summing up. On the facts, the evidence of identification contained in the depositions was not of such poor quality that it would have been unsafe to convict on it if the jury had received the appropriate guidance in the summing up. There were, accordingly, no grounds on which the trial judges could have exercised their discretion to exclude the admission of the depositions (see p 311 *f*, p 312 *c* *b* *j* and p 313 *a* to *g*, post); *R v Sang* [1979] 2 All ER 1222, *R v Blithing* (1983) 77 Cr App R 86 and *R v O'Loughlin* [1988] 3 All ER 431 considered.

(2) Where the sole evidence of identification connecting the defendant to the crime was uncorroborated, the trial judge should give the jury a clear warning of the danger of a mistaken identification and only in the most exceptional circumstances should a conviction based on uncorroborated identification evidence be upheld in the absence of *c* such a warning. The fact that the defendant had been picked out at an identification parade did not obviate the need for such a warning. In the circumstances the failure of the trial judge in each case to give the jury the appropriate warning vitiated the convictions. It followed therefore that the appeals would be allowed and the convictions quashed (see p 314 *g j* to p 315 *a c d* and p 316 *f*, post); *R v Turnbull* [1976] 3 All ER 549 applied.                                                                    *d*

**Notes**
For a witness's deposition as evidence, see 11 Halsbury's Laws (4th edn) para 427.

**Cases referred to in judgment**
*R v Blithing* (1983) 77 Cr App R 86, CA.                                    *e*
*R v Collins* [1938] 3 All ER 130, CCA.
*R v Linley* [1959] Crim LR 123, Leeds Assizes.
*R v O'Loughlin* [1988] 3 All ER 431, CCC.
*R v Sang* [1979] 2 All ER 1222, [1980] AC 402, [1979] 3 WLR 263, HL.
*R v Turnbull* [1976] 3 All ER 549, [1977] QB 224, [1976] 3 WLR 445, CA.      *f*
*R v White (Donald)* (1975) 24 WIR 305, Jamaica CA.
*R v Whylie* (1978) 25 WIR 430, Jamaica CA.
*Selvey v DPP* [1968] 2 All ER 497, [1970] AC 304, [1968] 2 WLR 1494, HL.
*Sutherland v The State* (1970) 16 WIR 342, Guyana CA.

**Appeals**                                                                   *g*
                                *Scott and anor v R*
Richard Scott and Dennis Walters appealed with special leave of the Judicial Committee of the Privy Council granted on 29 April 1986 against the decision of the Court of Appeal of Jamaica (Carberry, Carey and White JJA) on 20 December 1982 dismissing the appellants' applications for leave to appeal against their convictions and sentences on 25 September 1980 in the Home Circuit Court at Kingston before Campbell J and a jury for *h* murder. The facts are set out in the judgment of the Board.

                                *Barnes and ors v R*
Winston Barnes, Washington Desquottes and Clovis Johnson appealed with special leave of the Judicial Committee of the Privy Council granted on 5 November 1986 against the decision of the Court of Appeal of Jamaica (Carey, Ross JJA and Wright AJA) on 10 *j* February 1986 dismissing their applications for leave to appeal against their convictions and sentences on 24 November 1983 in the Home Circuit Court at Kingston before Parnell J and a jury for murder. The facts are set out in the judgment of the Board.

*Peter Thornton* and *Dennis Daley* (of the Jamaican Bar) for the appellants Scott and Walters.
*Justin Shale* for the appellants Barnes, Desquottes and Johnson.

*The Director of Public Prosecutions of Jamaica (Glen Roy Andrade QC) and Kent S Pantry (of the Jamaican Bar) for the Crown.*

13 March. The following judgment of the Board was delivered.

**LORD GRIFFITHS.** On 25 September 1980 the appellants Richard Scott and Dennis Walters were found guilty of murder and sentenced to death. Their appeals were dismissed by the Court of Appeal of Jamaica on 20 December 1982. On 24 November 1983 the appellants Winston Barnes, Washington Desquottes and Clovis Johnson were found guilty of murder and sentenced to death. They were refused leave to appeal by the Court of Appeal of Jamaica on 10 February 1986.

These appeals have been heard together because they raise a common issue of importance, namely whether a trial judge in a criminal case in Jamaica has a discretion to refuse to admit a sworn deposition of a witness who has died before the trial, and if so in what circumstances the discretion should be exercised. The appeals also require their Lordships to consider further grounds of appeal in each case with which they will deal after considering the common issue.

The prosecution case against Scott and Walters was that on 11 May 1978 the appellants shot Abraham Roberts, a special constable, with his own revolver in a bar at 9 Harris Street, Kingston. He died from his injuries on 15 May 1978. The only eye witnesses to the shooting were a woman who was in the company of the deceased and who was subsequently seen at the police station but who did not give evidence at the trial and David Ridley, the ten-year-old son of the owner of the bar, who had a good opportunity to see those who carried out the shooting but who failed to identify either of the appellants on a subsequent identification parade.

The only evidence of identification of the appellants was that contained in the deposition of Cecil Gordon who died before the trial. The deposition reads:

'This deponent Cecil Gordon, on his oath says as follows: "I am a sideman on a truck and live in the parish of Kingston. On 11th May, 1978, about 2.45 p.m. I was walking on Harris Street, Kingston 13, in the parish of Kingston, and after passing a bar saw two men standing at a gate about half chain from the bar. I walked past these men who were about an arm's length from me and went into the yard. I then went to my gate about two chains away at 2 Harris Street. As I opened the gate I heard an explosion like a gunshot coming from the direction of the bar. I turned around and looked in that direction and saw the two men I had passed on the road running from the bar. One of the men who I had known about five months before that day was running in front with a gun in his hand, the other man was running close behind him. They ran across Harris Street, turned down a cross street and disappeared from my sight. I then saw a woman holding up a man and taking him out of the bar. They passed me at my gate. I followed them down a Spanish Town Road and saw the man leaning against a wall. I went up to him and he raised up his shirt. I then saw a wound at his side. The lady had left him at the time. She returned shortly after in a taxi, the man was placed in the taxi which drove away with him and the lady. I went to the Denham Town Police Station and made a report. On the 19th of May, 1978, about 9.00 p.m., I was walking on Spanish Town Road and saw the two men sitting around a table on the sidewalk playing a game with other men. I went to the Denham Town Police Station and made a report. I went back with the police to Spanish Town Road and saw the two men still playing the game. In the presence and hearing of the two men I told a policeman that they were the two men who had shot the policeman at the bar. The men made no statement. The policeman took them to the Denham Police Station. I went with them. The two accused in the dock are the men I saw running from the bar and who were pointed out by me to the police. The accused Richard Scott is the man I knew before that day. He was the man running in front with the gun in his hand. The accused Walters was running behind the accused Richard Scott. I knew Scott as Owen. Immediately after hearing

the explosion I saw the two accused running from the bar and the lady holding the
man and coming out after them."

Cross-examined by Miss Benbow: "I used to live at 11 Harris Street before going
to 2 Harris Street. I do not know the number of the bar premises. I passed the bar
before reaching the gate at 11 Harris Street. There are other buildings between the
bar and 11 Harris Street. The buildings are houses. There is just one gate between
the bar premises and 11 Harris Street. The two men were standing in front of a gate
at 11 Harris Street. Other people are now living at 11 Harris Street. The two accused
men were standing against the gate column of 11 Harris Street and looking in the
direction of the bar. They were looking sideways down the road. I did not call to
them."

Cross-examined by Miss Lyer: "I have been living on Harris Street for a long time.
The gate of premises 11 Harris Street was open and the accused men were standing
behind the column of the gate. The column was taller than the men. I had turned
into the premises 11 Harris Street and saw the men by the column at the gate.
Premises No. 2 Harris Street is on the other side of the road from 11 Harris Street. I
was going to somebody at 11 Harris Street. I went into 11 Harris Street with the
intention of picking some ackees but they were not yet open. I just looked on the
ackee tree and turned back through the gate. I did not stop to speak to anyone. The
two accused men were still at the gate when I left the premises. I cannot say how
long it took me to walk from 11 Harris Street to 2 High Street. I saw the faces of the
two men when they were running."

To Court: "I did not know the lady who was holding up the man. I had never
seen her before. I saw her at the Denham Town Police Station later that day. I didn't
know the man with the wound before that day."

This is signed by the Resident Magistrate of the Gun Court.

REGISTRAR: Mr. B. L. Myrie, on the 25th of July, 1978 and it is also signed by the
witness Cecil Gordon.'

The appellants both gave evidence and their defence was that neither of them had
been in Harris Street on the day of the shooting and that at the time of their arrest they
were not singled out by Gordon but arrested with a number of other persons.

The prosecution case against Barnes, Desquottes and Johnson was that on the morning
of 3 December 1982 Horace Fowler was shot after stopping his Datsun van in Olympic
Way whilst on his way to his factory in Spanish Town Road and the $1,000 that he had
with him to pay his employees was stolen. The prosecution alleged that Barnes had
hidden in the back of the van and at a prearranged spot had shouted for the van to stop
and that when it stopped Clovis Johnson and Washington Desquottes approached the cab
of the van and Johnson shot and killed Fowler. It was then alleged that all three accused
ran off with Johnson carrying a bag containing the money.

There were two eye witnesses of the shooting, Percival Brown heard the gunshot and
looked in the direction of the van to see Fowler slumped over the wheel of the van. He
saw one man walking away from the van down Fourth Street but was unable to recognise
anyone.

Larkland Green was the other eye witness. He gave evidence at the preliminary
inquiry but was shot and killed before the trial. His deposition including cross-
examination reads as follows:

'This deponent Larkland Green on his oath saith as follows: I am a truck sideman
residing in the parish of St. Andrew. I knew the deceased Horace Fowler. He was
the manager for the Gypsum Factory on the Spanish Town Road. I used to see him
driving a motor van. I do not remember the colour. On 3rd December, 1982, I was
standing at the corner of Olympic Way and Sixth Street in Olympic Gardens and
saw the van driven by the deceased coming from the direction of the bank on
Olympic Way, and reaching near the corner of Sixth Street, near Mr. Austin shop, I

heard the accused Winston Barnes who lying on the floor of the van called out "Hold
on driver" and the driver Mr. Fowler stopped the van. I then saw two men who had
come along Sixth Street stopped at the corner. They were Clovis Johnson and
Washington Desquottes, otherwise called Budda. They are now in the dock. (witness
points to accused man). I saw Clovis Johnson went to the front of the van where the
driver Mr. Fowler was sitting and pushed a gun through the window. I heard an
explosion like a gun shot and saw the accused Clovis Johnson with the gun in his
hand running down Sixth Street, followed by the other two men. Clovis Johnson
had a bag in hand which he did not have when he went up to the van. After the
explosion I observed that Mr. Fowler was lying stretched out on the seat of the van.
A crowd gathered and a man went in the van and drove it away with Mr. Fowler. I
have known Clovis Johnson for more than twenty years. He used to live near to me
at Magesty Gardens. I have known Washington Desquottes, otherwise called Budda
for over one year. I knew him when living at Woodpecker Avenue. I have known
Winston Barnes, o/c Redman for about two years. I used to see him at the Gypsum
Factory. I heard something later that day. I never saw Mr. Fowler again. The
incident took place after lunch time. Lunch time was 12.00 midday.

Cross-examination by Mr. Green who also holds for Mr. Soutar. Clovis Johnson
was a boy when I first knew him. He was about ten years of age at the time. I have
been seeing him all along. He stopped talking to me from he turned away. I was
once a Home Guard. I knew that Johnson was once involved in politics. I do not
know what side he supported. I am a J.L.P. supporter. I was not a P.N.P. at the last
election. There was no bad blood between the accused Johnson and myself. I have
known the accused Barnes for about three years. I have never spoken to him. I was
standing about eight feet from the van when it stopped. (Witness points out
distance). I was standing at a gate. I was standing outside Mr. Austin's gate waiting
on a man that I worked with. People were walking on the road. More buses than
pedestrians passed that corner. Mr Austin's premises is a bar. The other two men
were standing at the corner when the van stopped. As the van stopped the men
went up to it. After the explosion some people ran away, others ran towards the
van. I didn't run away.

Cross-examined by Mr. Williams. The van stopped on Olympic Way. I was
standing on Olympic Way. I was at Mr. Austin's gate. The gate is about ten feet
from the corner. (Witness points out distance). I was not then working at the
Gypsum Factory. I saw the van drove up before seeing the two men. I have no idea
of the time. The men went up to the van as it stopped. The incident with the
accused putting his hand in the front of the van took place in a short time. After the
incident the three men ran down Sixth Street. I saw their backs while they were
running. I was standing on the left hand side of the van. I don't know if the van was
a left or right hand drive vehicle.

Larkland Green, His Mark.

B. L. Myrie,
Resident Magistrate
Gun Court
3.3.83.'

The defence of each defendant was an alibi. Barnes made an unsworn statement from
the dock supported by the sworn evidence of one witness. Desquottes made an unsworn
statement from the dock supported by the sworn evidence of his sister. Johnson gave
sworn evidence in support of his own alibi.

It will be seen from this brief recital of the facts that in each case the vital evidence of
identification was that contained in the sworn depositions of the deceased witnesses.
Without the evidence in the depositions there would have been insufficient evidence to
put any of the appellants on trial. The trial judges in each case admitted the depositions

in evidence pursuant to the provisions of s 34 of the Justices of the Peace Jurisdiction Act, the relevant part of which provides:

'... and if upon the trial of the person so accused as first aforesaid, it shall be proved by the oath or affirmation of any credible witness that any person whose deposition shall have been taken as aforesaid is dead, or so ill as not to be able to travel, or is absent from this Island or is not of competent understanding to give evidence by reason of his being insane, and if also it be proved that such deposition was taken in the presence of the person so accused, and that he, or his counsel or solicitor had a full opportunity of cross-examining the witness, then, if such deposition purport to be signed by the Justice by or before whom the same purports to have been taken, it shall be lawful to read such deposition as evidence in such prosecution, without further proof thereof, unless it shall be proved that such deposition was not, in fact, signed by the Justice purporting to sign the same: Provided, that no deposition of a person absent from the Island or insane shall be read in evidence under the powers of this section, save with the consent of the court before which the trial takes place.'

In its original form the section only provided for a deposition to be read in evidence if the deponent was dead or too ill to attend the trial. The power to read the deposition if the deponent was absent from the island or insane was added by amendment and it was at the same time provided that this power should be subject to the consent of the court. That this additional power should be made subject to the consent of the court is readily understandable. If absence from the island is temporary an adjournment may be more just than continuing without the presence of the witness and if the witness becomes insane it may cast grave doubt on the value of his evidence. But no similar statutory discretion is bestowed on the court if the witness is dead or gravely ill. The judgment of Carberry JA in the appeal of Scott and Walters contains a masterly analysis of the historical background of s 34 and the corresponding provisions contained in English statute and common law. Their Lordships accept his conclusion that no statutory discretion is bestowed on a judge by s 34 to exclude a deposition if a witness is dead or too ill to attend court. If such a statutory discretion had existed it would have been unnecessary to provide specifically for such a discretion when the two additional grounds of admissibility, namely absence from the island and insanity, were subsequently added to the statute.

There remains however the further question whether, even if a deposition is admissible under s 34, there exists at common law a power in a judge to refuse to allow the prosecution to adduce it in evidence.

Two recent cases in the House of Lords *Selvey v DPP* [1968] 2 All ER 497, [1970] AC 304 and *R v Sang* [1979] 2 All ER 1222, [1980] AC 402 contain numerous judicial dicta that refer to the discretion of a judge in a criminal trial to exclude admissible evidence if it is necessary in order to secure a fair trial for the accused. In *Selvey's* case the power was held to extend to exclude the admission of the character of the accused under s 1(f)(ii) of the Criminal Evidence Act 1898. In *R v Sang* the Court of Appeal certified the following question of law for the consideration of the House:

'Does a trial judge have a discretion to refuse to allow evidence, being evidence other than evidence of admission, to be given in any circumstances in which such evidence is relevant and of more than minimal probative value?'

The answer to that question contained in the speech of Lord Diplock, with which the rest of their Lordships agreed, was in the following terms ([1979] 2 All ER 1222 at 1231, [1980] AC 402 at 437):

'(1) A trial judge in a criminal trial has always a discretion to refuse to admit evidence if in his opinion its prejudicial effect outweighs its probative value. (2) Save with regard to admissions and confessions and generally with regard to evidence obtained from the accused after commission of the offence, he has no discretion to refuse to admit relevant admissible evidence on the ground that it was obtained by improper or unfair means. The court is not concerned with how it was obtained. It is no ground for the exercise of the discretion to exclude that the evidence was obtained as the result of the activities of an agent provocateur.'

The phrase 'prejudicial effect' is a reference to the fact that although evidence has been admitted to prove certain collateral matters there is a danger that a jury may attach undue weight to such evidence and regard it as probative of the crime with which the accused is charged. An example is the admission of the bad character of the accused if he has attacked the character of a prosecution witness. This evidence of the accused's bad character is admitted to assist the jury to decide how far they can rely on the allegations he makes against the prosecution witness and therefore what weight they should attach to the evidence of that prosecution witness. It is not admitted to prove that because the accused is a man of bad character he is more likely to have committed the crime because English law does not regard a propensity to commit crime as probative of the particular crime with which the accused is charged. Nevertheless, there may be a danger that knowledge of the accused's bad character may unduly prejudice the jury against him.

In the case of Barnes, Desquottes and Johnson it was submitted to the Court of Appeal that the prejudicial effect of the deposition outweighed its probative value. This was a misuse of the phrase. The evidence in the deposition was highly probative of the offence, it was the evidence of an eye witness well placed to see the events he described. It was only 'prejudicial' in the sense that it was on the face of it strong prosecution evidence that might well result in the conviction of the accused. The Court of Appeal, after citing R v Sang, rejected the submission, saying:

'In the instant case, as already pointed out, there was no question of the prejudicial effect of the evidence outweighing its probative value, the evidence had not been obtained from any of the applicants, and since the evidence was relevant and admissible the learned trial judge had no discretion to exclude it from the trial.'

Whilst agreeing with the Court of Appeal that the admission in evidence of the deposition did not fall within the rule that evidence may be excluded on the ground that its prejudicial weight excludes its probative value, their Lordships do not accept that because the deposition is relevant and admissible evidence a judge has *no* discretion to exclude it.

In R v Sang the House was not concerned to consider the problem of the admissibility of depositions and a number of their Lordships were careful to state that the discretion was not limited to cases where the prejudicial effect of evidence outweighed its probative value. In particular Lord Salmon said ([1979] 2 All ER 1222 at 1237, [1980] AC 402 at 445):

'I recognise that there may have been no categories of cases, other than those to which I have referred, in which technically admissible evidence proffered by the Crown has been rejected by the court on the ground that it would make the trial unfair. I cannot, however, accept that a judge's undoubted duty to ensure that the accused has a fair trial is confined to such cases. In my opinion the category of such cases is not and never can be closed except by statute. I understand that the answer given by my noble and learned friend, Lord Diplock, to the certified question accepts the proposition which I have just stated. On that basis, I respectfully agree with that answer.'

See also the speeches of Lord Fraser and Lord Scarman ([1979] 2 All ER 1222 at 1239, 1243, [1980] AC 402 at 447, 452).

There have been a number of decisions in which a deposition has been excluded. In R v Linley [1959] Crim LR 123 Ashworth J refused to allow the evidence of the victim of a robbery to be read. In *R v O'Loughlin* [1988] 3 All ER 431 Kenneth Jones J refused to permit the depositions of two witnesses and the statement of a police officer to be read in an IRA trial where this evidence constituted the sole evidence against the accused. It should however be noted that in that case the judge was exercising the statutory discretion recently bestowed by s 78(1) of the Police and Criminal Evidence Act 1984. In *R v Blithing* (1983) 77 Cr App R 86 the Court of Appeal allowed an appeal on the ground that the trial judge should have exercised his discretion to exclude a statement tendered in committal proceedings which is treated as equivalent to a deposition under the English statute. Again in parenthesis it is to be noted that the court assumed that the discretion existed under s 13(3) of the Criminal Justice Act 1925. The Court of Appeal held that the discretion should be exercised to ensure that the defendant received a fair trial and allowed the appeal because the judge had held that the discretion should only be exercised if it would be 'grossly unfair' to the accused to admit the statement. Their Lordships are very doubtful whether they would have exercised the discretion in the same way as the Court of Appeal on the facts of that case but do not dissent from the proposition that the discretion should be exercised to ensure a fair trial for the accused.

In *R v White (Donald)* (1975) 24 WIR 305 the Court of Appeal in Jamaica held that the trial judge had a common law discretion which he ought to have exercised on the particular facts of that case to exclude a deposition which contained the only evidence against the accused in an identification case. The Court of Appeal in Scott and Walters were critical of some of the reasoning of that decision, but did not go so far as to say it was wrongly decided in so far as it recognised the existence of the discretion at common law. In *Sutherland v The State* (1970) 16 WIR 342 the Court of Appeal in Guyana recognised a discretion at common law to exclude a deposition if its admission would be likely to produce injustice of a kind inconsistent with a fair trial; although on the facts of that case the Court of Appeal held the deposition had been properly admitted.

There is one further case to which reference is made in some of the authorities but which has little bearing on the problem raised in the present appeal. In *R v Collins* [1938] 3 All ER 130 the accused had indicated to the examining magistrates that he intended to plead guilty at his trial. The magistrates therefore bound over the witnesses for the prosecution conditionally under s 13 of the Criminal Justice Act 1925 as it appeared that no witnesses would be required at the trial. When the accused appeared at quarter sessions he changed his mind and pleaded not guilty. He asked for an adjournment to call witnesses to prove an alibi. His application for an adjournment was refused and the deputy chairman allowed the prosecution to prove their case by reading the depositions of the witnesses who had been conditionally bound. Humphreys J, in giving the judgment of the Court of Criminal Appeal, stated that the course adopted by the deputy chairman 'was not intended by the statute and . . . could never have been contemplated by Parliament' (at 132). This observation was manifestly correct: the power to bind over a witness conditionally was introduced to provide for the situation when the evidence of a witness is uncontroversial and unchallenged so that it can be read without putting the witness to the unnecessary inconvenience of attending the trial. In making this point Humphreys J naturally stressed the normal form of jury trial and the value of cross-examination; but his remarks in this context are no reliable guide to the considerations that should weigh with a judge when considering whether or not to exercise his discretion to admit a deposition.

In the light of these authorities their Lordships are satisfied that the discretion of a judge to ensure a fair trial includes a power to exclude the admission of a deposition. It is, however, a power that should be exercised with great restraint. The mere fact that the deponent will not be available for cross-examination is obviously an insufficient ground for excluding the deposition, for that is a feature common to the admission of all depositions which must have been contemplated and accepted by the legislature when it gave statutory sanction to their admission in evidence. If the courts are too ready to exclude the deposition of a deceased witness, it may well place the lives of witnesses at

risk particularly in a case where only one witness has been courageous enough to give
a evidence against the accused or only one witness has had the opportunity to identify the
accused. It will of course be necessary in every case to warn the jury that they have not
had the benefit of hearing the evidence of the deponent tested in cross-examination and
to take that into consideration when considering how far they can safely rely on the
evidence in the deposition. No doubt in many cases it will be appropriate for a judge to
develop this warning by pointing out particular features of the evidence in the deposition
b which conflict with other evidence and which could have been explored in cross-
examination; but no rules can usefully be laid down to control the detail to which a
judge should descend in the individual case. In an identification case it will, in addition,
be necessary to give the appropriate warning of the danger of identification evidence.
The deposition must of course be scrutinised by the judge to ensure that it does not
contain inadmissible matters such as hearsay or matter that is prejudicial rather than
c probative and any such material should be excluded from the deposition before it is read
to the jury.

Provided these precautions are taken it is only in rare circumstances that it would be
right to exercise the discretion to exclude the deposition. Those circumstances will arise
when the judge is satisfied that it will be unsafe for the jury to rely on the evidence in
the deposition. It will be unwise to attempt to define or forecast in more particular terms
d the nature of such circumstances. This much however can be said, that neither the ability
to cross-examine, nor the fact that the deposition contains the only evidence against the
accused, nor the fact that it is identification evidence will of itself be sufficient to justify
the exercise of the discretion.

It is the quality of the evidence in the deposition that is the crucial factor that should
determine the exercise of the discretion. By way of example, if the deposition contains
e evidence of identification that is so weak that a judge in the absence of corroborative
evidence would withdraw the case from the jury, then, if there is no corroborative
evidence, the judge should exercise his discretion to refuse to admit the deposition for it
would be unsafe to allow the jury to convict on it. But this is an extreme case and it is to
be hoped that prosecutions will not generally be pursued on such weak evidence. In a
case in which the deposition contains identification evidence of reasonable quality then
f even if it is the only evidence it should be possible to protect the interests of the accused
by clear directions in the summing up and the deposition should be admitted. It is only
when the judge decides that such directions cannot ensure a fair trial that the discretion
should be exercised to exclude the deposition.

In neither of the present appeals was the evidence of identification contained in the
depositions of such poor quality that it would be unsafe to convict on it if the jury had
g received the appropriate guidance in the summing up. There were, accordingly, no
grounds on which it would have been right to exercise the discretion to exclude the
admission of these depositions in evidence.

Their Lordships turn now to consider the additional grounds of appeal. In the case of
Scott and Walters it is submitted that the judge failed to give an adequate direction on
h the issue of identification. Experience has taught judges that no matter how honest a
witness and no matter how convinced he may be of the rightness of his opinion his
evidence of identity may be wrong and that it is at least highly desirable that such
evidence should be corroborated. It has however also been recognised that to require
identification evidence in all cases to be corroborated as a matter of law will tilt the
balance too far against the prosecution. The compromise of this dilemma arrived at in R
j v Turnbull [1976] 3 All ER 549, [1977] QB 224 is the requirement that a judge must warn
the jury in the clearest terms of the risk of a mistaken identification. Lord Widgery CJ
giving the judgment of the five-judge court said ([1976] 3 All ER 549 at 551–552, [1977]
QB 224 at 228):

'First, whenever the case against an accused depends wholly or substantially on the correctness of one or more identifications of the accused which the defence alleges to be mistaken, the judge should warn the jury of the special need for caution before convicting the accused in reliance on the correctness of the identification or identifications. In addition he should instruct them as to the reason for the need for such a warning and should make some reference to the possibility that a mistaken witness can be a convincing one and that a number of such witnesses can all be mistaken. Provided this is done in clear terms the judge need not use any particular form of words.'

In *R v Whylie* (1978) 25 WIR 430 at 432 the Court of Appeal in Jamaica, following *R v Turnbull*, said:

'Where, therefore, in a criminal case the evidence for the prosecution connecting the accused to the crime rests wholly or substantially on the visual identification of one or more witnesses and the defence challenges the correctness of that identification, the trial judge should alert the jury to approach the evidence of identification with the utmost caution as there is always the possibility that a single witness or several witnesses might be mistaken.'

Never can the importance of such a warning be greater than in a case such as the present where the sole evidence of identity is contained in the deposition of a deceased witness and where the quality of the identification may have been of the fleeting glance type, for in cross-examination the witness said he saw the men's faces as they ran from the bar. It is possible that he may have recognised the men as he passed them earlier in the street but he does not say so in the deposition and there will of course be no opportunity for investigating the matter at trial.

In dealing with the evidence of Gordon the judge never warned the jury that although Gordon may have been an honest witness his identification of the two accused might nevertheless be mistaken. On the contrary, the emphasis throughout is on the question of the adequacy of the opportunity that Gordon had for observing the two accused. These passages in the summing up, so far from conveying any warning of the danger of mistake, carry the clear implication that provided that the identifying witness had a sufficient opportunity to observe the accused the identification evidence may be safely relied on. The concluding paragraph in the passage dealing with the identification evidence again, so far from hinting at any danger in reliance on the identification evidence, suggests by implication that the confidence with which Gordon picked out the two accused when they were found amongst others at the bingo game in some way authenticates the identification itself. This of course is erroneous. The fact that an identifying witness has picked out the accused at an identification parade in no way obviates the need for a warning of the danger that his evidence may be mistaken.

The Court of Appeal considered that the judge's direction on identification was adequate and referred to the fact that he had pointed out the circumstances in which the identification was made and the handicap the jury suffered in not seeing the witness cross-examined. The Court of Appeal also said: 'The judge discussed with the jury . . . the danger of identification evidence.' With all respect to the Court of Appeal, the judge did not discuss with the jury the fundamental danger of identification evidence which is that the honest witness convinced of the correctness of his identity may yet be mistaken. Their Lordships have given anxious consideration to the question of whether this submission is fatal to the convictions. They take into account that the jury had the opportunity to see the accused give evidence and clearly rejected their alibis and that they took only 11 minutes to arrive at their verdict. Their Lordships have nevertheless concluded that if convictions are to be allowed on uncorroborated identification evidence there must be a strict insistence on a judge giving a clear warning of the danger of a mistaken identification which the jury must consider before arriving at their verdict, and that it would only be in the most exceptional circumstances that a conviction based

on uncorroborated identification evidence should be sustained in the absence of such a
*a* warning. In this capital offence their Lordships cannot be satisfied that the jury would
inevitably have convicted if they had received the appropriate warning in the summing
up and they will accordingly advise Her Majesty to allow the appeal of Scott and Walters.

The same point on lack of a proper direction on identification evidence is taken on
behalf of the appellants, Barnes, Desquottes and Johnson. The judge in this case gave no
direction of any kind on the issue of identification. He did not warn the jury of the
*b* danger of a mistaken identification nor did he draw attention to the circumstances in
which it was made or to the fact that it differed from the evidence of the other eye
witness, Brown.

The Court of Appeal in rejecting the appeal on this ground said:

*c*
> 'A failure to warn the jury of dangers inherent in visual identification cases, it
> must be borne in mind, is but one of the factors to be taken into consideration in
> determining the fairness and adequacy of a summing up.'

This passage gives too little weight to the recognised dangers of convicting on
uncorroborated evidence of identity. For the reasons already given a failure to give a
warning of the danger of identification evidence is generally to be regarded as a fatal flaw
in a summing up and almost inevitably so in a case such as the present where the sole
*d* evidence of identity is the uncorroborated deposition of a deceased witness. Their
Lordships are satisfied that the failure to give any direction on the issue of identity is a
sufficient reason to compel them to advise Her Majesty to allow the appeal in this case.

Barnes and Desquottes also appeal on the ground that no adequate direction was given
on whether or not they might be guilty of manslaughter rather than murder on the
ground that they were not party to a common enterprise to use a firearm in the robbery.
*e* In their Lordships' view the circumstances of this case did call for a direction on common
enterprise which would have left the issue of manslaughter to the jury, albeit there was
evidence on which the jury would be entitled to conclude that all three men were party
to a common enterprise to use the gun. However, as their Lordships are satisfied that the
appeal must be allowed on the issue of identification, they do not propose to go further
into this issue which depends solely on the particular circumstances of this case.
*f* Complaint was also made that the judge gave the impression to the jury that the
witness of identification had been deliberately liquidated to prevent him giving evidence.
Their Lordships are sure that the judge had no intention to convey any such impression,
nevertheless they have misgivings that the judge's choice of language may have
unwittingly sown the seed of such a suspicion in the minds of the jury. The judge in the
presence of the jury delivered a long ruling giving his reasons for admitting the
*g* deposition of the deceased witness, in the course of which he said:

> 'That application was based on the evidence that Larkland Green was a witness
> called at the preliminary inquiry into this charge, and that after giving evidence at
> the inquiry, and before the start of this trial, he was shot and killed.'

*h* And at a later stage in the ruling he said, discussing s 34:

> 'The other instance is where the witness, having given evidence at the preliminary
> inquiry and before the Circuit Court trial begins, has died. And it doesn't matter
> whether the witness was deliberately liquidated for the purpose of putting him out
> of the way so that he cannot give evidence, or he dies of natural causes, of a heart
> attack, for instance, it doesn't matter, once it is proved he has died.'

*j* And, finally, he finished his ruling by saying:

> 'It would be a serious thing. That was what I was trying to avoid from away back
> in 1974, for it to be authorised in Jamaica; for it to be believed in Jamaica; or that it
> should be the law in Jamaica, that a man can commit a serious offence and those

acting on his behalf, or even with his assistance, only have to eliminate the chief witness to secure his own acquittal. That if that were laid down to be the law in   *a* Jamaica, I shudder at what should happen. The evidence that we have is that of the chief witness—I make no further comment, it is the subject of police inquiry, and it would have to be, because the officer who gave the evidence saw the man dead on the street with a bullet in the head, to at least enforce the preliminary inquiry into the cause of death the police would have to inquire into it.'

In the course of the summing up the judge said:

> 'Now, witnesses were called on both sides but principal witness, Mr Larkland Green, who would have been called if he had been alive, is gone beyond, way beyond, and miracles are not being worked these days where you can raise a man from the dead, so you remember listening to that lengthy legal argument as to whether or not I should have allowed the deposition of this witness to be read ...   *c* the only eye witness to the incident, Larkland Green, who, at the preliminary examination, implicated the three accused, was shot to death on 11 May 1983. That was about two months after he had given evidence at the preliminary examination. That is not under any dispute.'

Larkland Green was found by the police shot dead in the street with a man named   *d* Bennett who had also been shot to death. Bennett had no connection with this case and there is no suggestion that Green's death was in any way connected with the accused or anyone acting in their interest. Their Lordships nevertheless feel considerable unease that the judge's remarks may have at least implanted in the jury's mind the suspicion that Green was killed to prevent him giving evidence that identified the accused. The judge should have heard the arguments of counsel and have given his ruling on the   *e* admissibility of the evidence in the absence of the jury and should have avoided language in the summing up that could be interpreted as carrying any implication that the witness had been killed to prevent him giving evidence. This then is another feature of the trial that contributes to the final decision of their Lordships humbly to advise Her Majesty that the interests of justice demand that the convictions of these appellants should be quashed and their appeal allowed.   *f*

*Appeals allowed. Convictions quashed.*

Solicitors: *Simons Muirhead & Burton* (for the appellants); *Charles Russell Williams & James* (for the Crown).

Mary Rose Plummer   Barrister.

*a*    # Mills and others v Winchester Diocesan Board of Finance and others

CHANCERY DIVISION
KNOX J
*b*    7, 8 DECEMBER 1988

*Charity – Proceedings – Parties – Charity Commissioners – Action in negligence against commissioners – Commissioners giving opinion or advice that local charity comprising educational trust had failed – Local inhabitants claiming that commissioners' opinion and advice erroneous and that commissioners had failed to exercise due care and skill in giving opinion and advice –*
*c*    *Whether commissioners owing duty of care to potential objects of charity – Whether action lying against commissioners in negligence – Charities Act 1960, ss 24, 28.*

*Negligence – Duty to take care – Existence of duty – Charity Commissioners – Action in negligence against commissioners – Commissioners giving opinion or advice that local charity comprising educational trust had failed – Local inhabitants claiming that commissioners' opinion and advice*
*d*    *erroneous and that commissioners had failed to exercise due care and skill in giving opinion and advice – Whether commissioners owing duty of care to potential objects of charity – Whether action lying against commissioners in negligence.*

In 1942 land and premises in a village were conveyed to the diocesan board of finance on trust to be used by the vicar of the village as a school or for other educational purposes if
*e*    they ceased to be used as a school. Thereafter the premises were used as a school under the control of the local education authority but in 1986 the authority decided to cease maintaining the school. The plaintiffs, who were inhabitants of the village, put forward proposals for the premises to be used as a nursery school and the diocesan board of finance sought the opinion or advice of the Charity Commissioners under s 24(1)ᵃ of the Charities Act 1960 but the commissioners rejected those proposals on the ground that they were
*f*    outside the powers of the trusts. The commissioners took the view that the trusts had failed and the diocesan board of finance, on the advice of the commissioners, proposed to sell the land and premises with planning permission and use the proceeds for diocesan purposes. Under s 28ᵇ of the 1960 Act there was provision for the validity of advice given by the commissioners under s 24 to be challenged by means of charity proceedings in which the determination of the court on the validity of that advice could be sought with
*g*    the leave of the commissioners or the court. The plaintiffs brought an action against the diocesan board of finance, the commissioners and the Attorney General alleging that the commissioners' opinion and advice were erroneous and that they had unreasonably frustrated the proposals for a nursery school. The plaintiffs sought declarations that the trusts had not failed, that the commissioners' opinion and advice were erroneous and that the establishment of a nursery school was within the trusts and also sought an order that
*h*    the commissioners bear the costs of the proceedings. On the application of the commissioners the master struck out the claim against them on the ground that it disclosed no cause of action against them. The plaintiffs brought a second action against the same parties in which they alleged that in giving an erroneous opinion and advice the commissioners had been negligent in failing to exercise due care and skill, and sought, inter alia, damages for negligence against the commissioners. On the application
*j*    of the commissioners the master also struck out that claim against them on the ground that it disclosed no cause of action against them. The plaintiffs appealed against both striking out orders.

---

*a*    Section 24 is set out at p 325 *c d*, post
*b*    Section 28, so far as material, is set out at p 325 *g h* and p 326 *b*, post

**Held** – The existence of a statutory right of appeal under s 28 of the 1960 Act in respect
of an erroneous opinion and advice given by the Charity Commissioners under s 24 of  *a*
that Act, the disadvantages of a negligence action against the commissioners proceeding
concurrently with charity proceedings under s 28 and the negative effect on the general
good of charities if the commissioners' decisions were open to attack by means of
negligence actions brought by such a wide class as potential objects of charity combined
to negative the existence of a duty of care owed by the commissioners to the potential
objects of charity. In any event it was doubtful whether there was sufficient proximity  *b*
between a potential object of a charity and the commissioners to give rise, if coupled
with damage, to a right to damages for negligence. Alternatively, having regard to those
factors it would not be just and reasonable for the commissioners to be under a duty of
care at common law to the potential objects of charity. Accordingly, the claim in
negligence against the commissioners had been rightly struck out. Without that claim
the proceedings were charity proceedings under s 28 and it would be contrary to the  *c*
settled practice of the court and would needlessly add to costs if the commissioners were
parties to those proceedings. Furthermore, neither the claim for costs nor the claim for a
declaration that the commissioners' opinion and advice were erroneous justified the
commissioners being parties to the proceedings and accordingly the other claims against
the commissioners had been rightly struck out (see p 326 *g h*, p 331 *h* to p 332 *d f* and
p 333 *a*, post).  *d*

> *Jones v Dept of Employment* [1988] 1 All ER 725 followed.
> *Ministry of Housing and Local Government v Sharp* [1970] 1 All ER 1009 and *Anns v
Merton London Borough* [1977] 2 All ER 492 considered.

**Notes**
For the general powers of the Charity Commissioners to authorise dealings with the  *e*
administration of a trust, and the giving of advice and opinion, see 5 Halsbury's Laws
(4th edn) paras 790–793, 795–796, and for cases on the subject, see 8(1) Digest (Reissue)
460–463, 2140–2143, 2150–2179.
For the Charities Act 1960, ss 24, 28, see 5 Halsbury's Statutes (4th edn) 726, 729.

**Cases referred to in judgment**  *f*
*Anns v Merton London Borough* [1977] 2 All ER 492, [1978] AC 728, [1977] 2 WLR 1024,
HL.
*Belling (decd), Re, Enfield London Borough v Public Trustee* [1967] 1 All ER 105, [1967] Ch
425, [1967] 2 WLR 382.
*Clarke v Bruce Lance & Co (a firm)* [1988] 1 All ER 364, [1988] 1 WLR 881, CA.
*Curran v Northern Ireland Co-ownership Housing Association Ltd (Stewart, third party)* [1987]  *g*
2 All ER 13, [1987] AC 718, [1987] 2 WLR 1043, HL.
*Davis Contractors Ltd v Fareham UDC* [1956] 2 All ER 145, [1956] AC 696, [1956] 3 WLR
37, HL.
*Donoghue (or M'Alister) v Stevenson* [1932] AC 562, [1932] All ER Rep 1, HL.
*Hauxwell v Barton-upon-Humber UDC* [1973] 2 All ER 1022, [1974] Ch 432, [1973] 3 WLR  *h*
41.
*Hedley Byrne & Co Ltd v Heller & Partners Ltd* [1963] 2 All ER 575, [1964] AC 465, [1963]
3 WLR 101, HL.
*Henley v Lyme Corp* (1828) 5 Bing 91, 130 ER 995; *affd* (1832) 3 B & Ad 77, 110 ER 29;
*affd* (1834) 1 Bing NC 222, [1824–34] All ER Rep 503, 131 ER 1103, HL.
*Home Office v Dorset Yacht Co Ltd* [1970] 2 All ER 294, [1970] AC 1004, [1970] 2 WLR  *j*
1140, HL.
*Jones v Dept of Employment* [1988] 1 All ER 725, [1989] QB 1, [1988] 2 WLR 493, CA.
*Lane v Cotton* (1701) 1 Ld Raym 646, [1558–1774] All ER Rep 109, 91 ER 1332.
*McLoughlin v O'Brian* [1982] 2 All ER 298, [1983] 1 AC 410, [1982] 2 WLR 982, HL.
*Ministry of Housing and Local Government v Sharp* [1970] 1 All ER 1009, [1970] 2 QB 223,
[1970] 2 WLR 802, CA.

*Peabody Donation Fund (Governors) v Sir Lindsay Parkinson & Co Ltd* [1984] 3 All ER 529,
a     [1985] AC 210, [1984] 3 WLR 953, HL.
*Saunderson v Baker and Martin* (1772) 3 Wils KB 309, 95 ER 1072.
*Sutherland Shire Council v Heyman* (1985) 60 ALR 1, Aust HC.
*Ultramares Corp v Touche* (1931) 255 NY 170, NY Ct of Apps.
*Yuen Kun-yeu v A-G of Hong Kong* [1987] 2 All ER 705, [1988] AC 175, [1987] 3 WLR 776,
        PC.

b

**Appeals**
By notices of appeal dated 17 June 1988 and 1 November 1988 respectively the first and
second plaintiffs, Rosamund Mary Mills and Derek Russell de Cowey Trasenter, in an
action brought with the third and fourth plaintiffs, Anita Lucie Fideline Taylor and Barry
Lawson Bays, against the Winchester Diocesan Board of Finance, the Charity
c    Commissioners and the Attorney General, appealed against two orders made by Master
Barratt on 13 June 1988 and 19 October 1988 respectively striking out the claims against
the commissioners. The facts are set out in the judgment of the court.


The first and second plaintiffs appeared in person.
d    *Peter Crampin* for the commissioners.
The other parties did not appear.


**KNOX J.** I have before me two appeals from orders of Master Barratt, one in each of
two actions. The actions are between the same parties and concern the same subject
e    matter. In each action there are four plaintiffs and at present, disregarding the order that
is being appealed, three defendants. The plaintiffs are all inhabitants of the village of
Upton Grey and it is in that capacity that they bring these proceedings. The defendants
are the Winchester Diocesan Board of Finance, the Charity Commissioners and Her
Majesty's Attorney-General. The issue before me today, put in a sentence, is whether the
orders made by the master striking out the second defendant, the Charity Commissioners,
f    in both actions, essentially on the ground that the pleaded cases against them disclosed
no cause of action in law, were correct.
    For the purposes of determining applications to strike out on the basis that no cause of
action in law is shown, the court assumes, without deciding, that the allegations of fact
contained in the statement of claim are true. I wish to emphasise that I am not deciding
whether what the plaintiffs plead to be the facts of this case are correct, although the basic
g    underlying historical facts are not seriously in dispute: I am making an assumption that
the pleaded facts are correct in order to test the question of whether, putting the case at
its highest in the plaintiffs' favour, it is proper for the commissioners to remain as parties
to the actions.
    The first action was started by writ on 7 April 1988. The statement of claim sets out
some of the terms on which a piece of land and premises at that village of Upton Grey in
h    Hampshire were conveyed to the first defendant, the diocesan board, by a conveyance
dated 28 January 1942. That conveyance is an admitted document and there are the
following provisions quoted from it in the statement of claim in the first action.
    Paragraph 3 of that statement of claim (as amended) reads:

        'By the said conveyance the Winchester Diocesan Board of Finance took the
j        premises upon the following trusts among others: (1) *Clause 8(b)* To be used by the
        Vicar for the time being of Upton Grey for all or any of the following purposes, that
        is to say ... "as a School or Schools for the Education of Children and Adults or
        Children only of the labouring manufacturing and other poorer classes in the Parish
        of Upton Grey aforesaid." and or "as a Class-Room Meeting Room or Lecture-Room
        for confirmation or Communicants' Classes or for other Religious Instruction or for
        Secular Instruction." (2) *Clause 11* The premises were to be in all respects under the

sole management and control of the Vicar who should from time to time direct for
what purpose or purposes and in what manner the same should be used. (3) *Clause*  *a*
13 That the Bishop of the Diocese shall have the powers of a Visitor over the trust
premises and over the management and control thereof and that the said Vicar shall `
in all things whatsoever pertaining to the said trust observe and carry out all
directions or orders from time to time made or to be made by the Bishop of the
Diocese. (4) *Clause 14* That if at any time the hereditaments cease to be used as
aforesaid, the same shall be held upon trust for some other purposes for the  *b*
education of poor persons in religious and useful knowledge.'

I can pass over the next two paragraphs of the statement of claim. I come then to para
6, which states what happened historically and is not, I understand, in serious dispute:

'Up to 1986 the said premises were in the possession and control of the Local
Education Authority and used as a school for the education of the children of Upton  *c*
Grey and surrounding neighbourhood. But in 1986 the Local Education Authority
published proposals to cease to maintain the school. The inhabitants submitted
objections and went in a Delegation to London. But the Department of Education
over-ruled their objections and gave approval to the closure of the school and it was
closed.'
                                                                                   *d*
Paragraph 7 again contains historical facts which I think are not in serious issue:

'In February 1987 the Plaintiffs with the support of many of the residents of
Upton Grey (expressed strongly at a large village meeting at which the Diocesan
Secretary was present) put forward proposals in writing for the premises to be used
as a school for the Under-Fives in Upton Grey.'
                                                                                   *e*
The plaintiffs say that the proposals are within the powers of the trusts.

Paragraph 8 sets out the attitude of the diocesan board as sympathetic, by reference to
a letter that it wrote, and it goes on as follows with regard to the commissioners:

'But the Charity Commissioners after a lapse of three months (in a letter dated 23
April but received on 11 May) rejected the proposals saying that they are not within  *f*
the powers of the trust: and that the trusts had failed and repeatedly asserted this
view . . .'

In consequence the diocesan board on the advice of the commissioners intend to sell the
premises with outline planning permission and use the whole or part of the proceeds for
diocesan benefit. The reasoning of the commissioners is set out in the letter that is
identified.                                                                         *g*

Then there are paragraphs that deal with the attitude of the Bishop of Winchester and
the vicar, and then there are further paragraphs which deal with the principal question
that will come before the court, but not today, namely what is the true construction of
the words that I have already read from the earlier part of the statement of claim,
'labouring manufacturing and other poorer classes' in cl 8(b) and possibly 'poor' in cl 14.  *h*

I can take the statement of claim for present purposes up at para 14, which states what
the locus standi of the plaintiffs is:

'The charity is a "local Charity." It was established for purposes which are directed
wholly for the benefit of the Parish of Upton Grey and neighbourhood. The
Plaintiffs are four of the inhabitants of the area. They are taking these proceedings
in good faith at their own expense for the benefit of the locality . . .' .          *j*

and there is a reference to the Charities Act, ss 28(1) and 45(1).

Paragraph 15 reads:

'These proceedings are brought under the Court's jurisdiction with respect to

a

trusts: in relation to the administration of a trust for charitable purposes. They are "charitable proceedings" (Section 28(8)).'

Then there are questions about joining the Attorney General about which I am not concerned, because he has now been joined, and that is not appealed from.

There is a statement that the plaintiffs are proceeding by writ because they want discovery and a statement that the commissioners have no right to veto the proceedings.

b

That is not in dispute because there is, of course, a right of appeal, as I shall mention later, in relation to the giving of consent to the bringing of charity proceedings. I can pick the matter up at para 19, which reads:

'The aforesaid letter of 10 February 1987 was a written application by the Charity Trustees to the Commissioners for their opinion and advice within Section 24 of the Charities Act 1960 [that is a reference to the application that was made by the

c

diocesan board to the commissioners, as mentioned at the beginning of para 8 of the statement of claim]: and the letter dated 23 April 1987 ... contained the opinion and advice of the Commissioners given under that section [that is s 24]. These were followed by other letters to the same effect including one from the Department of Education dated 8 January [1988] and of the Commissioners dated 3 February 1988. The opinion and advice of the Commissioners in those letters were erroneous in that

d

the Commissioners repeatedly said that the proposals for a nursery school were not within the powers of the trust and that the trusts had failed.'

That is the central allegation in this first statement of claim as against the commissioners. Paragraph 20 reads:

e

'Following on that opinion and advice (and another written application under Section 24) the Commissioners gave their opinion and advice that they would be prepared to make an order authorising the Board to sell the property ... Such an order would be made under Section 23 of the Act. It implied that the Charity Commissioners were of opinion that a sale was expedient in the interests of the charity and could be made without any [cy-près] scheme.'

f

I can then pass over the next few paragraphs, and go to the last paragraph, which sums up what the case against the commissioners is said to be and it introduces a claim in relation to costs in the following words:

'25. In all the circumstances aforesaid the Commissioners have unreasonably frustrated the proposals of the inhabitants for a nursery school at Upton Grey. Their opinion and advice were erroneous. It has brought about this litigation. They should

g

pay the costs of it.'

That is the whole of the statement of claim so far as is relevant to what I have to decide, but I should read what the relief is that the plaintiffs seek in this action. It is under four paragraphs. The first paragraph is for a declaration as to the meaning of the words '"labouring manufacturing and other poorer classes" in the Parish of Upton Grey' in the

h

1942 deed, as applicable today. The second is for a declaration that the establishment of a nursery school for under-fives in Upton Grey and neighbourhood is within the power of the trusts. The third is for a declaration that the trusts have not failed, and the fourth is for a declaration that the advice and opinion of the commissioners were erroneous.

In that action, therefore, there are three types of claim advanced: first of all, the questions of construction under the 1942 conveyance and whether the trusts thereof

j

have failed; second, a declaration is sought that the advice and opinion of the commissioners were erroneous; and, third, there is a claim that the commissioners should bear the cost of the proceedings. There is no claim in that action that the commissioners did more than give erroneous advice under s 24 of the 1960 Act. In particular, there is no allegation of negligence or claim to damages against them

In relation to that action, on 13 June 1988 the master made an order, inter alia, that the commissioners do cease to be a party to this action, and that para 4 of the prayer for *a* relief in the amended statement of claim be struck out on the grounds that the amended statement of claim discloses no reasonable cause of action against the commissioners, and that the plaintiffs do pay to the defendants their costs in both the said applications. From that decision, the plaintiffs appeal. The notice of appeal is dated 17 June 1988, and there is no question but that it was given in time. It is a notice that the plaintiffs intend to appeal against the orders that the commissioners cease to be parties in the action and that *b* para 4 of the prayer of relief be struck out, and against the order for costs.

The second action was started by writ on 17 June 1988, which is very shortly after the master gave that decision. Further questions of construction as to the meaning of the expression 'poor persons' in cl 14 are raised in the statement of claim, and the question is raised too whether a cy-près scheme could have been made and whether visitatorial powers could be exercised by the bishop in the circumstances that now obtain. I am not *c* concerned with any of those issues at this stage.

What is relevant for my purposes today is para 11 of that statement of claim in the second action, which reads as follows:

> 'The Plaintiffs repeat paragraphs 10, 11, 12, 14, 19, 20, 21, 24 and 25 of the said *d* amended Statement of Claim and say that in giving the erroneous opinion and advice the Charity Commissioners were negligent in that they failed to exercise due care and skill and thereby caused much damage, injury and distress to the Plaintiffs and the inhabitants of Upton Grey and neighbourhood. If they had given good and proper advice to the Diocesan Board in reply to their letter of 10 February 1987 a nursery school would in all probability before now have been established on the premises in pursuance of the scheme made by the Charity Commissioners them- *e* selves.'

There is then a withdrawal of what is described as a concession that the first action was a charitable proceeding, but I am not directly concerned with that today.

The relief that is claimed in the second action is contained in three declarations: first of all, in relation to the construction of the deed; second, the visitatorial powers of the *f* bishop; and third, in connection with a cy-près scheme. None of those is directly relevant. However, fourth, there is a claim to damages for negligence against the commissioners, which, of course, is highly relevant.

The second action, therefore, unlike the first action, contains a claim to damages for negligence. In common with the first action, it raises the question of construction and there are claims to declarations concerning the powers of the bishop and the making of a *g* scheme. In neither action is there any suggestion that the commissioners have acted mala fide or for improper motives. In the first action the plaintiffs plead that the commissioners were wrong in the advice that they gave, in the second that there were not only wrong, but negligent, and have thereby caused damage to the plaintiffs and the inhabitants of Upton Grey and neighbourhood.

In the second action the master made the order appealed against on 19 October 1988. *h* He ordered that the commissioners do cease to be parties to this action on the ground that having regard to the relief sought in the writ and the statement of claim against the first and third defendants, and having regard also to s 24(2) of the 1960 Act, the commissioners had been improperly made parties thereto. Second, he ordered that the writ and statement of claim be amended by striking out the commissioners as defendants, by striking out para 11 of the statement of claim, and further by striking out of the *j* prayer for relief set out at the end of the statement of claim the words 'against the Charity Commissioners', and para 4 of the prayer. He made no order as to costs.

The appeal against that order is as settled in writing in terms only against the orders that the commissioners cease to be parties and that para 4 of the prayer for relief be struck out, but it was obviously intended to include an appeal for the restoration of para 11 of

the statement of claim and I treat it as such. Indeed, a letter was sent indicating that that
*a* was the intention after the original notice was served.

The first two plaintiffs appeared before me in person. They made it clear to me that
they have no legal qualifications and for legal argument they relied effectively on some
notes on the law evidently prepared by a person not unfamiliar with the law, since it is
punctuated by quotations from reported cases, some old, some not so old, and with
references to statutes. I have had all the assistance that a judge rightly expects from a
*b* member of the Bar from counsel who appeared for the commissioners and who drew
my attention to all the material of which he was aware which was relevant to this appeal,
whether or not it was in favour of his clients. The fact remains that I have not had the
assistance of legal argument on both sides, which is unfortunate because a question of
considerable public importance is involved namely, whether an action for damages can
be brought against the commissioners for advice given in exercise of their statutory
*c* functions under s 24 of the 1960 Act if that advice is not only wrong but given
negligently and thereby loss is involved to potential objects of the trust. Because of the
public importance of the point, I heard the argument and I am giving judgment in open
court and not in chambers where this appeal would normally be heard.

The statements of claim in the two actions do not allege that the four individual
plaintiffs are members of the labouring, manufacturing and other poorer classes within
*d* the meaning of the 1942 conveyance. Indeed, para 14 of the first statement of claim
states that they are four of the inhabitants of the area and are taking the proceedings in
good faith at their own expense for the benefit of the locality. Nevertheless, both the first
and second plaintiffs made it clear that the construction which they support is one which
is wide enough to embrace them as potential objects of the charity. Therefore, I propose
for the purposes of this appeal to assume in their favour that this argument is well
*e* founded. I am not of course so deciding.

The functions of the commissioners are primarily stated in the 1960 Act. Although as
a body they were established in 1853, it is the 1960 Act that presently sets out their
functions. Section 1 of the 1960 Act, so far as material, provides:

*f*     '(1) There shall continue to be a body of Charity Commissioners for England and
      Wales, and they shall have such functions as are conferred on them by this Act in
      addition to any functions under any other enactment not repealed by this Act . . .
      (3) The Commissioners shall (without prejudice to their specific powers and
      duties under other enactments) have the general function of promoting the effective
      use of charitable resources by encouraging the development of better methods of
      administration, by giving charity trustees information or advice on any matter
*g*    affecting the charity and by investigating and checking abuses . . .'

There is a note to sub-s (3) in *Tudor on Charities* (7th edn, 1984) pp 496–497, which reads
as follows:

      'This subsection is new, and, by giving it statutory expression, makes clear and
*h*   emphasises the general function already carried out by the Commissioners. It is
      important, because its effect is to relieve the Commissioners, who are civil servants
      (see Sched. 1, para. 1(3)), from the obligation which a civil servant is normally under
      to obey the Secretary of State who appoints him and who is responsible to Parliament
      for him, unless there is a statutory power (such as this subsection) which gives him
      independence. The fact that the Act declares the positive and active role which the
*j*   Commissioners should take in advising and assisting charities enables the staff of the
      Charity Commissioners to volunteer advice in correspondence and interviews with
      trustees . . .'

The 1960 Act then sets out various specific powers and duties of the Charities
Commission. Section 4 requires them to maintain a register of charities and s 5(3)

provides for an appeal to the High Court against a decision of the commissioners to enter or not to enter any institution in the register.

Section 18 of the 1960 Act gives the commissioners concurrent jurisdiction with the High Court for certain purposes. Subsections (1) to (3) read:

'(1) Subject to the provisions of this Act, the Commissioners may by order exercise the same jurisdiction and powers as are exercisable by the High Court in charity proceedings for the following purposes, that is to say:—(a) establishing a scheme for the administration of a charity; (b) appointing, discharging or removing a charity trustee or trustee for a charity, or removing an officer or servant; (c) vesting or transferring property, or requiring or entitling any person to call for or make any transfer of property or any payment.

(2) Where the court directs a scheme for the administration of a charity to be established, the court may by order refer the matter to the Commissioners for them to prepare or settle a scheme in accordance with such directions (if any) as the court sees fit to give ...

(3) The Commissioners shall not have jurisdiction under this section to try or determine the title at law or in equity to any property as between a charity or trustee for a charity and a person holding or claiming the property or an interest in it adversely to the charity, or to try or determine any question as to the existence or extent of any charge or trust.'

The other qualification on the commissioners' power is contained in sub-s (9), which reads as follows:

'The Commissioners shall not exercise their jurisdiction under this section in any case (not referred to them by order of the court) which, by reason of its contentious character, or of any special question of law or of fact which it may involve, or for other reasons, the Commissioners may consider more fit to be adjudicated on by the court.'

Rights of appeal are conferred on the Attorney General by s 18(10), which I need not trouble with, but sub-ss (11) and (12) give rights of appeal to other persons. Subsections (11) and (12) read:

'(11) An appeal against any order of the Commissioners under this section may also, at any time within the three months beginning with the day following that on which the order is published, be brought in the High Court by the charity or any of the charity trustees, or by any person removed from any office or employment by the order (unless he is removed with the concurrence of the charity trustees or with the approval of the special visitor, if any, of the charity): Provided that no appeal shall be brought under this subsection except with a certificate of the Commissioners that it is a proper case for an appeal or with the leave of one of the judges of the High Court attached to the Chancery Division.

(12) Where an order of the Commissioners under this section establishes a scheme for the administration of a charity, any person interested in the charity shall have the like right of appeal under subsection (11) above as a charity trustee, and so also, in the case of a charity which is a local charity in any area, shall any two or more inhabitants of the area and the parish council of any rural parish comprising the area or any part of it.'

Similar appeal rights are given by s 20(7) in relation to actions taken to protect charities, for example the removal of trustees, as the result of an inquiry which has been instituted by the commissioners under s 6 of the Act.

All the above provisions are only relevant by way of background to the general scheme of the 1960 Act. The particular part of that Act with which the matter that I have to

decide is concerned is that contained in ss 23 to 28. Section 23 empowers the
a commissioners to authorise dealings with charity property. It will suffice if I read sub-s
(1):

> 'Subject to the provisions of this section, where it appears to the Commissioners
> that any action proposed or contemplated in the administration of a charity is
> expedient in the interests of the charity, they may by order sanction that action,
> whether or not it would otherwise be within the powers exercisable by the charity
b > trustees in the administration of the charity; and anything done under the authority
> of such an order shall be deemed to be properly done in the exercise of those powers.'

Section 24 is central to this appeal and I must read it in full:

> '(1) The Commissioners may on the written application of any charity trustee
> give him their opinion or advice on any matter affecting the performance of his
c > duties as such.
> (2) A charity trustee or trustee for a charity acting in accordance with the opinion
> or advice of the Commissioners given under this section with respect to the charity
> shall be deemed, as regards his responsibility for so acting, to have acted in
> accordance with his trust, unless, when he does so, either—(a) he knows or has
d > reasonable cause to suspect that the opinion or advice was given in ignorance of
> material facts; or (b) the decision of the court has been obtained on the matter or
> proceedings are pending to obtain one.'

It is, of course, evident that the immunity conferred by sub-s (2) is one conferred on
trustees who act in accordance with the opinion or advice of the commissioners under
sub-s (1) and not one which is conferred on the commissioners themselves.
e     The plaintiffs submit that an implication can be drawn from that fact that the
commissioners are liable for damage caused by advice if given negligently. That, of
course, is the matter which I have to decide. It will also be observed that s 24 contemplates
that the issue in question may be referred to the court for its decision and that, as soon as
proceedings are pending for that to be done, the immunity of the trustees ceases in
relation to advice previously given by the commissioners. The section does not say so,
f but it is clear that if the trustees act in accordance with the decision of the court when
given they will equally be protected against liability for so acting. The way in which
proceedings can be taken in relation to advice given by the commissioners under s 24
and in relation to action based on that advice is set out in s 28, which is the other
important section. Subsection (1) reads:

g > 'Charity proceedings may be taken with reference to a charity either by the
> charity, or by any of the charity trustees, or by any person interested in the charity,
> or by any two or more inhabitants of the area of the charity, if it is a local charity,
> but not by any other person.'

That contains two phrases which are the subject of specific definitions. 'Charity
h proceedings' are defined in s 28(8) in these terms:

> '. . . proceedings in any court in England or Wales brought under the court's
> jurisdiction with respect to charities, or brought under the court's jurisdiction with
> respect to trusts in relation to the administration of a trust for charitable purposes.'

A 'local charity' is defined in s 45(1) as meaning:

j > '. . . in relation to any area, a charity established for purposes which are by their
> nature or by the trusts of the charity directed wholly or mainly to the benefit of that
> area or of part of it.'

There is no doubt but that this is, in fact, a local charity. Equally, therefore, there is no

doubt that the plaintiffs, as inhabitants of the area of the charity, have a locus standi to
bring charity proceedings relating to the charity. Leave is needed, however, under sub-s  *a*
(2) or sub-s (5) of s 28. Subsections (2) and (5) read:

'(2) Subject to the following provisions of this section, no charity proceedings
relating to a charity (other than an exempt charity) shall be entertained or proceeded
with in any court unless the taking of the proceedings is authorised by order of the
Commissioners...

(5) Where the foregoing provisions of this section require the taking of charity  *b*
proceedings to be authorised by an order of the Commissioners, the proceedings
may nevertheless be entertained or proceeded with if after the order had been
applied for and refused leave to take the proceedings was obtained from one of the
judges of the High Court attached to the Chancery Division.'

There is no question of the commissioners being able to be judges in their own cause  *c*
in the matter of leave, because an appeal lies from any decision against giving leave to a
judge of the Chancery Division.

Charity proceedings as defined in s 28(8) do not include proceedings to resolve a bona
fide dispute whether a charitable trust has been declared (see Re Belling (decd), Enfield
London Borough v Public Trustee [1967] 1 All ER 105, [1967] Ch 425 and Hauxwell v Barton-
upon-Humber UDC [1973] 2 All ER 1022, [1974] Ch 432). A fortiori they would not  *d*
include an action in tort, such as is involved in asserting a claim to damages for negligent
advice causing loss. On the other hand, they would comprise proceedings to challenge
the accuracy of the commissioners' opinion or advice on any matter affecting the
performance of a charity trustee's duties under s 24(1) of the 1960 Act. There is, therefore,
machinery available to any person having the necessary locus standi to challenge the
validity of advice given by the commissioners under s 24 of the Act. Indeed, that is what  *e*
the plaintiffs are doing in both actions in those parts of the statements of claim in those
actions where they seek the determination of the court as to the construction of the 1942
conveyance.

I turn then to the question whether the commissioners are proper parties to the
proceedings in relation to the three types of claim which are raised: first of all, questions
of construction of the trusts and whether the trusts have failed; second, claims to damages  *f*
for negligence in giving advice; and, third, a claim in relation to costs.

As to the first, that is to say the question of construction, no argument has been
addressed to me in favour of the proposition that the commissioners are proper parties to
questions of construction and questions of whether trusts have failed. Such a joinder
would be contrary to the long-settled practice of the court and would merely engender
additional costs by adding an extra party without any corresponding benefit that I can  *g*
see to the charity. In my judgment it would plainly be wrong for them to be joined in
relation to those claims.

Equally clear to my mind is the issue in relation to joinder so as to recover costs. In my
judgment it is only proper to join a party as a defendant if the plaintiff seeks to assert a
legal right against the defendant. There is no right to costs save as an adjunct to the  *h*
resolution of the proceedings in question. That is not to say that there are not some
highly exceptional cases where the court has power to award costs against a person who
is not a party to the proceedings, but no such exceptional case is pleaded in either of these
actions.

That leaves the important issue in this appeal, namely whether the commissioners are
liable for advice given under s 24 if that advice is not only wrong but given negligently  *j*
and causes loss. The liability, if it exists, must be based on a breach of the common law
duty of care, and that is, indeed, the basis on which the notes on the law to which I
referred earlier, which the plaintiffs espoused, put the matter. It is stated in this way:

'Erroneous opinion or advice If the Commissioners negligently give erroneous *a*  opinion or advice under Section 24(1), they are liable under the principle stated by Best CJ in *Henly v Lyme Regis* ((1828) 5 Bing 91 at 108, 130 ER 995 at 1001): "If a man takes a reward for the discharge of a public duty, that instant he becomes a public officer: and if by any act of negligence or any act of abuse in his office, any individual sustains an injury, that individual is entitled to redress in a civil action." That was applied in *Ministry of Housing v Sharp* ([1970] 1 All ER 1009 at 1016, [1970] 2 QB 223 at 266) and is exemplified by *Dorset Yacht v Home Office* ([1970] 2 All ER

*b*  294, [1970] AC 1004). The Commissioners are also liable on the principle laid down by the House of Lords in *Hedley Byrne v Heller* ([1963] 2 All ER 575 at 594, [1964] AC 465 at 503), where Lord Morris of Borth-y-Gest said that "If a person takes it upon himself to give information or advice to, or allows his information or advice to be passed on to another person who, as he knows or should know, will place reliance upon it, then a duty of care will arise."'

*c*  The decision in *Henly v Lyme Corp* (1828) 5 Bing 91 at 107, 130 ER 995 at 1001 was put on very broad grounds indeed by Best CJ. He illustrated his general proposition—

'if a public officer abuses his office, either by an act of omission or commission, and the consequence of that, is an injury to an individual, an action may be maintained against such public officer'

*d*  by reference to refusals by bishops to hold an ecclesiastical court, thus preventing a grant of probate, and a refusal by a clergyman of the established church to administer the sacrament. I do not find that particular authority, which was concerned with liability to maintain a seawall ratione tenurae through acceptance of a grant on that condition, as of much direct assistance today. The liability of public authorities and officers has been

*e*  authoritatively considered by the House of Lords and the Court of Appeal in this century and it is to these modern authorities, rather than that isolated statement taken from the judgment of Best CJ in the Court of Common Pleas, that I turn for guidance.

A more modern decision which is referred to in the notes on the law as an application of the principle of Best CJ which is nearer home is *Ministry of Housing and Local Government v Sharp* [1970] 1 All ER 1009, [1970] 2 QB 223. That was an action which concerned

*f*  rights to compensation to a landowner in respect of a negligent failure to enter a matter which was susceptible of being registered in the local land charges register and which, if not so registered, permitted a purchaser to take free from the liability in question. That operated to the detriment of the landowner in the particular circumstances of that case.

The reference which is contained in the notes on the law to that case is a reference to a passage in the judgment of Lord Denning MR, and to understand what appears there it

*g*  is necessary to start where he said ([1970] 1 All ER 1009 at 1016, [1970] 2 QB 223 at 265–266):

'By requiring a search, a purchaser is entitled to know exactly what charges incumber it, and to adjust his price accordingly. If the registrar issues an official certificate, showing the land to be clear of any charge, that is conclusive in favour of

*h*  the purchaser, see s 17(3) of the Land Charges Act 1925. Suppose, now, that a clerk in the registry makes a mistake. He omits to enter a charge, or wrongly gives a clear certificate, with the result that the incumbrancer loses the benefit of it. Who is to suffer for the mistake? Is the incumbrancer to bear the loss without any recourse against anyone? Surely not. The very object of the registration system is to *secure* him against loss. The system breaks down utterly if he is left to bear the loss himself.

*j*  Who then is to bear the loss? The negligent clerk can, of course, be made to bear it, if he can be found and is worth the money, which is unlikely. Apart from the clerk himself, there is only one person in law who can be made responsible. It is the registrar. He must answer for the mistakes of the clerk and make compensation for the loss. He is a public officer and comes within the settled principle of English law that, when an official duty is laid on a public officer, by statute or by common law, then he is *personally* responsible for seeing that the duty is carried out. He may, and often does, get a clerk or minor official, to do the duty for him, but, if so, he is answerable for the transgression of the subordinate: see *Saunderson v Baker and Martin* (1772) 3 Wils KB 309 at 317, 95 ER 1072 where Blackstone J states the position of the sheriff. Sometimes it is an *absolute* duty, in which case he must see that it is performed *absolutely*: see the instances given by Sir John Holt in *Lane v Cotton* (1701) 1 Ld Raym 646 at 651, [1558–1774] All ER Rep 109 at 111–112. At other times it is only a duty to use due *diligence*, in which case he must see that due diligence is used: see the celebrated judgment of Best J in *Henly v Lyme Corp* (1828) 5 Bing 91 at 107–109, 130 ER 995 at 1001. But, in any event, if the duty is broken, and injury done thereby to one of the public, then the public officer is answerable. The injured person can sue him in the civil courts for compensation. It is not open to the public officer to say: "I get low fees and small pay. It is very hard to make me *personally* responsible." By law he is responsible. He will, of course, if he is wise, insure himself against his liability, or get the government to stand behind him. But liable he is to the person injured. Our English Law does not allow a public officer to shelter behind a droit administratif.' (Lord Denning MR's emphasis.)

Lord Denning MR came to the conclusion that there was an absolute liability in that particular case. In that respect, he was in a minority of one, because Salmon and Cross LJJ came to a contrary conclusion on the question of absolute liability. However, both Lord Denning MR and Salmon LJ came to the conclusion that in principle the clerk who made the search was under a duty of care to anyone he knew or ought to have known might be injured if he made a mistake, and the second defendants, who were in fact his employers, were liable for any negligence as their servant. That was a liability on the basis of vicarious responsibility of the employer for the employee's tort.

This is an authority, therefore, where there is a duty of care found to exist and to be owed not just as a matter of public law, but also to members of the public who come within the category of persons who were known by the person under the duty or ought to have been known to be persons who might be injured if a mistake was made. It is, of course, not an authority in the light of the majority decision for there being an absolute duty in the very wide terms in which Best CJ laid down his general proposition in 1828, but it illustrates the fact that there may well be a duty owed individually to a class of persons to perform a function which is called for by some statutory provision, if that is the conclusion that one draws on the construction of the Act in question. It is to be observed, of course, that it was a case where, if there was no such a duty owed, the aggrieved person was without a remedy, as that passage that I read from the judgment of Lord Denning MR makes eloquently clear.

The other modern authorities on this subject are conveniently collected in *Jones v Dept of Employment* [1988] 1 All ER 725, [1989] QB 1. The facts are stated in the headnote as follows [1989] QB 1 at 1–2):

'The plaintiff's claim for unemployment benefit was disallowed by an adjudication officer but allowed on appeal by the social security tribunal. Thereafter the plaintiff began an action in negligence in the county court against the defendant, the Department of Employment, alleging that the adjudication officer, as its employee, had reached his decision negligently and that the defendant had failed to review the decision on receiving further evidence from the plaintiff's solicitor. The defendant applied to strike out the proceedings as disclosing no cause of action on the ground that the adjudication officer's duties were of a judicial nature attracting immunity from suit under section 2(5) of the Crown Proceedings Act 1947. The judge held that no such immunity applied and refused the application. The defendant appealed on grounds not advanced in the county court, namely (1) that section 117(1) of the Social Security Act 1975, as amended, in providing that apart from the appellate

a    procedures set out in the Act the adjudication officer's decision on any claim was
     final, excluded any common law right of action in negligence relating to the making
     of a decision by an adjudication officer, and (2) that an adjudication officer owed no
     duty of care at common law to a person whose claim he was considering so as to
     found an action in negligence'

     The decision of the court, is only relevant on that latter point, and it is to be found in
b    the fourth of the holdings of the court, which is stated as follows ([1989] QB 1 at 2-3):

     'That the adjudication officer's duty lay in the field of public law, any breach of
     that duty giving rise to remedy by way of judicial review; that in consequence,
     having regard to the non-judicial nature of his duties and in particular to the
     legislation which provided an aggrieved claimant with an adequate remedy by way
     of appellate procedure, it was not just and reasonable to hold that the adjudication
c    officer or the defendant was under a common law duty of care; and that, accordingly,
     misfeasance apart, the adjudication officer's decision was not susceptible of challenge
     at common law . . .'

     The leading judgment was delivered by Glidewell LJ, who dealt with the earlier points
     with which I am not concerned, and turned to the question of whether there was a duty
d    of care, where he said ([1988] 1 All ER 725 at 734-735, [1989] QB 1 at 20-22):

     'The question we therefore have to decide is whether such a duty of care can exist.
     In Curran v Northern Ireland Co-ownership Housing Association Ltd [1987] 2 All ER 13
     at 17, [1987] 2 AC 718 at 724 Lord Bridge said: "My Lords, Anns v Merton London
     Borough [1977] 2 All ER 492, [1978] AC 728 may be said to represent the high-water
     mark of a trend in the development of the law of negligence by your Lordships'
e    House towards the elevation of the 'neighbourhood' principle derived from the
     speech of Lord Atkin in Donoghue v Stevenson [1932] AC 562, [1932] All ER Rep 1
     into one of general application from which a duty of care may always be derived
     unless there are clear countervailing considerations to exclude it." In his speech in
     Anns v Merton London Borough [1977] 2 All ER 492 at 498, [1978] AC 728 at 751 in a
     famous passage Lord Wilberforce said: "Through the trilogy of cases in this House,
f    Donoghue v Stevenson [1932] AC 562, [1932] All ER Rep 1, Hedley Byrne & Co Ltd v
     Heller & Partners Ltd [1963] 2 All ER 575, [1964] AC 465 and Home Office v Dorset
     Yacht Co Ltd [1970] 2 All ER 294, [1970] AC 1004, the position has now been reached
     that in order to establish that a duty of care arises in a particular situation, it is not
     necessary to bring the facts of that situation within those of previous situations in
     which a duty of care has been held to exist. Rather the question has to be approached
g    in two stages. First one has to ask whether, as between the alleged wrongdoer and
     the person who has suffered damage there is a sufficient relationship of proximity
     or neighbourhood such that, in the reasonable contemplation of the former,
     carelessness on his part may be likely to cause damage to the latter, in which case a
     prima facie duty of care arises. Secondly, if the first question is answered
h    affirmatively, it is necessary to consider whether there are any considerations which
     ought to negative, or to reduce or limit the scope of the duty or the class of person
     to whom it is owed or the damages to which a breach of it may give rise (see the
     Dorset Yacht case [1970] 2 All ER 294 at 297-298, [1970] AC 1004 at 1027, per Lord
     Reid)." In more recent authorities a somewhat different approach has been adopted.
     In Yuen Kun-yeu v A-G of Hong Kong [1987] 2 All ER 705 at 710, [1988] AC 175 at
j    191-192 Lord Keith commented on Lord Wilberforce's formulation. Lord Keith
     said: "Their Lordships venture to think that the two-stage test formulated by Lord
     Wilberforce for determining the existence of a duty of care in negligence has been
     elevated to a degree of importance greater than it merits, and greater perhaps than
     its author intended. Further, the expression of the first stage of the test carries with
     it a risk of misinterpretation. As Gibbs CJ pointed out in Sutherland Shire Council v

*Heyman* (1985) 60 ALR 1 at 13 there are two possible views of what Lord Wilberforce meant. The first view, favoured in a number of cases mentioned by Gibbs CJ, is that he meant to test the sufficiency of proximity simply by the reasonable contemplation of likely harm. The second view, favoured by Gibbs CJ himself, is that Lord Wilberforce meant the expression 'proximity or neighbourhood' to be a composite one, importing the whole concept of necessary relationship between plaintiff and defendant described by Lord Atkin in *Donoghue v Stevenson* [1932] AC 562 at 580, [1932] All ER Rep 1 at 11. In their Lordships' opinion the second view is the correct one. As Lord Wilberforce himself observed in *McLoughlin v O'Brian* [1982] 2 All ER 298 at 303, [1983] 1 AC 410 at 420, it is clear that foreseeability does not of itself, and automatically, lead to a duty of care. There are many other statements to the same effect. The truth is that the trilogy of cases referred to by Lord Wilberforce each demonstrate particular sets of circumstances, differing in character, which were adjudged to have the effect of bringing into being a relationship apt to give rise to a duty of care. Foreseeability of harm is a necessary ingredient of such a relationship, but is not the only one. Otherwise there would be liability in negligence on the part of one who sees another about to walk over a cliff with his head in the air, and forbears to shout a warning." In *Governors of the Peabody Donation Fund v Sir Lindsay Parkinson & Co Ltd* [1984] 3 All ER 529 at 534, [1985] AC 210 at 240 Lord Keith, having set out the passage quoted above from the speech of Lord Wilberforce in *Anns v Merton London Borough*, said: "There has been a tendency in some recent cases to treat these passages as being themselves of a definitive character. This is a temptation which should be resisted. The true question in each case is whether the particular defendant owed to the particular plaintiff a duty of care having the scope which is contended for, and whether he was in breach of that duty with consequent loss to the plaintiff. A relationship of proximity in Lord Atkin's sense must exist before any duty of care can arise, but the scope of the duty must depend on all the circumstances of the case. In *Home Office v Dorset Yacht Co Ltd* [1970] 2 All ER 294 at 307–308, [1970] AC 1004 at 1038–1039 Lord Morris, after observing that at the conclusion of his speech in *Donoghue v Stevenson* [1932] AC 562 at 599, [1932] All ER Rep 1 at 20 Lord Atkin said that it was advantageous if the law 'is in accordance with sound common sense' and expressing the view that a special relation existed between the prison officers and the yacht company which gave rise to a duty on the former to control their charges so as to prevent them doing damage, continued: 'Apart from this I would conclude that in the situation stipulated in the present case it would not only be fair and reasonable that a duty of care should exist but that it would be contrary to the fitness of things were it not so. I doubt whether it is necessary to say, in cases where the court is asked whether in a particular situation a duty existed, that the court is called on to make a decision as to policy. Policy need not be invoked where reason and good sense will at once point the way. If the test whether in some particular situation a duty of care arises may in some cases have to be whether it is fair and reasonable that it should so arise the court must not shrink from being the arbiter. As Lord Radcliffe said in his speech in *Davis Contractors Ltd v Fareham Urban District Council* [1956] 2 All ER 145 at 160, [1956] AC 696 at 728, the court is "the spokesman of the fair and reasonable man".' So in determining whether or not a duty of care of particular scope was incumbent on a defendant it is material to take into consideration whether it is just and reasonable that it should be so.'"

Glidewell LJ then finishes his judgment with the following observations:

'The question thus is whether, taking all these circumstances into account, it is just and reasonable that the adjudication officer should be under a duty of care at common law to the claimant to benefit. Having regard to the non-judicial nature of the adjudication officer's responsibilities, and in particular to the fact that the

statutory framework provides a right of appeal which, if a point of law arises, can
*a* eventually bring the matter to this court, it is my view that the adjudication officer
is not under any common law duty of care. In other words, I agree with counsel for
the department that his decision is not susceptible of challenge at common law
unless it be shown that he is guilty of misfeasance. Indeed, in my view, it is a general
principle that, if a government department or officer, charged with the making of
decisions whether certain payments should be made, is subject to a statutory right
*b* of appeal against his decisions, he owes no duty of care in private law. Misfeasance
apart, he is only susceptible in public law to judicial review or to the right of appeal
provided by the statute under which he makes his decision.'

It is to be observed that Glidewell LJ must have used the expression 'misfeasance' as
meaning something wider than negligence based on breach of common law duty of care,
*c* because that was the form of the action that was brought in *Jones v Dept of Employment*
and is the form of the action which is brought in one of these actions before me. There
is, therefore, no question of misfeasance within the meaning of that phrase as used by
Glidewell LJ before me.

Slade LJ agreed with Glidewell LJ and put his conclusion in the following words
([1988] 1 All ER 725 at 738–739, [1989] QB 1 at 25):

*d* 'If in the present case it be necessary or appropriate to consider whether it is just
and reasonable that the alleged duty of care should be held to exist . . . I hold without
hesitation that it would not be just and reasonable, if only for these reasons. First, as
counsel for the plaintiff more or less accepted, the appeal procedure provided for by
the 1975 Act and the 1980 Act itself for practical purposes provides a disappointed
*e* claimant with a perfectly adequate remedy for recovery of unemployment benefit
properly due to him though, it is true, without costs, interest and any general
damages for anxiety and distress. Second, as counsel for the plaintiff also accepted,
one logically inevitable consequence of holding that a common law duty of care
existed would be this. Immediately following an arguably negligent and erroneous
decision of an adjudication officer, a claimant would have the right to pursue an
*f* action in negligence against the adjudication officer and/or the department without
even pursuing his statutory rights of appeal (albeit at the risk of having any award
of damages reduced, though not necessarily eliminated, on the grounds that he had
not mitigated his damage by appealing). In the context of this legislation, under
which there are likely to be many thousands of citizens who rightly or wrongly
consider themselves aggrieved, it would seem to me to make no sense to hold that
*g* it is open to a disappointed citizen to challenge the decision in this particular
manner. In more general terms, I would agree with Glidewell LJ that ordinarily,
and subject of course to the particular provisions of the relevant statute, a government
officer or department who or which is charged by statute with deciding whether
certain payments should be made out of public funds and is subject to a statutory
right of appeal against such decisions, will owe no duty of care to potential recipients
*h* in private law. Misfeasance apart, I would agree that ordinarily it or he will only be
susceptible (in public law) to judicial review and also to the relevant rights of appeal.'

Taking those statements of law into account, it is my conclusion that the plaintiffs'
argument does not succeed even on the basis of the two-stage test derived from Lord
Wilberforce's speech in *Anns v Merton London Borough* [1972] 2 All ER 492 at 498, [1978]
*j* AC 728 at 751. I doubt whether there is sufficient proximity between a potential object
of a charity and the commissioners to satisfy the first stage in his two-stage approach, but
whether that be so or not I am clear that there are considerations which negative the
existence of a duty of care owed to the potential objects of a charity by the commissioners,
breach of which, if coupled with damage, gives rise to a right to damages for common
law negligence. Those reasons are as follows, and I would add also that they are also

factors which lead me to the conclusion that the just and reasonable test is not satisfied by the plaintiffs either. First and foremost, the statutory scheme of the 1960 Act, and in *a* particular ss 23 to 28, confers an effective right of appeal against the substance of the matter, that is to say against any action proposed to be taken on the basis of advice given by the commissioners which is claimed to be erroneous. There is, therefore, no question either of the commissioners being in any sense above the law or of aggrieved persons with a sufficient locus standi not having a remedy. The remedy is there in s 28, and indeed in this case is in fact being exercised because the questions of construction are *b* being brought before the court and it is in relation to those questions that it is alleged that the commissioners were wrong and negligently wrong.

Second, the concurrent exercise of rights in negligence actions at common law and of rights of appeal in charity proceedings could only multiply legal costs to the probable detriment of the charity concerned. I accept, of course, that the arguments that moved Slade LJ in particular in relation to a possible bypassing of the appeal procedure laid down *c* by the statute does not apply to the same extent in this particular case, but it would nevertheless still be the fact in actions of this type that there could simultaneously be an action in negligence against the commissioners for erroneous advice and an application by way of charity proceedings under s 28 of the 1960 Act. That would seem to me to be an unfortunate state of affairs.

Third, it would in my view be contrary to the general good of charities for the *d* commissioners' decision to be subject not only to appeal, which is entirely proper and provided for, but also to attack by so wide a class of persons as potential objects of charity. I was referred to Cardozo LJ's famous reference 'to a liability in an indeterminate amount for an indeterminate time to an indeterminate class' (see *Ultramares Corp v Touche* (1931) 255 NY 170 at 179 cited by Balcombe LJ in *Clarke v Bruce Lance & Co (a firm)* [1988] 1 All ER 364 at 370, [1988] 1 WLR 881 at 889. *e*

Fourthly, and least significant, there was no authority whatever cited to me for such an action in all the long history of the commissioners since 1853. By itself, that is not conclusive, for the categories of relationship which are capable of giving rise to a duty of care are not closed.

I should emphasise that I entirely accept that the statute does require the commissioners *f* to be careful in giving the advice that they do give pursuant to s 24. There is no question of the commissioners being under no obligation to treat their duties seriously and responsibly. The critical question in this case is to whom is that duty owed, and it is because I have come to the conclusion that there is no individual duty at common law owed to the potential objects of charity that I decide the way that I do.

I should also add, because the case is referred to in the notes on the law which I read, *g* that the decision in *Hedley Byrne & Co Ltd v Heller & Partners Ltd* [1963] 2 All ER 575, [1964] AC 465 is plainly distinguishable because there never was any question here of the plaintiffs relying on the commissioners' advice, which the plaintiffs have at all times consistently opposed and resisted, as of course is their right.

That only leaves the question of the declaration in the first action, that the commissioners' opinion was erroneous. In my judgment, that is not a declaration which *h* would be of any utility to anybody concerned to maintain as part of the proceedings because the heart of the matter and what really matters is going to be determined in relation to the rest of the proceedings. When a declaration has been made in one direction or the other on the first three heads of claim in the plaintiffs' prayer for relief in the first action and on the claims in the second action, other than in the fourth claim in damages, the real matters in dispute will have been decided by the court and it would be a work of *j* supererogation to go on and to say that the advice and opinion of the commissioners which they gave in their letter was erroneous. That fact would have been decided by the earlier decision, if the decision is that way, but no practical utility would be served by having a separate declaration to that effect. So there is no justification to be found in the plea for that declaration for joining the commissioners.

a   For all these reasons I dismiss the appeals. I have not dealt with certain arguments that
were advanced to me based on the plaintiffs' locus standi, because it is not in my
judgment necessary to do so.

*Appeals dismissed.*

b   Solicitors: *Treasury Solicitor.*

Evelyn M C Budd   Barrister.

c   # Capps v Miller

COURT OF APPEAL, CIVIL DIVISION
MAY, CROOM-JOHNSON AND GLIDEWELL LJJ
30 NOVEMBER 1988

d   *Negligence – Contributory negligence – Road accident – Crash helmet – Failure to fasten securely
– Defendant wholly to blame for accident – Plaintiff in part responsible for injuries – Plaintiff
riding a moped – Plaintiff failing to secure strap of crash helmet – Helmet coming off before
plaintiff's head striking road – Whether plaintiff contributorily negligent – Whether plaintiff's
damages should be reduced – Law Reform (Contributory Negligence) Act 1945, s 1 – Motor
Cycles (Protective Helmets) Regulations 1980, reg 4.*

e   The plaintiff suffered severe brain damage when a car driven by the defendant ran into
the plaintiff's moped. At the time of the accident the plaintiff was wearing a crash
helmet but with the chin strap unfastened, contrary to reg 4[a] of the Motor Cycles
(Protective Helmets) Regulations 1980. In subsequent criminal proceedings the defendant
pleaded guilty to driving with excess alcohol. The plaintiff brought a claim against the
f   defendant for damages for personal injury. The defendant admitted that liability for the
accident was wholly attributable to his negligent driving but claimed that the plaintiff
had been contributorily negligent in wearing an unfastened crash helmet. On the trial
of the issue of contributory negligence the judge found that because the crash helmet
had not been securely fastened it had come off before the plaintiff's head struck the road,
with the result that his injuries had been increased by 'some incalculable degree'.
g   However, the judge held that the defendant's responsibility for the plaintiff's injuries
had not been reduced to any significant extent and that accordingly the damages
recoverable by the plaintiff would not be reduced under s 1[b] of the Law Reform
Contributory Negligence Act 1945 by reason of the crash helmet not being securely
fastened. The defendant appealed against that decision.

h   **Held** – The plaintiff's failure to fasten the chin strap of his crash helmet securely or at
all in breach of reg 4 of the 1980 regulations had clearly contributed to the extent of the

---

a   Regulation 4, so far as material, provides:
      '(1) ... every person driving or riding ... on a motor bicycle when on a road shall wear
protective headgear ...
j         (3) In this Regulation ... "protective headgear" means headgear which—(a) is [a helmet] and
(b) if worn with a chin cup attached to or held in position by a strap or other fastening provided on
the helmet, is provided with an additional strap or other fastening (to be fastened under the
wearer's jaw) for securing the helmet firmly to the head of the wearer; and (c) is securely fastened
to the head of the wearer by means of the straps or other fastening provided on the headgear for
that purpose.'
b   Section 1, so far as material, is set out at p 337 b, post

injuries which he had suffered as a result of the accident notwithstanding that the defendant was wholly responsible for the accident. Since contributory negligence had *a* been established the court was required to assess the extent by which the damages should be reduced even though it was not possible to assess the extent to which the plaintiff's injuries had been increased because his crash helmet had come off. In making that assessment there was (per May and Glidewell LJJ) a distinction in the degree of blameworthiness between not wearing a helmet at all and wearing a helmet which was not securely fastened, and in those circumstances the plaintiff's damages should be *b* reduced by 10% (see p 340 *j* to p 341 *b e* to *g* and p 342 *b h* to p 343 *c e f*, post).

*O'Connell v Jackson* [1971] 3 All ER 129 distinguished.
*Froom v Butcher* [1975] 3 All ER 520 considered.

**Notes**
For the effect of contributory negligence generally and in traffic cases, see 34 Halsbury's *c* Laws (4th edn) paras 68, 75, and for cases on the subject, see 36(1) Digest (Reissue) 270–274, 1084–1112.

For reduction of damages on account of contributory negligence, see 12 Halsbury's Laws (4th edn) para 1212.

For the Law Reform (Contributory Negligence) Act 1945, s 1, see 31 Halsbury's Statutes (4th edn) 185. *d*

**Cases referred to in judgments**
*Davies v Swan Motor Co (Swansea) Ltd* [1949] 1 All ER 620, [1949] 2 KB 291, CA.
*Froom v Butcher* [1975] 3 All ER 520, [1976] QB 286, [1975] 3 WLR 379, CA; *rvsg* [1974] 3 All ER 517, [1974] 1 WLR 1297.
*Johnson v Tennant Bros Ltd* [1954] CA Transcript 329. *e*
*O'Connell v Jackson* [1971] 3 All ER 129, [1972] 1 QB 270, [1971] 3 WLR 463, CA.
*Smith v Blackburn* [1974] RTR 533.

**Case also cited**
*McLean v Bell* (1932) 147 LT 262, [1932] All ER Rep 421, HL.
*f*

**Appeal**
The defendant, Michael Ray Miller, appealed against the judgment of Henry J sitting in the Queen's Bench Division at Norwich on 14 March 1988 whereby, on the issue of contributory negligence, he gave judgment for the plaintiff, Robin Graham Capps (suing by his next friend David Graham Capps), in his claim for damages for injuries sustained by him when his moped was in collision with the defendant's motor car. The facts are *g* set out in the judgment of Croom-Johnson LJ.

*Michael Wright QC* and *H Jonathan Barnes* for the defendant.
*John Leighton Williams QC* and *John A Sabine* for the plaintiff.

**CROOM-JOHNSON LJ** (giving the first judgment at the invitation of May LJ). This *h* appeal arises out of an accident which took place on 2 March 1985 when the plaintiff, who was just a few days short of his seventeenth birthday, was on his moped near his home at about 11.20 pm. He had been out on his moped and he was stationary in the centre of the road about to turn right into the driveway of his home. While he was in that position he was run into from behind by a motor car which was being driven by the defendant, who had just overtaken another vehicle at a speed, according to the judgment *j* of Henry J, described by the passenger of that vehicle as being 'fast but not excessively so'. It is now common ground that it must have been between 30 and 40 miles per hour. He ran into the back of the plaintiff and in his statement to the police he told them that he had not seen the plaintiff. He also told the police at once that he had been drinking;

*a*  he was breathalysed and his breath-test reading recorded him at midnight as being 72%
over the limit. He pleaded guilty to a charge of driving with excess alcohol.

Unfortunately the injuries to the plaintiff were serious. I will come to the injuries in a
moment, but principally he received a blow to the head which resulted in brain damage
as the result of the accident.

There was an issue at the trial whether or not the plaintiff at the time of the accident
had his helmet on his head. There is no question that while he had been riding the
*b*  moped it had been on his head and that was what was required by the Motor Cycles
(Protective Helmets) Regulations 1980, SI 1980/1279. But reg 4(3) defines 'protective
headgear' as headgear which is securely fastened to the head of the wearer by means of
the straps provided for that purpose. The difficulty in the present case was, as the judge
was forced to find, that the helmet, although on his head, was not fastened by the straps.

There was a considerable issue at the trial whether, when the head injuries took place,
*c*  the helmet had been on his head or had already come off because it had not been fastened
on by the straps. There were two explanations. That which was put on behalf of the
plaintiff (for the plaintiff could remember little or nothing about the circumstances) was
that he had been thrown up in the air, a fact which was deposed to by the passenger in
the motor car of the defendant, and that he had come down on the bonnet of the car and
unquestionably his helmet had gone through and smashed the windscreen of that motor
*d*  car. The helmet was subsequently found on the lap of the passenger in the defendant's
motor car. On that basis, when the head injuries were caused, at the time when the blow
to the head took place his helmet, albeit unstrapped, was still on his head and therefore
no breach of the regulations would have been causative of the injury to his head.

The other explanation, which was that put forward on behalf of the defendant, was
that in the course of the blow by the motor car on the moped and in the course of the
*e*  plaintiff being thrown into the air the helmet had come off because it was not fastened
and had smashed the windscreen in the way I have described, but the plaintiff, by now
without any helmet on his head, had landed on his head on the road and so had suffered
the brain injuries which resulted.

The judge investigated these alternative explanations with great care. The explanation
depended in part on the fact that these helmets are specially designed so that if they
*f*  receive a hard blow with the wearer's head inside the helmet, the lining is of a self-
destructive type and therefore it absorbs the shock. In the present case there was found
to be absolutely no destruction or effect on the lining of the helmet and there was
nothing about the condition of the helmet which indicated that it had been on the
plaintiff's head at the time.

There was also an explanation put forward that the plaintiff must have landed on the
*g*  bonnet of the defendant's motor car and caused some damage to it. That was negatived
by evidence and the judge found that that had not happened. In the result he came to
the conclusion, and said so in terms, that he accepted the explanation given on behalf of
the defendant as to how the accident happened, namely that, because the helmet was not
strapped on, it had come off before his head hit the road and that was the explanation of
*h*  the brain injuries.

The brain injuries were dealt with in the evidence of Dr Anthony Roberts, a
neurosurgeon, who was called as a witness. In a long report, and on the assumption that
the accident happened in the way which ultimately the judge found that it had, he said:

*j*  'If this is what happened then I am quite sure his brain injuries were a good deal
more serious than they might have been had his helmet stayed on until his head
made contact with the road inside it. The concussive forces imparted to his brain
would have been substantially cushioned and he might well have escaped with no
more than residual impairment of his memory, concentration and perhaps temper
control, though possibly not even the latter.'

He then went on to give his explanation of what had happened to cause such injuries as
the plaintiff suffered. He said there had been impairment of the temporal and frontal *a*
lobes of the brain, worse on the right, and that was likely to have been caused by—

> 'the swelling of the bruised brain, subjected to shearing strains in its substance,
> and the swelling caused secondary damage by impairing blood flow and oxygen
> supply.'

He went on to say:                                                                         *b*

> 'Had the force of the impact been absorbed to any extent, as it is likely to have
> been by his crash helmet [I interpolate to say that means if it had been on his head
> at the critical moment], then I think it virtually certain that much of the shear-
> strain brain damage would not have occurred, secondary damage the result of brain
> swelling would not have been so severe, and in all probability he would not have *c*
> been so deeply unconscious for so long which impaired blood and oxygen supply to
> his brain further. This, of course, is all no more than assumption based on what is
> known about the value of helmets absorbing impact forces, and there is no way of
> measuring these so far as I know in the individual case in retrospect. I can only
> attempt as I have done to look at the type of brain damage he has sustained and offer
> a guess as to how much less it might have been on the basis of experience of the *d*
> after effects of less severe uncomplicated closed head injuries.'

He was cross-examined on that report, but what I have read in effect was the substance
of the medical evidence ultimately accepted by the judge.

On behalf of the plaintiff another neurosurgeon, Mr Holmes, was called. His evidence
was directed to a different issue, which was not to deal with the worsening effect of the
accident if it was caused without any helmet on the head, but more with the idea of *e*
showing that the helmet had been on the head and that the accident was therefore caused
in the way which the plaintiff put forward and which the judge ultimately rejected.

What the judge found as a matter of fact was this. After putting forward the two
contentions as to how the accident took place he said:

> 'It is a matter which does not admit of any certainty, there being serious difficulties *f*
> in each account. I am ultimately compelled to find that, on the balance of probability,
> the defendant's reconstruction of the accident is likely to be the correct one, namely
> that it was a blow to the unprotected head that caused the brain damage, that is to
> say a blow with the helmet off. [I interpolate to say that that necessarily means that
> he came down on the road and not on the motor car.] It seems to me also that the
> probability is that the extent of the injuries would have been to some incalculable *g*
> degree less had the helmet stayed on and it would have stayed on if the strap had
> been done up. Clearly, as I have said, it is a matter about which there can be no
> certainty, the case is one very close to the line either way, but on the balance of
> probabilities it seems to me that failure to do the strap up made some difference to
> the severity of the injuries sustained though it would be impossible to express a
> view as to what difference it would have made.'                                        *h*

I should add that the judge's finding that the strap had not been done up was reinforced
by the fact that there was no damage to the strap indicating that it had been done up, but
had broken or in some way been carried away in the course of the accident. The judge
then went on to say:

> 'As I have said, while the accident was in no sense the plaintiff's fault but was *j*
> entirely the fault of the defendant, the damage caused was caused partly as a result
> of the fault of the plaintiff in that the damage would have been likely to have been
> less if the chin strap of his crash helmet had been done up.'

On those facts as found by the judge there then arose the question of whether there

was contributory negligence on the part of the plaintiff, the negligence of the defendant
a being admitted and not in issue. That required consideration of the Law Reform
(Contributory Negligence) Act 1945. Section 1(1) reads:

'Where any person suffers damage as the result partly of his own fault and partly
of the fault of any other person or persons, a claim in respect of that damage shall
not be defeated by reason of the fault of the person suffering the damage, but the
b          damages recoverable in respect thereof shall be reduced to such extent as the court
thinks just and equitable having regard to the claimant's share in the responsibility
for the damage . . .'

There are three points to note about that subsection. The first is that it got rid of the
old common law rule that contributory negligence was a complete defence to the
plaintiff's claim. Second, that before it comes into force the plaintiff's injury must be
c the result partly of his own fault and partly the fault of any other person, and that
requires that his injury must have been caused by his fault. The last part is that, that
having been satisfied, the apportionment of damages and the apportionment of liability
then goes on to be considered under the last part of the subsection, which says that the
plaintiff's damages 'shall be reduced to such extent as the court thinks just and equitable
d having regard to the [plaintiff's] share in the responsibility for the damage'.
In the present case the contributory negligence as alleged was the breach of the
regulations in not wearing 'protective headgear' through not having fastened the strap.
Causation was established on the finding of the judge and therefore it was necessary to
have the next part of the inquiry to see what was the effect of the increase on the
plaintiff's injuries because of his negligence. What test is to be applied in those
e circumstances?
O'Connell v Jackson [1971] 3 All ER 129, [1972] 1 QB 270 came by way of appeal to this
court in a case where a moped driver was not wearing a crash helmet. In those days the
regulations enforcing the wearing of a crash helmet had not come into force, but the
question was: if the plaintiff was not wearing a helmet, was it foreseeable that he would
suffer injury and in those circumstances was he guilty of contributory negligence? This
f court said without hesitation that he would be guilty of contributory negligence and
adopted the test which had been laid down in Davies v Swan Motor Co (Swansea) Ltd [1949]
1 All ER 620, [1949] 2 KB 291. Davies v Swan Motor Co (Swansea) Ltd was a case where
there was a collision between a dust cart and an omnibus. The plaintiff was driving
neither: he was riding on the step of the dust cart in a somewhat unsafe position. The
Court of Appeal, having said that the responsibility as between the two motorists was to
g be apportioned as two-thirds and one-third, also had to go on to discuss whether the
plaintiff, Mr Davies, was guilty of contributory negligence. This court came to the
conclusion that he had not been taking proper care for his own safety in riding in the
manner he did and said that he was 20% to blame.
Returning to O'Connell v Jackson, the question then arose, applying Davies v Swan Motor
Co (Swansea) Ltd, as to how the 1945 Act was to be applied. Edmund Davies LJ, who gave
h the judgment of the court, said ([1971] 3 All ER 129 at 132, [1972] 1 QB 270 at 277):

'The plaintiff being entirely innocent in relation to the collision without which
he would not have been injured at all, the tests of blameworthiness and causative
potency commonly adopted since Davies v Swan Motor Co (Swansea) Ltd [1949] 1 All
ER 620, [1949] 2 KB 291 are not entirely easy to apply to the injury which in fact
j          followed. It seems to us that only a broad approach is possible. It must be borne in
mind that, for so much of the injuries and damage as would have resulted from the
accident even if a crash helmet had been worn, the defendant is wholly to blame,
and the plaintiff not at all. For the additional injuries and damage which would not
have occurred if a crash helmet had been worn, the defendant, as solely responsible
for the accident, must continue in substantial measure to be held liable, and it is

only in that last field of additional injuries and damage that the contributory negligence of the plaintiff has any relevance. It is not possible on the evidence to  *a* measure the extent of that field and then apportion that measure between the blameworthiness and causative potency of the acts and omissions of the parties. We can only cover the two stages in one stride and express the responsibility of the plaintiff in terms of a percentage of the whole. Giving the best consideration that we can to the whole matter, we assess the responsibility of the plaintiff in terms of 15 per cent of the whole, and allow the appeal to the extent of reducing the damages  *b* to that extent.'

The matter arose again with further development in *Froom v Butcher* [1975] 3 All ER 520, [1976] QB 286. That was not a crash helmet case. It was a case where the plaintiff was not wearing a seat belt at the time; he did not like them because of the risk of being trapped in the vehicle had he been wearing a seat belt. He suffered injuries in the accident  *c* from which he would not have suffered had he been wearing a seat belt. At that time seat belts, although fitted in most cars, were not compulsory objects to wear and again the question was: was it contributory negligence to avoid wearing one? The judgment of the court was given by Lord Denning MR, who said ([1975] 3 All ER 520 at 525, [1976] QB 286 at 292):

'In these seat belt cases, the injured plaintiff is in no way to blame for the accident  *d* itself. Sometimes he is an innocent passenger sitting beside a negligent driver who goes off the road. At other times he is an innocent driver of one car which is run into by the bad driving of another car which pulls out on to its wrong side of the road. It may well be asked: why should the injured plaintiff have his damages reduced? The accident was solely caused by the negligent driving by the defendant. Sometimes outrageously bad driving. It should not lie in his mouth to say: "You  *e* ought to have been wearing a seat belt." That point of view was strongly expressed in *Smith v Blackburn* [1974] RTR 533 at 536 by O'Connor J. He said: ". . . The idea that the insurers of a grossly negligent driver should be relieved in any degree from paying what is proper compensation for injuries is an idea that offends ordinary decency. Until I am forced to do so by higher authority, I will not so rule."'  *f*

Then in reference to O'Connor J's expression of opinion, Lord Denning MR went on to say: 'I do not think that is the correct approach.'

Since *Froom v Butcher* and *O'Connell v Jackson* the test of foreseeability in both crash helmet and seat belt cases is no longer of much relevance because they are both now the subject of statutory compulsion under regulations which require people to wear them where appropriate. Therefore the question arises as to how the apportionment of blame  *g* for the accident under the 1945 Act should be carried out. Lord Denning MR in *Froom v Butcher* [1975] 3 All ER 520 at 527, [1976] QB 286 at 295 said:

'Whenever there is an accident, the negligent driver must bear by far the greater share of responsibility. It was his negligence which caused the accident. It also was a prime cause of the whole of the damage. But insofar as the damage might have  *h* been avoided or lessened by wearing a seat belt, the injured person must bear some share. But how much should this be? Is it proper to enquire whether the driver was grossly negligent or only slightly negligent? or whether the failure to wear a seat belt was entirely inexcusable or almost forgivable? If such an enquiry could easily be undertaken, it might be as well to do it. In *Davies v Swan Motor Co* we said that consideration should be given not only to the causative potency of a particular  *j* factor, but also its blameworthiness. But we live in a practical world. In most of these cases the liability of the driver is admitted; the failure to wear a seat belt is admitted; the only question is: what damages should be payable? This question should not be prolonged by an expensive enquiry into the degree of blameworthiness on either side, which would be hotly disputed. Suffice it to assess a share of responsibility which will be just and equitable in the great majority of cases.

*a*    Sometimes the evidence will show that the failure made no difference. The damage would have been the same, even if a seat belt had been worn. In such cases the damages should not be reduced at all. At other times the evidence will show that the failure made all the difference. The damage would have been prevented altogether if a seat belt had been worn. In such cases I would suggest that the damages should be reduced by 25 per cent. But often enough the evidence will only

*b*    show that the failure made a considerable difference. Some injuries to the head, for instance, would have been a good deal less severe if a seat belt had been worn, but there would still have been some injury to the head. In such case I would suggest that the damages attributable to the failure to wear a seat belt should be reduced by 15 per cent.'

*c*    Although that is a seat belt case, now that both have been put on a statutory basis I see no reason to distinguish between seat belt cases and crash helmet cases and I would apply the dictum of Lord Denning MR to crash helmets just as he spoke of it in relation to seat belts. Just as the unfastened seat belt is not a way of wearing a seat belt, so an unfastened helmet will not be a way of wearing the statutory helmet.

It now remains to be seen how the judge treated these matters in his judgment. After

*d*    referring to Lord Denning MR's passage in *Froom v Butcher*, he went on to say:

> 'Pausing there from the citation of the authority, this is clearly the case where the driver of the car, the defendant, was grossly negligent and where I would view the plaintiff's failure to fasten his helmet as almost forgivable. One would not, when going out on one's moped, expect to be involved in an accident as severe as this one

*e*    > was.'

Having referred further to Lord Denning MR's judgment in *Froom v Butcher* the judge came to his conclusions in this way:

> 'Dealing with those two factors that one should look at in assessing responsibility under the statute, namely the factors of causative potency and blameworthiness, on

*f*    > the facts of this case, where the defendant's fault was the sole cause of the accident, it seems to me that responsibility, as it is used in the statute, is largely a matter of blameworthiness. It is clearly necessary to look at the importance of the failure to fasten the chin strap in causing the damage. Even having done that, responsibility, it seems to me, should here be decided principally on the matter of blameworthiness. Here the plaintiff was wearing a full face helmet, only likely to come off in a serious accident. It is probable, but there can be no certainty, that the damage would have

*g*    > been less if the helmet had not come off. The accident was catastrophic in its consequences. It was 100% the defendant's fault. His fault was considerably aggravated by the fact that he had been drinking before he drove. Indeed, the probability is that this accident would not have happened had he not been drinking. The probability, it seems to me, on the facts of this accident, where he did not even

*h*    > see the motor cyclist before he ran into him, is that the accident was caused solely by the effect of drink on this driver. The Court of Appeal has indicated that one should not make apportionments of contributory negligence for percentages less than 10%, that is to say that there should only be a reduction of the plaintiff's damages where his responsibility is significant, 10% or above. On that basis, I unhesitatingly reject the suggestion that I should find contributory negligence on

*j*    > the plaintiff's part here, in an accident of this severity caused by the driver in the defendant's state. The plaintiff being in no way responsible for the accident, it seems to me that the sole responsibility for the accident which the defendant has must in all the circumstances carry with it responsibility for the damage caused by the accident. The defendant's self-induced condition reduced his ability to drive to the point where it seems that he did not even see the plaintiff before he hit him. He hit him with such force that catastrophic injuries were likely and the fact that the actual injuries sustained might have been reduced had the chin strap been fastened does *a* not in my judgment reduce the defendant's responsibility for those injuries by any significant extent. Therefore, the issue of contributory negligence is decided in favour of the plaintiff.'

In my view in those passages the judge fell into error. First, in allocating responsibility for the damage, he seems to have concentrated mainly, if not entirely, on the responsibility *b* for the accident, which has to be taken into account, it is true, in assessing blameworthiness, but not to the exclusion of the plaintiff's own contributory negligence, and causative contributory negligence, in failing to secure his helmet. This was a breach of a statutory duty by the plaintiff, and moreover one which was a criminal offence, which had been passed into law not only for the purpose of inflicting fines but for the protection of motor cyclists and to prevent or lessen what injuries might be caused if not complied with. *c* What the judge seems to have taken into account is what might have been in the plaintiff's mind when he went out on his moped but did not comply with the regulation in fastening his helmet. When he said, 'One would not, when going out on one's moped, expect to be involved in an accident as severe as this one was', the judge was in my view taking into account something which was quite irrelevant. The whole point about wearing helmets is that you never know what is going to happen in an accident, or what *d* kind of accident you may unfortunately get involved in, albeit through no fault of your own, when you are on the road. The purpose of the regulation which requires the wearing of helmets is because they must be protection against whatever may happen, with a view to preventing or lessening the effect of head injury.

Second, the judge having come to the conclusion that the accident was unquestionably the governing factor in apportioning blameworthiness (and, applying Lord Denning *e* MR's judgment in *Froom v Butcher*, that must be clearly right), he did it to the extent where he entirely failed to take into account the plaintiff's breach of statutory duty. He applied what he took to be the rule that, if you were disposed to find a case of contributory negligence made out but with an apportionment of contributory negligence of something less than 10%, you would not give effect to any finding of contributory negligence whatsoever. This was a matter which after the passing of the 1945 Act did have, and may *f* still have in places, currency in the law of negligence, that if something was really de minimis here the judge would not give effect to it. We were referred, owing to the industry of junior counsel for the defendant, to the origin of that idea. It appears to have been in *Johnson v Tennant Bros Ltd* [1954] CA Transcript 329, decided in the Court of Appeal by Lord Goddard CJ, Hodson and Romer LJJ. What had happened in that case was that somebody had fallen through a hole in the factory floor in circumstances which *g* overwhelmingly represented negligence on his part, notwithstanding that the factory owner was in breach of s 25 of the Factories Act 1937, which said that the hole in the factory floor should be fenced. The finding was not the element of negligence or breach of statutory duty on the part of the factory owners at something less than 10%, but that in the circumstances of that particular case the breach of statutory duty was not the effective cause of the injury. If the court found that, then s 1 of the Law Reform *h* (Contributory Negligence) Act 1945 never came into play. But, be that as it may, the matter did apparently have some currency and was to the recollection of some members of this court applied in negligence cases at one time. It may have a good foundation in common sense not to enter into too fine a distinction in findings of negligence. But, where you have here an unquestionable breach of a statutory regulation, that kind of consideration is not in my view applicable and accordingly, in my view, the judge was *j* wrong in the present case when he said that he was not going to find any contributory negligence on the part of the plaintiff.

This was not a case which was de minimis that could be put on one side. It was quite clearly a case where the injured plaintiff had been out on his moped. The circumstances a in which there was no strapping of his helmet do not seem to have been investigated. All that happened was that it was known that the defendant had been driving when he had had too much to drink and obviously driving badly. What was also known, on the judge's findings, was that the plaintiff was in breach of his legal duty to see that his helmet was properly secured. Accordingly, in my view, there ought to have been a finding by the judge of contributory negligence on the part of the plaintiff with, to some extent, a consequent reduction of his damages. The question is how much?

b     If one takes Lord Denning MR's guidelines in *Froom v Butcher* [1975] 3 All ER 520 at 528, [1976] QB 286 at 296, one has to read in instead of seat belts 'an effectively secured helmet'. When Lord Denning MR says—

c         'we live in a practical world. In most of these cases the liabiliity of the driver is admitted; the failure to wear a seat belt is admitted; the only question is: what damages should be payable? This question should not be prolonged by an expensive enquiry into the degree of blameworthiness on either side, which would be hotly disputed,'

that is a description of the circumstances in which the present case came before the court.
    Lord Denning MR laid down guidelines. The question is whether it is right to depart from them and in what circumstances. My own view is that guidelines are there for a
d purpose and are to be complied with in the circumstances in which they are provided. One does not say that they should never be departed from, but ordinarily they should be adhered to because it is of the greatest importance that they should generally be kept to for the sake of the swift conduct, and it may be settlement, of litigation. I would myself say that here the conditions which had been postulated by Lord Denning MR in *Froom v Butcher* were complied with. If the presence of the helmet would have made no difference
e at all, then the damages should not be reduced. If it would have prevented his injuries altogether, they should be reduced by 25%. If the presence of the helmet on his head would have caused a less severe degree of injury, then the damages ought to be reduced by 15%.
    The judge did not make any finding, and he could not make any finding on the evidence, as to the amount by which the plaintiff's injuries have been made worse
f because his helmet had come off. It simply was not possible on the medical evidence and on the material available.
    In those circumstances I would apply the lower of Lord Denning MR's figures and say that the degree of the plaintiff's blameworthiness should be put at 15% and his damages reduced accordingly. As, however, May and Glidewell LJJ have come to the conclusion that the right figure would be 10% and not 15%, I do not propose to differ from that
g figure. I would allow this appeal and make the finding of contributory negligence accordingly.


    **GLIDEWELL LJ.** Everybody must have great sympathy for this plaintiff, who, at a quarter to eleven on the night of 2 March 1985 was a fit young man of nearly seventeen
h years of age, with a good job and good prospects and no doubt looking forward to a happy life. Five minutes later he sustained injuries which have left him so severely brain damaged that he will never be capable of holding or doing a proper job. It is doubtful whether he will ever be able to look after himself in any real sense. He will probably live most of his life in care and his emotions have been greatly affected.
    The temptation for a judge assessing the damages for those injuries, in a case in which
j it is now established beyond a peradvanture that the defendant by his atrocious driving was entirely responsible for the accident that caused the injuries, to award the plaintiff the full damages as if there were no question of contributory negligence must in such circumstances be considerable. Nevertheless, as the law stands, s 1 of the Law Reform (Contributory Negligence) Act 1945 requires that, when a person is proved to have

suffered damage partly as the result of his own fault, the court must assess the extent to
which it thinks it just and equitable, having regard to his share in the responsibility for   *a*
the damage, to reduce the amount of his damages. That is the exercise that the judge
undertook and he decided that they should not be reduced.

For the reasons that he has just given, I agree with Croom-Johnson LJ that the judge
fell into error. He should have concluded in the circumstances, where the plaintiff was
wearing a helmet which was either not fastened at all or was not securely fastened, and
where it was clear that the wearing of a securely fastened helmet would most probably   *b*
have substantially lessened the injuries which he suffered, that it was proper for the court
to assess a percentage by which the damages should be reduced. I therefore also agree
that the appeal must be allowed.

As Croom-Johnson LJ has indicated, we have differed as to the percentage. Counsel for
the defendant urges us to adopt the guidelines postulated in 1975 by Lord Denning MR
in *Froom v Butcher* [1975] 3 All ER 520, [1976] QB 286 as an exact analogy. Here the   *c*
evidence failed to establish with clarity, as must often be the case, the extent to which the
injuries would have been lessened if the young man's helmet had remained on his head
after the accident. Counsel for the defendant therefore urges us to say that this falls fairly
and squarely within the dictum of Lord Denning MR in *Froom v Butcher* [1975] 3 All ER
520 at 528, [1976] QB 286 at 296, where he said:

*d*

'. . . often enough the evidence will only show that the failure made a considerable
difference. Some injuries to the head, for instance, would have been a good deal less
severe if a seat belt had been worn, but there would still have been some injury to
the head. In such case I would suggest that the damages attributable to the failure to
wear a seat belt should be reduced by 15 per cent.'

That proportion coincides with the judgment of this court in *O'Connell v Jackson* [1971] 3   *e*
All ER 129 at 133, [1972] 1 QB 270 at 278, where at the conclusion of the judgment of
the court Edmund Davies LJ said:

'We can only cover the two stages in one stride and express the responsibility of
the plaintiff in terms of a percentage of the whole. Giving the best consideration
that we can to the whole matter, we assess the responsibility of the plaintiff in terms   *f*
of 15 per cent of the whole, and allow the appeal to the extent of reducing the
damages to that extent.'

*O'Connell v Jackson* was a crash helmet case, *Froom v Butcher* was a seat belt case. Counsel
for the defendant urges us to say that there is no practical difference and should be no
legal difference between not wearing a seat belt and not wearing a crash helmet or
wearing a crash helmet that is not properly fastened. In *O'Connell v Jackson* the plaintiff   *g*
was not wearing a crash helmet at all. The present regulations were not yet in force, but
the Highway Code recommended the wearing of a crash helmet and the plaintiff
admitted that he had read the Highway Code. For my part I agree that a failure by a
motor cyclist not to wear a crash helmet is equivalent to a failure by a car driver or front
seat passenger not to wear a properly fastened seat belt and I would normally think it   *h*
right to apply Lord Denning MR's guidelines in *Froom v Butcher* in such a case. But I
draw a distinction between a case where a motor cyclist is wearing a crash helmet but has
not fastened it or has not fastened it properly, and a case in which he is not wearing a
crash helmet at all.

Counsel for the defendant, in answer to a question from May LJ, accepted that there
was a factual difference, but said that that difference should have no legal consequence. I   *j*
disagree. It seems to me obvious that wearing, as this young man was, a close fitting
crash helmet, will in some accidents have the result that the helmet will remain on the
head and thus be effective either in reducing the effect or alternatively eliminating
damage to the head from the results of the accident. In my view the degree of

blameworthiness of a plaintiff, who puts on a crash helmet but fails to fasten it properly
*a* or at all, is less than that of one who does not put on his helmet at all. Counsel suggested
that blameworthiness really came in before one got to the stage of the 25% in Lord
Denning MR's guidelines for not wearing a seat belt where it is proved that the result of
that was that injuries, which would not have been sustained at all if a seat belt had been
worn, were worsened. I do not disagree with that proposition. It seems to me that in the
altered circumstances where a crash helmet is worn but not properly fastened, the whole
*b* scale of reduction, because of the lesser blameworthiness, should to an extent be less. It is
for that reason and in those circumstances that I think the appeal should be allowed but
to the extent of reducing the plaintiff's damages by 10% and attributing that degree of
causation of the damage to him.

**MAY LJ.** With respect to the trial judge I, too, agree that he erred in considering the
*c* question of contributory negligence in the respects referred to by Croom-Johnson LJ. Of
the authorities to which we have been referred in the course of the appeal, in my
judgment the most pertinent is that of *O'Connell v Jackson* [1971] 3 All ER 129, [1972] 1
QB 270. As Croom-Johnson and Glidewell LJJ have pointed out, that was a claim by a
moped rider who had not been wearing a crash helmet when he was involved in a road
accident, the responsibility for which accident had been solely that of the other road user.
*d* I respectfully agree with Glidewell LJ that factually that case can, and should be,
distinguished from the instant case in that in that case no helmet at all was being worn,
whereas in the present case a helmet was being worn, although not properly fastened.
     In the instant case I direct myself in accordance with the principles contained in the
last paragraph of the judgment of the court delivered by Edmund Davies LJ in *O'Connell
v Jackson* [1971] 3 All ER 129 at 132, [1972] 1 QB 270 at 277. I do not embark on the
*e* inquiry deprecated by Lord Denning MR in the passage from his judgment in *Froom v
Butcher* [1975] 3 All ER 520, [1976] QB 286, to which Croom-Johnson LJ has referred. I
merely give the best consideration that I can to the facts and circumstances of the instant
case and, doing so, I would agree with Glidewell LJ in assessing the contributory
negligence in this case at 10%. I would allow the appeal accordingly.

*f*   *Appeal allowed.*

Solicitors: *Daynes Hill & Perks*, Norwich (for the defendant); *Kenneth Bush & Co*, King's
Lynn (for the plaintiff).

                                        Carolyn Toulmin   Barrister.

# Garvin v Domus Publishing Ltd and another

CHANCERY DIVISION
WALTON J
15, 16, 17 JULY 1987

*Contempt of court – Defence – Self-incrimination – Criminal offence – Documents disclosed on execution of Anton Piller order – Application for leave to use documents obtained under Anton Piller order in contempt proceedings – Whether proceedings for contempt of court proceedings for a 'criminal offence' – Whether privilege against self-incrimination available as defence in contempt proceedings – Whether documents obtained under Anton Piller order can be used in contempt proceedings – Civil Evidence Act 1968, s 14(1)(a).*

The plaintiff, who was the managing director of the defendant companies and was entitled to a share of the profits, was dismissed. She brought an action for wrongful dismissal claiming damages, arrears of salary and an account of profits. In order to protect her position she obtained a Mareva injunction restraining the companies from removing out of the jurisdiction or transferring, charging or disposing of any assets except in the ordinary course of business. The plaintiff subsequently suspected that the companies were being run down, and she applied for an Anton Piller order to obtain and preserve documents which might show that the companies and those controlling them had breached the Mareva injunction. In her application the plaintiff made it clear that, if her suspicions that the Mareva injunction had been breached were well founded, she would bring proceedings for contempt. The judge hearing the Anton Piller application granted the order against the companies and their owner and the managing director of one of them subject to leave being obtained before any information obtained under the Anton Piller order was used in any proceedings for contempt. After executing the Anton Piller order the plaintiff applied for leave to use documents seized under the order to bring proceedings for contempt against the owner and the managing director for breaches of the Mareva injunction. The owner and the managing director contended that leave to use the documents ought not to be granted because the defendants ought not to be required to produce documents which might tend to incriminate them. The question arose whether the privilege against self-incrimination applied in proceedings for contempt of court, having regard to s 14(1)(a)[a] of the Civil Evidence Act 1968, which provided that the privilege applied in proceedings other than criminal proceedings 'only as regards criminal offences . . . and penalties'.

**Held** – Proceedings for contempt of court were not proceedings for a criminal offence for the purposes of s 14(1)(a) of the 1968 Act and therefore the privilege against self-incrimination did not apply to documents obtained under an Anton Piller order. It followed that the defendants could not oppose the plaintiff's use of the documents to bring contempt proceedings against them. The plaintiff would accordingly be granted the leave sought (see p 349 h j, p 351 f g and p 352 a f g, post).

*Pooley v Whetham* (1880) 15 Ch D 435 applied.

Dictum of Lord Denning MR in *Comet Products UK Ltd v Hawkex Plastics Ltd* [1971] 1 All ER 1141 at 1143–1144 not followed.

**Notes**

For civil contempt, see 9 Halsbury's Laws (4th edn) paras 52–86, and for cases on the subject, see 16 Digest (Reissue) 61–88, 598–857.

For the Civil Evidence Act 1968, s 14, see 17 Halsbury's Statutes (4th edn) 173.

---

a    Section 14(1), is set out at p 349 f, post

**Cases referred to in judgment**

a *Bramblevale Ltd, Re* [1969] 3 All ER 1062, [1970] Ch 128, [1969] 3 WLR 699, CA.

*Comet Products UK Ltd v Hawkex Plastics Ltd* [1971] 1 All ER 1141, [1971] 2 QB 67, [1971] 2 WLR 361, CA.

*Crest Homes plc v Marks* [1987] 2 All ER 1074, [1987] AC 829, [1987] 3 WLR 293, HL.

*Pooley v Whetham* (1880) 15 Ch D 435, CA.

*Redfern v Redfern* [1891] P 139, [1886–90] All ER Rep 524, CA.

b *Rio Tinto Zinc Corp v Westinghouse Electric Corp* [1978] 1 All ER 434, [1978] AC 547, [1978] 2 WLR 81, HL.

*Yianni v Yianni* [1966] 1 All ER 231, [1966] 1 WLR 120.


**Motion**

By motion dated 23 April 1987 the plaintiff, Sharon Denise Garvin, sought an order that
c she be at liberty to make use of documents seized pursuant to an Anton Piller order made
by Millett J on 3 March 1987 for the purpose of bringing proceedings for contempt of
court against Anthony Page and Barnett Bernhard for alleged breaches of a Mareva
injunction granted by Warner J on 16 December 1985 restraining the defendants,
Domus Publishing Ltd and Domus Publications Ltd, from removing out of the
jurisdiction or transferring, charging or disposing of any assets of the defendants except
d in the ordinary course of business as carried on prior to the order until after judgment or
further order in the action brought by the plaintiff against the defendants for damages
for wrongful dismissal, arrears of salary and an account of profits. The facts are set out in
the judgment.

*Ivan Krolick* for the plaintiff.
e *Nigel Tozzi* for the defendants.

**WALTON J.** The present is an application of a rather unusual nature, because it is for
leave to utilise a document discovered in consequence of the execution of an Anton Piller
order for the purpose of bringing proceedings for contempt. The way in which the
matter arises is this. The plaintiff in the action, Miss Sharon Denise Garvin, was formerly
f the managing director of both of the defendant companies, having been appointed to
that position on or about 8 July 1983. She was removed from that position, as she says,
wrongfully, and in consequence she has launched the present action. Her interest under
the terms of her agreement as managing director is not merely confined to the question
of earnings, but she is entitled thereunder to a share of profits and also in certain
circumstances to obtain shares in the company. She is therefore concerned that the
g companies should continue to exist and that they should continue to be profitable. The
action was started at the end of 1985 and virtually contemporaneously with the issue of
the amended writ the plaintiff moved for and obtained an ex parte Mareva injunction on
16 December 1985, which was then continued inter partes on 19 December 1985. The
order, which was made by Warner J, ordered that the defendants and each of them
should be restrained until after judgment or until further order in the mean time from
h doing, in the usual form—

    'the following acts or any of them that is to say (1) Removing from the jurisdiction
    of this Honourable Court or in any manner transferring charging or disposing of
    any of their assets SAVE in the usual course of business as carried on prior to the
    making of the order . . . (2) In the event that any business transaction exceeds or
j    forms part of a series which exceeds £10,000 removing from the jurisdiction or in
    any manner transferring or disposing of any part of the proceeds of sale thereof . . .'

and there was the usual proviso saving any rights the banks might have.

At some considerably later period, as a result of information received, at any rate in
part as a result of information received, from a bookkeeper in the companies, the plaintiff

became very apprehensive that the affairs of the companies were being run down and
that when she finally recovered judgment in the action she would be recovering *a*
judgment against an empty shell. With a view to ensuring that at any rate all the
documents relating to what she feared had been going on in the company should be
preserved, she applied for an Anton Piller order. But she made it perfectly clear in her
application for the Anton Piller order that if what she suspected might be the case should
turn out to be the case, namely that the terms of the inter partes Mareva injunction had
been breached, she would seek to bring proceedings for contempt against whoever was *b*
responsible for that matter. This posed Millett J, before whom the matter came,
something of a problem, because the purpose of an Anton Piller order is undoubtedly to
recover or preserve either physical goods as in the usual case of contraband, cassettes,
bottles of perfume or things of that nature, being passed off as genuine, or documents. It
is not simply and solely in any way directed to the question of discovering material for
contempt proceedings. So, Millett J, this double-headed matter being in front of him, *c*
was troubled as to what he should do, but finally he said that he proposed to grant the
order in the terms in which it was sought, subject of course to the minor amendments
which always arise in these matters and which he discussed with counsel, but to impose
the requirement that leave should be sought before any information obtained as a result
of the order could be used for any proceedings for contempt. It is pursuant to that
provision that counsel for the plaintiff has applied to me for the grant of such leave. I *d*
should make it clear in fact that the actual order as drawn up does not reflect that vital
part of Millett J's intention. However that came about, it is quite clear that the order does
not reflect it, purely as a result of some drafting or typist's error or some error of that
nature, and therefore I have directed that the order should be regarded as amended by
the inclusion of that restriction under the terms of the slip rule.

The Anton Piller order was granted against both defendants and against a Mr Anthony *e*
Page, who is now the managing director of the second defendants, and Mr Barnett
Bernhard, who is resident in the United States of America and who has taken no part in
these proceedings, who is or was the owner, I think indirectly, of both of the defendant
companies.

In the course of the execution of the Anton Piller order, an agreement, ostensibly dated
22 November 1985, has been discovered, which document appears to be a matter of *f*
some suspicion. I say 'appears', because in fact it is at the moment in the custody of the
court, Millett J having, by a separate order, on being apprised of the potential curiosity of
this document, directed that that is in fact what should happen.

On the face of that document it will be observed that the agreement therein expressed
was made before the Mareva injunction had been granted, the ex parte injunction having
been granted on 16 December and the inter partes on 19 December. One of the curiosities *g*
of the present matter is that the Mr Page therein referred to, the managing director of
the second defendant and one of the persons at any rate against whom it is proposed to
move a motion for contempt, has given the court an explanation of this document. The
explanation is as follows:

> 'In about September 1986 I approached my solicitors, Pothecary & Barratt, on *h*
> behalf of [a company which is interested, called Network] and asked them to draw
> up a formal document providing for the transfer of assets from Domus [I think that
> is the second defendant] to Network. I should point out that I did not mention the
> Plaintiff's proceedings nor the fact that she had obtained a Mareva Injunction . . .
> because I did not think it was relevant: the written agreement I wanted drawing up
> reflected events that had already occurred before the obtaining of the Mareva *j*
> Injunction. On the 11th December 1986 I was handed the Agreement. It was
> undated. I sent three copies to Mr. Bernhard for signature [still undated]. On their
> return I also signed them and then back-dated the Agreement to 22nd November
> 1985. If that was a wrong thing to do then I fully accept I should not have back-

dated the Agreement in that way and I apologise unreservedly. A true copy of the
Agreement is now produced and shown to me marked "ASP 2". However, I now
appreciate that a document drawn up after the grant of a Mareva Injunction but
which purports to be made before such grant appears to be a serious breach of the
Injunction. I was of course aware of the Mareva when I back-dated the Agreement.
But because of the background that I have described I honestly believed and continue
to believe that there has been no breach of the Mareva in this instance. The
Agreement was back-dated, but I consider that I was entitled to back-date it so that
it reflected the terms that had already been orally agreed and put into effect in
November 1985. I did not intend to mislead anybody thereby because the assets had
already been sold pursuant to the terms agreed orally and before the grant of the
Mareva Injunction. That there was, in fact, no breach of the Mareva is, I suggest,
highlighted by the openness with which the Agreement has continued to come into
effect.'

The astonishing thing now is that it is really Mr Page (although I shall have something
to say about this in a moment) who has opposed the grant of leave to the plaintiff to use,
inter alia, that document (and I think there is no gainsaying that that document is the
foundation of the plaintiff's possible case in contempt, whatever other supporting
documents there may be) on the ground, after the perfectly innocent explanation that
has been given in his affidavit, that it may tend to incriminate him. It seems a rather odd
stand for a person, who has a perfectly innocent explanation for that document and who
has given it, to take. Nevertheless of course he is entitled to take it.

There has recently been a decision in the House of Lords, *Crest Homes plc v Marks*
[1987] 2 All ER 1074, [1987] AC 829, in which Lord Oliver makes it perfectly plain that
documents which are obtained in the ordinary way by discovery, including discovery
which is effected as a result of an Anton Piller order, can be used without any restriction
whatsoever for the purpose of making a contempt application by the plaintiff if the
plaintiff so requires. But, as counsel for the defendants has pointed out, that may be (I
am not wholly convinced) based on the fact that in that case the defendants did not in
any way object or take exception to the discovery which had been made. In the present
case, when the matter came on originally before me, the second defendant did not play
any part. The second defendant had been represented down to some recent date, but the
solicitors have come off the record and there were no new solicitors on the record. There
then ensued, in consequence of that, an interesting debate between counsel for the
defendants and myself as to the person to whom the privilege, if there were any such
privilege, belonged.

The matter is not wholly untouched by authority, because in *Rio Tinto Zinc Corp v
Westinghouse Electric Corp* [1978] 1 All ER 434, [1978] AC 547 the point was discussed by
their Lordships, although not decided, as to what the position would be if a company
had the privilege in a document and it was then sought to obtain the contents of the
document, or the contents of the transaction recorded in the document, from servants or
agents of the company. The argument on the one side was that undoubtedly, under
those circumstances, the privilege of the company would be worth nothing if it could be
undermined in this way. The House of Lords, apart from noting that the point was an
interesting one, did not decide it. But here of course the matter would be vital, but the
other way round, that is to say it is quite clear that the document as a document is a
document of the company, and therefore the privilege, if there is any privilege at all,
belongs to the second defendant, and not to Mr Page. Therefore my view on the matter
was that Mr Page had no independent right to privilege, and that therefore, if the
company did not assert the right, and the company is not here to assert it, Mr Page
himself certainly could not take the point.

Between my last discussion of the matter with counsel for the defendants and this
morning, solicitors have been instructed on behalf of the second defendant and they have

now put themselves on the record. As a result of that, counsel for the defendants was enabled to appear for the second defendant and therefore that point is not a point which *a* arises any longer in the matter, because the second defendant now is taking the point that the document is the subject matter of privilege.

The first question therefore which arises is whether, so far as contempt of court proceedings are concerned, there is any privilege of the nature that counsel for the defendants and the company would seek to assert. Undoubtedly there are some expressions of opinion of Lord Denning MR in *Comet Products UK Ltd v Hawkex Plastics* *b* *Ltd* [1971] 1 All ER 1141 at 1143–1144, [1971] 2 QB 67 at 73–74 which tend to suggest that there indeed is:

'Although this is a civil contempt, it partakes of the nature of a criminal charge. The defendant is liable to punished for it. He may be sent to prison. The rules as to criminal charges have always been applied to such a proceeding. I see that Cross J in *Yianni v Yianni* [1966] 1 All ER 231, [1966] 1 WLR 120, so decided; and furthermore *c* we ourselves in this court, in *Re Bramblevale Ltd* [1969] 3 All ER 1062, [1970] Ch 128, said that it must be proved with the same degree of satisfaction as in a criminal charge. It follows that the accused is not bound to give evidence unless he chooses to do so. In this connection I quote what Bowen LJ said in *Redfern v Redfern* [1891] P 139 at 147, [1886–90] All ER Rep 524 at 528: "It is one of the inveterate principles *d* of English law that a party cannot be compelled to discover that which, if answered, would tend to subject him to any punishment, penalty, forfeiture . . . 'no one is bound to incriminate himself'." This was not always the law in the case of civil contempt. In the days of Sir William Blackstone, 200 years ago, civil contempt was an exception to the general principle. In those days a plaintiff was entitled to deliver interrogatories to the defendant, which the defendant was bound to answer on oath. *e* In his Commentaries, Sir William Blackstone said that—"this method of making the defendant answer upon oath to a criminal charge, is not agreeable to the genius of the common law in any other instance", and he went on to say that "by long and immemorial usage, [it] has now become the law of the land" (4 Bl Com (18th edn, 1829) 287–288). I am prepared to accept that such a rule did exist in the days of Sir William Blackstone. But I do not think it exists any longer today. The genius of the *f* common law has prevailed. I hold that a man who is charged with contempt of court cannot be compelled to answer interrogatories or to give evidence himself to make him provide his guilt. I reject the submission that the defendant is a compellable witness in the contempt proceedings against him.'

And of course I should make it perfectly clear, in case it has not been made already clear, that the company, whether or not it is made a respondent to any contempt proceedings, *g* would itself have been in contempt, and of course Mr Page would be in contempt, if there is a contempt, by reason of his having been the managing director of the company.

In fact counsel for the plaintiff took me through that case very carefully this morning, and it appears quite clear that that passage from Lord Denning MR's judgment is in fact wholly obiter. The question there was a very curious one indeed. If I may read the *h* headnote in order to point out what was in issue ([1971] 2 QB 67):

'The plaintiffs in a passing off action obtained an interim injunction restraining the defendants from passing off their product as the plaintiffs'. Before the trial of the action the plaintiffs alleged that the defendants were guilty of contempt of court in disobeying the injunction and applied for the committal of the second defendant to prison for his contempt. Affidavits were filed on each side and were read at the *j* hearing of the application. Cantley J. made an order allowing the cross-examination of the defendant upon his affidavit which had been read by counsel for the plaintiffs. On the defendant's appeal:—*Held*, allowing the appeal, that, since an application to commit for contempt had a quasi-criminal aspect and the proposed cross-a examination would be likely to cover broad issues in the action, as a matter of discretion the cross-examination ought not to be allowed.'

So what was in issue in that case was whether it was right to allow cross-examination of the defendant, Mr Hawkins, who had in fact filed an affidavit. That affidavit was on matters going outside the question of contempt, because counsel for the plaintiff made it perfectly clear to the Court of Appeal that he was undoubtedly going to try and go completely outside the contempt proceedings, pick up matters at a very much earlier
b stage and attempt to prove to the court that Mr Hawkins was thoroughly dishonest from the word go. So, so far from being an authority for the proposition that a man charged with contempt has some right of privilege, all that this decided was that he could, if he put in an affidavit (because of course if he had not put in an affidavit he would not be a compellable witness anyway in proceedings) and he was going to be cross-examined
c solely on matters arising in the contempt proceedings, he could not escape that cross-examination, but that if the cross-examination was intended to go wider then he could. So really at the end of the day, although of course one is always interested in Lord Denning MR's somewhat personal views as to the contents of the law, the case does not lay down any proposition which assists me in the present case in the slightest.

But, supposing it did, then I should be bound not to follow it. The reason I would be
d bound not to follow it is that nowhere in that case (and indeed I am not complaining or criticising anybody in any way because it did not involve the section at all) was any reference made to s 14 of the Civil Evidence Act 1968. That section came into effect on the passing of the Act on 25 October 1968 and therefore was in force at the date when the *Comet Products* case was decided. This whole Act was passed as a result of the Lord Chancellor's Law Reform Committee's 13th, 15th and 16th Reports (Cmnds 2964, 3391
e and 3472). Section 14 of the Act reads:

'(1) The right of a person in any legal proceedings other than criminal proceedings to refuse to answer any question or produce any document or thing if to do so would tend to expose that person to proceedings for an offence or for the recovery of a penalty—(a) shall apply only as regards criminal offences under the law of any part of the United Kingdom and penalties provided for by such law; and (b) shall include
f a like right to refuse to answer any question or produce any document or thing if to do so would tend to expose the husband or wife of that person to proceedings for any such criminal offence or for the recovery of any such penalty . . .'

So here we have a provision that, as from the date of that section, the right of a person to produce any document or thing if to do so would tend to expose that person to
g proceedings for an offence or for the recovery of a penalty '(a) shall apply only as regards criminal offences under the law of any part of the United Kingdom and penalties provided for by such law . . .' The crucial word there is 'only'. Whether or not it was so intended (as a member of the committee, I can testify, as appears from our report, that we never considered the question of privilege against self-incrimination so far as contempt was concerned), even if that was not in any way in the minds of the committee, one has
h to take the law as one finds it, and the Act says that it shall apply only as regards criminal offences and penalties.

Is a proceeding for contempt of court a criminal offence? To that, so far as I can see, there is only one answer, namely that it is not. Of course it is perfectly true that the standard of proof required in such a proceeding is the criminal standard of proof. That is understandable, because it is an extremely serious matter indeed for a person to be
j accused of contempt of court. As a result of that, one can find in the cases a good many expressions, like 'quasi-criminal', and expressions to the same effect. Indeed the mere fact that the word 'quasi-criminal' was used shows that it is not criminal, when one at any rate is dealing, as one is dealing here of course, with civil contempt. It seems to me that this is borne out by the only case I can find dealing with the matter and dealing with it

in a rather interesting setting, *Pooley v Whetham* (1880) 15 Ch D 435. The headnote reads as follows:

'An attachment issued by the High Court of Justice for disobedience of an order of the Court in a civil action is not an offence within the meaning of the 19th section of the *Extradition Act*, 1870. Therefore, where a party to an action in the Chancery Division was arrested in *Paris* for a crime under the *Extradition Act*, and while in prison in *England* under the warrant was served with an attachment for disobedience to an order in the action:—*Held* (affirming the decision of *Bacon*, V.C.), that the attachment was valid, and that the prisoner was not entitled to his discharge until he had cleared his contempt, although he had been acquitted of the criminal charge. The 19th section of the *Extradition Act* is not confined to political offences, but applies to all criminal charges.'

And then an example of the way in which one has to put glosses on even the plainest words:

'If a warrant under the *Extradition Act* is obtained, not for the *bonâ fide* purpose of punishing a person for a crime, but with the indirect object of making him amenable to an attachment in a civil action, the Court will relieve against such an abuse of the process of the Court.'

In the Court of Appeal, James LJ said (at 440):

'In my opinion, neither the words nor what is called the spirit of the Act of Parliament, that is to say, the true intent and meaning of the [Extradition Act 1870], have any reference to what is really in this case a mere civil process. Although it assumes the form of punishment for contempt of Court, it is a mere civil process to enforce obedience to an order of a civil Court to do something on behalf of or for the benefit of a private person, which has no reference whatever to any offence committed against the State or against the Sovereign of the State, which are the offences mentioned there. It appears to me that it is impossible to extend the words to an attachment for a contempt which is really only a process of coercion to compel the performance of the order of the Court in what, as I have said, is a civil matter.'

Brett LJ said (at 442–443):

'But then comes the next question, which is whether a contempt is, even though the contempt were committed before surrender, an offence such as is mentioned in the 19th section. Now the offence there mentioned is one which is thus described: "Where a person might be triable or tried for any offence." How is it possible to say that he was ever triable or tried for a contempt? It is not a matter which is a triable offence. It is a civil process under which he is detained, which he can get rid of at any time by purging his contempt, and it is not, in my opinion, a triable offence or an offence upon which a man can be tried at all. The real truth is that the word "offence" in the 19th section means a criminal act, whether a felony or a misdemeanor is immaterial, but an offence which would be triable in a criminal Court. Therefore it does not apply to civil processes, so that the objections which were founded on that reading of the statute all fail.'

Cotton LJ, who was the third member of the court, said (at 444–445):

'Now, it is difficult to see here what can be said to be the trial of Mr. *Pooley* when he was taken under the attachment; but I do not decide it on that ground. It is sufficient to say that in my opinion what is here forbidden is his being tried— whatever that may mean—for an offence against the criminal law. In a former part and in a subsequent part of that section mention is made of crimes in respect of which a person can be taken under the Act, and although the word "crime" is not

used where we find the prohibition, yet the offence there referred to, coupling it
a    with what goes before and what goes after must, in my opinion, mean an offence
against the criminal law, that is to say, a crime for which the offender can be tried,
in the ordinary sense of the word, under the criminal law. But here there was
nothing criminal. Incorrectly we say a man is guilty of gross contempt, that is to
say, he has disobeyed an order of the Court in a civil proceeding, but that is not a
crime or offence against the criminal law. It is one the Court is bound to deal with
b    by committing the man to prison; but that is simply for the purpose of enabling a
litigant who has got an order which has been disobeyed to obtain his civil rights,
and it is a mere process to enforce civil rights, and not any proceeding for punishing
a crime, as suggested. Therefore, in my opinion, the second objection fails.'

Now we have here of course the precise words 'criminal offences', so that, if any further
c   reinforcement of *Pooley v Whetham* (1880) 15 Ch D 435 was required, those words would
provide it.

Counsel for the defendants has an interesting submission, which he says is founded on
the word 'penalty'. He says that s 14(1)(*a*) of the Civil Evidence Act 1968 says that it does
apply in relation to penalties. I do not think that is quite right, because he is there trying
to read 'penalty' in an extremely wide sense, and to come extent he founds himself on
d   the Contempt of Court Act 1981, s 14, which says:

'(1) In any case where a court has power to commit a person to prison for
contempt of court and . . . no limitation applies . . . [the] fixed term . . . shall not . . .
exceed two years in the case of committal by a superior court, or one month in the
case of committal by an inferior court
e    '(2) In any case where an inferior court has power to fine a person for contempt
of court and (apart from this provision) no limit applies to the amount of the fine,
the fine shall not on any occasion exceed £1,000 . . .'

and he says that that recognises that contempt of court may end up in a fine and a fine is
a penalty. I think, with all respect to counsel, that that is quibbling with words. It is
quibbling with words, because of course in the widest possible way it is a penalty, in the
f    sense that a penalty is something which one suffers as a result of having done wrong.
But, if he would only look at the opening words of s 14(1) of the 1968 Act, he will see
that the person in question can refuse to produce any document or thing if to do so
would tend to expose that person to proceedings for the recovery of a penalty. That
makes it perfectly clear that the kind of penalty that the section has in mind is the sort
which is provided for by statute, whereby some person brings proceedings of whatever
g   nature to recover a penalty. Nobody ever brings contempt of court proceedings to recover
a penalty. The result at the end of the day may be that the court will impose a fine,
instead of sending the offender to prison. But nobody recovers a penalty or brings the
proceedings to recover the penalty. 'Penalty', in my judgment, in that section has the
narrow meaning of penalty recoverable under statute, and nothing wider than that.

Counsel for the defendants then made a separate submission to the effect that one of
h   the allegations which quite clearly may be made as a result of Mr Page not having told
the truth in his affidavit is that the disclosure of that document would tend to expose Mr
Page to a claim for forgery, because, to produce a document which tells a lie about itself,
if the date is material, as it undoubtedly is here, then putting on a false date can amount
to a claim for forgery under s 9(1)(*g*) of the Forgery and Counterfeiting Act 1981. The
answer to that seems to me to be something which I have really already discussed,
j    because, if there is any privilege here, the document is a document of the company and
the privilege is the privilege of the company and forgery is not something which the
company as a company can do. It must be done by the hand of somebody, and it is that
person who will be liable, and in this case it would be Mr Page. So I do not think he
would have any independent right to object to the production of that document. In any

event, what I am asked to do has nothing to do with criminal proceedings at all. I am only asked to release the documents discovered on the Anton Piller order for the purpose *a* of their being used in contempt proceedings.

The last point which counsel for the defendants took is an interesting point on s 18(5) of the Civil Evidence Act 1968. The first time one reads it, it undoubtedly gives one a bit of a shock. It is in the section 'General interpretation, and savings', and it says:

> 'Nothing in this Act shall prejudice—(a) any power of a court, in any legal *b* proceedings, to exclude evidence (whether by preventing questions from being put or otherwise) at its discretion . . .'

From the way in which that section is framed, it seems to me to be quite clear to be directed towards existing powers of the court, because the word is 'prejudiced' ('Nothing in this Act shall prejudice') and therefore what the Act is thinking about is existing powers of the court to exclude evidence, whether by preventing questions from being *c* put or otherwise. But, when one comes to think about it, it is in fact a power which the court frequently exercises by stopping counsel from putting perfectly useless questions or pursuing perfectly useless lines of argument and sometimes by tossing aside affidavits which really have nothing to do with the case and saying that one is not going to look at them at all. All that this is doing is preserving those sorts of powers of the court.

There are more interesting and difficult powers along the same lines. For example, *d* there are cases where one is dealing with confessions made to priests, and knowledge in the possession of a doctor as the medical adviser for one of the parties to the case, which sometimes it is proper to allow to come in for the purpose of doing justice and sometimes it is proper to exclude totally for the purpose of doing justice. So there is indeed quite a wide variety of circumstances where the court has this power and is accustomed to and does frequently exercise it. But it does not seem to me that that is intended to give the *e* court any power to do as it likes, as it were, in admitting or rejecting evidence. All such exercises of that power, as in the case of any other judicial power, must be exercised on a proper judicial basis. So far as any question here would arise on exercising it, I return to that with which I started. Mr Page has given me a perfectly innocent explanation for the document. He has even exhibited a copy of the document to his affidavit. Under those circumstances it would seem very odd indeed to say that that document should be *f* excluded from consideration by a court for what properly (because in fact I know that the plaintiff has not had an opportunity of having the document examined up to date) may be extracted from it in due course.

Putting all those matters together, it seems to me that this is a case where I ought to give leave to the plaintiff to use the documentation obtained on the Anton Piller discovery for the purpose of bringing contempt proceedings, and, for the avoidance of doubt, I will *g* declare, as appears, I think, quite clearly from *Crest Homes plc v Marks* [1987] 2 All ER 1074, [1987] AC 829, that no leave is required in relation to any other documents which have been discovered in the course of the action in the course of normal discovery.

*Leave granted.*
*h*

Solicitors: *John Byrne & Co* (for the plaintiff); *Pothecary & Barratt* (for the defendants).

Hazel Hartman　Barrister.

*a*

# Re H and another (minors) (adoption: putative father's rights)

COURT OF APPEAL, CIVIL DIVISION

LORD DONALDSON OF LYMINGTON MR, BALCOMBE AND NICHOLLS LJJ

11 APRIL 1989

*b*

*Child – Care – Local authority – Illegitimate child – Putative father applying for custody and access – Mother's parental rights vested in local authority – Local authority making application to free child for adoption – Father applying for custody and access – Right of putative father to be heard – Right of father to apply for parental rights order – Whether parental rights order interfering with local authority's exercise of their statutory rights over children – Family Law*
*c* *Reform Act 1987, s 4.*

The unmarried parents of two children lived together until February 1985, when the father left the home. Shortly afterwards a place of safety order was made in respect of the children and later, at the mother's request, the children were received into voluntary care by the local authority, which passed a parental rights resolution under s 3 of the Child
*d* Care Act 1980 in respect of the mother's rights. The children were fostered and were regularly visited by the father until November 1987, when the local authority terminated the parents' access to the children and applied to the county court to free both children for adoption. The father applied for custody of and access to the children under the Guardianship of Minors Act 1971 but the judge refused his application on the ground that the grant of custody and access to the father would have the effect of interfering
*e* with the statutory rights and duties entrusted to the local authority in respect of children in their care. The father appealed. Before the appeal was heard s 4[a] of the Family Law Reform Act 1987, which provided that if the putative father of an illegitimate child was granted parental rights under that section he was required to share those rights jointly with the mother, came into force. By s 7[b] of the 1987 Act an order freeing a child for
*f* adoption could not be made unless the court was satisfied that a putative father had no intention of applying for a parental rights order or that such an order was likely to be refused. The father indicated at the hearing of the appeal that he intended to apply for such an order. The local authority contended that since a parental rights order under s 4 of the 1987 Act would interfere with the local authority's exercise of their statutory rights over the children such an order could not be made while a parental rights resolution under s 3 of the 1980 Act remained in force.
*g*

**Held** – A parental rights order made under s 4 of the 1987 Act, unlike a custody order made under the 1971 Act, would not interfere with a local authority's exercise of their statutory rights over the children in their care but would merely give the putative father locus standi and place him in the same position as the parent of a legitimate child to
*h* make applications to the court, eg to discharge a parental rights resolution under s 5(4)(b) of the 1980 Act, to oppose an adoption order or an order freeing a child for adoption, or to be heard on access if the child was in care. Accordingly, the father's appeal against the refusal to grant him custody would be dismissed and the case would be remitted to the court below to be heard on the merits (see p 357 *h j* and p 358 *c* to *g*, post).

M v H [1988] 3 All ER 5 distinguished.

*j*

**Notes**

For a local authority's powers in relation to minors, see 24 Halsbury's Laws (4th edn) para 580.

For the assumption by a local authority of parental rights and duties, see ibid para 790.

---

*a*   Section 4 is set out at p 357 *a b*, post
*b*   Section 7 is set out at p 357 *c* to *e*, post

For freeing a child for adoption, see ibid para 659.
For the Guardianship of Minors Act 1971, see 6 Halsbury's Statutes (4th edn) 305.
For the Child Care Act 1980, ss 3, 5, see ibid 535, 539.

**Cases referred to in judgments**
M v H [1988] 3 All ER 5, [1988] 3 WLR 485, HL.
N (minors), Re (1989) Times, 1 March, CA.

**Appeal**
The putative father of two illegitimate children appealed with the leave of the judge
against the decision of his Honour Judge Marder QC sitting in Slough County Court on
25 October 1988 whereby he dismissed the father's application for custody of the children
under s 9 of the Guardianship of Minors Act 1971 and made a preliminary ruling of law
that the scope of the court's inquiry into the position of the putative father in a contested
freeing for adoption application in which there had been an assumption of the parental
rights of the mother by a local authority was limited solely to the issue of whether the
mother's agreement to the making of an adoption order should be dispensed with on one
of the grounds specified in s 16(2) of the Adoption Act 1976. The facts are set out in the
judgment of Balcombe LJ.

Robert J Seabrook QC and Sally Smith for the father.
Brian Jubb for the mother.
Anita M Ryan QC and Mhairi McNab for the local authority.

**BALCOMBE LJ** (delivering the first judgment at the invitation of Lord Donaldson
MR). This is an appeal with the leave of the judge from a decision of his Honour Judge
Marder QC given in the Slough County Court on 25 October 1988 on a preliminary
point of law on an application by a local authority to free two young children for
adoption. There is also before us by amendment an appeal by the putative father of these
children against a refusal of the judge to grant him custody of those children under the
Guardianship of Minors Act 1971.

The facts are these. In the spring of 1981 the parents of these two children met and
began to live together but they never married. On 18 October 1982 a boy was born and
on 27 December 1983 a girl was born, so the boy is now six and a half years old and the
girl is a little over five. They lived together as a family unit until February 1985, when
the father left the home, and on 24 March 1985 the mother left the children in the care
of her parents, who contacted the local authority's social services department. On
25 March 1985 a place of safety order was made in respect of both children.

On 23 May 1985 the local authority's application to the juvenile court for a care order
was refused, but then the children were received into voluntary care at the request of the
mother under s 2 of the Child Care Act 1980. In December 1985 the mother gave a 28-
day notice for the return of the children to her but she withdrew that notice on 6 January
1986. On 27 August 1987 the local authority passed a parental rights resolution in respect
of the mother's rights under s 3 of the Child Care Act 1980. It will, of course, be
appreciated that at that time the father had no parental rights as such because he and the
mother had not married.

In the mean time, the children, who have been in the care of foster parents, were
visited regularly by the father, with rather less regularity by the mother, and, indeed, by
other relatives as well. But the local authority, for reasons which no doubt seemed good
to them, decided that these children needed a more permanent base and, therefore, as a
preliminary to that, gave notice to the father on 4 November 1987 that his access to the
children would be terminated as from January 1988. Similarly, in December 1987 the
mother's access was also terminated.

In February 1988 the children were introduced to prospective adopters, but that
particular introduction broke down and the children went back to the original foster
parents. On 17 March 1988 the local authority made an application to the local county

court to free both children for adoption. On 24 May 1988 the father made an application
a  under the Guardianship of Minors Act 1971 for custody and access to both children. The
significance of that application will become apparent in a moment. Then in September
1988 introductions began for the children to a new adoptive family and on 1 October
1988 the children were placed with that new adoptive family. As far as I am aware, they
are still there.

The local authority's application to free the children for adoption and the father's
b  application under the 1971 Act for custody and access came before Judge Marder at the
Slough County Court on 25 October 1988.

With those introductory facts I turn now to consider the relevant statutory provision,
which is s 18 of the Adoption Act 1976. Subsection (1) of that section is to the following
effect:

c    'Where, on an application by an adoption agency [I pause there to interpolate that
a local authority is included in that phrase], an authorised court is satisfied in the
case of each parent or guardian of the child that—(a) he freely, and with full
understanding of what is involved, agrees generally and unconditionally to the
making of an adoption order, or (b) his agreement to the making of an adoption
order should be dispensed with on a ground specified in section 16(2), the court
d    shall make an order declaring the child free for adoption.'

As far as the mother is concerned, who was the only person at that stage who could be
called a parent, the local authority were and are applying that her agreement should be
dispensed with.

Then I turn to sub-s (7) as it was originally drafted:

e    'Before making an order under this section in the case of an illegitimate child
whose father is not its guardian, the court shall satisfy itself in relation to any person
claiming to be the father that either—(a) he has no intention of applying for custody
of the child under section 9 of the Guardianship of Minors Act 1971, or (b) if he did
apply for custody under that section the application would be likely to be refused.'

f  One needs to consider that subsection in conjunction with the definition section of the
1976 Act, namely s 72, and the definition of the word 'guardian' which under sub-s (1)(b)
of the definition as it was originally drafted read:

'"guardian" . . . (b) in the case of an illegitimate child, includes the father where
he has custody of the child by virtue of an order under section 9 of the Guardianship
of Minors Act 1971, or under section 2 of the Illegitimate Children (Scotland) Act
g    1930.'

So it can be seen how the provisions of s 18 dovetailed. If the father had a custody
order under the 1971 Act, he was deemed to be the guardian and, therefore, his consent
to the order freeing the child for adoption was either needed or had to be dispensed with
under s 16(2). But, if, at the time of the application, the matter had not proceeded that
h  far because he had no order under s 9 of the 1971 Act, sub-s (7) provided that the court
must first satisfy itself that he either had no intention of applying for custody or, if he
did apply for custody, it would have been likely to be refused. That was how the section
stood as at the date of the hearing before Judge Marder.

He was also referred to a recent decision of the House of Lords in M v H [1988] 3 All
ER 5, [1988] 3 WLR 485. I think I need refer only to the relevant part of the headnote
j  ([1988] 3 WLR 485):

'Held, dismissing the appeals, that the jurisdiction of the court under section 9 of
the Guardianship of Minors Act 1971, to entertain applications by the mother or
the father of a minor for the legal custody of, or access to, such minor, was not
limited to applications by one parent against the other but extended to applications
by one parent against a third party, including a local authority having the care of
the minor pursuant to a resolution made under section 3(1) of the Child Care Act

1980; but that, though the court had jurisdiction to entertain the father's applications for access and custody, it could not exercise that jurisdiction to review the merits of decisions made by the local authority in pursuance of their statutory powers to make decisions about the welfare of children in their care . . .'

The effect of that case, and that actually was also a case of a father of illegitimate children, was that, where the children are in the care of a local authority (in that case they happened to be in care pursuant to a parental rights resolution but it would be equally applicable if they had been in care under a care order), even though there is jurisdiction to entertain an application by the father for custody under the 1971 Act, that jurisdiction may never be exercised, because its effect would be, by granting the father custody, namely actual physical possession of the child, to interfere with the rights and duties which Parliament has entrusted to the local authority in the case of children in their care.

So, when this particular application came before Judge Marder, he took the view, which I must say seems to me inevitable, that in this case s 18(7) of the Adoption Act 1976 did not help this father because his application for custody under the 1971 Act must inevitably be refused because of the way the House of Lords had decided that that jurisdiction must be exercised. So he dismissed the father's application for custody, ruled on his position under the freeing for adoption provisions as a preliminary point of law and gave leave to appeal. He also adjourned the freeing application for other matters to be dealt with so that the position is that there has not, as yet, been any order freeing these children for adoption.

Counsel for the father before us in this court kept the custody point under the 1971 Act open. He did not concede that the judge's decision was incorrect although he accepted there were great difficulties in his way. So it is technically still open should he wish to take this matter further; but, for my part, I would say at once that I think the judge was quite right to deal with the matter in the way in which he did in the then state of the law.

However, as from 1 April of this year, namely ten days ago, the law has been changed because the Family Law Reform Act 1987 (Commencement No 2) Order 1989, SI 1989/382, brought into force a number of the provisions of the Family Law Reform Act 1987 which were not previously in force, and to that Act I now address myself.

Section 1(1) of the 1987 Act, which actually was one of the provisions already in force, is in the following terms:

'In this Act and enactments passed and instruments made after the coming into force of this section, references (however expressed) to any relationship between two persons shall, unless the contrary intention appears, be construed without regard to whether or not the father and mother of either of them, or the father and mother of any person through whom the relationship is deduced have or had been married to each other at any time.'

The title to the Act indicates that it is an Act to reform the law relating to the consequences of birth outside marriage, and the subsection which I have just read makes that point clear; but it does, as I have said, refer only to that Act and enactments passed and instruments made after the coming into force of the section.

However, s 2 deals with the construction of enactments relating to parental rights and duties already in force at the time of the passing of the 1987 Act and that section was one of those brought into force on 1 April. Subsection (1)(f) of that section is to the following effect:

'In the following enactments, namely . . . (f) the Child Care Act 1980 except Part I and sections 13, 24, 64 and 65 . . . references (however expressed) to any relationship between two persons shall be construed in accordance with section 1 above.'

Section 4 of the 1987 Act, also brought into force on 1 April, is headed 'Parental rights and duties of father':

'(1) Where the father and mother of a child were not married to each other at the time of his birth, the court may, on the application of the father, order that he shall have all the parental rights and duties with respect to the child.

(2) Where the father of a child is given all the parental rights and duties by an order under this section, he shall, subject to any order made by the court otherwise than under this section, have those rights and duties jointly with the mother of the child or, if the mother is dead, jointly with any guardian of the child appointed under the 1971 Act.'

Then one comes to s 7 of the 1987 Act, also brought into force on 1 April:

'(1) In section 18 of the Adoption Act 1976 (which relates to orders declaring a child free for adoption), for subsection (7) there shall be substituted the following subsection—"(7) Before making an order under this section in the case of a child whose father and mother were not married to each other at the time of his birth and whose father is not his guardian, the court shall satisfy itself in relation to any person claiming to be the father that either—(a) he has no intention of making—(i) an application under section 4 of the Family Law Reform Act 1987 for an order giving him all the parental rights and duties with respect to the child; or (ii) an application under any enactment for an order giving him a right to custody, legal or actual custody or care and control of the child; or (b) if he did make such an application, the application would be likely to be refused."

(2) In section 72(1) of that Act (interpretation), in the definition of "guardian" for paragraph (b) there shall be substituted the following paragraph—"(b) in the case of a child whose father and mother were not married to each other at the time of this birth, includes the father where—(i) an order is in force under section 4 of the Family Law Reform Act 1987 giving him all the parental rights and duties with respect to the child; or (ii) he has a right to custody, legal or actual custody or care and control of the child by virtue of an order made under any enactment."'

So it will be seen that the effect of the amendment which came into force on 1 April was to provide that, before the court can make an order freeing a child for adoption, in the case of a father of an illegitimate child, the court now has to be satisfied that he has no intention of making an application for parental rights and duties under s 4 of the 1987 Act or, if he did make such an application, the application would be likely to be refused. We were told by counsel for the father, as indeed would appear to be obvious from the course the father has pursued so far, that it is his intention now to make such an application. Prima facie, therefore, since as yet there has been no order freeing the children for adoption, when the case goes back to first instance it will be necessary for the judge who then considers it to consider the father's new postion.

However, counsel for the local authority sought to persuade us that the change in the law to which I have already referred made no difference because, she submitted, the effect of M v H [1988] 3 All ER 5, [1988] 3 WLR 485 still applied. In my judgment, that submission was mistaken because a parental rights order under s 4 of the 1987 Act will not interfere with the local authority's exercise of their statutory rights over the children, but will merely give the father a locus standi and place him in the same position as the parent of a legitimate child to make the necessary applications to court. That, it seems to me, is the difference between a parental rights order (giving locus standi) and a custody order (under the 1971 Act) which would, if given effect to, interfere with the council's rights in relation to children in their care.

If I follow that position through for a moment, it seems to me, though I do not think it is necessary for the purposes of this case to decide it, that the father, if granted a parental rights order, would not share those rights with the local authority so long as the parental rights resolution remains in force unless the order gives him, as well as parental rights, actual custody of the children. I reach that conclusion because of s 8(3) of the Child Care Act 1980, which took effect from 1 April:

'Where, in the case of a child whose father and mother were not married to each other at the time of his birth, an order is in force under section 4 of the Family Law *a* Reform Act 1987 by virtue of which actual custody is shared between the mother and the father, both the mother and the father shall be treated as parents of the child for the purposes of the provisions of this Part.'

It will be recalled that s 2(1)(*f*) of the 1987 Act otherwise excepted Pt I of the Child Care Act 1980.

So, as I say, at the moment it seem to me, without necessarily deciding it, that, even if *b* the father were successful in his application for a parental rights order under s 4, that would not of itself without more, 'more' being actual custody, give him shared parental rights with the local authority. But what it will do is give him a locus standi to be heard, for example on an application to discharge the parental rights resolution under s 5(4)(*b*) of the 1980 Act. It will also, so it seems to me, and for the purposes of this appeal I so *c* hold, give him the right to oppose an adoption order or an order freeing the children for adoption. Of course, he would have to make out his case on the merits, but at least he would have a locus standi. Finally, it would seem to me also to give him rights to be heard on access to a child in care under Pt IA of the 1980 Act.

It seems to me that this construction of the Act will remove the anomaly to which the courts have so often referred and, most recently, this court in the as yet unreported *d* decision of *Re N* (1989) Times, 1 March, where the father of children, the parents not having been married, who may have played a full part in their lives but, as I say, never married, is denied even the opportunity to be heard on matters vital to the future of those children.

In the result, so far as the appeal by the father against the refusal to grant him a custody order under the 1971 Act is concerned, I, for my part, would dismiss the appeal. So far as *e* the appeal on the preliminary point of law is concerned, since the point has become academic for the reasons I have endeavoured to give, I would make no order on that appeal, but would direct that the case should go back to the court of first instance to be dealt with on its merits under the new sub-s (7) of s 18. Since it would be the first time on which such an application would be dealt with by a court of first instance, and also to ensure that the application should be dealt with as speedily as possible, I would propose *f* that the matter be brought up into the Principal Registry and then direct that the application should be heard by a judge of the Family Division of the High Court as soon as possible.

**NICHOLLS LJ.** I agree.

*g*

**LORD DONALDSON OF LYMINGTON MR.** I also agree.

*Father's appeal against refusal to grant custody dismissed but case remitted to court below to be heard on the merits. No order as to costs.*

Solicitors: *Winter-Taylors*, High Wycombe (for the father); *Kidd Rapinet*, Maidenhead (for *h* the mother); *Griffiths Robertson*, Reading, agents for *D C H Williams*, Reading (for the local authority).

Mary Rose Plummer   Barrister.

a

# R v Norfolk County Council, ex parte M

QUEEN'S BENCH DIVISION (CROWN OFFICE LIST)
WAITE J
6, 7, 23 FEBRUARY 1989

b
Child – Child abuse – Child abuse register – Register maintained by local authority – Registration of alleged abuser – Child making allegations of sexual abuse against applicant – Local authority convening case conference to consider allegations – Case conference deciding to place applicant's name on register and secretly inform his employers – Applicant given no opportunity to rebut allegations – Whether case conference acting unfairly and contrary to natural justice.

c
Judicial review – Availability of remedy – Child abuse register – Register maintained by local authority – Registration of alleged abuser – Child making allegations of sexual abuse against applicant – Local authority convening case conference to consider allegations – Case conference deciding to place applicant's name on register and secretly inform his employers – Applicant given no opportunity to rebut allegations – Whether case conference's decision part of authority's internal administrative procedures – Whether case conference's decision subject to judicial review.

d
The applicant, M, was a 55-year-old married man of good character who was employed as a plumber. While he was working at the home of the parents of the complainant he allegedly indecently assaulted her and obscenely exposed himself. The complainant was a 13-year-old girl who had been recorded twice before by the local authority social services department as having been the victim of sexual abuse, and who dressed and behaved precociously and had an unsettled home life. The girl told her teacher that M
e
had behaved indecently towards her and both the police and the social services department were informed. The police arrested M but he denied the girl's allegations; the police decided to take no action because of the lack of evidence and released him. A few days later the girl complained of receiving improper advances from another man. The local authority convened a case conference consisting of a senior social worker, another social
f
worker, a police inspector, a clinical assistant, the girl's schoolteacher and a consultant child psychiatrist. The conference decided that the names of both M and the girl should be placed on the authority's child abuse register and that M's employer should be informed. M's name was accordingly entered on the register as a 'known/suspected abuser' and he was notified of that fact but not that his employer had been informed. His employer instituted an internal disciplinary inquiry and suspended him pending the
g
outcome. M applied for judicial review of the decisions made as the result of the case conference. The local authority opposed the application, contending that the decisions of the case conference and the registration of M on the child abuse register were not matters which were susceptible to judicial review because they formed part of the authority's internal administrative procedures.

h
**Held** – The decision of a child abuse case conference convened by a local authority social services department to register a person's name on its child abuse register as a child abuser was not simply a matter of the local authority's internal administrative procedures since it affected the rights of the alleged abuser. Accordingly, a case conference was required to act fairly when making a decision whether to enter the name of the alleged abuser on
j
its child abuse register and if it acted unfairly or unreasonably in deciding to enter a person's name on the register as a child abuser the court would grant judicial review of the decision. In all the circumstances the local authority's case conference had acted unfairly, unreasonably and in breach of natural justice by failing to consider whether the complainant's accusations might be a fantasy or fabrication, in deciding that M was guilty after a brief and one-sided investigation, in denying M the opportunity of objecting or

the decision, in maintaining its child abuse register in a slipshod manner without making
any distinction between known and suspected abusers and in deciding to put secret
pressure on M's employer. Accordingly, M would be granted an order of certiorari to
quash the case conference's decision (see p 364 *d e g* to p 365 *d f, p 366 a* to *e* and p 367
*a b*, post).

*Associated Provincial Picture Houses Ltd v Wednesbury Corp* [1947] 2 All ER 680 applied.

**Notes**
For care and welfare of children by local authorities, see 24 Halsbury's Laws (4th edn)
para 786.
   For judicial control of administrative action, see 1 ibid paras 46–52.
   For natural justice and the duty to act fairly, see ibid para 66.

**Cases referred to in judgment**
*Associated Provincial Picture Houses Ltd v Wednesbury Corp* [1947] 2 All ER 680, [1948] 1
   KB 223, CA.
*Council of Civil Service Unions v Minister for the Civil Service* [1984] 3 All ER 935, [1985] AC
   374, [1984] 3 WLR 1174, HL.

**Application for judicial review**
M applied, with the leave of Mann J given on 19 October 1987, for judicial review by
way of an order of certiorari to quash the decision of the respondent, the Norfolk County
Council acting by its social services department, to register M's name on the council's
register of child abusers following two case conferences on 10 June and 13 July 1987
convened by the social services department which had decided that M had sexually
abused a girl on or about 5 June 1987. The facts are set out in the judgment.

*Roger Gray QC* and *Timothy Townshend* for M.
*David Mellor* for the council.

*Cur adv vult*

23 February. The following judgment was delivered.

**WAITE J.** This judicial review application arises from a complaint made by a 13-year-
old girl to her schoolteacher that the plumber working in her parent's home had behaved
indecently towards her. The girl was interviewed by the police and a social worker to
whom she repeated the allegation. When the plumber was interviewed by the police he
strenuously denied it. The police took no further action.
   The local authority's social services department, without notice to or contact of any
kind with the plumber, convened a case conference. It recorded a finding that the
plumber had committed sexual abuse of the girl and resolved that both her name as
victim and his as abuser should be entered on their child abuse register.
   The plumber's first contact with the local authority was the receipt of a letter informing
him of that decision. He was later summoned by his employers to attend a disciplinary
interview, on the ground that his name appeared on the register as an abuser, and he was
suspended from his work in the mean time. That disciplinary interview has been
adjourned to await the outcome of these proceedings and the plumber has been allowed
to work in the interval on condition that he is never unaccompanied in occupied
premises.
   He has obtained leave to apply for judicial review of the case conference decision and
of his consequent registration as an abuser. The local authority oppose review on the
ground that neither the decision nor the registration are actions which are capable by

their nature of being reviewed judicially at all, or which, if reviewable, offend reason or
*a* infringe any applicable rule of natural justice.

These are issues of some importance, to which it is impossible to do justice without a
more detailed examination both of the child abuse registration system generally and of
the circumstances in which it was operated in the present case.

Child abuse registers (or child protection registers as the Department of Health and
Social Security (the DHSS) would prefer them to be called) have been in general use since
*b* the early 1970s. They have no statutory authority, but the basis of their operation has
been prescribed by a series of departmental circulars of which the most recent is
LASSL(80)4HN(80)20. They were intended initially as a register of children at risk from
physical or emotional suffering or deprivation through non-accidental injury or parental
inadequacy or neglect. That function was extended during the early 1980s to include
cases of sexual abuse, with the approval of the DHSS handbook 'Child Abuse—Working
*c* Together' published in draft in April 1986.

It has always been an essential feature of the registration system that no name can be
placed on the register without the authority of a case conference. That is a body described
in the handbook as an 'Inter-professional meeting'. It is normally chaired by a senior
social worker and attended by representatives of other agencies or professional disciplines.
The function of case conferences is stated in the handbook to be advisory, though one
*d* suspects that in practice their decisions are treated as mandatory. They certainly have at
least one directory function, because both the circular and the handbook stress that the
authorisation of a case conference is an essential preliminary to registration.

The circular and handbook also both emphasise the importance (save in exceptional
cases) of notification to and consultation with the parents or other carers before the name
of a child is entered on the register. No guidance appears to be given by either document
*e* as to the extent (if any) to which those whom it is proposed to register as abusers should
be entitled to notice or consultation.

Access to the information on the register is not restricted to the authority's own social
workers. Entries may also be inspected by a fairly wide but carefully defined section of
the public. It consists, broadly speaking, of the people or agencies whom one would
expect to find present or represented at a case conference. If either the registered victim
*f* or any registered abuser moves to the area of another authority, the receiving authority
is immediately notified and the relevant particulars are transferred to its own child abuse
register.

The register maintained by the respondent county council is, I understand, in more or
less standard form. It comprises a card index in which each victim's name appears on a
printed white card in which provision is made for particulars of parentage and so on.
*g* Each white card also has printed on it a box headed with the legend 'Identity of known/
suspected Abuser(s)'. There is also a supplementary register in which any person named
on one of the white cards as a known or suspected abuser is allocated a blue card giving
his name and other particulars including a cross-reference to the victim.

The card index has the administrative advantage that when a registered victim or
*h* abuser moves to the area of another authority the white or blue card (as the case may be)
can follow him and take its place in the equivalent index maintained by the receiving
authority. The council, in common with most other authorities, has published its own
pamphlet in a form approved by the DHSS and also by the Norfolk area review
committee, the body under whose delegated authority the council acts as custodian of
the register. The pamphlet is called 'Child Abuse' and is intended to give public guidance
*j* and information about child abuse procedures in the county. It contains an assurance
that the child abuse register is kept at County Hall 'under conditions of strict security'
and that its contents will only be disclosed to 'designated personnel'. These include the
police, probation and education welfare services, and all general practitioners in Norfolk.

The inherent confidentiality of the register was strongly relied on by the council at

this hearing as a ground of immunity from judicial review, with the support of an
affidavit by the director of social services in which he deposed:                            *a*

'No consequences flow from the mere fact that a name is entered in the Child
Abuse Register as that of an abuser unless and until access is sought to the Register
by some designated person having a proper interest in the management of the case
concerned . . .'

The events relevant to the present case began on 25 November 1985 when a white  *b*
card was entered in the council's child abuse register in respect of a girl whom I will call
'K'. She was born on 28 July 1973 and was therefore then 12. The card reports that she
had twice been the victim of sexual abuse perpetrated by two separate abusers, neither of
whom appears to have been a parent or custodian. The names of both of them were
entered in the box headed 'Identity of known/suspected abuser'. Nothing more is known
about the abuse then suffered by this child. It is not mentioned at all in the council's  *c*
evidence, and only came to light when production of the original registration documents
was requested in the course of the hearing.

On Thursday, 4 June 1987 (shortly before her fourteenth birthday) K arrived at school
in a distressed state and told her teacher that a plumber working at her parents' home
had behaved indecently towards her. She was interviewed by the police and by the social
worker, Ms Norgrove, who had been her key worker at the time of the earlier abuse.       *d*

K's account was that on the morning of the previous Monday, 1 June, she had been in
the living room in her nightdress putting on her make-up when the plumber arrived.
He had spoken to her in a familiar way and patted her bottom, saying how pretty she
was. When she returned to the living room after getting dressed he patted her bottom
again many times. She said she had told her mother about it later that day but had simply
been told to ignore the man.                                                             *e*

She then went on to give her account of the events of the day of her complaint,
Thursday, 4 June. She had woken in the morning, she said, to find the same man in the
bedroom which she shared with her 12-year-old brother. He left the room without
saying anything, returned later while she was dressing (still in her brother's presence)
and again said nothing and left. When she had dressed, she went down to the kitchen
and found the plumber there. He put his arm round her, touched her breasts through  *f*
her jumper, and also touched her bottom. Shortly after that she had to pass the toilet
twice before leaving for school. On both occasions the toilet door was open with the
plumber inside, and each time he coughed to draw her attention. On the first occasion
she saw him standing sideways (so as to be visible to her in profile) with his fly buttons
open and his penis out. On the second occasion he laughed and waved his penis at her in
what was described by the reporting social worker (presumably paraphrasing the girl's  *g*
actual words) as a masturbatory gesture. She then left for school without saying anything
to her mother, who had been in the house throughout. On her way to school she had
tried unsuccessfully to make a telephone call to Ms Norgrove's office, and had made a
complaint to the teacher soon after she reached school.

There had been a plumber working at K's house on the mornings of both 1 and 4 June.  *h*
I will call him 'M'. He is a married man aged 55, of good character. He was on the
permanent maintenance staff of the district council which owned K's house. His
employers (whom it is unnecessary to name) are a local authority entirely separate and
distinct from the respondent county council.

M was arrested that same day, 4 June, and was in police custody for three and a half
hours. He did not dispute that he had been in the house on the mornings in question,  *j*
but when K's allegations were put to him he firmly and consistently denied that there
was a word of truth in them.

The council's social services department convened a case conference for 10 June 1987.
It was chaired by Mr Arthurton, a senior social worker. The others present were Ms

Norgrove, a chief detective inspector of police, a clinical assistant, K's school teacher and
*a* a consultant child psychiatrist.

Ms Norgrove reported K's complaint in the terms already described. The inspector
reported on M's denials and said that the police had decided to take no further action for
lack of evidence, a decision which he was persuaded by others at the conference to hold
in abeyance for the time being. The psychiatrist expressed the view that both K and her
mother might need psychiatric help or counselling. It was agreed that a further case
*b* conference would be held on 13 July 1987. Mr Arthurton himself then made the
suggestion that he might in the mean time 'speak informally' (as he expressed it) to M's
employers. No one else present could see any impropriety in that step.

The six participants at the case conference then proceeded to record a number of
decisions of which it is material to quote two: '1. The conference was persuaded that [M]
had committed sexual abuse of [K] and both her name and his should therefore appear
*c* on the register.' The second decision was numbered 4: 'Mr Arthurton to satisfy himself
that the Housing Manager [of M's employers] is aware of the situation regarding his
employee.'

The first of those decisions is part of the subject matter of M's review application and
will be discussed later in this judgment. The other decision forms part of a very
disquieting background. It amounts to nothing less than a decision to inform on M to
*d* his employers behind his back. That shows up in a very poor light when placed beside
the published assertions of security in the council's own pamphlet, and it is worryingly
at variance with the assurances of confidentiality given in the affidavit sworn by the
director of social services. It should perhaps also be recorded that the fact that this
unfortunate decision had been taken at all did not come to light until a very late stage of
this review hearing when the case conference minutes were produced from the council's
*e* files at my own request.

The first decision was implemented on 26 June 1987, when K was allocated a further
white card (additional to the previous registered entry) on which M was named as her
'known/suspected abuser', and a blue card with a similar description was brought into
being for M himself.

*f* The first contact of any kind which M had with the council was when he received a
letter dated 26 June 1987. It was signed by a team leader in Mr Arthurton's area office
and marked as 'Strictly confidential'. It read in full as follows:

'Dear Mr. [M],
    Following various alleged incidents on the 1 and 4 June 1987 with a girl called
[K], a case conference was persuaded that sexual abuse had taken place. As a result,
*g* your name now appears on the Child Abuse Register, as an abuser.
                                                                Yours sincerely . . .'

M was distressed by the letter and took it straight away to his employers to ask for their
advice as to what he should do to clear his good name. He was not, of course, to know
that Mr Arthurton had already made a secret approach to them.

*h* The council's further case conference took place, as arranged, on 13 July 1987. There
were four people present this time: the psychiatrist, the police inspector, Ms Norgrove
and Mr Arthurton. It was reported by Ms Norgrove that a few days earlier (26 June) K
had made yet another complaint about sexual misconduct: a man in whose van she had
accepted a ride had made, she said, 'rude suggestions' to her. K's teacher had described
her to Ms Norgrove as being unsettled at school, where she appeared inappropriately
*j* dressed in tight jeans and high heels. Ms Norgrove herself described K as leading an
unsettled home life between her mother and other relatives or friends: 'flitting around
from living base to another', was her description.

The case conference then proceeded to record decisions that K and her mother should
both be referred for counselling, and that no further police action against M should be

taken. Mr Arthurton was directed nevertheless 'to have further contact with the abuser's
employer'.

*a*

M was told by the police on 15 July 1987 that no further action would be taken against
him. His relief was short-lived, however, because on 27 July he received a letter from his
employers summoning him to an inquiry instituted under their internal disciplinary
procedure on the ground that his name had been recorded in the council's register as an
abuser, following allegations made by a young girl in a property where he was working;
he was supended on full pay in the mean time. I have already mentioned that the *b*
disciplinary hearing has been held over to await the outcome of this case, and M has been
temporarily reinstated subject to a condition that he does not work in occupied premises
without a companion.

M instructed solicitors, who wrote to the director of social services protesting against
the registration and the manner in which it had been effected, and requiring his name to
be removed. That was refused, but he was offered the opportunity of attending, with or *c*
without representation, at a reconvened case conference at which he would be allowed to
'make his observations personally'. That was an offer to attend in person before a body
which had already condemned him in his absence. He refused it, and in my view had
every justification for doing so, in the light both of what he then knew and of what he
has since learnt.

That completes the account of the background to this application. Before turning to *d*
the principles of law involved, it seems to me appropriate to look generally at the
procedures adopted by the council leading up to M's registration as an abuser, in order to
see how far they accorded with good sense, fairness and sound social work practice. From
that standpoint, their procedures are, in my view, open to criticism in three significant
respects.

The first relates to the worrying circumstances of the child with whom they were *e*
dealing. K had already been registered as a child twice abused before the involvement of
M. She was dressing and behaving precociously and was leading an unsettled home life.
Within a few days after her accusations against M she was reported as having complained
of improper advances by yet another man. It is, of course, distressingly common for
abused children to become vulnerable to further abuse because their past sufferings have
made them sexually precocious or flirtatious. It is also by no means unusual, however, *f*
for a child, when once abused, to imagine or allege acts of further abuse supposedly
perpetrated by people who are demonstrably innocent. (One of the well-known hazards,
for example, of fostering abused children is that the child may come up with unfounded
allegations of abuse against the new carers.)

It is a particularly troubling feature of the present case that the possibility does not
appear even to have occurred to either case conference, or for that matter to any level of *g*
the council's social services, that K's accusations might be a fantasy or fabrication
proceeding directly from her own very evident emotional problems, and that, if there
was the least possibility that such might be the case, they were at risk of stigmatising an
innocent man as an abuser. That is a risk to which their minds could, of course, have
been immediately opened if M and his professional advisers had been allowed, before the *h*
registration was effected, an opportunity of informed comment on the material
considered by the two case conferences.

The second criticism relates to the form in which the first case conference expressed
the primary decision. Social workers are trained to forbear from passing judgments;
indeed it is through their use of it that the ungainly word 'non-judgmental' has found its
way into the English language. It is surprising, therefore, that the case conference should *j*
have thought it right or necessary to record a solemn finding of guilt against M after a
brief and one-sided investigation. It would surely have been sufficient for the conference
to have recorded simply that on the material at present available there appeared to be
sufficient evidence to justify registering the name of M as K's suspected abuser.

The third criticism is closely related to that. The council adopted what appears to me
a  to have been a dangerously slipshod approach to the formula 'identity of known/
suspected abuser(s)' printed on both the blue and the white card. When this formula was
first approved (as it must once presumably have been) by the DHSS, it must surely have
been the intention that the registering authority should delete one description or the
other and not leave both 'known' and 'suspected' to stand. A known abuser, one would
think, would be a person who had been found guilty by a civil or criminal court or who
b  had made a full confession; a suspected abuser would be someone in relation to whom
the evidence, though as yet untested in court proceedings, appeared sufficiently persuasive
to justify treating the alleged perpetrator as a potential threat to the registered child or to
other children. The distinction between the two is not drawn in either of the registrations
affecting K, which prompts the suspicion that it may have been omitted for other
children on the council's register as well.

c   When the flawed proceedings of the case conference are set alongside the council's
unworthy decision to put secret pressure on M's employers, the overall picture becomes
very disturbing. The courts are always slow to censure local authorities in cases of this
kind, because judges are aware of the difficulties (including resource problems) with
which social workers have to contend. Nevertheless, the circumstances of the present
case are exceptional and extreme. M is entitled to a finding, which I make regretfully,
d   that the council's conduct towards him was obtuse, unfeeling and unfair.

Its counsel understandably preferred to concentrate the council's resistence to judicial
review on pure grounds of law. His first submission was a courageous one. Neither the
case conference decision nor the consequent registration of M as an abuser were acts
capable of being reviewed judicially. They were, he claimed, purely clerical or ministerial
acts, internal to the council's own administrative procedures and simply part and parcel
e   of the general corpus of its casework notes and other confidential files and records. M's
rights and obligations in private law were, he claimed, unaffected by his registration as
an abuser, and the registration has not deprived him of any benefit or advantage which
the council had in the past permitted him to enjoy: see Council of Civil Services Unions v
Minister for the Civil Service [1984] 3 All ER 935 at 949, [1985] AC 374 at 408 per Lord
f   Diplock.

I have been wholly unable to accept that argument. The section of the public entitled
to access to the register is certainly limited, but it is a significant section and it includes
people with powers of choice and decision capable of working to M's disadvantage. In
the days when his name was not on any register of child abusers he enjoyed the advantage
of being able to compete on equal terms with others for employment in the educational
g   or social services or for positions of trust such as a child-minder or foster or adoptive
parent. By registering his name as an abuser on a register to which all potential employers
or selectors within any of those fields would have access, the council have deprived him
of that advantage. The absolute confidentiality of a child abuse register cannot, moreover,
be entirely guaranteed and the advantage of a good name, which M enjoyed before
registration, is now in daily jeopardy through the risk that inquisitive minds or wagging
h   tongues may breach the security of the register.

It is proper, in my judgment, to take into account also the fact that before the
registration M enjoyed peace of mind and a contented home life. Now he is in a state of
permanent distress which at times has affected his health, and his wife too has been very
upset. I am satisfied, for all these reasons, that it is not the law that local authorities are
free to exercise arbitrary control over the entry of names of alleged abusers on a child
j   abuse register with total immunity from supervision by the courts. Any such immunity
would seriously erode the rights of the citizen.

Counsel's second submission was founded on the premise, which is undoubtedly
correct, that the council's decision cannot (in the absence of bad faith or excess of
jurisdiction, neither of which is relied on by counsel for M) be reviewed in the courts

except on the basis of breach of natural justice or unreasonableness within the limited
sense of that term approved in *Associated Provincial Picture Houses Ltd v Wednesbury Corp*     *a*
[1947] 2 All ER 680, [1948] 1 KB 223.

Under the head of natural justice, counsel contends that in deciding to register M as an
abuser the council was not acting judicially, or even quasi judicially, but administratively,
and was accordingly exempt from any requirement to apply the natural justice rules to
its case conference proceedings.

I accept that a case conference deliberating whether or not to place a name on the     *b*
register as an abuser is not acting judicially so as to make the rules of natural justice
automatically applicable to its procedures as though it had been functioning as a tribunal.
Nevertheless, the consequences of registration for M were in my judgment sufficiently
serious (for the reasons I have already stated) to impose on the council a legal duty to act
fairly towards him. The council's case conference acted unfairly and in manifest breach
of that duty when it operated a procedure which denied him all opportunity of advance     *c*
warning of its intention, or of prior consultation, or of being heard to object, or of
knowing the full circumstances surrounding its decision.

As to unreasonableness, counsel contends that the onus is on M to show that the
council's conduct in relation to the registration was irrational to an extent verging on the
absurd, and that all the criticism that may fairly be made of his client does not add up to
unreasonableness in that restricted sense. I do not agree with that submission in its result.     *d*
The council's behaviour towards M offended not only the most basic notions of fair play
but was also so unreasonable as in my judgment to come well within the *Wednesbury*
principle.

Certiorari will therefore lie to quash the case conference decision of 10 July 1987 so far
as it purported to describe M as the abuser of K and also to quash the entries on the
council's child abuse register so far as they purport to identify him as the known or     *e*
suspected abuser of K.

I have referred to this as an anxious case. It is also in many ways an instructive one,
and it may therefore be worth mentioning the lessons which I believe should be drawn
from it.

Any system of registration designed to enable the names of known or suspected abusers     *f*
of children to be brought rapidly and with the minimum of inquiry to the attention of
the various agencies with responsibilities towards children, in any part of the country in
which the victim or the alleged perpetrator happen to be living at any one time, is bound
to have great potential as an instrument for the relief and prevention of suffering. A
child abuse register nevertheless remains (at all events as regards the abusers named on
it) in essence a blacklist, and as such it also has dangerous potential as an instrument of     *g*
injustice or oppression.

Social workers are not by nature either unjust or oppressive; they work selflessly for
the support of those least able to help themselves. For them the risk of oppression lies,
rather, in being drawn by enthusiasm into the single-minded pursuit of one good
objective to the total exclusion of all others. Child abuse is an undoubted, and disturbingly
prevalent, social evil; much criminal behaviour, drug and alcohol addiction, mental     *h*
stress or illness in adults can be traced directly back to it. Such abuse is often concealed
by fear and social taboos, giving it something in common with the social evil of witchcraft
which was an affliction to earlier and more credulous generations.

Considerable headway has been made in overcoming these inhibitions, and in
promoting the detection and treatment of child abuse generally, through the use of
simple maxims which everyone can understand, like 'A child has the right to be believed'.     *j*
Such expressions are dangerously emotive however, and if they were to be applied
mindlessly by the over-zealous or ruthlessly by the undertrained, there would be a real
risk of injustice to adults suspected of abuse through an unquestioning acceptance of the
complaints of their young accusers. That is a risk too chillingly reminiscent of seventeenth

*a* century Salem to be tolerated in a free society, and the interventionary powers of the High Court are the only means of keeping it at bay.

It has to be remembered, all the same, that Parliament has entrusted virtual autonomy to local authorities in the discharge of their statutory duties of child care, and the powers of judicial intervention have to be made to fit into that framework. I have held that it is the duty of a case conference (or other agency of local government) exercising a discretion whether or not to enter the name of an alleged abuser on the child abuse register to act

*b* fairly. Fairness is, and needs to be, a flexible concept, and circumstances are liable to vary widely as to the degree of advance notice or opportunity of objection or consultation which attention to fairness in particular cases requires. Thus cases involving a parent or other custodian may require very different treatment from those involving a stranger; and cases where there has been a civil or criminal finding or a confession may need to be treated differently from those that rest on suspicion alone. The choice of a fair procedure

*c* for any particular set of circumstances is a topic on which reasonable opinions may properly vary, and social workers ought to be allowed sensible latitude when deciding how the requirements of fairness are best to be satisfied in each case.

Such a decision will involve for them a weighing exercise, requiring them to balance their duty of fairness to the suspected abuser against their statutory duty to act as effectively as possible for the protection of children from injury or abuse. There will be

*d* many cases in which that will not be found an easy task, and the balance will turn out to be a very fine one.

It is not the function of the courts, vigilant though they will always be to restrain an oppressive use of these registers, to substitute their own view how such a balance is to be resolved for that of the informed and specialist authorities who have been charged by statute with the duty of resolving it. If, therefore, it can be demonstrated in future cases

*e* that the particular procedure or range of inquiry followed by a local authority in the course of registering the name of an alleged abuser has represented a genuine attempt, reasonable in all the circumstances, to reconcile the duty of child protection on the one hand and the duty of fairness to the alleged abuser on the other, it is unlikely that the courts will intervene through judicial review to strike the registration down.

*f* Meanwhile, the immediate and urgent concern must be to ensure that the duty to act fairly towards alleged or suspected abusers becomes sufficiently well known and understood for it to take a prominent place in the minds of the social workers who have to deal with these anxious and distressing cases. I trust that the unfortunate experiences of the present case will act as a spur to those who have the power and the authority to see that this is done.

*g* *Certiorari granted.*

Solicitors: *Cole & Co*, Norwich (for M); *T D W Molander*, Norwich (for the council).

Bebe Chua   Barrister.

# R v Brixton Prison Governor, ex parte Kahan

QUEEN'S BENCH DIVISION

MUSTILL LJ AND McCOWAN J

22, 23 NOVEMBER, 2 DECEMBER 1988

*Extradition – Fugitive offender – Persons liable to be returned – Offence committed in Commonwealth country – Fiji – Right to request return of fugitive – Fiji's membership of Commonwealth lapsing when Fiji became a republic – Fiji remaining a 'designated Commonwealth country' for purpose of requesting return of fugitive offenders – Detained Fijian fugitive applying for discharge – Whether Fiji entitled to request return of fugitive – Whether right to request return of fugitive qualified by Commonwealth membership requirement – Whether designated Commonwealth country entitled to request return of fugitive – Fugitive Offenders Act 1967, ss 1, 2(1), 5(1) – Fugitive Offenders (Designated Commonwealth Countries) (No 3) Order 1970, art 2.*

*Extradition – Fugitive offender – Restrictions on return – Political offence – Power of court – Divisional Court – Evidence on application not yet considered by magistrate – Whether Divisional Court having power to intervene in proceedings for return of fugitive – Whether Divisional Court should intervene before magistrate has made his decision on evidence – Fugitive Offenders Act 1967, s 4.*

The government of the Republic of Fiji applied for the return of K under s 1[a] of the Fugitive Offenders Act 1967. The Secretary of State issued an authority to proceed against K under s 5(1)[b] of the 1967 Act and K was arrested and detained in prison to await extradition proceedings before the Chief Metropolitan Stipendiary Magistrate. K applied for a writ of habeas corpus with a view to terminating the extradition proceedings, claiming, inter alia, that since Fiji's membership of the Commonwealth had lapsed when it became a republic it was not entitled to request the return of fugitive offenders because s 1(a) of the 1967 Act limited that right to 'a Commonwealth country', and therefore the Secretary of State had no power to issue the authority to proceed under s 5(1). The government of Fiji contended that although the Commonwealth leaders had published a statement in October 1986 that on the basis of established Commonwealth conventions Fiji's membership of the Commonwealth had lapsed when it became a republic it was nevertheless entitled to request the return of K since Fiji was still 'a designated Commonwealth country' as defined in s 2(1)[c] of the 1967 Act since it had not been removed by Order in Council from the list of 'Countries whose citizens are Commonwealth citizens' in Sch 3 to the British Nationality Act 1981 and there had been no amendment to the Fugitive Offenders (Designated Commonwealth Countries) (No 3) Order 1970, art 2[d] of which designated Fiji for the purposes of s 1 of the 1967 Act.

**Held** – The government of the Republic of Fiji was entitled to request the return of a fugitive offender since Fiji remained 'a designated Commonwealth country' within s 2(1) of the 1967 Act and all the powers, rights and duties created by that Act were expressed throughout in terms of 'the designated Commonwealth country' without any qualification or reference to that country being a member of the Commonwealth for the time being.

---

a Section 1 is set out at p 370 e f, post

b Section 5(1), so far as material, provides: 'Subject to the provisions of this Act relating to provisional warrants, a person shall not be dealt with thereunder except in pursuance of an order of the Secretary of State (in this Act referred to as an authority to proceed), issued in pursuance of a request made to the Secretary of State by or on behalf of the Government of the designated Commonwealth country . . . in which the person to be returned was accused or was convicted.'

c Section 2(1) is set out at p 370 f g, post

d Article 2 is set out at p 371 c, post

Accordingly, the Secretary of State was empowered to detain K with a view to his return
*a* to Fiji under the 1967 Act, and K's application would therefore be dismissed (see p 371 *j*,
p 372 *c d j* and p 374 *g h*, post).

Per curiam. Although the Divisional Court has power under s 4$^e$ of the 1967 Act to
intervene at any stage in proceedings for the return of a fugitive to a designated
Commonwealth country in order to determine whether the offence for which his return
is requested is of a political character, in practice the court should not enter on the factual
*b* inquiry necessary before the magistrate who under s 7(5)$^f$ of that Act has the responsibility
of weighing the evidence has made his decision (see p 374 *c* to *h*, post); *Schtraks v
Government of Israel* [1962] 3 All ER 529 distinguished.

### Notes

For the return of a fugitive offender to a Commonwealth country, see 18 Halsbury's
*c* Laws (4th edn) paras 247–273, and for cases on the subject, see 24 Digest (Reissue) 1152–
1171, *12253–12321*.

For the Fugitive Offenders Act 1967, ss 1, 2, 4, 5, 7, see 17 Halsbury's Statutes (4th edn)
518, 519, 521, 523, 524.

For the British Nationality Act 1981, Sch 3, see 31 ibid 171.

*d* ### Cases referred to in judgments

*Schtraks v Government of Israel* [1962] 3 All ER 529, [1964] AC 556, [1962] 3 WLR 1013,
HL.
*USA v Gaynor* [1905] AC 128, PC.

### Cases also cited

*e* *India (Government) and Mubarak Ali Ahmed, Re* [1952] 1 All ER 1060, DC.
*R v Governor of Pentonville Prison, ex p Cheng* [1973] 2 All ER 204, [1973] AC 931, HL; *affg*
[1973] 1 All ER 935, [1973] AC 931, DC.

### Motion

*f* Mohammed Rafiq Kahan applied, by notice of motion dated 18 October 1988, for an
order directing the issue of a writ of habeas corpus ad subjiciendum to the governor of
Brixton prison, where the applicant was detained awaiting extradition proceedings before
the Chief Metropolitan Stipendiary Magistrate, on the ground, inter alia, that, since the
Republic of Fiji which had requested his extradition under s 1 of the Fugitive Offenders
Act 1967 was no longer a member of the Commonwealth, the 1967 Act did not apply
and that, consequently, the Secretary of State for the Home Department had had no
*g* power to issue an authority to proceed against him under s 5(1) of that Act. The facts are
set out in the judgment of Mustill LJ.

*R Alun Jones* for the applicant.
*Clive Nicholls QC* and *Clare Patricia Montgomery* for the government of Fiji.
*h* *Duncan Ouseley* for the Secretary of State and the prison governor.

*Cur adv vult*

---

*e* Section 4, so far as material, is set out at p 373 *e*, post
*f* Section 7(5), so far as material, provides: 'Where an authority to proceed has been issued in respect
of the person arrested and the court of committal is satisfied, after hearing any evidence tendered
*j* in support of the request for the return of that person or on behalf of that person, that the offence
to which the authority relates is a relevant offence and is further satisfied—(a) where that person is
accused of the offence, that the evidence would be sufficient to warrant his trial for that offence if
it had been committed within the jurisdiction of the court . . . the court shall, unless his committal
is prohibited by any other provision of this Act, commit him to custody to await his return
thereunder; but if the court is not so satisfied or if the committal of that person is so prohibited,
the court shall discharge him from custody.'

2 December. The following judgments were delivered.

**MUSTILL LJ.** On 26 September 1988 the Secretary of State for the Home Department issued an authority to proceed against Mohammed Rafiq Kahan, pursuant to s 5(1) of the Fugitive Offenders Act 1967. Proceedings before the Chief Metropolitan Stipendiary Magistrate with a view to his commitment under s 7 of the 1967 Act are not yet formally in train, and the full hearing before the magistrates is unlikely to take place within the next two months. Mr Kahan, who is presently confined in Her Majesty's Prison Brixton, now applies for an order of habeas corpus with a view to terminating the entire process at the present stage.

Three·contentions are advanced on his behalf. First, that since the country which has requested his extradition is the Republic of Fiji, which is no longer a member of the Commonwealth, the 1967 Act does not apply. Second, the order which granted authority to proceed is irrational since it is absurd for the Secretary of State to apply the mechanisms of the 1967 Act to initiate an extradition to a non-Commonwealth country, since even if the words of the Act are wide enough to cover such a case, it is plain that the legislation was never intended to operate outside the network of relationships which bind nations together to form the Commonwealth. Third, the offences with which Mr Kahan has been charged in Fiji are so plainly of a political character that, in the light of s 4(1)(a) of the 1967 Act, an order for his return is out of the question, and, that this being so, it would be wrong to retain him in custody to face a wholly nugatory set of proceedings. I will consider these arguments in turn.

The first argument turns on ss 1 and 2 of the 1967 Act, of which the relevant parts read as follows:

'**1.** *Persons liable to be returned.* Subject to the provisions of this Act, a person found in the United Kingdom who is accused of a relevant offence in any other country being—(*a*) a Commonwealth country designated for the purposes of this section under subsection (1) of section 2 of this Act; or (*b*) a United Kingdom dependency as defined by subsection (2) of that section, or who is alleged to be unlawfully at large after conviction of such an offence in any such country, may be arrested and returned to that country as provided by this Act.

**2.** *Designated Commonwealth countries and United Kingdom dependencies.*—(1) Her Majesty may by Order in Council designate for the purposes of section 1 of this Act any country for the time being mentioned in Schedule 3 to the British Nationality Act 1981 (countries having separate citizenship), or any other country within the Commonwealth; and any country so designated is in this Act referred to as a designated Commonwealth country.

(2) In this Act the expression "United Kingdom dependency" means—(*a*) any colony (not being a colony for whose external relations a country other than the United Kingdom is responsible); (*b*) any associated state within the meaning of the West Indies Act 1967; and (*c*) any country outside Her Majesty's dominions (being a country in which Her Majesty has jurisdiction, or over which She extends protection, in right of Her Government in the United Kingdom) to which Her Majesty may by Order in Council apply this subsection, not being in any case a country which is or forms part of a designated Commonwealth country.

(3) Her Majesty may by Order in Council direct that this Act shall have effect in relation to the return of persons to, or in relation to persons returned from, any designated Commonwealth country or United Kingdom dependency subject to such exceptions, adaptations or modifications as may be specified in the Order.

(4) For the purposes of any Order in Council under subsection (1) of this section, any territory for the external relations of which a Commonwealth country is responsible may be treated as part of that country or, if the Government of that country so requests, as a separate country.

a
(5) Any Order in Council under this section, other than an Order to which subsection (6) applies shall be subject to annulment in pursuance of a resolution of either House of Parliament . . .'

The reference to Sch 3 to the British Nationality Act 1981 in s 2(1) was formerly to s 1(3) of the British Nationality Act 1948. With the introduction of Commonwealth citizenship, the list was reformulated in Sch 3 to the 1981 Act, under the title 'Countries whose citizens are Commonwealth citizens'.

b
The problem arising in the present case, which I cannot believe to have been foreseen by the framers of the Act, arises in the following way. By the Fiji Independence Act 1970 Fiji became a self-governing state and ceased to be a British colony, with effect from 10 October 1970, and Fiji was added to the list of Commonwealth countries having separate citizenship in the British Nationality Act 1948, called up by s 2(1) of the 1967 Act. On the same day there came into force the Fugitive Offenders (Designated Commonwealth

c
Countries) (No 3) Order 1970, SI 1970/1438, art 2 of which read as follows: 'Fiji is hereby designated for the purposes of section 1 of the Fugitive Offenders Act 1967.'

Although the details were not before us, it is clear that about this time Fiji must have applied for and been granted membership of the Commonwealth. At all events, there is no doubt that, whatever exactly s 1 of the 1967 Act may mean, the Act thereafter applied

d
to Fiji to the exclusion of the Extradition Acts 1870 to 1935. However, on 16 October 1986 the Commonwealth leaders published a statement which began with the following words:

'Commonwealth leaders acknowledged that, on the basis of established Commonwealth conventions, Fiji's membership of the Commonwealth lapsed with the emergence of the Republic on 15 October . . .'

e
It is common ground that from that date Fiji has not been a member of the Commonwealth. Nevertheless, Her Majesty has not yet by Order in Council removed Fiji from the list in Sch 3 to the 1981 Act (such an order being susceptible of annulment by a resolution of either House) or amended the 1970 designation order (which would require a positive resolution of each House). Hence the present problem. Is it sufficient

f
for the return of a fugitive for the requesting country to be a designated Commonwealth country, as defined in s 2(1) of the 1967 Act? If so, then the request by Fiji falls within the Act, since it is common ground that Fiji is still a country. Or is there an additional requirement, that the requesting country shall be a member of the Commonwealth? If so, then the request is invalid, since Fiji is no longer such a country.

This is a very short point of construction. One starts with the wording of the two

g
sections. The argument for the applicant is simple. The qualification for the right to request the return of a fugitive, set out in s 1(a) of the 1967 Act, begins with the words 'a Commonwealth country . . .' The draftsman must have inserted the word 'Commonwealth' for a purpose, and the only purpose which there can be is to ensure the country must still be in the Commonwealth, as well as still being designated, at the time when the arrest and return take place.

h
For the government of Fiji it is contended that this overlooks the fact that 'Commonwealth' is not a new word, since it already forms part of the expression defined in s 2(1). If the applicant's interpretation were correct, s 1(a) would have begun 'a Commonwealth designated Commonwealth country . . .' and this is not what it says. The different terminology in s 1(a) is accounted for by the necessity to accommodate the defined term within the grammatical structure of the paragraph.

j
As a matter of language, I prefer the government's interpretation. The drafting of both sections is rather odd. I find it hard to see why the draftsman should have created a formula in s 2(1) and described it as being for the purposes of s 1, when in fact it is a definition for all purposes, as the later part of s 2(1) and s 19 make clear, nor why it should have been thought necessary to refer forward from s 1(a) to the immediately

following s 2(1). Nevertheless, this is what the draftsman decided to do, and having done so he could not, I believe, have fitted 'designated', 'Commonwealth' and 'country' into s 1(a) without changing the order in which they appear. To my mind, I find this change in word order far too insubstantial to justify the inference that a further qualification was being added as a prerequisite to a call for the return of a fugitive. This conclusion is reinforced when one sees that the whole of the powers, rights and duties created by the Act are expressed throughout in terms of the 'designated Commonwealth country' or United Kingdom dependency. (Section 2(4), which is the only place where 'Commonwealth' appears otherwise than in association with 'designated', is expository in nature.) Thus, the identification of the relevant offences in s 3, the place to which the fugitive is to be returned in accordance with ss 4 and 4A, the origin of the request which founds the authority to proceed under s 5, and the evidence to be adduced under s 11 are all defined in terms of the designated Commonwealth country, without any qualification such as 'for the time being a member of the Commonwealth'. It would be absurd if the test for s 1 were different from that which applies everywhere else.

In response, it is submitted by the applicant that since s 1 sets the scene for what follows, the word 'Commowealth' must by implication be treated as tacked onto 'designated Commonwealth country' wherever it appears. But this would be strange drafting indeed; to create a partial definition in s 2(1), redefine it in s 19, add to it in s 1(a), and yet revert to the partial definition for the remainder of the Act, including, it may be noted, s 14, which is concerned with the return of fugitives to the United Kingdom from abroad, and has nothing to do with the subject matter of s 1. I cannot believe that this was intended, and the fact that the long title of the statute does refer to 'other Commonwealth countries' is not sufficient to compel the opposite conclusion.

In addition to the language of the 1967 Act itself, it is suggested that light is shed by consideration of broader issues of policy. For example, the government of Fiji submits that the word 'Commonwealth' is too lacking in precise content to have been chosen as a likely vehicle for adding an important qualification to the identification of the requesting state. I doubt whether this carries the question much further. That the Commonwealth exists is incontrovertible, the more so since this very Act employs the expression 'Head of the Commonwealth' in s 4(5). True, the word 'Commonwealth' is rarely if ever used in statute law on its own, rather than as part of an expression such as 'Commonwealth country' defined by reference to a list. Nevertheless, it would I believe be possible to put together a working definition from the declaration of principles contained in the final communiqué of the meeting of Commonwealth prime ministers dated 26 April 1949. There might be difficulties in determining exactly when membership terminates in an unusual case such as the present where the member does not itself elect to withdraw, but I would not regard these difficulties, no doubt hard to foresee in 1967, as sufficient to rule out the use of 'Commonwealth' as an extra qualification, if this is what the language of the 1967 Act really suggests.

On the other hand, I am also unimpressed by the argument that it is very unlikely that the up-to-date regime created by the 1967 Act for the benefit of Commonwealth countries would have been intended to continue to be available after the requesting country had left the Commonwealth. There must be quite a number of statutes, some of which have been drawn to our attention, which admit of the possibility that a state might continue to have some aspects of its relationships with the United Kingdom governed by what is essentially Commonwealth legislation during the interregnum between its leaving the informal association of members and having its ties formally severed by the amendment of the statute or Order in Council. Given the intangible, albeit real, nature of the Commonwealth bonds I do not find this at all surprising.

Thus I find nothing outside the 1967 Act to cast any doubt on the conclusion which I have reached by examining its terms. Notwithstanding the able argument of counsel for the applicant, I would hold that the government of Fiji was and remains entitled to request the return of the applicant under the 1967 Act.

The second question is whether the Secretary of State can be said to have acted
*a* irrationally in issuing the authority to proceed on the basis that, as the applicant asserts
in his grounds of application, 'the manifest intention of Parliament in 1967 was that the
Act should only be used in the case of Commonwealth members' (ground B). In my
judgment, this argument cannot stand in the light of the conclusion expressed on the
first point. If the 1967 Act, correctly construed, empowers the Secretary of State to return
a fugitive to a non-Commonwealth state, I am unable to see how Parliament can be said
*b* to have intended that it should not be used for that purpose. Since, on this limb of his
case it is not suggested that the applicant is in a different position from any other fugitive
whom it is sought to return to Fiji, or to a national of any other country which may in
the future find itself in the same anomalous position as Fiji in relation to United Kingdom
legislation, the applicant is in effect contending that the Secretary of State is bound to
refuse authority to proceed in every similar case. To write the discretion out of the Act
*c* in this way is to my mind impossible.

The third argument is on the following lines. The court has only to look at the
documents lodged with the Chief Metropolitan Stipendiary Magistrate in support of the
application to commit for it to be seen at once that the offence is of a political character.
This being so, the court should grasp the nettle, recognise that no order for return could
ever properly be made and by releasing the applicant at once spare him a long period in
*d* custody awaiting the completion of proceedings which are bound to end in his release.
The court has jurisdiction to decide this issue at the present stage, so the argument
continues, by virtue of s 4(1) of the 1967 Act, which begins as follows:

> 'A person shall not be returned under this Act to a designated Commonwealth
> country, or committed to or kept in custody for the purposes of such return, if it
*e* > appears to the Secretary of State, to the court of committal or to the High Court or
> High Court of Justiciary on an application for habeas corpus or for review of the
> order of committal—(*a*) that the offence of which that person is accused or was
> convicted is an offence of a political character . . .'

The applicant also prays in aid the following passage from the speech of Viscount
*f* Radcliffe in *Schtraks v Government of Israel* [1962] 3 All ER 529 at 536–537, [1964] AC
556 at 585–586:

> 'The issue whether the offence charged is an offence of a policital character raises,
> I think, different considerations. Having regard to the wording of s. 3(1) of the
> Extradition Act, 1870, this issue must be regarded as introduced by way of a special
> condition peculiar to the Act, in the sense that it has nothing to do with ordinary
*g* > committal proceedings not under the Act: and it seems to be the evident intention
> of the statute that the issue should be considered as a substantive matter at any stage
> by any authority, magistrate, court, or Secretary of State, which has a duty to
> perform in relation to the extradition. If it is so regarded, it seems to me proper to
> consider on its merits any evidence that is available at the time when consideration
> is required. I should not treat this procedure so much as depending on the court's
*h* > duty to inquire into the magistrate's jurisdiction as on the special conditions laid
> down by the Act for the carrying out of an extradition request.'

The response of the government of Fiji and of the Secretary of State is twofold. First, it
is said that when the Act is properly understood it is seen that the court has no jurisdiction
to intervene at the present stage, and that *Schtraks*'s case has no bearing on the point. As
*j* to the latter part of the argument, I agree. The issue in *Schtraks*'s case was whether the
Divisional Court and the House of Lords had the power to hear additional evidence
under s 3(1) of the Extradition Act 1870, after the magistrate had committed the fugitive
to await surrender, with a view to showing that, contrary to the magistrate's ruling, the
offence was of a political character and that, accordingly, the fugitive should be released
from custody. Under the 1967 Act, the position is made plain by s 8(4). The 1870 Act

contained no equivalent provision. Nevertheless, the House held that there was such a power under the old Act in cases where the political nature of the offence was before the court. I do not however read *Schtraks*'s case as saying anything about the power of the court to intervene ahead of any ruling by the magistrate.

Leaving *Schtraks*'s case aside, the government of Fiji still maintains that the structure of the 1967 Act compels the conclusion that there is no such power of intervention. Of this I am not so sure. The scheme of the Act undoubtedly contemplates, in the case of proceedings not launched by provisional warrant, a chain of decisions with three links: (i) the issuing by the Secretary of State of an authority to proceed; (ii) the committal by the magistrate of the fugitive to await return; and (iii) the decision by the Secretary of State to return him. As counsel for the Secretary of State and the governor of Brixton prison has pointed out, the first stage has already passed, without any challenge to the decision, except on the issue of construction previously discussed, whilst the second has not yet been reached. In one sense, therefore, there is nothing on which any proceedings for judicial review could fasten. On the other hand, the words of s 4 appear very plain, and do not seem to me, even when read in conjunction with s 8, to rule out the possibility of an application for habeas corpus before the magistrate has made his adjudication. That such an application can be made at a stage such as the present where the objection goes to the jurisdiction of the Secretary of State to issue the authority to proceed was not challenged in relation to the first of the grounds of application argued before us; and indeed it could not have been, given the words of s 5(3). I think it at least possible that other questions besides those of jurisdiction would in theory be open to a fugitive in relation to the exercise by the Secretary of State of his discretion to issue the authority to proceed.

I need not, however, express a concluded opinion on this question, for whatever may be the position in theory it seems to be absolutely plain that in practice the court should not now contemplate entering on a factual inquiry such as would be necessary before the question of granting any relief at the present stage could be addressed. An application for habeas corpus is not the proper vehicle for such an inquiry. The procedures of the Divisional Court are not adapted to this task. The evidence is far from complete. When it is ready, it should be brought before the magistrate who is charged with the responsibility under s 7(5) of weighing it to decide whether it has sufficient weight to justify committal, and who is specifically given jurisdiction under s 4(1) to rule on the political character of the offence in respect of which he is being asked to commit. For the Divisional Court to usurp the role of fact-finder, in place of its proper function as a court of review, would lead to just those adverse consequences which were foreshadowed in a similar context by the Judicial Committee in *USA v Gaynor* [1905] AC 128 at 138. In my judgment we should not take this untimely step.

I would therefore dismiss the application.

**McCOWAN J.** I agree.

*Application dismissed.*

Solicitors: *Victor Lissack & Roscoe* (for the applicant); *Crown Prosecution Service* (for the government of Fiji); *Treasury Solicitor.*

Dilys Tausz   Barrister.

# King v Weston-Howell

COURT OF APPEAL, CIVIL DIVISION
SIR NICOLAS BROWNE-WILKINSON V-C, PARKER AND NOURSE LJJ
15, 16 FEBRUARY, 8 MARCH 1989

*b* *Solicitor – Payment of costs by solicitor personally – Delay by solicitor – Payment into court – Defendant prevented from making payment into court because of delay by plaintiff's solicitors in providing particulars of damages claimed – Whether plaintiff's solicitors personally liable for costs for preventing defendant from making effective payment in – Whether late payment into court by defendant effective – RSC Ord 22, r 3, Ord 62, r 11.*

*c* The plaintiff brought an action against the defendant claiming damages for medical negligence. The trial was fixed for 22 April 1985. On 3 October 1984 the defendant admitted liability and 12 days before the trial on the issue of quantum was due to begin the plaintiff's solicitors provided particulars of the damages claimed. The defendant, who had been told by his insurers to settle for up to £290,000, considered on the basis of existing authority that it was then too late to seek instructions to make a payment in and *d* the trial on quantum proceeded on the date set down. On 30 April 1985 judgment was given for the plaintiff for £276,651·46. The judge ordered the defendant to pay the plaintiff's costs on a party and party basis. However, the defendant contended that part of the costs should be paid by the plaintiff's solicitors personally because they had provided particulars of the damages claimed less than 21 days before the hearing and had thereby deprived the defendant of the opportunity to make an effective payment into *e* court under RSC Ord 22. The judge held that a late payment into court was ineffective under Ord 22, r 3[a] to provide the defendant with any protection in costs and ordered (i) that the plaintiff was entitled to her costs up to and including 30 March 1985, ie 21 days before the hearing, (ii) that the costs as between the plaintiff and her solicitors be disallowed pursuant to Ord 62, r 11[b] as from 1 April 1985 and (iii) that the plaintiff's solicitors personally pay one-half of the defendant's costs incurred on or after 1 April *f* 1985, such costs to be taxed on an indemnity basis, and the defendant's costs of the application itself on the standard basis. The plaintiff's solicitors appealed.

**Held** – Since RSC Ord 22, r 1(1)[c] provided that in an action for a debt or damages a defendant could at any time make a payment in in satisfaction of the plaintiff's claim and since there was nothing in Ord 22 which provided that a payment in made less than *g* 21 days before trial was ineffective, if a payment in was made less than 21 days before the trial both the fact and the amount of the payment in had to be taken into account when costs were awarded, although the fact that the payment in was late might be relevant to the degree of its effectiveness as to costs. Accordingly, where a payment in in excess of the amount recovered would have been made more than 21 days before trial but for the default of the plaintiff, the defendant was prima facie entitled to the costs from the actual *h* date of payment in and could be awarded costs from an earlier date if the judge so decided. Since the defendant had been in a position to make a payment in by mid-April he was prima facie entitled to his costs from that date but, on the judge's findings, had he asked for costs from 1 April on the ground that he would have made a payment in earlier but for the plaintiff's default, he would probably have obtained such an order and therefore it could not be said that the defendant had been prevented from recovering *j* such costs but for the delay. In those circumstances the defendant had not been deprived of his protection in costs because his payment in was made less than 21 days before trial

---

*a*  Rule 3, so far as material, is set out at p 378 *j* to p 379 *d*, post
*b*  Rule 11, so far as material, is set out at p 383 *j* to p 384 *b*, post
*c*  Rule 1(1) is set out at p 378 *j*, post

and it followed that the plaintiff's solicitors could not be made personally liable for one-half of the defendant's costs incurred on or after 1 April 1985. The appeal would therefore be allowed, the judge's order set aside and the plaintiff awarded her costs of the action on the standard basis (see p 378 *h*, p 379 *f h j*, p 380 *a g* to *j*, p 381 *j* to p 382 *a*, p 383 *c d g h* and p 384 *c* to *h*, post).

Bowen v Mills & Knight Ltd [1973] 1 Lloyd's Rep 580 overruled.

**Notes**
For the liability of solicitors to pay costs, see 44 Halsbury's Laws (4th edn) paras 259–262, and for cases on the subject, see 44 Digest (Reissue) 421–422, 4587–4600.

**Cases referred to in judgments**
Banco Fonsecas E Burnay SARL v K O Boardman International Ltd [1985] 1 Lloyd's Rep 386.
Bowen v Mills & Knight Ltd [1973] 1 Lloyd's Rep 580.
Campbell (Donald) & Co Ltd v Pollak [1927] AC 732, [1927] All ER Rep 1, HL.
Findlay v Railway Executive [1950] 2 All ER 969, CA.
Wagman v Vare Motors Ltd [1959] 3 All ER 326, [1959] 1 WLR 853, CA.

**Cases also cited**
Davy-Chiesman v Davy-Chiesman [1984] 1 All ER 321, [1984] Fam 48, CA.
Mauroux v Sociedade Comercial Abel Pereira da Fonseca SARL [1972] 2 All ER 1085, [1972] 1 WLR 962.
Orchard v South Eastern Electricity Board [1987] 1 All ER 95, [1987] QB 565, CA.
Practice Direction (personal injuries action: particulars of special damage) [1984] 3 All ER 165, [1984] 1 WLR 1127.
R v Oxfordshire CC, ex p Wallace (1987) 137 NLJ 542, DC.
Sinclair-Jones v Kay [1988] 2 All ER 611, CA.
Ward v Chief Constable of Avon and Somerset Constabulary [1987] CA Transcript 780.
Wilsher v Essex Area Health Authority [1986] 3 All ER 801, [1987] QB 730, CA; rvsd [1988] 1 All ER 871, [1988] 2 WLR 557, HL.

**Appeal**
On 30 April 1985 Jupp J gave judgment for the plaintiff, Linda Carol King (suing by her next friend Hilda King), for £276,651·46 in an action brought by her against the defendant, Clifford Weston-Howell, for damages for personal injuries. Having given judgment the judge adjourned the question of costs and on 30 January 1987, having heard submissions from the plaintiff's solicitors, he ordered that (i) the costs as between the plaintiff's solicitors and the plaintiff be disallowed as from 1 April 1985, (ii) the defendant's solicitors be indemnified by the plaintiff's solicitors as to one-half of their costs after 1 April 1985 and (iii) the plaintiff pay the costs of the application in the matter. The plaintiff's solicitors appealed against the order made on 30 January 1987. The facts are set out in the judgment of Parker LJ.

Peter Sheridan QC and J F Holt for the plaintiff's solicitors.
Adrian Whitfield QC and Robert Francis for the defendant.
The plaintiff did not appear.

*Cur adv vult*

8 March. The following judgments were delivered.

**PARKER LJ** (giving the first judgment at the invitation of Sir Nicolas Browne-Wilkinson V-C). In January 1981 the plaintiff underwent a comparatively minor cosmetic operation. The defendant was the anaesthetist. The anaesthetic was negligently

administered with the tragic result that the plaintiff suffered severe brain damage. Suing
a by her next friend, Hilda King, she issued a writ against the defendant on 10 August
1982. In March 1984 the trial of the action was fixed for 22 April 1985. At that stage,
both liability and damages were in issue. The estimated length of trial was five days. On
3 October 1984 the defendant admitted liability. The estimated length of trial, the only
remaining issue being quantum of damages, was revised from five days to three days.
The trial, before Jupp J, duly began on 22 April 1985. On 30 April, the sixth day of the
b trial, judgment was given for the plaintiff for £265,606·41 and interest. The total
amount of the judgment inclusive of interest was £276,651·46.

The judge ordered that the defendant should pay the plaintiff's costs on a party and
party basis but this order was subject to two qualifications, only one of which is now
relevant. This arose from the fact that it was submitted on behalf of the defendant that
there should be an order that part of the costs should be paid by the plaintiff's solicitors
c personally. Stated broadly, the submission was that the solicitors' conduct, principally in
culpable delay in providing particulars of the damages claimed, had had the effect of
unduly prolonging the trial and depriving the defendant of the opportunity to make an
effective payment into court.

This question the judge adjourned into chambers so that the solicitors could be
represented, indicating that he had in mind that if an order were to be made against the
d solicitors, the amount of costs against the solicitors would be deducted from the amount
the plaintiff was entitled to receive under the order made against the defendant.

Having heard the application in chambers, the judge delivered his judgment in open
court and ordered (1) that the plaintiff be at liberty to enter judgment for her costs of the
action up to and including 30 March 1985, (2) that the costs as between the plaintiff and
her solicitors be disallowed pursuant to RSC Ord 62, r 11(1)(a)(iii) as from 1 April 1985
e and (3) that the plaintiff's solicitors personally pay to the defendant's solicitors one-half of
his costs of the action incurred on or after 1 April 1985 to be taxed on an indemnity basis
together with his costs of the application itself on the standard basis.

From that order the plaintiff's solicitors appeal.

Before the judge the defendant put his case on that basis which had been indicated
immediately after the trial but it is apparent from the judgment that the judge felt
f unable to make any order based on the prolongation of the trial. The order made was
clearly made on the ground that, due to culpable delay of the plaintiff's solicitors in
providing particulars of the damages claim, the defendant had been unable to make an
effective payment into court because he had not had the information necessary to enable
him to do so until less than 21 days before the trial.

In his judgment he said:
g

'. . . the Rules of the Supreme Court as to payment into court in Ord 22, r 3 and
the notes thereto limit the time within which a payment into court is effective. A
payment in by a defendant out of time does not give him any advantage in costs
such as is provided by the rules in the event of the plaintiff recovering less than the
amount paid into court. I was cited a judgment of Ashworth J in *Bowen v Mills &*
h *Knight Ltd* [1973] 1 Lloyd's Rep 580, where a payment in was made less than the
prescribed 14 days before trial, and was therefore completely ineffective in helping
the defendant in costs. The plaintiff's claim in that case was exaggerated. He
recovered less than a third of the sum which had been paid into court . . . In her
affidavit the defending solicitors' representative says that that accurate advice would
j have provided her with reasonable grounds to have made an effective payment into
court, but it was too late. The affidavit says: "I feel sure I would have obtained
instructions from the Medical Protection Society, for whom I acted on the Defendants
behalf, to pay into court a sum in excess of £280,000." It seems to me that that must
be right, as she had already been told to settle for up to £290,000. She went on:
"Had I been able to take that step, in the result the Defendant would have had a

valid claim for his costs incurred thereafter." . . . It was not until 10 April, 12 days
before the hearing, that sufficient documentation was handed to the defendant's  *a*
solicitors and some figures were agreed. In this kind of case, figures are usually
agreed as figures, before the trial begins . . . The information was insufficient and
given too late. The result was that the defendant was unjustly deprived of the
opportunity to take advantage of the rules of court as to payment in . . . I must
make an allowance for the possibility that an advantageous order for costs after
payment into court would not have been achieved, but my view is that the defendant  *b*
had a very good chance of succeeding and getting such an order. I must make
allowance for the fact that, though I have spoken of the possibility of a payment into
court, it does not follow as night follows day that the court would have followed the
normal rule as to costs, but again there was a very good chance. This is precisely the
kind of case where defendants, faced with what they consider to be an inordinate
claim, do pay into court. In my experience, when the parties are very near but not  *c*
sure of the proper size of the award, litigation is often conducted in a friendly sort
of way without payment into court. The parties, though close, often find it more
satisfactory to have a judgment. This is not that kind of case: it is one where what
was considered to be an exaggerated claim was made, and in the normal course
defendants would expect to meet that by a payment into court.'

*d*

I include the last passage only to show that the judge considered what might have
happened if a payment in 'in time' had exceeded the amount of the judgment. What he
did not consider at all was any possibility that a 'late' payment in could have resulted in
an order that the costs or part of the costs after payment in should be paid by the plaintiff
to the defendant. He regarded a 'late' payment in as completely ineffective to provide the
defendant with any protection in costs. The first and most crucial issue on this appeal is  *e*
whether he was right in this conclusion.

The determination of this issue requires an examination of the relevant rules and the
notes thereto. Order 22, r 1(1) provides:

> 'In any action for a debt or damages any defendant may *at any time* pay into court
> a sum of money in satisfaction of the cause of action in respect of which the plaintiff  *f*
> claims or, where two or more causes of action are joined in the action, a sum or
> sums of money in satisfaction of any or all of those causes of action.

Under r 1(3) he may also increase the amount of any payment in without leave.

On making or increasing payment in, the defendant must give notice in Ord 62, App
A, Form 23 to the plaintiff and any other defendant, and within three days of receipt of
the notice the plaintiff must send to the defendant written acknowledgment of receipt.  *g*

The notes to r 1 in *The Supreme Court Practice 1988* vol 1, para 22/1/9 include the
following statement:

> '. . . to be effective on the question of costs, the payment or last payment in made
> or increased before the beginning of the trial or hearing of the action must be made
> not less than 21 days before the trial or hearing of the action begins, or otherwise  *h*
> the plaintiff will not have the full time allowed to him by r. 3, in which to accept
> the money paid into court without leave. See *Bowen* v. *Mille & Knight Ltd.* ([1973] 1
> Lloyd's Rep 580). This of course is subject to the right of a party to make or increase
> a payment into court after the trial or hearing of an action has begun.'

There is nothing in r 1 to support the statement that to be effective a payment or
increase before trial must be made not less than 21 days before the trial or hearing begins. One  *j*
must therefore proceed to r 3, to which the note refers. So far as immediately relevant
that rule provides:

> '(1) Where money is paid into court under Rule 1, then subject to paragraph (2)
> within 21 days after receipt of the notice of payment or, where more than one

*a*  payment has been made or the notice has been amended; within 21 days after receipt of the notice of the last payment or the amended notice but, in any case, before the trial or hearing of the action begins, the plaintiff may—(a) where the money was paid in respect of the cause of action or all the causes of action in respect of which he claims, accept the money in satisfaction of that cause of action or those causes of action, as the case may be, or (b) where the money was paid in respect of some only of the causes of action in respect of which he claims, accept in satisfaction

*b*  of any such cause or causes of action the sum specified in respect of that cause or those causes of action in the notice of payment, by giving notice in Form No. 24 in Appendix A to every defendant to the action.

(2) Where after the trial or hearing of an action has begun—(a) money is paid into court under rule 1, or (b) money in court is increased by a further payment into court under that rule, the plaintiff may accept the money in accordance with

*c*  paragraph (1) within 2 days after receipt of the notice of payment or notice of the further payment, as the case may be, but, in any case, before the judge begins to deliver judgment or, if the trial is with a jury, before the judge begins his summing up . . .

(4) On the plaintiff accepting any money paid into court all further proceedings in the action or in respect of the specified cause or causes of action, as the case may

*d*  be, to which the acceptance relates, both against the defendant making the payment and against any other defendant sued jointly with or in the alternative to him shall be stayed . . .

(6) A plaintiff who has accepted any sum paid into court shall, subject to rules 4 and 10 and Order 80, rule 12, be entitled to receive payment of that sum in satisfaction of the cause or causes of action to which the acceptance relates.'

*e*

Paragraph (2) was introduced in 1966. The notes to r 3 contain (a) the statement that its effect was to enable an effective payment in to be made after the trial has begun and (b) similar notes to that already quoted under r 1 (see *The Supreme Court Practice 1988* vol 1, para 22/3/1).

*f*  Again the rule itself says nothing to limit the effectiveness or otherwise of payment in being made less than 21 days before trial or less than two days before the judge begins judgment or summing up.

It limits the time during which the plaintiff may accept the sum of money, with the result that all further proceedings are stayed, but no more. In respect of payments made 21 days or more before trial, he will have a full 21 days, but thereafter he will only have

*g*  the balance of the 21 days which remain before trial and, once the trial has begun, he will only have two days or the balance of that period between payment in and judgment or summing up.

If the payment in is before trial, whether 21 days or less than that, acceptance will have the further result that the plaintiff will be entitled, subject to exceptions not presently relevant, to receive the money paid in without further order. Where, however, the

*h*  money is paid in after the trial has begun, although the result of acceptance will be that further proceedings will be stayed, the plaintiff will under Ord 22, r 4(3) not be so entitled but must obtain an order of the court which must deal with the whole costs of the action.

The further provisions of Ord 22 contain nothing of relevance.

There is nothing in Ord 22 itself, therefore, which provides or in my judgment even

*j*  indicates that a payment in less than 21 days before trial is ineffective. Indeed, it seems clear that the reverse is the case. I can see no reason why a payment in on the first day of trial which must be accepted within two days should be effective but a payment in 20 days before trial which may be accepted at any time up to trial should be wholly ineffective. Furthermore, the time at which trial will begin or the judge commences his summing up or judgment cannot be predicted with certainty. Trials may be accelerated or delayed. A trial may take longer or shorter than is expected. Judgment may be given extempore or reserved. I find it prima facie unacceptable that the validity or effectiveness *a* of a payment in can be affected by chances such as this.

It is not necessary to consider certain of the provisions of Ord 62. I set out those immediately relevant. Rule 2(4) provides:

'The powers and discretion of the Court under section 51 of the [Supreme Court Act 1981] (which provides that the costs of and incidental to proceedings of the Supreme Court shall be in the discretion of the Court and that the Court shall have *b* full power to determine by whom and to what extent the costs are to be paid) and under the enactments relating to the costs of criminal proceedings to which this Order applies shall be exercised subject to and in accordance with this Order.'

Rule 3 provides:

(1) This rule shall have effect subject only to the following provisions of this *c* Order.

(2) No party to any proceedings shall be entitled to recover any of the costs of those proceedings from any other party to those proceedings except under an order of the Court.

(3) If the Court in the exercise of its discretion sees fit to make any order as to the *d* costs of any proceedings, the Court shall order the costs to follow the event, except when it appears to the Court that in the circumstances of the case some other order should be made as to the whole or any part of the costs . . .'

Rule 5 provides:

'(1) No order for costs is required in the circumstances mentioned in this rule . . . *e*
(4) Where a plaintiff by notice in writing in accordance with Order 22, rule 3, accepts money paid into court in satisfaction of the cause of action or of all the causes of action in respect of which he claims, or accepts money paid in satisfaction of one or more specified causes of action and gives notice that he abandons the others, he shall be entitled to his costs of the action incurred up to the time of giving notice of acceptance . . .' *f*

Rule 9(1) provides:

'The Court in exercising its discretion as to costs shall take into account . . . (b) any payment of money into court and the amount of such payment . . .'

It follows, in my view, from the foregoing that if a payment in is made, albeit after the 21 days mentioned in Ord 22, r 3, both the fact of payment in and the amount of *g* payment in *must* be taken into account. To ignore payments made less than 21 days before trial or two days before judgment appears to be directly contrary to r 9(1)(b). It might, I suppose, be argued that the fact of payment in is taken into account if the judge ascertains that it was less than 21 days before trial and then in the exercise of his discretion decides to ignore it, but, if that were right, he would still only have taken account of the fact of payment in and he must also take into account the amount. If the rules had *h* intended to provide that any payment in made less than 21 days before trial or two days before the commencement of judgment should be ineffective as to costs, they would in my view have made it clear.

So much for the rules themselves. Apart from authority, I would have no hesitation in concluding that a 'late' payment must be taken into account although the fact of lateness *j* might be relevant as to the degree of effectiveness.

I turn now to the authorities, and first those which establish the basis on which, where a payment in has been made but not accepted and the plaintiff recovers no more than the amount of the payment, the proper order, in the absence of special circumstances, is that the plaintiff has his costs to date of payment in and the defendant has his costs thereafter.

a
This is clearly stated in *Findlay v Railway Executive* [1950] 2 All ER 969, a case where, like the present case, liability was admitted. Somervell LJ said (at 971):

b

c

d
'The first point to be decided here is whether a defendant who has paid money into court which has not been taken out and exceeds the sum awarded to the plaintiff is a successful litigant or a successful party within those two statements of the law. I hold that he is, and that the principles there laid down apply. The main purpose of the rules for payment into court is the hope that further litigation will be avoided, the plaintiff being encouraged to take out the sum paid in, if it be a reasonable sum, whereas, if he goes on and gets a smaller sum, he will be penalised wholly or to some extent in costs. Once, therefore, the money has been paid in, the *lis* between the parties simply is: Is that sum sufficient to cover the damage which has been suffered. *Prima facie*, therefore, the defendants in the present case are entitled to be paid their costs as from the date of payment in, but, of course, as in other cases, there may be circumstances connected with the case which entitled the judge to make some order other than that of giving the successful litigant his costs, and counsel for the plaintiff submitted that there were such circumstances in this case. [HIS LORDSHIP referred to the submissions of counsel and the facts on which they were based, said that there were no circumstances entitling the judge to deprive the successful defendants of their costs, and concluded:] If I am right in holding that the defendants in the circumstances of this case are the successful litigants or parties then, on what I have read from the opinion of VISCOUNT CAVE, L.C., in the House of Lords [in *Donald Campbell & Co Ltd v Pollak* [1927] AC 732 at 809, 811, [1927] All ER Rep 1 at 40, 41], the learned judge went wrong in principle, and his order cannot stand, and this appeal, must be allowed.'

e
Reference may also be made, inter alia, to *Wagman v Vare Motors Ltd* [1959] 3 All ER 326, [1959] 1 WLR 853. There also liability was admitted and the defendants made a payment into court on 18 August 1958. Morris LJ said ([1959] 3 All ER 326 at 332, [1959] 1 WLR 853 at 860):

f

g
'. . . the real issue between the parties ever after Aug. 18, 1958, was whether £575 was or was not the right sum for the plaintiff to receive. After that date the plaintiff could have had £575. The plaintiff decided to go on with the litigation in the hope of getting more. The plaintiff was unsuccessful in his endeavour, but at all times after Aug. 18 he could have had the amount that was awarded by the learned judge. The defendants, therefore, were successful on the issue that was being contested before the learned judge.'

h

j
If the basis of the ordinary order is that, where the plaintiff recovers no more than the payment in the defendant is, from the date of payment in, the successful litigant and thus, in the absence of some sufficient reason to deprive him thereof, entitled to his costs, it follows in my view that, where a defendant has paid in, say, 16 days before trial and the plaintiff recovers no more than the payment, the defendant is prima facie entitled to his costs from that date. He suffers to some extent in that the time from which he is prima facie entitled to costs is later than it would have been had he paid in earlier, but I can see no valid reason for depriving him of all his costs. True, the plaintiff is given less time to take advantage of the payment, by accepting it and getting an order for his costs, but I cannot regard this as justifying an order which deprives him, although successful, of all the costs to which he would have been entitled had he paid in in time, particularly when the rules themselves allow for payment in *at any time*, not merely up to 21 days before trial and specifically limit the time for acceptance once trial has begun to two days.
Furthermore, where, as in the present case, the judge finds that a payment in, in excess of the amount recovered, would have been made more than 21 days before trial but for the default of the plaintiff, it would in my judgment be a very relevant factor and might

even lead a judge to award costs to the defendant from a point earlier than the payment in.

The authority relied on in the notes to Ord 22, rr 1 and 3, *Bowen v Mills & Knight Ltd* [1973] 1 Lloyd's Rep 580, must next be considered. In that case a payment in which exceeded the amount recovered was made one day short of the 14 days then provided by the rules instead of the 21 days which now prevails. The defendant applied for his costs from the date of payment in. The argument on costs is fully reported. For the defendant reliance was placed on Ord 62, r 5 (now Ord 62, r 9(1)(b)) and mention was made of a decision of Hinchcliffe J in which he was said, in the case of a 'late' payment in, to have awarded the defendant costs from date of payment in. For the plaintiff reliance was placed on a note in *The Supreme Court Practice* similar to those presently appearing, but at that stage unsupported by authority.

At the conclusion of the argument Ashworth J said (at 590):

> 'Prima facie, the plaintiff has got 14 days to accept, with the penalty that thereafter if he does not reach the sum he will have to pay the costs, but *prima facie* if he can bring himself to trial within the period after the payment-in he is free of that sanction, and, accepting what you say, even if R.S.C., Order 62, r. 5 gives me an overriding discretion I should not exercise it in this case.'

Notwithstanding this, he gave leave to appeal on the question of costs.

With respect to that very experienced judge, I am unable to regard the decision as being of any great weight in itself for it is apparent that the rules were not fully considered. Such weight as it has lies in the fact that it has stood for a long time as authority that a late payment in is ineffective to give *any* protection in costs. It is, however, not in truth authority for such a proposition.

The combined researches of counsel have been unable to uncover any further authority in point save the decision of Neill J in *Banco Fonsecas E Burnay SARL v K O Boardman International Ltd* [1985] 1 Lloyd's Rep 386. In that case the trial began on 17 October 1983. On 13 September the defendants' solicitors paid a cheque in foreign currency into the court funds office and informed the plaintiffs' solicitors to that effect. It was, however, not until 27 September that the defendants were able to give proper notice of payment in. This was because of delay in clearance of the cheque through the Bank of England. The plaintiffs acknowledged receipt on 29 September but reserved the right to contend that the moneys were paid in too late. Thereafter the plaintiffs, on 3 April 1984, accepted an offer by the defendants that notwithstanding that the time for so doing had expired they should take out the money in full and final settlement but without prejudice to the question whether the notice had been effectively given. This question came on for hearing before the judge on 18 April. It was argued on behalf of the bank that the payment in should be regarded as wholly ineffective because the notices of payment in were within the 21 day period before trial, reliance being placed on the decision of Ashworth J. Neill J said (at 388):

> 'I have come to the conclusion that I should take the following factors into account in deciding how I should exercise my discretion: (a) The rules provide a period of 21 days during which a plaintiff can decide whether or not to accept a payment into Court. That period is expressed to begin on the date of the receipt of the notice of payment in (O. 22, r. 3 (1)), and the notice referred to is that prescribed in O. 22, r. 1 (2). Strictly speaking therefore the solicitors for [the plaintiffs] were entitled to question the validity of the payment into Court having regard to the date fixed for trial, though they took the risk that owing to some unforeseen event the trial might have had to be postponed for a few days. (b) It was open to Boardman to have increased the sum in Court after the trial began by a small amount. They did not do so. (c) I am satisfied that in any event Boardman are entitled to the costs of and occasioned by the adjournment in October and of the hearing on Oct. 25. (d) Once the trial had begun it became clear that the real issue on the bills on which the U.K.

subsidiaries had defaulted was whether [the plaintiffs] could recover more than the
*a* Escudos sums advanced. Most of the time expended in October was taken up in
exploring ways in which the bank might be entitled to the profits arising from
changes in the rate of exchange. I have taken these factors into account. I have also
reminded myself of the evidence which was given and of the course of the trial.'

It is in my view clear that although the judge accepted that the payment in had been
made 'late' he did not regard it as ineffective and it is to be inferred that, in awarding the
*b* plaintiffs' costs only up to the second day of the trial and the defendants their costs
thereafter, he proceeded on the basis that there would be complete absurdity if it were so
regarded when the defendants could have made it fully effective by increasing the
amount by a token sum on the first day of the trial.

I respectfully agree that it was right to regard the payment in as affording prima facie
*c* some protection. But I would go further. Since, when a payment in exceeds the amount
recovered, the defendant has been successful the starting point of the discretion must be
that the defendant should have his costs from that date. Other circumstances may justify
a departure from the prima facie position, for example that the lateness was due to the
plaintiff's fault or that, although the payment was made 22 days before the date fixed,
the beginning of the trial was put forward for two days owing to the collapse of a
*d* previous case.

With this lengthy preliminary, which I have felt necessary in view of the time for
which Ashworth J's decision has appeared as authority that a late payment in is wholly
ineffective, I can return to the facts of the present case.

The judge has accepted that the defendant's solicitor could have obtained instructions
to pay £290,000 into court had she sought such instructions. He has also found that she
*e* was not in a position to seek such instructions until mid-April and that this was due to
the default of the plaintiff's solicitors. It is common ground that had such payment been
made, it would not have been accepted, but there is no evidence that the defendant was,
at the time, considering payment in.

Taking this position, the judge asked himself the question 'What would have been
likely to have happened had such payment been made in time?' He did not ask himself
*f* the question 'What would have been likely to happen had the payment in been made in
mid-April?' He simply assumed that any such payment would have been wholly
ineffective. In the light of the notes in *The Supreme Court Practice 1988* this is not
surprising, but with respect to both the judge and the authors of *The Supreme Court
Practice*, it is in my view wrong. Had such a payment been made, both the fact of such
payment and its amount were bound to be considered, and on principle the defendant
*g* would prima facie have been entitled to the costs from date of payment in.

I can see no basis on which he could have properly been deprived of such an order. If
this is right, the only possible effect of the payment in being made 'late' would have been
that the defendant would have got an order for costs from mid-April but not from some
earlier date. He could, however, have applied, in such circumstances, for the order to go
back further on the ground that he would have paid in earlier but for the plaintiff's
*h* default. I say the plaintiff's default rather than the plaintiff's solicitors' default for at that
stage the sole question would have been the proper order for costs inter partes. On the
basis of the judge's findings, which I do not set out in detail, it appears to me highly
probable that an application to date back to 1 April would have been successful.

The judge having, however, understandably, proceeded on a basis which in my
judgment was wrong in law, the order should be set aside.

*j* There remains for consideration whether this court has the necessary material on
which to exercise its own discretion on whether the matter should be remitted to the
judge for reconsideration. This brings me to Ord 62, r 11(1) under which the defendant's
application was made. It provides:

> 'Subject to the following provisions of this rule, where it appears to the Court that
> costs have been incurred unreasonably or improperly in any proceedings or have

been wasted by failure to conduct proceedings with reasonable competence and
expedition, the Court may—(*a*) order—(i) the solicitor whom it considers to be *a*
responsible (whether personally or through a servant or agent) to repay to his client
costs which the client has been ordered to pay to any other party to the proceedings;
or (ii) the solicitor personally to indemnify such other parties against costs payable
by them; and (iii) the costs as between the solicitor and his client to be disallowed;
or (*b*) direct a taxing officer to inquire into the matter and report to the Court, and
upon receiving such a report the Court may make such order under sub-paragraph *b*
(*a*) as it thinks fit.'

Since it is common ground that even if a payment in had been made it would not have
been taken out, all the costs actually incurred by both sides would have been incurred in
any event and it is not suggested that any can be said to have been incurred unreasonably
or improperly. Can it then be said that any costs have been wasted by failure on the part *c*
of the plaintiff's solicitors to conduct the proceedings with reasonable competence and
expedition? It was submitted for the defendant that the costs incurred by him from
1 April can be regarded as having been wasted because had he made a payment in by
31 March he would have recovered them from the plaintiff, but having been prevented
from making an effective payment in, he was unable to do so.

I have very considerable doubt whether this argument could succeed even if, contrary *d*
to my view, any payment in after 31 March would have been ineffective, but in my
judgment, it is unnecessary to decide the point in this case. The defendant was by mid-
April in a position to make a payment in. Had he then done so, it would have been
effective to enable him to recover costs from that date. The argument would, therefore,
only be available in respect of the period from 31 March to that date. I have, however,
already expressed the view that, had the defendant asked for costs as from 1 April on the *e*
ground that he would have made his payment then but for the plaintiff's delay in making
information available, he would, on the judge's findings, probably have obtained such an
order. This being so, it could not be said that he has been prevented from recovering any
costs which would have been recoverable but for the delay. Accordingly, I would allow
the appeal, set aside the judge's order and order that the plaintiff have her costs of the
action on the standard basis. *f*

By way of postcript I should, in fairness to the solicitors, say that while the judge was
in my view entirely justified in criticising them for delay I have no doubt that such
criticism could not have justified any order against them save on the basis which I hold
to have been wrong in law that they had prevented the defendant from making an
effective payment into court.

*g*

**NOURSE LJ.** I agree.

**SIR NICOLAS BROWNE-WILKINSON V-C.** I also agree.

*Appeal allowed.*

*h*

Solicitors: *Lipkin Gorman* (for the plaintiff's solicitors); *Le Brasseur & Monier-Williams* (for
the defendant).

Celia Fox    Barrister.

# Customs and Excise Commissioners v Diners Club Ltd and another

COURT OF APPEAL, CIVIL DIVISION
DILLON, RALPH GIBSON AND WOOLF LJJ
21, 22 FEBRUARY, 3 MARCH 1989

*Value added tax – Supply of goods and services – Supply – Credit card scheme – Taxpayers operating credit card schemes – Contractual agreements between taxpayers and cardholders and between taxpayers and retailers – Cardholders agreeing to pay taxpayers cost of goods and services received from retailers on presenting credit card – Taxpayers agreeing to purchase from retailers cost of providing cardholders with goods and services less discount or commission – Whether taxpayers supplying retailers with financial service for a consideration – Value Added Tax Act 1983, s 3(2)(b), Sch 6, Group 5, item 1.*

DC and CSL were companies which operated charge and credit card businesses. Under the scheme operated by DC a cardholder was liable to DC for all charges, which were defined as meaning all debts, incurred through use of the card. By a contract between DC and the retailers, DC agreed to purchase and the retailers agreed to sell and assign all accounts created by the use of the cards by the cardholders less a discount. Under the scheme operated by CSL, CSL agreed with a cardholder to buy from the relevant retailer any debt created by the purchase of goods or services by the use of the card and the cardholder was liable to pay CSL the full amount of such debt. Under the agreement between CSL and the retailers, a charge meant a debt incurred by use of a card, and the retailers agreed to sell at their face value less a commission deducted by CSL and CSL agreed to buy all charges properly incurred. The Commissioners of Customs and Excise claimed that the card companies made exempt supplies for the purposes of value added tax and that consequently they were only entitled to recover a reduced portion of the input tax on taxable supplies made to them. A value added tax tribunal rejected the claim, holding that the arrangements between the card companies and their respective retailers were factoring arrangements by which the card companies bought the rights of the retailers to receive cash payments for goods and services supplied to cardholders, and that accordingly neither card company made supplies to the retailers for the purposes of value added tax. The judge allowed an appeal by the Crown, holding that the card companies made exempt supplies of services to the retailers, namely the receipt of or dealing with money within item 1[a] of Group 5 of Sch 6 to the Value Added Tax Act 1983, for which the consideration within s 3(2)(b)[b] of that Act was the discount or the commission. The card companies appealed, contending (i) that, although a cardholder became indebted to a retailer when he used a card to purchase goods or services, that debt was not extinguished when the card was accepted by the retailer, notwithstanding that the cardholder himself was discharged from liability to pay the retailer, but remained in existence and was sold and assigned by the retailer to them and (ii) that the payments which they made to the retailers were for the purchase by them of those debts and therefore it was the retailers who made the supply. The Crown contended that the card companies supplied the retailers with the benefit of their credit card operations and the discount was the consideration for that supply.

**Held** – Where a card was accepted by a retailer, not only was the liability of the cardholder to the retailer extinguished but so also was the debt created by the use of the card, albeit that the debt was replaced by a new debt due from the cardholder to the card

---

*a*    Item 1 is set out at p 389 *a*, post
*b*    Section 3(2), so far as material, is set out at p 388 *e*, post

company. However, even if that was not so and there was an assignment by the retailer of that debt, that did not mean that there was not also a supply for the purposes of value *a* added tax by the card companies. Where a purchaser provided services in addition to making payment there was not necessarily only a single supply by the vendor. In such circumstances the precise position had to be resolved by examining the entire transaction, which in the case of the card companies' operations comprised not only the contract between the retailer and the card company but also the contract between the cardholder and the card company. When that was done it was clear that supplies were made by DC *b* and CSL, namely the making of the payment to the retailer pursuant to their contractual obligation to do so. That payment was not merely a payment for a supply by the retailer but was also the supply of a service by the card company to the retailer, and was for a consideration, namely the discount or commission, within s 3(2)(*b*) of the 1983 Act. Moreover, it fell within item 1 of Group 5 in Sch 6 to that Act and was therefore an exempt supply. Accordingly, the appeal would be dismissed (see p 394 *b* to *g*, p 395 *a* to *c* *j*, p 397 *b* to *e* and p 398 *a*, post).

Dictum of Ralph Gibson J in *Customs and Excise Comrs v Pippa-Dee Parties Ltd* [1981] STC 495 at 501 applied.

Decision of Kennedy J [1988] 2 All ER 1016 affirmed.

### Notes *d*

For the meaning of 'supply' for the purposes of value added tax, see 12 Halsbury's Laws (4th edn) para 871, and for cases on the subject, see 49 Digest (Reissue) 4–13, 5–33.

For exemption of financial dealings from value added tax, see 12 Halsbury's Laws (4th edn) para 900, and for a case on the subject, see 49 Digest (Reissue) 19, 58.

For the Value Added Tax Act 1983, s 3, Sch 6, Group 5, item 1, see 48 Halsbury's Statutes (4th edn) 603, 686. *e*

### Cases referred to in judgments

*British Railways Board v Customs and Excise Comrs* [1977] 2 All ER 873, [1977] 1 WLR 588, CA.

*Charge Card Services Ltd, Re* [1988] 3 All ER 702, [1988] 3 WLR 764, CA; *affg* [1986] 3 *f* All ER 289, [1987] Ch 150, [1986] 3 WLR 697.

*Customs and Excise Comrs v Oliver* [1980] 1 All ER 353.

*Customs and Excise Comrs v Pippa-Dee Parties Ltd* [1981] STC 495.

*Esso Petroleum Ltd v Customs and Excise Comrs* [1976] 1 All ER 117, [1976] 1 WLR 1, HL.

*Richardson (Inspector of Taxes) v Worrall, Westall v McDonald (Inspector of Taxes)* [1985] STC 693.

*g*

### Cases also cited

*Customs and Excise Comrs v Zinn* [1988] STC 57.

*Olds Discount Co Ltd v John Playfair Ltd* [1938] 3 All ER 275.

### Appeal

Diners Club Ltd and Cardholder Services Ltd (the taxpayer companies) appealed against *h* the decision of Kennedy J [(1988) 2 All ER 1016) on 12 February 1988 allowing an appeal by the Commissioners of Customs and Excise against a decision of a London value added tax tribunal (chairman Lord Grantchester QC sitting alone) ([1987] VATTR 10) released on 10 February 1987 whereby it was decided that the taxpayer companies were not making supplies which were exempt for the purposes of value added tax. The facts are set out in the judgment of Woolf LJ. *j*

*Rex Bretten QC* and *Fay Stockton* for the taxpayer companies.
*John Mummery* for the Crown.

*Cur adv vult*

3 March. The following judgments were delivered.

a

**WOOLF LJ** (giving the first judgment at the invitation of Dillon LJ). This is an appeal by the taxpayer companies, Diners Club Ltd (Diners) and Cardholder Services Ltd (CSL). CSL is an associated company of Diners and, as is well known, both companies operate charge and credit card businesses.

b  *The issue*
        The issue on this appeal is whether the taxpayer companies in conducting their respective businesses make exempt supplies for the purposes of value added tax when they make a payment to retailers of the amount of the charges, less a discount, incurred by holders of their cards when using those cards to acquire goods or services from retailers.
c        The Commissioners of Customs and Excise contend that they do make exempt supplies. The taxpayer companies contend they do not. The value added tax tribunal, in a decision given by its chairman, Lord Grantchester QC ([1987] VATTR 10), decided (accepting the argument of the taxpayer companies) that they do not do so, but the opposite view was taken by Kennedy J in his judgment of 12 February 1988 (see [1988] 2 All ER 1016) which is now under appeal.
d        The issue is of considerable practical importance to the taxpayer companies and other credit card companies, as is indicated by the amount involved in the three specimen assessments which are the subject of this appeal. Each of those assessments is dated June 1986. The first and second concern Diners and are respectively in the sums of £20,763·58 for the period 1 April to 30 June 1985 and £196,370·20 for the period 1 July 1985 to 31 March 1986. The third assessment relates to CSL and is in the sum of £8,824·57 in e        respect of the period 1 April to 30 June 1985.
        1 April 1985 is the date on which the Value Added Tax Act 1983 was amended to refer specifically in a note to credit card, charge card or similar payment card operations.
        The explanation for the commissioners adopting what at first sight appears to be a surprising role of seeking to establish that the supplies are exempt is explained by the fact that if the supplies are exempt this reduces the proportion of the input tax which the f        taxpayer companies are entitled to recover on taxable supplies made to them (see ss 14 and 15 of the 1983 Act and the Value Added Tax (General) Regulations 1985, SI 1985/886).
        When considering the relevant statutory provisions, it is helpful to have in mind, in general terms, the arguments of the taxpayer companies and the Commissioners of Customs and Excise. The taxpayer companies argue that the payments they make to the g        retailers are for the purchase by them of the debts incurred by their cardholders (members) when they use cards to pay for goods or services. The taxpayer companies do not pay the full amount of those charges but the charges less a discount, which is in accord with what happens under a factoring agreement where a factor acquires the debts of a retail company with a view to recovering those debts from a customer. On this h        argument the supply is not made by the taxpayer companies but by the retailers who sell the debts.
        The position is explained clearly in a short passage from the decision of Lord Grantchester in which he gives his reasons for rejecting an argument of the commissioners ([1987] VATTR 10 at 23):

j        'In my view, the arrangements between Diners and CSL and their respective Authorised Retailers are basically factoring arrangements. Diners and CSL buy the rights of the Authorised Retailers to receive cash payments for goods and services supplied. A sale of a debt for a payment in cash is prima facie, for tax purposes, in my opinion, a supply by the vendor and not by the purchaser. There appears to me to be nothing in the arrangements before me to indicate that such approach should not be adopted in this case.'

The commissioners, on the other hand, contend that the discount from the amount of the charges is the consideration for the taxpayer companies supplying the retailers with the benefits of their credit or charge card operations, which include assuring the retailers that they will receive payment and in fact making the payment of the money due in respect of goods or services which retailers have supplied to members who have used their cards for acquiring goods or services.

### The relevant statutory provisions

Turning to the statutory provisions to which it is necessary to refer, I commence with s 1 of the 1983 Act, which provides:

> 'A tax, to be known as value added tax, shall be charged in accordance with the provisions of this Act on the supply of goods and services in the United Kingdom . . .'

The scope of the tax is dealt with in s 2. It is only necessary to refer to sub-s (1), which provides:

> 'Tax shall be charged on any supply of goods or services made in the United Kingdom, where it is a taxable supply made by a taxable person in the course or furtherance of any business carried on by him.'

As there is a dispute between the parties whether there is any relevant supply made by the taxpayer companies, s 3 is important since it describes what is meant by a 'supply'. It is only necessary to cite sub-s (2):

> '. . . (a) "supply" in this Act includes all forms of supply, but not anything done otherwise than for a consideration; (b) anything which is not a supply of goods but is done for a consideration (including, if so done, the granting, assignment or surrender of any right) is a supply . . .'

As Griffiths J said in *Customs and Excise Comrs v Oliver* [1980] 1 All ER 353 at 354:

> 'There is no definition of "supply" in the Act itself, but it is quite clear from the language of the Act that "supply" is a word of the widest import.'

The width of what is a supply for value added tax purposes is made clear by s 3(2)(b) in so far as it refers to 'anything . . . done for a consideration'. However, I accept the submission of counsel for the taxpayer companies that the word 'supply' must still be read in the context of the other provisions of the Act and in particular s 1, and that, while it would be possible to regard any payment of money as being a supply, for the purpose of the tax the payment of money by itself as the consideration for the price of goods or services supplied to the payer does not normally constitute a supply by the payer. It follows that, if the transactions between the taxpayer companies and their retailers are correctly categorised in the way the taxpayer companies contend, then the taxpayer companies do not make a supply for a consideration to their retailers when they pay them the sum due for charges incurred by their retailers. It is the retailers who make a supply to them by assigning the debts, and the sums paid by the taxpayer companies are the consideration for those supplies.

So far as the time of supply is concerned, it is sufficient to refer to s 4(3), which states:

> '. . . a supply of services shall be treated as taking place at the time when services are performed.'

It is s 17 of the Act which deals with exempt supplies. It states that a supply will be exempt 'if it is of a description for the time being specified in Schedule 6 to this Act'. Schedule 6 is divided into various groups and it is Group 5, which is headed 'Finance', which is the group which is relevant. Group 5 is divided into seven items but it is only necessary to refer to item 1 and item 5 and note 4:

'Item No.

a          1. The issue, transfer or receipt of, or any dealing with, money, any security for money or any note or order for the payment of money . . .
          5. The making of arrangements for any transaction comprised in item 1 . . .

Notes . . .
          (4) This Group includes any supply by a person carrying on a credit card, charge card or similar payment card operation made in connection with that operation to a
b          person who accepts the card used in the operation when presented to him in payment for goods or services.'

It was note (4) which came into operation in 1985. The part played by notes in the Act is dealt with in s 48(6), which provides:

c          'Schedules . . . 6 to this Act shall be interpreted in accordance with the notes contained in those Schedules . . .'

The terms of note (4) make it clear that some payments by card companies to their retailers are intended to be treated as supplies which are exempt. However, the way the policy which is to be discerned from the note has been implemented means that the note only has effect when it can be properly said that there is something which is done for a
d consideration by a card company which, in accordance with s 3(2), is to be regarded as a supply for value added tax purposes.
          Counsel for the taxpayer companies in his clear, concise and helpful submissions argues that the agreements which the taxpayer companies made with their respective retailers and members make it clear that the taxpayer companies are not making such supplies. However, he recognises that if the taxpayer companies had chosen to conduct
e their operations in a different manner they could be regarded as making such supplies. It is therefore necessary to look with some care at the contractual arrangements which the taxpayer companies make with their retailers and members.

*The contractual arrangements*
f          In *Re Charge Card Services Ltd* [1988] 3 All ER 702, [1988] 3 WLR 764 the Court of Appeal had to consider the consequences of a charge card operator going into liquidation. Sir Nicolas Browne-Wilkinson V-C, in a judgment with which the other members of the court agreed, distinguished between the features common to credit card transactions generally and the particular features of individual schemes. He described the general features of credit card transactions as follows ([1988] 3 All ER 702 at 705, [1988] 3 WLR 764 at 768):
g
          '(A) There is an underlying contractual scheme which predates the individual contracts of sale. Under such scheme, the suppliers have agreed to accept the card in payment of the price of goods purchased; the purchasers are entitled to use the credit card to commit the credit card company to pay the suppliers. (B) That underlying scheme is established by two separate contracts. The first is made
h          between the credit company and the seller: the seller agrees to accept payment by use of the card from anyone holding the card and the credit company agrees to pay to the supplier the price of goods supplied less a discount. The second contract is between the credit company and the cardholder: the cardholder is provided with a card which enables him to pay the price by its use and in return agrees to pay the credit company the full amount of the price charged by the supplier. (C) The
j          underlying scheme is designed primarily for use in over-the-counter sales, ie sales where the only connection between a particular seller and a particular buyer is one sale. (D) The actual sale and purchase of the commodity is the subject of a third bilateral contract made between buyer and seller. In the majority of cases, this sale contract will be an oral, over-the-counter sale. Tendering and acceptance of the

credit card in payment is made on the tacit assumption that the legal consequences will be regulated by the separate underlying contractual obligations between the *a* seller and the credit company and the buyer and the credit company. (E) Because the transactions intended to be covered by the scheme would primarily be over-the-counter sales, the card does not carry the address of the cardholder and the supplier will have no record of his address. Therefore the seller has no obvious means of tracing the purchaser save through the credit company. (F) In the circumstances, credit cards have come to be regarded as substitutes for cash; they are frequently *b* referred to as "plastic money". (G) The credit card scheme provides advantages to both seller and purchaser. The seller is able to attract custom by agreeing to accept credit card payment. The purchaser, by using the card, minimises the need to carry cash and obtains at least a period of free credit during the period until payment to the card company is due.'

These general features exist in the case of the schemes operated by both taxpayer *c* companies. These schemes had, however, in addition, special features to which it is necessary to draw attention. Each of the taxpayer companies had more than one scheme. However, for the purposes of this appeal the parties have agreed that the court should only consider one typical scheme employed by each company as the other schemes which they operate would not be materially different. I will take the Diners scheme first and *d* then turn to the CSL scheme which is known as the Beefeater scheme.

*Particular features of the Diners scheme*

1. In order to become a cardholder the member had to fill in an application form which indicated that the annual subscription was currently £22·50, in addition to which an enrolment fee of £15 was payable. The member in the application form declared that *e* he agreed to abide by 'the rules of membership'.

2. The rules of membership included the following:

'1 . . . (f) The Member is liable to Diners Club for all charges which are incurred through use of the Card (and bought by Diners Club from Establishments), and for all acts and omissions of any Authorised Cardholder . . .

**2.** (a) Diners Club will send Statements for charges incurred through use of the *f* Card . . . (b) Statements must be settled in full on receipt in your billing currency . . . (c) Any charge which is not incurred in your billing currency will be converted at the rate applying on the day the charge is received by Diners Club at its head office in the United Kingdom. A conversion fee equal to 1% of the converted amount will be added . . . (d) If any amount is not received by Diners Club by the 40th day after the date of the Statement in which it first appears, a service charge *g* equal to 2% of that amount is payable to Diners Club. An additional service charge, equal to 3% of the unpaid balance, is payable for each period of 30 days after the 40th day until that balance is received. Diners Club may vary the rate of service charge from time to time by written notice to the Member or by publication. (e) If a Statement is not settled promptly you are liable to reimburse Diners Club for its *h* collection and legal costs. You are liable to a handling fee of £5 if any cheque or other remittance is not honoured on first presentation . . .

**3** . . . (b) You are liable for all loss suffered by Diners Club arising from any unauthorised use of the Card, unless you are covered by the Diners Club Card Loss Indemnity Scheme, although Diners Club may, at its discretion, limit this liability to the first £30 of loss suffered by Diners Club . . . *j*

**9.** In these Rules, unless the context otherwise requires . . . "charge" means a debt incurred through use of a Card at an Establishment . . . "Establishment" means a person who has entered into arrangements with the Diners Club International organisation for the supply of goods, tickets, services or cash to holders of Diners Club International charge cards . . . "Member" means the person at whose request a the Card is issued . . . and who agrees to be responsible for charges incurred through its use . . .'

3. The contract between Diners and its retailers (called 'Establishments') commences by stating:

'This agreement sets out the undertakings of each party in operating the system of Diners Club International Charge Cards . . .'

b The agreement then sets out certain conditions applying to the acceptance of cards, and goes on to deal with 'Purchase of charges':

'(a) The Diners Club Limited agrees to purchase and the Establishment agrees to sell and assign to us all accounts created by the use of a Diners Club International Charge Card for the sum stated less a discount as provided for in Schedule "B" such
c discount being calculated on the gross total of the charge. (b) All charges received at Diners Club by mid-day on Friday will be paid by cheque dated the following Friday sent first class post. (c) All charges should be submitted (weekly if possible) and not later than 30 days after signing. All other charges will only be accepted subject to collection from Members.'

d The next paragraph is headed 'Disputes'. It states:

'In the event of any charge disputed and not paid by a Member, whilst Diners Club will use every effort to aid a settlement the Establishment agrees to re-imburse Diners Club with such charges if no agreement is reached.'

Then there is a paragraph dealing with the provision of promotional material, first of
e all by the Establishment and secondly by Diners Club, who undertake—

'to publicise this affiliation with the Establishment by inclusion of relevant details of each Establishment in Directories circulated to Members.'

*Particular features of the Beefeater scheme*
f    CSL operated this scheme for Whitbread & Co plc (Whitbread) and it was primarily intended that the cards which were issued would be used by customers of Whitbread and its associated companies at their retail outlets.
The agreement between Whitbread and CSL has the following relevant terms:

'1. *Definitions* . . . (b) "Charge" means a debt (which term includes all gratuities and value added tax thereon) incurred in an Establishment on or after the
g Commencement Date by the use of a Card (as hereinafter defined) in accordance with the terms of this Agreement . .
2. *Management of The Scheme* (a) CSL will: (i) issue charge cards . . . (iii) operate the Scheme in an efficient and business-like manner; (iv) bear the expenses of operating the Scheme . . . (c) Each Card, shall be issued on the terms of the Conditions of
h Use . . .
3. *Promotion* (a) WHITBREAD shall procure that at its own expense all reasonable endeavours shall be made to promote the Scheme so as to maximise the number of Cardholders . . .
5. *Sale and Purchase of Charges* (a) Subject to the terms of this Agreement, WHITBREAD agrees to sell to CSL, and to procure that each of the Scheme Members
j sells to CSL, and CSL agrees to purchase from WHITBREAD and other Scheme Members all Charges properly incurred at their respective Establishments. (b) Each Charge will be sold at its full face value less the commission referred to in Clause 6 below . . . (e) Upon such payment the relevant Charge shall be deemed to have been assigned absolutely by the relevant Scheme Member to CSL, without recourse to the Scheme Member except as stated herein.

6. *Commission* . . . (b) Subject to (f) below, the commission ("Commission") shall be payable by Scheme Members to CSL calculated on the face value of Charges purchased by CSL hereunder during the relevant Month and determined on the basis of the Gross Turnover during the immediately preceding Rolling Twelve Month Period and shall be at the relevant rate set out in the Second Schedule hereto. (c) CSL shall be entitled to deduct Commission at such rate from the purchase price of each Charge purchased by it hereunder and from any other amounts due from CSL to the relevant Scheme Member or any other Scheme Member. (d) Where the gross revenue (excluding VAT) to CSL from Commission for any Month is less than £1,000, WHITBREAD shall, not later than 15 days after the end of such Month, but subject to receipt of an appropriate invoice, pay to CSL by way of additional commission an amount equal to the difference between the said gross revenue and £1,000. (e) Where the gross revenue (excluding VAT) to CSL from Commission and additional commission for any Twelve Month Period is less than £30,000, WHITBREAD shall, not later than 15 days after the end of such Twelve Month Period but subject to receipt of an appropriate invoice, pay to CSL by way of further additional commission an amount equal to the difference between the said gross revenue and £30,000.'

Paragraph 7, 'Qualifying Charges', sub-para (a) of this clause, sets out certain conditions as to qualifying charges, and then sub-para (b) goes on to provide:

'WHITBREAD will procure that each Charge submitted to CSL for purchase pursuant to Clause 5 above will qualify for purchase as stated above. Without prejudice to any other remedies of CSL, if any Charge does not so qualify; (i) CSL shall not be obliged to purchase such Charge; (ii) if CSL does purchase such Charge then (i) if CSL so requests within six months after the Charge was first submitted to CSL WHITBREAD shall procure that the relevant Scheme Member will forthwith re-purchase such Charge from CSL for a purchase price equal to its full face value payable on re-purchase, and (ii) so long as CSL has not so requested, the purchase of such Charge by CSL shall be with full recourse to the Scheme Member if such Charge is not paid to CSL in full for any reason whatsoever. Such right of recourse shall not be affected by any time, waivers, variations or other dealings on the part of CSL in good faith in relation to such Charge and shall apply notwithstanding the invalidity or unenforceability of such Charge.'

There are also provisions as to Whitbread securing the repurchase of charges by scheme members in other specified circumstances. Paragraph 11 is headed 'Recovery of Charges'. This paragraph places obligations on Whitbread to assist CSL in recovering charges.

The member to whom the card is issued agrees to conditions of use of the card. Condition 5a provides:

'CSL will purchase from the relevant Scheme Member any debt . . . created by the purchase of goods or services by the use of a Card . . . and the Customer shall be liable to pay to CSL the full amount of such debt. (Nothing herein shall be taken as relieving the Customer from his liability to pay such a debt to the relevant Scheme Member where CSL declines to purchase any debt or requires the relevant Scheme Member to repurchase any debt from it).'

Condition 6 states:

'CSL shall render monthly accounts to the Customer in respect of all Charges, which accounts shall be payable in full immediately upon presentation. A service charge of 2·0% will be charged on the balance remaining unpaid on any account at the end of 30 days after the date of such account and thereafter an additional service charge of 2·0% will be charged for each 30 days during which any balance remains unpaid . . .'

*Determination of the issue*

a   Counsel for the taxpayer companies submits that if the bilateral contracts between the taxpayer companies and their respective retailers and members are examined (whatever may be the position with regard to other card schemes), when a cardholder uses a card to purchase goods or services from an authorised retailer the cardholder becomes indebted to the retailer to the extent of the costs of those goods or services, notwithstanding the intention of the cardholder to settle the transaction by using his card. In support of this

b   contention he relies on the decision of Scott J in *Richardson (Inspector of Taxes) v Worrall* [1985] STC 693. In that case a card was used for buying petrol but the petrol would be placed in the vehicle before the card was tendered to the retailer. Scott J, basing himself on a dictum of Lord Simon in *Esso Petroleum Ltd v Customs and Excise Comrs* [1976] 1 All ER 117 at 123, [1976] 1 WLR 1 at 6, stated that a motorist who goes to a self-service station, at the time he puts petrol in the tank of his car or when he has petrol put in its

c   tank by a garage attendant, contracts to purchase the petrol at the price displayed on the pump. Scott J went on to categorise as nearly hopeless an argument that the contract or the contract binding on both parties was that payment would be made by means of a Barclaycard and then added (at 720):

> 'Credit card advertisements outside a garage may well be regarded as a standing
d   > offer to motorists to settle their liability by means of the advertised credit cards. But
> a motorist whether or not he intends to use a particular credit card does not put the
> petrol in his tank on the footing that he is obliged to use that card. The right to use
> the particular card, or to use any other advertised credit card, is a right of which he
> can avail himself if he wishes. He can, if he prefers, pay in cash. If an implied term
> of the contract regarding payment is to be spelled out it is, in my judgment, a term
e   > that payment will be made in cash but that if the motorist prefers he may settle his
> liability by a valid credit card of a sort displayed at the garage or by a cheque backed
> by an acceptable bank card. The underlying obligation, however, in lieu of an
> acceptable credit card or cheque and bank card is to make payment in cash.'

I agree with this reasoning of Scott J. It follows that in the sort of case with which Scott J was dealing, where the contract antedates payment, an indebtedness between the

f   cardholder and the retailer exists. The position, however, could in my view well be different (although I do not regard it as necessary to finally determine this for the purpose of the present appeal) in the case of transactions where the contract is not made until the customer hands his card to the retailer in payment and the retailer accepts the card. An example of the sort of situation I have in mind occurs in a bookshop when the customer hands the books he wishes to purchase and his credit card to the shop assistant and the

g   shop assistant there and then makes out the credit card slip which is signed by the customer. In this situation it appears to me unlikely that the customer is ever indebted to the retailer. My reasoning for distinguishing the latter situation is made clear by the decision of Millett J at first instance and of the Court of Appeal in *Re Charge Card Services Ltd* [1986] 3 All ER 289, [1987] Ch 150; *affd* [1988] 3 All ER 702, [1988] 3 WLR 764,

h   CA. As counsel for the taxpayer companies accepts, that decision is binding authority that where a card is produced by a cardholder and accepted by a retailer and the cardholder signs the sales voucher the cardholder is unconditionally discharged from liability to pay to the retailer the amount of the cost of the goods or services. Counsel for the taxpayer companies does not, however, accept, as counsel for the Crown contends, that this has the effect of extinguishing the debt. He submits that, having regard to the

j   terms of the bilateral contracts between the retailer and the taxpayer companies and the members and the taxpayer companies, the debts remain in existence but are sold and assigned by the retailers to the taxpayer companies and are then, in due course, collected by the taxpayer companies from the members, who instead of being liable to the retailers become liable to the taxpayer companies. I accept that there is support to be found for this submission in some of the individual terms of the bilateral contracts to which I have referred. However, I do not accept the submission. On the different facts of *Re Charge Card Services Ltd* [1988] 3 All ER 702 at 708, [1988] 3 WLR 764 at 772, which also *a* involved the supply of fuel, Sir Nicolas Browne-Wilkinson V-C said: 'One way of looking at the matter is to say that there was quasi–novation of the purchaser's liability', meaning thereby that the liability to the retailer was changed to a liability to the credit card company. On the different facts arising under the taxpayer companies' schemes, I consider that, where the member becomes indebted to the retailer on a card being accepted, not only is the liability of the cardholder to the retailer extinguished but so also *b* is the debt, albeit that the debt is replaced by a new debt due from the member to either Diners or CSL. I come to that conclusion, notwithstanding that some of the language used in the agreements points in a different direction, because any other result would be inconsistent with both sets of bilateral contracts when read as a whole, and in particular it is inconsistent with the different obligations which the member owes to the retailer before he uses his card to those which he owes to the credit card company under his *c* contract with that company after he has used the card. I need only give one example of the sort of term I mean, and that is the term which provides for interest on late payment. If subsequently one of the situations arise where the taxpayer companies are entitled to have recourse to the retailer, this is in respect of the indebtedness of the member to the taxpayer companies and not the debt, if any, which was owed to the retailer.

I would, therefore, reject the primary argument advanced by counsel for the taxpayer *d* companies for allowing this appeal. It is not possible when drafting the contracts by using labels which refer to assignments of debts to change the reality of what is created by the terms of the contracts as a whole. In saying this I am not putting any special meaning on the agreements for the purposes of value added tax but giving effect, as is clearly intended, to the language of both bilateral contracts under the schemes operated by each of the taxpayer companies. *e*

However, it is not on my rejection of this argument of counsel for the taxpayer companies that I would primarily decide this appeal. In my view, there is a much more fundamental basis for accepting the argument of the Crown. As counsel for the Crown contends, even if there was an assignment by the retailers of a debt created by the use of the cardholder's card for the purchase of goods or services this does not mean there was *f* not also a supply which is an exempt supply under the 1983 Act. Although in the case of an ordinary purchase or sale there will usually only be a single supply, namely a supply by the vendor, this is not necessarily the situation where the purchaser provides services in addition to making payment.

Where additional services are provided by the purchaser, the position is more complex and has to be resolved by the approach which was indicated by Ralph Gibson J in a value *g* added tax case dealing with a very different situation, namely *Customs and Excise Comrs v Pippa-Dee Parties Ltd* [1981] STC 495. Having referred to earlier authorities, and in particular *British Railways Board v Customs and Excise Comrs* [1977] 2 All ER 873, [1977] 12 WLR 588, Ralph Gibson J said (at 501):

> 'It is clear therefore that a technical analysis of one part of a transaction, or of one set of obligations within a contract, even though accurate in legal principle, which *h* is capable of explaining the service supplied, or the consideration given, in a restricted way, is not necessarily the right answer in law to the application of the provisions of this statute. I accept counsel for the Crown's submission that this approach does indicate that taxable transactions should not be artificially dissected so as to demonstrate as being the service provided, or the consideration given, something other or less than that which appears to have been the service provided *j* or consideration given upon examination of the entire transaction. The meaning of "entire transaction" for this purpose must be objectively determined upon the facts of the transaction by reference to the terms agreed.'

*a* When applying the approach which is indicated in that passage of Ralph Gibson J's judgment to this case, it is necessary not only to look at the contract between the retailer and the credit card company but the other bilateral contract between the member and the credit card company. They all form part of the entire transaction which has to be taken into account in deciding whether or not Diners and CSL make supplies to the retailer.

*b* When this is done it is clear that Diners and CSL undoubtedly do make supplies. They set up and operate their respective credit card operations. They provide a means by which the retailer can increase his business by holding himself out as being prepared to accept the credit cards of either Diners or CSL. They ensure that the retailer will receive payment, apart from in those exceptional cases referred to in the contracts. If Diners or CSL had charged the retailers an annual fee to become authorised retailers of the respective schemes, in my view it would be clear beyond doubt that Diners and CSL *c* were making supplies of services within the meaning of s 3(2)(b) and that those services were for a consideration, namely the annual fee. Does it make any difference that no annual fee is in fact charged? In my view, it does make a difference because of the impact of s 4(3), which defines the time of supply as when the service is performed, since there can be no relevant supply unless it is for a consideration. Because of this the operation of the schemes in general by the taxpayer companies can only be regarded as the background *d* against which a supply which can be relied on by the commissioners takes place. This supply is the making of the payments to the retailer pursuant to the contractual obligation to make that payment placed on Diners and CSL by their respective contracts with the retailer. Viewing that payment in accordance with the approach indicated by Ralph Gibson J, it is not a payment merely for a supply simpliciter by the retailer which would not also constitute a supply by the card company. The entire transaction when objectively *e* determined demonstrates that the payment is also the supply of a service to the retailer by Diners and CSL.

Is it, then, a service which is supplied for a consideration? The answer is Yes. If you seek to ascertain, from an examination of the terms of the entire transaction, why there is the provision for a discount (that is to ask what this consideration is for) the answer which the entire transaction provides is that it is for the benefits which the scheme *f* operated by the credit card company confers on the retailer, which include the service of providing the payment which is assured by the credit card company.

It only remains to consider whether the supply falls within Group 5. As to this, item 5 does not assist the Crown because that item would only be applicable to the overall arrangements where it is provided for a fee. It does not apply to the individual payments with which we are concerned and in respect of which the discount is given. However, *g* particularly when item 1 is read in conjunction with note (4), there is here clearly a supply in the form of the transfer of money to the retailer when a payment is made and therefore a supply which falls within item 1 of the group.

It follows that if this is the correct manner in which to determine the issue raised on this appeal, note (4) to Group 5 has the effect that is intended. The features of the schemes *h* of the taxpayer companies which result in this conclusion are not the specific features of their respective schemes but the general characteristics of credit card and charge card schemes described by Sir Nicolas Browne-Wilkinson V-C, that is the payment by the card company of the charges less discount in performance of the assurance by the card company that it will pay to the retailer the amount of the charges incurred by the cardholder to the retailer less the discount the retailer allows the company in consideration *j* of the services the retailer receives under the scheme.

For these reasons I would dismiss the appeal.

**RALPH GIBSON LJ.** I agree that the appeal should be dismissed for the reasons set out in the judgments of Dillon and Woolf LJJ.

**DILLON LJ.** The issue on this appeal is whether there has been a supply of services by the credit card companies, Diners Club Ltd (Diners) and its subsidiary Cardholder *a* Services Ltd (CSL), to approved establishments under the relevant charge card schemes even if only an exempt supply.

The complexities of value added tax law are at present enshrined in the Value Added Tax Act 1983. Section 17 provides that a supply of goods or services is an exempt supply if it is of a description for the time being specified in Sch 6 to the Act, and Sch 6 includes in Group 5 under the heading 'Finance':                                                      *b*

'. . . supply by a person carrying on a credit card, charge card or similar payment card operation made in connection with that operation to a person who accepts the card used in the operation when presented to him in payment for goods or services.'

It is not in dispute that Diners and CSL do carry on credit card or charge card operations and that the authorised establishments do accept the cards used in the relevant operations *c* when presented to them in payment for goods or services. Accordingly, the question is whether Diners and CSL make any supply to the authorised establishment in connection with the relevant credit card or charge card operation.

Section 1 of the 1983 Act provides for a tax to be known as value added tax to be charged on the supply of goods and services in the United Kingdom, including anything treated as such a supply. Section 2(2) provides that a taxable supply is a supply of goods *d* or services made in the United Kingdom other than an exempt supply. Section 3 provides, by sub-s (1), that Sch 2 shall apply for determining what is, or is to be treated as, a supply of goods or a supply of services, but no one has so far found anything in Sch 2 that assists in the present case. Section 3 goes on, however, to provide, by sub-s (2), as follows:
                                                                                        *e*
'. . . (a) "supply" in this Act includes all forms of supply, but not anything done otherwise than for a consideration; (b) anything which is not a supply of goods but is done for a consideration (including, if so done, the granting, assignment or surrender of any right) is a supply of services.'

The words in para (b) 'anything which . . . is done for a consideration' are prima facie *f* enormously wide and almost all-embracing. The Crown concedes, however, that the payment of money by the customer as the consideration for a supply of goods or a supply of services is not itself to be regarded either as a supply of goods or as a supply of services; it is not even an exempt supply within the phrase used in item 1 in Group 5 of Sch 6: 'The issue, transfer or receipt of, or any dealing with, money, any security for money or any note or order for the payment of money.' The concession extends, as I understand it, to the payment of the consideration or price for a supply of goods or services by cheque, *g* as well as to payment in cash by coin of the realm and banknotes.

The taxpayer companies, Diners and CSL, say that the Crown's concession is right because the scheme of the 1983 Act draws a distinction, particularly in ss 3(2) and 10, between the supply of goods or services and the consideration for the supply. It would be inconsistent with the scheme of the Act, it is suggested, for the consideration and the *h* supply both to rank as supplies. The taxpayer companies accordingly say that, under the schemes which they have set up, the authorised establishments make equitable assignments to the taxpayer companies of the rights which they had or would have had against the customers, the cardholders, if they, the establishments, had not accepted payment from the cardholders by the use of credit cards or charge cards. The taxpayer companies say that these equitable assignments constitute a supply of services by the *j* authorised establishments to the taxpayer companies, and that all else is but the consideration for that supply and therefore not itself a supply of services or supply of anything else.

Before, however, there were any such equitable assignments there was an antecedent

agreement between the card company and the establishment under which alone the
*a* establishment became entitled to take part in the credit card or charge card operation at
all. It is from that antecedent agreement that the position must be considered. What
happened is clearly shown, in CSL's case, by the terms of CSL's Beefeater scheme
established with Whitbread. There was an agreement between CSL and Whitbread under
which CSL agreed to issue charge cards in an agreed form to cardholders, to renew those
cards and to operate the scheme (ie a charge card scheme for Whitbread) in an efficient
*b* and businesslike manner at the expense, except as otherwise provided, of CSL and make
the appropriate discounted payments to scheme members. Each authorised establishment
had to become a scheme member and execute an accession agreement accepting the
terms of the master agreement. In those circumstances there was, in my judgment, a
supply of services by CSL in setting up and running the scheme and making discounted
payments to the scheme members and it was a supply to all the scheme members as well
*c* as to Whitbread. The value for value added tax purposes of the service supplied to the
authorised establishments as scheme members is properly to be taken, in my judgment,
as the amount of the discounts earned by CSL from operating the scheme with those
scheme members.

The agreement between Diners and an authorised establishment is less explicit than
the CSL scheme, because the Diners scheme is general and not specially designed for the
*d* requirements of a particular company and its subsidiaries or franchisees. But the legal
analysis is, in my judgment, the same. The starting point is the agreement between
Diners and the establishment, and there is no doubt at all, in my judgment, that Diners
provides services to the establishment under the agreement, including, but not limited
to, the payment of the discounted sums in advance of any payment by the cardholder to
Diners. The tripartite arrangement is of course beneficial to all three parties, Diners and
*e* the establishment and the cardholder; the benefits for the establishment are that it gets
the custom of the cardholder, who might have preferred to go elsewhere if the
establishment was not prepared to accept the Diners card, and also, if the amount of the
cardholder's bill exceeds the limit of a bank cheque card, that the establishment gets the
guarantee of discounted payment by Diners.

I therefore find it unnecessary to decide whether the notion embodied in the
*f* documents of an equitable assignment to the card company of the liability of the
cardholder to the establishment is capable of existing in law where the liability of the
cardholder only arises at the point of payment when at the same time he produces his
credit card or charge card. I have assumed that even in such circumstances there could
be an equitable assignment as claimed; but it makes no difference to the outcome. I
gratefully adopt the general analysis of credit card transactions by Sir Nicolas Browne-
*g* Wilkinson V-C in *Re Charge Card Services Ltd* [1988] 3 All ER 702, [1988] 3 WLR 764.
The credit card or charge card transaction differs fundamentally from the usual factoring
arrangement whereby a company factors its debts, in that under a credit card or charge
card arrangement the principal debtor, the cardholder, assumes direct liability to the card
company when he uses his card, to the exclusion of liability to the original creditor.

*h* Finally, I am somewhat chary of the words used by Kennedy J at the end of his
judgment ([1988] 2 All ER 1016 at 1023):

'For the purposes of value added tax it is the reality which matters and the taxation
authorities are not necessaily bound by the words used by the contracting parties.'

In any tax context such an approach is at best over-simplified. I much prefer the approach
*j* of Ralph Gibson J in *Customs and Excise Comrs v Pippa-Dee Parties Ltd* [1981] STC 495 at
501 when he said:

'The approach of the court was thus . . . to look at the entire transaction as revealed
by the terms of the contract . . . The meaning of "entire transaction" for this purpose

must be objectively determined upon the facts of the transaction by reference to the terms agreed.'

Accordingly, I too agree that this appeal should be dismissed.

*Appeal dismissed. Leave to appeal to the House of Lords refused.*

Solicitors: *Allen & Overy* (for the taxpayer companies); *Solicitor for the Customs and Excise.*

L I Zysman Esq    Barrister.

*Applied in* Robertson v Banham & Co (a firm)
[1997] 1 All ER 79

# Barclays Bank of Swaziland Ltd v Hahn

HOUSE OF LORDS

LORD KEITH OF KINKEL, LORD BRIGHTMAN, LORD TEMPLEMAN, LORD GRIFFITHS AND LORD LOWRY
27 APRIL, 18 MAY 1989

*Practice – Service – Service through letter box – Writ for service on defendant within jurisdiction – Defendant absent from jurisdiction when copy writ inserted through letter box – Defendant arriving within jurisdiction two hours later – Defendant learning that special messenger had delivered envelope to his flat – Defendant leaving country next day without picking up envelope – Whether defendant required to be within jurisdiction when service effected through letter box – RSC Ord 10, r 1(2)(b).*

*Practice – Service – Service through letter box – Date of service – Deemed date of service – Writ – Writ served through letter box deemed to be served on seventh day after date on which letter inserted through letter box 'unless the contrary is shown' – Defendant absent from jurisdiction when copy writ inserted through letter box – Defendant arriving within jurisdiction two hours later – Defendant learning that special messenger had delivered envelope to his flat – Defendant leaving country next day without picking up envelope – Whether deemed date of service displaced – RSC Ord 10, r 1(3)(a).*

The plaintiff bank issued a writ within the jurisdiction against the defendant, a South African national, to recover moneys under a guarantee. The defendant had a flat in England where he stayed for three months of the year on average and the bank purported to effect service of the writ on him under RSC Ord 10, r 1(2)(b)[a] by inserting it through the letter box of the flat. The defendant was out of the country at the time but two hours later he arrived at an airport in England where he was met by the caretaker of the flat, who informed him that a special messenger had called at the flat that afternoon and had put an envelope through the letter box. Instead of going to the flat as he had intended the defendant stayed at a nearby hotel. His wife went to the flat but did not open the envelope; she then joined her husband at the hotel. The defendant left the country the next day. The defendant contended that the writ had not been duly served on him because, in making provision for a 'writ for service on a defendant within the jurisdiction' to be served by inserting it through a letter box in a sealed envelope, Ord 10, r 1(2)(b) was referring to a defendant who was within the jurisdiction and the defendant had not been physically present within the jurisdiction at the time the envelope was inserted through his letter box. The master held that service had not been properly effected and on appeal by the bank his decision was affirmed by the judge. The bank appealed to the Court of Appeal, which allowed its appeal, holding that Ord 10, r 1(2)(b) did not require the presence of the defendant within the jurisdiction since the words 'A writ for service on a

---

a   Rule 1, so far as material, is set out at p 400 g to p 401 a, post

a defendant within the jurisdiction' were descriptive of the writ and its service and not of the defendant. The defendant appealed to the House of Lords.

**Held** – On its true construction RSC Ord 10, r 1(2)(*b*) required the defendant to be physically present within the jurisdiction at the time service was effected by inserting it through a letter box in a sealed envelope, since 'within the jurisdiction' in r 1(2) referred to the defendant and not to the writ or its service. However, since under Ord 10, r 1(3)(*a*)
b the date of service effected under r 1(2) was the seventh day after the date on which the copy writ was inserted through the letter box 'unless the contrary is shown', a plaintiff or a defendant could displace the deemed date of service by proving that the defendant had acquired knowledge of the writ at some other date. In the circumstances the bank had shown that the copy writ had come to the defendant's knowledge when he was within the jurisdiction, ie immediately after his arrival at the airport in England. If followed
c therefore that the writ had been properly served on him under Ord 10, r 1(2)(*b*) on that day. The appeal would therefore be dismissed (see p 399 *h*, p 402 *c* to *e g* to *j* and p 403 *a* to *f*, post).

Decision of the Court of Appeal [1989] 1 All ER 193 affirmed on other grounds.

**Notes**
d For service of process by insertion through letter box, see 37 Halsbury's Laws (4th edn) para 152, and for cases on substituted service, see 37(2) Digest (Reissue) 263, *1711–1714*.

**Appeal**
John Aneck Hahn appealed with the leave of the Appeal Committee of the House of Lords given on 16 January 1989 against the decision of the Court of Appeal (Fox, Parker
e and Croom-Johnson LJJ) ([1989] 1 All ER 193, [1989] 1 WLR 13) on 3 August 1988 allowing the appeal of the respondents, Barclays Bank of Swaziland Ltd (the bank), a company incorporated under the laws of Swaziland, against the order of Sir Neil Lawson sitting as a judge of the High Court in the Queen's Bench Division in chambers on 28 January 1988 whereby he dismissed the appellant's appeal from the order made by Deputy Master Ashton on 7 October 1987 declaring that a writ issued on 16 December
f 1986 by the bank against the appellant had not been duly served on the appellant and that therefore the court had no jurisdiction to hear the bank's claim. The facts are set out in the opinion of Lord Brightman.

*Winston Roddick QC* and *Michael Soole* for the appellant.
*Conrad Dehn QC* and *Michael Brindle* for the bank.
g
Their Lordships took time for consideration.

18 May. The following opinions were delivered.

h **LORD KEITH OF KINKEL.** My Lords, I have had the opportunity of considering in draft the speech to be delivered by my noble and learned friend Lord Brightman. I agree with it, and for the reasons given by him would dismiss the appeal.

**LORD BRIGHTMAN.** My Lords, the question before your Lordships is the validity of the service of a writ on the appellant, Mr Hahn. The mode of service adopted by the
j respondent bank's solicitors was the insertion of the copy writ through the letter box of the appellant's home at Amersham. At that particular moment it so happened that the appellant was outside the jurisdiction, though he came within the jurisdiction some two hours later. The appellant claims that such service was ineffective owing to his absence from the jurisdiction at the material time.

The appellant is a national of the Republic of South Africa. He has, however, a home

in England, consisting of a flat near Amersham in Buckinghamshire, which his wife has
rented since 1985. Having been accepted by the Revenue as a non-resident for tax *a*
purposes, the appellant does not stay in England for more than six months in any tax
year; on average he is here for some three months in the year, although sometimes
longer.

The respondents, Barclays Bank of Swaziland Ltd, claim that in 1982 the appellant
executed a deed guaranteeing the banking account of a company called Swaziland
Chemical Industries (Pty) Ltd. That company went into liquidation in 1984 owing (it is *b*
said) some £12m to the bank. The bank sought payment from the appellant and issued
proceedings against him in South Africa. Those proceedings were abandoned owing to
difficulties of service. On 16 December 1986 the bank issued a writ against the appellant
in this country for recovery of the money. In January 1987 leave was obtained to serve
the writ out of the jurisdiction but it did not prove possible to effect service. The bank
then sought to serve the appellant in England.                                          *c*

RSC Ord 10, r 1, to which I will refer in detail later, enables a writ, instead of being
served personally, in certain circumstances to be served by inserting through the letter
box of the defendant's usual or last-known address a copy of the writ enclosed in a sealed
envelope addressed to the defendant. On 14 April 1987 a person acting on behalf of the
bank's solicitors attended at the appellant's home with an envelope containing a copy of
the writ. The door was opened by Mr Symonds, the caretaker, who said that the appellant *d*
was not there but might be arriving later in the day. The solicitors' representative then
put the envelope containing the copy writ through the letter box and left. This occurred
at about 1530 hrs.

The appellant and his wife had left South Africa on 12 April en route for England and
were due to arrive at Heathrow at about 1730 hrs on 14 April. Mr Symonds and his wife
had already prepared the flat for occupation by them when the solicitors' representative *e*
called. Shortly thereafter Mr Symonds drove to the airport to fetch the appellant and his
wife. At the start of their journey home Mr Symonds told the appellant that a man had
called at the flat that afternoon and put through the letter box an envelope addressed to
him, which Mr Symonds stated he had not opened. On receiving this news the appellant
instructed Mr Symonds to drive to the White Hart Hotel at Beaconsfield, where the car *f*
dropped the appellant. The appellant's wife continued on to the flat, where she was
shown the envelope. She then returned to the White Hart at about 1945 hrs, and both of
them proceeded to the Holiday Inn near Heathrow for the night. The appellant left
Heathrow the following day for Geneva, without having visited the flat then or at any
later time in that year.

The terms of Ord 10, r 1, so far as material for present purposes, are as follows:    *g*

'(1) A writ must be served personally on each defendant by the plaintiff or his
agent.
(2) A writ for service on a defendant within the jurisdiction may, instead of being
served personally on him, be served—(*a*) by sending a copy of the writ by ordinary
first-class post to the defendant at his usual or last known address, or (*b*) if there is a *h*
letter box for that address, by inserting through the letter box a copy of the writ
enclosed in a sealed envelope addressed to the defendant. In sub-paragraph (*a*) "first-
class post" means first-class post which has been pre-paid or in respect of which
prepayment is not required.
(3) Where a writ is served in accordance with paragraph (2)—(*a*) the date of
service shall, unless the contrary is shown, be deemed to be the seventh day . . . after *j*
the date on which the copy was sent to or, as the case may be, inserted through the
letter box for the address in question; (*b*) any affidavit proving due service of the
writ must contain a statement to the effect that—(i) in the opinion of the deponent
(or, if the deponent is the plaintiff's solicitor or an employee of that solicitor, in the
opinion of the plaintiff) the copy of the writ, if sent to, or, as the case may be,

a

inserted through the letter box for, the address in question, will have come to the knowledge of the defendant within 7 days thereafter; and (ii) in the case of service by post, the copy of the writ has not been returned to the plaintiff through the post undelivered to the addressee . . .'

It is the appellant's claim that the writ was not duly served on him because on its true construction Ord 10, r 1(2)(b) requires that the defendant shall be physically present within the jurisdiction at the time of service, and the appellant was outside the jurisdiction

b

when the envelope was inserted through his letter box. Put shortly, it was argued on the appellant's behalf that the jurisdiction of the court to entertain an action in personam depended historically on the defendant being served personally with the King's writ. When the Rules of the Supreme Court were amended in 1979 to permit 'letter box service', it was not intended to alter the substantive jurisdictional requirement that the

c

defendant be physically present within the jurisdiction at the time of service, but merely to provide an alternative to the procedural requirement that the defendant be handed the process personally. Physical presence within the jurisdiction at the time of service remained an essential ingredient of valid service. Under para (2)(b) the time of service is the time when the envelope is inserted through the letter box. The appellant was not, at that time, in England. Therefore the writ was not duly served. This argument was

d

accepted by the master and upheld on appeal by the High Court judge. The result, your Lordships were told, would be the same even if contrary to the appellant's submission the writ were deemed to be served a week later by virtue of para (3)(c), since the appellant remained outside the jurisdiction.

The bank contended that, although a writ can be served on a defendant personally only if he is then physically present within the jurisdiction, nevertheless it does not

e

follow that physical presence within the jurisdiction is necessary for the validity of the alternative means of service provided by Ord 10, namely postal or letter-box service. In support of this argument it was contended that, in the opening words of para (2) 'A writ for service on a defendant within the jurisdiction may . . . be served' by post or letter box, the words 'within the jurisdiction' are not descriptive of 'a defendant' but of the nature of 'a writ for service', namely a writ which is in the form of a writ for service within the

f

jurisdiction as distinct from a writ which is in the form of a writ for service outside the jurisdiction. The former type of writ can properly be served on a defendant who is outside the jurisdiction provided that the requirements of the order are fulfilled, that is to say, in the case of letter-box service, the letter box must be located at the usual address of the defendant, or at his last known address, and the plaintiff must be in a position to depose when he seeks to prove service that in his opinion the copy writ will have come

g

to the knowledge of the defendant within seven days after such insertion.

The bank's argument was accepted by the Court of Appeal. As Fox LJ said ([1989] 1 All ER 193 at 195–196, [1989] 1 WLR 13 at 16–17):

'It seems to me that the words "A writ for service on a defendant within the jurisdiction" are descriptive of the writ and its service and not of the defendant. In

h

my opinion they are directed at the distinction between a writ for service within the jurisdiction and one for service out of the jurisdiction . . . The result, in my opinion, is that the language of Ord 10 does not require the presence of the defendant within the jurisdiction when the envelope containing a copy writ is put through the letter box or is posted . . . It is important to observe that we are not dealing with a situation in which service is effectively permissible on persons having no real connection with

j

this country. In this respect I am not troubled by the example of service through the letter box at the last-known address of a person who has not entered this country for, say, 20 years . . . These provisions [para (3)(b) of r 1 of Ord 10], it seems to me, protect the person who has ceased to have any real connection with the address at which the service is made. The opinion that is required to be sworn to on behalf of the plaintiff, involving, as it does, the likelihood that the writ will come to the knowledge of the defendant within seven days, assumes a substantial degree of contact with this country on the part of the defendant served.'

a

The absurdity which would flow from the appellant's argument was highlighted in the judgment of Parker LJ ([1989] 1 All ER 193 at 196, [1989] 1 WLR 13 at 18):

'. . . if one had a defendant living in the northern part of Cumbria, who was regularly in the habit of crossing the border for his lunch, it appears to me to make a complete nonsense of the whole matter if he were able to say that service had been b bad because at the time when the letter had been put through the letter box or at the time when it had been posted he had happened to be in the southern part of Scotland for no more than an hour.'

Before your Lordships the appellant sought to advance an alternative argument that a defendant on whom it is sought to effect service within the jurisdiction must be within c the jurisdiction at the time of the issue of the writ, when the appellant was also abroad. There is no judicial authority to support this novel proposition and it was not pressed.

My Lords, I accept the appellant's proposition that the defendant must be within the jurisdiction at the time when the writ is served, and I do not find it possible to agree the Court of Appeal's approach. This approach would mean that a writ could validly be served under Ord 10 on a defendant who had once had an address in England but had d permanently left this country and settled elsewhere by inserting the copy writ through the letter box of his last address, provided that the plaintiff was able within seven days to communicate to the defendant the existence of the copy writ; for in such circumstances the plaintiff could properly depose that the copy writ would have come to the knowledge of the defendant within seven days after it was left in the letter box of his last known address. This appears to me to outflank Ord 11 (relating to service of process outside the e jurisdiction) in every case where the defendant was formerly resident in this country and is capable of being contacted abroad within seven days. I feel no doubt that the words 'within the jurisdiction' apply to the defendant, and not to the writ for service.

My Lords, I entirely applaud the common sense of the decision of the Court of Appeal, but I prefer to reach the same destination by another route. I think that the clue to the problem is to be found in para (3)(a) of Ord 10, r 1. This provides, inter alia, that the date f of service is to be the seventh day after the date on which the copy writ was inserted through the letter box for the address in question 'unless the contrary is shown'. It follows from the exception that there may be circumstances where the date of service is not the date of letter-box insertion. I therefore ask myself: in what circumstances might a plaintiff or defendant be able to show that the seventh day after the date of insertion through the letter box was not the date of service; do such circumstances exist in the g present case; and, if so, what date of service takes the place of the deemed date of service?

My Lords, in the case of letter-box service I can think of nothing which is capable of giving content to the expression 'unless the contrary is shown' save that it refers to the defendant's knowledge of the existence of the writ, nor was the appellant's counsel able to suggest any other solution. Indeed, it is the obvious solution because the purpose of serving a writ is to give the defendant knowledge of the existence of proceedings against h him; that is exactly what a defendant acquires when a writ is served on him personally; and it is exactly what I would expect that procedural rules would require when service is impersonal and not personal.

So I answer the first question which I have posed by saying that a plaintiff or a defendant may displace the deemed date of service by proving that the defendant acquired knowledge of the writ at some other date. j

I turn therefore to my second question, and ask myself whether in the instant case the bank can 'show the contrary', ie establish that the deemed date of service (namely 21 April) ought to be displaced by some other date. In my opinion the answer is clearly Yes, and that date is 14 April. For on that day, after the appellant had landed at Heathrow,

he acquired knowledge of the copy writ. I appreciate that there is no admission by the
a appellant that he knew of the writ, and that there is no finding of fact to that effect. But
the existence of that knowledge is transparently clear. The appellant was intending to
drive to the flat. He is informed by Mr Symonds of the existence of the envelope and of
the circumstances of its delivery. He then changes course and does not go to the flat. But
his wife goes there, looks at the envelope but does not open it. The appellant stays the
night at a hotel near Heathrow and takes a flight out of England on the next day. Why
b did the appellant take such care to stay away from the envelope? Obviously an important
envelope, because it was to his knowledge delivered by special messenger. Why did he
not open the envelope or ask his wife to open it? Because he knew perfectly well what it
contained. There is no other conceivable reason nor was the appellant's counsel able to
suggest one.

In the result the bank is able to show the contrary, and establish without a scintilla of
c doubt that the copy writ came to the knowledge of the appellant late in the afternoon of
14 April, when he was within the jurisdiction. The writ was therefore properly served
on him under Ord 10, r 1(2)(b) on that day.

For the reasons which I have suggested to your Lordships, I would dismiss this appeal
with costs, although my reasoning differs from that of the Court of Appeal.

d **LORD TEMPLEMAN.** My Lords, for the reasons given in the speech of my noble
and learned friend Lord Brightman, I would dismiss this appeal.

**LORD GRIFFITHS.** My Lords, I have had the advantage of reading the speech of my
noble and learned friend Lord Brightman. I agree with it and would dismiss the appeal.

e **LORD LOWRY.** My Lords, I have had the advantage of reading in draft the speech of
my noble and learned friend Lord Brightman.

I agree with it and, for the reasons which he gives, I, too, would dismiss the appeal.

*Appeal dismissed.*

f Solicitors: *Hart Brown & Co*, Guildford (for the appellant); *Lovell White Durrant* (for the
bank).

Mary Rose Plummer    Barrister.

# Ali & Fahd Shobokshi Group Ltd v Moneim and others

*a*

CHANCERY DIVISION
MERVYN DAVIES J
20, 21, 22, 23 FEBRUARY, I MARCH 1989

*b*

*Practice – Pre-trial or post-judgment relief – Mareva injunction – Ex parte application – Duty of applicant to disclose material facts – Non-disclosure of material facts – Consequences of non-disclosure – Plaintiff company obtaining ex parte injunction against defendant alleging three instances of fraud – Plaintiff company and defendant engaging in complicated financial transactions over period of years – Plaintiff company not disclosing full extent of financial dealings between parties when applying for injunction – Plaintiff company applying inter partes for* c *continuation of injunction until after trial – Whether injunction should be continued – Whether complaint of non-disclosure and issue of appropriate relief should be considered as soon as defendant able to show material non-disclosure.*

The plaintiff was a Saudi trading company owned by two brothers. The defendant M was manager of its finance department. The plaintiff claimed that M had misappropriated *d* company funds during the course of his employment and it brought an action against him and others to recover the misappropriated money and for an account. The plaintiff subsequently applied ex parte for a Mareva injunction to restrain M from removing any of his assets out of the jurisdiction or dealing with any of his assets within the jurisdiction except to the extent that their value exceeded £250,000. The ex parte application was supported by evidence alleging three isolated instances of fraud totalling £271,904·24 *e* together with certain financial irregularities, but no explanation was given of the background of the financial dealings against which the three specific claims were made. On 21 September 1988 an injunction was granted in the terms sought until 19 October. The plaintiff then issued a notice of motion seeking to continue the injunction against M alone until after judgment except to the extent that his assets exceeded £621,904. At the *f* inter partes hearing of the motion the question arose whether continuation of a Mareva order should be refused on the grounds that the ex parte order had been obtained without proper disclosure of the material facts and, if so, whether any complaint of non-disclosure should be dealt with after the trial of the action, thereby limiting M's relief to damages for non-disclosure. M alleged that over the years a series of complicated accounting transactions had taken place between the plaintiff, M and the two brothers controlling *g* the plaintiff and that if an account was taken M might well be shown to be owed money by the plaintiff. M contended that it was misleading for the plaintiff to allege on the ex parte application three isolated instances of fraud without reference to the context in which those transactions had taken place.

**Held** – Where an applicant had obtained a Mareva injunction ex parte without proper *h* disclosure of material facts the court would refuse to continue the order if the non-disclosure was not innocent, in the sense that there had been an intention to omit or withhold material information, and the injunction would not have been granted if full disclosure had been made. Having regard to the fact that on the ex parte application the plaintiff had alleged three isolated instances of fraud without giving any account of the complex financial transactions which had been conducted between the parties over the *j* years, it was reasonable to conclude (a) that the plaintiff had intended not to disclose the fact that the plaintiff, M and the two brothers controlling the plaintiff had engaged in complex financial dealings and (b) that an injunction would not have been granted if a true picture of the parties' financial dealings had been given. Accordingly, the plaintiff's motion would be dismissed and the Mareva injunction discharged (see p 413 a to c and p 415 b c, post).

Dictum of Nourse LJ in *Behbehani v Salem* [1989] 2 All ER 143 at 156 applied.

*a*   Per curiam. As soon as a defendant can show non-disclosure of a substantial kind he should be at liberty to require the discharge of an ex parte Mareva injunction (without it being immediately reimposed) and to seek damages for non-disclosure without having to wait until after trial since at that point damages might be an entirely inadequate remedy (see p 414 *h j*, post); dicta of Donaldson LJ in *Bank Mellat v Nikpour* [1985] FSR 87 at 92 and of Sir John Donaldson MR in *Eastglen International Corp v Monpare SA* (1986)

*b*   137 NLJ 56 applied; *Dormeuil Frères SA v Nicolian International (Textiles) Ltd* [1988] 3 All ER 197 not followed.

### Notes

For Mareva injunctions, see 37 Halsbury's Laws (4th edn) para 362, and for cases on the subject, see 37(2) Digest (Reissue) 474–476, 2947–2962.

*c*

### Cases referred to in judgment

*Bank Mellat v Nikpour* [1985] FSR 87, CA.

*Behbehani v Salem* [1989] 2 All ER 143, CA.

*Brink's-MAT Ltd v Elcombe* [1988] 3 All ER 188, [1988] 1 WLR 1350, CA.

*Derby & Co Ltd v Weldon (No 1)* [1989] 1 All ER 469, [1989] 2 WLR 276, CA.

*d*   *Dormeuil Frères SA v Nicolian International (Textiles) Ltd* [1988] 3 All ER 197, [1988] 1 WLR 1362.

*Eastglen International Corp v Monpare SA* (1986) 137 NLJ 56, CA.

*Lloyds Bowmaker Ltd v Britannia Arrow Holdings plc (Lavens, third party)* [1988] 3 All ER 178, [1988] 1 WLR 1337, CA.

*R v Kensington Income Tax Comrs, ex p Princess Edmond de Polignac* [1917] 1 KB 486, CA.

*e*   *Thermax Ltd v Schott Industrial Glass Ltd* [1981] FSR 289.

*Yardley & Co Ltd v Higson* [1984] FSR 304, CA.

*Z Ltd v A* [1982] 1 All ER 556, [1982] QB 558, [1982] 2 WLR 288, CA.

### Cases also cited

*Bir v Sharma* (1988) Times, 7 December.

*f*   *EMI Records Ltd v Ian Cameron Wallace Ltd* [1982] 2 All ER 980, [1983] Ch 59.

*Ushers Brewery Ltd v P S King & Co (Finance) Ltd* [1971] 2 All ER 468, [1972] Ch 148.

### Motion

By writ issued on 19 September 1988 the plaintiff, Ali & Fahd Shobokshi Group Ltd (the group), a company incorporated in Saudi Arabia, brought an action against (1)

*g*   Mohammed Sayed Abdel Moneim, (2) his wife, Eitemad I A Khalil and (3) Ametry SA, a Swiss company alleged to be controlled by Mr Moneim, claiming money relief on the ground that Mr Moneim had appropriated moneys belonging to the group. Bank of America National Trust and Savings Association was added as a fourth defendant because of an account held at the bank by Mr Moneim. On 21 September 1988 Peter Gibson J heard an ex parte application by the group for a Mareva injunction and made an order

*h*   restraining Mr Moneim until 19 October 1988 from removing any of his assets out of the jurisdiction or dealing with any of his assets within the jurisdiction except and so far as the value of those assets exceeded £250,000. On 27 September 1988 the group subsequently brought an inter partes motion against Mr Moneim alone, seeking to continue the Mareva injunction until after judgment except and so far as the value of his assets exceeded £10m, later amended to read £621,904. The second, third and fourth

*j*   defendants took no part in the hearing of the motion. The facts are set out in the judgment.

*Vivian Chapman* for the group.
*Richard Slowe* for Mr Moneim.

*Cur adv vult*

1 March. The following judgment was delivered.

**MERVYN DAVIES J.** This is an inter partes hearing of a Mareva application. A writ was issued on 19 September 1988. The plaintiff is Ali & Fahd Shobokshi Group Ltd (the group), incorporated in Saudi Arabia. The original defendants were Mohammed Sayed Abdel Moneim, Eitemad·I A Khalil and a Swiss company said to be controlled by Mr Moneim, Ametry SA. A fourth defendant has been added, Bank of America National Trust and Savings Association (Bank of America). I am concerned only with the first defendant, Mr Moneim, since the principal notice of motion before me dated 27 September 1988 seeks Mareva relief only against that defendant. There is a second notice of motion before me dated 21 October 1988 where certain disclosure orders and the like are sought against the Bank of America; but that relief is opposed, at any rate for present and practical purposes, only by Mr Moneim. The claim in the writ is for money relief. Mr Moneim is said to have appropriated money belonging to the group. Various accounts are sought.

On 21 September 1988 Peter Gibson J heard an ex parte application for Mareva relief. The application was supported by an affidavit of Sheikh Fahd sworn on 20 September. Sheikh Fahd is a director of the plaintiff group. It appears that Mr Moneim became employed by the group in 1974. He was third in authority in the group following Sheikh Fadh and his brother, Sheikh Ali. He ceased to be employed by the group either in 1984 or in 1988. There is no clear evidence as yet on that point. However, over the years following 1974 Mr Moneim was manager for the group of its banking, investment and accounts department. Sheikh Fahd and his brother, Sheikh Ali, were content to entrust the control of banking, investment and accounting to Mr Moneim.

I have not been able to form a very clear idea of the group's activities but it seems that they have been extensive and in many parts of the world. In his affidavit Sheikh Fahd says that the group employed Mr Moneim until July 1988. At about that time the brothers became aware of Mr Moneim having been arrested in Egypt on various charges relating to taxation, customs duties and corruption. Mr Moneim is on bail in Egypt but is not allowed to leave that country. I am told that Mr Moneim strenuously contests the charges. At any rate the brothers then decided to investigate their accounts. These investigations have led the brothers to believe that Mr Moneim has appropriated three separate sums of money belonging to the group as well as committing other financial irregularities.

As to these separate sums there is first said to be a sum of £62,000. A cheque for that sum dated 19 September 1983 and drawn on the group is said to have been paid into Mr Moneim's private account with the Bank of America. The drawing of the cheque was authorised by Mr Moneim although signed by Mr Fawzi, another employee. The £62,000 is said to have related to moneys sent by the group to the group's account at Barclays Bank plc in London for the purpose of satisfying a loan in US dollars made by the Nordic Bank of Finland. The money sent was £1,274,922 and a further sum of £139,993. The loan was paid off in the sum of £1,319,368·47. In the result, taking account of interest and legal fees, it is said that £84,586·96 remained in the group's account. The £62,000 is said to have been drawn from that sum.

The second sum also concerns the Nordic Bank. The group had $US50,000 on deposit there. It is said that Mr Moneim instructed Mr Fawzi to draw a cheque on the account in favour of him (Mr Moneim). The money on deposit was remitted by Nordic to Barclays Bank and the sum equivalent in sterling to the amount of the deposit was paid into Mr Moneim's account by a cheque signed by Mr Fawzi and dated 13 February 1984. The amount was £37,204·24.

The third sum specified was £172,700, money owed to the group in connection with some transactions in shares in Croydon Hotel and Leisure Co Ltd. I need not express detail further than to say that the managing director of the Croydon company was

a
requested by telex dated 18 April 1984 to transmit £172,700 to Mr Moneim's account at the Bank of America. It is accepted, as I understand, that £100,000 of that £172,700 may have been repaid by Mr Moneim to the group.

Paragraph 14 of the affidavit then reads:

b
'The Group's claim in this Honourable Court's jurisdiction is that the first defendant has acted in breach of his contract of employment and in breach of his fiduciary obligations to the company in that the sums of £62,000, £72,700 and £37,204·24 have been taken from the Group by the first defendant without authorisation and not returned. Also there remains the investigation of the £100,000 referred to above.'

c
The affidavit then goes on to refer to other matters. It appears that the group is suing Mr Moneim in Saudi Arabia for 66,219,909 Saudi riyals (about £10m) based on 20 separate alleged misappropriations of funds belonging to the group. Proceedings were issued in Jeddah on 13 September 1988. There are also proceedings against Mr Moneim by the group in Switzerland. That fact does not appear in the affidavit but counsel for the group so informed Peter Gibson J. It is then said in the affidavit that Mr Moneim has, alone or with his wife, a number of bank accounts. These include four accounts with the Bank of America, three being in Cannon Street and one in Jersey, an account at Barclays

d
Bank in Langham Place, two accounts at Lloyd Bank International in London, together, it is believed, with accounts in London at Merrill Lynch, Manufacturers Hanover and the Swiss Bank Corp. The group expresses a belief that the money in those accounts is derived from its funds. As well, Mr Moneim's private residence in London, held in the name of Ametry SA (a company said to be wholly controlled by Mr Moneim), is said to have been purchased with funds derived from the group.

e
In para 22 the affidavit then discloses that the group and both the brothers are themselves the subject of Mareva orders. There is an order dated 29 January 1987 against the group and Sheikh Ali made at the instance of American Express Bank Ltd. There is an order against Sheikh Fahd dated 9 October 1986, as varied on 18 February 1987, this again at the instance of American Express. Those Mareva orders affect, as I understand, assets in England. That being so, and to support a cross-undertaking in damages for the

f
purposes of the present application, the group has caused funds outside England worth £25,000 to be paid into a Swiss account to stand security for any such damages. The account is now in joint names, with Mr Moneim's solicitors being one of the names.

There are 25 exhibits to the affidavit. I will mention some of them. The second is an accountant's report prepared in Saudi Arabia and dated 13 September 1988. It suggests misappropriation by Mr Moneim in the sum of 66,218,909 Saudi riyals. The third is a

g
report of an internal audit in London dated 19 September 1988. It draws attention to an alleged misappropriation of the three specific sums I have already mentioned. The eighteenth is a 29-page translation of a petition by the group to the authorities in Saudi Arabia with a view to Mr Moneim being taken to Saudi Arabia (from Cairo) for trial. The petition itemises 19 'facts' amounting to allegations of irregularities concerning 19 sums. Each of these sums is of a substantial amount: thus fact 1 mentions $US180,625,

h
fact 2 mentions $US1,200,515 and fact 3 $US800,000 etc. The twenty-fifth exhibit is a list of bank accounts worldwide said to be held by Mr Moneim in places such as London, Paris, Cairo, New Mexico, Geneva etc. I need not mention the other exhibits. I was told that Peter Gibson J had those documents overnight and while they were not all read in extenso before him I was told that counsel referred to them or some of them in the course of the ex parte application.

j
On that evidence (and some exhibits I need not mention) Peter Gibson J on 21 September 1988 made an ex parte order until 19 October 1988 restraining Mr Moneim from removing any of his assets from out of the jurisdiction or dealing with any of his assets inside the jurisdiction except and so far as the value of the assets exceeded £250,000.

Fifteen bank accounts were mentioned as subject to the order. It seems that sum of £250,000 was fixed by reference to the sum of the three specific amounts that I have mentioned (£271,904·24 less the £100,000 that may have been repaid) together with a margin for costs.

Following the making of the ex parte order the plaintiff group issued a notice of motion returnable on 19 October 1988. The motion in effect seeks the continuing of a Mareva order until after judgment except and so far as the value of Mr Moneim's assets exceed £10m. This is the motion now before me save to say that the £10m has been amended to read £621,904. The motion was before Knox J on 19 October 1988. A detailed order was made by consent continuing the Mareva order in force until the effective hearing of the motion.

After some other interlocutory applications which I need not mention there was an ex parte application before Vinelott J on 14 December 1988. The group sought to increase the sum of £250,000 already mentioned and to obtain a banker's trust order. The application failed. The judge was critical of the application and said it was wholly misconceived. He referred to the fact that Mr Moneim intended to apply for the Mareva order to be set aside altogether on the ground of non-disclosure. Since that time applications on various matters (such as security, time etc) have been before a number of judges. However, those need not now be considered. In the mean time and since that time affidavit evidence has been filed. There are on a quick count about 41 affidavits, with bulky exhibits, including five affidavits by Sheikh Fahd and another five by Mr Moneim. They appear before me in seven lever arch files. Viewing them I called to mind the words of Parker LJ in *Derby & Co Ltd v Weldon (No 1)* [1989] 1 All ER 469 at 475, [1989] 2 WLR 276 at 283 to the effect that very long interlocutory applications with documents of thousands of pages are unwarranted. I informed counsel that I felt unable to embark on any detailed consideration of the documents before the court in that the only issues were those specified by Parker LJ.

As the matter then proceeded, it became plain that the plaintiff group might well succeed before me on all three issues, that is to say (i) I might well find that the group had a good arguable case, if not for misappropriation, at any rate for an account, (ii) it was accepted that Mr Moneim had assets within the jurisdiction and (iii) there were grounds for supposing that there might be dissipation. I suggested to counsel for Mr Moneim that, for the purposes only of the motion, these issues might be conceded by him so that the only question left before the court would be whether or not a Mareva order should be refused inter partes by reason of any non-disclosures in the course of the ex parte application before Peter Gibson J. Counsel, responsibly if I may say so, fell in with my suggestion to the extent that he said he would not oppose for the purposes of the motion the propositions (i) that there was a good arguable case, at any rate for an account, (ii) that there was a risk of dissipation and (iii) that Mr Moneim has assets in England. Thus there was left for decision only the question that I have mentioned above.

I proceed to consider the non-disclosures complained of.

(1) A reading of the affidavit of Sheikh Fahd of 20 September 1988 suggests (and I think it is accepted) that the sums of £62,000, £37,204·24 and £172,700 I have mentioned were paid into Mr Moneim's private account at the Bank of America in London. Mr Moneim's complaint is that that account was used openly and extensively for the purposes of the group's business and yet this fact was not disclosed on the ex parte application. On the contrary, Sheikh Fahd says in para 3 of his first affidavit:

'The first defendant had no authority to use his private bank accounts in connection with any of the Group's financial dealings or to facilitate the transfer of moneys between the Group and other entities.'

As against that, para 7 of an affidavit of Mr Esmat sworn on 8 December 1988 and filed on behalf of the group says:

a
'I, and I believe others in my department and the accounts department, were aware of the private account of Mr. M. S. A. Moneim with Bank of America, London and that it was used for Group's purposes. I did not inform either Sheikh Fahd Shobokshi or Sheikh Ali Shobokshi of its use for Group's purposes until after 27th July 1988 when I agreed to be appointed to a committee of Group to investigate the conduct of Mr. M. S. A. Moneim. Nor am I aware that any other employee in my department or the accounts department did so whilst Mr. M. S. A. Moneim was
b
employed with Group.'

Those observations were made after Mr Moneim in his affidavit sworn on 22 November 1988 had asserted that his Bank of America account was used for group purposes. I was taken to various entries in some of the exhibited documents which certainly seem to show that the Bank of America account was used for group purposes.

c
(2) It seems that Mr Moneim gave to each of the brothers a general power of attorney so that either could operate the Bank of America account or any other account in the name of Mr Moneim. The translation of the power is not altogether easy to read but it is, as I understand, common ground that the brothers did have a power of attorney over Mr Moneim's assets. Mr Moneim's evidence in this regard includes para 7 of his affidavit sworn on 22 November 1988. That paragraph includes these words:

d
'Often the plaintiff company did not want to pay money into accounts where banks were pressing for reduction of loans and likewise was often up against a limit on lending, whereas I could borrow money in my personal name when the plaintiff company could not. One of the matters which the plaintiff had to guard against was, of course, if anything should happen to me or I was unavailable, it would be necessary for the Shobokshi brothers to operate my bank accounts. Accordingly, I
e
gave each of them a general power of attorney on 9th May 1978 and a certified copy thereof is now produced and shown to be marked "MSAM 3" together with a translation.'

The existence of the power of attorney was not disclosed on the ex parte application.

(3) In an affidavit sworn on 5 February 1989 Mr Moneim exhibits a schedule of
f
payments out of his Bank of America account over the period 24 August 1980 to 14 January 1985. The payments out total £5,264,175·88. I was taken through some calculations derived from Sheikh Fahd's second affidavit sworn on 5 December 1988 and an exhibit thereto which, it so appears, shows that the money paid into the account was £4,888,269. I do not feel able at present to accept the accuracy of either of those figures. There is also the fact that while the first figure is related to August 1980 to January 1985,
g
the second figure may relate to some other period. However that may be, it is of interest to see the substantial sums that were paid over the years into and out of the Bank of America account to or for the group. The three specific sums relied on for the purposes of the ex parte application should, I think, have been placed in the context of the extensive use that had been made of the Bank of America account not only by Mr Moneim but also for the group's purposes. In this connection also an exhibit to the
h
affidavit of Sheikh Fahd sworn on 21 February 1989 shows the mass of transactions that had taken place between Mr Moneim and the group.

(4) It is common ground that most, if not all, of the relevant bank statements were sent to Jeddah. In his first affidavit Mr Moneim says:

j
'8. I now turn to the three specific claims made in these proceedings. All three transactions concern moneys received in my account at the Bank of America. As already said this was among several accounts which I agree the company could also use for its transactions and indeed that was the principal use of this account. Accordingly, the account address was the plaintiff company's Post Office Box 5470 in Jeddah where, along with all post, the accounts and supporting documentation

were opened by the staff and passed to the plaintiff company's accounts department
for appropriate attention. A full record was kept of all transactions and plaintiff       *a*
company's accounts department produced a full reconciliation statement. There is
now produced and shown to me marked MSAM 4 copies of the bank statements
between 31st January 1983 and 31st October 1983 . . . together with pages 51–62 of
my personal journal showing the plaintiff company's accounts department's own
reconciliation of my Bank of America account up to December 1984.'

This quotation is of interest in that on reading the affidavit used on the ex parte       *b*
application it would not appear that the details of the Bank of America account were
available to the plaintiff group. I should add that the statements of account are themselves
not very informative but pp 19, 20 and 21 of the exhibit appear specifically to refer to
the three specific sums that have been referred to.

(5) The accounting position as between the group, each of the brothers and Mr       *c*
Moneim is, as I have indicated, on the present state of the evidence very unclear. It
becomes even more so when one is told of what has been called the Misrimpex account.
In his fourth affidavit sworn on 21 February 1989 Sheikh Fahd refers to Misrimpex
stating that that is the name of a business owned by Mr Moneim in Egypt and of which
he was the sole proprietor. The affidavit exhibits a translation of the relevant pages of
Moneim's private account with the group; the original (as exhibited) covers 259 pages.       *d*
Another exhibit is the accounts of Misrimpex with the group. In para 12 of the affidavit
Sheikh Fahd says:

> 'As appears from the private account and the Misrimpex account Moneim is in
> credit on his personal account in the sum of S.R.3,867,275·05 but in debit on the
> Misrimpex account in the sum of S.R.48,750,627·44.'       *e*

As to these matters Mr Moneim's attitude is, as I understand, that there is an issue
whether the Misrimpex business belongs to him or to the group or to the brothers or in
some shares between them. If it belongs to the group he says £606,000 is owing to him.
If it belongs to him then Mr Moneim owes £7m. Obviously these matters cannot be
examined, let alone decided, at this stage. However that may be, the group on the ex
parte application in effect alleged three instances of peculation as though they could be       *f*
treated as separate fraud charges. The background of complicated accountings between
the parties was not sufficiently alluded to. The Misrimpex account, in my view,
emphasises that fact. The same remark applies as respects what is called the Nadco loan.

(6) There are serious suggestions of the group's insolvency. Mr Moneim in his first
affidavit says in para 3 that in 1984 the group owed about $US400m. The group's assets,
he says, may be worth about $US150m. In an affidavit in reply sworn on 5 December       *g*
1988 Sheikh Fahd does not directly challenge those figures and accepts that in 1984 the
group sought from its creditor banks a moratorium. So far as I was told, the position of
the group has not noticeably improved. The group's financial position was not mentioned
in the evidence used on the ex parte application, save as to the reference to the Mareva
orders made against the group and the brothers (see para 22).       *h*

(7) Mr Moneim referred to para 4 of Sheikh Fahd's first affidavit sworn on 20
September 1988. The paragraph states (as I have mentioned) that Mr Moneim was.
arrested in Eygpt and charged with corruption and other offences. A reference is made
in the paragraph to a loss of 60,000,000 Egyptian pounds. This paragraph is complained
of as being prejudicial and unfair. Thus there is no reference to the fact, known to the
group, that Mr Moneim vehemently denied the charges. Furthermore, the amount for       *j*
which Mr Moneim was said to be responsible was, as counsel for the group accepted, not
60m Egyptian pounds but between 1 m and 2m Egyptian pounds. As I have read the
evidence, the para 4 mentioned was unfairly prejudicial for the purposes of an ex parte
application.

Counsel for Mr Moneim said that there were yet more matters that were not but ought a  to have been put before the judge. I regard the matters I have itemised as being sufficient for the purposes of considering counsel's submission that the application for a Mareva order, being now inter partes, ought to be refused by reason of non-disclosures at the time of the ex parte application.

The only evidence before Peter Gibson J was the evidence of Sheikh Fahd sworn on 20 September 1988 with 25 exhibits. I have already indicated their content. Now that there has been read much of the mass of evidence filed since that time it does seem to me that b  the judge may have received an inaccurate picture of the situation existing between the group, the brothers and Mr Moneim so far as their financial dealings are concerned. The ex parte application was on the footing that three isolated sums were abstracted. The truth is that over the years the most complicated accounting transactions have been conducted between the parties. If an account is taken it may be that Mr Moneim will be shown owing money. It is not inconceivable that he will be shown as a creditor. This c  overall picture was known to the brothers and yet they fixed on three items to allege fraud. It may be, I do now know, that fraud will at some time in the future be proved. But to allege three isolated instances of fraud without reference to the complex accounting systems to which the brothers and Mr Moneim were parties seems to me to be highly unsatisfactory.

In these circumstances I turn to the authorities concerning the consequences of non-d  disclosure during ex parte applications. In *R v Kensington Income Tax Comrs, ex p Princess Edmond de Polignac* [1917] 1 KB 486 at 509 Warrington LJ said:

'It is perfectly well settled that a person who makes an ex parte application to the Court—that is to say, in the absence of the person who will be affected by that which the Court is asked to do—is under an obligation to the Court to make the fullest e  possible disclosure of all material facts within his knowledge, and if he does not make that fullest possible disclosure, then he cannot obtain any advantage from the proceedings, and he will be deprived of any advantage he may have already obtained by means of the order which has thus wrongly been obtained by him.'

However, those words do not necessarily preclude a plaintiff from applying inter partes f  for the relief wrongly obtained ex parte if on the inter partes hearing full disclosure is made. An instance of this is *Yardley & Co Ltd v Higson* [1984] FSR 304. There it emerged that an ex parte order had been made in favour of a plaintiff who had failed to disclose a material fact. When the matter became inter partes a full explanation of the non-disclosure was given. The Court of Appeal felt able to continue the ex parte order (albeit in a limited form). Lawton LJ said (at 309–310):

g  'Reference has been made to [the *Polignac* case] and also to the judgment of Browne-Wilkinson J. in *Thermax Ltd* v. *Schott Industrial Glass Ltd.* ([1981] FSR 289). The submission was made that once it is established that material facts have not been disclosed, the court ought as a matter of law to refuse equitable relief. I do not find it necessary to go into the law about this matter in any way, because it is clear that in cases of injunctions, even if there has to be a discharge of one injunction h  because there has not been proper disclosure, that does not prevent a further application for an injunction being made. I will accept for the purposes of my judgment that before Nourse J. there was a failure to make full disclosure as should have been made and that the omissions were material omissions. But after that there was a further application, and when the matter came before Goulding J. on the further application he was apprised of all the material facts and he knew what the j  situation was with regard to the soap in cartons.'

It is to be noted that in that case the failure to disclose was innocent and was dealt with in subsequent evidence (see [1984] FSR 304 at 310 per Oliver LJ).

*Bank Mellat v Nikpour* [1985] FSR 87 is a case where a Mareva order was obtained ex parte without proper disclosure. Relief was refused when the matter became inter partes.

In the Court of Appeal Lord Denning MR quotes Robert Goff J in the court below (at 89):

> 'That being so I discharge the *Mareva* injunction granted in September of this year. I am not prepared to grant a new *Mareva* injunction today since it is impossible to judge whether the money would still be here if the injunction had not been granted on the basis of the Affidavit which I have described. It would be unfair to the defendant for the Court to enable the plaintiff to renew the injunction on further evidence.'

The Court of Appeal upheld that view, so that the consequence of the plaintiff's non-disclosure was to deprive him of all Mareva relief although sought inter partes.

In *Lloyds Bowmaker Ltd v Brittania Arrow Holdings plc (Lavens, third party)* [1988] 3 All ER 178 at 183, [1988] 1 WLR 1337 at 1343 Glidewell LJ accepted that despite any initial non-disclosure the court has a discretion whether to grant a second Mareva injunction at a stage when the whole of the facts are before it 'and may well grant such a second injunction if the original non-disclosure was innocent and if an injunction could properly be granted even had the facts been disclosed' (see also [1988] 3 All ER 178 at 187, [1988] 1 WLR 1337 at 1349 per Dillon LJ). However, in that case the discretion was not exercised to maintain the Mareva in existence. *Brink's-MAT Ltd v Elcombe* [1988] 3 All ER 188, [1988] 1 WLR 1350 went the other way, an ex parte order being continued in existence after an inter partes hearing despite an initial non-disclosure. The discretion I have mentioned was fully recognised, with Balcombe LJ stating that the discretion is one to be exercised sparingly (see [1988] 3 All ER 188 at 194, [1988] 1 WLR 1350 at 1358).

I now mention *Behbehani v Salem* [1989] 2 All ER 143. This was a case in the Court of Appeal where there were considered the circumstances in which it is appropriate for the court, having discharged a Mareva injunction for non-disclosure, immediately to regrant substantially the same injunction. Nourse LJ said (at 156):

> 'I agree that in order to get at the principles of discretion on which the court acts in a case of this kind we need not now look further than the decision of this court in *Brink's-MAT Ltd v Elcombe* [1988] 3 All ER 188 at 193, [1988] 1 WLR 1350 at 1357, where they are summarised in the passage in the judgment of Ralph Gibson LJ which Woolf LJ has read. In para (vii) of that summary we find that: "The court has a discretion, notwithstanding proof of material non-disclosure which justifies or requires the immediate discharge of the ex parte order, nevertheless to continue the order, or to make a new order on terms: '. . . when the whole of the facts, including that of the original non-disclosure are before it, [the court] may well grant such a second injunction if the original non-disclosure was innocent and if an injunction could properly be granted even had the facts been disclosed.' (See *Lloyds Bowmaker Ltd v Britannia Arrow Holdings plc (Lavens, third party)* [1988] 3 All ER 178 at 183, [1988] 1 WLR 1337 at 1343–1344 per Glidewell LJ.)" Although it would not be correct to treat Glidewell LJ's statement of the circumstances in which the court may exercise its discretion as being exhaustive, it is, I think, likely to have relevance in many of these cases, and it is certainly a useful starting point in this. I should add that in the *Brink's-MAT* case all three members of this court defined an innocent non-disclosure as one where there was no intention to omit or withhold information which was thought to be material. Since it is accepted both that the non-disclosure justified or required the immediate discharge of the ex parte order and that the whole of the facts are now before the court, the questions to which we should start by addressing ourselves are, first, whether it was innocent and, second, whether an injunction could properly have been granted if full disclosure had been made to Roch J.'

So I come to the conclusion that I must consider (a) whether the non-disclosure complained of was innocent and (b) whether an injunction could properly have been

granted if full disclosure had been made to Peter Gibson J. If (a) and (b) are answered in
*a*  the affirmative, then the court has a discretion.

As to (a) I cannot regard the non-disclosure as 'innocent' as that word is explained in
the quotation above. In fastening on three comparatively small sums as the principal
foundation of the ex parte application one may, I think, readily infer that there was an
intention not to disclose, at any rate at that stage, the fact that the group and the brothers
and Mr Moneim had been engaged together in the most complex financial transactions.
*b*  As to (b) I doubt whether an order would properly have been granted if a better and truer
picture of the parties' financial dealings had been painted. The whole story would have
smacked of the need for an account rather than seeking to assert three specific claims. A
Mareva injunction is granted only if it appears likely that the plaintiff will recover a
certain or approximate sum: see *Z Ltd v A* [1982] 1 All ER 556 at 572, [1982] QB 558 at
585.

*c*  Since (a) and (b) are answered in the negative I must refuse the plaintiff group's motion
for Mareva relief. I go on to say that if I am wrong in my answers to (a) or (b) I would
exercise my discretion by refusing Mareva relief. I would do so by reference to three
principal considerations: (i) when ex parte, the group gave a misleading impression of its
financial dealings and the part that Mr Moneim played therein; (ii) the group, when inter
parties, did not attempt to explain why it was that it launched the ex parte application
*d*  with evidence that failed to explain, in however limited a way, the background of
financial dealings against which the three specific claims were made; and (iii) the
discretion is, as Balcombe LJ says, to be exercised sparingly.

It remains to mention *Dormeuil Frères SA v Nicolian International (Textiles) Ltd* [1988] 3
All ER 197, [1988] 1 WLR 1362. The *Dormeuil* case was one in which the plaintiffs
complained of the defendants' use of the trade name Dormeuil. They obtained an Anton
*e*  Piller order. They then moved inter partes for a continuation of the interim injunction
in the Anton Piller order restraining the defendants from using the trade name pending
trial. By a cross-motion the defendants sought discharge of the Anton Piller order on the
grounds of non-disclosure. The entry and search part of the order had by then been
executed. The defendants did not object to an injunction pending trial in some limited
form. Sir Nicolas Browne-Wilkinson V-C said ([1988] 3 All ER 197 at 200–201, [1988] 1
*f*  WLR 1362 at 1369–1370):

> 'In my judgment, save in exceptional cases, it is not the correct procedure to apply
> to discharge an ex parte injunction on the grounds of lack of full disclosure at the
> interlocutory stage of the proceedings. The purpose of interlocutory proceedings is
> to regulate the future of the case until trial. Where an Anton Piller order has been
*g*  > made ex parte, in the vast majority of cases the order has been executed before the
> inter partes hearing. Setting aside the Anton Piller order cannot undo what has
> already been done. As to the injunction contained in the ordinary Anton Piller
> order, that is directed to last only until the inter partes hearing of the motion. The
> correct course, as the Court of Appeal decisions show, is to regulate the matter for
*h*  > the future on the basis of the evidence before the judge on the inter partes hearing.
> The sole relevance of the question "Should the ex parte order be set aside?" is, so far
> as I can see, to determine the question whether the plaintiff is liable on the cross-
> undertaking in damages given on the ex parte hearing. That is not an urgent matter.
> It is normally much better dealt with at the trial by the trial judge, who knows all
> the circumstances of the case and is able, after cross-examination, to test the veracity
*j*  > of the witnesses. Similar considerations apply in the case of an ex parte Mareva
> injunction. When the motion comes before the court inter partes, the court can
> then on the evidence before it from both sides decide what is the correct form of the
> Mareva relief to grant until trial. The question whether the earlier ex parte order
> should be set aside is not an urgent matter and is only relevant to the cross-
> undertaking in damages. Similar considerations apply in the case of ordinary ex

parte injunctions. In my judgment, therefore, in the ordinary case it is wrong on
the hearing of an inter partes motion to go into the huge complexities involved in
seeking to disentangle at that stage whether there was full disclosure when the ex
parte order was obtained. The matter should normally be dealt with at trial in the
way I have indicated. The right course, therefore, would normally be to adjourn an
application to set aside the ex parte order to be dealt with at the trial. That is the
course that I think is appropriate in this case, but neither the plaintiffs nor the
defendant are happy with that.'

Sir Nicolas Browne-Wilkinson V-C then stood over the motion to discharge; and, on the
plaintiffs' motion for an injunction to restrain the use of the trade name made an order
until trial. So Sir Nicolas Browne-Wilkinson V-C declined to deal with the motion to
discharge the Anton Piller order at that stage. He also said, as appears above, that 'Similar
considerations apply in the case of an ex parte Mareva injunction'.

Thus the question arises whether, in the light of this most recent decision, I should
have left the complaint of non-disclosure to be dealt with after trial with the defendant
then confined to seeking damages for non-disclosure (see [1988] 3 All ER 197 at 200–
201, [1988] 1 WLR 1362 at 1370). I do not think that would have been the right course.
I say that in reliance on the words of Robert Goff J as quoted in the *Bank Mellat* case [1985]
FSR 87 at 89. Those words appear to have been approved of by all the Lords Justices in
the Court of Appeal. Thus Donaldson LJ said (at 92):

'I think that the learned judge was abundantly right, and the furthest he could
conceivably have gone would have been to consider granting a *Mareva* injunction
upon the basis of the latest version of the plaintiffs' claim, but to suspend its
operation for a period so that the advantage of the previous, wrongly obtained,
*Mareva* injunction would become spent before the new injunction came into effect.
I do not know as a practical matter that that would have been the right way of
granting relief to the plaintiffs, and we certainly have not been asked to make such
an order.'

See also Slade LJ's judgment in the *Bank Mellat* case (at 93). There are some further words
of Sir John Donaldson MR in *Eastglen International Corp v Monpare SA* (1986) 137 NLJ 56
quoted by Glidewell LJ in the *Lloyds Bowmaker* case [1988] 3 All ER 178 at 183, [1988] 1
WLR 1337 at 1343:

'I stand by everything I said in the *Bank Mellat* case about the importance of full
and frank disclosure, and I would support any policy of the courts which was
designed to buttress that by declining to give anybody any advantage from a failure
to comply with that obligation. I would go further and say that it is no answer that
if full and frank disclosure had been made you might have arrived at the same
answer and obtained the same benefit. This is the most important duty of all in the
context of ex parte applications.'

So, as I see it, it would not be right to require a defendant to wait until after trial to
seek damages for non-disclosure. On the contrary, a defendant should be at liberty to
require the discharge of an ex parte Mareva order (without its immediate reimposition)
as soon as he can show non-disclosure of a substantial kind. The considerations which
lead me to this view are (a) if non-disclosure (when ex parte) is sought to be repaired
during an inter partes hearing it is unfair to keep the order in being without any interval
of time because to do that is to prejudice the defendant (see the words of Robert Goff J).
The parties should be restored to the position they were in prior to the ex parte
application, ie when no Mareva injunction was in force. No doubt this means that a
defendant will have the opportunity of making away with his assets but that is due to
the plaintiff's failure properly to make his initial application. (b) Damages for non-
disclosure awarded after trial may be an entirely inadequate remedy for a defendant who
has to suffer the oppression of a Mareva order up to trial.

It is perhaps unfortunate that I have felt obliged to reach these conclusions. Sir Nicolas
Browne-Wilkinson V-C has shown a commonsense way of disposing of interlocutory
conflicts concerning Anton Piller and Mareva orders which should in many cases be
satisfactory so far as concerns the parties and will result in a saving of court time (see the
*Dormeuil* case [1988] 3 All ER 197 at 200–201, [1988] 1 WLR 1362 at 1369–1370). I
would hope that that way will be followed in most cases. In recent years the court time
taken in the interlocutory conflicts I have mentioned is deplorable. However that may
be, in this case the exceptional facts coupled with the authorities I have mentioned
compel me to the conclusion I have mentioned. The situation calls, if I may say so, for
guidance from the Court of Appeal in this 'growth industry' of Mareva and Anton Piller
orders.

As I have indicated, the Mareva order made on 21 September 1988 is not to be
continued.

*Injunction discharged.*

Solicitors: *Simmons & Simmons* (for the group); *S J Berwin & Co* (for Mr Moneim).

Jacqueline Metcalfe    Barrister.

# Practice Note

QUEEN'S BENCH DIVISION
LORD LANE CJ, FARQUHARSON AND POTTS JJ
26 MAY 1989

*Criminal evidence – Tape recording – Tape recording of police interviews – Preparation for
proceedings in Crown Court – Notice of amendment or editing of record of interview or transcript
– Objection to amendment or editing – Production and proof of tape by interviewing officer –
Arrangements for operating tape machine – Costs where procedure not complied with – Police
and Criminal Evidence Act 1984, s 60 – Criminal Justice Act 1987, s 4(1)(c) – Code of Practice
on Tape Recording, para 5.4, note 5B.*

**LORD LANE CJ** gave the following direction (which is to have effect from 6 June
1989) at the sitting of the court.

1. Paragraph 5.4 and note 5B of the *Code of Practice on Tape Recording* issued in accordance
with s 60 of the Police and Criminal Evidence Act 1984 envisage that a case in the Crown
Court in which a tape recording of a police interview with a suspect has been made will
normally be conducted using a record of interview if such a record has been agreed by
the defence.

2. Sufficient notice must be given to allow consideration of any amendment to the
record of interview or the preparation of any transcript of a tape-recorded interview or
any editing of a tape for the purpose of playing it back in court. To that end, the
following practice should be followed.

(a) Where the defence is unable to agree a record of interview or transcript (where one
is already available) the prosecution should be notified no more than 21 days from the
date of committal or date of transfer with a view to securing agreement to amend. The
notice should specify the part to which objection is taken or the part omitted which the
defence consider should be included. A copy of the notice should be supplied to the court
within the period specified above.

(b) If agreement is not reached and it is proposed that the tape or part of it be played
in court, notice should be given to the prosecution by the defence no more than 14 days

after the expiry of the period in para 2(a) above in order that counsel for the parties may agree those parts of the tape that should not be adduced and that arrangements may be *a* made, by editing or in some other way, to exclude that material. A copy of the notice should be supplied to the court within the period specified above.

(c) Notice of any agreement reached under para 2(a) or (b) above should be supplied to the court by the prosecution as soon as is practicable.

(d) Alternatively, if, in any event, prosecuting counsel proposes to play the tape or part of it, the prosecution should, within 28 days of the date of committal or date of *b* transfer, notify the defence and the court and the defence should notify the prosecution and the court within 14 days of receiving the notice if they object to the production of the tape on the basis that a part of it should be excluded. If the objections raised by the defence are accepted, the prosecution should prepare an edited tape or make other arrangements to exclude the material part and should notify the court of the arrangements made. *c*

(e) Whenever editing or amendment of a record of interview or of a tape or of a transcript takes place, the general principles set out in *Archbold's Pleading, Evidence and Practice in Criminal Cases* (43rd edn, 1988) paras 4–186, 4–187 and 4–188 should be followed.

3. If there is a failure to agree between counsel under para 2 above, or there is a *d* challenge to the integrity of the master tape, notice and particulars should be given to the court and to the prosecution by the defence as soon as is practicable. The court may then, at its discretion, order a pre-trial review or give such other directions as may be appropriate.

4. If a tape is to be adduced during proceedings before the Crown Court, it should be produced and proved by the interviewing officer, or any other officer who was present at *e* the interview at which the recording was made. The prosecution should ensure that such an officer will be available for this purpose.

5. Where such an officer is unable to act as the tape machine operator, it is for the prosecution to make some other arrangement.

6. In order to avoid the necessity for the court to listen to lengthy or irrelevant *f* material before the relevant part of a tape recording is reached, counsel shall indicate to the tape machine operator those parts of a recording which it may be necessary to play. Such an indication should, so far as possible, be expressed in terms of the time track or other identifying process used by the interviewing police force and should be given in time for the operator to have located those parts by the appropriate point in the trial. *g*

7. Once a trial has begun, if, by reason of faulty preparation or for some other cause, the procedures above have not been properly complied with, and an application is made to amend the record of interview or transcript or to edit the tape, as the case may be, thereby making necessary an adjournment for the work to be carried out, the court may make at its discretion an appropriate award of costs. *h*

8. Where a case is listed for hearing on a date which falls within the time limits set out above, it is the responsibility of the parties to ensure that all the necessary steps are taken to comply with this practice direction within such shorter period as is available.

9. In para 2(a) and (d) above, 'date of transfer' is the date on which notice of transfer is given in accordance with the provisions of s 4(1)(c) of the Criminal Justice Act 1987. *j*

10. This practice direction should be read in conjunction with the *Code of Practice on Tape Recording* referred to above and with Home Office circular 76/1988 issued on 17 August 1988.

N P Metcalfe Esq   Barrister.

# Brunyate and another v Inner London Education Authority

HOUSE OF LORDS
LORD BRIDGE OF HARWICH, LORD GRIFFITHS, LORD ACKNER, LORD JAUNCEY OF TULLICHETTLE
AND LORD LOWRY
10, 11, 25 MAY 1989

*Education – Local education authority – Removal of governor – Discretion to remove governor of voluntary schools – Authority appointing 10 of 21 governors – Two of authority's appointees refusing to vote in accordance with wishes of authority – Authority removing non-compliant appointees as governors – Whether removal of governors lawful – Education Act 1944, s 21(1).*

A local education authority maintained two voluntary controlled schools in its area which were governed by a single governing body in accordance with an arrangement made by the authority under s 20 of the Education Act 1944 and articles of government made under s 17(3) of that Act. There were 21 school governors, ten of whom were appointed by the authority for a four-year term. In May 1988 the governing body of the schools decided to institute a process of consultation with interested parties concerning the future of the schools following the prospective abolition of the authority and the introduction of grant-maintained schools and city technology colleges by the Education Reform Act 1988. The three options under consideration were that the schools should remain voluntary controlled schools, should opt for grant-maintained status or should become city technology colleges. In July 1988 the governing body issued a consultation document inviting views on the merits of the three options by 17 December 1988. The authority wrote to the ten governors appointed by it asking them to indicate that they would support an extension of the consultation period and, during the consultation period, would provisionally support the authority's policy that the schools should retain their existing status as voluntary controlled schools. The applicants, who were two of those governors, refused to give that assurance and subsequently the governing body resolved not to extend the consultation period, the applicants voting with the majority. Because the applicants had not acceded to the authority's request and had failed to support its policy, the authority removed them from the governing body of the schools. The applicants applied for an order of certiorari to quash the authority's decision to remove them as governors but the Divisional Court dismissed their application on the ground that the authority was entitled to have a policy in relation to the affairs of a voluntary school and to exercise its statutory power under s 21(1)[a] of the 1944 Act to remove governors whom it had appointed as a means of promoting the implementation of that policy. The applicants appealed to the Court of Appeal, which allowed their appeal. The authority appealed to the House of Lords.

**Held** – The governors of voluntary schools had both the right and the duty, so long as they held office as such, to exercise the function of their office independently of the local education authority and in accordance with their own judgment, and therefore the discretion conferred on a local education authority by s 21(1) of the 1944 Act to remove from office a governor it had appointed could not be exercised in such a way as to usurp the governor's independent role. The removal of the applicants as governors on the grounds of their non-compliance with the wishes of the authority amounted to a usurpation of the applicants' independent function as governors under the 1944 Act and,

---

a   Section 21(1) provides: 'Any governor of a county school or of a voluntary school may resign his office, and any such governor appointed by a local education authority or by a minor authority shall be removable by the authority by whom he was appointed.'

accordingly, was an unlawful exercise of the power conferred by s 21(1). The appeal would therefore be dismissed (see p 420 *f* and p 421 *h* to p 422 *b f* to *h*, post).

*R v Trustee of Roman Catholic Diocese of Westminster, ex p Mars* (1987) 86 LGR 507 doubted.

### Notes

For governors of secondary schools and of special schools maintained by education authorities, see 15 Halsbury's Laws (4th edn) para 110.

For the Education Act 1944, ss 17, 20, 21, see 15 Halsbury's Statutes (4th edn) 121, 124, 125.

### Cases referred to in opinions

*Associated Provincial Picture Houses Ltd v Wednesbury Corp* [1947] 2 All ER 680, [1948] 1 KB 223, CA.

*R v Trustee of Roman Catholic Diocese of Westminster, ex p Mars* (1987) 86 LGR 507.

### Appeal

The Inner London Education Authority (the ILEA) appealed with leave of the Court of Appeal against the decision of the Court of Appeal (Kerr, Balcombe and Woolf LJJ) on 24 February 1989 allowing the appeal of the respondents, Margaret Isabel Brunyate and John Leonard Hunt (the applicants), from the decision of the Divisional Court of the Queen's Bench Division (Glidewell LJ and Pill J) on 2 February 1989 dismissing their application for judicial review by way of an order of certiorari to quash the decision of the ILEA on 17 January 1989 that they be removed as governors of the Haberdashers' Aske's Hatcham Schools, a declaration that it was unlawful and associated relief. The House of Lords gave the Secretary of State for Education and Science leave to be heard on the appeal. The facts are set out in the opinion of Lord Bridge.

*James Goudie QC* and *Alan Wilkie* for the ILEA.
*Anthony Scrivener QC* and *Ian Croxford* for the applicants.
*John Laws* and *Alison Foster* for the Secretary of State.

Their Lordships took time for consideration.

25 May. The following opinions were delivered.

**LORD BRIDGE OF HARWICH.** My Lords, the Haberdashers' Aske's Hatcham Boys' School and Girls' School (the schools) are voluntary controlled schools established in accordance with the provisions of ss 9 and 15 of the Education Act 1944. The school premises are the property of a charity of which the Haberdashers' Company are trustees (the foundation). The two schools are governed in accordance with an arrangement made under s 20 and articles of government made under s 17(3) of the 1944 Act by a single governing body. There are 21 governors, of whom seven are appointed by the foundation, two are teachers and two are parents, one teacher and one parent being elected by the bodies of teachers and parents at each school, and the remaining ten are appointed by the Inner London Education Authority (the ILEA), by whom the schools are maintained. I will refer to the last category as 'authority governors'. Authority governors are appointed for a term of four years. By convention authority governors have in the past been appointed in proportion to the representation of the main political parties on the ILEA. Prior to the events giving rise to the present litigation there were eight authority governors representing the Labour interest and two, the respondents to this appeal, representing the Conservative interest.

The Education Reform Act 1988 provides for the abolition of the ILEA on 1 April 1990 (s 162) and the introduction of two new types of schools, namely grant-maintained

schools (s 52) and city technology colleges (CTCs) (s 105). In May 1988 the governing
*a* body of the schools decided to institute a process of consultation with interested parties
concerning the future of the schools. There are three options open: first, that the schools
should remain voluntary controlled schools, which would mean that after 1 April 1990
they would be maintained by Lewisham London Borough Council; second, that the
schools should become grant-maintained schools, which would mean that they would be
maintained by the Secretary of State; third, that the schools should become CTCs. The
*b* first of these options is favoured by the ILEA, the third by the foundation. Unhappily
the issue, as so much in the field of education today, is one of acute political controversy.
  The governing body issued a consultation document in July 1988 describing the
implications of the three options and inviting views on their merits by 17 December
1988. The document indicated that the governors, in the light of views expressed in the
first stage of consultation, expected to identify the option they proposed to follow by
*c* mid-January 1989, so that interested parties could express further views on the chosen
option by 1 March 1989. The governors indicated that they would not feel able to
proceed with any option which was opposed by a clear majority of current parents and
staff. On 3 November 1988 the ILEA wrote to all authority governors asking them to
indicate that they would support an extension of the consultation period, and that,
*d* during the consultation period, they would provisionally support the ILEA's policy that
the schools should retain their existing status as voluntary controlled schools. The present
respondents (the applicants) declined to give either indication. On 13 December 1988
the governing body resolved not to extend the consultation period, the present applicants
voting with the majority to that effect. The ILEA continued to press the governing body
for an extension and on 22 December wrote to the applicants noting that they had not
*e* acceded to the authority's previous request and that they had voted against extending the
consultation period and indicating that the authority was minded to consider their
removal from the governing body. Both applicants replied that they had open minds
about the schools' future, which they would consider on the merits. On 17 January 1989
the ILEA resolved that the applicants be removed from the governing body of the
schools.
*f*   I have recounted this history in briefest summary form and have not found it necessary
to refer either to the correspondence exchanged between the clerk and legal adviser to
the ILEA and the applicants' solicitors, or to the various reports which were before the
sub-committees and committees of the ILEA on the basis of which the effective decisions
of the authority leading to the removal of the applicants as governors were taken. As
appears from the very much fuller examination of the history in the judgment of Woolf
*g* LJ in the Court of Appeal, the ILEA exercised its statutory power to remove the applicants
not merely because of the difference which arose with respect to the length of the
consultation period, but also because it believed it to be an appropriate means of seeking
to ensure that the authority's policy with respect to the future of the schools should
prevail. The question in the appeal is whether a local education authority's power to
remove a governor of a voluntary school during the term for which he has been
*h* appointed may lawfully be exercised for the sole purpose of securing the implementation
by the governing body of the local education authority's policy in relation to the affairs
of the school.
  The applicants applied to quash the decision to remove them as governors. The
Divisional Court (Glidewell LJ and Pill J) dismissed the application. It approached the
issue from the point of view of the reasonableness, in the *Wednesbury* sense, of the
*j* decision of the ILEA (see *Associated Provincial Picture Houses Ltd v Wednesbury Corp* [1947]
2 All ER 680, [1948] 1 KB 223). It held that a local education authority was entitled to
have a policy in relation to the affairs of a voluntary school and to exercise its statutory
power to remove governors whom it had appointed as a means of promoting the
implementation of that policy. In this it followed and applied the reasoning of Simon
Brown J in *R v Trustee of Roman Catholic Diocese of Westminster, ex p Mars* (1987) 86 LGR

507, who, in analogous circumstances, upheld the decision of the trustees of a Roman Catholic voluntary school, by whom the power of appointment and removal of foundation governors was exercisable, to remove a governor who refused to support the trustees' policy.

The Court of Appeal (Kerr, Balcombe and Woolf LJJ) reversed the decision of the Divisional Court by a majority (Balcombe LJ dissenting). It granted leave to appeal to your Lordships' House.

As so often happens the issue in the case by the time it reaches your Lordships' House has been considerably refined and narrowed. Section 21(1) of the 1944 Act gives to those who appoint governors of a voluntary school a power to remove them which is on its face quite unfettered. It is accepted, of course, that the power must be exercised reasonably, in the *Wednesbury* sense. But it is now also accepted, I think, that some further limitation on the power may be derived, as a matter of construction, from a consideration of the statutory machinery for the government of voluntary schools established by the 1944 Act. It is unnecessary to refer to the provisions of the Act in extenso to make good the proposition that local education authorities and the governing bodies of voluntary schools are entirely distinct and independent entities each having their own separate statutory duties and powers. This is most graphically illustrated by s 67(1) (as amended by the Education Act 1980, s 1, Sch 1, para 1 and the Secretary of State for Education and Science Order 1964, SI 1964/490, art 3(2)(a)), which provides:

> 'Save as otherwise expressly provided by this Act, any dispute between a local education authority and the governors of any school with respect to the exercise of any power conferred or the performance of any duty imposed by or under this Act, may, notwithstanding any enactment rendering the exercise of the power or the performance of the duty contingent upon the opinion of the authority or of the governors, be referred to the Secretary of State; and any such dispute so referred shall be determined by him.'

Just as the governing bodies of voluntary schools are independent of local education authorities, so also, it is accepted, individual governors, so long as they hold office as such, have both the right and the duty to exercise the function of their office independently in accordance with their own judgment. It follows implicity, though this was not in terms conceded, that the power of removal cannot be exercised in a way that would amount to a usurpation of the governors' independent role.

For present purposes the most important section in the 1944 Act is s 14, which provides machinery for the discontinuance of a voluntary school. In the instant case discontinuance of the schools as voluntary controlled schools would be a necessary preliminary step to be taken before they could be re-established as CTCs by agreement between the foundation and the Secretary of State for Education and Science under s 105 of the Education Reform Act 1988. Section 14 of the 1944 Act (as amended by the Education Act 1946, s 14(1), Sch 2, Pt II, the 1980 Act and the 1964 order) provides, so far as material:

> '(1) Subject to the provisions of this section, the governors of a voluntary school shall not discontinue the school except after serving on the Secretary of State and on the local education authority by whom the school is maintained not less than two years' notice of their intention to do so: Provided that, except by leave of the Secretary of State, no such notice as aforesaid shall be served by the governors of any voluntary school in respect of the premises of which expenditure has been incurred otherwise than in connection with repairs by the Secretary of State or by any local education authority or former authority. If the Secretary of State grants such leave, he may impose such requirements as he thinks just—(a) in regard to the repayment of the whole or any part of the amount of the expenditure so incurred by the Secretary of State; (b) where the Secretary of State is satisfied that the local education authority will require, for any purpose connected with education, any premises

a
which are for the time being used for the purposes of the school in regard to the conveyance of those premises to the authority; (c) in regard to the payment by the local education authority of such part of the value of any premises so conveyed as is just having regard to the extent to which those premises were provided otherwise than at the expense of the authority or a former authority; (d) where any premises for the time being used for the purposes of the school are not to be so conveyed, in regard to the payment to the authority by the governors of the school of such part

b
of the value of those premises as is just having regard to the extent to which they were provided at the expense of the authority or a former authority.

(2) No such notice as aforesaid shall be withdrawn except with the consent of the local education authority . . .

(5) Where any school is discontinued in accordance with the provisions of this section, the duty of the local education authority to maintain the school as a

c
voluntary school shall be extinguished.'

Thus it is clear that the institution of action to discontinue a voluntary school lies solely within the province of the governing body.

It is rightly and inevitably conceded by counsel for the ILEA that governors are in no sense delegates of the authority by whom they were appointed and cannot be required to

d
vote on any particular matter as the authority wishes. He concedes further that, if a local education authority were regularly to ask all the governors of a voluntary school in relation to the conduct of the affairs of the school to indicate their willingness to vote in accordance with the wishes of the authority and to remove those governors who declined to give the necessary indication, this would be an abuse of the power of removal. This, he says, would be unreasonable in the *Wednesbury* sense, but there is nothing, he submits,

e
either unreasonable or contrary to the policy which underlies the statutory scheme for the government of voluntary schools if the authority, on an issue of sufficient importance to the future of a school, removes governors who are unwilling to vote as the authority wishes.

The difficulty I find with this argument is to see where, if it is accepted, any line can be drawn by the courts to distinguish between lawful and unlawful exercise of the power

f
of removal. If a local education authority always requires an indication in advance from all governors appointed by it that they will vote as the authority wishes and removes them if they do not comply, the authority will wholly usurp the independent function of the governors. Counsel for the ILEA accepts that such an exercise of the power would, as he would put it, be unreasonable and therefore unlawful. But the lawfulness or unlawfulness of removal of the non-compliant governors cannot, it seems to me, depend

g
on the reasonableness or on the relative importance in any particular case of the view which the local education authority seeks to impose on the governing body. On all matters of education policy, whether of major or minor importance and whether affecting the day-to-day conduct or the long-term future of a voluntary school, the local education authority may perfectly reasonably entertain views which some of the governors it has appointed may not share. So far as reasonableness in the *Wednesbury*

h
sense is concerned, if it is reasonable for the authority to exercise the power of removal in one case, as a means of enforcing its own view, the courts cannot say that it is unreasonable in another. But I do not believe that this is a matter of reasonableness. The true view, in my opinion, is that to allow removal in any case of non-compliant governors on the grounds of their non-compliance with the wishes of the authority is inevitably to allow a usurpation of the governors' independent function, which, on the true

j
construction of the 1944 Act, is an unlawful exercise of the power conferred by s 21.

A further argument was addressed to your Lordships for the ILEA which sought to draw an analogy between a decision of the local education authority not to reappoint a governor on the expiry of his four-year term and a decision to remove him at any time during that term. The authority has a wholly unfettered discretion as to whom it will appoint or reappoint. This is clearly correct. Therefore, so ran the argument, towards the end of a governor's term the authority can ensure compliance by a threat not to reappoint and in substance this is equivalent to removal for non-compliance. The argument, with respect, seems to me fallacious and without substance. Precisely because the decision whether or not to reappoint is unfettered and unchallengeable, whereas the discretion to remove under s 21 must be exercised on lawful grounds, there is no analogy between the two situations.

Although it did not feature in the argument relied on by the ILEA, reference was made in the course of the argument to art 11(a) of the schools' articles of government, made under s 17(3) of the 1944 Act, which provides:

'The Local Education Authority shall determine the general educational character of the schools and their place in the local educational system. Subject thereto the Governors shall have the general direction of the conduct and curriculum of the schools.'

I express no opinion whether this provision in the articles of government confers any legally enforceable right on the local education authority, as such, which it might exercise in opposition to any action taken by the governing body to effect the discontinuance of the schools as voluntary controlled schools pursuant to s 14 of the 1944 Act. What it cannot do, in my opinion, is to enable the local education authority to exercise indirect control over discontinuance by an unlawful exercise of the power to remove authority governors under s 21(1) of the 1944 Act.

In the light of the views I have expressed, I find it difficult to see how the reasoning of Simon Brown J in *R v Trustee of Roman Catholic Diocese of Westminster, ex p Mars* (1987) 86 LGR 507 can be supported. However, that case arose from different facts and turned on different statutory provisions from those in question in this appeal. Your Lordships were told that leave has now been granted out of time to appeal against that decision. In the circumstances it would be inappropriate to express any concluded view as to its correctness.

I would dismiss the appeal.

**LORD GRIFFITHS.** My Lords, I have had the advantage of reading in draft the speech of my noble and learned friend Lord Bridge. I agree with it, and for the reasons that he gives I also would dismiss the appeal.

**LORD ACKNER.** My Lords, for the reasons contained in the speech of my noble and learned friend Lord Bridge I, too, would dismiss the appeal.

**LORD JAUNCEY OF TULLICHETTLE.** My Lords, I have had the advantage of reading in draft the speech of my noble and learned friend Lord Bridge. I agree with it and for the reasons which he gives I, too, would dismiss the appeal.

**LORD LOWRY.** My Lords, I have had the advantage of reading in draft the speech of my noble and learned friend Lord Bridge. I agree with it and for the reasons which he gives I, too, would dismiss the appeal.

*Appeal dismissed.*

Solicitors: *C L Grace* (for the ILEA); *Field Fisher Waterhouse* (for the applicants); *Treasury Solicitor.*

Mary Rose Plummer    Barrister.

*a* # Attorney General (ex rel Yorkshire Derwent Trust Ltd and another) v Brotherton and others

CHANCERY DIVISION
*b* VINELOTT J
28, 29, 30 JUNE, 1, 4–6, 8, 11–15, 18, 19 JULY, 19 DECEMBER 1988

*Water and watercourses – Navigation – Public right of navigation – Land covered by water – River – Right of navigation over river – Whether right of navigation a right of way over 'land covered with water' – Highways Act 1980, s 31(1)(11).*

*c* A charitable trust whose main object was the restoration of the River Derwent as a navigable river and the town council of Malton, a town on the bank of the river about 38 miles upstream from the junction of the river with the River Ouse, wished to preserve any public rights of recreation on the river that might exist and in particular wished to restore locks which, because of their disrepair, obstructed navigation. Accordingly, the *d* Attorney General, suing at the relation of the trust and the town council, commenced proceedings against the defendants, who were riparian owners owning land along the river bank and who wished the river to remain as a haven for wildlife undisturbed by river traffic. The relief sought was a declaration that a public right of navigation exercisable by all members of the public in any type or class of vessel capable of navigating the river existed along the course of the Derwent from the village of Sutton, which was *e* the limit of the tidal reaches of the Derwent, to Malton along and past the defendants' land. The trial of various preliminary issues was ordered, including whether public rights of navigation could be established under s 31(1)[a] of the Highways Act 1980 (which consolidated the legislation dealing with public rights of way). Under s 31(1) where a way 'over any land' had been actually enjoyed by the public as of right without interruption for 20 years the way was deemed to have been dedicated as a highway and *f* for that purpose 'land' included, by virtue of s 31(11)[b], 'land covered with water'. The question arose whether a right of navigation was a right of way 'over any land covered with water' for the purposes of s 31(1).

**Held** – Construing the 1980 Act and its predecessors in accordance with the ordinary usage of English language, a right of navigation would not be regarded as a right of way over land, and water which was navigated would not be regarded as a highway but as a *g* waterway. That construction was reinforced by the fact that s 31(3) of the 1980 Act made provision for the erection of notices visible to all users to negative an intention to dedicate a right of way as a highway, and since it would not always be possible to erect such a notice in respect of navigable water that indicated that the legislature did not intend the Act to apply to rights of navigation. Accordingly, on its true construction s 31 of the 1980 Act and its predecessors did not apply to public rights of navigation (see p 428 *h* to *h* p 429 *a* and p 430 *a* to *d*, post).

*Wills's Trustees v Cairngorm Canoeing and Sailing School Ltd* 1976 SC (HL) 30 considered.

Per curiam. The extension by s 31(11) of the 1980 Act of the reference to 'land' in s 31(3) to include 'land covered with water' was designed to make it clear that the 1980 Act may extend to fords and causeways covered in water at some stage of the tide (see *j* p 429 *b*, post).

---

*a*  Section 31(1) provides: 'Where a way over any land, other than a way of such a character that use of it by the public could not give rise at common law to any presumption of dedication, has been actually enjoyed by the public as of right and without interruption for a full period of 20 years, the way is to be deemed to have been dedicated as a highway unless there is sufficient evidence that there was no intention during that period to dedicate it.'

*b*  Section 31(11), so far as material, is set out at p 427 *f*, post

**Notes**

For rights of navigation in inland waters, see 49 Halsbury's Laws (4th edn) paras 891–     *a*
903, 909–913, and for cases on the subject, see 49 Digest (1986 reissue) 340–343, 2601–
2624.

For the Highways Act 1980, s 31, see 20 Halsbury's Statutes (4th edn) 176.

**Cases referred to in judgment**

*A-G v Antrobus* [1905] 2 Ch 188.
*Bernstein (Lord) of Leigh v Skyviews and General Ltd* [1977] 2 All ER 902, [1978] QB 479,     *b*
     [1977] 3 WLR 136.
*Bourke v Davis* (1889) 44 Ch D 110.
*Jones v Bates* [1938] 2 All ER 237, CA.
*Marshall v Ulleswater Steam Navigation Co Ltd* (1871) LR 7 QB 166.
*Orr Ewing v Colquhoun* (1877) 2 App Cas 839, HL; *rvsg* (1877) 4 R 344, Ct of Sess.     *c*
*Williams v Wilcox* (1838) 8 Ad & El 314, [1835–42] All ER Rep 25, 112 ER 857.
*Wills's Trustees v Cairngorm Canoeing and Sailing School Ltd* 1976 SC(HL) 30.

**Cases also cited**

*A-G and Newton Abbot RDC v Dyer* [1946] 2 All ER 252, [1947] Ch 67.
*Evans v Godber* [1974] 3 All ER 341, [1974] 1 WLR 1317, DC.
*Fairey v Southampton CC* [1956] 2 All ER 843, [1956] 2 QB 439, CA.     *d*
*K (decd), Re* [1985] 1 All ER 403, [1985] Ch 85; *affd* [1985] 2 All ER 833, [1986] Ch 180,
     CA.
*Merstham Manor Ltd v Coulsdon and Purley UDC* [1936] 2 All ER 422, [1937] 2 KB 77.

**Preliminary issues**     *e*

By an originating summons dated 10 May 1984, as amended, the Attorney General at
and by the relation of the Yorkshire Derwent Trust Ltd and the town council of Malton,
commenced proceedings against the defendants, namely, (1) David R Brotherton, (2)
Anne Henson sued as Anne Mears, (3) Roger St Clair Preston, (4), (5) and (6) John Philip
Starkey, John Fitzgerald Willcox Jenyns and Anne Gwendoline Luttrell, sued as the
trustees of the Huttons Ambo Estate, (7), (8) and (9) Geoffrey Mark Victor Winn, George     *f*
Roland Hill Cholmeley and Robin Anthony Langley Leach, sued as the trustees of the
Aldby Park Estate, and (10) the Yorkshire Wildlife Trust Ltd, seeking a declaration
against the defendants and each of them that a public right of navigation subsisted along
the course of the River Derwent in North Yorkshire and Humberside over along and past
the land of which the defendants and each of them respectively claimed to be the owners
which right was exercisable by all members of the public in any type or class of vessel     *g*
then or thereafter to be capable of navigating the same. On 25 July 1986 Millett J in
chambers directed that the following questions be determined as preliminary issues in
advance of the trial: (1) whether there was a public right of navigation along the course
of the River Derwent over along and past the land of which the defendants and each of
them respectively claimed to be the owners (the relevant land) immediately prior to the
enactment of the Act entitled 'AN Act for making the River Darwent in the County of     *h*
York navigable' (1 Anne c 14 (1702)), alternatively, immediately before completion in or
about 1723/5 of the several works undertaken pursuant to the powers conferred thereby;
(2) whether on the true construction of the 1702 Act that Act (a) by necessary implication
conferred a right on any person who wished to navigate the Derwent for commercial
(cargo carrying) purposes to do so on payment (if laden with cargo) of the appropriate
toll (the maximum toll being prescribed by s 5 of the 1702 Act) subject to natural or     *j*
necessary restrictions as to draught, length, beam, speed and similar matters and obliged
any riparian owner or occupier past whose land such navigation occurred to submit
thereto without compensation or satisfaction save as provided by the 1702 Act, or (b) by
necessary implication conferred a right on any person who wished to navigate the

a Derwent for any purpose to do so on payment (if laden with cargo) of the said appropriate toll therefore subject as aforesaid and obliged any riparian owner or occupier past whose land such navigation occurred to submit thereto as aforesaid, or (c) by necessary implication dedicated part of the bed and course of the River Derwent (including all parts downstream of the northernmost part of the relevant land) to the public as a highway by water, or (d) by necessary implication vested part of the bed and course of the River Derwent (including all parts downstream of the northernmost part of the

b relevant land) jointly in the undertakers named in the 1702 Act, or (e) had any two or more of the effects set forth at sub-paras (a) to (d) thereof inclusive, or (f) had any other (and, if so, what) effect in or towards the creation of a public right of navigation, or (g) created no public right of navigation; (3) whether a public right of navigation over and along and past the relevant land arose subsequent to the enactment of the 1702 Act but not solely by force of it and prior to the making of the River Derwent Navigation Act

c Revocation Order 1935, SR & O 1935/978, which right was subsisting immediately prior to the making of the 1935 order; (4) whether on the true construction of s 41 of the Land Drainage Act 1930 and the 1935 order and in the events which had happened by 21 September 1935 the 1935 order (a) revoked, varied or extinguished (i) all public rights of navigation (if any) over along and past the relevant land, or (ii) only such public rights of navigation (if any) as pre-existed the enactment and putting into execution of the 1702

d Act, or (iii) only such public rights of navigation (if any) as were created by or under or pursuant to the 1702 Act, or (iv) only such rights (if any) as arose after the putting of the 1702 Act into execution but not solely by force of it; or (b) did not revoke vary or extinguish any public rights of navigation over along and past the relevant land; (5)(i) whether all or any (and, if so, which) of the following provisions applied or apply to public rights of navigation, (a) s 1 of the Rights of Way Act 1932, (b) s 1 of the Rights of

e Way Act 1932 as amended by s 58 of the National Parks and Access to the Countryside Act 1949, (c) s 34 of the Highways Act 1959, (d) s 31 of the Highways Act 1980, and (ii) if the answer to (i) was in the affirmative, whether all or any (and, if so, which) of such provisions as might be held to have applied or apply to public rights of navigation applied or apply to navigation by members of the public over along and past the relevant land before the confirmation of the 1935 order. The report concerns question (5) only. The

f facts are set out in the judgment.

E W H Christie and C H Pymont for the plaintiff.
W D Ainger for the defendants.

*Cur adv vult*

g
19 December. The following judgment was delivered.

**VINELOTT J.** The issue in this case is whether there exists a public right of navigation over that part of the Yorkshire Derwent which lies between Malton and Sutton. The

h plaintiff is the Attorney General. He sues at the relation of the Yorkshire Derwent Trust Ltd and the town council of Malton. The Yorkshire Derwent Trust Ltd (the Derwent Trust) is a charitable body. Its main object is the restoration of the River Derwent as a navigable river, in particular the restoration of the lock cuts and locks round dams which presently obstruct the navigation of the river. The Derwent Trust is an offshoot of the Inland Waterways Association in the sense that its main object is a particular application

j of the more general objects of the association and that it acts in conjunction with the association, though there is, I understand, no legal link between them. Malton, which lies on the west bank of the Derwent about 38 miles from the junction of the Derwent with the River Ouse, is the only sizeable town on the Derwent. Its town council, like the Derwent Trust, is concerned to preserve any public rights of recreation on the river which may exist.

The defendants are all riparian owners. They own lands bordering the Derwent at various points between Malton and Sutton. I shall describe the precise situation of the *a* defendants' land later. I should, however, make it clear at the outset that their purpose in opposing the plaintiff's claim is not the selfish purpose of preserving the river for their own enjoyment and excluding the public. They take the view that it is in the public interest that this stretch of river, which is still comparatively unspoilt, should be preserved as a haven for the river wildlife for which it is famous, and that unrestricted public access along the river with motor boats and other pleasure craft would lead to the *b* rapid destruction of a precious national asset. But, of course, the feelings that have been aroused by this litigation are not the less intense because they do not arise from a conflict between economic or commercial interests but because of the parties' very different perceptions of what is truly in the public interest.

This is not the trial of the action. At an early stage Millett J directed that a number of preliminary issues should be determined in advance of the trial. In broad terms, the *c* issues fall under three heads. The first is whether any part of the Derwent between Sutton (which is the limit of the tidal part of the Derwent) and Malton was subject to a public right of navigation either before 1702 when an Act 'for making the River Darwent in the County of York navigable' (1 Anne c 14) was enacted or before the time when works of improvement under that Act to the stretch of the river between Malton and Sutton were completed in about 1725. The 1702 Act was repealed by the Derwent Valley *d* Water Act 1935 (25 & 26 Geo 5 c cv) and the second head is whether (a) the Act created a public right of navigation which endured so long as the Act remained unrepealed, but fell with the Act and with the right created by that Act for the undertakers who met the cost of improving and maintaining the navigation to charge tolls, leaving only those public rights of navigation which existed before the Act was enacted or before the works of improvement were completed or (b) the Act or the acquiescence of the riparian owners *e* in its enactment or in the improvement of the navigation and its subsequent use evidence an intention to dedicate and acceptance by the public of dedication of the river as a publicly navigable river in perpetuity. The third head is whether the user of navigation, in particular by non-commercial craft, over the years since the works of improvement were completed was capable of founding a presumption of a lost modern grant dedicating the river as a publicly navigable river or giving rise to public rights of navigation under *f* the Rights of Way Act 1932 and the statutes which have since amended and re-enacted the provisions originally so enacted. Those are the issues in outline.

[His Lordship then described the physical characteristics and history of the river and considered the legislation. He then considered the first four preliminary issues and found in favour of the defendants on each issue, answering question (1) No, except for the tenth defendant's land downstream of Sutton, question (2) in the sense of alternative (d), *g* question (3) No, and question (4) in the sense of alternative (a)(iii). His Lordship continued:]

Question 5

I turn, therefore, to what is, I think, the most substantial issue in this case. It is also one of considerable general importance. The question is: *h*

'(1) Whether all or any (and if so, which) of the following provisions applied or apply to public rights of navigation: (a) Section 1 of the Rights of Way Act 1932; (b) Section 1 of the Rights of Way Act 1932 as amended by Section 58 of the National Parks and Access to the Countryside Act 1949; (c) Section 34 of the Highways Act 1959; (d) Section 31 of the Highways Act 1980. (2) If the answer to (1) is in the affirmative, whether all or any (and is so, which) of such provisions as may be held *j* to have applied or apply to public rights of navigation applied or apply to navigation by members of the public over along and past the relevant land before the confirmation of the 1935 Order'.

The Rights of Way Act 1932 was described by counsel for the defendants aptly, I think,

as the long-delayed child of the famous Stonehenge case, *A-G v Antrobus* [1905] 2 Ch 188,
a   which drew into sharp relief the difficulties which lay in the way of establishing a public
right of way by long user. A private members Bill to ameliorate these difficulties was
introduced shortly after *A-G v Antrobus* had been decided. It failed, as did many other
similar private Bills introduced later until, in 1932, government time was made available.
As originally enacted, the 1932 Act provided for the acquisition of public rights of way
of 20-year user if there was some person in possession of the relevant land capable of
b   dedicating the way and 40-year user if there was not. It was amended by s 58(1) of the
National Parks and Access to the Countryside Act 1949, which assimilated the two
periods. Section 1 of the amended Act read as follows:

> '(1) Where a way, not being of such a character that user thereof by the public
> could not give rise at common law to any presumption of dedication, upon or over
> any land has been actually enjoyed by the public as of right and without interruption
c > for a full period of twenty years, such way shall be deemed to have been dedicated
> as a highway, unless there is sufficient evidence that there was no intention during
> that period to dedicate such way . . .
> (6) Each of the respective periods of years mentioned in this section shall be
> deemed and taken to be the period next before the time when the right of the public
d > to use a way shall have been brought into question by notice as aforesaid or
> otherwise . . .
> (8) For the purposes of this section, the expression "land" includes land covered
> with water.'

The 1932 Act as amended was re-enacted in s 34 of the Highways Act 1959 and that
section was in turn repealed and re-enacted in s 31 of the Highways Act 1980. The
e   language of the 1932 Act, as amended by the 1949 Act, was not materially altered when
it became in turn s 34 of the 1959 Act and s 31 of the 1980 Act, but some reliance was
placed by counsel for the defendants on other provisions in the 1980 Act. I will come
back to this point later. The central question is whether a right of navigation is a right of
way 'over any land' within what is now s 31(1) of the 1980 Act, which in turn must be
read together with s 31(11) of the 1980 Act (formerly s 1(8) of the 1932 Act): 'For the
f   purposes of this section "land" includes land covered with water.'
The case for the plaintiff can be shortly stated. A right of navigation over a river is a
right of way over the bed or alveus of the river. The owner of the bed of the river does
not have any exclusive right of property in the water in the river: flowing water in a
stream or river which runs through the land of more than one owner is publici juris.
However, he has the same right to object to the use of the river by others as he has to
g   object to any other invasion of the air space above his land, not, perhaps, usque ad coelum
but 'to such height as is necessary for the ordinary use and enjoyment of his land and the
structures on it' (see *Lord Bernstein of Leigh v Skyviews and General Ltd* [1977] 2 All ER 902
at 907, [1978] QB 479 at 488 per Griffiths J). A right to navigate along a river is thus a
right of way over the subjacent land and should be pleaded as such. That was recognised
h   by Lord Hatherley in *Orr Ewing v Colquhoun* (1877) 2 App Cas 839 at 846, where, speaking
of the River Leven in Scotland, a non-tidal river, he said: '. . . there are two totally distinct
and different things; the one is the right of property, and the other is the right of
navigation. The right of navigation is simply a right of way . . .'
Similarly, in *Bourke v Davis* (1889) 44 Ch D 110 at 120, where the question was whether
there was a public right of boating on the River Mole below Cobham Bridge, Kay J said:
j   'For all the purposes of this case the right claimed is similar to a right of highway on land
not covered by water.' Then, having cited the above passage in the speech of Lord
Hatherley and an observation by Lord Blackburn in *Orr Ewing v Colquhoun* (1877) 2 App
Cas 839 at 846, 848, he continued: 'I must treat the claim of the Defendant, therefore, as
if it were a claim to establish a right of highway on dry land.'
It is said that any doubt that might otherwise exist is removed by sub-s (11) of s 31 of

the 1980 Act. Read in conjunction with sub-s (11), sub-s (1) can be expanded to read, 'where a right of way over any land (including land covered by water) has been actually enjoyed by the public as of right . . .' and so expanded fits in precise terms the proper legal analysis of a public right of navigation. A river over which there is a public right of navigation is a highway and the way is properly described as a way over land covered with water.

I hope that I have adequately summarised counsel's argument for the plaintiff, which he developed with great skill and learning. I am not convinced by it. There is, of course, ancient authority for the claim that a publicly navigable river is one of the King's highways. Mr Flower in his introduction to *Public Works in Mediaeval Law* vol 2 (Selden Society vol 40 (1923)) pp xiv–xv, observes:

> 'It is probable that no hard and fast distinction between roads, bridges, rivers and other means of communication was recognised by the mediaeval lawyer. Even in comparatively modern times Hawkins [2 Hawk PC 152] stated that in books of the best authority a river common to all men is called a highway.'

In *Williams v Wilcox* (1838) 8 Ad & El 314 at 329, [1835–42] All ER Rep 25 at 27 Lord Denman CJ observed: 'It cannot be disputed that the channel of a public navigable river is a King's highway, and is properly so described . . .'

However, it has always been recognised that the analogy of a highway over land is not a complete one. Lord Denman CJ in *Williams v Wilcox* 8 Ad & El 314 at 330, [1835–42] All ER Rep 25 at 27 pointed to one of the differences; the user of a navigable river which becomes choked has no right to go extra viam and cut a new channel. And in the case of a public right of navigation there is in general no person who is obliged to keep it in repair, though there may be, by custom, an obligation on a manor or a parish to maintain the banks. Lord Wilberforce in *Wills's Trustees v Cairngorm Canoeing and Sailing School Ltd* 1976 SC (HL) 30 at 125, pointed to another difference when he said:

> 'The appellants invoked the analogy of a public right of way, or a highway overland. As to this they were able to cite authorities of some strength for the propositions that prescriptive use subject to technical rules is required to establish the right and that the right may be correspondingly lost by disuse for a prescriptive period. But I am in agreement with the Lord Ordinary that a public right of navigation in a non-tidal river and a public right of way on land are not necessarily governed by the same rules. A public right of way on highways is established by use over the land of a proprietor; its exact course must be shown, and it must be between public termini. A river on the other hand is permanently there as a natural feature, it has at least one terminus—the sea.'

That case is also authority for the proposition that, under Scottish law at least, a public right of navigation need not be a right of navigation between two public places. There is at least a doubt whether under English law this proposition is true of a right of way over land. Lord Fraser had this point in mind when, after referring to a passage in the judgment of the Lord President (Inglis) in the Court of Session in *Orr Ewing v Colquhoun* (1877) 4 R 344 explaining a right of navigation as analogous to a right of way, Lord Fraser added (1976 SC (HL) 30 at 167): 'It would not of course follow that the analogy was complete in every respect, and I do not think it is'.

The 1932 Act must be construed in accordance with the ordinary usage of English language and I do not think that an ordinary educated user of English language would regard a right of navigation as a right of way over land. Told that a person taking a day trip on a paddle steamer from London Bridge to Sheerness or sailing in Poole Harbour, or taking a motor boat up the navigable part of the Thames was using the King's highway or exercising a right of way as a member of the public, he would, I suspect, reply that is lawyers' language and archaic language at that or in a less hostile way that a highway

may be an analogy which is helpful in some contexts, but misleading in others. A right
*a* to navigate over the waters of a river is a right of way over water and commonly referred
to as a waterway. A person using it has no right to use or disturb the soil of the bed of the
river, except for the purpose of temporary anchorage or for wading ashore he owns or
has the right to use the adjoining bank (see *Marshall v Ulleswater Steam Navigation Co Ltd*
(1871) LR 7 QB 166). Nor does the express provision that the reference to land is to
include 'water over land' assist the plaintiff. For that extension is explicable as being read
*b* as designed to make it clear that the Act may extend to a ford or a causeway covered in
water at some states of the tide. It was said by Scott LJ in *Jones v Bates* [1938] 2 All ER 237
at 244–245 that the purpose of the 1932 Act was to assimilate English and Scottish law.
In the case of a right of way over land the practical effect of the 1932 Act is that the
ingredients that must be proved to establish a right of way by land user are largely if not
wholly assimilated to the requirement that must be proved to establish a right of way
*c* under Scottish law. But to infer that the purpose of the 1932 Act was to assimilate
English law to Scottish law as regards the acquisition of rights of navigation is to beg the
question whether a right of navigation is aptly described as a right of way over land.
There is in fact authority for the proposition that under Scottish law it is not. *Wills's*
*Trustees v Cairngorm Canoeing and Sailing School Ltd* 1976 SC (HL) 30 concerned the
principles under which, under Scottish law, a public right of navigation may be acquired
*d* by proof of physical capacity for public use and of 'actual public use for a period of which
the memory of man does not run to the contrary in practice for a period of 40 years, this
being capable of proof by evidence, and by *existimatio circumcolentium*' (per Lord
Wilberforce (at 126)). As I understand it, the rule was the same as regards the acquisition
of public rights of way over land before the enactment of the Prescription and Limitation
(Scotland) Act 1973. Section 3(3) of that Act provides:
*e*
'If a public right of way over land has been possessed by the public for a continuous
period of twenty years openly, peaceably and without judicial interruption, then, as
from the expiration of that period, the existence of the right of way as so possessed
shall be exempt from challenge.'

*f* Lord Fraser, having referred to s 3(3), added (at 165):

'That Act is concerned with *inter alia* the establishment by positive prescription of
positive servitudes and public rights of way over land but it does not, in my opinion,
apply to the period of use required to prove navigability of a river. In the latter
context I think "time immemorial" must return its customary meaning of 40 years,
though it is possible that proof of actual use for less than 40 years might suffice if
*g* there were proof that the river had long been regarded as a public channel of
communication by public opinion in the neighbourhood, what was called in Roman
law *existimatio circumcolentium* ...'

The decision of the House of Lords in the *Cairngorm School* case is not a binding
authority on the question whether a right of navigation is a right of way over land for
*h* the purposes of the 1932 Act and its successors. That case concerned a different Act which
has to be construed in the context of Scottish law where the foundations of public rights
of way and of navigation are very different. There is, so far as I have been able to discover,
nothing in the 1973 Act which corresponds to s 31(11). Moreover, the question whether
s 3(3) of the 1973 Act applies to public rights of navigation was not in issue and was not,
I think, adverted to in any of the other speeches in the House of Lords. What was in issue
*j* was whether a right of navigation (by floating logs down the River Spey) once established
by evidence of user from time immemorial had been lost by non-user for 40 years before
the action was brought. However, the passage in the speech of Lord Fraser is strong
persuasive authority for the proposition that a right of navigation over a river is not in
the ordinary sense of the word a right of way over land and, as I have said, the express

extension of the references to land to include land covered by water is capable of being interpreted as designed to include fords and causeways or to make it clear that they are *a* not excluded.

There is another provision in the 1932 Act repeated in its successors which indicates that the legislature did not intend that the Act should apply to rights of navigation.

Section 31(3) of the 1980 Act (which re-enacts precisely similar provisions in the earlier Acts) provides:

'Where the owner of the land over which any such way as aforesaid passes—(*a*) *b* has erected in such manner as to be visible to persons using the way a notice inconsistent with the dedication of the way as a highway, and (*b*) has maintained the notice after 1st January 1934, or any later date on which it was erected, the notice, in the absence of proof of a contrary intention, is sufficient evidence, to negative the intention to dedicate the way as a highway.'

*c*

In the case of a small stream or river it might be possible to place a notice visible to all using the stream or river for the purposes of navigation. In the case of a larger river it might not. Of course public rights of navigation have been established from time immemorial over most large rivers, even where not tidal. However, a right of navigation can exist over an island lake where it might be quite impractical to erect a notice visible to all, in particular to those diverging from the direct route because of the exigencies of *d* wind and weather. *Marshall v Ulleswater Steam Navigation Co Ltd* (1871) LR 7 QB 166 concerned a public right of navigation over Ulleswater.

Counsel for the defendants relied on other provisions in the 1980 Act in support of his submission. 'Highway' is defined in s 328(1) in terms which exclude a ferry or waterway and ss 108, 109 and 111 deal with the diversion of and other works to waterways which are there contrasted with highways. I find it unnecessary to explore the question whether *e* the provisions of the 1932 and 1949 Acts when re-enacted in substantially the same terms in subsequent Highway Acts should be differently construed because of changes in the legislative context and I express no opinion on that point.

Having regard to the clear conclusion I have reached on the first limb of question 5 and in view of the excessive length of this judgment, I do not propose to answer the *f* second limb of the question which, in the view I take, is wholly academic.

In my judgment, the defendants succeed on all the preliminary questions. The only remaining question is whether the plaintiff can rely on user of the river since 1935 to found the implication of dedication by lost modern grant. I will ask counsel to tell me whether the action is to be continued while that question is further litigated or whether the determination of the issues in the sense that I have decided them will be the end of this litigation, subject, of course, to any appeal.

*g*

[Counsel for the plaintiffs informed the judge that the action would proceed to trial.]

*Declaration that statutory provisions on rights of way, not applicable to public rights of navigation.*

*h*

Solicitors: *Payne Hicks Beach* (for the plaintiff); *Hepworth & Chadwick*, Leeds (for the defendants).

Jacqueline Metcalfe   Barrister.

a          # Reed and others v Madon and others

CHANCERY DIVISION
MORRITT J
20, 21, 22, 23, 24, 27, 28, 29, 30 JUNE, 1, 22 JULY 1988

b   *Burial – Burial rights – Exclusive rights to burial plot – Infringement of rights – Body of*
   *defendant's wife buried in plot reserved by plaintiff – Erection of memorial – Whether injunction*
   *would be granted requiring defendant to arrange exhumation of wife's body – Whether injunction*
   *would be granted requiring removal of memorial – Cemeteries Clauses Act 1847, s 48 – Burial*
   *Act 1857, s 25.*

c   The plaintiffs were three sisters and were Turkish Muslims. Shortly before their mother
   died the plaintiffs and their parents had agreed to purchase burial rights to enable all five
   of them to be buried together facing Mecca as was customary. In October 1975 their
   mother died and was buried in a plot purchased by the plaintiffs in a cemetery owned by
   the third defendant. In addition to the plot in which the mother was buried the plaintiffs
   purchased for £320 exclusive burial rights in four adjacent plots which they intended to
d   use for their father and themselves. A deed of grant dated 19 January 1976 was executed
   by the third defendant giving to the plaintiffs exclusive rights of burial for 30 years in
   the four reserved plots subject to the third defendant's rules. The deed of grant was
   entered in the third defendant's register of reserved plots. On 15 March 1976 the part of
   the cemetery containing the five plots purchased by the plaintiffs was conveyed by the
   third defendant to the fourth defendant, an associated company. In April 1976 the
e   plaintiffs' father died and was buried in the reserved plot next to his wife. In October
   1984 the first defendant's wife was buried in one of the plaintiffs' reserved plots. The first
   defendant paid £200 for the burial rights and received from the fourth defendant a deed
   of grant dated 26 October 1984 which was similar to the grant issued to the plaintiffs. In
   March 1985 the first defendant erected a memorial over his wife's grave which was larger
   than the plot in which she was buried and which, with certain plantings, encroached
f   onto the adjoining plot reserved to the plaintiffs. The plaintiffs issued a writ claiming
   that they had exclusive rights of burial in the reserved plots under s 48[a] of the Cemeteries
   Clauses Act 1847, which provided that 'No Body shall be buried in any Place wherein the
   exclusive Right of Burial shall have been granted by the Company . . .' The plaintiffs
   accordingly alleged infringement of their statutory right to the exclusive right of burial
   in their reserved plots, breach of duty, breach of contract and trespass, and sought
g   injunctions restraining the first defendant from trespassing on their reserved plots,
   restraining the third and fourth defendants from permitting any body to be buried in
   their reserved plots without their consent, requiring the defendants to make the necessary
   arrangements to exhume the body of the first defendant's wife and remove it and the
   memorial from their reserved plot, and damages. By a third party notice the first
h   defendant claimed an indemnity against the fourth defendant.

   **Held** – (1) The statutory right under s 48 of the 1847 Act to the exclusive right of burial
   in a reserved plot was to be equated with a right of property and therefore infringement
   of that right conferred a cause of action not only against the cemetery company but also
   against any infringer. Furthermore, the exclusive right of burial in a reserved plot
j   extended to the surface of the plot and necessarily included the right that no one else's
   memorial would be placed over the plot even if it did not contain a body and also the
   right to prevent other acts of encroachment over the reserved plot. Since the plaintiffs'
   statutory right to the exclusive right of burial in their reserved plots had been infringed

---

a   Section 48 is set out at p 434 c, post

when the body of the first defendant's wife was buried in one of the plaintiffs' reserved
plots the plaintiffs had a right of action against all the defendants, who were jointly and *a*
severally liable for the breach of duty constituted by the burial. They were also jointly
and severally liable for the infringement caused by the memorial, since the grant made
to the first defendant required him to obtain permission from the cemetery company for
the memorial and the third and fourth defendants had given permission for which they
charged and were paid £20, but only the first defendant was liable for the further
encroachments made by planting since that had been done without the permission of *b*
the third and fourth defendants (see p 436 *j* to p 437 *b d* to *g*, p 439 *j* to p 440 *b*, p 441 *c*
and p 443 *a*, post).

(2) Since a licence granted by the Home Secretary under s 25*b* of the Burial Act 1857
was required for the exhumation of a body and since such a licence would only be
granted in exceptional circumstances and would not be granted against the wishes of the
nearest living relative, it was unlikely that an injunction requiring the defendants to *c*
make the necessary arrangements to exhume the body of the first defendant's wife and
remove it and the memorial from their reserved plot would have any practical effect and
therefore the court would not grant such an injunction. Instead, the court would order
that the memorial be shifted to leave space for the burial of the plaintiffs in due course
and would make a declaration of the plaintiffs' rights to prevent any further infringement.
The plaintiffs were entitled to damages for loss of burial rights and distress, and the third *d*
and fourth defendants should indemnify the first defendant for his share of the damages
for loss of burial rights, half the cost of moving the memorial and three-quarters of his
share of the damages for distress (see p 440 *c* to *f*, p 441 *a b j* to p 442 *f* and p 443 *a*, post).

**Notes**
For the grant of exclusive right of burial in a cemetery, see 10 Halsbury's Laws (4th edn) *e*
para 1126, and for cases on the subject, see 7 Digest (Reissue) 567, 3268–3271.

For the Cemeteries Clauses Act 1847, s 48, see 5 Halsbury's Statutes (4th edn) (1989
reissue) 702.

For the Burial Act 1857, s 25, see ibid 719.

*f*

**Cases referred to in judgment**
*Ashby v Harris* (1868) LR 3 CP 523.
*Bryan v Whistler* (1828) 8 B & C 288, 108 ER 1050.
*Cutler v Wandsworth Stadium Ltd* [1949] 1 All ER 544, [1949] AC 398, HL.
*Hoskins-Abrahall v Paignton UDC* [1929] 1 Ch 375 [1928] All ER Rep 55, CA.
*London Cemetery Co v Cundey* [1953] 2 All ER 257, [1953] 1 WLR 786.
*McGough v Lancaster Burial Board* (1888) 21 QBD 323, CA.                          *g*
*Matthews v Jeffrey* (1880) 6 QBD 290.
*Nottingham General Cemetery Co, Re* [1955] 2 All ER 504, [1955] Ch 683, [1955] 3 WLR
   61.

**Cases also cited**                                                                *h*
*Andrews v Barnes* (1888) 39 Ch D 133, [1886–90] All ER Rep 758, CA.
*Archer v Brown* [1984] 2 All ER 267, [1985] QB 401.
*Beckett (Alfred F) Ltd v Lyons* [1967] 1 All ER 833, [1967] Ch 449, CA.
*East Suffolk Rivers Catchment Board v Kent* [1940] 4 All ER 527, [1941] AC 74, HL.

---

*b*   Section 25, so far as material, provides: 'Except in the cases where a body is removed from one   *j*
     consecrated place of burial to another by faculty granted by the ordinary for that purpose, it shall
     not be lawful to remove any body, or the remains of any body, which may have been interred in
     any place of burial, without licence under the hand of one of Her Majesty's Principal Secretaries of
     State, and with such precautions as such Secretary of State may prescribe as the condition of such
     licence ...'

*Hadley v Baxendale* (1854) 9 Exch 341, [1843–60] All ER Rep 461, 156 ER 145.
*Heywood v Wellers (a firm)* [1976] 1 All ER 300, [1976] QB 446, CA.
*Jarvis v Swans Tours Ltd* [1973] 1 All ER 71, [1973] QB 233, CA.
*Perry v Sidney Phillips & Son (a firm)* [1982] 3 All ER 705, [1982] 1 WLR 1297, CA.
*Spooner v Brewster* (1825) 3 Bing 136, 130 ER 465.
*R v Abney Park Cemetery Co* (1873) LR 8 QB 515.
*R v St Mary Abbot's, Kensington* (1840) 12 Ad & El 824, 113 ER 1026.
*Strutt v Whitnell* [1975] 2 All ER 510, [1975] 1 WLR 870, CA.
*Sutherland (Duke) v Heathcote* [1892] 1 Ch 475, CA.

## Action

By a writ and statement of claim dated 14 June 1985 the plaintiffs, Handan Iffet Reed, Neriman Grove and Nezih Simon, the daughters of Ahmed Essad and Fatma Essad (both deceased), sought (1) an injunction to restrain the first defendant, F S Madon, from erecting any structure or entering or otherwise trespassing on the allotments reserved for the first plaintiff in Brookwood cemetery or any part thereof, (2) an injunction to restrain the third and fourth defendants, Brookwood Cemetery Ltd and Brookwood Park Ltd, respectively and each of them from allowing any body to be buried in the reserved allotments without the consent of the first plaintiff, (3) an order that the defendants take all necessary steps, subject to obtaining the licence of the Secretary of State for the Home Department, to procure the exhumation and removal of the remains of the first defendant's wife from the reserved allotments and the removal of the memorial stone over her grave, (4) an order that the first defendant apply for and take all necessary steps within his power to obtain the licence of the Secretary of State pursuant to s 25 of the Burial Act 1857 for the exhumation and removal of his wife's remains from the reserved allotment, (5) alternatively, an order that the first defendant provide to or for the benefit of the plaintiffs his consent in writing for the remains to be exhumed and removed from the reserved allotment and to take all other necessary steps within his power to enable the plaintiffs to obtain such licence, (6) alternatively, damages in lieu of the order, and (7) further or alternatively, damages for trespass, interference with the plaintiffs' rights, breach of statute, breach of contract and/or breach of duty. The first defendant issued a third party notice against the third and fourth defendants claiming to be indemnified against the plaintiffs' claim. The action against the second defendant, Mr D J T Dally, a director of the defendant companies, was struck out by order of the court dated 30 October 1986. The facts are set out in the judgment.

*Frank Hinks* for the plaintiffs.
*Stephen Lloyd* for the first defendant.
*John Bryant* for the third and fourth defendants.

*Cur adv vult*

22 July. The following judgment was delivered.

**MORRITT J.** The third defendant, Brookwood Cemetery Ltd, was originally incorporated in 1852 with the name of the London Necropolis and Mausoleum Co by the Act 15 & 16 Vict c cxlix. By s 8 of that Act the Cemeteries Clauses Act 1847 and the Lands Clauses Consolidation Act 1845 were, with immaterial exceptions, incorporated therein. The Cemeteries Clauses Act 1847 provides, inter alia, as follows:

'XL. The Company may set apart such Parts of the Cemetery as they think fit for the Purpose of granting exclusive Rights of Burial therein, and they may sell, either in perpetuity or for a limited Time, and subject to such Conditions as they think fit, the exclusive Right of Burial in any Parts of the Cemetery so set apart, or the Right

of One or more Burials therein, and they may sell the Right of placing any
Monument or Gravestone in the Cemetery, or any Tablet or monumental Inscription     *a*
on the Walls of any Chapel or other Building within the Cemetery.

XLI. The company shall cause a Plan of the Cemetery to be made upon a Scale
sufficiently large to show the Situation of every Burial Place in all the Parts of the
Cemetery so set apart, and in which an exclusive Right of Burial has been granted;
and all such Burial Places shall be numbered, and such Numbers shall be entered in
a Book to be kept for that Purpose, and such Book shall contain the Names and     *b*
Descriptions of the several Persons to whom the exclusive Right of Burial in any
such Place of Burial has been granted by the Company; and no Place of Burial, with
exclusive Right of Burial therein, shall be made in the Cemetery without the same
being marked out in such Plan, and a corresponding Entry made in the said Book,
and the said Plan and Book shall be kept by the Clerk of the Company . . .

XLVIII. No Body shall be buried in any Place wherein the exclusive Right of     *c*
Burial shall have been granted by the Company, except with the Consent of the
Owner for the Time being of such exclusive Right of Burial.'

In 1935 the third defendant was registered under the Companies Act 1929. The
principal object set forth in cl 3(1) of its memorandum of association has at all material
times been:     *d*

'To make provision for the interment and/or cremation of the dead and to carry
on the business of undertakers in all its branches and any ancillary business in
accordance with and under the powers of the London Necropolis and National
Mausoleum Companies Act 1852 and Acts amending the same, and the Lands
Clauses Consolidation Act as incorporated, and to maintain, keep and use the
cemetery at or near Woking as thereby authorised and generally to comply with     *e*
and observe the provisions of the said Acts of Parliament so far as applicable to the
company.'

The third defendant was the owner of Brookwood Cemetery at all material times down
to at least March 1976.

The plaintiffs are sisters. They are, and their parents were, Turkish Muslims. On 11     *f*
October 1975 their mother, Mrs Essad, died and was buried in Brookwood Cemetery. In
addition to the plot in which Mrs Essad was buried, for reasons which I will describe
later, the plaintiffs at the same time purchased from the third defendant exclusive burial
rights in four plots adjoining the plot in which Mrs Essad was buried for the further sum
of £320.

By a deed of grant executed by the third defendant and dated 19 January 1976, in     *g*
consideration of the sum of £320, the third defendant granted to the first plaintiff (who
was wrongly described therein as 'Mr Reed')—

'The exclusive rights of burial for thirty years in the reserved grave sites numbered
RA 2838, 2839, 2840 and 2841 in the Company's books and measuring 9 feet by 4
feet each subject to the rules and regulations of the Company and to the obligation
to have the grave site maintained by the Company. A memorial stone or monument     *h*
may be erected only with the prior approval of the company, any such memorial
stone or monument to be kept in good repair at the expense of the grantee.'

This grant was duly entered in the register of reserved plots maintained by the third
defendant as '4 reserved allotments adjoining Grave No. 226132 (Essad) on bank on old
Moslem ground'. There is no evidence of what (if any) rules and regulations of the third     *j*
defendant were then in force.

It is common ground that the position of the four reserved allotments when viewed
from the adjacent road was one to the right and three to the left of Mrs Essad's grave. For
convenience I shall number these plots 1 to 5 from the left. Mrs Essad was buried in plot
4.

On 15 March 1976 the relevant part of the cemetery was conveyed by the third
*a* defendant to the fourth defendant, Brookwood Park Ltd, and on 20 May 1976 the fourth
defendant was registered as the proprietor with title absolute in HM Land Registry. The
fourth defendant was originally incorporated as the Stockport Borough Cemetery Co Ltd
under the Companies Act 1929. Its objects are appropriate for the carrying on of a
cemetery business. There is no evidence that it was ever given any special statutory rights
or powers.

*b* On 21 April 1976 the plaintiffs' father died, and on the next day he was buried in the
reserved plot to the left of his wife, that is to say plot 3, which was given the grave plot
number 226320.

On 19 October 1984 the wife of the first defendant died. In circumstances which I
shall describe in greater detail, on 24 October 1984 she was buried in the part of the
plaintiffs' reserved allotments which I have for convenience numbered plot 1. The first
*c* defendant paid £200 for the burial rights in this plot and obtained from the fourth
defendant a deed of grant dated 26 October 1984 in the same form as that obtained by
the plaintiffs, except that the specified period was 50 years, not 30, the word 'reserved'
was omitted and there was added at the end: 'It is strongly recommended that advice be
sought from the Company before commitment regarding memorials.'

On 13 March 1985 a memorial measuring in excess of the 9 feet by 4 feet plot to
*d* which the first defendant thought he had purchased exclusive burial rights was erected
on the first defendant's instructions. There is an issue whether the memorial extends
beyond the boundaries of plot 1 onto part of plot 2 as well. But it is not necessary to
consider this issue until after I have considered what causes of action the plaintiffs have
against which defendant.

The writ in this action was issued on 14 June 1985, the original second defendant,
*e* Mr D J T Dally, a director of the defendant companies, was subsequently struck out.

The plaintiffs' claims are put under four heads. (1) The plaintiffs claim a statutory right
under s 48 of the 1847 Act to the exclusive right of burial in plots 1 and 2 which they
claim to have been infringed by the first, third and fourth defendants. This is disputed
by the first defendant but not by the third or fourth defendants. (2) In the alternative
they claim that the grant of exclusive burial rights confers on them an interest in land in
*f* or over plots 1 and 2 which they claim has been infringed by the first, third and fourth
defendants. This is disputed by all the defendants. (3) The plaintiffs claim against the
third defendant and the fourth defendant damages for breach of duty imposed by s 41 of
the 1847 Act. The third and fourth defendants do not dispute their liability. (4) The
plaintiffs claim against the third defendant damages for breach of contract. The third
defendant does not dispute its liability.

*g* By a third party notice the first defendant claims against the fourth defendant an
indemnity against any liability he may have incurred to the plaintiffs and also damages
(including damages for distress) for negligence and breach of contract against the fourth
defendant. It is agreed between the first defendant, the third defendant and the fourth
defendant that no distinction should be drawn between the third and fourth defendants,
*h* and the first defendant has elected that any judgment to which he might be entitled
against either of them should be given against the fourth defendant.

In these circumstances I will consider, first, the question of liability under the first and
second heads of the plaintiffs' claim.

In the early years of the nineteenth century it was quite common for companies to be
incorporated by private Act of Parliament for the purpose of providing cemeteries
*j* otherwise than in a churchyard. The legal nature of a right to exclusive burial in a part
of a churchyard was by no means clear, as is shown by the various references in *Bryan v
Whistler* (1828) 8 B & C 288, 108 ER 1050, to 'interest in land', 'easement', 'incorporeal
hereditament' and 'privilege'. That case did not decide what the legal nature of such right
was.

The 1847 Act was enacted against this background. Sections 40 to 51 contained detailed provisions for the grant of exclusive burial rights in cemeteries to which that Act applied. Sections 40 and 41 I have already read. Section 42 provided for the form of grant which was contained in the schedule. Section 43 required the company to keep a register of grants. Section 44 provided:

> 'The exclusive Right of Burial in any such Place of Burial shall, whether granted in perpetuity or for a limited Time, be considered as the Personal Estate of the Grantee, and may be assigned in his Lifetime or bequeathed by his Will.'

Section 45 authorised the form of assignment contained in the schedule. Such form was an assignment by AB of:

> '... the exclusive Right of Burial ... granted to me ... in perpetuity [or as the Case may be]... and all my Estate, Title, and Interest therein, to hold the same unto the said C.D. in perpetuity [or as the Case may be ...]...'

Section 46 provides for a register of assignments. Section 47 requires the registration of probates of every will whereby an exclusive right of burial is bequeathed. Section 48 I have already read. Sections 49, 50 and 51 deal with consecrated ground and the regulation of monuments.

I have been referred to a number of cases decided after 1847, but in none of these was the effect of s 48 of the 1847 Act in point. They are, in chronological order, *Ashby v Harris* (1868) LR 3 CP 523, *Matthews v Jeffrey* (1880) 6 QBD 290, *McGough v Lancaster Burial Board* (1888) 21 QBD 323, *Hoskins-Abrahall v Paignton UDC* [1929] 1 Ch 375, [1928] All ER Rep 55, *London Cemetery Co v Cundey* [1953] 2 All ER 257, [1953] 1 WLR 786 and *Re Nottingham Cemetery Co* [1955] 2 All ER 504, [1955] Ch 683 (in which none of the earlier cases was cited).

The first defendant contends that on its true construction the 1847 Act provides for the regulation of the cemetery and casts duties on the cemetery company alone. The consequence, as alleged, is that there can be no duty on the first defendant which could confer on the plaintiffs a claim for breach of statutory duty against him.

The plaintiffs rely on *Cutler v Wandsworth Stadium Ltd* [1949] 1 All ER 544 at 547–548, [1949] AC 398 at 407, where Lord Simonds said:

> 'It is, I think, true that it is often a difficult question whether, where a statutory obligation is placed on A., B., who conceives himself to be damnified by A.'s breach of it, has a right of action against him. But on the present case I cannot entertain any doubt. I do not propose to try to formulate any rules by reference to which such a question can infallibly be answered. The only rule which in all circumstances is valid is that the answer must depend on a consideration of the whole Act and the circumstances, including the pre-existing law, in which it was enacted. But that there are indications which point with more or less force to the one answer or the other is clear from authorities which, even where they do not bind, will have great weight with the House. For instance, if a statutory duty is prescribed, but no remedy by way of penalty or otherwise for its breach is imposed, it can be assumed that a right of civil action accrues to the person who is damnified by the breach. For, if it were not so, the statute would be but a pious aspiration.'

The 1847 Act contains no penalties for the infringement of s 48. Accordingly, unless the Act confers on the owner of the exclusive right of burial a cause of action, his right is nugatory. The first defendant suggested that such right would be sufficiently protected by a cause of action against the cemetery company alone. It was suggested that if the right was infringed by a third party the cemetery company could sue in trespass and thereby protect the exclusive right which it had granted.

I am unable to accept this submission. The 1847 Act contemplates that the exclusive right of burial may exist in perpetuity and by devolution and assignment pass through a number of hands. It is equated with a right of property. In principle, the owner of such a a right can protect it by action against any infringer. Moreover, as the facts of this case show, the cemetery company might by its own acts vis-à-vis the third party preclude itself from suing the third party. Finally, s 48 is in general terms. Had it been intended that the obligation should be cast on the cemetery company alone it could so easily have been stated: cf ss 41, 43, 46, 47, 50 and 51. Accordingly, in my judgment, s 48 of the 1847 Act confers on the plaintiffs a cause of action against the first defendant as well as against the third and fourth defendants.

b The second issue, whether an exclusive right of burial is an interest in land, is of academic interest only. As counsel for the plaintiffs readily accepted, it would make no practical difference if I held, as I have, that the plaintiffs have a cause of action against the first defendant for breach of the statutory duty imposed by s 48 of the 1847 Act. Accordingly, I do not find it necessary to deal with this point.

The extent of the grant of exclusive burial rights falls to be determined by reference to c the 1847 Act and the deed of grant to the plaintiffs. The defendants contended that it conferred no rights over or control of the surface of the land at least until a corpse was buried thereunder. Thus, it was alleged, the plaintiffs could not object to the existence of Mrs Madon's memorial or further planting in extension of the site of her grave carried out on the first defendant's instructions or to the removal of shrubs and roses planted by the plaintiffs.

d Section 40 of the 1847 Act specifically authorised the third defendant to sell 'the Right of placing any Monument or Gravestone in the Cemetery . . .' The grant to the plaintiffs included the provision that 'A memorial stone or monument may be erected only with the prior approval of the Company'. It would be entirely inconsistent with the grant as a whole if the company were entitled to permit a memorial to a third party to be placed on a site in which it had granted exclusive burial rights. To do so would in practice e prevent the exercise of the right of burial and preclude the owner thereof from having any prospect of obtaining the company's permission to the erection of his own memorial. Thus in my judgment the rights granted to the plaintiffs must necessarily include the right that no one else's memorial shall be placed over the site in which they have exclusive burial rights.

f Further encroachment by extending the site of a grave by planting or fencing has the same effect. It would be deplorable if the due exercise of a right of exclusive burial involved the need to rip out cypress trees, turfing and fencing in extension of someone else's grave and memorial. Accordingly, in my judgment, the rights conferred on the plaintiffs necessarily include the right to prevent other acts which have the effect of extending an adjoining grave site onto land over which they have exclusive rights of g burial.

Before considering whether these rights have been infringed and, if so, by whom and what relief the plaintiffs are entitled to, I must set out the facts as I find them in greater detail.

A few months before the death of their mother in October 1975 the plaintiffs, their father and mother had discussed and agreed to purchase rights to a plot in which all five h of them could be buried side by side in due course. It was necessarily implicit in such agreement that each of them should be buried so as to face Mecca. This was a custom observed by Turkish families of their class, and the agreement was designed among other things to give comfort to their mother in the last few weeks of her life. Then, or shortly before their father's death, it was agreed between themselves and him that for reasons of family relationships the second plaintiff should be buried in plot 1, the third plaintiff in j plot 2, Mr Essad in plot 3 and the first plaintiff in plot 5. It was and is important to the plaintiffs that this plan should be carried out, not only because of the custom, but, more significantly, because of the promises given to their parents.

The plots, purchased in 1975 and 1976, were alleged by the plaintiffs to extend, when viewed from the road, from the left-hand edge of a path on the right for 20 feet with a depth of 9 feet. If this is right, it means that Mrs Essad's grave straddles plots 4 and 5 and

Mr Essad's grave straddles plots 3 and 4. The third and fourth defendants contend that
the graves should be assumed to be in the centre of their respective plots. I agree. The
path in question was not defined, but had been worn down by use. It could not be
sensibly regarded as a permanent marker. The only reasonable assumption, given that
the rights to all five plots were bought at the time of Mrs Essad's death, is that Mrs Essad
was correctly buried in the centre of plot 4 and that the other four plots should be
measured off on that assumption. The consequence is that Mrs Madon's grave and the
memorial subsequently put up by the first defendant is confined to plot 1 and does not
itself overlap on to plot 2. I should add that on this finding the boundaries, as contended
for by the third and fourth defendants on a marked plan, are not accurate in that the
boundaries on the 4-foot sides of the five plots need to be adjusted so that the coffins
of Mr and Mrs Essad are central with regard to those sides as well as with regard to the
9-foot sides.

Following the deaths of their parents the plaintiffs arranged for the entire site to be
maintained by the third defendant until July 1979. Some form of enclosure with small
pines was put round all five plots. The pines did not survive, and after 1979 some form
of enclosure consisting of shrubby honeysuckle was substituted. There were four small
stones to mark the four corners, and three rose bushes were planted. The plaintiffs, or
one of them, took it in turns to tend the plots by cutting the grass every three or four
weeks.

But partly due to the fact that larger pines overshadowed the site so that nothing grew
well, and partly due to vandalism, the plaintiffs' efforts to care for the plots were not very
successful. The plaintiffs allege that it ought to have been obvious when Mrs Madon
came to be buried in October 1984 that burial rights in plot 1 had already been granted
to someone else.

After Mrs Madon's death, Mr Reddy, a friend of Mr and Mrs Madon of many years'
standing, undertook the task of making arrangements for her funeral. He went to the
cemetery and inspected two sites. Having selected one of them, he took the first defendant
to see it. The first defendant approved, and arrangements were made for Mrs Madon's
burial in that plot. But the night before the funeral the cemetery foreman telephoned
Mr Reddy to inform him that the chosen site was not available and suggested plot 1
instead. Mr Reddy agreed. In their oral evidence both Mr Reddy and the first defendant
stated that they saw plot 1 for the first time on the day of the funeral. Mr Reddy said he
went a few hours earlier to make sure that the site was properly prepared.

This evidence conflicted with the defence of the first defendant and a proof of evidence
of Mr Reddy, as to which privilege was waived. In each of these documents the first
defendant and Mr Reddy said that plot 1 was the second site shown to Mr Reddy and to
the first defendant. The plaintiffs invite me to infer that both Mr Reddy and the first
defendant deliberately changed their evidence at a late stage, because they thought to do
so would assist the first defendant's case, and that the only reason for so thinking was that
they now realised that there were signs on plot 1 from which they should have, but did
not, deduce that the burial rights therein belonged to somebody else.

I do not draw that inference. If such signs had existed, I find it inconceivable that the
cemetery foreman would not actually have concluded that the burial rights might have
belonged to another and checked from the register which did exist. Thus if such signs
existed there is no reason to think that he would have suggested plot 1 when he
telephoned Mr Reddy the night before the funeral.

In my judgment the combined effect of the overshadowed nature of the site, the
consequences of vandalism and the fact that these events took place in late October is
such that there was no sufficient indication on plot 1 from which the first defendant
might have deduced that the burial rights had already been disposed of to another.
Nevertheless, in preparing Mrs Madon's grave, such honeysuckle or rose bushes as still
existed were removed. It was contended by the third and fourth defendants that the
plaintiffs had no right to maintain them on the site and did so merely by the licence of

the third and fourth defendants. But at the least revocation of such licence would require
a reasonable notice to the plaintiffs, which they were never given.

In late November 1984 the first defendant gave instructions to Mr Orgill of Patrick
Stonemasons for the making and erection of a memorial over his wife's grave. The
memorial was ultimately erected on 13 March 1985. Also in November 1984 the
plaintiffs discovered that Mrs Madon had been buried in plot 1, and on 10 December
1984 solicitors instructed by them wrote to the third defendant protesting. The plaintiffs
b claim that by 16 to 18 February 1985 the first defendant knew of their claim and
deliberately hastened the erection of the memorial in a bid to strengthen his position.
The first defendant contends that he did not know of their claim until about 7 March
1985 and that his concern was merely to have the memorial erected in time for certain
traditional ceremonies on the Iranian New Year, which fell on 21 March 1985. This issue
has been hotly contested, and I must deal with it in some detail. [His Lordship considered
c the evidence, concluded that on the balance of probabilities the first defendant had been
informed of the plaintiffs' claim to plot 1 on 27 February 1985, and continued:] Even if I
had reached the conclusion that the first defendant knew of the plaintiffs' claim on or
before 18 February, I would still not have concluded that the first defendant hurried on
the erection of the memorial to strengthen his position vis-à-vis the plaintiffs. The first
defendant's attitude throughout has been that he purchased burial rights from the fourth
d defendant. His wife was buried. He paid £6,000 for the memorial, 50% in November
1984 and the balance on 22 March 1985. He paid a fee to the fourth defendant for
permission to have the memorial erected. He regarded the plaintiffs' claim as nothing to
do with him. Moreover, no doubt was cast on his evidence that the Iranian New Year on
21 March is a very important date for the commemoration of the dead with appropriate
observances at the graveside.
e    Nevertheless, I have no doubt that the first defendant knew of the plaintiffs' claim two
weeks before the memorial was erected. He took no steps to contact the plaintiffs or their
solicitors. There is no suggestion that he sought or obtained any advice on the validity or
otherwise of their claims, nor did he tell Mr Orgill to delay the erection of the memorial.
Instead he wrote to Mr Orgill on 2 March stating that it was imperative that the memorial
should be erected by 17 March. In these circumstances he took the risk that his view that
f the plaintiffs' claim was nothing to do with him might be wrong.

After the erection of the memorial various works were undertaken on the instructions
of the first defendant by way of turfing and the planting of cypresses, which had the
effect of extending the site of Mrs Madon's grave further than the memorial and on to
plot 2.
g    It was contended on behalf of the first defendant that he had not in fact infringed the
plaintiffs' rights by the burial, because he had not caused or permitted his wife to be
buried in plot 1. It was argued that the third and fourth defendants chose the site and
that the first defendant had no property in Mrs Madon's corpse or duty to bury her.

This contention ignores the facts that the first defendant accepted the site offered by
the cemetery foreman, made arrangements through Mr Reddy for Mrs Madon's
h interment and purported to purchase the exclusive burial rights in plot 1 to enable the
interment of his wife in that plot. In doing so he infringed the plaintiffs' rights. Questions
of fault or blame are irrelevant as between him and the plaintiffs on the question of
infringement.

Accordingly, in my judgment all the defendants are jointly and severally liable to the
plaintiffs in respect of the breach of duty constituted by the burial of Mrs Madon.
j    In the case of the memorial the third and fourth defendants claim that they are not
responsible because it was left to the first defendant to decide how large it should be and
whether it should be erected and, if so, where. This submission ignores the terms of the
first defendant's grant, which required him to obtain permission from the company, Mr
Orgill's evidence to the effect that he obtained permission from Mr Dally and the fact
that the third and fourth defendants charged and were paid £20 for giving their

permission. Thus, in my judgment, all the defendants are jointly and severally liable for
this infringement also.
    The further encroachments by the turfing and fencing and planting of cypresses were
carried out on the first defendant's instructions without permission from the third and
fourth defendants, so that only he is liable therefore.
    Equally, the preparation of Mrs Madon's grave, whereby such plants as there were on
plots 1 to 5 were removed, was the responsibility of the third and fourth defendants
alone.
    I turn now to the question of what, if any, injunctive relief should be granted.
Throughout the pre-trial correspondence and in the statement of claim the plaintiffs'
principal claim was that the body of Mrs Madon should be exhumed and the memorial
and the various encroachments should be removed altogether.
    By s 25 of the Burial Act 1857 the exhumation of Mrs Madon would require the
licence of the Home Secretary. The Home Secretary has an absolute discretion whether
to grant such a licence or not. Evidence was given by an official from the Home Office
to the effect that only in exceptional circumstances would the Home Secretary grant a
licence without the consent of the nearest living relative of the deceased. Consent given
pursuant to a court order would not be regarded as 'improper'. But a licence would not
be granted against the wishes of the nearest living relative.
    Thus the most that the court could do would be to order the first defendant to apply
to the Home Secretary for a licence and, if granted, to procure the exhumation of his
wife's body. I do not think that it would be right to do so.
    First, the court would be unable, by way of enforcement of any such order, to achieve
the result of exhumation. In the light of the evidence as to the Home Secretary's practice
I have no doubt that an application for a licence submitted by the first defendant
following a period of imprisonment for contempt of court, or, more likely, an application
made by a master in the name of the first defendant pursuant to a further order of the
court, would be refused. Moreover, I am very doubtful whether any licence would be
granted on an application made by the first defendant without resort being made to the
court's coercive powers. Thus in making such an order the court would in all probability
be acting in vain.
    Second, as I have already held, there was no reason why the first defendant or Mr
Reddy should have realised in October 1984 that exclusive rights of burial in plot 1 had
already been granted to the plaintiffs. The first defendant was as much a victim of the
fourth defendant's incompetence as the plaintiffs.
    Third, in the light of other possible orders to which I shall shortly refer, the exhumation
of Mrs Madon is not necessary to enable substantial practical effect to be given to the
plaintiffs' rights and the promises to their parents. Thus to make such an order would
give rise to substantial hardship and distress to the first defendant without any sufficient
corresponding advantage to the plaintiffs.
    Fourth, to refuse such an order in the exercise of a judicial discretion is consistent with
the decision of Fry J in Matthews v Jeffrey (1880) 6 QBD 290.
    At the trial the plaintiffs, while not abandoning their claim to such relief, sought as
their principal claim an order on the first defendant to move the memorial 1ft 3in to the
left, so that, while still covering Mrs Madon's grave, it would leave space for the burial in
due course of the plaintiffs in accordance with their family agreement. This was opposed
by the first defendant on the ground that in accordance with their family agreement plot
1 was reserved for the second plaintiff. She is now 55, and the exclusive burial rights
expire in 17 years' time. Thus, so the argument ran, unless the second plaintiff died
before she was 73, Mrs Madon's memorial would have been moved to no purpose. On
behalf of the plaintiffs it was contended that in practice the exclusive burial rights would
continue, because there would be insufficient space to grant them to anyone else.
    I decline to enter into any speculation as to the second plaintiff's expectation of life.
The fact is that, as I have held, Mrs Madon's memorial was erected in full knowledge of

the plaintiffs' claim. I have concluded that its erection infringed the plaintiffs' rights.
*a* The evidence of Mr Orgill was that in all proability it can be moved within a day and
without damage. The third and fourth defendants consent to it being moved 1ft 3in to
the left, which will involve an encroachment to that extent onto their land to the left of
plot 1. If it is moved to that extent it will enable the plaintiffs to be buried in due course
in accordance with their family agreement, because the third and fourth defendants also
agree that two bodies may be buried in the space which would then be available between
*b* the right-hand side of Mrs Madon's memorial and the left-hand side of Mr Essad's grave.
I will make such an order. I will leave to further argument the form of such an order,
but subject to such argument I think para 1 of the draft submitted by the plaintiffs is
appropriate. The plaintiffs also seek injunctions restraining any further infringement of
their rights. They contend that the first defendant has continually infringed their rights
in the past. It is true that the first defendant has consistently taken the view that the
*c* plaintiffs had no rights. But I have no reason to think that if by court order those rights
are declared the first defendant would infringe them in the future. Accordingly, I will
make a declaration of the plaintiffs' rights in accordance with this judgment and give
liberty to apply for an injunction if need arises.

I turn then to the question of damages. The result of my judgment so far is that the
plaintiffs are now excluded for all time from plot 1. Their rights in plot 1 have no
*d* residual value. Thus the measure of damages is the cost of another plot with some
addition to account for diminution in value of the remaining four. The evidence suggests
that the cost of a plot in 1987 was about £622, to which I add a small percentage to bring
it up to date, reaching a figure of £650. The diminution in value of the remaining four
I assess as half of that sum, namely £325. Thus I assess the loss of burial rights in plot 1
at £975.
*e* Counsel for the third and fourth defendants contended that the plaintiffs had failed in
their duty to mitigate their damage by unreasonably refusing to accept the alternatives
offered to them. I ruled that this contention was not open to the third and fourth
defendants in the absence of a defence raising this issue. Leave was sought to amend by
reference to offers contained in two letters from the third and fourth defendants to the
*f* plaintiffs' solicitors, dated 20 December 1984 and the 11 July 1985. I gave leave to amend
because the reasonableness or otherwise of those offers was extensively canvassed in the
evidence, albeit then directed to the exercise of the court's discretion in making
mandatory orders. Thus no injustice would be caused by giving leave to amend after the
evidence had been concluded.

The question is, therefore, whether the plaintiffs acted unreasonably in refusing those
*g* offers when made. In my judgment they did not. First, to have accepted any of them
would have involved releasing their rights against the first defendant. Second, the offers
would not mitigate the very special loss which the plaintiffs would suffer by being unable
to implement the agreement with their parents.

The letter of 20 December 1984 contained two offers. The first was for exclusive burial
rights in a plot to the left of Mrs Madon's grave. This would, if accepted, have separated
*h* at least one member of the family from the rest. The second was for a five-plot family
burial ground elsewhere in the cemetery. But this would have involved the exhumation
of the bodies of Mr and Mrs Essad.

The letter of the 11 July 1985 offered either one or three plots between Mr and Mrs
Essad's graves and the road. But this ground was not made up and was liable to erosion.
Its proximity to the road made it likely that cars would from time to time run over the
*j* graves.

Thus there was, in my judgment, no breach by the plaintiffs of their duty to mitigate
their damage. Accordingly, I will give judgment against the first, third and fourth
defendants in the sum of £975 under this head.

The various encroachments by the first defendant on plot 2, to which I have referred,
by planting and fencing have not as such caused any damage to the plaintiffs in the past

(except for their distress, to which I shall refer later) and will give rise to none in the
future in the light of the injunction I will make. Thus no damages are recoverable in this *a*
respect. The removal by the third and fourth defendants of the plaintiffs' plants in the
course of preparing Mrs Madon's grave caused some, but minimal, damage, which I
assess at £10. Judgment will be entered against the fourth defendant for that sum.

The plaintiffs also claim damages for their distress. None of the defendants contended
that damages for distress are irrecoverable as a matter of law for breach of a statutory
duty or of a contract such as arises in this case. It is readily foreseeable and within the *b*
contemplation of the parties that if the body of a third party is buried in a plot in which
the plaintiffs are entitled to exclusive burial rights it is probable that distress will be
caused to the plaintiffs. It was common ground that damages for anxiety and
inconvenience due to involvement in litigation are not recoverable.

There is no doubt that each of the plaintiffs suffered considerable distress at the
discovery of the fact that Mrs Madon had been buried in plot 1 and further distress at the *c*
first defendant's subsequent encroachments, quite apart from any anxiety caused by this
action. The plaintiffs made it plain that their concern was not to recover money but to
be put in a position whereby the family agreement could be performed. Nevertheless,
their claims for damages for distress were not abandoned.

Damages under this head cannot be quantified by any process of valuation. I bear in
mind that the object of any such award is to compensate the plaintiffs and not to punish *d*
the defendants. In my judgment, justice would be done by an award in favour of the
plaintiffs of £750 each. Accordingly, there will be judgment against the defendants for
£2,250 under this head.

I turn now to the third party notice. There is no doubt that the original fault lay with
the third and fourth defendants. The subsequent erection of a memorial was, while
primarily the first defendant's responsibility, contributed to by the third and fourth *e*
defendants, both by the original grant of exclusive burial rights to the first defendant
and by giving permission to the first defendant to erect the memorial. In those
circumstances, in my judgment, the third and fourth defendants should indemnify the
first defendant against any part of the sum of £975 which he may be called on to pay,
and should contribute half the cost of the expense of moving the memorial in accordance *f*
with my order. In the case of the damages for distress which I have awarded the plaintiffs,
in my judgment, the third and fourth defendants should contribute 75% of anything the
first defendant is called on to pay.

The form of this order will require consideration. It is my intention that the third and
fourth defendants should ultimately bear the liability for the percentages I have
mentioned, irrespective of which defendant the plaintiffs turn to for enforcement of the *g*
judgments in their favour.

By his third party notice the first defendant also claimed against the fourth defendant
damages in negligence and for breach of contract for his distress. But, as was made plain
in the concluding passages of his cross-examination on behalf of the plaintiffs, his distress
was wholly due to being sued by the plaintiffs and anxiety as to what (if any) order the
court might make. Before he was sued his attitude had been that the dispute between *h*
the plaintiffs and the third and fourth defendants was nothing to do with him. In these
circumstances in my judgment the first defendant is not entitled to recover damages for
distress from the fourth defendant.

Finally, I should record that in the course of his submissions counsel for the plaintiffs
contended that the conveyance of the cemetery by the third defendant to the fourth
defendant in March 1976 was void and that the register should be rectified. I have not *j*
dealt with this submission, because I was unable to see how it could affect any question I
had to decide. If the first defendant had infringed the rights of the plaintiffs, it was
immaterial whether the grant he had obtained from the fourth defendant was valid or
not. Equally, if the fourth defendant was liable to the first defendant that was because it
had purported to grant him exclusive burial rights in plot 1, and it was irrelevant

a whether it had title to do so or not. Moreover, the question may well affect the rights of other persons who are not parties to this action.

In the result, therefore, there will be judgment in the action against all three defendants, and in the third party proceedings against the fourth defendant in accordance with my findings. I will hear counsel as to the form of the order.

*Orders accordingly. Leave to first defendant to appeal granted.*

b

Solicitors: *Marsh Regan* (for the plaintiffs); *Stocken & Lambert* (for the first defendant); *Robbins Olivey,* Woking (for the third and fourth defendants).

Hazel Hartman    Barrister.

c

# Practice Direction

QUEEN'S BENCH DIVISION

d

*Evidence – Foreign tribunal – Examination of witness in relation to matters pending before foreign tribunal – Depositions for transmission to requesting court – Depositions normally to be typewritten – Certified true copy typescript to accompany signed manuscript where impracticable to obtain signature to typescript – Evidence (Proceedings in Other Jurisdictions) Act 1975.*

e When witnesses are ordered to be examined before district registrars, examiners of the court or others by orders made under the Evidence (Proceedings in Other Jurisdictions) Act 1975, handwritten depositions of their evidence are sometimes tendered to the Senior Master for transmission to the requesting court. Decipherment of manuscript depositions is liable to cause difficulty and embarrassment to the foreign courts to which they are sent. Depositions should therefore be typewritten. If it is impracticable to obtain f the signature of a deponent to a typescript, there should be returned both a signed manuscript and a typescript certified to be a true copy of the manuscript.

IAN WARREN
9 May 1989                                                                     Senior Master.

# Janred Properties Ltd v Ente Nazionale Italiano per il Turismo

COURT OF APPEAL, CIVIL DIVISION
O'CONNOR, CROOM-JOHNSON AND NOURSE LJJ
17, 18, 19, 20, 23 MARCH, 19 MAY 1987

*Estoppel – Conduct – Conduct leading representee to act to his detriment – Acquisition of real property – Option granted to Italian state body to purchase long lease of office premises – Contract requiring approval of Italian minister – Contract not effective due to absence of minister's consent – Purchaser entitled under Italian law to avoid contract – Purchaser failing to complete by completion date but paying deposit and leading vendor to believe that purchase would be completed – Whether purchaser estopped from denying that it was bound by agreement.*

*Sale of land – Damages for breach of contract – Repudiation by purchaser – Interest – Claim for interest on purchase money from contractual completion date to date of purchaser's repudiation of contract – Contract entitling vendor to interest at specified rate from date fixed for completion until purchase actually completed – Whether vendor entitled to interest at contractual rate where contract repudiated.*

On 2 July 1982 the London manager of the defendant, the Italian state tourist office, purported to exercise an option granted by the plaintiff to purchase the underlease of an office building in London for £1·5m. Under the terms of the option, completion was set for 30 September and if the defendant failed to complete on that date it was liable to pay interest on the unpaid purchase price at the rate of 18% until the purchase was completed and if the delay in completion was due to its negligence or default the plaintiff was entitled to the income from the property. The defendant's president subsequently authorised payment of a deposit of £150,000 to the plaintiff but under the constitution of the defendant the approval of the Italian Minister of Tourism and Entertainment was required for the agreement. However, because the necessary funds had not been budgeted for, the minister did not give his approval and the defendant failed to complete on the completion date. Instead of repudiating the agreement the defendant's president made an offer to complete by deferred instalments but that was rejected by the plaintiff. Negotiations continued for a delayed completion to take place and the plaintiff kept the property off the market in the mean time. Eventually the plaintiff served on the defendant a 21-day notice to complete and when the defendant still failed to complete the plaintiff issued a writ against it and resold the property for £200,000 less than the amount agreed between the parties. Before trial the plaintiff accepted the defendant's repudiation of the agreement and elected to sue for damages only. The defendant denied liability, contending that the July agreement was ultra vires and void because it had no power to enter into it without the approval of the minister. The plaintiff contended that the contract was merely voidable and since the defendant had not avoided the contract it was estopped from denying that it was bound by it. There was expert evidence that the absence of the minister's consent had the effect in Italian law not of rendering the contract absolutely void but of rendering it voidable at the suit of the state with the consent of the Italian court although binding on and not voidable by the other party. The judge held that although no contract had ever come into existence because the approval of the minister had not been obtained the agreement was binding on the defendant by estoppel and he gave judgment for the plaintiff for damages to be assessed on the basis that the plaintiff was neither entitled to interest at the contract rate on the balance of the purchase price from the contractual date for completion to the date when the plaintiff accepted the defendant's repudiation of the July agreement nor to retain the rents of the property during that period. The defendant appealed. The plaintiff cross-appealed on the basis on which damages were to be assessed, contending that it was entitled to interest at the contract rate on the balance of the purchase price up to the date of repudiation and was also entitled to retain the rents of the property during that period.

**Held** – (1) Applying English conflict of laws rules, the capacity of the defendant to enter into the July agreement was governed both by its constitution, as interpreted and given effect to by Italian law, and also by English law in regard to limitations imposed by the general law on the capacity of corporations to do certain acts. On the facts, even if no contract, whether voidable or otherwise, had been effectively entered into on 2 July 1982, the subsequent acts of the defendant's president in authorising payment of the deposit and offering to complete the purchase by deferred instalments constituted under Italian law the ratification of the July agreement or the entry into a fresh contract on the same terms, and in either case the defendant (but not the plaintiff) could either avoid the agreement with the consent of the Italian court or ratify it by obtaining the approval of the minister. Since in the circumstances the defendant's actions had led the plaintiff to suppose that the defendant regarded itself as bound by the contract and intended to complete it as soon as its administrative difficulties were overcome, there was a sufficient representation and a sufficient detriment to the plaintiff for the defendant to be estopped from denying that it was bound by the July agreement. It followed therefore that the defendant's appeal would be dismissed (see p 451 *f g*, p 452 *a* to *e*, p 454 *c* to *g j* to p 455 *c*, p 457 *h* and p 458 *b* to *d j* to p 459 *d*, post); *Rhyl UDC v Rhyl Amusements Ltd* [1959] 1 All ER 257 distinguished.

(2) The defendant's liability to pay interest on the purchase price if the purchase was not completed on the completion date was, under the terms of the contract, contingent on actual completion taking place. Accordingly, since completion had not taken place and the property was resold, the plaintiff was only entitled to recover an amount equal to the loss on resale, plus the expenses of effecting the resale. The plaintiff's cross-appeal would therefore be dismissed (see p 456 *f* to p 457 *bfh* and p 459 *c d*, post); *London Chatham and Dover Rly Co v South Eastern Rly Co* [1893] AC 429 applied; *Johnson v Agnew* [1979] 1 All ER 883 considered.

## Notes

For actions for damages for breach of contracts for sale of land, see 42 Halsbury's Laws (4th edn) paras 265–272, and for cases on the subject, see 40 Digest (Reissue) 385–403, 3377–3596.

For estoppel by conduct, see 16 Halsbury's Laws (4th edn) para 1609, and for cases on the subject, see 21 Digest (Reissue) 197–204, 1430–1467.

For interest on purchase money, see 42 Halsbury's Laws (4th edn) para 128, and for cases on the subject, see 40 Digest (Reissue) 195–201, 1419–1454.

## Cases referred to in judgments

*Damon Cia Naviera SA v Hapag-Lloyd International SA, The Blankenstein, The Bartenstein, The Birkenstein* [1985] 1 All ER 475, [1985] 1 WLR 435, CA; *affg* [1983] 3 All ER 510.
*Johnson v Agnew* [1979] 1 All ER 883, [1980] AC 367, [1979] 2 WLR 487, HL.
*Kok Hoong v Leong Cheong Kweng Mines Ltd* [1964] 1 All ER 300, [1964] AC 993, [1964] 2 WLR 150, PC.
*London Chatham and Dover Rly Co v South Eastern Rly Co* [1893] AC 429, HL.
*Rhyl UDC v Rhyl Amusements Ltd* [1959] 1 All ER 257, [1959] 1 WLR 465.
*Royal British Bank v Turquand* (1856) 6 E & B 327, [1843–60] All ER Rep 435, 119 ER 886, Exch Ch.

## Appeal and cross-appeal

The defendant, Ente Nazionale Italiano per il Turismo (ENIT), the Italian State Tourist Office, appealed against the judgment of Knox J ([1986] 1 FTLR 246) given on 5 December 1985 whereby he held that ENIT was liable to the plaintiff, Janred Properties

Ltd (Janred), in damages for failing to complete the purchase of a long lease of an office
property in London and ordered an inquiry as to damages. There was a cross-appeal by    *a*
Janred on the question of damages. The facts are set out in the judgment of Nourse LJ.

*Stanley Brodie QC* and *Stephen Nathan* for ENIT.
*Gavin Lightman QC, Jonathan Crystal* and *Elizabeth Jones* for Janred.

*Cur adv vult*    *b*

19 May. The following judgments were delivered.

**NOURSE LJ** (giving the first judgment at the invitation of O'Connor LJ). This is an
appeal from a decision of Knox J ([1986] 1 FTLR 246) given on 5 December 1985 in a    *c*
vendor's action for damages arising out of a contract for the sale of a long lease of an office
property in London. The unusual features of the case derive from the status of the
purchaser, Ente Nazionale Italiano per il Turismo (ENIT), which is an organisation
created and regulated by Italian legislation as a state body supported largely, if not
entirely, by Italian public funds. Shortly stated, ENIT's claim is that the contract was
ultra vires its constitution and therefore void. The vendor, Janred Properties Ltd (Janred),    *d*
claims that the contract was no worse than voidable and that ENIT is estopped from
denying that it is bound by it. Having decided other issues in favour of ENIT, Knox J
decided that question in favour of Janred and ordered an inquiry as to damages. Against
that decision ENIT now appeals. There is also a cross-appeal by Janred on a question of
damages.
    The facts are comprehensively stated in the judgment of Knox J. I shall repeat them    *e*
only so far as is necessary to understand the questions which arise on this appeal:
    Immediately before 19 March 1982 Janred held 1 Princes Street and 6 Swallow Place,
London SW1 (the property) under an underlease which had nearly 79 years to run, being
due to expire on 29 December 2060. On 19 March 1982 two agreements were entered
into between Janred of the one part and ENIT of the other part. The first was for the
grant to ENIT of a sub-underlease of the property for 25 years at an initial rent of    *f*
£114,000 per annum. That agreement was eventually completed out of time on 11 June
1982. The second agreement (the option agreement) conferred on ENIT an option to
purchase Janred's underlease of the property at a price of £1·5m. The option was made
exercisable by notice in writing to Janred or its solicitors at any time until 30 June 1982.
It was provided that on exercising the option ENIT should pay to the solicitors as
stakeholders a deposit of £150,000. The date fixed for completion was 31 July 1982. The    *g*
National Conditions of Sale (19th edn) were incorporated so far as applicable to a sale by
private treaty with certain variations of which the following require mention. The
prescribed rate of interest referred to in general condition 1(4) and applied by general
condition 7 as the rate at which the purchaser was to pay interest on unpaid purchase
money 'if the purchase shall not be completed on the date fixed for completion' was the
higher of 18% and 5% over Barclays Bank base rate from time to time in force. It was    *h*
further provided that in the event of delay in completion due to ENIT's neglect or default
Janred should be entitled to be paid interest and also to enjoy the income of the property.
That involved an exclusion of general condition 7(1)(iii). The period for special notices to
complete under general condition 22 was reduced from 28 to 21 days. It was provided
that the option agreement should become void if either the option was not exercised on    *j*
or before 30 June 1982 or the agreement for the grant of the sub-underlease (the 25-year
lease) should become void.
    As will appear, it was a requirement of ENIT's constitution that its entry into the two
agreements should be approved by the Italian Minister of Tourism and Entertainment
(the minister). That approval was not given until 2 April 1982.

As stated earlier, the 25-year lease was granted out of time. Strictly speaking, the effect
*a*  of that was to make the option agreement void, but the judge found that the parties
continued to treat it as valid. However, the option was not exercised on 30 June 1982
and lapsed a second time. On the afternoon of 2 July 1982 there was an important
meeting at ENIT's London offices attended by two directors of Janred and its solicitor on
one side and by Mr Tomaso Tomba, ENIT's London manager, another employee and
ENIT's solicitor on the other side. The object of that meeting was to see if an agreement
*b*  to revive the option and exercise it could be reached. It went on for some 3½ hours and
there were various problems into which it is now unnecessary to go except to say that
ENIT did not have £150,000 cash with which to pay the deposit. Eventually, a further
agreement (the July agreement) was there and then prepared by Janred's solicitor.

The July agreement, which incorporated the provisions of the option agreement so far
as not varied, provided, so far as material, as follows. By cl 1 Janred extended the option
*c*  period to include 2 July 1982. Clause 2 read:

'Deposit of £150,000 to be paid by 14th July 1982 and cheque post-dated to 14th
July 1982 from ENIT to Janred handed over today.'

Clause 3 read:

*d*      'ENIT exercises option to purchase the lease as defined in Option Agreement
relating to "the property" today and agrees with Janred that completion date shall
be 30th September 1982 . . .'

By cl 4 the terms of the option agreement, other than the clause dealing with the
possibility of Janred extending its leasehold interest (something for which provision had
been made by the option agreement but which had not in fact happened), were to
*e*  continue to be effective as varied by the July agreement and the contract created by the
exercise of the option.

As the judge observed, there were three significant alterations which were made to the
option agreement by the July agreement. First, the time for the option to be exercised
was extended until 2 July. Second, the completion date was postponed from 31 July to
30 September. Third, the deposit was to be paid to Janred and not to stakeholders. It has
*f*  at all times been accepted by Janred that the July agreement, if valid, constituted a new
contract for the purposes of ENIT's constitution. It was signed by Mr Tomba on behalf
of ENIT and by a director on behalf of Janred. A postdated cheque for £150,000, also
signed by Mr Tomba, was duly handed over.

I will refer to ENIT's constitution hereafter. At this stage it is enough to say that
between 20 December 1980 and 18 October 1982 its president, Avvocato Gabriello
*g*  Moretti, was, by a series of decrees of the minister, invested with all the powers of the
president, the board of directors and the executive committee of ENIT. That meant that
all the powers of ENIT were vested in Mr Moretti, although he did not of course have
power to give or dispense with the minister's approval where that was necessary.

Knox J decided, first, that, because ENIT's entry into the July agreement was not
*h*  approved by the minister, Mr Moretti did not have power to authorise Mr Tomba to sign
it and thereby bind ENIT. He decided, second, that Mr Tomba was not in any event
authorised to sign it by the terms of a telex which Mr Moretti sent to him on 2 July.
Third, he decided that a power of attorney granted to Mr Tomba by Mr Moretti's
predecessor did not assist Janred, mainly because it was known both to Mr Tomba and to
Janred that specific authority outside the power of attorney was needed from Rome
*j*  before Mr Tomba could bind ENIT. Fourth, he decided that neither Mr Tomba nor
ENIT's solicitor had ostensible authority to sign the July agreement on behalf of ENIT.

Janred has not sought to impugn the correctness of the judge's decision of any of those
four questions. Accordingly, the matter must be approached on the footing that on
2 July 1982 there was no existing agreement by ENIT to purchase Janred's underlease.
Furthermore, it has throughout been common ground that the minister never gave his

approval to any such agreement. The important question which remains is whether, in the light of subsequent events, ENIT is estopped from denying that it is bound by such *a* an agreement. In order that that question may be determined it is first necessary to consider ENIT's constitution and then to set out the material events which occurred after 2 July 1982.

Since 14 November 1981 the constitution of ENIT has been regulated by Law 648, which came into force on that day. Article 1 gave it legal personality as a public subject and subjected it to the control of the ministry. Article 2 set out its objects and activity; in *b* the sixth paragraph are found these words: 'ENIT is empowered to set up, wind up and reorganise delegations and representations and information offices abroad . . .' It has at all times been agreed that the purchase of the property as premises for ENIT in London was within its objects as set out in art 2. Article 4 states ENIT's officers as (a) the president, (b) the board of directors, (c) the executive committee and (d) the board of auditors.

Article 7, which is of crucial importance in the case, is, so far as material, in the *c* following terms:

'Functions of the Board of Directors—The Board of Directors passes resolutions concerning: (a) the general policy of ENIT and the annual and pluriannual programmes of activity, taking into account the national economic programmes; (b) the budgets, their variations and the balance sheets; (c) the pluriannual financial *d* commitments; (d) the organisation and the services and the establishment of offices abroad and on the Italian borders; (e) the general regulations concerning the legal and economic treatment of ENIT personnel; (f) the general regulations of administration and accounting . . . The resolutions provided under letters (a) and (c) above must be approved by a provision of the Minister of Tourism and Entertainment to be taken within the term of thirty days from date of receipt of the relevant *e* documents, expiring which term, the resolutions become executive. The resolutions under letters (b) and (f) are submitted for the approval of the Minister of Tourism and Entertainment pursuant to article 30 of the law of the 20th March 1975 No. 70. The resolutions under letters (d) and (e) above are approved pursuant to the provisions of article 29 of the law mentioned in the preceding paragraph.'

Article 9, which is also of importance, is in these terms: *f*

'The Executive Committee—The Executive Committee is formed by the President, the Vice-President and five members of the Board of Directors. The Executive Committee passes the resolutions necessary to the realisation of ENIT programmes as determined by the Board of Directors pursuant to the last paragraph of article 6 herein, and particularly passes resolutions concerning: (a) the financial *g* commitments as determined by the Articles; (b) the acquisitions and sales of immovable properties and rents exceeding the duration of nine years; (c) the acceptance of inheritances and donations; (d) the litigations as plaintiff or defendant; (e) all other matters as determined by the Articles or delegated by the Board of Directors. The resolutions under letters (b), (c) and (d) are submitted for the Board of Directors' ratification during the first subsequent meeting.' *h*

It was common ground between the expert witnesses who gave evidence on Italian law at the trial that ENIT's entry into the July agreement involved the acquisition of immovable property and rents exceeding the duration of nine years within art 9(b) and thus required a resolution of the executive committee. Knox J, having considered the expert evidence, found as a fact that both a budget variation and a pluriannual financial *j* commitment within art 7(b) and (c) respectively were involved, so that not only a resolution of the board of directors was required but also the approval of the minister. During the period in which Mr Moretti exercised plenipotentiary powers he was both the executive committee and the board of directors and it appears to have been his practice when necessary to sign one composite resolution or 'delibera'. However, the

judge found that all that was needed was an expression of Mr Moretti's will for there to
a be a sufficient resolution to bind ENIT and that for that purpose no particular formality
was required or imposed by Italian law. I will state the steps which Mr Moretti took in
regard to the July agreement when I reach that point in the narrative, to which I now
return.

On the evening of 2 July, after the conclusion of the meeting, Mr Tomba sent a telex
to Rome, in which he reported that he had entered into a contract for the property and
b the sum of £150,000 would have to be paid by 14 July and the balance of £1·35 m on
30 September 1982. He did not draw attention to the change from payment of the
deposit to a stakeholder to payment to Janred itself. On 5 July Mr Tomba delivered a
letter by hand to Rome, which enclosed the July agreement and all the other relevant
documents. An order for the transfer of £150,000 to meet the postdated cheque was
signed in Rome by the acting director-general of ENIT, Mr Lattanzi, and another of its
c officers. The judge found that between 2 July and 23 or 24 September 1982 Mr Moretti
allowed Mr Lattanzi and Mr Bianchi, the director of the department of ENIT concerned
with foreign establishments, to deal with the matter on his behalf. There can therefore
be no doubt that the payment of the £150,000, which was duly made on presentation of
the postdated cheque, must be taken to have been made on the authority of Mr Moretti.
It was therefore the act of ENIT itself.

d The judge found that after 2 July the conveyancing procedures in London between
contract and completion proceeded normally. Requisitions on title were served and
replied to and a transfer was approved and sealed by Mr Tomba in escrow. On
9 September 1982 it was sent to Janred's solicitor to be sealed by Janred in anticipation of
completion on 30 September.

The judge found that Mr Moretti approved in general terms the acquisition of Janred's
e underlease by the delayed exercise of the option, but did not understand all the details of
the transaction and, in particular, the payment of the deposit to a stakeholder. He found
that Mr Moretti did not bother to inquire about the matter until 23 or 24 September.
On the latter date Mr Moretti, being away from Rome, saw for the first time a draft
delibera dated 27 July 1982 and signed on that day by Mr Bianchi and signed but not
f dated by Mr Lattanzi. It appeared on the face of the draft that a contract had been signed
on 2 July and that £150,000 had to be paid by 14 July 1982. There was, however, a blank
in that part of the draft which identified the item in the budget covering the £1·35 m
which was needed for completion and, as the judge observed, it was doubtless that which
brought about Mr Moretti's rather belated awakening to what had happened. In any
event, he refused to sign the delibera because there was no financial cover for that
amount.
g
Knox J continued as follows ([1986] 1 FTLR 246 at 256):

'Shortly after his return to Rome on 27 September, Mr Moretti met Mr Bianchi
and was told the whole story, notably as to the signature of the contract on 2 July
and the payment of the £150,000 on 14 July 1982. There followed a period of
somewhat hectic negotiations in Rome to try to save the deposit by assembling, by
h one means or another, the necessary £1,350,000. No attempt at all at this stage was
made in Rome to repudiate the July agreement although all the material necessary
to support such a repudiation was available to Mr Moretti from 29 September, if not
the 24th.'

The judge proceeded to refer to a second edition of the draft delibera of 27 July, but
j that was not signed by Mr Moretti either. On 30 September Mr Tomba relayed to Rome
the very firm advice of ENIT's solicitors that interest at 18% per annum would be payable
on the unpaid purchase price for every day's delay after that date. On 1 October Mr
Bianchi was sent to London to appraise the position, returning to Rome on 5 October.

Mr Moretti caused a further draft delibera dated 7 October to be prepared, which set
out the history of the matter in great detail. Between 29 September and 7 October he

had made a number of oral and written approaches to the minister or his officials with a
view to obtaining approval for the expenditure involved as well as the general approval
of the minister. On 8 October the minister's first private secretary wrote a letter to Mr
Moretti, the third paragraph of which was in these terms:

'In such circumstances, also because of instructions by the Minister, I can only
agree with the conclusions of your telephone call this morning, when you informed
me of your consistent intention to check personally in London the possibility of
delaying the completion of the contract, avoiding also the loss of the deposit already
paid.'

The judge thought, and I respectfully agree with him, that that paragraph specifically
approved Mr Moretti's suggestion made on the telephone that he should go to London
and seek to negotiate delay in completion and thus save the deposit. He continued as
follows (at 256):

'Here again, all the material needed to appreciate the possibility of repudiation of
the contract was available to the ministry, as it had been for over a week to Mr
Moretti, but no suggestion was made that an attempt to repudiate the contract as
not binding on ENIT should be made. On the contrary, a policy decision was taken
to try to negotiate a way out of the difficulty caused by the lack of cash. This was
motivated by the view then held that the purchase of Janred's underlease at a price
of £1,500,000 was more advantageous than to retain ENIT's [25-year lease].'

On 4 October Janred had served on ENIT a 21-day notice to complete under general
condition 22 as amended. On 14 October Mr Moretti went to London and held a meeting
at which Mr Tomba and a director of Janred were present, together with ENIT's solicitors
but not Janred's. There was a dispute at the trial whether the meeting was a 'without
prejudice' meeting or not, but the judge found that it was not. Mr Moretti said in
evidence that he specifically raised the question of the invalidity of the July agreement,
but the judge, who took an unfavourable view of Mr Moretti's testimony on several
important points, rejected that evidence. The judge found that there was not a trace in
all the written evidence that any claim of invalidity was advanced on 14 October, whereas
there was evidence that ENIT's solicitors continued to assure Janred's solicitors that
completion would take place and all that was needed was the resolution of bureaucratic
difficulties in Rome concerning the release of the necessary funds. He also found that at
the meeting on 14 October Mr Moretti made an offer to complete by deferred
instalments. Those proposals were not acceptable to Janred. On 28 October 1982, shortly
after the expiration of the 21-day period, the writ in this action was issued.

The remaining material facts can be shortly stated. The property had been kept off the
market by Janred after December 1981, when agreement in principle was reached, on
the strength successively of that agreement, the option agreement, the July agreement
and the continued negotiations for a delayed completion to take place with no suggestion
of a repudiation of the contract by ENIT. On 2 November 1982 it was put back on the
market, but it proved difficult to sell. Eventually, on 7 November 1983, after making
some rather complicated arrangements with the head lessee and the Crown as freeholder,
into the details of which it is unnecessary to go, Janred agreed to sell the property to
Clerical Medical Managed Funds Ltd. It is also unnecessary to go into the financial details
of the arrangements, because it is agreed that the loss to Janred on the resale was £200,000
against which, if the contract was valid, the deposit of £150,000 must be brought into
account.

Meanwhile, in Rome there was a hiatus in the control of ENIT after Mr Moretti's
plenipotentiary powers came to an end on 18 October 1982. Between then and
28 October efforts to assemble the balance of the purchase price continued, but nothing
effective was done. In January 1983 ENIT changed its London solicitors. It was not until
26 January that the new solicitors for the first time made a clear written statement of a

defence based on the assertion that Mr Tomba lacked the requisite authority to sign the
a  July agreement, a defence which had been foreshadowed in a telephone conversation a
few days earlier.

Janred applied under RSC Ord 86 for summary judgment for specific performance.
That application was granted by Warner J on 28 March 1983. Since the ground of his
decision was the same as that ultimately relied on by Knox J at the trial, it is desirable to
set out the material passage in Warner J's judgment:

b          '[Counsel for Janred] had, however, a number of alternative answers to [counsel
for ENIT's] argument and, on one of those, I have come to the conclusion that
[Janred] is entitled to succeed. It is estoppel, estoppel based, not on the representation
that Mr Tomba had authority to enter into the transaction on behalf of [ENIT], but
on the conduct of those acting for [ENIT] between 2 July 1982 and 26 January 1983,
from which those acting for [Janred] inferred, and were entitled to infer, that [ENIT]
c          regarded itself as bound by the transaction and fully intended to complete it as soon
as its internal administrative difficulties could be overcome. Nor was it ever
suggested on behalf of [ENIT] (until the evidence on its behalf was served on
15 February 1983) that those administrative difficulties included the absence of
compliance with the requirements of its constitution.'

d     On 14 July 1983 a division of this court consisting of Dunn and Slade LJJ allowed an
appeal by ENIT against Warner J's order on the ground that it was arguable that ENIT's
entry into the July agreement was ultra vires and void, so that there could be no estoppel
in Janred's favour (see [1983] CA Transcript 316). That was an argument which had not
been advanced before Warner J. ENIT was given unconditional leave to defend and the
action went to trial. Meanwhile, by a letter between solicitors delivered on 25 October
e  1983, Janred had accepted ENIT's repudiation of the July agreement and elected to sue
for damages.

In dealing with the question of estoppel, Knox J turned first to the question of
detriment to Janred. He referred to some grossly and culpably exaggerated evidence
which had been put in on behalf of Janred in support of the application under Ord 86.
However, he held that the fact that Janred kept the property off the market until
f  2 November 1982 as a result of ENIT's actions in signing the July agreement and
continuing thereafter to negotiate on the footing that there was a valid and binding
contract which it wished to complete out of time was sufficient detriment to ground an
estoppel, subject always to the effect of the ultra vires doctrine. It has not, as I understand
it, been suggested on behalf of ENIT that there was not sufficient detriment. On the
other side, it has not been suggested on behalf of Janred either that the rule in *Royal*
g  *British Bank v Turquand* (1856) 6 E & B 327, [1843–60] All ER Rep 435 applies to a
statutory corporation, whether English or Italian, or that s 9(1) of the European
Communities Act 1972 has any application to this case.

On the footing that there was no agreement in existence on 2 July 1982, it is not,
strictly speaking, appropriate to ask whether ENIT had power to enter into the July
h  agreement. The correct question to ask is whether it had power to ratify or affirm the
July agreement or to enter into a fresh contract on the same terms. However, the correct
question is a cumbersome one and I prefer, by way of a convenient shorthand, to ask the
question in the simpler form.

Counsel for ENIT submitted that this was a simple case where ENIT had no power to
enter into the July agreement without the approval of the minister, with the result that
j  it was ultra vires and void. He referred to authority, in particular to the decision of
Harman J in *Rhyl UDC v Rhyl Amusements Ltd* [1959] 1 All ER 257, [1959] 1 WLR 465,
for the proposition that a statutory body cannot be estopped from denying the validity
of an agreement which is void as being beyond its powers. If it were indeed correct to
say that ENIT's entry into the July agreement was, for want of the minister's approval,
ultra vires and void, then the submission of counsel for ENIT would doubtless be correct.

But the first and essential question is to decide whether the July agreement was, or should be treated as having been, of such a nature.

This question falls to be determined by an application of the rules of English private international law. Did ENIT have power to enter into the July agreement? Both sides relied on r 139 in Dicey and Morris *The Conflict of Laws* (10th edn, 1980) p 730:

'(1) The capacity of a corporation to enter into any legal transaction is governed both by the constitution of the corporation and by the law of the country which governs the transaction in question. (2) All matters concerning the constitution of a corporation are governed by the law of the place of incorporation.'

The July agreement, being one for the sale and purchase of English leasehold property, was governed by the law of England. Accordingly, if limbs (1) and (2) are read together and applied to this case, we have the following: the capacity of ENIT to enter into the July agreement is governed both by its constitution (as interpreted and given effect by Italian law) and by English law.

It follows that the first question to be asked is whether, under Italian law, ENIT was capable of entering into the July agreement and, if so, to what effect? Clearly the requirement that ENIT's capacity is to be governed also by English law cannot mean, as counsel for ENIT might like it to, that you take a second look at ENIT's constitution and determine its capacity as if it were an English corporation, because that would fly in the face of the requirement that all matters concerning the constitution of a corporation are to be governed by the law of the place of incorporation. The commentary to r 139 and the cases there cited make it clear that the requirement that ENIT's capacity is to be governed also by English law is directed towards limitations imposed by the general law on the capacity of corporations to do certain acts, for example on their capacity to hold land before the repeal of the Mortmain Acts.

Was ENIT capable under Italian law of entering into the July agreement without the approval of the minister and, if so, to what effect? That was a question which was fully canvassed in the evidence of the two expert witnesses on Italian law, Avvocato Storelli for Janred and Dr Pierantozzi for ENIT. It was a question which Knox J considered at length and with care, and it is worth emphasising that it was a question of fact to be decided on the evidence which was before him. That evidence was far more extensive than that which was before this court on the application under Ord 86. The reason for that may have been that the ultra vires point was only taken at a very late stage. On that occasion, after stating that it was common ground that the minister's consent had never been obtained, Slade LJ said:

'There is no evidence that Italian law would regard ENIT as having the capacity to enter into a contract for the acquisition of the premises in the absence of such consent or would regard any representative of ENIT as being capable of committing it to any such contract in the absence of such consent. The available evidence as to Italian law suggests rather the contrary, though such law is a question of fact which will, no doubt, have to be explained with care and in detail at the trial.'

Although there were differences of emphasis between the two experts, it seems to me that on this important question they were substantially at one. Knox J said ([1986] 1 FTLR 246 at 263):

'There was a large measure of agreement between them. First, they agreed that the results of the defects in the present case, absence of a proper *delibera* signed by the appropriate officers and no ministerial consent, was not to render the contract absolutely void but subject to what Dr Pierantozzi called *nullita relativa*. Avvocato Storelli said it would be more correct to call it *annullabilita relativa*. They agreed in attributing to *relativa* the meaning that the nullity in question was a feature that only the state entity could pray in aid.'

After reviewing further passages in the evidence of the two experts, the judge said (at
*a* 264):

> 'I find the Italian law to be as follows. Where there is a contract made by or on
> behalf of a public entity such as ENIT with a third party without requisite consent
> and made on the authority of persons to whom the requisite power is not given
> (here by Mr Tomba and Mr Lattanzi) the result is not a total nullity. The contract is
> voidable at the suit of the public authority and with the consent of the Italian court
> *b* and unlawful in the sense that it is contrary to provisions of the Italian law designed
> primarily to protect the Italian public revenue. The contract is binding upon and
> not voidable by the third party. *It is susceptible of ratification by the public entity on
> obtaining the requisite consent or otherwise curing the defect.*' (My emphasis.)

Having then considered a doctrine recognised by Italian law called 'culpa in
*c* contrahendo', the judge proceeded to ask himself whether, on the analysis which he had
made of the relevant Italian law, the defects in the formation of the July agreement were
such as to prevent the doctrine of estoppel from applying. He distinguished all the
authorities referred to by Slade LJ on the Ord 86 application, including *Rhyl UDC v Rhyl
Amusements Ltd* [1959] 1 All ER 257, [1959] 1 WLR 465, on the ground that they were
all cases in which there had either been a breach of a mandatory provision of the proper
*d* law or a lack of power in the body concerned. He said ([1986] 1 FTLR 246 at 265):

> 'In my judgment, the estoppel which English law as the proper law of the contract
> and the *lex fori* would apply is not excluded by the Italian legislation which results
> in applying *nullita relativa* to the July agreement for the following reasons. First, the
> badge of *ultra vires* is that it renders the relevant transaction a nullity incapable of
> *e* ratification and devoid of legal effect. That cannot be said of *nullita relativa* which
> renders a contract voidable only at the suit of one party and binding on the other.
> Secondly, the law which confronts the estoppel, to use Lord Radcliffe's phrase [in
> *Kok Hoong v Leong Cheong Kweng Mines Ltd* [1964] 1 All ER 300 at 308, [1964] AC
> 993 at 1016], is one designed to protect the Italian public revenue. While
> international comity requires proper regard to be paid to such considerations, it does
> *f* not in my judgment impose an imperative bar on what English law would otherwise
> treat as the just solution of a problem according to law. It may well be that different
> considerations would apply in relation to the grant of a decree of specific
> performance. Thirdly, there is no question but that ENIT itself, as opposed to the
> relevant officers, had power to enter into the July agreement which falls squarely
> within its objects. Fourthly, Italian law, if it had been the proper law, would have
> *g* been capable of providing protection to innocent third parties who in the context of
> *nullita relativa* affecting a contract with a public entity suffer loss from the improper
> conduct of the latter's officers. I have not found that Janred would have succeeded
> in establishing *culpa in contrahendo* in the present case for that is irrelevant, but the
> relevance of the doctrine is that the Italian doctrine of *nullita relativa* still leaves the
> third party who contracts with the public entity with legally protected rights arising
> *h* out of the transaction, as well, of course, as obligations, for he is bound.'

Finally, having rejected an argument of counsel for ENIT based on the proposition
that a voidable contract made by a minor cannot be made binding on him by estoppel,
the judge, for essentially the same reason as that which had appealed to Warner J, held
that the July agreement was binding on ENIT by estoppel.
*j*       Counsel for ENIT claimed that Knox J's decision on the estoppel question was contrary
to his decision on the very first of the questions which he had considered, namely that
because ENIT's entry into the July agreement was not approved by the minister Mr
Moretti did not have power to authorise Mr Tomba to sign it and thereby bind ENIT. I
see some force in that point, because, if ENIT had power, without any particular formality

for the expression of Mr Moretti's will and without the approval of the minister, to enter
into a voidable contract, there would seem to be no reason why Mr Moretti should not
have been able to authorise Mr Tomba to sign the July agreement and thereby bind ENIT
to such a contract. However, it seems that the judge decided this question on the footing,
first, that no contract, not even a voidable one, ever came into existence but, second, that
ENIT's power to enter into such a contract, moreover to ratify it on obtaining the
approval of the minister, was sufficient ground to let in the doctrine of estoppel.

Although I think that Knox J's approach to this question is perfectly acceptable, there
is a slightly different route to the same end, which may take a more positive view both
of his findings as to the effect of Italian law and of the material events after 2 July 1982.
For this purpose I assume that there was no contract, not even a voidable one, in existence
on that date, and I emphasise that it is only the judge's unappealed decision on that point
by which we are bound. However, there were two subsequent events of crucial
importance, each of which, in my judgment, can be regarded as having constituted a
ratification or affirmation by ENIT of the July agreement or an entry by it into a fresh
contract on the same terms. Moreover, on each occasion the act was clearly the act of
ENIT itself and not the unauthorised act of one of its officers. The only thing which was
still lacking was the approval of the minister.

The first of these events was the provision of the £150,000 to meet the postdated
cheque for the deposit on 14 July 1982. As I have already observed, there can be no doubt
that that payment must be taken to have been made on the authority of Mr Moretti, in
whom all the powers of ENIT were then vested. It is difficult to conceive of an act more
clearly calculated to ratify or affirm a previously unauthorised contract for the purchase
of land or to constitute an entry into a fresh contract on the same terms (it matters not
which) than the payment of the stipulated deposit. The second of these events was the
part played by Mr Moretti, still a plenipotentiary, at the meeting in London on
14 October, in particular his offer to complete the purchase by deferred instalments in
the face of the notice to complete which had by then been served. Again, it is difficult to
conceive of a more vivid act of ratification or affirmation, assuming, that is, that such an
act was still needed.

Knox J's findings as to the effect of Italian law must apply a fortiori to an act of ENIT
itself as opposed to an unauthorised act of one of its officers. In the circumstances it
would seem, as a matter of Italian law, that on 14 July, alternatively on 14 October 1982,
there came into existence a contract to purchase the property on the terms of the July
agreement. That contract was voidable at the suit of ENIT and with the consent of the
Italian court and was binding on and not voidable by Janred. It was susceptible of
ratification by ENIT on obtaining the minister's approval. If that is the position under
Italian law, I know of no principle, whether of public policy or otherwise, which requires
English law, as the law governing the contract, to take a different view of it. Admittedly
the doctrine of nullita relativa is unknown to our law. But that is not a sound reason for
denying to the contract the incidents resulting from the limited capacity of ENIT under
Italian law, being the law to which our law refers all questions on that subject. The only
reservation I would make is that the resultant contract must be one whose features can
be recognised by English law. That is not a difficulty which arises in the present case.

The estoppel question can therefore be approached by postulating that from 14 July,
alternatively from 19 October 1982 onwards, there was in existence a contract which
ENIT could either avoid with the consent of the Italian court or ratify by obtaining the
approval of the minister. I find myself in no doubt that that is enough to distinguish the
present case from all the authorities which were referred to by Slade LJ on the Ord 86
application. Again I see no reason, whether of public policy or otherwise, why the
doctrine of estoppel should not be capable of applying in this case.

Moreover, it is clear to me that ENIT acted in such a way as to lead Janred to suppose,
in the words of Warner J, that ENIT regarded itself as bound by the contract and fully

*a* intended to complete it as soon as its internal administrative difficulties (which Janred did not know included the absence of ministerial approval) could be overcome. For this purpose I need do no more than gratefully adopt the passages already quoted or referred to in that part of the judgment of Knox J which dealt with the material events between 14 July and 2 November 1982. Here again the events of 14 October seem to me to have been of particular significance, not least because the minister had specifically approved Mr Moretti's proposal that he should go to London to seek to negotiate a delay in

*b* completion and thus save the deposit. I do not suggest that there could have been any estoppel against the minister. I do suggest that his approval of Mr Moretti's proposed course of action could only have served to confirm ENIT's representations, expressed or implied, that it regarded itself as bound by the contract and fully intended to complete it.

For these reasons, which, in essential respects, are those relied on by Knox J, it being

*c* clear that there was a sufficient detriment to Janred, I conclude that ENIT is estopped from denying that it was bound by the July agreement. On that ground I would dismiss the appeal. I should add that counsel for Janred would if necessary have argued for an alternative liability of ENIT in tort based on an alleged breach of duty to inform Janred of the lack of Mr Tomba's authority. After counsel had dealt with the other questions we indicated that that was not one on which we wished to hear argument.

*d* I now turn to Janred's cross-appeal, with which I propose to deal far more briefly. Counsel for Janred submitted that the damages to which Janred is entitled in respect of ENIT's breach of contract include a sum equivalent to interest at the contract rate (effectively 18%) on the balance of the purchase price (£1·35m) between the contractual date for completion (30 September 1982) and the date on which Janred accepted ENIT's repudiation of the July agreement (25 October 1983). He also submitted that Janred is

*e* entitled to retain the rents of the property during the same period.

Knox J dealt with these submissions as follows ([1986] 1 FTLR 246 at 266):

'Both these questions turn on the same point; namely, whether the rights conferred on Janred by the option agreement to receive interest between the contractual date for completion and actual completion and to retain the net rents of

*f* the property as well as interest on the unpaid purchase price during the same period, constitute accrued rights which Janred continued to be entitled to notwithstanding and after the discharge of the contract by the acceptance by Janred of ENIT's breach of contract through failure to complete. In my judgment it is inaccurate to describe those rights as "accrued rights". The provisions of the contract entitling Janred to take both interest on the unpaid purchase price and to keep the rents of the property

*g* were still executory when Janred accepted ENIT's repudiation and the primary obligations under the contract were replaced by the secondary obligation to pay damages.'

Although counsel for ENIT did not adopt the judge's reasons, I myself have no reason to suppose that they are wrong. Counsel for Janred confined himself to answering the submissions of counsel for ENIT, which were not addressed to any question of accrued

*h* rights. We heard no argument on that. Since I think that the answer of counsel for ENIT is in any event correct, I will confine myself in the same way.

The contractual foundation for the submissions of counsel for Janred was cl 6(c) of the option agreement, which was in these terms:

*j* 'The prescribed rate of interest referred to in Condition 1(4) of the said National Conditions shall be five per cent above Barclays Bank Limited Base Rate from time to time in force with a minimum of 18% in every case and it is hereby expressly agreed that in the event of a delay in effecting completion owing to the neglect or default of the Board Janred shall be entitled both to be paid interest and to enjoy the income of the property.'

As for authority, counsel for Janred relied on the decision of the House of Lords in *Johnson v Agnew* [1979] 1 All ER 883 esp at 896, [1980] AC 367 esp at 400–401 in the *a* speech of Lord Wilberforce, and also on the decisions of Leggatt J and this court in *Damon Cia Naviera SA v Hapag-Lloyd International SA, The Blankenstein, The Bartenstein, The Birkenstein* [1983] 3 All ER 510; *affd* [1985] 1 All ER 475, [1985] 1 WLR 435, CA. He submitted that those decisions were authority for the proposition that you look at Janred's position, not on 30 September 1982 when the breach occurred, but on 25 October 1983 when the contract was lost. And so you ask yourself what sums Janred would have *b* received if the July agreement had been duly performed on the later date. The answer, said counsel for Janred, is that Janred would have received not only the balance of £1·35m, but also interest on that sum at the rate of 18% from 30 September 1982 onwards. It is therefore entitled to damages to compensate it for the loss of these sums, subject to bringing the deposit and the net proceeds of the resale into account. It is also entitled to retain the rents.                                                              *c*

The first point to be made here is that cl 6(c) of the option agreement is of no assistance to Janred. It is clear, as a matter of construction, that cl 6(c) could only have taken effect if the agreement had actually been completed. That, I think, is the same thing as saying that on 25 October 1983 Janred's rights under cl 6(c) were executory and not accrued. But, whether that be right or wrong, the position was governed by general condition *d* 7(1), which, subject to exceptions, provides:

> 'If the purchase shall not be completed on the completion date then ... the purchaser shall pay interest on the remainder of his purchase money at the prescribed rate from that date *until the purchase shall actually be completed*.' (My emphasis.)

It is clear, indeed it has never been doubted, that the purchaser's liability for interest *e* under such a condition is contingent on actual completion of the purchase. Moreover, the submissions of counsel for Janred would, so far as interest is concerned, apply to any common form contract containing a condition of that kind.

Accordingly, before we could accede to those submissions, we would have to think that the decision in *Johnson v Agnew* had altogether revolutionised the basis on which *f* damages are recoverable in a common form vendor's action for breach of a contract for the sale of land. I am entirely satisfied that that decision has not had that effect. We were not referred to any of the classical sources on the subject, eg *Williams on Vendor and Purchaser, Daniell's Chancery Forms* or *Seton's Judgments and Orders*, but such research as I have since been able to conduct has confirmed my belief that the standard form of order in such an action, where the property is resold, enables the vendor to recover an amount equal to the loss on the resale, plus the expenses of effecting it, and no more. He does not *g* recover quasi interest before acceptance of the repudiation: see, for example, 34 Court Forms (2nd edn) (1977 issue) 360, Form 20 (now ibid (1988 issue) 357, Form 21). The rule is, I believe, so well established that it ought hardly to be necessary to justify it. However, out of deference to the arguments which have been advanced in this case, I will attempt a brief exposition of the probable basis for it.

The essential fallacy in the submissions of counsel for Janred is that you look at the *h* vendor's position when the contract is lost. On the contrary, you look at it when the breach occurs, namely on the contractual date for completion. Lord Wilberforce himself recognised that that is the normal rule (see [1979] 1 All ER 883 at 896, [1980] AC 367 at 400). If the contract is completed on that date, the vendor receives the balance of the purchase price without any interest. It is perfectly true that the purchaser's default keeps *j* the vendor out of his money from then onwards, but here the vendor encounters the fundamental rule of the common law, which was finally established by the decision of the House of Lords in *London Chatham and Dover Rly Co v South Eastern Rly Co* [1893] AC 429, that quasi interest cannot be recovered by way of damages for non-payment of

money due. The exceptions which have recently been made to that rule have not been
a  made in a case such as this and I would think that one could only now be made by the
House of Lords in a case where the point arose directly for decision. Moreover, although
it is theoretically possible for the court to award actual interest on the balance of the
purchase price under the power which is now contained in s 35A(1) of the Supreme Court
Act 1981 from the contractual date for completion onwards (that being 'the date when
the cause of action arose'), I have never heard it suggested that that is something which
b  the court would do. The reason for that, I think, is that the vendor retains the benefit of
the property until the resale and an award of interest would give him a double benefit,
being one which is particularly marked in a case like the present where the property is
yielding a rack rent.

Counsel for Janred relied most strongly of all on the following words of Lord
Wilberforce in Johnson v Agnew [1979] 1 All ER 883 at 896, [1980] AC 367 at 401:
c
'In cases where a breach of contract for sale has occurred, and the innocent party
reasonably continues to try to have the contract completed, it would to me appear
more logical and just rather than tie him to the date of the original breach, to assess
damages as at the date when (otherwise than by his default) the contract is lost.'

I see the force of those words as a general statement of principle, but it is important to
d  remember that they were voiced in a case where the facts were somewhat unusual. There
the vendors had made a final election to sue for specific performance and had obtained a
decree to that effect. It was only when the vendors found that, for reasons outside their
control, they were unable to convey the property and thus perfect the decree that they
had to come back to the court and seek damages instead. In the present case, although it
might fairly be said that Janred 'reasonably continued to try to have the contract
e  completed', no final election to sue for specific performance was ever made and, if the
submissions of counsel for Janred are correct, I can see no reason why they should not
apply to every run of the mill case where the vendor tries for a while to get the purchaser
to complete and then gives up and elects to accept his repudiation of the contract instead.
As I have said, I think that only the House of Lords can say that Lord Wilberforce's
statement of principle applies to every such case.
f
For these reasons, I would have no hesitation in dismissing the cross-appeal. I am
fortified by the knowledge that Knox J arrived at the same conclusion. I infer that his
instinctive reaction to Janred's claim was the same as mine. The judge merely ordered an
inquiry as to damages. I would think it preferable for this court to make a declaration to
which regard can be paid when the inquiry is made. Broadly speaking, as I understand
the position, Janred is entitled to damages to compensate it for its loss on the resale after
g  bringing the deposit of £150,000 into account. It is also entitled to interest on the sum
found due from the date of the resale at what I believe both sides accept should be the
commercial court rate. Janred is entitled to retain the rents. Indeed, the contrary has
never been suggested.

h  **CROOM-JOHNSON LJ.** I have read the judgment of Nourse LJ and agree with it.
The trial judge found that no contract was concluded on 2 July 1982 on two grounds.
The first was that Mr Moretti did not have power to authorise Mr Tomba to sign the July
agreement and thereby bind ENIT. The reasoning on which he based that finding was
that the subject matter of the agreement was of a kind which requires ministerial consent
in order to fulfil the requirements of Law 648, art 7. Having held that art 7 applied, the
j  judge found that, if no prior consent was given, then that agreement was ultra vires, and
therefore void. That finding has supported the argument of counsel for ENIT that
accordingly the agreement cannot be validated by an estoppel, and he founds his case on
Rhyl UDC v Rhyl Amusements Ltd [1959] 1 All ER 257, [1959] 1 WLR 465. There was,
however, a second ground on which the judge found, which was that Mr Tomba never

was given any authority, or purported authority, to sign the agreement. Neither of these grounds has been the subject of any cross-appeal by Janred. We are therefore bound by *a* the judge's unappealed finding that there was no concluded July agreement. I entirely agree with the judge's finding that Mr Tomba did not have any authority. I do not agree with his reasoning that the lack of ministerial consent prevented Mr Moretti from having any power to authorise Mr Tomba to sign such an agreement and thereby to bind ENIT even provisionally. The evidence which the judge examined later, when he came to consider the question of estoppel, convinces me that he did.                                *b*

The argument on the issue of estoppel is founded, however, on a consideration of Italian law as it affected the contractual capacity of ENIT, by which the effect of the July agreement must be judged according to English law: see Dicey and Morris *The Conflict of Laws* (10th edn, 1980) r 139. For the purposes of this judgment I respectfully adopt the approach used by Nourse LJ where he says:

> 'On the footing that there was no agreement in existence on 2 July 1982, it is not, *c*
> strictly speaking, appropriate to ask whether ENIT had power to enter into the July agreement. The correct question to ask is whether it had power to ratify or affirm the July agreement or to enter into a fresh contract on the same terms. However, the correct question is a cumbersome one and I prefer, by way of a convenient shorthand, to ask the question in the simpler form.'
>                                                                                          *d*

Law 648 provides that the resolutions (delibera) which are relevant must be submitted to the minister for his approval. Presumably, he may approve or disapprove. If he does nothing or delays, then after 30 days from the receipt by him of the relevant documents 'the resolutions become executive'. What happened in the present case was that there never was a formal delibera signed by Mr Moretti and submitted by him to the minister. Nor was there approval, nor was there rejection.                                          *e*

The judge summarised the evidence of the two experts in Italian law ([1986] 1 FTLR 246 at 263):

> 'There was a large measure of agreement between them. First, they agreed that the results of the defects in the present case, absence of a proper *delibera* signed by the appropriate officers and no ministerial consent, was not to render the contract *f* absolutely void but subject to ... *nullita relativa* ... They agreed in attributing to *relativa* the meaning that the nullity in question was a feature that only the state entity could pray in aid. A third party, such as Janred, entering into a transaction affected by *nullita relativa*, to use Dr Pierantozzi's nomenclature, could not rely upon the defects and if the state entity so elected would be bound.'

The judge went on to say that the state entity could avoid the contract with the *g* sanction of the court. This is quite different from the *Rhyl UDC* situation, where the lease was void ab initio. It contemplates that the consent of the minister was not a requirement to be obtained before Mr Tomba signed the contract on 2 July, and it is not consistent with the judge's first finding that Mr Moretti had no power to authorise Mr Tomba to sign it. It is also consistent with what happened with the March contract, which was completed before the minister gave his consent retrospectively, although we have not *h* had argument addressed to us about that contract.

The judge later made his finding, referred to by Nourse LJ, that a contract made on 2 July would be voidable and not a total nullity. It was susceptible of ratification by the 'state entity' on obtaining the requisite consent or otherwise curing the defect. Accordingly, it would be valid unless and until it was avoided and if the minister did *j* nothing for 30 days it would become effective for all purposes. I see no reason why, if during the time that the contract was voidable at its option ENIT negotiated or performed obligations which amounted to representations that a valid contract existed and which were capable of raising an estoppel, ENIT should not be bound by them accordingly. It

would be estopped from denying that a valid contract existed. It would be independent
a of the question whether Mr Tomba had actual authority on 2 July, or whether a contract
had then been concluded. Here, ENIT clearly behaved towards Janred on the basis that it
considered that a valid and binding contract had been concluded, and there was no
suggestion put forward that it wished to repudiate the contract, in any manner, until
after these proceedings had begun. The alternative way of putting it, that it was affirming
or ratifying, comes to the same thing. The important point is that with knowledge of all
b the facts it was saying that it was content to be bound.

I agree with Nourse LJ that, by providing the money with which to meet the postdated
cheque, ENIT made a clear representation that it considered itself bound by a bargain
similar to that which Mr Tomba purported to make on 2 July. Furthermore, when Mr
Moretti arrived in London in October, authorised by the minister to negotiate with
Janred in order to avoid forfeiting the deposit, another clear representation was made.
c Neither of these acts was beyond the scope of the constitution of ENIT. Janred acted on
those representations to its detriment.

I also agree with the reasons given by Nourse LJ for dismissing the cross-appeal.

**O'CONNOR LJ.** I agree that both the appeal and the cross-appeal should be dismissed
for the reasons given in the judgments of Nourse and Croom-Johnson LJJ.
d

*Appeal and cross-appeal dismissed. Leave to appeal to the House of Lords refused.*

*25 November. The Appeal Committee of the House of Lords (Lord Keith of Kinkel, Lord Templeman
and Lord Griffiths) dismissed a petition by ENIT for leave to appeal.*

e Solicitors: *Colombotti & Partners* (for ENIT); *Howard Kennedy* (for Janred).

Mary Rose Plummer   Barrister.

# Suleman v Shahsavari and others                    a

CHANCERY DIVISION
ANDREW PARK QC SITTING AS A DEPUTY JUDGE OF THE HIGH COURT
14, 15 APRIL, 3, 4, 5 MAY, 17 JUNE 1988

*Sale of land – Damages for breach of contract – Measure of damages – Breach of contract caused* b
*by agent's want of authority – Vendors' solicitor signing contract for sale of house on behalf of*
*clients – Solicitor having no authority to sign for vendors – Purchaser unable to obtain specific*
*performance against vendors – Purchaser suing solicitor – Whether damages should be assessed*
*as at date of completion or at date of judgment.*

In 1985 the purchaser agreed to buy a house from the vendors, a married couple, for  c
£46,500. During the period prior to the exchange of contracts the vendors' solicitor dealt
almost exclusively with the wife since her husband was away in Iran for most of that
time. On 8 July the wife telephoned the solicitor to tell him that she was going to New
York and authorised him to sign the contract on behalf of herself and her husband. The
solicitor signed the contract but the vendors later refused to complete. The purchaser
brought an action seeking specific performance against the vendors or damages against  d
the solicitor for breach of warranty of authority. The judge found that there was no
binding contract between the vendors and the purchaser because the vendors' solicitor
had signed the contract on their behalf without authority and therefore the purchaser's
action against the vendors for specific performance failed, from which it followed that
the purchaser was entitled to damages against the vendors' solicitor for breach of warranty
of authority. The value of the house on the completion date was £56,000 and by the  e
time of the hearing had increased to £76,000. The question arose whether the damages
were to be calculated by reference to the difference between the contract price and the
market value of the house on the completion date or at the date of judgment.

**Held** – Having regard to the common law rule that where a purchaser lost his purchase  f
as the result of the vendor's default his damages could be assessed as at the date when he
lost his purchase if that was a more just measure of compensation and not on the basis of
the difference between the contract price and the market value on the completion date,
the purchaser was entitled to damages against the vendors' solicitor assessed on the basis
of the difference between the contract price and the market value of the house at the date
of judgment, since the date when he lost his purchase was when the judge held that he  g
could not enforce completion of the sale because the solicitor had signed the contract on
behalf of the vendors without authority (see p 463 *a d e g*, post).

**Notes**
For the authority of agents, see 1 Halsbury's Laws (4th edn) paras 728–735, and for cases  h
on the subject, see 1(1) Digest (Reissue) 443–451, *3101–3173*.
    For actions for damages for breach of contracts for sale of land, see 42 Halsbury's Laws
(4th edn) paras 265–272, and for cases on the subject, see 40 Digest (Reissue) 385–403,
*3377–3596*.

**Cases referred to in judgment**                                           j
*Bain v Fothergill* (1874) LR 7 HL 158, [1874–80] All ER Rep 83.
*Chitholie v Nash & Co (a firm)* (1973) 229 EG 786.
*Johnson v Agnew* [1979] 1 All ER 883, [1980] AC 367, [1979] 2 WLR 487, HL.
*Wroth v Tyler* [1973] 1 All ER 897, [1974] Ch 30, [1973] 2 WLR 405.

**Cases also cited**
a   *Malhotra v Choudhury* [1979] 1 All ER 186, [1980] Ch 52, CA.
*Radford v De Froberville* [1978] 1 All ER 33, [1977] 1 WLR 1262.

**Action**
Muhammad Suleman, by an amended summons dated 24 November 1986, brought an action against (1) Ebrahim Shahsavari and his wife, Ione Patricia Shahsavari, the vendors
b   of a house at 25 Tylecroft Road, London SW16, seeking specific performance of the contract of sale which had been signed by the vendors' solicitor, who purported to act on their behalf with the verbal authorisation of Mrs Shahsavari, damages for breach of contract and interest, and (2) M D Martinez & Co, a firm of solicitors of which Mr Martinez, the vendors' solicitor, was the sole proprietor, claiming damages for breach of warranty of authority and interest on the ground that Mr Martinez had had no authority
c   from Mr Shahsavari, either expressly or through his wife, to sign the contract on his behalf. Mr Martinez claimed an indemnity against Mrs Shahsavari if he was liable in damages to Mr Suleman. The case is reported only in respect of the quantum of damages to be awarded against Mr Martinez, the claim against Mr and Mrs Shahsavari having been dismissed. The facts are set out in the judgment.

d   *William Geldart* for Mr Suleman.
*Brian Hurst* for Mr and Mrs Shahsavari.
*Patrick Hamlin* for Mr Martinez.

*Cur adv vult*

e   17 June. The following judgment was delivered.

**ANDREW PARK QC.**

*Introduction*
25 Tylecroft Road, London SW16 is a three-bedroom terrace house in Norbury. This
f   case is about a sale of it which went comprehensively wrong and has ended up in this court. The facts are quite complex and partly in dispute. Several legal issues arise.
In the barest outline the case arises this way. The house was owned by Mr and Mrs Shahsavari, the first and second defendants. They put it on the market and Mr Suleman, the plaintiff, agreed to buy it. Contracts were exchanged, the vendors' part being signed by their solicitor, Mr Martinez, the third defendant, as their agent. Mr and Mrs Shahsavari
g   refused to complete. Mr Suleman claimed specific performance against them. They resisted the claim on the grounds that they had not signed the contract and Mr Martinez was not authorised by them to sign it as their agent. Mr Suleman then added a claim against Mr Martinez for damages for breach of warranty of authority. Mr Martinez says that he was the authorised agent of the Shahsavaris, but agrees that, if he was not, he is liable to Mr Suleman in damages. He says, however, that the damages should be the
h   difference between the contract price and the value of the house at the completion date, not (as Mr Suleman claims) the difference between the contract price and the value of the house at judgment. Mr Martinez also says that, if he is liable in damages to Mr Suleman, he is entitled to be indemnified by Mrs Shahsavari.
I therefore list the questions which I have to determine and, with a view to making the thread of this judgment more readily comprehensible, the conclusions which I have
j   reached on them. (1) Was there a contract binding Mr and Mrs Shahsavari to sell the house to Mr Suleman? Conclusion: No. Therefore Mr Suleman's claim against the Shahsavaris for specific performance or damages in lieu fails. (2) Is Mr Martinez liable in damages to Mr Suleman for breach of warranty of authority? Conclusion: Yes. Given my conclusion on (1) it is common ground that this follows. (3) Are the damages

calculated by reference to the difference between the contract price of the house and its market value at (i) the completion date, or (ii) the judgment date? Conclusion: the *a* judgment date. (4) Is Mr Martinez entitled to be indemnified by Mrs Shahsavari? Conclusion: No. As I indicate at the end of this judgment, there are aspects of these conclusions which leave me far less than happy. They are nevertheless the conclusions to which I believe I must come on the evidence and the law.

I shall next set out the facts more fully, and then I shall examine each of the questions *b* which I have to determine.

[His Lordship then set out the facts in detail and considered Mr Suleman's claim against Mr and Mrs Shahsavari. He found that Mr Martinez had dealt almost entirely with Mrs Shahsavari because Mr Shahsavari was in Iran for most of the time that the sale took place and that Mr Martinez had been authorised by Mrs Shahsavari to sign the contract on her behalf while she was in New York. His Lordship found that although Mr *c* Martinez had express authority from Mrs Shahsavari to sign the contract on her behalf he had no express authority from Mr Shahsavari to sign either directly or indirectly through Mrs Shahsavari and nor did he have implied or ostensible authority and in those circumstances Mr Suleman's claim against Mr and Mrs Shahsavari failed. He continued:]

*Mr Suleman's action against Mr Martinez*                                              *d*
If, as I have held is the case, the contract did not bind Mr and Mrs Shahsavari because Mr Martinez was not authorised to sign it, then Mr Suleman claims damages from Mr Martinez for breach of warranty of authority. It is agreed that, given my view on the previous point, this claim must succeed, but there is a significant question to be determined about the measure of damages. It arises in the following way.

The contract price was £46,500. The value of the house at the completion date, 5 *e* September 1986, is agreed at £56,000, £9,500 more than the contract price. The value just before the hearing is agreed at £76,000, £29,500 more than the contract price. Should the damages be £9,500 plus interest from September 1986 to judgment? Or should they be £29,500 but with no interest? (I should add that, since the failure to complete the sale is attributable to circumstances other than a defect in the title of Mr and Mrs Shahsavari, it is agreed that the damages are not limited to Mr Suleman's *f* abortive costs under the rule in *Bain v Fothergill* (1874) LR 7 HL 158, [1874–80] All ER Rep 83. He is entitled to damages for loss of bargain, but are they £9,500 or £29,500?)

In this connection counsel for the third defendant took me through a line of authorities beginning with *Wroth v Tyler* [1973] 1 All ER 897, [1974] Ch 30 and ending with *Johnson v Agnew* [1979] 1 All ER 883, [1980] AC 367. With scrupulous fairness he drew my *g* attention to passages which were unhelpful to his client Mr Martinez. I am indeed grateful to him. The cases, with one exception to which I will refer later, arose between purchaser and vendor, not between purchaser and an alleged agent for the vendor. I summarise the result of them as follows. (a) A purchaser who loses his purchase is entitled to damages at common law as well as to damages in lieu of specific performance under the Chancery Amendment Act 1858 (Lord Cairns's Act). (b) The usual measure of *h* damages at common law has in the past been the difference between the contract price and the price at completion, plus interest from completion until judgment. (c) This is not an absolute rule of law, and damages may be assessed by reference to the value at a different date if it would be more just to do so. (d) Where, as often in recent years, there have been dramatic changes in property values, it may be more just to assess damages at a different date. (e) That is particularly so where the innocent party reasonably continues *j* to try to have the contract completed; in such a case it is logical and just to assess damages as at the date when (otherwise than by his default) the contract is lost.

I should mention that *Johnson v Agnew* (the main source of the above summary) was not a case of a purchaser suing for damages where the value of the property has risen, but rather a case of a vendor suing for damages where the value of the property had fallen.

However, the same principles apply in each case.

a   If in this case I was assessing damages to be paid to Mr Suleman by Mr and Mrs Shahsavari, the vendors, I would certainly fix them at £29,500. £9,500 plus interest would not be adequate compensation to him. He has conducted himself entirely reasonably in seeking to obtain specific performance, for all that I have concluded that he cannot have it. He has been in no way dilatory over his claim and cannot be accused of having unreasonably failed to mitigate his damage.

b   Does it make any difference that Mr Suleman's damages are payable by Mr Martinez, not Mr and Mrs Shahsavari, and are for breach of warranty of authority, not for breach of contract to sell? Counsel for the third defendant, in submitting that it does, has referred me to the only case known where the point has been considered: *Chitholie v Nash & Co (a firm)* (1973) 229 EG 786. As in the present case, solicitors who, without authority, had signed a contract as agent for the vendor were liable in damages for breach of

c warranty of authority. Talbot J assessed the damages by reference to the value of the house at the completion date, not at judgment. Counsel for the third defendant says I should do the same in this case. He also points to the hardship to Mr Martinez of having to pay higher damages because he had to wait to see whether Mr Suleman's action for specific performance against the Shahsavaris would fail.

   I see the force of counsel's submissions, but I have nevertheless concluded that the

d damages should be £29,500, not £9,500. I distinguish *Chitholie v Nash & Co (a firm)* on two grounds. First, it was at all times agreed there that the solicitors had no authority to sign the contract, so the time when the plaintiff lost his purchase was the completion date. In this case Mr Suleman only loses his purchase by virtue of my judgment that he is not entitled to specific performance. Second, the basis of Talbot J's decision was that 'he was bound, as he saw it, to follow the normal common law rule as to the measure of

e damages for breach of a contract of sale'. That rule was, he believed, that damages were assessed by reference to the value at completion. However, at least since *Johnson v Agnew* [1979] 1 All ER 883, [1980] AC 367, decided by the House of Lords in 1979, I think that the common law rule is different. The rule now is that damages may, and perhaps even should, be assessed at the date when the plaintiff loses his purchase if that is a more just measure of compensation and the plaintiff has not unreasonably delayed his claim.

f   I agree with counsel for the plaintiff that it would be extraordinary if Mr Suleman was entitled to a lower amount of damages against Mr Martinez than he would have been awarded against Mr and Mrs Shahsavari, had he had a good claim against them. I sympathise with Mr Martinez over the increase in the damages attributable to Mr Suleman's unsuccessfully pursuing his claim for specific performance, but, as Lord Wilberforce said in *Johnson v Agnew* [1979] 1 All ER 883 at 896, [1980] AC 367 at 400:

g 'The general principle for the assessment of damages is compensatory.' Mr Suleman would not be adequately compensated by damages of £9,500 plus interest, however tough the higher damages might be on Mr Martinez.

   I therefore hold that, unless an application is made for a more up-to-date valuation to be adopted, the main damages for breach of warranty of authority are £29,500. There

h should be added £188·50 of lost conveyancing and other incidental costs suffered by Mr Suleman, but not £300 for a life insurance premium which he paid. As far as I could make out he still had the policy and may not have suffered any loss in that respect.

   Mr Martinez is still holding the deposit of £2,325 which Mr Suleman paid on exchange of contracts. He will no doubt repay it, with accrued interest, to Mr Suleman in the light of this judgment. Mr Suleman paid £250 of earnest money to Jackson Property Services.

j He must recover that from them. Mr Martinez has no liability for it.

*Mr Martinez's claim to be indemnified by Mrs Shahsavari*

   Mr Martinez contends that, if he is liable to Mr Suleman in damages for breach of warranty that he had authority from Mr and Mrs Shahsavari, he is entitled to be indemnified by Mrs Shahsavari because she is in breach of warranty to him that she had

authority from her husband. For quite some time in the course of the hearing I thought
that this must be right, but I have concluded otherwise.                                          *a*

An agent is presumed to warrant his or her authority, but the presumption can be
rebutted. In this case I believe it is, on Mr Martinez's own account of the circumstances
in which Mrs Shahsavari authorised him to sign the contract. This goes back to the
telephone conversation of 8 July, which I have described earlier. One problem dealt with
was: how to cope with the absence of Mr Shahsavari in Iran? Mr Martinez's evidence was
that he said to Mrs Shahsavari that she could sign the contract on behalf of herself and      *b*
her husband. The ultimate outcome that, though not signing the contract herself on
behalf of the two of them, she gave authority on behalf of the two of them to Mr
Martinez to sign the contract, all sprang from Mr Martinez's own suggestion. She did
not expressly say that she had her husband's authority, and Mr Martinez did not expressly
ask her. She therefore made no express representation to Mr Martinez, and I cannot
consider that, merely by falling in with Mr Martinez's suggestion that she could commit   *c*
her husband, she thereby represented or warranted to Mr Martinez that she was
authorised by her husband to commit him.

I can quite understand how Mr Martinez came to make his suggestion, and I have
considerable sympathy for him. All communications to him had always come from Mrs
Shahsavari, and he took it for granted, probably without giving it much thought, that if
she signed for her husband (or authorised Mr Martinez to sign for both of them) there   *d*
would be no problem. In ninety-nine cases out of a hundred he would have been right.
This, unfortunately, was the hundredth case.

I therefore conclude that Mr Martinez is not entitled to be indemnified by Mrs
Shahsavari.

*Conclusion*                                                                                       *e*

The final result is that Mr Martinez is the loser, and recovers nothing from either of
the Shahsavaris. In many respects I feel sorry about this. Mr Martinez had a difficult and
demanding client who wanted a solution to an intractable problem. As he said in a letter
to Mr Suleman's solicitors, written after everything had gone wrong: 'We endeavoured
to assist our clients.' It is very hard on him that his constructive efforts have rebounded   *f*
on him as they have, all the more so since, as I suspect (but do not know), Mr Shahsavari
might well have signed the contract himself (or given express authority to Mr Martinez
to sign it) if he had been in this country on 10 July.

However, Mr Martinez did take a risk. He could, perhaps, have said to Mrs Shahsavari
that he would only sign the contract and exchange it if he received a letter from her
instructing him to do so on behalf of herself and her husband and confirming that she
had her husband's authority. In his letter to Mr Suleman's solicitors he wrote:               *g*

'Whilst we understood or believed that we were receiving joint instructions and
spoke mainly to Mrs. Shahsavari, quite clearly it is open to Mr. Shahsavari to say that
he did not authorise an exchange of contracts.'

Unhappily for Mr Martinez, Mr Shahsavari has said precisely that. I believe on the   *h*
evidence and the law that it protects the Shahsavaris and leads to the unfortunate outcome
for Mr Martinez which I have described in this judgment.

For the reasons appearing in my judgment Mr Suleman's claim for specific performance
or damages against Mr and Mrs Shahsavari is dismissed. His claim for damages against
Mr Martinez succeeds, damages to be assessed as described in the judgment. Mr
Martinez's claim for an indemnity against Mrs Shahsavari fails.                                *j*

Solicitors: *Huntley Millard & Co* (for Mr Suleman); *M S Miller & Co*, South Croydon (for
Mr and Mrs Shahsavari); *Willey Hargrave* (for Mr Martinez).

Hazel Hartman    Barrister.

a   # C v C (minor: abduction: rights of custody abroad)

COURT OF APPEAL, CIVIL DIVISION
LORD DONALDSON OF LYMINGTON MR, NEILL AND BUTLER-SLOSS LJJ
13, 14 DECEMBER 1988
b

*Minor – Custody – Rights of custody – Foreign custody rights – Wrongful removal or retention
– Australian court giving custody of child to mother but providing that neither parent should be
entitled to remove child from Australia without consent of the other – Mother removing child to
England without father's consent – Father applying for order that child be returned to Australia
– Whether father's right to prevent child being removed from Australia without his consent
c   constituting a custody right – Whether return of child to Australia exposing child to grave risk of
psychological harm – Child Abduction and Custody Act 1985, Sch 1, arts 3, 5, 13.*

The mother, who was English, married the father, an Australian, in England in 1978 and
a year later they went to live in Australia. The child of the marriage, a boy, was born in
d   Australia in 1982. In 1985 the marriage broke down and divorce proceedings were
commenced in Australia. Agreement was reached over finance and the future
arrangements for the child and in November 1986 a consent order was made in the
Australian Family Court providing for the mother to have the custody of the child, for
the father and the mother to remain joint guardians and for neither parent to be entitled
to remove him from Australia without the other's consent. In August 1988 the mother
e   removed the child from Australia to England without the father's consent. The father
applied to the High Court in England under the Child Abduction and Custody Act 1985
for the return of the child to Australia, contending that his removal out of the jurisdiction
of the Australian court was 'wrongful removal or retention' under art 3[a] of the
Convention on the Civil Aspects of International Child Abduction as set out in Sch 1 to
the 1985 Act, since it had been done in breach of the father's rights of custody. By art 5[b]
f   of the convention 'rights of custody' included 'the right to determine the child's place of
residence'. The mother contended that, even if the removal of the child from Australia
had been wrongful, nevertheless there was a grave risk that if he was returned to Australia
he would be exposed to psychological harm within art 13[c] of the convention and therefore
should not be returned to Australia. The judge accepted that the child would suffer
psycological harm if he was returned to Australia without the mother and dismissed the
g   father's application. The father appealed.

**Held** – (1) Having regard to the international character of the 1985 Act and the
convention, the convention itself and the definitions contained in it were to be construed
according to their ordinary meaning and disregarding any special meaning which might
attach to them in the context of domestic legislation except in those instances where the
h   convention itself created an exception. Accordingly, the father's right to give or withhold
consent to any removal of the child from Austrialia, coupled with the implied right to
impose conditions, was to be recognised as a right of custody for the purposes of arts 3
and 5 of the convention, since it was a right to determine the child's place of residence. It
followed that the child had been wrongfully removed from Australia in contravention
of art 3 (see p 468 g j, p 471 f, p 472 b c f to j and p 473 a to d, post).
j       (2) Furthermore, art 13 of the convention did not preclude the return of the child to
Australia on the ground that the child would be exposed to grave risk of psychological

---

a   Article 3, so far as material, is set out at p 468 b, post
b   Article 5, so far as material, is set out at p 468 c, post
c   Article 13, so far as material, is set out at p 469 a b, post

harm, because the grave risk of harm to the child arose from the mother's refusal to return to Australia for her own reasons rather than for the sake of the child, and she **a** should not be allowed to create a situation which was psychologically harmful to the child and then rely on it in order to defeat the father's application. Moreover, the father was willing to give an undertaking to the court to ameliorate the rigours of the return of the child to Australia. The appeal would therefore be allowed (see p 469 *j* to p 470 *a*, p 471 *a* to *c e f* and p 472 *h*, post).

**b**

**Notes**
For return of children wrongfully removed, see Supplement to 8 Halsbury's Laws (4th edn) para 525A.

**Cases referred to in judgments**
*A (a minor) (abduction), Re* [1988] 1 FLR 365, CA.                            **c**
*E (a minor) (abduction), Re* [1989] 1 FLR 135, CA.

**Case also cited**
*B v B (minors: enforcement of access abroad)* [1988] 1 All ER 652, [1988] 1 WLR 526.

**Appeal**                                                                    **d**
The father of a minor appealed against the order of Latey J in chambers dated 14 October 1988 dismissing his application under the Child Abduction and Custody Act 1985 for the surrender of the child so that he might be returned to Australia. The facts are set out in the judgment of Butler-Sloss LJ.

*Anita M Ryan QC* and *Cherry Harding* for the father.                        **e**
*Michael Connell QC* and *E James Holman* for the mother.

**BUTLER-SLOSS LJ** (delivering the first judgment at the invitation of Lord Donaldson MR). This is an appeal from the order of Latey J made on 14 October 1988 on an application under the Child Abduction and Custody Act 1985 in respect of a boy called **f** Thomas, born on 27 July 1982. This Act gives statutory force to most of the articles of the Convention on the Civil Aspects of International Child Abduction (The Hague, 25 October 1980; TS 66 (1986); Cm 33).

The child was removed by his mother on 3 August 1988 from their home in Sydney, Australia, to England, where they are now living. The father before Latey J asserted and the mother denied that under the provisions of art 3 of the convention the removal and **g** retention of the child out of the jurisdiction of the Australian Family Court were wrongful. The mother further submitted that, if the removal or retention was found to be wrongful, nevertheless under the provisions of art 13 there was a grave risk that the return of the child would expose him to psychological harm. The judge dismissed the father's application under the 1985 Act and the father appeals from that order.

There are also wardship proceedings in respect of the child, the mother having issued **h** an originating summons on 11 August. Those proceedings were not before the judge nor are they before this court.

Further evidence was submitted to this court which has been taken into account only so far as it sets out the current proposals of the father if the child returns and the present financial position of the mother

The short facts are as follows.                                               **j**
The mother is 34 and English. In 1976 she went to Australia and met the father, who is 35 and Australian. They were married on 15 April 1978 in England, where they remained for a year before returning to make their home in Sydney. The one child was born in 1982. The marriage broke down in 1985 and the parents separated in July of that year. Divorce proceedings were commenced and agreement was reached over finance

and the future arrangements for Thomas. On 4 November 1986 the deputy registrar in
a  Sydney made a consent order including the following words:

> '(1) The wife to have custody of . . . the child of the marriage and the husband
> and the wife to remain joint guardians of the said child. (2) Neither the husband
> nor the wife shall remove the child from Australia without the consent of the other.'

During 1986 the mother, with the consent of the father, took the child for a holiday
b  to England.

The mother and child lived together in a suburb of Sydney until 3 August 1988, when
she left for England with the child, without first informing the father and without his
consent. As soon as the father learnt of the situation by a letter from the mother, he
applied to the Family Court in Sydney. The mother before her departure had applied to
vary the November 1986 consent order to delete the requirement for the father's consent
c  to the removal of Thomas from the jurisdiction.

Ross-Jones J heard the father's application on 8 and 10 August. On 10 August the
judge made orders for the return of the child and transferred the custody of Thomas to
the father on his return to the Australian jurisdiction. There was no provision made for
access to the mother in that eventuality. There was a further hearing before the judge on
23 August. The mother has appealed against the order transferring custody to the father.
d  The judge declined to stay the order transferring custody pending the hearing of the
appeal.

The mother has made in her affidavits various allegations against the father and has
given explanations for her action in removing Thomas from Australia. They are not, in
my judgment, relevant to an application under the 1985 Act, save as in so far as they may
affect the approach of the Australian authorities to the mother's return. From reading
e  the transcripts of the hearings and from the affidavits of the father, as well as the expert
evidence called on behalf of the mother, she is likely to be seen to be in contempt of court
in respect of the 1986 consent order and the orders made in August of this year. That
may be relevant to the considerations under art 13. The welfare of the child as the first
and paramount consideration is not, however, as Latey J correctly pointed out, the basis
f  of the Hague Convention and the Act incorporating it in the English law. Australia is a
signatory to the Hague Convention and enacted the relevant legislation in 1987.

The preamble to the Hague Convention sets out the intention of the states which
signed it:

> 'To protect children internationally from the harmful effects of their wrongful
> removal or retention and to establish procedures to ensure their prompt return to
g  > the state of their habitual residence, as well as to secure protection for rights of
> access.'

Article 1, which is not contained in Sch 1 to the 1985 Act, states that the objects of the
convention are—

> '(a) to secure the prompt return of children wrongfully removed to or retained
h  > in any contracting state; and (b) to ensure that rights of custody and access under the
> law of one contracting state are effectively respected in the other contracting state.'

As Nourse LJ said in Re A (a minor) (abduction) [1988] 1 FLR 365 at 368:

> 'These and other provisions of the Convention demonstrate that its primary
> purpose is to provide for the summary return to the country of their habitual
j  > residence of children who are wrongfully removed to or retained in another country
> in breach of subsisting rights of custody or access. Except in specified circumstances,
> the judicial and administrative authorities in the country to or in which the child is
> wrongfully removed or retained cannot refuse to order the return of the child,
> whether on grounds of choice of forum or on a consideration of what is in the best
> interests of the child or otherwise.'

Three questions arise in this case. (1) Was the removal of the child wrongful? (2) Is the retention of the child wrongful? (3) If the answer to either or both of the first two is Yes, does art 13 apply to stop the return of the child?

By art 3:

'The removal or retention of a child is to be considered wrongful where—(a) it is in breach of rights of custody attributed to a person, an institution or any other body, either jointly or alone, under the law of the State in which the child was habitually resident immediately before the removal or retention; and (b) at the time of removal or retention those rights were actually exercised, either jointly or alone, or would have been so exercised but for the removal or retention . . .'

By art 5:

'For the purposes of this Convention—(a) "rights of custody" shall include rights relating to the care of the person of the child and, in particular, the right to determine the child's place of residence . . .'

In respect of my first question, whether the removal was wrongful, Latey J heard argument as to the effect of the November 1986 order and in particular the effect of joint guardianship. He had before him the written opinion and oral evidence of an Australian Queen's Counsel. The judge's attention does not appear to have been sufficiently drawn to the effect on the definition in art 5 of the convention of cl 2 of the November 1986 order, that neither parent should remove the child from Australia without the consent of the other. Accordingly, the judge's attention was not drawn specifically to the question whether under Australian law cl 2 was capable of constituting a right of custody within the convention. In the absence of sufficient expert evidence on that point, this court must do its best to consider whether cl 2 comes within the definition given in art 5.

By cl 2 the father had, in my judgment, the right to determine that the child should reside in Australia or outside the jurisdiction at the request of the mother. In 1987 he gave his consent to the child coming to England for a specified holiday. One might consider the example of a parent wishing to leave the jurisdiction with the child for a longer period, say 12 months. The other parent, with cl 2 in the order, would have some control over not only the child leaving the jurisdiction but also as to the place to which the child was going, and not only the country: for instance, to live in London in suitable circumstances. If the child was retained under such an arrangement beyond the agreed date of return, it seems inconceivable to me that the convention could not effect the return of the child. But, if the argument so attractively advanced by counsel for the mother is right, there would be no instant redress by the justifiably aggrieved parent. The words of art 5 must, in my view, be read into art 3 and may in certain circumstances extend the concept of custody beyond the ordinarily understood domestic approach. Therefore in the present case there would be the general right of the mother to determine the place of residence within the Commonwealth of Australia, but a more limited right, subject to the father's consent, outside the jurisdiction of the Australian Family Court. The father does not have the right to determine the child's place of residence within Australia but has the right to ensure that the child remains in Australia or lives anywhere outside Australia only with his approval. Such limited rights and joint rights are by no means unknown to English family law and no doubt to Australian family law. Indeed, in art 3 rights of custody are specifically recognised as held jointly or alone. The convention must be interpreted so that within its scope it is to be effective. For my part I consider that the child was wrongfully removed from the jurisdiction in breach of cl 2 of the order of 4 November 1986.

It is not, therefore, necessary to look at the various Australian statutes or recent decisions or the expert opinion evidence proffered as additional evidence by the father.

The difficult question whether the retention of the child was to be considered wrongful

does not now arise and I do not propose to embark on a consideration of the effect of the
a  orders made in Sydney in August.

I turn, therefore, to the third question: whether art 13 applies. It states:

> '... the judicial or administrative authority of the requested State is not bound to
> order the return of the child if the person, institution or other body which opposes
> its return establishes that ... (b) there is a grave risk that his or her return would
> expose the child to physical or psychological harm or otherwise place the child in an
> b  intolerable situation ...'

In Re A (a minor) (abduction) [1988] 1 FLR 365 at 372 Nourse LJ considered the effect of
art 13(b) and said:

> 'The intendment of art. 13(b) cannot be that the judicial or administrative
> authority of the requested state is to be blinkered against a sight of the practical
> c  consequences of the child's return.'

The judge considered with great care the situation if the child was to return to Sydney
and we are rightly reminded by counsel for the mother that the judge heard the mother
give evidence and was impressed with her and the evidence which she gave. He was
satisfied that there was grave risk of psychological harm to Thomas. He pointed out:
d
> '... the mother had been the sole carer of Thomas. She has devoted herself to him
> and his care. Other than what she did in August there is no criticism of her. On the
> contrary [counsel for the father] paid a handsome tribute to her as an excellent
> mother. For his lifetime of six years she has been the centre of Thomas's life. His
> emotional tie, bonding, with her is the closest possible.'

e  He said also:

> 'I am satisfied that to remove Thomas back to Australia without his mother would
> create the gravest risk of very serious psychological harm, and that it would be
> wholly wrong to make an order which had that effect. Unless she had a home,
> financial support and the care of Thomas pending any further full investigation and
> f  decision, the risk of psychological harm would be little less even if the mother went
> with him.'

At that time the mother was in some danger of being dealt with under the contempt
of court. At that time there were no offers by the father to house her and the boy or
indeed any offer for the boy to remain with her pending proceedings or anything of the
sort which now has been presented to this court. But now matters have moved on, and
g  we have evidence that was not before the judge. The effect of that evidence is considerably
to ameliorate the rigours of the return of the child and his mother to Sydney.

The father's position now is that, in order to facilitate the return of the child, he will
gave certain undertakings to this court and to the Australian Family Court.

These undertakings are crucial to the welfare of the child, who has been sufficiently
h  disrupted in his removal from his home and his country and needs as a priority an easy
and secure return home. The mother has been the primary caretaker throughout his
short life, and since the parting of the parents when he was three for all but access periods
his sole caretaker. If possible, she should for his sake and not for hers be with him and
help him to readjust to his return. The father should not be instrumental in putting
obstacles in the way of that easy return, or make difficulties once the child is back. It is
j  essential that the judge hearing the future issues of custody and access or indeed the
Australian Family Court should have the opportunity to consider the welfare of the child
as paramount without emergency applications relating to the manner of the return of
the child.

The father has offered a number of undertakings. Those, as far as they go, are very
valuable, and, if I may say so, for my part, show the good intent that he has for the

welfare of his child and to return him to the jurisdiction of the Australian court. In my view, those undertakings should go somewhat further, and the undertakings that I for my part think should be required of this father, as a prerequisite of the return of the child, and without which I consider the child should not be expected to return, are as follows. (1) He will not seek to enforce against the mother the order for guardianship and custody dated 10 August 1988, and will not seek to remove Thomas from the care and control of the mother until the full adjudication by the Family Court in Sydney, Australia, on the merits on the contested issues of guardianship, custody and care and control of Thomas. (2) He will provide for the use of the mother a suitable motor car at his expense from the date of arrival for two months or until the adjudication, whichever may be the later. (3) He will obtain unfurnished accommodation within convenient distance of the school Thomas will attend, at a rental of not less than $A220 per week; and the mother shall pay the rent up to a limit of A$250 per week. The father will provide suitable and sufficient furniture. (4) He will use his best endeavours to secure for Thomas a place at a named preparatory school, and will pay for all fees, clothing and incidental expenses in relation to Thomas's education at that school. (5) He will provide air tickets and book seats for the mother and Thomas from London to Sydney, to travel on a day not before 1 January 1989, and will provide the sum of £50 to cover additional expenses of travel. (6) He will not institute or voluntarily support any proceedings for the punishment or committal of the mother in respect of any contempt of the Australian court that she may have committed prior to the date hereof. (7) Once Thomas's name has been removed from the mother's passport, he will not seek to have the mother's passport impounded. (8) He will pay maintenance for the mother and Thomas from the date of their arrival in Australia until adjudication, at the rate of $A650 per week, payable in advance. If the mother obtains employment, the sum of $A650 to be reduced by 50% of the salary that the mother receives. The first four weeks payment to be made on arrival in Australia and, thereafter, the fifth and subsequent payments to be made weekly in advance. (9) He will pay for any medical expenses reasonably incurred by the mother in respect of Thomas in Australia.

These undertakings cover, as far as I can see, all the entirely justifiable concerns of the judge. It will be a matter for the Australian Family Court as to with which parent in the future the child shall make his home, and nothing that I say in this judgment should be taken as in any way prejudging or affecting the decision that the Australian court may feel it necessary to make.

Counsel for the mother accepts that he cannot suggest other than that the Australian court will try the case in accordance with its approach to child cases, which appears to accord very closely to the approach of the courts of this country.

Nevertheless, the mother has said, for what appear to be emotional reasons, that she cannot go back. I am not sure that she is now saying that. But, if she does, what is to be done? The judge found, and I agree with him, that the mother is very important to the child. At the time of the hearing the mother was found by the judge to have reasonable grounds for refusing to return, and I would not disagree with him. Those grounds have now been removed by the undertakings which I expect will be given to this court, without which the child will not return, and through this court will be given to the Australian Family Court.

The mother has to rely on the Australian court for a decision as to the future home of the child. In the circumstances of this case, that is undoubtedly the right court to make that decision. She also has no family in Australia, a broken marriage and now, through her own actions and costly litigation, no assets.

She is responsible for the loss of her home, the spending of the proceeds of sale, the lack of job, car and money. None of these, in the light of the undertakings of the father, can be reasons to block the return of the child. The mother argues that if she does not return and the child is to return without her there is a grave risk of psychological harm to the child.

The grave risk of harm arises not from the return of the child, but the refusal of the
*a* mother to accompany him. The convention does not require the court in this country to
consider the welfare of the child as paramount, but only to be satisfied as to the grave risk
of harm. I am not satisfied that the child would be placed in an intolerable situation if
the mother refused to go back. In weighing up the various factors, I must place in the
balance and as of the greatest importance the effect of the court refusing the application
under the convention because of the refusal of the mother to return for her own reasons,
*b* not for the sake of the child. Is a parent to create the psychological situation, and then
rely on it? If the grave risk of psychological harm to a child is to be inflicted by the
conduct of the parent who abducted him, then it would be relied on by every mother of
a young child who removed him out of the jurisdiction and refused to return. It would
drive a coach and four through the convention, at least in respect of applications relating
to young children. I, for my part, cannot believe that this is in the interests of
*c* international relations. Nor should the mother, by her own actions, succeed in preventing
the return of a child who should be living in his own country and deny him contact with
his other parent. As Balcombe LJ said in *Re E (a minor) (abduction)* [1989] 1 FLR 135 at
142:

> *d* '... the whole purpose of this Convention is ... to ensure that parties do not gain
> adventitious advantage by either removing a child wrongfully from the country of
> its usual residence, or, having taken the child, with the agreement of any other party
> who has custodial rights, to another jurisdiction, then wrongfully to retain that
> child.'

If this mother will not accompany the child, despite the knowledge that his rightful
place is in New South Wales, then, on the facts before this court, I am not satisfied that
*e* art 13(*b*) applies and, in my judgment, the child should return to his father.
When the undertakings which I have set out are given on behalf of the father to this
court and, through this court, given to the Australian Family Court, I, for my part, would
allow this appeal, and order that Thomas do return to Sydney on the flight booked by the
father.

*f* **NEILL LJ.** I agree. I also agree with the orders proposed by Butler-Sloss LJ, provided
that the undertakings that she has set out in her judgment are given by the father both
to this court and to the Family Court of Australia.
I propose, however, to give a short judgment of my own on one aspect of the matter.
This case comes before the court in accordance with the Convention on the Civil
*g* Aspects of International Child Abduction (The Hague, 25 October 1982; TS 66 (1986);
Cm 33). The articles of the convention, which are set out in Sch 1 of the Child Abduction
and Custody Act 1985, have the force of law in the United Kingdom: see s 1(2) of the
1985 Act.
In the present case we are concerned in the first place with the question whether the
removal of the child by the mother from Australia was wrongful within the meaning of
*h* art 3 of the convention. That article, so far as it is material, provides as follows:

> 'The removal ... of a child is to be considered wrongful where—(*a*) it is in breach
> of rights of custody attributed to a person ... either jointly or alone, under the law
> of the State in which the child was habitually resident immediately before the
> removal ... and (*b*) at the time of removal ... those rights were actually exercised,
> either jointly or alone, or would have been so exercised but for the removal ... The
> *j* rights of custody mentioned in sub-paragraph (*a*) above may arise in particular by
> operation of law or by reason of a judicial or administrative decision, or by reason of
> an agreement having legal effect under the law of that State.'

The term 'custody' in relation to a child is a term which is used in many systems of
law. The meaning of the term may vary in different jurisdictions and in different

contexts in the same jurisdiction. The phrase 'rights of custody' may also have varying
meanings. For the purposes of the convention, however, the phrase 'rights of custody' is
given a particular definition. This definition is contained in art 5, which, so far as is
material, provides:

> 'For the purposes of this Convention—(a) "rights of custody" shall include rights
> relating to the care of the person of the child and, in particular, the right to
> determine the child's place of residence . . .'

The right to determine the child's place of residence is, therefore, included among the
rights of custody to which art 3 applies. Moreover, it appears from art 3 itself that this
right may be attributed to a person either jointly or alone, and it may arise by reason of,
inter alia, a judicial decision or by reason of an agreement having legal effect under the
law of the state in which the child was habitually resident immediately before the
removal.

With this introduction, I turn to the order dated 4 November 1986, made in Sydney,
in the Family Court of Australia. It was a consent order. By para 1 of the order it was
provided that the mother should have custody of the child and that the father and the
mother should remain as joint guardians. Paragraph 2 was in these terms:

> 'Neither the Husband nor the Wife shall remove the child from Australia without
> the consent of the other.'

The question for decision is whether para 2 gives to the father the right to determine
the child's place of residence. Plainly it is not an exclusive right. The mother has custody
of the child and can decide where in Australia they are to live. But the father's consent is
required before the child is removed by the mother from Australia. It seems clear that
this consent could be limited both as to the period of absence and as to the place to which
the child could be taken. Thus, to take an example, the father could consent to the child
residing with the mother for a period of a year or so in England or some other agreed
country or even at some particular address.

I am satisfied that this right to give or withhold consent to any removal of the child
from Australia, coupled with the implicit right to impose conditions, is a right to
determine the child's place of residence, and thus a right of custody within the meaning
of arts 3 and 5 of the convention. I am further satisfied that this conclusion is in
accordance with the objects of the convention and of the 1985 Act. Until last August this
child was habitually resident in Australia. In 1986 the Family Court of Australia made
orders relating to his custody, which included an agreed provision that he should not be
removed from Australia without the father's consent. In my judgment, the enforcement
of that provision falls plainly within the objects which the convention and the 1985 Act
are seeking to achieve.

**LORD DONALDSON OF LYMINGTON MR.** I agree that, for the reasons given
by Neill and Butler-Sloss LJJ, the removal of this child from the Commonwealth of
Australia was wrongful within the meaning of the Hague Convention which is set out in
Sch 1 to the Child Abduction and Custody Act 1985. I also agree with the terms of the
order proposed by Butler-Sloss LJ.

I give a separate judgment only because I wish to emphasise the international character
of this legislation. The whole purpose of such a code is to produce a situation in which
the courts of all contracting states may be expected to interpret and apply it in similar
ways, save in so far as the national legislatures have decreed otherwise. Subject then to
exceptions, such as are created by s 9 of the Act in relation to art 16 and s 20(4) of the Act
in relation to art 10(2)(b), the definitions contained in the convention should be applied
and the words of the convention, including the definitions, construed in the ordinary
meaning of the words used and in disregard of any special meaning which might attach
to them in the context of legislation not having this international character.

*a* We are necessarily concerned with Australian law because we are bidden by art 3 to decide whether the removal of the child was in breach of 'rights of custody' attributed to the father either jointly or alone under that law, but it matters not in the least how those rights are described in Australian law. What matters is whether those rights fall within the convention definition of 'rights of custody'. Equally, it matters not in the least whether those rights would be regarded as rights of custody under English law, if they fall within the definition.

*b* 'Custody', as a matter of non-technical English, means 'Safe keeping, protection; charge, care, guardianship' (I take that from the *Shorter Oxford English Dictionary*); but 'rights of custody' as defined in the convention includes a much more precise meaning, which will, I apprehend, usually be decisive of most applications under the convention. This is 'the right to determine the child's place of residence'. This right may be in the court, the mother, the father, some caretaking institution, such as a local authority, or it *c* may, as in this case, be a divided right, in so far as the child is to reside in Australia, the right being that of the mother but, in so far as any question arises as to the child residing outside Australia, it being a joint right subject always, of course, to the overriding rights of the court. If anyone, be it an individual or the court or other institution or a body, has a right to object, and either is not consulted or refuses consent, the removal will be *d* wrongful within the meaning of the convention. I add for completeness that a 'right to determine the child's place of residence' (using the phrase in the convention) may be specific, the right to decide that it shall live at a particular address, or it may be general, e g 'within the Commonwealth of Australia'.

We have also had to consider art 13, with its reference to 'psychological harm'. I would only add that in a situation in which it is necessary to consider operating the machinery of the convention, some psychological harm to the child is inherent, whether the child is *e* or is not returned. This is, I think, recognised by the words 'or otherwise place the child in an intolerable situation', which cast considerable light on the severe degree of psychological harm which the convention has in mind. It will be the concern of the court of the state to which the child is to be returned to minimise or eliminate this harm and, in the absence of compelling evidence to the contrary or evidence that it is beyond *f* the powers of those courts in the circumstances of the case, the courts of this country should assume that this will be done. Save in an exceptional case, our concern, ie the concern of these courts, should be limited to giving the child the maximum possible protection until the courts of the other country, Australia in this case, can resume their normal role in relation to the child.

*g* *Appeal allowed when undertakings have been given on behalf of the father; order that child do return to Sydney on flight booked by father; wardship to continue till child leaves jurisdiction. Leave to appeal to House of Lords refused.*

Solicitors: *Batchelors* (for the father); *Charles Russell Williams & James* (for the mother).

Mary Rose Plummer   Barrister.

# Robertson v Ridley and another

a

COURT OF APPEAL, CIVIL DIVISION
MAY, NOURSE AND WOOLF LJJ
8 NOVEMBER 1988

*Club – Members' club – Safety of premises – Club rules providing for chairman and secretary to*   b
*be responsible in law for conduct of club – Member injured by reason of condition of club premises*
*– Whether club liable under club rules for member's injuries – Whether club owing duty of care to*
*members to maintain club premises in reasonable state of safety and repair.*

*Negligence – Duty to take care – Club – Members' club – Member injured by reason of condition*
*of club premises – Whether club owing duty of care to members to maintain club premises in*   c
*reasonable state of safety and repair.*

The plaintiff, a member of an unincorporated members' club, was riding his motor cycle
out of the club grounds when he failed to see a pothole in the driveway, fell off and was
injured. He brought an action against the chairman and secretary of the club, as officers
of the club, claiming that they were liable for the injuries he had sustained by reason of   d
the condition of the club's premises, on the ground that the rules of the club, which
provided that the chairman and secretary 'were responsible in Law . . . for the conduct of
the Club', gave rise to a duty to maintain the premises in a reasonable state of safety and
repair. The judge dismissed the claim, holding that the club rules merely provided that
the two officers were to be responsible for those legal obligations already imposed on
members' clubs before the rules came into existence and did not give rise to any new   e
duty, with the result that the rules, as such, did not qualify the general common law rule
that individual members could not sue a club to which they belonged. The plaintiff
appealed.

**Held** – In so far as the rules of the club provided that two of its officers were to be   f
responsible in law for the conduct of the club then, in the absence of an express provision
that the officers were to be responsible for the condition of the club premises, the rules
did not give rise to a duty of care towards individual members to maintain the club
premises in a reasonable state of safety and repair and did not qualify the general common
law rule that there was no liability between a club or its members on the one hand and
individual members on the other. Accordingly, the plaintiff's claim failed and his appeal   g
would be dismissed (see p 475 h, p 477 d f to h and p 478 a to d, post).

*Shore v Ministry of Works* [1950] 2 All ER 228 followed.

*Prole v Allen* [1950] 1 All ER 476 considered.

**Notes**   h
For the liability of members of a club, see 6 Halsbury's Laws (4th edn) para 233, and for
cases on the subject, see 8(2) Digest (Reissue) 628–632, 81–110.

**Cases referred to in judgments**
*Prole v Allen* [1950] 1 All ER 476.   j
*Shore v Ministry of Works* [1950] 2 All ER 228, CA.

**Case also cited**
*Brown v Lewis* (1896) 12 TLR 455, DC.

**Appeal**

*a* The plaintiff, William Gardiner Robertson, a member of the Sale and Ashton-on-Mersey Conservative Club, appealed against the decision of McCullough J sitting in the Queen's Bench Division at Manchester on 10 March 1988 dismissing his action against that the defendants, Clifford Ridley and Lawrence Finch, the chairman and secretary of the club, for damages for personal injuries which he had sustained by reason of the condition of the club's premises. The facts are set out in the judgment of May LJ.

*b*
*Michael Redfern* for the plaintiff.
*Geoffrey Tattersall* for the defendants.

**MAY LJ.** On 20 April 1985 the plaintiff was riding his motor cycle out of the Conservative Club at Sale, of which he had been a member for a few months. He failed
*c* to see a pothole in the drive into which the motor cycle went. He fell off and injured himself. He suffered damage which has been agreed at full liability in the sum of £3,500 if liability there be.

He first issued proceedings against the club in its name, but then these were amended so that instead of the club the two individuals who were for the time being the chairman and secretary of the club became the defendants.
*d* In the court below the judge dismissed the plaintiff's claim on the basis, first, that there is in general no liability at common law on a club or its members on the one hand to individual members on the other and that in so far as the plaintiff relied on specific rules of the club to found liability, to which I shall refer in a moment, those could not assist him. Accordingly, he dismissed the plaintiff's claim and it is from that dismissal that the plaintiff now appeals.
*e* It is convenient to refer at the outset to the relevant rules to which our attention has been drawn. The club was in general run by a committee, but there were also two particular officers, a secretary and a chairman. By r 49(e) the secretary was responsible 'for the insurance of the Club against fire and burglary and in respect of liability for accidents occurring to the Club servants and for any other purposes directed by the
*f* Committee'. By r 49(n) he was 'responsible in Law, with the Chairman, for the conduct of the Club as a corporate body and is ex-officio a member of all sub-committees'. By r 50(c) the chairman was responsible in law with the secretary for the conduct of the club as a corporate body and was also ex officio a member of all sub-committees. For the sake of completeness I refer also to r 53(a), dealing with the trustees of the club, which provides:

*g* 'The property of the Club shall be vested in the Trustees. They shall deal with such property as directed by resolutions of the Committee (of which an entry in the minute book shall be conclusive evidence) and they shall be indemnified against risk and expense out of the Club's property.'

That is the brief context within which the facts of this case have to be determined.
*h* In so far as the judge held that in general there is no liability at common law on a club or its members on the one hand to individual members on the other hand, I respectfully agree. We have been referred, as was the judge, to *Prole v Allen* [1950] 1 All ER 476. That was an unincorporated members' club case. A member fell down a staircase which was unlighted. A question arose about the liability of the committee of the club and also the liability of the steward. Pritchard J said (at 477):

*j* 'With regard to the first defence—that the defendants owed no duty to the plaintiff—I think that that defence is well-founded in so far as it is raised on behalf of the defendants Allen, Short and Norman. They were members of the club as was the plaintiff, and, as such, they owed her no duties.'

But then the judge went on to consider the situation of the person appointed by the committee to be the steward of the club. He was also a member, but in relation to him the judge also said (at 477–478):

> 'In the case of the defendant, Andress, I think that the position is different. He, in addition to being a member of the club, a member of the committee, and one of the freeholders of the building, was the steward of the club, and I think that that relationship places him in a different position towards the plaintiff from that in which the other defendants are found. He was appointed by all the members, operating through the committee, and, in my judgment, he thereupon became the agent of each member to do reasonably carefully all those things which he was appointed to do, and in that way he came to owe a duty to each of the members to take reasonable care and to carry out his duties without negligence.'

Clearly, qua members, the members of the club owed no duty to other members, as in the instant case. Speaking for myself, I would express some reservation with regard to the liability of the member steward, Andress, whom the judge in that case found to be liable. But that question does not arise in the instant case.

In so far as the rules and their proper construction are concerned, the judge in his judgment found himself unable to put on them the construction for which counsel was contending on behalf of the plaintiff and he went on: '"He is responsible in law" means that he has the responsibility for such duties as the law already, ie before the rules come into existence, casts on the club.' There being no such duty, therefore, the rules could not make the chairman and secretary liable in respect of a breach of a non-existent duty.

In passing I would also wish to reserve the position of the responsibility of the chairman and secretary in the instant case and their responsibility for any duty which was specifically imposed on them by the rules, as distinct from common law. But to that again I shall come briefly in a moment.

We were also referred to *Shore v Ministry of Works* [1950] 2 All ER 228. That was again a members' club case. The plaintiff was a member and was struck by a brick which had been dislodged from the roof of the club and sustained personal injuries.

The case was tried at first instance by Lynskey J. When the matter came to this court, after the plaintiff's claim had been dismissed, in his judgment Tucker LJ referred to the terms of the plaintiff's membership in this way (at 230–231):

> 'She was admitted to membership on the terms of the rules governing the club, contained in the document called the "Constitution" which I have read. In that document are to be found all the matters which govern her relationship with the other members of the club, and the duties of the management committee and any authority which they derive from the body of members. There is nothing in the constitution which could impose on the committee the liability which the plaintiff seeks to put on them. After she had become a member of the club, whenever she attended this hall in the circumstances in which she was there on this occasion, she was merely one member of the club making use of premises of which the club as a whole were licensees, and I do not think that she has any remedy against the committee based on this contract.'

Tucker LJ then quoted with approval a passage from the judgment at first instance of Lynskey J in these terms (at 231):

> '. . . the management committee of the club were doing no more than acting as agents for all the members. They were elected by the members and they were exercising the powers of all the members as agents for those members. They were not a body which was contracting as a separate body with individual members nor had they any separate entity for the purpose of contracting with outsiders who came with members of the club . . .'

In the judgment of Jenkins LJ in this court we have a general statement of the position
*a* in this type of case (at 232):

> 'Once it appears, however, that this was a members' club and not a proprietary
> club, then it seems to me there is an end of the case, for the contract which the
> plaintiff made in October, 1946, was an ordinary contract of membership of a
> members' club, and the rights she acquired under it were simply those which she
> was entitled to enjoy in common with the other members, including the right from
> *b* time to time to use the club premises in accordance with the rules, with all their
> defects or imperfections. There was nothing in the nature of a special contract
> between the plaintiff and the committee of management. Her relationship to the
> committee of management was that of any other member. The persons from time
> to time elected to the committee of management were members elected by their
> *c* fellows to manage the affairs of the club on behalf of the general body of
> members . . .'

In my judgment those passages, particularly from the judgment in *Shore v Ministry of
Works*, to which I have referred, provide a complete answer, in so far as contract is
concerned, to the plaintiff's claim in this case. As the judge below said, there is in general
no liability at common law between a club or its members on the one hand and individual
*d* members on the other, and the rules to which I have referred are to be construed as
merely laying on the chairman and the secretary respectively those duties as the law
already at common law, and perhaps under the rules themselves, cast on the club, vis-à-
vis a member.

Realistically appreciating that that was clearly the position in contract, counsel for the
plaintiff argued below and before this court that the terms of the rules were such as to
*e* create such a relationship extra the contract between the chairman and the secretary on
the one hand and the plaintiff on the other as to lay on the former a duty to take
reasonable care in relation to the condition, inter alia, of the road in which the pothole
was and that, accordingly, providing a breach of that duty of reasonable care were shown,
there would be liability in those circumstances on the chairman and secretary.

For my part I have no doubt that the rules to which I have referred do not give rise to
*f* any such duty. It would in my judgment need very clear words in the rules of a members'
club to make the situation anything different from that to which in particular Jenkins LJ
referred in his judgment in *Shore v Ministry of Works*. Certainly, in the instant case,
merely to say that the secretary and the chairman shall be responsible in law for the
conduct of the club cannot lay any duty of care to the plaintiff on either the chairman or
the secretary in respect of the state of this roadway. In my opinion, therefore, the claim
*g* must fail both in contract and in tort and I would dismiss this appeal.

**NOURSE LJ.** I agree. The general rule of the common law is that membership of the
committee of a members' club does not per se carry with it any duty of care towards the
members. The authority cited for that proposition is *Prole v Allen* [1950] 1 All ER 476,
*h* where Pritchard J appears to have regarded the rule as settled. I agree that further support
for its existence is to be found in the passage from the judgment of Jenkins LJ in *Shore v
Ministry of Works* [1950] 2 All ER 228 at 232 which May LJ has read.

That being the general rule, the only other question is whether it has been modified
by the rules of this club. Counsel for the plaintiff sought to place some reliance on
rr 25(a) and (b) and 27, but they do not carry the matter any further. He has to rely
*j* wholly on rr 49(n) and 50(c), which provide that the secretary and the chairman
respectively are responsible in law for the conduct of the club 'as a corporate body'. That
is manifestly to misstate the status of a members' club, which is an unincorporated
association and not a corporate body. So what must be meant by those provisions is that
the two officers shall be responsible in law for the conduct of the members as a group, in

other words for observing the requirements of statute and regulation in the running of
the club and perhaps as regards liability towards third parties as well. On no view of *a*
those provisions can it be said that some new duty is constructed towards the members
themselves, a duty which, if it was to be cast on anyone, could be expected to be cast not
on the chairman and secretary alone but on all the members of the committee.

For these reasons, as well as for those stated by May LJ, I think that McCullough J
arrived at an entirely correct decision in this case and I too would dismiss the appeal.

*b*

**WOOLF LJ.** I agree that this appeal should be dismissed, and, save that I myself do not
have the same reservations about the judgment of Pritchard J in *Prole v Allen* [1950] 1 All
ER 476 indicated by May LJ, I agree that the appeal has to be dismissed for the reasons
given in the judgments of May and Nourse LJJ.

Prima facie the liability of a member of a members' club depends on the rules of the
club. In the absence of any provision in the rules or any action by an individual member, *c*
one member owes no duty to the other members of the club for the state of the club
premises. Here there was nothing in the rules which created any duty on the chairman
or the secretary and there was no evidence of any activity on their part which could create
a liability. Accordingly this appeal, in my view, must be dismissed.

*Appeal dismissed.* *d*

Solicitors: *Eden & Co*, Manchester (for the plaintiff); *Lace Mawer*, Manchester (for the
defendants).

Carolyn Toulmin   Barrister.

a

# Practice Note

QUEEN'S BENCH DIVISION
LORD LANE CJ, FARQUHARSON AND POTTS JJ
26 MAY 1989

b   *Legal aid – Criminal cases – Representation by counsel – Assignment of two counsel – Application*
   *for order for two counsel – Procedure – Legal Aid in Criminal and Care Proceedings (General)*
   *Regulations 1989, reg 48(3).*

**LORD LANE CJ** gave the following direction at the sitting of the court.

c   1. Regulation 48(3) of the Legal Aid in Criminal and Care Proceedings (General)
   Regulations 1989, SI 1989/344, empowers a High Court judge or a circuit judge to make
   a legal aid order to provide for the services of two counsel (a two counsel order) in
   proceedings in the Crown Court in the terms set out in that paragraph.
       2. An application for a two counsel order made to the Crown Court shall be placed
   before the resident or designated judge of that Crown Court (or, in his absence, a judge
d   nominated by a presiding judge of the circuit), who shall determine the application, save
   that where the application relates to a case which is to be heard before a named High
   Court judge or a named circuit judge he should refer the application to the named judge
   for determination.
       3. Paragraph 2 above shall not apply where an application for a two counsel order is
   made either during a pre-trial review or during a trial, when it shall be for the judge
e   seised of the case to determine the application.
       4. In the event of any doubt as to the proper application of this direction, reference
   shall be made by the judge concerned to a presiding judge of the circuit, who shall give
   such directions as he thinks fit.

N P Metcalfe Esq    Barrister.

# Practice Direction

*a*

SUPREME COURT TAXING OFFICE

*Costs – Taxation – Adjournment of appointment for taxation – Application for adjournment – Automatic adjournments not to be permitted – Notice to other parties – RSC Ord 62, r 30(1).*

*b*

Because of the waste of time caused by late adjournments, the understandable desire of parties to have their bills taxed with expedition and the application of the House of Lords decision in *Hunt v R M Douglas (Roofing) Ltd* [1988] 3 All ER 823, [1988] 3 WLR 975, the adjournment of appointments listed for taxation will not automatically be permitted, even by consent of the parties, unless an application to adjourn is made to the master concerned on a day not less than 14 working days prior to the appointment to be vacated. A very strong case would have to be made out for any later application, opposed or unopposed, to succeed. RSC Ord 62, r 30(1) requires not less than 14 days' notice of taxation to be given and the interests of other litigants awaiting an appointment must be borne in mind.

*c*

   This direction only applies to adjournments, not to cases where appointments are vacated because a settlement has been reached.

*d*

18 May 1989

F G BERKELEY
Chief Master.

*e*

# Practice Direction

QUEEN'S BENCH DIVISION

*Practice – Summons – Masters' summonses – Queen's Bench Division – Time summonses – Arrangements for issue – RSC Ord 32, r 3.*

*f*

The Practice Direction of 13 January 1978 ([1978] 1 All ER 723, [1978] 1 WLR 131) is revoked and the following direction substituted:

   1.  With a view to reducing the volume of business before the practice master, for a trial period starting 6 June 1989 a summons for hearing before a master of the Queen's Bench Division which seeks only the extension or abridgment of any period of time will *in term time* be issued for hearing before a deputy master at 10 am. *In vacation* there is normally no deputy master sitting, and existing arrangements will therefore continue, namely hearing before the practice master at 10.30 am.

*g*

   2.  Time summonses will be returnable, unless otherwise ordered, two days from the date of issue, excluding Saturdays, Sundays, bank holidays and any other days on which the Central Office is closed, and may be served on the day before the return day: see RSC Ord 32, r 3.

*h*

   3.  The issue or service of such a summons does not of itself operate to extend any period of time or to stay proceedings.

   4.  This practice direction does not apply to district registries.

*j*

19 May 1989

IAN WARREN
Senior Master of the
Queen's Bench Division.

a # R v Secretary of State for Transport, ex parte Pegasus Holidays (London) Ltd and another

QUEEN'S BENCH DIVISION (CROWN OFFICE LIST)

SCHIEMANN J

b 7 AUGUST 1987

*Natural justice – Hearing – Duty to hear parties – Opportunity to be heard – Secretary of State granting permit enabling Romanian pilots to operate charter aircraft to and from United Kingdom – Secretary of State provisionally suspending permit pending inquiry into Romanian licence requirements and pilots' ability to comply with them – Interested parties given no opportunity to be heard prior to suspension – Whether emergency involving safety of aircraft and passengers*
c *outweighing duty to hear parties – Whether Secretary of State's action reasonable.*

*Air traffic – International civil aviation – Permit to operate charter flights – Competency of pilots – Secretary of State granting permit enabling Romanian pilots to operate charter aircraft to and from United Kingdom – Pilots' licences issued by Romanian Civil Aviation Authority – Romanian*
d *licences required to be recognised as valid by United Kingdom under international convention – Five Romanian pilots failing United Kingdom Civil Aviation Authority examination – Secretary of State provisionally suspending permit pending inquiry into Romanian licence requirements and pilots' ability to comply with them – Whether suspension contrary to United Kingdom's obligations under convention – Whether Secretary of State entitled to suspend permit provisionally pending inquiry into whether Romanian licence requirements satisfying standards set by convention – Civil*
e *Aviation Act 1982, s 60(2) – Air Navigation Order 1985, arts 62(1), 83 – Chicago Convention 1944, arts 11, 33.*

The Secretary of State for Transport granted a permit to a Romanian organisation, T, under art 83[a] of the Air Navigation Order 1985 which enabled it to operate charter flights to and from the United Kingdom. The permit was subject to conditions which stipulated,
f inter alia, that the aircraft were to be operated by T's Romanian crews and that T was to ensure that the Romanian Civil Aviation Authority's licence requirements were complied with. P, a tour operator established in the United Kingdom, subsequently arranged for its charter flight passengers to travel on aircraft leased by A from T and operated by T. Five of T's pilots later took an examination set by the United Kingdom Civil Aviation Authority (the CAA), though there was no requirement for them to do so under the
g permit issued under art 83. Four of the pilots failed the test on flight rules and procedures and the fifth failed the written paper on aviation law. Those failures prompted the CAA to write a letter to the Department of Transport indicating serious grounds for concern regarding the ability of any of T's pilots to operate competently and in accordance with the standards required by the Romanian Civil Aviation Authority the aircraft leased by A. On the basis of that letter the Secretary of State concluded that T was in breach of the
h condition requiring it to ensure compliance with the Romanian licence requirements and he provisionally suspended T's permit under art 62(1)[b] of the 1985 order, pending an inquiry into and consideration of the Romanian licence requirements and the ability of T's pilots to comply with them. P and A sought judicial review of the Secretary of State's decision by way of an order of certiorari to quash the decision and suspension of the permit, on the grounds of (i) unfairness, in that no opportunity had been given to T or
j the other interested parties to make any representations to the Secretary of State prior to the suspension, (ii) irrationality and (iii) non-compliance with the Chicago Convention of 1944, because the decision, in effect, extended to all Romanian pilots and therefore the

---

a    Article 83, so far as material, is set out at p 484 *f*, post
b    Article 62(1) is set out at p 484 *h*, post

Secretary of State was calling into question and refusing to recognise the validity of any
Romanian licences and thereby acting contrary to art 33[c] of the convention, which *a*
provided that licences issued by contracting states, which included Romania, were to be
recognised as valid by other contracting states such as the United Kingdom, and also
contrary to art 11[d] of that convention, which prohibited any 'distinction as to nationality'
by one contracting state in respect of the validity of licences issued by another contracting
state.

*b*

**Held** – The application for judicial review would be dismissed for the following
reasons—

(1) The requirement of natural justice that a party affected by an administrative action
should have a reasonable opportunity of presenting his case could be waived where the
action contemplated was merely the provisional suspension of a licence or permit in an
emergency situation which might result in the loss of many lives if action was not taken. *c*
In the circumstances the Secretary of State had had good cause for alarm about the
competence of T's pilots and the safety of aircraft operated by it and passengers flying in
them and was justified in taking swift action to suspend T's permit provisionally pending
further inquiry, since the possible saving of life outweighed both the short-term financial
disadvantage to the parties and also the duty of fairness to provide the parties with an
opportunity to be heard. Accordingly, the applicants' challenge to the Secretary of State's *d*
action on the grounds of unfairness and irrationality failed (see p 489 *h j*, p 490 *b* to *d*,
p 491 *b* to *e* and p 494 *a b*, post); dicta of Tucker LJ in *Russell v Duke of Norfolk* [1949] 1
All ER 109 at 118 and of Lord Denning MR in *Lewis v Heffer* [1978] 3 All ER 354 at 364
considered.

(2) Under s 60(2)[e] of the Civil Aviation Act 1982, which provided that an air navigation
order might contain such provisions as appeared 'to be requisite or expedient ... for *e*
carrying out the Chicago Convention [and] any Annex thereto relating to international
standards and recommended practice', the powers conferred by the 1985 order were to
be exercised so as to give effect to and not conflict with the convention, and under the
proviso to art 33 of the convention the Secretary of State had power to undertake an
inquiry into the Romanian licence requirements and consider whether those requirements
met the minimum standards of competency established by the convention. Accordingly, *f*
the Secretary of State was entitled to act under art 62(1) of the 1985 order by provisionally
suspending T's permit pending an inquiry into the Romanian licence requirements and
consideration of whether those requirements met the minimum standards of competency
established by the convention, and he was also entitled to suspend the permit issued to T
in its entirety without acting contrary to the art 11 prohibition against discrimination on
the basis of nationality, because the permit applied to all Romanian pilots and not just *g*
the five who had failed the CAA examination. It followed that since the action taken by
the Secretary of State did not conflict with the provisions of the Chicago Convention, the
applicants' challenge on that ground also failed (see p 493 *a e g j* to p 494 *b*, post).

**Notes**

For the right to a hearing, see 1 Halsbury's Laws (4th edn) para 76, and for cases on the *h*
subject, see 1(1) Digest (Reissue) 200–201, 1172–1176.

For the Chicago Convention, see 2 ibid paras 802–807.

For the Civil Aviation Act 1982, s 60, see 4 Halsbury's Statutes (4th edn) 171.

For the Air Navigation Order 1985, arts 62, 83, see 3 Halsbury's Statutory Instruments
(Grey Volume) 117, 128.

*j*

**Cases referred to in judgment**

*Associated Provincial Picture Houses Ltd v Wednesbury Corp* [1947] 2 All ER 680, [1948] 1
KB 223, CA.

---

c  Article 33 is set out at p 492 *d e*, post
d  Article 11 is set out at p 492 *f g*, post
e  Section 60(2), so far as material, is set out at p 484 *b c*, post

*John v Rees* [1969] 2 All ER 274, [1970] Ch 345, [1969] 2 WLR 1294.
a  *Lewis v Heffer* [1978] 3 All ER 354, [1978] 1 WLR 1061, CA.
*R v Barnsley Metropolitan BC, ex p Hook* [1976] 3 All ER 452, [1976] 1 WLR 1052, CA.
*R v Civil Aviation Authority, ex p Northern Air Taxis Ltd* [1976] 1 Lloyd's Rep 344, DC.
*Russell v Duke of Norfolk* [1949] 1 All ER 109, CA.
*Wiseman v Borneman* [1969] 3 All ER 275, [1971] AC 297, [1969] 3 WLR 706, HL.

b  **Case also cited**
*Council of Civil Service Unions v Minister for the Civil Service* [1984] 3 All ER 935, [1985] AC
    374, HL.

**Application for judicial review**
Pegasus Holidays (London) Ltd and Airbro (UK) Ltd applied, with the leave of Ian
c  Kennedy J, sitting as the vacation judge in chambers on 5 August 1987, for judicial
review by way of an order of certiorari to quash a decision of the Secretary of State for
Transport made on 30 July 1987 under 62(1) of the Air Navigation Order 1985, SI 1985/
1643, to suspend provisionally permits granted to Tarom Romanian Air Transport
(Tarom) under art 83 of the 1985 order, under which Tarom was permitted to operate
charter aircraft on behalf of British airlines using its own Romanian crews, pending an
d  inquiry into and consideration of the Romanian Civil Aviation Authority's licence
requirements and the ability of Tarom's pilots to comply with them following the failure
by five of Tarom's pilots to pass the United Kingdom Civil Aviation Authority's
examination. The facts are set out in the judgment.

*Charles Flint* for the applicants.
e  *David Pannick* for the Secretary of State.
*Richard McManus* for the Civil Aviation Authority.

**SCHIEMANN J.** Pegasus Holidays (London) Ltd are travel operators. They are in the
business of arranging holidays for people going abroad from this country. They made
f  arrangements for their clients to travel on chartered Romanian aeroplanes flown by
Romanian pilots. This is only possible under our law if they have a permit from the
Secretary of State for Transport. They have such a permit. It came to the ears of the
Secretary of State, after this permit had been operating for a while, that five of the
Romanian pilots who were flying in this country (in part under permit and in part under
other similar permits) had failed a test which they had voluntarily undertaken which is
conducted by the Civil Aviation Authority (the CAA) to test the competence of pilots.
g  When the Secretary of State heard this, he provisionally suspended the permit that he
had given, causing of course a fair amount of chaos to the holiday-makers who were on
the point of leaving to go to their destinations because the plane could not fly, the permit
having been suspended. It is the suspension of that permit which is under attack in these
proceedings for judicial review, which were launched on 4 August 1987, earlier this
h  week, and the applicants obtained the leave of the single judge to take these proceedings
and various time limits normally applicable were abridged.
    Counsel appeared in front of me for the applicants, for the Secretary of State (who
issued and suspended the permit) and for the CAA, though the CAA is here more in case
one needs their help rather than as a specific party, although they were served under the
rules as a person interested. Before I go any further I ought to say that the case has been
j  argued in less than a day with brevity, succinctness and considerable ability, and I am
very much indebted to the short way in which counsel have put their points.
    The decision to suspend is under attack on three grounds: the first one is unfairness;
the second is irrationality; and the third is non-compliance with the Chicago Convention
which was signed in 1944 by a number of parties and to which both this country and
Romania are contracting parties (Convention on International Civil Aviation (Chicago, 7
December 1944; TS 8 (1953); Cmd 8742)).

The statutory background to the matter is as follows. Under the Civil Aviation Act 1982 the Secretary of State is by s 1(1)(c) charged with the general duty of organising, carrying out and encouraging measures for, amongst other things, the promotion of safety and efficiency in the use of civil aircraft. Section 60(1) of that Act provides:

'... Her Majesty may by Order of Council under this section (in this Act referred to as "an Air Navigation Order") make such provision as is authorised by subsections (2) and (3) below or otherwise by this Act or any other enactment.'

Subsection (2) provides:

'An Air Navigation Order may contain such provision as appears to Her Majesty in Council to be requisite or expedient—(a) for carrying out the Chicago Convention, any Annex thereto relating to international standards and recommended practices ... (b) generally for regulating air navigation.'

Under sub-s (3) of that section it is provided:

'Without prejudice to the generality of subsection (2) above ... an Air Navigation Order may contain provision ... (h) generally for securing the safety, efficiency and regularity of air navigation and the safety of aircraft and of persons and property carried therein, for preventing aircraft endangering other persons and property ... (n) as to the manner and conditions of the issue, validation, renewal, extension or variation of any certificate, licence or other document required by the Order (including the examinations and tests to be undergone), and as to the form, custody production, cancellation, suspension, endorsement and surrender of any such document ...'

As is well known, a series of air navigation orders have been made and the one currently in force, with which I am concerned, is the Air Navigation Order 1985, SI 1985/1643. Article 83 of that order provides:

'An aircraft registered in a Contracting State other than the United Kingdom [I interpose to say that Romania is such a contracting state], or in a foreign country, shall not take on board or discharge any passengers or cargo in the United Kingdom, being passengers or cargo carried or to be carried for hire or reward, except with the permission of the Secretary of State granted under this article to the operator or charterer of the aircraft ... and in accordance with any conditions to which such permission may be subject.'

Article 62(1) provides:

'The appropriate authority [I interpose to say that in the present case that is the respondent Secretary of State] may, if it thinks fit, provisionally suspend or vary any certificate, licence, approval, permission, exemption, authorisation or other document issued, granted or having effect under this Order, pending inquiry into or consideration of the case. The appropriate authority may, on sufficient ground being shown to its satisfaction after due inquiry, revoke, suspend or vary any such certificate, licence, approval, permission, exemption, authorisation or other document.'

I will come to the Chicago Convention provisions later in this judgment when I turn to consider the arguement based on them.

The facts of the matter are briefly these. In March 1987 one of the applicants leased two aircraft and in February 1987 an organisation known as British Island Airways plc (BIA) made an application to the Secretary of State for a licence under art 83 in which it is stated:

'. . . it is intended that the aircraft will be operated by Tarom flight deck crew
a    only and one Tarom senior cabin crew in addition to BIA's own cabin crew. Both
aircraft are Romanian registered.'

I interpose to say that Tarom is a Romanian organisation which was responsible for the
aircraft. Pursuant to that application a permit was in due course granted which reads, so
far as it is presently relevant:

b    '1. In pursuance of Article 83 of the Air Navigation Order 1985 the Secretary of
State hereby grants permission to Tarom Romanian Air Transport to take on board
and discharge passengers at points in the U.K., being passengers carried or to be
carried for hire or reward on charter flights.
2. This permit is granted subject to the following conditions: (a) Tarom Romanian
Air Transport may only operate flights pursuant to this permit on behalf of British
c    Island Airways Limited . . . (e) the aircraft shall be operated by Tarom Romanian
Air Transport crew; (f) Tarom Romanian Air Transport shall ensure that the
requirements of the Romanian Civil Aviation Authority relating to flight operations
and continuing airworthiness are complied with during the period of the lease.
3. This permit shall come into force on 8 April 1987 in respect of YR-BCL [one
of the aircraft] and 15 June 1987 in respect of YR-BCM and shall be valid until 2
d    November 1987 unless previously revoked or suspended.'

There is exhibited to one of the affidavits a letter from the CAA to the Department of
Transport dated 14 July complaining, in relation to aircraft operated by Tarom under the
BIA banner, of various alleged malpractices. Those concern the internal management
and deal with matters such as rubbish bags by the doors during landing. There is no
e    indication that those complaints have ever been drawn to the attention of BIA or indeed
the applicants, but neither is there any indication that those complaints played any part
in the consideration by the Secretary of State of his decision whether or not to revoke this
licence. In my judgment that letter is not really germane to the issues with which I am
concerned.
For reasons with which I need not lengthen this judgment, various Romanian pilots
f    took a CAA examination in aviation law, flight rules and procedures. Those tests were
taken in the middle of July of this year and it is right to say that there was no requirement
under the permit with which I am concerned that those tests be taken. They were taken
for a different purpose with which I am not concerned but for which the tests are
relevant. Of the five pilots who carried out tests, four failed the flying test part of the
examination on 16, 17 and 21 July, and the fifth, Capt N Bradis, failed the examination
g    on the air law written paper but passed on the flying test. However, at the end of the day
no pilot met the full requirements for the purpose for which these tests and examinations
were being done, namely for the conversion of his Romanian licence effectively into a
United Kingdom licence.
On the evening of 24 July 1987 the Department of Transport received a telephone call
from the CAA informing it that the CAA was urgently considering what advice to give
h    to the department as a result of doubts which had arisen on the ability of some Tarom
pilots to operate BAC-111 aircraft safely. I interpose to say that those are the aircraft with
which I am concerned. No details were given, but the CAA said that the department
could expect to receive a letter early in the following week.
Shortly after noon on 29 July 1987 the department received a letter dated 28 July from
the CAA. That letter dealt with a number of matters, but for present purposes it suffices
j    if I quote from that letter in which the writer says this:

'There is also the question of Tarom, which is currently operating BAC 1-11
aircraft under wet leases for BIA, LEA [London European Airlines] and Anglo
[Anglo Airlines Ltd]. I attach a copy of a letter which David Tomkins sent to
Warwick Smith on 14th July concerning the BIA operation. [I interpose to say that

that is the letter to which I referred.] As you may know, LEA and Anglo are
proposing to dry-lease Tarom aircraft and put them on the U.K. register. It is a   *a*
condition of the lease imposed by the lessor that a Tarom pilot should act as crew on
every flight and in order to enable this to be done the pilots' Romanian licences will
have to be validated. Last week validation tests were carried out on five of the pilots
who had been flying for LEA and Anglo. One passed, but the remaining four failed,
and failed badly. They showed poor airmanship and an inability to manoeuvre the
aircraft. It is the more worrying in that we have been told that the pilots tested are   *b*
Tarom training captains. They are, of course, still able to fly aircraft on the Romanian
register in and out of the U.K. The failure of the pilots to validate has thrown
Anglo's plans to dry-lease the aircraft into disarray and they are seeking an extension
of the permit currently granted to Tarom. LEA may follow suit. The operations I
have described are ones which CAA would not permit if the aircraft were being
operated by the British airlines which have wet-leased them. You will wish to   *c*
consider whether the permit issued by the Secretary of State should be withdrawn.'

That is all that I need read.

The reference to dry leases and wet leases are in substance to be construed, I understand,
as follows. Somebody who dry leases foreign aircraft wants to put them on the United
Kingdom register and therefore on the face of it their pilots have to comply with the   *d*
United Kingdom licencing requirements, whereas somebody who wet leases an aircraft
does not seek to put them on the United Kingdom register but keeps them on the register
of their native country with which they are registered. I am of course concerned with a
wet lease situation.

That letter came into the hands of the Secretary of State's officials shortly after noon on
29 July 1987. An affidavit from David Holmes, a deputy secretary in the Department of   *e*
Transport, contains the following:

'7 . . . The contents of the last two paragraphs of the CAA's letter [which are the
paragraphs I have read] caused the Department to consider that there were extremely
serious grounds for concern as to the ability of any Tarom pilots to operate BAC 1-
11 aircraft safely and competently in accordance with the standards required by the
International Civil Aviation Organisation (ICAO), of which Romania is a member   *f*
and to which Romanian standards conform. There were accordingly strong grounds
for concluding that condition 2(f) of the Article 83 permits was being breached.
The Secretary of State bore in mind not only the failure of four out of five Tarom
pilots tested to pass the CAA's validation tests, but also the CAA's advice that the
pilots tested were responsible for training other Tarom pilots.
          *g*
8. On the afternoon of 29th July 1987 the Department's safety adviser telephoned
the CAA to discuss the performance of the Tarom pilots in the CAA's tests, and the
CAA confirmed the points set out in the letter of 28th July. The Department then
gave urgent consideration to the steps which could lawfully be taken to protect
passengers, crew and the public in view of the information in its possession. Between
1 pm and 4.30 pm on 29th July Departmental officials telephoned LEA, BIA and   *h*
Anglo; BIA was telephoned at about 3.30 pm. All the airlines were advised that the
Department had been warned of serious problems by the CAA and was urgently
considering what action should be taken. It was made clear that any immediate
steps which might be needed such as requiring the airlines to refrain from using the
pilots who had failed the CAA tests were without prejudice to the decision of the
Secretary of State, which would be taken as quickly as possible . . .   *j*

10. On 30th July [the next day] the Secretary of State, having been advised by
officials, formed the view that immediate action was necessary in the interests of
aviation safety in the light of the contents of the CAA's letter of 28th July, and that
it was reasonable and proper to pay the closest regard to the risk to aviation safety
presented by the apparent failure of a number of Tarom pilots to operate BAC 1-11s
to the appropriate standards. The Secretary of State therefore decided on the

a    afternoon of 30th July provisionally to suspend the three Article 83 permits under which Tarom pilots were flying BAC 1-11 aircraft on behalf of British Airlines, pending due inquiry into and consideration of the case.

11. Following the Secretary of State's decision on 30th July to proceed to provisional suspension of the permits, Departmental officials telephoned Tarom's UK manager, LEA, BIA and Anglo to inform them that the Secretary of State was minded provisionally to suspend the Article 83 permits forthwith. All the airlines
b    were so notified between approximately 3 pm when officials were informed of the Secretary of State's intention, and 5.30 pm. At about 7.15 pm the provisional suspension orders were signed on behalf of the Secretary of State and immediately delivered by hand to Tarom's UK office. Copies were sent either by telex or facsimile transmission to LEA, BIA and Anglo at the same time and telexed to Tarom's head office in Bucharest.'
c
After reciting the existence of the permit granted on 8 April to which I have already referred, the order under attack reads as follows:

'2. Prima facie evidence has come to the notice of the Secretary of State that, in relation to the operation of BAC 1-11 aircraft, four Tarom training pilots have been
d    unable to satisfy standards equivalent to the minimum required by the International Civil Aviation Organisation, and hence have also been unable to comply with the requirements of the Romanian Civil Aviation Authorities as stipulated in Condition 2(f) of the said permit. By reason of this evidence he doubts and has cause to inquire into the ability of any Tarom pilots to comply with such requirements of the Romanian Civil Authorities in operating the BAC 1-11 aircraft YR-BCL and YR-
e    BCM for the purposes of the permit.
3. Pursuant to Article 62(1) of the Air Navigation Order 1985 the Secretary of State therefore hereby forthwith provisionally suspends the said permit pending inquiry into and consideration of the case.'

On the same day a restricted telex was sent to the United Kingdom Embassy in
f    Bucharest headed 'Safety problems with Tarom crew' which reads:

'On safety grounds we have suspended Tarom's permits pending further inquiries. Grateful if you would make the following self-explanatory points to the Romanian Civil Aviation Authorities.
2. We acknowledge our obligations under the Chicago Convention on International Civil Aviation to recognise the validity of the Romanian Civil Aviation
g    Authority's certificates of competence and airworthiness and we are not seeking to challenge Romanian Standards. We are sure that they would agree that safety is a fundamental consideration in air services matters and that all personnel and organisations involved in the provision of air transport should give utmost priority to the maintenance of safety standards and the prevention of accidents. In recent days we have had to take action on the grounds of safety in connection with Tarom
h    aircraft operated on behalf of the U.K. airlines.'

Then the telex sets out the background to the matter which I have already recited and then it continues:

'4. In these circumstances the U.K. authorities considered that there was a
j    reasonable doubt as to whether Tarom were complying with a condition of their operating permits issued by the Secretary of State for Transport that they should comply with the safety standards of the country of registration of the aircraft. We have therefore suspended those permits.
5. Her Majesty's Government urges the Romanian Civil Aviation Authorities to check that all Tarom pilots meet their standards of competency and to take such measures as they can to enforce the internationally recognised safety standards. We

would of course be prepared to consider any representations the Romanian authorities would wish to make before we reach a final decision on the revocation *a* of Tarom's temporary operating permits.

6. You may want to leave a text with the Romanian authorities for their further consideration. We also understand that the Romanians are aware of the problem and see it as a challenge to their safety standards. You should emphasise the point made in paragraph 2 that we are specifically not making such a challenge.'

*b*

On the next day, 31 July 1987, one of the other companies involved, LEA, came to an arrangement with the department in relation to the provisional suspension of the permit which affected them in the sense that they asked, and I think were granted, permission. I think that the suspension was terminated and their original temporary operating permit was varied so as to permit the aircraft to be operated by various named pilots and officers who, I am told, are all Irish and have an appropriate Irish licence.

*c*

On 4 August 1987 the Department of Transport wrote a letter to Tarom which included the following:

'In order to be able to restore the permit to its original form, the Secretary of State would need to be satisfied that any pilots holding Romanian licences who would operate the Romanian registered BAC 1-11s the subject of the permit are competent *d* to operate such aircraft to the internationally agreed standards to which the Romanian authorities adhere as members of ICAO and hence to comply with the requirements of the Romanian Civil Aviation Authority. The necessary evidence could for instance be obtained if further Romanian licenced pilots were to be tested by the CAA. The CAA have assured the Department that they will do all they can to expedite procedures to enable pilots presented for testing to take the requisite *e* tests. The Department is in any case in urgent touch with the Romanian authorities about the difficulties which have arisen.'

I interpose to say that I was told by counsel for the Secretary of State, on instructions, and of course I accept that the department invited the appropriate Romanian authorities to come over to this country last week, but for one reason or another that proved impracticable and they are going to be available for discussions next Monday, in three *f* days' time, with the department to consider this matter further.

The applicants' solicitors had meanwhile not been idle and had sent a letter of complaint dated 3 August to the Secretary of State for Transport, to which he replied on 4 August, which dealt with the points that they have made, but which I do not think I need read. That is the factual background to the matters with which I am concerned.

I turn now to consider the challenges and firstly look at the matter of unfairness. It is *g* conceded by counsel for the applicants that when one looks at art 62 of the 1985 order one sees a two-stage procedure. One stage is contained in the first sentence which I have read and the second one is contained in the second sentence. The first one deals with a provisional suspension, such as the one with which I am concerned, whereas the second deals with a longer term matter, be it revocation or a longer suspension. The second one, *h* as appears from the article, is a step that is not to be taken until due inquiry has been made and sufficient ground has been shown for the taking of the step to the satisfaction of the Secretary of State. However, counsel says that in circumstances such as the present, although there is no statutory requirement for any form of inquiry or for hearing the other side, none the less at common law any power to suspend must be exercised fairly where one has a situation in which the consequences for the permit holder are potentially *j* very severe and where there is no provision for compensation for such a suspension.

So far as the law is concerned, I do not think there is anything between the parties as to the principles to be applied. Those are conveniently set out in the leading case of *Wiseman v Borneman* [1969] 3 All ER 275 at 280, [1971] AC 297 at 311, where Lord Guest cites an earlier judgment by Tucker LJ in *Russell v Duke of Norfolk* [1949] 1 All ER 109 at 118, in which he opined:

a
'There are, in my view, no words which are of universal application to every kind of inquiry and every kind of domestic tribunal. The requirements of natural justice must depend on the circumstances of the case, the nature of the inquiry, the rules under which the tribunal is acting, the subject-matter that is being dealt with, and so forth. Accordingly, I do not derive much assistance from the definitions of natural justice which have been from time to time used, but, whatever standard is adopted, one essential is that the person concerned should have a reasonable opportunity of presenting his case.'

b

Counsel for the applicants accepts that the opportunity to state a case can in certain circumstances be excluded in relation to such provisional matters as those with which I am concerned, but they should not be excluded unless the situation genuinely demands it.

c
Counsel for the Secretary of State referred me to a Court of Appeal case of *Lewis v Heffer* [1978] 3 All ER 354, [1978] 1 WLR 1061 where there are discussions in the various unreserved judgments delivered by the court which are not precisely to the same effect in what they say. In particular he drew my attention to the following comments of Lord Denning MR. After having quoted Megarry J in *John v Rees* [1969] 2 All ER 274 at 305, [1970] Ch 345 at 397 where he said that—

d
'suspension is merely expulsion pro tanto. Each is penal, and each deprives the member concerned of the enjoyment of his rights of membership or office. Accordingly, in my judgment the rules of natural justice prima facie apply to any such process of suspension in the same way that they apply to expulsion.'

e
Lord Denning MR went on to say ([1978] 3 All ER 354 at 364, [1978] 1 WLR 1061 at 1073):

f
'Those words apply, no doubt, to suspensions which are inflicted by way of punishment, as for instance when a member of the Bar is suspended from practice for six months, or when a solicitor is suspended from practice. But they do not apply to suspensions which are made, as a holding operation, pending inquiries. Very often irregularities are disclosed in a government department or in a business house; and a man may be suspended on full pay pending inquiries. Suspicion may rest on him; and so he is suspended until he is cleared of it. No one, so far as I know, has ever questioned suspension on the ground that it could not be done unless he is given notice of the charge and an opportunity of defending himself and so forth. The suspension in such a case is merely done by way of good administration. A situation has arisen in which something must be done at once. The work of the department or the office is being affected by rumours and suspicions. The others will not trust the man. In order to get back to proper work, the man is suspended. At that stage the rules of natural justice do not apply . . .'

g

It is right to point out that the other Lords Justices tend not to go quite as far as Lord Denning MR in that formulation.

h
In the present case I am content to proceed on the basis that the rules of natural justice do apply but, in the words chosen by counsel for the Secretary of State, in such an emergency as the present, with a provisional suspension being all that one is concerned with, one is at the low end of the duties of fairness. He referred me in the course of his submissions on this point to *R v Civil Aviation Authority, ex p Northern Air Taxis Ltd* [1976] 1 Lloyd's Rep 344. That case, which was a Divisional Court case, was concerned with matters not dissimilar in some ways to the present. Natural justice as such was not argued; the matters were dealt with on the basis of the statutory requirements, but undoubtedly the result in the case does lend some support to the view that when one is dealing with this type of situation not much is required of the Secretary of State in order to act fairly.

j

The way the case is put by counsel for the applicants is this. He says that in the present case the Secretary of State could not reasonably decline to afford Tarom a short period to put its case as to why the permit should not be suspended, having regard to a number of matters which counsel identified. One of these is the lack of action on the letter of 14 *a* July which I have read. As I have indicated, I regard that letter as irrelevant. A second matter to which he drew my attention in this context was the time which the CAA took to refer the matter which he said was some indication as to its view of the urgency. I have set out the relevant dates. It is clear that the failing of the tests took place on 17 July and the Secretary of State was not informed until 29 July. That may or may not be a legitimate criticism of the CAA, but in my judgment, so far as the action of the Secretary *b* of State is concerned, it cannot be regarded as unfair in the circumstances of this case that he acted in the speedy way in which he did act. One has in the context of unfairness to bear in mind, on the one hand, the no doubt substantial economic damage to the applicants and perhaps the irritation and inconvenience which I do not doubt the passengers suffered. On the other hand, one has to bear in mind the magnitude of the risk, by which I mean not so much the high percentage chance of it happening but the *c* disastrous consequences of what would happen if something did happen. It is the old problem one has with nuclear power installations or vehicles, such as aeroplanes, carrying a large number of people that if something goes wrong then very many lives will be lost. While I do not doubt that different people, and maybe different Secretaries of State, would react differently to the same basic material, I am not prepared to say that the failure of the Secretary of State to permit more by way of representations than I have *d* indicated took place is a breach of the rules of natural justice. On that ground I would not quash this application.

It is right to say that I have borne in mind that Tarom have now had a full week to put forward arguments and so far, in any event from the arguments that the Secretary of State has had, he has not seen fit to change his mind. Of course to a degree it is a relevant consideration that the applicants do not complain of a failure to consult them but rather *e* of a failure to consult Tarom. Tarom is not party to this action, although I do bear in mind that it is fairly clear from the missives which have been received from Tarom that it is not content with what has happened. So much then for unfairness.

What about irrationality? The way counsel for the applicants puts the case is as follows. He says that notwithstanding that the suspension is only provisional, the Secretary of State is obliged to exercise the power reasonably. No issue is taken on that as a bald *f* proposition. Then, says counsel, one aspect of reasonableness is proportionality, that is, that the means adopted should be reasonable, having regard to the aim to be achieved and the effects of any course adopted. He referred me to what I think is the only case in which proportionality has been expressly adopted as part of a judgment in this country, namely *R v Barnsley Metropolitan BC, ex p Hook* [1976] 3 All ER 452 at 456, 461, [1976] 1 WLR 1052 at 1057, 1063. I will not read those passages because in the last analysis I do *g* not think counsel for the Secretary of State takes issue with the adoption of the principle of proportionality, save that he regards it in his submission as merely being an aspect of the *Wednesbury* rule: see *Associated Provincial Picture Houses Ltd v Wednesbury Corp* [1947] 2 All ER 680, [1948] 1 KB 223. It would perhaps be difficult for anyone appearing for the Government to take issue on the principle of proportionality being applied by *h* administrative authorities, bearing in mind recommendation R(80)2 of the committee of ministers concerning the exercise of discretionary powers by administrative authorities which was adopted by the Committee of Ministers of the Council of Europe on 11 March 1980 and which recommends governments of member states to be guided in their law and administrative practice by the principles annexed to this recommendation, one of which basic principles is that an administrative authority when exercising a discretionary *j* power should maintain a proper balance between any adverse effects which its decision may have on the rights, liberties or interests of persons and the purpose which it pursues. Counsel for the Secretary of State says that really what we are concerned with is only one particular manifestation of the *Wednesbury* rule.

Is there here such total lack of proportionality or lack of reasonableness? It is submitted by counsel for the applicants that the decision was unreasonable because it imposed a

total ban on all Tarom pilots regardless of whether they had failed a test. He points out
_a_  that the vast majority of Romanian pilots have not taken the CAA test and the only one
who has actually flown for BIA, Capt Bradis, indeed passed the flying part of the test. He
goes on to say that there is no indication in the evidence that the Secretary of State
considered the reasonable course of varying the permits so as to exclude as pilots those
who had failed or alternatively any pilot who had not passed or, if the Secretary of State
did consider that course, why it was rejected.

_b_  In my judgment the answer to that point is that what the Secretary of State was doing
here was suspending an existing permit. He was not being asked to vary it. He was
suspending it with immediate effect, leaving opportunities to those affected by the
suspension to make immediate approaches to him, such as indeed were made by LEA, to
get a new permit which will not be subject to such a provisional suspension. The permit
which the Secretary of State suspended was one which entitled any Romanian pilot to
_c_  fly. The Secretary of State was faced with a situation where a number of those Romanian
pilots, who would on the face of it be entitled to fly, had failed the test and indeed of the
five who had taken it all of them had failed the test in one respect or another. He
apparently took the view that this gave him some cause for alarm and while he was
investigating the matter people should not be flying around in aeroplanes being piloted
by what on the face of it was permitted in the licence, namely any Romanian pilot, some
_d_  of whom the Secretary of State was satisfied had given him cause for alarm. Subject to
the point which I shall come to in a moment in relation to the Chicago Convention, in
my judgment, one cannot say that this was irrational of the Secretary of State. He was in
a situation where he had to act extremely swiftly, but where the consequences of his
actions would be short-term financial disbenefit to the applicants and possible saving of
life.

_e_  In those circumstances, in my judgment, it was not unreasonable for the Secretary of
State to say on the afternoon that he came to the view: 'Well, I am putting a stop to things
while I find out a little bit more about it.' So in my judgment the challenge on
irrationality fails.

Now I turn to what in some ways I found the most difficult part of the case. That is
the argument in relation to the Chicago Convention, because here the parties are at odds
_f_  even as to the principles to be applied. Firstly, counsel for the applicants says that the
effect of s 60(1) of the 1982 Act is either to incorporate the convention into English law
or, alternatively, that the effect of that subsection is that the powers conferred by the
1985 order must be exercised so as to give effect to and not conflict with the provisions
of the convention and that it was Parliament's intention to apply that convention in this
country.

_g_  In riposte to this, counsel for the Secretary of State firstly made the point that if one
looks at s 60(2) it is provided that an air navigation order may contain such provisions as
appear to be requisite or expedient (a) for carrying out the Chicago Convention etc or (b)
generally for regulating air navigation. He says, and I accept, that it is not right to say
that the 1985 order is solely designed in order to incorporate the Chicago Convention
_h_  into English law. In my judgment, however, as a matter of construction of s 60,
Parliament did not authorise an air navigation order containing provisions which conflict
with the provisions of the convention. The 1985 order can go further, but it cannot
under the statute, in my judgment, run counter to the convention. That is a matter of
impression of s 60(2). If the subsection requires, as it does, that the order shall contain
such provision as appears to Her Majesty to be requisite or expedient for carrying out the
_j_  Chicago Convention, my interpretation of that is that it was not ·intended that Her
Majesty in Council should pick and choose which bits of the Chicago Convention should
be incorporated into the air navigation order.

An alternative way of approaching the problem is this, that the 1985 order should, in
my judgment, be construed, if it is possible, in such a way that its powers are to be
exercised in accordance with the country's obligations under the Chicago Convention.
That, as a submission, is accepted by counsel for the Secretary of State.

If one looks at art 62 of the 1985 order with its rather blanket reference to 'the
appropriate authority may, if it thinks fit, [do such and such]' or simply 'the appropriate   *a*
authority may, on sufficient ground being shown to its satisfaction after due inquiry . . .',
there is nothing in that article which indicates that the appropriate authority is not to be
guided by the country's obligations under the Chicago Convention. So, even if one
merely adopts the construction approach to the 1985 order, that, in my judgment, would
be sufficient to impose an obligation on the Secretary of State so to exercise his powers
that they are exercised consonant with the Chicago Convention. That of course does not   *b*
get counsel for the applicants home all the way because he has to look at the convention
and persuade the court that there is something in that convention which prevents the
Secretary of State from suspending provisionally the permit which he granted under
art 83 of the 1985 order.

The parts of the convention on which counsel for the applicants relies are essentially
arts 32 and 33. Article 32(*a*), headed 'Licences of personnel', provides:   *c*

> 'The pilot of every aircraft and the other members of the operating crew of every
> aircraft engaged in international navigation shall be provided with certificates of
> competency and licences issued or rendered valid by the State in which the aircraft
> is registered.'

It is agreed that para (*b*) does not apply. Article 33 provides:   *d*

> 'Certificates of airworthiness and certificates of competency and licences issued or
> rendered valid by the contracting State in which the aircraft is registered, shall be
> recognised as valid by the other contracting States, provided that the requirements
> under which certificates or licences were issued or rendered valid are equal to or
> above the minimum standards which may be established from time to time   *e*
> pursuant to this Convention.'

In essence counsel says that it would be contrary to the convention for a state to impose
a system of double checking on the competence of pilots of a certain nationality as a
condition of permitting flights. This he says would be discrimination contrary to the
terms of art 11 of the convention and contrary to the purposes of the convention as   *f*
evidenced by its preamble. Article 11 provides:

> 'Subject to the provisions of this Convention, the laws and regulations of a
> contracting State relating to the admission to or departure from its territory of
> aircraft engaged in international air navigation, or to the operation and navigation
> of such aircraft while within its territory, shall be applied to the aircraft of all
> contracting States without distinction as to nationality, and shall be complied with   *g*
> by such aircraft upon entering or departing from or while within the territory of
> that State.'

The preamble to the convention, on which he relies, contained the words:

> '. . . the undersigned governments having agreed on certain principles and
> arrangements in order that international civil aviation may be developed in a safe   *h*
> and orderly manner and that international air transport services may be established
> on the basis of equality of opportunity and operated soundly and economically. . .'

Counsel for the applicants says that, in the light of the passage in the Foreign Office's
telex which I have already read, it is clear that Her Majesty's government accept that the
Romanian authorities imposed ICAO standards, and indeed that was expressly accepted   *j*
in front of me by counsel for the Secretary of State. Counsel goes on to say that there is
no suggestion in the case that the crew did not meet those standards at the time they
were issued with licences by the Romanian authorities.

The answer that counsel for the Secretary of State makes to the second point is that the
whole purpose of the suspension procedure in the present case has been that the Secretary

of State wants to find out whether in the individual cases those standards were met, but
*a*  that he does not know and he does not concede that they were. He wants to find out and
he has, so it is submitted on his behalf, and I accept, a reasonable cause for making
investigation.

The submission by counsel for the applicants is that by his decision and subsequent
statements the Secretary of State is calling into question and refusing ro recognise the
validity of Romanian crew licences and that this can be the only explanation of the total
*b*  ban on Romanian pilots which in substance is the result of the temporary revocation.

In reply to that, on the face of it, forceful submission, counsel for the Secretary of State
makes a number of points, the first one of which was that the Romanians themselves
have not complained. I am not impressed by that because it is clear from the
correspondence that in any event the Romanians are not happy with it and that they are
concerned. Indeed, we have been told that they are flying over to London to try and sort
*c*  the matter out on Monday. A more impressive point is that it is legitimate for the
Secretary of State to draw a provisional inference that all Romanian pilots are not
competent because he has seen that such of them as have taken the test have failed it in
one respect or another. I emphasise that we are dealing here with a provisional inference
made on very limited information for a very short period of time. Counsel says that the
Secretary of State had to act in a hurry. I am not very much impressed by that, although
*d*  of course one has considerable sympathy with the Secretary of State. It would not give
him powers which he otherwise did not have, so one has to see whether or not he has
those powers. Is there anything in art 33 which prevents him from exercising the power
of provisional suspension which he has purported to exercise? It is clear from art 33 in
its proviso that in relation to any particular pilot or any particular certificate or licence,
power is foreseen in the convention for the appropriate authority, which in this case is
*e*  the Secretary of State, to see whether a particular requirement, under which certificates
or licences were issued, is up to the appropriate standard.

This to a degree I think, perhaps somewhat reluctantly, counsel for the applicants
conceded. Had it merely been a case of four pilots having their personal licences
withdrawn, then I think counsel would accept that the Secretary of State could take such
*f*  provisional measures while he saw whether indeed the licences had been properly issued
or whether something had gone wrong in the testing procedures of a particular person,
because he had fielded somebody who looked like him and who took the examination,
or had produced, as happens in some spheres, a perfectly good certificate in the name of
somebody with an identical name but who did not happen to be that person, although
he had the same name, or those sort of situations.

*g*  The real complaint that counsel for the applicants has is that in effect all Romanian
pilots are being blacked in this way. It is a forceful submission, but, in my judgment, it
is wrong and for this reason, that what has been suspended in the present case is a licence
under which any Romanian pilot was entitled to fly. It was reasonable, in my judgment,
to suspend the licence to fly in the case of the pilots who had failed the test and since the
licence that was being suspended applied to all Romanian pilots, the only way that licence
*h*  could be dealt with was by suspending it in its totality. Of course the same thing could
have been done, as was done indeed on the appropriate day in relation to LEA, namely
an application could be made for a new licence or a variation of the licence so as to permit
some other thing to be done, for instance for pilots to be allowed to fly who have passed
the examination by the CAA, or alternatively for any pilots save the five against whom,
as it were, a black mark lay. That could have been done and I am satisfied that these
*j*  matters will no doubt be discussed carefully at the Monday meeting. I am told that the
Secretary of State in principle is of course anxious that this question should be resolved.
Indeed it may be that the people who originally gave him cause for concern will after the
explanations on Monday no longer give him cause for concern.

I remind myself that I am dealing here with a provisional action on behalf of the
Secretary of State and I do not see anything in the convention which prevents him from

taking this provisional action in these particular circumstances. Whether he is entitled to
go further and take a more permanent form of action it is not for me to say, but I have
given some indication, which I hope will be of help to the parties of my view as to the
relevance of the convention.

For the reasons which I have given, this challenge fails. In consequence I have not had
to consider the arguments on discretion and I say nothing in this judgment about them.

*Application dismissed.*

Solicitors: *Landau & Scanlan* (for the applicants); *Treasury Solicitor*; *R J Britton* (for the
Civil Aviation Authority).

Raina Levy   Barrister.

# Essex County Council v Ellam (Inspector of Taxes)

COURT OF APPEAL, CIVIL DIVISION
PURCHAS, DILLON AND CROOM-JOHNSON LJJ
3, 23 FEBRUARY 1989

*Income tax – Annual payment – Payment out of profits etc already taxed – Annual payments
due under deed of covenant – Fees for training course – Requirement by course organisers that
students be sponsored by local authorities – Local authority sponsoring taxpayer's son as student
provided taxpayer entered into agreement to repay fees paid by it – Taxpayer entering into deed
of covenant to cover payment of fees – Payments made under covenant net of tax – Whether
covenanted payments made in return for services – Whether local authority entitled to refund of
tax already paid – Income and Corporation Taxes Act 1970, s 52(1).*

In 1980 S decided that G, his mentally handicapped son, would benefit from attending a
two-year residential training course at an institution run by a national charity. The
institution only acceped students sponsored by their local authorities, who were
responsible for their fees. S accordingly approached his local council and on 30 June 1981
entered into an agreement with the council by which he undertook that, if the council
would enter into contract with the charity to be responsible for G's fees, he would
reimburse the council for whatever fees it paid to the charity from time to time.
Subsequently, and without prior consultation with the council, S executed a deed under
which he entered into a seven-year deed of covenant in favour of the council. In a
covering letter sent with the deed of covenant S indicated to the council that the
covenanted sums (net of tax) and the tax repayments available to the council thereon
would equal the expected amount of the fees in question. He undertook to pay any
shortfall separately. Payments were then made by S to the council under the covenant. S
claimed to be entitled to deduct the tax from the payments by virtue of s 52(1)[a] of the

---

a   Section 52(1) provides: 'Where any annuity or other annual payment charged with tax under Case
III of Schedule D, not being interest, is payable wholly out of profits or gains brought into charge
to income tax—(b) the whole of the profits or gains shall be assessed and charged with income tax
on the person liable to the annuity or other annual payment, without distinguishing the annuity
or other annual payment, and (c) the person liable to make the payment, whether out of the profits
or gains charged with income tax or out of any annual payment liable to deduction, or from which
a deduction has been made, shall be entitled on making the payment to deduct and retain out of it
a sum representing the amount of income tax thereon, and (d) the person to whom the payment
is made shall allow the deduction on receipt of the residue of the payment, and the person making

(Continued on page 495)

*a* Income and Corporation Taxes Act 1970 as annual payments charged with income tax under Case III of Sch D. When the council sought repayment of the tax deducted the claim was refused on the basis that the payments were made by S in return for services, namely the training of G. On appeal, the council contended that the payments made under the covenant were pure income profit and were therefore annual payments within s 52. The Special Commissioner held that the payments under the covenant were payments under the agreement for which the council had given consideration by *b* entering into the agreement with the charity to pay G's fees and that accordingly they were not pure income profit and were therefore not annual payments within s 52. The judge upheld the Special Commissioner's decision. The council appealed.

**Held** – (1) In deciding whether payments under a deed of covenant were 'annual payments' within Case III of Sch D the court had to look beyond the mere terms of the *c* deed to see what the transaction was, in order to be able to determine what the nature of the payments was in the hands of the covenantee or to conclude whether in any particular case the payment received by the covenantee could be regarded as pure income of the covenantee without regard to some other expenditure or commitment of the covenantee (see p 498 *e g h*, p 500 *c* and p 503 *g*, post).

(2) In all the circumstances and in particular in view of the covering letter, which *d* clearly earmarked the net payments under the deed of covenant for meeting either directly or by reimbursement G's fees at the institution, it was impossible to regard the payments made by S under the deed of covenant as pure income of the council without regard to the obligation, which the council undertook at S's request, to pay those fees to the charity. Nor could the payments under the deed of covenant be considered as pure income profit of the council undiminished by any deduction, and treated as income of *e* the council subject to tax without deduction, since the covenanted payments could not, in the circumstances and in the light of the covering letter, be subject to tax in the council's hands, if the council were a taxpayer, without deduction of the fees payable by the council to the charity. The appeal would therefore be dismissed (see p 499 *a b*, p 500 *d g h* and p 503 *f g*, post); dicta of Scrutton LJ in *Earl Howe v IRC* [1918–19] All ER Rep 1088 at 1098, of Greene MR in *Re Hanbury (decd), Comiskey v Hanbury* (1939) 38 TC 588 *f* at 590 and *Campbell and anor (trustees of Davies's Educational Trust) v IRC* [1968] 3 All ER 588 applied; *IRC v Duke of Westminster* [1935] All ER Rep 259 and *IRC v City of London Corp (as Conservators of Epping Forest)* [1953] 1 All ER 1075 distinguished.

**Notes**

*g* For deduction of tax from annuities or other annual payments out of taxed profits, see 23 Halsbury's Laws (4th edn) para 584, and for cases on the subject, see 28(1) Digest (2nd reissue) 416–420, 2001–2016.

In relation to tax for the year 1988–89 and subsequent years of assessment and for companies' accounting periods ending after 5 April 1988 s 52 of the Income and Corporation Taxes Act 1970 was replaced by s 348 of the Income and Corporation Taxes *h* Act 1988. For s 348 of the 1988 Act, see 44 Halsbury's Statutes (4th edn) 419.

**Cases referred to in judgments**

*Campbell and anor (trustees of Davies's Educational Trust) v IRC* [1968] 3 All ER 588 , [1970] AC 77, [1968] 3 WLR 1025, HL.
*Ceylon Comr of Inland Revenue v Rajaratnam* [1971] TR 451, PC.
*j* *Hanbury (decd), Re, Comiskey v Hanbury* (1939) 38 TC 588, CA.
*Hawkins (Inspector of Taxes) v Leahy* [1952] 2 All ER 759.
*Howe (Earl) v IRC* [1919] 2 KB 336, [1918–19] All ER Rep 1088, CA.

(Continued from page 494)
the deduction shall be acquitted and discharged of so much money as is represented by the deduction, or if that sum had been actually paid, and (*e*) the deduction shall be treated as income tax paid by the person to whom the payment is made.'

*IRC v City of London Corp (as Conservators of Epping Forest)* [1953] 1 All ER 1075, [1953] 1
WLR 652, HL.
*IRC v Duke of Westminster* [1936] AC 1, [1935] All ER Rep 259, HL.
*IRC v National Book League* [1957] 2 All ER 644, [1957] Ch 488, [1957] 3 WLR 222, CA.
*Smith v Earl of Jersey* (1821) 3 Bli 290, 4 ER 610, HL.

**Cases also cited**
*Alan (W J) & Co Ltd v El Nasr Export & Import Co* [1972] 2 All ER 127, [1972] 2 QB 189,
CA.
*IRC v Mallaby-Deeley (personal representatives)* [1938] 4 All ER 818, CA.
*IRC v Plummer* [1979] 3 All ER 775, [1980] AC 896, HL.
*Prenn v Simmonds* [1971] 3 All ER 237, [1971] 1 WLR 1381, HL.

**Appeal**
Essex County Council appealed against the order of Hoffmann J ([1988] STC 370) dated
3 November 1987 dismissing their appeal by way of a case stated (set out at [1988] STC
371–383) from a determination of a Commissioner for the Special Purposes of the
Income Tax Acts that the inspector of taxes had correctly refused a claim for repayment
of tax made by the council in respect of sums paid to it under a deed of covenant. The
facts are set out in the judgment of Dillon LJ.

*G R A Argles* for the council.
*Alan Moses* for the Crown.

At the conclusion of the argument the court announced that the appeal would be
dismissed for reasons to be given later.

23 February. The following judgments were delivered.

**DILLON LJ** (delivering the first judgment at the invitation of Purchas LJ). The court
has before it an appeal by the Essex County Council against a decision of Hoffmann J
([1988] STC 370) given on 3 November 1987 whereby the judge dismissed an appeal by
case stated by the council against a decision in favour of the Crown by one of the Special
Commissioners for Income Tax, Miss Wix. Although brought by the council, the appeal
would, if successful, enure entirely for the benefit of a Mr David Skidmore.

The facts are fully set out in the case stated (see [1988] STC 370 at 371–383). They can
be summarised quite shortly for the purposes of this judgment. Mr Skidmore resides in
Essex. It is his misfortune that his son Graham who was born in May 1963 is mentally
handicapped. In 1980 Mr Skidmore decided that it would be of benefit to Graham if
Graham could for two years from 1 September 1981 (by which date Graham would of
course be of full age) attend a course in social training at an institution called Dilston Hall
at Corbridge in Northumberland. Dilston Hall is run by the well-known charity Mencap,
and it is the policy of Mencap not to accept students at Dilston Hall unless they are
sponsored by their local authorities. In particular, Mencap looks to the sponsoring local
authority to pay, on the usual termly basis, the fees for any child at Dilston Hall, leaving
it to the authority to make any appropriate arrangements for the child's parents to
reimburse or contribute to the fees for the child's terms at Dilston Hall.

Accordingly, as a resident in Essex Mr Skidmore approached the council for the council
to sponsor Graham at Dilston Hall. The council agreed to do so, provided that Mr and
Mrs Skidmore first agreed to pay the council the fees, and a provisional place was reserved
for Graham at Dilston Hall. Then, by a written agreement dated 30 June 1981, Mr and
Mrs Skidmore jointly and severally agreed with the council, in consideration of the
council entering into a contract with Mencap for Graham to go to Dilston Hall, that Mr
and Mrs Skidmore would reimburse the council any amount paid by the council under
the council's contract with Mencap.

a The council thereupon confirmed to Dilston Hall the place provisionally reserved for Graham for 1 September 1981, and confirmed its sponsorship of Graham. Graham therefore duly went to Dilston Hall in September for the two-year course.

Mr Skidmore was, not unnaturally, concerned at the high fees payable for Graham's time at Dilston Hall, and he asked whether the council would be prepared to contribute to the cost, but in its then financial circumstances the council felt unable to do so. Mr Skidmore accordingly, holding a view that under our tax law he could throw part of the

b costs of Graham's time at Dilston Hall onto the Commissioners of Inland Revenue, proceeded to put into effect an idea which had been briefly mentioned to the council at the very outset in March 1980, but not then explored: he executed a deed poll which is dated 18 September 1981 and which is a deed of covenant in favour of the council, and sent it to the council under cover of a letter of 21 September 1981, without any prior warning (save in so far as the mention of such a scheme in a tentative way in March 1980

c might be regarded as a warning).

By the deed of covenant he covenanted with the council to pay the council a gross amount of £1,333 on each 1 December, 1 March and 1 August for a period of seven years or for the period of the joint lives of Mr Skidmore and Graham or until Graham should cease to be receiving full-time education or social training at any university, college, school or other educational or social training establishment or until he should commence

d such education or social training in such establishment within the county of Essex (whichever should be the shortest period) the first payment to be made on 1 December 1981. In the covering letter of 21 September he said as follows:

'I would now like to deal with the financial matters arising out of Graham's stay at Dilston Hall and to limit the considerable expense which may arise, I would like

e to make payments to the County Council by way of a standard education covenant, suitably adapted to cover the special circumstances. My covenant is enclosed and should be retained for production to the revenue authorities at the end of the fiscal year. They occasionally wish to see it when the Form R185(AP) is made. The annual fee at Dilston Hall is approximately £5,000 p.a. but after taking supplementary benefits into account is more like £4,000 p.a. I have covenanted to pay £3,999. I

f will make out a standing order with my bank to remit £933·10 on the 1st December, March and August of each year. This totals £2,799·30. The balance, i.e. £1,199·70 is recovered by sending Form R185(AP) to the Inland Revenue. This payment is equal to 30% tax on the sum of £3,999. I will obtain the form which I have to complete and send it to you for you to submit. I have, of course, arranged to reimburse you for the full expense you incur on Graham's behalf and inasmuch as

g these arrangements fall short, I will discharge the liability by cheque. Please let me have full details of the account and the address to which I should direct my standing order.'

The council, on receipt of the deed of covenant and covering letter, sought confirmation from the Revenue that if payments were made by Mr Skidmore under the deed of

h covenant subject to deduction of tax the council would, in all the circumstances which were candidly put before the Revenue, be entitled to recover from the Revenue the tax deducted. Such confirmation was, however, not forthcoming. Consequently the council never agreed to accept the deed of covenant in satisfaction, to the extent of the gross sums thereby covenanted to be paid, of the obligations of Mr and Mrs Skidmore under the indemnity agreement of 30 June 1981. But Mr Skidmore made his payments to the

j council under the deed of covenant, net of tax at the standard rate, and the council accepted the sums paid, applied them towards settlement of Mr Skidmore's obligation to reimburse the council for Graham's fees at Dilston Hall, and then applied to the Revenue for the refund of the tax deducted by Mr Skidmore. That was refused by the Revenue. Consequently the council appealed against the refusal and the appeal came before the Special Commissioner; hence the appeal to the judge and now the present appeal. Clearly, however, the appeal would, if successful, enure entirely for the benefit of Mr Skidmore, since the council has an incontestable right under the indemnity agreement to recover from Mr and Mrs Skidmore whatever it fails to recover from the Revenue by these proceedings. That may have some connection with the fact, otherwise irrelevant, that the firm of solicitors of which Mr Skidmore is a partner act as solicitors for the council in these proceedings.

The statutory framework is not in dispute. Under s 353 of the Income and Corporation Taxes Act 1970 the council is exempt from all charge to income tax in respect of its income. The section further provides that, so far as the exemption from income tax calls for repayment of tax, effect shall be given thereto by means of a claim. That was the section under which the council claimed repayment of the tax deducted by Mr Skidmore from the gross payments payable under the deed of covenant. Mr Skidmore's claim to deduct the tax arose under s 52 of the 1970 Act, on the basis that the payments under the deed of covenant constituted an 'annuity or other annual payment charged with tax under Case III of Schedule D'. It is common ground that *if* the payments under the deed of covenant constituted 'an annuity or other annual payment charged with tax under Case III of Schedule D' Mr Skidmore was entitled to deduct tax and make the payments net as he did, and the tax so deducted was income of the council which the council is entitled to recover under s 353; but not otherwise. Case III of Sch D is set out in s 109(2) of the 1970 Act, but it is unnecessary to set out that subsection in this judgment. The key words are those already quoted, 'an annuity or other annual payment'.

The essence of the scheme for deduction of tax by the payer of an annual payment or annuity and reclaiming of the tax by the payee if the payee is exempt from income tax is that the annual payment or annuity is such as in law to be regarded as income of the payee. It is well established, however, that not all income qualifies, and the crucial question, as put by Lord Donovan in *Campbell and anor (trustees of Davies's Educational Trust) v IRC* [1968] 3 All ER 588 at 606 [1970] AC 77 at 112, is whether the payment is 'pure income' or 'pure profit income' in the hands of the payee as those terms have been used in the decided cases. That is the crucial question in the present case.

Counsel for the council submits, however, at some considerable length as a preliminary issue that as the deed of covenant is a deed the question whether the sums payable under the deed of covenant are 'pure income' or 'pure profit income' of the council has to be decided on the words of the deed of covenant alone and by itself, without regard to any evidence of surrounding circumstances, and in particular without regard to the terms of the covering letter of 21 September 1981 with which the deed of covenant was sent by Mr Skidmore to the council.

In support of this preliminary submission, counsel for the council relies on the general rule categorically stated in 12 Halsbury's Laws (4th edn) para 1478 and the footnotes thereto, by reference in particular to the opinion of Park J in *Smith v Earl of Jersey* (1821) 3 Bli 290 at 380, 4 ER 610 at 641 'that parol or extrinsic evidence cannot be admitted to contradict, vary, or add to the terms of a deed'. No case has however been cited to us in which the court, having to decide whether payments under a deed of covenant were annual payments within Case III of Sch D, has not looked beyond the mere terms of the deed of covenant to see what the transaction was, in order to be able to determine what the nature of the payment was in the hands of the covenantee. Indeed if the submissions of counsel for the council are correct it would seem that the decision of the House of Lords in *Campbell v IRC* and the decision of this court in *IRC v National Book League* [1957] 2 All ER 644, [1957] Ch 488 must have been given per incuriam: see especially the opening paragraphs of the speech of Lord Donovan in *Campbell v IRC* [1968] 3 All ER 588 at 604–605 [1970] AC 77 at 110.

Counsel for the council further submits that, if the council had not chosen to allocate Mr Skidmore's net payments under the deed of covenant towards his liability under the indemnity agreement to reimburse the council its expenditure to Mencap for Graham's time at Dilston Hall, Mr Skidmore would have had no option but to pay again. If, despite accepting his net payments under the deed of covenant, the council had chosen to sue Mr

Skidmore for the total sums paid to Mencap Mr Skidmore, in the submission of counsel
a for the council, would have had no defence to the action; the general rule referred to
above would have precluded him from setting up the net payments under the deed of
covenant as partial payments under the indemnity agreement.

For my part I find this preliminary submission by counsel for the council unarguable.
The covering letter clearly earmarked the net payments under the deed of covenant for
meeting either directly or by reimbursement Graham's fees at Dilston Hall. A condition
b was thereby imposed on the council which, if it took the payments, it could not ignore.
I entirely agree with the way Hoffmann J put it in his judgment, when he said ([1988]
STC 370 at 384):

'It is clear from that letter that the basis upon which he was sending the covenant
to the council was that payments under the covenant would be treated as discharging
c pro tanto the joint and several liability of himself and his wife under the agreement
of 30 June. The council was of course not obliged to accept payment in that form.
The agreement of 30 June provided for payment of the full amount which the
council had had to pay to Mencap within 28 days of the submission of invoices. But
in my judgment, if the council accepted payments under the covenant it could not,
in the light of the covering letter, afterwards say that those payments did not operate
d in discharge of the liability under the agreement. The council did in fact accept the
payments . . .'

I turn therefore to the substantive question whether the payments made by Mr
Skidmore under the deed of covenant were, or were not, in the circumstances of this case
and in view of the covering letter, annual payments by Mr Skidmore within Case III of
e Sch D, which depends, as I have mentioned, on whether the payments were 'pure income'
or 'pure profit income' in the hands of the council as payee.

In *Campbell v IRC* the payments made under a deed of covenant were held not to be
'pure income' in the hands of the covenantees, who were charitable trustees, because the
covenantees were bound to apply the covenanted payments towards buying certain
capital assets from the covenantors. The House of Lords approved two well-known
f passages in earlier authorities which give guidance as to what is or is not an annual
payment within Case III of Sch D.

The first is a passage in the judgment of Scrutton LJ in *Earl Howe v IRC* [1919] 2 KB
336 at 352–353, [1918–19] All ER Rep 1088 at 1098, a case concerned with a covenant
to pay premiums under a life insurance policy, where he said:

'It is not all payments made every year from which income tax can be deducted.
g For instance, if a man agrees to pay a motor garage 500l. a year for five years for the
hire and upkeep of a car, no one suggests that the person paying can deduct income
tax from each yearly payment. So if he contracted with a butcher for an annual sum
to supply all his meat for a year. The annual instalment would not be subject to tax
as a whole in the hands of the payee, but only that part of it which was profits . . .
These premiums are either payments of capital to obtain on the death a sinking
h fund—the policy moneys—or the price of such a payment or fund. They do not
seem to me to be annual payments ejusdem generis with annual interest or
annuities, and as income tax on them cannot be deducted against the recipient, I see
no reason why the person paying should deduct them from his taxable income.'

The second is a passage in the judgment of Greene MR in *Re Hanbury (decd), Comiskey
j v Hanbury* (1939) 38 TC 588 at 590 where he said:

'There are two classes of annual payments which fall to be considered for Income
Tax purposes. There is, first of all, that class of annual payment which the Acts
regard and treat as being pure income profit of the recipient undiminished by any
deduction. Payments of interest, payments of annuities, to take the ordinary simple

case, are payments which are regarded as part of the income of the recipient, and
the payer is entitled in estimating his total income to treat those payments as *a*
payments which go out of his income altogether. The class of annual payment
which falls within that category is quite a limited one. In the other class there stand
a number of payments, none the less annual, the very quality and nature of which
make it impossible to treat them as part of the pure profit income of the recipient,
the proper way of treating them being to treat them as an element to be taken into
account in discovering what the profits of the recipient are.'                               *b*

It is submitted that the essence of Scrutton LJ's instance is that the garage proprietor
and the butcher are carrying on trades, and so are only taxable on the profits of their
trades, and not on any gross receipts of the trades. It is said therefore that the oft-quoted
instances are only relevant where the covenantee is carrying on a trade. It seems to me
that the fact that the covenantees instanced by Scrutton LJ were carrying on trades is just *c*
one of several possible scenarios which would lead to the conclusion in a particular case
that the payment received by the covenantee cannot be regarded as pure income of the
covenantee without regard to some other expenditure or commitment of the covenantee.
In the present case it is impossible, in my judgment, in all the circumstances and in view
in particular of the covering letter, to regard the payments by Mr Skidmore under the
deed of covenant as pure income of the council without regard to the obligation, which *d*
the council undertook at Mr Skidmore's request, to pay Mencap the fees for Graham's
stay at Dilston Hall. One goes to cancel the other, and there is nothing left to support the
council's claim for repayment or to justify deduction of tax by Mr Skidmore under Case
III of Sch D.

I note that in *Campbell v IRC* [1968] 3 All ER 588 at 593, [1970] AC 77 at 96 Viscount
Dilhorne, after referring to *Howe v IRC* and *Re Hanbury*, said:                             *e*

'It follows from these decisions that the annual payments which are to be treated
as an element to be taken into account in computing the profits of the recipient, are
not to be regarded as annual payments coming within s. 169(1) and s. 447(1) of the
Act of 1952; but it does not follow that annual payments from which no deductions
fall to be made for the purpose of computing profits and gains are to be treated as *f*
"forming part of the income" of the recipient and as coming within these sections.
"The very quality and nature" of the payments may make it "impossible to treat
them as part of the pure profit income of the recipient" . . .'

Similarly Lord Upjohn referred to Greene MR's statement, 'pure income profit of the
recipient undiminished by any deduction', and treated it as meaning income of the
recipient which, by whatever method of assessment or collection the Act laid down, *g*
would be subject to tax without deduction (see [1968] 3 All ER 588 at 602–603, [1970]
AC 77 at 108). But in the present case the covenanted payments by Mr Skidmore could
not, in the circumstances and in the light of the covering letter, be subject to tax in the
council's hands, if the council was a taxpayer, without deduction of the fees payable by
the council to Mencap.

Counsel for the council seeks to get round this by referring us to various authorities. *h*
The first is the well-known case of *IRC v Duke of Westminster* [1936] AC 1, [1935] All ER
Rep 259. There the duke had entered into seven-year covenants with his gardener and
with various other employees. By the deed of covenant with the gardener the duke
covenanted to pay the gardener a specified weekly sum during their joint lives or for
seven years. By cl 3 it was expressly agreed that the payments were to be without
prejudice to such remuneration as the gardener would become entitled to in respect of *j*
such services (if any) as he might thereafter render to the duke. There was also a collateral
letter to the gardener, at which the court did not hesitate to look, from the duke's
solicitors, in which the solicitors recorded that they had read over the deed of covenant
to the gardener and that the payments under the deed were irrespective of any work the

gardener might do for the duke after the deed came into effect. The letter went on
*a* ([1936] AC 1 at 11–12, [1935] All ER Rep 259 at 264):

> 'We explained that there is nothing in the deed to prevent you being entitled to
> and claiming full remuneration for such future work as you may do, though it is
> expected that in practice you will be content with the provision which is being
> legally made for you so long as the deed takes effect, with the addition of such sum
> *b* (if any) as may be necessary to bring the total periodical payment while you are still
> in the Duke's service up to the amount of the salary or wages which you have lately
> been receiving. You said that you accepted this arrangement, and you accordingly
> executed the deed.'

The duke claimed to deduct the sums payable under the deeds of covenant from his
total income for surtax purposes on the footing that the sums payable were annual
*c* payments within Sch D. The Crown claimed, however, that the payments were not
within Sch D because they were payments of wages within Sch E from which tax was
not then deductible.

The majority in the House of Lords upheld the duke's claim. One of the majority,
Lord Macmillan, held that the effect of the deed and the letter was to embody an
*d* agreement between the gardener, or other covenantee, and the duke that so long as he
remained in the duke's employment the covenantee would be content with the
covenanted payments under the deed plus the difference between them and the wages
he was previously receiving. The other members of the majority were of the view that
there was no such binding agreement. All the majority agreed, however, that the
payments under the deed were not payments of wages and the duke was entitled to
*e* deduct them from his total income for surtax purposes: they were not payments of wages
because, as Lord Macmillan put it, it was agreed on all hands that the legal effect of the
deed was to give the covenantee thereafter for the period of its endurance the right to the
specified weekly payments irrespective of whether he remained in the duke's employment
or not (see [1936] AC 1 at 26, [1935] All ER 259 at 271). Indeed, on the evidence some of
the covenantees had retired before the case came on for hearing and had continued to
*f* receive their covenanted payments. Whether or not they could have claimed wages, in
addition to the covenanted payments, for service to the duke while the deeds were in
force was therefore a matter that did not affect the nature of the covenanted payments in
the recipient's hands. Therefore, in my judgment, the issues which arose in *Earl Howe v
IRC*, *Campbell v IRC* and *IRC v National Book League* did not arise in the *Duke of Westminster's*
case.

*g*      Counsel for the council referred also to the decision of Harman J in *Hawkins (Inspector
of Taxes) v Leahy* [1952] 2 All ER 759. In that case the court had to consider the National
Health Service (Superannuation) Regulations 1947, SR & O 1947/1755, which provided
that a doctor who had entered the national health service on the appointed day and who
then held life insurance policies could elect not to participate in the national health
service superannuation scheme, and to receive instead an annual sum, described as a
*h* contribution towards the maintenance of his policies, equal to 8% of his remuneration as
a practitioner. It was held that the doctor was taxable on these annual sums as annual
payments chargeable under Case III of Sch D. It was submitted, against this, that the
annual sums were not pure income profits, but merely contributions towards the doctor's
liability to the insurance company for the premiums. But Harman J rejected that, saying
tersely (at 763): '. . . the two things bear absolutely no relation to one another.' That
*j* being the ratio, the case, whether right or wrong, does not bear on the present case, since
in the present case the covenanted payments and the obligation of the council to pay the
fees for Graham to Mencap bear every relation to one another.

Counsel for the council then referred to the decision of the House of Lords in *IRC v
City of London Corp (as Conservators of Epping Forest)* [1953] 1 All ER 1075, [1953] 1 WLR

652. In that case the Corporation of London made annual payments for the upkeep of
Epping Forest for the public benefit. The corporation was itself the conservator of Epping     *a*
Forest, and in that capacity held it on charitable trusts. The corporation was bound by
statute, the Epping Forest Act 1878 (41 & 42 Vict c ccxiii), to contribute from time to
time to the capital and income of a fund to be called the Epping Forest fund such moneys
as should be necessary. The corporation claimed successfully to deduct tax from its
annual contributions to the Epping Forest Fund on the basis that these contributions
were annual payments within the meaning of Case III of Sch D; it followed, as the Epping     *b*
Forest fund was a charitable fund, that the corporation in its capacity of conservator was
entitled to recover the tax thus deducted. The case turned, as I read it, on a correct
appreciation of the corporation's position and obligations under the 1878 Act (see [1953]
1 All ER 1075 at 1083, [1953] 1 WLR 652 at 661–662 per Lord Normand). It was argued
for the Crown that no sum paid by the corporation under the Act could ever be profit in
the hands of the corporation as conservator because the amount of the sum payable was     *c*
measured by the amount of the Epping Forest fund's deficit and therefore the whole of
it had to go to pay expenses and no part could ever be profit. It was held, however, that
the true appreciation was that the payments by the corporation to the fund were
payments to enable the conservator to carry on its charitable functions under the Act,
and did not differ from the common case where a person enters into a seven-year
covenant to pay annual sums to a charity for its general purposes.     *d*

If that is a correct appreciation, the transaction in the *City of London* case was so different
from the transaction in the present case that the decision in the *City of London* case does
not, in my judgment, provide compelling guidance in the present case.

Counsel for the council had a further argument based on the wording of the deed of
covenant executed by Mr Skidmore. The events which on the wording of the deed would
bring Mr Skidmore's liability under the deed to an end are the death of Mr Skidmore or     *e*
Graham, the end of Graham's receipt of education or training or the commencement of
education or training for Graham in an establishment in Essex. That would leave the
liability continuing if Graham had left Dilston Hall, and had been sent, at Mr Skidmore's
expense without any sponsorship or liability on the part of the council, to a training
establishment in Worcestershire, or any other county but Essex. It is argued that in that
event the payments under the deed of covenant would necessarily be pure income or     *f*
pure profit income of the council since they would be unaffected by any obligation of
the council to pay fees for Graham or by any obligation of indemnity or reimbursement
of Mr and Mrs Skidmore. It is then said that the nature of the payments under the deed
of covenant cannot change as the facts change, just as in *IRC v Duke of Westminster* [1936]
AC 1, [1935] All ER Rep 259 the nature of the payments was held to have been the same
before as well as after the covenantee's departure from the duke's service.     *g*

In passing I would observe that it seems highly unlikely, in view of his comments on
the great expense of Dilston Hall, that Mr Skidmore would ever have been able to afford
Graham's fees at a training establishment in Worcestershire unless first released by the
council from his deed of covenant in the council's favour. I do not find it necessary,
however, to explore hypothetical cases. We are concerned with a claim by the council to     *h*
recover tax deducted by Mr Skidmore from payments made by him to the council while
Graham was at Dilston Hall, and therefore while the covering letter of 21 September
1981, the indemnity agreement by Mr and Mrs Skidmore and the council's obligation to
Mencap were all in force. I cannot accept that a correct appreciation of the position while
those documents and obligations were in force is governed by consideration of what the
position might have been if sums had been paid under the deed of covenant in other     *j*
circumstances after all these documents and obligations had terminated. To put the same
point another way, the payments under the deed of covenant would clearly have been
pure income of the council if they had not been earmarked as they were for the particular
purpose for which they were earmarked; one does not determine the effect in law of the

*a*   earmarking by considering hypothetical future payments under the same deed of covenant which, in a different scenario, would not be earmarked at all.

Finally and alternatively it is submitted for the council that even if the payments made by Mr Skidmore under the deed do not qualify as 'annual payments' within Case III of Sch D, they qualify as payments of an 'annuity' within Case III. It was submitted that the complexities about 'pure income' or 'pure profit income' which the courts have had to consider in relation to alleged 'annual payments' within Case III do not apply to payments

*b*   of an annuity. I do not agree. Mention was made by counsel for the council in argument of the decision of the Privy Council in *Ceylon Comr of Inland Revenue v Rajaratnam* [1971] TR 451. That case was concerned with a Ceylon Income Tax Ordinance which only used the word 'annuity' and not the phrase in Case III 'annuity or other annual payment'; the actual decision was that the word 'annuity' was not limited to annuities which had been purchased for a capital sum, and therefore payments to the covenantee under an ordinary

*c*   seven-year deed of covenant were payments of an 'annuity'. Lord Cross, who gave the opinion of the Judicial Committee, observed (at 454):

> 'In the United Kingdom as the Act contains the words "or other annual payment" the question whether any given payment which admittedly falls under one or other head should be described as "an annuity" or not is only of academic interest.'

*d*   Counsel for the council conceded in his skeleton argument that the factors which may cause a payment claimed as an annual payment to be treated otherwise than as pure income profit may be relevant, but not decisive, in determining whether a payment is an annuity properly so called. He offered no guidance, however, as to what degree of 'impurity' was sufficient to prevent a payment qualifying under Case III as an annual payment and yet not sufficient to prevent it qualifying as a payment of an annuity. In

*e*   my judgment in the sort of context with which we are concerned in the present case or with which the courts were concerned in *Campbell v IRC*, *Earl Howe v IRC* and *IRC v National Book League* the factors which prevent a series of payments coming within Case III as annual payments also prevent them being within Case III as payments of an annuity; in such a context the test is the same.

*f*   For the foregoing reasons, I agree with the conclusion of the Special Commissioner and of Hoffmann J and I would dismiss the appeal.

**CROOM-JOHNSON LJ.** I agree.

**PURCHAS LJ.** I also agree.

*g*   *Appeal dismissed. Leave to appeal to the House of Lords refused.*

Solicitors: *Robin Thompson & Partners*, Ilford (for the council); *Solicitor of Inland Revenue*.

Heather Whicher    Barrister.

# Roberts and another v J Hampson & Co (a firm)

QUEEN'S BENCH DIVISION AT MANCHESTER

IAN KENNEDY J

21, 22, 23, 24, 25 MARCH, 25 MAY 1988

*Negligence – Surveyor – Duty to take care – Surveyor making report to building society for mortgage application – Survey and valuation carried out negligently – Surveyor not following trail of suspicion when suspicions aroused as to defect – Purchaser relying on report – Surveyor knowing that purchaser likely to rely on report – Whether surveyor owing purchaser duty to exercise reasonable skill and care in carrying out valuation – Whether surveyor under duty to follow trail of suspicion – Whether surveyor liable for negligence.*

*Negligence – Professional person – Duty to exercise reasonable skill and care – Duty where work done for standard fee – Whether duty of care modified by fact that individual case may involve more time than expected or fee structure contemplated.*

The plaintiffs, an engaged couple of modest means, entered into a contract to purchase a bungalow for £19,000. They applied to a building society for a 95% mortgage to finance the purchase. The society arranged for a valuation to be carried out by the defendant surveyors and the property was inspected by a qualified surveyor employed by the defendants. The surveyor found on his inspection marked dampness in a skirting board along one wall in the main bedroom but he thought that it was residual dampness left over from a drainage problem which had been remedied and that it would eventually dry out. The surveyor traced the dampness along two-thirds of the skirting board but did not lift the carpet next to it or attempt to move a piece of furniture near the end of the skirting board where it joined the wall between the bedroom and the kitchen, nor did he check the corresponding skirting board in the kitchen. He stated in his report that a 'limited amount of dampness was noted in the external walls at the rear' and that a 'certain amount of rot was noted in the skirtings in [the main bedroom]'. He valued the property at the sale price of £19,000. A copy of his report was passed to the plaintiffs, who proceeded with the purchase. Shortly after the purchase the plaintiffs discovered that the wall between the main bedroom and the kitchen and also other parts of the house were heavily infested with dry rot, which it was estimated would cost more than £3,000 to eradicate. The plaintiffs brought an action for damages against the defendants, alleging that the defendants' surveyor had been negligent in carrying out his survey.

**Held** – Where a surveyor carrying out a building society inspection for valuation purposes had his suspicions aroused as to a defect in the property he was under a duty to take reasonable steps to follow the trail of suspicion, moving furniture or carpets if necessary, until he had all the information which it was reasonable for him to have before making his valuation of the property. Since the proximity between the defendants and the plaintiffs was such that the defendants ought reasonably to have recognised both the importance which the plaintiffs would attach to their valuation and their own answerability to the plaintiffs in making it, the defendants owed a duty to the plaintiffs to take reasonable care in making their valuation. The defendants were in breach of that duty because their surveyor's investigation of the property was inadequate in that when he discovered dampness in the skirting board in the main bedroom his suspicions ought to have been aroused and he ought to have lifted the carpet and moved the piece of furniture to follow the trail of suspicion. The plaintiffs were accordingly entitled to damages of £5,500 (see p 509 c d, p 510 e f, p 511 d e, p 512 f to h and p 513 a c d, post).

*Yianni v Edwin Evans & Sons (a firm)* [1981] 3 All ER 592 and *Harris v Wyre Forest DC* [1988] 1 All ER 691 considered.

*a* Per curiam. It is inherent in any standard-fee work that some cases will be 'winners' and others 'losers', from the professional man's point of view, but the fact that in an individual case he may need to spend two or three times as long as he would have expected, or as the fee structure would have contemplated, is something that he must accept. His duty to take reasonable care in carrying out his work remains the root of his obligation (see p 510 *c d*, post).

*b* **Notes**
For the duty of care generally, see 34 Halsbury's Laws (4th edn) para 5, and for cases on the subject, see 36(1) Digest (Reissue) 17–32, 34–103.

**Cases referred to in judgment**
*Anns v Merton London Borough* [1977] 2 All ER 492, [1978] AC 728, [1977] 2 WLR 1024,
*c* HL.
*Harris v Wyre Forest DC* [1988] 1 All ER 691, [1988] QB 835, [1988] 2 WLR 1173, CA.
*Hedley Byrne & Co Ltd v Heller & Partners Ltd* [1963] 2 All ER 575, [1964] AC 465, [1963] 3 WLR 101, HL.
*Ministry of Housing and Local Government v Sharp* [1970] 1 All ER 1009, [1970] 2 QB 223, [1970] 2 WLR 802, CA.
*d* *Yianni v Edwin Evans & Sons (a firm)* [1981] 3 All ER 592, [1982] QB 438, [1981] 3 WLR 843.
*Yuen Kun-yeu v A-G of Hong Kong* [1987] 2 All ER 705, [1988] AC 175, [1987] 3 WLR 776, PC.

**Action**
*e* The plaintiffs, Anthony Peter Roberts and Karen Roberts, by a writ dated 13 January 1986 and a statement of claim brought an action against the defendants, J Hampson & Co, a firm of chartered surveyors, claiming damages in respect of negligence in the preparation by the defendants, their servants or agents of a report and valuation on or about 31 May 1984 relating to a house known as and situated at Delfryn, Eglwysbach, Colwyn Bay in the county of Clwyd in reliance on which the plaintiffs purchased the
*f* property and suffered inconvenience, distress, loss and damage. The action was heard in Manchester, but judgment was given in London. The facts are set out in the judgment.

*Michael Black* for the plaintiffs.
*Rosen Peacocke* for the defendants.

*g*                                                                        *Cur adv vult*

25 May. The following judgment was delivered.

**IAN KENNEDY J.** In early 1984 Mr and Mrs Roberts were engaged to be married. (Mrs Roberts was then a Miss Iveson.) They wanted to buy a house against their
*h* forthcoming marriage. He was 22 and in a junior grade on the railways; she was 21 and a hairdresser. They went first to the Halifax Building Society in Llandudno for advice. They went to the Halifax because it was the biggest society and, to their minds, would therefore give the best advice and service. Mrs Roberts knew something of the deputy manageress, a Miss Wetherson, because she did Miss Wetherson's hair.

Mr and Mrs Roberts's means were very modest. When Miss Wetherson had made the
*j* necessary calculations she told them that the limit of any mortgage advance on their earnings would be in the order of £18,500. The Roberts had only a few hundred pounds saved. Miss Wetherson gave them a copy of the Halifax's leaflets and explanatory material, included in which was their advice on valuations and surveys. Mr and Mrs Roberts took the material away, read it and began to look for a house in their price range.

[His Lordship described how the mortgage form was filled in and continued:] It is agreed that Miss Wetherson had explained the procedure as to surveys and valuations either then or on the previous occasion. Mr and Mrs Roberts both understood it, of that there is no doubt.

The Halifax offered three schemes, as outlined in their brochure. In practice Miss Wetherson only discussed schemes 1 and 2 with her clients since so few of their predecessors had ever opted for scheme 3, the conventional full structural survey. I am satisfied that she did explain the two schemes properly, that she did, as she says she did, recommend scheme 2, and that the Roberts understood the position; they chose scheme 2.

In scheme 1 the valuer's client is the Halifax, though a copy of the valuation is provided to the purchaser; in scheme 2 the purchaser is the client, though a valuation is provided for the Halifax. This important difference is reflected in the administrative arrangements.

[His Lordship referred to another property which the plaintiffs were interested in purchasing and for which the defendants prepared a scheme 2 survey indicating that certain repairs would need to be made, the cost of which when added to the purchase price exceeded the plaintiffs' means. His Lordship continued:] The plaintiffs subsequently found a bungalow called Delfryn at Eglwysbach in the Conwy Valley, the property with which this case is concerned. It is described in the selling agent's particulars. Seemingly, it had been on the market for a little time, for the original asking price of £22,500 had been reduced, first, to £19,950 and then, by the time the plaintiffs saw the house, to £19,000. They made an offer of £19,000, again subject to contract, which was accepted. The plaintiffs returned to see Miss Wetherson, although on this occasion it was Miss Iveson who signed the mortgage application form. On this occasion they selected scheme 1, as the instructions to the valuers (the defendants) show. These instructions also show that the plaintiffs were seeking a 95% mortgage.

[His Lordship explained that the plaintiffs selected scheme 1 because they could not afford another scheme 2 survey which might be wasted. His Lordship also described Delfryn in more detail and continued:] The valuation was done by a Mr Jones, an assistant to the sole principal of the defendants. Mr Jones had obtained the degree of BSc in building studies in 1980 and had then done his professional training in a general practice in Liverpool. He passed his examinations for associate membership of the Royal Institute of Chartered Surveyors in the summer of 1983 in the building surveying division and joined the defendants in September 1983. In the eight months that he had been with the defendants the major part of his time had been spent on building society inspections and valuations.

The Halifax's instructions were dated 29 May 1984 and were received by Mr Jones on the following day. By chance, he was going to the area that day and he was able to make an appointment to see Delfryn at noon. He would have allowed for about half an hour at the property, an assessment not dissented from by either of the expert surveyors. He would have been equipped with damp-meter, fine screwdriver and a torch and would have had a clip board with pro formas, which are his working notes in the present case. On his return to his office he would have dictated his report and valuation, which was signed on the following day. The report and valuation is typed in triplicate. A copy is provided for the applicant. During the trial, to illustrate another point, a copy was handed in from the defendants' files to illustrate what would have been seen by the Halifax. The Halifax were told that the property was certified as suitable for a maximum advance. The Halifax sent the report and valuation in a folder under cover of their own letter. The folder repeats the caution about a scheme 1 valuation and gives certain further advice. I shall have to consider the valuation in detail later in this judgment but, for the present, I note only that it contained these words:

'A limited amount of dampness was noted in the external walls at the rear of the property. A certain amount of rot was noted in the skirtings within Bedroom 2 and we would recommend that an undertaking is obtained that a reputable timber Specialist is engaged to eradicate the rot. The purchase price for the property compares favourably with sale prices recently obtained for other similar bungalows in the area . . . Valuation of property £19,000.'

Comforted by the thought that the property was valued at the price they had agreed
*a* to pay, and by the absence of any reference to substantial defects or the insistence on a
retention, Mr and Mrs Roberts proceeded with their purchase. The details of the
conveyancing are substantially immaterial. I note, however, that in the inquiries before
contract in response to the question: 'Does the property have a damp proof course?' the
vendor replied: 'Yes, so far as the Vendor is aware—please arrange for a structural survey
to be carried out to confirm the foregoing.' And in response to the question: 'So far as the
*b* Vendors are aware, has the property been [affected] by any of the following:—
a) Structural or building defects? b) Subsidence? c) Dry or wet rot, rising damp,
woodworm or other infestation?' the reply was: 'The Vendor is not aware of any of these
matters having affected the property. The purchasers should, nonetheless, arrange for a
full structural survey to be carried out to ascertain whether the property has been so
affected. The purchasers should rely on such Survey.' The only point in these essentially
*c* formal questions and formal replies are that they did nothing to disabuse Mr and Mrs
Roberts of the view that they had taken. The purchase was completed on 20 August 1984
and the Roberts moved in to Delfryn virtually immediately.

Two or three months after they moved in, and therefore probably in the second half
of October, they found 'mushrooms', as they thought they were, on the wall and skirting
in the back lobby. [His Lordship described the infestation of dry rot and evidence of
*d* rising damp in more detail and continued:] I pass therefore to the details of Mr Jones's
inspection and the physical signs that would then have been available to him.

Mr Jones began by measuring the external walls, as his sketch shows (such
measurements were relevant to the valuation which he was asked to make). As he went
round he noted the condition of the exterior. The external decorations, the joinery and
the roof were all satisfactory. However, he noticed that there was high ground around
*e* the extension of bedroom 2 and that soil rested against the walls of that room above
damp-proof course level. A photograph attached to the report of Mr Caird, the surveyor
who gave evidence for the plaintiffs, illustrates where the high ground was, although the
photograph somewhat exaggerates the position. The soil was not as high as this
photograph would suggest and much of the apparent 'height' is long grass and other
*f* vegetation. It was generally agreed that Mr Jones was broadly right in his assessment that
there was high ground at the rear of the property and round the extension and that more
extensive high ground found by Rentokil's damp-proof surveyor was the result of an
over-enthusiastic definition of 'high ground'. Mr Jones said that he was untroubled by
the high ground against the extension because soil against the external leaf of a cavity
wall is not something of the first importance. Continuing on his journey round the
*g* house, Mr Jones came to the concrete path at the rear of the original building. What he
saw is illustrated by a photograph attached to the report of Mr Jackson, the damp-proof
surveyor. The first window, that with the waste pipe under it, is the kitchen window;
the second, which appears to abut on the return of the extension, is that of bedroom 1. It
is clear that the concrete path has, at some time, been broken away to produce the
channel shown in the photographs. The channel extends from the entrance to the back
*h* door to the return wall of the new extension and for a short distance along that wall. It
thus follows that it was likely that the channel had been cut when or after the extension
was built and therefore the cause for its being dug was in existence then.

That was the external evidence which, as Mr Jones agreed, he had to have in mind
when he went inside the house. The construction that Mr Jones put on this evidence has
to be seen in the light of his belief that the main walls were of solid construction. In
*j* reaching this conclusion he was mistaken, but he was mistaken without being negligent.
Indeed, Mr Caird, made the same mistake when he was engaged on a thorough survey of
the house to prepare himself to give evidence.

The external walls were rendered and the rendering was carried down to and beyond
the point at which the damp-proof course would have been. This was bad practice and
all the professional witnesses are agreed that the rendering should be cut back and
bullnosed at a point about six inches above the damp-proof course level. There was in
fact a damp-proof course in these walls, as Mr Jackson found. This damp-proof course

was not easily found and Mr Caird did not find it. Mr Jackson, who clearly made his
examination with the greatest care, was able to see traces of bitumen felt, as well as beads     **a**
of bitumen. Mr Jones told me that he believed that there was a damp-proof course
because of the age of the building but I am far from satisfied that he actually detected it
by observation; he certainly made no reference one way or the other in his notes or in his
report. I do not question Mr Jones's honesty but I have grave doubts as to the accuracy of
his evidence. He claimed to have a greater recollection of the events of this inspection
than I believe it is possible for him to have had, having regard to, firstly, the number of     **b**
such inspections which he carries out within any given week and, secondly, the fact that
concern about the particular house was not raised until a year later. I find that his
evidence is in large part based on reconstruction and contains a fully understandable
element of self-justification. If Mr Jones did believe that there was a damp-proof course,
he must have appreciated that it was possibly bridged, and almost certainly compromised,
by the level to which the rendering had been brought down. The rendering was in good     **c**
condition and unaffected by any spalling. This would have suggested, particularly in the
context of a supposedly solid wall, that the amount of rising dampness could not have
been very great for if it had been, it is likely that the frosts of winter would have produced
some spalling damage to the rendering.

When he went inside, Mr Jones followed his usual practice in such cases. He carried
out damp readings with his electric damp meter at three to four foot intervals along the     **d**
external walls and along the skirtings. He told me that he tested every three to four feet,
subject to furniture being in the way. Since the major problem is likely to be rising
damp, his practice was to test at about six inches above the skirting and then to retest
higher up if he found any evidence of dampness. No one criticises this procedure. He
was, he said, naturally concerned about the same rear wall. He had found dampness
along the rear of the main bedroom, to the left of and under the window. He said that     **e**
he found a limited amount of dampness which registered in the yellow area on his meter,
which meant 17% to 20% relative dampness. He said that the actual figure would have
been about 19%. It is this sort of precision which I believe to be unreliable at this distance
in time. Having found dampness, he would have tested upwards at three to four inch
raises and it is his evidence that the dampness extended upwards for about a foot. He
deemed it to be rising damp and in this he was right.     **f**

At this point a further qualification has to be introduced. When the paper was stripped
from these walls (and it is not suggested that Mr Jones should have done so) it was found
that they had been replastered to about dado height. The walls behind the new plaster
were very wet indeed but the new plaster had a damp-shielding element in it which
limited the amount of dampness which Mr Jones's test would have detected. This work
had been done by a skilled plasterer who had matched the new thickness to the old so     **g**
well that the tell-tale bump at the junction, which would ordinarily have been expected
to be visible through the wallpaper, was quite absent. Thus there was nothing to suggest
to Mr Jones that there had been any need for replastering. No one now knows whether
that replastering was done following the removal of a wooden dado, or because of the
same manifestation of damp which had led to the path on the other side of the wall being     **h**
cut away. This factor, therefore, explains why the wall would have seemed less damp to
Mr Jones than in fact it was and underlines that one further ground of suspicion was
denied him.

Mr Jones did, however, detect marked dampness within the skirting board under the
window of the bedroom. He told me that his judgment was that the rot was the result of
dampness which had been left in the wall since the time that the channel had been cut     **j**
and that this dampness had not completely resolved itself by the time of his inspection,
as his readings on the lower part of the wall tended to show. He further judged that the
rot in the skirting board was a local attack only. It is on the validity of this last conclusion
that the case, in essence, turns.

It is agreed that the terms on which such an inspection as that presently under
consideration are conducted do not require the surveyor to move furniture nor to lift

carpets where that cannot readily be done. If Mr Jones had lifted the carpet adjacent to
*a* the skirting board, and there is a dispute between Mr and Mrs Roberts and him whether
it was tacked down, it is, in my judgment, likely that he would have gained significantly
more information to aid his judgment. Mr Jackson has helpfully drawn a sketch which
illustrates how dampness was, in fact, bridging the damp-proof course (any question of
local defects in the damp-proof course membrane aside). His sketch is self-explanatory
but it shows that the bitumen layer on the concrete oversite was not in line with the
*b* damp-proof membrane in the walls, nor was there any upstand or flashing to make good
that defect. Thus the wood blocks which were butted against the exterior walls were
acting as a wick and transferring the general dampness from the foundations, across the
membrane to the higher parts of the wall. His sketch shows that the skirting board was
not flush with the wall itself but distanced from it by the thickness of the plaster. The
plaster had been brought down to the top of the skirting board and that board was held
*c* firmly by nails driven into the brickwork behind. The general dampness could and
would have reached the skirting board both from contact with the wood blocks and also
along the nails between the walls and the board. As Mr Jackson's sketch shows, about
one-and-a-half inches of the outermost blocks would be under the shadow of the skirting
board and the gap behind it. None the less it is self-evident, and I am prepared to find,
that if a damp meter had been used to take a reading from the wood blocks beneath the
*d* carpet and close up against the skirting board, a high figure would have been revealed
and, as I am satisfied, a very relevant and probably crucial piece of information obtained.
Such a reading would have told Mr Jones that the process was active and that he was not
seeing the mere working out of a problem which had essentially been remedied.
    Mr Jones said that the rot extended over about two-thirds of the length of the skirting
and that there was then a piece of furniture at the end towards the kitchen (he did not
*e* specify what that piece of furniture was). The layout of the room and the position of the
windows suggest that whatever it may have been, and I am not satisfied that Mr Jones's
recollection is necessarily correct, it is unlikely to have been a wardrobe or any other
substantial piece. Mr Jones did not speak of moving it or trying to move it. He did not
attempt to get a reading from the floor, although he knew (or was about to learn if he
had not yet been to bedroom 2) that this floor was a wood block floor. He knew, or he
*f* was to know, that because he lifted the carpet in that bedroom and saw the join between
the old wood blocks and the new asphalt floor. Equally, he did not go and specifically
check the corresponding piece of skirting board in the kitchen under the sink, where
broadly the same conditions obtained as obtained at the point where he had found rot.
    Mr Jones said that he did not mention the bridging of the damp-proof course by the
*g* rendering in his valuation because he knew that any specialist contractor called in to
remedy the rot would insist on the necessary cutting back and bullnosing of the rendering
as a condition of a guarantee. His omission to make any reference to this feature is one of
the factors which leaves me uncertain as to whether in truth he gave any close thought
whether or not there was a damp-proof course.
    In my view it is not necessary to consider the other matters which Mr Caird raised. If
*h* the plaintiffs' case does not succeed on the material which I have so far recited, it will not
succeed on the remainder. I should, however, say that I have the gravest doubts about
some of Mr Caird's figures for damp readings. If they were accurate and representative
of the position as it would have been found by Mr Jones, the carpets (and the house was
fully carpeted) would almost inevitably have been damp, mouldy and probably smelly:
they were none of these things. It may be that his figures are in part explained by the
*j* plaster having been removed from the walls and the long period of non-occupation of
the house. Equally, I do not believe that there is a great deal of importance in the
criticisms of the way that he expressed himself about the damp readings and the various
scales on his damp meter. Certainly any errors which he may have made were detected
in sufficient time so that they do not impinge on my judgment.
    Consonant with the view that he had formed, Mr Jones recommended 'that an
undertaking is obtained that a reputable timber Specialist is engaged to eradicate the rot'.

Mr Jones said that he had estimated that the cost of remedying the rot, together with the
ancillary work to the rendering, would not be above £350 and he would have  *a*
recommended a retention unless he thought the works would have cost above £500.

Those being the facts of the matter, I turn to consider whether they give rise to
liability.

The first question is: what is the extent of the service that a surveyor must provide in
performing a building society valuation? The service is, in fact, described in the Halifax's
brochure. It is a valuation and not a survey, but any valuation is necessarily governed by  *b*
condition. The inspection is, of necessity, a limited one. Both the expert surveyors who
gave evidence before me agreed that with a house of this size they would allow about
half an hour for their inspection on site. That time does not admit of moving furniture,
or of lifting carpets, especially where they are nailed down. In my judgment, it must be
accepted that where a surveyor undertakes a scheme 1 valuation it is understood that he
is making a limited appraisal only. It is, however, an appraisal by a skilled professional  *c*
man. It is inherent in any standard fee work that some cases will colloquially be 'winners'
and others 'losers' from the professional man's point of view. The fact that in an
individual case he may need to spend two or three times as long as he would have
expected, or as the fee structure would have contemplated, is something that he must
accept. His duty to take reasonable care in providing a valuation remains the root of his
obligation. In an extreme case, as Mr Caird said, a surveyor might refuse to value on the  *d*
agreed fee basis, though any surveyor who too often refused to take the rough with the
smooth would not improve his reputation. If, in a particular case, the proper valuation
of a £19,000 house needs two hours' work, that is what the surveyor must devote to it.

The second aspect of the problem concerns moving furniture and lifting carpets. Here
again, as it seems to me, the position that the law adopts is simple. If a surveyor misses a
defect because its signs are hidden, that is a risk that his client must accept. But, if there  *e*
is specific ground for suspicion and the trail of suspicion leads behind furniture or under
carpets, the surveyor must take reasonable steps to follow the trail until he has all the
information which it is reasonable for him to have before making his valuation. Thus, I
think it is entirely reasonable for Mr Jones to say that he took his damp readings along
the walls at intervals of three or four feet unless there was furniture in the way, but it  *f*
does not follow from that that he was relieved from moving furniture if an evident
defect extended behind it.

The next and central question is whether the defendants owed a duty to the plaintiffs
in respect of the care with which they performed the valuation. Counsel for the
defendants submits that the plaintiffs were outside the scope of the defendants' duty of
care. She submits that the scope of a duty is not to be found in any broad concept of  *g*
neighbourhood nor, now, in the test proposed by Park J in *Yianni v Edwin Evans & Sons
(a firm)* [1981] 3 All ER 592, [1982] QB 438. She submits that that case was wrongly
decided and should not be followed. She submits that the correct test is a tripartite one:
there must be proved the fact of reliance, the reasonableness of reliance and the
foreseeability of reliance. I will dispose at once of the fact of reliance for it is not in
question that the plaintiffs did rely on the valuation provided by the defendants.  *h*

*Yianni v Edwin Evans & Sons (a firm)* was discussed and distinguished by the Court of
Appeal in *Harris v Wyre Forest DC* [1988] 1 All ER 691, [1988] QB 835. The Court of
Appeal declined to consider whether *Yianni*'s case was correctly decided, although Kerr LJ
expressed certain reservations.

Park J had been guided in formulating his test by a passage in Lord Wilberforce's
speech in *Anns v Merton London Borough* [1977] 2 All ER 492 at 498–499, [1978] AC 728  *j*
at 751–752, among other statements of the law. That passage has since received detailed
analysis by the Privy Council in *Yuen Kun-yeu v A-G of Hong Kong* [1987] 2 All ER 705,
[1988] AC 175. In these circumstances and since part of the foundation of Park J's test
has been further explained, I believe that, notwithstanding the fact that *Yianni*'s case has
been followed in other cases, I should adopt the test framed by Nourse LJ in *Harris v
Wyre Forest DC* [1988] 1 All ER 691 at 696–697, [1988] QB 835 at 844. Having cited

from the speech of Lord Pearce in *Hedley Byrne & Co Ltd v Heller & Partners Ltd* [1963] 2
*a*  All ER 575 at 617, [1964] AC 465 at 539, Nourse LJ continued:

> 'That, I respectfully think, is a valuable statement because, in dealing with the
> first and perhaps less familiar kind of difficulty, it highlights a requirement which
> is common to all those cases where the necessary proximity has been found. The
> circumstances must be such that the maker of the statement ought reasonably to
> recognise both the importance which will be attached to it by the recipient and his
*b*  own answerability to the recipient in making it. In *Hedley Byrne & Co Ltd v Heller &
> Partners Ltd* itself and in other cases this requirement has been expressed as a
> voluntary assumption of responsibility or the like, but it has been held that in some
> circumstances the liability can extend to a case where the maker of the statement is
> under a duty to make it: see *Ministry of Housing and Local Government v Sharp* [1970]
*c*  1 All ER 1009, [1970] 2 QB 223. I would therefore frame the essential question
> which we have to decide in these terms: were the circumstances such that the
> defendants ought reasonably to have recognised both the importance which would
> be attached to Mr Lee's valuation by the plaintiffs and their own answerability to
> them in making it?'

Nourse LJ then addressed himself to the disclaimer of liability, as I shall have to consider
*d*  the suggested disclaimer in this case.

I believe, therefore, that counsel for the defendants is essentially right, although I
would prefer not to subdivide the question but rather take this test: were the
circumstances such that the defendants ought reasonably to have recognised both the
importance which would be attached to their valuation by the plaintiffs and their own
answerability to the plaintiffs in making it? Although the structure of the case was
*e*  different in *Harris v Wyre Forest DC* in that the plaintiffs there were suing the lenders,
with the lenders' servant as second defendant, there is no reason why the same test should
not apply here.

I turn first to the copy of the valuation which was provided to Mr and Mrs Roberts,
together with the covering notes. I have already remarked on the fact that a special copy
is provided for the applicant and that it is one page of a multipart set typed by the valuers.
*f*  The accompanying notes to which the applicants' attention is drawn are:

> '1. The enclosed report is a copy of the Valuers Report and Valuation For
> Mortgage prepared by the Society's Valuer solely for the use of the Society in
> assessing the adequacy of the proposed security for mortgage purposes and in
> determining the amount (if any) to be advanced on mortgage.
*g*      2. The report has been prepared in a form specifically designed to enable the
> Society to deal with your application as quickly as possible. The inspection by the
> Society's Valuer was not a survey and it is possible that there are defects in the
> property which were not discovered by the Valuer in the course of his limited
> inspection. There may also be defects which are not shown in the report as they are
> not significant to the Society in assessing the adequacy of the security for mortgage
*h*  purposes. *You should not therefore assume that the defects shown (if any) are the only defects
> which may be present in the property.*
>      3. If the valuer has suggested that the Society make a retention from the advance
> in respect of improvements or repairs you should satisfy yourself as to the cost of
> carrying out the necessary repair work as the cost of these works could exceed the
> amount of the suggested retention.
*j*      4. If you have not already done so, you should consider what steps you need to
> take to satisfy yourself as to the condition of the property. If you desire a survey for
> your own protection you should consult a surveyor on your own account. YOU ARE
> RECOMMENDED TO DO THIS. The valuer who prepared the report and valuation for the
> Society may be prepared to undertake a private survey on your behalf and if so the
> Society will be pleased to put you in touch with him if you wish to consider using
> his services for this purpose.

5. The valuation figure shown on the Valuers Report and Valuation For Mortgage is the valuer's opinion of the open market value of the property (in some cases adjusted to allow for works which are to be carried out). As the valuation has been carried out for mortgage purposes, it should not be regarded as the only valid valuation figure relating to the property, but nevertheless it is upon this valuation figure that the Society will make its assessment for mortgage purposes.

6. Where the property is being purchased no warranty is given that the purchase price is reasonable.

7. The Report and Valuation is for the Society's use and for your information only and is not to be disclosed to anybody except your own professional advisers.'

I was not told how the fee structure operated in the event that the applicant chose to go to the same valuer for a 'private survey', but I shall assume that he would be charged for a scheme 2 survey, being credited with the cost of the scheme 1 which had already been paid. In para 7 there is a contrast between 'the Society's use' and 'your information only'. I am not here dealing with a point of construction, but I think it is unlikely that the ordinary applicant would read any distinction into that contrast. The whole tenor of the warnings contained in the notes is as to the limited nature of the inspection on which the valuation was based and on the desirability of a survey proper being undertaken. However, any significance which there might be in the contrast is reduced when in the last paragraph there is contemplated a disclosure to professional advisers; this must be for the purpose of some use being made of the information, for it could scarcely be for light reading only. Stress is laid on the different needs of the society and the applicant, but in the final analysis both the society and the applicant are concerned whether the property is worth the amount that is proposed to be paid.

In *Yianni v Edwin Evans & Sons (a firm)* [1981] 3 All ER 592, [1982] QB 438 the evidence showed that between 10% and 15% only of purchasers who bought with the assistance of building societies had their own surveys. The evidence in the present case is, unsurprisingly, similar. Miss Wetherson said that at that time not many scheme 2 valuations were being taken up. Mr Jones, in describing the pattern of his work, said that in the average month he would do 35 to 40 scheme 1 valuations, 6 scheme 2 surveys and only 1 full survey. Thus in the Llandudno area some 13 to 15% of purchasers were having their own survey.

In my judgment there is clearly a sufficient proximity between the defendants and the plaintiffs in the present case. The defendants undoubtedly knew from the very fact that a scheme 1 survey was being undertaken that it was highly unlikely that the plaintiffs were relying on some other professionally based information as to the property. They knew clearly of the terms of the Halifax's notes to applicants and therefore that there was no disclaimer of liability. Mr Jackson, in the course of his evidence, said that in 1984 there was a realisation among surveyors that valuations were read and relied on by borrowers. I am fully satisfied that there has been here established a duty on the part of the defendants towards the plaintiffs to take reasonable care in the making of their valuation.

I turn to the question of breach. The only breach suggested is in relation to Mr Jones's assessment of the rot and its cause. His description is a laconic one: 'A certain amount of rot'. The likelihood is that the skirting board was badly infested in May 1984. Although the speed at which dry rot can spread is not accurately predictable, it can be as fast as 14 mm a week. There are no circumstances proved here which would suggest any reawakening of dormant rot. There was no installation of central heating, no flood or dripping pipe, no carpeting of a previously uncarpeted area. The house had been superficially well cared for. This does not appear to have been the case of a house whose previous occupiers could not afford to heat it, where the arrival of a new owner with the inclination and means to maintain a higher temperature may trigger the spread of rot. In any event, the months between the survey and the discovery of the outbreak were summer and autumn months when a change in the living pattern of the occupants would be of less significance.

Although I recognise that there were features suggesting residual dampness, particularly
*a* the absence of spalling and the fact that the new plaster which had been put on the lower
part of this wall made it the more difficult to detect the extent to which dampness was
rising up it, I consider that Mr Jones made inadequate investigations to determine
whether the rot was indeed so localised as he, as I believe, assumed. Mr Jackson agreed,
as it seems to me wholly correctly, that a surveyor must be conservative if there is
something present in a house which might be serious. He said that if there was evidence
*b* of past repairs and yet evidence of rot in one room there should be a conservative
approach, and that the surveyor should recommend further investigation. His own test
was that if the repairs were likely to cost 10% of the proposed purchase price he would
certainly have recommended a retention. He said that if he was uncertain as to the
position he would recommend a retention and further investigation. In that event, as he
described it, the building society would require quotations to be obtained before
*c* proceeding with the matter. In my judgment Mr Jones was wanting in that he did not
take any test of the wood blocks of the floor, a test which I am satisfied would have
revealed some dampness to put him on further inquiry, even if there were not traces of
rot itself. I was also very surprised by his evidence that he did not trace the rot further
because of the presence of a piece of furniture. In my judgment, he failed to appreciate
the difference between his ordinary duty in relation to parts of the structure which were
*d* hidden by furniture or by carpets and his duty where there was what I have called a trail
of suspicion. I am satisfied that there was in this case a lack of reasonable care, albeit
restricted to this one matter.

What is the quantum of the plaintiffs' damages? It is agreed from the evidence which
I have just recited and from the figures to which I now turn that in this case there ought
to have been the recommendation of a retention, with or without further investigations.
*e* I am satisfied that if a retention had been called for this purchase would not have gone
through, for the Roberts were unable to fund any part of the purchase themselves. I
cannot think that any other lender would offer any bridging facilities in the then existing
circumstances. It follows, therefore, that this purchase would not have gone through.

Before I turn to the question of quantum, I should record that the Roberts were treated
*f* with the greatest consideration and, indeed, generosity, by the Halifax when their plight
was known. They are now housed in another property, which they are purchasing
through the Halifax, but in the interim their position was very difficult. They stayed in
Delfryn for a total of 13 months and in August 1985 removed to Mrs Roberts's mother's
home. They had to do so because by then Mrs Roberts was having a baby and their advice
was that Delfryn was then no place for a young baby; I am sure this advice was right.
*g* They were staying with Mrs Roberts's mother when their first child was born on
14 October 1985 and remained there for about 12 months. Delfryn was finally sold by
the building society in July 1986 for £14,000.

There was much discussion before me whether this was a fair market price or not, and
whether it was influenced by the fact that the purchaser had relations in the immediate
vicinity, but I am satisfied that that was then its value. The dispute between the two
*h* surveyors as to the value of the house in 1984 is quite marked. Mr Caird said that it was
worth something in the order of £12,000 whereas Mr Jackson valued it at £17,000. In
the event the house was sold, as I have said, for £14,000 in July 1986. This is not
necessarily a good mark of its value two years earlier because the dry rot would
undoubtedly have extended a great deal in the interim and there was wage and cost
inflation which would have affected the remedying of the rot and of the associated
*j* defects. I am satisfied that there was no very great change in house prices in the area over
those two years, so that that element does not require particular consideration. I had
supposed that there must be an element of 'blight' in a house which had had so serious a
defect, but I am satisfied by the evidence that this is probably counteracted by the fact
that today one may be reasonably confident of eradicating dry rot and the execution of
substantial works always offers a purchaser an opportunity to give effect to his own ideas
of how he would like the house to be. It is clear, none the less, that the execution of these

repairs would, particularly in the case of the installation of a new chemical damp-proof
course, provide some element of amelioration.

[His Lordship then considered the evidence relating to the work that would have been
needed to put the house in good order and which therefore would be reflected in its
value, and continued:] I find that the value of Delfryn at the time of survey was £15,500.

The plaintiffs claim for disturbance and disruption. It is not submitted that there
cannot be such a claim, and such a claim was allowed by Park J in *Yianni v Edwin Evans &
Sons (a firm)* [1981] 3 All ER 592, [1982] QB 438. Each assessment must be made on the
facts of the individual case and there can be nothing in the nature of a conventional
award. In my judgment the disruption to this young couple was extreme and in the
result a particularly upsetting one. Whereas they might have hoped to bring their new
baby back to their home they were denied that and had instead to live with Mrs Roberts's
mother. There is no suggestion that they were not welcome there, although there were
the usual discords. In my judgment, the difference in their situation merits an award of
£1,500.

Accordingly, in my judgment, the plaintiffs are entitled to recover £5,500.

*Judgment for the plaintiffs for £5,500.*

Solicitors: *Cobbett Leak Almond*, Manchester (for the plaintiffs); *Pinsent & Co*, Birmingham
(for the defendants).

K Mydeen Esq   Barrister.

# Smith v Eric S Bush (a firm)
# Harris and another v Wyre Forest District Council and another

HOUSE OF LORDS

LORD KEITH OF KINKEL, LORD BRANDON OF OAKBROOK, LORD TEMPLEMAN, LORD GRIFFITHS AND
LORD JAUNCEY OF TULLICHETTLE

6, 7, 8, 9, 13, 14, 15, 16 FEBRUARY, 20 APRIL 1989

*Negligence – Surveyor – Duty to take care – Surveyor making report to building society or local
authority for mortgage application – Survey and valuation carried out negligently – Application
form and report containing disclaimer of responsibility for condition of property – Purchaser
relying on report – Surveyor knowing that purchaser likely to rely on report – Whether surveyor
owing purchaser duty to exercise reasonable skill and care in carrying out valuation – Whether
disclaimer reasonable – Whether disclaimer effective to exclude liability – Whether surveyor liable
for negligence – Unfair Contract Terms Act 1977, s 2(2).*

*Contract – Unfair terms – Exclusion of liability for negligence – Surveyor – Surveyor making
report to building society or local authority for mortgage application – Survey carried out
negligently – Application form and report containing disclaimer of responsibility – Factors to be
considered when considering reasonableness – Whether disclaimer reasonable – Unfair Contract
Terms Act 1977, s 2(2).*

In two cases the questions arose whether a surveyor instructed by a mortgagee to value a
house owed the prospective purchaser a duty in tort to carry out the valuation with
reasonable skill and care and whether a disclaimer of liability by or on behalf of the
surveyor for negligence was effective.

In the first case the respondent applied to a building society for a mortgage to enable
her to purchase a house. The building society, which was under a statutory duty to obtain
a written valuation report on the house, instructed the appellants, a firm of surveyors, to

inspect the house and carry out the valuation. The respondent paid the society an
a   inspection fee of £38·89 and signed an application form which stated that the society
would provide her with a copy of the report and mortgage valuation obtained by it. The
form contained a disclaimer to the effect that neither the society nor its surveyor
warranted that the report and valuation would be accurate and that the report and
valuation would be supplied without any acceptance of responsibility. In due course the
respondent received a copy of the report, which contained a disclaimer in terms similar
b   to those on the application form. The report, which valued the house at £16,500, stated
that no essential repairs were required. In reliance on the report and without obtaining
an independent survey the respondent purchased the house for £18,000, having accepted
an advance of £3,500 from the society. In their inspection of the house the appellants
had observed that the first floor chimney breasts had been removed but they had not
checked to see whether the chimneys above were adequately supported. Eighteen
c   months after the respondent purchased the house, bricks from the chimneys collapsed
and fell through the roof causing considerable damage. The respondent brought an
action against the appellants claiming damages for negligence. The judge held that the
appellants were liable and awarded the respondent damages. The Court of Appeal
affirmed his decision, holding that the disclaimer was not fair and reasonable and was
ineffective under the Unfair Contract Terms Act 1977. The appellants appealed to the
d   House of Lords.
    In the second case the appellants applied to the local authority for a mortgage to enable
them to purchase a house. The local authority, which was under a statutory duty to
obtain a valuation before advancing any money, decided to carry out the valuation
themselves and for that purpose instructed their valuation surveyor. The appellants
signed an application form which stated that the valuation was confidential and was
e   intended solely for the information of the local authority and that no responsibility
whatsoever was implied or accepted by the local authority for the value or condition of
the property by reason of the inspection and report. After receiving the surveyor's
valuation of the house at the asking price of £9,450, the local authority offered to advance
the appellants 90% of that sum subject to certain minor repairs being done to the house.
f   The appellants, assuming that the house was worth at least the amount of the valuation
and that the surveyor had found no serious defects, purchased the property for £9,000
without obtaining an independent survey. Three years later they discovered that the
house was subject to settlement, was virtually unsaleable and could only be repaired, if at
all, at a cost of more than the purchase price. The appellants brought an action against
the local authority and their surveyor claiming damages for negligence. The judge
g   upheld their claim but the Court of Appeal reversed his decision on the ground that the
notice had effectively excluded liability. The appellants appealed to the House of Lords.

**Held** – (1) A valuer who valued a house for a building society or local authority for the
purposes of a mortgage application for a typical house purchase, knowing that the
mortgagee would probably, and the mortgagor would certainly, rely on the valuation,
h   and knowing that the mortgagor was an intending purchaser of the house and had paid
for the valuation, owed a duty of care to both parties to carry out his valuation with
reasonable skill and care. It made no difference whether the valuer was employed by the
mortgagee or acted on his own account or was employed by a firm of independent
valuers since he was discharging the duties of a professional man on whose skill and
judgment he knew the purchaser would be relying. Furthermore, the fact that the local
j   authority or building society was under a statutory duty to value the house did not
prevent the valuer coming under a contractual or tortious duty to the purchaser. The
extent of the liability was, however, limited to the purchaser of the house and did not
extend to subsequent purchasers (see p 517 f to h, p 520 a b, p 522 j to p 523 a d to g,
p 526 a, p 529 f to h, p 526 c to 537 b, p 541 h c e to p 542 d and p 544 f g, post); dictum
of Denning LJ in Candler v Crane Christmas & Co [1951] 1 All ER at 433–434 applied;
Yianni v Edwin & Sons (a firm) [1981] 3 All ER 592 approved.

(2) However, the valuer could disclaim liability to exercise reasonable skill and care
by an express exclusion clause but such a disclaimer made by or on behalf of the valuer
constituted a notice which was subject to the 1977 Act and therefore had to satisfy the
requirement in s 2(2)*a* of that Act of reasonableness to be effective. In considering
whether a disclaimer might be relied on, the general pattern of house purchases and the
extent of the work and liability accepted by the valuer had to be borne in mind. Having
regard to the high costs of houses and the high interest rates charged to borrowers, it
would not be fair and reasonable for mortgagees and valuers to impose on purchasers the
risk of loss arising as a result of the incompetence or carelessness on the part of valuers. It
followed therefore the disclaimers were not effective to exclude liability for the negligence
of the valuers, and accordingly the first appeal would be dismissed and the second appeal
would be allowed (see p 517 *f* to *h*, p 524 *c d f*, p 526 *e* to *h*, p 527 *f j*, p 528 *d e*, p 529 *j*,
p 531 *b* to *j*, p 532 *c* to *e* and p 543 *b c*, post).

Per curiam. Where a surveyor is asked to survey industrial property, large blocks of
flats or very expensive houses for mortgage purposes, where prudence would seem to
demand that the purchaser obtain his own survey to guide him in his purchase it may be
reasonable for him to limit his liability to the purchaser or exclude it altogether (see
p 517 *f* to *h*, p 528 *d e*, p 531 *j* to p 532 *a* and p 543 *c*, post).

Decision of the Court of Appeal in *Smith v Eric S Bush (a firm)* [1987] 3 All ER 179
affirmed.

Decision of the Court of Appeal in *Harris v Wyre Forest DC* [1988] 1 All ER 691
reversed.

**Notes**

For the duty of care generally, see 34 Halsbury's Laws (4th edn) para 5, and for cases on
the subject, see 36(1) Digest (Reissue) 17–32, 34–103.

For agreements to exclude or restrict liability for negligence, see 34 Halsbury's Laws
(4th edn) para 67.

For the Unfair Contract Terms Act 1977, s 2, see 11 Halsbury's Statutes (4th edn) 217.

**Cases referred to in opinions**

*Anns v Merton London Borough* [1977] 2 All ER 492, [1978] AC 728, [1977] 2 WLR 1024,
   HL.
*Candler v Crane Christmas & Co* [1951] 1 All ER 426, [1951] 2 KB 164, CA.
*Cann v Willson* (1888) 39 Ch D 39.
*Curran v Northern Ireland Co-Ownership Housing Association Ltd* (1986) 8 NIJB 1, NI CA;
   *rvsd in part* [1987] 2 All ER 13, [1987] AC 718, [1987] 2 WLR 1043, HL.
*George v Skivington* (1869) LR 5 Exch 1.
*Hedley Byrne & Co Ltd v Heller & Partners Ltd* [1963] 2 All ER 575, [1964] AC 465, [1963]
   3 WLR 101, HL.
*Langridge v Levy* (1837) 2 M & W 519, [1835–42] All ER Rep 586, 150 ER 863; *affd*
   (1838) 4 M & W 337, [1835–42] All ER Rep 586, 150 ER 1458, Ex Ch.
*Ministry of Housing and Local Government v Sharp* [1970] 1 All ER 1009, [1970] 2 QB 223,
   [1970] 2 WLR 802, CA.
*Nocton v Lord Ashburton* [1914] AC 932, [1914–15] All ER Rep 45, HL.
*Odder v Westbourne Park Building Society* (1955) 165 EG 261.
*Phillips Products Ltd v Hyland* (1984) [1987] 2 All ER 620, [1987] 1 WLR 659, CA.
*Roberts v J Hampson & Co* [1989] 2 All ER 504.
*Ultramares Corp v Touche* (1931) 255 NY 170, NY Ct of Apps.
*Woods v Martins Bank Ltd* [1958] 3 All ER 166, [1959] 1 QB 55, [1958] 1 WLR 1018.
*Yianni v Edwin Evans & Sons (a firm)* [1981] 3 All ER 592, [1982] QB 438, [1981] 3 WLR
   843.

---

*a*   Section 2(2) is set out at p 519 *j*, post

## Appeals

a                              *Smith v Eric S Bush (a firm)*

The defendants, Eric S Bush (a firm) (the surveyors), appealed with the leave of the Appeal
Committee of the House of Lords given on 29 October 1987 against the decision of the
Court of Appeal (Dillon, Glidewell LJJ and Sir Edward Eveleigh) ([1987] 3 All ER 179,
[1988] QB 743) on 13 March 1987 dismissing an appeal by the surveyors against the
decision of Mr Gerald Draycott sitting as an assistant recorder in the Norwich County
b   Court on 17 April 1986 whereby in an action by the plaintiff, Jean Patricia Smith (Mrs
Smith), against the surveyors for damages for professional negligence in relation to a
survey carried out by their senior partner, Mr Cannell, in relation to 242 Silver Road,
Norwich, he awarded Mrs Smith the sum of £4,379·97 damages including interest. The
facts are set out in the opinion of Lord Templeman.

c                          *Harris and anor v Wyre Forest DC and anor*

The plaintiffs, Adam Charles Harris and Kim Harris (Mr and Mrs Harris), appealed with
the leave of the Court of Appeal against the decision of that court (Kerr, Nourse LJJ and
Caulfield J) ([1988] 1 All ER 691, [1988] QB 835) on 17 December 1987 allowing the
appeal of the defendants, Wyre Forest District Council and Trevor James Lee, against the
d   decision of Schiemann J ([1987] 1 EGLR 231) on 24 November 1986 whereby in an
action brought by Mr and Mrs Harris against the council and Mr Lee for damages for
negligence in relation to a valuation carried out by the latter in respect of 74 George
Street, Kidderminster, the judge awarded Mr and Mrs Harris the sum of £12,000
damages. The facts are set out in the opinion of Lord Templeman.

*Anthony D Colman QC, Malcolm Stitcher* and *David Platt* for Mr and Mrs Harris.
e   *Piers Ashworth QC* and *Nicholas J Worsley* for the council and Mr Lee.
*Nigel Hague QC* and *Jane Davies* for the surveyors.
*Robert Seabrook QC* and *Philip Havers* for Mrs Smith.

Their Lordships took time for consideration.

f   20 April. The following opinions were delivered.

**LORD KEITH OF KINKEL.** My Lords, I have had the opportunity of considering in
draft the speeches to be delivered by my noble and learned friends Lord Templeman,
Lord Griffiths and Lord Jauncey. I agree with them, and for the reasons they give would
allow the appeal in *Harris v Wyre Forest DC* and dismiss that in *Smith v Eric S Bush (a firm)*.
g

**LORD BRANDON OF OAKBROOK.** My Lords, for the reasons set out in the
speeches to be delivered by my noble and learned friends Lord Templeman, Lord
Griffiths and Lord Jauncey, I would allow the appeal in *Harris v Wyre Forest DC* and
dismiss the appeal in *Smith v Eric S Bush (a firm)*.

h   **LORD TEMPLEMAN.** My Lords, these appeals involve consideration of three
questions. The first question is whether a valuer instructed by a building society or other
mortgagee to value a house, knowing that his valuation will probably be relied on by the
prospective purchaser and mortgagor of the house, owes to the purchaser in tort a duty
to exercise reasonable skill and care in carrying out the valuation unless the valuer
j   disclaims liability. If so, the second question is whether a disclaimer of liability by or on
behalf of the valuer is a notice which purports to exclude liability for negligence within
the Unfair Contract Terms Act 1977 and is, therefore, ineffective unless it satisfies the
requirement of reasonableness. If so, the third question is whether, in the absence of
special circumstances, it is fair and reasonable for the valuer to rely on the notice
excluding liability.

In *Harris v Wyre Forest DC* the first appeal now under consideration, Mr and Mrs Harris wished to purchase 74 George Street, Kidderminster, and needed a mortgage. *a* They applied to the council. By s 43 of the Housing (Financial Provisions) Act 1958 (as amended by s 37 of the Local Government Act 1974), the council were authorised to advance money to any persons for the purpose of acquiring a house, provided:

'... (2) ... the local authority ... shall satisfy themselves that the house ... to be acquired is ... or will be made in all respects fit for human habitation ...
(3) ... (e) the advance shall not be made except after a valuation duly made on *b* behalf of the local authority ...'

Mr and Mrs Harris signed the application form supplied by the council and that form contained the following declaration and notice:

'I/WE enclose herewith the Valuation Fee & Administration Fee £22. I/WE *c* understand that this fee is not returnable even if the Council do not eventually make an advance and that the Valuation is confidential and is intended solely for the information of Wyre Forest District Council in determining what advance, if any, may be made on the security and that no responsibility whatsoever is implied or accepted by the Council for the value or condition of the property by reason of such inspection and report. (You are advised for your own protection to instruct your *d* own Surveyor/Architect to inspect the property) I/WE agree that the Valuation Report is the property of the Council and that I/WE cannot require its production ...'

The council decided to carry out their own valuation and for that purpose instructed their employee, the second respondent, Mr Lee. After receiving Mr Lee's valuation, the *e* council made a written offer to advance £8,505 to Mr and Mrs Harris to be secured on a mortgage of the house and subject to their undertaking to carry out within 12 months the works detailed in the schedule to the offer. The schedule was in these terms:

'ESSENTIAL REPAIRS (1) Obtain report for District Council from [Midlands Electricity Board] regarding electrics and carry out any recommendations. (2) Make *f* good mortar fillets to Extension.'

Mr and Mrs Harris assumed from the council's offer that, as was the case, the house had been valued at £8,505 at the least, and that the valuer had not found serious defects and they therefore accepted the offer and entered into a contract to purchase the house for £9,000. Three years later, Mr and Mrs Harris discovered that the house was defective; one builder quoted £13,000 to carry out work to make the house safe. Another builder *g* refused to tender for the work, which he regarded as impractical and unsafe. The damages suffered by Mr and Mrs Smith, including interest up to the date of trial, were agreed at £12,000. The trial judge was satisfied that Mr Lee did not exercise reasonable skill and care and that the council, as his employer, were vicariously liable for Mr Lee's failure and he therefore ordered the council to pay £12,000. The Court of Appeal allowed the appeal of the council on the grounds that by the notice contained in the application *h* form signed by Mr and Mrs Harris the council had avoided incurring liability. Mr and Mrs Harris now appeal.

In *Smith v Eric S Bush (a firm)*, the second appeal now under consideration, Mrs Smith wished to purchase 242 Silver Road, Norwich, and needed a mortgage. She applied to the Abbey National Building Society. By s 25 of the Building Societies Act 1962, now s 13 of the Building Societies Act 1986, the Abbey National was bound to obtain 'a written *i* report prepared and signed by a competent and prudent person who ... is experienced in the matters relevant to the determination of the value' of the house, dealing with the value of the house and with any matter likely to affect the value of the house (see s 25(2)(a)). Mrs Smith paid to the Abbey National an inspection fee of £36·89 and signed the application form, which contained the following declaration and notice:

a
'I/We accept that the Society will provide me/us with a copy of the report and mortgage valuation which the Society will obtain in relation to this application. I/We understand that the Society is not the agent of the Surveyor or firm of Surveyors and that I am making no agreement with the Surveyor or firm of Surveyors. I/We understand that neither the Society nor the Surveyor or the firm of Surveyors will warrant, represent or give any assurance to me/us that the statements, conclusions and opinions expressed or implied in the report and mortgage evaluation

b
will be accurate or valid and the Surveyor(s) report will be supplied without any acceptance of responsibility on their part to me/us'

The Abbey National instructed the appellant firm, Eric S Bush (the surveyors), to carry out the valuation. The surveyors valued the house at £16,500 and the report contained the following paragraph:

c
'11. REPAIRS RECOMMENDED AS A CONDITION OF MORTGAGE: No essential repairs are required. We noted a number of items of disrepair in the building which we have taken into account in our valuation, but which are not considered to be essential for mortgage purposes.'

A copy of the report was supplied to Mrs Smith by the Abbey National.

d
In reliance on the report, Mrs Smith accepted an advance of £3,500 from the Abbey National and entered into a contract to purchase the house for £18,000. Eighteen months later, bricks from the chimneys collapsed and fell through the roof into the loft and the main bedroom and ceilings on the first floor. The collapse was due to the fact that two chimney breasts had been removed from the first floor, leaving the chimney breasts in the loft and the chimneys unsupported. Mr Cannell, who carried out the inspection for

e
the surveyors and was a chartered surveyor, had observed the removal of the first floor chimney breasts but had not checked to see that the chimneys above were adequately supported.

The trial judge was satisfied that Mr Cannell had not exercised reasonable skill and care and that the surveyors were liable for his negligence to Mrs Smith and awarded her £4,379·97 damages including interest. The judge ignored the notice contained in the

f
application and signed by Mrs Smith whereby the Abbey National disclaimed liability on the part of the surveyors. The Court of Appeal (Dillon, Glidewell LJJ and Sir Edward Eveleigh) ([1987] 3 All ER 179, [1988] QB 743) held that the disclaimer was not fair and reasonable and was ineffective under the Unfair Contract Terms Act 1977; it accordingly affirmed the award of damages made by the judge. The surveyors now appeal.

As I have indicated therefore, the three questions involved in these appeals are, first,

g
whether the council's valuer was liable to Mr and Mrs Harris in negligence and whether the surveyors were liable to Mrs Smith in negligence, second, whether, if negligence applies, the notices excluding liability fall within the ambit of the Unfair Contract Terms Act 1977 and, third, whether it is fair and reasonable for the valuers to rely on the notices.

Section 1(1) of the 1977 Act defines 'negligence' as the breach—

h
'(a) of any obligation, arising from the express or implied terms of a contract, to take reasonable care or exercise reasonable skill in the performance of the contract; (b) of any common law duty to take reasonable care or exercise reasonable skill . . .'

Section 2 of the Act provides:

j
'(1) A person cannot by reference to any contract term or to a notice . . . exclude or restrict his liability for death or personal injury resulting from negligence.
(2) In the case of other loss or damage, a person cannot so exclude or restrict his liability for negligence except in so far as the term or notice satisfies the requirement of reasonableness.'

The common law imposes on a person who contracts to carry out an operation an obligation to exercise reasonable skill and care. A plumber who mends a burst pipe is

liable for his incompetence or negligence whether or not he has been expressly required
to be careful. The law implies a term in the contract which requires the plumber to
exercise reasonable skill and care in his calling. The common law also imposes on a
person who carries out an operation an obligation to exercise reasonable skill and care
where there is no contract. Where the relationship between the operator and a person
who suffers injury or damage is sufficiently proximate and where the operator should
have foreseen that carelessness on his part might cause harm to the injured person, the
operator is liable in the tort of negligence.

Manufacturers and providers of services and others seek to protect themselves against
liability for negligence by imposing terms in contracts or by giving notice that they will
not accept liability in contract or in tort. Consumers who have need of manufactured
articles and services are not in a position to bargain. The Unfair Contract Terms Act 1977
prohibits any person excluding or restricting liability for death or personal injury
resulting from negligence. The Act also contains a prohibition against the exclusion or
restriction of liability for negligence which results in loss or damage unless the terms of
exclusion or the notice of exclusion satisfies the requirements of reasonableness.

These two appeals are based on allegations of negligence in circumstances which are
akin to contract. Mr and Mrs Harris paid £22 to the council for a valuation. The council
employed, and therefore paid, Mr Lee, for whose services as a valuer the council are
vicariously liable. Mrs Smith paid £36·89 to the Abbey National for a report and
valuation and the Abbey National paid the surveyors for the report and valuation. In
each case the valuer knew or ought to have known that the purchaser would only
contract to purchase the house if the valuation was satisfactory and that the purchaser
might suffer injury or damage or both if the valuer did not exercise reasonable skill and
care. In these circumstances I would expect the law to impose on the valuer a duty owed
to the purchaser to exercise reasonable skill and care in carrying out the valuation.

In *Cann v Willson* (1888) 39 Ch D 39, approved by this House in *Hedley Byrne & Co Ltd
v Heller & Partners Ltd* [1963] 2 All ER 575, [1964] AC 465, a valuer instructed by a
mortgagor sent his report to the mortgagee, who made an advance in reliance on the
valuation. The valuer was held liable in the tort of negligence to the mortgagee for
failing to carry out the valuation with reasonable care and skill.

A valuer who values property as a security for a mortgage is liable either in contract or
in tort to the mortgagee for any failure on the part of the valuer to exercise reasonable
skill and care in the valuation. The valuer is liable in contract if he receives instructions
from and is paid by the mortgagee. The valuer is liable in tort if he receives instructions
from and is paid by the mortgagor but knows that the valuation is for the purpose of a
mortgage and will be relied on by the mortgagee.

In *Odder v Westbourne Park Building Society* (1955) 165 EG 261 a purchaser paid a survey
fee to a building society, the survey was carried out by the chairman of the building
society and in the result the purchaser purchased the house for £4,000 with the help of
an advance of £3,000. There were serious defects and the house was unsaleable. There
was a disclaimer of liability for negligence for the survey in the mortgage offer but
Harman J held that the disclaimer—

> 'did no more than to state what the legal position would be even if it were not
> there but it did emphasise the matter and took much of the sting out of the
> plaintiff's allegation, which was to the effect that once the building society had had
> a survey made and were willing to lend money, everthing was all right and that she
> would not have entered on the transaction if they had not kept silent about the
> defects or been negligent in not discovering them. In view of the warning in the
> proposal form that grievance, if it were one, lost any of its justification.'

Since 1955 a good deal of water has passed under the negligence bridge.

In *Candler v Crane Christmas & Co* [1951] 1 All ER 426, [1951] 2 KB 164 the accountants
of a company showed their draft accounts to and discussed them with an investor who,
in reliance on the accounts, subscribed for shares in the company. Denning LJ, whose

dissenting judgment was subsequently approved in the *Hedley Byrne* case, found that the
*a* accounts owed a duty to the investor to exercise reasonable skill and care in preparing the
draft accounts. Denning LJ said ([1951] 1 All ER 426 at 431, [1951] 2 KB 164 at 176):

> 'If the matter were free from authority, I should have said that they clearly did
> owe a duty of care to him. They were professional accountants who prepared and
> put before him these accounts, knowing that he was going to be guided by them in
> making an investment in the company. On the face of those accounts he did make
*b* > the investment, whereas if the accounts had been carefully prepared, he would not
> have made the investment at all. The result is that he has lost his money.'

Denning LJ rejected the argument that—

> 'a duty to take care only arose where the result of a failure to take care will cause
> physical damage to persons or property . . . I can understand that in some cases of
*c* > financial loss there may not be a sufficiently proximate relationship to give rise to a
> duty of care, but if once the duty exists I cannot think that liability depends on the
> nature of the damage.'

(See [1951] 1 All ER 426 at 432–433, [1951] 2 KB 164 at 178–179.)
The duty of professional men 'is not merely a duty to use care in their reports. They
*d* have also a duty to use care in their work which results in their reports' (see [1951] 1 All
ER 426 at 433, [1951] 2 KB 164 at 179). The duty of an accountant is owed—

> 'to any third person to whom they themselves show the accounts, or to whom
> they know their employer is going to show the accounts, so as to induce him to
> invest money or take some other action on them. I do not think, however, the duty
*e* > can be extended still further so as to include strangers of whom they have heard
> nothing and to whom their employer without their knowledge may choose to show
> their accounts . . . The test of proximity in these cases is: Did the accountants know
> that the accounts were required for submission to the plaintiff and use by him?'

(See [1951] 1 All ER 426 at 434, [1951] 2 KB 164 at 180–181.)
Subject to the effect of any disclaimer of liability, these considerations appear to apply
*f* to the valuers in the present appeals.
In the *Hedley Byrne* case a bank which supplied a reference for a customer was held to
owe a duty of care to a stranger who relied on the reference but the bank escaped liability
because in the reference the bank expressly disclaimed liability. Lord Reid said ([1963] 2
All ER 575 at 583, [1964] AC 465 at 486):

> 'A reasonable man, knowing that he was being trusted or that his skill and
*g* > judgment were being relied on, would, I think, have three courses open to him. He
> could keep silent or decline to give the information or advice sought: or he could
> give an answer with a clear qualification that he accepted no responsibility for it or
> that it was given without that reflection or inquiry which a careful answer would
> require: or he could simply answer without any such qualification. If he chooses to
*h* > adopt the last course he must, I think, be held to have accepted some responsibility
> for his answer being given carefully, or to have accepted a relationship with the
> inquirer which requires him to exercise such care as the circumstances require.'

Lord Devlin rejected the argument that the maker of a careless statement is only under
a duty to be careful if the duty, which is contractual or fiduciary or arises from the
*j* relationship of proximity, causes physical damage to the person or property of the
plaintiff (see [1963] 2 All ER 575 at 601, [1964] AC 465 at 515). Lord Devlin also said
([1963] 2 All ER 575 at 610, [1964] AC 465 at 528–529):

> '. . . the categories of special relationships, which may give rise to a duty to take
> care in word as well as in deed, are not limited to contractual relationships or to
> relationships of fiduciary duty, but include also relationships which . . . are

"equivalent to contract" that is, where there is an assumption of responsibility in circumstances in which, but for the absence of consideration, there would be a *a* contract.'

In the present appeals the relationship between the valuer and the purchaser is 'akin to contract'. The valuer knows that the consideration which he receives derives from the purchaser and is passed on by the mortgagee, and the valuer also knows that the valuation will determine whether or not the purchaser buys the house.

In *Ministry of Housing and Local Government v Sharp* [1970] 1 All ER 1009, [1970] 2 QB *b* 223 the local authority was held liable to the ministry because of the failure of an employee of the authority to exercise reasonable skill and care in searching for entries in the local land charges register. The search certificate prepared by the clerk negligently failed to record a charge of £1,828 11s 5d in favour of the ministry. Lord Denning MR rejected the argument—
*c*

'that a duty to use due care (where there was no contract) only arose when there was a voluntary assumption of responsibility... Lord Reid in *Hedley Byrne & Co Ltd v Heller & Partners Ltd* [1963] 2 All ER 575 at 583, [1964] AC 465 at 487 and ... Lord Devlin ([1963] 2 All ER 575 at 610–611, [1964] AC 465 at 529)... used those words because of the special circumstances of that case (where the bank disclaimed responsibility). But they did not in any way mean to limit the general principle. In *d* my opinion the duty to use due care in a statement arises, not from any voluntary assumption of responsibility, but from the fact that the person making it knows, or ought to know, that others, being his neighbours in this regard, would act on the faith of the statement being accurate.'

(See [1970] 1 All ER 1009 at 1018–1019, [1970] 2 QB 223 at 268.) *e*
Salmon LJ said ([1970] 1 All ER 1009 at 1027–1028, [1970] 2 QB 223 at 279):

'I do not accept that, in all cases, the obligation to take reasonable care necessarily depends on the voluntary assumption of responsibility. Even if it did, I am far from satisfied that the council did not voluntarily assume responsibility in the present case. On the contrary, it seems to me that they certainly chose to undertake the duty *f* of searching the register and preparing the certificate. There was nothing to compel them to discharge this duty through their servant.'

In the present proceedings by Mr and Mrs Harris the council accepted the application form and the valuation fee and chose to conduct their duty of valuing the house through Mr Lee. In the case of Mrs Smith the surveyors first accepted the valuation fee derived from Mrs Smith and undertook the duty of preparing a report which they knew would *g* be shown to and relied on by Mrs Smith.

Counsel for the council and Mr Lee relied on the decision of the Court of Appeal of Northern Ireland in *Curran v Northern Ireland Co-ownership Housing Association Ltd*) (1986) 8 NIJB 1. On a preliminary issue the court held that a mortgagee of a house owed no duty of care to the purchaser in respect of a valuation. The purchaser's action against the valuer remains to be determined. Gibson LJ said (at 14) that in the *Hedley Byrne* type of *h* case—

'there must be an assumption of responsibility in circumstances in which, but for the absence of consideration, there would be a contract. Responsibility can only attach if the defendant's actions implied a voluntary undertaking to assume responsibility.' *j*

I agree that, by obtaining and disclosing a valuation, a mortgagee does not assume responsibility to the purchaser for that valuation. But in my opinion the valuer assumes responsibility to both mortgagee and purchaser by agreeing to carry out a valuation for mortgage purposes knowing that the valuation fee has been paid by the purchaser and knowing that the valuation will probably be relied on by the purchaser in order to decide

whether or not to enter into a contract to purchase the house. The valuer can escape the
*a* responsibility to exercise reasonable skill and care by an express exclusion clause, provided
the exclusion clause does not fall foul of the Unfair Contract Terms Act 1977. The Court
of Appeal also decided in *Curran's* case that a local authority which provides a house-
owner with a grant to carry out works of extension to his house might owe a duty of care
to a subsequent purchaser of the house to ensure that the works of extension are carried
in a manner free from defect; this House reversed the Court of Appeal on this point (see
*b* [1987] 2 All ER 13, [1987] 1 AC 718) but the speech of Lord Bridge dealt with the ambit
of *Anns v Merton London Borough* [1977] 2 All ER 492, [1978] AC 728 and not with the
duty of care which arises when the proximity between tortfeasor and victim is akin to
contract.

It was submitted by counsel for the council and Mr Lee that the valuation was prepared
in fulfilment of the statutory duty imposed on the council by s 43 of the Housing
*c* (Financial Provisions) Act 1958. Similarly, the valuation obtained by the Abbey National
was essential to enable them to fulfil their statutory duty imposed by the Building
Societies Act 1962. But in *Candler v Crane Christmas & Co* [1951] 1 All ER 426, [1951] 2
KB 164 the draft accounts were prepared for the company, which was compelled by
statute to produce accounts.

In the present appeals the statutory duty of the council to value the house did not in
*d* my opinion prevent the council coming under a contractual or tortious duty to Mr and
Mrs Harris, who were cognisant of the valuation and relied on the valuation. The
contractual duty of a valuer to value a house for the Abbey National did not prevent the
valuer coming under a tortious duty to Mrs Smith, who was furnished with a report of
the valuer and relied on the report.

In general, I am of the opinion that in the absence of a disclaimer of liability the valuer
*e* who values a house for the purpose of a mortgage, knowing that the mortgagee will rely
and the mortgagor will probably rely on the valuation, knowing that the purchaser
mortgagor has in effect paid for the valuation, is under a duty to exercise reasonable skill
and care and that duty is owed to both parties to the mortgage for which the valuation is
made. Indeed, in both the appeals now under consideration the existence of such a dual
duty is tacitly accepted and acknowledged because notices excluding liability for breach
*f* of the duty owed to the purchaser were drafted by the mortgagee and imposed on the
purchaser. In these circumstances it is necessary to consider the second question which
arises in these appeals, namely whether the disclaimers of liability are notices which fall
within the Unfair Contract Terms Act 1977.

In *Harris v Wyre Forest DC* the Court of Appeal (Kerr, Nourse LJJ and Caufield J)
accepted an argument that the 1977 Act did not apply because the council by their
*g* express disclaimer refused to obtain a valuation save on terms that the valuer would not
be under any obligation to Mr and Mrs Harris to take reasonable care or exercise
reasonable skill. The council did not exclude liability for negligence but excluded
negligence so that the valuer and the council never came under a duty of care to Mr and
Mrs Harris and could not be guilty of negligence. This construction would not give effect
*h* to the manifest intention of the 1977 Act but would emasculate the Act. The construction
would provide no control over standard form exclusion clauses which individual
members of the public are obliged to accept. A party to a contract or a tortfeasor could
opt out of the 1977 Act by declining, in the words of Nourse LJ, to recognise 'their own
answerability to the plaintiff's (see [1988] 1 All ER 691 at 697, [1988] QB 835 at 845).
Caulfield J said that the Act 'can only be relevant where there is on the facts a potential
*j* liability' (see [1988] 1 All ER 691 at 704, [1988] QB 835 at 850). But no one intends to
commit a tort and therefore any notice which excludes liability is a notice which excludes
a potential liability. Kerr LJ sought to confine the Act to 'situations where the existence
of a duty of care is not open to doubt' or where there is 'an inescapable duty of care' (see
[1988] 1 All ER 691 at 702, [1900] QB 835 at 853). I can find nothing in the 1977 Act or
in the general law to identify or support this distinction. In the result the Court of Appeal
held that the Act does not apply to 'negligent misstatements where a disclaimer has

prevented a duty of care from coming into existence' (see [1988] 1 All ER 691 at 699–700, [1988] QB 835 at 848 per Nourse LJ). My Lords, this confuses the valuer's report    *a*
with the work which the valuer carries out in order to make his report. The valuer owed
a duty to exercise reasonable skill and care in his inspection and valuation. If he had been
careful in his work, he would not have made a 'negligent misstatement' in his report.

Section 11(3) of the 1977 Act provides that, in considering whether it is fair and
reasonable to allow reliance on a notice which excludes liability in tort, account must be
taken of 'all the circumstances obtaining when the liability arose or (but for the notice)    *b*
would have arisen'. Section 13(1) of the Act prevents the exclusion of any right or remedy
and (to that extent) s 2 also prevents the exclusion of liability 'by reference to . . . notices
which exclude . . . the relevant obligation or duty'. Nourse LJ dismissed s 11(3) as
'peripheral' and made no comment on s 13(1). In my opinion both these provisions
support the view that the 1977 Act requires that all exclusion notices which would in
common law provide a defence to an action for negligence must satisfy the requirement    *c*
of reasonableness.

The answer to the second question involved in these appeals is that the disclaimer of
liability made by the council on its own behalf in *Harris*'s case and by the Abbey National
on behalf of the appellant surveyors in *Smith*'s case constitute notices which fall within
the 1977 Act and must satisfy the requirement of reasonableness.

The third question is whether in relation to each exclusion clause it is, in the words of    *d*
s 11(3) of the 1977 Act—

'fair and reasonable to allow reliance on it, having regard to all the circumstances
obtaining when the liability arose or (but for the notice) would have arisen.'

The liability of the council for the breach by Mr Lee of his duty of care to Mr and Mrs    *e*
Harris arose as soon as Mr and Mrs Harris, in reliance on the valuation of £8,505, bought
the house for £9,000. The liability of the surveyors for the breach of their duty of care to
Mrs Smith in their valuation arose as soon as Mrs Smith, in reliance on the valuation of
£16,500, bought the house for £18,000. The damages will include the difference
between the market value of the house on the day when it was purchased and the
purchase price which was in fact paid by the purchaser in reliance on the valuation.    *f*

Both the present appeals involve typical purchases. In considering whether the
exclusion clause may be relied on in each case, the general pattern of house purchases and
the extent of the work and liability accepted by the valuer must be borne in mind.

Each year one million houses may be bought and sold. Apart from exceptional cases
the procedure is always the same. The vendor and the purchaser agree a price but the
purchaser cannot enter into a contract unless and until a mortgagee, typically a building    *g*
society, offers to advance the whole or part of the purchase price. A mortgage of 80% or
more of the purchase price is not unusual. Thus, if the vendor and the purchaser agree a
price of £50,000 and the purchaser can find £10,000 the purchaser then applies to a
building society for a loan of £40,000. The purchaser pays the building society a
valuation fee and the building society instructs a valuer who is paid by the building
society. If the valuer reports to the building society that the house is good security for    *h*
£40,000, the building society offers to advance £40,000 and the purchaser contracts to
purchase the house for £50,000. The purchaser, who is offered £40,000 on the security
of the house, rightly assumes that a qualified valuer has valued the house at not less than
£40,000.

At the date when the purchaser pays the valuation fee, at the date when the valuation
is made and at the date when the purchaser is offered an advance, the sale may never take    *j*
place. The amount offered by way of advance may not be enough, the purchaser may
change his mind or the vendor may increase his price and sell elsewhere. For many
reasons a sale may go off, and in that case the purchaser has paid his valuation fee without
result and must pay a second valuation fee when he finds another house and goes through
the same procedure. The building society, which is anxious to attract borrowers, and the

a purchaser, who has no money to waste on valuation fees, do not encourage or pay for detailed surveys. Moreover, the vendor may not be willing to suffer the inconvenience of a detailed survey on behalf of a purchaser who has not contracted to purchase and may exploit minor items of disrepair disclosed by a detailed survey in order to obtain a reduction in the price.

The valuer is and, in my opinion, must be a professional person, typically a chartered surveyor in general practice, who, by training and experience and exercising reasonable b skill and care, will recognise defects and be able to assess value. The valuer will value the house after taking into consideration major defects which are, or ought to be obvious to him, in the course of a visual inspection of so much of the exterior and interior of the house as may be accessible to him without undue difficulty. This appears to be the position as agreed between experts in the decided cases which have been discussed in the course of the present appeal. In *Roberts v J Hampson & Co (a firm)* [1989] 2 All ER 504 Ian c Kennedy J, after hearing expert evidence, came to the following conclusions concerning a valuation commissioned by the Halifax Building Society. I have no doubt the case is of general application. The judge, referring to the Halifax Building Society valuation, as described in the literature and as described by expert evidence, said (at 510):

d      'It is a valuation and not a survey, but any valuation is necessarily governed by condition. The inspection is, of necessity, a limited one. Both the expert surveyors who gave evidence before me agreed that with a house of this size they would allow about half an hour for their inspection on site. That time does not admit of moving furniture, or of lifting carpets, especially where they are nailed down. In my judgment, it must be accepted that where a surveyor undertakes a scheme 1 valuation it is understood that he is making a limited appraisal only. It is, however, e      an appraisal by a skilled professional man. It is inherent in any standard fee work that some cases will colloquially be "winners" and others "losers" from the professional man's point of view. The fact that in an individual case he may need to spend two or three times as long as he would have expected, or as the fee structure would have contemplated, is something that he must accept. His duty to take reasonable care in providing a valuation remains the root of his obligation. In an f      extreme case . . . a surveyor might refuse to value on the agreed fee basis, though any surveyor who too often refused to take the rough with the smooth would not improve his reputation. If, in a particular case, the proper valuation of a £19,000 house needs two hours' work, that is what the surveyor must devote to it. The second aspect of the problem concerns moving furniture and lifting carpets. Here again, as it seems to me, the position that the law adopts is simple. If a surveyor g      misses a defect because its signs are hidden, that is a risk that his client must accept. But, if there is specific ground for suspicion and the trail of suspicion leads behind furniture or under carpets, the surveyor must take reasonable steps to follow the trail until he has all the information which it is reasonable for him to have before making his valuation.'

h In his reference to 'a scheme 1 valuation' the judge was alluding to the practice of charging scale fees to purchasers and paying scale fees to valuers.

The valuer will not be liable merely because his valuation may prove to be in excess of the amount which the purchaser might realise on a sale of the house. The valuer will only be liable if other qualified valuers, who cannot be expected to be harsh on their fellow professionals, consider that, taking into consideration the nature of the work for j which the valuer is paid and the object of that work, nevertheless he has been guilty of an error which an average valuer, in the same circumstances, would not have made and, as a result of that error, the house was worth materially less than the amount of the valuation on which the mortgagee and the purchaser both relied. The valuer accepts the liability to the building society, which can insist on the valuer accepting liability. The building society seeks to exclude the liability of the valuer to the purchaser, who is not

in a position to insist on anything. The duty of care which the valuer owes to the building
society is exactly the same as the duty of care which he owes to the purchaser. The valuer    *a*
is more willing to accept the liability to the building society than to the purchaser because
it is the purchaser who is vulnerable. If the valuation is worthless the building society
can still insist that the purchaser shall repay the advance and interest. So, in practice, the
damages which the valuer may be called on to pay to the building society and the chances
of the valuer being expected to pay are less than the corresponding liability to the
purchaser. But this does not make it more reasonable for the valuer to be able to rely on    *b*
an exclusion clause which is an example of a standard form exemption clause operating
in favour of the supplier of services and against the individual consumer.

Counsel for the surveyors, who has great experience in this field, urged on behalf of
his clients in this appeal, and on behalf of valuers generally, that it is fair and reasonable
for a valuer to rely on an exclusion clause, particularly an exclusion clause which is set
forth so plainly in building society literature. The principal reasons urged by counsel for    *c*
the surveyors are as follows. (1) The exclusion clause is clear and understandable and
reiterated and is forcefully drawn to the attention of the purchaser. (2) The purchaser's
solicitors should reinforce the warning and should urge the purchaser to appreciate that
he cannot rely on a mortgage valuation and should obtain and pay for his own survey.
(3) If valuers cannot disclaim liability they will be faced by more claims from purchasers,
some of which will be unmeritorious but difficult and expensive to resist. (4) A valuer    *d*
will become more cautious, take more time and produce more gloomy reports, which
will make house transactions more difficult. (5) If a duty of care cannot be disclaimed the
cost of negligence insurance for valuers and therefore the cost of valuation fees to the
public will be increased.

Counsel for the surveyors also submitted that there was no contract between a valuer
and a purchaser and that, so far as the purchaser was concerned, the valuation was    *e*
'gratuitous', and the valuer should not be forced to accept a liability he was unwilling to
undertake. My Lords, all these submissions are, in my view, inconsistent with the ambit
and thrust of the 1977 Act. The valuer is a professional man who offers his services for
reward. He is paid for those services. The valuer knows that 90% of purchasers in fact
rely on a mortgage valuation and do not commission their own survey. There is great    *f*
pressure on a purchaser to rely on the mortgage valuation. Many purchasers cannot
afford a second valuation. If a purchaser obtains a second valuation the sale may go off
and then both valuation fees will be wasted. Moreover, he knows that mortgagees, such
as building societies and the council, in the present case, are trustworthy and that they
appoint careful and competent valuers and he trusts the professional man so appointed.
Finally, the valuer knows full well that failure on his part to exercise reasonable skill and
care may be disastrous to the purchaser. If, in reliance on a valuation, the purchaser    *g*
contracts to buy for £50,000 a house valued and mortgaged for £40,000 but, in fact
worth nothing and needing thousands more to be spent on it, the purchaser stands to
lose his home and to remain in debt to the building society for up to £40,000.

In *Yianni v Edwin Evans & Sons (a firm)* [1981] 3 All ER 592, [1982] QB 438 Mr and Mrs
Yianni decided that, if the Halifax Building Society would agree to advance £12,000,    *h*
they would buy a house for £15,000, otherwise they would let the house go as they had
no money apart from £3,000. The house was valued by a valuer on behalf of the Halifax
at £12,000, an advance of this amount was offered and accepted and the house was
bought and mortgaged. Mr and Mrs Yianni then discovered that the house needed
repairs amounting to £18,000. Park J found, on evidence largely derived from the chief
surveyor to the Abbey National, that the proportion of purchasers who have an    *j*
independent survey is less than 15%, that purchasers rely on the building society
valuation, that purchasers trust the building societies, that each purchaser knows that he
has paid a fee for someone on behalf of the society to look at the house:

'... the intending mortgagor feels that the building society, whom he trusts,
must employ for the valuation and survey competent qualified surveyors; and, if
the building society acts on its surveyor's report, then there can be no good reason

a  why he should not also himself act on it. The consequence is that if, after inspection by the building society's surveyor, an offer to make an advance is made, the applicant assumes that the building society has satisfied itself that the house is valuable enough to provide suitable security for a loan and decides to proceed by accepting the society's offer. So, if Mr Yianni had had an independent survey, he would have been exceptional in the experience of the building societies and of those employed to carry out surveys and valuations for them.'

b  (See [1981] 3 All ER 592 at 597, [1982] QB 438 at 445.)

Park J, following the Hedley Byrne case [1963] 2 All ER 575, [1964] AC 465, concluded that a duty of care by the valuers to Mr and Mrs Yianni would arise if the valuers knew that their valuation—

c  'in so far as it stated that the property provided adequate security for an advance of £12,000, would be passed on to the plaintiffs who, notwithstanding the building society's literature and the service of the notice under s 30 of the Building Societies Act 1962, in the defendants' reasonable contemplation would place reliance on its correctness in making their decision to buy the house and mortgage it to the building society . . . These defendants are surveyors and valuers. It is their profession

d  and occupation to survey and make valuations of houses and other property. They make reports about the condition of property they have surveyed. Their duty is not merely to use care in their reports, they have also a duty to use care in their work which results in their reports . . . Accordingly, the building society's offer of £12,000, when passed on to the plaintiffs, confirmed to them that 1 Seymour Road was sufficiently valuable to cause the building society to advance on its security 80%

e  of the purchase price. Since that was also the building society's view the plaintiffs' belief was not unreasonable.'

(See [1981] 3 All ER 592 at 604, [1982] QB 438 at 454–455.)

In Yianni's case there was no exclusion of liability on behalf of the valuer. The evidence and the findings of Park J, which I have set out, support the view that it is unfair and

f  unreasonable for a valuer to rely on an exclusion clause directed against a purchaser in the circumstances of the present appeals.

Counsel for the surveyors referred to a new Abbey National proposal resulting from a consideration Yianni's case. The purchaser is offered the choice between a valuation without liability on the valuer and a report which, as counsel for the surveyors agreed, did not involve any more work for the valuer but accepted that the valuer was under a

g  duty to exercise reasonable skill and care. The fee charged for the report as compared with the fee charged for the valuation represents an increase of £100 for a house worth £20,000, and £150 for a house worth £100,000, and £200 for a house worth £200,000. On a million houses, this would represent increases of income to be divided between valuers, insurers and building societies, of about £150m. It is hardly surprising that few purchasers have chosen the report instead of the valuation. Any increase in fees, alleged

h  to be justified by the decision of this House in these appeals, will no doubt be monitored by the appropriate authorities.

It is open to Parliament to provide that members of all professions or members of one profession providing services in the normal course of the exercise of their profession for reward shall be entitled to exclude or limit their liability for failure to exercise reasonable skill and care. In the absence of any such provision valuers are not, in my opinion,

j  entitled to rely on a general exclusion of the common law duty of care owed to purchasers of houses by valuers to exercise reasonable skill and care in valuing houses for mortgage purposes.

In the Green Paper Conveyancing by Authorised Practitioners (Cm 572) the government proposes to allow building societies, banks and other authorised practitioners to provide conveyancing services to the public by employed professional lawyers. The Green Paper includes the following relevant passages:

'3.10 There will inevitably be claims of financial loss arising out of the provision of conveyancing services. A bad mistake can result in a purchaser acquiring a property which is worth considerably less than he paid for it—because, for example, the conveyancer overlooked a restriction on use or the planning of a new motorway. The practitioner will be required to have adequate professional indemnity insurance or other appropriate arrangements to meet such claims.'

Annex para 12 states:

'An authorised practitioner must not contractually limit its liability for damage suffered by the client as a result of negligence on its part.'

The government thus recognises the need to preserve the duty of a professional lawyer to exercise reasonable skill and care so that the purchaser of a house may not be disastrously affected by a defect of title or an encumbrance. In the same way, it seems to me, there is need to preserve the duty of a professional valuer to exercise reasonable skill and care so that a purchaser of a house may not be disastrously affected by a defect in the structure of the house.

The public are exhorted to purchase their homes and cannot find houses to rent. A typical London suburban house, constructed in the 1930s for less than £1,000, is now bought for more than £150,000 with money largely borrowed at high rates of interest and repayable over a period of a quarter of a century. In these circumstances it is not fair and reasonable for building societies and valuers to agree together to impose on purchasers the risk of loss arising as a result of incompetence or carelessness on the part of valuers. I agree with the speech of my noble and learned friend Lord Griffiths and with his warning that different considerations may apply where homes are not concerned.

In the instant case of *Harris v Wyre Forest DC* I would allow the appeal of Mr and Mrs Harris, restore the order of the trial judge and order the costs of Mr and Mrs Harris to be borne by the council. In the case of *Smith v Eric S Bush (a firm)* I would dismiss the appeal with costs.

**LORD GRIFFITHS.** My Lords, these appeals were heard together because they both raise the same two problems. The first is whether the law places a duty of care on a professional valuer of real property which he owes to the purchaser of the property although he has been instructed to value the property by a prospective mortgagee and not by the purchaser. The second problem concerns the construction and application of the Unfair Contract Terms Act 1977.

*Smith v Eric S Bush (a firm)*
I shall deal with this appeal first because its facts are similar to hundreds of thousands of house purchases that take place every year. It concerns the purchase of a house at the lower end of the market with the assistance of finance provided by a building society. The purchaser applies for finance to the building society. The building society is required by statute to obtain a valuation of the property before it advances any money (see s 13 of the Building Societies Act 1986). This requirement is to protect the depositors who entrust their savings to the building society. The building society therefore requires the purchaser to pay a valuation fee to cover or, at least, to defray the cost of obtaining a valuation. This is a modest sum and certainly much less than the cost of a full structural survey; in the present case it was £36·89. If the purchaser pays the valuation fee, the building society instructs a valuer, who inspects the property and prepares a report for the building society giving his valuation of the property. The inspection carried out is a visual one designed to reveal any obvious defects in the property which must be taken into account when comparing the value of the property with other similar properties in the neighbourhood. If the valuation shows that the property provides adequate security for the loan, the building society will lend the money necessary for the purchaser to go

ahead, but prior to its repeal by the Building Societies Act 1986 would send to the
a purchaser a statutory notice pursuant to s 30 of the Building Societies Act 1962 to make
clear that by making the loan it did not warrant that the purchase price of the property
was reasonable.

The building society may either instruct an independent firm of surveyors to make
the valuation or use one of its own employees. In the present case, the building society
instructed the appellants, an independent firm of surveyors. I will consider whether it
b makes any difference if an 'in-house' valuer is instructed when I come to deal with the
other appeal. The building society may or may not send a copy of the valuer's report to
the purchaser. In this case the building society was the Abbey National and they did send
a copy of the report to the purchaser, Mrs Smith. I understand that this is now common
practice among building societies. The report, however, contained in red lettering and
in the clearest terms a disclaimer of liability for the accuracy of the report covering both
c the building society and the valuer. Again, I understand that it is common practice for
other building societies to incorporate such a disclaimer of liability.

Mrs Smith did not obtain a structural survey of the property. She relied on the valuer's
report to reveal any obvious serious defects in the house she was purchasing. It is
common ground that she was behaving in the same way as the vast majority of purchasers
of modest houses. They do not go to the expense of obtaining their own structural
d survey; they rely on the valuation to reveal any obvious serious defects and take a chance
that there are no hidden defects that might be revealed by a more detailed structural
survey.

The valuer's report said 'the property has been modernised to a fair standard . . . no
essential repairs are required' and it valued the property at £16,500. If reasonable skill
and care had been employed when the inspection took place, it would have revealed that
e as a result of removing the chimney breasts in the rooms the chimneys had been left
dangerously unsupported. Unaware of this defect and relying on the valuer's report, Mrs
Smith bought the house for £18,000 with the assistance of a loan of £3,500 from the
building society.

After she had been living in the house for about 18 months, one of the chimney flues
f collapsed and crashed through the bedroom ceiling and floor causing damage for which
Mrs Smith was awarded £4,379·97 against the surveyors who had carried out the
valuation.

Counsel for the surveyors conceded that on the facts of this case the surveyors owed a
duty of care to Mrs Smith unless they were protected by the disclaimer of liability. He
made this concession, he said, because the surveyors knew that their report was going to
be shown to Mrs Smith and that Mrs Smith would, in all probability, rely on it, which
g two factors would create the necessary proximity to found the duty of care. He submitted,
however, that, if the surveyor did not know that his report would be shown to the
purchaser, no duty of care would arise and that the decision in *Yianni v Edwin Evans &*
*Sons (a firm)* [1981] 3 All ER 592, [1982] QB 438 was wrongly decided. I shall defer
consideration of this question to the second appeal, for it does not arise on the facts of the
h present case. Suffice it to say, for the moment, that on the facts of the present case it is
my view that the concession made by counsel is correct.

At common law, whether the duty to exercise reasonable care and skill is founded in
contract or tort, a party is as a general rule free, by the use of appropriate wording, to
exclude liability for negligence in discharge of the duty. The disclaimer of liability in the
present case is prominent and clearly worded and, on the authority of *Hedley Byrne & Co*
j *Ltd v Heller & Partners Ltd* [1963] 2 All ER 575, [1964] AC 465, in so far as the common
law is concerned effective to exclude the surveyors' liability for negligence. The question
then is whether the Unfair Contract Terms Act 1977 bites on such a disclaimer. In my
view it does.

The Court of Appeal, however, accepted an argument based on the definition of
negligence contained in s 1(1) of the 1977 Act, which provides:

'For the purposes of this part of this Act "negligence" means the breach—(a) of any obligation, arising from the express or implied terms of a contract, to take reasonable care or exercise reasonable skill in the performance of the contract; (b) of any common law duty to take reasonable care or exercise reasonable skill (but not any stricter duty); (c) of the common duty of care imposed by the Occupiers' Liability Act 1957 or the Occupiers' Liability Act (Northern Ireland) 1957.'

It held that, as the disclaimer of liability would at common law have prevented any duty to take reasonable care arising between the parties, the Act had no application. In my view this construction fails to give due weight to the provisions of two further sections of the Act. Section 11(3) provides:

'In relation to a notice (not being a notice having contractual effect), the requirement of reasonableness under this Act is that it should be fair and reasonable to allow reliance on it, having regard to all the circumstances obtaining when the liability arose or (but for the notice) would have arisen.'

And s 13(1) provides:

'To the extent that this Part of this Act prevents the exclusion or restriction of any liability it also prevents—(a) making the liability or its enforcement subject to restrictive or onerous conditions; (b) excluding or restricting any right or remedy in respect of the liability, or subjecting a person to any prejudice in consequence of his pursuing any such right or remedy; (c) excluding or restricting rules of evidence or procedure; and (to that extent) sections 2 and 5 to 7 also prevent excluding or restricting liability by reference to terms and notices which exclude or restrict the relevant obligation or duty.'

I read these provisions as introducing a 'but for' test in relation to the notice excluding liability. They indicate that the existence of the common law duty to take reasonable care, referred to in s 1(1)(b), is to be judged by considering whether it would exist 'but for' the notice excluding liability. The result of taking the notice into account when assessing the existence of a duty of care would result in removing all liability for negligent misstatements from the protection of the Act. It is permissible to have regard to the second report of the Law Commission on *Exemption Clauses* (Law Com no 69), which is the genesis of the Unfair Contract Terms Act 1977, as an aid to the construction of the Act. Paragraph 127 of that report reads:

'Our recommendations in this Part of the report are intended to apply to exclusions of liability for negligence where the liability is incurred in the course of a person's business. We consider that they should apply even in cases where the person seeking to rely on the exemption clause was under no legal obligation (such as a contractual obligation) to carry out the activity. This means that, for example, conditions attached to a licence to enter on to land, and disclaimers of liability made where information or advice is given, should be subject to control . . .'

I have no reason to think that Parliament did not intend to follow this advice and the wording of the Act is, in my opinion, apt to give effect to that intention. This view of the construction of the Act is also supported by the judgment of Slade LJ in *Phillips Products Ltd v Hyland* [1987] 2 All ER 620, [1987] 1 WLR 659, when he rejected a similar argument in relation to the construction of a contractual term excluding negligence.

Finally, the question is whether the exclusion of liability contained in the disclaimer satisfies the requirement of reasonableness provided by s 2(2) of the 1977 Act. The meaning of reasonableness and the burden of proof are both dealt with in s 11(3), which provides:

'In relation to a notice (not being a notice having contractual effect), the requirement of reasonableness under this Act is that it should be fair and reasonable *a*     to allow reliance on it, having regard to all the circumstances obtaining when the liability arose or (but for the notice) would have arisen.'

It is clear, then, that the burden is on the surveyor to establish that in all the circumstances it is fair and reasonable that he should be allowed to rely on his disclaimer of liability.

I believe that it is impossible to draw up an exhaustive list of the factors that must be taken into account when a judge is faced with this very difficult decision. Nevertheless, the following matters should, in my view, always be considered.

*b*     (1) Were the parties of equal bargaining power? If the court is dealing with a one-off situation between parties of equal bargaining power the requirement of reasonableness would be more easily discharged than in a case such as the present where the disclaimer is imposed on the purchaser who has no effective power to object.

(2) In the case of advice, would it have been reasonably practicable to obtain the advice from an alternative source taking into account considerations of costs and time? In the *c*     present case it is urged on behalf of the surveyor that it would have been easy for the purchaser to have obtained his own report on the condition of the house, to which the purchaser replies that he would then be required to pay twice for the same advice and that people buying at the bottom end of the market, many of whom will be young first-time buyers, are likely to be under considerable financial pressure without the money to *d*     go paying twice for the same service.

(3) How difficult is the task being undertaken for which liability is being excluded? When a very difficult or dangerous undertaking is involved there may be a high risk of failure which would certainly be a pointer towards the reasonableness of excluding liability as a condition of doing the work. A valuation, on the other hand, should present no difficulty if the work is undertaken with reasonable skill and care. It is only defects *e*     which are observable by a careful visual examination that have to be taken into account and I cannot see that it places any unreasoable burden on the valuer to require him to accept responsibility for the fairly elementary degree of skill and care involved in observing, following up and reporting on such defects. Surely it is work at the lower end of the surveyor's field of professional expertise.

(4) What are the practical consequences of the decision on the question of *f*     reasonableness? This must involve the sums of money potentially at stake and the ability of the parties to bear the loss involved, which, in its turn, raises the question of insurance. There was once a time when it was considered improper even to mention the possible existence of insurance cover in a lawsuit. But those days are long past. Everyone knows that all prudent, professional men carry insurance, and the availability and cost of insurance must be a relevant factor when considering which of two parties should be *g*     required to bear the risk of a loss. We are dealing in this case with a loss which will be limited to the value of a modest house and against which it can be expected that the surveyor will be insured. Bearing the loss will be unlikely to cause significant hardship if it has to be borne by the surveyor but if it is, on the other hand, quite possible that it will be a financial catastrophe for the purchaser who may be left with a valueless house and no money to buy another. If the law in these circumstances denies the surveyor the right *h*     to exclude his liability, it may result in a few more claims but I do not think so poorly of the surveyors' profession as to believe that the floodgates will be opened. There may be some increase in surveyors' insurance premiums which will be passed on to the public, but I cannot think that it will be anything approaching the figures involved in the difference between the Abbey National's offer of a valuation without liability and a valuation with liability discussed in the speech of my noble and learned friend Lord *j*     Templeman. The result of denying a surveyor, in the circumstances of this case, the right to exclude liability will result in distributing the risk of his negligence among all house purchasers through an increase in his fees to cover insurance, rather than allowing the whole of the risk to fall on the one unfortunate purchaser

I would not, however, wish it to be thought that I would consider it unreasonable for professional men in all circumstances to seek to exclude or limit their liability for negligence. Sometimes breathtaking sums of money may turn on professional advice against which it would be impossible for the adviser to obtain adequate insurance cover *a* and which would ruin him if he were to be held personally liable. In these circumstances it may indeed be reasonable to give the advice on a basis of no liability or possibly of liability limited to the extent of the adviser's insurance cover.

In addition to the foregoing four factors, which will always have to be considered, there is in this case the additional feature that the surveyor is only employed in the first place because the purchaser wishes to buy the house and the purchaser in fact provides *b* or contributes to the surveyor's fees. No one has argued that if the purchaser had employed and paid the surveyor himself, it would have been reasonable for the surveyor to exclude liability for negligence, and the present situation is not far removed from that of a direct contract between the surveyor and the purchaser. The evaluation of the foregoing matters leads me to the clear conclusion that it would not be fair and reasonable for the surveyor to be permitted to exclude liability in the circumstances of this case. I *c* would therefore dismiss this appeal.

It must, however, be remembered that this is a decision in respect of a dwelling house of modest value in which it is widely recognised by surveyors that purchasers are in fact relying on their care and skill. It will obviously be of general application in broadly similar circumstances. But I expressly reserve my position in respect of valuations of quite different types of property for mortgage purposes, such as industrial property, large *d* blocks of flats or very expensive houses. In such cases it may well be that the general expectation of the behaviour of the purchaser is quite different. With very large sums of money at stake prudence would seem to demand that the purchaser obtain his own structural survey to guide him in his purchase and, in such circumstances with very much larger sums of money at stake, it may be reasonable for the surveyors valuing on behalf of those who are providing the finance either to exclude or limit their liability to *e* the purchaser.

*Harris v Wyre Forest DC*

The Housing (Financial Provisions) Act 1958 (as amended by the Local Government Act 1974) gave power to local authorities to lend money for house purchase. Section 43 *f* of the 1958 Act provided, inter alia, that before making the loan the local authority had to satisfy themselves that the house was, or would after repair, be fit for human habitation. The local authority were also required to secure the loan by way of a mortgage on the property and only to make the loan after they had obtained a valuation of the property made on their behalf.

The appellants, Mr and Mrs Harris, two young first-time buyers, applied to the first *g* respondent, Wyre Forest DC, for a loan to enable them to purchase a small old house in Kidderminster. The asking price of the house was £9,450. Mr and Mrs Harris completed an application form to the council seeking a loan of £8,950. The application form contained the following paragraphs:

'TO BE READ CAREFULLY AND SIGNED PERSONALLY BY ALL APPLICANTS                                *h*
I/WE enclose herewith Valuation Fee & Administration Fee £22·00. I/WE understand that this fee is not returnable even if the Council do not eventually make an advance and that the Valuation is confidential and is intended solely for the information of Wyre Forest District Council in determining what advance, if any, may be made on the security and that no responsibility whatsoever is implied or accepted by the Council for the value or condition of the property by reason of such *j* inspection and report. (You are advised for your own protection to instruct your own Surveyor/Architect to inspect the property). I/WE agree that the Valuation Report is the property of the Council and that I/WE cannot require its production . . .'

a When the council had received their application and their cheque for £22, they instructed the second respondent, Mr Lee, a valuation surveyor in the council's employment, to inspect and value the house. Mr Lee inspected the house and prepared a report in which he valued the property at the asking price of £9,450 and under the head 'Essential Repairs' he entered 'Obtain report for District Council from M.E.B. [Midland Electricity Board] regarding electrics and carry out any recommendations' and 'Make good mortar fillets to Extension'. We were told that the entry in respect of the electrical

b installation is one that is standard in all council's reports and it would seem the only other essential repair was a minor matter relating to mortar fillets in the extension. No other defects of any sort were noted on the report.

This report was not shown to Mr and Mrs Harris but, having received the report, the council made them an offer of a loan of £8,505 secured by a mortgage on the property on condition that they undertook to carry out the electrical work and the repair of the

c mortar fillets in the extension as recommended by the valuer to the satisfaction of the council. The Harrises accepted the offer and bought the house for £9,000.

Unfortunately, Mr Lee had failed to report that the house had suffered from serious settlement which required inspection by a structural engineer. When the Harrises tried to sell the house three years later, the prospective purchaser also applied to the council for a loan and Mr Lee was again sent to inspect the house. On this occasion he reported

d the settlement and recommended that a structural engineer's report should be obtained before any loan was made. In due course, a structural engineer's report revealed that the house was in a dangerous and unstable condition and that the cost of repairs would be many thousands of pounds. In fact, damages, subject to liability, were agreed at £12,000. Obviously, had Mr Lee reported in his first report in the same terms as he did in his second report, the Harrises would never have bought the house. The judge held that Mr

e Lee was negligent in the making of his first report and there is no appeal from that finding of fact.

For the reasons that I have already given, the disclaimer of liability must be disregarded when considering whether the council or Mr Lee owed any duty to care to Mr and Mrs Harris. Counsel for the council and Mr Lee has submitted that they did not because there

f was no voluntary assumption of responsibility on their part in respect of Mr Lee's inspection and report. He submits that *Yianni v Edwin Evans & Sons (a firm)* [1981] 3 All ER 592, [1982] QB 438 was wrongly decided. That case was the first of a number of decisions, at first instance, in which surveyors instructed by mortgagees have been held liable to purchasers for negligent valuations. The facts were that the plaintiffs, who wished to buy a house at a price of £15,000, applied to a building society for a mortgage.

g The building society engaged a firm of valuers to value the property for which the plaintiffs had to pay. There was no disclaimer of liability although the mortgage application form advised the plaintiffs to obtain an independent survey. They did not do so because of the cost involved. The surveyors valued the property at £15,000 and assessed it as suitable for maximum lending. The building society offered the plaintiffs a maximum loan of £12,000 with which they purchased the property. There was serious

h damage to the house caused by subsidence which should have been discovered by the surveyors at the time of their inspection and it was admitted that the surveyors had been negligent.

In that case there was no disclaimer of liability and the valuer's report was not shown to the purchaser. Ignoring the disclaimer of liability, the facts are virtually indistinguishable from the present case unless it can be said that the fact that Mr Lee was

j an in-house valuer can make a difference when considering the existence of his duty of care to the purchaser. Park J said ([1981] 3 All ER 592 at 604, [1982] QB 438 at 454):

'... I conclude that, in this case, the duty of care would arise if, on the evidence, I am satisfied that the defendants knew that their valuation of 1 Seymour Road, in so far as it stated that the property provided adequate security for an advance of

£12,000, would be passed on to the plaintiffs, who . . . in the defendants' reasonable contemplation would place reliance on its correctness in making their decision to *a* buy the house and mortgage it to the building society.'

Finding both these conditions satisfied, Park J held the surveyors to be liable.

Counsel for the council and Mr Lee drew attention to the doubts expressed about the correctness of this decision by Kerr LJ in the course of his judgment in the Court of Appeal, and submitted, on the authority of *Hedley Byrne & Co Ltd v Heller & Partners Ltd* *b* [1963] 2 All ER 575, [1964] AC 465, that it was essential to found liability for a negligent misstatement that there had been 'a voluntary assumption of responsibility' on the part of the person giving the advice. I do not accept this submission and I do not think that voluntary assumption of responsibility is a helpful or realistic test for liability. It is true that reference is made in a number of the speeches in the *Hedley Byrne* case to the assumption of responsibility as a test of liability but it must be remembered that those *c* speeches were made in the context of a case in which the central issue was whether a duty of care could arise when there had been an express disclaimer of responsibility for the accuracy of the advice. Obviously, if an adviser expressly assumes responsibility for his advice, a duty of care will arise, but such is extremely unlikely in the ordinary course of events. The House of Lords approved a duty of care being imposed on the facts in *Cann v Willson* (1888) 39 Ch D 39 and in *Candler v Crane Christmas & Co* [1951] 1 All ER *d* 426, [1951] 2 KB 164. But, if the surveyor in *Cann v Willson* or the accountant in *Candler v Crane Christmas & Co* had actually been asked if he was voluntarily assuming responsibility for his advice to the mortgagee or the purchaser of the shares, I have little doubt he would have replied: 'Certainly not. My responsibility is limited to the person who employs me.' The phrase 'assumption of responsibility' can only have any real meaning if it is understood as referring to the circumstances in which the law will deem *e* the maker of the statement to have assumed responsibility to the person who acts on the advice.

In *Ministry of Housing and Local Government v Sharp* [1970] 1 All ER 1009, [1970] 2 QB 223 both Lord Denning MR and Salmon LJ rejected the argument that a voluntary assumption of responsibility was the sole criterion for imposing a duty of care for the negligent preparation of a search certificate in the local land charges register. *f*

The essential distinction between the present case and the situation being considered in the *Hedley Byrne* case and in the two earlier cases is that in those cases the advice was being given with the intention of persuading the recipient to act on it. In the present case the purpose of providing the report is to advise the mortgagee but it is given in circumstances in which it is highly probable that the purchaser will in fact act on its contents, although that was not the primary purpose of the report. I have had considerable *g* doubts whether it is wise to increase the scope of the duty for negligent advice beyond the person directly intended by the giver of the advice to act on it to those whom he knows may do so. Certainly in the field of the law of mortgagor and mortgagee there is authority that points in the other direction. In *Odder v Westbourne Park Building Society* (1955) 165 EG 261 Harman J held that a building society owed no duty of care to purchasers in respect of the valuation report for mortgage purposes prepared by the *h* chairman of the society. From the tenor of the short report it appears that Harman J regarded it as unthinkable that a mortgagee could owe a duty of care to the mortgagor in respect of any action taken by the mortgagee for the purpose of appraising the value of the property. In *Curran v Northern Ireland Co-ownership Housing Association Ltd* (1986) 8 NIJB 1 the Court of Appeal in Northern Ireland held that the Northern Ireland Housing Executive, which had lent money on mortgage pursuant to powers contained in the *j* Housing Act (Northern Ireland) 1971, owed no duty of care to their mortgagor in respect of the valuation of the property. The claim against the executive had been struck out by the judge on the ground that the pleadings disclosed no cause of action. For the purpose of the appeal, the following facts were assumed: (1) that the executive had instructed an

independent valuer to prepare a valuation of the property; (2) that the valuation had
a  been negligently prepared; (3) that the executive had negligently instructed an
incompetent valuer; (4) that the valuer's report would not be shown to the purchaser; (5)
that the purchaser knew that the executive would not lend money without a valuation
to justify the loan; (6) that the executive knew that the purchaser would assume that the
valuation showed that the property was worth at least as much as the figure which the
executive was willing to advance on mortgage, and that the purchser would rely on the
b  valuation to that extent. Gibson LJ based his judgment on the absence of any acceptance
of responsibility on the part of the executive. In the course of his judgment he said (at
14):

> 'Responsibility can only attach if the defendant's act implied a voluntary
> undertaking to assume responsibility. Were it otherwise a person who offered to an
> expert any object for sale, making it clear that he was unaware of its value and that
c  > he was relying on the other to pay a proper price, could sue the other should he later
> discover that he had not received the full value even though the purchaser had made
> no representation that he was doing any more than look after his own interests. Nor
> can any class of persons who to the knowledge of another habitually fail to take
> precautions for their own protection in a business relationship cast upon another
> without his consent an obligation to exercise care for their protection in such
d  > transaction so as to protect them from their own lack of ordinary business prudence.
> Generally, a mortgage contract in itself imports no obligation on the part of a
> mortgagee to use care in protecting the interests of a mortgagor . . .'

Gibson LJ said (at 21):

e  > 'But in so far as the facts of this case are clearly within the area of contemplation
> in the *Hedley Byrne* case, I have no doubt that the condition precedent to liability is
> that the executive should have indicated to the plaintiffs, or so acted as to mislead
> them into believing, that the executive was accepting responsibility for its opinion.'

Commenting on *Yianni v Edwin Evans & Sons (a firm)* [1981] 3 All ER 592, [1982] QB
f  438, Kerr LJ in his judgment in the Court of Appeal in the present case said ([1988] 1 All
ER 691 at 701, [1988] QB 835 at 851–852):

> 'But its inherent jurisprudential weakness in any ordinary situation is clear.
> Suppose that A approaches B with a request for a loan to be secured on a property or
> chattel, such as a painting, which A is proposing to acquire. A knows that for the
> purpose of considering whether or not to make the requested loan, and of its
g  > amount, B is bound to make some assessment of the value of the security which is
> offered, possibly on the basis of some expert inspection and formal valuation. Then
> assume that B knows that in all probability A will not have had any independent
> advice or valuation and is also unlikely to commission anything of the kind as a
> check on B's valuation. B also knows, of course, that any figure which he may then
> put forward to A by way of a proposed loan on the basis of the offered security will
h  > necessarily be seen to reflect B's estimate of the minimum value of the offered
> security. Suppose that A then accepts B's offer and acquires the property or chattel
> with the assistance of B's loan and in reliance, at least in part, on B's willingness to
> advance the amount of the loan as an indication of the value of the property or
> chattel. Given those facts and no more, I do not think that B can properly be
> regarded as having assumed, or as being subjected to, any duty of care towards A in
j  > his valuation of the security. Even in the absence of any disclaimer of responsibility
> I do not think that the principles stated in *Hedley Byrne & Co Ltd v Heller & Partners
> Ltd* [1963] 2 All ER 575, [1964] AC 465 support the contrary conclusion. B has not
> been asked for advice or information but merely for a loan. His valuation was
> carried out for his own commercial purposes. If it was done carelessly, with the

result that the valuation and loan were excessive, I do not think that A can have any ground for complaint. And if B made a small service charge for investigating A's *a* request for a loan, I doubt whether the position would be different; certainly not if he were also to add a disclaimer of responsibility and a warning that A should carry out his own valuation.'

Kerr LJ, however, added ([1988] 1 All ER 691 at 701–702, [1988] QB 835 at 852):

'It may be, but I agree that we should not decide this general question on the *b* present appeal, that the particular circumstances of purchasers of houses with the assistance of loans from building societies or local authorities are capable of leading to a different analysis and conclusion.'

I have come to the conclusion that *Yianni*'s case was correctly decided. I have already given my view that the voluntary assumption of responsibility is unlikely to be a helpful *c* or realistic test in most cases. I therefore return to the question in what circumstances should the law deem those who give advice to have assumed responsibility to the person who acts on the advice or, in other words, in what circumstances should a duty of care be owed by the adviser to those who act on his advice? I would answer: only if it is foreseeable that if the advice is negligent the recipient is likely to suffer damage, that there is a sufficiently proximate relationship between the parties and that it is just and *d* reasonable to impose the liability. In the case of a surveyor valuing a small house for a building society or local authority, the application of these three criteria leads to the conclusion that he owes a duty of care to the purchaser. If the valuation is negligent and is relied on damage in the form of economic loss to the purchaser is obviously foreseeable. The necessary proximity arises from the surveyor's knowledge that the overwhelming probability is that the purchaser will rely on his valuation, the evidence was that *e* surveyors knew that approximately 90% of purchasers did so, and the fact that the surveyor only obtains the work because the purchaser is willing to pay his fee. It is just and reasonable that the duty should be imposed for the advice is given in a professional as opposed to a social context and liability for breach of the duty will be limited both as to its extent and amount. The extent of the liability is limited to the purchaser of the house: I would not extend it to subsequent purchasers. The amount of the liability *f* cannot be very great because it relates to a modest house. There is no question here of creating a liability of indeterminate amount to an indeterminate class. I would certainly wish to stress, that in cases where the advice has not been given for the specific purpose of the recipient acting on it, it should only be in cases when the adviser knows that there is a high degree of probability that some other identifiable person will act on the advice that a duty of care should be imposed. It would impose an intolerable burden on those *g* who give advice in a professional or commercial context if they were to owe a duty not only to those to whom they give the advice but to any other person who might choose to act on it.

I accept that the mere fact of a contract between mortgagor and mortgagee will not of itself in all cases be sufficient to found a duty of care. But I do not accept the view of the Court of Appeal in *Curran v Northern Ireland Co-ownership Housing Association Ltd* (1986) 8 *h* NIJB 1 that a mortgagee who accepts a fee to obtain a valuation of a small house owes no duty of care to the mortgagor in the selection of the valuer to whom he entrusts the work. In my opinion, the mortgagee in such a case, knowing that the mortgagor will rely on the valuation, owes a duty to the mortgagor to take reasonable care to employ a reasonably competent valuer. Provided he does this the mortgagee will not be held liable for the negligence of the independent valuer who acts as an independent contractor. *j*

I have already pointed out that the only real distinction between the present case and *Yianni*'s case is that the valuation was carried out by an in-house valuer. In my opinion this can make no difference. The valuer is discharging the duties of a professional man whether he is employed by the mortgagee or acting on his own account or is employed

by a firm of independent surveyors. The essence of the case against him is that he as a
professional man realised that the purchaser was relying on him to exercise proper skill
and judgment in his profession and that it was reasonable and fair that the purchaser
should do so. Mr Lee was in breach of his duty of care to the Harrises and the local
authority, as his employers, are vicariously liable for that negligence.

For reasons that are essentially the same as those I considered in the other appeal, I
would hold that it is not reasonable to allow the local authority or Mr Lee to rely on the
exclusion of liability. Accordingly, I would allow this appeal.

**LORD JAUNCEY OF TULLICHETTLE.** My Lords, these two appeals raise the
important issue of the extent to which a valuer instructed by a mortgagee owes a duty of
care to a potential mortgagor whom he knows will be shown in some shape or form the
results of his valuation prior to purchasing the property in question.

*Smith v Eric S Bush (a firm)*
(I) Mrs Smith applied to the Abbey National Building Society for a mortgage to enable
her to purchase a house. The building society in pursuance of its statutory duty under
s 25 of the Building Societies Act 1962 (now s 13 of the Building Societies Act 1986)
instructed the appellants, a firm of surveyors and valuers (the surveyors), to prepare a
written report as to the value of the house. Mrs Smith paid to the building society a fee
in respect of this report. Mrs Smith's application to the building society contained a
disclaimer of liability by them on behalf of the appellants, which disclaimer she
acknowledged. Thereafter the building society sent to Mrs Smith a copy of the report
and informed her that her application had been accepted. Both the copy report and the
letter drew attention to the fact that the report was not to be taken as a structural survey.
The report stated that the surveyor had made the report without any acceptance of
responsibility to Mrs Smith and the letter advised her to obtain independent professional
advice. Thereafter, without obtaining an independent valuation, Mrs Smith purchased
the house, which later proved to be structurally defective to a material extent. The
surveyor, who was a member of the appellant firm, was found to be negligent in failing
to discover and report on the defect. He was at all material times aware that his report
would be shown to Mrs Smith, that she would be likely to place reliance on it in deciding
whether to buy the house and that his fee derived from a payment by her to the building
society.

Three questions arise, namely: (1) whether in the absence of the disclaimers of liability
the appellants owed a duty to Mrs Smith; (2) if so, whether the disclaimers fell within
the ambit of the Unfair Contract Terms Act 1977; and (3) if they did, whether they
satisfied the requirements of reasonableness.

Since *Hedley Byrne & Co Ltd v Heller & Partners Ltd* [1963] 2 All ER 575, [1964] AC 465
it has been beyond doubt that in certain circumstances A may be liable to B in tort in
respect of a negligent statement causing economic loss to B. In considering whether such
circumstances exist in the present case I propose, before looking at *Hedley Byrne & Co Ltd
v Heller & Partners Ltd* to look at two earlier cases. In *Cann v Willson* (1888) 39 Ch D 39
an intending mortgagor, at the request of the solicitor of an intending mortgagee, applied
to a firm of valuers for a valuation of the property in question. The valuers sent the
valuation, which subsequently turned out to be wholly inept, to the mortgagee's solicitors
knowing that it was required for the purpose of an advance. When the mortgagor
defaulted the property was found to be worth far less than the valuation, whereby the
mortgagee suffered loss. In an action by the mortgagees against the valuer Chitty J said
(at 42–43):

'In this case the document called a valuation was sent by the Defendants direct to
the agents of the Plaintiff for the purpose of inducing the Plaintiff and his co-trustee
to lay out the trust money on mortgage. It seems to me that the Defendants

knowingly placed themselves in that position, and in point of law incurred a duty towards him to use reasonable care in the preparation of the document called a valuation.'

In *Candler v Crane Christmas & Co* [1951] 1 All ER 426, [1951] 2 KB 164 accountants were in the course of preparing the accounts of a company. They were instructed to press on and complete them so that they might be shown to the plaintiff, who, they were informed, was a potential investor. A clerk of the accountants prepared the accounts and at the request of the company discussed these with the plaintiff, who, relying thereon, invested money in the company. In the event the accounts gave a wholly misleading picture of the state of the company and the plaintiff sustained loss. In a dissenting judgment which was subsequently approved in *Hedley Byrne & Co Ltd v Heller & Partners Ltd* Denning LJ, after suggesting that professional persons such as accountants, surveyors and valuers, might in certain circumstances owe a duty apart from contract to use care in their reports and in the work from which they resulted, said ([1951] 1 All ER 426 at 434, [1951] 2 KB 164 at 180–181):

> 'Secondly, to whom do these professional people owe this duty? I will take accountants, but the same reasoning applies to the others. They owe the duty, of course, to their employer or client, and also, I think, to any third person to whom they themselves show the accounts, or to whom they know their employer is going to show the accounts so as to induce him to invest money or take some other action on them. I do not think, however, the duty can be extended still further so as to include strangers of whom they have heard nothing and to whom their employer without their knowledge may choose to show their accounts. Once the accountants have handed their accounts to their employer, they are not, as a rule, responsible for what he does with them without their knowledge or consent ... The test of proximity in these cases is: Did the accountants know that the accounts were required for submission to the plaintiff and use by him? That appears from *Langridge v. Levy* ((1837) 2 M & W 519, [1835–42] All ER Rep 586), as extended by CLEASBY, B., in *George v. Skivington* ((1869) LR 5 Exch 1 at 5), and from the decision of CHITTY, J., in *Cann v. Willson* ((1888) 39 Ch D 39) which is directly in point.'

Denning LJ said ([1951] 1 All ER 426 at 435, [1951] 2 KB 164 at 183):

> 'It will be noticed that I have confined the duty to cases where the accountant prepares his accounts and makes his report for the guidance of the very person in the very transaction in question. That is sufficient for the decision of this case. I can well understand that it would be going too far to make an accountant liable to any person in the land who chooses to rely on the accounts in matters of business, for that would expose him, in the words of CARDOZO, C.J., in *Ultramares Corpn. v. Touche* ((1931) 255 NY 170 at 179), to "... liability in an indeterminate amount for an indeterminate time to an indeterminate class."'

In *Hedley Byrne & Co Ltd v Heller & Partners Ltd* [1963] 2 All ER 575, [1964] AC 465 bankers who were asked about the financial stability of one of their customers gave favourable references but stipulated that these were 'without responsibility'. The plaintiffs on whose behalf the information had been sought relied on the references and thereby suffered loss. They sued the bank. Lord Reid said ([1963] 2 All ER 575 at 583, [1964] AC 465 at 486):

> 'A reasonable man, knowing that he was being trusted or that his skill and judgment were being relied on, would, I think, have three courses open to him. He could keep silent or decline to give the information or advice sought: or he could give an answer with a clear qualification that he accepted no responsibility for it or that it was given without that reflection or inquiry which a careful answer would require: or he could simply answer without any such qualification. If he chooses to

a   adopt the last course he must, I think, be held to have accepted some responsibility
    for his answer being given carefully, or to have accepted a relationship with the
    inquirer which requires him to exercise such care as the circumstances require.'

    Lord Reid said, with reference to *Candler v Crane Christmas & Co* [1951] 1 All ER 426,
    [1951] 2 KB 164: 'This seems to me to be a typical case of agreeing to assume responsibility
    ...' (see [1963] 2 All ER 575 at 583, [1964] AC 465 at 487). Lord Morris said ([1963] 2
b   All ER 575 at 588–589, [1964] AC 465 at 494–495):

        'My lords, it seems to me that if A assumes a responsibility to B to tender him
        deliberate advice there could be a liability if the advice is negligently given. I say
        "could be" because the ordinary courtesies and exchanges of life would become
        impossible if it were sought to attach legal obligation to every kindly and friendly
        act ... Quite apart, however, from employment or contract there may be
c       circumstances in which a duty to exercise care will arise if a service is voluntarily
        undertaken.'

    He further stated ([1963] 2 All ER 575 at 590, [1964] AC 465 at 497):

        'Leaving aside cases where there is some contractual or fiduciary relationship
        there may be many situations in which one person voluntarily or gratuitously
d       undertakes to do something for another person and becomes under a duty to
        exercise reasonable care. I have given illustrations. Apart from cases where there is
        some direct dealing, there may be cases where one person issues a document which
        should be the result of an exercise of the skill and judgment required by him in his
        calling and where he knows and intends that its accuracy will be relied on by
        another.'
e
    He further stated ([1963] 2 All ER 575 at 594, [1964] AC 465 at 502–503):

        'My lords, I consider that it follows and that it should now be regarded as settled
        that if someone possessed of a special skill undertakes, quite irrespective of contract,
        to apply that skill for the assistance of another person who relies on such skill, a duty
        of care will arise. The fact that the service is to be given by means of, or by the
f       instrumentality of, words can make no difference. Furthermore if, in a sphere in
        which a person is so placed that others could reasonably rely on his judgment or his
        skill or on his ability to make careful inquiry, a person takes it on himself to give
        information or advice to, or allows his information or advice to be passed on to,
        another person who, as he knows or should know, will place reliance on it, then a
        duty of care will arise.'
g
    Lord Devlin, after posing the question, 'Is the relationship between the parties in this
    case such that it can be brought within a category giving rise to a special duty?' (see
    [1963] 2 All ER 575 at 608, [1964] AC 465 at 525), referred to a number of cases, and
    continued ([1963] 2 All ER 575 at 610–611, [1964] AC 465 at 528–529):

h       'I think, therefore, that there is ample authority to justify your lordships in saying
        now that the categories of special relationships, which may give rise to a duty to take
        care in word as well as in deed, are not limited to contractual relationships or to
        relationships of fiduciary duty, but include also relationships which in the words of
        LORD SHAW in *Nocton v. Lord Ashburton* ([1914] AC 932 at 972, [1914–15] All ER
        Rep 45 at 62) are "equivalent to contract" that is, where there is an assumption of
j       responsibility in circumstances in which, but for the absence of consideration, there
        would be a contract. Where there is an express undertaking, an express warranty as
        distinct from mere representation, there can be little difficulty. The difficulty arises
        in discerning those cases in which the undertaking is to be implied. In this respect
        the absence of consideration is not irrelevant. Payment for information or advice is
        very good evidence that it is being relied on and that the informer or adviser knows

that it is ... I do not understand any of your lordships to hold that it is a
responsibility imposed by law on certain types of persons or in certain sorts of *a*
situations. It is a responsibility that is voluntarily accepted or undertaken either
generally where a general relationship, such as that of solicitor and client or banker
and customer, is created, or specifically in relation to a particular transaction. In the
present case the appellants were not, as in *Woods* v. *Martins Bank, Ltd.* ([1958] 3 All
ER 166, [1959] 1 QB 55) the customers or potential customers of the bank.
Responsibility can attach only to the single act, i.e., the giving of the reference, and *b*
only if the doing of that act implied a voluntary undertaking to assume
responsibility.'

Lord Devlin summarised his conclusions ([1963] 2 All ER 575 at 611, [1964] AC 465 at
530):

'I shall therefore content myself with the proposition that wherever there is a *c*
relationship equivalent to contract there is a duty of care. Such a relationship may
be either general or particular. Examples of a general relationship are those of
solicitor and client and of banker and customer ... Where, as in the present case,
what is relied on is a particular relationship created ad hoc, it will be necessary to
examine the particular facts to see whether there is an express or implied undertaking
of responsibility. I regard this proposition as an application of the general conception *d*
of proximity.'

There are a number of references in the speeches in the *Hedley Byrne* case to voluntary
assumption of responsibility. Although in that case the respondent bankers gave the
financial reference without payment, I do not understand that 'voluntary' was intended
to be equiparated with 'gratuitous'. Rather does it refer to a situation in which the *e*
individual concerned, albeit under no obligation in law to assume responsibility, elected
so to do. This is, I think, made clear by Lord Devlin's reference to the responsibility
voluntarily undertaken by a solicitor to his client.

Here the building society had a statutory duty under s 25 of the Building Societies Act
1962 to satisfy itself as to the adequacy of the security of any advance to be made and for
that purpose to obtain 'a written report prepared and signed by a competent and prudent *f*
person who ... is experienced in the matters relevant to the determination of the value
...' (see s 25(2)(a)). In pursuance of that duty the building society instructed the
surveyors, who, by accepting these instructions, not only entered into contractual
relations with the building society but also came under a duty in tort to it to exercise
reasonable care in carrying out their survey and preparing their report. To that extent
they were in no different position to that of any other professional person who has *g*
accepted instructions to act on behalf of a client. However, there were certain other
factors present which must be taken into account. In the first place the surveyors were
aware that their report would be made available to Mrs Smith. In the second place they
were aware that she would probably rely on the contents of the report in deciding
whether or not to proceed with the purchase of the house and that she would be unlikely *h*
to obtain an independent valuation. In the third place they knew that she had at the time
of the mortgage application paid to the building society an inspection fee which would
be used to defray their fee. In these circumstances would the surveyors in the absence of
disclaimers of responsibility have owed a duty of care to Mrs Smith?

In each of the three cases to which I have referred there was direct contact between the
negligent provider of information on the one hand and the plaintiff or his agent on the *j*
other. In *Cann v Willson* (1888) 39 Ch D 39 the sole purpose of the valuation was to enable
the intending mortgagor to obtain a mortgage over the property value. In *Candler v
Crane Christmas & Co* [1951] 1 All ER 426, [1951] 2 KB 164, although the accounts were
prepared for the benefit of the company, the discussion between the accountants' clerk
and the plaintiff was for the sole purpose of enabling the latter to decide whether or not

to invest in the company. Chitty J and Denning LJ referred to the valuation being sent
*a* and the accounts being shown and discussed for the purpose of inducing the plaintiff to
do something. In the *Hedley Byrne* case the information was provided to satisfy the
inquiry made on behalf of the plaintiff. In the present case there was no direct contact
between the surveyors and Mrs Smith and their sole purpose in preparing their report
was to enable the building society to fulfil its statutory obligation. There are thus points
of important distinction between the facts of this case and those of the other three.
*b* However, that does not necessarily mean that a different result must follow. The question
must always be whether the particular facts disclose that there is a sufficiently proximate
relationship between the provider of information and the person who has acted on that
information to his detriment, such that the former owes a duty of care to the latter.

It is tempting to say that in this case the relationship between Mrs Smith and the
surveyors was, in the words of Lord Shaw in *Nocton v Lord Ashburton* [1914] AC 932 at
*c* 972, [1914–15] All ER Rep 45 at 62 quoted by Lord Devlin in *Hedley Byrne & Co Ltd v
Heller & Partners Ltd* [1963] 2 All ER 575 at 610, [1964] AC 465 at 528–529, 'equivalent
to contract' inasmuch as she paid for the surveyors' report. However, I do not think that
Lord Devlin, when he used those words, had in mind the sort of tripartite situation
which obtained here, but rather was he considering a situation where the provider and
receiver of information were in contact with one another either directly or through their
*d* agents, and where, but for the lack of payment, a contract would have existed between
them. In the present case a contract existed between the building society and the
surveyors who carried out their inspection and produced their report in pursuance of
that contract. There was accordingly no room for a contract between Mrs Smith and the
surveyors. I prefer to approach the matter by asking whether the facts disclose that the
surveyors in inspecting and reporting must, but for the disclaimers, by reason of the
*e* proximate relationship between them, be deemed to have assumed responsibility towards
Mrs Smith as well as to the building society who instructed them.

There can be only an affirmative answer to this question. The four critical facts are
that the surveyors knew from the outset (1) that the report would be shown to Mrs
Smith, (2) that Mrs Smith would probably rely on the valuation contained therein in
*f* deciding whether to buy the house without obtaining an independent valuation, (3) that
if, in these circumstances, the valuation was, having regard to the actual condition of the
house, excessive Mrs Smith would be likely to suffer loss and (4) that she had paid to the
building society a sum to defray the surveyors' fee.

In the light of this knowledge the surveyors could have declined to act for the building
society, but they chose to proceed. In these circumstances they must be taken not only to
*g* have assumed contractual obligations towards the building society but delictual
obligations towards Mrs Smith, whereby they became under a duty towards her to carry
out their work with reasonable care and skill. It is critical to this conclusion that the
surveyors knew that Mrs Smith would be likely to rely on the valuation without
obtaining independent advice. In both *Candler v Crane Christmas & Co* [1951] 1 All ER
426, [1951] 2 KB 164 and *Hedley Byrne & Co Ltd v Heller & Partners Ltd* [1963] 2 All ER
*h* 575, [1964] AC 465 the provider of the information was the obvious and most easily
available, if not the only available, source of that information. It would not be difficult
therefore to conclude that the person who sought such information was likely to rely on
it. In the case of an intending mortgagor the position is very different since, financial
considerations apart, there is likely to be available to him a wide choice of sources of
information, to wit independent valuers to whom he can resort, in addition to the valuer
*j* acting for the mortgagee. I would not therefore conclude that the mere fact that a
mortgagee's valuer knows that his valuation will be shown to an intending mortgagor of
itself imposes on him a duty of care to the mortgagor. Knowledge, actual or implied, of
the mortgagor's likely reliance on the valuation must be brought home to him. Such
knowledge may be fairly readily implied in relation to a potential mortgagor seeking to
enter the lower end of the housing market but non constat that such ready implication

would arise in the case of a purchase of an expensive property whether residential or commercial. Counsel for the surveyors conceded that if there had been no disclaimer they must fail. For the reasons which I have just given I consider that this concession was rightly made.

I would only add three further matters in relation to this part of the case. In the first place the duty of care owed by the surveyors to Mrs Smith resulted from the proximate relationship between them arising in the circumstances hereinbefore described. Such duty of care was accordingly limited to Mrs Smith and would not extend to 'strangers' (to use the words of Denning LJ in *Candler v Crane Christmas & Co* [1951] 1 All ER 426 at 434, [1951] 2 KB 164 at 181) who might subsequently derive a real interest in the house from her. In the second place the fact that A is prepared to lend money to B on the security of property owned by or to be acquired by him cannot per se impose on A any duty of care to B. Much more is required. Were it otherwise a loan by A to B on the security of property, real or personal, would ipso facto amount to a warranty by A that the property was worth at least the sum lent. In the third place the sum sought by Mrs Smith as a mortgage was relatively small and represented only a small proportion of the purchase price. The house with all its defects was worth substantially more than that sum, and had the report merely stated that the house was adequate security for that sum Mrs Smith would have had no complaint. However, the report contained a 'mortgage valuation' of the house, which valuation wholly failed to reflect the structural defect. It is that valuation of which Mrs Smith is entitled to complain.

(II) The next question is whether the disclaimers by and on behalf of the surveyors fall within the ambit of the Unfair Contracts Act 1977. In *Hedley Byrne & Co Ltd v Heller & Partners Ltd* [1963] 2 All ER 575, [1964] AC 465 it was held that the disclaimer of responsibility made by the defendant bankers when giving the reference negatived any assumption by them of a duty of care towards the plaintiff. If the circumstances of this case had arisen before 1977 there can be no doubt that the disclaimers would have been effective to negative such an assumption of responsibility. Has the 1977 Act altered the position? The relevant statutory provisions are ss 2(2), 11(3) and 13(1):

'**2** . . . (2) In the case of other loss or damage, a person cannot so exclude or restrict his liability for negligence except in so far as the term or notice satisfies the requirement of reasonableness . . .

**11** . . . (3) In relation to a notice (not being a notice having contractual effect), the requirement of reasonableness under this Act is that it should be fair and reasonable to allow reliance on it, having regard to all the circumstances obtaining when the liability arose or (but for the notice) would have arisen . . .

**13.**—(1) To the extent that this Part of this Act prevents the exclusion or restriction of any liability it also prevents—(*a*) making the liability or its enforcement subject to restrictive or onerous conditions; (*b*) excluding or restricting any right or remedy in respect of the liability, or subjecting a person to any prejudice in consequence of his pursuing any such right or remedy; (*c*) excluding or restricting rules of evidence or procedure; and (to that extent) sections 2 and 5 to 7 also prevent excluding or restricting liability by reference to terms and notices which exclude or restrict the relevant obligation or duty . . .'

In the other appeal, *Harris v Wyre Forest DC*, the Court of Appeal held that the 1977 Act did not apply. Nourse LJ accepted the argument of the council and Mr Lee that a notice which prevented a duty of care from coming into existence was not one on which s 2(2) bit (see [1988] 1 All ER 691 at 699, [1988] QB 835 at 848). Kerr LJ said ([1988] 1 All ER 691 at 703, [1988] QB 835 at 854):

'For these reasons I agree with the judgments of Nourse LJ and Caulfield J that the effect of the 1977 Act on the disclaimer of responsibility and warning is of no relevance to the present case. One never reaches that issue, since it arises only if the existence of a duty of care and a breach of it have first been established.'

Counsel for the council and Mr Lee in the *Harris* appeal supported the reasoning of
*a* the Court of Appeal and argued that the Act only applied to a disclaimer which operated
after a breach of duty had occurred. Counsel for the surveyors in this appeal adopted his
argument.

My Lords, with all respect to the judges of the Court of Appeal, I think that they have
overlooked the importance of s 13(1). The words 'liability for negligence' in s 2(2) must
be read together with s 13(1), which states that the former section prevents the exclusion
*b* of liability by notices 'which exclude or restrict the relevant obligation or duty'. These
words are unambiguous and are entirely appropriate to cover a disclaimer which prevents
a duty coming into existence. It follows that the disclaimers here given are subject to the
provisions of the Act and will therefore only be effective if they satisfy the requirement
of reasonableness.

(III) I have had the advantage of reading in draft the speech of my noble and learned
*c* friend Lord Griffiths, and I gratefully adopt his reasons for concluding that the disclaimers
did not satisfy the statutory requirement of reasonableness. I cannot usefully add
anything to what he has said on this matter.

For the foregoing reasons I would dismiss this appeal.

*d* *Harris v Wyre Forest DC*

Mr and Mrs Harris, two young people who were at the time contemplating matrimony,
applied to the council for a mortgage over a house which they wished to buy. At the
time, local authorities were empowered by s 43 of the Housing (Financial Provisions) Act
1958 (as amended by s 37 of the Local Government Act 1974) to advance money up to a
sum not exceeding the value of the security for house purchase. Before making an
*e* advance the local authority was required to satisfy themselves that the house was or
would be made in all respects fit for human habitation and have a valuation made.

The Harrises submitted their application form together with a 'valuation fee and
administration fee' of £22. The form contained an acknowledgment that the council
accepted no responsibility for the value or condition of the house by reason of the
*f* inspection report. The council instructed the second respondent, Mr Lee, a valuer in
their employment, to inspect the house and report. Mr Lee valued the house at the
asking price of £9,450, recommended that the maximum loan should be 90% of the
value and under the heading of 'Essential repairs' stated: '(1) Obtain report for District
Council from M.E.B. [Midlands Electricity Board] regarding electrics and carry out any
recommendations. (2) Make good mortar fillets to Extension.' Mr Lee's report was not
*g* shown to the Harrises but they were subsequently offered, by the council, an advance of
£8,505 on condition, inter alia, that they carried out the essential repairs above referred
to. Relying on this offer and without obtaining other advice as to value, the Harrises
bought the house. Unfortunately there were present serious structural defects in the
house which Mr Lee had not referred to and which materially reduced its value. As a
result of the defects the Harrises suffered loss.

*h*    The foregoing is a summary of the relevant facts and I turn to examine in more detail
those facts which determine whether or not Mr Lee owed a duty of care to the Harrises.
He knew that the report would not be sent to the Harrises but that they would be told
the amount of any advance and would be told of any repairs which he considered to be
essential. He also knew that the Harrises were likely to be first-time buyers of modest
means. There is no finding by the judge that he was aware that the Harrises were likely
*j* to rely on his valuation in buying the house and that they were unlikely to obtain
independent advice. However, after referring to the position of a valuer acting for a
building society, Schiemann J said ([1987] 1 EGLR 231 at 236):

'Such a valuer has been held to be liable to the mortgagor in the *Yianni* case and I
see nothing on the grounds of policy or in the subsequent case law which should
prevent me from following that decision.'

In *Yianni v Edwin Evans & Sons (a firm)* [1981] 3 All ER 592, [1982] QB 438 the plaintiffs applied to a building society for a mortgage and paid a fee for the statutory valuation. The building society instructed the defendant surveyors to value the property and on receipt of their valuation offered to the plaintiffs a loan of 80% of the asking price of the house. The defendants' report was not made available to the plaintiffs. The application form advised the plaintiffs to obtain an independent survey and with the offer of the loan the plaintiffs received a notice under s 30 of the Building Societies Act 1962 indicating that an advance by the building society did not imply that the purchase price was reasonable. Consequent on the offer, the plaintiffs bought the house without obtaining an independent valuation. Some time later, structural defects were discovered which the defendants admitted that they should have found on their inspection. The plaintiffs sucessfully sued the defendants for negligence. However, the facts in that case differed in one material aspect from those in the present in that there was there unchallenged evidence from the chief surveyor of a very large building society that no more than 15% of persons applying to a building society for a mortgage instructed independent surveys. Park J concluded that the defendant surveyors, who had regularly carried out valuations for the building society, were aware that their figure of valuation would be passed on to the plaintiffs and were aware that the plaintiffs would rely on it when they decided to accept the offer of the building society. In the absence of such a specific finding of awareness in the present case I do not think that it can necessarily be assumed that the experience of a local authority valuation surveyor must be the same as that of an independent surveyor regularly acting on behalf of a large building society. The only other relevant piece of evidence in the extracts from the transcript is the following question by the judge to Mr Lee and the answer thereto:

'Q. You did know that if the list of essential repairs was passed on to the mortgagor he would take the view that these were, in your eyes, the essential repairs? A. That is right . . .'

My Lords, I have found this case very much more difficult than that of *Smith v Eric S Bush (a firm)*. I do not find it easy to infer from such findings as were made by Schiemann J and from the question and answer above quoted that Mr Lee was aware that the Harrises would be likely to buy on reliance on his valuation without obtaining further advice. However, I understand that your Lordships do not share this difficulty and in these circumstances I do not feel disposed to dissent from the majority view. I therefore conclude, albeit with hesitation, that Mr Lee would, but for the terms of the disclaimer in the application form, have owed a duty of care to the Harrises. In that situation the second and third question which I posed in the *Smith v Eric S Bush* appeal would arise and would fall to be answered in the same way as in that appeal. It therefore follows that this appeal should be allowed.

*Appeal in Harris v Wyre Forest DC allowed. Appeal in Smith v Eric S Bush (a firm) dismissed.*

Solicitors: *Thursfield Adams & Westons*, Kidderminster (for Mr and Mrs Harris); *Lawrence Graham*, agents for *Rowleys & Blewitts*, Birmingham (for the council and Mr Lee); *Barlow Lyde & Gilbert* (for the surveyors); *Hood Vores & Allwood*, Dereham (for Mrs Smith).

Mary Rose Plummer   Barrister.

# F v West Berkshire Health Authority and another (Mental Health Act Commission intervening)

HOUSE OF LORDS

LORD BRIDGE OF HARWICH, LORD BRANDON OF OAKBROOK, LORD GRIFFITHS, LORD GOFF OF CHIEVELEY AND LORD JAUNCEY OF TULLICHETTLE

27, 28 FEBRUARY 1, 2, 6, 7, 8, 9 MARCH, 4, 24 MAY 1989

*Sterilisation – Mentally handicapped person – Consent – Female voluntary in-patient at mental health hospital – Patient having sexual relations with male patient and operation required to be performed on her in her best interests – Whether operation can lawfully be carried out despite inability of patient to consent – Whether court having jurisdiction to give or withhold consent to operation – Appropriate procedure to be adopted.*

*Medical practitioner – Trespass to the person – Consent to operation – Operation on or other treatment of person unable to give consent – Lawfulness of operation or other treatment – Operation or other treatment in person's best interests – Whether operation or other treatment lawful – Whether lawful only if carried out to save life or to ensure improvement or prevent deterioration in physical or mental health.*

*Declaration – Jurisdiction – Declaration as to lawfulness of proposed conduct – Proposed medical treatment – Medical treatment of person unable to consent thereto – Mentally handicapped person – Sterilisation – Sterilisation in person's best interests – Whether declaration necessary to establish lawfulness of sterilisation – How application for declaration should be made – Who should be parties to application – RSC Ord 15, r 16.*

*Mental health – Patient – Management of property and affairs of patient – Management by judicial authorities – Affairs – Whether 'affairs of patient' extending to medical treatment or limited to business affairs etc – Mental Health Act 1983, s 93(1).*

The plaintiff, F, a woman aged 36, suffered from serious mental disability. She had the verbal capacity of a child aged two and the general mental capacity of a child aged four or five. Since the age of 14 she had been a voluntary in-patient at a mental hospital controlled by the defendant health authority. She had formed a sexual relationship with a male patient, P. There was medical evidence that, from a psychiatric point of view, it would be disastrous for her to become pregnant and since there were serious objections to all ordinary methods of contraception, either because she would be unable to use them effectively or because of a risk to her physical health, the medical staff in charge of F decided that the best course was for her to be sterilised. Because she was disabled by her mental capacity from giving her consent to the operation her mother, acting as her next friend, sought as against the health authority a declaration under RSC Ord 15, r 16[a] that the absence of her consent would not make sterilisation of her an unlawful act. It was conceded that the court had no power to give consent on behalf of F or to dispense with the need for such consent because the parens patriae jurisdiction in respect of persons suffering from mental incapacity no longer existed and there was no comparable statutory jurisdiction. The judge granted the declaration sought. The Official Solicitor appealed to the Court of Appeal, which affirmed the judge's decision, holding that the court had power to authorise such an operation. The Official Solicitor appealed to the House of Lords, contending that in the absence of a parens patriae jurisdiction sterilisation of an adult mental patient who was unable to give her consent to the operation could never be lawful.

---

*a*  Rule 16 is set out at p 570 *b c*, post

**Held** – The court had no jurisdiction either by statute or derived from the Crown as
parens patriae to give or withhold consent to a sterilisation operation on an adult woman *a*
disabled by mental inacpacity (as it would have in wardship proceedings in the case of a
minor) because the Crown's previous statutory and prerogative jurisdiction in lunacy
had been replaced by the provisions of the Mental Health Act 1983. Furthermore, the
jurisdiction conferred on the nominated judge under s 93(1)[b] of the 1983 Act to manage
'the affairs of patients' did not extend to questions relating to the medical treatment of a
patient but related solely to a patient's business affairs and the like. However, the court *b*
did have jurisdiction either under its inherent jurisdiction or under RSC Ord 15, r 16 to
make a declaration that the proposed operation was lawful on the ground that in the
circumstances it was in the best interests of the patient, and although (Lord Griffiths
dissenting) such a declaration was not necessary to establish the lawfulness of the
operation, because a doctor could lawfully operate on such a patient if it was in her best
interests, in practice the court's jurisdiction should be invoked whenever it was proposed *c*
to perform such an operation, since a declaration would establish by judicial process
whether the proposed operation was in the best interesinterests of the patient and
therefore lawful. In determining whether the proposed operation was in the best interests
of the patient the court should apply the established test of what would be accepted as
appropriate treatment at the time by a reasonable body of medical opinion skilled in that
particular form of treatment. The judge had accordingly been right to grant the *d*
declaration sought and the appeal would therefore be dismissed (see p 548 *d* to *f*, p 550 *h*,
p 552 *d*, p 553 *b*, p 554 *c* to *e*, p 556 *g* to p 557 *b e f*, p 558 *a*, p 560 *e* to *g*, p 561 *d e h j*,
p 562 *f*, p 563 *a*, p 565 *j* to p 566 *a f g*, p 567 *f* to *h*, p 568 *g* and p 571 *b d* to *f h*, post).
   *Bolam v Friern Hospital Management Committee* [1957] 2 All ER 118 applied.
   Per curiam. (1) Applications for a declaration that a proposed operation on, or medical
treatment for, a patient can lawfully be carried out despite the inability of such patient *e*
to give his consent to it should be made by way of originating summons issued out of
the Family Division of the High Court. The applicants should normally be those
responsible for the care of the patient or those intending to carry out the proposed
operation or other treatment if it is declared to be lawful. The patient must always be a
party and should normally be a respondent. In cases in which the patient is a respondent *f*
the patient's guardian ad litem should normally be the Official Solicitor. In any cases in
which the Official Solicitor is neither the next friend nor the guardian ad litem of the
patient nor an applicant he must be a respondent. With a view to protecting the patient's
privacy, but always subject to the judge's discretion, the hearing should be in chambers,
but the decision and the reasons for it should be given in open court (see p 548 *d f g*,
p 555 *d*, p 558 *c* to *f*, p 561 *d e*, p 568 *h*, p 569 *a* and p 571 *f*, post).
   (2) At common law a doctor can lawfully operate on or give other treatment to adult *g*
patients who are incapable of consenting to his doing so, provided that the operation or
treatment is in the best interests of such patients. The operation or treatment will be in
their best interests only if it is carried out in order either to save their lives or to ensure
improvement or prevent deterioration in their physical or mental health (see p 548 *d*,
p 549 *a b*, p 551 *c*, p 557 *e*, p 560 *e f*, p 561 *d e*, p 565 *j* to p 566 *a f g* and p 571 *f h*, post). *h*

**Notes**
For general powers and duties of guardians of mental health patients, see 30 Halsbury's
Laws (4th edn) para 1153.
   For the Crown as parens patriae, see 8 ibid para 901.
   For consent to medical treatment, see 30 ibid para 38, and for cases on the subject, see *j*
33 Digest (Reissue) 273, 2242–2243.
   For the court's powers to grant declarations, see 1 Halsbury's Laws (4th edn) para 185,
and for cases on the subject, see 30 Digest (Reissue) 189–211, 202–318.
   For the Mental Health Act 1983, s 93, see 28 Halsbury's Statutes (4th edn) 732.

---

*b*   Section 93(1), so far as material, is set out at p 553 *d*, post

**Cases referred to in opinions**

a  *A-G's Reference (No 6 of 1980), Re* [1981] 2 All ER 1057, [1981] QB 715, [1981] 3 WLR 125, CA.
*Australasian Steam Navigation Co v Morse* (1872) LR 4 PC 222.
*B (a minor) (wardship: sterilisation), Re* [1987] 2 All ER 206, [1988] AC 199, [1987] 2 WLR 1213, HL.
*Bolam v Friern Hospital Management Committee* [1957] 2 All ER 118, [1957] 1 WLR 582.
b  *Cole v Turner* (1704) Holt KB 108, 90 ER 958, NP.
*Collins v Wilcock* [1984] 3 All ER 374, [1984] 1 WLR 1172, DC.
*D (a minor) (wardship: sterilisation), Re* [1976] 1 All ER 326, [1976] Fam 185, [1976] 2 WLR 279.
*Eve, Re* (1986) 31 DLR (4th) 1, Can SC.
*Grady, Re* (1981) 85 NJ 235, NJ SC.
c  *Guaranty Trust Co of New York v Hannay & Co* [1915] 2 KB 536, [1914–15] All ER Rep 24, CA.
*Jane, Re* (22 December 1988, unreported), Aust Fam Ct.
*Marshall v Curry* [1933] 3 DLR 260, NS SC.
*Murray v McMurchy* [1949] 2 DLR 442, BC SC.
*Prager v Blatspiel Stamp & Heacock Ltd* [1924] 1 KB 566, [1924] All ER Rep 524.
d  *R v Coney* (1882) 8 QBD 534, CCR.
*R v Donovan* [1934] 2 KB 498, [1934] All ER Rep 207, CCA.
*Russian Commercial and Industrial Bank v British Bank for Foreign Trade Ltd* [1921] 2 AC 438, [1921] All ER Rep 329, HL.
*S v S, W v Official Solicitor* [1970] 3 All ER 107, [1972] AC 24, [1970] 3 WLR 366, HL.
*Schloendorff v Society of New York Hospital* (1914) 211 NY 125, NY Ct of Apps.
e  *Sidaway v Bethlem Royal Hospital Governors* [1985] 1 All ER 643, [1985] AC 871, [1985] 2 WLR 480, HL.
*T, Re* (14 May 1987, unreported), Fam D.
*T v T* [1988] 1 All ER 613, [1988] Fam 62, [1988] 2 WLR 189.
*Vine v National Dock Labour Board* [1956] 3 All ER 939, [1957] AC 488, [1957] 2 All ER 106, HL.
f  *Wilson v Pringle* [1986] 2 All ER 440, [1987] QB 237, [1986] 3 WLR 1, CA.
*X, Re* (1987) Times, 4 June.

**Appeal**

g  The Official Solicitor to the Supreme Court appealed with the leave of the Court of Appeal against the decision of that court (Lord Donaldson MR, Neill and Butler-Sloss LJJ) on 3 February 1989 dismissing his appeal brought pursuant to a direction given by the Lord Chancellor under s 90(3)(b) of the Supreme Court Act 1981 on 16 January 1989 ([1989] 1 All ER 764, [1989] 1 WLR 133) and by leave granted by the Court of Appeal on 8 December 1988 from the order dated 2 December 1988 of Scott Baker J sitting in chambers but giving judgment in open court whereby by an originating summons
h  issued on the application of the first respondent, F, by her mother and next friend against the second respondent, West Berkshire Health Authority, he ordered and declared that under RSC Ord 15, r 16 the sterilisation of F would not amount to an unlawful act by reason only of the absence of F's consent. The House of Lords allowed an application by the Mental Health Act Commission for England and Wales for leave to intervene in the appeal. The facts are set out in the opinion of Lord Brandon.

j
*James Munby QC* for the Official Solicitor.
*R F Nelson QC, Jean Ritchie* and *James Medd* for F.
*Adrian Whitfield QC, Robert Francis* and *Adrian Hopkins* for the health authority.
*Allan Levy* as amicus curiae.
*Duncan Ouseley* for the commission.

Their Lordships took time for consideration.

4 May. **LORD BRIDGE OF HARWICH** made the following announcement. My
Lords, I understand that your Lordships all agree on the appropriate disposal of this
appeal although not yet ready to state your reasons. In the circumstances it is obviously
desirable that the appeal should now be determined for reasons to be given later. I
accordingly propose that the appeal be dismissed but that there be substituted for the
order and declaration made by Scott Baker J an order in the following terms. (1) It is
declared that the operation of sterilisation proposed to be performed on the plaintiff
being in the existing circumstances in her best interests can lawfully be performed on
her despite her inability to consent to it. (2) It is ordered that in the event of a material
change in the existing circumstances occurring before the said operation has been
performed any party shall have liberty to apply for such further or other declaration or
order as may be just.

24 May. The following opinions were delivered.

**LORD BRIDGE OF HARWICH.** My Lords, I have had the advantage of reading the
speeches of my noble and learned friends Lord Brandon and Lord Goff. I concurred in
the dismissal of the appeal, subject to a variation of the terms of the order made by Scott
Baker J for the reasons given by them.

The appeal raised a number of difficult questions regarding both the jurisdiction and
the procedure of the court in relation to the lawfulness of the sterilisation of an adult
woman disabled by mental incapacity from giving her consent to the operation. These
issues are fully examined by Lord Brandon and Lord Goff and I further agree, for the
reasons they give, with the following conclusions: (1) that no court now has jurisdiction
either by statute or derived from the Crown as parens patriae to give or withhold consent
to such an operation in the case of an adult as it would in wardship proceedings in the
case of a minor; (2) that the court has jurisdiction to declare the lawfulness of such an
operation proposed to be performed on the ground that it is in the circumstances in the
best interests of the woman and that, although such a declaration is not necessary to
establish the lawfulness of the operation, in practice the court's jurisdiction should be
invoked whenever such an operation is proposed to be performed; (3) that for the future
the procedure to be used when applying for a declaration of the kind in question should
be regulated as proposed in the speech of my noble and learned friend Lord Brandon.

The issues canvassed in argument before your Lordships revealed the paucity of clearly
defined principles in the common law which may be applied to determine the lawfulness
of medical or surgical treatment given to a patient who for any reason, temporary or
permanent, lacks the capacity to give or to communicate consent to that treatment. It
seems to me to be axiomatic that treatment which is necessary to preserve the life, health
or well-being of the patient may lawfully be given without consent. But, if a rigid
criterion of necessity were to be applied to determine what is and what is not lawful in
the treatment of the unconscious and the incompetent, many of those unfortunate
enough to be deprived of the capacity to make or communicate rational decisions by
accident, illness or unsoundness of mind might be deprived of treatment which it would
be entirely beneficial for them to receive.

Moreover, it seems to me of first importance that the common law should be readily
intelligible to and applicable by all those who undertake the care of persons lacking the
capacity to consent to treatment. It would be intolerable for members of the medical,
nursing and other professions devoted to the care of the sick that, in caring for those
lacking the capacity to consent to treatment, they should be put in the dilemma that, if
they administer the treatment which they believe to be in the patient's best interests,
acting with due skill and care, they run the risk of being held guilty of trespass to the
person, but, if they withhold that treatment, they may be in breach of a duty of care

a owed to the patient. If those who undertake responsibility for the care of incompetent or unconscious patients administer curative or prophylactic treatment which they believe to be appropriate to the patient's existing condition of disease, injury or bodily malfunction or susceptibility to such a condition in the future, the lawfulness of that treatment should be judged by one standard, not two. It follows that if the professionals in question have acted with due skill and care, judged by the well-known test laid down in *Bolam v Friern Hospital Management Committee* [1957] 2 All ER 118, [1957] 1 WLR 582,

b they should be immune from liability in trespass, just as they are immune from liability in negligence. The special considerations which apply in the case of the sterilisation of a woman who is physically perfectly healthy or of an operation on an organ transplant donor arise only because such treatment cannot be considered either curative or prophylactic.

c **LORD BRANDON OF OAKBROOK.** My Lords, this appeal concerns the proposed sterilisation of an adult woman, F, who is disabled by mental incapacity from consenting to the operation. By an originating summons issued in the High Court, Family Division, on 20 June 1988, in which F by her mother and next friend was named as plaintiff and the West Berkshire Health Authority as defendant, F applied for (1) a declaration under RSC Ord 15, r 16 that to effect her sterilisation would not amount to an unlawful act by

d reason only of the absence of her consent or (2) the consent of the court under either its parens patriae or its inherent jurisdiction to her sterilisation. The application was heard by Scott Baker J in chambers with the assistance of counsel instructed by the Official Solicitor as amicus curiae. On 2 December 1988 the judge gave judgment in open court and by order of that date made the declaration sought under (1) above. Pursuant to a direction given by the Lord Chancellor under s 90(3)(b) of the Supreme Court Act 1981

e the Official Solicitor, being of opinion that it was in F's interests that the case should be considered by the Court of Appeal, obtained the leave of that court to appeal against the decision of Scott Baker J. By order dated 3 February 1989 the Court of Appeal (Lord Donaldson MR, Neill and Butler-Sloss LJJ) dismissed the Official Solicitor's appeal and gave him leave to appeal to your Lordships' House. Subsequently, the House allowed an application by the Mental Health Act Commission for England and Wales for leave to

f intervene in the appeal and your Lordships had the benefit of additional argument by counsel for them at the hearing.

The material facts relating to F, which are not in dispute, are these. She was born on 13 January 1953, so that she is now 36. She suffers from serious mental disability, probably as a consequence of an acute infection of the respiratory tract which she had when she was about nine months old. She has been a voluntary in-patient at Borocourt

g Hospital (a mental hospital under the control of the health authority) since 1967, when she was 14. Her mental disability takes the form of an arrested or incomplete development of the mind. She has the verbal capacity of a child of two and the general mental capacity of a child of four to five. She is unable to express her views in words but can indicate what she likes or dislikes, for example people, food, clothes and matters of

h routine. She experiences emotions such as enjoyment, sadness and fear, but is prone to express them differently from others. She is liable to become aggressive. Her mother is her only relative and visits her regularly. There is a strong bond of affection between them. As a result of the treatment which F has received during her time in hospital she has made significant progress. She has become less aggressive and is allowed considerable freedom of movement about the hospital grounds, which are large. There is, however,

j no prospect of any development in her mental capacity.

The question of F being sterilised has arisen because of a relationship which she has formed with a male patient at the same hospital, P. This relationship is of a sexual nature and probably involves sexual intercourse, or something close to it, about twice a month. The relationship is entirely voluntary on F's part and it is likely that she obtains pleasure from it. There is no reason to believe that F has other than the ordinary fertility of a woman of her age. Because of her mental disability, however, she could not cope at all with pregnancy, labour or delivery, the meaning of which she would not understand. Nor could she care for a baby if she ever had one. In these circumstances it would, from a psychiatric point of view, be disastrous for her to conceive a child. There is a serious objection to each of the ordinary methods of contraception. So far as varieties of the pill are concerned she would not be able to use them effectively and there is a risk of their causing damage to her physical health. So far as an interuterine device is concerned, there would be danger of infection arising, the symptoms of which she would not be able to describe so that remedial measures could not be taken in time.

In the light of the facts set out above Scott Baker J concluded that it would be in the best interests of F to have an operation for sterilisation by ligation of her fallopian tubes. The Court of Appeal unanimously affirmed that conclusion, and no challenge to its correctness was made on behalf of any party at the hearing of the appeal before your Lordships.

It might have been supposed that, with such complete agreement that it was in F's best interests that she should be sterilised, no difficulty about giving effect to that agreement would have arisen. Difficulty, however, has arisen because of doubts about three questions of law and legal procedure. The first question is whether it is necessary or desirable for the court to become involved in the matter at all. The second question is: if so, what jurisdiction does the court have to deal with the matter, and according to what principles should that jurisdiction be exercised? The third question is: assuming that the court has jurisdiction and is bound to exercise it in a particular manner, what procedure should be used for the invocation and subsequent exercise of that jurisdiction?

If F were a minor of say 17, instead of an adult of 36, and the same problem arose in relation to her, there would be no difficulty in answering these three questions. This is because your Lordships' House dealt authoritatively with a case involving the sterilisation of a girl just under 18, who suffered from mental disability closely comparable to F's, in *Re B (a minor) (wardship: sterilisation)* [1987] 2 All ER 206, [1988] AC 199. The answer to the first question would have been that, because of the seriousness of deciding whether the girl should be sterilised or not, the court, in the form of the High Court, Family Division, should be involved in the matter. The answer to the second question would be that the court could exercise its wardship jurisdiction, and, in doing so, would be bound to treat the welfare, or to use an expression with substantially the same meaning, the best interests of the minor, as the paramount consideration. The answer to the third question would be that the wardship jurisdiction of a court would be invoked by the issue by an interested party of an originating summons under RSC Ord 90, r 3, and the procedure then followed would be the ordinary procedure designed to bring all relevant expert and other evidence before the court so as to enable it to decide whether sterilisation was or was not in the best interests of the girl.

For reasons which will become apparent later, no court or judge has now any jurisdiction with respect to the person of an adult under mental disability comparable with the wardship jurisdiction of the High Court with respect to the person of a minor in a similar condition. Because of this, no ready answers are available to the three questions referred to above in the case of such an adult, and a separate examination of each of them has to be made.

(1) *The necessity or desirability of the court being involved*

Part IV of the Mental Health Act 1983 contains provisions, which it is not necessary to detail, imposing restrictions or conditions on the giving to mentally disordered persons of certain kinds of treatment for their mental disorder. The Act, however, does not contain any provisions relating to the giving of treatment to patients for any conditions other than their mental disorder. The result is that the lawfulness of giving any treatment of the latter kind depends not on statute but the common law.

At common law a doctor cannot lawfully operate on adult patients of sound mind, or

give them any other treatment involving the application of physical force however small
*a* (which I shall refer to as 'other treatment'), without their consent. If a doctor were to
operate on such patients, or give them other treatment, without their consent, he would
commit the actionable tort of trespass to the person. There are, however, cases where
adult patients cannot give or refuse their consent to an operation or other treatment. One
case is where, as a result of an accident or otherwise, an adult patient is unconscious and
an operation or other treatment cannot be safely delayed until he or she recovers
*b* consciousness. Another case is where a patient, though adult, cannot by reason of mental
disability understand the nature or purpose of an operation or other treatment. The
common law would be seriously defective if it failed to provide a solution to the problem
created by such inability to consent. In my opinion, however, the common law does not
fail. In my opinion, the solution to the problem which the common law provides is that
a doctor can lawfully operate on, or give other treatment to, adult patients who are
*c* incapable, for one reason or another, of consenting to his doing so, provided that the
operation or other treatment concerned is in the best interests of such patients. The
operation or other treatment will be in their best interests if, but only if, it is carried out
in order either to save their lives or to ensure improvement or prevent deterioration in
their physical or mental health.

Different views have been put forward with regard to the principle which makes it
*d* lawful for a doctor to operate on or give other treatment to adult patients without their
consent in the two cases to which I have referred above. The Court of Appeal in the
present case regarded the matter as depending on the public interest. I would not disagree
with that as a broad proposition, but I think that it is helpful to consider the principle in
accordance with which the public interest leads to this result. In my opinion, the
principle is that, when persons lack the capacity, for whatever reason, to take decisions
*e* about the performance of operations on them, or the giving of other medical treatment
to them, it is necessary that some other person or persons, with the appropriate
qualifications, should take such decisions for them. Otherwise they would be deprived
of medical care which they need and to which they are entitled.

In many cases, however, it will not only be lawful for doctors, on the ground of
necessity, to operate on or give other medical treatment to adult patients disabled from
*f* giving their consent: it will also be their common law duty to do so.

In the case of adult patients made unconscious by an accident or otherwise, they will
normally be received into the casualty department of a hospital, which thereby
undertakes the care of them. It will then be the duty of the doctors at that hospital to use
their best endeavours to do, by way of either an operation or other treatment, that which
is in the best interests of such patients.
*g*
In the case of adult patients suffering from mental disability, they will normally, in
accordance with the scheme of the Mental Health Act 1983, be either in the care of
guardians, who will refer them to doctors for medical treatment, or of doctors at mental
hospitals in which the patients either reside voluntarily or are detained compulsorily. It
will then again be the duty of the doctors concerned to use their best endeavours to do,
*h* by way of either an operation or other treatment, that which is in the best interests of
such patients.

The application of the principle which I have described means that the lawfulness of a
doctor operating on, or giving other treatment to, an adult patient disabled from giving
consent will depend not on any approval or sanction of a court but on the question
whether the operation or other treatment is in the best interests of the patient concerned.
*j* That is, from a practical point of view, just as well, for, if every operation to be performed,
or other treatment to be given, required the approval or sanction of the court, the whole
process of medical care for such patients would grind to a halt.

That is not the end of the matter, however, for there remains a further question to be
considered. That question is whether, in the case of an operation for the sterilisation of
an adult woman of child-bearing age who is mentally disabled from giving or refusing

her consent to it, although involvement of the court is not strictly necessary as a matter of law, it is nevertheless highly desirable as a matter of good practice. In considering that *a* question, it is necessary to have regard to the special features of such an operation. These features are: first, the operation will in most cases be irreversible; second, by reason of the general irreversibility of the operation, the almost certain result of it will be to deprive the woman concerned of what is widely, and as I think rightly, regarded as one of the fundamental rights of a woman, namely the right to bear children; third, the deprivation of that right gives rise to moral and emotional considerations to which many *b* people attach great importance; fourth, if the question whether the operation is in the best interests of the woman is left to be decided without the involvement of the court, there may be a greater risk of it being decided wrongly, or at least of it being thought to have been decided wrongly; fifth, if there is no involvement of the court, there is a risk of the operation being carried out for improper reasons or with improper motives; and, sixth, involvement of the court in the decision to operate, if that is the decision reached, *c* should serve to protect the doctor or doctors who perform the operation, and any others who may be concerned in it, from subsequent adverse criticisms or claims.

Having regard to all these matters, I am clearly of the opinion that, although in the case of an operation of the kind under discussion involvement of the court is not strictly necessary as a matter of law, it is nevertheless highly desirable as a matter of good practice.

There may be cases of other special operations to which similar considerations would *d* apply. I think it best, however, to leave such other cases to be examined as and when they arise.

(2) *The jurisdiction of the court and the principles on which it should be exercised*

In the course of the argument in this appeal your Lordships were invited to consider four kinds of jurisdiction by the exercise of which the court might become involved in *e* the decision whether F should be sterilised or not. These were: first, the parens patriae jurisdiction; second, jurisdiction under Pt VII of the Mental Health Act 1983; third, a jurisdiction which the Court of Appeal considered could be exercised under appropriate amendments to RSC Ord 80; and, fourth, the jurisdiction to make declarations. I shall examine each of these in turn.

I consider first the parens patriae jurisdiction. This is an ancient prerogative jurisdiction *f* of the Crown going back as far perhaps as the thirteenth century. Under it the Crown as parens patriae had both the power and the duty to protect the persons and property of those unable to do so for themselves, a category which included minors (formerly described as infants) and persons of unsound mind (formerly described as lunatics or idiots). While the history of that jurisdiction and the manner of its exercise from its inception until the present day is of the greatest interest, I do not consider that it would *g* serve any useful purpose to recount it here. I say that because it was accepted by the Court of Appeal, and not challenged by any of the parties to the appeal before your Lordships, that the present situation with regard to the parens patriae jurisdiction as related to minors survives now in the form of the wardship jurisdiction of the High Court, Family Division. Second, so much of the parens patriae jurisdiction as related to *h* persons of unsound mind no longer exists. It ceased to exist as a result of two events, both of which took place on 1 November 1960. The first event was the coming into force of the Mental Health Act 1959, s 1 of which provided:

'Subject to the transitional provisions contained in this Act, the Lunacy and Mental Treatment Acts, 1890 to 1930, and the Mental Deficiency Acts, 1913 to 1938, shall cease to have effect, and the following provisions of this Act shall have *j* effect in lieu of those enactments with respect to the reception, care and treatment of mentally disordered patients, the management of their property, and other matters related thereto.'

The second event was the revocation by warrant under the sign manual of the last

warrant dated 10 April 1956, by which the jurisdiction of the Crown over the persons
a and property of those found to be of unsound mind by inquisition had been assigned to
the Lord Chancellor and the judges of the High Court, Chancery Division.

The effect of s 1 of the 1959 Act, together with the warrant of revocation referred to
above, was to sweep away the previous statutory and prerogative jursidiction in lunacy,
leaving the law relating to persons of unsound mind to be governed solely, so far as
statutory enactments are concerned, by the provisions of that Act. So far as matters not
b governed by those provisions are concerned, the common law relating to persons of
unsound mind continued to apply. It follows that the parens patriae jurisdiction with
respect to persons of unsound mind is not now available to be invoked in order to involve
the court or a judge in the decision about the sterilisation of F.

I consider, second, jurisdiction under Pt VII of the Mental Health Act 1983. That part
of the Act has the heading 'Management of Property and Affairs of Patients' and comprises
c ss 93 to 113. The question which has to be considered is whether the expression 'the
affairs of patients', as used in the heading and various sections of Pt VII, includes medical
treatment such as an operation for sterilisation. In order to answer that question, it is
necessary to examine the following sections in Pt VII which are mainly relevant to it:

'**93.**—(1) The Lord Chancellor shall from time to time nominate one or more
d judges of the Supreme Court . . . to act for the purposes of this Part of this Act.

(2) There shall continue to be an office of the Supreme Court, called the Court of
Protection, for the protection and management, as provided by this Part of this Act,
of the property and affairs of persons under disability . . .

**95.**—(1) The judge may, with respect to the property and affairs of a patient, do
or secure the doing of all such things as appear necessary or expedient—(a) for the
e maintenance or other benefit of the patient, (b) for the maintenance or other benefit
of members of the patient's family, (c) for making provision for other persons or
purposes for whom or which the patient might be expected to provide if he were
not mentally disordered, or (d) otherwise for administering the patient's affairs.

(2) In the exercise of the powers conferred by this section regard shall be had first
of all to the requirements of the patient, and the rules of law which restricted the
f enforcement by a creditor of rights against property under the control of the judge
in lunacy shall apply to property under the control of the judge; but, subject to the
foregoing provisions of this subsection, the judge shall, in administering a patient's
affairs, have regard to the interests of creditors and also to the desirability of making
provision for obligations of the patient notwithstanding that they may not be legally
enforceable.

g **96.** Without prejudice to the generality of section 95 above, the judge shall have
power to make such orders and give such directions and authorities as he thinks fit
for the purposes of that section and in particular may for those purposes make orders
or give directions or authorities for—(a) the control . . . and management of any
property of the patient; (b) the sale, exchange, charging or other disposition of or
h dealing with any property of the patient; (c) the acquisition of any property in the
name or on behalf of the patient; (d) the settlement of any property of the patient,
or the gift of any property of the patient to any such persons or for any such purposes
as are mentioned in paragraphs (b) and (c) of section 95(1) above; (e) the execution
for the patient of a will making any provision . . . which could be made by a will
executed by the patient if he were not mentally disordered; (f) the carrying on by a
j suitable person of any profession, trade or business of the patient; (g) the dissolution
of a partnership of which the patient is a member; (h) the carrying out of any
contract entered into by the patient; (i) the conduct of legal proceedings in the name
of the patient or on his behalf; (j) the reimbursement out of the property of the
patient . . . of money applied by any person either in payment of the patient's debts
(whether legally enforceable or not) or for the maintenance or other benefit of the

patient or members of his family . . . (k) the exercise of any power (including a
power to consent) vested in the patient, whether beneficially, or as guardian or   *a*
trustee, or otherwise . . .'

The expression 'the affairs of patients', taken by itself and without regard to the context
in which it appears, is, in my view, capable of extending to medical treatment of patients
other than treatment for their mental disorder. There is further an obvious attraction in
construing that expression, as used in Pt VII of the 1983 Act, as having that extended   *b*
meaning (the wider meaning), since there would then be a judicial authority, namely a
judge nominated under s 93(1), who would have statutory power to authorise, or refuse
to authorise, the sterilisation of an adult woman of unsound mind such as F. There are
two passages in the sections of the Act set out above which, if they do not expressly
support the wider meaning, are at least consistent with it. The first is the passage in
s 95(1)(a) 'for the maintenance *or other benefit* of the patient'. The second is the passage in   *c*
s 96(1)(k) 'the exercise of any power *(including a power to consent)* vested in the patient,
whether beneficially, or as guardian or trustee, or otherwise'. It seems to me, however,
that, when one examines the general tenor of Pt VII of the Act, and more particularly the
context in which the two passages referred to above are to be found, the expression 'the
affairs of patients' cannot properly be construed as having the wider meaning. It must
rather be construed as including only business matters, legal transactions and other   *d*
dealings of a similar kind.

I would, therefore, hold that Pt VII of the 1983 Act does not confer on a judge
nominated under s 93(1) any jurisdiction to decide questions relating to the medical
treatment of a patient, such as the question of F's sterilisation in the present case.

I consider, third, the jurisdiction relied on by the Court of Appeal. Lord Donaldson
MR reached the conclusion that operations for the sterilisation of adult women, disabled   *e*
by mental disorder from giving their consent, as of minors, were in a special category,
and should not be performed without the approval of the court. He then turned to the
question of the procedure to be used for seeking that approval and said:

'This at once raised the question of how the court should be consulted and what
form its concurrence in the treatment of the patient should take. Thus far, apart   *f*
from the instant case, there have been three occasions on which proposed abortion
or sterilisation operations on adults who were incompetent to consent have been
brought before the court (*Re T* (14 May 1987, unreported) per Latey J; *Re X* (1987)
Times, 4 June per Reeve J and *T v T* [1988] 1 All ER 613, [1988] Fam 62 per Wood
J). In each case those who proposed that the operation be carried out sought and
obtained a declaration that to do so would be lawful. For my part, I do not think
that this is an appropriate procedure. A declaration changes nothing. All that the   *g*
court is being asked to do is to declare that, had a course of action been taken without
resort to the court, it would have been lawful anyway. In the context of the most
sensitive and potentially controversial forms of treatment the public interest requires
that the courts should give express approval before the treatment is carried out and
thereby provide an independent and broad based "third opinion". In the case of   *h*
wards of court, the performance of any such operation without first obtaining the
approval of the court would in any event constitute a very grave contempt of court.
In the case of other minors, the law will impose a very heavy burden of justification
on those who carry out the treatment without first ensuring that the minors are
made wards of court and the court's consent obtained. In the case of adults who are
themselves incompetent to consent, the law will impose an equally heavy burden of   *j*
justification if those who carry out the treatment do not first seek a determination
of the lawfulness of the proposed treatment by enabling the court to approve or to
disapprove. As this problem has only recently arisen, there is no specific procedure
laid down for obtaining the court's approval. RSC Ord 80 is that which is concerned

with persons under a disability and there should be little difficulty in framing a new rule under that order prescribing such a procedure. We trust that this will receive urgent attention from the Lord Chancellor and the Supreme Court Rule Committee. In the course of argument we were told that the Official Solicitor knows of a small number of other cases in which it is considered necessary that such an operation be performed on an adult patient, but in which the outcome of this appeal has been awaited. Clearly it would not be right that those patients should have to await the formulation and enactment of a new procedural rule. Fortunately the court has inherent jurisdiction to regulate its own proceedings where the rules make no provision and, pending the appearance of a new rule or a practice direction by the President of the Family Division of the High Court, we will direct as follows. (1) Applications for the court's approval of medical or surgical treatment where such approval is required should be by way of originating summons issuing out of the Family Division of the High Court. (2) The applicant should normally be those responsible for the care of the patient or those intending to carry out the treatment, if it is approved. (3) The patient must always be a party and should normally be a respondent. In cases in which the patient is a respondent the patient's guardian ad litem should normally be the Official Solicitor. In any cases in which the Official Solicitor is not either the next friend or the guardian ad litem of the patient or an applicant he shall be a respondent. (4) With a view to protecting the patient's privacy, but subject always to the judge's discretion, the hearing will be in chambers, but the decision and the reasons for that decision will be given in open court. As the procedure adopted in this case accorded with what at the time was thought to be appropriate and as the judge investigated the matter fully and reached a decision, the wisdom of which no one seeks to challenge, I would dismiss the appeal.'

Neill LJ said:

'There are, however, some operations where the intervention of a court is most desirable if not essential. In this category I would place operations for sterilisation and organ transplant operations where the incapacitated patient is to be the donor. The performance of these operations should be subject to outside scrutiny. The lawfulness of the operation will depend of course on the question whether it is necessary or not, but in my view it should become standard practice for the approval of the court to be obtained before an operation of this exceptional kind is carried out. Thus it is of the greatest importance to guard against any tendency for operations for sterilisation to be performed as a matter of convenience or merely to ease the burden of those who are responsible for looking after the patient. Each case needs to be looked at with especial care to ensure that the operation is indeed in the best interests of the patient. I consider that a special form of procedure should be provided so that the matter can be brought before the court in the simplest way possible. A claim for a declaration under RSC Ord 15, r 16 is not a satisfactory form of procedure because, if the claim were unopposed, as it often would be, the proceedings would be open to the technical objections that declarations are not in the ordinary way made by consent or where the defendant or respondent has asserted no contrary claim. Nevertheless, the purpose of the application to the court will be to satisfy the court that the operation which is to be performed will be necessary and lawful and the court's approval will be sought on this basis. If the court is so satisfied its decision will provide a safeguard for those who carry out the operation and an assurance to the public that the facts have been fully investigated in a court of law. If the court is not so satisfied, its approval will not be given and the operation will not go ahead. Of course, if there was any possibility that the operation was going to be proceeded with after approval had been withheld, which would be extremely unlikely, the court could grant an injunction. It may be that the most convenient method of prescribing the appropriate form of procedure will be by way of a new rule under RSC Ord 80, which is concerned with proceedings relating to those under a disability. I have had the advantage of reading in draft the judgment of Lord Donaldson MR. I agree with his proposals as to how the proceedings should be constituted and heard.'

Butler-Sloss LJ said:

'In my judgment, a decision as to sterilisation of a person under a disability ought not to be left entirely to the decision of the family and the medical profession alone. Public policy requires that there should be imposed the supervision of the courts in so important and delicate a decision. In the previous cases ... and in the present appeal the mechanism has been by declaration under RSC Ord 15, r 16. I agree that this is not an appropriate procedure. A declaration cannot alter the existing position and the granting of it at first instance may have limited efficacy in any subsequent litigation. The court by a declaration alone cannot give approval. The reverse application, an injunction, is also limited in its usefulness and, other than the Official Solicitor if notified, there may be no one with an interest available to apply for it. There is at present no mechanism providing for the approval of the court in the present case. It does, however, exist in the sphere of property by RSC Ord 80 for persons under a disability and by analogy I see no reason in principle why a rule should not be framed to prescribe such a procedure. I respectfully agree with Lord Donaldson MR as to the procedure that he has set out in his judgment and the participation of the Official Solicitor. Such a procedure is needed in those operations coming within the special category which includes sterilisation, in the public interest, in order to demonstrate that the operation will or will not be lawful and to give or withhold the approval of the court.'

My Lords, as I understand the judgments of all three members of the Court of Appeal, they took the same view with regard to the involvement of the court in a case such as F as I expressed earlier, namely that, although such involvement is not strictly necessary as a matter of law, it is highly desirable as a matter of good practice. They went on, however, to say that the court's involvement should take the form of giving or refusing its approval to the sterilisation operation proposed. They further considered that the procedure to be used for the making and determination of an application for approval could conveniently be prescribed by a new rule under RSC Ord 80.

I recognise that such a form of proceeding, if it were open to be adopted, would provide an admirable solution to the procedural problem which arises. With respect to the Court of Appeal, however, I cannot see how or on what basis the High Court, or any court or judge, can have jurisdiction to approve or disapprove a proposed operation. If the old parens patriae jurisdiction were still available with respect to persons of unsound mind, as it is with respect to minors who are wards, and if its exercise could be conferred on the judges of the High Court, Family Division, in the same way as the wardship jurisdiction has been conferred on them, there would be no difficulty. For the reasons which I gave earlier, however, the parens patriae jurisdiction with respect to adults of unsound mind no longer exists, and if that jurisdiction, or something comparable with it, is to be recreated, then it must be for the legislature and not for the courts to do the recreating. Rules of court can only, as a matter of law, prescribe the practice and procedure to be followed by the court when it is exercising a jurisdiction which already exists. They cannot confer jurisdiction, and, if they purported to do so, they would be ultra vires.

In my opinion, therefore, a jurisdiction to approve or disapprove an operation, which the Court of Appeal considered to be available to the High Court, and appropriate to be exercised in the present case, does not exist.

I turn, fourth and lastly, to the jurisdiction to make declarations. I do not think that it
*a* is right to describe this jurisdiction as being 'under RSC Ord 15, r 16'. The jurisdiction is
part of the inherent jurisdiciton of the High Court, and the rule does no more than say
that there is no procedural objection to an action being brought for a declaration whether
any other kind of relief is asked for or available or not.

There can, in my view, be no doubt that the High Court has jurisdiction, in a case like
the present one, to make a declaration with regard to the lawfulness of an operation for
*b* sterilisation proposed to be carried out. As appears, however, from the passages in the
judgments of the three members of the Court of Appeal which I set out earlier, they all
concluded that procedure by way of declaration, though used in the present case and
three previous cases similar to it, was not a satisfactory procedure to be adopted. Their
grounds of objection were these. First, that a declaration changes nothing (Lord
Donaldson MR and Butler-Sloss LJ). Second, that an application for a declaration might
*c* be unopposed and it was not the ordinary practice to grant declarations by consent or
where there is no contrary claim (Neill LJ). Third, that the public interest requires that
the court should give express approval to a proposed operation and a declaration does not
have that effect (Lord Donaldson MR, Neill LJ and Butler-Sloss LJ). Fourth, that a
declaration granted at first instance may have limited efficacy in any subsequent litigation
(Butler-Sloss LJ).
*d*     With respect to all three members of the Court of Appeal, I do not consider that these
objections are well founded. The first objection, that a declaration changes nothing,
would be valid if the substantive law were that a proposed operation could not lawfully
be performed without the prior approval of the court. As I indicated earlier, however,
that is not, in my view the substantive law, nor did the Court of Appeal, as I understand
the judgments, hold that it was. The substantive law is that a proposed operation is
*e* lawful if it is in the best interests of the patient, and unlawful if it is not. What is required
from the court, therefore, is not an order giving approval to the operation, so as to make
lawful that which would otherwise be unlawful. What is required from the court is
rather an order which establishes by judicial process (the 'third opinion' so aptly referred
to by Lord Donaldson MR) whether the proposed operation is in the best interests of the
*f* patient and therefore lawful, or not in the patient's best interests and therefore unlawful.
The second objection, that the application for a declaration might be unopposed and it
is not the ordinary practice to grant declarations by consent or where there is no contrary
claim, would only be valid in the absence of appropriate rules of procedure governing an
application of the kind under discussion. The same objection could be raised against the
procedure by way of application for approval of the proposed operation favoured by the
Court of Appeal, in the absence of rules of procedure such as those propounded by Lord
*g* Donaldson MR and agreed to by Neill and Butler-Sloss LJJ. I accept, of course, that no
such rules of procedure have so far been made. But, even without them, there would
have to be a summons for directions, preferably before a judge, and he could be relied on
to ensure that the application was not unopposed, and that all necessary evidence, both
for and against the proposed operation, were adduced before the court at the hearing.
*h*     The third objection, that the public interest requires that the court should give express
approval to a proposed operation and that a declaration does not have that effect, appears
to be largely semantic. By that I mean that, whichever of the two forms of procedure, if
both were available, were to be used, the nature of the inquiry which would have to be
made by the court, and of the reasoned decision which it would be obliged to give after
carrying out that inquiry, would be substantially the same.
*j*     The fourth objection, that a declaration granted at first instance may have limited
efficacy in any subsequent litigation, was not the subject matter of any argument before
your Lordships. My provisional view is that, whatever procedure were to be used, only
the parties to the proceedings and their privies would be bound by, or could rely on, the
decision made. In practice, however, I think that that would be enough.

For the reasons which I have given, I am of opinion that, having regard to the present limitations on the jurisdiction of the court, by which I mean its inability to exercise the *a* parens patriae jurisdiction with respect to adults of unsound mind, the procedure by way of declaration is, in principle, an appropriate and satisfactory procedure to be used in a case of this kind.

(3) *Procedure to be used when applying for a declaration*
The Court of Appeal, as I indicated earlier, considered that the correct form of *b* proceeding in a case of this kind was an application to the court for approval of the proposed operation. On that basis, as appears from a part of the judgment of Lord Donaldson MR which I quoted earlier, he formulated certain directions numbered (1) to (4) (with which both Neill and Butler-Sloss LJJ agreed) to govern such applications pending the making of appropriate amendments to RSC Ord 80 by the Supreme Court Rule Committee. On the basis of my conclusion that the correct form of proceeding is *c* an application for a declaration, it seems to me that, subject to certain alterations in the wording of directions (1) and (2), those directions would be equally appropriate to the latter kind of proceeding. I would alter directions (1) and (2) so as to read:

'(1) Applications for a declaration that a proposed operation on or medical treatment for a patient can lawfully be carried out despite the inability of such *d* patient to consent thereto should be by way of originating summons issuing out of the Family Division of the High Court.
(2) The applicant should normally be those responsible for the care of the patient or those intending to carry out the proposed operation or other treatment, if it is declared to be lawful.'

I would leave directions (3) and (4) as they are. *e*
Counsel for the intervener, the Mental Health Act Commission for England and Wales, invited your Lordships to say that further and more detailed directions with regard to evidence and other matters should be added to directions (1) to (4) above. In my opinion there will, in cases of this kind, have to be a summons for directions heard by a judge, and it should be left to him to decide, on the hearing of such summons, *f* whether any, and, if so what, further and more detailed directions should be given in the particular case before him.
I consider also that further consideration needs to be given, first, to the precise terms in which a declaration should be granted and, second, to the question whether any order supplementary to the declaration should be made.
The form of order and declaration made by Scott Baker J in the present case was this: *g*

'IT IS ORDERED AND DECLARED that under the Rules of the Supreme Court Order, 15, Rule 16 the sterilisation of the Plaintiff would not amount to an unlawful act by reason only of the absence of the Plaintiff's consent.'

In my view, three changes in the form of the order should be made. First, for the reasons which I gave earlier, I think that the reference to RSC Ord 15, r 16 is unnecessary and *h* should be omitted. Second, I think that the declaration should be amplified in two ways: (a) to show the finding of fact on the foundation of which it is made; and (b) to make it clear that it is made on the basis of existing circumstances only. Third, I think that provision should be made for the possibility of a change in the existing circumstances occurring before the declaration is acted on. Taking account of these three matters I consider that the order should be in the following form, or something broadly similar to *j* it: '(a) It is declared that the operation of sterilisation proposed to be performed on the plaintiff being in the existing circumstances in her best interests can lawfully be performed on her despite her inability to consent to it. (b) It is ordered that in the event of a material change in the existing circumstances occurring before the said operation has been performed any party shall have liberty to apply for such further or other

*a* declaration or order as may be just.'

Your Lordships were referred by counsel in the course of the hearing of the appeal to the way in which the problem raised in this case has been dealt with in other countries, whose legal systems were originally derived, to a large extent at any rate, from the common law of England. These countries were the United States of America, Canada and Australia, and a large file of reported cases decided in them was made available, to

*b* some of which specific reference was made. My Lords, the material so supplied was of compelling interest, and it is right to express gratitude to those concerned for the industry displayed in making it available. In my view, however, the way in which the problem has been dealt with in those other countries does not in the end assist your Lordships to any great extent in the determination of this appeal. This is because it is clear that, under their legal systems, the parens patriae jurisdiction with respect to persons of unsound

*c* mind is still alive and available for exercise by their courts. It follows that those courts have powers to deal with the problem concerned which are, unfortunately as I think, denied to the courts here. In these circumstances I do not consider that it would serve any useful purpose to examine and analyse this extensive body of American, Canadian and Australian law, and I trust that my omission to do so will not be regarded as indicating disrespect of any kind toward the legal systems of those countries.

*d* There is one further matter with which I think that it is necessary to deal. That is the standard which the court should apply in deciding whether a proposed operation is or is not in the best interests of the patient. With regard to this Scott Baker J said:

> 'I do not think they [the doctors] are liable in battery where they are acting in good faith and reasonably in the best interests of their patients. I doubt whether the
*e* test is very different from that for negligence.'

This was a reference to the test laid down in *Bolam v Friern Hospital Management Committee* [1957] 2 All ER 118, [1957] 1 WLR 582, namely that a doctor will not be negligent if he establishes that he acted in accordance with a practice accepted at the time by a responsible body of medical opinion skilled in the particular form of treatment in question.

*f* All three members of the Court of Appeal considered that the *Bolam* test was insufficiently stringent for deciding whether an operation or other medical treatment was in a patient's best interests. Lord Donaldson MR said:

> 'Just as the law and the courts rightly pay great, but not decisive, regard to accepted professional wisdom in relation to the duty of care in the law of medical negligence (the *Bolam* test), so they equally would have regard to such wisdom in
*g* relation to decisions whether or not and how to treat incompetent patients in the context of the law of trespass to the person. However, both the medical profession and the courts have to keep the special status of such a patient in the forefront of their minds. The ability of the ordinary adult patient to exercise a free choice in deciding whether to accept or to refuse medical treatment and to choose between treatments is not to be dismissed as desirable but inessential. It is a crucial factor in
*h* relation to all medical treatment. If it is necessarily absent, whether temporarily in an emergency situation or permanently in a case of mental disability, other things being equal there must be greater caution in deciding whether to treat and, if so, how to treat, although I do not agree that this extends to limiting doctors to treatment on the necessity for which there are "no two views" (per Wood J in *T v T* [1988] 1 All ER 613 at 621, [1988] Fam 52 at 62). There will always or usually be a
*j* minority view and this approach, if strictly applied, would often rule out all treatment. On the other hand, the existence of a signifcant minority view would constitute a serious contra-indication.'

Neil LJ said:

'I have therefore come to the conclusion that, if the operation is necessary and the proper safeguards are observed, the performance of a serious operation, including *a* an operation for sterilisation, on a person who by reason of a lack of mental capacity is unable to give his or her consent is not a trespass to the person or otherwise unlawful. It therefore becomes necessary to consider what is meant by "a necessary operation". In seeking to define the circumstances in which an operation can properly be carried out Scott Baker J said: "I do not think they are liable in battery where they are acting in good faith and reasonably in the best interests of their *b* patients. I doubt whether the test is very different from that for negligence." With respect, I do not consider that this test is sufficiently stringent. A doctor may defeat a claim in negligence if he establishes that he acted in accordance with a practice accepted at the time as proper by a responsible body of medical opinion skilled in the particular form of treatment in question. This is the test laid down in *Bolam v Friern Hospital Management Committee.* But to say that it is not negligent to carry out *c* a particular form of treatment does not mean that that treatment is necessary. I would define necessary in this context as that which the general body of medical opinion in the particular specialty would consider to be in the best interests of the patient in order to maintain the health and to secure the well-being of the patient. One cannot expect unanimity but it should be possible to say of an operation which is necessary in the relevant sense that it would be unreasonable in the opinion of *d* most experts in the field not to make the operation available to the patient. One must consider the alternatives to an operation and the dangers or disadvantages to which the patient may be exposed if no action is taken. The question becomes: what action does the patient's health and welfare require?'

Butler-Sloss LJ agreed with Neill LJ.

With respect to the Court of Appeal, I do not agree that the *Bolam* test is inapplicable *e* to cases of performing operations on, or giving other treatment to, adults incompetent to give consent. In order that the performance of such operations on, and the giving of such other treatment to, such adults should be lawful, they must be in their best interests. If doctors were to be required, in deciding whether an operation or other treatment was in the best interests of adults incompetent to give consent, to apply some test more stringent *f* than the *Bolam* test, the result would be that that such adults would, in some circumstances at least, be deprived of the benefit of medical treatment which adults competent to give consent would enjoy. In my opinion it would be wrong for the law, in its concern to protect such adults, to produce such a result.

For the reasons which I have given I would dismiss the appeal, subject to varying the order of Scott Baker J by substituting for the declaration made by him the amplified *g* declaration and further order which I formulated earlier.

**LORD GRIFFITHS.** My Lords, the argument in this appeal has ranged far and wide in search of a measure to protect those who cannot protect themselves from the insult of an unnecessary sterilisation. Every judge who has considered the problem has recognised that there should be some control mechanism imposed on those who have the care of *h* infants or mentally incompetent women of child bearing age to prevent or at least inhibit them from sterilising the women without approval of the High Court. I am, I should make it clear, speaking now and hereafter of an operation for sterilisation which is proposed not for the treatment of diseased organs but an operation on a woman with healthy reproductive organs in order to avoid the risk of pregnancy. The reasons for the anxiety about sterilisation which it is proposed should be carried out for other than *j* purely medical reasons, such as the removal of the ovaries to prevent the spread of cancer, are readily understandable and are shared throughout the common law world.

We have been taken through many authorities in the United States, Australia and Canada which stress the danger that sterilisation may be proposed in circumstances which are not truly in the best interests of the woman but for the convenience of those *a*  who are charged with her care. In the United States and Australia the solution has been to declare that, in the case of a woman who either because of infancy or mental incompetence cannot give her consent, the operation may not be performed without the consent of the court. In Canada the Supreme Court has taken an even more extreme stance and declared that sterilisation is unlawful unless performed for therapeutic reasons, which I understand to be as a life-saving measure or for the prevention of the spread of disease: see *Re Eve* (1986) 31 DLR (4th) 1. This extreme position was rejected by this

*b*  House in *Re B (a minor) (wardship: sterilisation)* [1987] 2 All ER 206, [1988] AC 199, which recognised that an operation might be in the best interests of a woman even though carried out in order to protect her from the trauma of a pregnancy which she could not understand and with which she could not cope. Nevertheless Lord Templeman stressed that such an operation should not be undertaken without the approval of a High Court judge of the Family Division. In this country *Re D (a minor) (wardship: sterilisation)* [1976]

*c*  1 All ER 326, [1976] Fam 185 stands as a stark warning of the danger of leaving the decision to sterilise in the hands of those having the immediate care of the woman, even when they genuinely believe that they are acting in her best interests.

I have had the advantage of reading the speeches of my noble and learned friends Lord Brandon and Lord Goff and there is much therein with which I agree. I agree that those charged with the care of the mentally incompetent are protected from any criminal or

*d*  tortious action based on lack of consent. Whether one arrives at this conclusion by applying a principle of 'necessity' as do Lord Brandon and Lord Goff or by saying that it is in the public interest as did Neill LJ in the Court of Appeal, appear to me to be inextricably interrelated conceptual justifications for the humane development of the common law. Why is it necessary that the mentally incompetent should be given treatment to which they lack the capacity to consent? The answer must surely be because

*e*  it is in the public interest that it should be so.

In a civilised society the mentally incompetent must be provided with medical and nursing care and those who look after them must do their best for them. Stated in legal terms the doctor who undertakes responsibility for the treatment of a mental patient who is incapable of giving consent to treatment must give the treatment that he considers

*f*  to be in the best interests of his patient, and the standard of care required of the doctor will be that laid down in *Bolam v Friern Hospital Management Committee* [1957] 2 All ER 118, [1957] 1 WLR 582. The doctor will however be subject to the specific statutory constraints on treatment for mental disorder provided by Pt IV of the Mental Health Act 1983. Certain radical treatments such as surgical destruction of brain tissue cannot be performed without the consent of the patient and if the patient is incapable of giving

*g*  consent the operation cannot be performed, however necessary it may be considered by the doctors. Other less radical treatment can only be given with the consent of the patient or, if the patient will not or cannot consent, on the authority of a second medical opinion. There are however no statutory provisions that deal with sterilisation.

I agree with Lord Brandon's analysis of the provisions of the Mental Health Act 1983 and, in particular, that in its context the expression 'the affairs of patients' in Pt VII cannot

*h*  be construed as including medical treatment and thus providing a substitute for the parens patriae jurisdiction previously vested in the Lord Chancellor and the judges of the High Court, Chancery Division, which was removed by warrant under sign manual dated 1 November 1960, contemporaneously with the passing of the Mental Health Act 1959.

Finally, I agree that an action for a declaration is available as a mechanism by which a

*j*  proposed sterilisation may be investigated to ensure that it is in the woman's best interests.

But I cannot agree that it is satisfactory to leave this grave decision with all its social implications in the hands of those having the care of the patient with only the expectation that they will have the wisdom to obtain a declaration of lawfulness before the operation is performed. In my view the law ought to be that they must obtain the approval of the court before they sterilise a woman incapable of giving consent and that it is unlawful to sterilise without that consent. I believe that it is open to your Lordships to develop a common law rule to this effect. Although the general rule is that the individual is the master of his own fate the judges through the common law have, in the public interest, imposed certain constraints on the harm that people may consent to being inflicted on their own bodies. Thus, although boxing is a legal sport, a bare knuckle prize fight in which more grievous injury may be inflicted is unlawful (see *R v Coney* (1882) 8 QBD 534), and so is fighting which may result in actual bodily harm (see *Re A-G's Reference (No 6 of 1980)* [1981] 2 All ER 1057, [1981] QB 715). So also is it unlawful to consent to the infliction of serious injury on the body in the course of the practice of sexual perversion (see *R v Donovan* [1934] 2 KB 498, [1934] All ER Rep 207). Suicide was unlawful at common law until Parliament intervened by the Suicide Act 1961.

The common law has, in the public interest, been developed to forbid the infliction of injury on those who are fully capable of consenting to it. The time has now come for a further development to forbid, again in the public interest, the sterilisation of a woman with healthy reproductive organs who, either through mental incompetence or youth, is incapable of giving her fully informed consent unless such an operation has been inquired into and sanctioned by the High Court. Such a common law rule would provide a more effective protection than the exercise of parens patriae jurisdiction which is dependent on some interested party coming forward to invoke the jurisdiction of the court. The parens patriae jurisdiction is in any event now only available in the case of minors through their being made wards of court. I would myself declare that on grounds of public interest an operation to sterilise a woman incapable of giving consent on grounds of either age or mental incapacity is unlawful if performed without the consent of the High Court. I fully recognise that in so doing I would be making new law. However, the need for such a development has been identified in a number of recent cases and in the absence of any parliamentary response to the problem it is my view that the judges can and should accept responsibility to recognise the need and to adapt the common law to meet it. If such a development did not meet with public approval it would always be open to Parliament to reverse it or to alter it by perhaps substituting for the opinion of the High Court judge the second opinion of another doctor as urged by counsel for the Mental Health Act Commission.

As I know that your Lordships consider that it is not open to you to follow the course I would take I must content myself by accepting, but as second best, the procedure by way of declaration proposed by Lord Brandon and agree to the dismissal of this appeal.

**LORD GOFF OF CHIEVELEY.** My Lords, the question in this case is concerned with the lawfulness of a proposed operation of sterilisation on the plaintiff, F, a woman of 36 years of age, who by reason of her mental incapacity is disabled from giving her consent to the operation. It is well established that, as a general rule, the performance of a medical operation on a person without his or her consent is unlawful, as constituting both the crime of battery and the tort of trespass to the person. Furthermore, before Scott Baker J and the Court of Appeal, it was common ground between the parties that there was no power in the court to give consent on behalf of F to the proposed operation of sterilisation, or to dispense with the need for such consent. This was because it was common ground that the parens patriae jurisdiction in respect of persons suffering from mental incapacity, formerly vested in the courts by royal warrant under the sign manual, had ceased to be so vested by revocation of the last warrant on 1 November 1960, and further that there was no statutory provision which could be invoked in its place. Before your Lordships, having regard to the importance of the matter, both those propositions were nevertheless subjected to close scrutiny, and counsel for the Official Solicitor deployed, with great ability, such arguments as can be advanced that the parens patriae jurisdiction is still vested in the courts as a matter of common law, and that the necessary statutory jurisdiction is to be found in Pt VII of the Mental Health Act 1983, and in

particular in ss 93, 95 and 96 of that Act. However, with the assistance of counsel, I for
*a* my part have become satisfied that the concessions made below on these points were
rightly made. On both points I find myself to be respectfully in agreement with the
opinion expressed by my noble and learned friend Lord Brandon, and I do not think it
necessary for me to add anything.

It follows that, as was recognised in the courts below, if the operation on F is to be
justified, it can only be justified on the applicable principles of common law. The
*b* argument of counsel revealed the startling fact that there is no English authority on the
question whether as a matter of common law (and if so in what circumstances) medical
treatment can lawfully be given to a person who is disabled by mental incapacity from
consenting to it. Indeed, the matter goes further, for a comparable problem can arise in
relation to persons of sound mind who are, for example, rendered unconscious in an
accident or rendered speechless by a catastrophic stroke. All such persons may require
*c* medical treatment and, in some cases, surgical operations. All may require nursing care.
In the case of mentally disordered persons, they may require care of a more basic kind,
dressing, feeding and so on, to assist them in their daily life, as well as routine treatment
by doctors and dentists. It follows that, in my opinion, it is not possible to consider in
isolation the lawfulness of the proposed operation of sterilisation in the present case. It is
necessary first to ascertain the applicable common law principles and then to consider
*d* the question of sterilisation against the background of those principles.

Counsel for the Official Solicitor advanced the extreme argument that, in the absence
of a parens patriae or statutory jurisdiction, no such treatment or care of the kind I have
described can lawfully be given to a mentally disordered person who is unable to consent
to it. This is indeed a startling proposition, which must also exclude treatment or care to
persons rendered unconscious or unable to speak by accident or illness. For centuries,
*e* treatment and care must have been given to such persons, without any suggestion that it
was unlawful to do so. I find it very difficult to believe that the common law is so
deficient as to be incapable of providing for so obvious a need. Even so, it is necessary to
examine the point as a matter of principle.

I start with the fundamental principle, now long established, that every person's body
*f* is inviolate. As to this, I do not wish to depart from what I myself said in the judgment
of the Divisional Court in *Collins v Wilcock* [1984] 3 All ER 374, [1984] 1 WLR 1172, and
in particular from the statement that the effect of this principle is that everybody is
protected not only against physical injury but against any form of physical molestation
(see [1984] 3 All ER 374 at 378, [1984] 1 WLR 1172 at 1177).

Of course, as a general rule physical interference with another person's body is lawful
*g* if he consents to it; though in certain limited circumstances the public interest may
require that his consent is not capable of rendering the act lawful. There are also specific
cases where physical interference without consent may not be unlawful: chastisement of
children, lawful arrest, self-defence, the prevention of crime and so on. As I pointed out
in *Collins v Wilcock* [1984] 3 All ER 374 at 378, [1984] 1 WLR 1172 at 1177, a broader
exception has been created to allow for the exigencies of everyday life: jostling in a street
*h* or some other crowded place, social contact at parties and such like. This exception has
been said to be founded on implied consent, since those who go about in public places,
or go to parties, may be taken to have impliedly consented to bodily contact of this kind.
Today this rationalisation can be regarded as artificial; and, in particular, it is difficult to
impute consent to those who, by reason of their youth or mental disorder, are unable to
give their consent. For this reason, I consider it more appropriate to regard such cases as
*j* falling within a general exception embracing all physical contact which is generally
acceptable in the ordinary conduct of everyday life.

In the old days it used to be said that, for a touching of another's person to amount to
a battery, it had to be a touching 'in anger' (see *Cole v Turner* (1704) Holt KB 108, 90 ER
958 per Holt CJ); and it has recently been said that the touching must be 'hostile' to have
that effect (see *Wilson v Pringle* [1986] 2 All ER 440 at 447, [1987] QB 237 at 253). I

respectfully doubt whether that is correct. A prank that gets out of hand, an over-friendly slap on the back, surgical treatment by a surgeon who mistakenly thinks that the patient *a* has consented to it, all these things may transcend the bounds of lawfulness, without being characterised as hostile. Indeed, the suggested qualification is difficult to reconcile with the principle that any touching of another's body is, in the absence of lawful excuse, capable of amounting to a battery and a trespass. Furthermore, in the case of medical treatment, we have to bear well in mind the libertarian principle of self-determination which, to adopt the words of Cardozo J (in *Schloendorff v Society of New York Hospital* *b* (1914) 211 NY 125 at 126), recognises that—

> 'Every human being of adult years and sound mind has a right to determine what shall be done with his own body; and a surgeon who performs an operation without his patient's consent, commits an assault . . .'

This principle has been reiterated in more recent years by Lord Reid in *S v S, W v Official* *c* *Solicitor* [1970] 3 All ER 107 at 111, [1972] AC 24 at 43.

It is against this background that I turn to consider the question whether, and if so when, medical treatment or care of a mentally disordered person who is, by reason of his incapacity, incapable of giving his consent can be regarded as lawful. As is recognised in Cardozo J's statement of principle, and elsewhere (see e g *Sidaway v Bethlem Royal Hospital Governors* [1985] 1 All ER 643 at 649, [1985] AC 871 at 882 per Lord Scarman), some *d* relaxation of the law is required to accommodate persons of unsound mind. In *Wilson v Pringle* the Court of Appeal considered that treatment or care of such persons may be regarded as lawful, as falling within the exception relating to physical contact which is generally acceptable in the ordinary conduct of everyday life. Again, I am with respect unable to agree. That exception is concerned with the ordinary events of everyday life, jostling in public places and such like, and affects all persons, whether or not they are *e* capable of giving their consent. Medical treatment, even treatment for minor ailments, does not fall within that category of events. The general rule is that consent is necessary to render such treatment lawful. If such treatment administered without consent is not to be unlawful, it has to be justified on some other principle.

On what principle can medical treatment be justified when given without consent? *f* We are searching for a principle on which, in limited circumstances, recognition may be given to a need, in the interests of the patient, that treatment should be given to him in circumstances where he is (temporarily or permanently) disabled from consenting to it. It is this criterion of a need which points to the principle of necessity as providing justification.

That there exists in the common law a principle of necessity which may justify action which would otherwise be unlawful is not in doubt. But historically the principle has *g* been seen to be restricted to two groups of cases, which have been called cases of public necessity and cases of private necessity. The former occurred when a man interfered with another man's property in the public interest, for example (in the days before we could dial 999 for the fire brigade) the destruction of another man's house to prevent the spread of a catastrophic fire, as indeed occurred in the Great Fire of London in 1666. The latter *h* cases occurred when a man interfered with another's property to save his own person or property from imminent danger, for example when he entered on his neighbour's land without his consent in order to prevent the spread of fire onto his own land.

There is, however, a third group of cases, which is also properly described as founded on the principle of necessity and which is more pertinent to the resolution of the problem in the present case. These cases are concerned with action taken as a matter of necessity *j* to assist another person without his consent. To give a simple example, a man who seizes another and forcibly drags him from the path of an oncoming vehicle, thereby saving him from injury or even death, commits no wrong. But there are many emanations of this principle, to be found scattered through the books. These are concerned not only with the preservation of the life or health of the assisted person, but also with the

preservation of his property (sometimes an animal, sometimes an ordinary chattel) and
*a* even to certain conduct on his behalf in the administration of his affairs. Where there is
a pre-existing relationship between the parties, the intervener is usually said to act as an
agent of necessity on behalf of the principal in whose interests he acts, and his action can
often, with not too much artificiality, be referred to the pre-existing relationship between
them. Whether the intervener may be entitled either to reimbursement or to
remuneration raises separate questions which are not relevant to the present case.

*b*     We are concerned here with action taken to preserve the life, health or well-being of
another who is unable to consent to it. Such action is sometimes said to be justified as
arising from an emergency; in Prosser and Keeton *Torts* (5th edn, 1984) p 117 the action
is said to be privileged by the emergency. Doubtless, in the case of a person of sound
mind, there will ordinarily have to be an emergency before such action taken without
consent can be lawful; for otherwise there would be an opportunity to communicate
*c* with the assisted person and to seek his consent. But this is not always so; and indeed the
historical origins of the principle of necessity do not point to emergency as such as
providing the criterion of lawful intervention without consent. The old Roman doctrine
of negotiorum gestio presupposed not so much an emergency as a prolonged absence of
the dominus from home as justifying intervention by the gestor to administer his affairs.
The most ancient group of cases in the common law, concerned with action taken by the
*d* master of a ship in distant parts in the intereests of the shipowner, likewise found its
origin in the difficulty of communication with the owner over a prolonged period of
time, a difficulty overcome today by modern means of communication. In those cases, it
was said that there had to be an emergency before the master could act as agent of
necessity; though the emergency could well be of some duration. But, when a person is
rendered incapable of communication either permanently or over a considerable period
*e* of time (through illness or accident or mental disorder), it would be an unusual use of
language to describe the case as one of 'permanent emergency', if indeed such a state of
affairs can properly be said to exist. In truth, the relevance of an emergency is that it may
give rise to a necessity to act in the interests of the assisted person without first obtaining
his consent. Emergency is however not the criterion or even a prerequisite; it is simply a
frequent origin of the necessity which impels intervention. The principle is one of
*f* necessity, not of emergency.

We can derive some guidance as to the nature of the principle of necessity from the
cases on agency of necessity in mercantile law. When reading those cases, however, we
have to bear in mind that it was there considered that (since there was a pre-existing
relationship between the parties) there was a duty on the part of the agent to act on his
principal's behalf in an emergency. From these cases it appears that the principle of
*g* necessity connotes that circumstances have arisen in which there is a necessity for the
agent to act on his principal's behalf at a time when it is in practice not possible for him
to obtain his principal's instructions so to do. In such cases, it has been said that the agent
must act bona fide in the interests of his principal (see *Prager v Blatspiel Stamp & Heacock
Ltd* [1924] 1 KB 566 at 572, [1924] All ER Rep 524 at 528 per McCardie J). A broader
statement of the principle is to be found in the advice of the Privy Council delivered by
*h* Sir Montague Smith in *Australasian Steam Navigation Co v Morse* (1872) LR 4 PC 222 at
230, in which he said:

'... when by the force of circumstances a man has the duty cast upon him of
taking some action for another, and under that obligation, adopts the course which,
to the judgment of a wise and prudent man, is apparently the best for the interest of
*j* the persons for whom he acts in a given emergency, it may properly be said of the
course so taken, that it was, in a mercantile sense, necessary to take it.'

In a sense, these statements overlap. But from them can be derived the basic requirements,
applicable in these cases of necessity, that, to fall within the principle, not only (1) must
there be a necessity to act when it is not practicable to communicate with the assisted

person, but also (2) the action taken must be such as a reasonable person would in all the circumstances take, acting in the best interests of the assisted person.                                    *a*

On this statement of principle, I wish to observe that officious intervention cannot be justified by the principle of necessity. So intervention cannot be justified when another more appropriate person is available and willing to act; nor can it be justified when it is contrary to the known wishes of the assisted person, to the extent that he is capable of rationally forming such a wish. On the second limb of the principle, the introduction of the standard of a reasonable man should not in the present context be regarded as  *b* materially different from that of Sir Montague Smith's 'wise and prudent man', because a reasonable man would, in the time available to him, proceed with wisdom and prudence before taking action in relation to another man's person or property without his consent. I shall have more to say on this point later. Subject to that, I hesitate at present to indulge in any greater refinement of the principle, being well aware of many problems which may arise in its application, problems which it is not necessary, for  *c* present purposes, to examine. But as a general rule, if the above criteria are fulfilled, interference with the assisted person's person or property (as the case may be) will not be unlawful. Take the example of a railway accident, in which injured passengers are trapped in the wreckage. It is this principle which may render lawful the actions of other citizens, railway staff, passengers or outsiders, who rush to give aid and comfort to the victims: the surgeon who amputates the limb of an unconscious passenger to free him  *d* from the wreckage; the ambulance man who conveys him to hospital; the doctors and nurses who treat him and care for him while he is still unconscious. Take the example of an elderly person who suffers a stroke which renders him incapable of speech or movement. It is by virtue of this principle that the doctor who treats him, the nurse who cares for him, even the relative or friend or neighbour who comes in to look after him will commit no wrong when he or she touches his body.                                    *e*

The two examples I have given illustrate, in the one case, an emergency and, in the other, a permanent or semi-permanent state of affairs. Another example of the latter kind is that of a mentally disordered person who is disabled from giving consent. I can see no good reason why the principle of necessity should not be applicable in his case as it is in the case of the victim of a stroke. Furthermore, in the case of a mentally disordered  *f* person, as in the case of a stroke victim, the permanent state of affairs calls for a wider range of care than may be requisite in an emergency which arises from accidental injury. When the state of affairs is permanent, or semi-permanent, action properly taken to preserve the life, health or well-being of the assisted person may well transcend such measures as surgical operation or substantial medical treatment and may extend to include such humdrum matters as routine medical or dental treatment, even simple care  *g* such as dressing and undressing and putting to bed.

The distinction I have drawn between cases of emergency and cases where the state of affairs is (more or less) permanent is relevant in another respect. We are here concerned with medical treatment, and I limit myself to cases of that kind. Where, for example, a surgeon performs an operation without his consent on a patient temporarily rendered unconscious in an accident, he should do no more than is reasonably required, in the best  *h* interests of the patient, before he recovers consciousness. I can see no practical difficulty arising from this requirement, which derives from the fact that the patient is expected before long to regain consciousness and can then be consulted about longer term measures. The point has however arisen in a more acute form where a surgeon, in the course of an operation, discovers some other condition which, in his opinion, requires operative treatment for which he has not received the patient's consent. In what  *j* circumstances he should operate forthwith, and in what circumstances he should postpone the further treatment until he has received the patient's consent, is a difficult matter which has troubled the Canadian courts (see *Marshall v Curry* [1933] 3 DLR 260 and *Murray v McMurchy* [1949] 2 DLR 442), but which it is not necessary for your Lordships to consider in the present case.

But where the state of affairs is permanent or semi-permanent, as may be so in the case
*a* of a mentally disordered person, there is no point in waiting to obtain the patient's
consent. The need to care for him is obvious; and the doctor must then act in the best
interests of his patient, just as if he had received his patient's consent so to do. Were this
not so, much useful treatment and care could, in theory at least, be denied to the
unfortunate. It follows that, on this point, I am unable to accept the view expressed by
Neill LJ in the Court of Appeal, that the treatment must be shown to have been necessary.
*b* Moreover, in such a case, as my noble and learned friend Lord Brandon has pointed out,
a doctor who has assumed responsbility for the care of a patient may not only be treated
as having the patient's consent to act, but also be under a duty so to act. I find myself to
be respectfully in agreement with Lord Donaldson MR when he said:

'I see nothing incongruous in doctors and others who have a caring responsibility
*c*   being required, when acting in relation to an adult who is incompetent, to excercise
a right of choice in exactly the same way as would the court or reasonable parents in
relation to a child, making due allowance, of course, for the fact that the patient is
not a child, and I am satisfied that that is what the law does in fact require.'

In these circumstances, it is natural to treat the deemed authority and the duty as
interrelated. But I feel bound to express my opinion that, in principle, the lawfulness of
*d* the doctor's action is, at least in its origin, to be found in the principle of necessity. This
can perhaps be seen most clearly in cases where there is no continuing relationship
between doctor and patient. The 'doctor in the house' who volunteers to assist a lady in
the audience who, overcome by the drama or by the heat in the theatre, has fainted away
is impelled to act by no greater duty than that imposed by his own Hippocratic oath.
Furthermore, intervention can be justified in the case of a non-professional, as well as a
*e* professional, man or woman who has no pre-existing relationship with the assisted
person, as in the case of a stranger who rushes to assist an injured man after an accident.
In my opinion, it is the necessity itself which provides the justification for the
intervention.

I have said that the doctor has to act in the best interests of the assisted person. In the
*f* case of routine treatment of mentally disordered persons, there should be little difficulty
in applying this principle. In the case of more serious treatment, I recognise that its
application may create problems for the medical profession; however, in making
decisions about treatment, the doctor must act in accordance with a responsible and
competent body of relevant professional opinion, on the principles set down in *Bolam v
Friern Hospital Management Committee* [1957] 2 All ER 118, [1957] 1 WLR 582. No doubt,
*g* in practice, a decision may involve others besides the doctor. It must surely be good
practice to consult relatives and others who are concerned with the care of the patient.
Sometimes, of course, consultation with a specialist or specialists will be required; and in
others, especially where the decision involves more than a purely medical opinion, an
inter-disciplinary team will in practice participate in the decision. It is very difficult, and
would be unwise, for a court to do more than to stress that, for those who are involved in
*h* these important and sometimes difficult decisions, the overriding consideration is that
they should act in the best interests of the person who suffers from the misfortune of
being prevented by incapacity from deciding for himself what should be done to his own
body in his own best interests.

In the present case, your Lordships have to consider whether the foregoing principles
apply in the case of a proposed operation of sterilisation on an adult woman of unsound
*j* mind, or whether sterilisation is (perhaps with one or two other cases) to be placed in a
separate category to which special principles apply. Again, counsel for the Official
Solicitor assisted your Lordships by deploying the argument that, in the absence of any
parens patriae jurisdiction, sterilisation of an adult woman of unsound mind, who by
reason of her mental incapacity is unable to consent, can never be lawful. He founded
his submission on a right of reproductive autonomy or right to control one's own

reproduction, which necessarily involves the right not to be sterilised involuntarily, on
the fact that sterilisation involves irreversible interference with the patient's most
important organs, on the fact that it involves interference with organs which are
functioning normally, on the fact that sterilisation is a topic on which medical views are
often not unanimous and on the undesirability, in the case of a mentally disordered
patient, of imposing a 'rational' solution on an incompetent patient. Having considered
these submissions with care, I am of the opinion that neither singly nor as a whole do
they justify the conclusion for which counsel for the Official Solicitor contended. Even
so, while accepting that the principles which I have stated are applicable in the case of
sterilisation, the matters relied on by counsel provide powerful support for the conclusion
that the application of those principles in such a case calls for special care. There are other
reasons which support that conclusion. It appears, for example, from reported cases in
the United States that there is a fear that those responsible for mental patients might
(perhaps unwittingly) seek to have them sterilised as a matter of administrative
convenience. Furthermore, the English case of *Re D (a minor) (wardship: sterilisation)*
[1976] 1 All ER 326, [1976] Fam 185 provides a vivid illustration of the fact that a highly
qualified medical practitioner, supported by a caring mother, may consider it right to
sterilise a mentally retarded girl in circumstances which prove, on examination, not to
require such an operation in the best interests of the girl. Matters such as these, coupled
with the fundamental nature of the patient's organs with which it is proposed irreversibly
to interfere, have prompted courts in the United States and in Australia to pronounce
that, in the case of a person lacking the capacity to consent, such an operation should only
be permitted with the consent of the court. Such decisions have of course been made by
courts which have vested in them the parens patriae jurisdiction, and so have power, in
the exercise of such jurisdiction, to impose such a condition. They are not directly
applicable in this country, where that jurisdiction has been revoked; for that reason alone
I do not propose to cite passages from the American and Australian cases although, like
my noble and learned friend Lord Brandon, I have read the judgments with great respect
and found them to be of compelling interest. I refer in particular to *Re Grady* (1981) 85
NJ 235 in the United States and, in Australia, to the very full and impressive consideration
of the matter by Nicholson CJ in *Re Jane* (22 December 1988, unreported), who in
particular stressed the importance of independent representation by some disinterested
third party on behalf of the patient (there a minor).

Although the parens patriae jurisdiction in the case of adults of unsound mind is no
longer vested in courts in this country, the approach adopted by the courts in the United
States and in Australia provides, in my opinion, strong support for the view that, as a
matter of practice, the operation of sterilisation should not be performed on an adult
person who lacks the capacity to consent to it without first obtaining the opinion of the
court that the operation is, in the circumstances, in the best interests of the person
concerned, by seeking a declaration that the operation is lawful. (I shall return later in
this speech to the appropriateness of the declaratory remedy in cases such as these.) In
my opinion, that guidance should be sought in order to obtain an independent, objective
and authoritative view on the lawfulness of the procedure in the particular circumstances
of the relevant case, after a hearing at which it can be ensured that there is independent
representation on behalf of the person on whom it is proposed to perform the operation.
This approach is consistent with the opinion expressed by Lord Templeman in *Re B (a
minor) (wardship: sterilisation)* [1987] 2 Ali ER 206 at 214–215, [1988] AC 199 at 205–206
that, in the case of a girl who is still a minor, sterilisation should not be performed on her
unless she has first been made a ward of court and the court has, in the exercise of its
wardship jurisdiction, given its authority to such a step. He said:

> 'No one has suggested a more satisfactory tribunal or a more satisfactory method
> of reaching a decision which vitally concerns an individual but also involves
> principles of law, ethics and medical practice.'

*a* I recognise that the requirement of a hearing before a court is regarded by some as capable of deterring certain medical practitioners from advocating the procedure of sterilisation; but I trust and hope that it may come to be understood that court procedures of this kind, conducted sensitively and humanely by judges of the Family Division, so far as possible and where appropriate in the privacy of chambers, are not to be feared by responsible practitioners.

*b* It was urged before your Lordships by counsel for the Mental Health Act Commission (the commission having been given leave to intervene in the proceedings) that a court vested with the reponsibility of making a decision in such a case, having first ensured that an independent second opinion has been obtained from an appropriate consultant of the appropriate speciality, should not, if that second opinion supports the proposal that sterilisation should take place, exercise any independent judgment but should simply follow the opinion so expressed. For my part, I do not think that it is possible or desirable *c* for a court so to exercise its jurisdiction. In all proceedings where expert opinions are expressed, those opinions are listened to with great respect; but, in the end, the validity of the opinion has to be weighed and judged by the court. This applies as much in cases where the opinion involves a question of judgment as it does in those where it is expressed on a purely scientific matter. For a court automatically to accept an expert opinion, simply because it is concurred in by another appropriate expert, would be a *d* denial of the function of the court. Furthermore, the proposal of the commission is impossible to reconcile with the American and Australian authorities which stress the need for a court decision after a hearing which involves separate representation on behalf of the person on whom it is proposed to perform the operation. Having said this, I do not feel that the commission need fear that the opinions of the experts will in any way be discounted. On the contrary, they will be heard with the greatest respect; and, as the *e* present case shows, there is a high degree of likelihood that they will be accepted.

I turn finally to the question of the procedure adopted in the present case, in which a declaration is sought. The relief claimed by the plaintiff in these proceedings is a declaration that to effect a sterilisation will not amount to an unlawful act by reason only of the absence of the plaintiff's consent. Scott Baker J granted the declaration as asked. The Court of Appeal dismissed the appeal and affirmed the order of Scott Baker J. Even *f* so, all members of the Court of Appeal expressed the opinion that procedure by way of declaration was not appropriate in a case such as this. Lord Donaldson MR said:

'For my part, I do not think that this is an appropriate procedure. A declaration changes nothing. All that the court is being asked to do is to declare that, had a course of action been taken without resort to the court, it would have been lawful *g* anyway. In the context of the most sensitive and potentially controversial forms of treatment the public interest requires that the courts should give express approval before the treatment is carried out and thereby provide an independent and broad based "third opinion".'

He then proceeded, with the concurrence of the other members of the court, to make *h* directions in respect of applications for the court's approval of medical or surgical treatment, pending the appearance of a new rule of the Supreme Court (to be added to RSC Ord 8o) or a practice direction of the President of the Family Division.

With all respect to the Master of the Rolls, in the absence of any parens patriae jurisdiction vested in the High Court I know of no jurisdictional basis on which any such rule of the Supreme Court or practice direction, still less directions such as he proposed, *j* could be founded. The course of action proposed by the Master of the Rolls presupposes the existence of a jurisdiction under which approval by the High Court is required before the relevant medical or surgical treatment is performed. There is at present no such jurisdiction; and the jurisdiction of the High Court cannot be expanded by a rule of the Supreme Court or practice direction or other direction. The present position is that the lawfulness of medical or surgical treatment cannot, in the case of adults, depend on the approval of the High Court. In my opinion, the course of action proposed by the Master of the Rolls would be ultra vires.

However, I do not altogether share the misgivings expressed by him (and shared by his other colleagues in the Court of Appeal) about the procedure for declaratory relief. First of all, I can see no procedural objection to the declaration granted by the judge, either as a matter of jurisdiction or as a matter of exercise of the discretion conferred by the relevant rule of the Supreme Court, Ord 15, r 16. Rule 16 provides:

'No action or other proceeding shall be open to objection on the ground that a merely declaratory judgment or order is sought thereby, and the Court may make binding declarations of right whether or not any consequential relief is or could be claimed.'

In *Guaranty Trust Co of New York v Hannay & Co* [1915] 2 KB 536, [1914–15] All ER Rep 24, a leading case in which an unsuccessful attack was mounted on the vires of the then Ord 25, r 5 (the predecessor of the present rule), forthright statements were made by both Pickford and Bankes LJJ as to the breadth of the jurisdiction conferred by the rule. Pickford LJ said ([1915] 2 KB 536 at 562, [1914–15] All ER Rep 24 at 35):

'I think therefore that the effect of the rule is to give a general power to make a declaration whether there be a cause of action or not, and at the instance of any party who is interested in the subject-matter of the declaration.'

And Bankes LJ said ([1915] 2 KB 536 at 572, [1914–15] All ER Rep 24 at 39):

'It is essential, however, that a person who seeks to take advantage of the rule must be claiming relief. What is meant by this word relief? When once it is established, as I think it is established, that relief is not confined to relief in respect of a cause of action it seems to follow that the word itself must be given its fullest meaning. There is, however, one limitation which must always be attached to it, that is to say, the relief claimed must be something which it would not be unlawful or unconstitutional or inequitable for the Court to grant or contrary to the accepted principles upon which the Court exercises its jurisdiction. Subject to this limitation I see nothing to fetter the discretion of the Court in exercising a jurisdiction under the rule to grant relief, and having regard to general business convenience and the importance of adapting the machinery of the Courts to the needs of suitors I think the rule should receive as liberal a construction as possible.'

There are of course some limits which have been established to the exercise of the discretion under the rules. In *Russian Commercial and Industrial Bank v British Bank for Foreign Trade Ltd* [1921] 2 AC 438 at 448, [1921] All ER Rep 329 at 332 Lord Dunedin said with reference to the ancient Scottish action of declarator:

'The rules that have been elucidated by a long course of decisions in the Scottish courts may be summarized thus: The question must be a real and not a theoretical question; the person raising it must have a real interest to raise it; he must be able to secure a proper contradictor, that is to say, someone presently existing who has a true interest to oppose the declaration sought.'

Subsequently, in *Vine v National Dock Labour Board* [1956] 3 All ER 939 at 943–944, [1957] AC 488 at 500, Viscount Kilmuir LC found this Scottish approach to be helpful; and indeed there is authority in the English cases that a declaration will not be granted where the question under consideration is not a real question, nor where the person seeking the declaration has no real interest in it, nor where the declaration is sought without proper argument, eg in default of defence or on admissions or by consent. In the present case, however, none of these objections exists. Here the declaration sought does indeed raise a real question; it is far from being hypothetical or academic. The plaintiff has a proper interest in the outcome, so that it can properly be said that she is

*a* seeking relief in the broad sense described by Bankes LJ. The matter has been fully argued in court, through the intervention of the Official Solicitor, and indeed with the benefit of assistance from an amicus curiae. I wish to add that no question arises in the present case regarding future rights: the declaration asked relates to the plaintiff's position as matters stand at present. In all the circumstances, I can see no procedural difficulty in the way of granting a declaration in the present case. In truth, the objection

*b* of the members of the Court of Appeal to the declaratory remedy was that it was not so appropriate as the exercise by the court of the parens patriae jurisdiction, had that still been available, by which the court would have considered whether or not to grant approval to the proposed treatment. This is a justifiable comment, in that (statute apart) only the exercise of the parens patriae jurisdiction can ensure, as a matter of law, that the approval of the court is sought before the proposed treatment is given. If, however, it

*c* became the invariable practice of the medical profession not to sterilise an adult woman who is incapacitated from giving her consent unless a declaration that the proposed course of action is lawful is first sought from the court, I can see little, if any, practical difference between seeking the court's approval under the parens patriae jurisdiction and seeking a declaration as to the lawfulness of the operation.

I am satisfied that, for the reasons so clearly expressed by the judge, he was right to

*d* grant the declarations sought by the plaintiff in the present case. I would therefore dismiss the appeal. My noble and learned friend Lord Brandon has proposed that certain alterations should be made to the declaration made by the judge. I for my part understand that the declaration was made on the basis of existing circumstances; but I am very content that this should be made clear in the order, and that express provision should be

*e* made for a liberty to apply, as proposed by my noble and learned friend.

**LORD JAUNCEY OF TULLICHETTLE.** My Lords, the difficult questions raised in this appeal have been fully examined in the speeches of my noble and learned friends Lord Brandon and Lord Goff and I entirely agree with their conclusions as to the manner in which this appeal should be disposed of and with their reasons for such disposal.

*f* My Lords, I should like only to reiterate the importance of not erecting such legal barriers against the provision of medical treatment for incompetents that they are deprived of treatment which competent persons could reasonably expect to receive in similar circumstances. The law must not convert incompetents into second class citizens for the purposes of health care.

There are four stages in the treatment of a patient, whether competent or incompetent.

*g* The first is to diagnose the relevant condition. The second is to determine whether the condition merits treatment. The third is to determine what the merited treatment should be. The fourth is to carry out the chosen form of merited treatment. In the case of a long-term incompetent, convenience to those charged with his care should never be a justification for the decision to treat. However, if such persons take the decision in relation to the second and third stages (supra) solely in his best interests and if their

*h* approach to and execution of all four stages is such as would be adopted by a responsible body of medical opinion skilled in the particular field of diagnosis and treatment concerned, they will have done all that is required of them and their actings will not be subject to challenge as being unlawful.

*Appeal dismissed.*

*j*
Solicitors: *Official Solicitor*; *Leighs* (for F); *Turner Kenneth Brown*, agents for *Clarks*, Reading (for the health authority); *Treasury Solicitor*.

                                        Mary Rose Plummer   Barrister.

# El Capistrano SA and another v ATO Marketing Ltd

COURT OF APPEAL, CIVIL DIVISION
KERR AND BALCOMBE LJJ
13 JANUARY 1989

*Contempt of court – Breach of court order – Defence of autrefois acquit – Availability in civil contempt proceedings – Contempt proceedings dismissed for procedural irregularity – Affidavit in support of notice of motion to commit defective – Defendants pleading irregularity as preliminary issue in proceedings – Affidavit struck out and notice of motion dismissed on basis that plaintiffs could issue fresh proceedings – Whether issue of fresh notice of motion could be defeated by plea of autrefois acquit – Whether defendants in peril of imprisonment on hearing of first motion – Whether first motion entailing investigation on merits.*

The plaintiffs alleged that the defendant company and one of its directors had committed breaches of undertakings they had given to the court in a passing-off action between the parties. Accordingly, the plaintiffs applied by notice of motion for sequestration of the assets of the defendant company and its director and also for the committal of the director to prison. The notice of motion complied with the rules of court and, as required by the rules, was accompanied by an affidavit in support of the application to commit. The affidavit relied on hearsay evidence to support the alleged breaches of the undertaking. The defendants applied by cross-motion to strike out the substantive parts of the affidavit on the ground that hearsay evidence was inadmissible in civil contempt proceedings. On the hearing of the motion and cross-motion the judge decided that the affidavit contained inadmissible evidence and should be removed from the file and since the motion to commit was thus left unsupported by evidence, contrary to the rules, the judge decided, on the basis that the plaintiff could issue fresh proceedings, to dismiss the motion without adjudicating on the merits rather than to adjourn it for amendment of the affidavit. The plaintiffs issued a fresh motion to commit which complied with the rules and in which they alleged the same contempt and relied on the same facts as had been alleged in the first motion. The defendants pleaded autrefois acquit or the rule against double jeopardy on the basis that they had been in peril of punishment on the hearing of the first motion since the first notice of motion itself had been a valid notice. The judge hearing the second motion upheld the defendants' contention and dismissed the motion. The plaintiffs appealed.

**Held** – The dismissal of civil process for a procedural irregularity was not necessarily equivalent to an acquittal in criminal proceedings for the purpose of applying the doctrine of autrefois acquit or the rule against double jeopardy. Furthermore, the question whether proceedings for civil contempt had been dismissed after an investigation 'on the merits' so that the doctrine of autrefois acquit could apply was to be determined on broad considerations of justice, having regard to the fact that in civil proceedings generally the phrase 'on the merits' had a wider meaning than in criminal law and ought not to be narrowly interpreted. In particular, it was not the case that it was only where civil contempt proceedings had been dismissed for a defect in the process that it could be said that the dismissal had not been on the merits. In all the circumstances, the defendant company and its director had not been in peril of punishment when the first notice of motion was heard since the defendants had not waived the alleged irregularity in the affidavit supporting the first notice of motion and, furthermore, had from the outset pleaded the irregularity as a preliminary issue which if determined in their favour would preclude any investigation into the merits of the first motion, as in fact had happened. It

followed that the defendants had not been entitled to plead autrefois acquit and the
a  appeal would therefore be allowed (see p 583 *h* to p 584 *e* and p 585 *e j*, post).

Dictum of Lush J in *Haynes v Davis* [1915] 1 KB 332 at 338–339 applied.

*Jelson (Estates) Ltd v Harvey* [1984] 1 All ER 12 applied.

**Notes**

For committal for civil contempt, see 9 Halsbury's Laws (4th edn) paras 92–93, 101, and
b  for cases on the subject, see 16 Digest (Reissue) 94–95, 927–937.

For autrefois acquit in criminal proceedings, see 11 Halsbury's Laws (4th edn) paras
241–244, and for cases on the subject, see 14(1) Digest (Reissue) 440–458, 3774–3899.

**Cases referred to in judgments**

*A-G v Times Newspapers Ltd* [1973] 3 All ER 54, [1974] AC 273, [1973] 3 WLR 298, HL.
c  *British Railways Board v Warwick* (17 June 1980, unreported), QBD.

*Broadbent v High* [1985] RTR 359, DC.

*Danchevsky v Danchevsky (No 2)* (1977) 121 SJ 796, CA.

*DPP v Porterhouse* (20 October 1988, unreported), DC.

*Grimble & Co v Preston* [1914] 1 KB 270, DC.

*Haynes v Davis* [1915] 1 KB 332, DC.
d  *J (an infant), Re* [1960] 1 All ER 603, [1960] 1 WLR 253.

*Jelson (Estates) Ltd v Harvey* [1984] 1 All ER 12, [1983] 1 WLR 1401, Ch D and CA.

*R v Swansea Justices, ex p Purvis* (1981) 145 JP 252, DC.

*Rossage v Rossage* [1960] 1 All ER 600, [1960] 1 WLR 249, CA.

*Savings and Investment Bank Ltd v Gasco Investments (Netherlands) BV* [1984] 1 All ER 296,
[1984] 1 WLR 271.
e  *Savings and Investment Bank Ltd v Gasco Investments (Netherlands) BV (No 2)* [1988] 1 All ER
975, [1988] Ch 422, [1988] 2 WLR 1212, CA.

**Interlocutory appeal**

By a notice of motion dated 22 December 1987 the plaintiffs, El Capistrano SA and El
Capistrano Villages Ltd, applied for a writ of sequestration of assets against the second
f  defendant, Asset Group Ltd, for contempt of court in breaching an undertaking given
by it to the court on 24 August 1987 in proceedings between the plaintiffs and the first
defendant, ATO Marketing Ltd, and the second defendant. The plaintiffs also applied in
the notice of motion for sequestration of the assets of Mr Richard King, a director of the
second defendant, or alternatively for Mr King's committal to prison for breaches of the
undertaking. In accordance with RSC Ord 52, r 4(2) the notice of motion was
g  accompanied by an affidavit in support of the application. By a cross-motion dated 25
January 1988 the defendants and Mr King applied to have the substantive parts of the
affidavit struck out on the ground that they consisted of hearsay evidence which was
irrelevant evidence in the contempt proceedings. On 28 January 1988 Harman J, after
reading the affidavit, directed that it should be removed from the file and dismissed the
h  plaintiffs' motion of 22 December 1987. On 6 April 1988 the plaintiffs issued a fresh
motion applying for writs of sequestration against the second defendant and Mr King,
alternatively for an order committing Mr King to prison for breaches of the undertaking
given on 24 August 1987. On the hearing of that motion the defendants pleaded autrefois
acquit in respect of the dismissal of the first motion. On 6 July 1988 Morritt J upheld
that plea and dismissed the second motion. The plaintiffs appealed. The grounds of the
j  appeal were that the judge erred in law in finding that the second defendant and Mr
King had stood in peril of punishment on the hearing of the first motion for the same
contempt as that alleged in the second motion. The facts are set out in the judgment of
Kerr LJ.

*Malcolm Knott* for the plaintiffs.

*Romie Tager* for the defendants.

**KERR LJ.** This is an appeal by the plaintiffs against the dismissal by Morritt J on 6 July 1988 of a motion for the sequestration of the defendants' assets and the committal of one *a* of its directors, Mr Richard King, on the ground of a civil contempt of court which Morritt J founded on the basis of the doctrine of autrefois acquit or double jeopardy. He concluded that in the circumstances of this case the defendants had already been in jeopardy in an earlier hearing before Harman J in relation to the same allegations, and that therefore the present motion must fail. It is a most unusual case which raises a novel point in the context of civil contempt and double jeopardy, a combination which has, as *b* far as the cases cited to us go, only arisen in one decision, a judgment of this court in 1983, to which I come later.

The history began with a writ in August 1987 complaining that the defendants were passing off their business as that of the plaintiffs. The companies on both sides are engaged in the promotion of time-sharing holiday properties in Spain. The plaintiffs, whose name includes the word 'Capistrano', complained that the defendants made use of *c* that word in various ways and claimed an injunction.

On 24 August 1987 there was a hearing of a motion which happened also to come before Harman J. The defendants then gave various undertakings until trial or further order which the plaintiffs accepted in lieu of pressing for an interlocutory injunction.

Subsequently the plaintiffs alleged that during September and October 1987 the defendants acted in breach of those undertakings in various respects. They accordingly *d* issued committal proceedings for breach of the undertakings by a notice of motion dated 22 December 1987. They claimed sequestration of the assets of the second defendant and the committal of the director to whom I have already referred.

The notice of motion concluded with the following paragraph:

'AND FURTHER TAKE NOTICE that the Plaintiffs intend to read and use in support of *e* this application the Affidavit of PETER HERBERT CHARLES MOODY and the exhibits thereto proving the said contempt, a copy of which is served with and accompanies this Notice of Motion.'

That paragraph was included to comply with RSC Ord 52, r 4(2). Indeed, it goes slightly further than that provision requires. What it requires is that— *f*

'the notice of motion, stating the grounds of the application and accompanied by a copy of the affidavit in support of the application, must be served personally on the person sought to be committed.'

The notice of motion was properly served and so was the affidavit to which it refers. Where this paragraph went further (though it does not really matter) was that it also *g* identified in the notice of motion the affidavit on which the plaintiffs proposed to rely.

Mr Moody was the solicitor acting for the plaintiffs. The feature of his affidavit which played a prominent part in what happened thereafter was that his evidence in support of the allegation of breaches of the undertakings was all given on the basis of information and belief, as is of course usual in interlocutory proceedings. The defendants took objection to this by issuing a cross-motion to strike out everything of substance in the *h* affidavit. When the matter came before Harman J there was also before the court an affidavit by a witness of fact, a Mr Catton. But that was not referred to in the notice of motion and, more importantly, had not been served on the defendants and therefore failed to comply with Ord 52, r 4(2). The point which the defendants took in para (4) of their notice of motion was in the following terms. They asked for an order that—

'all references in the Affidavit sworn herein by Peter Moody on the 22nd *j* December 1987 to the hearsay evidence of and to documents allegedly produced by one Steven Catton be struck out on the ground that such evidence is irrelevant and/ or oppressive and if relevant ought in the circumstances to have been given in an Affidavit sworn by the said Catton himself.'

The defendants' cross-motion, which also dealt with other matters, was supported by an
*a* affidavit sworn by Mr Glasner, their solicitor, in which he set out various grounds for
challenging the evidence given by Mr Moody, in particular because it was given on the
basis of hearsay or information and belief. In that regard Mr Galsner said:

> 'Counsel has advised the Second Defendant and Mr King that evidence should not
> be filed in direct reply to the secondhand hearsay evidence of Mr Catton until this
> Honourable Court has considered paragraph (4) of the Defendants' Notice of Motion
*b* > herein.'

It follows that right from the start the defendants were taking the line that they should
not be required to defend the plaintiffs' allegations on the merits, but that the plaintiffs'
evidence in support of their allegations should be struck out. That was the position when
the matter came before Harman J on the plaintiffs' motion for committal and on the
*c* defendants' cross-motion to strike out the plaintiffs' evidence in support of their motion.
What then happened is important to the outcome of this appeal and it is therefore
necessary to read much of the transcript of this hearing before Harman J. First we have
an extract from the proceedings. This begins with the last part of the opening remarks
by counsel for the plaintiffs, Mr Knott, who appeared for the plaintiffs below and in this
court, just before he came to deal with the evidence. No doubt what he had been saying
*d* until then was to remind the judge of the background and that he himself had been
concerned with the case in August 1988. The transcript begins as follows:

> '*Mr Knott.* The evidence of breach rests on three documents essentially which are
> exhibited to my instructing solicitor's affidavit, and this is, if I may say so, the
> troublesome affidavit with which my friend takes issue. Can I go to it at once,
*e* > asking your Lordship to look at it de bene esse.'

The reference to taking issue was to para (4) of the defendants' notice of motion.
Then Harman J said: '. . . Mr Knott, may we start by trying to see if I and you
understand the law in the same way.'
There was then some argument which has not been transcribed in which counsel
*f* presumably sought to rescue Mr Moody's affidavit from the defendants' objections. But
that was not accepted by the judge, who then gave judgment on that aspect of the
proceedings. I must read most of this:

> 'I have before me a motion, by notice given on 22 December 1987, for the
> sequestration of the assets of the second defendant to the action and for the
> sequestration of the assets of and/or the committal of a man said to be the sole
*g* > director of the second defendant. On the motion coming on for hearing today,
> notice having been given in the proper way by a paragraph on the notice of motion
> that the evidence in support was to be the affidavit of Mr Peter Herbert Charles
> Moody and the exhibits thereto served with the notice of motion, [counsel] for the
> defendants, respondents to the motion, objected to that evidence. [Counsel] takes
*h* > the point that the affidavit of Mr Moody is not firsthand evidence, it is largely in its
> substantial part hearsay and in part double hearsay. [Counsel for the defendants]
> further submits that this motion for committal and sequestration is not within the
> evidential rules applicable to interlocutory proceedings; that further evidence sought
> to be relied on in support of the motion, although not listed on the notice of motion
> as being relevant, or intended to be used on the hearing of the motion, including an
*j* > affidavit by one Stephen Paul Catton sworn on 26 January 1988, is also not properly
> before the court. Further evidence has been handed to me of which notice was not
> given in the notice of motion. That evidence does not appear to be objectionable in
> itself but it does not take the notice of motion any further.'

Pausing there, as I have already explained, there is in fact no requirement in Ord 52, r 4(2) that the affidavit must be identified in the notice of motion. But Mr Catton's affidavit had not been served and could, therefore, form no part of this motion.

The judgment went on:

> 'The objection to Mr Moody's evidence . . . is based on the well-known decisions in *Rossage v Rossage* [1960] 1 All ER 600, [1960] 1 WLR 249, the decision of Cross J in this division in *Re J (an infant)* [1960] 1 All ER 603, [1960] 1 WLR 253; and the decision of Peter Gibson J in *Savings and Investment Bank Ltd v Gasco Investments (Netherlands) BV* [1984] 1 All ER 296, [1984] 1 WLR 271.'

Pausing there, I should say that Harman J and both counsel were then unaware that the latter case had gone to this court and had resulted in an important decision on the admissibility of hearsay evidence in proceedings for civil contempt, to which I shall return.

Then the judge said:

> 'This is a motion, in broad terms, for contempt of court by alleged breaches of an order made in this division (by chance by me) on Monday, 24 August last [that was the order in which the undertakings were given]. Such matters raise most serious issues and require to be proved to a high standard. It is in my view clear that the court must be astute to ensure that only proper evidence is relied on in relation to such matters.'

Then he went on to make it clear that in his view the authorities precluded evidence of information and belief to be given in proceedings of this kind, because he regarded them as not being interlocutory proceedings in which such evidence is admissible under Ord 41, r 5(2).

I do not think I need to read this. Harman J then went on to say that these objections, which counsel had taken for the defendants as a preliminary matter, were fatal to the crucial parts of Mr Moody's affidavit and that without those there was in effect no evidence to support the alleged contempt.

Harman J then went on:

> 'In my view, none of the evidence referred to is properly on the file for the purposes of a motion for sequestration and committal such as this, and I shall direct that Mr Moody's affidavit of 22 December 1987 be removed from the file together with its exhibit and that Mr Catton's affidavit of 26 January 1988 likewise but for different reasons which I have given also be removed from the file. The remaining evidence, as I say, is merely formal and does not support the motion in any substance.'

So that was his judgment on the issue which is relevant to this appeal.

After that, going back to the transcript of the proceedings, we have the following exchange. Counsel then appearing for the defendants, who are today represented by different counsel, said: 'Will your Lordship provide for the costs of that part of the respondents' motion.' I think that he was referring to para (4) of the cross-motion because he had just heard a judgment in which that paragraph had been upheld. The other paragraphs dealing with other matters were dealt with in a second separate judgment which the judge gave later. Harman J said:

> 'I think I probably will but I am not sure what Mr Knott now wishes to do. He has a notice of motion served and expressly referring to an affidavit which has been taken off the file. I am not sure what he wants to do with the motion . . . Do you want it adjourned? *Mr Knott.* Yes.
> *Harman J.* Mr Knott, the difficulty is that the Court of Appeal has said that you must specify in the notice of motion for contempt the evidence on which you rely. I have held that the evidence relied on here is not properly on the file and cannot be

a referred to; the notice of motion is in some difficulty. *Mr Knott.* I should have to seek leave to amend the notice of motion.

*Harman J.* You would like to adjourn it for considering that? *Mr Knott.* My Lord, I would, if you please'.

Then Harman J called on counsel for the defendants, who said:

b 'In my submission, the convenient course would be for it to be started all over again.

*Harman J.* I would have thought so. Mr Knott, it does seem to me that you are not getting very much by saving the thing. One is left with a very limping document. You are entirely at liberty to serve a fresh one but referring to proper evidence.'

c Mr Knott then had a word with his instructing solicitors and again asked for the motion to be adjourned and not dismissed. He said:

'It might have this advantage, if your Lordship was prepared in due course to give me leave to amend dispensing with re-service then some costs will be saved, otherwise it does not matter ... So for that reason I do ask that the motion be adjourned in the hope of saving a little bit of money, that is all.

d *Harman J.* I am sorry, Mr Knott. I think the contempt motion ought not to be around in a form which is not proper because it is not supported by any evidence. I think the more convenient course (although it may cost your client a bit more money, I realise that) would be to say that there should be no order on the motion, save that it be dismissed.'

e He then dismissed the plaintiffs' motion for committal with costs and allowed the relevant part of the defendants' cross-motion, also with costs.

With hindsight one can now see that this has led to a position which is ironical in two respects. First, it was clearly envisaged by everyone that it made no difference, save in terms of the costs of re-service, whether the motion was dismissed or adjourned. The judge ultimately decided to dismiss it for procedural, if not cosmetic, reasons, because it f was unsupported by any evidence and could therefore not stand under the rules. It obviously never crossed anyone's mind that the dismissal of the motion might have the consequence that the plaintiffs would be precluded from issuing a fresh motion based on the same facts if it was supported by proper evidence. On the contrary, the transcript shows that both the judge and counsel considered that this course was clearly open to the plaintiffs and that they would no doubt in due course adopt it, as they did. The second g irony is that no one was then aware of the decision of this court in *Savings and Investment Bank Ltd v Gasco Investments (Netherlands) BV (No 2)* [1988] 1 All ER 957, [1988] Ch 422 in which judgment had been given on 12 November 1987 but which was not reported, at least not fully, until it appeared in the All England Law Reports in April 1988.

The relevance of that decision is that it shows that Harman J's view that the evidence of Mr Moody was objectionable on the ground of hearsay was not the law. This court, h consisting of Purchas, Nicholls and Russell LJJ, decided two points in relation to an application for committal for a civil contempt, analogous to the position in the present case. The first was that such an application is of an interlocutory nature and not final, with the result that Ord 41, 5(2) applies to it so as not to preclude hearsay evidence, provided proper grounds of information and belief are shown. That was contrary to the j narrow view which Harman J had formed of the meaning or scope of an interlocutory application in the context of proceedings for contempt, basing himself on older authorities. Second, the court concluded that not only were such proceedings interlocutory but that they were clearly civil proceedings and not analogous to criminal proceedings, with the result that the Civil Evidence Act 1968 and other rules relating to evidence in civil proceedings applied to these proceedings.

The irony is double in this sense. First, the defendants were undoubtedly in jeopardy if that decision had been known since the plaintiffs' motion was in fact supported by admissible evidence. In this court counsel for the defendants has sought to rely on that fact, which nobody then had in mind, as Morritt J recognised when he gave the judgment from which this appeal arises. But, since that point was never taken below, nor mentioned by Morritt J in his judgment, nor supported by any cross-notice in the appeal to this court, I put it on one side.

The second irony is that, since the evidence was admissible, there was no basis for dismissing the motion on the ground on which it was dismissed. The ironical result is that if the defendants' objection to the present fresh motion on the ground of autrefois acquit is well founded then they would indeed have been very lucky, in the most technical manner possible, because the dismissal of the first motion on which they base this contention should never have occurred. However, I equally put that out of my mind. I think that one has to proceed, as Morritt J did, on the basis on which the hearing before Harman J took place, and to that extent ignore the decision in *Savings and Investment Bank Ltd v Gasco Investments (Netherlands) BV (No 2)*. However, what that case clearly shows, and Morritt J did of course have it before him, is that it points away from any close analogy between proceedings for civil contempt on the one hand and criminal proceedings on the other.

Nevertheless, having said that, it is also clear that the rule against double jeopardy or the principle of autrefois convict or acquit both apply to proceedings for civil contempt. The authority frequently cited in support of that proposition is the decision of this court in *Danchevsky v Danchevsky (No 2)* (1977) 121 SJ 796. In that case the defendant had been committed to prison on several occasions, but on each occasion for the breach of a single order which had been made on 15 May 1974 that he should vacate the former matrimonial home. It was held that the subsequent committals should be quashed, because one must only be punished once for breach of a single order. Lord Denning MR is reported as having said: 'All three committal orders had been for failure to comply with the original order of 15 May 1974. Having been punished once for that offence the later orders were invalid.' Lawton LJ concurred and said that the husband could have pleaded autrefois convict. Goff LJ agreed. That principle has been accepted in this court and is clearly good law.

The question now is whether situations which in criminal proceedings would found a defence of autrefois acquit, or autrefois convict, apply equally in proceedings for civil contempt. The only reported case in which the application of the doctrine of double jeopardy, if I may so call it, has been considered in the context of proceedings for civil contempt is the decision of this court in *Jelson (Estates) Ltd v Harvey* [1984] 1 All ER 12, [1983] 1 WLR 1401. However, before coming to that I should refer to an important earlier decision in criminal committal proceedings which was considered by this court in the *Jelson* case. That was a decision of the Divisional Court in *Haynes v Davis* [1915] 1 KB 332. In that case an information was preferred against the appellant for having sold adulterated milk, but when the case came on for hearing it transpired that no certificate of analysis had been served with the summons as required by s 19(2) of the Sale of Food and Drugs Act 1899. The magistrates, accordingly, dismissed the summons and there was no investigation of the facts. A second summons was then taken out in respect of the same alleged offence and served together with the analyst's certificate. It was held by a majority, Lush J dissenting, that the appellant had been in peril of being convicted on the first summons and was therefore entitled to plead autrefois acquit to the second summons. Although it has been said by Donaldson LJ in *R v Swansea Justices, ex p Purvis* (1981) 145 JP 252 at 254, to which I shall come shortly, that in the result there was no real difference of view between the three members of the court (Ridley and Avory JJ in the majority and Lush J in the minority), I think that Lush J did take a very different view on the applicable principles, and it is that judgment which has been preferred by this court in *Jelson (Estates) Ltd v Harvey* [1984] 1 All ER 12, [1983] 1 WLR 1401. I

therefore begin by reading a substantial extract from the judgment of Lush J in *Haynes v*
*a* *Davis* [1915] 1 KB 332 at 338–339:

> 'It has been constantly laid down, perhaps in somewhat different terms, that there
> are three conditions which must be fulfilled before the plea of autrefois acquit can
> be successfully raised, those three conditions being stated in Russell on Crimes, vol.
> ii., p. 1982. There the author, after saying that "at common law a man who has once
> been tried and acquitted for a crime may not be tried again for the same offence if
> *b* he was 'in jeopardy' on the first trial," proceeds as follows: "He was so 'in jeopardy' if
> (1.) the Court was competent to try him for the offence; (2.) the trial was upon a
> good indictment, on which a valid judgment of conviction could be entered; and
> (3.) the acquittal was on the merits, ie by verdict on the trial, or in summary cases
> by dismissal on the merits, followed by a judgment or order of acquittal." I quite
> agree that "acquittal on the merits" does not necessarily mean that the jury or the
> *c* magistrate must find as a matter of fact that the person charged was innocent; it is
> just as much an acquittal upon the merits if the judge or the magistrates were to
> rule upon the construction of an Act of Parliament that the accused was in law
> entitled to be acquitted as in law he was not guilty, and to that extent the expression
> "acquittal on the merits" must be qualified, but in my view the expression is used
> *d* by way of antithesis to a dismissal of the charge upon some technical ground which
> had been a bar to the adjudicating upon it. That is why this expression is important,
> however one may qualify it, and I think the antithesis is between an adjudication of
> not guilty upon some matter of fact or law and a discharge of the person charged on
> the ground that there are reasons why the Court cannot proceed to find if he is
> guilty. ... In my opinion the statement that a man must not be twice placed in
> *e* peril or in jeopardy means that he must have been tried on the first occasion and
> that all the three conditions I have named have been fulfilled.'

Then Lush J referred to another authority, *Grimble & Co v Preston* [1914] 1 KB 270, and
went on as follows ([1915] 1 KB 332 at 340):

> *f* 'Grimble v Preston means this and only this, a person chooses to take his chance of
> being acquitted and waives his right to have this formality complied with [that is,
> the service of an analyst's certificate] he cannot afterwards be heard to say that the
> magistrate had no right to try him. The person charged in such circumstances
> always has the right at any moment, provided he does not do that which operates as
> a waiver, to insist that the magistrate should no longer proceed with the adjudication.
> That right the present appellant exercised, and I find it impossible to satisfy myself
> *g* that he ever was in peril. How is it possible to reconcile this statement that there
> was a fatal defect in these proceedings which prevented the magistrate going on to
> adjudicate, unless the person charged chooses to waive it, with the statement that
> the same person was running the risk of being properly convicted? I find it difficult
> to reconcile these two statements. In my view the appellant never was in peril.'

*h*
The question is how that is to be applied in the present case. Clearly the defendants
equally did not waive what they regarded, and Harman J agreed, was an irregularity
which made the plaintiffs' evidence inadmissible. On the contrary, they insisted on
taking it as a preliminary issue, on which they succeeded.

Against that background I come to *Jelson (Estates) Ltd v Harvey* [1984] 1 All ER 12,
*j* [1983] 1 WLR 1401. That was a motion for committal for a civil contempt of the same
kind as in the present case and Ord 52, r 4 was applicable to the motion. However, the
original notice of motion did not comply with it because it did not state the grounds of
the application by specifying the breaches complained of. On that being drawn to his
attention at the hearing of the motion Warner J made no order on the motion. He did
not read the evidence or consider the merits in any way. The plaintiff then served a

second notice of motion which complied with Ord 52, r 4 by setting out the alleged
breaches, which were the same as in the first case. The accompanying affidavit was also     *a*
the same. The defendants then raised a preliminary objection that the court should not
entertain the second motion on the ground of the doctrine of double jeopardy. Goulding
J rejected this objection and fined the defendants for contempt. Apart from a variation
in the amount of the fine that decision was upheld by this court, and it is clearly a case of
considerable importance for present purposes.

In the course of his judgment Goulding J said ([1984] 1 All ER 12 at 16, [1983] 1 WLR     *b*
1401 at 1405–1406):

> 'Where there is litigation of a certain question or issue before the court resulting
> in a final or substantial order which decides it, then it is well established that it is too
> late (save in exceptional cases) for a party to adduce in subsequent litigation against
> the same opponent, or one privy to him, a fact that might well have been brought     *c*
> forward on the previous occasion. That doctrine, however, does not apply where
> there is a mere procedural defect and the court has never gone into the merits,
> though both parties were before it. Here the judge himself, I think, recognised (if
> his remarks are correctly reported) that he was not deciding the question of the
> alleged contempt and that the plaintiffs, if they put their proceedings in order,
> might try again. Accordingly, the doctrine of res judicata, in its wider or more     *d*
> general form relied on by counsel for the defendant does not in my judgment avail
> him.'

Later on, having dealt with the possibility of amending the notice of motion, he said
([1984] 1 All ER 12 at 16, [1983] 1 WLR 1401 at 1406):

> 'However, I think that is attempting to read into Warner J's order something that     *e*
> is not there. I think that all that he decided was that he would not give relief on the
> notice of motion dated 11 April, leaving it entirely open to the plaintiffs to serve a
> proper notice of motion that the court could then consider on its merits.'

So one can see that the course adopted by the defendant before Warner J was similar to
what happened before Harman J in the present case, and that Goulding J's understanding     *f*
of the consequences (the plaintiffs' right to get their tackle in order and to start again)
coincided with that of Harman J.

However, counsel for the defendants says that there is one crucial distinction which
makes all the difference. In the *Jelson* case the notice of motion was in itself defective
because it did not specify the alleged breaches of the relevant order, whereas in this case
the defect lay in the inadmissibility of the evidence supporting it which must be served     *g*
with the motion under the rules. In order to test this submission, I must first continue
with the judgments in the *Jelson* case.

The judgment of Goulding J was in effect upheld by Cumming-Bruce and Dillon LJJ
in this court. In relation to *Haynes v Davis* Cumming-Bruce LJ said ([1984] 1 All ER 12 at
19, [1983] 1 WLR 1401 at 1409):

> 'But, for myself, having considered the judgments, I prefer the view taken in the     *h*
> minority judgment of Lush J, and, if it is necessary, I would hold that this court
> should follow the approach of Lush J rather than the approach of the majority. I
> take the view, however, that it is not necessary to determine that matter, because I
> am not satisfied that these proceedings, civil proceedings for contempt, are so close
> to the subject matter which the court was considering in *Haynes v Davis* (bound as
> they were to administer the law in accordance with the provisions of the Summary     *j*
> Jurisdiction Acts) as to make it necessary or even useful in this court to take the view
> that it should proceed in exactly the way that the Queen's Bench Divisional Court
> did when reviewing the case stated by the magistrate in *Haynes v Davis*. I would take
> the broader approach: accepting that these were proceedings for the punishment of

*a*  the defendant for breach of an injunction made in civil proceedings, when the judge observed the irregularity on the notice of motion and decided that it would be wrong, that is to say unfair, to proceed to adjudicate on the merits when the grounds had not appeared from the notice of motion so that the defendant had not had time specifically to consider those grounds, there was, in my view, no room in these proceedings for contempt for the application of the doctrine of autrefois acquit by analogy with criminal proceedings. I would take the view that the judge, when
*b*  making no order on the motion, never in fact allowed the defendant to be in any peril of any punishment on that notice of motion, and it seems to me wholly unreal to borrow from criminal law a doctrine which in the criminal law may properly be applied with greater strictness than is necessary in these civil proceedings. I can see nothing the least unfair in the course that Warner J took when he made no order on the summons, clearly with a view to enabling the plaintiffs to issue a second notice
*c*  of motion curing the irregularity by stating the grounds on which the plaintiffs relied.'

Then he said that Goulding J was right to proceed to inquire into the merits.

Dillon LJ agreed. He referred to *Danchevsky v Danchevsky (No 2)* (1977) 121 SJ 796 and quoted a phrase from Goulding J's judgment ([1984] 1 All ER 12 at 20, [1983] 1 WLR
*d*  1401 at 1411):

'"I am quite clear that if a man has been cleared of an alleged civil contempt on a proper investigation of the merits he should not be put in jeopardy a second time . . ." [He then went on as follows] With that I entirely agree. I think the question is whether on a true appreciation of the circumstances the defendant here
*e*  was ever in jeopardy a first time on the first notice of motion to commit him. The rules of court provide in RSC Ord 52, r 4 that the notice of motion by which an application for an order of committal is made must state the grounds of the application and must also be accompanied by a copy of the affidavit in support of the application. The notice of motion which came before Warner J, although it referred to the affidavit, did not state the grounds of the application. Therefore the
*f*  technical point was taken for the defendant, and was rightly acceded to by Warner J, that the notice of motion failed to comply with the rules and should not be investigated; it should be dismissed out of hand, as it was. Counsel for the defendant now says, "Oh, but the defect might have been waived. The court, had the defect been waived, would have had jurisdiction to investigate the merits, and so Mr Harvey [the defendant] was in jeopardy of committal." It seems to me that he never
*g*  was in jeopardy, because the point was firmly taken and accepted by the judge at the outset of the hearing. The merits were never gone into. It is not appropriate to look at what might theoretically have happened in a different scenario of the facts. It is necessary to consider in each case where the question is one of autrefois acquit what actually happened. So far as the authorities are concerned, counsel for the defendant has to rely on the decision of the majority of the Divisional Court in
*h*  *Haynes v Davis* [1915] 1 KB 332, to which Cumming-Bruce LJ has referred. For my part, I prefer the minority judgment of Lush J in that case (see [1915] 1 KB 332 at 339–340). I would regard the criterion as being that put by Lush J and interpreted by him in his judgment. A man who has been once tried and acquitted for a crime may not be tried again for the same offence if he was in jeopardy on the first trial; in considering whether he was in jeopardy, one of the factors is whether the acquittal
*j*  was on the merits, by verdict at the trial or, in summary cases, by dismisssal on the merits. Accepting the further explanation given by Lush J in that judgment as to what is meant by acquittal on the merits, it is quite clear that in the present case the defendant was not acquitted on the merits. Therefore the point of autrefois acquit is not available to him and I reject that ground of appeal.'

That is the nearest authority for present purposes. As I have said, it is clearly different, because in the present case the notice of motion was opened in a preliminary way and was not defective in itself. But the supposed defects in the evidence could have been cured by adjournment and amendment, or there could have been an appeal against the dismissal of the motion by Harman J. Counsel for the defendants says all that, and he also relies on the very wide powers of the court under Ord 2, r 1, which are there to preserve rather than to strike out or dismiss defective or irregular proceedings. He says that this motion was effective and dismissed on the merits. He also relies on a number of decisions of the Divisional Court in relation to criminal proceedings which considered whether the defence of autrefois convict or acquit applied.

The most helpful case to counsel's argument for the defendants in that connection is *R v Swansea Justices, ex p Purvis* (1981) 145 JP 252. What happened there and in at least one other subsequent case in this field was that in a criminal case before a magistrates' court the prosecution was not ready when the case came on but was refused an adjournment. In the absence of any evidence the magistrates dismissed the information. Then the question was whether they were entitled to hear a further information based on the same facts. They rejected a plea of autrefois acquit and convicted the defendant. He then applied to the Divisional Court to quash the conviction and succeeded on the ground that he had already been acquitted on the same charge.

Giving the leading judgment, Donaldson LJ said that the case was very simple and on all fours with a judgment of Lord Lane CJ in *British Railways Board v Warwick* (17 June 1980, unreported), in which he had said:

'Consequently one is left with this simple series of facts; there was an arraignment, there was an election to be tried summarily, there was a plea of not guilty, there was no evidence proffered by the prosecution, there was in effect a verdict of not guilty: and the case was dismissed.'

(See 145 JP 252 at 253.) He said that the position in that case was the same and therefore held that autrefois acquit was a defence to the second charge. He rejected a submission that a trial on the merits meant anything other than the description of a situation in which the defendant was in jeopardy of being convicted. Bingham J agreed.

A similar case in the Divisional Court was *Broadbent v High* [1985] RTR 359 but the defence of autrefois acquit there failed. Two virtually identical charges had been put forward by the prosecution. The defendant required an election between them. When the prosecution elected to proceed on no 2 the justices immediately dismissed no 1. The question was then whether that dismissal could found a defence of autrefois acquit to no 2. It was held, perhaps not surprisingly, that in that situation the doctrine of double jeopardy did not apply.

Finally, I should refer to the last case on which counsel for the defendants relied. That again was a decision of the Divisional Court in a criminal context, *DPP v Porterhouse* (20 October 1988, unreported), of which we have a transcript. The court consisted of May LJ and Ian Kennedy J. That was also a case of two charges being laid successively, but the first was defective because it referred to a combination of facts and statutory provisions which made no sense. On that being dismissed, the question was whether a conviction on the second charge, based on the same facts but correctly drafted, could proceed. The court followed *Broadbent v High* and held that it could proceed, but based themselves on the fact that the first information was 'so faulty in form and content that the respondent could never have been in jeopardy on it, and thus its dismissal could not give rise to any defence of autrefois acquit on the second information.'

Counsel for the defendants relies on that. Above all he relies on the point that in *Jelson (Estates) Ltd v Harvey* [1984] 1 All ER 12, [1983] 1 WLR 1401 the defect lay in the motion itself and not in the evidence in support of it, as here.

There is no doubt that if the analogy of the criminal cases applies in full to a defence

of autrefois acquit in the present context, then that defence must prevail. There is also
*a* no doubt, and this is the point on which Morritt J relied, that if what this court said in
the *Jelson* case is confined to situations in which the notice of motion is itself defective,
then again the defence of autrefois acquit must obviously apply in the present case. It is
that logic and narrow point of distinction which impressed the judge, and which he
accepted after reviewing the authorities. He founded himself on a narrow analysis of the
*Jelson* case. He noted in passing that the proceedings before Harman J had been decided
*b* on a wrong basis, because *Savings and Investment Bank Ltd v Gasco Investments (Netherlands)
BV (No 2)* [1988] 1 All ER 975, [1988] Ch 422 was unknown to all concerned. But he did
not found anything on that; nor, in my view, can this appeal be affected by that
consideration. Having reviewed the cases he said:

> 'These cases show that a respondent is not in peril in fact if the notice of motion
*c* or charge is defective and not proceeded with. If, though defective, the motion or
> charge is proceeded with, the respondent may be in peril in the particular
> circumstances of the case. The converse proposition is that a motion or charge which
> is not defective and which is proceeded with to a conclusion, does in fact imperil the
> respondent, and depending on the result would give rise to the subsequent defence
> of autrefois acquit or autrefois convict. A motion for committal may fail for a
*d* number of different legal or factual reasons. If it fails because of inadequate evidence,
> it may be (as in this case) because the material evidence was inadmissible, or it may
> be that it was not sufficiently cogent. But, either way, the respondent will have been
> imperilled in fact, even though the application did not succeed, the failure of the
> first application being implicit in the defence itself. I see no reason why the success
> or otherwise of the defence should depend on the reason why the evidence on the
*e* first application was found to be inadequate. Moreover, I do not see any basis for
> drawing a distinction based on the way the objection to the evidence is made. In
> this case the [defendants] very properly gave notice by their cross-motion, but on an
> application for committal they would have been entitled to object without prior
> notice when it was sought to read the affidavit in support. In either case, if the
> motion is dismissed, the [defendants] will have been acquitted of contempt of court.
*f* In this case there is no doubt that the plaintiffs' notice of motion complied with the
> rules, there was nothing defective about it, the plaintiffs' motion was moved, and
> Harman J read and considered all the evidence. Because of the defects in the evidence
> referred to in the judgment, the plaintiffs' motion was dismissed. In my judgment
> the [defendants] were in fact imperilled on the first application.'

*g* And he went on to say that therefore the present second application could not proceed
and dismissed it. That is the order under appeal.
  If I may say so, I fully appreciate the logic of that passage. But its logic is only
compelling if one is bound to place the same narrow interpretation on what was said in
this court in *Jelson (Estates) Ltd v Harvey* by confining that case to situations in which
there is a defect in the process itself. However, there is no authority which compels that
*h* conclusion, and the wide remarks of Cumming-Bruce and Dillon LJJ point in the
opposite direction on the question of what fairness and justice require in the context of
proceedings for civil contempt. Equally, there is no principle of justice which compels
this conclusion. No one could say here that the defendants were ever regarded by
Harman J as having been in peril of punishment, or as having been acquitted by him.
He clearly thought that it made no difference in principle whether he adjourned or
*j* dismissed the motion; he only dismissed it because he felt that it was procedurally tidier
to do so. Everyone in court envisaged that the plaintiffs could issue a fresh notice of
motion, and Harman J expressly founded his decision in part on their ability to do so.
The defendants on the other hand, going back to the judgment of Lush J in *Haynes v
Davis* [1915] 1 KB 332, made it clear that they were not prepared to waive what they

believed to be the procedural irregularities in the plaintiffs' evidence. Their line was that
these precluded the plaintiffs from reaching the stage of any trial on the merits. The *a*
defendants were saying: 'We are not obliged even to contest the merits in this case
because the plaintiffs' evidence is so defective that the motion cannot get off the ground.'
That was their line, and it succeeded.

In the same way as Lush J, I cannot see how that can be consistent with their having
been in jeopardy of being convicted of contempt of court. The reality, if one applies what
Cumming-Bruce and Dillon LJJ said, is that in substance there has never been any *b*
imperilment of the defendants in the present case. I would therefore decline to draw the
narrow procedural distinction between the situation in this case before Harman J and
that before Warner J in *Jelson (Estates) Ltd v Harvey*. I also think that in the context of
civil proceedings generally the phrase 'on the merits' may well have a wider connotation
than it has in the criminal law, and that the dismissal of a civil process is not by any
means necessarily equivalent to an acquittal in criminal proceedings. There is no *c*
authority or principle which requires a narrow interpretation of the express 'on the
merits', or of the doctrine of double jeopardy, in the law of civil contempt. We are
entitled to view such cases on a broad basis of justice, and in my view we should clearly
do so.

Accordingly, though with every respect for the analytical view taken by Morritt J, I
cannot agree with him and would allow this appeal. *d*

**BALCOMBE LJ.** I agree that, for the reasons given by Kerr LJ, this appeal should be
allowed, but since we are differing from the judge below I add a few words of my own.

Morritt J considered this case as raising an important point of principle; it was for that
reason that he gave leave to appeal to this court. This appeal turns on the question: how
far should the analogy of the criminal law be applied in dealing with a civil contempt of *e*
court? In this connection I would not, without further argument, be prepared to accept
the dictum of Lawton LJ in *Danchevsky v Danchevsky (No 2)* (1977) 121 SJ 796 that any
contempt of court is a common law misdemeanour. For a full discussion of the difference
between civil and criminal contempt, I refer to Borrie and Lowe *Law of Contempt* (2nd
edn, 1983) and to the speech of Lord Diplock in *AG v Times Newspapers Ltd* [1973] 3 All *f*
ER 54 at 71–72, [1974] AC 273 at 311–312.

Returning to the question about how far the analogy of the criminal law should be
applied when dealing with a civil contempt of court, I too refer to *Jelson (Estates) Ltd v
Harvey* [1984] 1 All ER 12, [1983] 1 WLR 1401. Kerr LJ has cited that case in some
detail, but there are one or two passages to which I would wish to refer or repeat. There
is a passage from the judgment of Goulding J at first instance which I find of assistance.
Goulding J said ([1984] 1 All ER 12 at 15, [1983] 1 WLR 1401 at 1405): *g*

> 'However, I have been referred by neither side to any authority showing how far
> and in what manner the doctrines of the criminal law about previous acquittal are
> applicable in a case of civil contempt. And although I am quite clear that if a man
> has been cleared of an alleged civil contempt on a proper investigation of the merits *h*
> he should not be put in jeopardy a second time, it does not seem to me that one
> should too readily draw procedural analogies between the contempt process and
> those either of indictment or summary prosecution. I think it is in accordance with
> the proper nature and application of the rule against double jeopardy that an
> applicant should not be prevented from renewing a complaint of contempt of court
> simply because of a procedural defect in his first attempt to do so; and I think it *j*
> would be generalising the authority of *Haynes v Davis* [1915] 1 KB 332 too much to
> apply it by analogy to the present case.'

I respectfully agree with that passage in its entirety.

Then I would repeat a brief passage from the judgment of Cumming-Bruce LJ, to

which Kerr LJ has already referred, where Cumming-Bruce LJ said ([1984] 1 All ER 12
at 19, [1983] 1 WLR 1401 at 1410):

> 'I would take the view that the judge [he refers there to Warner J in that case],
> when making no order on the motion, never in fact allowed the defendant to be in
> any peril of any punishment on that notice of motion, and it seems to me wholly
> unreal to borrow from criminal law a doctrine which in the criminal law may
> properly be applied with greater strictness than is necessary in these civil
> proceedings.'

Finally, a passage from the judgment of Dillon LJ in the same case, which again has been
mentioned by Kerr LJ ([1984] 1 All ER 12 at 20, [1983] 1 WLR 1401 at 1411):

> 'Counsel for the defendant now says, "Oh, but the defect might have been waived.
> The court, had the defect been waived, would have had jurisdiction to investigate
> the merits, and so Mr Harvey [the defendant] was in jeopardy of committal." It
> seems to me that he never was in jeopardy, because the point was firmly taken and
> accepted by the judge at the outset of the hearing. The merits were never gone into.
> It is not appropriate to look at what might theoretically have happened in a different
> scenario of the facts. It is necessary to consider in each case where the question is one
> of autrefois acquit what actually happened.'

In these circumstances, for my part I derive only limited assistance from the criminal
cases to which counsel for the defendants has referred us, because it seems to me to be
necessary for us to look at the substance of what happened before Harman J to see
whether in fact the second defendant and Mr King were ever really in jeopardy.

On the facts of this case in my judgment it is clear that Harman J never allowed the
second defendant or Mr King 'to be in any peril of any punishment on that' (ie the first
notice of motion; the quotation is taken from the judgment of Cumming-Bruce LJ in
*Jelson (Estates) Ltd v Harvey* [1984] 1 All ER 12 at 19, [1983] 1 WLR 1401 at 1410). I find
it unreal to borrow a further doctrine from criminal law to say that in fact the second
defendant and Mr King were effectively in jeopardy.

Kerr LJ has read the relevant passages from the judgment of Morritt J. The substance
of his finding is to be found in the transcript of his judgment where the judge said:

> 'I see no reason why the success or otherwise of the defence should depend on the
> reason why the evidence on the first application was found to be inadequate.
> Moreover, I do not see any basis for drawing a distinction based on the way the
> objection to the evidence is made. In this case the [defendants] very properly gave
> notice by their cross-motion, but on an application for committal they would have
> been entitled to object without prior notice when it was sought to read the affidavit
> in support. In either case, if the motion is dismissed, the [defendants] will have been
> acquitted of contempt of court.'

I accept the submission of counsel for the plaintiffs, made in his skeleton argument that
in that passage the judge effectively equated a successful preliminary objection to the
form of the proceedings with an acquittal, and I agree with him that there is, and in this
case there clearly was, a clear and important distinction between the two. The second
defendant and Mr King are of course entitled to take any technical point which is in their
favour, but the lack of merit in their approach is in fact highlighted by their counsel's
skeleton argument, where he said (at para 6): 'It is the respondent's case that the very
limping document [ie the first notice of motion] would have been a valid motion for the
purposes of O.52 r 4(2).' Harman J, and presumably both counsel before him, did not
appreciate that the rules of autrefois acquit or autrefois convict might apply. Had this
point been made by counsel for the plaintiffs, there is every likelihood that Harman J
would not have ordered the dismissal of the motion of 22 December 1987. It was as a
result of that dismissal that the defendants ceased to be in jeopardy on the first motion.

A court approaches a case of this kind in an attempt to do justice to both parties. For my part, I would add that had I taken a different view of the substance of the law I would *a* have been prepared to give favourable consideration to an application for leave to appeal out of time against the order of Harman J, but that question does not now arise.

*Appeal allowed. Leave to appeal to House of Lords refused.*

Solicitors: *Nathan Silman* (for the plaintiffs); *Maxwell Glasner & Co* (for the defendants). *b*

Wendy Shockett Barrister.

# R v Ensor *c*

COURT OF APPEAL, CRIMINAL DIVISION
LORD LANE CJ, KENNEDY AND HUTCHISON JJ
14 MARCH 1989

*Criminal law – Trial – Counsel's conduct of client's case – Counsel for accused making wrong* *d*
*decision in conduct of case – Counsel ignoring client's wishes as to how case should be conducted –*
*Counsel refusing to apply for severance of counts despite accused's wish that they be severed –*
*Whether counsel's conduct constituting material irregularity in conduct of trial.*

The appellant was accused of two counts of rape alleged to have been committed on two separate occasions against two different complainants. The two counts were quite *e* properly joined in the same indictment but the appellant wanted the two counts severed and made his wishes known to his solicitor and counsel. Since there was no similarity between the two offences an application for severance ought to have succeeded if it had been made. However, counsel appearing for the appellant at his trial decided that there were advantages in the two counts being heard together because in his opinion there was a good chance of an acquittal on one of the charges and that would enhance the possibility *f* of an acquittal on the other. Counsel accordingly decided not to apply for severance of the counts. Counsel did not inform the appellant of his decision or the reasons for it. On the trial of the second count both the fact of intercourse and the absence of consent were in issue but the judge gave a direction as to the need for corroboration only in respect of the lack of consent. The appellant was convicted on both counts. He appealed on the grounds, inter alia, that his counsel's conduct in not applying to sever the counts in the *g* indictment constituted a material irregularity in the conduct of the trial and that the judge should have directed the jury in regard to the second count on the need for corroboration of both the act of intercourse and lack of consent.

**Held** – Except in the case of flagrantly incompetent advocacy on the part of the accused's *h* counsel the court would not set aside a conviction on the ground that counsel had made a decision or pursued a course in the conduct of the trial which later appeared to have been mistaken or unwise, even if that decision or course of conduct was contrary to the accused's wishes. Since the decision of the appellant's counsel not to apply for severance of the counts, even if erroneous, had been carefully considered and could not be described as flagrantly incompetent advocacy the court would not set aside the convictions on the *j* ground that counsel had acted contrary to the appellant's wishes. However, the trial judge had been wrong not to have directed the jury on the need for corroboration of both the act of intercourse and lack of consent in regard in the second count and the conviction on that count would be quashed (see p 590 *f j* to p 591 *a* and p 593 *b* to *e g*, post).

*R v Irwin* [1987] 2 All ER 1085 doubted.

**Notes**

a For the authority of counsel to conduct a case, see 3(1) Halsbury's Laws (4th edn reissue) para 508.

For corroboration in rape cases, see 11 Halsbury's Laws (4th edn) para 458, and for cases on the subject, see 15 Digest (Reissue) 1216, 10426–10431.

**Cases referred to in judgment**

b R v Gautam (1987) Times, 4 March, CA.

R v Henry and Manning (1969) 53 Cr App R 150, CCA.

R v Irwin [1987] 2 All ER 1085, [1987] 1 WLR 902, CA.

R v Lucas [1981] 2 All ER 1008, [1981] QB 720, [1981] 3 WLR 120, CA.

R v Novac (1976) 65 Cr App R 107, CA.

R v Stewart (1986) 83 Cr App R 327, CA.

c R v Swain (12 March 1987, unreported), CA.

**Cases also cited**

R v West (1983) 79 Cr App R 45, CA.

R v Wilson (1973) 58 Cr App R 304, CA.

d **Appeal against conviction**

Maxie Angus Anderson Ensor appealed with the leave of the single judge against his conviction on 17 December 1986 in the Crown Court at Birmingham before his Honour Judge Ross QC and a jury on two counts of rape for which he was sentenced to five years' imprisonment on count 1 and four years' imprisonment on count 2, the sentences to run consecutively. The facts are set out in the judgment of the court.

e

David Jeffreys QC and Michael Wolkind (neither of whom appeared below) for the appellant.

B R Escott Cox QC and Timothy Raggatt for the Crown.

*Cur adv vult*

f 14 March. The following judgment of the court was delivered.

**LORD LANE CJ.** On 17 December 1986 in the Crown Court at Birmingham before his Honour Judge Ross QC and a jury the appellant was convicted on two counts of rape, as to the second by a majority of 11 to 1, and was sentenced on the first count to five years' imprisonment and on the second to four years' imprisonment to run consecutively,

g making a total of nine years' imprisonment. He now appeals against conviction by leave of the single judge.

The facts giving rise to the first count were these. The complainant, Miss P, aged 31, visited in the early hours of 12 February 1986 a club in Hockley, Birmingham. She had since 2.30 pm on the previous day spent most of the time drinking in the company of

h her girlfriend and two men. After a meal at about 10.30 pm they all went to the club. The other three went home at various times after midnight, leaving Miss P behind. The appellant was employed as a doorman or 'bouncer' at the club. She danced with him and he, eventually, so she said, offered to drive her home, an offer which she accepted, only to find that she was being taken to his home and not hers. She accepted his invitation to go in for coffee. The time by now was about 4.30 am.

j When she in due course sought to telephone for a taxi, he stopped her doing so, pushed her into the bedroom and ordered her to take off her clothes. He pushed her onto the bed and, according to her, raped her. She went to the bathroom and when she came out he took her back to the bedroom and then produced what she thought was a whip. She was terrified that she was going to be whipped, but instead of that he wound the lash round his private parts and had sexual intercourse with her again, this time from behind.

She was by now crying out for him to stop; he for his part was crying out at the self-inflicted pain he was suffering by reason of the ligature and it was in those circumstances *a* that he raped her for the third time. By this time it was about 7.30 am and she was able to telephone for a taxi, taking the address from a letter which had shortly before been delivered by the postman.

Very shortly after she got home she telephoned to her boyfriend. He went straight round to see her and to him she appeared very distressed, complaining that she had been raped. She was terrified and too scared, it was said, to go to the police in case the appellant *b* came after her. She told the boyfriend about the whip. She also rang her solicitor, who advised her to go to the police. It was not, however, until 25 February that she made a complaint to the police. That was after she had heard that the appellant had been arrested in respect of the second alleged rape. On 28 February she made a statement to the police, inter alia, describing the whip.

The appellant's account of this incident was that Miss P had been a willing participant *c* in everything that had happened, that she had been both willing and co-operative first in the performance of 'oral sex' and later when sexual intercourse proper had taken place, that it was true that he had put a ligature round his private parts in order, it seems, to engorge and enlarge his penis for his own satisfaction. The ligature was formed, however, not by any whip, he said, but by the cord from his track suit. Miss P could not have seen any whip; she must have imagined it. On 3 March police went to his house with a search *d* warrant and there they found two whips, one of which was of the sort described by the complainant, and also a number of potential accessories for paranormal sexual activities. The importance of the whip will become apparent when we turn to the amended notice of appeal.

The complainant in the second count was Miss H, aged 22. She was an employee at the same club as the appellant. In the early hours of 23 February she accepted a lift home *e* in the appellant's car. There had earlier been some horseplay in a jacuzzi upstairs in the club, in the course of which she had been soaked. As a result she was clad only in a blanket for the drive home. Once there, he accepted her invitation to a cup of coffee. As she was dressing in the bedroom, she said, he came in naked and took hold of her. She struggled. He pushed her down on her back, punched and slapped her face, probed her *f* private parts with his hands and raped her. She denied giving him encouragement. She admitted that she had given him her mother's telephone number in order, she said, to prevent any more violence.

She complained to a friend later that morning. The police were called and Miss H was examined by a doctor, who observed a number of scratches, abrasions and bruises on her and in particular a swelling below the left eye. Samples were taken to be examined for *g* semen, blood and pubic hairs. All the tests were negative. There was in short no scientific support for the allegation of rape. The appellant's account of this event was that he was too tired to achieve proper sexual intercourse. He performed 'oral sex' on Miss H with her consent. He could provide no acceptable explanation for her injuries.

We have gone into some detail as to the facts of the two counts in order to cast light on the submissions made to us by counsel for the appellant on the question of corroboration. *h*

Before we come to that aspect we turn to examine the facts which gave rise to the original notice of appeal. This was the subject of counsel's first submission to us, which was as follows.

Although the two counts of rape were properly joined in the same indictment, counsel who appeared for the appellant at the trial should have applied for the two counts to be severed. It is clear from the information available to us that the appellant himself wanted *j* such an application to be made, and made his wishes known to his lawyers. Counsel submitted that, if the application had been made, it ought to have succeeded, because there was no such similarity between the alleged offences as to enable the prosecution to rely on the facts of one to prove guilt in respect of the other. Indeed that was conceded by counsel for the Crown, who has appeared for the prosecution throughout.

At least for the purposes of argument we are prepared to accept further submission of
a counsel for the appellant that if the indictment had been severed the appellant's chances
of acquittal would have been improved, but, in fairness to both counsel who appeared
for the defence at the trial, it must be said that they did not overlook the possibility of
applying for the indictment to be severed. On the contrary they discussed that possibility
and concluded that if the application were to be made it would fail.

According to leading counsel, he also came to the conclusion that there was certain
b advantages to be gained by the defence if the two counts of rape were heard together, the
principal advantage being that it could be openly said to the jury of the first complainant,
with whom the appellant admitted having had sexual intercourse, that she made no
complaint to the police until ten days later and only then when she knew that the
appellant was in custody as a result of the second complainant alleging that she had been
raped. So the defence could rely on the first complainant's delay to allege that she
c consented, an allegation strengthened by the suggestion that she was only prepared to
pursue a false allegation of rape when she heard of the fresh rape charge. As the second
complainant's case against the appellant was apparently less strong than that of her
predecessor, if her case failed, so the appellant might well be acquitted on both counts.

In developing his first submission counsel for the appellant submitted that, although
it is not the obligation of counsel to discuss with his client every step which he proposes
d to take during the course of a criminal trial, it was here the duty of leading counsel to
inform the appellant of his decision not to apply for the indictment to be severed, and of
his reasons for that decision, and that his failure to take that step, coupled with his failure
to make the application, a failure of which the appellant was never aware until the end
of the trial, constitutes a material irregularity in the conduct of the trial the consequences
of which were such that this court ought now to intervene.

e Counsel for the Crown has submitted that, although on the evidence the appellant
right up to the end of the pre-trial consultation with his leading counsel clearly wanted
counsel to apply to sever the indictment, nevertheless it must be inferred that the
appellant tacitly accepted and acceded to counsel's decision not to make that application.
He says, with force, and we accept, that it is inconceivable that this appellant, who was
no stranger to court procedure, should have sat in the dock for days within a few feet of
f his legal representatives without ever inquiring whether the application had been made
and in the mistaken belief that it had been made and rejected.

But that does not deprive counsel for the appellant of his basic submission, which is
that leading counsel, contrary to what he must have known to be the wishes of his client,
declined to make an application in circumstances in which this court would normally
expect a successful application to have been made, and that in consequence a miscarriage
g of justice has occurred, which we should now correct.

We must therefore look a little more closely at the extent to which this court will
concern itself with what passes between an accused person and his legal representatives.

Counsel for the Crown contends that in a criminal trial defending counsel is only
obliged to seek specific instructions from his client in relation to two matters: first, as to
h plea, and second, as to whether the client himself wishes to give evidence. All other
decisions are for counsel, and it is for him to decide, as a matter of discretion, which
matters, if any, need to be discussed with the accused. The discretion is one, he submits,
which this court will not attempt directly to review, although it might, for example, in
a wholly exceptional case be prepared to consider whether compelling evidence which
was available but which defence counsel for no good reason refused to lead renders the
j conviction unsafe and unsatisfactory.

Counsel for the appellant relied heavily on R v Irwin [1987] 2 All ER 1085, [1987] 1
WLR 902, decided by another division of this court on 19 February 1987. That was a
case in which at a retrial counsel for the defence decided not to call alibi witnesses who
had given evidence at the earlier trial, which had ended in a disagreement. On appeal it
was said that the question was not whether counsel was right in thinking that the

witnesses should not be called but whether he was entitled to bind his client. The court
held that he was not entitled to do so, asserting that on this topic there is no authority to  *a*
be found in any criminal case (see [1987] 2 All ER 1085 at 1088, [1987] 1 WLR 902 at
905).

It seems that the court in *R v Irwin* was not referred to the decision of this court in *R v
Novac* (1976) 65 Cr App R 107. There the court was concerned with the topic we have to
consider in the present case, namely the question of severance. A number of defendants
each faced a conspiracy count and counts alleging specific offences, and one defendant,  *b*
Raywood, applied for the specific offence count against him to be severed from the
conspiracy count. The application was refused but his appeal succeeded on the basis that
the application ought to have been allowed, and Bridge LJ, giving the judgment of the
court, continued (at 112):

> 'It is surprising that no application similar to that made on behalf of Raywood  *c*
> should have been made on behalf of Novac or Andrew-Cohen to sever the specific
> offence counts against them. [Counsel] for Novac told us that he thought it pointless
> to make such an application after the application on behalf of Raywood had been
> refused. But we can see no basis which would have justified him assuming that the
> one application must necessarily be determined in the same way as the other. It was
> for him to make an application to sever on his own client's behalf if thought  *d*
> appropriate. *No such application having been made there can be no basis for complaint in
> this Court that the conspiracy and related counts were heard together in Novac's case with
> the specific offence count.*' (Our emphasis.)

In *R v Novac* the court does not seem to have considered it necessary to inquire whether
counsel in refraining from making an application to sever acted with or without the
express authority of his client, no doubt because generally speaking this court will always  *e*
proceed on the basis that what counsel does is done with the authority of the client who
has instructed counsel to conduct his case.

In *R v Gautam* (1987) Times, 4 March, which was decided by this court on 27 February,
a few days after the appeal in *R v Irwin* had been heard, Taylor J, said:

> '. . . it should be clearly understood that if defending counsel in the course of his  *f*
> conduct of the case makes a decision, or takes a course which later appears to have
> been mistaken or unwise, that generally speaking has never been regarded as a
> proper ground for an appeal.'

That was a shoplifting case in which counsel, for what were patently good reasons, had
declined to lead medical evidence at the trial until after the jury had returned a verdict.  *g*

On 12 March 1987 another division of this court heard the appeal in *R v Swain*
(unreported), where the appellant contended, with apparent justification, that his counsel,
by incompetent cross-examination, had introduced evidence which was prejudicial to
this case, which was then amplified by the witness in answer to a question put to him by
the judge. In an attempt to circumvent the difficulties which he faced arising out of
what was said in *R v Gautam*, counsel at the hearing of the appeal sought to rely mainly  *h*
on the intervention of the judge, but the court found that what was said in answer to the
judge added nothing to what had already been said by the witness to counsel. Various
other points were considered with which we need not now be concerned, but O'Connor
LJ said that, if the court had any lurking doubt that the appellant might have suffered
some injustice as a result of flagrantly incompetent advocacy by his advocate, then it
would quash the convictions, but in that particular case it had no such doubts.  *j*

We consider the correct approach to be that which was indicated by this court in *R v
Gautam*, subject only to the qualification to which O'Connor LJ referred in *R v Swain*. We
consider further that the decision in *R v Irwin*, even if it can be reconciled with *R v Novac*
(which we doubt), should be regarded as being confined to its own facts. This ground of
appeal accordingly fails, because counsel's carefully considered decision not to apply to

sever the charges, even if erroneous, cannot possibly be described as incompetent, let
a  alone flagrantly incompetent, advocacy.

As to corroboration, counsel for the appellant makes a number of criticisms of the
summing up.

First, he submits that the warning given by the judge to the jury was inadequate.
What the judge said was this:

b      'The essence of the offence is the absence of consent. In all offences of this sort,
       where it is alleged that a woman has been subjected, without her consent, to sexual
       familiarities of any kind, whether it be indecent assault or the full offence of rape, it
       is the duty of the judge to give you this warning. It is not safe to proceed to
       conviction of a case of this sort on the uncorroborated testimony of the woman who
       makes the complaint. That is not an element adverting on the female sex, it is
c      simply that the . . . courts, through years of experience, have come to the conclusion
       that unless the complaining woman's evidence is supported by other evidence,
       independent of her's, it simply is not safe to convict even though you may be
       satisfied in your own minds that she is telling the truth.'

In support of his general criticism, counsel for the appellant makes two points. He
argues that it would have been preferable for the judge to direct the jury that it was
d  dangerous to convict on the uncorroborated evidence of the complainant. Further, he
submits, the judge's language was too wide, and would, or could, have left the jury with
the impression that it was in relation to the truth of the complainant's evidence generally
rather than to the specific issues of the fact of intercourse and the absence of consent that
the warning was directed.

Delivering the judgment of this court in R v Stewart (1986) 83 Cr App R 327 at 335
e  Mustill LJ said:

       'Whilst the language in which the "full" warning on corroboration is expressed in
       the judgments has tended to follow a pattern, there is ample authority that no set
       formula is required, and indeed that the words "danger" or "dangerous" need not
       themselves be employed. At the same time, however, the courts have emphasised
f      that (as Salmon L.J. said in Henry and Manning ((1968) 53 Cr App R 160 at 163)),
       there must be clear and simple language that will without any doubt convey to the
       jury that it is really dangerous to convict on the evidence of the impugned witness
       alone . . .'

In our view the words used by the judge in the present case fulfilled this requirement.
g  Having told the jury that it was 'not safe' to convict on uncorroborated evidence, he
reinforced that warning with the words 'it simply is not safe to convict . . .' This plainly
would have conveyed to the jury that it was dangerous to convict in the absence of
corroboration.

As to the second limb of this submission, which is that the judge's language was too
wide and may not have been understood as referring to those vital ingredients of the
h  offences that were disputed, it is necessary to consider the two cases separately. So far as
count 1 is concerned, the fact of intercourse was admitted by the appellant, and the vital
issue was consent. The passage we have already cited began with the words 'The essence
of the offence is absence of consent . . .' When he began a few lines later to deal with the
facts, the judge said:

j      'In the case of [Miss P] . . . there is only one issue and that is the issue of consent . . .
       It is not disputed in her case that the defendant had intercourse with her, so the only
       issue that requires corroboration is the issue of consent.'

The jury can therefore have been in no doubt that it was to the issue of absence of
consent that the warning in relation to corroboration applied. We accordingly reject the
second limb of counsel's general criticism.

We now turn to the main submissions advanced by counsel on corroboration. His contention in relation to the first count was that the judge was wrong in stating that the *a* matter of the whip was capable of constituting corroboration of Miss P's assertion that she did not consent to intercourse. He directed the jury that it was the only matter capable of constituting corroboration and, having reminded the jury of the conflict of evidence whether it was a whip or merely a tracksuit cord which was produced and used in the manner already described, he said:

> 'On 28 February it is common ground that the statement that she then gave to *b*
> the police included a description of this leather dog whip and when the police went
> to the house and searched it they found a leather dog whip which resembled the
> thing that she was talking about. There you have something outside Miss P's
> evidence which you are entitled to bear in mind when asking yourselves: "Well,
> was she telling the truth about this or not?" That is really the only point where her *c*
> evidence is supported from something outside because ... she was describing
> something that the defendant denies he ever produced and it turns out in fact he
> possesses such a thing ...'

In this connection it is important to note that the evidence of Miss P was that when the whip was produced she thought the appellant was going to use it on her, and was terrified, although in the event what the appellant proceeded to do was to make use of it *d* in the way already described.

Counsel for the appellant submits that, whereas the finding of a whip such as the one described provided some general confirmation of her account, it did not in any way support her assertion of lack of consent. It was not suggested by her that he actually threatened her, or used the whip on her, to secure compliance. At most, submits counsel, it supports the conclusion that he was lying, and the way the judge dealt with it was in *e* effect to invite the jury to regard his lie as being capable of amounting to corroboration. Counsel for the appellant submits that such a lie does not satisfy the tests laid down in the well-known case of *R v Lucas* [1981] 2 All ER 1008, [1981] QB 720 and that in any event the judge did not, as he would have had to do had he been inviting the jury to consider a lie as possible corroboration, give them a direction in accordance with that *f* case.

We do not, however, accept that this was the way in which the jury were being told they might regard the matter. The evidence that required corroboration was Miss P's evidence that the admitted intercourse was without her consent. When she was describing the immediate circumstances of two of the acts of intercourse Miss P described the production of a whip which she said she thought the appellant was going to use on *g* her and which terrified her; so that, notwithstanding the fact that he did not expressly threaten her to use it, the whip was plainly an element and an important element in her submission to intercourse.

The appellant denied the production of such an article, and yet one, corresponding with Miss P's description, was found by the police in his house. No doubt, incidentally, that tended to show that he had been lying; but it also supported in a material particular *h* her assertion of lack of consent. In our view it was in the latter rather than the former sense that the judge invited the jury to consider it as possible corroboration. We find nothing in his language to suggest the contrary; and indeed it would be surprising if this very experienced judge, had he intended to invite the jury to treat a lie by the appellant as possible corroboration, had omitted to give them a *Lucas* direction.

We therefore reject the submissions of counsel for the appellant as to corroboration in *j* connection with the first count.

As to the second count, the vital thing to be remembered is that both the fact of intercourse and the absence of consent were in issue.

The general direction which the judge gave, and which we have already cited, plainly adverted only to the issue of consent. When he came to address the question of what

evidence was capable of amounting to corroboration, the judge directed the jury that if
*a* they were satisfied that Miss H came by her injuries when she was with the appellant
they were entitled to ask themselves 'whether they are or are not wholly consistent with
whatever went on between her and this man being with her consent'. He spoke of them
as something which might 'go to corroborate and support her'.

This direction was of course perfectly accurate in relation to the issue of lack of consent.
But the nature of the injuries was such that they were not capable of corroborating the
*b* fact of intercourse. Moreover, even had they been so capable, nowhere did the judge
direct the jury that they should, in the case of Miss H, look for corroboration of Miss H's
evidence that intercourse had occurred.

It is not necessary further to elaborate this point, because counsel for the Crown
accepted that nowhere did the judge refer to the need for corroboration of the act of
intercourse. He submitted, however, that given that the appellant's account in evidence
*c* was that there was oral intercourse to which Miss H readily consented, and that he was
unable sensibly to account for her injuries, it could be said that there was corroboration,
or that at least this was a case in which we should apply the proviso.

There is no doubt that, as the law stands, the warning as to the need to look for
corroboration and the danger of convicting without it must be given in relation to each
of the two ingredients of the offence, where both are in dispute. There was here a failure
*d* to give such a direction, which in our view constituted a material misdirection. We
might well have acceded to counsel for the Crown's invitation to apply the proviso had
there not been features of the evidence in relation to count 2, some of which appear from
the facts we have recited and others of which we have in mind but need not specifically
mention, which in our view make it impossible to say that, had they received a proper
direction, the jury would inevitably have convicted.
*e* Accordingly the appeal will be allowed in relation to count 2, and the conviction on
that count quashed.

There is one observation that we wish to add. Counsel for the Crown told us that, as
far as he could recall, the judge did not invite, nor did counsel volunteer, any submissions
in connection with corroboration. This was a case which was by no means straightforward
*f* in that respect, and we feel that the judge would have been assisted by submissions from
counsel, in the course of which there would have been explored, separately in relation to
each count, both aspects of the matter, namely (i) what were the ingredients of the
offences in respect of which the jury should be told to look for corroboration and (ii)
what evidence was there capable of amounting to corroboration. In almost all cases where
a direction on corroboration is required, it is desirable that the judge should, at the
*g* conclusion of the evidence, hear submissions from counsel (they will often be very brief)
on these two important matters. If this practice is followed, the sort of problems
exemplified by the present appeal will usually be avoided.

In the upshot the appeal against conviction is dismissed as count 1, and allowed as to
count 2, on which the conviction is accordingly quashed.

*h* *Appeal allowed in part; conviction on count 2 quashed.*

Solicitors: *Whitelock & Storr* (for the appellant); *Crown Prosecution Service*, Birmingham.

N P Metcalfe Esq    Barrister.

# Evans v Chief Constable of Surrey Constabulary (Attorney General intervening)

QUEEN'S BENCH DIVISION
WOOD J
30 NOVEMBER 1987, 20 JANUARY 1988

*Discovery – Privilege – Production contrary to public interest – Class of documents – Police report submitted to Director of Public Prosecutions in course of criminal investigation – Plaintiff bringing action for wrongful arrest and false imprisonment – Attorney General certifying that disclosure of report contrary to public interest – Whether chief constable entitled to withhold report on ground of public interest.*

In 1984 a young woman, C, was found murdered in a station car park. As a result of their investigations the police arrested the plaintiff, a friend of C, on 2 September and released him on 5 September, and arrested him again on 19 October and released him on 20 October. The plaintiff remained under suspicion and on 11 December the defendant chief constable submitted to the Director of Public Prosecutions a bundle of statements from potential witnesses and a covering report seeking his advice. On 25 March 1985 the Director of Public Prosecutions advised and authorised the defendant to charge the plaintiff with the murder of C. The next day a man arrested for another offence admitted to C's murder and was subsequently convicted of her murder. The plaintiff was never charged. He brought an action for damages and exemplary damages for wrongful arrest and false imprisonment and sought discovery of the report to the Director of Public Prosecution of 11 December though not the advice which was given as a result. The master, having read the report, ordered its disclosure. The defendant appealed and the Attorney General sought leave to intervene, certifying that the report should not be disclosed on the ground of public interest.

**Held** – (1) Public interest immunity was not a 'privilege', within the meaning normally given to that word when considering discovery, which could be waived. It was an issue which, if facts were disclosed on which it could arise, had to be considered, if necessary, by the court itself. Once public interest immunity was properly raised, the burden was on the party seeking disclosure to show why the documents should be produced for inspection by the court privately. Discovery involved two stages: disclosure of the existence of a document and production of that document for inspection. Normally the court would only order production in the first place, which order could be the subject of appeal, and it was only thereafter that the court would inspect the document. Before a question of public interest immunity could be raised, the document had to be disclosable within the rules of discovery normally applicable in litigation. If a public interest claim was raised, it was necessary for those who sought to overcome it to demonstrate the existence of a counteracting interest calling for disclosure of the particular documents involved. It was only then that the court could proceed to the balancing process (see p 596 j to p 597 a d e g, p 598 f g and p 600 d h j, post); *Burmah Oil Co Ltd v Bank of England and A-G* [1979] 3 All ER 700 and *Air Canada v Secretary of State for Trade (No 2)* [1983] 1 All ER 910 followed.

(2) On the facts, the plaintiff had not satisfied the court under the ordinary rules of discovery that the contents of the report were likely to help his case or damage that of the defendant. That was especially so as it was common ground that the Director of Public Prosecutions had advised that the plaintiff be charged with the murder and therefore must have considered that there was a prima facie case against him. It followed that the plaintiff had not established that he was entitled to production of the report (see p 601 g h, post); *Conway v Rimmer* [1968] 1 All ER 874 distinguished.

(3) Furthermore, it would be contrary to the public interest for the report to be the

subject of disclosure since it was important in the functioning of the process of criminal
*a* prosecution that there should be freedom of communication between police forces
around the country and the Director of Public Prosecutions in seeking his legal advice,
without fear that those documents would be subject to inspection, analysis and detailed
investigation at some later stage. It followed that the appeal would be allowed (see p 603
*e* to *h*, post); dictum of Glyn-Jones J in *Auten v Rayner* [1960] 1 All ER 692 at 696 applied.

*b* Notes
For withholding documents on the ground of public interest, see 13 Halsbury's Laws
(4th edn) paras 86–91, and for cases on the subject, see 18 Digest (Reissue) 154–160,
1265–1301.

Cases referred to in judgment
*c* *Air Canada v Secretary of State for Trade (No 2)* [1983] 1 All ER 910, [1983] 2 AC 394,
   [1983] 2 WLR 494, HL.
*Auten v Rayner* [1960] 1 All ER 692, [1960] 1 QB 669, [1960] 2 WLR 562.
*Burmah Oil Co Ltd v Bank of England and A-G* [1979] 3 All ER 700, [1980] AC 1090, [1979]
   3 WLR 722, HL.
*Cie Financière et Commerciale du Pacifique v Peruvian Guano Co* (1882) 11 QBD 55, CA.
*d* *Conway v Rimmer* [1968] 1 All ER 874, [1968] AC 910, [1968] 2 WLR 998, HL.
*D v National Society for the Protection of Cruelty to Children* [1977] 1 All ER 589, [1978] AC
   171, [1977] 2 WLR 201, HL.
*Glasgow Corp v Central Land Board* 1956 SC (HL) 1.
*Holtham v Comr of Police of the Metropolis* (1987) Times, 28 November, CA.
*Williams v Home Office* [1981] 1 All ER 1151.
*e* *Woodworth v Conroy* [1976] 1 All ER 107, [1976] QB 884, [1976] 2 WLR 338, CA.

Interlocutory appeal
The plaintiff, David Evans, sought against the defendant, the Chief Constable of Surrey
Constabulary, damages including exemplary damages, for wrongful arrest and false
imprisonment. In the course of the action the plaintiff sought disclosure of the police
*f* report sent to the Director of Public Prosecutions on 11 December 1984 relating to his
arrest. On 8 July 1987 Master Prebble ordered that the report be disclosed. The defendant
appealed and the Attorney General sought leave to intervene, certifying that it was in the
public interest that the report should not be disclosed. The appeal was heard in chambers
but judgment was given by Wood J in open court. The facts are set out in the judgment.

*g* Martin Russell for the defendant.
Jeremy P Maurice for the plaintiff.
John Laws for the Attorney General.

*Cur adv vult*

*h*
20 January. The following judgment was delivered.

WOOD J. In this action the plaintiff sues the defendant on a number of grounds, but
principally and materially for the present issue, for damages and exemplary damages for
wrongful arrest and false imprisonment during two periods, namely from about 3 pm
*j* on 2 September 1984 to about 3.30 pm on 5 September 1984 and from about 8.30 pm
on 19 October to about 3.30 pm on 20 October of the same year.
   The claim arises out of the following facts. On or about 30 August 1984 a young
woman, Glennys Leslie Coe, was found murdered in the car park adjoining London Road
Railway Station, Guildford, in Surrey. She was a friend of the plaintiff. Investigations
were started and a large number of statements were taken from potential witnesses. The
plaintiff was interviewed on more than one occasion. As a result of their investigations

the police arrested the plaintiff on 2 September and released him on 5 September, and
arrested him again on 19 October and released him on 20 October.                                    *a*

The plaintiff remained under suspicion, and on 11 December 1984 the defendant
submitted to the Director of Public Prosecutions a bundle of statements from potential
witnesses and a covering report, seeking his advice. On 25 March 1985 the Director of
Public Prosecutions advised and authorised the defendant to charge the plaintiff with the
murder of Miss Coe, from which it seems clear that in his opinion there existed a prima
facie case against the plaintiff.                                                                  *b*

The very next day, 26 March 1985, a man named Stephen Doyle was arrested in Essex
for an offence of rape, and after being interviewed by police officers from Surrey,
admitted to Miss Coe's murder. On 30 January 1986 Doyle was convicted of that murder.
The plaintiff was never charged.

In arresting the plaintiff on each of these two occasions the police officers concerned
were exercising their powers under s 2(4) of the Criminal Law Act 1967, which reads:      *c*

'Where a constable, with reasonable cause, suspects that an arrestable offence has
been committed, he may arrest, without warrant, anyone whom he, with reasonable
cause, suspects to be guilty of the offence.'

At a trial, therefore, it will be for the defendant to prove on the balance of probabilities   *d*
that the arresting officers had reasonable cause or grounds for suspecting that the plaintiff
had murdered Miss Coe. Section 2(4) of the 1967 Act was considered recently in the
Court of Appeal in *Holtham v Comr of the Police of the Metropolis* (1987) Times, 28
November. The court there emphasised that suspicion is a state of conjecture or surmise
where proof is lacking. It must not be confused with the provision of evidence.

In the defence, extensive particulars of the facts on which reliance is placed have been   *e*
pleaded, and no doubt the defendants will be restricted at trial to those primary facts.
The plaintiff will receive all the statements of the potential witnesses, that is the primary
evidence, and now seeks discovery and production of the report to the Director of Public
Prosecutions of 11 December, but not the advice which was given as a result.

On 8 July 1987 Master Prebble, having read the report, ordered its disclosure. The
defendant appeals from this order and the Attorney General has sought leave to intervene.  *f*
This was not opposed. It was also common ground between the parties before me that
the reasoning of the master was open to criticism, and thus in any event the whole issue
should be examined afresh. I was told that the defendant had waived any privilege he
might have in the report to the Director of Public Prosecutions, but this is not an issue of
privilege in the ordinary sense when discussing issues of discovery and production of
documents. This is a public interest immunity claim and it becomes my duty, in any    *g*
event, to consider the issue which now falls within the public rather than the private
domain.

In order to trace the general principles of law on which I should act, it is unnecessary
to look further back than *Conway v Rimmer* [1968] 1 All ER 874, [1968] AC 910 and the
main cases which followed, namely *D v National Society for the Prevention of Cruelty to
Children* [1977] 1 All ER 589, [1978] AC 171; *Burmah Oil Co Ltd v Bank of England and A-G*  *h*
[1979] 3 All ER 700, [1980] AC 1090, and *Air Canada v Secretary of State for Trade (No 2)*
[1983] 1 All ER 910, [1983] 2 AC 394. I shall refer to each of those cases by a shorthand
name hereafter.

The law on this topic is not standing still, and I believe that culminating in the *Air
Canada* case the principles now applicable may be stated as follows.

First, these issues are interlocutory, and my decision is one made within the discretion   *j*
or substantially within the discretion of a judge at first instance: see the *Burmah Oil* case
[1979] 3 All ER 700 at 704, [1980] AC 1090 at 1108 per Lord Wilberforce.

Second, public interest immunity is not a 'privilege' (within the meaning normally
given to that word when considering discovery) which can be waived. It is an issue
which, if facts are disclosed on which it could arise, must be considered, if necessary, by

a the court itself: see the *Air Canada* case [1983] 1 All ER 910 at 917, [1983] 2 AC 394 at 436 per Lord Fraser.

Third, once public interest immunity is properly raised, the burden is on the party seeking disclosure to show why the documents should be produced for inspection by the court privately: see the *Air Canada* case [1983] 1 All ER 910 at 914, [1983] 2 AC 394 at 433 per Lord Fraser, where he says:

b   'In the present case, then, we have documents which are admittedly relevant to the matters in issue, in the sense explained in *Compagnie Financière et Commerciale du Pacifique v Peruvian Guano Co* (1882) 11 QBD 55 at 63 per Brett LJ. I am willing to assume that they are, in the words of RSC Ord 24, r 13 "necessary . . . for disposing fairly of the cause" on the (perhaps not very rigorous) standard which would apply if this were an ordinary case in which public interest immunity had not been claimed. But it has been claimed, and the onus therefore is on the appellants, as the c   parties seeking disclosure, to show why the documents ought to be produced for inspection by the court privately.'

Fourth, discovery involves two stages, disclosure of the existence of a document and production of that document for inspection. In the *Air Canada* case it was decided that in the first place the court normally should only order production, which order can be the d subject of appeal, and it is only thereafter that the court should inspect the document: see also *Conway's* case [1968] 1 All ER 874 at 889, [1968] AC 910 at 953 per Lord Reid. There would seem to be two occasions where this sequence should not be followed. The first is where the court has 'definite grounds for expecting to find material of real importance to the party seeking disclosure' (see the *Air Canada* case [1983] 1 All ER 910 at 917, [1983] 2 AC 394 at 431 per Lord Fraser) and, second, where in exceptional cases e the court feels it necessary to inspect the document to verify the fact that a 'class' claim is validly made: see the *Burmah Oil* case [1979] 3 All ER 700 at 706–707, [1980] AC 1090 at 1111 per Lord Wilberforce, where he says:

   'A claim remains a class even though something may be known about the contents; it remains a class even if parts of documents are revealed and parts f   disclosed. Burmah did not, I think, dispute this. And, the claim being a class claim, I must state with emphasis that there is not the slightest ground for doubting that the documents in question fall within the class described; indeed the descriptions themselves and references in disclosed documents make it clear that they do. So this is not one of those cases, which anyway are exceptional, where the court feels it necessary to look at the documents in order to verify that fact. We start with a g   strong and well-fortified basis for an immunity claim.'

Fifth, before any question of public interest immunity can be raised the document must be disclosable within the rules of discovery normally applicable in litigation: see the *Burmah Oil* case [1979] 3 All ER 700 at 731, [1980] AC 1090 at 1141 per Lord Scarman, where he says:

h   'Foster J based his decision on the view which he formed that production of the documents for which immunity is claimed would not materially assist Burmah's case at trial. He was, I think, right, when faced with the public interest immunity objection to disclosure, to ask himself whether production could be said to be necessary for fairly disposing of the case. For, if it be shown that production was not necessary, it becomes unnecessary to balance the interest of justice against the j   interest of the public service to which the Minister refers in his certificate.'

I would also refer to the passage from the speech of Lord Edmund-Davies in the *Air Canada* case [1983] 1 All ER 910 at 921–922, [1983] 2 AC 394 at 441 where he says:

   'My Lords, I proceed to state the obvious. Under our Supreme Court practice, discovery of documents between parties to an action with pleadings (as in the present case) is restricted to documents "relating to matters in question in the action" (RSC Ord 24, r 1(1)), and no order for their inspection by the other party or to the *a* court may be made "unless the Court is of opinion that the order is necessary either for disposing fairly of the cause or matter or for saving costs" (Ord 24, r 13(1)). It is common sense that the litigant seeking an order for discovery is interested, not in abstract justice, but in gaining support for the case he is presenting, and the sole task of the court is to decide whether he should get it. Applying that test, any document which, it is reasonable to suppose, contains information which *may* enable the party *b* applying for discovery either to advance his own case or to damage that of his adversary, if it is a document which may fairly lead him to a train of inquiry which may have either of those two consequences, must be disclosed (see *Compagnie Financière et Commerciale du Pacifique v Peruvian Guano Co* (1882) 11 QBD 55 at 63 per Brett LJ). So it was that in *Glasgow Corp v Central Land Board* 1956 SC (HL) 1 at 18, 20 Lord Radcliffe spoke of the need that "a litigant who has *a case to maintain* should *c* not be deprived of the means of *its* proper presentation by anything less than a weighty public reason", and concluded, "Nor . . . do I feel any clear conviction that the production of the documents sought for is in any real sense *essential to the appellants' case*" (emphasis added). It follows that, at every stage of interlocutory proceedings for discovery, the test to be applied is: will the material sought be such as is likely to advance the seeker's case, either affirmatively or indirectly by *d* weakening the case of his opponent? To take but one more example out of many, such was again the test applied by the Court of Appeal in *Woodworth v Conroy* [1976] 1 All ER 107, [1976] 1 QB 884. It is accordingly insufficient for a litigant to urge that the documents he seeks to inspect are *relevant* to the proceedings. For, although relevant, they may be of merely vestigial importance, or they may be of importance (great or small) only to his opponent's case. And to urge that, on principle, justice is *e* most likely to be done if free access is had to all relevant documents is pointless, for it carries no weight in our adversarial system of law. So far, I have been speaking of legal practice and procedure in general.'

Sixth, if a public interest immunity claim is raised, and it is usually only raised on sound or solid ground, it is necessary for those who seek to overcome it to demonstrate *f* the existence of a counteracting interest calling for disclosure of the particular documents involved. It is then, and only then, that the court may proceed to the balancing process: see the *Burmah Oil* case [1979] 3 All ER 700 at 708, [1980] AC 1090 at 1113 per Lord Wilberforce.

When a court comes to the exercise of the balancing process, documents are usually placed in one of two classes, either the 'class' case of documents or the 'contents' case of *g* documents. In the latter the certificate would in many cases prove to be conclusive. Most of the reported cases are 'class' cases. There is a wide variation to be found between state or Cabinet documents and routine documents such as confidential reports on a probationary police constable. Nevertheless, the certificate provides a strong basis of objection and I must not forget that the onus is on the litigant claiming production.

As was stressed by Lord Fraser in the *Air Canada* case the circumstances may vary *h* greatly from case to case and it is not really possible to state a test in a form applicable to each case. I refer to his speech where he says ([1983] 1 All ER 910 at 917, [1983] 2 AC 394 at 435):

'My Lords, I do not think it would be possible to state a test in a form which could be applied in all cases. Circumstances vary greatly. The weight of the public interest *j* against disclosure will vary according to the nature of the particular documents in question; for example, it will in general be stronger where the documents are Cabinet papers than when they are at a lower level. The weight of the public interest in favour of disclosure will vary even more widely, because it depends on the probable evidential value to the party seeking disclosure of the particular documents, in almost infinitely variable circumstances of individual cases. The most that can a usefully be said is that, in order to persuade the court to inspect documents for which public interest immunity is claimed, the party seeking disclosure ought at least to satisfy the court that the documents are very likely to contain material which would give substantial support to his contention on an issue which arises in the case, and that without them he might be "deprived of the means of ... proper presentation" of his case: see *Glasgow Corp v Central Land Board* 1956 SCHL 1 at 18 per Lord Radcliffe. It will be plain that that formulation has been mainly derived

b from the speech of Lord Edmund-Davies in the *Burmah Oil* case [1979] 3 All ER 700 at 721, [1980] AC 1090 at 1129 and from the opinion of McNeill J in *Williams v Home Office* [1981] 1 All ER 1151 at 1154. It assumes, of course, that the party seeking disclosure has already shown in his pleadings that he has a cause of action, and that he has some material to support it. Otherwise he would merely be "fishing".'

c In this case, the Attorney General has provided a certificate, the relevant parts of which read as follows:

'The Report [that is the report to the Director of Public Prosecutions] contains, inter alia, evidence and material gathered by an investigating officer in pursuance of a murder investigation, together with his views thereon ...

d 5. I have formed the opinion that it is necessary in the public interest that the said Report be withheld from production in these proceedings for the reasons hereinafter set out.

6. (i) By Section 2(1) of the Prosecution of Offences Act, 1979, which was in force when this report came into existence, it is provided that "It shall be the duty of the Director, under the superintendence of the Attorney-General (b) to give such advice

e and assistance to chief officers of police ... concerned in any criminal proceedings respecting the conduct of those proceedings as may be prescribed ..." (ii) By Regulation 4 of the Prosecution of Offences Regulations, 1978, (SI 1978 No. 1357), it is provided that: "The Director of Public Prosecutions shall give advice whether on application by or on his own initiative to ... chief officers of police and such other persons as he may think right in any criminal matter which appears to him to

f be of importance or difficulty or which for any other reason appears to him to require his intervention by way of advice and any such advice may be given at his discretion either orally or in writing". (iii) By Regulation 6(1) of the said Regulations it is provided that: "The chief officer of police of every police area ... shall give to the Director of Public Prosecutions information with respect to any of the following offences, where it appears to him that there is a prima facie case for proceedings –

g (d) offences by homicide except offences of causing death by reckless driving."

7. By Section 2(2) of the Prosecution of Offences Act, 1985 (by which the Prosecution of Offences Act, 1979 is repealed) it is provided that: "It shall be the duty of the Director: (a) to take over the conduct of all criminal proceedings, other than specified proceedings, instituted on behalf of a police force ...; (b) to institute

h and have the conduct of criminal proceedings in any case where it appears to him that: (i) the importance or difficulty of the case makes it appropriate that proceedings should be instituted by him ... (e) to give, to such extent as he considers appropriate, advice to police officers on all matters relating to criminal offences ..."

8. In my view, it is essential for the proper enforcement of the criminal law and in particular for the proper fulfilment by the Director of Public Prosecutions and

j chief officers of police of their respective statutory and other duties that correspondence or other communications between them (or those acting on their behalf) relative to the seeking and giving of advice should be able to be made fully, frankly and in confidence and without fear that such correspondence, enquiries and communications may subsequently be disclosed in civil proceedings or be used for other purposes than the enforcement of the criminal law. Such advice may well involve questions of policy in relation to the conduct of the public services, and

include the formation of personal judgments by officers as to the appropriate course
to be taken. For documents of the kind hereinbefore referred to, which concern or
are made in connection with the proper discharge of the Director of Public
Prosecutions of his aforesaid duties and which are of an intrinsically confidential
nature, to be liable to disclosure in civil proceedings would, I believe, restrict and
inhibit communication and seriously impede the implementation of the functions
of the Director of Public Prosecutions and would, therefore, be contrary to the
public interest. In forming this judgment, I have had regard to the views expressed
on behalf of the Director of Public Prosecutions which are to the firm effect that
such material should be protected while, of course, the judgment I have made is
wholly my own.

9. I have personally considered the Report referred to in paragraph 3 of this
Certificate, and I am satisfied that it belongs to the class of documents referred to in
paragraph 8 hereof, which it is necessary to withhold from production for the
proper functioning of the public service. It is the duty of the Crown to assert a claim
for public interest immunity, and accordingly, I must and do object to the disclosure
or use of the said document.'

I therefore turn to the facts of the present case. The first thing to note is that, unlike
many of the cases, the onus here is on the defendant to prove 'reasonable cause to suspect'.
The pleadings show that unless that burden is discharged the plaintiff will succeed. The
second is that the facts on which the defendant will be entitled to rely are pleaded and
that the issues on primary facts are therefore limited. The third is to note that the
relevant time for establishing existence or non-existence of the suspicion is at the moment
of each arrest.

I have therefore first to decide whether under the ordinary rules of discovery the
plaintiff has established that he is entitled to production of the report to the Director of
Public Prosecutions, and in doing so I turn to the guidance given by Lord Edmund-
Davies in the passage referred to above in the *Air Canada* case [1983] 1 All ER 910 at 921,
[1983] 2 AC 394 at 441, the words to which he refers being those of Brett LJ in the well-
known passage in *Cie Financière et Commercial du Pacifique v Peruvian Guano Co* (1882) 11
QBD 55 at 63, which I just cite for convenience:

'It seems to me that every document relates to the matters in question in the
action, which not only would be evidence upon any issue, but also which, it is
reasonable to suppose, contains information which *may*—not which *must*—either
directly or indirectly enable the party requiring the affidavit either to advance his
own case or to damage the case of his adversary. I have put in the words "either
directly or indirectly," because, as it seems to me, a document can properly be said
to contain information which may enable the party requiring the affidavit either to
advance his own case or to damage the case of his adversary, if it is a document
which may fairly lead him to a train of inquiry, which may have either of these two
consequences . . .' (Brett LJ's emphasis.)

Those words read literally would lead to endless 'fishing expeditions', but the breadth
of the expression used by Brett LJ is limited by Lord Edmund-Davies to the phrase 'likely
to advance the applicant's case . . .' and to 'A reasonable probability of finding support',
an expression used by Lord Keith in the *Burmah Oil* case [1979] 3 All ER 700 at 726,
[1986] at AC 1090 at 1135. In any event, both expressions indicate that there must be
some sound basis beyond speculation for believing that the documents would advance
the case of the applicant or damage that of his opponent. It must go beyond a mere
'fishing expedition'.

The case for the defendant and for the Attorney General may be summarised as
follows. (1) The report to the Director of Public Prosecutions is not a document which
should be ordered to be produced under the ordinary rules relating to discovery, as it is
immaterial to what was going through the minds of the police officers at the time of the
arrests. The primary evidence is contained in the witness statements, and any view

expressed by the police officers in a report of December 1984 cannot help or hinder the
*a* plaintiff. The onus is on the defendant, and there is no sufficient likelihood or reasonable
probability of the contents of the report assisting the plaintiff's case or damaging that of
the defendant. It will not throw factual light on the reasons which the police had for
their suspicion and for the arrest. (2). If I should hold the document disclosable then in
carrying out the 'balancing exercise' I should in my discretion refuse to order production,
because the broad interest of justice does not require disclosure and there are no sufficient
*b* reasons shown why public interest would be served by disclosure rather than non-
disclosure.

The plaintiff naturally relied on *Conway v Rimmer* [1968] 1 All ER 874, [1968] AC 910
where it is said that a similar report was ordered to be produced. I find a number of
distinctions between that case and the present. In *Conway*'s case the parties both wanted
the document to be disclosed, and the causes of action were different in that malicious
*c* prosecution was being alleged in that case. The order for production was being considered
at the stage of the 'balancing exercise'.

However, the most obvious distinction is that the certificates were in very different
form. The relevant part of the Attorney General's certificate in that case reads in reference
to the report to the chief officer of police:

*d*      '... that the said document numbered 47 fell within a class of documents
         comprising reports by police officers to their superiors concerning investigations
         into the commission of crime. In my opinion the production of documents of each
         such class would be injurious to the public interest.'

(See [1968] 1 All ER 874 at 878, [1968] AC 910 at 913.)

There is no reference there to the Director of Public Prosecutions, and consideration of
*e* his position scarcely appears in any of the speeches. In the present case, stress is laid by
the Attorney General on the position of the Director of Public Prosecutions and the fact
that he is approached for and is giving advice of a legal nature. I therefore distinguish
*Conway v Rimmer* on its facts.

On the issue of production under the common law rules of discovery, the plaintiff
submits that he does not seek to see documents emanating from the Director of Public
*f* Prosecutions, but a report from investigating officers to a senior officer. Secondly, it is
submitted that as very little evidence was brought to light after the arrests and before the
submission of the report, the contents of that report are likely to show the state of mind
of the police at the time of the arrests. Thirdly, it was submitted that the production of
the report would enable the plaintiff to assess the strength of his own case, and enable
him, if so advised, to abandon his claim with a consequent saving in costs.

*g* Having considered all the facts before me and the submissions, I have reached the
conclusion that the plaintiff has not satisfied me that the contents of this report are likely
to help his case or damage that of the defendant. This seems to me to be more especially
to be so as it is common ground that the Director of Public Prosecutions advised that the
plaintiff be charged with the murder and therefore must have considered that there was
*h* a prima facie case against him. The material time is the time of arrest and the facts and
matters relied on have been pleaded. Malice is not material.

However, the issue of public interest immunity having been fully argued before me,
and lest I am held to be wrong on the prior issue, I will proceed to carry out the 'balancing
exercise'. In so doing, I base myself on the passages in the speech of Lord Fraser in the *Air
Canada* case [1983] 1 All ER 910 at 916–917, [1983] 2 AC 394 at 434–435 where he says:

*j*      'A great variety of expressions have been used in the reported cases to explain the
         considerations that ought to influence judges in deciding whether to order
         inspection.'

By this, I take him to mean production for inspection. And then later he says:

        '... the test is intended to be fairly strict. It ought to be so in any cases where a
        valid claim for public interest immunity has been made.'

It is of course to be emphasised that a document, by way of a report to the Director of
Public Prosecutions seeking advice, could be considered a routine document rather than    a
a document of state such as Cabinet papers. However, it seems to me that there is an
additional and relevant factor in that this document is seeking the legal advice of the
Director of Public Prosecutions. If a member of a public department were to communicate
with the legal adviser within his department seeking advice, then I venture to think that
the document would be covered by privilege in its normal usage in discovery. Here I am
considering a form of privilege in the public domain rather than the private domain and,    b
of course, police officers are not public servants.

The position of the Director of Public Prosecutions was considered in an earlier case to
which I was helpfully referred, namely *Auten v Rayner* [1960] 1 All ER 692, [1960] 1 QB
669. In that case the plaintiff sued a Colonel and Mrs Rayner and a Detective Sergeant
Bolongaro for damages for conspiracy, malicious arrest and prosecution, abusive process,
false imprisonment and injurious falsehood. Certain entries in diaries of the detective    c
sergeant had been sealed by order of the Home Secretary, who claimed Crown privilege.
The trial began on 18 January 1960, and during the trial application was made to Glyn-
Jones J to unseal the diary entries. However, the matter material to the present case is
that on 25 February, the day fixed for the application to unseal, a subpoena duces tecum
was served on the Director of Public Prosecutions requiring him to produce the following
documents ([1960] 1 All ER 692 at 694, [1960] 1 QB 669 at 671–672):    d

'1. All correspondence and other documents in Mr. MacDermott's possession
relating to the matters in issue in this suit and in particular to the investigations, the
preliminary proceedings, the seeking and inverviewing of potential witnesses, and
the trial in the prosecution R. v. *Auten*. 2. Reports of the defendant Bolongaro and of    e
other officers of the Metropolitan or other police forces. 3. Memoranda or notes of
interviews. 4. Relevant entries in your official diaries for the material period. 5.
Notes of conferences, your briefs and instructions to prosecuting counsel at the
Central Criminal Court, and any opinions from them. 6. Proofs of witnesses and all
other material accompanying your briefs.'

Objection was made on behalf of the Crown, a claim of Crown privilege being made    f
in respect of the first four classes of documents, and a claim of professional privilege in
respect of the last two classes.

The judge dealt with the issue of the documents mentioned in the subpoena in his
judgment, where he said ([1960] 1 All ER 692 at 696, [1960] 1 QB 669 at 679–681):

'So far as the "Reports of the defendant Bolongaro and of other officers of the
Metropolitan or other police forces" are concerned, these are the very reports in    g
respect of which Crown privilege has already been claimed, and in so far as they
were at one time, or in so far as any of them were at one time in possession of the
defendant Bolongaro, the Court of Appeal decided that he could not be called on to
produce them. They are the same documents still:—police reports by the defendant
Bolongaro to his superiors, or by other officers of the Metropolitan Police Force to
the Director or by members of any other police force to the Metropolitan Police    h
Force. The Attorney-General says that in so far as it is necessary for him to do so, he
would here and now claim Crown privilege, or, alternatively that the claim to
Crown privilege already made in respect of these documents so far as they were in
the possession of Bolongaro still applies to prevent their production. I am quite sure
that is right. If it should be necessary—I do not think it is—for any formal claim in
respect of the production of these documents by Mr. MacDermott to be made by    j
any other Minister of the Crown, I should undoubtedly have refused to order the
production of the documents for a sufficient time to enable the claim to be made.
So far as the documents in paras. 3 and 4 of the subpoena are concerned—"3.
Memoranda or notes of inverviews. 4. Relevant entries in your official diaries"—

that is, in Mr. MacDermott's official diaries—they are documents in respect of
which the Attorney-General himself here and now claims Crown privilege, and I
cannot go behind that claim. It is quite unnecessary to put the Attorney-General to
the trouble of swearing an affidavit. He is obviously entitled to come into court and
make his claim to Crown privilege in face of the court, and he has done so. Those
documents are not to be produced. So far as documents in paras. 5 and 6 of the
subpoena are concerned, the Attorney-General says that the Director of Public
Prosecutions is entitled to claim a professional privilege analogous to the privilege
claimed in respect of documents in the possession of a solicitor. There is perhaps a
little difficulty there, because the right to claim privilege is that of the client rather
than the solicitor. The Attorney-General says that for the purpose of such a claim to
privilege, the Director is his own client. I am not sure that there is a precise analogy
between the position of the Director and the position of a solicitor; but those rules
of public policy which have resulted in there being established a right of a client
and solicitor to claim privilege as to documents and statements in the possession of
the solicitor appear to me to apply with equal, if not greater, force to the position of
the Director of Public Prosecutions. I regret having to make such a ruling on the
spur of the moment, as it were, and without having had the benefit of that fuller
argument which I am sure I should have had if, as I say, the Attorney-General had
not been confronted with this document almost on his way to the court, but I think,
however full the argument, I should arrive at the same conclusion, and I should
much prefer to give my judgment straight away rather than cause any further delay
in this case which has already lasted long enough.'

The comments of Glyn-Jones J in that case seem to me to be pertinent to the
consideration of public interest immunity which I have to make, and by parity of
reasoning I see no reason why the factor of legal advice should not be a potent one in
reaching my own conclusion in the exercise of my discretion. It seems to me important,
and very important in the functioning of the criminal process of prosecution, that there
should be freedom of communication between police forces around the country and the
Director of Public Prosecutions in seeking his legal advice, without fear that those
documents will be subject to inspection, analysis and detailed investigation at some later
stage. The pressure on police forces in these days is enormous and, in my judgment, it
will be contrary to the public interest for such documents to be the subject of disclosure
in civil proceedings subsequently even though a prosecution has been completed,
whether successfully or not. I find the arguments in the Attorney General's certificate to
be convincing.

I have reminded myself of the principles set forth in the speeches in *Conway v Rimmer*
[1968] 1 All ER 874, [1968] AC 910, and taking into account the matters to which I have
already referred and seeking on the whole of the evidence to achieve a balance, and
bearing in mind that the burden on the applicant for production and inspection is not
light, I have reached the conclusion that it would be inappropriate in the present case to
accede to a request for an order for production, and I would allow this appeal from the
master and refuse the plaintiff's application.

*Appeal allowed. Application for discovery refused.*

Solicitors: *Sharpe Pritchard* (for the defendant); *Manches & Co* (for the plaintiff); *Treasury Solicitor*.

K Mydeen Esq   Barrister.

# Practice Note

QUEEN'S BENCH DIVISION
LORD LANE CJ, FARQUHARSON AND POTTS JJ
26 MAY 1989

*Criminal law – Costs – Power to award costs – Award out of central funds – Amount of costs to be paid – Defence costs – Private prosecutor's costs – Costs of witness, interpreter or medical evidence – Disallowance of costs – Award of costs against offenders and appellants – Costs incurred through unnecessary or improper act or omission – Award of costs against solicitors – Legal aid costs – Legal aid contributions – Advice on appeal – Criminal Appeal Act 1968, Pts I, II – Mental Health (Amendment) Act 1982, s 34(5) – Prosecution of Offences Act 1985, ss 16, 17, 18, 19, 20 – Costs in Criminal Cases (General) Regulations 1986, regs 3, 14 – Legal Aid in Criminal and Care Proceedings (Costs) Regulations 1989, Sch 1, Pt II, para 1.*

**LORD LANE CJ** gave the following direction at the sitting of the court.

PART I: INTRODUCTION

*Scope*

1.1 This direction shall have effect in the Crown Court, the Divisional Court of the Queen's Bench Division and the Court of Appeal, Criminal Division where the court in the exercise of its discretion considers an award of costs in criminal proceedings or deals with criminal legal aid costs and contributions.

*Power to award costs*

1.2 The powers enabling a court to award costs in criminal proceedings are contained in Pt II (ss 16–21) of the Prosecution of Offences Act 1985 and in regulations made under ss 19 and 20 of that Act, the Costs in Criminal Cases (General) Regulations 1986, SI 1986/1335.

1.3 Section 16 makes provision for the award of defence costs out of central funds. Section 17 provides for an award of costs to a private prosecutor out of central funds. Section 18 gives power to order a convicted defendant or unsuccessful appellant to pay costs to the prosecutor and s 19(1) and reg 3 provide for awards of costs between parties where costs have been wasted.

1.4 The court also has power under its inherent jurisdiction over officers of the court to order a solicitor personally to pay costs incurred as a result of an unnecessary or improper act or omission and may give directions relating to legal aid costs and contributions. (The procedure to be followed is set out below at Pt VIII.)

*Extent of orders for costs from central funds*

1.5 Where a court orders that the costs of a defendant, appellant or private prosecutor should be paid from central funds, the order will include the costs incurred in the proceedings in the lower courts unless for good reason the court directs that such costs are not included in the order.

*Amount of costs to be paid*

1.6 Except where the court has directed in an order for costs from central funds that only a specified sum shall be paid, the amount of costs to be paid shall be determined by the appropriate officer of the court. The court may, however, order the disallowance of costs out of central funds not properly incurred or direct the determining officer to consider whether or not specific items have been properly incurred. The court may also make observations regarding legal aid costs. The procedures to be followed when such circumstances arise are set out in this direction.

*a*   1.7   Where the court orders an offender to pay costs to the prosecutor, or orders one party to pay costs to another party, the order for costs must specify the sum to be paid.

1.8   Where the court is required to specify the amount of costs to be paid, the court cannot delegate the decision. Wherever practicable solicitors should provide counsel with details of costs incurred at each stage of the proceedings. The court may however require the appropriate officer of the court to make inquiries to inform the court as to the costs incurred and may adjourn the proceedings for inquiries to be made, if necessary.

*b*

PART II: DEFENCE COSTS FROM CENTRAL FUNDS

*In the Crown Court*

2.1   Where a person is not tried for an offence for which he has been indicted or committed for trial or has been acquitted on any count in the indictment, the court may *c*   make a defendant's costs order in his favour. Such an order should normally be made whether or not an order for costs inter partes is made, unless there are positive reasons for not doing so. Examples of such reasons are: (a) the defendant's own conduct has brought suspicion on himself and has misled the prosecution into thinking that the case against him is stronger than it is; (b) there is ample evidence to support a conviction but the defendant is acquitted on a technicality which has no merit.

*d*   2.2   Where a person is convicted of some count(s) in the indictment but acquitted on others the court may exercise its discretion to make a defendant's costs order but may order that only part of the costs incurred be paid. Where the court considers that it would be inappropriate that the defendant recovers all of the costs properly incurred, the amount must be specified in the order.

2.3   The court may make a defendant's costs order in favour of a successful appellant: *e*   see s 16(3).

*In the Divisional Court of the Queen's Bench Division*

2.4   The court may make a defendant's costs order on determining proceedings in a criminal cause or matter.

*f*   *In the Court of Appeal, Criminal Division*

2.5   A successful appellant under Pt I of the Criminal Appeal Act 1968 may be awarded a defendant's costs order.

2.6   On determining an application for leave to appeal to the House of Lords under Pt II of the Criminal Appeal Act 1968, whether by prosecutor or by defendant, the court may make a defendant's costs order.

*g*   2.7   In considering whether to make such an order the court will have in mind the principles applied by the Crown Court in relation to acquitted defendants (see para 2.1 above).

PART III: PRIVATE PROSECUTOR'S COSTS FROM CENTRAL FUNDS

3.1   There is no power to order the payment of costs out of central funds of any *h*   prosecutor who is a public authority, a person acting on behalf of a public authority, or acting as an official appointed by a public authority as defined in the Act. In the limited number of cases in which a prosecutor's costs may be awarded out of central funds, an application is to be made by the prosecution in each case. An order should be made save where there is good reason for not doing so, eg where proceedings have been instituted or continued without good cause.

*j*

PART IV: COSTS OF WITNESS, INTERPRETER OR MEDICAL EVIDENCE

4.1   The costs of attendance of a witness required by the accused, a private prosecutor or the court, or of an interpreter required because of the accused's lack of English or of an oral report by a medical practitioner are allowed out of central funds unless the court directs otherwise.

4.2　The Crown Court may order the payment out of central funds of such sums as appear to it to be reasonably sufficient to compensate any medical practitioner for the expenses, trouble or loss of time properly incurred in preparing and making a report on the mental condition of a person accused of murder: see the Mental Health (Amendment) Act 1982, s 34(5).

PART V: DISALLOWANCE OF COSTS OUT OF CENTRAL FUNDS

5.1　Where the court makes an order for costs out of central funds, it must (a) direct the appropriate authority to disallow the costs incurred in respect of any items if it is plain that those costs were not properly incurred; such costs are not payable under ss 16(6) and 17(1) of the Prosecution of Offences Act 1985, and it may (b) direct the appropriate authority to consider or investigate on taxation any items which may have been improperly incurred. Costs not properly incurred include costs in respect of work unreasonably done, eg if the case has been conducted unreasonably so as to incur unjustified expense, or costs have been wasted by failure to conduct proceedings with reasonable competence and expedition. The precise terms of the order for costs and of any direction must be entered in the court record.

5.2　Where the court has in mind that a direction in accordance with para 5.1(a) or (b) might be given it must inform any party whose costs might be affected or his legal representative of the precise terms thereof and give a reasonable opportunity to show cause why no direction should be given. This should normally be done in chambers at such time as the court thinks proper. If the court decides to give a direction it may announce the decision in open court if it is of the opinion that it is in the interests of justice to do so. If a direction is given under para 5.1(b) the court should inform the party concerned of his rights to make representations to the appropriate authority.

5.3　The appropriate authority may consult the court on any matter touching the allowance or disallowance of costs. It is not appropriate for the court to make a direction under para 5.1(a) when so consulted.

PART VI: AWARD OF COSTS AGAINST OFFENDERS AND APPELLANTS

6.1　The Crown Court may make an order for costs against a person convicted of an offence before it, against an offender otherwise before it and against an unsuccessful appellant. The court may make such an order payable to the prosecutor as it considers just and reasonable (s 18(1), reg 14).

6.2　The Court of Appeal, Criminal Division may order an unsuccessful appellant to pay costs to such person as may be named in the order. Such costs may include the cost of any transcript obtained for the proceedings in the Court of Appeal (s 18(2) and (6)).

6.3　An order should be made where the court is satisfied that the offender or appellant has the means and the ability to pay.

6.4　The amount must be specified in the order by the court.

PART VII: AWARD OF COSTS INCURRED AS A RESULT OF UNNECESSARY OR
IMPROPER ACT OR OMISSION

7.1　The Crown Court and the Court of Appeal, Criminal Division may order the payment of any costs incurred as a result of an unnecessary or improper act or omission by or on behalf of any party to the proceedings (s 19, reg 3).

7.2　The court must hear the parties and may then order that all or part of the costs so incurred by one party shall be paid to him by the other party.

7.3　The order must specify the amount of the costs to be paid.

7.4　Such an order is appropriate only where the failure is that of the defendant or of the prosecutor. Where the failure is that of the legal representative(s) the inherent jurisdiction (Pt VIII below) may be exercised.

PART VIII: AWARDS OF COSTS AGAINST SOLICITORS

*a*     8.1   In addition to the power under reg 3 of the Costs in Criminal Cases (General) Regulations 1986 to order that costs improperly incurred be paid by a party to the proceedings the Supreme Court (which includes the Crown Court) may in the exercise of its inherent jurisdiction over officers of the court order a solicitor personally to pay costs thrown away by reason of some improper act or omission on his part or that of his staff.

*b*     8.2   No such order shall be made unless reasonable notice has been given to the solicitor of the matter alleged against him and he is given a reasonable opportunity of being heard in reply. If the court considers it necessary to hold such a hearing in chambers, a shorthand note should be kept.

8.3   There is no power to award costs to be paid personally by counsel but where counsel acts under legal aid the court may make observations to the determining
*c*   authority (see Pt IX below).

PART IX: LEGAL AID COSTS

*In the Crown Court and the Court of Appeal, Criminal Division*

9.1   Where it appears to any judge of the Crown Court or the Court of Appeal,
*d*   Criminal Division, sitting in proceedings for which legal aid has been granted, that work may have been unreasonably done, eg if the legally assisted person's case may have been conducted unreasonably so as to incur unjustifiable expense, or costs may have been wasted by failure to conduct the proceedings with reasonable competence or expedition, he may make observations to that effect for the attention of the appropriate authority. The judge or the court, as the case may be, should specify as precisely as possible the item
*e*   or items, which the determining authority should consider or investigate on the determination of the costs payable pursuant to the legal aid order. The precise terms of the observations must be entered in the court record.

9.2   It is not the function of the judge or the court, to disallow or order the disallowance of fees and expenses. It is for the appropriate authority to decide whether any disallowance should affect any individual counsel or solicitor and the amount of any
*f*   such disallowance. His decision will depend on the circumstances of the case.

9.3   In the Crown Court, in proceedings specified in para 1 of Pt II of Sch 1 to the Legal Aid in Criminal and Care Proceedings (Costs) Regulations 1989, SI 1989/343, where standard fees would otherwise be payable, where the trial judge is dissatisfied with the solicitor's conduct of the case or he considers that, for exceptional reasons, the fees should be determined by the appropriate authority, he may direct that such determination
*g*   take place.

9.4   Where the judge or the court has in mind that observations under para 9.1 or that a direction under para 9.3 should be made the solicitor or counsel whose fees or expenses might be affected must be informed of the precise terms thereof and of his right to make representations to the appropriate authority and be given a reasonable opportunity to show cause why the observations or direction should not be made. This
*h*   should normally be done in chambers at such time as the judge or the court thinks proper. If it is decided to make the observations or direction the decision may be announced in open court if the judge or the court considers that it is in the interests of justice to do so.

9.5   Where such observations or direction are made the appropriate authority must afford an opportunity to the solicitor or counsel whose fees might be affected to make
*j*   representations in relation to them.

9.6   Whether or not observations under para 9.1 have been made the appropriate authority may consult the judge or the court on any matter touching the allowance or disallowance of fees and expenses, but if the observations then made are to the effect mentioned in para 9.1 the appropriate authority should afford an opportunity to the solicitor or counsel concerned to make representations in relation thereto.          *a*

PART X: LEGAL AID CONTRIBUTIONS

*In the Crown Court and the Court of Appeal, Criminal Division*

10.1   When a defendant who is acquitted on all counts or successfully appeals against his conviction has paid a contribution under a legal aid order the court should normally order the repayment of the contribution and remit any unpaid instalments due under *b* the order, unless there are circumstances which make such a course of action inappropriate. Details of any contribution order and payments should be given to the court before it considers what order should be made.

10.2   The exercise of the power to remit unpaid instalments regardless of the outcome of the trial or appeal will depend on the circumstances of each case.

*c*

PART XI: ADVICE ON APPEAL TO THE COURT OF APPEAL, CRIMINAL DIVISION

11.1   In all cases the procedure set out in *A Guide to Proceedings in the Court of Appeal Criminal Division* published by the Criminal Appeal Office with the approval of the Lord Chief Justice in 1989 should be followed. The reference to App 1 which follows is to App 1 to that guide.

11.2   This procedure requires written advice to be delivered to the defendant within *d* 21 days of conviction or sentence. In simple cases this will involve little or no expense. If the procedure is not followed and the work has not been done with due care, fees may be reduced accordingly. Counsel will have received instructions in the form of App 1 from the solicitor which specifically refer him to the guide. Counsel is required to complete App 1 immediately following the conclusion of the case and the solicitor should give a copy to the defendant at that stage. Where counsel's immediate and final view in App 1 *e* is that there are no reasonable grounds of appeal, no additional fees should be allowed. In any other circumstances counsel must further advise in writing within 14 days and where it was reasonable for counsel so to advise an allowance should be made for the advice.

11.3   When both (a) counsel or solicitor has given positive advice to appeal and (b) notice of application for leave to appeal or of appeal has been lodged with the Crown *f* Court on the strength of that advice, the Registrar of Criminal Appeals is the appropriate authority to determine the fees in respect of the work in connection with the advice and notice of application etc. The Crown Court should not determine those fees unless the solicitor confirms that the notice of application etc was not given on his or counsel's advice. Where no notice of application etc is given, either because of unfavourable advice or despite favourable advice, the appropriate authority is the appropriate officer for the *g* Crown Court.

11.4   If it appears that the defendant was never given advice the Crown Court should direct the solicitor's attention to this fact and if there is no satisfactory explanation as to why no advice was sent the determining officer should bear this in mind when determining the solicitor's costs and should draw the solicitor's attention to the 1989 *h* guide.

PART XII: REVOCATIONS

12.1   The Practice Directions listed below are hereby withdrawn:

[1968] 1 All ER 778, [1968] 1 WLR 389
[1977] 1 All ER 540, [1977] 1 WLR 181          *i*
[1977] 1 All ER 542, [1977] 1 WLR 182
[1980] 2 All ER 336, [1980] 1 WLR 697
[1981] 3 All ER 703, [1981] 1 WLR 1383
[1982] 3 All ER 1152, [1982] 1 WLR 1447.

N P Metcalfe Esq   Barrister.

# a Lonrho plc v Secretary of State for Trade and Industry

## and another appeal

HOUSE OF LORDS

b LORD KEITH OF KINKEL, LORD TEMPLEMAN, LORD GRIFFITHS, LORD ACKNER AND LORD LOWRY

12, 13, 17, 18, 19 APRIL, 18 MAY 1989

*Company – Investigation by Department of Trade and Industry – Affairs of company – Company involved in merger – Inspector's report – Publication – Discretion of Secretary of State whether and when to publish report – Secretary of State deferring publication of report until completion of investigations by Serious Fraud Office and Director of Public Prosecutions – Scope of Secretary of State's discretion – Whether Secretary of State acting unlawfully in withholding publication – Companies Act 1985, s 437(3)(c).*

*Monopolies and mergers – Reference to Monopolies and Mergers Commission – Discretion of d Secretary of State whether to make reference to commission – Whether Secretary of State entitled to act on advice of Director General of Fair Trading in deciding whether to refer bid to commission.*

In 1981 the appellant made a take-over bid for a public company (Fraser) which was referred to the Monopolies and Mergers Commission, which found that the merger would operate against the public interest. In November 1984 the appellant sold its e holding in Fraser to the F brothers, who, on 4 March 1985, through AIT, a company controlled by them, announced a full bid for the share capital of Fraser. The bid was not referred to the commission because of assurances given to the Secretary of State by the F brothers about the offer and their intentions with regard to Fraser. As a result of its bid AIT acquired the entire share capital of Fraser. In April 1987 the Secretary of State appointed inspectors to inquire into the affairs of AIT, pursuant to s 432(2) of the f Companies Act 1985, following allegations by the appellant that the statements and assurances given by the F brothers were false and had been fraudulently made and, accordingly, that they and their company were not suitable persons to control Fraser. On 23 July 1988 the inspectors submitted their report to the Secretary of State, who sent a copy of it to the Serious Fraud Office and the Director General of Fair Trading. The Secretary of State assured the appellant that he intended to publish the report as soon as g possible but on 29 September 1988 the Department of Trade and Industry announced in a press release that because the Serious Fraud Office required further time for investigation and consideration of the case publication of the report would be deferred. The same press release announced that the Director General of Fair Trading would be considering whether to advise the Secretary of State to refer the merger to the commission. The h appellant continued to press the Secretary of State to publish the inspectors' report but he refused, having been advised by the Director of the Serious Fraud Office that immediate publication would seriously inhibit the inquiries being made by him and cause serious prejudice to any trial which might take place thereafter. After considering further arguments from the appellant and from his own officials, the Secretary of State confirmed his decision not to publish the report. Meanwhile, on 25 November 1988 the Secretary j of State decided on the advice of the Director General of Fair Trading not to refer the merger to the commission. The appellant applied for judicial review of the Secretary of State's decision to defer publication of the report and his refusal to refer to the commission the merger relating to the acquisition of Fraser by AIT. The Divisional Court granted the application but the Court of Appeal reversed its decision. The appellant appealed to the House of Lords.

**Held** – (1) In exercising the discretion conferred on him by s 437(3)(c)[a] of the 1985 Act
to publish or withhold publication of the inspectors' report the Secretary of State was     **a**
required to act in the public interest after taking such advice as he considered appropriate.
In the circumstances the Secretary of State had properly exercised his discretion in
deciding to defer publication of the report on the ground that early publication might be
prejudicial to the Serious Fraud Office's investigation and to a fair trial, since in arriving
at his decision he had acted independently and only confirmed the decision after careful
consideration of the arguments of the appellant and of his own officials. Accordingly,     **b**
the appeal in respect of the publication decision would be dismissed (see p 615 c to e,
p 616 d to j and p 621 e to g, post).
(2) In exercising his discretion under the Fair Trading Act 1973 to decide which
mergers to refer to the commission the Secretary of State had to be guided, although he
was not fettered, by the advice of the Director General of Fair Trading. On the facts, no
useful purpose would have been served by a reference to the commission since no     **c**
competition or consumer issues were involved in the merger situation arising from the
bid by AIT for Fraser nor was there any indication that the particular expertise of the
commission was required to advise the Secretary of State on any aspects of the public
interest about which he was already fully informed. It followed therefore that the
Secretary of State had not acted irrationally in deciding, on the advice of the Director
General of Fair Trading, not to refer the bid to the commission. The appeal against his     **d**
refusal to make a reference to the commission would therefore be dismissed (see p 618 j
to p 619 c, p 620 g to j and p 621 a to g, post).

**Notes**
For appointment of inspectors to investigate affairs of company and the inspectors' report,     **e**
see 7(2) Halsbury's Laws (4th edn) paras 1221, 1225.
For the Fair Trading Act 1973, see 47 Halsbury's Statutes (4th edn) 125.
For the Companies Act 1985, s 437, see 8 ibid 481.

**Cases referred to in opinions**
*Associated Provincial Picture Houses Ltd v Wednesbury Corp* [1947] 2 All ER 680, [1948] 1     **f**
     KB 223, CA.
*Padfield v Minister of Agriculture Fisheries and Food* [1968] 1 All ER 694, [1968] AC 997,
     [1968] 2 WLR 924, HL.
*R v Lancashire CC, ex p Huddleston* [1986] 2 All ER 941, CA.

**Appeal**     **g**
Lonrho plc appealed with leave of the Court of Appeal given on 23 January 1989 against
the decision of that court (Dillon, Mustill and Stocker LJJ) on 20 January 1989 allowing
the appeal of the Secretary of State for Trade and Industry against the decision of the
Divisional Court of the Queen's Bench Division (Watkins, Mann LJJ and McCowan J) on
17 January 1989 granting Lonrho judicial review of (i) the decision of the Secretary of     **h**
State on 29 September 1988 and affirmed on 25 October 1988 deferring publication of
the report of the inspectors appointed by him to investigate the affairs of the House of
Fraser Holdings plc (Fraser) until investigations into the subject matter of that report by
the Serious Fraud Office and the Director of Public Prosecutions were completed on the
ground that the decision was ultra vires and unlawful and issuing an order of mandamus
requiring the Secretary of State to reconsider the matter according to law, and (ii) the     **j**
decision of the Secretary of State made on 25 November 1988 not to refer to the
Monopolies and Mergers Commission the merger relating to the acquisition in 1984 and
1985 by Al Fayed Investment and Trust (UK) plc of Fraser on the ground that it was ultra

---

[a]   Section 437(3), so far as material, is set out at p 615 b, post

_a_    vires and issuing mandam...
facts are set out in the opini...

John Beveridge QC, David Pannı...
David Oliver QC and Patrick Elia...
John Mummery and Laurence Rabin...

_b_    Their Lordships took time for consideration.

18 May. The following opinions were delivered.

**LORD KEITH OF KINKEL.** My Lords, in this appeal the appellant company (referred to hereafter as 'Lonrho') seeks to set aside two orders made by the Court of
_c_    Appeal (Dillon, Mustill and Stocker LJJ) on 20 January 1989 dismissing the application of Lonrho for judicial review of two decisions of the respondent (referred to hereafter as 'the Secretary of State'), namely: (1) his refusal made on 29 September 1988 and affirmed on 25 October 1988 to defer publication of the report of the inspectors appointed by him to investigate the affairs of House of Fraser Holdings plc (referred to hereafter as 'Holdings') until investigations into the subject matter of that report by the Serious Fraud
_d_    Office and the Director of Public Prosecutions are completed (and if those investigations led to prosecutions, until those prosecutions had been concluded). This is referred to hereafter as 'the publication decision'. The Divisional Court (Watkins, Mann LJJ and McCowan J) had on 17 January 1989 declared that this decision was ultra vires and unlawful and had issued an order of mandamus requiring the Secretary of State to reconsider the matter according to law; and (2) the decision of the Secretary of State made
_e_    on 25 November 1988 not to refer to the Monopolies and Mergers Commission (referred to hereafter as 'the MMC') the merger situation relating to the acquisition in 1984 and 1985 by Al Fayed Investment and Trust (UK) plc (referred to hereafter as 'AIT') of the House of Fraser plc (referred to hereafter as 'Fraser') notwithstanding that the report of the inspectors disclosed the existence of previously undisclosed material facts. The Divisional Court had held that this decision was ultra vires and mandamus was issued
_f_    requiring the Secretary of State to make this reference.
The orders of the Divisional Court were set aside by the Court of Appeal. Lonrho now appeal to this House.

_The material facts_
_g_    The material facts are not in dispute. In brief summary, they are as follows.
(1) In 1978 Lonrho, having acquired an investment in Scottish and Universal Investments Ltd (referred to hereafter as 'SUITS') which in turn held an interest in Fraser, made a bid for all the outstanding share capital in SUITS. This bid was referred to the MMC which, in March 1979, reported that the bid would not be against the public interest. In due course, and as a result of the bid, Lonrho acquired SUITS, thereby
_h_    securing a holding of 29·9% of the issued share capital of Fraser.
(2) In February 1981 Lonrho made a bid for Fraser which was referred to the MMC. Following its finding that the merger situation would operate against the public interest, Lonrho were asked to give, and gave to the then Secretary of State, an undertaking that it would not seek to increase its interest in Fraser above the 29·9% interest it already held.
(3) In late May 1984 an attempt by Lonrho to reconstitute the board of Fraser gave
_j_    rise to a merger situation which again resulted in a reference to the MMC. On 5 October the MMC sought and obtained an extension of time in which to investigate and report on the merger situation referred to it.
(4) In November 1984 Lonrho sold its 29·9% holding in Fraser to the Fayed brothers for approximately £138m.
(5) On 14 February 1985 the MMC reported to the then Secretary of State that the

612

not operate against the public interest.
...ublished and Lonrho remained subject to the  *a*
...C's report on the reference of February 1981.

*merger*...vehicle of the Fayed brothers, announced a full bid for

*However...* ...his offer was recommended by the Fraser board of directors.

*under...* 985 the MMC's report relating to Lonrho and received by the

*the ...* 14 February 1985 was published.

...arch 1985, it was announced that the merger situation caused by the AIT  *b*
...aser was not to be referred to the MMC. The Secretary of State gave, as among
...easons for not so referring on non-competition grounds, 'the statements made and
assurances given by the Fayed family about the offer and their intentions with regard to
the House of Fraser [and] the support given to those statements and assurances by
Kleinwort Benson Ltd'.

(9) Also on 14 March 1985 Lonrho was released from the undertaking given to the  *c*
Secretary of State not to increase its Fraser interest to 30% or more.

(10) AIT as a result of its bid announced on 4 March 1985 acquired 100% of the share
capital in Fraser. In due course, AIT changed its name to House of Fraser Holdings plc
(referred to hereafter as 'Holdings').

(11) On 9 April 1987, following a period in which representations had been made
principally by Lonrho concerning the circumstances in which Holdings had acquired  *d*
Fraser, the Secretary of State, pursuant to s 432(2) of the Companies Act 1985, appointed
inspectors to inquire into the affairs of Holdings and report thereon. The inspectors
appointed were Mr Philip Heslop QC and Mr Hugh Aldous FCA. Mr Heslop resigned his
appointment on 13 May 1987 and on 15 May 1987 Mr Henry Brooke QC was appointed
in his place. The allegations made by Lonrho were to the effect that the statements and
assurances were false, and had been fraudulently made by the Fayeds, with the object,  *e*
inter alia, of avoiding a reference to the MMC and that, on several grounds, the Fayeds
and Holdings were not suitable persons to control Fraser.

(12) On 23 July 1988 the inspectors submitted their report to the Secretary of State.
Six days later, on 29 July, the Secretary of State sent a copy of the inspectors' report to the
Serious Fraud Office (referred to hereafter as 'the SFO'). Under s 1(3) of the Criminal
Justice Act 1987 the Director of the SFO 'may investigate any suspected offence which  *f*
appears to him on reasonable grounds to involve serious or complex fraud'. On 19
August a copy of the report was sent to the Director General of Fair Trading, Sir Gordon
Borrie (referred to hereafter as the 'Director General').

(13) On 13 September 1988 the Secretary of State, in reply to a letter from Mr
Rowland, the chief executive of Lonrho, stated that 'As regards publication, our policy is
to publish unless there is a genuine and unavoidable impediment to doing so; this policy  *g*
will be applied to the report'.

(14) On 16 September 1988 the Secretary of State personally assured Lonrho's
representatives at a meeting that he intended to publish the report, as soon as possible,
and that this meant weeks, rather than years.

(15) On 29 September 1988 the Department of Trade and Industry (referred to  *h*
hereafter as 'the DTI') announced, in a press release, that, because the SFO required
further time for investigation and consideration of the case, 'the Secretary of State cannot
publish the report for the time being, but will do so as soon as circumstances permit'.
The same press release also announced that the Director General was considering whether
the report demonstrated the existence of new material facts and that, if so, he would
advise the Secretary of State whether to refer the merger to the MMC.

(16) On 5 October 1988, at a meeting attended by representatives of Lonrho and  *j*
officials of the DTI, Lonrho were given an opportunity to put forward submissions as to
why the inspectors' report should be published; in the alternative Lonrho submitted that
a copy of the report should be divulged to Lonrho. Mr Mallinson, the head of the
investigations division of the DTI, informed Lonrho that the Secretary of State still

wished to publish the report as soon as possible, but that the position was complicated
*a* because the inquiries of the SFO were continuing. Mr Mallinson said, inter alia:

> 'The needs of the SFO as to publication is a further intervening factor ... I am
> advised ... that the Director General is satisfied that he can put you in a position to
> make full submissions, without your seeing the report. I do not expect you to agree,
> but that is his view. Our discretion to provide the report is governed by the views
*b* of the SFO and the Director General.'

Lonrho's leading counsel said:

> 'In view of the press release ... I am asking the Secretary of State to say that he
> has misdirected himself. He can, and should, publish. There is nothing in the
*c* circumstances of the investigation justifying a decision not to publish. This factor
> does not justify the decision not to refer. In the context of judicial review, I make
> the argument to try to change his mind.

(17) On 12 October 1988 Lonrho submitted to the DTI a copy of a joint opinion
signed by three leading and two junior counsel which, so far as relevant, asserted that it
*d* was unlikely that the SFO would take statements from witnesses within one year, that 'a
trial must be several years away', that 'it appears that the Serious Fraud Office involvement
provides no reasons why' the Secretary of State should not publish the report and that
there were a number of enumerated public interest reasons, especially 'the public interest
in the uncovering of fraud', why the report should be published.

(18) On 20 October 1988 a memorandum of submissions on behalf of Lonrho was
*e* presented to the DTI reiterating and amplifying the view of Lonrho and the view of its
counsel. At 2.00 pm on 20 October 1988 a meeting took place between the deputy
Director General of Fair Trading and Lonrho's representatives. This was followed by a
meeting at the DTI attended by three counsel, two solicitors and three directors on behalf
of Lonrho. A prepared statement was read out by Mr Mallinson on behalf of the DTI.
This stated that the purpose of the meeting was for the DTI to state its position on
*f* publishing the report in the light of the issues raised by the opinion of counsel on behalf
of Lonrho which had been handed to the DTI; the DTI had carefully studied the opinion
and taken advice on it; the Secretary of State would be consulted on the matter following
the meeting and any further points which Lonrho or its advisers might wish to make at
the meeting would be noted and reported to the Secretary of State; given the Secretary of
State's firm intention to publish the report as soon as circumstances permit, the DTI
*g* considered it right and necessary to take account of all points that were made on the issue
of publication; all points made would be given the closest scrutiny by the Secretary of
State who continued to keep an open mind on the subject of publication; the decision
not to publish the report was taken by the DTI and not on the SFO's insistence; and the
decision not to publish was taken following advice from the SFO that immediate
publication would seriously inhibit the inquiries made by the SFO and cause serious
*h* prejudice to any trial which may take place thereafter. Mrs Chase, a representative of the
SFO, explained in brief the concerns of the SFO and was cross-examined by Lonrho's
counsel. The remarks of Mrs Chase at this meeting as recorded in a note made by
Lonrho's junior counsel and which are particularly relied on by Lonrho are:

> 'Those charged with prosecuting a case won't prosecute at all if there is any
*j* likelihood of an argument by the defendants that they have been prejudiced in any
> way. It would be monstrously unfair to bring proceedings at all if matters had
> already been tried in the public domain. That is why many cases are not tried: it is
> the decision of the prosecutor ... [If] there was any publication at all I would call off
> the investigation: there would be no point in committing further public resources
> to it.'

(19) On 24 October 1988 Mr Fordham, a partner in Messrs Stephenson Harwood, Lonrho's solicitors, referred Mr Mallinson of the DTI to a newspaper article 'and stated that it gave credence to his client's suggestion that this was all a political cover-up'.

(20) On 25 October Mr Mallinson wrote to Lonrho's solicitors affirming the decision which had been previously made on 29 September (see para 15, supra). The material part of the letter reads as follows:

'The Secretary of State has considered carefully the written and oral submissions which have recently been made by your firm, by counsel and by your clients to the effect that the report of the inspectors should now be published. The Secretary of State has seen the written submissions which were delivered to his officials on 12 and 20 October and he has been briefed on the meeting which took place with officials on 20 October. In particular, he has been briefed on the arguments which were raised by counsel for Lonrho at the meeting on 20 October to the effect that the current inquiries by the Serious Fraud Office are not a serious impediment to publication. These arguments have been put to, and discussed with, the Serious Fraud Office and the Department's own Counsel. Having taken all these matters into account, the Secretary of State has decided that there is no warrant for changing his earlier view that, in the present circumstances, it would not be proper for him to publish the report . . .'

(21) On 4 November 1988 Lonrho gave notice of an application to apply for judicial review of the decision of the Secretary of State 'dated 29 September 1988 and affirmed on 25 October 1988 . . . to refuse to publish the report of the inspectors . . .' The grounds on which the relief was sought included the following:

'(14) At a meeting on 20th October 1988, representatives of the SFO and of the Secretary of State informed representatives of the Applicant that the reasons for the Secretary of State's change of mind were submissions on the part of the SFO to the effect that the publication of the Report might: (1) impede a fair trial (by reason of publicity) if criminal charges were to be brought; (2) hinder the gathering of information and evidence relevant to the bringing of criminal charges . . .'

No reference was made in the grounds on which the relief was sought to any statements made by Mrs Chase in cross-examination at the meeting held on 20 October 1988.

(22) While this was going on, the question of whether to refer the merger situation to the MMC was being considered by the Office of Fair Trading. On 23 November 1988 representatives of Lonrho met the Secretary of State to make submissions as to why, in their view, the merger situation should be referred to the MMC. At that meeting the Secretary of State became involved in arguments and interjections with Mr Rowland and others about the decision of the Secretary of State not to publish the inspectors' report and not to supply Lonrho with a copy of the report. In the course of these exchanges the Secretary of State said:

'It is still my intention to publish but I can only do what has always been the policy of this Department and that is not to publish until any prosecution is over . . . I have listened to and considered the points you have made and have to consider the report I have . . . Only those who have read the report are in a position to judge: our view and our past practice is that if there is any prosecution, you do not publish.'

(23) On 25 November 1988 the DTI issued a press release stating that the Secretary of State had decided, in accordance with the advice of the Director General, not to refer the merger situation to the MMC. The press notice went on to say that the Secretary of State had decided, after considering representations made to him and the advice of the Director General, that a reference to the commission would not be appropriate, but that it might, in due course be appropriate for other steps to be taken in the light of the inspectors' report.

*The publication decision*

a        The Secretary of State is empowered, pursuant to s 432(2) of the Companies Act 1985, to appoint inspectors to investigate the affairs of a company in the circumstances there defined. By s 437 of the same Act, the Secretary of State is given wide powers to deal with an inspector's report. So far as publication of the report is concerned, s 437(3)(c) provides that 'the Secretary of State may, if he thinks fit . . . (c) cause any such report to be printed and published'.

b        It is contended on behalf of Lonrho, and indeed is not disputed by the Secretary of State, that the discretion of the Secretary of State whether, and when, to publish the report, must be exercised by him (and not at the dictation of another minister or body) by reference to relevant and not irrelevant considerations and in a manner which is not unreasonable, in the *Wednesbury* sense (see *Associated Provincial Picture Houses Ltd v Wednesbury Corp* [1947] 2 All ER 680, [1948] 1 KB 223).

c        The discretion of the Secretary of State to publish or withhold publication was exercisable in the public interest. The Secretary of State must decide, after taking such advice as he considered appropriate, whether in his view there were public interest grounds for early publication and, if so, whether those grounds were outweighed by public interest grounds in favour of postponing publication. The report had been referred to the SFO and must therefore have raised some suspicions of serious or complex fraud. The Secretary of State decided the report should not be published for the time being because he took the view that early publication would or might inhibit the SFO in its inquiries into fraud and prejudice the fair trial of anyone charged with fraud as a result of the SFO investigation. The exercise by the Secretary of State of his discretion to withhold publication for the time being can only be quashed by the court if the court is satisfied that the Secretary of State acted unlawfully. There are three grounds on which the legality of the minister's decision is attacked.

First, Lonrho submit that the Secretary of State treated himself as bound to follow the advice of the SFO and illegally delegated to the SFO the exercise of a discretion which was vested in the minister and not in the SFO. Lonrho relied on the press release dated 12 September which stated that the minister 'cannot' publish. Lonrho rely also on the remarks of Mr Mallison on 5 October 1988 and the observations of the Secretary of State on 23 November 1988. But the DTI made it clear that, though the Secretary of State attached importance and was entitled to attach importance to the views of the SFO, he was acting independently and confirmed his decision on 25 October only after careful consideration of the arguments advanced by Lonrho and after consulting his own officials and counsel.

Second, Lonrho submit that the decision of the Secretary of State was unlawful because he was or may have been influenced by incorrect advice. For this purpose, Lonrho claimed that on 20 October Mrs Chase asserted wrongly that in the past both investigations and prosecutions had been abandoned because of publicity and that early publication of the report would be bound to cause the SFO to abandon their investigation. But Mrs Chase made it clear that every case must be considered according to its own facts; it was indeed her view that in the particular circumstances of the report on Holdings early publication of the report would be fatal to further investigation and prevent any prosecution being launched but she was entitled to express her own personal view; she had read the report. The written statement furnished by the DTI on 5 October and the letter dated 25 October, however, make it clear that the Secretary of State made his decision because he had formed the view that early publication of the report would 'seriously inhibit' the SFO and 'in all likelihood prejudice a fair trial'. The views of the Secretary of State did not reflect either advice or a belief that the SFO would be bound to abandon their investigation if the report were published before the investigation were finished.

Third, Lonrho submit that the decision of the Secretary of State to withhold early publication was 'perverse' and 'irrational' and was a decision which no reasonable Secretary of State properly advised as to the facts and the law could have reached.

The Director of the SFO swore an affidavit in these proceedings on 16 December 1988 in which he advised that 'to publish the report would be likely to prejudice the *a* investigation' and 'would run the risk of preventing a fair trial'. The Director of the SFO gave reasons for his advice and he was supported by an affidavit which was also sworn on 16 December 1988 by the Director of Public Prosecutions. The Director of the SFO said in his affidavit:

'6. I adhere to the view that publication of the report would run the risk of *b* prejudicing a fair trial. The publicity given to the report might encourage those reading or interpreting it to regard as proved matters which have still to be proved at the criminal trial. This is particularly the case where, as here, the inspectors have been appointed pursuant to statutory powers and their report accordingly has a statutory basis.
7. It is also relevant to have regard to the amount of publicity the report, if *c* published, would receive. In the present case there has already been considerable discussion in the media of the events which are the subject of the report and the topic has aroused considerable public interest. With the publication of the report, this discussion and interest would be considerably fuelled and would increase, particularly where interested parties have ready access to the media and the means thereby to initiate and encourage publicity.' *d*

In these circumstances the attack on the rationality of the decision of the Secretary of State cannot be sustained; even without the evidence of the two directors, it seems to me that the Secretary of State was entitled to take the view that early publication might be prejudicial to the SFO and to a fair trial.

It is true that the Divisional Court took a different view of the effect of early publication but the members of the Divisional Court had not read the report and knew nothing of *e* the investigations of the SFO. The Divisional Court was also confident of the ability of a jury on the instructions of a judge to forget everything they had read and seen before the trial. But the Secretary of State, who had read the report and was advised by the SFO and officials and counsel of the DTI, who had also read the report, was obliged to consider the possible risks stemming from the early publication of this particular report relating to a notorious controversy which was bound to continue between Mr Rowland and the Fayed *f* brothers.

The judgments of the Divisional Court illustrate the danger of judges wrongly though unconsciously substituting their own views for the views of the decision-maker who alone is charged and authorised by Parliament to exercise a discretion. The question is not whether the Secretary of State came to a correct solution or to a conclusion which meets with the approval of the Divisional Court but whether the discretion was properly *g* exercised. The Secretary of State considered the advice he received from the SFO about the effect of early publication and the contrary advice of counsel for Lonrho. The Secretary of State also considered the disadvantages urged by Lonrho of postponing publication. No fault can be found with the decision-making process of the Secretary of State and he was entitled and bound to make up his own mind to publish or postpone *h* publication in the public interest. Any attack on the good faith of the Secretary of State was expressly disclaimed by counsel for Lonrho. The correspondence and memoranda of the negotiations between the DTI and Lonrho show a scrupulous anxiety on the part of the DTI to act fairly and to give proper consideration to the problems posed by the contents of the report.

The appeal in respect of the publication decision therefore fails. *j*

*Effect of negotiations between Lonrho and the Department of Trade and Industry*
A study in chronological order of all the negotiations and correspondence between Lonrho and the DTI discloses that Lonrho sought properly to change the mind of the Secretary of State but improperly to bully the DTI by threats of judicial review, to

intimidate the DTI by insinuations of a political 'cover up' and to obtain and exploit
a observations which, distorted and taken out of context, might lend some support to an
application for judicial review. Judicial review is a protection and not a weapon. The
only effect of Lonrho's conduct is to discourage decision makers from affording oral
interviews. In some cases an oral interview will remove misunderstandings and provide
clarification and new information. In the present case there never was excuse or
justification for a meeting, let alone four meetings, although the DTI was understandably
b anxious to demonstrate its fairness. It was clear from beginning to end that the Secretary
of State intended to publish the report as soon as possible and took the view that the
public interest in early publication of the report was outweighed by the risk that early
publication might hamper or prevent the institution, or prejudice the outcome, of a
criminal prosecution. Lonrho's arguments that early publication would have no adverse
effect and that there were overwhelming public interest reasons in favour of early
c publication could be and were fully set forth and explained in written submissions of
inordinate length to which oral representations added nothing.

*The reference to the Monopolies and Mergers Commission*
d    Before considering the merits of Lonrho's challenge to the decision of the Secretary of
State not to refer the bid by AIT for Fraser to the MMC it is first necessary to consider the
statutory background to the decision.
     The Fair Trading Act 1973 makes provision for a measure of control to be imposed by
government on commercial activity which is considered to be 'against the public interest'.
The 'public interest' is not defined but it is apparent from the long title of the Act, the
e structure of the Act and in particular s 84 of the Act, which sets out the particular matters
which the MMC must take into account when considering the public interest, that the
Act is primarily concerned with the impact of commercial activity on the economy as a
whole including questions of competitiveness, consumer protection and employment. It
is also apparent that whether or not a particular commercial activity is or is not in the
'public interest' is very much a matter of political judgment and the Act is structured to
f bring under direct parliamentary scrutiny any action proposed by the Secretary of State
to interfere with commercial activity which he considers to be against the public interest.
The Secretary of State is only empowered to take action against a merger if the MMC has
advised in a report laid before both Houses of Parliament that the merger is or may be
against the public interest and the Secretary of State must act by a draft order laid before
Parliament in accordance with the provisions of Sch 9 to the Act. These provisions ensure
g that a decision which is essentially political in character will be brought to the attention
of Parliament and subject to scrutiny and challenge therein, and the courts must be
careful not to invade the political field and substitute their own judgment for that of the
minister. The courts judge the lawfulness, not the wisdom, of the decision.
     The bid by AIT for Fraser in March 1985 was a merger to which the Act applied
because the capital value of Fraser exceeded £30m and although the bid was not referred
h to the MMC at that time, it is common ground that the inspectors' report may indicate
the existence of previously undisclosed facts which would give a discretion to the
Secretary of State to refer the merger to the MMC provided he did so within six months
of receiving the report.
     Section 76 of the 1973 Act imposes a duty on the Director General of Fair Trading to
advise the Secretary of State on merger situations. It provides:
j
         'It shall be the duty of the Director—(a) to take all such steps as are reasonably
     practicable for keeping himself informed about actual or prospective arrangements
     or transactions which may constitute or result in the creation of merger situations
     qualifying for investigation, and (b) to make recommendations to the Secretary of
     State as to any action under this Part of this Act which in the opinion of the Director

it would be expedient for the Secretary of State to take in relation to any such arrangements or transactions.'

On 19 August the Secretary of State sent a copy of the inspectors' report to the Director General. On 29 September 1988 a press release from the DTI announced that the Director General was considering whether the report demonstrated the existence of new material facts and that, if so, he would advise the Secretary of State whether to refer the merger to the MMC. In the course of considering what advice he should give the Secretary of State the Director General received submissions from both Lonrho and the Fayed brothers. After considering the inspectors' report and these submissions, the Director General advised the Secretary of State against a reference to the MMC.

On 25 November 1988 the DTI published the following press release announcing the decision of the Secretary of State not to refer the merger to the MMC:

'The Secretary of State for Trade and Industry has decided, in accordance with the advice of the Director General of Fair Trading, not to refer the following merger situations to the Monopolies and Mergers Commission: Acquisition in 1984 and 1985, by Al Fayed Investment and Trust U.K. Plc., of House of Fraser Plc. This decision was made in the light of the report of inspectors appointed under section 432(2) of the Companies Act 1985 to investigate the affairs of House of Fraser Holdings Plc. This report which is not being published for the time being owing to enquiries by the prosecution authorities, indicates the existence of previously undisclosed material facts about the transactions. As a result, the Secretary of State has discretion under the Fair Trading Act 1973 to make a reference to the M.M.C. After considering representations made to him, the advice of the Director General, and the findings of the inspectors' report (in particular on the circumstances surrounding the acquisition of shares in House of Fraser in 1984 and 1985), the Secretary of State has concluded that a reference to the M.M.C. would not be appropriate. However it may be appropriate in due course for other steps to be taken in the light of the inspectors' report.'

Before arriving at this decision the Secretary of State had not only received the inspectors' report and the advice of the Director General but had also had representations made to him on behalf of Lonrho by a legal team and by Mr Rowland personally at meetings with both the Secretary of State himself and with the officials of his department. The Secretary of State must have received a unique amount of advice on the issue of whether or not he should exercise his discretion to refer the matter to the MMC.

Despite the fact that the Secretary of State has acted in accordance with the advice which Parliament has directed that he should receive from the Director General, Lonrho assert that he has acted unlawfully and in breach of his statutory duty under the Act. It is said that in following the advice of the Director General not to refer the bid to the MMC, the Secretary of State has acted so irrationally that his decision should be quashed and that he should be ordered to make a reference. Irrationality is the sole ground on which the Secretary of State's decision was challenged; there is no suggestion that the decision was taken in bad faith or for any improper reason such as a cover-up of political or departmental ineptitude.

The Divisional Court found in Lonrho's favour on this issue because they regarded it as the policy of the Act that there should be a reference to the MMC on the ground that—

'when a merger situation is complicated by factors which are best understood by men rich in experience of the business world, their powers of investigation should be enlisted and their advice invited.'

I cannot accept this interpretation of the Act. The Act vests a discretion in the Secretary of State to decide whether to seek the advice of the MMC, which is one of the three statutory bodies created by the Act to give advice to the Secretary of State. The approach

of the Divisional Court is to convert this discretion into a duty and it also ignores the
a   expertise of the Director General of Fair Trading and his department, who are also rich
in experience of merger situations and under a duty to give advice whether or not to
make a reference to the MMC. If every complicated merger that qualified for a reference
under s 64 and which potentially affected the public interest had to be referred to the
MMC the whole system would break down under the weight of the work. In 1988 260
merger situations were considered in the office of the Director General of which only 11
b   were ultimately referred to the MMC. If all 260 mergers had been referred, the MMC
could not possibly have carried out their statutory duty to investigate and report within
the time limit of six months required by the Act. The Secretary of State must exercise
his discretion to decide which mergers to refer and it is clearly the policy of the Act that
his discretion should be guided, although not fettered, by the advice of the Director
General.

c       The decision in *Padfield v Minister of Agriculture Fisheries and Food* [1968] 1 All ER 694,
[1968] AC 997 was relied on by Lonrho to support two limbs of their argument. First, it
was said to support a construction of the Act that imposed a duty on the Secretary of State
to make a reference to the MMC, and second, the fact that the Secretary of State had
given no reason for his decision not to make a reference was said to lead to the conclusion
that no rational reason existed for his decision. In my view that case does not support
d   either limb of the argument. The decision in *Padfield* turned on the construction of the
Agricultural Marketing Act 1958. The headnote reads ([1968] AC 997 at 997–998):

> 'The Agricultural Marketing Act, 1958, contained (inter alia) provisions relating
> to the milk marketing scheme. By section 19: "(3) A committee of investigation
> shall— . . . (b) be charged with the duty, if the Minister in any case so directs, of
> considering, and reporting to the Minister on . . . any . . . complaint made to the
e   > Minister as to the operation of any scheme which, in the opinion of the Minister,
> could not be considered by a consumers' committee. . . . (6) If a committee of
> investigation report to the Minister that any provision of a scheme or any act or
> omission of a board administering a scheme is contrary to the interests of consumers
> of the regulated products, or is contrary to the interests of any persons affected by
f   > the scheme and is not in the public interest, the Minister, if he thinks fit to do so
> after considering the report—(a) may by order make such amendments in the
> scheme as he considers necessary or expedient for the purpose of rectifying the
> matter; (b) may by order revoke the scheme; (c) in the event of the matter being one
> which it is within the power of the board to rectify, may by order direct the board
> to take such steps to rectify the matter as may be specified in the order. . . ." Under
g   > the scheme, producers had to sell their milk to the Milk Marketing Board, which
> fixed the different prices paid for it in each of the eleven regions into which England
> and Wales were divided. The differentials reflected the varying costs of transporting
> the milk from the producers to the consumers, but they had been fixed several years
> ago, since when transport costs had altered. The South-Eastern Region producers
> contended that the differential between it and the Far-Western Region should be
h   > altered in a way which would incidentally have affected other regions. Since the
> constitution of the board, which consisted largely of members elected by the
> individual regions, made it impossible for the South-Eastern producers to obtain a
> majority for their proposals, they asked the Minister of Agriculture, Fisheries and
> Food to appoint a committee of investigation and when he refused applied to the
> court for an order of mandamus.'

j
The minister gave among his reasons for refusing to appoint a committee of
investigation that the complaint was unsuitable for investigation because it raised 'wide
issues' and the minister owed no duty to producers in any particular region. It was held
that these were bad reasons for refusing to appoint a committee and showed that the
minister had misunderstood the policy and intention of the Act, which was that genuine
and substantial complaints of this nature should be investigated by a committee of

investigation. I can find no parallel between the appointment of a committee to
investigate a specific complaint that individuals are suffering injustice and a reference to *a*
the MMC to enable a wide-ranging inquiry to determine whether a commercial situation
is or may be operating against the public interest. The two situations are entirely different
and the construction placed on the Agricultural Marketing Act 1958 throws no light on
the construction of the Fair Trading Act 1973.

Turning now to the question of reasons, Sir Dingle Foot QC, instructed on behalf of
the minister, submitted in the course of his argument in *Padfield's* case that the minister *b*
can refuse to act on a complaint without giving any reasons and in such a case a
complainant would have no remedy and the decision cannot be questioned. Not
surprisingly this submission was rejected. Lord Pearce said ([1968] 1 All ER 694 at 714,
[1968] AC 997 at 1053–1054):

> 'I do not regard a Minister's failure or refusal to give any reasons as a sufficient *c*
> exclusion of the court's surveillance. If all the prima facie reasons seem to point in
> favour of his taking a certain course to carry out the intentions of Parliament in
> respect of a power which it has given him in that regard, and he gives no reason
> whatever for taking a contrary course, the court may infer that he has no good
> reason and that he is not using the power given by Parliament to carry out its
> intentions. In the present case, however, the Minister has given reasons which show *d*
> that he was not exercising his discretion in accordance with the intentions of the
> Act of 1958.'

See also passages to the like effect in the speeches of Lord Reid, Lord Hodson and Lord
Upjohn ([1968] 1 All ER 694 at 701, 712, 719, [1968] AC 997 at 1032, 1049, 1061).

Although reference was made to the judgment of Sir John Donaldson MR in *R v
Lancashire CC, ex p Huddleston* [1986] 2 All ER 941, in which he referred to the desirability *e*
of proceedings for judicial review being conducted with the cards face up on the table, it
was not submitted to your Lordships that there was any general duty to give reasons for
a decision in all cases, nor was it submitted that this Act imposed a particular duty on the
Secretary of State to give reasons for his refusal to make a reference to the MMC; and it is
not the practice of the Secretary of State to give reasons when he decides not to make a
reference to the MMC. *f*

The absence of reasons for a decision where there is no duty to give them cannot of
itself provide any support for the suggested irrationality of the decision. The only
significance of the absence of reasons is that if all other known facts and circumstances
appear to point overwhelmingly in favour of a different decision, the decision-maker
who has given no reasons cannot complain if the court draws the inference that he had
no rational reason for his decision. *g*

It is difficult to see what useful purpose would have been achieved by a reference to
the MMC other than as a step towards enabling the Secretary of State to exercise his
powers under Sch 8 to order Holdings to divest themselves of their shares in Fraser, in
other words, to take Harrods away from the Fayed brothers, which is, of course, Lonrho's
principal objective in these proceedings. No competition or consumer issues are involved *h*
in the present situation and there is no indication that the particular expertise of the
MMC is required to advise the Secretary of State on any aspect of the public interest. It
can of course be said that it is contrary to the public interest in its widest sense that the
Director General and the Secretary of State should be deceived during the investigation
of a merger and that there is a public interest in pursuing and punishing those who do
so. But on this aspect of the public interest the Secretary of State has already received the *j*
inspectors' report and further public resources are being committed in the investigation
by the SFO and the DPP. The Secretary of State does not need the assistance of the MMC
to clarify these aspects of the public interest about which he is already fully informed.

The measures that the Secretary of State can take under Sch 8 pursuant to a finding by
the MMC that a merger is contrary to the public interest are designed to prevent or

*a*  correct damage to the economy as a consequence of an undesirable merger rather than as punitive measures against individuals. If the Director General and the Secretary of State who has acted on his advice take the view that in present circumstances it is unnecessary to take the power to order Holdings to divest themselves of their shares in Fraser and therefore unnecessary to have a reference to the MMC, I can see nothing irrational in such a decision. If the current investigation should warrant proceedings for serious fraud no doubt the criminal law will take its course. Furthermore, there are extensive powers

*b*  available under the Company Directors Disqualification Act 1986 which would, if circumstances justified it, enable the Fayed brothers to be removed from control of Fraser. Looking at the matter from the point of view of the overall health of the economy, which is the manifest purpose for which the Secretary of State is given his powers under the 1973 Act, I find it impossible to say that it was irrational to decide not to launch the MMC on an inquiry that would cover ground already investigated by the

*c*  inspectors and which is being further investigated by the SFO and the DPP. I agree with the judgments of Dillon and Mustill LJJ, and adopting the language of Dillon LJ, I reach, without hesitation, the conclusion that Lonrho has not made a case that no reasonable Secretary of State could have refused to make a reference to the Monopolies and Mergers Commission.

*d*  For these reasons I would dismiss the appeal against the refusal to make a reference to the MMC and, in consequence, the provisional reference, ordered by the Court of Appeal to preserve the power to make a reference within the six months' time limit pending the hearing of this appeal, becomes void.

*e*  **LORD TEMPLEMAN.** My Lords, I have had the advantage of reading in draft the speech delivered by my noble and learned friend Lord Keith, I agree with it and for the reasons which he gives would dismiss the appeal.

**LORD GRIFFITHS.** My Lords, I have had the opportunity of considering in draft the speech of my noble and learned friend Lord Keith. I agree with it and for the reasons given by him would dismiss the appeal.

*f*  **LORD ACKNER.** My Lords, for the reasons contained in the speech of my noble and learned friend Lord Keith I, too, would dismiss the appeal.

**LORD LOWRY.** My Lords, I have had the advantage of reading in draft the speech of my noble and learned friend Lord Keith.

*g*  I agree with it and, for the reasons which he gives, I too would dismiss the appeal.

*Appeal dismissed.*

Solicitors: *Stephenson Harwood* (for Lonrho); *Herbert Smith* (for Fraser); *Treasury Solicitor.*

Mary Rose Plummer    Barrister.

# Pittalis and another v Grant and another

*a*

COURT OF APPEAL, CIVIL DIVISION
SLADE, NOURSE AND STUART-SMITH LJJ
20, 23 JANUARY, 10 MARCH 1989

*Court of Appeal – Ground of appeal – Point of law not argued in court below – Appeal from* *b*
*county court – Whether appellant entitled to argue new point of law on appeal – County Courts*
*Act 1984, s 77(1).*

*Rent restriction – Subtenancy – Determination of superior tenancy – Business premises – Flat*
*above shop – Subtenancy of flat forming part of property let as business premises – Whether*
*property constituting 'premises' – Whether on determination of superior tenancy of business* *c*
*premises residential subtenancy of part of property continuing to qualify for statutory protection*
*– Rent Act 1977, s 137(3).*

In 1977 the then head lessees granted the first defendant a subtenancy of a flat above a
shop for a term of three years at a rent of £26 per month. The shop itself was let on a
business tenancy. In 1979 the head lessees assigned the headlease to assignees. In 1980 *d*
the subtenancy of the flat expired by effluxion of time but the first defendant and his
wife, the second defendant, continued in occupation of the flat as statutory tenants. On
15 June 1987 the assignees of the headlease surrendered it to the freehold owners, who
shortly afterwards brought an action in the county court against the defendants for
possession of the premises. The question arose whether the defendants continued to be
protected tenants when the headlease was surrendered and the freehold owners became *e*
their landlords, having regard to s 137(3)[a] of the Rent Act 1977, which provided that
where a dwelling house which was subject to a protected tenancy under the 1977 Act
formed 'part of premises' which had been let as a whole on a superior tenancy which was
not a protected tenancy under the Act the dwelling house continued to be subject to the
protected tenancy when the superior tenancy came to an end. The judge held that
s 137(3) applied to the defendants' tenancy of the flat so that the freehold owners were *f*
not entitled to possession and dismissed their claim. The freehold owners appealed to the
Court of Appeal and sought to raise at the hearing of the appeal a point of law not raised
below, namely that the property was not 'premises' within s 137(3) and that, therefore,
s 137(3) did not apply to protect the defendants' tenancy of the flat. Accordingly, the
further question arose whether, contrary to existing authority, the freehold owners were
entitled to appeal from the county court to the Court of Appeal on a point of law which *g*
had not been raised below.

**Held** – (1) The rule of law that an appeal did not lie from the county court to the Court
of Appeal on a point of law not raised below was obsolete and ought no longer to be
followed, since the rule had been established when the only right to appeal from a
decision of the county court was on a point of law. However, that restriction on the right *h*
of appeal, which was the basis for the rule, had been removed by the Supreme Court Act
1981 and a general right of appeal from the county court to the Court of Appeal on both
law and fact was provided for by s 77(1)[b] of the County Courts Act 1984 (see p 632 b to f,
post); *Smith v Baker & Sons* [1891–4] All ER Rep 69 not followed.

(2) For the purposes of s 137(3) of the 1977 Act the word 'premises' referred to
premises which were dwelling houses for the purposes of that Act and, accordingly, *j*
where the headlease which was surrendered was a lease of business premises part of
which was used for residential purposes, the subtenancy of the residential part did not

---

*a* Section 137(3) is set out at p 624 h j, post
*b* Section 77(1) is set out at p 631 h, post

a   form 'part of premises' which had been let as a whole on a superior tenancy to which s 137(3) applied and therefore the residential subtenancy was not protected under s 137(3) when the superior tenancy was surrendered. The appeal would accordingly be allowed and the freehold owners granted possession of the flat (see p 625 g to p 626 c g h and p 632 g, post); *Maunsell v Olins* [1975] 1 All ER 16 applied.

### Notes

b   For appeals from a county court on a question of law only, see 10 Halsbury's Laws (4th edn) para 658, and for cases on the subject, see 13 Digest (Reissue) 510–516, 4230–4271.

For protection under the Rent Acts of a subtenant of premises forming part of a superior letting, see 27 Halsbury's Laws (4th edn) paras 583–585, and for cases on the subject, see 31(2) Digest (Reissue) 1001–1007, 1012–1016, 7984–8019, 8040–8067.

For the Rent Act 1977, s 137, see 23 Halsbury's Statutes (4th edn) 505.

c   For the County Courts Act 1984, s 77, see 11 ibid 473.

### Cases referred to in judgment

*Boyer v Warbey* [1952] 2 All ER 976, [1953] 1 QB 234, CA.
*Cadogan (Earl) v Henthorne* [1956] 3 All ER 851, [1957] 1 WLR 1.
*Clarkson v Musgrave & Sons* (1882) 9 QBD 386, DC.
d   *Cousins v Lombard Deposit Bank* (1876) 1 Ex D 404, DC.
*Davies v Warwick* [1943] 1 All ER 309, [1943] KB 329, CA.
*Firth, Ex p, re Cowburn* (1882) 19 Ch D 419, [1881–5] All ER Rep 987, CA.
*Jackson (Francis) Developments Ltd v Stemp* [1943] 2 All ER 601, CA.
*Jones v Dept of Employment* [1988] 1 All ER 725, [1989] QB 1, [1988] 2 WLR 493, CA.
*Legge v Matthews* [1960] 1 All ER 595, [1960] 2 QB 37, [1960] 2 WLR 620, CA.
e   *Macdougall v Knight* (1889) 14 App Cas 194, HL.
*Maunsell v Olins* [1975] 1 All ER 16, [1975] AC 373, [1974] 3 WLR 835, HL.
*Oscroft v Benabo* [1967] 2 All ER 548, [1967] 1 WLR 1087, CA.
*Rhodes v Liverpool Commercial Investment Co* (1879) 4 CPD 425, DC.
*Seymour v Coulson* (1880) 5 QBD 359, CA.
*Sharrock v London and North Western Rly Co* (1875) 1 CPD 70, CA.
f   *Smith v Baker & Sons* [1891] AC 325, [1891–4] All ER Rep 69, HL.
*Snell v Unity Finance Ltd* [1963] 3 All ER 50, [1964] 2 QB 203, [1963] 3 WLR 559, CA.
*Tasmania (owners) v City of Corinth (owners), The Tasmania* (1890) 15 App Cas 223, HL.
*Whall v Bulman* [1953] 2 All ER 306, [1953] 2 QB 198, [1953] 3 WLR 116, CA.

### Cases also cited

g   *Cow v Casey* [1949] 1 All ER 197, [1949] 1 KB 474, CA.
*Wright v Arnold* [1946] 2 All ER 616, [1947] KB 280, CA.

### Appeal

The plaintiffs, Kyriacos John Pittalis and Erato Pittalis who were the freehold owners of
h   92 High Road, London N2, appealed against the decision of his Honour Judge Goldstone sitting in the Barnet County Court on 2 December 1987 whereby he dismissed their claim for possession of the upper part of 92 High Road (a flat) which was occupied by the defendants, John Forsyth Grant and his wife, as statutory tenants on the ground of a point of law which was not raised below, namely that the property was not 'premises' within s 137(3) of the Rent Act 1977 and that, therefore, s 137(3) did not apply to protect
j   the defendants' tenancy of the flat. The facts are set out in the judgment of the court.

*Philip Engelman* (who did not appear below) for the plaintiffs.
*David J Reade* for the defendants.

*Cur adv vult*

10 March. The following judgment of the court was delivered.

**NOURSE LJ.** This is a Rent Acts case in which the substantive question is whether, on *a* the determination of a superior tenancy, a statutory subtenancy of part of the premises continued to qualify for protection under s 137(3) of the Rent Act 1977: cf *Maunsell v Olins* [1975] 1 All ER 16, [1975] AC 373. The point which is now relied on by the landlords was not raised before the county court judge. And so we must also decide whether it can be raised now: cf *Smith v Baker & Sons* [1891] AC 325, [1891–4] All ER *b* Rep 69.

By a headlease dated 9 December 1882 the dwelling house and shop now known as 92 High Road, East Finchley, London N2 (the property) was demised to the lessee therein named for a term of 99 years from 29 June 1882 at a yearly rent of £10. The headlease contained a lessee's covenant against carrying on or permitting to be carried on the trade or business of a tavern-keeper, innkeeper, victualler or beerhouse-keeper, but no other *c* covenant against user. It did not contain any covenant against assigning, subletting or parting with possession of the property or any part thereof.

By an agreement in writing made on 17 August 1977 the then head lessees, Bartons (Basildon) Ltd, granted to the first defendant, Mr John Forsyth Grant, a subtenancy of the upper part of the property (the flat) for a term of three years from 1 February 1977 at a monthly rent of £26. On 17 May 1979 Bartons assigned the headlease to Porter Nash *d* Ltd, who were still the owners thereof when it expired by effluxion of time on 23 June 1981. It is agreed that the property then included premises (ie the lower part) which were occupied by Porter Nash for the purposes of a business carried on by it, so that the tenancy created by the headlease was subject to the provisions of Pt II of the Landlord and Tenant Act 1954.

Porter Nash duly acquired a new lease of the property under the 1954 Act, but on *e* 15 June 1987 they surrendered it to the freehold owners of the property, the plaintiffs, Mr Kyriacos John Pittalis and Mrs Erato Pittalis. Meanwhile, on 31 January 1980 the subtenancy of the flat had expired by effluxion of time and the first defendant continued in occupation as the statutory tenant thereof. He and his wife are still in occupation. It is agreed that their occupation was protected by the Rent Acts while Porter Nash remained the head lessees of the property. But the effect of the surrender of the headlease was to *f* bring them into a direct relationship with the plaintiffs. The substantive question is whether the effect of s 137(3) of the 1977 Act was to continue the defendants' protection as against the plaintiffs.

On 13 August 1987 the plaintiffs commenced proceedings against the defendants in the Barnet County Court, seeking possession of the flat and mesne profits from the date of the surrender of the headlease. The action came on for trial before his Honour Judge *g* Goldstone, by whom it was dismissed on 27 November 1987. The plaintiffs now appeal to this court.

Section 137(3) of the Rent Act 1977, as amended by the Agricultural Holdings Act 1986, is in these terms:

> 'Where a dwelling-house—(a) forms part of premises which have been let as a *h* whole on a superior tenancy but do not constitute a dwelling-house let on a statutorily protected tenancy; and (b) is itself subject to a protected or statutory tenancy, then, from the coming to an end of the superior tenancy, this Act shall apply in relation to the dwelling-house as if, in lieu of the superior tenancy, there had been separate tenancies of the dwelling-house and of the remainder of the premises, for the like purposes as under the superior tenancy, and at rents equal to *j* the just proportion of the rent under the superior tenancy.
>
> In this subsection "premises" includes, if the sub-tenancy in question is a protected or statutory tenancy to which section 99 of this Act applies, an agricultural holding within the meaning of the Agricultural Holdings Act 1986.'

As to this provision, there has at all times been agreement on two points. First, the
a property, while it was let as a whole under the head lease, did not constitute a dwelling
house let on a statutorily protected tenancy. That was because the tenancy created by the
headlease was one to which Pt II of the 1954 Act applied: see s 24(3) of the 1977 Act.
Second, the flat was itself a dwelling house subject to a statutory tenancy. However, in
the court below it was conceded by counsel who then appeared for the plaintiffs that the
property was 'premises' within the contemplation of s 137(3)(a). His only argument was
b one which was rejected by Judge Goldstone, in our view correctly, as being contrary to
the decision of Hallett J in *Cadogan (Earl) v Henthorne* [1956] 3 All ER 851, [1957] 1 WLR
1, a decision which was approved by this court in *Legge v Matthews* [1960] 1 All ER 595,
[1960] 2 QB 37. The judge therefore had no alternative but to hold that s 137(3) applied
to the flat and to dismiss the plaintiffs' claim for possession accordingly.

Counsel who now appears for the plaintiffs has argued that the property is not
c 'premises' within the contemplation of s 137(3) at all, so that the subsection does not
apply to the flat and does not protect the defendants' occupation of it. He seeks to
withdraw the concession made below and to amend the plaintiffs' notice of appeal
accordingly. It is clear, as counsel for the plaintiffs fully accepts, that he seeks to raise a
question of law which was not raised and submitted to the county court judge at the
trial. Although his ability to do so is, strictly speaking, a preliminary question, the more
d convenient course is to deal first with the substantive question. Once that question has
been identified it will be easier to decide whether it is one which can be raised in this
court or not.

Counsel for the plaintiffs has relied on the decision of the House of Lords in *Maunsell v
Olins* [1975] 1 All ER 16, [1975] AC 373, which was not cited below. That case was
decided on s 18(5) of the Rent Act 1968, which was for all material purposes in identical
e terms to those of s 137(3), except that the last paragraph of the later subsection was not
included. It was held that the 'premises' to which s 18(5) related included any premises
'which, as a matter of fact, applying accepted principles, would be held to be a dwelling-
house for the purposes of the Act' (see [1975] 1 All ER 16 at 24, [1975] AC 373 at 389 per
Lord Wilberforce, with whom the other members of the majority agreed). That case was
concerned with the subtenancy of a cottage on a farm which had been let on an
f agricultural tenancy. The head tenancy having been determined, the freeholder succeeded
in his claim for possession of the cottage against the subtenants on the ground that the
farm was not 'premises' within Lord Wilberforce's test. The effect of that decision in
regard to agricultural holdings has now been reversed by the final paragraph of s 137(3),
but its authority continues in full force and effect in regard to other types of property.

The question then is whether, on 15 June 1987, the property fell within Lord
g Wilberforce's test or not. Counsel in a clear and tenacious argument on behalf of the
defendants contended that the question depended on whether the property was, as a
matter of fact and applying accepted principles, a dwelling house or not. He submitted
that that was a question which was not decided by the judge and could only have been
decided on evidence which was not before him, a submission which is of cardinal
h importance in relation to the plaintiffs' ability to raise the substantive question in this
court.

We do not think that counsel's submission is correct. It ignores the requirement that
the property must be held to be a dwelling house 'for the purposes of the Act'. The
supremacy of that requirement becomes clearer from an earlier passage in Lord
Wilberforce's speech where, after stating the narrowest view of 'premises', he turned to
j the narrower view which he favoured ([1975] 1 All ER 16 at 23–24, [1975] AC 373 at
388–389):

'A less narrow view would be to say that "premises" includes not only dwelling-
houses in the normal popular sense, but premises, which, for the purposes of the
Rent Act 1968, are treated as dwelling-houses. Everybody knows, and the draftsman

must be taken to have known, that protection under the Rent Acts is given not merely to single, identifiable, pure dwelling-houses or dwelling units, but also to *a* units of a mixed character—houses let with a garden or a yard or a garage or a paddock, houses part (even a substantial part) of which is used for business purposes.'

The same point is made in the speeches of Lord Reid and Viscount Dilhorne (see [1975] 1 All ER 16 at 18, 19, [1975] AC 373 at 383, 384). The converse of Lord Wilberforce's last example is business premises, part (even a substantial part) of which is used for *b* residential purposes. That seems to be what we are concerned with here. Admittedly we do not know the precise facts. But what we do know is that on 15 June 1987 the tenancy of the premises was one to which Pt II of the 1954 Act applied. The consequence, under s 24(3) of the 1977 Act, was that it was not a regulated tenancy. It necessarily follows that the property, whatever its actual state may have been, was not to be treated as a dwelling house for the purposes of the 1977 Act and for that reason was not 'premises' within the *c* contemplation of s 137(3).

There is a further objection to counsel's argument for the defendants. Even if the view which we have expressed as to 'premises' were incorrect, he would still have to show that the new notional tenancy of the flat was to be for residential purposes, because otherwise the application of the 1977 Act for which s 137(3) provides would not assist the defendants. Here he encounters the difficulty that the Act is to apply as if there had been *d* separate tenancies of the flat and the lower part of the property 'for the like purposes as under the superior tenancy'. Counsel for the defendants submitted that the word 'purposes' is to be construed distributively, so that you look at the purposes for which each part of the property was used on the material date, it being clear that the flat was then used for residential purposes. That is another submission which we are unable to accept. What have to be regarded are the purposes under the superior tenancy, not the *e* purposes under the subtenancy of the flat nor the use to which it was actually being put. The purposes under the superior tenancy were those under the headlease, which described the property as a dwelling house and shop and, broadly speaking, prohibited it from being used as a public house. And so the purposes under the superior tenancy were partly business and partly residential and it is for those *dual* purposes that the notional separate tenancies of each part of the property would be deemed to be granted if it constituted *f* premises within the contemplation of s 137(3). Counsel would say that that would be a very bizarre result. But it would, we think, be the result of the words which Parliament has used. If, on the other hand, the view which we have expressed as to 'premises' is correct, then everything falls into place and there is nothing bizarre about it at all. Indeed, we think that the real utility of this second point is to confirm the view that 'premises' are limited to premises, which, for the purposes of the 1977 Act, are to be *g* treated as dwelling houses. Authoritative support for the view that the draftsman of the subsection did not have in mind any superior tenancy other than one for residential purposes is to be found in the observations of Lord Reid in *Maunsell v Olins* [1975] 1 All ER 16 at 18, [1975] AC 373 at 382–383.

For these reasons we are of the opinion, first, that the substantive question is a pure *h* question of law which does not depend on evidence as to the actual state of the property at the material date and, second, that if it is open to the plaintiffs to raise it in this court, it ought to be decided in their favour.

The stance which an appellate court should take towards a point not raised at the trial is in general well settled: see *Macdougall v Knight* (1889) 14 App Cas 194 and *Tasmania (owners) v City of Corinth (owners), The Tasmania* (1890) 15 App Cas 223. It is perhaps best *j* stated in *Ex p Firth, re Cowburn* (1882) 19 Ch D 419 at 429, [1881–5] All ER Rep 987 at 991 per Jessel MR:

'... the rule is that, if a point was not taken before the tribunal which hears the evidence, and evidence could have been adduced which by any possibility would

a
prevent the point from succeeding, it cannot be taken afterwards. You are bound to take the point in the first instance, so as to enable the other party to give evidence.'

Even if the point is a pure point of law, the appellate court retains a discretion to exclude it. But where we can be confident, first, that the other party has had opportunity enough to meet it, second, that he has not acted to his detriment on the faith of the earlier omission to raise it and, third, that he can be adequately protected in costs, our usual
b
practice is to allow a pure point of law not raised below to be taken in this court. Otherwise, in the name of doing justice to the other party, we might, through visiting the sins of the adviser on the client, do an injustice to the party who seeks to raise it.

If the present case were governed by the general rule, we would hold that these three requirements were satisfied, so that the plaintiffs should be allowed to raise the substantive question in this court. But ever since the decision of the House of Lords in *Smith v Baker*
c
*& Sons* [1891] AC 325, [1891–4] All ER Rep 69 a special rule has been established in regard to appeals from the county court. It has been held that there is no right of appeal on a question of law, even on a pure question of law, which was not raised and submitted to the county court judge at the trial. Although exceptions have from time to time been allowed, the existence of the rule was recognised in this court as recently as 1987 in a case in which another exception was made: see *Jones v Dept of Employment* [1988] 1 All ER
d
725, [1989] QB 1. But Glidewell LJ said ([1988] 1 All ER 725 at 730, [1989] QB 1 at 14–15):

> '*Smith v Baker & Sons* was of course decided at a time when effectively the only right to appeal from a decision of the county court was on a point of law. Now that the right of appeal from the county court on questions of fact has been substantially extended, the scope of the rule in *Smith v Baker & Sons* may be open to future
e
> consideration.'

Counsel for the plaintiffs would be well content that we should make yet another exception now, if such we can properly do. But encouraged no doubt by the words of Glidewell LJ, he has asked us to reconsider the rule in principle and, if we may, to sweep it away altogether. That has set us on a careful examination of the provisions of successive
f
County Courts Acts, of the authorities which gave rise to the rule and of those which have succeeded it.

It was provided by s 14 of the County Courts Act 1850 that if either party should be dissatisfied with the determination or direction of the court 'in Point of Law, or upon the Admission or Rejection of any Evidence' such party might appeal and, by s 15, that such appeal should be in the form of a case agreed on by both parties and, if they could not
g
agree, that the judge of the county court should settle the case and sign it. In *Sharrock v London and North Western Rly Co* (1875) 1 CPD 70 it was held, perhaps more accurately it was confirmed, by this court that s 14 gave no right of appeal on a question of fact. With the passage of time it was found that the system of appeal by way of special case was unsatisfactory. Accordingly, it was provided by s 6 of the County Courts Act 1875:

h
> 'In any cause, suit, or proceeding, other than a proceeding in bankruptcy, tried or heard in any county court, and in which any person aggrieved has a right of appeal, it shall be lawful for any person aggrieved by the ruling, order, direction, or decision of the judge . . . to appeal against such ruling . . . by motion to the court to which such appeal lies, instead of by special case . . . And at the trial or hearing of any such cause, suit, or proceeding, the judge, at the request of either party, shall make a note
j
> of any question of law raised at such trial or hearing, and of the facts in evidence in relation thereto, and of his decision thereon, and of his decision of the cause, suit, or proceeding . . .'

There was also provision for the note to be signed by the judge. In *Cousins v Lombard Deposit Bank* (1876) 1 Ex D 404 it was held by the Divisional Court of the Exchequer

Division that that section was procedural only, giving an alternative right of appeal; and that it had not extended the substantive right of appeal, which remained an appeal in *a* point of law only.

In that case it was unnecessary to decide what was the effect of that part of s 6 which provided for the making of a note by the judge and it seems that it would have been well arguable, as a matter of construction, that it was not made a condition precedent to the right of appeal that a note should be made. However, in *Rhodes v Liverpool Commercial Investment Co* (1879) 4 CPD 425 it was held by the Divisional Court of the Common Pleas *b* Division that where the judge actually took a note of the evidence, but was not requested to make a note of any question of law raised at the trial and did not do so, no appeal could be brought in relation to such a question. In *Seymour v Coulson* (1880) 5 QBD 359 it was held by this court that it was unnecessary for the request to be made at the trial, if the judge had in fact noted the question of law and the evidence in relation thereto and the note was available to the higher court. That was thought to have thrown some doubt on *c* the authority of *Rhodes v Liverpool Commercial Investment Co*, but in *Clarkson v Musgrave & Sons* (1882) 9 QBD 386 it was held by the Divisional Court of the Queen's Bench Division that that was not so. It was held in terms that it was a condition precedent to the right to appeal under s 6 of the 1875 Act that the question of law on which it was desired to appeal should have been raised before the county court judge at the trial.

Those were the principal decisions under the County Courts Acts 1850 to 1875. *Smith* *d* *v Baker & Sons* [1891] AC 325, [1891–4] All ER Rep 69 was decided under the County Courts Act 1888, s 120 of which was to the same effect as s 6 of the 1875 Act. In that case the decision in *Clarkson v Musgrave & Sons* was expressly approved and thus the rule became firmly established.

At this stage it is helpful to understand how it had come about that the raising of the question of law at the trial was a condition precedent to the right of appeal. The rule *e* cannot, we think, have been rested solely on the language of s 6 which did not express the right of appeal to depend on the making of the judge's note. Rather it was the product of what the judges who decided those cases thought to be a necessary practice, influenced as they no doubt were by the difficulties, not to say injustices, which would or might have arisen if material questions of law were not identified at the only level of *f* decision at which the facts could be found. Remember also that in those days there were no pleadings in the county court and the facts were often found by juries.

The first of these considerations finds expression in many of the judgments in the early cases. In *Rhodes v Liverpool Commercial Investment Co* (1879) 4 CPD 425 the plaintiff, a trustee in bankruptcy, sought to recover a sum which he alleged had been paid to the defendants by the debtor by way of fraudulent preference. Before the county court judge *g* evidence was adduced only on behalf of the plaintiff. The question was whether the facts established by that evidence amounted in law to a fraudulent preference. At the close of the plaintiff's case the defendants did not ask for a nonsuit, but argued the case on the facts. Although the judge made a note of the plaintiff's evidence, he was not requested to make, and he did not make, a note of any question of law. Judgment having been given against the defendants, they appealed, unsuccessfully, on the ground that the facts *h* disclosed in the judge's notes of the evidence did not entitle the plaintiff to a verdict. It was held that that was a question of law which, not having been raised at the trial, could not be raised on appeal. Grove J said that the object of s 6 was—

'to prevent that which would work manifest injustice, viz. persons taking their chance of the decision of the county court judge being in their favour, and afterwards, on finding the decision against them, taking advantage of a mistake in *j* some point of law to which the attention of the judge had never been called.'

(See 4 CPD 425 at 429–430.)

In *Clarkson v Musgrave & Sons* (1882) 9 QBD 386 the plaintiff claimed compensation for injuries under the Employers' Liability Act 1880. The jury found that the accident

occurred through the negligence of the defendants. The judge was requested to take a
note of the evidence, but he was not requested to make a note of any question of law, nor
did the defendants contend at the trial that there was no evidence to go to the jury as to
the question of liability under the 1880 Act. It was held that they could not advance that
contention on appeal. Field J said (at 391):

> 'The object of the provisions of s. 6, is clearly to let the opponent of the party who
> asks for the note to be taken know what the question of law is, and to give him the
> opportunity of meeting it by necessary evidence. The judge must be asked to decide
> the question of law, and it is of great importance that he should be asked to take a
> note of the evidence relating thereto, both in the interest of the opponent, and in
> order that this Court on appeal should have a complete and clear record of what the
> point raised at the trial was, and of the judge's decision upon it.'

Cave J said (at 393):

> 'All the cases, including *Seymour* v. *Coulson*, recognise this at least—that the point
> must be taken at the trial, when it might be cured by evidence, and ought not to be
> taken for the first time on appeal, upon notes sent up to this Court for the purpose
> of raising another and a distinct point of law.'

In *Smith v Baker & Sons* [1891] AC 325, [1891–4] All ER Rep 69 the plaintiff again
claimed compensation under the Employers' Liability Act 1880. At the close of his case
the defendants, relying on the principle volenti non fit injuria, unsuccessfully asked for
a nonsuit. The jury, having then heard the evidence adduced on behalf of the defendants,
found that they had been negligent, that there had been no contributory negligence on
the part of the plaintiff and that he did not voluntarily take a risky employment with a
knowledge of its risks. There was an appeal on the volenti issue to the Divisional Court,
which dismissed it but gave leave for a further appeal to be brought to this court, where
it was allowed on an entirely new ground of law, namely that there had been no evidence
of negligence on the part of the defendants to go to the jury. It was held by the House of
Lords that that question, not having been raised at the trial, could not be raised on appeal.
It is interesting to note that counsel for the plaintiff relied not only on *Clarkson v Musgrave
& Sons*, but also on a submission that the same principle had been applied by the House
to actions in the High Court, for which purpose he referred to *The Tasmania* (1890) 15
App Cas 223 and *Macdougall v Knight* (1889) 14 App Cas 194; at the same time, counsel
for the defendants did not argue that *Clarkson v Musgrave & Sons* was wrongly decided
(see [1891] AC 325 at 329, 331).

Lord Halsbury LC said ([1891] AC 325 at 333, [1891–4] All ER Rep 69 at 73):

> 'My Lords, this was an action originally tried in the county court, and it is very
> important to bear in mind that only a limited appeal is allowed by law in actions so
> tried. There is no power to review the decision of fact arrived at in the country court
> by any other tribunal than the county court itself. A matter of law can be made the
> subject of appeal, but then only when the point has been raised at the trial before
> the learned judge ... My Lords, I think there are good reasons for the enactment
> which has so limited an appeal, and in truth even where written pleadings render
> such precautions as the statute has enforced in the county court less necessary, the
> same precaution has been constantly enforced where applications for a new trial
> have been made in the Superior Courts. It is obvious that it would be unjust to one
> of the parties if the other could lie by and afterwards, having failed on the contention
> that he in fact set up, be permitted to rely on some other point not suggested at the
> trial, but which if it had been suggested might have been answered by evidence: see
> *McDougall v. Knight*.'

Lord Herschell, after saying that he saw no reason to think that the decision in *Clarkson v*

*Musgrave & Sons* was erroneous, continued ([1891] AC 325 at 358, [1891–4] All ER Rep 69 at 86):

a

'It would, in my opinion, be very mischievous if an appeal from a decision of a county court could be sustained on the ground that there was no evidence to go to the jury when that point had not been raised before the county court judge.'

These observations, when read in context, suggest that the primary objective of the founders of the rule was to prevent injustice in a case where, if the point had been raised when it ought to have been, the other side would or might have been able to adduce evidence to answer it. In such a case protection would be given by the general rule. Especially significant is Lord Halsbury LC's reference to *Macdougall v Knight* which, as has been shown, is one of the leading authorities on the general rule. But because none of the early cases was clearly one where the new question was a pure question of law, the judges who decided them did not have to ask themselves whether a distinction ought to have been made in such a case. We do not say positively that it ought to have been. Unless anything could have been made of the words 'and of the facts in evidence in relation thereto' as suggesting that only questions of law which depended on evidence were in view, the distinction was not made by s 6, which was otherwise expressed to apply to all questions of law alike. The more significant point is that the rule in regard to questions of law was established as an adjunct to the implied statutory prohibition against any appeal on a question of fact. The important question which we may have to decide is whether, now that the prohibition has gone, there is any sound basis for the perpetuation of the adjunct.

b

c

d

In none of the many reported decisions since *Smith v Baker & Sons* have we been able to discover that any examination of the origins of the rule was made. Apart from the exceptions which have from time to time been allowed, it has been taken to apply to all questions of law alike, whether they depend on evidence or not. By 1952 it had been clearly recognised that in this respect county court appeals differed from High Court appeals: see *Boyer v Warbey* [1952] 2 All ER 976 at 977, [1953] 1 QB 234 at 239 per Evershed MR. At that time the County Courts Act 1934 was in force, which was in all material respects to the same effect as the 1888 Act. The rule was given renewed vigour by the decision of this court in *Oscroft v Benabo* [1967] 2 All ER 548, [1967] 1 WLR 1087. By that time a limited right of appeal on questions of fact had been given by the County Courts Act 1959, but the possible consequences of that were not considered. Before coming to the more recent legislation, we find it convenient to deal next with the exceptions to the rule which have so far been established and then to consider whether they support a further exception in this case.

e

f

The first exception is where the county court has acted without jurisdiction, for example by making an order for possession of premises which are protected by the Rent Acts (see e g *Davies v Warwick* [1943] 1 All ER 309 at 313, [1943] KB 329 at 336 per Goddard LJ and *Francis Jackson Developments Ltd v Stemp* [1943] 2 All ER 601 at 602–603) or by making an order on a false hypothesis of fact (see *Whall v Bulman* [1953] 2 All ER 306, [1953] 2 QB 198, as explained by Diplock LJ in *Oscroft v Benabo* [1967] 2 All ER 548 at 556, [1967] 1 WLR 1087 at 1099). The second is where the county court has enforced an illegal contract: see *Snell v Unity Finance Ltd* [1963] 3 All ER 50, [1964] 2 QB 203. The third is where the plaintiff's proceedings are liable to be struck out as disclosing no cause of action: see *Jones v Dept of Employment* [1988] 1 All ER 725, [1989] QB 1. In that case Glidewell LJ was of the opinion that the question was in any event one of jurisdiction (see [1988] 1 All ER 725 at 731, [1989] QB 1 at 15).

g

h

Counsel for the plaintiffs has submitted that here we have another case in which the county court judge has acted without jurisdiction. He said that the judge had refused to make an order for possession when he ought to have done so. But we agree with counsel for the defendants in thinking that that is not a matter of jurisdiction at all. It is altogether different from a case where, without the power to make it, an order for

j

possession is made. It is a case where the judge has acted (through no fault of his own) on
a a mistaken view of the law. That distinction was made very clear by Diplock LJ in *Oscroft
v Benabo* [1967] 2 All ER 548 at 557, [1967] 1 WLR 1087 at 110 where, after observing
that a court may, among other examples, lack jurisdiction to make the kind of order
made, eg an order for possession of premises protected by the Rent Acts, he continued:

> 'A mere error of law, however, made by a county court judge on an application
b of a kind which he is entitled to entertain between parties between whom he is
> entitled to adjudicate, resulting in an order of a kind which he is entitled to make,
> does not affect his "jurisdiction" to make the order. It is an erroneous determination
> in point of law . . .'

Then it was said that, as in *Whall v Bulman*, the judge had been asked to decide the case
on the false hypothesis that the property was 'premises' within the contemplation of
c s 137(3) of the 1977 Act. But that was a false hypothesis not of fact but of law and, as
Diplock LJ pointed out, that makes all the difference (see [1967] 2 All ER 548 at 557,
[1967] 1 WLR 1087 at 1101).

For these reasons, we are of the opinion that the present case does not fall within any
of the established exceptions to the rule, which perhaps can be loosely described as being
d restricted to illegality and lack of jurisdiction or the next best thing. If the rule is to be
upheld, we are bound by authority to hold that the present case is within it. And so
everything depends on whether we ought to accede to the broader submission that, the
substratum having gone, there is nothing left to uphold it.

We turn then to the County Courts Act 1959. Section 107 contained a general
provision to the effect that no judgment or order of a county court, nor any proceedings
therein, sould be removed by appeal, motion, certiorari or otherwise into any other court,
e except in accordance with the 1959 Act. Section 108 retained the pre-existing right of
appeal to this court on questions of law. Section 109(1) introduced, for the first time, a
right of appeal to this court on questions of fact in the proceedings mentioned in sub-s
(2), eg certain actions founded on contract or tort, or for money recoverable by statute,
and certain actions for the recovery of land. Section 110(1) introduced a right of appeal
f to this court on questions of fact in admiralty proceedings. Section 112 retained the
provisions as to the judge's note on appeal in much the same form as they had taken in
ss 120 and 121 of the 1888 Act and then in s 108 of the 1934 Act.

By the Supreme Court Act 1981, ss 107, 109 and 110(1) of the 1959 Act were repealed
and s 108 was amended so as to give a general right of appeal on both law and fact,
subject to the leave either of the county court judge or of this court in certain classes of
g proceedings from time to time prescribed by order made by the Lord Chancellor. Section
112 was also amended in minor respects. The amended s 108 has now been re-enacted as
s 77 of the County Courts Act 1984, sub-s (1) of which is in these terms:

> 'Subject to the provisions of this section and the following provisions of this Part
> of this Act, if any party to any proceedings in a county court is dissatisfied with the
> determination of the judge or jury, he may appeal from it to the Court of Appeal in
h such manner and subject to such conditions as may be provided by the rules of the
> Supreme Court.'

The amended s 112 has now been re-enacted as s 80 of the 1984 Act, which is in these
terms:

> '(1) At the hearing of any proceedings in a county court in which there is a right
j of appeal [or from which an appeal may be brought with leave], the judge shall, at
> the request of any party, make a note—(a) of any question of law raised at the
> hearing; and (b) of the facts in evidence in relation [to any such question]; and (c) of
> his decision [on any such question] and of his determination of the proceedings.
> (2) Where such a note has been taken, the judge shall (whether notice of appeal

has been served or not), on the application of any party to the proceedings, and on payment by that party of such fee as may be prescribed by the fees orders, furnish *a* him with a copy of the note, and shall sign the copy, and the copy so signed shall be used at the hearing of the appeal.'

The words in square brackets show the minor amendments which had been made by the 1981 Act.

The broad effect of ss 77 and 80 of the 1984 Act is this. A party to proceedings in the *b* county court may appeal on law or on fact or on both. Although leave is required in certain classes of proceedings, no distinction is for that purpose made between questions of law and questions of fact. In relation to questions of law, the county court judge is still required, on request, to make the note which he has been required to make ever since the enactment of s 6 of the 1875 Act. Although there is now an equal right of appeal on questions of fact, the judge is not required to make a note of any question of fact raised *c* at the hearing. That may be no more than an oddity or it may suggest that s 80 is now an outdated survival from more primitive times. Certainly it would seem that the provisions now embodied in that section have in practice been overtaken by the modern developments in pleading in the courty court, by the virtual disappearance of juries there and by the judge's inherent duty to make a note of the proceedings coupled with the provisions of RSC Ord 59, r 19(4). None of us has ever known of a case where the parties *d* have made a formal request to the judge, either at the hearing or afterwards, pursuant to s 80 or its predecessors.

We would therefore think that, even without the equal right of appeal on questions of fact, s 80, the representative of s 6 of the 1875 Act, had become an unsure foundation for the rule in *Smith v Baker & Sons*. But when account is taken of the ability of this court now to overturn the county court on fact as much as on law, there is seen to be no *e* foundation for the rule at all. The statutory prohibition as an adjunct to which it was established has gone. There is no longer any good ground for a distinction between county court and High Court appeals and the general rule should apply to both.

For these reasons we hold that the rule in *Smith v Baker & Sons* ought no longer to be applied. We are conscious that it may seem a strong thing for this court to hold thus of a rule established by the House of Lords, albeit one enfeebled by exceptions, the statutory *f* support which gave it life at last turned off. But, where it can see that the decision of the higher court has become obsolete, the lower court, if it is not to deny justice to the parties in the suit, is bound to say so and to act accordingly.

We allow the substantive question to be raised in this court and we decide it in favour of the plaintiffs. We therefore allow the appeal and, subject to submissions as to the date when it should take effect, we will make an order for possession of the flat. *g*

*Appeal allowed. Leave to appeal to the House of Lords refused.*

Solicitors: *Simon Wakefield & Co* (for the plaintiffs); *Henry Wimborne* (for the defendants).

Celia Fox    Barrister.

a          # E F Hutton & Co (London) Ltd v Mofarrij

COURT OF APPEAL, CIVIL DIVISION
KERR LJ AND EWBANK J
21 FEBRUARY 1989

b    *Practice – Service out of the jurisdiction – Action to enforce, rescind, dissolve, annul or otherwise affect a contract – Otherwise affect – Claim under foreign contract – Claim on dishonoured Greek cheque given as security for indebtedness incurred under English brokerage contract – Whether claim in respect of Greek cheque directly 'affecting' contract governed by English law – Whether good arguable case that rules for service out of jurisdiction complied with – RSC Ord 11, r 1(1)(d)(iii).*

c
As part of a brokerage contract governed by English law made between the plaintiffs, an English company, and the defendant, a foreign commodity trader trading in Athens and elsewhere, the parties agreed that the defendant would provide security by a bank guarantee for any indebtedness he incurred under the brokerage contract. Pending the issue of the guarantee the defendant drew a cheque in Greece on a Greek bank for
d    $US300,000 payable to the plaintiffs in Greece and delivered it to their representative there as security. It was an implied term of the brokerage contract that the plaintiffs would not present the cheque for payment unless the defendant's indebtedness under the contract exceeded $US300,000 and conversely that the defendant's liability under the brokerage contract would immediately and directly be reduced pro tanto on payment of the cheque. The defendant's account under the brokerage contract went into deficit in
e    excess of $US300,000 and the plaintiffs presented the Greek cheque for payment in Greece but the cheque was dishonoured. The plaintiffs brought proceedings in England against the defendant claiming damages for breach of the brokerage contract and were given leave to serve the writ on the defendant outside the jurisdiction under RSC Ord 11, r 1(1)(d)(iii)[a], which provided for service out of the jurisdiction where the claim was brought to 'enforce . . . or otherwise affect . . . a contract . . . governed by English law'.
f    Later the plaintiffs obtained leave to amend the writ to claim in addition damages for breach of the contract arising on the Greek cheque and to serve the amended writ outside the jurisdiction. The defendant appealed against those orders, contending that there was no jurisdiction either to amend the writ, because the claim on the Greek cheque, being a claim on a foreign contract, did not fall within Ord 11, r 1(1)(d)(iii), or to serve the amended writ outside the jurisdiction even if the claim on the cheque consequentially
g    'affected' the English brokerage contract. The plaintiffs contended that the claim on the Greek cheque had been brought to enforce or 'otherwise affect' the brokerage contract, alternatively that the dishonouring of the Greek cheque also constituted a breach of the English brokerage contract or, in the further alternative, that even if the claim on the Greek cheque did not clearly 'affect' the brokerage contract within r 1(1)(d)(iii) there was a good arguable case that it did so sufficiently to confer jurisdiction to serve the amended
h    writ out of the jurisdiction.

**Held** – The defendant's obligations under the English brokerage contract had been directly affected by his breach of the Greek cheque contract since if the Greek cheque had not been dishonoured the amount due from the defendant under the brokerage contract would have been immediately and directly reduced by $US300,000. It followed that the
j    claim on the Greek cheque contract was brought to 'otherwise affect' the English brokerage contract within RSC Ord 11, r 1(1)(d)(iii). Alternatively, the claim brought on the Greek cheque 'otherwise affected' the English brokerage contract because the breach

---

a    Rule 1(1), so far as material, is set out at p 637 e f, post

of the cheque contract had also been a breach of the brokerage contract and, furthermore, the defendant's promise to honour the cheque had formed part of his consideration *a* under the brokerage contract for the plaintiffs' obligations thereunder. It followed that the claim on the Greek cheque had been a proper claim for which to give leave to amend the writ and leave under Ord 11, r 1(1)(d)(iii) to serve the amended writ out of the jurisdiction (see p 638 *a b g* to p 639 *b* and p 640 *d* to *f*, post).

BP Exploration Co (Libya) Ltd v Hunt [1976] 3 All ER 879 applied.

Per Kerr LJ. A plaintiff can only rely on having a good arguable case for serving process *b* outside the jurisdiction under Ord 11 where the issue whether there should be leave to serve out of the jurisdiction leaves room for further investigation of questions of fact or mixed fact and law. Where the test of a good arguable case for service out of the jurisdiction does fall to be applied, because a decision on the issue whether leave should be granted under Ord 11 cannot be decided on the affidavit material then available to the court, the appropriate test is whether it appears to the court on that material that the *c* plaintiff has a good arguable case in regard to all the relevant issues, including those which may not need to be further investigated at the trial (see p 639 *e f j* to p 640 *a*, post); dicta of Lord Porter in Tyne Improvement Comrs v Armement Anversois SA, The Brabo [1949] 1 All ER 294 at 299 and of Parker LJ in Islamic Arab Insurance Co v Saudi Egyptian American Reinsurance Co [1987] 1 Lloyd's Rep 315 at 317 considered.

*d*

### Notes

For service of a writ out of the jurisdiction in respect of a claim in contract, see 37 Halsbury's Laws (4th edn) para 178, and for cases on the subject, see 37(2) Digest (Reissue) 285–301, 1831–1911.

*e*

### Cases referred to in judgments

BP Exploration Co (Libya) Ltd v Hunt [1976] 3 All ER 879, [1976] 1 WLR 788.
Hagen, The [1908] P 189, [1908–10] All ER Rep 21, CA.
Islamic Arab Insurance Co v Saudi Egyptian American Reinsurance Co [1987] 1 Lloyd's Rep 315, CA. *f*
Nova (Jersey) Knit Ltd v Kammgarn Spinnerei GmbH [1977] 2 All ER 463, [1977] 1 WLR 713, HL.
Spiliada Maritime Corp v Cansulex Ltd, The Spiliada [1986] 3 All ER 843, [1987] AC 460, [1986] 3 WLR 972, HL.
Tyne Improvement Comrs v Armement Anversois SA, The Brabo [1949] 1 All ER 294, [1949] AC 326, HL.
*g*
Vitkovice Horni a Hutni Tezirstvo v Korner [1951] 2 All ER 334, [1951] AC 869, HL.

### Application for leave to appeal

The defendant, Abdul Ghani Mofarrij, applied for leave to appeal against the order of Hirst J made on 20 May 1988 giving the plaintiffs, E F Hutton & Co (London) Ltd, leave *h* to amend their writ of summons and points of claim indorsed thereon to claim against the defendant damages for breach of a Greek cheque contract, as well as damages under an English brokerage contract, and leave to serve the amended writ and points of claim outside the jurisdiction under RSC Ord 11, r 1(1). On 14 October 1988 Kerr LJ adjourned the defendant's ex parte application for leave to appeal for hearing by the full court. The grounds of the appeal were that the judge did not have jurisdiction either to amend the *j* writ and points of claim or to give leave to serve them out of the jurisdiction because the new cause of action on the Greek cheque was not one in respect of which process could be served out of the jurisdiction, since the cheque, which was drawn in Greece on a Greek bank, created obligations subject to Greek law which were performable in Greece and the cheque, if dishonoured, had been dishonoured in Greece, and thus the contract *a* arising from the Greek cheque was a foreign contract. The facts are set out in the judgment of Kerr LJ.

*Timothy Young* for the defendant.
*Jonathan Gaisman* for the plaintiffs.

**KERR LJ.** Having just reminded ourselves that this is an application for leave to appeal
*b* by the defendant, we think that in the light of the submissions we should give him leave to appeal, and we now give judgment on the appeal.

This arises from a decision of Hirst J under RSC Ord 11 in the Commercial Court on 20 May 1988. He had before him a claim on an English commodity contract against the defendant, who is resident in Greece or Saudi Arabia or both. Leave to serve him abroad on account of a breach of that English contract had previously been granted ex parte by
*c* Staughton J and the writ had been served.

The plaintiffs were minded to proceed under Ord 14 for summary judgment. However, in circumstances which I shall mention in a moment in the context of that contract, the defendant had also given them a Greek cheque by way of security which had been presented and dishonoured by him. Hirst J was faced with an application by the plaintiffs to amend their statement of claim by relying on the dishonour of the
*d* cheque as well as on the breach of the English contract. They asked for leave to re-serve the amended statement of claim on the defendant by relying on the cheque as well. Hirst J granted leave almost as a matter of course without giving elaborate reasons. He said:

*e* 'I consider this to be a perfectly proper case for leave to serve out of the jurisdiction. I therefore give leave to serve out pursuant to RSC Ord 11. I also think that this is a perfectly proper case for leave to amend the Writ.'

However, it is common ground that Hirst J was not referred to the cheque which he permitted the plaintiffs to introduce into these proceedings in this manner. As I have already indicated, the cheque was Greek. If he had known that, I think that he would
*f* have appreciated that the position is considerably more complex than he thought. I say all that by way of background to this appeal, which now raises a novel point on Ord 11.

The plaintiffs are a well-known firm of commodity brokers in London. They are or were owned by an associated company with the same or a similar name in New York. We are concerned with E F Hutton & Co (London) Ltd.

The defendant was, and may still be, a commodity trader trading in Saudi Arabia and
*g* Athens. Through a Mr Badran, a representative of the plaintiffs, he entered into agreements for the opening of commodity accounts, which have been called brokerage contracts, for sugar in London and New York and grain in Chicago, the latter two being concluded with the American company. We are concerned with a sugar contract in London. This was opened by the plaintiffs in favour of the defendant through Mr Badran.

*h* The contract was dated 14 April 1986. It contained in cl 6, among other terms, the following provision: '. . . All monies which the undersigned owes to you at any time shall be repayable to you at your principal office in London.' Quite apart from that provision, it has never been contested that the brokerage contract was governed by English law. For present purposes I shall therefore refer to it as 'the English brokerage contract'.

*j* Under the umbrella and as part and parcel of the English brokerage contract it was also agreed that there should be security for any indebtedness by the defendant under the contract. Such indebtedness could of course take the form of a deficit on the account or of a liability for margin or interest.

Pending the issue of a bank guarantee which never materialised, the agreement was that the defendant would deliver a cheque to the plaintiffs for $US300,000. This was obviously subject to the implied condition that the plaintiffs would have no right to present the cheque unless and until such indebtedness under the English brokerage contract should arise. The reasons for handing over the cheque, which happened in Greece, are set out in the affidavits without any substantial difference between the parties. The defendant deposed as follows:

'I said, however [this was to Mr Badran, who had come to see the defendant in Athens], that the cheque should not be presented without proper notice because I did not keep sums of that order in that account which was a current account. He reassured me that there was no question of presenting it and that it was only security to file with E. F. Hutton until I provided my guarantee, which would in due course be finalised for US$300,000 but about which there was no particular urgency.'

On behalf of the plaintiffs Mr Bacon, the solicitor dealing with this matter, said the following:

'In my first affidavit I state the fact, as is the case, that the cheque the subject matter of the amended writ was delivered to the plaintiffs for any deficit in the defendant's account with the plaintiffs. It has been confirmed to me by Mr Badran that the obtaining of the cheque from the defendant was and was understood by the defendant to be a condition of the operation of the defendant's account with the plaintiffs.'

One then comes to the cheque itself. It was dated 30 April 1986 for $US300,000 and stated to have been issued at Athens. It was made payable to the order of the plaintiffs, E F Hutton (London) Ltd and drawn on the branch at Citibank in Athens. It provided on the front: 'THIS CHECK IS PAYABLE IN GREECE BYSIGHT DRAFT IN NEW YORK FUNDS.'

The plaintiffs claim that the defendant's account went into deficit in excess of $US300,000. It remains to be seen whether, and if so on what grounds, it is disputed that they became entitled to present the cheque. But it is not disputed that the plaintiffs have at least a good arguable case on that. The cheque was duly presented in Athens for payment but was dishonoured. On 8 October 1986 notice of dishonour was duly given to the defendant both in Saudi Arabia and Athens.

As I mentioned at the beginning, the plaintiffs' original claim against the defendant was based solely on the English brokerage contract. They closed out the defendant's open position after the cheque had been dishonoured and are now claiming over $US420,000 by way of debt or damages. That was the claim in the original writ for which they had obtained leave to serve out under Ord 11. When Hirst J granted leave to add a claim on the cheque he was almost certainly unaware that it was a Greek cheque in all respects. We now know that it was drawn in Greece on a Greek bank, payable in Greece and had been delivered to a representative of the plaintiffs in Athens. What is now said is that leave should not have been given to amend the writ and to re-serve it on the defendant. There is no challenge to the exercise by Hirst J of his discretion in this matter. Or, perhaps more accurately, it is not contested that if a claim on the cheque could properly be brought within the ambit of Ord 11, then it is not denied that it would be proper for this court, now that it knows the full facts, to exercise the discretion to permit re-service under Ord 11. Indeed, it would be surprising if this were not so. Given that the underlying, or umbrella, contract is clearly the English brokerage contract, which clearly falls within Ord 11 on the ground that it is governed by English law and that it has been broken here, the transaction as a whole is manifestly within the spirit of Ord 11. No doubt that is what led Hirst J to say what he did.

However, it is of course also trite law that there can be no leave to amend a writ which has been served out of the jurisdiction by the addition of a cause of action which does not qualify under Ord 11. Accordingly, the writ and statement of claim could only be permitted to be amended in this case if the claim on the cheque can also be brought within Ord 11. Everything depends on that.

When the matter came before Hirst J, there was a defect in the supporting affidavit on
a behalf of the plaintiffs because the deponent did not identify the provision of Ord 11 on
which he relied, as he should have done. That has now been rectified and nothing turns
on it. What we are concerned with is the question whether or not there is any provision
of Ord 11, or any other principle, which covers the inclusion of the claim on the cheque.

We were referred to the well-known rules applicable to Ord 11, which are collected in
*The Supreme Court Practice 1988* vol 1, para 11/1/6 under the heading 'Principles upon
b which leave to serve outside the jurisdiction is granted'. Principle 1 contains the following
statements:

> 'The applicant for leave must show that his case falls clearly within one or other
> of the sub-paragraphs of r. 1(1) or (2). In the application of this principle . . . (c) any
> ambiguity in the constructon of the rules will be resolved in favour of the foreigner
> . . .'

c

and there is a reference to *The Hagen* [1908] P 189, [1908–10] All ER Rep 21. There is
also a sweeping up note at the end: 'The degree of proof of compliance with these
requirements is, generally speaking, that of "a good arguable case".'

The well-known authorities cited are *Vitkovice Horni a Hutni Teẑirstvo v Korner* [1951]
d 2 All ER 334, [1951] AC 869 and *Tyne Improvement Comrs v Armement Anversois SA, The
Brabo* [1949] 1 All ER 294, [1949] AC 326.

That is the background. The first and main way in which counsel for the plaintiffs
puts this matter is by relying on Ord 11, r 1(1)(*d*)(iii) in certain respects. Paragraph (iii)
refers to contracts which are by their terms, or by implication, governed by English law.
In the present case that is certainly true of the English brokerage contract. Leaving out
most of the immaterial words, the plaintiffs therefore submit that the case falls within
e r 1(1)(*d*)(iii) on the following basis. They rely on the words in r 1(1)(*d*):

> '. . . service of a writ out of the jurisdiction is permissible with the leave of the
> Court if in the action begun by the writ . . . (*d*) the claim is brought to enforce,
> rescind, dissolve, annul or otherwise affect a contract, or to . . . obtain other relief in
> respect of the breach of a contract, being . . . a contract which . . . (iii) is by its terms,
f > or by implication, governed by English law . . .'

Although I have read most of that provision to set the context, the important words
are that the action is begun by a writ in which a claim is brought to affect a contract
governed by English law. What the plaintiffs submit is that the claim on the cheque is a
claim which affects the English brokerage contract. Counsel for the defendant strongly
challenges that. He points out that the contract contained in and evidenced by the
g cheque, to which I will refer as 'the cheque contract', is separate and distinct from the
English brokerage contract. And so it manifestly is. He accepts that there is no authority
which precludes the construction on which the plaintiffs rely. But he submits that there
has never been a case, and certainly we have not been referred to any, in which a claim
was brought on one contract, a foreign contract, which, viewed in isolation, could not
h have been the subject of leave to serve out of the jurisdiction under Ord 11, where that
claim affects an English contract. He submits that to allow such a claim to proceed under
Ord 11 would open what he referred to as 'Pandora's box', and I think he mentioned the
floodgates in the same breath. He points out by reference, for instance, to *Nova (Jersey)
Knit Ltd v Kammgarn Spinnerei GmbH* [1977] 2 All ER 463, [1977] 1 WLR 713 that a bill
of exchange given as security is independent from the underlying contract. He referred
j in particular to the remarks of Lord Russell which stressed that in an action on a bill of
exchange a breach of the underlying contract for which the bill was given cannot be
invoked as a set-off (see [1977] 2 All ER 463 at 479, [1977] 1 WLR 713 at 732). That is
perfectly true. But it is always open to the court to examine the circumstances in which
a bill of exchange was given and these may well raise a defence.

Take the present case as an illustration. As I have already said, it was clearly a term of

the English brokerage contract that the plaintiffs would have no right to present this
cheque for payment unless an indebtedness exceeding $US300,000, the amount of the  *a*
cheque, had arisen under that contract. If it had been presented prematurely a claim on
the cheque could have been resisted. Conversely, payment of the cheque would
immediately and directly reduce the defendant's liability pro tanto under the English
brokerage contract. In my view it is that feature, that direct link between the cheque and
the English brokerage contract, which entitles the court to hold that the claim on the
cheque is one which affects a contract governed by English law and which is, accordingly,  *b*
within Ord 11, r 1(1)(*d*)(iii).

In *BP Exploration Co (Libya) Ltd v Hunt* [1976] 3 All ER 879 at 885, [1976] 1 WLR 788
at 795, I considered the meaning of the words 'otherwise affect' and said that those words
were almost as wide as they could be. That decision was recently mentioned with
approval by Lord Goff in *Spiliada Maritime Corp v Cansulex Ltd, The Spiliada* [1986] 3 All
ER 843 at 859, [1987] AC 460 at 481. It is, of course, perfectly true that in *BP Exploration*  *c*
*Co (Libya) Ltd v Hunt* only one contract was under consideration. As I have said, I know of
no case in which the present issue has arisen in the context of more than one contract in
the sense that the claim which is said to affect an English contract is a claim under a
foreign contract, albeit between the same parties. Counsel for the defendant therefore
says with considerable force that it would indeed be opening Pandora's box if a plaintiff
could use these provisions of Ord 11 for the purpose of bringing a clearly foreign claim  *d*
within the jurisdiction on the ground that it has some consequence for, or repercussion
on, and in that sense affects, an English contract for which leave to serve out of the
jurisdiction would be granted. I accept that. One could take two examples which were
mentioned in the course of argument. First, suppose that an English company has two
contracts with a contractor. The first is a foreign contract for some prefabrication which
is entirely outside Ord 11. The second is a construction contract to be performed in this  *e*
country by means of the materials to be prefabricated abroad under the foreign contract.
Suppose that there is then a breach of the foreign contract. I quite agree that it could not
possibly be right that the company could obtain leave to serve abroad a claim under the
foreign prefabrication contract merely on the ground that its breach has had some
consequences for, or repercussions on, the due performance of the English contract.
Similarly, if a plaintiff alleges that the defendant has committed a tort abroad which has  *f*
had consequences on an English contract between the parties to be performed in this
country, I would not for one moment accept that leave to serve the defendant out of the
jurisdiction for the commission of the tort would be permissible under Ord 11,
r 1(1)(*d*)(iii).

But the position in the present case is different, not only because the plaintiffs' claims  *g*
fall manifestly within the spirit of Ord 11. The claim on the cheque affects the English
brokerage contract directly and not merely consequentially. The obligations under that
contract are directly affected by the performance or breach of the cheque contract. If the
cheque had been honoured then the amount alleged to be due under the brokerage
contract would immediately and directly have been reduced from $US420,000 to
$US120,000. That would not be a case of some indirect consequence or repercussion. It  *h*
would be the direct effect of the defendant meeting his obligations under the cheque.
On that basis, I consider that the present case can be brought within the words 'otherwise
affect a contract governed by English law'.

There is another way in which the plaintiffs' contention can be put on which their
counsel relied in the alternative. It leads to the same conclusion and is another facet of
the same point. Since the cheque was given as part and parcel of the English brokerage  *j*
contract and as security for the performance by the defendant of his obligations under it,
it must have been an implied term of the brokerage contract that the cheque would be
honoured if it was properly presented. The promise to honour the cheque, if it became
due to be paid because of the situation under the brokerage contract, must have formed
part of the consideration given by the defendant for the plaintiffs' obligations under the

brokerage contract. In addition to being a breach of the cheque contract in Greece, the
*a* dishonour of the cheque in such circumstances must also have been a breach of the
brokerage contract in England. In a sense that is no more than putting the contention
based on the words 'otherwise affects' in a different and simpler way.

There were other submissions made by counsel for the plaintiffs which I do not accept.
He also relied on the subsequent words 'or to obtain other relief in respect of the breach
of a contract' with reference to the English brokerage contract. But that adds nothing to
*b* the second way of putting the plaintiffs' contention, viz that the dishonour of the cheque
was itself breach of the brokerage contract as well as of the cheque contract.

For the same reasons, I do not think that counsel for the plaintiffs gains anything by
relying on Ord 11, r 1(1)(e). This refers to claims—

> *c* 'brought in respect of a breach committed within the jurisdiction of a contract
> made within or out of the jurisdiction, and irrespective of the fact ... that the
> breach was preceded or accompanied by a breach committed out of the jurisidiction
> ...'

The history and wording of that provision show that the breaches in question must have
been breaches of the same contract. It therefore adds nothing to the second way discussed
above.
*d*    In the alternative counsel submitted that the cheque contract was also governed by
English law. He pointed out that he was able to escape from the provisions of s 72 of the
Bills of Exchange Act 1882 because everything concerning the cheque had happened in
Greece and therefore did not fall within its conflict of law provisions. But I do not accept
that. Viewed in isolation the cheque contract was clearly governed by Greek law.

Finally, counsel submitted that even if he was not clearly right on the effect of the
*e* words 'or otherwise affects', with which I dealt first, nevertheless he had 'a good arguable
case' that he was right, and that was sufficient. This submission raises a point of some
general importance and I should make it clear that I would equally not accept it. It seems
to me that a plaintiff can rely on the concept or test of a good arguable case only in
situations which leave room for further investigation of issues of fact or of mixed fact
and law as to whether or not some requirement of Ord 11 is satisfied. That appears to
*f* have been the view of Lord Porter in *The Brabo* [1949] 1 All ER 294 at 299, [1949] AC
326 at 341 and also of Parker LJ in *Islamic Arab Insurance Co v Saudi Egyptian American
Reinsurance Co* [1987] 1 Lloyd's Rep 315 at 317, where he said:

> *g* 'The question is whether the plaintiffs have a good arguable case that English law
> is the proper law. If they have, then there is jurisdiction to give leave. It may well
> be that there is also a good arguable case for some other law being the proper law
> and that, if the action goes forward, that case will prevail at the trial. That is not to
> the point, at all events unless it is clear that the question of proper law cannot be
> further illuminated at the trial. In the present case it clearly can.'

In the case before us, however, it clearly cannot. We are faced with a succinct problem
*h* concerning the correct construction and application of provisions of Ord 11 to a succinct
situation, the terms of the English brokerage contract to be considered in combination
with the cheque contract. Although the answer may not be simple, that is a situation
which cannot realistically involve or require any further investigation. It follows in my
view that it will not do for the plaintiffs to say that even if they cannot bring themselves
within both the letter and spirit of Ord 11, they nevertheless have a good arguable case.
*j* They are either right or wrong and the court must decide the issue here and now even if
it is difficult, as in *The Brabo* and *BP Exploration Co (Libya) Ltd v Hunt* [1976] 3 All ER 879,
[1976] 1 WLR 788.

For the sake of completeness I would only add this. In situations where the test of a
good arguable case on the part of the plaintiff falls to be applied, because a decision on
the issue cannot be taken further on the material available at the stage of the application

under Ord 11, this test applies both to issues which will or may, and to issues which will not or may not, be further investigated at the trial. The *Islamic Arab Insurance* case *a* provides a good example, among many others. The first issue, as to where the contract was made, will probably have disappeared from sight by the trial on the ground that it is irrelevant to the outcome. But the issue as to the proper law may well remain alive for decision. In either event, however, the test at the stage of the Ord 11 application is whether or not it appears to the court that the plaintiffs have a good arguable case on the limited affidavit material which is then available. *b*

The present case is not in the same category. But in my view the plaintiffs just get home on its unusual facts. It should certainly be a source of satisfaction that they can do so, particularly in the light of what counsel for the plaintiffs called 'the post-*Spiliada* world'. There can be no doubt, taking the case as a whole, that this country is the appropriate forum, and the only appropriate forum, for resolving the disputes between the plaintiffs and the defendant. It would be lamentable if the action on the brokerage *c* contract had to be brought here and, as counsel for the defendant submits, the action on the cheque had to be brought in Greece, even though the issues and the defences open to the defendant would be the same in both places.

Accordingly, I conclude that this was indeed a proper case for leave to amend the statement of claim and to allow the amended state of claim, including the claim on the cheque, to be served on the defendant outside the jurisdiction. *d*

Accordingly, I would dismiss this appeal.

**EWBANK J.** In my view the claim on the Greek cheque affects the English brokerage contract in the sense that if the claim on the cheque succeeds, the claim on the brokerage contract will be substantially and obviously affected.

Accordingly, in my view, the claim on the cheque satisfies the provisions of RSC *e* Ord 11, r 1(1)(*d*)(iii).

I am also of the view that there is an obvious inference in the brokerage contract that the Greek cheque which was given as security would be met and not dishonoured. The dishonour of the cheque was, accordingly, in my judgment, a breach of the brokerage contract. *f*

I too would dismiss the appeal.

*Appeal dismissed.*

Solicitors: *Middleton Potts* (for the defendant); *Simmons & Simmons* (for the plaintiffs).

Wendy Shockett    Barrister.

# Tate & Lyle Industries Ltd v Davy McKee (London) Ltd

QUEEN'S BENCH DIVISION (COMMERCIAL COURT)

HIRST J

19, 21 DECEMBER 1988

*Arbitration – Award – Leave to appeal against award – Hearing of application for leave to appeal – Hearing of application by official referee – Jurisdiction – Whether Commercial Court judge having power to direct that application for leave to appeal be heard by official referee rather than High Court judge – Whether application for leave to appeal constituting official referees' business – Whether official referee having same jurisdiction as High Court judge to hear application – RSC Ord 36, rr 1(2)(b), 4(1), Ord 73, rr 3(2)(a), 6.*

A commercial judge has power under RSC Ord 73, rr 3(2)(a)[a] and 6[b] to direct that an application for leave to appeal under s 1(3) of the Arbitration Act 1979 on a question of law arising out of an award made by an arbitrator in construction industry or other building cases be heard by an official referee rather than a High Court judge, because such an application is a 'cause or matter commenced in the . . . Queen's Bench Division . . . for which trial by an official referee is desirable in the interests of one or more of the parties on grounds of expedition, economy or convenience' and therefore falls within the broad definition of official referees' business in Ord 36, r 1(2)(b)[c] since a 'trial' for the purposes of r 1(2)(b) is synonymous with a determination which decides a point at issue and, as such, includes the procedure whereby the court may grant or refuse leave to appeal in the exercise of its discretion, and, on the basis that the application is properly to be treated as official referees' business, the official referee has the 'same jurisdiction, powers and duties (including the power of committal and discretion as to costs) as a judge' by virtue of Ord 36, r 4(1)[d], with the result that he has the same jurisdiction to hear the application for leave to appeal as a High Court judge (see p 644 d to j, post).

## Notes

For reference for trial before an official referee, see 37 Halsbury's Laws (4th edn) para 477.

For the powers of the Commercial Court or judges in arbitration proceedings, see ibid para 598.

For the Arbitration Act 1979, s 1, see 2 Halsbury's Statutes (4th edn) 609.

## Cases referred to in judgment

*Munday v Norton* [1892] 1 QB 403.

*Northern Regional Health Authority v Derek Crouch Construction Co Ltd* [1984] 2 All ER 175, [1984] QB 644, [1984] 2 WLR 676, CA.

## Application

The plaintiff, Tate & Lyle Industries Ltd, issued a summons in the Commercial Court on 14 December 1988 under s 1 of the Arbitration Act 1979 for leave to appeal on a question of law arising out of an interim award made the arbitrator, Mr Henry Maurice Rowson, on 18 November 1987 in respect of a contract for the construction or reconstruction of a sugar refinery plant made between the plaintiff and the defendant, Davy McKee (London)

---

a   Rule 3(2) is set out at p 642 j, post
b   Rule 6 is set out at p 642 j to p 643 a, post
c   Rule 1(2) is set out at p 643 b c, post
d   Rule 4(1) is set out at p 643 d t, post

Ltd. On 5 February 1988 Hirst J transferred the summons to be heard by a judge hearing
official referees' business. The application was heard by his Honour Judge Lewis Hawser  *a*
QC, who refused leave to appeal on 4 October 1988. The plaintiff applied to the
Commercial Court on 30 November 1988 for the summons to be relisted in the
Commercial Court for a hearing de novo, on the grounds that (i) Judge Hawser had had
no jurisdiction to hear the application since, by virtue of RSC Ord 73, rr 3(2)(*a*) and 6, it
could only be heard by a Commercial Court judge or a High Court judge and (ii) the
application did not fall within the ambit of official referees' business as defined in Ord 36,  *b*
r 1(2). The application was heard in chambers but judgment was given by Hirst J in open
court. The facts are set out in the judgment.

*David Gardam QC* and *Nicholas Padfield* for the plaintiff.
*Donald Keating QC* and *Rupert Jackson QC* for the defendant.

*c*

*Cur adv vult*

21 December. The following judgment was delivered.

## HIRST J.
*d*
*Introduction*
   This case raises an important question concerning the powers of the Commercial Court
to refer to the official referees' court applications under s 1(3) of the Arbitration Act 1979
for leave to appeal on a question of law arising out of an award made by an arbitrator in
construction industry or building cases.
   This has been the practice of the Commercial Court for several years, but it is now  *e*
challenged by the plaintiff, Tate & Lyle Industries Ltd, as being ultra vires the Rules of
the Supreme Court. The matter is thus one of considerable importance and it is for that
reason I have decided to give my judgment in open court.

*The history of the proceedings*
   On 18 November 1987 Mr Henry Maurice Rowson made an interim award in an  *f*
arbitration under a contract concerning the construction or reconstruction of a plant in
the sugar-refining industry between the plaintiff and the defendant, Davy McKee
(London) Ltd. The amount at stake exceeds £3m.
   On 14 December 1987 a summons for leave to appeal was issued in the Commercial
Court by the plaintiff. On 5 February 1988 I made an order transferring the summons to
the official referees' court.  *g*
   On 4 October 1988 his Honour Judge Lewis Hawser QC heard the application and
refused leave to appeal.
   The plaintiff now alleges that the order for transfer was ultra vires, and the decision of
Judge Hawser consequently a nullity. It therefore asks me to relist the summons in the
Commercial Court for hearing de novo.
*h*
*Relevant provisions of the Rules of the Supreme Court*
   So far as applications for leave to appeal are concerned, the relevant provisions are
contained in RSC Ord 73, r 3(2)(*a*) and r 6. Rule 3(2) provides:

   'Any application (*a*) for leave to appeal under section 1(2) of the Arbitration Act
   1979, or (*b*) under section 1(5) of that Act (including any application for leave), or (*c*)  *j*
   under section 5 of that Act, shall be made to a judge in chambers.'

   Rule 6 provides:

   '(1) Any matter which is required, by rule 2 or 3, to be heard by a judge, shall be
   heard by a Commercial Judge, unless any such judge otherwise directs.

(2) Nothing in the foregoing paragraph shall be construed as preventing the powers of a Commercial Judge from being exercised by any judge of the High Court.'

The powers of official referees are laid down by Ord 36, rr 1 and 4 as follows:

'*Application and interpretation*
1.—(1) This Order applies to official referees' business in the Chancery Division or Queen's Bench Division, and the other provisions of these rules apply to such business subject to the provisions of this Order.

(2) In this Order official referees' business includes, without prejudice to any right to a trial with a jury, any cause or matter commenced in the Chancery Division or Queen's Bench Division, being a cause or matter—(a) which involves a prolonged examination of documents or accounts, or a technical scientific or local investigation such as could more conveniently be conducted by an official referee or (b) for which trial by an official referee is desirable in the interests of one or more of the parties on grounds of expedition, economy or convenience or otherwise . . .

*Powers, etc. of official referees*
4.—(1) Subject to any directions contained in the order referring any matter to an official referee—(a) the official referee shall for the purpose of disposing of any cause or matter (including any interlocutory application therein) or any other business referred to him have the same jurisdiction, powers and duties (including the power of committal and discretion as to costs) as a judge, exercisable or, as the case may be, to be performed as nearly as circumstances admit in the like cases, in the like manner and subject to the like limitations; and (b) every trial and all other proceedings before an official referee shall, as nearly as circumstances admit, be conducted in the like manner as the like proceedings before a judge.

(2) Without prejudice to the generality of paragraph (1) but subject to such directions as are mentioned therein, an official referee before whom any cause or matter is tried shall have the like powers as the Court in respect to claims relating to or connected with the original subject-matter of the cause or matter by any party thereto against any other person, and Order 15, rule 5(2) and Order 16 shall with any necessary modifications apply in relation to any such claim accordingly . . .'

In *Northern Regional Health Authority v Derek Crouch Construction Co Ltd* [1984] 2 All ER 175 at 192, [1984] QB 644 at 675, which was a case concerning the powers of an official referee to open up, review or revise architects' certificates, Sir John Donaldson MR concluded his judgment with a comment concerning the need to reduce delays in the disposal of official referees' business as follows:

'If this reduction in the length of the lists does not occur or seems unlikely to occur, urgent consideration should be given to conferring upon the official referees a power analogous to that contemplated by s 92 of the County Courts Act 1959 to enable the official referees, whether sitting as such or as arbitrators, to refer, or sub-refer, the "nuts and bolts" of the suit to a suitably qualified arbitrator for enquiry and report. This would result in the official referees becoming, in effect, the construction industry court, having the same relationship to the construction industry as the Commercial Court has to the financial and commercial activities of the City of London. It could decide questions of principle which are of general interest, leaving it to the individual arbitrators to apply those principles to the details of individual disputes.'

The editors of *The Supreme Court Practice 1988* vol 1, para 36/1–9/10 describe the 'Courts of the Official Referees' as follows:

'Each of the Official Referees in London has a permanent court and chambers in the Royal Courts of Justice. The Court is a Court of the High Court and a trial before an Official Referee is a trial in the High Court, and a judgment which the Official Referee directs to be entered is a judgment of the High Court. This is so *a* notwithstanding that the Official Referees are nominated circuit judges, deputy circuit judges or recorders, although an official referee should be addressed as "Your Honour" when sitting in court or chambers (see *Practice Direction ( Judges: Modes of Address)* ([1982] 1 All ER 320, [1982] 1 WLR 101). The trial of an action before an Official Referee is not an arbitration and his decision and direction for judgment is not an award, certificate or report *(Munday v. Norton* ([1892] 1 QB 403)).' *b*

Counsel for the plaintiff submits that an official referee can only exercise High Court jurisdiction when either (i) he is requested by the Lord Chancellor to sit as a High Court judge under s 9 of the Supreme Court Act 1981 (which, as is common ground, does not apply in the present case) or (ii) when he is conducting official referees' business as defined by Ord 36, r 1.

The ambit of Ord 36, r 1, he submits, on its proper construction, is confined to the *c* matters defined in r 1(2)(*a*) and (*b*), neither of which cover an application for leave to appeal against an arbitration award, since the propriety of an arbitrator's decision on a point of law does not involve the matters laid down in sub-para (*a*) and is not a 'trial' within sub-para (*b*). As to the latter point, counsel submits that the procedure for the grant or refusal of leave to appeal in the exercise of the court's discretion cannot constitute *d* a trial, and in support of this argument he notes the contrast between Ord 32, dealing with applications and proceedings in chambers, and Ords 33 to 35 which deal with various aspects of trials.

Counsel for the defendant submits that Ord 36, r 1 should be accorded a broad construction in the light of the word 'includes'. More specifically, he submits that the word 'trial' extends to any determination which decides a point at issue, and that in *e* consequence this application falls fairly and squarely within r 1(2)(*b*) on the ground that trial by an official referee is desirable in the interests of expedition, economy or convenience. This construction, he submits, is borne out by the provisions of Ord 36, r 4.

*Conclusion* *f*

In my judgment Ord 6, r 1, on its proper interpretation, does not bear the narrow construction put forward by counsel for the plaintiff. Taking r 1(2)(*b*) first, the question is whether the proceeding in question is a *cause or matter* for which trial by an official referee is desirable for the reasons given. The words 'cause or matter' are very wide, and in my judgment fully apt to cover an application for leave to appeal against the decision of an arbitrator. The word 'trial' in this context does not, therefore, in my judgment bear *g* the narrow connotation sought by counsel, but is synonymous with 'determination'. Thus in my judgment, even without recourse to the word 'includes', this application for leave to appeal against an award of an arbitrator in a construction contract case like the present is official referees' business as defined in r 1(2)(*b*), since trial or determination by an official referee is desirable in the interests described in the sub-paragraph for the reasons given by Sir John Donaldson MR in the *Crouch* case. This view is, in my *h* judgment, reinforced by the use of the word 'includes', which shows that Ord 36, r 1 is not to be restrictively interpreted; this is borne out by the phraseology of Ord 36, r 4(1), which refers to 'any cause or matter (including any interlocutory application therein) or *any other business* referred to him . . .'

As already noted, once it is held that the cause or matter in question is properly to be treated as official referees' business, counsel for the plaintiff does not dispute that, by *j* virtue of Ord 36, r 4(1), the official referee has the powers of a High Court judge, as stated in the above-quoted note in *The Supreme Court Practice 1988.*

It follows that a commercial judge, pursuant to his power to direct that such an appeal be heard otherwise than by a commercial judge, has power in construction industry or building cases like the present to direct that the application shall be heard by an official referee.

*a*    Consequently my order dated 5 February 1988 was intra vires the Rules of the Supreme Court, and this application for a new hearing will be dismissed.

*Application dismissed.*

Solicitors: *Simmons & Simmons* (for the plaintiff); *Masons* (for the defendant).

*b*                                                                              K Mydeen Esq   Barrister.

*c*

# Practice Direction

SUPREME COURT TAXING OFFICE

*d*  *Costs – Taxation – Review of taxation – Criminal proceedings – Review of decision of taxing authority – Procedure – Notice of appeal – Documents to be forwarded with notice of appeal – Appeals to High Court – Originating summons – Form of notice of appeal – Legal Aid in Criminal Proceedings (General) Regulations 1968, reg 14D – Legal Aid in Criminal Proceedings (Costs) Regulations 1982 – Costs in Criminal Cases (General) Regulations 1986 – Legal Aid in Criminal Proceedings (Costs) Regulations 1988 – Legal Aid in Criminal and Care Proceedings (Costs)*
*e*  *Regulations 1989 – Legal Aid in Criminal and Care Proceedings (General) Regulations 1989, reg 54.*

1. Solicitors and counsel dissatisfied with the determination of costs under the Costs in Criminal Cases (General) Regulations 1986, SI 1986/1335, or under the Legal Aid in Criminal Proceedings (Costs) Regulations 1982, SI 1982/1197, the Legal Aid in Criminal
*f*  Proceedings (Costs) Regulations 1988, SI 1988/423, and the Legal Aid in Criminal and Care Proceedings (Costs) Regulations 1989, SI 1989/343, may apply to the appropriate authority (or his determining officer) for a review of the determination. Appeal against a decision on such a review may be made to a taxing master. Written notice of appeal must be given to the Chief Taxing Master within 21 days of receipt of the reasons given for the decision, or within such longer time as the Chief Taxing Master may direct.
*g*    2. The notice of appeal shall be in the Form A annexed hereto, setting out in separate numbered paragraphs each fee or item of costs or disbursement in respect of which the appeal is brought, showing the amount claimed for the item, the amount determined and the grounds of the objection to the decision on the taxation or determination. It shall be accompanied by a cheque for the appropriate fee made payable to 'HM Paymaster General'. The notice must state whether the appellant wishes to appear or to be
*h*  represented or whether he will accept a decision given in his absence.
       Such of the following documents as are appropriate should be forwarded with the notice of appeal: (a) a legible copy of the bill of costs showing the allowances made; (b) counsel's brief and papers, instructions to and opinions of counsel; (c) counsel's fee claim, fee note and any memorandum by counsel submitted to the determining authority; (d) a copy of the appellant's representations made to the determining authority; (e) the
*j*  reasons of the taxing officer or determining officer; (f) the solicitors' correspondence files, attendance notes and time records; (g) a copy of the legal aid order and of any authorities given under reg 14D of the Legal Aid in Criminal Proceedings (General) Regulations 1968, SI 1968/1231 (as amended by SI 1983/1863), or reg 54 of the Legal Aid in Criminal and Care Proceedings (General) Regulations 1989, SI 1989/344; (h) a copy of the indictment; (i) the depositions and witness statements (exhibits should be lodged only if relevant). If any of the relevant documents are not immediately available the

giving of the notice of appeal should not be delayed on that account but should be accompanied by a note setting out the missing documents and an undertaking to lodge *a* them within a time, not exceeding 28 days, specified in the undertaking.

3. Appellants are reminded that it is their responsibility to procure the lodgment of the relevant papers even if they are in the possession of the Crown Court or other persons. Appeals may be listed for dismissal if the relevant papers are not lodged with the notice of appeal or within the time set out in the undertaking.

4. Delays frequently arise in dealing with appeals by counsel because the relevant *b* papers have been returned by the court to the solicitor, whose file may not be readily available or who may have destroyed the papers. These problems would be avoided if counsel's clerk were, immediately on his lodging with the court a request for redetermination, to ask his instructing solicitor to retain safely the relevant papers.

*Appeals to the High Court* *c*

5. An appellant desiring to appeal to a judge from the decision of the taxing master should, within 21 days of receipt of the master's decision, request him to certify that a point of principle of general importance (specifying the same) is involved. An appeal is instituted by originating summons in the Queen's Bench Division within 21 days of the receipt of the master's certificate. The times may be extended by a taxing master or the High Court, as the case may be. *d*

6. The judge by whom appeals against decisions of taxing masters in respect of costs in criminal matters are to be heard and determined will be nominated by the Lord Chief Justice each term and will ordinarily be the judge nominated to hear reviews of taxations pursuant to RSC Ord 62, r 35.

7. The originating summons by which such appeal is to be instituted shall be issued by the Supreme Court Taxing Office and shall be in the form prescribed by the taxing *e* masters and shall contain full particulars of the item or items or the amount allowed in respect of which the appeal is brought. After the issue of the summons the appellant shall forthwith lodge with the Clerk of Appeals, Supreme Court Taxing Office, all the documents used on the appeal to the taxing master.

8. The summons is to be served within three days after issue returnable on a day to be appointed and shall be indorsed with an estimate of the length of hearing. The Chief *f* Clerk of the Supreme Court Taxing Office will obtain from the nominated judge a date for hearing and will notify the parties.

9. After the appeal has been heard and determined the Chief Clerk shall obtain the documents, together with a sealed copy of any order of the judge which may have been drawn up, and shall notify the court concerned of the result of the appeal. *g*

10. The practice directions listed below are hereby withdrawn:

[1972] 2 All ER 984, [1972] 1 WLR 1020
[1972] 2 All ER 985, [1972] 1 WLR 1021
25 July 1976, unreported (Chief Taxing Master)
[1977] 2 All ER 541, [1972] 1 WLR 610

*h*

11. This practice direction is issued with the concurrence of the Lord Chief Justice.

F G BERKELEY
26 May 1989 Chief Taxing Master.

FORM A

*Form of Notice of Appeal*

APPEAL PURSUANT TO THE COSTS IN CRIMINAL CASES (GENERAL) REGULATIONS 1986/THE LEGAL AID IN CRIMINAL PROCEEDINGS (COSTS) REGULATIONS 1982 AND 1988/THE LEGAL AID IN CRIMINAL AND CARE PROCEEDINGS (COSTS) REGULATIONS 1989

CROWN COURT AT              /DIVISIONAL COURT/COURT OF APPEAL, CRIMINAL DIVISION

Regina v

Appeal of

Case no

To: The Chief Taxing Master and to the appropriate authority of the Crown Court at /Divisional Court/Court of Appeal, Criminal Division

The appellant                    appeals to a taxing master against the redetermination of the costs in the above matter.

The following are the items in respect of which the appellant appeals:

| Item | Description | Amount claimed | Amount allowed | Grounds of objection |
|------|-------------|----------------|----------------|----------------------|
| 1 | | | | |
| 2 | | | | |
| 3 | | | | |
| [etc] | | | | |

The appellant intends/does not intend to attend the hearing of the appeal and will accept a decision in his absence.

Dated the              day of              19 .

[Signed]

Appellant/Solicitor for the Appellant

[Address]

[Tel no]

[Ref]

See accompanying notes which must be complied with.

*Notes*

1. The notice of appeal must be lodged with

    The Clerk of Appeals
    Supreme Court Taxing Office
    Royal Courts of Justice
    Strand
    London WC2A 2LL

within 21 days of the date of receipt of the determining officer's reasons.

2. Any fee payable, if by cheque made payable to 'HM Paymaster General', must accompany the form.

3. A copy of the notice of appeal must be sent to the Crown Court/Registrar of Criminal Appeals on the same day as it is lodged with the Clerk of Appeals.

4. The following documents must be lodged with the notice of appeal: (a) a legible copy of the bill of costs showing the allowances made; (b) counsel's brief and papers, instructions to and opinions of counsel; (c) counsel's fee claim, fee note and any memorandum by counsel submitted to the determining authority; (d) a copy of the appellant's representations made to the determining authority; (e) the reasons of the taxing officer or determining officer; (f) the solicitors' correspondence files, attendance notes and time records; (g) a copy of the legal aid order and of any authorities given

under reg 14D of the Legal Aid in Criminal Proceedings (General) Regulations 1968 or reg 54 of the Legal Aid in Criminal and Care Proceedings (General) Regulations 1989; (h) a copy of the indictment; (i) the depositions and witness statements (exhibits should be lodged only if relevant).

5. If any of the above documents are not available the procedure set out in para 2 of the practice direction dated 26 May 1989 ([1989] 2 All ER 645) should be followed.

# Jet Holdings Inc and others v Patel

COURT OF APPEAL, CIVIL DIVISION
NICHOLLS AND STAUGHTON LJJ
7, 9 MARCH 1988

*Conflict of laws – Foreign judgment – Enforcement – Fraud – Foreign judgment obtained by fraud – Whether foreign judgment obtained by fraud enforceable – Whether foreign court's views on allegation of fraud relevant.*

A foreign judgment will not be enforced at common law if it has been obtained by fraud even though the allegation of fraud has been investigated and rejected by the foreign court, since the foreign court's decision on whether there was fraud is neither conclusive nor relevant and nor is it relevant whether the alleged fraud goes directly to the cause of action or is collateral fraud (see p 652 c d g h, p 653 c and p 655 a, post); *Abouloff v Oppenheimer & Co* [1881–5] All ER Rep 307 and *Vadala v Lawes* [1886–90] All ER Rep 853 applied.

If a foreign plaintiff wishes to avoid the possibility of having an issue of fraud tried all over again when attempting to enforce a foreign judgment at common law he should in the first place bring his action where he expects to be able to enforce his judgment (see p 652 e and p 655 a, post).

### Notes
For impeachment of foreign judgments, see 8 Halsbury's Laws (4th edn) paras 726–727, and for cases on the subject, see 11 Digest (Reissue) 601–603, *1473–1486*.

### Cases referred to in judgments
*Abouloff v Oppenheimer & Co* (1882) 10 QBD 295, [1881–5] All ER Rep 307, CA.
*DPP v Humphrys* [1976] 2 All ER 497, [1977] AC 1, [1976] 2 WLR 857, HL.
*Jacobson v Frachon* (1928) 138 LT 386, CA.
*Pemberton v Hughes* [1899] 1 Ch 781, CA.
*Vadala v Lawes* (1890) 25 QBD 310, [1886–90] All ER Rep 853, CA.

### Cases also cited
*Codd v Delap* (1905) 92 LT 510, HL.
*Israel Discount Bank of New York v Hadjipateras* [1983] 3 All ER 129, [1984] 1 WLR 137, CA.
   *Manger v Cash* (1889) 5 TLR 271.
*Meyer v Meyer* [1971] 1 All ER 378, [1971] P 298.
*Robinson v Fenner* [1913] 3 KB 835.
*Svirskis v Gibson* [1977] 2 NZLR 4, NZ CA.
*Syal v Heyward* [1948] 2 All ER 576, [1948] 2 KB 443, CA.

### Interlocutory appeal
The defendant, Bachu Patel, appealed against the decision of Patrick Bennett QC sitting as a deputy judge of the High Court in the Queen's Bench Division on 23 July 1987 whereby he dismissed an appeal by Mr Patel from the order of Master Trench of 3 March 1987 giving summary judgment under RSC Ord 14 for the plaintiffs, Jet Holdings Inc,

Jet Executive Travel Inc and Princess Productions Inc, in their action brought to enforce
a a judgment of the Superior Court of the State of California for Los Angeles County. The
facts are set out in the judgment of Staughton LJ.

*Lionel Swift QC* and *Donald Cryan* for Mr Patel.
*Michael Burton QC* and *Edward Cohen* for the plaintiffs.

b **STAUGHTON LJ** (giving the first judgment at the invitation of Nicholls LJ). This
action is brought to enforce a foreign judgment, that is to say a judgment of the Superior
Court of the State of California for Los Angeles County. The defence is, first, that the
judgment was obtained by fraud. Alternatively, it is said that the proceedings in which
the judgment was obtained were opposed to natural justice. The present proceedings are
for summary judgment in the English action under RSC Ord 14. The defendant, Mr
c Patel, says that he should have leave to defend on those grounds or that, in terms of Ord
14, r 3, there ought for some other reason to be a trial of the action.

The facts are on any view unusual. From 1980 or 1981 until 1983 Mr Patel worked as
an accountant in California for the three companies which are plaintiffs in this action.
Mr Don Arden is the president of those companies, and appears to be in charge of their
affairs. He has an address in Wimbledon, London SW19. The companies were engaged
d in the popular music business. In November 1983 Mr Arden claimed that Mr Patel had
wrongfully misappropriated large sums of money from the companies, and summarily
dismissed him. Mr Patel denies that there had been any wrongful misappropriation.

There followed, according to Mr Patel, three occasions when actual or threatened
violence was directed at him by or on behalf of Mr Arden, with the object of inducing
him to repay money to the companies. I need not state the details of those three occasions
e at any length, but only the broad outline. The first was in November 1983, in California.
Mr Patel says that Mr Arden pulled a gun from his brief case and threatened to shoot
him. He also threatened to frighten Mr Patel's parents and said that he would send his
'friends' over to the United Kingdom. He made it clear that his 'friends' were members
of the New York Mafia. Mr Arden is also said to have thrown several objects at Mr Patel
and punched him in the face.
f The second occasion was in England, where Mr Patel promptly went after the first
occasion, on 7 December 1983. Mr Patel says that he was taken from his parents' house
by threats to Mr Arden's address in Wimbledon and there, as he says, he was threatened
and beaten up by Mr Arden and forced to sign a document instructing his bank to release
the equivalent of $100,000.

The third incident also occurred in England, on 14 February 1984. At 9 o'clock in the
g morning Mr Patel says that he was persuaded by threats to go to the plaintiffs'
headquarters in London. He says that there he was threatened, hit and punched by Mr
Arden and his associates, and kept captive until the following morning. Eventually he
was released on his promise to pay the sum of £10,000 in one month's time.

All that is strenuously denied by Mr Arden. Mr Patel did not pay the second sum of
h £10,000, instead he went to the police. As a result, Mr David Arden, the son of Mr
Arden, and two gentlemen who were accountants were prosecuted at the Central
Criminal Court. At that stage Mr Arden senior was not prosecuted. The accountants
were acquitted, but Mr David Arden, under his actual name of David Levy, was convicted
of (1) conspiracy to make an unwarranted demand with menaces and (2) false
imprisonment. He was sentenced to two years' imprisonment, of which one year was to
j be suspended. Much later Mr Arden senior was also prosecuted; he was acquitted.

Meanwhile, on 30 May 1984, the plaintiff companies commenced their action in the
Californian court against Mr Patel. Their monetary claim amounted to $168,000, and
they also sought punitive damages in the sum of $2m. Mr Patel's first response was to
start an action in England against Mr Arden and the two accountants, claiming the return
of his $100,000 or the sterling equivalent. A statement of claim was served against the
accountants only, Mr Arden not having been served with the writ. That was signed by

counsel and alleged conspiracy, assault, false imprisonment and conversion. The action has not since proceeded. Then, on 23 July 1984, Mr Patel entered an appearance in the American action, and served an answer to the plaintiffs' complaint. He says that he did this on the advice of his English solicitors and counsel, who were different from those representing him today. That was a most important step, since it acknowledged the jurisdiction of the American court. If it had not been taken, I presently do not see any ground on which the American judgment could have been enforced in this country. But, as it was, an appearance was entered, an answer was filed and, on 26 November 1984, Mr Patel filed a cross-claim there against the present plaintiffs, Mr Arden and a number of others.

In the proceedings that ensued, there are three particular matters to note. First, on 7 November 1984 the American court heard an application that Mr Patel's deposition be taken in Los Angeles. The application was made on behalf of the plaintiffs. It was opposed, with evidence from Mr Patel that he did not wish to visit the United States because, if he did so, he would be in fear of his life owing to the violence and threats which he had suffered previously. There was, however, at the same time an assertion by his American lawyer that he would be present later at the trial. It is not altogether easy to reconcile that statement with Mr Patel's assertion that he was afraid to go to the United States. No doubt he could be cross-examined about that, if it were ever material. On that occasion the judge refused the application. We have no note as such of the judge's reasons, but there is some indication that he did pay regard to Mr Patel's fears.

Nearly a year later, on 25 October 1985, the American court made an order that Mr Patel attend two doctors in Los Angeles for physical and medical examination on 7 and 8 January 1986. That was no doubt relevant to the assertion in his cross-complaint that he had suffered injury which was continuing. The order which the court made on that occasion continued:

'3. The expense of BACHU PATEL's travel to Los Angeles, including air fare, motel and meals, is to be borne by Plaintiffs and Cross-Defendants, who shall make the necessary arrangements in advance.

4. If BACHU PATEL desires, he may select a security guard to guard him during his stay in Los Angeles, the expense of which shall be borne by Plaintiffs and Cross-Defendants.'

Mr Patel did not comply with that order. His explanation was as follows:

'On January 5, 1986, I telephoned British Airways in order to verify the existence of a prepaid ticket in my name paid for by Jet Executive Travel for passage from London to Los Angeles, California. I was advised that no such prepaid ticket existed. In view of that fact, I did not go to Heathrow Airport on January 6, 1986, as I had previously planned.'

There is evidence which suggests that this explanation was untrue. On 10 February 1986 the American court made an order excluding evidence that Mr Patel had suffered any physical or mental injury at the hands of the plaintiffs.

The question of the deposition of Mr Patel in Los Angeles was raised again before the American court by the plaintiffs on 27 February 1986. It was again opposed on his behalf on the ground that he should not be forced to endanger his life by going to Los Angeles. On this occasion an order was made for the deposition to be taken in Los Angeles on 28 and 29 April 1986. The plaintiffs were again to bear the cost involved, including the cost of a security guard. Mr Patel did not attend. He claimed, for the second time, that an air ticket had not been provided. There is again evidence which suggests that this explanation was untrue. As counsel for Mr Patel points out, the American court had ruled against his submission that he ought not to be obliged to put his life in danger, so it may be Mr Patel

felt that some other reason must be found to justify his not having complied with the
a  court's order.

By that time Mr Patel's American lawyers had ceased to act for him and had been
removed from the record. He says in his affidavit that he did not have the means to
instruct them adequately, since the plaintiffs had extorted the sterling equivalent of
$100,000 from him by violence and threats.

Eventually, on 11 June 1986, the American court ordered (1) that the cross-complaint
b  be dismissed, (2) that the answer be stricken and (3) that default be entered against Mr
Patel. On that occasion the judge read and considered, as he noted on the document, a
declaration by Mr Patel, in which he again gave brief details of the threats and violence
which he had suffered, stated that he had no money left to pay his lawyers and repeated
that airline tickets had not been provided on the two occasions when he had failed to
attend in Los Angeles. We have no direct evidence whether the judge did or did not
c  accept the truth of what Mr Patel was saying when he came to make his orders.

On 9 September 1986 the damages were assessed in California. A declaration by Mr
Arden disclosed that he or his companies had received $100,000, and offered to take that
into account, but claimed an additional sum of $86,000 in respect of hotel expenses
incurred by Mr Patel. Judgment was entered against Mr Patel for $168,940, which was
the sum originally claimed, without regard to the credit of $100,000 or the additional
d  claim of $86,000. There was also judgment for $2,463·50 costs and punitive damages in
the sum of $500,000. It is that judgment which the plaintiffs now seek to enforce here.
They have not been able to proceed under any of the statutory provisions relating to the
registration of foreign judgments. Instead, they sue on the judgment at common law.

On 3 March 1987 Master Trench gave summary judgment for the plaintiffs, under
Ord 14, in respect of the amount claimed and interest. There was an appeal from that
e  order which was heard by Mr Patrick Bennett QC sitting as a deputy judge of the High
Court in the Queen's Bench Division on 23 July 1987. The appeal was dismissed. Mr
Patel now appeals from that order of the deputy judge.

The enforcement of foreign judgments at common law is set out clearly and concisely
in Dicey and Morris *The Conflict of Laws* (11th edn, 1987) rr 42–46. Those provide as
follows:
f

'Rule 42.—A foreign judgment which is final and conclusive on the merits and
not impeachable under any of Rules 43 to 46 is conclusive as to any matter thereby
adjudicated upon, and cannot be impeached for any error either (1) of fact; or (2) of
law.

Rule 43.—(1) A foreign judgment is impeachable if the courts of the foreign
g          country did not, in the circumstances of the case, have jurisdiction to give that
judgment in the view of English law in accordance with the principles set out in
Rules 37 to 41 inclusive . . .

Rule 44.—A foreign judgment relied upon as such in proceedings in England is
impeachable for fraud. Such fraud may be either (1) fraud on the part of the party
in whose favour the judgment is given; or (2) fraud on the part of the court
h          pronouncing the judgment.

[I need not read rule 45, which deals with public policy.]

Rule 46.—A foreign judgment may (*semble*) be impeached if the proceedings in
which the judgment was obtained were opposed to natural justice.'

On the threshold of the argument for Mr Patel is the point that the foreign court's
j  own view whether the judgment was obtained by fraud is not conclusive or indeed
relevant. The deputy judge seems to have taken the contrary view. In his judgment he
said:

'The US court was fully cognisant of the issue whether the failure to attend was or
might have been because of improper pressures. The services of a bodyguard were

offered at the plaintiffs' expense. On the evidence before me I cannot see that the US judgment was obtained by fraud even using the wider meaning of that term. The *a* US court considered the matter. [Mr Patel] was represented and the issue was resolved against him. This was not a case where r 42 of Dicey and Morris *The Conflict of Laws* was avoided by the exception that there was fraud.'

The judge then went on to consider the alternative case relating to natural justice and, after referring to *Pemberton v Hughes* [1899] 1 Ch 781 and the comment on r 46 in *Dicey* *b* *and Morris*, he said:

'. . . the objection could have been and was taken before the foreign court. That issue having been raised, argued and adjudicated on, in my view there was no denial of natural justice.'

Where the objection to enforcement is based on jurisdiction, that is r 43, it is to my *c* mind plain that the foreign court's decision on its own jurisdiction is neither conclusive nor relevant. If the foreign court had no jurisdiction in the eyes of English law, any conclusion it may have reached as to its own jurisdiction is of no value. To put it bluntly, if not vulgarly, the foreign court cannot haul itself up by its own bootstraps. Logically the same reasoning must apply where enforcement is resisted on the ground of fraud, r 44. If the rule is that a foreign judgment obtained by fraud is not enforceable, it cannot *d* matter that in the view of the foreign court there was no fraud. But this doctrine makes a great inroad into the objective, which is generally desirable, of enforcing foreign judgments where in the eyes of English law the foreign court had jurisdiction. The defendant may have been served in the foreign country, entered an appearance, given evidence, been disbelieved and had judgment entered against him. If he asserts that the plaintiff's claim and evidence were fraudulent that issue must be tried all over again in *e* enforcement proceedings. The lesson for the plaintiff is that he should in the first place bring his action where he expects to be able to enforce a judgment.

That doctrine has encountered criticism from academic writers: see *Dicey and Morris* p 469, footnote 66. A possible view which is taken by some is that the fraud relied on must be extraneous or collateral to the dispute which the foreign court determines. But in my judgment it is a hundred years too late for this court to take that view. The *f* decisions in *Abouloff v Oppenheimer & Co* (1882) 10 QBD 295, [1881–5] All ER Rep 307 and *Vadala v Lawes* (1890) 25 QBD 310, [1886–90] All ER Rep 853 show that a foreign judgment cannot be enforced if it was obtained by fraud, even though the allegation of fraud was investigated and rejected by the foreign court.

Counsel for the plaintiffs seeks to distinguish those authorities on the ground that in them the court was concerned with fraud going directly to the cause of action, and not *g* with some aspect of procedural fraud. I cannot accept that there is any such distinction to be drawn. If there is a difference, collateral fraud is a stronger case where the English court should be more ready to investigate anew matters which were considered by the foreign court than in the case of fraud going directly to the cause of action which was adjudicated on by the foreign court. So I would conclude that the foreign court's views on fraud are neither conclusive nor relevant whether the fraud is said to be fraud going *h* directly to the cause of action or collateral fraud, on the authorities as they have stood for a hundred years.

I have said that in the alternative Mr Patel also relies on r 46 in *Dicey and Morris*. The rule itself refers to proceedings opposed to natural justice. In the comment to that rule (at p 474) the authors cite the observations of Lindley MR in *Pemberton v Hughes* [1899] 1 *j* Ch 781 at 790:

'If a judgment is pronounced by a foreign Court . . . English courts never investigate the propriety of the proceedings in the foreign Court, unless they offend against English views of substantial justice.'

The way counsel for Mr Patel puts the point is that the proceedings in this case, he says,
a 'offended against English views of substantial justice'.

Once again one would expect that the foreign court's views would logically be neither conclusive nor relevant as to the propriety of its own proceedings. If the English court considers that the foreign court did not observe the rules of natural justice, for example the rule audi alteram partem or nemo judex in rem suam, why should it make any difference that the foreign court thought that it was observing the rules of natural justice?
b But *Dicey and Morris* p 475 takes the contrary view in a passage which says that a foreign judgment cannot be impeached on this ground if the objection could have been and was taken before the foreign court. The authority cited to support that is *Jacobson v Frachon* (1928) 138 LT 386. It is by no means clear to me that that case is authority for the proposition stated in *Dicey and Morris*. But I do not find it necessary to decide this appeal on the basis of r 46 or on procedural failure to comply with the rules of natural justice or
c with, as Lindley MR puts it, English views of substantial justice. It can be decided in my judgment on r 44, fraud. It is plain, as I have said, that when considering fraud the English courts have to consider the facts afresh without regard to the decision of the foreign court.

Mr Patel's case before us was not that there was fraud in the cause of action itself. He
d does not resist enforcement on the ground that he had misappropriated none of the plaintiffs' money, and that the plaintiffs were fraudulent in asserting that he had misappropriated money. So, in a sense, his allegation here is of collateral fraud. He asserts that the plaintiffs' conduct was fraudulent in (1) assaulting him with violence and threats, so that he was afraid to go to California, (2) obtaining $100,000 from him by those means, so that he was unable to afford continuing legal representation in California, and
e (3) failing to invite the American court to take that $100,000 into account against the plaintiffs' claim. Factually ground (3) seems to be not supported by the evidence. Alternatively, Mr Patel says that the American court was misled by the plaintiffs as to the true reason for his default.

For Ord 14 purposes, we must take the facts to be as deposed to by Mr Patel in his affidavit, unless what he says is plainly untrue. There are good grounds for questioning
f Mr Patel's credibility in relation to the two occasions when he says that no air ticket was available for him. Documentary evidence suggests that on each occasion an air ticket was available. Counsel for the plaintiffs also argues that Mr Patel cannot any longer have had any fear of going to California by the time of the three interlocutory proceedings which I have mentioned, for this reason. The incidents of threats and violence relied on had all taken place before the American action was commenced. Yet Mr Patel entered an
g appearance in that action when he need not have done so, and served an answer and served a cross-complaint. Hence we are urged to conclude that any apprehension he may have previously felt about going to America must have subsided. Against that, it must be remembered that Mr Patel was a potential witness against Mr David Arden, until he was convicted on 19 March 1986, and, therefore, could have thought that he was regarded with animosity by the Arden family. He was also a potential witness against Mr Arden
h senior, until 20 November 1987 when he was acquitted. Thirdly, counsel for the plaintiffs relies on the occasion when Mr Patel's lawyer asserted that he would attend the trial in the United States, at the same time as producing evidence from Mr Patel that he was afraid to attend for a deposition.

However, there is also independent evidence to support the conclusion that Mr Patel was subject to mistreatment by the plaintiffs or their associates. First and most obviously,
j there is the conviction of Mr David Arden for a conspiracy to make an unwarranted demand with menaces, and for false imprisonment. Secondly, one of the two accountants said in an affidavit about the incident of 7 December 1983:

'Both the third defendant and I can only conclude that these proceedings against us result from a malicious intention to embroil us in proceedings resulting from an act of violence, to which we were unwitting and unwilling spectators.'

That seems to be an admission or an assertion that an act of violence took place. I am firmly of the view that the evidence of Mr Patel cannot, for Ord 14 purposes, be rejected as wholly untruthful.

It is, I think, clear that the plaintiffs' American lawyers were asserting to the court implicitly, and even to some extent expressly, that Mr Patel's account of violence, threats and fear was untrue. If in fact it was true, that assertion, together with the actual incidents relied on, is capable of amounting to fraud in this context: see the speech of Viscount Dilhorne in *DPP v Humphrys* [1976] 2 All ER 497 at 506–507, [1977] AC 1 at 21, where he quotes a passage from Spencer Bower and Turner *Res Judicata* (2nd edn, 1969) p 323 with approval:

'The fraud necessary to destroy a *prima facie* case of estoppel by *res judicata* includes every variety of *mala fides* and *mala praxis* whereby one of the parties misleads and deceives the judicial tribunal.'

Although that was said in the context of estoppel by res judicata, I cannot see that it is any the less applicable in the context of enforcement of a foreign judgment; nor apparently did Viscount Dilhorne, since in that passage he also cited *Abouloff v Oppenheimer & Co* and *Vadala v Lawes*.

But counsel for the plaintiffs submits that the American court was not deceived. This is the heart of the matter. He invites us to conclude that the American court was prepared to assume the facts on which Mr Patel relied, but concluded that it was still right to make the orders that it did make, and perhaps also that it had no option but to make those orders.

For my part I would not accept, without express evidence, that an American or any other judge, believing or assuming on 11 June 1986 that Mr Patel had on three occasions been subject to threatened and actual violence, that he had been forced to hand over $100,000, that in consequence he had no money left to pay his lawyers and that he was in genuine fear in going to the United States, would nevertheless have given judgment against him in default for the sum of $168,000 and $500,000 punitive damages. Nor would I accept, without express evidence, that an American judge, believing or assuming some or all of those facts, would have made the orders for a medical examination or for Mr Patel's deposition in Los Angeles, relying only on such protection as might be afforded by a security guard. There were other orders that could have been made, for example an order could have been made for the examination of Mr Patel in England by a doctor who was qualified to practice medicine in this country, or an order could have been made for taking evidence from Mr Patel in England, although it may well be that in the absence of consent the process which would have had to have been employed might not have been wholly satisfactory. Of course, if Mr Patel had refused his consent to a process which was the equivalent of what would have happened in the United States the judge would have taken that into account.

In my judgment there is an issue to be tried in this case whether Mr Patel is entitled to resist enforcement, at any rate on the ground of fraud. Accordingly, this appeal should be allowed, and the judgment set aside. The action must go to trial. In the course of this judgment I have expressed views both on the facts and the law. Those views will be in no way binding on the judge who tries the action.

There is one other matter. Counsel for the plaintiffs said that, if the judgment were set aside, still there should be some interim protection for his clients. Presently they have a charging order on Mr Patel's house, although it ranks after two other charging orders. In the ordinary way that charging order would go if the judgment on which it is founded were set aside, as it must be. We invited counsel to address us on whether instead there should be a *Mareva* injunction or some similar order. Counsel for Mr Patel said that his client was content that the charging order should remain, with liberty to apply. Counsel a  for the plaintiffs is also content that that should be the case if the appeal is allowed. So that would be the order that I would make.

**NICHOLLS LJ.** I agree.

*Appeal allowed. Judgment set aside.*

b  Solicitors: *T Cryan & Co,* Wealdstone (for Mr Patel); *Tarlo Lyons Randall Rose* (for the plaintiffs).

Celia Fox    Barrister.

c

# Hammersmith and Fulham London Borough Council v Top Shop Centres Ltd
d # Hammersmith and Fulham London Borough Council v Glassgrove Ltd

CHANCERY DIVISION
WARNER J
e  22–25, 28–30 NOVEMBER, 1, 2, 4, 5, 19 DECEMBER 1988

*Landlord and tenant – Relief against forfeiture – Underlessee – Vesting order – Effect of vesting order – Lessee subleasing and mortgaging property – Landlord obtaining forfeiture against lessee – Mortgagee of lease obtaining vesting order granting new lease – Whether vesting of new lease in mortgagee automatically reinstating underlessee's leases – Law of Property Act 1925, s 146(4).*

f
*Landlord and tenant – Relief against forfeiture – Right of re-entry – Rent – Entitlement to rent – Lessee subleasing and mortgaging property – Receivers appointed by mortgagee to collect rents from underlessees – Landlord obtaining forfeiture against lessee – Landlord obtaining order excluding mortgagees and receivers from demanding and receiving rent from underlessees – Whether landlord's receipt of rents from underlessees constituting full enforcement of right of re-*
g  *entry – Whether underlessee's right to apply for relief against forfeiture ending when landlord obtaining exclusive entitlement to demand and receive rent – Law of Property Act 1925, s 146(4).*

In 1961 the trustees of an estate leased it to P, a development company, for a term of more than 100 years under a lease which contained a provision entitling the trustees to re-enter the property and forfeit the lease if P went into liquidation. P mortgaged its
h  lease and developed the site and then granted underleases to various tenants including the plaintiff council, which was granted two underleases in 1970 for the residue of the term of P's lease less ten days. P later went into liquidation. When the trustees became aware of the winding up of P they served a writ on P claiming forfeiture of the headlease on the ground of the liquidation. In 1984 the Court of Appeal made an order of forfeiture in the trustees' favour. As a result of the forfeiture of P's headlease all interests derived
j  from that lease, including the mortgages and the council's underleases, ceased to exist. However, neither the trustees nor the mortgagees formally apprised the underlessees of the situation, and the receivers who had been appointed by the third mortgagee to manage the property and collect rents from the underlessees continued to do so as though the underleases granted by P still subsisted. The trustees obtained injunctions restraining the receivers and mortgagees from demanding or receiving rents from the underlessees

or from managing the estate, which injunctions continued until the court made a vesting
order under s 146(4)[a] of the Law of Property Act 1925 granting the first mortgagee a *a*
new lease for the term of P's lease less one day. The first mortgagee subsequently
purchased the freehold of the estate from the trustees and sold it to T together with the
lease, which was sold subject to the underleases granted by P in so far as they still subsisted
or had been affirmed. T transferred the freehold to two of its subsidiaries, the first and
second defendants, and the lease was surrendered. Following that transfer a dispute arose
over the status of the council's tenancy. The defendants asserted that the council's *b*
underleases no longer subsisted and that its tenancy was on a year-to-year basis terminable
on six months' notice, and sought, in effect, to enforce a right which was part of the
trustees' original right of re-entry. In response the council sought a declaration as against
the defendants that its tenancy was on the same terms as set out in the underleases
granted by P or, alternatively, relief from forfeiture under s 146(4) of the 1925 Act. The
council contended, inter alia, (i) that the vesting of the new lease in the first mortgagee *c*
had automatically reinstated the council's underleases as interests to which the lease was
subject and the subsequent surrender of the lease left the freehold subject to the
underleases and (ii) that the council had not lost the right to apply for relief from
forfeiture under s 146(4) when the trustees became entitled to receive the rents and
profits of the estate, since the mere receipt of rent did not amount to an assertion of their
right of re-entry. *d*

**Held** – (1) The court had a wide discretion under s 146(4) of the 1925 Act to make an
order vesting a new lease in a party claiming an estate or interest in the demised property
as an underlessee on such conditions as it thought appropriate to the circumstances of the
case subject only to the term of the new lease not exceeding that of the original lease.
Accordingly, all interests deriving from the original lease would not be automatically *e*
reinstated if the court vested a new lease in an underlessee, since those interests might
not fit into the provisions of the new lease ordered by the court (see p 664 *d e j* to p 665 *c
g*, post); dictum of Romer LJ in *Ewart v Fryer* [1901] 1 Ch 499 at 515–516 and of Scott J
in *Official Custodian for Charities v Mackey* [1984] 3 All ER 689 at 701 followed; *Chelsea
Estates Investment Trust Co Ltd v Marche* [1955] 1 All ER 195 distinguished.
(2) Once a headlease had been forfeited an underlessee was in relation to the freeholder *f*
a trespasser against whom the freeholder's right of re-entry could be effectively asserted
by compelling the underlessee to take a new lease or give up possession, but not by
merely receiving rent payable under the erstwhile underlease. Accordingly, since the
trustees had not actively sought to enforce their right of re-entry against the council
following the forfeiture of P's lease and the order entitling them to demand and receive
rents, but had merely received the rent payments when due, the council had not lost its *g*
right to apply for relief from forfeiture. The council would not, however, be granted
relief under s 146(4) because instead it was entitled to succeed on the basis of an equitable
estoppel, since the first mortgagee in whom the new lease was vested had, with the co-
operation of the trustees, encouraged the council to assume to its detriment that its
underleases still existed and it would be unconscionable for the defendants, who were *h*
bound by the conduct of those parties as their successors in title, to be permitted to deny
that. The council would accordingly be granted declaration to that effect (see p 669 *e f*,
p 670 *h j* and p 672 *e*, post); *Ashton v Sobelman* [1987] 1 All ER 755 applied.

---

*a*   Section 146(4), so far as material, provides: 'Where a lessor is proceeding by action or otherwise to   *j*
      enforce a right of re-entry or forfeiture under any covenant, proviso, or stipulation in a lease . . .
      the court may . . . make an order vesting, for the whole of the term of the lease or any less term,
      the property comprised in the lease or any part thereof in any person entitled as under-lessee to
      any estate or interest in such property upon such conditions . . . as the court in the circumstances
      of each case may think fit, but in no case shall any such under-lessee be entitled to require a lease
      to be granted to him for any longer term than he had under his original sub-lease.'

**Notes**

*a*  For the underlessee's right to relief from forfeiture, see 27 Halsbury's Laws (4th edn) para 441, 443, and for cases on the subject, see 31(2) Digest (Reissue) 838–843, 6932–6961.
For the Law of Property Act 1925, s 146, see 37 Halsbury's Statutes (4th edn) 273.

**Cases referred to in judgment**

*American Cyanamid Co v Ethicon Ltd* [1975] 1 All ER 504, [1975] AC 396, [1975] 2 WLR
*b*    316, HL.
*Ashton v Sobelman* [1987] 1 All ER 755, [1987] 1 WLR 177.
*Basham (decd), Re* [1987] 1 All ER 405, [1986] 1 WLR 1498.
*Cadogan v Dimovic* [1984] 2 All ER 168, [1984] 1 WLR 609, CA.
*Central Estates (Belgravia) Ltd v Woolgar (No 2)* [1972] 3 All ER 610, [1972] 1 WLR 1048,
      CA.
*c*  *Central London Property Trust Ltd v High Trees House Ltd* (1946) [1956] 1 All ER 256,
      [1947] KB 130.
*Chatsworth Properties Ltd v Effiom* [1971] 1 All ER 604, [1971] 1 WLR 144, CA.
*Chelsea Estates Investment Trust Co Ltd v Marche* [1955] 1 All ER 195, [1955] Ch 328,
      [1955] 2 WLR 139.
*Dendy v Evans* [1910] 1 KB 263, [1908–10] All ER Rep 589, CA.
*d*  *Egerton v Jones* [1939] 3 All ER 889, [1939] 2 KB 702, CA.
*Ewart v Fryer* [1901] 1 Ch 499, CA; *affd* [1902] AC 187, [1900–3] All ER Rep 577, HL.
*Greasley v Cooke* [1980] 3 All ER 710, [1980] 1 WLR 1306, CA.
*Grundt v Great Boulder Pty Gold Mines Ltd* (1937) 59 CLR 641, Aust HC.
*Habib Bank Ltd v Habib Bank AG Zurich* [1981] 2 All ER 650, [1981] 1 WLR 1265, CA.
*Jones d Cowper v Verney* (1739) Willes 170, 125 ER 1115.
*e*  *Keith v R Gancia & Co Ltd* [1904] 1 Ch 774, CA.
*Knights v Wiffen* (1870) LR 5 QB 660.
*Lowenthal v Vanhoute* [1947] 1 All ER 116, [1947] KB 342.
*Moorgate Mercantile Co Ltd v Twitchings* [1975] 3 All ER 314, [1976] QB 225, [1975] 3
      WLR 286, CA; *rvsd* [1976] 2 All ER 641, [1977] AC 890, [1976] 3 WLR 66, HL.
*f*  *Official Custodian for Charities v Mackey* [1984] 3 All ER 689, [1985] Ch 168, [1984] 3
      WLR 915.
*Official Custodian for Charities v Mackey (No 2)* [1985] 2 All ER 1016, [1985] 1 WLR 1308.
*Official Custodian for Charities v Parway Estates Development Ltd* [1984] 3 All ER 679, [1985]
      Ch 151, [1984] 3 WLR 525, CA.
*Quilter v Mapleson* (1882) 9 QBD 672, CA.
*g*  *Ramsden v Dyson* (1866) LR 1 HL 129.
*Rogers v Rice* [1892] 2 Ch 170, [1891–4] All ER Rep 1181, CA.
*Taylor Fashions Ltd v Liverpool Victoria Trustees Co Ltd* [1981] 1 All ER 897, [1982] QB 133,
      [1981] 2 WLR 576.
*Stroud Building Society v Delamont* [1960] 1 All ER 749, [1960] 1 WLR 431.

*h*  **Cases also cited**

*Abbey National Building Society v Maybeech Ltd* [1984] 3 All ER 262, [1985] Ch 190.
*Belgravia Insurance Co Ltd v Meah* [1963] 3 All ER 828, [1964] 1 QB 436, CA.
*Blyth v Dennett* (1853) 13 CB 178, 138 ER 1165.
*Clarke v Grant* [1949] 1 All ER 768, [1950] 1 KB 104, CA.
*Denn d Brune v Rawlins* (1808) 10 East 261, 103 ER 774.
*j*  *Dixon v Kennaway & Co* [1900] 1 Ch 833.
*Doe d Cheny v Batten* (1775) 1 Cowp 243, [1775–1802] All ER Rep 594, 98 ER 1066
*Doe d Hughes v Bucknell* (1838) 8 C & P 566, 173 ER 620.
*Doe d Tucker v Morse* (1830) 1 B & Ad 365, 109 ER 822.
*Doe d Prior v Ongley* (1850) 10 CB 25, 138 ER 11.
*Doe d Pennington v Taniere* (1848) 12 QB 998, 116 ER 1144.

*Gill v Lewis* [1956] 1 All ER 844, [1956] 2 QB 1, CA.

*Great Western Rly Co v Smith* (1876) 2 Ch D 235, CA; *affd* (1887) 3 App Cas 165, HL.          *a*

*Greenwood v Martins Bank Ltd* [1933] AC 51, [1932] All ER Rep 318, HL.

*Jenkins d Yate v Church* (1776) 2 Cowp 482, 98 ER 1199.

*Jump v Payne* (1899) 68 LJQB 607.

*Ladup Ltd v Williams & Glyn's Bank plc* [1985] 2 All ER 577, [1985] 1 WLR 851.

*Lee v Smith* (1854) 9 Exch 662, 156 ER 284.

*Martin v Smith* (1874) LR 9 Exch 50.          *b*

*Pakwood Transport Ltd v 15 Beauchamp Place Ltd* (1978) 36 P & CR 112, CA.

*Public Trustee v Westbrook* [1965] 3 All ER 398, [1965] 1 WLR 1160, CA.

*Roe d Jordan v Ward* (1789) 1 H BL 97, 126 ER 58.

*Smith v Metropolitan City Properties* [1986] 1 EGLR 52.

          *c*

**Originating summonses**

By two originating summonses dated 7 January 1988 the Hammersmith and Fulham London Borough Council sought as against each of the defendants, Top Shop Centres Ltd and Glassgrove Ltd, who were the successors in title to the freehold of property at Shepherd's Bush Green, London W12 (known as Shepherd's Bush Centre and formerly the Charecroft Estate), a declaration that the council was the tenant of part of the property          *d*
on the same terms as contained in two underleases dated 2 December 1970 made between Parway Estates Developments Ltd (Parway) and the council for the residue of Parway's lease less ten days or, alternatively, relief from forfeiture under s 146(4) of the Law of Property Act 1925. The action arose following the forfeiture of Parway's headlease and the defendants' assertion that the council's underleases no longer subsisted and that its tenancy was on a year-to-year basis terminable on six months' notice. The facts are set          *e*
out in the judgment.

*Nigel Hague QC* and *D A Hochberg* for the council.

*Edward Nugee QC* and *Presiley Baxendale* for the defendants.

          *f*
                                        *Cur adv vult*

19 December. The following judgment was delivered.

**WARNER J.** These two actions were begun by originating summonses issued on 7 January 1988. In each of them the plaintiffs are the mayor and burgesses of the London          *g*
Borough of Hammersmith and Fulham, and in each of them the defendant is a subsidiary of Tops Estates plc. In the first action that subsidiary is Top Shop Centres Ltd; in the second action it is Glassgrove Ltd.

The actions are about underleases to the Hammersmith and Fulham London Borough Council of parts of a substantial development on the south side of Shepherd's Bush Green in Hammersmith. That development is on two sites, one on the eastern side and the          *h*
other on the western side of Rockley Road. The eastern site is much the larger of the two.

Omitting immaterial details, and there are many, the history of those sites and of that development is this. The two sites together constitute what was at one time called, and sometimes still is called, the Charecroft estate (the estate). The freehold of that estate was formerly owned by the trustees of the Campden Charities (the trustees).

On 10 August 1961 the trustees granted a building lease of the estate to Parway Estates          *j*
Development Ltd (Parway). That was a lease for 107½ years from 25 March 1961 at a rent (after the first two and a half years) of £15,000 pa, subject to provisions for its review. The only review that took place was in 1968, when the rent was increased to £27,500. The lease contained a proviso for re-entry in common form which was to take effect in,

*a*  inter alia, the event of the tenant going into liquidation, whether compulsorily or voluntarily, otherwise than for the purpose of reconstruction or amalgamation. I will call that lease 'Parway's lease'.

Pursuant to that lease, Parway carried out the development in question. On the eastern side that development consisted, and it consists, of a comparatively small office block called Atlantic House which fronts on Rockley Road and, on the greater part of the site, of a shopping centre at ground and basement level, a car park at first floor level, the roof

*b*  of which constitutes what is called an amenity deck (it is, I understand, a roof garden) and two tower blocks of residential flats. On the western site there were and are two more tower blocks of residential flats, car parks and a service station fronting on Shepherd's Bush Green. The whole development was completed in about 1970. It became known as the Shepherd's Bush Centre.

As the development was completed in successive phases, Parway granted underleases

*c*  of the many parts of it to appropriate tenants. In particular, on 2 December 1970, Parway granted two underleases to the council pursuant to the Housing Act 1957. One was an underlease of the two tower blocks and of the amenity deck on the eastern site. The other was an underlease of the two tower blocks and of a car park on the western site. Each of those underleases was expressed to be made in consideration of the expense incurred by the council in connection with the erection of the demised buildings, of the rent reserved

*d*  by the underlease and of the covenants by the council therein contained. In each case the underlease was for a term beginning on 2 December 1970 and continuing for the residue of the term of Parway's lease less the last ten days thereof. In other words, the underleases were to continue until 15 September 2068.

In each case the underlease reserved a yearly rent payable quarterly on the usual quarter days. That rent in the case of the first underlease was £8,000 pa. In the case of

*e*  the second underlease it was £7,000 pa. There was no provision for rent reviews. In each case the covenants by the council included full repairing covenants and a covenant to insure the demised buildings.

At various dates from 1968 to 1974, Parway mortgaged its lease. In the result, that lease became subject to a first charge in favour of the London and Manchester Assurance Co Ltd and its subsidiary, London and Manchester (Pensions) Ltd, jointly (I will call them

*f*  'the London and Manchester companies'), to a second charge in favour of Slater Walker Ltd, to a third charge in favour of the Royal Bank of Scotland plc and to a fourth charge in favour of Slater Walker Ltd again. Slater Walker Ltd played no further active part in the story and my references hereafter to the mortgagees are references to the London and Manchester companies and the Royal Bank of Scotland.

*g*  On 22 October 1976 the Royal Bank of Scotland appointed two partners in the firm of Messrs Ernst & Whinney, namely Mr Mackey and Mr Hamilton, to be joint receivers in respect of the property comprised in Parway's lease. The receivers arranged for agents, Messrs J Trevor & Sons (Trevors), to collect the rents from the underlessees and to manage the estate. Trevors paid the rent due under Parway's lease to the trustees.

On 26 February 1979 the Companies Court made a compulsory winding-up order

*h*  against Parway on the petition of the Inland Revenue Commissioners. However, Trevors continued to manage the estate as before. The trustees did not become aware of the winding up until July 1981. Thereafter they refused to accept further rent. On 10 December 1981 they applied to the Companies Court for leave to take proceedings against Parway for forfeiture of its lease. That leave was granted on 24 June 1982. On 6 July 1982 the trustees issued a writ claiming forfeiture of the lease on the ground of

*j*  Parway's liquidation and mesne profits until possession should be delivered up. The only defendant in that action, 'the forfeiture action', was Parway. The writ was served on 19 July 1982.

Parway defended the forfeiture action on the ground that the trustees should be held, for various reasons, to have waived their right to forfeit. Alternatively, it counterclaimed

for relief from forfeiture. That defence and counterclaim were undertaken by the
liquidator at the request of the receivers and on their indemnity against costs. The Royal *a*
Bank of Scotland stood behind the receivers for the purposes of that indemnity. The
liquidator took the view, rightly, as it turned out, that the charges on the lease exhausted
its value and that there was no equity in it for Parway.

On 23 May 1983, before the forfeiture action came on for trial, the mortgagees issued
summonses in that action seeking to be joined as parties to it and, if necessary, relief
under s 146(4) of the Law of Property Act 1925. That relief would be necessary if the *b*
trustees succeeded against Parway in forfeiting the lease. The summonses were adjourned
by the master to the judge to be heard immediately after the forfeiture action.

The forfeiture action came on for trial before Mr Vivian Price QC sitting as a deputy
judge of the High Court in the Chancery Division. He gave judgment on 27 July 1983.
He held that the trustees had not waived their right to forfeiture. He could not grant
Parway relief from forfeiture under s 146 of the 1925 Act because, more than a year *c*
having gone by since Parway went into liquidation, sub-s (10) of that section precluded
him from doing so. However, he held that he had power to grant Parway such relief
under the general equitable jurisdiction of the court, and he did so. That meant that he
did not need to deal with the mortgagees' summonses for relief under s 146(4) and those
summonses were not proceeded with before him.

The judgment of the deputy judge was the subject of an appeal and cross-appeal to the *d*
Court of Appeal. The decision of the Court of Appeal thereon was given on 18 April
1984: see *Official Custodian for Charities v Parway Estates Development Ltd* [1984] 3 All ER
679, [1985] Ch 151. The Court of Appeal affirmed the judge's judgment in so far as he
had held that the trustees had not waived their right to forfeiture. The Court of Appeal
held, however, that the judge had been wrong to grant Parway relief from forfeiture
under the general equitable jurisdiction of the court. It held that the effect of sub-ss (9) *e*
and (10) of s 146 was to oust any such jurisdiction where a lessor was enforcing a right to
forfeit a lease because of the bankruptcy or liquidation of the lessee.

The mortgagees' summonses for relief under s 146(4) were not before the Court of
Appeal but it was recognised in the Court of Appeal that, as a result of s 1 of the Law of
Property (Amendment) Act 1929, the mortgagees' applications for such relief would not
be subject to the one-year time limit. Counsel for the trustees accepted that the *f*
mortgagees (or one of them) would be entitled to relief subject only to consideration of
the terms on which such relief should be granted.

The order of the Court of Appeal declared that Parway's lease had been forfeited on 19
July 1982, the date of the service of the writ on the forfeiture action. The Court of Appeal
refused Parway leave to appeal to the House of Lords. Parway petitioned the House of
Lords for such leave. The Appeal Committee of the House of Lords dismissed its petition *g*
on 28 June 1984 (see [1984] 3 All ER 679 at 680, [1985] Ch 151 at 167).

It is not in doubt and it is not now disputed that, as a result of the forfeiture of Parway's
lease, all interests derived therefrom, including the mortgages and the council's
underleases, ceased to exist. However, neither the trustees nor the mortgagees took any
formal step to apprise the underlessees of the situation. They acted as though rents were *h*
still collectable from the underlessees under their underleases. While Parway's petition
to the House of Lords was pending, a dispute arose between the trustees and the
mortgagees as to who should manage the estate and receive those rents. To resolve that
dispute the trustees, on 18 May 1984, issued a writ against the receivers and the
mortgagees and, on the same day, launched a motion for interlocutory injunctions in the
action begun by that writ, which I shall call 'the trustees' second action'. *j*

The motion came before Scott J. He gave judgment on it on 15 June 1984: see *Official
Custodian for Charities v Mackey* [1984] 3 All ER 689, [1985] Ch 168. At that time the
receivers were still collecting the rents from the former underlessees and managing the
estate through Trevors. The mortgagees' summonses for relief under s 146(4) were still

pending and in addition the mortgagees had issued writs claiming such relief. However,
a  the mortgagees' advisers regarded it as inappropriate to proceed with their applications
for relief until it was certain that Parway's lease would remain forfeited. That still
depended on the outcome of the proceedings in the House of Lords.

The trustees claimed that, unless and until the House of Lords reversed the decision of
the Court of Appeal or the mortgagees obtained relief under s 146(4), they were entitled
as freeholders to receive the rents and profits of the estate and to manage it. It was
b  accepted on their behalf, as it had been in the Court of Appeal, that, if the order of the
Court of Appeal stood, the mortgagees would obtain relief under s 146(4). It was,
however, contended on behalf of the trustees that any relief under s 146(4) could only
take the form of an order vesting in the mortgagees a new lease taking effect from the
date of the order. That was accepted on behalf of the mortgagees but it was contended
on their behalf that the court making that order would have power to order also that the
c  rents and profits of the estate accruing between the date of the forfeiture of Parway's lease
and the date of the order should belong to the mortgagees. Scott J held that that was not
so. He therefore rejected arguments put forward on behalf of the mortgagees, based on
*American Cyanamid Co v Ethicon Ltd* [1975] 1 All ER 504, [1975] AC 396, that the balance
of convenience lay in favour of maintaining the status quo by allowing the receivers to
go on collecting the rents of the estate and managing it.
d    He made a complicated order designed to take account of all possible eventualities. He
granted the trustees an interlocutory injunction restraining the receivers and the
mortgagees from demanding or receiving any moneys or rents payable by occupiers or
sublessees of the estate and, on an undertaking by the trustees to instruct Trevors as their
agents in respect of the estate, a further interlocutory injunction restraining the receivers
and the mortgagees from managing or interfering with the management of the estate.
e  He ordered that both injunctions should be discharged in the event of the House of Lords
allowing Parway's appeal or in the event of a vesting order being made in favour of any
of the mortgagees under s 146(4). Lastly, on the receivers' undertaking that, in the event
of the House of Lords refusing Parway leave to appeal or dismissing its appeal, they
would account to the trustees for all rents and other moneys received by them from
f  occupiers or sublessees, he suspended both injunctions until, in effect, the determination
by the House of Lords of that appeal. Scott J also directed that the mortgagees' actions for
relief under s 146(4) should be consolidated with the trustees' second action.

In the result, Trevors continued to manage the estate and to collect the rents and profits
of it but, as from 28 June 1984, as agents for the trustees.

In October 1984 the trial of the trustees' second action took place before Nourse J.
g  During that trial, on 29 October 1984, Nourse J made by consent, on the mortgagees
agreeing to give such undertakings as the court should think fit to require as a condition
of granting relief from forfeiture, an order than the estate should vest in the London and
Manchester companies jointly for the residue of the term granted by Parway's lease, less
one day, at such rent and subject to such covenants, conditions and agreements as should
be settled by the court. On the same day the London and Manchester companies
h  instructed Trevors to continue to manage the estate on their behalf.

On 21 December 1984 Nourse J gave judgment in the trustees' second action: see
*Official Custodian for Charities v Mackey (No 2)* [1985] 2 All ER 1016, [1985] 1 WLR 1308.
There were further proceedings before him (as Nourse LJ sitting as an additional judge
of the Chancery Division) on 30 July 1985, when he settled the terms of his order (see
[1985] 1 WLR 1308 at 1318). The main question that he had to deal with was whether
j  the trustees could recover from the receivers sums paid to them by occupiers of the estate
as rent during the period between the service of the writ in the forfeiture action and the
order of Scott J. Those sums amounted to about £1m after there had been deducted from
them sums that had been received by the trustees in respect of mesne profits for that
period at the rate of £27,500 pa. Nourse J held that the trustees could not recover that

£1m or thereabouts either as money had and received by the receivers to their use or in
equity or as mesne profits for the receivers' own trespass.                                   *a*

Nourse J dealt also with the terms on which the new lease to the London and
Manchester companies should be granted pursuant to the order he had made on 29
October 1984. He directed that the new lease should be at an initial rent of £27,500 and
that it should otherwise reproduce the terms of Parway's lease. He required an
undertaking from the London and Manchester companies to use their best endeavours
to execute by 29 January 1986 certain works of repair, the details of which had been   *b*
agreed during the trial and were set forth in a schedule to his order. And he required the
London and Manchester companies to undertake to pay the whole of the trustees' costs
of the forfeiture action on the common fund basis in so far as those costs should not be
recovered in the liquidation of Parway. His order referred to the draft of a lease which
the London and Manchester companies were to execute, and contained a declaration that
that lease should be subject to the charges created by Parway during the years 1968 to   *c*
1974 in favour of the mortgagees and of Slater Walker Ltd.

On 23 September 1985 a lease in the terms ordered by Nourse J was executed by the
trustees and by the London and Manchester companies. I will call that lease 'the London
and Manchester lease'.

The London and Manchester companies then set about marketing the estate. For that
purpose they instructed Messrs Healey & Baker.                                          *d*

On 28 February 1986 contracts were exchanged firstly for the sale by the trustees to
the London and Manchester companies of the freehold of the estate for £2·5m and
secondly for the sale by the London and Manchester companies to Tops Estates plc of
both that freehold and the London and Manchester lease for a total of £6,450,000.

Between 29 October 1984 and 28 February 1986 the London and Manchester
companies had themselves granted underleases of some of the shops in the shopping   *e*
centre. The sale by the London and Manchester companies to Tops Estates plc was
expressly subject to those underleases. As regards the underleases granted earlier by
Parway, including the council's underleases, the contract for that sale contained a clause
stating that the vendors believed them to have been forfeit but that in so far as they were
still subsisting or had been affirmed by the vendors the London and Manchester lease   *f*
was sold subject to and with the benefit of them.

Completion of those contracts took place on 25 March 1986 by a series of instruments.
The effect of those instruments (I am still omitting immaterial details) was that (1) the
freehold of the eastern site was transferred to Top Shop Centres Ltd, (2) the freehold of
the western site was transferred to Glassgrove Ltd and (3) the London and Manchester
lease was surrendered.

I understand that the net proceeds of sale of the London and Manchester lease were   *g*
sufficient to pay off the London and Manchester companies' first charge, Slater Walker
Ltd's second charge and part of the Royal Bank of Scotland's third charge, but no more.

After completion Top Shop Centres Ltd and Glassgrove Ltd (the defendants) terminated
Trevors' instructions and instructed other agents to manage the estate. Thereafter
disputes arose between the defendants and some of the occupiers of the estate, including   *h*
the council, about the fate of the latter's erstwhile underleases. It was to resolve those
disputes, so far as it was concerned, that the council issued the present originating
summonses.

Throughout the period during which Trevors had managed the estate, successively on
behalf of the receivers, of the trustees and of the London and Manchester companies,
they had done so on the footing that the underleases subsisted. In particular they   *j*
demanded and received rents on that footing. The defendants contend that, in
consequence, the council now has tenancies from year to year terminable on six months'
notice of the property demised to it by its underleases on the terms of those underleases
so far as applicable to a tenancy from year to year. However the defendants say that they
have no desire to recover possession from the council, save of some small pieces of land

on the western site which the council does not need and which Glassgrove Ltd could put
*a*  to good use. Otherwise what the defendants wish to do is to negotiate with the council
for the grant of new leases to the council. Top Shop Centres Ltd also wishes to ensure
that the council carries out repairs to the amenity deck, which is admittedly in such a
state of disrepair that rainwater is leaking through it into shops below.

The council contests the defendants' view in three ways. First, it contends that the
order of Nourse J vesting the London and Manchester lease in the London and Manchester
*b*  companies had the effect of automatically reinstating the council's erstwhile underleases
as underleases to which that lease was subject. On well-known principles the subsequent
surrender of the London and Manchester lease did not extinguish those underleases but
left the freehold subject to them.

Alternatively, the council contends that the conduct of the trustees and of the London
and Manchester companies in demanding and receiving rent, and in other ways which I
*c*  have not yet referred to, gave rise to an estoppel which is binding on the defendants and
precludes them from denying that the council's underleases are still subsisting.

In the further alternative, the council contends that it is still entitled to apply for relief
from forfeiture under s 146(4) of the 1925 Act. The defendants contend that the council's
right to apply for such relief came to an end on 28 June 1984 when, as a result of Scott J's
order, the trustees became entitled to receive the rents and profits of the estate and to
*d*  manage it. However, the defendants concede that, if I should reject the council's first and
second contentions but accept its third, I should grant it relief from forfeiture.

There was before me a good deal of evidence, much of it oral, directed to the question
on what terms I should in that event grant relief. I did not, however, hear counsels'
submissions on that evidence because, before they were due to make them, agreement
was reached between the parties as to what (except as regards costs) those terms should
*e*  be.

The council's first contention raises a point of law on which there appears to be no
authority save dicta of Scott J in the judgment that he delivered on 15 June 1984, where
he said ([1984] 3 All ER 689 at 701, [1985] Ch 168 at 188):

*f*  '... it is clear that a vesting order in favour of the mortgagees under s 146(4)
could not reinstate the various subleases. Such reinstatement would require
agreement between sublessees and the relevant lessor although a measure of
reinstatement could be effected by s 146(4) vesting orders made on the application
of the sublessees.'

The point was not however argued before Scott J. I was told by counsel for the defendants,
*g*  who was there on behalf of the receivers and the Royal Bank of Scotland, that everyone
assumed the law to be as Scott J stated it, but of course no one was there to argue on
behalf of the underlessees.

Counsel for the council put forward a most attractive argument to the effect that
Scott J was wrong. He pointed out that where relief is granted to a lessee under sub-s (2)
of s 146 the effect is automatically to reinstate all derivative interests: see *Dendy v Evans*
*h*  [1910] 1 KB 263, [1908–10] All ER Rep 589. The effect, he said, should be the same as
far as possible where relief is granted under sub-s (4). Counsel accepted that, whereas the
grant of relief under sub-s (2) restores the original lease as if there had been no forfeiture,
the grant of relief under sub-s (4) creates a new lease as from the date of the court's order:
see *Chelsea Estates Investment Trust Co Ltd v Marche* [1955] 1 All ER 195, [1955] Ch 328,
*Cadogan v Dimovic* [1984] 2 All ER 168, [1984] 1 WLR 609 and the judgment of Scott J
*j*  ([1984] 3 All ER 689 at 696–701, [1985] Ch 168 at 181–187). He submitted, however,
that that new lease was obtained by the applicant in substitution for his original
underlease and should not give him something materially different. If the new lease
were free from derivative interests to which the original underlease had been subject, it
might be either more valuable or more onerous than that underlease, depending on the
characteristics of those derivative interests. Counsel drew my attention to dicta of

Vaughan Williams LJ in *Ewart v Fryer* [1901] 1 Ch 499 at 512, where he said that s 4 of
the Conveyancing Act 1892, the ancestor of s 146(4), only carried a little further the    *a*
common law principle that, where a lease was subject to an underlease, no surrender of
the lease or other arrangement between the lessor and lessee could defeat the interest or
estate of the underlessee. Counsel also relied strongly on the *Chelsea Estates* case, where
Upjohn J held that the mortgagee of a lease which had been forfeited held a new lease
vested in him under s 146(4) subject to the equity of redemption of the mortgagor.

Much as I would like to do so, I find it impossible to extend the principle of Upjohn J's    *b*
decision to the present case. An equity of redemption is, as its name indicates and as is
well known, a creature of equity. Although Upjohn J clearly felt that the case before him
was a difficult one, because his decision could give rise to anomalies and hardship
whichever way it went, there was logic in his holding that that equity attached to the
new lease obtained by the mortgagee. There is no similar equity here. As counsel for the
defendants submitted, the rights of the former underlessees depend entirely on common    *c*
law and statute. If I am to give effect to counsel's argument for the council, it can only be
by way of interpretation of s 146(4) itself.

Both counsel referred to anomalies that would arise if I decided this question in the
way the other urged me to do. To that extent I am faced with the same sort of problem
as was Upjohn J. The factor that seems to me decisive is this. As was emphasised in *Ewart
v Fryer* [1901] 1 Ch 499 particularly by Romer LJ, what is now s 146(4) confers on the    *d*
court a wide discretion. The court may not under that subsection vest in the applicant a
new lease beginning before the date of its order or ending later than the original
underlease would have done; but the discretion of the court is otherwise unfettered. In
*Ewart v Fryer* (at 515–516) Romer LJ said:

'Now, s. 4 of the Act of 1892, in my opinion, ought not to be cut down or unduly    *e*
hampered by giving a restricted meaning to each word that is used in it. The section
is to my mind purposely framed generally, so as to give the utmost liberty to the
Court to do what is just as between the parties. I think that the section gives the
most ample discretion to the Court to say upon what conditions and terms the
property comprised in the original lease should be vested in the underlessee—a
discretion absolutely unfettered by any limitation, except that contained in the    *f*
words at the end of the section. That section did not, to my mind, of necessity
contemplate that the terms of the original lease should be kept alive, either all or
any of them, though no doubt, speaking generally, regard would be had to them,
and most of them probably would be kept alive in the new lease that had to be fixed
as between the original lessor and the underlessee; but, as a matter of fact, it is not
necessary that in the new lease there should be inserted any term of the original    *g*
lease. The section is perfectly general. For example, the Court is not bound to give
to the lessee the whole of the term of his underlease. Probably it generally would do
so, but it is not bound of necessity to do it. It is bound to have regard to the words
at the end of the section, and not to give him a longer term than the term of his
underlease. The terms of the lease with respect to the covenants and so forth are, in
my opinion, left open to be dealt with according to what is thought just by the    *h*
Court, having regard to all the circumstances. That is contained in the provision as
to the execution of any deed or other document which the Court shall think fit.
Then there are these important words—"payment of rent, costs, expenses, damages,
compensation, giving security or otherwise." Does that mean that the Court is
restricted in saying what rent shall be the rent of the new lease? In my opinion, No.    *j*
It does not follow that the rent must of necessity be either the rent fixed by the
original lease or the rent fixed by the underlease. It is to be such a rent as will do
justice between the parties under the circumstances.'

Thus the court may, under s 146(4), order that the new lease should be at a rent

different from that reserved by the original underlease, as it did in *Ewart v Fryer*. It may
*a* order that the new lease should be for a term ending sooner than the term granted by the
original underlease. It may order that the new lease should contain different covenants
and it may, on my reading of the subsection, order that the new lease should comprise a
lesser part of the property demised by the forfeited lease than was comprised in the
original underlease.

That being so, it seems to me impossible to attribute to Parliament, when it enacted
*b* s 4 of the 1892 Act or when it re-enacted that provision as s 146(4) of the 1925 Act, an
intention implicitly to enact that, on the court making an order vesting a new lease in a
former underlessee, all interests derived from his original underlease should automatically
be reinstated. Those interests might not fit into the provisions of the new lease ordered
by the court. An underlease could be for a term extending beyond the term of the new
lease. It could be at a rent incompatible with that reserved by the new lease. It could
*c* require compliance with covenants different from those in the new lease and it could
comprise property not comprised in the new lease.

Counsel for the council sought to escape from that conclusion in two ways. First, he
said that it was hard to imagine circumstances in which the court would think it right to
order relief on terms inconsistent with any relevant underlease. Second, he said that the
wide discretion of the court under s 146(4) would enable it to adjust the terms of any
*d* such underlease. The latter submission is inconsistent with the concept of automatic
reinstatement and involves implying even more provisions into the subsection. Both
submissions overlook the fact that the court might not know of the existence let alone
the terms of every derivative interest. RSC (Amendment No 2) 1986, SI 1986/1187,
which came into force on 1 October 1986, amended RSC Ord 6, r 2 by adding to it para
(1)(c)(iii) and (2), with the result that a writ in a forfeiture action must now be indorsed
*e* with the name and address of, and be sent to, any person whom the plaintiff knows to be
entitled to claim relief against forfeiture under s 146(4) or in accordance with s 38 of the
Supreme Court Act 1981 as underlessee or mortgagee. That would have applied in the
present case to the trustees' forfeiture action. Whether it would have ensured that the
owners of all interests derived from Parway's lease were before the court is by no means
certain. I was told that, counting all the council's tenants, the shopkeepers and so forth,
*f* there are some 500 of them. At all events, until that amendment of Ord 6, r 2, there was
no obligation on anyone to inform the court of derivative interests. (Consider *Egerton v
Jones* [1939] 3 All ER 889, [1939] 2 KB 702 and what actually happened in the present
case.) There is still no such obligation on an applicant under s 146(4).

I therefore reject the council's first contention. I think that on that point Scott J was
*g* right.

I turn to the council's second contention, that based on estoppel. In his opening
submissions counsel for the council relied on an equitable estoppel, a proprietary estoppel.
He accepted that, if he could not succeed in establishing such an estoppel, he could not
succeed on the basis of a common law estoppel. In his closing submissions he put forward
an alternative argument, based on *Stroud Building Society v Delamont* [1960] 1 All ER 749,
*h* [1960] 1 WLR 431 and *Chatsworth Properties Ltd v Effiom* [1971] 1 All ER 604, [1971] 1
WLR 144, to the effect that, in circumstances such as those of this case, a landlord may
be precluded from denying the existence of a new tenancy on the same terms in all
respects as those of the old tenancy without the tenant having to show that he relied to
his detriment on the landlord's conduct.

I will consider first the council's case based on equitable estoppel. As to that, the
*j* principle on which counsel relied was that expressed in two passages in the judgment of
Oliver J in *Taylor Fashions Ltd v Liverpool Victoria Trustees Co Ltd* [1981] 1 All ER 897,
[1982] QB 133. The first was the passage, expressly approved by the Court of Appeal in
*Habib Bank Ltd v Habib Bank AG Zurich* [1981] 2 All ER 650 at 666, [1981] 1 WLR 1265 at
1285, where Oliver J said ([1981] 1 All ER 897 at 915–916, [1982] QB 133 at 151–152):

'Furthermore, the more recent cases indicate, in my judgment, that the application
of the *Ramsden v Dyson* (1866) LR 1 HL 129 principle (whether you call it proprietary    *a*
estoppel, estoppel by acquiescence or estoppel by encouragment is really immaterial)
requires a very much broader approach which is directed to ascertaining whether,
in particular individual circumstances, it would be unconscionable for a party to be
permitted to deny that which, knowingly or unknowingly, he has allowed or
encouraged another to assume to his detriment rather than to inquiring whether
the circumstances can be fitted within the confines of some preconceived formula    *b*
serving as a universal yardstick for every form of unconscionable behaviour.'

The second was the citation by Oliver J ([1981] 1 All ER 897 at 918, [1982] QB 133 at
154–155) from the judgment of Lord Denning MR in *Moorgate Mercantile Co Ltd v
Twitchings* [1975] 3 All ER 314 at 323, [1976] QB 225 at 241, where Lord Denning MR
said:                                                                                *c*

'Estoppel is not a rule of evidence. It is not a cause of action. It is a principle of
justice and of equity. It comes to this. When a man, by his words or conduct, has
led another to believe in a particular state of affairs, he will not be allowed to go back
on it when it would be unjust or inequitable for him to do so. Dixon J [in *Grundt v
Great Boulder Pty Gold Mines Ltd* (1937) 59 CLR 641 at 674] put it in these words:    *d*
"The principle upon which estoppel *in pais* is founded is that the law should not
permit an unjust departure by a party from an assumption of fact which he has
caused another party to adopt or accept for the purpose of their legal relations." In
1947, after the *High Trees* case [*Central London Property Trust Ltd v High Trees House
Ltd* (1946) [1956] 1 All ER 256, [1947] KB 130], I had some correspondence with
Dixon J about it, and I think I may say that he would not limit the principle to an    *e*
assumption of fact, but would extend it, as I would, to include an assumption of fact
or law, present or future. At any rate, it applies to an assumption of ownership or
absence of ownership. This gives rise to what may be called proprietary estoppel.
There are many cases where the true owner of goods or of land had led another to
believe that he is not the owner, or, at any rate, is not claiming an interest therein,
or that there is no objection to what the other is doing. In such cases it has been held    *f*
repeatedly that the owner is not to be allowed to go back on what he has led the
other to believe. So much so that his own title to the property, be it land or goods,
has been held to be limited or extinguished, and new rights and interests have been
created therein. And this operates by reason of his conduct—what he had led the
other to believe—even though he never intended it.'

                                                                                     *g*
Turning back to the facts to the present case, there is ample evidence, the details of
which I need not go into because this is not in dispute, that it was at all times the policy
of the mortgagees and in particular of the London and Manchester companies to conceal,
so far as they could, from the underlessees the fact that Parway's lease had been forfeited.
The reason was that they wished to avoid 'problems' in the management of the estate. In
particular they feared that some of the underlessees, if they knew of the forfeiture, would    *h*
be glad to be rid of what they might regard as onerous underleases. It also appears that
the trustees were content, at least from the time of the hearing before Scott J, to co-
operate in that policy. That is why, throughout the period when Trevors managed the
estate, they did so on the footing that the underleases subsisted, even to the extent of
arranging for the grant of licences to assign underleases and of conducting rent reviews
in the case of such underleases as provided for them.                                *j*
     Counsel for the council accepts, however, that the council knew of the forfeiture. [His
Lordship considered the evidence about the extent of the council's knowledge and about
representations by the London and Manchester companies that the council's underleases
subsisted, and continued:]
     Counsel for the defendants, in, if I may say so, a characteristic display of learning, took

me through a long line of cases starting with *Jones d Cowper v Verney* (1739) Willes 170,
a  125 ER 1115 and ending with *Central Estates (Belgravia) Ltd v Woolgar (No 2)* [1972] 3 All
ER 610, [1972] 1 WLR 1048, which I will for convenience call 'the yearly tenancy cases',
although that is not an entirely adequate description of them. From those cases the
following propositions may be deduced.

(1) Where a lease is voidable, for instance because there has been a breach of covenant
by the tenant entitling the landlord to forfeit the lease, subsequent acceptance of rent by
b  the landlord operates as an election by him to treat the lease as subsisting.

(2) Where, on the other hand, a lease is or has become void, for instance because,
under the old law, it was granted by a tenant for life for a period exceeding his own life,
or because it did not comply with the statutory requirements for the creation of a long
lease, or because it was granted by a mortgagor in excess of his powers, or because it has
been determined by a valid notice to quit, the subsequent acceptance of rent at the rate
c  reserved by the void lease cannot operate to restore that lease. Such acceptance of rent is,
however, a fact from which the court may infer the creation of a new tenancy from year
to year on the terms of the void lease so far as applicable to such a tenancy. Whether that
inference should be drawn was, in the days of trial by jury, a matter for the jury. It is
now a question that should be approached by the judge as a juryman would. The better
view seems to be that where the inference is drawn the creation of the new tenancy rests
d  on an implied agreement between the parties rather than on an estoppel.

Counsel for the defendants also drew my attention to 27 Halsbury's Laws (4th edn)
paras 178 and 202, from which it appears that the implication of a tenancy from year to
year will arise only where the rent reserved by the void lease was a yearly rent, albeit
payable quarterly or at other intervals. Where the void lease reserved a monthly rent, the
implication will be of a monthly tenancy. Likewise, where the void lease reserved a
e  weekly rent, the implication will be of a weekly tenancy.

It was on those authorities that counsel relied in support of the defendants' contention
that in the present case the council is entitled and entitled only to tenancies from year to
year on the terms of its former underleases so far as applicable to such tenancies. The
difficulty in counsel's way was that in none of the yearly tenancy cases, except two, did
the landlord do more than either simply accept, or demand and receive, rent. The
f  exceptions were *Lowenthal v Vanhoute* [1947] 1 All ER 116, [1947] KB 342 and *Stroud
Building Society v Delamont* [1960] 1 All ER 749, [1960] 1 WLR 431. In *Lowenthal v
Vanhoute* estoppel was not and could not have been relied on. *Stroud Building Society v
Delamont* is, as I have already mentioned, a case that is relied on also by counsel for the
council. I will advert to it in more detail later. Suffice it to say at this stage that it is, on
the present point, neutral.

g  Counsel for the defendants was thus driven to argue that this case was no different in
essence from the yearly tenancy cases because the matters other than the receipt of rent
relied on by counsel for the council were not inconsistent with the council having
tenancies from year to year on the terms of its former underleases. As regards the
correspondence in April and May 1985 between Mr Harrow (the underwriting manager
h  of London and Manchester Assurance Co Ltd) and Mr Harvey (the litigation manager in
the legal department of London and Manchester Group plc) on the one hand and Mr
Dauncey (the council's insurance officer) on the other hand, counsel for the defendants
pointed out that those terms would include the council's obligations to insure as expressed
in its underleases. There was therefore nothing in that correspondence that was
inconsistent with the defendants' contention. Likewise, those terms would include the
j  council's obligations to repair as expressed in its underleases, so that the notices under
s 146(1) served in October 1985 were also consistent with that contention. True the
reference in para 4 of each of those notices to the Leasehold Property (Repairs) Act 1938
was inapposite, but that was trivial and merely a result of the fact that whoever drew up
the notices was completing a printed form.

To my mind, those submissions were unrealistic. Against the background of the

London and Manchester companies' policy, to which the trustees conformed from June 1984 onwards, the only conclusion that can reasonably be reached is that the trustees *a* knowingly allowed and the London and Manchester companies knowingly encouraged the council to assume that it still held its underleases. In saying that, I do not overlook the letter of Mr Lucas (the clerk to the trustees) of 30 April 1984 to Mr Dauncey, which was of course written before that policy was put into effect. However, that letter itself stated that the precise implications of the forfeiture of Parway's lease were not yet known, and itself implied that the council's obligations to insure the four tower blocks continued. *b*

Any estoppel to which that conduct on the part of the trustees and of the London and Manchester companies gave rise of course binds their successors in title, including the defendants. That is not disputed. However, such an estoppel can only arise if the council in fact assumed that its underleases were still subsisting and in reliance on or as a result of that belief acted to its detriment either positively or by failing to take a step that it would otherwise have taken.        *c*

There is no doubt that the council assumed that its underleases were still subsisting. It continued to do so until well after the acquisition of the estate by the defendants. There was a conflict of evidence as to when precisely the council was first informed of the defendants' contention that its underleases had ceased to exist and been replaced by tenancies from year to year. However, I do not think that the exact date matters. It was at the earliest in April 1986 and at the latest in October of that year.        *d*

Counsel for the council instanced three ways in which the council acted to its detriment as a result of its belief in the continued existence of its underleases.

First and foremost, the council did not seek to negotiate with the London and Manchester companies for the grant of new underleases or apply for relief under s 146(4). As I have already mentioned, the London and Manchester companies did grant some *e* underleases during the currency of their lease. It also appears that, at the time of the sale to Tops Estates plc, the London and Manchester companies had agreed to grant a new underlease to a bank which occupied one of the shops in the shopping centre and which had become aware that there was a doubt about the status of its underlease.

As to the council's failure to apply for relief under s 146(4), counsel for the defendants submitted that the council was in a dilemma. Either the defendants' contention on the *f* third issue in this case was sound, so that the council lost its right to apply for relief under s 146(4) on 28 June 1984, which was before there was any representation by the trustees or by the London and Manchester companies, or that contention was unsound and it was still open to the council to apply for relief. In any case, it was still open to the council to negotiate for new underleases.

I do not think that it would be satisfactory to determine the present issue on the basis *g* of that dilemma. I therefore turn now, as it were parenthetically, to counsel's arguments on the third issue.

Those arguments centred on the opening words of s 146(4): 'Where a lessor is proceeding by action or otherwise to enforce a right of re-entry or forfeiture under any covenant, proviso, or stipulation in a lease . . .' There is no material difference between those words and the opening words of s 146(2), the ancestor of which, s 14(2) of the *h* Conveyancing and Law of Property Act 1881, was considered by the Court of Appeal in two contrasting cases, *Quilter v Mapleson* (1882) 9 QBD 672 and *Rogers v Rice* [1892] 2 Ch 170, [1891–4] All ER Rep 1181.

In *Quilter v Mapleson* a lessor had obtained judgment for possession in an action brought under a proviso for re-entry but the lessee had been granted a stay of execution. *j* It was held that the lessor was still proceeding to enforce his right of re-entry so that it was not too late for the lessee to apply for relief against the forfeiture.

In *Rogers v Rice* the lessor had obtained a similar judgment but no stay of execution had been sought and the lessor had been given possession by the sheriff. It was held that it was too late for the lessee to apply for relief from forfeiture: the lessor's 'proceeding' to enforce his right of re-entry was at an end.

In neither of those cases was there any underlease. There was an underlease in *Ashton v*
*a*  *Sobelman* [1987] 1 All ER 755, [1987] 1 WLR 177, a decision of Mr John Chadwick QC
sitting as a deputy judge of the High Court. In that case a lessor claimed to have peaceably
re-entered by changing the lock on the demised premises and handing the key of the
new lock to the underlessee. The lessor made it clear, however, to the underlessee that he
was to continue in occupation under his existing underlease. The judge held that, that
being so, there had been no effective re-entry, the continuance of the underlease being
*b*  inconsistent with the forfeiture of the headlease. It would have been otherwise if the
lessor had agreed to grant the underlessee a new lease.

Counsel for the defendants accepts that *Ashton v Sobelman* was rightly decided but says
that it is distinguishable. He submits that, where, as here, a freeholder takes proceedings
to forfeit a headlease at a time when there are underlessees in occupation, the forfeiture
is complete when the headlessee is excluded from receipt of the rents and profits of the
*c*  demised premises. Counsel says that that necessarily follows from the nature of the
headlessee's interest and from the form of the order made against him, because 'possession'
in the context of a headlease and underleases means receipt of the rents and profits. Thus,
he says, in the present case, the trustees' proceedings for forfeiture were at an end when,
on the dismissal by the House of Lords of Parway's petition for leave to appeal, Scott J's
order took effect enabling the trustees to exclude the receivers and the mortgagees, who
*d*  derived their title from Parway, from receipt of the rents and profits and from managing
the estate.

In my opinion, the fallacy underlying that argument is, as counsel for the council
pointed out, that it overlooks the fact that once the headlease has been forfeited, the
underlessees are, vis-à-vis the freeholder, trespassers. The freeholder is entitled to turn
them out of possession. The mere receipt from them of the rents payable under their
*e*  erstwhile underleases is not an assertion of the freeholder's right of re-entry as against
them. So long as the freeholder has not effectively asserted that right, for instance by
compelling the underlessees to take new leases or give up possession, he has not fully
enforced his right of re-entry. The position today, as I see it, is that the defendants, who
are persons deriving title under the trustees and therefore, by virtue of sub-s (5) of s 146,
included in the expression 'lessor' in sub-s (4), are asserting against the council a right
*f*  which was part of the trustees' original right of re-entry. That right is the foundation of
their claim that the council now has only tenancies from year to year. It follows, in my
opinion, that the council's right to apply for relief from forfeiture was not lost on 28 June
1984 but still subsists, unless of course the council is entitled to succeed on the estoppel
issue.

I turn back to that issue. On the view that I have just expressed, the way in which the
*g*  council acted to its detriment as a result of its belief in the continued existence of its
underleases was correctly described by counsel for the council as being that it did not
seek to negotiate with the London and Manchester companies for the grant of new
underleases or apply for relief under s 146(4). The two of course go together because the
possibility of the council making an application for such relief would have been a
*h*  bargaining factor in any negotiations between it and the London and Manchester
companies. The question is whether it is a sufficient answer to that point that it is still
open to the council to negotiate, albeit with the present defendants, and to apply for
relief against forfeiture. On that question counsel referred me to *Knights v Wiffen* (1870)
LR 5 QB 660. In that case the plaintiff was lulled by a statement made by the defendant
into thinking that he need not demand payment of a sum of money to which he was
*j*  entitled from a person who was on the verge of bankruptcy. Blackburn J, with whom
Mellor and Lush JJ agreed, observed (at 665): '. . . very likely he might not have derived
much benefit if he had done so; but he had a right to do it.' They held the defendant
estopped from denying the truth of his statement. In my opinion, similar considerations
apply here. It may be that the council would have been no better off negotiating with
the London and Manchester companies than with the defendants; about that one can
only speculate, but it had a right to do it.

Counsel for the council, rightly in my view, did not in the end rely at all heavily on the second way in which he said that the council had acted to its detriment in the belief *a* that its underleases subsisted. He described it as 'only a little bit of a makeweight'. This was that the council in July and August 1985 spent £51,310 in replacing light fittings on the landings and staircases of the four tower blocks. That was not just repair, it was to some extent improvement because the original fittings had been flimsy whereas the new ones were vandal-resistant. The suggestion was that the council might not have carried out that improvement if it had thought that it had only yearly tenancies or was a *b* trespasser. There was, however, no direct evidence to that effect. It appears, moreover, that over 50% of the original fittings were broken beyond repair and that spares for them could not be obtained. I think that the council might, if it had known the true position about is underleases, have tried to defer the work until it had obtained new leases.

The third fact on which counsel relied on this part of the case was the grant by the council on 18 June 1985 to a company called Company Cars Rental Ltd of a ten-year sub- *c* underlease of the car park on the western site. I heard a good deal of argument on the question whether the grant of that sub-underlease could entail any detriment to the council. Counsel for the defendants, pointing to an admission by one of the council's witnesses in cross-examination that the sub-underlease had been granted on the best terms the council could have been obtained, argued that, so long as the council's yearly tenancies continued, the fact that it had no sufficient interest to support the sub- *d* underlease could give rise to no right of action in Company Cars Rental. If the council's yearly tenancies should be determined and Company Cars Rental be in consequence evicted, that company would have no remedy against the council under the covenant for quiet enjoyment in its sub-underlease because, as was accepted by counsel for the council, that covenant had been so framed as not to apply in the case of eviction by title paramount. Nor, said counsel for the defendants, would Company Cars Rental have any *e* remedy under the other covenants to which counsel for the council referred, such as covenants to repair, because the council could not incur liability under those covenants after the sub-underlease had been determined. At this point in the argument I was left thinking that the council was at least at risk of a dispute and possibly of litigation with Company Cars Rental. Then counsel for the council cited *Keith v R Gancia & Co Ltd* [1904] 1 Ch 774, which seems to me to show that the grant by an underlessee of a sub- *f* underlease is a sufficient alteration of his position to support an estoppel without it being necessary to examine the terms of the sub-underlease. Counsel for the defendants, rightly in my view, refrained from taking the point that the sub-underlease to Company Cars Rental affected only the western site, or the point that its grant antedated the service of the s 146 notices on the council.

There was no direct evidence that the council, in acting as it did in any of the three *g* ways relied on by counsel for the council, did so in reliance on a belief induced by the conduct of the trustees and of the London and Manchester companies. But there was no evidence to the contrary either. There is authority that in those circumstances such reliance may be presumed: see *Greasley v Cooke* [1980] 3 All ER 710, [1980] 1 WLR 1306 and *Re Basham (decd)* [1987] 1 All ER 405, [1986] 1 WLR 1498. The council is in my *h* opinion entitled to the benefit of that presumption.

In the result I think that counsel has made good the council's contention based on equitable estoppel. In a nutshell, I think that, the London and Manchester companies having, with the co-operation of the trustees, encouraged the council to assume to its detriment that its underleases subsisted, it would be unconscionable for the defendants now to be permitted to deny it. *j*

The alternative argument put forward by counsel for the council in his final submissions points to a shorter route whereby a substantially similar result may be reached, albeit perhaps a technically different one. That argument was, as I mentioned, based on *Stroud Building Society v Delamont* [1960] 1 All ER 749, [1960] 1 WLR 431 and *Chatsworth Properties Ltd v Effiom* [1971] 1 All ER 604, [1971] 1 WLR 144.

In the *Delamont* case a mortgagor without the consent of the mortgagee, a building
*a*  society, granted a weekly tenancy of the mortgaged premises. Because of that lack of
consent, the tenancy was not binding on the society. The mortgagor became bankrupt
and the society appointed its secretary to be receiver under s 109 of the Law of Property
Act 1925. He, by virtue of sub-s (2) of that section, was deemed to be the agent of the
mortgagor. The receiver requested the tenant to pay the rent due in respect of her
tenancy to him. In reply to an inquiry from the tenant as to the terms of the tenancy, the
*b*  society's solicitors wrote to her saying that they were the same as those between her and
the mortgagor. She then paid rent to the society. Subsequently, the society's solicitors
gave her notice to quit, referring to her as tenant of the society. The question was
whether she had become the tenant of the society. It was common ground that, if she
had, the notice was bad because the premises were business premises and the notice did
not comply with the statutory requirements. Cross J said ([1960] 1 All ER 749 at 751,
*c*  [1960] 1 WLR 431 at 434):

> 'When a mortgagor has granted a tenancy which is not binding on the mortgagee,
> the latter can, instead of treating the tenant as a trespasser, consent to treat him as
> his own tenant or he may act in such a way as precludes him from saying that he
> has not consented to take him as a tenant. Such an acceptance by the mortgagee of
> *d*   the mortgagor's tenant, whether express or implied, or operating by way of estoppel,
> must, I think, amount to a creation of a new tenancy between the parties. The
> tenancy between the mortgagor and the tenant is not one which is merely voidable
> by the mortgagee if he chooses not to accept it, but which he can confirm by waiving
> his right to avoid it. It is a nullity as against the mortgagee and so, if the mortgagee
> is to lose his right to treat the mortgagor's tenant as a trespasser, it must be because
> *e*   the tenant has become the mortgagee's tenant under a new tenancy.'

Then, after considering the facts of the case and the arguments of counsel for the society,
he concluded ([1960] 1 All ER 749 at 752–753, [1960] 1 WLR 431 at 436):

> 'It may well be that if one takes each point which may be said to tell in favour of
> the creation of a tenancy in isolation from the rest, each can be explained away on
> *f*   those lines, but I must look at the picture as a whole. So far as I know there is
> nothing in point of law to prevent a mortgagee who has appointed a receiver of
> mortgaged premises from creating, by virtue of his legal estate in the land, the
> relationship of landlord and tenant between himself and a tenant of the mortgagor
> without previously terminating the receivership . . . On that footing, I have to say
> whether (looking at the facts as a whole and putting myself in the position of a
> *g*   juryman) the society had consented to accept Mrs. Waller as tenant notwithstanding
> the receivership or whether they had not. In my judgment the right inference to
> draw from all the facts is that the society had consented to accept Mrs. Waller as a
> tenant. No doubt the society never deliberately abandoned any right which they
> had to treat Mrs. Waller as a trespasser. They never appreciated that they had any
> such right, and, if they had appreciated it, they might well have acted differently.
> *h*   This is, however, irrelevant to the question that I have to decide. In the result,
> therefore, I must refuse this application with costs.'

The facts of *Chatsworth Properties Ltd v Effiom* were similar so far as material. The
approach of Cross J in the *Delamont* case was expressly approved and followed by the
Court of Appeal (see [1971] 1 All ER 604 at 606, 608, [1971] 1 WLR 144 at 147, 149).
*j*     Counsel for the defendants, as I said earlier, classified the *Delamont* case among what I
have called the yearly tenancy cases. He was in my opinion right to do so. (He did not
include the *Effiom* case among those cases, but I imagine that that was because, apart from
the approval of the Court of Appeal, it adds little to the *Delamont* case. He told me that he
had made a selection.)
The distinctive feature of the *Delamont* and *Effiom* cases is that in neither of them could

a tenancy have been inferred from the payment of rent alone because the rent was
payable to a receiver who was the mortgagor's agent. That is clearer in the *Effiom* case  *a*
than in the *Delamont* case. What was crucial in both cases was what had been written to
the tenant by the mortgagee's solicitors. From that the court in each case, looking at the
picture as a whole as a juryman would, inferred that a new tenancy had been created
between the mortgagee and the mortgagor's erstwhile tenant.

Now, neither in the *Delamont* case nor in the *Effiom* case could there be any question
what kind of tenancy it was. It could only be a weekly tenancy. But, if the approach of  *b*
Cross J in the *Delamont* case and of the Court of Appeal in the *Effiom* case is adopted in a
case where, as here, the tenant formerly had a long lease and the communications
received by him from the mortgagee's solicitors were consistent with the continuance of
that lease rather than with a periodic tenancy, the inference to be drawn must, it seems
to me, be the creation of a fresh tenancy on the terms of that lease. It cannot, to my
mind, weaken the tenant's case that the rent is paid not to a receiver but to the  *c*
mortgagee's agent.

Neither Cross J nor the Court of Appeal thought it necessary to decide whether the
new tenancy arose as a result of an express or implied agreement or by estoppel. As I
mentioned earlier, the better view seems to be that, where the creation of a tenancy is
inferred in accordance with the principles established by the yearly tenancy cases, it rests
on an implied agreement between the parties. If, as I think, what I am now considering  *d*
is a logical extension or development of those principles, it would follow that what was
to be implied was an agreement for the grant of a new lease on the terms of the former
one. The practical consequences of that would be different from those of an estoppel. For
instance, it would presumably be necessary for a fresh deed to be executed in pursuance
of the agreement. However, in view of the conclusion I have reached that the council is
entitled to succeed on the basis of an equitable estoppel, I need not pursue that question.  *e*

I mentioned earlier that the parties had reached agreement about the terms on which
I should grant the council relief under s 146(4) if I concluded that such relief was its only
remedy. It occurs to me that those terms ought perhaps to be recorded in an agreed form
in case a higher court should take a different view from mine of the law. I will hear
counsel on this as well as on the form of the declaration that I should make.  *f*

*Declarations accordingly.*

Solicitors: *Mackenzie Mills* (for the council); *Paisner & Co* (for the defendants).

Evelyn M C Budd    Barrister.

# Securities and Investments Board v Pantell SA and another

CHANCERY DIVISION
SIR NICOLAS BROWNE-WILKINSON V-C
7, 8 MARCH 1989

*Practice – Pre-trial or post-judgment relief – Mareva injunction – Application by party having no beneficial interest in assets and no private cause of action against defendant – Application by Securities and Investments Board – Board suspecting that Swiss company carrying on investment business in United Kingdom without authority – Board applying for Mareva injunction to freeze company's London bank account – Whether board entitled to Mareva injunction – Financial Services Act 1986, ss 3, 6.*

The defendant company sent advertisements from Switzerland offering investment advice to United Kingdom investors and stressing the impartiality of the advice offered. The advertisements recommended shares in a United States company, describing it as the 'share of 1988' and stating that it was publicly owned and traded. In fact the shares were not listed or traded on any stock exchange and the president of the company was one of the two directors of the defendant. On 7 March 1989 the Securities and Investments Board (the SIB) learnt from the public prosecutor of Lugano in Switzerland that he had taken action to close the defendant down and had instituted criminal proceedings against the managers of the defendant for swindling and breaches of Swiss banking laws. The SIB was also informed that the defendant had sent cheques from United Kingdom investors to a London bank for credit to an account in the name of the defendant. The SIB immediately started an investigation into the defendant's affairs and sought a Mareva injunction to freeze the defendant's London bank account. Under s 6[a] of the Financial Services Act 1986 the SIB could obtain a court order requiring a company which had carried on an investment business without authority in contravention of s 3[b] of that Act to pay to the SIB for the benefit of persons affected by the company's activities such sum as the court deemed just.

**Held** – Where there was a strongly arguable case that a company which was under investigation by the SIB had been carrying on an investment business without authority in contravention of s 3 of the 1986 Act the court had jurisdiction to grant, in support of the SIB's statutory right of action under s 6 for the benefit of investors, a Mareva injunction in favour of the SIB restraining the company from dissipating its assets, notwithstanding that the SIB itself had no beneficial interest in the assets and no private cause of action against the company. Accordingly, since there was a strongly arguable case that the defendant had been carrying on an investment business without authority in contravention of s 3 of the 1986 Act the court would grant the injunction sought (see p 676 c d and p 677 e f h j, post).

*Chief Constable of Leicestershire v M* [1988] 3 All ER 1015 distinguished.

## Notes

For Mareva injunctions, see 37 Halsbury's Laws (4th edn) para 362, and for cases on the subject, see 37(2) Digest (Reissue) 474–476, 2947–2962.

For the Financial Services Act 1986, ss 3, 6, see 30 Halsbury's Statutes (4th edn) 262, 264.

## Cases referred to in judgment

*Chief Constable of Leicestershire v M* [1988] 3 All ER 1015, [1989] 1 WLR 20.
*Derby & Co Ltd v Weldon (No 2)* [1989] 1 All ER 1002, [1989] 2 WLR 412, CA.

---

a   Section 6, so far as material, is set out at p 676 e to p 677 a, post
b   Section 3 is set out at p 675 e f, post

*Siskina (cargo owners) v Distos Cia Naviera SA, The Siskina* [1977] 3 All ER 803, [1979] AC
210, [1977] 3 WLR 818, HL.                                                                              *a*

**Motion**
The Securities and Investments Board (the SIB) applied ex parte for Mareva injunctions
restraining the defendants, Pantell SA and Swiss Atlantic Holdings Ltd, both of which
were Swiss companies, from removing their assets out of the jurisdiction or dealing with
those assets within the jurisdiction or in the Channel Islands. The motion was heard in   *b*
camera but judgment was given by Sir Nicolas Browne-Wilkinson V-C in open court.
The facts are set out in the judgment.

*John Brisby* for the SIB.
The defendants did not appear.

                                                                                                        *c*
**SIR NICOLAS BROWNE-WILKINSON V-C.** Yesterday evening I granted the
Securities and Investment Board (the SIB) ex parte interlocutory injunctions against a
Swiss company, Pantell SA, and another company, Swiss Atlantic Holdings Ltd (Swiss
Atlantic). The injunctions restrain the defendants from dealing with their assets in this
country and in Guernsey. The order was made in camera, but since the case is the first
brought under the Financial Services Act 1986 I am giving my reasons in open court.          *d*
    The background facts are shortly as follows. Pantell has over a period of months at
least been sending advertisements of its services from overseas addresses to individuals in
this country and offering them investment advice. The advertisements offered the
investment services of Pantell to United Kingdom investors and stressed, amongst other
things, the impartiality of the advice offered. The advertisements recommended shares
in a United States company, Euramco, describing them as 'The share of 1988'. The shares   *e*
were said to be publicly owned and traded. The evidence indicates that a Dr Axel H
Schubert is one of the two directors of Pantell.
    Inquiries made by the SIB of the Securities and Exchange Commission in the United
States disclosed that Euramco shares are not listed or traded on any stock exchange. The
evidence further suggests that it would be illegal for a United States dealer to trade in   *f*
Euramco shares which had been issued in Europe. Further, it has been discovered that
Dr Schubert, far from being independent and impartial, is apparently the president of
Euramco.
    In December 1988 and January 1989 there was correspondence between the SIB and
solicitors acting for Pantell. Pantell's solicitors agreed that the advertisements were
unlawful since Pantell was neither authorised under the Financial Services Act 1986 nor
exempted from its provisions. It was further alleged that Pantell had many customers in   *g*
this country. On 20 February 1989 Pantell's solicitors informed the SIB that Pantell
would not distribute any further advertisements in the United Kingdom.
    The SIB have been in contact with the Swiss authorities since December of last year.
Early yesterday morning, Tuesday, 7 March, a representative of the SIB spoke on the
telephone with the public prosecutor in Lugano. He was told that the public prosecutor   *h*
had taken action to close down the business of Pantell because of violations of Swiss
banking law and of the law relating to fiduciary firms. The public prosecutor had entered
the premises and seized documents and records from which he had learnt that Pantell
had done business with, and received money from, investors from many countries but
mostly from the United Kingdom. In addition, it was apparent to the public prosecutor
that Pantell were sending cheques from United Kingdom investors to a branch of Barclays   *j*
Bank in London for credit to an account apparently in the name of Pantell. It was further
explained by the public prosecutor that the action he had taken in Switzerland did not
put an end to the legal existence of Pantell nor otherwise prevent its directors or staff
from continuing to give instructions to Barclays Bank in respect of that account.
    Following that telephone call the representative of the SIB sought the approval of the

board to institute statutory investigations into the affairs of Pantell, and in particular into
a  any account which it has or has had with Barclays Bank. A Mr King and others of the SIB
staff were appointed to investigate yesterday morning. Information was received
yesterday from Mr King that Pantell had a sterling account with Barclays Bank, 68
Knightsbridge, which had been opened on 27 January. It is estimated that about
£200,000 in total has been credited to that account to date, with payments out amounting
to over £100,000, including some substantial payments to a gentleman who is named,
b  and transfers to Swiss Atlantic in Guernsey. The present balance on the account is
apparently some £68,000 in credit, of which some £49,000 is in cleared funds. It appears
that Pantell has given standing instructions to Barclays Bank about transferring credit
balances on the account to Swiss Atlantic in Guernsey.

The evidence before me also contained a press release by the public prosecutor in
Lugano stating that it had initiated criminal proceedings against the managers of Pantell
c  for repeated and continuing instances of professional swindling, breaches of the federal
banking and saving laws and violations of canton law on the obligations of fiduciaries.
The press announcement noted that Pantell and other company associates operating on
an international level have led many investors in Great Britain and other parts of the
world to buy shares in private companies at a price vastly in excess of their value. In
d  particular, customers were persuaded to buy shares in Euramco Washington, which was
supposed to be involved in mining business in Panama.

Swiss Atlantic appears to be, or to have been, the parent company of Euramco. It is
therefore associated, at least indirectly, with Dr Schubert, one of the directors of Pantell.

In the circumstances it was apparent that if any assets of Pantell or its associate, Swiss
Atlantic, were to be kept available in this country it was necessary to ensure that they
e  were not removed from the banks in this country and in Guernsey. The question is
whether the court has power to grant such relief at the behest of the SIB.

Under s 3 of the 1986 Act it is provided as follows:

'No person shall carry on, or purport to carry on, investment business in the
United Kingdom unless he is an authorised person under Chapter III or an exempted
f  person under Chapter IV of this Part of this Act.'

Pantell is neither authorised nor exempted within the meaning of that section.

Investment business is defined in s 1(2) of the Act as meaning:

'the business of engaging in one or more of the activities which fall within the
paragraphs in Part II of that Schedule and are not excluded by Part III of that
g  Schedule.'

Part II of Sch 1, cross-headed 'Activities constituting investment business', includes the
following paragraphs:

h  '12. Buying, selling, subscribing for or underwriting investments or *offering* or
agreeing to do so, either as principal or as an agent.

13. Making, or *offering* or agreeing to make—(a) arrangements with a view to
another person buying, selling, subscribing for or underwriting a particular
investment; or (b) arrangements with a view to a person who participates in the
arrangements buying, selling, subscribing for or underwriting investments . . .

j  15. Giving, or *offering* or agreeing to give, to persons in their capacity as investors
or potential investors advice on the merits of their purchasing, selling, subscribing
for or underwriting an investment, or exercising any right conferred by an
investment to acquire, dispose of, underwrite or convert an investment.'

I stress the word 'offering' in these paragraphs.

I should also at this stage note s 57(1) of the Act, which provides:

'Subject to section 58 below, no person other than an authorised person shall issue *a* or cause to be issued an investment advertisement in the United Kingdom unless its contents have been approved by an authorised person.'

Section 207(3) provides:

'For the purposes of this Act an advertisement or other information issued outside *b* the United Kingdom shall be treated as issued in the United Kingdom if it is directed to persons in the United Kingdom or is made available to them otherwise than in a newspaper, journal, magazine or other periodical publication published and circulating principally outside the United Kingdom or in a sound or television broadcast transmitted principally for reception outside the United Kingdom.'

The question that arose was whether, by sending circular advertisements from outside *c* the United Kingdom to persons within the United Kingdom, Pantell and its associates were or were not carrying on an investment business in the United Kingdom. In my judgment it is plainly arguable that they were. They were carrying on an investment business within the definition either by offering to deal, or arrange deals, in investments or by offering to give investment advice here, or by in fact dealing here in investments; dealing has arguably taken place by them taking customers' money in this country. *d* Therefore in my view there is a strongly arguable case that Pantell's activities in circularising and dealing with customers in the United Kingdom, though conducted from overseas, was in breach of s 3 of the Act.

Section 6 of the Act provides, so far as material, as follows:

'... (2) If, on the application of the Secretary of State, the court is satisfied that a *e* person has entered into any transaction in contravention of section 3 above the court may order that person and any other person who appears to the court to have been knowingly concerned in the contravention to take such steps as the court may direct for restoring the parties to the position in which they were before the transaction was entered into.

(3) The court may, on the application of the Secretary of State, make an order *f* under subsection (4) below ... if satisfied that a person has been carrying on investment business in contravention of section 3 above and (*a*) that profits have accrued to that person as a result of carrying on that business; or (*b*) that one or more investors have suffered loss or been otherwise adversely affected as a result of his contravention of section 47 or 56 below or failure to act substantially in accordance with any of the rules or regulations made under Chapter V of this Part of this Act. *g*

(4) The court may under this subsection order the person concerned to pay into court, or appoint a receiver to recover from him, such sum as appears to the court to be just having regard—(*a*) in a case within paragraph (*a*) of subsection (3) above, to the profits appearing to the court to have accrued; (*b*) in a case within paragraph (*b*) of that subsection, to the extent of the loss or other adverse effect; or (*c*) in a case within both paragraphs (*a*) and (*b*) of that subsection, to the profits and to the extent *h* of the loss or other adverse effect.

(5) The court may under this subsection order the person concerned to pay to the applicant such sum as appears to the court to be just having regard to the considerations mentioned in paragraphs (*a*) to (*c*) of subsection (4) above.

(6) Any amount paid into court by or recovered from a person in pursuance of *j* an order under subsection (4) or (5) above shall be paid out to such persons or distributed among such persons as the court may direct, being a person or persons appearing to the court to have entered into transactions with that person as a result of which the profits mentioned in paragraph (*a*) of subsection (3) above have accrued

a to him or the loss or other adverse effect mentioned in paragraph (b) of that subsection has been suffered . . .

(9) Nothing in this section affects the right of any person other than the Secretary of State to bring proceedings in respect of any of the matters to which this section applies.'

b Under the Financial Services Act 1986 (Delegation) Order 1987 SI 1987/942, the Secretary of State has transferred certain of his functions pursuant to the Act to the SIB, including in particular the power to apply to the court under s 6 of the Act.

It therefore follows that under s 6 the SIB has the right to obtain an order from the court requiring Pantell, which has been carrying on investment business in contravention of s 3, either to pay a sum of money to the SIB under sub-s (5) or otherwise to secure moneys representing profits accrued to Pantell. The sums so paid to the SIB, or otherwise c secured, would then, under s 6, be available for distribution amongst the persons who had been affected by Pantell's activities. Such an order can arguably be made also against Swiss Atlantic, who, it is said, was a person who had been knowingly concerned in the contravention of s 3. In the normal case such orders under s 6 could not properly be made without giving Pantell the opportunity to be heard, and indeed the SIB are not at this stage seeking any such order.

d What the SIB were seeking was this. With a view to subsequently pursuing rights to relief against Pantell and Swiss Atlantic under s 6, they applied for Mareva relief, being an injunction seeking to ensure that assets of Pantell and Swiss Atlantic available within the jurisdiction or in the Channel Islands are not dissipated pending the determination by the court of the question whether any and if so what order should be made against them under s 6 of the Act.

e In the ordinary case the court grants Mareva relief (ie injunctions restraining the dissipation of assets pending trial of an action) at the suit of an individual who has a private right to damages or other relief (that is to say a private cause of action): see *Siskina (cargo owners) v Distos Cia Naviera SA, The Siskina* [1977] 3 All ER 803, [1979] AC 210. In this case the SIB itself has no beneficial interest in the moneys nor, apart from the statute, any cause of action against Pantell or Swiss Atlantic. But in my judgment the statutory f right of action for the benefit of investors conferred on the SIB by s 6 is as much a right of action as any normal right of action in common law. It follows that in my judgment the SIB is as much entitled to apply for protection by way of Mareva relief on behalf of the investors adversely affected by breach of the Act as would an ordinary private individual be entitled in an ordinary action.

Since granting the order yesterday I have considered whether my decision was g inconsistent with a recent decision of Hoffmann J in *Chief Constable of Leicestershire v M* [1988] 3 All ER 1015, [1989] 1 WLR 20. In that case the judge refused interim relief by way of Mareva injunction to the chief constable, who was seeking to restrain the defendant, a person facing a criminal trial for fraud, from disposing of property so as to ensure that there would be property available out of which a fine, if any, imposed by the criminal court could be paid. In that case the moneys in question were not those in h which any person defrauded had a legal interest. There was therefore no traceable interest in any private individual. Nor in that case was there any statutory right of action such as that conferred on the SIB by s 6 of the Act. In my judgment that is the feature which distinguishes the two cases. Parliament, by giving the Secretary of State (that is to say the SIB) a statutory cause of action, has invested the Secretary of State and the SIB with the necessary locus standi to apply for relief. In my judgment the court has the incidental j powers, including the power to grant Mareva relief, necessary to prevent such statutory right of action being rendered abortive by the dissipation of assets.

The order I made extended to assets in the Channel Islands. The Channel Islands have individual jurisdictions separate from that exercised by this court. The reason I made that order was as follows. The information available suggests that the money has been transferred from the London account to an account of Swiss Atlantic in Guernsey and *a* that that account is also held with Barclays Bank plc. As I have said, Swiss Atlantic, being associated through Dr Schubert with Pantell, may well have been knowingly a party to the breach of the statutory provisions contained in s 3. It would follow that an order under s 6 may in future be made against Swiss Atlantic. The injunction relating to assets in Guernsey was expressly made subject to the proviso suggested by Lord Donaldson MR in *Derby & Co Ltd v Weldon (No 2)* [1989] 1 All ER 1002 at 1015, [1989] 2 WLR 412 at *b* 429, which reads as follows:

'Provided that, in so far as this order purports to have any effect outside England and Wales, no person shall be affected by it or concerned with the terms of it until it shall have been declared enforceable or shall have been recognised or registered or be enforced by a foreign court (and then it shall only affect such person to the extent *c* of such declaration or ... enforcement) unless that person is (a) a person to whom this order is addressed or an officer or an agent appointed by power of attorney of such a person, or (b) a person who is subject to the jurisdiction of this court and who (i) has been given written notice of this order at his or its residence or place of business within the jurisdiction and (ii) is able to prevent acts or omissions outside the jurisdiction of this court which assist in the breach of the terms of this order.' *d*

The result of that proviso in the present case is to ensure that my order has no operation within the Channel Islands and does not trespass on the jurisdiction of the Guernsey court. However, if the branch of Barclays in Guernsey is holding moneys belonging to either of the defendants, the bank (being a bank locally resident in England) will, after service of the order, be required not to part with such moneys from the accounts held with the bank with their Guernsey branch. *e*

I should make it clear that, although I in fact decided this case on the basis that I have mentioned (namely on the basis of ss 3 and 6 of the Act), my researches overnight suggest that an alternative, and possibly clearer, route would be under s 57 of the Act, which deals specifically with advertisements, in relation to which s 61 confers on the Secretary of State (and therefore on the SIB) powers which are very similar to those contained in s 6 *f* of the Act, which I have considered.

Finally, I should point out that these orders do not in any way preclude customers of Pantell individually from enforcing their rights against any assets of Pantell: see ss 6(9) and 61(9) of the Act.

*Order accordingly.*
*g*

Solicitors: *Booth & Blackwell* (for the SIB).

Celia Fox    Barrister.

a
# Re Spence (deceased)
# Spence v Dennis and another

CHANCERY DIVISION
MORRITT J
8, 9, 16 FEBRUARY 1989
b

*Legitimacy – Child of void marriage – Bigamous marriage – Child born before ceremony of marriage between parents –One parent reasonably believing marriage valid – Whether person born before void marriage could be treated as legitimate – Legitimacy Act 1976, s 1(1).*

c
In 1895 A married L and in 1911 gave birth to the first defendant. Shortly thereafter A left L, taking the first defendant with her, and went to live with S. A subsequently gave birth to J in 1912 and to the plaintiff in 1916. A's marriage to L was never dissolved, but in 1934 she went through a form of marriage with S which was void, although S, at least, reasonably believed that the marriage was valid. A died in 1949, L in 1953 and S in 1957. J died intestate in 1985 and following his death the first defendant obtained a grant of letters of administration to his estate claiming to be the lawful sister of J. The plaintiff
d
contested the claim and issued a writ against the first defendant and the Treasury Solicitor seeking, inter alia, an order that letters of administration to J's intestate estate be granted to him on the ground that he was the legitimated brother of the whole blood of J and solely entitled to his estate by virtue of s 1(1)[a] of the Legitimacy Act 1976, which provided that the 'child of a void marriage, whenever born, shall . . . be treated as the legitimate child of his parents if at the time of the act of intercourse resulting in the birth (or at the time of the celebration of the marriage if later) both or either of the parties reasonably
e
believed that the marriage was valid'. The plaintiff contended that s 1(1) applied to an illegitimate child born before a void marriage took place. The Treasury Solicitor counterclaimed, contending that s 1(1) only applied to a child born after his parents had entered into a void marriage and that, since therefore neither the plaintiff nor the first
f
defendant was a legitimate brother or sister of the whole blood of the intestate, the latter's estate devolved on the Crown as bona vacantia on his death. On the trial of the question whether a person could be treated as legitimate under s 1(1) of the 1976 Act notwithstanding that he was born before his parents entered into a void marriage as a preliminary issue,

g
**Held** – A person could not be treated as legitimate under s 1(1) of the 1976 Act if he or she was born before his parents entered into a void marriage since, on its true construction, s 1(1) had the effect of placing the child of a void marriage in the same position as the child of a lawful marriage, that is to say legitimate at birth, and consequently it would be inappropriate to describe as the 'child of a void marriage' an illegitimate child born before the void marriage took place because at the time of his birth he was not the child of such
h
a marriage but simply the child of his parents, and to hold otherwise would involve a change of status during his life which the Act did not recognise and for which it made no provision. Accordingly, s 1(1) applied only to a child born after his parents had entered into a void marriage (see p 683 b d e h j, post).

**Notes**
j
For legitimation of child of a void marriage, see 1 Halsbury's Laws (4th edn) para 604.
     For the Legitimacy Act 1976, s 1, see 6 Halsbury's Statutes (4th edn) 432.
     As from 4 April 1988 the Family Law Reform Act 1987 has reformed the law relating to the consequences of birth outside marriage and amended s 1 of the 1976 Act.

---

a   Section 1(1) is set out at p 682 b c, post

**Cases referred to in judgment**
C v C [1947] 2 All ER 50, sub nom Colquitt v Colquitt [1948] P 19, DC.                    *a*
Wicks's Marriage Settlement, Re, Public Trustee v Wicks [1940] Ch 475.

**Cases also cited**
Edmondson's Will Trusts, Re [1972] 1 All ER 444, [1972] 1 WLR 183, CA.
Farrell v Alexander [1976] 2 All ER 721, [1977] AC 59, HL.
Galloway v Galloway [1955] 3 All ER 429, [1956] AC 299, HL.                               *b*
Minister of Home Affairs v Fisher [1979] 3 All ER 121, [1980] AC 319, PC.
Packer v Packer [1958] 2 All ER 127, [1954] P 15, CA.
Tom's Settlement, Re [1987] 1 All ER 1081, [1987] 1 WLR 1021.

**Preliminary issue**
The plaintiff, Richard Thomas Spence, issued a writ against the first defendant, Violet  *c*
Adeline Dennis, and the Treasury Solicitor in respect of the estate of John Spence who
died intestate on 21 March 1985, seeking, inter alia, orders to revoke the grant of letters
of administration to the intestate's estate made to the first defendant on 11 July 1985 in
the Oxford District Probate Registry and that a grant of letters of administration be made
to him on the ground that he was the legitimated brother of the whole blood of the
intestate and solely entitled to his estate by virtue of s 1(1) of the Legitimacy Act 1976  *d*
which, he claimed, enabled an illegitimate child born before his parents entered into a
void marriage to be treated as legitimate. The Treasury Solicitor served a counterclaim
in the action on 12 May 1988 claiming that s 1(1) only applied to a child born after a void
marriage and that since neither the plaintiff nor the first defendant was a legitimate
sibling of the whole blood of the intestate, the latter's estate devolved on the Crown as
bona vacantia on his death. On 21 July 1988 his Honour Judge Paul Baker QC sitting as  *e*
a judge of the High Court in the Chancery Division in chambers ordered the following
question to be tried as a preliminary issue in the action: whether a person could be treated
as legitimate under s 1(1) of the 1976 Act notwithstanding that he was born before his
parents entered into a void marriage. The first defendant took no part in the hearing of
the preliminary issue. The facts are set out in the judgment.                              *f*

*Philip Rossdale* for the plaintiff.
*Peter Crampin* for the Treasury Solicitor.
The first defendant did not appear.

                                                                        *Cur adv vult*
                                                                                          *g*
16 February. The following judgment was delivered.

**MORRITT J.** This is the trial of a preliminary issue. The question raised is:

> 'WHETHER a person may be treated as legitimate under Section 1(1) of the
> Legitimacy Act 1976 NOTWITHSTANDING that he was born before his parents entered
> into the void marriage therein referred to.'                                            *h*

The question is raised in relation to the succession on intestacy to the estate of John
Spence who died in 1985. The intestate, the plaintiff, Richard Thomas Spence, and the
first defendant, Violet Adeline Dennis, were all children of Addy Elizabeth Pidwell (to
whom I shall refer as 'the mother'). The question in the action is whether either or both
the plaintiff and the first defendant were a brother or sister of the whole or half blood of  *j*
the intestate, for, if neither was, there are no next of kin of the intestate and his estate
devolves on the Crown as bona vacantia. Thus, the second defendant is the Treasury
Solicitor. For reasons given in a letter dated 6 December 1988 from solicitors then acting
for the first defendant, the first defendant was not represented and took no part in the
hearing of the preliminary issue; but on this issue her position is no different from that
of the plaintiff.

a
In 1895 the mother married a Mr Frederick William Love. Their marriage was never dissolved during their joint lives. In 1911 the mother gave birth to twins, one of whom is the first defendant. Shortly thereafter the mother left Mr Love, taking the first defendant but not the other twin (of whom nothing further seems to be known) with her, and went to live with Mr Thomas Spence.

The mother gave birth to the intestate on 1 December 1912 and to the plaintiff on 24 June 1916. On 5 September 1934 the mother and Mr Thomas Spence went through

b
a form of marriage ceremony. Both of them were domiciled in England at the time. For the purpose of this preliminary issue I assume that Mr Thomas Spence, at least, reasonably believed that that marriage was valid.

The mother died in 1949, Mr Love in 1953 and Mr Thomas Spence in 1957. Following the death of the intestate in March 1985, in July the first defendant obtained a grant of letters of administration claiming to be a sister of the whole blood.

c
In March 1988 the plaintiff issued the writ in this action. He claims to be a legitimate brother of the whole blood of the intestate and the only person entitled to the estate of the intestate. The Treasury Solicitor claims that neither the plaintiff nor the first defendant is a legitimate brother or sister of the whole or half blood.

By s 1 of the Legitimacy Act 1926 it was provided:

d
'(1) Subject to the provisions of this section, where the parents of an illegitimate person marry or have married one another, whether before or after the commencement of this Act, the marriage shall, if the father of the illegitimate person was or is at the date of the marriage domiciled in England or Wales, render that person, if living, legitimate from the commencement of this Act, or from the date of the marriage, whichever last happens.

e
(2) Nothing in this Act shall operate to legitimate a person whose father or mother was married to a third person when the illegitimate person was born . . .'

Those provisions and the marriage ceremony in 1934 had no effect on the status of the mother's three children. First, at the time of their respective births the mother was married to Mr Love so that s 1(2) applied. Second, the marriage ceremony was bigamous and therefore not a legally valid marriage so as to come within s 1(1).

f
The law was amended in both respects by the Legitimacy Act 1959. Section 1 provided:

'(1) Subsection (2) of section one of the Legitimacy Act 1926 (which excludes the operation of that Act in the case of an illegitimate person whose father or mother was married to a third person at the time of the birth) is hereby repealed.

g
(2) In relation to an illegitimate person to whom it applies by virtue of this section, the Legitimacy Act, 1926, shall have effect as if for references to the commencement of that Act there were substituted references to the commencement of this Act.'

Thus the fact that the mother was married to Mr Love when the three children were born was no longer an obstacle. Section 2 provided:

h
'(1) Subject to the provisions of this section, the child of a void marriage, whether born before or after the commencement of this Act, shall be treated as the legitimate child of his parents if at the time of the act of intercourse resulting in the birth (or at the time of the celebration of the marriage if later) both or either of the parties reasonably believed that the marriage was valid.

j
(2) This section applies, and applies only, where the father of the child was domiciled in England at the time of the birth or, if he died before the birth, was so domiciled immediately before his death . . .'

Subsection (5) contained the definition of the expression 'void marriage' in the following terms:

'"Void marriage" means a marriage, not being voidable only, in respect of which

the High Court has or had jurisdiction to grant a decree of nullity, or would have or
would have had such jurisdiction if the parties were domiciled in England.'          *a*

Thus the fact of a marriage being void was no longer an obstacle to legitimacy in the
circumstances to which that section applied. These provisions and others were
consolidated into the Legitimacy Act 1976.

Section 1 of the 1976 Act provides:

'(1) The child of a void marriage, whenever born, shall, subject to subsection (2)    *b*
below and Schedule 1 to this Act, be treated as the legitimate child of his parents if
at the time of the act of intercourse resulting in the birth (or at the time of the
celebration of the marriage if later) both or either of the parties reasonably believed
that the marriage was valid.
(2) This section only applies where the father of the child was domiciled in
England and Wales at the time of the birth or, if he died before the birth, was so    *c*
domiciled immediately before his death.'

It is common ground that the 1934 marriage was a void marriage within the definition
contained in s 10 of the 1976 Act. The issue between the parties is clearly reflected in the
preliminary issue. Is it necessary that the birth of the child in question should follow the
void marriage, as the Treasury Solicitor contends, or may those events occur in either    *d*
order, as the plaintiff contends?

Before considering the words of sub-s (1) it is convenient to consider the structure and
context of the 1976 Act as a whole.

Section 2 provides for the legitimation of a person by the subsequent valid marriage of
his parents. A child of the parents so marrying 'shall, if the father of the illegitimate
person is at the date of marriage domiciled in England or Wales, render that person, if    *e*
living, legitimate from the date of the marriage'.

Section 3 deals with cases where the father is domiciled not in England or Wales but
in a country by the law of which an illegitimate child may be legitimated by virtue of
his parents' subsequent marriage. In the event of a subsequent marriage of the parents in
that country, the child, if living, 'shall in England and Wales be recognised as having
been so legitimated from the date of the marriage'.    *f*

Section 10 contains a definition of 'legitimated person' which applies except where the
context otherwise requires. That definition provides:

'"Legitimated person" means a person legitimated or recognised as legitimated—
(a) under section 2 or 3 above; or (b) under section 1 or 8 of the Legitimacy Act
1926; or (c) except in section 8, by a legitimation (whether or not by virtue of the
subsequent marriage of his parents) recognised by the law of England and Wales    *g*
and effected under the law of any other country; and cognate expressions shall be
construed accordingly.'

Thus, in the circumstances where s 1(1) does apply, the child is to 'be treated as the
legitimate child of his parents' but is not a legitimated person for the purposes of other
sections of the Act. Accordingly, s 5(3), (4) and (6) and ss 8 and 9 do not apply to a person    *h*
treated as legitimate under s 1(1). Both ss 5(3) and 8 point to a contrast in requiring the
legitimated person to be treated 'as if he had been born legitimate'.

There are therefore clear distinctions between 'a legitimated person' and a person
'treated as the legitimate child of his parents'. In the case of the former, legitimation
operates from the date of the subsequent marriage but for some specific purposes he is
treated as if he had been born legitimate. Rights of succession are expressly conferred by    *j*
s 5. The parents of the legitimated person are required to reregister the child within
three months of the date of the marriage (s 9).

By contrast, in the case of a person required by s 1(1) to be treated as the legitimate
child of his parents, no rights of succession are expressly conferred. Paragraphs 3 and 4
of Sch 1 assume rights of succession to exist equivalent to the rights of a child born of a

lawful marriage but exclude or limit those rights in specific cases or by reference to the
*a* commencement of the 1959 Act. There is no obligation to reregister comparable to s 9, and s 1(1) does not say in terms that the child is to be treated as the legitimate child of his parents from the date of the void marriage.

It is noticeable that s 1(2) refers to the domicile of the father at the time of the birth of the child, whereas ss 2 and 3 apply by reference to domicile at the date of the parents' marriage.

*b* In the light of those considerations I accept the submission of the Treasury Solicitor that the words in s 1(1) 'shall be treated as the legitimate child of his parents' operate so as to put that child in the same position, that is to say legitimate at birth, as the child of a lawful marriage.

The Treasury Solicitor's argument then proceeds to point out that the 1976 Act does not contemplate any change in such a child's status during its lifetime so that the void
*c* marriage must (it is argued) precede the birth.

Against that, the plaintiff contends that the phrase 'child of a void marriage' embraces a child born before the ceremony, that 'whenever born' means what it says and that the condition 'if at the time of the act of intercourse resulting in the birth (or at the time of the celebration of the marriage if later)' recognises that the birth may precede the marriage.

*d* The phrase 'child of a marriage' would comprise the children born in lawful wedlock and, in some contexts, those previously legitimated by the marriage (cf *Re Wicks's Marriage Settlement, Public Trustee v Wicks* [1940] Ch 475 and *C v C* [1947] 2 All ER 50, sub nom *Colquitt v Colquitt* [1948] P 19). But in the context of s 1(1) it would be inappropriate to describe as 'the child of a void marriage' an illegitimate child born before the void marriage took place. At the time of his birth he is not the child of a void
*e* marriage. At the time of the void marriage he is not the child of such a marriage: he is the child of his parents. If the section operates, he is treated as the legitimate child of his parents. If it does not, he remains the illegitimate child of his parents. Accordingly, in my judgment, this phrase, properly construed, supports the argument of the Treasury Solicitor.

*f* I accept, as the plaintiff submitted, that the word 'whenever' means 'at any time' and therefore the birth may be at any time. But this does not advance the argument, because the requisite birth is not of any child but is of the 'child of a void marriage'. The meaning of that phrase is not enlarged by the words 'whenever born'.

The condition to which I have referred recognises that conception may precede the void marriage. But it does not in terms recognise that the birth may. The later of the two events is taken as the time at which to test the reasonableness of the belief of either
*g* or both parents as to the validity of the marriage for good and obvious reasons; but it does not, in my judgment, require the inference that the birth may precede the void marriage particularly when such an inference would be inconsistent with the phrase 'the child of a void marriage'.

Accordingly, the structure and context of the 1976 Act as a whole, which differentiates
*h* between a child to whom s 1(1) applies and a legitimated person as defined and the words used in s 1(1) all point to the conclusion that s 1(1) only applies to a child born after the void marriage. Such a child when born is treated as the legitimate child of his parents. To hold otherwise would involve a change of status during his life which the Act does not recognise and for which it makes no provision.

Accordingly, I answer the preliminary issue in the negative.

*j*
*Order accordingly.*

Solicitors: *Owen White*, Ashford, Middlesex (for the plaintiff); *Treasury Solicitor*.

Hazel Hartman    Barrister.

# Sheikh v Chief Constable of Greater Manchester Police

COURT OF APPEAL, CIVIL DIVISION
O'CONNOR, CROOM-JOHNSON AND BALCOMBE LJJ
27, 28 FEBRUARY, 21 MARCH 1989

Police – Dismissal – Constable – Special constable – Discrimination on grounds of race – Whether special constable holding office of constable – Whether special constable deemed to be in employment as constable – Whether special constable entitled to protection against unlawful discrimination in employment on racial grounds – Race Relations Act 1976, ss 4, 16.

A special constable holds the office of constable, and accordingly is entitled to the protection of s 4[a] of the Race Relations Act 1976, which makes acts of discrimination by an employer unlawful, since by virtue of being a constable he is deemed by s 16[b] of the Act to be in employment and entitled to the protection of s 4 (see p 690 d e j and p 691 g h, post).

## Notes
For special constables, see 36 Halsbury's Laws (4th edn) paras 208–210, and for cases on the subject, see 37(1) Digest (Reissue) 323–324, 2088–2093.

For discrimination in employment on the ground of race, see 4 Halsbury's Laws (4th edn) para 1038.

For the Race Relations Act 1976, ss 4, 16, see 6 Halsbury's Statutes (4th edn) 770, 779.

## Cases referred to in judgments
A-G for New South Wales v Perpetual Trustee Co Ltd [1955] 1 All ER 846, [1955] AC 457, [1955] 2 WLR 707, PC.
Comr of Metropolitan Police v Hancock [1916] 1 KB 190, DC.
Fisher v Oldham Corp [1930] 2 KB 364, [1930] All ER Rep 96.

## Case also cited
Donaghey v P O'Brien & Co [1966] 2 All ER 822, [1966] 1 WLR 1170, CA.

## Appeal
Arshad Sheikh appealed against the decision of the Employment Appeal Tribunal (Wood J, Mr G A Peers and Mr S R Corby) ([1988] ICR 743) on 4 July 1988 dismissing his appeal from the decision of an industrial tribunal (chairman Mr W G Senior) sitting at Manchester on 23 October 1987 to refuse to hear out of time an application by the appellant that the respondent, the Chief Constable of the Greater Manchester Police, had unlawfully discriminated against the applicant by refusing him employment in the Greater Manchester Police Force and by dismissing him from his appointment as a special constable with the force. The facts are set out in the judgment of Croom-Johnson LJ.

Benet Hytner QC and G H K Meeran for the appellant.
Geoffrey Tattersall for the respondent.

Cur adv vult

21 March. The following judgments were delivered.

**CROOM-JOHNSON LJ** (giving the first judgment at the invitation of O'Connor LJ). This case has run a peculiar course. The appellant was born in Pakistan and came to this

---

a   Section 4, so far as material, is set out at p 685 b d, post
b   Section 16 is set out at p 687 d to j, post

country in 1969 as a child. He formed a desire to join the police force, but it seems he
a was too young, and so after passing an exam and being interviewed he was on 16 April
1986 appointed as a special constable. With a view to joining the regular police force he
attended a weekend assessment on 7 November 1986, but on that occasion he failed. On
29 May 1987 he was asked to resign and on 11 June 1987 his period of service as a special
constable was terminated.

He alleges that both events were due to racial discrimination, and applied to the
b industrial tribunal. The application in respect of refusal of entry to the police force was
made under the Race Relations Act 1976, s 4(1), which says:

'It is unlawful for a person, in relation to employment by him at an establishment
in Great Britain, to discriminate against another . . . (c) by refusing or deliberately
omitting to offer him that employment.'

c The application was made out of time but under s 68(6) of the 1976 Act the tribunal
could agree to hear it, if it considered it just and equitable to do so. The tribunal indicated
that it would refuse to exercise its discretion and promised to give reasons but did not do
so. It was therefore agreed before the Employment Appeal Tribunal that the issue of
refusal of entry must be returned to the same tribunal to be dealt with, and that was so
ordered.

d The dispute as to dismissal from the special constabulary was rejected on a preliminary
point that the tribunal did not have jurisdiction to entertain the application. Section 4(2)
of the 1976 Act states:

'It is unlawful for a person, in the case of a person employed by him at an
establishment in Great Britain, to discriminate against that employee . . . (c) by
e dismissing him, or subjecting him to any other detriment.'

Section 78 defines 'employment' as:

'employment under a contract of service or of apprenticeship or a contract
personally to execute any work or labour, and related expressions shall be construed
accordingly.'

f Before the tribunal it was urged that service as a special constable was a contract to
execute work or labour, notwithstanding that a special constable receives no remuneration.
What was said to be consideration moving from the chief constable, sufficient to support
a contract of employment, was a £20 boot allowance and subsistence allowances, the loan
of a uniform, the right to a pension in the event of illness or injury contracted while on
duty and exemption from jury service. The tribunal found there was no contract, and
g declined jurisdiction.

The appellant appealed, alleging that:

'The Tribunal had misdirected itself as to the proper test to be applied in
determining the question whether the appellant was employed under a contract of
service [and] as to the proper interpretation of the words "a contract personally to
h execute any work or labour" in section 78(1) . . .'

That, and the grounds supporting it, was the only matter put before the Employment
Appeal Tribunal.

It is clear from the judgment that the rejection of the 'contract' alleged was the only
ground of decision by the appeal tribunal, a decision which was reached by a majority.
j But the appeal tribunal went on to say ([1988] ICR 743 at 750):

'However, the majority are greatly exercised by the seeming unfairness of the
situation in which the [appellant] finds himself. By section 16 of the Race Relations
Act 1976, a regular police constable and a police cadet can bring proceedings alleging
gross racial discrimination, but a special constable cannot . . .'

and had carried out further research on its own. Section 16 can be loosely labelled a provision for deemed employment. The appeal tribunal concluded, again by a majority, that there were no provisions of the 1976 Act which enabled him to do so.

There has been some difference of opinion before us as to whether these other matters were even mentioned, let alone relied on, before the appeal tribunal. Counsel for the appellant has told us that they were referred to. Counsel for the respondent disagrees. I cannot help concluding that since any point on s 16 was not included in the grounds of appeal from the industrial tribunal, and it did not form part of the judgment of the appeal tribunal, if it was mentioned it can only have been a passing reference. Nevertheless, the point based on s 16 figures in the notice of appeal to this court, and counsel for the appellant has asked that in any event it should be argued here and considered by us. Counsel for the respondent objected. We have a discretion to allow it to be taken. It is a pure point of law. As will appear, our decision on the alternative point of counsel for the appellant obviously has relevance to the issue which has already been sent back to the industrial tribunal concerning the failure to enrol the appellant as a member of the regular police force. We considered that, since the whole matter is also one of general public importance, it would be wrong for this case to go off on the 'contract' point alone, and granted the application of counsel for the appellant, allowing a suitable short adjournment.

Section 1 of the 1976 Act defines discrimination for the purposes of the Act as racial discrimination.

Part II of the Act deals with discrimination in the employment field, and is itself divided into three sections: discrimination by employers, discrimination by other bodies, and police. Section 4 sets out what discrimination is unlawful. The main point of counsel for the appellant is that a special constable is included in s 16.

Special provision had to be made for the police, because it is trite law that the police are not 'employed' in the usual legal sense of that word. They are holders of a public office under the Crown and their authority is exercised by virtue of that office: see *A-G for New South Wales v Perpetual Trustee Co Ltd* [1955] 1 All ER 846 at 858, [1955] AC 457 at 489 per Viscount Simonds. Therefore, unless they were deemed to be in employment by s 16, the 1976 Act would have no application to police forces.

At common law, a constable is employed by nobody. The local corporation whose watch committee had established a police force was not vicariously liable for any torts committed by a member of that force: see *Fisher v Oldham Corp* [1930] 2 KB 364, [1930] All ER Rep 96. Nor is the chief constable. Nor is the Crown. It was therefore necessary for vicarious liability to be established by special statutory provision. This is contained in the Police Act 1964. Section 48(1) makes the chief constable liable for torts committed by a constable under his direction 'in like manner as a master is liable in respect of torts committed by his servants in the course of their employment . . .' Section 48(2) provides for any damages awarded against the chief constable 'in any proceedings brought against him by virtue of this section' to be met out of the police fund for that police area. This section thus provides a remedy for the innocent victim of a tortious constable, but it does not change the constitutional position.

Accordingly, s 4 of the 1976 Act, which deals with discrimination in relation to employment, cannot be used to apply to a police constable by making use of the definition of 'employment' set out in s 78, because the type of contract which is there referred to is a contract of employment which does not cover him. That definition, drawn in the way in which it is, covers not only the ordinary contract of service, but includes contracts for services which are performed by contractors 'employed' in the wider sense. It was urged before the industrial tribunal, the Employment Appeal Tribunal, and us, that a special constable engages 'personally to execute any work or labour', and time was devoted to itemising the duties of a special constable and those details of his engagement which are capable of amounting to consideration which can support such a contract. To my mind, this is a misconceived application of ss 4 and 78 because, if a special constable can be brought within s 4 by this device, the same reasoning

can be used to bring a police constable who is a member of a regular force within it. But
*a* the 1976 Act has recognised that in order to apply to police constables a special deeming
section, s 16, is needed.

Having said that, it only remains to say what has been put forward as the 'consideration'
which might bring a special constable within the extended definition of 'employment'
in s 78 is not capable of doing so. In my view, the industrial tribunal and Employment
Appeal Tribunal correctly rejected the submissions.

*b* It is the chief constable who engages a special constable. There are terms on which he
engages him, but they do not create a contract. They are all at the discretion of the chief
constable, save for exemption from jury service. As to this, special constables are made
ineligible by the Juries Act 1974. Counsel for the appellant was driven to submitting
that if the chief constable has a contract with a special constable (and, presumably, with a
police constable) it would be open to the chief constable to sue for damages for breach of
*c* contract if the 'special' failed to turn up for duty, a suggestion which cannot be entertained
for a moment.

The real point in this appeal is the new one, which is whether a 'special' is brought
within the 1976 Act by the deeming s 16, which provides:

'(1) For the purposes of this Part, the holding of the office of constable shall be
*d* treated as employment—(*a*) by the chief officer of police as respects any act done by
him in relation to a constable or that office; (*b*) by the police authority as respects
any act done by them in relation to a constable or that office.

(2) There shall be paid out of the police fund—(*a*) any compensation, costs or
expenses awarded against a chief officer of police in any proceedings brought against
him under this Act, and any costs or expenses incurred by him in any such
*e* proceedings so far as not recovered by him in the proceedings; and (*b*) any sum
required by a chief officer of police for the settlement of any claim made against
him under this Act if the settlement is approved by the police authority.

(3) Any proceedings under this Act which, by virtue of subsection (1), would lie
against a chief officer of police shall be brought against the chief officer of police for
the time being or, in the case of a vacancy in that office, against the person for the
*f* time being performing the functions of that office; and references in subsection (2)
to the chief officer of police shall be construed accordingly.

(4) Subsection (1) applies to a police cadet and appointment as a police cadet as it
applies to a constable and the office of constable.

(5) In this section—"chief officer of police"—(*a*) in relation to a person appointed,
or an appointment falling to be made, under a specified Act, has the same meaning
*g* as in the Police Act, (*b*) in relation to any other person or appointment, means the
officer who has the direction and control of the body of constables or cadets in
question; "the Police Act" means, for England and Wales, the Police Act 1964 or, for
Scotland, the Police (Scotland) Act 1967; "police authority"—(*a*) in relation to a
person appointed, or an appointment falling to be made, under a specified Act, has
the same meaning as in the Police Act, (*b*) in relation to any other person or
*h* appointment, means the authority by whom the person in question is or on
appointment would be paid; "police cadet" means any person appointed to undergo
training with a view to becoming a constable; "police fund" in relation to a chief
officer of police within paragraph (*a*) of the above definition of that term has the
same meaning as in the Police Act, and in any other case means money provided by
the police authority; "specified Act" means the Metropolitan Police Act 1829, the
*j* City of London Police Act 1839 or the Police Act.'

The whole question under the section is whether a 'special' holds 'the office of
constable'.

It will be noticed that there is no reference in s 16 to special constables, and it was
initially because of that omission that the Employment Appeal Tribunal, in its 'researches',

declined to apply s 16 to them. It also relied on the provisions dealing with 'employment' in the Employment Protection Act 1975 and Employment Protection (Consolidation) *a* Act 1978 which contain exemptions for people in police service. With respect to the appeal tribunal, the employment protection legislation is an unsafe guide, because it is providing protection which cannot in any event be given to police constables. It is dealing with a different problem. For the for same reason, I am unwilling to place reliance on the provisions of the Sex Discrimination Act 1975, where s 17 contains provisions which are clearly analogous to those of the Race Relations Act 1976, but which *b* are not of direct application, and on which counsel for the appellant relied. The problem, in my view, is to be solved by construing s 16.

The office of constable is of great antiquity, and his duties have always included the keeping and enforcement of the King's and Queen's peace. This power was local. Special constables, on the other hand, were first put on a statutory basis by the Special Constables Act 1831. By s 1, in time of tumult, riot or felony, any two justices of a parish or *c* township, if they considered that there were insufficient ordinary officials appointed for preserving the peace, were given power to appoint—

> 'so many as they shall think fit of the Householders or other Persons (not legally exempt from serving the Office of Constable) residing in such Parish, Township, or Place as aforesaid, or in the Neighbourhood thereof, to act as Special Constables, for *d* such Time and in such Manner as to the said Justices respectively shall seem fit and necessary, for the preservation of the Public Peace . . .'

Although the appointment was compulsory, the duties were essentially part-time. The justices were authorised to administer to every person so appointed an oath spelt out in the section, whereby he swore to serve the King 'in the Office of Special Constable'. The requirement that the 'special' should not be 'legally exempt from serving the office of *e* constable', while a pointer, is not by itself conclusive of the nature of the office of special constable.

At this time, the development of police forces, comprising constables, had not really begun. There were two more statutes dealing with special constables, in 1835 and 1838. The County Police Act 1839, sometimes called the Police Act 1839, by its preamble *f* recited the 1831 Act and stated that it was not expedient further to enlarge the powers of justices for appointing constables. It allowed the appointment of a chief constable who would appoint the petty constables, and gave him power to dismiss them. In this way the modern police constable grew out of the 1831 Act, as did the full-time paid police force in the modern sense. In the mean time, special constables were only removable by the justices under s 9 of the 1831 Act, a state of affairs which continued until 1914. While a police constable attested as such, 'specials' continued to use the oath or declaration *g* in the form prescribed by s 1 of the 1831 Act. When the Municipal Corporations Act 1882, s 191 empowered boroughs to appoint more borough constables, the oath was that appropriate to a constable, and he was liable to dismissal, under the Police Act 1839, by both the justices and the chief constable. Section 196, on the other hand, empowered the borough justices to appoint special constables, who took the different oath for 'specials' as *h* laid down by s 1 of the 1831 Act.

The 1914–18 war brought about a change. The Special Constables Act 1914 provided that by Orders in Council regulations might be made in respect of the appointment and position of special constables appointed under the 1831 Act. The Special Constables Order 1914, SR & O 1914/1375, in effect applied to them a number of the provisions of the Police Act 1839, two of which gave the chief constables of the police areas the *j* direction and control over them, and also the power to dismiss them. In *Comr of Metropolitan Police v Hancock* [1916] 1 KB 190 the issue was whether the regulations were ultra vires, so as to allow dismissal by the chief constable. The Divisional Court, presided over by Lord Reading CJ, held that the regulations were intra vires. The Special Constables Act 1914 applied only 'during the present war'. The Special Constables Act

1923 deleted those words, and the regulations were thus perpetuated. The position has
*a* therefore been that since then special constables while on duty have been under the
operational control of the appropriate chief constable, and liable to dismissal by him,
although they are not, be it noted, members of his police force.

By 1964 the reorganisation of the police forces in this country had reached such an
extent that a streamlining and simplification was necessary. The long title of the Police
Act 1964 is:

*b*
'An Act to re-enact with modifications certain enactments relating to police forces
in England and Wales, to amend the Police (Scotland) Act 1956, and to make further
provision with respect to the police.'

It is unquestionably an amending Act. While there are references throughout to
'constables', the word is used, according to context, in the primary meaning of a 'constable'
*c* in the historic sense, and in the secondary meaning as denoting a particular rank in a
police force.

Special constables are dealt with by s 16:

'(1) The chief officer of police of the police force maintained for any police area
may, in accordance with regulations under Part II of this Act, appoint special
*d* constables for that area.
(2) Subject to such regulations as aforesaid, all special constables for a police area
(including persons appointed as such before the commencement of this Act) shall
be under the direction and control of, and subject to dismissal by, the chief officer
of police.'

The reference to regulations is to the power of the Secretary of State conferred by s 34
*e* to 'make regulations as to the government, administration and conditions of service of
special constables.' Section 17 deals with police cadets.

The whole of the Special Constables Acts of 1831, 1835 and 1838, which had remained
in force all this time, were repealed. So was that part of the Municipal Corporations Act
1882 dealing with the appointment of special constables.

*f* Section 18 deals with the attestation of constables, which has always been the moment
at which they assume their powers and privileges. It requires:

'Every member of a police force maintained for a police area and every special
constable appointed for a police area shall, on appointment, be attested as a constable
by making a declaration in the form set out in Schedule 2 to this Act . . .'

*g* That form says:

'I,            of            do solemnly and sincerely declare and affirm
that I will well and truly serve Our Sovereign Lady the Queen in the office of
constable . . .'

In other parts of the Police Act 1964 the use of the terms 'constable' and 'special
*h* constable' is not entirely consistent. Reference has already been made to the provision in
s 48(1) for the chief constable to be vicariously liable for 'torts committed by constables
under his direction', and by s 48(2) for the payment of damages or costs so incurred out
of the police fund. Section 48(4), however, authorises the police authority (which controls
the police fund) to make such payments of damages and costs awarded 'against a member
of the police force . . . or any special constable . . .' This appears to suggest that a special
*j* constable is not included in the term 'constable' in s 48(1).

These provisions are imitated by s 16 of the Race Relations Act 1976 in providing for
the payment of compensation, costs and expenses payable under that Act, without
making express reference to special constables.

It is also to be noted that in regulations made by the Secretary of State under s 34 of
the Police Act 1964 reference is made to the 'office as a special constable' (see the Special

Constables (Injury Benefit) Regulations 1987, SI 1987/159) and 'the office of special constable' (see the Special Constables (Pensions) Regulations 1973, SI 1973/431). In the *a* Special Constables Regulations 1965, SI 1965/536, there is provision for disciplinary suspension 'from his office as constable'. There are other examples where the differences between the types of constables are spelt out, but it is not necessary to refer to them all.

But in s 19 of the Police Act 1964, which deals with the jurisdiction of constables, sub-s (1) says that a member of a police force shall have all the powers and privileges of a constable throughout England and Wales, whereas sub-s (2) provides that a special *b* constable shall have all the powers and privileges of a constable in the police area for which he is appointed. Pro tanto, the powers and privileges are the same. The child has now taken over the parent.

In my view, any special constable appointed under the 1831 Act, when he took the precribed oath, assumed the office of a constable for the area in which he was appointed and for so long as he was on duty. When by the Special Constables Act 1914 Parliament *c* authorised the making of regulations to bring 'specials' within the provisions of the Police Acts 1839 to 1910, it was recognising that different kinds of holders of the office of constable were to a large extent being brought into line. No other explanation can be given for the regulations, two of which are (for ease of reference) set out in *Comr of Metropolitan Police v Hancock* [1916] 1 KB 190 at 193. It was clearly assumed that when a 'special' was acting under the control of the chief constable he was exercising the office of *d* a constable. The Police Act 1964 proceeded on the same basis, and so did s 16 of the Race Relations Act 1976.

Moreover, the rules laid down by Pt II of the Race Relations Act 1976 clearly apply to part-time employment as well as to full-time employment, and when one looks at the 'deeming' s 16 one can see no reason why the part-time constable should have been left out. A special constable is, after all, a constable, although of a special kind, and once he *e* has attested he has assumed (and always did) that office.

I would therefore allow this appeal, and order that the appellant's complaint be remitted to the same industrial tribunal for hearing on its merits.

**BALCOMBE LJ.** This appeal raises a single issue of law: is a special constable within *f* those provisions of the Race Relations Act 1976 which relate to discrimination in the employment field?

Subsections (1) and (2) of s 4 of the Race Relations Act 1976 make certain acts of racial discrimination in the employment field unlawful; the particular complaint in the present case is discriminatory dismissal under s 4(2)(c). The industrial tribunal never investigated whether there had been unlawful discrimination because it accepted the respondent's contention that there was no jurisdiction to hear the complaint. *g*

It is long established that a police officer is not an employee of any person or body, be it the chief constable or the police authority: he is the holder of an office. However, s 16(1) of the 1976 Act provides that for the purposes of Part II of the Act (which includes s 4)—

> 'the holding of the office of constable shall be treated as employment—(a) by the *h* chief officer of police as respects any act done by him in relation to a constable or that office; or (b) by the police authority as respects any act done by them in relation to a constable or that office.'

So the short point is: does a special constable hold the office of constable? I entertain no doubt that he does. Whatever may have been the position before the coming into *j* force of the Police Act 1964 (the judgment of Croom-Johnson LJ deals fully with that position) that Act leaves no room for any doubt on this point. Some confusion may have arisen because the Act uses the term 'constable' in two senses: (1) as the lowest rank which may be held by a member of a police force, and it is common ground that a special constable is not a member of a police force and (2) as an office (one of the oldest in the

kingdom: Dogberry and Verges in Shakespeare's *Much Ado About Nothing* were constables)
*a* which is held by every member of a police force, from the highest rank to the lowest.

Section 16 of the Police Act 1964 is now the statutory authority for the appointment of special constables. Section 18 of the same Act provides for the attestation of constables and, so far as relevant, is in the following terms:

*b* 'Every member of a police force maintained for a police area *and every special constable appointed for a police area* shall, on appointment, be attested *as a constable* by making a declaration in the form set out in Schedule 2 to this Act . . .'

Schedule 2 sets out the form of declaration as follows:

*c* 'I,          of          do solemnly and sincerely declare and affirm that I will well and truly serve Our Sovereign Lady the Queen *in the office of constable* . . . and that while I continue to hold the said office I will to the best of my skill and knowledge discharge all the duties thereof faithfully according to law.' (My emphasis.)

In the light of these provisions it seems to me that the question is susceptible of only one answer.

*d* Certainly the draftsman of the Sex Discrimination Act 1975, with which the Race Relations Act 1976 is intended to correspond (see the title to the latter Act), considered that a special constable was the holder of the office of constable. I refer to s 17 of the 1975 Act, and in particular to the reference to special constables in s 17(2)(c). It is clear that the draftsman considered that special constables hold the office of constable, whereas police cadets have to be treated differently (see s 17(1)(3)(6)).

*e* I do not understand why so obvious a point was not raised at all before the industrial tribunal, was not raised in the notice of appeal to the Employment Appeal Tribunal and was only argued (if at all) very much as a line of last resort before the appeal tribunal, and counsel for the appellant has not given us any explanation. I can understand the frustration of counsel for the respondent in finding it raised, for the first time, as the leading point in this court. Nevertheless, there is no issue of fact on which it depends, *f* and it would have been quite wrong for this court to have decided this appeal on an entirely false basis, merely because the point had not been taken below. I also feel sympathy for the members of the two tribunals below who find their decisions reversed on a ground that was either not argued at all or, at best, only faintly argued, before them.

In the result I would allow this appeal on the simple ground that a special constable holds the office of constable and is therefore entitled to the protection of the Race *g* Relations Act 1976. It is unnecessary to deal with the alternative way in which counsel for the appellant put his case, and which was the way it was argued in both tribunals below, since he accepted that the 'work and labour' point arose only if he failed on the 'office of constable' point.

**O'CONNOR LJ.** I agree that this appeal should be allowed for the reasons given by *h* Croom-Johnson LJ.

*Appeal allowed.*

Solicitors: *Cuff Roberts North Kirk*, Liverpool (for the appellant); *R C Rees*, Salford (for the respondent).

Raina Levy   Barrister.

# Factortame Ltd and others v Secretary of State for Transport

HOUSE OF LORDS

LORD BRIDGE OR HARWICH, LORD BRANDON OF OAKBROOK, LORD OLIVER OF AYLMERTON, LORD GOFF OF CHIEVELEY AND LORD JAUNCEY OF TULLICHETTLE

17, 18, 19, 20, 24, 25, 26, 27 APRIL, 18 MAY 1989

*Injunction – Interlocutory – Jurisdiction – Injunction restraining enforcement of legislation pending reference to European Court – Applicants seeking injunction restraining Secretary of State from enforcing legislation against applicants pending reference to European Court – Legislation not requiring assistance from court for its enforcement – Legislation unambiguous – Whether court having jurisdiction to disapply legislation pending reference to European Court – Merchant Shipping Act 1988, Pt II, s 14(1) – Merchant Shipping (Registration of Fishing Vessels) Regulations 1988.*

*Crown – Relief against the Crown – Interlocutory relief – Jurisdiction – Injunction against officer of the Crown – Interim injunction – Judicial review proceedings – Application for interim injunction protecting Community rights claimed by applicants pending preliminary ruling from European Court – Interim injunction restraining Secretary of State from enforcing legislation against applicants pending ruling – Whether court having jurisdiction to grant injunction against Crown – Crown Proceedings Act 1947, ss 21(2), 23(2)(b) – Supreme Court Act 1981, s 31(2) – RSC Ord 53, r 1(2).*

Following the fixing of quotas for national fishing fleets under the European Economic Community's common fishing policy to prevent overfishing, the United Kingdom Parliament enacted the Merchant Shipping Act 1988, Pt II of which was intended to protect British fishing interests by restricting the number of vessels whose catch could be considered part of the United Kingdom's quota. Under the 1988 Act the Secretary of State was empowered to make regulations for a new register of British fishing vessels and in the exercise of those powers he promulgated the Merchant Shipping (Registration of Fishing Vessels) Regulations 1988, under which fishing vessels registered as British under the existing register of British fishing vessels were required to reregister under the 1988 Act as from 1 March 1988. Vessels could only qualify for entry on the new register if their owners or, in the case of companies, their shareholders were British citizens or were domiciled in Britain. The applicants were English companies which owned or managed 95 deep sea fishing vessels registered as British under the existing register of British fishing vessels but most of their directors and shareholders were Spanish nationals and consequently the applicants were unable to comply with the conditions for registration set out in s 14(1)[a] of the 1988 Act and could not qualify for entry on the new register. The applicants sought, by means of an application for judicial review, to challenge the validity of the legislation, contending that it contravened the provisions of the EEC Treaty by depriving the applicants of their Community law rights. The Secretary of State contended that Community law did not restrict a member state's right to decide who was entitled to be a national of that state or what vessels were entitled to fly its flag and that the 1988 legislation, being designed to achieve Community purposes, namely the common fisheries policy, conformed with Community law. The Divisional Court decided to request a preliminary ruling from the Court of Justice of the European Communities under art 177 of the Treaty on the substantive questions of Community law to enable it to determine the application, and pending the European Court's ruling it granted interim relief to the applicants in the form of orders that pending final

---

a    Section 14(1) is set out at p 696 *d*, post

judgment the operation of Pt II of the 1988 Act and the 1988 regulations were to be
a disapplied and the Secretary of State restrained from enforcing those provisions in respect
of the applicants. The purpose of the interim relief was to grant interim protection of
the applicants' Community law rights so as to enable them to continue to operate their
95 vessels as if they were duly registered British fishing vessels. It was anticipated that it
would take at least two years from the making of the reference before the European
Court would be able to make a ruling. The Secretary of State appealed against the interim
b relief granted, contending that the court had no jurisdiction to grant relief in the form
of an order disapplying a statute or restraining the Secretary of State from enforcing it.
The Court of Appeal allowed the appeal and set aside the order for interim relief. The
applicants appealed to the House of Lords.

**Held** – (1) The court had no power to make an order postponing the coming into force
c of a statute pending a reference to the European Court to determine its validity.
Accordingly, the Divisional Court had had no power to make the interim order
disapplying the provisions of Pt II of the 1988 Act until some uncertain future date, since
those provisions required no assistance from the court for their enforcement and were
unambiguous in their terms. Moreover, if the applicants failed to establish the rights
d they claimed before the European Court, the grant of the interim relief would have had
the effect of conferring on them rights directly contrary to Parliament's sovereign will
and of depriving British fishing vessels, as defined by Parliament, of a substantial
proportion of the United Kingdom quota of fish stocks protected by the common fisheries
policy (see p 702 j to p 703 c and p 710 h to p 711 b, post); F Hoffmann-La Roche & Co AG v
Secretary of State for Trade and Industry [1974] 2 All ER 1128 distinguished.
　　(2) Moreover, the court had no power to grant an interim injunction against the
e Crown in judicial review proceedings because injunctions had never been available at
common law in proceedings on the Crown side and that position had been effectively
preserved by ss 21(2)<sup>b</sup> and 23(2)(b)<sup>c</sup> of the Crown Proceedings Act 1947. Furthermore,
s 31(2)<sup>d</sup> of the Supreme Court Act 1981 had not conferred a new jurisdiction on the court
to grant interim injunctions against the Crown in judicial review proceedings and RSC
f Ord 53, r 1(2)<sup>e</sup>, which was in identical terms, could not extend the jurisdiction of the
court in that respect (see p 705 g, p 706 b to d, p 708 b to d f g, p 709 a b and p 710 h to
p 711 b, post); dicta in IRC v Rossminster [1980] 1 All ER 80 disapproved; R v Secretary of
State for the Home Dept, ex p Herbage [1986] 3 All ER 209 and R v Licensing Authority, ex p
Smith Kline & French Laboratories Ltd (Generics (UK) Ltd intervening) (No 2) [1989] 2 All ER
113 overruled.
g　　(3) However, the question whether, irrespective of the position under national law,
there was an overriding principle of Community law that a national court was under an
obligation to provide an effective interlocutory remedy to protect rights having direct
effect under Community law where a seriously arguable claim of entitlement to such
rights was advanced and the party claiming those rights would suffer irremediable
damage if he was not effectively protected during the interim period pending
h determination of the existence of those rights would be referred to the European Court
for a preliminary ruling under art 177 of the EEC Treaty (see p 710 c to f h to p 711 b,
post); Srl CILFIT v Ministry of Health Case 283/81 [1982] ECR 3415 applied.

b  Section 21(2) is set out at p 705 j, post
c  Section 23(2), so far as material, is set out at p 706 e, post
j
d  Section 31(2) is set out at p 703 j to p 704 a, post
e  Rule 1(2), so far as material, provides: 'An application for a declaration or an injunction . . . may be
made by way of an application for judicial review, and on such an application the Court may grant
the declaration or injunction claimed if it considers that, having regard to—(a) the nature of the
matters in respect of which relief may be granted by way of an order of mandamus, prohibition
or certiorari, (b) the nature of the persons and bodies against whom relief may be granted by way
of such an order, and (c) all the circumstances of the case, it would be just and convenient for the
declaration or injunction to be granted on an application for judicial review.'

**Notes**
For restrictions on granting injunctions against an officer of the Crown, see 11 Halsbury's   *a*
Laws (4th edn) para 1435.

For judicial review, see 37 ibid paras 567–583, for prerogative orders, see 11 ibid 1451,
and for cases on the subject, see 16 Digest (Reissue) 321–435, 3362–4797.

For references to the Court of Justice of the European Communities, see 51 Halsbury's
Laws (4th edn) paras 2·172–2·193.

For the Crown Proceedings Act 1947, ss 21, 23, see 13 Halsbury's Statutes (4th edn) 30,   *b*
32.

For the Supreme Court Act 1981, s 31, see 11 ibid 782.

For the EEC Treaty, art 177, see 50 ibid 325.


**Cases referred to in opinions**
                                                                          *c*
*American Cyanamid Co v Ethicon Ltd* [1975] 1 All ER 504, [1975] AC 396, [1975] 2 WLR
316, HL.
*Bourgoin SA v Ministry of Agriculture Fisheries and Food* [1985] 3 All ER 585, [1986] QB
716, [1985] 3 WLR 1027, CA.
*Firma Foto-Frost v Hauptzollamt Lubeck-Ost* Case 314/85 [1988] 3 CMLR 57, CJEC.
*Granaria BV v Hoofdproduktschap voor Akkerpbouwprodukten* Case 101/78 [1979] ECR 623.   *d*
*Hoffmann-La Roche (F) & Co AG v Secretary of State for Trade and Industry* [1974] 2 All ER
1128, [1975] AC 295, [1974] 3 WLR 104, HL; *affg* [1973] 3 All ER 945, [1975] AC
295, [1973] 3 WLR 805, CA.
*Hutton v Secretary of State for War* (1926) 43 TLR 922, HL.
*IRC v Rossminster Ltd* [1980] 1 All ER 80, [1980] AC 952, [1980] 2 WLR 1, HL.
*Merricks v Heathcoat-Amory* [1955] 2 All ER 453, [1955] Ch 567, [1955] 3 WLR 56.   *e*
*O'Reilly v Mackman* [1982] 3 All ER 1124, [1983] AC 237, [1982] 3 WLR 1096, HL.
*Pesca Valentia Ltd v Minister for Fisheries and Forestry* [1985] IR 193, Ir SC.
*R v Licensing Authority, ex p Smith Kline & French Laboratories Ltd (Generics (UK) Ltd
intervening) (No 2)* [1989] 2 All ER 113, [1989] 2 WLR 378, CA.
*R v Ministry of Agriculture Fisheries and Food, ex p Agegate Ltd* Case 3/87 (18 November
1988, unreported), Adv Gen.   *f*
*R v Ministry of Agriculture Fisheries and Food, ex p Jaderow Ltd* Case 216/87 (18 November
1988, unreported), Adv Gen.
*R v Secretary of State for the Home Dept, ex p Herbage* [1986] 3 All ER 209, [1987] QB 872,
[1986] 3 WLR 505.
*Srl CILFIT v Ministry of Health* Case 283/81 [1982] ECR 3415.
*Tamaki v Baker* [1901] AC 561, PC.   *g*


**Appeal**
By a notice of motion dated 22 December 1988 Factortame Ltd, Rawlings (Trawling) Ltd
and 93 others, who were the owners or managers of fishing vessels or the shareholders
and directors of the owners and managers, applied for judicial review of (1) the decision   *h*
of the Secretary of State for Transport, as contained in reg 66 of the Merchant Shipping
(Registration of Fishing Vessels) Regulations 1988, SI 1988/1926, that in the case of
fishing vessels owned, controlled and/or managed by nationals of member states of the
European Communities and duly registered as British fishing vessels under Pt IV of the
Merchant Shipping Act 1984 immediately before 1 December 1988, their continued
registration as such British fishing vessels (as provided by s 13(3) of the Merchant   *j*
Shipping Act 1988) should cease after 31 March 1989, unless the conditions for eligibility
as set out in Pt II of the 1988 Act and Pt VII of the 1988 regulations were satisfied, (2) the
decision of the Secretary of State, as contained in the 1988 regulations and, in particular,
Pt VII thereof, to render the applicants' fishing vessels and any British fishing vessels
which were or would be owned, chartered or operated by them or managed on their

behalf ineligible to be registered as British fishing vessels under Pt II of the 1988 Act,
a unless the conditions of eligibility set out in Pt II of the 1988 Act and Pt VII of the 1988
regulations were satisfied, (3) Pt II of the 1988 Act and, in particular (but without
prejudice to the generality of the foregoing), ss 12 to 18 and 22 to 25 thereof, and Pt VII
of the 1988 regulations to the exent that they rendered ineligible the applicants' fishing
vessels duly registered under Pt IV of the 1894 Act and any other British fishing vessels
which were or would be owned, chartered or operated by them or managed on their
b behalf to be registered as British fishing vessels under Pt II of the 1988 Act, unless the
conditions therein set out were satisfied. The relief sought was (1) a declaration that (i)
the decision of the Secretary of State, as embodied in particular in the provisions of Pt VII
of the 1988 regulations, to render ineligible for continued registration as British fishing
vessels after 31 March 1989 any existing British fishing vessels duly registered under
Pt IV of the 1894 Act which were now or might in the future be owned, chartered or
c operated by the applicants or managed on their behalf on the ground that such vessels
were (a) not British owned for the purposes of s 14 of the 1988 Act and/or (b) not
managed, directed and controlled from within the United Kingdom for the purposes of
s 14 thereof and/or (c) chartered, managed or operated by a person or company other
than a qualified person or company for the purposes of s 14 thereof, and/or (ii) the
provisions of Pt II of the 1988 Act and/or (iii) the provisions of Pt VII of the 1988
d regulations might not be applied to the applicants on grounds that such application was
contrary to EEC law as given effect by the European Communities Act 1972, in particular,
(a) arts 7, 34, 40, 48 to 66 and 221 of the EEC Treaty, (b) Council Regulations (EEC) 101/
76, 2796/81 and 170/83 relating to the common fisheries policy, (c) the principles of
proportionality, protection of legitimate expectation, acquired rights, non-retroactivity,
non-discrimination and equal treatment and respect for fundamental rights recognised
e and protected by EEC law and (d) the Treaty of Accession of the Kingdom of Spain to the
European Communities, (2) an order of prohibition prohibiting the Secretary of State
from treating the existing registration of the applicants' fishing vessels under Pt IV of the
1894 Act as having ceased on 1 April 1989, unless the applicants satisfied the conditions
of eligibility as set out in Pt II of the 1988 Act and Pt VII of the 1988 regulations, (3)
f damages and interest thereon pursuant to s 35A of the Supreme Court Act 1981, (4)
further or other relief, including a stay or interim relief pending final determination of
this matter and (5) costs. By order dated 10 March 1989 the Divisional Court (Neill LJ
and Hodgson J) decided to seek a preliminary ruling from the Court of Justice of the
European Communities pursuant to art 177 of the EEC Treaty on the substantive
questions of Community law which it considered necessary to enable it finally to
determine the application and pending final judgment or further order directed that the
g operation of Pt II of the 1988 Act and the 1988 regulations be disapplied and the Secretary
of State restrained from enforcing the same in respect of any of the applicants and any
vessel now owned (in whole or in part), managed, operated or chartered by any of them
so as to enable registration of any such vessels under the 1894 Act and the/or the Sea
Fishing Boats (Scotland) Act 1886 to continue in being. The Secretary of State appealed
h against so much of the order as granted the applicants interim relief pending the
reference to the European Court. On 16 March 1989 the Court of Appeal (Lord
Donaldson MR, Bingham and Mann LJJ) for reasons given on 22 March 1989 allowed
the appeal and set aside the interim order of the Divisional Court. The applicants appealed
with leave of the Court of Appeal to the House of Lords. The facts are set out in the
opinion of Lord Bridge.

j  *David Vaughan QC, Gerald Barling* and *David Anderson* for the first 94 applicants.
*Nicholas Forwood QC* for the 95th applicant, Rawlings (Trawling) Ltd.
*The Solicitor General (Sir Nicholas Lyell QC), John Laws* and *Christopher Vajda* for the Secretary
  of State.

Their Lordships took time for consideration.

18 May. The following opinions were delivered.

**LORD BRIDGE OF HARWICH.** My Lords, the applicants are a number of companies incorporated under the laws of the United Kingdom and also the directors and shareholders of those companies, most of whom are Spanish nationals. The applicant companies between them own or manage 95 deep sea fishing vessels, which were until 31 March 1989 registered as British fishing vessels under the Merchant Shipping Act 1894. Of these vessels 53 were originally registered in Spain and flew the Spanish flag. These 53 vessels were registered under the 1894 Act at various dates from 1980 onwards. The remaining 42 vessels had always been British fishing vessels. These vessels were purchased by the applicants at various dates, mainly since 1983.

The statutory regime governing the registration of British fishing vessels was radically altered by Pt II of the Merchant Shipping Act 1988 and the Merchant Shipping (Registration of Fishing Vessels) Regulations 1988, SI 1988/1926, both of which came into force on 1 December 1988. The following are the critical provisions of the Act which affect the applicants:

'**14.**—(1) Subject to subsections (3) and (4), a fishing vessel shall only be eligible to be registered as a British fishing vessel if—(a) the vessel is British-owned; (b) the vessel is managed, and its operations are directed and controlled, from the within the United Kingdom; and (c) any charterer, manager or operator of the vessel is a qualified person or company.

(2) For the purposes of subsection (1)(a) a fishing vessel is British-owned if— (a) the legal title to the vessel is vested wholly in one or more qualified persons or companies; and (b) the vessel is beneficially owned—(i) as to not less than the relevant percentage of the property in the vessel, by one or more qualified persons, or (ii) wholly by a qualified company or companies, or (iii) by one or more qualified companies and, as to not less than the relevant percentage of the remainder of the property in the vessel, by one or more qualified persons . . .

(7) In this section—"qualified company" means a company which satisfies the following conditions, namely—(a) it is incorporated in the United Kingdom and has its principal place of business there; (b) at least the relevant percentage of its shares (taken as a whole), and of each class of its shares, is legally and beneficially owned by one or more qualified persons or companies; and (c) at least the relevant percentage of its directors are qualified persons; "qualified person" means—(a) a person who is a British citizen resident and domiciled in the United Kingdom, or (b) a local authority in the United Kingdom; and "the relevant percentage" means 75 per cent. or such greater percentage (which may be 100 per cent.) as may for the time being be prescribed.'

Fishing vessels previously registered as British under the 1894 Act require to be reregistered under the 1988 Act, subject to a transitional period prescribed by the 1988 regulations which permitted their previous registration to continue in force until 31 March 1989.

At the time of the institution of the proceedings in which this appeal arises, the 95 fishing vessels in question failed to satisfy one or more of the conditions for registration under s 14(1) of the 1988 Act, and thus failed to qualify for registration, by reason of being managed and controlled from Spain or by Spanish nationals or by reason of the proportion of the beneficial ownership of the shares in the applicant companies in Spanish hands. The applicants sought by application for judicial review to challenge the legality of the relevant 1988 legislation on the ground that it contravened the provisions of the EEC Treaty and other rules of law given effect thereunder by the European Communities Act 1972 by depriving the applicants of rights of the kind referred to in s 2(1) of the 1972 Act as enforceable Community rights. It will be convenient to use the expression 'Community law' as embracing the EEC Treaty, subordinate legislation of

institutions of the European Economic Community (the EEC) and the jurisprudence
a developed by the Court of Justice of the European Communities and to use the expression
'directly enforceable Community rights' as referring to those rights in Community law
which have direct effect in the national law of member states of the EEC. The defence of
the Secretary of State to the applicants' challenge was and is, first, that Community law
does not in any way restrict a member state's right to decide who is entitled to be a
national of that state or what vessels are entitled to fly its flag and, second, that, in any
b event, the new legislation is in conformity with Community law and, indeed, is designed
to achieve the Community purposes enshrined in the common fisheries policy.

The applicants' application for judicial review was heard by the Divisional Court (Neill
LJ and Hodgson J), which, in judgments delivered on 10 March 1989, decided to request
a preliminary ruling from the European Court in accordance with art 177 of the EEC
Treaty on the substantive questions of Community law which it considered necessary to
c enable it finally to determine the application. The precise terms of the questions proposed
to be referred by the Divisional Court have not yet been settled. The Divisional Court
went on to consider an application by the applicants for interim relief and made an order
for the interim protection of the directly enforceable Community rights claimed by the
applicants in the following terms:

d      'IT IS ORDERED that: 1) Pending final judgment or further order herein the
       operation of Part II of the Merchant Shipping Act 1988 and the Merchant Shipping
       (Registration of Fishing Vessels) Regulations 1988 be disapplied and the Secretary of
       State be restrained from enforcing the same in respect of any of the Applicants and
       any vessel now owned (in whole or in part) managed operated or chartered by any
       of them so as to enable registration of any such vessel under the Merchant Shipping
e      Act 1894 and/or the Sea Fishing Boats (Scotland) Act 1886 to continue in being . . .'

An appeal against this order was heard by the Court of Appeal (Lord Donaldson MR,
Bingham and Mann LJJ), which on 16 March 1989 allowed the appeal, set aside the order
for interim relief and granted leave to appeal to your Lordships' House, giving its reasons
for its decision on 22 March.
f     Since the only issue before your Lordships on the appeal relates to the grant of interim
relief, your Lordships have not been called on to examine in any detail the rival
arguments of the parties on the substantive issues of Community law which will
determine the final outcome of the application for judicial review, or to consider the
voluminous affidavit evidence which was fully examined by the Divisional Court. In
these circumstances I shall gratefully adopt so much of the admirably lucid judgment of
g Neill LJ in the Divisional Court as is necessary to appreciate the nature of these arguments
and the factual and historical background against which the substantive issues fall to be
determined.
    Having set out the terms of the principal articles of the EEC Treaty relied on by the
applicants, Neill LJ continued:

h      'On the basis of these articles it was argued on behalf of the applicants that they
       had a number of relevant rights under Community law, including the following:
       (a) the right not to be discriminated against on the grounds of nationality (art 7);
       (b) the right in the case of the individuals to establish a business anywhere in the
       EEC (art 52) (including the right to carry on fishing at sea) and, in the case of the
       companies, [to be treated in the same way as natural persons who are nationals of
       member states] (art 58); and (c) the right in the case of the individual applicants to
j      participate in the capital of the applicant companies (art 221). It was further argued
       that these provisions of Community law were provisions which had direct effect
       and that the applicants' rights would be infringed by the application to them of the
       1988 Act and the 1988 regulations. It was submitted that these rights were
       fundamental rights which could not be swept away or submerged by the common

fisheries policy and that all provisions of the common fisheries policy had to be read
subject to these fundamental provisions. On behalf of the Secretary of State, on the  *a*
other hand, it was argued that the provisions of the Treaty were of no direct
relevance in this case because each member state has a sovereign right to decide
questions of nationality, that is who are permitted to be nationals and who are
permitted to fly the national flag. In the alternative, it was argued, the whole matter
was governed by the common fisheries policy, which was established to cope with
the special problems in the fishing industry and which recognised the importance,  *b*
and the need for protection, of national fishing fleets and national fishing
communities, and that the legislation merely gave effect to the common fisheries
policy and was therefore wholly consistent with the Community law.'

The judgment then traces the history of the common fisheries policy from its origins
before the accession of the United Kingdom to the Common Market through various  *c*
Community regulations up to the establishment of the system laid down for the
conservation of stocks of certain fish and the allocation of quotas to member states in
1983 which is embodied in the relevant Council regulations now applicable. The
judgment continues:

'The system adopted by the Council to ensure fair distribution was by the  *d*
establishment of national quotas. These national quotas were directly linked to
vessels flying the flag or registered in the individual member state. As I have already
observed, in art 10 of [Council Regulation (EEC) 2057/82] and art 11 of [Council
Regulation (EEC) 2241/87], all relevant fish caught by vessels flying the flag counted
against the quota of that state. In order to decide how to share out the available fish
between member states the Council took into account the quantities of fish which  *e*
had been caught, on average, by the fishing fleets of the relevant state between 1973
and 1978. Once the area governed by the common fisheries policy was extended as
from 1 January 1977 to a range of 200 miles from the coastline of member states,
the common fisheries policy began to make an impact on areas of the eastern
Atlantic, including the Western Approaches, which had traditionally been fished by
Spanish fishing vessels. Prior to the accession of Spain to the Community in 1986,  *f*
the rights of Spain to fish in the waters of the member states was governed by an
agreement reached between the EEC and Spain in 1980. This agreement laid down
strict limits on fishing by Spanish-registered boats. The principle of national quotas
was incorporated into the Act of Accession of 1985 whereby Spain and Portugal
became members of the EEC. The Act of Accession prohibited more than 150
Spanish fishing vessels in specified areas. From about 1980 onwards the applicants  *g*
and others began to register vessels which had formerly been Spanish fishing vessels
(that is vessels which had formerly flown the flag of Spain) as British fishing vessels
under the Merchant Shipping Act 1894. Some 53 of these vessels are those owned
by the applicants. In addition, the applicants and others bought British fishing
vessels with a view to using them for fishing in the area covered by the common
fisheries policy. The fish were, in the main, destined for the Spanish market. As  *h*
time went by the United Kingdom government became concerned at the growth of
the practice whereby Spanish interests were either buying British fishing vessels or
reregistering Spanish vessels under the 1894 Act. The United Kingdom government
therefore decided to make use of the powers contained in s 4 of the Sea Fish
(Conservation) Act 1967 to impose some additional conditions for the licences which
are required before fishing for stocks which are subject to quotas under the common  *j*
fisheries policy by vessels of 10 metres length and over. These new conditions were
announced on 6 December 1985. The conditions were of three kinds: operating,
crewing and social security. The conditions were described by Mr Noble [on behalf
of the Secretary of State] in his first affidavit in para 22, and can be summarised as
follows. The operating conditions were designed to ensure that the vessels concerned

had a real economic link with the United Kingdom ports. That link was to be
*a*   demonstrated in one of two ways: first, by selling a portion of the catch in the
United Kingdom (the landing test) or, second, by making a specified number of
visits to the United Kingdom (the visiting test). The crewing condition required
that at least 75% of the crew should be made up of EEC nationals (excluding, for a
period, nationals of Spain, Greece and Portugal) ordinarily resident in the United
Kingdom. The social security condition required that all the crew should contribute
*b*   to the United Kingdom's national insurance scheme. These conditions came into
force in January 1986. They have been challenged by Spanish interests in the
European Court in Luxembourg. It has been contended that they are contrary to
Community law. The decision of the European Court in the two relevant references
is now awaited. The cases have been brought, respectively, at the suit of a company
called Agegate Ltd and another company called Jaderow Ltd (see *R v Ministry of*
*c*   *Agriculture Fisheries and Food, ex p Agegate Ltd* Case 3/87 (18 November 1988) and *R*
*v Ministry of Agriculture Fisheries and Food, ex p Jaderow Ltd* Case 216/87 (18 November
1988)). In the course of the argument we were referred to the opinions in these two
cases of Mr Advocate General Mischo, in which he expressed views about the validity
of the conditions. In summary, his opinion was this: that the crewing and social
security conditions were valid, that the visiting test would be valid provided it did
*d*   not interfere with exports, but that the landing test (included as part of the operating
conditions) was in breach of art 34 of the EEC Treaty. It should be remembered that
earlier I referred to the terms of art 34. It has been the contention of the Secretary
of State that these conditions have not been observed by the applicants and that the
further measures prescribed in the 1988 Act and the 1988 regulations have been
necessary to secure that the purposes of the common fisheries policy are duly carried
*e*   out, and also to ensure that proper policing and safety control are improved. Such
then, in summary, is the background to this case and these are the relevant provisions
both of the Treaty and of the common fisheries policy to which our attention was
particularly directed.'

*f*   I add a footnote to this summary to observe that the preliminary rulings of the European
Court in the *Agegate* and *Jaderow* cases referred to by Neill LJ had still not been given at
the conclusion of the argument of this appeal before your Lordships.

Against this background and in view of the nature of the questions of Community
law involved, the discretionary decision of the Divisional Court to seek a preliminary
ruling from the European Court under art 177 was, it seems to me, unquestionably
*g*   right. The questions are of great difficulty and depend, I would think, on a wide range
of considerations which only the European Court has the competence to assess.

Having indicated his reasons for the conclusion that the case called for a reference
under art 177, Neill LJ said in considering the application for interim relief:

'For my part, I do not propose to express even a tentative view of the likely result
in the present reference, but neither side's arguments in my judgment can be
*h*   described as weak. They both merit the most careful scrutiny. The applicants'
contentions invoke the support of fundamental principles of the EEC Treaty. The
Solicitor General relies on sovereign rights over nationality, and on the special
provisions of the common fisheries policy. In these circumstances I think it is right
to look at the matter on the basis that the cogent and important arguments put
forward on behalf of the applicants are to be set against arguments of a like weight
*j*   urged with equal force on behalf of the Secretary of State.'

Hodgson J expressed the view that the applicants had 'a strong prima facie case' and was
critical of some of the arguments advanced on behalf of the Secretary of State. Your
Lordships have not, however, been invited to make your own independent assessment of
the relative strengths of the rival contentions on the substantive issues of Community

law which arise, and I think both sides accept that, in relation to the grant of interim relief, nothing turns on any difference between the assessments made by Neill LJ and Hodgson J.

It is estimated that the preliminary ruling requested by the Divisional Court from the European Court will not be given for two years from the date when the reference is made. The applicants claim that unless they are protected during this period by an interim order which has the effect of enabling them to continue to operate their 95 vessels as if they were duly registered British fishing vessels (which would be necessary to enable them to continue to hold licences to fish against the British quota of controlled stocks of fish) they will suffer irreparable damage. The vessels are not eligible to resume the Spanish flag and fish against the Spanish quota. To lay the vessels up pending the ruling of the European Court would be prohibitively expensive. The only practical alternative would be to sell the vessels or the Spanish holdings in the companies owning the vessels in what would be a glutted market at disastrously low prices. In addition many of the individual applicants are actively engaged in the operation and management of the vessels and would lose their livelihood. No doubt has been cast on the factual accuracy of these claims and I approach the question of interim relief on the footing that they are well founded. Moreover, as the law presently stands on the authority of *Bourgoin SA v Ministry of Agriculture Fisheries and Food* [1985] 3 All ER 585, [1986] QB 716 the applicants would have no remedy in damages for losses suffered pending the ruling of the European Court.

It is more difficult to assess, in practical terms, the adverse consequences of granting interim relief if the preliminary ruling of the European Court is in the event given in favour of the Secretary of State. Certainly there is no question of requiring from the applicants a cross-undertaking in damages, since it would be impossible to identify any damage sustained by individuals in the British fishing industry as a result of the continued operation of the applicants' vessels. But it is right to recognise that the policy of Her Majesty's government indorsed by Parliament in Pt II of the 1988 Act is to ensure that the quota of controlled stocks of fish allocated to the United Kingdom in accordance with the common fisheries policy, of which a sizeable proportion is presently taken by the applicants, should be fully available to be enjoyed by those engaged in the British fishing industry.

The familiar situation in English law in which the question arises whether or not an interim injunction should be made to protect some threatened right of the plaintiff or applicant for judicial review is one in which the facts on which the right depends are in dispute and the court cannot proceed immediately to the trial which will resolve that dispute. In this situation the court has a discretion to grant or withhold interim relief which it exercises in accordance with the principles laid down by your Lordships' House in *American Cyanamid Co v Ethicon Ltd* [1975] 1 All ER 504, [1975] AC 396. In deciding on a balance of convenience whether or not to make an interim injunction the court is essentially engaged in an exercise of holding the ring. In private law as between private parties the plaintiff will be required, if granted interim relief, to give a cross-undertaking in damages and the court is thus enabled to make a pragmatic decision as to who is likely to suffer the greater injustice, the plaintiff on the one hand if interim relief is withheld and he eventually establishes his right but is left to his remedy in damages or the defendant on the other hand if he is wrongly restrained in the interim and he is left to his remedy in damages on the plaintiff's cross-undertaking.

The situation which arises in the present case is fundamentally different from this familiar situation in two respects. The first which I wish to examine is that the dispute on which the existence or non-existence of the rights for which the applicants claim protection depends is one of law, not of fact, and the postponement of the resolution of that dispute arises, of course, from the necessity to seek a preliminary ruling from the European Court under art 177.

By virtue of s 2(4) of the 1972 Act Pt II of the 1988 Act is to be construed and take effect subject to directly enforceable Community rights and those rights are, by s 2(1) of

the 1972 Act, to be 'recognised and available in law, and ... enforced, allowed and
a  followed accordingly ...' This has precisely the same effect as if a section were
incorporated in Pt II of the 1988 Act which in terms enacted that the provisions with
respect to registration of British fishing vessels were to be without prejudice to the
directly enforceable Community rights of nationals of any member state of the EEC.
Thus it is common ground that, in so far as the applicants succeed before the European
Court in obtaining a ruling in support of the Community rights which they claim, those
b  rights will prevail over the restrictions imposed on registration of British fishing vessels
by Pt II of the 1988 Act and the Divisional Court will, in the final determination of the
application for judicial review, be obliged to make appropriate declarations to give effect
to those rights.

   It is difficult to envisage a parallel situation arising out of the disputed construction of
an English statute not involving any question of Community law which would call for a
c  decision whether or not the court could grant interim relief of the kind which the
applicants are seeking here. Suppose that an English statute contained two sections
allegedly in conflict with each other, one clear and unambiguous in its terms, the other
of doubtful import. If an English court were faced with a claim by a party litigant to
rights granted by the doubtful section which were denied by the unambiguous section,
   the court confronted with the issue at any level would decide it and no question of
d  interim relief could possibly arise.

   The nearest parallel arises where subordinate legislation which in its terms is clear and
unambiguous is challenged as ultra vires and a question arises as to the enforcement of
the subordinate legislation before the challenge to the vires has been resolved. This
indeed was the question which arose in F Hoffmann-La Roche & Co AG v Secretary of State
   for Trade and Industry [1974] 2 All ER 1128, [1975] AC 295, but it is important to
e  appreciate the context in which it arose. The Secretary of State had made a statutory
order under the Monopolies and Restrictive Practices (Inquiry and Control) Act 1948
which had been approved by both Houses of Parliament and which had the effect of
restricting the price at which Hoffmann-La Roche could sell certain drugs. It was
Hoffmann-La Roche who brought proceedings against the Secretary of State for a
f  declaration that the statutory order was ultra vires on the ground that the proceedings
before the Monopolies Commission and the findings of the Monopolies Commission on
which the statutory order was based were vitiated by breaches of the rules of natural
justice. Under the provisions of the 1948 Act the only means by which the statutory
order could be enforced was by injunction to restrain Hoffmann-La Roche from selling
the drugs in question above the stipulated price. The Secretary of State accordingly
g  moved for such an injunction and the motion was heard as if made in Hoffmann-La
Roche's action. The primary question in issue was whether the Secretary of State could
be required to give an undertaking in damages as a condition of the grant of an interim
injunction pending trial of the action at which the issue as to the validity of the statutory
order would be determined. But the House also had to determine whether it was
appropriate to grant an interim injunction to enforce the terms of the statutory order at
h  a time when a challenge to the vires of the order had not been resolved.

   The House in the Hoffmann-La Roche case affirmed by a majority (Lord Wilberforce
dissenting) the decision of the Court of Appeal ([1973] 3 All ER 945, [1975] AC 295) that
the interim injunction should be granted without requiring the Secretary of State to give
any cross-undertaking. The Solicitor General relies on passages in the speeches of the
majority as establishing the principle that the unambiguous terms of delegated legislation,
j  and, as he would say, a fortiori of an Act of Parliament, must be presumed to be the law
and must be enforced as such unless and until declared to be invalid in the one case or
declared to be incompatible with Community law on the other. Lord Reid said ([1974] 2
All ER 1128 at 1134, [1975] AC 295 at 341):

   'It must be borne in mind that an order made under statutory authority is as
   much the law of the land as an Act of Parliament unless and until it has been found

to be ultra vires . . . But I think that it is for the person against whom the interim
injunction is sought to show special reason why justice requires that the injunction     a
should not be granted or should only be granted on terms.'

Lord Morris said ([1974] 2 All ER 1128 at 1140, [1975] AC 295 at 349):

'The order then undoubtedly had the force of law. Obedience to it was just as
obligatory as would be obedience to an Act of Parliament.'

b

Lord Diplock said ([1974] 2 All ER 1128 at 1153–1154, [1975] AC 295 at 365):

'Unless there is such challenge and, if there is, until it has been upheld by a
judgment of the court, the validity of the statutory instrument and the legality of
acts done pursuant to the law declared by it, are presumed.'

Counsel for the applicants relies on passages in the speeches of the majority and in the     c
dissenting speech of Lord Wilberforce as qualifying the proposition that legislation
whose validity is called in question must in all circumstances be enforced unless and
until invalidated: see per Lord Morris, Lord Diplock, Lord Cross and the dissenting view
of Lord Wilberforce ([1974] 2 All ER 1128 at 1141, 1155, 1158, 1148, [1975] AC 295 at
350, 367, 371, 358). I do not find it necessary to set out these passages, since I accept that
the court may in its discretion properly decline to exercise its jurisdiction to grant an     d
interim order in aid of the enforcement of disputed legislative measures in a situation
where, as in the *Hoffmann-La Roche* case, it is necessary to invoke the court's jurisdiction
in order to secure their enforcement.

The application of this principle in relation to the enforcement of the provisions of
Pt II of the 1988 Act admits of a simple illustration. Section 22, as its sidenote indicates,
creates certain 'offences relating to, and liabilities of, unregistered fishing vessels'. If any     e
of the applicants were to be prosecuted for an offence in relation to an unregistered
fishing vessel or if proceedings for forfeiture of the vessel were instituted under s 22 and
the rights under Community law now claimed were relied on in defence, it is very
properly conceded by the Solicitor General that the court before which the prosecution
or forfeiture proceedings were brought, if it decided to refer questions of Community
law to the European Court, could grant a stay of the prosecution or forfeiture proceedings     f
pending the preliminary ruling of the European Court. This would be a proper case of
the court staying its hand until the issue as to the claim of Community rights was settled.
The prosecution or the forfeiture proceedings would not be frustrated but suspended. If
eventually the claimed Community rights were not upheld by the European Court, there
could still be a conviction or a forfeiture of the vessel. Precisely the same principle
underlies the decision of the Irish Supreme Court in *Pesca Valentia Ltd v Minister for*     g
*Fisheries and Forestry* [1985] IR 193, on which counsel for the applicants relies, where a
prosecution for an offence in contravention of Irish legislation regulating fisheries alleged
to be incompatible with Community law was stayed.

In the light of these considerations I do not believe that the *Hoffmann-La Roche* case
provides the conclusive answer, as a matter of English law, to the applicants' claim for     h
interim relief. But this brings me to what I believe to be the nub of the appeal, in so far
as it depends on English law, and to the second critical distinction between the claim to
interim relief advanced by the applicants and any claim to interim relief which an
English court has ever previously entertained. Unlike the statutory order which the
Secretary of State for Trade and Industry sought to enforce by interim injunction against
Hoffmann-La Roche, the provisions of Pt II of the 1988 Act require no assistance from     j
the court for their enforcement. Unambiguous in their terms, they simply stand as a
barrier to the continued enjoyment by the applicants' vessels of the right to registration
as British fishing vessels. In this situation the difficulty which confronts the applicants is
that the presumption that an Act of Parliament is compatible with Community law
unless and until declared to be incompatible must be at least as strong as the presumption

that delegated legislation is valid unless and until declared invalid. But an order granting
a the applicants the interim relief which they seek will only serve their purpose if it
declares that which Parliament had enacted to be the law from 1 December 1988, and to
take effect in relation to vessels previously registered under the 1894 Act from 31 March
1989, not to be the law until some uncertain future date. Effective relief can only be
given if it requires the Secretary of State to treat the applicants' vessels as entitled to
registration under Pt II of the 1988 Act in direct contravention of its provisions. Any
b such order, unlike any form of order for interim relief known to the law, would
irreversibly determine in the applicants' favour for a period of some two years rights
which are necessarily uncertain until the preliminary ruling of the European Court has
been given. If the applicants fail to establish the rights they claim before the European
Court, the effect of the interim relief granted would be to have conferred on them rights
directly contrary to Parliament's sovereign will and correspondingly to have deprived
c British fishing vessels, as defined by Parliament, of the enjoyment of a substantial
proportion of the United Kingdom quota of stocks of fish protected by the common
fisheries policy. I am clearly of the opinion that, as a matter of English law, the court has
no power to make an order which has these consequences.

It follows that this appeal must fall to be dismissed unless there is, as the applicants
contend, some overriding principle derived from the jurisprudence of the European
d Court which compels national courts of member states, whatever their own law may
provide, to assert, and in appropriate cases to exercise, a power to provide an effective
interlocutory remedy to protect putative rights in Community law once those rights
have been claimed and are seen to be seriously arguable, notwithstanding that the
existence of the rights is in dispute and will not be established unless and until the
European Court so rules. But before turning to consider the applicants' submissions on
e this aspect of Community law, a further and, as some may think, narrower and more
technical question of English law has to be decided.

The Solicitor General accepted in the courts below that it was not open to him to argue
that the court had no jurisdiction to grant an interlocutory injunction against the Crown
in the light of the majority judgments of the Court of Appeal in *R v Licensing Authority,
ex p Smith Kline & French Laboratories (Generics (UK) Ltd intervening) (No 2)* [1989] 2 All ER
f 113, [1989] 2 WLR 378 (the *SKF* case) affirming the previous judgment of Hodgson J in
*R v Secretary of State for the Home Dept, ex p Herbage* [1986] 3 All ER 209, [1987] QB 872.
The point was kept open for argument in your Lordships' House. Strictly speaking, I
think that the views expressed in the two cases referred to were obiter, since in neither
case did the court act on its view by proceeding to make an interim injunction against
the Crown. But this matters not. The question for your Lordships is whether Hodgson J
g in *Herbage*'s case and Woolf and Taylor LJJ, who were the majority in the *SKF* case, were
right in the conclusion they reached that, although the court has no jurisdiction to grant
an interim injunction against the Crown in proceedings begun by writ, it has such a
jurisdiction in proceedings on application for judicial review.

The question at issue depends, first, on the true construction of s 31 of the Supreme
h Court Act 1981, which provides, so far as material:

> '(1) An application to the High Court for one or more of the following forms of
> relief, namely—(a) an order of mandamus, prohibition or certiorari; (b) a declaration
> or injunction under subsection (2) ... shall be made in accordance with rules of
> court by a procedure to be known as an application for judicial review.
j
> (2) A declaration may be made or an injunction granted under this subsection in
> any case where an application for judicial review, seeking that relief, has been made
> and the High Court considers that, having regard to—(a) the nature of the matters
> in respect of which relief may be granted by orders of mandamus, prohibition or
> certiorari; (b) the nature of the persons and bodies against whom relief may be
> granted by such orders; and (c) all the circumstances of the case, it would be just and

convenient for the declaration to be made or the injunction to be granted, as the
case may be.                                                                          *a*

(3) No application for judicial review shall be made unless the leave of the High
Court has been obtained in accordance with rules of court; and the court shall not
grant leave to make such an application unless it considers that the applicant has a
sufficient interest in the matter to which the application relates.

(4) On an application for judicial review the High Court may award damages to
the applicant if—(a) he has joined with his application a claim for damages arising    *b*
from any matter to which the application relates; and (b) the court is satisfied that,
if the claim had been made in an action begun by the applicant at the time of
making his application, he would have been awarded damages . . .'

The essence of the reasoning leading to the conclusion that this section on* its true
construction confers a jurisdiction which never existed before to grant injunctions against   *c*
the Crown appears from the following passage in the judgment of Woolf LJ in the *SKF*
case [1989] 2 All ER 113 at 122–123, [1989] 2 WLR 378 at 390–391:

'Turning to consider the provisions of the 1981 Act, it is important to note that
there is a distinction between the way that the Act deals with the power of the courts
to grant relief by way of injunction or by way of declaration from that which exists
in relation to damages. Here, s 31(2) and (4) is important. [The judgement then sets    *d*
out the provisions of s 31(2).] The effect of s 31(2), read literally, is that the court has
a discretion to grant a declaration or grant an injunction at least in that class of cases
where it was the practice previously to grant an order of mandamus, prohibition or
certiorari, subject to the qualification that the application is against the type of body
or persons in relation to whom those orders normally would be available. This is a
different basis of jurisdiction from that which previously existed. [The judgment       *e*
then sets out the provisions of s 31(4).] The position with regard to a claim for
damages, therefore, is quite distinct from that in relation to a claim for a declaration
or injunction because in respect of a claim for damages it has to be a situation where
if the claim had been included in an action damages would be awarded. The key to
the distinction between sub-s (2) and sub-s (4) is that sub-s (2) has the innovative     *f*
effect of making a declaration or injunction for the first time a public law remedy
in addition to being a private law remedy which could be used to obtain relief on
the same basis against private bodies and public bodies, which was the position prior
to the coming into force of the new procedure of judicial review. However, in the
case of damages the situation is otherwise. Damages could previously only be
obtained in private law proceedings against a public body if private law, common       *g*
law or statutory rights were breached and now the same restrictions apply in judicial
review, that is public law proceedings, where damages are claimed. In my view,
looking at the language of s 31 alone, it is quite clear that the court's jurisdiction
was being extended in relation to declarations and injunctions, but the court's
jurisdiction was not being extended in relation to damages, and in relation to
damages all that has happened is that there is a procedural change, whereas in         *h*
relation to declarations and injunctions not only has there been a procedural change,
there has also been a jurisdictional change ... Against that background to the
statutory provisions I ask myself whether or not there is a power to grant an
injunction against the Crown, and subject to what I have to say hereafter I conclude
that there clearly is such a power under the new procedure.'

The question at issue depends, second, on the true construction of RSC Ord 53,     *j*
r 3(10)(b), which provides:

'Where leave to apply for judicial review is granted, then ... (b) if any other relief
is sought, the Court may at any time grant in the proceedings such interim relief as
could be granted in an action begun by writ.'

Proceeding from the premise that s 31(2) of the 1981 Act confers jurisdiction by statute
*a* in judicial review proceedings to grant injunctions against the Crown, the view of the
majority in the *SKF* case affirming Hodgson J in *Herbage's* case was that this provision in
the rules, on its true construction, enables that statutory jurisdiction to be exercised to
grant an interim injunction.

In my opinion, it is impossible to construe s 31 of the 1981 Act except in the light of
the relevant preceding history. In much that follows I am indebted to the submissions
*b* on this part of the case made on behalf of the Secretary of State by Mr Laws.

Before the passing of the Crown Proceedings Act 1947 the only means by which the
Crown might be impleaded in court were by petition of right, action against the Attorney
General for a declaration and action against certain ministers or government departments
which had been made liable to suit by statute. None of these procedures involved claims
for injunctions. Officers of the Crown, acting as such, were likewise immune from suit.
*c* An exception to this proposition is said by counsel for the 95th applicant, who presented
the argument for the applicants on this part of the case, to be established by *Tamaki v
Baker* [1901] AC 561, where the defendant Baker was the New Zealand Commissioner of
Crown Lands. Lord Davey, delivering the judgment of the Privy Council, said (at 576):

> 'Their Lordships hold that an aggrieved person may sue an officer of the Crown
*d*   to restrain a threatened act purporting to be done in supposed pursuance of an Act
> of Parliament, but really outside the statutory authority.'

But the exception is apparent, not real. The same passage from Lord Davey's judgment
was relied on by counsel for the plaintiff in *Hutton v Secretary of State for War* (1926) 43
TLR 106 in seeking to resist a preliminary point taken by the Attorney General that an
*e* action against the Secretary of State for War, as such, would not lie. Referring to this
passage in his judgment, Tomlin J said (at 107):

> 'The plaintiffs' contention really received no support from the passage referred to
> when it was read in its context. What Lord Davey was really saying was that in a
> case where an official was sued as an individual for a wrongful act it was no defence
*f*   to say that the wrongful act was done by him as an officer of the Crown. The
> argument that an action would lie against a Crown official, as such, when a wrong
> had been done which purported to be an exercise of a statutory authority, entirely
> failed.'

Injunctions were never available in proceedings on the Crown side invoking the
*g* ancient jurisdiction to issue the prerogative writs of mandamus, prohibition and
certiorari, which were transformed by s 7 of the Administration of Justice (Miscellaneous
Provisions) Act 1938 into orders to the same effect.

The 1947 Act by s 1 gives the right to sue the Crown in tort and in s 2 defines the
scope of the Crown's liability in tort. Section 21 provides, so far as material:

*h*
> '(1) In any civil proceedings by or against the Crown the court shall, subject to
> the provisions of this Act, have power to make all such orders as it has power to
> make in proceedings between subjects, and otherwise to give such appropriate relief
> as the case may require: Provided that:—(a) where in any proceedings against the
> Crown any such relief is sought as might in proceedings between subjects be granted
> by way of injunction or specific performance, the court shall not grant an injunction
*j*   or make an order for specific performance, but may in lieu thereof make an order
> declaratory of the rights of the parties . . .
> (2) The court shall not in any civil proceedings grant any injunction or make any
> order against an officer of the Crown if the effect of granting the injunction or
> making the order would be to give any relief against the Crown which could not
> have been obtained in proceedings against the Crown.'

By definition in s 38(2):

> '"civil proceedings" includes proceedings in the High Court or the county court  *a*
> for the recovery of fines or penalties, but does not include proceedings on the Crown
> side of the King's Bench Division . . .'

In the light of this definition, Hodgson J was, in my view, clearly right in *R v Secretary of State for the Home Dept, ex p Herbage* [1986] 3 All ER 209, [1987] QB 872 to reject an argument that proviso (*a*) to s 21(1) should be construed as extending to Crown side  *b* proceedings. The ambit of the words 'any proceedings' in the proviso can be no wider than the ambit of the words 'any civil proceedings' in the body of the subsection to which the proviso applies. Dicta to the contrary effect in *IRC v Rossminster Ltd* [1980] 1 All ER 80, [1980] AC 952, on which Mr Laws relied with undisguised lack of enthusiasm, must be regarded as having been expressed per incuriam. But, having said that, it is important to add that the absence from the 1947 Act of any express prohibition of the grant of  *c* injunctions against the Crown in proceedings on the Crown side is of no significance since, as already stated, injunctions were not available in Crown side proceedings and such a prohibition would have been otiose.

The previous common law position where an injunction is sought against an officer of the Crown is, in my view, effectively preserved by the combined effect of s 21(2) and the definition of the phrase 'civil proceedings by or against the Crown' in s 23(2)(*b*), which  *d* provides:

> 'Subject to the provisions of this section, any reference in this Part of this Act to
> civil proceedings against the Crown shall be construed as a reference to the following
> proceedings only . . . (*b*) proceedings for the enforcement or vindication of any right
> or the obtaining of any relief which, if this Act had not been passed, might have  *e*
> been enforced or vindicated or obtained by an action against the Attorney General,
> any Government department, or any officer of the Crown as such . . . and the
> expression "civil proceedings by or against the Crown" shall be construed
> accordingly.'

In *Merricks v Heathcoat-Amory* [1955] 2 All ER 453, [1955] Ch 567 the plaintiffs sought  *f* a mandatory injunction against the defendant requiring him to withdraw a draft scheme under the Agricultural Marketing Acts 1931 to 1949 which had been laid before both Houses of Parliament but was alleged to be ultra vires. It was argued that the defendant was not acting as a representative of the Crown but either in an official capacity as a person designated to perform statutory functions or in an individual capacity. Upjohn J rejected the argument. He said ([1955] 2 All ER 453 at 456–457, [1955] Ch 567 at 575):  *g*

> 'It seems to me that from start to finish he was acting in his capacity as an officer
> representing the Crown. That being so, it is conceded that no injunction can be
> obtained against him, and therefore the motion falls in limine. I am not at all
> satisfied that it is possible to have the three capacities which were suggested. Of
> course there can be an official representing the Crown and that is plainly this case.  *h*
> But if he were not, it was said that he was a person designated in an official capacity
> but not representing the Crown. The third alternative was that his capacity was
> purely that of an individual. I understand the conception of the first and the third
> categories, but I confess I find it very difficult to see how the second category can fit
> into any ordinary scheme. It is possible that there may be special Acts where named
> persons have special duties to perform which would not be duties normally fulfilled  *j*
> by them in their official capacity; but in the ordinary case where the relevant or
> appropriate Minister is directed to carry out the function or policy of some Act, it
> seems to me that he is either acting in his capacity as a Minister of the Crown
> representing the Crown, or is acting in his personal capacity, usually the former. I
> find it very difficult to conceive of the middle classification.'

This judgment has been subject to academic criticism (see Wade *Administrative Law* (6th
a edn, 1988) p 589), and counsel for the 95th applicant has submitted that *Merricks'* case
was wrongly decided. It seems to me, however, that the judgment of Upjohn J accords
entirely with the position in law before 1947, as explained in the judgment of Tomlin J
in *Hutton v Secretary of State for War* (1926) 43 TLR 106, which, as I have said, the 1947
Act appears to me to be specifically intended to preserve.

The new RSC Ord 53 was introduced in 1977 following the Law Commission's *Report
b on Remedies in Administrative Law* (Law Com no 73) (1976). The relevant recommendations
are set out in Pt V, headed 'Recommendations for Reform'. Under the sub-heading
'(a) An application for judicial review', para 43 reads:

> 'Our basic recommendation is that there should be a form of procedure to be
> entitled an "application for judicial review". Under cover of the application for
> judicial review a litigant should be able to obtain any of the prerogative orders, or,
c > in appropriate circumstances, a declaration or an injunction . . .'

Under the later sub-heading '(h) Interim relief on an application for judicial review, with
special reference to the Crown' the Law Commission addressed as a quite distinct problem
the lack of jurisdiction to grant interim injunctions against the Crown and set out its
reasoning and recommendation in this regard in para 51 as follows:
d
> 'We have pointed out that, where an application is being made for certiorari or
> prohibition, the Court can give interim relief preserving the *status quo* pending a
> final decision under Order 53, rule 1(5); and where an injunction is being sought
> such interim relief can be obtained by means of an interlocutory injunction.
> However, an injunction cannot be obtained against the Crown although it is possible
e > in such a case to get a declaration. But there is at present no form of interim
> declaration which in effect preserves the *status quo* pending the final declaration. We
> think it desirable that there should be a form of relief which would have this interim
> effect where a declaration is being sought against the Crown. We therefore
> recommend that section 21 of the Crown Proceedings Act 1947 should be amended
> to provide that, in addition to the power there given to make a declaratory order in
f > proceedings against the Crown, there is also power to declare the terms of an interim
> injunction which would have been granted between subjects. In spite of the judicial
> doubts which have been expressed as to the logical character of a provisional
> declaration, we see no reason to doubt that the Crown would respect a declaration
> of the terms of an interim injunction in the same way as it respects a final declaratory
> order.'
g
The Law Commission appended to its report a draft Bill by which it proposed that its
recommendations should be implemented. The recommendation that interim relief
should be available against the Crown was proposed to be implemented by cl 3(2) of the
draft Bill in the following terms:

> 'In section 21 of the Crown Proceedings Act 1947 (nature of relief in civil
h > proceedings by or against Crown), for paragraph (*a*) of the proviso to subsection (1)
> there shall be substituted the following paragraph:—"(*a*) the court shall not grant
> an injunction, or order specific performance, against the Crown but may in lieu
> thereof—(i) in a case where the court is satisfied that it would have granted an
> interim injunction if the proceedings had been between subjects, declare the terms
> of the interim injunction that it would have made; or (ii) make an order declaratory
j > of the rights of the parties".'

The decision taken following the report to proceed by amendment of the Rules of the
Supreme Court rather than by primary legislation limited to extent to which it was
possible to implement the recommendations of the Law Commission, since the Rule
Committee is only empowered to legislate in matters of practice and procedure and

cannot extend the jurisdiction of the High Court. Accordingly, the new Ord 53 proceeded to implement the recommendation in para 43 of the report (and cll 1 and 2 of the proposed draft Bill) but did not, as it could not, seek to implement the recommendation in para 51 (and cl 3(2) of the proposed draft Bill). The terms of Ord 53, r 1(1) and (2) are, and were when the order was first promulgated in 1977, in all relevant respects identical with the terms subsequently enacted by s 31(1) and (2) of the 1981 Act.

If s 31 of the 1981 Act were to be construed in isolation, I would see great force in the reasoning set out in the judgment of Woolf LJ in the *SKF* case [1989] 2 All ER 113 at 122–123, [1989] 2 WLR 378 at 390–391 which I have cited. But in the light of the history it seems to me that there are three reasons why it is impossible to construe s 31(2) as having the effect attributed to it by Woolf LJ of conferring a new jurisdiction on the court to grant injunctions against the Crown. First, s 31(2) and Ord 53, r 1(1) being in identical terms, the subsection and the paragraph must have the same meaning and the paragraph, if it purported to extend jurisdiction, would have been ultra vires. Second, if Parliament had intended to confer on the court jurisdiction to grant interim injunctions against the Crown, it is inconceivable, in the light of the Law Commission's recommendation in para 51 of its report, that this would not have been done in express terms either in the form of the proposed cl 3(2) of the Law Commission's draft Bill or by an enactment to some similar effect. There is no escape from the conclusion that this recommendation was never intended to be implemented. Third, it is apparent from s 31(3) that the relief to which s 31(2) applies is final, as opposed to interlocutory, relief. By s 31(2) a declaration may be made or an injunction granted 'where an application for judicial review . . . *has* been made . . .' But by s 31(3) 'No application for judicial review *shall* be made unless the leave of the High Court *has* been obtained in accordance with rules of court . . .' Under the rules there are two stages in the procedure: first, the grant of leave to apply for judicial review on ex parte application under Ord 53, r 3, and, second, the making of the application for judicial review which by r 5 is required to be by originating motion or summons duly served on all parties directly affected. Section 31(2) is thus in terms addressed to the second stage, not the first, and is in sharp contrast with the language of Ord 53, r 3(10), which by its terms enables appropriate interim relief to be granted by the court at the same time as it grants leave to apply for judicial review. This point appeared to me at first blush to be one of some technicality. But on reflection I am satisfied that it conclusively refutes the view that s 31(2) was intended to provide a solution to the problem of the lack of jurisdiction to grant interim injunctions against the Crown. The form of final relief available against the Crown has never presented any problem. A declaration of right made in proceedings against the Crown is invariably respected and no injunction is required. If the legislature intended to give the court jurisdiction to grant interim injunctions against the Crown, it is difficult to think of any reason why the jurisdiction should be available only in judicial review proceedings and not in civil proceedings as defined in the 1947 Act. Hence, an enactment which in terms applies only to the forms of final relief available in judicial review proceedings cannot possibly have been so intended.

Counsel for the 95th applicant, replying for the applicants to Mr Laws's submissions on this part of the case, did not address any of the issues to which I have referred in the foregoing paragraph, but submitted instead that the power to grant interim injunctions against the Crown in judicial review proceedings derived from a purely procedural change effected by the introduction of the new Ord 53 in 1977 which involved no extension of the court's jurisdiction and which it was within the power of the Rule Committee to make. I note that this submission runs entirely counter to the reasoning of Woolf LJ in the *SKF* case in the passage from his judgment which I have cited. Counsel for the 95th applicant relied in support of the submission on passages from the speeches delivered in your Lordships' House in *IRC v National Federation of Self-Employed and Small Business Ltd* [1981] 2 All ER 93, [1982] AC 617 and *O'Reilly v Mackman* [1982] 3 All ER 1124, [1983] 2 AC 237. I do find in those passages anything which supports the

submission, since it is clear from the context that none of their Lordships had addressed
a their minds to the question of injunctions against the Crown.

I have accordingly reached the conclusion that the views expressed by Hodgson J in *R
v Secretary of State for the Home Dept, ex p Herbage* [1986] 3 All ER 209, [1987] QB 872 and
by the majority of the Court of Appeal in the *SKF* case were erroneous and that, as a
matter of English law, the absence of any jurisdiction to grant interim injunctions against
the Crown is an additional reason why the order made by the Divisional Court cannot be
b supported.

I turn finally to consider the submission made on behalf of the applicants that,
irrespective of the position under national law, there is an overriding principle of
Community law which imposes an obligation on the national court to secure effective
interim protection of rights having direct effect under Community law where a seriously
arguable claim is advanced to be entitled to such rights and where the rights claimed will
c in substance be rendered nugatory or will be irremediably impaired if not effectively
protected during any interim period which must elapse pending determination of a
dispute as to the existence of those rights. The basic propositions of Community law on
which the applicants rely in support of this submission may be quite shortly summarised.
Directly enforceable Community rights are part of the legal heritage of every citizen of a
member state of the EEC. They arise from the EEC Treaty itself and not from any
d judgment of the European Court declaring their existence. Such rights are automatically
available and must be given unrestricted retroactive effect. The persons entitled to the
enjoyment of such rights are entitled to direct and immediate protection against possible
infringement of them. The duty to provide such protection rests with the national court.
The remedy to be provided against infringement must be effective, not merely symbolic
or illusory. The rules of national law which render the exercise of directly enforceable
e Community rights excessively difficult or virtually impossible must be overridden.

Counsel for the applicants, in a most impressive argument presented in opening this
appeal, traced the progressive development of these principles of the jurisprudence of the
European Court through a long series of reported decisions on which he relies. I must
confess that at the conclusion of his argument I was strongly inclined to the view that, if
f English law could provide no effective remedy to secure the interim protection of the
rights claimed by the applicants, it was nevertheless our duty under Community law to
devise such a remedy. But the Solicitor General, in his equally impressive reply, and in
his careful and thorough analysis of the case law, has persuaded me that none of the
authorities on which counsel for the applicants relies can properly be treated as
determinative of the difficult question, which arises for the first time in the instant case,
g of providing interim protection of putative and disputed rights in Community law
before their existence has been established. This is because the relevant decisions of the
European Court, from which the propositions of Community law asserted by counsel for
the applicants are derived, were all made by reference to rights which the European
Court was itself then affirming or by reference to the protection of rights the existence
of which had already been established by previous decisions of the European Court.

h    In the light of the course which I propose that your Lordships should take, it would
serve no useful purpose for me to attempt an analysis of the voluminous Community
case law to which the main arguments have been directed. It is significant to note,
however, that Community law embodies a principle which appears closely analogous to
the principle of English law that delegated legislation must be presumed to be valid
unless and until declared invalid. In *Granaria BV v Hoofdproduktschap voor Akkerpbouwpro-*
j *dukten* Case 101/78 [1979] ECR 623 the validity of a regulation made by the EEC Council
was challenged in proceedings before the court of a member state. In answering questions
referred to it under art 177 of the EEC Treaty the European Court held that every
regulation which is brought into force in accordance with the Treaty must be presumed
to be valid and must be treated as fully effective so long as a competent court has not
made a finding that it is invalid. On the other hand, in *Firma Foto-Frost v Hauptzollamt*

*Lübeck-Ost* Case 314/85 [1988] 3 CMLR 57 at 80 the Court of Justice said in giving
judgment, again on a reference under art 177:

> 'It should be added that the rule that national courts may not themselves declare
> Community acts invalid may have to be qualified in certain circumstances in the
> case of proceedings relating to an application for interim measures; however, that
> case is not referred to in the national court's question.'

In the light of these two authorities and in application of the principles laid down by
the European Court in *Srl CILFIT v Ministry of Health* Case 283/81 [1982] ECR 3415, I do
not think that it is open to your Lordships' House to decide one way or the other whether,
in relation to the grant of interim protection in the circumstances of the instant case,
Community law overrides English law and either empowers or obliges an English court
to make an interim order protecting the putative rights claimed by the applicants. It
follows, I think, that your Lordships are obliged under art 177 of the Treaty to seek a
preliminary ruling from the European Court. I would propose that the questions to be
referred should read as follows:

> '(1) Where—(i) a party before the national court claims to be entitled to rights
> under Community law having direct effect in national law (the rights claimed), (ii)
> a national measure in clear terms will, if applied, automatically deprive that party
> of the rights claimed, (iii) there are serious arguments both for and against the
> existence of the rights claimed and the national court has sought a preliminary
> ruling under art 177 whether or not the rights claimed exist, (iv) the national law
> presumes the national measure in question to be compatible with Community law
> unless and until it is declared incompatible, (v) the national court has no power to
> give interim protection to the rights claimed by suspending the application of the
> national measure pending the preliminary ruling, (vi) if the preliminary ruling is
> in the event in favour of the rights claimed, the party entitled to those rights is
> likely to have suffered irremediable damage unless given such interim protection,
> does Community law either (a) oblige the national court to grant such interim
> protection of the rights claimed or (b) give the court power to grant such interim
> protection of the rights claimed?
> (2) If question 1(a) is answered in the negative and question 1(b) in the affirmative,
> what are the criteria to be applied in deciding whether or not to grant such interim
> protection of the rights claimed?'

The adjournment of further consideration of the appeal, which must necessarily follow
is, I recognise, a most unsatifactory result from the applicants' point of view, and I
venture to express the hope that the European Court will, so far as their procedures
permit, treat the reference made by your Lordships' House as one of urgency to which
priority can be given.

**LORD BRANDON OF OAKBROOK.** My Lords, I agree with the speech delivered
by my noble and learned friend Lord Bridge. I also agree that further consideration of
the appeal should be adjourned until the Court of Justice of the European Communities
has given a preliminary ruling on the questions formulated by my noble and learned
friend for reference to it.

**LORD OLIVER OF AYLMERTON.** My Lords, I have had the advantage of reading
in draft the speech of my noble and learned friend Lord Bridge, with which I am in
entire agreement. I also agree that the questions posed in the speech of my noble and
learned friend must be referred to the Court of Justice of the European Communities
pursuant to art 177 of the EEC Treaty and that, pending the preliminary ruling of that
court, the further consideration of the appeal should be adjourned.

**LORD GOFF OF CHIEVELEY.** My Lords, I agree with the speech to be delivered
*a* by my noble and learned friend Lord Bridge. I also agree that further consideration of
the appeal should be adjourned until after the questions posed by my noble and learned
friend have been considered by the Court of Justice of the European Communities.

**LORD JAUNCEY OF TULLICHETTLE.** My Lords, I agree with the speech to be
delivered by my noble and learned friend Lord Bridge. I also agree that further
*b* consideration of the appeal should be adjourned until after the questions posed by my
noble and learned friend have been considered by the Court of Justice of the European
Communities.

*Questions referred to Court of Justice of the European Communities for preliminary ruling
accordingly. Appeal adjourned.*
*c*

Solicitors: *Thomas Cooper & Stibbard* (for the applicants); *Treasury Solicitor.*

Mary Rose Plummer    Barrister.

*d*

# Re St Martin le Grand, York
# Westminster Press Ltd v St Martin with St
# Helen, York (incumbent and parochial
*e* # church council) and others

YORK CONSISTORY COURT
CHANCELLOR THOMAS CONINGSBY QC
15, 16, 17, 29 FEBRUARY 1988

*f* *Easement – Right of way – Ecclesiastical property – Right of way over ecclesiastical property –
Right of way for pedestrian access – Existence of right of way – Law to be applied – Whether
secular or ecclesiastical law to be applied – Whether right of way over consecrated ground a right
of a secular or ecclesiastical nature – Whether ecclesiastical court having jurisdiction to make
rulings on scope of rights of way of a secular nature – Whether ecclesiastical court having
jurisdiction to grant faculty for pedestrian access more extensive than church bodies willing to
g agree to – Ecclesiastical Jurisdiction Measure 1963, s 6(1)(e).*

*Easement – Right of way – Prescription – Lost modern grant – Ecclesiastical property –
Presumption of grant of faculty – Right of way over churchyard – User as of right – Whether
presumed lost faculty deemed to be faculty for licence or for easement – Whether faculty could
confer easement or only licence of indefinite duration – Whether existing licence only terminable
h by further faculty – Prescription Act 1832, s 2.*

*Ecclesiastical law – Faculty – Secular use of consecrated ground – Licence to use churchyard for
secular purpose – Right of way to adjoining premises – Purpose for which churchyard originally
consecrated no longer possible – Whether court having discretion to allow limited secular use of
churchyard – Whether court should grant faculty for right of way over churchyard – Whether
j right of way should extend to licensees and visitors of occupiers of adjoining premises.*

*Ecclesiastical law – Consecrated ground – Right of way over consecrated ground – Right given
without grant of faculty – Nature of right – Whether right amounting to more than licence for
duration of grantor's incumbency – Whether right binding on grantor's successor.*

The petitioners owned and occupied a printing works adjacent to a church and claimed that for many years they had enjoyed certain rights to pass over the churchyard between the church and the printing works. The petitioners sought (i) confirmation of a presumed grant of a right of way on foot with laden or unladen trolleys for the benefit of the petitioners and their successors or the grant of a licence conferring such a right or a confirmatory faculty validating, so far as it related to pedestrian access with laden or unladen trolleys, an agreement entered into in 1967 between the then incumbent and the petitioners for a very limited vehicular use of the churchyard in cases of emergency and for the moving of machinery and (ii) confirmation of the grant of a similar right of way with motor vehicles subject to the conditions in the 1967 agreement. The incumbent and the parochial church council, who were concerned to maintain the churchyard as a peaceful place to which the public at large did not have general access and over which the church retained control, opposed any vehicular use of the churchyard by the petitioners (notwithstanding the 1967 agreement) and did not admit even the existence of a pedestrian right of way over the churchyard. Furthermore, although the parties opponent accepted that by a temporary arrangement with the petitioners there was de facto pedestrian access for the petitioners and their employees, they disputed that the petitioners exercised that use as of right. Moreover, even if the petitioners had exercised the pedestrian access as of right, the parties opponent contended that any such right did not extend to the petitioners' licensees or visitors, such as business suppliers, customers or relatives and friends of the petitioners' staff bringing messages. The petitioners contended that references in the 1967 agreement to 'the Company' were to be construed as meaning the petitioners' enterprise or business and indicated that the right of way included a right for the petitioners' licensees and visitors to visit the printing works. The questions arose (i) whether the ecclesiastical court had jurisdiction to allow consecrated ground to be applied to secular uses, (ii) if it did, whether in its discretion the court should allow a limited secular use of the churchyard to the extent proposed and (iii) if there was a right of pedestrian access, whether it was an easement or a licence.

**Held** – (1) A right of way for pedestrian access was similar to any other right of way, and the principles which the court had to apply were not affected by the fact that the right of way was over ecclesiastical property, the court having to apply the ordinary secular law rather than any specifically ecclesiastical law. Moreover, the rights with which the court was concerned were not exclusively or even substantially of an ecclesiastical nature but were rights existing wholly in the secular field, and accordingly it was not a case where the court should exercise its residual jurisdiction under s 6(1)(e)[a] of the Ecclesiastical Jurisdiction Measure 1963. Although the issue as to the legal status of the right required consideration of the law relating to the effects of consecration of land such as a churchyard, that was an area of law which could be considered as well in a secular court as in an ecclesiastical court, and was insufficient to justify the court regarding the issues as a whole which the court had to decide as being issues relating to ecclesiastical rather than secular rights. The court did not have jurisdiction to make rulings about the scope of rights of way of a basically secular nature unless to do so was necessarily ancillary to an application for a faculty of a kind which it would be possible for the court to grant; but it did have jurisdiction, if it considered it right to do so on the merits, to grant a faculty for a more extensive pedestrian access than that to which the church bodies were willing to agree, since as a result of consecration of the churchyard the fee was in abeyance and the right to deal with the fee (including the right to grant a right of way) was vested in the ordinary on whose behalf the consistory court could act (see p 721 *d e j*, p 722 *b* to *d*, p 723 *g h*, p 724 *a* and p 733 *j*, post).

(2) A full legal easement of way could not have been acquired by the petitioners under the doctrine of lost modern grant, there being a presumption of the grant of a faculty at

---

*a*    Section 6(1), so far as material, is set out at p 721 *g*, post

such time, because as a matter of law a faculty could not have conferred an easement but

_a_ only a licence of indefinite duration. Moreover, on the true construction of s 2$^b$ of the Prescription Act 1832 the lost faculty which was to be presumed because of the user as of right was to be deemed to be a faculty for a licence and not an easement. Furthermore, the licence which was in existence was terminable only by a further faculty application (see p 731 _h j_ and p 732 _d f_, post).

(3) Since in practical terms it was no longer possible to carry out the purpose for which

_b_ the churchyard was originally consecrated, viz for burials, and since in fact it was closed for burials, it was open to the court in its discretion to allow a limited secular use of the churchyard to the extent proposed. On the evidence, a pedestrian way, with or without trolleys, had been exercised for at least 100 years, and the use of that pedestrian access was of a kind and quality which gave rise to a right of way by prescription under the doctrine of lost modern grant (including a presumed faculty) rather than by use from

_c_ time immemorial. Furthermore, on its true construction the 1967 agreement entitling 'the Company' from time to time to pass with vehicles over the churchyard extended to entitle not only the petitioners to exercise the right of way but also their servants and their licensees having a legitimate business in coming to the petitioners' premises and persons such as friends and relatives of the petitioners' employees who were allowed by the petitioner to come to the premises from time to time to bring messages and the like

_d_ (see p 720 _b c_, p 727 _c e_ to _g_, p 728 _b_, p 730 _j_ to p 731 _a_ and p 732 _f g j_ to p 733 _a_, post); dictum of the deputy chancellor in _Re St John's, Chelsea_ [1962] 2 All ER 850 at 856 applied.

(4) In the circumstances the court would exercise its discretion in favour of granting a faculty for the very limited and short-term vehicular use of the churchyard which was proposed by the petitioners and agreed to by the parties opponent. The faculty and licence would be in similar terms to the 1967 agreement but limited as to time and

_e_ subject to a condition that the petitioners make good all damage caused by them to the churchyard or the church by the exercise of the rights of vehicular access (see p 720 _f g_, post).

Per curiam. (1) A right given to a person to pass over consecrated land cannot, without the grant of a faculty, amount to more than a licence granted by the incumbent for the duration only of his incumbency, and cannot be binding on his successors in title to the

_f_ freehold (see p 718 _a b_, post).

(2) The principle that consecrated land should be protected from secular use is not an absolute one (see p 720 _e_, post); _Morley BC v St Mary the Virgin, Woodkirk (vicar and churchwardens)_ [1969] 3 All ER 952 applied.

## Notes

_g_ For rights of way generally, see 14 Halsbury's Laws (4th edn) paras 144–161, and for cases on the subject, see 19 Digest (Reissue) 122–154, _859–1098_.

For prescription under the doctrine of lost modern grant, see 14 Halsbury's Laws (4th edn) paras 89–96, and for cases on the subject, see 19 Digest (Reissue) 78–82, _509–526_.

For matters within the residuary jurisdiction of consistory courts, see 14 Halsbury's Laws (4th edn) para 1344.

_h_ For the use of consecrated ground for secular purposes, see ibid para 1073, and for a case on the subject, see 19 Digest (Reissue) 447, _3541_.

For the Prescription Act 1832, s 2, see 13 Halsbury's Statutes (4th edn) 595.

For the Ecclesiastical Jurisdiction Measure 1963, s 6, see 14 ibid 284.

## Cases referred to in judgment

_j_ _Baxendale v North Lambeth Liberal and Radical Club Ltd_ [1902] 2 Ch 427.

_Bideford Parish, Re, ex p Rector and churchwardens and Bideford Corp_ [1900] P 314, Arches Ct.

_Butt v Jones_ (1829) 2 Hag Ecc 417, 162 ER 909, Arches Ct.

_h_  Section 2, so far as material, is set out at p 732 _a b_, post

*Hammond v Prentice Bros Ltd* [1920] 1 Ch 201.
*Hilcoat v Archbishops of Canterbury and York* (1850) 10 CB 327, 138 ER 132.
*Keith v Twentieth Century Club Ltd* (1904) 73 LJ Ch 545, [1904–7] All ER Rep 164.  *a*
*Liddell v Rainsford* (1868) 38 LJ Eccl 15, Con Ct.
*Linnell and Walker v Gunn* (1867) LR 1 A & E 363, Arches Ct.
*London (Mayor etc) v Cox* (1867) LR 2 HL 239.
*Martin v Mackonochie* (1878) 3 QBD 730, DC; *rvsd* (1879) 4 QBD 697, CA; *affd* sub nom
  *Mackonochie v Lord Penzance* (1881) 6 App Cas 424, HL.
*Morley BC v St Mary the Virgin, Woodkirk (vicar and churchwardens)* [1969] 3 All ER 952,  *b*
  [1969] 1 WLR 1867, Con Ct.
*Proud v Price* (1893) 63 LJQB 61, CA.
*St Andrew's, North Weald Bassett, Re* [1987] 1 WLR 1503, Con Ct.
*St Benet Sherehog, Re, re St Nicholas Acons* [1893] P 66, Con Ct.
*St Gabriel, Fenchurch St (rector and churchwardens) v City of London Real Property Co Ltd*  *c*
  [1896] P 95, Con Ct and Arches Ct.
*St John's, Chelsea, Re* [1962] 2 All ER 850, [1962] 1 WLR 706, Con Ct.
*St Mary Abbots, Kensington (vicar and churchwardens) v St Mary Abbots, Kensington (inhabitants)*
  (1873) Trist 17, Con Ct.
*St Mary of Charity, Faversham, Re* [1986] 1 All ER 1, [1986] Fam 143, [1985] 3 WLR 924,
  Comm Ct.  *d*
*St Paul's, Covent Garden, Re* [1974] Fam 1, [1973] 1 WLR 464, Con Ct.
*St Peter's, Bushey Heath, Re* [1971] 2 All ER 704, [1971] 1 WLR 357, Con Ct.
*Thornton v Little* (1907) 97 LT 24.
*Walter v Mountague and Lamprell* (1836) 1 Curt 253, [1835–42] All ER Rep 433, 163 ER
  85, Con Ct.
*Wood v Saunders* (1875) LR 10 Ch App 582, LJJ.  *e*
*Woodhouse & Co Ltd v Kirkland (Derby) Ltd* [1970] 2 All ER 587, [1970] 1 WLR 1185.

**Petition for faculty**
By a petition dated 13 November 1986 as subsequently amended Westminster Press Ltd
sought faculties (1) confirming the presumed grant to the petitioners' predecessors in  *f*
title of a right of way on foot and with laden or unladen trolleys over the churchyard of
the parish church of St Martin le Grand, York between the petitioners' printing works
and the public highway in Coney Street and enuring for the benefit of the petitioners
and their successors or in the alternative granting a licence conferring such rights, (1A)
alternatively confirming the grant to the petitioners' predecessors in title of a right of
way on foot and with laden or unladen trolleys over the churchyard pursuant to a deed  *g*
dated 4 October 1967 between the Rev Noel Francis Porter, Canon of York, vicar of St
Martin's church, Coney Street, York of the one part and Yorkshire Herald Newspaper Co
Ltd of the other part, (2) confirming the grant to the petitioners' predecessors in title of a
similar right of way with motor vehicles on the conditions set out in the deed dated
4 October 1967 whether arising by presumed grant by reason of long user as of right or
by the purported grant by the court of a licence conferring such rights and (3) for the  *h*
removal of the barrier erected at the entrance to the churchyard and completed on
3 February 1986. The parties opponent to the petition were the incumbent of the
benefice of All Saints Pavement with St Crux and of St Martin with St Helen and St
Denys, York, the parochial church council of the parish of St Martin with St Helen, York,
the feoffees of St Helen's and St Martin's and 22 individual objectors. The facts are set out
in the judgment.  *j*

*Michael Douglas* for the petitioners.
*John Bullimore* for the parties opponent.

*Cur adv vult*

29 February. The following judgment was delivered.

*a*

## THE CHANCELLOR.

NATURE OF THE PROCEEDINGS

These are proceedings under the Faculty Jurisdiction Measure 1964 in relation to the churchyard of the church of St Martin le Grand in Coney Street, which is part of the central area of the City of York. The petitioners, Westminster Press Ltd, own and occupy
*b* a printing works which lie partly between the church and the river Ouse and partly alongside the churchyard with a frontage onto Coney Street. The petitioners' premises are basically in the shape of an L with the longer side fronting onto the river Ouse. The layout of their premises and of the church and churchyard are shown on a scale plan prepared for the purposes of the hearing. The churchyard consists of the area between the church and the printing works and extends round to the rear or west end of the
*c* church. The entrances from the printing works onto the churchyard are mainly in that part of the yard. The petitioners' case is that they have had certain rights to pass over the churchyard for many years and in the proceedings they seek rulings as to the extent of those rights and, where necessary, they seek a faculty to ensure the future use of those rights, to ensure that a gate erected by the parochial church council of St Martin's (the
*d* PCC) across the Coney Street entrance to the yard should be of such construction as not to interfere with their use of the yard, and (again so far as necessary) to extend their use of the yard to cover use by their licensees and other visitors coming to and from their premises for purposes connected with their business or their staff. The basic position of the parties opponent is that they are concerned to maintain the churchyard as a peaceful place to which the public at large do not have general access and over which the church
*e* retains control. Prior to the erection of the gate in late 1985 or early 1986 the PCC and team vicar having responsibility for St Martin's had become much concerned over the parking of cars and other vehicles in the churchyard, that having occurred at a time when a previous 'gate' in the form of a chain and movable post had fallen into disuse. The parties opponent opposed any vehicular use of the churchyard by the petitioners (notwithstanding an agreement in 1967 between the then incumbent and the petitioners
*f* for a very limited vehicular use of the churchyard in cases of emergency and for the moving of machinery); they did not admit the existence of any right of way over the churchyard, even a pedestrian way and, although it was accepted that by a temporary arrangement with the petitioners there was de facto pedestrian access for the petitioners and their employees, it was disputed that the petitioners exercised this use as of right and the PCC asserted their own right to maintain a gate across the Coney Street entrance so as
*g* to prevent all access to the churchyard other than by permission of the PCC or clergy.

The pleadings in the case consist of a number of documents. The petition for faculty is dated 13 November 1986. The schedule of works contained in that petition was subsequently amended by insertion of an additional para 1A. It asks in para 1 for confirmation of a presumed grant of a right of way on foot with laden or unladen trolleys for the benefit of the petitioners and their successors. In the alternative it asks for the
*h* grant of a licence conferring such rights. In the alternative (by the new para 1A) the petitioners in effect ask for a confirmatory faculty to validate the agreement made in October 1967 in so far as it related to pedestrian access with laden or unladen trolleys. By para 2 of the amended schedule the petitioners seek 'confirmation' of the grant of a similar right of way with motor vehicles subject to the conditions set out in the 1967 agreement. Again I construe this as a prayer for a confirmatory faculty. Paragraph 2
*j* pleads that the vehicular right exists by virtue either of presumed grant by reason of long user as of right or by purported grant by the court of a licence. That is presumably a reference to the doctrine of prescription by lost modern grant. Finally the amended schedule asks for 'The removal of the barrier erected at the entrance to the said Churchyard (and completed on 3rd February 1986)'. I read this ao an application for a faculty to remove the barrier and it was conceded by both counsel at the hearing that

once the barrier had been erected (whether lawfully or not) a faculty would be required for its subsequent removal. The petition was accompanied by a letter dated 13 November 1986 from Messrs Lee Bolton & Lee (acting for the petitioners) to the registrar of the court. This letter became part of the evidence at the hearing and it contains a material admission to the effect that the 1967 deed was not by itself effective to confer new rights of a permanent nature in the absence of a faculty, it being further conceded that no such faculty was asked for or obtained. The letter also gives further information about the petitioners' claim to pedestrian and trolley access having arisen by prescription. The case of the individual objectors is set out in a large number of letters received at the registry from those persons following citation of the petition. Subsequently all these individual objectors (except Mrs Robinson) agreed to be represented by Messrs Harland & Co, who by that time were also representing the incumbent, the team vicar and the PCC, and also the feoffees of St Helen's and St Martin's, being the trustees, inter alia, of certain lands or their proceeds of sale, and probably certain other assets, previously connected with the church of St Martin's. On 19 November 1987 Harland & Co wrote a letter to the registrar setting out the objections in detail of the individual objectors. On the same date they wrote another letter to the registrar setting out the detailed objections of the feoffees. These letters have also been taken for the purpose of the proceedings as setting out any objections of the PCC, church wardens and clergy of the team ministry. Lee Bolton & Lee supplied an answer dated 11 December 1987 to the two letters of objection. As far as directions are concerned I gave directions on 20 January and 5 March 1987 (as indorsed on the backsheet of the petition) and some further directions were given by consent at a directions appointment which was held before the registrar on 13 November 1987, when a formal order for directions was drawn up. In the event the issues which arose at the hearing were somewhat different from those raised in the pleadings. To some extent this was due to certain concessions made on either side and to certain agreements between the parties as to some of the issues. In particular the parties had virtually reached an agreement, prior to the opening of the case, as to the limited extent of any vehicular access to the churchyard in future, subject to my being satisfied that a faculty should issue to implement such agreement. Also and by the same stage the parties opponent had come to accept the petitioners' case that they had in fact been using the churchyard for access on foot and by trolley for themselves and their servants, so that broadly speaking the main issues relating to pedestrian access were (a) whether a right of pedestrian way was limited to the petitioners and their servants or extended to licensees such as suppliers and customers and (b) whether such right amounted to an easement or merely to a licence. The parties opponent were no longer opposing all use by the petitioners of the yard, but were conceding pedestrian access as above and were also prepared to grant a limited amount of vehicular access (in case of emergency only) for a period of not more than 30 months. That period was put forward as reasonable on the basis of the petitioners' statement that their printing and newspaper business which they carried on from their premises would be coming to an end within such period of time. The question of the future form of the gate, and who should have a key to it, would fall to be decided in the light of the other issues. In the background there was a problem about the future development of the petitioners' site and the implications which would arise as to future use of the yard by pedestrians and vehicles in relation to the site as developed. It became clear that the attitudes of both sides in relation to the existing position were coloured by their wishes and fears in relation to the position as it would be after redevelopment. Although it appeared to me after the opening of the case that some of the issues which I was being asked to decide were not fully pleaded by the petitioners and that as a result I might need to make decisions in certain areas where the amended schedule of the petition did not indicate that this would occur, I nevertheless decided that it was not necessary to adjourn the proceedings for the purposes of amendment of the schedule or for recitation of the amended petition. That was because I was not asked to do this by either counsel and it seemed to me that all the possible parties opponent a who might have an interest in the new issues were either before the court or had received a sufficient general notification as to the scope of the issues likely to be decided at the hearing.

[The Chancellor then referred to the history of the church, which was built in the fifteenth century but seriously damaged in the 1939–45 war and only partially rebuilt. Regular church services were not held but there were special services on three days in the year and the church was used for retreats and counselling. There was also a parish office

b and lunch-time coffee room. The churchyard was consecrated and had been used for burials in the past but not in the last 130 years. The churchyard had been paved over since at least 1935 and probably for a considerable time before that. The Chancellor made a finding that the churchyard had been in fact closed for burials since at least the turn of the century. A public right of way was granted under faculty in 1949 over a small area of the churchyard nearest to the road but that had never been used due to the closing up

c of a door in the building adjacent to the churchyard to which the public right of way was to lead. The petitioners had used the yard for pedestrian access, for their employees, their suppliers and their customers, since at least 1935 and had brought vans in and out of the yard for about twenty years. In 1950 they brought heavy printing equipment into their premises by lifting it over the walls which then stood between the street and the yard. They had no other means of getting such equipment into their premises due to the

d layout of the relevant part of their buildings and lack of other access from the street. The Chancellor continued:]

THE ISSUES

*Vehicular access*

Prior to the opening of the case substantial agreement had been reached between the

e parties as to (a) the extent of any vehicular use up to the date of the hearing and (b) what vehicular use should be allowed subsequently. There had been no agreement at the time of the pleadings. What emerged from the evidence was that no vehicular access was possible prior to 1965, when the small walls and railings at the Coney Street end were removed for the purposes of building work on the church. It was common ground between witnesses on each side that during the course of the building works vehicles

f were able to come into the yard and were in fact brought in. Some of the vehicles related to the building works, some to the petitioners' business and some may even have belonged to members of the public taking advantage of the position. As the building works were nearing a conclusion both sides desired to regularise the position with regard to future use of the yard and eventually, after much discussion in meetings and in correspondence, an agreement (by deed) was entered into on 4 October 1967. In relation

g to vehicular access there was an agreement (in cl 3) that the petitioners should be entitled from time to time to pass with motor vehicles of a laden weight not exceeding 15 tons over the churchyard to and from their premises for the purpose of bringing into or taking out of the premises any equipment, apparatus or machinery. By cl 4 there was an agreement that they should—

h        'be permitted on first obtaining on each and every occasion the written consent of the Incumbent . . . which consent shall not be unreasonably refused in case of emergency to pass with motor vehicles over [the] Churchyard . . . for the purpose of collecting newspapers for delivery'

and it was agreed that an emergency should be—

j        'deemed to include a situation in which by virtue of abnormal congestion of traffic in Coney Street . . . the collection . . . of newspapers for delivery from [the petitioners'] normal collection point [should be] prevented or affected to a substantial degree.'

By cl 5 it was provided that the resurfacing of St Martin's churchyard (which was about to take place) should be carried out in such a way as to bear the weight of vehicles of up to 15 tons. The petitioners agreed to pay a sum of £300 towards the resurfacing of the churchyard and by a separate agreement (in correspondence) they agreed to pay a further *a* £1,500 to York Civic Trust (a charitable body concerned in the restoration of St Martin's). The clauses relating to vehicular traffic clearly gave the petitioners additional rights in the yard but in law such rights without a faculty could not amount to more than a licence granted by the incumbent for the duration only of his own incumbency, and could not be binding on his successors in title to the freehold. That was conceded on behalf of the petitioners at the hearing, a faculty for any more extensive rights not having been sought *b* at the time.

After that agreement the PCC had a light removable gate fitted at the entrance to the yard, this being in the form of a metal chain supported on three or four wooden posts, the wooden posts being removable. The chain was padlocked but a key was either given to or was available for the petitioners. From time to time the petitioners exercised their rights under the agreement in relation to vehicular access, but certainly as far machinery *c* was concerned the use was very infrequent. Canon Porter ceased to be the incumbent of St Helen and St Martin in 1975 and my finding is that, in law, the vehicular rights conferred by the agreement came to an end at that point. The parties did not give consideration to the legal position and the petitioners may have thought that the rights were continuing, notwithstanding that they were advised by their own solicitors at the time of the agreement that the absence of a faculty might well make the agreement for *d* vehicular access unenforceable. By the mid-1980s it appears that the clergy, church wardens and PCC of St Martin's did not have any clear recollection of the 1967 agreement. The evidence showed that the chain and posts were gradually damaged and by 1985 when the Rev Peter Dodson arrived only one wooden post remained and the lock on the chain was broken so that it was no longer effective. Not long afterwards the posts and chain fell into disuse altogether and for a time there was no means of preventing *e* vehicular access to the yard. For about a year the number of vehicles using the yard gradually increased. These seem sometimes to have been vehicles belonging to church people, sometimes vehicles going to the petitioners' business premises and sometimes vehicles of members of the public. On occasions cars blocked the only entrance to the south aisle of the church. At a special Remembrance Day service (probably in 1985) *f* someone, whose car had been blocked in, noisily interrupted the service, asking for a car to be moved. The PCC became very concerned about the number of vehicles illegally using the churchyard. Certainly the public had no right to park there and likewise the petitioners had no right to park vehicles. Early in 1986 the PCC therefore erected the present gate and it was that act which led to the proceedings being taken later in the year. A temporary accommodation was arrived at whereby the PCC agreed to permit *g* temporary use of the churchyard to the extent set out in cll 3 and 4 of the 1967 agreement on the undertaking of the petitioners to bring and pursue faculty proceedings for the purposes of deciding the disputed issues between the parties, and pending the adjudication. On that basis the petitioners were provided with a key to the new gate and they have had access across the yard for pedestrians and for trolleys to bring paper in and printed matter out (as before) and they have also had access for vans up to the size of a *h* transit van in the emergency situation of cl 4. On the other hand the present gate is erected in such a way as to prevent lorries entering the churchyard and heavy machinery could not be brought in and out as envisaged in cl 3. The entrance gap is barely 14 feet wide in total and not all that width can be safely used by vehicles without risk of damaging either the buttress on the corner of the church or the corner of an ancient building on the other side of the entrance way. The existing gate consists of a horizontal *j* pole with metalwork beneath it and this is supported on a pole at either end, the poles being fixed permanently into the ground. The horizontal gate is padlocked into the pole at one end and (I think) fixed at the other end but capable of hinging like a gate. The gap between the pole and the corner of the ancient building is about 3 feet and the gap between the other pole and the corner of the church is somewhat less. The petitioners' a   trolleys are 2ft 6in wide, so that they can pass through the existing gap on the building side, but if the load overhangs the side of the trolley there is difficulty. Happily it was agreed between the parties at the conclusion of the hearing that the gate will be altered to widen the pedestrian and trolley access of the petitioners, and in view of an agreement which has been reached (subject to my being able to grant a faculty in relation to it) the poles will also be moved in such a way as to widen the space for a vehicle, thereby allowing the petitioners during a limited period of time to be able to bring lorries into

b   the yard for the purposes of transporting machinery.

As the matter of vehicular access developed at the hearing in the light of the imminent move of the petitioners' printing business to another site in York, it became clear that the petitioners' interest is limited to ensuring vehicular access along the lines of cll 3 and 4 of the 1967 agreement for the remainder of their time at the present premises. During the opening counsel were able to announce that there was agreement between the parties to

c   such rights being conferred for a maximum period of 30 months should the petitioners not have moved during that time, but for a period of time up to the completion of their move should they move within 30 months. The only difference between the parties was that the petitioners asked for liberty to apply for an extension of time beyond 30 months whereas the parties' opponent did not wish any extension. Eventually however, during closing speeches, a formula was agreed whereby there should be liberty to apply to me

d   for an extension of time, but on the basis that a good case would have to be made out for an extension of time and that it was accepted that I might not grant it. In relation to vehicular access the only matter which remains to be considered is whether the court has legal jurisdiction to grant a limited vehicular access of this kind, for a limited period of time, over land which is consecrated, but which has clearly not been used for burials for at least 100 years.

e

*Jurisdiction to grant faculty for vehicular access*

Any faculty will be for a licence for a fixed period of time and no question arises of granting an easement, quasi-easement or licence of indefinite duration. There have been a number of faculty cases where a licence has been granted for a private right of way over

f   consecrated land. In *Re St Benet Sherehog, re St Nicholas Acons* [1893] P 66 Chancellor Dr Tristram QC granted faculties to the London Electric Lighting Co to construct flights of steps in portions of two disused churchyards for the purposes of their employees gaining access to electricity substations underneath public streets adjoining the churchyards. He said:

> 'The Court has undoubtedly jurisdiction to grant by faculty the user of a way
g     across a churchyard for public convenience or to an individual for private convenience, provided no detriment will thereby accrue to the parishioners.'

He granted licences for 21 years in each case. In *St Gabriel, Fenchurch St (rector and churchwardens) v City of London Real Property Co Ltd* [1896] P 95 the same chancellor confirmed a previous grant by him (a year or so earlier) of a right of passage on foot across

h   a consecrated churchyard (closed for burials by Order in Council) for the benefit of the occupiers of an adjoining property and this was done by a licence for 80 years. He declined to grant a faculty for a similar right of way in favour of the occupiers of another adjoining property, which right of way would have interfered with the one which he had previously sanctioned. Dr Tristram's decision was approved on appeal to the Dean of the Arches. In *Re Bideford Parish, ex p Rector and churchwardens and Bideford Corp* [1900]

j   P 314 a faculty was granted for a portion of a disused consecrated burial ground to be thrown into the adjoining public highway. It was argued that the ecclesiastical court had no authority to allow consecrated ground to be applied to secular uses but the Dean of the Arches said that in the case of a churchyard closed for burials an ecclesiastical court had the discretionary power to make an order of the kind asked for It is clear that the purpose of the faculty was that the piece of land to he transferred to the mayor, aldermen and burgesses of the town of Bideford should be used for the passage of vehicular traffic. In *Re St John's, Chelsea* [1962] 2 All ER 850 at 856, [1962] 1 WLR 706 at 714 Deputy *a* Chancellor Newson QC reviewed some of the earlier cases and said that, in deciding whether or not to allow consecrated land to be used for secular purposes, the central question was: 'Can the purpose for which the ground was originally consecrated no longer be lawfully carried out?' If so a faculty may issue for a secular use. If not the faculty may only issue for an ecclesiastical use, except in the limited case of a wayleave. Seeking to apply that dictum to the present case I have reached the conclusion that in *b* practical terms it is no longer possible to carry out the purpose for which the churchyard was consecrated, namely for burials, and that it is in fact closed for burials. That was the effect of the evidence given to me by the parties opponent and a visual examination of the site shows that in practice it would be impossible to bury people there. I consider that it is therefore open to me in my discretion to allow a limited secular use of the churchyard to the extent proposed, particularly having regard to the time limit of 30 *c* months, the fact that the licence will not allow vehicles to remain parked in the yard, and that it will allow vehicles into the yard only on rare occasions and on permission first being obtained from the incumbent, the team vicar or his deputy. This conclusion is further supported by *Morley BC v St Mary the Virgin, Woodkirk (vicar and churchwardens)* [1969] 3 All ER 952, [1969] 1 WLR 1867, where the deputy auditor, R O C Stable QC, granted a faculty for a strip of graveyard measuring 260 yards by some 12 yards to be *d* transferred to the borough council for the purpose of road widening, thereby allowing secular use of consecrated land, and this was done notwithstanding the opposition of the vicar, churchwardens and parochial church council concerned. Parts of the graveyard were still in use for burials. The deputy auditor granted the faculty because he was satisfied that it was in the public interest to do so. The land was required to widen an existing road into a dual carriageway, this being part of a very substantial road-widening *e* scheme stretching over many miles. The case can be distinguished from the present one in relation to the public interest factor but it illustrates the proposition that the principle whereby consecrated land should be protected from secular use is not an absolute one. Having considered these authorities I have reached the conclusion that I should exercise my discretion in favour of granting a faculty for the very limited and short-term vehicular use of St Martin's churchyard which is proposed by the petitioners and agreed *f* to by the parties opponent. The faculty and the licence will be in the terms of cll 3 and 4 of the 1967 agreement but limited as to time in the manner agreed between the parties and with the words 'incumbent or team vicar having responsibility for St Martin's' in substitution for the word 'incumbent' in cl 4. Further, the licence will be subject to a condition similar to cl 5 of that agreement, that is to say the petitioners are to make good all damage caused by them to St Martin's churchyard or to the church of St Martin's by *g* reason of the exercise of their rights of vehicular access above referred to.

[The Chancellor then dealt with the use of the churchyard by employees of the petitioners for parking bicycles and motorcycles in an area behind the church which was not visible from the street. The 1967 agreement made provision for that and the Chancellor said that his order would include a permission to continue that arrangement *h* in the form of a licence. The Chancellor continued:]

*Pedestrian access*

In discussing this matter it can be taken that the phrase 'pedestrian access' includes that form of access in conjunction with the use of trolleys. It was common ground between the parties at the hearing that the use of trolleys had gone on over the years as an adjunct *j* to pedestrian access. The petitioners claim a right of way for pedestrians (with or without trolleys) arising from long-standing user as of right. They claim this either by prescription at common law or by prescription under the doctrine of lost modern grant. They contend that the existence of a faculty should be presumed. They ask me to find that such a right exists and that it exists as an easement. Failing that they ask me to say that it is a quasi

easement, and failing that they ask me to say that it is a licence intended to be of
a permanent duration, such that it cannot be terminated without a further order of the
court (which would be in effect a faculty to terminate the existing right). The parties
opponent agree that the petitioners have exercised a right of pedestrian access for very
many years and they do not dispute the evidence of Mr Wade, the former assistant
manager of Herald Printers, that the right was being exercised when he started work at
the premises in 1935. The petitioners then asked me to determine the scope of the right
b and they contend that it extends to the petitioners' licensees, such as its business suppliers,
its customers (for example, people wanting printing work carried out), representatives of
companies seeking to do business with it and other persons having reason to come to the
premises, such as relatives and friends of staff of the petitioners coming to leave messages
or to meet members of staff at lunch break and the like. The parties opponent contended
from the start that any right of pedestrian access should not extend to licensees or visitors,
c but only extend to the petitioners themselves and their staff, and the parties opponent
maintained that position throughout the hearing and asked me to find that the pedestrian
access is limited to the petitioners and their servants.

*Jurisdiction as to pedestrian access*
    The first question which I have to decide in relation to this aspect of the case is whether
d I have jurisdiction in the consistory court to decide these questions relating to the
existence, legal status and scope of a right of way. Basically the nature of the right of way
claimed is similar to any other right of way and the principles applicable to the decision
which I have to make are not affected by the fact that the right of way happens to be over
ecclesiastical property. The law which I have to apply in reaching a conclusion is the
ordinary secular law rather than any specifically ecclesiastical law. It was conceded by
e counsel for the petitioners that the relief which he sought in relation to the pedestrian
access could equally well have been sought in the secular court, but he contended that it
was convenient for me to deal with it in the ecclesiastical court and he maintained that I
had jurisdiction. Clearly it is necessary to ensure that the ecclesiastical court does not
trespass on the secular court's jurisdiction and there have been numerous cases
(particularly in the last century) where the writ of prohibition has been used in the
f secular court to prevent the ecclesiastical court determining issues which ought to have
been raised in the secular court. I have considered whether I might have jurisdiction
under s 6(1)(e) of the Ecclesiastical Jurisdiction Measure 1963, which includes in the
original jurisdiction of the consistory court of the diocese—

g      'any proceedings . . . which, immediately before the passing of this Measure, [the
       consistory court] had power to hear and determine, not being proceedings
       jurisdiction to hear and determine which is expressly abolished by this Measure.'

This residual jurisdiction is referred to in 14 Halsbury's Laws (4th edn) para 1344. A
footnote says that the third edition of Halsbury's Laws (in which the law stated was in
general that in force on 1 October 1955) contained a statement to the effect that in some
h cases civil rights in connection with ecclesiastical property or with the recovery of money
applicable to ecclesiastical purposes could be tried and decided in the ecclesiastical courts,
although such proceedings were uncommon (see 13 Halsbury's Laws (3rd edn) para
1056). Reference was made to *Butt v Jones* (1829) 2 Hag Ecc 417, 162 ER 909, *Linnell and
Walker v Gunn* (1867) LR 1 A & E 363, *Liddell v Rainsford* (1868) 38 LJ Eccl 15 and *Proud
v Price* (1893) 63 LJQB 61 at 64–66. Having looked at these cases I am satisfied that it
j would not be right for me to attempt to deal with the questions which arise in relation
to the right of way in the present case by seeking to rely on the residual jurisdiction
provision of the 1963 Measure. Some of the cases cited in the third edition of Halsbury's
Laws are faculty applications in which a preliminary issue arose to be decided, and these
are therefore in the category of cases to which I will refer in due course. There are only
one or two examples of decisions involving civil rights or the recovery of moneys not

connected with the faculty jurisdiction. *Liddell v Rainsford* related to a dispute as to which of two clergymen should be entitled to retain and use communion alms for distribution *a* to the poor of the parish. The right to administer communion alms was clearly a matter of ecclesiastical law, not appropriate to be litigated in a secular court. *Proud v Price* related to a dispute over whether pews could be altered by the incumbent and churchwardens without the concurrence of a member of the congregation who claimed to be entitled to the exclusive use of the pews. Neither counsel has invited me to decide the issues about the right of way as a matter within my residual jurisdiction under the 1963 Measure and *b* it is my independent view that I should not do so because the rights with which I am concerned are not exclusively or even substantially of an ecclesiastical nature but are rights existing wholly in the secular field. For the purpose of determining whether the rights are of an ecclesiastical nature, so that they could be determined under the residual jurisdiction, I consider that it is purely incidental that in the present case rights are claimed in respect of ecclesiastical property, ie the churchyard of St Martin's. The issues *c* as to the existence and scope of the rights would be the same whether the rights were claimed in respect of ecclesiastical property or secular property. The issue as to the legal status of the right requires some consideration of the law relating to the effects of consecration on land such as a churchyard, but it is an area of law which can be considered as well in a secular court as in an ecclesiastical court. The fact that in relation to this one aspect of the case the secular court would have to take into account the law relating to *d* consecration and the existence of the faculty procedure is in my view insufficient to justify me in regarding the issues as a whole which I have to decide as being issues relating to ecclesiastical rather than secular rights.

I am urged, however, to decide these issues on the basis that they are ancillary to the petitioners' application for a faculty. If the petitioners do not have an existing pedestrian right of way (with or without trolleys) they ask for a faculty granting them such right of *e* way. If they have a right of way which does not extend to licensees they ask for a faculty granting such extension. It is argued that in order for me to decide whether faculties are required for these purposes I must first decide what the petitioners' existing rights are, so that the jurisdiction in deciding these issues is genuinely incidental to the faculty jurisdiction. The parties opponent do not argue against those submissions. I accept that *f* there is a long-standing practice whereby the ecclesiastical court will determine matters of a temporal nature which are incidental to the main ecclesiastical jurisdiction being exercised. In Phillimore *Ecclesiastical Law* (2nd edn, 1895) vol 2, p 1115 the following view is expressed:

> 'In case the principal matter belong to the cognizance of the spiritual court all matters incidental (though otherwise of a temporal nature) are also cognizable there; *g* no prohibition will lie provided they proceed in the trial of such temporal incident according to the rules of the temporal law . . .'

In relation to the latter part of this quotation I can confirm that the law which has been argued before me and which I shall apply in relation to the rights claimed by the petitioners is the temporal law. In *Phillimore* p 1116 it is said that where a custom or *h* prescription is put in issue prohibition may run if the ecclesiastical law is different from the civil law, and the cases quoted (at p 1119) in support of this proposition are *Mayor etc of London v Cox* (1867) LR 2 HL 239 and *Martin v Mackonochie* (1878) 3 QBD 730, DC; *rvsd* (1879) 4 QBD 697, CA; *affd* (1881) 6 App Cas 424, HL. I therefore direct myself that I must apply the temporal law.

In deciding whether to treat these issues as incidental to the faculty jurisdiction I take *j* the view that I must first be satisfied that this is a case in which I could (if satisfied on the merits) grant the faculty sought. Relevant to that is the question of whether the court has power to grant a faculty for a right of way (or an extension to a right of way) in circumstances where the incumbent, churchwardens and parochial church council do not concur. Such non-concurrence will obviously be a matter of importance in relation

to the merits, but does it remove the court's jurisdiction? The petitioners referred me to
*a* *Re St Andrew's, North Weald Bassett* [1987] 1 WLR 1503, a decision of Chancellor Cameron
QC. There a secular parish council petitioned for a faculty for a licence to pass and repass
over a churchyard for the purpose of access to a proposed cemetery. The petition was
opposed by the incumbent, churchwardens and parochial church council. Chancellor
Cameron discussed the implications of the opposition by these persons and bodies (at
1506). She referred to *Walter v Mountague and Lamprell* (1836) 1 Curt 253 at 260, [1835–
*b* 42] All ER Rep 433 at 435, where Chancellor Dr Lushington said:

> 'I think the consent of the rector is necessary by reason of his common law right;
> but I do not say whether or not, if the rector be called upon to shew cause, and he
> obstinately opposes a faculty, the Court may grant it. That point I consider it is not
> necessary to decide.'

*c* Chancellor Cameron concluded that Chancellor Lushington had left the point open. She
then referred to *St Gabriel, Fenchurch St (rector and churchwardens) v City of London Real
Property Co Ltd* [1896] P 95, where the question of overriding the opposition of the rector
did not arise but Chancellor Tristram QC made some general observations about
churchyards and the position of the incumbent. He said (at 101–102):

*d*    '... churchyards are by the law placed under the protection and control of the
> Ecclesiastical Courts and the freehold of the churchyard is in the rector, the fee
> being in abeyance; but the freehold is vested in him for the use (in so far as may be
> required) of the parishioners. Subject to that use, he is entitled to receive the profits
> arising from the churchyard; but he cannot by law make any appropriation of the
> soil of the churchyard. Such appropriation can only be made for limited purposes
*e*    by a faculty issued from the Ecclesiastical Court.'

Chancellor Tristram's judgment was upheld on appeal to the Court of Arches, where the
Dean of Arches, Lord Penzance, in no way demurred from anything that the chancellor
had said. Chancellor Cameron then referred to *Re St Paul's, Covent Garden* [1974] Fam 1
at 4, where Chancellor Newsom QC referred to the above-quoted passage from the *St
Gabriel* case and said that as churchyards were under the protection and control of the
*f* consistory court he took the view that he had jurisdiction to grant a faculty which would
override the views of an incumbent should it be right to do so. He said (at 5):

> 'No doubt if the company were to petition me without the incumbent or parochial
> church council approving, I might very well refuse the faculty. I should not do so
> because I have no power to grant it but upon the merits.'

*g*
I am prepared to follow the reasoning in the three cases to which I have referred and I
consider that I have jurisdiction, if I consider it right to do so on the merits, to grant a
faculty for a more extensive pedestrian access than that to which the church bodies are
willing to agree. This arises from the fact that, as a result of consecration of the
churchyard, the fee is in abeyance and the right to deal with the fee (including the right
*h* to grant a right of way) is vested in the ordinary on whose behalf the consistory court
may act. Having concluded that I do have jurisdiction in an appropriate case to grant a
faculty, I am able also to conclude that if some issue is genuinely ancillary to the question
whether or not such faculty should be granted I have jurisdiction to decide such issue. A
further example of the consistory court deciding issues as ancillary to the faculty
jurisdiction is *Re St Mary of Charity, Faversham* [1986] 1 All ER 1, [1986] Fam 143, a
*j* decision of Commissary General his Honour Judge John Newey QC. There the petition
was for the sale of a flagon so that the proceeds could be used to carry out urgent repairs
to the church. Appearance was entered by several bodies, some of which contended that
the parish did not own the flagon and also that the Commissary Court had no jurisdiction
to determine their ownership. The Commissary General held that an ecclesiastical court
does have jurisdiction to determine ownership of chattels when it is essential to do so in

order to decide whether to grant a faculty in respect of the chattels. As already indicated I conclude that I have jurisdiction on the basis that these issues are ancillary to my faculty *a* jurisdiction.

Counsel for the petitioners urged on me as a further basis for my taking jurisdiction over these issues the fact that the petitioners' case that they are entitled to pedestrian access, with or without trolleys and for the benefit of licensees, is based, inter alia, on the doctrine of prescription by lost modern grant and that it is inherent in that doctrine (when applied to a way over a churchyard) that the grant of a faculty at some time in the *b* past must be presumed. He then said that it would be necessary for the court to construe that faculty (even though no document exists and the doctrine assumes that it has been lost) and he argued that this exercise of construction is one for the ecclesiastical court and not the secular court. He referred to the *St Gabriel* case as an example of a chancellor taking jurisdiction to construe a previous faculty (in that case one granted by himself). He referred to the headnote in the report ([1896] P 95 at 96). As I have decided to accept *c* jurisdiction on a different basis it is not necessary for me to decide whether I would have jurisdiction to decide issues as to existing rights of way and their scope because of the presumed existence of a faculty and I therefore leave that question open.

*The issues*

In relation to the existence, nature and scope of any existing right of pedestrian way I *d* have to decide three questions. (a) Is user as of right proved by the evidence, so as to establish a prescribed right either at common law or under the doctrine of lost modern grant? (b) What is the scope of the right and in particular does it extend to use of the way by licensees (for example, customers, suppliers, representatives of companies wishing to do business with the petitioners, other persons having business dealings with the petitioners and friends or relatives of members of the petitioners' staff wishing to speak *e* to members of staff or to leave items for them as a matter of convenience)? (c) Does any such right amount in law to an easement or to a licence, and if it is a licence is it determinable by any of the church bodies concerned either at will or on any particular grounds, or is it determinable only by the consistory court? This third question is largely a question of law, whereas the first two questions are largely questions of fact and depend *f* on the evidence given at the hearing and contained in documents and correspondence placed before me.

*Documentary evidence*

[The Chancellor referred to documents of 1763, 1949 and 1950 and continued:] In the bundle of correspondence there is a letter dated 24 September 1948 written by Mr H E Harrowell to a firm of chartered surveyors, Messrs Hollis & Webb. Mr Harrowell was *g* the solicitor and partner in a firm of Messrs H E Harrowell & Brown but he was writing this letter in his capacity as clerk to the feoffees of St Martin's. The letter was in connection with the proposed sale of the almshouses to the Yorkshire Newspaper Co Ltd, for whom Hollis & Webb were acting. At the end of the letter Mr Harrowell wrote:

'The Newspaper Company already have right of way over the passage way lying *h* between the Church of St. Martin and the land coloured pink and blue and leading to their premises adjacent to the River Ouse.'

The plan referred to in that letter is not available but I read this passage in the letter as strong evidence of the existence of a right of way over the full length of the churchyard because of the reference to 'premises adjacent to the River Ouse'. It has to be noted that *j* the letter was written on behalf of the feoffees and not on behalf of other persons who are now parties opponent, but the letter is clearly of great importance because the feoffees, as owners of the almshouses and owners or former owners of pieces of land in the general area (or the proceeds of sale of such land), were in a good position to know the existing position as to rights of way. There is no suggestion in this letter of the right of way being

otherwise than 'as of right'. Since no information is given as to the origin of the right it
*a* is reasonable to infer that it was considered to be a right of long standing.

Then there is a letter written on 3 September 1949 by the solicitors of the feoffees to
the then rural dean, of which the second paragraph contains the following words: 'The
Company already has a private right of way over the Churchyard . . .' A similar letter
was written to the then Archdeacon of York. Then there is a letter by the same solicitors
to the registrar dated 31 October 1949. It accompanied the petition for faculty in relation
*b* to the public right of way. The letter refers to 'new works to be carried out by the
Yorkshire Herald' and the evidence at the hearing showed that in about 1950 the
Yorkshire Herald, having acquired the almshouses, pulled down those almshouses and
constructed the present three-storey building on the site. The letter of 31 October 1949
refers to the extra use which would be made of the churchyard and refers to this as 'their
excessive user of their right of way'. The documents and correspondence alone would
*c* provide substantial evidence of the existence of a way for pedestrians, to and from the
petitioners' premises, used as of right, for a considerable time prior to 1949 and
continuing in use up to and beyond the 1967 agreement, but in addition there was
considerable oral evidence.

*d* *Oral evidence*[1]

Mr Wade, the former assistant manager of Herald Printers, said that he started work
at the petitioners' printing works in 1935 and at that time his employers already had a
practice of using the yard to bring in paper on hand trolleys and to take out finished
products on the same trolleys. The trolleys were 5 or 6 feet long and $2\frac{1}{2}$ feet wide and
could carry about half a ton. They were used everyday and were pushed manually. The
*e* people who came in and out of the yard consisted mostly of employees of the petitioners
but in addition there were such people as representatives from paper companies and of
other companies with whom the petitioners did business.

Mr Smallwood, the services manager of Yorkshire Press, said that he joined the
company in 1951 and had been continuously employed since then except for two years'
*f* national service. Employees of the petitioners used the yard to get to and from work and
customers and other persons having business with the petitioners also came across the
yard. Contractors who undertook cleaning for the petitioners such as the cleaning of
overalls, towels and clothes came across the churchyard from time to time to make
deliveries and collections.

Mr Platt, a general maintenance worker for York County Press since 1977, said that
*g* about 50 or 60 people per day used the churchyard to gain access to the printing works.
Some 40 or so other people came into the churchyard apparently to look at the outside of
the church or to go into the church as visitors or tourists.

I admitted a statement by Mr Walter Smith, who died in November 1987 after the
date of the directions appointment before the registrar. His statement said that he
worked for York County Press and its predecessor Yorkshire Herald from 1938 until his
*h* retirement in 1962, by which time he was manager of the Yorkshire Herald Printing
Works. He said that he was never in any doubt that the company had a right of access on
foot from Coney Street to the company's premises across the churchyard and that this
was used by the company's employees and people doing business with the company.
There was also a right to take trolleys over the churchyard.

On behalf of the parties opponent Canon John Armstrong said that he was the
*j* incumbent of All Saints from 1971 onwards and the team rector of the York central team
ministry from 1975 onwards. He did not dispute the existence of a right of way on foot
and for trolleys. Much of his evidence was to do with the consequences to St Martin's of
any substantial increase in the number of pedestrians using the churchyard and I will

---

1    This section of the judgment has been abridged by the Chancellor for the purposes of this report.

deal with that aspect later in this judgment. The Rev Peter Dodson said that he was team
vicar with responsibility for St Helen's and St Martin's and had held the position for three　*a*
years. He said that St Martin's church was open during the daytime and people came in
to meditate and to be quiet, particularly during the lunch period. On about two days per
week retreats were conducted in the church. Although there was a certain amount of
noise from the street this was muffled and acceptable when inside the church. There
were restrictions in Coney Street as to vehicles, the period during which vehicles were
prohibited being between 11.30 am and 4.00 pm. When he first arrived as team vicar　*b*
the churchyard was being used for parking of vehicles to an unacceptable degree. Some
of the vehicles belonged to or related to the petitioners' business but others belonged to
members of the public who were taking advantage of the position. On occasions quite
large vehicles backed into the churchyard and sometimes there were vehicles parked
close up against the door of the church. It was in those circumstances that the church
decided to erect the present barrier at the beginning of 1986. He did not dispute the　*c*
existence of a pedestrian right of way from Coney Street to the petitioners' printing
works but he said that he was very concerned about increase in the use of the churchyard
by pedestrians. The church wished to retain control of how the churchyard is used and
he said: 'We are trying to provide a place of peace and tranquility where counselling can
be provided and people can come to meditate; many people in the city centre value this.'
He was very concerned about the effects of a commercial development of the printing　*d*
works site if that meant that the public would have access to the churchyard.

Mr David Robinson, churchwarden of St Martin's since 1986 and vice-chairman of the
PCC of St Helen's and St Martin's, said that he had attended St Helen's and St Martin's for
the last three and a half years. He was concerned about the uncertainty arising from the
proposed development of the site and such matters as maintaining the cleanliness of the
churchyard, responsibility for any damage to it, controlling the behaviour of the public　*e*
and ensuring that noise or other nuisance was not caused by any of the retail outlets.

Miss Roberta Green said that she had been concerned with St Martin's since 1943,
when it was in a ruinous state, and she had been on the PCC of St Helen's and St Martin's
for 30 years and a churchwarden between 1981 and 1987. She was concerned about the
legal duty of churchwardens to keep order in churchyards and the legal obligations on　*f*
the PCC.

The Archdeacon of York said that the reason for the parish putting up the present gate
was to deal with the parking problem which had arisen. He did not favour any vehicular
use of the churchyard if that could be avoided because of risk of damage to the buttresses
of the church wall and the building on the left of the entrance. The churchyard should
not become a busy place but should remain a quiet courtyard providing a buffer between
the church (in its use for retreats and meditation) and the busy street outside. These were　*g*
the views of the members of the diocesan advisory committee, of which he is a member,
and they were also his own views as archdeacon. In cross-examination he said that he
could see that a retail user for the printing works site was in many ways a logical
development and visually might result in an improvement, but he would be concerned
about problems of noise and nuisance and the large numbers of people who might want　*h*
to go to the new retail outlets and he said that unfortunately members of the public in
York did not always behave in an orderly manner but were sometimes noisy and ill-
behaved.

Mr Hackman, the group property adviser to the holding company of the petitioners,
gave evidence about the proposals for use of the site when the petitioners ceased business
there in a little over one year's time. He said that the site was zoned in the York city plan　*j*
for retail purposes and that he, as the person responsible for realising the asset (with a
view to paying for the costs of the new printing works), would seek a development for
retail purposes. The petitioners would be likely to dispose of their interest in the site and
would therefore be unlikely to have long-term responsibility for what occurred there.
He said that he understood that 'the planners' welcomed the concept of retail development

in principle. Retail development would involve bringing back the line of the buildings
*a* round the churchyard so as to provide a larger space for shop frontages and entrances. He
said that any development would be of the highest class because of the existing high level
of rents of premises in Coney Street. All the buildings on the site would be demolished
except the listed buildings on the Coney Street frontage. The space behind the church
would be widened. If for some reason retail development of the site were not permitted
the petitioners would propose to let the existing buildings for light industrial use to a
*b* number of different tenants, each holding a different part of the building. Each tenancy
having a frontage onto the churchyard would need a right of access across it. The
petitioners would try to improve the general environment of the church and it would be
in their interests to do so.

FINDINGS
*c* My findings are as follows.
(a) *A pedestrian way*, both with and without trolleys, has been exercised over this
churchyard for very many years. It has been exercised since well before 1935 and I
conclude for at least the last 100 years. The age of each of the buildings known to have
stood around the churchyard was not established but some of them have been there for
at least 100 years and it seems to me undeniable that the occupiers of the buildings
*d* around the churchyard have had a pedestrian access to Coney Street. I find that it has not
been restricted to any particular route across the churchyard. I further find that it has
been exercised as of right, that is to say nec vi, nec clam, nec precario. The 1949
correspondence in particular seems to establish user as of right, since if it had been
otherwise than by right I think that Mr Harrowell, the clerk to the feoffees of St Martin's
at the time, would have said so. I think that the user has been for the benefit of the
*e* petitioners and their predecessors in title as fee simple owners of the printing works
buildings and I am satisfied that the use was never furtive or secret but was entirely open.
I find that the use was of a kind and quality capable of giving rise to a right by way of
prescription. The period of user as of right required under the Prescription Act 1832, s 2
is 20 years next before the commencement of the proceedings and I am satisfied that
such use has taken place for a considerably longer period than 20 years prior to the
*f* commencement of the faculty proceedings. Because of the legal principles to which I
have already referred as to the right to grant a right of way being in the ordinary and not
in the incumbent (as freeholder for the time being) or any other body or person, I
conclude that the appropriate form of prescription in relation to the present case is that
under the doctrine of lost modern grant (including a presumed faculty) rather than by
use from time immemorial. I am therefore satisfied that a right of way on foot, both
*g* with and without trolleys, over the whole of the churchyard from Coney Street at one
end to the printing works at the other has been established.
(b) *How extensive is the right?*  Does it extend only to the petitioners and their servants
or does it also extend to licensees? The evidence of Mr Wade, Mr Smallwood and Mr
Platt and the statement of Mr Smith all provide substantial evidence that the right of way
*h* was exercised by and for licensees as well as servants of the company. The 1949
correspondence does not indicate that, in the view of the feoffees, the right of way was
not available to licensees. The inherent probabilities point to the right of way being for
licensees as well as the company and its servants. It would be very difficult to operate a
business from these printing works without being able to receive calls there from
customers, suppliers and other persons having a business interest, since geographically
*j* there is no realistic access to the premises otherwise than through the churchyard. The
large sign 'Herald Printers' which was clearly visible from the street would in my view
indicate to customers and suppliers that they could cross the yard to reach those premises.
When the almshouses were conveyed in 1950 the feoffees included a right of way from
the entrance to the almshouses across the churchyard to the street and I think it is plain
that such right of way must have included a right in the occupiers in the almshouses to

receive visits from licensees, including such people as their friends, relatives, tradespeople
and the doctor. It was conceded by counsel for the parties opponent that the pedestrian *a*
right of way for the almshouses must have included, and did include, a right in respect
of licensees. If that is the case in relation to the almshouses, it is difficult to see why it
should not be the case also in relation to the commercial premises, since there are
powerful practical reasons in both cases for the right being required for licensees,
although the classes of people requiring to come to the premises would clearly vary as
between residential property and commercial property. Thus far there would appear to *b*
be substantial evidence to support the petitioners' case on this point.

However, it is necessary to consider with some care the wording of and inferences to
be drawn from the 1967 deed between Canon Porter and the petitioners. Counsel for the
parties opponent argued that this deed evidences a more limited right of way, not
extending to licensees and he said that the petitioners could not go behind what they
agreed to in 1967. The deed is dated 4 October 1967 and it is clear from bundle 2 of the *c*
correspondence that it resulted from a great deal of prior discussion. The original draft
had to be considered and amended before its terms were agreeable on both sides. Counsel
points to cl 2 of the recital, which says that one of the purposes of the agreement is to
'remove any doubts or uncertainties which may exist as to the rights of the Company
over St. Martins Churchyard'. I agree with him that it follows that the intention of the
agreement was to record accurately the extent of the existing right. This is dealt with in *d*
cl 2 of the main part of the agreement, which reads as follows:

> '*The* parties desire to record that for many years past the Company and its servants
> have enjoyed and shall continue at all times hereafter to enjoy a right of way on foot
> and with laden or unladen trolleys over St. Martins Churchyard to and from Coney
> Street to and from the Company's printing works shown coloured red on the plan.' *e*

The parties opponent say that cl 2 defines the right of pedestrian access as being for 'the
Company and its servants' only. It is argued that if it had been understood that the right
was also for the benefit of licensees this would have been stated because of the degree of
care which was being used in drawing up the wording of this document as a record of
the existing position.

Those are powerful arguments but they have to be set against the findings which I *f*
have already made as to the way in which the yard was being used for pedestrian access
right up to the time of the 1967 agreement, i e that customers, suppliers and other people
having business with the petitioners were openly crossing the yard on foot.

Counsel for the petitioners argued for a different interpretation of the 1967 deed in a
way not inconsistent with the other evidence of a right extending to licensees and the
issue thus joined is the one which I have to decide. I think that the following matters are *g*
of particular relevance.

(1) The correspondence in bundle 2 leading up to this deed shows that it was the
intention on both sides that the existing rights with regard to the use of the churchyard
should continue. The deed should be interpreted in the light of its purpose, indicated by
cl 2 of the recital, 'to remove any doubts or uncertainties' as to existing rights, and *h*
indicated in the prior correspondence. Counsel for the parties opponent agreed that the
purpose of the document was relevant to its interpretation. The following letters and
documents in bundle 2 are significant. In the minutes of a diocesan committee under
the heading 'St. Martin's Churchyard, Coney Street, York' there is the entry: 'Canon N. F.
Porter, as the vicar of St. Martin's Church, had acknowledged the company's rights to
take trolleys carrying goods . . . over the churchyard . . .' The entry goes on to record *j*
Canon Porter's agreement to the emergency vehicular use which eventually appeared as
cll 3 and 4 of the deed. There is no mention in the entry of the right of pedestrian way
being limited to the company and its servants. It is of general relevance to the matter
that the petitioners obtained these additional vehicular rights in 1967 (having not had
them prior to that time) and there is nothing to indicate that a reduction in the extent of

the pedestrian access was a quid pro quo for the additional vehicular rights. On the
*a* contrary a letter from the petitioners' London office of Westminster Press Provincial
Newspapers Ltd to Mr Bradbury, the petitioners' director and general manager in York,
shows that in all the petitioners were paying £1,800 towards the costs of resurfacing the
churchyard in 1967. £300 of this was referred to in the deed and the balance of £1,500
was, on the evidence which I heard, paid by the petitioners to the York Civic Trust,
which was the charitable body providing the funds, or part of the funds, for the
*b* restoration of the church and churchyard. Throughout the correspondence during 1967
there is no mention at all of the petitioners giving up a pedestrian right of access for
licensees. In a letter from the York Diocesan Re-organisation Committee to Canon Porter,
in effect giving consent to the terms of the draft deed, it says in relation to the clause
dealing with pedestrian access: 'Item 2 has been allowed, and should continue.' This
would imply that whatever had hitherto been the extent of the pedestrian access was
*c* intended to continue and that the writer of the letter assumed that the wording of the
draft achieved that end. Finally there is a letter dated 1 October 1986, a letter written
after the present issue had been joined. Although this letter is partly expressed to be
'without prejudice' it was included in the agreed bundle on the basis that I should see it.
It is written by the solicitor to the parties opponent to the solicitor for the petitioners and
the material part reads:

*d*
> 'I am authorised to say, without prejudice, that my clients would be likely to
> accept that your client Company has a licence for its servants or agents to pass over
> the yard with or without trollies.'

This of course goes beyond the words of the 1967 deed and the words 'or agents' may, in
the context, be intended to refer to licensees.

*e*      (2) The essential contention of counsel for the petitioners is that the word 'Company'
should be construed as meaning the enterprise or business of the petitioners', so that it
would include all pedestrian use of the churchyard connected with that enterprise or
business. He supports this interpretation by referring to the word 'enjoyed' and argues
that the phrase 'for many years past the Company . . . [has] enjoyed and shall continue at
all times hereafter to enjoy' indicates that the company was to benefit from the right of
*f* way and it is to be inferred that such benefit included a right for its licensees to visit its
premises. This seems to me to be a powerful argument.

(3) Counsel for the petitioners referred me to a passage in *Gale on the Law of Easements*
(15th edn, 1986) p 292 where it is said: '. . . the maxim that a grant must be construed
most strongly against a grantor must be applied' and there is reference to *Wood v Saunders*
(1875) LR 10 Ch App 582 at 584n. While that passage is relating to a grant rather than
*g* (as in the present case) the recital of an existing situation, it seems to me that the same
principles of construction apply. The passage in *Gale* continues: 'In particular, in
construing a grant the court will consider (1) the *locus in quo* over which the way is
granted; (2) the nature of the *terminus ad quem*; and (3) the purpose for which the way is
to be used.' These references seem to me to support the petitioners' case.

(4) Counsel for the petitioners then draws my attention to cl 3 of the deed, which
*h* confers the right for vehicles of a laden weight not exceedings 15 tons to be brought onto
the churchyard for the purpose of bringing in or taking out of the petitioners' premises
any equipment, apparatus or machinery. He argues that it must in common sense have
been envisaged that on occasions such vehicles would belong not to the petitioners
themselves but to some other company or individual who agreed to take away machinery
no longer required at the premises or who was supplying new machinery. It is highly
*j* improbable that all new equipment, apparatus and machinery would be transported on
the company's own vehicles. On that basis it is significant that the express wording of
this clause, if narrowly construed, would limit the company in such a way that the
vehicles of any other company or person could not come onto the churchyard. That
points towards a wide interpretation of the word company', similar to that for which

counsel contends in relation to the preceding clause, that is to say that the word 'Company' means the enterprise or business activity of the petitioners. Perhaps an alternative way of *a* arriving at the same result is to say that if permission is given to a company to exercise a right over a churchyard this will be construed as including licensees unless the contrary is stated. Here there was clearly an opportunity to say that the company's rights did not include its visitors but that was not stated.

I find the petitioners' arguments compelling and I think that there is some judicial authority in support of them. In *Gale on the Law of Easements* (15th edn, 1986) p 307 *b* reference is made to *Hammond v Prentice Bros Ltd* [1920] 1 Ch 201 at 216, where Eve J said:

> 'After all the grant is appurtenant to the dominant tenement, and in my opinion in the absence of special circumstances ought to be so construed as to secure to the grantee all that is necessary for the reasonable enjoyment of the dominant tene- *c* ment . . .'

*Gale* continues:

> 'Words in a grant mentioning certain persons as entitled to use, e.g. tenants, visitors and the like, are generally to be regarded as illustrative and not as restrictive.'

Both counsel referred me to *Baxendale v North Lambeth Liberal and Radical Club Ltd* [1902] *d* 2 Ch 427, where it was held that the grant, contained in a lease, of full right 'for the lessee, his executors, administrators, and assigns, undertenants and servants' at all times and for all purposes connected with the use and enjoyment of the premises to use a way extended to members and honorary members of, and all other persons going lawfully to and from, a working men's club afterwards established on the premises. Swinfen Eady J said that it could not be doubted that, in the ordinary case of a right of way to a house *e* and premises which could only be used as a private dwelling house, the right would extend not only to the grantee, but to members of his family, his servants, visitors, guests and tradespeople, even though none of those persons was expressly mentioned in the grant, and that the necessary or reasonable user of the club premises as a club required that there should be liberty of passing over the way in question for the persons and vehicles shown to have used it. It seems to me that in effect Swinfen Eady J was *f* construing the word 'lessee' as including the lessee's family, visitors, guests and tradespeople going lawfully to his premises. The petitioners in the present case asked me to construe the word 'Company' in a similar way.

There are two cases referred to in *Gale* where the court was more reluctant to put a wide interpretation on documents creating rights of way. In *Thornton v Little* (1907) 97 *g* LT 24 a right of way was granted so as to be annexed to premises then used as a school to the grantee, her administrators and assigns, 'and her and their tenants, visitors, and servants'. Kekewich J seemed inclined to regard the enumeration of permitted persons as exhaustive but he did hold that he could interpret the words in the light of the circumstances and therefore the word 'visitors' included pupils. In *Keith v Twentieth Century Club Ltd* (1904) 73 LJ Ch 545, [1904–7] All ER Rep 164 the right to use a London *h* square garden was held not to apply to the residents of a club when the house for the benefit of which the right had been granted was converted into a residential club. Buckley J declined to extend the words of grant, 'heirs executors administrators and assigns and his and their lessees and sub-lessees or tenants (being occupiers for the time being of the house . . .) and for his and their families and friends', to residents of the club. It seems to me that this case turned to a considerable degree on the fact that the dwelling *j* house was no longer being used in the way envisaged at the time of the grant and that the language of the grant, particularly the part about use by families and friends, was no longer apt to deal with the new situation of a residential club. This is an illustration of the words of the deed being construed in the light of the circumstances. Applying that principle in the present case, and particularly having regard to *Baxendale*'s case, I consider

that the decided cases support the petitioners' contention that I should construe the word
'Company' widely so as to cover the company's licensees having a lawful business interest
in coming to the premises. I therefore reach the conclusion that the right of pedestrian
way was in fact exercised by the petitioners throughout the period not only by themselves
and their servants but also by and for their licensees having a legitimate business interest
in coming to their premises.

(c) *Easement or licence*   The remaining question is what is the legal status of the
pedestrian right. Counsel for the petitioners has argued that it is an easement but counsel
for the parties opponent says that it is a licence. I have already made some reference to
the effects of consecration and the putting into abeyance of the fee. In 14 Halsbury's
Laws (4th edn) para 1073 there appears this statement:

'When consecrated a church or churchyard ceases to be the property of the donor,
who, by dedicating his property to God, voluntarily sacrifices it for the attainment
of sacred objects. Thereafter, in strictness only the authority of an Act of Parliament
or Measure of the Church Assembly or General Synod can divest it of its sacred
character, and a faculty should not be granted for applying it to secular purposes
[except in relation to certain recognised deviations].'

The authority cited is *Hilcoat v Archbishops of Canterbury and York* (1850) 10 CB 327 at
347, 138 ER 132 at 140. Halsbury's Laws continues (para 1074):

'It is not possible to alienate consecrated land or buildings completely from sacred
uses and to appropriate them permanently to secular uses without the authority of
an Act of Parliament or a Measure of the Church Assembly or General Synod . . .
Except in the pursuance of [such] powers . . . it is not lawful to sell, lease or otherwise
dispose of any church . . . or the site . . . of [it] or any consecrated land belonging or
annexed to a church . . .'

There are a few exceptions to this principle, for example, the road widening cases to
which I have already referred. In *St Gabriel, Fenchurch St (rector and churchwardens) v City
of London Real Property Co Ltd* [1896] P 95 a pedestrian right of way was granted in the
form of a licence for 80 years and it was assumed by all parties and by the chancellor that
it was not appropriate to grant an easement.

In *Re St Peter's, Bushey Heath* [1971] 2 All ER 704, [1971] 1 WLR 357 the petitioners,
the incumbent and churchwardens, petitioned for a faculty to authorise them to enter
into an agreement for the granting of a right of way across part of the unconsecrated
curtilage of the parish church. Chancellor G H Newsom QC granted a faculty authorising
the user, subject to conditions, for 99 years. Originally the petitioners had asked for a
more extensive right, not limited to 99 years. The chancellor said ([1971] 2 All ER 704
at 706, [1971] 1 WLR 357 at 359–360):

'Counsel for the petitioners . . . conceded, and in my judgment correctly, that it
is impossible to create a legal estate in consecrated land, save under the authority of
an Act of Parliament or a Measure . . .'

He referred to *St Mary Abbots, Kensington (vicar and churchwardens) v St Mary Abbots,
Kensington (inhabitants)* (1873) Trist 17. Chancellor Newsom in granting a faculty for a
licence directed that the legal estate in the land should remain in the incumbent. My
conclusion is that a full legal easement of way could not have been acquired in the present
case. I have previously indicated my view that the case falls to be considered under the
doctrine of prescription by lost modern grant, there being a presumption of the grant of
a faculty at some time. I consider that as a matter of law such a faculty could not have
conferred an easement, but it could have conferred a licence of indefinite duration.
Counsel for the petitioners did not concede this but he agreed that in practical terms an
indefinite licence would have the same effect as an easement and he was disposed to refer
to such a licence as a 'quasi easement' for that reason. He did refer me to the Prescription

Act 1832, s 2 in support of his primary contention that there can be an easement of way
over consecrated land and I must refer to that section. The relevant parts read:

> 'No Claim which may be lawfully made at the Common Law, by Custom,
> Prescription, or Grant, to any Way or other Easement . . . to be enjoyed or derived
> upon, over, or from any Land or Water of our said Lord the King . . . or being the
> Property of any Ecclesiastical or Lay Person, or Body Corporate, when such Way or
> other Matter as herein last before mentioned shall have been actually enjoyed by
> any Person claiming Right thereto without Interruption for the full Period of
> Twenty Years, shall be defeated or destroyed by shewing only that such Way or
> other Matter was first enjoyed at any Time prior to such Period of Twenty years . . .'

It is argued that since this section speaks of 'any Way or other Easement . . . over . . . the
Property of any Ecclesiastical . . . Person' it must be implying that an easement of way
can exist over ecclesiastical property. I do not believe that is a necessary interpretation of
this section because I think that the reference to ecclesiastical property is clearly wide
enough to include land which is not consecrated and in respect of which an easement can
therefore be acquired. I do not read the section as intending to alter the rule of law about
consecrated land which clearly existed in and prior to 1832 whereby an easement over
consecrated land cannot be created. In those circumstances the lost faculty which is to be
presumed because of the user as of right to which I have already referred must be deemed
to be a faculty for a licence and not an easement.

*Terms of the licence*

Counsel for the parties opponent agreed that the licence for a pedestrian way was of
indefinite duration and was not terminable by the parties opponent. I agree with that
concession. However, just as the acquisition of the licence is deemed to have been by
faculty (the fee and control of the land being in the ordinary), so the licence can be
terminated by faculty if the ordinary (acting through the consistory court) is put on
notice that the licence is being abused and if the consistory court considers that the
licence should be terminated. The procedure would involve an application for a further
faculty to terminate the existing licence. I find therefore that the licence which is in
existence is one which is terminable only by a further faculty application. It extends to
persons having a lawful business interest in attending the petitioners' premises and it also
extends to such people as friends and relatives of members of staff who may be allowed
by the petitioners to come to the premises from time to time to bring messages and the
like.

In relation to the question whether the quality of the petitioners' use of the right of
way, in so far as it related to licensees, was 'as of right' counsel for the parties opponent
urged me to take the view that the use by licensees had been secret. He said that it would
not have been possible for anyone on behalf of the church authorities to know whether a
particular person walking across the churchyard was a member of the petitioner company
or one of its servants, or contrariwise was a licensee. That may be so in practice, although
I think that the church authorities could have called for a list of employees and members
of the company so as to be able to identify them, and distinguish them from licensees, if
it had wished to do so, and that clearly did not occur. But be that as it may, I do not think
the test of 'secrecy' is whether the church authorities could in practice distinguish
between servants and other people, but it is a question of whether there was any lack of
openness or concealment being practised by or on behalf of the petitioners. I am satisfied
that there was not and that the petitioners allowed their customers, suppliers and other
visitors to come to them openly across the churchyard. The presence of the large sign
facing towards the road seems to me to make that clear because, if there had been any
intention of secrecy, it would have been most unwise to display that sign in such an
obvious manner and over such a long period of time. I have reached the conclusion that
the 1967 agreement should be construed on the basis that the word 'Company' is wide

enough to include licensees. Counsel for the parties opponent did suggest to me at the
*a* end of his submissions that the agreement might amount to an estoppel by deed. That
argument cannot arise in the light of my construction of the relevant clause.

*Agents*

Having reached a conclusion that the right of way is to be used by persons having a
legitimate business interest to come to the premises I conclude also that if there are
*b* circumstances in which the petitioners genuinely appoint an agent for the purposes of
carrying out some part of their business, so that that person needs to come to the premises
on foot, he becomes a licensee within the class of persons who has a business interest to
come to the premises. To that extent therefore agents are within the class of person
covered by the right of way. An agent not connected with the petitioners' business would
in my view be outside the class.

*c* Having reached these conclusions in relation to the existing right of pedestrian way it
clearly becomes unnecessary for me to consider the petitioners' application that, in the
absence of such a right, I should grant a faculty to provide it.

[The Chancellor then dealt with the proposals of the parties for alterations to the gate
at the street end of the churchyard and indicated the directions he would give. Those
directions would allow a permanently open gap wide enough to allow access by
*d* pedestrians and trolleys and a gate capable of being opened to allow access by vehicles on
occasions to be notified by the petitioners in advance. In view of the petitioners' proposals
to develop their site those arrangements would be for 30 months. The Chancellor
continued:]

*Future of the site*

*e* I have already referred to the evidence given on this aspect. Until almost the end of his
final speech counsel for the petitioners was asking me to deal in my judgment with the
situation as it will be when a development takes place either for retail use (as is likely) or
for subdivision of the existing premises for a number of light industrial uses (as is
unlikely). The concern of the petitioners is to know the extent of pedestrian access which
will be permitted over the churchyard when development takes place. It is clear that if
*f* there is a major retail development this courtyard would be very valuable for purposes
of access to the new shopping area. There is even the possibility of this yard being used
as an access to a mall or further pedestrian way passing into and through the shopping
area and possibly even to areas which are now on adjacent sites. I can readily see that it is
of some importance to the petitioners to have an indication as to the possible future scope
of the pedestrian access as this may be of relevance to their plans. When counsel for the
*g* petitioners was dealing with this aspect of the case I told him that I considered that I did
not have jurisdiction to deal with it at the present time. One factor is that it is not in any
way raised in the petition and the schedule of works and as a result the citation of the
proceedings has not given notice to any interested party that I might adjudicate on a
future position which is very materially different from the present one. Technically that
*h* difficulty could possibly be overcome by an adjournment and recitation of an amended
petition. But having reached that situation a better procedure would probably be to leave
this aspect of the case to be dealt with at a later stage and under a fresh petition. If the
matter does come before me in due course I certainly consider that a fresh petition will
be required because of the need to particularise the faculty being sought and/or the issues
to be decided, so that proper notice of these matters can be given at the time of citation.

*j* However, my reason for declining to deal with future aspects at this stage is not any
procedural problem in relation to the petition and citation, but is a question of
jurisdiction. As I have said earlier in this judgment, I do not consider that I have
jurisdiction to make rulings about the scope of rights of way of a basically secular nature
unless to do so is necessarily ancillary to an application for a faculty of a kind which it
would be possible for me to grant. In relation to the development proposals it is possible

that when the proposals are clear a faculty application could be made asking the court to grant a faculty for an extension of the existing right of way so that it covers the extended *a* class of licensees (both in quality and quantity) which the petitioners will say should be allowed to use the churchyard. I thing it might well be a matter necessarily ancillary to such an application for me to decide at that stage whether this increased class of visitors is or is not within the existing pedestrian right of way. I am satisfied, however, that at the present time any adjudication whether the existing right of way extends to a large number of customers visiting a retail outlet (and members of the public window- *b* shopping) could not be necessarily ancillary to any faculty application which I could at present consider. I could not consider a faculty application relating either to a development for retail business or a development for the division of the existing premises into a number of light industrial businesses until particulars of the proposals are clear. I cannot consider matters ancillary to such a faculty application until the faculty application itself is properly constituted. *c*

It is clear that if a stage is reached where those issues have to be decided there will be a great deal more information which will be needed by the court. There will need to be evidence as to the number of customers and members of the public likely to be wanting to use the churchyard and this will depend to a substantial extent on what other access there may be to the proposed redeveloped premises. If there is no other main access to those premises one could envisage a situation where the present 50 or 60 pedestrians *d* using this yard to get to the printing works might increase to many hundreds per day. The question would then arise whether such use could or could not fall within the existing right. As far as non-employees are concerned the existing right has related to a relatively small number of customers, suppliers and others having a business interest to come to the premises. The vast increase in numbers of customers might be outside the existing use. Also there might well be a change in the quality of the use as well as a *e* change in the quantity of it because the people coming into the churchyard would not only be customers but would also be people who simply wanted to walk round looking in shop windows, or perhaps entering the shops without intending to buy, and they would thereby be more in the category of ordinary members of the public than the category of customers. It would be a use considerably wider than the existing one where *f* all the licensees are persons having a business interest in going to the petitioners' premises and are not going to those premises as tourists or window-shoppers or for some other non-business purpose.

It would also be necessary to have information as to the extent of any nuisance caused in other retail areas of the City of York by noise from shops, bad behaviour by the public and/or people such as buskers and street vendors. It has to be borne in mind that this site *g* is in an extremely busy area in the centre of York and in the summer months in particular vast numbers of people visit the city. The situation in the Coppergate Centre, although no doubt different in detail, might provide some indication of how the public would use a new retail outlet on the printing works site. It would then be necessary for considerable thought to be given to the question of safeguards for the church and how the use of the churchyard could be controlled and monitored. It would have to be borne in mind that *h* the churchwardens and the PCC both have legal responsibilities in respect of the churchyard. The question of making good any damage in the churchyard caused by customers or members of the public would have to be considered. Again there would be a question of who should maintain insurance against the risk of people using the churchyard being injured.

The question of whether as a matter of law the existing right for customers to use the *j* churchyard could extend to a very much larger number of customers as a result of the development may well turn out to be complex. Prior to my informing counsel for the petitioners that I felt unable to proceed into this area (and of his agreement that I should not do so) he referred me to certain authorities and counsel for the parties opponent also did so. For the record it may be of value to list some of these. I was referred to Jackson

*Law of Easements and Profits* (1978) pp 146–148 in relation to whether an increase in user
a   if very great can of itself amount to excessive user. It is possible that a change in quantity
might be so vast as to amount to a change in quality: see *Woodhouse & Co Ltd v Kirkland
(Derby) Ltd* [1970] 2 All ER 587, [1970] 1 WLR 1185. I was also referred in this context
to *Keith v Twentieth Century Club Ltd* (1904) 73 LJ Ch 545, [1904–7] All ER Rep 164,
where the right to use the garden in the square was held not to apply to the residents of a
club following the conversion of the house. Plainly these are difficult questions and I
b  have indicated the way in which they might come within my jurisdiction if the issue
raised by them is necessarily ancillary to a faculty application which I would in turn have
jurisdiction to grant.

I express my gratitude to both counsel for the great amount of research done by both
of them in order to place the legal arguments and authorities before me and for the
clarity of those arguments. As I am delivering this judgment in written form it will not
c  be possible for the usual post-judgment discussion to take place as to the precise terms of
my order. I will provide a written order but I will direct that the order will not be drawn
up for 14 days after copies of it (and of this judgment) are sent to the parties' solicitors, so
as to enable counsel to contact the registrar if any alteration is needed in the form of the
order. Otherwise the order should be drawn up in the form in which I have drafted it.

d  ### Costs

I heard argument from both counsel in relation to costs, but of course the argument
was on a provisional basis. Counsel for the parties opponent argued that, whatever my
decision on the central and most disputed area of the case (the extent of the pedestrian
access), I should order the petitioners to pay all the costs, that is to say all the costs of the
parties opponent and all the court costs. He said that I should do this because it is the
e  petitioners who will benefit from the proceedings and he pointed to the fact that until
the very end of the hearing they had been seeking to obtain a ruling from me about
access by customers to the site as it will be after the development and that they had only
abandoned the attempt when I made it clear that I did not have jurisdiction to deal with
the matter. He also said that the parties opponent had always acted reasonably and that
f   their only interest was to preserve the quietness of the churchyard and the control over it
which they were entitled to exercise in their capacity as clergy, churchwardens and PCC.
The individual objectors supported the church bodies and were in a similar position.
Counsel for the petitioners said that, by concession, his clients would not be seeking that
any of their costs should be paid by the parties opponent in the event of the petitioners
succeeding on the major point in the case. On the other hand, the petitioners did not
g  accept that they should pay any of the costs of the parties opponent. He did not accept
that the parties opponent had been entirely reasonable at all stages and pointed to the
suggestion by the PCC that the petitioners should pay a substantial annual sum for the
restoration in 1985 and 1986 of their rights in the churchyard. He also said that the
erection of the present gate was more than a technical infringement of the petitioners'
existing right of pedestrian access.

h  The question of costs is entirely in my discretion, but I must exercise it judicially. I do
not take the view that either side has acted in any substantial way unreasonably and I
think that the issues which had to be decided in these proceedings were difficult ones. I
think it is not surprising that a consistory court had to be held in order to resolve these
matters since the law relating to them is not at all easy. I think there is force in the
argument of counsel for the parties opponent that it is the petitioners who ultimately
j   stand to benefit from the proceedings, whereas the church parties will not benefit either
commercially or in terms of the use and enjoyment of the church. I think it is likely that
the impact on the petitioners' financial position of having to meet costs of proceedings
will be less than the impact on the position of the parties opponent. I have come to the
conclusion that it would be right for the petitioners to make a contribution towards the
costs of the parties opponent, but since the petitioners have succeeded on one of the

major points in the case I do not think they should pay all the costs of the parties opponent. In deciding on an appropriate proportion I have in mind that a court hearing *a* lasting the better part of one day would in any event have been required in this case even if the issue about the extent of the right of way (for licensees) had been agreed. That is because the faculty for vehicular access during the next 30 months would have required consideration by me on oral evidence and I would have considered it right for the petitioners to pay the costs of that issue because it is a right which they seek and from which they will benefit. It is a right of considerable value to them to be able to have *b* access over this yard for the purposes of removing what I imagine will be a large quantity of machinery and other equipment when they leave the premises. Having considered these and all the other factors with regard to costs which were mentioned to me in argument and the contents of a letter from counsel for the parties opponent dated 18 February 1981, I have come to the conclusion that the petitioners ought to pay two-thirds of the costs of the parties opponent. If these costs cannot be agreed there will have *c* to be a taxation by the registrar and the petitioners must pay the appropriate proportion pursuant to my order. There is also the matter of court costs. These must be paid by the petitioners. The petitioners wanted to establish the position with regard to their legal rights in the churchyard and it is primarily for their benefit that the proceedings have been taken. Legal aspects of the use of the churchyard have not been adequately dealt with in the past. I refer to the lack of clarity of the 1967 deed, the failure to apply for a *d* faculty in 1967 and allowing a state of affairs to exist over a long period of time without clarifying its legal implications. I am satisfied that the predominant reason for having a court hearing has been the petitioners' desire to clarify these matters for commercial reasons connected with the proposed development. The matter of the gate could have been resolved without a hearing. However, I stated to counsel at the conclusion of the hearing that the order for costs would not be drawn up for 14 days after this judgment *e* was sent to the respective solicitors, thereby to give an opportunity to either side to argue the question of costs before me on a further occasion if they wish to do so.

Before leaving the case I would like to commend both sides in this dispute for the measure of agreement which they were able to reach prior to the opening of the case and certain further agreements which were reached during the course of the hearing. This *f* has not been an easy situation for either side, and there are difficult decisions which lie ahead. I have been impressed however by the good sense and reasonableness of everyone involved and I am sure that the existing atmosphere of co-operation will continue. The church of St Martin's is important not only for people likely to use the church but also as a symbol in the centre of the city. The printing works site is also important in terms of its future development and the amenities of the city. There is a real need for such co-operation as will lead to the enhancement of both the church and the site. For *g* geographical reasons the future of each of them is inextricably entwined with the other and it is clear to me that all those who took part in the hearing before me fully appreciated this.

*Faculties accordingly. Petitioners to pay court costs and two-thirds of costs of parties opponent.* *h*

Solicitors: *Lee Bolton & Lee* (for the petitioners); *Harland & Co*, York (for the parties opponent).

N P Metcalfe Esq    Barrister.

a

# Ipswich Borough Council v Fisons plc

CHANCERY DIVISION
SIR NICOLAS BROWNE-WILKINSON V-C
17 MAY 1989

b
*Arbitration – Award – Leave to appeal against award – Factors to be considered by court when deciding whether to grant leave – Award affecting parties' rights for the future – Construction of terms of lease – Appeal against arbitrator's decision on construction of terms of lease – Test to be applied in deciding whether to grant leave – Arbitration Act 1979, s 1(3)(b).*

By an agreement made in 1955 between the corporation and the tenant the tenant agreed
c to construct an office block on a site made available to it by the corporation and the corporation agreed to grant the tenant a 99-year lease from 29 September 1955. There was no provision for rent reviews. Clause 25 of the agreement provided that the corporation would offer to the tenant a lease of approximately 1,400 sq yd of land for use as a permanent car park, such lease to expire concurrently with the lease of the office building. There was part performance of cl 25 by the provision of a considerably smaller
d area of land for car parking. In December 1982, the time for compliance with cl 25 having expired, the parties entered into a further agreement whereby they extended the time for making an offer of the remaining land for the car park. In October 1986 the corporation offered certain land to the tenant but differences arose between the parties because the corporation claimed that the lease of the car park should be at a current open market rent and on such terms as might be agreed between the parties at that date, including a provision for rent reviews. The tenant contended that since the offer was
e made pursuant to the obligation contained in cl 25 of the 1955 agreement the rent and other terms of the lease should be such as would have been agreed in 1955, which would not include any provision for rent reviews. The dispute was referred to arbitration and the arbitrator held that the terms and conditions of the lease of the car park were to be determined on the basis of the rent and other terms which the parties would have agreed
f in 1955. The corporation applied for leave to appeal under s 1(3)[a] of the Arbitration Act 1979.

**Held** – When considering an application under s 1(3)(b) of the 1979 Act for leave to appeal against an arbitrator's award where the subject matter of the arbitration regulated the future property rights of the parties, the test whether to grant leave from the
g arbitrator's decision was not whether the court was satisfied that there was a strong prima facie case that the arbitrator was wrong in law but whether, after hearing submissions, the court was left in real doubt whether the arbitrator was right in law. On the facts, since the subject matter of the arbitration would affect the future legal relationship of the parties until 2054 and since the court was left in real doubt whether the arbitrator was right, leave to appeal would be granted (see p 740 j, p 741 c h j and p 742 c to f, post).
h    *Pioneer Shipping Ltd v BTP Tioxide Ltd, The Nema* [1981] 2 All ER 1030, *Antaios Cia Naviera SA v Salen Rederierna AB, The Antaios* [1984] 3 All ER 229, *Lucas Industries plc v Welsh Development Agency* [1986] 2 All ER 858 and dictum of Lord Donaldson MR in *Seaworld Ocean Line Co SA v Catseye Maritime Co Ltd, The Kelaniya* [1989] 1 Lloyd's Rep 30 at 32 considered.

j **Notes**
For appeals to the High Court from an arbitrator's award, see 2 Halsbury's Laws (4th edn) para 615.
    For the Arbitration Act 1979, s 1, see 2 Halsbury's Statutes (4th edn) 609.

---

a    Section 1, so far as material, is set out at p 740 b c, post

**Cases referred to in judgment**

*Antaios Cia Naviera SA v Salen Rederierna AB, The Antaios* [1984] 3 All ER 229, [1985] AC  *a*
191, [1984] 3 WLR 592, HL.

*Lucas Industries plc v Welsh Development Agency* [1986] 2 All ER 858, [1986] Ch 500, [1986]
3 WLR 80.

*Pioneer Shipping Ltd v BTP Tioxide Ltd, The Nema* [1981] 2 All ER 1030, [1982] AC 724,
[1981] 3 WLR 292, HL.

*Seaworld Ocean Line Co SA v Catseye Maritime Co Ltd, The Kelaniya* [1989] 1 Lloyd's Rep 30,  *b*
CA.

*Warrington and Runcorn Development Corp v Greggs plc* [1987] 1 EGLR 9.

**Application for leave to appeal**

By a summons dated 11 November 1988 Ipswich Borough Council (the corporation)
sought leave to appeal against the interim award of the arbitrator, Mr David R Crome,  *c*
dated 21 October 1988 in arbitration proceedings between Fisons plc as applicants and
the corporation as respondents. The facts are set out in the judgment.

*Kirk Reynolds* for the corporation.
*David Grant* for Fisons.

*d*

**SIR NICOLAS BROWNE-WILKINSON V-C.** This is an application for leave to
appeal from a decision of an arbitrator under s 1(3) of the Arbitration Act 1979.

By an agreement made in 1955 between the mayor, aldermen and burgesses of the
Borough of Ipswich (the corporation) and Fisons Ltd, the corporation made available a
site in Ipswich for the construction by Fisons of an office block. Fisons were to erect the
building on the site and were then to be granted a 99-year lease from 29 September 1955  *e*
at a rent of £530 per annum. That was plainly an unimproved ground rent. The terms
of the lease to be granted were set out in a schedule; it contained no provision for rent
review. Clause 25 of the 1955 agreement provides as follows:

'THE Corporation hereby undertake with the Tenant that they will within twenty-
one years from the date hereof offer to the Tenant a Lease of approximately One  *f*
thousand four hundred square yards of land in the vicinity of the said land for use
as a permanent car park for a term to expire concurrently with the Lease referred to
· in Clause 13 hereof but otherwise upon such terms and conditions as may be
mutually agreed between the Corporation and the Tenant'.

Fisons constructed the office block and the lease was duly granted. Clause 25 was partly  *g*
performed by providing a smaller area for car parks and other interim arrangements.
However, by the time within which cl 25 was to be complied with, namely 1976, there
had not been a full compliance with cl 25.

In December 1982 the corporation and Fisons entered into a further agreement which,
after reciting the 1955 agreement (including cl 25), that time for compliance with cl 25
had expired and that the parties had agreed to extend the time for making the offer for  *h*
the remaining land, provided as follows:

'1. The Landlord shall on or before the 9th December 1984 offer to the Tenant a
lease of approximately 918 square yards of land in accordance with Clause 25 of the
agreement. 2. If the Tenant does not accept such offer within a period of 28 days
then the determination of the terms of the new lease shall be referred to an  ·
independent expert appointed in default of agreement by the President for the time  *j*
being of the Royal Institute of Chartered Surveyors who shall receive representation
from the parties but whose decision shall be final and binding. The terms so fixed
by the independent expert shall be open for acceptance by the tenant for a period of
28 days. The costs of the independent expert shall be borne as he may direct.'

*a*  On 24 October 1986 the corporation made an offer of certain land for car parking. They set out in a letter the terms on which a lease was offered. The proposed lease of the car park was to expire contemporaneously with the lease of the office building, but they proposed a rent of £7,500 per annum with provision for rent review every three years. On receipt of that offer differences arose between the corporation and Fisons. The corporation took the view that the lease of the car park should be at a current open market rent (though it is not clear to me whether it is contended that the rent should be

*b*  at 1982, 1984 or 1986 figures) and also that the lease should contain terms which would be such as would be agreed between landlord and tenant at that date, including in particular a provision for rent review. Fisons, on the other hand, took the view that the offer was being made pursuant to the obligation contained originally in cl 25 of the 1955 agreement, that it was part and parcel of the building agreement relating to the office block, that accordingly the rent should be fixed on the basis of what would have been

*c*  agreed in 1955 and that the terms of the lease should be such as would have been agreed in 1955, which, they submit, would exclude any rent review provision.

The parties agreed to refer the matter to arbitration. Originally a surveyor was suggested as the arbitrator. But it was eventually agreed that a solicitor, Mr Crome, should be appointed. In due course he gave a fully reasoned interim award. In the award he stated that the issues put to him for determination were:

*d*

'5.1 Whether upon their true construction the provisions of clause 25 of the 1955 Agreement together with the provisions of the 1982 Agreement give rise to legally enforceable obligations between the parties and 5.2 Upon a true construction of the documents referred to what should be the true basis on which rent and the other terms appropriate to a Lease now proposed by the Respondent to the Applicant in

*e*  respect of a site for use as a car park comprising 918 square yards . . . should be determined.'

He determined that there was no legally enforceable obligation under the 1955 agreement, but that there was a legally enforceable contract in the terms of cll 1 and 2 of the 1982 agreement. In the third paragraph of his award he said:

*f*

'In concluding the consideration to be paid and in deciding the terms of the covenant against assignment the expert will apply a subjective test and will decide the matter on the basis of rent and terms which the parties themselves would have agreed at the time of the 1955 Agreement had the presently proposed site then been available and shall have regard to the following matters in particular . . .'

*g*

He then ruled that the terms of the lease should be the terms of the lease of the office block and that there should be no rent review. Having made that determination as to the legal basis of the expert's determination, he left it to another expert to resolve, he not being a valuer.

In those circumstances there is a slight oddity in the submission to arbitration. The

*h*  1982 agreement provided for one expert to settle the terms and plainly envisaged that the expert would be a surveyor. In fact what the parties have done is to approach the matter in two stages, first, by submitting questions of law to a solicitor as arbitrator and then presumably going forward to the second stage of determination by an expert on the basis of the solicitor's legal decision. I think it is common ground between the parties that there has in any event been an implied submission to Mr Crome, the arbitrator, of

*j*  the questions which he set out in his award.

The decision of the arbitrator being unacceptable to the corporation, they have applied for leave to appeal against the award. The question of law, as explained to me by counsel for the corporation in opening this application, is this: whether the arbitrator was right in determining that the rent payable under and the terms of the lease should be such as would have been agreed between the parties in 1955, as opposed to December 1984. Again, there is some doubt as to the relevant date, but nothing turns on that date for present purposes.

The Arbitration Act 1979, s 1, deals with judicial review of arbitration awards. Subsection (1) abolished the jurisdiction of the court to set aside or remit an award on the ground of errors of fact or law on its face. Subsection (2) then provided a right of appeal to the High Court on any question of law arising out of an award made on an arbitration agreement. Subsections (3) and (4) provide:

> '(3) An appeal under this section may be brought by any of the parties to the reference . . . (b) subject to section 3 below, with the leave of the court.
>
> (4) The High Court shall not grant leave under subsection (3)(b) above unless it considers that, having regard to all the circumstances, the determination of the question of law concerned could substantially affect the rights of one or more of the parties to the arbitration agreement . . .'

I have no doubt that the requirement of sub-s (4) is satisfied. Plainly the terms on which a lease expiring in 2054 is to be granted will substantially affect the rights of both parties.

The question which arises is whether, under the discretion in s 1(3)(b), the leave of the court should be given for an appeal. The words of sub-s (3)(b) are entirely general: Parliament has not itself imposed any fetter on the exercise of that discretion. However, the House of Lords has on two occasions given indications as to how, at least in the area of commercial and shipping contracts, that discretion should be exercised: see *Antaios Cia Naviera SA v Salen Rederierna AB, The Antaios* [1984] 3 All ER 229, [1985] AC 191 and *Pioneer Shipping Ltd v BTP Tioxide Ltd, The Nema* [1981] 2 All ER 1030, [1982] AC 724. As the House of Lords indicated, the purpose of the changes introduced by the 1979 Act was to seek to avoid the practice which had arisen of allowing so-called points of law to be used to delay and cause further expense in arbitrations in commercial or shipping contracts. The words of the House of Lords are, in my judgment, directed to those types of commercial contract. In that context the House of Lords has drawn a distinction between arbitration relating to a standard form of commercial contract and arbitration relating to a contract which is a one-off contract involving no general question of standard form contract. Where there are standard terms of commercial contract, the House of Lords indicated that leave to appeal from the arbitrator should be given if there was a strong prima facie case that the arbitrator was wrong in law. In a case which is concerned with a one-off contract, the House of Lords indicated that the judge should only give leave if he was satisfied that the arbitrator was obviously wrong.

The question is how far those guidelines are applicable outside cases involving commercial or shipping contracts. The problem has previously arisen in relation to rent review clauses. Such a case came before me in *Lucas Industries plc v Welsh Development Agency* [1986] 2 All ER 858, [1986] Ch 500. I held that the detailed approach laid down by the House of Lords in commercial and shipping contracts was not directly applicable to arbitration on the construction of rent review clauses for three reasons: first, that there was in that context nothing corresponding to the standard commercial contract clause; second, that on rent review clauses there were or could be points which were of general application under the general law; third, and in my judgment most importantly, that the true construction of a rent review clause on any one rent review would arise again on each subsequent review and that a decision by the arbitrator on the first review, if not appealed, would probably give rise to an issue estoppel on the second and subsequent rent reviews. On those grounds I thought a rather different test appropriate: if after hearing submissions the judge was left in real doubt whether the arbitrator was right in law, it was appropriate to grant leave so that the law regulating the future relationship of the parties could be authoritatively determined by the court.

My decision in that case, I believe, has subsequently been applied in relation to other rent review cases by other judges in this division. In *Warrington and Runcorn Development*

*Corp v Greggs plc* [1987] 1 EGLR 9 Warner J extended the decision to a case where the
a  point arising on a rent review clause might well not have been a question of construction
of the clause but related to the way in which the arbitrator had conducted the fixing of
the revised rent.

The question which arises, therefore, is whether the test in *The Antaios* and *The Nema* is
the appropriate test to apply in considering whether I should give leave to appeal in this
case. If that test does apply then, on any footing, leave must be refused. The questions
b  which arise in this case and which were remitted to the arbitrator are difficult questions
of construction arising in unusual circumstances. Neither the construction of the
agreements nor the events will ever recur. I am very far from satisfied that the arbitrator
was clearly wrong, or even that there is a strong prima facie case that he was wrong. In
my judgment the case is one where different minds could form different views. However,
the question is one on which, in my judgment, the arbitrator may well have reached the
c  wrong conclusion. Applying the test I adopted in the *Lucas Industries* case, I am left in
real doubt whether the arbitrator was right; I am not altogether happy about some of the
reasoning which led him to his conclusion.

The question, therefore, is what is the appropriate test to apply in deciding whether to
grant leave to appeal in the circumstances of this case? None of the factors which led me
in the *Lucas Industries* case to depart from *The Antaios* test are present in this case. This is
d  truly a one-off contract in a one-off set of circumstances, leading to the fixing of the terms
of the lease once and for all. It raises, so far as I can see, no general question of law. There
is no question of an issue estoppel arising since it is a one-off event. Therefore this case
does not fall within the grounds of decision in the *Lucas Industries* case.

In my judgment, the correct test to apply is not an easy matter. The underlying
philosophy of the 1979 Act was to prevent the delay and expense involved in testing
e  arbitrators' decisions in the High Court and beyond. In *Seaworld Ocean Line Co SA v
Catseye Maritime Co Ltd, The Kelaniya* [1989] 1 Lloyd's Rep 30 at 32 Lord Donaldson MR
said that the whole purpose of the 1979 Act was to give primacy to finality over legality
(meaning the correct legal answer) in cases where parties had chosen arbitration. He
went on to say:

f       'If it is a one-off case in which the general market and the Commercial fraternity
has no interest (it merely affects the rights of the particular parties), then the fact
that they have chosen their own dispute settlor weighs very heavily in the balance.
They have accepted him for better or for worse in relation to all questions of fact,
and there is a strong presumption that they have also accepted him for better or for
worse in relation to questions of law.'

g  In a case such as the present, it can fairly be said that the corporation has determined and
agreed to remit to the arbitrator the decision of these points of law and should abide by
his decision. To permit the matter to be further litigated by way of appeal in such a case
is to run counter to the policy of the Act designed to ensure speediness and cheapness of
arbitration.

h      On the other side there are also forceful arguments. The points of law that arise in this
case will have a major impact on the terms of a lease which will last until the year 2054.
It regulates the future legal relationship of the parties. In addition to the rent, the other
terms of the lease will have to be determined, including in particular the rent review
clause. The presence of a rent review every three years up to 2054 would be a major
imposition on Fisons. It is extremely hard, if the arbitrator's decision is erroneous in law,
j  that the corporation should be left with a tenant for many decades holding on the terms
of a lease which in law they should not be enjoying.

I find these considerations nicely balanced. I do not regard the decision of the House
of Lords in *The Nema* [1981] 2 All ER 1030, [1982] AC 724 and *The Antaios* [1984] 3 All
ER 229, [1985] AC 191 as being decisive in this sort of case. The House of Lords was
plainly laying down guidelines in relation to commercial and shipping contracts. In *The*

*Nema* [1981] 2 All ER 1030 at 1037, [1982] AC 724 at 739 Lord Diplock said:

> 'The judicial discretion conferred by sub-s (3)(*b*) [of s 1 of the 1979 Act] to refuse  *a*
> leave to appeal from an arbitrator's award in the face of an objection by any of the
> parties to the reference is in terms unfettered; but it must be exercised judicially;
> and this, in the case of a dispute that parties have agreed to submit to arbitration,
> involves deciding between the rival merits of assured finality on the one hand and
> on the other the resolution of doubts as to the accuracy of the legal reasoning  *b*
> followed by the arbitrator in the course of arriving at his award, *having regard in that*
> *assessment to the nature and circumstances of the particular dispute.*' (My emphasis.)

It seems to me entirely consistent with that approach to say that the conflicting demands
of finality and legality may vary according to the subject matter of the arbitration.

    I have, with considerable hesitation, come to the conclusion that in the present case
leave to appeal should be given. The crucial distinction, in my judgment, is between, on  *c*
the one hand, arbitrations designed to resolve existing disputes arising out of conflicts as
to liability for events which have happened in the past and arbitrations or decisions of an
expert in a case such as the present, where the function of the expert or arbitrator is to
regulate the future relationship of the parties. In the latter type of case it seems to me
that the hardship of inflicting a decision which may be erroneous in law on one party is
capable of outweighing the loss of speed and certainty. For myself, I think in a case where  *d*
the subject matter of the arbitration regulates the future property rights of the parties
the right approach to the giving of leave to appeal is the same as that which I adopted in
*Lucas Industries plc v Welsh Development Agency* [1986] 2 All ER 858, [1986] Ch 500,
namely that if, after hearing submissions, the judge is left in real doubt whether the
arbitrator was right in law leave should be given. That should not be taken as a charter
for ingenious lawyers to think up ingenious points of law with no real merit; I emphasise  *e*
that what has to exist is a real, not an imaginary or remote, doubt.

    As I am left in real doubt whether the arbitrator was right, I propose to give leave to
appeal in this case. I have given my reasons at length since, in my judgment, there is
here a question of principle involved.

    I will give leave to appeal under s 1(6A). It is not clear whether or not a certificate is in  *f*
addition required under s 1(7) as being an appeal from a decision of the High Court 'on
an appeal under this section'. If such certificate is required I give it. I certify that the
question of law to which my decision on leave to appeal relates is one which for some
other special reason should be considered by the Court of Appeal, such special reason
being that there is doubt as to how far the principles laid down by the House of Lords in
relation to commercial and shipping contracts are applicable in the case of arbitrations  *g*
outside those fields.

*Leave to appeal granted.*

Solicitors: *Westhorp Ward & Catchpole*, Ipswich (for the corporation); *Birketts*, Ipswich (for
Fisons).

Celia Fox     Barrister.

a # ROFA Sport Management AG and another v DHL International (UK) Ltd and another

COURT OF APPEAL, CIVIL DIVISION
MAY, NEILL AND RALPH GIBSON LJJ
12 JANUARY, 2 MARCH 1989

b

*Practice – Compromise of action – Discontinuance of action – Stay of action – Settlement agreed before hearing of action – Terms of settlement embodied in consent order staying action – Application by intervener for joinder after settlement concluded – Whether consent order staying action amounting to discontinuance of action – Whether action still in being when application made by intervener for joinder – RSC Ord 15, r 6(2).*

c

The plaintiffs held exclusive rights to appoint companies as official suppliers to and sponsors of the International Football Federation (FIFA) World Cup in 1986. Another company (the licensor) held exclusive commercial rights relating to all marks and designs of FIFA. The defendant claimed to be entitled to describe itself as the 'Official Worldwide Courier to the FIFA World Cup 1986' under a licence granted by the licensor. By a writ d and summons issued on 26 July 1985 the plaintiffs sought to restrain the defendant from using the description 'Official Worldwide Courier to the FIFA World Cup 1986'. The licensor heard about the action and informed the plaintiffs that they intended to apply to be joined as co-defendants, but before they had taken any formal steps to be joined a settlement was reached between the plaintiffs and the defendant which was embodied in a consent order dated 14 August 1985 staying the proceedings. The licensor issued a e summons applying to intervene pursuant to RSC Ord 15, r 6(2)[a]. The plaintiffs resisted the application on the ground that there was no action in existence after 14 August 1985 and the court had no jurisdiction to entertain the licensor's application. The master and on appeal the judge held that a stay was not the same as a dismissal or discontinuance and ordered the licensor to be joined. The plaintiffs appealed against the order.

f **Held** – An action which had been stayed, even though an order of the court was required before it could proceed further, was nevertheless still technically in being and was to be distinguished from an action which had been discontinued or dismissed and which was incapable of being revived. The consent order of 14 August 1985 embodying the settlement between the plaintiffs and the defendant was in effect a stay of the action, and was expressed to be so, and therefore the court had jurisdiction to entertain the application g of the licensor to be joined pursuant to RSC Ord 15, r 6(2). Accordingly, the appeal would be dismissed (see p 747 f, p 748 j, p 749 j and p 750 e, post).

Dictum of Wills J in *Selig v Lion* [1891] 1 QB 513 at 515, *Green v Rozen* [1955] 2 All ER 797 and *Empson v Smith* [1965] 2 All ER 881 considered.

Per curiam. For the sake of clarity and certainty the word 'stay' in an order should not h be used as a possible equivalent of a dismissal or a discontinuance (see p 749 h and p 750 e, post).

### Notes
For settlement or compromise of an action, see 37 Halsbury's Laws (4th edn) para 388, and for cases on the subject, see 37(3) Digest (Reissue) 11–13, 3015–3022.
For the effect of a stay of proceedings, see 37 Halsbury's Laws (4th edn) para 438.

j

### Cases referred to in judgments
*Castro v Murray* (1875) LR 10 Ex 213.
*Cooper v Williams* [1963] 2 All ER 282, [1963] 2 QB 567, [1963] 2 WLR 913, CA.

---

*a   Rule 6(2), so far as material, is set out at p 746 j to p 747 a, post*

*Dawkins v Prince Edward of Saxe-Weimar* (1876) 1 QBD 499, DC.
*Duke of Buccleuch, The* [1892] P 201, CA.
*Empson v Smith* [1965] 2 All ER 881, [1966] 1 QB 426, [1965] 3 WLR 380, CA.
*Green v Rozen* [1955] 2 All ER 797, [1955] 1 WLR 741.
*Hadmor Productions Ltd v Hamilton* [1982] 1 All ER 1042, [1983] 1 AC 191, [1982] 2 WLR 322, HL.
*Metropolitan Bank Ltd v Pooley* (1885) 10 App Cas 210, [1881–5] All ER Rep 949, HL.
*Selig v Lion* [1891] 1 QB 513, DC.

**Cases also cited**
*Ardandhu, The* (1886) 11 PD 40, CA.
*Hearn, Re, de Bertodano v Hearn* (1913) 108 LT 452; *affd* 108 LT 737, CA.
*McCallum v Country Residences Ltd* [1965] 2 All ER 264, [1965] 1 WLR 657, CA.

**Interlocutory appeal**
The plaintiffs, ROFA Sport Management AG and ISL Marketing AG, appealed from an order of Rougier J made on 25 February 1988 whereby he dismissed their appeal from an order of Master Lubbock made on 22 January 1986 adding, pursuant to RSC Ord 15, r 6(2), Sport-Billy Productions R Deyhle as second defendants to an action brought by the plaintiffs against the first defendants, DHL International (UK) Ltd. The facts are set out in the judgment of Neill LJ.

*Stuart Isaacs* for the plaintiffs.
*Peter Irvin* for the second defendants.
The first defendants were not represented.

*Cur adv vult*

2 March. The following judgments were delivered.

**NEILL LJ** (giving the first judgment at the invitation of May LJ). This is an appeal by the plaintiffs from the order of Rougier J dated 25 February 1988, whereby he dismissed an appeal from the order of Master Lubbock dated 22 January 1986 by which the master ordered that Sport-Billy Productions R Deyhle (Sport-Billy) be added as second defendants to the action pursuant to RSC Ord 15, r 6(2).

The plaintiffs in the action are ROFA Sport Management AG (ROFA) and ISL Marketing AG (ISL). By a written agreement dated 11 July 1982, made between the Fédération Internationale de Football Association (FIFA) and ROFA, ROFA were granted the exclusive right to appoint certain companies as official suppliers/sponsors for the FIFA World Cup which was due to be held in Mexico in the summer of 1986. In due course ROFA appointed ISL as their exclusive marketing agents. Both ROFA and ISL are Swiss companies.

In about May 1985 it came to the attention of ROFA that DHL International (UK) Ltd (DHL) were describing themselves as the 'Official Worldwide Courier to the FIFA World Cup 1986'. ROFA's solicitors wrote a letter of complaint dated 21 May 1985, stating that in the light of an agreement between FIFA and ROFA, DHL were not entitled so to describe themselves. DHL replied that they were entitled to use this description because they had been granted a licence by Sport-Billy, who were the transferees from FIFA of 'the exclusive commercial rights relating to all marks and designs of FIFA'. There was then some further correspondence but it proved inconclusive.

On 26 July 1985 ROFA and ISL issued a writ against DHL and also a summons seeking an interlocutory injunction. The date for the hearing of the summons was later fixed for 23 August 1985. The main relief claimed in the writ was as follows:

a   '1. An injunction to restrain the Defendants, whether acting by themselves, their directors, servants or agents or otherwise howsoever from describing themselves or holding themselves out in any way whatsoever as being the official worldwide courier to the FIFA World Cup, 1986. 2. Damages for interference by the Defendants with the contractual relations between the plaintiffs and FIFA and for passing off by reason of the Defendants' use of the description of themselves as the Official Worldwide Courier to the FIFA World Cup, 1986'.

b   On the same day, 26 July 1985, Sport-Billy became aware of the proceedings. Their solicitor got in touch with DHL's solicitors and a few days later told them that Sport-Billy would apply to be added as co-defendants. Before, however, Sport-Billy had taken any formal steps to be added as co-defendants, the plaintiffs and DHL had achieved a settlement. A consent order, dated 14 August 1985, was made in the following terms:

c   'Upon the parties agreeing terms AND BY CONSENT IT IS ORDERED that all further proceedings in this action be stayed, the parties having agreed terms of settlement, and it is further ordered that there be no Order as to costs'.

The order bore the written consent of DHL's solicitors dated 13 August.

d   On 15 August DHL's solicitors informed the solicitors for Sport-Billy of the settlement. It seems that the solicitors for Sport-Billy expressed surprise as they had previously understood that the summons for an interlocutory injunction was due to be heard on 23 August. On 16 August Sport-Billy issued a summons to be heard before the judge in chambers on 23 August seeking to be joined as parties in the action. This summons was later replaced by a summons issued on 20 August for hearing before a master.

e   The later summons came before Master Lubbock on 22 January 1986 when he ordered that Sport-Billy should be added as second defendants in the action. The purpose of such joinder was explained by Mr Peter Armstrong, a partner in the firm of solicitors acting for Sport-Billy, in an affidavit sworn on 22 August 1985, in these terms:

f   'The Interveners have a substantial interest in the matters in dispute in these proceedings, namely the question of the extent of their contractual rights obtained from FIFA compared with those obtained from FIFA by the Plaintiffs. The Interveners have granted sub-licences to other organisations operating in the UK and wish to grant similar rights in respect of other goods or services to others. Those clients and potential clients are all potential subjects of similar attack by the Plaintiffs under circumstances where the commercial pressure of such an attack may be wholly disproportionate to the legal strengths of the Plaintiffs' claim. Furthermore,

g   the Plaintiffs' attack on the Defendants as bona fide sub-licensee of the Interveners may give rise to issues between the Interveners and the Defendants and I submit that it is wholly appropriate for the Interveners to have an opportunity of ventilating the true underlying issues in this action.'

h   The plaintiffs appealed against Master Lubbock's order. The appeal was heard by Rougier J on 6 March 1987 when he dismissed the appeal. Though by then the 1986 World Cup had taken place the matter remained a live issue between the parties because of disputes which were likely to arise in relation to the next World Cup in 1990.

It was argued on behalf of the plaintiffs before the judge that though the consent order was in form an order for a stay, it was in fact an order for the discontinuance of the

j   action. Accordingly, it was argued, the action came to an end on 14 August 1985, and the court had therefore no jurisdiction to entertain any summons issued after that date or to make an order under Ord 15, r 6(2). In the alternative it was submitted that it was a wrong exercise of any discretion vested in the court under this rule to make an order in the circumstances of this case where the previous parties had already finally disposed of their differences and had reached a binding settlement.

The judge rejected both these arguments. We have been provided with a note of his judgment which he approved on 12 June 1988. On the question of jurisdiction the judge　*a* said that he was attracted by the master's approach, namely that because there are two different methods of arresting proceedings, one by a stay and the other by discontinuance, they must mean different things. He concluded that the action was still alive.

On the question of discretion, the judge said that he was not impressed by the argument that the plaintiffs would suffer prejudice. He continued:

　*b*

'I was at one point concerned whether the intervener was equally protected by being able to sue in Switzerland but it is here that Sport-Billy's name has been impugned. I am not attracted by the plaintiffs taking a swipe at a sub-licensee of the main licensee and then claiming that the main licensee cannot defend himself here. It would be unjust not to allow them to defend.'

It seems, however, that at some stage during the hearing counsel for the plaintiffs　*c* raised the further question whether the consent order of 14 August 1985 correctly reflected the agreement which had been reached between the plaintiffs and DHL, and whether the order should be rectified. The judge therefore expressed his conclusion on the appeal in these terms:

'Therefore I find . . . that the action remains alive and . . . subject to the question　*d* of rectification, I would exercise my discretion to allow the interveners to intervene.'

On 10 March 1987 the plaintiffs issued a summons for rectification of the order of 14 August 1985 so that the word 'discontinued' should be substituted for the word 'stayed', and that the words 'all further proceedings in' should be deleted. On 12 October 1987 this summons was heard by Master Lubbock and was dismissed. Finally, on 25 February 1988 an order was made by consent giving effect to the decision of Rougier J on 6 March　*e* 1987, in the light of the subsequent dismissal of the claim for rectification. By this order the plaintiffs were given leave to appeal to this court.

The principal argument in this court on behalf of the plaintiffs was directed to the question of jurisdiction. The argument was developed on these lines: (1) that the court could not make an order under Ord 15, r 6(2)(b) unless proceedings were still on foot in　*f* the cause or matter; (2) that there were no such proceedings if there was nothing left to be done in the case; (3) that it is necessary to look not only at the form of the consent order but also at its substance, (4) that an unconditional consent order to stay all further proceedings may operate as a discontinuance or dismissal of the action; (5) that in the present case the consent order to stay was made pursuant to the settlement of the whole dispute between the plaintiffs and DHL; the order was unconditional and nothing　*g* remained to be done in the case; (6) that the order did not contain any liberty to apply, and that even if it had done the presence of these words would not necessarily have kept the action alive; (7) that as from 14 August 1985 there were no proceedings and no cause or matter in existence in which an order under Ord 15, r 6(2)(b) could be made. In support of these submissions we were referred to a number of authorities including the decision of Slade J in *Green v Rozen* [1955] 2 All ER 797, [1955] 1 WLR 741, where the　*h* various methods of settling an action were described and analysed.

In order to examine these submissions it is necessary to consider methods other than a stay whereby the progress of an action can be brought to a halt by order of the court made before trial. These methods are dismissal and discontinuance. First, I should refer to the relevant parts of Ord 15, r 6(2), which is in these terms:

'Subject to the provisions of this rule, at any stage of the proceedings in any cause　*j* or matter the Court may on such terms as it thinks just and either of its own motion or on application . . . (b) order any of the following persons to be added as a party, namely— (i) any person who ought to have been joined as a party or whose presence before the Court is necessary to ensure that all matters in dispute in the cause or matter may be effectually and completely determined and adjudicated upon, or (ii)

a  any person between whom and any party to the cause or matter there may exist a
question or issue arising out of or relating to or connected with any relief or remedy
claimed in the cause or matter which in the opinion of the Court it would be just
and convenient to determine as between him and that party as well as between the
parties to the cause or matter.'

b  It will be seen from the opening words of r 6(2) that the order can be made 'at any
stage of the proceedings in any cause or matter'. The question for determination,
therefore, is whether there were any proceedings in existence in this action on 22 January
1986 when Master Lubbock made his order, or even on 20 August 1985 when the
summons seeking joinder was issued.                                                                        '

It was not in dispute that if the action had been dismissed by consent and the order

c  had been drawn up the court would have had no jurisdiction thereafter to make any
order under Ord 15, r 6(2). It is not necessary, however, for the purpose of the present
appeal to consider what differences exist between the dismissal of an action on the merits
and a dismissal for a failure to comply with some rule of procedure. Once an action has
been dismissed then, subject to any rights of appeal or, in certain circumstances, the right
to bring a fresh action, it is at an end.

d  It was also not in dispute that if the action had been discontinued by an order made
under Ord 21, r 3 and the order had been drawn up the action would have been at an
end and no order could be made thereafter under Ord 15, r 6(2). Order 21, though with
amendments, can be traced through Ord 20 of the 1962 rules to Ord 26 of the 1883 rules.
It provides a complete code relating to the discontinuance of an action. It also deals with
cases where a party wishes to withdraw part of a claim or counterclaim. In the present

e  case, however, the order did not provide for discontinuance under Ord 21, r 3 and the
application for the rectification of the order of 14 August 1985 has been dismissed.

I turn, therefore, to consider the nature and effect of an order for the stay of all further
proceedings in an action.

It is plain that in some cases where an order for a stay is made the action undoubtedly

f  remains alive. Thus, for example, an order to stay proceedings pending the provision of
security is intended to be and takes effect as a temporary brake on proceedings while the
party against whom the order is made finds the necessary security. Once the security has
been provided the brake is removed and the action proceeds. In the present case, however,
the only operative part of the order was the order for a stay. Nothing remained to be
done by either party after 14 August 1985 when the consent order was made and entered.

g  Looking at the substance of the matter, it was argued, the action after 14 August was as
dead as if it had been dismissed or discontinued by an order made under Ord 21, r 3. The
proceedings came to an end and therefore the order for joinder had not been made 'at
any stage of the proceedings' as required by Ord 15, r 6(2).

In this connection our attention was drawn to the decision in The Duke of Buccleuch
[1892] P 201. In that case an application was made in an Admiralty action to substitute

h  the cargo owners for their agents as plaintiffs. The application was made after the trial. It
was made under Ord 16 (the predecessor of the present Ord 15), which by r 11 provided
for the joinder of fresh parties 'at any stage of the proceedings'. The Court of Appeal
upheld the judge's decision to allow the substitution on the basis that the action was
clearly not at an end because the judge had only determined the issue of liability and the
damages had still to be assessed. Fry LJ gave as his reasons for dismissing the appeal (at

j  212):

'I base my decision upon the words "at any stage of the proceedings." It has been
argued that the rules do not apply after final judgment. They apply, in my opinion,
as long as anything remains to be done in the case. In this case there remains the
assessment of damages.'

In reliance on this decision counsel for the plaintiffs submitted that the order was not made at a 'stage of the proceedings' because after 14 August 1985 nothing remained to  **a** be done. In my judgment, however, this submission is only decisive if a stay can properly be regarded as equivalent to a discontinuance or dismissal. If the action remains in being it is still at a 'stage' albeit a dormant stage.

I turn next, therefore, to the judgment of Wills J in the Divisional Court in *Selig v Lion* [1891] 1 QB 513. In that case the plaintiff was a discharged bankrupt. Having purchased the assets in the bankruptcy from the trustee he applied for the removal of a stay of  **b** proceedings which had been stayed unconditionally during his bankruptcy without opposition from the trustee. The appeal against the refusal of the application was dismissed on the ground that as the trustee had elected not to proceed with the action the plaintiff as assignee of the assets was barred too. But in the course of his judgment Wills J said (at 515):

> **c**
> 'Two views may be taken of the nature of a stay; first, that it is a discontinuance, in which case cadit quæstio; and secondly, that it is not equivalent to a discontinuance, but may be removed if proper grounds are shewn. The latter is a possible view; but the mere fact that a right of action, hampered by a stay, is transmitted to another person cannot entitle the assignee to have the stay removed; the election made by his assignor would be a sufficient answer to such a contention.'  **d**

In *Green v Rozen* [1955] 2 All ER 797 at 800–801, [1955] 1 WLR 741 at 746 Slade J referred to the two schools of thought as to the effect of a stay and described it as an interesting point of law for resolution in some future case. He also referred to the note in *The Annual Practice 1955* p 3182. It may be observed that there are passages to the same effect in *The Supreme Court Practice 1988* vol 2, para 5208.  **e**

It seems clear that before rules were made under the Supreme Court of Judicature Act 1873 the courts of common law had an inherent jurisdiction to stay an action. In *Castro v Murray* (1875) LR 10 Ex 213 the Court of Exchequer stayed the plaintiff's action under its inherent jurisdiction on the basis that the action was frivolous and vexatious and an abuse of the process of the court. In the following year in *Dawkins v Prince Edward of Saxe-Weimar* (1876) 1 QBD 499 Blackburn and Mellor JJ stayed an action in the Queen's  **f** Bench Division on the ground that the action was hopeless and bound to fail. Here again the order for a stay was made under the inherent jurisdiction of the court.

In *Metropolitan Bank Ltd v Pooley* (1885) 10 App Cas 210 at 214, [1891–5] All ER Rep 949 at 951 the Earl of Selborne LC made reference to the earlier practice in these terms:

> 'Before the Rules were made under the Judicature Act, the practice had been established to stay a manifestly vexatious suit which was plainly an abuse of the  **g** authority of the Court, although so far as I know there was not at that time either any statute or rule expressly authorizing the Court to do it. The power seemed to be inherent in the jurisdiction of every Court of Justice to protect itself from the abuse of its own procedure. Another reason why that should have been very rarely done before the recent rules is this, that if the objection was one which could be raised  **h** upon the face of the pleadings, that always might be done by demurrer.'

It is interesting to notice that in that case Lord Selborne LC came to the conclusion that the action should be 'absolutely stayed' as frivolous and vexatious, and that Lord Blackburn concluded that the action ought to be 'stayed altogether'. Nevertheless, it is clear from the form of order which was made that the action was, in fact, dismissed (see 10 App Cas 210 at 220, 224, 228, [1881–5] All ER Rep 949 at 954, 956, 958.)  **j**

It seems to me, therefore, to be possible to argue from the earlier practice and the language used in the cases decided shortly after the Supreme Court of Judicature Act 1873 that a distinction can be drawn between an absolute order to stay which is equivalent to a discontinuance or dismissal, and a conditional order to stay which by its terms contemplates the continuance of the action if the condition is fulfilled.

I have come to the clear conclusion, however, that it would not be satisfactory at the
present day to seek to draw a line between stays which were absolute and stays which
were conditional and then to equate absolute stays with orders for dismissal or
discontinuance. Stays are granted in many different circumstances. Moreover, the width
of the jurisdiction is underlined by the wording of s 49(3) of the Supreme Court Act
1981, which provides:

'Nothing in this Act shall affect the power of the Court of Appeal or the High
Court to stay any proceedings before it, where it thinks fit to do so, either of its own
motion or on the application of any person whether or not a party to the proceedings.'

In addition to its inherent jurisdiction the court has power to stay proceedings under a
number of different rules of court. Moreover, there is power to stay proceedings or
execution under particular statutes. It seems to me that there are many instances where
the court has power to grant a stay where the order is not conditional in any ordinary
sense of the term but where a change of circumstances may make a further application
to the court desirable. For example, an action may be stayed under s 4 of the Arbitration
Act 1950, or on the ground that the action should be tried in a foreign court. In such
cases the chances of the action proceeding to trial in England may be remote, but
difficulties in the arbitration or a decision by a foreign court to decline jurisdiction may
make it desirable to revive and continue the stayed action. An illustration of such a
revival is provided by the decision in *Empson v Smith* [1965] 2 All ER 881, [1966] 1 QB
426. In that case the action had been stayed by a county court registrar in April 1963
following the issue of a certificate that the defendant was a member of the official staff of
the High Commissioner for Canada in the United Kingdom. On 31 July 1964 the
Diplomatic Privileges Act 1964 came into force. This Act had the effect of removing
diplomatic immunity from members of the administrative and technical staff in relation
to acts performed outside the course of their duties. The plaintiff applied for the removal
of the stay and the defendant applied for a dismissal of the action on the basis that it was
a nullity. The deputy county court judge dismissed the plaintiff's action as a nullity, but
the Court of Appeal allowed her appeal. Diplock LJ explained the matter as follows
([1965] 2 All ER 881 at 886, [1966] 1 QB 426 at 437):

'If the defendant had applied before the commencement of the Diplomatic
Privileges Act 1964, to have the plaintiff's action dismissed there would have been
no answer to his application, but he delayed until November 1964. By that date his
right to immunity from civil suit had been curtailed by that Act . . .'

The case was sent back to the county court to determine the issue whether the acts of
which the plaintiff complained were performed by the defendant outside the course of
his duties. The case illustrates, however, the distinction between a stay of proceedings
and the dismissal or setting aside of proceedings. The plaintiff's action could have been
dismissed at the time when the stay was imposed. In any ordinary sense it was an absolute
stay. Nevertheless, the action was not brought to an end and it was capable of being
revived when the law was changed about 16 months after the registrar had made his
order.

In my judgment, for the sake of clarity and certainty the word 'stay' in an order should
not be treated as a possible equivalent of a dismissal or a discontinuance. There may well,
of course, be cases, however, where the person who wishes to have the stay removed will
face great difficulties. An action which has been stayed by consent following a
compromise provides an obvious example. But, as it seems to me, the action following a
stay remains technically in being. The action cannot proceed or resume its active life
without an order of the court, but I do not consider that it can properly be regarded as
dead in the same way as an action which has been dismissed or discontinued by order.

In these circumstances, I consider that the judge had jurisdiction to make the order
which he did.

I turn next to the question of discretion, with which I can deal very shortly. The
circumstances in which an appellate court can interfere with the exercise by a judge of a      *a*
discretion vested in him were explained by Lord Diplock in a well-known passage in his
speech in *Hadmor Productions Ltd v Hamilton* [1982] 1 All ER 1042 at 1046, [1983] 1 AC
191 at 220. In broad terms such interference is only permissible where the judge has
misunderstood the law or the facts or has taken into account irrelevant matters or ignored
matters which were plainly relevant to his decision. It seems to me to be clear that the
judge in this case directed himself correctly both on the law and the facts. Moreover, it is      *b*
certainly not a case that falls into that residual class where the judge can be said to have
reached an unreasonable conclusion. Other judges might have decided the case
differently, but that is no reason for this court to interfere.

It will be necessary, however, to protect the settlement which was reached between
the plaintiffs and DHL. Counsel for the second defendants, Sport-Billy, recognised this. I
would therefore dismiss the appeal but vary the order in such a way as to ensure that the      *c*
settlement which has been reached between the plaintiffs and DHL is not disturbed.
There is a precedent for an order which protects the interests of a party who has already
reached a settlement. In *Cooper v Williams* [1963] 2 All ER 282, [1963] 2 QB 567 a widow
was allowed to intervene in an action under the Fatal Accidents Acts in which a settlement
had already been reached between the defendant and the infant plaintiff. The Court of
Appeal approved the decision of the judge to allow this intervention but on terms that      *d*
such intervention should not prejudice the interests of the infant.

The action will proceed but effectively only between Sport-Billy and the plaintiffs, or
perhaps only between Sport-Billy and ROFA. The exact form of the order will need to be
carefully drafted.

**RALPH GIBSON LJ:** I agree.      *e*

**MAY LJ.** I also agree.

*Appeal dismissed. Leave to appeal to the House of Lords refused.*

Solicitors: *Theodore Goddard* (for the plaintiffs); *Daynes Hill & Perks*, Norwich (for the      *f*
second defendants).

Carolyn Toulmin    Barrister.

a
# Singh and another v Observer Ltd

QUEEN'S BENCH DIVISION
MACPHERSON J
27, 28 FEBRUARY 1989

b  *Costs – Order for costs – Jurisdiction – Order against person maintaining action – Plaintiff's*
*action for libel supported financially by anonymous person – Plaintiff's solicitor agreeing not to*
*reveal identity of maintainer of action – Defendant newspaper applying for judgment with costs*
*on indemnity basis – Whether court having jurisdiction to order costs against party maintaining*
*action – Whether costs order restricted to order made against party to proceedings – Whether*
*person maintaining plaintiff's action liable for defendant's costs – Whether plaintiff's solicitor*
c  *could be ordered to disclose identity of maintainer – Criminal Law Act 1967, s 14 – Supreme*
*Court Act 1981, s 51.*

The plaintiff brought an action against a newspaper claiming damages for libel. Prior to
the trial of the action the newspaper applied for and was granted security for costs in the
sum of £35,000. The plaintiff complied with the order to provide security for costs by
d  means of a personal undertaking given by the plaintiff's solicitor backed by a guarantee
given to the solicitor by an unknown person or persons. Two further orders requiring
the plaintiff to provide security for costs were made following the adjournment of the
hearing on the plaintiff's failure to appear in court, both in the sum of £10,000, and
were complied with in exactly the same manner. In subsequent cross-examination on
his means the plaintiff indicated that another person or persons who had no interest in
e  his litigation against the newspaper were financing him, both directly by providing the
funds necessary to meet his costs and indirectly through the guarantees. When the
plaintiff was pressed to disclose the identity of his financial supporters his solicitor
objected, claiming that the guarantees were given to him and not the plaintiff and that
he had given his word to the guarantors that their identity would not be revealed. The
plaintiff again failed to appear in court and the newspaper, which estimated that its costs
f  then amounted to £110,000, applied for judgment with costs on an indemnity basis and
an order that the plaintiff and his solicitor disclose the identity of the person or persons
who had provided the guarantees or otherwise supported the plaintiff's action. The
plaintiff contended that the court had no jurisdiction to order costs against any person
maintaining an action and therefore it was unnecessary for the court to order disclosure
of the persons who had maintained the plaintiff's action, since (i) s 51[a] of the Supreme
g  Court Act 1981 and RSC Ord 62 contemplated orders for costs being made only against a
party to the proceedings or from trust funds or by a party's solicitor personally and (ii) an
order against a person maintaining an action was precluded by s 14[b] of the Criminal Law
Act 1967 because such an order would, in effect, revive the tort of maintenance which
had been abolished by that section.

h  **Held** – The court had power to order a party who was financially supporting a plaintiff's
action without himself having any interest in the litigation to pay the defendant's costs if
the action failed, since it would be contrary to public policy and justice to restrict the
operation of s 51 of the 1981 Act, which conferred on the court 'full power to determine
by whom and to what extent the costs are to be paid', by imposing a limitation on the
court's power to make a costs order against the maintainer of an action, particularly in
j  view of the fact that it would be unjust if an action was kept going purely by the outside
financing of persons who had no interest in the litigation and who would otherwise not
be liable for any of the other party's costs if the action failed. A corollary of that power to

---

a   Section 51, so far as material, is set out at p 755 a b, post
b   Section 14 is set out at p 756 c, post

order the maintainer of an action to pay the costs was that the court also had a power to order disclosure of the maintainer's identity which, given the public interest that justice *a* should be done in respect of the cost of litigation, overrode any undertaking of confidentiality given by the plaintiff or his solicitor, to the guarantor or maintainer, who was not the solicitor's client. Moreover, the abolition of maintenance as a crime or tort did not exclude the possible liability for costs of a maintainer. Accordingly, judgment with costs on an indemnity basis would be given for the newspaper and the plaintiff and his solicitor would be ordered to disclose the identity of the party or parties who had *b* maintained the action (see p 755 *c d* and p 756 *a b j* to p 757 *a c d f* to *h*, post).

Dicta of Lord Denning MR in *Hill v Archbold* [1967] 3 All ER 110 at 112, of Lord Denning MR in *Trendtex Trading Corp v Crédit Suisse* [1980] 3 All ER 721 at 741 and of Lord Goff in *Aiden Shipping Co Ltd v Interbulk Ltd, The Vimeira* [1986] 2 All ER 409 at 413, 416–417 applied.

*c*

**Notes**
For jurisdiction to award costs, see 37 Halsbury's Laws (4th edn) para 713, and for cases on the subject, see 37(3) Digest (Reissue) 230–233, 4273–4289.

For the discretion of the court to award costs, see 37 Halsbury's Laws (4th edn) paras 714–716, 721, and for cases on the subject, see 37(3) Digest (Reissue) 240–243, 4350–4378.	*d*

For agreements involving maintenance and what amounts to maintenance, see 9 Halsbury's Laws (4th edn) paras 400–401.

For the Criminal Law Act 1967, s 14, see 45 Halsbury's Statutes (4th edn) 652.

For the Supreme Court Act 1981, s 51, see 11 ibid 809.

**Cases referred to in judgment**
*Aiden Shipping Co Ltd v Interbulk Ltd, The Vimeira* [1986] 2 All ER 409, [1986] AC 965, *e*
	[1986] 2 WLR 1051, HL.
*Bartlett v Barclays Bank Trust Co Ltd (No 2)* [1980] 2 All ER 92, [1980] Ch 515, [1980] 2
	WLR 430.
*Bowen Jones v Bowen Jones* [1986] 3 All ER 163.
*EMI Records Ltd v Ian Cameron Wallace Ltd* [1982] 2 All ER 980, [1983] Ch 59, [1982] 3	*f*
	WLR 245.
*Hill v Archbold* [1967] 3 All ER 110, [1968] 1 QB 686, [1967] 3 WLR 1218, CA.
*Orme v Associated Newspapers Group Ltd* [1980] CA Transcript 809.
*Pascall v Galinski* [1969] 3 All ER 1090, [1970] 1 QB 38, [1969] 3 WLR 626, CA.
*Trendtex Trading Corp v Crédit Suisse* [1980] 3 All ER 721, [1980] QB 629, [1980] 3 WLR
	367, QBD and CA; *affd* [1981] 3 All ER 520, [1982] AC 679, [1981] 3 WLR 766, HL.	*g*

**Application**
The plaintiff, Kunwar Chander Jeet Singh, and a company in which he held the controlling interest, London Venture Capital Market Ltd, issued a writ on 15 March 1985 against the defendant newspaper proprietor, The Observer Ltd, claiming damages for libel. The Observer subsequently applied for an order pursuant to RSC Ord 23, *h* r 1(1)(a) and/or (c) that the plaintiff provide security for its costs in the sum of £35,000. The order was granted by Master Trench on 3 April 1987 and security was provided by an undertaking given to the court by the plaintiff's solicitor, Richard Christopher Martyn Sykes, which was backed by a guarantee from an unknown party or parties. Two further orders requiring the plaintiff to provide security for costs were made by Garland J on 8 February 1988 and Tudor Evans J on 4 May 1988 both in the sums of £10,000, each *j* following an adjournment of the hearing on the plaintiff's failure to appear in court, and each of which was complied with in the same manner. The plaintiff failed to appear in court again on 27 February 1989. On the same day the Observer applied for judgment with costs on an indemnity basis and an order that the plaintiff and his solicitor disclose the identity of the party or parties who had given the guarantees or otherwise maintained

a the plaintiff's action. Proceedings by the plaintiff's company had been stayed on 9 June 1987 on the application of the Official Receiver. The facts are set out in the judgment.

*P Milmo QC* and *Andrew Monson* for the plaintiff.
*Charles Gray QC* and *Desmond Browne* for the Observer.

**MACPHERSON J.** Kunwar Singh and his company, which bears, according to taste,
b the dependable or risky name of London Venture Capital Market Ltd and which is said to be an issuing house, sued The Observer Ltd for damages for libel in March 1985. The allegation was that the plaintiff had been defamed by an article alleging that he had bribed those compiling a financial newsletter in the United States of America to write a favourable article about some shares called Bio-Isolate Holdings so that the plaintiff could make a financial killing. By its defence the Observer pleaded 'no libel' and also, and
c perhaps more in point, it pleaded justification. The matter will never now be resolved since the plaintiff is not here to make good his claim.

I have been taken through the unedifying history of this case and also that of a parallel case in which a company called Ravendale Group plc and the plaintiff were involved. There is no need to repeat that history here. However, the position is that the Ravendale action stands dismissed with costs because of the plaintiff's failure to provide security for
d costs in the sum of £125,000.

The plaintiff is also involved in other matters, including debts of £1·26m owed by an organisation called the City Investment Centre. There are visible in the case the hallmarks of financial instability.

In three stages the plaintiff has, in the present case, been ordered to provide £55,000 security for costs. This is not surprising when the evidence in support of those applications
e is read. It is all amongst the papers which I have considered.

The case has three times been adjourned. On 8 February 1988 Garland J doubted whether the plaintiff was genuinely unable to attend the trial on that day and doubted whether the plaintiff had any intention so to do. He ordered £10,000 security to be provided within seven days. On 4 May the matter was again adjourned by Tudor Evans J. It was said that the plaintiff had had trouble with the Indian immigration authorities
f over leaving India. On 26 May Tudor Evans J ordered some documents to be produced and he ordered further security and ordered that the plaintiff, who was in England but did not come to sustain his case, be examined as to his means.

It is of much importance to note that all the security thus ordered, £55,000, was provided, not by payment into court, but by the personal solicitor's undertaking of Mr Richard Sykes, who acts for the plaintiff. This procedure has apparently been approved
g by the court. I am bound to say that I doubt its wisdom but perhaps that is not strictly a matter for me today. These undertakings are backed by guarantees from an unknown person or persons. I assume that no solicitor in his senses would give his undertaking without such cover and without assessing the cover to be watertight.

On 27 May and 12 July a solicitor, Mr Harrison, and a barrister, Mr Desmond Browne, respectively cross-examined the plaintiff on behalf of the Observer. I believe that it is not
h unfair to say that the plaintiff gave unsatisfactory and largely unhelpful answers to the questions put. But, amongst other things, the plaintiff agreed that his litigation was being financed by others. He said that 'family and friends contribute'. And when pressed, quite rightly, by Master Warren to name the contributors, he named Mr and Mrs Chopra as the people involved. Mr Sykes had raised an objection to that question, indicating that the security was being guaranteed and that the guarantee was privileged. This position
j Mr Sykes maintains today. Through counsel he argues that the identity of the guarantor is privileged or is a matter of confidentiality.

At the second part of the examination on 12 July, the plaintiff admitted that he was incorrect about the Chopras and he said that a Mr Nahegu and others were involved in assisting him. At no time did he or Mr Sykes indicate that any of the persons named had any interest in the litigation against the Observer, so that there can be no doubt but that another or others are financing the plaintiff indirectly through those guarantees, and directly by providing the money necessary to finance his own costs. Otherwise, Mr Sykes could not act, because I am quite certain that he would not take on speculative litigation. That would be quite wrong.

Mr Sykes confirms this unusual guarantee arrangement and I refer to his letter of 20 July 1988 to the Observer's solicitors. There he indicates that the guarantee is given to him and not to the plaintiff and he says that the secrecy which he wishes to maintain is because the person involved does not wish to be involved in publicity about the case and Mr Sykes says that he has given his word to the guarantor that his name would not be mentioned. Today the plaintiff again failed to come to court. Mr Sykes has no instructions from him; nor has his counsel, who has argued the matter before me today. However, it seemed to me to be right to hear counsel, and I am grateful to him and to counsel for the Observer for their clear submissions.

Counsel for the plaintiff has helped me very much by putting his client's and his solicitor's case. I put the matter in that way because today the Observer applies for three things: first, for judgment in this action; second, for costs on an indemnity basis; and, third, for an order that the plaintiff and his solicitor disclose the name of the person or persons maintaining these proceedings.

As to judgment, there is no dispute. As to the costs, the only dispute is whether or not they should be ordered on an indemnity basis. Counsel for the plaintiff refers me to two cases in this regard: *Bartlett v Barclays Bank Trust Co Ltd (No 2)* [1980] 2 All ER 92, [1980] Ch 515 and *Bowen Jones v Bowen Jones* [1986] 3 All ER 163. I accept and am guided by the principles there set out. Only in exceptional circumstances or special cases should the court depart from the standard basis of costs. I am wholly satisfied that this is a special or exceptional case. The matter has only been kept alive by Mr Sykes's undertakings. Each judge who has so far dealt with the matter has doubted the good faith and the intentions of the plaintiff for reasons which appear to me to be palpable. Here we are in 1989 again with the plaintiff absent and his solicitor without instructions. In my judgment, it would be most unjust to the Observer to award costs on the standard basis against the plaintiff. Different considerations arise in connection with Mr Sykes's security. But, as to the plaintiff, it seems to me clear that costs should be ordered which could, if they are ever recovered from the elusive plaintiff, cover the Observer's actual expenses; and in my discretion I so order.

I am glad to think that a case of this kind and its conduct by the plaintiff is exceptional. In my judgment it is well outside the ordinary run of cases and, without doubt, special. I note the words of Megarry V-C in the case of *EMI Records Ltd v Ian Cameron Wallace Ltd* [1982] 2 All ER 980, [1983] Ch 59. He stressed the particular need for an award of indemnity costs in that case and in other contempt cases. But the principle is of wider application than that, as that case and the others cited show.

I turn, then, to the question of disclosure of the name of the maintainer of these proceedings. I stress at once that I will of course make no order against him or her, or them, should there be more than one, without allowing full opportunity to him, her or them to put before the court the full position and to argue whether any, and if so what, order should be made. For example, if the degree of maintenance is limited to a private and personal guarantee to Mr Sykes, the matter may go no further than that and it may not be proper to make any order at all, or some limited order.

If, however, it is shown that the whole edifice of this litigation has been maintained, then a full order for costs could be made. At present I strongly suspect that the latter is the true position and the plaintiff's reticence and his own answers given before Master Warren suggests strongly that this is so.

I deal with the interlocking arguments separately.

1. Has the court power to order a maintainer to pay costs? Counsel for the plaintiff argues that even if a maintainer exists the court could not order costs against him. He points to s 51 of the Supreme Court Act 1981, which reads as follows:

'(1) Subject to the provisions of this or any other Act and to rules of court, the
costs of and incidental to all proceedings in the civil division of the Court of Appeal
and in the High Court, including the administration of estates and trusts, shall be in
the discretion of the court, and the court shall have full power to determine by
whom and to what extent the costs are to be paid . . .

(3) Provision may be made by rules of court for regulating any matters relating
to the costs of proceedings in the civil division of the Court of Appeal or in the High
Court, including the administration of estates and trusts.'

RSC Ord 62 is the relevant costs rule. Counsel argues that the rule contemplates orders
for costs only against another party or from various funds or, exceptionally, for example,
against solicitors under the provisions of Ord 72, r 10. He argues that it is untenable to
say that other persons shall pay costs, and he says that since there are no rules or
procedures governing the position of any party who might be so affected, the court is
unable to order costs against, for example, any person maintaining an action in any
circumstances. In my judgment, this is a restrictive view of s 51.

In particular, I refer to the plain wording of s 51 and to a case cited by counsel for the
Observer in support of his argument that if the circumstances justify it, costs can be
awarded outside the categories set out by counsel for the plaintiff. The case is *Aiden
Shipping Co Ltd v Interbulk Ltd, The Vimeira* [1986] 2 All ER 409, [1986] AC 965. That is of
course a case involving arbitration and interlocking charterers, sub-charterers and owners.
But in my judgment the decision is of general application. Lord Goff traced the history
of the legislation as to costs and pointed out that the words of s 51 are indeed wide. I
quote the following passages from his speech ([1986] 2 All ER 409 at 413, 416–417,
[1986] AC 965 at 975, 981):

'It is, I consider, important to remember that s 51(1) of the 1981 Act is concerned
with the *jurisdiction* of the court to make orders as to costs. Furthermore, it is not to
be forgotten that the jurisdiction conferred by the subsection is expressed to be
subject to rules of court, as was the power conferred by s 5 of the 1890 Act. It is
therefore open to the rule-making authority (now the Supreme Court Rule
Committee) to make rules which control the exercise of the court's jurisdiction
under s 5(1). In these circumstances, it is not surprising to find the jurisdiction
conferred under s 51(1), like its predecessors, to be expressed in wide terms. The
subsection simply provides that "the court shall have full power to determine *by
whom* . . . the costs are to be paid". Such a provision is consistent with a policy under
which jurisdiction to exercise the relevant discretionary power is expressed in wide
terms, thus ensuring that the court has, so far as possible, freedom of action, leaving
it to the rule-making authority to control the exercise of discretion (if it thinks it
right to do so) by the making of rules of court, and to the appellate courts to establish
principles on which the discretionary power may, within the framework of the
statute and the applicable rules of court, be exercised. Such a policy appears to me, I
must confess, to be entirely sensible. It comes therefore as something of a surprise
to discover that it has been suggested that any limitation should be held to be *implied*
into the statutory provision which confers the relevant jurisdiction . . . Courts of
first instance are, I believe, well capable of exercising their discretion under the
statute in accordance with reason and justice. I cannot imagine any case arising in
which some order for costs is made, in the exercise of the court's discretion, against
some person who has no connection with the proceedings in question. If any
problem arises, the Court of Appeal can lay down principles for the guidance of
judges of first instance; or the Supreme Court Rule Committee can propose
amendments to the Rules of the Supreme Court for the purpose of controlling the
exercise of the statutory power vested in judges subject to rules of court.' (Lord
Goff's emphasis.)

I refer also to a further passage in Lord Goff's speech without reading it (see [1986] 2 All
ER 409 at 415–416, [1986] AC 965 at 979–980).

Looking at Ord 62, I find no restriction which would prevent the court's jurisdiction extending, in proper circumstances, to somebody proved to be maintaining an action. *a* Indeed, it seems to me that it would be wrong to impose such a limitation on the court's powers. I am glad to be able to say that the court would not be helpless to make an order, should it be proved that an action has truly been kept going purely because of outside financing, and thus to have been maintained, without the maintainer having any interest whatsoever in the litigation, and by persons who hope never to be made liable for a penny of the other side's costs, should their action fail. It would surely be contrary to *b* justice so to restrict the operation of s 51.

2. Does s 14 of the Criminal Law Act 1967 preclude an order for costs against a maintainer? Section 14 reads as follows:

'(1) No person shall, under the law of England and Wales, be liable in tort for any conduct on account of its being maintenance or champerty as known to the common *c* law, except in the case of a cause of action accruing before this section has effect.

(2) The abolition of criminal and civil liability under the law of England and Wales for maintenance and champerty shall not affect any rule of that law as to cases in which a contract is to be treated as contrary to public policy or otherwise illegal.'

Counsel for the plaintiff argues that s 14 of that Act abolished maintenance. He says *d* that it would be reviving the tort of maintenance to contemplate an order for costs in a case of this kind. Counsel says that cases subsequent to 1967 make it plain that this is so. In my judgment, here again counsel's arguments for the Observer prevail. He refers particularly to *Orme v Associated Newspapers Group Ltd* [1980] CA Transcript 809 (the Moonies case) and to two cases there cited, *Hill v Archbold* [1967] 3 All ER 110, [1968] 1 QB 686 and *Trendtex Trading Corp v Crédit Suisse* [1980] 3 All ER 721, [1980] QB 629. I *e* quote from the judgment of Lord Denning MR in *Orme's* case:

'For centuries the law has said that every person must bring his suit on his own behalf and at his own expense. No third person is allowed to support him by paying the costs of it unless he has some legitimate interest sufficient to warrant his interference in it. Maintenance is no longer a criminal offence. But it is still contrary *f* to the civil law. It is still contrary to public policy. I tried to explain it in *Hill v Archbold* [1967] 3 All ER 110 at 112–113, [1968] 1 QB 686 at 695, and in the recent case of *Trendtex Trading Corp v Crédit Suisse* [1980] 3 All ER 721 at 741, [1980] QB 629 at 653. The result of it all is that: "It is perfectly legitimate today for one person to support another in bringing or resisting an action (as by paying the costs of it) provided that he has a legitimate and genuine interest in the result of it and the *g* circumstances are such as reasonably to warrant his giving his support", and this is an important addition, "provided always that the one who supports the litigation, if it fails, pays the costs of the other side."'

It is true that in *Orme's* case the ratio of the case was that the plaintiffs were held to be nominal plaintiffs and were simply ordered to provide security for costs on those grounds. *h* But in my judgment the reference to costs and the obligation of the maintainer to pay them is important.

*Hill v Archbold* was a pre-1967 case, but *Trendtex* was not. Lord Denning MR in *Trendtex* [1980] 3 All ER 721 at 741, [1980] QB 629 at 653 refers both to the effect of the 1967 Act and to maintenance in post-1967 cases. He accepted of course that the crime and tort of maintenance were struck down as such, but he stressed that as a matter of *j* public policy the Act did not strike down the cases which declare that maintenance of another's action is legitimate only if the maintainer has a legitimate and genuine interest in the result of it and the circumstances are such as to warrant his giving his support. Lord Denning MR then quoted from *Hill v Archbold* [1967] 3 All ER 110 at 112, [1968] 1 QB 686 at 694. In my judgment that is good law and eminently good sense. I do not

accept that the abolition of maintenance as a crime or a tort is an obstacle to the Observer's
a  application today. Whether or not an injunction would go to restrain a maintainer is not
for decision here. Counsel for the plaintiff argues that since there is no longer such a
cause of action, no relief would be granted. But that does not, in my judgment, exclude
the possible liability for costs of a maintainer in circumstances such as those before me.

During argument reference was made to common circumstances in which others pay
for the litigation of a party, for example legally aided cases, insurance cases and union-
b  assisted cases which make up much of today's non-jury list. But legal aid is statutory and
so are the restrictions on recovery of costs from the fund. The legal aid authorities can
control the hardship which may be caused to successful litigants, who may not recover
their costs, by requiring counsel to give fearless opinions as to the merits of a case as a
condition of continuing legal aid. Insurance companies are subrogated to their insured's
rights, and both they and unions invariably pay the costs of unsuccessful litigation.
c  Otherwise, injustice could certainly result and I do not believe that if, for example,
unions decided simply to refuse to pay costs in these cases, the court would not step in.

3. Does the confidentiality of Mr Sykes's arrangement prevent the court from ordering
him to disclose the maintainer's name and should the solicitor be ordered to disclose the
name? In my judgment it does not, and he should. The guarantor and the maintainer
are not the solicitor's clients. It may be that in the end the whole arrangement will be
d  shown to be such that the maintenance is limited. But, as I said above, that must await
the maintainer's reaction and argument. That is the penalty of choosing to be secret.

I see no ground for holding that any privilege of confidentiality exists which is not
overridden by the public interest in seeing that justice is done as to the expenses and costs
of litigation. In different fields the court has been ready to order a solicitor to disclose, for
example, the name of his client where it was both relevant and necessary (see *Pascall v*
e  *Galinski* [1969] 3 All ER 1090, [1970] 1 QB 38) There seems to me to be no doubt but
that if Mr Sykes were to be subpoenaed to give evidence on the question of liability or
quantum of costs he could be compelled to disclose the name of his guarantor. It is surely
thus impractical and unnecessary to have to take the roundabout step of issuing a
subpoena when a simple order for disclosure of the name of the person involved will
have the same effect with less time and cost involved.
f
I understand and respect Mr Sykes's unwillingness to act without an order of the court.
But in my judgment the time has come when, in the court's exercise of its inherent
powers, Mr Sykes and the plaintiff should be ordered to disclose the name or names of
those who have guaranteed to cover the £55,000 which Mr Sykes has undertaken to pay,
and the name or names of any person who has financed or is financing Mr Singh's
litigation against the Observer.
g
If this topic is a nettle, then in my judgment it should be grasped. It would, in my
judgment, be unjust that the Observer, in all the circumstances of this case, should not
be able to know who is behind this litigation, and, if so advised, to ask them to come to
court to show cause why they should not pay the Observer's costs. Otherwise, it seems
likely that the sum of £55,000, which I am told would be the sum irrecoverable over
and above the £55,000 which is available, will surely never be recovered from the
h  plaintiff, judging by his reticence in the matter of this and other cases.

In conclusion I simply say that I do not believe that these courts are powerless to order
investigation and, if necessary, to order a maintainer to pay the successful party's costs. I
will make such orders as achieve this just result.

j  *Order accordingly.*

Solicitors: *Richard C M Sykes* (for the plaintiff); *Turner Kenneth Brown* (for the Observer).

K Mydeen Esq    Barrister.

# R v Royal Pharmaceutical Society of GB, ex parte Association of Pharmaceutical Importers and others
# R v Secretary of State for Social Services, ex parte Association of Pharmaceutical Importers and others

### (Joined cases 266 and 267/87)

COURT OF JUSTICE OF THE EUROPEAN COMMUNITIES

JUDGES DUE (PRESIDENT), JOLIET, O'HIGGINS, GRÉVISSE (PRESIDENTS OF CHAMBERS), SLYNN, MANCINI, SHOCKWEILER, MOITINHO DE ALMEIDA AND RODRÍGUEZ IGLESIAS

ADVOCATE GENERAL M DARMON

12 JANUARY, 10 MARCH, 18 MAY 1989

*European Economic Community – Imports – Prohibition on imports – Quantitative restrictions on imports from another member state – Measures having equivalent effect – Pharmaceutical products – Parallel imports – Prescriptions – Professional and national rules prohibiting pharmacist from supplying medicinal product having trade mark or proprietary name other than that specified in prescription – Rule preventing pharmacist dispensing therapeutically equivalent imported parallel products – Whether rules constituting 'measures' having equivalent effect to quantitative restrictions on imports – Whether rules justified on grounds of protection of public health – National Health Service (General Medical and Pharmaceutical Services) Regulations 1974, Sch 4, Pt I, para 2(1) – EEC Treaty, arts 30, 36.*

The Royal Pharmaceutical Society of Great Britain, which was the pharmacists' professional body, adopted a code of ethics which, inter alia, prohibited a pharmacist from substituting, except in an emergency, any other product for a product specifically named in the prescription, even if he believed that the therapeutic effects and quality of that other product were identical. In 1986 the society's council published an official statement confirming that that rule applied to imported medicines as well as to those produced for the United Kingdom market. Under the national health service, which supplied about 95% of pharmaceutical products supplied on prescription, doctors generally had freedom to prescribe proprietary medicinal products under their proprietary name, although they were encouraged to prescribe such products under their generic names. Under para 2(1)[a] of the Terms of Service for Chemists as set out in Pt I of Sch 4 to the National Health Service (General Medical and Pharmaceutical Services) Regulations 1974 pharmacists were required to supply the products specified in prescriptions, so that where a doctor prescribed a product by its proprietary name only the product bearing that name could be supplied by the pharmacist. The Association of Pharmaceutical Importers, which was a trade association whose members' principal activity was the importation from other countries of the European Economic Community of 'parallel' pharmaceutical products (ie products imported from EEC member states in which their

a  Paragraph 2(1) provides: 'A chemist shall supply with reasonable promptness, to any person who presents on a prescription form—(a) an order for drugs, not being Scheduled drugs or appliances signed by a doctor or by his deputy or assistant; (b) an order for a drug specified in Schedule 3B to the regulations signed by, and endorsed on its face with the reference 'S3B' by, a doctor or by his deputy or assistant; (c) an order for listed drugs and medicines, signed by a dentist or his deputy or assistant, such drugs as may be so ordered and such of the appliances so ordered as he supplies in the normal course of his business.'

marketing was authorised and which had no differences in therapeutic effect from
*a* products covered by product licences granted in the United Kingdom and which were
made by the same manufacturer or by a member of the same group of companies as the
product covered by the licence or by a licensee of the manufacturer), contended that the
society's rule and the national health service terms of service, so far as they prohibited
pharmacists from supplying products other than those specified in prescriptions,
infringed art 30[b] of the EEC Treaty on the ground that their effect was equivalent to
*b* imposing quantitative restrictions on the importation of parallel pharmaceutical products.
In the course of proceedings brought by the association against the society and the
Secretary of State for Social Services, the Court of Appeal referred to the Court of Justice
of the European Communities the questions whether the society's rule and the national
health service terms of service were inconsistent with art 30 and, if they were, whether
they were justifiable under art 36[c] of the Treaty on grounds of the protection of, inter
*c* alia, public health.

**Held** – (1) Measures adopted by a professional body such as the society, which laid down
rules of ethics applicable to the members of the profession and which had a committee
on which national legislation had conferred disciplinary powers that could involve the
removal from the register of persons authorised to exercise the profession, could
*d* constitute 'measures' within the meaning of art 30 of the EEC Treaty (see p 779 *j* to p 780
*a* and p 781 *f g*, post).
   (2) In the absence of any Community legislation regulating the relationship between
doctors and pharmacists and in particular regulating the attending doctor's freedom to
prescribe any product he chose or the possibility of the pharmacist dispensing a medicinal
product other than that prescribed in the prescription, it was for the member states to
*e* decide, within the limits laid down by art 36 of the EEC Treaty, the degree to which they
wished to protect human health and life and how that degree of protection was to be
achieved. Furthermore, there was no evidence that a rule prohibiting pharmacists from
substituting another medicinal product for one designated by name in the prescription,
even if the other product had the same therapeutic effect, went beyond what was
*f* necessary to achieve the objective in view, namely to leave the entire responsibility for
the treatment of the patient in the hands of the doctor treating him; in particular, the
reasons, based on psychosomatic phenomena, for which a specific proprietary medicinal
product might be prescribed rather than a generic product or any other proprietary
medicinal product having the same therapeutic effect could not be discounted. Moreover,
there was no evidence that the application of such a general rule to products imported
*g* from other member states in which they were marketed lawfully constituted a means of
arbitrary discrimination or a disguised restriction on trade between member states within
art 36. It followed therefore that a national rule of a member state which required a
pharmacist, in response to a prescription calling for a medicinal product by its trade mark
or proprietary name, to dispense only a product bearing that trade mark or proprietary
name could be justified under art 36 on grounds of the protection of public health even
*h* where the effect of such a rule was to prevent the pharmacist from dispensing a
therapeutically equivalent product licensed by the competent national authorities and
manufactured by the same company or group of companies or by a licensee of that
company but bearing a trade mark or proprietary name applied to it in another member
state which differed from the trade mark or proprietary name which appeared in the

---

*j*  *b*   Article 30, so far as material, is set out at p 780 *b*, post
    *c*   Article 36, so far as material, provides: 'The provisions of Articles 30 to 34 shall not preclude
         prohibitions or restrictions on imports, exports or goods in transit justified on grounds of . . . the
         protection of health and life of humans . . . Such prohibitions or restrictions shall not, however,
         constitute a means of arbitrary discrimination or a disguised restriction on trade between Member
         States.'

prescription (see p 780 *j* to p 781 *d g h*, post); *de Peijper* Case 104/75 [1976] ECR 613 considered.

*a*

## Notes

For the elimination of quantitative restrictions on imports and of measures having equivalent effect within the European Economic Community, see 52 Halsbury's Laws (4th edn) paras 12·55–12·111, and for cases on the subject, see 21 Digest (Reissue) 249–250, 1662–1663.

*b*

For chemists' terms of service, see 33 Halsbury's Laws (4th edn) para 104.

For the supply of medicinal products by pharmacists, see 30 ibid para 643.

For the EEC Treaty, arts 30, 36, see 50 Halsbury's Statutes (4th edn) 276, 278.

## Cases cited

*Blesgen v Belgium* Case 75/81 [1982] ECR 1211.

*c*

*Centrafarm BV v American Home Products Corp* Case 3/78 [1978] ECR 1823.

*Centrafarm BV v Sterling Drug Inc* Case 15/74 [1974] ECR 1147.

*Centrafarm BV v Winthrop BV* Case 16/74 [1974] ECR 1183.

*de Peijper* Case 104/75 [1976] ECR 613.

*Dundalk Water Supply Scheme, Re, EC Commission v Ireland* Case 45/87 [1989] 1 CMLR 225, CJEC.

*d*

*Duphar BV v Netherlands* Case 238/82 [1984] ECR 523.

*EC Commission v Ireland* Case 249/82 [1982] ECR 4005.

*Hoffmann-La Roche & Co AG v Centrafarm Vertriebsgesellschaft Pharmazeutischer Erzeugnisse mbH* Case 102/77 [1978] ECR 1139.

*Merck & Co Inc v Stephar BV* Case 187/80 [1981] ECR 2063.

*Parke Davis & Co v Probel* Case 24/67 [1968] ECR 55.

*e*

*Pfizer Inc v Eurim-Pharm GmbH* Case 1/81 [1981] ECR 2913.

*Procureur du Roi v Dassonville* Case 8/74 [1974] ECR 837.

*Rewe-Zentral AG v Bundesmonopolverwaltung für Branntwein* Case 120/78 [1979] ECR 649.

*van Luipen (F) en Zn BV* Case 29/82 [1983] ECR 151.

*Vereniging van Vlaamse Reisbureaus v Sociale Dienst van de Plaatselijke en Gewestelijke Overheidsdiensten* Case 311/85 [1989] 4 CMLR 213, CJEC.

*f*

## Reference

By a judgment on 30 July 1987 and order dated 7 August 1987 the Court of Appeal (Kerr, Ralph Gibson and Russell LJJ) ([1987] 3 CMLR 939) referred to the Court of Justice of the European Communities for a preliminary ruling under art 177 of the EEC Treaty certain questions (set out at p 763 *b* to *g*, post) on the interpretation of arts 30 and 36 of the Treaty in order to enable it to determine whether certain national measures concerning pharmaceutical products supplied only on prescription were compatible with those provisions. The questions arose in the course of an appeal to the Court of Appeal by the Association of Pharmaceutical Importers and its members (the association) against the refusal of the Divisional Court of the Queen's Bench Division (May LJ and Simon Brown J) ([1987] BTLC 196) on 10 April 1987 to grant the association's application for judicial review by way of declarations (1) that a statement of the Council of the Royal Pharmaceutical Society of Great Britain published in the Pharmaceutical Journal on 12 July 1986 in relation to the dispensing on prescription of certain proprietary medicines, particularly those imported from other EEC countries, and its decision as set out in a letter of 12 August 1986 not to revoke the statement and (2) that the failure of the Secretary of State for Social Services to amend the Terms of Service for Chemists contained in Pt I of Sch 4 to the National Health Service (General Medical and Pharmaceutical Services) Regulations 1974, SI 1974/160, and the Medicines (Labelling) Regulations 1976, SI 1976/1726, constituted measures having an equivalent effect to a quantitative restriction on imports of those medicines within art 30 of the EEC Treaty and were

*g*

*h*

*j*

unlawful void and unenforceable. By order of 11 November 1987 the court decided to
*a* join the cases for the purposes of the written procedure, the oral procedure and the
judgment. The association, the society, the United Kingdom, the Kingdom of Belgium,
the Kingdom of Denmark and the Commission of the European Communities submitted
written observations to the court. The language of the cases was English. The facts are
set out in the report for the hearing presented by the Judge Rapporteur.

*b* **The Judge Rapporteur (O Due)** presented the following report for the hearing.

I—FACTS AND WRITTEN PROCEDURE
  The appellants in the main proceedings, the Association of Pharmaceutical Importers
and other parties (hereinafter referred to as 'the association'), are a trade association
incorporated in the form of a company limited by guarantee and the members of the
*c* said association. Their principal activity is the importation from other countries in the
EEC of so-called 'parallel' pharmaceutical products and their marketing in the United
Kingdom.
  In these proceedings, the association's contention is that the measures introduced by
the respondents in the main proceedings, the Secretary of State for Social Services
(hereinafter referred to as 'the Secretary of State') and the Royal Pharmaceutical Society
*d* of Great Britain (hereinafter referred to as 'the society'), which is the pharmacists'
professional body in the United Kingdom, infringe art 30 of the EEC Treaty on the
ground that their effect is equivalent to imposing quantitative restrictions on the
importation of some of the parallel pharmaceutical products in which the association
deals.
  After the association's contention had been rejected on 10 April 1987 by the Divisional
*e* Court of the Queen's Bench Division of the High Court of Justice ([1987] BTLC 196), the
association appealed to the Court of Appeal against that decision.
  The marketing in the United Kingdom of proprietary medicinal products, that is to
say medicinal products prepared in advance and marketed under special names, is subject
to the issue of a licence under the Medicines Act 1968 and Council Directive (EEC) 65/
*f* 65 of 26 January 1965 on the approximation of provisions laid down by law, regulation
or administrative action relating to proprietary medicinal products. In order to comply
with the judgment of the Court of Justice in *de Peijper* Case 104/75 [1976] ECR 613, the
Department of Health and Social Security introduced in May 1984 a simplified procedure
applicable to parallel imports of proprietary medicinal products. The licence granted
under that procedure is known as a product licence (parallel import) (hereinafter referred
to as a 'PL(PI) licence').
*g*
  The grant of such a licence is subject to certain conditions, namely that the product
must be imported from an EEC member state in which it has already obtained a
marketing authorisation under art 3 of Council Directive (EEC) 65/65, that it has no
differences, having therapeutic effect, from a product covered by a product licence
already granted in the United Kingdom and that it must be made by the same
*h* manufacturer or by a member of the same group of companies as the product covered
by the United Kingdom licence, or by a licensee of such manufacturer. In the event of
the grant of a PL(PI) licence satisfying those requirements, the scope of the grant was
defined as follows:

  'A PL(PI) issued in accordance with the application, allows the holder to import
  the product it covers into the United Kingdom and to arrange for its sale or supply
*j*  in this country. It allows him to procure the assembly (i.e., labelling and, if necessary,
  packaging) of the product but does not authorise him to procure its manufacture.'

PL(PI) licences covering about 220 products have been granted. The incentive for the
importation into the United Kingdom of proprietary medicinal products is that in many
instances the licensed products are at present marketed in other EEC member states at

considerably lower prices. In most cases the parallel imports have the same brand name as the United Kingdom domestic product. However, about 50 of the products are marketed under a different brand name from that of the product already marketed in the United Kingdom. In a number of cases, both within the category of products marketed under a different name, and the remainder of about 170 which have identical names, the parallel products may vary from the United Kingdom product in their appearance, such as their colour, size, shape or packaging.

Section 58 of the Medicines Act 1968, concerning medicinal products on prescription only, gives the appropriate ministers power to specify by order descriptions or classes of medicinal products. According to sub-s (2), concerning the scope of the provisions, no person is to sell by retail, or supply in circumstances corresponding to a retail sale, a medicinal product of a description, or falling within a class, specified in an order under s 58 except in accordance with a prescription given by an appropriate practitioner. Furthermore, no person is to administer any such medicinal product unless he is an appropriate practitioner or a person acting in accordance with the directions of an appropriate practitioner.

Under para 2(1) of the Terms of Service for Chemists as set out in Pt I of Sch 4 to the National Health Service (General Medical and Pharmaceutical Services) Regulations 1974, SI 1974/160 (as substituted by SI 1985/290), which are regulations adopted under the authority of the Secretary of State, a chemist is to supply to any person who presents on a prescription form an order for drugs such drugs as may be so ordered. Any breach of those terms must be investigated by the pharmacist's local pharmaceutical service committee and reported to his local family practitioner committee, which can then take disciplinary action against the pharmacist. 95% of all prescriptions are issued by doctors in the national health service.

Nearly all pharmaceutical products have an approved non-proprietary name which is the name given by the competent authorities to the formulation of drugs which the product contains. The manufacturer of a product may market it either using the appropriate approved non-proprietary name or using a particular name chosen by him. Although the competent authorities encourage doctors to prescribe generically, doctors are generally free to prescribe by specifying a named proprietary product.

Paragraph 1.4(ii) and (iv) of a code of ethics adopted by the society in 1984 and the accompanying guidance notes provide as follows;

> 'A pharmacist should not substitute (except with approval of the prescriber or a hospital drug and therapeutics committee or in an emergency) any other product for a specifically named product even if he believes that the therapeutic effect and quality of the other product is identical. There will be situations of emergency when a pharmacist finds it necessary to substitute another product for a specifically named product prescribed by a practitioner; in such cases reasonable steps should be taken to ensure that the effect and quality of the substitute so far as can be ascertained is identical to that prescribed . . .
> A pharmacist should not deviate from the prescriber's instructions when dispensing a prescription except where necessary to protect the patient . . .'

On 12 July 1986 the society published an official statement which drew attention, inter alia, to the relevant parts of the guidance notes and continued as follows:

> 'The Council confirms that the above provisions apply to imported medicines as well as those produced for the United Kingdom market.'

On 12 August the society rejected a request from the association to revoke the above-mentioned statement.

Noting that, according to the association, the said statement and the corresponding interepretation of the terms of service applied at the same time by the authorities acting on behalf of the Secretary of State had caused imports of parallel products bearing a name

different from the corresponding product initially authorised practically to dry up, the
a   Court of Appeal decided that such measures could be contrary to arts 30 and 36 of the
EEC Treaty (see [1987] 3 CMLR 939). It therefore decided to stay proceedings in *R v
Royal Pharmaceutical Society of GB, ex p Association of Pharmaceutical Importers* Case 266/87
and referred the following questions to the Court of Justice for a preliminary ruling:

'1. Is a national rule of a Member State inconsistent with Article 30 of the EEC
b       Treaty where it requires a pharmacist, in response to a prescription calling for a
medicinal product by its trade-mark or proprietary name, to dispense only a product
bearing that trade-mark or proprietary name where the effect of such a rule is to
prevent the pharmacist from dispensing a therapeutically equivalent product
licensed by the competent national authorities pursuant to rules adopted in
conformity with the judgment of the Court of Justice in Case 104/75 [*de Peijper*
c       [1976] ECR 613] and manufactured by the same company or group of companies
or by a licensee of that company but bearing a trade-mark or proprietary name
applied to it in another Member State which differs from the trade-mark or
proprietary name appearing in the prescription?
2. In the event of the first question being answered in the affirmative is such a
national rule justifiable on grounds of protection of public health or the protection
d       of industrial or commercial property?
3. In either event was the statement of the Council of the Pharmaceutical Society
of Great Britain published in the Pharmaceutical Journal on 12 July 1986 or its
decision as set out in its letter of 12 August 1986 not to revoke that statement a
"measure" within the meaning of Article 30 of the EEC Treaty?'

On the basis of the same arguments, the Court of Appeal stayed the proceedings in *R v
e   Secretary of State for Social Services, ex p Association of Pharmaceutical Importers* Case 267/87
and referred the following questions to the Court of Justice for a preliminary ruling:

'1. Is Article 30 of the EEC Treaty to be interpreted as prohibiting a national rule
which requires a pharmacist, in response to a doctor's prescription identifying a
pharmaceutical product by its trade-mark, to dispense only a product bearing that
f       trade-mark where the effect of the rule is to prevent the dispensing of a
therapeutically equivalent product licensed by the competent national authorities
pursuant to rules adopted in conformity with the judgment of the Court of Justice
in Case 104/75 [*de Peijper* [1976] ECR 613] but which bears a trade-mark applied to
it in another Member State differing from the name used in the prescription?
2. If so, in what circumstances is such a rule justifiable on the grounds set out in
g       Article 36 of the EEC Treaty?'

The orders for reference were received at the court registry on 7 September 1987.
By order of 11 November 1987 the court decided to join Cases 266/87 and 267/87 for
the purposes of the written procedure, the oral procedure and the judgment.
In accordance with art 20 of the Protocol on the Statute of the Court of Justice, written
h   observations were submitted to the court by the appellants in the main proceedings, the
Association of Pharmaceutical Importers and other parties, represented by David Vaughan
QC, assisted by Derrick Wyatt, barrister, instructed by Stephen Kon of S J Berwin & Co,
solicitors, London, by the respondent in the main proceedings in Case 266/87, the Royal
Pharmaceutical Society of Great Britain, represented by Robert Webb, barrister, instructed
by E J R Hill of Walker Martineau, solicitors, London, by the United Kingdom,
j   represented by S J Hay, of the Treasury Solicitor's Department, acting as agent, assisted
by John Laws and Nicholas Paines, barristers, by the Kingdom of Belgium, represented
by A Reyn, Director of European Affairs in the Ministry of Foreign Affairs, acting as
agent, by the Kingdom of Denmark, represented by Jørgen Molde, Legal Adviser at the
Ministry for Foreign Affairs, acting as agent, and by the Commission of the European
Communities, represented by Eric L White, a member of its Legal Department, acting
as agent.

On hearing the report of the Judge Rapporteur and the views of the Advocate General, the court decided to open the oral procedure without any preparatory inquiry. However, *a* the court requested the Commission to submit a synopsis of the relevant rules governing the relations between doctors and pharmacists in the other member states, except Denmark, the situation in that country being dealt with in the observations of the Danish government.

By letter of 26 August 1988 the Commission replied to that question as follows;

*b*

'In the majority of Member States, the pharmacist is usually required to dispense to the patient the medicinal product which has been prescribed by the doctor exactly in accordance with the terms of the doctor's prescription. The pharmacist may not substitute a product which he considers to be therapeutically equivalent to the one prescribed. If the product prescribed by the doctor is not available, the pharmacist may, as a general rule, only substitute an equivalent product with the permission of *c* the doctor concerned. In cases of emergency, however, or, in certain Member States, in case of hospital use, substitution may be permitted on the responsibility of the pharmacist. In Spain and the Netherlands the situation is different. The pharmacist may dispense any other medicinal product which has the same active ingredient(s), the same pharmaceutical form and the same strength as the product prescribed without the consent of the doctor. In Spain, however, the consent of the patient is *d* required before the pharmacist may substitute. Following the judgment of the Court in Case 104/75 *de Peijper* ([1976] ECR 613), the Federal Republic of Germany, the Netherlands, the United Kingdom and Ireland (as well as Denmark) have established schemes to verify the therapeutic equivalence of parallel imports. For economic reasons, the other Member States have not yet received a significant volume of parallel imports of medicinal products, and appear therefore not to have *e* found it necessary to establish such schemes. In the Federal Republic of Germany, the pharmacist may dispense a parallel import, notwithstanding that its name is different from the product on the national market, provided that the prescribing doctor has expressly left him this option. In Ireland, the marketing authorization for parallel imports of a medicinal product is granted under the name of the product as it is ordinarily on the market in Ireland. The parallel importer is obliged to state *f* this name on the label of the product. Thus the pharmacist is able to verify that the parallel import, which may originally have had a different name, is therapeutically equivalent to the product which is ordinarily on the market and the pharmacist may dispense any product which carries that proprietary name. Finally, in the Netherlands, because of the general rule in favour of substitution, the pharmacist may dispense any parallel import which is therapeutically equivalent to the product *g* on the national market, notwithstanding that its name is different.'

II—WRITTEN OBSERVATIONS

The *Association of Pharmaceutical Importers* claims that the decisions adopted by the society and the Secretary of State amount to 'measures' within the meaning of art 30 of *h* the EEC Treaty and observes, with reference to the judgment of the court in *F van Luipen en Zn BV* Case 29/82 [1983] ECR 151, that art 30 applies to bodies established under private law where such bodies exercise public functions or act in reliance on national law.

Referring to the settled case law of the court, in the first place, the judgment *Procureur du Roi v Dassonville* Case 8/74 [1974] ECR 837, the association observes that the prohibition in art 30 extends beyond frontier formalities and restrictions to any national measure *j* capable of affecting the marketing prospects of imported products, that is to say those which have an indirect effect on imports.

The association adds that decisions such as those at issue in the proceedings before the national court constitute restrictions on imports contrary to art 30 of the EEC Treaty because of their discriminatory effects. Decisions such as those at issue prevent the

product which is prescribed from being dispensed whenever it bears a trade name used
*a* in another member state which is different from the domestic trade name.

The association also claims that the decisions at issue do not fall outside the scope of art
30 on the ground that they give effect to consumer choice. The choices involved are not
for the most part made by independent commercial operators or by customers but by
doctors employed under public law who take no account of commercial considerations
in taking their decisions.

*b* The association also points out that in its judgment in *Duphar BV v Netherlands* Case
238/82 [1984] ECR 523 the court recognised the special nature of the market in
pharmaceutical products in member states where that market is subject to supervision
and control for reasons of social policy. The applicable test under art 30 in such a context
is whether the rules in question permit imports to compete in price on the national
market. The effect of the decisions of the society and the Secretary of State is virtually to
*c* exclude from the market imported products which are therapeutically identical to, or
without distinction from, domestic products made by the same company or group of
companies, or under licence, and which differ only in bearing a trade name which is
different from the domestic trade name.

The association contends that no therapeutic grounds could possibly exist for preferring
a product bearing a United Kingdom trade name over the same product or a product
*d* without therapeutic distinction made by the same manufacturer bearing a non-United
Kingdom trade name. Prescribing by the United Kingdom trade name authorises the
dispensing of the United Kingdom product, or of a product bearing a name affixed in
another member state which happens to be the same.

The association claims that the national rule at issue in these proceedings has had the
same effect as revocation of a valid marketing authorisation. It also emphasises that for
*e* all purposes material to the present proceedings PL(PI) products are to be treated as
identical to or without distinction in regard to their domestic counterparts, irrespective
of whether the trade name they bear is the same as or different from the domestic name.

With regard to the possible application of art 36 of the EEC Treaty in order to
safeguard national trade mark rights, the association argues that there are no grounds
*f* whatsoever based on the enjoyment of national trade mark rights which would justify
the national rule at issue in these proceedings. It is difficult to see on what basis the
society can claim an interest in protecting trade mark rights of commercial operators.

With regard to the possible application of the same article on public health grounds,
the association argues that exceptions to the free movement of goods are to be construed
strictly and cannot be justified if other measures, less burdensome to freedom of trade,
are capable of achieving the same aim (see the judgment of the court in *de Peijper* Case
*g* 104/75 [1976] ECR 613. On the basis of the same judgment, the association adds that the
burden of establishing that measures derogating from art 30 can be justified lies on the
national authorities. Furthermore, a derogation is permissible only if it can be established
that there is a sufficiently serious threat to public health to justify a restriction on imports
or sales and, even if it can, the measure taken must be proportionate. Even on grounds
*h* of public health, it-is not open to national authorities to differentiate between medical
products which are recognised as being therapeutically identical or without distinction.

In any event, the association contends that the possible loss of placebo effect and the
remote risk of patient anxiety if the patient received a drug with a name other than that
indicated by his doctor cannot amount to a sufficiently serious threat to public health to
justify a restriction on the free movement of goods. In any event, national restrictions on
*j* the importation of PL(PI) products bearing a name different from the United Kingdom
name could never be justified on grounds of public health under art 36 of the EEC Treaty
since they would amount to a disguised restriction on trade between member states
within the meaning of the second sentence of art 36 of the Treaty.

Consequently, the association proposed that the court should reply as follows to the
first question in both Case 266/87 and Case 267/87: art 30 is to be interpreted as

prohibiting a national rule which requires a pharmacist, in response to a doctor's
prescription identifying a pharmaceutical product by its trade name, to dispense only a
product bearing that trade name where the effect of the rule is to prevent the dispensing
of a product licensed by the competent national authorities pursuant to rules adopted in
conformity with the judgment of the Court of Justice in *de Peijper* Case 104/75 [1976]
ECR 613 as therapeutically identical or without distinction but which bears a trade name
differing from the name used in the prescription.

The association proposes that the court should reply to the second question in Case
266/87 as follows: such a rule cannot be justified under art 36 of the EEC Treaty in order
to safeguard national trade mark rights, or in order to safeguard public health.

The association proposes that the court should reply to the second question in Case
267/87 as follows: such a rule cannot be justified under any of the grounds set out in art
36 of the EEC Treaty.

The association contends that the third question referred by the Court of Appeal in
Case 266/87 should be answered in the affirmative both with regard to the statement in
the Pharmaceutical Journal of 12 July 1986 and to its letter of 12 August 1986.

The *Royal Pharmaceutical Society of Great Britain* contends, in regard to the first question,
that its statement of 12 July 1986 does not discriminate against licensed imported drugs
but makes it clear that pharmacists should treat them in the same way as other licensed
drugs, imported or domestic. The principle is that, if a medicinal product is prescribed
by its product's name, the pharmacist should dispense the product marketed under that
name.

The society is not against the policy of encouraging prescribing by generic or non-
proprietary name. When a drug is so prescribed, the pharmacist may dispense any
medicinal product meeting the requirements of the prescription. It is for the prescriber
to choose the drug, or the actual product which contains it. In either event what the
pharmacist is doing is dispensing the prescription, not altering it, for example, to a
generic version of a drug, when the prescriber has made a specific choice of product.

Referring to the judgment of the court in *Duphar BV v Netherlands* Case 238/82 [1984]
ECR 523, the society remarks that national provisions such as those in this case are
compatible with art 30 of the EEC Treaty if there is no discrimination between domestic
goods and parallel imports. It adds that, if importers wish to import more goods, all they
have to do is persuade the doctors, dentists or veterinarians, who are the exclusive
'market', to prescribe them.

The society proposes that the reply to the first question should be in the negative.

With regard to the second question, the society points out that it asks only whether a
rule is 'justifiable' as opposed to being 'justified'. It adds that the association has put in no
evidence to contradict the authoritative and detailed evidence of the potential danger to
health.

Any anxiety caused to the patient through the dispensing of a drug of quite a different
name to that expected, or by the expected name on the container not matching that on
the tablets themselves, could effect compliance with the dose regimen and hence
treatment, to the detriment of the health of the patient.

If there be a restriction on imports, then any such restriction is justifiable because
without it a doctor cannot be so sure that his patient receives what he prescribes and,
unless he can be so sure, the evidence shows that patients' confidence may be lost and
treatment adversely affected.

As regards the protection of property, the society points out that it has a legitimate
interest in protecting its pharmacist members from numerous actions for breach of trade
mark. According to the court's judgment in *Centrafarm BV v American Home Products
Corp* Case 3/78 [1978] ECR 1823, drug companies have the right to preserve their trade
mark within the various jurisdictions of the European Community, even where a single
company may be the proprietor of both marks.

The society proposes that the court should reply in the affirmative to the second
question.

With regard to the third question, the society points out that it operates as a body
*a* independent of Parliament. Under the Pharmacy Act 1954, Parliament has set up a
statutory disciplinary committee of the society, which acts autonomously. It does not
report or make recommendations to the council of the society. Moreover, the 1954 Act
allows the committee to remove pharmacists from the register for, inter alia, 'misconduct',
but what constitutes misconduct is solely for the committee to determine.

The contested statement does no more than confirm a long-standing practice of many
*b* years, by which pharmacists are to dispense, without discrimination, whichever drug or
product it be, general or specific, which a prescriber has chosen to prescribe for a patient,
whose clinical details he will know, but the dispenser may not.

The society therefore proposes that the court should decide that its statement does not
constitute a 'measure' within the meaning of art 30 of the EEC Treaty.

In conclusion, it argues that if there is a 'measure' it does not have an effect equivalent
*c* to a restriction on imports. It is non-discriminatory and applies only to the supply of a
product once prescribed. It does not affect the question of what is prescribed (imported
or not). If there is such a restriction, it is not only justifiable but in fact justified on
grounds of the protection of health and of trade marks.

The *United Kingdom* observes, in regard to the scope of art 30, that the dispensing of
pharmaceutical products is in essence a commercial supply of goods by a private supplier.
*d* However, it has certain important characteristics: first, the selection of the particular
goods to be supplied is a skilled operation; second, the task of selecting the goods is
entrusted to the doctor, and is one of a number of decisions which the doctor has to make
concerning the treatment of the patient; third, the person who chooses the goods is
different from the person who consumes them.

Furthermore, art 30 does not call into question the principle in a commercial
*e* transaction that the supplier must supply what has been ordered, a principle which must
apply, in particular, when it is a doctor who chooses and prescribes the medicine for a
patient.

The contested rules do not themselves restrict imports. The products in question can
at present be imported and dispensed against a 'generic' prescription or a prescription
*f* using the name under which they are marketed.

The contested rules are not the cause of the pharmacists' inability to dispense the
parallel imported product. The real reason lies in the fact that the imported product bears
a trade mark other than that indicated on the doctor's prescription and, as the court
decided in *Centrafarm BV v American Home Products Corp* Case 3/78 [1978] ECR 1823, the
law of trade marks prevents importers from placing such marks on products which they
import.
*g* The United Kingdom does not consider that it is obliged to set up a special system in
order to increase imports of particular products by enabling them to circumvent the
effects of trade mark law as interpreted by the Court of Justice.

Such a system would be artificial because it would involve discrimination in favour of
one particular category of imports and, moreover, would be unsatisfactory and even
*h* dangerous from the point of view of public health.

It would be artificial inasmuch as it would permit pharmacists to dispense a product
named 'B' on the basis of a prescription ordering product 'A'. It would also be inconsistent
with the requirements of the regulations on labelling, which require the dispensed
product to be labelled with the name used by the doctor on the prescription.

It would be discriminatory inasmuch as it would favour 'parallel' products over other
*j* proprietary medicinal products which are therapeutically equivalent to those prescribed
by the doctor.

It would be unsatisfactory and dangerous because of the confusion on the part of the
patient which would result therefrom and which might well lead him not to take the
product dispensed even though failure to do so might well cause him harm.

The United Kingdom submits that, if the contested rules fall within the scope of art 30
at all, the considerations referred to above constitute a justification of the rules either as

being necessary to satisfy mandatory requirements of the sort recognised by the court in *Rewe-Zentral AG v Bundesmonopolverwaltung für Branntwein* Case 120/78 [1979] ECR 649 *a* (*Cassis de Dijon*) or on grounds of the protection of health under art 36 of the EEC Treaty. Those objectives cannot be achieved by other means.

Finally, the United Kingdom contends that the special system which the association seeks to have introduced would violate the essential subject matter of trade marks. It observes that, according to the judgment of the court in *Centrafarm BV v American Home Products Corp* Case 3/78 [1978] ECR 1823, the essential function of the trade mark is to *b* guarantee the identity of the origin of the trade marked product to the consumer or ultimate user. A situation in which the product supplied would not even bear the trade mark selected by the doctor would frustrate the attainment of the objectives which it is the essential function of the trade mark to secure.

With regard to the third question in Case 266/87, the United Kingdom observes that the society is a body composed of members of the pharmaceutical profession and is not *c* under government control, although certain statutory functions are entrusted to it.

The United Kingdom submits that the answers to be given to the questions raised in this reference are as follows.

In Case 266/87, question 1: a national rule of a member state is consistent with art 30 of the EEC Treaty where it requires a pharmacist, in response to a prescription calling for a medicinal product by its trade mark or proprietary name, to dispense only a product *d* bearing that trade mark or proprietary name; questions 2 and 3: in the light of the answer to be given to question 1, questions 2 and 3 do not call for a reply. Alternatively, the answer to be given to question 2 is as follows: such a rule is justifiable on grounds of the protection of public health and the protection of industrial and commercial property.

In Case 267/87, question 1: art 30 of the EEC Treaty does not prohibit a national rule which requires a pharmacist, in response to a doctor's prescription identifying a *e* pharmaceutical product by its trade mark, to dispense only a product bearing that trade mark; question 2: in the light of the answer given to question 1 it is unnecessary to reply to question 2. Alternatively, the answer to be given to question 2 is: such a rule is justifiable on the grounds set out in art 36 of the EEC Treaty where it guarantees to the consumer the authenticity of the product supplied to him and protects him from *f* confusion about the identity of that product.

The *Government of the Kingdom of Belgium* emphasises that in Belgium a pharmacist must dispense exactly the same drug prescribed in the prescription. To authorise the pharmacist to dispense another medicinal product would open the door to all kinds of substitution of more or less identical or similar products. Furthermore, a right of substitution would not re-establish fair competition between parallel imported products and other products. The problems raised in these cases can be resolved only by *g* Community action to harmonise prices, if necessary supplemented in the long term by harmonisation of the trade marks and names of medicinal products.

The *Danish Government* points out first of all that, by insisting that the pharmacist must only dispense precisely the product indicated by the doctor in the prescription, responsibility towards the patient is unequivocally laid on the doctor. Furthermore, the *h* fact that the doctor, being the best qualified person, himself makes the choice which he is best placed to make excludes any danger of confusion or anxiety on the part of the patient if the pharmacist, motivated, possibly, by a direct economic interest, was free to dispense products other than the one prescribed.

When a doctor issues a prescription for certain pharmaceutical products, he is making a choice which may be influenced by advertising but is based both on his knowledge of *j* the patient and of the various pharmaceutical products, and which takes no account of economic considerations.

The Danish government adds that in many member states, including Denmark, pharmacists have a duty to supply, and at the same time an exclusive right to sell, medicinal products for which a prescription is necessary. Furthermore, Danish a pharmacists may themselves be producers of medicinal products both through their own businesses and to some extent through the manufacturing business that is jointly owned by them, which could give rise to doubt whether they have made an unbiased consumer choice.

The situation under discussion in no way falls within the scope of art 30 of the EEC Treaty because the rules are applied without distinction to imported and nationally produced medicinal products. The only question is therefore who makes the choice.

b If the court should none the less find that the rules at issue in this case are incompatible with art 30, the Danish government considers that they are fully justified on the grounds mentioned in art 36, namely, inter alia, grounds of public health.

The *Commission* points out first of all that, although the society is not a state body, certain public law supervisory functions conferred on it by statute are measures attributable to the state.

c Consequently, the Commission is of the opinion that the positions taken by the society and the Secretary of State, who is part of the government of the United Kingdom, constitute measures for the purposes of art 30 of the EEC Treaty.

With regard to the compatibility of the contested measures with art 30 of the Treaty, the Commission points out that they apply to all pharmaceutical products, whether imported or not, but that they are capable of favouring domestic production.

d The Commission points out that doctors prescribing medicines under the national health service are acting as agents of a state body. In that regard, the Commission draws attention to the second sentence of art 7(2) of Council Directive (EEC) 77/62 of 21 December 1976 co-ordinating procedures for the award of public supply contracts, according to which the indication of trade marks is prohibited unless the product cannot otherwise be described, in which case the words 'or equivalent' are to be added.

e The Commission does not accept the argument that the contested measures are no more than an 'expression of the normal rule of commerce that the supplier must supply what has been ordered'. In so far as the customer is considered to be the patient who will consume the product, the contested measures go further than the 'normal rule of commerce'. The customer is entitled to accept an identical product to that prescribed, even if it bears a different name and has a different trade mark, and, in that case, the

f supplier is not of course obliged to supply the trade marked product. However, the contested measures constitute an instruction from an authority of the state to the pharmacist, backed up with the threat of disciplinary action, requiring him to supply the trade marked product even if the patient would have been prepared to accept the identical product with a different trade mark.

The Commission is therefore of the opinion that the contested measures constitute

g measures of having an effect equivalent to quantitative restrictions within the meaning of art 30 of the Treaty.

The Commission accepts, with regard to the possible justification of the contested measures, that the prevention of anxiety and the maintenance of the confidence of a patient in his treatment are justified objectives coming within the protection of the life

h and health of humans under art 36 of the Treaty. The problem arises in particular in the case of older patients and those who receive long-term treatment. According to the Commission, those objectives could well justify a decision by a doctor to specify a particular trade marked product in certain circumstances. However, the Commission considers that the measures adopted in this case are more restrictive than necessary to achieve that objective. It can conceive of two methods of achieving those objectives

j which would be less restrictive.

First, it would be a simple matter to provide that all national health service prescription forms contain a notice advising the pharmacist that where a medicine is specified by a trade mark he is free to dispense an alternative medicine which has been officially recognised as presenting no differences having therapeutic effect from the specified trade marked product. The prescribing doctor should be free to strike out this notice if he

considers that the equivalent product would not be suitable for his patient for some
reason. In such a case the pharmacist would be required to dispense only the product  *a*
with the specified trade mark.

The second solution would be to allow a pharmacist to dispense a therapeutically
equivalent product against a prescription specifying a trade marked product but to
require him in such circumstances clearly to bring to the attention of the patient (for
example through the affixing of a label) that the dispensed medicine may differ in name
(and possibly colour, taste and shape) from that prescribed or that to which the patient  *b*
has become accustomed, but that the therapeutic effect is identical.

With regard to the question whether the contested measures may be justified on
grounds related to the protection of industrial and commercial property rights, the
Commission points out that the contested measures not only amount to an instruction to
pharmacists not to infringe trade mark rights but also prohibit pharmacists from
providing an alternative product even where the proprietor of the trade mark permits or  *c*
acquiesces in such action or where the exercise of the trade mark right would be
incompatible with the EEC Treaty. In so far as the measures go further than is necessary
to protect actual trade mark rights which can be legally exercised, they cannot be justified
on the grounds of the protection of industrial and commercial property.

For the reasons set out above the Commission concludes that the court should reply to
the questions of the Court of Appeal as follows. (1) A national rule of a member state  *d*
which prevents a pharmacist, in response to a prescription calling for a medicinal product
by its trade mark or proprietary name, from dispensing a therapeutically equivalent
product licensed by the competent national authorities pursuant to rules adopted in
conformity with the judgment of the Court of Justice in *de Peijper* Case 104/75 [1976]
ECR 613 and manufactured by the same company or group of companies or by a licensee
of that company but bearing a trade mark or proprietary name applied to it in another  *e*
member state which differs from the trade mark or proprietary name appearing in the
prescription constitutes a measure of equivalent effect to a quantitative restriction on
imports within the meaning of art 30 of the EEC Treaty. (2) (a) Such a rule may only be
justified for the protection of public health if there exist no other equally effective means
of protection which are less restrictive of trade between member states. (b) Such a rule is  *f*
not justified for the protection of industrial and commercial property rights to the extent
that they prohibit actions which would not infringe those rights or which are permitted
by the proprietor of those rights or against which those rights could not be exercised by
virtue of Community law (arts 30 and 86 of the EEC Treaty). (c) The file before the court
does not indicate any other ground of justification known to Community law for such a
national rule. (3) Actions taken by the Pharmaceutical Society of Great Britain within the  *g*
ambit of its public law supervisory function over pharmacists constitute measures for the
purpose of art 30 of the EEC Treaty.

*David Vaughan QC* and *Derrick Wyatt* for the association.
*Robert Webb QC* for the society.
*Eric L White* for the Commission.  *h*
*John Laws* and *Nicholas Paines* for the United Kingdom.
M A *Fiestra* for the Netherlands.

10 March. **The Advocate General (M Darmon)** delivered the following opinion[1]. Mr
President, Members of the Court,
1. The case law of the court on the free movement of goods bears witness to its  *j*
determination to achieve the objectives of integration in that domain. But this
voluntarism, to which I firmly subscribe, naturally encounters a limit, that of common
sense, and a constraint, that of the way in which public opinion, be it lay or informed,

---

1   Translated from the French

perceives the direction in which the developments inspired by the court's judgments are
a pointing. And it is in my opinion those limitations which it is today proposed that the
court should cast aside when its indorsement is sought for an implied alteration of the
respective roles of doctor and pharmacist as understood in almost all the member states
of the Community. I would ask the court not to judge me too harshly for expressing my
feelings even before mentioning the difficulties facing it. I am aware that I am departing
here from established practice but my purpose in so doing is to draw attention at once to
b the very sensitive subject about to be considered.

2. These two sets of preliminary questions from the Court of Appeal require the court
to consider once again 'parallel' imports of medicinal products (see in particular *Parke
Davis & Co v Probel* Case 24/67 [1968] ECR 55, *Centrafarm BV v Sterling Drug Inc* Case 15/
74 [1974] ECR 1147, *Centrafarm BV v Winthrop BV* Case 16/74 [1974] ECR 1183, *de
Peijper* Case 104/75 [1976] ECR 613, *Hoffmann-La Roche & Co AG v Centrafarm
c Vertriebsgesellschaft Pharmazeutischer Erzeugnisse mbH* Case 102/77 [1978] ECR 1139,
*Centrafarm BV v American Home Products Corp* Case 3/78 [1978] ECR 1823, *Merck & Co
Inc v Stephar BV* Case 187/80 [1981] ECR 2063 and *Pfizer Inc v Eurim-Pharm GmbH* Case 1/
81 [1981] ECR 2913).

3. In order to comply with the court's judgment in *de Peijper* Case 104/75 [1976] ECR
613 the United Kingdom introduced in May 1984 a system under which a product
d licence (parallel import) (hereinafter referred to as a 'PL(PI) licence') is granted. It would
be as well to recall the principal features of that system. The issue of a PL(PI) licence is
subject to the following conditions: the product must be imported from a member state
in which it has already obtained a marketing authorisation; it must not have any
differences, having therapeutic effect, from a product covered by a licence already granted
in the United Kingdom; it must be made by the same manufacturer or by a member of
e the same group of companies as the product covered by the United Kingdom licence, or
by a licensee of such manufacturer.

Once obtained, the PL(PI) licence authorises its holder to import and market the
product concerned in the territory of the United Kingdom.

4. I will point out immediately that the dispute in the main proceedings has arisen
f from the situation where the PL(PI) product has a different trade mark from that
applying in the United Kingdom.

5. The contested measures, namely para 1.4(ii) and (iv) of the code of ethics of the
Pharmaceutical Society of Great Britain (hereinafter referred to as 'the Pharmaceutical
Society') and the interpretation thereof (see the statement of 12 July 1986 confirmed by a
letter of 12 August 1986 rejecting a request to revoke that statement) as well as para 2(1)
g of the Terms of Service for Chemists as set out in Pt I of Sch 4 to the National Health
Service (General Medical and Pharmaceutical Services) Regulations 1974, SI 1974/160 (as
substituted by SI 1985/290) as interpreted by the Secretary of State for Social Services,
prohibit pharmacists from supplying a product having a trade mark or name different
from that prescribed by the doctor. Those general measures also apply where the PL(PI)
product has a trade mark different from that borne by the product prescribed by the
h doctor.

6. In order to explain clearly all the aspects of the dispute, I should point out first of
all that, according to the court's judgment in *Centrafarm BV v American Home Products
Corp* Case 3/78 [1978] ECR 1823 at 1841–1842 (paras 15, 20–22), the registering in two
member states of two different trade marks in respect of the same product is not in itself
contrary to the EEC Treaty. Therefore, the proprietor of a trade mark may prevent an
j unauthorised third party from affixing to a product lawfully bearing one of the trade
marks the other mark concerned. However, the court expressed a reservation with regard
to the case where two trade marks are registered with the intention of partitioning
markets.

7. I should explain next that British doctors generally prescribe products using a name
which is familiar to them, that is to say the name used in the United Kingdom. Where

that name is the same as the trade mark of the PL(PI) product, the contested measures will not prevent the supply of that product. This is not the case where the two trade *a* marks are different. In that case, existing United Kingdom law prohibits the pharmacist from supplying the PL(PI) product, just as for that matter it prohibits him from supplying any product not bearing the trade mark prescribed by the doctor.

8. Approximately 220 products have so far been granted a PL(PI) licence and 50 or so have a different trade mark. 19 of the latter products are among the 300 drugs most widely prescribed in the United Kingdom.                                                           *b*

9. Before the adoption of the contested measures, the volume of trade in PL(PI) products had become considerable because pharmacists were supplying them proprio motu even if they bore a different trade mark and even when they had received a prescription prescribing the United Kingdom brand. The reason for this was simple: since he is reimbursed on the basis of the scale laid down for the national product, the pharmacist obtains a substantial profit which encourages 'substitution' (I use this term in *c* my opinion for the sake of convenience; to my mind, it is clear that such usage does not reflect any reservations about the equivalence between the prescribed product and the product supplied in such a case). It is the prohibition of such 'substitution' that the Association of Pharmaceutical Importers (API), an association of parallel importers, has challenged before the national court in order to obtain a declaration that it is a measure having equivalent effect within the meaning of art 30 of the EEC Treaty.          *d*

10. That, in outline, is the background to the dispute which has led to this reference for a preliminary ruling.

11. The first United Kingdom court before which the contested measures were brought considered that they did not constitute rules contrary to art 30 (see [1987] BTLC 196). It is now for the court to state the criteria which will enable the Court of Appeal to uphold or invalidate that view.                                                                *e*

12. In order to assist the court in that task, I will not adhere strictly to the order of the questions adopted by the Court of Appeal. In my view, it is necessary to examine first of all whether the statement of the Pharmaceutical Society, which was later confirmed, constitutes, having regard to the nature of that body, a measure of the kind prohibited by art 30 of the EEC Treaty.                                                            *f*

13. The Pharmaceutical Society was created by a royal charter in 1843. It maintains a register on which a pharmacist must be entered in order to be able to practise. It may bring disciplinary proceedings, which may result in fines, suspensions or even removal from the register. Appeals against such decisions are brought before the High Court of Justice. The pursuit of the pharmacist's profession is based on the observation of professional rules, in particular a code of ethics of which the statement in question is an *g* illustration.

14. In my view, three essential features must be emphasised: the regulation of the profession, the issuing of rules of ethics and the exercise of disciplinary powers to ensure that those rules are observed. The Pharmaceutical Society therefore constitutes a professional body having as its task the provision of a *public service* which it performs in the *public interest*. The compulsory nature of admission to its register and its disciplinary *h* powers are characteristic of *rights and powers derogating from the generally applicable rules of law*. Such rights and powers are radically different from those of ordinary private bodies.

15. In order to dispel any doubt, I would point out that the court has held that the conduct of a local authority (see *Re Dundalk Water Supply Scheme, EC Commission v Ireland* Case 45/87 [1989] 1 CMLR 225, legally distinct from the state in municipal law, and even the conduct of a body constituted under private law, supported by the state, may be *j* attributed to the state for the purposes of the application of art 30 (see *EC Commission v Ireland* Case 249/82 [1982] ECR 4005). It is not therefore the legal nature of the Pharmaceutical Society which would be sufficient to prevent its actions from being classified as 'public measures' (see *Vereniging van Vlaamse Reisbureaus v Sociale Dienst van de Plaatselijke en Gewestelijke Overheidsdiensten* Case 311/85 [1989] 4 CMLR 213) and

therefore to remove them from the scope of art 30 if their effects on intra-Community
*a* trade infringed the prohibition laid down in that provision.

16. With that difficulty resolved, let us go on to consider the provisions in question in
the light of the prohibition of measures having equivalent effect. It is complained that
the rule against substitution excludes from the market imported products which are,
from the therapeutic point of view, identical or equivalent to the national products
manufactured by the same company or group of companies or under licence and which
*b* differ from the national products only in their trade name.

17. The first point to be made here is that, if there were no such rules, purchases of
PL(PI) products by pharmacists would probably increase, as the situation prior to 1986
shows. However, is it automatically to be assumed, on the basis of a reading of the court's
judgment in *Procureur du Roi v Dassonville* Case 8/74 [1974] ECR 837, that the measures
in question must be considered contrary to art 30? On a close analysis of the situation, I
*c* firmly reject that view. Let us consider for that purpose first of all the judgments of the
court which seem to me to be the most relevant in this regard.

18. In its judgment in *Blesgen v Belgium* Case 75/81 [1982] ECR 1211 esp at 1229
(para 9) the court held that the prohibition on the sale of spirits of an alcoholic strength
exceeding 22° in drink retailing establishments was not incompatible with art 30. It
stated that such a measure, applicable to national and imported products alike, had *no
d connection with imports* and, *for that reason*, was not of such a nature as to impede trade
between member states. More recently, in its judgment in *Duphar BV v Netherlands* Case
238/82 [1984] ECR 523 the court held that a prohibition on reimbursing the costs of
certain medicinal products in order to maintain a balanced health care budget, *in a
national context where most of the medicinal products consumed are imported*, was not a
measure having equivalent effect either. The court stated that such a measure 'cannot *in
e itself be regarded* as constituting a restriction on the freedom to import guaranteed by
Article 30 of the Treaty' if the list in question was drawn up in a non-discriminatory
manner as regards imported products (at 541 (para 20); my emphasis).

19. Let me say right away that, considered in the light of that case law, the contested
measures are not, in my view, to be regarded as constituting a barrier to trade.

*f* 20. The Divisional Court considered that the measures involved in this case expressed
'the normal rule of commerce'. The appellants in the main proceedings and the
Commission challenge that view: they argue that the rule that the supplier must supply
what has been ordered is irrelevant in this context; the market in medicinal products is
quite special; doctors are not independent economic agents, since they are governed by
public law and are not subject to commercial necessities.

*g* 21. In my view, that argument is not in any way inconsistent with the proposition
that what the doctor prescribes must be supplied.

22. First of all, I think that it is not difficult to show that in an ordinary commercial
transaction the principle pacta sunt servanda cannot be considered to be a measure having
equivalent effect. This may be illustrated by a very simple example. Two member states
in southern Europe each have a distinct make of vehicles whose ranges were, until quite
*h* recently, identical. Let us suppose that car dealers in one of those states fulfil orders for
cars of the national make by supplying identical vehicles of the other state's make. This
would clearly stimulate imports. However, if such practices were brought before the
courts, they would undoubtedly be declared unlawful under the law of obligations. No
one would imagine that the rule pacta sunt servanda could be declared contrary to art 30.
It would simply be a matter of drawing the inferences from the customers' choices.
*j* However, the volume of imports would vary, depending on whether or not the
contractual principles were observed. Yet clearly those principles are in themselves
unconnected with the imports.

23. Although doctors, as such, are not economic agents or consumers, their writing of
prescriptions, unlike the individual choices of consumers, involves personal and ethical
responsibility which in some cases may lead to judicial sanctions. That fact, far from

weakening the comparison with the private consumer, reinforces it. At issue here are the rules for ensuring that doctors' decisions are respected.

24. In 10 out of 12 member states it is for doctors alone to decide which pharmaceutical products to prescribe and their choice must be strictly respected. The absolute nature of that choice is, in my view, no more qualified by the various rules in force in the United Kingdom referred to in the proceedings ('black list', the obligations to prescribe a generic name in certain cases) than is the judge's independence by the provisions of law determining the powers and duties of his office. That right of choice must be compared with the sole right of choice that the patient may exercise: whether to have the products he has been prescribed supplied to him or not. The Treaty has no injurious effect on the conceptions which underlie those rules and which the member states have sanctioned in adopting such arrangements. In that regard, the Commission's argument suggesting that under the normal rule of commerce the patient may accept a product different from the one prescribed must be rejected. It ignores the fact that, in the national systems, a medicinal product is obtained on the decision of the doctor alone. Although the patient may tell the doctor of his preferences and apprehensions, it is the doctor alone who finally takes the decision on his own responsibility. I am surprised that at the hearing distinctions were drawn according to whether a medicinal product is to be supplied under the national health service or as a part of private treatment. The unicity of ethical rules cannot be servered according to the manner in which the financial costs are borne. Could one imagine the lawyer's duty to maintain professional confidentiality varying in strictness depending on whether or not his fees are covered by legal aid?

25. More generally, the argument concerning the public law status of doctors practising in the national health service seems to me to be beside the point: the question put by the Court of Appeal is not whether the conduct of British doctors should be regarded as constituting a set of 'public measures' infringing art 30, nor is it whether the requirements of Community law are disregarded at the stage when the choice is made by the doctor: the question is whether *compliance with that choice* is itself contrary to the Treaty.

26. As it stands at present, Community law cannot deprive the member states of their powers relating to the definition of the roles of professional persons providing health care. The effect of the national rules described above is that the consumption of medicinal products obtainable on prescription, and therefore pharmacists' demand for them, is determined by decisions taken by doctors. That is why the pharmaceutical companies' extensive efforts to provide and distribute information and the campaigns to increase the awareness of social security institutions in order to try to rationalise expenditure on health care are directed at the medical profession. The peculiar standpoint adopted by the API therefore appears to be this: since the prescribing of PL(PI) products by doctors is insufficient, the rules of the game must be changed by giving pharmacists the possibility of 'interpreting' prescriptions. Now, whilst that possibility may, in the British context, stimulate imports, it seems wrong to me to deduce from it a contrario that compliance with prescriptions itself creates a restriction incompatible with art 30. However, that is the deduction which the API invites the court to make.

27. In its observations the API argues that PL(PI) products must be able to compete with national brands. My own view could not be better expressed: to compete with national brands supposes competition at the point where it *must* take place. Let me be more explicit. If the API considers that the equivalence of the imported products with national brands involves requirements other than the formal equality of access to the market provided by the PL(PI) system, then it is for the API to take steps, where necessary, to ensure that they are observed both as regards the products (taking action against any abuses of trade mark rights) and as regards the context of prescriptions (taking action against possible obstacles to advertising, for example). But, because the concept of a measure having equivalent effect supposes that such a measure in itself restrict imports, art 30 certainly cannot be prayed in aid in order to obtain a change in the rules applicable

to the dispensing of prescriptions. The postman, it is said, is not responsible for bad news.

*a*   I therefore consider that the contested measures constitute 'the ancillary links in the chain', to repeat an expression used at the hearing.

28. As regards the rules in question, I firmly maintain that the only requirement which Community law must impose here is that the rules applicable to the dispensing of medical prescriptions must be absolutely neutral, regardless of the product prescribed. If this is the case, as in this instance, the prohibition of 'substitution' 'cannot *in itself* be

*b*   regarded as constituting a restriction on the freedom to import guaranteed by Article 30 of the Treaty' (see *Duphar BV v Netherlands* Case 238/82 [1984] ECR 523 at 541 (para 20); my emphasis).

29. In order to avoid any ambiguity, let me make it clear that my approach is not based on the concept of 'mandatory requirements' as defined in *Rewe-Zentral AG v Bundesmonopolverwaltung für Branntwein* Case 120/78 [1979] ECR 649 (*Cassis de Dijon*) and

*c*   in subsequent judgments. 'Mandatory requirements' apply to measures which constitute obstacles to trade. I hope that I have shown that this is not the position in the case of the contested measures now under consideration.

30. If the court decides to adopt the view I have proposed, it will not have to consider whether the measures at issue may possibly be justified under art 36.

31. For my part, I will be brief on this point, in view of the very clear arguments

*d*   which seem to me to preclude the contested measures from being regarded as contrary to art 30. If, however, the court should consider that they are contrary to art 30, could it regard them as justified on the grounds of the protection of public health or the protection of industrial and commercial property?

32. In my view, there can be no doubt that a precise definition of the doctor's and pharmacist's roles represents a guarantee for the patient. Faithfulness in dispensing a

*e*   prescription is the corollary of the doctor's responsibility and no doubt the patient's confidence in the treatment prescribed by him largely depends on it. More particularly, it cannot be ruled out that the loss of the 'placebo effect' or the presence of the 'anxiety factor' give rise to risks which the prohibition of 'substitution' is intended to prevent.

33. The Commission, however, contends that other, less restrictive, means could

*f*   safeguard the aims in question. It mentions the possibility of obtaining the patient's agreement to 'substitution' or of providing information to the patient and, secondly, the introduction of prescription forms all bearing the letters 'PL(PI)' which the doctor could cross out if he wished.

34. As regards the patient's agreeing to 'substitution', I would point out that such an arrangement would be very formalistic and would take no account of the specific situation of the patient, who in most cases is not able to appreciate the significance of

*g*   such consent when faced with a pharmacist, a professional person, who is urging him to accept a brand different from that prescribed by his doctor. Moreover, and most important of all, I think that it would be dangerous to open by implication the way to a situation where the substantial profit resulting from 'substitution' alone would be the pharmacist's main motive for bringing it about.

*h*   35. The second possibility would amount to introducing a presumption of an 'alternative' prescription for the PL(PI) product which the doctor could rebut by crossing out the relevant words or letters printed on the prescription form. The formal responsibility of the practitioner would thus be formally respected.

36. At this juncture I must raise two queries designed to warn against the disadvantages of such a solution, which to my mind is more appealing than convincing.

*j*   37. The first is prompted by the observations of the United Kingdom: would not the position in which PL(PI) products would thus be placed prove to be discriminatory in relation to that of other products, perhaps imported directly, that are strictly equivalent?

38. The second is my own: can we treat as a matter of no account how such a 'presumption' would be viewed in medical ethics? In my opinion, the establishment by decisions of this court of a questionable hierarchy of the relevant values is something that

should be avoided. The court has accepted that on the ground of the protection of trade mark rights two different trade marks may be affixed to the same product. That is the *a* source of the dispute before the national court. In order to safeguard the requirements of the free movement of goods which de facto is hindered by that protection of trade marks, would it be comprehensible for the court to adopt a solution which would implicitly but necessarily lead to a change in the arrangements governing medical prescriptions?

39. Finally, it remains to consider whether the prohibition of substitution is justified by the protection of trade mark rights in the event (which was discussed in these *b* proceedings) that trade mark rights would be contravened under national law if a product bearing a trade mark different from that prescribed by the doctor was supplied.

40. The court takes the view that the exercise of rights which national law confers on the proprietor of a trade mark in order to protect its 'specific subject-matter' is not contrary to Community law. In its judgment in *Centrafarm BV v American Home Products Corp* Case 3/78 [1978] ECR 1823 at 1840 (para 11) the court stated: *c*

'. . . the specific subject-matter is in particular the guarantee to the proprietor of the trade-mark that he has the exclusive right to use that trade-mark for the purpose of putting a product into circulation for the first time and therefore his protection against competitors wishing to take advantage of the status and reputation of the mark by selling products *illegally bearing that trade-mark.*' (My emphasis.) *d*

The court explained (at 1840 (paras 12–13)):

'. . . the essential function of the trade-mark . . . is to guarantee the identity of the origin of the trade-marked product to the consumer or ultimate user . . . This guarantee of origin means that *only the proprietor may confer an identity upon the product by affixing the mark.*' (My emphasis.) *e*

The court went on to state (at 1841 (para 17)):

'The right granted to the proprietor to prohibit any unauthorized affixing of his mark to his product accordingly comes within the specific subject-matter of the trade-mark.'

41. If a prescription for product A is dispensed by the supply of product B, the *f* economic interests of the proprietor of trade mark A will certainly be affected. However, if product B is supplied under trade mark B without having been relabelled so as to bear trade mark A, the exclusive right to use the latter trade mark is not called in question at all.

42. In other words, if the 'substitution' of products is not accompanied by any physical *g* operation whereby a third party has usurped—

'the right to affix one or other mark to any part whatsoever of the production or to change the marks affixed by the proprietor to different parts of the production'

(see *Centrafarm BV v American Home Products Corp* Case 3/78 [1978] ECR 1823 at 1841 (para 15)), art 36 of the EEC Treaty cannot profitably be relied on in order to justify the *h* prohibition of the measure in question. In such a case, the product's guarantee of origin cannot in fact be compromised since the medicinal product will be supplied bearing the original marking used by the proprietor of the right.

43. Although I do not believe that I need dwell any longer on this aspect of the case, I would simply point out that the argument calling in aid the protection of trade mark rights as justification for the measure in question, in the event that the court should *j* consider the measure contrary to art 30, would give the 'prescribed' brand an undue competitive advantage.

44. I indicated earlier what was essentially at stake in the problem submitted to the court. Nevertheless, I am fully aware of the risks entailed in the prescribing by doctors, and therefore the actual importation, of parallel products. The difficulty is quite clearly

this: does Community law include requirements other than formal equality of access to
a   the market in the case of products such as those covered by a PL(PI) licence?

45. When considering this question it is necessary to bring to mind what is clearly at
the root of the proceedings brought before the national court: first of all, the difficulty
for PL(PI) products to establish themselves on a market characterised by the prescribing
habits of national medical practitioners. In this regard, the assertion that advertising
directed towards national practitioners is ineffectual is, I think, questionable. Doctors'
b   lack of commercial interest is the same in the case of all medicinal products, whether
imported or not, and yet it does not appear that companies are abandoning the promotion
of their products. It was indeed contended at the hearing that the advertising of PL(PI)
products by parallel importers is unlawful in domestic law. In any event, the course
chosen by the API has not given us any cause to test any such restrictions against the
requirements of Community law.

c   46. However, as I have said, it is in trade mark rights that the real difficulty lies. The
Commission, which has devoted more than half of its observations to this subject, tells
the court that if the possibilities of relabelling were open to parallel importers, the
problems of this case would be resolved. It also invites the court to clarify its judgment
in *Centrafarm BV v American Home Products Corp* Case 3/78 [1978] ECR 1823 as regards
the question whether the exercise of trade mark rights, and more precisely the registering
d   of two different trade marks in respect of the same product, is contrary to Community
law if it leads to the partitioning of markets, or whether it is necessary for such an effect
to be intended, as that judgment appears to suggest.

47. Having regard to the terms of the reference now before it, the court clearly does
not have to consider that question in order to confirm or qualify the terms of the decision
in *Centrafarm BV v American Home Products Corp*. I would merely observe that the API's
e   strategy is not so much expressly to call that decision in question as to attempt to use it
in order to prove an intention to partition markets. Obviously I shall be careful not to
assess the chances of success of any actions which may be brought on the latter basis.

48. In conclusion, I propose that the court should answer the questions put to it by
the Court of Appeal as follows: the adoption, by a body created by the state and possessing
f   rights and powers derogating from the generally applicable rules of law, of an ethical
rule the non-observance of which may lead to disciplinary proceedings may constitute a
public measure for the purpose of art 30 of the EEC Treaty; a national provision whereby
a pharmacist is in all events required, when dispensing a prescription designating a
medicinal product by its trade mark or its registered name, to supply exclusively a
product bearing that mark or name is not incompatible with art 30 of the EEC Treaty
g   even where it precludes the supply by the pharmacist of a product of equivalent value,
authorised by the national authorities under provisions adopted in accordance with the
judgment in *de Peijper* Case 104/75 [1976] ECR 613 and manufactured by the same
company or the same group of companies, or by the owner of a licence from that
company, but bearing a mark or a name used for that product in a member state which
is different from that mentioned in the prescription.

h

18 May. **THE COURT OF JUSTICE** delivered the following judgment.

1. By orders of 30 July 1987, which were received at the court registry on 7 September
1987, the Court of Appeal of England and Wales referred to the court for a preliminary
ruling under art 177 of the EEC Treaty three questions on the interpretation of arts 30
j   and 36 of the Treaty in order to enable it to determine whether certain national measures
concerning pharmaceutical products supplied only on prescription are compatible with
those provisions.

2. The questions arose in two sets of proceedings between, on the one hand, the
Association of Pharmaceutical Importers and its members, who carry out parallel imports
of pharmaceutical products from other member states which they then market in the

United Kingdom, and, on the other, the Pharmaceutical Society of Great Britain (Case 266/87) and the Secretary of State for Social Services (Case 267/87).

3. In order to comply with the judgment of the court in *de Peijper* Case 104/75 [1976] ECR 613, the United Kingdom introduced a simplified procedure for granting marketing authorisations for parallel imports of proprietary medicinal products having the same therapeutic effects as a product already authorised in the United Kingdom and produced by the same manufacturer or group of manufacturers or by a person licensed by the manufacturer of the product already authorised.

4. It appears from the documents before the court that of the 220 or so products in respect of which licences have been issued under the simplified procedure about 50 are marketed under a brand name which differs from that of the equivalent product previously authorised in the United Kingdom. It is also not in dispute that, even in such cases, pharmacists have often supplied the parallel import when dispensing a prescription specifying the brand of product previously authorised. That practice is explained by the fact that the parallel imports cost pharmacists less and thus enable them to obtain a higher profit margin.

5. Section 58(2) of the Medicines Act 1968 prohibits the sale by retail, or the supply in circumstances corresponding to a retail sale, of certain pharmaceutical products except in accordance with a prescription issued by a practitioner (a doctor, a dentist or a veterinary practitioner). As a general rule, a practitioner is free either to prescribe the medicinal product in question by its generic name or to prescribe a proprietary medicinal product by its brand name.

6. The Pharmaceutical Society of Great Britain, which is the pharmacists' professional body, has adopted a code of ethics and guidance notes which, inter alia, prohibit a pharmacist from substituting, except in an emergency, any other product for a product specifically named in the prescription, even if he believes that the therapeutic effect and quality of the other products are identical. The same rules also provide that a pharmacist should not deviate from the prescriber's instructions when dispensing a prescription except where this is necessary in order to protect the health of the patient.

7. Having regard to the above-mentioned practice of some pharmacists of dispensing products which were the subject of parallel imports and which bear a brand name other than that indicated in the prescription, the council of the society published an official statement on 12 July 1986 confirming that the above-mentioned rules of professional ethics 'apply to imported medicines as well as those produced for the United Kingdom market'. It is that statement, which the society refuses to revoke, which is the subject of the main proceedings in Case 266/87.

8. According to a statement agreed by the parties to the main proceedings in Case 267/87 and submitted by the Court of Appeal, approximately 95% of the pharmaceutical products supplied on prescription are supplied under the national health service. Under that service, the United Kingdom government gives doctors the freedom, subject to certain exceptions, to prescribe proprietary medicinal products under their proprietary name, although it encourages them to prescribe them under generic names. Under the Terms of Service for Chemists as set out in Pt I of Sch 4 to the National Health Service (General Medical and Pharmaceutical Services) Regulations 1974, SI 1974/160 (as substituted by SI 1985/290), pharmacists are required to supply the products specified in prescriptions. If a doctor has used his freedom to prescribe a product by its proprietary name, only the product bearing that name may therefore be supplied by the pharmacist. It is the application of that rule to parallel imports of proprietary medicinal products which is the subject of the main proceedings in Case 267/87.

9. After noting, following the publication of the above-mentioned statement by the Pharmaceutical Society of Great Britain and the simultaneous application of the terms of service to imported products, that parallel imports of proprietary medicinal products bearing a brand name different from that of the product previously authorised in the United Kingdom had practically ceased, the Association of Pharmaceutical Importers and

its members challenged those two measures before the Divisional Court ([1987] BTLC
*a* 196) and, when their application was dismissed, they then appealed to the Court of
Appeal (see [1987] 3 CMLR 939).

10. The Court of Appeal stayed the proceedings and referred the following questions
to the court for a preliminary ruling in Case 266/87:

'1. Is a national rule of a Member State inconsistent with Article 30 of the EEC
*b* Treaty where it requires a pharmacist, in response to a prescription calling for a
medicinal product by its trade-mark or proprietary name, to dispense only a product
bearing that trade-mark or proprietary name where the effect of such a rule is to
prevent the pharmacist from dispensing a therapeutically equivalent product
licensed by the competent national authorities pursuant to rules adopted in
conformity with the judgment of the Court of Justice in Case 104/75 [*de Peijper*
*c* [1976] ECR 613] and manufactured by the same company or group of companies
or by a licensee of that company but bearing a trade-mark or proprietary name
applied to it in another Member State which differs from the trade-mark or
proprietary name appearing in the prescription?

2. In the event of the first question being answered in the affirmative is such a
national rule justifiable on grounds of protection of public health or the protection
*d* of industrial or commercial property?

3. In either event was the statement of the Council of the Pharmaceutical Society
of Great Britain published in the Pharmaceutical Journal on 12 July 1986 or its
decision as set out in its letter of 12 August 1986 not to revoke that statement a
"measure" within the meaning of Article 30 of the EEC Treaty?'

*e* 11. In Case 267/87 the Court of Appeal referred for a preliminary ruling two questions
which are essentially identical to the first two questions in Case 266/87. For that reason,
the court decided, by order of 11 November 1987, to join the two cases for the purposes
of the written procedure, the oral procedure and the judgment.

12. Reference is made to the report for the hearing for a fuller account of the facts of
the main proceedings, the applicable national rules, the course of the procedure and the
*f* observations submitted to the court, which are mentioned or discussed hereinafter only
in so far as is necessary for the reasoning of the court.

*Third question*

13. Before the question whether the measures at issue fall under the prohibition in art
30 of the EEC Treaty or whether they are justified under art 36 of the Treaty is considered,
*g* the point raised by the national court's third question, which is whether a measure
adopted by a professional body such as the Pharmaceutical Society of Great Britain may
come within the scope of the said articles, should be resolved.

14. According to the documents before the court, that society, which was incorporated
by royal charter in 1843 and whose existence is also recognised in United Kingdom
legislation, is the sole professional body for pharmacy. It maintains the register in which
*h* all pharmacists must be enrolled in order to carry on their business. As can be seen from
the order for reference, it adopts rules of ethics applicable to pharmacists. Finally, United
Kingdom legislation has established a disciplinary committee within the society which
may impose disciplinary sanctions on a pharmacist for professional misconduct; those
sanctions may even involve his removal from the register. An appeal lies to the High
Court from decisions of that committee.

*j* 15. It should be stated that measures adopted by a professional body on which national
legislation has conferred powers of that nature may, if they are capable of affecting trade
between member states, constitute 'measures' within the meaning of art 30 of the EEC
Treaty.

16. The reply to the third question should therefore be that measures adopted by a
professional body, such as the Pharmaceutical Society of Great Britain, which lays down

rules of ethics applicable to the members of the profession and has a committee on which national legislation has conferred disciplinary powers that could involve removal from *a* the register of persons authorised to exercise the profession may constitute 'measures' within the meaning of art 30 of the EEC Treaty.

*The first two questions*

17. It should be pointed out that under art 30 of the Treaty 'Quantitative restrictions on imports and all measures having equivalent effect shall . . . be prohibited between *b* Member States'. As the court has consistently held (see, in the first place, the judgment in *Procureur du Roi v Dassonville* Case 8/74 [1974] ECR 837), any measure which is capable of hindering, directly or indirectly, actually or potentially, intra-Community trade constitutes a measure having an effect equivalent to a quantitative restriction.

18. According to the order for reference in Case 266/87, it is common ground between the parties to the main proceedings that the 50 or so products imported in parallel, which *c* have brand names different from those of the equivalent products previously authorised in the United Kingdom, were marketed in that member state in significant quantities for several years but their importation practically ceased during the summer of 1986, which is the time when the Pharmaceutical Society of Great Britain published its statement drawing attention to the ethical rule prohibiting pharmacists from substituting another product for a specifically named product even if the other product has identical *d* therapeutic effect and confirming that that rule applied to imported products as well as to domestic products.

19. In those circumstances, and although the existence of a causal link is a matter of dispute between the parties, the court cannot exclude the possibility that, in the particular circumstances of the case, the said rule is capable of hindering intra-Community trade. For that reason, and without there being any need to decide whether a rule prohibiting a *e* pharmacist from substituting another product with the same therapeutic effect for the medicinal product prescribed by the doctor treating the patient generally constitutes a measure having equivalent effect within the meaning of art 30 of the EEC Treaty, it is necessary to consider whether such a rule may be justified under art 36 (second question).

20. In that regard, it should be noted that among the grounds of public interest set *f* out in art 36, only the protection of health could be relevant. A rule prohibiting a trader from substituting, even with the consumer's consent, another product for the brand ordered would go beyond what could be necessary for the protection of industrial and commercial property. It should also be added that, although the court in its judgment in *Centrafarm BV v American Home Products Corp* Case 3/78 [1978] ECR 1823 considered that the proprietor of a trade mark which is protected in one member state is justified under *g* art 36 in preventing a product from being marketed by a third party under the mark in question even if previously that product had been lawfully marketed in another member state under another mark held in the latter state by the same proprietor, it made an express reservation as regards cases in which the practice of using different marks for the same product is for the purpose of artificially partitioning the markets.

21. On the other hand, the rules concerning the relationship between doctors and *h* pharmacists and in particular those rules relating to the attending doctor's freedom to prescribe any product he chooses and to any possibility which the pharmacist may have to dispense a medicinal product other than that prescribed in the prescription are part of the national public health system. As long as those matters have not been regulated by Community legislation, it is for the member states, within the limits laid down in art 36, to decide on the degree to which they wish to protect human health and life and how *j* that degree of protection is to be achieved.

22. There is no evidence in this case to justify a conclusion by the court that a rule prohibiting pharmacists from substituting another medicinal product for one designated by name in the prescription, even if the other product has the same therapeutic effect, goes beyond what is necessary to achieve the objective in view, which is to leave the entire responsibility for the treatment of the patient in the hands of the doctor treating

*a* him. In particular, the court finds itself unable to discount the reasons, based on psychosomatic phenomena, for which, according to the observations submitted by the Pharmaceutical Society of Great Britain and by the governments of several member states, a specific proprietary medicinal product might be prescribed rather than a generic product or any other proprietary medicinal product having the same therapeutic effect.

23. Furthermore, the arguments put forward by the Association of Pharmaceutical Importers do not disclose any evidence that the application of such a general rule to *b* products imported from other member states, in which they may be marketed lawfully, constitutes a means of arbitrary discrimination or a disguised restriction on trade between member states within the meaning of the last sentence of art 36.

24. The reply to the first two questions should therefore be that a national rule of a member state requiring a pharmacist, in response to a prescription calling for a medicinal product by its trade mark or proprietary name, to dispense only a product bearing that *c* trade mark or proprietary name may be justified under art 36 of the EEC Treaty on grounds of the protection of public health even where the effect of such a rule is to prevent the pharmacist from dispensing a therapeutically equivalent product licensed by the competent national authorities pursuant to rules adopted in conformity with the judgment of the Court of Justice in *de Peijper* Case 104/75 [1976] ECR 613 and manufactured by the same company or group of companies or by a licensee of that *d* company but bearing a trade mark or proprietary name applied to it in another member state which differs from the trade mark or proprietary name appearing in the prescription.

*Costs*

25. The costs incurred by the Belgian, Danish and Netherlands governments, the United Kingdom and the Commission of the European Communities, which have *e* submitted observations to the court, are not recoverable. As these proceedings are, in so far as the parties to the main proceedings are concerned, a step in the proceedings pending before the national court, the decision as to costs is a matter for that court.

On those grounds, the court, in answer to the questions submitted to it by the Court of Appeal of England and Wales by orders of 30 July 1987, hereby rules: (1) measures *f* adopted by a professional body such as the Pharmaceutical Society of Great Britain, which lays down rules of ethics applicable to the members of the profession and has a committee on which national legislation has conferred disciplinary powers that could involve the removal from the register of persons authorised to exercise the profession, may constitute 'measures' within the meaning of art 30 of the EEC Treaty; (2) a national rule of a member state requiring a pharmacist, in response to a prescription calling for a medicinal *g* product by its trade mark or proprietary name, to dispense only a product bearing that trade mark or proprietary name may be justified under art 36 of the EEC Treaty on grounds of the protection of public health even where the effect of such a rule is to prevent the pharmacist from dispensing a therapeutically equivalent product licensed by the competent national authorities pursuant to rules adopted in conformity with the *h* judgment of the Court of Justice in *de Peijper* Case 104/75 [1976] ECR 613 and manufactured by the same company or group of companies or by a licensee of that company but bearing a trade mark or proprietary name applied to it in another member state which differs from the trade mark or proprietary name appearing in the prescription.

Agents: *S J Berwin & Co* (for the association); *Walker Martineau* (for the society); *Eric L* *j* *White*, Legal Department of the EC Commission (for the Commission); *Susan Hay*, Treasury Solicitor's Department (for the United Kingdom); *A Reyn*, Director of European Affairs at the Ministry of Foreign Affairs, Foreign Trade and Co-operation with Developing Countries (for the Belgian government); *J Molde*, Legal Adviser at the Ministry of Foreign Affairs (for the Danish government).

Mary Rose Plummer      Barrister.

# Re C (a minor) (wardship: medical treatment)

COURT OF APPEAL, CIVIL DIVISION

LORD DONALDSON OF LYMINGTON MR, BALCOMBE AND NICHOLLS LJJ

19, 20 APRIL 1989

*Ward of court – Jurisdiction – Medical treatment – Terminally ill baby – Nature of medical treatment to be administered to ward – Whether aim of treatment should be to ease suffering or to achieve short prolongation of life.*

A baby was made a ward of court shortly after her birth because the local authority's social services department considered that her parents would have great difficulty in looking after her. Soon after being made a ward it was discovered that the baby had been born seriously brain damaged, that she was severely handicapped and was terminally ill. The question arose as to the appropriate treatment for the baby, the extent to which the medical staff looking after her should seek to prolong her life and whether the baby should receive treatment appropriate to a child who was not handicapped or treatment appropriate to her condition. The local authority applied to the court for directions in the wardship proceedings. The Official Solicitor, as the baby's guardian ad litem, obtained a specialist's report which stated that the aim of treatment of the baby should be to ease her suffering rather than achieve a short prolongation of her life. The judge directed that leave be given to the hospital authorities to treat the ward in such a way that she ended her life peacefully with the least pain, suffering and distress and that the hospital authorities were not required to treat any serious infection which the baby contracted or to set up any intravenous feeding system for her. The Official Solicitor appealed against the terms of the order, contending, inter alia, that the judge had been wrong to direct that treatment of serious infections and intravenous feeding were not necessary.

**Held** – Where a ward of court was terminally ill the court would authorise treatment which would relieve the ward's suffering during the remainder of his or her life but would accept the opinions of the medical staff looking after the ward if they decided that the aim of nursing care should be to ease the ward's suffering rather than achieve a short prolongation of life, and in such circumstances it would be inappropriate to include in the court's directions any specific instructions as to how the ward was to be treated. Accordingly, the Official Solicitor's appeal would be allowed to the extent that the judge's direction that treatment of serious infections and intravenous feeding were not necessary would be deleted (see p 784 *f g*, 788 *e* to *h*, p 789 *a* to *c* and p 790 *c d*, post).

Per curiam. In applications for directions concerning the medical treatment of terminally ill wards of court the court, in giving judgment, should make clear what it is doing and why, what are the reasons leading to the court's decision and what kind of treatment is to be followed or not, as the case may be (see p 788 *j* and p 790 *b d*, post).

## Notes

For the court's jurisdiction over wards of court, see 24 Halsbury's Laws (4th edn) para 576, and for cases on the subject, see 28(2) Digest (Reissue) 911–916, 2220–2248.

For the duties of the Official Solicitor, see 10 Halsbury's Laws (4th edn) para 950, and for cases on the subject, see 16 Digest (Reissue) 238, 2347–2348.

## Cases referred to in judgments

*B (a minor) (wardship: medical treatment), Re* [1981] 1 WLR 1421, CA.

*B (a minor) (wardship: sterilisation), Re* [1987] 2 All ER 206, [1988] AC 199, [1987] 2 WLR 1213, HL.

a  D (a minor) (wardship: sterilisation), Re [1976] 1 All ER 326, [1976] Fam 185, [1976] 2
   WLR 279.
   S D, Re [1983] 3 WWR 618, BC SC; rvsg [1983] 3 WWR 597, BC Prov Ct.

**Appeal**
The Official Solicitor, as guardian ad litem of the second defendant, a baby, C, appealed
from the order made by Ward J on 14 April 1989 on the application of the plaintiffs, the
b  local authority in whom C's care and control were vested, for directions in wardship as to
the appropriate treatment for the ward. The first defendant was C's mother. The facts
are set out in the judgment of Lord Donaldson MR.

Andrew Kirkwood QC for the Official solicitor.
John Leslie for the local authority.
c  Martin J Wood for the mother.

**LORD DONALDSON OF LYMINGTON MR.** Before coming to the substance of
the appeal there is one preliminary matter with which I should deal. Experience suggests
that it is no longer possible to rely on good sense, taste and sensitivity to protect parents
from the invasion of their personal grief in a situation such as this. Nor does this protect
d  health and local authorities and their officers from being harrassed when making difficult
decisions. For this reason the judge imposed a wide ranging injunction in the interests of
C forbidding any inquiries directed to ascertaining the identity of C, her parents, the
local authority, the area health authority and the hospital medical practitioners and staff
having, or having had, care of C. This injunction also extended to restraining the media
by itself, its servants, agents or otherwise from publishing any material which will
e  identify or assist in identifying any of those persons or bodies.
   I personally regret the necessity for any such injunction but have no doubt of its need.
That being so, I have to say that the names of the solicitors involved should not be
published at the present stage because such publication would or might identify the area
in which they practise and suggest, rightly or wrongly, the area in which the relevant
local and area health authorities operate. If, of course, that situation changes, the court
f  will be only too happy to authorise disclosure of that information[1].
   Turning now to the substance of the appeal, I have, most regretfully, to start with one
fundamental and inescapable fact. Baby C is dying and nothing that the court can do,
nothing that the doctors can do and nothing known to medical science can alter that fact.
   The problem of how to treat the terminally ill is as old as life itself. Doctors and nurses
have to confront it frequently, but it is never easy. Parents and relatives have to confront
g  it less often and that makes it all the more difficult for them. Judges are occasionally
faced with it when terminally ill children are wards of court. It is an awesome
responsibility only made easier for them than for parents to the extent that judges are
able to approach it with greater detachment and less emotional involvement.
   The present case is one of the saddest which can be imagined. Not only are we
concerned with a very young baby, but one who became terminally ill before she was
h  even born, a fact which only became apparent at a later date.
   C was born prematurely on 23 December 1988. She is now 16 weeks old. At birth she
was found to be afflicted with a much more serious condition than the usual type of
hydrocephalus. There was not merely a blockage of cerebral spinal fluid within the brain,
but as a result the brain structure itself was poorly formed. Her progress since then and
further examinations have revealed how exceptionally she has been affected, and to that
j  I will return.
   But first I must explain how the court came to be involved. Some time before C was
born and at a time when no one anticipated that she would be born handicapped, the

1   Editor's note. Such an order was subsequently made: see Re C (a minor) (wardship: medical treatment)
    [1989] 2 All ER 791

social services were in possession of information which showed that the parents would have great difficulty in caring for her. This aspect was the subject of long and anxious *a* consideration and it was decided that when she was born an application should be made to make her a ward of court. I must emphasise that this decision was quite unrelated to C's medical condition, which was neither known nor suspected at the time at which it was made. When C was born and it became apparent that she was brain damaged, the only change of plan was a decision to apply for a 14-day place of safety order under the Children and Young Persons Act 1969 to preserve the position until C could be made a *b* ward of court. Once C had become a ward, which happened on 5 January 1989, two weeks after her birth, the court became charged with the obligation of making decisions in the interests of the welfare of C which would otherwise have been solely a matter for her parents.

One of the first decisions which the court had to make was whether or not to agree to the child being operated on to relieve pressure on the brain. This is often done in cases of *c* hydrocephalus with good results, but alas in the case of C all that could be hoped for was that it would prevent her head becoming so enlarged that nursing would become impossible. The damage to her brain had been done before birth and was irreparable.

Those who, understandably, have been moved by the story of C, but who have no personal involvement, have publicly commented that this operation should have been performed. I am bound to say that I think it might have been better if they had first *d* made sure of the facts. In fact, the registrar of the court readily consented to its being undertaken and it was. The actual order was dated 11 January 1989 and it required that C 'who is suffering from congenital hydrocephalus, receive such treatment, including surgical treatment, as is considered medically appropriate' to her condition. It was pursuant to this order that the doctors operated on C and inserted a shunt to relieve pressure on her brain. *e*

At all times since her birth C has received the finest and most caring medical and nursing attention which this country has to offer. However, the time came when a decision had to be made on what further treatment should be provided. In a critical situation such as this such decisions should not be, and are not, taken without wide consultation. And so it came about that the local authority's medical and social services *f* departments became involved. The essential problem was what treatment should be given in the best interests of C if, as sooner or later was inevitable, she suffered some infection or illness over and above the handicaps from which she was already suffering. In the middle of last month a social worker expressed the view that in such a situation the court would expect the doctors to embark on 'treatment appropriate to a non handicapped child'. The legal department of the local authority, on the other hand, expressed the view that C should 'receive such treatment as is appropriate to her *g* condition'.

For my part, I have no doubt that the legal department was right and the social worker was wrong. You do not treat a blind child as if she was sighted, or one with a diseased heart as if she was wholly fit. But this difference of opinion created a problem for Dr W, the physician in charge of C, for his paediatric colleague, Dr S, and for the nursing staff. *h* Sooner or later he or the local authority would have been bound to seek instructions from the court because, as Heilbron J said in *Re D (a minor) (wardship: sterilisation)* [1976] 1 All ER 326 at 335, [1976] Fam 185 at 196:

'... once a child is a ward of court, no important step in the life of that child, can be taken without the consent of the court ...'

*j*

In the circumstances, and quite rightly, the local authority decided to consult the court sooner rather than later. In previous correspondence, which was of course made available to the judge, Dr W had raised the question of what he should do if the time came when it proved impossible to feed C through a syringe, in itself a procedure fraught with difficulty. In such circumstances should he resort to the use of a nasal-gastric tube? If C vomited, should he set up an intravenous drip? If C developed a terminal respiratory

infection, should she be given antibiotics? All these were legitimate and difficult
*a* questions, given the sad but fundamental truth that C was dying and the only question
was how soon this would happen.

Faced with these problems, the judge invited the intervention of the Official Solicitor,
who asked one of the nation's foremost paediatricians to examine C and to make
recommendations. I do not name him, simply because it might serve to identify where
C is being treated; I refer simply to 'the professor'. The professor reported as follows and
*b* I read from his report:

'The records revealed that at birth she had a much more serious condition than
the usual type of hydrocephalus. The detailed investigations which were done
showed that there was not merely a blockage of cerebro-spinal fluid within the
brain, but that the brain structure itself was poorly formed. Thus the operation that
*c* was done to relieve the pressure within the brain was no more than a palliative
procedure to prevent her head from becoming so excessive large that nursing would
be impossible. The operation could not be expected to restore brain function. [C's]
appearance is of a tiny baby. Although she is 16 weeks old, she is the size of a 4 week
baby apart from her head, which is unusually large by way of being tall and thin—
squashed because of sleeping on her side. She lies quiet until handled and then she
*d* cries as if irritated. Her eyes move wildly in an uncoordinated way and she does not
appear to see. (Her pupils do not respond to light so it is most unlikely that the
mechanism for vision is present). She did not respond to very loud noises that I
made, though the nurses said that she sometimes seems startled to their loud noises.
However, my impression was that she did not hear, or had very poor hearing. She
holds her limbs in a stiff flexed position. More detailed examination suggested that
*e* she had generalised spasticity of all her limbs as a result of the brain damage. The
only social response she makes is the irritable crying when handled, though
sometimes she can be pacified by stroking her face. She does not smile and does not
respond in any other way. The only certain evidence of her feeling or appreciating
events is the report of her quietening when her face is stroked. Thus she does not
have the developmental skills and abilities of a normal new born baby. It is
*f* inconceivable that appreciable skills will develop, bearing in mind that there has
been no progress during the past four months. She has severe brain damage. She is
very thin and has not gained weight despite devoted nursing care at [the hospital].
She is receiving regular small doses of the sedative Chloral. If she does not receive
that she crys "as if in pain", though the carers are unsure where the pain originates.
I do not believe that there is any treatment which will alter the ultimate prognosis,
*g* which appears to be hopeless. She has massive handicap as a result of a permanent
brain lesion. Her handicap appears to be a mixture of severe mental handicap,
blindness, probable deafness and spastic cerebral palsy of all four limbs. In addition,
although given a normal amount of food, her body is not absorbing or using it in
the normal way so that she is not growing. I do not believe that she can be said to be
enjoying her life and I find it hard to know if she is experiencing very much, though
*h* the reports of irritable crying suggest that certain things upset her. She is receiving
outstandingly devoted care . . . which could not be replicated in many children's
units, or in many homes. The high standard of care makes it difficult to forecast
how long she will live . . . In the event of her acquiring a serious infection, or being
unable to take feeds normally by mouth I do not think it would be correct to give
antibiotics, to set up intravenous fusions or nasal-gastric feedings regimes. Such
*j* action would be prolonging a life which has no future and which appears to be
unhappy for her. However, the opinions of the local nurses and carers should be
taken into account for they know her well, show great love to her, and have a feeling
for her needs that an outsider cannot have. Thus if they believed she was in pain or
would suffer less by a particular course of action, it would be correct to consider that
course of action, always bearing in mind the balance between short-term gain and
needless prolongation of suffering.'

It will be seen that the professor took the view that the goal should be to ease the suffering of C rather than to achieve a short prolongation of her life. But he did not rule *a* out the giving of antibiotics, intravenous fusions or nasal-gastric feeding if this would achieve this result. Above all, he felt that, in reaching decisions as events unfolded, the opinions of the local nurses and carers should be given the greatest possible weight.

In giving the reasons for his decision Ward J said:

'That poor baby has now been nursed and attended by the hospitals with a degree *b* of devotion to duty which deserves the very highest commendation, and I pay tribute to those who have had part in the care of this ward, and I give my thanks to those for so looking after my ward on my behalf. I have had the advantage of a report by an eminent professor of paediatrics, instructed by the Official Solicitor, whom I caused to become involved in this matter to represent the interests of the baby. The professor observes in his report that the outstandingly devoted care she *c* has received could not be replicated in many children's units or in many children's homes, and it is important that that should receive its proper tribute and its proper commendation. Sadly, notwithstanding that devotion this child has not prospered. I have had the benefit of reading the report and hearing the evidence of Dr W, who is the consultant physician at the hospital, a physician of 21 years' experience, and I give him my thanks for the assistance he has given me. He reports to me that this *d* baby has made virtually no progress since her birth.'

I omit some other matters and quote again from the judge's judgment, where he said: 'The damage which she has suffered is quite exceptionally severe.' Then he set out the evidence in support of that proposition and continued:
*e*

'The medical evidence satisfies me that the damage to the cortex of the brain is gross and abnormally severe. The cortex of the brain is that part of the brain which serves the higher functions; those functions of intellect which make human life distinguishable, perhaps, from other forms of life. That damage, moreover, is irreparable, and about that all the medical witnesses are wholly agreed. There is, *f* therefore, no prospect of a happy life for this child, sadly; no prospect whatever. The prognosis, in the conclusion of [the professor], is that it is inconceivable that appreciable skills will ever develop, and that is, of course, confirmed by the total ·failure of progress in these few short weeks of her life. There is, in the united opinion of the medical experts, no treatment which will alter that prognosis, and the prognosis is therefore one of hopelessness. I am therefore dealing with a child *g* massively handicapped by a mixture of severe or permanent brain lesions, blindness, probable deafness and generalised spastic cerebral palsy of all four limbs.'

The judge then referred to the decision of this court in *Re B (a minor) (wardship: medical treatment)* [1981] 1 WLR 1421. There the facts were very different. The child suffered from Down's Syndrome and would be very handicapped mentally and physically. *h* Nevertheless, she could have a life expectancy of 20 to 30 years. She developed an intestinal blockage which would be fatal within a few days unless operated on, but could be cured by operation. There was a difference of medical opinion on whether, in all the circumstances, it was in B's best interests to operate. The parents, who were consulted, thought that it would not. At an earlier stage the judge had taken the view that the operation should be performed but later, when the difference of medical opinion *j* emerged, the judge felt that he should accept the view of the parents. This court disagreed. It held that the judge's duty was to have regard solely to what was in the best interests of the child and that it was not for the court to decide that the child should not have the chance of the normal life span of a mongoloid child with the handicap, defects and life of such a child.

C does not have any such option. She is, as I have already said, dying, and there is no
*a* medical or surgical treatment which can alter this fact. The judge continued in his
judgment, saying:

> 'But here I am quite satisfied that the damage is severe and irreparable. In so far
> as I can assess the quality of life, which as a test in itself raises as many questions as it
> can answer, I adjudge that any quality to life has already been denied to this child
> because it cannot flow from a brain incapable of even limited intellectual function.
*b* Inasmuch as one judges, as I do, intellectual function to be a hallmark of our
> humanity, her functioning on that level is negligible if it exists at all. Coupled with
> her total physical handicap, the quality of her life will be demonstrably awful and
> intolerable . . . Asking myself what capacity she has to interact mentally, socially,
> physically, I answer none. This is her permanent condition.'

*c*      It was shortly after this that the judge, in a brief passage in his judgment, failed to
express himself with his usual felicity. He said:

> 'Putting the interests of this child first and putting them foremost so that they
> override all else, and in fulfilment of the awesome responsibility which Parliament
> has entrusted on me, I direct that leave be given to the hospital authorities to treat
*d* the ward to die, to die with the greatest dignity and the least of pain, suffering and
> distress.'

No judge giving an extempore judgment has not, at one time or another, realised that
he has not expressed himself as he intended. For this reason, and because the reasons for
a decision in one case are published and are rightly taken into account in deciding others,
it has long been the practice for judges in appropriate cases to make small revisions in the
*e* wording of their judgments when they receive a transcript from the shorthand writers.
So it was in this case. The judge revised the first sentence of that passage to read:

> 'I direct that leave be given to the hopsital authorites to treat the ward in such a
> way that she may end her life and die peacefully with the greatest dignity and the
> least of pain, suffering and distress.'

*f*
Unfortunately, the formal order also contained the misleading phrase 'treat the minor
to die'. Such orders are not seen by the judge unless he specifically asks to approve its
wording, and the judge was at first unaware of its phraseology. When it was drawn to
his attention, he at once exercised his powers under the slip rule to amend that part of
the order to read: 'the hospital authority be at liberty to allow her life to come to an end
peacefully and with dignity.'
*g*
     The Official Solicitor in appealing to this court does not take issue on this part of the
judge's order. Nor do the local authority or the mother, both of whom have been
represented. All concerned accept that the judge correctly directed himself that the first
and paramount consideration was the well-being, welfare and interests of C as required
by the decision of this court in *Re B (a minor) (wardship: medical treatment)* and by the
*h* House of Lords in a later and different case with the same name, *Re B (a minor) (wardship:
sterilisation)* [1987] 2 All ER 206 at 211, [1988] AC 199 at 202 per Lord Hailsham LC.
     Counsel for the local authority nevertheless felt it his duty to direct our attention to a
decision of the British Columbia Supreme Court in *Re SD* [1983] 3 WWR 618, while
submitting that the facts were very different. In so doing he was fulfilling the
fundamental duty of members of the legal profession to assist the courts in the
*j* administration of justice, regardless of the views or interests of their client. He was
wholly right so to do. In the event, I am fully satisfied that it does nothing to cast doubts
on the correctness of his clients', and the judge's, view that the advice of the professor
should be accepted. It was another case in which a child suffered from hydrocephalus,
but the child concerned was very much older. The child had twice been operated on to
implant a shunt and the question was whether he should now undergo a third operation.

He was undoubtedly severely handicapped, but not as severely as some in his class at the
hospital school. If a third operation were to be performed he would probably continue *a*
to live as he had done before and would do so for some years. The parents thought that
there should be no operation and that he should be allowed to die at once. The higher
court authorised the operation, saying it was too simplistic to say, as did the parents, that
the child would be allowed to die in peace. There was a real possibility that, without the
operation, the child would endure in a state of progressive disability and pain. That is a
wholly different case.                                                                    *b*
     The Official Solicitor in bringing this appeal had three objectives. The first was to
question the propriety of an order expressed to be 'liberty to treat the minor to die'. As I
hope I have made clear, neither Ward J nor anyone else would uphold such phraseology
and he himself amended it. Second, the Official Solicitor wished to question that part of
the order of the judge which appeared to provide that in no circumstances should certain
treatment be undertaken. To that I will return in a moment. Third, the Official Solicitor *c*
wished to allay anxieties in some quarters that the hospital staff were treating C in a way
designed to bring about her death. These anxieties, while no doubt sincerely felt, were
wholly without foundation and, when expressed, were deeply wounding to the dedicated
staff caring for C who, as the professor said, were providing C with devoted care which
could not be replicated in many children's units.
     Let me make it clear that, in my judgment, the Official Solicitor has been quite right *d*
to adopt this course. His first objective was achieved by the judge himself, but the Official
Solicitor was not to know that this would occur. His third objective has, I hope, now
been achieved. There remains only the second objective.
     In para (4) of his order the judge ordered:

     'The hospital authority do continue to treat the minor within the parameters of *e*
     the opinion expressed by [the professor] in his report of 13.iv.1989 which report is
     not to be disclosed to any person other than the hospital authority.'

However, in para (3) he had ordered:

     '. . . but it shall not be necessary either, (a) to prescribe and administer antibiotics *f*
     to treat any serious infection which the minor might contract; or (b) to set up
     intravenous fusions or nasal gastric feeding regimes for the minor.'

     These two parts of the order are inconsistent with one another because the professor
did not wholly rule out these steps if the local nurses and carers took a different view
when the question arose for decision. He merely said that he did not think that such
measures were correct if the object was simply to prolong a life which had no future and *g*
appeared to be unhappy for C. I have no doubt that he would have considered revising
his opinion, and indeed would have revised it, if the local nurses and carers had thought
that such treatment would relieve C's suffering during such life as remained for her.
     The second difficulty which arises out of this part of the order is the ban on any
publication of the professor's advice. This was one of those comparatively rare cases of *h*
special difficulty and sensitivity in which the public interest requires that, subject to
maintaining the privacy of those concerned, the court's decision and the reasons for it
should be open to public scrutiny. The formal order itself will not be likely to be very
informative, and in any event it would require considerable editing to remove any clues
as to the identity of those concerned. What is required in such cases is that the judge
should give judgment in open court, taking all appropriate measures to preserve the *j*
personal privacy of those concerned. However, such a judgment can set out all the
relevant facts and the medical and other considerations of which the judge has taken
account. Thus, in this judgment I have quoted extensively from the professor's advice
without, I hope, giving any clue as to his identity or that of C, her parents or the authority
involved.

a No new principle is involved in this appeal. I would allow the appeal to the extent of deleting the whole of para (3) of the judge's order. I do so for two reasons. First, the inclusion of specific instructions as to treatment is potentially inconsistent with para (4), which adopts the professor's advice. Second, para (3) of the order as amended starts with these words:

b  'The hospital authority be at liberty to treat the minor to allow her life to come to an end peacefully and with dignity and, pursuant to such leave, it is directed that the hospital authority shall administer such treatment to the minor as might relieve her from pain, suffering and distress inter alia by sedation . . .'

Now, the specific references to treatment are, of course, amply covered by the professor's advice. But the opening words seem to me to have a potential for giving rise to misunderstanding and are, therefore, much better avoided and now deleted. To that c extent I would allow the appeal.

**BALCOMBE LJ.** This is a case where baby C was made a ward of court for reasons wholly unconnected with her present state of health. Nevertheless, once a child is a ward of court, no major step in his or her life may be taken without the leave of the court. It is clear that the issue with which the judge was, and with which this court is now, faced d involves such a major step: should the doctors persevere with treatment to prolong a life which, in the words of the professor, 'has no future and which appears to be unhappy for her'?

This is a problem of a kind with which, as a result of advances in medical science, the courts in this and other jurisdictions are increasingly being faced. We have been referred to an English case in this court, *Re B (a minor) (wardship: medical treatment)* [1981] 1 WLR e 1421, where a similar problem arose. On the facts of that case the court decided that the quality of life prospectively open to the child was such that the child's welfare required the court to authorise an operation to remove an intestinal obstruction to a 10-day-old mongoloid child, without which operation she would have died. But Templeman LJ recognised (at 1424) that there might be cases of severe proved damage where the future is so certain and where the life of the child is so bound to be full of pain and suffering f that the court might be driven to a different conclusion. A court can only act on the evidence before it, and I agree with the judge that the evidence here, which has been fully rehearsed by Lord Donaldson MR, establishes that this is indeed such a case.

We were also referred to the Canadian case of *Re SD* [1983] 3 WWR 618, where the court was concerned with the case of a seven-year-old boy with severe brain damage caused by meningitis. The question there was whether an operation to revise a 'shunt', a g plastic tube which drains excess cerebrospinal fluid away from the brain, which had become blocked, should be performed. The evidence there was that, without the shunt revision, which the boy's parents opposed on the ground that he should be allowed to die with dignity rather than to continue to endure a life of suffering, the boy would not necessarily die but might live for months or years. Thus, as McKenzie J said (at 629) that h case was—

  'not a "right to die" situation where the courts are concerned with people who are terminally ill from incurable conditions. Rather it is a question of whether S. has the right to receive appropriate medical and surgical care of a relatively simple kind which will assure to him the continuation of his life, such as it is.'

j The evidence in the present case shows, I repeat, that this is the case of a child terminally ill since, as the professor says in his report: 'I do not believe that there is any treatment which will alter the ultimate prognosis, which appears to be hopeless.'

Courts in the United States of America have also been faced with similar cases and the problem has been the subject of discussion at legal conferences. Nevertheless, neither in this country nor, so far as I know, elsewhere has the legislature attempted to lay down

guidelines for the courts or others faced with a problem of the type that arises in this
case.

For my part, I agree that the judge applied the right test and on the evidence came to a
decision in substance (although initially worded in a way which led to misinterpretation)
not only to which he was entitled to come in the exercise of his discretion, but with
which I agree and believe was right in the circumstances of this case. In a case of this type
it is essential that the court, in giving judgment, should make it clear what it is doing
and why: what are the reasons which lead to the court's decision and what course of
treatment is to be followed, or not, as the case may be. So far as the form of the order is
concerned, it should usually be sufficient to refer to the medical report where, as in the
present case, it is apparent that there are considerations to be taken into account, for
example the opinions of the local nurses and carers, which cannot be conveniently
reduced into a simple form of words contained in the order itself. However, this is a
matter of detail and not of substance; what is important is that the court should make it
clear why it considers the case is one where life-prolonging treatment should be given or
withheld as the case may be. This the judge has done in this case and I agree with his
decision.

I would therefore allow the appeal only to the extent indicated by Lord Donaldson
MR.

**NICHOLLS LJ.** I agree with both judgments.

*Appeal allowed in part. No order for costs.*

Solicitors: *Official Solicitor; A R Sykes,* Bradford (for the local authority); *T I Clough & Co,*
Bradford (for the mother).

                                                        Frances Rustin   Barrister.

*a*

# Re C (a minor) (wardship: medical treatment) (No 2)

COURT OF APPEAL, CIVIL DIVISION

LORD DONALDSON OF LYMINGTON MR, BALCOMBE AND NICHOLLS LJJ

21, 26 APRIL 1989

*b*

*Ward of court – Jurisdiction – Protection of ward – Freedom of publication – Publication of matter likely to be harmful to ward – Jurisdiction of court to restrain publication – Ward terminally ill baby – Court giving directions as to treatment of ward – Newspaper wishing to identify and interview those involved in care and treatment of ward and to publish details of her care and treatment and family background – Whether injunction should be granted prohibiting*

*c* *identification of ward, her parents, hospital where she was being treated or persons having or who had had care of ward or prohibiting soliciting or publication of information about ward or parents.*

The Court of Appeal made an order authorising the treatment of a brain damaged, severely handicapped and terminally ill baby who was a ward of court which would ease

*d* the ward's suffering during the remainder of her life rather than achieve a short prolongation of life and stated that the court would accept the opinions of the medical staff and those looking after the ward at the hospital where she was being cared for as to the appropriate treatment for her. The court also made an injunction prohibiting the publication of material which identified the ward, the parents, the hospital at which she was being treated or any person having care of the ward or who had cared for her, prohibiting the soliciting of information about the ward or her parents from the parents,

*e* the hospital staff or any person having care of the ward or who had cared for her, and prohibiting the publication of such information. The applicant newspaper challenged the imposition of an injunction in such wide terms on the ground that it inhibited informed discussion and comment on an important issue of legitimate public interest. In particular, the newspaper, while accepting that the ward and the parents should not

*f* be identified, asserted that it should be free to publish photographs of and interview those who were involved in the care and treatment of the ward.

**Held** – Since publicity about the medical treatment of the ward of court could affect the quality of care given to her, the public interest in ensuring that the quality of care she was receiving did not suffer required the court, in the interests of the ward, to issue an

*g* injunction prohibiting identification of the ward, the parents, the hospital at which she was being treated or any person having care of the ward or who had cared for her, and the soliciting or publication of information about the ward or her parents, notwithstanding that the ward herself was incapable of being affected by any publicity. Moreover, such an injunction would reinforce the duty of confidentiality owed by those caring for her. Furthermore, the injunction against identifying the parents was justified in order to

*h* protect the wardship jurisdiction since parents might refuse to make a child a ward of court if they thought that they might be identified and singled out for media attention (see p 794 *c* to *j*, p 795 *f j*, p 797 *j* to p 798 *e* and p 800 *b* to *f*, post).

**Notes**

For the court's jurisdiction over wards of court, see 24 Halsbury's Laws (4th edn) para

*j* 576, and for cases on the subject, see 28(2) Digest (Reissue) 911–916, 2220–2248.

**Cases referred to in judgments**

A-G v Newspaper Publishing plc [1987] 3 All ER 276, [1988] Ch 333, [1987] 3 WLR 942, Ch D and CA.

C *(a minor) (wardship: medical treatment), Re* [1989] 2 All ER 782, CA.

X *(a minor) (wardship: restriction on publication), Re* [1975] 1 All ER 697, [1975] Fam 47, *a*
[1975] 2 WLR 335.

X *CC v A* [1985] 1 All ER 53, sub nom *Re X (a minor) (wardship: injunction)* [1984] 1 WLR
1422.

### Application

Mail Newspapers plc, the proprietors of the Daily Mail and the Mail on Sunday, applied *b*
to the Court of Appeal to review the width and terms of the injunctions ordered by Ward
J on 14 April 1989 and reaffirmed by the Court of Appeal on 20 April 1989 restraining,
inter alia, any person from making or causing or permitting to be made any inquiry
directed to ascertaining the identity of a ward of court who was the subject of directions
given by the court as to her treatment, the parents of the ward, the local authority, the
local health authority, hospital or medical practitioners or staff having or who had had *c*
care of the ward. It was further ordered that an injunction be issued to restrain the media
from publishing any material which would identify or assist in identifying any of the
persons or bodies referred to in the first injunction. The facts are set out in the judgment
of Lord Donaldson MR.

*Charles Gray QC* and *Heather Rogers* for the applicants.                                              *d*
*James Munby QC* for the Official Solicitor.
*Angus Moon* for the mother.
*John Leslie* for the local authority.

At the conclusion of the argument the court announced that the injunction would be
substituted for reasons to be given later.                                                             *e*

26 April. The following judgments were delivered.

**LORD DONALDSON OF LYMINGTON MR.** This application is, in a sense, a
postscript to that which we heard and determined on 20 April: see *Re C (a minor)*          *f*
*(wardship: medical treatment)* [1989] 2 All ER 782. However, it would be a mistake to
think that it is not equally important in its own right. It comes to us in the form of an
application rather than an appeal because, due to the urgency of the situation, we were
already seised of the matter by reason of the Official Solicitor's appeal. Had the matter
not already come to this court, the newspaper should and would have applied to the
judge who made the order about which they complain.                                                    *g*
The order of Ward J included the following wide-ranging injunction:

> 'IT IS ORDERED THAT an injunction be made restraining any person from making
> or causing or permitting to be made any enquiry directed to ascertaining the
> identity of 1) The Ward 2) The parents 3) The Local Authority 4) The Area Health
> Authority, hospital or medical practitioners or staff having or having had care of the
> ward. IT IS FURTHER ORDERED THAT an injunction be made restraining the media by  *h*
> itself, servants, agents or otherwise from publishing any material which will identify
> or assist in identifying any of the persons or bodies mentioned in the aforementioned
> injunction.'

None of the parties to the main appeal raised any objection to this injunction and I
only referred to it in my judgment because one of the law reporters sensibly and helpfully  *j*
inquired whether they would be 'publishing any material which will identify or assist in
identifying any of the persons or bodies mentioned in the aforementioned injunction' if,
in reporting our judgments, they identified the solicitors and counsel who had appeared
on the appeal. One of the counsel had a practice which was concentrated in the Leeds
area where Ward J had heard the case and given judgment and the solicitors, other than

the Official Solicitor, had local addresses. After seeking the assistance of counsel and the
a solicitors concerned, we concluded that, as is not unusual in wardship cases, the names of
the solicitors should not be included in any law report, but that there were no sufficient
grounds for extending this anonymity to counsel, which would have represented a
departure from the settled practice. On the other hand, in the light of the fact that C's
expectation of life was short and that the injunction had been imposed in the interests of
her welfare, I said that the point could be looked at again at a later date.

b        After we had given judgment, Mail Newspapers plc, the proprietors of the Daily Mail
and of the Mail of Sunday, to whom I will refer as 'the Mail', applied to us to review the
width and terms of the injunction. Since they were bound by it and had not been heard
in opposition to it, we readily agreed to their being heard and expedited the hearing,
which took place less than 24 hours after we had given judgment on the main appeal. In
the light of that application we reconsidered the injuctive order by Ward J and substituted
c one in different terms. At the same time we announced that, in the light of the
importance of our ruling, we proposed to put our reasons into writing and give them at
a later date. This we now do.

The new injunction which we imposed was in the following terms:

'It is further ordered that an injunction be made restraining, until further Order,
d        any person, whether by himself, his servants or agents or otherwise howsoever, or
in the case of a company, whether by its directors or officers, servants or agents or
otherwise howsoever from: 1. Publishing the name or address or otherwise
identifying: (a) the Ward; (b) the Parents; (c) any Hospital at which the Ward is
being or has been treated; or (d) any natural person having or who has had the care
of the Ward. 2. Soliciting any information relating to the Ward or her parents (other
e        than information already in the public domain) from the parents of the Ward, any
staff at any such hospital as mentioned in para 1(c) above or any such person as is
mentioned in para 1(d) above, provided that no breach of this Order shall be
committed by any person who does no more than enquire of another person as to
whether that person is a person comprised in para 1(d) above; 3. Publishing any
such information as is referred to in para 2 above obtained directly or indirectly
f        from any person referred to in para 2 above.'

The basis of the Mail's application was that the matters dealt with by Ward J and by
this court on appeal raised important issues of legitimate public interest and that the Mail
wished to report the facts and background of the case as fully and accurately as possible
so that discussion and comment could be properly informed and soundly based. While
it was accepted that neither C nor her parents should be identified, it was submitted that
g all newspapers and radio and television media ought to be free to publish photographs of
all who were or had been involved in the care and treatment of C, to make inquiries of
them and others as to her care and treatment and as to the circumstances which led to
her being made a ward of court and to publish the results of those inquiries.

In considering this application it is of fundamental importance to distinguish between
h the public interest and the public's curiosity. The public interest may demand the
overriding of rights to which the courts would otherwise give effect. The public's
curiosity, understandable and indeed in some circumstances admirable though it may
be, can never have this effect. So far as the media are concerned, the public interest in
investigation, publication and comment may in some circumstances override the rights
of individuals to confidentiality, but an understandable and sometimes reasonable desire
j to satisfy the public's curiosity never can.

The origin of the wardship jurisdiction is the duty of the Crown to protect its subjects
and particularly children who are the generations of the future. It is exercised by the
courts on behalf of the Crown (see Latey J in Re X (a minor) (wardship: restriction on
publication) [1975] 1 All ER 697 at 700–701, [1975] Fam 47 at 52). The machinery for its
exercise is an application to make the child a ward of court. Thereafter, the court is

entitled and bound in appropriate cases to make decisions in the interests of the child
which override the rights of its parents. Furthermore, the court is entitled, and bound in
appropriate cases, to make orders affecting third parties which the parents could not
themselves have made. Obvious examples are orders forbidding the publication of
information about the ward or the ward's family circumstances. Consistently with this,
applications to the court in wardship proceedings are made within the privacy of the
court sitting in chambers and the decision of the court and its reasons for that decision
are not normally given in open court.

In the exceptional circumstances of this case, Ward J took the view that the public
interest required that he disclose his decision and the reasons for that decision. In this he
was clearly right. On appeal we varied his decision in one respect and decided that there
was a public interest in slightly greater disclosure of the facts. For this reason, I disclosed
in my judgment the greater part of the opinion of the professor who had examined baby
C at the request of the Official Solicitor.

I now have to consider whether there is any public interest in further disclosure. I also
have to give the reasons which in my opinion justify the exercise of the court's jurisdiction
to prohibit identification, the soliciting of information and the publication of information
in the terms of the injunctive order which we have made.

The nature of C's treatment and its objectives have been fully disclosed. There remain
the family circumstances which led, quite independently of her medical condition, to
her being made a ward of court. Those circumstances are no different from many other
situations in which it is right that a child should be made a ward of court but which, in
accordance with the settled practice of the courts, are not disclosed to the public. I cannot
accept that there is any public interest which requires their disclosure in this particular
case.

I consider that the information disclosed in the judgment of Ward J and of this court
on the main appeal provides all necessary material for discussion and comment on the
sole issue of genuine public interest, namely the vitally important question of how a
child should be cared for and treated in the tragic situation of baby C.

However, this conclusion does not of itself justify the injunction which the judge
imposed or that which we substituted. Unless the public interest or a private right
enforceable by the courts requires an injunction, the courts cannot intervene. On the
facts of this case such intervention can only be justified on one or other or a combination
of two bases. These are (1) that the injunction is necessary for the welfare of C or for
safeguarding her rights and (2) that the injunction is necessary in the interests of the
administration of justice.

The judge I think approached the matter on the basis that, while the public interest
required that he give judgment in open court in order to disclose his decision and the
factual and legal basis for that decision, he ought so far as possible to maintain the normal
position in wardship that the proceedings are essentially private to the parties. He
therefore sought to achieve a total ban on making any inquiries or publishing any matter
which went beyond what was revealed in his judgment.

On this application I have approached the matter from a slightly different direction.
As was rightly pointed out to us, C's medical condition is such that she will always remain
in total ignorance of anything which is said or written about her. This is an unusual
feature which distinguishes this from most other wardship cases. However, she is utterly
dependent on those who care for her. If media identification of those carers or inquiries
as to their identity, what they are doing for her and why they are doing it will or may
affect the quality of that care, her welfare requires that such a course be prohibited, unless
the public interest otherwise requires. I can see no grounds for thinking that the public
interest so requires and I am wholly satisfied that such identification and inquiries would
add significantly to the emotional and other stress to which those caring for C are subject.
Against this it is said that they are professionals and will be able to overcome such stress.
If anyone can, I am sure that they will, but I am not satisfied that they will be able to do
so.

This is not, however, a justification for an injunction forbidding the identification of
*a* those who have cared for C in the past or inquiries as to their identity, what they have
done for her and why they did it, assuming, which in the case of the medical carers is a
big assumption, that they may not hereafter have to care for her. Here a different aspect
of the court's jurisdiction comes into play. Each one of these carers has in fact been
involved with C in a professional capacity and, as such, owed C a duty of confidentiality.
This is not denied by counsel for the Mail. However, he submits that this is no
*b* justification for a prohibition on their identification and that in any event it is for them
in pursuance of their professional obligation to refuse to give any information. If in
breach of that obligation any of them provide third parties with information, it should
be permissible to publish it.

I disagree. In the absence of a compelling public interest pointing in the other
direction, in my judgment the court is entitled and bound to safeguard C's right to
*c* confidentiality by reinforcing the former carers' professional obligation and creating an
obstacle to third parties' possible attempts to induce them to breach it and to the
exploitation of any such breaches. In this context, I should mention that in this particular
case the carers are likely to be approached not only by the media, but also by pressure
groups who may not display even the consideration and sense of responsibility which
one always hopes for in representatives of the media.

*d* I have dealt with the justification for that part of the revised injunction which deals
with carers and former carers for C in relation to their treatment of C. However, the
injunction also extends to identifying any hospital at which C is being or has been treated
and to soliciting information about C from any staff at such a hospital. The justification
for this extension is as follows. (1) In its absence there will be a real risk that those seeking
information will gather outside the hospital and interrogate all who are entering it or
*e* leaving it, possibly desisting from further questioning if they find that the people
concerned are carers or former carers for C, but persisting in questioning others. This
will have serious effects on the efficient running of the hospital and, in so far as the
hospital is one at which C is still being cared for, might well affect her. (2) All the staff at
these hospitals owe C a duty of confidentiality in relation to information acquired by
them as such staff, irrespective of whether they themselves are or have been carers of C.
*f* (3) If the fact that a sick child is a ward of court and that in the public interest the court
gives a judgment in open court relating to the child leads to the work of hospitals being
disrupted, there will be a strong disincentive to anyone, and in particular local and
hospital authorities, making or supporting applications for wardship. In a word, the
justification for this extension rests on a combination of the need to safeguard the welfare
of C and her right to confidentiality and the need to maintain free and unfettered access
*g* to the wardship jurisdiction of the court.

There remains only that part of the injunction which restrains the identification of the
parents and soliciting information from them about themselves or C and from hospital
staff about C's parents. The parents undoubtedly owe C a duty of confidentiality, save in
so far as C's welfare otherwise requires, and those who care or have cared for C and the
*h* staff at the hospitals concerned probably have no information about the parents otherwise
than in the context of C's presence as a patient, with its attendant duty of confidentiality.
However, this does not justify an injunction prohibiting identification of the parents or
soliciting information from them about themselves or about each other or publishing
such information. For my part, I regard this part of the injunction as justifiable and
justified in protection of the wardship jurisdiction. Many parents would not willingly
*j* make or agree to a child being made a ward of court if they thought that this might lead
to their being identified and singled out for special attention by the media.

The substantial difference between the new injunction and that imposed by Ward J is
that the local authority and the local health authority can now be identified. If they or
any of their officers who fall outside the scope of the injunction are asked questions about
this case, I am confident that they will answer them with discretion, if at all.

Since the hearing another problem has been brought to our attention by a different

national newspaper. It arises in this way. Where a non-identification injunction is granted, it is usual for the solicitors to the party which obtained it to notify the main    a
organs of the press, radio and television of its terms. However, the media are in real difficulty in complying if neither the order nor the notification identifies the ward whose identification is prohibited.

I am grateful to this national newspaper for raising the point, which is of general application. Sir Stephen Brown, the President of the Family Division, tells me that he will be considering what can best be done to meet it in future cases. Meanwhile, I agree    b
that in this case the problem shall be dealt with as suggested by Balcombe LJ, whose judgment I have read.

**BALCOMBE LJ.** Baby C was born on 23 December 1988. Her parents are unmarried and their circumstances and history are such that the local authority had already, before C's birth, decided to apply to have the baby, when born, made a ward of court. That    c
decision was clearly right and was duly implemented on 5 January 1989. However, when C was born, it transpired that she had hydrocephalus and her brain was severely damaged. An operation performed to relieve the pressure within the brain was no more than palliative, and the unanimous evidence of all the doctors is that her life has no future and appears to be unhappy for her.

It was in these circumstances that the local authority applied to the court for directions    d
as to what treatment should be given to baby C. That application came before Ward J sitting in chambers at Leeds. He authorised the hospital to treat baby C so as to allow her life to come to an end peacefully and with dignity. Quite correctly, in view of the seriousness of the decision he had to make, he gave judgment in public so that all might know the reasons for his decision. This of course had the result that what might otherwise have remained private became a matter of public knowledge. In order to preserve the    e
confidentiality of the matter, he granted the following injunctions by an order headed 'In the matter of BABY C' and omitting the name of the district registry in which the action was proceeding and the names of the parties (being the local authority, the mother and the ward):

'. . . restraining any person from making or causing or permitting to be made any    f
enquiry directed to ascertaining the identity of 1) The Ward 2) The parents 3) The Local Authority 4) The Area Health Authority, hospital or medical practitioners or staff having or having had care of the ward [and] restraining the media [sic] . . . from publishing any material which will identify or assist in identifying any of the persons or bodies mentioned in the aforementioned injunction.'

g
The Official Solicitor, as guardian ad litem of baby C, appealed against the substantive order of Ward J. His reasons for doing so were explained by Lord Donaldson MR in his judgment given on 20 April 1989: see Re C (a minor) (wardship: medical treatment) [1989] 2 All ER 782. On that occasion this court, while expressing approval of what the judge had done in substance, varied the form of his order so as to allow the hospital a discretion to treat baby C in accordance with the advice of the professor of paediatrics who had    h
reported on her case. In effect, this authorised the hospital to withhold life-prolonging treatment for baby C. At the same time, we confirmed the injunctions granted by Ward J and extended them to the extent of prohibiting reporting the names of solicitors for the parties, since this would have identified the district where they practice, and hence the local authority and the area health authority.

However, on the following day, 21 April, the Mail on Sunday newspaper applied to    j
this court for a modification of these injunctions so as to permit the fullest possible report of a case of very great public interest. Although such an application would normally be made to the court of first instance, in the particular circumstances of this case we entertained the application without objection by the other parties concerned. In his affidavit in support of the application, the editor of the Mail on Sunday made it clear that he would not wish to identify baby C or, without their consent, her parents. However,

both in his affidavit and in the course of submissions of counsel for the applicants, it was
*a* made clear that the newspaper would wish to be able to identify the medical practitioners
and other staff having the care of baby C, as well as the local and area health authorities
concerned.

Certain matters were common ground. It was accepted that the Mail on Sunday, being
affected by the injunctions, had a right to apply for their modification: see *A-G v
Newspaper Publishing plc* [1987] 3 All ER 276 at 304, [1988] Ch 333 at 375. It was also
*b* accepted that 'the media', whatever might be included in that expression, could not alone
be restrained by the second injunction, which should, like the first, extend to the whole
world. It was not contested that the court exercising wardship jurisdiction had power to
make an order binding on the world at large: see *X CC v A* [1985] 1 All ER 53, [1984] 1
WLR 1422. Finally, it was accepted that whatever modifications were made to the
injunctions had to be done generally and could not be limited to the Mail on Sunday.

*c*    Counsel for the Official Solicitor, supported by counsel for the local authority, sought
to persuade us that we had jurisdiction to grant these injunctions extending beyond the
jurisdiction in wardship. Without ruling out the possibility that there may be cases in
which a wider jurisdiction exists, for my part I am quite satisfied that our only jurisdiction
in this case is the wardship jurisdiction, ie to do whatever is considered necessary for the
welfare of the ward, baby C: see *Re X (a minor) (wardship: restriction on publication)* [1975]
*d* 1 All ER 697, [1975] Fam 47. However, as the majority of this court (Roskill LJ and Sir
John Pennycuick) held in that case, the exercise of that jurisdiction involves holding a
balance between the protection of the ward and the rights of outside parties, in particular
the right of free publication generally enjoyed by outside parties.

The facts of this case differ widely from the other reported cases concerning the
exercise of this jurisdiction. Thus in *Re X (a minor) (wardship: restriction on publication)* the
*e* ward was a girl aged 14, who might herself be gravely damaged psychologically if she
were to read material in a book about to be published containing explicit description of
the aberrant sexual behaviour of her dead father. In *X CC v A* (the Mary Bell case) the
ward's mother had, when herself a child, been convicted of the murder of two young
children. She had, after release on licence, assumed another name. If her true identity
were disclosed, it would damage the fragile stability she had achieved and thereby
*f* endanger the well-being of her own infant child.

Here it is common ground that baby C herself cannot now and will not survive to be
aware of any publicity about her case. She will have to stay in hospital for what remains
of her life, so that the effect of publicity on her parents could have no direct effect on her.
But, as a result of the court's order to which I have already referred, baby C's welfare is
entirely dependent on the doctors and staff of the hospital where she is being cared for
*g* with devotion. It seems to me to be inescapable that, in the particular circumstances of
this tragic case, any outside pressure on them could directly affect C's welfare. Thus, to
quote from the professor's report:

'In the event of her acquiring a serious infection, or being unable to take feeds
normally by mouth I do not think it would be correct to give antibiotics, to set up
*h*    intravenous fusions or nasal-gastric feedings regimes. Such action would be
prolonging a life which has no future and which appears to be unhappy for her.
However, the opinions of the local nurses and carers should be taken into account
for they know her well, show great love to her, and have a feeling for her needs that
an outsider cannot have. Thus if they believed she was in pain or would suffer less
by a particular course of action, it would be correct to consider that course of action,
*j*    always bearing in mind the balance between short-term gain and needless
prolongation of suffering.'

These will be awesome decisions for anyone to make. They should be able to make
them solely in the interests of baby C, and free from any pressure to which they would
be subject if they knew that their identity was known and that they might be the subject
of attack from those who objected to their decision. Indeed, they should be able to make

them free from interference by telephone calls asking them for their views, from being approached by reporters or photographers as they enter or leave the hospital, or being *a* otherwise harassed in the many ways possible. So I am satisfied that, bearing in mind the balance to which I have already referred, and bearing in mind also that sufficient information has been given in the judgment below and in the judgments of this court to enable proper public discussion of the very important issues that arise in this case to take place, the welfare of baby C, and the protection of the confidentiality to which she, as much as any other patient, is entitled concerning her medical treatment, requires that *b* those caring for her be protected from being identified publicly, or from being subjected to solicitation for information about her.

The position of the parents is not quite so straightforward. As I have said, they do not have the care of C. Nevertheless, any identification of, or pressure on, them might well affect the professional carers of C. Thus, to take a not impossible example, the mother, who has since the birth of C played virtually no part in her life, or in the subject of her *c* treatment, might well be persuaded by outside pressure or inducement to take such a part and then to seek to persuade the professional carers to take a course other than that which, in C's interest, they were proposing to take.

So in my judgment, in the exercise of the wardship jurisdiction, the welfare of the court's ward, baby C, does not require injunctions as wide as those granted by the judge, who sought to put a 'ring fence' around her and all connected with her; it does require *d* that there be a prohibition against the identification of the ward, her parents, the hospital where she is being cared for, and the medical practitioners and other staff (eg nurses, hospital staff and social workers) who have, or have had, the care of baby C. Such persons should also be protected from having information about baby C sought from them. At the conclusion of the hearing on 21 April we announced this conclusion (with reasons to be given later) and the form of the order which was then agreed between counsel as *e* giving effect to our decision is set out as an appendix to this judgment. Further, it is necessary that the injunction order, as well as the order continuing the wardship, giving care and control of the ward to the local authority and authorising her treatment, should be entitled (by reference to a schedule) with the real name of the ward, and not just as 'In the matter of baby C' and should name the district registry and the parties (the defendants *f* being named only in the schedule), otherwise the persons to whom the order is addressed will not know whom it is they are restrained from identify or soliciting.

APPENDIX

*Re C*

IT IS ORDERED that the injunction granted by Ward J on 14 April 1989 as varied and *g* continued by this court on 20 April 1989 be discharged; and in substitution therefore the following order be made:

'IT IS FURTHER ORDERED that an injunction be made restraining, until further order, any person, whether by himself, his servants or agents or otherwise howsoever, or in the case of a company, whether by its directors or officers, servants or agents or *h* otherwise howsoever from: (1) publishing the name or address or otherwise identifying: (a) the ward; (b) the parents; (c) any hospital at which the ward is being or has been treated; or (d) any natural person having or who has had the care of the ward; (2) soliciting any information relating to the ward or her parents (other than information already in the public domain) from the parents of the ward, any staff at any such hospital as mentioned in para (1)(c) above or any such person as is *j* mentioned in para (1)(d) above, provided that no breach of this order shall be committed by any person who does no more than inquire of another person whether that person is a person comprised in para (1)(d) above; (3) publishing any such information as is referred to in para (2) above obtained directly or indirectly from any person referred to in para (2) above.'

**NICHOLLS LJ.** It is, of course, a fundamental principle in this country that justice
*a* should be administered in public. The public are entitled to know, and should know,
what matters are being brought before the judges, what decisions and orders are being
made by judges, and the reasons for those decisions and orders. In reporting on such
matters the press have an indispensable function as the eyes and ears of the public.
Moreover, and as part of the freedom of the press in this country, responsible investigative
journalism has a role of great importance.

*b*      Nevertheless, there are occasions when the administration of justice in public would
be self-defeating: the public identification of the parties, or even the hearing of the
matter in public at all, may be attended by a real risk that such publicity would defeat
the purpose which the court proceedings are properly intended to achieve. In such cases
the court has an inherent power to conduct its process in such a way as will prevent that
result. Proceedings relating to the welfare of minors are an example of this. The court is
*c* concerned to see that the welfare of the child which the court is seeking to promote is
not jeopardised by publicity.

In the present case the court is faced with the application of these established principles
to a particular factual situation. The case concerns the welfare of a baby girl who was
made a ward of court for reasons unconnected with her medical condition. In the normal
way court proceedings relating to her welfare would be conducted in private, and the
*d* court's findings and conclusions would also be announced in private. But in this case the
baby is dying. There is, naturally and properly, a high degree of public interest and
concern in the nature of the medical treatment to which the court has given its approval.
It is eminently right and proper that, although this case concerns the welfare of a minor,
that fact should not be allowed to hinder informed public debate.

It was for this reason that the judge gave a full, carefully reasoned judgment in open
*e* court. It was for this reason that on appeal this court, whose judgments were also given
in open court, included in the first judgment lengthy verbatim extracts from the report
of the leading paediatrician who has been consulted and whose recommendations
regarding treatment have been approved by the court: see *Re C (a minor) (wardship:
medical treatment)* [1989] 2 All ER 782. These extracts set out full details of baby C's
medical condition and the recommended treatment. It can be seen, therefore, that the
*f* judge and this court have throughout been alive to the need for the public to be kept
fully informed. At each stage the court has taken steps to see that all the facts material to
informed discussion of any ethical, legal and medical issues involved have been brought
firmly into the public domain. The press and, through the press, the public already have
access to all these facts.

The Mail on Sunday wishes to go further than this. It wishes to be able to bring more
*g* information into the public domain. The newspaper has made it clear that it has no
intention of naming or identifying the baby or her parents. But through counsel it
submitted that the injunction protecting baby C should go no wider than this, for the
reasons set out in an affidavit made by the editor, Mr Steven:

'I see no possibility that Baby C could suffer any damage from publicity about her
*h* in "The Mail on Sunday", or the media generally. Baby C is not now, nor will she
ever be, capable of understanding anything written about her. Nothing that "The
Mail on Sunday" could write would harm her. The fundamental reason for the
power of a Court exercising wardship jurisdiction to make an order about publicity
is not present. Even if damage to Baby C was possible, I cannot see that any harm
could be caused to her by the identification of the local authority, health authority,
*j* hospital, medical practitioners, staff having care of her, or the solicitors for the
parties. There is a danger that the Order will protect from criticism or comment
public authorities which should be accountable to the public for the decisions they
take. Further, by prohibiting inquiries in the form it does, the Order prevents "The
Mail on Sunday" from carrying out part of its legitimate function.'

Counsel for the applicants made plain that the Mail on Sunday wishes to be free to
identify and publish photographs of the professor whose report I have mentioned and of    *a*
the doctors and other medical staff who have the care of baby C. It wishes to be able to
interview the parents and the social workers and the medical staff; although, as the case
proceeded, the newspaper indicated that it would not object to a ban on soliciting
information about the baby from medical practitioners and others currently having
direct care of her.

I am unable to accept this. Those who have the charge of baby C have, in all conscience,    *b*
a task which is sufficiently difficult and emotionally draining without the pressures on
them, as they carry out their work and make their medical decisions day by day, being
increased by the massive personal publicity which would be likely in the absence of an
appropriately framed injunction. The promotion of baby C's welfare requires that those
caring for her should not have to cope with this additional burden. Nor, for the same
reason, should they be faced with the additional burden of any comments from the    *c*
parents which might be induced by the press.

But baby C's interests do not stop there. Those who have previously been involved in
her care, as social workers or as medical staff, owe a duty of confidence to her in respect
of the information they have acquired about her and her background. Likewise, all the
staff at the hospital where baby C is being cared for. Such information could not properly
be disclosed by any of these individuals to the media. That being so, I can see no    *d*
disadvantage and considerable advantage in this position being made abundantly clear,
by the protective injunction being framed in terms which include a prohibition on
soliciting such information from such persons and from publishing any such information.

It was for these reasons that I agreed that an order should be made last Friday in the
terms stated by Lord Donaldson MR. These terms represent a sensible balance, in a case
of considerable general public importance, between, on the one hand, the right of the    *e*
public to be kept informed of what is going on in court and, on the other hand, the need
for the welfare of baby C not to be put at risk by public indentification of her, her parents
and those who are or have been involved in her care.

*Application granted in part. Injunctions discharged and fresh injunction substituted. No order*    *f*
*for costs. Leave to appeal to the House of Lords refused.*

Solicitors: *Swepstone Walsh* (for the applicants); *Official Solicitor ; T I Clough & Co*, Bradford
(for the mother); *A R Sykes*, Bradford (for the local authority).

Frances Rustin    Barrister.

# Thetford Corp and another v Fiamma SpA and others

## (Case 35/87)

COURT OF JUSTICE OF THE EUROPEAN COMMUNITIES

JUDGES LORD MACKENZIE STUART (PRESIDENT OF CHAMBER), BOSCO, DUE, MOITINHO DE ALMEIDA (PRESIDENTS OF CHAMBERS), KOOPMANS, EVERLING, BAHLMANN, GALMOT, KAKOURIS, O'HIGGINS AND SHOCKWEILER

ADVOCATE GENERAL M J MISCHO

I MARCH, 28 APRIL, 30 JUNE 1988

European Economic Community – Freedom of movement – Goods – Restriction of freedom – Restrictions justified on grounds of protection of industrial and commercial property – Goods infringing United Kingdom patent – Patent lacking novelty but for rule excluding 50-year-old specifications from consideration – Restriction on importation – Whether restriction justified on ground of protection of industrial and commercial property – Patents Act 1949, s 50(1) – EEC Treaty, arts 30, 36.

European Economic Community – Freedom of movement – Goods – Restriction of freedom – Restrictions justified on grounds of protection of industrial and commercial property – Goods infringing United Kingdom patent – Patent lacking novelty but for rule excluding 50-year-old specifications – Whether injunction prohibiting importation available to patent holder – Whether relief limited to reasonable royalty or other monetary award – EEC Treaty, arts 30, 36.

The plaintiffs were the owners of two United Kingdom patents relating to an invention for portable toilets granted pursuant to the Patents Act 1949 which but for s 50(1)[a] of that Act, which excluded 50-year-old specifications from consideration, would have lacked novelty. The defendants manufactured such toilets in Italy and imported them into the United Kingdom although they had no licence from the plaintiffs. The plaintiffs brought an action against the defendants alleging infringement of their patents. The defendants denied infringement and contended that the plaintiffs' patents were invalid on grounds of lack of novelty and inventive step and that, even if they were valid, relief was limited to a royalty or other monetary award since the grant of an injunction would be a quantitative restriction on imports or a measure having equivalent effect under art 30[b] of the EEC Treaty and was not justified under art 36[c] of the Treaty on grounds of the protection of industrial and commercial property. The Patents Court struck out the latter defence from the pleadings as disclosing no reasonable defence. The defendants appealed to the Court of Appeal, which referred to the Court of Justice of the European Communities for a preliminary ruling the questions (i) whether a subsisting patent which had been granted under the 1949 Act in respect of an invention which but for s 50 of that Act would have lacked novelty constituted 'industrial or commercial property' entitled to protection under art 36 and (ii) if such a patent was entitled to such protection whether the only relief justified under art 36 would be an order for the payment of a reasonable royalty or other monetary award but not an injunction.

---

a · Section 50(1), so far as material, is set out at p 814 g h, post

b · Article 30 provides: 'Quantitative restrictions on imports and all measures having equivalent effect shall, without prejudice to the following provisions, be prohibited between Member States.'

c · Article 36, so far as material, provides: 'The provisions of Articles 30 to 34 shall not preclude prohibitions or restrictions on imports, exports or goods in transit justified on grounds of . . . the protection of industrial and commercial property. Such prohibitions or restrictions shall not, however, constitute a means of arbitrary discrimination or a disguised restriction on trade between Member States.'

**Held** – (1) Since the existence of patent rights was a matter solely of national law, a member state's patent legislation was covered in principle by the derogations from the prohibition on quantitative restrictions on imports and all measures having equivalent *a* effect in art 30 which were provided for by art 36 even though a patent granted for an invention under that legislation might not be declared invalid by reason only of the fact that the invention appeared in a patent specification filed more than 50 years previously. Furthermore, since s 50(1) of the 1949 Act did not give rise to any discrimination, and applied equally to foreign and United Kingdom nationals, and since its objects were to *b* foster creativity on the part of inventors in the interests of industry and to reward by the grant of a patent the rediscovery of inventions more than 50 years old, the application of the 50-year rule was not a means of arbitrary discrimination or a disguised restriction on trade between member states within art 36. Accordingly, the plaintiffs' patents constituted industrial and commercial property entitled to protection under art 36 (see p 815 *h* to p 816 *d* and p 817 *a*, post). *c*

(2) Furthermore, since the right of the proprietor of a patent to prevent importation and marketing of products manufactured under compulsory licence was part of the substance of patents law, where national law normally provided for the issue of an injunction to prevent any infringement that measure was justified under art 36, particularly where no licence had been granted by the proprietor of the patent in the country of manufacture (see p 816 *g h* and 817 *b*, post). *d*

**Notes**

For early patent specifications, see 35 Halsbury's Laws (4th edn) para 48.

For the freedom of movement of goods in the European Economic Communities and justification for restrictions on trade between member states, see 52 ibid paras 12.55–12.111. *e*

For the Patents Act 1949, s 50, see 33 Halsbury's Statutes (4th edn) 54.

For the EEC Treaty, arts 30, 36, see 50 ibid 276, 278.

**Cases cited**

*Allen & Hanburys Ltd v Generics (UK) Ltd* Case 434/85 [1988] 2 All ER 454, [1989] 1 WLR *f* 414, CJEC.

*Centrafarm BV v Sterling Drug Inc* Case 15/74 [1974] ECR 1147.

*de Peijper* Case 104/75 [1976] ECR 613.

*Deutsche Grammophon Gesellschaft mbH v Metro-SB-Großmärkte GmbH & Co KG* Case 78/70 [1971] ECR 487.

*EC Commission v Germany* Case 12/74 [1975] ECR 181. *g*

*Keurkoop BV v Nancy Kean Gifts BV* Case 144/81 [1982] ECR 2853.

*Merck & Co Inc v Stephar BV* Case 187/80 [1981] ECR 2063.

*Parke Davis & Co v Probel* Case 24/67 [1968] ECR 55.

*Pharmon BV v Hoechst AG* Case 19/84 [1985] ECR 2281.

**Reference** *h*

By an order lodged on 5 February 1987 the Court of Appeal referred to the Court of Justice of the European Communities for a preliminary ruling under art 177 of the EEC Treaty two questions (set out at p 814 *c d*, post) concerning the interpretation of art 36 of the Treaty with a view to the assessment of the compatability with the rules on the free movement of goods of certain provisions of United Kingdom patent law and especially the principle of relative novelty. The questions were raised in the course of an appeal to *j* the Court of Appeal (Fox, Stephen Brown and Parker LJJ) ([1987] 3 CMLR 266) on 27 November 1986 by the defendants, Fiamma SpA and Fiamma UK (Fiamma), against the order of Falconer J on 30 July 1985 in the Patents Court striking out certain defences to an action brought against them by the plaintiffs, Thetford Corp (USA) and Thetford (Aqua) Products Ltd (Thetford), for infringement of two United Kingdom patents owned a  by Thetford. Thetford, Fiamma, the United Kingdom and the Commission of the European Communities submitted written observations to the court. The language of the case was English. The facts are set out in the report for the hearing presented by the Judge Rapporteur.

**The Judge Rapporteur (Giacinto Bosco)** presented the following report for the hearing.

b

I—FACTS AND PROCEDURE

In two actions for patent infringement, Thetford Corp, which is the owner of two United Kingdom patents relating to inventions for portable toilets, is suing Fiamma SpA, a manufacturer of such toilets in Italy, and Fiamma UK (hereinafter referred to as 'Fiamma'), which imports them into the United Kingdom. Fiamma has no licence from

c  Thetford Corp in Italy, the United Kingdom or anywhere else. According to the documents before the court, the products in question are not patented in any other member state of the EEC.

Before the Patents Court Fiamma denied the patent infringement and argued that Thetford Corp's patent was void on the grounds of lack of novelty and lack of inventive step. It also contended that, even if the patent were valid, arts 30 and 36 of the EEC

d  Treaty limited the relief which the courts of the United Kingdom ought to grant to the patent holder.

On an application by Thetford Corp, the Patents Court struck out the latter defence from the pleadings, whereupon Fiamma appealed to the Court of Appeal, which decided that, bearing in mind that there was no direct authority of the Court of Justice on the points raised by the defendants, the allegations disclosed an arguable case. Thus it decided

e  that the relevant paragraphs of the defences should not be struck out at that stage but that two questions should be referred to the Court of Justice for a preliminary ruling (see [1987] 3 CMLR 266). By way of preliminary the Court of Appeal states that for the purpose of deciding the questions of law posed it is necessary to assume that (a) patent 235 is a valid patent under United Kingdom law, (b) patent 235 would be invalid under the laws of other member states, except possibly Ireland, because of the seven cited patent

f  specifications published more than 50 years before the priority date but excluded from consideration in the United Kingdom under s 50 of the Patents Act 1949, (c) the exclusion of 50-year-old specifications under s 50 of the 1949 Act does not apply to patents granted under the Patents Act 1977, (d) the plaintiffs have not sought to obtain any corresponding patent in any other member state and (e) the alleged infringing articles were manufactured in Italy and imported and sold in the United Kingdom.

g  The Court of Justice of the European Communities is accordingly requested to give a preliminary ruling on the following questions:

'(1) Whether a subsisting patent which has been granted in the United Kingdom under the provisions of the Patents Act 1949 in respect of an invention which but for the provisions of section 50 of that Act would have been anticipated (lacked

h  novelty) by a specification as is described in paragraphs (a) or (b) of section 50(1) of that Act constitutes industrial or commercial property entitled to protection under Article 36 of the Treaty of Rome?

(2) If such a patent is entitled to such protection as aforesaid whether as contended by the Defendants Fiamma in this case the only relief justified under Article 36 of the Treaty would be an order for the payment of a reasonable royalty (or other

j  monetary award) but not an injunction.

Pursuant to art 20 of the Protocol on the Statute of the Court of Justice, written observations were submitted by: Thetford Corp and another, the plaintiffs in the main proceedings, represented by Clifford Chance; Fiamma SpA and others, the defendants in the main proceedings, represented by Messrs Evershed & Tomkinson; the United

Kingdom of Great Britain and Northern Ireland, represented by Nicholas Pumfrey; and the Commission of the European Communities, represented by Eric White, a member *a* of its legal department, acting as agent.

On hearing the report of the Judge Rapporteur and the views of the Advocate General the court decided to open the oral procedure without any preparatory inquiry. The court put a written question to the United Kingdom and the Commission on the 50-year rule under the Patents Act 1949.

*b*

II—WRITTEN OBSERVATIONS SUBMITTED TO THE COURT

*The first question*

*Thetford Corp and another*, the plaintiffs in the main proceedings (hereinafter referred to as Thetford), argue in the first place that it is well established in Community law that patents granted under the national laws of member states constitute 'industrial or *c* commercial property' within the meaning of art 36 of the Treaty (see *Parke Davis & Co v Probel* Case 24/67 [1968] ECR 55, *Centrafarm BV v Sterling Drug Inc* Case 15/74, [1974] ECR 1147 and *Merck & Co Inc v Stephar BV* Case 187/80 [1981] ECR 2063).

Although steps have been taken towards the harmonisation of patent law in the EEC, that objective had not been achieved when the patent in question was granted and still has not been achieved today. Consequently, the existence and the validity of patents *d* must depend on the national law under which they were granted.

The patent in question was properly granted under the national law of the United Kingdom, and the fact that the invention may not be patented or patentable in other member states is not material. It would not be practically possible to consider the validity or the enforceability of every patent by reference not only to the national law of the member state granting it, but also by reference to the national laws of the other member *e* states. Even if such an inquiry were feasible, the question would arise in the event of inconsistency between the laws of two or more member states as to which should benefit from the provisions of art 36 and which should not. As at the date when the patent in question was applied for, the laws of the member states differed widely, in particular with regard to the 'novelty of a patent application'.

After giving several examples of the purported absurdity of the defendants' submission, *f* Thetford suggests that the court should answer the first question as follows:

> 'Such a patent constitutes "industrial or commercial property" within the meaning of art 36 of the Treaty, because it is an ordinary patent granted under the national law of the United Kingdom. There is no ground for objection under EEC law to a provision such as that found in s 50 of the Patents Act 1949. The patent is therefore *g* entitled to protection under art 36.'

The *United Kingdom* maintains, first, that under the Convention for the Protection of Industrial Property (Paris, 20 March 1883) (London revision 1934) (TS 55 (1938); Cmd 5833), a patent can be recognised as such regardless of the detailed criteria adopted by the national law for determining validity.

*h*

The legislation applicable at the time when the patent in question was granted, namely the Patents Act 1949, provided that any document relied on as depriving an invention of novelty must be published in the United Kingdom, and any patent specification must additionally be less than 50 years old. The reasons for that concept of 'relative novelty', which was introduced by the Patents Act 1902, lie in the fact that it was considered that the requirement of absolute novelty was not necessarily in the public interest. In *j* particular, a very old document lodged at the Patent Office 'should not ... be used to defeat a meritorious contribution to the industry of the country'.

Second, the existence of a national patent right is not affected by Community rules and, at the present stage of development of Community law, the criteria according to which a member state grants patent rights are a matter for the national law of that *a* member state. In the present case, the criteria followed by a member state for granting a national patent affect the existence of national patent rights, which, according to the case law of the court, is a matter for the national law. Community law merely requires that the measure go no further than is justified by the protection of the interest in question. That is not the case as regards the protection given by United Kingdom law to a patent issued under the circumstances described by the Court of Appeal.

*b* The United Kingdom therefore suggests that the first question should be answered as follows:

*c* 'The specific subject matter of the patent right, which is industrial or commercial property whose protection is justified by art 36 of the EEC Treaty, includes the guarantee that the patentee, to reward the creative effort of the inventor, has the exclusive right to use an invention with a view to manufacturing industrial products and putting them into circulation for the first time, as well as the right to oppose infringements. It is for the national law of a mamber state to determine the degree of creative effort on the part of the patentee which is to be rewarded by the grant of a patent, and to determine the circumstances in which the right will be granted.'

*d* The *Commission* considers that the answer to the first question can be deduced from the court's judgment in *Keurkoop BV v Nancy Kean Gifts BV* Case 144/81 [1982] ECR 2853 at 2871 (para 18), in which the court stated that 'in the absence of Community standardization or of a harmonization of laws the determination of the conditions and procedures under which protection of designs is granted is a matter for national rules . . .'

*e* The patent in question was issued under the Patents Act 1949, which constitutes legislation for the protection of industrial and commercial property, and the 50-year rule comes within the scope of the conditions and procedures which are to be determined by member states' legislation. If, however, the court considers that it is necessary for those conditions and procedures to be justified under art 36, then the Commission takes the view that the exclusion of patent specifications over 50 years old from consideration in the examination of a patent application and in revocation or infringement proceedings could be justified in the interests of simplifying proceedings.

*f* The Commission, therefore, suggests that the first question should be answered as follows:

*g* 'In the present state of development of Community law, national patent legislation is not incompatible with arts 30 and 36 of the EEC Treaty merely because it provides that a patent may be granted in respect of an invention, and such a patent may not be revoked, even though the invention is described in a patent specification filed more than 50 years earlier.'

*Fiamma SpA and others*, the defendants in the main proceedings (hereinafter referred to as 'Fiamma'), consider that the two questions put by the national court are closely linked, and ask the court to bear that in mind.

*h* Fiamma argues essentially that the court's case law with regard to the application of art 36 to patents cannot be relied on in this instance. The previous decisions of the court relate to inventions, characterised by the fact that they were new and involved an inventive step. On the other hand, the Thetford patent is in respect of matter which was made available to the public many years ago. The patent is in respect of 'insubstantial' subject matter which Thetford has not sought to protect or enforce in other member states of the EEC. The effect of the patent is therefore to isolate the United Kingdom

*j* from the rest of the EEC, where the products in question may be freely manufactured and sold.

Fiamma argues, in particular, that it is not enough that a national law calls a particular right a 'patent' for it necessarily to follow that 'industrial or commercial property' is involved. On the contrary, regard must be had to whether the right in question has the 'minimum characteristics' of a patent and can therefore derogate from the fundamental principle of the free movement of goods. The question therefore arises as to what is the 'area of discretion' available to national patent laws in the present state of development of $a$ Community law. Fiamma identifies the *following three tests* which, in its view, should be applied to delimit that discretion: (i) the greater the steps which have been taken towards harmonisation, the smaller the area of discretion must be; (ii) whilst it is true that at present Community law has not yet laid down an exhaustive regime and hence the procedures for obtaining a national patent are a matter for national laws, those procedures must nevertheless fall within the limits which are necessary to give effect to the $b$ requirements of the free movement of goods; (iii) certain matters are fundamental to particular industrial property rights (for example, the rule that patents should be granted only for inventions). In relation thereto, the area of discretion should be smaller than that which is justified in the case of procedural rules.

On the basis of those three tests, Fiamma reaches the conclusion that the patent in question is outside the area of discretion, since it is in the field of patents that *the most* $c$ *progress* has been made towards *harmonisation* (the Convention on the Unification of Certain Points of Substantive Law on Patents for Invention (Strasbourg, 27 November 1963; TS 70 (1980); Cmnd 8002); the Convention on the Grant of European Patents (the European Patent Convention) (Munich, 5 October 1973; TS 20 (1978); Cmnd 7090); the Convention for the Patent for the Common Market (the Community Patent Convention) (Luxembourg, 15 December 1975; EC 18 (1976); Cmnd 6553), which is not yet in force, $d$ and the resolution annexed to the latter); 'novelty' is the fundamental requirement of a patent. Neither of the conventions places a restriction on which published documents form part of the state of the art; the justification for the 50-year rule in the Patents Act 1949 was probably administrative convenience (to ease the burden of the examination of patents). It therefore offers no justification for preventing those alleged to have infringed the patent from relying on all relevant material which has been published. $e$

Fiamma therefore proposes that the court should answer the first question as follows:

> 'It is an essential requirement of a patent that it be granted in respect of novel subject matter. Therefore, it is not justified to grant relief which will have the effect of restricting imports from another member state in respect of a patent granted in the circumstances set out in the first question asked by the Court of Appeal.' $f$

*The second question*

Thetford, the United Kingdom and the Commission reach the same conclusions and propose a similar answer on the basis of the court's case law, and, in particular, of the aforementioned judgments in *Centrafarm BV v Sterling Drug Inc* Case 15/74 [1974] ECR 1147 and *Merck & Co Inc v Stephar BV* Case 187/80 [1981] ECR 2063 and of the judgment $g$ in *Pharmon BV v Hoechst AG* Case 19/84 [1985] ECR 2281.

Thetford argues essentially that there is no reason why in the present case it should not obtain an injunction in order to protect the specific subject matter of its patent. In particular the court has never held that the mere absence of a patent in another member state debars the owner of a property right from contesting the importation of goods from that member state into the state in which his protection does exist. $h$

Thetford therefore suggests the following answer:

> 'No. The specific object of a patent is the guarantee that the patentee has the exclusive right to use the invention and to put the industrial products into circulation for the first time. Thetford are therefore entitled to all the relief normally accorded to a patentee, including the right to seek an injunction to prevent further $j$ infringement.'

The *United Kingdom* considers that the measures which may be taken to protect the specific subject matter of the patent are those which are prescribed by national law. Since the national law applies without distinction to both domestically produced and imported goods, there can be no justification for limiting the available remedies.

It therefore proposes that the second question should be answered as follows:

a    'If the national law normally provides for an injunction for the purpose of opposing all infringements, that relief is justified under art 36.'

The *Commission* considers that the availability of an injunction to prevent infringement of the patent by importation is justified under art 36. It stresses, in particular, that this case differs from the request for a preliminary ruling in *Allen & Hanburys Ltd v Generics*
b    *(UK) Ltd* Case 434/85 [1988] 2 All ER 454, [1989] 1 WLR 414, where the Commission stated in its written observations that to limit the availability of an injunction to cases of imports is not justified under art 36 and that the only protection which is justified in such a case is the right to a royalty. In this case there is no suggestion that the products involved were put on the market by or with the consent of Thetford or any person connected therewith. If, however, Fiamma has not applied for a licence of right, the
c    grant of an injunction is justified to prevent infringement of the patent.

The Commission suggests that the second question should be answered as follows:

'The order making the reference does not disclose any facts which might justify the contention that the only relief justified under Article 36 of the Treaty would be an order for the payment of a reasonable royalty (or other monetary award) but not
d    an injunction.'

*Fiamma* argues that the 'rule of proportionality' set out by the court in *de Peijper* Case 104/75 [1976] ECR 613 also applies to the area of industrial and commercial property. There is nothing to oblige the court to adopt an 'all or nothing' approach. There is a whole spectrum of measures which may be justified under art 36, ranging from a total ban on imports to purely formal procedures which cause almost no expense or delay to
e    an importer. Fiamma maintains that there are reasons of expediency for extending to the sphere of industrial property the concept of a 'range of measures' which has already been applied by the court in connection with other grounds of justification under art 36.

Fiamma points out that the majority of cases which have come before the court involving the relationship between arts 30 and 36 have been concerned with the exhaustion of rights. They have therefore not been concerned with the question of
f    justification of relief falling short of an injunction. Consequently, Fiamma asks the court to consider whether, in relation to this kind of patent (namely 'a monopoly which is called a "patent", but which is granted in respect of subject matter which is old'), the specific subject matter includes the right to obtain reward for the marketing of the product, but not necessarily a right to an injunction.

g    Fiamma suggests that the court should answer the second question as follows:

'If the answer to question 1 is that such a patent is entitled to some protection under art 36, this protection does not extend to the grant of an injunction where the importer of products which are covered by the patent and which originate in another member state has indicated a willingness to pay a reasonable royalty to the patentee in respect of such imports.'

h

III—ANSWERS TO QUESTION PUT BY THE COURT
The court asked the United Kingdom and the Commission to provide additional explanations of the rationale of the principle of 'relative novelty' in the light of the written observations submitted to the court.

In its answer, the *Commission* acknowledges that the precise reason for the existence of
j    the 50-year rule is more complex and less satisfactory as regards art 36 of the EEC Treaty than it suggested in its written observations.

In particular, the Commission considers that an aspect of the 50-year rule is contrary to arts 30 and 36, namely the provision whereby use or publication of an invention outside the United Kingdom during the 50 years prior to the lodging of the application would not defeat the claim to novelty. The effect of that requirement, since abolished by the Patents Act 1977, was that it allowed a patent to be obtained in the United Kingdom in respect of an invention which was freely used or published in another member state at the time of the application but not if it was used or published in the United Kingdom at that time.

Although there is nothing in this case to suggest that the invention in question was used or published in another member state during the 50 years preceding the grant of the patent, the Commission considers that the court should make it clear that it is not justified to limit the examination to use or publication in the United Kingdom to the exclusion of use or publication in other member states.

The *United Kingdom* traces the history of the principle of 'relative novelty' and points out that prior to 1902 the Patent Office did not examine patent applications for novelty. By enacting the recommendations of the Committee of Inquiry chaired by Sir Edward Fry *(Report on the Patent Acts* (Cd 506, 530) (1901)), the Patents Act 1902 provided for the examination of applications for prior publication in the specification of United Kingdom patents less than 50 years old. It laid down that an invention is not to be taken as anticipated by reason only of its publication in a specification of a United Kingdom patent more than 50 years old.

The 50-year limitation seems to have been adopted for practical reasons connected with the cost of searches at the Patent Office. Also, it was considered that obsolete patents which had never been worked and never published except in patent specifications should not be available as anticipations, since they had provided no public utility.

Lastly, the United Kingdom emphasises that the rule in question applied only to inventions published in patent specifications. If an invention had been used, however long ago that use had taken place, it was grounds for invalidating the patent.

*Guy Burkill* for Thetford.
*Michael Hicks* for Fiamma.
*Nicholas Pumfrey* for the United Kingdom.
*Eric L White* for the EC Commission.

28 April. **The Advocate General (M J Mischo)** delivered the following opinion[1]. Mr President, Members of the Court,

1. This request for a preliminary ruling relates to a patent infringement action in which Thetford Corp (USA) and Thetford (Aqua) Products Ltd (UK) (which I will refer to as 'Thetford') are suing Fiamma SpA and Fiamma UK (which I will refer to as 'Fiamma'). The latter are, respectively, the manufacturers in Italy and the importers into the United Kingdom of portable toilets patented by Thetford in the United Kingdom, and in that member state alone. Thetford, from which Fiamma has no licence whether in the United Kingdom, in Italy or elsewhere, is relying in particular on a patent (which I will refer to as 'patent 235') issued under the Patents Act 1949, which continues to govern the patent despite its having been replaced by the Patents Act 1977.

2. The Court of Appeal of England and Wales, before which the main proceedings are pending, asks this court to make the following assumptions: (a) patent 235 is a valid patent under United Kingdom law; (b) patent 235 would be invalid under the laws of other member states, except possibly Ireland, because seven patent specifications were published more than 50 years before the priority date but excluded from consideration in the United Kingdom under s 50 of the Patents Act 1949; (c) the exclusion of 50-year-old specifications under s 50 of the 1949 Act does not apply to patents granted under the Patents Act 1977; (d) the plaintiffs have not sought to obtain any corresponding patent in any other member state; (e) the alleged infringing articles were manufactured in Italy and imported and sold in the United Kingdom.

---

1 Translated from the French

*The first question*

a    3. The first of the two questions referred to the court by the Court of Appeal is as follows:

'Whether a subsisting patent which has been granted in the United Kingdom under the provisions of the Patents Act 1949 in respect of an invention which but for the provisions of section 50 of that Act would have been anticipated (lacked novelty) by a specification as is described in paragraphs (*a*) or (*b*) of section 50(1) of

b    that Act constitutes industrial or commercial property entitled to protection under Article 36 of the Treaty of Rome?'

4. Section 50(1) of the Patents Act 1949 provides as follows:

'An invention claimed in a complete specification shall not be deemed to have been anticipated by reason only that the invention was published in the United

c    Kingdom—(*a*) in a specification filed in pursuance of an application for a patent made in the United Kingdom and dated more than fifty years before the date of filing of the first-mentioned specification; (*b*) in a specification describing the invention for the purposes of an application for protection in any country outside the United Kingdom made more than fifty years before that date . . .'

d    5. Consequently, it is not possible in United Kingdom law to base an action for the revocation of a patent on a specification issued in the United Kingdom or in any other country more than 50 years before.

6. The first question put by the Court of Appeal therefore seeks to establish whether the derogation from arts 30 to 34 of the EEC Treaty which is set out in the first sentence of art 36 necessarily applies to all patents or whether, on the contrary, that exception does

e    not apply to patents which, were it not for s 50(1) of the Patents Act 1949, would be liable to be revoked, that is to say patents granted by virtue of the principle of relative novelty.

7. The defendant in the main proceedings (Fiamma) considers that the freedom which, according to the court (see, in particular, *Centrafarm BV v Sterling Drug Inc* Case

f    15/74 [1974] ECR 1147 at 1162 (para 7)), the member states have to define the conditions for the existence of intellectual and commercial property rights must necessarily be subject to limits and not exceed a certain area of discretion. Accordingly, it considers that a right granted by a national legislature does not constitute a patent and cannot qualify for the protection afforded on that ground by art 36 unless certain fundamental conditions are fulfilled. In particular, a 'patent' granted in the absence of novelty or an inventive step could not be regarded as industrial and commercial property.

g    8. However, in its judgment in *Keurkoop BV v Nancy Kean Gifts BV* Case 144/81 [1982] ECR 2853 the court made it clear that in the state of Community law then obtaining it would not examine the precise conditions laid down by national law for the grant of an intellectual property right. The question at issue in that case was whether art 36 of the Treaty permitted the application of a national law which, like the Uniform Benelux Law

h    on Designs (the terms of which were adopted by the convention of 25 October 1966 (Tractatenblad 1966, No 292, p 3)), gave an exclusive right to the first person to file a design, without persons other than the author or those claiming under him being entitled, in order to challenge such an exclusive right or defend an action for an injunction brought by the holder of the right, to contend that the person filing the design was not the author of it, the person who commissioned the design from him or

j    his employer. The court stated (at 2871 (para 18)):

'. . . in the present state of Community law and in the absence of Community standardization or of a harmonization of laws the determination of the conditions and procedures under which protection of designs is granted is a matter for national rules . . .'

9. Moreover, despite the fact that the Uniform Benelux Law afforded protection to a product which in fact had not been commonly known in the industrial and commercial *a* circles concerned *in the Benelux territory* during the 50 years prior to the filing of the design (at 2870 (para 15), the court ruled (at 2874 (operative part of judgment, para 1)):

'In the present state of its development Community law does not prevent the adoption of national provisions of the kind contained in the Uniform Benelux Law, as described by the national court.'          *b*

10. However, Fiamma further argues that whereas there has been little harmonisation in the field of designs, with which the *Keurkoop* case was concerned, the same cannot be said of patents. There has been significant progress towards harmonisation of national laws regarding patents, and at Community level agreement has even been reached on matters of substantive patent law, including novelty. Account should therefore be taken *c* of that development.

11. What is the actual position? The Convention for the Patent for the Common Market (the Community Patent Convention) (Luxembourg, 15 December 1975; EC 18 (1976); Cmnd 6553) has still not entered into force.

12. The Convention on the Unification of Certain Points of Substantive Law on Patents for Invention (Strasbourg, 27 November 1963; TS 70 (1980); Cmnd 8002) and *d* the Convention on the Grant of European Patents (European Patent Convention) (Munich, 5 October 1973; TS 20 (1978); Cmnd 7090) also incorporate the principle of absolute novelty, but those conventions are not part of the Community legal order.

13. Furthermore, they did not enter into force until after the patent in question was granted to Thetford (the Strasbourg Convention on 1 August 1980 and the Munich Convention, as far as the United Kingdom was concerned, on 7 October 1977).          *e*

14. Lastly, both the Munich Convention and the Luxembourg Convention allow national patents to continue to exist alongside European patents. Since Thetford's patent was not applied for under the Munich Convention, it is purely national and continues to be governed by the provisions of United Kingdom law.

15. In sum, I therefore consider that the judgment in the *Keurkoop* case does in fact *f* constitute a relevant precedent, and that there is no reason for not applying in this case the court's ruling to the effect that the definition of the conditions for the existence of industrial and commercial property rights is a matter for the member states (see, in particular, *Centrafarm BV v Sterling Drug Inc* Case 15/74 [1974] ECR 1147 at 1162 (para 7), even if the resulting differences between national laws creates obstacles to the free movement of goods. Thus, in *Parke Davis & Co v Probel* Case 24/67 [1968] ECR 55 at 71 *g* and *Deutsche Grammophon Gesellschaft mbH v Metro-SB-Großmärkte GmbH & Co KG* Case 78/70 [1971] ECR 487, Dutch and German law made provision for industrial or commercial property rights which were unknown in Italy and in France respectively. However, the court did not call in question the member states' freedom to grant industrial or commercial property rights within the meaning of art 36, even though differences between those rights were the source of a potential barrier to the free movement of *h* goods.

16. Those are the observations which, in my view, are called for with regard to the first sentence of art 36, which, in the opinion of the representatives of the United Kingdom and Thetford, is the only provision to which the Court of Appeal intended to refer.

17. However, in my view the appraisal of the issue would be incomplete were we to *j* ignore the second sentence of art 36. The national court asks not only whether a patent granted under the conditions described constitutes industrial or commercial property, but whether it constitutes industrial or commercial property entitled to protection under art 36 of the EEC Treaty.

18. It would not be entitled to protection if the prohibition or restriction on imports

based on the existence of a patent constituted a means of arbitrary discrimination or a
*a* disguised restriction on trade between member states within the meaning of the second
sentence of art 36.

19. In fact, it could be that an injunction prohibiting the importation of a product,
issued in view of the existence of a patent, may constitute such discrimination or such a
restriction simply because the patent was granted in circumstances indicative of a
protectionist intention.

*b*    20. Therefore, in this case the court is not called on to consider, as Fiamma asks it to
do, whether a patent such as the one granted to Thetford constitutes a genuine patent
(under United Kingdom law that is in fact the case), but to consider whether in the light
of the circumstances in which the patent was granted (that is to say despite the existence
of specifications going back more than 50 years) the prohibition on the importation of
products of the type in question constitutes arbitrary discrimination or a disguised
*c* restriction on trade.

21. It is from that point of view that Fiamma's example of the grant of a patent for a
perfectly ordinary football may be helpful. If a member state were in fact to grant a
patent for such an article in everyday use, without any doubt its motive would be to
reserve a monopoly for a national manufacturer, thereby imposing a disguised restriction
on trade within the meaning of the second sentence of art 36.

*d*    22. It was, moreover, on the basis of the second sentence of art 36 that the court held
in the 'Sekt and Weinbrand' case (see *EC Commission v Germany* Case 12/74 [1975] ECR
181 at 199 (para 16), which Fiamma cites in support of its argument, that art 30 of the
Treaty had been infringed because German law granted the protection provided for
indications of origin to appellations which, at the time when such protection was granted,
were merely generic in nature.

*e*    23. Can the protection of a patented product against imports from another member
state despite the relative novelty of the invention likewise constitute arbitrary
discrimination or a disguised restriction on imports?

24. Certainly, according to the established case law of the court, the specific subject
matter of a patent consists in—

*f*        'according the inventor an exclusive right of first placing the product on the
        market so as to allow him to obtain the *reward for his creative effort*.' (My emphasis.)

(See, most recently, *Pharmon BV v Hoechst AG* Case 19/84 [1985] ECR 2281 at 2298
(para 26).)

25. Consequently, where there is no effort to reward, a prohibition on importation
can scarcely be anything other than the expression of a discriminatory or protectionist
*g* attitude (the example of the football).

26. The United Kingdom and the Commission argue that there is reward for an effort
in this case, namely the effort put in by the author of the 'reinvention', who makes a
forgotten invention available once again to the country. This reasoning seems to me to
be valid, especially since *only patent specifications* going back more than 50 years are
*h* excluded from the state of the art by s 50 of the Patents Act 1949. In other words,
publication in forms other than patent specifications and previous use going back more
than 50 years may be relied on in order to obtain the revocation of the patent. (I would
observe that the national court asked us to assume simply as a working hypothesis that
Thetford's patent is valid under United Kingdom law.) Anticipation is ignored only
where the old invention exists only in the form of old documents lodged at the Patent
*i* Office. In that context it seems to me to be possible to speak of reinvention and rewarding
reinvention, whether the 'inventor' was wholly ignorant of the old specifications and
made an invention quite independently of them or whether he discovered them on the
shelves of the Patent Office and developed a modern product from them.

27. Other arguments tend to show that this is not one of the cases covered by the
second sentence of art 36. First, paras (*a*) and (*b*) of s 50(1) of the Patents Act 1949 make

no distinction between specifications describing an invention lodged in connection with a patent application in the United Kingdom and those lodged in connection with a patent application in another country: in both cases specifications which are more than 50 years old are not taken into consideration. (Moreover, it was not contested that specifications relating to patent applications made abroad are available at the United Kingdom Patent Office.)

28. It is also uncontested that foreign nationals applying for a patent in the United Kingdom have the same rights as British nationals in regard to the 50-year rule. Hence, if Fiamma had lodged its patent application before Thetford and if its product had not been described in a publication available in the United Kingdom Fiamma would have obtained a United Kingdom patent. It would have been able to enforce that patent both with respect to imports (except imports of its own products marketed with its consent in other member states) and with regard to any infringers of that patent in the territory of the United Kingdom.

29. It may be concluded, therefore, that a prohibition or restriction on imports granted with a view to protecting the exclusive rights of the holder of a patent issued in respect of an invention the novelty of which in the absence of the 50-year rule could have been contested would not constitute arbitrary discrimination or a disguised restriction on trade between member states within the meaning of the second sentence of art 36.

30. It remains for me to say a few words about a related issue raised by the Commission in answering the questions put by the court. Under the Patents Act 1949 it was possible to obtain a patent in the United Kingdom for an invention which was freely used or published (and could therefore be freely used) in another member state at the time of the application. Like the Commission, I take the view that if such legislation still existed now a prohibition on importation granted in order to protect a patent obtained on that basis would constitute arbitrary discrimination or a disguised restriction on trade between member states. The question whether the Treaty could now be invoked in order to deprive the holder of a patent which was validly granted in 1969, that is to say before the United Kingdom became a member of the Community, of the right to oppose imports, in my view raises very complex problems involving, inter alia, concepts such as the transitional period, legal certainty, legitimate expectations and vested rights. There can be no question of the court's dealing with them by way, so to speak, of an obiter dictum when the Court of Appeal has not even raised the matter.

31. For all the reasons set out above I propose, therefore, that the first question should be answered as follows:

> 'A subsisting patent which was granted in the United Kingdom under the provisions of the Patents Act 1949 in respect of an invention which but for the provisions of s 50 of that Act would have been anticipated (lacked novelty) by a specification as is described in para (a) or (b) of s 50(1) of that Act constitutes industrial or commercial property entitled to protection under art 36 of the EEC Treaty.'

*The second question*

32. In its second question the Court of Appeal asks whether, if a patent such as Thetford's is entitled to the protection of art 36, the only relief justified under that article would, as Fiamma has argued, be an order for the payment of a reasonable royalty (or other monetary award) but not an injunction.

33. According to the established case law of the court (see, most recently, *Pharmon BV v Hoechst AG* Case 19/84 [1985] ECR 2281 at 2298 (para 26)):

> '... the substance of a patent right lies essentially in according the inventor an exclusive right of first placing the product on the market so as to allow him to obtain the reward for his creative effort. It is therefore *necessary* to allow the patent proprietor to *prevent the importation* and marketing of products manufactured under

a     a compulsory licence in order to protect the substance of his exclusive rights under his patent.' (My emphasis.)

34. There is all the more reason to reach such a conclusion where there is not even a compulsory licence in the country of manufacture or any form of consent on the part of the patentee to the marketing of the product concerned (cf *Merck & Co Inc v Stephar BV* Case 187/80 [1981] ECR 2063, *Centrafarm BV v Sterling Drug Inc* Case 15/74 [1974] ECR
b     1147).

35. Consequently, prohibiting importation is the normal method of protecting the specific subject matter of the patentee's right and there is no room for considerations based on the principle of proportionality. Moreover, it would be paradoxical to require United Kingdom law to tolerate the importation of products manufactured abroad without the patentee's consent whereas if the products were manufactured in the United
c     Kingdom it would be possible to restrain the manufacturer's activity by means of an injunction.

36. In contrast, the situation would be quite different if, all other things being equal, an infringer established in the country in question could only be ordered to pay royalties but could not be restrained by injunction from manufacturing. In that case an injunction issued against importers alone would constitute an arbitrary discrimination within the
d     meaning of the second sentence of art 36. This follows from the court's judgment in *Allen & Hanburys Ltd v Generics (UK) Ltd* Case 434/85 [1988] 2 All ER 454 at 474, [1989] 1 WLR 414 at 430 (para 23 of judgment; see also para 22) where the court ruled that—

'arts 30 and 36 of the Treaty must be interpreted as precluding the courts of a member state from issuing an injunction prohibiting the importation from another member state of a product which infringes a patent endorsed "licences of right"
e     against an importer who has undertaken to take a licence on the terms prescribed by law where no such injunction may be issued in the same circumstances against an infringer who manufactures the product in the national territory.'

37. For all those reasons I propose the following answer to the second question:

f     'Article 36 permits the courts of a member state to issue an injunction prohibiting the importation and marketing of a product infringing a patent issued in that state where, in the same situation, an injunction could be issued against an infringer manufacturing the product in the national territory.'

30 June. **THE COURT OF JUSTICE** delivered the following judgment.

g     1. By an order which was lodged at the court registry on 5 February 1987 the Court of Appeal, London, referred to the court for a preliminary ruling under art 177 of the EEC Treaty two questions concerning the interpretation of art 36 of the EEC Treaty with a view to the assessment of the compatibility with the rules on the free movement of goods of certain provisions of national patent law and especially the principle of 'relative
h     novelty'.

2. Those questions were raised in proceedings brought by Thetford Corp and Thetford (Aqua) Products Ltd (hereinafter referred to as 'Thetford'), the owners of several United Kingdom patents relating to portable toilets, against Fiamma SpA, a manufacturer of such toilets in Italy, and Fiamma UK, which imports them into the United Kingdom (hereinafter together referred to as 'Fiamma').

j     3. It appears from the order of the national court that Thetford sued Fiamma for infringement of two United Kingdom patents, granted pursuant to the Patents Act 1949, namely Patent no 1226235 and Patent no 1530155. The articles alleged to constitute an infringement of those patents are portable toilets manufactured in Italy and sold in the United Kingdom. Fiamma has no licence from Thetford in the United Kingdom, in Italy or anywhere else.

4. Before the Patents Court Fiamma denied the patent infringement and argued, on
the one hand, that Thetford's patent was invalid on grounds of lack of novelty and  *a*
inventive step and, on the other, that even if the patent were valid, arts 30 and 36 of the
EEC Treaty limited the relief which the courts of the United Kingdom ought to grant to
the proprietor of the patent.

5. After the Patents Court had granted Thetford's application, Fiamma appealed to the
Court of Appeal, which decided that, bearing in mind that there was no direct authority
of the Court of Justice on the points raised by the defendants, the allegations disclosed an  *b*
arguable case. It therefore decided to refer the following questions to the Court of Justice
for a preliminary ruling:

> '1. Whether a subsisting patent which has been granted in the United Kingdom
> under the provisions of the Patents Act 1949 in respect of an invention which but
> for the provisions of section 50 of that Act would have been anticipated (lacked  *c*
> novelty) by a specification as is described in paragraphs (*a*) or (*b*) of section 50(1) of
> the Act constitutes industrial or commercial property entitled to protection under
> Article 36 of the Treaty of Rome?
> 2. If such a patent is entitled to such protection as aforesaid whether as contended
> by the defendants Fiamma in this case the only relief justified under Article 36 of
> the Treaty would be an order for the payment of a reasonable royalty (or other  *d*
> monetary award) but not an injunction?'

6. Reference is made to the report for the hearing for a fuller description of the facts,
the applicable national legislation and the observations submitted to the court, which are
mentioned or discussed hereinafter only in so far as is necessary for the reasoning of the
court.
                                                                                    *e*

*The first question*

7. The Court of Appeal's first question seeks to establish whether the derogation from
arts 30 to 34 of the EEC Treaty which is set out in the first sentence of art 36 necessarily
applies to any patent granted pursuant to the legislation of a member state or whether,
on the contrary, it does not apply to patents granted by virtue of the principle of relative  *f*
novelty.

8. The principle of relative novelty, as adopted at the material time by the legislation
of the United Kingdom, is the result of s 50(1) of the Patents Act 1949, which provided
as follows:

> 'An invention claimed in a complete specification shall not be deemed to have
> been anticipated by reason only that the invention was published in the United  *g*
> Kingdom—(*a*) in a specification filed in pursuance of an application for a patent
> made in the United Kingdom and dated more than fifty years before the date of
> filing of the first-mentioned specification; (*b*) in a specification describing the
> invention for the purposes of an application for protection in any country outside
> the United Kingdom made more than fifty years before that date . . .'
                                                                                    *h*
Consequently, it was not possible under the 1949 Act to base an action to have a patent
declared invalid on a specification issued in the United Kingdom or any other country
more than 50 years previously.

9. It should be observed in limine that, as the parties acknowledged at the hearing,
the question put by the Court of Appeal hinges on the question of relative novelty, in so
far as it was not possible under the Patents Act 1949 to have a patent declared invalid  *j*
solely on the ground that its specification was published prior to a period of time fixed
by statute.

10. In that connection, it must be pointed out that the effect of the provisions of the
Treaty on the free movement of goods, in particular art 30, is to prohibit as between
member states restrictions on imports and all measures having equivalent effect.

According to art 36, however, those provisions do not preclude prohibitions or restrictions
a on imports justified on grounds of the protection of industrial and commercial property.
However, such prohibitions or restrictions must not constitute a means of arbitrary
discrimination or a disguised restriction on trade between member states.

11. Fiamma argues that the derogation provided for in art 36 can apply only if a
patent right granted pursuant to national legislation fulfils certain fundamental
conditions. In particular, a patent granted in the absence of novelty or an inventive step
b cannot be regarded as being covered by the expression 'protection of industrial and
commercial property'.

12. In that regard, it must be observed, as the court held in *Keurkoop BV v Nancy Kean
Gifts BV* Case 144/81 [1982] ECR 2853 at 2871 (para 18) on the protection of designs,
that—

c       'in the present state of Community law and in the absence of Community
         standardization or of a harmonization of laws the determination of the conditions
         and procedures under which protection ... is granted is a matter for national
         rules ...'

13. However, Fiamma contends that the court's case law on designs may not be
transposed to the field of patents in view of the higher degree of harmonisation of
d national legislation which has already been achieved in that field and the existence of
international conventions based on the principle of absolute novelty.

14. That argument cannot be upheld. Firstly, no harmonisation of the patents
legislation of the member states has yet been effected by virtue of measures of
Community law. Secondly, none of the international conventions in force on patents is
capable of supporting Fiamma's argument. The entry into force of the Convention on
e the Grant of European Patents (the European Patent Convention) (Munich, 5 October
1973; TS 20 (1978); Cmnd 7090), which is based on the principle of absolute novelty,
did not affect the existence of national legislation on the granting of patents. Article 2(2)
of that convention expressly provides that 'The European patent shall, in each of the
Contracting States for which it is granted, have the effect of and be subject to the same
conditions as a national patent granted by that State'. As for the Convention on the
f Unification of Certain Points of Substantive Law on Patents for Invention (Strasbourg, 27
November 1963; TS 70 (1980); Cmnd 8002), it must be pointed out that, since that
convention entered into force after the patent in question had been granted, it cannot
serve as a determining factor for the purposes of the interpretation of Community law.
The only instrument the provisions of which might afford support for Fiamma's point
of view with regard to the recognition in the Community legal order of the principle of
g absolute novelty is the Convention for the Patent for the Common Market (the
Community Patent Convention) (Luxembourg, 15 December 1975; EC 18 (1976);
Cmnd 6553), which has close links with the aforementioned Munich Convention but
which has not yet entered into force.

15. It follows that, as the court held in *Parke Davis & Co v Probel* Case 24/67 [1968]
h ECR 55, since the existence of patent rights is at present a matter solely of national law, a
member state's patents legislation, such as the legislation at issue, is covered in principle
by the derogations from art 30 which are provided for in art 36.

16. It must next be considered whether the application of the principle at issue may
not constitute a means of arbitrary discrimination or a disguised restriction on trade
between member states within the meaning of the second sentence of art 36.

j      17. As regards the first possibility, namely whether a means of arbitrary discrimination
is involved, it is sufficient, in order to refute that argument, to point out that before the
court the agent of the United Kingdom stated, without being contradicted by the other
parties, that the application of s 50(1) of the Patents Act 1949 does not give rise to any
discrimination. On the one hand, that rule prevents consideration from being given to a
specification disclosing an invention whether it was filed in the United Kingdom or in

another state; secondly, there is no discrimination based on the nationality of applicants for patents: foreign nationals applying for patents in the United Kingdom have the same *a* rights as United Kingdom nationals.

18. It must further be considered whether the application of the principle in question may not give rise to a disguised restriction on trade between member states.

19. In that regard, the justification for the rule of relative novelty, as given in the documents before the court, discloses that the objective pursued by the United Kingdom legislature in introducing the '50-year rule' in 1902 was to foster creative activity on the *b* part of inventors in the interest of industry. To that end, the 50-year rule aimed to make it possible to give a reward, in the form of the grant of a patent, even in cases in which an 'old' invention was 'rediscovered'. In such cases the United Kingdom legislation was designed to prevent the existence of a former patent specification which had never been utilised or published from constituting a ground for revoking a patent which had been validly issued.          *c*

20. Consequently, a rule such as the 50-year rule cannot be regarded as constituting a disguised restriction on trade between member states.

21. In view of the foregoing considerations, the answer to the national court's first question must be that, in the present state of Community law, art 36 must be interpreted as not precluding the application of a member state's legislation on patents which provides that a patent granted for an invention may not be declared invalid by reason *d* only of the fact that the invention in question appears in a patent specification filed more than 50 years previously.

*The second question*

22. In its second question the Court of Appeal asks essentially whether the national court is free to choose from among the various forms of relief available under national *e* law in cases of infringement or whether the only relief justified under art 36 of the Treaty is an order for the payment of a reasonable royalty (or other monetary award) but not an injunction prohibiting the importation of the infringing article from another member state.

23. Fiamma maintains in that connection that the 'rule of proportionality' as defined *f* in the case law of the court and, in particular, by *de Peijper* Case 104/75 [1976] ECR 613 should also be applied in the field of industrial and commercial property. In particular, in view of the particular features of the case at issue, in which the protection conferred by art 36 relates to a patent obtained by virtue of the rule of relative novelty, the specific subject matter of the patent is already adequately protected by conferring on the proprietor of the patent the right to obtain reward for the marketing of the patented *g* article without going so far as to give him the right to obtain an injunction.

24. However, it must be observed in that connection that according to the case law of the court (most recently in *Pharmon BV v Hoechst AG* Case 19/84 [1985] ECR 2281) the right of the proprietor of a patent to prevent the importation and marketing of products manufactured under a compulsory licence is part of the substance of patents law. There is all the more reason for that conclusion to apply in a case such as this where no licence *h* has been granted by the proprietor of the patent in the country of manufacture.

25. Consequently, the answer to the second question must be that, where national law normally provides for the issue of an injunction to prevent any infringement, that measure is justified under art 36.

*Costs*          *j*

26. The costs incurred by the United Kingdom and the Commission of the European Communities, which have submitted observations to the court, are not recoverable. Since these proceedings are, in so far as the parties to the main proceedings are concerned, in the nature of a step in the proceedings pending before the national court, the decision as to costs is a matter for that court.

*a*  On those grounds, the court, in reply to the questions submitted to it by the Court of Appeal, London, hereby rules: (1) in the present state of Community law, art 36 does not preclude the application of a member state's legislation on patents which provides that a patent granted for an invention may not be declared invalid by reason only of the fact that the invention in question appears in a patent specification filed more than 50 years previously; (2) where national law normally provides for the issue of an injunction to prevent any infringement, that measure is justified under art 36.

*b*

Agents: *Clifford Chance* (for Thetford); *Evershed & Tomkinson*, Birmingham (for Fiamma); *Susan Hay*, Treasury Solicitor's Department (for the United Kingdom); *Eric L White*, Legal Department of the EC Commission (for the Commission).

Mary Rose Plummer    Barrister.

*c*

# J Sainsbury plc and another v Enfield London Borough Council

*d*

CHANCERY DIVISION

MORRITT J

12, 13, 14, 15 DECEMBER 1988, 16 JANUARY 1989

*Restrictive covenant affecting land – Annexation of benefit – Retained land – Intention that benefit*
*e* *of purchaser's covenants be annexed to retained land – Restrictive covenant in conveyance preventing purchasers or their successors using land for building purposes other than houses or for trade or business – No reference in conveyance to retained land or to vendor's successors in title – Vendor not living on retained land – Whether benefit of purchaser's covenants annexed to retained land – Conveyancing and Law of Property Act 1881, s 58(1).*

*f*  In 1881 W purchased an estate which was inherited by his son, AW, in 1882. Neither W nor AW ever lived on the estate and in 1882 AW entered into a contract to sell the whole estate but the sale was never completed because the purchasers went bankrupt. On 5 April 1894 AW sold part of the land to the predecessors in title of the second plaintiffs by way of a conveyance which contained restrictive covenants preventing the use of the land by the purchasers or their successors in title for, inter alia, building purposes other *g*  than houses, or for trade or business. Under s 58(1)[a] of the Conveyancing and Law of Property Act 1881 the covenants were deemed to have been made 'with the covenantee, his heirs and assigns' and had effect as if such heirs and assigns were expressed in the conveyance. AW sold further parts of the estate to other purchasers and after his death in 1898 his executors sold the remainder of the land. In 1985 the second plaintiffs entered into a contract for the sale of the land in the 1894 conveyance to the first plaintiffs subject *h*  to a condition that the land was no longer subject to the restrictive covenants. The plaintiffs applied together for a declaration to that effect. The application was opposed by the successors in title of the land retained by AW when the land in the 1894 conveyance was sold.

**Held** – The declaration would be granted because, construing the conveyance in the
*j*  light of the surrounding circumstances, it could not be inferred from the conveyance that the benefit of the purchaser's covenants was intended to be annexed to the land

*a*  Section 58(1) provides: 'A covenant relating to land of inheritance, or devolving on the heir as special occupant, shall be deemed to be made with the covenantee, his heirs and assigns, and shall have effect as if heirs and assigns were expressed.'

retained by AW when the land in the 1894 conveyance was sold, since it was clear that
AW intended to sell the estate as and when he could rather than retain it for himself and *a*
there was no express reference in the conveyance to the retained land or to his successors
in title. Furthermore, the deemed incorporation of AW's heirs and assigns into the
conveyance by s 58(1) of the 1881 Act was not as such sufficient to give rise to the
annexation of the benefit of the purchaser's covenants to the retained land, nor did s 58
cause the benefit of the covenants to run with that land and be annexed to it. Accordingly,
the 1894 conveyance did not annex the benefit of the purchaser's covenants to the *b*
retained land and there were no longer any persons entitled to the benefit of the
purchaser's covenants (see p 822 *a b*, p 823 *d* to *h*, p 824 *a b* and p 826 *h j*, post).

Renals v Cowlishaw [1874–80] All ER Rep 359, Reid v Bickerstaff [1908–10] All ER Rep
298 and Federated Homes Ltd v Mill Lodge Properties Ltd [1980] 1 All ER 371 distinguished.

**Notes**	*c*
For annexation of a restrictive covenant to retained land, see 16 Halsbury's Laws (4th
edn) para 1353.

For the Conveyancing and Law of Property Act 1881, s 58, see 37 Halsbury's Statutes
(4th edn) 60.

Section 58 of the 1881 Act was repealed by the Law of Property Act 1925, s 207, Sch 7,
but by s 78(2) thereof the repeal does not affect covenants to which that section applied. *d*
As to covenants made after 1925, see s 78(1) of the 1925 Act.

**Cases referred to in judgment**
Federated Homes Ltd v Mill Lodge Properties Ltd [1980] 1 All ER 371, [1980] 1 WLR 594,
CA.
Forster v Elvet Colliery Co Ltd [1908] 1 KB 629, CA; affd sub nom Dyson v Forster [1909] *e*
AC 98, [1908–10] All ER Rep 212, HL.
Ives v Brown [1919] 2 Ch 314.
Kumar v Dunning [1987] 2 All ER 801, [1989] QB 193, [1987] 3 WLR 1167, CA.
Mann v Stephens (1846) 15 Sim 377, 60 ER 665, LC.
Marten v Flight Refuelling Ltd [1961] 2 All ER 696, [1962] Ch 115, [1961] 2 WLR 1018. *f*
Newton Abbot Co-op Society Ltd v Williamson & Treadgold Ltd [1952] 1 All ER 279, [1952]
Ch 286.
Reid v Bickerstaff [1909] 2 Ch 305, [1908–10] All ER Rep 298, CA.
Renals v Cowlishaw (1878) 9 Ch D 125, [1874–80] All ER Rep 359; affd (1879) 11 Ch D
866, [1874–80] All ER Rep 359, CA.
Rogers v Hosegood [1900] 2 Ch 388, [1900–3] All ER Rep 915, CA.
Shropshire CC v Edwards (1982) 46 P & CR 270.	*g*
Union of London and Smith's Bank Ltd's Conveyance, Re, Miles v Easter [1933] Ch 611, [1933]
All ER Rep 355, CA.
Zetland (Marquess) v Driver [1938] 2 All ER 158, [1939] Ch 1, CA.

**Case also cited**	*h*
Roake v Chadha [1983] 3 All ER 503, [1984] 1 WLR 40.

**Originating summons**
By originating summons dated 13 May 1988 the plaintiffs, J Sainsbury plc and Haringey
London Borough Council, applied for (1) a declaration that freehold property situate at
Winchmore Hill in Enfield, London, which was comprised in a conveyance dated 5 April *j*
1894 made between Alfred Walker junior of the first part, Alfred Walker junior and
Henry Brown of the second part, and Samuel West, Anthony Alfred Bowlby and Thomas
William Shore of the third part was no longer subject to the restrictive covenants as to
user contained in the conveyance or (2) alternatively a declaration whether the restrictive
covenants in the conveyance were enforceable and, if so, by whom. The defendant to the

a summons was Enfield London Borough Council, which was appointed to represent all
persons who were successors in title to Alfred Walker jnr in respect of land retained by
him when the 1894 conveyance was entered into. The facts are set out in the judgment.

*Gavin Lightman QC* and *Elizabeth Jones* for the plaintiffs.
*Anthony Scrivener QC* and *Geoffrey Stephenson* for the defendant.

b                                                                                    *Cur adv vult*

16 January. The following judgment was delivered.

**MORRITT J.** By this originating summons the plaintiffs seek a declaration pursuant to
c   s 84(2) of the Law of Property Act 1925 that certain freehold land at Winchmore Hill in
the London borough of Enfield is no longer subject to restrictive covenants contained in
a conveyance of 5 April 1894.
        The land in question was formerly part of the Highfield House estate and is now
registered in Her Majesty's Land Registry under title no MX 70079. The second plaintiff,
Haringey London Borough Council, is the registered proprietor and has contracted to sell
d   the land to the first plaintiff, J Sainsbury plc, subject, inter alia, to the condition that a
declaraton, as sought by this originating summons, is made.
        By the conveyance of 5 April 1894 the purchasers of the land entered into certain
covenants with the vendor, Alfred Walker junior. The question for determination is
whether the benefit of those covenants was annexed to certain land retained by the
vendor so as to be enforceable by successors in title to such retained land. By an order
e   made on 29 July 1988 the defendant, Enfield London Borough Council, was appointed
to represent all persons being successors in title of Alfred Walker junior to that retained
land.
        The Highfield House estate was bought by Alfred Walker senior on 30 May 1881. The
boundaries of the estate were Hoppers Road to the west, Compton Road to the north and
Green Lanes to the east. Apart from Highfield House itself, the estate was undeveloped.
f   By his will dated 10 November 1881 Alfred Walker senior appointed his son, Alfred
Walker junior, and Henry Brown to be his executors, and after bequeathing certain
legacies left all his real and personal estate to his son Alfred Walker junior. Alfred Walker
senior died on 19 July 1882 and probate of his will was granted to Alfred Walker junior
and Henry Brown on 4 September 1882. Alfred Walker senior never lived at Highfield
House nor did his son.
g       On 20 October 1882 Alfred Walker junior contracted to sell the whole estate to G & N
Hempsted for a price payable by instalments. G & N Hempsted assigned their interest in
the contract to North London Freehold Land and House Co Ltd. For some reason, not
apparent from the evidence, on 28 January 1883 Alfred Walker junior and G & N
Hempsted conveyed Highfield House, but not the rest of the estate, to Peregrine Purvis
h   as nominee subject to the terms of the contract.
        In November 1883 the Hempsted's went bankrupt and North London Freehold Land
and House Co Ltd went into liquidation. On 27 October 1887 Alfred Walker junior duly
determined the contract for sale. On 9 March 1894 Alfred Walker junior sold a small
plot of land adjacent to the Congregational Chapel and on 4 April 1894 Peregrine Purvis
reconveyed Highfield House to Alfred Walker junior.
j       The conveyance in question was executed on 5 April 1894. It was made between
Alfred Walker junior of the first part, Alfred Walker junior and Henry Brown, described
as a builder, of the second part, and S West, A M Bowlby and T W Shore, called, 'the
purchasers', of the third part. In the margin of the conveyance is a plan which shows,
coloured green, the part of the Highfield estate being thereby conveyed. That part is a
square on the south-east corner of the estate. The eastern boundary is Green Lanes. The

western boundary is described as 'proposed road' and the surrounding land to the west
and the north is described as 'other land belonging to Alfred Walker Esq'.

The conveyance recites the purchase of the estate by Alfred Walker senior, his will,
death, the grant of probate and the progress with the administration of his estate. It then
recites:

'AND WHEREAS the said Alfred Walker has agreed with the Purchasers for the sale
to them of the hereditaments hereinafter described and the inheritance thereof in
fee simple free from incumbrances but subject to the conditions and stipulations as
to user thereof hereinafter contained at the price of four thousand two hundred
pounds.'

The operative part provides:

'... the said Alfred Walker and Henry Brown as trustees do hereby release and
the said Alfred Walker as beneficial owner hereby conveys unto the Purchasers ALL
that piece of ground part of the Highfield House Estate situate on the west side of
Green Lanes at Winchmore Hill in the Parish of Edmonton in the county of
Middlesex containing ten acres and with the measurements and boundaries thereof
more particularly described in the plan drawn in the margin of these presents and
thereon coloured green TO HOLD the same subject to the conditions and stipulations
as to user thereof hereinafter contained UNTO AND TO the use of the Purchasers in fee
simple ...'

Thereafter Alfred Walker junior acknowledged the right of the purchasers to
production of the documents specified in the schedule and covenanted with the
purchasers to redeem the tithe rentcharge and in the mean time to indemnify the
purchasers. There was then a covenant in the following terms:

'AND the said Alfred Walker so as to bind the owners for the time being of that
portion of the said Highfield House Estate not hereby conveyed and shown on the
said plan and thereon marked "other land belonging to Alfred Walker Esq.," doth
hereby covenant with the purchasers that he the said Alfred Walker or his successors
in title shall not so long as the land hereby conveyed is used as a recreation ground
and not for building purposes make or permit to be made on or over any portion of
the strip of land coloured yellow on the said plan (being a strip of land one foot wide
along the western boundary of the land hereby conveyed) any road or footway
whatsoever and shall not at any time make any road or footway within one [and
then a word appears which is illegible] the land hereby conveyed ...'

This is the only reference in the conveyance, apart from the operative part itself, to the
'other land belonging to Alfred Walker Esq.' shown on the plan. There followed two
provisos enabling the purchasers to acquire the strip of land referred to, the only relevance
of which is that they contain two references to Alfred Walker or his successors in title.

The covenants with which I am directly concerned are in the following terms:

'AND the purchasers so as to bind themselves and their successors in title whilst
the land hereby conveyed shall remain vested in them and to the intent to bind all
future owners thereof but not so as to incur any personal liability after they shall
have parted with the land hereby conveyed do hereby covenant with the said Alfred
Walker that in the event of the land hereby conveyed being at any time used for
building purposes no building shall be erected thereon other than houses each of a
net rental value of not less than £35 per annum and to be used as private
dwellinghouses only and that no trade business or manufacture of any kind shall at
any time be carried on upon any part of the land hereby conveyed and particularly
that no part of the land hereby conveyed shall at any time be used as a hospital
infirmary sanitorium or place for the care or treatment of persons afflicted with

infectious or non-infectious diseases or of unsound mind but the fact that charges
may be made for admission to the land hereby conveyed for the purpose of
witnessing or taking part in cricket matches athletic sports or other entertainments
of a like character shall not be deemed to be the carrying on of business within the
meaning of this covenant AND that the Purchaser shall not dig clay for or make or
burn bricks on the land hereby conveyed or do or permit to be done thereon
anything which may be or become a nuisance annoyance or disturbance to the
occupiers of neighbouring or adjacent premises but the use of burnt clay in the
construction of tennis courts running paths or a recreation ground shall not be
deemed to be a breach of this covenant AND also that the Purchasers shall erect and
maintain suitable fences on the boundaries of the land shown by red lines and
marked thus (T) on the said plan for enclosing the land hereby conveyed such fences
not to exceed 6 feet 6 inches in height AND further that no buildings or erections
shall be placed nearer than 15 feet to the line of the proposed road A.B. shown on
the said plan.'

Thereafter Alfred Walker junior sold six further parts of the Highfield House estate
prior to his death on 23 March 1898. The remainder of the estate was sold by his
executors after his death.

The land retained in 1894 has now been developed, but the land then conveyed has
not been. It is not alleged that there was a building scheme or that there was any
assignment of the benefit of the covenant. The only question is whether the benefit of
the covenants given by the purchasers in the conveyance dated 5 April 1894 was annexed
to the land then retained by Alfred Walker junior so as to pass with that land on the
subsequent disposition thereof. The defendant did not contend before me that the benefit
of the covenants passed on subsequent sales under s 6 of the Conveyancing and Law of
Property Act 1881 because of the decision in *Kumar v Dunning* [1987] 2 All ER 801,
[1989] QB 193. The plaintiffs did not contend before me that if the benefit of the
purchasers' covenants was annexed to the retained land of Alfred Walker junior that it
was annexed only to the whole of it and not to each and every part thereof because of the
decision in *Federated Homes Ltd v Mill Lodge Properties Ltd* [1980] 1 All ER 371, [1980] 1
WLR 594. However, both points were reserved for argument on any appeal.

The purchasers' covenants related to land of inheritance and consequently, pursuant to
s 58(1) of the 1881 Act, are 'deemed to be made with the covenantee, his heirs and assigns
and shall have effect as if heirs and assigns were expressed'. Thus the material part of the
conveyance reads as follows:

'The purchasers, so as to bind themselves and their successors in title, whilst the
land hereby conveyed shall remain vested in them and to the intent to bind all
future owners thereof but not so as to incur any personal liability after they shall
have parted with the land hereby conveyed, do hereby covenant with the said Alfred
Walker, his heirs and assigns, that . . .'

As I have already recorded, it is not contended that in this case there was a building
scheme or that the benefit of the purchasers' covenants was expressly assigned on the
subsequent sales of the retained land. It is common ground that the retained land was
capable of being benefited by the covenants and was sufficiently identified so as to enable
annexation of the benefit of the covenants if annexation was intended. The requisite
intention is that the covenants should enure for the benefit of the retained land: cf *Re
Union of London and Smith's Bank Ltd's Conveyance, Miles v Easter* [1933] Ch 611 at 628,
[1933] All ER Rep 355 at 364.

The issues between the parties are as follows. (1) From what facts or by what documents
may such intention be inferred or expressed? (2) Is the requisite intention manifested by
such facts or documents as may be considered? (3) Irrespective of intention, was the

benefit of the covenants annexed to the retained land by virtue of s 58 of the 1881 Act? I
will deal with the issues in that order.

On the first issue the plaintiffs contend that the intention must be manifested in the
conveyance in which the covenant was contained when construed in the light of the
surrounding circumstances, including any necessary implication in the conveyance from
those surrounding circumstances. The defendant claims that such intention may be
inferred from surrounding circumstances which fall short of those which would
necessitate an implication in the conveyance itself.

The defendant relies on the points that the land intended to be benefited may be
ascertained from surrounding circumstances alone (see *Marten v Flight Refuelling Ltd*
[1961] 2 All ER 696, [1962] Ch 115) and that in some reported cases the possibility of
inferring the relevant intention wholly from the surrounding circumstances is envisaged.

Thus, in *Renals v Cowlishaw* (1878) 9 Ch D 125 at 129 Hall V-C stated:

> 'A purchaser may also be entitled to the benefit of a restrictive covenant entered
> into with his vendor by another or others where his vendor has contracted with him
> that he shall be the assign of it, that is, have the benefit of the covenant. And such
> covenant need not be express, but may be collected from the transaction of sale and
> purchase. In considering this, the expressed or otherwise apparent purpose or object
> of the covenant, in reference to its being intended to be annexed to other property,
> or to its being only obtained to enable the covenantee more advantageously to deal
> with his property, is important to be attended to.'

However, the reference to the 'otherwise apparent purpose or object or the covenant' is
equally consistent with the plaintiffs' submissions.

Similarly in *Rogers v Hosegood* [1900] 2 Ch 388 at 407–408, [1900–3] All ER Rep 915
at 921 the Court of Appeal stated:

> 'When, as in *Renals* v. *Cowlishaw*, there is no indication in the original conveyance,
> or in the circumstances attending it, that the burden of the restrictive covenant is
> imposed for the benefit of the land reserved, or any particular part of it, then it
> becomes necessary to examine the circumstances under which any part of the land
> reserved is sold, in order to see whether a benefit, not originally annexed to it, has
> become annexed to it on the sale, so that the purchaser is deemed to have bought it
> with the land, and this can hardly be the case when the purchaser did not know of
> the existence of the restrictive covenant.'

Again, this statement appears to me to be equally consistent with the plaintiffs' approach.

However, the other authorities to which I have been referred show, in my judgment,
that the plaintiffs' submission is correct. Thus in *Reid v Bickerstaff* [1909] 2 Ch 305 at 320,
[1908–10] All ER Rep 299 at 300 Cozens-Hardy MR stated:

> 'It is irrelevant to urge that the performance of the covenant would be greatly for
> the benefit of the adjoining land. The benefit of a covenant capable of being annexed
> to land, but not expressed to be so annexed, either by the deed containing the
> covenant or by some subsequent instrument executed by the covenantee, does not
> pass as an incident of land on a subsequent conveyance. *Renals* v. *Cowlishaw* and
> *Rogers* v. *Hosegood* seem to me to bear out what I have said.'

In *Miles v Easter* [1933] Ch 611 at 628, [1933] All ER Rep 355 at 364 in the passage to
which I have already referred, the Court of Appeal stated that the intention must be
shown in the conveyance itself. There is a similar statement by the Court of Appeal in
*Marquess of Zetland v Driver* [1938] 2 All ER 158 at 161, [1939] Ch 1 at 8.

In *Newton Abbot Co-op Society Ltd v Williamson & Treadgold Ltd* [1952] 1 All ER 279 at
283, [1952] Ch 286 at 289 Upjohn J stated:

> 'In this difficult branch of the law one thing, in my judgment, is clear, *viz*., that

a

in order to annex the benefit of a restrictive covenant to land so that it runs with the land without express assignment on a subsequent assignment of the land, the land for the benefit of which it is taken must be clearly identified in the conveyance containing the covenant.'

When contrasted with a later passage in his judgment 9[1952] 1 All ER 279 at 286–288, [1952] Ch 286 at 294–297) it is plain that he considered that the intention to benefit the retained land must be apparent from the conveyance.

b

Finally, in *Shropshire CC v Edwards* (1982) 46 P & CR 270 at 277–278 his Honour Judge Rubin, sitting as a judge of the High Court, concluded:

c

'But it is not necessary, though highly desirable, that express words should be used to annex the benefit of the covenant to the land with which it is to run. If, on the construction of the instrument creating the restrictive covenant, both the land which is intended to be benefited and an intention to benefit that land, as distinct from benefiting the covenantee personally, can be clearly established, then the benefit of the covenant will be annexed to that land and run with it notwithstanding the absence of express words of annexation.'

d

In these circumstances, in my judgment, I have to construe the conveyance of 5 April 1894 in the light of the relevant circumstances to see whether the purchasers' covenants were given for the benefit of the retained land. I turn therefore to the second issue.

It seems plain that Alfred Walker junior never intended to retain the Highfield House estate for his own use and enjoyment. Within weeks of obtaining probate of his father's will he had entered into the contract to sell the entire estate to the Hempsteds. He recovered possession on the determination of that contract in October 1887. Two years

e

after the 1894 conveyance he was selling other parts of the estate and parts unsold at his death were sold shortly thereafter by his executors. It seems reasonable to infer that by 1894 Alfred Walker junior intended to sell off the estate as and when opportunity occurred. However, this does not, in my judgment, necessarily give rise to an inference that the benefit of the purchasers' covenant was intended to be annexed to the retained land. An estate owner might equally well intend the benefit of the covenants to remain

f

with him, so that he might exploit them in due course either by express assignment to particular purchasers or by exacting further payments from the owners of the land bound by them as the price for their release wholly or partially.

There is no indication in the covenant itself that it was made with Alfred Walker junior in his capacity as owner of the retained land. Indeed, other parts of the conveyance indicate the contrary. Thus in the covenant by Alfred Walker junior there is express

g

reference to the other land belonging to him as shown on the plan. In that covenant and the provisos which followed it express reference is made to the successors in title of Alfred Walker junior to that land.

If it had been intended to annex the benefit of the purchasers' covenants to the retained land it is remarkable that there is no reference to the retained land or to Alfred Walker junior's successors in title in that covenant.

h

Moreover, the reference to Alfred Walker junior's heirs and assigns deemed to be incorporated by s 58 of the 1881 Act is not, as such, sufficient to give rise to any annexation. Thus in *Renals v Cowlishaw* (1878) 9 Ch D 125, [1874–80] All ER Rep 359 the covenant was with the covenantees 'their heirs, executors, administrators and assigns'. But the reference to 'assigns' was not sufficient to effect annexation. Likewise in *Reid v Bickerstaff* [1909] 2 Ch 305, [1908–10] All ER Rep 298 the covenant in favour of the

j

covenantees 'their heirs and assigns' did not effect any annexation. Nor in *Ives v Brown* [1919] 2 Ch 314 was the benefit of a covenant with the covenantee 'his heirs and assigns' thereby annexed to the land. *Miles v Easter* [1933] Ch 611, [1933] All ER Rep 355 is to the same effect. The only authority to the contrary is *Mann v Stephens* (1846) 15 Sim 377, 60 ER 665, where the covenant was with 'B his heir and assigns', but in that case the only point argued was whether a successor in title of the covenantor was liable on the covenant. It was not argued that the successor in title to the land of the original covenantee was not *a* entitled to the benefit.

Accordingly, in my judgment, the conveyance of 1894 did not, on its true construction, annex the benefit of the purchasers' covenants to the retained land. There are no words in the conveyance indicating any such intention, nor do the surrounding circumstances necessitate any implication. Accordingly, I pass to the third issue.

In *Federated Homes Ltd v Mill Lodge Properties Ltd* [1980] 1 All ER 371, [1980] 1 WLR *b* 594 the Court of Appeal decided that in the case of a covenant relating to land of the covenantee in the sense that it touched and concerned that land the effect of s 78 of the Law of Property Act 1925 was to cause the benefit of the covenant to run with that land and be annexed to it. Section 78 of the 1925 Act provides as follows:

'(1) A covenant relating to any land of the covenantee shall be deemed to be made *c* with the covenantee and his successors in title and the persons deriving title under him or them, and shall have effect as if such successors and other persons were expressed. For the purposes of this subsection in connexion with covenants restrictive of the user of land "successors in title" shall be deemed to include the owners and occupiers for the time being of the land of the covenantee intended to be benefited. *d*

(2) This section applies to covenants made after the commencement of this Act, but the repeal of section fifty-eight of the Conveyancing Act, 1881, does not affect the operation of covenants to which that section applied.'

In his judgment in *Federated Homes Ltd v Mill Lodge Properties Ltd* [1980] 1 All ER 371 at 379, [1980] 1 WLR 594 at 604–605 Brightman LJ stated:
*e*

'The first point to notice about s 78(1) is that the wording is significantly different from the wording of its predecessor, s 58(1) of the Conveyancing and Law of Property Act 1881. The distinction is underlined by sub-s (2) of s 78, which applies sub-s (1) only to covenants made after the commencement of the Act. Section 58(1) of the earlier Act did not include the covenantee's successors in title or persons deriving title under him or them, nor the owners or occupiers for the time being of *f* the land of the covenantee intended to be benefited. The section was confined, in relation to realty, to the covenantee, his heirs and assigns, words which suggest a more limited scope of operation than is found in s 78. If, as the language of s 78 implies, a covenant relating to land which is restrictive of the user thereof is enforceable at the suit of (1) a successor in title of the covenantee, (2) a person deriving title under the covenantee or under his successors in title, and (3) the owner *g* or occupier of the land intended to be benefited by the covenant, it must, in my view, follow that the covenant runs with the land, because ex hypothesi every successor in title to the land, every derivative proprietor of the land and every other owner and occupier has a right by statute to the covenant. In other words, if the condition precedent of s 78 is satisfied, that it so say, there exists a covenant which *h* touches and concerns the land of the covenantee, that covenant runs with the land for the benefit of his successors in title, persons deriving title under him or them and other owners and occupiers.'

The defendant seeks to argue from this decision, and notwithstanding the reasoning expressed in it, that s 58 of the 1881 Act had the same effect. The same point was taken in *Shropshire CC v Edwards* (1982) 46 P & CR 270 but was not decided. *j*

In *Renals v Cowlishaw* (1878) 9 Ch D 125, [1874–80] All ER Rep 359 and *Reid v Bickerstaff* [1909] 2 Ch 305, [1908–10] All ER Rep 298 the covenants to which I have referred were entered into before s 58 of the 1881 Act came into force on 31 December 1881. Thus, this point was not of relevance in those cases. But in view of the date of the decision in *Renals v Cowlishaw* it would be very surprising if by enacting in s 58(1) of the 1881 Act that—

'A covenant . . . shall be deemed to be made with the covenantee, his heirs and assigns, and shall have effect as if heirs and assigns were expressed'

Parliament intended to effect annexation when the Court of Appeal had already decided that such words if expressed did not suffice.

Between the 1881 Act and the 1925 Act the covenants in *Ives v Brown* [1919] 2 Ch 314 and *Miles v Easter* [1933] Ch 611, [1933] All ER Rep 355 were entered into. But s 58 of the 1881 Act was not referred to in either case.

In *Forster v Elvet Colliery Co Ltd* [1908] 1 KB 629 the Court of Appeal did refer to s 58 of the 1881 Act. The case was not concerned with annexation of the benefit of covenants relating to freehold land. Cozens-Hardy MR said (at 635):

'The word "lessee" is by the definition at the beginning of the lease to include also "his executors, administrators and assigns, unless such construction be excluded by the sense or the context." And by s. 58 of the Conveyancing Act, 1881, words of limitation are to be read into the covenant, assuming it to be a covenant "relating to land." Now, under the old law, it is settled that the owner of the surface, not being mentioned as a party to the deed, could not have sued on the covenant.'

Fletcher Moulton LJ said (at 637–638):

'It is true that none of the plaintiffs in these actions were either owners or occupiers of any portion of these superjacent lands at the date of the lease. But the plaintiffs are successors in title of the then owners of portions of such lands by reason of being their assignees, and they urge that s. 58, sub-s. 1, of the Conveyancing and Law of Property Act, 1881, applies to such a covenant as we have in this case, and that it must accordingly be deemed to have been made with the covenantee, his heirs and assigns. In other words, they say that, although the intention of the parties may have been to make a separate and direct covenant with each future owner, the fact that such a covenant would not be effectual does not prevent the present plaintiffs from claiming under the covenant made with their predecessors in title, who were owners of the lands at the date of the lease, and with whom, therefore, the lessee could and did effectually covenant.'

And Farwell LJ said (at 641):

'In the present case the lessors of the minerals and the owners of the surface are different persons. In my opinion, therefore, the owners for the time being mean, primarily at any rate, the owners at the date of the deed; and by s. 58, sub-s. 1, of the Conveyancing and Law of Property Act, 1881, the covenant is made with them, their heirs and assigns. If any other owner not claiming as owner at that date, or as heir or assign of such owner, were to sue, the dictum of Sir George Jessel would apply to him. Some difficulty is created by the additon of the words "occupier or occupiers"; this is used in contradistinction to owner, and the Conveyancing and Law of Property Act, 1881, would therefore read into the covenant "his or their executors, administrators or assigns" instead of heirs and assigns. Such a covenant could not run with the land, but I do not think that this can affect the right of the owners, as it has not been suggested that the covenants are with owners and occupiers jointly.'

On the subsequent appeal to the House of Lords no reference was made to s 58 of the 1881 Act (sub nom *Dyson v Forster* [1909] AC 98, [1908–10] All ER Rep 212).

The Law of Property Act 1922 was an amendment Act. Section 96 provides so far as material:

'. . . (2) Every covenant running with the land entered into before the commencement of this Act shall take effect subject to the provisions of this Act, and accordingly the benefit or burden of every such covenant shall, subject as aforesaid,

vest in or bind the persons who by virtue of this Act succeed to the title of the
covenantee or the covenantor, as the case may be.

*a*

(3) The benefit of a covenant relating to land entered into after the commencement
of this Act may be made to run with the land without the use of the words "heirs"
if the covenant is of such a nature that the benefit could have been made to run with
the land before the commencement of this Act, and if an intention that the benefit
shall pass to the successors in title of the covenantee appears from the deed containing
the covenant.

*b*

(4) For the purposes of this section, a covenant runs with the land when the
benefit or burden of it, whether at law or in equity, passes to the successors in title
of the covenantee or the covenantor, as the case may be.'

The section was, no doubt, passed to cater for the fact that succession rights had been
altered. But it did not otherwise affect the operation of s 58 of the 1881 Act in relation to
covenants entered into prior to the commencement of the 1922 Act.

*c*

The Law of Property (Amendment) Act 1924 was also, as its title indicates, an
amending Act. Section 3 provided:

'The amendments and provisions, for facilitating the consolidation of the statute
law relating to conveyancing and property, contained in the Third Schedule to this
Act, shall have effect.'

*d*

And in Sch 3, Pt I, para 11, it is stated:

'The following provision shall be inserted at the end of section fifty-eight of the
Conveyancing Act, 1881:—"For the purposes of this section in connexion with
covenants restrictive of the user of land 'successors in title' shall be deemed to include
the owners and occupiers for the time being of the land of the covenantee intended
to be benefited."'

*e*

That Act was to come into force on 1 January 1926 (see s 12(3)) but was in fact superseded
by the Law of Property Act 1925, which came into force on the same day and repealed
s 3 of and Sch 3 to the 1924 Act.

It may be that, as submitted, one purpose of para 11 of Pt I of Sch 3 to the 1924 Act
was to cater for the difficulty expressed by Farwell LJ in *Forster v Elvet Colliery Co Ltd* to
which I have referred. But the overall effect of the amendments made by the 1922 and
1924 Acts was much wider than that. Thus, s 78 of the Law of Property Act 1925, which
only applies to covenants entered into after 1 January 1926, was in radically different
terms from s 58 of the 1881 Act, as Brightman LJ pointed out in *Federated Homes Ltd v
Mill Lodge Properties Ltd* [1980] 1 All ER 371 at 379, [1980] 1 WLR 594 at 604. The
principle of that case cannot be applied to s 58 of the 1881 Act. There are no words in
s 58 capable by themselves of effecting annexation of the benefit of a covenant. All that
section did was to deem the inclusion of words which both before and after the enactment
of s 58 had, with the exception of *Mann v Stephens* (1846) 15 Sim 377, 60 ER 665, been
consistently held to be insufficient without more to effect annexation of the benefit of a
covenant.

*f*

*g*

*h*

Accordingly, in my judgment, there are now no persons entitled to the benefit of the
purchasers' covenants contained in the 1894 conveyance. I will therefore make a
declaration in the terms of para 1 of the originating summons, subject to any point of
detail on the precise wording which counsel may wish to raise.

*Declaration accordingly.*

*j*

Solicitors: *Denton Hall Burgin & Warrens* (for the plaintiffs); *G F Smith*, Enfield (for the
defendant).

Hazel Hartman   Barrister.

# Thorpe v Chief Constable of the Greater Manchester Police

COURT OF APPEAL, CIVIL DIVISION
DILLON, NEILL AND MUSTILL LJJ
23 FEBRUARY, 21 MARCH 1989

*Discovery – Production of documents – Similar cases – Relevance – Discovery directed solely to credit – Similar fact evidence – Adjudications of guilt in police disciplinary proceedings – Plaintiff arrested by police officers – Police officers' conduct investigated – Plaintiff bringing civil action against police and applying for discovery of certificates of convictions or adjudications of guilt in police disciplinary proceedings – Whether documents to be used solely for examination as to credit as witness discoverable – Whether certificates of convictions or adjudications of guilt in police disciplinary proceedings discoverable.*

The plaintiff was arrested by police officers while attending a demonstration against the Home Secretary at Manchester University on 1 March 1985. He was charged with and convicted in the magistrates' court of obstructing the highway but on appeal to the Crown Court the conviction was quashed. In the course of the appeal the judge stated that it appeared that one, if not both, of the police officers involved in the plaintiff's arrest had given false evidence before the magistrates. As the result of the judge's comments and complaints by other persons concerned in the demonstration an investigation was carried out by investigating officers into the actions of the two officers. The plaintiff brought an action against the chief constable, as being vicariously liable for torts committed by the two officers, claiming damages for assault, unlawful arrest, false imprisonment and malicious prosecution. The plaintiff applied to the district registrar for, and was granted, discovery of the custody records of all persons arrested by the two officers at the demonstration but the registrar refused further discovery. On appeal by the plaintiff against the refusal of further discovery the judge granted the plaintiff discovery of, inter alia, certificates of previous convictions or adjudications of guilt in police disciplinary proceedings arising out of the plaintiff's arrest or which although not arising out of the demonstration might be evidence of similar facts. The chief constable appealed against the judge's order in so far as it required him to produce any adjudications of guilt in police disciplinary proceedings.

**Held** – The court would not order discovery of material which would be used solely for cross-examination of a witness as to credit since it would be oppressive if a party was obliged to disclose any document which might provide material for cross-examination as to his credibility as a witness. Furthermore, the court would not order discovery of material which would be evidence of similar facts if that evidence would merely show a disposition to commit the conduct alleged and was not required to rebut a defence of accident or coincidence or to prove a system of conduct. Although certificates of convictions in criminal courts relating to the events of 1 March 1985 would plainly be admissible under s 11 of the Civil Evidence Act 1968 and therefore discoverable, s 11 did not apply to adjudications of guilt in police disciplinary proceedings, which therefore, being outside s 11, were not probative of anything. The chief constable's appeal would accordingly be allowed (see p 830 *b c d*, p 831 *b* to *e*, p 833 *e g h* and p 834 *f*, post.

**Notes**
For disclosure of documents, see 13 Halsbury's Laws (4th edn) paras 37–38, and for cases on the subject, see 18 Digest (Reissue) 12, 48–51, 48 52, 338–360.

For the Civil Evidence Act 1968, s 11, see 17 Halsbury's Statutes (4th edn) 169.

**Cases referred to in judgments**

*Ballantine (George) & Son Ltd v F E R Dixon & Son Ltd* [1974] 2 All ER 503, [1974] 1 WLR 1125.

*Berger v Raymond Sun Ltd* [1984] 1 WLR 625.

*Blakebrough v British Motor Corp Ltd* (1969) 113 SJ 366, CA.

*Board v Thomas Hedley & Co Ltd* [1951] 2 All ER 431, CA.

*Boardman v DPP* [1974] 3 All ER 887, [1975] AC 421, [1974] 3 WLR 673, HL.

*Kennedy v Dodson* [1895] 1 Ch 334, CA.

*Mood Music Publishing Co Ltd v De Wolfe Ltd* [1976] 1 All ER 763, [1976] Ch 119, [1976] 2 WLR 451, CA.

**Interlocutory appeal**

The Chief Constable of the Greater Manchester Police appealed with the leave of the judge against the order of Hodgson J sitting in the Queen's Bench Division in Manchester on 17 and 19 February 1988 and dated 10 May 1988 allowing the appeal of the plaintiff, Kevin Thorpe, against the decision of Mr District Registrar Gee on 26 November 1987 to the extent that the chief constable was ordered to disclose to the plaintiff any documents containing any criminal convictions or adjudications of guilt in disciplinary proceedings against two police officers who were witnesses in an action brought by the plaintiff against the chief constable claiming damages for assault, unlawful arrest, false imprisonment and malicious prosecution. The facts are set out in the judgment of Dillon LJ.

*Shokat Khan* for the plaintiff.
*Eric Shannon* for the chief constable.

*Cur adv vult*

21 March. The following judgments were delivered.

**DILLON LJ.** The Chief Constable of Greater Manchester, the defendant in this action, appeals by leave of the judge against the interlocutory ruling in relation to discovery in the action which was given by Hodgson J on 19 February 1988.

The background to the action is as follows. On 1 March 1985 the plaintiff, Mr Thorpe, attended what he says was a peaceful demonstration outside the students' union building of Manchester University on the occasion of a visit of the Home Secretary to that building. The plaintiff was arrested by the police and taken to a local police station and detained for a while. He was charged with an offence of obstruction of the highway and was convicted in the magistrates' court. His conviction was however quashed on appeal to the Crown Court presided over by the Recorder of Manchester, his Honour Judge Prestt QC, and we were told that there were comments by the Recorder to the effect that it appeared that the magistrates' court had been deceived by false evidence given by at least one, if not both, of the two police officers who were concerned with the plaintiff's case. The plaintiff therefore sues the chief constable, as the person vicariously liable for torts committed by the two officers in the course of their duties, claiming damages for assault, unlawful arrest, false imprisonment and malicious prosecution. From the nature of the case it is likely that it will be tried by a judge and jury and not by a judge alone.

As a result of complaints by persons other than the plaintiff there was an investigation of the events of 1 March 1985 by the Avon and Somerset Constabulary, and because of the Recorder's comments the investigating officers opened a file in respect of the two police officers in their relationship with the plaintiff.

There was an application by the plaintiff's solicitors for further discovery. That came initially before the district registrar. He made an order for discovery of (a) the custody records relating to all persons arrested by the two police officers in the vicinity of the

University of Manchester students' union on 1 March 1985, (b) the record sheets which
a    recorded the reception into police vans of the aforesaid persons after their arrest and (c)
any documents pertaining to or relating to the arrest of such persons. He declined,
however, to grant the plaintiff any further relief. The plaintiff accordingly appealed, and
his appeal came before Hodgson J, who ordered further discovery under two headings.
The first, as to which there is no appeal, covers—

b          'all evidence taken by the investigation by the Avon and Somerset Police with
regard to the two police officers who gave evidence against the [plaintiff] in the
Magistrates Court and Crown Court proceedings save for the report of the
investigating officer and prosecuting Counsel's memorandum.'

The second, against which the chief constable now appeals, is expressed in the order of
the judge as drawn up as follows:
c
'All documents relating to any previous convictions and/or adjudications of guilt
against the two police officers who were allegedly involved in the arrest and
detention of the [plaintiff] on the evening of the 1st March 1985.'

It is common ground between the parties, and is borne out by the note of the judge's
judgment, that the words 'all documents relating to' etc are intended to mean no more
d    than the certificates of any convictions in any criminal courts and the comparable
documents recording adjudications of guilt in police disciplinary proceedings.
It is conceded for the plaintiff that, even so, the disputed part of the judge's order is too
wide in that it would cover matters which have no conceivable relevance to any issue in
the present action. That is obvious. What the plaintiff actually seeks can be put under
two headings, viz (1) certificates of conviction and adjudications of guilt on charges
e    arising out of the incidents of 1 March 1985 so far as such incidents involved the plaintiff
or on charges arising out of the evidence given by the two officers against the plaintiff
and (2) certificates of conviction and adjudications of guilt on charges, not necessarily
relating to 1 March 1985, which might support a 'similar facts' line of inquiry or
evidence. I refer to these as 'heading (1)' and 'heading (2)'.
Conversely, the chief constable concedes that if there are certificates of conviction by
f    criminal courts within heading (1) they would be and should be disclosed. Such
certificates of conviction would directly affect the issues in the action, in that under s 11
of the Civil Evidence Act 1968 they would be admissible in evidence at the trial and the
officers would be taken to have committed the offences unless the contrary were to be
proved. Section 11 does not apply, however, to adjudications of guilt in police disciplinary
proceedings, and the chief constable's concession does not extend to such adjudications;
g    counsel for the chief constable submits that a document recording an adjudication of
guilt in police disciplinary proceedings would be unintelligible without the investigating
officer's report and that report would be protected by public interest immunity from
production at the trial or any earlier stage in the course of these proceedings.
Discovery is to be given, under RSC Ord 24, r 2, of all documents 'relating to any
h    matter in question' between the parties in the action. It is very well established, however,
as explained in *The Supreme Court Practice 1988* vol 1, para 24/2/5 that the words 'relating
to any matter in question between them [the parties]' refer not to the subject matter of
an action but to the questions in the action, and that any document must be disclosed
which it is reasonable to suppose contains information which may enable the party
applying for discovery either to advance his own case or to damage that of his adversary
j    or which may fairly lead him to a train of inquiry which may have either of these two
consequences. Discovery is thus not necessarily limited to documents which would be
admissible in evidence. Counsel for the plaintiff refers also to Ord 24, r 8, where there is
a reference, in a discovery context, to 'disposing fairly of the cause or matter' and he
submits that fairness requires that the chief constable, who has ready access to information
about the criminal convictions (if any) of the plaintiff whether or not relevant to any

issue in the action, should disclose certificates of convictions (if any) of the two police officers on what broadly can be described as 'similar facts' charges as mentioned in *a* heading (2) above.

There are, however, a number of relevant limitations on the principles which I have mentioned.

The first is that the court should not order discovery, or interrogatories which are a form of discovery, on matters which would go solely to cross-examination as to credit. I think that Walton J was right in *George Ballantine & Son Ltd v F E R Dixon & Son Ltd* *b* [1974] 2 All ER 503, [1974] 1 WLR 1125 to deduce that limitation from the judgment of A L Smith LJ in particular in *Kennedy v Dodson* [1895] 1 Ch 334, although the actual decision in the *George Ballantine* case is better put on the different ground that the discovery sought was in itself oppressive. It would indeed be an impossible situation in my view if discovery had to be given of every document, not relevant to the actual issues in the action, which might open up a line of inquiry for cross-examination of the litigant *c* solely as to credit.

In the second place, while, as Lord Herschell LC pointed out in *Kennedy v Dodson* (at 338), there are cases in which the evidence of what happened in one transaction may be relevant to the question of what happened in another, where that is not so to order discovery in respect of what may turn out to be similar fact transactions would be likely to be oppressive and so the order should not be made. That is very much emphasised in *d* the judgments of Lord Herschell LC and Lindley LJ in *Kennedy v Dodson*. That fully justifies the decision in *George Ballantine & Son Ltd v F E R Dixon & Son Ltd*, where the plaintiffs in their pleading alleged passing off by the defendant in the supply of whisky in named countries, and sought discovery of documents relating to the defendant's supply of whisky, and it would seem gin, to other countries.

Instances, to which we were referred in argument, of cases in which evidence of what *e* happened in one transaction was relevant to the question of what happened in another are *Board v Thomas Hedley & Co Ltd* [1951] 2 All ER 431 and *Blakeborough v British Motor Corp Ltd* (1969) 113 SJ 366. In those cases the issue was whether certain goods supplied by the defendants were dangerous or unfit for use and discovery was ordered of documents relating to complaints by other purchasers about similar goods supplied from the same source and to the investigation of such complaints. Similarly, in an action for *f* damages for negligence which has caused personal injury, evidence that to the defendant's knowledge there had been similar previous accidents in the same premises to other persons would be relevant to show the defendant's knowledge of the risk, and discovery of complaints of these previous injuries would be relevant. But in an action for damages for professional negligence against a solicitor evidence of other claims for negligence made or established against the defendant by other clients in respect of other matters *g* would be irrelevant and inadmissible, and discovery in respect of such other matters would be oppressive; a plaintiff charging a solicitor with negligence in one matter could not investigate other areas of his practice in an endeavour to establish that he had a propensity to be careless.

The reconciliation between this principle and the rule in *The Supreme Court Practice* *h* 1988 vol 1, para 24/2/5 that there should be discovery of documents which may fairly lead the applicant for discovery to a train of inquiry which may advance the litigant's own case or damage that of his adversary is, in my judgment, that a train of inquiry which can only lead to matters which would not be admissible in evidence (save solely in cross-examination as to credit) does not lead to either of those two desirable ends.

The test of the admissibility of evidence of similar facts is in general the same in civil *j* and in criminal cases: see *Berger v Raymond Sun Ltd* [1984] 1 WLR 625 at 630 per Warner J. Lord Denning MR has suggested, in the passage from his judgment in *Mood Music Publishing Co Ltd v De Wolfe Ltd* [1976] 1 All ER 763, [1976] Ch 119 which is set out in the judgment of Neill LJ, which I have had the advantage of reading in draft, that in civil cases the courts have not been so chary of admitting such evidence as in criminal

cases, but I apprehend that Lord Denning MR was thinking of civil cases tried by a judge
*a*  alone. Where there is a jury the court must be more careful about admitting evidence
which is in truth merely prejudicial than is necessary where there is a trial by a judge
alone who is trained to distinguish between what is probative and what is not. By the
test in criminal cases the evidence of similar facts should be excluded unless it has a really
material bearing on the issues to be decided; to be admissible, therefore, the evidence
must be related to something more than isolated instances of the same kind of offence:
*b*  see *Boardman v DPP* [1974] 3 All ER 887 at 893, [1975] AC 421 at 439 per Lord Morris.

Applying these principles, my conclusion so far as regards adjudications of guilt in
police disciplinary proceedings (as opposed to certificates of convictions in criminal
courts) within heading (1) is that they do not lead to any train of inquiry, since the
plaintiff will be getting the available statements of evidence under the undisputed part
of the judge's order, and, being outside s 11 of the 1968 Act, the adjudications of guilt
*c*  are not probative of anything. It would indeed be quite wrong that they should be
admitted in evidence in a jury trial because of the danger that the jury might regard
them as probative of the matters which the jury themselves have to decide. These
adjudications of guilt (if any) should not therefore be disclosed.

So far as documents within heading (2) are concerned, these could of course lead to
fresh trains of inquiry into matters not at present known to the plaintiff. But I cannot see
*d*  that evidence, eg that one or both of the two police officers used excessive violence in
effecting an arrest of some other person in some other circumstances, can be probative
that he or they used excessive violence against the plaintiff on 1 March 1985; so likewise
if there was a past finding of guilt in relation to an attempt to deceive the court (though
if that were so I cannot conceive that the officer or officers would have still been in the
force at 1 March 1985). Therefore documents within heading (2) lead to nothing that
*e*  would be admissible in evidence, save solely cross-examination as to credit. Such
documents are not therefore, in my judgment, discoverable.

Accordingly I would, for my part, allow this appeal, and set aside the order of the
judge, in so far as it is challenged in this appeal, save only as to certificates of conviction
within heading (1).

*f*
**NEILL LJ.** The plaintiff brings this action against the Chief Constable of the Greater
Manchester Police for damages for assault, unlawful arrest, false imprisonment and
malicious prosecution. So much is clear from the form of the writ. The claim arises out
of an incident which took place on 1 March 1985 when the plaintiff was arrested during
a demonstration at Manchester University on the occasion of a visit by the then Home
*g*  Secretary.

After his arrest the plaintiff was prosecuted in the magistrates' court on a charge of
obstruction. He was convicted, but he then appealed to the Crown Court. His appeal was
heard by the Recorder of Manchester, his Honour Judge Prestt QC. In allowing the
appeal Judge Prestt commented on the evidence given on behalf of the prosecution by
two police officers. I understand that these comments amounted to a finding that the
*h*  court had been deceived by the two officers.

Following the demonstration a number of complaints were made against the police by
persons other than the plaintiff under s 49 of the Police Act 1964. These complaints led
to an investigation by the Avon and Somerset Constabulary. Later, after the plaintiff's
conviction had been set aside on appeal, the investigating officers opened a file to include
the dealings between the two police officers and the plaintiff.

*j*  On 6 October 1986 the plaintiff issued a writ. Pleadings were then served. On 20 May
1987 the defendant served his list of documents but the extent of this discovery was
considered to be unsatisfactory by those advising the plaintiff.

An application was made on behalf of the plaintiff for specific discovery. This
application was supported by an affidavit sworn by the plaintiff's solicitor dated 8 October
1987 in which he set out six classes of documents which he said should have been

disclosed. We are concerned with only one of these classes. On 10 December 1987 the
district registrar made an order in respect of three of the classes and there was no appeal
from this part of his order. There was an appeal, however, by the plaintiff from the
refusal by the district registrar to make an order in respect of the three remaining classes,
which included the class with which we are concerned.

The appeal was heard by Hodgson J on 19 February 1988 in Manchester. He refused
the application for further discovery in relation to one of the classes but allowed the
appeal in relation to the other two. His order was for the discovery of:

'(i) all evidence taken by the investigation by the Avon and Somerset Police with
regard to the two police officers who gave evidence against the [plaintiff] in the
Magistrates Court and Crown Court proceedings save for the report of the
investigating officer and prosecuting Counsel's memorandum. (ii) All documents
relating to any previous convictions and/or adjudications of guilt against the two
police officers who were allegedly involved in the arrest and detention of the
[plaintiff] on the evening of the 1st March 1985.'

There has been no appeal against the first part of the order, though it may be noted
that it was conceded on behalf of the plaintiff that the documents excluded from this
part of the order were protected by privilege. The appeal in this court is concerned only
with the documents in para (ii).

The area of debate has now been further restricted. It is common ground that the
form of the order did not accurately reflect the judge's decision. The order was not
intended to cover 'All documents *relating to* any previous convictions' etc, but, as is made
clear in the notice of appeal, was to comprise 'any documents containing any criminal
convictions or adjudications of guilt in disciplinary proceedings against [the two police
officers]'. Two further matters are also now common ground: (a) the order is in any
event too wide because it could cover adjudications in relation to an infringement, e g a
misuse of petrol, which could have no relevance to any issue in these proceedings; and
(b) it is accepted on behalf of the chief constable that any certificate of conviction by a
criminal court relating to the events on 1 March 1985 would be admissible in evidence
under s 11 of the Civil Evidence Act 1968 and is therefore plainly discoverable.

The plaintiff's application for further discovery is now restricted to two sub-classes of
documents which can be identified as follows: (1) any document containing an
adjudication of guilt in disciplinary proceedings arising out of the incidents on 1 March
1985 or based on the evidence given by the two officers against the plaintiff; and (2) any
document containing a certificate of conviction or an adjudication of guilt on charges
relating to other occasions where the charges might provide evidence or support a line of
inquiry of 'similar facts'.

I seems clear that before the judge the case for the plaintiff was conducted rather
differently than before us. Indeed I have not been able to detect in the judge's judgment
any reference to an argument that certain documents might be relevant as containing
evidence of 'similar facts'. Before the judge the argument was confined, it seems, to the
contention that other convictions and adjudications could be used in cross-examination
as to credit. The judge, who was referred to none of the authorities apart from the notes
in *The Supreme Court Practice* 1988, dealt with this contention as follows:

'. . . the one thing which is clearly within this civil litigation is that the credit of
the plaintiff and the credit of the two police officers is absolutely fundamental to the
proceedings. In those circumstances it does seem to me that if there had been, and
there may well not have been, against either of the police officers, and I say that
because the Chief Constable of the Greater Manchester Police takes the point on a
matter of principle rather than from any contents point of view, then it seems to
me that their disclosure, as limited to adjudications and convictions, would be
necessary for the fair disposal of the action in that they would undoubtedly advance

a the plaintiff's case. They would clearly damage the defendant's case which is based on vicarious liability for the two police officers, and they might lead the plaintiff to further investigations which might prove fruitful for his case.'

In this court we allowed the plaintiff to advance his claim for discovery both on the basis of cross-examination as to credit and on the basis of possible 'similar fact' evidence. I shall consider the matter under these two headings.

b *The credit of the two police officers*

A party to an action is required to give discovery in accordance with RSC Ord 24, r 2 of all documents 'relating to any matter in question' between the parties. It is clearly established, however, that the 'matters in question' cover wider ground than the issues as disclosed in the pleadings. Thus a party is obliged to disclose any document which it is reasonable to suppose contains information which may enable the party applying for

c discovery either to advance his own case or to damage that of his adversary or which may fairly lead to a train of inquiry which may have either of these two consequences. It follows that discovery is not necessarily limited to documents which would be admissible in evidence.

It is further to be observed that in imposing a limitation on discovery Ord 24, r 8

d refers to documents which are necessary 'for disposing fairly of the cause or matter . . .'

At first sight there is some force in the argument that documents which may contain material to impugn the credit of one party might well enable the other party to advance his case. So too it can be said that in a case such as the present, where the chief constable has access to police records and other material which might be useful for the cross-examination of the plaintiff, fairness requires that the chief constable should give

e discovery of any documents which relate to the 'characters' of the two police officers.

I am satisfied, however, that it has been the long-standing practice not to order discovery which is directed solely to credit. It is sufficient to refer to the decision of the Court of Appeal in *Kennedy v Dodson* [1895] 1 Ch 334 and to the decision of Walton J in *George Ballantine & Son Ltd v F E R Dixon & Son Ltd* [1974] 2 All ER 503, [1974] 1 WLR 1125.

f The existence of this limitation on the right to discovery is also recognised in Ord 26, r 1(4), which is concerned with discovery by means of interrogatories. This paragraph is in the following terms:

'A proposed interrogatory which does not relate to [any matter in question between the applicant and the other party in the cause or matter] shall be disallowed notwithstanding that it might be admissible in oral cross-examination of a witness.'

g
The reason for this limitation on discovery is plain. Discovery in an action would become gravely oppressive and time-consuming if there were an obligation on a party to disclose any document which might provide material for cross-examination as to his credit-worthiness as a witness. The present practice is a salutary one which helps to keep discovery within reasonable and sensible bounds.

h *Evidence of 'similar facts'*

I have found this part of the case, which was not developed, even if it was mentioned, before the judge, more difficult.

The leading modern authority on 'similar fact' evidence in civil proceedings is *Mood Music Publishing Co Ltd v De Wolfe Ltd* [1976] 1 All ER 763, [1976] Ch 119. In that case

j the plaintiffs wished to adduce evidence of music which they claimed was very similar to music of which they owned the copyright. Lord Denning MR said ([1976] 1 All ER 763 at 766, [1976] Ch 119 at 127):

'The admissibility of evidence as to "similar facts" has been much considered in the criminal law. Some of them have reached the highest tribunal, the latest of them being *Boardman v Director of Public Prosecutions* [1974] 3 All ER 887, [1975] AC 421. The criminal courts have been very careful not to admit such evidence unless *a* its probative value is so strong that it should be received in the interests of justice: and its admission will not operate unfairly to the accused. In civil cases the courts have followed a similar line but have not been so chary of admitting it. In civil cases the courts will admit evidence of similar facts if it is logically probative, that is if it is logically relevant in determining the matter which is in issue; provided that it is not oppressive or unfair to the other side; and also that the other side had fair notice *b* of it and is able to deal with it . . . The matter in issue in the present case is whether the resemblances which "Girl in the Dark" bears to "Sogno Nostalgico" are mere coincidences or are due to copying. On that issue it is very relevant to know that there are these other cases of musical works which are undoubtedly the subject of copyright, but yet the defendants have produced musical works bearing close resemblance to them. Whereas it might be due to mere coincidence in one case, it *c* is very unlikely that there would be coincidences in four cases.'

Evidence of 'similar facts' is relevant both in criminal and in civil cases to rebut defences such as accident or coincidence or sometimes to prove a system of conduct. Such evidence is not admissible, however, merely to show that the party concerned has a disposition to commit the conduct alleged. In the present case there is no reason to *d* suppose that any defence of accident or coincidence is likely to be raised. Nor on the present material is there any basis for an argument that evidence or other convictions or adjudications might be relevant to prove a 'system' of, for example, violence towards demonstrators. It is also to be remembered that this is an application for specific discovery where a prima facie case of possession must be made out: see Ord 24, r 7.

I have therefore come to the conclusion that on the present pleadings it would be *e* contrary to the established practice to make an order for disclosure which *might* provide evidence of 'similar facts' or lead to further inquiries on these lines.

There may be cases where such an order would be justified, but I do not consider that such an order, which in the instant case would be purely speculative, could be properly made in this case. I would allow the appeal.

*f*

**MUSTILL LJ.** I have had the benefit of reading in draft the judgments prepared by Dillon and Neill LJJ and agree with them both.

*Appeal allowed in part. Leave to appeal to the House of Lords refused.*

Solicitors: *Rhys Vaughan*, Manchester (for the plaintiff); *Sharpe Pritchard*, agents for *R C* *g* *Rees*, Salford (for the chief constable).

Celia Fox    Barrister.

a # Re Gilmartin (a bankrupt), ex p the bankrupt v International Agency and Supply Ltd

CHANCERY DIVISION
HARMAN J
1, 2, 7 NOVEMBER 1988

b

*Insolvency – Appeal – Appeal from registrar – Appeal to judge – Debtor appealing against bankruptcy order made by registrar – Whether appeal amounting to true appeal or rehearing – Insolvency Rules 1986, r 7.48(2).*

An appeal under r 7.48(2)[a] of the Insolvency Rules 1986 from an order made by a county
c court or by a registrar of the High Court to a single judge of the High Court is a true appeal, the purpose of which is to consider whether the jurisdiction below has been properly exercised, and is not a rehearing. Accordingly, where a bankruptcy registrar makes a bankruptcy order against a debtor after properly determining on the evidence before him that there is no prospect of the debt being repaid within a reasonable time and that there has not been an unreasonable refusal by the petitioning creditor and
d supporting creditors of an offer made by the debtor within s 271(3) of the Insolvency Act 1986, an appeal by the debtor against the order will be dismissed on the ground that the registrar has not made an error in law in the exercise of his discretion (see p 837 *f j* and p 838 *b c e f*, post).

*Re Rolls Razor Ltd (No 2)* [1969] 3 All ER 1386 distinguished.

e ## Notes
For an appeal from a decision of a bankruptcy registrar, see 3(2) Halsbury's Laws (4th edn reissue) paras 723, 725–728.

For the Insolvency Act 1986, s 271, see 4 Halsbury's Statutes (4th edn) (1987 reissue) 913.
f For the Insolvency Rules 1986, r 7.48, see 3 Halsbury's Statutory Instruments (Grey Volume) 442.

## Cases referred to in judgment
*Debtor (No 59 of 1987, Newcastle upon Tyne), Re a* (1988) Independent, 1 February.
*Evans v Bartlam* [1937] 2 All ER 646, [1937] AC 473, HL.
g *Ladd v Marshall* [1954] 3 All ER 745, [1954] 1 WLR 1489, CA.
*Practice Note* [1905] WN 128.
*Rolls Razor Ltd, Re (No 2)* [1969] 3 All ER 1386, [1970] Ch 576, [1970] 2 WLR 100.

## Cases also cited
*Cooper v Cooper* [1936] WN 205, CA.
h *Debtor, Re a, ex p petitioning creditor* (1920) 89 LJKB 432, DC.
*Debtor (No 452 of 1948), Re a, ex p the debtor v M R Le Mee-Power* [1949] 1 All ER 652, CA.
*Field (a debtor), Re, ex p the debtor v H & J Quick Ltd* [1978] 2 All ER 981, [1978] Ch 371, DC.

## Appeal
j Patrick Joseph Gilmartin appealed against the decision of Mr Registrar Dewhurst given on 6 July 1988 whereby a bankruptcy order was made against him on the application of

---

a    Rule 7.48 (2) provides: 'In the case of an order made by a county court or by a registrar of the High
Court, the appeal lies to a single judge of the High Court, and an appeal from a decision of that
judge on such an appeal lies, with the leave of that judge or the Court of Appeal, to the Court of
Appeal.'

the petitioning creditor, International Agency and Supply Ltd, seeking an order that the bankruptcy order be set aside on the ground, inter alia, that the registrar erred in law in concluding that there was no unreasonable refusal by the petitioning creditor and supporting creditors of an offer made by the debtor within s 271(3) of the Insolvency Act 1986. The creditor's application resulted from the debtor's failure to settle a debt of £28,544·02 incurred through his business as an investment and insurance consultant which was carried out at 123 Sydney Street, London SW3. The facts are set out in the judgment.

*Edward Evans-Lombe QC* and *Barry Stancombe* for the debtor.
*Martin Keenan* for the creditor.

**HARMAN J.** I have before me an appeal against the decision of Mr Registrar Dewhurst given on 6 July 1988 when he made a bankruptcy order against the appellant debtor, Patrick Joseph Gilmartin. The grounds of the appeal were that the registrar had erred in law in concluding that there was no unreasonable refusal by the petitioner and supporting creditors within s 271(3) of the Insolvency Act 1986.

The appeal was opened to me on the basis that there was to be a complete rehearing of the matter without regard to the decision of the registrar. I expressed doubt about that and the matter was rather intermittently argued as to the nature of an appeal against the making of a bankruptcy order under the new Insolvency Rules 1986, SI 1986/1925. Such an appeal by r 7.48(2) lies from a registrar to a single judge of the High Court. That rule also applies to appeals from orders made by a county court, that is either by a county court judge or by a registrar of the county court, on bankruptcy petitions. The rule is immediately following and closely analogous to r 7.47, which provides for appeals in the exercise of the winding-up jurisdiction over companies. Both in winding up and in bankruptcy, appeals from a county court or a registrar of the High Court lie to a single judge of the High Court. These rules were made pursuant to s 375 of the 1986 Act itself and they replace the old proceedings in bankruptcy whereby appeals from county courts, whether the decision was of the registrar or judge, went to a Divisional Court of the Chancery Division with two judges sitting together and appeals from the bankruptcy registrars in the High Court went direct to the Court of Appeal.

The question raised was very neatly expressed by counsel for the creditor in this matter as being whether the alteration had merely been an alteration as to the tribunal which heard the appeal or whether it had been an alteration as to the nature of the appeal. Counsel for the debtor has submitted that, as on appeal from masters to a High Court judge, whether in the Queen's Bench Division or in the Chancery Division, the judge has the whole jurisdiction, hears the matter entirely de novo and concludes by exercising his own discretion without regard to the discretion exercised below, so here the registrar of the High Court was in an equivalent position to a master of the High Court. He pointed out, correctly, that in the Queen's Bench Division the qualifications for the office of master are much the same as the qualifications for the registrar in bankruptcy or companies registrar. That fact supported the conclusion that the judge was to hear the matter wholly de novo as he would an appeal from a master and to proceed to exercise his own discretion.

Counsel for the creditor observed that the old forms of appeal in these matters were what one would call true appeals, that is that the decision below stood unless the appellate tribunal was persuaded it was wrong, and in so far as the decision was discretionary it could only be upset either for error of law or by the appellate court, whether the Divisional Court in Chancery or the Court of Appeal, being satisfied that the tribunal below had wholly misconceived the matter or wholly failed to exercise a proper discretion. Such tests are of course substantially more severe than a matter of simply the exercise of the court's own discretion. The true appeal can lead to the court saying, 'Well, we would not have exercised our discretion in the same manner but the proper matters

*a*  were taken into account, no error of principle or law can be seen and therefore we cannot and should not upset the decision below.'

Counsel for the debtor pressed me with such decisions as that of Megarry J in *Re Rolls Razor Ltd (No 2)* [1969] 3 All ER 1386 esp at 1396, [1970] Ch 576 esp at 591. As one would expect from that extremely learned judge the judgment is exhaustive and deals in great detail with every possible view of the matter. Megarry J in his judgment referred

*b*  to the decision in *Evans v Bartlam* [1937] 2 All ER 646, [1937] AC 473, which established that the appeal in Queen's Bench chambers to the judge in chambers is one where the judge in chambers has the discretion and the master's discretion is, as it were, ignored (see [1969] 3 All ER 1386 at 1395, [1970] Ch 576 at 590). The judge went on to consider the position in Chancery and the history of the Chancery masters and further considered the position under *Practice Note* [1905] WN 128 (see [1969] 3 All ER 1386 at 1396, [1970]

*c*  Ch 576 at 591). He referred to various other matters and then observed that in his view the difference in machinery between the Chancery and the Queen's Bench and, as it then was, the Probate, Divorce and Admiralty Divisions was not something that affected the matter and observed that—

*d*  'what is made is an order of the High Court; and in that court the judge and the registrar both hold office. A litigant who moves from one to the other remains within the court. He is not moving to a different court, as he would be if he went to the Court of Appeal. What the order of the High Court is to be in any case is to be determined by the officer of the court who exercises the jurisdiction of the court. If the matter stays with the registrar, he is that officer; if it is brought before the judge, it is him; and if it is the judge, then it should be his discretion.'

*e*  (See [1969] 3 All ER 1386 at 1395–1396, [1970] Ch 576 at 590.)

Those observations I should treat with great care and weight because they are the observations of a judge of great learning in the history of the courts and the procedures of the courts. However I have come to the conclusion that they are not applicable today in the new situation created by the 1986 Act. Here one has, contrary to those points which Megarry J made in *Re Rolls Razor Ltd (No 2)*, appeals to the single judge of the

*f*  High Court from both the county court, a completely different court, and the registrar, either the companies registrar in a winding up or the bankruptcy registrar in bankruptcy matters. In bankruptcy both are substitutes for procedures that were from different courts to a different court, in the old days from the county court to the Divisional Court in Chancery or from the bankruptcy registrar to the Court of Appeal. The combination nowadays in the single High Court judge of jurisdiction to hear appeals from a different

*g*  court and from an officer of his own court in a very closely related matter persuade me that I should look more carefully at the matter than to simply say, 'What is the court that is deciding it?'

There cannot in my view be different bases of approach for bankruptcy appeals from county courts to the single judge from the bases of approach applicable to appeals from

*h*  bankruptcy registrars to the single judge, or I would add, though it is not directly before me, from the companies registrar in winding up to the single judge. Further, I notice that the whole of this new machinery has been designed to make the single judge the determining judge for these matters since any appeal from him lies only with his leave or perhaps the leave of the Court of Appeal. That introduces a limitation on appeals and that in my view makes it the more likely that the appeal to the single judge is to be a true

*j*  appeal, trying to consider whether the jurisdiction below has been properly exercised, rather than a complete hearing de novo, which would in effect mean there would be but one hearing and without leave, there would be no appeal in the true sense at all.

I also bear in mind the observations of Knox J in *Re a debtor (No 59 of 1987, Newcastle upon Tyne)* (1988) Independent, 1 February. There Knox J decided that a bankruptcy appeal to the single judge, in that case from a county court registrar, was a true appeal. It followed that evidence on the appeal could only be admitted on what are commonly *a* called *Ladd v Marshall* [1954] 3 All ER 745, [1954] 1 WLR 1489 grounds. Those grounds are that on appeal the only proper evidence is the evidence below and that special reasons have to be shown to justify the admission of fresh evidence. That is quite unlike an appeal by way of complete rehearing. That decision to my mind supports the proposition that this is a true appeal and accords with my own impression of the whole matter.

I therefore conclude that it is for the appellant to show in these appeals that the *b* bankruptcy registrar or county court judge (or, in winding up, the companies registrar) has erred in principle or erred in law in the way in which he has applied or exercised his discretion. Having so said I consider Mr Registrar Dewhurst's decision and I find that his quite short judgment held that there was a series of offers (counsel for the creditor before me analysed them as being six different offers) over a period during which the bankruptcy petition was before the court on six different occasions between April and July 1988, that *c* the circumstances were such that the offer which was before the court was one which required 40 months for the debt which was claimed in the bankruptcy petition to be settled, that the security offered had been agreed in principle and according to the debtor was to be executed by him but no steps whatever had been taken by the debtor to prepare and execute and tender the securities which he said he was willing to offer, and that the whole conduct of the debtor was one which the registrar thought, and for my part I *d* would have come to the same conclusion but anyhow it cannot be said he erred in so thinking, showed a course of conduct of constantly postponing the evil day. The registrar observed that a petitioning creditor is entitled to be paid his debt in full on the hearing of a petition unless it is adjourned on the ground that there is a reasonable prospect of him being paid within a reasonable time. In the circumstances of this case I think he was correct to take that as the basic test and to say that the prospects of the debt being paid *e* within a reasonable time were not such as anybody could say were reasonable prospects.

I therefore conclude that there is no error of law nor one of principle in the exercise of the discretion which the registrar had and I for my own part would have come to precisely the same conclusion. For those reasons I shall dismiss the appeal.

*Appeal dismissed.* *f*

Solicitors: *Jon Snelling & Co* (for the debtor); *Rayner de Wolfe* (for the creditor).

Evelyn M C Budd    Barrister.

# R v Johnson

a

COURT OF APPEAL, CRIMINAL DIVISION
WATKINS LJ, McCOWAN AND JUDGE JJ
11, 21 APRIL 1989

b
*Criminal law – Murder – Provocation – Self-induced provocation – Defendant inducing provocative acts in others leading him to lose self-control and stab deceased – Whether self-induced provocation a good defence to charge of murder – Homicide Act 1957, s 3.*

The appellant while drinking in a nightclub began to behave in an unpleasant manner and made violent threats towards the deceased and his girlfriend. A tense atmosphere developed in which the appellant was taunted by the deceased's girlfriend and the
c deceased seized hold of the appellant and pinned him to the wall while holding a glass. Other people in the club told the deceased to drop the glass and when he did so the appellant suddenly produced a flick knife and stabbed the deceased to death. The appellant told the police that he had been 'glassed' and mugged before and was terrified of being 'glassed' again and carried the knife for his own protection. He was charged with murder and pleaded self-defence. At his trial his counsel was unwilling to raise the
d defence of provocation because it ran counter to the defence of self-defence but he submitted that the judge ought specifically to leave the issue of provocation to the jury. The judge declined to do so on the ground that provocation which was self-induced could not be a defence for the purposes of s 3[a] of the Homicide Act 1957. The appellant was convicted. He appealed, contending that the issue of provocation should have been left to the jury.
e

**Held** – Since anything said or done which provoked a defendant to lose his self-control could amount to provocation for the purposes of s 3 of the 1957 Act a defendant was entitled to rely on 'self-induced provocation', ie a reaction by another caused by the defendant's conduct which in turn led him to lose his own self-control, as a defence to a
f charge of murder and accordingly if there was evidence which might lead the jury to find provocation, whether self-induced or not, such a defence had to be left to the jury by the trial judge. Since the appellant had been deprived of having his defence of provocation considered by the jury the appeal would be allowed, the conviction for murder would be quashed and a verdict of manslaughter substituted (see p 841 *j* to p 842 *a f* to *j*, post).
g
   Dictum of Lord Diplock in *DPP v Camplin* [1978] 2 All ER 168 at 173 applied.
   Dictum of Lord Pearson in *Edwards v R* [1973] 1 All ER 152 at 158 explained.

**Notes**
For provocation as a defence to murder, see 11 Halsbury's Laws (4th edn) para 1163, and for cases on the subject, see 15 Digest (Reissue) 1122–1128, 9426–9489.
h

**Cases referred to in judgment**
*DPP v Camplin* [1978] 2 All ER 168, [1978] AC 705, [1978] 2 WLR 679, HL.
*Edwards v R* [1973] 1 All ER 152, [1973] AC 648, [1972] 3 WLR 893, PC.
*R v Cascoe* [1970] 2 All ER 833, CA.

j  **Case also cited**
*R v Doughty* (1986) 83 Cr App R 319, CA.

**Appeal against conviction**
Christopher Richard Johnson appealed with the leave of the single judge against his

---
a  Section 3, so far as material, is set out at p 841 *d*, post

conviction for murder in the Crown Court at Sheffield before Ognall J and a jury on 18 February 1988 for which he was sentenced to life imprisonment. The facts are set out in $a$ the judgment of the court.

*P J Kelson* (assigned by the Registrar of Criminal Appeals) for the appellant.
*Michael Slater* for the Crown.

*Cur adv vult* $b$

21 April. The following judgment of the court was delivered.

**WATKINS LJ.** On 18 February 1988 in the Crown Court at Sheffield before Ognall J the appellant was convicted by a jury of the murder of Derek Roberts. He was sentenced to life imprisonment. He appeals against conviction with the leave of the single judge.

The deceased died during the night of 18–19 May 1987 in a nightclub in Sheffield $c$ when the appellant stabbed him in the chest with a knife. The blade of the knife, 3·8 inches long, penetrated the chest to the heart. The wound, there was but one, travelled from the deceased's left to right parallel with the ground. There were no defensive wounds on the deceased.

During the evening both the appellant and the deceased had been drinking at the nightclub. The appellant was carrying a knife. It was a flick or 'swish' knife. The deceased $d$ was unarmed. A tense atmosphere developed in the club when the appellant started to behave in an unpleasant way. Threats of violence were made by him to a female friend of the deceased and then to the deceased himself. This woman and the deceased became extremely annoyed. A struggle developed between the two men during the course of which the stabbing occurred.

As is inevitable in an incident of this kind, various witnesses saw different parts of the $e$ fatal incident and there were some inconsistencies in their evidence. However, in a manner of which no possible complaint can be made, the judge, in the course of the summing up, carefully summarised the evidence of each witness, the appellant included, for the jury's consideration.

Save for what it is said of that evidence later in relation to provocation, we do not see $f$ the need to rehearse it here in any detail. Suffice it to say that when he was seen by the police the appellant maintained that he had been terrified of being 'glassed'. That had happened to him before. He was in fear of it happening again. He had also in the past been mugged. He therefore carried the knife for his own protection. He further said that when the incident happened in the club he sought to protect himself because he thought he was about to be 'glassed' again, so he took his knife out of his jacket pocket $g$ and pushed it at the deceased.

In his evidence he reiterated that he opened his knife because he believed he was going to be 'glassed'. He did not speak expressly of any loss of self-control.

The case for the Crown was that the appellant had lost his temper and deliberately struck the deceased. He intended either to kill him or to do him some really serious bodily harm. The defence was that the appellant, believing that he was about to be $h$ attacked by the deceased with a glass, did no more than act in reasonable self-defence. This defence was obviously rejected by the jury.

Counsel for the appellant did not invite the jury to consider 'provocation'. The judge gave no direction to the jury on this issue.

The ground for the present appeal is that the judge should have directed the jury to consider provocation. $j$

At the conclusion of the evidence and before the summing up, counsel for the appellant, in the absence of the jury, submitted that he either would not or could not, seeing that he was depending on self-defence, address the jury on provocation but that that issue should be left to them by the judge. The judge said, in effect, that if there was any evidence of provocation he was well aware that he should leave that issue to the jury and the fact that counsel for the appellant did not intend to advance it was irrelevant.

The principle governing such a matter has been set out, and a judge's duty in that
a  respect emphasised, in a number of reported cases. It is usefully summarised in *R v Cascoe*
[1970] 2 All ER 833 at 837, where it was said: 'Whether the issue [of provocation] is
raised at the trial or not, if there is evidence which might lead the jury to find provocation,
then it is the duty of the court to leave that issue to the jury.'

In the course of the submissions from both counsel for the defence and counsel for the
Crown, the judge raised the matter of 'self-induced' provocation. He said: 'It is rather
b  difficult to see how a man who excites provocative conduct can in turn rely on it as
provocation in the criminal law.'

He was referring there to the unpleasant threatening behaviour by the appellant at the
start of the incident. No authority on this point was cited to the judge. The concept of
self-induced provocation was not analysed. Counsel for the Crown did not rely on it and,
in giving his ruling, the judge did not refer to it. In his conclusion the judge agreed with
c  the submission of the Crown that it would be inappropriate, having regard to the
evidence, to leave provocation to the jury. Hence the lack of direction to the jury on this
issue.

Section 3 of the Homicide Act 1957 provides:

'Where on a charge of murder there is evidence on which the jury can find that
d    the person charged was provoked (whether by things done or by things said or by
both together) to lose his self-control, the question whether the provocation was
enough to make a reasonable man do as he did shall be left to be determined by the
jury . . .'

In *DPP v Camplin* [1978] 2 All ER 168 at 173, [1978] AC 705 at 716 Lord Diplock said
that this section—

e
'makes it clear that if there was any evidence that the accused himself at the time
of the act which caused the death in fact lost his self-control in consequence of some
provocation however slight it might appear to the judge, he was bound to leave to
the jury the question . . . whether a reasonable man might have reacted to that
provocation as the accused did.'

f      It was accepted before us by counsel for the Crown that the evidence before the jury
included the following. Before the stabbing incident the appellant had been taunted by
a woman who called him a 'white nigger'. Apparently, although a white man himself,
he affected at times a West Indian accent. He reacted to that abuse. It upset him. It made
him angry. There were high words between him and others, the deceased included.
Seemingly to leave the club or that part of it, the appellant walked away towards the exit.
g  The deceased, however, followed him and poured beer over him. The deceased then
removed his jacket. The appellant did not. The deceased by placing his arm across the
appellant's chest or throat seized hold of the appellant and pinned him against a wall.
While he was thus pinned against the wall the woman who had described him as a 'white
nigger' attacked him by punching his head and pulling his hair. There were shouts from
some of the others present that the deceased should drop the glass which he held in his
h  hand. He did so. Until this moment the appellant had not retaliated. But his attitude to
being held captive suddenly changed. He somehow bent down and produced the knife
and lunged at the deceased with it. He lunged again, so it was said, but failed to make
contact. He was restrained by one of his friends. His explanation for his conduct was, as
has been stated, a fear of being 'glassed'. He did not, as has also been stated, claim that he
had lost his self-control.
j      Nevertheless, if the jury rejected, as they did, his account that he was acting in self-
defence they might, in our judgment, very well have inferred from all that evidence that
there had indeed been a sudden loss of self-control.

That evidence may not have been powerfully suggestive of provocation. But it was, in
our view, rather more than tenuous. It is easily conceivable, we think, that the jury, if
directed on the issue, would have come to the conclusion that the appellant was so

provoked as to reduce murder to manslaughter. Therefore, subject only to the question of self-induced provocation referred to by the judge, in our judgment this defence should *a* have been left to the jury.

There was undoubtedly evidence to suggest that, if the appellant had lost his self-control, it was his own behaviour which caused others to react towards him in the way we have described.

We were referred to the decision of the Privy Council in *Edwards v R* [1973] 1 All ER 152 at 158, [1973] AC 648 at 658, where the trial judge had directed the jury thus:      *b*

'. . . in my view the defence of provocation cannot be of any avail to the accused in this case . . . It ill befits the accused . . . having gone there with the deliberate purpose of blackmailing this man—you may well think that it ill befits him so say out of his own mouth that he was provoked by any attack. In my view the defence of provocation is not one which you need consider in this case.'
     *c*

The Full Court in Hong Kong held that this direction was erroneous. The Privy Council agreed with the Full Court. On the particular facts of the case Lord Pearson, giving the judgment of the Board, said ([1973] 1 All ER 152 at 158, [1973] AC 648 at 658):

'On principle it seems reasonable to say that (1) a blackmailer cannot rely on the *d* predictable results of his own blackmailing conduct as constituting provocation . . . and the predictable results may include a considerable degree of hostile reaction by the person sought to be blackmailed . . . (2) but if the hostile reaction by the person sought to be blackmailed goes to extreme lengths it might constitute sufficient provocation even for the blackmailer; (3) there would in many cases be a question of degree to be decided by the jury.'
     *e*

Those words cannot, we think, be understood to mean, as was suggested to us, that provocation which is 'self-induced' ceases to be provocation for the purposes of s 3 of the 1957 Act.

The relevant statutory provision being considered by the Privy Council was in similar terms to s 3. In view of the express wording of s 3, as interpreted in *DPP v Camplin*, *f* which was decided after *Edwards v R*, we find it impossible to accept that the mere fact that a defendant caused a reaction in others, which in turn led him to lose his self-control, should result in the issue of provocation being kept outside a jury's consideration. Section 3 clearly provides that the question is whether things done or said or both provoked the defendant to lose his self-control. If there is any evidence that it may have done, the issue must be left to the jury. The jury would then have to consider all the circumstances of the incident, including all the relevant behaviour of the defendant, in deciding (a) *g* whether he was in fact provoked and (b) whether the provocation was enough to make a reasonable man do what the defendant did.

Accordingly, whether or not there were elements in the appellant's conduct which justified the conclusion that he had started the trouble and induced others, including the deceased, to react in the way they did, we are firmly of the view that the defence of *h* provocation should have been left to the jury.

Since it is not possible for us to infer from their verdict that the jury inevitably would have concluded that provocation as well as self-defence had been disproved, the verdict for murder will be set aside. A conviction for manslaughter on the basis of provocation will be substituted.

     *j*

*Appeal allowed. Verdict for murder quashed. Conviction for manslaughter substituted. Sentence of eight years' imprisonment imposed.*

Solicitors: *Crown Prosecution Service*, Sheffield.

N P Metcalfe Esq    Barrister.

a
# R v University of London Visitor, ex parte Vijayatunga

COURT OF APPEAL, CIVIL DIVISION
LORD DONALDSON OF LYMINGTON MR, BINGHAM AND MANN LJJ
27, 28 FEBRUARY, 9 MARCH 1989
b

*University – Visitor – Jurisdiction – Refusal by university to award degree – Academic staff appointing examiners to assess thesis – Applicant claiming examiners not qualified to assess thesis – Applicant petitioning visitor – Visitor refusing to intervene – Visitor concluding that prescribed procedures for appointing examiners had been followed and that choice of examiners involving exercise of expert academic judgment with which visitor should not interfere – Whether visitor's*
c *decision wrong in law – Whether court's jurisdiction over visitor supervisory or appellate – Whether court can interfere with visitor's exercise of discretion or ·judgment or confined to correcting errors of law.*

The applicant, who was a student for the degree of Doctor of Philosophy at a university, submitted a thesis at the end of her studies. The thesis was considered by two examiners
d appointed by the university's academic staff in accordance with the relevant statutes and regulations. Following consideration of the thesis and a re-examination the university refused to award the applicant a doctorate but offered her a lower degree, which she declined. The applicant petitioned a committee of the Privy Council acting for Her Majesty in Council as the visitor of the university, challenging the refusal to award her a
e doctorate, on the ground that the appointed examiners had not been properly qualified to assess her thesis because they did not specialise in her academic discipline, with the result that her thesis had been misjudged. The committee declined to intervene on the ground that it was no part of its duty to interfere in matters of scientific or technical judgment and that it would not be proper to express a view as to the choice of examiners or to criticise the university's decision on such a choice save where, which was not the
f case, it was apparent that the appointed examiners were plainly not qualified to perform their task. The petition was accordingly dismissed. The applicant sought judicial review of the committee's decision, contending that the selection of examiners did not involve a pure exercise of academic judgment and that the evident mismatch between the appointed examiners' fields of specialisation and the subject of the applicant's thesis raised an obvious question for inquiry and that by failing to make such an inquiry the
g committee had abdicated its role as visitor by deferring to the body whose conduct it was its duty to investigate. The Divisional Court dismissed the application on the grounds that the examiners had been appointed in accordance with the rules and academic practices of the university and that their appointment involved an exercise of academic judgment not shown to be clearly wrong. The applicant appealed to the Court of Appeal.

h **Held** – Whatever the committee's correct approach in ruling on the applicant's petition, the court's jurisdiction was supervisory and not appellate; its role was to confine itself to correction of demonstrated errors of law and it could not properly interfere with any exercise of discretion or judgment by the committee unless it was of the opinion that it was wrong in law. In the circumstances the committee had been entitled, if not bound, to conclude that the university's prescribed procedures for appointing examiners had
j been followed, and accordingly there had not been any manifest procedural impropriety. Furthermore, the committee had been entitled to conclude that the choice of examiners involved an exercise of expert or academic judgment into which it should not intrude, there being no reason to think that that judgment had been improperly exercised. It followed that the applicant had not shown that the committee had made a decision

which was wrong in law and the appeal would therefore be dismissed (see p 849 *h j*,
p 850 *e f j* to p 851 *a d f g* and p 852 *a*, post).

Decision of the Divisional Court [1987] 3 All ER 204 affirmed.

*a*

**Notes**

For the nature of visitatorial powers, and for a visitor's powers and jurisdiction, see 5
Halsbury's Laws (4th edn) paras 872–873, 877, 879–885, and for cases on the subject, see
8(1) Digest (2nd reissue) 641–643, 646–647, 5112–5124, 5172–5184.

*b*

**Cases referred to in judgments**

*Associated Provincial Picture Houses Ltd v Wednesbury Corp* [1947] 2 All ER 680, [1948] 1
KB 223, CA.

*Race Relations Board v Associated Newspapers Group Ltd* [1978] 3 All ER 419, [1978] 1
WLR 905, CA.

*c*

*Thomas v University of Bradford* [1987] 1 All ER 834, [1987] AC 795, [1987] 2 WLR 677,
HL.

**Cases also cited**

*A-G v Atherstone Free School (Governors)* (1834) 3 My & K 544, 40 ER 207, LC.

*A-G v Talbot* (1748) 3 Atk 662, 26 ER 1181, LC.

*d*

*Council of Civil Service Unions v Minister for the Civil Service* [1984] 3 All ER 935, [1985] AC
374, HL.

*Kirkby Ravensworth Hospital, Ex p* (1808) 15 Ves Jun 305, 33 ER 770, LC.

*Philips v Bury* (1694) Skin 447, [1558–1774] All ER Rep 53, 90 ER 198, HL.

*R v Dunsheath, ex p Meredith* [1950] 2 All ER 741, [1951] 1 KB 127, DC.

*Thomson v University of London* (1864) 33 LJ Ch 625.

*e*

**Appeal**

The applicant, Janaki Vijayatunga, appealed against the judgment of the Divisional Court
of the Queen's Bench Division (Kerr LJ and Simon Brown J) ([1987] 3 All ER 204, [1988]
QB 322) on 13 May 1987 whereby it refused her application for judicial review by way
of (1) orders of certiorari and/or prohibition to quash decisions of a committee of the
Privy Council acting for Her Majesty in Council as visitor of the University of London
dismissing petitions submitted by the applicant in November 1981 and May 1984 in
which the applicant sought to challenge the university's refusal to award her the degree
of Doctor of Philosophy, (2) orders of mandamus to grant her petitions and (3) declarations
that the committee's decisions were ultra vires and void and/or that her case had not been
fully heard. The facts are set out in the judgment of Bingham LJ.

*f*

*g*

*Stephen Sedley QC* and *Philip Engelman* for the applicant.

*John Laws* and *Robert Jay* for the visitor.

*George Newman QC* and *Michael Lazarus* for the university.

*h*

*Cur adv vult*

9 March. The following judgments were delivered.

*j*

**BINGHAM LJ** (giving the first judgment at the invitation of Lord Donaldson MR). On
13 May 1987 a Queen's Bench Divisional Court (Kerr LJ and Simon Brown J) ([1987] 3
All ER 204, [1988] QB 322) dismissed an application by the applicant Miss Vijayatunga,
for judicial review of two decisions of a committee of the Privy Council acting for Her
Majesty in Council as visitor of the University of London. I shall call this 'the committee'.
The applicant now appeals against the order of the Divisional Court. But in this court the

argument has somewhat narrowed and it is now only one decision of the committe, that
*a* made on 16 March 1983, which the applicant seeks to challenge.

Strictly, the committee did not make a decision but expressed an opinion for the guidance of Her Majesty in Council, but for ease of reference it has been found convenient to treat the committee as if it were itself the visitor. I shall continue to do so. It has been accepted that the identity of the visitor does not preclude an order of judicial review if an order is otherwise appropriate.

*b* The facts have been clearly and comprehensively stated by Kerr LJ in judgment (see [1987] 3 All ER 204 at 206–208, [1988] QB 322 at 325–328). This relieves me of the need to give more than the barest summary necessary to raise the legal issue argued before us.

In October 1975 the applicant registered as a student of Bedford College to read for a Doctorate of Philosophy in zoology. She was at that time a research assistant to Professor Dales, head of the department of zoology at Bedford College and a professor in the *c* university, who became her supervisor. Under his supervision she prepared a thesis entitled 'Lysosomes in the coelomocytes of three species of polychaete annelids with particular reference to Nereis diversicolor'. In lay terms, the subject matter was a study of cell constituents in the free cells found in the body cavity of three species of ragworm, in particular the species nereis diversicolor. The subject was one which Professor Dales approved.

*d* In July 1979 the applicant's thesis was nearing completion. The secretary to the board of studies in zoology asked Professor Dales to put forward nominees for appointment as examiners. Having spoken to a lecturer in zoology at the applicant's college he put forward the names of Professor Gahan and Professor Holt. Professor Bullough, the chairman of the higher degrees sub-committee of the board of studies in zoology, accepted the nomination and made the appointments, later accepted by the sub-*e* committee. Both before the appointments were made and just after the applicant expressed the clear opinion that neither of these professors was qualified to examine in the specialised field covered by her thesis.

On 5 November 1979 the applicant was orally examined by Professors Gahan and Holt. After an unhappy incident fully discussed by the committee and Kerr LJ but not *f* now material, the applicant was told on 14 December 1979 that she had been unsuccessful in her examination for the degree of PhD. She did not, for understandable reasons, accept the offer of a lesser degree but instead applied to be re-examined. She was re-examined in May 1980 by a board composed of three new examiners in addition to the original two, but was again unsuccessful.

In November 1981 the applicant petitioned Her Majesty in Council as visitor of the *g* University under the statutes scheduled to the University of London Act 1978 (c ii). It is this petition, heard on 25 February and dismissed on 16 March 1983, with which alone this appeal is now concerned. The applicant did, however, thereafter seek redress by complaint, held inadmissible, to the European Commission of Human Rights, and by further petition, also unsuccessful, to the committee. In her application for judicial review the applicant seeks, in effect, a declaration that the committee's decision of 16 *h* March 1983 was reached on an incorrect basis in law.

In her petition to the committee what is now the applicant's crucial complaint was put thus:

'3. Your Petitioner contends that the appointment of the said examiners was wrong and ought to be set aside alternatively that the said examiners were not proper or competent examiners by reason of the following . . . (b) The said examiners *j* were not Zoologists specialising in the field to which the said thesis related, Professor P. B. Gahan was a Professor of Botany and had been awarded a Doctorate in Histochemistry; Professor S. J. Holt was a Professor at the Courtauld Institute of Biochemistry and had been awarded a Doctorate in Chemistry.'

The nub of the applicant's grievance was elaborated in a letter to the Vice-Chancellor of the University to which she made reference in her petition:

'1. .... It follows that I did not have any zoologist as my examiner, despite the
fact that I had presented my thesis to the Board of Studies in Zoology. With a *a*
botanist (Histochemist), Professor P.B. Gahan, and a chemist (Histochemist),
Professor S. J. Holt, I had two histochemists to assess a piece of work which
contributed to the field of zoology (comparatively [sic] zoology). The major part of
my work consisted of morphological studies on the coelomocytes.

2. As a result of this bias towards histochemistry, the examiners tended to
concentrate on that aspect of my work, to the detriment of the other, more *b*
important contributions I have made. And yet I only applied standard histochemical
methods, to further elucidate the morphological findings. I have not made any
contributions to the field of histochemistry, e.g., by devising a new histochemical
staining method. Most of my contributions to the field of zoology may not have
been appreciated. In support of this statement I would like to cite one of the
questions which Professor P. B. Gahan asked me at the viva examination regarding *c*
my comparing the coelomocytes to vertebrate leucocytes instead of (say) to liver
cells. He went on to add that this had proved to be my greatest pitfall. In reply to
this I re-iterated what I have already stated in my thesis (please see pp.    of my
thesis), namely that coelomocytes are "free" cells and not attached cells and hence
may be compared to leucocytes. Further this comparison is perfectly valid and that
I was not the first to remark on this analogy. Numerous scientists have compared *d*
coelomocytes to insect haemaocytes and in turn to vertebrate leucocytes. (Please see
Enc.,    ). A zoologist would have recognised the validity of such a comparison and
would have considered it one more plus point in my favour, as I have conclusively
shown such a similarity to exist'.

The university in its answer said:                                                    *e*

'In answer to paragraph 3 of the Petition the University denies that the
appointment of Professors Gahan and Holt as Examiners was wrong and ought to
be set aside, and it denies that they were not proper or competent examiners ... (b)
(i) Professors Gahan and Holt were put forward as possible Examiners of the *f*
Petitioner to the Secretary of the Board of Studies in Zoology following the
Secretary's request for nominations made to Professor Dales as the Petitioner's
supervisor. Professor Dales put forward their names after discussion with Dr.
Thorndyke, the Senior Lecturer in Zoology at Bedford College. Their qualifications
were: *Professor Gahan.* Professor of Botany at Queen Elizabeth College. He obtained
his Ph.D in 1964 in, according to the University's Records, Zoology – Histochemistry. *g*
He is (and was) a member of the Board of Studies in Zoology. Histochemistry is a
subdiscipline of the three main biological subjects of anatomy, botany and zoology.
*Professor Holt.* Professor of Experimental Biochemistry at the Courtauld Institute of
Biochemistry. He obtained his Ph.D. in 1948 in Organic Chemistry. He holds a
degree of D.Sc. in Cytochemistry. The further grounds on which it was considered
that they were suitable to examine the Petitioner were as follows. The thesis was a *h*
cytochemical and ultrastructural study of the phagocytes in several species of
polychaete annelids. Although entirely within the purview of the Board of Studies
in Zoology, the appropriate examiners were those with particular knowledge of cell
structure, cytochemical techniques, electron microscopy and indentification of
lysosomal enzyme activity by histochemical means, using both light microscopy
and electron microscopy. The two examiners appointed fulfilled completely these *j*
requirements. Professor Holt had worked for many years on the histochemistry of
lysosomal enzymes, and especially on ultrastructural and cytochemical studies
employing electron microscope methods for enzyme localization and the application
of these methods to problems in cell biology. Professor Gahan was and is one of the

a   leading cell biologists in the University and has worked particularly with lysosomes and cytochemistry of lysosomal enzymes.'

The applicant did not serve any reply to the university's answer and no oral evidence was called before the committee. The essential materials for its decision were those I have identified. It should, however, be mentioned that Dr Thorndyke was a lecturer at Bedford College and the university were wrong to describe him as a senior lecturer.

b   The passage in the committee's decision on which, for purposes of this appeal, our attention has been concentrated, is this:

'The Committee will deal first with the petitioner's complaint that Professors Gahan and Holt were not zoologists specialising in the field of zoology to which the petitioner's thesis related. She submitted that both examiners were primarily histochemists and therefore would tend to concentrate on the histochemistry aspect
c   of her work, to the detriment of the important contributions which she was seeking to make to the field of comparative zoology. The petitioner says that she only applied histochemical methods in order to elucidate her morphological findings, and did not seek to make any contributions to the field of histochemistry. Thus her thesis was misjudged. While appreciating the nature of the petitioner's complaint, the Committee desire to emphasise, as has been observed in other cases, that it is no
d   part of their duty to interfere in matters of scientific or technical judgment. It would not be proper for the Committee to express a view of their own as to the choice of examiners, or to criticise the decision on such matters of the University authorities, save in a case, which is far from the instant case, where it is apparent from the facts that the examiners appointed by the University were plainly not qualified to perform their task. The Committee are of the opinion that the petitioner
e   is not entitled to any relief by reason of this complaint.'

Any summary of the excellent argument addressed by counsel for the applicant will do it injustice but I must try. It was to this effect. In a case such as the present the visitor is the sole source of justice between a member and the university. Where complaint is made the visitor must make such investigation as is in the circumstances appropriate. If,
f   in the absence of bad faith or obvious mistake, a complaint concerns a pure exercise of academic judgment, such as assessment of a candidate's academic performance, the visitor will not substitute his judgment for that of the academic authorities. But the selection of suitably qualified examiners does not involve a pure exercise of academic judgment, and the evident mismatch in this case between the examiners' fields of specialisation and the subject of the applicant's thesis raised an obvious question for
g   inquiry. Had the inquiry been properly and fully made the question might have been adequately answered and the apparent anomaly explained, but the committee failed to inquire and so abdicated its role as visitor, deferring to the body whose conduct it was its duty to investigate. In so acting the committee misdirected itself and its decision is, on familiar principles, amenable to judicial review.

The Divisonal Court had the benefit of the speeches made by Lord Griffiths and Lord
h   Ackner in *Thomas v University of Bradford* [1987] 1 All ER 834, [1987] AC 795, and as a result the broad principles governing exercise of visitatorial jurisdiction were not in issue before the Divisional Court or before us. But I think counsel to the applicant was right to detect some difference, at least of emphasis, in the interpretation and application of these principles by the two judges in the Divisional Court.

Kerr LJ referred to counsel's submission that it was incumbent on the committee to
j   investigate the applicant's complaints and the university's answer in sufficient depth to satisfy the committee personally that the appointments of examiners was reasonable, or at any rate not unreasonable, given the subject matter and nature of the applicant's thesis on the one hand and the examiners' qualifications on the other, and he continued ([1987] 3 All ER 294 at 313, [1900] QB 322 at 333–334):

'But I regret that I cannot for one moment accept any such mandatory prescription governing the mode of the exercise of visitatorial powers. These fall to be exercised *a* in an almost infinite variety of situations, and the mode of their exercise must necessarily be left to the discretion of the visitor, provided of course that he acts judically. Thus, far from concluding that the exercise of a merely supervisory jurisdiction is wrong in all cases, as counsel for the applicant appears to submit, it seems to me that in some cases it may well be the only proper exercise of visitatorial powers. In many situations, for example, it might be an abuse of power, and a *b* justifiable source of grievance on the part of the foundation, if the visitor entered on matters which, by the statutes of the foundation, were expressly left in the discretion of specially designated officers or members. Thus, counsel for the applicant himself accepted that the question whether or not the thesis and viva voce examination of the applicant satisfied the standard required for a PhD was solely a matter for her examiners. He accepted this, because that was clearly the effect of the relevant *c* statutes and regulations. However, as explained below, these equally prescribe the procedures for the appointment of the examiners themselves. They lay down no requirements as to their qualifications. The effect of the regulations is to leave these in the discretion of those members of the academic staff in whom the power and duty to appoint the examiners is vested, obviously having regard to the knowledge and experience which is to be expected from holders of their posts in the academic *d* hierarchy. Accordingly, if the visitor declines to interfere with their decisions on matters which depend on academic or scientific or other technical judgment, then it seems to me quite impossible to say that he has committed any error of law, unless the decisions in question are so plainly irrational or fraught with bias or some other obvious irregularity that they clearly cannot stand. Prima facie, by enrolling as a candidate for a PhD at a particular university, the candidate accepts that his or her *e* fitness for that degree will be judged by examiners appointed in accordance with the rules and academic practices of the chosen university. The powers of review possessed by the visitor of the university do not form part of the structure of academic judgment on which the candidate's enrolment is based. It is merely an instance of last resort in exceptional circumstances, and not, as the submissions of counsel for the applicant implied, an integral part of something in the nature of an *f* appellate structure. For these reasons I cannot for one moment accept that the committee in the present case was bound to investigate the applicant's grievances to the extent of satisfying itself directly that the appointment of these particular examiners was not unreasonable in the circumstances, let alone that they were suitable to be appointed.'

*g*

Thus Kerr LJ, while acknowledging that the visitor's role would depend on the circumstances in which his jurisdiction was invoked, regarded his role as supervisory where powers or duties were under the statutes of the univeristy conferred or imposed on designated officers. It was primarily because the examiners here were appointed in accordance with the rules and academic practices of London University that Kerr LJ *h* approved the decision of the committee.

Simon Brown J also delivered a judgment, to which counsel for the applicant paid a tribute in which I fully join. The judge summarised the competing submissions of counsel for the applicant and counsel for the committee, giving reasons for preferring the former. He then said, in a passage which despite its length merits quotation ([1987] 3 All ER 204 at 220–221, [1988] QB 322 at 344–345):

*j*

'I conclude therefore that the visitor enjoys untrammelled jurisdiction to investigate and correct wrongs done in the administration of the internal law of the foundation to which he is appointed: a general power to right wrongs and redress grievances. And if that on occasion requires the visitor to act akin rather to an appeal

court than to a review court, so be it. Indeed there may well be occasions when he
could not properly act other than as an essentially appellate tribunal. The difference
between visitatorial and this court's supervisory jurisdiction may be illustrated thus.
It will often be inappropriate for this court in the exercise of its review jurisdiction
to investigate the facts underlying the legal dispute before it. Equally, this court
must from time to time leave undisturbed a decision on the merits which it believes
to be wrong because it recognises that there is properly room for two views on the
point. But in my judgment there are no such limitations on the visitor's jurisdiction:
he may, indeed should, investigate the basic facts to whatever depth he feels
appropriate and he may interfere with any decision which he concludes to be wrong,
even though he feels unable to categorise it as *Wednesbury* unreasonable [see
*Associated Provincial Picture Houses Ltd v Wednesbury Corp* [1947] 2 All ER 680, [1948]
1 KB 223]. Generally speaking, therefore, I prefer the approach urged on us by
counsel for the applicant. But it nevertheless remains important to recognise that
many decisions giving rise to dispute will be subject to considerations which quite
properly inhibit the visitor from embarking on any independent fact-finding role. I
agree with Kerr LJ that this is as plainly true of the appointment of examiners as of
the decision of such examiners on the standard attained by a candidate. But in both
cases this seems to me less because the university statutes expressly entrust those
decisions to the discretion of particular members of the university than that these
members are peculiarly fitted by their eminence, experience and expertise to arrive
at proper decisions. This, indeed, was the essential burden of the submissions of
counsel on behalf of the university. And it must be remembered that even courts
exercising an unlimited appellate jurisdiction on occasions recognise that the
tribunal appealed from may have an expertise which particularly qualifies it to
decide a given question and will accordingly decline to intervene, save only if
satisfied that such tribunal was clearly wrong (see for instance the Court of Appeal
decision in *Race Relations Board v Associated Newspapers Group Ltd* [1978] 3 All ER
419, [1978] 1 WLR 905). My final conclusion, therefore, is that the visitor's role
cannot properly be characterised either as supervisory or appellate. It has no exact
analogy with that of the ordinary courts. It cannot usefully be defined beyond
saying that the visitor has untrammelled power to investigate and right wrongs
arising from the application of the domestic laws of a charitable foundation;
untrammelled, that is, save only and always that the visitor must recognise the full
width of his jurisdiction and yet approach its exercise in any given case reasonably
(in the public law sense). I wholly share Kerr LJ's conclusions on the instant
application that, in regard to each petition, the committee did indeed both recognise
the full width of their visitatorial jurisdiction and approach its exercise entirely
properly.'

Of this passage counsel for the applicant made only one criticism: the visitor should, he
said, investigate to whatever depth *is* appropriate, not to whatever depth he *feels*
appropriate (see [1987] 3 All ER 204 at 221, [1988] QB 322 at 344). Plainly this is what
the judge meant. The tenor of the judgment is that the visitor should investigate the
basic facts to the extent that in the exercise of a proper judgment he concludes to be
appropriate. The ground on which Simon Brown J declined to interfere with the
committee's decision was, if I understand him aright, that the appointment of examiners
to assess the applicant's thesis involved an exercise of expert judgment not shown to be
clearly wrong.

Leaving their application to the instant case on one side for the moment, I wholly
agree with the general principles which Simon Brown J laid down. The correct approach
can, I think, be illustrated by a hypothetical case involving facts remote from the present:
I suppose a college whose statutes empowered it to terminate a student's membership,
inter alia, if (1) he or she failed after receiving 28 days' written notice to do so to pay any

sum owed to the college or (2) was guilty of persistent insobriety such as, in the opinion
of the college, to render him or her unfit to remain a member or (3) failed in the opinion *a*
of the college to attain the academic standard required of students of the college. I also
suppose an appeal to the visitor by students whose membership had been determined
under (1), (2) and (3) respectively. In case (1) the visitor's role (although characterised, one
hopes, by the cheapness, lack of formality and procedural flexibility applauded by Lord
Griffiths in *Thomas v University of Bradford* [1987] 1 All ER 834 at 849, [1987] AC 795 at
824) would be essentially that of a first instance judge, that is he would hear and *b*
determine any disputed issue whether the debt was owed, whether notice was given,
whether there was a failure to pay and whether any defence of estoppel or a promise of
extra time was made out. He would be the judge of the facts and the law. In case (2) his
role would be a little different. Here, he would, I think, satisfy himself (if it were in issue)
that there was reliable evidence of persistent insobriety not of a trivial kind. He would
further wish to be satisfied, if there were any reason to doubt, that the college's decision *c*
was taken in good faith and not for any extraneous reason. If satisfied on those points he
would not, even if it were different, substitute his own opinion on fitness for that of the
college. That is because his responsibility is to see that the college acts lawfully in
accordance with the statutes, not to act as an independent arbiter of matters entrusted by
the statutes to the judgment of the college and on which its judgment is likely to be
better, because better informed and more experienced, than his. In case (3) the visitor *d*
would, again, satisfy himself (if it were in doubt) that there was reliable evidence of poor
academic performance and that the college's decision had not been tainted by bad faith
or extraneous motivation. If so satisfied, he would go no further, for the same reasons as
in (2). He could not legitimately override the college's bona fide assessment, based on
reliable evidence, of the student's academic performance. Both judges in the Divisional
Court would, I hope, agree with this analysis. *e*

I return to the applicant's case, reminding myself that whatever the committee's
correct approach in ruling on her petition there is no doubt about the role of this court,
which is to confine itself to correction of demonstrated errors of law. We could not
properly interfere with any exercise of discretion or judgment by the committee unless
of opinion that it was wrong in law. *f*

Despite the compelling argument of counsel for the applicant, I am not, for my part,
of that opinion. My reasons are these. (1) The committee was entitled, if not bound, to
conclude that the university's prescribed procedures for appointing examiners had been
followed. This was not therefore a case of manifest procedural impropriety. Following
the right procedures does not of course prevent mistakes being made, but it does reduce
the chances of error because decisions are made by those thought to be competent to
make them. (2) The committee knew that the examiners appointed had been suggested *g*
by Professor Dales, a very senior zoologist who had approved the subject of the applicant's
thesis and acted as her supervisor throughout. The committee saw a document suggesting
that Professor Dales had done no more than glance at the finished thesis. That may no
doubt be so, but there was nothing before the committee to rebut the inference one
would ordinarily draw, that during nearly four years of supervision the professor had *h*
become fully aware of what the applicant was working on. It is hard to see how anyone
could have been better placed than the professor to suggest appropriate examiners. This
remains true even if, as is said, relations between him and the applicant were not entirely
happy, since no imputation has been made against his competence, integrity or good
faith. (3) The committee took the view, with which I agree, that the choice of examiner
may well, and in this case did, involve an exercise of expert judgment. An appropriate *j*
examiner could not be appointed unless the appointor had some understanding (a) of the
specialist field to which the thesis related and (b) of the scientific knowledge and
experience of those who might be asked to assess it. No one without that understanding
could reliably have made an appointment in the present case. Unless there was some
reason to think that this expert judgment was improperly exercised here, the committee

was in my judgment entitled to treat this as an area into which it should not intrude. (4)

a  The committee did not, I infer, regard the appointment of two professors neither of whom was, at any rate primarily, a zoologist as in itself so anomalous or surprising or obviously inappropriate as to suggest that the appointor's expert judgment had been improperly exercised. I do not think it was wrong to take that view. However convenient it may sometimes be for teachers, textbook writers and educational administrators to treat fields of study as discrete and well-defined, if somewhat arbitrary, areas, like the

b  mid-western states of the American union, scholars and scientists are not in their pursuit of knowledge in the real world to be confined within such artificial frontiers. The same problem may engage the attention of the mathematician, the physicist and the astronomer, or, in a more familiar field, the lawyer, the philosopher and the political theorist. Labels are not decisive, or even perhaps very significant. The material before the committee did not, it is true, suggest that the examiners' own research duplicated

c  that of the applicant. Had it done so she might in any event have been refused her degree for want of originality. But I think the material did suggest that the examiners were expert in fields closely related to the applicant's field of research. To throw doubt on their qualifications it would in my view have been incumbent on the applicant to show an arguable case that their specialised fields were so far removed from her own as to disable them from fairly and expertly assessing her work, even if this involved some work by

d  them. The committee did not consider such a case to have been raised, and I agree. It may not be wholly without significance (a) that neither of the examiners asked to be excused the exacting task of examining, as I would expect any responsible scientist to do if he felt insufficiently expert to make a fair and reliable assessment and (b) that although only one of the three additional examiners appointed for the applicant's re-examination was, as I understand, a zoologist, she has not at any time questioned the fitness of any one

e  of the three.

Material has been placed before the court which shows the high esteem in which the applicant's scientific work has been held by disinterested assessors in the past, and her recent work has, we are told, attracted financial support from a most prestigious quarter. This is impressive testimony to the applicant's qualities as a scientist, and makes one

f  regret that the events of 1979–80 turned out as they did. We, however, have only the limited task defined above. Like the Divisional Court I am not persuaded that the committee made a decision which was wrong in law, and I would accordingly dismiss the appeal.

**MANN LJ.** The court has a supervisory but not an appellate jurisdiction in regard to

g  the visitor of the University of London. The issue in this case was whether the examiners appointed by the university to examine the applicant's thesis were competent so to do. The choice of examiners was initiated by the applicant's own supervisor after a discussion with the lecturer in zoology at the applicant's college. It is deposed on behalf of the university in the following terms:

h     'The thesis was a cytochemical and ultrastructural study of the phagocytes in several species of polychaete annelids. Although entirely within the purview of the Board of Studies in Zoology, the appropriate examiners were those with particular knowledge of cell structure, cytochemical techniques, electron microscopy and identification of lysosomal enzyme activity by histochemical means, using both light microscopy and electron microscopy. The two examiners appointed fulfilled

j     completely these requirements. Professor Holt had worked for many years on the histochemistry of lysosomal enzymes, and especially on ultrastructural and cytochemical studies employing electron microscope methods for enzyme localization and the application of these methods to problems in cell biology. Professor Gahan was and is one of the leading cell biologists in the University and has worked particularly with lysosomes and cytochemistry of lysosomal enzymes.'

This seems to me wholly a matter of academic judgment in which this court should not interfere.                                                                              *a*

**LORD DONALDSON OF LYMINGTON MR.** I agree with both judgments.

*Appeal dismissed. Leave to appeal to the House of Lords refused.*

Solicitors: *Davis Walker & Co*, Chalfont St Peter (for the applicant); *Treasury Solicitor;*  *b*
*Clifford Chance* (for the university).

Frances Rustin   Barrister.

*c*

# Lord Advocate v Scotsman Publications Ltd and others

HOUSE OF LORDS
LORD KEITH OF KINKEL, LORD TEMPLEMAN, LORD GRIFFTHS, LORD GOFF OF CHIEVELEY AND LORD   *d*
JAUNCEY OF TULLICHETTLE
15, 16, 17 MAY, 6 JULY 1989

*Confidential information – Injunction against disclosure of information – Information relating to
security service – Public interest in preventing disclosure – Book written by former member of
security services – Book not containing material prejudicial to public interest – Limited publication*  *e*
*of book – Newspaper publishing article about book – Crown seeking interim interdict to prevent
further publication of contents of book – Whether in public interest that further publication of
contents of book should be restrained.*

In 1987 C, a member of the British security service (MI6) from 1948 to 1953 who had   *f*
remained on close terms with members of the security service, in particular the head of
the service from 1973 to 1977, sought authorisation from the Crown to publish a book
of memoirs about his service with MI6 and to publish in it material disclosed to him by
other members of the service. When authorisation to publish the book was refused C
published 500 copies of the book privately and distributed 279 copies to various private
individuals in December 1987. Following representations made to him on behalf of the   *g*
Crown C gave an undertaking on 30 December 1987 not to distribute any more copies
of the book without first giving 14 days' notice of his intention to do so. However, a copy
of the book came into the possession of the Sunday Times newspaper, which published
an article about it on 27 December 1987. On 2 January 1988 the Attorney General
obtained an injunction in England restraining that newspaper from publishing any
further information from the book concerning the British intelligence and security   *h*
services. A copy of the book was also handed over to the Scotsman newspaper by one of
the original recipients and on 5 January 1988 the Scotsman published an article about
the book. The Lord Advocate requested the publishers of the Scotsman to give an
undertaking not to publish any material which if published in England would be in
breach of the injunction against the Sunday Times but they refused to give such an
undertaking. The Lord Advocate thereupon presented a petition against the publishers   *j*
and editor of the Scotsman (the first and second respondents) for an interim interdict
restraining them and any person having notice of the interdict from disclosing or
publishing any information obtained by C in the course of his employment with the
British security and intelligence services. The first and second respondents, together with
the third and fourth respondents, who were interested in publishing material from the
book, opposed the petition. The Lord Ordinary refused the Lord Advocate's application

and on appeal his interlocutor was affirmed by the Second Division of the Court of
*a* Session. The Lord Advocate appealed to the House of Lords. The Lord Advocate conceded
that the book did not contain any information the disclosure of which was capable of
damaging national security but contended that C as a former member of the security
intelligence service remained under a lifelong obligation of confidentiality owed to the
Crown as regards information which came into his possession, and that as regards
information communicated to him by other members of the service after his retirement
*b* he was under the same obligation of confidentiality as affected those other members.

**Held** – A third party who came into possession of security information which was
originally confidential but which had been revealed by a Crown servant in breach of his
duty of confidence would not be restrained from publishing that information if it was
not damaging to national security and the third party was not involved in the Crown
*c* servant's breach of his duty of confidentiality, since the public interest would not require
that publication be restrained in such circumstances. Accordingly, although C as a
former member of the British security and intelligence services owed a lifelong duty of
confidentiality to the Crown which rendered him liable to be restrained by injunction or
interdict from revealing information which came into his possession in the course of his
work and although a publisher or other person acting on his behalf was under a similar
*d* restraint, the Crown was not entitled to an injunction or interdict restraining publication
by a third party, such as the Scotsman, of such information unless such restraint was
required in the public interest. Furthermore (per Lord Templeman and Lord Jauncey),
that reasoning accorded with the Official Secrets Act 1989, which when it came into
force would make it an offence for any employee or former employee of the security
services to disclose any information about the security services whereas a third party
*e* would be guilty of an offence only if he disclosed information about the security services
which was damaging. Since the Crown had conceded that the book did not include
material damaging to national security and since publication had already taken place the
Lord Advocate had not established a good arguable prima facie case that further
publication by the respondents would be prejudicial to the public interest. The Lord
Ordinary and the Second Division had therefore been right to refuse interim interdict
*f* and the appeal would be dismissed (see p 858 *g h j* to p 859 *b g h*, p 861 *d f* to *j*, p 862 *j* and
p 863 *a* to *d j* to p 864 *b e f*, post).

*A-G v Guardian Newspapers Ltd (No 2)* [1988] 3 All ER 545 applied.

**Notes**
*g* For injunctions restraining disclosure of confidential information, see 24 Halsbury's Laws
(4th edn) para 1014, and for cases on the subject, see 28(2) Digest (Reissue) 1081–1090,
868–917.
     For proceedings to protect a public right, see 24 Halsbury's Laws (4th edn) paras 1030–
1031.

**Cases referred to in opinions**
*h*
*A-G v Guardian Newspapers Ltd (No 2)* [1988] 3 All ER 545, [1988] 3 WLR 776, HL; *affg*
     [1988] 3 All ER 545, [1988] 2 WLR 805, CA; *affg* [1988] 3 All ER 545, [1988] 2 WLR
     805.
*A-G v Jonathan Cape Ltd* [1975] 3 All ER 484, [1976] QB 752, [1975] 3 WLR 606.
*Commonwealth of Australia v John Fairfax & Sons Ltd* (1980) 147 CLR 39, Aust HC.
*j* *Handyside v UK* (1976) 1 EHRR 737, E Ct HR.
*Sunday Times v UK* (1979) 2 EHRR 245, E Ct HR.

**Appeal**
The Lord Advocate appealed with leave of the Second Division of the Inner House of the
Court of Session in Scotland against an interlocutor of the Second Division (the Lord
Justice Clerk (Ross), Lord Dunpark and Lord McDonald) (1988 SLT 490) dated 8 April

1988 refusing a reclaiming motion by the Lord Advocate against an interlocutor dated
23 February 1988 pronounced by the Lord Ordinary (Coulsfield) refusing the Lord   *a*
Advocate's application for interim interdict to restrain the first and second respondents,
Scotsman Publications Ltd and Magnus Linklater, the proprietor and the editor
respectively of the Scotsman newspaper, and any person having notice of the interdict,
from disclosing and publishing certain information obtained by Anthony Cavendish in
the course of his employment with the British security and intelligence services which
he had published in the book *Inside Intelligence*. The third respondent, Scottish Television   *b*
plc, and the fourth respondent, George Outram & Co Ltd, publishers of the Glasgow
Herald, appeared as persons having notice of the interdict. The facts are set out in the
opinion of Lord Keith.

J A Cameron QC (Vice-Dean of Faculty) and N F Davidson (both of the Scottish Bar) for the
    Lord Advocate.                                                                                *c*
W A Nimmo Smith QC and J A Peoples (both of the Scottish Bar) for the first and second
    respondents.
R N M MacLean QC (of the Scottish Bar) and Desmond Browne for the third and fourth
    respondents.

Their Lordships took time for consideration.                                                      *d*

6 July. The following opinions were delivered.

**LORD KEITH OF KINKEL.** My Lords, Mr Anthony Cavendish was employed by
the British secret intelligence service (MI6) from 1948 to 1953. After leaving the service
he remained on close terms with some continuing members of it, in particular Sir   *e*
Maurice Oldfield, who was head of MI6 from 1973 to 1977. In 1987 Cavendish sought
authorisation from the government for publication of a book of memoirs which included
some information about his period of service with MI6 and his association with Sir
Maurice Oldfield. The book was called *Inside Intelligence*. Authorisation to publish it was
refused. Mr Cavendish then had 500 copies of the book printed at his own expense, and   *f*
at Christmas 1987 distributed 279 copies of it to various private individuals. Following
representations made to him on behalf of the Crown, Mr Cavendish on 30 December
1987 gave an undertaking not to distribute any more copies of the book without first
giving 14 days' notice.
    Apparently a copy of the book came into the hands of the Sunday Times newspaper,
which published an article about it on 27 December 1987. On 2 January 1988 the
Attorney General was granted by the High Court of Justice an injunction against Times   *g*
Newspapers Ltd (the publishers of the Sunday Times) restraining them from publishing
any information obtained by Mr Cavendish concerning the British security and
intelligence services. The injunction also bore to restrain similarly 'any person having
notice of this order'. On 15 January 1988, following a hearing inter partes, the injunction
was modified to the effect, inter alia, of permitting the publication of parts of *Inside*   *h*
*Intelligence* which remained undeleted in an expurgated copy placed before the court,
amounting to about two-thirds of the book.
    A copy of *Inside Intelligence* also came into the possession of the Scotsman newspaper,
having apparently been handed over to it by the one of the original recipients. On
5 January 1988 the Scotsman published an article which included some of the material
contained in the book. The first respondents, the publishers of the Scotsman, were   *j*
requested on behalf of the Lord Advocate to give an undertaking that they would not
publish any material which if published in England would be in breach of the injunction
granted against Times Newspapers Ltd. They refused to give such an undertaking, and
thereupon the Lord Advocate launched the present petition against the publishers and
the editor of the Scotsman in the Court of Session, by the amended prayer of which he
asked the court—

a
'to interdict the respondents or either of them or their agents, servants or anyone acting on their behalf or any person having notice of said interlocuter from disclosing or publishing or causing or permitting to be disclosed or published to any person all or any material or information obtained by Anthony Cavendish in the course of his employment with the British Security and Intelligence Services or obtained by other officers of those services in the course of their employment with them and given by such officers to Anthony Cavendish being information

b
concerning the British Security and Intelligence Services or their activities or any other British Security organisation or its activities provided that there shall not be prohibited publication of the following (a) information contained in articles previously published by the Sunday Times; (b) information contained in the document entitled "Inside Intelligence", No 27 of process, but only insofar as such information is not obscured to any extent by being lined through in the text;

c
(c) information comprised in (i) fair and accurate reporting of proceedings in Open Court in the United Kingdom; (ii) fair and accurate reporting of proceedings in either House of Parliament whose publication is not prohibited by that House; and for interdict *ad interim* . . .'

After sundry procedure which included the lodging of answers to the petition not

d
only by the publishers and editor of the Scotsman but also by Scottish Television plc and George Outram & Co Ltd, the publishers of the Glasgow Herald, who objected to the proposal that any interdict granted should bind any person having notice of it, the Lord Ordinary on 23 February 1988, following a lengthy hearing, refused the Lord Advocate's application for interim interdict. His interlocuter was affirmed by the Second Division (the Lord Justice Clerk (Ross), Lord Dunpark and Lord McDonald) (1988 SLT 490) on

e
8 April 1988. The Lord Advocate now appeals, with leave of the Second Division, to your Lordships' House.

The grant or refusal of interim interdict is a discretionary matter, so that in order to succeed the Lord Advocate must demonstrate that the courts below in some way misdirected themselves in law or that their discretion was exercised unreasonably. The ground on which the Lord Advocate seeks interdict is that of confidentiality. It is averred

f
that Mr Cavendish as a former member of the secret intelligence service remains under a lifelong obligation of confidentiality owed to the Crown as regards information which came into his possession as such a member, and further, that as regards information communicated to him after his retirement by other members of the service he is under the same obligation of confidentiality as affected those other members. The Scotsman's article of 5 January 1988 is said to contain material revealed by Mr Cavendish in breach

g
of his obligation. The Lord Advocate goes on to aver, in statement 7 of his petition:

'That the petitioner is reasonably apprehensive that it is likely that the respondents will publish further information obtained by Anthony Cavendish concerning the British Security and Intelligence Services or their activities or any other British Security organisation or its activities or other security service or its activities. Further

h
the petitioner is apprehensive that standing the nature of the material and information that others will seek to disclose or publish said material to the prejudice of the administration of justice. Disclosure or publication of said material and information is prejudicial to the interests of the Crown. It is prejudicial to national security. It is prejudicial to said interests in the following respects:—(a) the intelligence and security services of friendly foreign countries with which the

j
British Security and Intelligence Services are in liaison would be likely to lose confidence in their ability to protect classified information; (b) the British Security and Intelligence Services depend upon the confidence and co-operation of other organisations and persons which confidence would be likely to suffer serious damage should Mr Cavendish reveal information of the nature described above; (c) there would be a risk that other persons who are or have been employed in the British Security and Intelligence Services who have had access to similar information might

seek to publish it; (d) there would be likely to be a serious adverse effect in the future on the morale and discipline of members of the British Security and Intelligence Services if the disclosure of said information were allowed in breach of said duty of confidentiality; (e) in the absence of interdict pressure would be likely to be exerted by the media on other members or ex-members of the British Security and Intelligence Services to give their views on matters referred to by Mr Cavendish; (f) detriment will be likely to flow from the publication of information about the methodology and personnel and organisation of the British Security and Intelligence Services.'

It is the Lord Advocate's case that the duty of confidence which was incumbent on Mr Cavendish in relation to relevant information contained in his book is incumbent also on the respondents, who received that information knowing that it had been revealed by Mr Cavendish in breach of his own obligation.

In the course of the argument for the Lord Advocate before the Second Division it became clear, as apparently it had not been before the Lord Ordinary, that the Crown did not maintain that *Inside Intelligence* contained any information disclosure of which was capable of damaging national security. From that point of view the whole contents of the book were entirely innocuous. So the grounds on which the Second Division refused interim interdict were different from those relied on by the Lord Ordinary, which in the circumstances need not be examined. The judges of the Second Division, having considered such authorities on the law of confidentiality as existed in the Scottish corpus juris, came to the conclusion that Scots law in this field was the same as that of England, in particular as respects the circumstances under which a person coming into possession of confidential information knowing it to be such, but not having received it directly from the original confider, himself comes under an obligation of confidence. That conclusion was, in my opinion, undoubtedly correct. While the juridical basis may differ to some extent in the two jurisdictions, the substance of the law in both of them is the same. If it had not been for the acceptance by counsel for the Lord Advocate that further publication of the information contained in the book would not be prejudicial to national security, the Second Division would have been disposed to grant interim interdict. They would not, at the interlocutory state, have been prepared to hold that such limited publication as had already taken place had placed the contents of the book in the public domain to such an extent that a restriction on further publication would serve no useful purpose. But in the face of the concession about absence of prejudice to national security the Second Division were unable to find that a prima facie case for permanent interdict had been pleaded. The Lord Justice Clerk said, under reference to statement 7 of the petition (1988 SLR 490 at 505):

'Bearing in mind that this is avowedly a non-contents case, I am of opinion that the Lord Advocate has failed to make out a prima facie case. Heads (a) to (f) might have been relevant if this had been a contents case. This is because heads (a) to (f) are all expressed as being referable to information, i.e. the contents of the book. But since this is a non-contents case, they are irrelevant. This can be seen clearly if each of the heads is examined separately. So far as (a) is concerned, it could not be contended that foreign security services would be likely to lose confidence in the ability of the British security and intelligence services to protect classified information unless it were being asserted that the book contained classified information. It is nowhere averred that there is classified information in the book, and in the context of a non-contents case this could not arise. So far as (b) is concerned the same comment can be made. The same is true of (c) since "similar information" must be a reference back to classified information. The same is true of (d). So far as (e) is concerned what is said to be apprehended is that the media would exert pressure upon members or ex-members of the British security and intelligence services to give their views "on matters referred to by Mr Cavendish". This must be a reference

a
to what is in the book, and cannot be material to a non-contents case. What appears to lie behind (a) to (e) is that if Mr Cavendish is allowed to publish his memoirs there will be a loss of confidence in the British security and intelligence service and a risk of further disclosures. One can readily understand that once it is known that there has been disclosure by Mr Cavendish, these results will ensue. The trouble is that it is now known widely that Mr Cavendish has made these disclosures and accordingly the anticipated results must have occurred. That being so, there is no

b
way in which the loss of confidence referred to and the reduction in morale can be averted by an order of the court. I would stress that in this context it is not the degree of publication which is important but the fact that there has been publication at all. As junior counsel for the first respondents put it: "Once the leak occurs, the damage is done". As soon as it becomes known that there has been disclosure or publication on the part of Mr Cavendish, the damaging consequences referred to in

c
paras. (a) to (e) are inevitable. Paragraphs (a) to (e) might well have been convincing considerations if an interdict were being sought before any publication or disclosure by Mr Cavendish had taken place. However, since such publication and disclosure have taken place, granting interdict now would indeed be closing the proverbial stable door after the horse had bolted. I would only add, under reference to (c) and (d), that I doubt in any event whether the court would be justified in granting

d
interdict if the purpose of the interdict was not to stop a wrong but was to deter others and to maintain morale. On this aspect I respectfully agree with what Lord Oliver said in *Att. Gen.* v. *Guardian Newspapers Ltd.* ([1987] 3 All ER 316 at 373-374, [1987] 1 WLR 1248 at 1318). So far as (f) is concerned it appears to me that this head would only be relevant in the context of a contents case. It clearly envisages publication of the contents of the book which might then enable the reader to learn

e
something about the methodology, personnel and organisation of the British security and intelligence services. But we know nothing about the contents of the book, and there is no suggestion that it contains information on these matters. In the context of a non-contents detriment case, I am of opinion that head (f) can have no proper relevance, and counsel for the petitioner appeared ultimately to recognise this.'

f
Similar views were expressed by Lord Dunpark and Lord McDonald.

At the time of the decision by the Second Division the *Spycatcher* case had passed through the stages of trial before Scott J and appeal to the Court of Appeal: see *A-G v Guardian Newspapers Ltd (No 2)* [1988] 3 All ER 545, [1988] 2 WLR 805. The decision on

g
appeal to your Lordships' House, which affirmed the Court of Appeal, was given on 13 October 1988 (see [1988] 3 All ER 545, [1988] 3 WLR 776). That decision authoritatively established that a member or former member of the British security or intelligence services owes a lifelong duty of confidentiality to the Crown which renders him liable to be restrained by injunction or interdict from revealing information which came into his possession in the course of his work. Disclosure of such information is by

h
its nature damaging to national security and there is no room for close examination of the precise manner in which revelation of any particular information would cause damage. A publisher or other person acting on behalf of the member or former member of the service was held to be subject to similar restraint. It was the prospect of damage to the public interest which necessistated the fetter on freedom of speech, and the House accepted the principle that in general the Crown was not in a position to insist on

j
confidentiality as regards governmental matters unless it could demonstrate the likelihood of such damage being caused by disclosure. I said ([1988] 3 All ER 545 at 640, [1988] 3 WLR 776 at 782-783):

'In so far as the Crown acts to prevent such disclosure or to seek redress for it on confidentiality grounds, it must necessarily, in my opinion, be in a position to show that the disclosure is likely to damage or has damaged the public interest. How far the Crown has to go in order to show this must depend on the circumstance of each *a* case. In a question with a Crown servant himself, or others acting as his agents, the general public interest in the preservation of confidentiality, and in encouraging other Crown servants to preserve it, may suffice. But, where the publication is proposed to be made by third parties unconnected with the particular confidant, the position may be different. The Crown's argument in the present case would go the length that in all circumstances where the original disclosure has been made by a *b* Crown servant in breach of his obligation of confidence, any person to whose knowledge the information comes and who is aware of the breach comes under an equitable duty binding his conscience not to communicate the information to anyone else irrespective of the circumstances under which he acquired the knowledge. In my opinion that general proposition is untenable and impracticable, in addition to being unsupported by any authority. The general rule is that anyone *c* is entitled to communicate anything he pleases to anyone else, by speech or in writing or in any other way. That rule is limited by the law of defamation and other restrictions similar to those mentioned in art 10 of the Convention for the Protection of Human Rights and Fundamental Freedoms (Rome, 4 November 1950; TS 71 (1953); Cmd 8969). All those restrictions are imposed in the light of considerations of public interest such as to countervail the public interest in freedom of expression. *d* A communication about some aspect of government activity which does no harm to the interests of the nation cannot, even where the original disclosure has been made in breach of confidence, be restrained on the ground of a nebulous equitable duty of conscience serving no useful practical purpose.'

This passage recognises that there may be some circumstances under which a third *e* party may come into possession of information, originally confidential, which has been revealed by a Crown servant in breach of his own duty of confidence, and yet may not be liable to be restrained from passing it on to others. In *Spycatcher* itself the circumstances which resulted in the defendant newspapers not being restrained from publishing and commenting on material contained in the book were that it had been disseminated worldwide to the extent of over one million copies and that it was freely available in this *f* country. In that situation it was impossible for the Crown to demonstrate that further publication by the defendants would add to any extent to the damage to the public interest which had already been brought about.

One particular circumstance of the present case, which gives it a peculiar and perhaps unique character, is the abandonment by the Lord Advocate of any contention that the contents of *Inside Intelligence* include any material damage to national security. The other *g* most relevant circumstance is that the book has been distributed by Mr Cavendish to 279 recipients. These two circumstances in combination must lead inevitably to the conclusion that the Lord Advocate has not pleaded a good arguable prima facie case that further publication by the respondents would do any material damage to the public interest. If a proof were allowed, any opinion evidence on the lines of statement 7 of the petition, such as was given by Sir Robert Armstrong in the *Spycatcher* case, would be *h* given on the basis that the contents of the book were innocuous. The court would not be proceeding on the normal prima facie footing that any book about his work by a former member of the security or intelligence services was directly prejudicial to national security. Further, as the Lord Justice Clerk pointed out, the sort of indirect prejudice which is described in paras (a) to (e) of statement 7 is brought about by the known fact of publication by a former member of the service, not by its extent. *j*

It was argued for the Lord Advocate that dismissal of this appeal would have the effect that any newspaper which received an unsolicited book of memoirs by a present or former member of the security or intelligence services would be free to publish it. That is not so. If there had been no previous publication at all and no concession that the a  contents of the book were innocuous the newspaper would undoubtedly itself come under an obligation of confidence and be subject to restraint. If there had been a minor degree of prior publication, and no such concession it would be a matter for investigation whether further publication would be prejudicial to the public interest, and interim interdict would normally be appropriate.

My Lords, I can find no material misdirection in law in the opinions of the judges of the Second Division, nor anything unreasonable in the manner of exercise of their
b  discretion. I would accordingly dismiss the appeal and find it unnecessary to deal with the argument of the third and fourth respondents regarding the form of the interim interdict asked for.

**LORD TEMPLEMAN.** My Lords, in this appeal the Lord Advocate, acting on behalf of the Crown, claims to restrain the respondent newspapers and television companies
c  from disclosing certain information contained in a book written by one Cavendish, that information having been obtained by him in the course of his employment with the British security and intelligence services.

Any such restraint is an interference with the right of expression safeguarded by the Convention for the Protection of Human Rights and Fundamental Freedoms (Rome, 4 November 1950; TS 71 (1953); Cmd 8969) to which the United Kingdom government
d  adheres. Article 10 of the convention is in these terms:

'(1) Everyone has the right to freedom of expression. This right shall include freedom to hold opinions and to receive and impart information and ideas without interference by public authority and regardless of frontiers . . .

(2) The exercise of these freedoms, since it carries with it duties and responsibilities,
e  may be subject to such formalities, conditions, restrictions or penalties as are prescribed by law and are necessary in a democratic society, in the interests of national security, territorial integrity or public safety, for the prevention of disorder or crime, for the protection of health or morals, for the protection of the reputation or rights of others, for preventing the disclosure of information received in confidence, or for maintaining the authority and impartiality of the judiciary.'
f

The question therefore is whether the restraint sought to be imposed on the respondents is 'necessary in a democratic society in the interests of national security'. Similar questions were considered in *A-G v Guardian Newspapers Ltd (No 2)* [1988] 3 All ER 345, [1988] 3 WLR 776 (the *Spycatcher* case) but at that time Parliament had not provided any answer to the questions posed by the conflict between the freedom of
g  expression and the requirement of national security.

In my opinion it is for Parliament to determine the restraints on freedom of expression which are necessary in a democratic society. The courts of this country should follow any guidance contained in a statute. If that guidance is inconsistent with the requirements of the convention then that will be a matter for the convention authorities and for the United Kingdom government. It will not be a matter for the courts.
h  The guidance of Parliament has now been provided in the Official Secrets Act 1989, which was enacted on 11 May 1989 and will be brought into force on such date as the Secretary of State may by order appoint. By the 1989 Act certain categories of persons will be guilty of a criminal offence if they disclose information relating to security or intelligence in the circumstances specified in the Act but not otherwise. In my opinion
j  the civil jurisdiction of the courts of this country to grant an injunction restraining a breach of confidence at the suit of the Crown should not, in principle, be exercised in a manner different from or more severe than any appropriate restriction which Parliament has imposed in the 1989 Act and which, if breached, will create a criminal offence as soon as the Act is brought into force.

Section 1 deals with a person who is or has been a member of any of the security and intelligence services. Such a person, who may, for want of a better expression, be described as a security employee, is by s 1(1)—                                                    *a*

> 'guilty of an offence if without lawful authority he discloses any information, document or other article relating to security or intelligence which is or has been in his possession by virtue of his position as a member of any of those services . . .'

By s 7 a disclosure by a Crown servant is made with lawful authority if, and only if, it is made in accordance with his official duty and a disclosure by any other person is made   *b* with lawful authority if, and only if, it is made in accordance with an official authorisation duly given by a Crown servant. Cavendish is not now a Crown servant and he has failed to obtain official authorisation for some parts of his book. Cavendish has made disclosures which would infringe s 1 if the 1989 Act were in force.

Section 5 deals with third parties, that is to say, generally speaking persons who are not and have not been members of the security and intelligence services. Section 5(1) applies   *c* where—

> '(a) any information, document or other article protected against disclosure by the foregoing provisions of this Act has come into a person's possession as a result of having been—(i) disclosed (whether to him or another), by a Crown servant . . . without lawful authority . . .'                                                              *d*

In my opinion the respondents fall into the category described by s 5 notwithstanding that Cavendish had retired from his employment and was not a Crown servant at the date when information protected against disclosure was disclosed by Cavendish and came into the possession of the respondents. The restrictions imposed by the 1989 Act on third parties are less onerous than the restrictions placed on Cavendish and other security employees. By s 5(2), subject to s 5(3), a third party into whose possession confidential   *e* information has come—

> 'is guilty of an offence if he discloses it without lawful authority knowing, or having reasonable cause to believe, that it is protected against disclosure by the foregoing provisions of this Act and that it has come into his possession as mentioned in subsection (1) above.'                                                                     *f*

In the present case the respondents are well aware that the information derived from Cavendish is protected against disclosure and came into their possession as a result of a disclosure by Cavendish. But by s 5(3):

> 'In the case of information or a document or article protected against disclosure by sections 1 to 3 above, a person does not commit an offence under subsection (2)   *g* above unless—(a) the disclosure by him is damaging; and (b) he makes it knowing, or having reasonable cause to believe, that it would be damaging . . .'

By s 1(4) the disclosure by the respondents of the protected information derived from Cavendish will be damaging if—

> '(a) it causes damage to the work of, or of any part of, the security and intelligence   *h* services; or (b) it is of information or a document or other article which is such that its unauthorised disclosure would be likely to cause such damage or which falls within a class or description of information, documents or articles the unauthorised disclosure of which would be likely to have that effect.'

The information derived from Cavendish which the respondents may wish to publish   *j* and disclose is information embedded in a book of memoirs by Cavendish. Part of that book relates to the period between 1948 and 1953 when Cavendish was a security employee and is protected against disclosure by s 1 of the 1989 Act. The Crown concede, however, that publication of that information by the respondents will not cause or be likely to cause damage to the work of the security or intelligence services, presumably

because the information is inaccurate or unenlightening or insignificant. The information
*a*  itself does not fall within a class or description of information the unauthorised disclosure
of which would be likely to be damaging. Nevertheless, the Crown contend that it is
entitled to restrain the respondents from publishing this harmless information because
the information is contained in the memoirs of a security employee. It is said that the
publication of harmless information derived from a former security employee and
protected by s 1 against disclosure by him, though not damaging in itself, would cause
*b*  harm by encouraging other security employees to make disclosures in breach of s 1 of
the 1989 Act and by raising doubts as to the reliability of the security service.

My Lords, it is well known, at home and abroad, that every security service suffers
from time to time from an employee who is disloyal for idealogical or other reasons
which may derive from the desire for profit or notoriety. The motives of Cavendish are
irrelevant if he is in breach of the duty of lifelong confidence of security employees
*c*  accepted in the *Spycatcher* case and imposed by s 1 of the 1989 Act. If the 1989 Act had
been in force when Cavendish circulated his book to a chosen band of readers, he would
have committed an offence under s 1 of the Act notwithstanding that the information
disclosed in his book is harmless. But it does not follow that third parties commit an
offence if they disclose harmless information. Were it otherwise, the distinction between
an offence by a security employee and an offence by a third party which appears from
*d*  the 1989 Act would be eradicated. A security employee can commit an offence if he
discloses any information. A third party is only guilty of an offence if the information is
damaging in the sense defined by the Act.

If the Crown had asserted that future publication by the Scotsman would be likely to
damage the work of the security services, then difficult questions might have arisen as to
the nature of the damage feared, whether an injunction was necessary within the
*e*  meaning attributed to that expression by the European Court of Human Rights and
whether the restriction on freedom of expression constituted by the injunction sought
was 'proportionate to the legitimate aim pursued' as required by the European Court of
Human Rights in *Handyside v UK* (1976) 1 EHRR 737 and *Sunday Times v UK* (1979) 2
EHRR 245. These difficult questions do not, however, arise since the Crown conceded
that future publication would not be likely to cause damage other than the indirect
*f*  damage which I have already rejected.

In the present case the respondents did not instigate or encourage or facilitate any
breach by Cavendish of his obligations. They did not solicit a copy of the Cavendish book
or any information from him or derived from him. They did not commit an offence at
common law in connection with an offence or attempted offence by Cavendish. It may
be that there are circumstances in which a third party might be liable to be restrained
*g*  from publishing protected information even though the publication by the third party
might itself be harmless. It is unnecessary, however, to consider this possibility in the
present instance.

I would affirm the decision of the Court of Session and dismiss the appeal of the
Crown.

*h*
**LORD GRIFFITHS.** My Lords, I have had the advantage of reading the speech of my
noble and learned friend Lord Keith, and for the reasons he gives I would dismiss this
appeal.

**LORD GOFF OF CHIEVELEY.** My Lords, I have had the advantage of reading the
*j*  speech of my noble and learned friend Lord Keith, and for the reasons he gives I would
dismiss this appeal.

**LORD JAUNCEY OF TULLICHETTLE.** My Lords, Anthony Cavendish, a former
member of the security services from 1948 to 1953, wrote a book of his memoirs entitled
*Inside Intelligence* and sought leave of the Crown to publish it. Leave was refused.

Thereafter Cavendish had 500 copies printed, and in December 1987 distributed some
279 as 'Christmas cards'. One of these 'Christmas cards' was sent to a Scottish member of
Parliament who passed it to the editor of the Scotsman. Proceedings were initiated in
England by the Attorney General against the Observer and the Sunday Times newspapers
and interim injunctions were granted by Kennedy J on 1 and 2 January 1988 against
their publishing information supplied directly or indirectly by Cavendish in breach of
his duty of confidence owed to the Crown. The terms of these injunctions were
subsequently modified when the Crown restricted its initial refusal of leave to publish to
certain parts (the blue-pencilled parts) of the book. The Lord Advocate, on behalf of the
Crown, also presented a petition for suspension and interdict in the Court of Session
against the Scotsman and its editor, and interim interdict against publication was granted
by Lord Coulsfield on 5 January 1988, but after sundry procedure, involving a recall of
the interdict of consent, interim interdict was refused by him on 23 February 1988 (see
1988 SLT 490). The Lord Advocate proceeded against the Scotsman after the editor had
refused to give an undertaking not to publish any material which could, if published in
England, be in breach of Kennedy J's injunction. The Lord Advocate reclaimed the Lord
Ordinary's interlocuter but the Second Division on 8 April 1988 adhered thereto (see
1988 SLT 490). It is to be noted that the hearing before the Second Division took place
some time before the hearing of *A-G v Guardian Newspapers Ltd (No 2)* [1988] 3 All ER
545, [1988] 3 WLR 776 (the *Spycatcher* case) in your Lordship's House.

The Lord Advocate concedes that there is nothing in the blue-pencilled parts of the
book which would endanger national security if published. Furthermore, he does not
aver that the Scotsman or its editor had any responsibility for Cavendish's publication of
the book or for their receipt of it. He takes his stand on the proposition that since there
is a lifelong duty of non-disclosure on anyone who has been a member of the security
services, any unauthorised disclosure of information, however innocuous, deriving from
such a member by a person who is aware that the disclosure is unauthorised is against
the public interest and should be restrained. This must, at any rate, be the position at an
interlocutory stage and was the basis on which Millett J granted an interim injunction in
the *Spycatcher* case. The Lord Advocate is thus relying on the act of publication by the
respondents and not on the character of the information which they propose to publish.
The respondents, while accepting that Cavendish is subject to such a lifelong duty,
maintain that the public interest does not require that anyone fortuitously acquiring
confidential information derived from him which does not endanger national security
should be restrained from publishing.

My Lords, the Lord Advocate's contention was decisively rejected in this House in the
*Spycatcher* case and it is sufficient to refer to the speech of Lord Keith ([1988] 3 All ER
545 at 640, [1988] 3 WLR 776 at 782–785). Counsel for the Lord Advocate sought to get
round this difficulty by submitting that the present case was different from the *Spycatcher*
case in that there had been no worldwide publication of the material. I agree with the
Lord Justice Clerk that 'There is all the difference in the world between a case such as
*Spycatcher* where about 1,000,000 copies of the book had been published and distributed
and the present case where such publication as there had been was clearly limited' (see
1988 SLT 490 at 504). However, the fact that this book is not generally available to the
public does not necessarily render inapplicable the principles enunciated in the *Spycatcher*
case.

It is now beyond doubt that the Crown can only restrain the publication of confidential
information if the public interest requires such restraint. This principle was enunciated
in *A-G v Jonathan Cape Ltd* [1975] 3 All ER 484 at 495, [1976] QB 752 at 770–771 by Lord
Widgery CJ and in *Commonwealth of Australia v John Fairfax & Sons Ltd* (1980) 147 CLR
39 at 51–52 by Mason J and was expressly approved in this House in the *Spycatcher* case.
It is also clear from that case that any attempt by a member, past or present, of the
security services to publish without authority information which he acquired in the
course of his work will be restrained regardless of the character of the information. The

public interest requires that members should not breach their duty of confidence. This
*a*   is what Lord Griffiths described as the 'brightline rule' in the *Spycatcher* case [1988] 3 All
ER 545 at 650, [1988] 3 WLR 776 at 795. In the present case the respondents accepted
that this rule would apply in any proceedings against Cavendish in the United Kingdom.

To what extent a third party receiving information which he knows to be disclosed in
breach of confidence will be restrained from publication thereof must depend on the
circumstances. If the information is likely to be damaging to national security he will
*b*   almost certainly be restrained. So far as confidential information which is not so
damaging is concerned, it would be inappropriate in this appeal to attempt an exhaustive
definition. Suffice it to say that an agent publishing on behalf of the confidant would
probably be restrained (see the *Spycatcher* case [1988] 3 All ER 545 at 642–643, [1988] 3
WLR 776 at 786 per Lord Keith) as would anyone in the 'direct chain from the confidant'
(see [1988] 3 All ER 545 at 652, [1988] 3 WLR 776 at 797 per Lord Griffiths). I would
*c*   consider that anyone who was directly involved in the disclosure by the confidant of the
information sought to be published should be restrained and there might be circumstances
in which a person deriving a right to publish from such a person should similarly be
restrained. In such cases the public interest in requiring members of the security services
not to breach their duty of confidence overrides the public interest in the freedom of
speech. However, Cavendish's unauthorised disclosure and hence his breach of duty
*d*   occurred when he posted his book to the member of Parliament. When the book reached
the respondents there had already occurred a breach of duty in which they had been in
no way involved.

To quote the words of Lord Keith in the *Spycatcher* case [1988] 3 All ER 545 at 640,
[1988] 3 WLR 776 at 783:

*e*       'The general rule is that anyone is entitled to communicate anything he pleases to
anyone else, by speech or in writing or in any other way. That rule is limited by the
law of defamation and other restrictions similar to these mentioned an art 10 of the
Convention for the Protection of Human Rights and Fundamental Freedoms (Rome,
4 November 1950; TS 71 (1953) Cmd 8969). All those restrictions are imposed in
the light of considerations of public interest such as to countervail the public interest
*f*       in freedom of expression.'

Article 10 identifies 'the interests of national security' and 'preventing the disclosure of
information received in confidence' as grounds on which restraint may be imposed on
freedom of expression. The Crown accepts that the interests of national security do not
require that publication of this book be restrained but maintain that the matters set out
in statement 7 of the petition and which are fully set out in the speech of my noble and
*g*   learned friend Lord Keith constitute sufficient detriment to the public interest to
outweigh the interest in preserving freedom of expression. In my view, this proposition
is unsound. The six matters relied on in statement 7 are almost identical to matters relied
on as national security factors by Sir Robert Armstrong in the *Spycatcher* case: see the
judgment of Scott J ([1988] 3 All ER 545 at 590–592, [1988] 2 WLR 805 at 860–862).
*h*   Scott J concluded that having regard to the worldwide publication of *Spycatcher* further
damage to national security on any of the grounds advanced by Sir Robert Armstrong
would not take place and he therefore refused to grant a permanent injunction. In this
House Lord Griffiths expressed his broad agreement with Scott J's assessment of Sir
Robert Armstrong's grounds (see [1988] 3 All ER 545 at 654, [1988] 3 WLR 776 at 800).
If the Lord Advocate's argument in this appeal is correct, it would appear to follow that
*j*   Scott J in the *Spycatcher* case should have granted a permanent injunction on the basis
that for the reasons given by Sir Robert Armstrong the public interest required restraint
of publication notwithstanding the fact no further damage to national security would
have resulted therefrom, and that the majority of the Court of Appeal and your Lordships
should have come to a similar conclusion. This is not a realistic approach. National
security is not in issue, the respondents were not involved in Cavendish's breach of duty,

and it therefore follows that the public interest in freedom of expression outweighs any public interest there may be in restraining the mere act of publication by the respondents. To put the matter another way, the Lord Advocate has made no relevant averments of such detriment to the public interest as would entitle him to an inquiry and ad interim to an interdict restricting the right of freedom of expression. The Second Division's approach to and refusal of the reclaiming motion was correct and I would therefore dismiss the appeal.

My Lords, during the course of argument reference was made to the Official Secrets Act 1989 which has not yet come into force. It is interesting to give a brief summary of certain of its provisions which relate specifically to members of the security services. Section 1(1) makes it an offence for a past or present member of the security services to disclose confidential information without lawful authority. Section 5(2) makes it an offence for a person into whose possession information has come in the manner indicated in s 5(1) to disclose without lawful authority knowing, or having reasonable cause to believe, that it is protected against disclosure by, inter alia, s 1(1). Section 5(3) provides that an offence under s 5(2) is not committed unless the disclosure is damaging and the offender makes it knowing or having reasonable cause to believe that it would be damaging. Section 5(1) provides that s 5(2) applies where, inter alia, any information has come into a person's possession as a result of having been disclosed by a Crown servant without lawful authority. Section 5(1) does not refer to past Crown servants, as does s 1(1) and (3), but s 5(3) applies to information 'protected against disclosure by sections 1 to 3'. On the assumption that s 5 was intended to apply to confidential information deriving from past as well as present members of the security services, an assumption which may well be unjustified having regard to the obscurity of the language, the pattern of the Act appears to be that disclosure of any such information by such a person is a statutory offence but that disclosure by third parties is only such an offence if the disclosure is damaging. Thus, just as the first and second respondents cannot be interdicted from publishing at common law so they could not have been prosecuted under the 1989 Act had it been in force in respect of such publication.

My Lords, an argument was advanced by the third and fourth respondents in relation to the inclusion in any interdict which might be pronounced of the words 'or any person having notice of said interlocuter'. In view of the way in which I propose that this appeal should be disposed of, I do not find it necessary to deal with this matter.

*Appeal dismissed.*

Solicitors: *Treasury Solicitor*, agent for *Solicitor to the Secretary of State for Scotland*, Edinburgh (for the appellant); *Allen & Overy*, agents for *Dundas & Wilson CS*, Edinburgh (for the first and second respondents); *Lovell White Durrant*, agents for *John G Gray & Co*, Edinburgh, agents for *Levy & McRae*, Glasgow (for the third respondents) and for *Haig-Scott & Co WS*, Edinburgh, agents for *Bannatyne Kirkwood France & Co*, Glasgow (for the fourth respondents).

Mary Rose Plummer     Barrister.

# R v Watson

*a*

COURT OF APPEAL, CRIMINAL DIVISION
LORD LANE CJ, FARQUHARSON AND POTTS JJ
23, 26 MAY 1989

*b*

*c*

*Criminal law – Manslaughter – Causing death by unlawful act – Unlawful act – Death occurring after burglary – Defendant entering victim's flat at night with intent to steal – Victim an elderly man with heart trouble living alone – Victim woken up and verbally abused by defendant – Police and council workmen arriving shortly after burglary – Victim dying hour and a half after burglary – Jury directed that defendant responsible for victim's death even if heart attack brought on by arrival of police or council workmen – Whether knowledge of victim to be attributed to defendant confined to knowledge which defendant acquired when first entering house – Whether knowledge of victim to be attributed to defendant including knowledge gained during whole of his stay in house – Whether defendant guilty of manslaughter.*

*d*

*e*

The appellant and another man entered the home of an 87-year-old man late at night by breaking a window with intent to commit burglary. The occupant, who lived alone and suffered from a serious heart condition, was woken up by the appellant and his accomplice and verbally abused but the appellant and his accomplice made off without stealing anything. Shortly after the burglary the police arrived to investigate and council workmen came to board up the broken window and then, an hour and a half after the burglary, the occupant had a heart attack and died. The appellant was later arrested and charged with burglary and manslaughter of the occupant of the house and was convicted. He appealed against his conviction for manslaughter.

*f*

*g*

**Held** – Where a defendant had entered a house as a burglar and confronted an elderly occupant who had a heart attack some time after discovering the defendant, the knowledge of his victim to be attributed to the defendant for the purposes of a charge of manslaughter was not confined to the knowledge which the defendant acquired when he first entered the house but included knowledge gained during the whole of his stay in the house since his unlawful act comprised the whole of his burglarious intrusion. Accordingly, since the appellant must have become aware of the occupant's frailty and old age in the course of his intrusion he ought to have realised that his unlawful act would subject the occupant to a risk of harm. However, since the appellant's counsel had not been given the opportunity to make submissions before the judge directed the jury to the effect that if the arrival of the police or the council workmen had caused the occupant's heart attack the burglary was still responsible for the occupant's death regardless of which of those events actually precipitated the attack, the conviction for manslaughter would be quashed (see p 867 *e* and 868 *c d*, post).

*h*

**Notes**
For manslaughter and killing by an unlawful act, see 11 Halsbury's Laws (4th edn) paras 1161, 1169, and for cases on the subject, see 15 Digest (Reissue) 1136–1140, 9609–9656.

**Cases cited**
*R v Dawson* (1985) 81 Cr App R 150, CA.
*j*   *R v Roberts* (1971) 56 Cr App R 95, CA.

**Appeal against conviction**
Clarence Archibald Watson appealed with the leave of the single Judge against his conviction on 24 February 1988 in the Central Criminal Court before his Honour Judge

Herrod QC and a jury on, inter alia, a charge of manslaughter for which he was sentenced to four years' imprisonment. The facts are set out in the judgment of the court.  *a*

*Michael West QC* and *David Radford* (assigned by the Registrar of Criminal Appeals) for the appellant.
*Roy Amlot QC* and *Nigel Sweeney* for the Crown.

*Cur adv vult*  *b*

26 May. The following judgment of the court was delivered.

**LORD LANE CJ.** On 24 February 1988 in the Central Criminal Court the appellant was convicted of manslaughter. He had already pleaded guilty to burglary. He was sentenced on the following day as follows: in respect of the manslaughter, four years'  *c* imprisonment; in respect of the burglary, two years' imprisonment to run concurrently. He was also in breach of two suspended sentences of three months' and six months' imprisonment respectively, which were ordered to take effect unaltered and consecutively to the other sentences. The total sentence was therefore one of four years and nine months' imprisonment.

He now appeals against conviction by leave of the single judge.  *d*

The facts of the case, in so far as they are relevant, were as follows. Late at night on 11 December 1986 two men, one of whom was the appellant, broke into the home of a man called Harold Moyler. Mr Moyler was 87 years old and suffered from a serious condition of the heart. He lived alone. The two men first threw a brick through the window and, having made entry to the house, confronted Mr Moyler as he woke up, abused him verbally and then made off without stealing anything.  *e*

Mr Moyler died an hour and a half later as the result of a heart attack. The case for the Crown was that the heart attack was a direct consequence of the unlawful actions of the appellant and his colleague.

The defence put forward by the appellant was that he was not responsible for the death. Mr Moyler's heart condition could have caused his death at any time, quite apart  *f* from any question of excitement or shock. Furthermore, there were two events subsequent to the burglary, either of which might have precipitated the heart attack: first, the arrival of the police and, second, the arrival of council workmen to board up the broken window. Any adverse effect of the burglary, it was suggested, would have ceased long before the death occurred.

There was a sharp conflict of evidence on the medical issue. Dr West, who was called on behalf of the prosecution, had performed the autopsy. He was sure that the burglary  *g* was the cause of death. He described for the benefit of the jury how excitement causes the production of adrenalin, making the heart beat faster. The heart therefore needs more blood and oxygen but is unable to obtain it if there is a chronic heart disease, as there was here, with the result that the arteries leading to the heart are substantially narrowed. The heart then begins to beat irregularly, it eventually stops beating and thus  *h* death ensues.

He said that his opinion was that this chain of events began with the burglary and continued up to the time of death. The initial shock caused by the burglary could last for a considerable period of time, and certainly for the one and a half hours which was the length of time involved in the present case.

At the close of the prosecution case counsel for the appellant submitted, unsuccessfully,  *j* that there was no case for the appellant to answer.

The appellant himself did not give evidence, but Dr Matterson was called to give evidence on his behalf. His opinion was that the excitement and stress caused by the burglary could not have been a subsisting and operating cause of death one and a half hours later. If any extraneous incident was responsible for the heart attack, it must have

been the arrival of the police or that of the council workmen. However, the victim's
*a* condition was such that a heart attack could have occurred at any time without the
necessity of any excitement or shock.

It is accepted that the judge correctly defined the offence of manslaughter as it applied
to the circumstances as follows:

*b* 'Manslaughter is the offence committed when one person causes the death of
another by an act which is unlawful and which is also dangerous, dangerous in the
sense that it is an act which all sober and reasonable people would inevitably realise
must subject the victim to the risk of some harm resulting whether the defendant
realised that or not.'

The first point taken on behalf of the appellant is this. When one is deciding whether
the sober and reasonable person (the bystander) would realise the risk of some harm
*c* resulting to the victim, how much knowledge of the circumstances does one attribute to
the bystander? The appellant contends that the unlawful act here was the burglary as
charged in the indictment.

The charge was laid under s 9(1)(*a*) of the Theft Act 1968, the allegation being that the
appellant had entered the building as a trespasser with intent to commit theft. Since that
offence is committed at the first moment of entry, the bystander's knowledge is confined
*d* to that of the defendant at that moment. In the instant case there was no evidence that
the appellant, at the moment of entry, knew the age or physical condition of Mr Moyler
or even that he lived there alone.

The judge clearly took the view that the jury were entitled to ascribe to the bystander
the knowledge which the appellant gained during the whole of his stay in the house and
so directed them. Was this a misdirection? In our judgment it was not. The unlawful act
*e* in the present circumstances comprised the whole of the burglarious intrusion and did
not come to an end on the appellant's foot crossing the threshold or windowsill. That
being so, the appellant (and therefore the bystander) during the course of the unlawful
act must have become aware of Mr Moyler's frailty and approximate age, and the judge's
directions were accordingly correct. We are supported in this view by the fact that no
one at the trial seems to have thought otherwise.
*f* The second ground of appeal arises in the following way. The prosecution, as already
indicated, based their case on the proposition advanced by Dr West that the burglary had
caused the heart attack to occur one and a half hours later. The judge had correctly
directed the jury on these lines, setting out Dr West's opinion and the conflicting opinion
of Dr Matterson, to the effect that the stress caused by the burglary would have subsided
in 20 minutes and that the fatal heart attack was therefore either spontaneous or the
*g* result of the arrival of the police or the council workmen.

Finally on this point, the judge said:

'So, what do you do? You must consider all these opinions very carefully. You
must say to yourselves, where you have someone as skilled and experienced as Dr
Matterson expressing the views as he did, it might be very difficult for you to reject
*h* his opinion out of hand. If you do say to yourselves: "Well, Dr Matterson is right",
or "He may be right", that is all you need to say to yourself. If he may be right it
would be proper for you to return a verdict of not guilty in this case.'

That, like the rest of his directions to the jury prior to their retirement, was simple,
concise and clear.
*j* However, after the jury had been in retirement for some time, they returned with two
questions. The second of the two questions was not easy to understand, but the effect was
to ask what should be the verdict if the victim's heart beat had returned to normal after
the burglary but the arrival either of the police or of the council workmen had caused a
second crisis which resulted in death 'as a direct result of the emotional stress which was
continuing in the victim'.

A discussion took place in the absence of the jury as to how the judge should deal with this difficult matter. The judge was clearly minded at first to direct the jury to acquit if *a* that was the conclusion at which they had arrived.

Counsel for the prosecution, however, by a submission, which he tells us he now regrets, persuaded the judge to change his mind and in the upshot the following further direction was given:

'Now, if you were to say to yourself: "Well, I am sure that the heart rate had *b* returned to normal some 20 minutes afterwards, but the two succeeding incidents did cause a further increase in the heart rate, and it was one or other, or both, of those incidents which caused death", the burglary would still be responsible for the death, provided that you are satisfied that the two subsequent incidents were natural consequences of the burglary. That would be a matter for your determination.'

That was introducing a fresh dimension into the jury's task, namely a consideration of *c* whether it could be said that as a matter of logic the burglary was the cause of the police arriving and of the necessity to board up the window and so for the arrival of the council workmen and so for the heart attack, whichever of the three matters may have been the precipitating event.

It may be that counsel for the appellant would have been able to say little of assistance to his client had he had the opportunity to address the jury on this fresh topic. *d* Nevertheless, the fact that he was deprived of that opportunity, coupled with the fact that the jury were not, it seems, wholly convinced that Dr West's opinion was correct, lead us, not without some hesitation, to say that this verdict of guilty of manslaughter is unsatisfactory. The conviction is accordingly quashed.

*Conviction for manslaughter quashed.*

*e*

Solicitors: *Crown Prosecution Service.*

N P Metcalfe Esq    Barrister.

# Hurditch v Sheffield Health Authority

*a*

COURT OF APPEAL, CIVIL DIVISION
PURCHAS, NOURSE LJJ AND SIR ROUALEYN CUMMING-BRUCE
17, 18 NOVEMBER, 16 DECEMBER 1988

*b*   *Damages – Personal injury – Provisional damages – Order for provisional damages – Offer to submit to award – Defendants making offer in respect of provisional damages but rejecting part of plaintiff's medical evidence – Whether sufficient agreement to satisfy requirements for award of provisional damages – Supreme Court Act 1981, s 32A – RSC Ord 37, r 9.*

*c*

The plaintiff had been exposed to asbestos both in his employment with the defendant health authority and in his previous employment. He brought an action against the health authority for damages for personal injuries and also sought provisional damages under s 32A[a] of the Supreme Court Act 1981. The health authority claimed that at least part of his condition was attributable to his previous employment. On 20 October 1986 the health authority wrote to the plaintiff making an offer of £2,500 in respect of a provisional figure for damages. On 12 November 1986 the offer was accepted by the

*d*   plaintiff, and he subsequently applied under RSC Ord 37, r 9(3)[b] for an order for an award of provisional damages. In January 1987 the health authority denied that its letter of 20 October was an offer to pay a sum of money pursuant to Ord 37, r 9. The master held that the letter of 20 October was an offer within the terms of Ord 37 and that it had been accepted by the plaintiff on 12 November, and that accordingly the plaintiff was entitled to an award in the agreed sum. The health authority appealed to the judge, who allowed the appeal, dismissed the plaintiff's summons and set aside the master's order. The

*e*   plaintiff appealed to the Court of Appeal.

**Held** – The health authority's offer contained in its letter of 20 October and the plaintiff's acceptance on 12 November constituted an agreement that the case was one in which an award of provisional damages was appropriate and accordingly the plaintiff was under a

*f*   duty to apply for an order under RSC Ord 37, r 9. Furthermore, the medical reports which were available to the master showed areas of agreement which would satisfy the requirements of s 32A of the 1981 Act and Ord 37, namely the identification of those diseases which were asbestos-related and which might arise in the future and that there was a risk of serious deterioration in the plaintiff's physical condition. Accordingly, the master had available to him not only the figure for an award of provisional damages but

*g*   also the identification of the disease in respect of which serious deterioration might result and that was all that was required to make an award. Moreover, the area of dispute between the parties, namely the causation of future disease and the basis on which future damages might be assessed, did not affect the assessment of a sum in respect of the plaintiff's existing condition. It followed that the master had jurisdiction to make the order. The appeal would therefore be allowed (see p 876 *e f*, p 877 *g* to p 878 *e* and p 879

*h*   *a* to *d f h* to p 880 *a*, post).

**Notes**

For provisional damages, see Supplement to 37 Halsbury's Laws (4th edn) para 364A.
     For the Supreme Court Act 1981, s 32A, see 11 Halsbury's Statutes (4th edn) 785.

*j*   **Case referred to in judgments**

*Jones v Griffith* [1969] 2 All ER 1015, [1969] 1 WLR 795, CA.

---

*a*   Section 32A, so far as material, is set out at p 872 *j* to p 873 *b*, post
*b*   Rule 9 is set out at p 873 *f g*, post

**Cases also cited**

*Bryce v Swan Hunter Group plc* [1987] 2 Lloyd's Rep 426.

*Hotson v East Berkshire Area Health Authority* [1987] 2 All ER 909, [1987] AC 750, HL.

*McGhee v National Coal Board* [1972] 3 All ER 1008, [1973] 1 WLR 1, HL.

**Interlocutory appeal**

By a writ issued on 28 November 1985 the appellant, Brian Hurditch, brought an action against the respondents, Sheffield Health Authority, claiming, inter alia, damages for personal injuries and/or physical harm and consequential loss and/or breach of statutory duty sustained while employed by the authority. On 30 June 1986 the statement of claim was amended to include a specific claim for provisional damages under s 32A of the Supreme Court Act 1981 in respect of pain and suffering and loss of amenity suffered by the appellant up to the date of trial. On 20 October 1986 the authority made an offer of £2,500 in respect of a provisional figure for damages. On 12 November 1986 the offer was accepted by the appellant, and by a summons dated 13 November 1986 he sought leave to enter judgment pursuant to RSC Ord 37, r 9(3). By a letter dated 28 January 1987 the authority denied that the letter of 20 October constituted an offer to pay a sum of money subject to Ord 37, r 9. On 19 May 1987 Master Turner held that the letter of 20 October was an offer within the terms of Ord 37, r 7 and that it had been accepted by the appellant's letter of 12 November and that accordingly the appellant was entitled to an award in the sum agreed. The authority appealed and on 7 December 1987 on the hearing of the summons and the appeal Kennedy J sitting in the Queen's Bench Division at Sheffield allowed the appeal, dismissed the summons and set aside the master's order. The appellant appealed, pursuant to leave granted by Dillon LJ, on the ground that the judge had wrongly held that the letters of 20 October and 12 November did not constitute sufficient agreement for the purpose of s 32A of the 1981 Act and Ord 37. The facts are set out in the judgment of Purchas LJ.

*Jeffrey Burke QC* and *Vivienne Gay* for the appellant.

*Richard Maxwell QC* and *P M Beard* for the authority.

*Cur adv vult*

16 December. The following judgments were delivered.

**PURCHAS LJ.** This appeal raises an important point on the powers of the court to make a provisional award of damages in personal injury cases under the provisions of s 32A of the Supreme Court Act 1981 which was added to that Act under the provisions of s 6(1) of the Administration of Justice Act 1982 and which came into force on 1 July 1985. The provisions were enacted to remedy a serious defect, which had long been recognised, in the powers of the court to award damages for personal injuries in cases where there was a known risk of a further development either by way of a new disease, eg the onset of epilepsy, or a serious deterioration of a presently existing and detected condition: see *Jones v Griffiths* [1969] 2 All ER 1015, [1969] 1 WLR 795 per Sachs LJ.

The circumstances can be shortly stated. The appellant, Brian Hurditch, was born on 11 April 1940. He had two relevant periods of employment during which it is common ground he was at substantial risk owing to exposure to asbestos. The first period was when employed by the Royal Navy as an engineer concerned with the lagging of heating pipes and boilers etc between 1957 and 1972. The second period, which is still current, commenced in 1972 when the appellant was first employed by the respondent health authority. In 1983 the appellant for the first time suffered breathlessness caused by an asbestos-related disease or condition. He continued to be employed by the authority but a statement of claim was served on his behalf on 19 December 1985, to which a defence was served on 28 January 1986. Besides formal denials of liability, the defence raised a defence of limitation and asserted that any condition suffered by the appellant was

attributable to his earlier period of exposure. Although there is a large measure of
*a* agreement between the medical experts consulted by the appellant and the authority
there are areas where opinions vary. However, there seems to be common ground that
the appellant's present condition, although mainly referable to the earlier period, is also
referable to the current employment. The emphasis on the earlier period is because
medical experience at present indicates that it takes 10 to 15 years for the effect of
exposure to asbestos to become manifest in any serious way. Another feature over which
*b* there may still be an area for dispute is whether and to what extent in each of the two
relevant periods of employment the appellant was exposed to a type of asbestos known as
blue asbestos in distinction from white or brown asbestos. This is of particular significance
not to the present condition of the appellant but to the risk of development of serious
conditions also being asbestos-related, namely bronchial carcinoma or mesothelioma.
Neither of these conditions has been detected at the moment and it is in relation to these,
*c* amongst other developments, that the award for provisional damages is particularly
appropriate. There is also a third complicating factor, namely the possible carcinogenic
effects of the appellant's habit of smoking tobacco.

In the statement of claim served on 19 December 1985 the particulars of injury make
reference to the two particular diseases as well as asbestosis and asbestos pleural disease;
but it was not until 30 June 1986 that the statement of claim was amended to include a
*d* specific claim for provisional damages under s 32A of the 1981 Act. By this time further
and better particulars of the statement of claim had been delivered on 24 April 1986.

After the delivery of pleadings solicitors acting for the two parties were in contact by
way of negotiation. It is necessary to refer to some of these negotiations. There is in the
papers an attendance note of a conversation between a Mr Tagg, a legal executive acting
for the solicitors representing the authority, and a Mr Solomons, a partner in the firm of
*e* solicitors acting for the appellant. The note made by Mr Solomons is as follows:

> 'He has in mind making an offer to submit of £2,000. I thought this was far too
> little and said it should be at least £5000. He points out that we are entitled only to
> the proportion which relates to Sheffield Health Authority and not the proportion
> which relates to the Navy and that according to their doctor, whose report I have,
*f* the bulk of the symptoms relate to the Navy exposure. He is awaiting instructions.'

This was followed up by a letter written by Mr Tagg headed 'Without Prejudice' and
dated 20 October 1986 which read as follows:

> 'We refer to our recent discussions with Mr. Solomons of your office concerning
> this case. Following our discussions we advised our clients with regard to this case
*g* and we have instructions on a without prejudice basis to make an offer of £2,500 in
> respect of a provisional figure for damages which we think, given the circumstances
> of this case, is more than generous. As you are aware and, we believe, concede, there
> was substantial exposure before the plaintiff joined the defendants' employment
> and our medical argument is that such symptoms as are currently displayed are
> wholly attributable to the previous exposure. Such symptoms as the plaintiff may
*h* seek to attribute to his exposure whilst in the defendants employment are minimal
> but, that said, the defendants would not wish to cause any additional worries to the
> plaintiff and on that basis are prepared to put forward this offer. Perhaps you would
> take your clients instructions and come back to us in due course. We would be
> prepared to deal with the matter on a consent basis if this figure can be agreed.'

*j* On 3 November Mr Tagg, as a result of a telephone request from Mr Solomons,
extended the time for acceptance to the end of the year. The content of this conversation
is significant when the provisions of the rules made under s 32A are considered. RSC Ord
37, r 9(3) provides that an offer under r 9 must be accepted within 21 days. On 12
November Mr Solomons formally accepted the offer extended in the letter of 20 October
in these terms:

'We refer to our telephone conversation with your Mr. Tagg on 3 November and are most grateful to him for very kindly extending our time for acceptance of your clients' offer to submit until the end of this year. We now have instructions from our client and the offer is accepted. We are issuing a Summons for leave to enter judgment in accordance with R.S.C. Order 37, Rule 9(3) and Rule 8(2) and this will be served shortly. Meanwhile we enclose draft agreed statement of facts and shall be obliged to hear whether it may be agreed.'

The draft judgment provided for the payment of £2,500 by way of immediate damages—

'upon the assumption that the plaintiff will not at a future date as a result of the act or omission of the defendants ... develop either of the following diseases, namely bronchial carcinoma or mesothelioma or suffer deterioration in his physical condition of the following type, namely, any substantial deterioration in his physical condition due to asbestos induced disease ...'

Paragraph 2 provided for costs. Paragraph 3 provided that the appellant should have leave to apply for further damages in respect of the disease or type of deterioration specified and that no period within which such an application may be made was to be specified. Paragraph 4 provided for a list of documents to be produced to the court. The purpose of these documents was to form an evidential basis against which the court could entertain a future application for further damages and consisted of a copy of the judgment, a copy of the order giving leave to enter judgment, a copy of the pleadings, an agreed statement of facts and a bundle of agreed medical reports being both those obtained by the plaintiff and by the defendant.

Up to the letter of 12 November 1986 the appellant's solicitors had not submitted their medical reports to the authority's solicitors. Mr Tagg replied to Mr Solomons's letter by letter dated 14 November which stated:

'We are bespeaking a cheque from our clients and will pay this into court in the near future. We are not prepared to agree the draft statement of facts disclosed by you.'

On 17 November 1986 Mr Solomons issued a summons for an appointment for leave to enter judgment and served this on Mr Tagg. This was acknowledged by the latter in a letter dated 26 November 1986 in which Mr Tagg said that he was taking instructions and made a number of comments about the brief statement of facts. Although there were complaints about the statement of facts in detail, there was no suggestion from Mr Tagg that he objected in principle to the summons seeking a provisional order for damages. Further correspondence passed between the parties.

The matter came to a head in a letter written by Mr Tagg dated 28 January 1987. In this letter it was, for the first time, denied that the letter of 20 October constituted an offer to pay a sum of money subject to Ord 37, r 9. It was further asserted that Mr Solomons could not reasonably regard the letter as such an offer 'because the sum of money referred to could not be assessed on "the assumption that the injured person will not develop the disease or suffer the deterioration as in s. 32A"'. It will be necessary to consider in more detail subsequently the contentions being proposed by the defendants at the stage of their letter of 28 January 1987.

It is convenient at this stage to refer to the statutory provisions against which this appeal has to be considered. Section 32A of the 1981 Act provides:

'(1) This section applies to an action for damages for personal injuries in which there is proved or admitted to be a chance that at some definite or indefinite time in the future the injured person will, as a result of the act or omission which gave rise to the cause of action, develop some serious disease or suffer some serious deterioration in his physical or mental condition.

a
(2) Subject to subsection (4) below [which is not relevant], as regards any action for damages to which this section applies in which a judgment is given in the High Court, provision may be made by rules of court for enabling the court, in such circumstances as may be prescribed, to award the injured person—(a) damages assesed on the assumption that the injured person will not develop the disease or suffer the deterioration in his condition; and (b) further damages at a future date if he develops the disease or suffers the deterioration.

b
(3) Any rules made by virtue of this section may include such incidental, supplementary and consequential provisions as the rule-making authority may consider necessary or expedient . . .'

The rules which have so far been made under the powers in s 32A are to be found in RSC Ord 37, rr 7 to 10. The following rules are relevant for the present purposes:

c
'7 . . . (2) In this Part of this Order "award of provisional damages" means an award of damages for personal injuries under which—(a) damages are assessed on the assumption that the injured person will not develop the disease or suffer the deterioration referred to in section 32A; and (b) the injured person is entitled to apply for further damages at a future date if he develops the disease or suffers the deterioration.

d
8.—(1) The Court may on such terms as it thinks just and subject to the provisions of this rule make an award of provisional damages if—(a) the plaintiff has pleaded a claim for provisional damages, and (b) the Court is satisfied that the action is one to which section 32A applies.

(2) An order for an award of provisional damages shall specify the disease or type of deterioration in respect of which an application may be made at a future date, and shall also, unless the Court otherwise determines, specify the period within which such application may be made . . .

e
9.—(1) Where an application is made for an award of provisional damages, any defendant may at any time (whether or not he makes a payment into court) make a written offer to the plaintiff—(a) to tender a sum of money (which may include an amount, to be specified, in respect of interest) in satisfaction of the plaintiff's claim for damages assessed on the assumption that the injured person will not develop the disease or suffer the deterioration referred to in section 32A; and (b) to agree to the making of an award of provisional damages.

f
(2) Any offer made under paragraph (1) shall not be brought to the attention of the Court until after the Court has determined the claim for an award of provisional damages.

(3) Where an offer is made under paragraph (1), the plaintiff may, within 21 days after receipt of the offer, give written notice to the defendant of his acceptance of the offer and shall on such acceptance make an application to the Court for an order in accordance with the provisions of rule 8(2).'

g

h
The first date (16 February 1987) for the hearing of the summons under Ord 37, r 9(3) was adjourned by consent and the matter came back before Master Turner on 16 and 29 April 1987. On the first occasion the master ordered the authority to pay the sum of £2,500 to the appellant. The master delivered a judgment and made his order on 19 May. By this time reports both from Mr Hutchcroft, a consultant physician who was reporting on behalf of the appellant, and from Mr P Howard, the consultant physician reporting on behalf of the authority, were available. Although there was no dispute on the existing condition of the appellant, nor that this was referable to asbestos-related conditions, there was a difference of opinion whether the X-rays disclosed an existing condition of asbestosis or not. Whether this was a relevant medical distinction for the present purposes may be very debatable. It could not, however, be said that the medical reports were agreed although, as counsel for the appellant has submitted, the area of

j

disagreement was marginal. The gravity of the difference rested in the future dispute which might well arise should either bronchial carcinoma or mesothelioma arise. This would raise the question whether the disease was caused by the condition of work and in which employment, and to what extent the appellant was exposed to asbestos, including especially blue asbestos. It had nothing to do with the sum assessed for damages in relation to the appellant's existing condition. It was, however, relevant to what has been called 'the threshold', ie the datum point from which a court in the future would consider such damages as might be awarded for either the new diseases whch had originated or the serious deterioration which had occurred, subject in both cases, however, to causation being established, as it would have to be established were it to be disputed in the second stage of the assessment of damages.

Master Turner concluded that the letter of 20 October was an offer within the terms of Ord 37, r 9 and that it was accepted by the letter of 12 November 1986 and that, therefore, an application to the court for an order in accordance with the provisions of Ord 37, r 8(2) was something which the appellant was obliged to do under the provisions of Ord 37, r 9(3). The material part of the master's judgment reads as follows:

'RSC Ord 37, rr 8 and 9 do not require the parties to agree the requirements of Ord 37, r 8(2) as a precondition of the making of an offer under Ord 37, r 9(1) and its acceptance under Ord 37, r 9(3). All that is necessary is for the defendants to admit that the plaintiff is entitled to an award of provisional damages and to quantify their assessment of its quantum. In this respect the defendants are pre-empting the decision of the court under Ord 37, r 8(1)(a) and (b). Of course, if the parties can agree the two requirements of Ord 37, r 8(2), so much the better but Ord 37, r 9(3) does not make it a precondition of the making of an application for any such order in accordance with the provisions of Ord 37, r 8(2) that these two requirements shall have been agreed. The Practice Directions of the Lord Chief Justice are made under the inherent authority of the holders of his office to prescribe and regulate the procedures of the High Court and are in addition to the Rules of the Supreme Court. However, it was provided by Parliament that it was "the rule making authority" (s 32A(3)) which was to provide for the provisions necessary to satisfy the making of such an award and that authority is the Rule Committee. The Lord Chief Justice's directions merely lay down the general practice to be followed but do not necessarily cater for every eventuality.'

At this stage it is necessary to refer to the relevant parts of *Practice Note* [1985] 2 All ER 895, [1985] 1 WLR 961:

'A. *Judgments for provisional damages after trial*
The following practice will be followed.

1. *Trial proceedings*
The oral judgment of the judge will specify the disease or type of deterioration: (a) which, for the purpose of the award of immediate damages, has been assumed will not occur; (b) which will entitle the plaintiff to further damages if it occurs at a future date.

2. The material parts of the associate's certificate and the judgment entered pursuant to it will be in the following or similar form with such variations as may be necessary under RSC Ord 37, r 8: "The judge awarded to the plaintiff by way of immediate damages [*set out the award, differentiating between general and special damage, in the usual way*] on the assumption that the plaintiff would not at a future date as a result of the act or omission giving rise to the cause of action develop the following disease, namely [*specify it*] [*or suffer deterioration in his physical or mental condition of the following type* [*specify it*]]. And the judge further ordered that if

a the plaintiff at a future date so develop such disease [or did so suffer such deterioration] he should be entitled to apply for further damages."

3. The judge will normally specify the period within which the application for further damages must be made and this will be set out in the associate's certificate and the judgment.

### 4. Documents: case file

b The judge will also direct what documents are to be lodged and preserved as material for any further assessment. These documents are hereinafter called the case file. Subject to his directions the case file will normally include: (a) a copy of the associate's certificate; (b) a copy of the judgment drawn up on it; (c) the pleadings; (d) a transcript of the judge's oral judgment; (e) all medical reports placed before the court; (f) a transcript of such parts of the plaintiff's own evidence as to his physical c condition and of the medical evidence as the judge may think necessary . . .

### B. Orders without trial

Section 32A of the Supreme Court Act 1981 requires that immediate damages and provisional damages must be the subjects of awards by the court if they are to be enforced under that section. Accordingly the following practice shall be followed in relation to settlements under that section.

d 10. Application shall be made by summons for leave to enter judgment by consent in the terms of a draft annexed to the summons. If the plaintiff is under a disability, the approval of the court should be asked for in the summons and recited in the draft judgment.

11. The draft shall contain the particulars in paras 1 to 3 hereof. It shall also contain a direction as to the documents to be placed on the case file. These will e normally be: (a) a copy of the order made on the summons; (b) a copy of the judgment; (c) pleadings, if any; (d) an agreed statement of the facts; (e) agreed medical reports. The contents of the case file shall be scheduled to the order and to the judgment. The terms of the order and judgment shall be subject to the court's approval . . .'

f     The authority contended before the master that although the offer made in the letter of 20 October was an offer within the context of Ord 37, because all the matters set out in Part B of the practice note could not be agreed there was no right to make an application to the court under Ord 37, r 9(3). The master held against this contention:

'I am satisfied that so long as the conditions of Ord 37, r 9(1)(a) and (b) are satisfied g and the plaintiff has made an acceptance in writing as required by Ord 37, r 9(3), then he is entitled to seek an order of the court under Ord 37, r 8(2). If the parties cannot agree all the matters set out in Part B of the practice note, then the court must determine the issues that remain. It would be quite unjust that a plaintiff should be deprived of a judgment for provisional damages merely because the details of necessary supporting documents cannot be agreed.'

h     The master accordingly ordered that the summons before him be transferred to a single judge for hearing in open court so that the outstanding matters could be determined by the judge. He directed an exchange of medical reports and, in the event of their not being agreed, that medical evidence should be called before the judge, limited to one witness for each side. He referred to his order of 16 February 1987 for the j payment by the authority to the appellant of £2,500 and acknowledged in his judgment that this payment had been incorrectly described as an interim payment and confirmed that the sum was an award of provisional damages within the provisions of Ord 37, r 8(2). In contravention of his order, however, the authority had paid the sum into court, which, it is conceded by leading counsel who appeared for them on the appeal, was incorrect. On the appellant's application it was subsequently paid out to him.

The matter came before Kennedy J at Sheffield on 7 December 1987. The judge acceded to the submissions made by junior counsel for the authority that an order under *a* Ord 37, r 8(2) should not have been made:

> 'It seems to me to be plain beyond peradventure that there was not that degree of agreement which is the necessary precondition for the matter to come before the court pursuant to Ord 37, r 9. There was a tender of a sum of money but there was not an offer to submit to an award of provisional damages. However if I am wrong *b* as to that, as a matter of discretion I would not make the order which is sought. There are too many loose ends. There is no disadvantage to the plaintiff. The matter can be and has been dealt with by the payment of interim damages. Where there is lack of agreement concerning the matters within Ord 37, rr 8 and 9 that is the proper course rather than the plaintiff asking the court to make decisions about matters which can only properly be made at a full hearing.'
> *c*

On appeal counsel for the appellant submitted that the exchange of correspondence in October and November 1986 constituted a binding agreement and that this agreement was all that was required to satisfy Ord 37, r 9 and that thereafter it was incumbent on the appellant to issue a summons so as to bring the matter before the court within the provisions of Ord 37, r 8. Counsel for the authority, whilst not contending that the letter of 20 October was an offer to make an interim payment, which was the stance adopted *d* by solicitors for the authority in their letter of 28 January 1987, nevertheless submitted that it was an inadequate offer for the purposes of Ord 37 and that the appellant was not entitled to accept the offer accordingly. Bearing in mind that the two firms of solicitors involved are experienced in this type of litigation, one is constrained to ask what was the real purpose of the offer made on 20 October if it was not intended to be accepted for the purpose of Ord 37, r 9? Notwithstanding the skill with which counsel for the authority *e* endured this forensically uncomfortable position, I regret having to say that I found his arguments wholly unimpressive. It may well have been that the authority's solicitors, although meaning to achieve an agreement within Ord 37, r 9, had misunderstood the legal position, but it did not lie in their mouth to be saying that they made an offer which they appreciated would not be adequate for the purpose and one moreover on which *f* they relied in its inadequacy for the contention that the appellant had no business to accept it knowing that it was so inadequate. Having said this, I do not find it necessary to make any further comment on or to analyse the submission of counsel for the authority on this aspect of the case.

The important and central issues, however, are (a) whether the judge was correct in his attitude that there was not a sufficient agreement to satisfy Ord 37, r 9, (b) whether Master Turner was correct in holding that there was and (c) whether there was jurisdiction *g* to give directions for a 'hybrid trial' or, as I would rather put it, a trial of outstanding issues as ordered by Master Turner.

The intention disclosed in s 32A is that the power to award damages previously limited to a 'once for all' award was in certain circumstances to be extended to a two stage process. Before this process could be adopted it had to be proved or admitted that there was 'a *h* chance that at some definite or indefinite time in the future the injured person will as a result of the act or omission which gave rise to the cause of action develop some serious disease or suffer some serious deterioration'. Section 32A(2) provides that in any action for damages to which the section applies and in which a judgment is given in the High Court provision may be made by rules of court to enable the court to adopt the two stage process as defined in sub-ss (a) and (b). It was under this subsection that RSC Ord 37 was *j* made. Section 32A(3), however, gives power to the rule-making authority to make rules to include 'incidental supplementary and consequential provisions'. I have little doubt that should the rule-making authority have considered it necessary, there was power under this section to make rules to provide for the trial of outstanding issues in respect of which consent could not be attained but which were necessary for the proper operation

of the power granted in s 32A. There may, however, be a question raised whether this
rule-making power has or has not been exercised.

The underlying jurisdiction, therefore, granted to the court under s 32A is 'triggered'
by the delivery of a judgment in the qualifying circumstances. Quite obviously this may
be a judgment after a trial of all or even some of the issues, or it may be a judgment
reached by consent as to all the issues necessary for an order under s 32A(2)(a). This leaves
s 32A(2)(b). Since the disease or deterioration, of which there is proved or admitted to be
a chance of future development, is not a matter at large, its nature is clearly a parameter
which Parliament assumed would be identified before an order for provisional damages
could be made.

Turning now to the provisions of Ord 37, there is clearly no problem when a trial has
taken place before, presumably, a single judge of the High Court. He will have necessarily
determined both the medical condition resulting from the breach of duty or tort which
gives rise to the necessity of an immediate award of damages and furthermore he will
have considered and satisfied himself of the existence of 'the chance of such further
disease or deterioration'. Thus the prerequisites for an award of provisional damages will
have been established. The rule-makers had, however, to consider what was the position
where the parties had reached an accord. Clearly it was highly desirable within the
concept of economic and efficient administration of justice that such accords could be
translated into awards for provisional damages, otherwise such cases would invariably
have to be litigated at length. Here again no problem arises when the accord is complete
as to the existence of a chance to satisfy s 32A(1) as well as the identification of the
conditions to which the chance applied to satisfy s 32A(2)(a) and (b). The problem arises
when the parties are agreed as to the essential criteria under s 32A(1) that an order for
provisional damages should be made but have not succeeded in reaching a full agreement
so that there are still some 'nuts and bolts to be tightened'. So far as s 32A is concerned, I
have no doubt that Parliament intended that the facility to award provisional damages,
including as it does the opportunity to return to the court for a further assessment of
damages, would extend not only to those cases where there was a full trial of all issues or
full agreement on all issues but also to the position where the parties were agreed
substantially on some issues and some issues were left to be determined by the court. The
question is whether the rule-making authority, exercising its powers under s 32A(2) and
(3), have covered what, for the want of a better term, I will describe as the hybrid
position. This requires a careful consideration of the words of Ord 37, r 9. Clearly the
basic requirements of s 32A must be satisfied, namely agreement that the case is one
appropriate for an award of provisional damages. That position having been reached, the
next requirement is that there should be a sum agreed to represent the first stage, namely
under s 32A(2)(a). This, as I read the provisions of Ord 37, r 9, is all that is required before
the plaintiff is under a duty to apply for a summons so that an order in the form of Ord
37, r 8(2) can be made. I have formed the view, therefore, that the submissions of counsel
for the authority that this position had not been reached are not acceptable. In my
judgment, the offer in the letter of 20 October was without any question the indication
of a view that the case was one appropriate for an award of provisional damages and that
the figure to be awarded for the first stage was £2,500. There was nothing said or done
to withdraw this offer before it was formally accepted by the letter of 16 November.
There was, therefore, a completed agreement first that the case was one appropriate for
an award of provisional damages and secondly that the first stage payment should be
£2,500. This, in my judgment, satisfied Ord 37, r 9(1)(a) and (b).

The next question, therefore, is: what powers were open to the master when the
summons came before him? Counsel for the authority submitted that it was impossible
to comply with the provisions of the practice note until there had been an agreement
over medical evidence. I cannot agree with this submission and regretfully I must express
the view that Kennedy J was wrong to be persuaded by the presence of what he described
as 'loose ends' as being a ground for refusing to act under Ord 37, r 9 or indeed Ord 37,

r 8(2). As to his alternative approach based on a purported exercise of a discretion not to make an order on the same grounds, I must respectfully say that I cannot support this as *a* a proper exercise of discretion in the circumstances of this case, for the same reasons.

In my judgment Master Turner's assessment of the significance of the practice note was correct. Its purpose is clear, namely to give advice as to what steps should be taken to ease the burden placed on the court should an eventuality arise in the future which will bring into operation the second stage of assessment of damages under the order for an award of provisional damages. By no stretch of the jurisdictional imagination can these *b* provisions restrict or inhibit, or indeed for that matter extend, the powers given to the court under s 32A and the rules made thereunder. Happily in this case the medical reports which were available to Master Turner showed areas of agreement which would satisfy the requirements of s 32A(1) and (2) and Ord 37, r 8(2), namely identifying those diseases which were asbestos-related and which might arise in the future, namely pleural carcinoma or mesothelioma although there was a dispute as to the degrees of probability *c* or otherwise of the development of either. There was also agreement that there was a risk of serious deterioration of the appellant's presently admitted asbestos associated condition, whether it be formally described as asbestosis or not. What the 'chance' was in mathematical terms was nihil ad rem. The master, therefore, had to hand reports which showed that the parties' advisers agreed on the necessary medical foundation for an order of provisional damages; but even this was not necessary because having made the offer *d* in the letter of 20 October that the present case was one suitable for an award of provisional damages, it would not lie in the mouth of the defendants to deny this before the master on a hearing under Ord 37, r 8(2). The master, therefore, had not only the figure for the present award of damages but also the necessary identification of the diseases which were envisaged as possible developments and the condition in respect of which serious deterioration might result, which was all that was required under the rules *e* and the section to make an order. The fact that he was not in a position to comply fully with the recommendations of the practice note did not affect the jurisdiction to make the order.

I now turn to consider whether or not Master Turner was justified in ordering a trial of the outstanding medical issues. In the circumstances of the present case I have come to the conclusion that it was not strictly necessary. There was so little area of dispute *f* between the doctors that almost certainly the medical reports would have been agreed; but even if they were not, then it is perfectly open by analogy with the provisions under Part A of the practice note to file medical reports from each side so as to form the basis of future consideration. On such an occasion the whole question of causation of the new disease or serious deterioration would be open to argument both as to attributability as between one or other of the periods of exposure to asbestos and also to the carcinogenic *g* dangers resulting from the appellant's smoking habits. Such a trial would involve considerable areas of dispute. Although I understand the submission of counsel for the authority that the resolution of such issues would be more difficult if proper investigation were not undertaken at this stage, I am not impressed that this can be a reason for not making an award of provisional damages. I can see, however, a difficulty arising in *h* another case where there was a serious dispute as to the identification of the new diseases which might in the future be attributed to the wrong which gave rise to the judgment in the first place or as to the period in which any future application ought to be made. I am not wholly satisfied that Ord 37 as presently drawn would allow the master to order the trial of an issue on the Ord 37, r 8(2) summons, there having been an area of limited agreement satisfying Ord 37, r 9. Clearly there is jurisdiction granted by the section and *j* had it been necessary in the present case I would have been minded to agree that there was jurisdiction to order the trial of a limited area of dispute as a separate issue in the way that Master Turner ordered on the occasion the matter was before him. In the circumstances of the present case, however, in my judgment he would have been justified in dealing with the matter himself without referring it to a single judge and entering

judgment under s 32A in accordance with Ord 37, r 8(2) for £2,500 reserving the right
a  to the appellant to reapply in the future for a further award of damages within the
provisions of the order. For these reasons I would allow this appeal and order that there
should be judgment for the sum of £2,500 as provisional damages with an order,
unlimited as to time, providing for the appellant to seek a further award of damages in
relation to an onset of bronchial carcinoma or mesothelioma or the serious deterioration
of his present asbestos-related condition. So as to comply, so far as is appropriate in the
b  circumstances of this case, with para 11 of the practice direction, the following documents
should be placed on the court file: (1) a copy of the order; (2) the pleadings; (3) a
statement of those facts in respect of which the parties are in agreement; (4) an agreed
medical report, but in the event of failure to agree, medical reports from both parties. I
shall be prepared to consider submissions from counsel if any variation of this part of the
judgment is sought.

c
**NOURSE LJ.** I agree that this appeal must be allowed for the reasons given by Purchas
LJ. Because we differ from the view of Kennedy J, I add some observations of my own.
   The judge thought that there was a tender of a sum of money, but not an offer to
submit to an award of provisional damages. I respectfully disagree. My own view of the
matter is perfectly expressed in the following extract from the judgment of Master
d  Turner:

> 'I am quite satisfied that the letter of 22 October 1986 was intended by the
> defendants to be an offer under RSC Ord 37, r 9(1): it could not have been anything
> else. To have made such an offer I am in no doubt that they accepted and agreed
> that an award of provisional damages was appropriate in this case. I am satisfied that
e > they accepted that there was a chance that at some definite or indefinite time in the
> future the plaintiff would, as a result of the acts or omissions of the defendants
> which gave rise to this cause of action, develop some serious disease or suffer some
> serious deterioration in his physical or mental condition.'

   The offer having been made, it was duly accepted by the appellant's solicitors' letter of
f  12 November 1986. The appellant was thereupon obliged by Ord 37, r 9(3) to make an
application to the court for an order 'in accordance with the provisions of r 8(2)', which
is in these terms:

> 'An order for an award of provisional damages shall specify the disease or type of
> deterioration in respect of which an application may be made at a future date, and
> shall also, unless the Court otherwise determines, specify the period within which
g > such application may be made.'

   Although r 8(2) thus provides for only two matters to be specified in the order, it was
submitted by counsel for the authority, in my view correctly, that it is still an order
within r 8(1), which may therefore be made 'on such terms as [the court] thinks just'.
But I do not think that those words give the court some wide ranging discretion to refuse
h  to make an order in a case where there has been an offer and acceptance within r 9. In
particular, the court should not accede to an attempt by one of the parties to escape the
consequences of such an offer and acceptance by saying that there has been no agreement
on matters which do not need to be agreed, for example on every aspect of the medical
history and prognosis. The object of r 9, a very worthy one, is to encourage these cases to
be disposed of by agreement. Doubtless the court has its own interest in seeing that its
j  orders are as clear and workable as they can be. But, generally speaking, it has no interest,
beyond the requirements of r 8(2), in clarifying matters which the parties are content to
leave unclear. True it may make the task of the judge at the later trial that much more
difficult, but not more difficult than the decision of other questions which often arise in
this kind of case.
   I therefore agree with Purchas LJ that Kennedy J was wrong in thinking that there

were too many loose ends for the court to act. I think that we can and ought to make an order in the form proposed by Purchas LJ and there is nothing which I wish to add on that aspect of the case.

**SIR ROUALEYN CUMMING-BRUCE.** For the reasons given by Purchas and Nourse LJJ I agree that this appeal should be allowed. I also agree with the form of order proposed.

*Appeal allowed. Leave to appeal to the House of Lords refused.*

Solicitors: *Brian Thompson & Partners* (for the appellant); *Keeble Hawson*, Sheffield (for the authority).

Radhika Edwards    Barrister.

# Ogwr Borough Council v Dykes

COURT OF APPEAL, CIVIL DIVISION
PURCHAS AND RALPH GIBSON LJJ
7, 9 NOVEMBER 1988

*Landlord and tenant – Tenancy – Tenancy distinguished from licence – Intentionally homeless person having priority need – Local authority required to provide accommodation for sufficient period to enable homeless person to find other accommodation – Local authority providing temporary accommodation in discharge of statutory function – Homeless person being granted exclusive possession of accommodation – Whether tenancy or licence created – Housing Act 1985, s 65(3).*

An intentionally homeless person who is provided with accommodation for a limited period by a local authority, in fulfilment of the authority's obligation under s 65(3)[a] of the Housing Act 1985 to provide an intentionally homeless person who has a priority need with accommodation for a sufficient period to enable him to find other accommodation, occupies the accommodation under a licence determinable at the local authority's discretion, and not under a secure tenancy, if the right to occupy is on terms which specifically and definitively negative any intention to create a tenancy, notwithstanding that the homeless person is granted exclusive possession for a fixed term at a fixed rent (see p 886 g to j and p 887 d e, post).

Dictum of Lord Templeman in *Street v Mountford* [1985] 2 All ER 289 at 300 applied.

**Notes**

For the general principles for determining whether an agreement creates a tenancy or a licence, see 27 Halsbury's Laws (4th edn) para 6, and for cases on the subject, see 31(1) Digest (Reissue) 202–203, 1692–1698.

For the Housing Act 1985, s 65, see 21 Halsbury's Statutes (4th edn) 92.

**Cases referred to in judgments**

*AG Securities v Vaughan* [1988] 2 All ER 173, [1988] 2 WLR 689, CA; *rvsd* [1988] 3 All ER 1058, [1988] 3 WLR 1205, HL.

*Dresden Estates Ltd v Collinson* [1987] 1 EGLR 45, CA.

---

a    Section 65(3) is set out at p 883 *b*, post

*Eastleigh BC v Walsh* [1985] 2 All ER 112, [1985] 1 WLR 525, HL.

a *Hadjiloucas v Crean* [1987] 3 All ER 1008, [1988] 1 WLR 1006, CA.

*South Holland DC v Keyte* (1985) 84 LGR 347, CA.

*Street v Mountford* [1985] 2 All ER 289, [1985] AC 809, [1985] 2 WLR 877, HL; *rvsg* (1985) 49 P & CR 324, CA.

**Cases also cited**

b *Cocks v Thanet DC* [1982] 3 All ER 1135, [1983] 2 AC 286, HL.

*Southgate BC v Watson* [1944] 1 All ER 603, [1944] KB 541, CA.

**Appeal**

The defendant, Rosemary Dykes, appealed against the order of his Honour Judge ap

c Robert made in the Bridgend County Court on 28 April 1988 granting an order for possession of the property at 24 Beach Road, Pyle, Bridgend, in favour of the plaintiffs, Ogwr Borough Council, against the defendant. The facts are set out in the judgment of Purchas LJ.

*Roger Garfield* for the defendant.

d *Geoffrey Stephenson* for the council.

**PURCHAS LJ.** This is an appeal from a possession order made on 28 April 1988 by his Honour Judge ap Robert in the Bridgend County Court against the defendant, Rosemary Dykes.

The order related to premises, 24 Beach Road, Pyle, Bridgend, which were part of the

e housing stock of Ogwr Borough Council (to whom I shall refer as 'the council') which had been occupied by the defendant and her four dependent children as tenants. Generally, the facts are not in dispute and can be shortly stated.

The defendant and her husband were joint tenants of the council. Their marriage clearly came into difficulties and, in March 1986, the council had obtained a possession order against both Mr and Mrs Dykes, which they physically enforced by eviction on or

f about 10 March 1986. This, it is common ground, determined any pre-existing joint tenancy.

Although the husband was away from home on 10 March 1986, he returned to live there subsequently but left finally in July 1987 after which his marriage with the defendant was dissolved.

The events of 10 March are important. According to the defendant's evidence, she and

g her children were evicted and immediately let back into the premises on terms which are central to this appeal. First, there was a letter of that date from the council, as follows:

'HOUSING (HOMELESS PERSONS) ACT 1977.

LICENCE TO OCCUPY TEMPORARY ACCOMMODATION:

1. In compliance with the duty imposed upon them by Section 4(3) of the

h Housing (Homeless Persons) Act, 1977, the Ogwr Borough Council ("the Council") hereby grant you a licence to occupy for a period of thirteen weeks commencing with the date specified above the dwelling known as 24 Beach Road, Pyle. 2. The purpose of making temporary accommodation available to you is to give you a reasonable opportunity to secure permanent accommodation elsewhere for you and your family. *After the thirteen week period mentioned above has expired the Council will*

j *require you to vacate the temporary accommodation which they have made available to you and they will be under no further duty to provide you with accommodation.'* (The letter's emphasis.)

I need not read the rest of that letter, which deals with the terms on which the occupation was to proceed. Of the same date (I suspect, although we have not been formally told, typed by the council but for signature by the defendant) there is a letter with a similar heading, which reads as follows:

*a*

'I acknowledge receipt of your letter of 10th March 1986 granting me licence to occupy the above property temporarily in fulfilment of the Council's duty to me under Section (3) of the Housing (Homeless Persons) Act, 1977. I have read the letter carefully and have understood what is contained in it. I undertake to comply with the terms and conditions upon which the licence has been granted to me in every respect.

*b*

Yours faithfully,
[signed] Mrs Dykes.'

At the same time, and with the same date, there is a form with the defendant's name and address on the top and reference to the reduction of arrears of rent in the sum of just over £200 by regular instalments starting on 13 March, and, above the signature of the *c* defendant, there is this statement:

'I promise to keep to the above agreement. If at any time I default on the agreement, I understand that proceedings will be taken to take possession of the property without further notification.'

The family remained in occupation. Small amounts were paid, but nothing that is *d* relative to that agreement to which I have just referred, and the arrears steadily accumulated until a much later date when (and the details are not important to this appeal) the payment of the rent was made under the social services arrangements by the Department of Health and Social Security.

In passing I should refer to a letter that was written by the council on 9 October 1986. I do not propose to read it. It is agreed between the parties that it was a misconceived *e* letter. It purported to discharge some duties under the then homeless persons legislation, but it does not concern the issues raised on this appeal.

Finally, by a letter dated 19 February 1987, the council purported to determine the licence. That is addressed to Mr and Mrs Dykes. It is quite consistent with the history of this case that Mr Dykes might still well have been in occupation. It reads as follows:

*f*

'HOUSING ACT 1985
You are aware that you occupy your present accommodation under a Licence granted to you to discharge the Council's duty towards you following intentional homelessness, as defined by the Housing Act 1985. I am therefore instructed to demand that you deliver vacant possession of 24 Beach Road, Pyle, Bridgend to the Council by not later than 9.00 a.m. on the 4th March, 1987.'

*g*

Then there is a warning that, if vacant possession were not given, process would be taken. The significance of the date 4 March 1987 is that it is a little short of 12 months from the date when the occupation under the Housing (Homeless Persons) Act 1977 commenced.

It is now convenient to refer very shortly to the statutory provisions with which this appeal is concerned. The notice and, as I have already said, the original letter of 10 March *h* were written, and rightly written, under the provisions of the Housing (Homeless Persons) Act 1977. The relevant provisions of that Act were replaced by provisions in the Housing Act 1985, which came into effect on 1 April 1986. The terms of those provisions in the 1985 Act, for the purposes of this appeal, are equivalent to those under the 1977 Act and, for convenience sake and with the agreement of the parties, the court has considered the terms of the latter Act only.

*j*

There is no dispute that the defendant was homeless, having been evicted as a result of the determination of the earlier joint tenancy. Furthermore, having four dependent children, she had a priority need for the purposes of the appropriate legislation and had become (and this is not being disputed) intentionally homeless as a result of a persistent refusal to pay rent and fell to be dealt with under, first of all, the provisions of s 4(3) and

4(2)(*b*) of the 1977 Act but which now can be studied in the form of s 65 of the Housing
*a* Act 1985. The relevant provisions of that Act are to be found in sub-s (3), which reads as
follows:

'Where they [the council] are satisfied that he has a priority need but are also
satisfied that he became homeless intentionally, they shall—(*a*) secure that
accommodation is made available for his occupation for such period as they consider
will give him a reasonable opportunity of securing accommodation for his
*b* occupation, and (*b*) furnish him with advice and such assistance as they consider
appropriate in the circumstances in any attempts he may make to secure that
accommodation becomes available for his occupation.'

It is clear from the wording of that section that it is open to the council responsible under
these provisions to comply with its duty under s 65(3)(*a*) in any way that appropriately
*c* fulfils that duty. It is clearly open to them in appropriate cases to grant a tenancy, to
grant a licence to occupy or to provide lodgings without exclusive possession, such as in
a hotel or boarding house.

Before parting with these statutory provisions, for convenience sake I refer at this stage
to para 4 of Sch 1 to the 1985 Act. Schedule 1 refers to tenancies for the purposes of the
Housing Act provisions which are not secure tenancies, and para 4, under the heading
*d* 'Accommodation for homeless persons', provides:

'(1) A tenancy granted in pursuance of ... (*b*) section 65(3) (duty to house
temporarily person found to have priority need but to have become homeless
intentionally) ... is not a secure tenancy before the expiry of the period of twelve
months beginning with the date specified in sub-paragraph (2), unless before the
*e* expiry of that period the tenant is notified by the landlord that the tenancy is to be
regarded as a secure tenancy ...'

As a subjective matter between the council and the defendant, there can be little doubt
that the intention was that a licence should be granted for a fixed period of 13 weeks,
which, at the time of writing the letter, the council clearly considered was a period of
*f* time which would give the defendant and her family a reasonable opportunity of
securing other accommodation. The judge held that this agreement was such a licence
for such a limited period, and that it did not fall to be construed as creating a tenancy
under the authority of *Street v Mountford* [1985] 2 All ER 289, [1985] AC 809 but was
the type of case to which Lord Templeman was referring (see [1985] 2 All ER 289 at 300,
[1985] AC 809 at 826). While dealing with *Street v Mountford* I wish to refer to one other
short passage from Lord Templeman's speech ([1985] 2 All ER 289 at 293, [1985] AC
*g* 809 at 818):

'If on the other hand residential accommodation is granted for a term at a rent
with exclusive possession, the landlord providing neither attendance nor services,
the grant is a tenancy; any express reservation to the landlord of limited rights to
enter and view the state of the premises and to repair and maintain the premises
*h* only serves to emphasise the fact that the grantee is entitled to exclusive possession
and is a tenant.'

Then, having referred to exclusive occupation, he continued ([1985] 2 All ER 289 at 299–
300, [1985] AC 809 at 826–827):

*j* 'But in addition to the hallmark of exclusive occupation of residential
accommodation there were the hallmarks of weekly payments for a periodical term.
Unless these three hallmarks are decisive, it really becomes impossible to distinguish
a contractual tenancy from a contractual licence save by reference to the proffered
intention of the parties or by the judge awarding marks for drafting. Slade LJ was
finally impressed by the statement at the foot of the agreement by Mrs Mountford

"I understand and accept that a licence in the above form does not and is not intended to give me a tenancy protected under the Rent Acts." Slade LJ said (49 *a* P & CR 324 at 330): ". . . it seems to me that if [Mrs Mountford] is to displace the express statement of intention embodied in the declaration, she must show that the declaration was either a deliberate sham or at least an inaccurate statement of what was the true substance of the real transaction agreed between the parties . . ." My Lords, the only intention which is relevant is the intention demonstrated by the agreement to grant exclusive possession for a term at a rent. Sometimes it may be *b* difficult to discover whether, on the true construction of an agreement, exclusive possession is conferred. Sometimes it may appear from the surrounding circumstances that there was no intention to create legal relationships. Sometimes it may appear from the surrounding circumstances that the right to exclusive possession is referable to a legal relationship other than a tenancy. Legal relationships to which the grant of exclusive possession might be referable and which would or *c* might negative the grant of an estate or interest in the land include occupancy under a contract for the sale of the land, occupancy pursuant to a contract of employment or occupancy referable to the holding of an office. But where as in the present case the only circumstances are that residential accommodation is offered and accepted with exclusive possession for a term at a rent, the result is a tenancy.'

The judge referred to the judgment of Sir John Donaldson MR in *South Holland DC v Keyte* (1985) 84 LGR 347. This case dealt with action taken under the Housing (Homeless Persons) Act 1977. It is necessary to read only one short extract from the judgment (at 352):

'I do not find it necessary to decide whether it was or was not a tenancy, but for my part I would like to make it absolutely clear that I do not accept it as being *e* axiomatic that a relationship which purports to be between a licensor and a licensee creates a tenancy, even if it gives exclusive possession, where the licensor is a local authority performing their duty under the Housing (Homeless Persons) Act 1977. Lord Templeman, who gave the leading judgment in *Street v Mountford* said . . . [Then the quotation which I have already mentioned is set out.] It seems to me that it is at least possible that in these cases the relationship is referable to something *f* other than a tenancy, namely, a licence which has been given in fulfilment of a statutory duty under the Act. If that is a live issue in some other case, it can then be raised, properly and gone into after full argument.'

Counsel for the defendant submitted that the letter of 10 March complied with the three criteria set out in *Street v Mountford*, a fixed term, exclusive occupation and a fixed *g* rent, and, as a matter of the operation of law, must be considered as a tenancy. He referred to *Eastleigh BC v Walsh* [1985] 2 All ER 112, [1985] 1 WLR 525 and relied on the speech of Lord Bridge in that case. It establishes the proposition (which it is not necessary to enlarge on in this judgment) that the duties carried out by a local authority in the housing context generally may and do fall into two quite separate categories: their public duty to carry out the provisions of the statute in deciding whether or not a person is *h* entitled to relief at their hands under the provisions of the statute, but that thereafter, having once taken that decision, in the steps that they take they are acting in the area of private law and are subject to the ordinary law that prevails in that area. In other words, as I have already indicated in this judgment, it is open to a local authority to create a tenancy or a licence, or to take such other steps as it thinks appropriate in the discharge of its duty. *j*

However, the operation of para 4 of Sch 1 to the Housing Act 1985 has an important effect on the position of a tenancy, or indeed a licence which otherwise would be considered as a tenancy under the provisions of that Act, where an authority is acting under the duties imposed on it in the homeless persons legislation.

a   Counsel for the defendant submitted that, notwithstanding the provisions of this schedule, the tenancy which he said was created under the authority of *Street v Mountford* was for a fixed term of 13 weeks, that that was the period announced by the council as being a reasonable period for the discharge of its duties under s 65(3), and that, in holding it over after that, in effect the tenancy was taken out of the protecting provisions of Sch 1 to the 1985 Act and became a perfectly normal week-to-week tenancy for which there has been exclusive occupation, a fixed rent and a fixed period by the week. Therefore,
b   counsel submitted, the defendant and her children became protected under the provisions of the 1985 Act.

Counsel for the defendant also argued that, even if the letter of 10 March 1986 did not create a tenancy, then a tenancy was created by the council allowing the defendant to remain in exclusive possession in the circumstances which I have just described.

As a third leg he argued that, even if it were only a licence, then, if it was no longer
c   granted in pursuance of the duties under s 65(3) which, for the reasons I have already described in referring to his submissions, came to an end after the 13-week period, then s 79(3) of the 1985 Act would afford the same protection to a licensee as to a tenant and therefore, again, a possession order ought not to have been made.

In passing, it should be noted that under the provisions of para 4 of Sch 1, even if s 65(3) continued to bear on the licence or the tenancy, within another week, or just
d   under, the 12 months would have passed and, again, the defendant would have a protected status.

The notice given on 19 February 1987, it was submitted by counsel for the council, brought the licence to an end and, although proceedings were not in fact started for a possession order until August 1987, it was not seriously to be argued that this further act of leniency on the part of the council could prejudice its position by extending the period
e   of occupation to one in excess of 12 months and leaving, as it were, the rump of an arrangement which would attract protection as a secured tenancy.

This point was not argued in the court below, counsel for the defendant very frankly told us that, but we allowed him to raise it during the course of his submissions. Having considered his submissions, we did not consider that there was anything in the point and
f   that fell from the argument.

Notwithstanding the able submissions of counsel for the defendant, I find that I cannot accept his submissions, which really depended on establishing through *Street v Mountford* that there was a tenancy created in the first place. Unless he could establish this, as counsel fairly and frankly more or less conceded in his reply, his other arguments would not be of great strength.

g   *Street v Mountford* [1985] 2 All ER 289, [1985] AC 809 has been considered in two subsequent cases in this court, and I wish to refer very shortly to each of them. The first one was *Hadjiloucas v Crean* [1987] 3 All ER 1008, [1988] 1 WLR 1006. I wish only to go to the start of my judgment, which refers to the submissions made by counsel for the appellant who was repeating submissions made to the judge which had been rejected. I said ([1987] 3 All ER 1008 at 1012, [1988] 1 WLR 1006 at 1011):

h   'At the core of counsel's argument lies a reading of the speech of Lord Templeman in *Street v Mountford* on which he founds a submission that in all cases involving residential premises the occupier must either be a tenant or a lodger and that there is no room for a person enjoying some intermediate interest in the premises. In considering the issue of status counsel for the appellant submitted that the court must inquire into the true nature of the agreement between the parties, and in
j   doing so should ask itself as a matter of established fact and by reference to the circumstances and conduct of the parties the following questions. (1) Are there *premises* intended to be used as residential accommodation? (2) Is there a *person*, or are there *persons*, who, it is intended, should alone or between them occupy those premises as residential accommodation? (3) Is there a sum of *money* which is, or

sums of *money* which together are, identified or identifiable as being for the
occupation of those premises? (4) Is the sum of money referred to in (3) referable to    **a**
a term, whether fixed or periodic? If all these factual questions are answered in the
affirmative, tenancy follows as a matter of law, save where (5) "lodging" as defined
by Lord Templeman applies or (6) the case falls into one of the classes of exceptional
circumstances as illustrated by Lord Templeman.' (My original emphasis.)

As appears subsequently in my judgment, I was unable to accept all of those submissions,    **b**
although some of them were acceptable. The proposition that, as a matter of law, if the
first four criteria are satisfied a tenancy was established was one which, with respect to
counsel for the appellant, I was not able to accept and nor, indeed, has my position
changed today. In *AG Securities v Vaughan* [1988] 2 All ER 173 at 178, [1988] 2 WLR 689
at 695 Fox LJ set out the principles that he derived from *Street v Mountford* which were
relevant to the case with which he was concerned. For the purposes of this judgment I    **c**
gratefully agree with and adopt the first two of the criteria and do not in any way dissent
from any of the other criteria, merely to comment that they do not apply in the
circumstances of this case. The first two principles are:

'(1) Exclusive possession is of the first importance in deciding whether an
occupier is a tenant ... (2) Exclusive possession is not decisive because there are
circumstances in which an occupier who has exclusive possession is not a tenant.    **d**
Thus, he may be an owner in fee simple, a trespasser, a mortgagee in possession, an
object of charity or a service occupier ...'

The propositions established in *Street v Mountford*, and accepted by this court, clearly
demonstrate that exclusive occupation is of primary importance although it is not
exclusively decisive. Lord Templeman recognised that exclusive occupation could be    **e**
referable to a legal relationship other than a tenancy, and Fox LJ also recognised that
there are circumstances in which a person may enjoy exclusive possession but yet not be
a tenant. Of course, no one has written the possibility of a licence existing out of the law
of England in this context. By its very nature a licence, if it is proved to exist in
appropriate conditions, negates the concept of exclusive possession.

The existence of a licence is acknowledged in the appropriate legislation, and, as I have    **f**
already indicated in this judgment, attracted special protection under s 3(2A) of the
Protection from Eviction Act 1977, as imposed in that Act by the 1980 Act, and under
the provisions of s 79(3) of the Housing Act 1985. Once one admits of the possibility of a
person with apparent exclusive possession not being a tenant, even if his occupation is
for a fixed term and for a fee, then in my judgment it is probably not possible to attempt
to define a category of exceptions. The contract under which occupation is granted must    **g**
be construed objectively and of course, as appears from the authorities to which I have
already referred, this does not mean necessarily according to the express words included
in the documents. If all that is disclosed is the granting of exclusive possession for a fixed
term for payment of a rental fee, then, in the absence of any feature indicating to the
contrary, the intention of the parties as expressed by their agreement must be to create a
tenancy. If, however, the context in which the right to exclusive occupation is granted    **h**
specifically and definitively negatives an intention to create a tenancy, then some other
interest appropriate to the intention established by that context will be created.

The background to the present case, namely the provision by the council of limited
accommodation in the discharge of its function under s 65(3) of the Housing Act 1985
(that function being limited in the terms I have already cited in this judgment) and the
acknowledgment of this situation by the defendant, in my judgment negatives any    **j**
inference that a tenancy was intended as an objective creation by the relationship under
which the council allowed the defendant and her children to repossess the home. This
approach is not inconsistent either with the passages cited from the speech of Lord
Templeman in *Street v Mountford* nor with the principles enunciated by Fox LJ in the *AG*

*Securities v Vaughan,* and is consistent with the judgment of Glidewell LJ in *Dresden*
*a* *Estates Ltd v Collinson* [1987] 1 EGLR 45 and the approach of the court in *Hadjiloucas v*
*Crean.*

For these reasons, in my judgment, Judge ap Robert correctly held that there was a
licence granted for 13 weeks which was allowed to run on as a licence in the discharge of
their duties under s 65(3) of the 1985 Act, but that it was determined, and lawfully
determined, as a licence by the letter of 19 February 1987. Had it been a tenancy the
*b* period in that letter, being less than four weeks, would not have been effective; but, to
determine a licence of the nature created by this relationship, it was effective to determine
any rights granted to the defendant in the discharge of the council's duty under the Act.
Thereafter the defendant enjoyed no rights in the property. There is no evidence of any
receipt of rent, and she continued in occupation of the property at risk.

Throughout the period of the occupation under licence the council was under the
*c* protection of para 4 of Sch 1, since the clear inference to be drawn from the circumstances
is that the defendant and her family were allowed to remain in the property in pursuance
of an extension of the reasonable time which it was the duty of the council to allow for
her obtaining alternative accommodation under s 65(3).

I would accordingly dismiss this appeal.

*d* **RALPH GIBSON LJ.** The making of the agreement and the rights given by it to the
defendant under which the defendant occupied the dwelling house are referable, in my
judgment, to the legal relationship of duty between the defendant and the council
created by the Housing (Homeless Persons) Act 1977. The court therefore can, for the
reasons explained by Purchas LJ, and in my judgment should, hold that the council was
able in law to grant a licence only and not a tenancy of the dwelling house,
*e* notwithstanding the fact that exclusive possession of the dwelling house was thereby
given for a term and included provision for payment of money for the use of the
dwelling house. By the document used that effect was achieved.

I therefore agree that this appeal should be dismissed.

*f* *Appeal dismissed. No order for costs. Leave to appeal to the House of Lords refused. Stay of*
*possession order until 28 days from last day on which open to petition to House of Lords.*

Solicitors: *Whittinghams,* Bridgend (for the defendant); *J G Cole,* Bridgend (for the council).

Raina Levy    Barrister.

# Kelly v Norwich Union Fire Insurance Society Ltd

COURT OF APPEAL, CIVIL DIVISION
CROOM-JOHNSON, BINGHAM AND TAYLOR LJJ
4, 5 APRIL 1989

*Insurance – Property insurance – Perils insured against – Escape of water from mains – Escape occurring before policy taken out – Loss or damage to property resulting from escape occurring during period of policy – Insurers agreeing in policy to indemnify insured in respect of 'events' occurring during period of insurance – Whether 'events' referring to occurrence of perils insured against or to loss or damage resulting from insured peril – Whether policy protecting insured against damage occurring during period of policy but resulting from peril occurring before policy came into effect.*

In October 1977 the plaintiff insured his house with the defendant insurance company under a home insurance policy which provided for the defendants to indemnify the plaintiff against loss or damage to the house caused by any of the insured perils specified in the policy, which included burst water mains. The final clause of the policy stated that the defendants would indemnify the plaintiff in respect of 'events occurring during the period of insurance' provided the plaintiff had paid the premiums due under the policy. The water supply to the house came direct from the water main in the road and in the summer of 1977, ie before the commencement of the policy, the pipe running from the main to the house burst, causing a prolonged discharge of water from the pipe before it was repaired. The leakage caused damage to occur to the house during the period of the policy. The plaintiff made a claim under the policy but the defendants refused to pay. The plaintiff then brought an action against the defendants contending that he was entitled to be indemnified under the policy for the damage because it had been caused by an insured peril, namely a burst water main, and the consequential loss or damage was an event which had occurred during the period of the policy and therefore fell within the final clause of the policy. The defendants contended that they were only liable to indemnify the plaintiff for an insured peril which occurred during the period of the policy. The judge dismissed the plaintiff's claim. The plaintiff appealed.

**Held** – On the true construction of the policy, the 'events' referred to in the final clause of the policy were the happening of any of the specified insured perils and not the loss or damage to the house caused by any of those perils. Accordingly, the defendants' liability to indemnify the plaintiff could only be brought about by the occurrence of one of the insured perils during the period of the policy. The policy therefore protected the plaintiff against specified perils occurring during the period of insurance and not against damage occurring during the period of the insurance but resulting from a peril which had occurred before the policy came into effect. Since the water main had burst before the policy came into effect and it was only the loss or damage consequential on the burst main which had occurred during the period of the policy, the plaintiff was not entitled to be indemnified under the policy for the loss or damage. The appeal would therefore be dismissed (see p 895 *c* to *e* and p 896 *c e j* to p 897 *a*, post).

**Notes**
For the peril insured against in non-marine insurance, see 25 Halsbury's Laws (4th edn) paras 443–444, 448.

**Case referred to in judgment**
*Hutchins Bros v Royal Exchange Assurance Corp* [1911] 2 KB 398, CA.

**Cases also cited**

a   *Buchanan & Co v Faber* (1899) 15 TLR 383.
   *Bufe v Turner* (1815) 6 Taunt 338, 128 ER 1065.
   *Ellerbeck Collieries Ltd v Cornhill Insurance Co Ltd* [1932] 1 KB 401, CA.
   *Hough & Co v Head* (1885) 55 LJQB 43, CA.
   *Knight v Faith* (1850) 15 QB 649, 117 ER 605.
   *Lockyer v Offley* (1786) 1 Term Rep 252, 99 ER 1079.
b   *Mitsui v Mumford* [1915] 2 KB 27.


**Appeal**

By a writ indorsed with a statement of claim issued on 1 August 1985 the plaintiff, Nicholas Christopher Kelly, claimed against the defendants, Norwich Union Fire Insurance Society Ltd (the Norwich Union), the costs of repairing damage to Mr Kelly's
c   bungalow at 21 Castleton Road, Wickford, Essex under Home Plus policies Mr Kelly had taken out with the Norwich Union. The Norwich Union by their defence denied that Mr Kelly was entitled to claim under the policies in respect of the loss or damage in question. At the trial of the action on 16 March 1987 his Honour Judge Butler QC sitting as a judge of the High Court dismissed Mr Kelly's claim. Mr Kelly appealed. The facts are set out in the judgment of Croom-Johnson LJ.
d

*Anthony Speaight* for Mr Kelly.
*John E A Samuels* QC and *Andrew Burr* for the Norwich Union.

**CROOM-JOHNSON LJ.** A bungalow was erected at 21 Castledon Road, Wickford in Essex in the 1920s. In 1940 a Mr and Mrs Manzi moved into it, and in 1961 the plaintiff,
e   Mr Kelly, went to live there as a lodger and he stayed as such until 1969. In 1971 he bought the bungalow from Mrs Manzi, who lived there until 1975. After 1975 Mr Kelly, who is a builders' labourer, lived there on his own. In about 1977 he painted and decorated the bungalow and put in some new floorboards. He said that he observed no cracks or trouble with the structure. He decided to insure it, and he did so, through brokers, with the defendants, Norwich Union Fire Insurance Ltd (the Norwich Union).
f   The insurance policy began on 29 October 1977. It lasted for 12 months until 28 October 1978. He insured the building for £15,000 and also the contents for a lesser sum.
   The policy he took out was in two parts. The first part referred to the buildings; the second part referred to the contents. The cover which was given to the buildings begins in this way:

g      'The Company will indemnify the Insured by payment reinstatement replacement or repair as provided below
      1 *The Buildings* Loss or damage to the buildings caused by any of the insured perils.'

There were other matters included, to which it is unnecessary to refer.
h      The rest of this part of the policy, dealing with the insurance of the buildings, covers loss of rent and the cost of alternative accommodation, accidental damage by external means to underground services, the breakage of glass and sanitary fixtures, and cl 5 provides cover against the property owner's liability at law for accidental bodily injury or accidental loss of, or damage to, material property, and there are various exclusions. That part of the policy is described as the 'Cover'.
j      There is then a section marked B, giving the special exclusions, to which I need not refer. There is then section C, which defines what the buildings are, and section D is of importance. It is headed 'Definition of Insured Perils' and it goes through altogether 11 kinds of insured peril, beginning with fire and explosion and continuing with storm and flood, riot, civil commotion and matters of that kind. It is necessary to refer only to two of them. Number (5) reads.

'Bursting or overflowing of water tanks apparatus or pipes (forming part of the domestic fixed water system) washing machines or water mains . . .'    *a*

and no (10) is:

'Landslip or subsidence of the site on which the building stands'

with certain exclusions.

There is also a clause at the end of the definition of insured perils, which reads as    *b*
follows:

'The cover in respect of the Insured perils (3) [that is riot or civil commotion] (5) *bursting or overflowing of water tanks apparatus or pipes* forming part of the domestic fixed water system or washing machines or water mains and (6) *theft or any attempt thereat* shall be inoperative when the private dwelling is unfurnished other than when there is a change of occupier when the cover shall apply whilst the    *c*
premises are unfurnished for a period(s) not exceeding 30 days during any one period of insurance such period(s) to commence on the date when the outgoing occupier vacates the private dwelling.'

There are two other sections of the first part of the policy, to which it is unnecessary to make any reference.    *d*

Th second part of the policy deals with the cover for the contents; instead of dealing with the building, as does the first part, it deals with the contents of the insured private dwelling. It deals with the contents which are temporarily removed; it provides under para 4 cover for the tenant's liability, namely all sums for which the insured is liable as tenant not as owner. Also, under para 6, it provides cover for personal and employers' liability at law for damages and claimants' costs in respect of accidental bodily injury,    *e*
with various terms and conditions and exclusions. Under para 7 it deals with compensation for the death of the insured or his or her spouse. There are again, in this part of the policy dealing with the contents, special exclusions; there is a definition of what is meant by 'Contents' and there is a definition of the insured perils. After these first two sections of the policy there is a section dealing with special safety precautions which the insured is advised to take, as to how to prevent burst pipes and how to prevent theft.    *f*

At the end of the policy there are also incorporated some general conditions. For present purposes it is only necessary to deal with one, which is general condition 3, which reads:

'On the happening of any event likely to give rise to a claim under this policy the Insured shall (a) immediately report in writing to the Company and provide all    *g*
particulars and evidence and do all such things as the Company may reasonably require Unless notice in writing is received by the Company within 30 days of the happening of such event the Company will not be liable (b) immediately forward all correspondence legal process or any other document to the Company unanswered (c) refrain from discussing liability with any third party.'

The whole policy document finishes up with the clause on which this appeal principally    *h*
depends. It reads as follows:

'The Company named in the schedule will in the terms of this policy indemnify or pay the Insured in respect of events occurring during the period of insurance or any subsequent period for which the Insured pays and the Company agrees to accept a renewal premium.'    *j*

There is then a provision that the proposal is the basis of, and forms part of, the contract.

That was the first of two policies taken out by Mr Kelly. It was renewed at the end of the year, on 29 October 1978, to expire on 28 October 1979. The next renewal, at a

slightly increased sum, was on 29 October 1979 for a 12-month period. It was not the
a  same policy; on this occasion the company substituted a different policy for both the
building and the contents. The wording was slightly different; the only relevant
difference, which is not significant, was that the insured peril no (5) was in respect of the
'Escape of water from the domestic fixed water system . . . or water mains . . .' It also had
the description of landslip or subsidence as an insured peril. The clause at the end, which
I have already read out, namely 'The Company named in the schedule will in the terms
b  of this policy indemnify' and so on, remained the same.

The last renewal was of the second policy; it took place on 29 October 1980 and
expired on 28 October 1981.

During those years there were certain facts which were found by the judge and which
must be recorded. The bungalow was built on clay. From the years 1974 to 1976 there
was a period of dry weather and an exceptionally hot summer in 1976. All this led to the
c  dessication of the site by the drying of the clay. The bungalow had no storage tank
inside; the water supply was direct from the mains in the roadway. In 1977 there was
observed what I shall call 'the first break' in a pipe coming to the bungalow from the
main. There was a lead pipe leading to a stopcock just inside the garden, and from there
to another pipe which was two metres outside the wall of the house. At that point the
lead pipe joined a copper pipe, which was then the main supply into the bungalow. It
d  seems that that was not a satisfactory way of running those pipes, because there is a
difficulty in joining two such substances (that is to say lead to copper) satisfactorily. Mr
Kelly first noticed that there was a fall-off in the pressure from taps in the bungalow.
According to an answer which he gave to the judge and which the judge adopted, he did
not call a plumber for some months, but he did eventually call a plumber, who made a
repair at the joint where the two pipes met and had come apart. At that point it seems
e  that he himself dug a trench to enable the repair to be carried out. All that happened
before he took out the first policy of insurance.

In 1978 there was a second break at the same point; it seems that the repair had not
been a satisfactory job. Again Mr Kelly noticed a loss of water pressure, and he then saw
a pool of water at the point where the break had taken place. On this occasion, as the
judge found, he called in a plumber very quickly and the repair was done immediately.
f  On the plumber's advice Mr Kelly then stopped using the water at full pressure. This was
to avoid a third break which might have been caused had he gone on using the water at
full pressure.

The next date which requires mention is in February 1980, when a contractor
employed by Mr Kelly did some pebble-dashing on the outside of the bungalow. The
only significance of that at this stage, about which there was some dispute, was that when
g  it was done it would have been apparent if cracks in the structure had by then developed,
but it seems that there were none.

In 1980 there was a third escape of water. There was a leak at the stopcock and a leak
at the joint of the two pipes and thereafter, when water was not required by Mr Kelly, he
simply turned it off at the stopcock. He noticed at that time that in the trench round the
h  stopcock there was water tending to lie.

He made his first claim against the Norwich Union under the policy with which we
are concerned on 23 March 1981. He described the date on which he had discovered the
damage as the morning of 23 March 1981, but I think that was really the date on which
he was making the claim. In describing fully what happened he said:

'I noticed hairline cracks appearing in the walls over the past few months. I went
j  away to a friends for a while & when I returned the cracks had opened up, the door
step has fallen away and the tiles on the roof are parting. Windows have been
broken by the pressure & [I] had to take locks off of doors before I could open them'.

It does appear that there was then serious displacement of the building.

On 30 April 1981 a claims controller from the Norwich Union, a Mr Anderson, visited the premises. He was told by Mr Kelly that the damage had been taking place since about October or November 1979, and Mr Anderson's view was that this was damage due to subsidence.

In June 1981 the Norwich Union sent a Mr Rudkins, a civil engineer, to the premises. He appears to have been puzzled by what he found and to have been uncertain what the cause was, but he was inclined to say that it was not subsidence. The result was that a soil investigation was carried out by experts, and it was found that the soil was highly susceptible to volumetric change when there was a change in the moisture content. The result of that was that Mr Rudkins still considered that there had been no subsidence.

In July 1982 a structural engineer, Mr Kelsey, attended and carried out an examination for Mr Kelly. He came to the conclusion that this was damage caused by subsidence. I think at that time he was inclined to blame some trees as having absorbed the moisture from the subsoil, making it dry; that was his view. As it turned out, and as I shall explain later on, the theory that this was subsidence was all wrong.

The Norwich Union were refusing to pay out on the claim for reasons which are obscure but which seem to have been detailed much later by their eventual amendment to the defence in this action. They were alleging that Mr Kelly was in breach of conditions in the policy because he had not immediately reported in writing within 30 days, that he had wrongly said in his proposal that the building was in good condition and would be so maintained by him, which was wrong, and that the water main was defective and that he had not repaired it, and that therefore, for that and possibly other reasons as to which one does not speculate, liability under the policy was repudiated.

Meanwhile, Mr Kelly had begun an action based on the damage having been caused, as Mr Kelsey had said, by subsidence. It is right to say that the allegations made in the amended defence were negatived at the trial by the judge.

The case came on for trial on 10 November 1986. Counsel for Mr Kelly asked the judge to have a view, which took place. One of the things which I think was exercising him was that by now Mr Kelsey was puzzled about whether the damage was caused by subsidence. What had puzzled Mr Kelsey was that the effect on the soil seemed only to be underneath the house and not outside it, and there were other inconsistencies in the nature of the damage which puzzled him. As a result of a further inspection he had now decided that the damage had been caused, not by subsidence but by what is known as 'heave'. Heave is the opposite of subsidence; instead of the soil being let down, it is the soil rising up and causing damage to the structure on top of it. If, of course, there has been something like desiccated clay at the site of the house, caused by very dry weather, and then the incursion into the site of a lot of water, the clay will swell up and it may well be that with clay of the type on which this bungalow was built it will overdo itself and rise up much too much. At all events, as a result of the visit to the site in November 1987, and a further report by Mr Kelsey, there was a reamendment, with the permission of the judge, on 12 December 1986, after the trial had begun; that denoted that this was not a case of subsidence but was a case of heave. It was after that that the Norwich Union put in their defence with a great deal more, as I have mentioned, in the way of merely putting Mr Kelly to proof.

When Mr Kelsey went back to the site on his second visit in November or December 1986 he found something which had not been discovered before. Lying under the ground between the stopcock and very close to the wall of the bungalow he found a totally disconnected lead pipe. It was what was referred to throughout the case and in this court as 'the coiled pipe'. Apparently at some stage it had formed part of the way of bringing water to the bungalow, but it had been disconnected and instead of being removed it had remained under ground all this time. I do not think it was ever established when that was done, but at all events it was certainly there by 1977 and it was something which could possibly have been there even longer. It was something which was unknown to Mr Kelly.

a    The result of it, as tested by Mr Kelsey, the engineer, was that he was able to establish that, when the stopcock was turned on in its trench just inside the garden wall, the effect of it was to fill the little trench by the stopcock, either from a leak or for some other reason, and the water would then run from that trench, through the coiled pipe, which acted as a kind of conduit from the stopcock trench to just in front of the house, and Mr Kelsey was of the view, which I think was accepted by the judge, that this coiled pipe must have been the means of producing quantities of additional water onto the clay

b    subsoil under the bungalow when the stopcock was turned on or when it was leaking. What the judge found on those facts was that by the time the trial eventually took place both Mr Rudkins and Mr Kelsey agreed that this was a case of heave and not a case of subsidence. The judge found that between 1974 and 1976 there had been a desiccation of the clay site, that subsequently to that water had been entering the clay and causing it to expand.

c    In the course of his judgment he made some findings of fact as to how the water got there. I quote from his judgment:

'From the evidence it is apparent that this might have occurred in a number of ways and at different times. Firstly, there was the lengthy discharge at mains pressure in the summer of 1977; secondly, there was the water leak that was repaired
d    in 1978; thirdly, there was, beginning early in 1980, the overflow from the trench at the stopcock and the consequential discharge from the coil of pipe by the front door. But it was only in the summer of 1977 that water escaped into the clay for a prolonged and uninterrupted period at full mains pressure. And, putting on one side the consequential discharge from the coil of pipe, the overflow from the trench at the stopcock was of minimal effect. Mr Kelsey said that there would have been
e    no significant discharge of water from the stopcock into the clay under the house without the presence of the coil. Nor, on the evidence, would there have been any significant or substantial discharge as a consequence of the leak that necessitated the 1978 repair. So there remain, as the significant or substantial causes of water entering the clay and causing "heave", firstly the discharge of water in the summer of 1977 and secondly the discharge of water from the coil from early 1980. Neither
f    of the experts has attempted to apportion the relative contribution of these causes. Perhaps it is impossible to do so. The importance of this will shortly be apparent.'

He went on in his judgment to make one further finding. He said:

'I accept that heave commenced immediately consequent on the summer 1977 burst and continued thereafter throughout the period of insurance.'

g    In this action Mr Kelly has relied on both the 1977 burst and the 1980-onwards incursion of water from the coiled pipe. The 1977 burst was what one can roughly call pre-policy water, and the other, in 1980, was the incursion of water after the insurance had begun. The judge found that the circumstances of both incursions of water came within the wording of insured peril no (5) in the policy which was in force at the time when the incursion took place, and the contrary has not been argued before us. The
h    judge found that the 1977 incursion, not having happened during the currency of the insurance, was not an 'insured peril' within the meaning of the policy at that time, notwithstanding that it caused loss or damage to the buildings after the insurance had begun in October 1977.

In coming to that conclusion he relied on *Hutchins Bros v Royal Exchange Assurance Corp*
j    [1911] 2 KB 398. We have been referred to that case, but with respect to the judge I do not think that that case supports the conclusion that he had come to. It was a case on a somewhat different point, but in the end that does not affect the decision of this appeal.

There can be no dispute that the incursion of water from the coiled pipe in 1980, and the damage which it caused, was an insured peril and caused loss or damage within the meaning of the policy. The damage to the building began in 1980, or perhaps late 1979;

it continued; if it had been possible to say how much of it was due to the 1977 incursion and its continuing effects, and how much was due to the further incursion which began *a* early in 1980, it might have been possible to ask the judge to apportion the blame between the two. However, such an apportionment was not asked for by counsel for Mr Kelly for the excellent reason that it was not possible for it to have been done. As the judge said in his judgment:

> 'Can I apportion here? I think not. The only event within the policy with which *b* I am concerned is that relating to the discharge through the coil of pipe. I have no evidence whatsoever which would allow me to make an assessment of the damage caused by this event, or the extent of its contribution to the "heave". In appropriate circumstances I would have thought it right to adopt such an approach, although I have been referred to no English case where this has been done. Indeed, I was never invited by counsel for Mr Kelly so to apportion, and there has been no argument *c* about it.'

Of course, the 'excellent reason' was that the two experts, Mr Rudkins and Mr Kelsey, had both said that they were totally unable to apportion the responsibility for the final damage to the bungalow to whichever of the two causes which the judge found were operative. *d*

Counsel who has appeared for Mr Kelly both in the court below and in this court has accordingly conceded that in order to succeed in this court he must succeed on the 1977 burst as well as on the 1980 leak. The way he puts his argument is attractively simple. He said that in the first part (and for present purposes I take the first policy) the words

> 'The Company will indemnify the Insured by payment reinstatement replacement *e* or repair as provided below
> 1 *The Buildings* Loss or damage to the buildings caused by any of the insured perils'

mean that all he has to do is to point to loss or damage which occurs during the currency of the policy and to prove that it was caused by one of the insured perils. It is submitted *f* that Mr Kelly was then entitled to his indemnity notwithstanding that the insured peril, that is to say the escape of water from the mains, occurred before the policy was taken out. In other words it is submitted that it is the loss or damage that is the event which has to occur during the period of insurance in order to comply with the clause at the end of the policy. This would have the result, perhaps a surprising one, that, as here, the insurers on granting the policy would be taking on a potential liability which might become actual in the future and about which no one knew anything at the time; but if *g* that is what the policy means, so be it.

The alternative argument, put on behalf of the Norwich Union, is that the events which must have occurred during the period of insurance are the events which are the happening of the insured perils, that those are matters which will be apparent and of which there must be, or would normally be, knowledge of when they take place. There *h* is only one other place in the policy where the words 'event' or 'events' are used, and that is in general condition 3, which I have already read. It is submitted on behalf of the Norwich Union that the word 'events' there used suggests that an event is something which is known, or at least knowable. In my own view, I get no assistance at all from general condition 3. It does not deal with matters like underground water or anything of that kind. In my view it is there in order that the insured may give information to the *j* insurance company of events 'likely to give rise to a claim', because to my mind that is dealing with third party liability, a matter which is covered under both sections of both policies. That reasoning of the Norwich Union does not deal satisfactorily with the insured peril of subsidence of the site. That is something which may well take place

unknown to anybody, without immediately causing damage to the building, and
*a* therefore counsel for Mr Kelly submits that accordingly the only safe meaning to be
given to the word 'events' during the period of insurance, in the final clause, is the
happening of the loss or damage, about which there can be no ignorance, so as to enable
the insured householder to make his claim.

Curiously enough, the industry of counsel, which has provided us with a number of
authorities, has not enabled them to find any direct authority in any branch of insurance
*b* which has dealt directly with this point. Accordingly, in my view it is necessary to return
to first principles.

This policy is a contract in writing. It contains, as one would expect, an effective clause
which defines the date on which the insurer will come on risk, the risks that he is
accepting and the circumstances in which he becomes liable to indemnify. It does that
by reference to the terms of the policy, the schedule and so on. Until that time (when he
*c* becomes liable) arrives, the insurer is liable for nothing. The rest of the policy defines
and limits his liability when any liability does attach and the construction of the
remainder of the policy is subject to that effective clause. In this policy the liability is
brought about by the happening of one of the insured perils, and the very description of
the peril as being an insured peril means that at the time when it becomes fact the
insurance is already effective, in other words, that the insurance period has begun when
*d* that event takes place. The words of indemnity on which Mr Kelly relies must be subject
to the words in the effective clause, and the risk must take place, as an event, during the
period of the insurance. The later occurrence of the damage is not in my view an 'event'
within the meaning of the policy. Accordingly, in my view the meaning of the word
'events' contended for by the Norwich Union is the correct one. It is referring to any of
the events which brings about the liability of the insurance company once the policy has
*e* become effective, and does not deal simply with the occurrence of the damage as counsel
for Mr Kelly submits.

Mention was made during the argument as to what effect this clause might have on
certain hypothetical sets of circumstances. One such was a leaking of the water main
which set in train a process of dry rot which might only result in loss or damage after the
period of insurance, or any subsequent period for which the insurance was renewed, had
*f* expired. It is not necessary to express any view on that problem in this appeal. Problems
such as that, and others that were instanced, can be dealt with if and when they ever '
arise.

Accordingly, I would dismiss this appeal.

*g* **BINGHAM LJ.** An insurance policy of the kind here under consideration is a contract
of indemnity. By it the insurer undertakes to indemnify the insured against loss or
damage to the subject property caused by certain perils specified in the policy.

The leakage of water which took place in 1978 was quickly remedied and was held to
be of no significance. That finding has not been challenged.

The leakage of water during 1980 is accepted as a peril specified in the policy then
*h* current, and occurred during the policy term. But the insured cannot show that his
house suffered any quantifiable loss or damage as a result of that leakage alone. It is
accordingly accepted on his behalf that he must, to make good his claim against these
insurers, show that they agreed to indemnify him against loss or damage suffered by his
house during the four policy years when the insurer was on risk as a result of the water
leakage in 1977. It is accepted that that leakage was a peril specified in the policies, and
*j* despite the argument of counsel for the Norwich Union to the contrary I am satisfied
that the judge found the resulting damage to have occurred during the cumulative term
of the policies. The insured's problem is that the 1977 leakage admittedly began and
ended before the term of the first policy began.

The insured argues that under the policies he is entitled to be indemnified if damage caused by a specified peril occurs during the cumulative term of the policies, even though the peril occurred before that term began.

The insurers argue that the insured is under the policies entitled to be indemnified if the insured peril occurs during the term of one or other policy and causes damage, even though the damage may occur, or become evident, after expiry of the term of any policy or the cumulative term of all the policies.

Neither party contends that the right to indemnity is dependent on the occurrence of both the specified peril and the resulting damage during the term of one or all of the policies, and neither party contends that there can be a right to indemnity if neither the specified peril nor the resulting damage occurs during the term of one or all of the policies.

In agreement with Croom-Johnson LJ I am of the clear opinion that under these policies the insured's right to indemnity is dependent on his showing that the specified peril in question occurred during the term of one or other policy. I give five reasons for that conclusion. (1) The reference to 'events occurring during the period of insurance' in the insurers' crucial contractual undertaking most aptly applies to the occurrence of specific perils and not to the occurrence of damage resulting therefrom. (2) Subsidence is specified as an insured peril. Heave is not. Heave is not a phenomenon of which I was formerly aware, but one should not assume that the insurers were similarly ignorant. It is noticeable that, whereas the insured warranted in his initial proposal that the house had not been damaged by subsidence, the insurers are not similarly protected in the case of heave. The two cases are not the same, since even on the insured's argument he can recover for damage caused by heave only where that is caused by a specified peril, whereas subsidence of itself founds a claim unless its cause is one of those specifically excluded. But, if this policy had intended to cover an insured against loss or damage to the house caused by heave caused by a specified peril occurring before the policy began, I think it overwhelmingly likely that an appropriate warranty would have been exacted from the insured at the outset. (3) I think it contrary to common understanding that an event may qualify as an insured peril if occurring before the policy term. This common understanding is reflected in the traditional language of the Lloyd's ship and goods voyage policy scheduled to the Marine Insurance Act 1906:

'Touching the adventures and perils which we the assurers are contented to bear and do take upon us in this voyage: they are of the seas . . .' etc.

It would be somewhat startling if a claim would lie for damage suffered during a voyage as a result of perils which had occurred before the insurers came on risk, or if (in the non-marine field) an insurer were liable for dry or wet rot which became apparent during his policy term although caused by an escape of water years earlier when another insurer, or no insurer, had been on risk. (4) If asked what he had insured against during the policy year, an insured under a policy such as these (if he knew the policy terms) would in my view reply 'fire, explosion, lightning, earthquake, storm, flood . . .' etc not 'loss or damage caused by fire, explosion, lightning, earthquake, storm, flood . . .' etc. This is in my view a case where the colloquial response accurately reflects the legal reality. (5) The researches of counsel unearthed no reported case in which an insurer had been held liable to indemnify the insured although the specified peril occurred before the insurer came on risk. While ultimately all must turn on the wording of the policy in question, it would in my view need compelling language of a kind not found here to lead to so unusual a result.

The insurers may well be right to accept that if the specified peril occurs during the policy term it makes no difference that the resulting damage occurs after, perhaps well after, its expiry. But the point does not arise for decision here and I think it is best not to decide it until it does.

My conclusion is in all essentials the same as that of the judge, as also of Croom-Johnson LJ. I too would dismiss the appeal.

**TAYLOR LJ.** I agree, and would add only one further reference to the policy in support
*a*   of the construction favoured by Croom-Johnson and Bingham LJJ.

Under section D of the first policy there is a heading 'Definition of Insured Perils'.
Thereafter there are the eleven tabulated headings to which Croom-Johnson LJ has
already referred. There follows a provision in each of the two policies which is very
similar; I read it from the second policy:

*b*   'The cover in respect of the insured perils (3) loss or damage by *malicious persons*
(5) *escape of water* and (6) *theft* or *attempted theft* will not operate when (a) the private
dwelling is unfurnished or (b) the private dwelling is unoccupied because of a
change of occupier. In the event of a change of occupier cover will apply for a period
not exceeding 30 days during any one period of insurance such period to commence
on the date when the outgoing occupier vacates the private dwelling.'

*c*   That provision clearly envisages that the insured peril will occur during the operational
period of the policy; moreover, it could not sensibly apply to the occurrence of an insured
peril prior to the commencement of that period.

I too would dismiss this appeal.

*Appeal dismissed. Leave to appeal to House of Lords refused.*
*d*

Solicitors: *Gepp & Sons*, Chelmsford (for Mr Kelly); *Budd Martin Burrett*, Chelmsford (for
the Norwich Union).

Wendy Shockett    Barrister.

*e*

# R v Bath Licensing Justices, ex parte Cooper
*f* # and another

QUEEN'S BENCH DIVISION
WOOLF LJ AND SAVILLE J
7 APRIL 1989

*Natural justice – Magistrates – Bias – Fair hearing not possible – Member of local licensing*
*g* *committee sitting on appeal from committee's decision – Applicants applying for full liquor licence*
*– Application refused by local licensing committee – Applicants making unsuccessful second*
*application again and then appealing to Crown Court – Appeal heard by bench which included*
*justice who had been member of licensing committee which dismissed applicants' first application –*
*Whether reasonable suspicion that applicants would not have fair hearing of appeal.*

*h*
The applicants were the licensees of a wine bar the licence for which excluded spirits.
The applicants applied for a full on-licence to enable them to sell spirits. That application
was refused by the local licensing committee. Six months later the applicants again
applied for a full on-licence and again their application was dismissed. The applicants
then appealed to the Crown Court against the second dismissal. The appeal was heard by
*j* a bench which included one of the licensing justices who had heard and dismissed the
applicants' first application. The Crown Court dismissed the applicants' appeal. The
applicants applied for judicial review of the Crown Court's decision on the ground that it
was contrary to natural justice for a licensing justice who had heard the applicants' first
application also to sit on the appeal to the Crown Court since justice could not be seen to
be done in those circumstances.

**Held** – The test of whether an appellate body could have the same membership as the
body which adjudicated on the matter below was whether a reasonable and fair-minded  *a*
person sitting in court and knowing all the facts would have a reasonable suspicion that
the appellant would not have a fair hearing of the appeal because a fair hearing would
not be possible. Applying that test, the applicants had established that a fair hearing of
their appeal was not possible, since the issues on the appeal to the Crown Court on the
second application were the same as those in the first application and just as justice would
not have appeared to have been done if the licensing justice who had heard the applicants'  *b*
first application had sat on the appeal to the Crown Court on that application justice
could not be seen to be done when he sat on the appeal to the Crown Court on the second
application. The application for judicial review would therefore be granted (see p 902 *d*
to *g* and p 905 *h*, post).

Per curiam. Clearly there can be situations where after a period of time there can be
no objection taken to a justice who has earlier adjudicated on a similar matter concerning  *c*
a particular party to proceedings before the bench subsequently sitting on an appeal in
respect of a later decision. The dividing line between a fair hearing being possible or not
possible is a matter of fact and degree to be determined according to the circumstances
of the particular case. However, as a rough and ready working rule in licensing cases a
fair hearing should be possible if more than 12 months have elapsed between the hearings
of the licensing committee (see p 903 *b c g* to *j* and p 905 *h*, post).              *d*

**Notes**

For test of disqualificaton by bias, see 29 Halsbury's Laws (4th edn) paras 257, 259, and
for cases on the subject, see 33 Digest (Reissue) 73–75, 83, 259–271, 342–349.

**Cases referred to in judgments**                                          *e*

*Hannam v Bradford City Council* [1970] 2 All ER 690, [1970] 1 WLR 937, CA.
*Metropolitan Properties Co (FGC) Ltd v Lannon* [1968] 3 All ER 304, [1969] 1 QB 577,
   [1968] 3 WLR 694, CA.
*R v Liverpool City Justices, ex p Topping* [1983] 1 All ER 490, [1983] 1 WLR 119, DC.
*R v Oxford Regional Mental Health Review Committee, ex p Mackman* (1986) Times, 2 June.  *f*
*R v Uxbridge Justices, ex p Burbridge* (1972) Times, 21 June, DC.

**Application for judicial review**

John William Charles Cooper and Susan Cooper, joint licensees of Shades Wine Bar at 4
Edgar Buildings, Bath, applied with the leave of Popplewell J given on 16 January 1989
for judicial review of the decision of the Crown Court at Bristol (his Honour Judge
McCarraher and justices) on 23 September 1988 dismissing their appeal from the decision  *g*
of the Bath licensing justices on 8 April 1988 not to grant a full on-licence for Shades
Wine Bar. The relief sought was an order of mandamus to compel the Crown Court to
hear and determine the appeal of the applicants impartially and according to law. The
facts are set out in the judgment of Woolf LJ.

                                                         *h*

*Ian D Glen* for the applicants.
*Nigel Pleming* for the Crown Court.
The licensing justices did not appear.

**WOOLF LJ.** This is an application for judicial review by Mr and Mrs Cooper to quash a
decision of the Crown Court on 23 September 1988 sitting to hear an appeal from a  *j*
decision of the petty sessional division of Bath. The principal point which arises on the
application is one which is of some significance to licensing committees of justices, and
the court is fortunate in having had the benefit (on a point which is by no means easy to
resolve) of exceedingly able arguments both by counsel for the applicants and counsel for
the Crown Court.

The facts giving rise to the application are relatively short and appear clearly from the
a  affidavit filed on behalf of the applicants by Mr Cooper. He and his wife are the joint
licensees of Shades Wine Bar, which carries on business at 4 Edgar Buildings, Bath. This
is in the central area of Bath and enjoys a busy trade. It operates as a restaurant at lunch
time, and apparently there are other wine bars operated in that way, but no doubt in the
evening its trade is somewhat different. That is not revealed in the affidavits. The wine
bar was licensed in 1980. The licence was a general on-licence, except that it was limited
b  to all types of liquor except spirits. All the other central wine bars are licensed to sell
spirits, though in a few cases it is said there are restrictions as to beer sales. It is said in the
affidavit (and, for the purposes of this application, I will assume this is correct) that all
restaurants, and of course public houses, can sell spirits, though presumably in the case
of restaurants they will frequently be limited to holding a restaurant licence.

In 1987 the applicants, being unhappy about the limitation with regard to spirits,
c  decided to make a new licence application. They went through the appropriate
formalities and on 6 November 1987 their application came before the Bath licensing
committee. That licensing committee was in effect hearing an application by the
applicants for a full on-licence, which would be equivalent to a public house licence. One
of the members of the licensing committee which heard that application was a Mr Fortt.
Witnesses were called, including those presenting the application and customer witnesses
d  who indicated that they wished to purchase spirits. The application was dismissed.
Although no reasons may have been given initially, in fact, contrary to what was said in
the affidavit, reasons were thereafter given by the justices.

The applicants were dissatisfied with the result and so they went to different legal
advisers, who, in consequence of their investigations, decided that instead of making an
appeal to the Crown Court it would be preferable if a fresh application was made. A fresh
e  application was therefore made, which came on for hearing on 8 April 1988,
approximately six months later. The application was unopposed but it was dismissed,
and, on this occasion, the applicants decided to appeal to the Crown Court sitting at
Bristol.

The appeal was heard on 23 September 1988, when the court was presided over by one
of the circuit judges, his Honour Judge McCarraher. One of the justices he was sitting
f  with was in fact one of the justices who had taken part in the adjudication of 6 November
1987 as a member of the justices licensing committee sitting on that day, namely Mr
Fortt. The appeal was unsuccessful, the court indicating in giving its reasons for the
appeal being unsuccessful that it did not consider there was sufficient evidence of need
before the court. The judge gave as an example of the sort of situation where he would
regard there being sufficient need a case where there was an application for a public
g  house licence on a new housing estate.

During the hearing it had been appreciated by the applicants that Mr Fortt was sitting
at the Crown Court, and that he was not only sitting on the appeal but also that he had
sat on 6 November 1987. They had, however, no advance notice that this was going to
be the situation and they said nothing about it to their legal advisers because they did not
appreciate the significance of this, nor did it occur to them that they had any right to
h  object. However, having taken advice after they had been disappointed with the result
of their appeal, they made an application to this court. The preliminary point which they
have taken on this application was that, Mr Fortt having sat on 6 November 1987, it was
not right for him to sit on the hearing of the appeal ten months later on 23 September
1988. They take a subsidiary point, which was also advanced in argument before us, and
that is that the Crown Court misdirected itself in its approach to the question of need
j  and that on that basis this court should intervene by way of judicial review.

It is right that I should make it clear that counsel for the Crown Court has not (and, in
my view, has correctly not) advanced any argument before this court to suggest that in
the circumstances of this case, assuming that the applicants were otherwise entitled to
succeed on the first point, because the applicants did not during the hearing raise the

point they would not be entitled to succeed. I say that merely because there could be some cases, where the facts are different from this case, where it might be said that if an *a* applicant stood by and allowed a situation to occur to which he objects he is not entitled, as a matter of discretion, to be granted relief by this court.

There is a second matter that I should make clear straight away. No one makes in this case any criticism whatsoever of Mr Fortt. If I may say so, he behaved with commendable responsibility. If matters have gone wrong, it is certainly not due to any departure from the proper standards which are to be expected of a magistrate on the part of Mr Fortt. On *b* two occasions he raised the question of the propriety of his sitting with the clerk to the justices. We are told he had in mind the provisions of rules which I am going to come to in a moment. He wished therefore to have confirmation that it was proper for him to sit, because when he was asked to attend the Crown Court he appreciated that he had sat on the application which was heard on 6 November 1987. He was assured, and that assurance was confirmed as a result of his second inquiry, that it was in order for him to sit. It was *c* only on the basis of those assurances that he did not raise the matter at the Crown Court. This is unfortunate. If the matter had been raised I have little doubt that the present problems would not have arisen and this application would not have occurred. As I hope I have made clear, this is again certainly not a matter for which Mr Fortt can be criticised in any way.

The argument is advanced in relation to the first point in two different ways by counsel *d* for the applicants. He submits, first of all, that when the relevant statutory provisions are examined Mr Fortt was in fact disqualified from sitting in the Crown Court. If he does not succeed on that contention then he argues, and perhaps this is the argument to which he attaches most importance, that this is a situation where justice has not been seen to be done: because Mr Fortt sat as a member of the licensing committee on 6 November 1987 justice was not seen to be done when he sat again on the hearing of the appeal on 23 *e* September 1988.

Although the second manner in which the argument advanced is the more important, it is convenient to look first of all at the first way in which the point is put. That is put primarily on the basis of r 5 of the Crown Court Rules 1982, SI 1982/1109, which provides: *f*

> 'A justice of the peace shall not sit in the Crown Court on the hearing of an appeal in a matter on which he adjudicated or of proceedings on committal of a person to the Court for sentence under section 37 or 38 of the Magistrates' Courts Act 1980 by a court of which he was a member.'

In general terms the facts on the first hearing before the licensing committee on 6 *g* November 1987 were exactly the same as the facts that the licensing committee had to consider on 8 April 1988. Therefore, in general terms, the facts which the Crown Court had to consider on the appeal from the decision of 8 April 1988 were the same as those which were before the licensing committee on 6 November 1987. I emphasise the words 'generally the same' because, of course, there were differences. The evidence was different. Even on the appeal, as that was a rehearing, the evidence would not have been the same *h* as that on 8 April 1988. For the purposes of the argument it is sufficient to say that the evidence was generally the same.

What counsel for the applicants says (bearing in mind the language of r 5) is that when Mr Fortt sat on 6 November 1987 he was adjudicating on the same matter on which he had adjudicated on 23 September 1988. Speaking for myself, I do not consider that submission is one of any substance, because the word 'matter' as it appears in r 5 is, in my *j* view, referring to the same proceedings as are the subject of the adjudication of the appeal. The term 'matter' is a broad term, because the Crown Court Rules 1982 deal with various types of procedures. The fact that there are different proceedings where the same sort of issues are inquired into on different occasions, only one of which is the subject of

appeal, does not make the other proceedings which are not the subject of appeal the same
*a* matter for the purposes of that rule.

The other relevant provision which it is necessary to look at with regard to
disqualification is not contained in the 1982 Rules but is contained in s 22 of the
Licensing Act 1964. That section contains procedural provisions as to appeals. Section
22(7) provides:

*b*    'A justice shall not act in the hearing or determination of an appeal under section
      21 of this Act from any decision in which he took part.'

Counsel for the applicants did not rely on this other statutory provision for the purposes
of his first argument on the question of Mr Fortt's ability to sit on the appeal. In my view
he was correct not to do so, because it is clear from the language of s 22(7) that all that is
being referred to is a prohibition of a justice sitting on the hearing or determination of
*c* an appeal from the very decision which is under appeal.

It is therefore possible to proceed straight away to the second way the argument is put
on behalf of the applicants. This has, in my view, very much more substance than the
first way in which it is argued. It depends on the general rule, which can be described as
a common law rule, as to justice being seen to be done. There are a considerable number
of authorities now on this subject. They are conveniently collected in *R v Liverpool City*
*d* *Justices, ex p Topping* [1983] 1 All ER 490 at 494, [1983] 1 WLR 119 at 123. In that
judgment Ackner LJ refers to the very well known case of *Metropolitan Properties Co*
*(FGC) Ltd v Lannon* [1968] 3 All ER 304 at 310, [1969] 1 QB 577 at 599 where Lord
Denning MR set out a test, and then he goes on to deal with the view of Cross LJ in
*Hannam v Bradford City Council* [1970] 2 All ER 690 at 700, [1970] 1 WLR 937 at 949 as
follows:
*e*
      'If a reasonable person who has no knowledge of the matter beyond knowledge
      of the relationship which subsists between some members of the tribunal and one
      of the parties would think that there might well be bias, then there is in his opinion
      a real likelihood of bias. Of course, someone else with inside knowledge of the
      character of the members in question might say: "Although things don't look very
*f*    well, in fact there is no real likelihood of bias." But that would be beside the point,
      because the question is not whether the tribunal will in fact be biased, but whether
      a reasonable man with no inside knowledge might well think that it might be
      biased.'

Having referred to that quotation, Ackner LJ goes on in his judgment to refer to an
approach adopted by Lord Widgery CJ in *R v Uxbridge Justices, ex p Burbridge* (1972)
*g* Times, 21 June and he then concludes in this way ([1983] 1 All ER 490 at 496, [1983] 1
WLR 119 at 125):

      'In the affidavits put in on behalf of the justices, there is no suggestion that they
      are incapable of controlling their computer. The chief constable, who was
      represented on this application, provided us with no information to suggest that
*h*    there cannot be put before the justices the limited material as occurred in the pre-
      computer era. To our mind there is a real danger that administrative convenience is
      being given greater priority than the requirements of justice. We therefore repeat
      that in our judgment the practice of putting before the justices' court sheets
      expressed in this fashion is most undesirable. Can it also be said to be wrong in law?'

*j* Ackner LJ goes on to deal with his conclusions with regard to the facts of that particular
case. I refer to that passage in Ackner LJ's judgment dealing with administrative
convenience because, before this court, counsel for the Crown Court has (for reasons
which will become apparent later in this judgment) argued strongly that in this case
undesirable administrative consequences would follow from a decision adverse to the

Crown Court, which he submits this court should have in mind in deciding this application.

The only other authority to which I need make reference is *R v Oxford Regional Mental Health Review Committee, ex p Mackman* (1986) Times, 2 June. That case is not fully reported but we have been provided with a transcript. That case is of some interest for two reasons. First of all, the court was there concerned with a situation that can happen within the mental health area where there are successive applications to a mental health review tribunal and a question arises whether it is appropriate for the same members of the tribunal to sit on more than one application. I need say no more about that case so far as the facts are concerned, because there is in my view a difference between a tribunal hearing successive applications which has common membership and an appellate body having the same membership as the body which adjudicated on the matter in the court below. What I have to say hereafter I recognise may not necessarily be applicable to the former situation with which we are not presently dealing. The second reason I refer to that case is because McNeill J in my view, in the course of his judgment, in a sentence put forward a test which can be readily applied to this case in deciding whether or not matters have been correctly dealt with by the Crown Court, having regard to the fact that Mr Fortt was sitting both in the Crown Court and as a member of the licensing committee, albeit the licensing committee that was sitting in November 1987 and not on the second application in April 1988. What McNeill J said was:

> 'But at the end of the day, could the reasonable and fair-minded person sitting in court and knowing all the facts have a reasonable suspicion that this applicant would not have a fair hearing, that a fair hearing would not be possible?'

For the purposes of this application, that test is, in my view, the appropriate test, albeit that it is necessary to insert after the words 'a fair hearing' the words 'of an appeal'. Asking myself that question, I have come to the conclusion that, although I regard this case as being near the borderline, these applicants have established that the reasonable and fair-minded person sitting in the court and knowing all the facts would have a reasonable suspicion that this applicant did not have a fair hearing of his appeal and that a fair hearing was not possible.

Basically, the issues on the appeal to the Crown Court on 23 September 1988 were identical with the issues which would have arisen on that appeal if it had been an appeal from the decision of 6 November 1987. There is no doubt, and no dispute, that quite apart from any statutory provision it would not have been just for Mr Fortt to have sat on the hearing of 8 April 1988 and on the appeal of 23 September 1988. Does it make what would otherwise be unjust, just if the fact is that, instead of sitting on 8 April 1988, he was sitting on 6 November 1987? The conclusion which I would come to is that the position is the same since a reasonable person would take the view that just as he would have been tainted if he had sat on 8 April 1988, so he was tainted because he sat on 6 November 1987.

For reasons that I have explained, Mr Fortt did not raise the matter at the hearing. I anticipate (and I am merely giving my own assessment of the situation) that, if he had not had the assurances which he did, he would have thought it right to mention the matter at the hearing on 23 September 1988 if the matter was not raised by the applicant. If he had raised it, then it may well be, we do not know, that the applicants would have waived any objection to Mr Fortt sitting. If they had waived their objection then they could not apply to this court. But they did not have, in my view, an opportunity of making an objection in the circumstances here. They are entitled to say that there is here the appearance of injustice albeit, as I am quite confident myself, that Mr Fortt adjudicated on the matter every bit as fairly as those other justices who were sitting on 23 September 1988 and who were not part of either of the previous hearings. It is not a question of whether Mr Fortt was able to put out of his mind his view of what happened on 6

November 1987; the question is whether he succeeded in doing so from an appearance

*a* point of view, bearing in mind that the statutory legislation presupposes that a person is to have a right of appeal and that the intent of the legislation is that a person is to have a right of appeal by a different tribunal from that which adjudicated on the matter on the first occasion. So far as this case is concerned, it is true that the body from which he had his statutory right to appeal, which he exercised, was different. But, because of the history to which I have made reference, the position was very much the same with regard to the

*b* hearing of 6 November 1987 as it was at 8 April 1988 and, in my view, it is difficult to distinguish between the two situations.

Clearly, however, there can be situations where, after a period of time has elapsed, there can be no reasonable objection taken to a magistrate who has adjudicated on a similar matter earlier concerning a particular party to proceedings before the magistrates sitting on an appeal in respect of a later decision. Where the dividing line is to be drawn

*c* will be very much a matter of fact and degree to be determined on the particular circumstances of the case.

However, I am very mindful of the submissions which counsel for the Crown Court made as to the practicalities which I will come to more specifically when dealing with later arguments which I have to consider in giving my conclusions on this application. I consider it is right for this court to try and help justices' clerks and others who have the

*d* task of assisting persons in Mr Fortt's situation.

As to that, the first piece of assistance that I can perhaps give (and I venture assistance with a degree of caution, because circumstances can be very different) is that, if there is any doubt whether the situation is one where it is appropriate for a particular justice to sit on appeal when he has been involved in any way in the matter in the court below, the best solution to adopt is for it to be mentioned at the outset to the parties so that they can

*e* make submissions to the appellate court and the matter can be considered in the light of those submissions. In the vast majority of cases, if that is done that will solve the problem. It could not be dealt with in that way in this case because of the assurance which Mr Fortt had received.

In addition to that assistance, the only other piece of assistance that I can offer (and I do

*f* say it with particular caution here, because the facts can vary a great deal) is to draw attention to the implication which flows from the facts of this case itself. On the facts I have indicated I regard it as being close to the borderline. The period of time between the two hearings before the licensing committee was six months. The period between the first hearing before the licensing committee and the hearing before the Crown Court was ten months. I would suggest that if more than 12 months had elapsed between the

*g* hearing before the licensing committee on the first occasion and that on the second occasion the problems that we are faced with in this case would in practice not have arisen. After that period of time, in the ordinary way, one would expect that a member of a licensing committee would have heard so many facts with regard to other applications that the earlier hearing will no longer be materially in his mind so as to adversely affect the outcome. Certainly it would be my view that after a period of 12 months a reasonable

*h* and fair-minded person, sitting in court and knowing all the facts, in the ordinary case would not have a reasonable suspicion that the appellant would not have a fair hearing of his appeal.

That, as I indicated, is very much guidance of a general nature. It is not meant to be laying down a legal principle and it should not be so regarded. In cases of doubt the first piece of advice which I have offered should be followed, but, for administrative purposes,

*j* it may be helpful just to have a very rough and ready working rule and that is why I have proffered the second piece of advice.

Counsel for the Crown Court argues that, although the court comes to an adverse conclusion to him, on considering the general position at common law, as indicated by the authorities to which I have made reference, in this case it would not be right to apply those authorities in the way that I have indicated. He submits that here the Licensing Act 1964 and the provisions of the Crown Court Rules 1982 to which I have made *a* reference have laid down the precise circumstances in which a magistrate is disqualified from sitting on an appeal. If it is a case falling outside that provision and the rules, then the situation is that the justice is entitled to sit because it is Parliament's intention (and the intention of those who are responsible for drafting the rules) to codify the circumstances in which a justice is and is not entitled to sit on an appeal.

This argument counsel for the Crown Court regards as particularly important, because, *b* he submits, were the situation otherwise there could be very real practical difficulties, not difficulties which he submits are insurmountable, but very real difficulties. They arise out of the fact that at the material time the statutory maximum of licensing justices was 15. That statutory maximum has now been extended to 20. But, in relatively small petty sessional divisions, it is quite common for there to be less justices who are members of the licensing committee than the statutory maximum. In the case of Bath at the *c* relevant time, the actual number of justices who were members of the licensing committee was 12.

Counsel for the Crown Court then draws attention to the provisions of the Act dealing with the constitution of the Crown Court on an appeal from licensing justices. Those provisions are contained in r 3(2) of the Crown Court Rules 1982 which provides:

*d*

'On the hearing of an appeal against a decision of licensing justices under the Licensing Act 1964, the Crown Court shall consist of a judge sitting with four justices, each of whom is a member of a licensing committee appointed under Schedule 1 to that Act and two (but not more than two) of whom are justices for the petty sessions area in which the premises to which the appeal relates are situated.'

Counsel for the Crown Court draws attention to the fact that, bearing in mind that you *e* can have up to six applications in the course of a year to the same licensing committee raising the same issue, although this is unlikely to happen, one can readily see that, when a division only has a 12-member licensing committee, taking into account the members of the committee who become tainted as a result of successive applications, the number of licensing members who are available to sit could soon be exhausted. Indeed, it is clear from the affidavit of the clerk to the justices in this case that even with two applications *f* there were problems in finding justices to sit at the Crown Court for the hearing in September 1988.

In answer to this submission, counsel for the applicants drew the court's attention to the provisions which contain the power for dispensation in r 4. Those powers provide for the two justices to whom I have referred in appropriate circumstances, so as to avoid unreasonable delay, to be reduced to one. Also there is a proviso that the justices may sit *g* without any justice on the committee below in a case where the parties appearing at the hearing of the appeal agree.

However, notwithstanding that dispensationary power, it is right to acknowledge that administrative problems could arise, and the question this court has to consider is whether or not the general approach which is adopted in this case by the common law in *h* the authorities to which I have referred should be regarded as being excluded by the statutory provisions of s 22(7) of the Licensing Act 1964 and the provisions of r 5 of the Crown Court Rules 1982, which it is clear, in my view, do not apply to this case. So far as that is concerned it is my view that to accept what would otherwise be regarded as an unjust result from the normal consequence requires a clear intent to that effect to be shown by the Act of Parliament or the Crown Court Rules. In my view the proper *j* approach to the section of the Act and the rules is to regard them as laying down a standard which must be complied with in regard to fairness, but not an exhaustive standard. It is still possible in the appropriate circumstances for that standard to be expanded by the provisions of the common law so as to accord with the well-established

principles to which I have earlier made reference. Counsel for the applicants helpfully
referred the court to Wade *Administrative Law* (6th edn, 1988) pp 478–479, in which
there is reference to the fact that there can be situations where, to quote the editor, Sir
William Wade:

> 'Natural justice then has to give way to necessity; for otherwise there is no means
> of deciding and the machinery of justice or administration will break down.'

I cannot believe that in the circumstances which exist on appeals from licensing justices
we would ever get to such a situation of necessity. If it did arise then, of course, the
position would have to be disclosed to the appellant and he would have to decide whether
or not he wished to proceed. If he was not prepared to proceed and take advantage of the
dispensation powers which are contained in the Act where agreement occurs, then it
would be a situation where he, by his own acts, would bring about a situation where the
appeal would not be possible. I cannot believe myself that in practice such a situation
would arise and, if there was any difficulty, I am confident that a practical solution will
be achieved which will ensure the minimum standards of fairness generally in the law
could be applied to a hearing of the appeal. I therefore come to the conclusion that the
applicants on the principal ground on which they rely are entitled to succeed.

I will therefore deal extremely shortly (and I hope counsel for the applicants will
recognise that no discourtesy is intended to his argument if I deal with the matter in that
way) with the second argument with regard to need which he advanced. He submitted
that this was a case where, bearing in mind that there was an existing business and all
that was being asked for was to extend to spirits what already existed in relation to other
forms of alcoholic beverages, only very limited evidence of need should have been
necessary to establish the case before the justices licensing committee and, indeed, the
Crown Court. He submitted that the example given by the Crown Court judge, and the
way they phrased their reasons for dismissing the matter in relation to need, clearly
indicates that they must have applied some wrong standard in coming to the conclusion
that the appeal was not entitled to succeed. I am afraid I find that submission is wholly
without foundation. It is for the Crown Court to say in the ordinary case what material
it requires before it is satisfied that it is an appropriate case to grant what was, after all, a
new licence which was equivalent to a public house licence. The Crown Court said that
the evidence which was called before it was not enough to satisfy it that there should be
such a licence granted, and I for my part consider that on the material which was before
it it was entitled to come to the conclusion that the application should not be granted on
the appeal. It could, of course, have come to the opposite conclusion but, as to what
decision it came to, that was for it to decide and this decision is one which there are no
grounds established before this court which would justify the court interfering.

Accordingly I would, speaking for myself, allow this application for judicial review on
the first ground alone.

Counsel have not had an opportunity of addressing us as to what form of relief would
be appropriate and I merely confine myself to saying that the application succeeds at this
stage.

**SAVILLE J.** I agree, and I would only add this. Counsel for the Crown Court drew
attention to what he suggested would be great, perhaps even insurmountable, difficulties
in finding sufficient justices to deal with licensing appeals if the applicants' submission
on natural justice were accepted. I am not persuaded that the difficulties, although
undoubtedly they may well exist or arise in the future, are likely to be quite as great or
insurmountable as counsel would perhaps have us believe. What I am persuaded of is the
overriding and constant need to guard against the danger to which Ackner LJ drew
attention in *R v Liverpool City Justices, ex p Topping* [1983] 1 All ER 490 at 496, [1983] 1

WLR 119 at 125 of administrative convenience being given greater priority than the interests of justice.

*Application allowed. Decision quashed and case remitted to Crown Court to rehear appeal.*

Solicitors: *Thrings & Long*, Bath (for the applicants); *Treasury Solicitor.*

Raina Levy   Barrister.

# Note
# Re H and another (minors) (adoption: putative father's rights)

COURT OF APPEAL, CIVIL DIVISION
LORD DONALDSON OF LYMINGTON MR, BALCOMBE AND NICHOLLS LJJ
21 JULY 1989

**LORD DONALDSON OF LYMINGTON MR** issued the following statement of the court. At an earlier hearing of this case (see [1989] 2 All ER 353, [1989] 1 WLR 551) the court's attention had not been drawn to para 1 of Sch 3 to the Family Law Reform Act 1987, which provides:

> 'This Act (including the repeals and amendments made by it) shall not have effect in relation to any application made under any enactment repealed or amended by this Act if that application is pending at the time when the provision of this Act which repeals or amends that enactment comes into force.'

It follows that, whilst the court's decision is authority as regards the new Act, it should not be treated as any authority in relation to cases to which the transitional provisions did apply.

The local authority indicated that it was withdrawing its present application, thus giving the father the right to make representations on any further applications.

Frances Rustin   Barrister.

# R v Civil Service Appeal Board, ex parte Bruce (Attorney General intervening)

COURT OF APPEAL, CIVIL DIVISION

DILLON, TAYLOR LJJ AND SIR JOHN MEGAW

29, 30 NOVEMBER 1988

*Judicial review – Refusal of relief – Discretion – Dismissal of civil servant – Appeal to Civil Service Appeal Board – Complaint also made to industrial tribunal – High Court action commenced to enforce alleged compromise of industrial tribunal proceedings – Civil Service Appeal Board concluding that dimissal fair – Board giving no reasons for its decision – Application for judicial review of board's decision – Divisional Court dismissing application in view of other remedies being pursued – Whether Divisional Court properly exercising its jurisdiction in dismissing application.*

*Appeal – Fresh point – Point abandoned in court below – Point abandoned on advice of counsel – Court of Appeal refusing to allow point to be resuscitated – Whether wrong to admit further evidence on the point.*

*Civil Service Appeal Board – Decision – Reasons for decision – Decision setting out parties' contentions and board's conclusion thereon – Decision not setting out reasons for board's conclusion – Whether board should include reasons in its decision.*

In 1982 the applicant was offered employment in the Civil Service as an executive officer in the Inland Revenue enforcement office. He remained in that employment until his service was terminated in 1985. He appealed to the Civil Service Appeal Board to consider the fairness of the termination of his service. In August 1985 the applicant also commenced proceedings in an industrial tribunal complaining of unfair dismissal, but those proceedings were postponed. Nevertheless the applicant contended that his application to the industrial tribunal had been compromised and in March 1986 he issued a writ in the High Court seeking to enforce that compromise. Meanwhile the Civil Service Appeal Board, by a written decision in January 1986 in which it set out, inter alia, the applicant's contentions and those of the employing department, concluded that the decision to terminate the applicant's employment was fair but, as was the board's practice, it refrained from giving reasons for its conclusion. The applicant applied for judicial review of the board's decision on the ground that it had failed to give sufficient or any reasons for its decision. The Divisional Court decided that in all the circumstances and in view of the other proceedings which were being pursued by the applicant it was not appropriate to grant him judicial review and it dismissed his application. The applicant appealed to the Court of Appeal.

**Held** – Not only had the applicant failed to show that the Divisional Court had been so plainly wrong in the exercise of its discretion that the Court of Appeal should interfere, but in all the circumstances and on the particular facts the Divisional Court's exercise of its discretion had plainly been right. The appeal would therefore be dismissed (see p 912 *h j*, p 913 *c e f* and p 914 *a* to *c*, post).

Per curiam. (1) Where in the exercise of its discretion and in the circumstances of the case the Court of Appeal refuses to allow a party to resuscitate a point deliberately abandoned on the advice of counsel in the court below, it would be wrong to admit further evidence on the point (see p 910 *h j*, p 913 *f* and p 914 *c*, post).

(2) It would give a greater sense of fairness if the Civil Service Appeal Board added to its written decisions a short and factual statement of the reasons for its conclusion (see p 913 *d f* and p 914 *b c*, post).

Decision of the Divisional Court [1988] 3 All ER 686 affirmed.

**Notes**
For judicial control of administrative action, see 1 Halsbury's Laws (4th edn) paras 46– *a*
47.
   For a civil servant's right of appeal against dismissal, see 8 ibid paras 1303, 1309.

**Cases referred to in judgments**
*Alexander Machinery (Dudley) Ltd v Crabtree* [1974] ICR 120, NIRC.
*R v Immigration Appeal Tribunal, ex p Khan (Mahmud)* [1983] 2 All ER 420, [1983] QB 790, *b*
   [1983] 2 WLR 759, CA.

**Cases also cited**
*Breen v Amalgamated Engineering Union* [1971] 1 All ER 1148, [1971] 2 QB 175, CA.
*Council of Civil Service Unions v Minister for Civil Service* [1984] 3 All ER 935, [1985] AC
   374, HL.                                                                                    *c*
*Kleinwort Benson Ltd v Malaysia Mining Corp Bhd* [1988] 1 All ER 714, [1988] 1 WLR 799.
*R v Chief Constable of the Merseyside Police, ex p Calveley* [1986] 1 All ER 257, [1986] QB
   424, CA.
*R v East Berkshire Health Authority, ex p Walsh* [1984] 3 All ER 425, [1985] QB 152, CA.
*R v Mental Health Review Tribunal, ex p Pickering* [1986] 1 All ER 99.
*R v Secretary of State for Home Dept, ex p Benwell* [1984] 3 All ER 854, [1985] QB 554.    *d*
*Street v Mountford* [1985] 2 All ER 289, [1985] AC 809, HL.
*West Midlands Co-op Society v Tipton* [1986] 1 All ER 513, [1986] AC 536, HL.
*Westminster City Council v Great Portland Estates plc* [1984] 3 All ER 744, [1985] AC 661,
   HL.

**Appeal**                                                                                  *e*
The applicant, Vaughan Maurice Synnott Bruce, appealed against the decision of the
Divisional Court of the Queen's Bench Division (May LJ and Roch J) ([1988] 3 All ER
686) on 19 June 1987 whereby it dismissed his application for judicial review of the
decision of the Civil Service Appeal Board made on 8 January 1986 that the decision of
the Commissioners of Inland Revenue to terminate his employment as an executive  *f*
officer was fair. The Attorney General was given leave to intervene as second respondent.
The facts are set out in the judgment of Dillon LJ.

*Eldred Tabachnik QC* and *Richard Drabble* (neither of whom appeared below) for the
   applicant.
*Nigel Pleming* for the board was not called on.
*John Laws* for the Attorney General was not called on.                                     *g*

**DILLON LJ.** The court has before it an appeal by Mr Bruce (the applicant) against an
order of a Divisional Court of the Queen's Bench Division (May LJ and Roch J) ([1988] 3
All ER 686) made on 19 June 1987 whereby his substantive application for judicial
review of a decision of the Civil Service Appeal Board was dismissed.                        *h*
   The factual history of the matter is that the applicant was born in 1951 and
unfortunately as a result of an illness he has been severely disabled since he was about
five years old. In November 1982 he was offered employment in the Civil Service as an
executive officer in the Inland Revenue enforcement office at Worthing. He remained
in that engagement until his service was terminated with effect from 14 September 1985.
He appealed, as he was entitled to, to the Civil Service Appeal Board, a body established  *j*
under the Crown prerogative, to consider the fairness of the termination of his service.
There were submissions on each side and a hearing by the board in December 1985 as a
result of which the board by a written decision of 8 January 1986 concluded that the
department's decision to terminate the applicant's appointment was fair. He therefore
applied for leave to seek judicial review of the decision of the board, and that leave was

ultimately granted in February 1986. After various procedural interludes, which I need
a not further mention, the application for judicial review of the decision of the board came
before May LJ and Roch J for hearing in April 1987 and their reserved judgment was
delivered, as I have mentioned, on 19 June 1987.

The ground on which the decision of the board was challenged in argument before
the Divisional Court was solely that the board had failed to give sufficient or any reasons
for its decision. Apart from the application for judicial review the applicant started
b proceedings before an industrial tribunal, complaining of unfair dismissal. These
proceedings were started on 15 August 1985. They have so far remained in abeyance. He
also, on 21 March 1986, issued a writ in the High Court alleging that the proceedings
before the industrial tribunal had been compromised and claiming to enforce the
compromise. That action is still proceeding, but in October 1986 he was granted leave to
amend the proceedings and has amended them, claiming additionally a declaration that
c his employment was terminated wrongfully and unlawfully and without reasonable
cause, and further, or alternatively, damages for wrongful and unlawful dismissal, and
alternatively damages for breach of an implied term in his contract that the job offered
to him would be suitable in the light of his disability. In that action the applicant appears
in person and the action is of course brought against the Commissioners of Inland
Revenue, who were the employing department, and not against the Civil Service Appeal
d Board or, for that matter, the Attorney General, who has been given leave to intervene in
these proceedings. The action is still pending.

At the hearing before the Divisional Court many points were argued, but the
substantive point on which the case was decided was that as a matter of discretion in all
the circumstances and in view of the other proceedings which were being pursued by
the applicant it was not appropriate to grant him judicial review on the ground which
e alone was relied on, that no reasons for the decision had been given by the board. The
Divisional Court did not therefore reach any conclusion on whether there was a duty on
the board to give reasons, or on the effect as a matter of natural justice of inadequacy of
the reasons given. It did, in the course of the judgment, reach the conclusion that the
employment of the applicant in the Civil Service was under the prerogative and not
under a contract of employment and also that, other things being equal, a decision of the
f board was susceptible of being reviewed by judicial review. The decision whether or not
the employment was under a contract of employment seems to have been in the result
obiter. We have been asked by counsel for the Attorney General to hear argument in
support of the view of the Attorney that there was a contract of employment, but since,
on the view we take, this appeal must anyhow fail, anything we said on that topic would
be obiter and we have therefore declined to hear argument on it. It does not affect the
g proceedings by the applicant in the industrial tribunal because there is statutory provision
making that procedure applicable to employment under the Crown.

When the appeal was first mentioned there was a question whether the appeal had
become academic because the parties had composed their differences. But it was explained
to us that though there have been discussions and certain terms, which I need not
h mention, have been agreed in principle no agreement had been actually concluded, nor
had any terms been signed. We accept therefore that this case is not academic.

Also when the case was opened counsel for the applicant sought leave to amend the
notice of appeal to raise a fresh point not raised in the notice of appeal so far, and not
canvassed before the Divisional Court. This concerned certain documents and the broad
question was whether there were grounds for criticising the procedures of the board
j because matters were so handled that the applicant was not able to put before the board
certain documents which he had wished to put in. We ruled against allowing any
amendment, but deferred giving our reasons at that stage. I do not propose to go through
the history of this document issue in detail. It is absolutely clear that the point was taken
in the original Form 86A which was lodged by the applicant seeking leave to apply for
judicial review and it was elaborated in a supplemental notice of application for leave,

settled by counsel and issued on 10 April 1987. When the hearing before the Divisional
Court came on the applicant agreed to abandon the point on the advice of leading and      *a*
junior counsel of great experience then appearing for him. We have been supplied with
an affidavit of the solicitor then acting who explains that when the applicant and his
solicitor arrived at court both junior and leading counsel advised the applicant in the
strongest terms not to pursue the documents point:

> 'The Applicant stated that he wished this aspect of his case to be argued but both      *b*
> Counsel made it plain that they were not prepared to do so at public expense. The
> Applicant then instructed . . . Counsel to abandon the documents argument which
> he did.'

The solicitor goes on to say that he—

> 'wished Counsel to reconsider the matter as the advice had been given under           *c*
> pressure of time at the door of the Court'

and so a facsimile transmission was sent to junior counsel stressing the applicant's
continued concern at the abandonment of the documents point in its entirety. Counsel
was asked to reconsider the documents contained in the bundles before the court and the
aspects of the documents point. There was then a further conference with junior counsel
before the next day's hearing in the Divisional Court on 30 April when counsel confirmed    *d*
that he had reconsidered the matter fully, but remained of the view that the documents
argument was untenable. The applicant reluctantly accepted that advice. The whole of
the documents argument therefore in all its limbs was abandoned by the applicant in the
court below.

Having now changed solicitors and counsel he seeks to resuscitate the point.

The decision of the Divisional Court was given, as I have said, on 19 June 1987. The      *e*
notice of appeal was given on 3 December 1987. The appeal was fixed for hearing this
week as long ago, we were told, as July 1988. The notice seeking to amend the notice of
appeal to resuscitate the documents point and supported by an application to admit
further evidence on appeal in relation to that point was only issued on 1 November 1988.
The further evidence sought to be introduced is an affidavit sworn on 30 April 1987, but    *f*
it is an affidavit which was not supplied to the other side before November 1988.

In support of the application to resuscitate the documents point it is said that the
advice given by counsel which led to the abandonment of the point was founded on a
misunderstanding, namely that the documents sought to be introduced were documents
to be produced by the Inland Revenue, whereas in truth they were copies in the
applicant's possession of documents on the files of the Inland Revenue. There is no
evidence of any misunderstanding by counsel and I am wholly unpersuaded that counsel   *g*
did not fully appreciate the correct position. That appears from the papers then before
the court. Whether the copies to be used were already in the possession of the applicant,
or had to be produced by the Inland Revenue, was irrelevant to the issue whether they
should be admitted, which turned on quite other considerations, namely questions of
confidentiality and questions of relevance of the documents to the issues before the     *h*
board, whatever the source of the documents. It is also said that as the board was prepared
to meet the point in the Divisional Court in April 1987 it is no hardship if it has to meet
it in this court now. My view is emphatically that, as a matter of the discretion of this
court in the circumstances of these proceedings and this case, it would be wholly wrong
to allow the applicant to resuscitate a point deliberately abandoned on the advice of
counsel in the court below; a fortiori it would be wrong to admit further evidence on     *j*
that point.

Accordingly I proceed to consider the substantive appeal. There the applicant has two
points to deal with: firstly and foremostly that the court below decided the case as a
matter of discretion; and secondly the reasons point, as it has been called, namely that
there were no adequate reasons given for the decision of the board. The written decision

is a carefully prepared document. It sets out that there had been the written submissions
a presented to the board, the notification of appeal with supporting documents, the
applicant's main statement of appeal with supporting documents, the department's
statement with supporting documents, and further comments from the applicant with
supporting documents received shortly before the hearing. The decision then sets out
over several pages in numbered paragraphs the contentions on behalf of the applicant by
a representative of his union, and sets out again in detail in subsequent paragraphs the
b arguments put forward for the employing department justifying the dismissal and
dealing with the applicant's contentions.

The conclusion at the end of the report in the final paragraph is put shortly thus:

> 'Having considered very carefully the written statements and the oral submissions
> made at the hearing the Board conclude that the Department's decision to terminate
> [the applicant's] appointment was fair.'
c

It has apparently been the practice of the board to refrain from giving reasons for its
conclusions, but to set out as carefully as it can what the issues were and the course of the
proceedings. So far as this court is concerned the law on the giving of reasons by a
tribunal is conveniently set out in *R v Immigration Appeal Tribunal, ex p Khan (Mahmud)*
[1983] 2 All ER 420, [1983] QB 790. The judgment of the court was given by Lord Lane
d CJ and Ackner and Oliver LJJ agreed. Lord Lane CJ set out certain views expressed by
Donaldson P as president of the National Industrial Relations Court in *Alexander
Machinery (Dudley) Ltd v Crabtree* [1974] ICR 120 (see [1983] 2 All ER 420 at 422, [1983]
QB 790 at 793). Donaldson P stressed that the basis of the proposition that reasons should
be given is that in the absence of reasons it is impossible to determine whether or not
there has been an error of law. Donaldson P had then gone on to say in the *Alexander
e Machinery* case (see [1983] 2 All ER 420 at 422, [1983] QB 790 at 793): 'Failure to give
reasons therefore amounts to a denial of justice and is itself an error of law.' Lord Lane
CJ said ([1983] 2 All ER 420 at 423, [1983] QB 790 at 794):

> 'Speaking for myself, I would not go so far as to indorse the proposition set forth
> by Donaldson P that any failure to give reasons means a denial of justice and is itself
f > an error of law. The important matter which must be borne in mind by tribunals
> in the present type of circumstances is that it must be apparent from what they state
> by way of reasons first of all that they have considered the point which is at issue
> between the parties, and they should indicate the evidence on which they have come
> to their conclusions. Where one gets a decision of a tribunal which either fails to set
> out the issue which the tribunal is determining either directly or by inference, or
g > fails either directly or by inference to set out the basis on which it has reached its
> determination on that issue, then that is a matter which will be very closely regarded
> by this court, and in normal circumstances will result in the decision of the tribunal
> being quashed. The reason is this. A party appearing before a tribunal is entitled to
> know, either expressly stated by it or inferentially stated, what it is to which the
> tribunal is addressing its mind. In some cases it may be perfectly obvious without
h > any express reference to it by the tribunal; in other cases it may not. Second, the
> appellant is entitled to know the basis of fact on which the conclusion has been
> reached. Once again in many cases it may be quite obvious without the necessity of
> expressly stating it, in other cases it may not.'

In the present case the board has set out the issues and contentions to which it was
j addressing itself, and its conclusion in the paragraph that I have quoted must essentially
be an acceptance in whole or in part of the contentions for the Inland Revenue. Therefore
the question which the Divisional Court had to decide, if it was going to grant judicial
review and a quashing of the decision of the board, was whether the reasons given, if
indeed it is accepted that reasons ought to be given, were sufficient as an acceptance of
the whole of the contentions of the Inland Revenue, or whether it should have indicated

precisely which contentions it accepted, if it did not accept all, and to some extent why it accepted them. But it is accepted that there is no obligation to go into lengthy reasoning, examining all points in detail, or anything of that sort. Then the Divisional Court would also have had to consider whether, in so far as the reasons given were insufficient, that had the effect of producing an error of law or a miscarriage of justice which would warrant the quashing of the decision and a rehearing before the board. That is the background to the exercise by the Divisional Court of its discretion by way of refusing judicial review.

At the end of his judgment May LJ dealt with the crucial question of discretion as follows ([1988] 3 All ER 686 at 696–697):

'Even if the failure of the board in the instant case to give any reasons for its decision did mean that in law that decision was open to challenge by way of judicial review I have no doubt whatever that it would be a wholly wrong exercise of this court's discretion to grant the present applicant any relief. Simultaneously with his application to us he has not only started proceedings before an industrial tribunal, but also, as he alleges, he has compromised those proceedings with the board itself and has then started and continued to prosecute civil proceedings in the High Court based on that alleged compromise. In my opinion the right course for us to take is to leave the applicant to the other remedies which he seeks in those other proceedings.'

Roch J concurred in that and said ([1988] 3 All ER 686 at 697):

'Let me say at once that I agree with May LJ, that the answer to the second question in the present case is that the applicant's claim to relief should not proceed by way of judicial review; that the discretion which the court has in deciding to grant or withhold relief by way of judicial review should in this case be exercised against the granting of relief, because the applicant has a sufficient opportunity for redress, if indeed he has been wronged, in the proceedings which he has started before the industrial tribunal, or, if those proceedings have been compromised, as the applicant now contends, in the High Court action which the applicant has commenced to enforce the alleged settlement.'

Counsel for the applicant has taken us to leading textbooks, Wade *Administrative Law* (6th edn, 1988) and *de Smith's Judicial Review of Administrative Action* (4th edn, 1980), to stress the difference between a procedure for judicial review and an appellate procedure, and he has submitted that there is certainly no rule that other remedies must be fully exhausted before any application is made for judicial review; if, for instance, it is obvious that a decision reached by an administrative tribunal was reached in flagrant breach of natural justice, then it would be appropriate to quash that decision by way of judicial review without waiting for appeal procedures to be first exhausted. Even before the Divisional Court, the question was not as straightforward as that.

The question before us, however, is, as it seems to me, very different, namely a question of the discretion of the Divisional Court. It is its discretion which the court was exercising in refusing to grant what is essentially discretionary relief. It is not a question whether we, had we been sitting in the Divisional Court, would have taken the same view. It has to be shown that on a matter which was decided entirely as one of discretion the Divisional Court reached a conclusion which was plainly wrong. In my judgment counsel for the applicant falls a very long way short of that. This was a decision which the Divisional Court was in all the circumstances of this case fully entitled to take. I do not seek to express any view on any general proposition that judicial review should not be granted if there is an alternative remedy before an industrial tribunal. It is only necessary to consider this particular case in the light of the nature of the complaint that was made in the judicial review proceedings which I have indicated, and of the variety of other claims which the applicant has launched.

There is one point I would add, however. It was urged by counsel for the applicant
a  that the applicant's aim was to be reinstated in the Civil Service either in his previous
department or in some other position. I can well see that he would wish indeed to be
reinstated in work. But though the board could, if there were a quashing of the decision
and a rehearing, recommend reinstatement if it thought that appropriate, or recommend
some other solution, its recommendation would not be binding on the Inland Revenue,
let alone on other Civil Service departments. The only decision of the board on an appeal
b  to it which would be binding is as to the amount of compensation to which the applicant
would be entitled in the view of the board if his dismissal had been unfair. It is pointed
out that even on that there is a difference between the remedy of the applicant before the
board and his remedy before an industrial tribunal in that there is a limit to the amount
that the industrial tribunal can award, whereas there is no prescribed limit to the amount
that the board could award. Even so, however, I am not persuaded that there is any basis
c  at all for saying that the Divisional Court erred in the exercise of its discretion, and
accordingly on the ground of discretion, as stated in the passages I have read from the
judgments of May LJ and Roch J, I would dismiss this appeal.
    I would add, however, that I support the view of Roch J expressed in the final
paragraph of his judgment where he said ([1988] 3 All ER 686 at 702):

d      'The addition of one or two equally short paragraphs stating in outline the reasons
       which must have existed for that conclusion [ie the conclusion of the board at the
       end of its judgment] would ask little of the board, would give a greater sense of
       fairness and, if the reasoning is stated shortly and factually, would avoid the creation
       of a body of precedent, which, I would agree with Mr Forman [the chairman of the
       board], is a result devoutly to be wished.'

e      However, this court does not find it necessary to decide the reasons point. The decision
of the Divisional Court is affirmed as a decision made in exercise of its discretion in the
circumstances of the case.
    The appeal is dismissed.


f  **TAYLOR LJ.** I agree.
    Counsel for the applicant has emphasised the distinction between appeal and review.
He submits that where a grievance relates to the substance or merits of the case it is
appropriate for the aggrieved party to use whatever appeal procedures are available to it,
rather than seeking judicial review. Where, however, what is at issue is the legality or
fairness of the process leading to the impugned decision judicial review should not be
g  refused simply because an avenue of appeal is open to the applicant. Here counsel for the
applicant submits that the question whether the Civil Service Appeal Board ought to give
reasons is not one concerning the merits of the applicant's case, but is appropriate to the
judicial review procedure whereby the court exercises a supervisory jurisdiction over the
proceedings of inferior tribunals, their legality and fairness.
    I recognise that the distinction drawn by counsel for the applicant is a valid one, and
h  that in a proper case an application for judicial review should be entertained
notwithstanding the existence of other remedies by way of appeal. In the present case
had the applicant come straight and solely for judicial review I, for my part, would have
felt much force in his argument that if other issues were decided in his favour he should
not fail merely on discretion. But he did not adopt that course. He also brought
j  proceedings in the industrial tribunal for unfair dismissal. Furthermore there is no
question of those proceedings having been stayed or hanging fire. He claims they were
concluded by way of compromise and indeed he has launched a High Court action by
writ to enforce the terms of the alleged compromise, adding, by leave, a claim for
wrongful dismissal. In those circumstances both members of the Divisional Court
considered that its discretion should be exercised against granting a remedy by way of

judicial review and that the applicant should be left to such remedies as he seeks in his High Court action.

For this court to take a different view would require it to be shown that that exercise of discretion was so plainly wrong that the court should interfere. In my view that is not shown. Indeed I consider that on the particular facts of this case it was plainly right.

I would support the view expressed by Roch J in the Divisional Court and indorsed by Dillon LJ in his judgment that, whatever might be the legal requirements of the board, as a matter of policy and discretion it would be appropriate for short reasons to be given in the terms suggested by Roch J.

I too would dismiss this appeal.

**SIR JOHN MEGAW.** I agree that this appeal should be dismissed. I agree with the reasons given by Dillon and Taylor LJJ. I would only add one sentence. I am unable myself to see that the requirements of natural justice have been infringed in any relevant respect.

*Appeal dismissed. No order for costs.*

Solicitors: *Sharpe Pritchard*, agents for *Whitehead Monckton & Co*, Maidstone (for the applicant); *Treasury Solicitor*.

Raina Levy    Barrister.


# James v Eastleigh Borough Council

COURT OF APPEAL, CIVIL DIVISION

SIR NICOLAS BROWNE-WILKINSON V-C, PARKER AND NOURSE LJJ

13, 14 FEBRUARY, 26 APRIL 1989

*Sex discrimination – Provision of goods, facilities or services – Entry to swimming pool – Pensioners admitted free to pool – Plaintiff and his wife both aged 61 – Wife admitted free because she had reached pensionable age for women of 60 – Plaintiff required to pay because he had not reached pensionable age for men of 65 – Whether plaintiff unlawfully discriminated against on grounds of sex – Sex Discrimination Act 1975, ss 1(1)(a), 29.*

The plaintiff and his wife, who were both aged 61, visited a swimming pool run by the defendant council, which had adopted a policy of providing free swimming facilities for persons who had reached the age for a state retirement pension. In accordance with that policy the plaintiff was charged 75p because he had not reached the pensionable age for men of 65, while his wife was admitted free because she had reached the pensionable age for women of 60. The plaintiff brought an action in the county court against the council claiming that it had unlawfully discriminated against him on the grounds of sex, contrary to s 29[a] of the Sex Discrimination Act 1975, because the refusal to provide him with free swimming while providing it for his wife amounted to less favourable treatment and therefore discrimination within s 1(1)(a)[b] of that Act. The judge dismissed the claim and the plaintiff appealed.

---

a    Section 29, so far as material, is set out at p 917 c d, post
b    Section 1(1) is set out at p 917 a b, post

**Held** – For the purposes of determining whether a defendant's treatment of a plaintiff
*a* amounted to discrimination within s 1(1)(*a*) of the 1975 Act what was relevant was
whether, subjectively, the defendant had treated the plaintiff less favourably because of
his or her sex and not whether there was a causative link between the less favourable
treatment received by the plaintiff and the defendant's behaviour. Accordingly, where
the defendant's reason for affording less favourable treatment to the plaintiff was neither
overtly nor covertly related to the plaintiff's sex it could not be said that the defendant
*b* had acted 'on the grounds of . . . sex' for the purposes of s 1(1)(*a*) even though his action
resulted in a disparate impact as between men and women. Since the council had not
intended to discriminate between men and women in the provision of free swimming
but had intended to provide free swimming to pensioners it had not been guilty of
unlawful discrimination merely because the difference in pensionable age between men
and women resulted in the plaintiff and his wife being treated differently when they
*c* visited the council's swimming pool. The plaintiff's appeal would accordingly be
dismissed (see p 918 *h j*, p 919 *b c* and p 920 *b f g*, post).

Dictum of Woolf J in *R v Commission for Racial Equality, ex p Westminster City Council*
[1984] ICR 770 at 776–777 applied.

*Equal Opportunities Commission v Birmingham City Council* [1989] 1 All ER 769 considered.

*d*
**Notes**
For sex discrimination generally, see 16 Halsbury's Laws (4th edn) para 771:2.

For the Sex Discrimination Act 1975, ss 1, 29, see 6 Halsbury's Statutes (4th edn) 699,
719.

*e* **Cases referred to in judgments**
*Equal Opportunities Commission v Birmingham City Council* [1989] 1 All ER 769, [1989] 2
    WLR 520, HL.
*Hampson v Dept of Education and Science* [1989] ICR 179, CA.
*Owen & Briggs v James* [1982] ICR 618, CA.
*R v Commission for Racial Equality, ex p Westminster City Council* [1984] ICR 770; *affd in*
*f*    *part* [1985] ICR 827, CA.
*Showboat Entertainment Centre Ltd v Owens* [1984] 1 All ER 836, [1984] 1 WLR 384, EAT.

**Cases also cited**
*Amin v Entry Clearance Officer, Bombay* [1983] 2 All ER 864, [1983] 2 AC 818, HL.
*g* *Charter v Race Relations Board* [1973] 1 All ER 512, [1973] AC 868, HL.
*Dockers' Labour Club and Institute Ltd v Race Relations Board* [1974] 3 All ER 592, [1976]
    AC 285, HL.
*Duke v GEC Reliance Ltd* [1988] 1 All ER 626, [1988] AC 618, HL.
*Garland v British Rail Engineering Ltd* [1979] 2 All ER 1163, [1979] 1 WLR 754, CA; *rvsd*
    [1982] 2 All ER 402, [1983] 2 AC 751, CJEC and HL.
*h* *Grieg v Community Industry* [1979] ICR 356, EAT.
*Horsey v Dyfed CC* [1982] ICR 755, EAT.
*Kassam v Immigration Appeal Tribunal* [1980] 2 All ER 330, [1980] 1 WLR 1037, CA.
*Kidd v DRG (UK) Ltd* [1985] ICR 405, EAT.
*i* *Marshall v Southampton and South West Hampshire Area Health Authority (Teaching)* Case
    152/84 [1986] 2 All ER 584, [1986] QB 401, CJEC.
*j* *Ministry of Defence v Jeremiah* [1979] 3 All ER 833, [1980] QB 87, CA.
*Ojutiku v Manpower Services Commission* [1982] ICR 661, CA.
*Perera v Civil Service Commission (No 2)* [1983] ICR 428, CA.
*Roberts v Tate & Lyle Food and Distribution Ltd* [1983] ICR 521, EAT.
*Roberts v Tate & Lyle Industries Ltd* Case 151/84 [1986] 2 All ER 602, CJEC.
*Seide v Gillette Industries Ltd* [1980] IRLR 427, EAT.

**Appeal**

The plaintiff, Peter James, appealed with leave of the judge against the decision of his      *a*
Honour Judge Tucker QC sitting in the Southampton County Court on 28 October 1987,
whereby he dismissed Mr James's claim that the Eastleigh Borough Council had
discriminated against him contrary to s 29 of the Sex Discrimination Act 1975. The facts
are set out in the judgment of Sir Nicolas Browne-Wilkinson V-C.

*Anthony Lester QC* and *Michael Kent* for Mr James.      *b*
*Peter J H Towler* for the council.

*Cur adv vult*

26 April. The following judgments were delivered.

      *c*
**SIR NICOLAS BROWNE-WILKINSON V-C.** In November 1985 the plaintiff, Mr
Peter James, and his wife went to the Fleming Park Leisure Centre swimming pool in
the borough of Eastleigh. Both were aged 61 years. Mr James had retired from his
employment some years before. Mrs James was admitted free of charge; Mr James had
to pay an admission fee of 75p. This was because the council had adopted a policy under
which free swimming was allowed 'for children under three years of age and persons      *d*
who have reached the state pension age'. Pensionable age is the age at which a person can
first be paid a state pension. By virtue of s 27(1) of and Sch 22 to the Social Security Act
1975, pensionable age is 65 for men and 60 for women. It was for this reason that Mr
James was required to pay whereas his wife of the same age was not required to pay.

The swimming facilities were provided by the council under s 19 of the Local
Government (Miscellaneous Provisions) Act 1976, sub-s (2) of which permits differential      *e*
rates to be charged for facilities provided by the council.

Mr James, supported by the Equal Opportunities Commission, started these proceedings
against the council. He claimed a declaration that under the Sex Discrimination Act 1975
it was unlawful to discriminate against men who have attained the age of 60 by refusing
to provide them with a concession of free swimming at the Fleming Park Leisure Centre
and damages limited to £300. The claim was dismissed by his Honour Judge Tucker      *f*
QC. Mr James appeals to this court.

It may be thought that the sum of 75p does not warrant such lengthy and expensive
litigation. But the Equal Opportunities Commission take the view that the widespread
practice of providing facilities either free or at concessionary rates to those who have
reached state pension age is discriminatory and unlawful. They have therefore pursued
this as a test case.      *g*

As the facts of this case demonstrate, there is no doubt that the council's policy has a
discriminatory impact as between men and women who are over the age of 60 but under
the age of 65. Women of that age enjoy the concession; men of the same age do not. But
not all conduct having a discriminatory effect is unlawful; discriminatory behaviour has
to fall within the statutory definition of discrimination and to have occurred in a context      *h*
(eg in relation to employment or the provision of facilities) in which the Sex
Discrimination Act 1975 renders such discrimination unlawful.

The 1975 Act is drafted on the basis that sex discrimination will operate as against
women not against men. Section 2 of the 1975 Act provides, so far as relevant for present
purposes, that its provisions are to be read as applying equally to the treatment of men. I
will therefore quote the provisions of the Act, after making the necessary modifications,      *j*
as they apply to discrimination against men.

Section 1(1) of the 1975 Act defines discrimination to which the Act applies.
Discrimination is of two kinds, normally referred to as direct discrimination (dealt with
by sub-s (1)(*a*)) and indirect discrimination (dealt with by sub-s (1)(*b*)). Section 1(1) reads
as follows:

a   'A person discriminates against a [man] in any circumstances relevant for the
purposes of any provision of this Act if—(*a*) on the grounds of [his] sex he treats
[him] less favourably than he treats or would treat a [woman], or (*b*) he applies to
[him] a requirement or condition which he applies or would apply equally to a
[woman] but— (i) which is such that the proportion of [men] who can comply with
it is considerably smaller than the proportion of [women] who can comply with it,
and (ii) which he cannot show to be justifiable irrespective of the sex of the person
b   to whom it is applied, and (iii) which is to his detriment because [he] cannot comply
with it.'

Part II of the 1975 Act deals with discrimination in the employment and related fields;
Pt III (which includes s 29) deals with discrimination in other fields. Section 29(1)(*b*)
provides:

c   "It is unlawful for any person concerned with the provision (for payment or not)
of goods, facilities or services to the public or a section of the public to discriminate
against a [man] who seeks to obtain or use those goods, facilities or services . . . (*b*) by
refusing or deliberately omitting to provide [him] with goods, facilities or services
of the like quality, in the like manner and on the like terms as are normal in [her]
case in relation to [female] members of the public or (where [he] belongs to a section
d   of the public) to [female] members of that section.'

Applying s 29 to the facts of this case, Mr James says that the council, which is
concerned with the provision of a facility (ie swimming) to the public has discriminated
against him in refusing to provide him (being a person over 60 but under the age of 65)
with the facility on the like terms as are normal in relation to female members of the
e   public of that age (ie free).
In the court below it was common ground that the council's policy was discriminatory
within the meaning of s 1 of the 1975 Act. There was no consideration of the question
whether such discrimination was direct or indirect, a fundamental point to which I will
have to return. Both below and in this court the council accepts that there was no
statutory defence to this claim if it properly fell within s 29; in particular, the council
f   accepts that the various exemptions from the Act affecting provisions in relation to death
or retirement do not apply to this case since there is no such exception affecting s 29 of
the Act.
The council's principal defence below was that the case does not fall within s 29. The
council was providing the facility to 'a section of the public' to which Mr James belongs,
ie those not of pensionable age; women in the same section of the public (ie women not
g   of pensionable age) are provided with the facility on exactly the same basis (ie at a charge
of 75p); therefore the charging policy is not unlawful. The judge accepted this argument.
I cannot agree for two reasons. First the point was not open on the pleadings. Paragraph
1 of the particulars of claim alleges that the council was providing swimming facilities to
the public. This was admitted by the defence, obviously correctly. Once it is accepted
that facilities were being provided for the public (as opposed to a section of the public)
h   any discriminatory failure to provide those facilities on the same basis to comparable
males and females on the same terms comes within the exact words of the section. The
discriminatory provision of facilities is unlawful if those facilities are provided *either* for
the public *or* for a section of the public. Mr James as a member of the public was
discriminated against; it is irrelevant whether, when treated as a member of a section of
the public, there was or was not discrimination.
j   Moreover, in my judgment it is not permissible for a defendant in such a case to seek
to define the section of the public to which it offers services in terms which are themselves
discriminatory in terms of gender. If this were not so it would be lawful, for example, to
provide free travel for men but not for women on the grounds that the facility of free
travel is only being provided for a section of the public comprising men. Whatever else

may be meant by a 'section of the public', in my judgment it cannot mean a class defined
by reference to sex or, under the Race Relations Act 1976, by reference to race: cf *Showboat*
*Entertainment Centre Ltd v Owens* [1984] 1 All ER 836 at 842, [1984] 1 WLR 384 at 391.

    Therefore in my judgment the judge was wrong to reject the claim on the grounds
that the discriminatory conduct did not fall within s 29. A new and much more
fundamental point arose during the course of the argument in this court. There is no
suggestion that the reason for the council adopting its policy was a desire to discriminate
against men. The council's reason for giving free swimming to those of pensionable age
was to give benefits to those whose resources would be likely to have been reduced by
retirement. The aim was to aid the needy, whether male or female, not to give preference
to one sex over the other. Moreover the condition which had to be satisfied in order to
qualify for free swimming did not refer expressly to sex at all. The condition was simply
that the applicant had to be of pensionable age. The undoubtedly discriminatory effect
of that condition only emerges when one gets to the next question, ie at what age do
men and women become pensionable? The question is whether the council's policy
amounts to direct discrimination 'on the ground of his sex' within s 1(1)(*a*) or indirect
discrimination within s 1(1)(*b*) by reason of the council having imposed a condition on
men and women alike with which a considerably smaller proportion of men than
women can comply.

    The point is potentially of great importance since it affects the legality of many
concessions which are given to those of pensionable age or in receipt of pensions. If such
concessions amount to direct discrimination, such discrimination cannot be justified;
any discrimination on the ground of sex is unlawful if it falls within Pts II and III of the
1975 Act. But if such concessions are only indirectly discriminatory within s 1(1)(*b*) the
defendant is given an opportunity to show that the imposition of the condition is
'justifiable' irrespective of sex. Thus in the present case the council might be able to show
that the only reasonable way of giving benefits to senior citizens is by reference to
pensionable age and argue that the discriminatory impact of such a condition is justifiable.
The Equal Opportunities Commission, through counsel, say that that is not so and that
many organisations now operate concessionary arrangements for the elderly which do
not have a sexually discriminatory impact. There is therefore a real issue whether such a
condition is justifiable. But if, as the Equal Opportunities Commission contend, the
giving of such concessions by reference to pensionable age amounts to direct
discrimination, the question of justifiability will never arise.

    Counsel for Mr James forcefully submitted that there is direct discrimination in this
case. He submitted that discrimination is 'on the ground of' sex within s 1(1)(*a*) if the sex
of the plaintiff is a substantial cause of the less favourable treatment. In this context, he
says, the correct question is: what would the position have been but for the sex of the
plaintiff? If the position would be different if the plaintiff's sex were different, that is
direct discrimination.

    I do not accept that construction of s 1. In my judgment s 1(1)(*a*) is looking to the case
where, subjectively, the defendant has treated the plaintiff less favourably because of his
or her sex. What is relevant is the defendant's reason for doing an act, not the causative
effect of the act done by the defendant. As counsel for the council pointed out, s 1(1) is
referring throughout to the activities of the alleged discriminator. In the case of direct
discrimination 'a person discriminates against a man . . . if on the ground of his sex he
treats him less favourably . . .' Those words indicate that one is looking, not to the
causative link between the defendant's behaviour and the detriment to the plaintiff, but
to the reason why the defendant treated the plaintiff less favourably. The relevant
question is 'Did the defendant act on the ground of sex?' not 'Did the less favourable
treatment result from the defendant's actions?' Thus, if the overt basis for affording less
favourable treatment was sex (eg an employer saying 'no women employees') that is
direct discrimination. If the overt reason does not in terms relate to sex (eg in selection
for redundancy, part-time employees are the first to go) that is not on the face of it direct

discrimination since sex does not come into the overt reason given for the action. If, but
a  only if, it is shown that the overt reason is not the true reason but there is a covert reason
why the employer adopted those criteria (eg to get rid of his female employees) will it be
direct discrimination. In such a case the true reason for the policy is the desire to treat
women less favourably than men; the employer is therefore acting on that ground.

But, in a case where neither the overt condition imposed nor any covert reason relates
directly to the sex of the plaintiff, in my judgment it cannot be said that the defendant
b  afforded less favourable treatment 'on the ground' of sex. He acted not on the ground of
sex but on other grounds. The result of his acting on grounds other than sex may produce
a disparate impact on men and women; if so, his actions may constitute unlawful indirect
discrimination. He has not acted on the ground of the plaintiff's sex, since that was not
his reason for adopting the policy he has adopted.

Counsel for Mr James submitted that the view I have expressed is tantamount to
c  holding that an intention to discriminate is necessary in order for there to be direct
discrimination, a view which is shown to be wrong by the decision of the House of Lords
in *Equal Opportunities Commission v Birmingham City Council* [1989] 1 All ER 769, [1989] 2
WLR 520. In that case the council provided substantially fewer places for girls than boys
in single sex secondary schools. The council had no intention or desire to discriminate
against girls but the discrimination was overtly on the grounds of sex. That case
d  demonstrates that, if a requirement or condition is imposed which overtly applies sexual
criteria to the availability of some benefit, that is direct discrimination on the grounds of
sex even though the defendant has no desire to prefer one sex over the other. Having
expressly adopted such overtly sex-based criteria, the defendant cannot be heard to say
that he has not acted on the ground of sex: manifestly, sex is the ground of his actions
whatever his intentions. The grounds for my decision in this case are the reasons I am
e  seeking to give, not my intention or desire to administer the law correctly.

That is not to say that intentions or motive are irrelevant for the purpose of discovering
the defendant's reason for behaving as he has. In a case where the defendant has not
applied expressly sex-based criteria but it is shown that his true reason was based on the
sex of the plaintiff, he may well have had an intention to discriminate on the ground of
sex; indeed it is hard to think of a case in which such intention will not be present. But
f  even in the case of such overt discrimination, the legally determinant matter is the true
reason for the defendant's behaviour, not his intention or motive in so behaving. In my
judgment there is a clear distinction between the ground or reason for which a person
acts and his intention in so acting.

There is a further objection to counsel's construction of the section. If there is direct
discrimination in every case where there is a substantial causative link between the
g  defendant's treatment and the detriment suffered by the plaintiff as a result of his sex I
can see no room for the operation of sub-s (1)(b). In every case in which a sexually neutral
condition in fact operates differentially and detrimentally to one sex as opposed to the
other, the imposition of such a condition would be a substantial cause of detriment to
the plaintiff by reason of his or her sex, ie it would fall within counsel's causation test and
therefore constitute direct discrimination under sub-s (1)(a). This plainly was not the
h  intention of Parliament, which was drawing a clear distinction between, on the one
hand, those cases where the defendant expressly or covertly acts by reference to the sex
of the plaintiff and, on the other, those cases where the defendant acted on grounds not
expressly or covertly related to sex but his actions have caused a disparate impact as
between the sexes.

j  I can see nothing in the authorities to which we were referred which is inconsistent
with the view I have expressed. In *Owen & Briggs v James* [1982] ICR 618 at 622 Cairns
LJ was plainly looking to the subjective reason why the respondent refused to appoint a
black applicant for a job; her colour 'was an important factor in his failure to consider
her application further'. See also per Stephenson LJ (at 620). This is to look at the reason
why something was done not the causative effect of what had been done.

In *R v Commission for Racial Equality, ex p Westminster City Council* [1984] ICR 770, it was held that there was direct discrimination within s 1(1)(*a*) if the substantial or effective, though not necessarily the sole or intended, reason was the person's race. Woolf J treated the relevant question as being whether what was done was 'because' of the colour of the applicant (at 776–777). He treated intention as being relevant, though not an essential requirement, in determining 'why an action was taken'. Therefore again he was looking to the reason why some action was taken by the defendant and not to the effect of such action on the plaintiff.

Accordingly, in my judgment Mr James cannot succeed on a claim based on direct discrimination. He might have succeeded on a claim pleaded and based on indirect discrimination within s 1(1)(*b*). This would have required him to plead and prove that the proportion of men who can show they are of pensionable age is considerably smaller than the proportion of women who are and also that as a result he has suffered a detriment. No such case was pleaded or made in the court below. It was suggested that we should remit the case to be reheard on the right basis. However in my judgment that is not the correct course. Mr James has failed to plead the case in the only way it could succeed and justice does not require him to be given leave to amend at this late stage. If Mr James and the Equal Opportunities Commission wish to pursue the point of principle, there is no reason why Mr James should not again seek to gain free entry to the swimming pool and, if refused, to start fresh proceedings on the right basis.

We were asked to give general guidance as to the principles which would be applicable on any remitted or future case based on indirect discrimination. I do not think it is desirable to give such guidance since, as it seems to me, the essential question will be whether the council has justified its policy within the meaning of s 1(1)(*b*)(ii). Statistical evidence that nationally a larger proportion of women than men are of pensionable age would, in the absence of evidence to the contrary, lead to the inevitable conclusion that such is the position in Eastleigh. The payment of the 75p entry fee is a detriment. Therefore, the crucial question will be whether the council can show that the differential impact of its policy is justifiable. As that is a question of fact to be determined on evidence not before us and in accordance with the principles recently stated by this court in *Hampson v Dept of Education and Science* [1989] ICR 179, it is undesirable for this court to express any views on it.

**PARKER LJ.** I agree.

**NOURSE LJ.** I also agree.

*Appeal dismissed. No order for costs. Leave to appeal to the House of Lords refused.*

Solicitors: *Ewing Hickman & Clark*, Southampton (for Mr James); *N R Smith*, Eastleigh (for the council).

Celia Fox    Barrister.

a     # Lanford v General Medical Council

PRIVY COUNCIL
LORD BRIDGE OF HARWICH, LORD BRANDON OF OAKBROOK AND LORD LOWRY
18 MAY, 26 JUNE 1989

b     *Medical practitioner – Professional misconduct – Using obscene and indecent language and behaving improperly to two female patients – Corroboration – Admissibility of similar fact evidence – Similar obscene language used to both patients – No striking similarity in what was done to patients – Whether evidence of what was said to one patient capable of corroborating evidence of indecency by other patient.*

c     *Medical practitioner – Professional misconduct – Charge of serious professional misconduct – Misconduct in course of medical examination of two female patients – Charge founded on complaints of both patients – Whether complaints on which charge founded ought to have been heard separately.*

d     The appellant, a registered medical practitioner, was charged by the Professional Conduct Committee of the General Medical Council with using obscene and indecent language and behaving improperly to two female patients in the course of professional consultations and examinations. The incidents were said to have taken place about six days apart. In one case the appellant allegedly used obscene language and indecently assaulted the patient when conducting an internal inspection to check the position of a coil. In the other case the appellant allegedly used obscene language and behaved improperly towards the patient when she consulted him about an infected toe. The language and acts

e     complained of had no relevance to the medical examination itself. There was a striking similarity in what the appellant allegedly said to both patients but not in what he did to them. The legal assessor directed the committee on corroboration by stating that the evidence of each patient was capable of amounting to corroboration of the other's account if they gave independent evidence of separate incidents involving the appellant, the circumstances were such as to exclude any danger of a jointly fabricated account and

f     there was such a striking similarity or similarities in each account as to be probative. The committee found the appellant guilty of serious professional misconduct and ordered that his name be erased from the register. The appellant appealed to the Privy Council, contending (1) that the legal assessor had misdirected the committee on the question of corroboration since he should have warned them against treating one incident as corroboration of the other because the admitted similarity in what the appellant allegedly

g     said to each patient could not properly be relied on by the prosecution where there was no striking similarity in what he allegedly did to them and (2) that the complaints on which the charge was based ought to have been heard separately.

**Held** – (1) Similar fact evidence was admissible if its similarities were either unique, in

h     which event its probative value would approach that of a fingerprint, or striking, when the probative value would vary depending on how striking the similarity was. Since the evidence of what the appellant said before and after his examination of the patients tended, if believed, to prove that the relevant physical contact when examining them was indecent and improper the evidence of what he allegedly said in one case was capable of corroborating the evidence of indecency in the other, provided a striking similarity

j     was found between the two cases (see p 927 *h* to p 928 *a*, post); *Boardman v DPP* [1974] 3 All ER 887 applied.
      (2) Since there was a striking similarity between the two complaints it was eminently proper and in the interests of justice for the two complaints to be heard together. It followed therefore that the appeal would be dismissed (see p 928 *b c*, post).

Per curiam. (1) The onus and standard of proof in disciplinary proceedings before the Professional Conduct Committee of the General Medical Council and the relevant legal *a* principles are those applicable to a criminal trial (see p 925 *e*, post).

(2) Where a charge of professional misconduct is founded on two or more separate incidents, those incidents should each be made the subject of a separate charge of professional misconduct instead of being listed as particulars of one offence of professional misconduct. Such a practice should be followed even when the prosecutor intends to have the charges heard together, as he may properly do in many cases (see p 928 *d e*, *b* post).

## Notes

For serious professional misconduct by a medical practitioner, see 30 Halsbury's Laws (4th edn) paras 123, 125, and for cases on the subject, see 33 Digest (Reissue) 294–297, 2360–2368.                                                                                                *c*

For the admissibility of evidence of similar offences and acts of the accused, see 11 Halsbury's Laws (4th edn) paras 375–381, and for cases on the subject, see 14(2) Digest (Reissue) 509–521, 4167–4248.

## Cases referred to in judgment

*Boardman v DPP* [1974] 3 All ER 887, [1975] AC 421, [1974] 3 WLR 673, HL.       *d*
*DPP v Kilbourne* [1973] 1 All ER 440, [1973] AC 729, [1973] 2 WLR 254, HL.
*Harris v DPP* [1952] 1 All ER 1044, [1952] AC 694, HL.
*Makin v A-G for New South Wales* [1894] AC 57, [1891–4] All ER Rep 24, PC.
*Moorov v HM Advocate* 1930 JC 68, HC of Just.
*R v Ball* [1911] AC 47, HL.
*R v Sims* [1946] 1 All ER 697, [1946] 1 KB 531, CCA.                                  *e*
*R v Smith* (1915) 84 LJKB 2153, 11 Cr App R 229, [1914–15] All ER Rep 262, CCA.
*R v Straffen* [1952] 2 All ER 657, [1952] 2 QB 911, CCA.

## Appeal

Dr Elliott Hugh Lanford appealed against the determination of the Professional Conduct *f* Committee of the General Medical Council of 7 December 1988 that by reason of serious professional misconduct his name should be erased from the Register of Medical Practitioners. The facts are set out in the judgment of the Board.

*Philip Cox QC* and *Roderick Adams* for the appellant.
*Robin Simpson QC* and *Rosalind Foster* for the committee.
                                                                                        *g*

26 June. The following judgment of the Board was delivered.

**LORD LOWRY.** This appeal by Dr Elliott Hugh Lanford arises from a hearing on 6 and 7 December 1988 before the Professional Conduct Committee of the General Medical Council (the committee) at which the appellant was charged in the following terms:      *h*

> 'That being registered under the Medical Act, (a) on 6 August 1987 in the course of a professional consultation with Mrs A at your surgery premises you (i) used obscene and indecent language and made improper remarks of a sexual nature to Mrs A and (ii) behaved improperly towards her; (b) on 12 August 1987 in the course of a professional consultation and examination of Mrs B at your surgery premises you (i) used obscene and indecent language and made improper remarks of a sexual *j* nature to Mrs B and (ii) behaved improperly towards her. And that in relation to the facts alleged you have been guilty of serious professional misconduct.'

The committee found that the facts alleged in the charge had been proved and that the appellant had been guilty of serious professional misconduct, and ordered that his name a be erased from the register of medical practitioners and that his registration be suspended forthwith in accordance with s 38 of the Medical Act 1983. Announcing the committee's decision, the chairman stated that they had determined that the facts alleged in the charge had been proved to their satisfaction.

Counsel for the appellant, who was not instructed at the original hearing, submitted to their Lordships (1) that the legal assessor had misdirected the committee on the question of corroboration and (2) that the complaints of Mrs A and Mrs B on which the
b charge of professional misconduct was based ought to have been heard separately. Both submissions involve some discussion of what may be called the similar facts rule of evidence. It is therefore necessary first to summarise the facts alleged (and found to have been proved) regarding each incident and to see what directions the legal assessor gave to the committee.

Mrs A, aged 24 and a patient of the appellant since she was 5, was fitted with a coil in
c 1985. She went to the hospital in 1987 with a vaginal infection and was referred to the appellant who prescribed in July for the infection. On 6 August 1987 she came back, as requested, for him to check the position of the coil. For this purpose she removed her underclothing so far as was necessary and lay on the doctor's couch. The appellant parted her legs saying 'This is the best position for a screw'. He then used a metal speculum to conduct an internal inspection. Having done this, he took a plastic glove out of a wrapper,
d described it as a french letter and blew it up. He said, 'I cannot get the fucking thing on' and put on another rubber glove. He then put his hand on Mrs A's vagina 'in the clitoris position', as she described it, and his hand moved up and down. Next he said, 'I am going to check your pussy' and put his hand into her vagina. He found that the coil was correctly in place and, having done so, said, according to Mrs A, 'And oh, what a lovely pussy it is.' According to Mrs A, the movement of the doctor's hand on her clitoris and
e the insertion of his hand into the vagina were two separate movements, the first being 'a deliberate, repetitive motion', as a member of the committee put it in a question to Mrs A. Mr A was waiting with his car outside. On reaching the car, Mrs A burst into tears and in answer to her husband's questions explained what had happened. They then drove to a police station and thence to a citizens' advice bureau.

f Mrs B, aged 28, had registered with the appellant in February 1987 and had consulted him a number of times. On 12 August 1987 she went to the appellant's surgery because she was having trouble with her left big toe which was 'weeping'. She explained her problem, took off her shoe (she was not wearing stockings or tights) and, as requested, lifted her foot to put it on the front of the swivel-chair of the appellant, who had turned to face her. He said, 'Don't put it on my balls, because you will hurt them.' He examined Mrs B's foot and she then took it away. Treatment was discussed (she had a year earlier
g been to a different doctor who had given her cicatrin powder) and this led to the mention of her registration with the appellant, who asked Mrs B what her name was and whether she was 'Miss' or 'Mrs'. She said, 'Miss, I am getting married in six weeks' and he replied, 'So you are going to get screwed, then.' When asked what her attitude to that comment was, Mrs B said, 'I wanted to leave the surgery . . . I just said, "What do you want me to
h do about my toe?"' After a further short discussion Mrs B let the appellant see her toe again, but 'I would not lift my foot up, so he leant forward'. He put one hand underneath her heel and his right hand was round her ankle and he then slid it up her skirt 'about halfway, between my knee and my thigh'. In cross-examination Mrs B refuted the suggestion that the appellant's hand was supporting her leg and said that it was 'more at the side because his hand travelled up the side of my leg'. At this point the appellant said,
j according to Mrs B, 'You have got nice feet, nice thighs and a nice pussy.' She pulled her skirt down, stood up, put her shoe on and walked out. She walked across the road to a telephone box 'feeling terrible'. A friend, Mrs S, saw Mrs B from the top of a bus, looking distressed, telephoned her that night to see what was wrong and was then told by Mrs B what had happened to her. The next day Mrs B telephoned 'the Family Practitioners or the Medical Council, I cannot remember which one first'.

When the evidence concluded and counsel had made their submissions, the legal _a_
assessor, at the request of the chairman, advised the committee. This is what he said:

'The committee should look for corroboration of the evidence of each complainant
in view of the nature of the allegations made by each. I should warn you that it is
dangerous to act on the evidence of this nature of allegation if it is uncorroborated,
but the committee can do so if, keeping that warning in mind, the committee is
sure in either case that the complainant was telling the truth. Corroboration consists _b_
of evidence which confirms in some material particular that the matters complained
of occurred and that it was Dr Lanford who said and did the things alleged.
Corroborative evidence must come from a source which is independent of the
complainant. Evidence of a complaint by a complainant shortly after the alleged
events is not capable of being corroboration, neither is it evidence of the facts
complained of. It is simply evidence which may show a consistency of conduct by a
complainant with the account given by her of her sworn evidence. The evidence _c_
given by Mr. A or Mrs. A's complaints and distress—in particular the distress—the
evidence given by Mr. A of the distress immediately after the alleged event and
whilst in the close vicinity of the doctor's surgery is capable of amounting to
corroboration, but little, if any weight, should in practice be attached to it if the
Committee finds that it was only part and parcel of the complaint which she was _d_
then making to Mr. A. The same principles apply to the evidence as to Mrs. B's
distress in that such evidence is capable of constituting corroboration in the same
circumstances. Greater weight could be attached to that evidence in her case, if the
Committee were to find that it was not part of the complaint being made to another
person, the evidence having come from the lady on the bus at a time some hours
before the complaint was made to her. The evidence of each complainant, Mrs. A _e_
and Mrs. B, is capable of amounting to corroboration of the other's account if they
give independent evidence of separate incidents involving the doctor and the
circumstances are such as to exclude any danger of a jointly fabricated account and
you find in each account such striking similarity or similarities as to be probative.
However, I should warn you that, as there are only two instances, you should
proceed with great caution before finding any evidence of a system and using one _f_
account to corroborate the other.'

Before coming to the matters in controversy, their Lordships note with satisfaction the
legal assessor's introductory direction on corroboration which is strictly in accordance
with the authorities. The same can be said of his treatment of the doctrine of recent
complaint and his approach to evidence of distress, including his caution with regard to
distress which is 'part and parcel of the complaint'. _g_

The sole criticism made by counsel for the appellant of the legal assessor's advice was
directed to the penultimate paragraph:

'The evidence of each complainant, Mrs. A and Mrs. B, is capable of amounting
to corroboration of the other's account if they give independent evidence of separate
incidents involving the doctor and the circumstances are such as to exclude any _h_
danger of a jointly fabricated account and you find in each account such striking
similarity or similarities as to be probative.'

Counsel acknowledged that, as the legal assessor had emphasised, it was important in
cases featuring similar fact evidence to exclude the possibility of joint fabrication and also
conceded that, as the prosecuting counsel had taken pains to establish in this case, there _j_
was no real risk of collusion here. But, while admitting that evidence which requires
corroboration can both provide and receive corroboration to and from other evidence
which requires corroboration (_DPP v Kilbourne_ [1973] 1 All ER 440, [1973] AC 729), he
argued that the committee should not have been allowed to treat one incident as

corroborating the other, on the ground that there was no striking similarity in what the
a appellant allegedly *did*, as distinct from what he *said*, in each case: the committee could
have been wrongly influenced to find corroboration in the absence of what he described
as the necessary similarity or unity between the alleged indecent acts. Therefore, he
contended, so far from dwelling on the possibility of finding 'in each account such
striking similarity or similarities as to be probative', the legal assessor should have warned
the committee against using one incident as corroboration of the other. Counsel's next
b point, as their Lordships can understand, was the logical consequence of that argument,
assuming it to be sound; that the complaints, instead of being dealt with together, ought
to have been heard separately by different committees because, unless there was a true
similar fact situation, to hear them together would be unfair to the appellant.

Alongside these main arguments had been a collateral submission that it was
incumbent on the legal assessor to specify the similarities on which the committee might
c possibly rely. As it appears to their Lordships, the similarities started with the not very
striking, yet linking, feature of an examination of two women patients within a short
time (six days), both examinations being preceded and accompanied by heartily obscene
and sexually suggestive language. What is additionally significant is the use of the words
'screw' and 'pussy', particularly when it is recalled that, in relation to Mrs B, these words
had no relevance to the medical examination itself. So striking, indeed, was the similarity
d of the appellant's utterances in this last-mentioned respect that, both at the hearing by
the committee and before their Lordships, the respective counsel then representing the
appellant were constrained to admit the existence of that striking similarity in express
terms.

Counsel for the appellant (rightly, as their Lordships consider) submitted that the onus
and standard of proof in these disciplinary proceedings and the relevant legal principles
e were those applicable to a criminal trial. And his main contention must be viewed in the
light of the rules which govern the use of similar fact evidence as corroboration. There is
no magic about this word. As was pointed out in *DPP v Kilbourne* [1973] 1 All ER 440 at
448, 463, 456, [1973] AC 729 at 741, 758, 750: '[it] means no more than evidence tending
to confirm other evidence', per Lord Hailsham LC; it is 'evidence which renders other
f evidence more probable', per Lord Simon; and, to quote from the speech of Lord Reid:

'There is nothing technical in the idea of corroboration. When in the ordinary
affairs of life one is doubtful whether or not to believe a particular statement one
naturally looks to see whether it fits in with other statements or circumstances
relating to the particular matter; the better it fits in, the more one is inclined to
believe it. The doubted statement is corroborated to a greater or lesser extent by the
g other statements or circumstances with which it fits in.'

Similar fact evidence has different uses, to establish identity by reference to a
distinguishing characteristic, or to rebut a defence of accident or coincidence as in *R v
Smith* (1915) 84 LJKB 2153, [1914–15] All ER Rep 262, or to add probative force to
evidence which directly tends to prove an offence or one of its ingredients (for example,
h indecent intent, as allegedly in this case). In *Boardman v DPP* [1974] 3 All ER 887 at 896,
[1975] AC 421 at 443 Lord Wilberforce said:

'This is simply a case where evidence of facts similar in character to those forming
the subject of the charge is sought to be given in support of the evidence on that
charge.'

j Under this heading similar fact evidence is a branch of corroboration evidence, but with
this special feature, that it has to pass a test (in the first place imposed by the judge and
ultimately by the jury, if there is one) of striking similarity before it can be admitted and
then accepted as such. Also in *Boardman's* case [1974] 3 All ER 887 at 897, [1975] AC 421
at 444 Lord Wilberforce said:

'The basic principle must be that the admission of similar fact evidence (of the kind now in question) is exceptional and requires a strong degree of probative force. *a* This probative force is derived, if at all, from the circumstance that the facts testified to by the several witnesses bear to each other such a striking similarity that they must, when judged by experience and common sense, either all be true, or have arisen from a cause common to the witnesses or from pure coincidence. The jury may, therefore, properly be asked to judge whether the right conclusion is that all are true, so that each story is supported by the other(s).'                                          *b*

In the same case Lord Morris said ([1974] 3 All ER 887 at 894–895, [1975] AC 421 at 441):

'It is always for a jury to decide what evidence to accept. If told that they may take one incident into consideration when deciding in regard to another it will be entirely for them to decide what parts of the evidence they accept *and how far they* *c* *are assisted by one conclusion in reaching another.* It will be for the judge in his discretion to rule whether the circumstances are such that evidence directed to one count becomes available and admissible as evidence when consideration is being given to another count.' (Our emphasis.)

As their Lordships have already noted, the argument advanced for the appellant was *d* that the admitted similarity in what he allegedly *said* to Mrs A and Mrs B respectively could not properly be relied on by the prosecution when there was no striking similarity in what he allegedly *did* to them. (For the purpose of considering this argument their Lordships will ignore, as they would have to do in an ordinary criminal case, the fact that what the appellant allegedly said could itself constitute serious professional misconduct, even if less serious than that actually found against him.) Their Lordships do not have *e* far to seek for a convincing refutation of the appellant's contention. In the famous case of *R v Smith*, as reported in 11 Cr App R 229 at 238; cf [1914–15] All ER Rep 262 at 264, referred to above Lord Reading CJ, delivering the judgment of the Court of Criminal Appeal, said:

'The second point taken is that even assuming that evidence of the death of the *f* other two women was admissible, the prosecution ought only to have been allowed to prove that the women were found dead in their baths. For the reasons already given in dealing with the first point, it is apparent that to cut short the evidence there would have been of no assistance to the case. In our opinion it was open to the prosecution to give, and the judge was right in admitting, evidence of the facts surrounding the deaths of the two women.'
                                                                                                           *g*
The surrounding facts, which did not relate to the manner in which the women met their deaths, included the fact that the accused had recently gone through a form of marriage with each of them in turn and the fact that he had insured their lives and stood to benefit by their deaths. Their Lordships have also noted in *Boardman v DPP* [1974] 3 All ER 887 at 895, 900, 904, 912, 914, [1975] AC 421 at 442, 447, 452, 461, 463 the careful attention paid, in the quest for corroborative evidence, by Lord Morris, Lord *h* Hailsham, Lord Cross and Lord Salmon to the similarity in the accused's conduct and statements when making the visits to the school dormitories which preceded and led to the offences which he later committed elsewhere. One may also refer in this connection to the facts of *Makin v A-G for New South Wales* [1894] AC 57, [1891–4] All ER Rep 24, the leading case on similar facts, and to the classic opinion of this Board delivered by Lord Herschell LC, where he said ([1894] AC 57 at 65, [1891–4] All ER Rep 24 at 25– *j* 26):

'In their Lordships' opinion the principles which must govern the decision of the case are clear, though the application of them is by no means free from difficulty. It a   is undoubtedly not competent for the prosecution to adduce evidence tending to shew that the accused has been guilty of criminal acts other than those covered by the indictment, for the purpose of leading to the conclusion that the accused is a person likely from his criminal conduct or character to have committed the offence for which he is being tried. On the other hand, the mere fact that the evidence adduced tends to shew the commission of other crimes does not render it inadmissible if it be relevant to an issue before the jury, and it may be so relevant if

b   it bears upon the question whether the acts alleged to constitute the crime charged in the indictment were designed or accidental, or to rebut a defence which would otherwise be open to the accused. The statement of these general principles is easy, but it is obvious that it may often be very difficult to draw the line and to decide whether a particular piece of evidence is on the one side or the other.'

c   In that case the similar facts which supported the proof of guilt consisted partly of antecedent circumstances.

In *Harris v DPP* [1952] 1 All ER 1044 at 1046, [1952] AC 694 at 705 Viscount Simon said:

d   'In my opinion, the principle laid down by LORD HERSCHELL, L.C., in *Makin's* case remains the proper principle to apply, and I see no reason for modifying it. *Makin's* case was a decision of the Judicial Committee of the Privy Council, but it was unanimously approved by the House of Lords in *R. v. Ball* ([1911] AC 47) and has been constantly relied on ever since. It is, I think, an error to attempt to draw up a closed list of the sort of cases in which the principle operates. Such a list only provides instances of its general application, whereas what really matters is the

e   principle itself and its proper application to the particular circumstances of the charge that is being tried.'

The point is clearly made by Lord Hailsham in *Boardman v DPP* [1974] 3 All ER 887 at 904, [1975] AC 421 at 452 where, having adverted to *R v Smith* and *R v Straffen* [1952] 2 All ER 657, [1952] 2 QB 911, he continued:

f   'The permutations are almost indefinite. In *Moorov* [*Moorov v HM Advocate* 1930 JC 68] coincidence of story as distinct from coincidence in the facts was held to be admissible and corroborative, and this, after some fairly agonised appraisals, was what was thought in *Kilbourne* [*DPP v Kilbourne* [1973] 1 All ER 440, [1973] AC 729]. The fact is that, although the categories are useful classes of example, they are not closed (see per Viscount Simon in *Harris v Director of Public Prosecutions* ([1952]

g   1 All ER 1044 at 1046, [1952] AC 694 at 705), and they cannot in fact be closed by categorisation. The rules of logic and common sense are not susceptible of exact codification when applied to the actual facts of life in its infinite variety.'

The conclusion from what has been said is that, just as corroboration is found in any evidence which confirms other evidence, so also similar fact evidence, a type of

h   corroboration, appears in an infinite variety of forms. For the evidence to be admitted, its similarities must be either unique, in which event its probative value will approach that of a fingerprint, or striking, when its probative value will vary depending on how striking the similarity is. But similar fact evidence cannot be defined by a degree of similarity measurable on a scale or by reference to the place or time at which it appears. It follows that, in their Lordships' view, the legal assessor's advice to the committee was

j   perfectly correct. Ordinarily a doctor may properly make relevant physical contact when examining a patient with the patient's consent. But the evidence of each patient was that the contact was indecent and improper. The evidence of what the appellant said before and after his examination tended, if believed, to prove that the contact was indecent And the evidence of what the appellant allegedly said in one case (provided a striking similarity was found between the two cases) was capable of corroborating the evidence of indecency in the other. Their Lordships were also interested to note that, there being *a* only two instances, the legal assessor cautioned the committee with regard to using one account to corroborate the other, following almost word for word the observation of Lord Cross in *Boardman v DPP* [1974] 3 All ER 887 at 911, [1975] AC 421 at 460.

The claim that the complaints of Mrs A and Mrs B ought to have been tried separately falls to be decided on the same principles as are applicable to the criticism of the legal assessor's direction on corroboration. This point is illustrated by Lord Wilberforce's *b* observations in *Boardman v DPP* [1974] 3 All ER 887 at 896, [1975] AC 421 at 443. And it has been accepted at least since *R v Sims* [1946] 1 All ER 697, [1946] KB 531 that, where two or more charges have been included in one indictment, an application for a separate trial of different counts ought to be acceded to if the evidence to be adduced on one count in the indictment is considered unlikely to pass the similar fact test in relation to another count in the same indictment.　　　　　　　　　　　　　　　　　　　　　　*c*

In the present case, so far from suggesting that the complaints of Mrs A and Mrs B be heard separately, counsel then representing the appellant appeared to favour a joint hearing. But the important consideration, having regard to their Lordships' expressed view of the similar fact evidence, is that this was a case in which it was eminently proper and in the interests of justice for the two complaints to be heard together.

For these reasons their Lordships will humbly advise Her Majesty that this appeal *d* should be dismissed. The appellant must pay the committee's costs before this Board.

Finally, it may provide guidance for the future if their Lordships now state that, where a charge of professional misconduct is founded on two or more separate incidents, those incidents should each be made the subject of a separate charge of professional misconduct instead of being listed as particulars of one offence of professional misconduct, as in the present case. This practice should be followed even when the prosecutor intends, as he *e* may properly do in many cases, to have the charges heard together. It will serve as a reminder that the evidence tendered with reference to one aspect of an accused person's alleged misconduct is not necessarily admissible in relation to another aspect, and it will be more convenient in cases where an accused applies successfully for separate hearings.

*Appeal dismissed.*　　　　　　　　　　　　　　　　　　　　　　　　　　　　*f*

Solicitors: *Hempsons* (for the appellant); *Waterhouse & Co* (for the committee).

Mary Rose Plummer　　Barrister.

# Finnish Marine Insurance Co Ltd v Protective National Insurance Co

QUEEN'S BENCH DIVISION
ADRIAN HAMILTON QC SITTING AS A DEPUTY JUDGE OF THE HIGH COURT
21, 22, 23 DECEMBER 1988, 11 JANUARY 1989

*Practice – Service out of the jurisdiction – Action to enforce, rescind, dissolve, annul or otherwise affect a contract – Otherwise affect – Action for declaration that no contract between plaintiff and defendant – Agents of reinsurers issuing two reinsurance policies for defendant – Plaintiff insurer claiming reinsurance without authority and denying existence of contract of reinsurance with defendant – Plaintiff obtaining leave to serve writ out of jurisdiction on ground that its claim affected contract between reinsurers and their agents – Whether court having jurisdiction to uphold service of writ – Whether plaintiff required to show that his claim affected a contract between himself and defendant – Whether sufficient for plaintiff to show that his claim affected contract between himself and third party – RSC Ord 11, r 1(1)(d)(ii)(e).*

*Practice – Stay of proceedings – Foreign defendant – Jurisdiction – Foreign defendant applying for stay of proceedings pending reference to arbitration – Whether application to stay amounting to voluntary submission to jurisdiction of court to decide merits – Whether court having jurisdiction to consider application to stay but no jurisdiction to decide merits – Arbitration Act 1975, s 1(1).*

The London branch of a Guernsey firm of underwriters, acting as agents for reinsurers, issued two reinsurance policies for the defendant, a Nebraskan corporation. On slips setting out the essential details of the risk of each policy the agents wrote lines representing a percentage of the insured value which they were willing to underwrite on behalf of the reinsurers 'subject to confirmation' by their head office in Guernsey, which confirmation was later given. The plaintiff, as the successor in title to the reinsurers' business, issued a writ against the defendant seeking a declaration that the reinsurers' agents had written the lines without authority and that therefore it was not party to any contract of reinsurance with the defendant, and further claiming an account of sums paid by the agents on the reinsurers' behalf to the defendant's brokers in London and repayment of those sums. The plaintiff subsequently applied for and was granted leave under RSC Ord 11 to serve the writ out of the jurisdiction on the defendant in Nebraska on the basis that its claim fell within the scope of r 1(1)(d)(ii)[a], which concerned claims brought 'to rescind, dissolve, annul or otherwise affect a contract . . . made by or through an agent trading or residing within the jurisdiction', and r 1(1)(e), which concerned claims brought in respect of breaches of contract occurring within the jurisdiction regardless of where the contract was made. The defendant first applied to set aside service of the writ on the ground that Ord 11, r 1(1)(d)(ii) or (e) presupposed the existence of a contract between the plaintiff and the defendant and therefore did not permit a plaintiff to obtain leave to serve a writ out of the jurisdiction while denying that a contract ever existed, and then applied for a stay of the proceedings under s 1(1)[b] of the Arbitration Act 1975. The

---

a   Rule 1(1), so far as material, provides: '. . . service of a writ out of the jurisdiction is permissible with the leave of the court if in the action begun by the writ . . . (d) the claim is brought to enforce, rescind, dissolve, annul or otherwise affect a contract . . . which—(i) was made within the jurisdiction, or (ii) was made by or through an agent trading or residing within the jurisdiction on behalf of a principal trading or residing out of the jurisdiction . . . (e) the claim is brought in respect of a breach committed within the jurisdiction of a contract made within or out of the jurisdiction . . .'

b   Section 1(1), so far as material, provides: 'If any party to an arbitration agreement to which this section applies . . . commences any legal proceedings in any court against any other party to the agreement . . . in respect of any matter agreed to be referred, any party to the proceedings may at any time after appearance, and before delivering any pleadings or taking any other steps in the proceedings, apply to the court to stay the proceedings . . .'

plaintiff contended (i) that the court had jurisdiction to uphold service of the writ because
in order to bring its claim within the scope of r 1(1)(d)(ii) or (e) it was sufficient for it to
show that the claim affected a contract between the plaintiff and a third party rather than
a contract between the plaintiff and the defendant so that the contract between the
reinsurers (and therefore the plaintiff) and their agents sufficed to found jurisdiction,
and (ii) that even if the contractual claim failed it was entitled to succeed by virtue of a
quasi-contractual claim founded on the claims for an account and repayment of the sums
paid on behalf of the reinsurers to the defendant. The plaintiff further contended that
the defendant, by applying for a stay of proceedings under s 1 of the 1975 Act, had
voluntarily submitted to the jurisdiction of the court to determine the claim.

**Held** – (1) In order to bring a claim within the scope of RSC Ord 11, r 1(1)(d)(ii) or (e) it
was not sufficient for a plaintiff to show that there was a contract between himself and a
third party. Instead, he had to show that there was a contract between himself and the
defendant and that there was a good arguable case that the claim affected the contract.
Accordingly, since the plaintiff denied the existence of any contract with the defendant
and sought a declaration to that effect, its claim had not been brought to 'affect' a contract
but to prove that no such contract ever existed and, as such, the claim did not fall within
the scope of r 1(1)(d)(ii) or (e). It followed that service of the writ out of the jurisdiction
could not be justified on the basis of the plaintiff's contractual claim, nor could it be
justified on the basis of the quasi-contractual claim also advanced because even if the
plaintiff could prove that sums had been paid on behalf of the reinsurers to the defendant's
brokers in London and that those sums were recoverable in quasi contract the application
for leave to serve out of the jurisdiction would have had to have been founded on
r 1(1)(d)(i), and not on r 1(1)(d)(ii) or (e), since the quasi contract would have been 'made'
when the money was received. The defendant's application to set aside service of the writ
would therefore be allowed (see p 933 e f, p 934 b to e j, p 935 b to f and p 938 a, post);
dicta of Lord Simon and Lord Wright in *Heyman v Darwins Ltd* [1942] 1 All ER 337 at
343, 360 and *Cia Naviera Micro SA v Shipley International Inc, The Parouth* [1982] 2 Lloyd's
Rep 351 applied; dictum of Kerr J in *BP Exploration Co (Libya) Ltd v Hunt* [1976] 3 All ER
879 at 885 considered.

(2) An application for a stay of proceedings under s 1 of the 1975 Act was a method of
renouncing the jurisdiction of the court to decide the merits of the claim forming the
subject matter of the proceedings in favour of arbitration, since it served to invoke the
jurisdiction of the court to consider the application and determine whether the stay
should be granted but not jurisdiction to decide the merits. Accordingly, the defendant
had not voluntarily submitted to the jurisdiction of the court to decide the merits when
it issued the s 1 summons. The defendant would however be given leave to withdraw
the summons since there was sufficient evidence that it had been issued by mistake (see
p 937 a d to p 938 a, post); dicta of Robert Goff LJ in *Astro Exito Navegacion SA v Hsu, The
Messiniaki Tolmi* [1984] 1 Lloyd's Rep 266 at 270 and of Staughton and Parker LJJ in *Metal
Scrap Trade Corp v Kate Shipping Co Ltd, The Gladys* [1988] 3 All ER 32 at 39–40, 44
applied; *Williams & Glynn's Bank plc v Astro Dinamico Cia Naviera SA* [1984] 1 All ER 760
considered.

## Notes

For service of a writ outside the jurisdiction with leave in respect of a contractual claim,
see 37 Halsbury's Laws (4th edn) paras 171, 178, and for cases on the subject, see 37(2)
Digest (Reissue) 279–282, 285–291, 1801–1813, 1831–1849.

For contracts of reinsurance, see 25 Halsbury's Laws (4th edn) paras 209–215.

For the Arbitration Act 1975, s 1, see 2 Halsbury's Statutes (4th edn) 603.

## Cases referred to in judgment

*A and B v C and D* [1982] 1 Lloyd's Rep 166.

*Astro Exito Navegacion SA v Hsu, The Messiniaki Tolmi* [1984] 1 Lloyd's Rep 266, CA.

a  *Bowling v Cox* [1926] AC 751, HL.

*BP Exploration Co (Libya) Ltd v Hunt* [1976] 3 All ER 879, [1976] 1 WLR 788.

*Cia Naviera Micro SA v Shipley International Inc, The Parouth* [1982] 2 Lloyd's Rep 351, CA.

*Cromie v Moore* [1936] 2 All ER 177, CA.

*Dulles's Settlement Trusts, Re, Dulles v Vidler* [1951] 2 All ER 69, [1951] Ch 842, CA.

*Firth v John Mowlem & Co Ltd* [1978] 3 All ER 331, [1978] 1 WLR 1184, CA.

b  *Hagen, The* [1908] P 189, [1908–10] All ER Rep 21, CA.

*Harris v Taylor* [1915] 2 KB 580, [1914–15] All ER Rep 366, CA.

*Henry v Geopresco International Ltd* [1975] 2 All ER 702, [1976] QB 726, [1975] 3 WLR 620, CA.

*Heyman v Darwins Ltd* [1942] 1 All ER 337, [1942] AC 356, HL.

*Insurance Corp of Ireland v Strombus International Insurance Co Ltd* [1985] 2 Lloyd's Rep

c  138, CA.

*Jogia (a bankrupt), Re, ex p the trustee v D Pennellier & Co Ltd* [1988] 2 All ER 328, [1988] 1 WLR 484, CA.

*Metal Scrap Trade Corp Ltd v Kate Shipping Co Ltd, The Gladys* [1988] 3 All ER 32, [1988] 1 WLR 767, CA.

*Nominal Defendant v Motor Vehicle Insurance Trust of Western Australia* (1983) 50 ALR 511,

d  NSW SC.

*Rousou (a bankrupt) (trustee) v Rousou* [1955] 2 All ER 169, [1955] 1 WLR 545.

*Somportex Ltd v Philadelphia Chewing Gum Corp* [1968] 3 All ER 26, CA.

*Spiliada Maritime Corp v Cansulex Ltd, The Spiliada* [1986] 3 All ER 843, [1987] AC 460, [1986] 3 WLR 972, CA.

*Sydney Express, The* [1988] 2 Lloyd's Rep 257.

e  *Tyne Improvement Comrs v Armement Anversois SA, The Brabo* [1949] 1 All ER 294, [1949] AC 326, HL.

*Williams & Glyn's Bank plc v Astro Dinamico Cia Naviera SA* [1984] 1 All ER 760, [1984] 1 WLR 438, HL.

f  **Summonses**

The plaintiffs, Finnish Marine Insurance Co Ltd, a Finnish insurance company which was the successor in title to the business of another Finnish insurance company, Omsesidiga, issued a writ on 29 December 1987 against the defendants, Protective National Insurance Co, a Nebraskan corporation, seeking (1) a declaration that the London branch of Accolade Underwriting Agency (Accolade) of Guernsey, acting as agents for

g  Omsesidiga, had written lines of 2·5% and 10% on two reinsurance policies issued to the defendants without the actual or apparent authority of Omsesidiga and that therefore the plaintiffs were not parties to any contract of reinsurance with the defendants, (2) an account of the sums paid on behalf of Omsesidiga by Accolade to the defendants' London brokers, Messrs Fielding & Partners, and (3) an order for repayment of those sums. On 20 June 1988 Hirst J gave leave under RSC Ord 11 to serve the writ out of the jurisdiction.

h  By a summons dated 18 August 1988 the defendants applied for a stay of proceedings under s 1 of the Aribration Act 1975 and by a second summons dated 27 October 1988 applied for an order setting aside the service of the writ. The summonses were heard in chambers but judgment was given by Adrian Hamilton QC in open court. The facts are set out in the judgment.

j

*Gordon Langley QC* and *T Howe* for the plaintiffs.
*Jonathan Gaisman* for the defendants.

*Cur adv vult*

11 January. The following judgment was delivered.

**ADRIAN HAMILTON QC.** Both parties have asked me to deliver judgment in open
court. There are two summonses before me: (1) a summons by the defendants to
discharge the order of Hirst J dated 20 June 1988 and to set aside service of a writ served
abroad thereunder; and (2) a summons, also by the defendants, for a stay of proceedings
under s 1 of the Arbitration Act 1975.

The plaintiffs are a Finnish corporation, whose address is in Helsinki. They are the
successors in title to Omsesidiga, another Finnish insurance company. The defendants
are a Nebraskan corporation, whose address is in Omaha, Nebraska. Omsesidiga (whom
for ease of reference I shall include in the expression 'the plaintiffs') had an underwriting
agency agreement with Accolade Underwriting Agency of Guernsey, Channel Islands.
For reasons familiar to the courts, Accolade wrote lines in London 'subject to confirmation'
by Accolade in Guernsey.

The current dispute involves two contracts of reinsurance: (1) a 90% quota share treaty
for the primary $US250,000; on this Accolade wrote a line of 2½% on behalf of the
plaintiffs 'subject to confirmation'; (2) a casualty excess of loss for $US750,000 in excess
of $US250,000. On this Accolade wrote a line of 10% on behalf of the plaintiffs, 'subject
to confirmation'. In each case: (1) the defendants' brokers, placing the risk on their
behalf, were Fielding & Partners, London brokers, who used a standard London slip and
form; (2) each slip was subject to 'Intermediary Clause naming Fielding & Partners'; and
(3) it was common ground that the line was confirmed by Accolade in Guernsey.

*The dispute*

The substantial dispute between the parties is that raised by the declaration claimed by
the plaintiffs, namely whether Accolade wrote these lines without any actual or apparent
authority of the plaintiffs. If so, they are not parties to any contract with the defendants
at all. On the resolution of that dispute would depend the issue whether the defendants
are entitled to enforce their rights under the contracts. No claim to enforce the contracts
against the plaintiffs has been made by the defendants in this country, by counterclaim
or separate action or by arbitration. If the slips were written without authority, then the
plaintiffs would seek to enforce their claim for an 'account' in para (2) of the indorsement
on the writ, and the order for payment under para (3). I must refer in more detail to this
claim later in this judgment.

The natural plaintiffs are the present defendants. As the risks cover a United States
casualty account, there is a reasonable inference that there have been substantial losses,
but I have no evidence of the extent to which losses have arisen and been paid by the
plaintiffs. There is a paucity of evidence, but it appears that the defendants appointed an
arbitrator on 20 November 1987. There is an issue whether there is an arbitration clause.
The only information I have is contained in an exhibit to the affidavit of Mr Webster (of
the plaintiffs' original solicitors), in a letter dated 12 August 1988 which suggests that
there were treaty wordings, which included an arbitration clause providing for arbitration
in Omaha, Nebraska. On this material, obviously no stay could be granted, but this does
not matter because all that the defendants want to do is to withdraw the summons.

Whether as a riposte or not, the plaintiffs issued the present writ on 29 December
1987.

*The RSC Ord 11, r 1 application*

Hirst J had before him the writ, an affidavit of Mr Grant (of the defendants' solicitors)
dated 16 June 1988, and an exhibit containing copies of the Accolade underwriting
agency agreement, the two slips and an inconclusive exchange of telexes about possible
service. The affidavit raises the issue that the plaintiffs claim that Accolade had written
this business without authority, and that the defendants' brokers, Fielding & Partners,
were aware of this absence of authority. The provisions relied on were Ord 11, r 1(1)(d)(ii),

which concerns a 'claim . . . brought to . . . rescind, dissolve, annul or otherwise affect a
*a*   contract . . . which . . . was made by or through an agent trading or residing within the
jurisdiction . . .' or Ord 11, r 1(1)(e), which concerns a 'claim . . . brought in respect of a
breach committed within the jurisdiction of a contract made within or out of the
jurisdiction . . .' There is nothing in any of the documents before Hirst J which suggests
that leave is being sought in respect of a quasi-contractual claim.

Hirst J granted leave to serve out of the jurisdiction on 20 June 1988.

*b*
*The application to set aside*
   Certain principles are well known. The jurisdiction under Ord 11 is 'exorbitant' and
'extraordinary' (*Spiliada Maritime Corp v Cansulex Ltd, The Spiliada* [1986] 3 All ER 843 at
858, [1987] AC 460 at 481 per Lord Goff) and ambiguities in the rules are to be resolved
in favour of the foreigner (*The Hagen* [1908] P 189 at 201, [1908–10] All ER Rep 21 at
*c*   26).
   I shall deal first with the grounds on which, as I see it, Hirst J based his order. As to
them, the arguments before me raise two points as to the 'contract' on which the plaintiffs
rely: (1) does the contract have to be between the plaintiffs and the defendants? and (2)
can a plaintiff base a claim for service out of the jurisdiction on a claim that no contract
has ever come into existence?
*d*
*Is it sufficient to say that a contract between the plaintiff and a third party is affected?*
   Counsel for the plaintiffs says that the contract does not need to be between the
plaintiffs and the defendant and that it is sufficient for him to show that the claim affects
the plaintiffs' contract with Accolade. If he is right, this is a point which has been
regularly overlooked by distinguished lawyers.
*e*   In my judgment, however, it is clearly wrong. It is probably sufficient to construe
Ord 11, r 1(1)(d) alone. It seems to me clear that all the earlier grounds ('enforce, rescind,
dissolve, annul') can only relate to a contract between plaintiff and defendant. There is
nothing to indicate that a different type of contract becomes available when the claim is
to 'affect' a contract. In each case the word 'contract' means a contract between plaintiff
and defendant. This seems to have been assumed in *Cromie v Moore* [1936] 2 All ER 177.
*f*   I do not regard the New South Wales case of *Nominal Defendant v Motor Vehicle Insurance
Trust of Western Australia* (1983) 50 ALR 511 as sufficiently close on the facts to be of
assistance. In the leading case of *Tyne Improvement Comrs v Armement Anversions SA, The
Brabo* [1949] 1 All ER 294 at 298, [1949] AC 326 at 338 Lord Porter said:

   'Primarily the jurisdiction of the courts in this country is territorial in the sense
*g*     that the contract or tort sued on must have some connection with this country . . .'

I regard this rule as clear, but if there is any doubt it should be resolved in favour of the
foreigner.

*Does the rule allow a plaintiff to get leave while denying that a contract ever existed*
*h*   *between the plaintiff and the defendant?*
   This is a difficult and important point and, surprisingly, there is no direct authority.
Dicey and Morris *Conflict of Laws* (11th edn, 1987) p 316 expresses the opinion that 'if, on
the plaintiff's own showing, no such contract as he alleges was made with the defendant,
leave will not be granted', but the authorities cited, *Cromie v Moore* and *Nominal Defendant
v Motor Vehicle Insurance Trust of Western Australia*, do not seem to support the text. The
*j*   authorities show that a claim for a declaration that a contract has been discharged by
rescission for misrepresentation, as in *Insurance Corp of Ireland v Strombus International
Insurance Co Ltd* [1985] 2 Lloyd's Rep 138 at 142, or has been discharged by frustration,
is within the rule as a claim within the meaning of 'or otherwise affect a contract': see *BP
Exploration Co (Libya) Ltd v Hunt* [1976] 3 All ER 879 at 885, [1976] 1 WLR 788 at 795
per Kerr J, where he said:

'The words "or otherwise affect" are very wide; indeed, almost as wide as they can
be. A claim for a declaration that a contract has become discharged, whether as a
result of frustration, repudiation, or otherwise, is in my view a claim which affects
the contract in question. The contrary construction would have serious and highly
inconvenient consequences.'

Counsel for the plaintiffs argues that the same considerations apply if the claim is that
there has never been a contract at all. I cannot accept that this is correct. There is a clearly
recognised distinction between the case where there has been a contract, which has later
been discharged by an accepted repudiation, frustration or rescission, and a 'contract'
which has never been entered into at all: see *Heyman v Darwins Ltd* [1942] 1 All ER 337
at 343, 360, [1942] AC 356 at 366, 384 per Lord Simon and Lord Wright.

In the present case the plaintiffs say that there never was a contract at all. If they are
right there never was any contract to 'affect', in distinction to the contract that did exist,
but had been frustrated, in *BP Exploration v Hunt*.

I do not consider that the plaintiffs escape from this difficulty because the defendants
sought a stay on the basis of an arbitration clause, which presupposes a contract. There is
no evidence before me of such a contract. The mere issue of a summons does not provide
evidence that it is soundly based. The defendants now seek to withdraw their summons.
It is for the plaintiffs to demonstrate that their claim is brought to 'affect' a contract. They
only have to show a good arguable case, but I do not consider they can do this by denying
the existence of a contract at all: see *Dicey and Morris on Conflict of Laws* (11th edn, 1987)
p 316 and *Cia Naviera Micro SA v Shipley International Inc, The Parouth* [1982] 2 Lloyd's
Rep 351. The plaintiffs' claim for a declaration is, therefore, not brought to 'affect' a
contract, but to prove that no contract ever existed. In my judgment, this is not within
the rule.

### Good arguable case

Had I reached the conclusion that the plaintiffs' claim was within the sub-paragraphs
of the rule relied on, I would have held that they had a good arguable case that Accolade
acted without authority. Counsel for the defendants does not dispute that there is a good
arguable case in the case of the excess of loss treaty, but denies that there is a good
arguable case in relation to the primary quota share treaty.

In relation to the quota share treaty I say no more than that the line of $US6,250
exceeds the maximum retained line of £1,000 for any one risk imposed by the first
addendum to the underwriting agency agreement. There is no evidence of excess of loss
reinsurance being affected limiting the retained line to this figure.

Although there is no doubt much to argue about, both as to the law and the facts, I am
satisfied that the plaintiffs would have a good arguable case. I would not have held that
the fact that the plaintiffs claimed only a negative declaration prevented them having a
good arguable case in a case where the issue is an important one for the parties, and there
are no proceedings anywhere else to decide that issue.

### Quasi-contractual relief

Counsel for the plaintiffs then says that in any case he can succeed, because claims (2)
and (3) of the indorsement on the writ set up a quasi-contractual claim which provides
an independent ground on which to support Hirst J's decision.

It is not challenged that a 'contract' in the rule includes a quasi contract: see *Bowling v
Cox* [1926] AC 751 and *Re Jogia (a bankrupt), ex p the trustee v D Pennellier & Co Ltd* [1988]
2 All ER 328 at 337, [1988] 1 WLR 484 at 495.

However, (1) I do not consider that claims (2) and (3) on the writ set up a proper claim
in quasi contract. They set up a claim for an account which seems to me misconceived. I
do not think that the fact that a claim could have been based on quasi contract, makes it
a claim in quasi contract, within the rule.

(2) The evidence before Hirst J now relied on to support a claim in quasi contract was
a  in para 6 of Mr Grant's affidavit as follows:

> 'It was an express and/or implied term of the said agreement that payment of
> premiums and claims by the Defendants/Plaintiffs respectively and/or agents acting
> on their behalf should be made in London . . .'

There was no contrary evidence by the defendants. Nevertheless, I do not regard this as
b  sufficient evidence for the plaintiffs to be able to prove that their claim based on quasi
contract comes within the rules. There is no evidence of how accounting actually took
place. Even with the evidence in two affidavits of Mr Fleming (of the defendants'
solicitors), sworn after Hirst J gave leave, the plaintiffs' case does not seem to prove a case
based on quasi contract, although one can speculate that there may be one.
   (3) The application before Hirst J was, as I have said, expressly based on Ord 11,
c  r 1(1)(d)(ii) and Ord 11, r 1(1)(e). This is pursuant to the requirement that a plaintiff
must make clear which sub-paragraph of r 1(1) is relied on: see *The Supreme Court Practice
1988* vol 1, para 11/4/3. I do not see how the claim in quasi contract can be brought
within either of these sub-paragraphs. If I assume that the plaintiffs have sufficiently
proved that moneys were paid in London on their behalf (although they say that Accolade
were not their agents in this transaction) to Fieldings on behalf of the defendants, and
d  that those moneys are recoverable in quasi contract, the sub-paragraph which could be
involved would be Ord 11, r 1(1)(d)(i) on the basis that the quasi contract was 'made' or
'arose' when the money was received: see *Re Jogia* [1988] 2 All ER 328 at 338, [1988] 1
WLR 484 at 495–496 per Sir Nicolas Browne-Wilkinson V-C. (I think that where Sir
Nicolas Browne-Wilkinson V-C refers ([1988] 2 All ER 328 at 337, [1988] 1 WLR 484 at
495) to Ord 11, r 1(f), he must have meant to refer to Ord 11, r 1(1)(d), which is in fact
e  the equivalent of Ord 11, r 1(1)(e) at the time of Danckwerts J's decision in *Trustee of
Rousou (a bankrupt) v Rousou* [1955] 2 All ER 169, [1955] 1 WLR 545.)
   The plaintiffs obviously could not rely on Ord 11, r 1(1)(d)(i) in relation to the
'contracts' in the slips, because those were 'made' when confirmed in Guernsey.
   For these reasons I do not consider that the plaintiffs can rely on the claims made in (2)
and (3) of the indorsement on the writ to justify Hirst J's leave.
f

*Conclusion on jurisdiction under Ord 11*
   Accordingly the plaintiffs have not satisfied me that their claim comes within Ord 11,
on any of the bases relied on.

*Discretion*
g
   This does not strictly arise for my consideration, but I should indicate what my views
would have been, if I had found I had jurisdiction. Had I concluded that the plaintiffs'
claim for a declaration that they were not bound by the contracts between the plaintiffs
and the defendants was within the sub-paragraphs of Ord 11, r 1 relied on, I would have
exercised my discretion to allow service out of the jurisdiction. The forum conveniens
h  for the resolution of this dispute would appear to be the English courts, for the reasons
relied on by the plaintiffs. The defendants have appointed an arbitrator, but there is no
proper evidence before me of an arbitration clause. If English law applied, it is extremely
unlikely that the arbitration clause would be wide enough to allow the arbitrator to
decide if there was a contract, and I have no reason to assume that any other relevant law
would approach this issue differently (see *Heyman v Darwins Ltd* [1942] 1 All ER 337 at
j  343, [1942] AC 356 at 366). I do not think that the claim for a declaration is objectionable
as a pre-emptive strike, when there is no evidence that the defendants are taking steps to
have the issue of whether there are binding contracts determined in any other
jurisdiction. It is with reluctance that I have decided that there is no jurisdiction under
Ord 11 to uphold the service in Nebraska on the basis already set out, but my decision
deprives me of any discretion.

If I had concluded that the quasi-contractual claim alone had been brought within the rule, I would not have exercised my discretion to uphold service. This is ancillary to the main dispute whether there are binding contracts, and should be tried in the same jurisdiction.

### Submission to the jurisdiction

That is not, however, the end of the matter, because the plaintiffs say that the defendants have voluntarily submitted to the jurisdiction by the issue of a summons to stay under s 1 of the Arbitration Act 1975. For those not familiar with *Henry v Geopresco International Ltd* [1975] 2 All ER 702, [1976] QB 726, this would appear a startling conclusion. The summons seeks to stop the English action, so that the arbitration can proceed. It does not indicate any wish to have the English courts try the merits of the dispute, quite the contrary.

*Henry v Geopresco International Ltd* was a controversial decision in which the Court of Appeal followed the earlier controversial decision of *Harris v Taylor* [1915] 2 KB 580, [1914–15] All ER Rep 366. The essence of the decision was that an application to the Alberta courts for a stay of proceedings on the ground of an arbitration clause was a submission to the jurisdiction of the Alberta courts, so as to make the ultimate decision of those courts enforceable in England. Roskill LJ, giving the judgment of the court, said ([1975] 2 All ER 702 at 720–721, [1976] QB 726 at 749):

> 'For our part, we think that where any issues arise for decision at any stage of the proceedings in the foreign court and that court is invited by the defendant as well as by the plaintiff to decide those issues, "the merits" are voluntarily submitted to that court for decision so that that submission subsequently binds both parties in respect of the dispute as a whole, even if both would not have been so bound in the absence of that voluntary submission.'

This decision has been reversed by statute by s 33 of the Civil Jurisdiction and Judgments Act 1982. That section does not, however, have any effect on the issue whether there has been a voluntary submission to the English courts, and counsel for the plaintiffs says that the reasoning of the Court of Appeal provides authority for saying that the mere issue of the summons to stay under the 1975 Act is a voluntary submission.

I do not accept this submission. The Court of Appeal stressed that its decision was as to the enforcement of foreign judgments: see, for example, where Roskill LJ said ([1975] 2 All ER 702 at 717, [1976] QB 726 at 746):

> '. . . on no view is *Re Dulles' Settlement Trusts (No 2)* [1951] 2 All ER 69, [1951] Ch 842 a decision regarding the enforceability of foreign judgments by action in the courts of this country and we think the decision (whether right or wrong on its facts) leaves the authority of *Harris v Taylor* [1915] 2 KB 580, [1914–15] All ER Rep 366 wholly unshaken. It can fairly be said that *Harris v Taylor* is not a decision the underlying principles of which should be extended. That we unhesitatingly accept.'

Now that the direct effect of *Henry v Geopresco International Ltd* has been reversed by statute, I see no basis for extending the principles applied to issues of voluntary submission to the English courts. What is such a voluntary submission depends on its facts. I adopt the test of the Court of Appeal in *Astro Exito Navegacion SA v Hsu, The Messiniaki Tolmi* [1984] 1 Lloyd's Rep 266 at 270:

> 'Now a person voluntarily submits to the jurisdiction of the Court if he voluntarily recognises, or has voluntarily recognised, that the Court has jurisdiction to hear and determine the claim which is the subject matter of the relevant proceedings. In particular, he makes a voluntary submission to the jurisdiction if he takes a step in proceedings which in all the circumstances amounts to a recognition of the Court's jurisdiction in respect of the claim which is the subject matter of those proceedings.'

a
In my judgment an application for a stay under the 1975 Act does not recognise the
court's jurisdiction in respect of the claim: it challenges such jurisdiction. It challenges it
in the same way as an application for a stay under s 49(3) of the Supreme Court Act 1981
(*Williams & Glyn's Bank plc v Astro Dinamico Cia Naviera SA* [1984] 1 All ER 760, [1984] 1
WLR 438) or under an exclusive jurisdiction clause (*The Sydney Express* [1988] 2 Lloyd's
Rep 257). There is a helpful passage in Mustill J's judgment in *A and B v C and D* [1982]
1 Lloyd's Rep 166 at 171–172:

b
'Indeed, one not infrequently finds that a London arbitration clause is relied upon
to found jurisdiction under R.S.C., O.11 on the ground that the presence of the
clause signifies an implied choice of English law. The position is, however, quite
different where the defendant is entitled to a stay, as of right, under the [Arbitration
Act 1975], and makes it plain that this is a right which he intends to assert. Here,
c
the upholding of the leave granted ex parte is an empty formality as it will
immediately be followed by a successul application to stay. The difference between
accepting jurisdiction over the claim and then renouncing it in favour of arbitration,
and renouncing it directly, is one of form alone; in this instance, there is no practical
distinction between a summons to set aside a leave granted ex parte, and a summons
to stay under the 1975 Act.'

d
This passage was cited with approval by the Court of Appeal in *Metal Scrap Trade Corp v
Kate Shipping Co Ltd, The Gladys* [1988] 3 All ER 32 at 39–40, 44, [1988] 1 WLR 767 at
776–777, 781–782 per Staughton and Parker LJJ. These passages seem to confirm that an
application for a stay, particularly a mandatory stay, under the Arbitration Acts is merely
a method of renouncing the jurisdiction of the courts.
Counsel for the plaintiffs seeks to distinguish *Williams & Glyn's Bank plc v Astro
e
Dinamico Cia Naviera SA* on the grounds that the two applications were issued
simultaneously. That is true, but I do not think that this was a fact essential to the
decision. I think that the crucial point was that the invoking of the jurisdiction to stay
was the invoking of the court's jurisdiction to decide if it had jurisdiction to decide on
the merits, not the invoking of the latter jurisdiction, ie to decide on the merits. I
consider that the same considerations apply to an application to stay under the 1975 Act.
f
Finally counsel for the plaintiffs says that the application for a stay necessarily involves
the jurisdiction of the court to decide if there is a contract, which is the very issue that
falls to be decided on the merits of their declaration. I do not, however, consider that that
fact changes the nature of the jurisdiction invoked by the application to stay. It remains
the invocation of the court's jurisdiction to decide if it has jurisdiction, not the jurisdiction
to decide the merits.
g
Accordingly, I find that there has been no submission to the jurisdiction.

*Withdrawal of summons to stay*
If I am wrong on that, there is sufficient evidence that the summons to stay was issued
by mistake. On my findings there was no mistake by the defendants' previous solicitors,
h
let alone their present solicitors who were not then involved. If I am wrong, however,
then in my judgment there was a mistake. I think that in this context a mistake can be a
mistake of law. What has to be shown is that the minds of the defendants or their
advisers were affected by something that can properly be called a 'mistake': see *Somportex
v Philadelphia Chewing Gum Corp* [1968] 3 All ER 26 and *Firth v John Mowlem & Co Ltd*
[1978] 3 All ER 331 at 334–335, [1978] 1 WLR 1184 at 1188–1189. I think that this is
j
shown. I see no prejudice to the plaintiffs in the issuing of the summons, which has
never been pressed. The authorities show that the rule gives a complete discretion,
although, of course, one which must be exercised judicially: see *Firth v John Mowlem &
Co Ltd* [1978] 3 All ER 331 at 334, [1978] 1 WLR 1184 at 1100 per Megaw LJ.
In my discretion, I give leave for the summons to be withdrawn.

*Conclusion*

(1) I give the defendants leave to withdraw their summons for a stay. (2) I direct that *a* the order of Hirst J herein dated 20 June 1988 be discharged and service of the writ herein be set aside. Finally I express my gratitude to counsel on both sides for their helpful and concise but comprehensive arguments on several points of real difficulty.

*Order accordingly.*

*b*

Solicitors: *D J Freeman & Co* (for the plaintiffs); *Holman Fenwick & Willan* (for the defendants).

K Mydeen Esq    Barrister.

*c*

# Customs and Excise Commissioners v Faith Construction Ltd and other appeals

*d*

COURT OF APPEAL, CIVIL DIVISION
PARKER, BINGHAM AND MANN LJJ
26, 27, 28 APRIL, 26 MAY 1989

*Value added tax – Tax avoidance scheme – Zero-rating – Building work – Supply in the course* *e* *of construction, alteration or demolition of building – Standard-rating of alteration work as from 1 June 1984 – Transitional rules for zero-rating of alteration work if paid for before 1 June 1984 – Taxpayer companies entering into arrangement with owners of properties for payment in advance for work to be done on properties – Taxpayer companies then making loans to or depositing equivalent amount with owners before 1 June 1984 – Owners repaying loans or releasing deposits in stages against architects' certificates after 1 June 1984 – Transactions* *f* *discharging owners' liabilities to taxpayer companies – Whether payment received by taxpayer companies before 1 June 1984 or on presentation of architects' certificates – Whether works zero-rated or liable to tax at standard rate – Value Added Tax Act 1983, s 5(1).*

On 13 March 1984 it was announced that from 1 June 1984 supplies of building alteration works, which until then had been zero-rated for value added tax purposes, would be charged with tax at the standard rate. Under s 5(1)[a] of the Value Added Tax *g* Act 1983, if the person making the supply received a payment in respect of it, the supply would, to the extent covered by the payment, be treated as taking place at the time the payment was received. The Commissioners of Customs and Excise raised assessments on four separate building companies for value added tax on the supply of building alteration works carried out after 1 June 1984 but for which financial arrangements for payments *h* had been made by the building owners (the customers) before 1 June 1984. In two cases the moneys paid were directly or indirectly lent back to the customers and the loans were repaid in stages against architects' certificates as the works proceeded. In the other two cases the moneys paid into the builders' deposit accounts by the customers were only released against architects' certificates. All the repayments or releases occurred after 1 June 1984. The building companies were assessed to value added tax on the repayments *j* or releases. Value added tax tribunals allowed appeals by the first two building companies on the ground that the transactions were genuine and that the companies had received payment within s 5(1) of the 1983 Act before 1 June 1984; appeals by the Crown were

---

*a*  Section 5(1) is set out at p 941 *e, post*

dismissed by the High Court. Value added tax tribunals dismissed appeals by the other
*a* two building companies on the ground that the deposits themselves did not constitute
payments and that payment within s 5(1) was not received until after 1 June 1984 when
the architects' certificates were presented; appeals by the building companies were
allowed by the High Court. The Crown appealed to the Court of Appeal in all four cases,
contending that the building companies had not received payment for the building
alteration works until the loans repaid or the moneys were released.

*b*
**Held** – The transfer of funds by the customers to the building companies under the
financial arrangements entered into before 1 June 1984 had discharged the customers'
liabilities to the taxpayer companies under the building contracts and thereafter the
building companies had no right to sue for payment. Accordingly, in each case the
arrangements amounted to good contractual payments. As the payments were received
*c* before 1 June 1984 it followed that the supplies of the building works had been made
before 1 June 1984 by virtue of s 5(1) of the 1983 Act and consequently were zero-rated
for the purposes of value added tax. The appeals would therefore be dismissed (see p 943
*c d h j*, p 944 *e f*, p 945 *j* to p 946 *c g h* and p 947 *c* to *e g*, post).
Decisions of Simon Brown J [1988] 1 All ER 919, of Henry J [1988] STC 443, [1989]
STC 192 and of McNeill J [1988] STC 735 affirmed.
*d*

**Notes**
For zero-rating in relation to the construction or alteration of buildings, see 12 Halsbury's
Laws (4th edn) paras 904, 912, and for cases on the subject, see 49 Digest (Reissue) 22–
24, 71–79.
*e*    For the time of supply for value added tax purposes, see 12 Halsbury's Laws (4th edn)
para 874, and for cases on the subject, see 49 Digest (Reissue) 13, 31–32.
For the Value Added Tax Act 1983, s 5, see 48 Halsbury's Statutes (4th edn) 605.

**Cases referred to in judgments**
*Craven (Inspector of Taxes) v White* [1988] 3 All ER 495, [1988] 3 WLR 423, HL.
*f* *Furniss (Inspector of Taxes) v Dawson* [1984] 1 All ER 530, [1984] AC 474, [1984] 2 WLR
226, HL.
*IRC v Burmah Oil Co Ltd* [1982] STC 30, HL.
*IRC v Duke of Westminster* [1936] AC 1, [1935] All ER Rep 259, HL.
*Ramsay (WT) Ltd v IRC* [1981] 1 All ER 865, [1982] AC 300, [1981] 2 WLR 449, HL.

*g* **Cases also cited**
*Brimnes, The, Tenax Steamship Co v Brimnes (owners)* [1974] 3 All ER 88, [1975] QB 929,
CA.
*Customs and Excise Comrs v Diners Club Ltd* [1989] 2 All ER 385, CA; *affg* [1988] 2 All ER
1016.
*Customs and Excise Comrs v Pippa-Dee Parties Ltd* [1981] STC 495.
*h* *Garforth (Inspector of Taxes) v Newsmith Stainless Ltd* [1979] 2 All ER 73, [1979] 1 WLR
409.
*Gisborne v Burton* [1988] 3 All ER 760, [1988] 3 WLR 921, CA.
*Ingram v IRC* [1985] STC 835, [1986] Ch 585.
*Parkside Leasing Ltd v Smith (Inspector of Taxes)* [1985] STC 63, [1985] 1 WLR 310, 58 TC
282.
*j* *Street v Mountford* [1985] 2 All ER 289, [1985] AC 809, HL.

**Appeals**
*Customs and Excise Comrs v Faith Construction Ltd*
The Crown appealed with the leave of the judge against the decision of Simon Brown J
([1988] 1 All ER 919, [1989] QB 176) on 6 November 1987 whereby he dismissed the

Crown's appeal against the decision of a London value added tax tribunal (chairman Lord
Grantchester QC) dated 26 March 1986 whereby it was decided that an agreement      *a*
between Delmon Property Co (1983) Ltd (Delmon) and the respondents, Faith
Construction Ltd (the taxpayer company), that Delmon would pay the contract price for
works of alteration to a property at 36–38 Church Road, Burgess Hill, that the taxpayer
company would then lend an amount equal to the contract price back to Delmon and
that the arrangement would be carried out by the exchange of cheques was a genuine
transaction and that accordingly supplies rendered by the taxpayer company to Delmon   *b*
should be treated as having been made prior to 1 June 1984. The facts are set out in the
judgment of Parker LJ.

*Customs and Excise Comrs v West Yorkshire Independent*
*Hospital (Contract Services) Ltd*

The Crown appealed with the leave of the judge against the decision of Henry J ([1988]   *c*
STC 443) on 10 March 1988 whereby he dismissed the Crown's appeal against the
decision of a Manchester value added tax tribunal (chairman Mr A W Simpson) ([1986]
VATTR 151) dated 7 August 1986 whereby it allowed an appeal by the respondents,
West Yorkshire Independent Hospital (Contract Services) Ltd (the taxpayer company),
and held that certain payments to the taxpayer company for procuring the completion
of the design and erection of the extension of a clinic were not made after 1 June 1984   *d*
and thus were not liable to value added tax at the standard rate. The facts are set out in
the judgment of Parker LJ.

*Dormers Builders (London) Ltd v Customs and Excise Comrs*

The Crown appealed with the leave of the judge against the decision of McNeill J ([1988]
STC 735) on 12 April 1988 whereby he allowed an appeal by the respondents, Dormers   *e*
(Builders) Ltd (the taxpayer company), against a decision of a London value added tax
tribunal (chairman Mr Neil Elles) on 9 April 1987 confirming a decision by the
Commissioners of Customs and Excise that certain supplies of goods and services were
taxable to value added tax at the standard rate. The facts are set out in the judgment of
Parker LJ.                                                                              *f*

*Nevisbrook Ltd v Customs and Excise Comrs*

The Crown appealed with the leave of the judge against the decision of Henry J ([1989]
STC 192) on 2 December 1988 whereby he allowed an appeal by the respondents,
Nevisbrook Ltd (the taxpayer company), against a decision of a London value added tax
tribunal (chairman Mr Neil Elles) released on 8 July 1987 confirming an assessment    *g*
dated 25 July 1985 to value added tax in the sum of £5,073·32 made on the taxpayer
company. The facts are set out in the judgment of Parker LJ.

The appeals were heard together.

*John Mummery* and *Guy Sankey* for the Crown.                                          *h*
*Roderick Cordara* for the taxpayer companies.

*Cur adv vult*

26 May. The following judgments were delivered.                                         *j*

**PARKER LJ.** We have before us four appeals in respect of value added tax. The
appellants are, in each appeal, the Commissioners of Customs and Excise. The respondents
are four building companies, named respectively Faith Construction Ltd (Faith), West
Yorkshire Independent Hospital (Contract Services) Ltd (West Yorkshire), Dormers
Builders (London) Ltd (Dormers), and Nevisbrook Ltd (Nevisbrook).

The four judgments from which the commissioners appeal are: as to Faith by Simon
*a* Brown J ([1988] 1 All ER 919, [1989] QB 179), as to West Yorkshire by Henry J ([1988]
STC 443), as to Dormers by McNeill J ([1988] STC 735) and as to Nevisbrook by Henry J
([1989] STC 192). In the cases of Faith and West Yorkshire, appeals by the commissioners
against decisions of a value added tax tribunal in favour of the taxpayer companies were
dismissed. In the cases of Dormers and Nevisbrook, appeals by the two taxpayer
companies from decisions of a value added tax tribunal in favour of the commissioners
*b* were allowed.

The background to each appeal is the same. On 13 March 1984 the Chancellor of the
Exchequer announced in his budget speech that, as from 1 June 1984, value added tax in
respect of building alteration services, which at that time were zero-rated, would be
charged at the standard rate. Section 1 of the Value Added Tax Act 1983 provides that
value added tax shall be charged on any supply of goods or services and s 2(3) that tax on
*c* the supply of goods or services is the liability of the person making the supply and
(subject to provisions about accounting and payment) becomes due at the time of supply.
Sections 4 and 5 deal with the ascertainment of the time of supply. So far as immediately
material they provide:

*d* '**4.**—(1) The provisions of this section and section 5 below shall apply for
determining the time when a supply of goods or services is to be treated as taking
place for the purposes of the charge to tax . . .
(3) Subject to the provisions of section 5 below, a supply of services shall be
treated as taking place at the time when the services are performed.
**5.**—(1) If, before the time applicable under subsection (2) or subsection (3) of
section 4 above, the person making the supply issues a tax invoice in respect of it or
*e* if, before the time applicable under paragraph (*a*) or (*b*) of subsection (2) or subsection
(3) of that section, he receives a payment in respect of it, the supply shall, to the
extent covered by the invoice or payment, be treated as taking place at the time the
invoice is issued or the payment is received . . .'

The purpose of s 5(1) is plainly to accelerate the date for payment of tax. It is, in the
*f* absence of a change in rating, for the benefit of the Revenue in that it will recover tax
earlier. It will also be for the benefit of the Revenue if, subsequent to tax invoice or
receipt of payment by the supplier, the rate of tax is reduced. If, however, the rate goes
up between receipt of payment and performance, whilst the Revenue will still get the
benefit of early payment, it will lose the amount of the increase and the supplier of the
services and the building owner will benefit to the extent of the increase.

In the present cases the four taxpayer companies sought, not surprisingly, to achieve
*g* the benefit of advance payment and receipt. The question for determination is whether
they have succeeded in doing so.

As the facts of all cases are fully set out in the reports of the judgments under appeal, I
do not propose to rehearse them here. I shall state only the bare essentials. In each case it
is common ground that, prior to 1 June 1984, the building owner paid money into a
*h* bank account of the builder in respect of building services to be supplied thereafter. In
two cases, Faith and West Yorkshire, the money was so paid pursuant to arrangements
whereby the same amount was either directly or indirectly to be and was in fact forthwith
lent back either to the building owner or to a company closely associated with the
building owner, the loan to be repayable against architects' certificates as the work
proceeded. In the other two cases, Dormers and Nevisbrook, the money was paid into a
*j* deposit account of the builder under arrangments whereby it was only to be released to
the builder against architects' certificates. In the former two cases the loan was in fact
repaid against architects' certificates and in the latter two cases the moneys in the deposit
accounts were in fact released against architects' certificates. All such repayments and
releases occurred after 1 June 1984.

The foregoing statement represents a considerable simplification of complicated

arrangements but is sufficient for present purposes, for the dispute between the parties
falls within a narrow compass. Counsel for the Crown put the matter this way in his *a*
skeleton argument:

> '3. The central features of the contractual arrangements made in each case before
> the 1st June 1984 were that (1) a sum of money was credited before the 1st June
> 1984 to a bank account bearing the name of the builder, but subject to terms and
> conditions; (2) no sums would be released to the builder in respect of the services
> supplied by him until architects' certificates were produced in respect of the services *b*
> performed by him after the 1st June 1984.
> 4. The Commissioners' contention is that no payments were received by the
> builders in respect of the services performed by them until the relevant sums in
> respect of those services were in fact released to the builder on production of the
> architects' certificates.
> 5. All "payments" by way of credit into a bank account in the name of the builder *c*
> before the 1st June 1984 were conditional or qualified only and were not therefore
> payments received by the builder in respect of services supplied until those payments
> became unconditional or unqualified.'

In the course of argument the submission was refined somewhat and put in the
following form: a payment in respect of a supply is not a payment received by the person *d*
making the supply within the meaning of s 5(1) of the 1983 Act to the extent that it is
conditional on the moneys not being available for use by or for the benefit of the person
making the supply until the supply has been made.

The point at issue is a short one depending wholly on the construction of s 5(1) of the
1983 Act. Before considering it, I should mention that no criticism was or could be made
of either the builders or the contractors for attempting to take advantage of the *e*
continuance of zero-rating up to 1 June by making advance payment for services to be
supplied thereafter. Not only was it apparent from the budget speech and the terms of
s 5(1) that the opportunity to do so existed and would be to their mutual benefit but, in
addition, the commissioners had at the same time issued a notice which was a positive
invitation to do so. Paragraph 14 of that notice was in the following terms: *f*

> 'The transitional rules for registered builders not using a retail scheme are as
> follows: (a) *Work completed before 1 June.* You need not charge tax even if you do not
> invoice your customer until after that date. (b) *Work not started before 1 June.* This is
> liable to the tax except to the extent that the customer pays *before 1 June.* (The issue
> of an invoice prior to 1 June for work which, if carried out before that date, would
> have been zero-rated is not a tax invoice and has no effect.) (c) *Work in progress at* *g*
> *1 June.* Provided that you can apportion the supply in a realistic way, you are entitled
> to zero rate that part of the job done before 1 June and charge at 15% for the balance.
> Alternatively if your customer agrees to pay for the whole job *before* 1 June, then
> the whole job attracts the zero rate.'

The accuracy of the words in parenthesis in sub-para (b) is questionable and the last *h*
sentence of sub-para (c) was admitted by counsel for the Crown to be wrong but no point
arises on this on these appeals. What is of some importance is that the notice brought
home to builders the benefit of securing payment from the customer before 1 June in
respect of work to be done thereafter.

I turn to the construction of s 5(1). I have already observed that it is clearly designed
for the benefit of the Revenue by the advancement of the tax point. It is also important *j*
to note that the issue of a tax invoice is an alternative to receipt of payment for the
purpose of accelerating point of supply. Assuming for the moment that the words in
parenthesis in sub-para (b) of para 14 of the notice are correct, the alternative was not
available in the present cases. If, however, there had been, for example, a change, not
from zero to standard rate but from one rate to a higher rate, the mere issue of a tax

invoice would have been enough to accelerate the incidence of tax and thus enable the
a supplier to take advantage of the lower rate. The section is not therefore concerned, at
least in part, with real transactions but with the artificial advancement of the tax point.

It is, in my view, convenient to consider the position which would or might have
obtained had the increase been from a lower rate to the standard rate and the Revenue
being aware of a payment for the services having been made on, say, 29 May immediately
sought to recover tax on the whole of a contract price, say £1m, which would otherwise
b only have become payable a year later. Would it have been any answer to such a claim
for the builder to say, 'True I have received the money and my customer is under no
further liability under the building contract, but he only paid on condition that I would
lend him back the money, so I have not really received payment and will not do so until
he repays the loan'? Such an answer would, in my view, be open to serious objection.
The true legal effect of what had occurred would be that the builder's right to payment
c for the services had been discharged and in place of it he had acquired a cause of action
for money lent and nothing else. Thus the answer could only be good if receipt of
repayment of the loan, which was the only enforceable right left to the builder, is by
some process of alchemy converted into payment for services for which payment had
already been made and in respect of which the builder no longer had any enforceable
right.
d    Again, consider a case where a builder with financial problems wishes to reassure both
his bankers and actual sub-contractors that he will be able to complete a particular
contract. If such a person can persuade his customer to pay for the whole of the works in
advance, but undertakes to his bankers that he will only use the money to pay his own
workforce and material obligations and his sub-contractors, the payment when made is
subject to a fetter but it is accepted that it would be a payment received within s 5(1).
e Can it make any difference that the customer exacts a similar undertaking? I am unable
to see why it should.

For the taxpayer companies it was submitted that since, in each case, payments were
in fact made by the customer, were received by the builder and discharged the liability
under the contracts, the words of the statute are complied with and it is nothing to do
with the Revenue what the builder thereafter does with the money whether by agreement
f with his bankers or his customer or anyone else. As it was submitted before the tribunal
in one of the appeals, if the payment was made, as it was, it cannot have disappeared into
a black hole. It must have been received by someone and the only possible recipient is in
each case the builder. Had the builder not received it he could not, in the cases of Faith
and West Yorkshire, have made the loan.

g    We were referred to authorities on the meaning of payment in other contexts but they
do not, in my judgment, assist. It is simply a case of the construction of a simple
subsection in its own context and enacted for the plain purpose of accelerating the
moment at which the supplier's liability occurs.

Given that the payments, although made under arrangements which fettered the
recipient's use of the money received, discharged the liability of the customer under the
building contract and left the recipient with no right to sue for payment thereunder, I
h can see no alternative but to conclude that in each case payment was made before 1 June
and accordingly that the Crown's contention that payment was not received until, in the
cases of Faith and West Yorkshire, there was partial repayment of the loan and, in the
cases of Dormers and Nevisbrook, the money was released from the deposit account, is
unsustainable.

j    That conclusion is sufficient to dispose of the appeals in the Dormers and Nevisbrook
cases, both of which in my judgment should be dismissed.

In the cases of Faith and West Yorkshire, however, a further matter arises, at least
theoretically. In those cases it was submitted that the principles derived from W T
Ramsay Ltd v IRC [1981] 1 All ER 865, [1982] AC 300, IRC v Burmah Oil Co Ltd [1982]
STC 30, Furniss (Inspector of Taxes) v Dawson [1984] 1 All ER 530, [1984] AC 474 and

*Craven (Inspector of Taxes) v White* [1988] 3 All ER 495, [1988] 3 WLR 423 were applicable in the present case and would result in the conclusion that, even if viewed alone the *a* payments made would be received prior to 1 June, the true legal result of the arrangements, viewed as one composite transaction or a preordained series of transactions, was that payment was only received when the loans were repaid against architects' certificates. I say 'at least theoretically' for counsel for the Crown, in my view rightly, frankly accepted that, if he failed on the construction point, it was at least doubtful if he would be much assisted by the first three of these cases as elucidated in the fourth.          *b*

Reliance was principally placed on Lord Keith's speech in *Craven (Inspector of Taxes) v White* [1988] 3 All ER 495 at 500, [1988] 3 WLR 423 at 430 where he said:

> 'My Lords, in my opinion the nature of the principle to be derived from the three cases is this: the court must first construe the relevant enactment in order to ascertain. its meaning; it must then analyse the series of transactions in question, regarded as a whole, so as to ascertain its true effect in law; and finally it must apply the *c* enactment as construed to the true effect of the series of transactions and so decide whether or not the enactment was intended to cover it. The most important feature of the principle is that the series of transactions is to be regarded as a whole. In ascertaining the true legal effect of the series it is relevant to take into account, if it be the case, that all the steps in it were contractually agreed in advance or had been *d* determined on in advance by a guiding will which was in a position, for all practical purposes, to secure that all of them were carried through to completion. It is also relevant to take into account, if it be the case, that one or more of the steps was introduced into the series with no business purpose other than the avoidance of tax.'

I have already dealt with the true construction of the section. I have also, in the process, in effect analysed the true effect of the series of transactions regarded as a whole and *e* concluded that its true effect in law was not that payment was received for the supplies as and when the loan was repaid. It accordingly follows that the respective builders are not liable to value added tax on that basis which is that for which the Crown contends.

In the result I would reject the alternative argument and dismiss the appeals in these two cases also.          *f*

**BINGHAM LJ.** Value added tax is chargeable on the supplier of services. It becomes due at the time of supply. A supply of services is treated as taking place at the time when the services are performed, save that if before that time the supplier receives a payment in respect of the supply such supply is treated as taking place at the time the payment is received (see the Value Added Tax Act 1983, ss 2(1) and (3), 4(3) and 5(1)).          *g*

During periods when the value added tax regime is stable, questions of timing are unlikely to cause difficulty. If, for example, a builder does work chargeable to value added tax under a typical contract providing for stage payments against periodical architect's certificates, he will become liable to pay the tax in respect of the works covered by each certificate when payment under it is made, since the service is not treated as supplied until the works are completed.          *h*

The problem common to the four present appeals arises because building work carried out for the alteration of buildings, previously zero-rated, became subject to value added tax at the standard rate with effect from 1 June 1984. This change, announced by the Chancellor in his budget speech two and a half months earlier, gave builders and their customers the opportunity to seek to arrange matters so that building works, although done after 1 June, would not be subject to the tax. They both had an obvious incentive *j* to do so, the customer because the work would be cheaper, the builder because an increase in the price might cost him the contract. Tax would not be chargeable if, before the work was done and before 1 June, the builder received a payment in respect of the work. Whether, within the meaning of s 5(1), the taxpayer companies did so receive a payment is the question at issue in these appeals.

The taxpayer companies (Faith, West Yorkshire, Dormers and Nevisbrook) were all
building companies. They all contracted before 1 June to carry out alteration works for
customers (ie Delmon, the hospital company, Wharf and Batleyville). In three cases the
customer was closely associated with its contracting building company. (The exception
was Batleyville, but even in that case a high degree of confidence existed, as is shown by
the agreement made.) In each case funds were transferred by customer to the building
company before 1 June in respect of works to be carried out thereafter. But these were
not out-and-out payments with no strings attached. In two cases, the customer (Delmon
and the hospital company) borrowed the money to pay the building company (Faith and
West Yorkshire) and made the payment on terms that the building company would
immediately lend the money back to the customer to repay its original borrowing. In
the other two cases, the customer (Wharf and Batleyville) paid the money into an account
in the building company's name but on terms that it should not be available for use by
the building company until a condition had been fulfilled.

In all four cases the building company would gain unfettered beneficial enjoyment of
the money representing the price of the works only when and as architects' certificates
were periodically issued certifying the value of work done. In the first two cases such
certificates would trigger the repayment of the building company's loan to the customer,
to the extent certified. In the other two cases they would give the building company the
right to draw or procure the drawing of funds, to the extent certified, from the account
in the company's name.

In the first two cases, where money was lent back to the customers and repaid to the
building companies, the value added tax tribunals found for the building companies and
were upheld by the judge (Simon Brown and Henry JJ). In the other cases, where money
was paid to the building companies' accounts and released on the issue of architects'
certificates, the tribunals found against the building companies and were reversed by the
judge (McNeill and Henry JJ).

The question for decision can be simply stated: when money was transferred by the
customer to the building company before 1 June 1984 did the building company
thereupon receive a payment in respect of the supply of building services to be made
thereafter?

The main thrust of counsel's excellent argument for the Crown was that the transfers
of money which undoubtedly took place before 1 June in each case did not amount to
payments within the meaning of s 5(1) and, if they were payments, the building
companies did not receive the payments within the meaning of the subsection. His
reason for so submitting was that in no case did the building company obtain beneficial
enjoyment of the funds transferred at the time of transfer, because either it was
committed to relending the money at once to the transferor or it could not draw on the
funds transferred until a condition (the issue of an architect's certificate) had been
fulfilled.

I find nothing in s 5(1) to indicate that Parliament intended the concept of making or
receiving a payment to have any meaning other than that which the law would ordinarily
give it. I cannot, certainly, suppose that the draftsman was anxious to prevent parties
accelerating an event which would in the ordinary way accelerate a tax liability. There is
of course much law as to what in the absence of agreement amounts to payment, but in
the contractual context my understanding is that A pays the price to B when he does that
which B agrees to accept as payment of the price. This assumes that the transaction is
genuine, not a sham, and that A and B are not taking part in a charade, but in all these
cases the Crown accepts that the transaction is genuine and not a sham.

In the Faith and West Yorkshire cases I am persuaded that the transfer of funds made
before 1 June was a payment received by the building companies. First, it is common
ground that this transfer was accepted in full and final satisfaction of the building
companies' right to be paid for the work they were to do. If thereafter the customers had
failed to repay the building companies' loans against architects' certificates, the building

companies could have sued for breach of contract but could not have sued for the price because according to their agreement they had already been paid it. Second, if it be *a* correct that the customers had paid, I do not think it can be said that the building companies had not received the payment, since the making of a payment necessarily involves the receipt of a payment and it is not suggested that anyone other than the building companies received these payments.

I have felt more doubt about the Dormers and Nevisbrook cases, but in the end conclude that the same answer must apply there also. The effect of the agreements, *b* genuinely made, appears to have been that the transfers into accounts in the names of the building companies should be accepted in full and final payment of the price, the funds thereafter being the property of the building companies, who would be absolutely entitled to interest earned on the sums deposited. Had funds not been released thereafter according to the agreements the building companies could have sued for breach of contract but could not, as I understand the facts, have sued for the price because again, *c* according to their agreements, they had received it.

I therefore think that the main argument of counsel for the Crown must be rejected. In the first two cases (Faith and West Yorkshire), but not in the other two, however, he had an alternative argument based on *Craven (Inspector of Taxes) v White* [1988] 3 All ER 495, [1988] 3 WLR 423 and the explanation which the majority of the House of Lords there gave of the cases culminating in *Furniss (Inspector of Taxes) v Dawson* [1984] 1 All *d* ER 530, [1984] AC 474. Founding himself in particular on the passage in Lord Keith's speech in *Craven v White* [1988] 3 All ER 495 at 500, [1988] 3 WLR 423 at 430, counsel for the Crown argued that one should look at the whole series of preordained events and ask what the true effect in law of the series of events was and then determine whether there was, as a matter of construction, a payment received within the meaning of the 1983 Act. So viewed, the events which occurred here did not amount to payment. I shall *e* deal with this argument shortly because, even if it be assumed that the *Furniss v Dawson* principle applies to value added tax and that we are here dealing with a preordained series of transactions as opposed to a single transaction, the argument cannot in my view succeed. If we were entitled to disregard the legal effect of what was done here and give effect to the underlying substance, it might be possible to say that these payments were *f* not really payments because they were made for the purpose of avoiding value added tax and without any (or any other) commercial justification. But that is an approach which Lord Tomlin's well-known speech in *IRC v Duke of Westminster* [1936] AC 1 at 19–21, [1935] All ER Rep 259 at 267–268 roundly condemned where the transaction in question is genuine and I do not understand the principle there laid down, described as 'cardinal' by Lord Wilberforce in *W T Ramsay Ltd v IRC* [1981] 1 All ER 865 at 871, [1982] AC 300 *g* at 323, to have been diluted or abrogated by later decisions. If the payments are to be disregarded the Crown would, I think, have to show them to be a sham, and this it has not sought to do. If, as I have concluded, these were in law good contractual payments, then I do not think we are entitled to disregard their legal effect and treat them as something else. The judges below were, in my view, right in reaching the conclusions they did. *h*

For these reasons, as well as those given more fully by Parker LJ (which I have had the advantage of reading in draft and with which I agree), I would dismiss all these appeals.

**MANN LJ.** I gratefully adopt the statement of essential facts contained in the judgment of Parker LJ.

The issue in each of these appeals involves a single and short point of statutory *j* construction. The provision to be construed is s 5(1) of the Value Added Tax Act 1983. The section has the shoulder note 'Further provisions relating to time of supply'. So far as is now material, the subsection provides as follows:

'If, before the time applicable under . . . subsection (3) of section 4 above, the person making the supply . . . receives a payment in respect of it, the supply shall, a    to the extent covered by the . . . payment, be treated as taking place at the time . . . the payment is received.'

If that subsection is inapplicable, then the time of supply is the time when services are performed (s 4(3) of the 1983 Act). It is common ground that sums of money were transferred to the four building companies before the companies had performed the building works which they were engaged to perform. The transfers took place before building works, which were works of alteration (as was the nature of the works in each

b    of the four cases), became subject to value added tax on 1 June 1984.

It is obvious that each transfer was made with the object of avoiding payment of value added tax by taking advantage of the accelerative provisions of s 5(1). The commissioners concede that none of the transactions was a sham. The transactions are therefore to be approached on the basis that they are what they appear to be. The question is thus simply: did each of the building companies 'receive a payment'? Counsel for the Crown

c    very persuasively argued that the answer is No. I find myself able to resist his persuasiveness.

The core of the argument of counsel for the Crown was that there could not be a payment received by the person who is to make the supply where that person does not have the beneficial use of the moneys prior to performance of the services. This seems to

d    me to gloss simple words. Payments were made and payments made must have a recipient and who else could that be but the building companies? How could Faith and West Yorkshire have made the loans to their employers had they not received the moneys transferred? The repayment of the loan by stages when architects' certificates were issued could be enforced not by an action for moneys due under the building contract but by an action for breach of the loan agreement. As to the cases of Dormers and Nevisbrook,

e    the companies are the only possible recipients of the moneys, they were entitled to the interest on the deposit and, if a release was not authorised against an architect's certificate, then the claim would not lie under the building contract but would be for breach of the arrangement concerning release.

In the cases of Faith and West Yorkshire, counsel for the Crown drew our attention to a number of cases and in particular relied on a passage in the speech of Lord Keith in

f    *Craven (Inspector of Taxes) v White* [1988] 3 All ER 495 at 500, [1988] 3 WLR 423 at 430. I do not rehearse the passage, which is set out in the judgment of Parker LJ. I observe of it that the construction of the statute is such that the transactions gave rise to a payment received and that the two transactions were genuine and were found by the tribunal to have commercial reasons albeit the object was to avoid the payment of value added tax (see [1988] 1 All ER 919 at 926, [1989] QB 179 at 188 (Faith) and [1986] VATTR 151 at

g    164 (West Yorkshire)).

I have had the advantage of reading in draft the judgments of Parker and Bingham LJJ. I agree with them and for their reasons, and those which I have shortly expressed, I also would dismiss these appeals.

h    *Appeals dismissed. Leave to appeal to the House of Lords refused.*

Solicitors: *Solicitor for the Customs and Excise*; *H H Mainprice* (for Faith, Dormers and Nevisbrook); *Hammond Suddards*, Bradford (for West Yorkshire).

Heather Whicher   Barrister.

# R v Smith (Ian)                                                                    *a*

COURT OF APPEAL, CRIMINAL DIVISION
LORD LANE CJ, KENNEDY AND HUTCHISON JJ
9 JUNE 1989

*Drugs – Drug trafficking – Confiscation order – Proceeds of drug trafficking – Any payments or*   *b*
*other rewards received in connection with drug trafficking – Whether 'proceeds' of drug trafficking*
*referring to net or gross proceeds – Whether confiscation order can be made in respect of aggregate*
*of all payments received from drug trafficking – Whether severity of confiscation order can be*
*mitigated – Drug Trafficking Offences Act 1986, ss 2(1), 4(3).*

For the purposes of s 2(1)[a] of the Drug Trafficking Offences Act 1986 'any payments or   *c*
other rewards' received in connection with drug trafficking refers to any payment
whatsoever in money or kind and not just the net profit derived from drug trafficking
after the deduction of expenses, whether the expenses relate to the purchase of drugs,
travelling, entertainment or otherwise. Accordingly, in making a confiscation order
under the 1986 Act in respect of the 'proceeds' of drug trafficking derived from a number
of transactions the trial judge is entitled to aggregate all payments received without   *d*
making any allowance for the fact that the payment received from each transaction or
part thereof might have been reinvested in the next transaction, since s 2 is deliberately
drafted to avoid the necessity of the trial judge having to enter into an accountancy
exercise. However, it is open to the judge under s 4(3)[b] of the 1986 Act to mitigate the
severity of a confiscation order if the amount of money available to the defendant to
satisfy the order is less than the amount which the court decides was the value of the   *e*
proceeds of his drug trafficking (see p 951 *b* to *d f*, post).

**Notes**
For confiscation of proceeds of drug trafficking, see Supplement to 11 Halsbury's Laws
(4th edn) para 1099A.3.
                                                                                    *f*
**Case referred to in judgment**
*R v Aramah* (1982) 76 Cr App R 190, CA.

**Appeal against sentence**
Ian Smith appealed against a confiscation order in the sum of £14,000 made by the judge
on 6 May 1988 under the Drug Trafficking Offences Act 1986 following his conviction   *g*
on 26 January 1988 in the Crown Court at Portsmouth before his Honour Judge Brodrick
and a jury on a charge of conspiracy to supply cannabis for which he was sentenced to
five years' imprisonment in addition to the confiscation order. The appeal first came
before the court (Lord Lane CJ and Henry J) on 17 March 1989 when the court dismissed
the appeal against the sentence of imprisonment but adjourned the appeal against the
confiscation order for consideration by a court of three judges. The facts are set out in the   *h*
judgment of the court.

*David Swinstead* (assigned by the Registrar of Criminal Appeals) for the appellant.
*Michael Vere-Hodge* for the Crown.

**LORD LANE CJ.** On 26 January 1988 in the Crown Court at Portsmouth before his   *j*
Honour Judge Brodrick and a jury, this appellant, Ian Smith, was convicted of conspiracy

---

*a*   Section 2(1) is set out at p 950 *g*, post
*b*   Section 4(3) is set out at p 951 *e*, post

to supply cannabis. Sentence was adjourned after the hearing in order to consider the
a making of a confiscation order under the Drug Trafficking Offences Act 1986. That
hearing took three days to complete in May 1988. In the upshot the appellant was
sentenced to five years' imprisonment and a confiscation order in the sum of £14,000
under the 1986 Act was made.

He appealed against that sentence by leave of the single judge. The matter was heard
originally by a two-judge court, of which I was one of the members, on 17 March 1989.
b We dismissed the appeal so far as the imprisonment of five years was concerned, and we
adjourned the matter to a court of three judges in order to try the more complicated
matter of the confiscation order under the 1986 Act. We have now had the matter argued
before us most helpfully, if we may say so, by both counsel who have appeared before us
today.

It is perhaps necessary for me to repeat some of the judgment which was delivered in
c the earlier hearing before the two-judge court in order to set the scene of the facts so far
as this case is concerned.

The prosecution case was this. Over a period of time prior to 1 May 1987 this appellant
used to travel from Portsmouth to an address in Feltham on a number of occasions where
one of his co-accused called Murrell had his home. He sometimes travelled with a man
called Fisher, who was also a co-accused, and sometimes with another co-accused called
d Palmer. The object of the journeys was to obtain cannabis for resale in Hampshire.

The police were alerted to what was going on and they kept observation on the
appellant and the various co-accused. It was not a continuous operation of surveillance,
and some of the journeys made by the appellant were not observed, but the dates on
which the material journeys were made were these: an unknown occasion before 6 April;
6 April itself, when the appellant was observed to visit Murrell's house; 13 April, when
e the appellant drove Palmer to London, where they met Fisher; 17 April, which was an
occasion admitted by the appellant himself; 28 April, when the appellant visited Murrell's
house alone; and finally on 1 May, when the appellant collected Palmer and drove to
Murrell's address. When they came out Palmer was carrying a white package. They
drove to Woking railway station. They were arrested there. In a holdall at Palmer's feet
was found an envelope containing 2 kg of cannabis resin. In the appellant's pocket was
f an envelope containing £380. Murrell was arrested shortly afterwards. At his house was
found a kilogramme of cannabis resin together with the paraphernalia of the drug dealer,
and four brown envelopes containing a total of almost £4,500, the notes being packed in
a manner precisely the same as the notes which were found on the appellant himself. At
the appellant's house when it was searched were found a set of weights and other
incriminating articles.
g The first point taken by the appellant concerns both aspects of the appeal, the sentence
of five years which we upheld on the previous occasion and the confiscation order. It is
this. The judge in delivering his judgment said:

'So, out of six trips, it seems to me that I can properly assume that drugs changed
hands on four of them. I think I am entitled to assume that it was in the region of
h 2 kg per trip. So, a total of 8 kg came into his possession which was available for
resale. I propose to make a further assumption, which is perhaps more favourable
to [the appellant] than it ought to be, and I propose to assume that he only disposed
of 1 kg from each trip.'

It is suggested by counsel for the appellant that those calculations were based on a
j misapprehension of the evidence, a point which he did not take on the first hearing of
this appeal, but we allowed him to take it on this occasion, because it does affect both
legs, the imprisonment leg (if I may call it that) and the confiscation leg. It is this, that
the occasion on which the cannabis resin was actually found in the possession of the
defendant was one in which the resin was in a plastic bag being carried. We are now
provided with photographs, which we were not on the previous occasion, which show

the way in which the cannabis resin was, so to speak, packed. Each piece is in the exact shape of a cake of soap. The cannabis which was being carried on the final occasion was *a* in that form in a plastic bag.

It seems that on the other occasions when the police carried out the observation, there was nothing being carried by the appellant. The officers were questioned and gave answers to the effect that there was nothing apparently bulky being carried on the person of the appellant so far as they could tell. The point is therefore taken that it was quite wrong for the judge to do as he did, namely to assume that 2 kg were being carried on *b* each occasion, when to carry 2 kg would have involved carrying a large number of these cakes.

What the judge did was not to act strictly according to observation. He was making an assumption, the words he used were: 'I think I am entitled to assume that it was in the region of 2 kg per trip.' In the judgment of this court he was entitled to make that assumption for a number of different reasons. First of all it might very well be that there *c* were on the person of the appellant these cakes of cannabis which could have been carried in various pockets without any necessary bulging or observable bulging of the clothes. Second, there were all sorts of other ways in which these cakes of cannabis could have been dealt with without the necessity of the police being in a position when carrying out their observation of being able to observe anything peculiar which would indicate that cannabis of this quantity was on the person of the appellant. *d*

In our judgment the judge was perfectly entitled to make that assumption as he did. As also indicated, he made deductions from those assumed figures in fairness to the appellant. Those deductions likewise, in the judgment of this court, were properly made.

So far as the first point is concerned, that fails. That means that the sentence of five years' imprisonment was clearly based on the guideline judgment of *R v Aramah* (1982) 76 Cr App R 190 on the basis of a correct assumption of the amount of cannabis which *e* this man had in fact been dealing with.

The next point is a point taken on the meaning of the 1986 Act. The way in which this ground of appeal is put forward is this. The judge wrongly applied the provisions of s 2 of the Act in basing his calculation on the assumption that £3,500 had been received from each successful sale, whereas that £3,500 consisted partly of the same sum of money which was reinvested in each transaction. The calculation, goes on the submission, should *f* have been based on the profit made from each transaction.

Section 2(1) of the 1986 Act reads as follows:

> 'For the purposes of this Act—(*a*) any payments or other rewards received by a person at any time (whether before or after the commencement of section 1 of this Act) in connection with drug trafficking carried on by him or another are his *g* proceeds of drug trafficking, and (*b*) the value of his proceeds of drug trafficking is the aggregate of the values of the payments or other rewards.'

What the judge did, as already indicated, was to find as a fact that there were four occasions on which payments were received by the appellant in connection with drug trafficking carried on by him. On each he found that there were payments of at least *h* £2,500 and these were accordingly his 'proceeds' of drug trafficking. He then aggregated the values of those payments, as he conceived he was enjoined to do by s 2(1)(*b*): 4 × £2,500 = £10,000, and he declared that to be the value of the proceeds.

That is wrong, submits counsel for the appellant, because the majority of each sum received as payment would be invested in purchasing the next consignment for sale, and so on. Therefore, goes the argument, so far as a charge of this nature is concerned, namely *j* a charge of conspiracy when a number of transactions are in question, the judge should only have taken into account the profit element of each successful trip.

Whether that submission is correct depends simply on the wording of s 2. But before proceeding to consider that argument, it is worth noting, as counsel for the Crown rightly pointed out to the court, that there was absolutely no evidence that money had

been 'rolled over' in this way, if one can use that expression, because from first to last the
*a* appellant had denied that he was dealing in cannabis in the way the prosecution
contended that he was. There was absolutely no evidence that he had rolled over any
money in the way alleged.

Leaving aside that factual difficulty in the way of the appellant, we turn to consider
the question from the legal aspect, namely the meaning of s 2(1).

The words 'any payments' are on the face of them clear. They must mean, indeed it is
*b* clear from the wording, any payment in money or in kind. It does not mean, in the
judgment of this court, net profit derived from the payment after the deduction of
expenses, whether the expenses are those of purchase, travelling, entertainment or
otherwise. The same consideration applies to the words 'other rewards'. They also have
to be valued. If for example the receiver of the drugs had rewarded the appellant by
providing him with an expensive holiday or an expensive motor car, it would not, we
*c* think, the legitimate to construe the words 'value of the rewards' as meaning the value of
the holiday or motor car less the business expenses involved in earning the reward.

It seems to us that the section is deliberately worded so as to avoid the necessity, which
the appellant's construction of the section would involve, of having to carry out an
accountancy exercise, which would be quite impossible in the circumstances of this case.
It may be that the wording is draconian, and that it produces a draconian result. But it
*d* seems to us that, if that is the case, it was a result intended by those who framed the Act.

That interpretation of the Act is to some extent, in the view of this court, mitigated in
its severity by the provisions of s 4(3) of the 1986 Act, which reads as follows:

> 'If the court is satisfied that the amount that might be realised at the time the
> confiscation order is made is less than the amount the court assesses to be the value
> *e* of his proceeds of drug trafficking, the amount to be recovered in the defendant's
> case under the confiscation order shall be the amount appearing to the court to be
> the amount that might be so realised.'

Counsel for the appellant seeks to support his argument that s 2 is dealing with profits
and not the receipts by relying on that subsection. We do not consider that his
interpretation is correct. It seems to us that what that subsection is doing is saying simply
*f* that, if in the upshot the amount of money available to the defendant to satisfy a
confiscation order is less than the amount which the court finds he should pay, then the
court is entitled to mitigate the amount ordered to take account of that fact.

We have perhaps said enough to indicate that in our view the judge in this very clear
judgment of his, which has all marks of preparation, careful consideration and correct
interpretation of the Act, is correct. There is no proper ground for complaint either with
*g* regard to the sentence of imprisonment which was imposed or with regard to the amount
which was ordered to be paid under the 1986 Act by way of confiscation. Consequently
this appeal must be dismissed.

*Appeal dismissed.*

*h* Solicitors: *Crown Prosecution Service*, Portsmouth.

N P Metcalfe Esq    Barrister.

# Banque Financière de la Cité SA v Westgate Insurance Co Ltd

COURT OF APPEAL, CIVIL DIVISION

SLADE, LLOYD AND RALPH GIBSON LJJ

13–15, 18, 19, 21, 22, 25–28 APRIL, 3–6, 9, 10, 12, 13, 18–20, 23, 24 MAY, 28 JULY 1988

*Insurance – Disclosure – Duty to disclose – Duty of utmost good faith – Reciprocal nature of duty – Failure to disclose material facts – Insurer's duty of disclosure – Banks making loans to companies guaranteed by credit insurance policies arranged by broker – Broker's employee dishonestly issuing cover notes when part of cover missing – Banks lending large sums in reliance on cover notes – Insurers aware of broker's employee's deception – Insurers not informing banks of deception – Companies defaulting on loans – Whether duty of utmost good faith reciprocal – Whether insurers in breach of duty of utmost good faith.*

*Insurance – Disclosure – Duty to disclose – Duty of utmost good faith – Breach of duty – Damages for breach – Breach by insurer – Whether insured entitled to damages or merely avoidance of contract of insurance and return of premium.*

*Misrepresentation – Disclosure – Duty to disclose – Duty of utmost good faith – Failure to disclose material facts – Whether silence amounting to misrepresentation – Whether misrepresentation 'made' to other party if there is a failure to disclose material facts – Misrepresentation Act 1967, s 2(1).*

*Negligence – Duty to take care – Insurer – Duty owed by insurer to insured – Banks making loans to companies guaranteed by credit insurance policies arranged by broker – Broker's employee dishonestly issuing cover notes when part of cover missing – Banks lending large sums in reliance on cover notes – Insurers aware of broker's employee's deception – Whether insurers owing duty of care to disclose broker's employee's deception to banks.*

*Misrepresentation – Negligent misrepresentation – Pre-contractual negotiations – Silence in course of pre-contractual negotiations – Effect of silence – Banks making loans to companies guaranteed by credit insurance policies arranged by broker – Broker's employee dishonestly issuing cover notes when part of cover missing – Banks lending large sums in reliance on cover notes – Insurers aware of broker's employee's deception – Whether insurers owing duty of care to disclose broker's employee's deception to banks – Whether party's right to withhold material fact during pre-contractual negotiations preventing duty of care arising.*

Between 1979 and 1981 various syndicates of banks advanced large sums of money by way of loans to four companies controlled by B. The loans were made on the security of gemstones and credit insurance policies covering failure by the borrowing companies to repay the loans. The credit insurance policies were arranged by L, a branch manager of a reputable insurance broker, who negotiated and arranged to place part of the primary insurance cover for the first and subsequent loans with the insurers through its senior underwriter, D. Each policy contained a clause excluding the insurer's liability in the event of fraud. Each loan agreement was made on condition that the banks would only advance the money when they were satisfied that the security for the loan was in place. L was unable to place with following insurers the full amount of risk for the first loan by the due date in January 1980, and in order to enable the loan (of 26·25m Swiss francs) to go through he arranged with D to underwrite the loan on a 14-day 'held covered' basis but represented to the banks that the insurance was complete and issued false cover notes to that effect even though, after the expiry of the 14 days, part of the cover was then missing. D became aware of L's deception in June 1980 but did not inform the insurers a  (his own employers) or the brokers (L's employers) or the banks of the deception. In fact D continued to underwrite the further loans (of 53·75m Swiss francs) on the same basis, knowing that L was providing incomplete cover for the banks. The borrowing companies subsequently defaulted on all the loans, the gemstones proved to be practically worthless in relation to the amounts borrowed and B disappeared with the money advanced by the banks. The banks brought an action to recover the moneys from the insurers. The banks conceded that they could not recover under the insurance policies because the loss to

b  which the policies related had been caused by B's fraud and the insurers were entitled to rely on the fraud exclusion clause, but they contended that, because the insurers owed them a common law duty of care or because contracts of insurance were contracts uberrimae fidei, the insurers were under a duty to disclose to them the deceit being practised on them by their brokers (through L) as soon as the insurers, acting through D, became aware of that deception. The banks claimed, and the insurers accepted, that the

c  banks would not have advanced the loans if they had known of L's deception in issuing false cover notes. The judge held (i) that the duty of utmost good faith existing between an insurer and an insured was reciprocal and required the insurers, acting through D, to disclose L's deception to the banks, who were entitled to damages in respect of that breach, (ii) that it was reasonably foreseeable that D's failure to disclose L's deception would create a risk of financial loss to the banks and it was just and reasonable to impose

d  a duty of care on the insurers in the circumstances and (iii) that the insurers' breach of their duty of utmost good faith and duty of care was an effective cause of the banks' losses and therefore the banks were entitled to recover damages from the insurers. The insurers appealed, contending, inter alia, (i) that they had not acted in breach of their duty of utmost good faith but, if they had, that breach did not give rise to a claim in damages, (ii) that the banks could not found their claim for damages on the fact of non-disclosure

e  or on a claim that the non-disclosure amounted to a breach of contract or a misrepresentation, (iii) that the banks could not found their damages claim in negligence because the cause or extent of the banks' loss as the result of L's deception was not reasonably foreseeable since the cause and extent of the loss was dependent on the fraud perpetrated by B and that was not reasonably foreseeable, and (iv) furthermore, the insurers did not owe a duty of care to the banks because a mere failure to speak did not

f  give rise to liability under the principles relating negligent misstatements.

**Held** – The appeal would be allowed for the following reasons—
    (1) Since the common feature of a contract of the utmost good faith was that by the very nature of the contract one party was likely to have command of means of knowledge not available to the other, the obligation to disclose material facts was a mutual and

g  absolute obligation imposing reciprocal duties on both insurer and insured, and in the case of the insurer required him to disclose all facts known to him which were material either to the nature of the risk sought to be covered or the recoverability of a claim under the policy which a prudent insured would take into account when deciding whether to place with that insurer the risk for which he was seeking cover. In failing to disclose L's

h  deception the insurers, acting through D, were in breach of their duty of utmost good faith owed to the banks, who on discovering the non-disclosure would have had the right to rescind the contract of insurance and recover the premiums paid. However, the duty of full disclosure, being neither contractual, tortious, fiduciary or statutory in character but founded on the jurisdiction originally exercised by the courts of equity to prevent imposition, did not give rise to a claim in damages. Furthermore, a claim for damages

j  did not arise by reason of any misrepresentation since failure to make disclosure in breach of the duty to disclose did not amount to a misrepresentation that full disclosure had been made and in the absence of any disclosure there had been no misrepresentation 'made' to the banks and none made with the intention that they should act on it, with the result that s 2(1)[a] of the Misrepresentation Act 1967 did not apply (see p 988 d,

_a_   Section 2(1) is set out at p 1003 _f g_, post

p 989 *a c d*, p 990 *e*, p 991 *c d*, p 993 *f g*, p 995 *e g h*, p 996 *a b e*, p 997 *f g*, p 1002 *b c* and
p 1003 *b* to *e j* to p 1004 *b*, post); *Carter v Boehm* [1558–1774] All ER Rep 183, *Merchants'*    *a*
*and Manufacturers' Insurance Co Ltd v Hunt* [1941] 1 All ER 123 and *Container Transport
International Inc v Oceanus Mutual Underwriting Association (Bermuda) Ltd* [1984] 1 Lloyd's
Rep 476 applied.

(2) It was not a necessary element of liability in negligence for economic loss resulting
from the act of an independent third party that the manner and means by which the
particular loss was caused or the extent of the loss be reasonably foreseeable. Accordingly,    *b*
where reasonable foresight of the relevant kind of loss was proved it was not necessary to
prove reasonable foresight of the manner in which the loss was suffered or the extent of
the loss. It followed that although B's fraud was not reasonably foreseeable the danger to
which the banks were exposed was the danger of financial loss resulting from entering
into the loan transaction induced by L's deception and that danger was a reasonably
foreseeable consequence of D's failure to disclose L's deception to the banks    *c*
notwithstanding that the particular means by which the loss caused included B's
fraud. However, although a mere failure to speak could give rise to a liability in
negligence under the principles relating to negligent misstatements provided there was
a voluntary assumption of responsibility and reliance on that assumption, D had not
voluntarily assumed any responsibility towards the banks in respect of L's honesty and
the banks had not relied on any assumption of responsibility by D. Even if the law were    *d*
in rare cases, because of the special circumstances and the relationship between the
parties, to treat a defendant as having assumed a responsibility to the plaintiff capable of
giving rise to a claim for damages for pure economic loss even in the absence of evidence
of any actual voluntary assumption of responsibility and reliance on that assumption, the
insurers would still not fall into that category, since the basic principle of the law of
contract that there was no obligation to disclose a material fact during pre-contractual    *e*
negotiations before entering into an ordinary commercial contract prevented a duty of
care arising on the part of the insurers to the banks and to hold the insurers liable in
negligence for their failure to disclose L's deception would be contrary to that basic
principle (see p 986 *e* to *g*, p 987 *c d f* to *h*, p 1005 *c d h*, p 1006 *a*, p 1007 *c d j*, p 1008 *c*,
p 1009 *c d*, p 1010 *d* to *f*, p 1011 *d e*, p 1012 *d* to  *g* and p 1015 *a* to *h*, post); dicta of    *f*
Blackburn J in *Smith v Hughes* [1861–73] All ER Rep 632 at 637, and of Lord Atkin in *Bell
v Lever Bros Ltd* [1931] All ER Rep 1 at 30–31, *Hughes v Lord Advocate* [1963] 1 All ER 705
and *Yuen Kun-yeu v A-G of Hong Kong* [1987] 2 All ER 705 applied; *Hedley Byrne & Co Ltd
v Heller & Partners Ltd* [1963] 2 All ER 575 considered.

Decision of Steyn J sub nom *Banque Keyser Ullmann SA v Skandia (UK) Insurance Co Ltd*
[1987] 2 All ER 923 reversed.
   *g*

## Notes

For the duty of utmost good faith, the duty to make disclosure and the duties of an
insurer in general, see 25 Halsbury's Laws (4th edn) paras 365–366, 378, and for cases on
the subjects, see 29 Digest (Reissue) 50–51, 74–79, 381–386, 666–715.

For the duty to take care, see 34 Halsbury's Laws (4th edn) paras 5, 18–53, and for cases
on the subject, see 36(1) Digest (Reissue) 17–55, 34–117.    *h*

For the Misrepresentation Act 1967, s 2, see 29 Halsbury's Statutes (4th edn) 725.

## Cases referred to in judgment

*Al-Kandari v J R Brown & Co (a firm)* [1988] 1 All ER 833, [1988] QB 665, [1988] 2 WLR
    671, CA.
*American Express International Banking Corp v Hurley* [1985] 3 All ER 564.    *j*
*Anns v Merton London Borough* [1977] 2 All ER 492, [1978] AC 728, [1977] 2 WLR 1024,
    HL.
*Bank of Nova Scotia v Hellenic Mutual War Risks Association (Bermuda) Ltd, The Good Luck*
    [1988] 1 Lloyd's Rep 514.
*Bell v Lever Bros Ltd* [1932] AC 161, [1931] All ER Rep 1, HL.
*Black King Shipping Corp v Massie, The Litsion Pride* [1985] 1 Lloyd's Rep 437.

*Blackburn Low & Co v Vigors* (1887) 12 App Cas 531, HL; *rvsg* (1886) 17 QBD 553, CA.

*a*   *Bolton v Stone* [1951] 1 All ER 1078, [1951] AC 850, HL.

*Candlewood Navigation Corp Ltd v Mitsui OSK Lines Ltd, The Mineral Transporter, The Ibaraki Maru* [1985] 2 All ER 935, [1986] AC 1, [1985] 3 WLR 381, PC.

*Carter v Boehm* (1766) 3 Burr 1905, [1558–1774] All ER Rep 183, 97 ER 1162.

*Container Transport International Inc v Oceanus Mutual Underwriting Association (Bermuda) Ltd* [1984] 1 Lloyd's Rep 476, CA.

*b*   *Curran v Northern Ireland Co-ownership Housing Association Ltd* [1987] 2 All ER 13, [1987] AC 718, [1987] 2 WLR 1043, HL.

*Donoghue (or M'Alister) v Stevenson* [1932] AC 562, [1932] All ER Rep 1, HL.

*Esso Petroleum Co Ltd v Mardon* [1976] 2 All ER 5, [1976] QB 801, [1976] 2 WLR 583, CA.

*Glasgow Assurance Corp Ltd v William Symondson & Co* (1911) 16 Com Cas 109.

*Hedley Byrne & Co Ltd v Heller & Partners Ltd* [1963] 2 All ER 575, [1964] AC 465, [1963]
*c*   3 WLR 101, HL.

*Heskell v Continental Express Ltd* [1950] 1 All ER 1033.

*Hughes v Lord Advocate* [1963] 1 All ER 705, [1963] AC 837, [1963] 2 WLR 779, HL.

*Ionides v Pender* (1874) LR 9 QB 531, DC.

*Iron and Steel Holding and Realisation Agency v Compensation Appeal Tribunal* [1966] 1 All ER 769, [1966] 1 WLR 480, DC.

*d*   *Lamb v Camden London BC* [1981] 2 All ER 408, [1981] QB 625, [1981] 2 WLR 1038, CA.

*Lee v Jones* (1864) 17 CBNS 482, 144 ER 194.

*Leigh & Sillavan Ltd v Aliakmon Shipping Co Ltd, The Aliakmon* [1986] 2 All ER 145, [1986] AC 785, [1986] 2 WLR 902, HL.

*Leon v Casey* [1932] 2 KB 576, [1932] All ER Rep 484, CA.

*Lishman v Northern Maritime Insurance Co* (1875) LR 10 CP 179.

*e*   *Lister v Romford Ice and Cold Storage Co Ltd* [1957] 1 All ER 125, [1957] AC 555, [1957] 2 WLR 158, HL.

*London Assurance v Mansel* (1879) 11 Ch D 363.

*London General Omnibus Co Ltd v Holloway* [1912] 2 KB 72, [1911–13] All ER Rep 518, CA.

*March Cabaret Club and Casino Ltd v London Assurance* [1975] 1 Lloyd's Rep 169.

*f*   *Merchants' and Manufacturers' Insurance Co Ltd v Hunt* [1941] 1 All ER 123, [1941] 1 KB 295, CA.

*Minister of Pensions v Chennell* [1946] 2 All ER 719, [1947] KB 250.

*Ministry of Housing and Local Government v Sharp* [1970] 1 All ER 1009, [1970] 2 QB 223, [1970] 2 WLR 802, CA.

*Moens v Heyworth* (1842) 10 M & W 147, 152 ER 418.

*Moorgate Mercantile Co Ltd v Twitchings* [1976] 2 All ER 641, [1977] AC 890, [1976] 3
*g*   WLR 66, HL.

*National Bank of Greece SA v Pinios Shipping Co No 1, The Maira* [1989] 1 All ER 213, [1989] 3 WLR 185, CA.

*Overseas Tankship (UK) Ltd v Morts Dock and Engineering Co Ltd, The Wagon Mound (No 1)* [1961] 1 All ER 404, [1961] AC 388, [1961] 2 WLR 126, PC.

*h*   *Peabody Donation Fund (Governors) v Sir Lindsay Parkinson & Co Ltd* [1984] 3 All ER 529, [1985] AC 210, [1984] 3 WLR 953, HL.

*Perl (P) (Exporters) Ltd v Camden London BC* [1983] 3 All ER 161, [1984] QB 342, [1983] 3 WLR 769, CA.

*Polemis and Furness Withy & Co Ltd, Re* [1921] 3 KB 560, [1921] All ER Rep 40, CA.

*Povey v Secretary of State for the Environment* (1986) Times, 17 July, [1986] CA Transcript
*j*   678.

*Rivaz v Gerussi Bros & Co* (1880) 6 QBD 222, CA.

*Rondel v Worsley* [1967] 3 All ER 993, [1969] 1 AC 191, [1967] 3 WLR 1666, HL.

*Ross v Caunters (a firm)* [1979] 3 All ER 580, [1980] Ch 297, [1979] 3 WLR 605.

*Rozanes v Bowen* (1928) 32 Ll L Rep 98, CA

*Simaan General Contracting Co v Pilkington Glass Ltd (No 2)* [1988] 1 All ER 791, [1988] QB 758, [1988] 2 WLR 761, CA.

*Smith v Hughes* (1871) LR 6 QB 597, [1861–73] All ER Rep 632, DC.

*Smith v Littlewoods Organisation Ltd (Chief Constable, Fife Constabulary, third party)* [1987] 1 **a**
    All ER 710, [1987] AC 241, [1987] 2 WLR 480, HL.

*Tai Hing Cotton Mill Ltd v Liu Chong Hing Bank Ltd* [1985] 2 All ER 947, [1986] AC 80,
    [1985] 3 WLR 317, PC.

*Tradax Export SA v Dorada Cia Naviera SA, The Lutetian* [1982] 2 Lloyd's Rep 140.

*Wagon Mound, The (No 2), Overseas Tankship (UK) Ltd v Miller Steamship Co Pty* [1966] 2
    All ER 709, [1967] 1 AC 617, [1966] 3 WLR 498, PC.                                **b**

*Woods v Martins Bank Ltd* [1958] 3 All ER 166, [1959] 1 QB 55, [1958] 1 WLR 1018.

*Yorkshire Dale Steamship Co Ltd v Minister of War Transport, The Coxwold* [1942] 2 All ER
    6, [1942] AC 691, HL.

*Yuen Kun-yeu v A-G of Hong Kong* [1987] 2 All ER 705, [1988] AC 175, [1987] 3 WLR 776,
    PC.

                                                                                      **c**

## Appeal

The defendants, Westgate Insurance Co Ltd (formerly Hodge General and Mercantile
Insurance Co Ltd), appealed against the decision of Steyn J sub nom *Banque Keyser Ullmann
SA v Skandia (UK) Insurance Co Ltd* [1987] 2 All ER 923, [1987] 2 WLR 1300, [1987] 1
Lloyd's Rep 69 on 30 September 1986 giving judgment for the plaintiffs, Banque
Financière de la Cité SA (formerly Banque Keyser Ullmann en Suisse SA) (Keysers), in  **d**
their action for damages against the defendants and others for breach of the defendants'
duty of utmost good faith in respect of certain credit insurance policies issued by them
to indemnify losses arising on certain loans made by the plaintiffs. Other appeals arising
out of the same action, namely an appeal by Skandia (UK) Insurance Co Ltd against
Keysers, Slavenburg's Banque (Suisse) SA, American Fletcher (Suisse) SA and Chemical
Bank, were settled on 20 May 1988 during the hearing of the appeal. The facts are set out **e**
in the judgment of the court.

Sydney Kentridge QC, Crawford Lindsay QC and Charles Cory-Wright for Skandia (until 20
    May).

Mark Waller QC, Jonathan Gaisman (until 20 May) and Charles Cory-Wright (from 20 May) **f**
    for Hodge.

Nicholas Strauss QC, Nicholas Stadlen and Kenneth Maclean for Chemical Bank (until 20
    May).

John Griffiths QC, Mark Hapgood and Hodge Malek for the other banks.

                                                              *Cur adv vult*
                                                                                      **g**

28 July. The following judgment of the court was delivered.

**SLADE LJ.** This is the judgment of the court, to which all its members have contributed,
on an appeal from a judgment of Steyn J delivered on 30 September 1986 (see sub nom
*Banque Keyser Ullmann SA v Skandia (UK) Insurance Co Ltd* [1987] 2 All ER 923, [1987] 2 **h**
WLR 1300, [1987] 1 Lloyd's Rep 69). The appellant is an insurance company which is
now named Westgate Insurance Co Ltd, but was formerly named Hodge General and
Mercantile Insurance Co Ltd, and will be referred to in this judgment as 'Hodge'. That
judgment was delivered in four commercial actions, namely action 1983 B No 813 (the
Ultron action), action 1983 S No 762 (the Deminter action), action 1983 S No 764 (the
HSG action) and action 1982 B No 3436 (the ESG action).                               **j**

There were orginally before this court appeals in all four actions. The principal
appellant in the Ultron action was Hodge. The appellant in the other three actions was
another insurance company, Skandia (UK) Insurance Co Ltd (Skandia). It was also an
appellant in the Ultron action in relation to an order for costs. However, at a late stage in
the course of the hearing, Skandia, which was separately represented, withdrew its

appeals in all four actions. Accordingly, in the event judgments on the appeals in the
*a* Deminter, HSG and ESG actions are no longer required. This judgment relates solely to
the Ultron action.

Four Swiss banks in all were joined as respondents to the appeals. Nearly all of them
have changed their names since the proceedings began, but it will be convenient to refer
to them by the names by which they are called in the documentation before the court.
The respondents to Hodge's appeal in the Ultron action are Banque Keyser Ullmann en
*b* Suisse SA (Keysers). The respondents to Skandia's appeal in the Deminter action were
Slavenburg's Banque (Suisse) SA (Slavenburgs), American Fletcher Bank (Suisse) SA
(American Fletcher) and Chemical Bank. The respondents to Skandia's appeal in the HSG
action were American Fletcher and Chemical Bank. Keysers were respondents to Skandia's
appeal in the ESG action. In this court Keysers, Slavenburgs and American Fletcher
appeared by the same counsel, but Chemical Bank was separately represented.

*c* The four actions raise issues of fact and law of considerable complexity and interest.
The trial in the court below took some three months and was followed by a very full,
clear and careful judgment of the judge, to which we pay tribute. The hearing of the
appeals has occupied about 24 working days. We gratefully acknowledge the care and
skill with which the cases have been presented on all sides.

It is necessary briefly to explain the course of the hearing. It began with counsel
*d* presenting Skandia's appeals. On day 8 counsel begin his opening of Hodge's appeal. In
doing so he adopted the submissions of counsel for Skandia so far as they applied to the
case on the appeal of Hodge, but added substantial submissions of his own. On day 11
counsel for Chemical Bank began responding to Skandia's appeals. On day 19 counsel for
the other three respondent banks began his address. In doing so he adopted in general
terms the entirety of the submissions of counsel for Chemical Bank both on the facts and
*e* the law.

On day 21 of the hearing counsel announced that Skandia was withdrawing its appeals.
An order was accordingly made by consent whereby, on certain terms relating to costs
and to the dismissal of a cross-appeal by Keysers against Skandia in the Ultron action, all
Skandia's appeals were dismissed. Counsel for Skandia and Chemical Bank then withdrew
*f* from the court.

Counsel then proceeded with and completed their submissions on behalf of Keysers in
response to Hodge's appeal in the Ultron action. Finally, on day 23, counsel for Hodge
began his reply in support of this appeal, which he concluded on the following day.

In the result there remains before this court for adjudication only Hodge's appeal in
the Ultron action. A cross-appeal by Keysers against Hodge in that action has been
*g* abandoned. This curtailment of the number of appeals has done little or nothing to
reduce the difficult and important issues of law with which we have to deal. These have
been more or less common to all four appeals. It has somewhat reduced the contentious
issues of fact. For, while the causes of action in the Ultron action are based primarily on
events occurring up to September 1980, the causes of action in the Deminter, HSG and
ESG actions were based on events occurring up to later dates. However, we think it
*h* necessary to include a brief reference to the events which gave rise to those three actions,
since these formed an important part of the background against which the issues in the
Ultron action fell to be dealt with at the trial.

As will appear, a number of other banks besides those already mentioned have from
time to time been interested as participators in making the various loans with which
these actions are concerned. For the sake of convenience, where precise identification of
*j* the particular bank or banks concerned appears unnecessary, we will from time to time
use the expression 'the banks' to refer to one or more of the respondent banks and these
other participators. Also, for the sake of convenience, with all due respect to the
arguments submitted to us, we do not propose in every instance to differentiate between
them by reference to the names of counsel who presented them. In referring to
submissions made by counsel for Hodge, we intend to include both the submissions

made by counsel for Hodge and those made by counsel for Skandia, which so far as
applicable were adopted by counsel for Hodge. In referring to submissions made by *a*
counsel for Keysers, we intend to include both the submissions made by counsel for
banks other than Chemical Bank and those made by counsel for Chemical Bank which,
so far as applicable, were adopted by them. Since by arrangement between the parties
the address of counsel for Skandia preceded that of counsel for Hodge and the address of
counsel for Chemical Bank preceded that of counsel for the other banks, it was inevitable
that in some respects the principal burden of the argument should fall on counsel for *b*
Skandia and Chemical Bank, though in the event they had both left the court before the
end of the hearing.

*The nature of the case*
The story, as the judge said, is one of fraud on a massive scale. During the years 1979 *c*
to 1981 a Spanish citizen, Mr Jaime Ballestero, persuaded various combinations of the
above-named banks, together with other banks, to make loans amounting in all to 80m
Swiss francs (approximately £30m at present rates of exchange) to four Liechtenstein or
Swiss companies, all of which he controlled. The securities offered in respect of the loans
included gemstones and credit insurance policies. Mr Ballestero, together with other *d*
persons who produced fraudulent valuations of the gemstones, perpetrated frauds both
on the lending banks and the insurers, who included Hodge and Skandia. The banks
suffered heavy losses. Whether or not they attempted to do so, they did not succeed in
obtaining any redress from Mr Ballestero and his fraudulent associates. In the first
instance they attempted to obtain recoupment of their losses under the policies, but
eventually were driven to accept that claims of this nature were unsustainable because all *e*
the policies contained clauses expressly excluding liability for claims arising out of fraud.
However, the banks found themselves in a position to attack the insurers on another
front. The insurances were throughout arranged by Ernest Notcutt & Co Ltd (Notcutts),
a reputable firm of Lloyd's brokers with offices in London, Beckenham and Cardiff. Mr
Roy Lee of that firm negotiated and arranged all the relevant insurances, acting for Mr
Ballestero and the banks. In 1979 he was the manager of the firm's Cardiff office. In 1980 *f*
he had become their regional development manager. He had left the firm in late 1981.
Mr Lee had been guilty of dishonest conduct from an early stage in the transactions.
Neither he nor his employer nor the insurers are shown to have been involved in any
way with the fraud perpetrated by Mr Ballestero and his associates, or to have been aware
of them at any material time. As to Mr Lee, the most relevant features of his misconduct
consisted in the issue at an early stage of cover notes in which he represented to the *g*
interested banks that 100% cover was in place before it had in fact been fully placed and
in permitting them thereafter unwittingly to remain with only partial cover for a period
of several months.
The banks asserted that in June 1980 Mr A C Dungate, who was then employed by
Hodge and subsequently by Skandia, became aware of such misconduct on the part of
Mr Lee and failed to disclose it to them. They claimed that if it had been disclosed to *h*
them, no further sums would have been lent by them and correspondingly no further
losses would have occurred. In short they said that if disclosure had been made they
would have avoided the loss to which the fraud of Mr Ballestero and his associates
subsequently subjected them. Mr Dungate is thus a key figure in these proceedings.
The judge acceded to these claims. He found that Hodge and Skandia were liable to
the banks in damages effectively in an amount equivalent to that which would have been *j*
recoverable under the policies in respect of these subsequent loans. No allegation of fraud
was made against Mr Dungate or his employers. The liability was held to arise in
negligence at common law and on the further ground that Hodge and Skandia were in
breach of a duty to the banks of the utmost good faith. Hodge now challenges the judge's
decision on a number of grounds of fact and of law, which will be explained later in this
judgment.

Brief particulars of the loan transactions are as follows:

| Description of loan | Borrower | Date of loan | Amount (Swiss francs) |
|---|---|---|---|
| (1) The first Ultron loan | Ultron SA (Ultron) | 23 January 1980 | 26·25m |
| (2) The second Ultron loan | Ultron | 2 September 1980 | 10·75m |
| (3) The Deminter loan | Deminter SA (Deminter) | 17 November 1980 and 15 December 1980 (in two tranches) | 17m |
| (4) The HSG loan | Holdings St Georges SA (HSG) | 6 January 1981 | 13m |
| (5) The ESG loan | Etablissement St Georges (ESG) | 18 March 1981 | 13m |
| | | | 80m |

Each of the loans was for a period of two years. The object of the Ultron loans, as presented to the banks by Mr Ballestero, was to finance the development of a tourist complex in Menorca referred to as Shangri-La. The object of the other three loans, as presented by him, was to provide finance for a Chilean fruit exporting company, Cia Frutera Sud-Americana SA (Safco) which he controlled.

All the lending banks had great, and as it turned out, wholly misplaced confidence in Mr Ballestero. They found his personality very impressive and he produced good references, so far as they went. However, the banks also required and were offered security. The principal securities offered by him in respect of each loan were a deposit of gemstones (emeralds, sapphires and rubies) and a credit insurance policy. The value of the gemstones was certified by a valuer put forward by Mr Ballestero, the Gemmologisch Instituut-Antwerpen (GIA) which was managed by Mr F Verbruggen and acted on behalf of the borrowing companies. Professor Jurgen Pense of the Johannes-Gutenburg University of Mainz, who also acted on behalf of those companies, issued certificates that the gemstones were as described in GIA's certificates. The lending banks also obtained further advice on their own behalf from a valuer, Mr Eric Demuth, a Zurich jeweller, and former chairman of the Swiss Association of Gemmology.

On the face of it, the values of the pledged gemstones had been satisfactorily established and they represented substantial security. In the case of each loan the stones pledged were valued at more than double the capital amount of the loan. However, as the judge found, the lending banks primarily relied on the benefit of the credit insurance. The substantial purpose of each policy was to insure the banks against loss in the event of the borrower defaulting and the proceeds of sale of the gemstones not sufficing to pay the amount of the outstanding debt. In the case of the ESG loan the policy named the lending banks as the insured. In the case of the other three loans the borrowing companies were named as the insured. However, the banks were either named as co-insured or to the insurers' knowledge were to be the assignees under the policies.

Each policy contained a 'fraud exclusion' clause.

*The events of December 1979 to January 1980: the first Ultron loan*

Ultron was a Liechtenstein company controlled by Mr Ballestero. The first Ultron loan, like all the subsequent loans, was negotiated between Mr Ballestero and the banks' representatives in Switzerland. It was made available to Ultron by Keysers (18·75m Swiss francs), American Fletcher (4·50m Swiss francs) and by Banca Unione Di Credito (3m Swiss francs) on or about 23 January 1980. The last-mentioned banks are not parties to Hodge's appeal because their claims in respect of the first Ultron loan have been assigned to Keysers. Keysers acted as agent for the participating banks. Subsequently there were certain variations in the participations and certain sub-participations, but these do not matter for present purposes. The same observation applies to the later loans.

The first Ultron loan was ultimately dealt with by a written loan agreement dated 23 January 1980, of which the opening words recorded the granting of the loan 'subject to all the necessary security being lodged'. The agreement summarised the 'purpose of the loan' by reference to the Shangri-La project. It provided for an extendible fixed term loan for two years from 20 December 1979. It provided for guarantees consisting of three items, namely:

> '1. Pledging of a parcel of precious stones ... the replacement of which in the opinion of experts is estimated at Frs. 75,000,000 2. Assignment with modification by ULTRON A.G. of an insurance policy of the English insurance group, the lead company of which is [Hodge] ... for an amount of Frs. 37,000,000.— guaranteeing, in the event of the borrower defaulting, payment to the Banks of any outstanding sum after realisation of the pledge. 3. The share capital ... of your company, pledged in favour of the Banks by its owner.'

The loan agreement provided for payment of interest six months in arrears, payable for the first time on 20 June 1980. it reserved to the banks the right to demand repayment of capital and interest on the occurrence of certain specified events which included the default for over ten days in the payment of capital or interest due.

As the judge found in relation to this and all the subsequent loan agreements, the banks were only prepared to advance the money once they were satisfied that the securities were properly in place. All the necessary arrangements therefore had had to be made before the loan agreement was signed and the loan was made (see [1987] 2 All ER 923 at 936, [1987] 2 WLR 1300 at 1316).

The pledge of shares in Ultron was always regarded as of minimal value. Though the banks would enjoy the security, such as it was, of the deposited gemstones, the judge found that they relied on the credit insurance as their principal security. Mr Ballestero introduced Mr Lee to the banks and Mr Lee undertook to arrange the necessary insurance in regard to the first Ultron loan (see [1987] 2 All ER 923 at 936, [1987] 2 WLR 1300 at 1317).

Mr Lee approached Hodge to take the lead. He did so through Mr Dungate, who was then employed as Hodge's senior underwriter and had experience in contingency insurance.

It was initially contemplated by Mr Lee and Mr Dungate that the necessary insurance cover for the first Ultron loan should be provided for as a single risk and that Hodge would take a 25% line on the cover of 37m Swiss francs. On 11 December 1979 Mr Dungate, on behalf of Hodge, signed a slip taking a 25% line. The material provisions of this slip, which with some variations appeared in later slips, were as follows:

'Insured:     Ultron AG
Period:       24 months at date to be advised Leading Underwriter only
Interest:      Precious stones
Location:    Whilst held in one of the following banks in Geneva ...
Conditions: This insurance is to indemnify the Insured in the event of Non Repayment of the line of credit granted at the end of the period of 24 months. In the event of the sale of the security not realising the full balance of the credit outstanding, Underwriters agree to reimburse the banks to whom the policy has been assigned the amount of the difference between the full sale proceeds and the amount outstanding on the loan and that the maximum amount of indemnity will be 50% of the valuation of the stones at the time of deposit or Sw. Fcs. 37,000,000 whichever is the smaller.

*Subject to:* a) The banks satisfying themselves regarding ownership and the right of the borrower to place the stones as security b) The banks' responsibility to ascertain that at the time of depositing the stones, the valuation fairly reflects the market value of the stones and that the stones listed in the valuation are those held on deposit.

*Excluding*: any claims arising out of:—1) Directly or indirectly fraud, attempted fraud, misdescription and deception by any party. 2) Directly or indirectly from faulty title, or wrongful ownership or inability to pledge the security. 3) Physical loss or damage and/or the consequences thereof.

*Warranted*: a) That the client has arranged a line of credit to be extended for a period of 24 months from the commencement of this policy and that the maximum amount of the credit including Accumulated Interest will be Sw. Fcs. 37,000,000 b) That the client will deposit with the bankers security in the form of precious stones as outlined in the valuation and appraisal issued by the Gemological Institute of Antwerp dated      and that the appraised value of these stones will be not less than Sw. Fcs. 75,000,000 c) The stones are held to the joint names of the Insured Bankers and Insurerers and not to be released without written consent of all parties . . .

Insd. Advice:Under Swiss banking law, precious stones are not allowed to be shown in the banks' balance sheets as security against a loan and for this reason this insurance is security as a bond against the Insured's loan.'

The judge found that the statement as to Swiss banking law contained in this slip, and repeated in several cover notes subsequently issued, was to Mr Lee's knowledge untrue and that he continued to repeat it even though Mr Verkooyen, a joint manager of Keysers concerned with the Ultron loans, told him that the statement was nonsense. Its importance, as the judge said, was that it was calculated to create the impression in the insurers that but for the Swiss legal position, the pledge of gemstones would be sufficient security (see [1987] 1 Lloyd's Rep 69 at 82).

On 12 December 1979, having regard to the terms of the proposed insurance, Mr Verkooyen sent to Mr Lee a telex informing him of the proposed location of the gemstones and the procedure as to their valuation. The telex was initialled by Mr Dungate 'seen and approved 12/12/79'.

Mr Lee found himself in difficulties because it was not possible to carry out his original intention of providing for the insurance cover as a single risk. He therefore decided to place the insurance of 37m Swiss francs in three layers, namely: (1) a primary layer of 9·25m Swiss francs, (2) a first excess layer of 9·25m Swiss francs in excess of 9·25m Swiss francs and (3) a second excess layer of 18·5m Swiss francs in excess of 18·5m Swiss francs.

On 17 December Mr Dungate, on behalf of Hodge, initialled a slip taking a 100% line on the primary layer for the two-year period, this slip being intended to replace the earlier slip which he had signed. The provisions of the slip were in all material respects the same as those of the earlier one, save that a sentence was added at the end of condition (b), stating: 'The procedure regarding valuation see telex 12.12.79 seen and agreed by Leading Underwriter.'

On 18 December 1979 Notcutts issued a cover note confirming the arrangement of the insurance by Hodge for the primary layer. That cover note was in proper form and no point arises on it.

However, Mr Lee still had to make arrangements for the first excess layer and the second excess layer. There was some urgency because the first Ultron loan was due for completion in January 1980. As the judge found, Mr Lee realised that unless he could complete those layers quickly, the Ultron loan would not be completed. He and his firm would lose the commission and anticipated future business from Mr Ballestero would not materialise (see [1987] 2 All ER 923 at 932, [1987] 2 WLR 1300 at 1312).

Mr Lee therefore sought Mr Dungate's further help. Mr Dungate, as the judge found regarded the transaction as attractive; it was the largest contingency risk he had ever underwritten (see [1987] 2 All ER 923 at 932, [1987] 2 WLR 1300 at 1312). He was not in a position to take any further substantial line on the excess layers. However, according to Mr Dungate's evidence, Mr Lee told him on 15 January 1980 that he (Lee) had written confirmation on the insurance slip for 80% of the first excess layer and that he had arranged the cover for the remaining 20%, though he had not yet received written confirmation. On 15 January 1980 Mr Dungate initialled the back of the slip for the first excess layer '20% Hodge A.C.D. 15/1/80'. He did so without affixing Hodge's stamp on it. As the judge found, this was intended as 14 days' temporary cover only (see [1987] 2 All ER 923 at 936, [1987] 2 WLR 1300 at 1317).

Thereupon, on 15 January 1980, Notcutts issued a cover note for the first excess layer. It was signed both by Mr Lee and by Mr Trevor Wilkinson, who was the joint managing director of Notcutts. It had attached to it a schedule headed 'Security' which purported to show the percentages for which the respective underwriters had committed themselves. The schedule, which was signed by Mr Lee and Mr Wilkinson, showed Hodge as committed for 19% instead of 20%. More importantly, it untruly represented that Hodge had taken this line for the two-year period of the loan, while Hodge had only agreed to hold covered (for 20%) for up to 14 days.

On 28 January 1980 Mr Dungate was told by Mr Lee that the cover for the first excess layer was complete. By an appropriate deletion he cancelled his indorsement on the first excess layer slip. The judge found that the first layer was effectively completed by 30 January 1980 (see [1987] 2 All ER 923 at 932, [1987] 2 WLR 1300 at 1312).

However, the second excess layer remained to be completed. This presented a major problem for Mr Lee. The Prudential signed a slip for 5% as leading underwriter in respect of that layer on 28 January 1980. That same day Mr Lee told Mr Dungate that he was still awaiting written confirmation, mainly from abroad, of the balance of the cover but that it was all there. In the meantime he asked Mr Dungate to hold cover for 73·5% on the second excess layer for just 14 days. Mr Dungate agreed to do so. On 28 January 1980, on behalf of Hodge, he wrote on the back of the slip 'H/C 73·5% 14 days 28/1/80 Hodge A.C.D.'.

Mr Dungate's evidence as to the extent of the authority conferred on him by Hodge to accept risks on their behalf was somewhat confused. However, it appears to be common ground that he would have had no authority to accept risks beyond 10m Swiss francs, at least until such risks were reinsured. He admitted that he did not reinsure, but asserted that he had no need to do so because Hodge was not really on risk at all.

The judge, however, found that in fact the second excess layer was substantially incomplete towards the end of January 1980 as some promised lines had not been confirmed, and a substantial part of the cover had not been placed at all (see [1987] 2 All ER 923 at 932, [1987] 2 WLR 1300 at 1312). On the basis of this finding, it seems clear that Mr Dungate was acting beyond his authority in committing Hodge, even to the limited extent to which he intended to commit it, by signing the slip on 28 January 1980.

On the same day, 28 January 1980, Notcutts issued a cover note to Keysers as the lead bank, which purported to show that the full cover on the second excess layer for the two-year period was completed. It was signed by Mr Wilkinson and Mr Lee and bore the date 28 January 1980. There was subsequently attached to it a list headed 'Security' which was dated 29 January 1980 and was signed by Mr Lee alone. This list purported to show the names of the underwriters who had together agreed to provide the full cover for the second excess layer for the two-year period and the percentages for which they had respectively committed themselves. It showed the names of the Prudential as the leading underwriter (5%) and of five other underwriters, of whom the last-named was Hodge, which was shown as being on cover for 78·25%. This cover note, which is of great importance on these appeals, was to Mr Lee's knowledge false in two material respects because it represented (1) that the cover on the second excess layer was complete, while, as the judge found, as at 28 January 1980 it was substantially incomplete; (2) that Hodge was on cover for 78·25% for the full two-year period, while in truth it had merely committed itself to a 'hold covered' arrangement for only 73·5% for up to 14 days.

As to the gemstones, which formed part of the security for the first Ultron loan, Mr Ballestero placed before Keysers certificates and valuations by GIA, signed by Mr Verbruggen and Mr Fuhrmann, and certificates signed by Professor Pense that the

gemstones were as described in the certificates of GIA. Professor Pense, in handing over
a the certificates, orally assured Keysers that GIA's valuations were correct. The banks' own
expert, Mr Demuth, examined random samples of the gemstones selected by a Keysers
official and certified that the details corresponded with the GIA certificates.

At the trial it was common ground that the GIA certificates and valuations were
fraudulent. The real value of the gemstones never exceed about 5m Swiss francs. The
judge concluded that Professor Pense's oral statement confirming the correctness of the
b GIA certificates must have been made fraudulently or recklessly. The judge made no
finding in regard to Mr Demuth's honesty or otherwise. It seems that he was not invited
to do so (see [1987] 2 All ER 923 at 936, [1987] 2 WLR 1300 at 1317).

In reliance on the three cover notes issued to them by Notcutts and on the purported
expert evidence produced to them concerning the gemstones, the banks in January 1980
parted with the sum of 26·25m Swiss francs for the first Ultron loan in ignorance that
c the cover on the second excess layer was substantially incomplete and that the gemstones
were relatively worthless.

*The events of February to May 1980*

During the succeeding months Notcutts set about completing the cover for the second
excess layer for the first Ultron loan. They produced a new slip, intended to replace the
d slip which the Prudential had signed on 28 January 1980. On 27 February 1980 the
Prudential signed this new slip for 5%. It shows the stamps of a large number of other
underwriters for varying percentages. All the other stamps bear dates later than
27 February 1980. The majority of the dates fall in March or April 1980. The latest of
them is the stamp of Federated Insurance Co Ltd (Federated) which bears the date 11 June
1980. There are also shown in manuscript on the slip a number of entries, all in the same
e handwriting (presumably that of Mr Lee), headed 'Overseas placements'. The underwriters
named in this list include nine who are described in the slip as 'direct' insurers. They also
include four, namely Aachener Ruck of Germany, Folksam of Sweden, CER of France
and Imperio of Portugal who are described in the slip as reinsurers. These last four
underwriters (the four foreign underwriters) are shown as having accepted the risk for
f percentages totalling 6%.

The judge heard no evidence from Mr Lee or those who had signed the slip as to the
dates on which the second excess layer was completed. He therefore regarded the slip
itself as the best evidence in this context. The dates on the slip revealed coverage of only
12% by 19 March 1980 and 52·5% by 22 April 1980. As the judge said, it was not clear
when the missing lines were completed. However, he found on a balance of probabilities
g that, save for the 6% line of Federated, the missing lines were added between April and
early June and that the last 6% was only placed on or about 9 June 1980. Specifically he
found that the cover was substantially incomplete in the period 11 February 1980 (when
the 'hold covered' agreement for the second excess layer expired) to the beginning of May
1980.

The policy for the primary layer was issued by Hodge on 16 May 1980. The insured
h was expressed to be 'Ultron . . . . . or the bank or banks to which this policy has been or
may be assigned'. Hodge was named as insurer. The sum insured was stated to be 'Swiss
Francs: 9,250,000 (part of Swiss Francs 37,000,000)'. The premium was 555,000 Swiss
francs. The period of insurance was stated to be '24 months at 20th December 1979'. The
policy recited that—

j       'the Insured has made to The Insurers a proposal which shall mean any signed
proposal form and declaration and/or any information in connection with this
insurance supplied by or on behalf of The Insured in addition to or in substitution
thereof all of which is declared to be the basis of this Contract and has paid THE
PREMIUM stated herein . . .'

The insurers thereby agreed subject to certain provisions and qualifications to
indemnify the insured—

'in the event of and to the extent of the non-repayment by or on behalf of Ultron
A.G. at or by the end of 24 (twenty-four) calendar months from the inception of the
line of credit granted to Ultron A.G. by the Bank or Banks to whom this Policy has
been or may be assigned to the extent only of such balance of the line of credit
remaining unpaid up to a limit of Swiss Francs 9,250,000'

The policy contained a warranty (inter alia) that the maximum amount of the credit
should not exceed the sum of 37m Swiss francs.

The fraud exclusion clause in the policy (different from the terms of the slip) read as
follows:

'The Insurers shall not be liable hereunder for (i) Any claim or claims arising
directly or indirectly out of or caused directly or indirectly by fraud attempted fraud
misdescription or deception by any person firm organisation or company.'

Since Keysers no longer sues on the policy further reference to its terms is unnecessary.

*The amendment of the Ultron primary layer policy*

In early May 1980 Mr Lee came to see Mr Dungate to ask him whether as lead
underwriter for the primary layer he would agree to an increase in the total sum insured
so as to enable the borrowers to raise a fresh loan on the security of a third excess layer.
He represented that the value of the gems had increased from 75m Swiss francs to 95m
Swiss francs and produced letters from GIA, Professor Pense and Mr Demuth to this
effect. Hodge was also asked to agree to an extension of the period of the cover. In due
course, in consideration of the payment of an additional premium, Mr Dungate agreed
to permit an increase of 10m Swiss francs in the total sum insured and to an extension of
the period of insurance. He also obtained the agreement of Ennia UK Ltd and the
Prudential, who were respectively the leading underwriters for the first and second excess
layers, to such amendments.

On 11 June 1980 Mr Dungate accordingly signed an indorsement by way of
amendment to the Ultron primary layer policy. That indorsement was replaced by a
further indorsement signed by him on 24 June 1980 which, in consideration of an
additional premium of 150,000 Swiss francs, provided (inter alia) that (a) the period of
insurance should be extended to 10 February 1982, (b) the total limit of the insurance
should be increased from 37m Swiss francs to 47m Swiss francs, (c) the individual limit
of 9·25m Swiss francs under the policy should, however, remain unaltered. Whether or
not in view of (c), (b) effectively increased the insurers' risk, (a) certainly did so.

As will appear, having obtained such consents, Ultron in due course (in September
1980) obtained a fresh loan of 10·75m Swiss francs on the security of a third excess layer
by way of further insurance. However, save as already mentioned, neither Hodge nor
Mr Dungate played any part in the insurance arrangements for this third excess layer.

The additional premiums of 150,000, 75,000 and 50,000 Swiss francs due respectively
to Hodge, Ennia UK Ltd and the Prudential were not paid until about 4 September 1980.
However, in our judgment, as indeed we think is now common ground, the contract
between the banks and Hodge providing for the amendment of the Ultron primary layer
policy had been concluded on 24 June 1980 and no contractual arrangements between
Hodge and the banks relevant for the purpose of this appeal were concluded after that
date. The identification of this date is material because if a duty of disclosure fell on
Hodge, through Mr Dungate, it would prima facie have continued up to that date but
not beyond it.

*The events of June 1980: the first discovery of Mr Lee's dishonesty*

It was suggested at the trial that Mr Lee became a conspirator with Mr Ballestero in his
scheme to defraud the banks. The judge did not accept this suggestion, observing that
suspicion is no substitute for evidence. His conclusion was that Mr Lee's motive was to
obtain for himself and for his firm substantial brokerage in the transactions brought to

a   him by Mr Ballestero. It must be stressed that it has not been proved that in any material respects they were acting in association with one another.

Nevertheless, the judge found that Mr Lee was a dishonest broker who was prepared to deceive those who dealt with him whenever he regarded it as necessary for the attainment of his objectives (see [1987] 2 All ER 923 at 940, [1987] 2 WLR 1300 at 1324). Further instances of his dishonesty will appear later in this judgment. However, no one in Hodge or the banks appears even to have suspected it before June 1980, when by
b   chance Mr Dungate first learned about the issue of the two false cover notes.

In the normal course of things, Hodge, as underwriter, might never have found out about the cover notes inasmuch as they had been issued by Mr Lee as broker and agent of the insured banks. But Hodge was a company in the Standard Chartered Group. The group included a company based in Zurich, Standard Chartered AG which by arrangement with Keysers, was a participant in the first Ultron loan. Standard Chartered
c   AG, as participant, received copies of the three cover notes dated 18 December 1979, 15 January 1980 and 28 January 1980. Mr Jekyll, its managing director, noticed Hodge's apparent exposure on each of the three layers (100%, 19% and 78·25%). He raised the matter with Mr Dungate in a telephone conversation and in a letter dated 28 May 1980, which read as follows:

d       'Three Cover Notes totalling SFr. 37,000,000—issued by Ernest A. Notcutt
          & Company Ltd., indemnifying Ultron AG, Geneva.

        As agreed in our telephone conversation today I am enclosing copies of the above Cover Notes for your perusal. The benefits of the underlying insurances have been assigned to a group of lending bankers, in which we are participating, headed by Banque Keyser Ullmann en Suisse S.A., Geneva, and my purpose in forwarding
e       Notcutt's Cover Notes to you is to assist in establishing the exact extent of your exposure on Ultron AG in these insurances. I look forward to receiving your further advices in due course.'

When Mr Dungate received this letter and the cover notes on 2 June 1980 he was surprised and annoyed. He immediately telephoned Mr Lee and on the same day Mr Lee
f   had a telephone conversation with Mr Verkooyen of Keysers. Also, on the same day a Mr Stetler of Standard Chartered AG, having been contacted by Keysers, telephoned Mr Dungate and confirmed that the limit of Hodge's exposure was accepted as being 9·25m Swiss francs.

Subsequently Mr Lee wrote to Mr Verkooyen a letter bearing the date 4 June 1980. Since the letter bears a stamp showing the date of receipt as being 12 June 1980, it appears
g   likely that it was posted some days after 4 June. It read as follows:

    'Re: ULTRON AG
        Further to our telephone conversation 2nd June 1980, I would confirm our mutual understanding of the security which has been placed on cover. As advised initially, Hodge General and Mercantile Insurance Company are the complete security for the first loss primary cover of 9,250,000 Swiss Francs. This Company
h       were also shown as security on the first excess and second excess layers, but as advised only on a provisional basis to be replaced either by direct or reinsurers lines. I apologise for not advising you in writing of the Companies who replaced Hodge General and Mercantile Insurance Company Limited, on both of these layers, but now enclose a complete list of security for your retention, and would confirm that the only involvement of Hodge General and Mercantile Insurance Company
j       Limited, is for the primary layer of 9,250,000.00 Swiss Francs. No doubt you will take whatever steps you think fit to advise the various participating Companies of the complete security as per the attached lists.'

In the course of his evidence Mr Verkooyen denied that Mr Lee had ever advised him that the cover of Hodge on the first and second excess layers was provisional in the sense of being limited to 14 days.

Enclosed with this letter to Mr Verkooyen were what purported to be complete lists of the underwriters who had respectively given cover in respect of each of the three layers. *a* These lists did not show the name of Hodge in connection with the first excess layer or the second excess layer. Nor did they show the names of the four foreign underwriters referred to above. They did, however, show the name of Federated for 6%, though its stamp was not placed on the slip until 11 June.

The judge found that this letter to Mr Verkooyen was not intended to alert him or Keysers to Mr Lee's deception and the gap in the insurance cover and that it did not in *b* fact do so (see [1987] 2 All ER 923 at 939, [1987] 2 WLR 1300 at 1320).

Mr Lee wrote to Mr Dungate a letter, which also bore the date 4 June 1980. It appears that it was delivered not by post but by hand. It read:

'Re: ULTRON AG

I am enclosing a copy of a letter sent today to Mr Verkooyen of Banque Keyser *c* Ullmann en Suisse, Geneva, giving the revised lists of security on the first excess and second excess layers for the above cover. I am sorry that the fact that we did not advise Keyser Ullmann in writing of the revised security, prior to this day, may have caused you an inconvenience. I am also bring [sic] with me, for your inspection, the slips showing the full hundred percent cover on both excess layers. I now trust that this matter can be resolved satisfactorily and look forward to dealing with the *d* endorsement increasing the total Sum Insured with you at the same time.'

Mr Dungate's immediate and primary concern was to make certain that Hodge was on risk only for the 9·25m Swiss francs on the first layer and for nothing on either of the other two layers. On or shortly after 4 June 1980 Mr Lee brought along the slips for his inspection. By examining them, Mr Dungate obtained confirmation that Hodge was on risk only to this limited extent. *e*

On any footing Mr Lee should at an earlier stage have issued revised cover notes. These would have shown that Hodge was no longer on risk in respect of either of the two excess layers. He apologised to Mr Dungate for not having done so and in fact sent new cover notes to Keysers. However, he never offered Mr Dungate an explanation of his deception of the banks by the issue of false cover notes. No excuse could be offered for it. *f*

By a letter of 9 June 1980, Mr Dungate replied to Mr Jekyll as follows:

'Three Cover Notes totalling SFr. 37,000,000— issued by Ernest A. Notcutt & Company Limited., indemnifying Ultron AG, Geneva.

Thank you for your letter of the 28th May, together with enclosures for which I am extremely obliged. I would refer to our subsequent telephone [sic] and take the opportunity copy [sic] of enclosing letter received from Notcutts together with *g* various documents received with the letter. After considerable enquiries with the various Underwriters concerned, I have satisfied myself that the cover has been correctly placed, but this does not in any way detract from the unprofessional manner in which Notcutts have acted, and would probably have never been brought to my notice had it not been for your kindness in drawing my attention to same. May I express my appreciation of your highlighting a situation which should never *h* have arisen.'

On 20 June 1980, with the object of reassuring Keysers, Mr Lee wrote to Keysers a letter deliberately misrepresenting the effect of the fraud exclusion clause. The judge accepted Mr Dungate's evidence that he did not authorise the false statement contained in this letter, but found that Mr Lee made it intending that Keysers should rely on it and *j* Keysers in fact relied on it.

*The judge's finding as to Mr Dungate's knowledge in June 1980 of Mr Lee's misconduct and as to the action (if any) taken by him in consequence*

In his capacity as an underwriter, Mr Dungate was not responsible for completing the cover on the second excess layer. That was the responsibility of the brokers. However,

Hodge's associated company, Standard Chartered AG, as participant in the first Ultron
*a* loan was interested in the completeness of the insurance cover for that loan. Mr Dungate's
evidence was to the effect that by examination of the slips he satisfied himself that the
cover was complete in June 1980; that he did not notice the dates of the lines on the slip,
being only interested in the extent of the cover; that while he knew in June 1980 that
Mr Lee had dishonestly failed to show the 14-day limitation on the cover note issued on
28 January 1980, he believed that the cover had in fact been replaced within the 14 days,
*b* so that there was no gap; that the failure to issue replacement cover notes after the 14
days had been due to an 'administrative error'; that the banks had never been exposed to
serious risk of loss and that any such risk had by June 1980 long since disappeared; that
since what Mr Lee had done was bound to be discovered he had acted stupidly rather
than dishonestly; and that Mr Lee's prompt reaction when the matter came to light
enabled him to have trust and confidence in him in the future. Mr Dungate further gave
*c* evidence to the effect that in early June 1980 in two telephone conversations with Mr
Lee's superior, Mr Wilkinson, the managing director of Notcutts, he reported to Mr
Wilkinson the facts relating to the slip, the cover notes and Mr Lee's conduct and
suggested to him that Mr Lee should be more closely supervised thereafter by Notcutts'
chief broker, Mr Fowler. He stated that on a number of occasions thereafter, though not
always, Mr Fowler did accompany Mr Lee to meetings.
*d*    Mr Dungate accepted in evidence that, if he had known of serious dishonesty on the
part of Mr Lee, it would have been his professional duty to bring the facts fairly to the
notice of the interested banks and not to deal further with any new transaction. However,
he sought to justify his failure to bring Mr Lee's misconduct to their attention
substantially on the grounds summarised in the immediately preceding paragraph.
Detailed findings as to the extent of Mr Dungate's knowledge of Mr Lee's dishonest
*e* conduct and as to the views which he formed in respect of such conduct are to be found
in the judgment of Steyn J (see [1987] 2 All ER 923 at 933–934, 937–938, 940, [1987] 2
WLR 1300 at 1313–1314, 1319, 1324).
    The judge found in effect that (a) in early June 1980 Mr Dungate, having seen the
cover notes of 15 and 28 January 1980, became aware that in January 1980 Mr Lee had
deliberately deceived the banks by the issue of two false cover notes, both of which
*f* showed Hodge as being on cover for two years, while in fact it had committed itself for
only up to 14 days, and the second of which showed it as being on cover for 78·25%,
while in fact it had committed itself for only 73·5%; (b) on seeing the slips in early June
1980 Mr Dungate further became aware that 6% of the cover on the second excess layer
was still missing; (c) the last 6% was, to Mr Dungate's knowledge, not obtained until
*g* about 9 June 1980 (see [1987] 2 All ER 923 at 933–934, [1987] 2 WLR 1300 at 1313–
1314; see also [1987] 1 Lloyd's Rep 69 at 86).
    It was apparent that Mr Lee's false cover notes had caused the banks no loss. No claim
had as yet been made in respect of the first Ultron loan and on the face of it no claim
could have been made, since the first payment of interest due under the loan agreement
was not due until 20 June 1980. As soon as the cover was completed in June 1980 the
*h* insurance position was rectified. The judge, however, found that Mr Lee's dishonesty
had left the banks 'seriously exposed' over the period February to June 1980 and that Mr
Dungate knew this.
    While Mr Lee had offered an explanation to Mr Dungate of what he termed the
'administrative error' (and the judge termed 'the minor sin') consisting of the failure to
send replacement cover notes during the completion of the cover, the judge found that
*j* he had never explained his dishonest conduct in issuing the false cover notes. The judge
said ([1987] 1 Lloyd's Rep 69 at 87):

> 'Mr. Lee's letter of June 4, 1980, to [Keyser] . . . again confessed to the supposed
> minor sin and suppressed the fact of Mr. Lee's deceit and the exposure of the banks
> caused by the gap in the insurance cover over several months. Mr. Dungate saw that
> letter. He forwarded it to Mr. Jekyll. He actively assisted Mr. Lee is passing the
> matter off as an administrative error. In my judgment the inference is irresistible

that Mr. Dungate knew that Mr. Lee had been guilty of deceiving his employers, the underwriters and the banks.'

He found (at 87) that Mr Dungate 'appreciated the quality of Mr Lee's dishonesty.'

It was common ground that Mr Dungate, on discovering Mr Lee's misconduct, gave no report of it to his superiors in Hodge or to any of the banks or underwriters concerned. The judge, accepting Mr Wilkinson's evidence on this point in preference to that of Mr Dungate, also found that Mr Dungate did not report it to Mr Wilkinson. He found that his decision to keep the matter to himself served to protect himself, because he had acted beyond his authority in entering into the 'held covered' arrangements in January 1980. Moreover, he considered, Mr Dungate realised that if he were to report it to Notcutts and the banks, that would have spelt the end of further profitable underwriting business with Mr Ballestero's companies.

Such, according to the judge's findings, were the motives which actuated Mr Dungate in continuing to do business with Mr Lee. The judge found that after June 1980 on behalf of Hodge and subsequently Skandia, he underwrote lines on insurances which served as securities in support of bank loans amounting in the aggregate to 53·75m Swiss francs and that the total premiums earned by Hodge in respect of the Ultron loan transactions were 1,417,500 Swiss francs (see [1987] 1 Lloyd's Rep 69 at 81).

In the course of describing the next five stages in the chronology, we will gratefully adopt, largely verbatim, a number of passages from the equivalent sections of the judge's judgment.

### The second Ultron loan: 2 September 1980

Before June 1980 Mr Ballestero had already been pressing for an increase in the Ultron loan. A further loan was eventually made on 2 September 1980. The further sum advanced was 10·75m Swiss francs. The original participants in the loan were Arbuthnot Latham & Co Ltd, Kredietbank (Suisse) SA and A Sarasin & Cie in differing proportions. The claims of these three participants have been assigned to Keysers. The terms of the loan were similar to those which we have already set out in respect of the first Ultron loan. The principal securities were gemstones, now fraudulently revalued at about 95m Swiss francs, and an increase of the credit insurance limit from 37m Swiss francs to 47m Swiss francs. The security in the form of an increase of the credit insurance constitutes the third excess layer. It was for 10m Swiss francs in excess of 37m Swiss francs.

For the insurance in relation to the third excess layer, Mr Lee turned to individuals who purported to act on behalf of the Californian branch of a Bolivian entity known as Cia Americana de Seguros y Reaseguros SA. There was well-founded doubt as to the soundness or even existence of this branch. Since the policy contained a cut-through clause entitling the insured in the event of insolvency to sue the reinsurer, the standing of the insurer was less important so long as there existed satisfactory and enforceable reinsurance. Mr Lee assured Keysers that he had inspected the reinsurance treaties, but he had not done so. In relation to the third excess layer, he also acted in wilful disregard of his explicit instructions from Notcutts in issuing a cover note without a director's approval.

### Mr Dungate leaves Hodge and joins Skandia: 1 October 1980

In late 1980 the Standard Chartered Group decided to sell Hodge. There was a risk that the new parent company of Hodge might wish the company to cease writing contingency business. In these circumstances Mr Dungate was approached by Skandia to join them as senior underwriter of their contingency business. Mr Dungate accepted the offer, and on 1 October 1980 he commenced employment at Skandia, with his assistant, Mr Robin Wood. By an indorsement no 4 to the Ultron policy, Hodge, acting on its own behalf and on behalf of the following market, assigned their interest, responsibilities and liabilities in the policy to Skandia and the banks consented to the assignment. From October 1980 Mr Lee dealt with Mr Dungate as Skandia's underwriter, viz in relation to the Deminter, HSF and ESG transactions.

*The Deminter loan of 17 November and 15 December 1980*

a      Deminter was a Liechtenstein company. It was also the alter ego of Mr Ballestero. Two loan agreements were concluded by it with the banks. The first tranche, lent by Slavenburgs and American Fletcher, was covered by an agreement of 17 November 1980. The second tranche, lent by Chemical Bank, was covered by an agreement of 15 December 1980. The total sum advanced was 17m Swiss francs.

The scheme of the transaction was similar to that of the Ultron transaction. The b principal securities were a pledge of gems and an insurance policy. As in the Ultron transaction, the banks received a fraudulent GIA valuation, a certificate from Professor Pense as to the genuineness of the gems and a further certificate of Mr Demuth. The existence of the insurance cover was verified by a cover note issued by Notcutts. On behalf of Skandia, Mr Dungate wrote a 25% line on this insurance. Relying on these documents, the banks parted with their money and Mr Ballestero appropriated it.

c      After 17 November 1980, when Slavenburgs and American Fletcher advanced their tranche of the Deminter loan, but before 15 December 1980, when Chemical Bank advanced its tranche, Chemical Bank received a number of very unfavourable references which seriously questioned both the expertise and the integrity of GIA and Mr Verbruggen. Chemical Bank did not communicate the terms of the reports themselves to Slavenburgs and American Fletcher, but by telexes of 9 December 1980 its vice-d president, Mr Berti, informed those two banks that their checkings on GIA were 'not entirely satisfactory'. Notwithstanding this information, Chemical Bank proceeded to lend 10m Swiss francs to Deminter on 15 December 1980 and subsequently Chemical Bank and American Fletcher proceeded to lend respectively 11m Swiss francs and 2m Swiss francs under the HSG loan transaction on 6 January 1981. At the trial this constituted one of the grounds of the allegation of contributory negligence on the part of e Chemical Bank and American Fletcher.

On 11 December 1980 American Fletcher wrote to Notcutts asking them to take note that after the issue of the cover note of 17 November 1980 Chemical Bank had received checkings on GIA which were 'not entirely satisfactory'. Despite American Fletcher's request to do so, Mr Lee dishonestly failed to pass on this information to the underwriters.

f      In relation to the Deminter loan and subsequent HSG loan, there was further deception on the part of Mr Lee. In the case of these loans, the banks took the attitude, which they made clear to him, that they did not wish to take the responsibility for the valuation of the gemstones or to warrant the correctness of such valuation. Mr Dungate's attitude, however, was that the banks must give such warranties. Mr Lee met this problem by misleading both sides. He informed the banks that Mr Dungate had agreed to their g approach. To Mr Dungate, however, he represented that the banks were content that the policy should contain the warranties which he required. The policies issued by Mr Dungate in the case of the Deminter and HSG loans accordingly contained warranties of this nature. But, when Mr Lee gave copies of the policies to the banks, he had excised those warranties and retyped the relevant pages so that they stated that the banks took no responsibility for the valuations. The banks only discovered these machinations in July h 1981 when they compared policies with Skandia.

*The HSG loan of 6 January 1981*

By a loan agreement of 6 January 1981 HSG, another company which was the later ego of Mr Ballestero, borrowed 13m Swiss francs from American Fletcher and Chemical j Bank. The principal security for the loan was again a pledge of gemstones and insurance cover. At the closing transaction the banks were satisfied as to the fulfilment of the conditions for their protection by a fraudulent certificate of GIA and certificates by Professor Pense and Mr Demuth as to the value of the gemstones and by a Notcutts cover note as to the insurance cover. Mr Dungate again wrote a 25% line on behalf of Skandia. Relying on these closing documents, the banks paid 13m Swiss francs to HSG, which was immediately appropriated by Mr Ballestero.

*The ESG loan of 18 March 1981*

Under a loan agreement of 18 March 1981 ESG, another company of Mr Ballestero, borrowed 13m Swiss francs from three banks, namely Keysers, Banque Arabe et Internationale d'Investissements of Paris and Arbuthnot Latham & Co Ltd of London.

As before, the offer of security in the form of a pledge of gemstones and insurance cover induced the banks to grant the loan. As before, a fraudulent GIA certificate and certificates from Professor Pense and Mr Demuth persuaded the banks that the value of the gems was as represented. A cover note from Notcutts recorded that the insurance was in place. In reliance on the closing documents, the banks paid over 13m Swiss francs, which went into Mr Ballestero's pocket. During a period of some 15 months he had thus cheated the banks out of a capital sum of 80m Swiss francs. The part of this sum advanced after Mr Dungate became aware in June 1980 of Mr Lee's fraud in the Ultron transaction was 53·75m Swiss francs.

*Mr Lee's dishonest acts up to March 1981*

Mr Lee was represented by counsel on the first day of the trial but his counsel then withdrew. He chose not to give evidence. He has not been a party to the appeals before this court.

Approaching Mr Lee's role with the caveat that he had not heard Mr Lee's own account of the matter, the judge found that, in addition to issuing the two false cover notes of 15 and 28 January 1980, Mr Lee had been guilty of, inter alia, the following acts of fraud. (1) The misrepresentation as to Swiss banking law contained in the slip presented to Mr Dungate for signature on 11 December 1979 and repeated in subsequent cover notes, despite Mr Verkooyen's advice to Mr Lee that the statement was nonsense. (2) The misrepresentation as to the effect of the fraud exclusion clause contained in Mr Lee's letter to Keysers to 20 June 1980 relating to the Ultron loans. (3) The misrepresentation referred to above concerning the reinsurance arrangements in respect of the second Ultron loan. (4) The issue to the banks, as mentioned above, of policies in relation to the Deminter and HSG loans, including wording which placed the responsibility for the valuation of the gemstones on the insurers, while supplying the insurers with policies including wording to the opposite effect. (5) The failure to pass on to Skandia at American Fletcher's request the highly material information that Chemical Bank's check-ups on GIA had proved not entirely satisfactory.

In the context of these frauds two unconnected observations should be made at this stage. First, while some of them endangered the insurance cover which the banks thought they were getting, having regard to the fraud exclusion clauses in the policies the loss actually suffered in the event by the banks, due to Mr Ballestero's fraud, would never have been covered by the policies. Second, the judge did not find that Mr Dungate was aware of any of the five matters listed above until some time after the conclusion of the last of the loan transactions. Keysers' charge against Mr Dungate (and through him against Hodge) is based on his knowledge alleged by Keysers (and found by the judge) of the falsity of the two cover notes of 15 and 28 January 1980 and of the gap in the banks' insurance cover on the first Ultron loan up to May or June 1980.

The judge also found ([1987] 1 Lloyd's Rep 69 at 81):

'On some occasions, particularly after Notcutts became a little restive about Mr. Lee's activities in the second half of 1980, Mr. Lee attended meetings accompanied by Mr. John Fowler, who was Notcutts' senior non-marine broker in their London office. But the inference is irresistible that Mr. Fowler's involvement in the transactions was spasmodic, and was little more than a perfunctory and ineffectual "brake" on Mr. Lee's entrepreneurial activities. Mr. Fowler was (I find) unaware of any wrongdoing on Mr. Lee's part. On the broking side Mr. Lee was in effect in sole charge. He resigned from Notcutts in late 1981, but a form of cooperation, and profit-sharing, continued between Mr. Lee and Notcutts in relation to the transactions in question.'

*The events after March 1981 up to and including trial*

a      Initially payments of interest under the loans were duly made. After the ESG loan in March 1981 Mr Ballestero tried to borrow further sums from the banks. Gradually suspicions were aroused. Mr Ballestero's attempts to borrow money were rejected. In the second half of 1981 the borrowing companies defaulted on all the loans. The banks' money had gone. In the context of the sums in question the value of the gemstones was found to be negligible (less than 10% of the valuation figures). The valuations of the b      gemstones by which Mr Ballestero had satisfied them were found to have been fraudulent. The subsidiary forms of security held by the banks, such as the shares of the borrowing companies and the personal guarantee of Mr Ballestero and an associate were worthless. Mr Ballestero and the moneys which he had extracted from the banks had disappeared. The banks claimed reimbursement under the insurance policies which they had always regarded as their principal security. The insurers denied liability in reliance on the fraud c      exclusion clauses.

      Four separate actions were instituted in the Commercial Court relating respectively to the Ultron loans, the Deminter loans, the HSG loan and the ESG loan. Notcutts were joined as defendants, as being vicariously liable for the frauds of Mr Lee. Very shortly before the trial, which began on 13 May 1986, all the issues between the banks and Notcutts in all four actions were settled. One of the terms of the settlement was that d      Notcutts would co-operate with the banks, so far as they could, in prosecuting their claims against Hodge and Skandia. Under the settlement Notcutts accepted liability in the sum of £10·5m. This figure was the sum in respect of which Notcutts were protected by liability insurance cover.

      The banks also sought judgment against Mr Lee in fraud, but as has already been explained, he took no active part in the trial and in the outcome the judge, having stated e      that he was satisfied that Mr Lee deceived the banks on a number of occasions, stood over their claims against him for subsequent adjudication (see [1987] 2 All ER 923 at 960, [1987] 2 WLR 1300 at 1349).

      This left the banks and the insurance companies as protagonists at the trial. Initially the banks had contended that the insurers were liable to them under the policies. Chemical Bank was the first to admit (in November 1985) that the fraud exclusion clause f      rendered any such claim unsustainable. The other banks made no such concession until the trial. Having abandoned their claims under the policies at the trial, they proceeded with claims of a different nature against the insurers. These other claims were founded on Mr Dungate's alleged failure to report to anyone the issue of the two false cover notes by Mr Lee and the fact (if it was the fact) that for several months before June 1980 the banks participating in the first Ultron loan had had no proper insurance cover in respect g      of the second excess layer. The banks' submission, accepted by the judge, was that as soon as he acquired knowledge of these matters he should have reported them to the banks or to Mr Wilkinson, his superior, at Notcutts. He accepted that a report to Mr Wilkinson, if made, would have sufficed. But the banks' contention, which the judge also accepted, was that no such report was ever made (see [1987] 2 All ER 923 at 954, [1987] 2 WLR h      1300 at 1342).

      The banks asserted that Hodge, and subsequently Skandia through their employee Mr Dungate, owed a duty of care to the lending banks and that a continuing breach of this duty occurred on account of his failure to inform either Notcutts or the banks of these matters in and after June 1980. They asserted that this failure constituted negligence on the part of Mr Dungate and that the negligence caused loss, for which his employer's (the j      insurers) were vicariously liable in tort on each occasion after June 1980 when an insured bank made an advance to one of the four borrower companies in ignorance of Mr Lee's prior dishonesty. Keysers further asserted that if disclosure had been made they would not have permitted the first Ultron loan, which had been made before June 1980, to remain outstanding. They claimed recoupment for their losses in respect of the first Ultron loan as well as the second Ultron loan.

      The banks' claims, however, were not based merely on negligence at common law.

They also contended that the insurers, first Hodge and later Skandia, were bound by the *a* principle of uberrima fides, as it applies to insurance contracts, to disclose Mr Lee's dishonesty to the banks. They claimed that that non-disclosure entitled them to damages, or alternatively (as a last resort) to the return of their premiums.

In relation to the loss on the Ultron loans, Hodge was said to be vicariously liable for Mr Dungate's omission to report. In relation to the loss on the Deminter, HSG and ESG loans, Skandia was said to be liable.

There were certain other heads of claim which were rejected by the judge and will be *b* referred to later in this judgment. However, as he said, the banks always put in the forefront of their submissions the allegations that the insurers were in breach of the common law duty of care, or alternatively the duty of the utmost good faith (see [1987] 2 All ER 923 at 941, [1987] 2 WLR 1300 at 1326).

*The judgment of Steyn J*                                                                            *c*
Most of the judge's crucial findings of fact have already been mentioned. We turn now to his conclusions of law. He rejected Keysers claims to recoupment of their losses in the first Ultron loan and for return of the insurance premiums paid by them to Hodge in respect of the Ultron loans (see [1987] 2 All ER 923 at 954, [1987] 2 WLR 1300 at 1342). A cross-appeal by Keysers in the Ultron action in respect of these two matters has not been pursued, so that it is no longer necessary to consider them. In the event, this court *d* is thus concerned solely with Keysers claims to recoupment of their losses in respect of the second Ultron loan.

The judge rejected these claims of Keysers and similar claims of the other plaintiff banks in so far as they were based on fiduciary duties said to be owed by the insurers to the banks and on s 50 of the Supreme Court Act 1981. Though Keysers challenged such rejection in a respondent's notice, the challenge has not been pursued in this court. He *e* further rejected the claims of Keysers and similar claims of the other banks in so far as they were based on s 2 of the Misrepresentation Act 1967. He declined to hold that there had been any misrepresentation.

The judge nevertheless held that Hodge was liable to Keysers in respect of their losses on the second Ultron loan and Skandia was liable to the interested banks in respect of the *f* losses on the subsequent loans. His conclusions which led him to this decision were substantially as follows.

(1) Reciprocal duties of good faith are owed to one another by an insurer and an insured (see [1987] 2 All ER 923 at 942, [1987] 2 WLR 1300 at 1327–1328). That conclusion had not been challenged in this court.

(2) The body of rules described as the uberrima fides principle are rules of law *g* developed by the judges; the relevant duties apply before the contract comes into existence; it is incorrect to categorise these duties as implied terms of the insurance contract or to say that the rules become applicable by way of collateral contract; the following market of insurers accordingly could not be liable to the banks (see [1987] 2 All ER 923 at 944, [1987] 2 WLR 1300 at 1329).

(3) There was a duty on Mr Dungate to disclose the relevant facts known to him *h* concerning Mr Lee's dishonesty to the banks, either directly or through Notcutts (see [1987] 2 All ER 923 at 945, 954, [1987] 2 WLR 1300 at 1330–1331, 1342).

(4) The liability (if any) for the non-disclosure in respect of the two Ultron loans rested with Hodge and in respect of the subsequent loans rested with Skandia (see [1987] 2 All ER 923 at 945, [1987] 2 WLR 1300 at 1331).

(5) In principle an insured can claim damages from an insurer arising from loss *j* suffered by the insured as a result of the breach of the obligation of the utmost good faith by the insurer provided that the insured can prove that the non-disclosure induced him to enter into the contract (see [1987] 2 All ER 923 at 945–947, [1987] 2 WLR 1300 at 1331–1333).

(6) The banks had established a duty of care at common law on the part of the insurers

which obliged them to make disclosure to the banks of Mr Lee's dishonesty so far as it

a  was known to them (see [1987] 2 All ER 923 at 947–954, [1987] 2 WLR 1333–1341).

(7) On the basis of the judge's earlier findings of fact, breaches of the insurers' duty of utmost good faith and of their common law duty of care had been established (see [1987] 2 All ER 923 at 954, [1987] 2 WLR 1300 at 1342).

(8) In the context of causation, if a full disclosure of the facts relating to Mr Lee's dishonesty in issuing the false cover notes had been made, none of the banks would have

b  entered into any further loans after June 1980 (see [1987] 2 All ER 923 at 954, [1987] 2 WLR 1300 at 1342).

(9) While the element of reasonable foreseeability was a factor in the context of issues relating to duty, breach, causation and remoteness, Mr Lee had committed the very kind of frauds in and about the insurance transactions which were reasonably foreseeable by an underwriter in Mr Dungate's position in June 1980 or subsequently (see [1987] 2 All

c  ER 923 at 955, [1987] 2 WLR 1300 at 1343).

(10) While Mr Ballestero's fraud was not foreseeable in June 1980, it was a cause of the banks' losses. On the other hand, the insurers' breach of duty was also a cause of the banks' losses because, if they had disclosed Mr Lee's dishonesty, the banks would not have suffered them. Mr Ballestero's fraud and the insurers' breach of duty (based on the uberrima fides principle or the tort of negligence) were two causes of equal 'efficacy' of

d  the banks' losses and this sufficed to sustain the banks' claims on this aspect. The banks' carelessness in and about the negotiation of the loan transactions, even if established, did not negative the causal connection between the insurers' breach of duty and the banks' resultant losses (see [1987] 2 All ER 923 at 955–956, [1987] 2 WLR 1300 at 1343–1344).

(11) The banks' losses were not too remote in law to be recoverable (see [1987] 2 All ER 923 at 956–957, [1987] 2 WLR 1300 at 1344).

e  (12) The judge rejected an argument advanced on behalf of the insurers, not repeated in this court, to the effect that the banks through their brokers (ie through Mr Lee) misrepresented the risk to the insurers, or failed to disclose material facts to the insurers, who in turn were entitled to recover damages against the banks in a like amount as the banks were entitled to recover from the insurers (see [1987] 2 All ER 923 at 957–958,

f  [1987] 2 WLR 1300 at 1344–1346).

(13) While the insurers submitted that the banks were entitled to no damages or to substantially reduced damages by reason of contributory negligence of each of the banks, this defence was held to fail on the grounds that the relevant provisions of the Law Reform (Contributory Negligence) Act 1945 do not cover a case where a defendant is held liable on the basis of a breach of the duty of the utmost good faith (see [1987] 2 All

g  ER 923 at 958–959, [1987] 2 WLR 1300 at 1346–1347).

(14) In any event, save in the case of Chemical Bank, none of the pleaded allegations of contributory negligence were made out and each of them failed against each of the banks (see [1987] 2 All ER 923 at 959, [1987] 2 WLR 1300 at 1347–1348).

(15) There had been contributory negligence on the part of Chemical Bank so that if, contrary to the judge's view, the insurers were liable to the banks solely on the basis of

h  breaches of the common law duty of care, it would be just and equitable, within the meaning of s 1(1) of the 1945 Act, that Chemical Bank's damages should be reduced by 50% (see [1987] 2 All ER 923 at 960, [1987] 2 WLR 1300 at 1348).

As things were, the judge made orders in the four actions on the basis that Hodge was liable to Keysers in respect of their losses on the second Ultron loan, but not the first Ultron loan, Skandia was liable to the interested banks in respect of their losses on the

j  Deminter, HSG and ESG loans, the banks' claims against Mr Lee and all questions of quantum of damages should be stood over for subsequent adjudication.

*Common ground on this appeal*

Hodge, like Skandia, in its lengthy notice of appeal has challenged many of the judge's findings of fact, as well as a number of his conclusions of law. To mention only some, the following findings of primary fact are disputed, namely (i) that Mr Dungate realised in early June 1980 that the cover on the second excess layer slip had been substantially incomplete for several months after the end of January, (ii) that Mr Dungate appreciated that (if it was the fact) the second excess layer slip was not complete when he saw it in early June, (iii) that the banks had been exposed to serious loss during that period, (iv) alternatively, that Mr Dungate realised this, (v) that Mr Dungate did not report Mr Lee's conduct to Mr Wilkinson, (vi) that Mr Dungate 'fully appreciated' the quality of Mr Lee's dishonesty, (vii) that, had the banks known at any time that Mr Lee's January 1980 cover notes were false, none of them would have had any further dealings with Mr Ballestero, (viii) that Mr Dungate was actuated by the motives of obtaining further business from Mr Lee, or of avoiding investigation by his own employers, and (ix) that the losses actually suffered by the banks or losses of the same general nature were reasonably foreseeable by Mr Dungate.

A number of other findings or inferences of fact made by the judge are under attack and a substantial amount of counsel's arguments were occupied in taking us through various aspects of the facts, on occasions in meticulous detail. We shall, of course, deal with all those issues of fact canvassed before us which we regard as material to our decision, but will intend no disrespect to the arguments if we do not deal with all of them, for we think that they fall into a fairly narrow compass.

Most of them in one way or another relate to what Mr Dungate knew and did (or failed to do) in and after June 1980. As to Mr Dungate's knowledge, we think it is by now common ground, and, if not, it is clearly established on the evidence, that by early June 1980 Mr Dungate knew at least the following facts: (a) Mr Lee had issued the cover note for the first excess layer in respect of the first Ultron loan on 15 January 1980, showing Hodge to be on cover for 19% of 9·25m Swiss francs for two years while in truth Hodge had agreed to give cover for only up to 14 days (and for 20%); (b) Mr Lee had issued the cover note for the second excess layer on 28 January 1980 showing Hodge to be on cover for 78·25% of 18.5m Swiss francs for two years while in truth Hodge had agreed to be on cover for only up to 14 days and for only 73·5%; (c) the banks would not have lent without full cover; (d) Mr Lee had on these two separate occasions issued the cover notes intending that the banks should be deceived into lending without the full cover shown on the cover notes, thereby acting dishonestly towards the insured, the insurers and his own employers; (e) in reliance on the dishonest cover notes, the banks had not only lent large sums but had paid to Notcutts insurance premiums totalling 462·5m Swiss francs; (f) the reason why Mr Lee had deceived the banks and did not simply tell them to wait until the cover was completed was that he feared that if there was delay the transaction might fall through and the brokers' commission might be lost; (g) Mr Lee had in his letter to Mr Verkooyen of 4 June 1980 told the lie that Hodge had agreed to give cover 'on a provisional basis to be replaced either by direct or reinsurers lines'.

As to Mr Dungate's knowledge, substantially what remains in issue on this appeal is whether he knew that Mr Lee had in fact failed to replace the cover for the second excess layer until June 1980, so that for several months there had been a gap during which the banks had no insurance cover at all. As to Mr Dungate's actions, substantially what remains in issue is whether or not he reported what he knew to Mr Lee's superior at Notcutts, Mr Wilkinson. The factual issues concerning the part played by Mr Dungate in the history of this matter, while of great importance, are thus fairly limited in scope.

*Keysers' respondent's notice*

By their respondent's notice in the Ultron action, Keysers submit that the judgment of Steyn J should be affirmed on the additional grounds:

'1. That the implied representation made by Mr Dungate to Mr Verkooyen in December 1979 that there were no material facts known to [Hodge] which cast doubt upon the suitability and trustworthiness of Mr Lee as a broker was a a continuing representation, and/or a representation which was made afresh by [Hodge] to the [Keysers] upon and by reason of each subsequent dealing between Mr Dungate and Mr Lee, which representation was false at all times after 2nd June 1980, and accordingly [Hodge] are liable to [Keysers] for damages for misrepresentation and/or negligent misstatement and/or negligence 2. That [Hodge] induced [Keysers] to enter into the Ultron and ESG policies of insurance by the misrepresentation that they had disclosed all material facts and/or [Hodge]

b committed a breach of warranty to like effect . . .'

While the submission made in the first limb of para 1 has not been pursued in this court, the submissions made in the second limb of para 1 and in para 2 have been advanced on behalf of Keysers.

c *The issues on Hodge's appeal*
     In the light of the foregoing and of the course of the argument, it appears to this court that the following are the principal issues which arise for consideration on Hodge's appeal. (1) Did Mr Dungate in early June 1980 realise that the cover on the second excess slip had been substantially incomplete for several months after the end of January 1980? To what extent did he at that time and thereafter appreciate the quality of Mr Lee's

d dishonesty? (2) What (if any) information concerning Mr Lee's dishonesty did Mr Dungate give to Mr Wilkinson in or after June 1980? (3) What damage could Mr Dungate reasonably have foreseen as likely to be suffered by the banks in the event of his failure to disclose to them the information possessed by him as to Mr Dungate's dishonesty? (4) It being common ground that the contracts between the banks and the insurers were contracts uberrimae fidei, was Hodge in breach of its duty to the banks of

e the utmost good faith? (5) If so, (a) were such breaches capable in law of giving rise to a claim for damages and (b) does the 1945 Act apply to any such claim? (6) Did Hodge induce the banks to enter into the amended insurance contract concluded with Hodge on 24 June 1980 by any misrepresentation? (7) If so, does such misrepresentation give rise to a claim for damages under the Misrepresentation Act 1967? (8) Did Hodge owe the banks a duty under the common law of negligence not to cause them the type of

f damage suffered by them? (9) If so, was Hodge in breach of such duty? (10) (a) Did any such breach of duty or misrepresentation as is referred to in issues (4) or (6) or (8) above cause the banks loss? (b) If so, is such loss too remote to be recoverable in law? (11) Do the damages (if any) recoverable by Keysers fall to be reduced on the grounds of contributory negligence, and if so by how much?

g *Issue (1)*
     Before answering the questions of fact raised by issue (1), it is as well to consider why the issue is relevant. It was common ground between the parties that Mr Dungate knew in June 1980 that Mr Lee had issued two dishonest cover notes. In those circumstances it might fairly be asked why any further investigation of Mr Dungate's state of mind and knowledge should be necessary. The judge posed the same question in the course of his

h judgment ([1987] 1 Lloyd's Rep 69 at 83):

'Is it necessary to examine oral evidence when the primary facts seem to be agreed? Is it not simply a question of law whether the insurer owed a duty to the banks to disclose Mr. Lee's dishonesty?'

j If the correct view on the expert evidence is that Mr Lee's dishonesty in issuing false cover notes was a material fact which ought to have been disclosed, under the principles governing contracts uberrimae fidei, then Mr Dungate's *perception* of Mr Lee's dishonesty, a topic which absorbed much of the argument before us, becomes irrelevant for the purpose of applying those principles. For if Mr Dungate knew the facts which ought to have been disclosed, then the *materiality* of those facts was not for him to judge: see *Container Transport International Inc v Oceanus Mutual Underwriting Association (Bermuda)*

*Ltd* [1984] 1 Lloyd's Rep 476. On that view the insurers would be under a duty to disclose Mr Lee's admitted dishonesty, and if Hodge's claim was founded simply on the principles *a* governing contracts uberrimae fidei we could go straight on to consider whether they were in breach of that duty, and if so, what would be the appropriate remedy.

Unfortunately, we cannot take that short cut. Although knowledge by Mr Dungate of the issue of the dishonest cover notes would be sufficient to ground a claim for non-disclosure, based on those principles, that is not, as we have seen, the only way in which the banks put their case. They put it also in negligence, and under the Misrepresentation *b* Act 1967. It is these alternative claims that require us to look into the facts, and consider in particular whether Mr Dungate became aware that a gap had existed in the banks' security for several months after the expiry of the 14-day cover granted by Mr Dungate on 28 January 1980. If Mr Dungate continued to believe, as he said in his evidence, that the second excess layer was complete by 12 February 1980, then it is possible to understand, even if we cannot share, his view that the issue of the false cover notes should *c* be, as he put it, condoned. Mr Lee would have committed the minor sin of issuing false cover notes for a limited period and then failing to issue fresh cover notes when the limited period had expired. But, if Mr Dungate knew that there was a gap in the cover, the matter at once becomes more serious. For Mr Lee would have committed the major sin of issuing false cover notes for an indefinite period, without the alternative security having been put in place. Knowledge of the major sin might justify the imposition of a *d* duty of care in negligence, whereas knowledge of the minor sin might not. So it becomes necessary for us to examine the oral and documentary evidence in detail.

Before the judge it was argued that it had not been proved that there had been any gap in the cover at all. But no such argument was advanced before us. Counsel for Skandia conceded at the outset that the cover on the second excess layer was substantially incomplete for several months after 12 February; and counsel for Hodge did not argue *e* the contrary. The only question is whether Mr Dungate knew it. The judge found that he did. He based his finding on two grounds. First he found it improbable in the extreme that Mr Dungate did not read the slip, and, in reading it, did not notice the dates on which the following market added their stamps. Second, he found that there was still a gap of 6% in the cover when Mr Lee showed Mr Dungate the slip on or shortly after 4 June 1980. We will take each of these points in turn. But it is important to notice at *f* the outset that the judge would have found that Mr Dungate knew of the gap, ie knew that the banks' security had been substantially incomplete for several months, even if he were wrong about the last 6%.

As to the first point, Mr Dungate was adamant that if he noticed the dates on which the following market placed their stamps on the slip he attached no importance to them. His only concern was whether there was 100% cover. 'I was not counting up dates,' he *g* said, 'I was counting up percentages.' Counsel for Skandia argued that this was understandable. A slip is not necessarily initialled as soon as an insurer agrees to accept a line. There may be an interval between the placement (if oral) and the written confirmation, and a further interval between the written confirmation and the initialling of the slip. Moreover, we know that there was at least one other slip going round the *h* market, and perhaps others as well. The dates appearing on the final slip seen by Mr Dungate would be the dates when the stamps were transferred from the original slip, and not the date when the original slip was initialled. Counsel for Hodge illustrated this point by a schedule comparing the dates when cover was first confirmed, and the dates appearing in the first and second excess layer slips. In the light of all these points counsel submitted that it would be 'unfair' to pin Mr Dungate with knowledge of the gap in *j* June 1980. He added that the judge had to be satisfied that Mr Dungate knew for certain that there had been a gap in the cover. Nothing less would suffice.

We agree that, for the present purposes, the judge had to be satisfied on the balance of probabilities that Mr Dungate was aware of the gap in the cover. But we do not agree with the submission of counsel for Hodge that the judge had to be satisfied that Mr

Dungate knew *for certain*, or beyond reasonable doubt, that the gap had existed. The
*a* certainty or otherwise of Mr Dungate's knowledge adds nothing to the fact of knowledge,
save possibly that the more certain he was of the gap, the easier it would be for the banks
to establish that he was under a duty of care in negligence. Was the judge then entitled
to find that Mr Dungate was aware of the gap? In our view he was.

In the first place there was the expert evidence. Mr Merrett, a marine underwriter of
long experience, said that in his view the broad range of dates shown on the slip indicated
*b* that the slip had been placed over an extended period of time. Mr Outhwaite, the
underwriter called by the insurers, agreed that on a cursory examination the most likely
explanation would be that the insurers came on risk at about the time they initialled the
slip.

Second, there are the inherent probabilities. The judge found it improbable in the
extreme that Mr Dungate did not read the slip. For he was annoyed with Mr Lee, and
*c* had demanded an explanation. In those circumstances it seems as improbable to us, as it
must have seemed to the judge, that Mr Dungate would have accepted Mr Lee's word
that the temporary cover granted by Hodge had been replaced within 14 days, while *not*
accepting his word, without checking, that the cover added up to 100%.

Third, there is the statement in Mr Dungate's proof furnished in November 1982 that
the second excess layer slip showed that some of the cover had not been placed until mid-
*d* April. If that was Mr Dungate's reaction when shown the slip in November 1982, it is
difficult to see why he would not have drawn the same inference when he saw the slip in
June 1980.

For the reasons we have given, there was evidence to justify the judge's finding that
Mr Dungate became aware of the gap in June 1980. We agree with his conclusion. But
even if we had been in doubt, we would have been most reluctant to disturb his finding,
*e* based as it was, in part at least, on his impression of Mr Dungate as a witness. The judge
did not regard Mr Dungate as a good witness. On critical issues he found him 'extremely
defensive and unreliable'. It is difficult for us to judge such matters from a perusal of the
transcript. But we have been taken through a substantial part of Mr Dungate's evidence
and there are a number of passages in it which to us bear out the judge's impression.
*f* Counsel for Skandia accepted that the burden of persuading us to reverse the judge's
finding as to Mr Dungate's state of knowledge was a heavy one. Nevertheless he
submitted that the judge had been unduly harsh in his assessment of Mr Dungate as a
witness. We bear that submission in mind. Nevertheless, the present case falls far short
of the sort of case in which we would feel justified in disturbing the judge's finding of
fact. We were referred to some recent commercial cases in which the Court of Appeal
has reversed the trial judge on a question of fact, where the credibility of witnesses has
*g* been in issue. But such cases remain the exception. We would hold, in agreement with
the judge, that Mr Dungate became aware in June 1980 that there had been a substantial
gap in the banks' security after the expiry of the 14-day cover.

We turn to the second ground on which the judge found against Mr Dungate, namely
that there was still a gap of 6% when he saw the slip in June 1980. It will be remembered
*h* that the last of the stamps placed on the slip was that of Federated. According to the
judge's finding, Federated accepted a line of 6% on or about 9 June. The stamp was placed
on the slip on 11 June. At first sight therefore, the slip must have been incomplete when
Mr Dungate first saw it at the beginning of June. Yet Mr Dungate was insistent that the
lines added up to 100%. What was his explanation?

We have already mentioned the four foreign underwriters who appear in the list of
*j* overseas placements. They accepted 'as reinsurers' for a total of 6%. On the original of
the slip their names are crossed out in pencil. Mr Dungate said that they had not been
crossed out when he first saw the slip in June. If the four foreign underwriters are
included, and Federated excluded, the total comes to 100%. Yet the judge found
specifically that 6% was still missing. By inference therefore he must have found that,
contrary to Mr Dungate's evidence, the names of the four foreign underwriters had

already been crossed out in pencil when he first saw the slip, or alternatively, that he would have known that they should not be included in the total since they had accepted *a* as reinsurers only.

Counsel for Skandia made the strong point that Mr Lee would never have been so foolish as to write to Mr Dungate on 4 June that he would be bringing with him a slip showing the full 100%, if the slip did not indeed show 100%. Whether he in fact had 100% or merely pretended that he had, is another matter. It was said that in the circumstances the judge had no grounds for rejecting Mr Dungate's evidence as to the *b* crossing out, and no basis for his finding that there was still a gap when Mr Dungate first saw the slip in June.

We do not think it possible to come to a firm conclusion on the judge's second ground. The judge makes no express finding about when or how the names of the four foreign underwriters were crossed out. The matter was not fully explored in evidence, and we are left with too many uncertainties and loose ends. Thus the only evidence as to when, *c* in practice, the reinsurers' names would have been crossed out came from Mr Dungate himself. He said that the broker would normally cross out the reinsurers' names when he obtained someone to front for them. Now the 6% taken by Federated was never (so far as we know) reinsured at all. The four foreign underwriters reinsured National Transit Co, not Federated. It was not until 4 July 1980 that Notcutts informed National Transit that they had arranged reinsurance for them in accordance with their instructions. *d* Yet National Transit had signed their line *before* Federated signed on 11 June.

A further difficulty is that it looks from the original of the slip as if the National Transit line was reduced at some time from 17½% to 11½%—again a difference of 6%. Whether this was part of the process of marking down, or how it came about, we do not know, since Mr Lee never gave evidence.

Yet another difficulty is that it was never suggested to Mr Dungate that he was not *e* entitled to count in the four foreign underwriters (assuming they had not been crossed out) on the ground that they had accepted lines as reinsurers only.

The judge may well have been right in inferring that the last 6% was not yet in place at the beginning of June; indeed he probably was. He may even have been right in inferring that Mr Dungate knew it. But having regard to the uncertainties, some only of which we have mentioned, we would prefer to rest our view that Mr Dungate knew of *f* the gap on the first of the judge's grounds, rather than the second.

The remaining matter for consideration under the first issue is whether Mr Dungate 'appreciated the quality of Mr Lee's dishonesty'. We use that language because it is the language used by the judge, and it is the finding which is specifically challenged in the insurers' notice of appeal. By 'the quality of Mr Lee's dishonesty' the judge meant, we think, the extent of his dishonesty, its nature and possible consequences. The significance *g* of the finding goes, as we have already said, to the issues of negligence and misrepresentation rather than non-disclosure.

A recurring theme in Mr Dungate's evidence was that, although he realised in June 1980 that Mr Lee had acted stupidly, and indeed dishonestly, in issuing the false cover notes, he did not regard him as a dishonest man. Counsel for Skandia sought to justify *h* that attitude. He submitted that it is easy for us now, looking back, to see that Mr Lee was dishonest through and through. But looking at it as Mr Dungate did in June 1980, Mr Lee's conduct may have seemed more venial. He was anxious that the business should go through. He took a risk. In due course the truth would in any event have come to light. By the middle of June 1980 he had, on any view, obtained 100% cover. The banks were never seriously exposed or imperilled. Why then should Mr Dungate be under any *j* obligation to report the matter? Why should he not turn a blind eye on the ground that no harm had actually been done?

We are conscious, as always, of the dangers of being wise after the event. But there is a short answer to the argument of counsel for Skandia. Mr Dungate's evidence that he did not regard Mr Lee as a dishonest man, but as being guilty only of an isolated act of dishonesty, was predicated, as the judge pointed out, on the assumption that he did not

know of the gap in the cover. But the judge has found that he did know of the gap, and
*a* we have upheld that finding. In the course of his cross-examination Mr Dungate accepted
that if he had been aware of the gap in the cover it would have been his duty to inform
the banks. In our view that answer is in itself sufficient to justify the judge's finding that
Mr Dungate was fully aware of the quality of Mr Lee's dishonesty.

As for the judge's finding that the banks were 'seriously exposed', it was pointed out
on behalf of the insurers that for loss to result the value of the alleged gemstones would
*b* have had to drop very greatly below their supposed value; the loss would have had to
extend beyond the first layer of 9·25m Swiss francs and the first excess layer of 9·25m
Swiss francs and into the second excess layer of 18·5m Swiss francs to reach that point at
which any part of the cover was lacking. Nevertheless, it remains true that the banks
were over the period February to June 1980 exposed to a risk which was certainly not
negligible, and Mr Dungate must have realised this.

*c* But counsel for Skandia had another string to his bow. The judge found that Mr
Dungate actively assisted in passing off Mr Lee's dishonesty as an administrative error.
His motive was to prevent an investigation of his own conduct in the matter, that is to
say, his agreement to hold the banks covered for 14 days when he had no authority to do
so. Counsel for Skandia submitted that the judge misinterpreted Mr Dungate's motive,
and thereby fell into error. If Mr Dungate was involved in a 'cover up', the last thing he
*d* would have done would be to send on to Mr Jekyll, of Standard Chartered AG, a copy of
Mr Lee's letter to Mr Verkooyen of 4 June 1980, with its reference to Hodge having
provided cover 'on a provisional basis to be replaced . . .' As counsel for Hodge pointed
out in his reply, provisional cover until replaced (which might be never) would be far
more likely to prompt an investigation at the instance of Standard Chartered AG than
cover for 14 days.

*e* There is force in these points. But there is also much which remains unexplained in
Mr Dungate's actions in the early part of June. In his letter to Mr Jekyll he wrote: 'After
considerable enquiries with the various Underwriters concerned, I have satisfied myself
that the cover has been correctly placed . . .'

In his evidence he referred only to inquiries of the Prudential and Ennia. If what he
said in this letter was true, and he had made other inquiries as well, for example of
*f* Commercial Union, he would have been bound to discover the gap in the cover and
would, on his own evidence, have been under a duty to disclose Mr Lee's dishonesty to
the banks. If on the other hand what he says in his evidence was true, why did he refer
in his letter to 'considerable enquiries'? Either way there was material on which the
judge could find that he had 'actively assisted in passing off Mr Lee's dishonesty as an
administrative error' within the organisations of Hodge and Notcutts.

*g* We consider below, under issue (6), whether the 'active assistance' amounted in law to
a misrepresentation to the banks. We are presently concerned only with Mr Dungate's
motive. Whether his motive was to avoid an investigation of his own conduct, or
whether he simply wished to play down what had happened in order that Mr Lee should
continue to bring him valuable business is, in our view, of marginal significance.
*h* Whatever his precise motive, the judge was, as we have already said, justified on the
evidence in finding that Mr Dungate was 'fully aware of the quality of Mr Lee's
dishonesty'. We would therefore reject Hodge's argument on issue (1).

*Issue (2)*

Once again we start by asking why the issue is relevant. The answer is that it was
*j* common ground at the trial, as before us, that if the insurers were under a duty to
disclose Mr Lee's dishonesty, that duty would have been discharged by their informing
Notcutts. It was not suggested that they had informed the banks. Nor was it suggested
(for what it may have been worth) that they had informed Mr Ballestero. But Mr
Dungate's evidence was that he had two telephone conversations with Mr Wilkinson, a
director of Notcutts, in June 1980. According to his evidence, he informed Mr Wilkinson
of what had happened, criticised Mr Lee's conduct in issuing false cover notes, and asked

that in future when Mr Lee came to see him he should be accompanied by Mr John
Fowler, a senior broker from Notcutts office. Mr Wilkinson had no recollection of any          *a*
such conversations. The judge found that no such conversations ever took place. He
rejected Mr Dungate's evidence as untruthful, and preferred Mr Wilkinson's evidence
where they differed. He found Mr Wilkinson to be conspicuously careful, truthful and
reliable.

Counsel for Skandia attacked these findings. He submitted that, just as the judge had
been over-harsh to Mr Dungate, he was over-generous to Mr Wilkinson. There was much          *b*
in Mr Wilkinson's conduct, he said, which called for explanation. Thus, as we have
already mentioned, the cover note dated 28 January 1980 was signed by Mr Wilkinson
as well as Mr Lee. Yet within a short time Mr Wilkinson was actively engaged in finding
cover to replace Hodge. A possible inference would be that he, like Mr Lee, was aware
that the cover note was false. Yet counsel for Skandia declined to ask us to draw any such
inference, no doubt because it was never put to Mr Wilkinson in cross-examination. In          *c*
the course of his evidence Mr Wilkinson was asked a number of questions about how he
came to sign the cover note. The gist of his evidence was that he could not remember,
but that he must have been relying on information given to him by Mr Lee or Mr Fowler
or both of them and that Mr Lee probably misled him. There was no satisfactory
explanation anywhere in his evidence of how he came to sign the cover note. At one
point it looked as if counsel for Hodge was going to submit that Mr Wilkinson knew as          *d*
much about the false cover notes as Mr Lee; if so, there could be no duty to disclose to
him what he already knew. But counsel for Hodge conceded that, much as he would like
to take the point, he could not do so without leave. In the event he sought no such leave.
Both he and counsel for Skandia relied on Mr Wilkinson's knowledge for the limited
purpose of explaining why he did not react more violently when he was told (if he was
told) of the false cover notes in June. If he already knew that the cover notes were false it          *e*
would explain why he did not recall the conversation with Mr Dungate.

As to Mr Dungate's evidence that Mr Lee was to be accompanied in future by Mr
Fowler, counsel for Skandia submitted that the obvious way for the banks to deal with
the suggestion was to call Mr Fowler himself. Yet they never did so. Another strong
point made in that connection turned on the wording of an internal memorandum dated          *f*
5 June 1980, sent to Mr Wilkinson by Mr Mackeson-Sandbach, the chairman of Notcutts.
The memorandum starts with Mr Mackeson-Sandbach saying that he was very concerned
about Mr Lee's activities. Paragraph 4 of the memorandum reads:

'I understand from Andrew [Douglas] that there are some comings and goings on
the jewellery contingency. We must not over-extend ourselves on this tricky type
of insurance and we must be satisfied that there is adequate security available from          *g*
Insurers. No cover notes or acceptance of cover can possibly be issued by Roy Lee.'

Counsel for Skandia submitted that the occasion for sending the memorandum must
have been Mr Dungate's discovery of the false cover notes, which he must then have
communicated to someone at Notcutts. It would be too much of a coincidence to suppose          *h*
that Mr Mackeson-Sandbach had independent grounds for being concerned about Mr
Lee, at precisely the same time.

Finally, counsel for Skandia relied on a passage from Mr Dungate's proof furnished in
November 1982. After referring to the events of June 1980, the proof continues:
'Thereafter Notcutt's instructions to Mr. Lee were that Fowler had to be present at all
times.' Counsel for Skandia argued that in the context the word 'thereafter' had a          *j*
causative as well as a temporal significance. It was because Mr Lee had issued the false
cover notes that Notcutts gave instructions for Mr Fowler to be present at all times.

By these arguments counsel for Skandia and Hodge built up a strong case. But there
are strong arguments the other way. Thus the argument based on Mr Dungate's proof is
undermined, or at any rate weakened, by the fact that nowhere in Mr Dungate's proof is
there any reference to any conversation with Mr Wilkinson. Indeed the point was not

a raised at all until a fortnight before the trial. This may suggest that it was something of an afterthought on Mr Dungate's part.

But the major obstacle in the Hodge's path is the fact that the judge accepted both Mr Mackeson-Sandbach and Mr Wilkinson as witnesses of truth. Mr Mackeson-Sandbach was asked about his memorandum of 5 June 1980. His evidence was clear that he was not aware that Mr Lee had issued any cover notes at all. He did not regard himself as withdrawing authority from Mr Lee to issue cover notes because no such authority had
b ever been given. He merely wished to make his instructions clear that Mr Lee was in no circumstances to issue them.

Where a witness, whom the judge accepted as a witness of truth, has stated categorically that the memorandum was not prompted by the discovery of the false cover notes but by other considerations, it would require an overwhelmingly strong case for this court to disbelieve him. Furthermore, the reference in Mr Mackeson-Sandbach's memorandum
c to 'comings and goings on the jewellery contingency' could well be explained by the contents of a memorandum of 4 June 1980 addressed by Mr Lee to Mr Wilkinson in which Mr Lee referred to journeys to various parts of the world which he had already undertaken and proposed to undertake in relation to the insurance arrangements for the third excess layer.

There is another difficulty facing the insurers. Both Mr Wilkinson and Mr Mackeson-
d Sandbach said that if they had been told about the false cover notes they would have suspended or dismissed Mr Lee on the spot. They did not do so. It seems to us more or less inconceivable that if Mr Wilkinson had been told of Mr Lee's dishonesty he would not have passed on this information to Mr Mackeson-Sandbach at a time when Mr Lee's 'comings and goings' were already causing some anxiety in Notcutts. Of course, it could be said that Mr Wilkinson and Mr Mackeson-Sandbach were lying, or that their reaction
e at the time might have been different. There is certainly a risk that they are exaggerating what would have been their reaction at the time in the light of their current knowledge of Mr Lee's subsequent dishonesty. But the fact remains that they do not seem to have reacted at all. This is inexplicable save on the basis that they were ignorant. It is not enough to say that the judge was over-generous to Mr Wilkinson. We could not find that he had been over-harsh to Mr Dungate without rejecting the whole thrust and substance
f of Mr Wilkinson's evidence. This we are unwilling to do. It follows that we would reject Hodge's arguments on issue (2) as well as on issue (1).

Before leaving these issues and turning to the issues of law, we should record that counsel for Chemical Bank addressed us on the facts for the best part of five days and his skeleton argument on the facts was a very full one. We shall be returning to the facts later in this judgment, when we come to consider causation under issue (10). But at this
g stage we would only say that we mean no discourtesy to counsel for Chemical Bank or to counsel for the other banks, who adopted most of his arguments and added others of his own, if we have not followed them down every by-way. If we had been against them on the facts, we would have dealt with their arguments on the facts more fully. As it is, we are in their favour.

h
*Issue (3)*

What damage could Mr Dungate reasonably have foreseen as likely to be suffered by the banks in the event of his failure to disclose to them the information possessed by him as to Mr Lee's dishonesty?

This issue is relevant to two aspects of the case: first, Steyn J described it as the threshold
j question for proof of the existence of a duty of care under the principle stated by Lord Wilberforce in *Anns v Merton London Borough* [1977] 2 All ER 492, [1978] AC 728; and, second, it will determine, at least so far as concerns the claim in negligence, whether the loss suffered by the banks on the second Ultron loan was in law too remote for it to be treated as caused by any breach of duty on the part of Hodge. The facts on which this issue is to be decided are provided by the answers to issues (1) and (2) and the facts which are stated above as being common ground.

Since the appeal by Hodge against the findings of fact of Steyn J on issues (1) and (2) has failed, it followed that the judge addressed the question of foreseeability on the correct factual basis. The question whether on that basis of fact a reasonable underwriter in the position of Mr Dungate was bound to anticipate as probable that, if he took no steps to inform Notcutts or the banks of Mr Lee's deception, the banks would suffer the kind of loss suffered by them as a result of making the second Ultron loan was a matter of fact for the judge to determine and, if he determined it on the correct basis, this court on appeal should be slow to interfere with that determination: see per Lord Mackay in *Smith v Littlewoods Organisation Ltd (Chief Constable, Fife Constabulary, third party)* [1987] 1 All ER 710 at 719, [1987] AC 241 at 258 in a judgment with which Lord Keith and Lord Griffiths agreed. The main questions of law are whether, having regard to the nature of this case, the judge directed himself correctly as to the meaning of 'probable' in the concept of anticipating something as probable, or having reasonable foresight of it, and as to the relevant 'kind' of damage of which reasonable foresight was required to be established.

The principle of law which insists on reasonable foreseeability of damage, both for the existence of a duty of care and for recoverability of damage as caused by any breach, was intended to limit within reasonable bounds the circumstances in which an act or omission may be held to give rise to liability and the consequences of any act or omission in respect of which damages may be awarded. The law is concerned with the foreseeability of the particular damage suffered and in respect of which the claim is made; thus, in *Overseas Tankship (UK) Ltd v Morts Dock and Engineering Co Ltd, The Wagon Mound (No 1)* [1961] 1 All ER 404 at 415, [1961] AC 388 at 425 Viscount Simonds, giving the judgment of the Privy Council, said:

> '... [in negligence] there can be no liability until the damage has been done. It is not the act but the consequences on which tortious liability is founded. Just as (as it has been said) there is no such thing as negligence in the air, so there is no such thing as liability in the air. Suppose an action brought by A for damage caused by the carelessness (a neutral word) of B, for example a fire caused by the careless spillage of oil. It may, of course, become relevant to know what duty B owed to A, but the only liability that is in question is the liability for damage by fire.'

The Privy Council declined to follow the decision of this court in *Re Polemis and Furness Withy & Co Ltd* [1921] 3 KB 560, [1921] All ER Rep 40, which had held that, if the defendant was guilty of negligence, he was responsible for all the consequences whether reasonably foreseeable or not, provided that the consequences were 'direct'. Viscount Simonds said ([1961] 1 All ER 404 at 413, [1961] AC 388 at 423):

> '... if some limitation must be imposed on the consequences for which the negligent actor is to be held responsible—and all are agreed that some limitation there must be—why should that test (reasonable foreseeability) be rejected which, since he is judged by what the reasonable man ought to foresee, corresponds with the common conscience of mankind and a test (the "direct" consequences) be substituted which leads to nowhere but the never ending and insoluble problems of causation.'

Nevertheless, notwithstanding the rejection of the limitation based on direct consequences in preference for reasonable foreseeability, it was their Lordships' opinion that, in probability, not many cases would for that reason have a different result. The reason for that view was that, although the court is required to concentrate on the particular damage suffered, the essential factor in determining liability was said to be whether the damage is of such a *kind* as the reasonable man should have foreseen. The extent to which the limitation of reasonable foreseeability restricts the liability of a defendant must depend on the way in which the 'kind' of damage is defined in a particular case (see [1961] 1 All ER 404 at 413, 415, [1961] AC 388 at 422, 426).

So far as concerns physical injury the principle of reasonable foreseeability has not
*a* imposed any significant limitation because, once it is proved that some form of physical
injury is foreseeable, the defendant is liable for all consequences which in fact occur even
though unforeseeable in the manner of their happening or in the extent suffered and the
defendant must take the victim as he turns out to be and pay for the consequences.

In *Hughes v Lord Advocate* [1963] 1 All ER 705, [1963] AC 837 an eight-year-old
plaintiff was injured when he entered a tent which had been left by workmen over an
*b* open manhole in the street. The tent was unguarded but surrounded by paraffin lamps.
The boy caused a lamp to fall into the manhole. An explosion of paraffin vapour caused
the boy to fall into the manhole and he suffered injuries from burns. The plaintiff was
denied relief on the ground that the accident was not such as could be reasonably
foreseen. On appeal to the House of Lords it was held that the damage was caused by a
type of occurrence which had arisen from a known source of danger, the lamp, and was
*c* reasonably foreseeable. The defendants were liable although the source of danger had
acted in an unforeseeable way. Lord Reid rejected the contention that the mere fact that
the way in which the accident happened could not be anticipated was enough to exclude
liability although there was a breach of duty and that breach of duty caused danger of a
kind that could have been anticipated. In short, the injury to the plaintiff was caused by
a known source of danger but caused in a way which could not have been foreseen and
*d* that afforded no defence (see [1963] 1 All ER 705 at 707–708, [1963] AC 837 at 846–
847).

The contest in this case on the definition of the type of loss, for the purposes of the test
of reasonable foreseeability, turns on the fact that at most Mr Dungate, the underwriter
employed by Hodge, could only foresee that Mr Lee might repeat the sort of deception
which he had practised on the banks with reference to the insurers' security for the first
*e* Ultron loan and, if he did, the banks might suffer financial loss as a result of being
induced by Mr Lee's fraud to enter into a transaction of loan, into which they would not
otherwise have entered, and in which the insurance cover, as against the various insurers,
might turn out to be wholly or partly unenforceable because of the fraud of Mr Lee. But
the loss suffered by the banks on the second Ultron loan, once it was made, did not result
only from the fact that the cover was unenforceable because of the fraud of Mr Lee. The
*f* banks could have recovered nothing on the policies, assuming there to have been no
fraud by Mr Lee, because the fraud of Mr Ballestero, which was not foreseeable, was a
cause of loss which the banks had expressly agreed to exclude from the policy cover.

Is the type of loss which must be shown to have been reasonably foreseeable in this
case to be defined as loss resulting from the fraud of Mr Ballestero, who was the insured
and the borrower from the bank, or in some wider terms, such as loss resulting from
*g* entering into a transaction of loan induced by fraud?

Steyn J dealt with foreseeability as follows. After reference to the two-stage test
described by Lord Wilberforce in *Anns v Merton London Borough* [1977] 2 All ER 492,
[1978] AC 728 he considered three features of the case relied on by Hodge as precluding,
as a matter of legal principle, a ruling that a duty of care existed. Those features were,
*h* first, the contractual setting between the insurers and the banks, second, the fact that in
the submission of Hodge the breach of duty alleged against them was 'pure omission'
and, third, the fact that the breach of duty alleged involved the making of a judgment
by Mr Dungate about whether a third party, Mr Lee, would in future attempt to deceive
the banks. Steyn J held that no one of the three features, in so far as they existed on the
facts of the case, precluded a ruling that Hodge owed a duty of care to the banks.
*j* Nevertheless, on the matter of the interposition of a third party in the alleged duty
situation, Steyn J added that it 'requires most careful consideration. And in particular it
will be necessary to consider what the requirement of reasonable foresight comprehends
in such a case' (see [1987] 2 All ER 923 at 952, [1987] 2 WLR 1300 at 1340).

Steyn J then turned to the question of reasonable foreseeability and set out his
conclusions in the following words ([1987] 2 All ER 923 at 952, [1987] 2 WLR 1300 at
1340):

'In a case such as the present it is, in my judgment, insufficient, in order to
establish liability, that it was in the reasonable contemplation of the insurers that a    *a*
failure to disclose Mr Lee's dishonesty might possibly result in financial harm to the
banks. A bare possibility is not enough. In my judgment it must be shown that it
was reasonably foreseeable by the insurers that there was a manifest and obvious
risk that a failure to disclose would lead to financial loss by the banks. That is how I
approach the matter. No purpose would be served in repeating or summarising the
findings of fact which I have already made. I am entirely satisfied that it was    *b*
reasonably foreseeable that, if Mr Lee's dishonesty was not disclosed to the banks,
there was a manifest and obvious risk that the banks might suffer financial loss as a
result of Mr Lee's future dishonesty. That, in my judgment, is the foresight which
a reasonable underwriter would have had. But I am also satisfied that Mr Dungate
in fact distrusted Mr Lee, and realised that there was a substantial risk that Mr Lee
might again deceive the banks to their financial detriment. He chose to ignore the    *c*
banks' position, and was content to proceed on the basis that, exercising "care", he
could look after his employers' interests. In all the circumstances I am satisfied that
the banks have satisfied the threshold requirement of proximity and neighbourhood.'

He returned to the question of foreseeability again in dealing with the issue of
remoteness and causation. It had been submitted that Mr Lee's frauds after June 1980    *d*
were different in kind from the fraud perpetrated by the issue of the false cover notes.
Steyn J said ([1987] 2 All ER 923 at 955, [1987] 2 WLR 1300 at 1342–1343):

'I repeat my finding that it was reasonably foreseeable by the insurers from June
1980 that there was a manifest and obvious risk that Mr Lee would again deceive
the banks and insurers in and about the insurance transactions, thereby affording
the insurers with a complete defence to any claim on the policies. In so far as it was    *e*
argued that Mr Lee's subsequent frauds were different in kind from the fraud
perpetrated by him in the first Ultron transaction, I disagree. It is, of course, true
that the precise manner of his future fraudulent conduct was not foreseeable. But
Mr Lee's subsequent frauds were of the same general character as his earlier fraud.
Mr Lee committed the very kind of frauds in and about the insurance transactions    *f*
which were reasonably foreseeable by an underwriter in Mr Dungate's position in
June 1980 or subsequently.'

Steyn J did not in terms define the kind of loss in fact suffered by the banks or discuss
the question whether that loss was of a kind which was reasonably foreseeable by Mr
Dungate.
Before us, the submissions for Hodge on this issue were directed both to the proper    *g*
inferences to be drawn from the facts as established and to the relevant principles of law.
As to the inferences of fact counsel contended that an underwriter in the position of Mr
Dungate could not reasonably foresee (a) any danger of fraud on the part of Mr Ballestero
merely because of his knowledge of the fraud of Mr Lee, (b) any danger that Mr Lee,
having been found out, would lie again so as to defraud the banks, (c) any danger that, if
Mr Lee should again defraud the banks, that fraud would damage the banks by providing    *h*
a defence to the insurers in respect of any claim on the policies and (d) any prospect that,
if Mr Dungate reported Mr Lee's prior deception, whether it resulted in the dismissal of
Mr Lee or not, such report would cause the second Ultron loan not to proceed.
As to the law, counsel for Hodge submitted (i) for proof of reasonable foresight of
economic loss resulting from the fraud of a third party it was not sufficient to prove only
foresight of the type of loss to the exclusion of foresight of cause or extent; reliance was    *j*
placed on the speech of Lord Pearce in *Hughes v Lord Advocate* [1963] 1 All ER 705 at
715–716, [1963] AC 837 at 857–858, (ii) in this sort of case the banks must prove
reasonable foresight either of the fraud of Mr Ballestero, which caused the loss at least in
the sense of rendering Mr Lee's frauds of no account, or of a likely connection between
Mr Lee's fraud and that of Mr Ballestero and (iii) further, the proper approach on the

a  question of reasonable foresight is to consider whether the loss suffered, ie loss from Mr
Ballestero's fraud, which was a loss irrecoverable under the policy by reason of the express
terms of the policy, was 'the very type of thing' which was reasonably foreseeable as the
consequence of not performing the duty to disclose Mr Lee's deception. On the facts the
only consequence which was foreseeable as the 'very type of thing', which disclosure
might avoid, was repetition by Mr Lee of his fraud in issuing cover notes in respect of
which real cover did not exist or, at its widest, some loss resulting from further and
b  different frauds by Mr Lee. Reliance was placed on the speech of Lord Goff in *Smith v
Littlewoods Organisation Ltd* [1987] 1 All ER 710, [1987] AC 241.

Before considering the submissions directed to the inferences of fact it is necessary to
consider the submission on the law of counsel for Hodge and to determine whether
Steyn J reached his conclusions on the facts on the correct basis. We emphasise that we
are dealing here with the issue of reasonable foreseeability only. It is the first stage of the
c  inquiry, that is to say in Lord Wilberforce's words in *Anns v Merton London Borough* [1977]
2 All ER 492 at 498, [1978] AC 728 at 751 whether—

'there is a sufficient relationship of proximity or neighbourhood such that, in the
reasonable contemplation of [the alleged wrongdoer], carelessness on his part may
be likely to cause damage to [the person who has suffered damage] . . .'

d  In Lord Goff's words, the problems in this case cannot be solved 'simply through the
mechanism of foreseeability': see *Smith v Littlewoods Organisation Ltd* [1987] 1 All ER 710
at 735, [1987] AC 241 at 279.

*Smith*'s case was concerned with the question whether an occupier of property owed a
duty of care to adjoining occupiers in respect of acts of trespass on his property resulting
in damage by fire to adjoining properties. Lord Mackay noted ([1987] 1 All ER 710 at
e  720, [1987] AC 241 at 259):

'It is plain from the authorities that the fact that the damage, on which a claim is
founded, was caused by a human agent quite independent of the person against
whom a claim in negligence is made does not, of itself, preclude success of the claim,
since breach of duty on the part of the person against whom the claim is made may
f  also have played a part in causing the damage.'

Next, after reference to *Lamb v Camden London BC* [1981] 2 All ER 408, [1981] QB 625
and to the judgment of Oliver LJ, Lord Mackay continued ([1987] 1 All ER 710 at 721,
[1987] AC 241 at 261):

'. . . where the only possible source of the type of damage or injury which is in
g  question is agency of a human being for whom the person against whom the claim
is made has no responsibility, it may not be easy to find that as a reasonable person
he was bound to anticipate that type of damage as a consequence of his act or
omission. The more unpredictable the conduct in question, the less easy to affirm
that any particular result from it is probable and in many circumstances the only
way in which a judge could properly be persuaded to come to the conclusion that
h  the result was not only possible but reasonably foreseeable as probable would be to
convince him that, in the circumstances, it was highly likely. In this type of case a
finding that the reasonable man should have anticipated the consequence of human
action as just probable may not be a very frequent option. Unless the judge can be
satisfied that the result of the human action is highly probable or very likely he may
have to conclude that all that the reasonable man could say was that it was a mere
j  possibility. Unless the needle that measures the probability of a particular result
flowing from the conduct of a human agent is near the top of the scale it may be
hard to conclude that it has risen sufficiently from the bottom to create the duty
reasonably to foresee it. In summary I conclude, in agreement with both counsel,
that what the reasonable man is bound to foresee in a case involving injury or
damage by independent human agency, just as in cases where such agency plays no

part, is the probable consequences of his own act or omission, but that, in such a case, a clear basis will be required on which to assert that the injury or damage is more than a mere possibility.'

Then, after considering other cases relating to fires decided in Scotland and the cases in this court of *Lamb v Camden London BC* [1981] 2 All ER 408, [1981] QB 625 and *P Perl (Exporters) Ltd v Camden London BC* [1983] 3 All ER 161, [1984] QB 342, Lord Mackay took up the question of the meaning of the word 'probable' as used in the authorities concerned with reasonable foresight of damage arising from the acts of third parties. After setting out a passage from the opinion of the Board in *The Wagon Mound (No 2)*, *Overseas Tankship (UK) Ltd v Miller Steamship Co Pty* [1966] 2 All ER 709 at 718, [1967] 1 AC 617 at 642–643, in which Lord Reid referred to *Bolton v Stone* [1951] 1 All ER 1078, [1951] AC 850, Lord Mackay continued ([1987] 1 All ER 710 at 727, [1987] AC 241 at 269):

> 'In my opinion this observation demonstrates that, when the word "probable" is used in this context in the authorities, it is used as indicating a real risk as distinct from a mere possibility of danger. It is not used in the sense that the consequence must be more probable than not to happen, before it can be reasonably foreseeable.'

It is clear in our view that Steyn J directed himself that, in a case of economic loss resulting from the deliberate and dishonest conduct of a third party, it was necessary to show more than an awareness of a bare possibility of harm from such a cause but awareness of what he called a 'manifest and obvious risk' of financial loss to the banks from Mr Lee's future dishonesty. Those words, in the context of his judgment as a whole, indicate, and either adjective would suffice, the same sense as that conveyed by the words 'real risk as distinct from a mere possibility of danger' as used by Lord Mackay in the passage cited above from *Smith v Littlewoods Organisation Ltd*. Further there was in the evidence a clear basis to support the judge's conclusion. There was no error in that regard.

As to the point raised by counsel for Hodge with reference to foresight of immediate cause and of extent of damage we do not therein find any basis for holding that Steyn J misdirected himself. We cannot accept the submission that, in the case of economic loss resulting from the act of an independent third party, there is to be introduced into the concept of reasonable foreseeability of damage a requirement of foresight of the manner and means by which the particular loss was caused or of the extent of the loss suffered. When the judge considers whether reasonable foresight of the relevant kind of loss has been proved, he is entitled and required to consider all the circumstances of the case. We can, however, find in Lord Pearce's speech in *Hughes v Lord Advocate* [1963] 1 All ER 705 at 715–716, [1963] AC 837 at 857–858 no support for the submission that, where reasonable foresight of the relevant kind of loss is proved, the court is required further to be satisfied that there was reasonable foresight of the manner in which the loss was suffered or the extent of it.

Next, there is in our view no principle of law which requires in this case proof of reasonable foresight of damage arising from the fraud of Mr Ballestero, or proof of awareness of the fact that the prior fraud of Mr Lee indicated in some way the risk of fraud by Mr Ballestero. To cover the point, in case it should be accepted by the court, counsel for Keysers contended, as did counsel for Chemical Bank, that the discovery by Mr Dungate of the past fraud of Mr Lee should reasonably have caused Mr Dungate to anticipate that there might be fraud going on in which both Mr Lee and Mr Ballestero were concerned. It was said, for example, that Mr Dungate should have suspected that Mr Ballestero was bribing Mr Lee. Reliance was placed on the terms in which Mr Lee represented to Mr Dungate the merits both of Mr Ballestero and of his Menorcan scheme. Steyn J made no finding to this effect. We did not find these submissions persuasive and if it had been necessary for the banks to prove that Mr Dungate should reasonably have foreseen that the banks were exposed to danger from fraud *on the part of Mr Ballestero* we would have held that the banks on that ground should fail.

It seems to us that the principle stated in *Hughes v Lord Advocate* is applicable to this
*a* case and was correctly applied by Steyn J. That principle requires the court to consider in
what terms the damage in fact suffered by the plaintiffs may fairly be categorised by type
for the purpose of the test of reasonable foreseeability. The process of categorisation must
be determined by the purpose for which it is carried out, namely to test whether there is
a sufficient relationship of proximity or neighbourhood such that in the reasonable
contemplation of the alleged wrongdoer carelessness on his part may be likely to cause
*b* damage to the person who has suffered damage: see *Anns v Merton London Borough* [1977]
2 All ER 492 at 498, [1978] AC 728 at 751 per Lord Wilberforce. It is for the plaintiff to
point to a categorisation of the loss suffered by him, which the court on examination can
accept as appropriate and accurate, and which the plaintiff can demonstrate was
reasonably foreseeable by the defendant.

The judge held, as we think rightly, that the fraud of Mr Ballestero was not foreseeable.
*c* The banks however submitted to Steyn J, and repeated the submission in this court, that
the kind of damage suffered by them was financial loss caused by Mr Lee's dishonesty, in
particular loss caused by being induced by the *fraud of Mr Lee* to enter into a transaction
of loan into which, but for that dishonesty, they would not have entered. It seems to us
that that is an accurate description of the kind of loss suffered by the banks. The second
Ultron loan was made, as Steyn J found on the strength of a cover note sent by Mr Lee
*d* (see [1987] 2 All ER 923 at 939, [1987] 2 WLR 1300 at 1321). The insurer was said in the
cover note to be a Californian entity bearing the name 'Compania Americana de Seguros'.
The Californian entity was a bogus company. The policy had a 'cut through clause'
enabling the banks to claim against the reinsurers but Mr Lee had not satisfied himself
that satisfactory and enforceable reinsurance existed. He assured Keysers that he had
inspected the reinsurance treaties which he could not have done since they were in La
*e* Paz. Further, Mr Lee had also misrepresented the effect of the fraud exclusion clause to
Keysers in terms which were wholly untrue to the knowledge of Mr Lee. On the judge's
findings, therefore, the banks were induced to enter into the transaction of the second
Ultron loan as a result of the fraud of Mr Lee and suffered loss in consequence.

The judge held that that kind of loss was reasonably foreseeable because it was caused
by the same kind of fraud which Mr Lee had perpetrated against the banks with reference
*f* to the first Ultron loan and of which Mr Dungate in June 1980 had knowledge. That
finding of the judge cannot, in our view, be faulted. The danger to which the banks were
exposed was, therefore, danger of financial loss caused by the fraud of Mr Lee. The
damage suffered in the second Ultron loan was caused by that danger notwithstanding
the fact that the particular means by which it was caused included the fraud of Mr
Ballestero, and notwithstanding the fact that the extent of the loss suffered, namely the
*g* whole of the amount of the loan and interest on it, resulted from the fraud of Mr
Ballestero and not of Mr Lee. The reason for that is obvious: but for Mr Lee's fraud the
loan would not have been made.

That conclusion, if right, is an answer to all the points of law put forward by counsel
for Hodge. The 'very type of thing' which, in the judge's findings, Mr Dungate could
*h* foresee as the consequence of not disclosing Mr Lee's deception was loss resulting from
the repetition of that kind of deception, namely fraud on the part of Mr Lee inducing
the banks to enter into the second Ultron loan transaction, and the damage suffered in
that transaction was of that kind. It follows that Steyn J not only addressed the question
of reasonable foreseeability on the correct factual basis but also determined it on the
correct basis in law. The submission of counsel for Hodge as to the proper inferences of
*j* fact to be drawn were powerful. There was, in our view, force in the submission that Mr
Dungate may well have thought it unlikely that, having been found out, Mr Lee would
again resort to fraud to deceive the banks. But Mr Lee was only found out in fact by Mr
Dungate, and not by anyone else, because Mr Dungate chose to tell no one else. Mr
Dungate did not know what was going to happen about the insurance cover for the
second Ultron loan. He was not going to write it and would have no part in it. We are

not persuaded by any of the matters put forward by counsel that Steyn J was wrong to reach the conclusion which he did.

In the event the appeal on the issue of foreseeability fails.

*Issue (4)*

We begin with a statement of basic principle of the English law of contract:

> 'Ordinarily the failure to disclose a material fact which might influence the mind of a prudent contractor does not give the right to avoid the contract. The principle of caveat emptor applies outside contracts of sale. There are certain contracts expressed by the law to be contracts of the utmost good faith, where material facts must be disclosed; if not, the contract is voidable. Apart from special fiduciary relationships, contracts for partnership and contracts of insurance are the leading instances. In such cases the duty does not arise out of contract; the duty of a person proposing an insurance arises before a contract is made, so of an intending partner.'

(See *Bell v Lever Bros Ltd* [1932] AC 161 at 227, [1931] All ER Rep 1 at 32 per Lord Atkin.)

The common features of contracts which are classified by the law as contracts uberrimae fidei is that by their very nature one party is likely to have the command of means of knowledge not available to the other. In the leading case of *Carter v Boehm* (1766) 3 Burr 1905 at 1909, [1558–1774] All ER Rep 183 at 184 Lord Mansfield CJ described the relationale behind the duty of disclosure falling on the insured in the case of contracts of insurance as follows:

> 'Insurance is a contract upon speculation. The special facts, upon which the contingent chance is to be computed, lie most commonly in the knowledge of the *insured* only: the under-writer trusts to his representation, and proceeds upon confidence that he does not keep back any circumstance in his knowledge, to mislead the under-writer into a belief that the circumstance does not exist, and to induce him to estimate the risque, as if it did not exist. The keeping back such circumstance is a *fraud*, and therefore the policy is *void*. Although the suppression should happen through *mistake*, without any fraudulent intention; yet still the under-writer is *deceived*, and the policy is *void*; because the risque run is really different from the risque understood and intended to be run, at the time of the agreement.' (Lord Mansfield CJ's emphasis.)

The law relating to marine insurance was codified by the Marine Insurance Act 1906. Section 17 provides:

> 'A contract of marine insurance is a contract based upon the utmost good faith, and, if the utmost good faith be not observed by either party, the contract may be avoided by the other party.'

Section 18 defines the duties of disclosure falling on the insured. The first two subsections provide:

> '(1) Subject to the provisions of this section, the assured must disclose to the insurer, before the contract is concluded, every material circumstance which is known to the assured, and the assured is deemed to know every circumstance which, in the ordinary course of business, ought to be known by him. If the assured fails to make such disclosure, the insurer may avoid the contract.
>
> (2) Every circumstance is material which would influence the judgment of a prudent insurer in fixing the premium, or determining whether he will take the risk.'

It has been common ground on these appeals that there is no relevant difference between the obligations of disclosure falling on the parties to a contract of non-marine insurance by virtue of the common law and those falling on the parties to a contract of marine insurance by virtue of the 1906 Act.

That Act did not define the duties of disclosure falling on the insurer. In our judgment,
*a* however, there is no doubt that the obligation to disclose material facts is a mutual one
imposing reciprocal duties on insurer and insured. In the case of marine insurance
contracts, s 17 in effect so provides. The occasions where disclosure by the insurer is
required may in practice be rare since the circumstances material to the insurance will
ordinarily be known only to the proposed insured. Nevertheless, such occasions may
arise. The mutuality of the duty under the common law was recognised by Lord
*b* Mansfield CJ himself in *Carter v Boehm* (1766) 3 Burr 1905 at 1909, [1558–1774] All ER
Rep 183 at 184, where he gave this example:

> 'The policy would equally be void, against the *under-writer*, if *he* concealed; as, if
> he insured a ship on her voyage, which he privately knew to be arrived: and an
> action would lie to recover the premium.' (Lord Mansfield CJ's emphasis.)

*c* According to more recent authority the word 'void' in this passage should read 'voidable':
see 25 Halsbury's Laws (4th edn) para 377 and the cases there cited.
It is no less clear that where there is obligation to disclose material facts it is an absolute
one which is not negatived by the absence of fraud or negligence. The law requires a
party to an insurance contract to state not only all those material circumstances within
his knowledge which he believes to be material, but those which are in fact so: see eg
*d* *London Assurance v Mansel* (1879) 11 Ch D 363 and *Container Transport International Inc v
Oceanus Mutual Underwriting Association (Bermuda) Ltd* [1984] 1 Lloyd's Rep 476. Thus,
the mrely accidental failure to disclose facts, if material facts, will involve a breach of
duty.
The authorities show that, in relation to the duty of disclosure falling on the insured,
every fact is material which would influence the judgment of a prudent insurer (not the
*e* particular insurer: see the *Container Transport* case) in deciding whether to accept the
particular risk for the particular insured and, if so, at what premium. Thus:

> 'Any fact is material which leads to the inference, in the circumstances of the
> particular case, that the subject matter of insurance is not an ordinary risk, but is
> exceptionally liable to be affected by the peril insured against . . . Any fact is material
*f* > which leads to the inference that the particular proposer is a person, or one of a class
> of persons, whose proposal for insurance ought to be subjected to special
> consideration before it can be decided whether it should be accepted at all or
> accepted at normal rate. This is usually referred to as the moral hazard.'

(See 25 Halsbury's Laws (4th edn) paras 368–369.)
*g* In some earlier cases it was considered that no concealment would vitiate a policy
unless it was a concealment of a fact concerning the specific risk insured. That, however,
is not the correct rule. As Blackburn J said in *Ionides v Pender* (1874) LR 9 QB 531 at 539:

> '. . . the rule laid down in Parsons on Insurance ((1868) vol 1, p 495), that all
> should be disclosed which would affect the judgment of a rational underwriter
> governing himself by the principles and calculations on which underwriters do in
*h* > practice act, seems to us a sound one.'

This court took the same view in *Rivaz v Gerussi Bros & Co* (1880) 6 QBD 222.
In the context of issue (4), the principal debate in this court has concerned the proper
test of materiality when the court is considering the duty of disclosure falling on the
insurer, as opposed to the insured. Not surprisingly, counsel have been able to cite very
*j* little authority giving direct guidance on this point. The process of adapting the well-
established principles relating to the duty of the insured to the obverse case of the insurer
is not wholly easy.
Steyn J dealt with this point thus ([1987] 2 All ER 923 at 944, [1987] 2 WLR 1300 at
1330):

> 'In considering the ambit of the duty of the disclosure of the insurers, the starting
> point occurs to me as follows: in a proper case it will cover matters peculiarly within

the knowledge of the insurers, which the insurers know that the insured is ignorant
of and unable to discover but which are material in the sense of being calculated to $a$
influence the decision of the insured to conclude the contract of insurance. In
considering whether the duty of disclosure is activated in a given case a court ought,
in my judgment, to test any provisional conclusion by asking the simple question:
did good faith and fair dealing require a disclosure?'

In our judgment, with respect to the judge, the test of materiality adumbrated by him $b$
is not an entirely satisfactory one. True it is that all contracts of insurance are (in the
words of s 17 of the 1906 Act applicable to contracts of marine insurance) based on the
utmost good faith. However, in the case of commercial contracts, broad concepts of
honesty and fair dealing, however laudable, are a somewhat uncertain guide when
determining the existence or otherwise of an obligation which may arise even in the
absence of any dishonest or unfair intent; they are not the tests embodied in s 18 of the $c$
1906 Act. More importantly, in our judgment, it would be too broad a proposition to
state that any fact is material if it is 'calculated to influence the decision of the insured to
conclude the contract of insurance'. To give one example, it might well be that in a
particular case proposed insurers would be aware of another reputable underwriter who
would be prepared to underwrite the same risk at a substantially lower premium. In our
judgment the mere existence of the relationship of insurers and insured would not place $d$
on them the duty to inform the insured of this fact.

In adapting the well-established principles relating to the duty of disclosure falling on
the insured to the obverse case of the insurer himself, due account must be taken of the
rather different reasons for which the insured and the insurer require the protection of
full disclosure. In our judgment, the duty falling on the insurer must at least extend to
disclosing all facts known to him which are material either to the nature of the risk $e$
sought to be covered or the recoverability of a claim under the policy which a prudent
insured would take into account in deciding whether or not to place the risk for which
he seeks cover with that insurer.

It is common ground that the acquisition by Mr Dungate in June 1980 of knowledge
of Mr Lee's dishonesty did not place him under any obligation to make disclosure to the
banks *by virtue of the already subsisting contract of insurance*: cf *Lishman v Northern Maritime* $f$
*Insurance Co* (1875) LR 10 CP 179. It is, however, submitted on behalf of Keysers that a
duty of disclosure rested on Hodge (through Mr Dungate) during the negotiations for
the amendment of the Ultron primary layer policy which preceded the second Ultron
loan. These negotiations, as has already appeared, resulted in the conclusion of a further
contract of insurance between Hodge and the insured on 24 June 1980. In our judgment,
the question whether or not Hodge discharged its duty of full disclosure must be $g$
determined by reference to the point of time immediately before the conclusion of that
further contract.

It was submitted on behalf of Hodge that there had been no failure to discharge any
such duty. Counsel submitted (and we are disposed to accept) that Mr Lee's dishonest
conduct could not be said to be material to the additional risk to which Hodge was
subjecting itself by the amendment to the Ultron primary layer policy provided for by $h$
the further contract of 24 June 1980. He went on to submit that this dishonest conduct
was equally not material to the recoverability of a claim under the amended policy, on
the grounds that it would not by itself have entitled the insurers either to avoid the policy
or to invoke the fraud exclusion clause.

In our judgment, however, this approach to the question of materiality is too narrow. $j$
In the section of this judgment headed 'Common ground on this appeal' and under issue
(1) we have set out certain facts which we consider that Mr Dungate knew in June 1980
and onwards. These facts by themselves must have sufficed to make Mr Dungate aware
that the broker through whom the banks had been dealing had not only committed acts
of serious dishonesty towards all parties concerned over the past few months but was well
capable of committing other acts of deception in the future. We think it clear that such

facts were material to the recoverability of a claim under the amended Ultron first layer
*a* policy which, if disclosed to him, a prudent insured would have taken into account in
deciding whether or not to make the new arrangements for insurance with Hodge in
June 1980. The reason is that he would have recognised a possible danger that the policy,
either in its original form or in its amended form, might in the future prove to be
unenforceable because of the fraud exclusion clause, or voidable, if Mr Lee's dishonesty
were found to have extended to the arrangements for the original placing of the insurance
*b* policy with Hodge or its amendment.

The facts known by Mr Dungate demonstrating the dishonesty of the broker through
whom the banks were negotiating with him were thus material facts which it was his
duty to disclose to them before they concluded the contractual arrangements with the
insurers which were concluded on 24 June 1980.

It follows that in our judgment (a) Hodge, through Mr Dungate, was in breach of this
*c* duty of disclosure owed to the banks in June 1980, (b) in the absence of supervening
events depriving them of this right, the banks, on discovering the non-disclosure, would
have had the right to rescind the further contract of insurance concluded on 24 June
1980 and to demand the return of the further premium paid by them in September
1980.

However, this is not the relief arising out of the non-disclosure which Keysers seek. A
*d* claim for the return of the premium raised in its respondent's notice has not been
pursued in this court. Instead, Keysers seek damages for breach of the obligation of
disclosure. To this claim we now turn.

*Issue (5)*

*e* If the failure of Mr Dungate in June 1980 and afterwards to disclose to the banks the
information possessed by him as to Mr Lee's dishonest past conduct had itself constituted
the tort of deceit, the banks would have had a claim for damages against Mr Dungate's
employers in the ordinary way. However, the general rule is that, subject to certain
exceptions, mere passive non-disclosure of the truth, however deceptive, does not amount
*f* to deceit in law: see *Salmond and Heuston on the Law of Torts* (19th edn, 1987) pp 435–436.
None of the exceptions apply in the present case. Keysers have not advanced any claim
in deceit and they have no statutory right to disclosure. They have therefore been obliged
to seek other routes by which to pursue their claims to monetary compensation.

The first of these routes rests on the submission that the breach of a party to a contract
uberrimae fidei of his obligation of disclosure is itself capable of giving rise to an action
*g* for damages in an appropriate case. This is a novel claim as yet entirely unsupported by
any decision of the courts of this country beyond the judgment of the judge. And indeed
we have been told that after research no authority of any common law court has been
discovered which supports it.

Lord Mansfield CJ, in the example given by him in *Carter v Boehm* (1766) 3 Burr 1905
at 1909, [1558–1774] All ER Rep 183 at 184 concerning the underwriter who insured a
*h* ship for a voyage when he privately knew that it had already arrived, described the
remedy as an action to recover the premium. The legal position is stated thus in Spencer
Bower *Actionable Non-Disclosure* (1915) para 223:

> 'In substance, the right of any party complaining who elects to avoid a contract in
> the negotiation for which material facts have been withheld from him is to have the
> contract judicially annulled, or judicially treated as a nullity. And this is his only
*j* > right. He is not entitled to recover damages against the party charged, unless the
> non-disclosure assumes the character of fraudulent concealment, or amounts to
> fraudulent misrepresentation, or is otherwise founded on, or characterized and
> accompanied by, fraud, and his case is so put (whether alternatively or not), and
> proved: in any of which events, however, the damages are recoverable for a fraud,
> and not for the non-disclosure as such.'

The authority given by Spencer Bower for his proposition that the complaining party has no right to recover damages, which he describes in a footnote as 'a very familiar and well-established rule', is a statement of the law by Scrutton J in *Glasgow Assurance Corp Ltd v William Symondson & Co* (1911) 16 Com Cas 109. In that case an insurance company brought an action to avoid a contract of reinsurance and certain policies issued thereunder as being obtained by fraudulent representation and by concealment of material facts. The concealment alleged related in substance to the intention of the broker to declare as assured his own underwriting partners who would make a profit by difference of premiums (at 120). Scrutton J held that the material facts which had to be disclosed to the underwriter were as to the subject matter, the ship and the perils to which the ship was exposed and that the concealment alleged did not amount to concealment of a material fact. However, he went on to observe (at 121):

'If I had found concealment of a material fact, the plaintiffs would have had to face the question, to which in my opinion they gave no satisfactory answer, as to how they could cancel the policies when underwriters, parties to them ... were not before the Court; for non-disclosure is not a breach of a contract giving rise to a claim for damages, but a ground of avoiding a contract.'

In the present case Steyn J rightly described this dictum as obiter and, while no less rightly describing Scrutton J as a matchless commercial lawyer, thought that he should not give undue weight to it for reasons expressed by him (see [1987] 2 All ER 923 at 946, [1987] 2 WLR 1300 at 1332).

However, while the 1906 Act and the judgments in many reported cases specifically refer to avoidance of the contract as the remedy for the breach of the obligation of disclosure in contracts of insurance, neither the 1906 Act nor any reported case or textbook cited to us suggests that a remedy by way of damages may also be available.

Keysers claim under the present head may thus perhaps at first sight appear a bold one. Nevertheless, as was submitted on behalf of the banks, the entire absence of any authority directly supporting (or indeed rejecting) a claim of this nature is not perhaps entirely surprising. By the very nature of insurance cases allegations of non-disclosure of material facts are more likely to be made by the insurers than by the insured; in the ordinary course insurers will know of no material facts of which the insured himself is ignorant. And in the ordinary course the right to avoid the policy will be an adequate remedy for the aggrieved insurer.

In the rare case where there has been non-disclosure of a material fact by the insurer the position may be rather different. Avoidance of the policy and the return of the premium may well constitute entirely sufficient relief for the insured if he becomes aware of the non-disclosure before the occurrence of the contingency against which he has intended to insure. If, however, he becomes aware of it only after the occurrence of the contingency, relief of this nature may be quite inadequate.

Considerations such as these led the judge to conclude that an action for damages lies for breach of the obligation of the utmost good faith in an insurance context. He said ([1987] 2 All ER 923 at 946, [1987] 2 WLR 1300 at 1332):

'Once it is accepted that the principle of the utmost good faith imposes meaningful reciprocal duties, owed by the insured to the insurers and vice versa, it seems anomalous that there should be no claim for damages for breach of those duties in a case where that is the only effective remedy. The principle ubi jus ibi remedium succinctly expresses the policy of our law.'

He pointed out that on the facts of the present case an order for the return of the insurance premiums, even if still available, would be a derisory remedy in relation to the true loss if there had been a breach of duty by the insurers which caused the loss. He observed ([1987] 2 All ER 923 at 947, [1987] 2 WLR 1300 at 1333):

'Occasionally judges have to apply an existing remedy to a new situation when a a right already recognised by the law is not adequately protected . . . justice and policy considerations combine in requiring me to rule that in principle an insured can claim damages from an insurer arising from loss suffered by the insured as a result of a breach of the obligation of the utmost good faith by the insurer.'

Counsel for the other banks made forceful submissions to the same effect. However, the principle ubi jus ibi remedium cannot, in our judgment, by itself justify a decision b to give the remedy of damages in a novel situation not covered by previous authority unless this is preceded by an analysis of the origin and nature of the right in question. The question whether or not the remedy of damages is available may well depend on the nature of the right and of the corresponding duty of the other party. With all respect to the judge's very careful judgment, we do not think that it contained any such analysis. He clearly did not regard the right as being one which existed in tort, because he c considered that any claim for damages for its breach would not fall to be reduced by virtue of the Law Reform (Contributory Negligence) Act 1945. However, he apparently did not regard it as a duty existing in contract. Earlier in his judgment he had summarised the arguments of the parties in this context as follows ([1987] 2 All ER 923 at 943, [1987] 2 WLR 1300 at 1329):

d '. . . on behalf of the banks the utmost good faith principle was said to be an implied term of an insurance contract, while the insurers submitted that it was simply a rule, or more accurately a set of rules, of positive law.'

He expressed his conclusion on this point ([1987] 2 All ER 923 at 944, [1987] 2 WLR 1300 at 1329):

e '. . . the body of rules which are described as the uberrima fides principle are rules of law developed by the judges. The relevant duties apply before the contract comes into existence, and they apply to every contract of insurance. In my judgment it is incorrect to categorise them as implied terms, in the sense in which the banks seek to do so. I also reject the contention that these rules become applicable by way of a collateral contract.'

f Steyn J also rejected an argument (not repeated in this court) based on alleged fiduciary duties owed by the insurers to the banks (see [1987] 2 All ER 923 at 954, [1987] 2 WLR 1300 at 1342). If the banks' right to full disclosure of material facts is founded neither on tort nor on contract nor on the existence of a fiduciary duty nor on statute, we find it difficult to see how as a matter of legal analysis it can be said to found a claim for damages.

g Counsel for Chemical Bank, implicitly recognising this difficulty, relied on contract. He submitted that it is an implied term of all contracts of insurance that each party shall observe the utmost good faith and that the duty of disclosure is simply one facet of that duty. In support of this submission he referred us first to the wording of s 17 of the 1906 Act. If a contract of marine insurance is 'based upon the utmost good faith' it is, in his submission, natural to treat the fundamental obligation of disclosure as an implied term h of the contract. The same principles must apply to non-marine insurance contracts: see London Assurance v Mansel (1879) 11 Ch D 363 at 368–369 per Jessel MR. In our judgment, however, the wording of s 17, if anything, goes against, rather than supports, the banks' submission, inasmuch as it explicitly confers on the other party, in a case where the utmost good faith has not been observed, the right to avoid the contract but makes no mention of damages, as we would have expected if the legislature had regarded j the duty as arising out of an implied term of the contract. We will revert to this section below.

Counsel for Chemical Bank further relied on a line of decisions which show that, while the general rule is that the duty to disclose ceases to exist as soon as the contract of insurance is made, the duty is in some circumstances capable of arising even after that time. Thus, in Black King Shipping Corp v Massie, The Litsion Pride [1985] 1 Lloyd's Rep

437 Hirst J held that the insured was in breach of this duty in failing to disclose to the
underwriters the fact that a ship was entering a dangerous area which would attract a
higher premium. He accepted the argument of the underwriters by analogy with s 18(2)
of the 1906 Act that there was continuing duty on the insured throughout the voyage to
disclose to the underwriters any circumstance which if known and believed would
'influence him in any relevant decision he had to make, e.g., the fixing of AP [additional
premium], or whether to pay, compromise, or resist a claim' (at 510–511). In support of
the underwriters' argument in that case particular reliance was placed (at 509–510) on
the rationale underlying the old practice prior to 1936 governing orders for the disclosure
of ships' papers, as laid down in authorities such as *Leon v Casey* [1932] 2 KB 576 at 579,
[1932] All ER Rep 484 at 485. Counsel for Chemical Bank submitted that this post-
contractual duty of disclosure can only have its origin in an implied term in the original
contract that each party should observe the utmost good faith, and that this lends support
to his submission that in all cases the duty of utmost good faith is based on such implied
term.

We did not find this line of argument compelling. It may be that on the particular
facts of some cases (though by no means necessarily all) the duty of post-contractual
disclosure can be said to arise under the terms of the preceding contract. However, it by
no means follows that the duty of pre-contractual disclosure arises under the contract
rather than the general law.

It was further argued on behalf of the banks that, unless the bilateral duty of disclosure
gives rise to a remedy in damages, the contract is 'unbalanced', since rescission of the
policy, while an adequate remedy for the insurer, is no adequate remedy for the insured.
We are not convinced that rescission of the policy is necessarily an adequate remedy even
for the insurer, if, for example, the non-disclosure has led him to accept a risk at a far
lower premium than he would otherwise have charged. In any event, in our judgment,
the so-called lack of balance of the contract throws no further light on the legal origin of
the right of either party to demand full disclosure.

Counsel for Chemical Bank submitted that the duty of disclosure is one example of a
well-recognised category of implied term, namely a term imposed as a matter of general
law on contracts of a particular kind, in this case contracts of insurance. In this context
he referred us to *Lister v Romford Ice and Cold Storage Co Ltd* [1957] 1 All ER 125 at 134,
143, [1957] AC 555 at 579, 594 per Viscount Simonds and Lord Tucker. He invited us to
follow an obiter dictum of Parke B in *Moens v Heyworth* (1842) 10 M & W 147 at 157–
158, 152 ER 418 at 423 (not an insurance case), where it was said:

'. . . those instruments [policies of insurance] are made upon an implied contract
between the parties, that everything material known to the assured should be
disclosed by them. That is the basis upon which the contract proceeds . . .'

There are other obiter judicial dicta to the same effect. If the duty of disclosure were
founded on an implied term of the contract of insurance that each party had made full
disclosure of all material facts to the other, we could see no reason in principle why the
breach of such implied term should not give rise to a claim for damages. In our
judgment, however, the weight of authority and of principle is against any such
conclusion.

In his dissenting judgment in the Court of Appeal in *Blackburn Low & Co v Vigors*
(1886) 17 QBD 553 at 561 Lord Esher MR rejected the view of *Duer on Marine Insurance*
(1846) that it is part of the contract of insurance that full disclosure shall be made as well
as that every representation shall be accurate, observing:

'But if this be correct, the contract should never be set aside or treated as void on
the ground of concealment; the contract should stand and be treated as broken by
the assured. This view would raise new complications which have never yet been
urged.'

Lord Esher MR summarised his conclusions (at 562):

a       'The freedom from misrepresentation or concealment is *a condition* precedent to
the right of the assured to insist on the performance of the contract, so that on a
failure of the performance of the condition the assured cannot enforce the contract.'
(Lord Esher MR's emphasis.)

The decision of the majority of the Court of Appeal in *Blackburn Low & Co v Vigors* was
b   reversed on appeal (see (1887) 12 App Cas 531). Lord Halsbury LC said (at 536):

'I doubt very much whether the solution of the controversy as to what is the true
principle upon which the contract of insurance is avoided by concealment or
misrepresentation, whether by considering it fraudulent or as an implied term of
the contract, helps one very much in deciding the present case.'

c   However, Lord Watson, echoing the words of Lord Esher MR, said (at 539):

'It is, in my opinion, a condition precedent of every contract of marine insurance
that the insured shall make a full disclosure of all facts materially affecting the risk
which are within his personal knowledge at the time when the contract is made.'

Lord FitzGerald (at 542) said that he was prepared to adopt the judgment of Lord Esher
d   MR. Lord Macnaghten (at 542), following Lord FitzGerald, began by saying that he
agreed and then added observations which have no relevance to the point now under
discussion.
Four only of their Lordships were sitting in *Blackburn Low & Co v Vigors*. We do not
find it necessary to consider whether the speeches of Lord Watson and Lord FitzGerald
read together with the concurring words of Lord Macnaghten, constitute binding
e   authority in support of Lord Esher MR's view that it is a *condition precedent* to the right
of the insured to insist on performance of the contract that the insured shall have made
full disclosure of all facts materially affecting the risk which are within his knowledge.
At least these speeches are of very high authority in support of the view, which is met by
no binding authority to the contrary.
f       The word 'condition', as used by English lawyers, is capable of bearing different senses.
In *Chitty on Contracts* (25th edn, 1983) para 752 a distinction is, in our judgment, correctly
drawn between what is there termed a 'promissory' condition, being a promise or
assurance for the non-performance of which a right of action accrues to the innocent
party, and a 'contingent condition', ie a provision that on the happening of some
uncertain event an obligation shall come into force or that an obligation shall not come
g   into force until such an event happens. It is pointed out that in the latter case the non-
fulfilment of the condition gives no right of action for breach but simply suspends the
obligations of one or both of the parties.
In our judgment is it clear that Lord Esher MR, in using the phrase 'condition
precedent', was using it in the sense of a contingent, rather than a promissory, condition
and was rejecting *Duer*'s suggestion that in the case of a contract of insurance uberrimae
h   fidei the parties are to be treated as having promised that full disclosure has been or
would be made.
In our judgment, support for this view may also be derived from a consideration of
the origin of the powers of the court to give relief in the cases of innocent pre-contractual
misrepresentation by a party to a contract uberrimae fidei. In *Merchants' and
Manufacturers' Insurance Co Ltd v Hunt* [1941] 1 All ER 123 at 136, [1941] 1 KB 295 at
j   318 Luxmoore LJ (with whom Scott LJ agreed on this point (see [1941] 1 All ER 123 at
128, [1941] 1 KB 295 at 312) said:

'Whatever may be the decision with regard to non-disclosure, as to which I say
nothing, I am satisfied that in a case of positive misrepresentation the right to avoid
a contract, whether of insurance or not, depends not on any implied term of the

contract, but arises by reason of the jurisdiction originally exercised by the Courts of Equity to prevent imposition.'

Though Scott and Luxmoore LJJ found it unnecessary to decide this further point, we think that the right to avoid a contract uberrimae fidei in the case of non-disclosure must be founded on the same jurisdiction. Scott LJ pointed out ([1941] 1 All ER 123 at 128, [1941] 1 KB 295 at 313):

'Even the common law duty of disclosure I find difficult to explain fully on the theory of its resting only on an implied term of the contract. If it did, it would not arise until the contract had been made, and then its sole operation would be to unmake the contract.'

The view that the duty of disclosure arises entirely outside the contract uberrimae fidei has the weighty support of Lord Atkin's dictum in *Bell v Lever Bros Ltd* [1932] AC 161 at 227, [1931] All ER Rep 1 at 32 cited above.

Much more recently, in *March Cabaret Club and Casino Ltd v London Assurance* [1975] 1 Lloyd's Rep 169 at 175 May J, after a review of the authorities, said:

'Bearing in mind the basis of the rule, however, which is as Lord Justice Scrutton pointed out [in *Rozanes v Bowen* (1928) 32 Ll L Rep 98 at 102] the fact that there is a disparity in negotiating position between the intending assured and insurers, in my judgment the duty to disclose is not based upon an implied term in the contract of insurance at all; it arises outside the contract . . .'

If, however, this obligation does not arise under contract or statute and no fiduciary relationship between the parties is asserted, a breach of the obligation must, in our judgment, itself constitute *a tort* if it is such as to give rise to a claim for damages.

There is no authority whatever to support the existence of such a tort and, quite apart from such lack of authority, there are in our judgment at least four reasons why this court should not by its present decision create a novel tort of this nature. First, we have already concluded that the powers of the court to grant relief where there has been non-disclosure of material facts in the case of a contract uberrimae fidei stems from the jurisdiction originally exercised by the courts of equity to prevent imposition. The powers of the court to grant relief by way of rescission of a contract where there has been undue influence or duress stem from the same jurisdiction. Since duress and undue influence as such give rise to no claim for damages, we see no reason in principle why non-disclosure as such should do so.

Second, the decision in *Container Transport International Inc v Oceanus Mutual Underwriting Association (Bermuda) Ltd* [1984] 1 Lloyd's Rep 476 establishes that, where an underwriter is seeking the conventional remedy of avoidance of the policy, the actual effect of the non-disclosure on his mind is irrelevant. The effect of the non-disclosure on the mind of a notional prudent underwriter, judged objectively, is the relevant criterion. The same approach must, in our judgment, apply in a case where an insured is seeking avoidance of the policy. The court will be concerned not so much with the effect of the non-disclosure on *his* mind as that of the mind of a prudent notional insured in his position. Steyn J rightly recognised the difficulties involved in translating this approach to a case where the insured is seeking damages. He said ([1987] 2 All ER 923 at 947, [1987] 2 WLR 1300 at 1333):

'Assuming therefore that . . . the test is the effect on the notional insured only, it could legitimately be asked how *damages* could be awarded if the non-disclosure had no effect on the insured. In my judgment the only conceivable answer is that the requirements for avoidance are less than for an action for damages.' (Steyn J's emphasis.)

We agree that this is the only conceivable answer, but think that the problem posed by

the judge is another illustration of the conceptual difficulties involved in a decision that
*a* a remedy by way of damages lies in this class of case.

Third, s 17 of the 1906 Act, which imposes reciprocal obligations of good faith on both
parties to such a contract, specifically gives the injured party the remedy of avoidance of
the contract (and no other remedy). Likewise, s 18(1), which specifically defines the duty
of disclosure falling on the assured, concludes by stating the insurer's remedy as follows:
'If the assured fails to make such disclosure, the insurer may avoid the contract.' There is
*b* not a suggestion in any of the succeeding provisions of the 1906 Act that a breach of the
obligation of good faith will, as such, give rise to a claim for damages. Section 91(2), it is
true, provides that: 'The rules of the common law including the law merchant, save in
so far as they are inconsistent with the provisions of this Act, shall continue to apply to
contracts of marine insurance.' Nevertheless, we think the clear inference from the 1906
Act is that Parliament did not contemplate that a breach of the obligation would give rise
*c* to a claim for damages in the case of such contracts. Otherwise it would surely have said
so. It is not suggested that a remedy is available in the case of non-marine policies which
would not be available in the case of marine policies.

Fourth, as we have already stated, in the case of a contract uberrimae fidei, the
obligation to disclose a known material fact is an absolute one. It attaches with equal
force whether the failure is attributable to 'fraud, carelessness, inadvertence, indifference,
*d* mistake, error of judgment, or even to [the] failure to appreciate its materiality': see
Ivamy *General Principles of Insurance Law* (5th edn, 1986) p 156 and the cases there cited.
A decision that the breach of such an obligation in every case and by itself constituted a
tort if it caused damage could give rise to great potential hardship to insurers and even
more, perhaps, to insured persons. An insured who had in complete innocence failed to
disclose a material fact when making an insurance proposal might find himself
*e* subsequently faced with a claim by the insurer for a substantially increased premium by
way of damages before any event had occurred which gave rise to a claim. In many cases
warranties give by the insured in the proposal form as to the truth of the statements
made by him might afford the insurers the same remedy, but by no means in all cases.
In our judgment it would not be right for this court by way of judicial legislation to
create a new tort, effectively of absolute liability, which could expose either party to an
*f* insurance contract to a claim for substantial damages in the absence of any blameworthy
conduct.

No relevant breach of contract has been established and fraud is not alleged against Mr
Dungate or Hodge. We accordingly hold that, if the breach by Hodge, through Mr
Dungate, of its duty of full disclosure is to give rise to a claim for damages at the suit of
Keysers, this claim must be based on (innocent) misrepresentation or the tort of
*g* negligence.

We answer issue (5)(a) in the negative sense. Issue (5)(b) does not arise.

*Issue (6)*

The issue of misrepresentation (which the judge found against the banks) is of
*h* importance in two separate contexts on this appeal, namely the claim under the
Misrepresentation Act 1967 and the claim in negligence.

In any case where a claim based on alleged misrepresentation falls to be considered by
this court, close attention must, in our view, be directed to the claimant's pleading. The
reasons are not merely technical. Justice to any person faced with an allegation of this
nature demands that he should be informed before the trial fairly and squarely precisely
*j* what claim he has to meet, most particularly if the misrepresentation is said to have
arisen from his conduct, not from words spoken or written. Furthermore, the state of
the pleadings will throw light on the course of the trial in the court below, because the
presumption must be that the judge would not have permitted a case to be put which
was not covered by the pleadings without requiring their amendment.

The judge made an explicit finding that Mr Dungate 'was in no way involved in Mr Ballestero's fraud and was not an active participant in Mr Lee's deception of the banks' *a* (see [1987] 2 All ER 923 at 934, [1987] 2 WLR 1300 at 1314). Nevertheless, in the course of his judgment he did say that Mr Dungate, in forwarding a copy of Mr Lee's letter of 4 June 1980 to Mr Jekyll, the managing director of Standard Chartered, 'actively assisted Mr Lee in passing the matter off as an administrative error' (see [1987] 1 Lloyd's Rep 69 at 87). Furthermore, apparently by reference to that earlier finding, he said: 'I have found that Mr Dungate assisted Mr Lee in June 1980 in covering up Mr Lee's dishonesty . . .' *b* (see [1987] 2 All ER 923 at 947, [1987] 2 WLR 1300 at 1347). From time to time during the course of argument in this court there have been similar assertions of a cover-up by Mr Dungate.

However, the effect of the judge's findings referred to in the preceding paragraph must not be misunderstood. They do not amount to a finding of any misrepresentation made *to Keysers*. Mr Dungate's letter dated 9 June 1980 to Mr Jekyll is not even referred *c* to in Keysers' pleading. As it happened, Standard Chartered had become interested in the first Ultron loan and the insurance cover for that loan because in January 1980 Keysers had assigned sub-participations in part of the loan of 18·75m Swiss francs made by it to a group of bankers of which Standard Chartered was one. This was how Standard Chartered had come to receive copies of the three cover notes relating to the first Ultron loan. However, Mr Jekyll had made the inquiries contained in the letter to Mr Dungate of *d* 28 May 1980, to which Mr Dungate's letter of 9 June was a response, not because Standard Chartered was a participant in the loan, but because Hodge had provided part of the insurance cover and Standard Chartered, as a company associated with Hodge, was together with Hodge simply concerned with ascertaining the extent of Hodge's exposure on such insurance. Counsel for the banks other than Chemical Bank expressly accepted that Mr Dungate's letter of 9 June 1980 to Mr Jekyll could not be regarded as a *e* misrepresentation to the interested banks and that Keysers could not rely on this letter to support their claim of misrepresentation.

Nor, despite the passing references in the judgment and in argument to a cover-up, does Keysers' pleading suggest that Mr Dungate in June 1980, or at any other time, conducted himself in any way with the intention of inducing Keysers mistakenly to believe in Mr Lee's honesty and to act on the assumption that Mr Lee was an honest *f* broker. If such conduct had been pleaded and proved and the banks could have shown that they had been misled by it, we can see no reason why Hodge, as Mr Dungate's employer, should not have been liable to Keysers in damages for deceit. However, it cannot be too strongly stressed that no allegation of deceit of this kind was either made or established at the trial. If the banks had been able to allege and prove fraudulent misrepresentation, if only by conduct, on the part of Mr Dungate, the legal position *g* would have been quite different from that which we have to consider on this appeal.

As things were, the misrepresentation on the part of Mr Dungate alleged by Keysers in their pleading fell within a narrow compass. Paragraph 32 of their reamended pleading covered their claims both in misrepresentation and in negligence. We find it advisable to quote this paragraph in full, save for sub-para (11), which raised a claim *h* based on warranty which was rejected by the judge and has not been proceeded with in this court:

'1) In or about mid December 1979 Mr Verkooyen of [Keysers] contacted Mr Dungate of [Hodge] direct by telephone in order to obtain his confirmation that the original primary layer slip initialled by Mr Dungate on 11th December 1979 constituted a binding obligation of [Hodge]. 2) Mr Dungate declined to provide *j* such confirmation and instead told Mr Verkooyen to address all communications through Mr Lee. 3) [Hodge] thereby impliedly represented that there were no material facts known to [Hodge] which cast doubt upon the suitability and trustworthiness of Mr Lee as broker. 4) In its nature the said representation was a representation to [Keysers] and the other participating banks which continued (unless corrected or withdrawn) for so long as [Hodge] and [Keysers] continued to

communicate through Mr Lee; alternatively [Hodge] made the said representation
afresh upon and by reason of each dealing with Mr Lee subsequent to the said
telephone conversation. 5) The said representation became false and untrue on, at
the latest, 2nd June 1980 by reason of the knowledge then acquired by Mr Dungate
of Mr Lee's conduct in relation to the procuring and issuing of the first and second
excess layer cover notes, as pleaded in paragraph 30 herein and the Further and
Better Particulars thereof. 6) Further, by letter dated 4th June 1980, Mr Lee sent Mr
Dungate a copy of his letter of even date to Mr Verkooyen, which, as was obvious to
Mr Dungate, a) failed to disclose to [Keysers] the existence of the fraudulent
misrepresentations contained in the first and second excess layer cover notes; and
b) contained a further fraudulent misrepresentation that [Hodge] had in fact been
on cover until replaced by other insurers. 7) [Hodge] owed the participating banks
a duty to take reasonable care to correct or withdraw their said representation in the
event that it became false and/or a duty of care in the continued making thereof,
but in breach of duty they negligently failed to correct or withdraw the same at any
time on or after 2nd June 1980 and instead continued the making thereof. 8) Further
or alternatively in or about early May 1980 Mr Dungate and Mr Lee entered into
negotiations for an increase in the primary layer policy limits from Sw.Fr.37,000,000
to Sw.Fr. 47,000,000. [Keysers] were advised by Mr Lee of such negotiations by
letter dated 14th May 1980. 9) By an agreement evidenced by endorsements dated
24th June 1980 and 11th September 1980 [Hodge] agreed to the said increase (and
various consequential amendments to the primary layer policy) in consideration of
a premium of Sw.Fr. 150,000, which was paid by [Keysers] on or about
3rd September 1980. 10) Throughout the period from May 1980 to 11th September
1980 ("the material times") [Hodge] represented to the participating banks that
there were no material facts to disclose. [Hodge] so represented by their failure to
disclose any material facts in circumstances where, by reason of their duty of utmost
good faith, they owed a duty of disclosure . . . 12) The acts of Mr Lee referred to in
sub-paragraphs 5 and 6 hereof were material facts in relation to the Ultron
insurances, and at all material times the participating banks had no knowledge
thereof. 13) [Hodge] did not at any material time disclose the material facts to the
participating banks and accordingly the said warranty was broken and the said
representation was false. 14) Further and alternatively [Hodge] owed the participating banks a duty at law throughout the material times to use reasonable care to
disclose the material facts, such duty arising from:—a) [Hodge's] voluntary
assumption, by entering into negotiations with Mr Lee for an increase in the
primary policy limits, of a duty to disclose material facts; b) the practice in the
London insurance market that insurers and insureds do not deal directly with one
another, but that all dealings should take place through brokers; c) Mr Dungate's
refusal to deal directly with Mr Verkooyen, and his insistence instead on using Mr
Lee as the channel of communication; d) Mr Dungate's decision in late May 1980 to
investigate Mr Lee's conduct in relation to the Ultron first and second excess layer
cover notes and the knowledge of the material facts thereupon acquired by [Hodge];
e) [Hodges'] knowledge that the participating banks were unaware of the material
facts; f) the tripartite nature of the loans and insurances known to [Hodge]; 15) In
breach of duty [Hodge] negligently failed to disclose to [Keysers] any of the material
facts. 16) Further or alternatively, throughout the material times it was reasonably
foreseeable by [Hodge] (through Mr Dungate) that if they (a) failed to disclose the
material facts and/or (b) continued to deal with Mr Lee in relation to the Ultron
insurances, the participating banks would suffer injury. 17) Notwithstanding their
knowledge that the participating banks were unaware of the said risk of injury,
[Hodge] continued to deal with Mr Lee in relation to the Ultron insurances in and
after June 1980. 18) In the premises [Hodge] owed the participating banks a duty to
take reasonable care to avoid the said risk of injury. 19) In breach of duty [Hodge]
negligently failed to advise the participating banks of the material facts and

continued to deal with Mr Lee on the Ultron insurances without taking any steps, whether by warning or otherwise, to avoid the said risk of injury. 20) But for the making of the representations pleaded in this paragraph the participating banks would not have made the second Ultron loan of Sw.Fr. 10,750,000, nor would they have permitted the first Ultron loan to remain outstanding. 21) By reason of [Hodge's] said misrepresentations and/or breaches of duty, the participating banks suffered loss and damages as particularised in paragraph 31 hereof.'

As is stated in *Chitty on Contracts* (25th edn, 1983) para 402:

'Representations are treated for many purposes as continuing in their effect until the contract between the parties is actually concluded. This is one reason why a statement which is true when made, but which ceases to be true to the knowledge of the representor before the contract is concluded, is treated as a misrepresentation unless the representor informs the representee of the change in circumstances.'

One head of alleged misrepresentation originally relied on by Keysers in their pleading will be seen to have been to the following effect. Mr Dungate, it was said, in the telephone conversation of December 1979, made an implied representation to Mr Verkooyen that Mr Lee was, so far as he (Mr Dungate) knew, a suitable and trustworthy broker. This representation, it was claimed, fell to be treated as a misrepresentation from 2 June 1980 onwards, when Mr Dungate learnt of its untruth but nevertheless failed to inform the banks of its untruth. The judge, however accepted Mr Dungate's evidence that he did not remember this conversation, which, according to Mr Verkooyen, lasted only some 15 seconds. He found it unrealistic and unfair to suggest that Mr Dungate should have remembered the conversation in June 1980. He accordingly rejected the claims arising out of that telephone conversation (see [1987] 2 All ER 923 at 947, [1987] 2 WLR 1300 at 1333). Conceivably, such claims might have been open to a rather different analysis either on the facts or on the law. However, though they are repeated in Keysers' respondent's notice (the first limb of para (1)), they have not been pursued in this court.

Two, and only two, pleaded allegations of misrepresentation have been pursued by Keysers in this court. The first is that (even disregarding the telephone conversation with Mr Verkooyen of December 1979) on each occasion when Mr Dungate dealt with Mr Lee as broker for the banks after December 1979, Mr Dungate made an implied representation to the banks that Hodge knew of no marterial facts casting doubt on the suitability and trustworthiness of Mr Lee as a broker. We can deal with this claim quite shortly.

Indisputably, on particular facts, it is possible for a representation to be implied from a person's conduct, even though he has not spoken or written a single word by way of representation. To quote a familiar dictum, a representation can, for example, be made 'by a nod or wink or a shake of the head or a smile'.

In support of their allegation of misrepresentation in the present case, Keysers, having discarded Mr Dungate's telephone conversation with Mr Verkooyen of December 1979, can rely on no active conduct whatever on the part of Mr Dungate (not even a nod or a wink) save his continued dealings with Mr Lee, accompanied by no disclosure to the banks. On behalf of the banks, however, reliance was placed on a principle stated thus in *Spencer Bower and Turner on Estoppel by Representation* (3rd edn, 1977) pp 49–50 (applied by Bingham J in *Tradax Export SA v Dorada Cia Naviera SA, The Lutetian* [1982] 2 Lloyd's Rep 140 at 156–158):

'... each [party to a transaction] is entitled to suppose that the other has fully discharged all such obligations (if any) of disclosure or action himself as may have been created by the circumstances. If, therefore, he receives from that other no intimation, by language or conduct, of the existence of any fact which, if existing, it would have been the latter's duty, having regard to the relation between them, the nature of the transaction, or the circumstances of the case, to reveal, he has

a
legitimate ground for believing that no such fact exists, or that there is nothing so abnormal or peculiar in the nature of the transaction, or in the circumstances of the case, as to give rise to any duty of disclosure, and to shape his course of action on that assumption; in other words, he is entitled to treat the representor's silence or inaction as an implied representation of the non-existence of anything which would impose, or give rise to, such a duty, and, if he alters his position to his detriment on the faith of that representation, the representor is estopped from afterwards setting

b
up the existence of such suppressed or undisclosed fact.'

This principle, it was submitted, is capable of applying both during negotiations and after a contract is concluded. In this case, as the judge found, Mr Dungate knew that the banks were relying on Mr Lee as their broker in the insurance contracts and that they were acting on the assumption that he was the trustworthy representative of Notcutts,

c
when in truth he was not. In these circumstances, it was argued, following the principles set out in *Spencer Bower and Turner*, the banks were entitled to treat Mr Dungate's silence concerning Mr Lee as an implied representation that he knew of nothing materially reflecting on Mr Lee's probity.

However, a brief reference to the facts of *The Lutetian* [1972] 2 Lloyd's Rep 140 will, in our judgment, show how different they were from those of the present case. There the

d
owners of a vessel sought to rely on the charterers' deduction of four days' anticipated off-hire as grounds for withdrawal. As Bingham J found (at 157):

'Nothing could have been easier or more natural than to tell the charterers why, in the owners' view, the deduction was improper ... Instead they went to some lengths to impede the charterers in ascertaining the reason.'

e
He found it impossible to resist the conclusion that 'the owners were bent not on securing performance of the charter-party but on stage-managing a very profitable withdrawal' (at 158). He said:

'The relationship of owner and charterer is not one of the utmost good faith. One must be careful not to impute unrealistically onerous obligations to those who may choose to conduct their relations in a tough and uncompromising way. There is

f
nonetheless a duty not to conduct oneself in such a way as to mislead. I have no doubt that the owners knew that the charterers believed they had paid the right amount. It was their duty, acting honestly and responsibly, to disclose their own view to the charterers. They did not do so and indeed thwarted the charterers' attempts to discover their views. Their omission to disclose their own calculation led the charterers to think, until a very late stage, that no objection was taken to the

g
calculation. It would in my view be unjust in the circumstances if the owners could rely on the incorrectness of a deduction which they had every opportunity to point out at an earlier stage and which their failure to point out caused the charterers to overlook.'

On these findings of fact Bingham J, if we may say so, not surprisingly held that the

h
owners were estopped or precluded from relying on the charterers' deduction as grounds for withdrawal. There had been both a failure to disclose their views as to the deduction and a deliberate thwarting of the charterers' attempts to discover their views. The charterers had relied on this conduct on the part of the owners and therefore assumed that no objection was taken to the calculation.

We will assume in favour of Keysers, without deciding, that any conduct which is

j
capable of giving rise to an estoppel by conduct is capable of giving rise to a claim for misrepresentation. Nevertheless, if a person is to base a defence on estoppel by conduct or a claim for misrepresentation said to have been made by conduct, he must, in our judgment, at very least show that he relied on the representation in question. In the present case Keysers have not shown either (a) that they were led by Mr Dungate to believe that he was making any representation as to Mr Lee's honesty or (b) that they

relied on any such representation. So far as we are aware, no evidence was called on behalf of any of the banks suggesting that Mr Dungate in any way led them to understand *a* that he was vouching for Mr Lee's honesty. This, in our judgment, is the short answer to the claim based on this first head of alleged misrepresentation. In our judgment Steyn J was clearly right to reject it.

That first head had to be and was necessarily based on the particular facts of the case. The second head pursued by Keysers in this court is reflected in para 32(10) of their pleading and is of a different character. The submission, as developed in argument, is *b* that in the case of any contract of insurance there is deemed to be an implied representation by each party that he has made full disclosure of all material facts. The representation is said to arise *by operation of law* in every such case. As counsel for Chemical Bank pithily put the point in argument, 'Where there is a duty to disclose silence in law constitutes a misrepresentation.' Accordingly, it is submitted, Hodge must be treated as having induced the banks to enter the new insurance arrangements of June *c* 1980 by the untrue representation that it had made disclosure of this nature.

A number of textbook writers, having stated that silence or non-disclosure on its own does not constitute misrepresentation, go on to state as a matter of general principle that it will constitute a misrepresentation in a case where the contract requires the utmost good faith: see e g *Cheshire Fifoot and Furmston's Law of Contract* (11th edn, 1986) pp 260–262 and *Chitty on Contracts* (25th edn, 1983) paras 399, 460.        *d*

Counsel who presented the main argument for the banks on misrepresentation, submitted that this statement of general principle derives support from judicial dicta in insurance cases. For example in *Carter v Boehm* (1766) 3 Burr 1162 at 1165, [1558–1774] All ER Rep 183 at 185 Lord Mansfield CJ referred to concealment as 'fraudulent, if designed'. In *Blackburn Low & Co v Vigors* (1886) 17 QBD 553 at 561 Lord Esher MR referred with approval to a statement in Arnould *Marine Insurance* (2nd edn, 1857) in *e* which the author described suppression of the truth arising from a wilful intention to deceive for the assured's own benefit as suppression arising 'from the fraud of the assured'. In the submission of counsel for Chemical Bank, there can be no fraud without a misrepresentation. We accept that without a misrepresentation there can be no fraud in the sense of giving rise to a claim for damages in tort. In our judgment, however, the *f* references to 'fraud' in the passages in those and other insurance cases relied on by counsel for Chemical Bank were made in a quite different context and are simply intended to refer to dishonest conduct. They lend no support to the proposition that non-disclosure involves an implied representation in such cases.

Counsel, however, submitted that more explicit support for the proposition is to be derived from certain cases concerning contracts of suretyship, such as *Lee v Jones* (1864) *g* 17 CBNS 482 at 503–504, 144 ER 194 at 203, in which Blackburn J in the course of his judgment said:

'. . . when the creditor describes to the proposed sureties the transaction proposed to be guaranteed (as in general a creditor does), that description amounts to a representation, or at least is evidence of a representation, that there is nothing in the transaction that might not naturally be expected to take place between the parties to *h* the transaction such as that described. And, if a representation to this effect is made to the intended surety by one who knows that there is something not naturally to be expected to take place between the parties to the transaction, and that this is unknown to the person to whom he makes the representation, and that, if it were known to him, he would not enter into the contract of suretyship, I think it is evidence of a fraudulent representation on his part.'        *j*

In such a case, counsel submitted, Blackburn J was saying that there was an implied representation to the intended surety that there was nothing in the transaction of suretyship which he would not naturally expect to be there.

We do not think that any assistance is to be derived from these cases relating to

contracts of suretyship. Though they may on particular facts give rise to limited
*a* obligations of disclosure they are not contracts uberrimae fidei which give rise to a
general obligation to disclose. As Blackburn J himself said (17 CBNS 486 at 506, 144 ER
194 at 204):

> 'I think that it must in every case depend upon the nature of the transaction,
> whether the fact not disclosed is such that it is impliedly represented not to exist;
> and that must generally be a question of fact proper for a jury.'

*b*

In our judgment that case and a further decision of this court relied on by counsel
relating to a suretyship for the fidelity of a servant (*London General Omnibus Co Ltd v
Holloway* [1912] 2 KB 72, [1911–13] All ER Rep 518) lend no support whatever to the
proposition that a breach of the duty of disclosure in the case of contracts uberrimae fidei
always as a mater of law falls to be treated as constituting a misrepresentation.
*c* The proposition, if correct, could have far-reaching consequences. The supposed
misrepresentation might presumably fall to be treated as made not only to the parties to
a written contract but to other persons who would in the future be relying on its terms
as recorded in the contract. The proposition, however, is in our judgment untenable. It
derives no support from authority. If the legislature had regarded it as well founded, the
1906 Act, which specifically states that 'promissory warranties' are to be treated as
*d* incorporated by law in a contract of marine insurance (see ss 33 to 41), would have taken
a very different form. Most of the reasons which we have stated for rejecting the
proposition that the failure to disclose a material fact constitutes a breach of an implied
term of a contract uberrimae fidei support, mutatis mutandis, the rejection of the
proposition that such failure constitutes a misrepresentation deemed to arise by operation
of law.
*e* We reject this proposition and answer issue (6) in the negative.

*Issue (7)*

Section 2(1) of the Misrepresentation Act 1967, which is the subsection relied on by
Keysers, provides:

*f* 'Where a person has entered into a contract after a misrepresentation has been
made to him by another party thereto and as a result thereof he has suffered loss,
then, if the person making the misrepresentation would be liable to damages in
respect thereof had the misrepresentation been made fraudulently, that person shall
be so liable notwithstanding that the misrepresentation was not made fraudulently,
unless he proves that he had reasonable ground to believe and did believe up to the
*g* time the contract was made that the facts represented were true.'

Under issue (6) we have referred to the two heads of alleged misrepresentation still
pursued by Keysers and have concluded that neither head has been established as a matter
of fact or law. If these conclusions be correct, Keysers' claims for damages based on the
1967 Act must necessarily fail for that reason, if no other, and issue (7) does not arise.
*h* There are, however, at least two further reasons why these heads of claim could, in our
judgment, give rise to no claim for damages under the 1967 Act, even if the
misrepresentation alleged had been proved.
First, as the wording of s 2(1) shows, one of the conditions which has to be satisfied if a
remedy under that subsection is to be available is that 'the person making the
misrepresentation would be liable to damages in respect thereof had the misrepresentation
*j* been made fraudulently'. Thus, in the words of counsel for Hodge, the ingredients of a
fraudulent misrepresentation have to be present save for the ingredient of dishonesty.
However, one of the essential ingredients of a misrepresentation if it is to give rise to a
cause of action for deceit is that it should be made with the intention that it should be
acted on by the other party (see *Clerk and Lindsell on Torts* (15th edn, 1982) para 17–32).
It was never alleged against Mr Dungate, let alone proved, that he made any

misrepresentation to the banks with the intention that they should act on it. This, in our judgment, would be an answer to both heads of claim based on the 1967 Act.

As regards the second head of claim, we think there would be a further answer. If s 2(1) is to apply at all, a misrepresentation has to have been 'made' to the complainant by the other party. The expression 'misrepresentation... made' (which is repeated in several later sections of the 1967 Act) would, in our judgment, on the ordinary meaning of words be inapt to refer to a misrepresentation which had not been made in fact but was (at most) merely deemed by the common law to have been made. If it had been the intention of the legislature that a mere failure to discharge the duty of disclosure in the case of a contract uberrimae fidei would fall to be treated as the 'making' of a representation within the meaning of the 1967 Act, we are of the opinion that the legislature would have said so.

We accordingly answer issue (7) in the negative.

*Issue (8)*

We now come to what counsel for Skandia called the heart of the case. Did Hodge owe the banks a common law duty of care in negligence? The judge was held that they did.

He dealt first with the three special features on which the insurers relied to negative a duty of care. These were (i) that the court ought not to impose liability in tort when the parties are in a contractual relationship, (ii) that this was a case of omission to act on the part of Mr Dungate, and the courts have always been reluctant to impose liability for a pure omission, and (iii) that the banks' case involves the proposition that Mr Dungate had to make a judgment whether a third party (Mr Lee) would in future attempt to deceive the banks. The judge concluded that none of these three considerations prevented a duty of care from arising on the facts of the present case. He went on to hold that there was a manifest and obvious risk that the failure to disclose Mr Lee's dishonesty would lead to financial loss on the part of the bank, that what he called the threshold requirement of proximity was therefore satisfied and that it was just and reasonable in all the circumstances that the insurers should be under a duty of care. The judge clearly had in mind not only Lord Wilberforce's two-stage test in *Anns v Merton London Borough* [1977] 2 All ER 492, [1978] AC 728, but also the cautionary observations on that test made by Lord Keith in *Governors of the Peabody Donation Fund v Sir Lindsay Parkinson & Co Ltd* [1984] 3 All ER 529 at 534, [1985] AC 210 at 240–241, where he said:

'There has been a tendency in some recent cases to treat these passages as being themselves of a definitive character. This is a temptation which should be resisted. The true question in each case is whether the particular defendant owed to the particular plaintiff a duty of care having the scope which is contended for, and whether he was in breach of that duty with consequent loss to the plaintiff. A relationship of proximity in Lord Atkin's sense [see *Donoghue v Stevenson* [1932] AC 562 at 580, [1932] All ER Rep 1 at 11] must exist before any duty of care can arise, but the scope of the duty must depend on all the circumstances of the case . . . So in determining whether or not a duty of care of particular scope was incumbent on a defendant it is material to take into consideration whether it is just and reasonable that it should be so.'

The judge gave judgment on 30 September 1986. Since then there have been many further authorities in the same field. As a result we find ourselves approaching the problem of duty of care from a slightly different angle. The courts have continued to place emphasis on the observations of Lord Keith in the passages cited above: see per Bingham LJ in *Simaan General Contracting Co v Pilkington Glass Ltd (No 2)* [1988] 1 All ER 791 at 797, [1988] QB 758 at 773 and the cases cited by him. It must therefore be right to take into consideration, as did the judge, whether it is just and reasonable in all the circumstances of the present case that the insurers should be held to be under a duty of care to the banks. But that is not the end of the inquiry, as many authorities illustrate.

However just and reasonable it might seem at first sight, the court is not free to hold that
a the insurers were under any duty of care to Keysers if so to hold would run counter to
established principles of the law of contract or tort or both. We must bear in mind the
observations of Lord Brandon in *Leigh & Sillavan Ltd v Aliakmon Shipping Co Ltd, The
Aliakmon* [1986] 2 All ER 145 at 153, [1986] AC 785 at 815, quoted by the judge. In
commenting on the two-stage process described by Lord Wilberforce in *Ann's* case, Lord
Brandon said:

b          '... Lord Wilberforce was dealing ... with the approach to the questions of the
        existence and scope of a duty of care in a novel type of factual situation which was
        not analogous to any factual situation in which such a duty had already been held to
        exist. He was not, as I understand the passage, suggesting that the same approach be
        adopted to the existence of a duty of care in a factual situation in which the existence
        of such a duty had repeatedly been held not to exist.'
c
Our conclusion will be that we are not free to hold that the insurers were under a duty of
care in the present case.

We start with foreseeability. We are in agreement with the judge, for the reasons
mentioned under issue (3), that economic loss of the type actually suffered by the banks
was a reasonably foreseeable consequence of the failure to Mr Dungate to report Mr Lee's
d dishonesty.

In going on to consider justice and reasonableness, and all the other circumstances of
the case, the starting point must be that this is a case of what is now called 'pure economic
loss', that is to say financial loss not arising from injury to person or property. In such
cases it is well established that 'some limit or control mechanism has to be imposed on
the liability of a wrongdoer towards those who have suffered economic damage in
e consequence of his negligence': see *Candlewood Navigation Corp Ltd v Mitsui OSK Lines Ltd,
The Mineral Transporter, The Ibaraki Maru* [1985] 2 All ER 935 at 945, [1986] AC 1 at 25
per Lord Fraser. The control mechanism operates, he said, at the second stage of Lord
Wilberforce's two-stage approach. But, in the light of Lord Keith's opinion in *Yuen Kun-
yeu v A-G of Hong Kong* [1987] 2 All ER 705, [1988] AC 175, it may be more correct to
regard the control mechanism as operating at the first stage of the two-stage approach.
f Lord Keith preferred to regard the second stage as being very narrow in scope. It could
only arise, he said, when public policy required that there should be no liability. A rare
example would be in a case like *Rondel v Worsley* [1967] 3 All ER 993, [1969] 1 AC 191.
If Lord Keith's view is followed, then the control mechanism operates at the first stage,
with the consequence that there is lacking the necessary degree of proximity in Lord
Atkin's sense.
g    In the *Candlewood Navigation* case itself, as in the subsequent decision of the House of
Lords in *The Aliakmon* [1986] 2 All ER 145, [1986] AC 785, an obligatory control
mechanism was imposed by the long-established rule that in the case of physical damage
to property, whether damage to goods (as in the latter case) or damage to a ship (as in the
former), the law does not recognise a claim in negligence by a person whose only rights
h in relation to the property are contractual. If he is to recover for any injury which he had
suffered he must have had either the legal ownership of, or a possessory title to, the
property concerned.

In our judgment there is just such a control mechanism in the present case which we
will later identify.

The decision of the House of Lords in *Hedley Byrne & Co Ltd v Heller & Partners Ltd*
j [1963] 2 All ER 575, [1964] AC 465 and subsequent decisions founded on its principles
establish that, where in the particular circumstances of a case one party is shown to have
assumed a voluntary responsibility to another, the court may hold that a special
relationship exists between them giving rise to a duty of care, the breach of which is
capable of giving rise to a claim for damages for purely economic loss.

The facts of the *Hedley Byrne* case, which arose out of a negligent misrepresentation, are too well known to require repetition. While that case established that economic loss resulting from a negligent misrepresentation may be recovered in tort, there are two  *a* conditions for recoverability. The first is that the defendant should have assumed a voluntary responsibility towards the plaintiff in making the statement or representation. The second is that the plaintiff should have relied on it. As Lord Devlin said in summarising what he understood to be the decision of the House of Lords ([1963] 2 All ER 575 at 610–611, [1964] AC 465 at 529):

> 'I do not understand any of your lordships to hold that it is a responsibility  *b* imposed by law on certain types of persons or in certain sorts of situations. It is a responsibility that is voluntarily accepted or undertaken either generally where a general relationship, such as that of solicitor and client or banker and customer, is created, or specifically in relation to a particular transaction. In the present case the appellants were not, as in *Woods* v. *Martins Bank, Ltd.* ([1958] 3 All ER 166, [1959] 1 QB 55) the customers or potential customers of the bank. Responsibility can attach  *c* only to the single act, i.e., the giving of the reference, and only if the doing of that act implied a voluntary undertaking to assume responsibility. This is a point of great importance because it is, as I understand it, the foundation for the ground on which in the end the House dismisses the appeal.'

Recently, in *Yuen Kun-yeu v A-G of Hong Kong* [1987] 2 All ER 705 at 714, [1988] AC  *d* 175 at 196, Lord Keith confirmed that the *Hedley Byrne* decision 'turned on the voluntary assumption of responsibility towards a particular party, giving rise to a special relationship'; see also *Simaan General Contracting Co v Pilkington Glass Ltd (No 2)* [1988] 1 All ER 791 at 805, [1988] QB 758 at 784 per Dillon LJ.

Now if the facts of the present case had been that Mr Dungate had carelessly misrepresented to the banks that Mr Lee was an honest man, the *Hedley Byrne* principles  *e* would, in our judgment, plainly have applied, subject to the conditions we have mentioned, even though the misrepresentation was made in a pre-contractual setting.

On the facts of many cases, the conclusion of a contract will preclude the parties from relying on the law of tort to provide them with any greater protection than that which the contract itself has expressly or impliedly conferred on them: see *Tai Hing Cotton Mill Ltd v Liu Chong Hing Bank Ltd* [1985] 2 All ER 947, [1986] AC 80 and *National Bank of*  *f* *Greece SA v Pinios Shipping Co No 1, The Maira* [1989] 1 All ER 213, [1989] 3 WLR 185. However, the decision of this court in *Esso Petroleum Co Ltd v Mardon* [1976] 2 All ER 5, [1976] QB 801 establishes that in appropriate circumstances liability in tort may be imposed on one contracting party to another for misrepresentations made before the signing of a written contract. As Shaw LJ succinctly put it ([1976] 2 All ER 5 at 26, [1976]  *g* QB 801 at 832–833):

> 'It is difficult to see why, in principle, a right to claim damages for negligent misrepresentation which has arisen in favour of a party to a negotiation should not survive the event of the making of a contract as the outcome of that negotiation. It may, of course, be that the contract ultimately made either expressly or by implication shows that, once it has been entered into, the rights and liabilities of the  *h* parties are to be those and only those which have their origin in the contract itself. In any other case there is no valid argument apart from legal technicality for the proposition that a subsequent contract vitiates a cause of action in negligence which had previously arisen in the course of negotiation.'

It would have been possible for the parties in the *Esso Petroleum* case to make express  *j* provision as to the effect of the pre-contractual representations in their contract. Indeed such provision is not uncommon in commercial contracts. But that possibility was held not to exclude liability in tort. By the same token, in the present case it would have been possible, though highly unlikely, for the parties in concluding the contract of 24 June 1980 to have included an express warranty by Hodge as to the honesty of the broker's

employee. Like the judge, we would not regard that possibility as sufficient in itself to
a  exclude a duty of care in tort, if we were otherwise minded to find such a duty.

Accordingly, if Mr Dungate had carelessly misrepresented to the banks that Mr Lee
was an honest man, the *Hedley Byrne* principles would, in our judgment, have enabled
Keysers to succeed in their claim in negligence if, though only if, they could have proved
a voluntary assumption of responsibility in respect of such representation by Mr Dungate
coupled with reliance by the banks. It is to be observed that in the *Esso Petroleum* case
b  [1976] 2 All ER 5 at 15, 22, [1976] QB 801 at 820, 828 Lord Denning MR and Ormrod
LJ specifically referred to an assumption of responsibility by the defendant. In many
cases where a misrepresentation has been made to another person, particularly by a
professional man acting in the course of his profession, the assumption of responsibility
may be readily inferred.

But on the view of the facts taken by the judge and by this court there has been no
c  misrepresentation in the present case. The essence of the banks' case is that they are
seeking to recover damages for economic loss which they say they suffered as the result
of Mr Dungate's *failure* to inform them of Mr Lee's dishonesty.

Can a mere failure to speak ever give rise to liability in negligence under *Hedley Byrne*
principles? In our view it can, but subject to the all-important proviso that there has been
on the facts a voluntary assumption of responsibility in the relevant sense and reliance on
d  that assumption. These features may be much more difficult to infer in a case of mere
silence than in a case of misrepresentation. But that they can be inferred is shown by a
recent decision of this court in *Al-Kandari v J R Brown & Co (a firm)* [1988] 1 All ER 833,
[1988] QB 665 (though *Hedley Byrne* itself does not appear to have been there cited).

In that case solicitors for a husband in custody proceedings had agreed to hold the
passport of the husband and the two children of the marriage (who were in the custody,
e  care and control of the plaintiff wife) to the order of the court. This court, in the words
of Lord Donaldson MR, held ([1988] 1 All ER 833 at 836, [1988] QB 665 at 672):

> 'In voluntarily agreeing to hold the passport to the order of the court, the solicitors
> had stepped outside their role as solicitors for their client and accepted responsibilities
> towards both their client and the plaintiff and the children.'

f  It held that the solicitors were in breach of their duty to the plaintiff in, inter alia,
failing to inform her or her solicitors that the Kuwaiti Embassy had retained the passport
or that arrangements had been made for the husband to attend the embassy on the
following day in the absence of any representative of the defendants (see [1988] 1 All ER
833 at 837, [1988] QB 665 at 674). The plaintiff's claim in negligence succeeded.

We can see no sufficient reason on principle or authority why a failure to speak should
g  not be capable of giving rise to liability in negligence under *Hedley Byrne* principles,
provided that the two essential conditions are satisfied.

A hypothetical example may illustrate the point. Suppose that a father employs an
estate agent for a fee to advise his son on the proposed purchase of a house and the estate
agent negligently fails to inform the son that a motorway is shortly to be constructed
within a few hundred yards of the property. We would not doubt that in such a case the
h  son, knowing of the estate agent's duty and relying on it, could have a claim in negligence
under *Hedley Byrne* principles. To draw a distinction on those particular facts between
misinformation and a failure to inform would be to perpetuate the sort of nonsense in
the law which Lord Devlin condemned in the *Hedley Byrne* case [1963] 2 All ER 575 at
603, [1964] AC 465 at 517.

j  So in so far as Keysers' case is based on *Hedley Byrne* principles, the question comes to
this. Did Mr Dungate in fact assume responsibility towards the banks? If so, did the
banks rely on that assumption of responsibility? The answer to each part of the question
must surely be No.

We can see no justification for holding that Mr Dungate, who made no representation,
assumed any responsibility at all in relation to Mr Lee's honesty or dishonesty. Counsel

for the banks other Chemical Bank argued that a voluntary assumption of responsibility is to be found in Mr Dungate's voluntary conduct in continuing to deal with Mr Lee. We *a* do not agree. The phrase 'voluntary assumption of responsibility' in this context means what it says: conduct by the party signifying that he assumes responsibility for taking due care in respect of the statement or action. No doubt, in deciding whether there has been such an assumption of responsibility the conduct of the party may be objectively construed. To deal in the ordinary way with an agent without any relevant communication to his principal cannot, we think, be held to be an assumption of responsibility because *b* the party has done nothing which signifies assumption of responsibility in the relevant sense.

Nor is there any evidence that the banks relied on any assumption of responsibility by the insurers in respect of Mr Lee's honesty. We need not repeat what we have already said in that connection under issue (6). It must follow that, in the absence of any voluntary assumption of responsibility and reliance by the banks, no duty of care on the *c* part of the insurers can be established under *Hedley Byrne* principles.

But counsel for the banks other than Chemical Bank had an alternative submission. He argued that, although voluntary assumption of responsibility, coupled with reliance, is a condition for the existence of a duty of care in some cases of pure economic loss, it is not a condition of every such case; a duty of care not to cause economic loss may be owed without it. As authority he relied on Lord Keith's opinion in *Yuen Ken-yeu v A-G of Hong* *d* *Kong* [1987] 2 All ER 705, [1988] AC 175. The whole thrust of Lord Keith's opinion, according to counsel, is that the existence of a duty of care depends, not on voluntary assumption of responsibility, but on a sufficient degree of proximity between the parties; and by proximity he meant, not just foreseeability of harm, but the whole concept of the necessary relationship between plaintiff and defendant giving rise to a duty of care in the particular case. It is the directness and closeness of the relationship which matters. Lord *e* Keith, according to this submission, only mentioned the voluntary assumption of responsibility as an example of a factual situation giving rise to a direct and close relationship, and when dealing, at the end of his opinion, with a particular argument based on the *Hedley Byrne* case itself.

In the course of his argument counsel referred us to the decision of this court in *f* *Ministry of Housing and Local Government v Sharp* [1970] 1 All ER 1009, [1970] 2 QB 223, the decision of Megarry V-C in *Ross v Caunters (a firm)* [1979] 3 All ER 580, [1980] Ch 297 (which was referred to without disapproval by Lord Donaldson MR in *Al Kandari v J R Brown & Co (a firm)* [1988] 1 All ER 833, [1988] QB 665) and the decision of Mann J in *American Express International Banking Corp v Hurley* [1985] 3 All ER 564 as representing in his submission the best examples of cases where plaintiffs have recovered damages in *g* negligence for pure economic loss, albeit in the absence of any voluntary assumption by the defendant of responsibility towards the particular plaintiff.

While the decision in none of those cases was explicitly founded on any such voluntary assumption of responsibility, the nature and dates of the three decisions submitted as the three best examples indicate that the cases falling into this category are at least rare. Further, the nature of those cases with reference to the relationship between the claimant *h* and the defendant was, we think, very different from this case. In *Sharp's* case the duty on the local authority with reference to the search was imposed by statute; and the plaintiff ministry's claim was upheld against that local authority, whose clerk had negligently failed to mention in the certificate, given in response to a local land charge search made by an intending purchaser, that the ministry had a charge on the land in question, despite the fact that the ministry had placed no reliance on any statement by *j* the local authority. In *Ross v Caunters* the defendant solicitors had undertaken to their client, the testator, to act with care with reference to the effective making of the testator's will, including the conferring of a benefit on a named beneficiary. That beneficiary was held entitled to recover against the solicitors in respect of the benefit lost through the solicitors' negligence although there had been no direct assumption of responsibility by

the solicitors to the beneficiary or reliance by the beneficiary. In the *American Express*
a case mortgagees were held liable for the breach of the duty imposed by the law to take
reasonable care to obtain the true market value of the mortgaged property on realisation
in the exercise of a power of sale; and that liability was held to extend to the guarantor of
the mortgagor's debt. In each of these cases there was an act negligently performed as
opposed to pure omission. In each case the relevant duty was imposed by statute or by
law or clearly assumed; and it was held that the law did not require demonstration of
b reliance by the claimant on careful performance by the defendant.

On one reading of Dillon LJ's judgment in *Simaan General Contracting Co v Pilkington
Glass Ltd (No 2)* [1988] 1 All ER 791 at 805, [1988] QB 758 at 784 it would appear that he
may have regarded the recoverability of damages for negligence for pure economic loss
as being dependent in every case on the voluntary assumption of responsibility.
Nevertheless, in the light of counsel's analysis of Lord Keith's speech in *Yuen Kun-yeu v
c A-G of Hong Kong* [1987] 2 All ER 705, [1988] AC 175 and the three other decisions on
which he relies, we are prepared to accept, for the purposes of this judgment, that in
some cases (if rare) of pure economic loss the court may be willing to find the existence
of a duty of care owed by a defendant to a plaintiff even in the absence of evidence of any
actual voluntary assumption by the defendant of such duty and/or of any reliance on
such assumption. We shall accordingly proceed on the basis that, on appropriate facts,
d the court may be willing to hold that, having regard to the special circumstances and the
relationship between the parties, a defendant should be treated *in law* (even though not
in fact) as having assumed a responsibility to the plaintiff which is capable of giving rise
to a claim for damages for pure economic loss. The remaining question, therefore, is
whether Hodge should be so treated in this case.

In this context we attach importance to the distinction to which the judge in our view
e gave insufficient weight. For better or worse, our law of tort draws a fundamental
distinction between the legal effects of acts on the one hand and omissions on the other.
Lord Goff in *Smith v Littlewoods Organisation Ltd* [1987] 1 All ER 710 at 729, [1987] AC
241 at 271 stated as a general principle that 'common law does not impose liability for
what are called pure omissions'. Similarly, in *Yuen Kun-yeu's* case [1987] 2 All ER 705 at
f 710, [1988] AC 175 at 192 Lord Keith said:

> 'Foreseeability of harm is a necessary ingredient of such a relationship, but it is
> not the only one. Otherwise there would be liability in negligence on the part of
> one who sees another about to walk over a cliff with his head in the air, and forbears
> to shout a warning.'

g Lord Bridge referred to the important distinction between acts and omissions in
*Curran v Northern Ireland Co-ownership Housing Association Ltd* [1987] 2 All ER 13 at 17,
[1987] AC 718 at 724, where he said:

> '. . . *Anns v Merton London Borough* may be said to represent the high-water mark
> of a trend in the development of the law of negligence by your Lordships' House
> towards the elevation of the "neighbourhood" principle derived from the speech of
h > Lord Atkin in *Donoghue v Stevenson* [1932] AC 562, [1932] All ER Rep 1 into one of
> general application from which a duty of care may always be derived unless there
> are clear countervailing considerations to exclude it. In an article by Professor J C
> Smith and Professor Peter Burns, "Donoghue v Stevenson—The Not So Golden
> Anniversary" (1983) 46 MLR 147, the trend to which I have referred was cogently
> criticised, particularly in its tendency to obscure the important distinction between
j > misfeasance and non-feasance.'

The example given by Lord Keith is of a failure to prevent physical harm. But the
same reluctance on the part of the courts to give a remedy in tort for pure omission
applies, perhaps even more so, when the omission is a failure to pevent economic harm.
As will appear below, a corresponding distinction is drawn by the law of contract which

in general imposes no liability by virtue of a failure to speak as opposed to a misrepresentation.

In an important passage of his judgment the judge said that he did not regard the present case as 'a case of pure omission.' He gave two reasons (see [1987] 2 All ER 923 at 951, [1987] 2 WLR 1300 at 1338–1339):

> 'The relationship between the parties involved obligations of good faith and fair dealing. Moreover, the alleged duty arises in the context of insurers who had an established business relationship with the banks, and continued to transact further with the banks (and to make profits) in the knowledge that a risk, viz further dishonesty by Mr Lee, which was obvious to the insurers, was not appreciated by the banks and could not be discovered by them. It is a situation essentially different from pure omission cases. In my judgment the fact that the duty relied on by the banks required affirmative action on the part of the insurers (unless they simply decided in the circumstances not to insure) does not preclude a ruling that such a duty existed.'

We take first his point that there was here an established business relationship with the banks, and the insurers continued to do business with the banks, even though they knew of the risk resulting from Mr Lee's dishonesty, while the banks did not.

In our judgment, to hold that these factors by themselves gave rise to a duty on the part of Mr Dungate to report Mr Lee's dishonesty to the banks, capable of exposing him or his employers to a liability in tort, would undermine basic principles of our law of contract.

Throughout this case it has to be borne in mind that the period in June 1980 in which it is said that Mr Dungate's duty to report arose and continued was one during which he was in the course of conducting contractual negotiations with the banks on behalf of his employers.

The general principle that there is no obligation to speak within the context of negotiations for an ordinary commercial contract (though qualified by the well-known special principles relating to contracts uberrimae fidei, fraud, undue influence, fiduciary duty etc) is one of the foundations of our law of contract, and must have been the basis of many decisions over the years. There are countless cases in which one party to a contract has in the course of negotiations failed to disclose a fact known to him which the other party would have regarded as highly material, if it had been revealed. However, ordinarily in the absence of misrepresentation, our law leaves that other party entirely without remedy. Lord Atkin gave some striking examples in *Bell v Lever Bros Ltd* [1932] AC 161 at 224, [1931] All ER Rep 1 at 30–31 (we have added the numbering to his examples):

> '[1] A. buys B.'s horse; he thinks the horse is sound and he pays the price of a sound horse; he would certainly not have bought the horse if he had known as the fact is that the horse is unsound. If B. has made no representation as to soundness and has not contracted that the horse is sound, A. is bound and cannot recover back the price. [2] A. buys a picture from B.; both A. and B. believe it to be the work of an old master, and a high price is paid. It turns out to be a modern copy. A. has no remedy in the absence of representation or warranty. [3] A. agrees to take on lease or to buy from B. an unfurnished dwelling-house. The house is in fact uninhabitable. A. would never have entered into the bargain if he had known the fact. A. has no remedy, and the position is the same whether B. knew the facts or not, so long as he made no representation or gave no warranty. [4] A. buys a roadside garage business from B. abutting on a public thoroughfare: unknown to A., but known to B., it has already been decided to construct a byepass road which will divert substantially the whole of the traffic from passing A.'s garage. Again A. has no remedy.'

Example 2 is common mistake. In examples 1, 3 and 4, B, if he had directed his mind

to the matter, either might well have realised that A was proceeding under a
*a* misapprehension or knew that that was so, and that this misapprehension was likely to
cause a loss. Nevertheless, in our judgment, it would be wholly contrary to principle to
suggest, at least in the case of an ordinary contract made between persons in an ordinary
relationship, that B, having undertaken no relevant contractual obligation to A, should
be treated as having assumed a responsibility which could give rise to a liability to A in
tort. To reach such a decision as to the effect of a non-disclosure in the course of
*b* contractual negotiations would run counter to the general principle of caveat emptor on
which our law of contract is founded. As Blackburn J said in *Smith v Hughes* (1871) LR 6
QB 597 at 607, [1861–73] All ER Rep 632 at 637:

'... even if the vendor was aware that the purchaser thought that the article
possessed [some particular] quality, and would not have entered into the contract
unless he had so thought, still the purchaser is bound, unless the vendor was guilty
*c* of some fraud or deceit upon him, and ... a mere abstinence of disabusing the
purchaser of that impression is not fraud or deceit; for, whatever may be the case in
a court of morals, there is no legal obligation on the vendor to inform the purchaser
that he is under a mistake, not induced by the act of the vendor.'

By the same token we would hold that no legal obligation on the part of Mr Dungate
*d* to inform the banks of Mr Lee's dishonesty arose, either in contract or in tort, merely
because there was an 'established business relationship' between the parties, and because
the insurers continued to transact further business with the banks. That factor does not
turn a pure omission into a misrepresentation, in tort any more than in contract. It
would not justify the court treating Mr Dungate as having assumed a duty or
responsibility to speak, in tort, which was not imposed on him by the law of contract. In
*e* this context the following observations of Lord Scarman in *Tai Hing Cotton Mill Ltd v Liu
Chong Hing Bank Ltd* [1985] 2 All ER 947 at 957, [1986] AC 80 at 107 are apposite:

'Their Lordships do not believe that there is anything to the advantage of the
law's development in searching for a liability in tort where the parties are in a
contractual relationship. This is particularly so in a commercial relationship.
*f* Though it is possible as a matter of legal semantics to conduct an analysis of the
rights and duties inherent in some contractual relationships including that of banker
and customer either as a matter of contract law ... or as a matter of tort law ...
their Lordships believe it to be correct in principle and necessary for the avoidance
of confusion in the law to adhere to the contractual analysis: on principle because it
is a relationship in which the parties have, subject to a few exceptions, the right to
*g* determine their obligations to each other, and for the avoidance of confusion because
different consequences do follow according to whether liability arises from contract
or tort ...'

The judge was, if we may say so, somewhat dismissive of this passage in Lord Scarman's
opinion. He said that the views expressed were tentative in character, and not intended
*h* to be of general application. We do not share that view. Lord Scarman's opinion contains
a valuable warning as to the consequences of an ever-expanding field of tort. It should be
no part of the general function of the law of tort to fill in contractual gaps. If the nature
of the contract of 24 June 1980 had not been one of the utmost good faith, then, in the
absence of any fraud or misrepresentation by Mr Dungate, we would in the end have
regarded the banks' case in negligence as almost unarguable.
*j* We turn now to the judge's other reason for regarding this case as not being one of
pure omission, namely that 'The relationship between the parties involved obligations of
good faith and fair dealing' (see [1987] 2 All ER 923 at 951, [1987] 2 WLR 1300 at 1338),
by which we understand him to refer to the nature of the contracts of insurance as being
one of the utmost good faith.
This brings us to what was, in our view, the most forceful submission made on behalf

of the banks. It ran on the following lines. As is common ground the negotiations between Hodge and the banks which resulted in the contract of insurance of 24 June 1980 imported mutual obligations of disclosure at least for the purpose of the application of the principle of *Carter v Boehm* (1766) 3 Burr 1905, [1558–1774] All ER Rep 183. Hodge, through Mr Dungate (as we have held), was in breach of this obligation because early in June 1980 he became aware but failed to disclose to the banks that the broker through whom they had been dealing had committed acts of serious dishonesty towards all parties concerned over the past few months. Furthermore (as we have held) it was a conscious act on the part of Mr Dungate not to transmit the information to anyone, knowing the facts of Mr Lee's untrustworthiness and knowing the risks to the banks arising therefrom. Why on those facts should the court not treat Hodge as having in law voluntarily assumed responsibility to make full disclosure of all material facts to the banks, not only for the purpose of the principles of *Carter v Boehm*, but also for the purpose of the law of negligence in tort? The very nature of the contract which was being negotiated, it is said, gives rise to a special relationship between the negotiating parties which justifies the imposition of a duty of care.

We see the force of the points summarised in the last paragraph, but cannot accept the conclusion to which they are directed. We do not think that the nature of the contract as one of the utmost good faith can be used as a platform to establish a common law duty of care. Parliament has provided that in the case of marine insurance the consequence of a failure to disclose a material fact, and by inference the *only* consequence, is that the contract may be avoided. It is not suggested that the consequences in non-marine insurance should be different. In those circumstances it is not, we think, open to the court to assist the banks by providing a supplementary remedy in tort. No doubt, on the very unusual facts of the present case, the statutory remedy of rescission seems inadequate. This is unfortunate for the banks. But the banks' misfortune is of the same kind as the misfortune suffered by the injured party in the various instances given by Lord Atkin in *Bell v Lever Bros Ltd* [1932] AC 161 at 224, [1931] All ER Rep 1 at 30–31, where the law affords no remedy at all. What the banks cannot do in our judgment is to invoke the nature of the contract as one of good faith, with its limited contractual remedy, to bridge the gap so as to give them a cause of action in tort. The error in the submission made for the banks is that it ignores the nature of the special obligation imposed in contracts of utmost good faith. The obligation does not, if we are right, create a duty to speak for breach of which the law attaches the consequences which flow from an ordinary breach of duty, whether statutory or otherwise. It is a rule of law which provides, and provides only, that certain stated consequences (namely the insured party's right to avoid the contract) will follow if utmost good faith be not observed.

Furthermore, despite the eloquent submissions of counsel for the banks other than Chemical Bank in this context, we are not satisfied that justice and reasonableness imperatively require the finding of a duty of care owed by Hodge to Keysers. This is not a case in which the denial to the banks of a cause of action in negligence will mean that the banks are left without any remedy at all. For Notcutts, the firm of brokers by whom Mr Lee was employed, and on whom the banks placed reliance for the honesty of Mr Lee, were vicariously liable for the actions of Mr Lee; and Mr Ballestero and his fraudulent associates were also liable for the loss which they directly caused to the banks. It is true that Mr Ballestero and his associates have either disappeared or are not worth suing. But Notcutts were well worth suing and were sued, although in the event the banks chose to settle their claims against them on the terms which we have already mentioned. This, therefore, is far from being a case where the invocation of the law of tort against the banks was the only way by which the courts could have afforded them a remedy. It is possible to exaggerate the hardship which Keysers will suffer if this court declines to give them a remedy against Hodge.

This having been said, we can well understand the banks' desire to demonstrate that, by failing to take any action with reference to Mr Lee's known dishonesty, the insurers

failed to prevent the wrongs subsequently inflicted on the banks by Mr Ballestero.
*a* Counsel made much of the fact that what we are concerned with here was dishonesty on the part of Mr Lee, and dishonesty which was proven, not merely suspected. It was said that it ought to be the policy of the law to promote honesty and probity in business dealings, particularly in the insurance market. We accept that Mr Dungate's failure to inform the banks of Mr Lee's dishonesty was morally reprehensible. By any decent standards of commercial morality the disclosure should have been made. This view of
*b* contemporary morality was supported by the expert witnesses who said that it was part of Mr Dungate's professional duty to inform the banks.

But this, to our minds, is one of those many cases where the legal obligation falls short of the moral imperatives. No doubt liability for negligence is based 'upon a general public sentiment of moral wrongdoing for which the offender must pay' (see *Donoghue v Stevenson* [1932] AC 562 at 580, [1932] All ER Rep 1 at 11). But it must be remembered
*c* that Lord Atkin went on to say, in the very next sentence, that—

> 'acts or omissions which any moral code would censure cannot in a practical world be treated so as to give a right to every person injured by them to demand relief.'

*d* The law cannot police the fairness of every commercial contract by reference to moral principles. It frequently appears with hindsight, as in this case, that one contracting party had knowledge of facts which, if communicated to the other party, would have protected him from loss. However, subject to well-recognised exceptions, the law does not and should not undertake the reopening of commercial transactions in order to adjust such losses.

Though a well-recognised exception might have enabled the court at an earlier date to
*e* afford Keysers a remedy by way of rescission of the contract of 24 June 1980 there is, in our judgment, no such exception which would enable it to grant Keysers a remedy against Hodge by way of damages in tort. To do so would be to cut across all the principles of our law of contract relating to the effect of silence in the course of pre-contractual negotiations. This is the relevant control mechanism in regard to the present
*f* claim for damages for economic loss.

One feature of the judge's judgment is the repeated reference to the novelty of the claim put forward by the banks. He said that this factor did not trouble him. He said ([1987] 2 All ER 923 at 947, [1987] 2 WLR 1300 at 1334):

> 'The novelty of the case has never, in itself, been any obstacle or disincentive to declaring that a duty arises. Precedents are not exhaustive of duty situations but
*g* merely illustrations of cases where the courts have held a duty to exist.'

We agree, of course, that novelty is never in itself a good answer to a claim. In one sense the facts of every case coming before the courts are unique. But, with all respect to him, the judge's anxiety not to be deterred by the supposed novelty of the claim led him, we think, to pay too much regard to the facts of the particular case *in isolation*, and less
*h* than proper regard to the *type* of case with which he was dealing, namely one of a failure to speak in the course of pre-contractual negotiations causing pure economic loss. Just as in *Candlewood Navigation Corp Ltd v Mitsui OSK Lines Ltd, The Mineral Transporter, The Ibaraki Maru* [1985] 2 All ER 935, [1986] AC 1 and in *Leigh & Sillavan Ltd v Aliakmon Shipping Co Ltd, The Aliakmon* [1986] 2 All ER 145, [1986] AC 785 other established principles precluded the finding of a duty of care in tort, so in the present case the
*j* principles relating to a failure to speak in the course of pre-contractual negotiations preclude the finding of such a duty, at least in a case where the damage consisted of pure economic loss; and the banks must be content with the remedies provided by the law against the other parties on whom long-established duties are imposed.

We are conscious that we have only dealt with a small proportion of the cases cited to us in relation to the duty of care. We cannot refer to them all. However, before leaving this issue we should briefly refer to the decisions of the House of Lords in *Moorgate Mercantile Co Ltd v Twitchings* [1976] 2 All ER 641, [1977] AC 890 and of Hobhouse J in *Bank of Nova Scotia v Hellenic Mutual War Risks Association (Bermuda) Ltd, The Good Luck* [1988] 1 Lloyd's Rep 514. We do not propose to summarise the facts of the latter case. Suffice it to say that Hobhouse J held that the defendants were liable in damages to the plaintiff bank for breach of certain letters of undertaking, but in the course of a long and very careful judgment he went on to consider, obiter and inter alia, whether the defendants were alternatively liable to the plaintiff for breach of a 'duty to speak' consisting of a failure by the defendants to inform it that a vessel, security for a loan granted by the bank, was trading in the Persian Gulf and thus uninsured against war risks. In this context Hobhouse J said (at 548):

> '... following the approach of the House of Lords in *Moorgate v. Twitchings*, I consider that, in principle, wherever the Courts have recognized a duty to speak sufficient to give rise to the remedy of estoppel they should also, in the absence of some special circumstance, be treated as having recognized a duty to speak which can result in a liability in damages ... In *Moorgate v. Twitchings* ([1976] 2 All ER 641 at 646, [1977] AC 890 at 903), Lord Wilberforce set out the factors which he considered would give rise to the relevant duty. These were summarized by Mr. Justice Bingham in *The Lutetian* ([1982] 2 Lloyd's Rep 140 at 157), as the proposition: "The duty necessary to found an estoppel by silence or acquiescence arises where a reasonable man would expect the person against whom the estoppel is raised, acting honestly and reasonably, to bring the true facts to the attention of the other party known by him to be under a mistake as to their respective rights and obligations."'

Applying this test, together with the principle which he had extracted from *Moorgate Mercantile Co Ltd v Twitchings*, Hobhouse J considered that the defendants should be held to have been under a duty to speak which was capable of giving rise to a liability in damages in tort.

We have been told that *The Good Luck* is under appeal[1]. In all the circumstances we think it neither desirable nor necessary to say more about it beyond paying tribute to the depth of the legal analysis contained in it and making the following brief observations.

We are content to assume, without deciding, that *Moorgate Merchantile Co Ltd v Twitchings* is good authority for the proposition that a failure by A to give information to B which is capable of affording B a plea of estoppel may also in some cases be capable of giving rise to a claim by B against A for damages in tort. In particular, the failure to give information may involve a positive misrepresentation by conduct. Such is our view of the facts of *The Lutetian* [1982] 2 Lloyd's Rep 140, where Bingham J found that there had been a deliberate thwarting of the charterer's attempts to discover the owner's views. It may be that the conclusion of Hobhouse J in *The Good Luck* on the issues of estoppel by silence and negligence can be justified on the basis that the failure to inform the plaintiff that the vessel was trading in the Gulf was in all the circumstances positively misleading and itself led the plaintiff into an erroneous belief. However, the facts of the present case are very different from those of *The Lutetian* and *The Good Luck*. There was no question of the banks making any assumptions as to Mr Lee's honesty or otherwise because of Mr Dungate's conduct. As we have explained under issue (6), in our judgment he made no misrepresentation; nor was there any reliance by the banks. His silence could not have given rise to any estoppel against Hodge. Accordingly, in our judgment, the references in argument to *Moorgate Mercantile Co Ltd v Twitchings* and *The Good Luck* do not assist Keysers.

For the sake of clarity, in view of the legal importance of this issue, albeit by way of

---

1   Subsequent to the decision reported herein *The Good Luck* was reversed by the Court of Appeal: see (1989) Times, 20 April

prolonging a very lengthy judgment, we summarise our reasons for holding that the
insurers were under no duty of care to the banks in the present case, and for venturing to
disagree with the judge's conclusion on this point, as follows.

(1) We agree with the judge that (a) economic loss of the type actually suffered by the
banks was a reasonably foreseeable consequence of Mr Dungate's failure to report Mr
Lee's dishonesty, (b) the fact that the negotiations of June 1980 culminated in a contract
between Hodge and the banks would not by itself have prevented the banks from relying
on *Hedley Byrne* principles, *if* there had been a misrepresentation, and (c) the third of the
special features referred to at the start of this section of our judgment, namely the
foresight required as to the future action by a third party, did not by itself negative a
duty of care.

(2) However, contrary to the judge's view, we regard this case, in the absence of any
misrepresentation as factually a case of pure omission: see below.

(3) We accept that even a pure omission consisting of a failure to speak would be
capable of giving rise to a liability in negligence under *Hedley Byrne* principles provided
that there had on the facts been a voluntary assumption of responsibility by the insurer
and there had been reliance on that assumption by the banks. However, on the facts, Mr
Dungate did not voluntarily assume any responsibility in respect of Mr Lee's honesty and
the banks did not rely on any such assumption.

(4) We accept that in some cases (if rare) of pure economic loss the court may, even in
the absence of any evidence of such assumption and of any such reliance, be prepared to
find the existence of a duty of care and to treat the defendant *in law* as having assumed a
responsibility or duty to the plaintiff which is capable of giving rise to a claim for
damages for such loss. However, Hodge cannot, in our judgment, be so treated for the
reasons summarised below.

(5) The period in June 1980 during which it is said that Mr Dungate's duty to report
arose and continued was one during which he was in contractual negotiations with the
banks. The general principle of our law, qualified by certain recognised exceptions, is
that there is no obligation to speak within the context of negotiations for an ordinary
commercial contract.

(6) The mere fact that there was an existing business relationship between the parties
and that the insurers continued to transact further business with the banks would not
justify the court in holding that the insurers had assumed a duty or responsibility to
speak, in tort, which was not imposed on them by the law of contract.

(7) Likewise, the fact that the negotiations between Hodge and the insurers which
resulted in the contract of 24 June 1980 imported mutual obligations of disclosure for
the purpose of the principles of *Carter v Boehm* (1766) 3 Burr 1905, [1558–1774] All ER
Rep 183 would not justify the court in holding that the insurers had assumed such a
duty in tort.

(8) Justice and reasonableness do not imperatively require the finding of a duty of care
owed by Hodge to Keysers which gives rise to such a cause of action, particularly since
other remedies have been available to the banks against other persons, including the
claim against Notcutts which they saw fit to settle.

(9) To grant Keysers a remedy against Hodge in tort would be to cut across the
principles of our law of contract relating to the effect of silence in the course of pre-
contractual negotiations.

(10) Like the judge we deplore the fact that we live in a world in which commercial
dishonesty, such as that of Mr Lee, is rampant. Like him we wish it could be eliminated,
particularly from the insurance markets of the world, and not least the London insurance
market. But we cannot regard our decision in the present case as an appropriate
instrument for seeking to achieve that purpose.

*Issue* (9)
   In view of our answer to issue (8), issue (9) does not arise.

*Issue* (10)

For the reasons given above we have already decided that Keysers have no cause of
action against Hodge. On this footing the further issues relating to causation, remoteness    *a*
and contributory negligence do not strictly call for any decision. However, we think it
right to state our views on these issues because they have been very fully argued, they
raise some important and difficult questions of fact and law and this is a case in which
obviously a further appeal may be pursued.

Before dealing first with these questions of fact, we make these general observations.    *b*
If, contrary to our view, the failure of Mr Dungate to disclose Mr Lee's dishonesty had
been capable of giving rise to a cause of action in tort, the issue of causation would be
of fundamental importance in the consideration of Keysers' claim against Hodge.
For while the banks could have no difficulty in establishing a causative link between
the fraud of Mr Ballestero and their losses, the link between Mr Dungate's failure and
their losses is much less clear. The judge held that Mr Lee had not been shown to be    *c*
a co-conspirator of Mr Ballestero in his scheme to defraud them. The dishonesty of
Mr Lee was not shown by itself to have caused any loss to the banks although it had led
the banks to enter into the transactions in which they were defrauded by Mr Ballestero.
The banks' case against the insurers has throughout been based on the fundamental
proposition of fact that if Mr Dungate had made the disclosure which the banks claim
he should have made they themselves would have made no further loans to Mr    *d*
Ballestero's companies.

Steyn J held this proposition of fact to have been made out. He accepted that the
insurers' duty of disclosure could have been fulfilled if Mr Dungate had disclosed Mr
Lee's dishonesty (see [1987] 2 All ER 923 at 954, [1987] 2 WLR 1300 at 1342). However,
he considered that to Mr Dungate's knowledge, Notcutts, on receiving such information,
would undoubtedly have dismissed Mr Lee and that 'that would have been the end of    *e*
such business' (see [1987] 1 Lloyd's Rep 69 at 88). He had already found that 'Mr
Ballestero could not have obtained the Ultron [or any other loans] without Mr Lee's
assistance' (see [1987] 2 All ER 923 at 934, [1987] 2 WLR 1300 at 1314). Furthermore,
he considered that, also to Mr Dungate's knowledge, 'if he reported the matter to the
banks, or if they learnt about it from the insurers or brokers, a major investigation would
have followed, which would also have spelt the end of such business' (see [1987] 1 Lloyd's    *f*
Rep 69 at 88).

Even after they had learnt of Mr Lee's dishonesty it would clearly have been open to
the banks to carry on with the loan transactions, if necessary through brokers other than
Notcutts. The judge, however, thought that they would not have done so. He listed the
ten bankers who had given evidence and recorded that he found them all to have been
entirely truthful and the general terms of their evidence to have been reliable. The    *g*
general thrust of the evidence of all the banking witnesses was, he said, that, if Mr Lee's
dishonesty in issuing the false cover notes had been disclosed to the banks, 'that would
have spelt the end of the negotiations in respect of all loan transactions after June, 1980'
(see [1987] 1 Lloyd's Rep 69 at 103). The judge accepted that that was so and his first
ground of decision on causation was his acceptance of the bankers' evidence. Secondly,
he accepted that disclosure of Mr Lee's dishonesty to the banks would have spelt the end    *h*
of the negotiations because that consequence was in accordance with his view of the
inherent probabilities. Deception and fraud are, he said, strong words in banking parlance
and 'In a case where the dishonesty related to the banks' primary security ... the
disincentive to dealing further with the broker or to continuing the loan negotiations
would have been overwhelming' (see [1987] 1 Lloyd's Rep 69 at 103).

So far as the issue of causation depends on the judge's findings of fact, the most    *j*
important of the submissions of counsel for Hodge (as they appeared to us) can be
conveniently dealt with under four headings, namely (A) the effect of a report to Notcutts,
(B) 'refusing to deal with Mr Lee', (C) the effect of a report to Keysers and (D) the 'but if
only' argument.

*(A)  The effect of a report to Notcutts*

a    Steyn J, as we have said, accepted that the insurers' duty of disclosure could have been fulfilled if Mr Dungate had disclosed Mr Lee's deceit to Mr Wilkinson. It was accordingly submitted for Hodge that the judge's conclusion was faulted at a stage before any question arose how the banks themselves would have responded to a report of Mr Lee's deception on the first Ultron loan. If Mr Wilkinson had been told by Mr Dungate of what Mr Lee had done, it was argued, the probability was that Mr Wilkinson would have

b    told not the banks but Notcutts' clients, namely Ultron or Mr Ballestero. There was in June 1980 no reason to doubt the integrity of Mr Ballestero. Instructions had come from Mr Ballestero and it was both reasonable and sufficient to inform him. Further, in connection with the placing of the third excess layer for the purposes of the second Ultron loan, when the directors of Notcutts considered that Cia Americana, the insurers proposed by Mr Lee, were not satisfactory, the information was passed not to the banks

c    but to Mr Ballestero by a letter of 11 June 1980 written to him by Mr Lee with Mr Wilkinson's approval. If the report had been made to Mr Ballestero it would, said counsel for Hodge, have gone no further.

There are no express findings of fact by the judge on these matters. The reason is that, as counsel for Hodge acknowledged, the point was not specifically argued below and was not put to Mr Wilkinson. On this crucial point, however, the evidence of Mr Wilkinson

d    was clear and unqualified. He said that he would have told the banks. It is objected that his answer was given in reply to what was, in the circumstances, a leading question. The criticism of the question is justified; but Mr Wilkinson's evidence was tested by a skilful and detailed cross-examination; and Steyn J, who heard his evidence, held that, if Mr Wilkinson had been given the information, the banks would have been informed about it by him or by another director of Notcutts.

e    As to the cover placed with Cia Americana and the fact that the report was made to Mr Ballestero and not direct to the banks, the point is well made and was, no doubt, seen as having some force by Steyn J if made to him. It does not appear to have been effectively explored in evidence for this purpose. The effective answer to it, however, is that at that stage there was no suggestion of fraud practised on the banks by Mr Lee or by anybody else; the grounds of suspicion about Cia Americana were as to financial capacity and not

f    as to the honesty of their agents. The fact that Mr Wilkinson was content with a report to Mr Ballestero in June 1980 with reference to Cia Americana does not demonstrate that the judge was wrong to find on Mr Wilkinson's evidence that Mr Wilkinson, if told of Mr Lee's previous dishonesty, would have caused that fact to be reported to the banks. It is impossible to hold on these grounds that the judge's conclusion on the facts with reference to causation is shown to have been wrong.

g

*(B)  Refusing to deal with Mr Lee*

A second reason was advanced on behalf of Hodge for submitting that the judge's conclusion as to causation was faulted at a stage before any question arose as to how the banks would have responded to a report of Mr Lee's deception on the first Ultron loan.

h    Mr Dungate, it is said, could have discharged any obligation arising from his knowledge of such deception by refusing to deal further with Mr Lee instead of passing on the information either to Mr Lee's employers or to the banks. If he had chosen simply to refuse to deal further with Mr Lee, it is argued, the second Ultron loan would still have been made; so the chain of causation is not established.

We will assume in favour of Hodge, without deciding the point, that a mere refusal to

j    deal with Mr Lee would in all the circumstances have released Mr Dungate from any obligation arising from his knowledge of that deception. However, no evidence was sought from witnesses as to what was likely to have happened if Mr Dungate had refused to deal with Mr Lee without explanation of his refusal. There is no evidence directed to showing that insurance cover was likely to have been available on terms acceptable to the banks from any other insurers and through a different servant of Notcutts or other brokers. However, the conclusive answer to the point is, in our judgment, that it is not open to Hodge. Assuming that a refusal of Mr Dungate to deal with Mr Lee would have been an effective discharge of any obligation laid on Mr Dungate, and assuming that such refusal to deal would have resulted in the obtaining of insurance cover by other means and thereby the making of the second Ultron loan, the fact is that Mr Dungate did not refuse to deal with Mr Lee but chose to deal with him in negotiating the necessary amendment of the insurance cover provided by Hodge. Having taken the course of dealing with Mr Lee, it is irrelevant to the issue of causation to speculate as to what might have happened if Mr Dungate had taken a different course.

The factual issue of causation, therefore, must be considered by this court on the basis on which it was considered by Steyn J, namely: was it proved that, if given information of Mr Lee's fraud with reference to the insurance cover for the first Ultron loan, the banks would not have made the second Ultron loan?

*(C)  The effect of a report to Keysers*
In reaching his conclusion that the banks would have lent no more money to Mr Ballestero's companies if they had known of Mr Lee's dishonesty the judge attached considerable importance to the evidence of the banking witnesses. A substantial part of the argument of counsel for Hodge on the issue of causation correspondingly was directed to discounting, both in general and particular terms, the reliability and weight of this evidence. The judge had acknowledged the great danger in dealing with a group of witnesses collectively, but saw no use in summarising the evidence of each witness, since all of them had impressed him as 'conscientious bankers who gave, by and large, reliable evidence' (see [1987] 1 Lloyd's Rep 69 at 103). The submission for Hodge was that the crucial factual issue of causation could not be properly approached or decided in this way and that detailed examination of the evidence of these witnesses showed that the judge's conclusion was wrong.

Counsel for Hodge submitted that the judge's acceptance of the evidence of the banks' witnesses confirmed no more than that they then honestly believed that, if given certain information, they or their banks would have acted as they asserted that they would have acted; but the witnesses were speaking with hindsight about hypothetical events; their assertions were contrary to the probabilities demonstrated by the indisputable facts; and, it was said, this court is in as good a position to assess those probabilities as was the judge at the trial. Therefore this court could and should set aside the judge's findings on causation.

Furthermore, counsel submitted, the circumstances in which the claim in respect of the second Ultron loan came to be advanced by Keysers made it necessary that the evidence of Keysers' witnesses should be approached with all the greater caution. Keysers were the agent bank when the loan was made. After the discovery of Mr Ballestero's fraud claims were made against Keysers by the banks which had participated in the Ultron loans and the other loans, on the ground that Keysers had been negligent. The claims against Keysers were settled on terms that they acquired the parts of the Ultron loans due to the other participating banks by paying a proportion only of the sums due and by granting in some cases a right in the plaintiff banks to receive a small proportion of any sums recovered by Keysers. The effect of the arrangement is that Keysers, which were charged with negligence by the participating banks, would, if they retained the judgment given in their favour by Steyn J in respect of the second Ultron loan, retain more than they lost on the loan. The submission was that Keysers' witnesses had very strong incentives to convince themselves that, if told of Mr Lee's deception, Keysers at once would have called in the first Ultron loan (which the judge rejected) and would have made no further loans (which the judge accepted).

There is, in our judgment, nothing of substance in these points by way of general criticism of the evidence of Keysers' witnesses. The difficulty for witnesses in giving objective, fair and accurate evidence when speaking with hindsight of matters which

affect their employer's financial interest and their personal professional reputation was
*a* explored in evidence and must have been fully taken into account by the judge. By itself
those points indicate no error on his part. Whether taken by themselves or with the
other issues of fact discussed below, they do not show that this court could properly
interfere with his findings of fact.

As to the details of the evidence of the banks' witnesses, we have considered the
transcripts of the evidence of Mr Magnenat, Keysers' chairman, of Mr Naggar, the vice-
*b* chairman, of Mr Verkooyen and Mr Martin, managers, and of Mr Reist, assistant
manager. Mr Magnenat and Mr Naggar both gave evidence that, if told of Mr Lee's
deceit, Keysers would have called in the first Ultron loan and made no further loans.
Both were cross-examined in detail and at length to the effect that, having regard to their
trust in Mr Ballestero and to the fact that the gap in the insurance cover had been fully
covered without harm done, it would have appeared unfair to Mr Ballestero and
*c* unnecessary in commercial prudence so to act. Consideration was given to whether there
would have appeared to be any good ground in law to call in the first Ultron loan in the
absence of any apparent default. It was said that Keysers would have taken legal advice.
Steyn J, who accepted their evidence as given fairly and honestly, must have rejected
their contention that they would have called in the first Ultron loan, on the basis that, in
the light of the uncertain position in law on the known facts, it was not proved that
*d* Keysers would have taken that course.

The evidence of Mr Verkooyen, who was in general charge of the business with Mr
Ballestero, was the subject of particularly searching analysis by counsel for Hodge. Mr
Verkooyen was not asked any questions as to how he would have acted if told of Mr Lee's
deceit by Mr Wilkinson. However, counsel argued that, on the evidence, the probability
was that any report from Mr Wilkinson would have gone to Mr Verkooyen and that Mr
*e* Verkooyen would have told no one else, because it would not have appeared to him to be
of any significance. Mr Wilkinson, in making a full and candid report, would have
emphasised that Mr Lee had intended to cause no harm to the banks and had believed
that none would result. Furthermore, the submission that Mr Verkooyen would have
taken no action was based partly on the fact that Mr Verkooyen stated in evidence that in
December 1979 he had been told by Mr Lee that, although the cover note stated that
*f* Hodge was committed without qualification for the full term of the insurance cover, the
cover provided by Hodge was provisional. Mr Verkooyen understood that to mean that
Hodge had taken the remaining amount of the cover until replaced. Counsel contended
that Mr Verkooyen must be taken as having known that the cover note was misleading
in an important sense in that, contrary to the obligations apparently recorded by the
cover notes, Hodge might be replaced by other insurers in whom the banks might have
*g* less confidence. Nevertheless, he had told no one else of that fact.

Further, counsel pointed to the fact that Mr Verkooyen was aware that, after Mr Lee
had been told that the statement about Swiss law was nonsense, that statement continued
to appear in documents dealing with the insurance cover and Mr Verkooyen therefore
knew that Mr Lee was making fraudulent misrepresentations. There was, therefore, no
*h* reason to suppose that Mr Verkooyen would have attached any importance to the
revelation of the past deception by Mr Lee with reference to the cover notes, when the
matter had been fully put right.

In our judgment, however, the judge's conclusion on the causation issue cannot be
faulted on the basis that a report to Mr Verkooyen would not have been passed on by
him to Mr Naggar and Mr Magnenat. Such a possibility was not suggested at the trial. If
*j* it had been suggested to Mr Verkooyen, we think it clear that he would have repudiated
it. The Ultron loan was for Keysers a loan of a very large amount and of an unusual
nature. Keysers owed duties to participating banks. It is inherently unlikely that he
would have kept to himself or regarded as unimportant a report that the lending banks
had been deceived as to the state and extent of the principal security for a large loan. It
appears that it was never clearly suggested to Mr Verkooyen in cross-examination, or

accepted by him, that he was aware that Mr Lee had been guilty of any deliberate deception. We think that the short answer to this suggestion which is now made is that, if Mr Verkooyen was an honest witness, as the judge held him to be, he cannot have been aware of such deception; if he had been aware of it he would have taken action on the information.

On merely reading the documents and transcripts of the evidence of Keysers' witnesses, we are bound to say that we would not find it so easy to assess the probable reactions of the banks if they had been informed of Mr Lee's deception, as apparently did the judge. The confidence of the assertions by their witnesses, in particular by Mr Magnenat and Mr Naggar, appears not to fit with complete consistency alongside the response of Mr. Verkooyen, as an experienced banker, to the 'provisional' nature of Hodge's commitment under the cover notes or to the repetition of the statement as to Swiss law or as to other matters. However, we have not had the great advantage of seeing and hearing the many witnesses give their evidence.

Counsel has submitted that it was for the banks to prove that, with reference to the second Ultron loan which had been approved in principle by the banks in May 1980, alternative insurance from other underwriters would not have been available in the market on terms acceptable to the banks. In our view the main issue of fact does not depend on the burden of proof about the availability of alternative cover. The banks set out to prove that, if given the information about Mr Lee's deception, the negotiations for further loans would have been terminated. The judge accepted their evidence to that effect. It was, in our view, open to the judge to reach that conclusion on the evidence and his conclusion has not been shown to be wrong.

It has, therefore, been proved that, if Hodge had, in performance of any duty laid on them, passed on the information about Mr Lee's deception, whether to Notcutts or direct to the banks, the second Ultron loan would not have been made.

### (D)	The 'but if only' argument

Counsel for Hodge, however, submitted that it still does not follow that the failure to pass on such information in fact caused the banks' losses. He listed some of the many incidents of which, he said, it was possible fairly to say of the banks: 'But if only you, as a prudent banker, had acted differently, the fraud which caused the losses would in fact have been prevented.' They were referred to as the 'but if only' incidents. The purpose, apart from attempting to show the banks' negligent disregard of their own interests, was first to submit that, if the law placed a duty on Mr Dungate, for breach of which the insurers are to be held vicariously liable, that liability is not in accordance with a commonsense view of what caused the banks' losses or of what justice should require. Next, it was to demonstrate that any breach of duty by Mr Dungate was of such little significance that it could not reasonably be held to have been a cause of equal efficacy with the fraud of Mr Ballestero.

Counsel's list contained 13 incidents. Three of them related to the failure of the banks to carry out any check on the truth of Mr Ballestero's assertions about the Menorcan project. Five of them related to various precautions in relation to the gem valuations which the banks could have taken but failed to take. One of them concerned the willingness of Keysers to pass on to another participating bank the dishonest representations made by Mr Ballestero without checking them. Another related to the failure of Mr Verkooyen to take any action despite his knowledge of the misrepresentation as to Swiss banking law referred to in the section of this judgment dealing with Mr Lee's dishonest acts. Another arose out of the failure of Mr Wilkinson, who had signed the cover notes for the first Ultron loan, to make effective inquiries into why and in what circumstances Notcutts were still in February to May 1980 seeking to complete the insurance cover supposedly provided by those cover notes. Another concerned the failure of Mr Verkooyen or anyone else in Keysers to take note of the warning signs in relation to British Bank Corp and Cia Americana, through which Mr Lee put forward insurance cover for the last layer required for the second Ultron loan. The tenth incident arose out

a
of the failure of Mr Verkooyen or anyone else in Keysers to question with the insurers the terms in which Mr Lee had made an assertion that the insurers had authorised him to state that the fraud exclusion clause would not apply to the gem valuations, but nevertheless were not prepared to issue an indorsement to that effect.

This, on the face of it, is a formidable list. Counsel pertinently reminded us of Lord Griffiths's cautionary reference in *Smith v Littlewoods Organisation Ltd* [1987] 1 All ER 710 at 713, [1987] AC 241 at 251 to the fable of the prince who lost his kingdom but for the
b want of a nail for the shoe of his horse. It should be noted that the pleaded case of Hodge on contributory negligence does not extend to all the matters covered by the 'but if only' incidents. Nevertheless, in counsel's submission, they show that it would defy common sense to attribute the banks' losses to the non-disclosure complained of.

The 'but if only' argument gives rise to questions of law as well as fact. We will refer further to the legal implications of the argument below. Suffice it to say at this stage that,
c so far as it is a submission of fact, while we see its force, we cannot agree with it. As we have already indicated, there are in our view no sufficient grounds to disturb the judge's finding that, if Hodge had in performance of any duty laid on it passed on the information about Mr Lee's deception, whether to Notcutts or direct to the banks, the second Ultron loan would not have been made. Once this is accepted, we think it is clear that as a matter of fact the failure to pass on the information was *a* cause of Keysers' losses.

d

*(E)  Remoteness and causation in law*
We turn now to the legal issues arising in the context of causation. It was submitted for Hodge that, if the appeal on the factual issue failed, still the only cause in law of the banks' losses on the second Ultron loan was the fraud of Mr Ballestero. If that submission were rejected, there would still remain the issue of remoteness, that is to say whether the
e particular losses suffered are within the protection provided by the law to the banks in respect of any breach of duty proved against Hodge. That question, as was common ground, is to be determined by reference to reasonable foreseeability and has already been dealt with under issue (3) above.

The assumption on which consideration of the issue of causation in law proceeds is that Hodge was under a duty at common law to inform the brokers or the banks of the
f deception practised by Mr Lee and was guilty of a tortious wrong in failing to do so. The alternative grounds of alleged liability, namely breach of duty of utmost good faith, or for actionable misrepresentation, will be mentioned separately below. The references hereafter to breach of duty by Hodge are references to that duty which for these purposes is assumed to exist.

On the basis of a proved duty arising in tort, and breach of it, Steyn J applied the
g principles stated by Devlin J in *Heskell v Continental Express Ltd* [1950] 1 All ER 1033 at 1047:

'Where the wrong is a tort, it is clearly settled that the wrongdoer cannot excuse himself by pointing to another cause. It is enough that the tort should be a cause and it is unnecessary to evaluate competing causes and ascertain which of them is
h dominant ...'

As already stated above Steyn J held that the test was satisfied on the ground that, although the second Ultron loan would not have been made if Mr Ballestero had not carried out his frauds, so also that loan would not have been made if Hodge had discharged the duty laid on them. There were thus, in his view, two causes of equal
j efficacy.

Counsel's submissions, apart from those directed to foreseeability and remoteness, were that the breach of duty, if it is to give rise to liability, must be an effective cause of the loss, and it was not an effective cause in this case because other causative acts, both preceding and following the breach of duty, were of such a nature and of such potency that the original breach of duty ceased to be effective.

As to the concept of effective cause, counsel referred to the judgment of Denning J in

*Minister of Pensions v Chennell* [1946] 2 All ER 719, [1947] KB 250. That was a pension
case in which foreseeability was irrelevant and the issue was whether the interference by
a young boy, who moved and caused an unexploded incendiary bomb to explode in a *a*
public place so as to injure the plaintiff, was an intervening or extraneous event of so
powerful a causative effect, that the dropping of the bomb was relegated to no more than
a part of the history or circumstances in or on which the interference of the boy operated.
It was held that the action of the boy was not of such a nature as to cause the dropping of
the bomb to be so regarded. That decision of Denning J has been approved and applied *b*
by this court in cases where issues of causation have arisen under statutory provisions
considered to be similar for that purpose: see *Iron and Steel Holding and Realisation Agency
v Compensation Appeal Tribunal* [1966] 1 All ER 769, [1966] 1 WLR 480 and *Povey v
Secretary of State for the Environment* (1986) Times, 17 July.

In *Yorkshire Dale Steamship Co Ltd v Minister of War Transport, The Coxwold* [1942] 2 All
ER 6, [1942] AC 691 it was decided that the cause of a loss has to be ascertained by the *c*
standard of common sense of the ordinary man: see the citation of that case by Devlin J
in the passage from *Heskell v Continental Express Ltd* [1950] 1 All ER 1033 at 1048, cited
by Steyn J in his judgment in this case, in considering causation in contract. That
principle, in our view, is equally applicable to the ascertainment of an effective cause of
loss in tort.

Counsel's contentions with reference to the 'but if only' incidents were directed to this *d*
issue. In our judgment, however, the judge was right to hold that the failure by Hodge
to cause the banks to be informed of Mr Lee's deception was (subject to the issue of
remoteness based on unforeseeability) an effective cause of the banks' losses on the second
Ultron loan. For reasons further explained in dealing below with contributory negligence,
the banks were not the authors of their own misfortune in the sense that their own
negligence with regard to their own interests must be taken as the sole cause of their *e*
losses. They were not in respect of any of the incidents listed by counsel, or in any other
respect, proved to have been guilty of any negligence at all. One incident was concerned
not with acts or omissions of the banks but of Mr Wilkinson, who was a servant of
Notcutts. All the incidents are matters of omission and did not involve any breach by the
banks of the self-regarding duty to protect their own interests. They were, indeed, no
more than the circumstances in which the breach of duty of Hodge operated. *f*

The assumed duty on Hodge was to cause information to be provided to the banks
which Hodge knew was relevant to the making of the decision by the banks whether to
enter into the transaction of the second Ultron loan on the terms proposed. Performance
of that duty at any time down to the making of the loan would have caused the loan not
to be made. It was, in short, a case of a continuing breach of the obligation.

It is impossible in these circumstances by the standards of common sense to regard the *g*
breach of duty by Hodge, performance of which would have prevented the loss, as
reduced to a mere part of the history, simply because the fraud of Mr Ballestero was also
a necessary cause of the loss. Down to the moment when the second Ultron loan was
made, performance of the duty would have prevented the loss which Mr Ballestero's
fraud caused to the banks. Failure by Hodge to perform that duty is, in our judgment, to *h*
be treated as an effective cause and not as a mere part of the preceding history.

The issue would be answered in the same way if the supposed breach on the part of
Hodge were breach of the duty of utmost good faith, or if the basis of the claim were the
making of a misrepresentation which induced the banks to enter into the second
insurance contract which was to provide the main security for the second Ultron loan.

The last aspect of this issue, of course, is remoteness based on a submission that the loss *j*
suffered by the banks on the second Ultron loan was a kind of loss not reasonably
foreseeable. That has already been dealt with under issue (3) above, which we have
decided in favour of Keysers.

*Issue (11)*

Hodge's pleading in relation to contributory negligence was contained in the points of

defence and counterclaim of the first, second and third defendants, in their finally
a amended form, as incorporated into the pleading of Hodge. In substance, the points
alleged and pursued on this appeal were (taking the lettering from the pleading): (a)
failure to investigate the 'moral risk' (which we understand to mean the creditworthiness)
of Mr Ballestero; (b) failure to investigate Mr Ballestero's assertions with reference to the
development in Menorca, and in particular the capacity of the project to generate funds
to repay the borrowings.

b    Apart from one finding with reference to Chemical Bank the judge held that no
contributory negligence had been made out. He dealt with the matter in general terms.
After setting out all the allegations which had been raised before him in respect of all the
loans against all the participating banks, he said ([1987] 2 All ER 923 at 959, [1987] 2
WLR 1300 at 1347–1348):

c        'This is not an exhaustive catalogue of the allegations but it gives the flavour of
        the case of the insurers on contributory negligence against the banks, other than
        Chemical Bank. The answer to the allegations of contributory negligence is, in my
        view, quite simple. While I have considered the evidence in relation to each bank
        separately, I can deal with the position of the banks, other than Chemical Bank, at
        the same time. On the oral and documentary evidence I am satisfied that each of the
d        banks was entitled to regard Mr Ballestero as an honest and reliable borrower.
        Secondly, I am satisfied that the banks, in accordance with the then current banking
        practice, regarded the loans as falling into two broad classes; crédit financière (an
        asset-backed loan) and crédit commerciale (a loan dependent on the success of
        underlying commercial projects). In the case of loans in the latter category prudent
        banking practice required investigation of the borrower and the underlying
e        transaction. But in my view the banks rightly regarded the loans as falling into the
        first category. The banks viewed the loans as being asset-backed, viz by a pledge of
        gemstones and by 100% credit insurance which (subject to the fraud exclusion
        clause) they regarded as virtually equivalent to a bank guarantee. Against this
        background I have come to the conclusion that none of the pleaded allegations of
        contributory negligence against the banks are established.'

f    Part of the attack on this conclusion of the judge was directed to his acceptance of the
reasonableness of the banks' view that the second Ultron loan was asset-backed. The
submission was that, since the credit insurance was subject to the fraud exclusion clause,
it would not reasonably be regarded as equivalent to a bank guarantee. It was submitted
that, if there is a bank guarantee of a loan, in ordinary unqualified terms, it is no defence
g    to the guarantor bank that the loan was induced by fraud. In our judgment, the validity
of the judge's acceptance of the reasonableness of the banks' view about the nature of the
loan transaction depends on his finding that the banks were entitled to regard Mr
Ballestero as an honest and reliable banker. The banks had made inquiries about him.
There was no evidence of an experienced banker to say that, according to ordinary
prudent banking practice, some additional form of inquiry should in the circumstances
h    have been carried out which would in probability have revealed the fraudulent purposes
of Mr Ballestero or that he was not to be trusted. The only evidence of an experienced
banker which criticised the conduct of any of the banks was elicited from Mr Keller of
American Fletcher, to which evidence we refer below. That evidence had nothing to do
with prior checking of the honesty or reliability of Mr Ballestero. Steyn J was entitled on
the evidence to find, as he did, that the banks had good and sufficient reason as prudent
j    bankers to accept Mr Ballestero as honest and reliable. Having reached that conclusion,
Steyn J was also entitled, in our view, to find that the banks reasonably regarded the
second Ultron loan as asset-backed so far as concerned any need, in ordinary commercial
prudence, to make any further inquiries than they did about the project which Mr
Ballestero had put forward as the enterprise in which the loans would be invested. The
banks had no reason to suppose that the insurance was not effective according to its
terms. That conclusion amounts in our view to an effective answer, as Steyn J held it to

be, to the remaining allegations of contributory negligence which have been pursued on
this appeal.

The evidence of Mr Keller was directed to an allegation made by solicitors acting for
American Fletcher in respect of claims made by American Fletcher against Keysers which
were eventually included in the settlement between Keysers and the other banks which
we have described above in general terms. The allegations were set out in a telex of
December 1983, and claims were advanced in respect of the participation by American
Fletcher in the first Ultron loan and in the Deminter and HSG loans with which this
appeal is no longer concerned. In summary, the contention was that Keysers became
aware through the Autotrain transaction, a separate matter with which Mr Lee was
concerned, of suspicious circumstances regarding Cia Americana who were to be the
insurers in the Autotrain transaction and who were also the fronting insurers for the
additional excess layer required for the second Ultron loan (see p 968, ante), that American
Fletcher should have been advised of those circumstances and that Keysers would have
been in a position to take American Fletcher out of the Ultron syndicate. Mr Keller
confirmed that in his view that allegation was fairly made. As developed by counsel for
Hodge this point went to the issue of causation in fact, as tending to show that an
indication of fraud by a person connected with the transaction would not in probability
have caused the banks to terminate negotiations. This matter was never specifically
pleaded as an act of contributory negligence relevant to the making of the second Ultron
loan, and the evidence of Mr Keller provides no ground for holding that the judge's
rejection of the allegation of contributory negligence on the part of Keysers was mistaken.

*Conclusions*

To summarise our conclusions. (1) Hodge's appeal on issues (1), (2), (3) and (4) fails. (2)
Hodge's appeal on issue (5) succeeds. (3) Keysers' cross-appeal on issue (6) fails. (4) Issue
(7) does not arise, but if it had arisen we would have upheld the judge's decision on this
point. (5) Hodge's appeal on issue (8) succeeds. (6) Issues (9), (10) and (11) do not arise,
but if they had arisen we would have upheld the judge's decision on these issues.

In the final result we allow this appeal from the judgment of Steyn J of 30 September
1986. We propose to set aside his order and order that judgment be entered for Hodge in
the action. We dismiss Keysers' cross-appeal. Subject to further submissions, we propose
to adjourn any argument on the question of costs for hearing after the parties have had a
fuller opportunity to consider the contents of this wide-ranging judgment.

*Appeal allowed. Order of Steyn J set aside. Judgment for Hodge. Keysers' cross-appeal dismissed.*
*Leave to appeal to the House of Lords granted.*

Solicitors: *Herbert Smith* (for Skandia); *Richards Butler* (for Hodge); *Slaughter & May* (for
Chemical Bank); *Hopkins & Wood* (for the other banks).

Vivian Horvath    Barrister.

# Government of Canada and another v Aronson

HOUSE OF LORDS
LORD BRIDGE OF HARWICH, LORD ELWYN-JONES, LORD GRIFFITHS, LORD JAUNCEY OF TULLICHETTLE
AND LORD LOWRY
8, 9, 10 MAY, 20 JULY 1989

*Extradition – Fugitive offender – Relevant offences – Corresponding United Kingdom offence – Offence against law of designated Commonwealth country – Act or omission constituting the offence – Whether ingredients of Commonwealth country's offence must establish that fugitive offender guilty of corresponding United Kingdom offence – Whether sufficient if totality of evidence of Commonwealth country's offence would prove fugitive offender guilty of corresponding United Kingdom offence – Fugitive Offenders Act 1967, ss 3(1)(c), 7(5)(a).*

The respondent was alleged to have committed 77 offences of dishonesty in Canada between 1983 and 1986. He was arrested in England and the Canadian government sought his return to Canada under the Fugitive Offenders Act 1967 to stand trial for those offences. The chief metropolitan stipendiary magistrate held that the evidence produced by the Canadian government established that the offences were 'relevant offences' within s 3(1)(c)[a] of the 1967 Act and that the evidence was sufficient to warrant the trial of the respondent for those offences if he had committed them in England and he accordingly committed the respondent to custody to await his return to Canada. The respondent applied for habeas corpus on the ground that he had been wrongly committed on 69 of the offences because they were not relevant offences since 'the offence' for the purposes of the 1976 Act meant the offence of which the fugitive was accused in the Commonwealth country and accordingly 'the act or omission constituting the offence' in s 3(1)(c) meant the criminal conduct specifically alleged against him in the Commonwealth country's warrant. The government of Canada and the governor of the prison where the respondent was detained (the appellants) contended that s 3(1)(c) referred to the criminal conduct of the fugitive constituting an offence against the law of the United Kingdom as demonstrated by the evidence before the magistrate, even if the ingredients which went to make up that criminal conduct did not always correspond with the ingredients of the criminal conduct alleged in the Commonwealth country's warrant. The Divisional Court granted the application and quashed the magistrate's order in respect of the 69 offences. The appellants appealed to the House of Lords.

**Held** (Lord Griffiths and Lord Jauncey dissenting) – When a designated Commonwealth country sought the return under the 1967 Act of a person accused or convicted of an offence against the law of that country that offence was only a 'relevant offence' under s 3(1)(c) of that Act, for which the fugitive offender was liable to be returned, if the ingredients of the Commonwealth country's offence, as disclosed by the particulars of the offence in the charge, would, if proved, establish that the fugitive offender was guilty of a corresponding United Kingdom offence. Accordingly, the mere fact that the totality of the evidence relied on to prove the Commonwealth country's offence would, if accepted, prove that the fugitive offender was guilty of a corresponding United Kingdom offence was not sufficient to establish a 'relevant offence' for the purposes of s 3(1)(c), since the issue which the examining magistrate had to decide was whether the evidence was sufficient to warrant the trial of the fugitive in the United Kingdom for what he was alleged by the requesting country to have done wrong and not just for what he appeared to have done wrong according to English law. Since the definition of the 69 offences under the Canadian Criminal Code did not contain all the ingredients of the

---

a   Section 3(1) is set out at p 1029 *g h*, post

corresponding English offences it followed that the appeal would be dismissed (see p 1027 *c* to *h*, p 1028 *c* to *e*, p 1042 *f* to p 1043 *a*, p 1044 *f g* and p 1049 *h*, post).

R *v Governor of Brixton Prison, ex p Gardner* [1968] 1 All ER 636 considered.

Per Lord Bridge, Lord Elwyn-Jones and Lord Lowry. The Secretary of State, when issuing an authority to proceed, must give the magistrate enough information to decide whether the Commonwealth offence is a relevant offence and whether there is enough evidence to commit for trial on the Commonwealth offence in accordance with s 7(5)(*a*)[b] of the 1967 Act (see p 1028 *c* to *e*, p 1043 *h j* and p 1049 *h*, post).

**Notes**

For 'relevant offences' for extradition purposes, see 18 Halsbury's Laws (4th edn) paras 256–259, and for cases on the subject, see 24 Digest (Reissue) 1158, 12274–12279.

For the Fugitive Offenders Act 1967, ss 3, 7, see 17 Halsbury's Statutes (4th edn) 520, 524.

As from a day to be appointed s 3 of the 1967 Act (which defines 'relevant offence') is to be substituted by the Criminal Justice Act 1988, s 1(9), Sch 1, para 6, which Act introduces similar codes for extradition between the United Kingdom and foreign states and for the return and surrender of fugitive offenders between the United Kingdom and Commonwealth countries or colonies of the United Kingdom. As from 27 September 1989 s 3 (as so substituted) and s 7 of the 1967 Act are to be replaced by ss 2 and 9 of the Extradition Act 1989 (wherein 'relevant offences' are termed 'extradition crimes').

**Cases referred to in opinions**

*A-G's Reference (No 1 of 1988)* [1989] 2 All ER 1, [1989] 2 WLR 729, HL.
*Arton, Re (No 2)* [1896] 1 QB 509, DC.
*Bellencontre, Re* [1891] 2 QB 122, DC.
*Black-Clawson International Ltd v Papierwerke Waldhof-Aschaffenburg AG* [1975] 1 All ER 810, [1975] AC 591, [1975] 2 WLR 513, HL.
*Government of Denmark v Nielsen* [1984] 2 All ER 81, [1984] AC 606, [1984] 2 WLR 737, HL; *affg* (1983) 79 Cr App R 1, DC.
*Hanlon v Law Society* [1980] 2 All ER 199, [1981] AC 124, [1980] 2 WLR 756, HL.
R *v Governor of Brixton Prison, ex p Gardner* [1968] 1 All ER 636, [1968] 2 QB 399, [1968] 2 WLR 512, DC.
R *v Governor of Pentonville Prison, ex p Budlong* [1980] 1 All ER 701, [1980] 1 WLR 1110.
R *v Governor of Pentonville Prison, ex p Myers* (6 December 1972, unreported), DC.
*Tarling v Government of the Republic of Singapore* (1979) 70 Cr App R 77, HL.

**Appeal**

The Government of Canada and the governor of Her Majesty's Prison, Pentonville, appealed with the leave of the Divisional Court of the Queen's Bench Division against the decision of that court (Bingham LJ and Leggatt J) on 20 December 1988 whereby, on the application of the respondent, Richard Allen Aronson, for a writ of habeas corpus ad subjiciendum, it ordered that the order of the Chief Metropolitan Stipendiary Magistrate sitting at Bow Street Magistrates' Court on 2 August 1988 committing the respondent to prison under s 7 of the Fugitive Offenders Act 1967 in respect of 77 offences listed in the schedule to that order to await return to Canada under that Act be quashed in respect of 69 of those offences, on the ground that they were not 'relevant offences' within the meaning of s 3 of the 1967 Act. The facts are set out in the opinion of Lord Lowry.

*Clive Nicholls QC* and *Michael Birnbaum* for the appellants.
*R Alun Jones QC* and *Clare Patricia Montgomery* for the respondent.

---

*b*    Section 7, so far as material, is set out at p 1042 *a* to *c*, post

Their Lordships took time for consideration.

*a*

20 July. The following opinions were delivered.

**LORD BRIDGE OF HARWICH.** My Lords, this appeal turns on the construction of
s 3(1)(c) of the Fugitive Offenders Act 1967. When a designated Commonwealth country
*b*  seeks the return from the United Kingdom of a person who is accused or has been
convicted of an offence against the law of that country (a Commonwealth offence), that
offence is only a 'relevant offence' if—'the act or omission constituting the offence . . .
would constitute an offence against the law of the United Kingdom if it took place within
the United Kingdom . . .'. What does this phrase mean? Does it mean that the ingredients
of the Commonwealth offence, as disclosed by the particulars of the offence in the charge,
*c*  would, if proved, establish guilt of a corresponding United Kingdom offence (the narrow
construction)? Or does it mean that that totality of the evidence relied on to prove the
Commonwealth offence would, if accepted, prove guilt of a corresponding United
Kingdom offence (the wide construction)? I have reached the clear conclusion that the
narrow construction is to be preferred.
    The issue arises when the Commonwealth offence may be established by particularising
*d*  and proving ingredients A, B and C, but the nearest corresponding United Kingdom
offence requires that the prosecution prove ingredients A, B, C and D. It is submitted for
the government of Canada and the governor of Her Majesty's Prison Pentonville (the
appellants) that if, in a particular case, the evidence relied on to prove the Commonwealth
offence would be sufficient, if accepted, to establish ingredient D in addition to
ingredients A, B and C this is sufficient to satisfy the requirements of s 3(1)(c). Whether
*e*  the extra ingredient necessary to prove the United Kingdom offence, over and above the
ingredients which constitute the Commonwealth offence, is a physical or mental element,
the wide construction leads to startling results. Two men are accused of the identical
Commonwealth offence particularised against them in identical terms. The committing
magistrate must decide whether the offence with which each is charged is a 'relevant
offence': see s 7(5). If the evidence establishes ingredients A, B and C against both men
*f*  but ingredient D against the first man only, the magistrate must commit the first man,
but not the second, to custody to await his return to the designated Commonwealth
country. Yet so much of the evidence that is relied on to establish ingredient D, or any
inference drawn from the evidence to establish ingredient D, will be irrelevant to his
trial for the Commonwealth offence after his return. The anomaly is even more striking
in relation to a fugitive whose return is sought as a convicted offender. Neither the jury's
*g*  verdict of guilty nor his own plea of guilty to the Commonwealth offence as charged will
be sufficient to resolve the question whether the Commonwealth offence of which he
was convicted was a 'relevant offence'. The committing magistrate will have to go behind
the verdict or the plea and the convicted offender's liability to return will presumably
depend on the magistrate's own view whether the evidence establishes all the ingredients
*h*  of the corresponding United Kingdom offence. I do not think the language of the statute
fairly admits of the wide construction. The short answer is that neither the additional
ingredient, nor the evidence which is said to establish that ingredient, forms any part of
the material 'constituting' the Commonwealth offence. But, if the language is ambiguous,
the narrow construction is to be preferred in a criminal statute as the construction more
favourable to the liberty of the subject.
*j*     The basic fallacy in the appellants' argument, as set out in paras 1 to 5 under the
heading 'Question 1' in their written case, lies in the attempt to assimilate the
requirements of the 1967 Act to the requirements of the Extradition Act 1870. The
attempt fails because the structure and machinery of the two Acts are entirely disparate.
An 'extradition crime' under the 1870 Act is one of the specific English crimes set out in
the 'List of Crimes' in Sch 1. The introductory paragraph reads:

'The following list of crimes is to be construed according to the law existing in England, or in a British possession (as the case may be), at the date of the alleged *a* crime, whether by common law or by statute made before or after the passing of this Act . . .'

Nowhere in the 1870 Act is there any provision which has the effect of imposing a double-criminality rule, though such a rule may be introduced into the extradition machinery by the provisions of particular treaties. By contrast, Sch 1 to the 1967 Act sets *b* out a list of returnable offences described in broad categories and reproducing in terms the list found in Annex 1 to the *Scheme relating to the Rendition of Fugitive Offenders within the Commonwealth* (Cmnd 3008 (1966)) agreed between Commonwealth law ministers in 1966. Legislating to give effect to the scheme, it was necessary to provide that a returnable offence should both fall within one of those broad categories and satisfy the 'double-criminality rule' laid down in cl 10 of the scheme. That explains why the definition of *c* 'relevant offence' in s 3(1) requires that, in relation to a designated Commonwealth country, both paras (*a*) and (*c*) should be satisfied.

For these reasons, and for those given by my noble and learned friend Lord Lowry, with whose speech I fully agree, I would dismiss the appeal.

**LORD ELWYN-JONES.** My Lords, this appeal involves construction of s 3(1)(*c*) of *d* the Fugitive Offenders Act 1967, which created a stricter and more demanding scheme of extradition than its predecessor the Fugitive Offenders Act 1881. I have had the advantage of reading in draft the speeches of my noble and learned friends Lord Bridge and Lord Lowry. I agree with them and with 'the narrow construction' of the words in the section. To the extent that the section is ambiguous, as the 1967 Act imposes criminal liability, it should, in my opinion, be construed in the narrow sense in favour of the *e* liberty of the subject. I would dismiss the appeal.

**LORD GRIFFITHS.** My Lords, the Canadian government wish to extradite the respondent to stand trial in Canada on a large number of offences of dishonesty which he is alleged to have committed in Canada between 1983 and 1986. The Chief Metropolitan Stipendiary Magistrate was satisfied by evidence produced by the Canadian government *f* that the offences were relevant offences within the meaning of s 3 of the Fugitive Offenders Act 1967 and that the evidence was sufficient to warrant the trial of the respondent for those offences if he had committed them in England. The magistrate therefore committed respondent to custody to await his return to Canada to stand trial on 77 offences.

The respondent applied for habeas corpus and before the Divisional Court submitted *g* that he had been wrongly committed on 69 of the offences. The Divisional Court if it had felt free to do so would have upheld the magistrate; however, it felt constrained by authority to apply a construction of the 1967 Act which it clearly considered incorrect and which forced it to quash the committal in respect of 69 of the offences. In my opinion the Divisional Court's preferred construction of the 1967 Act is correct and the respondent should be committed on all 77 charges. Furthermore, I do not think that the *h* earlier authorities cited by the Divisional Court in fact compelled it to adopt a construction of the Act which it did not believe to be right.

The 1967 Act was introduced to give effect to a *Scheme relating to the Rendition of Fugitive Offenders within the Commonwealth* (Cmnd 3008) presented to Parliament by the Secretary of State for the Home Department by command of Her Majesty in May 1966. It is, I think, worth setting out the foreword to the scheme: *j*

'At the Meeting of Commonwealth law Ministers, held at Marlborough House, London, from 26th April to 3rd May 1966, the arrangements for the extradition of fugitive offenders within the Commonwealth were reviewed in the light of the constitutional changes which have taken place since the passing of the Fugitive a Offenders Act 1881. The following extract from the communiqué issued at the conclusion of the Meeting explains the purpose of the Scheme, the text of which is reproduced at pages 1–8:—"The Meeting considered that Commonwealth extradition arrangements should be based upon reciprocity and substantially uniform legislation incorporating certain features commonly found in extradition treaties, e.g. a list of returnable offences, the establishment of a *prima facie* case before return, and restrictions on the return of political offenders. The Meeting accordingly

b formulated a Scheme setting out principles which could form the basis of legislation within the Commonwealth and recommended that effect should be given to the Scheme in each Commonwealth country. The Scheme does not apply to Southern Rhodesia".'

This was a radically different scheme from that which had previously applied to the extradition of fugitive offenders under the Fugitive Offenders Act 1881. Under that Act
c a fugitive was returnable if he had committed any crime in a part of Her Majesty's dominions punishable with imprisonment for more than 12 months regardless of whether or not his conduct amounted to a crime in that part of Her Majesty's dominions where he was arrested. The new scheme proposed that a fugitive should only be returned for a returnable offence and proposed the introduction of what it described as the double-
d criminality rule. The relevant paragraphs read as follows:

'*Returnable offences*
2.—(1) A fugitive will only be returned for a returnable offence.
(2) For the purposes of this Scheme a returnable offence is an offence described in Annex 1 (whatever the name of the offence under the law of the countries and territories concerned, and whether or not it is described in that law by reference to
e some special intent or any special circumstances of aggravation), being an offence which is punishable by a competent court in the country or territory to which return is requested by imprisonment for twelve months or a greater penalty.

*Double-criminality rule*
10. The return of a fugitive offender will either be precluded by law or be subject
f to refusal by the competent executive authority if the facts on which the request for his return is grounded do not constitute an offence under the law of the country or territory in which he is found.'

The definition of a relevant offence in s 3 of the 1967 Act provides:

'(1) For the purposes of this Act an offence of which a person is accused or has been convicted in a designated Commonwealth country or United Kingdom
g dependency is a relevant offence if—(a) in the case of an offence against the law of a designated Commonwealth country, it is an offence which, however described in that law, falls within any of the descriptions set out in Schedule 1 to this Act, and is punishable under that law with imprisonment for a term of twelve months or any greater punishment; (b) in the case of an offence against the law of a United Kingdom
h dependency, it is punishable under that law, on conviction by or before a superior court, with imprisonment for a term of twelve months or any greater punishment; and (c) in any case, the act or omission constituting the offence, or the equivalent act or omission, would constitute an offence against the law of the United Kingdom if it took place within the United Kingdom or, in the case of an extra-territorial offence, in corresponding circumstances outside the United Kingdom.
j (2) In determining for the purposes of this section whether an offence against the law of a designated Commonwealth country falls within a description set out in the said Schedule 1, any special intent or state of mind or special circumstances of aggravation which may be necessary to constitute that offence under the law shall be disregarded.
(3) The descriptions set out in the said Schedule 1 include in each case offences of

attempting or conspiring to commit, of assisting, counselling or procuring the
commission of or being accessory before or after the fact to the offences therein
described, and of impeding the apprehension or prosecution of persons guilty of
those offences.

(4) References in this section to the law of any country (including the United
Kingdom) include references to the law of any part of that country.'

Section 3(1)(a) and (b) and (2) of the Act correspond to cl 2 of the scheme. The schedule
to the Act is identical to Annex 1(A) of the scheme and s 3(3) of the Act to Annex 1(B) of
the scheme. Section 3(1)(c) enacts the double-criminality rule contained in cl 10 of the
scheme.

This introduction brings me to the short point of construction raised by this appeal.
For convenience I set out again s 3(1)(c):

> 'in any case, the act or omission constituting the offence, or the equivalent act or
> omission, would constitute an offence against the law of the United Kingdom if it
> took place within the United Kingdom or, in the case of an extra-territorial offence,
> in corresponding circumstances outside the United Kingdom.'

The question is what is meant by the words 'the act or omission constituting the offence'.
Do these words refer to the conduct of the accused so that s 3(1)(c) is satisfied if what he
did would constitute a crime if committed in this country? Or do the words refer to the
ingredients of the Canadian offence, so that s 3(1)(c) is only satisfied if the definition of
the offence in the Canadian Criminal Code contains all the ingredients in the definition
of a corresponding English offence? The Divisional Court would have adopted the
former construction but reluctantly felt constrained by the decision of the Divisional
Court in R v Governor of Pentonville Prison, ex p Myers (6 December 1972, unreported) to
adopt the latter construction, with the result that the man against whom there is evidence
that he committed 69 offences of dishonesty for which he could be tried in this country
cannot be tried in Canada on any of them.

I have no hesitation in construing the words 'act or omission constituting the offence'
as a reference to the conduct of the accused. I cannot reconcile the alternative construction
with s 3(1)(a), which by its language shows that what is required is broad similarity, not
exact correspondence, of offence, a factor emphasised by s 3(2), which directs that
questions of special intent or state of mind or aggravating circumstances shall be
disregarded when considering whether an offence in a Commonwealth country is within
a description of crime contained in Sch 1. To adopt the alternative construction is to look
for exact correspondence between the definition of the crimes in the two countries and
no scheme of extradition based on such a premise will ever be workable, as has been
recognised since the early days of the operation of extradition laws.

We should, so far as we are able, construe this Act to give effect to the Commonwealth
scheme on which it was founded. The double-criminality rule in cl 10 of the scheme is
clear enough: a fugitive is not to be returned if 'the facts on which the request for his
return is grounded do not constitute an offence' in this country. The facts can only be a
reference to the facts established by evidence which comprise the conduct of the accused.
If the evidence is that the accused has committed crimes which are in the broad
description contained in Sch 1 (and in this case it is not disputed that that is so), I can see
no injustice in returning him to Canada if what he is alleged to have done would also
have been criminal in this country, which is also not disputed in this case. This was the
intention of the scheme and I can see no reason why Parliament should not have wished
to implement it.

I can find no support in the authorities to which the Divisional Court referred for the
construction that the Divisional Court felt compelled to place on s 3(1)(c). As I understand
its judgment, the Divisional Court held that the court should look at the Canadian
offence as framed in the Canadian code and that, if that offence lacked any ingredient of

the corresponding English offence, then the fugitive could not be extradited regardless
of the fact that the particulars of the charge revealed conduct that constituted the English
offence. This the Divisional Court believed to be the effect of *R v Governor of Brixton
Prison, ex p Gardner* [1968] 1 All ER 636, [1968] 2 QB 399 and *R v Governor of Pentonville
Prison, ex p Myers*. But as I read these authorities they were concerned not with the
construction of s 3(1)(c) but with the way in which the particulars of the offence should
be established for the purposes of the committal proceedings. It is axiomatic that a person
charged with a crime is entitled to know not only the offence with which he is charged,
be it a statutory or common law crime, but also to have particulars of the conduct which
it is alleged constituted the offence. The difficulty that confronted the New Zealand
government in *Ex p Gardner* was that the only particulars of the offence for which
extradition was requested were those contained in the New Zealand warrant attached to
the authority to proceed, and, that they alleged a false pretence as to a future event, which
is not a crime under English law. It was therefore clear that it was the intention of the
New Zealand government to prosecute the accused for conduct which did not amount to
a crime in this country. This offended against the double-criminality rule and it was for
this reason that extradition was refused. There was no discussion of alternate constructions
of s 3(1)(c) and the case appears to me to have proceeded on the assumption that s 3(1)(c)
required the courts to examine the conduct alleged against the accused.

In *Ex p Myers* the court faced the same problems, in that the only particulars of the
offence were those contained in the Canadian warrant and that from the wording of the
Canadian charge it appeared that it might be the intention to prosecute the accused in
Canada for conduct that would not be criminal in this country. Again, there is no
discussion of alternate constructions of s 3(1)(c). Lord Widgery CJ said:

> 'The problem as it seems to me throughout this case has been: how is one to
> identify the act or omission constituting the offence charged against the law of
> Canada . . .?'

There then follows a long discussion of the construction that should be put on the
wording of the charge, ie the particulars of the offence. This is, of course, necessary if
one is attempting to discover the conduct alleged against the accused but is wholly
unnecessary if one is comparing the definitions of the Canadian and English crimes. I
read this authority as proceeding on the construction of s 3(1)(c) preferred by the
Divisional Court and not, as it thought, as support for the alternative constructive it felt
compelled to adopt.

In *Ex p Gardner* Edmund Davies LJ recognised that it might in some cases be necessary
to look at the evidence in the depositions to determine whether the particulars disclosed
a relevant offence. Despite the difficulties of construction with which the court was faced
in *Ex p Myers* Lord Widgery CJ decided not to look at the evidence as an aid to the
construction of the charge in the Canadian warrant. In my view if any difficulty arises in
determining 'the acts or omissions' on which the requesting country relies the magistrate
should look at the evidence in the depositions and, if necessary, allow amendment to the
particulars in the charge to make it quite clear that he is committing on a relevant
offence, ie one that would be a criminal offence in this country. If, of course, the
depositions show that the acts or omissions would not constitute criminal behaviour in
this country, the magistrate will not commit on that charge.

There was some discussion before your Lordships about whether the magistrate
commits for the Canadian or the English offence. In my view neither formulation is
correct. The magistrate commits if he is satisfied that the authority to proceed discloses a
relevant offence and that the evidence discloses a prima facie case: see s 7(5)(a). It is
important that the warrant of committal should contain clear particulars of each relevant
offence to ensure that the accused will only be tried in the requesting country for a
criminal offence founded on the acts or omissions identified in the particulars, in order
to comply with the requirements of s 4(3):

'A person shall not be returned under this Act to any country, or committed to or *a*
kept in custody for the purposes of such return, unless provision is made by the law
of that country, or by an arrangement made with that country, for securing that he
will not, unless he has first been restored or had an opportunity of returning to the
United Kingdom, be dealt with in that country for or in respect of any offence
committed before his return under this Act other than—(a) the offence in respect of
which his return under this Act is requested; (b) any lesser offence proved by the
facts proved before the court of committal; and (c) any other offence being a relevant *b*
offence in respect of which the Secretary of State may consent to his being so dealt
with.'

I read 'offence' in this subsection as a reference to the offence as particularised in the
magistrate's warrant of committal, and this protects the accused from trial for any alleged
criminal action other than that for which he has been returned.

It was submitted that this construction of s 3(1)(c) would lead to difficulty when a *c*
request was made for the return of a prisoner who had escaped after conviction because
of the difficulty of knowing on what finding of fact a jury might have convicted him. I
believe that in the vast majority of cases there would be no difficulty in showing whether
or not the crime for which the accused was convicted was founded on facts that constitute
an English crime. I can conceive of the very rare case where there might be some doubt *d*
on which of two alternate bases a jury convicted where one view of the facts showed the
commission of a crime under English law and the other did not. I accept that in such a
case the accused could not be returned to finish his sentence. I believe such a situation to
be more hypothetical than real, and one hopes that not many requests for return will be
necessary because the authorities in the requesting country have allowed the prisoner to
escape: by far the most common situation is a request for the return of a ciminal who has *e*
fled the country before arrest. I prefer to accept the very limited difficulty that may arise
in such cases to the alternative of adopting a construction of the Act that will make it
nigh unworkable.

I would allow the appeal and restore the order of the magistrate.

**LORD JAUNCEY OF TULLICHETTLE.** My Lords, I have had the advantage of *f*
reading in draft the speech of my noble and learned friend Lord Griffiths. Subject to one
minor qualification, to which I shall refer later, I entirely agree with his reasoning and
conclusion and I, also, would allow the appeal. I only wish to add a few observations of
my own to those of my noble and learned friend.

I, too, have no hesitation in construing the words 'act or omission constituting the
offence' as a reference to the conduct of the accused. An offence against the law of a *g*
designated Commonwealth country is a relevant offence for the purposes of the Fugitive
Offenders Act 1967 if it satisfies the requirements of paras (a) and (c) of s 3(1). Paragraph
(a) refers to 'an offence' and requires that such offence falls within any of the descriptions
set out in Sch 1. It requires not identity of offence but rather broad similarity, no doubt
recognising that conduct of a similar type will not necessarily be given an identical label
in every Commonwealth country. Paragraph (c), on the other hand, refers to 'the act or *h*
omission constituting the offence', which words it is reasonable to assume were intended
to have a different meaning to 'the offence' or 'an offence'. If those words were intended
to refer to such conduct as would in the law of the designated Commonwealth country
constitute an offence without regard to the actual conduct of the accused it would be a
pointless exercise first to bring the Commonwealth offence under the broad umbrella of
similarity in para (a) and then go on to see whether it was also covered by the parasol of *j*
identity of ingredients in para(c). Such a result could have been achieved by one
paragraph which provided that an offence was a relevant offence if the ingredients
required to constitute it in the designated Commonwealth country also constituted an
offence in the United Kingdom. The fact that the two paragraphs rather than one were

included in the subsection suggests, almost irresistibly, that Parliament intended that the
a second paragraph should apply to the actual conduct of the accused and not to the
ingredients required by the law of the designated Commonwealth country to constitute
the offence. In the Divisional Court Bingham LJ said that if the matter were free from
authority he would have concluded—

b
'that the task of an English court of committal in determining whether an offence
was a relevant offence under s 3 was: (a) to determine whether or not the designated
Commonwealth country offence (with or without additional ingredients) fell within
any of the descriptions set out in the schedule; (b) to determine whether or not the
designated Commonwealth country offence was punishable under the law of the
designated Commonwealth country with 12 months' imprisonment or more; and
(c) to determine whether the accused person's conduct, relied on as constituting an
c
offence under the law of the designated Commonwealth country, would be criminal
in England if the conduct had occurred here. In performing task (c) I would expect
the court to review the evidence adduced by the designated Commonwealth country
in support of its application for the return of the accused person in order to decide
whether, and to what extent, the accused person's conduct disclosed in the evidence
would found criminal charges in England. I would therefore expect an inquiry into
d
the accused person's conduct and an analysis of it in terms of English criminal law,
not the comparison of legal definitions. If, of course, the designated Commonwealth
country and English crimes were identical the only inquiry (subject to s 3(1)(a)
would be as to the sufficiency of the evidence.'

I would indorse this approach to the application of s 3.
e      I turn to consider the authorities by which the Divisional Court considers itself to be
bound. *R v Governor of Brixton Prison, ex p Gardner* [1968] 1 All ER 636, [1968] 2 QB 399
did not, in my view, preclude the Divisional Court from adopting its preferred
construction of s 3. In that case it was apparent from the terms of the New Zealand
warrant that the offences with which the applicant was charged would not constitute
offences in English law. Lord Parker CJ said ([1968] 1 All ER 636 at 641, [1968] 2 QB
f 399 at 416):

'If one then looks at the offences set out and considers them in the light of
s. 3(1)(c), it seems to me perfectly clear that the acts complained of in the offences
with which the applicant was charged would not constitute offences under the law
of this country.'

g When the Lord Chief Justice used the words 'acts complained of' in that sentence, he
was, in my view, referring to the actual conduct relied on in the charges and not to the
ingredients required by the law of New Zealand to constitute the offences. In these
circumstances Lord Parker CJ found it unnecessary to consider further the details of the
case. However, Edmund Davies LJ, after rejecting a submission that s 7(5) obliged the
committing magistrates in every case to consider the contents of the depositions, said
h ([1968] 1 All ER 636 at 642, [1968] 2 QB 399 at 417):

'Such a task may, indeed, be necessary for the removal of doubts whether the
offence to which the authority relates is a relevant offence. If, however, as in the
present case, the other "evidence tendered in support of the request" makes it clear
that that offence is not a relevant offence, nothing contained in the depositions can
j
cure that fatal flaw, and their consideration therefore becomes otiose.'

*Ex p Gardner* did not decide, as a matter of principle and indeed did not require to decide,
that the act or omission constituting the offence in s 3(1)(c) must be determined solely by
reference to the ingredients required in the laws of the designated Commonwealth
country to constitute the offence.

Bingham LJ described the effect of the decision in *R v Governor of Pentonville Prison, ex p Myers* (6 December 1972, unreported) as being—

'that in deciding whether an offence is a relevant offence the court of committal should not look at the conduct alleged against the accused person and ask if that would be criminal if done here but should rather look at the charge formulated by the designated Commonwealth country under its own law and ask whether it would permit the accused person to be convicted here.'

In that case, as in the present case, the Divisional Court had to consider whether an offence charged under s 338(1) of the Criminal Code of Canada was a relevant offence for the purposes of s 3 of the 1967 Act. Lord Widgery CJ, after mentioning that s 338(1) was wider in scope than s 15 of the Theft Act 1968, said:

'... one really is driven to the conclusion that if this man is sent back to Canada to be tried on charge 1 of the authority to proceed, he may very well find himself faced with a charge within the scope of s 338, but outside the scope of s 15 of the Theft Act 1968. In other words, it seems to me that the act or omission constituting the offence, so far as that act or omission can be discovered in the terms of the charge, is too wide to satisfy s 3(1)(c). Whether that deficiency would be in any way made good by looking at the depositions, I do not feel disposed to say. For my part I think one ought to follow the *Gardner* principle here, and taking the view that I do, that on its face illuminated by the section of the Criminal Code to which I have referred, charge 1 does rely on acts or omissions as constituting the offence which acts or omissions one cannot positively say are within the scope of the English criminal law. It seems to me, therefore, that [leading counsel for the applicant] succeeds in regard to the first charge on that issue which has been the one which has given us the most difficulty.'

If I understand Lord Widgery CJ correctly, he was saying that, because Myers might ultimately be convicted in Canada under s 338(1) on facts which would not found a conviction in England under s 15 of the 1968 Act, the requirements of s 3(1)(c) were not satisfied. I do not find the reference to the *Gardner* principle easy to understand. If any principle is to be deduced from that case it can only be that where it appears ex facie of a Commonwealth warrant that the acts complained of in the offences charged would not constitute offences in England the requirements of s 3(1)(c) are not satisfied.

In *Ex p Myers*, however, the facts outlined by Lord Widgery CJ would almost certainly have constituted an offence under s 15 of the 1968 Act. The difficulty was created not by the character of the acts relied on by the Canadian authorities but by the terms of the relevant Canadian section. To such a situation I do not consider that *Ex p Gardner* has any application. I therefore conclude that Lord Widgery CJ was in error, both as to his understanding of what the *Gardner* principle was and also as to his application thereof to the case before him. It follows that *Ex p Myers* was wrongly decided. It is to this extent alone that I differ from the views expressed by my noble and learned friend Lord Griffiths.

**LORD LOWRY.** My Lords, this is an appeal on the part of the government of Canada and the governor of Her Majesty's Prison at Pentonville by leave of the Divisional Court of the Queen's Bench Division (Bingham LJ and Leggatt J) from an order made by that court on 20 December 1988 whereby it was ordered that a magistrate's order committing the respondent to prison under s 7 of the Fugitive Offenders Act 1967 in respect of 77 offences listed in a schedule to that order to await his return to Canada under the Act should be quashed in respect of 69 of those offences, on the ground that they were not 'relevant offences' within the meaning of s 3(1) of the Act. The Divisional Court at the same time ordered that the respondent should remain in custody in respect of the remaining eight offences pending a decision by the Secretary of State under s 9(1) of the

Act whether to return him to Canada or not, and no question arises as to those eight

*a* offences, which are admitted to be relevant offences.

In the case which is now before your Lordships the government of Canada, which is a designated Commonwealth country for the purposes of the Act, made a request to the Secretary of State for the return of the respondent to that country.

On 22 October 1987 a provisional warrant for the arrest of the respondent, who was then serving a prison sentence, was issued, and on 15 January 1988, having completed

*b* his sentence, he was arrested in Manchester. On 23 March 1988 the Secretary of State issued an authority to proceed which was addressed to the Chief Metropolitan Stipendiary Magistrate in the following terms:

'A request having been made to the Secretary of State on behalf of the Government of Canada for the return to that country of Richard Allen Aronson, also known as Richard Soderlind and Aaron Rubens, who is accused of the offences of obtaining

*c* property by deception, attempting to obtain property by deception, theft, forgery, using false instruments and having articles designed or adapted for making false instruments, as set out in the attached schedule: The Secretary of State hereby orders that a metropolitan stipendiary magistrate proceed with the case in accordance with the Fugitive Offenders Act 1967.'

*d* The schedule contained details of 78 offences said to have been committed in Canada, each in contravention of a specified section of the Criminal Code of Canada.

On 11 May 1988 a magistrate heard preliminary argument on the question whether the offences of which the respondent was accused were 'relevant offences' as defined by s 3(1) of the Act, the importance of that point being that, as provided by s 1, the liability to be returned to the requesting country affects only a person found in the United

*e* Kingdom who is accused of a *relevant offence* in that country. The magistrate ruled that the offences in the schedule to the authority to proceed were relevant offences, and on 1 and 2 August 1988 the Chief Metropolitan Stipendiary Magistrate heard evidence to determine whether there was sufficient evidence to commit the respondent. He held that there was such evidence, except in regard to the offence numbered 75 (about which no further argument arises), and issued a warrant of commitment in respect of the other

*f* 77 offences. The question now for your Lordships is whether the 69 offences in respect of which the Divisional Court (the members of which regarded themselves as bound by authority) quashed the magistrate's order are in point of law relevant offences or not. If they are, it is conceded by the respondent that the evidence for committal on each of them was sufficient. It is common ground that the answer depends on the true interpretation of s 3(1) of the Act, which reads as follows:

*g*

'For the purposes of this Act an offence of which a person is accused or has been convicted in a designated Commonwealth country or United Kingdom dependency is a relevant offence if—(a) in the case of an offence against the law of a designated Commonwealth country, it is an offence which, however described in that law, falls within any of the descriptions set out in Schedule 1 to this Act, and is punishable

*h* under that law with imprisonment for a term of twelve months or any greater punishment; (b) in the case of an offence against the law of a United Kingdom dependency, it is punishable under that law, on conviction by or before a superior court, with imprisonment for a term of twelve months or any greater punishment; and (c) in any case, the act or omission constituting the offence, or the equivalent act or omission, would constitute an offence against the law of the United Kingdom if

*j* it took place within the United Kingdom or, in the case of an extra-territorial offence, in corresponding circumstances outside the United Kingdom.'

This subsection will have to be considered in its statutory context and also against the historical background. I mention it now for the purpose of identifying the question which falls to be decided by your Lordships. What is meant by the words 'the act or

omission constituting the offence'? The government of Canada and the governor of Her
Majesty's Prison Pentonville (the appellants) contend that the words mean the criminal  *a*
conduct of the fugitive constituting an offence against the law of the United Kingdom,
as demonstrated by the evidence before the magistrate, even if the ingredients which go
to make up that criminal conduct do not always correspond with the ingredients of the
criminal conduct alleged in the Commonwealth country's warrant. The respondent, on
the other hand, says that 'the offence' means the offence of which the fugitive is accused
in the Commonwealth country and accordingly that 'the act or omission constituting the  *b*
offence' means the criminal conduct specifically alleged against him in the Commonwealth country's warrant. Thus, he argues, the magistrate cannot commit the fugitive
unless the Commonwealth offence charged against him would also constitute an offence
against the law of the United Kingdom *and* (by reference to s 7(5) of the Act) unless the
evidence before the magistrate would be sufficient to warrant the fugitive's trial for that
offence *if it had been committed* within the jurisdiction of the court.  *c*

I take as an illustration the facts of *R v Governor of Brixton Prison, ex p Gardner* [1968] 1
All ER 636, [1968] 2 QB 399, by which the Divisional Court, albeit with reluctance, felt
itself constrained to decide the present case in favour of the respondent. Warrants were
issued in New Zealand for the arrest of Gardner on charges which alleged that he had
obtained money by false pretences with regard to the future (an offence in New Zealand
but not one then recognised by English law). The Secretary of State issued an authority  *d*
to proceed which stated, inter alia, that Gardner was accused of offences of obtaining
money by false pretences. The magistrate considered the authority to proceed, found
that it related to offences of obtaining money by false pretences and, having read the
evidence in the form of New Zealand depositions, found a prima facie case of false
pretences as to the present, contrary to the law of the United Kingdom, and committed
the fugitive under s 7 to await his return to New Zealand. On the fugitive's application  *e*
for a writ of habeas corpus the Divisional Court (Lord Parker CJ, Edmund Davies LJ and
Widgery J) held that the words 'act or omission constituting the offence' meant the act or
omission constituting the offence of which the person was accused in the Commonwealth
country and that the Secretary of State's authority to proceed related to that offence, in
the instant case to the offences of which the fugitive was accused in New Zealand, as
disclosed in the warrants: accordingly, since the acts constituting those offences as so  *f*
disclosed would not, if they took place within the United Kingdom, constitute offences
against the law of the United Kingdom, the authority to proceed did not relate to 'relevant
offences'.

Before turning to the problem of construction, it will be helpful to look at the basis on
which, if *Ex p Gardner* is applied, the disputed 69 offences fall to be treated as not
relevant. Bingham LJ has precisely and clearly analysed this point in his judgment,  *g*
dividing the charges into six groups.

*Group 1* consists of 32 offences against s 338(1) of the Criminal Code of Canada, which
provides:

> 'Everyone who, by deceit, falsehood or other fraudulent means, whether or not it
> is a false pretence within the meaning of this Act, defrauds the public . . . is guilty  *h*
> of an indictable offence.'

As to this Bingham LJ observed:

> 'It is apparent that under this provision, contrary to the law here, a defendant
> could be convicted even if he had perpetrated no deception and in the absence of an
> intention to deprive the victim permanently of the goods or money obtained. Thus  *j*
> the Canadian offence not only has ingredients additional to those required here but
> lacks ingredients which the English criminal law treats as essential. If a conviction
> were obtained in this country on a charge so framed it would plainly have to be
> quashed. The same result must in my view follow so far as the committal on these

a
counts is concerned. It is pointed out that some of these charges, although not all, do allege false representations (as by giving false information or by passing worthless cheques) and that the facts show a clear intention premanently to deprive. The authorities to which I have referred in my view preclude us from giving effect to these submissions. The Canadian law would permit conviction even if no false representation and no intention to deprive permanently were established. The Canadian offence is one of "fraud", which here gives rise to no criminal liability of
b
itself in the absence of conspiracy. I fell bound to quash the committal on these counts.'

Group 2 consists of six offences under s 320(1) of the code, which provides:

'Everyone commits an offence who (a) by a false pretence . . . obtains anything in respect of which . . . theft may be committed . . .'

c
The Canadian offence, however, does not require proof of an intention permanently to deprive, which is an essential ingredient in England, and therefore the respondent could be convicted in Canada on facts which would not support a conviction in this jurisdiction.

Group 3 consists of 19 charges under s 326(1)(a) of the code, which provides:

'Everyone who, knowing that a document if forged, (a) uses, deals with, or acts
d
upon it . . . as if the document were genuine, is guilty of an indictable offence.'

But, to convict under s 3 of the Forgery and Counterfeiting Act 1981, it is necessary to prove that the defendant used the false instrument—

'with the intention of inducing somebody to accept it as genuine, and by reason of so accepting it to do or not to do some act to his own or any other person's
e
prejudice.'

These ingredients need not be alleged or proved in order to convict under the Canadian provision.

Group 4 consists of six offences under s 326(1)(b) of the code, which provides:

'Everyone who, knowing that a document is forged . . . (b) causes or attempts to
f
cause any person to use, deal with, or act upon it, as if the document were genuine, is guilty of an indictable offence.'

The Canadian offence does not require proof of an intention that the person induced to accept the document as genuine should do so to his own or another's prejudice, but this is an essential ingredient under English law.

g
Group 5 contains two charges under s 361(a) of the code, which provides:

'Everyone who fraudulently personates any person, living or dead, (a) with intent to gain advantage for himself or another . . . is guilty of an indictable offence.'

Here again it is clear that the Canadian offence does not require proof of the intention to cause prejudice needed by s 3 of the 1981 Act or the intention permanently to deprive
h
demanded by s 15 of the Theft Act 1968.

Group 6 consists of four offences under s 361(b) of the code, which provides:

'Everyone who fraudulently personates any person living or dead . . . (b) with intent to obtain any property or an interest in any property . . . is guilty of an indictable offence . . .'

j
But the Canadian offence does not require proof of the intent necessary under s 2 of the 1981 Act or the intention permanently to deprive needed by s 15 of the 1968 Act.

Before the 1967 Act came into force (on 1 September 1967) the return of fugitive offenders within Her Majesty's dominions was governed by the Fugitive Offenders Act 1881. I would draw your Lordships' attention to ss 2, 5 and 9:

'**2.** Where a person accused of having committed an offence (to which this part of this Act applies) in one part of Her Majesty's dominions has left that part, such *a* person (in this Act referred to as a fugitive from that part) if found in another part of Her Majesty's dominions, shall be liable to be apprehended and returned in manner provided by this Act to the part from which he is a fugitive. A fugitive may be so apprehended under an endorsed warrant or a provisional warrant.

**5.** A fugitive when apprehended shall be brought before a magistrate, who (subject to the provisions of this Act) shall hear the case in the same manner and *b* have the same jurisdiction and powers, as near as may be (including the power to remand and admit to bail), as if the fugitive were charged with an offence committed within his jurisdiction. If the endorsed warrant for the apprehension of the fugitive is duly authenticated, and such evidence is produced as (subject to the provisions of this Act) according to the law ordinarily administered by the magistrate, raises a strong or probable presumption that the fugitive committed the offence mentioned *c* in the warrant, and that the offence is one to which this Part of this Act applies, the magistrate shall commit the fugitive to prison to await his return, and shall forthwith send a certificate of the committal and such report of the case as he may think fit, if in the United Kingdom to a Secretary of State, and if in a British possession to the governor of that possession. Where the magistrate commits the fugitive to prison he shall inform the fugitive that he will not be surrendered until *d* after the expiration of fifteen days, and that he has a right to apply for a writ of habeas corpus, or other like process. A fugitive apprehended on a provisional warrant may be from time to time remanded for such reasonable time not exceeding seven days at any one time as under the circumstances seems requisite for the production of an endorsed warrant.

**9.** This Part of this Act shall apply to the following offences, namely, to treason *e* and piracy, and to every offence, whether called felony, misdemeanour, crime, or by any other name, which is for the time being punishable in the part of Her Majesty's dominions in which it was committed, either on indictment or information, by imprisonment with hard labour for a term of twelve months or more, or by any greater punishment; and for the purposes of this section, rigorous imprisonment, and any confinement in a prison combined with labour, by whatever *f* name it is called, shall be deemed to be imprisonment with hard labour. This Part of this Act shall apply to an offence notwithstanding that by the law of the part of Her Majesty's dominions in or on his way to which the fugitive is or is suspected of being it is not an offence, or not an offence to which this Part of this Act applies; and all the provisions of this Part of this Act, including those relating to a provisional warrant and to a committal to prison, shall be construed as if the offence were in *g* such last-mentioned part of Her Majesty's dominions an offence to which this Part of this Act applies.'

The magistrate's duty under s 5 was to decide whether the evidence raised a strong or probable presumption that the fugitive had committed the offence mentioned in the warrant, and by s 9 the Act applied to an offence notwithstanding that by the law of the *h* place where the fugitive was it was not an offence to which the Act applied; therefore in discharging his duty the magistrate was concerned only with the substantive criminal law of the place where the charge was laid and not with that of his own jurisdiction. This scheme contrasted with that of the Extradition Act 1870, as amended by the Extradition Act 1873, which governed and, as further amended, still governs the extradition of foreign criminals to a foreign state, where an arrangement has been made and an Order *j* in Council has applied the Act. Section 3 of the 1870 Act prohibits surrender if (1) the offence in respect of which surrender is demanded is of a political character or the purpose of the requisition is to try or punish the fugitive for such an offence or (2) the fugitive can be detained or tried for any offence other than the extradition crime proved by the facts on which the surrender is grounded. Section 10 (as amended by the Administration of Justice Act 1964, s 39(2) and Sch 3, para 9) provides:

'In the case of a fugitive criminal accused of an extradition crime, if the foreign warrant authorising the arrest of such criminal is duly authenticated, and such evidence is produced as (subject to the provisions of this Act) would, according to the law of England, justify the committal for trial of the prisoner if the crime of which he is accused had been committed in England, the police magistrate shall commit him to prison, but otherwise shall order him to be discharged. In the case of a fugitive criminal alleged to have been convicted of an extradition crime, if such evidence is produced as (subject to the provisions of this Act) would, according to the law of England, prove that the prisoner was convicted of such crime, the police magistrate shall commit him to prison, but otherwise shall order him to be discharged. If he commits such criminal to prison, he shall commit him, there to await the warrant of a Secretary of State for his surrender, and shall forthwith send to a Secretary of State a certificate of the committal, and such report upon the case as he may think fit.'

It deals with the extradition of persons convicted, as well as those accused, of an 'extradition crime', which is defined in s 26 as 'a crime which, if committed in England or within English jurisdiction, would be one of the crimes described in the first schedule to this Act'.

The legislation I have described formed the historical background to a meeting of Commonwealth law ministers which was held in London from 26 April to 3 May 1966 avowedly to review the arrangements for the extradition of fugitive offenders within the Commonwealth in the light of the constitutional changes which had taken place since the passing of the 1881 Act and at which a *Scheme relating to the Rendition of Fugitive Offenders within the Commonwealth* (Cmnd 3008) was formulated. The purpose was explained in the foreword:

'The Meeting considered that Commonwealth extradition arrangements should be based upon reciprocity and substantially uniform legislation incorporating certain features commonly found in extradition treaties, e.g. a list of returnable offences, the establishment of a *prima facie* case before return, and restrictions on the return of political offenders. The Meeting according formulated a Scheme setting out principles which could form the basis of legislation within the Commonwealth and recommended that effect shall be given to the Scheme in each Commonwealth country. The Scheme does not apply to Southern Rhodesia.'

The terms of the Act when passed clearly show that it was intended to follow very closely the principles of the scheme, as might indeed be expected of legislation giving effect to a scheme which represented an agreed recommendation. On the authority of *Black-Clawson International Ltd v Papierwerke Waldhof-Aschaffenburg AG* [1975] 1 All ER 810, [1975] AC 591 (recently applied in your Lordships' House in *A-G's Reference (No 1 of 1988)* [1989] 2 All ER 1 at 6, [1989] 2 WLR 729 at 734–735), it is permissible to look at circumstances preceding the legislation in order to see what was considered to be the mischief in need of a remedy and (I would add) the steps proposed to effectuate the remedy. I consider that the scheme is of more than usual assistance for this purpose and would refer in particular to the following paragraphs:

'*Returnable offences*
2.—(1) A fugitive will only be returned for a returnable offence.
(2) For the purposes of this Scheme a returnable offence is an offence described in Annex 1 (whatever the name of the offence under the law of the countries and territories concerned, and whether or not it is described in that law by reference to some special intent or any special circumstances of aggravation), being an offence

which is punishable by a competent court in the country or territory to which
return is requested by imprisonment for twelve months or a greater penalty.
                                                                              *a*

*Warrants, other than provisional warrants*
   3.—(1) A fugitive offender will only be returned if a warrant for his arrest has
been issued in that part of the Commonwealth to which his return is requested and
either—(*a*) that warrant is endorsed by a competent judicial authority in the part in
which he is found (in which case, the endorsed warrant will be sufficient authority
for his arrest), or (*b*) a further warrant for his arrest is issued by the competent *b*
judicial authority in the part in which he is found, not being a provisional warrant
issued as mentioned in clause 4 . . .

*Committal proceedings*
   5 . . . (4) Where a warrant has been endorsed or issued as mentioned in clause
3(1) the competent judicial authority may commit the fugitive to prison to await *c*
his return if—(*a*) such evidence is produced as establishes a *prima facie* case that he
committed the offence of which he is accused, and (*b*) his return is not precluded by
law, but, otherwise, will order him to be discharged . . .

*Double-criminality rule*
   10. The return of a fugitive offender will either be precluded by law or be subject
to refusal by the competent executive authority if the facts on which the request for *d*
his return is grounded do not constitute an offence under the law of the country or
territory in which he is found . . .

*Return of escaped prisoners*
   14.—(1) In the case of a person who—(*a*) has been convicted of a returnable
offence by a court in any part of the Commonwealth and is unlawfully at large *e*
before the expiry of his sentence for that offence, and (*b*) is found in some other part
of the Commonwealth, the provisions set out in this Scheme, as applied for the
purposes of this clause by paragraph (2), will govern his return to the part of the
Commonwealth in which he was convicted.
   (2) For the purposes of this clause this Scheme shall be construed, subject to any
necessary adaptations or modifications, as though the person unlawfully at large *f*
were accused of the offence of which he was convicted and, in particular—(*a*) any
reference to a fugitive offender shall be construed as including a reference to such a
person as is mentioned in paragraph (1), and (*b*) the reference in clause 5(4) to such
evidence as establishes a *prima facie* case that he committed the offence of which he
is accused shall be construed as a reference to such evidence as establishes that he has
been convicted.
                                                                              *g*
   (3) The references in this clause to a person unlawfully at large shall be construed
as including references to a person at large in breach of a condition of a licence to be
at large.'

   The Act, quite clearly, was intended to give effect to the scheme. Its most important
provisions for present purposes are ss 3, 4(3), 5, 6(1) and (2) and 7(5):          *h*

   3.—(1) For the purposes of this Act an offence of which a person is accused or has
been convicted in a designated Commonwealth country or United Kingdom
dependency is a relevant offence if—(*a*) in the case of an offence against the law of a
designated Commonwealth country, it is an offence which, however described in
that law, falls within any of the descriptions set out in Schedule 1 to this Act, and is
punishable under that law with imprisonment for a term of twelve months or any *j*
greater punishment; (*b*) in the case of an offence against the law of a United Kingdom
dependency, it is punishable under that law, on conviction by or before a superior
court, with imprisonment for a term of twelve months or any greater punishment;
and (*c*) in any case, the act or omission constituting the offence, or the equivalent act
or omission, would constitute an offence against the law of the United Kingdom if

it took place within the United Kingdom or, in the case of an extra-territorial offence, in corresponding circumstances outside the United Kingdom.

(2) In determining for the purposes of this section whether an offence against the law of a designated Commonwealth country falls within a description set out in the said Schedule 1, any special intent or state of mind or special circumstances of aggravation which may be necessary to constitute that offence under the law shall be disregarded.

(3) The descriptions set out in the said Schedule 1 include in each case offences of attempting or conspiring to commit, of assisting, counselling or procuring the commission of or being accessory before or after the fact to the offences therein described, and of impeding the apprehension or prosecution of persons guilty of those offences.

(4) References in this section to the law of any country (including the United Kingdom) include references to the law of any part of that country.

**4** . . . (3) A person shall not be returned under this Act to any country, or committed to or kept in custody for the purposes of such return, unless provision is made by the law of that country, or by an arrangement made with that country, for securing that he will not, unless he has first been restored or had an opportunity of returning to the United Kingdom, be dealt with in that country for or in respect of any offence committed before his return under this Act other than— (a) the offence in respect of which his return under this Act is requested; (b) any lesser offence proved by the facts proved before the court of committal; or (c) any other offence being a relevant offence in respect of which the Secretary of State may consent to his being so dealt with . . .

**5.**—(1) Subject to the provisions of this Act relating to provisional warrants, a person shall not be dealt with thereunder except in pursuance of an order of the Secretary of State (in this Act referred to as an authority to proceed), issued in pursuance of a request made to the Secretary of State by or on behalf of the Government of the designated Commonwealth country, or the Governor of the United Kingdom dependency, in which the person to be returned is accused or was convicted.

(2) There shall be furnished with any request made for the purposes of this section on behalf of any country—(a) in the case of a person accused of an offence, a warrant for his arrest issued in that country; (b) in the case of a person unlawfully at large after conviction of an offence, a certificate of the conviction and sentence in that country, and a statement of the amount if any of that sentence which has been served, together (in each case) with particulars of the person whose return is requested and of the facts upon which and the law under which he is accused or was convicted, and evidence sufficient to justify the issue of a warrant for his arrest under section 6 of this Act.

(3) On receipt of such a request the Secretary of State may issue an authority to proceed unless it appears to him that an order for the return of the person concerned could not lawfully be made, or would not in fact be made, in accordance with the provisions of this Act.

**6.**—(1) A warrant for the arrest of a person accused of a relevant offence, or alleged to be unlawfully at large after conviction of such an offence, may be issued— (a) on the receipt of an authority to proceed, by a metropolitan stipendiary magistrate or by sheriff principal or sheriff of Lothian and Borders; (b) without such an authority, by a metropolitan stipendiary magistrate or a justice of the peace in any part of the United Kingdom, upon information that the said person is or is believed to be in or on his way to the United Kingdom; and any warrant issued by virtue of paragraph (b) above is in this Act referred to as a provisional warrant.

(2) A warrant of arrest under this section may be issued upon such evidence as would, in the opinion of the magistrate or justice, authorise the issue of a warrant for the arrest of a person accused of committing a corresponding offence or, as the

case may be, of a person alleged to be unlawfully at large after conviction of an
offence, within the jurisdiction of the magistrate or justice ...

**7** ... (5) Where an authority to proceed has been issued in respect of the person
arrested and the court of committal is satisfied, after hearing any evidence tendered
in support of the request for the return of that person or on behalf of that person,
that the offence to which the authority relates is a relevant offence and is further
satisfied—(a) where that person is accused of the offence, that the evidence would
be sufficient to warrant his trial for that offence if it had been committed within the
jurisdiction of the court; (b) where that person is alleged to be unlawfully at large
after conviction of the offence, that he has been so convicted and appears to be so at
large, the court shall, unless his committal is prohibited by any other provision of
this Act, commit him to custody to await his return thereunder; but if the court is
not so satisfied or if the committal of that person is so prohibited, the court shall
discharge him from custody.'

I have said that the crucial provision is s 3(1), and in particular para (c); 'the offence' in
the phrase 'the act or omission constituting the offence' must be the offence (in the case
of a designated Commonwealth country) mentioned in para (a), that is the offence of
which the fugitive is accused in that country. This conclusion seems unavoidable when
one also has regard to ss 4(3)(a) (to which I will return) and 5(2) and to the opening words
of s 6(1). Similarly, in s 7(5) the offence to which the Secretary of State's authority to
proceed relates (as to which see s 5(3)) must be the offence of which the fugitive is accused
in the Commonwealth country because the court of committal needs to be 'satisfied ...
that the offence to which the authority relates is a relevant offence' (see s 3(1)) and—

'further satisfied—(a) where that person is *accused* of the offence, that the evidence
would be sufficient to warrant his trial *for that offence if it had been committed* within
the jurisdiction of the court; (b) where that person is alleged to be unlawfully at
large after conviction *of the offence*, that he has been so convicted and appears to be so
at large.'

The 'act or omission constituting the offence' cannot in my opinion mean 'the conduct,
as proved by evidence, on which the charge is grounded', because the evidence of such
conduct could prove something more than what has been charged. In such a case the
conduct proved would not be the act or omission constituting the offence of which the
fugitive is accused in the Commonwealth country; and that, if I may venture to remind
your Lordships, is the 'relevant offence', the offence described in s 3(1). For example, in
*R v Governor of Brixton Prison, ex p Gardner* [1968] 1 All ER 636, [1968] 1 QB 399 the act
constituting the offence of which the fugitive was accused was a false pretence as to the
future. Therefore it would not have helped the Crown to show the magistrate that
Gardner's conduct had also involved a false pretence as to the present. The words
'constituting the offence' must be read as 'constituting the offence of which the person is
accused'. If a further clue to the meaning of these words is needed, I suggest that it is
found in s 3(2). Again we are dealing with 'an offence against the law of a designated
Commonwealth country' and the subsection provides:

'... any special intent or state of mind or special circumstances of aggravation
which may be necessary to constitute that offence under the law shall be disregarded.'

The subsection contains the only express exception from the need to have regard to the
ingredients of the relevant Commonwealth offence and it also shows what is meant by
'constitute' and 'constituting'. One may paraphrase the effect of s 3(1)(c) by asking: 'what
is the essence of the Commonwealth offence? and would that be an offence against the
law of the United Kingdom? That is quite a different thing from looking at the course of
conduct revealed by the evidence and asking whether that conduct (as distinct from the
conduct of which the person is accused) would constitute an offence against the law of
the United Kingdom.

*a*    Contrary to what was submitted in argument, I see no difficulty in the use of the word 'necessary' in s 3(2). The difference in language between that subsection and s 3(1)(c) arises because in the latter the situation is actual and s 3(2) is dealing with a requirement. The word 'necessary' does not alter the meaning of the word 'constitute'.

   While the singular includes the plural, in speaking of 'the act or omission' one is not describing a course of conduct; one is speaking of the essential ingredients of an offence. This is not the same thing as the facts relied on to prove the offence, but, even on this
*b*    basis, one must deal with what proves the Commonwealth offence and not with the evidence generally from which one might deduce the commission of an English offence. The question must be: if the accused person did in England what it is alleged he did in Canada, would the evidence be sufficient to warrant his trial in England for that offence?

   The forms authorised for use in connection with extradition are found in Sch 2 to the 1870 Act. Those for use in connection with the return of fugitive offenders are contained
*c*    in the schedule to the Fugitive Offenders (Forms) Regulations 1967, SI 1967/1257, which came into operation on the same day as the Act. Having regard to what was said in *Hanlon v Law Society* [1980] 2 All ER 199 at 218–219, [1981] AC 124 at 193–194, it may be permissible to derive some slight assistance from the latter, although they are not part of the Act. Form 2, the warrant of arrest under s 6(1)(a), recites that the magistrate has received from the Secretary of State an order to proceed and that there is evidence that
*d*    the offence is a relevant offence as defined in s 3 and contains the following further recital:

> 'And there being in my opinion such evidence as would justify the issue of a warrant for the arrest of a person accused of committing [a] corresponding offence[s] ...'

*e*
The words 'corresponding offence' reflect the same words in s 6(2). I refer also to Form 4, the warrant of commitment under s 7(5), which contains a recital that the magistrate is satisfied—

> 'that the following offence[s] [of which the defendant is accused in               ],
> namely            , being [an] offence[s] to which the authority to proceed relates,
*f*    is/are [a] relevant offence[s] as defined in section 3 of that Act . . .'

These forms are also adapted for use in conviction cases.

   The continual reference to 'relevant offences' ensures that the magistrate's attention is directed to the requirements of s 3 and contrasts with the wording of the forms under the 1870 Act.

*g*    Section 5(2) is important not merely as an aid for the interpretation of the word 'offence'. The warrant issued in the Commonwealth country must be accompanied by particulars of the person whose return is requested and of the facts on which and the law under which he is accused or was convicted *and* evidence sufficient to justify the issue of a warrant for his arrest under s 6. It can be seen from this subsection that, in contrast to the treaty list of offences for the purpose of the 1870 Act (Sch 1), the description of the
*h*    relevant offence required by s 5(2) must be specific as to the Commonwealth law as well as the facts. And, although the Act is silent on this point, it seems clear to me that the Secretary of State, when issuing an authority to proceed, must give the magistrate enough information to decide whether the Commonwealth offence is a relevant offence and whether there is enough evidence to commit for trial on the Commonwealth offence in accordance with s 7(5)(a).

*j*    To return the fugitive on the Commonwealth charge involves the magistrate in finding a prima facie case on that charge, just as was required under s 9 of the 1881 Act, with the added requirement of double criminality that the evidence would be sufficient to warrant the fugitive's trial for that offence if it had been committed within the jurisdiction of the court (see s 7(5)). Therefore, knowledge of the constituent elements of the relevant offence is requisite.

I would further suggest that consideration of the case of a person unlawfully at large after conviction of an offence provides a strong argument for the narrower and more definite construction of s 3(1)(c). The court is not there dealing with prima facie evidence of a United Kingdom offence, but is asking whether a person convicted of a Commonwealth offence has been convicted of a *relevant* offence. Assuming that the act or omission constituting that offence would not constitute an offence in the United Kingdom, it would be pointless to rake over the evidence given at the trial, assuming that this was practicable, in order to find material which, if proved, would constitute an offence against the law of the United Kingdom. It would be impossible to amend the particulars of the Commonwealth offence of which the fugitive had been convicted or to predicate what facts the jury had found against the accused beyond the facts necessary to convict him of the Commonwealth offence with which he had been charged. There will, of course, be many cases, no doubt the vast majority, in which the difficulty which I have mentioned will not arise; but I am of the opinion that the probable rarity of the situation which I envisage (and to which no ready solution was presented in argument) does not justify a construction of the words 'relevant offence' which could be applied successfully to accusation cases but which admittedly could not be applied to a proportion of conviction cases which may have involved Commonwealth offences of exactly the same kind.

The mention of double criminality brings me back to the ministers' scheme of 1966 which, I may say, appeared to be quite strongly relied on by the appellants on the ground, as they contended, that it replaced the 1881 Act criterion by a test in conformity with the 1870 Act, as explained in *Government of Denmark v Nielsen* [1984] 2 All ER 81, [1984] AC 606. Clause 2 of the scheme dealt with 'returnable offences' and was reflected by ss 1 and 3(1)(a) and (b) and (2) of the Act. Clause 5(4), in which I draw attention to the words 'the offence of which he is accused', is reflected in s 7(5), and cl 10, headed 'Double-criminality rule', is reflected in s 3(1)(c). I would particularly stress in this paragraph the words:

'if the facts *on which the request for this return is grounded* do not constitute an offence under the law of the country or territory in which he is found.'

Clause 14 of the scheme also repays study. It is reflected in the provisions of the Act which deal with the return of convicted persons.

In my opinion the words to which I have drawn special attention in cll 5(4) and 10 of the scheme serve to emphasise that ss 3(1)(c) and 7(5) (which must be intended to give effect to those clauses) have the meaning which I have ascribed to them. They have nothing in common with the scheme of the 1870 Act and they require the magistrate to ask himself whether the evidence before him is sufficient to warrant the fugitive's trial in the United Kingdom for what he is *alleged* by the requesting country to have done wrong and not just for what he appears to have done wrong according to the English law.

The question of double criminality is discussed in an instructive judgment by Griffiths J in *R v Governor of Pentonville Prison, ex p Budlong* [1980] 1 All ER 701, [1980] 1 WLR 1110, an 1870 Act case, but before coming to it I must go back to *R v Governor of Brixton Prison, ex p Gardner* [1968] 1 All ER 636, [1968] 2 QB 399, the main authority against the appellants.

In that case the particulars in the New Zealand warrants, which were before the magistrate, described the false pretences as representations concerning the future, and the point taken on behalf of the fugitive was that the charges did not disclose an offence known to English law. Lord Parker CJ said ([1968] 1 All ER 636 at 639, [1968] 2 QB 399 at 412):

'... this provision is going further than the similar provisions in the Extradition Act, 1870, and is providing that to be a relevant offence not only must the offence a      fall within the general description of the words in Sch. 1, but also the act or omission constituting the offence must constitute an offence against the law of the United Kingdom.'

The Lord Chief Justice then referred to the relevant provisions of the Act and to the arguments on either side. He then continued ([1968] 1 All ER 636 at 641, [1968] 2 QB 399 at 415–416):

b          'In my judgment, counsel for the New Zealand government's arguments gives really no effect to the provisions of s. 3(1)(c). It seems to me that what is clearly contemplated here is that a request coming forward to the Secretary of State must set out in some form, and no doubt the most usual form is the warrant or warrants for arrest, the offence or offences of which the fugitive is accused, in this case in New Zealand. Not only must it supply a general description which will fulfil the

c      provisions of s. 3(1)(a), but it must condescend to sufficient detail to enable the matter to be considered under s. 3(1)(c). Similarly, as it seems to me, it is contemplated that the Secretary of State, in giving his authority to proceed under s. 5(1), should again set out the offences to which his authority is to relate in sufficient detail for the matter to be considered again not only under para. (a) but also under para. (c) of s. 3(1) ... It seems to me, however, perfectly plain that this

d      authority to proceed, albeit in general terms, must be taken as relating to the offences of which this applicant was accused in New Zealand, and on which the request was made for his return. That being so, one asks oneself: what were the offences of which the applicant was accused in New Zealand? In the absence of any indication in the authority to proceed, it seems to me that one must assume what is only natural in these cases, that the offences of which he was accused in New Zealand

e      were those set out in the warrants which accompanied the request to the Secretary of State. If one then looks at the offences and considers them in the light of s. 3(1)(c), it seems to me perfectly clear that the acts complained of in the offences with which the applicant was charged would not constitute offences under the law of this country.'

f   Edmund Davies LJ referred to s 3(1)(c) and said ([1968] 1 All ER 636 at 642, [1968] 2 QB 399 at 416–417):

          '"The offence" there referred to must mean the offence charged in New Zealand, and "the act or omission" refers to the manner or means whereby the offence so charged in New Zealand was committed. This involves examination of the particulars of the offence charged in New Zealand, and in the present case that

g      examination in turn necessitates consideration of the New Zealand warrants. It is conceded that those warrants particularise the offences laid in words which, were they incorporated in an information or indictment in this country, would allege no contravention of our criminal law. Section 7(5) requires to be demonstrated that the offence to which the authority to proceed relates is a relevant offence, and it is true that for that purpose the court of committal has to consider "any evidence tendered

h      in support of the request for the return" of the arrested person. As at present advised, however, I do not accept the submission of counsel for the New Zealand government that this obliges the committing magistrate in every case to consider the contents of the depositions. Such a task may, indeed, be necessary for the removal of doubts whether the offence to which the authority relates is a relevant offence. If, however, as in the present case, the other "evidence tendered in support of the request" makes

j      it clear that that offence is not a relevant offence, nothing contained in the depositions can cure that fatal flaw, and their consideration, therefore, becomes otiose.'

*Ex p Gardner* does not appear to say that a magistrate would never be justified in

committing a fugitive under s 7(5)(a) to face trial on a New Zealand charge of false
pretences just because a person *could* be convicted under New Zealand law by reason of a
false pretence as to the future, whereas it would in 1968 have required proof of a false
pretence as to the present in order to justify conviction in England. It concentrates
attention on what is charged in the warrant. I conceive that, if the particulars of the
offence given in or annexed to the warrant had alleged a false pretence as to the present,
the magistrate could then properly have committed the fugitive to await his return to
New Zealand, since the charge specified in the warrant and the particulars given therein
or annexed thereto constitute the offence in respect of which the fugitive's return is
requested. By virtue of s 4(3), the fugitive would be protected against the risk of being
convicted after his return by virtue of a false pretence as to the future. If this were not so,
the particulars could be altered in any case after the fugitive's return, perhaps to allege
the murder of a different victim on a different date and at a different place from those
originally alleged.

In *R v Governor of Pentonville Prison, ex p Myers* (6 December 1972 unreported) the
fugitive was accused in Canada of having advertised a bogus electrical slimming
treatment. The actual charges were 'obtaining property by deception and conspiracy to
obtain property by deception, as set out in the attached schedule'. The offence, like the
32 offences in group 1 in the present case, was laid under s 338(1) of the Criminal Code
of Canada. In the course of his judgment Lord Widgery CJ said:

'Now one comes to the difficulty. The problem as it seems to me throughout this
case has been: how is one to identify *the act or omission constituting the offence charged
against the law of Canada*, because . . . only if the act or omission constituting that
offence is itself a criminal offence in England does the offence become a relevant
offence under s 3.' (My emphasis.)

After referring to *Ex p Gardner*, he continued:

'Much of the difficulty in this case, I feel bound to say, is that the first charge has
been drafted in a form which is wholly foreign to English practice. Of course, the
Canadian government and those responsible for the administration of [the] criminal
law in Canada obviously have their own rules about these matters, but if they seek
to obtain the return of a fugitive from England under the 1967 Act, it seems to me
that the first duty on them in practice is to see that their charge is framed in a
manner which would suit not only the laws of Canada but also is susceptible of
being looked at by an English lawyer to see what is the act or omission on which it
is based.'

This passage appears to give countenance to my observation that the particulars of the
false pretences charge in *Ex p Gardner* might have been framed so as to satisfy s 3(1)(c),
but in the case now before your Lordships the situation is different. As appears from the
analysis of Bingham LJ, the substance of all 69 charges, however one expresses the
particulars, lacks a vital element without which s 3(1)(c) cannot be satisfied. With regard
to the offences in group 1, it would be of no avail to allege a false pretence, if that course
were warranted by the evidence, since the intention permanently to deprive would be
missing in any event.

Bingham LJ commented on *Ex p Myers* as follows:

'The effect of this decision is, I think inescapably, that in deciding whether an
offence is a relevant offence the court of committal should not look at the conduct
alleged against the arrested person and ask if that would be criminal if done here,
but should rather look at the charge formulated by the designated Commonwealth
country under its own law and ask whether it would permit the arrested person to
be convicted here. The facts outlined by Lord Widgery CJ would, I think without
doubt, have supported a conviction under s 15 of the Theft Act 1968 [for obtaining
by deception]; but the committal was quashed.'

As to this, I must point out that there was no means of alleging in the Canadian charge
a   under s 338(1) an intention permanently to deprive.

On the construction of s 3(1)(c) I think it is also worth noting that in *Tarling v
Government of the Republic of Singapore* (1979) 70 Cr App R 77 at 111 Lord Wilbeforce,
while making it clear (at 110) that his observation would be obiter, said:

> 'None of this, in my opinion, amounts to a case of the convoluted conspiracy to
b   defraud which is alleged and (see again GOVERNOR OF BRIXTON, *ex parte* GARDNER) it
> is not possible for the Government of Singapore to go outside the particulars of the
> alleged offence which, as it is required to do, it provided; and which were included
> in the authority to proceed.'

I have referred to *R v Governor of Pentonville Prison, ex p Budlong* [1980] 1 All ER 701,
[1980] 1 WLR 1110 in connection with double criminality. But I would first note that
c   in that case the applicants for habeas corpus had tried to rely on *Ex p Gardner* and *Ex p
Myers*. Griffiths J commented ([1980] 1 All ER 701 at 708, [1980] 1 WLR 1110 at 1117):

> 'I can see no reason why these decisions should be applied to proceedings under
> the 1870 Act. They turn on the construction of the Fugitive Offenders Act 1967,
> the shape and provisions of which are not in any way on all fours with the 1870 Act.
d   However, the applicants submit that because art III of the treaty [the United States
> of America (Extradition) Order 1976, SI 1976/2144] requires similar information to
> be submitted to the Secretary of State by the country requesting extradition to that
> required to be submitted by a Commonwealth country under s 3 of the 1967 Act, it
> follows that the Secretary of State's order under the 1870 Act shall contain the same
> particulars as, pursuant to *Gardner's* case, are required to be set out in the authority
e   to proceed under the 1967 Act. I cannot see why that result should necessarily
> follow, but the conclusive answer to the submission is to be found in the terms of
> s 20 of the 1870 Act which expressly provides that the order shall be valid if it
> follows the form prescribed in Sch 2, which form does not require the order to do
> other than state the general description of the crime for which extradition is asked.'

f   I most respectfully agree with those observations of Griffiths J. He then observed
([1980] 1 All ER 701 at 708, [1980] 1 WLR 1110 at 1118):

> 'Because, in my view, the *Gardner* and *Myers* cases do not support the applicants'
> argument, it is not necessary to consider if they were correctly decided. But I would
> not wish anything I have said to be taken as expressing my own endorsement of the
> decisions. It seems to me that they lead to the surprising conclusion that the success
g   or failure of a Commonwealth country to extradite a criminal who has offended
> against their laws may depend on the drafting of particulars in a document, namely,
> the authority to proceed, for which they are not responsible.'

As to that point, I would venture to suggest, having regard to what Lord Widgery CJ
said in *Ex p Myers*, that the relevant drafting of particulars of the offence ought to be that
h   undertaken by the Commonwealth country's lawyers when preparing their own warrant
for dispatch under s 5(2).

The principle of double criminality is instructively discussed (see 1980] 1 All ER 701
at 708–712, [1980] 1 WLR 1110 at 1118–1123). What is said to be required is not
identity of definition but correspondence of substance. It was pointed out that the law of
extradition depends not on any common law principles but on statute, and I would take
j   the opportunity of emphasising the differences between the 1967 Act and the 1870 Act
(see [1980] 1 All ER 701 at 709, [1980] 1 WLR 1110 at 1118). There is a reference to '*the
actual facts of the offence* which are all important rather than the definition of the crime in
the foreign law' (see [1980] 1 All ER 701 at 710, [1980] 1 WLR 1110 at 1120; my
emphasis). I would adapt this phrase to a fugitive offender situation by substituting the
words 'the actual facts of the offence charged in the Commonwealth country'. The

discussion concluded thus ([1980] 1 All ER 701 at 712, [1980] 1 WLR 1110 at 1122–1123):

> 'I therefore summarise by saying that double criminality in our law of extradition is satisfied if it is shown: (1) that the crime for which extradition is demanded would be recognised as substantially similar in both countries, and (2) that there is a prima facie case that the conduct of the accused amounted to the commission of the crime according to English law.'

Again I would adopt this statement but, in view of s 3(1)(c), would substitute for 'the conduct of the accused' in (2) the words 'the offence of which the person is accused in the Commonwealth country'.

My Lords, there is just one further case I must consider. That is *Nielsen v Government of Denmark* [1984] 2 All ER 81, [1984] AC 606. Just as the applicants in *Ex p Budlong* wrongly (and in vain) relied on *Ex p Gardner* and *Ex p Myers*, so the appellants here seem to me to have represented to your Lordships the paramount position of *Nielsen's* case, not only in relation to extradition, concerning which it is of course the leading authority, but also in regard to the return of fugitive offenders. I need not trouble your Lordships with the facts. For present purposes the importance of the case lies in the emphatic statement by Lord Diplock (affirming the judgment of Robert Goff LJ in the Divisional Court: see (1983) 79 Cr App R 1 at 10–11) that the committing magistrate is concerned only with the law of his own jurisdiction and not with that of the foreign state, even to the limited extent which might theretofore have been inferred from such cases as *Re Bellencontre* [1891] 2 QB 122, *Re Arton (No 2)* [1896] 1 QB 509 and *Ex p Budlong*. He pointed out that 'the crime of which he is accused' in s 10 of the 1870 Act means the crime specified in the Secretary of State's order to the magistrate. He continued ([1984] 2 All ER 81 at 87, [1984] AC 606 at 619):

> 'Under the principal treaty, the documents accompanying the requisition for the surrender of a fugitive criminal in an accusation case will state the "acts" on account of which the fugitive is demanded by the Danish government. It is for the Secretary of State to make up his mind what crime those acts would have amounted to according to the English law in force at the time they were committed if they had been committed in England.'

Lord Diplock said ([1984] 2 All ER 81 at 91, [1984] AC 606 at 624–625):

> 'At the hearing, ss 9 and 10 [of the 1870 Act] require that the magistrate must first be satisfied that a foreign warrant (within the definition in s 26 that I have already cited) has been issued for the accused person's arrest and is duly authenticated in a manner for which s 15 provides. Except where there is a claim that the arrest was for a political offence or the case is an exceptional accusation case, the magistrate is not concerned with what provision of foreign criminal law (if any) is stated in the warrant to be the offence which the person was suspected of having committed and in respect of which his arrest was ordered in the foreign state. The magistrate must then hear such evidence, including evidence made admissible by ss 14 and 15, as may be produced on behalf of the requisitioning foreign government, and by the accused if he wishes to do so; and at the conclusion of the evidence the magistrate must decide whether such evidence would, *according to the law of England*, justify the committal for trial of the accused for an offence that is described in the 1870 list (as added to or amended by subsequent Extradition Acts) provided that such offence is also included in the extraditable crimes listed in the English language version of the extradition treaty. In making this decision it is English law alone that is relevant. The requirement that he shall make it does not give him any jurisdiction to inquire into or receive evidence of the substantive criminal law of the foreign state in which the conduct was in fact committed.' (Lord Diplock's emphasis.)

a
My Lords, I hope I have said enough to show that, according to the wording of ss 3(1)(c), 5(2) and 7(5) of the 1976 Act, such an approach could not validly be adopted in a fugitive offender's case.

Another contrast with the procedure under s 5(2) of the 1976 Act is that in an 1870 Act case the treaty with the foreign state does not require the warrant of arrest to specify the particular provision of that state's criminal code which is alleged to have been infringed (see Nielsen's case [1984] 2 All ER 81 at 86, [1984] AC 606 at 618). The

b
accusation is general and not specific.

The 1966 scheme was formulated against a long-standing background of concern with the foreign state's law based on the practice followed in Re Bellencontre and Re Arton (No 2), which seems to me to reinforce the interpretation of the 1976 Act which I prefer. Moreover, one of the objects of the scheme was reciprocity, which must be easier to achieve if a specific, as distinct from a general, approach to the Commonwealth offence

c
is adopted.

I come back to the judgment appealed from. Bingham LJ said:

d
'Section 3(1)(c) is intended to ensure that an arrested person (AP) will not be returned to a designated Commonwealth country (DCC) if *the conduct of which he is accused* would not have been an offence against the law of England if it had taken place here ... Were the matter free from authority I should conclude that the task of an English court of committal in determining whether an offence was a relevant offence under s 3 was: (a) to determine whether or not the DCC offence (with or without additional ingredients) fell within any of the descriptions set out in [Sch 1]; (b) to determine whether or not the DCC offence was punishable under the law of the DCC with 12 months' imprisonment or more; and (c) to determine whether the

e
AP's conduct, relied on as constituting an offence under the law of the DCC, would be criminal if the conduct had occurred here. In performing task (c) I would expect the court to review the evidence adduced by the DCC in support of its application for the return of the AP in order to decide whether, and to what extent, the AP's conduct disclosed in the evidence would found criminal charges in England. I would therefore expect an inquiry into an AP's conduct and an analysis of it in terms

f
of English criminal law, not the comparison of legal definitions. If, of course, the DCC and English crimes were identical the only inquiry (subject to s 3(1)(a)) would be as to the sufficiency of the evidence.' (My emphasis.)

g
My respectful comment on this reasoning is the same as that of Lord Parker CJ on counsel's argument in R v Governor of Brixton Prison, ex p Gardner [1968] 1 All ER 636 at 641, [1968] 2 QB 399 at 415, namely that it appears to me to give no effect to the provisions of s 3(1)(c) (to which no provision of the 1870 Act corresponds). '(a)' and '(b)' above correspond to s 3(1)(a) of the Act, but '(c)' is a reflection not of s 3(1)(c), but of s 10 of the 1870 Act.

Finally, while I regard the meaning of s 3(1)(c) as reasonably clear, the very most that the appellants could in my opinion hope to say is that it is genuinely ambiguous, in

h
which case the point would have to be decided in favour of the subject.

My Lords, for the reasons which I have given, I would dismiss the appeal.

*Appeal dismissed.*

Solicitors: *Crown Prosecution Service*; *Sheridans* (for the respondent).

Mary Rose Plummer    Barrister.

# R v Ealing Magistrates' Court, ex parte Dixon

QUEEN'S BENCH DIVISION
WOOLF LJ AND SAVILLE J
4, 19 APRIL, 3 MAY 1989

*Criminal law – Proceedings – Duties of Director of Public Prosecutions – Undertaking conduct of proceedings – Private prosecution – Defendants charged by police – Private prosecutor signing charge sheet – Private prosecutor invited to conduct proceedings – Magistrates dismissing charges at committal proceedings – Whether police obliged to conduct proceedings – Whether magistrates correct in dismissing charges – Police and Criminal Evidence Act 1984, ss 37, 38 – Prosecution of Offences Act 1985, s 3(2).*

Search warrants obtained by the police under s 21A(1) of the Copyright Act 1956 were executed at the defendants' premises by police officers accompanied by two investigators from a copyright owners' federation, one of whom was the applicant. The defendants were subsequently charged at the police station with copyright offences, the charges being read out by the custody officer and the charge sheet being signed by the custody officer and the applicant, who signed as the 'person charging'. The custody officer informed the defendants' solicitor that the defendants were being charged on behalf of the copyright owners' federation and the police intended that the prosecution would be conducted by the federation. When the defendants were brought before the magistrates the prosecution was represented by a solicitor instructed by the federation. The case against the defendants was dismissed on the grounds that since the charges had been brought by the police and no informations had been laid on behalf of the federation the proper procedure for bringing a private prosecution had not been followed and the applicant had no standing as a prosecutor. The applicant applied for judicial review of the magistrates' decision.

**Held** – A police officer carrying out the duties imposed on him by ss 37[a] and 38[b] of the Police and Criminal Evidence Act 1984 when charging an arrested person had no power to perform those duties on behalf of a private individual or to entrust the subsequent prosecution to a private individual, since under s 3(2)[c] of the Prosecution of Offences Act 1985 it was the duty of the Director of Public Prosecutions or the Crown Prosecution Service on his behalf to take over the conduct of all criminal proceedings instituted on behalf of a police force. Accordingly, since the charges against the defendants had been laid by the police custody officer the prosecution against them had to be conducted by the Crown Prosecution Service and not by the copyright owners' federation. The application for judicial review of the magistrates' decision would therefore be dismissed (see p 1053 g h, p 1054 d to f h j and p 1055 h, post).

**Notes**

For the initiation of criminal proceedings, see 11 Halsbury's Laws (4th edn) paras 96–97, and for cases on the subject, see 14(1) Digest (Reissue) 185–188, 1320–1342.

For the Copyright Act 1956, s 21A, see 11 Halsbury's Statutes (4th edn) 283.

For the Police and Criminal Evidence Act 1984, ss 37, 38, see 12 ibid 986, 988.

For the Prosecution of Offences Act 1985, s 3, see ibid 1050.

**Case referred to in judgments**

*Rubin v DPP* [1989] 2 All ER 241, DC.

---

a    Section 37, so far as material, is set out at p 1053 c to e, post
b    Section 38, so far as material, is set out at p 1053 f, post
c    Section 3(2), so far as material, is set out at p 1054 b, post

**Cases also cited**

a   *Allman v Hardcastle* (1903) 89 LT 553, DC.
*Chic Fashions (West Wales) v Jones* [1968] 1 All ER 229, [1968] 2 QB 299, CA.
*Dixon v Wells* (1890) 25 QBD 249, DC.
*Duchesne v Finch* (1912) 107 LT 412, DC.
*Fox v Chief Constable of Gwent* [1985] 3 All ER 392, [1986] AC 281, HL.
*Ghani v Jones* [1969] 3 All ER 1700, [1970] 1 QB 693, CA.
b   *Giebler v Manning* [1906] 1 KB 709, DC.
*Harrington v Roots* [1984] 2 All ER 474, [1984] AC 743, HL.
*Lund v Thompson* [1958] 3 All ER 356, [1959] 1 QB 283, DC.
*Malz v Rosen* [1966] 2 All ER 10, [1966] 1 WLR 1008.
*R v Alladice* (1988) Times, 11 May, CA.
*R v Brentford Justices, ex p Catlin* [1975] 2 All ER 201, [1975] QB 455, DC.
c   *R v Derby Crown Court, ex p Brooks* (1984) 80 Cr App R 164, DC.
*R v Hughes* (1879) 4 QBD 614, CCR.
*R v Lushington, ex p Otto* [1894] 1 QB 420, DC.
*R v Millard* (1853) Dears 166, 169 ER 681.
*R v Shaw* (1865) Le & Ca 579, 169 ER 1522, CCR.
*Snodgrass v Topping* (1952) 116 JP 332, DC.
d   *Turner v Postmaster General* (1864) 5 B & S 756, 122 ER 1011, DC.
*Wandsworth Board of Works v Pretty* [1899] 1 QB 1, DC.

**Application for judicial review**

Reginald Dixon applied, with the leave of Simon Brown J given on 14 September 1988
for judicial review by way of an order of mandamus directed to the Ealing justices
e   ordering them to hold committal proceedings against the defendants, George Michael
Pollen, Christopher Richard Machay and Thomas Glen Everett, in respect of charges of
conspiracy to contravene s 21 of the Copyright Act 1956 which had been preferred
against the defendants at Ealing police station on 29 June 1988. The facts are set out in
the judgment of Woolf LJ.

f   *Michael Worsley QC* for the applicant.
*Dennis Naish* for the defendants Pollen and Machay.
*Jeremy Gompertz QC* and *Stuart Sleeman* for the Director of Public Prosecutions.
The defendant Everett did not appear.

g                                                                          *Cur adv vult*

3 May. The following judgments were delivered.

**WOOLF LJ.** This is an application for judicial review by Reginald Dixon, who is the
senior investigating officer of the Federation Against Copyright Theft Ltd (FACT), and
h   on behalf of that company, which has among its objects:

> 'To protect and advance the interests of its members and others in the United
> Kingdom of Great Britain and Northern Ireland in the copyright in cinematograph
> films, television programmes and all forms of audio-visual recording.'

The application relates to the decision of the Ealing justices to discharge the defendants,
j   George Michael Pollen, Christopher Richard Machay and Thomas Glen Everett, for want
of prosecution.
Counsel for the applicant contends that, in reaching this decision, the justices were not
acting lawfully and he seeks an order of mandamus directing the justices to proceed with
the committal proceedings against the defendants.
The principal issue which the application raises is whether a private prosecutor is

entitled to take over a prosecution when a defendant has been arrested and charged by
the police except with the authority and on behalf of the Crown Prosecution Service.     *a*

We first heard the application on 4 April 1989. However, because this case could have
wide implications for private prosecutions and the proper application of the Police and
Criminal Evidence Act 1984 and the Prosecution of Offences Act 1985, we adjourned
before the conclusion of the hearing in order to have the assistance of the argument on
behalf of the Director of Public Prosecutions.

At the resumed hearing on 19 April 1989 this assistance was provided by counsel for     *b*
the Director of Public Prosecutions, to whom we are most grateful. We are also grateful
to counsel for the defendants and counsel for the applicant for the arguments which they
advanced.

The facts giving rise to the application may be summarised as follows. On 25 May
1988 the police sought assistance of FACT with regard to the execution of a search
warrant which had been granted to the police under s 21A of the Copyright Act 1956.     *c*
That warrant could only be issued on the information of a constable. The search warrant
was duly executed and a considerable amount of material was recovered which ultimately
resulted in the defendants being charged with offences of conspiracy and offences of
infringing the 1956 Act. If the applicant is correct, the defendants have been engaged in
committing offences of this nature on a large scale. In the course of executing the warrant
the police, who were accompanied by the applicant and another employee of FACT,     *d*
arrested the defendants.

The defendants were not charged immediately but were granted 'police bail' and they
returned to the police station on 29 June 1988, when they were charged. Not surprisingly,
there is some doubt as to precisely what occurred when the defendants were charged, but
it is not disputed that a police officer, who would be the custody officer for the purposes
of s 37 of the Police and Criminal Evidence Act 1984, read out the charges and that the     *e*
defendants were granted bail to attend the Ealing Magistrates' Court on 27 July 1988. It
is also not in dispute that the applicant was present when the defendants were charged
and signed the charge sheet as the 'person charging', the charge sheet also being signed
by the custody officer as the officer taking the charge. According to the applicant, the
officer informed Mr Lindsay, the defendants' solicitor, that the complainant in the case
was FACT and that he, the applicant, of that organisation, was present and would sign     *f*
the charge sheet as prosecutor. According to Mr Lindsay, he asked the custody officer by
whom they were being charged and the officer replied by solicitors on behalf of FACT.

Initially, at the Ealing Magistrates' Court on 27 July, the defendants, on the advice of
their solicitors, remained out of court, but subsequently they entered the court at the
request of the justices, but it is not suggested that their absence from court had any     *g*
significance.

What happened before the justices is somewhat confused. However, it appears that an
argument was advanced on behalf of the defendants that the act of granting bail by the
police was a nullity, that the police had indicated that they were not bringing charges
and FACT had not followed the proper procedure for bringing a private prosecution and
that the solicitor who was there to represent FACT had therefore no standing as     *h*
prosecutor. The chairman of the justices states that it was not made clear to the bench
that the person charging was the applicant. The charge sheet was not produced and from
the arguments they heard the justices understood the police officer had signed the charge
sheet.

There was apparently a representative of the Crown Prosecution Service present in
court in relation to other matters and his assistance was sought, but he knew nothing     *j*
about the case. It was in these circumstances that the justices came to the decision which
is challenged, the justices indicating that their decision would not prevent further
informations being laid by FACT. This was not done at that time, but subsequently an
information was taken out.

In the course of his detailed argument counsel for the applicant advanced a number of

submissions supported by numerous authorities which would no doubt have been
*a* impeccable statements of the law prior to the passing of the Police and Criminal Evidence
Act 1984 and the Prosecution of Offences Act 1985, but in my view those submissions
and authorities are no longer relevant having regard to the fundamental changes made
in criminal procedure by the 1984 and 1985 Acts. The 1984 Act sets out a code of practice
which the police are required to follow, inter alia, where a suspect is arrested and taken
into custody. This is made clear by the provisions of Pt IV of the 1984 Act. For the
*b* purposes of the present application it is sufficient to refer to the following provisions of
ss 37 and 38 of the 1984 Act:

'**37.**—(1) Where—(*a*) a person is arrested for an offence—(i) without a warrant;
or (ii) under a warrant not endorsed for bail, or (*b*) a person returns to a police station
to answer to bail, the custody officer at each police station where he is detained after
his arrest shall determine whether he has before him sufficient evidence to charge
*c* that person with the offence for which he was arrested and may detain him at the
police station for such period as is necessary to enable him to do so.
(2) If the custody officer determines that he does not have such evidence before
him, the person arrested shall be released either on bail or without bail, unless the
custody officer has reasonable grounds for believing that his detention without
*d* being charged is necessary to secure or preserve evidence relating to an offence for
which he is under arrest or to obtain such evidence by questioning him.
(3) If the custody officer has reasonable grounds for so believing, he may authorise
the person arrested to be kept in police detention . . .
(7) Subject to section 41(7) below, if the custody officer determines that he has
before him sufficient evidence to charge the person arrested with the offence for
*e* which he was arrested, the person arrested—(*a*) shall be charged; or (*b*) shall be
released without charge, either on bail or without bail.
(8) Where—(*a*) a person is released under subsection (7)(*b*) above; and (*b*) at the
time of his release a decision whether he should be prosecuted for the offence for
which he was arrested has not been taken, it shall be the duty of the custody officer
so to inform him . . .
*f* **38.**—(1) Where a person arrested for an offence otherwise than under a warrant
endorsed for bail is charged with an offence, the custody officer shall order his
release from police detention, either on bail or without bail, unless—(*a*) . . . (iii) the
custody officer has reasonable grounds for believing that the person arrested will fail
to appear in court to answer to bail . . .'

*g* Counsel for the applicant submits in this case that the custody officer was charging the
defendants on behalf of the applicant of FACT and the applicant or FACT were the
prosecutors although the charges were being read over by the custody officer and bail
was being granted by that officer. He says that this is clear on the description of what
happened which I have set out above. I do not accept this submission. The officer was
performing the duties imposed on him by ss 37 and 38 of the 1984 Act, and he has no
*h* power to perform those duties on behalf of a private individual. There can be no doubt
that the Metropolitan Police in this case intended that subsequently the prosecution
would be conducted by FACT. The nature of the offences required that there should be
available to the prosecution technical expertise which FACT had and it may well be that
it was reasonable to conclude that the interests of justice would be best served if FACT
were allowed to conduct the prosecution. It was probably for this reason that the
*j* applicant was allowed to sign the charge sheet. This was the practice used in the past (but
which in my view is inappropriate now) to indicate the involvement of a private
individual in the prosecution. However, neither the signing of the charge sheet nor what
was said at the time about who was to prosecute would affect the substance of what took
place when the defendants were charged and then granted bail to appear at the
magistrates' court. Indeed, in relation to the granting of bail, counsel for the applicant at

the first hearing rejected the suggestion that the granting of bail was a nullity; he
submitted that the defendants were lawfully bailed to appear at the magistrates' court   *a*
and did appear in consequence of the bail knowing that the applicant and/or FACT were
prosecuting.

However, it is not the granting of bail which is important but the charging of the
defendants. The reason for this is that the 1985 Act makes the Director of Public
Prosecutions responsible for the conduct of certain criminal proceedings. Section 3(2) of
the 1985 Act provides:                                                                   *b*

'It shall be the duty of the Director—(*a*) to take over the conduct of all criminal
proceedings, other than specified proceedings, instituted on behalf of a police force
(whether by a member of that force or by any other person) . . .'

For the purposes of Pt I of the 1985 Act (which includes s 3(2)) s 15(2) states that—
                                                                                         *c*
'proceedings in relation to an offence are instituted . . . (*c*) where a person is
charged with the offence after being taken into custody without a warrant, when he
is informed of the particulars of the charge . . .'

In relation to this case s 15(2) describes precisely what happened when the defendants
were charged on 29 June 1988. Accordingly, as is submitted by counsel for the Director
of Public Prosecutions and counsel for the respondent defendants, the Director then   *d*
became under a duty to take over the conduct of the criminal proceedings. If the
Metropolitan Police, on whose behalf the custody officer was acting, did not wish this to
be the situation, then, instead of charging the defendants, the defendants should have
been released without being charged in accordance with s 37(7)(*b*) of the 1985 Act and
the officer would then have had to comply with s 37(8)(*b*).

Counsel for the applicant submits that the fact that the Director is required to take   *e*
over the conduct of the proceedings did not necessarily mean that the applicant was not
entitled to prosecute. Again, I disagree. Section 3(2) requires the Director 'to take over
the conduct of *all* criminal proceedings'. Furthermore, I regard the language of s 6 of the
1985 Act and the manifest object of the Act, which is to make the Director responsible
for the conduct of prosecutions which he is under a duty to take over, wholly inconsistent   *f*
with these submissions. Section 6 provides:

'(1) Subject to subsection (2) below, nothing in this Part shall preclude any person
from instituting any criminal proceedings or conducting any criminal proceedings
to which the Director's duty to take over the conduct of proceedings does not apply.
(2) Where criminal proceedings are instituted in circumstances in which the
Director is not under a duty to take over their conduct, he may nevertheless do so at   *g*
any stage.'

In this regard I also refer to s 23(2), (3) and (4) with regard to the Director's power to
discontinue proceedings.

The effect of these provisions is clear and so on 27 July 1988 the Crown Prosecution
Service on behalf of the Director was the only person entitled to conduct proceedings   *h*
unless the Director had exercised his power to appoint someone else to take over the
conduct of proceedings under s 5 of the 1985 Act, which had not happened here. It
follows therefore that the justices were correct to come to the conclusion that the solicitor
for the applicant and FACT was not able to conduct the committal proceedings. No one
was present on behalf of the Crown Prosecution Service in connection with the
defendants' committal proceedings for the simple reason that the Crown Prosecution   *j*
Service had never been informed of the proceedings because the police intended them to
be conducted by the applicant and FACT. However, once the defendants had been
charged, the police had no power to entrust anyone other than the Crown Prosecution
Service with the conduct of the proceedings.

Counsel for the defendants rightly concedes that, if an oral application had been made
to the justices for an information to be laid on behalf of the applicant, committal
proceedings could have taken place after the justices had discontinued the existing

proceedings. The jurisdiction of the justices to hear the committal proceedings is set out

*a* in s 2(3) of the Magistrates' Courts Act 1980, which provides:

> 'A magistrates' court . . . shall have jurisdiction as examining justices over any offence committed by a person who appears or is brought before the court . . .'

For the purposes of the magistrates' jurisdiction to hear committal proceedings the means by which the attendance of the defendants was obtained would not be relevant.

*b* However, no application for the committal proceedings to be heard on this basis was made to the justices, but as the chairman of the magistrates made clear to the applicant the justices' decision did not prevent him from commencing a further prosecution. This is a course still open to the applicant.

Counsel for the applicant, in the course of his submissions, contended that, if the decision of the justices was right, this would create great difficulties for the many private

*c* prosecutions which take place for shoplifting as well as the private prosecutions which take place in connection with offences of the type with which the defendants are charged. This submission naturally caused the court concern. However, in connection with shoplifting offences, counsel for the Director of Public Prosecutions put before us an instruction issued to the Metropolitan Police in consequence of the Prosecution of Offences Act 1985 which makes it clear that they will now be dealt with by the Crown

*d* Prosecution Service in cases where the police decide to prosecute and, if the police decide not to prosecute and 'the loser or his representative then insist on a private prosecution, they should be referred to the magistrates' court to apply for process'. Counsel for the Director of Public Prosecutions does not know of the existence of any similar instruction in relation to copyright prosecutions but he indicated that obviously the question of whether instructions should be given in this class of case will now be given urgent

*e* consideration.

The final matter to which I should refer does not directly arise in view of the conclusions to which I have already come. However, we did hear argument on the point and I will therefore, shortly, refer to it. The question is whether, in any event, it would be appropriate for FACT, a limited company, to conduct a private prosecution. As to this,

*f* we were referred to the decision of this court in *Rubin v DPP* [1989] 2 All ER 241. That case involved the issue as to the appropriateness of an information being preferred by 'the Thames Valley Police'. This court came to the conclusion that it was not appropriate for an information to be laid in the name of a police force in this way. Distinctions can be drawn between that situation and where it is a limited company which is seeking to prosecute. However, passages in the judgment of Watkins LJ could be regarded as indicating that a prosecution has to be by an individual rather than a corporate person.

*g* Having heard the argument which was advanced before us, I have reservations as to the reasoning which would lead to this conclusion. However, I do not propose to indicate a final view on the issue because it does not arise expressly for decision in this case and, in any event, in agreement with Watkins LJ, I would regard it as preferable for an individual to be the informant albeit that he is acting on behalf of a body corporate.

*h* I would, for these reasons, dismiss this application.

**SAVILLE J.** I agree.

*Application dismissed. The court refused leave to appeal to the House of Lords but certified, under s 1(2) of the Administration of Justice Act 1960, that the following point of law of general public*

*j* *importance was involved in the decision: whether a private prosecutor is entitled to take over a prosecution when a defendant has been arrested and charged by the police except with the authority and on behalf of the Crown Prosecution Service.*

Solicitors: *Knowles Cave & Co*, Luton (for the applicant); *Claude Hornby & Cox* (for the defendants Pollen and Machay); *Crown Prosecution Service.*

Dilys Tausz   Barrister.

# Green v Broadcasting Corp of New Zealand

*a*

PRIVY COUNCIL

LORD BRIDGE OF HARWICH, LORD ACKNER, LORD GOFF OF CHIEVELEY, LORD JAUNCEY OF TULLICHETTLE AND LORD LOWRY

5, 18 JULY 1989

*b*

*Copyright – Dramatic or musical performance – Script – Television show – Talent contest – Scripts claimed for standard introduction of competitors and same catch phrases used throughout show – No written text of shows put in evidence – Whether standard introductions and catch phrases amounting to 'scripts' – Whether use of standard introductions and catch phrases amounting to 'dramatic format'.*

*c*

The appellant was a well-known entertainer who, between 1956 and 1978, wrote, presented and compèred a television talent contest in England entitled 'Opportunity Knocks'. In 1975 and 1978 the respondent broadcast a similar television show under the same title in New Zealand. The appellant commenced proceedings against the respondent in the High Court of New Zealand for damages for passing off and infringement of copyright, claiming that copyright subsisted in the 'scripts and dramatic format' of the television show as broadcast in England. No scripts were produced in evidence, but in the course of examination the appellant claimed that he wrote the scripts of the shows, such as they were, by having the same form of introduction for each competitor and using the same stock or catch phrases throughout the show. In addition there was the use of a device called a 'clapometer' to measure audience reaction to competitors' performances. The trial judge held that there was no evidence that any part of the show was reduced to a written text which could be properly called a script, and dismissed the action. On appeal, the Court of Appeal of New Zealand accepted that the evidence established the existence of scripts but concluded that the scripts, such as they were inferred to be from the evidence, did not themselves do more than express a general idea or concept for a talent quest and hence were not the subject of copyright. The court accordingly dismissed the appeal. The appellant appealed to the Privy Council.

*d*

*e*

*f*

**Held** – The evidence as to the nature of the scripts and what their text contained was exiguous in the extreme, and accordingly, in the absence of precise evidence as to what the scripts contained the Court of Appeal had been correct to conclude that they were not the subject of copyright. Furthermore, it was stretching the use of the word 'format' to use it to describe the features of a television series such as a talent, quiz or game show which was presented in a particular way, with repeated but unconnected use of set phrases and with the aid of particular accessories. The protection which copyright gave created a monopoly and there had to be certainty in the subject matter of that monopoly in order to avoid injustice to the rest of the world, but the subject matter of the copyright claimed by the appellant for the 'dramatic format' of his television show was conspicuously lacking in certainty. Moreover, a dramatic work had to have sufficient unity to be capable of performance, and the features claimed as constituting the 'format' of a television show, being unrelated to each other except as accessories to be used in the presentation of some other dramatic or musical performance, lacked that essential characteristic. The appeal would therefore be dismissed (see p 1058 *d* to *h*, post).

*g*

*h*

Dictum of Farwell LJ in *Tate v Fullbrook* [1908] 1 KB 821 at 832–833 applied.

*j*

**Notes**

For what constitutes a dramatic or musical performance, see 9 Halsbury's Laws (4th edn) paras 834, 840, and for cases on the subject, see 13 Digest (Reissue) 66–67, 74–75, 636–642, 670–682.

**Case referred to in judgment**

*a*  *Tate v Fullbrook* [1908] 1 KB 821, CA.

Hugh Hughes Green appealed by leave of the Court of Appeal of New Zealand (Cooke, Hardie Boys and Wylie JJ) given on 10 May 1989 from the decision of that court (Somers and Casey JJ, Gallen J dissenting) on 22 September 1988 affirming the decision of the High Court of New Zealand (Ongley J) on 23 December 1983 dismissing his action
*b*  against the respondent, Broadcasting Corp of New Zealand, claiming damages for passing off and infringement of copyright in a television show entitled 'Opportunity Knocks' of which the appellant was the author, presenter and compère in England between 1956 and 1978. The facts are set out in the judgment of the Board.

*Hugh Laddie QC* and *Christopher Finlayson* (of the New Zealand Bar) for the appellant.
*c*  *David Baragwanath QC* and *J B Thomson* (both of the New Zealand Bar) for the respondent.

18 July. The following judgment of the Board was delivered.

**LORD BRIDGE OF HARWICH.** The appellant is a well-known personality in the
*d*  entertainment world. Between 1956 and 1978 he was the author, presenter and compère of a television show entitled 'Opportunity Knocks' in England. The show was in essence a talent contest. In 1975 and 1978 the respondent broadcast a similar television show under the same title in New Zealand. The appellant commenced proceedings in the High Court of New Zealand claiming damages for passing off and infringement of copyright. His action was dismissed by Ongley J on 23 December 1983. The judgment
*e*  was affirmed by the Court of Appeal (Somers, Casey and Gallen JJ) on 22 September 1988. The appellant now appeals to Her Majesty in Council by leave of the Court of Appeal. The only issue arising in the appeal relates to the claim of copyright. The Court of Appeal decided against the appellant by a majority, Gallen J dissenting.

The copyright alleged to have been infringed was claimed to subsist in the 'scripts and dramatic format' of 'Opportunity Knocks' as broadcast in England. The appellant's
*f*  primary difficulty arises from the circumstance that no script was ever produced in evidence. Ongley J concluded:

'There was really no evidence that any part of the show was reduced to a written text which could properly be called a script . . .'

He later added:

*g*  'No writing has been produced in evidence in this action in which, in my view, copyright could subsist.'

The Court of Appeal differed from the trial judge to the extent that it accepted that the evidence established the existence of scripts. But the evidence as to the nature of the scripts and what their text contained was exiguous in the extreme. It is to be found in
*h*  two short passages from the evidence given by the appellant himself. He said in the course of examination-in-chief:

'In the year 1956 I wrote the scripts of "Opportunity Knocks" shows, such as they were, because we would have what we would call the introductions, our stock phrases like "For So-and-So, Opportunity Knocks", phrases such as "This is your
*j*  show, folks, and I do mean you". The other part of the writing dealt with interviews with the people and one could not really call it writing because you were really only finding out what the artists wanted to talk about.'

He said in cross-examination:

'The script of "Opportunity Knocks" has continuously been the same for the catch phrases, the interviews each week with the artists had differed, the script for the past 17 years and long before 1975 contained particularly the end of the show beginning with the words "make your mind up time" using the clapometer and bringing back the five people.'

On the basis of this evidence Somers J concluded:

'. . . the scripts as they are inferred to be from the description given in evidence did not themselves do more than express a general idea or concept for a talent quest and hence were not the subject of copyright.'

In the absence of precise evidence as to what the scripts contained, their Lordships are quite unable to dissent from this view.

The alternative formulation of the appellant's claim relies on the 'dramatic format' of 'Opportunity Knocks', by which their Lordships understand is meant those characteristic features of the show which were repeated in each performance. These features were, in addition to the title, the use of the catch phrases 'for [name of competitor] opportunity knocks', 'this is your show folks, and I do mean you' and 'make up your mind time', the use of a device called a 'clapometer' to measure audience reaction to competitors' performances and the use of sponsors to introduce competitors. It was this formulation which found favour with Gallen J.

It is stretching the original use of the word 'format' a long way to use it metaphorically to describe the features of a television series such as a talent, quiz or game show which is presented in a particular way, with repeated but unconnected use of set phrases and with the aid of particular accessories. Alternative terms suggested in the course of argument were 'structure' or 'package'. This difficulty in finding an appropriate term to describe the nature of the 'work' in which the copyright subsists reflects the difficulty of the concept that a number of allegedly distinctive features of a television series can be isolated from the changing material presented in each separate performance (the acts of the performers in the talent show, the questions and answers in the quiz show etc) and identified as an 'original dramatic work'. No case was cited to their Lordships in which copyright of the kind claimed had been established.

The protection which copyright gives creates a monopoly and 'there must be certainty in the subject-matter of such monopoly in order to avoid injustice to the rest of the world': see *Tate v Fullbrook* [1908] 1 KB 821 per Farwell LJ at 832–833. The subject matter of the copyright claimed for the 'dramatic format' of 'Opportunity Knocks' is conspicuously lacking in certainty. Moreover, it seems to their Lordships that a dramatic work must have sufficient unity to be capable of performance and that the features claimed as constituting the 'format' of a television show, being unrelated to each other except as accessories to be used in the presentation of some other dramatic or musical performance, lack that essential characteristic.

For these reasons their Lordships will humbly advise Her Majesty that the appeal should be dismissed. The appellant must pay the respondent's costs of the appeal to the Board.

*Appeal dismissed*

Solicitors: *Alan Taylor & Co* (for the appellant; *Macfarlanes* (for the respondent).

Mary Rose Plummer    Barrister.

*a* # Publishers Association v EC Commission

## (Case 56/89 R)

COURT OF JUSTICE OF THE EUROPEAN COMMUNITIES
JUDGE DUE (PRESIDENT)
*b* 12 MAY, 13 JUNE 1989

*European Economic Community – Rules on competition – Agreements preventing, restricting or distorting competition – Sale of books – Net book agreement – Commission deciding agreement infringed rules on competition – Commission requiring immediate termination of agreement – Parties to agreement seeking annulment of decision – Application for interim measure suspending*
*c* *operation of commission's decision pending court's decision on annulment – EEC Treaty, arts 85(1)(3), 185, 186 – Rules of Procedure of the Court, art 83 – Commission Decision (EEC) 89/ 44.*

*European Economic Community – Commission – Decision – Suspension of operation of decision –*
*d* *Application for suspension of operation of commission's decision pending outcome of proceedings for annulment of decision – Case which applicant must establish – Urgent and prima facie case – Net book agreement – Price fixing agreement – Competent national court concluding in 1962 that agreement for public benefit – Agreement notified to Commission on accession to European Communities in 1973 – Commission deciding in 1988 that agreement infringed rules on competition – Commission requiring immediate termination of agreement infringing rules on*
*e* *competition – Parties to agreement seeking annulment of decision – Parties applying for interim measure suspending operation of decision – Whether case for interim measure established – EEC Treaty, arts 185, 186 – Rules of Procedure of the Court, art 83 – Commission Decision (EEC) 89/44.*

*f* The Publishers Association was an association comprising the majority of book publishers in the United Kingdom, the objects of which were to promote and protect the interests of its members, to encourage the widest possible dissemination of books and, for that purpose, to administer the Net Book Agreement made in 1957, and enforce and secure its observance by all lawful means. Under that agreement members of the association and signatories to the agreement undertook to apply standard conditions of sale to the
*g* sale in the United Kingdom and Ireland of all 'net books' (ie books which could not be sold to the public below a price fixed by the publisher or distributor for the book in question). The association had also adopted a number of decisions and rules which, directly or indirectly, related to the marketing of 'net books'. Although the agreements did not provide for any sanctions to be applied to signatories who did not observe them, compliance by booksellers with the standard conditions of sale were enforced by means
*h* of an injunction. About 75% of books sold in the United Kingdom or exported by United Kingdom publishers to Ireland were marketed as 'net books'. In 1962 and 1968 the Restrictive Practices Court concluded that the abrogation of the agreements would deny to the public, as purchasers, consumers or users of books, specific and substantial benefits or advantages enjoyed by them by virtue of the agreements and that the public would
*j* not suffer any significant detriment through continuation of the agreements as compared with the detriment that would result from their abrogation. The agreements, documents and rules were notified to the EC Commission in 1973 on the accession of the United Kingdom and Ireland to the European Communities. In December 1988 the Commission adopted Decision (EEC) 89/44, in which it concluded that the agreements, decisions and

rules constituted an infringement of art 85(1)[a] of the EEC Treaty. The Commission also refused an exemption for them under art 85(3) of the Treaty and required the association to take all steps necessary for bringing the infringement to an end forthwith. The association applied to the Court of Justice of the European Communities for annulment of the Commission's decision, and at the same time applied to the court, under arts 185[b] and 186[c] of the Treaty and art 83[d] of the Rules of Procedure of the Court, for an interim measure suspending the operation of the Commission decision in its entirety until the court had delivered judgment on the application in the main proceedings.

**Held** – (1) In order to determine whether there were circumstances giving rise to urgency and factual and legal grounds establishing a prima facie case for an interim measure under arts 185 and 186 of the EEC Treaty and art 83 of the Rules of Procedure of the Court ordering the suspension of the operation of a decision of the Commission, it was well established that the urgency of the application for suspension had to be assessed in relation to the necessity for an order granting interim relief in order to prevent serious and irreparable damage to the party requesting suspension (see p 1063 j, post).

(2) It was apparent that the competent court, viz the Restrictive Practices Court, had, in conformity with the applicable national legislation, evaluated the advantages accruing not only from fixed prices as such but also from the agreements laying down standard conditions of sale and had concluded that the agreements were indispensable in order to maintain those prices in practice. It followed therefore that the application did not appear to be devoid of all foundation and accordingly the requirement that a prima facie case be established was satisfied (see p 1064 f g, post).

(3) There were serious grounds for believing that abrogation or amendment of the agreements in a marketing system as extensive and complex as the 'net book' system on the United Kingdom and Irish markets might cause the economic operators concerned the serious and irreparable damage which the association claimed would occur. Since a balance was to be struck between that risk and the Commission's interest in bringing to an end forthwith the infringement of the competition rules contained in the EEC Treaty

---

a   Article 85, so far as material, provides:
     '1. The following shall be prohibited as incompatible with the common market: all agreements between undertakings, decision by associations of undertakings and concerted practices which may affect trade between Member States and which have as their object or effect the prevention, restriction or distortion of competition within the common market, and in particular those which: (a) directly or indirectly fix purchase or selling prices or any other trading conditions . . .
     3. The provisions of paragraph 1 may, however, be declared inapplicable in the case of: —any agreement or category of agreements between undertakings: —any decision or category of decisions by associations of undertakings; —any concerted practice or category of concerted practices; which contributes to improving the production or distribution of goods or to promoting technical or economic progress, while allowing consumers a fair share of the resulting benefit, and which does not: (a) impose on the undertakings concerned restrictions which are not indispensable to the attainment of these objectives; (b) afford such undertakings the possibility of eliminating competition in respect of a substantial part of the products in question.'
b   Article 185 provides: 'Actions brought before the Court of Justice shall not have suspensory effect. The Court of Justice may, however, if it considers that circumstances so require, order that application of the contested act be suspended.'
c   Article 186 provides: 'The Court of Justice may in any cases before it prescribe any necessary interim measures.'
d   Article 83, so far as material, provides:
     '1. An application to suspend the operation of any measure adopted by an institution, made pursuant to . . . Article 185 of the EEC Treaty . . . shall be admissible only if the applicant is challenging that measure in proceedings before the Court. An application for the adoption of any other interim measure referred to in . . . Article 186 of the EEC Treaty . . . shall be admissible only if it is made by a party to a case before the Court and relates to that case.
     2. An application of a kind referred to in paragraph 1 of this Article shall state the subject matter of the dispute, the circumstances giving rise to urgency and the factual and legal grounds establishing a prima facie case for the interim measures applied for . . .'

which it claimed to have ascertained, and since the agreements, decisions and rules in
a question had set up a marketing system which had applied since 1957 and been duly
notified to the Commission in 1973, the Commission's interest in 1989 in bringing the
infringement to an end could not override the association's interest in not running the
risk of jeopardising that system before the court had delivered judgment in the main
proceedings. Furthermore, the advantages which the Restrictive Practices Court had
found to be conferred on the public by the agreements, particularly as regards ensuring
b an adequate and varied supply of books of all kinds, might be irreversibly compromised
by immediate implementation of the contested decision. It followed therefore that the
condition concerning urgency was also to be regarded as satisfied (see p 1065 *b* to *e*, post).

(4) Since the association had established both a prima facie case and the condition
concerning urgency it followed that, although the association had not established that it
was necessary to suspend the operation of the contested decision in its entirety, it was
c appropriate to order the suspension of the operation of those parts of the decision which
refused the grant of an exemption under art 85(3) of the EEC Treaty for the agreements,
decision and rules and which required the association to take all steps necessary to bring
the infringement to an end forthwith (see p 1065 *g h* and p 1066 *a*, post).

**Notes**
d For the rules on competition within the European Communities, see 52 Halsbury's Laws
(4th edn) paras 19·01–19·03.

For applications for the suspension of operation of contested measures, see 51 ibid para
2·245.

For the EEC Treaty, arts 85, 185, 186, see 50 Halsbury's Statutes (4th edn) 293, 326.

e **Cases cited**
*Net Book Agreement 1957, Re* [1962] 3 All ER 751, LR 3 RP 246, [1962] 1 WLR 1347,
RPC.
*Net Book Agreements 1957, Re* (1 March 1968, unreported), RPC.

**Application**
f By an application lodged at the court registry on 27 February 1989 the Publishers
Association applied, pursuant to arts 185 and 186 to the EEC Treaty and art 83 of the
Rules of Procedure of the Court for an interim measure suspending in its entirety the
operation of Commission Decision (EEC) 89/44 of 12 December 1988 relating to
proceedings under art 85 of the Treaty (IV/27.393 and IV/27.394, Publishers Association—
Net Book Agreements) until the Court of Justice of the European Communities had
g delivered judgment on the association's application under the second paragraph of art 173
of the Treaty for the annulment of the decision. The Commission submitted written
observations to the court. The language of the case was English. The facts are set out in
the order.

h *Jeremy Lever QC* for the association.
*Nicholas Forwood QC* and *Berend Jan Drijber* for the Commission.

13 June. **THE PRESIDENT OF THE COURT OF JUSTICE** made the following
order.
j
1. By an application lodged at the court registry on 27 February 1989 the Publishers
Association brought an action under the second paragraph of art 173 of the EEC Treaty
for the annulment of Commission Decision (EEC) 89/44 of 12 December 1988 relating
to a proceeding under art 85 of the EEC Treaty (IV/527.393 and IV/27.394, Publishers
Association—Net Book Agreements) (OJ 1989 L22, p 12).
2. Article 1 of that decision states that certain agreements, decisions and rules adopted

by the applicant association, listed in paras (*a*) to (*f*) of that article and described below, constitute an infringement of art 85(1) of the EEC Treaty to the extent to which they cover the book trade between member states.          *a*

3. Article 2 of the decision refuses to grant an exemption under art 85(3) of the Treaty for those agreements, decisions and rules.

4. Article 3 of the decision requires the applicant association to take all steps necessary to bring the infringement to an end forthwith and art 4 of the decision requires it to inform the undertakings concerned, in particular booksellers, of those measures, stating          *b*
the practical effects which they will have.

5. By a separate document lodged at the court registry, also on 27 February 1989, the applicant applied, pursuant to arts 185 and 186 of the EEC Treaty and art 83 of the Rules of Procedure of the Court, for an interim measure suspending the operation of the above-mentioned decision in its entirety until the court has delivered judgment on the application in the main proceedings.          *c*

6. The defendant Commission submitted its written observations on 30 March 1989. The parties presented oral argument on 12 May 1989, a hearing set for that purpose on 21 April 1989 having been deferred at the request of the applicant.

7. Before considering whether the application for an interim order is well founded, it is appropriate to describe briefly the content and context of the agreements, decisions and rules to which the contested decision relates.          *d*

8. The Publishers Association is an association comprising the majority of the publishers established in the United Kingdom. The objects of the association are, in addition to promoting and protecting the interests of its members, to encourage the widest possible dissemination of books and, for that purpose, to administer and enforce and secure the observance by all lawful means of the agreement known as the 'Net Book Agreement 1957'.          *e*

9. Under that agreement, to which art 1(*a*) of the contested decision refers, firms which are members of the association and signatories to the agreement undertake to apply, for the sale of 'net books', the standard conditions of sale (known as the 'Standard Conditions of Sale of Net Books') laid down by the agreement. Those conditions apply to all sales to the public in the United Kingdom or Ireland by a wholesaler or retailer where the person publishing or distributing the book in question chooses to market it at an          *f*
imposed price the ('net price') and fixes that price.

10. Under those standard conditions of sale, no 'net book' may in principle be sold, offered for sale or permitted to be sold to the public below the 'net price'.

11. The standard conditions of sale provide that a 'net book' may be sold at a discount to such libraries, book agents and quantity buyers as have been previously authorised by the association, the amount and conditions of such discount being laid down in the          *g*
authorisation.

12. Pursuant to that provision, the association laid down rules determining the conditions for granting authorisation to libraries, limiting the discount to 10% and specifying the conditions which libraries must meet, rules on quantity discounts, fixing a scale of discounts, and, finally, rules for discounts to book agents. Article 1(*b*) of the          *h*
contested decision refers to those rules.

13. In the event of a breach of contract by a person selling or offering for sale to the public a 'net book', the signatories undertake, by virtue of the agreement, to enforce their contractual rights and the rights conferred on them by the Resale Prices Act 1976, if the association asks them to do so and provided that they are indemnified by the latter for the costs thereby incurred by them.          *j*

14. An agreement which is identical, except as regards indemnification by the association in the event of legal proceedings in respect of breaches of contract, has been concluded between a large number of publishers who are not members of the association. Article 1(*a*) of the contested decision also covers that agreement.

15. The association has also adopted a number of decisions and rules which, directly

*a* or indirectly, relate to the marketing of 'net books'. Those decisions and rules are enumerated in art 1(*c*) to (*f*) of the contested decision.

16. A 'Code of Allowances' contains provisions concerning reduced 'net prices', decided on by the publisher, for new editions and cheap editions which must be announced beforehand in the trade press and which may give rise to individual reductions of the 'net price' for copies held in stock by the bookseller.

*b* 17. Book club regulations apply to special editions intended for book clubs. They apply to books the trade editions of which are published as 'net books' and allow for special editions for book clubs registered with the association as having agreed to comply with the regulations. Those regulations lay down, in particular, the conditions which book clubs must satisfy regarding club membership and govern the advertising which they may undertake for their books.

*c* 18. A decision of the association governs an annual national book sale. Booksellers are allowed, within the limits and under the conditions laid down in the decision, to sell their overstocks and, as the case may be, to dispose of wholesalers' and publishers' overstocks for less than the 'net price'.

19. Finally, a directory of booksellers, which is brought up to date every two months, is published by the association, listing the booksellers who satisfy certain requirements and undertake to observe the standard conditions of sale of 'net books'.

*d* 20. The above-mentioned agreements do not provide for any sanctions to be applied to signatories who do not observe the agreement. Compliance with the standard sales conditions by booksellers in enforced, according to the association, where appropriate, by means of an injunction. In order to obtain such relief in Ireland and the United Kingdom, it is generally incumbent on the publisher to prove a contractual relationship with the bookseller. In the United Kingdom, however, the publisher may also rely on s 26 of the

*e* Resale Prices Act 1976, which enables him to enforce conditions concerning a resale price without having to prove a contractual relationship, provided that the bookseller in question has notice of those conditions.

21. It is apparent from the contested decision that the number of new titles published each year by the publishing industry in the United Kingdom is about 40,000, of which

*f* above 80% are produced by members of the association, the total value of annual production being around £1,700m. 65% of the books published in the United Kingdom are sold on the United Kingdom market, and the rest are exported. About a quarter of the exports go to other member states; 4·5% of the exports go to Ireland, where they represent more than 50% of total book sales.

22. It is undisputed as between the parties that around 75% of the books sold in the

*g* United Kingdom or exported by United Kingdom publishers to Ireland are marketed as 'net books'.

23. The agreements, decisions and rules to which the contested decision relates were notified, at the time of the accession of the United Kingdom and Ireland to the Communities, to the Commission on 12 June 1973, pursuant to art 25(2) of EEC Council Regulation 17 of 6 February 1962, the first regulation implementing arts 85 and 86 of

*h* the EEC Treaty, as amended by art 29 of the Act of Accession (1972).

24. Under art 185 of the EEC Treaty, actions brought before the Court of Justice are not to have suspensory effect. The court may, however, if it considers that the circumstances so require order that the operation of the contested acts be suspended.

25. Pursuant to art 83(2) of the Rules of Procedure of the Court, a decision ordering suspension may not be adopted unless there are circumstances giving rise to urgency and

*j* factual and legal grounds establishing a prima facie case for such a decision. As the court has consistently held, the urgency of an application for suspension must be assessed in relation to the necessity for an order granting interim relief in order to prevent serious and irreparable damage to the party requesting suspension.

26. It is necessary to consider whether those conditions are fulfilled in this case.

27. As regards, in the first place, the requirement of a prima facie case, the applicant

points out that, in its application in the main proceedings, it seeks in particular the annulment of the contested decision in so far as it rejects the application for an exemption under art 85(3) of the EEC Treaty. That exemption was refused, it claims, solely because the agreements, decisions and rules notified do not satisfy the condition laid down in art 85(3)(a) because they impose on the undertakings concerned restrictions which are not indispensable to the attainment of their objectives.

28. In that connection the applicant claims in particular that the contested decision does not contain an adequate statement of the reasons on which it is based and infringes art 85(3). It states that the agreements to which the decision relates are as unrestrictive as possible, in so far as each publisher is free to decide whether or not to become a signatory, to decide whether a book is to be marketed as a 'net book', to fix the 'net price', to choose the booksellers through which the book is to be sold and to negotiate the price that they are to pay, and that the use of standard type conditions is dictated by reasons of practicality. It also states in particular that the agreements, decisions and rules to which the contested decision relates were on two occasions, in 1962 and 1968, considered in depth by the national court having jursidiction in competition matters, the Restrictive Practices Court, which, after a long hearing and despite the fact that the fixing of sales prices is in principle prohibited by the national legislation, concluded that abrogation of the agreements would deny to the public, as purchasers, consumers or users of books, specific and substantial benefits or advantages enjoyed by them by virtue of the agreements and that the public would not suffer any significant detriment through continuation of the agreements, as compared with the detriments that would result from their abrogation (see *Re Net Book Agreement 1957* [1962] 3 All ER 751, LR 3 RP 246 and *Re Net Book Agreements 1957* (1 March 1968, unreported)).

29. It must be pointed out that in para 71 of the preamble the decision states that the arguments put forward by the association in support of its application for exemption are the same as those put forward within the context of the national proceedings referred to above but that those proceedings concerned not so much the necessity of a common application of standard conditions but much more the question whether fixed book prices as such were indispensable in order to attain their alleged objectives. Considering that those two aspects must be considered separately, the Commission then proceeds (in paras 72 to 86) to consider the indispensability of the agreements in question without taking account of the appraisal made by the above-mentioned national court.

30. It appears, however, from the national decisions referred to that the competent court proceeded, in conformity with the applicable national legislation, to evaluate the advantages accruing not only from fixed prices as such but also from the agreements laying down standard conditions of sale, the said agreements being, according to that national court, indispensable in order to maintain those prices in practice.

31. In those circumstances, it must be stated that, at the present interlocutory stage, the application does not appear to be devoid of all foundation and that accordingly the requirement that a prima facie case must be established is satisfied.

32. It must however be added that that finding relates only to the Commission's refusal to grant an exemption under art 85(3) of the EEC Treaty (art 2 of the contested decision). In fact, the applicant itself admits that, in principle, the system applied to 'net books' is contrary to art 85(1) of the Treaty to the extent to which it applies to trade between member states (art 1 of the contested decision).

33. As regards the requirement of urgency, the applicant association claims that in order to comply with the contested decision, in particular arts 3 and 4 thereof, it would have either to abrogate the agreements and the marketing system established by them or to amend the agreements and the system so that they cease to cover the book trade between member states. Abrogation of the agreements would, as the national court with jurisdiction in competition matters held, entail the consequence that there would be fewer stockholding bookshops, fewer and less varied titles would be published and the

prices of books would be higher overall. Those consequences would, for the members of
*a* the association, cause considerable commercial damage and lead to a development on the
United Kingdom and Irish book markets which it would be impossible subsequently to
reverse. Amendment of the agreements in the manner required by the Commission
would result in the abolition of the system established on the Irish market with the
above-mentioned consequences and, as regards the United Kingdom market, would in
particular entail the consequence that library suppliers and mail order suppliers would
*b* be liable to transfer their businesses to Ireland. Those consequences would, even in the
short term, lead to the elimination of the existing system.

34. It must be observed that there are serious grounds for believing that a change of
the kind mentioned above in a marketing system as extensive and complex as the 'net
book' system on the United Kingdom and Irish markets might cause the economic
operators concerned the serious and irreparable damage which it is claimed would occur.
*c*     35. A balance must be struck, in particular, between that risk and the Commission's
interest in bringing to an end forthwith the infringement of the competition rules
contained in the Treaty which it claims to have ascertained. Since the agreements,
decisions and rules in question set up a marketing system which has applied since 1957
and were duly notified to the Commission in 1973, the Commission's interest, in 1989,
in bringing the infringement to an end cannot override the applicant association's interest
*d* in not running the risk of jeopardising that system before the court has delivered
judgment in the main proceedings. In that context, it must also be observed that,
according to above-mentioned national decisions, the agreements in question confer
advantages on the public, particularly as regards ensuring an adequate and varied supply
of books of all kinds, which might be irreversibly compromised by immediate
implementation of the contested decision.
*e*     36. It follows that the condition concerning urgency must also be regarded as satisfied.
37. In the event of suspension of the operation of the contested decision being granted,
the Commission claims that the suspension should not cover art 1 of the decision. The
effect of such a suspension would be to restore the provisional validity of the agreements,
which would go beyond the scope of the jurisdiction of the Court of Justice in the matter
*f* of an application for interim relief. For its part, the applicant association contends that
the case law relied on by the Commission in that connection relates only to cases where
the agreement in question enjoyed no provisional validity before the Commission
decision and the applicant relies on the fact that the court recognised the provisional
validity of certain agreements by reason of the indivisibility of the prohibition provided
for in art 85(1) and of the possibility of exemption provided for in art 85(3).
*g*     38. It is unnecessary to consider those arguments at this stage; it need merely be
pointed out that a prima facie case has been established only with respect to the refusal to
grant an exemption (art 2 and, consequently, arts 3 and 4 of the contested decision) and
be stated that the applicant has not established that in order to avoid serious and
irreparable damage it is necessary to suspend the operation of the contested decision in
its entirety.
*h*     39. It must be observed that, at the hearing, the applicant emphasised the fact that no
sanctions against signatory undertakings which do not comply with the agreements in
question are provided for in the latter or applied in practice by the applicant association.
Moreover, it is apparent from the documents before the court that in Ireland, where the
consequences of the abolition of the standard conditions of sale in question would be
more serious, in particular for the watertightness of the system, observance of those
*j* conditions by booksellers can be ensured only by the establishment of a contractual
relationship between the publisher and the bookseller. However, that vertical relationship
is not, according to the explanations provided by the Commission at the hearing, affected
by the contested decision. In those circumstances, it appears at first sight that the
suspension of the obligation to proceed with the measures required by arts 3 and 4 of the

contested decision and the fact that the application for exemption referred to in art 2
thereof is still pending, the effects of that article likewise being suspended, are sufficient
to avoid the damage feared by the applicant.

40. In view of the foregoing, it is appropriate to order the suspension of the operation
of arts 2 to 4 of the contested decision.

On those grounds, the President hereby orders as follows: (1) the operation of arts 2 to
4 of Commission Decision 89/44 (EEC) of 12 December 1988 relating to a proceeding
under art 85 of the EEC Treaty (IV/27.393 and IV/27.394, Publishers Association—Net
Book Agreements) is suspended; (2) for the rest, the application is dismissed; (3) the costs
are reserved.

Agents: *Robin Griffith* of *Clifford Chance* (for the association); *Anthony McClellan*, legal
adviser, and *Berend Jan Drijber*, Legal Department of the EEC Commission (for the
Commission).

Mary Rose Plummer   Barrister.

# The Deichland

COURT OF APPEAL, CIVIL DIVISION
NEILL, STUART-SMITH LJJ AND SIR DENYS BUCKLEY
8, 9, 10 FEBRUARY, 20 APRIL 1989

*Admiralty – Jurisdiction – Action in rem – Claim for loss of or damage to cargo carried in ship –
Writ served on ship but ship not arrested on undertaking being given to pay amount adjudged to
be due – Charterers of ship a Panamanian company controlled from Germany – Charterers
named in writ as defendants – Charterers contesting jurisdiction of court on ground that company
domiciled in Germany and action against them should be brought there – Whether High Court
having jurisdiction over charterers in respect of claim – Civil Jurisdiction and Judgments Act
1982, s 42(3), (6), Sch 1, arts 2, 57 – International Convention for the Unification of Certain
Rules relating to the Arrest of Sea-going Ships 1952, art 7.*

The plaintiffs issued a writ in rem against a ship to recover damages in respect of damage
to their cargo occurring in the course of a voyage in 1986. The writ named the charterers
of the vessel at the relevant time as defendants and alleged breaches of contract and/or
breach of duty in relation to the plaintiffs' cargo. When the writ was served on the ship
an undertaking was given by the charterers' P & I club to pay such sums as might be
adjudged to be due by any competent court, with the result that the ship was not arrested.
The charterers were a Panamanian corporation whose central management and control
was in Germany. They applied, inter alia, for a declaration that the court had no
jurisdiction over them in respect of the subject matter of the claim, on the grounds that
under art 2[a] of the 1968 Convention on Jurisdiction and the Enforcement of Judgments
in Civil and Commercial Matters, as set out in Sch 1 to the Civil Jurisdiction and
Judgments Act 1982, they ought to be sued in Germany because they were domiciled
there. The plaintiffs contended, and the judge held, that while the action remained solely
in rem the charterers were not defendants and therefore art 2 did not apply. The
charterers appealed. The questions arose (i) whether the 1968 convention applied to an
Admiralty action in rem while it remained solely in rem, (ii) whether the charterers were
domiciled in Germany for the purposes of art 2, as they contended, or in Panama, as the

---

[a] Article 2 is set out at p 1073 *d e*, post

plaintiffs contended, and (iii) whether in any event the High Court had jurisdiction by
*a* virtue of art 57$^b$ of the 1968 convention, which provided that the convention did not
affect any other conventions governing jurisdiction, including the 1952 International
Convention for the Unification of Certain Rules relating to the Arrest of Sea-going Ships
which regulated the arrest of ships and the giving of security and which by art 7$^c$
provided that the courts of the country in which a ship was arrested had jurisdiction to
determine the merits of the claim.

*b*

**Held** – The appeal would be allowed for the following reasons—
(1) Having regard to the purpose of the 1968 convention, which was, inter alia, to
regulate the circumstances in which a person domiciled in one contracting state might
be brought before the courts of another contracting state in civil and commercial matters,
all forms of proceedings in civil and commercial matters were intended to be covered by
*c* the convention, except in so far as some special provision might otherwise prescribe.
Accordingly, assuming that the charterers were domiciled in Germany, the 1968
convention applied to the plaintiffs' Admiralty action in rem since the charterers would
wish to contest liability and the plaintiffs would wish to proceed in personam against
them if an appearance was entered even though the charter had ended, and therefore in
reality the charterers were being 'sued' in the proceedings within the meaning and intent
*d* of art 2 of the convention even though the proceedings remained solely in rem.
Furthermore, if the charterers entered an appearance the action would thereafter proceed
as an action in personam (see p 1074 *a* to *g*, p 1083 *a b* and p 1086 *a* to *c e g*, post).
(2) Furthermore, since s 42(3) and (6)$^d$ of the 1982 Act made it clear that for the
purposes of the Act a corporation could satisfy the statutory test of domicile set out in
s 42 in relation to more than one state, and since the seat of the charterers' company was
*e* in Germany because that was where their central management and control were situated,
the charterers were domiciled in Germany for the purposes of art 2 of the convention by
virtue of s 42(6)(*b*) (see p 1075 *e f*, p 1078 *e* to *h*, p 1084 *j* to p 1085 *a* and p 1086 *g*, post).
(3) Moreover, jurisdiction was not afforded to the English court by art 57 of the 1968
convention, read with art 7 of the 1952 convention, except in the case of an arrest and
since the ship had not been arrested, those provisions had no application. The High Court
*f* therefore did not have jurisdiction to try the action (see p 1077 *a* to *f*, p 1079 *g* to *j*,
p 1080 *g* to *j*, p 1083 *h j* and p 1086 *g*, post).

**Notes**
For the Admiralty jurisdiction of the High Court, see 1 Halsbury's Laws (4th edn) paras
*g* 301–307.
For the Civil Jurisdiction and Judgments Act 1982, ss 42, Sch 1, art 57, see 22
Halsbury's Statutes (4th edn) 366, 387 and for Sch 1, art 2 of the 1982 Act, see 11 ibid
929.

**Cases referred to in judgments**
*h* *August 8, The* [1983] 2 AC 450, [1983] 2 WLR 419, PC.
*Banco, The, Monte Ulia (owners) v Banco (owners)* [1971] 1 All ER 524, [1971] P 137, [1971]
      2 WLR 335, CA.
*Beldis, The* [1936] P 51, [1935] All ER Rep 760, CA.
*Broadmayne, The* [1916] P 64, CA.
*Burns, The* [1907] P 139, CA.
*j* *Dictator, The* [1892] P 304, [1891–4] All ER Rep 360.
*Gatoil International Inc v Arkwright-Boston Manufacturers Mutual Insurance Co* [1985] 1 All
      ER 129, [1985] AC 255, [1985] 2 All ER 74, HL.

---

*b*    Article 57 is set out at p 1073 *j*, post
*c*    Article 7, so far as material, is set out at p 1076 *d e*, post
*d*    Section 42, so far as material, is set out at p 1075 *a b*, post

*Gemma, The* [1899] P 285, [1895–9] All ER Rep 596, CA.
*Jade, The, The Eschersheim, Erkowit (owners) v Jade (owners), Erkowit (cargo owners) v* **a**
    *Eschersheim (owners)* [1976] 1 All ER 920, [1976] 1 WLR 430, HL.
*Letang v Cooper* [1964] 2 All ER 929, [1965] 1 QB 232, [1964] 3 WLR 573, CA.
*Linda, The* [1988] 1 Lloyd's Rep 175.
*Mersey Docks and Harbour Board v Turner, The Zeta* [1893] AC 468, HL.
*Monica S, The* [1967] 3 All ER 740, [1968] P 741, [1968] 2 WLR 431.
*Nordglimt, The* [1988] 2 All ER 531, [1988] QB 183, [1988] 2 WLR 338.        **b**
*R v Judge of the City of London Court* [1892] 1 QB 273, CA.
*Read v Brown* (1888) 22 QBD 128, CA.
*Sydney Express, The* [1988] 2 Lloyd's Rep 257.
*Williams & Glyn's Bank plc v Astro Dinamico Cia Naviera SA* [1984] 1 All ER 760, [1984] 1
    WLR 438, HL.

**c**

**Cases also cited**
*DSV Silo- und Verwaltungsgesellschaft mbH v Sennar (Owners), The Sennar* [1985] 2 All ER
    104, [1985] 1 WLR 490, HL.
*Freccia del Nord, The* [1989] 1 Lloyd's Rep 388.
*Nautik, The* [1895] P 121.
*River Rima, The* [1988] 2 All ER 641, [1988] 1 WLR 758, HL.        **d**

**Appeal**
Deich Navigation SA (Deich), the former demise charterers of the ship Deichland,
appealed with leave of the judge against the order of Sheen J ([1988] 2 Lloyd's Rep 454)
dated 19 July 1988 dismissing Deich's motion dated 27 June 1988 for an order that
service of the writ of summons issued out of the Admiralty registry of the High Court **e**
and served on the vessel within the jurisdiction by the plaintiffs, the owners of cargo
damaged during carriage in the Deichland claiming damages for breach of contract and/
or duty in and about the loading, handling, custody, care and discharge of the plaintiffs'
cargo and the carriage thereof on board the Deichland in 1986, be set aside and/or that all
further proceedings in the action be stayed and that pursuant to RSC Ord 12, r 8 the **f**
court decline jurisdiction and/or declare that it had no jurisdiction over Deich in respect
of the subject matter of the claim in the action. The facts are set out in the judgment of
Neill LJ.

*Charles Priday* for Deich.
*Richard Aikens QC* and *Julian Malins* for the plaintiffs.
                                                                                **g**

                                                            *Cur adv vult*

20 April. The following judgments were delivered.

**NEILL LJ.** This is an appeal by Deich Navigation SA (Deich) from an order of Sheen J **h**
dated 19 July 1988 whereby he dismissed their motion brought pursuant to RSC Ord 12,
r 8(1) and (3)(a) to contest the jurisdiction of the High Court. Certain consequential relief
was also sought.
    Deich contended that the action should have been brought in the Federal Republic of
Germany where, it was alleged, they were domiciled. Reliance was placed on the Civil
Jurisdiction and Judgments Act 1982 and, in particular, on art 2 of the 1968 Convention **j**
on Jurisdiction and the Enforcement of Judgments in Civil and Commercial Matters,
which is set out in Sch 1 to the 1982 Act.
    The writ in the action was issued from the Admiralty Registry of the High Court on
30 January 1987. The action was described in the writ as an 'Admiralty action in rem
against the ship Deichland'. The plaintiffs were named as 'The Owners of cargo lately

laden on board the ship "Deichland"'. The defendants were named as 'The Owners and/
*a*  or Demise Charterers of the ship "Deichland"'. In 1986 and at the date of the issue of the
writ Deich were the demise charterers of the ship, which has now been renamed the
Baracuda.

It is clear that the writ followed the form prescribed in RSC Ord 75, r 3(1) and in Form
1 in Appendix B to the rules. The claim was stated to be—

*b*       'for damages for breach of contract and/or duty in and about the loading,
handling, custody, care and discharge of the Plaintiffs' cargo and the carriage thereof
on board the Defendants ship "Deichland" in the year 1986.'

It is common ground that unless Deich can invoke the provisions of the 1982 Act and
the 1968 convention the High Court has jurisdiction to try this action in rem. The
Admiralty jurisdiction of the High Court is set out in s 20 of the Supreme Court Act
*c*  1981. By s 20(1)(a) and (2)(g) and (h) this jursidiction includes jurisdiction to hear and
determine 'any claim for loss of or damage to goods carried in a ship' and 'any claim
arising out of any agreement relating to the carriage of goods in a ship or to the use or
hire of a ship'.

The mode of exercise of the Admiralty jurisdiction is prescribed in s 21 of the 1981
*d*  Act. Section 21(4) provides:

'In the case of any such claim as is mentioned in section 20(2)(e) to (r), where—(a)
the claim arises in connection with a ship; and (b) the person who would be liable
on the claim in an action in personam ("the relevant person") was, when the cause
of action arose, the owner or charterer of, or in possession or in control of, the ship,
an action in rem may (whether or not the claim gives rise to a maritime lien on that
*e*  ship) be brought in the High Court against—(i) that ship, if at the time when the
action is brought the relevant person is either the beneficial owner of that ship as
respects all the shares in it or the charterer of it under a charter by demise; or (ii) any
other ship of which, at the time when the action is brought, the relevant person is
the beneficial owner as respects all the shares in it.'

*f*  It is not necessary to refer to any of the other provisions of s 21 save to notice that the
present claim could also have been brought against Deich by way of an action in
personam: see s 21(1).

The facts giving rise to this action can be stated quite shortly. In January 1986 a cargo
of steel coils was loaded on the vessel for carriage from Glasgow to La Spezia in Italy. At
that time the disponent owners of the vessel were Deich who were the demise charterers
*g*  for a period of two years (30 days less charterers' option) under a bareboat charter dated 6
May 1985. The plaintiffs contend that when the steel coils were delivered at La Spezia on
or about 1 February 1986 they were found to be wet-stained and rusted. In the action the
plaintiffs are seeking to recover damages in respect of the loss which they allege they
have suffered.

The writ in rem was issued on 30 January 1987. On 23 November 1987 a trainee legal
*h*  executive in the employment of the plaintiffs' solicitors served the writ on the vessel at
Erith Deep wharf at Erith in Kent by affixing the original writ on the window near the
ship's bridge for a short time and then, on removing the original writ, leaving the sealed
service copy in its place, accompanied by an appropriate form of acknowledgment of
service. By that date, however, the demise charter of the ship had ended, the ownership
of the ship had changed and the ship had been renamed.

*j*  When the writ in rem was served on the ship the ship was not arrested. On 27
November 1987, however, Deich's P & I club in Hamburg sent the plaintiffs a letter in
the following terms:

'In consideration of your refraining from arresting the MV "BARACUDA" ex
"DEICHLAND" or any other vessel in the same ownership, associated ownership or

management for the purpose of founding jurisdiction and/or obtaining security in any part of the world in respect of the above mentioned claim against Deich Navigation SA, bareboat charterers of the above named ship at the material time concerning damage to cargo, we the undersigned P and I Club, hereby guarantee to pay to your Solicitors on your behalf such sums as may be adjudged or found due to you by any competent Court or Tribunal or as may be agreed between the parties in respect of the said claim provided always that our liability hereunder shall not exceed the sum of £54,000,—(Pounds Sterling fifty four thousand) plus interest and costs, providing always in the event that the shipowners can establish before the competent Court their right to limit their liability pursuant to any applicable convention or legislation, such lesser sum as may represent the vessel's limit of liability.'

On 27 June 1988 Deich issued their notice of motion seeking, inter alia, a declaration that the court had no jurisdiction over the defendants in respect of the subject matter of the claim. The motion was heard by Sheen J on 30 June and 1 July 1988. He gave judgment on 19 July 1988 dismissing the motion with costs but gave leave to appeal to this court (see [1988] 2 Lloyd's Rep 454).

Before the judge Deich contended, as they have contended in this court, that they are domiciled in Germany and therefore the matter should be tried in Germany in accordance with art 2 of the 1968 convention. The judge rejected this contention on the basis that the 1968 convention did not apply to an Admiralty action in rem while it remained solely in rem. He said (at 458):

'This action is an action in rem and remains solely in rem until the demise charterers submit to the jurisdiction of this Court. Insofar as they wish on this motion to contest the jurisdiction of the Court they can only contest the jurisdiction in rem. On this motion they have not sought to do so. The ground of the application is "the defendants are domiciled in The Federal Republic of Germany". But while the action is solely in rem there are no "defendants", despite the words of the writ. The demise charterers must decide whether they will submit to the jurisdiction of this Court or allow the action in rem to proceed by default.'

*The issues on the appeal*

The issues which fall to be decided on this appeal can be stated as follows: (1) whether the 1968 convention has any application at all to an Admiralty action in rem while it remains solely in rem; (2) if the 1968 convention applies to the action, whether, for the purposes of art 2 of the 1968 convention, Deich are domiciled in Germany (as they contend) or in Panama (as the plaintiffs contend); (3) if the 1968 convention applies to the action and Deich are domiciled in Germany for the purposes of art 2, whether nevertheless the High Court has jurisdiction by reason of the combined effect of art 57 of the 1968 convention, s 9 of the 1982 Act and the provisions of the International Convention for the Unification of Certain Rules relating to the Arrest of Sea-going Ships (Brussels, 10 May 1952; TS 47 (1960); Cmnd 1128).

I propose to deal first with issue (1) which is the only aspect of the matter on which the judge expressed a conclusion in his judgment.

At the beginning of his submissions in this court counsel for the plaintiffs did not seek to support the judge's reasons for his decision, but later he changed his position and contended strongly that the judge was right. I make no criticism whatever of this change in stance. Clearly the point merits the most careful consideration.

*Issue (1)*

The case for Deich on this issue is based on art 2 of the 1968 convention which, so far as is material, is in the following terms:

a    'Subject to the provisions of this Convention, persons domiciled in a Contracting State shall, whatever their nationality, be sued in the courts of that State . . .'

Deich claim to be domiciled in the Federal Republic of Germany and contend that they should therefore be sued in Germany.

The plaintiffs argue on the other hand that, while the action remains solely an action in rem, Deich are not defendants and that therefore art 2 has no application. Accordingly, the plaintiffs seek to support the decision of the judge.

b    The plaintiffs' case is based on the proposition that an action in rem is an action against the ship itself and that the owners or charterers, as the case may be, of the ship only incur some personal liability if they enter an appearance. In that event the action will proceed both as an action in rem and as an action in personam: see The August 8 [1983] 2 AC 450. Unless and until an appearance is entered, however, the claim is against the res alone and

c    Deich are not defendants in a relevant sense although so described in the writ.

This is an important submission because, if it is right, it means that Deich are faced with the choice of either allowing the action to proceed undefended or of submitting to the jurisdiction by entering an appearance.

The origin and development of Admiralty actions in rem have been considered in numerous cases since the jurisdiction of the High Court of Admiralty was extended by

d    the Admiralty Court Act 1840. It is sufficient to mention The Dictator [1892] P 304, [1891–4] All ER Rep 360, R v Judge of City of London Court [1892] 1 QB 273, Mersey Docks and Harbour Board v Turner, The Zeta [1893] AC 468, The Beldis [1936] P 51, [1935] All ER Rep 760, The Monica S [1967] 3 All ER 740, [1968] P 741, and The Banco, Monte Ulia (owners) v Banco (owners) [1971] 1 All ER 524, [1971] P 137.

It seems clear from these and other authorities that the Admiralty action in rem had

e    its origin in the form of process whereby the property of a defendant was arrested as a means of compelling his appearance and bail or of providing a fund for securing compliance with the judgment. Once the defendant had appeared in the action it could then proceed in personam. In due course the action in rem was developed whereby the Admiralty Court was entitled to enforce its judgments against the arrested property to the extent of the claim and the claim was enforceable even if the property had passed

f    into the hands of an innocent purchaser.

In the present case, however, we are concerned with the statutory jurisdiction of the court and with statutory rights of action in rem. Thus, although the High Court of Admiralty had jurisdiction over contracts of affreightment before 1650 (see Scrutton on Charterparties (15th edn, 1948) p 478) it seems clear that this jurisdiction passed to the common law courts during the next two centuries. The Admiralty Court Act 1861

g    extended the statutory jurisdiction given to the High Court of Admiralty by the Admiralty Court Act 1840 and included a provision relating to contractual claims in respect of damage to imported cargo: see s 6. By s 35 of the 1861 Act it was provided that the jurisdiction conferred by the Act might be exercised either by proceedings in rem or by proceedings in personam.

A wider statutory jurisdiction over contracts of affreightment was introduced by the

h    Administration of Justice Act 1920. By that time the jurisdiction of the High Court of Admiralty had been vested in the High Court of Justice by s 16 of the Judicature Act 1873. Section 6 of the 1861 Act was repealed by the 1920 Act (s 21(2) and the Schedule) and was replaced by s 5(1) of the 1920 Act. Section 5(2) provided that the jurisdiction conferred by the section might be exercised either by proceedings in rem or by proceedings in personam.

j    As, however, s 6 of the 1920 Act was soon repealed and replaced by very similar provisions in the Supreme Court of Judicature (Consolidation) Act 1925 it is sufficient to refer to the relevant sections in the 1925 Act. Section 22(1) provided:

'The High Court shall, in relation to admiralty matters, have the following

jurisdiction ... that is to say—(*a*) Jurisdiction to hear and determine any of the
following questions or claims ... (xii) Any claim—(1) arising out of an agreement *a*
relating to the use or hire of a ship; or (2) relating to the carriage of goods in a ship;
or (3) in tort in respect of goods carried in a ship; unless it is shown to the court that
at the time of the institution of the proceedings any owner or part owner of the ship
was domiciled in England ...'

By s 33(2) it was provided that the jurisdiction might be exercised either in proceedings *b*
in rem or in proceedings in personam.

I come next to Pt I of the Administration of Justice Act 1956. Section 1 of the 1956
Act replaced s 22 of the 1925 Act and redefined the Admiralty jurisdiction of the High
Court in the light of the 1952 convention. The wording of s 1(1)(*g*) and (*h*) differed from
that of the corresponding provisions in s 22(1) of the 1925 Act and s 5(1) of the 1920 Act,
but, as the wording in these paragraphs is the same as that in s 20(2)(*g*) and (*h*) of the 1981 *c*
Act (see above), I do not need to set them out. I do propose, however, to set out the
relevant provisions of s 3(4) of the 1956 Act even though they are substantially reproduced
in s 21(4) of the 1981 Act. Section 3(4) provided:

> 'In the case of any such claim as is mentioned in paragraphs (*d*) to (*r*) of subsection
> (1) of section one of this Act, being a claim arising in connection with a ship, where
> the person who would be liable on the claim in an action in personam was, when *d*
> the cause of action arose, the owner or charterer of, or in possession or in control of,
> the ship, the Admiralty jurisdiction of the High Court ... may (whether the claim
> gives rise to a maritime lien on the ship or not) be invoked by an action in rem
> against—(*a*) that ship, if at the time when the action is brought it is beneficially
> owned as respects all the shares therein by that person; or (*b*) any other ship which,
> at the time when the action is brought, is beneficially owned as aforesaid.' *e*

The 1952 convention, which preceded the enactment of Pt I of the 1956 Act, achieved
an important compromise between English law and the law of many other European
countries as to the circumstances in which a ship might be arrested. English law had
hitherto restricted the right to arrest a ship to cases where a 'maritime' claim was made.
Moreover, the power of arrest did not extend to other ships in the same ownership as the *f*
ship concerned with the claim: see *The Beldis* [1936] P 51, [1935] All ER Rep 760. In
some Continental countries, however, the power of arrest could be exercised in respect
of any claim whether maritime or non-maritime and against any ship in the same
ownership. The 1952 convention reached a solution which restricted the power of arrest
to 'maritime claims' as defined in the convention. In substance the convention adopted
the approach of English law. *g*

I shall have to return later to refer to art 7 of the 1952 convention. At this stage it is
sufficient to observe: (a) that the manner in which the Admiralty jurisdiction of the High
Court could be invoked by an action in rem was extended as a result of this international
convention; (b) that, as appears from some of the documents which we were shown
during the hearing of the appeal recording the negotiations which led up to the
conclusion of the convention, specific attention was drawn in the course of the *h*
negotiations to the existence and nature of an Admiralty action in rem; and (c) that it has
been held that if the meaning of the 1956 Act is not clear the court may look at the terms
of the 1952 convention to assist in the construction of the Act; see *The Banco* [1971] 1 All
ER 524, [1971] P 137.

I come finally to the 1982 Act and to the relevant provisions of the 1968 convention.

It is provided by s 2(1) of the 1982 Act that the 1968 convention, the 1971 Protocol *j*
and the Accession Convention (whereby the United Kingdom acceded to the 1968
convention and the 1971 protocol) 'shall have the force of law in the United Kingdom,
and judicial notice shall be taken of them'. Section 3 contains provisions relating to the
interpretation of the conventions and is in these terms:

*a*  '(1) Any question as to the meaning or effect of any provision of the Conventions shall, if not referred to the European Court in accordance with the 1971 Protocol, be determined in accordance with the principles laid down by and any relevant decision of the European Court.

(2) Judicial notice shall be taken of any decision of, or expression of opinion by, the European Court on any such question.

*b*  (3) Without prejudice to the generality of subsection (1), the following reports (which are reproduced in the Official Journal of the Communities), namely—(a) the reports by Mr. P. Jenard on the 1968 Convention and the 1971 Protocol; and (b) the report by Professor Peter Schlosser on the Accession Convention, may be considered in ascertaining the meaning or effect of any provision of the Conventions and shall be given such weight as is appropriate in the circumstances.'

*c*  As appears from the preamble to the 1968 convention one of its objects was 'to determine the international jurisdiction' of the courts of the six states who were the original signatories.

Title I of the convention defined its scope. Article 1 provided that the convention should 'apply in civil and commercial matters whatever the nature of the court or tribunal'.

*d*  Title II was concerned with jurisdiction. Section 1 of this title contained general provisions and provided in art 2:

'Subject to the provisions of this Convention, persons domiciled in a Contracting State shall, whatever their nationality, be sued in the courts of that State. Persons who are not nationals of the State in which they are domiciled shall be governed by
*e*  the rules of jurisdiction applicable to nationals of that State.'

Article 3 provided:

'Persons domiciled in a Contracting State may be sued in the courts of another Contracting State only by virtue of the rules set out in Sections 2 to 6 of this Title . . .'

*f*  This article in addition set out a number of provisions under which the individual contracting states (including the three countries including the United Kingdom which acceded later) claimed jurisdiction over persons domiciled abroad, which were expressly stated not to be applicable as against persons domiciled in a contracting state.

Section 2 of Title II contained provisions conferring a special jurisdiction in a number of specific cases. It is only necessary to refer to part of art 5 in section 2. Nor is it necessary
*g*  to refer to any of the rules set out in sections 3 to 6 of Title II. The following provision in art 5 is, however, of importance:

'A person domiciled in a Contracting State may, in another Contracting State, be sued . . . (7) as regards a dispute concerning the payment of remuneration claimed in respect of the salvage of cargo or freight, in the court under the authority of which the cargo or freight in question: (a) has been arrested to secure such payment,
*h*  or (b) could have been so arrested, but bail or other security has been given; provided that this provision shall apply only if it is claimed that the defendant has an interest in the cargo or freight or had such an interest at the time of salvage.'

Finally, I should refer to part of art 57 in Title VII of the 1968 convention. This article provided:

*j*  'This Convention shall not affect any conventions to which the Contracting States are or will be parties and which, in relation to particular matters, govern jurisdiction or the recognition or enforcement of judgments . . .'

It is clear therefore that the 1968 convention does not affect any jurisdiction given to the High Court under the 1952 convention. I shall return to examine this point further in relation to the third issue.

The question for determination at this stage is whether, assuming for the moment that Deich are domiciled in the Federal Republic of Germany, they are being 'sued' in the High Court in England in the present proceedings, that is, while the action remains an action solely in rem.

I have come to the conclusion that the right approach when one is considering the effect of an international convention is to take account of the purpose or purposes of the convention. Plainly the 1968 convention was intended, inter alia, to regulate the circumstances in which a person domiciled in one contracting state might be brought before the courts of another contracting state 'in civil and commercial matters'. Accordingly, it seems to me that all forms of proceedings in civil and commercial matters were intended to be covered except in so far as some special provisions such as art 57 might otherwise prescribe. Furthermore, it seems to me that para (7) in art 5, which confers a special jurisdiction in the case of claims for remuneration in respect of the salvage of cargo or freight, contemplates that this special jurisdiction may be exercised by proceedings either in rem or in personam.

It is true that in the present case the vessel is no longer chartered to Deich and that the jurisdiction to entertain the action in rem is based on the provisions of s 21 of the 1981 Act. But looking at the reality of the matter it is Deich who are interested in contesting liability and against whom the plaintiffs would wish to proceed in personam if an appearance is entered. The position might have been different if the parties to the 1968 convention and to the Accession Convention had had no knowledge of the Admiralty jurisdiction of the High Court, but it is quite clear from paras 121 and 122 of Professor Schlosser's report on the Accession Convention (OJ 1979 C59, pp 108–109) that detailed consideration was given to the exercise of jurisdiction in maritime matters by the courts of the United Kingdom.

In these circumstances I find it impossible to conclude that on the proper construction of arts 2 and 3 of the 1968 convention Deich are not being 'sued' in these proceedings even though at this stage the proceedings are solely in rem. Deich are liable to be adversely affected by the result of the proceedings and wish to contest the merits of the plaintiffs' claim. By English law an Admiralty action in rem has special characteristics though, as has been seen, these characteristics were modified by the 1956 Act in line with the 1952 convention. I do not consider, however, that the rules relating to such actions and governing the rights of a plaintiff to levy execution can affect the substance of the matter when the court is faced with an international convention designed to regulate the international jurisdiction of national courts.

I would decide the first issue in favour of Deich.

*Issue* (2)

It is argued on behalf of the plaintiffs that even if art 2 can apply to an action in rem while it remains solely in rem Deich are unable to rely on this article because they are domiciled in the Republic of Panama.

Article 53 of the 1968 convention provides:

'For the purposes of this Convention, the seat of a company or other legal person or association of natural or legal persons shall be treated as its domicile. However, in order to determine that seat, the court shall apply its rules of private international law.'

It is therefore necessary to turn to the relevant provisions of the 1982 Act. Section 42 is concerned with the domicile and seat of a corporation or association and, so far as is material, provides:

'(1) For the purposes of this Act the seat of a corporation or association (as determined by this section) shall be treated as its domicile.

a
(2) The following provisions of this section determine where a corporation or association has its seat—(a) for the purposes of Article 53 (which for the purposes of the 1968 Convention equates the domicile of such a body with its seat) . . .

(3) A corporation or association has its seat in the United Kingdom if and only if—(a) it was incorporated or formed under the law of a part of the United Kingdom and has its registered office or some other official address in the United Kingdom; or (b) its central management and control is exercised in the United Kingdom . . .

b
(6) Subject to subsection (7), a corporation or association has its seat in a state other than the United Kingdom if and only if—(a) it was incorporated or formed under the law of that state and has its registered office or some other official address there; or (b) its central management and control is exercised in that state.

(7) A corporation or association shall not be regarded as having its seat in a Contracting State other than the United Kingdom if it is shown that the courts of
c
that state would not regard it as having its seat there.'

The relevant facts are not in dispute. Deich were incorporated in the Republic of Panama. The central management and control of Deich, however, are exercised in the Federal Republic of Germany. It is also common ground that the Federal Republic of Germany would regard Deich as having their seat there.

d
It is argued on behalf of the plaintiffs that a corporation can only have one seat and that if the test set out in s 42(6)(a) is satisfied there is no need to consider the alternative test in s 42(6)(b). Accordingly, it is said, Deich have their seat and are domiciled in Panama and therefore art 2 of the 1968 convention has no application.

I am not persuaded by this argument. It seems to me to be quite clear from s 42(3) and (6) that for the purposes of the 1982 Act a corporation may satisfy the statutory test in
e
relation to more than one state. Indeed, s 42(3) plainly covers the case of a corporation which has been incorporated abroad but where the central management and control of the corporation is exercised in the United Kingdom. For the purpose of art 53 such a corporation has its seat in the United Kingdom and can therefore be sued there. Furthermore, as was pointed out in argument, arts 21 and 22 of the 1968 convention are designed to deal with cases where related actions are brought in the courts of different
f
contracting states.

I am satisfied that for the purpose of art 2 Deich are domiciled in the Federal Republic of Germany (and would be so regarded by the courts of that state) because the seat of the company is in Germany by virtue of the alternative test prescribed in s 42(6)(b) of the 1982 Act.

g
*Issue (3)*

The plaintiffs further argue that even if a German court would otherwise have jurisdiction by reason of the provisions of Title II of the 1968 convention the High Court in England can exercise jurisdiction by virtue of art 57 of the 1968 convention when read in conjunction with art 7 of the 1952 convention and s 9 of the 1982 Act.

Article 57 of the 1968 convention is in these terms:

h
'This Convention shall not affect any conventions to which the Contracting States are or will be parties and which, in relation to particular matters, govern jurisdiction or the recognition or enforcement of judgments . . . (*Article 25(2) of the Accession Convention provides:* "With a view to its uniform interpretation, paragraph 1 of Article 57 shall be applied in the following manner: (a) The 1968 Convention as amended shall not prevent a court of a Contracting State which is a party to a
j
convention on a particular matter from assuming jurisdiction in accordance with that convention, even where the defendant is domiciled in another Contracting State which is not a party to that convention. The court shall, in any event, apply Article 20 of the 1968 Convention as amended . . .").'

It is therefore necessary to turn to art 7 of the 1952 convention to determine whether

or not the High Court has jurisdiction by reason of the provisions of that article. At the
same time, it is necessary to take account of the provisions of s 9 of the 1982 Act. This *a*
section, so far as material, provides:

> '(1) The provisions of Title VII of the 1968 Convention (relationship between
> that convention and other conventions to which Contracting States are or may
> become parties) shall have effect in relation to—(a) any statutory provision,
> whenever passed or made, implementing any such other convention in the United
> Kingdom; and (b) any rule of law so far as it has the effect of so implementing any *b*
> such other convention, as they have effect in relation to that other convention
> itself . . .'

I come next to art 7 of the 1952 convention. It will be remembered that the 1952
convention was concluded for the purpose of determining by agreement between the
contracting states certain uniform rules of law relating to the arrest of sea-going ships. It *c*
will also be remembered that a compromise solution was reached whereby the power to
arrest was confined to maritime claims as understood in English law but that the power
was extended, in accordance with the law of a number of continental countries, to
include a right to arrest a vessel in the same ownership. Article 7 of the 1952 convention,
so far as material, provides:

*d*

> '(1) The Courts of the country in which the arrest was made shall have jurisdiction
> to determine the case upon its merits [a number of conditions are then set out].
> (2) If the Court within whose jurisdiction the ship was arrested has not jurisdiction
> to decide upon the merits, the bail or other security given in accordance with Article
> 5 to procure the release of the ship shall specifically provide that it is given as security
> for the satisfaction of any judgment which may eventually be pronounced by a *e*
> Court having jurisdiction so to decide; and the Court or other appropriate judicial
> authority of the country in which the arrest is made shall fix the time within which
> the claimant shall bring an action before a Court having such jurisdiction . . .'

It was argued on behalf of the plaintiffs that though the word 'arrest' was used in art 7
the High Court nevertheless had jurisdiction because the usual undertaking had been *f*
given by a P & I club to prevent arrest, and because the High Court had jurisdiction to
try the matter under the 1956 Act which was passed to implement the 1952 convention.
Our attention was drawn to other articles in the 1952 convention which referred in
terms to security being given to prevent or avoid an arrest. In this context we were
referred to: (a) art 3(3), which provides:

> 'A ship shall not be arrested, nor shall bail or other security be given more than *g*
> once in any one or more of the jurisdictions of any of the Contracting States in
> respect of the same maritime claim by the same claimant; and, if a ship has been
> arrested in any one of such jurisdictions, or bail or other security has been given in
> such jurisdiction either to release the ship or to avoid a threatened arrest, any
> subsequent arrest of the ship or of any ship in the same ownership by the same
> claimant for the same maritime claim shall be set aside . . .' *h*

and (b) art 6, which provides:

> 'All questions whether in any case the claimant is liable in damages for the arrest
> of a ship or for the costs of the bail or other security furnished to release or prevent
> the arrest of a ship, shall be determined by the law of the Contracting State in whose *j*
> jurisdiction the arrest was made or applied for . . .'

In addition emphasis was placed on the common practice whereby ships are not
actually arrested but some security or undertaking is furnished to prevent an arrest.
I see the force of the argument that in the light of the 1956 Act the jurisdiction given
by art 7 of the 1952 convention should not be confined to cases where an arrest has

actually been effected. I have come to the conclusion, however, that the argument must
a   be rejected for the following reasons.

(1) It is clear, as I have already indicated, that the 1952 convention was only concluded
after long and detailed negotiations had taken place and the final wording represented a
compromise. One must be very careful therefore before accepting an argument that the
word 'arrest' in art 7 is capable of including a process which falls short of an actual arrest.

(2) The word 'arrest' is defined in art 1(2) as meaning the 'detention of a ship by
b   judicial process to secure a maritime claim, but does not include the seizure of a ship in
execution or satisfaction of a judgment'.

(3) In arts 3 and 6 respectively reference is made to 'bail or other security' given or
furnished 'to avoid a threatened arrest' or to 'prevent the arrest'. There are no comparable
words in art 7.

(4) Professor Schlosser in paras 122 and 123 of his Report on the Accession Convention
c   (OJ 1979 C59, pp 108–109) commented on the wording of art 5(7) of the 1968 convention
relating to jurisdiction in connection with the arrest of salvaged cargo or freight. He
explained that art 5(7)(b) introduced an extension of jurisdiction not expressly modelled
on the 1952 convention. He added:

> 'After salvage operations—whether involving a ship, cargo or freight—arrest is
d   > sometimes ordered, but not actually carried into effect, because bail or other security
> has been provided. This must be sufficient to confer jurisdiction on the arresting
> court to decide also on the substance of the matter.'

It seems to me that this comment or explanation is at least consistent with the view that
art 7 did not confer jurisdiction where bail or other security was given to avoid arrest.

(5) It is common ground that if it were not for the 1968 convention the High Court
e   would have jurisdiction to try this action and that this jurisdiction is derived from ss 20
and 21 of the 1981 Act (formerly ss 1 and 3 of the 1956 Act). In my view, however, as
the jurisdiction given by art 7 of the 1952 convention is governed by the word 'arrest' it
is not permissible for the purpose of applying s 9 of the 1982 Act to treat any part of the
High Court's jurisdiction other than the 'arrest' jurisdiction as being based on a statutory
f   provision implementing the 1952 convention.

I would therefore decide this issue also in favour of Deich.

Accordingly, I would allow the appeal. It will be necessary to hear further argument
on the form of order which should now be made.

**STUART-SMITH LJ.** Two questions arise for determination in this appeal. (1) For
g   the purpose of the Civil Jurisdiction and Judgments Act 1982 and the Convention on
Jurisdiction and Enforcement of Judgments in Civil and Commercial Matters signed at
Brussels on 27 September 1968, where are the appellant corporation, Deich Navigation
SA (Deich), domiciled? (2) If Deich are domiciled in the Federal Republic of Germany,
one of the contracting states under the 1968 convention, is the general requirement that
Deich must be sued in the courts of that state, as provided by art 2 of the 1968 convention,
h   affected by the fact that the plaintiffs have brought their claim by an action in rem in the
English Admiralty Court?

I turn to consider the first question. The 1968 convention has the force of law in the
United Kingdom (s 2(1) of the 1982 Act). Article 53 of the 1968 convention provides:

> 'For the purposes of this Convention, the seat of a company . . . shall be treated as
j   > its domicile. However in order to determine that seat, the court shall apply its rules
> of private international law.'

In English law those rules are to be found in s 42 of the 1982 Act, which provides by
sub-ss (6) and (7):

> '(6) Subject to subsection (7), a corporation or association has its seat in a state

other than the United Kingdom if and only if—(a) it was incorporated or formed under the law of that state and has its registered office or some other official address there; or (b) its central management and control is exercised in that state.

(7) A corporation or association shall not be regarded as having its seat in a Contracting State other than the United Kingdom if it is shown that the courts of that state would not regard it as having its seat there.'

It is common ground that (a) Deich were incorporated in Panama and have their registered office or some other official address there; (b) the central management and control of Deich are exercised in the Federal Republic of Germany; and (c) the courts of the Federal Republic of Germany would regard Deich as having their seat there. Counsel for Deich submits that under s 42(6) a corporation can have two seats: he accepts that they have a seat in Panama; he contends that they also have a seat in the Federal Republic of Germany. Counsel for the plaintiffs submits that they can have only one, and that is Panama. He points to the use of the singular 'seat' in s 42(1) to (7) and the fact that in s 5(3), (4) and (5) it seems clear that only one seat is contemplated. He submits that the construction of s 42(6) is that if para (a) is satisfied the court must look no further; it is only if both the requirements of para (a), that is to say incorporation or formation *and* presence of its registered office or official address, are not satisfied that the court needs to look at para (b). While I recognise the force of the argument based on the use of the singular, it seems to me that that construction requires the introduction after the word 'or' of some such words as 'if there is no such state', unless it can be said that these words are implicit from the use of the singular 'seat', instead of 'seat or seats'; and in my view they are not. Nor do I accept the submission of counsel for the plaintiffs that since s 42(6) is concerned with both corporations and associations, para (a) is related to one and para (b) to the other.

Since s 42 is concerned with jurisdiction and not the applicable or proper law to be applied, there seems to me no fundamental objection if two contracting states have jurisdiction. Indeed, this is clearly contemplated by the provisions of arts 5 to 15 (which deal with special jurisdiction, jurisdiction in matters relating to insurance and consumer contracts) and arts 21 and 22 (which deal with proceedings involving the same cause of action and related actions brought in the courts of different contracting states).

Deich's construction is supported by the opinion of Professor Schlosser, whose report on the Accession Convention may be considered in ascertaining the meaning or effect of any provision of the convention: see s 3(3)(b) of the 1982 Act and para 162 of Professor Schlosser's report (OJ 1979 C59, p 120). It also has the support of the learned editor of Dicey and Morris *Conflict of Laws* (11th edn, 1987) vol 1, p 285 and see the illustrations at p 287. Moreover, this construction seems to me to be consistent with the policy of the 1968 convention that defendants should be sued where they are domiciled, if that is in one of the contracting states. It also makes practical sense that a corporation can be sued where, to use the phrase of counsel for Deich, 'it puts up its brass plate or has its nerve centre'. Accordingly, I would hold that Deich is domiciled in the Federal Republic of Germany.

I turn then to the second question. The central principle of the 1968 convention is that in matters to which the convention applies, defendants are to be sued in the courts of the state in which they are domiciled. Article 1 provides that the convention shall apply in civil and commercial matters whatever the nature of the court of tribunal. There are then enumerated certain exceptions which do not apply. In my view the present claim falls within art 1. I must set out art 2, which provides:

'Subject to the provisions of this Convention, persons domiciled in a Contracting State shall, whatever their nationality, be sued in the courts of that State . . .'

The remainder of art 2 is not material. Article 3 provides:

'Persons domiciled in a Contracting State may be sued in the courts of another *a* Contracting State only by virtue of the rules set out in Sections 2 to 6 of this Title. In particular the following provisions shall not be applicable as against them . . . in the United Kingdom: the rules which enable jurisdiction to be founded on . . . (b) the presence within the United Kingdom of property belonging to the defendant; or (c) the seizure by the plaintiff of property situated in the United Kingdom.'

*b* It seems to me to be plain that, if an Admiralty action in rem is within art 2 at all, and the plaintiffs argue that it is not, it is caught by the words in (b) and (c) of art 3 relating to the United Kingdom. None of the exceptions in ss 2 to 6 are relevant to the present claim. I have already briefly mentioned arts 5 to 15 which constitute ss 2 to 4. Section 5 (art 16) confers exclusive jurisdiction regardless of domicile in certain matters, for example immoveable property. Section 6 (arts 17 and 18) is concerned with prorogation of jurisdiction where there is agreement between the parties that the courts of a

*c* contracting state are to have jurisdiction.

There is however a further exception to be found in art 57 of the 1968 convention. This provides:

'This Convention shall not affect any conventions to which the Contracting States are or will be parties and which, in relation to particular matters, govern jurisdiction . . .'

*d* It is common ground that the International Convention for the Unification of Certain Rules Relating to the Arrest of Sea-going Ships (Brussels, 10 May 1952; TS 47 (1960); Cmnd 1128), is one such convention. Both the United Kingdom and the Federal Republic of Germany are parties to that convention. Article 7 provides:

*e* '1. The Courts of the country in which the arrest was made shall have jurisdiction to determine the case upon its merits:—if the domestic law of the country in which the arrest is made gives jurisdiction to such Courts . . .'

'Arrest' is defined in art 1(2) as—

'the detention of a ship by judicial process to secure a maritime claim, but does *f* not include the seizure of a ship in execution or satisfaction of a judgment.'

'Maritime claim' is defined in art 1(1) as—

'a claim arising out of one or more of the following . . . (e) agreement relating to the carriage of goods in any ship whether by charterparty or otherwise; (f) loss of or damage to goods including baggage carried in any ship.'

*g* The present action is a maritime claim. Counsel for Deich accepts, as he is bound to do, that if the Deichland had been arrested, the English Admiralty Court would have merits jurisdiction. But she was not arrested. And he submits that on the plain wording of the article, it cannot be extended to a case where the ship might have been arrested, but is not. I do not understand counsel for the plaintiffs to dispute this. In my judgment *h* counsel for Deich is right. There are a number of points, in addition to the plain words of the article, which show that this is so. Article 3(3) of the 1952 convention draws a distinction between 'arrest . . . nor bail or other security . . . given . . . either *to release the ship or to avoid a threatened arrest*' (my emphasis). The 1968 convention makes the same distinction: see art 5(7) and the comments of Professor Schlosser at para 123 (OJ 1979 C 59, p 109) and art 36 of the Accession Convention. Furthermore, it is clear from the *j* travaux préparatoire that the question was raised whether the jurisdiction should be extended to cases where security was given to avoid arrest, and it was rejected. If need be, though in this case I consider there is no need since the meaning is plain, resort can be had to this discussion: see per Lord Wilberforce in *Gatoil International Inc v Arkwright-Boston Manufacturers Mutual Insurance Co* [1985] 1 All ER 129 at 132, [1985] AC 255 at 264.

Counsel for the plaintiffs argues that that is not the end of the matter. He submits that the jurisdiction for proceedings in rem is founded on s 21(2) of the Supreme Court Act 1981 (which re-enacted similar provisions in s 3 of the Supreme Court Act 1956). These statutory provisions were enacted to implement the 1952 convention: see per Lord Diplock in *The Jade, The Eschersheim* [1976] 1 All ER 920 at 923, [1976] 1 WLR 430 at 434. Section 21 of the Supreme Court Act 1981 provides:

> '(1) Subject to section 22, an action in personam may be brought in the High Court in all cases within the Admiralty jurisdiction of that Court.'

I pause only to say that it is common ground that an action in personam would now undoubtedly be subject to the provisions of the 1968 convention and triable only in the German courts. Section 21 continues:

> '(4) In the case of any such claim as is mentioned in section 20(2)(*e*) to (*r*), where— (*a*) the claim arises in connection with a ship; and (*b*) the person who would be liable on the claim in an action in personam ("the relevant person") was, when the cause of action arose, the owner or charterer of, or in possession or in control of, the ship, an action in rem may (whether or not the claim gives rise to a maritime lien on that ship) be brought in the High Court against—(i) that ship . . .'

The present claim falls within s 20(2)(*g*) being a claim for loss of or damage to goods carried in a ship. Fundamental to the argument of counsel for the plaintiffs on this point is s 9(1) of the 1982 Act. This provides:

> 'The provisions of Title VII of the 1968 Convention (relationship between that convention and other conventions to which Contracting States are or may become parties) shall have effect in relation to—(*a*) any statutory provision, whenever passed or made, implementing any such other convention in the United Kingdom; and (*b*) any rule of law so far as it has the effect of so implementing any such other convention, as they have effect in relation to that other convention itself.'

I do not find this the easiest section to construe. No doubt the need for this section arises, at any rate so far as the 1952 convention is concerned, because that convention was not adopted as such as the law of this country, for example by incorporating the convention in a schedule to the Act, as was done with the 1968 convention and the 1982 Act, but by implementing it in the Administration of Justice Act 1956 and the Supreme Court Act 1981. Counsel for the plaintiffs argues that since these Acts did implement the 1952 convention, everything enacted in the relevant sections, including s 21 of the 1981 Act, is now the law of this country by virtue of s 9(1).

I cannot accept this submission. In the first place, it seems to me extraordinary that jurisdiction which is not within the express terms of art 7 of the 1952 convention, and is expressly outside the provisions of arts 1, 2 and 3 of the 1968 convention, can creep in by the back door. Second, it seems to me plain from the wording of s 9 that the statutory provisions are only to be given effect so far as they implement the 1952 convention and not otherwise, no other convention being relevant for this purpose. Third, it is accepted that much of the jurisdiction given by s 21 of the 1981 Act is affected by the 1968 convention, eg Admiralty actions in personam and actions in rem in relation to aircraft (s 21(1) and (3)). Why, it may be asked, should not an action in rem relating to a ship be similarly affected save to the extent that it is preserved by the 1968 or 1952 conventions? I conclude therefore that jurisdiction is not afforded to the English court by art 57 of the 1968 convention or s 9(1) of the 1982 Act, except in the case of an arrest.

The alternative argument of counsel for plaintiffs is that an action in rem is not within art 2 of the 1968 convention at all, because persons are not being sued, the action being solely against the ship. This was the ground on which the judge decided the case in favour of the plaintiffs. At first counsel for the plaintiffs said that he was not seeking to uphold the judge's reasoning; but it seems to me that he is doing so in this submission

and he later accepted that he was. This has the rather startling result that a defendant
*a* cannot contest the jurisdiction of the English court in an action in rem. Since, if he
acknowledges service, he submits to the jurisdiction; if he does not, the action must go
undefended and by default. This is a curious result and not one, as it seems to me that is
contemplated either by the 1968 convention or the Rules of the Supreme Court. The
convention, by art 18, provides:

*b*
'Apart from jurisdiction from other provisions of this Convention, a court of a
Contracting State before whom a defendant enters an appearance shall have
jurisdiction. This rule shall not apply where appearance was entered solely to contest
the jurisdiction . . .'

The rules, by the combined effect of r 8(6) and (7) of Ord 12, provides:

*c*
'A defendant who makes application under paragraph (1) [to contest the
jurisdiction] shall not be treated as having submitted to the jurisdiction of the court
by reason of his having given notice of intention to defend the action; and if the
Court makes no order on the application or dismisses it, the notice shall cease to
have effect, but the defendant may subject to rule 6(1) lodge a further
acknowledgement of service and in that case . . . the acknowledgement . . . shall . . .
*d* be treated as a submission by the defendant to the jurisdiction . . .'

There is clear authority that an action in rem, being an action against the ship, is not
against the owners and is different in kind from an action in personam against the
owners. Fletcher Moulton LJ said in *The Burns* [1907] p 137 at 149–150:

*e*
'I am, therefore, of opinion that the fundamental proposition of the argument of
the appellants' counsel fails, and that the action in rem is an action against the ship
itself. It is an action in which the owners may take part, if they think proper, in
defence of their property, but whether or not they will do so is a matter for them to
decide, and if they do not decide to make themselves parties to the suit in order to
defend their property, no personal liability can be established against them in that
action. It is perfectly true that the action indirectly affects them. So it would if it
*f* were an action against a person whom they had indemnified . . . The only possible
support, in my opinion, for the proposition put forward by counsel for the appellants
is to be found in the language of the writ itself by which the action in rem is now
commenced; but I am of opinion that this ought not to weigh with us. If the old
form of warrant is looked at by which the arrest of a ship used to be made, the
language in no way supports the contention of the appellants. On the contrary, it is
*g* evident from the language of that warrant that the process was regarded then as
being directed against the ship itself. That old form was abandoned, and a new form
of writ was employed, by direction of those who were responsible for drawing up
the Forms under the Judicature Act. I think it was in 1883 that the rule was passed
which directed the present form of writ to be issued in Admiralty actions in rem.
The direction itself shows that, whether the language was felicitous for the purpose
or not, the writ was intended to apply to the old-established Admiralty action in
*h* rem, and was not intended to have the effect of creating a new type of action or
altering the nature of the action; and when we turn to the form which was at the
same time prescribed for the writ of possession in an Admiralty action in rem,
where there had been a default of appearance, we find that the language is quite
suitable, and shews that the proceeding is against the ship itself.'

*j*
This passage was followed by Hobhouse J in *The Nordglimt* [1988] 2 All ER 531 at 544–
545, [1988] QB 183 at 200.
However, once the shipowner acknowledges service, the action becomes an action in
personam. There are conflicting dicta whether or not it also continues as an action in
rem. Counsel for Deich has pointed out that the cases where it has been said that the

action continues both in personam and in rem are cases where the res was still under the
control of the court, because it was under arrest, as in *The August 8* [1983] 2 AC 450 at          *a*
456 per Lord Brandon where he cited a dictum from the judgment of A L Smith LJ in
*The Gemma* [1899] P 285 at 292, [1895–9] All ER Rep 596. In that case it was said that an
action in rem became an action in personam on appearance by the defendant; but in fact
bail had been put up by the defendant and was in court.

This view was clearly expressed by Sheen J in *The Linda* [1988] 1 Lloyds Rep 175 at
179:          *b*

'I have already said that this action was commenced as an action in rem against
*Linda*, but is now an action in personam and no longer in rem. In case it is thought
there is any conflict between this judgment and that of Mr. Justice Hobhouse in *The
Nordglimt* ([1988] 2 All ER 531, [1988] QB 183), let me emphasize the point that an
action in rem retains the characteristics of such an action only so long as it remains          *c*
an action against a ship or against the proceeds of sale of the ship. In *The Nordglimt*,
the ship remained under arrest. The action accordingly remained in rem. But there
are many occasions on which (a) solicitors offer to give contractual security and
undertake to accept service of a writ or to acknowledge service of it in order to avoid
the threatened arrest of a ship, or (b) a ship under arrest is released because security
to the satisfaction of the plaintiffs has been given. In such circumstances the action          *d*
proceeds as an action in personam regardless of the form of the writ. As was said by
Lord Justice A. L. Smith in *The Gemma* ([1899] P 285 at 292 [1895–9] All ER Rep
596 at 598): "The action, though originally commenced in rem, becomes a personal
action against the defendants upon appearance." While a ship is under arrest, or the
proceeds of sale of a ship are in Court, the action continues as an action in rem. If
service of the writ has been acknowledged, the action continues also in personam.          *e*
But if a ship is not arrested, or is released after arrest, there is no "res" against which
the plaintiff, or any other interested person, can proceed.'

Sheen J in the present case, after citing part of this passage from his previous judgment,
sought to distinguish it. He said ([1988] 2 Lloyd's Rep 454 at 458):

'I was, of course, applying my mind only to the practical reality of the proceedings.          *f*
The special purpose of an action in rem is to induce the owner of the res to submit
to the jurisdiction of this Court by acknowledging service of the writ and giving
notice of intention to defend. Once the owner has done so the plaintiff has the
advantage of being able to obtain a judgment in personam. But in the very
exceptional case such as *The Broadmayne* ([1916] P 64) in which the plaintiff could
not arrest the ship while it was requisitioned, and thereby belonged to His Majesty,          *g*
there remained a residual right to arrest when the requisition ceased. It did not cross
my mind when I was considering *The Linda* that there might be an occasion on
which the plaintiff might wish to obtain a judgment against the ship in
circumstances in which the ship had not been arrested and the plaintiff had agreed
not to arrest the ship or any other ship in the same ownership. But the instant case
may be just such a case. I have not been called upon to decide whether the guarantee          *h*
given by Trampfhart on Nov. 27, 1987 will enable the plaintiffs to obtain satisfaction
of a judgment in rem.'

But with all respect to the judge I cannot see that this is a valid distinction. In *The Linda*
the defendants had only submitted to the jurisdiction of the court to the extent of
arguing the issue of jurisdiction. As in this case the matter was raised by application          *j*
under Ord 12, r 8.
There is a clear distinction between submitting to the merits jurisdiction of the court
and submitting to its jurisdiction solely for the purpose of the court deciding its
jurisdiction: see *Williams & Glyn's Bank plc v Astro Dinamico Cia Naviera SA* [1984] 1 All

ER 760 at 763, [1984] 1 WLR 438 at 443 per Lord Fraser, applied by Sheen J in *The*
*a*  *Sydney Express* [1988] 2 Lloyds Rep 257. It seems to me inherent in the reasoning in both
*The Linda* and *The Sydney Express* that notwithstanding that the action is begun as an
action in rem a defendant can contest the court's jurisdiction on convention grounds and
is not to be taken to have submitted to the merits jurisdiction of the English court, and
he is not obliged so to submit or see the action against the ship go by default.

In my judgment the 1982 Act and the 1968 convention provide a comprehensive
*b*  code. If a defendant is domiciled in a contracting state he must be sued in that state
unless the case falls within the exceptions contained in ss 2 to 6 of the 1968 convention
or under the provisions of art 57, which for the purpose of this case means the 1952
arrest convention. Articles 1, 2, 3 and 57 are clearly intended as it seems to me to apply
to actions in rem.

The practical consequences of allowing this appeal do not seem to me to be as far
*c*  reaching as counsel for the plaintiffs suggested. If a plaintiff for some reason is determined
to litigate in the English Admiralty Court he can easily secure this; either he arrests the
ship, or he secures express agreement by the defendant owner or demise charterer to
submit to the jurisdiction of the English court to avoid arrest, no doubt at the same time
obtaining security. In the present case the plaintiffs did neither of these things.

I would allow the appeal.
*d*

**SIR DENYS BUCKLEY.** Article 2 of the Convention on Jurisdiction and the
Enforcement of Judgments in Civil and Commercial Matters signed at Brussels on 27
September 1968 provides that, subject to its other provisions, persons domiciled in a
contracting state shall be sued in the courts of that state. It is not suggested that any other
provision of that convention (apart may be from art 57) excludes the present case from
*e*  that general requirement. The United Kingdom and the Federal Republic of Germany
are both contracting states. Consequently (subject may be to art 57), if for the purposes
of the 1968 convention the appellant demise charterers (Deich) of the ship Deichland are
to be regarded as domiciled in Germany they can in accordance with art 2 be sued only
in Germany by any party bound by that article.

Section 2 of the Civil Jurisdiction and Judgments Act 1982 gives the 1968 convention
*f*  the force of law in the UK. The convention is consequently binding on the plaintiffs.
Accordingly, if Deich are to be regarded as domiciled in Germany, this appeal should
succeed if Deich can accurately be said to be 'sued' in this action notwithstanding that the
action is in form exclusively an action in rem against the ship.

Article 57 of the 1968 convention provides that that convention shall not affect any
conventions to which contracting states are parties and which govern jurisdiction or the
*g*  recognition or enforcement of judgments. When the United Kingdom acceded to the
1968 convention it was, and still is, a party to what has been referred to as the arrest
convention (the International Convention for the Unification of Certain Rules relating to
the Arrest of Sea-going Ships (Brussels, 10 May 1952; TS 47 (1960); Cmnd 1128)). That
convention regulates the arrest of ships in the jurisdictions of contracting states and the
*h*  furnishing of bail and other forms of security in respect of certain maritime claims
including any claim arising out of loss or damage to goods carried in any ship. Article 7
thereof provides that courts of the country in which a ship is arrested shall have
jurisdiction to determine the case on its merits. It seems to me, however, that nothing in
that convention can have any application to the present case because the Deichland has
not been arrested. Consequently, in my judgment art 57 of the 1968 convention does
*j*  not affect the present case.

So we are, I think, left with two questions: (1) whether Deich are 'domiciled' within
the meaning of that term in the 1968 convention in Germany; and (2) whether the
instant action is one in which Deich are 'sued' within the meaning of art 2 of that
convention as that article is given effect in English law by the 1982 Act.

(1) *Domicile*

Article 53 of the 1968 convention (omitting superfluous words) provides: 'For the *a* purpose of this Convention, the seat of a company . . . shall be treated as its domicile . . .' Section 42(1) of the 1982 Act is to the same effect. So for the purposes of art 2 of the 1968 convention we must inquire whether Deich are 'domiciled' in Germany, ie whether they have their seat there.

Article 53 of the 1968 convention provides that, in order to determine where that seat is situated, 'the court shall apply its rules of private international law'. Section 42(3), (4) *b* and (5) of the 1982 Act defines or describes a company which for the purposes of that Act, and so of art 53, has its seat in the United Kingdom. It cannot be suggested that Deich are such a company. Section 42(6) provides:

'Subject to subsection (7) a corporation . . . has its seat in a state other than the United Kingdom if and only if—(*a*) it was incorporated . . . under the law of that *c* state and has its registered office or some other official address there; or (*b*) its central management and control is exercised in that state.'

It is common ground that Deich were incorporated in the Republic of Panama (which is not a contracting state) and has their registered office there, but that their central management and control have always been conducted from Hamburg in Germany (which is a contracting state). Section 42(7) of the 1982 Act provides: *d*

'A corporation . . . shall not be regarded as having its seat in a Contracting State other than the United Kingdom if it is shown that the courts of that state would not regard it as having its seat there.'

The evidence establishes that the German courts would regard Deich as having a seat in Germany. It is noteworthy that s 42(7) refers exclusively to a contracting state and does *e* not extend to any other state. I find this entirely understandable, bearing in mind that the purpose of the 1968 convention is to regulate the mutual rights and obligations of contracting states bound by that convention and does not affect any other state.

It has been debated in argument on this appeal whether in consequence of the disjunctive 'or' between paras (*a*) and (*b*) of s 42(6) of the 1982 Act a company may in *f* some circumstances have a multiplicity of seats. For example a company might have been incorporated in Italy and have its registered office there, but might be centrally managed and controlled in Germany. This might cause problems where, as in the example, each of those two states is a contracting state, but I think that no such problem arises in the present case where the Republic of Panama is not a contracting state. For my part I do not consider it to be necessary to decide this question on this appeal. If there is *g* on the true construction of the subsection a possibility of a multiplicity of seats, the fact that the Deich were incorporated in Panama and have a registered office there cannot negate the possibility of their also having a seat in Germany. The possibility of their having a seat in Panama would, in my judgment, be irrelevant, Panama not being a contracting state. On the other hand, if on the true construction of the subsection the expression 'that state' must be understood as applying only to a contracting state or states, *h* para (*a*) of this subsection cannot apply to the present case.

I think it may be better to leave this question unresolved because analogous questions may hereafter arise under s 42(3), (4) and (5) to which different considerations may possibly apply which we have not explored. If I thought it necessary to decide this question on s 42(6) at this stage, I should, as at present advised, be inclined to do so in Deich's favour. The plaintiffs' argument, in my view, involves an implication that *j* s 42(6)(*b*) is to be construed as applying only if no seat can be identified within s 42(6)(*a*). That is not, in my opinion, a natural interpretation of the language used. I gain no assistance in connection with this problem from the inclusion of the words 'or association' in the subsection, on which counsel for the plaintiffs placed some reliance.

Accordingly, on the question of domicile I reach the conclusion that on the true

interpretation of both the 1968 convention and the 1982 Act Deich are for the relevant
a purposes 'domiciled' in Germany.

(2) *Article 2 of the convention*
    Sheen J, who is very experienced in this part of our law, held, rightly in my view, that
Deich by entering an appearance to the writ under protest contesting the jurisdiction of
the court had not submitted to the jurisdiction. There can be no doubt that, apart from
b the effect of the 1968 convention and of the 1982 Act, this action being one relating to
damage to goods carried in the Deichland, and the ship being within the territorial limits
of the Admiralty jurisdiction of the High Court when the writ was served, the action was
one in respect of which the court could exercise that jurisdiction. The question is whether
the combined effects of that convention and that Act was not to limit and exclude that
jurisdiction from the commencement of the Act in respect of claims against parties
c domiciled in other contracting states.
    I do not doubt that the court's Admiralty jurisdiction in an action in rem against a ship
is invoked, if not when the writ is issued, at the latest as soon as it is served on the ship. It
does not follow that it has been rightly invoked. I see no reason why it should not be as
permissible for a party who, if he were to enter an unconditional appearance to a writ in
rem, would become liable in personam to the claim on which the writ is based to enter a
d conditional appearance contesting the jurisdiction of the court as it is for a defendant in
any action in personam. In the present case Deich contend that the jurisdiction of the
court was not properly invoked because Deich are a company domiciled in another
contracting state and so are within art 2 of the 1968 convention. The judge disposed of
this point very tersely in his judgment ([1988] 2 Lloyd's Rep 454 at 458):

e          'The ground of the application is "the defendants are domiciled in the Federal
        Republic of Germany". But while the action is solely in rem there are no
        "defendants", despite the wording of the writ.'

There can be no doubt that in referring in their notice of motion of 27 June 1988 to the
'defendants' Deich were referring to themselves, the demise charterers of the ship. The
f substance of the application is that by reason of the 1968 convention and the 1982 Act it
was impermissible to bring the action elsewhere than in Germany.
    So, in my view, the next question for consideration is whether Deich have sufficient
locus standi in relation to the ship and in relation to the plaintiffs' claim which is the
substratum of the action to permit Deich to make that application.
    What art 2 of the 1968 convention says is that persons domiciled in another contracting
g state shall be sued in the courts of that state, which imports, in my opinion, that they
shall not be sued elsewhere. Can Deich accurately be said to be 'sued' in the instant
action? It is true that in an action in the High Court which is exclusively in rem against
a ship, the plaintiff cannot recover any relief against the party who could be made liable
on the same ground of complaint in an action in personam unless that party elects to
enter an appearance to the writ in rem. If he does enter such an appearance
h unconditionally he becomes liable in that action as though it had been commenced in
personam. This is a peculiarity of our rules of procedure and practice. The underlying
complaint, however, is the same whether the action be framed in personam or in rem.
To use an English term, the cause of action, that is to say those essential facts all of which
the plaintiff must establish, if disputed, to support his right to the judgment of the court
(*Read v Brown* (1988) 22 QBD 128 at 131 per Lord Esher MR), must be the same. The
j issue of a writ in rem makes available to the claimant, that is to say the plaintiff, different
and more limited remedies in some respects from those which would become available
to him in an action in personam founded on the same complaint, but the object of each
type of action is to recover, or to obtain security for, compensation for one and the same
complaint (see also *Letang v Cooper* [1964] 2 All ER 929 at 934 ff, [1965] 1 QB 232 at
242 ff per Diplock LJ). Moreover, any relief obtained by a plaintiff in an action in rem

only will be just as truly at the expense of the party against whom the underlying complaint is made as relief against that party in an action in personam would be. In *a* reality, distinguished from formal aspects, the instant action is, in my judgment, as much a suit against Deich as would be an action in personam against them founded on the same complaint. It is, I suggest, for this underlying reason that, if the owner or charterer of a ship against which an action in rem is brought enters an appearance to the writ, the action thenceforward and without being reconstituted or amended proceeds as though it were an action in personam against that owner or charterer and had been so ab *b* initio.

Reference to the statement of claim in this action makes very clear that the basis of the action against the Deichland consists of alleged breaches of contract and/or duty on the part of Deich and other alleged defaults on their part. The cause of action alleged is precisely that which would be alleged in an action in personam against Deich in respect of the same ground of complaint. *c*

The 1968 convention is a document binding on all contracting states and its language should consequently, in my judgment, not be construed by reference to domestic considerations of English law. The United Kingdom was not a contracting state when the convention first became operative. Consequently, I think that the word 'sued' in art 2 of the convention should be liberally interpreted in a sense consistent with the policy of the convention and the intention of the original contracting states. The mere act of *d* giving the convention the force of law in the United Kingdom cannot, in my opinion, alter the intent and effect of art 2 so ascertained.

The function of the 1982 Act is to implement the 1968 convention in the United Kingdom, that is to give it the force of law in the United Kingdom. So this appeal, in my judgment, depends primarily not on the 1982 Act or English law but on the true interpretation of the 1968 convention and, in particular, of art 2 of it. *e*

In these circumstances and for these reasons I would hold that in this action the plaintiffs are seeking to 'sue' Deich, and are 'suing' Deich, within the meaning and intent of art 2 of the 1968 convention and so of the 1982 Act. The contrary conclusion reached by the judge and supported in this court by the plaintiffs seems to me to conflict with the policy of the convention, which I take to be that (save where otherwise provided in *f* the convention) disputes of a litigious character between parties domiciled in different contracting states shall be resolved in the courts of the state in which that party is domiciled against whom a complaint is made.

I have now had an opportunity of reading the judgments of both Neill and Stuart-Smith LJJ, with both of which I agree. They have both entered into matters discussed in the course of the argument in greater detail than I have felt it necessary to do, but I do *g* not think I need cover any of that ground again in this judgment.

In these circumstances and for these reasons I would allow this appeal.

*Appeal allowed. No order for costs up to date of issue of the notice of motion of 27 July 1988; thereafter defendants' costs in Court of Appeal and below. Leave to appeal to the House of Lords granted.* *h*

Solicitors: *Ingledew Brown Bennison & Garrett* (for Deich); *Clyde & Co* (for the plaintiffs).

Mary Rose Plummer   Barrister.

*a*

# Mailer v Austin Rover Group plc

HOUSE OF LORDS

LORD MACKAY OF CLASHFERN LC, LORD BRIDGE OF HARWICH, LORD BRANDON OF OAKBROOK, LORD GOFF OF CHIEVELEY, LORD JAUNCEY OF TULLICHETTLE

*b* 2, 3 MAY, 27 JULY 1989

*Health and safety at work – Employer's duties – Premises made available for use by others – Duty to other person's employees – Duty to provide safe system of work – Respondents using spray painting booth and sump in car assembly plant – Independent contractor employed to clean booth and sump – Contractor's employees ignoring contractor's instructions for working in booth and*
*c* *sump – One of contractor's employees killed in flash fire while working in sump – Whether respondents guilty of failing to take reasonable measures to ensure so far as reasonably practicable that premises safe and without risk to health – Whether duty to guard against unknown and unexpected events – Health and Safety at Work etc Act 1974, s 4(2).*

The respondents' car assembly plant contained a spray painting booth beneath which was
*d* a large sump which was used to collect excess paint and thinners during painting operations. The booth contained a piped supply of highly inflammable thinners for use in painting. Thinners were also used as solvents to clean the booth. The respondents employed an independent contractor to clean the booth at times when there was no production. The contractor's system of work required that nobody should be in the sump when anyone was working in the booth above, that the contractor's employees should
*e* not use the piped supply of thinners in the booth but should use their own supplies, that thinners used in the course of cleaning the booth should not be tipped into the sump but should be dumped outside the booth, and that only a safe electric lamp should be taken into the sump. In the course of cleaning the booth one of the contractor's employees entered the sump to clean it while another employee was cleaning the booth above. A flash fire occurred in the sump and the employee cleaning it was killed. After the fire it
*f* was discovered that the employee in the booth above had been using the respondents' piped supply of thinners and had allowed it to overflow into the sump, that he had also been dumping used thinners into the sump instead of outside the booth and that the employee in the sump had been using an unsafe lamp. The contractor was prosecuted and convicted of failing to provide a safe system of work for its employees. The respondents, as the person in control of the non-domestic premises where the deceased
*g* was working at the time of the accident, were also prosecuted by an inspector of factories with failing to take such measures as were reasonable for them to take to ensure so far as reasonably practicable that the sump and piped thinners were safe and without risks to health, contrary to s 4(2)[a] of the Health and Safety at Work etc Act 1974. They were convicted by the magistrates and fined £2,000. They appealed by way of case stated to the Divisional Court which allowed their appeal. The inspector appealed to the House of
*h* Lords.

**Held** – Once it was proved in a prosecution under s 4(2) of the 1974 Act (a) that premises which had been made available for use by others were unsafe and constituted a risk to health (that being an absolute duty, breach of which was to be determined by reference to the time when the premises were being used rather than when they were made
*j* available), (b) that the defendant had a degree of control over those premises and (c) that, having regard to his degree of control and (Lord Goff dissenting) his knowledge of the likely use, it would have been reasonable for him to take measures which would ensure

---

*a* Section 4(2) is set out at p 1089 *c* to *e*, post

that the premises were safe and without risks to health, the onus lay on the defendant to show that, weighing the risk to health against the means, including cost, of eliminating *a* the risk, it was not reasonably practicable for him to take those measures. If the premises were not a reasonably foreseeable cause of danger to persons using the premises in a manner or in circumstances which might reasonably be expected to occur, it was not reasonable to require any further measures to be taken to guard against unknown and unexpected events which might imperil their safety. Since it was not reasonable for the respondents to take measures to make the spray painting booth and sump safe against *b* the unanticipated misuse of those premises by the contractor's employees the magistrates had been wrong to convict the respondents. The inspector's appeal would accordingly be dismissed (see p 1088 *j* to p 1089 *b*, p 1090 *g h*, p 1091 *j* to p 1092 *a d* to *f*, p 1093 *c* to *e h j*, p 1097 *h* and p 1098 *b c g* to p 1099 *f*, post).

Per Lord Goff. The duty under s 4(2) of the 1974 Act to ensure that premises are safe and without risks to health is, subject to the statutory qualifications, an absolute duty *c* regardless of whether the nature of the defect which makes the premises unsafe is unknown or unforeseeable (see p 1090 *c* to *e*, post); *Allen v Avon Rubber Co Ltd* [1986] ICR 695 doubted.

## Notes

For the duty of persons concerned with premises to persons other than employees, see 16 *d* Halsbury's Laws (4th edn) para 781.

For the Health and Safety at Work etc Act 1974, s 4, see 16 Halsbury's Statutes (4th edn) 618.

## Cases referred to opinions

*Allen v Avon Rubber Co Ltd* [1986] ICR 695, CA.      *e*
*Coltness Iron Co Ltd v Sharp* [1937] 3 All ER 593, [1938] AC 90, HL.
*Close v Steel Co of Wales Ltd* [1961] 2 All ER 953, [1962] AC 367, [1961] 3 WLR 319, HL.
*Edwards v National Coal Board* [1949] 1 All ER 743, [1949] 1 KB 704, CA.
*Hindle v Birtwistle* [1897] 1 QB 192, [1895–9] All ER Rep 175.
*Marshall v Gotham Co Ltd* [1954] 1 All ER 937, [1954] AC 360, [1954] 2 WLR 812, HL.
*Summers (John) & Sons Ltd v Frost* [1955] 1 All ER 870, [1955] AC 740, [1955] 2 WLR *f* 825, HL.

## Appeal

John Patrick George Mailer, an inspector of factories, appealed against the decision of the Divisional Court of the Queen's Bench Division (Woolf LJ and Hutchison J) on 5 May 1988 allowing an appeal by way of case stated by the respondents, Austin Rover Group *g* Ltd, against their conviction on 25 September 1987 by the justices for the county of Oxford acting in and for the petty sessional division of Oxford City on a charge brought by the appellant that they had failed to take such measures as were reasonable for them to take to ensure so far as reasonably practicable that a sump and piped solvent supplies were safe, contrary to s 4(2) of the Health and Safety at Work etc Act 1974, for which they were fined £2,000. The facts are set out in the opinion of Lord Jauncey.      *h*

Nigel Pleming for the inspector.
Charles Harris QC and Julian Waters for the respondents.

Their Lordships took time for consideration.

27 July. The following opinions were delivered.      *j*

**LORD MACKAY OF CLASHFERN LC.** My Lords, I have had the advantage of reading in draft the speech of my noble and learned friend Lord Jauncey. I agree with it and for the reasons he gives I would dismiss the appeal.

**LORD BRIDGE OF HARWICH.** My Lords, I have had the advantage of reading in
*a* draft the speech of my noble and learned friend Lord Jauncey. I agree with it and for the
reasons he gives I would dismiss the appeal.

**LORD BRANDON OF OAKBROOK.** My Lords, I have had the advantage of
reading in draft the speech prepared by my noble and learned friend Lord Jauncey. I
agree with it, and for the reasons which he gives I would dismiss the appeal.
*b*

**LORD GOFF OF CHIEVELEY.** My Lords, the background to the present appeal is
set out in the speech of my noble and learned friend Lord Jauncey whose account I
gratefully adopt. The case is concerned with the construction of s 4(2) of the Health and
Safety at Work etc Act 1974. Section 4 provides, so far as material, as follows:
*c*

> '(1) This section has effect for imposing on persons duties in relation to those who
> (*a*) are not their employees; but (*b*) use non-domestic premises made available to
> them as a place of work or as a place where they may use plant or substances
> provided for their use there, and applies to premises so made available and other
> non-domestic premises used in connection with them.
> *d* (2) It shall be the duty of each person who has, to any extent, control of premises
> to which this section applies or of the means of access thereto or egress therefrom or
> of any plant or substance in such premises to take such measures as it is reasonable
> for a person in his position to take to ensure, so far as is reasonably practicable, that
> the premises, all means of access thereto or egress therefrom available for use by
> persons using the premises, and any plant or substance in the premises or, as the case
> *e* may be, provided for use there, is or are safe and without risks to health . . .
> (4) Any reference in this section to a person having control of any premises or
> matter is a reference to a person having control of the premises or matter in
> connection with the carrying on by him of a trade, business or other undertaking
> (whether for profit or not).'

Section 4(2) makes provision, therefore, for the duty of a person who has, to any extent,
*f* control of the relevant premises or of the relevant plant or substance. That duty is defined
in a passage, three parts of which have been the subject of discussion before your
Lordships. These may be segregated as follows (my emphasis): (1) *to take such measures as
it is reasonable for a person in his position to take to ensure*; (2) *so far as is reasonably practicable*;
(3) that the relevant premises, plant or substance is or are *safe and without risks to health*.
I shall consider each of these three expressions in turn, though obviously they cannot
*g* be properly understood unless they are read as part of the subsection (and indeed the Act)
in which they are found.
I find it convenient to consider first the third expression, 'safe and without risks to
health'. Counsel for the respondents submitted that, for present purposes, premises
should be regarded as 'safe and without risks to health' if they are in such condition as to
*h* be unlikely to be the cause of injury, harm or risk to health to persons who are, or who
may reasonably be expected to be, in them. This interpretation he derived from certain
authorities concerned with the construction of s 14(1) of the Factories Act 1937 (now
s 14(1) of the factories Act 1961), which requires that dangerous parts of machinery shall
be securely fenced. In a series of leading cases it has become established that, for the
purposes of that subsection, machinery is to be regarded as dangerous if it is a reasonably
*j* foreseeable cause of injury to anybody acting in a way in which a human being may be
reasonably expected to act in circumstances which may be reasonably expected to occur:
see *Hindle v Birtwistle* [1897] 1 QB 192 at 195–196, [1895–9] All ER Rep 175 at 177 per
Wills J; *John Summers & Sons Ltd v Frost* [1955] 1 All ER 870 at 882, [1955] AC 740 at
765–766 per Lord Reid; *Close v Steel Co of Wales Ltd* [1961] 2 All ER 953, [1962] AC 367.
Furthermore, in *Allen v Avon Rubber Co Ltd* [1986] ICR 695 the definition of 'dangerous'

in the foregoing cases was invoked by the Court of Appeal for the purpose of interpreting the word 'safe' in s 29(1) of the 1961 Act, which provides as follows:

> 'There shall, so far as is reasonably practicable, be provided and maintained safe means of access to every place at which any person has at any time to work, and every such place shall, so far as is reasonably practicable, be made and kept safe for any person working there.'

Stocker LJ, with whose judgment the other members of the court agreed, expressed the opinion that, for the purpose of the appeal then before the court and probably in many, if not at all, other cases, this test seemed to be as apt in respect of a place of work as it was to the safety of a machine (see 703). Counsel for the respondents, very understandably, invoked *Allen v Avon Rubber Co Ltd* as authority for the proposition which he advanced before your Lordships.

This proposition I am, however, unable to accept. To me, the words 'safe and without risks to health' mean, prima facie, what they say, though no doubt they have to be related to the use for which the relevant premises are made available. Take the example of premises which, owing to an unknown and indeed unforeseeable defect, are in fact unsafe for such use; or a substance which, unforeseeably, possesses a characteristic which likewise renders it unsafe for such use. I do not for my part see how the unforeseeable nature of the defect or of the characteristic can nevertheless mean that the premises or substance are safe. The duty is to take such measures as it is reasonable for a person in the position of the defendant to take to ensure, so far as is reasonably practicable, that the relevant premises or substance is or are safe. It may be that if the danger in question is not foreseeable, the defendant will not be held to have been in breach of his duty; but, if so, that will not be because, in the examples I have given, the premises or substance are to be regarded as safe, but because the qualified nature of the duty may not give rise to any liability in the particular circumstances. The cases concerned with the fencing of 'dangerous' machinery do not, in my opinion, provide any assistance. It was inevitable that a qualified meaning of the word 'dangerous' would have to be adopted in those cases, otherwise any part of any machinery which happened to cause injury would, if not fenced, give rise to liability. That was obviously not the intention of Parliament, and so the courts interpreted the word 'dangerous' in that context in the manner I have indicated. But no such qualification is called for in respect of the word 'safe' in s 4(2) of the 1974 Act, nor, in my opinion, in respect of the same word in s 29(1) of the 1961 Act. To that extent, I am unable to accept the reasoning of the Court of Appeal in *Allen v Avon Rubber Co Ltd*.

I turn next to the second expression in s 4(2) of the 1974 Act which I have segregated, 'so far as is reasonably practicable'. These words have received authoritative interpretation in previous cases. It is now established that, in cases concerned with a statutory duty which is qualified by those words, the risk of accident has to be weighed against the measures necessary to eliminate the risk, including the cost involved. If, for example, the defendant establishes that the risk is small, but that the measures necessary to eliminate it are great, he may be held to be exonerated from taking steps to eliminate the risk on the ground that it was not reasonably practicable for him to do so. For this purpose, the onus of proof rests on the defendant, as is recognised in the 1974 Act: see s 40 of the Act. In *Edwards v National Coal Board* [1949] 1 All ER 743 at 747, [1949] 1 KB 704 at 712 Asquith LJ said:

> '..."reasonably practicable" is a narrower term than "physically possible" and seems to me to imply that a computation must be made by the owner, in which the *quantum* of risk is placed on one scale and the sacrifice involved in the measures necessary for averting the risk (whether in money, time or trouble) is placed in the other, and that, if it be shown that there is a gross disproportion between them— the risk being insignificant in relation to the sacrifice—the defendants discharge the

a

onus on them. Moreover, this computation falls to be made by the owner at a point of time anterior to the accident. The questions he has to answer are: (a) What measures are necessary and sufficient to prevent any breach of [the section]? (b) Are these measures reasonably practicable?'

In *Marshall v Gotham Co Ltd* [1954] 1 All ER 937, [1954] AC 360, a case concerned with the death of a workman caused by the fall of a roof in a gypsum mine, the fall being the result of an unusual geological condition known as 'slickenside' which had not been

b found in the mine for 20 years and which was not detectable by any known means before the fall, the mine owners were exonerated from liability on the ground that they had proved that it was not reasonably practicable to ensure the mine's safety from such a danger. Lord Oaksey said ([1954] 1 All ER 937 at 939, [1954] AC 360 at 369–370):

c

'I agree with the Court of Appeal that it was not reasonably practicable to take such steps when slickenside had never occurred in the mine for the last twenty years. The position before the accident and the position after the accident are two quite different things. The question is not simply whether it was practicable as a matter of engineering, but whether it was reasonably practicable when no such thing as slickenside had occurred in the mine for at any rate twenty years, or even been heard of by many experienced miners although it is a known geological fault.

d I agree with the speech of Lord Atkin in *Coltness Iron Co., Ltd.* v. *Sharp* ([1937] 3 All ER 593, [1938] AC 90 at 93–94), where he said: "In the facts of this case, where the dangerous machinery was exposed for only a few minutes, as the only means of effecting necessary repairs in a part of the mine where it was unlikely that any workman, other than the engineer engaged in the work of repair, would be exposed to risk of contact with the machine, I am unable to take the view that it was

e reasonably practicable by any means to avoid or prevent the breach of s. 55 [of the Coal Mines Act, 1911]. The time of non-protection is so short, and the time, trouble and expense of any other form of protection is so disproportionate, that I think the defence is proved." That is to say, what is "reasonably practicable" depends on a consideration whether the time, trouble and expense of the precautions suggested are disproportionate to the risk involved. It is conceded, in the present case, that it

f was not reasonably practicable to make the roof secure by timbering, and to have attempted to make it secure by hydraulic props in some places and by leaving it unmined in others when no slickenside had ever occurred for a period of twenty years was not, in my judgment, reasonably practicable.'

Lord Reid said ([1954] 1 All ER 937 at 941, [1954] AC 360 at 371):

g

'The only way to make a roof secure against a slickenside fall appears to be to shore it up, and, as the presence of slickenside cannot be detected in advance, full protection against this danger would require that every roof under which men have to pass or to work should be shored up or timbered. There is evidence that this is never done in gypsum mines and that, in this mine, the cost of doing it would be so

h great as to make the carrying on of the mine impossible. Ultimately, it was not maintained by counsel for the appellant that timbering was reasonably practicable, and I think that it is proved that it was not reasonably practicable to comply fully with the requirement of reg. 7 (3) so as to make the roof secure against this particular danger.'

j It follows from the passages which I have quoted that, for the purpose of considering whether the defendant has discharged the onus which rests on him to establish that it was not reasonably practicable for him, in the circumstances, to eliminate the relevant risk, there has to be taken into account, inter alia, the likelihood of that risk eventuating. The degree of likelihood is an important element in the equation. It follows that the effect is to bring into play forseeability in the sense of likelihood of the incidence of the relevant risk, and that the likelihood of such risk eventuating has to be weighed against the means, including cost, necessary to eliminate it.

This is, in my opinion, an important matter to bear in mind when considering the meaning of the first group of words which I have segregated, 'to take such measures as it is reasonable for a person in [the defendant's] position to take to ensure . . .' I have come to the conclusion that it is not a function of the word 'reasonable' in this passage to qualify the duty of the defendant with reference to reasonable foreseeability by him of the incidence of risk to safety. This is because the question of reasonable foreseeability in the sense of likelihood arises at a later stage, by the introduction of the qualifying words 'so far as is reasonably practicable', words which introduce a qualification to the duty of a strictly limited nature, in respect of which the onus of proof rests on the defendant. It must, in my opinion, be inconsistent with the limited nature of this qualification to read the previous words as qualifying the duty imposed on the defendant with reference to a broad criterion of reasonable foreseeability, because, where liability is imposed subject to the limited qualification 'so far as reasonably practicable', the element of likelihood of the risk eventuating is taken account of in the balancing exercise involved in deciding whether or not it was reasonably practicable to ensure the safety of the premises for the relevant use. Furthermore, if the function of the phrase 'to take such measures as it is reasonable for a person in his position to take' was to introduce a broad criterion of foreseeability of risk, the words 'in his position' in that phrase would serve no useful purpose. In my opinion, the phrase is concerned only to qualify the defendant's duty with reference to the extent of control which he has of the relevant premises, so as not to impose on him a greater duty than is reasonable having regard to the extent of his control.

Subject to the limited qualification embodied in the phrase 'so far as is reasonably practicable', it seems to me that the duty imposed on the defendant to ensure that the relevant premises are safe and without risk to health for any use for which they are made available is prima facie absolute. In other words, the complainant has only to prove that the defendant has failed to ensure (so far as he can reasonably do so, having regard to the extent of his control) that the relevant premises are safe and without risks to health in the sense I have described: the onus then pases to the defendant to prove, if he can, that it was not reasonably practicable for him to eliminate the relevant risk. It is at this stage that reasonable foreseeability becomes relevant, in the sense that there has to be an assessment of the likelihood of the incidence of risk. I wish to add that this reading of s 4(2) renders it, in my opinion, consistent with the general duties imposed under the immediately preceding ss 2 and 3 of the Act (concerned respectively with general duties of employers to their employees, and general duties of employers and self-employed to persons other than their employees), and the immediately succeeding ss 5 and 6 (concerned with general duties of persons in control of certain premises in relation to harmful emissions into the atmosphere, and general duties of manufacturers and others as regards articles and substances for use at work). This I regard as significant. The duty under s 4 is concerned only with non-domestic premises made available to persons as a place of work, and the duty is imposed only on a person who has to any extent control of the premises 'in connection with the carrying on by him of a trade, business or other undertaking (whether for profit or not)' (see s 4(4)). In these circumstances, there is no discernible reason why, as a matter of policy, any less heavy a duty should be imposed under s 4 than is imposed under the other sections.

With these principles in mind I turn to consider the findings of the magistrates. The two matters of complaint before them were that, in breach of their duty under the subsection, the respondents failed to ensure that thinners did not enter the booth, and that there was sufficient ventilation in the sump when the cleaning operations were being carried out. As to the former, it was submitted by the inspector that the respondents could have achieved the desired result either by capping off the pipe so that it could not be turned on, or by closing the valve outside the booth. As to the latter it was submitted

that since natural ventilation was inadequate, the respondents could have achieved the
*a* desired result either by switching on the ventilation unit in the booth, or by equipping
the sump with an independently powered ventilation unit. These submissions were
accepted by the magistrates.

It was the duty of the respondents, under the subsection, to ensure that the premises
were safe for the use for which they were made available to the employees of Wesleyshire
Industrial Services Ltd, ie the cleaning of the booth including the sump. The magistrates
*b* had therefore to consider whether the premises, and also the thinners stored there, were
safe for that use.

So far as the thinners were concerned, the magistrates concluded that, having regard
to their highly flammable nature, the respondents were under a duty to ensure that they
did not enter the sump; and they further concluded that the respondents had failed to
discharge that duty by closing the valve at the pipe and by turning off the pump 'because
*c* these measures did not ensure that thinners would not enter the sump'. That was not,
however, the correct question to which they should have addressed their minds. They
should have asked themselves the question whether, in the circumstances, the respondents
had ensured that the thinners (being a substance in the premises) were safe, ie safe having
regard to the use of the premises by the employees of Wesleyshire in cleaning the sump.
In establishing the nature of that use, the magistrates should have taken into account the
*d* fact that Wesleyshire were required to supply their own thinners for the purpose of
cleaning, as indeed they did, their employees being instructed not to use the respondents'
thinners for that purpose. There does not appear to have been, in the circumstances, any
reason why the relevant use of the premises should have involved any interference by
Wesleyshire's employees with thinners stored on the premises. It follows, in my opinion,
that on this issue the magistrates misdirected themselves in point of law.
*e* Turning to the issue of ventilation, the magistrates had to consider the question
whether the sump, without artificial ventilation, was safe for the relevant use. In effect
they concluded that it was not, since they held that the respondents' duty had not been
discharged because the available ventilation was not sufficient safely to disperse fumes
should thinners enter the sump. It appears that even if Wesleyshire's employees had
*f* acted in accordance with their instructions, they would have used their own thinners in
the sump; but there is no finding of fact to indicate that such use would have led to the
introduction of thinners into the sump in anything like the quantity which occurred
through the unauthorised conduct of Wesleyshire's employees. Not only did they make
use of the respondents' thinners by draining them from the pipe into a drum, but (1)
they tipped used thinners into the sump, contrary to instructions that they should be
*g* dumped outside 75 yards away from the booth; (2) the drum into which they were
draining the respondents' thinners was found to be completely full, with the liquid
thinners running out over the top of the drum; and (3) thinners were found in the sump
which had either been tipped there contrary to instructions, or had accumulated in the
sump from the over-filling of the drum. Again, there is no reason why the use of the
premises for cleaning by Wesleyshire's employees should have involved any such
*h* misconduct. Moreover, there is no finding by the magistrates that, in the absence of any
such misconduct, the cleaning of the sump with Wesleyshire's own thinners would have
been liable to cause fumes in such quantity as to give rise to any appreciable risk to safety.
In my opinion, by failing to direct their minds to these matters, the magistrates again
erred in law.

For these reasons, I would dismiss the appeal. The three questions posed for your
*j* Lordships' consideration are:

'(1) Where the prosecutor has proved under s 4(2) of the Health and Safety at
Work Act 1974 that the defendant had control of the premises and that there was a
danger or risk to health must the prosecutor further prove that the existence of such
danger or risk to health was reasonably foreseeable by the defendant? (2) Is a

requirement of foreseeability of risk contained within the phrase "such measures as it is reasonable for a person in his position to take" in s 4(2) of the 1974 Act? (3) Does the duty owed under s 4(2) of the 1974 Act by those in control of the premises relate only to the safety of the premises or the safety of activities which may be carried on by persons within the premises?'

I would answer those questions as follows: (1) No; (2) No; (3) the duty relates to the safety of the premises for the use for which they are made available.

**LORD JAUNCEY OF TULLICHETTLE.** My Lords, this appeal arises out of a prosecution by the appellant, one of Her Majesty's inspectors of factories, of the respondents, Austin Rover Group Ltd, in respect of an alleged contravention of s 4(2) of the Health and Safety at Work etc Act 1974. The relevant part of the information was in the following terms:

'... being a person in control of non-domestic premises within the meaning of the Health and Safety at Work etc Act 1974, namely the sump beneath No. 2 Sealer Booth which was made available for use as a place of work to Brian Eldridge now deceased, and being also in control of the piped solvent supplies in the vicinity of the said sump, did fail to take such measures as were reasonable to take to ensure, so far as reasonably practicable, that the sump and piped solvent supplies were safe, contrary to section 4(2) of the said Act ...'

After a hearing lasting three days the justices for the County of Oxford acting in and for the petty sessional division of Oxford City convicted Austin Rover and fined them £2,000 with costs of £750. Austin Rover appealed by way of stated case to the Divisional Court which allowed the appeal and quashed the conviction. The inspector now appeals to this House and the questions of law certified by the Divisional Court are as follows:

'(1) Where the prosecutor has proved under s 4(2) of the Health and Safety at Work Act 1974 that the defendant had control of the premises and that there was a danger or risk to health must the prosecutor further prove that the existence of such danger or risk to health was reasonably foreseeable by the defendant? (2) Is a requirement of foreseeability of risk contained within the phrase "such measures as it is reasonable for a person in his position to take" in s 4(2) of the 1974 Act? (3) Does the duty owed under s 4(2) of the 1974 Act by those in control of the premises relate only to the safety of the premises or the safety of activities which may be carried on by persons within the premises?'

Section 4 of the Act of 1974 is in the following terms:

'(1) This section has effect for imposing on persons duties in relation to those who—(a) are not their employees; but (b) use non-domestic premises made available to them as a place of work or as a place where they may use plant or substances provided for their use there, and applies to premises so made available and other non-domestic premises used in connection with them.

(2) It shall be the duty of each person who has, to any extent, control of premises to which this section applies or of the means of access thereto or egress therefrom or of any plant or substance in such premises to take such measures as it is reasonable for a person in his position to take to ensure, so far as is reasonably practicable, that the premises, all means of access thereto or egress therefrom available for use by persons using the premises, and any plant or substance in the premises or, as the case may be, provided for use there, is or are safe and without risks to health.

(3) Where a person has, by virtue of any contract or tenancy, an obligation of any extent in relation to—(a) the maintenance or repair of any premises to which this section applies or any means of access thereto or egress therefrom; or (b) the safety or the absence of risks to health arising from plant or substances in any such

premises; that person shall be treated, for the purposes of subsection (2) above, as
a    being a person who has control of the matters to which his obligation extends.

(4) Any reference in this section to a person having control of any premises or
matter is a reference to a person having control of the premises or matter in
connection with the carrying on by him of a trade, business or other undertaking
(whether for profit or not).'

b    The circumstances giving rise to the prosecution, as found by the justices, may be
summarised as follows. Austin Rover had in their Cowley works a number of paint spray
booths, including no 2 sealer booth (' the booth'). The floor of the booth sloped
downwards towards centrally positioned downpipes which led into a sump beneath. The
floor was covered with a metal grid and excess paint and solvents from the spraying
operation together with water used in connection therewith found their way into the
c    sump by way of the downpipe. In one of the walls of the booth was a projecting pipe
which supplied thinners under pressure from a ring main for use during painting. There
was on this projecting pipe a lever operated valve which controlled the flow of thinners.
There was a further valve on the pipe outside the booth which could also shut off the
flow. When the ring main was not under pressure, thinners would flow by gravity at a
reduced rate from the pipe in the booth if both values were open. The thinners were
d    highly inflammable. The booth was equipped with a mechanical ventilation system
which, when operating, effected rapid changes of air in the sump. Space in the sump was
restricted and it had neither light nor a ventilation system independent of that of the
booth.

The booth and sump required to be regularly cleaned and this was normally done at
weekends when the plant was shut down and the ventilation system switched off. Until
e    1982 this cleaning was carried out by Austin Rover employees, but in that year Austin
Rover entered into a contract with Wesleyshire Industrial Services Ltd who thereafter
carried out the work. On 30 August 1986 one of Wesleyshire's employees, Brian
Eldridge, went into the sump to clean it, while a fellow employee, James Mackie, was
working in the booth above. Some time afterwards a sudden flash fire erupted in the
sump as a result of which Brian Eldridge died. The ventilation system was switched off
f    at the time. Wesleyshire were prosecuted under s 2 of the 1974 Act, pleaded guilty, and
were fined £2,000.

In terms of the current contract between Austin Rover and Wesleyshire, the latter
were required to and did provide their own thinners for cleaning purposes. Furthermore,
Wesleyshire's employees were instructed (1) not to use Austin Rover's thinners from the
g    projecting pipe, (2) not to enter the sump when other cleaning operations were taking
place in the booth above, and (3) only to enter the sump with an approved safety lamp.
After the accident it was discovered (1) that thinners were flowing from the projecting
pipe by way of an attached rubber hose into a drum belonging to Wesleyshire. The valve
inside the booth was partially open and thinners were running slowly over the top of the
drum. Mackie had rigged up this arrangement some hours earlier; (2) that there were
h    thinners in the sump which had either come from the overflowing drum or had been
tipped there by Mackie contrary to instructions; and (3) that the lamp used by the
deceased in the sump was not an approved safety lamp. Samples from the thinners found
in the sump were found to flash at two degrees centigrade.

The justices also found that Austin Rover were in control of the Cowley works and
that all plant isolation procedures including those for the thinners pipe and the ventilation
j    were controlled and operated by Austin Rover employees. This latter finding must, of
course, be taken together with the finding as to Mackie's exercise in relation to the
projecting pipe. The justices concluded that Austin Rover were under a duty to ensure
that the thinners did not enter the sump and that there was sufficient ventilation in the
sump when the cleaning operations were being carried out. I understand the duty as to
ventilation to be related to the presence of thinners in the sump and not to be a duty to

be performed in all circumstances. They went on to conclude (1) that effective isolation of the thinners from the sump could have been achieved either by capping off the projecting pipe so that it could not be turned on or by closing the valve outside the booth, and (2) that effective ventilation of the sump could have been provided either by switching on the ventilation unit in the booth or by providing the sump with an independent ventilation unit. The foregoing precautions 'would have been reasonable measures and reasonably practicable for a person like' Austin Rover. Accordingly, Austin Rover had failed to take reasonable measures to ensure that the pipe thinners in the booth and the sump below were safe.

The Divisional Court concluded that the reasoning of the justices could be faulted in only one respect, namely that, in the absence of any finding as to whether or not it was foreseeable by a person in Austin Rover's position that there would be inteference with the valve on the projecting pipe, they were under no duty to take further precautions. Woolf LJ said:

'The matter was one of fact for the magistrates and one in respect of which their findings of fact are silent. They came to a conclusion that thinners entered the sump, because they had either been tipped into the sump by an employee of the contractor, or had accumulated in the sump from overspilling. But they made no finding as to whether that was something which the [respondent] company either knew of or was likely or should have reasonably been foreseen. If this risk was not reasonably foreseeable by a person in the [respondents'] position, the [respondents were] not under a duty to take further precautions. Having regard to the terms of s 4, there is no duty to take precautions against risks which are not reasonably foreseeable.'

Hutchison J said:

'The vital words on which I would place emphasis are the words "such measures as it is reasonable for a person in his position to take". In the light of the matters which Woolf LJ has mentioned, it seems to me inescapable that while the justices made findings which plainly involved that there were steps which the [respondents] could have taken, which would in fact have averted the fire and the unhappy consequences that flowed from it, they made no findings which justified the conclusion that it had been proved that those steps were steps it would have been reasonable for a person in the [respondents'] position to take.'

Counsel for the inspector submitted that at the time of the fire the premises were unsafe in two respects, namely (1) that the thinners had not been isolated, and (2) that the sump was not being mechanically ventilated while the deceased was working therein. Austin Rover had total control of the premises and modest measures were available to them to make the premises and the thinners far safer. Having failed to take those measures, they were in breach of their statutory duty under s 4, and it mattered not that they could not foresee the particular circumstances of the accident which occurred. Counsel for the respondents contended that so far as Austin Rover were concerned, the premises were at the material time safe and that in any event, it would not have been reasonable for them to have taken any further steps to that end. It was not contended that if it were reasonable for Austin Rover to take steps to ensure the safety of the sump and the thinners, it would not have been reasonably practicable for them to have done so.

My Lords, before turning to consider in detail the provisions of s 4, reference must be made to the preceding sections of the 1974 Act. Section 1 provides, inter alia:

'(1) The provisions of this Part shall have effect with a view to—(a) securing the health, safety and welfare of persons at work; (b) protecting persons other than persons at work against risks to health or safety arising out of or in connection with

the activities of persons at work; (c) controlling the keeping and use of explosive or
highly flammable or otherwise dangerous substances, and generally preventing the
unlawful acquisition, possession and use of such substances . . .

(3) For the purposes of this Part risks arising out of or in connection with the
activities of persons at work shall be treated as including risks attributable to the
manner of conducting an undertaking, the plant or substances used for the purposes
of an undertaking and the condition of premises so used or any part of them.'

Section 2 imposes duties on an employer in relation to his employees and by sub-s (1)
provides:

'It shall be the duty of every employer to ensure, so far as is reasonably practicable,
the health, safety and welfare at work of all his employees.'

Subsection (2) contains detailed provisions in relation to, inter alia, the provision and
maintenance of safe plant, systems of work and working environment. Section 3(1),
which imposes duties on employers in relation to persons who are not their employees,
is in the following terms:

'It shall be the duty of every employer to conduct his undertaking in such a way
as to ensure, so far as is reasonably practicable, that persons not in his employment
who may be affected thereby are not thereby exposed to risks to their health or
safety.'

Subsection (2) imposes similar duties on self-employed persons in relation to themselves
as well as to persons who are not their employees. Failure to discharge a duty imposed by
ss 2, 3 or 4 constitutes an offence (s 33) but does not give rise to civil liability (s 47). The
onus of proving that it was not reasonably practicable to perform any duty imposed by
ss 2, 3 or 4 is placed upon the accused (s 40).

Sections 2 and 3 impose duties in relation to safety on a single person, whether an
individual or a corporation, who is in a position to exercise complete control over the
matters to which the duties extend. An employer can control the conditions of work of
his employees and the manner in which he conducts his undertaking. However, s 4,
which imposes duties in relation to the safety of premises and plant and substances
therein, recognises that more than one person may have a degree of control of those
premises at any one time and hence be under a duty in relation thereto. The words 'to
any extent' and 'to take such measures as it is reasonable for a person in his position to
take' ('the middle words') point to the distinction between the unified control
contemplated in ss 2 and 3 and the possible divided control contemplated in s 4.

Two main questions of construction were involved in the arguments before your
Lordships, namely (1) what is meant by the words 'safe and without risks to health' in
the context of the premises and substances to which s 4 refers, and (2) what factors may
be taken into account in determining what measures it is reasonable for an accused to
take to ensure safety.

In relation to the first question, counsel for the inspector submitted that regard must
be had to the use to which the premises were being put at the relevant time. If it was
reasonably foreseeable that such use involved risks to health the premises were then
unsafe. Counsel for the respondents on the other hand argued that 'premises' were safe
when they were in such a condition as to be unlikely to be the cause of injury, harm or
risk to health to persons using premises for the purpose for which they were made
available. The difference between these submissions lay in the fact that counsel for the
inspector looked at safety at the time when the risk to health arose, which in the present
case was immediately prior to the fire, whereas counsel for the respondents looked at it
when the premises were first made available for non-employees to work in.

Safety of premises is not an abstract concept. It must be related to the purposes for
which the premises are being used at any one time. Some premises may be unsafe for

any normal use, for example because of large unguarded holes in the floor or unstable walls. Other premises may be completely safe for the purpose for which they were designed but completely unsafe for other purposes. For example an upper floor warehouse designed to a loading capacity of x lbs per square foot is safe when used within the capacity but would become unsafe if loaded to 2x lbs per square foot. If A makes available a warehouse to B who uses it within the designed loading capacity it could not be said that the warehouse was unsafe and a risk to health for the purposes of s 4(2) because B might at some future date exceed the designed loading capacity contrary to A's instructions. If, however, B in fact overloaded the floor the premises would thereby become unsafe for the purposes of the subsection.

In my view the submission of counsel for the inspector on this matter is correct. It would be not only to place too narrow a construction on s 4(2) to consider the safety of premises only at the time of their being made available but would be to ignore reality when a danger arose because of supervening events.

I turn now to consider the second main question. Counsel for the inspector argued that in determining what measures it was 'reasonable for a person in his position to take to ensure' safety regard should be had only to the extent of his control. Total control meant total measures. Counsel for the respondents on the other hand maintained that not only control but other considerations such as knowledge and foresight should be taken into account. Counsel for the inspector argued with some force that if more general factors had to be considered in determining what measures were reasonable, little content would be left for the succeeding words 'so far as is reasonably practicable', since it was difficult to envisage a situation in which it would be reasonable for a person to take measures but not reasonably practicable for him so to do. I was initially attracted by this argument, but have come to the conclusion that it is unsound.

The ambit of s 4 is far wider than that of ss 2 and 3. It applies to anyone who is in occupation of non-domestic premises and who calls in tradesmen to carry out repairs, it applies to those tradesmen in relation to the employees of others, and it applies to anyone who makes the premises available on a temporary basis for others to carry out work in. Thus organisations varying from multi-national corporations to the village shop are brought under the umbrella of the section. In the example of the warehouse to which I have already referred, it would be contrary to common sense and justice that A should be prosecuted if B had acted contrary to his instructions and without his knowledge. Indeed, if A were to be guilty of an offence in such circumstances, criminal liability would arise solely ex dominio. I do not consider that such a result was intended by Parliament, particularly in a provision capable of such broad application. In my view, it was to deal with such a situation as I have exemplified that the middle words were included in s 4(2). These words require consideration to be given not only to the extent to which the individual in question has control of the premises, but also to his knowledge and reasonable foresight at all material times. Thus when a person makes available premises for use by another, the reasonableness of the measures which he requires to take to ensure the safety of those premises must be determined in the light of his knowledge of the anticipated use for which the premises have been made available and of the extent of his control and knowledge, if any, of the actual use thereafter. If premises are not a reasonably foreseeable cause of danger to anyone acting in a way in which a human being may be reasonably expected to act in circumstances which may reasonably be expected to occur during the carrying out of the work or the use of the plant or substance for the purpose of which the premises were made available, I think that it would not be reasonable to require an individual to take further measures against unknown and unexpected events towards their safety. Applying this test to the warehouse example, A would escape liability under s 4(2) because it would not be reasonable for him to take further measures against B's unauthorised use, whereas B would incur liability because he must have foreseen the consequences of his overloading.

I would stress that in the middle words 'reasonable' relates to the person and not to the

measures. The question is not whether there are measures, which themselves are
a reasonable which could be taken to ensure safety and the absence of risk to health but
whether it is reasonable for a person in the position of the accused to take measures with
these aims. The emphasis is on the position of the accused. Thus while only one yardstick
determines whether premises are safe at any one time the measures to ensure the safety
required of each person having a degree of control may vary. Approaching the matter in
this way, content may be given to the words 'so far as reasonably practicable'. It could,
b having regard to his degree of control and knowledge of likely use, be reasonable for an
individual to take a measure to ensure the safety of premises, but it might not be
reasonably practicable for him to do so having regard to the very low degree of risk
involved and the very high cost of taking the measure.

My Lords, I shall summarise the approach as I see it to a successful prosecution under
s 4. The prosecutor must first prove that the premises are unsafe and constitute risks to
c health. If he so proves he must then go on to prove what persons have at that time any
degree of control of those premises. Thereafter he must prove that it would be reasonable
for one or more of the persons having a degree of control to take measures which would
ensure safety. If he proves these three matters the onus shifts to the accused to prove that
it was not reasonably practicable to take the measures in question.

My Lords, prior to the outbreak of fire in the sump, a number of events took place
d which should not have taken place if Wesleyshire or their servants had acted as they
should have done in accordance with the contract or their instructions. In the first place,
Mackie drew off thinners into the drum from the projecting pipe in the booth. In the
second place, he tipped thinners from time to time into the sump. In the third place, the
deceased went into the sump when Mackie was working in the booth above. In the
fourth place, he went into the sump with a lamp which was not an approved safety lamp.
e The justices made no findings that any of these four events should have been foreseen by
Austin Rover. In the absence of any such findings, I do not see how it could be said that
it was reasonable for Austin Rover to have taken measures to make the premises safe
against this unanticipated misuse thereof. I consider that the Divisional Court were
correct both in their reasoning and in their conclusion to allow the appeal.

I would therefore refuse the appeal. The questions as put do not truly reflect the issues
f which have been raised in this appeal and which I have already discussed. In these
circumstances I do not consider that any useful purpose would be served by attempting
to answer them.

*Appeal dismissed.*
Solicitors: *Treasury Solicitor* (for the inspector); *Henmans* (for the respondents).

Mary Rose Plummer    Barrister.

# Re Lonrho plc and others

HOUSE OF LORDS APPELLATE COMMITTEE
LORD KEITH OF KINKEL, LORD TEMPLEMAN, LORD GRIFFITHS, LORD ACKNER AND LORD LOWRY
10, 12, 20 APRIL, 22 MAY 1989
LORD BRIDGE OF HARWICH, LORD GOFF OF CHIEVELEY AND LORD JAUNCEY OF TULLICHETTLE
6, 7, 8, 12 JUNE, 27 JULY 1989

*Contempt of court – Interference with course of justice – Attempt to influence House of Lords – Respondent seeking judicial review of Secretary of State's decision not to publish inspectors' report on rival take-over – Respondent successful in Divisional Court – Divisional Court's decision reversed by Court of Appeal – Respondent appealing to House of Lords – Before appeal heard newspaper owned by respondent publishing inspectors' report – Respondent sending copies of newspaper to law lords listed to hear appeal in judicial review proceedings – Whether respondent acting in contempt of House of Lords – Contempt of Court Act 1981, s 2(2).*

The respondent company, in competition with the F brothers, was the unsuccessful bidder for a well-known London department store. Following its unsuccessful bid the respondent, supported by a national newspaper owned by it, mounted a sustained campaign to reverse the successful take-over of the department store's holding company by the F brothers and as the result of pressure exerted by the respondent the Secretary of State in 1985 appointed inspectors under the Companies Act 1985 to inquire into the take-over by the F brothers. The inspectors submitted their report to the Secretary of State in July 1988. The Secretary of State sent the report to the Director of the Serious Fraud Office and the Director of Public Prosecutions and in September he decided that he could not publish the report until the Serious Fraud Office had completed its investigation and any prosecutions arising therefrom had been completed. In November 1988 the Secretary of State decided, without giving reasons, that it would not be appropriate to refer the F brothers' take-over to the Monopolies and Mergers Commission. The respondent applied to the Divisional Court for judicial review of the Secretary of State's decisions. The Divisional Court granted the application but on appeal by the Secretary of State the Court of Appeal dismissed the application. The respondent appealed to the House of Lords. Prior to the hearing of the appeal by the House of Lords a copy of the inspectors' report came into the possession of the chief executive of the respondent who passed it to the editor of the newspaper owned by the respondent. The newspaper published a special edition on 30 March 1989 containing extracts from the inspectors' report. The Secretary of State obtained an injunction preventing distribution of the special edition as soon as he became aware of its existence but some 200,000 copies were sold before the injunction was obtained. In addition 2,000 to 3,000 copies were supplied to the respondent which, as part of its campaign against the F brothers' take-over, sent them by post to persons on a mailing list of persons to whom the respondent had been sending literature in the course of its campaign. The mailing list included members of both Houses of Parliament, and four of the five law lords who were listed to hear the respondent's appeal in the judicial review proceedings received a copy of the special edition of the newspaper. The question arose whether the respondent and those associated with it responsible for mailing the special edition of the newspaper to the law lords had committed a contempt. That question was referred to an appellate committee of the House for decision.

**Held** – (1) Since a publication referring to particular legal proceedings was less likely to be held to create a substantial risk that the course of justice in those proceedings would

be seriously impeded or prejudiced and therefore a contempt of court under s 2(2)[a] of
a the Contempt of Court Act 1981 if the proceedings were to be heard by a judge rather
than tried by a jury and since the possibility that an appellate court would be influenced
was even more remote and it was unlikely that the Secretary of State would be deterred
from contesting the appeal, it could not be said that the respondent was guilty of
contempt by causing to be published material which prejudged the issue in the appeal
proceedings pending before the House of Lords (see p 1116 j to p 1117 c f g, post); A-G v
b Times Newspapers Ltd [1973] 3 All ER 54 distinguished.
(2) A litigant who sought a judicial remedy to compel a particular course of action
was not guilty of contempt of court under s 2(2) of the 1981 Act if he resorted to self-
help to obtain the remedy without the assistance of the courts, since the fact that the
litigant thereby pre-empted the decision of the courts did not amount to impeding or
prejudicing the course of justice. Accordingly, the respondent was not guilty of contempt
c by causing to be published material which pre-empted the decision in the House of Lords
appeal proceedings. It followed that no case of contempt had been made out against the
respondent and those associated with it (see p 1118 h to p 1119 g and p 1120 e, post); A-G
v Newspaper Publishing plc [1987] 3 All ER 276 distinguished.

**Notes**
d For contempt of court in relation to pending proceedings, see 9 Halsbury's Laws (4th
edn) paras 8–9, and for cases on the subject, see 16 Digest (Reissue) 19–33, 193–342.
For the Contempt of Court Act 1981, s 2, see 11 Halsbury's Statutes (4th edn) 182.

**Cases referred to in reasons for advice**
A-G v Newspaper Publishing plc [1987] 3 All ER 276, [1988] Ch 333, [1987] 3 WLR 942,
e   Ch D and CA.
A-G v Times Newspapers Ltd [1973] 3 All ER 54, [1974] AC 273, [1973] 3 WLR 298, HL:
rvsg [1973] 1 All ER 815, [1973] QB 710, [1973] 2 WLR 452, CA.
Lonrho plc v Secretary of State for Trade and Industry [1989] 2 All ER 609, [1989] 1 WLR
525, HL.
R v D [1984] 1 All ER 574, CA.
f   R v Flower (1799) 8 Term Rep 314, 101 ER 1408.
R v Tibbits and Windust [1902] 1 KB 77, [1900–3] All ER Rep 896, CCR.
Sunday Times v UK (1979) 2 EHRR 245, E Ct HR.

**Proceedings for contempt**
By an order of the House of Lords made on 13 April 1989 there was referred to the
g Appellate Committee of the House to whom had been referred for their consideration
the consolidated appeals in the cause Lonrho plc v Secretary of State for Trade and Industry
[1989] 2 All ER 609, [1989] 1 WLR 525 the question whether the circumstances in
which a special edition of the Observer newspaper was published on 30 March 1989
constituted a contempt. The respondents to the proceedings were Lonrho plc, Mr R W
Rowland, the chief executive of Lonrho, Sir Edward du Cann, Mr P G Spicer and Mr F P
h Dunlop, directors of Lonrho, The Observer Ltd and Mr D Trelford, the editor of the
Observer newspaper, Mr J M Fordham of Stephenson Harwood, Lonrho's solicitors and
Mr A F S Fletcher of counsel who had advised Lonrho. The facts are set out in the report
of the committee.

Philip Havers as amicus curiae.
j Alan Rawley QC, Anthony Arlidge QC, David Pannick and Mark Shaw for Lonrho.
Gordon Pollock QC, Robert Wright QC, Michael Beloff QC, David Pannick and Mark Shaw for
the directors of Lonrho.
Gavin Lightman QC and Desmond Browne for the Observer.
John Chadwick QC, David Eady QC and John Rowland for Lonrho's legal advisers.

_____
a   Section 2(2) is set out at p 1113 g, post

22 May. The following reasons for the decision to advise the House that the contempt
proceedings be heard by a differently constituted committee were given by the Appellate
Committee (Lord Keith of Kinkel, Lord Templeman, Lord Griffiths, Lord Ackner and
Lord Lowry).

**THE APPELLATE COMMITTEE.** The principal events of relevance prior to the
start of the hearing on 22 May 1989 are as follows.

(1) From about 1978 onwards the company Lonrho was desirous of acquiring House
of Fraser plc which in turn controlled Harrods department store. In 1985 Fraser was
acquired by the Al Fayed brothers. Since then Lonrho has conducted a campaign to
establish that the Al Fayed brothers were guilty of fraud and deceit and to secure that, by
one means or another, the Al Fayed brothers shall be obliged to sell and Lonrho shall be
offered an opportunity to purchase the Fraser assets or some of them. The campaign
conducted by Lonrho included the distribution of campaign literature such as letters and
pamphlets to some 3,000, and in certain instances many more, recipients with the object
of obtaining support for Lonrho's views.

(2) Lonrho and the Al Fayed brothers became involved in a number of legal
proceedings. On 9 March 1987 an Appellate Committee of this House heard an appeal
involving, directly or indirectly, Lonrho and the Al Fayed brothers. The Appellate
Committee was presided over by Lord Keith of Kinkel. At the outset he drew attention
to the fact that over a considerable period the Lords of Appeal had been in receipt of
campaign literature and that some documents had been received while the appeal was
pending and even up to within a few days of the hearing, and expressed the view that
this was improper.

(3) On 9 April 1987, as a result of Lonrho's campaign, the Secretary of State for the
Department of Trade and Industry appointed inspectors to investigate and report on the
acquisition by the Al Fayed brothers of Fraser.

(4) On 23 July 1988 the inspectors appointed by the Secretary of State reported to him.
On 29 July 1988 the Secretary of State sent a copy of the inspectors' report to the Serious
Fraud Office which is empowered to investigate any suspected offence which may include
serious or complex fraud.

(5) The Secretary of State desired to publish the inspectors' report as soon as possible
but decided against immediate publication on the grounds that the investigations of the
Serious Fraud Office might be hindered and that a fair trial of anyone charged as a result
of the investigation might be prejudiced. He also decided, following advice tendered to
him by the Director of Fair Trading, not to refer the Al Fayed take-over of Fraser to the
Monopolies and Mergers Commission.

(6) Lonrho began judicial review proceedings for an order on the Secretary of State to
publish the inspectors' report and also to refer the Al Fayed take-over to the Monopolies
and Mergers Commission. Lonrho continued to circulate campaign literature directed
against the Al Fayed brothers and also questioning the integrity of the Secretary of State.

(7) In December 1988 Lonrho were advised by their solicitors not to send campaign
literature to any judge. This advice was repeated on 30 January 1989 as a result of a
remark by Mustill LJ made in the course of Lonrho's proceedings which indicated that
he had received such literature, and specific reference to law lords was included.

(8) On 17 January 1989 the Divisional Court ordered the Secretary of State to publish
the inspectors' report but on 20 January 1989 their decision was reversed by the Court of
Appeal. Lonrho appealed to this House. On 15 March 1989 Lonrho were again advised
by their solicitors not to send campaign literature to the Lords of Appeal.

(9) On about 23 March 1989 Mr Rowland, the chief executive of Lonrho, came into
possession of two unauthorised copies, one only partially complete, of the inspectors'
report. He caused these to be photocopied, and had a meeting with Mr Trelford, editor
of the Observer newspaper, which is owned by Lonrho. As a result of that meeting the
Observer on 30 March published a special issue containing extracts from and a summary

of and comments on the inspectors' report. The Secretary of State for Trade and Industry obtained an injunction against the Observer too late to prevent a wide distribution of copies. On the same day Lonrho posted 3,000 copies of the special issue to various recipients, including some of the Lords of Appeal. On 7 April further campaign literature, attacking the Al Fayed brothers, was circulated by Lonrho and received by some of the Law Lords.

(10) On 10 April 1989 the Appellate Committee met to hear Lonrho's appeal. Before the appeal was called on, the presiding Lord of Appeal made a statement in which he said, inter alia:

'It is for consideration whether the sending of these documents to the Lords of Appeal was designed to influence them in their approach to the appeal due to be heard today, and whether it may constitute a contempt of the House of Lords. It is further for consideration whether the partially successful publication by the Observer newspaper of its special issue did not in itself constitute a contempt of this House and, if so, whether that publication was instigated and brought about by Lonrho or Mr Rowland who would, if so, be parties to the contempt, the seriousness of which would be much aggravated by the existence of the pending appeal.'

The proceedings were adjourned until later in the day. Counsel for Lonrho then stated that the sending to the law lords of the Observer newspaper and the document of the 7 April was due to an administrative error and unreservedly apologised on behalf of Lonrho. Counsel sought and was granted a further two days' adjournment to obtain information and instructions.

(11) When the Appellate Committee met on 12 April explanatory affidavits on behalf of Lonrho were read by counsel. There was some discussion of the law and procedure relating to contempt of court and after the committee had conferred, it was announced:

'Having considered the affidavits which have been made available by Lonrho, their Lordships propose to proceed with the hearing of the appeal. At the conclusion of the arguments in the appeal, their Lordships will wish to hear submissions as to whether or not the conduct of Lonrho in bringing about the publication in the special issue of the Observer of extracts from the inspectors' report constitutes contempt in respect of which the taking of proceedings should be considered.'

(12) On 13 April the House ordered that the Appellate Committee to whom were referred the consolidated appeals in the cause Lonrho plc v Secretary of State for Trade and Industry ([1989] 2 All ER 609, [1989] 1 WLR 525) should consider whether the circumstances in which a special edition of the Observer newspaper was published on 30 March 1989 constituted a contempt.

(13) The hearing of Lonrho's appeal against the Secretary of State was completed on Wednesday, 19 April. On 20 April the Appellate Committee provided counsel with a statement which, after setting forth the terms of the order of the House dated 13 April, continued:

'Their Lordships are provisionally of the view that the following questions may arise on the above reference. (1) Was there a contempt of the House by Lonrho (or its directors) in procuring the distribution to Lords of Appeal in Ordinary of copies of the special issue of the Observer newspaper of 30 March 1989. (2) Was contempt of court under the Contempt of Court Act 1981, or otherwise, constituted by the general publication of that special issue? (3) If the answer to question (2) is in the affirmative, are any, and if so, which of the following responsible for it: (a) Lonrho; (b) Sir Edward Du Cann; (c) Mr Rowland and the other directors of Lonrho; (d) the Observer newspaper; (e) Mr Trelford, editor of that newspaper. Their Lordships would be assisted by the submissions of counsel upon the following matters: (1) whether the questions formulated above are expressed in the manner best suited for resolving the matter referred to them; (2) whether any further affidavit evidence, additional to that already available on the matter, is desired to be furnished to their Lordships by any person who may be affected; (3) whether it is appropriate and desired by any such person or counsel for the Attorney General that the deponent to any affidavit shall be subject to cross-examination; (4) the general procedure which should be adopted by their Lordships for dealing with the matter referred to them.'

At the request of the Appellate Committee the Attorney General had nominated counsel to assist the committee as amicus curiae and counsel appearing as amicus was in attendance on 20 April. In the course of discussion with counsel it was made clear that persons liable to be affected must be named, served with notice and a statement of charges, that they would be at liberty to file such evidence and affidavits as they thought fit, that deponents would be liable to be cross-examined and that after a consideration of the statement of charges and the affidavit evidence a hearing would take place. Counsel for Lonrho welcomed a suggestion that the statement of charges to be drafted by counsel appearing as amicus should be approved by the Appellate Committee before service and reserved the position of Lonrho with regard to discovery and legal privilege. After consideration by the Appellate Committee it was announced that—

'their Lordships will require counsel appearing as amicus to carry out the role of prosecutor. He will make available a formal statement on the usual lines which will be approved by their Lordships and served within seven days. The particular individuals who will be required to account are Mr Rowland, Sir Edward du Cann, Mr Spicer, Mr Fordham and Mr Trelford. It does not appear that any of the directors of Lonrho are particularly involved; although if it does emerge that they are counsel appearing as amicus can no doubt take steps. Of course, the companies Lonrho and the Observer are also to be called. Seven days after the serving of the statement, affidavits are to be lodged, and then a further seven days will be available for reply at the hearing, which will be postponed now until 22 May . . . All parties are entitled to be represented by counsel, whether jointly or separately is up to them to decide. Discovery will be expected to be given, and if there are any difficulties about that, then an application can be made to the House. At the hearing itself counsel appearing as amicus will open, and any person who has sworn an affidavit will attend for cross-examination unless notified by counsel appearing as amicus that they are not required to do so. If any of the parties desire a witness to attend for cross-examination they will notify counsel appearing as amicus who will arrange it. At the close of the evidence counsel appearing as amicus will make submissions to their Lordships on the law and the facts, and counsel for the parties affected will be in a position to do the same . . .'

(14) Later Mr Fletcher, junior counsel for Lonrho, most commendably volunteered that he had personally, on the instructions of Mr Fordham, a partner in the firm of solicitors acting for Lonrho, conveyed to the Observer offices the copies of the inspector's report from which the special issue was compiled. The amicus added his name to the list of persons required to account for their actions.

(15) On 24 April 1989 Lord Keith of Kinkel received through the post a document called *Birds of a Feather*. This had been despatched by Lonrho on 10 April. The document contained a serious attack on the good faith of the Secretary of State for Trade and Industry, stating that he had 'suppressed' the inspectors' report and accusing him of dishonourable conduct. The document also implied that Mr Dennis Thatcher, husband of the Prime Minister, was in some way mixed up in the matter in as much as both he and the Secretary of State were involved with certain allegedly sinister characters said to be close associates of the Al Fayed brothers. The document thus flatly contradicted the statement by counsel for Lonrho in the course of the hearing of the appeal, to the effect that the good faith of the Secretary of State was not impugned by his clients.

(16) Affidavit evidence was offered on behalf of Lonrho. This included accounts of
*a* consultations with and among Lonrho's legal advisers prior to the publication of the
special issue of the Observer, and of the advice given. From these it appeared that on 29
March 1989, at a meeting attended by Mr Rowland and other directors of Lonrho,
Lonrho was advised by Mr Robin Simpson QC and Mr Bevan of counsel that publication
of the inspectors' report in the Observer newspaper would be a contempt of the House.
However, in a later written opinion dated 3 April 1989 by five counsel, including Mr
*b* Simpson, the view was expressed that publication did not constitute contempt, though
Mr Simpson entered a caveat that proceedings might well be taken and might well
succeed.

(17) It was the general view of counsel advising Lonrho that the inspectors' report
should not be published in the Observer, on the ground that to do so would create a risk
of irreparable damage to Lonrho's prospects of success in their appeal.

*c* (18) Mr Spicer, a director of Lonrho, lodged an affidavit stating that the sending to
Lord Keith of *Birds of a Feather* was due to an administrative error, though a different
one, apparently, from that which had resulted in the sending to Lords of Appeal of the
special issue of the Observer.

On 22 May counsel for all the respondents except Mr Fletcher and Mr Fordham made
preliminary applications. The first application was that the hearing should not be
*d* proceeded with. Several suggestions were made as to alternative methods of dealing with
the possibility that contempt had been committed.

First, it was suggested that the Attorney General should be invited to consider whether
the charges of contempt should be brought. If he thought fit to bring charges, he should
prepare an indictment which would be considered by the magistrates and, if they
thought fit, referred for trial in the Crown Court by judge and jury. Second, it was
*e* suggested that the Attorney General might decide to proceed by way of motion in the
Divisional Court of the Queen's Bench Division. Third, it was suggested that the Attorney
General might recommend proceedings to take place before an Appellate Committee of
this House in accordance with the present instructions of the Appellate Committee.

There are obvious and insuperable objections in the present case to allowing the matter
to be referred to the discretion of the Attorney General. The suggested contempt relates
*f* to proceedings before this House in its judicial capacity and it is not for the Attorney
General to decide whether cognisance should be taken of such possible contempt or not.
Moreover, any decision by the Attorney General to proceed would be liable to be
questioned by Lonrho on the ground that he and the Secretary of State, who was
respondent to the appeal by Lonrho, were members of the same governmental
administration which was or could have been affected by the contempt.

*g* There are also insuperable objections in the present case to contempt proceedings
taking place otherwise than in this House. It is admitted that the normal and natural
forum for the hearing of contempt relating to proceedings before this House is the House
itself. If any authority be required, it can be found in *R v Flower* (1799) 8 Term Rep 314
at 323, 101 ER 1408 at 1413 per Lord Kenyon CJ. Of course, when a contempt of the
*h* House also involves a separate and independent crime, then the House may well take no
action in relation to the contempt, allowing or directing the ordinary criminal process to
take place. For example, in 1812 a Prime Minister, Mr Spencer Perceval, was shot in the
precincts of the House of Commons and his murderer was tried by the Assize Court. But
this is not such a case; the suggested contempts are contempts of court relating to
proceedings before this House and no other crime is alleged. There is no authority that
*j* vests in the Divisional Court of the Queen's Bench Division or any other court jurisdiction
to deal with the present matters in dispute.

That is enough to dispose of the suggested reference to the Attorney General. But,
because the first proposal to your Lordships was for prosecution on indictment, it is
appropriate to take the opportunity, thereby indorsing the statement in *Archbold's
Criminal Pleading, Evidence and Practice* (43rd edn, 1988) vol 2, para 24-22 and approving

the observations of the Court of Appeal in *R v D* [1984] 1 All ER 574 at 583, of saying that, given the jurisdiction, the proper and convenient remedy in the case of alleged *a* contempt of court by the media is by way of committal proceedings in the High Court. The last reported example of a prosecution of a newspaper for contempt was *R v Tibbits and Windust* [1902] 1 KB 77, [1900–3] All ER Rep 896 and this method of proceeding ought not to be revived.

The respondents other than Mr Fletcher and Mr Fordham then made alternative submissions about the composition of the Appellate Committee. It was argued that all *b* five members should be replaced, that alternatively, three named members should be replaced and that, alternatively, one named member should be replaced. The only objection of any possible substance was that, since the contempt proceedings had been initiated by those who were proposing to hear and adjudicate upon them, an objective observer might think that their Lordships were predisposed to decide against Lonrho and that in fact Lonrho did think so. Other objections were of a trivial and trifling *c* character. Thus there was a refusal to admit that any rebuke had been administered by the committee at the outset of proceedings on 9 March 1987. This was based on the expressed inability of counsel for Lonrho then present to remember any rebuke. Notwithstanding the presence of an affidavit by the Dean of the Faculty of Advocates, counsel for the respondents in the proceedings in question, to the effect that he clearly remembered the rebuke in question being addressed to Lonrho's counsel, it was suggested *d* that those of their Lordships who had been members of the committee on the occasion in question were in the position of witnesses. It was also submitted that the circumstance that the father of one of their Lordships had been Mr Rowland's dentist many years ago made him an unsuitable member of the committee though it was not suggested that he had ever known Mr Rowland personally. Further, the criticism which had been made by their Lordships, when dismissing Lonrho's appeal against the Secretary of State for *e* Trade and Industry, that Lonrho had employed against the Secretary of State bullying and intimidatory tactics was prayed in aid as indicating that their Lordships were in general likely to regard (or at least to be thought to regard) Lonrho and its directors unfavourably.

It is a curious quirk that a litigant which has engaged in conduct capable of being *f* regarded by an objective observer as of such a nature as to be likely to affront or antagonise the tribunal before which the litigant is appearing should be in a position to rely upon that conduct, whether it be deliberate or resulting from administrative inefficiency, as a ground for having the matters in issue referred to another tribunal. Fortunately those who administer justice in this country are not prone to feeling affront or antagonism.

It is irrelevant that the conduct in question might be thought likely to cause affront. *g* The only issue presented by the proceedings is whether the activities of Lonrho and the Observer interfered with or prejudiced the due administration of justice. The circumstances urged by Lonrho would not in fact have influenced their Lordships in considering and deciding this issue. But their Lordships were reluctant to leave Lonrho with a sense of grievance, however misguided, by insisting on hearing the proceedings *h* themselves. Accordingly, the House was advised to reconstitute the committee.

The question was accordingly referred to a differently constituted Appellate Committee.

*John Laws* and *Philip Havers* as amici curiae.
*Alan Rawley QC, Anthony Arlidge QC, David Pannick* and *Mark Shaw* for Lonrho. *j*
*Gordon Pollock QC, Robert Wright QC, Michael Beloff QC, David Pannick* and *Mark Shaw* for the directors of Lonrho.
*Gavin Lightman QC* and *Desmond Browne* for the Observer.
*John Chadwick QC, David Eady QC* and *John Rowland* for Lonrho's legal advisers.

a   At the conclusion of argument their Lordships announced that no case of contempt had
    been made out and that they would give their reasons later.

    27 July. The following report on the question of contempt was delivered by the Appellate
    Committee (Lord Bridge of Harwich, Lord Goff of Chieveley and Lord Jauncey of
    Tullichettle).

b   **THE APPELLATE COMMITTEE.**

    *The factual and procedural background*
        1.1  In March 1985 the Al Fayed brothers, through the instrumentality of Al Fayed
    Investment and Trust (UK) plc (AIT), acquired House of Fraser plc and thereby gained
    control of the Knightsbridge department store Harrods. The name of AIT was
c   subsequently changed to House of Fraser Holdings plc. This takeover frustrated an earlier
    attempt to acquire control of Harrods by Lonrho plc (Lonrho). The circumstances in
    which the takeover was achieved have ever since been the subject of a vigorous publicity
    campaign by Lonrho and its managing director and chief executive, Mr R W Rowland,
    supported by the Observer newspaper, published by Lonrho's wholly owned subsidiary
    The Observer Ltd, alleging fraud in the methods used to achieve the takeover and
d   attacking the Al Fayed brothers. We shall refer to this as 'the Lonrho campaign'. The
    ultimate object of the Lonrho campaign was to secure that, by one means or another, the
    Al Fayed brothers should be obliged to sell and Lonrho should have the opportunity to
    acquire shares giving control of House of Fraser plc and hence of Harrods. In April and
    May 1987 the Secretary of State for Trade and Industry appointed inspectors under s 432
    of the Companies Act 1985 to inquire into the affairs of House of Fraser Holdings plc.
e   The inspectors submitted their report to the Secretary of State on 23 July 1988. We shall
    hereafter refer to this as 'the inspectors' report'. Certain matters which were the subject
    of the inspectors' report were referred by the Secretary of State to the Serious Fraud Office
    and the Director of Public Prosecutions. The question whether to publish the report was
    one for the discretion of the Secretary of State under s 437(3)(c) of the 1985 Act.
    Notwithstanding vigorous representations by Lonrho urging immediate publication of
f   the inspectors' report, the Secretary of State decided to defer publication while
    investigations by the Serious Fraud Office and the Director of Public Prosecutions were
    continuing. The Secretary of State also decided not to exercise the discretion which arose
    in the light of the inspectors' report to make a reference to the Monopolies and Mergers
    Commission under s 64 of the Fair Trading Act 1973 of the 'merger situation qualifying
    for reference' constituted by the takeover of House of Fraser by AIT in 1985.
g       1.2  On 2 December 1988 Lonrho sought and obtained leave to make two applications
    for judicial review of the Secretary of State's decisions. We shall refer to these two
    applications as 'the publication application' and 'the reference application' respectively.
    The principal relief sought in the publication application was an order of mandamus
    requiring the Secretary of State to publish the inspectors' report. The principal relief
h   sought in the reference application was an order of mandamus requiring the Secretary of
    State to make a reference to the Monopolies and Mergers Commission. On 8 December
    1988, in the course of the judicial review proceedings before the Divisional Court,
    Lonrho unsuccessfully sought to obtain discovery of the inspectors' report. The judicial
    review applications were heard by the Divisional Court, who gave judgment on 17
    January 1989. On the publication application the court declared that the Secretary of
j   State's decision to defer publication of the inspectors' report was ultra vires and unlawful
    and remitted the matter to him 'for reconsideration as to publication of the said report'.
    On the reference application the court declared the Secretary of State's decision not to
    make a reference to the Monopolies and Mergers Commission to have been ultra vires
    and unlawful and ordered him to make such a reference. On 20 January 1989 the Court

of Appeal allowed the Secretary of State's appeals and set aside the Divisional Court's
orders in both cases, but gave Lonrho leave to appeal to the House of Lords. Lonrho duly *a*
presented petitions of appeal to the House. Before the end of the Hilary sittings of the
House the hearing of the appeals was fixed to begin on Monday 10 April.

1.3 On 23 March a copy of the inspectors' report came into the possession of Mr
Rowland. On 28 March two meetings were held at Mr Rowland's London home and at
his invitation attended by Sir Edward Du Cann, the chairman of Lonrho, Mr P G Spicer
and Mr F P Dunlop, two other directors of Lonrho, and by Mr J M Fordham, a partner in *b*
Stephenson Harwood, Lonrho's solicitors. The afternoon meeting was attended in
addition by Mr N Mitchell, the managing director of The Observer Ltd, Mr D Trelford,
the editor of the Observer, and by leading and junior counsel appearing for Lonrho in
the judicial review proceedings. At the second meeting on 28 March it was decided that
a copy of the inspectors' report should be made available to Mr Trelford for publication
in a special mid-week edition of the Observer on 30 March. The annual general meeting *c*
of Lonrho's shareholders was to be held on 30 March commencing at 11.45 am. It was
intended that disclosure of the contents of the report should be made to shareholders by
Sir Edward Du Cann in his chairman's speech to the meeting concurrently with disclosure
to the public by the special edition which was to be timed to go on sale at noon. The
special edition was prepared and printed, and arrangements were made for its distribution,
in conditions designed to achieve the maximum secrecy. Nevertheless it came to the *d*
attention of officers of the Department of Trade and Industry at about 10.30 am on 30
March that copies of a special edition of the Observer containing extracts from the
inspectors' report had been widely distributed to newsagents. As a result application was
made ex parte to Tudor Evans J on behalf of the Secretary of State for an injunction to
restrain Lonrho and The Observer Ltd from publishing or disclosing the report or any
extracts from it, which he granted at about 11.50 am. Shortly after noon the officer of *e*
the Department of Trade and Industry in charge of the matter telephoned to the
Grosvenor House Hotel where the Lonrho annual general meeting was being held and
was, after some minutes, able to speak to Mr Fordham and tell him of the injunction. It
was then too late to prevent sale of the copies of the special edition already distributed.
Nearly 200,000 copies were sold. In addition, between 2,000 and 3,000 copies of the
special edition were supplied by the Observer to Lonrho who distributed them by post *f*
to persons named on a mailing list to whom Lonrho had been regularly sending
propaganda literature in the course of the Lonrho campaign. The mailing list included
members of both Houses of Parliament; four of the five Lords of Appeal in Ordinary
who were to hear the appeals in the judicial review proceedings received copies of the
Observer special edition by post.

1.4 On Monday, 10 April Lonrho's appeals came on for hearing before an Appellate *g*
Committee (the first Appellate Committee) comprising Lord Keith of Kinkel, Lord
Templeman, Lord Griffiths, Lord Ackner and Lord Lowry. At the outset Lord Keith
made a statement raising the questions whether the publication of the Observer special
edition and sending copies of it to members of the first Appellate Committee might have
amounted to a contempt of the House of Lords by Lonrho and Mr Rowland, whether *h*
Lonrho had disqualified itself from pursuing the appeals and whether or not proceedings
for contempt of the House of Lords should be instituted and, if so, against whom. The
proceedings were thereupon adjourned to enable counsel and parties to consider their
position.

1.5 Upon resumption later in the day counsel for Lonrho said with reference to the
copies of the Observer special edition sent to members of the first Appellate Committee: *j*

> 'I am instructed unreservedly to apologise to your Lordships in respect of this
> matter. It is accepted that, whether intentional and whether or not amounting to a
> contempt, your Lordships ought not to have been sent these documents, and I take
> the earliest opportunity of apologising, as I am sure I shall be instructed to repeat

*a* more fully when the facts are known, for the fact it occurred, and the members of the board, as I am told, have expressly given those instructions.'

Following submissions and an indication by counsel for Lonrho that he intended to present evidence by affidavit, Lord Keith indicated the matters which, in the view of the first Appellate Committee, it would be appropriate for the affidavit evidence to cover. The proceedings were then adjourned to Wednesday, 12 April.

*b* 1.6 At the resumed hearing on 12 April the first Appellate Committee, after considering affidavit evidence put before them on behalf of both Lonrho and the Secretary of State, including affidavits previously sworn in the course of the Secretary of State's action against The Observer Ltd and Lonrho in which the interlocutory injunction had been granted, decided to proceed with the hearing of the appeals.

1.7 On Thursday, 13 April an order of the House was made—

*c* 'that the Appellate Committee to whom were referred the consolidated appeals in the cause *Lonrho plc v Secretary of State for Trade and Industry* ([1989] 2 All ER 609, [1989] 1 WLR 525) should consider whether the circumstances in which a special edition of the Observer newspaper was published on 30 March 1989 constituted a contempt.'

*d* This order instituted what it will be appropriate to refer to as 'the contempt proceedings'. The order was drawn to the attention of the parties in the course of the hearing of the appeals on Tuesday, 18 April. The argument of the appeals was concluded on Wednesday, 19 April. On Thursday, 20 April the first Appellate Committee sat again pursuant to the order of 13 April to consider, with the assistance of counsel for the parties in the appeal and counsel appointed by the Attorney General to act as amicus curiae, the procedure to *e* be followed in the conduct of the contempt proceedings, and at the conclusion of the hearing the first Appellate Committee gave directions in that regard.

1.8 Judgment in the judicial review proceedings was delivered by the House on 18 May dismissing Lonrho's appeals ([1989] 2 All ER 609, [1989] 1 WLR 525). The first Appellate Committee sat again on 22 May to consider the contempt proceedings, but preliminary objections were made by those who had been charged as respondents that *f* the members of the first Appellate Committee, having heard Lonrho's appeal and instituted the contempt proceedings ought not to adjudicate upon them. The first Appellate Committee allowed these objections and recused themselves. On 25 May the House ordered—

*g* 'That the Order of the 13th April last be discharged and that the question whether the circumstances in which a Special Edition of the Observer newspaper was published on 30th March 1989 constitute a contempt should be considered by an Appellate Committee consisting of members other than those appointed by that Order.'

*Preliminary observations*

*h* 2.1 Against this factual and procedural background consideration of the question referred to us by the House imposed on us, as an Appellate Committee, a novel and unique task. The contempt proceedings were brought by the House of its own motion as a 'superior court' within the definition in s 19 of the Contempt of Court Act 1981. The prosecution of the proceedings was conducted by counsel as amicus curiae pursuant to the procedural directions given by the first Appellate Committee. The respondents *j* identified were The Observer Ltd, Mr Trelford, Lonrho plc, Mr Rowland, Sir Edward Du Cann, Mr Spicer, Mr Dunlop, Mr Fordham and Mr A F S Fletcher. Mr Fletcher was one of the junior counsel instructed on behalf of Lonrho in the judicial review proceedings. The charges against the respondents were formulated in a document headed 'Amended Statement' to which we shall later have to refer in detail. If any of the respondents were guilty of contempt, this would expose them to criminal penalties. In these circumstances we were acutely conscious of being in the unenviable position of being both a tribunal of first instance and a tribunal of last resort.

2.2  The reason why we sat as an Appellate Committee of three was that, in the light of certain additional grounds of objection raised to members of the first Appellate Committee adjudicating on the contempt proceedings, two other Lords of Appeal in Ordinary thought it appropriate also to recuse themselves.

2.3  There was before us a very large volume of affidavit and other documentary evidence relating to the circumstances in which a copy of the inspectors' report came into Mr Rowland's possession, the circumstances in which the decision by Lonrho and the Observer was taken to publish extracts from the inspectors' report and as to the relevant legal advice which had been taken. Much of this evidence was produced in response to procedural directions given by the first Appellate Committee. It is to be noted that, in filing affidavits and in making discovery of documents, Lonrho and its directors waived privilege in respect of the legal advice which they had sought and obtained. Some question was raised before us as to whether in contempt proceedings the alleged contemnor can properly be required to give evidence and to make discovery, and whether in this case the affidavits had been filed and discovery given in response to directions which were compulsive in their effect. We noted that the affidavits had certainly been filed and discovery had been given without demur and that the waiver of privilege had been entirely voluntary. In the event we found that nothing turned on this point.

2.4  Mr Rowland gives an account of the circumstances in which a copy of the inspectors' report came into his possession which, if true, shows that it came from an anonymous and unidentified source and was not solicited by him or anyone else on behalf of Lonrho. That evidence was not tested in cross-examination because it was not relevant to any issue before us to determine the nature of any criminal offence or civil wrong which may have been committed in the disclosure to Mr Rowland of the contents of the inspectors' report. On any view, however, it must have been clear to all concerned that publication of extracts from the report in the Observer special edition was prima facie tortious as involving both a breach of copyright and a disclosure of material obtained from a person acting in breach of an obligation of confidence owed to the Secretary of State. It was clearly appreciated that if the Department of Trade and Industry had notice of the intended publication, they would immediately seek and almost certainly obtain an interim injunction. The possibility that the publication would, in the circumstances of the pending appeal to the House of Lords, be a contempt of the House was present to the minds of those who took the decision to publish, and they sought and obtained advice about it from a number of leading and junior counsel representing a wide range of legal expertise in the relevant fields of law. The advice they obtained was not unanimous. The inference we draw from the totality of the evidence is that the directors of Lonrho concerned in the decision to publish and Mr Trelford were prepared to take any risk there might be of the publication being condemned as contemptuous on the footing that the risk of any individual being sentenced to imprisonment was sufficiently remote to be discounted and that any financial penalties imposed would be a price worth paying to achieve the objective of making public without further delay material contained in the report which was seen as a vindication of the Lonrho campaign. In these circumstances, if the publication amounted in law to a contempt, it could not be regarded as other than serious and the difficult question whether it did amount to a contempt called for full investigation.

2.5  Mr Fordham and Mr Fletcher, apart from their role as legal advisers which is not criticised, played some part in the physical transmission of the copy of the inspectors' report from Lonrho to the offices of the Observer which was used in the compilation of the Observer special edition. If the publication amounted in law to a contempt, and if Mr Fordham and Mr Fletcher aided and abetted it, their offence was a very venial one and they have offered full apologies for it. We think it right to record that we do not regard their conduct as in any way dishonourable or discreditable.

2.6 The law relating to contempt of court is fraught with difficulties and uncertainties.
*a*  If an appeal in this area of the law came before the House in the ordinary way from the
decision of a lower court and fell to be determined by an Appellate Committee of five, it
would almost certainly call for an attempt to expound and clarify the relevant principles
applicable as widely as the subject matter of the appeal allowed. But in the circumstances
to which we have drawn attention in paras 2.1 and 2.2 above, two factors inhibit us from
making any such attempt. First, it may be open to question whether the report of an
*b*  Appellate Committee made otherwise than in the exercise of the appellate jurisdiction of
the House is of binding authority. Secondly, it would in any event be inappropriate for
an Appellate Committee of three, lacking the advantages which accrue from the
refinement of issues occurring in the course of the appellate process and the consideration
of the views expressed by judges in the courts below, to attempt any wider exposition of
the law than is strictly necessary for the decision of the specific issues arising for
*c*  determination in the contempt proceedings.

*The charges*
  3. The Amended Statement sets out the charges in the following terms:

  '1. The publication by the "Observer" newspaper, of which The Observer Ltd is
*d*   the proprietor and Donald Trelford the editor, of the special edition on 30 March
    1989, which publication was procured by or aided and abetted by Lonrho plc, Mr
    Rowland, Sir Edward Du Cann, Mr P Spicer, Mr R Dunlop, Mr J Fordham and Mr
    A Fletcher (a) obstructed and/or impeded or may have obstructed and/or impeded
    the House in the discharge of its judicial functions or had a tendency or may have
    had a tendency to produce such a result or was an attempt so to obstruct or impede
*e*   the House and/or; (b) created a substantial risk that the course of justice in the appeal
    proceedings would be seriously impeded or prejudiced and/or; (c) was calculated
    and was intended to interfere with the due administration of justice; in that: (1) the
    function of the Appellate Committee to decide, inter alia, the issue of publication or
    no of the inspectors' report was or may have been thereby usurped and the decision
    of the Appellate Committee on this issue was or may have been thereby pre-empted;
*f*   (2) the position of the other parties to the appellate proceedings was or may have
    been thereby prejudiced and the position of Lonrho plc in those proceedings was or
    may have been thereby improved; (3) the circumstances in which the Appellate
    Committee would or may have had to exercise its discretion whether to grant
    judicial review of the decision of the Secretary of State complained of were or may
    have been thereby altered with the result that the exercise by the Appellate
*g*   Committee of that discretion would or may have been thereby prejudiced; (4) the
    confidentiality in the report of the inspectors which the Court of Appeal had earlier
    preserved and which had yet to be decided upon by the Appellate Committee was
    thereby damaged and part of the subject matter of the appellate proceedings was or
    may have been thereby damaged or destroyed.
*h*   2. The distribution of copies of the special edition, inter alia, to four members of
    the Appellate Committee by Lonrho plc, and its directors Mr Rowland, Sir Edward
    Du Cann and Mr Spicer (a) may have obstructed and/or impeded the House in the
    performance of its judicial functions or had a tendency or may have had a tendency
    to produce such a result and/or; (b) was an attempt so to obstruct and/or impede the
    House and/or; (c) was calculated and was intended to interfere with the due
*j*   administration of justice; in that: (1) the distribution was an attempt to influence
    the members of the Appellate Committee; (2) the function of the Appellate
    Committee to decide whether the report should be received as evidence in the
    course of the appellate proceedings, as Lonrho plc contended, may have been thereby
    usurped and the decision of the Appellate Committee on this issue may have been
    thereby pre-empted.

3. The transmission of a document entitled "Birds of a Feather" sent by post on the 10th April 1989 to Lord Keith of Kinkel (a) may have obstructed and/or impeded *a* the House in the performance of its judicial functions or had a tendency or may have had a tendency to produce such a result and/or; (b) was an attempt so to obstruct and/or impede the House and/or; (c) was calculated and was intended to interfere with the due administration of justice; in that the distribution was an attempt to influence the members of the Appellate Committee.'

*b*

*The decision not to proceed on charges 2 and 3*

4.1 At the beginning of the hearing, submissions were made to us that both charges 2 and 3 fell outside the ambit of the question referred to us by the order of the House dated 25 May. We decided not to proceed on these charges for the following reasons.

*Charge 2*                                                                                              *c*

4.2 The question whether this charge falls within the terms of the order of 25 May turns upon the meaning of the phrase 'the circumstances in which a special edition of the "Observer" newspaper was published on 30 March 1989'. The submission for Lonrho and its directors was that copies of the Observer special edition sent by post to four members of the first Appellate Committee were not 'published' until they were received by post on 31 March 1989. This is a point of considerable technicality, but we did not *d* find it necessary to resolve the question of construction which it raised.

4.3 The effect of the affidavit evidence put before the first Appellate Committee on 12 April bearing upon the subject matter of charge 2 may be summarised as follows. The mailing list of persons to whom Lonrho regularly distributed propaganda literature in the course of the Lonrho campaign originally included members of both Houses of Parliament and Her Majesty's judges. Mr Fordham deposed with considerable *e* particularity to the circumstances in which, following the institution of the judicial review proceedings, he advised Lonrho that Her Majesty's judges and all Lords of Appeal in Ordinary should be excluded from future distributions. Mr Spicer, the director who was responsible for distribution of material in the course of the Lonrho campaign, deposed that the Board of Lonrho accepted Mr Fordham's advice and that he gave *f* instructions to his secretary to take the necessary steps to ensure that the relevant names were excluded from the mailing list. It was not, he says, until 10 April, when Lord Keith made his statement, that it was appreciated that the instructions had not been effectively acted on. Mr Spicer's secretary, Miss Halls, explained with elaborate particularity the system whereby the names on the Lonrho mailing list are stored in a word processor which automatically produces rolls of labels, the steps which she took to comply with Mr *g* Spicer's instructions to exclude the names of Lords of Appeal in Ordinary from rolls of labels awaiting use and from the word processor, and how it came about through an oversight on her part that rolls of labels from which the names of Lords of Appeal in Ordinary had not been removed were used in subsequent distributions. Mr Spicer and Sir Edward Du Cann both repeated in their affidavits sworn on 12 April the unreserved apology which had been made by counsel on 10 April for the fact that copies of the *h* Observer special edition had inadvertently been sent to members of the first Appellate Committee. They accepted that this was quite improper.

4.4 Counsel conducting the prosecution of the contempt proceedings as amicus curiae pursuant to the procedural directions given by the first Appellate Committee, conceded in argument that, if the dispatch to members of the first Appellate Committee of copies of the Observer special edition had occurred in the way indicated by the affidavit *j* evidence, charge 2 would not add anything of substance to the contempt alleged by charge 1. He nevertheless submitted that the evidence should be tested by cross-examination. It seemed to us that charge 2 would only add a significant additional factor to the contempt alleged by charge 1 if we were satisfied to the criminal standard of proof that copies of the Observer special edition were sent to the Lords of Appeal in Ordinary

in a deliberate attempt by directors of Lonrho to influence the minds of those who were
a to hear Lonrho's appeals in the judicial review proceedings, and that we could not arrive
at that conclusion unless we first rejected at least the evidence of Mr Spicer and Miss Halls
as perjured and concocted. We entertained doubts as to whether, in summary proceedings
for contempt, it would be appropriate to require deponents to submit to cross-
examination on material contained in affidavits sworn in the course of other proceedings
before the contempt proceedings were begun. Moreover, in the absence of any extraneous
b factor casting doubt on the evidence, we considered that cross-examination seeking to
establish that the evidence was perjured was of doubtful propriety and could not, in any
event, be expected to establish an affirmative case beyond reasonable doubt. We
concluded for these reasons that it would not be appropriate to proceed on charge 2.

*Charge 3*
c 4.5 As is clear on its face, charge 3 does not fall within the terms of the order of 25
May. The circumstances in which this charge came to be included in the Amended
Statement were not wholly clear. We did not consider it appropriate for us to take the
initiative in inviting the House to make a further order expressed in terms apt to embrace
charge 3 which might amount to the institution of fresh contempt proceedings beyond
the scope of those instituted on the initiative of the first Appellate Committee.
d

*Charge 1 : contempt of the House*
5. Paragraphs (a), (b) and (c) of charge 1 allege respectively contempt of the House of
Lords as such, a statutory contempt of court and a common law contempt of court. It
was common ground that contempt of the House as such could not be established unless
the ingredients of either a statutory or a common law contempt of court were made out
e in relation to the judicial review proceedings pending before the Appellate Committee
which was to exercise the appellate jurisdiction of the House.

*Statutory contempt of court*
6.1 Sections 1 and 2 of the Contempt of Court Act 1981 provide as follows:

f     '**1.** In this Act "the strict liability rule" means the rule of law whereby conduct
may be treated as a contempt of court as tending to interfere with the course of
justice in particular legal proceedings regardless of intent to do so.
      **2.** (1) The strict liability rule applies only in relation to publications and for this
purpose "publication" includes any speech, writing, broadcast or other communication in whatever form, which is addressed to the public at large or any section of the
g     public.
      (2) The strict liability rule applies only to a publication which creates a substantial
risk that the course of justice in the proceedings in question will be seriously
impeded or prejudiced.
      (3) The strict liability rule applies to a publication only if the proceedings in
question are active within the meaning of this section at the time of the publication.
h     (4) Schedule 1 applies for determining the times at which the proceedings are to
be treated as active within the meaning of this section.'

It is not disputed that the Observer special edition was a publication within the meaning
of s 2(1) and was published at a time when the appellate proceedings were active in
accordance with para 15 of Sch 1 to the 1981 Act. Thus, those responsible for the
j publication were guilty of contempt under the strict liability rule if, and only if, the
publication created a substantial risk that the course of justice in Lonrho's appeals to the
House of Lords would be seriously impeded or prejudiced.
      6.2 The Observer special edition, as well as containing extensive verbatim extracts
from the inspectors' report is presented editorially in such a way as to give maximum
impact to the support derived from it for the Lonrho campaign and also contains on its

front page an editorial written by Mr Trelford entitled 'Why We Are Publishing Today' which in terms accuses the Secretary of State of bad faith. This accusation was not only never advanced but was expressly disclaimed by Lonrho in the judicial review proceedings.

6.3 As the case of statutory contempt was argued before us, we think that the issues canvassed can be considered most conveniently under the two headings 'prejudgment' and 'pre-emption'.

*Prejudgment*

7.1 The concept of prejudgment as a contempt is closely allied to that of 'trial by newspaper'. The essential authority on which counsel appearing as amicus relies under this heading is *A-G v Times Newspapers Ltd* [1973] 3 All ER 54, [1974] AC 273. At a time when litigation was pending (but would not have been 'active' in terms of Sch 1 to the 1981 Act) between parents of children born with gross deformities caused by the drug thalidomide and Distillers Co (Biochemicals) Ltd, the manufacturers of thalidomide, the Sunday Times began to publish a series of articles in which both the moral and the legal merits of the litigation were discussed. The Attorney General sought an injunction to restrain publication of further articles in the series. The decision of the Divisional Court to grant the injunction was reversed by the Court of Appeal but restored by the House of Lords. As far as it is possible to summarise the reasoning in their Lordships' speeches, it is well summarised in the headnote which reads ([1974] AC 273 at 274):

'*Held*, that it was a contempt of court to publish material which prejudged the issue of pending litigation or was likely to cause public prejudgment of that issue, and accordingly the publication of this article, which in effect charged the company with negligence, would constitute a contempt, since negligence was one of the issues in the litigation.'

Lord Reid said ([1973] 3 All ER 54 at 64–65, [1974] AC 273 at 300):

'There has long been and there still is in this country a strong and generally held feeling that trial by newspaper is wrong and should be prevented. I find for example in the report of Lord Salmon's committee dealing with the law of contempt with regard to Tribunals of Inquiry (Cmnd 4078) a reference to the "horror" in such a thing. What I think is regarded as most objectionable is that a newspaper or television programme should seek to persuade the public, by discussing the issues and evidence in a case before the court, whether civil or criminal, that one side is right and the other wrong. If we were to ask the ordinary man or even a lawyer in his leisure moments why he has that feeling, I suspect that the first reply would be—well look at what happens in some other countries where that is permitted. As in so many other matters, strong feelings are based on one's general experience rather than on specific reasons, and it often requires an effort to marshall one's reasons. But public policy is generally the result of strong feelings, commonly held, rather than of cold argument. . . I think that anything in the nature of prejudgment of a case or of specific issues in it is objectionable not only because of its possible effect on that particular case but also because of its side effects which may be far reaching. Responsible "mass media" will do their best to be fair, but there will also be ill-informed, slapdash or prejudiced attempts to influence the public. If people are led to think that it is easy to find the truth disrespect for the processes of the law could follow and, if mass media are allowed to judge, unpopular people and unpopular causes will fare very badly. Most cases of prejudging of issues fall within the existing authorities on contempt. I do not think that the freedom of the press would suffer, and I think that the law would be clearer and easier to apply in practice if it is made a general rule that it is not permissible to prejudge issues in pending cases.'

Lord Morris said ([1973] 3 All ER 54 at 67–68, [1974] AC 273 at 303–304):

*a*
'Though on behalf of the respondents it was accepted that there must be no "scandalising" of a court nor conduct either in relation to the court or to the parties or to witnesses which amounts to inteference with the course of justice it was contended that discussions of the issues in a pending action will only be objectionable if it appears that such discussions may influence or appear to influence the decision of the court or may affect the minds of witnesses. Here lies one of the central issues

*b*
raised in the present case. To what extent may there be in the press or on television or, for example, in a public meeting a detailed discussion of and pronouncement on the issues which are raised in pending proceedings? It is said that in some circumstances such discussions or such pronouncements could take place without affecting or influencing either the court or the parties or any witnesses. While this, in some circumstances, could be so it would be very difficult in any particular case

*c*
to be sure that the effects of publicity were so limited and confined. Who could define with any confidence the boundaries of influence of a determined and sustained campaign in advancement of some particular issue between parties to litigation? But apart from this—is it right and is it appropriate, when parties to a dispute have submitted their dispute and the issues raised within it to the

*d*
arbitrament of the courts that there should be elaborate public debate and explicit expressions of opinions as to what the decision of the court ought to be and as to where the merits and the rights lie? For one thing it would usually be difficult, pending the findings of the court as to what were the material facts, to have any firm or satisfactory basis on which to begin to form opinion. But even apart from this is it not contrary to the fitness of things that there should be unrestricted

*e*
expressions of opinion whether the merits lie with one party to litigation rather than with another? Even if some expressions of opinion were the result of honestly attempted sound reasoning how easy it would be for later statements by others to amount simply to advocacy inspired by partisan motives for the cause of one party, and how difficult it would be then to stem the tide of public clamour for the victory of one side or the other. Though a judge would hope to be resistant to any pre-trial

*f*
soundings of the trumpet it must surely be contrary to public policy to allow them full blast. Furthermore, not only is it from the public point of view unseemly that in respect of a cause awaiting the determination of a court there should be public advocacy in favour of one particular side or some particular points of view but also the courts, I think, owe it to the parties to protect them either from the prejudices of prejudgment or from the necessity of having themselves to participate in the

*g*
flurries of pre-trial publicity. In this connection I agree with Lord Denning MR when he said ([1973] 1 All ER 815 at 821–822, [1973] 2 WLR 452 at 460)—"We must not allow 'trial by newspaper' or 'trial by television' or trial by any medium other than the courts of law."'

Lord Cross said ([1973] 3 All ER 54 at 84, [1974] AC 273 at 322–323):

*h*
'... we should maintain the rule that any "prejudging" of issues, whether of fact or of law, in pending proceedings—whether civil or criminal—is in principle an interference with the administration of justice although in any particular case the offence may be so trifling that to bring it to the notice of the court would be unjustifiable. It is easy enough to see that any publication which prejudges an issue in pending proceedings ought to be forbidden if there is any real risk that it may

*j*
influence the tribunal—whether judge, magistrates or jury, or any of those who may be called on to give evidence when the case comes to be heard. But why, it may be said, should such a publication be prohibited when there is no such risk? The reason is that one cannot deal with one particular publication in isolation. A publication prejudging an issue in pending litigation which is itself innocuous

enough may provoke replies which are far from innocuous but which, as they are replies, it would seem unfair to restrain. So gradually the public would become *a* habituated to, look forward to, and resent the absence of, preliminary discussions in the "media" of any case which aroused widespread interest. An absolute rule—though it may seem to be unreasonable if one looks only to the particular case—is necessary in order to prevent a gradual slide towards trial by newspaper or television.'

7.2 How far these passages from the speeches of their Lordships may still be relied *b* upon as accurate expressions of the law is extremely doubtful, certainly in relation to the kind of contempt which is the subject matter of the strict liability rule under ss 1 and 2 of the 1981 Act. The judgment of the House of Lords in *A-G v Times Newspapers Ltd* was delivered in July 1974. In December 1974 the Report of the Committee on Contempt of Court ('the Phillimore Report') (Cmnd 5794) was presented to Parliament. The 'prejudgment' test propounded in the speeches in *A-G v Times Newspapers Ltd* is heavily *c* criticised by the Phillimore Report at paras 106 to 111. The decision in *A-G v Times Newspapers Ltd* was also challenged before the European Court of Human Rights by the Sunday Times as an infringement of the right to freedom of expression guaranteed under art 10 of the European Convention on Human Rights (see *Sunday Times v UK* (1979) 2 EHRR 245). Article 10(2) of the convention provides that the exercise of the right to freedom of expression may be subject to such restrictions 'as are prescribed by law and *d* are necessary in a democratic society . . . for maintaining the authority and impartiality of the judiciary'. The court held by a majority of eleven votes to nine that the restriction imposed on the Sunday Times by the injunction which had been affirmed by the House of Lords was not justified by a 'pressing social need' and could not therefore be regarded as 'necessary' within the meaning of art 10(2). Since the European Convention on Human Rights is no part of our municipal law, we cannot resort to the decision of the European *e* Court of Human Rights as direct authority, but the 1981 Act, on any point on which any doubt arises as to its construction, may be presumed to have been intended to avoid future conflicts between the law of contempt of court in the United Kingdom and the obligations of the United Kingdom under the convention. Moreover, the definition of contempt of court under the strict liability rule in s 2(2) of the Act is derived directly from the recommendations contained in the Phillimore Report. *f*

7.3 The only safe course, we think, is to apply the test imposed by the statutory language according to its ordinary meaning, without any preconception derived from *A-G v Times Newspapers Ltd* as to what kind of publication is likely to impede or prejudice the course of justice. The question whether a particular publication, in relation to particular legal proceedings which are active, creates a substantial risk that the course of justice in those proceedings will be seriously impeded or prejudiced is ultimately one of *g* fact. Whether the course of justice in particular proceedings will be impeded or prejudiced by a publication must depend primarily on whether the publication will bring influence to bear which is likely to divert the proceedings in some way from the course which they would otherwise have followed. The influence may affect the conduct of witnesses, the parties or the court. Before proceedings have come to trial and before *h* the facts have been found, it is easy to see how critical public discussion of the issues and criticism of the conduct of the parties, particularly if a party is held up to public obloquy, may impede or prejudice the course of the proceedings by influencing the conduct of witnesses or parties in relation to the proceedings. If the trial is to be by jury, the possibility of prejudice by advance publicity directed to an issue which the jury will have to decide is obvious. The possibility that a professional judge will be influenced by *j* anything he has read about the issues in a case which he has to try is very much more remote. He will not consciously allow himself to take account of anything other than the evidence and argument presented to him in court.

7.4 After an action has been tried or an application for judicial review determined and when proceedings are pending on appeal from the decision of first instance or, as here,

from the Court of Appeal to the House of Lords, the possibility that a publication which
*a* discusses the issues arising on the appeal or the merits of the decision appealed against or
of the conduct of the parties in relation thereto will impede or prejudice the course of
justice in those proceedings is very much narrower. In the ordinary case, as here, there
will be no question of influencing witnesses. In general terms the possibility that the
parties will be influenced is remote. When a case has proceeded so far it is unlikely, save
in exceptional circumstances, that criticism would deter an appellant from pursuing his
*b* appeal or induce a respondent to forego the judgment in his favour or to reach a
compromise of the appeal. So far as the appellate tribunal is concerned, it is difficult to
visualise circumstances in which any court in the United Kingdom exercising appellate
jurisdiction would be in the least likely to be influenced by public discussion of the
merits of a decision appealed against or of the parties' conduct in the proceedings.
Discussion and criticism of decisions of first instance or of the Court of Appeal which are
*c* subject to pending appeals are a commonplace in legal journals, but on matters of more
general public interest examples also readily spring to mind of criticism in the general
press directed against, for example, criminal convictions, sentences imposed, damages
awarded in libel actions and other court decisions which arouse public controversy. No
case was drawn to our attention in which public discussion of the issues arising in, or
criticism of the parties to, litigation already decided at first instance has been held to be a
*d* contempt on the ground that it was likely to impede or prejudice the course of justice in
proceedings on appeal from that decision.

7.5 The publication in the Observer special ediction of extracts from the inspectors'
report falls for consideration as possible contempt under the heading of 'pre-emption'.
The vice at which the strictures in the speeches in *A-G v Times Newspapers Ltd* against
'trial by newspaper' and 'prejudgment' were directed is exhibited, if at all, in the editorial
*e* comment, in particular the accusation that the Secretary of State acted in bad faith in
deciding to defer publication of the inspectors' report. The issues arising in the appeals
were (1) whether the Secretary of State lawfully exercised his discretion under s 437(3)(c)
of the Companies Act 1985 in deciding to defer publication, no allegation of bad faith in
that decision being made, and (2) whether he exercised his discretion lawfully under s 64
of the Fair Trading Act 1973 in deciding not to make a reference to the Monopolies and
*f* Mergers Commission of the takeover of House of Fraser by AIT in 1985. Having heard
full argument, we do not consider that the editorial comment in the Observer special
edition, however intemperate the language in which it was expressed may have been,
created any risk that the Secretary of State, having succeeded in the Court of Appeal in
both appeals, would be deterred from seeking to uphold those decisions in opposition to
the appeals or deflected from the course he would otherwise have followed in relation to
*g* the appellate proceedings. Nor was the publication in this regard capable of exerting any
influence on the decision of the Appellate Committee on either appeal.

*Pre-emption*
8.1 The argument under this heading is really at the heart of the contempt proceedings
*h* and raises the most difficult question for decision. Lonrho's object in the publication
application for judicial review was to compel the publication of the inspectors' report. By
securing publication in advance of the decision of the House on Lonrho's appeal in
relation to that application, Lonrho and its directors may be said to have taken the law
into their own hands. In one sense, after publication of the substance of the report, the
question whether or not the Secretary of State lawfully decided to defer publication was
*j* rendered academic. If the Secretary of State had not intervened to restrain by injunction
the further publication of the Observer special edition after the initial sales, a circumstance
which Lonrho can hardly pray in aid in defence, the substance of the report would have
been fully in the public domain and the reasons which prompted the Secretary of State
to defer publication would no longer have been applicable. The confidentiality of the
report having been breached, it would no longer be of practical importance, save in

relation to the costs of the judicial review proceedings, whether or not the Secretary of State had acted lawfully in his previous decision to maintain that confidentiality. It is in this sense that it is contended that the decision of the Appellate Committee on the appeal was pre-empted and that the subject matter of the appellate proceedings was damaged or destroyed. The argument is a cogent one.

8.2 The only authority which throws light on this issue is *A-G v Newspaper Publishing plc* [1987] 3 All ER 276, [1988] Ch 333. In actions against the publishers of the Guardian and the Observer newspapers, the Attorney General obtained interloctory injunctions to restrain the publication of extracts from the book *Spycatcher* on the ground of their confidentiality. At a time when these injunctions were in force and the Attorney General's action was pending, the Independent newspaper published extracts from *Spycatcher*. The Attorney General brought proceedings against the publishers for contempt. The Court of Appeal held on a preliminary issue that the interim injunctions had been granted to preserve the confidentiality of the *Spycatcher* material and that publication by any other newspaper than those enjoined, by destroying the subject matter of the pending action, amounted to the actus reus of contempt. This judgment is likely, we understand, to be challenged in a future appeal to the House of Lords, but for present purposes we assume it to have been correct. All three judgments emphasise the importance of the injunctions indicating the court's intention to preserve the subject matter of the pending action as an essential ingredient of the contempt committed by a party not subject to those injunctions.

8.3 Here there was no injunction to restrain publication of the inspectors' report until after the initial publication of the Observer special edition, and the confidentiality of the inspectors' report was not directly in issue in the appellate proceedings, but rather the lawfulness of the Secretary of State's decision which had the effect of preserving that confidentiality. *A-G v Newspaper Publishing plc*, therefore, gives no support to the submissions of counsel appearing as amicus curiae under this heading, and the question whether they can be sustained or not must be determined as a matter of principle. Again, it is appropriate to ask whether the publication of extracts from the inspectors' report created a risk either that the Secretary of State would be deflected from the course he would otherwise have followed as respondent to the appeal in relation to the publication application or that the Appellate Committee would be influenced to decide any issue arising in that appeal otherwise than they would have done if there had been no such publication. Suppose that the Secretary of State, in the light of the publicity given by the Observer special edition to the substance of the inspectors' report, had felt obliged to accept that the reasons underlying his own previous decision to defer publication no longer applied, that all the damage which could be done to prejudice the investigations by the Serious Fraud Office and the Director of Public Prosecutions and any proceedings which might ensue from those investigations had already been done and that, therefore, it was pointless to seek an injunction and he must accept the publication as a fait accompli. In these circumstances, we see no reason to think that the Secretary of State would have been induced to concede that his previous decision to defer publication was unlawful or to abandon his resistance to Lonrho's appeal in relation to the publication application if Lonrho still pursued it. Again, this situation would not, we think, have affected in any way the approach of the Appellate Committee to the decision in that appeal as to whether the Secretary of State's original decision to defer publication had been lawful. If it had been held to be unlawful, in the situation envisaged, there would have been no remedy granted by order to quash the decision or to remit it for reconsideration because these would have become academic. In this situation it may well be that Lonrho, unless they had wished to pursue the appeal in relation to the publication application on the subject of costs alone, would have taken steps to withdraw it. The question must be asked, therefore, whether Lonrho and its directors, having created a situation in which they achieved by extraneous means the objective which the judicial review proceedings were designed to achieve, so that it was no longer necessary to pursue

the judicial review proceedings, may be said to have impeded or prejudiced the course of
*a*  justice in those proceedings. Lonrho, one may take it, would only have been permitted
to withdraw their appeal on terms of paying all the costs. If the appeal had been
withdrawn before publication of the Observer special edition, that publication could not
have been a contempt as creating a risk that the course of justice would be impeded or
prejudiced in proceedings which had already terminated. So it is difficult to see how the
publication could amount to a contempt if the appeal was withdrawn immediately
*b*  following publication. Similarly, if the copy of the inspectors' report obtained by Mr
Rowland had not come into his possession until after the hearing of the appeal and the
Observer special edition had been published in the very week in which the House
delivered judgment, the logic of the argument of counsel appearing as amicus curiae on
pre-emption would lead to the conclusion that publication on the day before judgment
was delivered would amount to a contempt as a pre-emption of the decision, but that
*c*  publication on the day after would not.
    8.4 In the light of these apparent anomalies we must ask whether there is any support
in principle or authority for the proposition that a litigant who seeks a judicial remedy
compelling a certain course of action creates a risk that the course of justice in the
proceedings in which the remedy is sought would be impeded or prejudiced if he takes
direct action to secure for himself the substance of the remedy sought without the
*d*  assistance of the court. The example was put in the course of argument of the plaintiff
who complains that his neighbour has built a wall obstructing his right of way and seeks
an injunction to have it removed. He succeeds at first instance, loses in the Court of
Appeal and appeals to the House of Lords. While the appeal is still pending he loses
patience and knocks the wall down. In this example, if the plaintiff succeeds in the
appeal, he will no longer need a mandatory injunction. If he loses, he will have rendered
*e*  himself liable in damages and possibly criminally. In either event, however deplorable
his conduct, it is difficult to see how the course of justice, in determining the legal rights
of the parties is likely to have been impeded or prejudiced in any way. It is easy to think
of many other examples of litigants resorting to this kind of self-help. In all or nearly all
of them their conduct may involve a breach of civil or criminal law or both. But so far as
*f*  we are aware, no case has ever been before the court in which conduct of this character
has been held to amount to contempt of court. We think that it would be a novel
extension of the law of contempt to hold that direct action taken by a litigant to secure
the substance of a remedy which he was seeking in judicial proceedings amounted to a
contempt in relation to those proceedings, and that the publication of extracts from the
inspectors' report in the Observer special edition did not create any risk that the course of
*g*  justice in the appellate proceedings challenging the lawfulness of the Secretary of State's
decision to defer publication would be impeded or prejudiced.

*The s 5 defence*
    9. Section 5 of the 1981 Act provides:

*h*      'A publication made as or as part of a discussion in good faith of public affairs or
    other matters of general public interest is not to be treated as a contempt of court
    under the strict liability rule if the risk of impediment or prejudice to particular
    legal proceedings is merely incidental to the discussion.'

This defence was relied on by the respondents. Having decided that the Observer special
edition created no risk of impediment or prejudice to the proceedings on Lonrho's
*j*  appeal, we do not need to consider it.

*Common law contempt*
    10. Section 6 of the 1981 Act provides:

    'Nothing in the foregoing provisions of this Act . . . (c) restricts liability for

contempt of court in respect of conduct intended to impede or prejudice the
administration of justice.'

Counsel appearing as amicus curiae submitted that the publication of the Observer
special edition, if not amounting to a statutory contempt under the strict liability rule,
might be shown by cross-examination of the witnesses on the affidavits sworn in the
contempt proceedings to have been intended to impede or prejudice the administration
of justice. We noted that the particulars relied on in support of the allegations of statutory
and common law contempt in charge 1, as set out in paras (1) to (4), were the same and
all alleged impediment or prejudice to the course of justice in the proceedings on
Lonrho's appeal, not to any wider aspect of the administration of justice. If the publication
of the Observer special edition did create a risk that the course of justice in Lonrho's
appeal would be impeded or prejudiced, there would be no difficulty in inferring that
those responsible for the publication intended that consequence. But if the publication
created no such risk, as we concluded in considering the question of statutory contempt,
common law contempt within the ambit of the particulars relied on in support of charge
1 could only be established if those responsible for the publication intended it to have
consequences affecting the appellate proceedings which it neither achieved nor was ever
likely to achieve. In the absence of any material in the evidence before us suggesting
such an intention, we could see no prospect that cross-examination could satisfy us
beyond reasonable doubt that such an intention was entertained. We accordingly decided
that no purpose would be served by requiring witnesses to submit to cross-examination.

*Decision*

11. It was for these reasons that we announced at the end of the hearing our unanimous
conclusion that no case of contempt had been made out.

*Costs*

12. It was accepted at the hearing on behalf of all respondents that we could not
recommend, since the House would have no power to make, any order relating to the
costs of the contempt proceedings. After the hearing a submission in writing was made
to us on behalf of the respondents that the payment of their costs by the Treasury might
be brought about by one or other of two courses of action, viz (1) an invitation to the
Lord Chancellor to recommend to the Financial Secretary to the Treasury that he should
in turn recommend on behalf of the Crown a motion to the House of Commons for such
payment; (2) a resolution recommending such payment analogous to such recommendations as may be made by Select Committees of the House of Commons for the payment
of the expenses of witnesses or experts. Our impression is that it would be quite
unconstitutional for us to take either suggested course of action. But we have not found
it necessary to examine this question further, since we are of opinion that the publication
of the Observer special edition was, in all the circumstances, such as to call for full inquiry
as to whether those responsible therefor had committed a contempt and that accordingly
it would be inappropriate that their costs should be paid out of public funds.

*Order discharged. No order for costs.*

Solicitors: *Treasury Solicitor*; *Simmons & Simmons* (for Lonrho and the directors); *Turner
Kenneth Brown* (for The Observer); *Stephenson Harwood* (for Lonrho's legal advisers).

Mary Rose Plummer    Barrister.